The B-17 Flying Fortress STORY

B-17G-20-BO 42-31614, named *Minnie The Mermaid* in the 533rd Bomb Squadron, 381st Bomb Group, flies with the chin turret turned to lessen the bitterly cold airflow through the gun apertures, some of which found its way into the nose compartment. Badly damaged by flak over Merseburg, this Fortress was written off in a crash-landing in liberated territory. (USAF)

The B-17 Flying Fortress Story

DESIGN – PRODUCTION – HISTORY

Roger A. Freeman

with

David R. Osborne

ARMS AND ARMOUR

This book is dedicated to
Kerrie (née Osborne) Hansey, 1965–1985

ARMS & ARMOUR PRESS
An imprint of the Cassell Group
Wellington House, 125 Strand, London WC2R 0BB

Distributed in the USA by Sterling Publishing Co. Inc.,
387 Park Avenue South, New York, NY 10016-8810

© Roger A Freeman, 1998
All rights reserved. No part of this book may be reproduced or transmitted
in any form or by any means electronic or mechanical including photocopy-
ing recording or any information storage and retrieval system without
permission in writing from the Publisher.

British Library Cataloguing-in-Publication data:
A catalogue record for this book is available from the British Library.

ISBN 1 85409 301 0

Edited and designed by Roger Chesneau/DAG Publications Ltd

Printed and bound in Great Britain

Contents

	Introduction	7
1	The Boeing Enterprise	9
2	Model 299: Design and Production	12
3	Changes, Alterations and Modifications	38
4	The Wright R-1820 Cyclone	57
5	B-17 Performance	58
6	Post-War Fortresses	60
7	Individual B-17 Histories	70
	Select Bibliography	320

Introduction

Boeing is one of the most successful aircraft manufacturing companies; possibly *the* most successful if gross financial figures are the yardstick. For more than fifty years its bomber aircraft were the backbone of the United States strategic forces, and since the middle of this century its commercial transports have been dominant in the world's airlines. While the highly successful 747 'jumbo jet' may be the best-known of Boeing products through its service to millions of air travellers over thirty years, the company's most famous design is almost certainly the Flying Fortress, the B-17 bomber of the Second World War. In the first instance the name 'Flying Fortress' captured the public's imagination and was given substance by the combat employment of the bomber, particularly in the mass daylight intrusions over Germany and the occupied countries of the Nazi regime. On some of these the most prolonged and ferocious air battles of the war took place. As to the Fortress and its crews' achievement, it has to be fairly said that other aircraft types and their employment can be seen to have made a greater contribution to victory, notably its more versatile running mate the B-24 Liberator. However, fame is not necessarily allied to achievement, and in this case it arose through the endurance of the bomber and its crews against often massive opposition. For the United States Army Air Forces the B-17 became its prime symbol of rugged inveteracy.

Not a small measure of this association with endurance were the occasions when Fortresses sustained extraordinary battle damage yet returned and landed safely at their bases when most contemporaries would have had to be abandoned in the air. Such incidents added to the legend, but the underlying factors were the sound construction and good flying characteristics of the aircraft. The B-17's inherent stability led to its employment in a number of civil roles following the Second World War, culminating a half century on in more airworthy examples remaining than any other type of heavy bomber from that conflict, their purpose now to entertain.

Only the Spitfire fighter has more published works in its honour than the Fortress. If the personal memoirs of those who served with the Fortress are included, the number of its published titles now runs into three figures. This addition to the host has been compiled with the purpose of giving a straightforward and comprehensive reference on the aircraft, its design and production history, service modifications and civilian adaptations. Additionally, there is a lengthy appendix with a brief history of all 12,731 Fortresses (more correctly Boeing Model 299s) built. Other than in these individual histories, the operational and combat service of the aircraft is not covered herein. Broadly, this is what might be termed a 'nuts and bolts' study, being concerned with mechanics rather than service history.

ACKNOWLEDGEMENTS

David Osborne undertook the considerable task of compiling the individual aircraft histories presented in this book. It represents an immense effort in diligence and research. Data and photographs have been drawn from many sources, chiefly Boeing publications, USAAF documents and USAF archives. Technical material reproduced herein was obtained chiefly from the US Air Force Museum and the Boeing Company. Among many bibliographical references the author wishes to cite the work of two former Boeing employees, Peter M. Bowers and Alwyn T. Lloyd. Pete Bowers is renowned as 'Mr B-17', and among his many works his *Fortress In The Sky* is recommended to anyone seeking an in-depth study of the Flying Fortress. The three volumes of Lloyd's *B-17 Flying Fortress in Detail and Scale* provide excellent pictorial material, particularly on the various adaptations of the type.

Individuals who have provided assistance and material for this work are Steve Birdsall, Ian Mactaggart, Dave Menard, George Pennick, Bruce Robertson, Joe Rotelli and Bob Sturges. Bruce Robertson has also given valued editorial advice. To all I offer my sincere thanks.

Roger A. Freeman
June 1997

1. The Boeing Enterprise

William E. Boeing was a prosperous entrepreneur of the north-western United States in the early years of the twentieth century. Timber was his major business, based on extensive forestry ground that he held in the Seattle area, wood still being the principal material for most construction requirements in both homes and commerce. Boeing's great delight in leisure hours was sailing, and he had acquired a small yacht-building shipyard on the Duwamish river, south of the city. The advent of powered flight intrigued many affluent gentlemen, and in Boeing's case sufficiently to be taken aloft as a passenger when the opportunity arose in 1914. He was so enthused by this experience that he later took pilot instruction and purchased an early Martin seaplane. But this was more than a rich man's indulgence, for with a Navy friend, Commander Conrad Westervelt, the plan was to design and build seaplanes at Seattle, a special building for this purpose being erected offshore on the city's Union Lake. Westervelt's naval duties saw him transferred to the Atlantic seaboard before the first flight, but, undeterred, Boeing continued with the venture, giving it company status. As with other emergent aircraft producers, the United States' entry into the First World War soon elevated Boeing's company from what many saw as a fanciful enterprise to a sound manufacturing concern with a good order book. Twenty days after the United States' declaration of war, in April 1917, Boeing reorganised the business as the Boeing Airplane Company, lending his name to what would eventually become the most widely known aircraft manufacturer in the world.

Apart from its own floatplane designs sold to the US Navy as trainers, Boeing's business acumen led him to seek outside work, and he soon secured a government contract to licence-build Curtiss flying boats. The Union Lake premises were not large enough for this expansion, so aircraft production was switched to the yacht yard on the Duwamish river, where additional assembly shops were erected. Peace brought a reversal of fortunes, with manufacturing contracts cancelled and little interest in the company's own designs for either military or civilian use, principally due to the large surplus of wartime aircraft available at give-away prices. To keep the factory in being Boeing had to divert the labour force to furniture and boat production—or anything else where spruce could be profitably used. But, if the company was to live up to its name in the future, it was essential to obtain federal contracts for Army and Navy requirements. These, few and far between in the early post-war days, were subject to fierce competition from others in the industry when specifications were put out to tender.

Holding the design rights for the aircraft models it procured, the US government was not bound to employ the company of origin: the lowest bidder usually obtained the contract, particularly in those dollar-starved days of military appropriations. Despite the company's somewhat isolated location in the north-western corner of the country, which could add a disadvantage through freight travel for manufacturing supplies from distant industrial areas, Boeing's aggressive tendering obtained contracts for modifying and updating 300 De Havilland DH4s, the most prevalent Army type at the end of the First World War, and another to build 200 Thomas-Morse fighters (then termed 'pursuits'). Small contracts were also obtained for aircraft repair and modification.

Through competitive tendering and good workmanship the Boeing Airplane Company was able to sustain a reasonably profitable business while developing its own design and engineering expertise. While his timber holdings may have played a part in 'Bill' Boeing's entry into aircraft manufacture, the way ahead was in light metals. Throughout the 1920s the company advanced its capabilities in this sphere, initially with tubular steel frame fuselages for the refurbished DH4s and then tubular-truss wing spars and the use of aluminium alloys.

While the company's main source of income was contracts for Army and Navy aviation, there was a growing market in the commercial airlines, the vast distances between major US cities encouraging air travel for both passenger and light cargo. Competition among manufacturers was no less forceful in this field, but in 1927 Boeing made a shrewd move by providing his own customer, Boeing Air Transport, which established itself in the multi-engine air transport market with the Boeing Model 80 trimotor biplane flying a Chicago–San Franciso route. Despite the stock market crash of 1929 and the severe economic depression that followed, when many industrial companies were bankrupted and the Boeing Airplane Company was also under financial stress, the firm's design and engineering staff were still able to advance their skills in metal construction.

Particularly successful was the Model 247 of 1932. A twin-engine, ten-seat, all-metal, low-wing monoplane, with retractable main wheels, it was a considerable improvement on the biplane transports then in airline service. Once again Boeing had an advantage by having an allied customer, through the reorganisation of Boeing Air Transport as the principle element of United Airlines, who provided an order for 60 Model 247s. This pooling of interests resulted in an alignment of several companies under the United Aircraft and Transport Corporation (UATC), including the aero engine manufacturer Pratt & Whitney and Hamilton propellers. UATC's Chairman was William E. Boeing. This corporation, soon to include other aircraft and component manufacturers, came to be viewed by government as a cartel. Anti-trust laws, passed in 1934, made it illegal for an aircraft manufacturer to own or be financially tied to an airline. With the break-up of the holding organisation William E. Boeing chose to let the Boeing Airplane Company go its own way, resigning from the Board and leaving Claire Egtvedt as Vice-President and General Manager.

Reorganised as the Boeing Aircraft Company, the Seattle manufacturing plant was again faced with an uncertain future unless more military contracts were forthcoming. The Model 247 airliner was being outclassed by Douglas designs which provided better payloads, and Boeing had no satisfactory successor to the 247. Government contracts remained the life-blood of the aviation industry, and competition to secure them was no less intense as the national economy began to recover from the Depression.

The method of acquisition remained little changed. Following an Army or Navy identi-

Above: With the XB-15, Boeing's first heavy bomber venture, the sheer size and complexity of the design, plus engineering problems, delayed its completion. The first flight took place exactly 26 months after that of the Model 299. It had a span of 149ft and grossed 70,706lb, and its four Pratt & Whitney R-1830-11 engines, each rated at 850hp, produced insufficient power to give this giant a good performance. It was regarded as purely experimental long before it flew. (Boeing)

fication of a service requirement and the availability of funds, the procedure was to issue a general specification to the industry inviting design proposals and costing. This amounted to a competition for the adjudged best design at the best price. The US Army, while maintaining that its aircraft were for the support of ground forces, was increasingly interested in extending the range of both reconnaissance and bombing types. There were, however, many Air Force officers who cherished the idea of air power as a separate entity, independent of both army and navy as was Britain's Royal Air Force. Similarly, the key to such establishment was the recognition of the bomber aircraft as a strategic weapon, capable of bringing destruction to an enemy's war-making capacity in his own homeland. The nurturing of such a doctrine was suppressed by the traditionalist Army hierarchy for much of the inter-war period, although some of the approved contracts for experimental and production projects were providing aircraft that could be used to fulfil this strategic role. Despite few production orders, funds were allocated for aeronautical research and experimentation.

Aware that the Europeans were developing large multi-engine aircraft capable of many hours' endurance, Wright Field, Ohio, the Army Air Corps test and experimental centre, was similarly motivated. On 14 April 1934 the commissioning agency issued a requirement for 'a long-range airplane suitable for military purposes' to the interested parties, Boeing and Martin. Of the two preliminary designs submitted, Boeing's response, the Model 294, impressed the adjudicating panel sufficiently for a contract to be awarded the following June for mock-up with design data and wind-tunnel tests. On the strength of these a single experimental prototype was ordered a year later. The Model 294 amounted to the construction of the largest and heaviest military aircraft to be built in America up to that time. It featured four 2,000hp Allison liquid-cooled engines, a wing span of 149ft and a gross weight of 70,000lb. It has been said that a good element of service prestige was involved in the acquisition of this giant, designated XBLR-1 (Experimental Bomber Long Range) by the Army.

While components for this aircraft could be and were constructed at Boeing's existing plant on the Duwamish river, another site had to be found for erection, the obvious choice being the King County airport, which had opened at Seattle in 1928 and was being increasingly used by the company for flying. The airfield was some two miles from the existing factory, and a large new building was erected on the west side in 1936. It was intended that completed sections of the bomber, redesignated XB-15 in the summer of that year, would be shipped by barge up the river for final assembly. The new factory, known as Plant No 2, covered 60,000 square feet. It featured a 200ft by 300ft single unobstructed assembly area with overhead monorails for the installation of engines and heavy sub-assemblies. Electricity and compressed air lines for power-operated tools were carried in channels under the flooring. In total, with the two plants, Boeing had some 400,000 square feet of factory floor by 1937.

In line with the development of military aircraft by European powers, the Model 294, subject to security measures, was first known as Project A at the Boeing factory. At an early stage it was evident that the 24-cylinder Allison engines originally planned for the aircraft would not be available, so less powerful but proven Pratt & Whitney radials were substituted. Design and engineering problems connected with Project A soon showed that a long development period would ensue before the prototype was ready to fly. While Project A was initially seen as an experimental venture, and the more so as the months passed, the Army Air Corps would within a few years need a replacement for the twin-engine Martin B-10 currently being produced for its bomber squadrons (the service life of a military aircraft being considered about five years at this time). Six weeks after the contract for Project A had been signed, on 8 August 1934, the Army circulated another document for a multi-engine aircraft capable of a 1,200-mile range with normal loads. Boeing's entry for the design competition was the Model 299, the first of the B-17 Flying Fortress family, a parallel project to the XB-15 and destined to fly more than two years before that experimental giant.

The advances in aircraft design and construction brought a growing sophistication and complexity which in turn brought greater financial investment. Despite its recognised expertise, the Boeing Aircraft Company was never far from the profit-or-loss equation during the 1930s: in 1936, for example, the company's profit stood at 7.3 per cent of sales, but two years later there was a deficit of 27.7 per cent. Nevertheless, the composite figure showed a general increase in overall profit between 1935 and 1941, although there were periods when the financial situation was so critical that part of the workforce had to be laid off. Not until 1940, with a substantial order for B-17s and a contract from the French to build Douglas DB-7 light bombers, was Boeing's place finally assured as a major aircraft manufacturer. From experience with the XB-15 and B-17 came the B-29 Superfortress, and its transport variant the C-97, which was sold post-war in a civil version as the Stratocruiser.

Between the two world wars the workforce fluctuated, falling to just over 700 in 1933, climbing to exceed 3,000 in 1939 and coming close to 45,000 during peak employment in 1944. The extension of the Seattle facility in 1940, a subsidiary at Vancouver, Canada, and government-financed plants in Wichita, Kansas, and Renton, Washington, enabled Boeing to produce 18,519 military and naval aircraft during the Second World War. Other manufacturers built 6,917 of its designs—B-17s and B-29s.

Thereafter, from 1945, Boeing bomber and transport designs would dominate in American services for nearly half a century. While the B-47 and, later, B-52 jet bombers were the backbone of the United States aerial deterrent force for many years, parallel to these military designs Boeing produced the Model 700 series jet airliners. Beginning with the 707, followed by the very successful 727, 737 and 747 and reinforced by the 757, 767 and 777, Boeing achieved the premier position in the world's commercial aviation market. At the end of the twentieth century, the United States' oldest uninterrupted manufacturer of aircraft had become the world's dominant producer of airliners. But the most famous product, and the aircraft that more than any other established the company's commercial success, was the Model 299, the legendary Flying Fortress.

Below: The roll-out of the Model 299, 16 July 1935: Boeing employees and invited guests admire the shining machine that was the world's first all-metal, four-engine, monoplane bomber. Some of the gun positions are covered or blacked out, although the nose was later exposed to public viewing when the cowlings had been installed on the four Hornet engines. Defensive armament blisters and bumps, which disrupted the sleek lines of the aircraft, caused a news editor of the *Seattle Times* to coin the descriptive term 'flying fortress'. (Roger Besecker)

2. Model 299: Design and Production

The First World War boosted the advance of aviation technology but the momentum was not sustained during the following decade. The 1930s witnessed a revival, at first through competition for markets and then the threat of another major war. Following the break-up of United Aircraft and Transport, where Boeing had enjoyed an advantage in orders from the corporation's airline, survival depended more than ever on winning military contracts. In both this and the civil field the need was to be ahead of the competition by offering advanced designs. Although successful in obtaining a contract from the Army for the Model 294, the giant XLRB-1 (alias Project A), this would not swell the company's funds significantly. Boeing's principals, more interested in production runs of substantial numbers of aircraft, looked to the likely future requirements of both the Army and Navy. The Navy, however, was unlikely to be interested in multi-engine aircraft, with which Boeing, through its recent designs (notably the Model 247 twin-engine airliner), had developed significant expertise. A replacement for the Army's main bomber force was the obvious target, and this had occupied much study time since Boeing's entry for the last design competition had lost out to the Martin B-10. The word from Wright Field was that another design competition would be issued later in 1934.

THE FIRST 134
The Army Air Corps bombers were for support of the land forces and the current-service Martin B-10 series were twin-engine, with a range of around 500 miles carrying a 2,000lb bomb load at a maximum speed of about 200mph. Engine power was the major factor in performance: the larger the airframe the heavier the load, so high speed and rate of climb were reduced. Streamlining to cut down drag helped, but if specified range and load requirements had to be met all competing manufacturers would come up with entries having a similar performance. The proven engines preferred by the Air Corps at this time were the Pratt & Whitney and Wright air-cooled radials, both makes developing 600–700hp. Seeking extra power, Boeing considered using four instead of two of these engines for a bomber development, with a parallel project for civil use having a passenger/freight-carrying fuselage. These ideas were given substance in design studies for the Models 299 and 300, the former military, the latter an airliner.

The design was given impetus by Boeing's receipt in August 1934 of Army Circular Proposal 35-356, the official solicitation. Submissions were invited for a multi-engine aircraft capable of flying 2,000 miles with a 2,000lb load at 200mph. Boeing's Chairman, Claire Egtvedt, made some discreet enquiries at Wright Field as to the meaning of the ambiguous term 'multi-engine' and was assured that this meant two or more. The way was clear for design work to begin in earnest, and in three weeks the basic drawings were available for review by the Boeing board. The design team under Egtvedt consisted of Project Engineer E. G. Emery, with E. C. Wells as his assistant, and a nine-man group of specialists. On 26 September 1934 the Board authorised $275,000 for the project—which was a sizeable part of the company's resources. As work progressed the Model 299 demanded a much larger investment, to a point where, if no order were to be forthcoming, Boeing's future would be in jeopardy.

In simple terms the Model 299 was to be a four-engine medium bomber with dimensions not significantly greater than those of a twin-engine model. The hoped-for advantage over its competitors would be in speed and range. As with every established manufacturer, the design engineers drew on previous proven structures, in this case a frame of square-sectioned spars with corrugated dural sheet covering inside the surface skin, main landing wheels that retracted into faired engine nacelles, welded wing fuel tanks and a monocoque frame-and-stringer fuselage. The designers incorporated recent advances in control by including wing flaps to aid take-off and landing and trim tabs on movable flight surfaces for fine adjustments. The comparatively recent controllable-pitch propeller allowed a low pitch setting to utilise full power and engine rpm for take-off and could be adjusted to a higher pitch for good flight characteristics. The main landing gear was retractable through mechanical movement and electric actuation. All crew positions were to be enclosed, the radial engines were to be smoothly cowled and a generally streamlined fuselage configuration was to be maintained.

Construction of the prototype began in December 1934 at the Duwamish river works. The fuselage was fabricated in four parts: the nose section forward of the cockpit, where gunner and bombardier were to be positioned; the main section holding the wing roots and containing the cockpit, with the standard Air Corps requirement for two pilot positions, provision for a navigator behind the pilots, a vertical-stack bomb bay and a radio operator's compartment; the section between the wing root trailing edge and the tail, which had three defensive positions; and the rear section to which the empennage was to be fixed. The four sections were then mated and the complete fuselage was transported to the hangar at Boeing Field (as the King County airport was known). Each wing was in two main sections, the inner containing the engine nacelles and fuel tanks. Taper pins held the wing sections together and the wings to the fuselage. The basic construction material was aluminium alloy, with flight surfaces fabric-covered for lighter control forces. The empennage had fabric-covered rudder and elevators over metal framing. Like the fuselage, these components were transported by barge and road to the hangar at Boeing Field for final assembly.

During the construction period several detail changes were made, the most significant being the adoption of the recently developed Hamilton Standard constant-speed propeller. Via a hydraulic governor, this automatically adjusted blade pitch to meet the engine setting and provided more efficient operation. Among other alterations, the tail wheel was made hydraulically retractable and the form of main wheel braking was improved. The engines selected were the latest Pratt & Whitney model Hornet 9-cylinder radials, each offering some 850hp for take-off. They were concealed in tight cowlings streamlined with the nacelles and fed by remote fuel pumps from welded aluminium tanks holding 1,700 US gallons. To meet the

MODEL 299: DESIGN AND PRODUCTION 13

military requirements the bomb bay could hold a 4,800lb maximum load, made up of four 600lb HE bombs placed each side of a narrow walkway. Emplacements for five hand-held machine guns for defence were situated in the nose and four blister-shaped structures covered the rear of the aircraft.

The assembly of the Model 299 was completed in July 1935 and the aircraft was wheeled out for display to the press and dignitaries on the 16th of that month. Boeing had by now invested more than 153,000 man-hours and over $400,000 of its reserves in this venture, with the knowledge that if no production order was forthcoming it could be in dire financial straits. Good publicity was needed, for while the Army adjudication at Wright Field would be decided by aviation engineers, trumpeting superlatives across the nation could do nothing but good for Boeing's image. And, that afternoon, Richard L. Williams, a journalist on the editorial staff of the *Seattle Times,* provided Boeing with the most telling comment that would eventually do much to make their latest design known both nationally and internationally. The copy that appeared in the following day's issue of the newspaper commented on the numerous gun positions and described the new bomber as a 'fifteen ton flying fortress'. A considerable degree of hyperbole resulted, but, this aside, the Model 299 was the first all-metal, four-engine, monoplane bomber in the world.

Engine and taxi trials conducted during the next few days highlighted a few problems, the most troubling being the oscillation of the tail wheel at high speeds. The shimmy was not easily rectified as the wheel still had to be steerable, and much time was expended in obtaining the correct amount of friction damping. The maiden flight was made on 28 July 1935, under a year since true design work had been commenced. Afterwards, when asked what it was like to fly such a large aircraft, Boeing test pilot Leslie R. Tower replied, 'Just like a little ship, only a little bigger'. Various adjustments and minor engineering work allowed only a total of 14 hours 15 minutes' flight time before the aircraft was sent to Wright Field on 20 August. The 2,100-mile flight there, taking 9 hours 3 minutes at an average speed of 233mph, earned more media kudos for the project in being a record. During the next few weeks tests went reasonably well, although there was an anxious time when one of the aircraft's engines had to be changed and a problem with power settings arose.

Overall, the Model 299's performance proved to be far superior in almost every respect to that of the two other entries. One was the Martin 146, a development of the Martin B-10 currently serving the Air Corps bombardment squadrons, and the other the Douglas DB-1, basically a bomber version of that company's very successful transport. Both types had similar performance and range, which in the case of top speed was 30mph slower than the Boeing's for the Martin and about 20mph for the Douglas. But it was in range that the Model 299 really excelled, being capable of more than 2,000 miles with a normal fuel load and double that of each competitor. There was no doubt which type impressed the Wright Field technicians and

Above: Typical wing structure.

Below: Pride of the Air Corps: Y1B-17 36-151, seen while assigned to the 49th Bombardment Squadron, 2nd Bombardment Group, in 1938. The most notable differences from the prototype were the Wright 1820 engines and the redesigned main landing gear, offering easier maintenance. The basic wing form was unchanged throughout the production of Model 299s—testament to its fundamentally sound design. (USAF)

those Air Corps officers imbued with the potential of bombing.

Then, on 30 October, came tragedy. With Major Ployer 'Pete' Hill, Chief of the Wright Field Flight Test Section, at the controls, the aircraft took off, immediately went into a steep climb, stalled at 200ft and crashed, despite last-minute efforts by the pilot to recover. Major Hill was killed and Leslie Tower, the Boeing test pilot who had made the first flight with the aircraft at Seattle, later died of injuries sustained. The co-pilot, Lieutenant Donald Putt, and two other men on board survived the burning wreck. The cause was established as the failure of the pilot to disengage the elevator locks which prevented damage from wind gusting when on the ground. The control was actuated by a lever in the cockpit and, ironically, was considered one of the good ideas introduced on the aircraft.

This was a black day for Boeing as it resulted in disqualification from the competition as there were still outstanding tests. However, the Air Corps leaders, apart from finding the B-299 (as it was identified in the Wright Field tests) by far the best bomber, were aware that aircraft manufacturers could not sustain the increasingly high development costs of a modern warplane knowing that elimination from a competitive trial would result in heavy loss on that particular project. But lobbying for Boeing and the B-299 was only partly successful in that the Army General Staff were inclined to follow the views of many in Congress that the funds appropriated should not be spent on expensive aircraft models if this reduced the strength in numbers. This could be seen as preference for quantity rather than quality, although the fact was that the Army hierarchy did not see any great need for extended range when any operations would be confined to support of the ground forces. Moreover, the Air Corps' advocates of a separate role for air power through the strategic use of the bomber would be encouraged by investment in an aircraft with the potential of the B-299.

The outcome of the evaluation could result in the purchase of up to 185 production units, and with the disqualification of the Boeing entry the Douglas DB-1 was considered the most worthy machine. The Air Corps made plain a preference for the Boeing and wanted a production order for 65 examples of an improved B-299 instead of a much larger number of the Douglas aircraft. The manufacturer's bids for 25 DB-1s was $99,150 each, against $196,730 each for a batch of 25 B-299s. The prices, less engines, submitted for production runs of 220 units were $58,500 each for the Douglas and $99,620 for the Boeing. As far as the Army

Top: The elaborate gun positions of the prototype were costly in man-hours to construct and wanting in both manipulation by and outlook for the gunners. (USAF)
Above: The Y1B-17 dispensed with the framing and gave better visibility by employing a Plexiglas moulding. Even so, swivelling the gun was cumbersome. (USAAF)

General Staff were concerned, they could have two Douglas bombers for every one Boeing, thus maintaining force strength, numbers being the yardstick. However, the lobby for the Boeing was sufficiently strong to persuade the Army hierarchy to allow an order for a small number of B-299s for further evaluation, and on 17 January 1937 an Army contract was awarded Boeing for fourteen, one of which was to be a static test airframe. Douglas received an order for 82, later increased to 133 B-18s, the Army designation for their DB-1.

The Boeing Model 229 was distinguished as the B-17, indicating the seventeenth bomber type in the form of designations in use by the Army Air Corps at that time. In the case of this initial order the aircraft were further identified as YB-17s, the 'Y' indicating a service test status, similarly to the 'X' prefix for an experimental prototype. There was no XB-17 as the unfortunate prototype was the property of Boeing and not the US government, although official literature would often refer to the aircraft by that designation. Before any of the YB-17s had been completed the designation was amended to Y1B-17, a piece of bureaucratic nonsense that had nothing to do with any changes to the aircraft or their employment but to the special funds used for their purchase.

The Y1B-17 was the Model 299B in the manufacturer's system. The major difference between this model and the prototype was the engines. The Pratt & Whitney Hornet had undergone a number of upgrades, and it was unlikely that further power increases could be obtained. The Wright Cyclone radial, also 9-cylinder but longer-stroked, currently offered higher power and had greater development potential. Both Boeing and Wright Field agreed that the Wright would be a better power unit for the Y1B-17, and all thirteen aircraft were delivered with the R-1820-39 version, rated at 930hp for take-off. The new engine improved all-round performance over

Above: The nose armament of a single .30-calibre Browning had a reasonable field of fire, if requiring the gunner to be something of a contortionist. The nose cone revolved and the gun cupola moved in azimuth, but far too slowly to meet a fast pass by a fighter. Britain's Air Vice-Marshal Harris commented in a report after inspecting a Y1B-17 that the contraption was 'More appropriately located in an amusement park than a war aeroplane'. This aircraft, being serviced at the 2nd Bombardment Group base on a morning in June 1937, shows the under-nose cut-in for the bombardier's position and the ungainly radio mast aft of the cockpit. (USAF)

the prototype, although this could partly be attributed to a better understanding of the relationship between the constant-speed propellers, the automatic fuel mixture controls and power settings. Among other changes was a new main landing gear. The prototype had a yoke-type structure supporting the oleos which functioned perfectly. The problem had been wheel changing, which entailed the removal of the axle while jacking under the wing—a difficult and lengthy procedure. The redesign featured a stub axle which allowed much easier servicing.

There were a number of detail changes, notably revised wing fuel tankage and rubber de-icer boots on the leading edges of the flight surfaces. Visually the Y1B-17 and its forebear were very similar, the most notable differences being the long carburettor air scoops on the top of the engine nacelles and gun 'blisters' less encumbered with framing to provide better visibility for gunners. The armament remained the same and was normally a .30 Browning in the nose and under positions and .50 calibre Brownings in the remainder. The fields of fire and manoeuvrability of the weapons in these enclosed cupolas were subject to some criticism, and Wright Field carried out experimental work on improvements.

The first flight of a Y1B-17 took place on 2 December 1936 and all thirteen aircraft were delivered to the Army Air Corps between January and August 1937. One was retained by Wright Field for experimental work and the others were assigned to the 2nd Bombardment Group at Langley Field, Virginia, the Air Corps' premier bombing formation and part of the General Headquarters Air Force, a command charged with rapid response to an emergency. It was in this command that the major enthusiasts of the quest for a means to prove air power were to be found, if their voices were muted. The Y1B-17 was just the tool for establishing the trade in which they believed, and over the next two years every effort was made to highlight the potential of the 'Flying Fortress', albeit as a far-ranging bomber to defend America's shores. During those two years the 2nd Bomb Group's twelve Y1B-17s flew 9,293 hours, covering 1,800,000 miles without serious mishap. Various records were set for speed and distance, including goodwill endurance flights to faraway South American countries. A friendly interception of the Italian liner *Rex* out in the Atlantic received a good amount of attention from United States' news media but irritated the US Navy, whose admirals considered the oceans their exclusive province. Their voices were added to those of the politicians, who objected to the big bombers for either financial or isolationist policy reasons.

Although the GHQ Air Force 'strongly recommended' that only B-17s be procured, it was not to get its way. In April 1937 the chairman of the Appropriations Sub-Committee, which handled War Department estimates, put on record that he deplored the unwise tendency of the Air Corps to demand larger and more expensive bombers such as the B-17. In the face of governmental criticism the 1937 expenditure on new bomber aircraft was for 177 improved Douglas B-18s and nothing for the nimble Boeing, on which the Materiel Division annual report commented, 'the exceedingly interesting military possibilities of this type reported last year have been well demonstrated.'

Behind the scenes, the Air Corps' enthusiasts for a strategic bombing doctrine were interested in putting the bomber at a higher altitude, where the lower air density would provide less drag on an airframe and higher speeds could be obtained. Another advantage would be a degree of safety for the bomber in being further removed from any anti-aircraft artillery fire encountered. Indeed, as the Y1B-17s were faster than the current pursuit types in the fighter squadrons, there was also the possibility that at high altitude enemy fighters might have difficulty intercepting. Much work had been done by Wright Field on the three main technical advances to make this possible—engine supercharging to get an aircraft into the sub-stratosphere, oxygen supply and regulation for the crews they carried, and a precision bomb sight for accurate strikes from such altitudes.

It was not surprising that Air Corps interest in high-altitude operations was soon directed to the potential of the four-engine Boeing, and while the YB-17s were still under construction arrangements were made with the manufacturer to complete the static test airframe as a flight test-bed for a turbo-supercharged version. Negotiations on the additional finance for this aircraft were fraught, particularly when the whole turbo-supercharger set-up had to be reworked. Boeing were to suffer a substantial loss on this venture due to the intransigence of the Air Corps Materiel Division over the matter of extra funding.

Given the Army designation Y1B-17A, Boeing's project Model 299F received a contract in May 1937 for construction to proceed, but various problems and changes delayed completion and the first flight, in April 1938, was more than three months behind schedule. In simple terms, a turbo-supercharger utilises the exhaust gases of an engine to drive a turbine which feeds a compressed volume of air to the engine. In the rarefied air at high altitudes an internal combustion engine would be unable to develop full power without supercharged air. The turbo-supercharger units, made by General Electric, were installed above the wing at the rear of the engine nacelles at the exhaust exits. As the units could not be buried in the wing they were housed in faired, 1ft high shrouds. Not only did this spoil the neat lines of engine nacelles in flight, but severe air flow turbulence was produced, causing vibration every time the turbos were engaged. The solution was to re-route the exhausts to the underside of the nacelles, where the turbo units could be successfully 'buried'. The revised supercharger arrangement was first flown in October 1938, but it took several weeks of modification and adjustment to perfect. Eventually the Y1B-17A was able to climb to over 35,000ft and achieve its top speed, 295mph, at 25,000ft; this was some 40mph faster at nearly twice the height of the Y1B-17. A practical demonstration of the aircraft's capability was the July 1939 flight from Los Angeles to New York, which Major Stanley Umstead, Chief of the Materiel Division Flying Branch, made in 9 hours, 14 minutes and 30 seconds at 26,000ft, averaging 265mph.

The results of the Y1B-17A tests heightened GHQ Air Force's enthusiasm for the potential of high-altitude bombing, and the addition of turbo-supercharging to new B-17 production models was approved. However, because of budgetary and political restraints, further B-17s were a long time arriving. The name of the game in successful military air-

Right: Visually, the most notable difference between the B-17B and the Y1B-17 concerned the nose. The deficiencies of the ungainly gun emplacement had been recognised and it had been replaced by a contoured structure in which the bombardier also acted as a gunner, using a .30-calibre weapon through a socket in the upper right side of the Plexiglas framing. The B-17B's main feature was engine turbo-supercharging, giving excellent high-altitude performance. These units, placed under the nacelles, required a rearrangement of the engine exhausts, which, on the inboard engines, were passed along the outboard sides to avoid the landing gear well. This is the command B-17B of the 19th BG at March Field, California, in November 1940. (USAAF)

Below: A Y1B-17 exhibiting the distinctive tailplane shape of the early Flying Fortresses, incorporating flight trimming tabs, which became a feature of most US warplanes during the following decade. Boeing claimed to have introduced this design feature. (USAF)
Bottom: The Y1B-17A at Wright Field following the repositioning of the engine turbo-supercharger. (Air Force Museum)

MODEL 299: DESIGN AND PRODUCTION

craft manufacture was advancement, and while the YB-17s were under construction Boeing engineers were working on improved designs for the hoped-for ensuing production model. This started out as the 299E, but despite an Air Corps specification that could only be met in competition by a four-engine bomber, as mentioned earlier, no B-17s were ordered during the fiscal year 1937 (which ran from 1 July to 30 June), the Army General Staff preferring more Douglas B-18 variants—177 of which were ordered. Not until August 1937 was the Air Corps Materiel Divison persuaded to issue a contract for ten production aircraft, to be designated B-17B.

By this time so many changes had been made to the original Boeing Model 299E submission that in its final form the design was re-designated 299M. The most significant change was the addition of turbo-superchargers, even though these had yet to be satisfactorily proved on the Y1B-17A. Other changes were a larger rudder for better directional control at altitude, and a new nosepiece, the bulbous turret structure being replaced with a nicely faired arrangement enhancing the type's elegance. The navigator's room in the Y1B-17 proved too remote for visual navigating and this crew member was repositioned in the nose, at a work table to the rear on the left side. Frontal defence was afforded by a flexible socket fitting in the upper right side of the nosepiece framing to take a .30 machine gun. Further to improve defence, a transparent bubble moulding in the top of the flight compartment at the rear was for use in fire control by an observer, there being two seats for additional crewmen or an aircraft commander aft of the pilots. Although the wing dimensions and structure remained the same, the inner section with the engine nacelles was extended, providing more room for turbo-supercharger intercooler fittings and allowing longer flaps to aid take-off and landing runs. Hydraulics were substituted for the more temperamental pneumatic actuation of the brakes on previous models. All B-17Bs and following Boeing-produced B-17s were built at the new Boeing Field factory, which became known as Plant 2.

The B-17B order was soon raised to thirteen, the number of aircraft considered necessary to equip and maintain a squadron. Before the first aircraft was completed two further increases of thirteen were funded, for a total of 39. To some extent this purchase reflected a concern in both the US military and the US government about developments in Europe, where the threat of the bomber dominated in war fears. While any talk of using long-range bombers for offensive purposes was still taboo, more people in authority were coming round to the view that the type should be on the inventory. A few weeks following the final addition to the contract, the Munich Crisis of September 1938 had a profound effect on American foreign policy, President Roosevelt making quite clear his disquiet about Nazi activities and the need to strengthen the nation's armed forces. Boeing, eager to capitalise on securing the resulting orders, had earlier recalled the newspaperman's description of the Model 299 and on 26 April 1938 copyrighted the name 'Flying Fortress' for use in further publicity.

The B-17Bs were delivered between October 1939 and March 1940. Despite being a

Below: The B-17C had more practical, flush gun emplacements, the fuselage blisters being replaced by removable windows, giving the gunner a better view and greater freedom of movement. The forward part of the 'waist window' had an extendable wind deflector. The under gunner was also given more room, with an extended bathtub-like emplacement, although the field of fire was still restricted to an area below the tail. Additional ball-and-socket fixtures were placed in the nose—in the upper left side and lower right of the bombardier's Plexiglas, the centre left-hand side window and the front right-hand side window. The two side window fixtures were for the use of the navigator. Wright Field retained B-17B 38-211 to develop improved defensive positions, but, apart from extra nose gun sockets and changes in the waist gun positions, it appeared little different from a B-17C. (USAAF)

Left, upper: A programme of camouflage finish—olive drab upper and grey lower surfaces—was introduced in 1941 for US Army combat aircraft, as on this B-17C of the 7th Bomb Group dropping practice bombs 'in train'. The large swing-open bomb bay doors were drag-inducing, and, though there were experiments with other types, these were never introduced into production. The 'bathtub' under gun emplacement shows well in this photograph. (USAAF)

Left, lower: The twenty B-17Cs withdrawn from USAAC service for supply to Britain were delayed awaiting the installation of bladder-type self-sealing fuel tanks. The 'silver' finish was short-lived as a coat of water-soluble olive paint was applied before their transatlantic ferry flights. AN528, seen here over the north-western United States with the incorrect identification AM528, was destroyed on the ground in England in July 1941 as the result of an engine fire. (USAAF)

near-$1m dollar contract, Boeing actually incurred a loss on the overall programme. Fortunately, by the time all these sums were done the company had secured orders that firmly established its financial position. With the Roosevelt administration's encouragement of military and naval expansion, the Army Air Corps was given a major role and the hierarchy's opposition to big bombers diminished. In March 1939 the Army issued a tender for up to 250 four-engine bombers and in September, while Hitler's forces had been subjugating Poland, Boeing received a contract for 38 B-17Cs, improved versions of the B-17B. With further appropriations the contract was changed in March 1940 to increase the order to 80 aircraft. Contract changes frequently diminished Boeing's profit on a project through Air Corps Materiel Command's frugality over such amendments, and the B-17C proved to be yet another example.

The B-17C started out as Boeing's Model 229H design study, specifically aimed at improving the defensive armament. The teardrop-shaped gun cupolas had been found to have restrictive fields of fire. These structures on the fuselage top and sides were eliminated and in their place removable windows allowed post-mounted machine guns more flexibility. The lower teardrop was replaced with a longer structure, likened to a bath tub, which allowed a kneeling gunner to operate a Browning against low attack from the rear. All guns were now the heavier .50in calibre Brownings, excepting the .30 nose weapon for which two more sockets were added in the framing so that the bombardier could reposition the gun to increase his field of fire. The two rear fuselage side positions—which became known as 'waist windows'—and the underside emplacement were provided with

MODEL 299: DESIGN AND PRODUCTION

Above: RAF Fortress I AN518 was handed back to the USAAF in India in 1942 to become B-17C 40-2079 again. Photographed here while in the Middle East and serving with No 220 Squadron, it had at times conducted solo combat sorties at between 30,000 and 35,000ft.

a small amount of armour plate for the gunners' protection.

There were several detail changes to fuel, electrical and oxygen systems and further brake improvements. The B-17C also had upgraded Cyclone engines and improved turbo-superchargers, raising the high-altitude top speed to well over 300mph, one service test putting the maximum as 323mph. Difficulty had been encountered in the B-17Bs with supercharger failure due to inadequate lubrication, all units having to be replaced early in 1940. The replacements raised the B-17B's performance, but there is no doubt that the B-17C's improvement in that respect also resulted from the reduced drag occasioned by the removal of gun cupolas. Deliveries were made between August and November 1940, but owing to the volume of additional changes required on the last 42 aircraft of the contract the Air Corps bestowed a new designation, B-17D, although the Boeing model identity remained the same. The principal difference between the B-17C and B-17D was the latter's non-metallic, self-sealing fuel tanks, a fixture already proved essential by British and German bombers in combat over Europe. Made by Goodrich, the rubber-compound bladder tanks could quickly seal a bullet or shell splinter hole.

There were more than thirty detail changes on the B-17D, mostly to fuel, oxygen and electrical systems. A greater demand for electrical power brought a change from 12 to 24 volts, with greater reliability. High-altitude flight with the B-17B had highlighted engine cooling difficulties in some situations, so another feature of the B-17D was the introduction of adjustable flaps round the rear of the engine cowling. These also provided one of the chief visual differences in distinguishing the B-17D from the C model. Another difference was the deletion of the fuselage camera window just aft of and below the rear of the wing root. With more attention to combat capability, rear defence was increased by placing two .50-calibre machine guns in both the under emplacement and the radio compartment position. While this may have made the B-17 more qualified for its popular name, the fields of fire from both these positions left much to be desired. Suitable power-operated turrets were under development by Sperry, but these were still some way from production. B-17D deliveries were made between February and May 1941 and, with a few B-17Cs returned to the factory for the installation of self-sealing tanks and other modifications to D model standard, were equipping new heavy bombardment squadrons.

From the spring of 1940 the British and French were involved in heavy investment in the USA for war materials, notably aircraft. The French were soon out of the picture, their contracts being taken up by the British, including one for 140 Douglas DB-7 light bombers which Boeing would build under licence. Anxious to obtain any worthy US warplane, the British showed interest in the B-17 and, although they were critical of its small bomb load and defensive armament, if made available it could be usefully employed. With a British order in mind, Boeing had explored the RAF's requirements under a design study labelled Model 299U. However, the Army Air Corps, soon to be the Army Air Forces, had no intention of losing production aircraft to a foreign power when it was intent on building its own force of heavy bombers. Here national politics entered the picture. Through Boeing's and the Air Corps' persistent courtship of the news media for their own purposes, the Flying Fortress was well known abroad as the bright star in America's air arsenal. The British, eager to draw on United States aid, were appreciative that by committing this type to battle good publicity could ensue in America. Similarly the Roosevelt administration, keen to justify the enormous investment being made in the nation's air arms, saw the use of the Flying Fortress by the British as a useful means to this end. The rhetoric of generals and other enthusiasts aside, the Air Corps were doubtful as to how the current model B-17 would fare against modern fighters such as the British and Germans had in service. Nevertheless, twenty B-17Cs were released for sale to Britain, where the type was to be known as the Fortress Mk I.

Below: Externally, the B-17D was distinguished from the B-17C by engine cowling flaps. However, many B-17Cs later received such flaps as a modification. Basically the same model, the D was more war-worthy, with both protective and defensive improvements, but the type was nearing the limit of such development. The nose ball-and-socket fittings providing alternative positions for the bombardier's .30-calibre machine gun are prominent in this photograph taken in Hawaii in March 1942. (USAAF)

Top: Boeing modified B-17C 40-2042 to take a Sperry upper turret in developing the installation for the B-17E, where it was placed further aft on the flight deck. This experimental aircraft had the under gun position removed with the intention of having a Bendix remotely controlled power turret installed. (PA of Canada)

Above: First of the big-tail Fortresses, 41-2393, the prototype B-17E, made its maiden flight on 6 September 1941 in bare metal finish. The bulkhead join at Station 6 can be clearly seen at the trailing edge of the wing root. Apart from the Sperry turret, the forward part of the aircraft was basically as the B-17D. (Boeing)

The RAF required certain changes, in particular the installation of Goodrich self-sealing fuel tanks. As these were still in short supply and being used in B-17D production which could not be disrupted, the twenty B-17s withdrawn from the Army Air Corps were returned to Boeing and put in temporary storage at McChord Field, Tacoma, Washington, until modifications could be accomplished. As the Norden bomb sight and autopilot was not released by the US Navy, similar Sperry equipment was substituted, most of this work being carried out at McClellan Field, near Sacramento, California. These and other minor modifications delayed the aircraft's delivery to Britain until April and May 1941. Before their transatlantic flights a coat of water-based olive green paint was applied to the bare metal finish, being replaced in the UK by the appropriate RAF camouflage scheme for high-altitude daylight operations.

The US Army Air Corps' doctrine of high-altitude precision attack had been developed primarily with the B-17. Basically, it involved a force of bombers in close formation operating at an optimum 20,000–25,000ft, the formation helping to mass defensive fire against any attacker. Having seen that operating its medium and heavy bombers in daylight brought prohibitive losses, RAF Bomber Command had turned its main force to night raids. Operational analysts considered B-17 formations no more likely to survive, particularly as their defensive armament was considered poor. Where the RAF thought the Fortress might succeed was at the then very high altitudes it could achieve: if operational flight could be sustained at 35,000ft, the Fortress would be above anti-aircraft artillery fire and enemy interceptors would probably have great difficulty reaching it. Close formations were thought impractical at this altitude, apart from there being insufficient aircraft in operational condition. The brief RAF combat use of the Fortress between July and October 1941 achieved little apart from valuable information on operating the type in a high-altitude European environment. Although *Luftwaffe* fighters did make successful interceptions, these all occurred at under 30,000ft. When the B-17s were able to maintain altitudes above this level they evaded interception, the chief obstacle to achieving the desired altitudes being engine problems—noticeably severe oil loss through the breathers. Gun freezing had also been a problem, and the Sperry precision bomb sight was not up to accurate attack from over 30,000ft. The surviving Fortress Is were split between RAF Coastal Command for sea-search duties and a small bombing contingent in the Middle East. The latter moved to India, and one surviving Fortress I was eventually returned to the USAAF.

BIG ASS BIRDS

By the spring of 1940 Boeing designers were aware that the Model 299 was reaching the end of viable development as a combat aircraft without radical changes in its configuration. A new design for a 'super bomber' had been proposed and was under consideration by Army Air Corps agencies, but even if accepted and put under contract it would require at least two years to get into production. With the possibility of the United States becoming involved in hostilities and requiring heavy bombers in a hurry, the only model on a production line was the B-17.

There had been a number of basic design studies on Model 299 variants, including one with a tricycle landing gear and another featuring power-operated gun turrets. The most criticised aspects of the B-17 were the small bomb load and its defensive armament. Nothing could be done about the internally carried bomb load because of the limitations of the bomb bay, designed to the Air Corps standard specification at the time of the original Model 299 conception. Defensive armament had been subject to continual improvement, but there was little scope to take this further. The British claimed that a power-operated gun turret behind the tail was essential for bomber defence and such could not be installed in the current fuselage. Such a heavy item would adversely affect the centre of gravity unless a completely new fuselage were designed, which was not a practical proposition in view of production-line tooling and other factors. Instead the Boeing designers concentrated on the rear fuselage aft of the wing trailing edge which, apart from the tail wheel unit and being a conduit for tail flight controls, was comparatively uncomplicated.

The new rear fuselage was cylindrical with moderate taper, allowing room for a hand-held gun position aft of the tail. The side gun 'waist' positions were retained and given a rectangular shape both to improve outlook and to simplify production. To obtain the best all-round field of fire the Sperry twin-gun power turret which was to be utilised had to be placed at the rear of the raised flight deck above the area previously occupied by additional crew seating. Anticipating that the turret would create turbulence, and also to improve directional stability at altitude which had proved wanting in the B-17B, a long, faired fin was employed. This feature led to the new model being irreverently referred to as 'the big ass bird' when it first appeared on USAAF airfields.

The Model 300 version of the 299 had eventually entered production as the Model 307, still virtually a 299 with an airliner fuselage. To advance airline travel the passenger cabin was pressurised for high-altitude flight, where inclement weather was less likely to be encountered. The bulbous fuselage necessary to encompass 33 passengers and five crew members had a diameter some 4ft greater than the B-17's and was found to give an air flow pattern which made the aircraft difficult to trim for smooth flight. The solution was an extension of the fin along the top of the fuselage, and this feature was utilised again on the 299, employing parts of the same specially designed structure. To counter movement of the centre of gravity aft and improve the B-17's longitudinal stability, the span of the tailplane was increased by approximately 10ft. In place of the 'bath tub' underfuselage position the design would incorporate a periscope-sighted, remote-controlled, two-gun turret under development by Bendix. The new model would boast an armament of nine or ten machine guns to become a true 'flying fortress'.

The usual Materiel Division procrastination and cost deliberations denied Boeing a contract until August 1940. When it came it was for 277 aircraft. Then, just over two weeks later, another 235 were added for an all-up order of 512. In view of the radical redesign a new Army designation was justified, but as Boeing distinguished it as a Model 299-O the Army kept with B-17, making it the E model. The stimulation of the United States' aviation industry by Britain and France and the nation's own rearmament programme brought production delays in raw materials and components during 1940–41, the first B-17E being delivered 150 days late. Following the Japanese attack on the Hawaiian bases and Germany's declaration of war, America's giant industrial capacity was soon getting into its stride. With fewer bottlenecks in production and a reduction in man-hours per airframe, the last of the 512 B-17Es was delivered in late May 1942, nearly 50 days ahead of schedule.

Forty-five B-17Es were offset to Britain under Lend-Lease arrangements and were used principally by RAF Coastal Command in the anti-U-boat war. Like all previous models, the E was subject to detail changes during the production run, the most significant being the introduction of the Sperry-manned under turret in place of the remote-control Bendix from B-17E 41-2505 onwards. The Bendix, periscope-sighted from a small transparent 'blister' to the rear of the turret, had been found impractical, the gunner having great difficulty in locating his target. The ingenious manned turret, popularly known as 'the ball', demanded a cramped position for the gunner but it proved highly effective in combat.

The B-17E was first flown in September 1941. In the matter of performance, it was, being heavier than the D model and because of the drag of the turrets, slower both in climb and top speed. Its high-altitude handling was better, although the service ceiling—that point where climb rate falls off to below 100ft a minute—was reduced. Later, in November 1942, a B-17E in which pressure breathing equipment was tested climbed to 42,900ft.

With the prospect of hostilities, the order book situation went from one extreme to the other, finance was no longer an obstacle and the Army Air Corps wanted all the B-17s it could get. With Boeing fully committed, the US government looked for production capacity with other manufacturers and was successful in persuading Lockheed Vega and Douglas to licence-build the B-17E. To unify activities a coordinating committee was estab-

Top: The Sperry top turret as fitted on the B-17E was squat and included metal panels that obscured the gunner's view. The nose section armament remained as with the C and D models. Both left and right side window ball-and-socket fixtures show in this photograph of 41-2600 serving as a trainer at Ephrata, Washington. (Boeing)

Above: The Bendix remote-control under turret was operated by a gunner lying prone to its rear and sighting on a target through a system using mirrors housed in the small transparent blister. Two low slit windows were provided on both sides of the fuselage for outlook. The arrangement was found impractical, chiefly because of the gunner's difficulty in locating a fast-moving target. Despite claims, it is doubtful if a Japanese fighter was ever hit by fire from this installation on any of the B-17Es that saw combat in the SWPA or Central Pacific area. The aircraft depicted served with the 7th Bomb Group and was photographed in India. (E. Walker)

Top left: The Sperry 'ball turret' was cramped but very effective when in the control of an accomplished gunner. It was, however, not for the squeamish as a parachute could not normally be worn by the gunner and time-consuming entry and exit were made via the fuselage when airborne. The .50 calibre gun barrels have been removed from their blast tubes on the turret in the photograph. The reflector gun sight is above and behind the man examining the bullet-proof glass panel, a modification made on UK-based B-17s. (USAAF)

Top right: One of the reasons for the redesign of the rear end of the Fortress was to provide a tail gun position, considered essential for the defence of all heavy bombers. Popularly known as the 'tail stinger', the twin .50 guns were manually operated and aimed with a ring-and-bead sight, seen outside the gunner's rear window, linked to the movement of the weapons. The guns had 30 degrees of movement in both elevation and depression, and 30 degrees to both left and right in azimuth. The normal ammunition provision was 500 rounds per gun. (USAAF)

Above left: Waist gun windows on the B-17E were rectangular with a retractable wind deflector. The gun could be swung in when not in use, and the window closed with a sliding cover. The gun in the photograph has an armour plate section attached, but this was soon dispensed with as it added to the difficulty of handling this heavy weapon. (Flight)

Above right: Two gunners demonstrating waist window armament and showing how they tended to get in each other's way. The ammunition was originally fed from cans holding only 500 rounds, but this aircraft has been modified to have trace feed. (USAAF)

Below: B-17Es sent to the UK in the summer of 1942 had .50-calibre nose side window guns installed at the Cheyenne modification centre, and these became a feature on most B-17s sent to combat areas. B-17E 41-9045 also has an additional ball-and-socket higher in the nose to keep the .30 gun further away from the bomb sight. (USAAF)

MODEL 299: DESIGN AND PRODUCTION

Above left: The interior of a B-17E nose, showing .50 guns high right and high left and a .30 gun in the lower right ball-and-socket, with the other ball-and-socket fittings stuffed with paper to stop draughts. The covered bomb sight is beyond the bombardier's seat, and the operating panel for bomb selection etc. is on the left. (*The Aeroplane*)

Above right: Liquid-cooled Allison engines powered the XB-38, ex-B-17E 41-2401.

Below: The B-17F was the designation of the standard Boeing Model 299-O built by three plants. The R-1820-97 engines introduced with this version gave improved high-altitude performance. The chief visual difference from the B-17E was the frameless Plexiglas nosepiece, as seen on this Boeing-built F serving with the 99th Bomb Group in 1943.(USAF)

lished in May 1941 which became known as BVD, the initials of the three manufacturers.

Influential advocates of liquid-cooled engines persuaded Wright Field procurement officers to investigate these powerplants as a means of improving B-17 performance. Apparently Boeing were not enthusiastic about this and the work was conducted by Lockheed Vega on B-17E 41-2401 that had been received for sample analysis during the tool-up for production at Burbank. The Wright Cyclones were replaced by four Allison V-1710-89, twelve-cylinder engines rated at 1,425hp, driving 12ft 1in diameter propellers, 7in greater than those on the radials. Engine mounts were redesigned and the coolant radiators placed in the leading edge of the wings between the two nacelles. The oil coolers, removed to effect this installation, were then placed low in the engine nacelles with appropriate cooling air ducting. The work was conducted largely by Lockheed engineers who had experience with these engines and assessories in the P-38 fighter. In line with USAAF policy on major engine changes, the aircraft was given a completely new designation, XB-38. Although beautifully streamlined, it weighed a ton more than when fitted with radial engines and performance was not as good as anticipated in the few hours experienced before an in-flight engine fire terminated the aircraft's existence. The cause was believed to be exhaust flame leakage in the conduit which had previously been subject to modifications. Two additional aircraft ordered with Allisons were cancelled when no great advantage could be seen in this engine change.

By the time Lockheed Vega and Douglas had tooled up for production the B-17E had been superseded by the F model. The B-17F was the designation for the standard model built by three factories, incorporating the same detail changes initiated for the B-17E. Visually the only major difference between the E and the F was the moulded nose piece without the bracing of the former. From an operational viewpoint the chief advantage of the F over the E was the improved Wright Cyclones, which provided greater maximum horsepower at the optimum combat altitude, 25,000ft, where 325mph by a test aircraft made this the fastest of all production Fortresses. Among many detail changes were important improvements in armament, with ammunition trace feed in place of containers, and additional armour protection for crew members and engines, all of which increased weight. In fact, from the 27,500lb of the unladen B-17D and the 32,250lb for the B-17E, the B-17F's additions took the total up to 34,000lb. A full load could add another ten tons, with the given limit 56,500lb, although

THE B-17 FLYING FORTRESS STORY

Above: A Douglas-built B-17F-60-DL prepares to take off from Framlingham, England, in October 1943. It has the standard nose and side window installations and the high-dome Sperry upper turret. Main wheel cover discs were dispensed with as unnecessary weight. (USAAF)

in practice combat loads would often increase this figure by another 10,000lb.

Contractual agreements for the B-17E were converted to the F model, of which 3,735 were produced between May 1942 and September 1943. Of these, 1,105 came from the two California plants, 605 from Douglas at Long Beach and 500 from Lockheed at Burbank. Both took some time to get into full production, the first B-17F from Long Beach requiring 100,000 man-hours of direct labour. The BVD pool had more than its share of problems with the time-consuming and often frustrating effort put into coordination of product details. The changes introduced at one factory could, for varying reasons, not be introduced at another at the same time. While changes were notified in technical publications with the serial numbers of the aircraft to which they applied, it was felt that more precise model identities, acknowledging differences, would be helpful. Each run of production aircraft incorporating the same specified changes would be identified by a block number. This would increase by units of five, the numbers in between being left for use by service organisations making required modifications at later dates.

In the case of B-17s, the model block number from one factory did not indicate that aircraft with the same block number from another factory were identical. To emphasis this point, a two-letter factory code was used as a suffix. The first Boeing-built B-17F was identified as a B-17F-1-BO and the first from Douglas and Vega as a B-17F-1-DL and a B-17F-1-VE, but they differed in respect of item changes. There were 27 different B-17F change blocks from Seattle, seventeen for the Douglas model and eleven with Vega during the course of production. The three plants used prefabricated sub-sections from the Boeing Wichita factory and other contractors but, despite using the same drawings and engineering data, each had its own methods of assembly and inevitably some minor differences arose between what were otherwise supposedly identical airframes. Douglas-built B-17s had strengthened main wing sections. Vega production had a similar wing section and reinforcement of the fuselage. AAF engineering officers claimed that in addition to being heavier and bringing a slight change in flight attitude, the Vega B-17Fs suffered from stress constrictions where two sections of the fuselage were joined at the radio room. The wings from Douglas or Vega B-17s would not fit a Boeing-built aircraft due to the former two having been built in a higher-temperature environment. The Douglas and Vega products also cost more, approximately an additional $37,000 and $27,000 per aircraft respectively.

From an operational standpoint the most important change made during B-17F production was an increase in fuel capacity from 1,730 to 2,810 US gallons. This was made possible by inserting nine bladder fuel cells in each wing outboard of the engines. Popularly known as 'Tokyo Tanks', they allowed

Right, upper: The second B-17F, 41-24341, was used by Lockheed Vega for conversion to the XB-40 bomber escort gun platform prototype. It is shown here shortly after completion. The main increase in armament was amidships, with twin waist guns each side and a Martin power turret in the former radio room gun hatch position. The XB-40 was later modified to have the fuselage decking forward of the Martin turret reduced to allow the guns full traverse, and the ball turret was no longer partly retractable. (Boeing)

Right, lower: The first batch of YB-40s had other refinements. These were Vega B-17Fs, but the modification work was carried out by Douglas at their Tulsa plant. (Boeing)

range to be extended by almost 1,000 miles under some combat conditions. Tokyo Tanks were installed with the B-17F-80-BO at Seattle, B-17F-25-DL at Long Beach and B-17F-30-VE at Burbank. Among many other changes incorporated in production B-17Fs was the installation of a gun position on either side of the nose for frontal defence. Staggered right forward, left back, the .50-calibre Brownings were for use by the navigator and bombardier respectively. These gun positions had previously only been installed on earlier production B-17s at modification centres. They appeared on Seattle-production Fortresses with the B-17F-55-BO, at Long Beach with the B-17F-15-DL and at Burbank with the B-17F-25-VE.

The side guns in the nose did not rectify the poor frontal defence of the Fortress, which was eventually met by the so-called chin turret. A Bendix remote-controlled two gun unit, this was located under the nose directly aft of the bombardier's Plexiglas. The computing sight was suspended at the top of this nosepiece and the turret movement controls and gun firing trigger were attached to a column support that could be folded to stow on the right. Spoiling the clean nose lines of the Fortress, the turret was a significant enough feature for the Army Air Forces to bestow a new model designation, B-17G, although, because no new contractual agreements were involved, Boeing still chose to consider this development just one more detail change to what as far as they were concerned was still the Model 299-O. However, the chin turret had made its début on an earlier B-17 variant.

The persistent belief that a large, tight formation of B-17s could fight off the most persistent fighter opposition led to proposals for a very heavily armed and armoured version to be used as an escort. By placing these aircraft, which would carry no bomb load, in the most exposed positions of a formation it was assumed that they could afford substantial protection to the bombers. Conversion work, carried out by Lockheed Vega, started in July 1942 using the second Boeing-built B-17F as the prototype. This was designated the XB-40, even though the aircraft would not be used in a bombing role. The 'chin turret' was a development of the remote-control ventral turret that had been tried on the early B-17Es. In place of the radio-room hand-held .50-calibre weapon a two-gun Martin power turret, similar to that used on B-26 Marauders, was placed in this position. The waist window positions were each given twin guns, to make the total number fourteen, all .50-calibre. Ammunition was increased threefold over the standard B-17, the bomb bay being used as a central store for a stated 11,135 rounds. Conversion work took four months, and after Wright Field approval a batch of thirteen test models was ordered under the designation YB-40. Because Vega B-17Fs had yet to incorporate some of the latest production changes these were used for the conversions which were carried out by Douglas at their Tulsa, Oklahoma, plant.

The work was completed by the end of April 1943 with several improvements on the prototype. The waist window on the right side

Below: The Bendix 'chin turret' as finally configured for the B-17 first appeared on the XB-40 and was controlled and sighted remotely by a gunner in what was the bombardier's position in standard Fortresses. The chin turret was a planned feature for all B-17s, but there were development problems to overcome before this became standard. (Boeing)

Above: The final production and most numerous Fortress model, the B-17G, was distinguished by the so-called 'chin turret'. This B-17G-1-BO also shows bare metal leading edges where rubber de-icing boots have been removed, the location of the supercharger turbines, the wing intakes for intercooler air, and the fuel booster pump and drain cock blister shields. (USAAF)

of the fuselage was moved forward to give gunners more room, and the twin gun mounts for both waist positions and the tail 'turret' had hydraulic boost for easier manipulation. To give the second top turret a better field of fire, the fuselage decking forward of its location was reduced. Formed into a special squadron, the YB-40s were sent to England in May 1943 where 'cheek' gun positions were added in the noses to make the total weaponry sixteen .50-calibre Brownings. Ten more conversions to YB-40s were put in hand at Tulsa; three with improved turrets were sent to the UK for evaluation but were never used in combat.

The YB-40 project was a failure. Despite careful weight distribution within the aircraft the centre of gravity moved aft, creating control difficulties. Once the B-17 formation had released its bombs the YB-40, still laden with ammunition, struggled to keep up and often failed, being 4,000lb heavier than a standard B-17F even when empty. In any case, by the summer of 1943 the USAAF advocates of 'go it alone bombers' had reluctantly to accept that a large, comparatively slow aircraft with .50-calibre machine guns was no match for a small interceptor fighter with heavy cannon. A sluggish YB-40 was probably less able to survive in a hostile environment than a conventional Fortress.

The Bendix chin turret had its teething troubles but was recognised as the answer to the complaint of combat commanders about inadequate frontal defence. However, it was August 1943 before the chin turret could be introduced on production lines, Douglas being the first. In fact, 80 aircraft left the factory as B-17F-80-DLs before the G model designation was finalised, later to be re-marked as B-17G-DLs. All told, 8,680 B-17Gs were manufactured between September 1943 and July 1945, when all production was finally terminated. There was no lessening of block changes, with 23 at Boeing and Lockheed Vega and 20 at Douglas.

The chin turret was not the only YB-40 feature that found its way to the B-17G. A few months into production staggered waist gun windows were introduced in answer to a complaint, first registered nearly two years before, that gunners got in each other's way when swinging their weapons. A further complaint about the exposure experienced by gunners at these open stations was also met, with Plexiglas encasing and special gun mounts that preserved the field of fire. With the introduction of the chin turret the two 'cheek' guns were eliminated from production. However, both the Eighth and Fifteenth Air Forces in Europe had these fitted at modification centres and requested reintroduction at the factory. The radio-room gun was given an improved field of fire in January 1944 by an enclosed hood with a K-5 mount that allowed 90 degrees' movement of the gun in zenith. A further improvement to armament was a revised tail gun emplacement originally developed at the B-17 Modification Centre at Cheyenne, Wyoming. The so-called 'tail stinger' emplacement introduced with the B-17E, while effective, had a limited field of fire and was not easy for the gunner to manipulate. The new structure helped to overcome both these shortcomings and was introduced into production during spring 1944.

As far as combat pilots were concerned the most beneficial change in B-17 production was the replacement of hydraulically actuated engine supercharger controls by electronics. The extremely low temperatures experienced with high-altitude operations in Europe caused hydraulic oil to become sluggish unless the controls were regularly exercised—not always possible or desirable. Supercharger control problems often precipitated loss of control and malfunction of the unit. A defunct supercharger meant loss of engine power and an inability to maintain formation, and a straggler in the hostile environment of enemy airspace was lucky to survive. Electronic controls, giving positive and relatively trouble-free operation, were first installed on B-17s in production at the end of 1943 and early 1944.

The B-17 was gradually withdrawn from the Pacific war fronts in favour of the longer-ranged B-24. Thereafter, in a bombing role, the Fortress was solely committed to operations over Europe. The highest USAAF inventory of B-17s was in August 1944, when 4,574 were on hand at the end of the month. Of these 2,263 were overseas. In the following months numbers held in the USA steadily declined while the overseas total rose to a peak of 3,006 in March 1945, of which 2,891 were in the European and Mediterranean war

Below: The Cheyenne tail gun position, which increased the all-round field of fire by 15 per cent, was available in kit form from the spring of 1944. The installation was particularly popular with the Fifteenth Air Force, which had many of its Fortresses so modified. B-17G-30-BO 42-31852, seen here on a bomb run while assigned to the 463rd Bomb Group, was an early recipient. This aircraft also has the enclosed waist gun windows which were not introduced on the production line until the 50-BO block. (USAAF)

theatres. The RAF also acquired B-17Gs, most of their 85 being used by specialist Bomber and Coastal Command units.

With the demise of Nazi Germany in prospect, production was tailed off, Boeing delivering its 4,035th and last B-17G on 13 April 1945. The final B-17G from Long Beach, the 2,395th, was rolled out in July 1945 and the Lockheed Vega line was the last to close with its 2,250th aircraft delivered on 4 August 1945. At peak production, reached early in 1944, the three factories were between them producing an average sixteen and a half B-17s each day. This was in March, and the rate was sustained at nearly this figure until July, when it began to reduce, with labour and materials for the B-29 and other new types having priority. By the spring of 1944 the time required to assemble each aircraft had come down to about 1,600 hours, and in consequence the average price of a B-17G had decreased by some $71,000 compared to that of the far less sohphisticated B-17E of 1942. The number of B-17 parts, less those in units like engines, propellers and equipment supplied by the government from other sources, has been given as 31,253 by one official source, although this must have been variable. The total number of man-hours required to produce a B-17 at Seattle in 1942 was 54,800, reducing to 35,400 in 1943, and the average for each B-17G in 1944 was only 18,600 man-hours. This was principally achieved by advances in construction techniques and improved manufacturing equipment. In consequence the unit cost also fell, from an average of $258,949 in 1942 to $187,742 for the last B-17Gs in 1945.

Right, top: This close-up view of the Cheyenne tail gun position reveals a sheet of armour plate bolted to the exterior as protection against low-velocity shell splinters—an in-the-field modification on an Eighth Air Force B-17G made acceptable through weight reductions elsewhere in the aft fuselage. (D. Collyer/W. Hadcraft)

Right, centre: B-17G-70-BO 43-37716 was Boeing's 5,000th Fortress built at Seattle, and it completion was marked by allowing the workforce to autograph the aircraft. Serving with the 96th Bomb Group in England, the aircraft was conspicuous for the mass of predominantly black and red signatures with addresses that covered all but the control surfaces. It gained a Cheyenne tail gun position while in the UK. (96th BG Assn)

Right, bottom: B-17G-40-VE 42-98021 became Fortress III HB791 with the British, and was serving in RAF Coastal Command's No 220 Squadron when this photograph was taken in the Azores. It was modified with a Cheyenne tail gun position and enclosed waist windows at the Denver modification centre before delivery. The ball turret has been replaced with a radome housing an AN/APS-15 scanner.

GENERAL ARRANGEMENT
B-17F

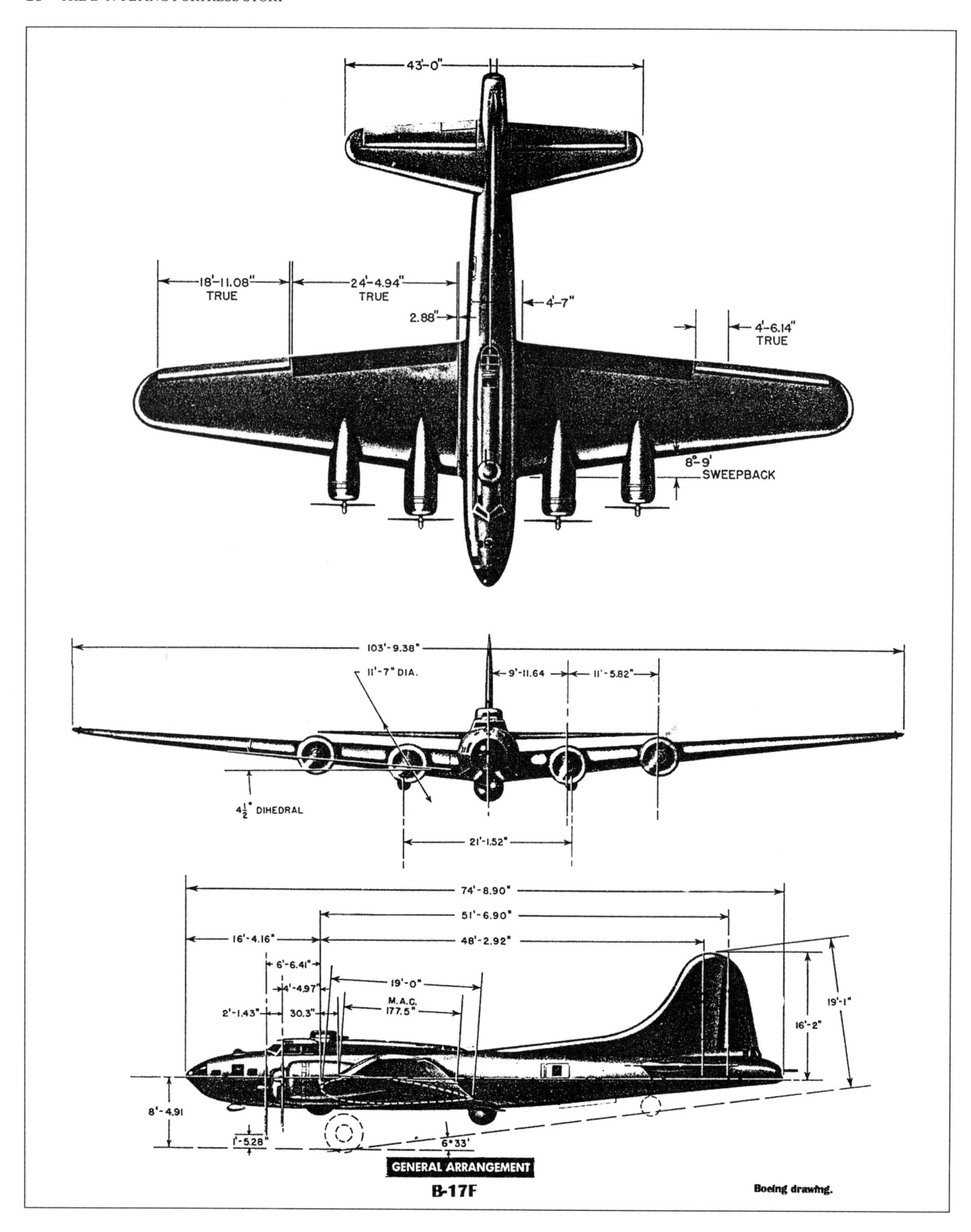

Boeing drawing.

MODEL 299: DESIGN AND PRODUCTION 29

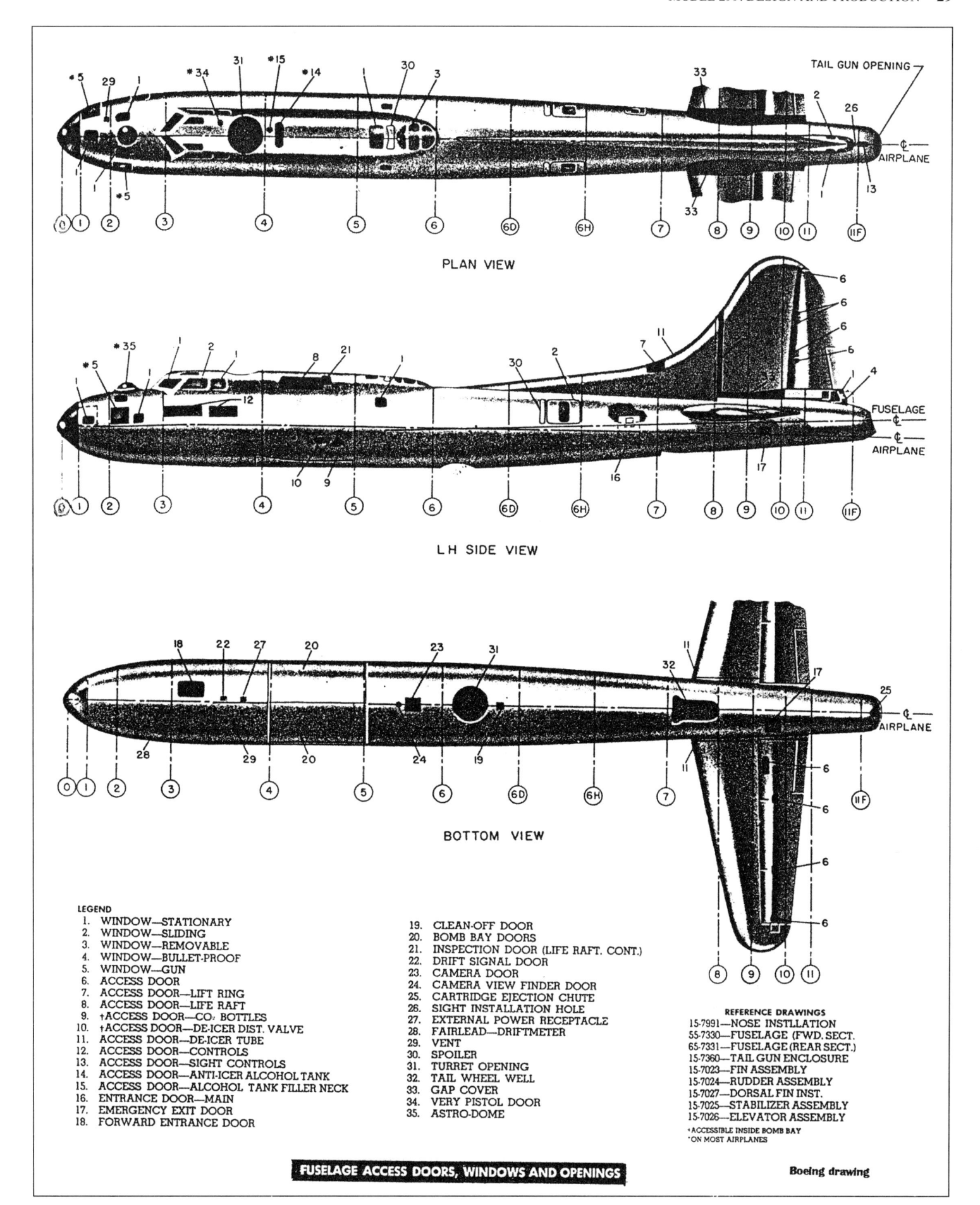

PLAN VIEW

LH SIDE VIEW

BOTTOM VIEW

LEGEND
1. WINDOW—STATIONARY
2. WINDOW—SLIDING
3. WINDOW—REMOVABLE
4. WINDOW—BULLET-PROOF
5. WINDOW—GUN
6. ACCESS DOOR
7. ACCESS DOOR—LIFT RING
8. ACCESS DOOR—LIFE RAFT
9. †ACCESS DOOR—CO₂ BOTTLES
10. †ACCESS DOOR—DE-ICER DIST. VALVE
11. ACCESS DOOR—DE-ICER TUBE
12. ACCESS DOOR—CONTROLS
13. ACCESS DOOR—SIGHT CONTROLS
14. ACCESS DOOR—ANTI-ICER ALCOHOL TANK
15. ACCESS DOOR—ALCOHOL TANK FILLER NECK
16. ENTRANCE DOOR—MAIN
17. EMERGENCY EXIT DOOR
18. FORWARD ENTRANCE DOOR
19. CLEAN-OFF DOOR
20. BOMB BAY DOORS
21. INSPECTION DOOR (LIFE RAFT. CONT.)
22. DRIFT SIGNAL DOOR
23. CAMERA DOOR
24. CAMERA VIEW FINDER DOOR
25. CARTRIDGE EJECTION CHUTE
26. SIGHT INSTALLATION HOLE
27. EXTERNAL POWER RECEPTACLE
28. FAIRLEAD—DRIFTMETER
29. VENT
30. SPOILER
31. TURRET OPENING
32. TAIL WHEEL WELL
33. GAP COVER
34. VERY PISTOL DOOR
35. ASTRO-DOME

REFERENCE DRAWINGS
15-7991—NOSE INSTLLATION
55-7330—FUSELAGE (FWD. SECT.
65-7331—FUSELAGE (REAR SECT.)
15-7360—TAIL GUN ENCLOSURE
15-7023—FIN ASSEMBLY
15-7024—RUDDER ASSEMBLY
15-7027—DORSAL FIN INST.
15-7025—STABILIZER ASSEMBLY
15-7026—ELEVATOR ASSEMBLY

† ACCESSIBLE INSIDE BOMB BAY
* ON MOST AIRPLANES

FUSELAGE ACCESS DOORS, WINDOWS AND OPENINGS

Boeing drawing

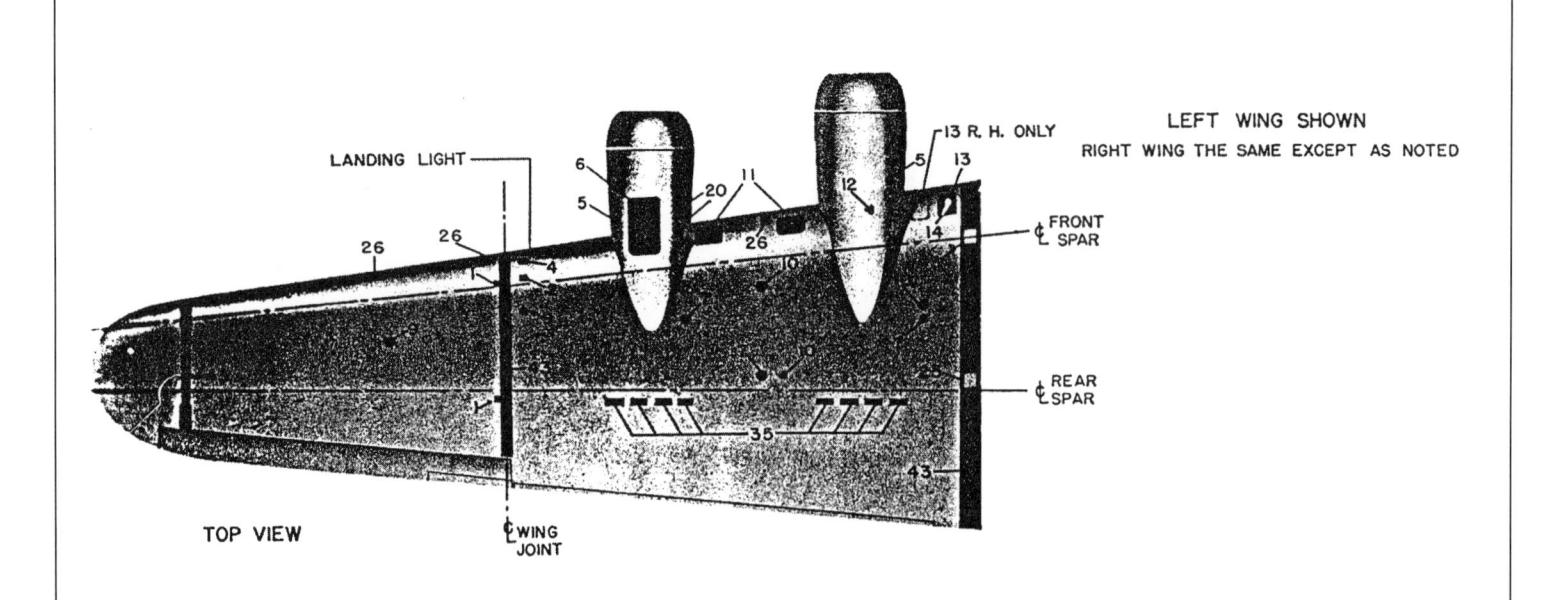

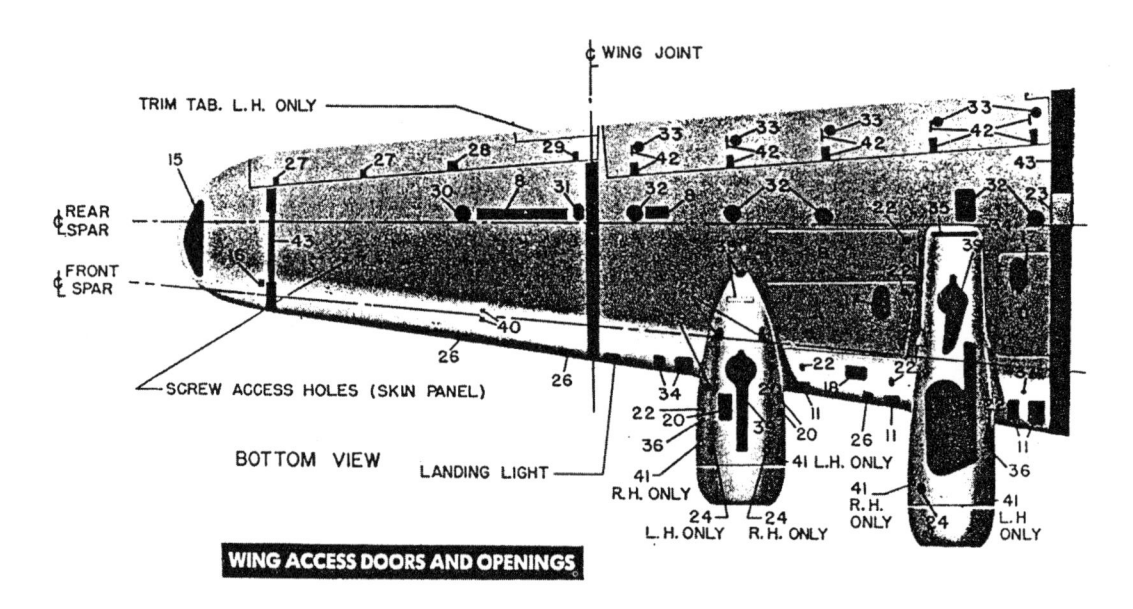

THE B-17 FLYING FORTRESS STORY

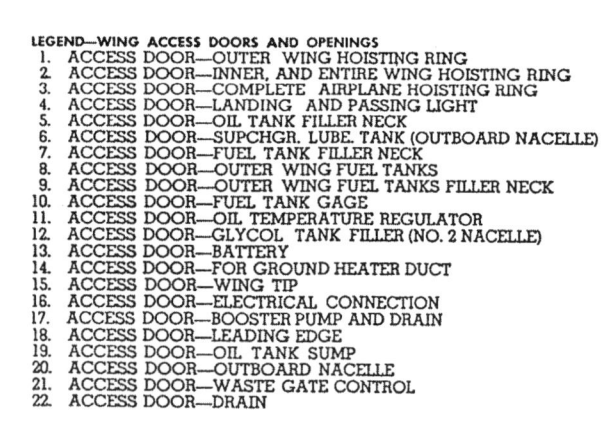

LEFT WING SHOWN
RIGHT WING THE SAME EXCEPT AS NOTED

TOP VIEW

BOTTOM VIEW

WING ACCESS DOORS AND OPENINGS

LEGEND—WING ACCESS DOORS AND OPENINGS
1. ACCESS DOOR—OUTER WING HOISTING RING
2. ACCESS DOOR—INNER, AND ENTIRE WING HOISTING RING
3. ACCESS DOOR—COMPLETE AIRPLANE HOISTING RING
4. ACCESS DOOR—LANDING AND PASSING LIGHT
5. ACCESS DOOR—OIL TANK FILLER NECK
6. ACCESS DOOR—SUPCHGR. LUBE. TANK (OUTBOARD NACELLE)
7. ACCESS DOOR—FUEL TANK FILLER NECK
8. ACCESS DOOR—OUTER WING FUEL TANKS
9. ACCESS DOOR—OUTER WING FUEL TANKS FILLER NECK
10. ACCESS DOOR—FUEL TANK GAGE
11. ACCESS DOOR—OIL TEMPERATURE REGULATOR
12. ACCESS DOOR—GLYCOL TANK FILLER (NO. 2 NACELLE)
13. ACCESS DOOR—BATTERY
14. ACCESS DOOR—FOR GROUND HEATER DUCT
15. ACCESS DOOR—WING TIP
16. ACCESS DOOR—ELECTRICAL CONNECTION
17. ACCESS DOOR—BOOSTER PUMP AND DRAIN
18. ACCESS DOOR—LEADING EDGE
19. ACCESS DOOR—OIL TANK SUMP
20. ACCESS DOOR—OUTBOARD NACELLE
21. ACCESS DOOR—WASTE GATE CONTROL
22. ACCESS DOOR—DRAIN
23. ACCESS DOOR—WING TERMINAL
24. ACCESS DOOR—ENGINE HEATING AND PROPANE STARTING
25. ACCESS DOOR—CARBURETOR ANTI-ICER TANK FILLER NECK
26. COVER—DE-ICER BOOT CONNECTION
27. ACCESS OPENING—AILERON HINGE
28. ACCESS OPENING—AILERON HINGE AND CONTROL
29. ACCESS OPENING—AILERON HINGE AND TRIM TAB
30. INSPECTION DOOR—AILERON CONTROL
31. INSPECTION DOOR—AILERON TRIM TAB CONTROL
32. INSPECTION DOOR—LANDING FLAP CONTROL
33. INSPECTION DOOR—LANDING FLAP SUPPORT
34. AIR INTAKE
35. AIR OUTLET
36. PLUG—OIL IMMERSION HEATER
37. RECEPTACLE—EXTERNAL BOMB RACK ELEC. CONTROL
38. LANDING WHEEL WELL
39. TURBO SUPERCHARGER WELL
40. MOORING WELL
41. CUTOUT—STARTER CRANK
42. SWING CUTOUT—LANDING FLAP
43. GAP COVER

ARMAMENT AND ARMOUR – B-17F-100-BO

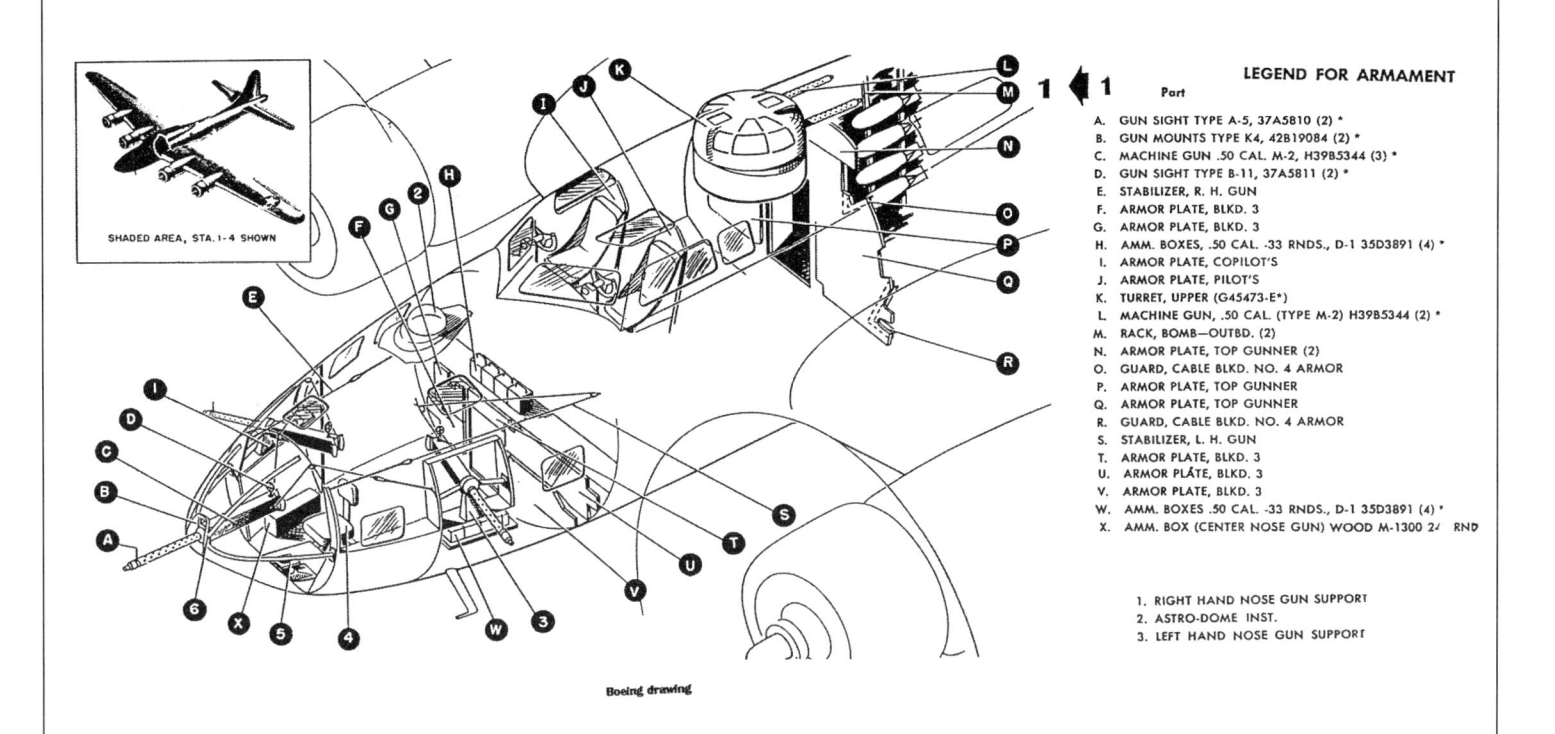

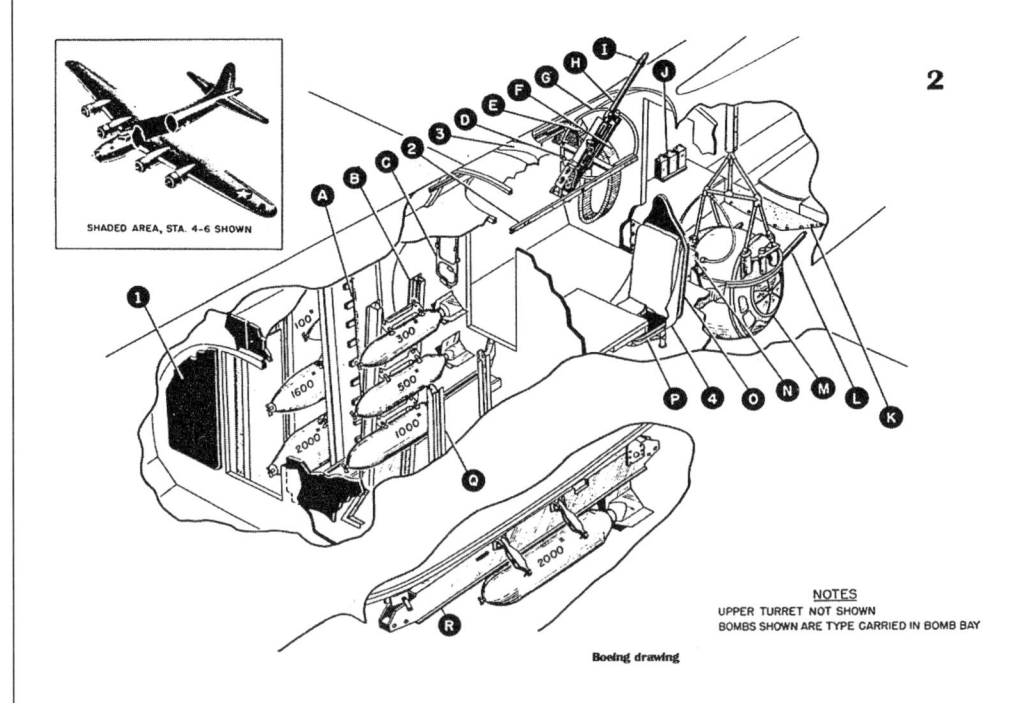

LEGEND FOR ARMAMENT

1

Part

- A. GUN SIGHT TYPE A-5, 37A5810 (2) *
- B. GUN MOUNTS TYPE K4, 42B19084 (2) *
- C. MACHINE GUN .50 CAL. M-2, H39B5344 (3) *
- D. GUN SIGHT TYPE B-11, 37A5811 (2) *
- E. STABILIZER, R. H. GUN
- F. ARMOR PLATE, BLKD. 3
- G. ARMOR PLATE, BLKD. 3
- H. AMM. BOXES, .50 CAL. -33 RNDS., D-1 35D3891 (4) *
- I. ARMOR PLATE, COPILOT'S
- J. ARMOR PLATE, PILOT'S
- K. TURRET, UPPER (G45473-E*)
- L. MACHINE GUN, .50 CAL. (TYPE M-2) H39B5344 (2) *
- M. RACK, BOMB—OUTBD. (2)
- N. ARMOR PLATE, TOP GUNNER (2)
- O. GUARD, CABLE BLKD. NO. 4 ARMOR
- P. ARMOR PLATE, TOP GUNNER
- Q. ARMOR PLATE, TOP GUNNER
- R. GUARD, CABLE BLKD. NO. 4 ARMOR
- S. STABILIZER, L. H. GUN
- T. ARMOR PLATE, BLKD. 3
- U. ARMOR PLATE, BLKD. 3
- V. ARMOR PLATE, BLKD. 3
- W. AMM. BOXES .50 CAL. -33 RNDS., D-1 35D3891 (4) *
- X. AMM. BOX (CENTER NOSE GUN) WOOD M-1300 24 RND

1. RIGHT HAND NOSE GUN SUPPORT
2. ASTRO-DOME INST.
3. LEFT HAND NOSE GUN SUPPORT

SHADED AREA, STA. 1-4 SHOWN

Boeing drawing

2

Part

- A. GUARD, BOMB RELEASE MECHANISM (2)
- B. BOMB RACKS (INBD.) (2)
- C. HOIST FRAME, BOMB (STOWED)
- D. SIGHT, FOLDING RING
- E. AMMUNITION BOX, .50 CAL. MACHINE GUN
- F. CHUTE, FLEXIBLE FEED, .50 CAL. AMM.*
- G. YOKE, GUN MOUNT
- H. MACHINE GUN, .50 CAL. TYPE M-2 H39B5344*
- I. SIGHT, FOLDING POST
- J. AMMUNITION BOXES, .50 CAL. MACHINE GUN (3)
- K. RETAINER, SHELL, AFT OF LOWER TURRET
- L. MACHINE GUNS, .50 CAL. TYPE M-2 H39B5344 (2)*
- M. TURRET, LOWER SPHERICAL 645849J*
- N. RETAINER, SHELL, BLK. 6
- O. ARMOR PLATE, RADIO OPERATOR'S SEAT
- P. ARMOR PLATE, RADIO OPERATOR'S SEAT
- Q. BOMB RACKS (OUTBD.) (2)
- R. BOMB RACKS, EXTERNAL (2)

* GOVERNMENT FURNISHED EQUIPMENT

SHADED AREA, STA. 4-6 SHOWN

NOTES
UPPER TURRET NOT SHOWN
BOMBS SHOWN ARE TYPE CARRIED IN BOMB BAY

Boeing drawing

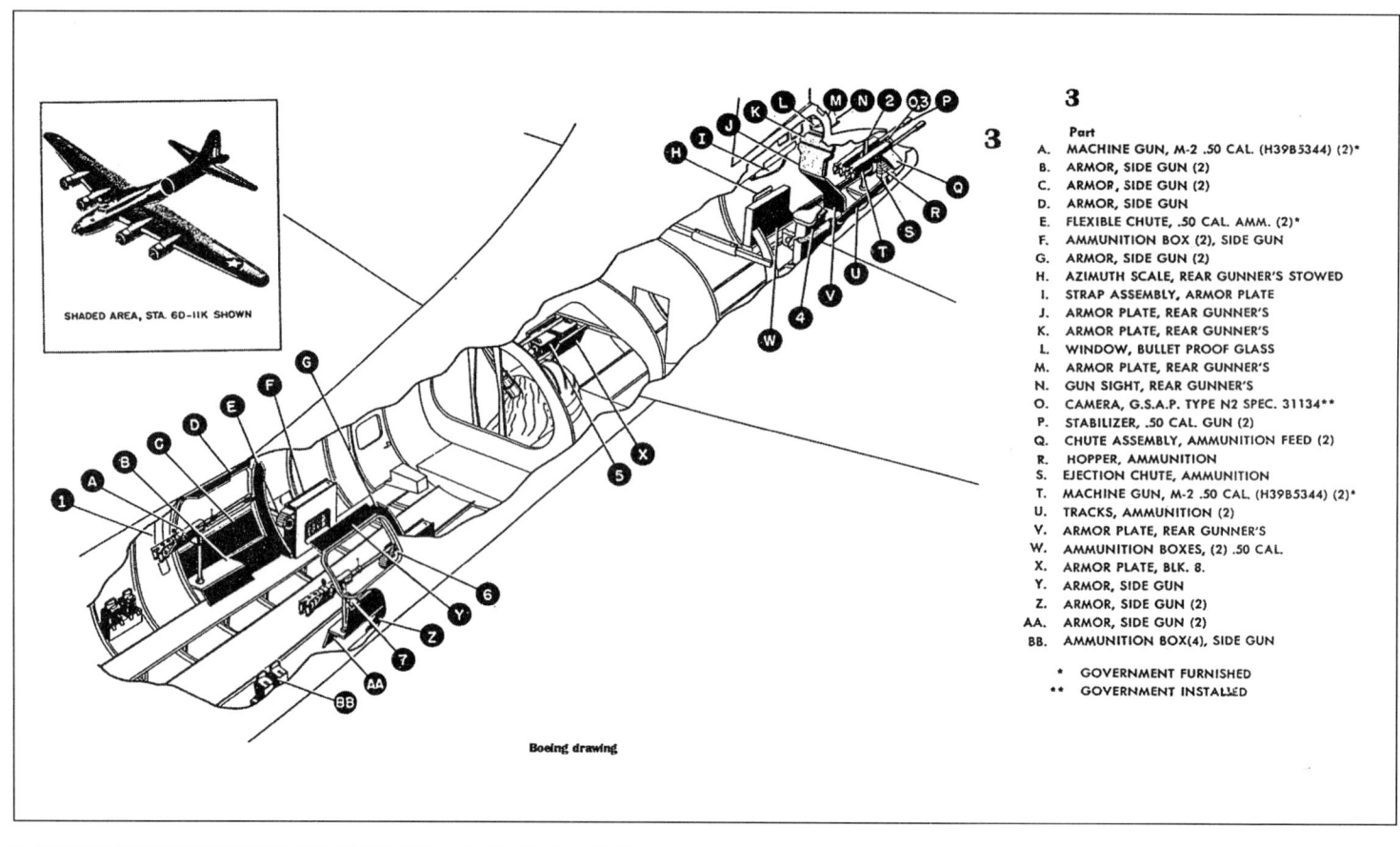

32 THE B-17 FLYING FORTRESS STORY

SHADED AREA, STA. 6D-11K SHOWN

Part

- A. MACHINE GUN, M-2 .50 CAL. (H39B5344) (2)*
- B. ARMOR, SIDE GUN (2)
- C. ARMOR, SIDE GUN (2)
- D. ARMOR, SIDE GUN
- E. FLEXIBLE CHUTE, .50 CAL. AMM. (2)*
- F. AMMUNITION BOX (2), SIDE GUN
- G. ARMOR, SIDE GUN (2)
- H. AZIMUTH SCALE, REAR GUNNER'S STOWED
- I. STRAP ASSEMBLY, ARMOR PLATE
- J. ARMOR PLATE, REAR GUNNER'S
- K. ARMOR PLATE, REAR GUNNER'S
- L. WINDOW, BULLET PROOF GLASS
- M. ARMOR PLATE, REAR GUNNER'S
- N. GUN SIGHT, REAR GUNNER'S
- O. CAMERA, G.S.A.P. TYPE N2 SPEC. 31134**
- P. STABILIZER, .50 CAL. GUN (2)
- Q. CHUTE ASSEMBLY, AMMUNITION FEED (2)
- R. HOPPER, AMMUNITION
- S. EJECTION CHUTE, AMMUNITION
- T. MACHINE GUN, M-2 .50 CAL. (H39B5344) (2)*
- U. TRACKS, AMMUNITION (2)
- V. ARMOR PLATE, REAR GUNNER'S
- W. AMMUNITION BOXES, (2) .50 CAL.
- X. ARMOR PLATE, BLK. 8.
- Y. ARMOR, SIDE GUN
- Z. ARMOR, SIDE GUN (2)
- AA. ARMOR, SIDE GUN (2)
- BB. AMMUNITION BOX(4), SIDE GUN

* GOVERNMENT FURNISHED
** GOVERNMENT INSTALLED

Boeing drawing

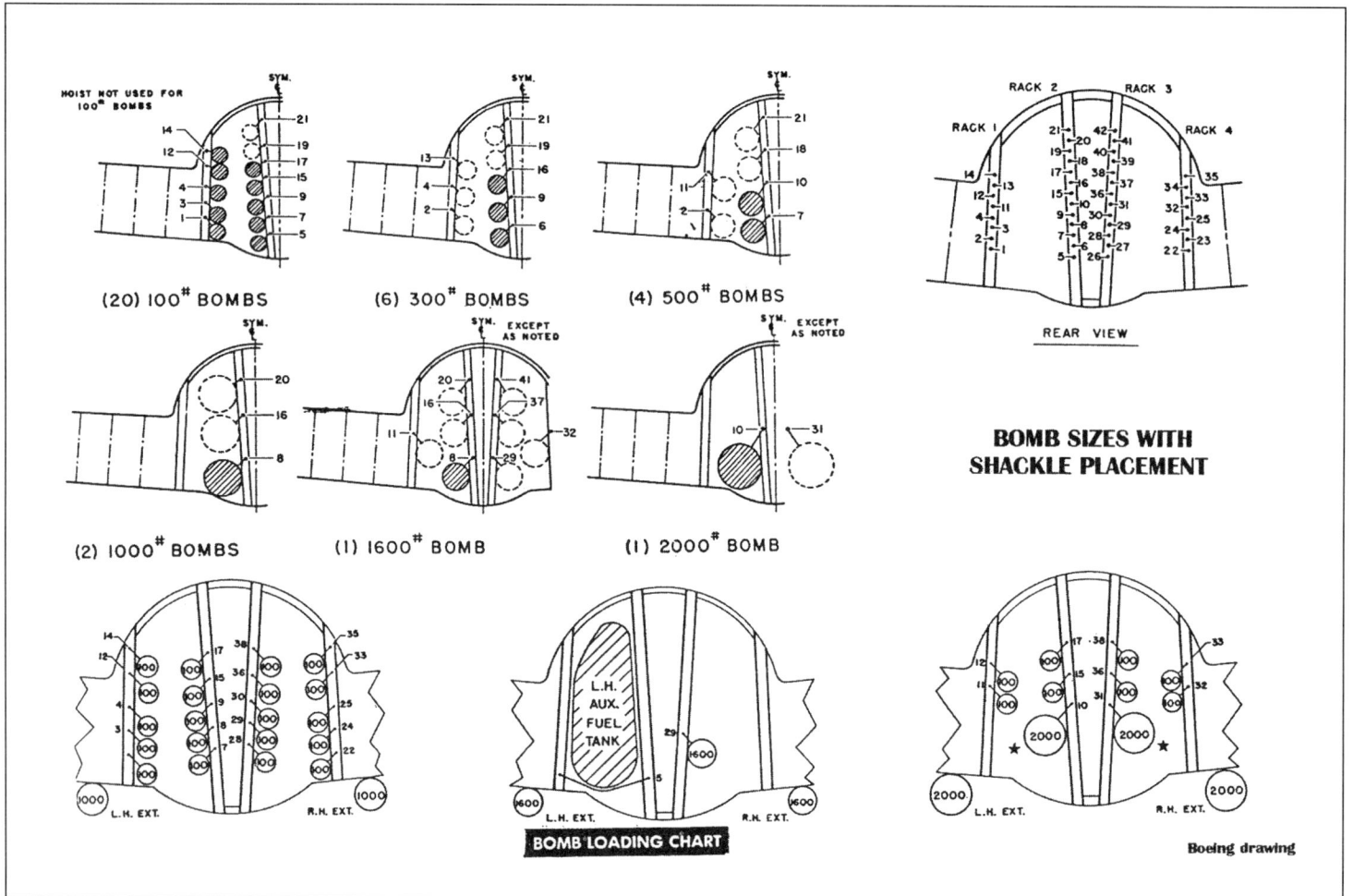

(20) 100# BOMBS — HOIST NOT USED FOR 100# BOMBS

(6) 300# BOMBS

(4) 500# BOMBS

(2) 1000# BOMBS

(1) 1600# BOMB

(1) 2000# BOMB

REAR VIEW

BOMB SIZES WITH SHACKLE PLACEMENT

BOMB LOADING CHART

Boeing drawing

MODEL 299: DESIGN AND PRODUCTION   33

EQUIPMENT LOCATION — B-17F-100-BO

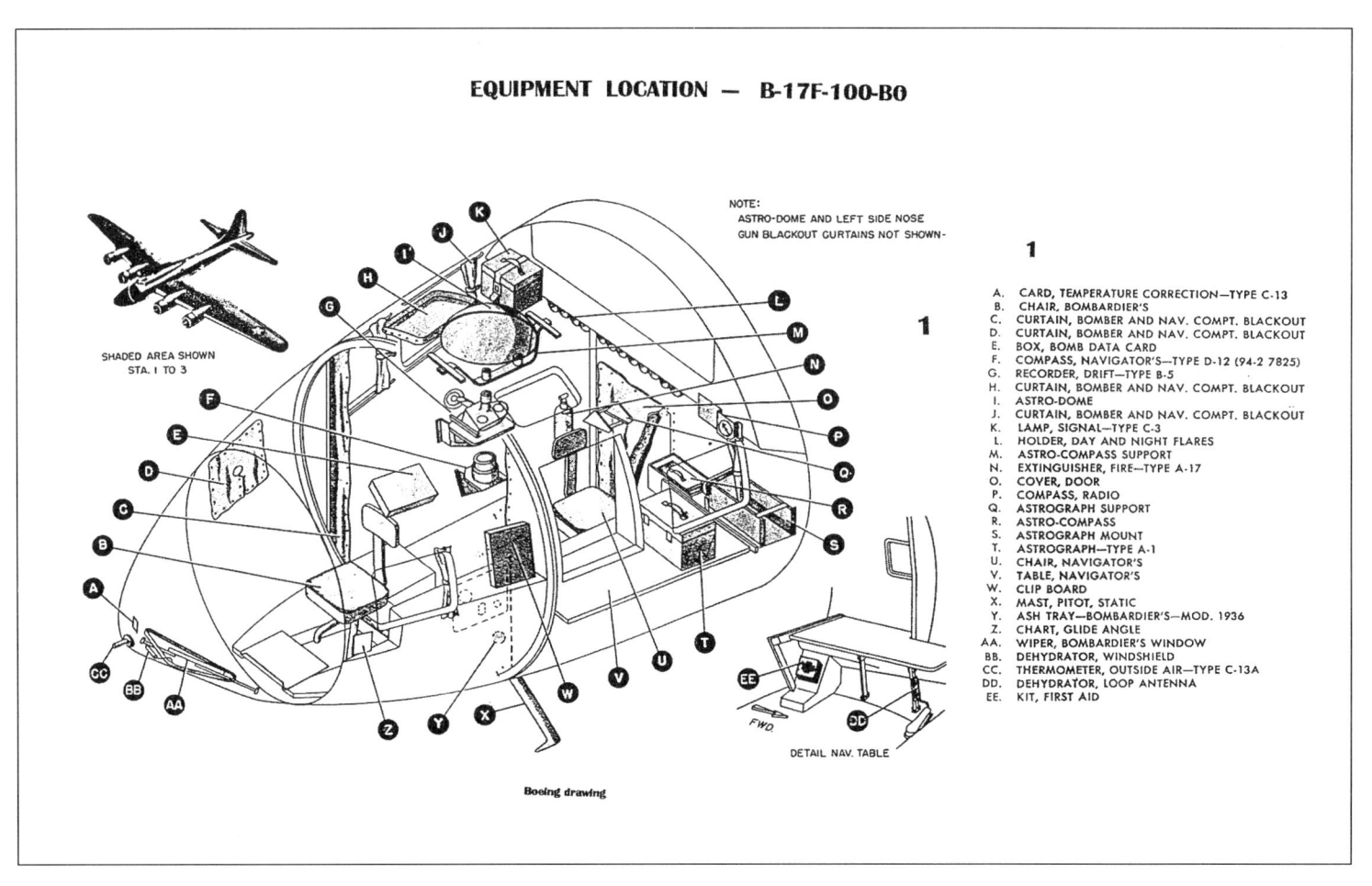

NOTE: ASTRO-DOME AND LEFT SIDE NOSE GUN BLACKOUT CURTAINS NOT SHOWN

SHADED AREA SHOWN STA. 1 TO 3

DETAIL NAV. TABLE

Boeing drawing

1

- A. CARD, TEMPERATURE CORRECTION—TYPE C-13
- B. CHAIR, BOMBARDIER'S
- C. CURTAIN, BOMBER AND NAV. COMPT. BLACKOUT
- D. CURTAIN, BOMBER AND NAV. COMPT. BLACKOUT
- E. BOX, BOMB DATA CARD
- F. COMPASS, NAVIGATOR'S—TYPE D-12 (94-2 7825)
- G. RECORDER, DRIFT—TYPE B-5
- H. CURTAIN, BOMBER AND NAV. COMPT. BLACKOUT
- I. ASTRO-DOME
- J. CURTAIN, BOMBER AND NAV. COMPT. BLACKOUT
- K. LAMP, SIGNAL—TYPE C-3
- L. HOLDER, DAY AND NIGHT FLARES
- M. ASTRO-COMPASS SUPPORT
- N. EXTINGUISHER, FIRE—TYPE A-17
- O. COVER, DOOR
- P. COMPASS, RADIO
- Q. ASTROGRAPH SUPPORT
- R. ASTRO-COMPASS
- S. ASTROGRAPH MOUNT
- T. ASTROGRAPH—TYPE A-1
- U. CHAIR, NAVIGATOR'S
- V. TABLE, NAVIGATOR'S
- W. CLIP BOARD
- X. MAST, PITOT, STATIC
- Y. ASH TRAY—BOMBARDIER'S—MOD. 1936
- Z. CHART, GLIDE ANGLE
- AA. WIPER, BOMBARDIER'S WINDOW
- BB. DEHYDRATOR, WINDSHIELD
- CC. THERMOMETER, OUTSIDE AIR—TYPE C-13A
- DD. DEHYDRATOR, LOOP ANTENNA
- EE. KIT, FIRST AID

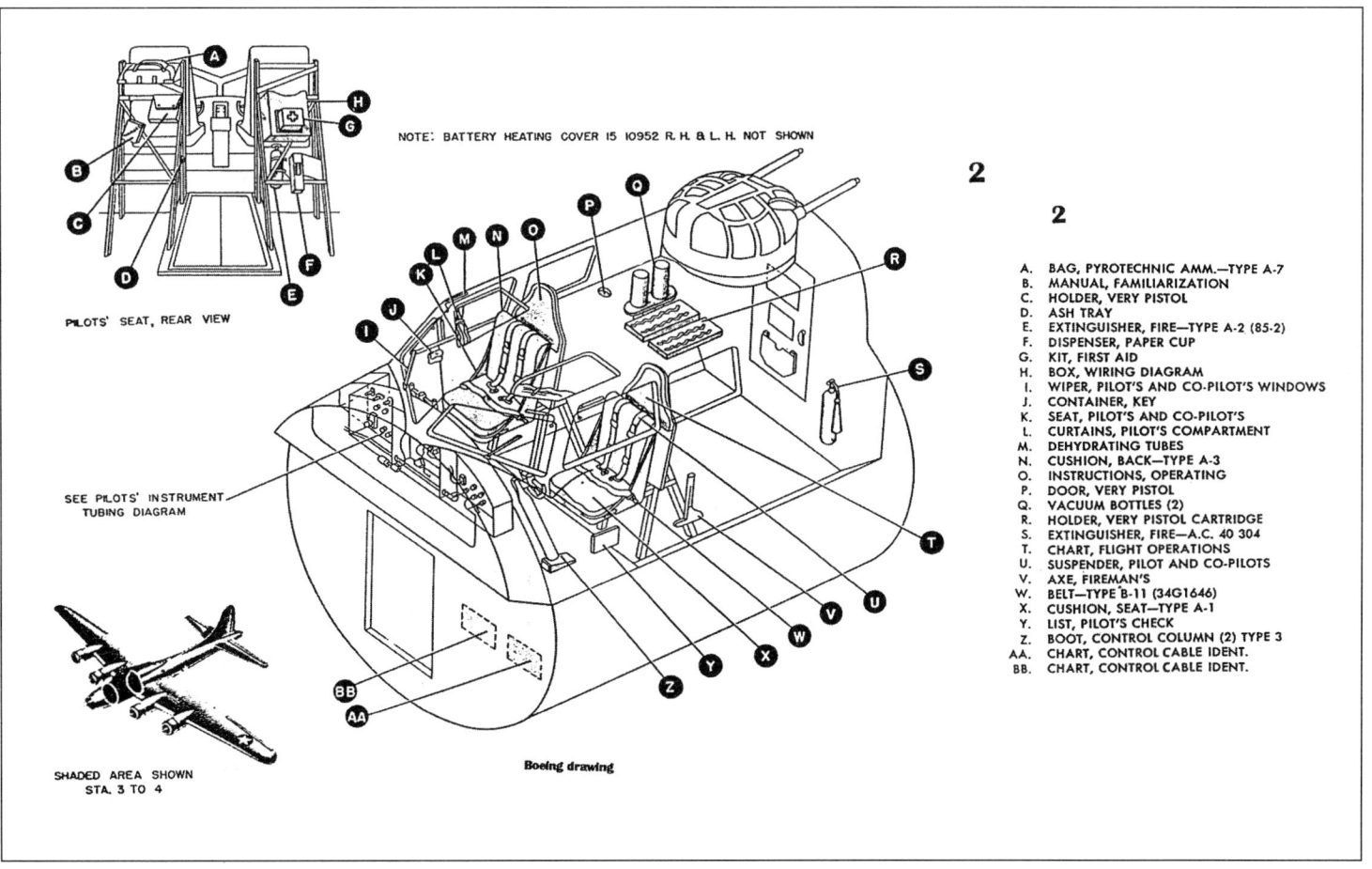

PILOTS' SEAT, REAR VIEW

NOTE: BATTERY HEATING COVER 15 10952 R.H. & L.H. NOT SHOWN

SEE PILOTS' INSTRUMENT TUBING DIAGRAM

SHADED AREA SHOWN STA. 3 TO 4

Boeing drawing

2

- A. BAG, PYROTECHNIC AMM.—TYPE A-7
- B. MANUAL, FAMILIARIZATION
- C. HOLDER, VERY PISTOL
- D. ASH TRAY
- E. EXTINGUISHER, FIRE—TYPE A-2 (85-2)
- F. DISPENSER, PAPER CUP
- G. KIT, FIRST AID
- H. BOX, WIRING DIAGRAM
- I. WIPER, PILOT'S AND CO-PILOT'S WINDOWS
- J. CONTAINER, KEY
- K. SEAT, PILOT'S AND CO-PILOT'S
- L. CURTAINS, PILOT'S COMPARTMENT
- M. DEHYDRATING TUBES
- N. CUSHION, BACK—TYPE A-3
- O. INSTRUCTIONS, OPERATING
- P. DOOR, VERY PISTOL
- Q. VACUUM BOTTLES (2)
- R. HOLDER, VERY PISTOL CARTRIDGE
- S. EXTINGUISHER, FIRE—A.C. 40 304
- T. CHART, FLIGHT OPERATIONS
- U. SUSPENDER, PILOT AND CO-PILOTS
- V. AXE, FIREMAN'S
- W. BELT—TYPE B-11 (34G1646)
- X. CUSHION, SEAT—TYPE A-1
- Y. LIST, PILOT'S CHECK
- Z. BOOT, CONTROL COLUMN (2) TYPE 3
- AA. CHART, CONTROL CABLE IDENT.
- BB. CHART, CONTROL CABLE IDENT.

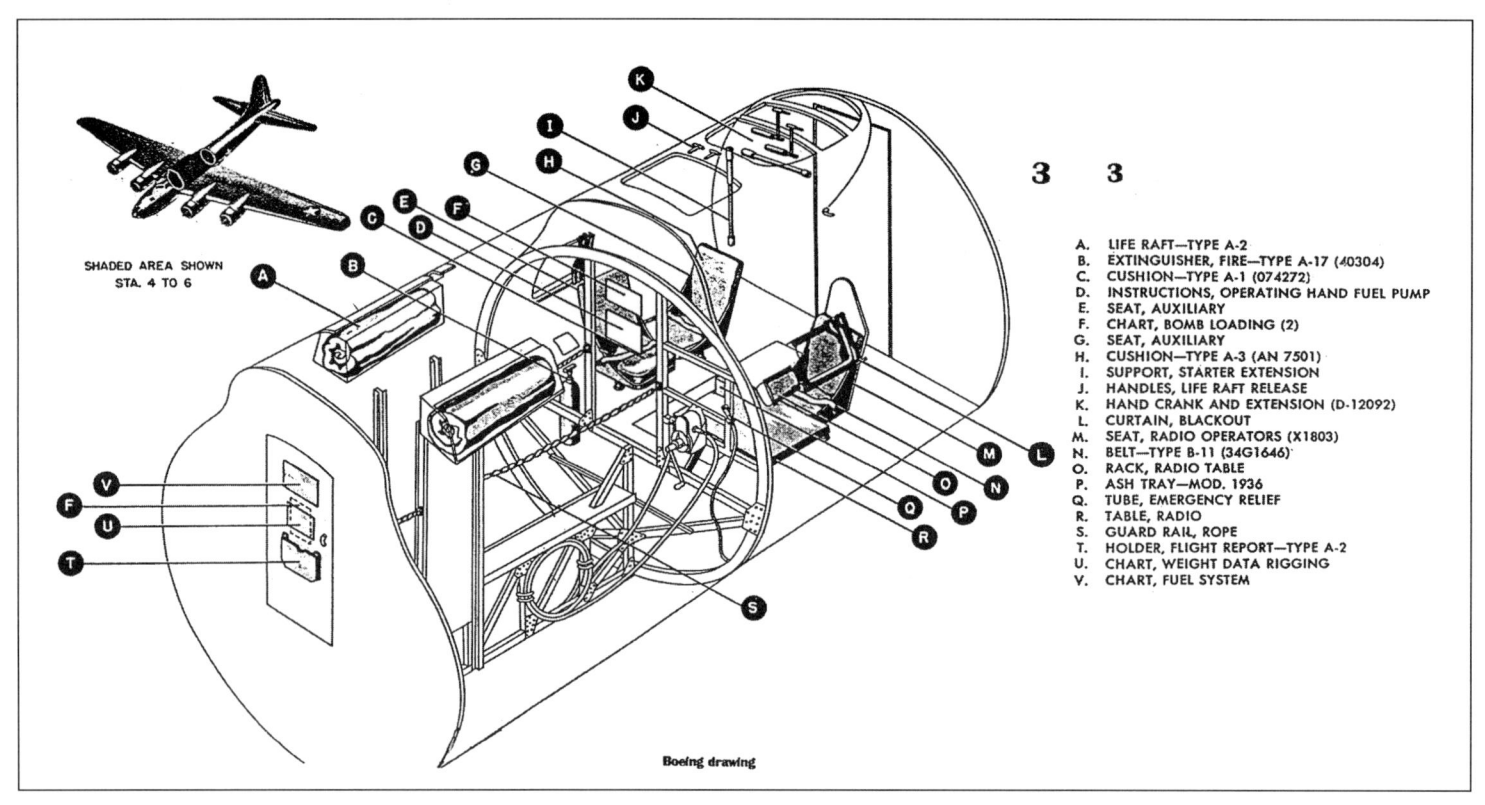

34 THE B-17 FLYING FORTRESS STORY

SHADED AREA SHOWN
STA. 4 TO 6

3

A. LIFE RAFT—TYPE A-2
B. EXTINGUISHER, FIRE—TYPE A-17 (40304)
C. CUSHION—TYPE A-1 (074272)
D. INSTRUCTIONS, OPERATING HAND FUEL PUMP
E. SEAT, AUXILIARY
F. CHART, BOMB LOADING (2)
G. SEAT, AUXILIARY
H. CUSHION—TYPE A-3 (AN 7501)
I. SUPPORT, STARTER EXTENSION
J. HANDLES, LIFE RAFT RELEASE
K. HAND CRANK AND EXTENSION (D-12092)
L. CURTAIN, BLACKOUT
M. SEAT, RADIO OPERATORS (X1803)
N. BELT—TYPE B-11 (34G1646)
O. RACK, RADIO TABLE
P. ASH TRAY—MOD. 1936
Q. TUBE, EMERGENCY RELIEF
R. TABLE, RADIO
S. GUARD RAIL, ROPE
T. HOLDER, FLIGHT REPORT—TYPE A-2
U. CHART, WEIGHT DATA RIGGING
V. CHART, FUEL SYSTEM

Boeing drawing

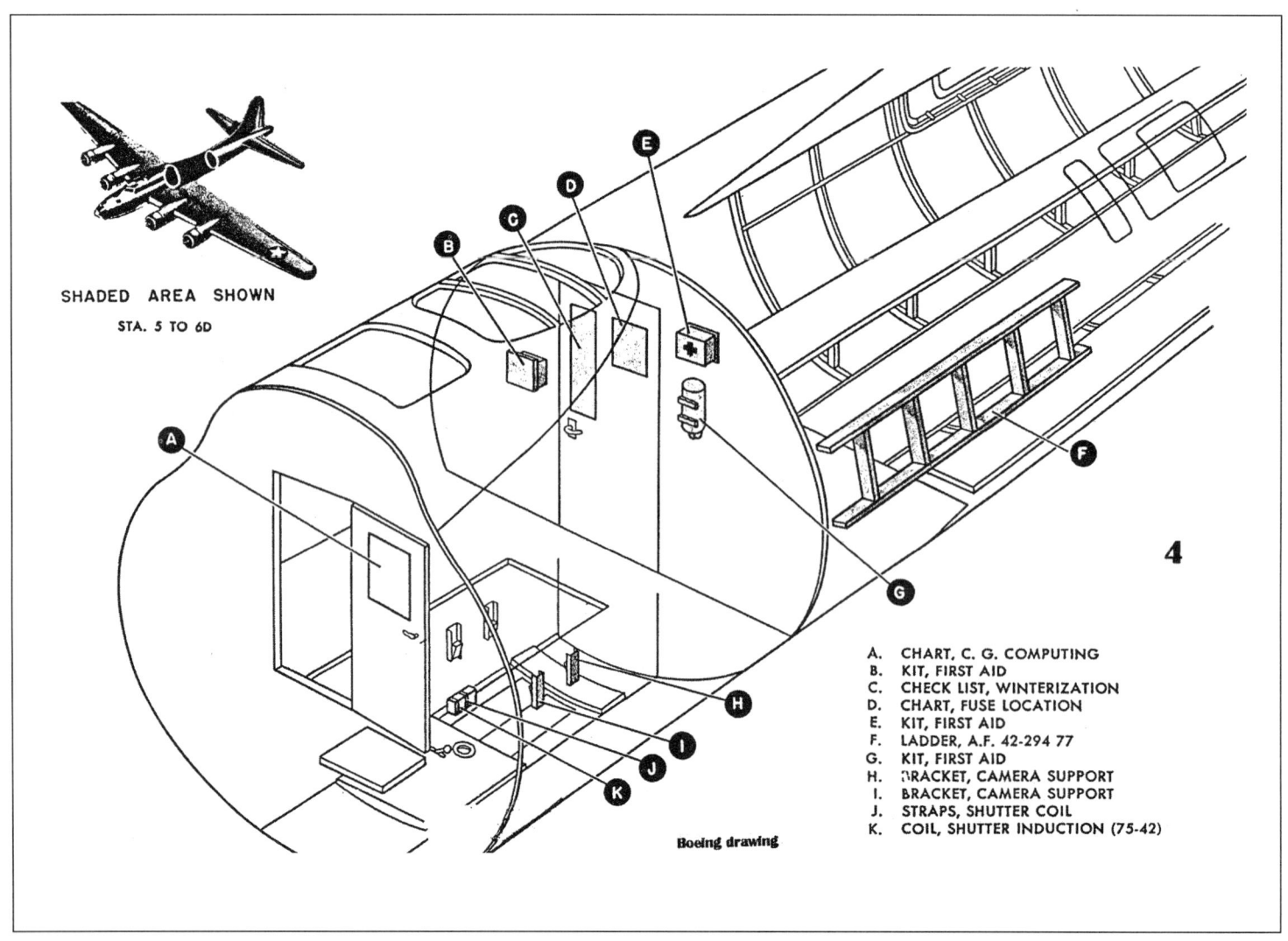

SHADED AREA SHOWN
STA. 5 TO 6D

4

A. CHART, C. G. COMPUTING
B. KIT, FIRST AID
C. CHECK LIST, WINTERIZATION
D. CHART, FUSE LOCATION
E. KIT, FIRST AID
F. LADDER, A.F. 42-294 77
G. KIT, FIRST AID
H. BRACKET, CAMERA SUPPORT
I. BRACKET, CAMERA SUPPORT
J. STRAPS, SHUTTER COIL
K. COIL, SHUTTER INDUCTION (75-42)

Boeing drawing

MODEL 299: DESIGN AND PRODUCTION   35

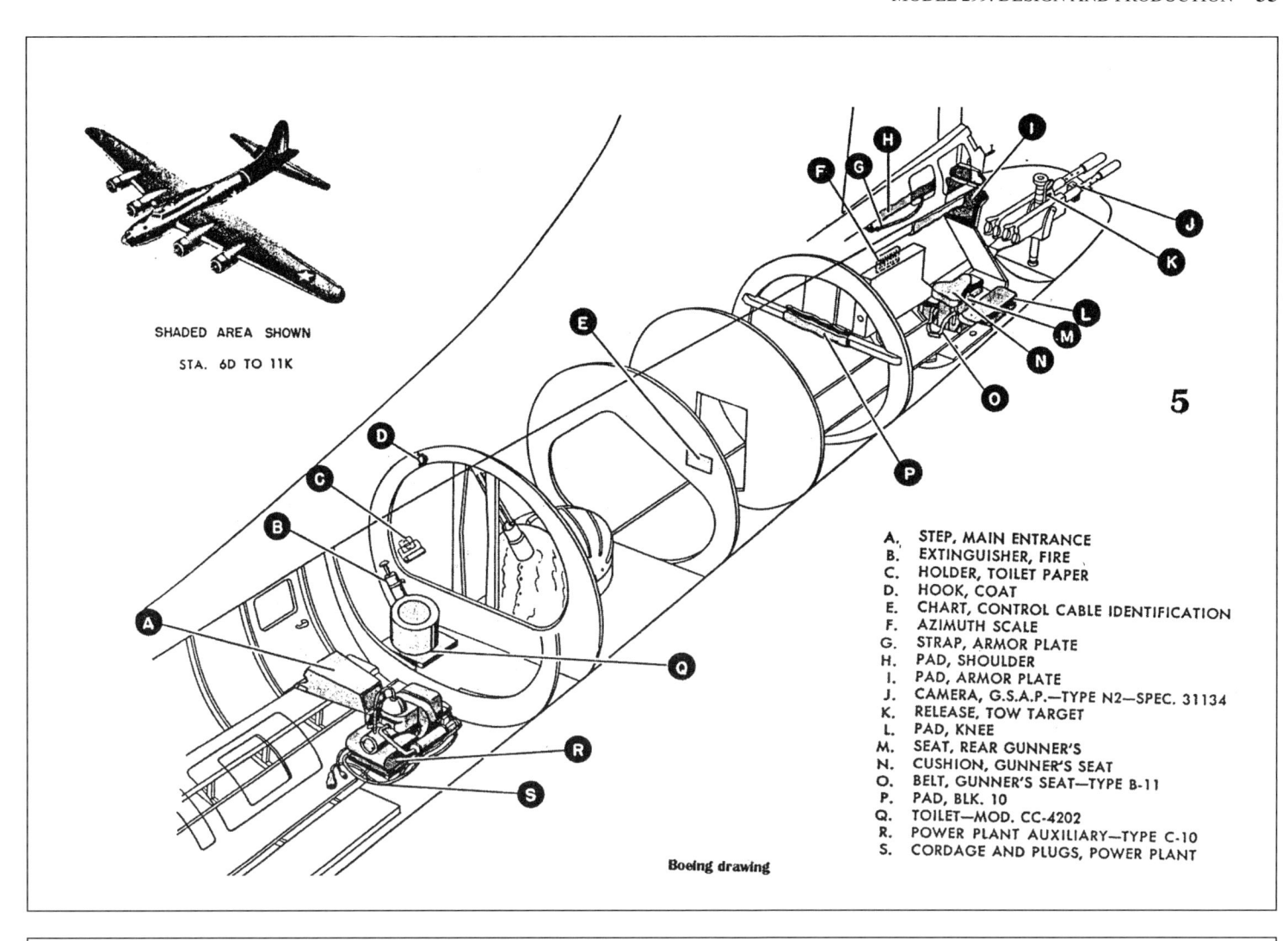

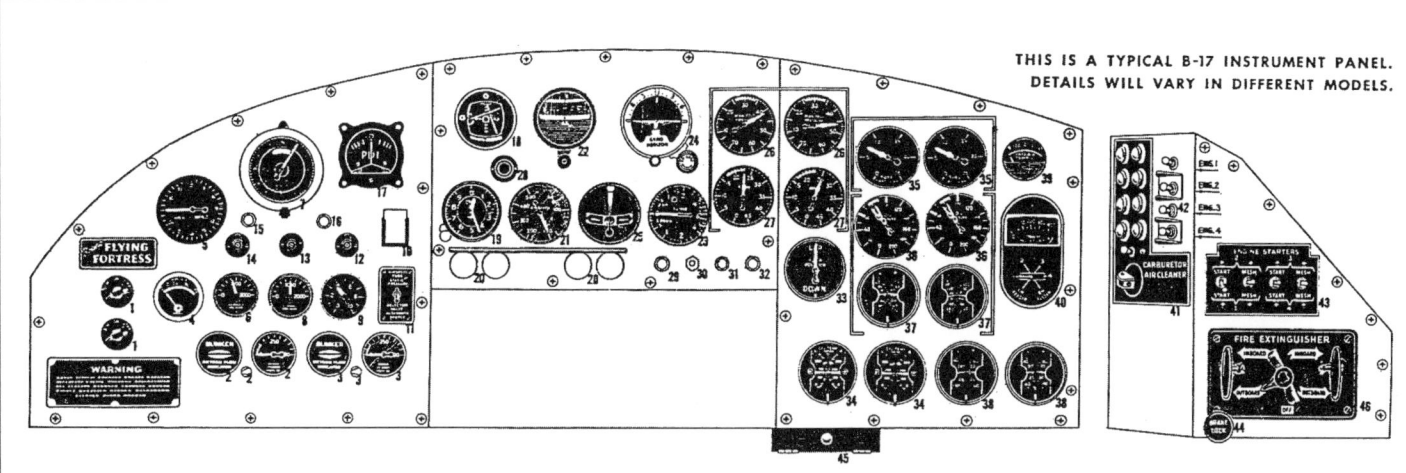

SHADED AREA SHOWN
STA. 6D TO 11K

A. STEP, MAIN ENTRANCE
B. EXTINGUISHER, FIRE
C. HOLDER, TOILET PAPER
D. HOOK, COAT
E. CHART, CONTROL CABLE IDENTIFICATION
F. AZIMUTH SCALE
G. STRAP, ARMOR PLATE
H. PAD, SHOULDER
I. PAD, ARMOR PLATE
J. CAMERA, G.S.A.P.—TYPE N2—SPEC. 31134
K. RELEASE, TOW TARGET
L. PAD, KNEE
M. SEAT, REAR GUNNER'S
N. CUSHION, GUNNER'S SEAT
O. BELT, GUNNER'S SEAT—TYPE B-11
P. PAD, BLK. 10
Q. TOILET—MOD. CC-4202
R. POWER PLANT AUXILIARY—TYPE C-10
S. CORDAGE AND PLUGS, POWER PLANT

Boeing drawing

THIS IS A TYPICAL B-17 INSTRUMENT PANEL.
DETAILS WILL VARY IN DIFFERENT MODELS.

1. Fluorescent light switches
2. Pilot's oxygen flow indicator, warning light and pressure gage
3. Copilot's oxygen flow indicator, warning light and pressure gage
4. Voltmeter (AC)
5. Radio compass
6. Emergency oil pressure gage (Not on G)
7. Flux gate compass
8. Hydraulic oil pressure gage
9. Suction gage
10. Altimeter correction card
11. Airspeed alternate source switch
12. Vacuum warning light
13. Main system hydraulic oil warning light
14. Emergency system hydraulic oil warning light (Not on G)
15. Bomb door position light (Not on G)
16. Bomb release light
17. Pilot's directional indicator
18. Pilot's localizer indicator
19. Altimeter
20. Propeller feathering switches
21. Airspeed indicator
22. Directional gyro
23. Rate-of-climb indicator
24. Flight indicator
25. Turn-and-bank indicator
26. Manifold pressure gages
27. Tachometers
28. Marker beacon light
29. Globe test button
30. Bomber call light
31. Landing gear warning light
32. Toilwheel lock light
33. Flap position indicator
34. Cylinder-head temperature gages
35. Fuel pressure gages
36. Oil pressure gages
37. Oil temperature gages
38. Carburetor air temperature gages
39. Free air temperature gage
40. Fuel quantity gage
41. Carburetor air filter switch
42. Oil dilution switches
43. Starting switches
44. Parking brake control
45. Spare fuse box
46. Engine fire extinguisher controls (on some airplanes)

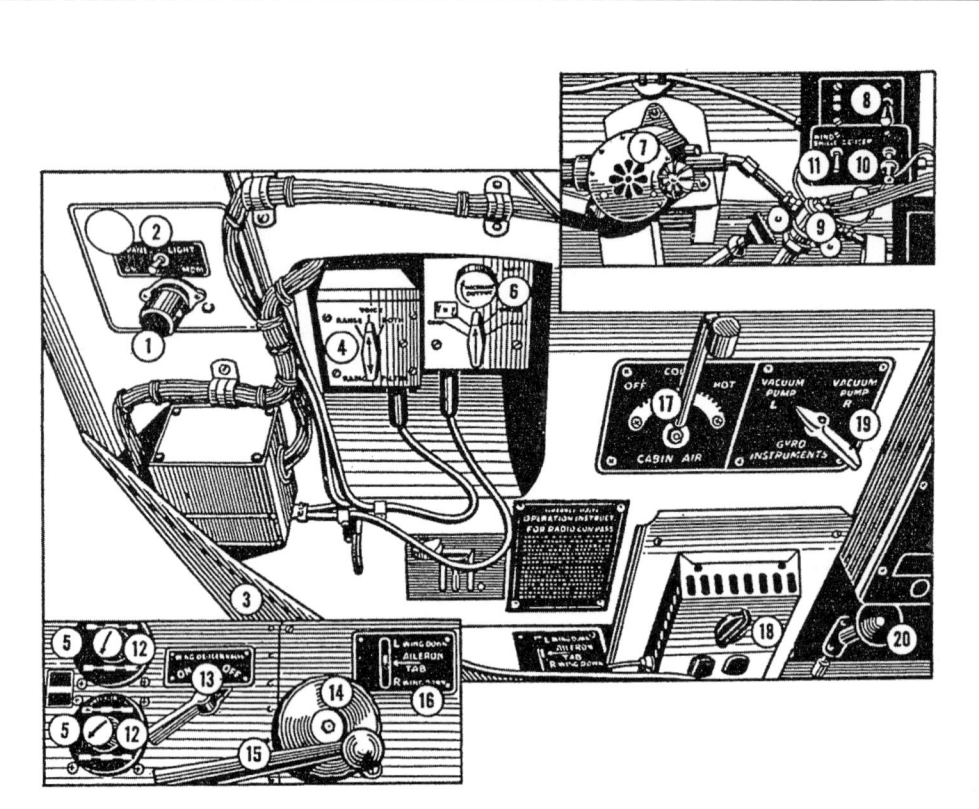

CONTROLS AT PILOT'S LEFT

1. Panel light
2. Panel light switch
3. Pilot's seat
4. Filter selector switch
5. Propeller anti-icer switch
6. Interphone jackbox
7. Oxygen regulator
8. Windshield wiper controls
9. Portable oxygen unit recharger
10. Windshield anti-icer switch
11. Windshield anti-icer flow control
12. Propeller anti-icer rheostats
13. Surface de-icer control
14. Aileron trim tab control
15. Pilot's seat adjustment lever
16. Aileron trim tab indicator
17. Cabin air control
18. Suit heater outlet
19. Vacuum selector valve
20. Emergency bomb release

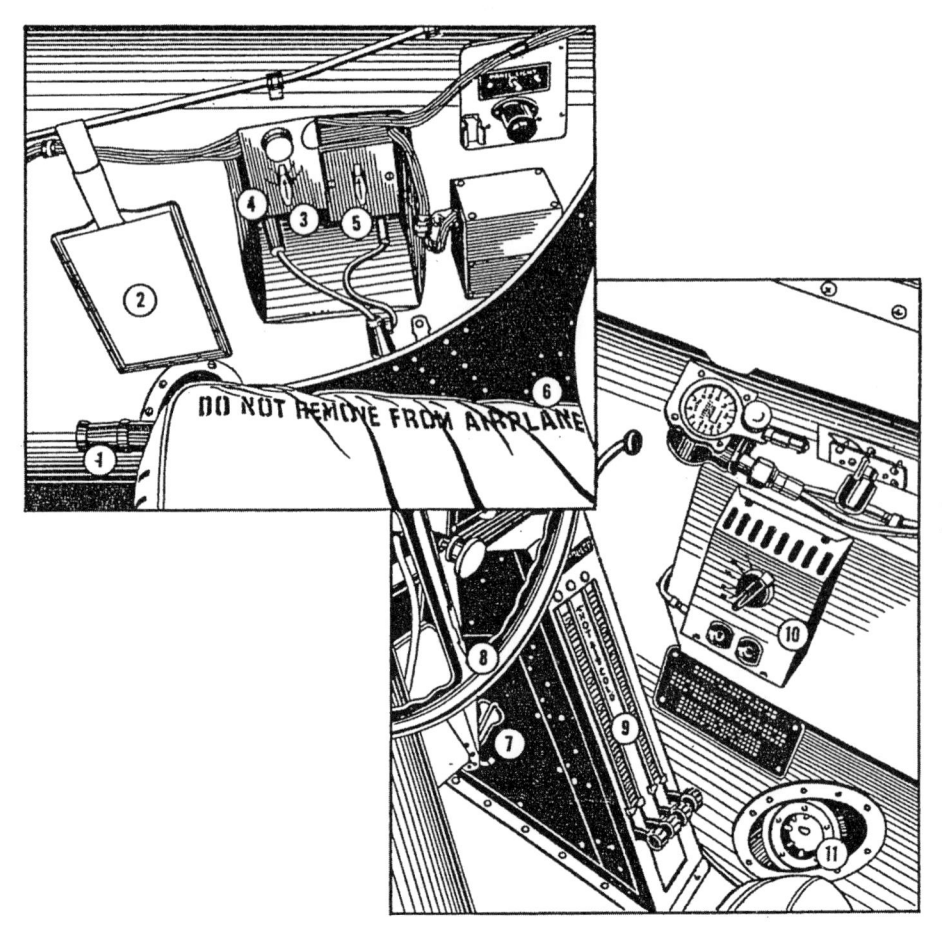

CONTROLS AT COPILOT'S RIGHT

1. Hydraulic hand pump
2. Checklist
3. Interphone selector switch
4. Interphone jackbox
5. Filter selector switch
6. Copilot's seat
7. Rudder pedal adjustment
8. Copilot's control wheel
9. Intercooler controls
10. Suit heater outlet
11. Engine primer

PILOT'S OPERATIONAL EQUIPMENT

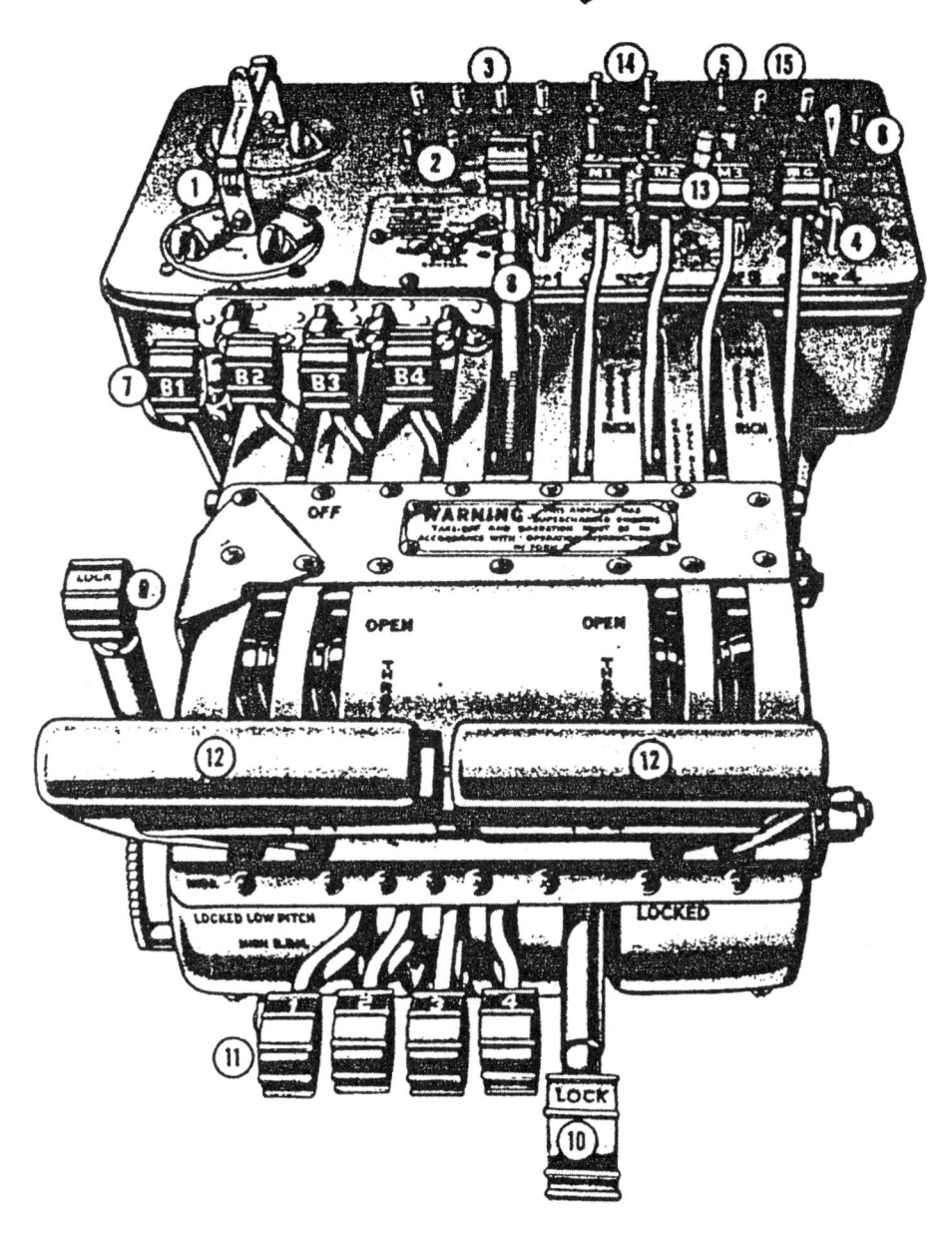

CONTROL PANEL AND PEDESTAL

1. Ignition switches
2. Fuel boost pump switches
3. Fuel shut-off valve switches
4. Cowl flap control valves
5. Landing gear switch
6. Wing flap switch
7. Turbo-supercharger controls (B-17F)
8. Turbo and mixture control lock
9. Throttle control lock
10. Propeller control lock
11. Propeller controls
12. Throttle controls
13. Mixture controls
14. Recognition light switches
15. Landing light switches

3. Changes, Alterations and Modifications

To advance the capabilities and reliability of an existing military aircraft it is subject to modification throughout its useful employment. These modifications come through corrections or improvements which, if the type is still being manufactured, will be introduced on the production line. In the days before the Second World War when there was a dearth of orders for new machines, Boeing, like other aircraft manufacturers, welcomed modification work. The changed US political climate of 1940, encouraging the sudden upturn in orders from Britain and France as well as increasing those for its own services, put considerable pressure on companies such as Boeing, which were seemingly expected to expand overnight. Following the hasty task of replacing B-17B superchargers which had suffered insufficient lubrication, the release of twenty B-17Cs for the RAF brought the next major priority modifications. The B-17Cs which had already been delivered to the Army Air Corps were recalled for modifications to RAF requirements which involved two major items. Self-sealing fuel cells were required, and these, apart from being in short supply, took several man-hours to install; and the Norden automatic pilot needed to be replaced with the older A-2 Sperry type together with the Sperry O-1 bomb sight. The RAF would have liked to have taken the Norden bomb sight and autopilot, but the US Navy, responsible for developing this advanced equipment, would not give permission for its release. Boeing engineers carried out the first autopilot change at Seattle and the rest of the aircraft were so modified at the Sacramento air depot. Boeing had been asked to put its factory on to 24-hour operation to be able to deal with this work. Following the RAF B-17Cs, those remaining in Army Air Forces service also received Goodrich self-sealing bladder fuel tanks to bring them up to B-17D standard. The continuing demand for modifications to existing aircraft could partly be met by expanding the use of air depots, but these had their limitations.

With the B-17E and the welter of modifications demanded once the United States found itself at war, it was essential that production should not be hindered by introducing changes. Even a relatively simple change could slow a production line, its introduction invariably posing problems with materials and labour skills. The answer was to carry out the desired changes at a special centre after an aircraft had been accepted from the factory, thus allowing their introduction on the production line to take place when this could be achieved without disruption. Many changes were only required for aircraft going to a particular war theatre—for example, special equipment and modifications for operating in extreme cold as faced in Alaska. Others might be required for special duties: photographic reconnaissance instead of bombing is an example that applied to the B-17. Providing such modification centres was another matter as the facilities with special skills and equipment could not be brought together quickly. However, a solution was found by enlisting the help of the major airlines, which already had maintenance bases with staff and tools, and these became the nuclei of modification centres. They were set up in January 1942, the United Airlines facility at Cheyenne, Wyoming, being earmarked principally for B-17 work. The Douglas plant at Tulsa, Oklahoma, became a secondary location for B-17 modifications, usually the more specialised tasks.

The list of modifications required for B-17s sent to Cheyenne varied almost from week to week as new items were added and others removed once they had been accepted on the production line. Although aircraft within each production block were intended to incorporate the same changes, this was not always the case with those made at modification centres. Nor did modification centres always indicate the special changes they had made to a particular model by amending the existing block number on the aircraft. There were literally hundreds of different changes made to wartime B-17s, although many were of no great significance from an operational standpoint. Indeed, the B-17 was the most modified of all USAAF warplanes.

USAAF air depots specialising in the repair of B-17s in the USA were set up at Fairfield, Oklahoma City and Warner Robins airfields. Their customers were aircraft from the dozen B-17 training bases in the Second and Third Air Force areas.

AGAINST JAPAN

Most modification requirements stemmed from the experiences of B-17 operatives in combat areas, the first coming from the South West Pacific Area (SWPA), the official term for the theatre of operations which included northern Australia, New Guinea and the Philippines. Surviving B-17Ds were withdrawn from operational use at an early date and B-17Es and Fs served in small numbers until replaced by B-24s. From the outset the main complaint was poor frontal defence and the need for a powered turret in the nose. The Brisbane air depot partly met the demand for

Below: Standard late-production B-17Gs from all three sources featured the Cheyenne tail position and clear Plexiglas waist windows with sill gun mounts. The radio room hatch gun, visible on this 60-DL of the 463rd Bomb Group, was deleted from later production. (USAF)

CHANGES, ALTERATIONS AND MODIFICATIONS   39

Above left: SWPA field-improvised mountings of three .50-calibre guns in B-17E 41-2463 of the 19th Bomb Group. Original ball-and-sockets for .30 weapons were bored to take the wider barrels, except those in side windows that remain unused. (USAF)

Above right: The standard side gun nose armament as fitted to B-17Es at US modification centres. The left centre and right forward windows were replaced with larger fittings with an aperture for a .50 Browning. The gun swivel mount was supported by a bracket with a stop to prevent the gunner, usually the navigator, firing into the aircraft's propellers or engines. B-17E 41-9103 went to the UK with the 97th Bomb Group in 1942 and, like many other combat B-17Es, operated with two .30 guns in the nosepiece. (USAAF)

Above left: Interior view of paired .50-calibre guns in the nose of a 19th Bomb Group B-17E. Intensive use fractured the Plexiglas, and internal brace supports to the ball-and-sockets were added to prevent this. (USAAF)

Above right: One of the three ball-and-socket fittings, intended for .30-calibre weapons in the noses of early Eighth Air Force B-17Fs, was often machined to take a .50, as on 42-5077 of the 91st Bomb Group. (USAAF)

Right: The bombardier's view from 42-5077, showing a .30 gun on the left and a .50 on the right. To avoid damage to the Plexiglas from the recoil of the more powerful weapon, three tubular support struts held the mounting. A banjo cord or strap kept the guns out of the bombardier's way when not in use. (USAAF)

Top left: The standard VIII Air Service Command twin .50 gun modification for B-17Fs. The weapons were mounted on a braced structure within the nosepiece and fired through a large aperture in the Plexiglas. A fireproof fabric around the blast tubes prevented air blast in the gunner's face. B-17Fs with twin nose guns did not carry a bomb sight and generally flew as wing aircraft to the leader, bombing on his signal. B-17F 42-29761 served with the 381st Bomb Group. (USAAF)

Top right: The standard B-17F fitting for a single .50-calibre gun in the upper part of the nose Plexiglas was first fitted at modification centres in the UK and then in the USA, as with 42-30783 of the 390th Bomb Group. (USAAF)

Above left: The original standard US modification centre nose side gun assembly for B-17Fs was similar to that used on B-17Es on Boeing and Douglas production lines. This view of the right side of an early aircraft—with ball-and-socket fittings in the nose Plexiglas—is unusual in that the bomb sight is not covered as it is in most early photographs of this then-secret instrument. (USAAF)

Above right: B-17F-60-BO 42-29723 of the 306th Bomb Group, with standard left-hand nose gun window. The right side gun barrel can be seen through Plexiglas over the covered bomb sight. (USAAF)

Left: Vega-built B-17Fs had a different arrangement of nose gun positions. That on the right occupied the centre position, and the left hand position replaced the forward window. The barrels have been removed from the blast tubes for cleaning on this 385th Bomb Group B-17F-35-VE, 42-5913. (USAAF)

improved forward firepower by replacing the .30-calibre machine guns, in ball-and-socket mounts offset 18in from the centreline of the nosepiece, with twin .50-calibre weapons firing through an aperture made in the upper part of the Plexiglas. The recoil of these weapons made them difficult to handle and the heavy supports required impeded the bombardier. For this reason B-17Es and Fs so equipped were normally flown as wing aircraft and dropped bombs on the signal of the leading aircraft which had a bomb sight. An alternative arrangement was a single .50 in the upper nose aperture and another .50 positioned to fire through the nose ventilating door to cover the downward area that the higher gun could not reach, but the field of fire was very limited. The displaced .30-calibre gun was often used in a ball-and-socket mounted in a spider frame replacing the forward escape hatch, although this was not popular owing to the updraught it created.

A number of other modifications relating to armament were effected on Fortresses at Brisbane. The B-17E ammunition boxes at the waist guns were found impracticable because of the small quantity of ammunition held. To increase the supply an ammunition can able to hold 300 rounds was designed with a false bottom to be used in conjunction with ammunition feed guides. The false bottom was mounted on springs, raising the ammunition as it was used and reducing the drag and weight which would otherwise be added to the feeding mechanism. Similar modifications were made to the ammunition feed for early B-17F waist guns. The Sperry upper turret was generally held to be the most effective defensive position but the early turrets had some difficulties highlighted in combat. The ammunition sometimes failed to feed when the guns were elevated at high angles. This was corrected by a coiled spring and a roller extension in the ammunition box. The original cables that charged the guns continually broke through being too small. Brisbane replaced these with a very flexible $^1/_8$in cable, that was also an inch longer, to allow the gun to return into function before the charging handle hit its stop. The opening and shutting of the machine-gun cover caused the firing solenoid cable to wear, and this was corrected by the use of a 90-degree cannon plug.

The Sperry ball turret also had its problems. Considerable trouble was experienced with the ammunition trace links jamming in the chutes that guided them out of the turret, occasionally causing gun stoppage. The chutes had to be enlarged to let the links fall freely. The door of the ball turret was the back rest for the gunner and the hinges proved to be insufficiently robust. Twisting of the hinges made the door difficult to close and on a few occasions the door had come open during flight, leaving the gunner held only by his safety straps. The Brisbane depot overcame this weakness by making new hinges out of heavy steel and both bolting and welding the hinge to the turret armour plate. Scorching of aircraft skin through gunfire brought the installation of blast tubes on turret guns. The telescopic sights fitted to the flexible guns on B-17Es were found to be impracticable as a result of limited vision and misting. These were replaced with the preferred ring-and-post sights.

Brisbane also carried out modifications to improve bomb-related problems. As designed, the bomb rack selector switch, situated in the bomb bay, had to be changed manually if an auxiliary fuel tank was being carried and there was a requirement to jettison it in an emergency. A situation could arise where there was insufficient time for a crew member to go into the bomb bay to operate this switch and avert a catastrophe. For this reason the switch was relocated on the bombardier's panel in the aircraft's nose. Much trouble was also experienced with the A-2 model release units failing to release bombs, although this could only be prevented by careful maintenance and ground checks to see that they functioned properly. The failure of bomb bay doors to open was traced to the grease on the operating screws freezing at high altitude. All grease was removed and graphite was substituted as a lubricant.

AGAINST GERMANY

The United Kingdom was the main location of B-17 deployment and an extensive programme of modifications was carried out throughout the aircraft's period of use. The main centre for this work was Burtonwood, near Liverpool, which eventually had facilities comparable to a factory installation with a staff of some 16,000. The first B-17Es arrived in the UK in July 1942 and were immediately given radio modifications to permit them to conform with British communication procedures. These included the installation of Mk 2 IFF (Identification Friend or Foe) and SBA (Standard Beam Approach) receivers. SBA, based on the Lorenz system used in the US, was available at many UK airfields and it was only necessary to remove the marker beacon antenna on the B-17 and install the SBA antenna in its place. The RAF had already suggested fourteen items on the B-17E which needed installation or modification. Apart from radio equipment, they felt that the bomb racks should be capable of holding British bombs, that downward recognition lights should be fitted and that fire extinguishers and additional equipment for the liferaft should be added.

The first few missions using B-17Es highlighted a number of weaknesses, namely a lack of sufficient forward firepower, a tail-heavy balance condition, difficulties with the ball turret and an inadequate oxygen supply for turrets. After only weeks in operational use the B-17E was withdrawn from first-line units and thereafter assigned to an operational training organisation.

One of the B-17Es was set aside for experimental modification and was extensively re-worked at Bovingdon. The first step was to alter the shape of the nose in order to place the bombardier and bomb sight where they would not be impeded by the forward defensive armament. As had been found in the SWPA, heavier armament in the nose could only be satisfactorily installed if the bomb sight were removed. The bomb sight on the experimental aircraft was placed further back in the compartment in a specially formed emplacement under the nose. The bombardier's instrument panel was relocated 6in forward from the rear partition of the compartment on the left side, under the radio compass receiver, and the bomb door lever placed opposite on the right. An oxygen regulator was mounted nearby on the rear wall and the bombardier's seat in the doorway to the flight deck was positioned on the left side of the compartment. The duties of bombardier and navigator were to be combined and the radio operator and all his equipment placed in the nose, where the radio operator would also man the front turret. B-17E radio equipment included a trailing antenna which was reeled in and out. This was eliminated and replaced by a wire running from the mast above No 3 bulkhead to the top of the fin and thence to a point roughly midway along the left wing.

The movement of the radio operator and equipment to the nose gave a better balance condition with the aircraft's centre of gravity at 28 per cent of the mean aerodynamic chord. The forward safe limit of the centre of gravity on a B-17E and F was 22 per cent of the mean aerodynamic chord, and the rear safe limit 32 per cent. The centre of gravity of a standard B-17E or F with full load was near the rear safe limit at 31 per cent and required the use of elevator trim tabs to correct for level flight. This caused structural strain and had a speed and altitude penalty.

Another serious problem with the B-17E was the inadequate oxygen supply to the turret gunners, the supply being exhausted after approximately 1°–2 hours. An enhanced supply for the top turret was provided by replacing the original F-1 model oxygen bottle in the top turret with a larger G-1 model. This, with an enlarged securing strap and brace, plus two pairs of the small D-2 bottles, installed on the outer sides of the two vertical turret supports, furnished 5 hours' supply for the gunner.

The oxygen supply to the ball turret was similarly increased to give 5 hours by replacing the small bottle with two full-size bottles, in the course of extensive modification. It was recognised that only men of small stature, wearing the heavy protective clothing necessary at high altitudes, could man and operate this turret successfully. Such were the space limitations that a parachute could not be worn, and in the event of the aircraft being abandoned in flight it was necessary for the gunner to rotate the turret to the position where he could open the door and climb into the fuselage to retrieve his parachute—an even more time-consuming task if the electrical power failed and the turret had to be hand-cranked. It was clear that if the aircraft was out of control at the time the gunner had little chance of escape—and the possibility of such a situation did not help his morale. Other difficulties experienced were the jamming of the ammunition link ejection chutes (as had been found in the SWPA), the failure of the trace to feed from the ammunition compartments due to dislodgement through the rolling of the turret, and the tangling of oxygen, earphone and throat microphone cords by the gunner's movement as each plugged in at a different place in the turret.

The turret was modified to provide more room for the gunner by removing the original ammunition compartments and replacing them with two tail-gun position boxes and mounting them on a yoke above the turret. The ammunition was fed to the guns by means of flexible chutes. The original link chutes were replaced by an attachment that ejected the links directly from each gun out of the turret. Rearrangement of the other equipment in the turret not only allowed a much larger operator to be accommodated but also permitted a backpack parachute to be worn in the turret. In an emergency all the gunner had to do was to bring his guns to the horizontal position, release the turret door and safety straps and bale out.

The engineering section at Bovingdon also wished to install B-24-type power turrets in the nose and tail of the B-17E involved, serial number 41-9112, but this and other modifications were beyond the capabilities of this organisation. Impressed by the improvements that had been made, in February 1943 the Eighth Air Force arranged for the aircraft to be flown back to the United States and taken to Wright Field for incorporation of the other modifications proposed. Consolidated power turrets were placed in the nose and tail positions, allowing the guns 70 degrees of elevation, 40 degrees of depression and 180 degrees in azimuth. A lighter Martin turret was substituted for the Sperry upper turret. The Martin was more compact, was some 120lb lighter and also had a seat whereas the gunner had to stand in the Sperry. The waist gun positions were eliminated and instead a power-boosted twin .50 gun installation was positioned in the former radio room. This was raised sufficiently to enable the guns to be deflected at 45 degrees on either side of the

Below left: The left side of 306th Bomb Group, Vega-built B-17F 42-5970 shows the stepped-out window moulding that allowed the gunner to direct his fire more to the front than from the side windows of the Boeing- or Douglas-built B-17Fs. (USAAF)

Below right: In the spring of 1943 a new type of nose 'cheek gun' fixture was put into production, initially available to modification centres and then incorporated in factory assembly lines. This featured a framed lip projection holding the gun mount and allowing greater forward cover than with the previous arrangements. The Plexiglas was moulded to meet the frame. This is B-17F-55-DL 42-3400 of the 95th Bomb Group. (USAAF)

Opposite top left: The left-hand side of B-17F-120-BO 42-30829, showing the redesigned standard cheek gun attachment. All three factories changed to this type. (USAAF)

Opposite top right: Wright Field authorities believed that, with the introduction of the chin turret, cheek guns would no longer be necessary for frontal defence. The combat air forces thought otherwise and demanded reinstatement. Early B-17Gs had visibly 'clean' noses, as had this 20-DL, 42-37839, of the 388th Bomb Group. (USAAF)

Opposite centre left: As a stop-gap, some combat units placed .50s through the small nose windows, as on B-17G-5-DL 42-3537 of the 94th Bomb Group. (USAAF)

Opposite centre right: Other early B-17Gs had the standard B-17F cheek gun fittings installed in the UK, utilising the same positions as on the B-17F. One such was B-17G-10-DL 42-37776, which served with the 384th Bomb Group. (W. T. Larkins)

Opposite bottom left: The nose side gun mounts were slightly modified for the B-17G and the positions reversed—left forward, right central—as with the original Vega production positions. This was to bring the right-hand gun further from the chin turret operating column. Before the cheek guns were reintroduced on the production lines US modification centres did the work, as on B-17G-30-BO 42-31917 of the 385th Bomb Group. The chin turret on this aircraft has extra long blast tubes on the guns to prevent damage to the nose Plexiglas if fired at maximum elevation. (USAAF)

Opposite bottom right: The left-hand fitting on B-17G-5-BO 42-31185 of the 447th Bomb Group. All production B-17Gs had the cheek guns in these locations. (USAAF)

CHANGES, ALTERATIONS AND MODIFICATIONS 43

44 THE B-17 FLYING FORTRESS STORY

fuselage, elevated to 78 degrees and swung a full 180 degrees in azimuth. The gunner in this open position was protected by a windshield. A new bombardier compartment with an unobstructed outlook was fashioned beneath the nose, reminiscent of the 'bath tub' lower gun position of the early B-17 models. The duties of bombardier and navigator were combined and the radio operator served as nose gunner. The original bombbay doors, which caused drag and restricted the ball turret gunner's fire when open, were replaced with folding panel doors which, when fully open, extended only 8in below the fuselage. A completely revised oxygen system was installed which provided each crewman with an independent supply by double lines, the intention being to make the system as invulnerable as possible. Battle damage to the oxygen system of standard B-17s had often been life-threatening.

The various changes resulted in an aircraft with a centre of gravity at near the ideal point and more than 1,000lb lighter than a standard B-17F through the reduction of the crew from ten to eight and the elimination of the waist guns and some armour. Top speed and handling qualities were said to be an improvement on those of the B-17F. Known as the Reed Project B-17, the aircraft was returned to the UK for evaluation in October 1943, although there is no record of it being used operationally. By this date the B-17G was coming into service with its effective chin turret, and the radical changes made on the Reed aircraft were deemed too extensive to incorporate on the production lines without severe interruption of deliveries—something that could not be countenanced at this time. Moreover, not everyone viewed these changes with approval, particularly the transfer of the radio equipment and operator to the nose and the combining of the bombardier's and navigator's duties. An additional reason why these improved features were not adopted was the expectation that B-29s and B-32s would soon replace the B-17s and B-24s on production lines.

In Europe, as in the SWPA, the major deficiency was in frontal armament. The first B-17Es to arrive had side nose gun installations carried out in the United States. B-17Fs were received with a ball-and-socket mount in the nose side windows to take a .30-calibre weapon. This was in the front window on the right side, for use by the bombardier, and in the rear window on the left, for use by the navigator. A priority was to install mounts able to take .50-calibre weapons in these positions, which involved substantial supports to the nose formers as the original Plexiglas mounts were not strong enough to take the recoil from 'point fifties'. By March 1943 200 early B-17Fs had received these modifications in the UK while 80 had single and 24 had twin gun installations firing through the upper part of the nose Plexiglas in similar fashion to the SWPA arrangements. No bomb sights were carried in the aircraft with these twin-gun nose mounts, and aircraft so equipped were intended to fly on the wing of a squadron or group leader doing the bomb aiming to afford extra forward firepower. Such was the 'kick' of these guns that holding accurate aim was extremely difficult. A single .50 gun in the upper nose was a more manageable alternative, and this could be held out of the way to permit a bomb sight to be used.

The first single .50 nose installations were offset to the right in most cases to allow the bombardier more room, the support structure and mounts being fabricated in the UK and supplied to combat groups in kit form for installation by their engineering personnel. By February 1943 a standard fitment had been agreed for this weapon to be centrally placed, and a request was sent to the United States for the installation to be made in production or at a modification centre. Most of this early work was done at the Honington, Suffolk, air depot. The service groups at this airfield also reinforced all ball turret doors in work similar to that performed on the Reed B-17E, as well as adopting the radio antenna changes made on that aircraft. By late March the same base was ready to change Mk II IFF sets for Mk III on all B-17s in the UK.

STAGING LISTS

Operational experience brought a growing number of unsatisfactory reports from combat units in the European Theatre of Operations (ETO), and by May 1943 a standard depot modification list had been prepared which ran to no fewer than 59 items! The list involved nineteen pertaining to armament, including the nose guns, resiting of the waist gun mounts, enlarging ammunition boxes to carry more rounds, collectors for ejected trace links to avoid fouling, mountings on the guns for reflector sights, the replacement of the metal panel in the top turret with Plexiglas and the removal of a metal bar in the same turret which obstructed the sight. Nine items were for additional or repositioned armour plate or bullet-proof glass. Three items pertained to the electrical system. Two concerned engine accessories, the exhaust flame dampers and a supercharger regulator. Eight dealt with radio and allied items, modification of the antenna and the installation of various equipment including a remote reading compass. There were seven requirements for structural changes or reinforcements and, finally, seven miscellaneous items such as oxygen detail, emergency air–sea rescue equipment and heating in the bomb bay. It was apparent that, with the current facilities and trained service manpower, in no way could all these requirements be met when the attrition in combat units demanded that replacement aircraft be made available as soon as possible. Moreover, there was a sudden influx of new B-17 groups at this time, increasing the workload threefold.

In late May it became necessary to define twelve first-priority modifications that had to be carried out before newly arrived aircraft could be flown operationally. These were the nose gun installations, the charging handle in the Sperry upper turret which jammed, a section made from 2°in armour plate behind the cockpit instrument panel, modifications to allow increased ammunition supply for the

---

Opposite top left: An in-the-field experiment by the 385th Bomb Group placed a 20mm cannon in the ultimate single nose gun fitting of a B-17F. Although the weapon's mount was well supported by a strong yoke (the bolts securing the end plates to the aircraft's skin can be seen), when the gun was fired the recoil compromised the safety of the nose compartment. The aircraft employed was B-17F-30-VE 42-5897. (USAAF)
Opposite top right: The 20mm cannon *in situ*, August 1943. It was found difficult for a gunner to control because of its weight and the recoil. (USAAF)
Opposite centre left: A 20mm cannon in the tail position of the 97th Bomb Group's B-17G 42-38090, one of at least five such installations made by this group in the spring of 1944. The sight was a ring-and-bead on the end of the long rod attached to the gun barrel. As M/Sgt Morley Russell, who worked on this installation, commented, 'The sight sure was a real Rube Goldberg type, but it worked well.' (Morley L. Russell)
Opposite centre right: Another 'in-the-field'-generated gun arrangement was the 384th Bomb Group's fixed battery of .50-calibre weapons under the nose of B-17G 42-31435. This battery, fired by the pilot, was devised to meet mass head-on attack. It was installed when this aircraft had to have major nose repairs following an accident. It was flown operationally for a few sorties in early July 1944, but there was no opportunity to use the guns prior to a crash-landing in the UK. (George Sheehan)
Opposite bottom: B-17G 42-38090, on a mission in July 1944, displays the 20mm cannon installation. Because of the limited movement of the gun it had a poor field of fire, but its purpose was to counter the enemy fighters that fired rockets from outside the range of the normal .50-calibre armament. B-17s with these tail cannon were flown at the rear of formations, and the weapon was considered more of psychological than destructive value. (Steve Birdsall)

46 THE B-17 FLYING FORTRESS STORY

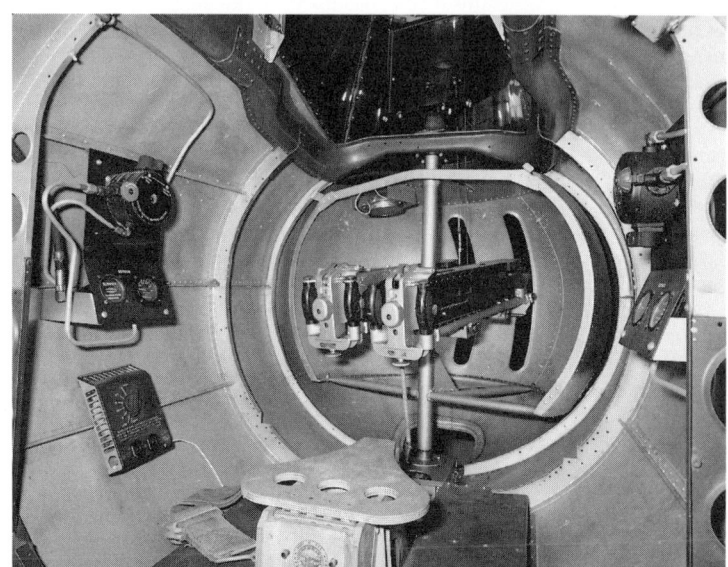

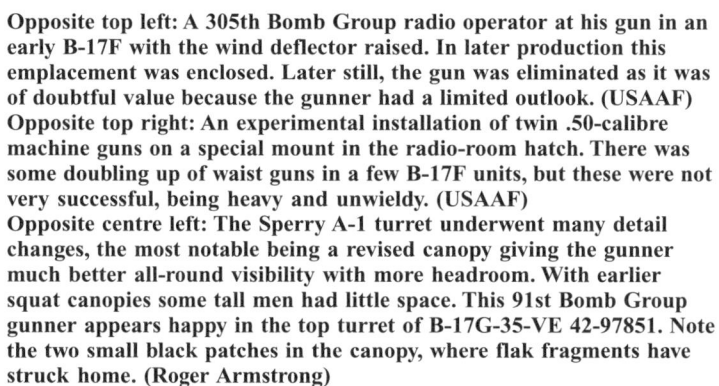

Opposite top left: A 305th Bomb Group radio operator at his gun in an early B-17F with the wind deflector raised. In later production this emplacement was enclosed. Later still, the gun was eliminated as it was of doubtful value because the gunner had a limited outlook. (USAAF)
Opposite top right: An experimental installation of twin .50-calibre machine guns on a special mount in the radio-room hatch. There was some doubling up of waist guns in a few B-17F units, but these were not very successful, being heavy and unwieldy. (USAAF)
Opposite centre left: The Sperry A-1 turret underwent many detail changes, the most notable being a revised canopy giving the gunner much better all-round visibility with more headroom. With earlier squat canopies some tall men had little space. This 91st Bomb Group gunner appears happy in the top turret of B-17G-35-VE 42-97851. Note the two small black patches in the canopy, where flak fragments have struck home. (Roger Armstrong)
Opposite centre right: A 303rd Bomb Group gunner demonstrating the cramped position in the ball turret, where movement was actuated by foot pedals. (USAF)
Opposite bottom left: A view of the ball turret interior, showing the reflector-type gun sight and installed guns either side of the gunner's position. For safety, a gunner never entered the turret until the B-17 was airborne. (IWM)
Opposite bottom right: The interior of a Cheyenne tail gun position, showing jockey seat (less cushion), oxygen regulator and supply lines (left and right). The switch gear at lower left is the electric rheostat for the gunner's heated suit. The twin .50-calibre guns were hand-operated. Armour protection has been removed from this aircraft. (IWM)
Above left: A 'clean' B-17G rear fuselage with full glazed waist windows and K-5 sill-mounted guns in the staggered positions. The ball turret, with door uppermost, is in its yoke support, and beyond is the open radio-room door. (IWM)
Above right: The flight deck from below the top turret, showing the 'crawlway' to the nose just aft of and below the pilots' seats. The aircraft's main oxygen supply was situated in this area. (IWM)

radio compartment gun, radio antenna changes and a better supply of oxygen to the ball and top turrets. These last were based on the Reed B-17 experiments. The other priority items were the installation of Mk III IFF sets and a remote indicating compass, modifications to prevent premature release of the liferaft and the provision of emergency equipment.

A list of eight second-priority requirements addressed the need for twin waist guns (soon eliminated as untenable in the circumstances), bullet proof glass for the pilots' windshields and side windows, the mounting bracket for the N-3A reflector sight on all .50 calibre guns (another requirement largely ignored), placing the waist gun mounts on the sills to provide wide fields of fire, the installation of Gee navigational sets, additional oxygen system modifications, a change of supercharger regulator and the collectors for ejected links and cases. There were eleven items for a third priority: armour plate protection for the bomb sight, the navigator's position and the under part of the cockpit floor adjacent to the pilots, frost-proofing of the cockpit windshields to improve visibility, reinforcement of the ball turret doors, modification to allow the ball turret to fire forward when the bomb bay doors were open, reinforcement to the fuselage structure in three places and additional special radio equipment. There was a fourth priority covering minor items for which work was requested at US modification centres before the aircraft were despatched overseas.

Further to clarify the procedure, in July 1943 so-called staging lists were introduced, identifying the various stages of modification on B-17s. These listed 101 items, although 42 were not modifications but instructions for inspections and the removal of equipment such as bomb-bay fuel tanks, de-icer boots, entry steps and extra seats when new aircraft arrived from the United States. Stage 1, the priority modifications, covered eight armament items, including the nose gun installation, increased ammunition supply for the flexible guns with flexible feed arrangements replacing ammunition magazines, the harmonisation of turret guns, reworking the charging handles in the Sperry top turret, changing the firing solenoid in the top and ball turrets to the improved G-4 type, the replacement of gaskets in the hydraulic mechanisms of the ball turret with more substantial material to stop oil leaks which were commonly experienced, and the retightening of all parts in the ball turret, particularly the door hinges. Two radio items were the substitution of Mk III IFF for Mk II and Command (short range) and Liaison (long range) antennae to fin and wing. Five items related to the Wright engines and accessories, but these were maintenance matters, requiring the changing of spark plugs for the British type, draining and replacing sump oil, cleaning filters and servicing the propeller governors. Five items pertained to structure, cutting down part of the armour that was found to obstruct the pilots, drilling holes in the radio room door for pressure relief and modifying the liferaft and installing a better

Above left: Flight decks were heated by glycol boilers which gained heat from their location in the engine exhaust collector, as seen on this B-17E nacelle. (*Flight*)

Above right: A view forward from between the pilots' seats, showing the distinctive throttle levers allowing individual or multi-engine adjustment with one hand. This Eighth Air Force B-17G has switches and instruments for additional combat equipment along the windshield sill. The crudely marked 'Y' in the centre of the instrument panel is the aircraft's call-letter. (USAAF)

Left: The attachment brackets for the taper pins holding the wing to the fuselage were difficult to reach and made wing changing a difficult task for maintenance crews. To ensure a true and safe fit, new pins and reamed holes had to be used. The exposed conduit was part of the de-icer system. (USAAF)

release for it. Eight miscellaneous minor items concerned among other things additional oxygen supply equipment, rescue equipment, flares and safety and stencilling instructions. Eleven items of equipment removal and maintenance made up this requirement, after which, if a replacement were urgently needed, a B-17F could be sent to a combat group without receiving Stage 2 modifications.

Many of the items in Stage 1 were in fact already being covered by the US modification centres at this time, and it was essential to check their inclusion. Stage 2 of the list provided for fuselage reinforcement to prevent cracking caused by gun blast from the top turret, repositioning the waist gun mounts to pivot clear of the fuselage skin line to provide a wider field of fire, installing a distance reading compass, adding armour plate to protect the instrument panel and replacing the metal panels in the top turret with Plexiglas. Stage 3 included the planned supercharger regulator change, the mounting bracket for reflector sight Mk IIIA on all .50 inch calibre guns, bullet-proof glass in the pilot's compartment and collectors for ejected bullet cases and links. Stage 4 covered only items for special duty aircraft such as those engaged in leaflet-dropping or radar developments.

Stage 5 listed fifteen items, work on which was by this date supposed to be carried out at the US modification centres but could be done in the UK if not evident on newly arrived aircraft. These concerned additional armour plate installations for the waist gunners, windshield frostproofing, the reinforcement of ball turret doors, modifications to the bomb-bay doors, the addition of bullet-proof glass for the ball turret, the installation of flexible ammunition feeds, a change in the tail gun sight control cable, the removal of the cross bar obstructing the top turret sight and the installation of 200-amp electrical generators on the outboard engines. A problem afflicting the B-17E and F at high altitude was the failure of brushes in the electrical generators, and these were replaced by a new type that would function in these conditions.

A frequent complaint from the ETO and MTO was the time taken to effect priority requirements at US modification centres. For example, two months elapsed after a .50-calibre nose gun mount was notified as urgent before a B-17F with this installation arrived in the UK. Upper turrets on B-17Fs were still arriving with a blind spot four months after this deficiency was pointed out.

The staging lists were updated at regular intervals throughout hostilities and although the number of required theatre modifications declined there was no lack of technical problems requiring a 'fix'. One of the first was the liferaft releasing in flight, catching on the tail surfaces and so endangering the aircraft. In a water landing the impact caused the raft door in the upper fuselage to open, but the mechanism was complicated and difficult to adjust correctly on the B-17E and F, resulting in the modifications mentioned. However, from opening too easily instances were reported when the raft door failed to open in a ditching, leading to the addition of an external means of release. Electric faults were not uncommon on B-17s in the UK due primarily to damp causing corrosion. Many instances of interphone system failure were experienced during the summer of 1943. These were traced to several causes, chiefly poor contact between the bushes and slip rings located in the hub of the pilots' control wheels and the binding of the push to operate buttons located on these wheels. The joints in engine ignition systems became corroded for the same reason, allowing the system to act as a crude radio transmitter and disrupting radio communications unless corrective action were taken.

Many modifications to B-17 radio equipment concerned improving reception and transmission. In October 1943 a programme to simplify the operation of Command and VHF sets was commenced, but the succession of radio changes continued to the end of hostilities. Apart from Command-required modifications, many originated in combat or service units, often as 'one-offs'. The quest for heavier armament saw the 385th Bomb Group install a 20mm cannon in the nose of a B-17F, but this was found to threaten the safety of the compartment when fired. A battery of six fixed .50 machine guns was tried out by the 384th Bomb Group, while in Italy the 97th Bomb Group used a 20mm cannon in the tail gun position on a number of its aircraft.

LONG-RANGE FUEL TANKS

The most significant factory change on the B-17F was the introduction of the so-called 'Tokyo Tanks' in the outer wing sections. Owing to a shortage of the self-sealing fuel cells used, several aircraft modified to take them were despatched overseas before the installation was made. The tanks drained by gravity to the main fuel tanks of the inner wing sections and were thus emptied first on long missions. While the additional fuel extended range and allowed distant targets to be attacked from the UK, the tanks were posing a hazard in that when they were empty and fume-filled an incendiary bullet could ignite an explosion sufficient to blow off the wing section. A study of losses revealed that 36 per cent of bombers went down on fire and that 20 per cent of these were fires in the outer wing sections. A further analysis showed that 15 per cent of bombers were lost to explosions and in 45 per cent of these the explosion occurred in the wings. Some experiments were carried out in the UK in pumping inert gases into the empty tanks, but this was found not to be a viable proposition. Some reduction of this hazard was achieved by incorporating small vents in the outer wing section to allow fresh air to drive out the fumes that accumulated around these tanks if they were badly holed and leaked—a modification that originated with the Italian-based B-17 groups.

Prior to the Tokyo Tanks, early B-17Fs had to carry a bomb-bay tank for extended range which, through its proximity to their stations, was not popular with crews, apart from its lessening the bomb load.

B-17G AND OPERATIONAL PROBLEMS

With the arrival of the B-17G in combat theatres it was found that the nose side gun positions had been discontinued. Apparently, so favourable were the reports of the chin turret that Materiel Command considered the side guns no longer necessary for frontal defence. The operational air forces took a different view and modification centres were soon busy installing the positions on the early B-17Gs until they were again included in US modification centre work. A standard mount for these positions had been produced in kit form during the spring of 1943 and featured a projecting lip and integral bracing to the fuselage side which did away with the interior braces of the early mounts but produced more drag, taking a few miles per hour off top performance. The chin turret, although acclaimed, was found to crack the nose Plexiglas when its guns were fired at maximum elevation. Eighteen-inch long blast tubes on the guns provided the solution.

Shortly after the first B-17Gs arrived in the UK, in September 1943, an experimental YB-40 was flown over for evaluation. This aircraft, 42-5833, had been completed to meet the many objections found with the trial YB-40s during the previous summer. The engines had good armour plate protection, but that in the rear of the aircraft had been reduced to improve flight characteristics. A weight reduction exercise had brought about an improvement to the empty state, although the aircraft was still substantially heavier than the B-17G. The most significant change was an entirely new type of tail gun position in which the two weapons, although still hand-held, were brought closer to the gunner and held in a cupola which moved in azimuth. In place of the post-and-bead sight of the production B-17G, an N-8 reflector sight was installed. This new arrangement, not only easier to handle, provided a wider cone of fire. Although this aircraft was not used operationally and was eventually returned to the USA, a favourable report was given on the revised tail gun position. This was eventually fabricated as a kit and installed on many B-17Gs by the Cheyenne modification centre to become generally known as the Cheyenne tail turret. The kits were also made available in the UK and Italy for use where the original tail gun position was damaged beyond economical repair. The 'Cheyenne turret' was introduced on production B-17Gs in the summer of 1944.

Left: A late production B-17G-85-DL, showing the radio-room hatch changes and the staggered waist gun positions. Main fuel filler caps and inner wing section vents also show clearly. (USAAF)
Below: Vents to allow fuel vapours trapped in the wing tips to escape originated with a Fifteenth Air Force experiment and were later available as a kit modification. This B-17G-85-DL had them installed during production. (USAF)

Top: The Reed Project B-17E after return to the UK. The twin .50s, manually operated with hydraulic boost, can be seen in the well normally occupied by the radio-room hatch. (USAAF)

Above left: The Convair power turret in the bulged fuselage end. The cut-out at the bottom of the rudder was necessary to prevent the guns fouling when the turret was turned with the guns at maximum elevation. (USAAF)

Above right: This view shows the bombardier's compartment below the nose, the folding bomb-bay doors and the modified ball turret. (USAAF)

Left: An interior view of the nose, with the turret doors at the top and the walkway above the bombardier's compartment in the foreground. The top of the bombardier's windshield can be seen beyond the latter. (USAAF)

Opposite, upper: Underwing racks were available for the B-17 and allowed much heavier loads to be carried, but only at a considerable penalty in endurance. Because of this they were rarely used, and only selected aircraft were fitted with the two locating brackets necessary for holding the racks. Two 1,000lb high-explosive bombs form the external load for this B-17F. (USAF)

Opposite, lower: The underwing racks were used for a variety of loads, including the parachute containers, the US version of the German flying bomb, Disney rocket bombs, TV-guided bombs and, in this case, glide bombs (standard 1,000lb bombs fitted with wings and empennage). (USAF)

CHANGES, ALTERATIONS AND MODIFICATIONS 51

The empty B-17G was a ton heavier than the B-17F despite continuing studies to eliminate accessories that were deemed unnecessary. Unfortunately, some of the items eliminated were very necessary. When the additional wing fuel cells were added to the B-17F it was decided to discontinue the individual engine fire extinguisher systems to save weight. These extinguishers consisted of a ring of CO_2-dispensing jets between the rear of the engine and the firewall. They had proved successful in extinguishing several engine fires in B-17Es and early F models, the value of this equipment being made apparent by the increasing number of later models that succumbed to engine fires. The extinguisher systems became another task for US modification centre installation until they were reintroduced on production lines in the spring of 1944.

An even costlier instance of an ill-chosen weight-saving measure was the deletion of a simple standpipe in each 37 US gallon oil tank situated in the engine nacelles. The purpose of this standpipe was to hold back sufficient oil if the tank were suddenly depleted to enable feathering of the propeller still to take place. If a propeller could not be feathered—that is, if it could not have its blades turned edge-on to the direction of flight so that they remained stationary—it would windmill, overspeeding the engine and causing intense vibration that could threaten the safety of the aircraft. Apparently, the weight-saving study initiated prior to the Tokyo Tanks installation concluded that there should always be sufficient oil for feathering if the supply were monitored efficiently. But in operational circumstances a rapid diminishing of the oil supply was often not noticed quickly enough for the propeller feathering button to be pushed and have the desired effect. A growing number of 'unable to feather' incidents, when fractured engine sumps lost oil, caused the Eighth Air Force to have a standpipe kit designed and supplied to service organisations.

Difficulty in obtaining the right materials in the UK during the winter of 1943–44 led to a delay with supplying kits, and the task appears to have been sidelined in favour of more pressing problems. However, in the summer of 1944 a report compiled through interviews with B-17 aircrew evadees and returned disabled prisoners of war highlighted the fact that in 43 per cent of cases failure to feather a propeller was the direct or indirect cause of loss. This revelation caused alarm, and urgent requests were made for the reintroduction of the standpipe on production aircraft and for kits to be made in the US and despatched to England and Italy. B-17Gs with the installation did not arrive overseas until September 1944 and modification kits later. Unfortunately, modification was a time-consuming task as it was also necessary to change an oil line. Further study of the feathering problem revealed that another source of failure was oil congealing in the extreme cold at high altitudes, and experiments were conducted in admitting hydraulic oil to the feathering duct-line to act as a dilutant. Other experiments involved the use of high-pressure nitrogen instead of oil, but these measures never went beyond the experimental stage.

Weaknesses often took time to be recognised, particularly when they appeared in a hitherto trouble-free component. Oil radiator leakage was not unknown, but during the winter of 1943–44 a sudden and alarming increase occurred. The copper core fractured and there were instances where the leakage was so serious that engines were starved of lubrication. Literally hundreds of these oil radiators had to be changed during this period. Changes in the manufacturing process had resulted in radiators that were insufficiently robust to resist the hydrostatic pressures, extreme temperatures and vibration. This problem was not satisfactorily solved until the early spring of 1944.

From the outset of operations the rubber de-icing boots along the leading edges of the flight surfaces were removed owing to the risk of their becoming damaged and dislodged in combat and fouling the flight surfaces. In their place a de-icing compound supplied by the British was used by the Eighth Air Force. In April 1944 a project was initiated for thermal de-icing of the wing by funnelling warm air up behind the leading edge. Many B-17Gs intended for this feature were delivered without the necessary primary engine heat exchangers because the intended design proved unsatisfactory. The 1,735 B-17Gs delivered without the heat exchangers—including 44 that did not even have the glycol heaters which the new type were supposed to re-

Above left: The 'Aphrodite' project's Castor radio-controlled 'flying bomb' B-17s produced the only open-cockpit Fortress. B-17F 42-30595 had the upper decking removed for a special operation which was cancelled. Thereafter the aircraft was used for training, remaining in the open-cockpit state. (USAF Museum)

Above right: Castor B-17s had numerous modifications. The nose hatch door was removed and a windshield was installed to enable fast and easy egress. The tank suspended under the fuselage dispensed smoke as a marker for the director B-17 guiding the drone aircraft. (USAF)

place—were fitted retroactively from December 1944 onwards.

In the summer of 1944 25 B-17Gs were modified in the United States for special squadrons given the task of testing the Azon guided bomb. This was a 1,000lb HE weapon fitted with a special tail containing a radio apparatus for controlling the bomb in azimuth during its free fall. As the successful use of this weapon required attack from half the usual bombing height, and the delivery aircraft was particularly vulnerable to anti-aircraft artillery fire if a long bomb run was involved, these B-17Gs featured so-called snap bomb-bay doors and heavy armour protection on the engines. The snap bomb bay opened and closed within a matter of seconds, the idea being to minimise the time the drag-creating doors were down on a target run. No use was made of the Azon weapon with Eighth Air Force B-17s, and these were employed in normal bombing operations where the sudden opening of the doors adversely affected speed and control during the bomb run. The engine armour included a curved section round the under lip of the cowl ring and extending 6in back and protection for the propeller governors, ignition harness, sump, carburettors, fuel strainers, oil temperature regulators and booster pump covers—in all, some 120lb per engine. The weight was in the right area but was considered a burden that produced a sluggish performance and placed more strain on the engines.

The continuing problem of added weight through equipment changes and guarding against the rearward movement of the centre of gravity was met by the elimination of one waist gunner, the deletion of the radio compartment gun and the halving of ammunition at the waist positions with the other half stored forward in the radio room for re-supply. Introduced from May 1944, the changes moved the centre of gravity forward 7in to within 5in of the desired position. This was deemed permissible because of the reduced activity of enemy fighters after the spring of that year. In the following spring some combat groups were flying without waist guns and others without chin and ball turrets in the belief that high speed through less drag was of greater benefit when flak was the principal antagonist. A further weight-saving move involved the replacement of some crew armour plate with 'flak curtains', laminated steel plates in canvas similar in make-up to body armour. These curtains were suspended or attached in locations where they could shield crew members from low-velocity shell splinters. Armour plate continued to be fixed to the floor below the bombardier and his sight, the navigator and the passage from the nose to the flight deck and behind the instrument panel, the work on new aircraft usually being carried out at sub-depots.

Necessity being the mother of invention, there was one piece of corrective action that would have appalled the designers of the B-17. An investigation into the cause of a number of top-turret fires in aircraft that had

Left: British Mk II and IIA (B-17F and E respectively) Fortresses were employed by RAF Coastal Command in oceanic reconnaissance. The Fortress IIAs were notable for displaying both their USAAF and British serials when delivered. FK209, alias 41-9203, has ASV radar search antennae above the nose and under both wings. (Canadian Archive)

been in service for some months found that the rotation of the turret frayed the electric cables that ran up the hollow central post, resulting in a fire and ignition of the oxygen lines that came up the same tube. The immediate solution was to fill the turret spigot tubes of older B-17s with concrete to seal the cables and lines and prevent their movement.

The Fortress, like other aircraft, revealed idiosyncrasies that had escaped the designers' attention. One such example was the fluxgate compass with its sensing apparatus located in the rear fuselage. Many reports of this instrument showing an inaccurate reading were puzzling, until it was discovered that if the compass were recalibrated while on the ground the retraction of the tail wheel in flight upset the magnetic field. The solution was to carry out the calibration during a test flight.

PRODUCTION BLOCK CHANGES

With the introduction of the block system of recording production changes, charts were compiled listing the changes made with each new block. The system was introduced with the B-17F and continued until the termination of production. The following extracts from the Production Change Charts for the B-17 illustrate the variation between the different manufacturers' blocks. A new block number did not necessarily mean changes. For example, the Vega plant made a practice of using a new block number for every hundred aircraft produced from the last B-17F batch to the end of production. Vega changes were often introduced within a block. Boeing and Douglas also batched production but, usually, did wait to introduce changes with a new block number, or gave a new number when changes were made.

B-17F-1-BO 41-24340 to 41-24389: R-1820-97 engines. Frameless Plexiglas nose. Wide-blade propellers and leak-proof oil tanks added. Oxygen system change. Engine cowlings modified to allow unimpeded propeller feathering.

B-17F-1-VE 42-5705 to 42-5709: Similar to B-17F-20-BO with A-11 supercharger regulator and P-1 model generators change.

B-17F-1-DL 42-2964 to 42-2966: Similar to B-17F-20-BO with A-11 supercharger regulator.

B-17F-5-BO 41-24390 to 41-24439: Circumferential armour at waist guns added and No 3 bulkhead armour deleted.

B-17F-5-VE 42-5710 to 42-5724: SCR-269G radio compass added and oxygen system changes.

B-17F-5-DL 42-2967 to 42-2978: Improved carburettor air filters and fuel transfer switch changes.

B-17F-10-BO 41-24440 to 41-24489: Modified tail wheel structure.

B-17F-10-VE 42-5725 to 42-5744: SCR-535 radio and bomb selector switch added. B-3 drift meter deleted plus minor changes.

B-17F-10-DL 42-2979 to 42-3003: Emergency brake lines, bomb selector switch, SCR-269G radio compass, circumferential armour for waist guns and armour plate for tail servo motors added. .30 nose gun deleted.

B-17F-15-BO 41-24490 to 41-24503: Minor detail changes.

B-17F-15-VE 42-5745 to 42-5764: Improved brakes, astrodome, A-12 oxygen regulators, alcohol de-icing windshield spray system all added.

B-17F-15-DL 42-3004 to 42-3038: Flexible gun mount in radio-room hatch, two .50-calibre staggered nose side guns, flexible ammunition feed for waist guns, astrodome and astrocompass, provision for Lorenz blind approach equipment, vacuum-operated instrument air filters, pyrotechnic signals and pistol stowage and A-12 oxygen regulators all added.

B-17F-20-BO 41-24504 to 41-24539: Ball-and-socket gun mounts in Plexiglas nose deleted and improved propeller governor added.

B-17F-20-VE 42-5765 to 42-5804: External bomb rack controls added.

B-17F-20-DL 42-3039 to 42-3073: External bomb rack controls, improved brakes and B-5 drift recorder added.

B-17F-25-BO 41-24540 to 41-24584: Minor detail changes.

B-17F-25-VE 42-5805 to 42-5854: Engine fire extinguisher system deleted. Detail electrical changes.

B-17F-25-DL 42-3074 to 42-3148: Outer wing section fuel tanks ('Tokyo') and B-4 starter and battery relays added.

B-17F-27-BO 41-24585 to 41-24639: Strengthened landing gear drag strut. Bladder-type main fuel tanks from 41-24606. .30 machine gun deleted from 41-24603 on.

B-17F-30-BO 42-5050 to 42-5078: Ball-and-socket gun mounts in nose side deleted and linking controls for external bomb racks added.

B-17F-30-VE 42-5855 to 42-5904: Fuel tanks in outer wing sections, reinforced wing flaps, heavy-duty brakes and improved main wheels, D-16 fuel pump and improved attachment of elevator fabric added. Bomb-bay fuel tanks deleted.

B-17F-30-DL 42-3149 to 42-3188: Engine fire extinguisher system deleted. D-16 fuel pump added.

Below: Fortress IIA FK185, which had served with No 220 Squadron on Atlantic patrol, was used for an experimental installation of a Vickers 40mm S gun in the nose. The intended role was low-level attack on U-boats or enemy shipping. It is not known if this aircraft was ever employed operationally with the weapon, and no other conversions are known. (Crown)

Above: Officially an F-9, 41-24440 continued to carry 'B-17F' as its designation while in service. Camera windows under and obliquely inclined on both sides of the lower nose were the F-9's distinguishing features. (USAF)

B-17F-35-BO 42-5079 to 42-5149: Tail gun armour deleted.

B-17F-35-VE 42-5905 to 42-5954: Nose gun mounts added.

B-17F-35-DL 42-3189 to 42-3228: Improved brakes and main landing gear, cockpit windshield wipers and increased hydraulic system capacity added.

B-17F-40-BO 42-5150 to 42-5249: Minor detail changes.

B-17F-40-VE 42-5955 to 42-6029: New landing gear motor added and minor electrical changes made.

B-17F-40-DL 42-3229 to 42-3283: Changes to tail gun sight linkage. Bomb-bay fuel tanks deleted.

B-17F-45-BO 42-5250 to 42-5349: Demand oxygen system and B-5 drift meter added.

B-17F-45-VE 42-6030 to 42-6104: A-3 oxygen flow indicators added. D-16 fuel pump deleted.

B-17F-45-DL 42-3284 to 42-3338: Reinforcement of nose in side-gun area, rudder structural changes, improved elevator fabric attachment, modified horizontal stabilisers for interchangeability, B-4 hydraulic pump and solenoid added.

B-17F-50-BO 42-5350 to 42-5484: Flexible trace feed for waist guns and direct-reading thermometer added. Heavy-duty brakes from 42-5459. Temperature indicator deleted.

B-17F-50-VE 42-6105 to 42-6204: Modified liferaft hatch and inspection window, plus modified tail stabilisers to give interchangeability.

B-17F-50-DL 42-3339 to 42-3393: Landing gear motor change and P-8 starter relay added.

B-17F-55-BO 42-29467 to 42-29531: Two .50 staggered side nose guns, revision of bomb release controls, increased hydraulic capacity, elevator down-spring and windshield de-icer alcohol spray system added.

B-17F-55-DL 42-3394 to 42-3422: Provision for auxiliary powerplant to operate main electrical system, B-3 bomb release control and AN5790 thermometer added.

B-17F-60-BO 42-29532 to 42-29631: Minor detail changes.

B-17F-60-DL 42-3423 to 42-3448: Revised Plexiglas nose added. Bombardier's window wiper, extra SCR-287 radio units, D-16 fuel transfer pump deleted.

B-17F-65-BO 42-29632 to 42-29731: Reinforcement of outer wing panels and new model P-1 electrical generators added.

B-17F-65-DL 42-3449 to 42-3482: Fittings and controls for external bomb racks and A-12 demand oxygen system added. Emergency hydraulic brake system removed.

B-17F-70-BO 42-29732 to 42-29831: New model D-16 emergency fuel pump added.

B-17F-75-BO 42-29832 to 42-29931: Radio compartment upper hatch gun, reinforcement of nose section at side guns and provision for use of auxiliary powerplant to operate electrical system added.

B-17F-80-BO 42-29932 to 42-30031: Fuel tanks ('Tokyo') in outer wing sections, tail wheel up limit switch and electrical motor changes added. Engine fire extinguisher system and bomb-bay fuel tanks deleted.

B-17F-85-BO 42-30032 to 42-30131: Improved brake and main wheel assembly and provision for remote reading compass added.

CHANGES, ALTERATIONS AND MODIFICATIONS 55

B-17F-90-BO 42-30132 to 42-30231: Improved Automatic Flight Control equipment and elevator fabric attachment added.

B-17F-95-BO 42-30232 to 42-30331: Reinforcement of radio room fuselage in gun mount area, modified tail stabilisers to give interchangeability and new model JH-3R starters added. External bomb racks deleted.

B-17F-100-BO 42-30332 to 42-30431: Changes to rudder balance, tail gun ammunition holder and minor electrical items added.

B-17F-105-BO 42-30432 to 42-30531: Remote reading compass and fuel valve change added. Landing gear warning horn deleted.

B-17F-110-BO 42-30532 to 42-30616: Flexible ammunition containers for tail guns and thermometer change added.

B-17F-115-BO 42-30617 to 42-30731: Carburettor air filter gasket revision and spare SCR-287 radio units deleted.

B-17F-120-BO 42-30732 to 42-30831: Modified liferaft hatch door and inspection window, oxygen A-3 flow meters and provision for revised bomb sight mount added. D-16 fuel transfer pump and emergency braking system deleted.

B-17F-125-BO 42-30832 to 42-30931: Low-temperature-proof hydraulic hoses added and changes in gyro flux gate compass mount made.

B-17F-130-BO 42-30932 to 42-31031: Reinforcement of lower nose for chin turret added and provision for change in bomb release equipment made.

B-17G-1-BO 42-31032 to 42-31131: Bendix chin turret, new Plexiglas nose, A-1 bomb control system, wiring for electric supercharger controls and induction vibrator starting coil added. Nose Plexiglas screen wiper deleted.

B-17G-1-VE 42-39758 to 42-39857: Bendix chin turret, Plexiglas nose change, wing tip reinforcement, reinforced fuselage aft of radio room, remote reading compass and B-3 bomb release interval control added. Bombardier's windshield wiper and No 3 bulkhead armour deleted.

B-17G-1-DL 42-3483 to 42-3503: Redesignated B-17F-70-DL. No 3 bulkhead armour omitted and Bendix chin turret added.

B-17G-5-BO 42-31132 to 42-31231: Additional oxygen supply for ball turret and fuel valve changes added.

B-17G -5-VE 42-39858 to 42-39957: Electronic turbo-supercharger regulator and emergency hydraulic brake system deleted. National insignia change incorporated.

B-17G-5-DL 42-3504 to 42-3563: Redesignated B-17F-75-DL. Bendix chin turret, A-3 oxygen flow indicator and induction vibrator starter coil added.

B-17G-10-BO 42-31232 to 42-31331: Provision in nacelles for electronic supercharger regulators, provision for SCR-595 or SCR-695 radio, and revised bomb sight mount wiring added. National insignia change incorporated.

B-17G-10-VE 42-39958 to 42-40057: Revised A-2A ball turret and British-type blind approach radio added.

B-17G-10-DL 42-37714 to 42-37803: Fuselage reinforcement aft of radio room against damage from the gun discharge, oil cooler drain cock and AN hose fittings added.

B-17G-15-BO 42-31332 to 42-31431: Provision for improved A-2 model ball turret, increased-capacity (600 rounds) ammunition boxes at waist guns.

B-17G-15-VE 42-97436 to 42-97535: Circumferential waist gun armour deleted from 42-97445. Oil reserve for propeller feathering system on 42-97447 only. SCR-695 radio (SCR-535 alternative), revised bomb sight wiring and wing tip light change added. Camouflage finish discontinued.

B-17G-15-DL 42-37804 to 42-37893: Electronic turbo-supercharger, SCR-522 VHF radio, SCR-595 radio (SCR-535 alternative), fuel valve changes and increased waist gun ammunition storage added.

B-17G-20-BO 42-31432 to 42-31631: A-2A model ball turret with oxygen line changes added.

B-17G-20-VE 42-97536 to 42-97635: Revised tail gun ammunition storage added.

B-17G-20-DL 42-37894 to 42-37988: Removable cockpit windshield panel added. National insignia change incorporated.

B-17G-25-BO 42-31632 to 42-31731: Revised carburettor air filters added.

B-17G-25-VE 42-97636 to 42-97735: B-22 high-speed, high-altitude supercharger added.

B-17G-25-DL 42-37989 to 42-38083: Circumferential waist gun armour deleted at 42-38064. Staggered nose side gun positions and staggered enclosed waist gun positions added, plus provision for Localise receiver RC-103.

B-17G-30-BO 42-31732 to 42-31931: Additional crew microphone and headset and minor electrical changes.

B-17G-30-VE 42-97736 to 42-97835: Oil reserve for propeller feathering system, starting with 42-97765, and fuel valve change added.

B-17G-30-DL 42-38084 to 42-38213: Provision for SCR-521 radio deleted. A-2A revised ball turret added.

Below: A General Electric B-2 turbo-supercharger on No 4 engine of a B-17E, showing the 'bucket wheel' which could glow red when the turbos were run for ground tests. The device centrally below the bucket wheel is the cooling cap which directed slipstream air to the rim of the bucket wheel. The dome of the cooling cap kept the wheel hub cool by preventing exhaust gases from blowing over the turbine wheel and by dissipating heat by radiation. The waste gate in the waste pipe controlled the amount of exhaust gas bypassing the bucket wheel and spilling into the atmosphere. Closing the gate increased pressure in the tail stack and thereby the speed of the bucket wheel to provide more boost. To hold a steady power setting, the waste gate was controlled by an automatic regulator, originally hydraulic but electronic in later production. (*Flight*)

B-17G-35-BO 42-31932 to 42-32116: B-22 high-speed turbo-supercharger and revised elevator trim tabs added. Camouflage finish discontinued from 42-32044.

B-17G-35-VE 42-97836 to 42-97935: Two staggered side nose guns added.

B-17G-35-DL 42-106984 to 42-107253: Homogeneous armour added. B-22 turbo-supercharger for high altitude added from 42-107109. B-10 bomb shackles added when available. Bomb hoist assembly deleted. Camouflage finish discontinued.

B-17G-40-BO 42-97058 to 42-97172: External access to life-raft release and RC-43B marker beacon added.

B-17G-40-VE 42-97936 to 42-98035: Stowage positions for extra SCR-274N radio units added from 42-98015. Reduced number of supercharger fixing bolts. Ball turret disconnect switch added.

B-17G-40-DL 44-6001 to 44-6125: Electrical bomb control system, oil reserve for propeller feathering system and D-5 fuel valve added and fuel tank hose changes.

B-17G-45-BO 42-97173 to 42-97407: Electrical bomb control system and A-8 signal container added. Changes to SCR-281 radio.

B-17G-45-VE 44-8001 to 44-8100: Homogeneous armour added from 44-8037. Electrical bomb control system and B-10 bomb shackles added. Parachute static lines at both exit doors added from 44-8088. Fuel tank fitting changes. Bomb-bay fuel tank fittings deleted.

B-17G-45-DL 44-6126 to 44-6250: Provision for bomb-bay tanks and stowage provision for extra SCR-274N radios deleted. Trailing static discharge wire at tail wheel added.

B-17G-50-BO 42-102379 to 42-102543: Circumferential waist gun armour deleted. Staggered enclosed waist guns with K-5 mount, engine fire extinguisher system and fuel valve change added.

B-17G-50-VE 44-8101 to 44-8200: Enclosed staggered waist gun positions with K-5 mounts. Outside release handles for liferaft added from 44-8105. Changes to hot air heating and provision for RC-103 radio added.

B-17G-50-DL 44-6251 to 44-6500: Enclosed radio gun compartment with K-5 mount, Cheyenne tail gun position with N-8 sight, engine fire extinguisher system, five modified oxygen regulators, additional stowage in liferaft compartment, outside release handles for liferaft, parachute static lines at exits and hot air heating. Provision for SCR-515 radio deleted. Lorenz blind approach equipment deleted from 44-6376 and G-1 oxygen signal deleted from 44-6401.

B-17G-55-BO 42-102544 to 42-102743: Main landing gear safety switch added.

B-17G-55-VE 44-8201 to 44-8300: Additions of enclosed radio-room gun with K-5 mount from 44-8287, Cheyenne tail gun with N-8 sight from 44-8287, fire extinguisher system from 44-8301, SCR-522 VHF radio from 44-8301. More stowage in liferaft compartment from 44-8208. Revised chin turret with provision for hand-charging added. Deletion of G-1 oxygen signal from 44-8268, provision for SCR-515 radio and Lorenz blind approach equipment.

B-17G-55-DL 44-6501 to 44-6625: Glide path radio receiver AN/ARN-5A Group 'A' and 'B' parts and RC-103 Group 'B' parts added.

B-17G-60-BO 42-102744 to 42-102978: Two staggered nose side guns with K-5 mounts from 42-102944. Provision for RC-103 from 42-102844. Stowage positions for extra SCR-274N radio units deleted from 42-102844.

B-17G-60-VE 44-8301 to 44-8400: Localiser receiver RC-103 Group 'B' parts, Group 'A' parts for TR-1335, Group 'A' parts for AN/ARN-5 glide path receiver, B-3 bomb release interval control, five extra oxygen regulators, engine fire extinguisher system and duplication of bomb sight wiring added.

B-17G-60-DL 44-6626 to 44-6750: Not traced.

B-17G-65-BO 43-37509 to 43-37673: Starter gearbox change, provision for SCR-521 radio deleted from 43-37648, additional storage in liferaft compartment from 43-37672.

B-17G-65-VE 44-8401 to 44-8500: AN/ARN-7 radio compass added and radio room gun deleted.

B-17G-65-DL 44-6751 to 44-6875: Not traced.

B-17G-70-BO 43-37674 to 43-37873: Oil reserve for propeller feathering system incorporated from 43-37728. Five additional oxygen regulators from 43-37774. Radio compass antenna, landing gear motor change and trailing wire static discharger added.

B-17G-70-VE 44-8501 to 44-8600: Changes to supercharger regulator electrics.

B-17G-70-DL 44-6876 to 44-7000: RCM equipment AN/APT-2 and AN/APQ-9 Group parts added from 44-6900.

B-17G-75-BO 43-37874 to 43-38073: Homogeneous armour from 43-38024. Parachute static lines added.

B-17G-75-VE 44-8601 to 44-8700: No major changes.

B-17G-75-DL 44-83236 to 44-83360: Radio compartment gun deleted. Interphone AN/AIC-2 (same as RC-36B except high-altitude amperage) added.

B-17G-80-BO 43-38074 to 43-38273: Additions of enclosed radio compartment gun with K-5 mount from 43-38274, Cheyenne tail gun with N-8 sight from 43-38473, SCR-522 VHF radio from 43-38174, RC-103 Group 'B' parts from 43-38174, outside release handles for liferaft, cockpit hot air heating system, duplication of bomb release wiring, changes to landing gear retracting units, AN/ARN-7 radio compass and Group 'A' parts AN/ARN-5 glide path receiver added.

B-17G-80-VE 44-8701 to 44-8800: AN/AIC-2 interphone (same as RC-36B except high altitude amperage) added.

B-17G-80-DL 44-83361 to 44-83485: Flak curtains in place of cockpit armour and flak curtains on upper half of bulkhead No 3.

B-17G-85-BO 43-38274 to 43-38473: G-1 oxygen signal deleted from 43-38363. Escape aid equipment changes.

B-17G-85-VE 44-8801 to 44-8900: Radio compartment gun deleted from 44-8817.

B-17G-85-DL 44-83486 to 44-83585: Not traced.

B-17G-90-BO 43-38474 to 43-38673: Revised oil coolers, changes to bomb door operation and supercharger regulator electrics added.

B-17G-90-VE 44-8901 to 44-9000: Armour in cockpit replaced by flak curtains. RCM equipment (AN/APT-2 and AN/APQ-9 'A' parts) added.

B-17G-90-DL 44-83586 to 44-83685: Not traced.

B-17G-95-BO 43-38674 to 43-38873: B-3A bomb release interval control, engine fire extinguisher changes and bomb rack modifications.

B-17G-95-VE 44-85492 to 44-85591: Flak curtains on upper half of bulkhead No 3 added.

B-17G-95-DL 44-83686 to 44-83885: Not traced.

B-17G-100-BO 43-38874 to 43-39073: Flak curtains on upper half of bulkhead No 3 added from 43-39009. Glide path radio receiver AN/ARN-5A Group 'B' parts added from 43-38923.

B-17G-100-VE 44-85592 to 44-85691: Not traced.

B-17G-105-BO 43-39074 to 43-39273: Cockpit armour replaced by flak curtains from 43-39109. Radio compartment gun deleted from 43-39206.

B-17G-105-VE 44-85692 to 44-85791: Not traced.

B-17G-110-BO 43-39274 to 43-39508: Not traced.

B-17G-110-VE 44-85792 to 44-85841: Not traced.

4. The Wright R-1820 Cyclone

The Fortress's powerplants were extremely robust units considering the environment in which they were operated and what was demanded of them in wartime. The Cyclone 9-cylinder air cooled radial first appeared in 1929 and was developed from an earlier model. With a longer stroke than the Pratt & Whitney R-1830 of similar size and power, it was considered better for high-altitude supercharging. The R-1830 Twin Wasp which powered the B-24 Liberator was similarly rated to the Cyclone but the latter, at 1,333lb dry, was 127lb lighter.

It was originally rated at 575hp for take off and normal flight but this was eventually more than doubled. The R-1820-39 of the Y1B-17 was rated at 850hp at 2,100rpm, and the R-1820-51 that powered the B-17B had 1,000hp at 2,300rpm. The B-17C, D and E models had the similarly rated R-1820-65 producing 1,200hp, supercharger-boosted for take-off. The standard combat Fortresses, the F and G models, had the R-1820-97 with a 16:9 crankshaft-to-propeller shaft ratio, giving improved high-altitude output. The bore of this model was 6.125in and the stroke 6.875in, with a piston displacement of 1,823in^3. When a water injection facility was added, the so-called War Emergency power it produced was rated at 1,380 hp. Available in kit form in combat areas from July 1944, water injection added an extra 17mph to the top speed of a B-17G at 20,000ft.

The Cyclone had a reputation for throwing oil through the breathers at high altitude, and while modifications limited this escape it was a 'dirty' engine under operational conditions. Rocker cover leaks were also common, the neoprene gasket being too thick and a poor seal. Thinner gaskets went some way towards improving matters, but with 80psi pressure on the rocker cover under full load the leaks often reappeared. The crews of Liberators with their cleaner Pratt & Whitney radials joked about Fortress airfields being easily identified from the air by the oil stained hard standings, which was often true. Excessive oil consumption was the principal reason for engine changes in operational units and arose from a number of causes, though mostly cylinder wear. The normal recommended time for engine change was 375 hours maximum for the B-17B, C and D models, but where a B-17 was employed in undemanding flight higher hours were achieved. Such were the harsh operating conditions of the SWPA that, although the maximum number of hours for the R-1820-65s on B-17Es was 350, many never reached half that figure. The R-1820-97s of the B-17F and G models had a recommended change period of 500 hours, but many engines went for near double this time in Europe. An engine change was considered to involve six men and take five hours. Often only two men were involved and it then took two days.

Ignition problems occurred at high altitudes. The early magnetos had a trailing contact for starting engines at slow rotation which worked well for this purpose. However, it was found that in the humid, rarefied air of some operational environments the spark would jump to the trailing contact, causing misfiring. This was cured by eliminating the trailing contact and installing a booster coil in the system, which was only used for starting. The ingress of moisture into electrical systems also occurred on the ground, particularly in England where the atmosphere was persistently damp in winter. The ignition harness was shielded to prevent the disruption of radio signals, but moisture often collected inside the shielding, requiring a small hole drilled in the lower part to act as a drain.

The major problem with engine operation was the turbo-supercharger, which had given no undue concern until exposed to the very humid, intensely cold, rarefied environment as found five miles high over Europe. Over-boosting an engine with supercharged power could, and did, cause carburettor ducting and exhaust manifolds to crack through the extremes of heat and cold, the former often causing loss of power. However, the main problem with superchargers was their hydraulic controls. So low were the temperatures at operational altitudes over Europe that the oil in the hydraulic lines would start to congeal, causing lagging response. Moreover, the supercharger and its regulator on the two inboard engines were set further back in the nacelles than on the outboard, and the oil in the longer lines to these tended to congeal more readily, producing erratic regulation and a power imbalance. This in turn would often lead to turbine over-speeding, damage and critical power loss. Changing a turbo unit was a difficult and unpopular task for mechanics. It was held in the nacelle by a large number of 7/16th bolts which were difficult to reach, and, on average, two men took five hours to complete the job. To minimise the risk of oil congealing it was necessary for pilots to exercise the turbo regulator controls every few minutes, which apart from being tiresome did not help for smooth engine operation.

The answer was electronic regulator controls in place of hydraulic, and these, a Minneapolis-Honeywell product, were introduced on production B-17Gs late in 1943. However, as often happened with such changes, many aircraft continued to have hydraulic regulators installed even though they were wired for the electronic system. More than one experienced B-17 pilot has declared that of all the many changes made to the B-17, electronic turbo-supercharger regulator control was the most significant and advantageous.

In order to economise on fuel many pilots had a habit of running engines with too lean mixtures. This raised engine temperatures and burnt out valves. Engine overheating was also caused by incorrect setting of the engine cowl flaps, which if fully opened under full power acted as air brakes, causing unnecessary drag. Overall, misuse was the one of the main contributory factors to engine malfunction, and 55 per cent of all combat losses involved engine failure.

In addition to production from the Wright plant at Patterson, New Jersey, R-1820 engines were from 1941 licence-built by the Studebaker Corporation at a South Bend, Indiana, factory. In fact, although at first mostly found on Douglas and Vega models, the majority of engines used in B-17s came from this source, although the early products were considered inferior to those from Wright. Malfunctions experienced with Studebaker engines led to a generally held bias for Wright products among B-17 pilots and mechanics, although, once manufacturing difficulties had been overcome, the Studebaker engine was equally reliable and gave good service.

5. B-17 Performance

Many factors determine the performance of an aircraft, power, drag, load, altitude, wind force and air temperature being critical. A number of tables of performance assessment exist for the B-17 and are notable for their differences. This is to some extent accounted for by the variation found in identical models and common to all production aircraft. In the type of operational employment favoured by the USAAF these differences were not crucial as a formation had set speeds and rates of climb and descent well removed from the maximum. In Europe the advised climb rate for a B-17F was 145 to 155 Indicated Air Speed (IAS) and cruise at 150 to 160 IAS. These speeds were slower than those for the B-24D, which climbed at between 155 and 165 IAS and cruised at 170 to 175 IAS. Operationally speed assessments were in IAS as shown on the instruments. As a rule of thumb, for every thousand-foot increase in altitude the IAS was another 2 per cent removed from true air speed. Thus a B-17 showing 150 IAS at 25,000ft had a true air speed of 225mph, or 240mph if at 160 IAS. The average rate of climb of a B-17F was from 300 to 400ft/min to reach the optimum operational height of 25,000ft, and for planning purposes this was taken as three minutes per 1,000ft of climb.

Although official publications gave the B-17E and early F models a range of 2,000 miles, in high-altitude operational employment 640 miles was the realistic figure, giving a radius of action of 320 miles. This was based on an all-up weight of 55,000lb at engine start with 1,760 US gallons of fuel. When the bomber had taxied, taken off and climbed to 25,000ft, occupying an hour, it would have consumed 380 gallons of fuel and weight would have decreased by 2,000lb. By the time 5,000lb of bombs had been dropped on the target the total weight was down to 43,700lb and 1,075 gallons had been consumed. The five-hour mission would leave 115 gallons in the tanks on return to base, at which time the total weight would be down to 41,030lb. For targets beyond this radius of action it was necessary for these model B-17s to make use of one or two auxiliary tanks in the bomb bay, which had capacities of 410 gallons each and doubled range, though at the expense of a reduced bomb load.

Table 1 shows top speeds for the early B-17F weighing 56,500lb, including a full fuel load at 1,730 US gallons and 6,000lb of bombs. At maximum continuous power it was calculated that the B-17F had an endurance of only 3.8 hours and a range of 900 miles, whereas with the same loading the endurance was 5.9 hours and the range 1,250 miles at cruise speed of 225mph at 25,000ft. With a reduction in weight top speed was greatly improved, and at just over 40,000lb gross 325mph could be attained at this altitude. This, however, did not take into consideration combat operational factors. Table 2, for the early B-17F at 56,500lb, illustrates how performance varied with changes in altitude.

The fitting of the so-called 'Tokyo Tanks' in the later B-17F and G nearly doubled range and radius of action, the additional 1,080 US gallons of fuel increasing the tactical radius of action to 700 miles. The additional weight did not affect handling qualities too adversely, apart from reducing performance in the early stages of a mission.

The B-17G loaded to gross 55,000lb, and with the drag-inducing chin turret required more power to climb at 145 IAS and flew at a slower speed in formation when using the same power settings as were common on early B-17F operations. On average the B-17G was 12mph slower at top speed than the B-17F, although combat operational speeds were normally far removed from top speeds—usually some 80 to 100mph less.

Table 1

Altitude (ft)	Top speed (max power	Top speed (max continuous power
30,000	298 mph	280 mph
25,000	299 mph	274 mph
20,000	288 mph	266 mph
15,000	274 mph	255 mph
10,000	263 mph	245 mph
5,000	252 mph	236 mph

Table 2

Altitude (ft)	Full power Top speed (mph)	Full power Rate of climb (ft/min)	Maximum continuous power Speed (mph)	Maximum continuous power Rate of climb (ft/min)	Maximum continuous power Time of climb (min)
30,000	298	400	280	225	52.0
25,000	299	725	274	450	36.2
20,000	288	850	266	550	25.7
15,000	274	950	255	675	17.3
10,000	263	1,050	245	750	10.2
5,000	252	1,125	236	1,125	4.0

B-17 PERFORMANCE

Table 3

Model	Engine rating: bhp/alt take-off / War Emergency / military / normal	Speed: max/hp/alt / landing (all at design wt)	Climb (min): time to alt / serv ceiling	Take-off/landing (ft): design wt over 50ft obstacle	Specimen range: miles/mph/alt ferry / normal / design	fuel (US gal): max / built-in / design	bombs: none / normal / design	weight: ferry / normal / design	Dimensions (ft): span / length / height / wing area	Weight (lb): empty / design / gross	Crew	Armament: guns: no/cal/rds bombs: no/size (lb)
YB-17	930 / – / – / 850/5,000	256/3,100/14,000 / 72	6.5/10,000 / 30,800	1,515 / 3,400	3,400/178/10,000 / 2,400/178/10,000 / 1,300/178/10,000	2,492 / 1,700 / 850	– / 4,000 / 2,000	43,650 / 42,500 / 34,873	103.9 / 68.4 / 19.3 / 21.0 / 1,425	24,460 / 34,873	6	5/.30/2000 or 5/.50/1000 / 4 × 2,000 (internal/external)
B-17A	1,000 / – / – / 800/25,000	295/3,200/25,000 / 78	7.8/10,000 / 38,000	1,700 / 2,500	3,600/176/10,000 / 2,400/230/25,000 / 1,300/230/25,000	2,492 / 1,700 / 850	– / 4,000 / 2,400	45,650 / 44,500 / 37,000	As above	26,520 / 37,000	6	As above
B-17B	As above / As above	292/3,400/25,000 / 80	7.0/10,000 / 38,000	1,775 / 2,500	3,600/176/10,000 / 2,400/230/25,000 / 1,300/230/25,000	2,492 / 1,700 / 850	– / 4,000 / 2,400	46,650 / 45,500 / 38,000	103.9 / 67.11 / 15.5 / 21.2 / 1,420	27,650 / 38,000	6	1/.30/500, 6/.50/3,000 / 4 × 2,000 (internal/external)
B-17C and B-17D	1,200 / – / 1,200/25,000 / 1,000/25,000	323/4,760/25,000 / 84	7.5/10,000 / 37,000	1,850 / 2,700	3,400/180/10,000 / 2,000/250/25,000 / 625/245/25,000	2,492 / 1,700 / 544	– / 4,000 / 2,000	49,650 / 48,500 / 39,320	As above	30,600 / 39,320	6	1/.30/500, 6/.50/3,000 / 2 × 2,000
B-17E	As above	317/4,800/25,000 / 88	7.1/10,000 / 36,500	2,150 / 2,700	3,200/180/10,000 / 2,000/224/15,000 / 500/250/25,000	2,520 / 1,730 / 404	– / 4,000 / 2,000	53,000 / 51,000 / 40,260	103.9 / 73.10 / 19.2 / 21.2 / 1,420	32,250 / 38,260	10	1/.30/500, 8/.50/3,600 / 2 × 2,000
B-17F BO (1–75) DL (1–20) VE (1–25)	1,200 / 1,380/25,000 / 1,200/25,000 / 1,000/25,000	299/4,800/25,000 / 90 (at 55,000lb)	25.7/20,000 / 37,500 (at 55,000lb design wt)	3400 / 2900 (55,000lb)	2,880/152/10,000 / 1,300/200/10,000 / 240/250/25,000	2,550 / 1,730 / 181 normal	– / 6,000 / 2,000	56,500 / 56,500 / 40,437	103.9 / 74.9 / 19.1 / 21.2 / 1,420	34,000 / 36,000 / 38,200 normal	10	11/.50/4,430 / 6 × 1,600 and 2 × 4,000 external
B-17F BO (80–130) DL (25–80) VE (30–50)	As above	As above	As above	As above	3,800/165/10,000 / 2,200/200/10,000 / –	3,630 / 2,810 / 1,168 (max)	– / 6,000 / 4,000	65,500 / 65,500 / 48,726	As above	34,000 / 38,000 / 44,560 max	10	As above
B-17G BO (1–110) DL (1–95) VE (1–110)	As above except new turbo increased critical altitude	287/4,800/25,000 / 90	37.0/20,000 / 35,600 (at 55,000lb design wt)	As above	3,400/180/10,000 / 2,000/182/10,000 / –	3,630 / 2,810 / 770	– / 6,000 / 4,000	65,500 / 65,500 / 48,726	As above; length 74.4 late models	36,135 / 38,000 / 44,560	10, later 9	12/.50/6,380 / 6 × 1,600 and 2 × 4,000 external
XB-40 YB-40	1,200 / – / 1,200/25,000 / 1,000/25,000	292/4,800/25,000 / 94	48.1/20,000 / 25,100 (at 60,500lb)	4,600 / 3,300	2,460/192/– / 2,260/196/– / –	2,520 / 1,700 / 2,261	– / – / –	63,300 / 54,400 / 58,000	103.9 / 74.9 / 19.1 / 21.2 / 1420	38,235 / 58,000	9	14/.50/11,200 / – / –

6. Post-War Fortresses

During and after hostilities the B-17 was adapted for duties other than its original purpose of bombing. This was due to the good handling characteristics of the aircraft, making it a first choice to carry a variety of special equipment. A prime vehicle for various radar and radar countermeasures devices, it had also been used by both the RAF and US Navy with sea-search radars. The type's inherent strength and lifting capability found it employed in carrying glide bombs, rocket bombs, flying bombs and other underwing stores. Old B-17s had even been loaded with 20,000lb of high explosive and used as radio-controlled missiles. The Fortress was also chosen to carry the US airborne lifeboat, and it was in a search and rescue capacity that it endured in USAF service until the mid-1950s.

B-17Es and Fs were employed for combat transport duties in the SWPA. Once Fortresses were declared no longer fit for bombing operations many were converted to transports. Devoid of power turrets, armour and war equipment, these B-17s were some 10,000lb lighter than the combat configuration. The type became a favourite conveyance for generals, several aircraft being given plush interiors to meet the expectations of senior ranks. B-17s were also favourites for testbeds, being used to carry special equipment or power units for trials. Again, because of the type's inherent stability, B-17s were used for radio-control operations, chiefly as targets for controlled missiles, the Fortress's last military use. All these adaptations from different employment required modifications to the original bomber configuration. The work was carried out by Boeing in some cases but more often by USAF depots or other manufacturers and civilian agencies.

Right, upper: The camera caught this lifeboat a second after its release from an SB-17G of the post-war Air Rescue Service during a demonstration. The cable still attached operated the parachute released when the boat was well clear of the aircraft. (USAF)
Right, lower: A Higgins boat installed under SB-17G 44-83585, showing the approximately 2ft ground clearance. The propellers, in protective screens, can be seen projecting from the hull.

POST-PRODUCTION DESIGNATION CHANGES

The variety of these special adaptations and uses brought a large number of official redesignations. The simplest forms were prefix letters to the original designation, which came into practice in 1942 and were added to when the need arose until the regulations were revised in June 1948. A prefix 'T' indicated that the B-17 served as a trainer and 'R' that it was considered obsolete and restricted to non-combat duties ('Z' had served this purpose at an earlier date but there is no evidence that it was ever applied to a B-17). 'E' stood for 'exempt' and was a late wartime prefix for B-17s in use by organisations outside the military for experimental or development work and which were not subject to the technical order requirements that might be issued by military agencies. 'M' was the prefix used for B-17Gs fitted with wing racks to carry the JB-2, the US version of the V-1 flying bomb.

Wartime and immediate post-war adaptations which had been specifically government-funded received designations in line with their purpose. The photographic reconnaissance versions of the B-17 were F-9s, although these were all modification-centre adaptations of existing models and in many cases still paraded with the B-17 designations on their data panels. Sixteen B-17Fs became officially recorded as F-9s, and 25 as F-9As and F-9Bs, varying in camera installations. An unspecified number of F-9Cs were camera-equipped B-17Gs. The Eighth Air Force 'Castor' project B-17Fs and Gs which were used as radio-controlled flying bombs were officially designated BQ-7, but in practice this was no more than a book-keeping label. C-108 was the designation given to the transport version of the B-17, although it only applied to four experimental and test aircraft officially funded for conversion. The XC-108 was B-17E 41-2593 stripped of armour and armament and fitted out for VIP passenger transport use, eventually being sent for use by General Douglas MacArthur, the senior US commander in the Pacific war zones. YC-108, originally B-17F 42-6036, was a similarly configured 'generals' buggy'. XC-108A, ex-B-17E 41-2595, was modified for cargo with a large, upward-opening door fitted on the left of the fuselage where the waist gun window had been positioned. XC-108B, 42-30196, featured fuel cells totalling 2,000 gallons' capacity in the fuselage as an experimental air tanker.

With the end of the war in Europe there was no longer any requirement for Fortresses in the bomber role and the type became available for a variety of duties. For major modification programmes, with specially allocated funding, the B-17Gs involved were given a new prefix designation. More than a hundred, re-worked to carry the Higgins A-1 airborne lifeboat with sea-search radar supplanting the chin turret, were re-designated B-17H. However, only a dozen are actually known to have carried this designation, for the majority continued as B-17Gs by their technical data panels. This applied to other post-war variants where the revised designation may have been carried on documentation but was not actually applied on the aircraft concerned.

In June 1948 revised regulations were issued covering USAF aircraft designations with a completely new series of prefix letter identifications. CB-17G was in force for transport conversions. DB-17G was a director misson featuring radio equipment for controlling unmanned aircraft. EB-17G by then indicated aircraft equipped with electronic countermeasures or search equipment. FB-17G supplanted F-9 for photographic versions. QB-17G was for unmanned, radio-controlled Fortresses used for missile targets. RB-17G indicated a reconnaissance mission. SB-17G replaced the B-17H for lifeboat-carrying and sea-search aircraft. TB-17G continued to identify Fortresses used for training purposes. VB-17G was for administrative staff transport conversions but came to represent VIP service. WB-17G covered aircraft used for weather reconnaissance. Additions in 1955 were JB-17G for aircraft temporarily modified for testing equipment and NB-17G for those permanently modified for test purposes. To differentiate between some models with different equipment in the radio-controlled target programme, in August 1955, QB-17Gs became QB-17Ls and QB-17Ns and DB-17Gs became DB-17Ps.

The surplus of new B-17Gs in the summer of 1945 enabled the US Navy to acquired 47 which received the designation PB-1 (Patrol, Boeing, Model 1). Seventeen of these were later transferred to the US Coast Guard as PB-1Gs and the 30 retained became PB-1Ws for anti-submarine patrols.

MODIFICATIONS

Numbers of B-17Gs with a little more use than their delivery hours were taken for a variety of military tasks during the immediate post-war years, sea-search and rescue being a major role. The pioneering use of the Higgins A-1 airborne lifeboat had been by the 5th Emergency Rescue Squadron in England during the closing months of the war in Europe. The B-17Gs used were war-weary aircraft and initially had only the modifications necessary to carry the boat, principally four suspension cables attached to bomb shackles in the bay and released by the salvo mechanism. The cables passed through apertures in the bomb bay doors. The boat, constructed largely of plywood, weighed 3,300lb

Left: The first Fortress obtained by the US Navy was B-17F 42-3521. Given the Navy Bureau number 34106, it was used by the Philadelphia experimental station for various projects. Here it carries a quarter-scale model of the F8F Bearcat to release for obtaining aerodynamic data. This aircraft was apparently still referred to as a B-17 in US Navy service and not by the PB-1 designation. (USN)
Below: Boeing PB-1W 77237 left the Douglas plant as B-17G-95-DL 44-83874. US Navy modifications included the deletion of all armament and the installation of an AN/APS-20 sea-search radar package in and under the bomb bay. These aircraft were employed as target vessels for strike aircraft to attack. (Harold G. Martin)

and was 27ft long. While well within the B-17G's lift capability, it imposed a performance penalty by demanding higher power settings to compensate for the additional drag. In service the chin turrets were removed and APS-3 radar scanners were fitted in this location under the nose. Some forty late-production B-17Gs were taken for modification as sea-search lifeboat carriers early in 1945 and used to equip the emergency rescue squadrons in the Pacific war theatres. These all had APS-3 radars with the scanner in an undernose radome. Initially the full armament, apart from the waist positions, was retained, but at the end of hostilities the top and under turrets were removed. The B-17H/SB-17G continued in rescue squadron service until the spring of 1956, when the last aircraft, 44-83701, was withdrawn from the Azores unit. SB-17Gs were also used by the Portuguese and Brazilian air arms. It was SB-17G 44-83885 of the 3rd Air Rescue Squadron that flew, albeit inadvertently, the first sortie of the Korean War on 25 June 1950 when endeavouring to return a senior officer to his command base.

The PB-1G Fortresses operated by the US Coast Guard from 1946 to October 1959 were configured much as the B-17H, with APS-3 sea-search radar and provision for carrying

Left, top to bottom: Originally supplied to the RAF, B-17G 42-97108 suffered accident damage and after repair was converted to a CB-17G for transport duties with USSTAF Air Service Command. General Eisenhower is known to have been conveyed in this aircraft, which had all turrets and armament removed. (Harry Holmes)
The XC-108A experimental cargo conversion made on a B-17E featured a large, upward-opening door on the left side of the fuselage. The limitations on loadings to avoid movement of the aircraft's centre of gravity too far aft did not encourage further experiments; nevertheless, after the war a number of B-17s converted as civil transports had similar cargo doors. (Boeing)
While many B-17s were stripped of combat equipment and converted to transport use, few of these aircraft had previously seen extensive combat service. An exception was B-17F 42-30227, which flew some two dozen missions with the 96th Bomb Group during the second half of 1943 and was returned to the US for training purposes the following year, only to be converted to a personnel transport and used by the Air Transport Command in the Pacific areas. (Bruce Robertson)
B-17G-65-BO 43-37550, another 96th Bomb Group aircraft, was written off as salvage after the *Luftwaffe* bombing of Poltava, USSR, on the night of 21 June 1944. However, US engineers gave it another life, by using undamaged components from other B-17s, and '550' served as a transport for Eastern Command. Unusually, the full serial number has been applied to the fin.

the Higgins lifeboat. All turrets and armament were removed. During their service period there were changes in radio and radar equipment. A few aircraft were later employed in coastal survey and mapping work, the last PB-1G in service being 77254, formerly 44-85828. PB-1Ws were used by the US Navy for vessel location, primarily submarines, and were fitted with AN/APS-20 radar. The scanner was housed in a very large streamlined radome positioned under the bomb bay area. P-38 type auxiliary tanks were carried on underwing pylons just outboard of Nos 1 and 4 engines to provide an additional 300 US gallons of fuel for enhanced endurance. Modification was carried out by a US Navy agency and the original armament was soon discarded. The auxiliary fuel tanks were also deleted in later service. At least one PB-1W had the radar scanner experimentally repositioned on the top of the fuselage.

B-17s had been used for reconnaissance flights from the introduction of the earliest models into service. The good high-altitude capability made the type attractive as a camera vehicle, with the designation F-9 bestowed on those aircraft modified for photographic reconnaissance. Although some forty B-17Fs were labelled as F-9, F-9A and F-9B, dependent on camera equipment, many more B-17Gs were employed in long-range photographic reconnaissance towards the end of Second World War and the immediate post-war period than the ten officially recorded as F-9Cs. The ten were the result of special work carried out at the Cheyenne Modification Center in 1944, where the chin turret was replaced by a projecting structure for a trimetrogen camera arrangement. Camera ports were also made in the radio room for three more cameras and there were a number of internal detail changes to aid the photographic mission. Apart from the chin turret, the standard armament was retained on these F-9Cs. Other B-17Gs converted for the photographic role simply had the chin turret removed and camera installations in the nose as well as the radio room. These aircraft were employed on the large-scale photo-mapping programme undertaken by USAAF squadrons at this time. F-9s became RB-17s in 1948, although many had never carried the F-9C identification.

Apart from the four official C-108 conversions to passenger-carrying transports, there were literally scores of B-17s retired from combat service that were modified for use in such duties during the closing months of the Second World War. In most cases the modifications were limited to the removal of all armament, turrets and armour, and the installation of improvised seating in the fuselage compartments aft of the wing. Much of this work was carried out by the service groups supporting combat units operating B-17s or by air depot groups. The degree of modification varied considerably, and while a few aircraft were re-marked as TB-, CB- or RB-17s on their technical data blocks, the majority had no such adjustment made to the original designation stencilled on the left-hand side of the nose. Many late-production B-17Gs were converted to CB-17Gs in the immediate post-war years for command use, with particularly elaborate interiors for those intended for senior generals, elevating the designation to VB-17G. There was no common standard for these conversions: the fairing-over of tail gun positions differed in detail and a few aircraft had an extended cone added. The cheek gun window retained on some CB-17Gs was removed on others, while additional fuselage windows were a feature occasionally seen. In short, each conversion was very much individually tailored.

The VB-17G was close to the XC-108 concept, with kitchen facilities in the bomb bay, the radio operator's position moved to the flight deck, plush seating for up to twelve persons and a swing-down rear entry door. At least ten B-17Gs are known to have been converted by Boeing to VB-17Gs for high command use and an unknown number of less extensive conversions elsewhere were also given this designation. The selection of the Fortresses for this use, at a time when purpose-built transports were available, is said to be due to a combination of four-engine reliability, speed and range. A number of CB- and VB-17Gs served as commanders' communication aircraft during the Korean War, 1950–53.

Another prominent military use of B-17s in the immediate post-war years and one that continued until 1960 was unmanned operations such as atomic fall-out penetration and missile targets. Once again, the flight stability of the type made it a prime choice for radio-control applications, which had their operational beginnings with the Castor 'flying bomb' project conducted by the Eighth Air

Top: In the immediate post-war years Fortresses were favourite long-range transports for high-ranking officers. VB-17G-75-DL 44-83257, used by General Carl Spaatz in 1946, carries a four-star display below the cockpit, plus 'Boops', a favourite nickname for his daughter, on the nose. (Roger Besecker)

Above: General George C. Kenney's B-17G-80-DL had creature comforts in the rear compartment, including waist window curtains, but retained tail, nose, side and top turret armament in the summer of 1945. (Steve Birdsall)

Top: Two of the 'drone' B-17s used in the Bikini atom-bomb tests were afterwards employed in an experimental flight from Hawaii to Muroc, California, on 6 August 1946. Covering 2,600 miles, this was at the time the longest flight made by remotely controlled aircraft, taking 14 hours 55 minutes from take-off to touch-down. B-17G-110-VE 44-85819, officially a BQ-7 at this date, was photographed soon after being despatched. The atomic bomb cloud insignia can just be distinguished on the nose. (USAF)

Above: The RCAF's six Fortresses in No 168 Squadron carried mail and urgent supplies across the Atlantic to its forces in Europe. Fortress II 9205, alias B-17E 41-9142, was unusual in having a special metal drop-down nose for loading. (RCAF)

Force from an airfield in England during the second half of 1944. Development of radio control apparatus and technique was continued in the United States with the use of four drone aircraft in the atomic detonation tests at Bikini Atoll in the Pacific. These radio-controlled aircraft were stripped of war equipment and fitted with monitoring apparatus which varied among the four, depending on the duties to be performed. Television and still cameras, air pressure recorders, air sample collectors and storage and radio test transmitters were the major items in the drones, which were controlled by other B-17Gs with monitoring equipment. Both drone and control aircraft were conspicuous for the number of antenna sported. The most distinctive feature of the control or 'mother' aircraft was the radome for the AS-154/APS-10 transmitter antenna located under the ball turret well (but longer and slimmer than that used for the once usual H2X in this position).

The use and development of remotely controlled aircraft continued, with their principal employment in hazardous environments. In 1948 the BQ-7 designation was discontinued and replaced by QB-17, although aircraft modified for the radio-control programme apparently retained the original B-17 designation. Two distinct types of drone evolved, that with a television camera in the nose and assorted monitoring equipment for investigative missions which became the QB-17L, and an airborne target drone with telemetering systems (transmission of instrument data) which became the QB-17N. Both models were subject to modifications as new equipment or new missions were introduced. Most eventually finished their days as 'live' targets for guided missiles, notably the Bomarc surface-to-air interceptor. Aircraft used for this purpose were fitted with 'Scoring Camera Stores' in streamlined wing-tip pods. Each pod normally contained four motion film cameras placed to give a complete photographic record of an interception. To minimise expense a near miss was programmed for the missile, but if the aircraft was hit and destroyed the wing-tip pod was released and brought safely to ground by the parachute contained therein. These replacement wing-tip structures reduced the overall span to 102ft. B-17s equipped for the control of B-17L and B-17N drones were designated DB-17P. A large external guidance antenna was their only distinguishing feature. The principal operator of QB-17s was the 3205th Drone Group with its HQ at Eglin Field, Florida.

POST-WAR B-17s IN OTHER SERVICES

Britain's Royal Air Force had more than a hundred Fortresses in service at the end of hostilities, used by Coastal Command for oceanic patrol and weather reconnaissance and by Bomber Command for radio countermeasures; however, having been supplied under Lend-Lease, they were replaced by indigenous types in 1946. The Royal Canadian Air Force had used six B-17E and F models for transatlantic mail delivery during 1944–45 and the survivors were soon retired. Brazil was given twelve SB-17Gs, which endured until the early 1970s, and Portugal received ten. There was, however, a B-17 unit in the Soviet Union about which little was known in the West.

During the war the Soviet Union had requested four-engine bombers from the United States. The Russian aid programme, though generous, never included heavy bombers. Frustrated and with strategic bombing ambitions, the Soviets collected together several USAAF B-17s that had crashed or force-landed in territory under their control. The first such acquisition was in the spring of 1944, and by the end of that year more than a score were in hand, many an amalgamation of parts from several Eighth and Fifteenth Air Force Fortresses. By the beginning of July 1945 the 890th Regiment of the 45th Division had seventeen B-17s on strength, most G models. These remained in service until replaced by the Soviet built copy of the B-29, the Tu-4. Their fate is not recorded, but one report mentions a B-17 in Russia in the early 1980s.

The French acquired B-17F 42-30177 from the USAAF in December 1944, a gift from General Eisenhower for use by General Pierre Koenig. Already adapted for passenger use with six seats in the rear fuselage, the aircraft was later refurbished by the French for use as a VIP transport until 1956.

There were reports of B-17s being employed in South American civil wars, but the most notable use of the type in belligerent activity after 1945 was by the Israeli Air Force, which used three with hastily improvised armament in the war with Egypt. These B-17Gs were smuggled out of the United States in 1948. A fourth was impounded in the Azores en route to Israel.

TEST-BED FORTRESSES

Of the many B-17 airframes for carrying experimental equipment, the first radically modified were two late-production Vega B-17Gs used as aerial test-beds for turboprop engines. The main modifications were carried out by Boeing who, for contractual purposes, gave these aircraft the company model designation 299Z. The first, 44-85813, went to the Wichita plant and was used by Wright to flight-test their XT-35 Typhoon from 1948, the installation being made in the nose. The same aircraft was used to test the TC-18 turbo compound engine in 1949, the J-65 jet in 1952 and the XT-49 turboprop in 1955, and two years later it was fitted with an R-3350. In order to retain the correct balance and crew protection, the flight deck was moved 4ft further back. Other modifications included stainless steel skin on the underside of the forward fuselage to protect against exhaust burn.

Right, top to bottom: Improvised tail defence on one of the three B-17Gs operated by the Israeli Air Force—a .50-calibre machine gun in an open emplacement. The aircraft were devoid of armament when received and were also in bare metal finish. The elaborate camouflage in shades of brown and green was embellished with a Mickey Mouse motif on this aircraft. (IAF)

Among the many strange modifications to which the B-17 was host during the decade following the Second World War, one of the most unusual was the streamlined pods on the wing tips of 44-85784. On a bailment contract to General Electric, these were allegedly to test the possibilities of manned defensive positions on a larger aircraft. This B-17G-105-VE eventually became the famous *Sally B*, an air show star in Europe.

The Pratt & Whitney-powered Boeing 299Z with the propellers on the four standard R-1820-97s feathered and the XT-34 turbo-prop keeping ex-44-85734 airborne. In addition to the repositioned flight deck, windows were placed in the former bomb bay area. (Harold G. Martin)

The Wright test-bed, 44-85813, finished its days of trials with a conventional R-3350 radial. Photographed here in May 1957, the five-engine Fortress was said to have topped 350mph in level flight. The combined engine ratings of this aircraft gave a formidable 7,000hp. (Smalley)

66 THE B-17 FLYING FORTRESS STORY

The second 299Z, 44-85734, was for the rival engine manufacturer Pratt & Whitney to test their XT-34 turboprop. The modification work, carried out at Boeing Seattle, was similar in scope to that previously performed at Wichita, although the flight deck was rebuilt some 6in further back. In 1957 a third Vega-built B-17G, 44-85747, was used by General Motors' Allison Division for a similar test installation with the T-56 turboprop. As this was a much lighter and less powerful engine it was not necessary to move the flight deck aft. Both the Wright and Allison testbeds were originally on government bailment contracts, the former aircraft being purchased by Wright in 1957. The Pratt & Whitney aircraft was owned by the company from the outset of the programme, having been acquired for $2,700 in 1947.

It was the nose of the B-17 that usually suffered in the course of modifications for specialised duties. A programme of cloud investigation known as the Cloud Physics Project involved three USAF TB-17Gs fitted with a thimble radome and numerous sensors forward of the flight deck. A civil-operated B-17G used to test aerial pick-up and delivery gear for clandestine CIA activities suffered 20ft lattice booms projecting from the nose area.

CIVIL FORTRESSES

Despite the limitations of its fuselage, particularly regarding the carriage of personnel or cargo, the B-17 found extensive use in civil roles. This was because of its excellent flight characteristics and the fact that war surplus aircraft were to be had at prices a fraction of the production cost. However, the first B-17s converted for civil transportation came free of charge.

A number of Eighth Air Force Fortresses were landed in Sweden during bombing missions over northern Germany. These aircraft were mostly battle-damaged, and, with little hope of regaining England, their crews chose to seek sanctuary in a neutral country. Needing equipment for its international airline, SILA, Sweden made use of selected B-17s and at the end of the war in Europe was presented with five by the US government for services rendered, plus two more for use by Denmark and two for spares. All seven 14-seat passenger transport conversions were made by SAAB and featured a galley, toilet, heating and soundproofing. The bomb bay was used for cargo loads of up to two metric tons. The Plexiglas nose was replaced on most with a 3ft long pointed fairing, and windows were fashioned in that part of the rear fuselage section with passenger seating.

The first aircraft to be taken for civil use by the Swedes was B-17F 42-3543, which

Top: The giant spinner and propeller on the XT-35 Typhoon turbo-prop development by Wright Aeronautical. As the aircraft, 44-85813, was still government property and let to Wright on a bailment contract, it was designated JB-17G. (Via Hugh Cowin)
Above: B-17G 42-32076 was one of the aircraft modified for airline work by the Swedes and transferred to the Danes. A 'solid' streamlined nose replaced the original Plexiglas structure and the tail gun position was also faired over. The aircraft later found its way to the French IGN organisation and eventually the USAF Museum at Dayton, Ohio, where it reposes in similar configuration and paintwork to that when the aircraft force-landed in Sweden in May 1944.
Below: The first civil transport Fortress in the United States was B-17G 44-85728, which Boeing modified for TWA and designated Model 299AB. It was also the first to be given a limited licence—hence the NL-1B registration. (Peter M. Bowers)

was serving with the 96th Bomb Group when it failed to return from a mission on 9 October 1943. It was entered on the Swedish civil register as SE-BAH on 24 January 1944. Three of the B-17s used were F models and four were Gs. One, 42-32076, a 91st Bomb Group aircraft entered on the Swedish register on 2 November 1945 as SE-BAP, was passed to the Danes and survives in the USAF Museum at Dayton, Ohio, having been returned to a bomber configuration. The B-17, a thirsty aircraft with a small payload, was quite unsuited for profitable airline service, so SILA withdrew them from the late summer of 1946.

The first Fortress registered for civil use in the United States was acquired in February 1946 by the famed film stunt flier Paul Mantz. This B-17F, 42-3360, becoming NC67974, was used in two war films but the demand from Hollywood studios was not as anticipated simply because it was much less expensive to 'hire' from the military services than employ a civilian source for 'movie' aircraft. Initially the scrap value of a B-17 for its metal was put at $1,000 in 1946, albeit that actual scrap prices ranged far below this figure. Appreciating that there was a small market for the commercial use of B-17s, an official War Assets Administration asking price of $13,750 was set for a complete aircraft. Few were sold for this figure, and the first was a low flight-time B-17G which TWA obtained in June 1946 for conversion to a long-range executive transport. One of the last from Vega, 44-85728 sent to Boeing for modification, emerged as Boeing contract model 299AB with plush accommodation for up to sixteen passengers and manned by a crew of five. The aircraft was used primarily for company executive travel and route pioneering, being uneconomical for regular passenger service. After a year's service TWA presented the 299AB to the Shah of Persia. Externally, 299AB was much like other disarmed Fortresses, four small windows each side of the fuselage 'waist' and another two in the former radio room being the only notable additions.

Other sales followed with similar conversions for transport use, and prices fell as low as $1,000 at WAA auctions. Non-profit organisations such as schools and municipal administrations that desired a B-17 as a memorial were able to purchase one from the WAA for $1,500. Many static display aircraft were later acquired by dealers and sold for refurbishment to flying status at a considerable profit. Airframes originally sold to scrap metal firms, for as little as $500, were also retrieved by dealers. Between 1946 and 1986 a total of 75 different B-17s were registered for civil operation in the USA.

Top: The most advantageous commercial use of this Second World War bomber was in high-altitude photographic mapping and survey work. Two US-based organisations, a third in Canada and a fourth in France did much of this work under contract to governments or other agencies. B-17G 44-83814 served Kenting Aviation Limited for this work during the period 1953–55. After other civil use it eventually became a museum piece. (George Pennick)
Above: The availability of several B-17s in serviceable condition led to their use in a number of war movies during the second half of the twentieth century. One such production was Columbia's *The War Lover*, for which most of the flying sequences were made with four B-17Gs brought together at Bovingdon, England, early in 1962. The aircraft were obtained from civil sources, and turrets, both real and fake, were installed and reasonably authentic decor was applied. B-17G 44-83877, with a bogus tail number, is shown with quite realistic fake battle damage—apart from the row of 'bullet holes' on the tail gun position, which could only have been achieved with a Tommy gun from a few feet away. (G. R. Mortimer)

B-17s, with their turbo-supercharged engines, were popular with cargo and passenger transport organisations using the high-altitude airports in some South American countries. At one time or another 23 were in civil use in Bolivia during the 1950s and 1960s, most operated by Lloyd Aereo Boliviano. A few transport B-17s also appeared on the civil registers of Peru, Columbia, Mexico and Nicaragua.

Of the several uses for civil Fortresses, photographic survey work proved viable from a commercial standpoint. Universal Aviation, of Tulsa, Oklahoma, commenced using B-17s for high-level aerial photographic mapping in 1947 under contract, and the Aero Service Corporation of Philadelphia was also involved in this work for several years, its three B-17s photographing more than two million square miles of terrain, mostly in South America and the Middle and Far East. Operations were carried out with various items of camera equipment at an optimum 32,000ft. A Canadian firm also used a B-17E and later a G for similar photographic survey work.

In 1948 the French Institut Géographique National (IGN) began to collect and operate B-17Gs in world-wide photographic map-

68 THE B-17 FLYING FORTRESS STORY

POST-WAR FORTRESSES 69

Left, upper: The first of thirteen airworthy and one ground-spares Fortresses operated by the Institut Géographique National over four decades was B-17G-100-VE 44-85643. Registered in France as F-BEEA in June 1948, it also became the last in service, sadly being burnt out after a take-off accident in July 1989 at Binbrook, England, during the making of the Warner Brothers *Memphis Belle* film. Fortunately, only minor injuries were incurred by crew and passengers. (IGN)

Left, lower: Although similarly configured, the task equipment carried by IGN B-17s varied over the years. F-BGSP was externally little different from the other B-17s at Criel, near Paris, an airfield that had been bombed several times by Fortresses during the war. However, this aircraft, originally 44-8846, was one of the few surviving B-17s that had been involved in combat missions, flying eight in April 1945 with the 511th Bomb Squadron, 351st Bomb Group, out of Polebrook, England. It had remained in Europe after the war, serving with the 45th Reconnaissance Squadron in Germany for a number of years until pensioned off and returned to the USA for disposal. Acquired by IGN in 1954, it was operated by that organisation for nearly thirty years. Re-registered F-AZDX, the aircraft was operated on the European air show circuit during the final years of the century, the only remaining airworthy B-17 that had taken part in the Second World War. The aircraft also appeared in the Warner Brothers *Memphis Belle* movie and in television dramas. (IGN)

Right, top: One of last commercial uses to which the B-17 was put was 'fire bombing'—the carrying and release of fire-suppressant material on forest fires. A prime operator on America's West Coast—where such fires are, unfortunately, a frequent occurrence in dry seasons—was the Aero Union Corporation of Chico, California. The three aircraft in service in April 1972, when this photograph was taken, were N5233V (44-83863), N3509G (44-83884) and N5230V (44-85778). Visually the most significant modification was the pointed nose cone replacing the Plexiglas piece. (Dave Menard)

Right, centre: From the 1970s, remaining B-17s eventually ended their days as museum pieces, mostly static with a few in airworthy condition. Revenue for upkeep and flight often came from use in fictional productions for TV or Hollywood. Once a DB-17P, 44-83684, operated by Planes of Fame, Buena Park, California, took part in the 1962–65 TV series called *12 O'Clock High*. It was later a static exhibit. When photographed at Alton, Illinois, in May 1971 the aircraft was painted up in the colours of the Eighth Air Force's 452nd Bomb Group. (Dave Menard)

Right, bottom: The famous *Sally B*, 44-85784, in one of its fictional roles. The decor was used for the 1981 TV 'soap opera' *We'll Meet Again*. At this time gun turrets were fibre glass and plastic look-alike, but in later years authentic items were obtained for some locations. Towards the end of the twentieth century a dozen B-17s were still airworthy. (George Pennick)

ping. As with North American companies, the type was chosen because it was relatively cheap to acquire and had excellent high-altitude performance, and, being unpressurised, photography could be conducted without intervening windows to cause distortion. IGN retained B-17s for this work until the 1970s. In total, thirteen different B-17Gs are known to have served IGN at Criel at one time or another during the 25 years this type was favoured.

The B-17's bomb bay was used to accommodate tanks for spraying operations with insecticides and fire-suppressant liquids over forest areas, spray booms being fitted under the wings when required. Tank arrangements varied, but a total of 2,400 US gallons was the maximum load. The tank used in fire-fighting B-17s had four compartments with watertight doors to allow direct selective release. Hoppers were also employed for dispersing granular material in agricultural use. The 'air tanker' B-17s were the last of the type in commercial service and endured for some 25 years until withdrawn in the early 1980s. One aircraft, ex-B-17F 42-6107, had its Cyclones replaced by Rolls-Royce Dart 510 turboprops in 1970, only to be destroyed in a crash later that year. All four engines failed, due, it is believed, to heavy ingestion of smoke from a forest fire.

From the 1980s the remaining airworthy Fortresses were in the hands of enthusiasts for the aircraft and flown for pleasure, the air show circuit being the source of most fuel funding. All have been restored to near their original configuration less war equipment. A total of ten were still flying in 1997.

7. Individual B-17 Histories

The primary identity of individual production-line aircraft is the manufacturer's construction number. Whatever military or civil numbers or registrations are subsequently applied by operators, the manufacturer's number remains inviolate. But each manufacturer applies his own range of numbers, and in the case of the B-17, coming from three different manufacturers, there was some duplication. All, except the prototype, were built on US government contracts and received US Army aircraft serial numbers, which became the dominant identification, for, apart from there being no duplication regardless of manufacturing source, from 1941 a slightly abbreviated form was carried boldly on tail fins and applied during production. The main identity in the following listing of the 12,731 B-17s built is the US Army serial.

Other military operators preferred their own serial numbers, notably the US Navy and the British. Unfortunately, no document giving a complete linking of USAAF serials to those carried by Royal Air Force Fortresses appears to exist, but individual examples known show that the British serials did not run consecutively with those of the B-17C and B-17E.

The main source of information for the individual histories was the individual record cards held by the USAF Historical Research Center. It will be noted that some entries are blank, and this indicates that the record card is missing. The details on the cards only cover an aircraft's base assignments while in the United States. Nothing was normally recorded of overseas service other than the date of final deletion from the records if appropriate. Additional details have been obtained from Missing Aircrew Reports, Loss Listings, and many other official documents and photographs. Some 40 published works were also consulted. Manufacturer's construction numbers matched with those of the US Army are as shown in Table 4.

Table 4

Model	Manufacturer's	USAAF serial numbers
299	1963	None
Y1B-17	1973 to 1985	36-149 to 36-161
Y1B-17A	198	37-369
B-17B	2004 to 2016	38-211 to 38-223
	2017 to 2029	38-258 to 38-270
	2030 and 2031	38-583 and 38-584
B-17C	2043 to 2080	40-2042 to 40-2079
B-17D	2087 to 2128	40-3059 to 40-3100
B-17E	2204 to 2480	41-2393 to 41-2669
	2483 to 2717	41-9011 to 41-9245
B-17F-BO	3025 to 3324	41-24340 to 41-24639
	3589 to 4023	42-5050 to 42-5484
	4581 to 6145	42-29467 to 42-31031
B-17G-BO	6146 to 7230	42-31032 to 42-32116
	7531 to 7880	42-97058 to 42-97407
	7881 to 8480	42-102379 to 42-102978
	8487 to 10486	43-37509 to 43-39508
B-17F-DL	7900 to 8499	42-2964 to 42-3563
B-17G-DL	8500 to 8999	42-37714 to 42-38213
	21899 to 22148	42-106984 to 42-107233
	22224 to 23223	44-6001 to 44-7000
	31877 to 32526	44-83236 to 44-83885
B-17F-VE	6001 to 6500	42-5705 to 42-6204
B-17G-VE	6501 to 6800	42-39758 to 42-40057
	6801 to 7400	42-97436 to 42-98035
	7401 to 8400	44-8001 to 44-9000
	8401 to 8750	44-85492 to 44-85841

Right: Y1B-17 36-156 sporting the white cowling bands that distinguished aircraft of the 20th Bombardment Squadron in the 2nd Bombardment Group at Langley Field. (USAF)

LEGEND:—
AA = anti-aircraft artillery (flak); AAB = Army Air Base; acc = accident; AF = Air Force; afd = airfield; ass = Assigned; b/d = battle damage; BG = Bombardment Group; BS = Bombardment Squadron; BU = Base Unit; BW = Bombardment Wing; CCRC = Combat Crew Replacement Center; c/l = crash landing; cr = crashed; c/t/o = crashed on take off; del = delivered; e/a = shot down by enemy aircraft; dest = destroyed; EVD = evaded; f/l = force landing; flak = flak hit; Flts = Flights; GR = German rocket; KAS = killed active service; KIA = killed in action; m = no of missions; MACR = Missing Air Crew Report; MD = Material Division; MIA = missing in action; n/b/d = non battle damage; POW = Prisoner of War; rep = repaired; retUS = returned United States; RFC = Reclamation Finance Centre (sold for scrap metal in USA); RS = Recon Squadron; sal = salvaged (destroyed/scrapped beyond economical repair); s/d = shot down; tran = transferred; TCS/Gp = Transport Command Squadron/Group; TD = temporary duty; w/ = with; WO = written off.

XB-15
35-277 Delivered to US Air Corps Jan '37; completed first test flight Oct 15; to 49BS/2BG at Langley, Va. Jan '38 for affiliation; on 4/2/39 flew to Chile with medical supplies after earthquake; took part in secret bombing test in the Canal Zone; photo-recon trip to Galapagos Is 9/5/40; late 1940 to Duncan Fd, Fl., for removal of armament; to San Antonio for conversion to transport aircraft and transferred to 6AF in March 1943, now designated XC-105 and assigned 20th Troop Carrier Squadron, at Howard Fd, CZ on 6/5/43. Fondly known as 'Grandpappy', carried all sorts of cargo around Caribbean airfields, before assigned to Panama Air Depot 18/12/44; in late 1945 was dismantled and taken to Diablo Dump, Albrook Fd, CZ, where it was buried.

Model 299 The first Fortress. Ordered 26/9/34. First flew 28/7/35 from Boeing Fd with Les Tower pilot. Many other test flights completed, then following October crashed at Wright Fd killing pilot Major Pete Hill. Other engineers etc taken to hospital, where observer Les Tower died later of his injuries. Fault found to be control surfaces still locked when taking off. Reg. N13372. Boeing number 1963.

Y1B-17
36-149 Del 49BS/2BG Langley 1/3/27; Amarillo 2/11/42; 71 flts; WO 11/12/42.
36-150 Del 96BS/2BG Langley 11/3/37; f/l March due to engine failure 8/10/40; Albuquerque 16/7/42; 66 flts; WO 30/12/42. [a/c No. 60]
36-151 Del 49BS/2BG Langley 28/3/37; took part in goodwill trip to South America 1938; Amarillo 21/11/42; 64 flts; WO 15/1/43. [a/c No. 80]
36-152 Del 20BS/2BG Langley 27/3/37; Sebring 6/2/42; 65 flts; WO 13/4/42. [a/c No. 50]
36-153 Del 2BG Langley 10/5/37; return to Langley 17/12/41; 58 flts; WO 22/6/43.
36-154 Del 49BS/2BG Langley 16/5/37; took part in goodwill trip to South America 1938; Amarillo 12/11/42; c/l March 1/12/40; 59 flts; WO 15/1/43. [a/c No. 81]
36-155 Del 2BG/HQ Langley 1/6/37; used by CO Major Bob Olds from 28/5/37; took part on goodwill trip to South America 1938; Amarillo 12/11/42; 56 flts; WO 29/1/43. [a/c No. 10.]
36-156 Del 20BS/2BG Langley 17/6/37; public relations trip to Grand Union High School, McClelland Fd 4/7/43; 66 flts; WO 2/4/42. [a/c No. 51]
36-157 Del 2BG Langley 6/6/37; cr east of San Jacinto, Cal. on 46th flt 18/12/40. Sal.
36-158 Del 49BS/2BG Langley 30/6/37; Amarillo 13/10/42; 65 flts; WO 18/12/42. [a/c No. 82]
36-159 Del 20BS/2BG Langley 14/9/37; Amarillo 19/11/42; 65 flts; WO 15/1/43. [a/c No. 52]
36-160 Del 2BG Langley 28/7/37; c/l 8/10/40 (rep); Amarillo 19/11/42; 64 flts; WO 5/1/43.
36-161 Del 49BS/2BG Langley 8/8/37; trans MD, Wright Fd for test purposes 16/9/41; Amarillo 9/10/42; 63 flts; WO 18/12/42. [a/c No. 89]

YB-17A
37-369 First flew 29/4/38, turbo chargers fitted, and used for other static tests such as stress; March Fd 3/10/40 and others, to Geiger 7/2/42.

B-17B
38-211 Del Wright Fd for armament testing 2/8/39; others before West Palm Beach, Fl. 28/9/42. WO 2/12/43.
38-212 Del 2BG Langley 10/3/39; Robins 21/7/42; WO 23/1/43.
38-213 Del Langley 27/8/39; Lowry 29/7/42; WO 25/11/42.
38-214 Del March 5/9/39; cr Davis Monthan, burned out, all crew killed 6/4/42. Sal 8/4/42.
38-215 Del March 6/11/39; 36BS/28BG Ladd Fd (Alaska) 12/10/40; Umnak 5/5/42.
38-216 Del March 28/9/39; 36BS/28BG Ladd Fd 4/10/40; shot down by Japanese Rufe, cr into mountain in fog on Kiska mission w/Jack Marks 18/7/42. (called OLD SEVENTY)
38-217 Del Langley 5/10/39; 36BS/28BG Ladd Fd; cr Lovelock, Nevada, 6/2/42. Sal 26/2/42.
38-218 Del Langley 16/10/39; Tucson, 2/2/42; cr Milford, 6/2/42. Sal 14/5/42.
38-219 Del Langley 21/10/39; 6AF Rio Hato (Panama) 3/6/41; Santa Lucia 24/10/41; Howard Fd (Guatemala) 22/3/42; Salinas (Ecuador) 4/7/42; sal 7/1/44.
38-220 Del March 23/10/39; ass 7RS/9BG Albrook (Panama) 3/6/41; David (Trinidad) 29/10/41; cr Guatemala, 25/7/42. Sal 3/8/42.
38-221 Del March 20/10/39; ass 32BS Albrook 3/6/41; France Fd (Panama) 19/8/41; David 16/10/42; WO 27/10/43.
38-222 Del March 5/10/39; ass 3BS/6BG France Fd. 3/6/41. Lost 2/8/41.
38-223 Del March 10/11/39; W Palm Beach 24/3/42; WO 24/4/42. 22/9/42; WO 9/2/42.
38-258 Del Langley 23/11/39; Sebring
38-259 Del Hamilton 21/11/39; Denver 17/7/43; WO 16/5/44.
38-260 Del Langley 1/12/39; Sioux Falls 21/7/43. WO 9/8/43.
38-261 Del Langley 3/11/39; Sioux Falls 21/7/43. WO 9/8/43.
38-262 Del Langley 7/12/39; Sebring 13/6/42. WO 26/3/43.
38-263 Del March 10/12/39; 3BS/6BG Albrook 3/6/41; retUS Baltimore, Md. 11/9/43. WO 27/8/44.
38-264 Del March 12/12/39; 7BS Albrook 3/6/41; Trinidad 2/10/41; c/t/o 12/1/42; sal 26/1/42.
38-265 Del March 18/12/39; 3BS/6BG Albrook 2/6/41; retUS Lowry 11/7/43; WO 27/7/45.
38-266 Del March 20/12/39; 44BS Albrook 3/6/41; Atkinson (Br Guiana) 20/8/41; retUS, cr Comfort, Tx, 14/2/42.
38-267 Del March 7/2/40; Spokane 18/12/41; WO 6/3/42.
38-268 Del March 7/2/40; Amarillo 7/8/43; WO 6/43.
38-269 Del Wright Fd 19/1/41; Sebring 20/6/42; WO 1/12/42.
38-270 Del Hamilton 7/2/40; Argentia (Nfld) 21/8/41; Sioux Falls 15/7/43; WO 5/10/43.
38-583 Del Salt Lake City 7/9/40; Scott 24/7/43; WO 6/12/43.
38-584 Del Salt Lake City 7/9/40; Lowry 24/7/43; WO 17/10/43.
38-610 Del Salt Lake City 7/9/40; Scott 17/7/43; WO 5/10/43.

B-17B
39-1 Del Hamilton 15/12/40; Lowry 7/12/42; WO 3/9/43.
39-2 Del Salt Lake City 6/40; Sebring 11/3/41; WO 4/8/41.
39-3 Del Hamilton 9/2/40; Amarillo 14/9/42; WO 24/9/43.
39-4 Del March 3/4/41; 6AF Panama 3/6/41; Trinidad 7/3/42; retUS 11/9/43; WO 26/1/45.
39-5 Del March 6/3/41; McDill 3/3/42; cr out of limits of continental USA; WO 6/8/42.
39-6 Del March 23/2/40; Amarillo 15/7/42; WO 4/8/42.
39-7 Del Salt Lake City 7/9/40; MAAD for de-icing equipment fitted 11/11/41; Amarillo 16/7/43; WO 7/8/43.
39-8 Del Salt Lake City 7/9/40; Argentia 28/8/41; cr North Reading, Ma. 13/8/42; sal.
39-9 Del Salt Lake City 3/9/40; Argentia 29/8/41; cr base 16/1/42, sal. Pilot 1st Lt Bartram C. Martin.
39-10 Del Salt Lake City 17/10/40; Amarillo 21/7/43; WO 4/8/43.

B-17C
40-2042 Del Air Force 21/7/40, then back to Boeing for two years, before returning to AF. WO 29/1/43.
40-2043 Del RAF 90sq Polebrook, UK 5/41
40-2044 Del RAF 90sq Polebrook, UK 5/41
40-2045 Del 5AF 14BS/19BG Clark Fd, Philippines 11/2/40; s/d Luzon 10/12/41, first B-17 lost in actual combat.
40-2046 Del Wright Fd 24/11/40; Eglin 16/5/42 for testing two 20mm cannon in nose; Chanute 18/12/43; RFC Altus 4/10/45.
40-2047 Del Strategic Air Depot 9/9/40; Salt Lake City 27/6/41; cr Georgetown, Cal. 2/11/41 w/Lt Leo Walker. Sal.
40-2048 Del 19BG 2/9/40; Clark Fd, Phil. 6/2/41; strafed on ground 8/12/41. Sal.
40-2049 Del 38 Recon Sq Salt Lake City 15/1/41; Albuquerque 4/12/41.
40-2050 Del SAD 3/9/40; Salt Lake City 19/5/41; overshot McClelland Fd 11/6/41. Sal 6/5/42.
40-2051 Del RAF 90sq Polebrook, UK 4/41
40-2052 Del RAF 90sq Polebrook UK4/41
40-2053 Del RAF 90sq Polebrook 5/41.
40-2054 Del 38 Recon Sq SAD 29/11/40; Albuquerque 10/12/41.
40-2055 Del RAF 90sq [AN537 WP-L] Polebrook 23/7/41; 220 Sq 12/2/42 (NR-L)
40-2056 Del RAF 90sq Polebrook 5/41.
40-2057 Del RAF 90sq Polebrook 4/41.
40-2058 Del SAD 3/10/40; Salt Lake City 24/12/40; Patterson 30/12/40; cr Fort Douglas, Utah; 4/2/41. Sal.
40-2059 Del SAD 14/10/40; Sunset Fd 21/6/41; Langley 14/11/41; ass Copper (Hickam Fd, Hawaii) 6/1/42; retUS Long Beach 25/10/42; Smyrna 15/12/42; Hendricks 25/12/42; Sebring 1/6/43. WO

4/8/43.
40-2060 Del RAF 90sq Polebrook 5/41.
40-2061 Del RAF 90sq Polebrook 5/41.
40-2062 Del 93BS/19BG Clarke Fd, Phil 20/10/41; Malang 30/12/41; s/d over Java 3/2/42.
40-2063 Del SAD 30/11/40; Salt Lake City 22/5/41; Sunset Fd 14/6/41; ass 38 Rec Sq Langley 14/11/41; WO 29/5/43.
40-2064 Del RAF 90sq Polebrook 4/41.
40-2065 Del RAF 90sq Polebrook 5/41.
40-2066 Del RAF 90sq [AN532 WP-J] Polebrook 9/8/41; tran 220sq (MB-J); Egypt & India. Ret USAAF 1/12/42; burnt out.
40-2067 Del Salt Lake City 13/2/41; Albuquerque 1/10/41; ass 19BG Clark Fd 2/11/41; strafed 8/12/41. Sal.
40-2068 Del RAF 90sq Polebrook 5/41.
40-2069 Del RAF [believed AN524], damaged on delivery; retUS Sebring, Fl. 1/12/42; cr Hendricks 3/1/43. Sal.
40-2070 Del Hawaii; dest in Jap attack on Hickam Fd, Pearl Harbor 7/12/41. Sal.
40-2071 Del RAF 90sq Polebrook 4/41.
40-2072 Ass 19BG Clarke Fd, Phil; damaged in attack 25/12/41, but repaired and used as transport.
40-2073 Del RAF 90sq Polebrook 4/41. UK
40-2074 Del Langley 14/11/41; tran 38RS, Hickam Fd. Sal.
40-2075 Del RAF 90sq Polebrook 5/41.
40-2076 Del RAF 90sq Polebrook UK 5/41.
40-2077 Del 50RC/11BG; Strafed Hickam Fd. Sal 8/12/41. (a/c No. 80).
40-2078 Del Salt Lake City 17/3/41; return Boeing; Salt Lake City 24/6/41; SAD 19/9/41; cr Duncan Fd, Texas 11/10/41. Sal.
40-2079 Del RAF 90sq (AN518 WP-B) Polebrook 13/5/41; tran 220sq Egypt; India; ret USAAF; to USA 26/9/43; WO 1/9/44.

B-17D
40-3059 Del Albuquerque 7/6/41; Salt Lake City 17/7/41; ass 19BG Clarke Fd, Phil. 17/10/41; strafed 8/12/41. Sal.
40-3060 Del Hamilton; ass 42BS/11BG Hawaii 14/5/41; dest Hickam 7/12/41. Sal. (a/c No. 61).
40-3061 Del Hamilton; ass 14BS/11BG Hawaii 14/5/41; tran 19BG 30/12/41; tran 19BG 30/12/41; dest Malang, Java, 28/2/42 in evacuation.
40-3062 Del March 6/5/41; ass 93BS/19BG Clarke Fd

Above: B-17C 40-2055, alias AN537, shepherding a convoy while in service with No 220 Squadron of RAF Coastal Command. (Crown)

2/11/41; blown up by terrorists Pasirian, Java 22/2/42. Sal.
40-3063 Del Albuquerque 11/6/41; ass 19BG Clarke Fd 17/10/41; hit by P-40 10/12/41. Sal.
40-3064 Del March 5/6/41; ass 93BS/19BG Clarke Fd 20/10/41; Malang 30/12/41; ground accident Malang, Java 16/1/42. Sal.
40-3065 Del Wright Fd 19/3/41; Geiger 19/12/41; Tucson 7/2/42; Sebring 20/6/42; Hobbs, NM. 7/11/42; Biggs 20/11/42; ass 93 Advan Trng Gp Patterson 4/4/43; RFC 11/5/45.
40-3066 Del Patterson 27/3/41; ass 14BS/19BG Clarke Fd 17/10/41; Malang 30/12/41; blown up by terrorists Pasirian, Java 22/2/42. Sal.
40-3067 Del Patterson 11/4/41; ass 30BS/19BG Clarke Fd 20/10/41; Malang 30/12/41; cr on take off Batchelor Fd, Australia 28/1/42. Sal.
40-3068 Del Patterson 16/4/41; ass 19BG Clarke Fd 17/10/41; strafed on ground 8/12/41. Sal.
40-3069 Del Salt Lake City 17/9/41; coll w/C-39 (early Dakota) No. 38-512 McClelland Fd 10/9/41 (rep); ass 19BG Clarke Fd 20/10/41; strafed on ground 8/12/41. Sal.
40-3070 Del Salt Lake City 29/9/41; ass 93BS/19BG Clarke Fd 17/10/41; Malang 30/12/41; blown up by terrorists Parisian, Java 22/2/42. Sal.
40-3071 Del Hawaii 14/5/41; ass 4RS/5BG Hickam Fd; dest 7/12/41. Sal. (a/c No. 90).
40-3072 Del Albuquerque SAD 6/5/41; ass 93BS/19BG Clarke Fd 17/10/41; blown up by terrorists Parisian, Java 22/2/42. Sal.
40-3073 Del Albuquerque SAD 6/5/41; ass 93BS/19BG Clarke Fd 20/10/41; s/d Masbate, Phil. 14/1/42.
40-3074 Del Albuquerque SAD 11/6/41; ass 93BS/19BG Clarke Fd 17/10/41; Malang 30/12/41; strafed Malang, Java 3/2/42. Sal.
40-3075 Del Albuquerque SAD 3/5/41; ass 19BG Clarke Fd 17/10/41; strafed on ground 8/12/41. Sal.
40-3076 Del Albuquerque SAD 5/6/41; ass 19BG Clarke Fd 17/10/41; strafed on ground 8/12/41. Sal.
40-3077 Del Hawaii 14/8/41; ass 50BS/11BG Hickam Fd; dest 7/12/41. Sal. (a/c No. 80).
40-3078 Del Hawaii 11/5/41; ass 14BS/19BG Malang,

Below: B-17D 40-3092 was assigned to the 5th Bomb Group in Hawaii at the time of the Japanese attack on Pearl Harbor. It survived to undertake many oceanic patrols, eventually ending its days as an instructional airframe at Yale University, where this photograph was taken.

Java 30/12/41; strafed on ground 3/2/42. Sal.
40-3079 Del Hamilton; ass 19BG Hawaii 14/5/41; Malang 30/12/41; on transport trip c/l Daly Waters, Australia with two engines out 14/3/42. Sal.
40-3080 Del Hamilton; ass 23BS/5BG Hickam Fd 14/5/41; dest 7/12/41. Sal. (a/c No.20).
40-3081 Del SAD 4/1/41; ass Hickam 14/5/41.
40-3082 Ass 5BG Long Beach 23/10/42; Love Fd 25/11/42; Smyrna 16/12/42; Lockburn 15/1/43; New Haven 15/7/43. WO 19/7/43.
40-3083 Ass 50BS/11BG Hawaii; dest Hickam Fd 7/12/41; sal. (a/c No. 81)
40-3084 Ass Hickam 14/5/41; WO 16/10/43. (a/c No. 41).
40-3085 Ass 5BG Hawaii 14/5/41; retUS Long Beach 23/10/42; March 29/11/42; Sebring 21/12/42; Lockburn 15/1/43; Sioux Falls 14/7/43; WO 21/7/43. (a/c No.1).
40-3086 Ass 14BS/19BG Hawaii 14/5/41; Ditched off Zamboanga 10/12/41.
40-3087 Del Albuquerque SAD 5/6/41; ass 93BS/19BG Clarke Fd 20/10/41; Damaged ground accident Del Monte 12/12/41. Sal.
40-3087 Del Albuquerque 5/6/41; ass 19BG Clarke Fd 17/10/41; Strafed on base 8/12/41. Sal.
40-3089 Ass 20BS/5BG Hickam 14/5/41. (a/c No.52)
40-3090 Ass 11BG Hickam 14/5/41. (a/c No.60)
40-3091 Ass 14BS/19BG Hickam 14/5/41; Clarke Fd 22/9/41. b/d Darwin, Aus 27/12/41. Sal.
40-3092 Ass 5BG Hickam 14/5/41; (a/c No.41) RetUS Long Beach 22/10/42; Love Fd 23/11/42; Smyrna 2/1/43; Lockburn 23/1/43; cr Newark 15/7/43; sal. Ended as trainer for Aviation Engineering Cadet Detachment at Yale Univ. 1944-45.
40-3093 Ass 14BS/19BG Hickam 14/5/41; Clarke Fd 17/10/41; strafed Del Monte 12/12/41. Sal.
40-3094 Ass 19BG Hickam 14/5/41; Clarke Fd 17/10/41; strafed on base 8/12/41. Sal.
40-3095 Ass 19BG Hickam 14/5/41; Clarke Fd 17/10/41; strafed on base 8/12/41. Sal.
40-3096 Ass 19BG Hickam 14/5/41; Clarke Fd 17/10/41.
40-3097 Ass 19BG Hickam 14/5/41; Java 30/12/41; retUS 17/11/44; RFC Kingman 24/11/46. Was personal hack for Gen George M.Brett, and later a VIP transport. Currently in Smithsonian Institute, longest serving B-17 in USAAF. THE SWOOSE.
40-3098 Del Albuquerque 5/6/41; ass 19BG Hickam 14/5/41; Clarke Fd 17/10/41; c/t/o Del Monte, Phil. 12/12/41. Sal.
40-3099 Del Albuquerque 11/6/41; ass 19BG Hickam 14/5/41; Clarke Fd 17/10/41; strafed on base 8/12/41. Sal.
40-3100 Ass 19BG Clarke Fd 21/10/41; damaged by P-40 on base 9/12/41. Sal.

B-17E

41-2393 Del Wright Fd 3/10/41; Eglin 10/10/41; Langley 28/12/41; Newfoundland (Argentia?) 8/1/42; cr 9/1/42. Sal.
41-2394 Del Patterson 2/12/41; March 18/12/41; McDill 18/1/42; West Palm Beach, (Mercury 6AF) 4/3/42; Pendleton 3/8/42; Ogden 2/9/42; Boise 9/10/42; Oklahoma City 6/2/43; Hendricks, 6/7/43; RFC Albuquerque 9/6/45. HANGAR QUEEN.
41-2395 Del Wright Fd 20/10/41 and used as static test a/c before WO 12/10/42.
41-2396 Del SAD 1/12/41; ass Hickam Fd 8/8/42; ass Poppy (13AF) 18/9/42; WO 15/6/44.
41-2397 Del SAD 2/12/41; ass Hickam Fd 1/6/42; ass Poppy (13AF) 25/10/42; WO 31/10/44.
41-2398 Del Wright Fd 13/10/41; ass 36BS/28BG Elmendorf 3/3/42; Kodiak 21/3/42; Lockburn, OH. 21/4/42; retUS Tinker 17/7/43; RFC Altus 9/10/45.
41-2399 Del Boeing as experimental a/c flight testing 4/5/42; also at Oseola and Selfridge, MI. Fds. RFC Stillwater 19/9/45.
41-2400 Del Douglas Aircraft Corp. as model; WO 30/9/44; Recl Comp 20/3/46.
41-2401 Del Douglas (Vega) as XB-38 Allison engine product; c/l Tipton, Cal. 16/6/43 due to engine fire and one passenger killed. Sal.
41-2402 Del Salt Lake SAD 20/11/41; ass Hickam Fd 1/6/42; cr 40 m Sth Kauai Is 27/12/41, all killed. A/c on search/attack mission.
41-2403 Del SAD 8/11/41; ass 42BS/11BG Hickam/Wheeler 20/10/42; ditched 26/1/43 w/Gen Nathan Twining aboard, w/Woodruff; WO 16/1/44.
41-2404 Del Salt Lake SAD 24/11/41; ass Hickam 4/3/42; WO 15/6/44.
41-2405 Del Salt Lake SAD 24/11/41; March 18/12/41; Langley 11/1/42; Bolling 29/11/42; Langley 10/12/42; Olmstead 22/2/43; Langley 6/3/43; Mitchell 8/6/43; Cherry Pt 5/7/43; Mitchell 11/7/43; RFC Kingman 19/10/45.
41-2406 Del Salt Lake SAD 26/11/41; ass Java 13/1/42; c/l Madera Is, 25/2/42 w/Hobson. WO 31/10/44.
41-2407 Del/Ass Wright Fd, Air Material Command as test a/c. RFC Davis-Monthan 10/4/45.
41-2408 Del Salt Lake SAD 8/1/42; ass 40BS/19BG; used in Gen MacArthur rescue attempt 25/3/42; ass 43RS/ Wheeler; sal 14/10/44.
41-2409 Del Salt Lake SAD 12/1/41; ass 11BG Hickam 30/1/42; c/l Guadalcanal 25/11/42; WO 20/9/43. OLE MAID.
41-2410 Del Salt Lake SAD 12/1/41; ass March 28/12/41; Langley 11/1/42; Jacksonville,Fl. 9/5/42; Presque Is 19/3/42; Occident 11/5/43; Mitchell 6/6/43; Smoky Hill, 3/6/44; San Bernardino, 31/12/45; Recl Comp 30/4/46.
41-2411 Del Salt Lake SAD 10/10/41; ass 44BS/40BG 20/12/41; Panama, CZ. 25/12/41; Guatemala 15/4/42; SAAD 28/7/42; Guatemala 5/12/42; cr t/o 21/1/43.
41-2412 Del Salt Lake SAD 10/11/41; ass 6AF 25/12/41; SAAD 21/3/42; Guatemala 4/10/42; retUS Tinker 3/8/44; RFC Arledge, 23/11/44.
41-2413 Del Salt Lake SAD 30/11/41; ass 42BS/11BG Hickam 30/1/42; tran 5AF 31/8/44; WO 11/6/45.
41-2414 Del Salt Lake SAD 9/11/41; cr burned out Ft Douglas 12/11/41. Sal.

Above: B-17E 41-2393 in camouflage finish. The remotely controlled power turret and the sighting blister can be seen under the centre of the fuselage. (Roger Besecker)

41-2415 Del Salt Lake SAD 28/11/41; ass Hickam 10/11/42; WO 11/5/44.
41-2416 Del Salt Lake SAD 9/11/41; ass 40BS/19BG Hickam SAN ANTONIO ROSE; tran 88RS/ ; Damaged Townsville, Aus 22/2/42; WO 31/1/44.
41-2417 Del Salt Lake SAD 19/1/41; ass 19BG Hawaii; tran Project X 26/12/42; Java 19/2/42; cr Queensland, Aus 6/7/42 w/Thompson. Sal. SAN ANTONIO ROSE II.
41-2418 Del Salt Lake SAD 26/11/41; ass 6AF 25/12/41; Panama 1/6/42; Puerto Rico 11/7/42; Guatemala 10/8/42; retUS Brownsville 3/10/42; Guatemala 8/1/43; Gen. Brett's CB-17C; WO 26/6/46.
41-2419 Del Salt Lake SAD 20/11/41; Java 13/1/42; c/l Palembang 22/2/42 w/Hughes; WO 9/1/45.
41-2420 Del Salt Lake SAD 20/11/41; ass 42BS/11BG 15/12/41; Hickam 22/7/42; Ditched Doma Cove, Guadalcanal 24/9/42 w/Norton; found by Seebees Jan/44. BESSIE THE JAP BASHER.
41-2421 Del Salt Lake SAD 26/11/41; ass 40BS/19BG Australia; cr Horn Is 16/7/42 w/McPherson; WO 31/10/44.
41-2422 Del Salt Lake SAD 24/11/41; ass 3BS/6BG 27/2/42; Guatemala 15/5/42; cr en route David Fd 5/8/43, 12 KAS.
41-2423 Del Salt Lake SAD 28/11/41; March 18/12/41; Project X McDill/Bakers Fd 25/12/41; cr Clewiston, 5/1/42. Sal.
41-2424 Del Salt Lake SAD 1/12/41; ass 6AF 27/12/41; Guatemala 15/4/42; retUS Tinker 25/6/42, RFC Altus 20/8/45.
41-2425 Del Salt Lake SAD 26/11/41; ass 6AF Panama 30/12/41; Guatemala 15/4/42; Puerto Rico 31/7/42; Guatemala 10/9/42; Panama 23/11/42; retUS Tinker 22/7/44; RFC Albuquerque 2/8/45.
41-2426 Del Salt Lake SAD 16/11/41; ass 43BS/11BG 17/8/42 [a/c No.42]; 5AF /8/43; retUS Hendricks 12/2/44; Recl Comp 31/12/45.
41-2427 Del Salt Lake SAD 25/11/41; ass Java Project X 28/1/42; strafed Singasari 3/2/42. Sal, WO 31/10/44.
41-2428 Del Salt Lake SAD 26/11/41; ass 98BS/11BG Hickam-Clarke 26/10/42. OL' SHASTA.
41-2429 Del Salt Lake SAD 26/11/41; ass 93BS/19BG Hickam-Clarke; s/d Rabual PNG 7/8/42 in MacArthur rescue attempt, w/Earp (RAAF); 2 crew survived but later executed; pilot Harl Pease MOH; WO 15/6/44.
41-2430 Del Salt Lake SAD 30/11/41; ass 88RS/7BG Hickam during Jap raid 7/12/41; tran 19BG; 43BG;

s/d Vunakanau 26/6/43 w/nav Holguin only POW; WO 28/6/43. NAUGHTY BUT NICE.

41-2431 Del Salt Lake SAD 30/11/41; ass 43BG Wheeler-Hickam 19/11/42; tran 5BG /2/43; retUS 11/1/44 (known as a gas hog!); Scott 17/1/45; Chanute 21/1/45; RFC Walnut Ridge 12/10/45.

41-2432 Del Salt Lake SAD 30/11/41; ass 88RS/7BG, landed Pearl Harbor 7/12/41; tran 40RS-28BS/7BG; 19BG; 43BG; 443TCG 8/12/43; WO 12/1/45. THE LAST STRAW.

41-2433 Del Salt Lake SAD 30/11/41; ass 88RS/7BG Hickam 22/5/42; retUS 1/9/44 Hendricks; Yuma 31/10/44; RFC Albuquerque 25/6/45.

41-2434 Del Salt Lake SAD 30/11/41; ass 28BS/19BG Hickam; Ditched off Cairns, en route Aus 17/8/42, w/Hoevet; WO 31/10/44.

41-2435 Del Salt Lake SAD 30/11/41; ass 40BS/19BG Hickam; s/d off Buna 12/8/42 w/Watson; WO 31/10/44.

41-2436 Del McDill 25/12/41; Project X 29/2/42; retUS Bolling 16/8/42; Langley 9/7/44; Selfridge 6/7/45; RFC Altus 24/9/45.

41-2437 Del Salt Lake SAD 2/12/41; ass 98BS/11BG Hickam 25/10/42; WO 15/6/44. (Figured in Midway TV Documentary.)

41-2438 Del Salt Lake SAD 2/12/41; ass 40RS/19BG Hickam 26/12/41; retUS Tinker 16/12/43; ass RCAF 168th Heavy Transport Sq Rockcliffe, Ont (No. 9206); Used for VIPs and mail to Prestwick, Scotland.

41-2439 Del Salt Lake SAD 2/12//41; ass Project X 22/2/42; Mobile 16/11/42; Sebring 4/1/43; RFC Albuquerque 25/6/45.

41-2440 Del Salt Lake SAD 21/1/41; ass 40RS/19BG Hickam 26/12/41; tran /11BG; retUS Lambert, MO. 7/3/44; Chanute 1/2/45; Recl Comp 15/7/46.

41-2441 Del Salt Lake SAD 3/12/41; ass 6AF Howard, Panama 27/12/41; Guatemala 6/3/42; cr in sea 7/1/43, all equip lost.

41-2442 Del Salt Lake SAD 3/12/41; ass 42BS/11BG Hickam 22/7/42; cr Shortland Bay 1/2/43 w/Hensley. YOKOHAMA EXPRESS.

41-2443 Del McChord 4/12/41; ass 42BS/11BG Hickam 15/12/41; MIA Hawaii 5/4/42 w/Cox.

41-2444 Del McChord 4/12/41; ass 42BS/11BG Hickam 18/10/42; retUS 17/10/43; WO 8/10/44.

41-2445 Del Sacramento 3/12/41; ass 42BS/11BG Hickam 22/7/42; tore off tail in taxi accident 9/12/42; WO 15/6/44. SO SOLLY PLEASE.

41-2466 Del Sacramento 8/12/41; ass 22BS/7BG Australia; f/l Popondetta, PNG 23/3/42 w/Eaton; retUS 31/10/44; restored at Travis AFB, the oldest E model in the world. SWAMP GHOST.

41-2447 Del Sacramento 8/12/41; ass 19BG Hickam; used in second MacArthur rescue attempt; bombed on Del Monte Fd 12/4/42 w/Bostrom. Sal. WO 31/10/44. SAN ANTONIO ROSE II.

41-2448 Del Sacramento 8/12/41; ass 6AF 27/12/41; Guatemala 12/4/42; retUS Tinker 8/7/44; WO 9/2/45.

41-2449 Del Sacramento 17/12/41; McDill 7/1/42; ass 19BG Hickam; strafed Broome, Aus 3/3/42; WO 30/10/44.

41-2450 Del Sacramento 17/11/41; McDill 5/1/42; Project X 18/1/42; ass 6AF Panama 4/3/42; Guatemala 15/4/42; WO in ground accident 1/8/43.

41-2451 Ass 6AF Panama 17/12/41, cr south of Rio Hato w/Scott 1/6/42; Guatemala 7/7/42; retUS Tinker 8/7/44; RFC Altus 24/8/45. Parts used to restore B-17G 44-83812 at Grass Valley, Cal 1969. AZTEC'S CURSE.

41-2452 Del Bakersfield 30/12/41; ass 93BS/19BG Java 10/2/42; used in MacArthur's first rescue attempt; ditched off New Guinea 10/8/42 w/Hawthorne.

41-2453 Del McDill 25/12/41; Hamilton 19/11/42; Pocatello 28/11/42; Oklahoma City 12/12/42; Pyote, 19/1/43; taxi accident 19/2/43 w/Nardi; damaged again Lockburn 26/11/43; RFC Altus 9/10/45.

41-2454 Del McDill 25/12/41; ass 19BG Java 18/1/42; strafed Broome Fd 3/3/42; sal.

41-2455 Del McDill 25/12/41; ass 19BG Java 26/1/42; strafed Singasari 20/2/42; sal.

41-2456 Del McChord 17/12/41; ass 19BG Java 18/1/42; s/d at sea 8/2/42 w/Dufrane.

41-2457 Del Sacramento 17/12/41; ass 19BG Java 20/3/42; Nasal (10AF?) 20/5/43; retUS Memphis,TN. 2/8/44; Eglin 5/11/44; Recl Comp 31/10/45.

41-2458 Del Sacramento 17/12/41; ass 28BS/19BG Java 30/1/42; tran 65BS/43BG; 317TCG Dobodura 11/43; WO 27/1/45. YANKEE DIDD'LER.

41-2459 Del Sacramento 17/12/41; ass 19BG Java 14/1/42; strafed Kendari, Borneo 16/1/42, sal.

41-2460 Del McDill 25/12/41; ass 19BG Java 15/1/42; c/l Mareeba, Aus 27/7/42 w/Becktold. Sal.

41-2461 Del McDill 25/12/41; ass 19BG Java 13/1/42; strafed Port Moresby 25/4/42. Sal.

41-2462 Del Geiger 22/12/41; ass 93BS/19BG Java 11/2/42 TOJO'S JINX; strafed Port Moresby 25/12/41. Became hack for L/Gen Krueger 6th Army, called BILLY, then WO 3/6/45.

41-2463 Del Geiger 28/12/41; ass 19BG Hickam 13/12/42; WO 13/8/43. YANKEE DOODLE.

41-2464 Del McChord 22/12/41; ass 7BG Hawaii; tran 93BS/19BG Java 21/1/42; 64BG/43BG Australia as hack named QUEENIE w/5AFSC; MIA Nadzab/Biak 8/7/44 w/19 aboard, no trace.

41-2465 Del McDill 30/12/41; ass Projext X 4/1/42; Nasal (10AF?) 20/5/42; WO 30/6/43.

41-2466 Del Geiger 25/12/41; ass 19BG Java 21/1/42; strafed Bandoeng, DEI 19/2/42; sal.

41-2467 Del McChord 22/12/41; Geiger 27/12/41; Hamilton 28/1/42; ass Hickam 16/2/42; retUS 21/10/43; WO 4/12/43.

41-2468 Del Sacramento 20/12/43; ass 19BG Java 18/1/42; c/l Madera Is, DEI. 25/1/42 w/ Northcutt; WO 3/8/43.

41-2469 Del McChord 23/12/41; ass 19BG Java 21/1/42; c/l Selembo 3/2/42 w/Swanson. Sal.

41-2470 Del McDill 7/1/42; ass 19BG Java 30/1/42; strafed Singasari 3/2/42; sal.

41-2471 Del McChord 20/12/41; ass 19BG Java 18/1/42; burnt out Jogjakarta 28/2/42; sal.

41-2472 Del McChord 24/12/41; ass 7BG Java 15/1/42; tran 19BG Australia; tran /43BG; over 200 missions; WO 31/8/44. GUINEA PIG.

41-2473 Del McChord 24/12/41; Project X 25/12/41; Langley 9/2/42; Palm Beach 11/3/42; Langley 13/5/42; Olmstead 1/2/43; Occident 29/4/43; retUS Mitchell 8/6/43; Gt Bend 16/7/44; Chanute 4/12/46; Recl Comp 20/8/46.

41-2474 Del McChord 23/12/41; Project X 20/2/42; Magpie 12/6/42; Glen 12AF 21/6/42; Oham 15AF 8/7/44; WO 12/11/44.

41-2475 Del Sacramento 27/12/41; Langley 4/1/42; McDill 7/1/42; c/l 20/4/42. Sal 7/8/43.

41-2476 Del McChord 24/12/41; ass 19BG Java 26/1/42; s/d at sea 29/1/42 w/Sparks.

41-2477 Del Sacramento 29/12/43; Langley 3/1/42; Project X 14/1/42; retUS Tyndall 12/11/43, converted to RB-17Q; Atlanta 6/10/44; Rome 12/12/44; RFC Walnut Ridge 8/1/46.

41-2478 Del Sacramento 26/12/41; ass 19BG Java 28/1/42; strafed Singasari 20/2/42; sal.

41-2479 Del Sacramento 27/11/41; Langley 7/1/42; McDill 16/1/42; cr in sea 20/2/42.

41-2480 Del Sacramento 26/12/41; Portland 29/12/41; Langley 3/1/42; McDill 6/1/42; Project X 11/1/42; WO 1/5/42.

41-2481 Del Sacramento 26/12/41; ass 19BG Java 14/2/42; tran 43BG; c/t/o Port Moresby 27/8/43; WO 30/10/43. TOPPER.

41-2482 Del Sacramento 28/12/41; Project X 13/1/42; c/t/o Boeing Fd, 20/12/42; sal.

41-2483 Del Sacramento 28/12/41; ass 19BG Java 31/1/42; blown up on evacuation Madioen 28/2/42.

41-2484 Del Langley 31/12/41; ass 19BG Java 9/2/42; strafed Singasari 20/2/42.

41-2485 Del McChord 31/12/41; Langley 3/1/42; McDill 6/1/42; Project X 6/3/42; retUS Tinker 5/6/42; Des Moines 22/7/44; Romulus 1/9/44; Stout 2/11/44; Recl Comp 29/6/45.

41-2486 Del Langley 31/12/41; ass 64BS/43BG Java 7/2/42 LADY LOU; (used in MacArthur's first rescue attempt—aborted); trans Daly Waters, Aus 5/42; retUS 10/42; RFC Altus 4/10/45.[a/c m/card Project X 20/2/42; Nasal 20/5/42; Hamilton 19/11/42; Pocatello 28/11/42; Pyote 30/1/43; La Junta, Col. 1/8/43; Lockburn 7/8/43; RFC Altus 4/10/45.

41-2487 Del Langley 30/12/41; Duncan 19/1/42; Hamilton 27/1/42; ass 42BS/11BG Hickam 21/2/42; tran 42BS 28/10/44; WO 11/6/45.

41-2488 Del McChord 30/12/41; ass 19BG Java 6/2/42; strafed Singasari 20/2/42. Sal.

41-2489 Del McDill 4/1/42; ass 93BS/19BG Java 7/2/42 SUZY Q; took part in all Pacific battles except Midway; claimed 26 enemy a/c; Mareeba, Aus, 9/42; retUS Hamilton 23/10/43; Peterson 8/6/44; Smoky Hill 12/7/44; San Bernadino 31/12/45; Recl Comp 15/7/46. SUZY-Q.

41-2490 Del Sacramento 10/1/42; Cr nth of Pendleton Fd 17/1/42. Sal.

41-2491 Del Boeing SAD 18/1/42; McDill 23/1/42; Nasal 20/5/42; Middle East 11/7/43; Central Africa /6/44; retUS Boeing 17/6/44 mod to RB-17; WO 30/11/45.

41-2492 Del McDill 4/1/42; ass 19BG Java 5/2/42; s/d at sea 8/2/42 w/Prichard.

41-2493 Del Sacramento 18/1/42; ass 19BG Java 5/2/42; strafed Bandoeng 19/2/42. Sal.

41-2494 Del McDill 3/1/42; ass 19BG Java 7/2/42; c/l Malang 8/2/42 w/Lorance. Sal.

41-2495 Del Portland 14/1/42; McDill 22/1/42; Palm Beach 26/4/42; Sebring 13/9/42; 2137 BU Hendricks 14/5/42; WO 5/7/44.

41-2496 Del Patterson 15/1/42; Wright 1/3/42; Minneapolis 13/4/42; Wright 10/6/42; Patterson 17/6/42; Biggs 15/5/43; 2511 BU Bryan 5/12/43; RFC Walnut Ridge 5/10/45.

41-2497 Del McDill 26/1/42; ass 19BG Java 17/2/42; tran 43BG Aus; sal Horn Is /9/43; TOJO'S NIGHTMARE.

41-2498 Del McDill 3/1/42; 19BG Java 9/2/42; strafed Singosari 20/2/42; sal.

41-2499 Del San Antonio 10/1/42; Nasal 20/5/42; retUS Hendricks 14/6/43; 4121 BU Kelly 23/9/44; 3018 BU Kingman 18/10/44; RFC Albuquerque 25/6/45.

41-2500 Del 5/1/42 Langley; ass 7BG Java 19/2/42; strafed Bandoeng, DEI 24/2/42. Sal.

41-2501 Del Sacramento 18/1/42; McDill 25/1/42; ass 5AF, c/l 20/2/42. Sal.

41-2502 Del Portland 14/1/42; McDill 10/2/42; Sebring 6/9/42; Brookley 25/3/43; Hendricks 2/4/43; 3036 BU Yuma 13/11/43; RFC Albuquerque 26/5/45.

41-2503 Del McDill 25/1/42; ass 7BG Java 19/2/42;

s/d over Bandoeng, DEI., 19/2/42 w/Franklin; sal.

41-2504 Del McDill 6/2/42; West Palm Beach 20/2/42; ass 6AF Howard, Panama 4/4/42; Guatemala 15/4/42; canal patrol & anti-sub duties; Mitchell 11/11/43; Mat Com Wright Fd; 4136 BU Tinker 2/1/45; Recl Comp 9/2/42.

41-2505 Del Portland 14/1/42; ass 19BG Java 10/2/42; MIA New Guinea 25/4/42 w/Fagan,8 KIA; First Sperry ball turret.

41-2506 Del Portland 14/1/42; McDill 25/1/42; ass 5AF; WO 31/10/44.

41-2507 Del 14/1/42; ass 19BG Java 20/2/42; used in first MacArthur rescue; ditched Mindanao 12/3/42 w/Godman.

41-2508 Del Albany 24/1/42; McDill 30/1/42; Sebring 3/2/42; Maxwell 17/3/42; Hendricks 13/5/42. WO 5/10/44.

41-2509 Del Albany 22/1/42; McDill 30/1/42; Sebring 3/2/42; Hendricks 29/7/42. RFC Albuquerque 15/6/45.

41-2510 Del Albany 22/1/42; Sebring 30/1/42; McDill 5/2/42; Cheyenne 9/5/42; Luke 28/12/42; Hendricks 4/3/43; WO 5/7/44.

41-2511 Del Albany 22/1/42; Sebring 23/1/42; McDill 13/2/42; Hendricks 16/4/42; WO 3/5/44.

41-2512 Del Cheyenne 27/1/42; RCAF Dorval, Montreal 13/3/42, to GB Defense Aid.

41-2513 Del Cheyenne 27/1/42; via RCAF Dorval 24/3/42 to GB (FK184)

41-2514 Del Ogden 23/1/42; Cheyenne 15/2/42; RCAF Dorval 24/3/42 to GB (FK185) 220Sq.

41-2515 Del Ogden 23/1/42; Cheyenne 2/3/42; Wayne Co. 5/4/42; RCAF Dorval 8/4/42 to GB (FK186)

41-2516 Del Ogden 20/1/42; Cheyenne 2/3/42; RCAF Dorval 24/3/42 to GB (FK187).

41-2517 Del Ogden 23/1/42; Cheyenne 15/2/42; RCAF Dorval 19/3/42 to GB (FK188)

41-2518 Del Ogden 23/1/42; Cheyenne 15/2/42; Wright 24/3/42; Wayne Co. 10/10/42; RCAF Dorval 18/10/42 to GB (FK189)

41-2519 Del Ogden 25/1/42; Cheyenne 10/2/42; Wayne Co. 31/3/42; RCAF Dorval 1/4/42 to GB (FK190)

41-2520 Del Ogden 20/1/42; Cheyenne 9/4/42; Lowry 5/5/42; Hamilton 27/5/42; ass 7AF Hawaii 28/5/42; retUS 2/9/44; Recl Comp 14/8/45. JAP HAPPY.

41-2521 Del Ogden 25/1/42; Hill 18/2/42; Cheyenne 12/4/42; Lowry 8/5/42; Hamilton 29/5/42; ass 7AF Hawaii 30/5/42; tran 5AF 15/6/44. G. I. ANGEL.

41-2522 Del Ogden 25/1/42; Cheyenne 21/3/42; Wayne Co. 11/4/42; Clewiston 30/11/42.

41-2523 Del Ogden 30/1/42; ass 98BS/11BG Hawaii; tran 5BG, on ops for 38 consecutive days; ditched ex-Kahili off Russell Is. 20/3/43 w/Col Unrul, 5BG CO, all crew rescued. GOONIE.

41-2524 Del Ogden 20/1/42; Hill 15/2/42; Cheyenne 12/4/42; Lowry 2/5; Hamilton 23/5/42; ass 5AF Hawaii 23/5/42; retUS Brookley 8/12/43; Hendricks 28/8/44; RFC 22/5/45.

41-2525 Del Ogden 25/1/42; Hill 15/2/42; Cheyenne 11/4/42; Lowry 5/5/42; Hamilton 27/5/42; ass 98BS/11BG Hawaii; tran 31BS/5BG; WO Kahilia 6/6/43. MADAM X.

41-2526 Del Ogden 25/1/42; Hill 15/2/42; Cheyenne 30/3/42; Wayne Co. 17/4/42; RCAF Dorval 22/4/42 to GB.

41-2527 Del Ogden 25/1/42; Portland 27/1/42; Ogden 17/2/42; Cheyenne 10/4/42; Lowry 6/5/42; ass 5AF Hawaii 21/5/42; WO 15/6/44.

41-2528 Del Patterson 25/1/42; Wright 15/2/42; Tallahassee 13/3/42; Eglin 18/4/42; Patterson, OH. 29/7/42; Alamogordo 21/8/42; Biggs 7/9/42; Alamogordo 2/10/42; Boise 10/11/42; Columbus, Oh. 19/3/43; RFC Altus 6/9/45.

41-2529 Del Patterson 25/1/42; Lowry 27/2/42; SAAD 16/5/42; ass Sumac 5AF 8/8/42.

41-2530 Del Cheyenne 27/1/42; Sebring 15/5/42; Hendricks 3/4/43, c/l 30/7/43, rep; RFC Albuquerque 24/6/45.

41-2531 Del Sebring 29/1/42; Geiger 29/3/42; Cheyenne 14/5/42; Wendover 27/5/42; WO 25/5/44. BUZZ KING.

41-2532 Del Sebring 8/3/42; Brookley 11/2/43; Hendricks 25/2/42; RFC Walnut Ridge 9/10/45.

41-2533 Del Sebring 27/1/42; missing from Hendricks 15/4/42 (at sea?). WO 21/4/42

41-2534 Del Sebring 27/1/42; Cheyenne 20/5/42; Eglin 29/11/42; c/l Hendricks 10/4/43. Sal 5/2/44.

41-2535 Del McDill 23/1/42; Tucson 31/1/42; ass 10AF Nasal 20/5/42; New Castle, DEL. 29/5/42; Wilmington 30/8/42; WO 5/6/44.

41-2536 Del McDill 29/1/42; ass 28BS/19BG Hawaii 3/42; tran 43BG Melbourne ; damaged Rabual 7/8/42; MIA 12/11/42.

41-2537 Del Wright Fd 29/1/42; Midland 5/1/42; Wright 21/1/43; Biggs 10/3/43; Wright 13/3/43; Oklahoma City 23/4/43; Wright 29/4/43. Recl Comp 20/3/46.

41-2538 Del Geiger 29/1/42; Tucson 7/2/42; Cheyenne 1/5/42; Salt Lake City 1/6/42; Wendover, Ut. 10/6/42; Westover 11/8/42; Boise 12/8/42; Memphis 6/9/42; Pyote 14/1/43; Barksdale, La. 27/2/43; RFC Albuquerque 14/7/45.

41-2539 Del Wright Fd 26/1/42; Muroc 12/7/42; Wright 17/7/42; Bolling 10/12/42; Wright 26/3/43; mid-air refuelling tests; Eglin 24/4/43; Tinker 13/5/43; RFC Walnut Ridge 15/11/45.

41-2540 Del Geiger 29/1/42; Tucson 7/2/42; 97BG Sarasota 29/3/42; Bangor 26/6/42; Westover 28/6/42; Long Beach 15/7/42; McDill 26/8/42; Tarrant 1/10/42; Love 14/3/43. WO 8/5/43.

41-2541 Del Geiger 29/1/42; Tucson 7/2/42; Cheyenne 14/5/42; Westover 23/5/42; Wendover 11/8/42; Biggs 29/8/42; Alamogordo 2/10/42; cr burned 6/10/42. Sal.

41-2542 Del Geiger 29/1/42; Tucson 10/2/42; Cheyenne 4/5/42; Wendover 10/6/42; Alamogordo 16/9/42; McChord 20/11/42; Oklahoma City 2/12/42; Hill 3/1/43; Napier 3/3/43; Hendricks 13/3/43. WO 5/7/44.

41-2543 Del Tucson 4/2/42; Geiger 12/2/42; Cheyenne 9/5/42; Wendover 12/5/42; Ephrata 4/6/42; Wendover 22/8/42; Westover 11/8/42; Boise 20/8/42; Topeka 28/10/42; Sioux Falls 21/11/42; Smyrna 28/2/43. WO 18/11/43.

41-2544 Del McDill 13/2/42; ass 6AF 2/3/42; Guatemala 15/4/42; SAAD 3/7/42; San Antonio 8/11/42; Guatemala 1/12/43; retUS Tinker 8/7/44. RFC Walnut Ridge 14/9/45.

41-2545 Del Tucson 4/2/42; Geiger 12/2/42; Cheyenne 12/4/42; Wendover 8/5/42; Ogden 10/8/42; Pocatello 6/11/42; Boise 20/12/42; Lockburn 21/2/43; wrecked in taxi accident with truck McDill 17/9/43, brakes failed w/Preinerich; RFC Walnut Ridge 12/12/45.

41-2546 Del Tucson 4/2/42; Las Vegas 6/2/42; McDill 15/2/42; Cheyenne 21/3/42; Memphis 11/6/42; Walla Walla 19/7/42; Topeka 30/8/42; Albuquerque 16/10/42; Lowry 19/10/42; Topeka 2/11/42; cr Randolph, UT. 29/11/42. Sal.

41-2547 Del Pendleton 5/2/42; 34BG Tucson 14/5/42; Rapid City 5/12/42; Walla Walla 14/1/43; Lockburn 9/4/43. RFC Albuquerque 14/7/45.

41-2548 Del Pendleton 5/2/42; Boise 17/2/42; Salt Lake City 24/6/42; Biggs 30/10/42; Pueblo 28/1/43. Recl Comp 19/10/45.

41-2549 Del Pendleton 4/2/42; Boise 15/2/42; Cheyenne 5/4/42; Wendover 9/6/42; Ogden 10/7/42; Alamogordo 20/8/42; Biggs 5/11/42; Hendricks 3/4/43; WO 1/9/44.

41-2550 Del Pendleton 4/2/42; Boise 25/2/42; Alamogordo 19/6/42; St Joseph 21/12/42; Nashville 1/5/43; Presque Is 1/7/43; Flushing 20/12/43; RFC Bush Fd 6/6/45.

41-2551 Del Pendleton 4/2/42; Boise 20/3/42; Cheyenne 19/5/42; Alamogordo 19/6/42; WO 21/7/42. (Two taxi accidents Hill 23/2 and Gowen 26/2/42).

41-2552 Del Pendleton 4/2/42; Boise 18/2/42; Cheyenne 3/5/42; Alamogordo 18/6/42; Bowman, KY. 26/6/42; Boise 20/8/42; Lockburn 22/3/43. RFC Altus 20/8/45.

41-2553 Del Pendleton 5/2/42; Boise 30/3/42; Cheyenne 6/5/42; Alamogordo 18/6/42; Westover 2/7/42; Wendover 21/7/42; Westover 11/8/42; Sebring 12/9/42; Hillsboro 23/6/43; Sebring 4/7/43. RFC Albuquerque 28/6/45.

41-2554 Del Pendleton 5/2/42; Salt Lake City 27/3/42; Wendover 8/4/42; Cheyenne 14/5/42; Wendover 28/5/42; Ogden 28/7/42; Westover 1/8/42; Biggs 19/8/42; Boise 14/9/42; Gowen 31/1/43; Hendricks 11/8/43. WO 11/7/44.

41-2555 Del Pendleton 5/2/42; Tucson 23/5/42; Geiger 30/5/42; c/t/o 20/8/42. Sal.

41-2556 Del Pendleton 5/2/42; Alamogordo 3/8/42; cr 10/8/42. Sal.

41-2557 Del Pendleton 5/2/42; Geiger 30/4/42; Tucson 26/5/42; Ephrata 4/6/42; Muroc 5/7/42; Geiger 1/9/42; Boise 8/10/42; Pueblo 11/1/43. RFC Altus 14/9/45.

41-2558 Del Pendleton 5/2/42; Cheyenne 14/5/42; Wright 15/6/42; Blythe 2/7/42; Geiger 1/9/42; Topeka 28/9/42; Oklahoma 27/11/42; Lockburn 30/3/43; cr 22/6/43. Sal.

41-2559 Del Pendleton 5/2/42; cr south of field 16/3/42 w/Neighbors. Sal.

41-2560 Del Pendleton 5/2/42; Boise 9/2/42; Salt Lake City 23/6/42; Biggs 13/9/42; Lockburn 1/5/43. RFC Altus 4/9/45.

41-2561 Del Pendleton 5/2/42; cr sth Gowen Fd 16/3/42. Sal.

41-2562 Del Pendleton 6/2/42; cr 15 miles nw of fd 26/3/42. Sal.

41-2563 Del Pendleton 6/2/42; Boise 19/2/42; Ogden 3//9/42; Boise 16/10/42; Oklahoma City 5/12/42; Wendover 5/1/43; Lockburn 8/4/43; WO 11/3/44.

41-2564 Del Pendleton 6/2/42; Cheyenne 2/5/42; Wendover 18/6/42; 305BG Muroc 5/7/42; Walla Walla 6/9/42; Rapid City 1/10/42; Topeka 18/11/42; Hendricks 15/5/43. RFC Albuquerque 8/8/45.

41-2565 Del 34BG Pendleton 6/2/42; cr Meacham, sw of fd 3/4/42 6 dead inc pilot Lt Laycock. Sal.

41-2566 Del McDill 6/2/42; cr 6 miles w of Orlando, 20/4/42, coll w/P-40, all killed. Sal.

41-2567 Del Pendleton 6/2/42; Cheyenne 9/4/42; Tucson 12/5/42; Ephrata 4/6/42; Muroc 5/7/42; St Joseph 9/8/42; MAD 8/9/42; St Joseph 1/10/42; Gore Fd 17/8/43. RFC Stillwater 25/8/45.

41-2568 Del Barksdale 9/2/42; Cheyenne 23/5/42; Boise 21/6/42; McChord 20/7/42; Boise 12/8/42; Oklahoma City 5/12/42; Pyote 11/1/43; Tinker 31/1/43; Lockburn 30/3/43; RFC Albuquerque 14/7/45.

41-2569 Del McDill 6/2/42; West Palm Beach 22/2/42; ass 6AF Panama 27/3/42; Guatemala 2/4/42; SAAD 13/6/42; Guatemala 24/6/42; SAAD 2/11/42;

Guatemala 1/12/42; Panama 19/3/43; WO 2/10/43.

41-2570 Del McDill 11/2/42; 97BG Sarasota 29/3/42; McDill 29/4/42; Sarasota 23/6/42; Bangor 29/6/42; Wendover 14/7/42; Westover 3/8/42; Sebring 28/12/42; RFC Albuquerque 9/8/45.

41-2571 Del McDill 10/2/42; Cheyenne 13/5/42; Sarasota 20/6/42; Westover 28/6/42; Wendover 14/7/42; Ogden 4/8/42; Rapid City 17/10/42; Pocatello 6/11/42; Oklahoma City 6/12/42; Gowen 7/2/43; Lockburn 31/3/43; Columbus 27/4/43; WO 21/5/44.

41-2572 Del McDill 17/2/42; Sarasota 25/6/42; Westover 28/6/42; 369BS/306BG Wendover 19/7/42; Westover 11/8/42; Sebring 24/9/42; Bolling 12/1/43; Hendricks 29/4/43; Recl Comp 29/1/46.

41-2573 Del Barksdale 7/2/42; Cheyenne 1/5/42; Orlando 22/6/42; Westover 28/6/42; 367BS/3206BS Wendover 15/8/42; Walla Walla 24/8/42; RFC Walnut Ridge 17/1/46.

41-2574 Del McDill 20/2/42; Cheyenne 10/5/42; Ogden 26/7/42; Wendover 6/8/42; Boise 30/12/42; Hendricks 25/3/43; RFC Walnut Ridge 19/12/45.

41-2575 Del McDill 14/2/42; c/l 20/4/42 w/Wright. Sal.

41-2576 Del Barksdale 9/2/42; Cheyenne 21/5/42; Walla Walla 30/7/42; Rapid City 1/10/42; Pocatello 6/11/42; Topeka 12/12/42; Wendover 6/1/43; Lockburn 30/3/43; RFC Altus 18/8/45.

41-2577 Del Barksdale 9/2/42; Cheyenne 10/5/42; Walla Walla 29/6/42; Pendleton 11/8/42; Boise 26/10/42; Topeka 1/12/42; 384BG Wendover 2/1/43; RFC Altus 9/10/45.

41-2578 Del Pendleton 18/2/42; ass 11 CCRC Bovingdon, UK; 340BS/97BG Polebrook, UK /5/42 BUTCHER SHOP; tran 326BS/92BG Bovingdon; tran 457BG Glatton, UK 3/3/44; on first 8AF mission w/Paul Tibbetts. Became hack for Col Wilson 77FS/20FG [LC-Z] Kings Cliffe, UK; sal 6/8/45. Oldest B-17 in 8AF. BIG TIN BIRD.

41-2579 Del Barksdale 8/2/42; McDill 2/3/42; Boise 18/8/42; March 15/11/43; Tinker 4/2/43; Gowen 24/2/43; Lockburn 21/3/43; RFC Altus 9/10/45.

41-2580 Del McDill 14/2/42; 97BG Sarasota 29/3/42; Bangor 26/6/42; Muroc 11/8/42; Walla Walla 5/9/42; 96BG Pocatello 6/11/42; Gowen 15/2/43; Hill 20/3/43; Lockburn 23/3/43; RFC Altus 9/10/45.

41-2581 Del Pendleton 18/2/42; Cheyenne 13/5/42; Biggs 27/6/42; Alamogordo 11/8/42; Lockburn 29/6/43; tran RCAF Rockcliffe, Ont. 14/12/43.

41-2582 Del Pendleton 18/2/42; Tucson 12/5/42; Ephrata 4/6/42; Alamogordo 16/8/42; Boise 13/11/42; Hendricks 3/4/43; Yuma 18/10/43; RFC Albuquerque 25/6/45.

41-2583 Del McDill 17/2/42; Cheyenne 8/5/42; Boise 21/6/42; Ogden 17/7/42; Gowen 17/2/43; Lockburn 1/4/43; RFC Altus 14/9/45.

41-2584 Del Barksdale 20/2/42; McDill 13/3/42; Cheyenne 21/5/42; Boise 27/6/42; coll w/B-17 in taxi accident 26/9/42. Sal.

41-2585 Del Barksdale 21/2/42; Cheyenne 156/5/42; Boise 21/6/42; Eglin 10/8/42; Oklahoma City 5/12/42; Pueblo 5/1/43; Lockburn 11/3/43; RFC Altus 6/9/45.

41-2586 Del Barksdale 22/2/42; 97BG Sarasota 29/3/42; Cheyenne 18/5/42; Walla Walla 17/8/42; 96BG Pocatello 4/11/42; Hendricks 24/3/43; WO 29/12/43.

41-2587 Del Barksdale 22/2/42; McDill 1/3/42; Sarasota [97BG] 29/3/42; McDill 18/4/42; Cheyenne 21/5/42; Orlando 11/8/42; Walla Walla 7/8/42; Rapid City 1/10/42; Pocatello [96BG] 4/11/42; Hendricks 24/3/43, WO 29/12/43.

41-2588 Del McDill 28/2/42; ass 340BS/97BG Sarasota 29/3/42; c/l Presque Is 28/6/42. Sal. Parts used on 41-9022.

41-2589 Del Barksdale 21/2/42; McDill 5/3/42; Boise 21/6/42; Yuma 18/10/42; c/l Gowen u/c failed 20/11/42, rep; Hendricks 31/3/43; RFC Albuquerque 10/6/45.

41-2590 Del McDill 24/2/42; Cheyenne 14/5/42; Walla Walla 26/6/42; Eglin 3/8/42; Wright 25/9/42; Lockburn 22/4/43; RFC Walnut Ridge 18/10/45.

41-2591 Del Pendleton; Tucson 12/5/42; Alamogordo 19/6/42; Biggs 7/11/42; Boise 9/1/43; Lockburn 24/2/43; Atlanta 11/8/43; RFC Altus 9/10/45.

41-2592 Del Pendleton; Cheyenne 6/5/42; Alamogordo 19/6/42; Eglin 18/8/42; Pyote 11/1/43; cr 22/2/43, WO.

41-2593 Del McDill 24/2/42; ass 91BG Walla Walla 21/6/42; MAAD 18/6/42 mod as XC-108 as taxi for Gen MacArthur, called BATAAN; later used by Gen Eichelberger as MISS EM; RFC Walnut Ridge 30/10/45.

41-2594 Del McDill 24/2/42; Cheyenne 23/5/42; ass 91BG Walla Walla 21/6/42; Pocatello 6/11/42; 19BG Pyote 11/1/43; 1497 AF Gp Lockburn 25/2/43; RFC Walnut Ridge 13/11/45.

41-2595 Del McDill 28/2/42; 97BG Sarasota 29/3/42; Ogden 7/7/42; 383BG Ainsworth 19/3/43; Wright Fd 17/8/43, modified to XC-108A cargo a/c. ATC in CBI; retUS. 1379BU Maine; sal Dow Fd 12/45. Remains to Marengo, Ill, 1985 for restoration. DESERT RAT.

41-2596 Del McDill 24/2/42; 97BG Sarasota 29/3/42; Westover 28/6/42; Wendover 20/7/42; Walla Walla 20/8/42; 452 AF Sq Hendricks 19/2/43; RFC Albuquerque 26/5/45.

41-2597 Del McDill 20/2/42; missing w/crew 6/5/42, cr at sea?

41-2598 Del Barksdale 24/2/42; 97BG Sarasota 29/3/42; Walla Walla 28/6/42; cr & burned 15/7/42. Sal.

41-2599 Del Lowry 26/2/42; Hamilton 7/6/42; ass 93BS/19BG Hawaii; tran 65BS/43BG; ditched 16/1/43; Took part in Midway battle. TUGBOAT ANNIE.

41-2600 Del Tucson 3/3/42; Cheyenne 14/5/42; Ephrata 4/6/42; Muroc 5/7/42; Davis Monthan 31/1/43; Hendricks 15/5/43; WO 5/7/45. ESMERELDA.

41-2601 Del Tucson 24/2/42; West Palm Beach 29/4/42; 29BG Boise 22/9/42; dam in coll w/B-17 29/9/42, rep; Hendricks 23/3/43; WO 21/11/44.

41-2602 Del Tucson 25/2/42; West Palm Beach 17/4/42; ass 12AF 29/4/43; retUS Memphis 10/4/44; Morrison 8/7/44; RFC Bush Fd 2/6/45.

41-2603 Del Tucson 26/2/42; Muroc 5/7/42; Eglin 18/8/42; Geiger 2/9/42; Boise 1/12/42; Lockburn 21/4/43; RFC Altus 9/10/45.

41-2604 Del Tucson 1/3/42; Salt Lake City 19/4/42; 306BG Wendover 18/4/42, cr in desert, all killed, 8/7/42. Sal.

41-2605 Del McDill 28/2/42; Cheyenne 21/5/42; Edgewood 18/10/42; Wendover 1/2/43; Hendricks 31/3/43; WO 5/7/44.

41-2607 Del McDill 26/2/42; Cheyenne 1/5/42; Sarasota 23/6/42; Wendover 15/7/42; Westover 11/8/42; WO 26/3/43.

41-2608 Del Ogden 22/2/42; Cheyenne 25/3/42; Wayne Co. 14/4/42; RCAF Dorval 20/4/42 to GB.

41-2609 Del Lowry 8/5/42; Hamilton 28/5/42; ass 19BG Hawaii 13/7/42; tran 43BG; retUS Hamilton 22/7/44; Tinker 14/9/44; Recl Comp 9/2/45.

41-2610 Del Ogden 22/2/42 (for RAF KH998); Cheyenne 27/3/42; ass 7AF Hawaii 22/5/42; WO 15/6/44.

41-2611 Del Ogden 22/2/42 (for RAF KH999); Lowry 4/5/42; ass 7AF Hawaii 16/8/42; retUS Tyndall 17/1/44; Kingman 20/11/44; RFC Albuquerque 16/6/45. (Shown on Midway TV documentary).

41-2612 Del Ogden 22/2/42 (for RAF); Lowry 4/5/42; ass 7AF 26/5/42; WO 15/6/44.

41-2613 Del Ogden 22/2/42 (for RAF); Cheyenne 29/5/42; ass 7AF Hawaii 3/6/42; WO 31/10/44.

41-2614 Del Ogden 22/2/42; Cheyenne 28/3/42; Wayne Co. 27/5/42; RCAF Dorval 19/6/42 to GB.

41-2615 Del Ogden 22/2/42; Cheyenne 26/3/42; Wayne Co. 11/4/42; RCAF Dorval 14/4/42 to GB.

41-2616 Del Ogden 22/2/42 (for RAF); ass 98BS/11B Hawaii 24/5/42; hit by flak over Guadalcanal 29/9/42 w/Lt Waskowicz. (painted blue all over). THE BLUE GOOSE.

41-2617 Del Minneapolis 7/3/42; ass 19BG Hawaii 13/5/42; c/t/o Port Moresby 7/8/42 w/Hillhouse; WO 31/10/44.

41-2618 Del Ogden 22/2/42; Cheyenne 30/3/42; Wayne Co. 21/5/42; RCAF Dorval 25/6/42 for GB.

41-2619 Del Ogden 3/3/42; Cheyenne 29/3/42; Wayne 10/6/42; RCAF Dorval 15/6/42 for GB.

41-2620 Del Ogden 7/3/42; Cheyenne 29/3/42; Wright 28/4/42; coll w/truck at Mitchell 29/5/42, rep; Wayne Co. 4/7/42; RCAF Dorval 8/7/42 for GB.

41-2621 Del Lowry 14/3/42; Boise 1/4/42; ass 93BS/19BG Hawaii 8/7/42; c/l Mareeba, Aus. 26/8/42 w/Casper; WO 31/10/44. THE DAYLIGHT LIMITED.

41-2622 Del Ogden 1/3/42; Cheyenne 26/3/42; Wayne Co. 16/5/42; RCAF Dorval 18/10/42 for GB.

41-2623 Del Ogden 1/3/42; Cheyenne 25/3/42; Wayne Co. 17/4/42; RCAF Dorval 24/4/42 for GB.

41-2624 Del Ogden 1/3/42 (for RAF); Cheyenne 27/3/42; Lowry 13/5/42; cr 10 m N of Wendover 15/5/42, lost control in a snowstorm; crew baled and all found except pilot Lt Payne.

41-2625 Del Ogden 1/3/42; Cheyenne 28/3/42; RCAF Dorval 8/5/42 for GB.

41-2626 Del McDill 1/3/42; ass 341BS/97BG Polebrook 4/42; tran 407BS/92BG Bovingdon 8/42; c/l Gatwick, UK, 9/10/42; sal. ROKELL'S RAIDER.

41-2627 Del Lowry 3/3/42; ass 19BG; tran 43BG; cr Schwimmer Fd, Laloki, NG, 26/12/43. Sal. R.F.D.TOJO.

41-2628 Del McDill 1/3/42; dam in taxi acc w/another a/c 19/4/42, rep; ass 341BS/97BG Polebrook 4/42; tran 92BG Bovingdon 8/42; CCRC 1/43; retUS 4104 BU Rome 25/8/44; Recl Comp 14/8/45.

41-2629 Del McDill 7/3/42; ass 340BS/97BG Polebrook 3/42; tran 305BG Grafton Underwood 5/11/42; 100BG Thorpe Abbotts /43; 92BG Bovingdon /43; retUS 121 BU Bradley 5/7/45; RFC Altus 6/8/45.

41-2630 Del Lowry 5/3/42; Sacramento 11/4/42; ass 7AF Hawaii 16/4/42; tran Nandi, Fiji Is 27/12/42; RFC Altus 10/9/45.

41-2631 Del Lowry 5/3/42; ass 19BG Hawaii 16/4/42; cr Chartres Towers, Aus, 7/5/42 w/Jacques, sal.

41-2632 Del Lowry 5/3/42; Boise 7/4/42; ass 7AF Hawaii 28/5/42; retUS Hendricks 21/12/43; RFC Albuquerque 9/8/45. (Shown in Midway TV documentary).

41-2633 Del Lowry 3/3/42; ass 93BS/19BG Hawaii 22/4/42; later used as taxi for Lt Gen George Kenny 5AF CO, WO 3/5/45. SALLY.

41-2634 Del Lowry 3/3/42; ass 19BG Hawaii 18/5/42; WO 5/8/43. TOJO'S PHYSIC.

41-2635 Del Lowry 3/3/42; ass 19BG Hawaii 28/5/52; s/d Solomon Is 1/11/42.

41-2636 Del Lowry 5/3/42; ass 19BG Hawaii 1/4/42;

ditched off Horn Is 13/7/42 w/Holdredge.

41-2637 Del Lowry 3/3/42; Boise 4/4/42; ass 19BG Hawaii 18/4/42; tran 43BG; retUS Tyndall 6/11/43; RFC Albuquerque 25/6/45.

41-2638 Del Lowry 9/3/42; Boise 1/4/42; ass 19BG Hawaii 23/4/42; tran 43BG; retUS Kelly 24/11/43; RFC Walnut Ridge 1/2/46.

41-2639 Del Lowry 5/3/42; Boise 4/4/42; ass 19BG Hawaii 27/5/42; WO 19/1/43.

41-2640 Del Lowry 5/3/42; ass 93BS/19BG Hawaii 22/4/42; Coll Horn Is, N Aus. 13/7/42 w/O'Bryan. Hit by a/c on ground sheering nose off 27/7/43, sal. TOJO'S PHYSIC.

41-2641 Del Lowry 5/3/42; ass 19BG Hawaii 1/4/42; WO 1/8/42.

41-2642 Del Lowry 2/3/42; Boise 1/4/42; ass 19BG Hawaii 22/4/42; tran 5AF; retUS Maxwell, ALA. 10/6/44; Bolling 16/6/44; Hendricks 5/7/44; RFC Walnut Ridge 13/10/45.

41-2643 Del Lowry 2/3/42; ass 19BG Hawaii 26/5/42; tran 93BS/43BG; s/d off New Britain 10/8/42 w/Grandman.

41-2644 Del Lowry 7/3/42; Boise 6/4/42; ass 30BS/19BG Hawaii 22/4/42; damaged Rabual 7/8/42, rep; retUS 31/8/44; WO 19/10/44.

41-2645 Del Lowry 2/3/42; ass 19BG Hawaii 20/5/42; tran 43BG; WO 6/12/42.

41-2646 Del Lowry 5/3/42; SAD 25/3/42; WO 4/4/42.

41-2647 Del AMC Wright 1/6/42; Newark 15/4/43; Wright 22/4/43; ASF Phillips,MD. 22/4/46.

41-2648 Del Lowry 5/3/42; ass 19BG Hawaii 23/5/42; tran 43BG; RFC Walnut Ridge 8/11/46. (shown in Midway TV documentary). LITTLE BUSTER UPPER.

41-2649 Del Lowry 4/3/42; ass 19BG Hawaii 13/4/42; tran 43BG 22/5/42; Brookley 17/5/43; tran 15AF? 20/1/45; sal North Africa 23/8/45.

41-2650 Del Minneapolis 7/3/42; ass 19BG Hawaii 5/5/42; cr New Guinea 18/9/42 w/Burky. Sal.

41-2651 Del Lowry 5/3/42; c/t/o 22/3/42 w/Howard, rep; Boise 13/9/42; Biggs 3/11/42; Wendover 9/12/42; 2137 BU Hendricks 28/5/43. WO 5/7/44.

41-2652 Del Lowry 5/3/42; ass 19BG Hawaii 13/4/42; c/l Ewan, Aus. 7/5/42 w/Habberstad; WO 17/10/44.

41-2653 Del Lowry 5/3/42; caught fire 20 miles nth Bakersfield, Cal. crew baled OK. Sal but no date given.

41-2654 Del Lowry 5/3/42; cr Hamilton 24/3/42. Sal (shown in Midway TV documentary).

41-2655 Del Lowry 5/3/42; ass 19BG Hawaii 1/4/42; Ditched off Horn Is 13/7/42 w/Lindsey.

41-2656 Del Lowry 7/2/42; ass 435BS/19BG Hawaii 29/5/42; MIA recon mission 19/8/42 w/Cook. CHIEF SEATTLE.

41-2657 Del Lowry 5/3/42; ass 19BG Hawaii 7/4/42; tran 30BS/43BG 22/5/42; sal 21/6/45. OLD FAITHFUL.

41-2658 Del Minneapolis 7/3/42; ass 19BG Hawaii 9/5/42; WO 15/6/44.

41-2659 Del Minneapolis 7/3/42; ass 19BG Hawaii 22/5/42; tran 43BG Port Moresby 13/7/42; WO 31/10/44. FRANK BUCK (BRING 'EM BACK ALIVE).

41-2660 Del Minneapolis 7/3/42; Salt Lake City 13/5/42; ass 19BG Hawaii 26/5/42; sal 22/4/45.

41-2661 Del Minneapolis 7/3/42; ass Hawaii 15/5/42; tran 5AF 21/7/42; WO 31/10/44.

41-2662 Del Minneapolis 7/3/42; ass 30BS/19BG Hawaii 21/5/42; tran 64BS/43BG 13/7/42; damaged Rabual 7/8/42, rep; 55TCS/375TCG Dobodura 11/43; RFC Ontario 4/6/45. SPAWN OF HELL.

41-2663 Del Minneapolis 7/3/42; ass 19BG Hawaii 5/5/42; cr south Buna 14/9/42 w/Erb. WO 31/10/44.

41-2664 Del Minneapolis 9/3/42; ass 30BS/19BG Hawaii 6/5/42; tran 64BS/43BG; c/t/o Port Moresby 14/6/43, 8k. Sal. THE JERSEY SKEETER.

41-2665 Del Minneapolis 7/3/42; ass 93BS/19BG Hawaii 14/5/42; tran 6SR Clark Fd, Philippines. LULU.

41-2666 Del Minneapolis 9/3/42; ass 19BG Hawaii 5/5/42; tran 43BG; retUS 4134 BU Spokane 22/3/44; 423 BU Walla Walla 4/7/44; 2137 BU Hendricks 29/7/44; RFC Albuquerque 9/8/45.

41-2667 Del Minneapolis 7/3/42; ass 7AF Hawaii 6/5/42; tran 5AF 22/5/42; WO 31/10/44.

41-2668 Del Minneapolis 9/3/42; ass 19BG Hawaii 5/5/42; retUS 3137 BU Hendricks 21/10/43; WO 13/7/44; Recl Comp 20/3/46.

41-2669 Del Minneapolis 11/3/42; ass 19BG Hawaii 4/5/42; retUS Pocatello 28/11/42; Oklahoma City 12/12/42; Pyote 19/1/43; Lockburn 26/2/43; RFC Altus 9/10/45.

41-9011 Del Minneapolis 11/3/42; ass 19BG Hawaii; tran 43BG; WO 22/5/42.

41-9012 Del Minneapolis; ass 19BG Hawaii 3/2/42; burned on ground Mareeba, Aus. 5/11/42. Sal.

41-9013 Ass 341BS/97BG 3/42; courier trip to N.Africa 18/12/42; tran 327BS/92BG (UX-V) Bovingdon 27/8/43; 482BG Alconbury 27/8/43; 94BG Rougham 10/11/43; retUS 4136 BU Tinker 22/5/44; Recl Comp 9/2/45.

41-9014 Del Minneapolis 11/5/42; ass 19BG Hawaii 5/5/42; ground accident Batchelor, Aus. 12/8/42 w/Smith. Sal.

41-9015 Del Minneapolis 11/5/42; ass 19BG Hawaii 6/5/42; tran 43BG; WO 19/2/43.

41-9016 Del 97BG McDill 12/3/42; Glen 5/4/43; To 16PMS/68RG Tunisia; MIA France 5/12/43, 12 KIA.

41-9017 Ass 342BS/97BG Polebrook 4/42 HEIDI HO; on first 8AF mission to Rouen-Sotteville 17/8/42; tran 305BG Grafton Underwood 6/11/42; 92BG Bovingdon 6/12/42; 482BG Alconbury; sal 20/5/45.

41-9018 Ass 341BS/97BG Polebrook 3/42; tran 327BS/92BG Bovingdon 8/42; MIA Lille 9/10/42 w/Chorak; ditched Channel 1 EVD 5KIA 3POW; MACR 15218.

41-9019 Ass 414BS/97BG 3/42 as LI'L SKUNKFACE; tran 305BG Grafton Underwood 6/11/42; 381BG Ridgewell 11/6/43; 327BS/92BG Bovingdon [UX-V] 10/7/43; 482BG Alconbury 27/8/43; WO 21/8/45.

41-9020 Ass 340BS/97BG Polebrook 3/42 as PHYLLIS; col w/41-9051, rep; 92BG Bovingdon 8/42; 303BG Molesworth 1/5/43; 2SAD Lt Staughton 19/7/44; sal n/b/d 26/7/44. TUGBOAT ANNIE.

41-9021 Ass 414BS/97BG 3/42 THE BIG BITCH; tran 390BG Framlingham 27/6/42 HANGAR QUEEN; 327BS/92BG Bovingdon 24/8/42; AFSC 9/10/42; on first 8AF mission 17/8/42; WO 31/5/45.

41-9022 Ass 341BS/97BG Polebrook 3/42; ALABAMA EXTERMINATOR; 92BG Bovingdon 8/42, used as ferry navigation a/c; 546BS/384BG [BR-L] Grafton Underwood 4/6/43; 1 BAD Burtonwood 27/7/44; WO 25/5/45.

41-9023 Ass 414BS/97BG Polebrook 3/42 YANKEE DOODLE; on first 8AF mission, carried Gen Ira Eaker; 92BG Bovingdon 24/8/42; 323BS/91BG [LG-X] Bassingbourn 30/3/43; sal 26/7/45.

41-9024 Ass 414BS/97BG Polebrook 3/42; c/l base 1/8/42; first a/c Sal. KING CONDOR.

41-9025 Ass 341BS/97BG Polebrook 3/42; 327BS/92BG Alconbury 29/6/42 LITTLE JOHN; Bovingdon /8/42; 11 CCRC 2/43; on courier trip to N/Africa 23/12/43; WO 2/6/45.

41-9026 Ass 342BS/97BG Polebrook 3/42 BABY DOLL; on first 8AF mission 17/8/42; 327BS/92BG Bovingdon /8/42; ditched Channel 6/9/42, w/Stewart 9KIA; MACR 16489.

41-9027 Del McDill 16/3/42; W Palm Beach 30/3/42; HQ Sq Glen, (Tangier); cr 8/10/43.

41-9028 Del McDill 17/3/42; W Palm Beach 30/3/42; WO 31/6/43.

41-9029 Del McDill 17/3/42; W Palm Beach 30/3/42; WO 21/11/45.

41-9030 Ass 414BS/97BG Polebrook 3/42; 92BG Bovingdon 4/12/42; 305BG Chelveston /11/43; 27 ATG; 3 SAD Watton, WO 25/5/45. BIG PUNK.

41-9031 Del McDill 18/3/42; W Palm Beach 30/3/42; WO 7/8/43.

Below: B-17E 41-9025, an original combat aircraft of the 341st Bomb Squadron, 97th Bomb Group, endured as a trainer and hack to be broken up in England at the end of hostilities in Europe. While the framed nosepiece was the most notable feature distinguishing the E from the F model, the E could also be identified by the narrow-blade propellers. (USAAF)

41-9032 Ass 414BS/97BG Polebrook; f/l Greenland 26/6/42, w/Stinson; sal. MY GAL SAL.

41-9033 Del Sebring 19/3/42; Pyote 18/4/42; Hendricks 19/4/42; WO 5/7/44.

41-9034 Del Sebring 21/3/42; 3017 BU Hobbs 11/10/42. Recl Comp 13/11/45.

41-9035 Del Sebring 20/3/42; 4136 BU Tinker; Recl Comp 7/6/46.

41-9036 Del Palm Beach 22/3/42; ass 6AF Panama 7/4/42; 5BG Gautemala 15/4/42; SAD 17/7/42; Guatemala 31/7/42; WO 28/9/42.

41-9037 Del Palm Beach 22/3/42; ass 6AF Panama 6/6/42; Puerto Rico 8/6/42; Guatemala 4/9/42; SAD 11/12/42; Guatemala 8/2/43; WO 15/10/43.

41-9038 Del Palm Beach 22/3/42; ass 6AF Panama 7/4/42; Guatemala 4/9/42; Panama 16/10/42; Guatemala 20/10/42; WO 7/1/44.

41-9039 Del Palm Beach 20/3/42; ass 44BS Panama 7/4/42; Guatemala 3/7/42; cr off Galapagos 6/1/43, 2 KAS.

41-9040 Del Palm Beach 22/3/42; ass 6AF Panama 4/7/42; /6BG Guatemala 15/6/42; SAD 17/7/42; Guatemala 31/7/42; San Antonio 5/11/42; Guatemala 15/1/43.

41-9041 Del Palm Beach 22/3/42; ass 6AF 21/4/42; Panama 14/6/42; Guatemala 6/7/42; retUS 9/8/45; RFC Altus 4/9/45.

41-9042 Del/?; ass 34BS/97BG Polebrook 3/42; tran 325BS/92BG [NV-T/B] Bovingdon 9/42; 359BS/303BG [BN-V] Molesworth as RIDGE RUNNER; Honington RG 22/4/43; 403 AD RG Langford Lodge 6/5/43; AFSC 26/7/43; WO 20/5/45. THE BERLIN SLEEPER.

41-9043 Ass 342BS/97BG Polebrook 3/42 PEGGY D; on first 8AF mission 17/8/42; 92BG Bovingdon /9/42; 534BS/381BG [GD-A1] Ridgewell 7/43; base hack, used to collect bodies from Isle of Man tragedy 25/4/45; RFC Altus 29/10/45. LITTLE ROCK-ETTE.

41-9044 Ass 341BS/97BG Polebrook 3/42; 325BS/92BG Bovingdon 9/42; cr Chivenor, ex-Portreath 14/2/43. Sal.

41-9045 Ass 414BS/97BG Polebrook 3/42 as TENNESSEE BELLE; 92BG Bovingdon 24/8/42; c/l Athenny, Ireland, ex N/Africa after taking part in 1st Prov Grp of Gen Brereton in Eritrea (as No 8.) 15/1/43; sal. STINKY.

41-9046 Del McDill 26/3/42; W Palm Beach 19/4/42; ass 6AF; c/l during violent thunderstorm in Belem (Brit. Honduras), killing two natives, 24/4/42, rep; Westover 28/6/42; Ogden 24/7/42; Wendover 5/9/42.

41-9047 Del McDill 26/3/42; W Palm Beach 19/4/42; ass 5AF New Britain 27/4/42; retUS 4124 BU Altus 4/12/42; 2114 BU Lockburn 14/8/44; RFC Altus 9/11/47.

41-9048 Del Sebring 26/3/42; MAD 15/6/42; Hendricks 19/3/43; Williams 14/1/44; La Junta 6/4/44; WO 19/9/44. RFC Walnut Ridge 7/12/45.

41-9049 Del Sebring 26/3/42; Hendricks 18/9/42; McDill 2/5/43; Hendricks 10/5/43 as TB-17 (No.01); WO 19/7/44.

41-9050 Del Sebring 26/3/45; Hendricks 17/3/43; Chicago Munc Apt 9/5/43; Hendricks 7/7/43; WO 7/7/44.

41-9051 Ass 342BS/97BG Polebrook 3/42; 326BS/92BG Bovingdon, then 326BS [UX-O] (?407) /9/42; col w/41-9021, rep; 813BS/482BG Alconbury; cr Keswick, Cumb. 14/9/43; WO 21/1/44.

41-9052 Del McDill 97BG 25/3/42, Cheyenne 5/5/42; Sarasota 3/6/42; Westover 26/6/42; Muroc 29/5/42; Ogden 16/8/42; 11AF Kodiak 13/1/43; retUS 20/12/44; RFC Bush Fd 7/6/45.

41-9053 Del Boise 303BG 27/3/42; cr mile south of Briggs, Id. 4/4/42 w/Jim Walker and crew killed, cause unknown; sal.

41-9054 Del Boise 303BG 28/3/42; Lowry 29/5/42; Hamilton 7/6/42; ass 5/7AF Hawaii 8/6/42; retUS Rome 18/7/45; Recl Comp 14/8/45.

41-9055 Del Boise 303BG 28/2/42; Ephrata 4/6/42; Muroc 3/7/42; Geiger 2/9/42; Rapid City 1/10/42; cr 17/10/42; sal. NIPPON MISS.

41-9056 Del Boise 303BG 28/3/42; Lowry 29/5/42; Hamilton 7/6/42; ass 7AF Hawaii 9/6/42; WO 15/6/44.

41-9057 Del Boise 303BG 27/3/42; Alamagordo 18/6/42; Gt Falls 27/8/42; Biggs 3/9/42; Alamogordo 2/10/42; Boise 25/1/43; Hill 2/2/43; Lockburn 11/3/43; RFC Altus 14/9/45.

41-9058 Del Geiger 301BG 30/3/42; Alamogordo 8/6/42; Westover 2/7/42; Alamogordo 3/8/42; Biggs 5/11/42; Wendover 9/12/42; Tinker 27/2/43; Lockburn 10/3/43; Patterson 23/10/43; RFC Altus 9/10/45.

41-9059 Del Boise 29/3/42; Lowry 29/5/42; ass 7AF Hawaii 7/6/42; WO 11/6/43.

41-9060 Del Boise 26/3/42; Lowry 29/5/42; ass 7AF Hawaii 7/6/42; WO 31/10/44.

41-9061 Del Wright Fd 3/2/42; Eglin 17/5/42; Wright 3/6/42; Phillips 21/6/42; Tinker 19/9/42; Patterson 19/2/43; RFC Altus 20/12/45.

41-9062 Del Geiger 301BG 30/3/42; Wendover 23/5/42; ass 11AF Bronze 5/6/42; Wendover 11/7/42; Westover 11/8/42; Oklahoma City 5/12/42; Boise 31/12/42; WO 18/2/43.

41-9063 Del Geiger 301BG 1/4/42; Alamogordo 18/6/42; Westover 2/7/42; Harlingen 5/8/42; Las Vegas 28/8/42; Harlingen 27/9/42; Memphis 9/10/42; Las Vegas 15/12/42; c/t/o Los Angeles 13/4/43, w/Capt Woodruff; sal 20/4/43.

41-9064 Del Geiger 301BG 30/3/42; Alamogordo 18/6/42; Westover 2/7/42; retained USA 16/8/42; Recl Comp 2/10/45.

41-9065 Del Geiger 301BG 30/5/42; Alamogordo 18/6/42; Westover 2/7/42; Long Beach 1/9/42; Ft McAndrew 19/9/42; Presque Is 31/1/43; Mitchell 8/6/43; Cherry Point 26/7/43; RFC Ontario 12/10/45.

41-9066 Del Geiger 301BG 2/4/42; Alamogordo 18/6/42; Westover 2/7/42; Wendover 20/7/42; Walla Walla 15/8/42; Topeka 3/9/42; Chanute 18/12/42; Recl Comp 19/3/45.

41-9067 Del Geiger 301BG 3/4/42; Alamogordo 18/6/42; Westover 2/7/42; Lowry 19/8/42; Boise 19/9/42; Oklahoma 18/12/42; Gowen 5/12/43; 2137 BU Hendricks 31/3/43; WO 7/7/44; Recl Comp 3/1/46.

41-9068 Del Geiger 301BG 3/4/42; Alamogordo 18/6/42; Westover 2/7/42; New Castle 1/9/42; Presque Is 20/4/43; Mitchell 8/6/43; Cherry Pt 26/7/43; Lakeland 30/9/44; Hillsboro 31/10/42; Red Bluff 22/2/45; 461 BU Seymour 30/8/45; RFC Ontario 31/10/45.

41-9069 Del Geiger 301BG 3/4/42; Alamogordo 18/6/42; Westover 2/7/42; Wendover 16/7/42; Westover 11/8/42; Sebring 2/9/42; Tarrant Fd 22/6/43; Hendricks 26/7/43; WO 23/10/43.

41-9070 Del Geiger 301BG 1/4/42; Alamogordo 18/6/42; Westover 2/7/42; Las Vegas 26/7/42; Roswell 6/6/43; Lockburn 19/7/43; RFC Altus 9/10/45.

41-9071 Del Geiger 301BG 5/4/42; Lowry 1/6/42; ass 42BS/11BG Hawaii 10/6/42; MIA Rendowa Is 8/9/42, w/Richards and crew all killed.

41-9072 Del Boise 303BG 4/5/42; Geiger 26/6/42; ass 11AF Kodiak 3/6/42; Umnak 4/6/42; retUS New Castle 29/4/43; Gore 21/8/43; Wilmington 16/9/43; Reno 30/6/44; RFC Albuquerque 25/6/45.

41-9073 Del Boise 359BS/303BG 4/4/42; Presque Is 31/5/42; Houlton 20/6/42; u/c retracted 27/6/42 w/Lt Sheeler, no injuries; WO 4/12/42.

41-9074 Del Boise 359BS/303BG 10/4/42; Presque Is 31/5/42; Slated 94BG; tran 340BS/97BG Polebrook 28/7/42; 303BG Molesworth 28/7/42; sal BD 7/9/42.

41-9075 Del Boise 303BG 4/4/42; Salt Lake City 17/5/42; Ephrata 4/6/42; 305BG Muroc 17/8/42; Biggs 11/9/42; Rapid City 3/12/42; Oklahoma City 24/2/43; Pueblo 1/9/43; RFC Albuquerque 5/7/45.

41-9076 Del Boise 303BG 6/4/42; Lowry 29/5/42; ass 7AF Hawaii 9/6/42; WO 15/6/44.

41-9077 Del Geiger 301BG 6/4/42; Alamogordo 18/6/42; Westover 2/7/42; Tyndall 14/8/42; Sebring 20/9/42; Eglin 16/11/42; Las Vegas 21/12/42; McClelland 17/2/43; WO 24/11/43; Recl Comp 3/1/46.

41-9078 Del Boise 303BG 4/4/42; Salt Lake City 17/5/42; Ephrata 4/6/42; Muroc 21/7/42; Geiger 2/9/42; 1174 Pilot Trng Sq Lockburn 22/2/43; RFC Altus 9/10/45.

41-9079 Del Geiger 301BG 5/4/42; Muroc 30/5/42; Alamogordo 19/6/42; Biggs 19/8/42; Boise 15/9/42; Hendricks 23/3/43; 3017 BU Hobbs 21/1/44; RFC Albuquerque 25/6/45.

41-9080 Del Geiger 301BG 6/4/42; ass 11AF Bronze 5/6/42; Kodiak 11/7/42; Gore 14/3/43; New Castle 6/4/42; Olmstead 17/5/43; Wilmington 30/8/43; RFC Bush Fd 19/6/45.

41-9081 Del Geiger 301BG 6/4/42; Alamogordo 18/6/42; Westover 2/7/42; New Castle 1/9/42; Mitchell 6/6/43; Cherry Pt 27/6/43; Selfridge 6/10/43; RFC Altus 29/8/45.

41-9082 Del Geiger 419BS/301BG 7/4/42; tran 97BG 7/42 (used by F/M Montgomery at times); 92BG /9/42; WO 22/6/43.

41-9083 Del Boise 303BG 7/4/42; Salt Lake City 17/5/42; Geiger 24/6/42; Muroc 305BG 5/7/42; Biggs 11/7/42; cr 4/11/42 w/Lt Byrd, 3 killed, a/c burned. Sal.

41-9084 Del Boise 303BG 7/4/42; Geiger 28/5/42; ass 11AF Alaska 5/6/42.

41-9085 Del Boise 359BS/303BG 7/4/42; 97BG Polebrook 9/42; tran 92BG Bovingdon /9/42; sal 26/6/45. JARRIN' JENNY.

41-9086 Del Boise 303BG 7/4/42; Alamogordo 18/6/42; Westover 2/7/42; Sebring 6/9/42; Yuma 31/10/42; RFC Albuquerque 12/6/45.

41-9087 Del Boise 303BG 10/4/42; Alamogordo 18/6/42; Westover 2/7/42; Wendover 27/7/42; Walla Walla 18/8/42; Boise 5/9/42; WO 4/1/43.

41-9088 Del Geiger 301BG 8/4/42; Alamogordo 18/6/42; Westover 2/7/42; Wendover 10/7/42; Walla Walla 18/8/42; c/t/o 25/9/42, rep; WO 4/1/43.

41-9089 Del Sarasota 15/4/42; ass 414BS/97BG Polebrook 4/42; on first 8AF mission 17/8/42 when co-pilot KIA, the first 8AF heavy bomber fatality of WWII; tran 92BG Bovingdon 24/8/42; 96BG Snetterton as tow target ship in /43; Recl Comp 27/11/45. JOHNNY REB.

41-9090 Del McDill 11/4/42; ass 342BS/97BG Sarasota 26/4/42; Presque Is 29/5/42; Ditched Narsassuaq Fjord, 35 miles SW Bluie West One, Greenland 26/6/42 w/Maj Chambers, 7 killed. THE SOONER.

41-9091 Del Geiger 301BG 8/4/42; Muroc 29/5/42; Alamogordo 18/6/42; Westover 2/7/42; Wendover 20/7/42; Biggs 19/8/42; cr Las Cruces, NM. 24/8/42, in thunderstorm; 7 killed, inc one EM.

41-9092 Del Geiger 301BG 8/4/42; Alamogordo

18/6/42; Westover 2/7/42; Wendover 10/7/42; Westover 11/8/42; Sebring 11/9/42; Lockburn 15/1/43; Las Vegas 17/10/43; RFC Albuquerque 26/5/45.

41-9093 Del Geiger 301BG 8/4/42; Lowry 31/5/42; ass 72BS/5BG Hawaii 7/6/42; retUS 2138 BU Tyndall 27/12/43; Kingman 22/10/44; RFC Albuquerque 25/6/45. SPOOK!

41-9094 Del Boise 303BG 10/4/42; Geiger 28/5/42; ass 11AF Bronze Kodiak 3/6/42; Umnak 4/6/42; retUS Spokane 20/5/43; Bismarck 10/8/43; Spokane 22/2/44; Long Beach 26/8/44; Courtland 16/11/44; RFC Ontario 4/6/45.

41-9095 Del Sarasota 97BG 14/4/42; West Palm Beach 22/4/42; Gt Britain 14/5/42 (error); sal Duko (MTO) 28/5/45.

41-9096 Del Boise 303BG 10/4/42; Wendover 13/5/42; Ogden 17/6/42; Westover 11/8/42; Sebring 3/9/42; 2137 BU Hendricks 17/4/43; Tarrent 8/7/43; Wright Mat Com 17/7/43; WO 25/7/44.

41-9097 Del Boise 303BG 16/4/42; West Palm Beach 17/4/42; Gt Britain 9/5/42; India; Con Inv 30/6/43.

41-9098 Del Boise 359BS/303BG 10/4/42; cr Llanthawdr Mtn, UK 11/8/42, all killed. Sal.

41-9099 Del Sarasota 97BG 12/4/42; West Palm Beach 22/4/42; ass Gt Britain 9/5/42; Sumac (5AF) 26/6/42; retUS Mines Fd 28/2/44; RFC Searcy Fd 7/8/45.

41-9100 As 414BS/97BG Polebrook 11/4/42 BIRMINGHAM BLITZKREIG; on first 8AF mission 17/8/42; tran 92BG Bovingdon 24/8/42; CCRC 1/43; 525BS/379BG Kimbolton, UK as formation a/c; RAF Clunto, NI. 8/2/44; sal 18/6/45.

41-9101 Del McDill 97BG 13/4/42; cr Greenland ice cap 15/6/42 (found 1/89); BIG STOOP.

41-9102 Del McDill 97BG 13/4/42; Bangor 26/6/42; Wendover 15/7/42; Biggs 19/8/42; Topeka 25/9/42; Oklahoma 20/11/42; Hendricks 1/4/43; RFC Walnut Ridge 19/12/45.

41-9103 Ass 414BS/97BG Polebrook 11/4/42; DIXIE DEMO; on first 8AF mission 17/8/42; tran 92BG Bovingdon 24/8/42; 91BG Bassingbourn 3/3/43; retUS 23/6/44; RFC Walnut Ridge 19/12/45.

41-9104 Del McDill 97BG 13/4/42; West Palm Beach 19/4/42; ass Gt Britain 8/5/42 (error); WO 31/11/43.

41-9105 Del McDill 341BS/97BG; Presque Is 31/5/42; cr Greenland ice cap 15/6/42; DODO.

41-9106 Del Sarasota 97BG 13/4/42; West Palm Beach 24/4/42; Bangor 26/6/42; Boise 2/8/42; ass 11AF Bronze 22/9/42; Umnak 1/2/43; RFC Walnut Ridge 14/9/45.

41-9107 Ass 340BS/97BG Polebrook 15/4/42; tran 390BG Framlingham 29/6/42; 407BS/92BG [PY-N] Bovingdon /9/42; 401BS/91BG [LL-X] Bassingbourn 22/7/43; 613BS/401BG [IN-P] Deenethorpe, Nth. 6/11/43; /390BG Framlingham, 6/11/43; 600BS/398BG Nuthampstead 29/8/44; sal 2/8/45.

41-9108 Del Sarasota 342BS/97BG 15/4/42; Presque Is 31/5/42; cr Greenland 26/6/42.

41-9109 Del Sarasota 97BG 18/4/42; West Palm Beach 27/4/42; ass Gt Britain 26/5/42 error; 10AF DAUB 13/9/42; 12AF GLEN 11/1/43; 15AF OHAM 30/9/44; Grenier 18/10/44; RFC Walnut Ridge 10/10/45.

41-9110 Del SAAD 24/4/42; Langley 20/5/44; Olmstead 1/2/43; Lowry 28/2/43; Presque Is 20/3/43; Mitchell 8/6/43; Westover 28/9/43; Roswell 8/1/44; WO 14/9/44; RFC Altus 9/10/45.

41-9111 Del Sarasota 97BG 15/4/42; McDill 24/6/42, hit when parked, by 41-2628, rep; Smyrna 21/11/42; Lockburn 22/1/43; Las Vegas 17/10/43; RFC Albuquerque 5/7/45.

41-9112 Del Geiger 419BS/301BG 20/4/42; experimental armaments a/c at Bovingdon; never involved in combat; retUS 14/2/43 for Project Reed; RFC Kingman 7/10/46. DREAMBOAT.

41-9113 Del Sarasota 97BG 18/4/42; burnt out base 9/5/42, pilot Lt Leland. Sal.

41-9114 Del Sarasota 341BS/97BG 18/4/42; tran 92BG /9/42; CCRC 14/2/43; courier trip to N Africa 14/2/43; sal 9/11/44.

41-9115 Ass 345BS/97BG Polebrook 10/4/42; cr Elvedon, practice flight 14/8/42; sal 26/10/42.

41-9116 Del Geiger 301BG 18/4/42; Alamogordo 18/6/42; Westover 2/7/42; Wendover 17/7/42; Walla Walla 18/8/42; Oklahoma City 24/11/42; Smyrna 25/2/43; Lockburn 30/3/43; Las Vegas 17/10/43; RFC Albuquerque 5/7/45.

41-9117 Del Geiger 301BG 18/4/42; Alamogordo 18/6/42; Westover 2/7/42; Rapid City 1/10/42; Pocatello 6/11/42; Ogden 20/12/42; Hendricks 19/2/43; WO 20/11/43.

41-9118 Del Geiger 301BG 18/4/42; Lowry 31/5/42; ass 7AF Hawaii 9/6/42; WO Solomon Is 4/10/43.

41-9119 Ass 419BS/301BG Chelveston 18/4/42; tran 97BG Polebrook 8/42; 92BG Bovingdon /9/42; CCRC /1/43; retUS 10/5/44; RFC Altus 11/9/45.

41-9120 Del SAAD 23/4/42; Langley 20/5/42; Olmstead 1/3/43; Presque Is 6/4/43; Mitchell 8/6/43; Cherry Pt 12/7/43; Brownsville 16/8/43; Kelly 21/9/43; Greenwood 7/11/43; RFC Walnut Ridge 18/10/45.

41-9121 Ass 359BS/303BG Molesworth 21/4/42; 97BG Polebrook /8/42; 92BG Bovingdon /9/42; /1/43 CCRC; sal 29/5/45. THE BIG BITCH.

41-9122 Del 303BG Boise 21/4/42; Lowry 21/5/42; ass 72BS/11BG Hawaii 9/6/42; tran 13AF 1/9/42; WO 15/6/44. EAGER BEAVERS.

41-9123 Del 303BG Boise 20/4/42; Wendover 25/5/42; Ephrata 4/6/42; Westover 5/8/42; Sebring 9/9/42; WO 17/3/44.

41-9124 Del Boise 303BG 20/4/42; Lowry 29/5/42; ass 98BS/11BG Hawaii 7/6/42; tran 31BS/5BG; bombed on Henderson Fd by 'Washing Machine Charlie' 23/3/43. Sal. BUZZ KING.

41-9125 Ass 359BS/303BG Molesworth 21/4/42; tran 342BS/97BG Polebrook /8/43; on first 8AF mission 17/8/42; courier flights to N Africa 2/5/43 as tow target a/c. PROWLER.

41-9126 Del Boise 303BG 21/4/42; Geiger 29/5/42; ass 36BS/28BG 11AF (Bronze); Kodiak 11/7/42; WO 28/8/42.

41-9127 Del Boise 303BG 21/4/42; Presque Is 24/5/42; overshot field at Houlton, Me. 30/6/42; rep but stayed in US; Boise 4/9/42; Rapid City 1/10/42; Smyrna 28/2/43; 2110 BU Lockburn 6/9/42; 3021 BU Las Vegas 17/10/42; RFC Albuquerque 5/7/45.

41-9128 Del Boise 28/4/42; Lowry 29/5/42; ass 7AF Hawaii 7/6/42; tran 13AF (Poppy); WO Solomon Is 27/3/43.

41-9129 Ass 359BS/303BG Molesworth 21/4/42; slated 388BG, tran 97BG Polebrook 8/42; 327BS/92BG [UX-R] Bovingdon 9/42; 305BG Grafton Underwood 6/11/42; 96BG Snetterton

Below: B-17E 41-9122, named *Eager Beavers*, taxiing in at Henderson Field, Guadalcanal, while serving with the 11th Bomb Group. It had an improvised mount for a .50 gun in the upper nosepiece. (USAAF)

11/8/43; sal 22/6/45.

41-9130 Del Boise 303BG 21/4/42; Salt Lake City 12/5/42; Wendover 9/8/42; Biggs 25/11/42; emergency landing 25/11/42; sal.

41-9131 Del SAAD 25/4/42; Langley 25/5/42; Olmstead 18/2/43; Langley 5/3/43; Mitchell 6/6/43; Cherry Pt 7/7/43; Grand Is 23/9/43; 1 MPC Culver 1/1/44.

41-9132 Ass 359BS/303BG Molesworth 21/4/42; 97BG Polebrook 8/42; 92BG Bovingdon /9/42; sal n/b/d 1/11/43.

41-9133 Del SAAD 26/4/42; Westover 27/5/42; Olmstead 18/2/43; Mitchell 8/6/43; Tinker 9/7/43; Robins 20/12/43; Patterson 21/2/44; Cincinnati 11/7/44; RFC Altus 29/8/45.

41-9134 Del SAAD 26/4/42; Langley 26/5/42; Mitchell 29/6/42; Olmstead 1/2/43; Presque Is 19/3/43; Mitchell 6/6/43; Cherry Pt 4/7/43; Chanute 16/9/43; RFC Altus 9/10/45.

41-9135 Del Cheyenne 27/4/42; Wayne 14/6/42; Minneapolis 31/7/42; Gt Falls 17/9/42; Wright Fd 11/11/42; RAF Gt Britain 30/11/42 (via Dorval, Canada?).

41-9136 Del Cheyenne 24/4/42; Wayne 13/6/42; RAF Gt Britain 17/6/42 (via Dorval?).

41-9137 Del McDill 29BG 1/5/42; Boise 21/6/42; Ogden 6/7/42; Oklahoma City 19BG 14/12/42; Pyote 11/1/43; WO 4/5/43.

41-9138 Del Cheyenne 24/4/42; Wayne 19/6/42; RAF Gt Britain 23/6/42 (via Dorval?).

41-9139 Del McDill 29BG 1/5/42; Lawson 11/5/42; Sarasota 23/6/42; Boise 3/8/42; ass 11AF Alaska Kodiak 4/2/43; Memphis 15/6/43; WO 10/6/44; Recl Comp 13/3/46.

41-9140 Del McDill 29BG 1/5/42; ass 11AF Bronze 5/6/42; Bangor 28/6/42; Walla Walla 2/8/42; Gt Falls 24/9/42; Elmendorf 26/9/42; retUS Buckley 15/2/44; RFC Walnut Ridge 14/9/45.

41-9141 Del Geiger 301BG 1/5/42; Alamogordo 18/6/42; Westover 2/7/42; Walla Walla 12/8/42; Boise 26/10/42; Lockburn 4/4/43; Las Vegas 17/10/43; RFC Albuquerque 5/7/45.

41-9142 Del Pendleton 34BG 2/5/42; Wright Fd 16/6/42; Geiger 11/7/42; Wendover 31/7/42; Westover 11/8/42; Walla Walla 20/9/42; Hill 2/10/42; Alamogordo 19/12/42; Lockburn 1/4/43; RCAF 168th Heavy Transport Sq, Rocklifffe, Ont. (No. 9205); Used for VIP and Mail to Prestwick; mid air coll with Wellington, f/l Predannack, UK 14/3/44.

41-9143 Del Boise 303BG 4/5/42; Alamogordo 18/6/42; Westover 2/7/42; Pocatello 6/11/42; RFC Altus 29/10/45. (refs. made of c/l Tadji, PNG?.

41-9144 Del Tucson 2/5/42; Alamogordo 18/6/42; Westover 2/7/42; Alamogordo 7/8/42; Biggs 28/11/42; Oklahoma City 11/12/42; Pueblo 4/1/43; WO 30/4/43.

41-9145 Del Geiger 301BG 1/5/42; Lowry 31/5/42; ass 7AF Hawaii 7/6/42; tran 13AF Poppy 22/7/42; WO 31/10/44.

41-9146 Del Geiger 301BG 28/4/42; ass 11AF Bronze 6/6/42; Ft Glen, Alaska 29/6/42; WO Umnak 18/7/42.

41-9147 Del SAAD 28/4/42; Langley 27/5/42; Olmstead 1/2/43; Presque Is 19/3/43; Mitchell 9/6/42; Cherry Pt 9/7/43; WO 14/9/44.

41-9148 Del Boise 359BS/303BG 25/4/42; 97BG Polebrook /6/42; 92BG Bovingdon /42 BOOMERANG; 369BS/306BG [WW-T] Thurleigh as T/T a/c 1/5/43; sal 22/6/45.

41-9149 Del Geiger 301BG 30/4/42; Alamogordo 15/6/42; Westover 2/7/42; Alamagordo 18/8/42; Biggs 7/11/42; Oklahoma City 7/12/42; Boise 1/8/43;

2137 BU Hendricks 18/8/43; 335 BU Del Marbry 20/11/43; Recl Comp 3/8/45.

41-9150 Del Geiger 301BG 29/4/42; Alamogordo 18/6/42; Westover 2/7/42; Wendover 30/11/42; 19BG Pyote 21/1/43; Hendricks 28/6/43; RFC Albuquerque 9/6/45.

41-9151 Del Geiger 301BG 25/4/42; Lowry 31/5/42; ass 42BS/11BG Hawaii 7/6/42; tran 13AF 22/7/42; s/d 1/2/43 w/Lt Hall.

41-9152 Del Geiger 301BG 28/4/42; Alamogordo 18/6/42; Westover 8/7/42; Tucson 24/8/42; March 4/9/42; Boise 14/10/42; Pocatello 6/11/42; Gowen 6/2/43; Hendricks 25/3/43; WO 29/4/43.

41-9153 Del Geiger 301BG 29/4/42; Lowry 31/5/42; ass 7AF Hawaii 7/6/42; tran 13AF Poppy 22/7/42; WO Solomon Is 19/7/43.

41-9154 Del Geiger 419BS/301BG 28/4/42; ass 97BG Polebrook 8/42; 327BS/92BG [UX-S] Bovingdon /9/42 as T/T a/c; WO 26/6/44. THE BAT OUTA HELL.

41-9155 Del Geiger 301BG 30/4/42; Lowry 31/5/42; ass 42BS/11BG 7AF Hawaii 7/6/42; tran 13AF Poppy 22/7/42; WO 15/6/44.

41-9156 Del Geiger 301BG 30/4/42; Lowry 31/5/42; ass 7AF Hawaii 7/6/42; tran 13AF Poppy 22/7/42; 7AF Hawaii 10/1/43; 13AF Poppy 4/5/43; WO Oahu 11/6/45. UNCLE BIFF.

41-9157 Del SAAD 25/4/42; Langley 25/5/42; Olmstead 17/2/43; tran 19AF Occident 29/4/43; Mitchell 8/6/43; 204 BU Smoky Hill 13/6/43; 244 BU Harvard 28/7/43; 610 BU Eglin 22/12/43; Recl Comp 31/10/45.

41-9158 Del SAAD 2/5/42; Langley 27/5/42; Olmstead 4/2/43; Presque Is 19/3/43; Mitchell 8/6/43; Cherry Pt 5/7/43; 246 BU Pratt 25/7/43; 3705 BU Lowry 26/10/43; WO 21/12/44. Recl Comp 2/10/45.

41-9159 Del Geiger 301BG 30/4/42; Alamogordo 18/6/42; Westover 2/7/42; Ogden 10/8/42; Walla Walla 3/9/42; Boise 3/11/42; cr Spence Fd 10/1/43, col mid air with another a/c w/Lt Lawrence; WO 7/3/43.

41-9160 Del SAAD 2/5/42, Mitchell 29/6/42; Langley 1/7/42; Bolling 6/12/42; Olmstead 18/2/43; Wilmington 16/6/43; Mitchell 4/7/43; RFC Ontario 11/4/45.

41-9161 Del Pendleton 34BG 11/5/42; Muroc 16/5/42; Alamogordo 19/6/42; Biggs 9/8/42; Alamogordo 2/10/42; cr 15/10/42 burned. Sal 18/12/43.

41-9162 Del McDill 29BG 6/5/42; Westover 28/6/42; Bangor 14/7/42; Ogden 28/8/42; ass 11AF Elmendorf 24/9/42; March 29/6/43; Long Beach 14/7/43; RFC Walnut Ridge 7/12/45.

41-9163 Del Wright 2/5/42; Patterson 5/5/42; Boca Raton 31/12/42; Wright 29/4/43; Eglin 15/9/43; Minneapolis 17/6/43; Ft Dix 2/12/44; Boca Raton 22/5/44; RFC Altus 29/2/45.

41-9164 Del Sebring 4/5/42; wrecked 1/6/42, a/c ground looped into concrete mixer at Hendricks, w/Freeman; WO 4/12/42.

41-9165 Del Sebring 4/5/42; MAAD 15/5/42; Sebring 13/7/42; 2137 BU Hendricks 29/11/42; RFC Albuquerque 9/10/45.

41-9166 Del Sebring 4/5/42; Henderichs 27/43; Hobbs 16/11/43; RFC Albuquerque 16/6/45.

41-9167 Del Sebring 4/5/43; wrecked 50 miles south of Appalachicola, Fl, 12/5/42 w/Tate; 2137 BU Hendricks 12/6/43; 3017 BU Hobbs 3/12/43; RFC Albuquerque 25/6/45.

41-9168 Del Sebring 5/5/42; Amarillo 17/3/43; Brookley 28/6/43; Hendricks 12/7/43; RFC Albuquerque 16/6/45.

41-9169 Del Sebring 451 Adv Fly Gp 5/5/42; Love Fd

29/5/42; 2137 BU Hendricks 8/6/43; WO 5/7/44; Recl Comp 13/3/46.

41-9170 Del McDill 29BG 7/5/42; Bangor 26/6/42; Muroc 29/7/42; Geiger 1/9/42; Alamogordo 2/10/42; Boise 7/11/42; Hendricks 25/2/43; WO 1/5/43.

41-9171 Del Sebring 5/5/42; WO 14/6/44.

41-9172 Del 29BG McDill 7/5/42; Bangor 29/6/42; Walla Walla 2/8/42; c/l Redmond, Or, 15/8/42. Sal 9/9/42.

41-9173 Del Sebring 5/5/42; Hendricks 16/5/43; o/s runway Morgantown, WV, 27/12/42 w/Hall, cause - gusty wind. WO 18/11/43.

41-9174 Del 29BG McDill 7/5/42; ass 340BS/97BG Polebrook 6/42; tran 92BG Bovingdon 9/42; CCRC 1/43; c/t/o 6/43; sal 25/6/43.

41-9175 Del McDill 29BG 7/5/42; ass 340BS/97BG Polebrook /6/42; 92BG Bovingdon /9/42; CCRC /43; sal n/b/d 6/10/44. (? first B-17 to c/l ELG Manston, UK 24/8/42?).

41-9176 Del McDill 29BG 14/5/42; Cr in Sarasota Bay 12/6/42.

41-9177 Del Pendleton 34BG 7/5/42; Muroc 16/5/42; Alamogordo 18/6/42; SAAD 12/7/42; ass 19AF Occident 8/9/42; Ft McAndrew 19/9/42; wrecked Sidney, Nova Scotia 11/11/42. Sal.

41-9178 Del Pendleton 34BG 8/5/42; Westover 2/7/42; WO 26/8/42.

41-9179 Del Pendleton 34BG 11/5/42; Lockburn 12/5/43; RFC Altus 9/10/45.

41-9180 Del Pendleton 34BG 9/5/42; Westover 10/7/42; Recl Comp 28/11/45.

41-9181 Del Pendleton 34BG 9/5/42; Westover 2/7/42; damaged when parked at Patterson 8/10/42 by B-17 41-24582, rep; WO 22/1/43.

41-9182 Del Pendleton 34BG 9/5/42; Hendricks 30/3/43; RFC Albuquerque 9/10/45.

41-9183 Del 34BG Pendleton 9/5/42; Westover 2/7/42; RFC Albuquerque 15/6/45.

41-9184 Del Pendleton 11/5/42; Westover 2/7/42; RFC Albuquerque 5/7/45.

41-9185 Del 34BG Pendleton 11/5/42; 305BG Muroc 57/42; RFC Albuquerque 15/6/45.

41-9186 Del 34BG Pendleton 11/5/42; Westover 2/7/42; c/t/o Rapid City 9/10/42; WO 30/1/43.

41-9187 Del McDill 92BG 12/5/42; Lockburn 28/3/43; WO 21/1/44.

41-9188 Del McDill 92BG 12/5/42; Westover 14/7/42; WO 26/8/42.

41-9189 Del McDill 92BG 11/5/42; Wendover 15/7/42; RFC Bush Fd 22/5/45.

41-9190 Del McDill 92BG 11/5/42; Wendover 369BS/306BG 15/7/42; RFC Albuquerque 26/5/45.

41-9191 Del McDill 92BG 12/5/42; Hendricks 24/6/43; RFC Albuquerque 12/6/45.

41-9192 Del McDill 92BG 12/5/42; Lockburn 29/2/43; Recl Comp 17/2/45.

41-9193 Del Lowry 18/5/42; ass 5AF Hawaii 7/6/42; WO 26/5/43.

41-9194 Del Lowry 18/5/42; ass 5AF Hawaii 7/6/42; WO 3/12/42.

41-9195 Del Cheyenne 15/5/42; Wayne 22/6/42; Gt Britain 1/7/42; ass RAF 220Sq [NR-T], SOC (WO) 4/9/45.

41-9196 Del Cheyenne 15/5/42; ass 5AF Hawaii 7/10/42; MIA New Britain w/Hareman 5/10/42.

41-9197 Del Cheyenne 16/5/42; Wayne 10/6/42; Gt Britain 2/7/42; ass RAF 220Sq [NR-M], SOC 22/12/45.

41-9198 Del Cheyenne 16/5/42; Wayne 27/6/42; Gt Britain 28/6/42; ass RAF 220Sq, cr Ballykelly, N Ireland 8/42. Sal.

41-9199 Del Cheyenne 16/5/42; Wayne 25/6/42; Gt

INDIVIDUAL B-17 HISTORIES

Britain 24/6/42; (FK211) Ass RAF 224Sq, SOC 4/3/47.
41-9200 Del Cheyenne 16/5/42; Wayne 22/6/42; Gt Britain 1/7/42; ass RAF 220Sq , ditched off Azores 21/12/43.
41-9201 Del Cheyenne 27/5/42; Wayne 7/6/42; Gt Britain 1/7/42; ass RAF 220Sq, cr Nutts Corner, N. Ire. /8/42. Sal.
41-9202 Del Cheyenne 17/5/42; Wayne 25/6/42; Gt Britain 25/8/42; ass RAF 206Sq [VX-B], cr Gibraltar, sal 30/11/43.
41-9203 Del Cheyenne 16/5/42; Wayne 23/6/42; Gt Britain 25/6/42; (FK209) Ass RAF 220Sq, cr Ballykelly, rep; MIA 25/3/43.
41-9204 Del Cheyenne 27/5/42; Wayne 23/6/42; Gt Britain 25/6/42; ass RAF 206Sq, SOC 11/3/45.
41-9205 Del Cheyenne 24/5/42; ass 11AF Kodiak 2/6/42; cr Lake Bennett, Carcross, Yukon Terr. w/McWilliams 16/10/43. WO.
41-9206 Del Lowry 19/5/42; ass 5AF Hawaii 7/6/42; f/l New Guinea w/Newton, 24/9/42, sal.
41-9207 Del Lowry 19/5/42; ass 5AF Hawaii 6/6/42; tran 43BG; WO 6/6/43.
41-9208 Del Lowry 20/5/42; ass 19BG Hawaii 7/6/42; c/t/o Port Moresby w/Price 19/9/42, sal.
41-9209 Del Lowry 19/5/42; ass 19BG Hawaii 22/9/42; tran 43BG; WO 15/4/43.
41-9210 Del Minneapolis 21/5/42; Wright 30/6/42; Minneapolis 11/10/42; Wright 5/3/43; Midland 21/6/43; 1454 BU Minneapolis 21/9/43; 4000 BU Wright 30/5/44; RFC Minneapolis 29/10/45. Canada CF-1CB (Civil 9920N/5842N); Bolivia CP-753 at La Paz; Fort Lauderdale for restoration.
41-9211 Del Cheyenne 22/5/42; ass 98BS/11BG Hawaii (flew at Guadalcanal Jan 43); retUS 901 BU Orlando 14/12/45. TYPHOON McGOON.
41-9212 Del Cheyenne 22/5/42; ass 7AF Hawaii 3/6/42; WO 8/8/42.
41-9213 Del Cheyenne 22/5/42; ass 42BS/11BG Hawaii 3/6/42; MIA Guadalcanal 24/9/42. JAP BASHER.
41-9214 Del Cheyenne 22/5/42; ass 98BS/11BG Hawaii 3/6/42; tran 23BS/5BG; retUS Tyndall 27/12/43; RFC Albuquerque 12/6/45. THE SKIPPER.
41-9215 Del Cheyenne 22/5/42; ass 98BS/11BG Hawaii 5/6/42; tran 13AF (Poppy) 22/7/42; WO 15/6/44. GALLOPIN' GUS.
41-9216 Del Cheyenne 23/5/42; ass 42BS/11BG Hawaii 4/6/42; tran 31BS-23BS/5BG 22/7/42; WO 15/6/44. ALLEY OOP.
41-9217 Del Cheyenne 22/5/42; ass 7AF Hawaii 7/6/42; retUS Tinker 16/6/43; Patt- erson 19/2/44; RFC Altus 18/9/45.
41-9218 Del Cheyenne 23/5/42; ass 7AF Hawaii 4/6/42; ditched (no fuel) 12/9/42 w/Coffield.
41-9219 Del Cheyenne 23/5/42; ass 7AF Hawaii 5/6/42; tran 13AF Poppy 22/5/42; WO 15/6/44. HELLZAPOPPIN.
41-9220 Del Cheyenne 22/5/42; ass 7AF Hawaii 5/6/42; tran 13AF Poppy 22/7/42; WO 15/6/44.
41-9221 Del Cheyenne 26/5/42; ass 42BS/11BG Hawaii 4/6/42; tran 13AF Poppy 22/7/42; MIA 6/8/42 w/Lt Stone.
41-9222 Del Cheyenne 23/5/42; ass 7AF Hawaii 5/6/42; retUS 21/10/43; RFC Altus 4/10/45.
41-9223 Del Cheyenne 23/5/42; ass 7AF Hawaii 6/6/42; tran 13AF Poppy 18/9/42; WO 4/11/42.
41-9224 Del Cheyenne 23/5/42; ass 98BS/11BG Hawaii; MIA 7/8/42 w/Loder.
41-9225 Del Cheyenne 28/5/42; Wayne 26/6/42; RAF 4/7/42 as FL455. 519Sq [Z9-A]; cr Westerdale, Wick, UK 1/2/45. Sal.
41-9226 Del Cheyenne 23/5/42; ass 7AF Hawaii 7/6/42; tran 13AF Poppy 22/7/42; WO 11/9/42.
41-9227 Del Cheyenne 23/5/42; ass 11BG Hawaii 6/6/42; tran 43BG; cr Pacific TO on liquor ride 31/12/44. YANKEE DOODLE JR.
41-9228 Del Cheyenne 26/5/42; Wayne 30/6/42; Gt Britain 1/7/42.
41-9229 Del Cheyenne 26/5/42; Wayne 30/6/42; Gt Britain 4/7/42.
41-9230 Del Cheyenne 26/5/42; Wayne 8/7/42; Gt Britain 14/7/42.
41-9231 Del Cheyenne 24/5/42; Wayne 28/5/42; Gt Britain 6/7/42.
41-9232 Del Cheyenne 27/5/42; Wayne 17/6/42; Gt Britain 30/6/42.
41-9233 Del Cheyenne 1/4/42; Boeing AC 9/6/42; WO 9/10/43; 3098 BU Burbank 31/1/44; Recl Comp 29/1/46.
41-9234 Del Cheyenne 30/5/42; ass /19BG Hawaii 21/8/42; tran 43BG; cr New Guinea 9/1/43, WO; (RAF FL461).
41-9235 Del Cheyenne 26/5/42; ass 19BG Hawaii 6/8/42; ditched off Cooktown, Aus.29/9/42 w/Linberg.
41-9236 Del Cheyenne 28/5/42; Wayne 6/7/42; Gt Britain 8/7/42.
41-9237 Del Cheyenne 28/5/42; Wayne 14/7/42; Gt Britain 28/6/42.
41-9238 Del Cheyenne 28/5/42; Wayne 5/7/42; Gt Britain 6/7/42.
41-9239 Del Cheyenne 28/5/42; Wayne 5/7/42; Gt Britain 11/7/42.
41-9240 Del Cheyenne 28/5/42; Wayne 28/7/42; Gt Britain 2/7/42.
41-9241 Del Cheyenne 1/6/42; Wayne 30/6/42; Gt Britain 10/7/42.
41-9242 Del Cheyenne 1/6/42; Wayne 3/7/42; Houlton 7/7/42; 726BS/451BG (B-24s?) Fairmont 11/11/43.
41-9243 Del Cheyenne 2/6/42; Wayne 25/6/42; Gt Britain 11/7/42.
41-9244 Del Cheyenne 29/5/42; ass 19BG Hawaii 6/8/42; tran 43BG; s/d Rabual 21/5/43 to night fighter. HONIKUU OKOLE.
41-9245 Del Cheyenne 1/6/42; Wayne 1/7/42; Gt Britain 7/7/42.

B-17F- BO

41-24340 Del Mat Com Boeing 26/6/42, first a/c with large paddle props; cr Puget Sound, Wa. 13/3/43.
41-24341 Del Cheyenne 11/6/42; Tulsa 26/11/42; Mat Com HQ Wright Fd as XB-40 armament test bed 15/9/43; 3704 BU Keesler 22/11/43; Recl Comp 4/4/45.
41-24342 Ass 92BG Bovingdon 8/42; 414BS/97BG Polebrook 24/8/42; tran Maison Blanche, Alg. 20/11/42; MIA Foggia 9/7/43 w/Bispham; MACR 642. STINKY JR.
41-24343 Ass 92BG Podington 13/7/42; tran 343BS/97BG Polebrook 8/42; Maison Blanche 22/11/42; tran 414BS; sal 15/3/43. PEGGY D Jr.
41-24344 Ass 326BS/92BG Bovingdon /42; 414BS/97BG Polebrook 8/42; MIA L'Orient, 97th's first mission 21/10/42, w/Bennett, cr Morlaix, Fr.
41-24345 Ass 326BS/92BG Bovingdon /42; 342BS/97BG Polebrook 8/42; Maison Blanche, 20/11/42; 20BG/2BG Massicault, 14/11/43; MIA Athens {5m} 20/12/43 w/Slaughter; 2 engines afire, 9 baled. MACR 1514.
41-24346 Ass 419BS/301BG 7/7/42; tran 12AF 11/42 {54m}; 348BS/99BG Tortorella, 12/43; retUS Tinker 3/6/44; RFC Arledge Fd 23/11/44. AVENGER.
41-24347 Ass 352BS/301BG Chelveston 7/42; c/l Church Lawford, UK 9/8/42 (crew OK), first a/c sal in UK. DOC STORK.
41-24348 Ass 353BS/301BG Chelveston 1/7/42; Tarafaroui 24/11/42; {41m} sal 24/9/44.PEGASUS.
41-24349 Del Middletown AAD 23/6/42; cr Bellefonte, Pa. 26/6/42 w/Fitzgerald. Sal.
41-24350 Ass 352BS/301BG Chelveston 7/42; Tafaraoui 24/11/42; exploded mid air on return from depot, all killed w/Sloulin 30/11/42 {8m} MACR 16242. DUMBO.
41-24351 Ass 353BS/301BG Chelveston 12/7/42; Tafaraoui 24/11/42, as HEINIE HEADHUNTERS {52m}; 416BS/99BG Tortorella 12/43 {21m} TAIL END CHARLIE; 840BS/483BG Tortorella 31/3/44; retUS 13/6/44; RFC Albuquerque 17/7/45.
41-24352 Ass 352BS/301BG Chelveston 7/42; Tafaraoui 24/11/42; c/l Mateur 9/5/43 {40m} w/Peabody; flak damage 6/11/43; retUS 22/10/43; RFC Walnut Ridge 31/10/45. HOLEY JOE.
41-24353 Del Cheyenne 28/6/42; ass 63BS/43BG Hawaii 31/7/42; trans 69/433 TCGps, New Guinea; sal 31/4/45. CAP'N & THE KIDS.
41-24354 Del Cheyenne 28/6/42; ass 7AF Hawaii 5/9/42; s/d Milne Bay, Aus. 26/8/42 w/Webb.
41-24355 Del Cheyenne 28/6/42; ass 5AF Hawaii 23/7/42; WO 21/9/43.
41-24356 Del Cheyenne 28/6/42; ass 5AF Hawaii 21/8/42; WO 4/3/43. DOUBLE TROUBLE.
41-24357 Del Cheyenne 28/6/42; ass 43BG Hawaii 30/7/42; tran 41TCS/317TCG 11/43; WO 7/12/45. THE SUPER CHIEF.
41-24358 Del Cheyenne 28/6/42; ass 63BS/43BG Hawaii 31/7/42; became hack at Nadzab, New Guinea, when war weary. Sal 13/9/45. LULU BELLE.
41-24359 Ass 301BG Westover 8/9/42; Chelveston 6/8/42; 813BS/305BG Grafton Underwood/Chelveston 25/11/42; 325BS/92BG [NV-F] Podington 24/4/43; 813BS/482BG Alconbury 25/8/43 {4m}; retUS Eglin 11/6/44; RFC Walnut Ridge 19/12/45.
41-24360 Ass 419BS/301BG Westover 7/42; Podington 6/8/42; Tafaraoui 24/11/42; {101m}; RFC Altus 27/8/45. HELL'S KITCHEN.
41-24361 Ass 301BG Westover 18/7/42; Podington 6/8/42; Tafaraoui 24/11/42; 96BS/2BG Massicault {38m}; 348BS/99BG Oudna 28/3/44 {52m}; 840BS/483BG Tortorella 31/3/44; retUS 11/6/44; RFC Altus 20/8/45. WABASH CANNON BALL.
41-24362 Ass 419BS/301BG Westover 6/8/42; Podington 6/8/42; ditched Channel on return from Lille 9/10/42 {3m} w/Swenson; crew saved, first such 8AF rescue.
41-24363 Ass 301BG Westover 7/42; Podington 6/8/42; Tafaraoui 24/11/42; MIA {6} Bizerte, Tun 28/11/42 w/Bruce; MACR 16197. BAD PENNY.
41-24364 Ass 353BS/301BG Westover 6/8/42; Podington 6/8/42; Tafaraoui 24/11/42 {64m}; 2BG Massicault 14/11/43; Amendola 9/12/43; MIA Fano, It. 15/1/44. MACR 1814.
41-24365 Ass 92BG Bangor 28/6/42; damaged f/l Bangor 20/7/42, rep; tran 364BS/305BG [WF-E/Z] /43 for training; retUS Grenier 18/1/44.
41-24366 Ass 353BS/301BG Westover 7/7/42; Podington 6/8/42 {6m}; Tafaraoui 24/11/42; 346BS/99BG Navarin 3/4/43; tran 429BS/2BG {5m}; ret 99BG; Le Senia, It. depot 3/44; c/l 19/8/44. Sal. K.O.
41-24367 Ass 419BS/301BG Westover 7/7/42; Podington 6/8/42; Tafaraoui 24/11/42; bombed by Luftwaffe at Biskra base 10/1/43. {20m} sal.
41-24368 Ass 352BS/301BG Westover 7/42; Podington 6/8/42; Tafaraoui 26/11/42; Maison

Above: B-17F-1-BO 41-24370 was claimed as the first B-17 flying in the European and Mediterranean war theatres to complete 100 combat sorties. Early B-17Fs had the low domed Sperry turret. (USAF)

Blanche 5/12/42; c/l Bone {6m} 8/12/43 w/Brasher; sal. MAVERICK.
41-24369 Ass 32BS/301BG Westover 6/7/42; Podington 6/8/42; Tafaraoui 26/11/42; c/l Maison Blanche, Alg. 5/12/42; BD {5m} Bizerte 15/12/42; sal. SPECIAL DELIVERY.
41-24370 Del Cheyenne Mod Cen 24/6/42; 92BG /6/42 as PALE FACE; 342BS/97BG Polebrook /8/42; Maison Blanche 20/11/42; {103m}; retUS Eglin 12/10/43; BERLIN SLEEPER II.
41-24371 Ass 353BS/301BG Westover 23/6/42; Podington 7/42; Tafaraoui 26/11/42; Maison Blanche, Alg. 5/12/42; Biskra 16/12/42; Ain M'Lila 17/1/43; St Donat 6/3/43; MIA {39m} Palermo, It. 18/4/43 w/Godwin, s/d by ME 110s, all killed. MACR 16508. DEVILS FROM HELL.
41-24372 Ass 352BS/301BG Westover 23/6/42; Chelveston/Podington 9/8/43; Tafaraoui 26/11/42; Maison Blanche 5/12/42; Biskra 16/12/42; Ain M'Lila 17/1/43; St Donat. 6/3/43; flak damage 11/4/43; {27m} sal. HELL'S BATTLEWAGON.
41-24373 Ass 326BS/92BG Bangor 15/7/42; 341BS/97BG Alconbury 8/42; 429BS/2BG Massicault 14/11/43; sal 31/1/44. PEACHES II.
41-24374 Ass 353BS/301BG Westover 23/6/42; Podington 6/8/42; Tafaraoui 24/11/42; MIA {4m} Bizerte 28/11/42 w/Maher; all POW, MACR 16038.
41-24375 Del MAD Salt Lake City 23/6/42; c/l 23/6/42 severe damage, parts used for stock. Sal.
41-24376 Ass 92BG Bangor 14/7/42; 341BS/97BG Polebrook 8/42; Maison Blanche 13/11/42; bombed by Luftwaffe on take off 20/11/42 w/Hughes; all killed.
41-24377 Ass 92BG Bangor 14/7/42; tran 342BS/97BG Maison Blanche 5/11/42; Used by Gen Mark Clark to Gibraltar 19/10/42; retUS Tinker 14/7/43; RFC Arledge 22/11/44. BOOMERANG II.
41-24378 Ass 92BG Bangor 24/6/42; 342BS/97BG Polebrook /8/42; Maison Blanche 13/11/42; Tafaraoui, Alg. 22/11/42; Biskra 25/12/42; Château-du-Rhumel 8/2/43 {125m}; tran 99BG Tortorella 11/43 {12m}; retUS Morrison 18/5/44 {137m}; RFC Bush Fd, 19/5/45. WAR EAGLE.
41-24379 Ass 92BG Bangor 24/6/42; 341BS/97BG Polebrook 17/8/42; 301BG St Donat 4/43 {18m} sal 9/11/44.
41-24380 Ass 92BG Bangor 24/6/42; c/l 26/6/42 w/Wingel, rep; 340BS/97BG Polebrook 26/7/42; Maison Blanche 10/11/42; sal 30/11/45. SUPERMAN.
41-24381 Del Cheyenne 26/6/42; ass 63BS/43BG Hawaii 30/7/42; Port Moresby; tran 54TCGp 11/43; FEPAB? 10/4/47.
41-24382 Ass 92BG Bangor 26/6/42; 341BS/97BG Polebrook 8/42; {100m}; sal 5/6/44. MIGHTY MIDGETS.
41-24383 Del Cheyenne 26/6/42; ass 5AF Sumac 31/7/42; WO 30/4/45.
41-24384 Del Cheyenne 26/6/42; ass 5AF Sumac 31/7/42; Con Miss 17/9/42. SNOOPY.
41-24385 Ass 326BS/92BG Bangor 19/7/42; 340BS/97BG Maison Blanche 13/11/42; Carried all commanders for Operation 'Torch' to Gibraltar 5/11/42; MIA Tripoli 18/1/43 w/Wilkin, WO 31/10/44.
41-24386 Ass 353BS/301BG Westover 7/42; Chelveston 9/8/42; Tafaraoui 26/11/42; Maison Blanche 5/12/42; Biskra 16/12/42; b/d La Goulette, Tun {20m} 2/1/43, w/Evans, left at base when group moved on to Ain M'Lila. 17/1/43. QUEEN BEE-17.
41-24387 Del Boeing Seattle Mat Com 9/7/42; WO 8/10/43; Recl Comp 20/11/45.
41-24388 Ass 92BG Bangor 31/7/42; 340BS/97BG Polebrook 8/42; damaged UK 7/9/42, rep; flew Gens Doolittle & Lemnitzer to Gibraltar 6/11/42; Maison Blanche 13/11/42; Tafaraoui 22/11/42; badly damaged again by enemy ground attack Biskra 10/1/43; sal 14/1/43.
41-24389 Del Westover 8/7/42 for UK, but switched to Air Material Command; Windsor Locks 3/9/42; Syracuse 1/10/42; Wright Fd 10/2/43; Recl Comp 3/4/46.
41-24390 Ass 419BS/301BG Westover 8/7/42; Chelveston/Podington 6/8/42; Tafaraoui 26/11/42; Maison Blanche 5/12/42; Biskra 16/12/42; Ain M'Lila 17/1/43; St Donat 6/3/43; Oudna 6/8/43; Cerignola,It. 7/12/43; Lucera 1/2/44; {60m} sal 20/2/45.
41-24391 Del Cheyenne 28/6/42; ass 93BS/19BG Mareeba, Aus (first a/c in) 3/8/42; tran 63BS/43BG; Con Acc 13/9/42. HOOMALIMALI.
41-24392 Ass 92BG Bangor 13/7/42; 414BS/97BG Polebrook 24/8/42; Maison Blanche 20/11/42; Tafaraoui 22/11/42; Biskra 25/12/42; Château-du-Rhumel 8/2/43; Pont-du-Fahs 1/8/43; Depienne 15/8/43; 2BG Massicault 14/11/43; sal 6/5/44. HELL'S KITCHEN.
41-24393 Ass 419BS/301BG Westover 8/7/42; tran 96BS/2BG Maison Blanche 13/11/42; Tafaraoui 22/11/42; Biskra 25/12/42; Château-du-Rhumel 8/2/43 {14m}; 483BG Tortorella 31/3/44; retUS Olmstead 24/7/43; RFC Bush Fd 4/6/45. EAGER BEAVER.
41-24394 Ass 353BS/301BG Westover 7/42; Chelveston 6/8/42; Tafaraoui 24/11/42; Maison Blanche 5/12/42; Biskra 16/12/42; Ain M'Lila 17/1/43; St Donat 6/3/43; MIA Castelventrano {21m} 13/4/43 w/Thomas. HOCKAMOLOCK JOCK VI BB.
41-24395 Ass 353BS/301BG Westover 8/7/42; Chelveston 9/8/42; tran Tafaraoui 26/11/42; Maison Blanche 5/12/42; Biskra 16/12/42; Ain M'Lila 17/1/43; St Donat 6/3/43; (traded for 42-30125 15/7/43); Oudna 6/8/43 {54m}; trans Massicault 49BS/2BG 14/11/43; MIA Laviarano (s/d) 30/1/44 w/Taylor, no chutes seen. MACR 2060. I DO DIT.
41-24396 Ass 419BS/301BG Westover 8/7/42; Chelveston 9/8/42 THE RELUCTANT GREMLIN; tran Tafaraoui 26/11/42; Maison Blanche 5/12/42; Biskra 16/12/42; Ain M'Lila 17/1/43; St Donat 6/3/43; Oudna 6/8/43 {52m}; tran 346BS/99BG Tortorella 14/11/43 {28m}; retUS Rome Fd 28/4/44 w/O'Carroll orig pilot who took it home for war bond tour; RFC Searcy Fd 31/7/45. EIGHT BALL.
41-24397 Ass 352BS/301BG Westover 8/7/42; Chelveston 9/8/42; c/l RAF Gatwick 2/10/42. Sal BD. Nose cut off to release crewman; 16 cannon holes, over 300 bullet holes plus flak damage. PHYLLIS.
41-24398 Ass 419BS/301BG Westover 8/7/42; Chelveston 9/8/42; c/l Newmarket 3/10/42. Sal.
41-24399 Ass 323BS/91BG [OR-V] Bangor 13/7/42; Bassingbourn 23/9/42; MIA Kassel 30/7/43 w/McCammon; cr Opijnen, Hol; 8KIA 2 POW. MACR 148. MAN O' WAR.
41-24400 Ass 92BG Bangor 13/7/42; tran 414BS/97BG Polebrook 24/8/42; Maison Blanche 13/11/42; Tafaraoui 22/11/42; damaged 21/10/42; sal. LITTLE BILL. (Margaret White,LIFE magazine, first US woman to fly combat mission,22/1/43.)
41-24401 Del Cheyenne 29/6/42; ass 5AF Sumac

3/8/43, not del; ass 398BG Rapid City 29/1/43; Dalhart 12/9/43; RFC Kingman 13/11/45.
41-24402 Del Cheyenne 30/6/42; ass 5AF Sumac 31/7/42; Con accident 17//11/42.
41-24403 Del Cheyenne 30/6/42; ass 30BS/19BG Mareeba, Aus. 21/8/42; Port Moresby 15/9/42; tran 65BS-63BS/43BG; as transport hack in later years. BLITZ BUGGY re-named Jan '43, THE OLD MAN. (used by Gen Whitehead Advon 5AF)
41-24404 Ass 352BS/301BG Westover 14/7/42; Polebrook 24/8/42; flew group first mission 5/9/42; tran Tafaraoui 26/11/42; Maison Blanche 5/12/42; Biskra 16/12/42; Ain M'Lila 17/1/43; St Donat 6/3/43; Oudna 6/8/43; c/l 11/9/43. {17m} sal. CAROL JEAN III.
41-24405 Ass 353BS/301BG Westover 12/7/42; Chelveston 9/8/42; Tafaraoui 26/11/42; Maison Blanche 5/12/42; Biskra 16/12/42; Ain M'Lila 17/1/43; St Donat 6/3/43; Oudna 6/8/43 {56m}; tran 96BS/2BG Massicault 14/11/43; Bizerte 2/12/43; Amendola 9/12/43; MIA {22m} Klagenfurt 19/3/44, w/Lavine, s/d 6 chutes seen, cr Cilli, It; MACR 3287.
41-24406 Ass 92BG Bangor 13/7/42; tran 414BS/97BG Polebrook 8/42; rammed by FW190 1/2/43, rep; tran 353BS/301BG {3m} St Donat 6/3/43; sal 6/3/45. ALL AMERICAN.
41-24407 Ass 352BS/301BG Westover 13/7/42; Chelveston 9/8/42; Tafaraoui 26/11/42; Maison Blanche 5/12/42; Biskra 16/12/42; Ain M'Lila 17/1/43; St Donat 6/3/43; Oudna 6/8/43 {48m}; 346BS/99BG Oudna 10/43 {34m}; to depot 3/44; retUS 9/5/44 Amarillo; RFC Walnut Ridge 5/12/45 THE GOON.
41-24408 Ass 32BS/301BG Westover 10/7/42; Chelveston 9/8/42; Tafaraoui 26/11/42; Maison Blanche 5/12/42; Biskra 16/12/42; Ain M'Lila 17/1/43; St Donat 6/3/43; Oudna 6/8/43 {42m}; tran 49BS/2BG Massicault 14/11/43; tran 483BG 29/4/44; retUS 11/12/44; RFC Albuquerque 28/6/45; PLUTOCRAT.
41-24409 Ass 352BS/301BG Westover 10/7/42; tran 32BS Chelveston 9/8/42; Tafaraoui 26/11/42; Maison Blanche 5/12/42; Biskra 16/12/42; Ain M'Lila 17/1/43; St Donat 6/3/43; Oudna 6/8/43 {35m}; tran 416BS/99BG Oudna 14/11/43 {39m}; tran 816BS/483BG Tortorella 31/3/44; retUS Olmstead 4/7/44; RFC Altus 11/9/45.
41-24410 Del SAD 29/6/42; Langley 20/7/42; Westover 1/9/42; New Castle 4/10/42; Salina 22/12/42; Rapid City 9/4/43; Geiger 22/6/43; RFC Albuquerque 25/6/45.
41-24411 Ass 325BS/92BG Bangor 13/7/42; 97BG Polebrook 8/42; sal n/b/d 21/10/42. DOTTIE.
41-24412 Ass 301BG Westover 30/6/42; 92BG Bangor 8/42; 340BS/97BG Polebrook /8/42; Maison Blanche 13/11/42; Tafaraoui 22/11/42; Biskra 25/12/42; Château-du-Rhumel 8/2/43; Pont-du-Fahs 1/8/43; De Pienne 15/8/43; Cerignola 20/12/43; Amendola 16/1/44; retUS 23/11/44; Recl Comp 6/7/45. FLYING FLIT GUN.
41-24413 Ass 92BG Bangor 14/7/42; tran 414BS/97BG Polebrook 24/8/42; Maison Blanche 13/11/42; Tafaraoui 22/11/42; Biskra 25/12/42; MIA Bizerte 26/12/42 w/Borders; direct flak, exploded, no survivors; BIRMINGHAM BLITZKREIG.
41-24414 Ass 92BG Bangor 14/7/42; tran 342BS/97BG Polebrook 8/42; Maison Blanche 13/11/42; Tafaraoui 22/11/42; Biskra 25/12/42; Château-du-Rhumel 8/2/43; Pont-du-Fahs 1/8/43; De Pienn 15/8/43; tran 49BS/2BG Massicault 14/11/43; retUS 21/4/44; RFC Altus 9/10/45. JARRIN' JENNY II.

41-24415 Ass 92BG Bangor 14/7/42; 414BS/97BG Polebrook 24/8/42; Maison Blanche 13/11/42; Tafaraoui 22/11/42; Biskra 25/12/42; Château-du-Rhumel 8/2/43; coll mid air w/25147, prop sheared part of tail off, crew man baled out over Med. Sea, pilot Holmes c/l at base 9/5/43. Sal. MACR 16254. YANKEE DOODLE II.
41-24416 Ass 326BS/92BG Bangor 16/7/42; 95BG Horham /43; 359BS/303BG [BN-V] Molesworth, 17/6/43 BLACK DIAMOND EXPRESS; retUS Sheppard 5/7/44; RFC Walnut Ridge 26/10/45.
41-24417 Ass 92BG Bangor 14/7/42; 97BG 24/8/42; dam 21/10/42; BAD 24/10/42; 369BS/306BG [WW-M] Thurleigh /10/42; ditched off Cromer 24/7/43 w/Maresh, all rescued. DIXIE DEMO II.
41-24418 Ass 352BS/301BG Westover 12/7/42; Chelveston 9/8/42; flew group's first mission 5/9/42; Tafaraoui 26/11/42; as MICKEY FINN {11m}; tran 32BS and renamed SPECIAL DELIVERY II {79m}; retUS Rapid City 398BG (training) 10/11/43; WO 20/10/44.
41-24419 Ass 92BG Bangor 14/7/42; 341BS/97BG Polebrook 8/42; Maison Blanche 13/11/42; Tafaraoui 22/11/42; Biskra 25/12/42; bombed on base by Luftwaffe 10/1/43; sal.
41-24420 Del Cheyenne 8/7/42; Hamilton 13/8/42; ass 5AF Sumac 21/8/42; WO 23/7/46.
41-24421 Ass 92BG Bangor 14/7/42; c/l Dow Fd, 15/7/42, rep; 341BS/97BG Polebrook 8/42; Maison Blanche 17/11/42; Tafaraoui 22/11/42; Biskra 25/12/42; Château-du-Rhumel 8/2/43; Pont-du-Fahs 1/8/43; De Pienn 15/8/43; 347BS/99BG Oudna 14/11/43 {16m}; depot 3/44; 483BG Tortorella 31/3/44; retUS Homested 24/6/44; RFC Stillwater 4/10/45. WONGO.
41-24422 Ass 352BS/301BG Westover 14/7/42; Chelveston 9/8/42; Tafaraoui 26/11/42; Maison Blanche 5/12/42; Biskra 16/12/42; Ain M'Lila 17/1/43; St Donat 6/3/43; Oudna 6/8/43; Cerignola 7/12/43; Lucera 1/2/44; {61m} sal 1/7/45. DICKIE DOODLE II.
41-24423 Ass 353BS/301BG Westover 12/7/42; Chelveston 9/8/42; Tafaraoui 26/11/42; Maison Blanche 5/12/42; Biskra 16/12/42; Ain M'Lila 17/1/43; St Donat 6/3/43; cr 28/5/43 {42m} sal. ITZABITCH.
41-24424 Del Cheyenne 1/7/42; ass 19BG Hawaii 6/8/42; accident 17/3/43, sal?,HELL FROM THE HEAVENS.
41-24425 Del Cheyenne 1/7/42; ass 5AF Sumac 21/8/42; s/d 19/4/43.
41-24426 Del Cheyenne 1/7/42; ass 7AF Hawaii 9/12/42; retUS Hamilton 28/7/44; WO 21/8/44.
41-24427 Del Cheyenne 1/7/42; ass 5AF Sumac 21/8/42; MIA 19/9/42 w/Williams.
41-24428 Del Cheyenne 1/7/42; ass 5AF Sumac 21/8/42; cr Mareeba, Aus. 7/9/42 w/Humrichouse; sal.
41-24429 Del Cheyenne 1/7/42; ass 5AF Sumac 3/8/42; MIA 5/12/42.
41-24430 Del Cheyenne 1/7/42; Bolling 12/8/42; ass Poppy (PTO) 1/9/42; WO 31/10/44.
41-24431 Ass 401BS/91BG [LL-G] Bangor 27/8/42; Bassingbourn 11/10/42; c/t/o 16/2/43; {5m} sal. THE SAINT.
41-24432 Ass 401BS/91BG [LL-E] Bangor 2/9/42; Bassingbourn 1/10/42; tran 324BS [DF-E]; MIA Rouen {11m} 20/12/42 w/Carson; e/a, cr Vascoeuil, Fr; 9KIA 1POW. MACR 5381.DANELLEN
41-24433 Del Middleton AD 9/7/42; Bolling 20/7/42; Westover 3/10/42; ass 15PRS/3PRG Membury UK 7/9/42; Steeple Morden, UK 27/10/42; tran 12AF La

Senia, Alg. 6/12/42; Algiers 25/12/42; Le Kroub, Alg. 5/6/43; La Marsa, Tun. 28/6/43; Grottaglie, It. 4/10/43; Bari 28/12/43; sal 1/5/44.
41-24434 Del Middleton AD 9/7/42; Bolling 28/7/42; Westover 3/10/42; ass 15PRS/3PRG Membury, Wilt. 7/9/42; Steeple Morden, UK 27/12/42; tran 12AF La Senia, Alg. 6/12/42; Algiers 25/12/42; Le Kroub, Alg. 5/6/43; La Marsa, Tun. 28/6/43; retUS Homestead 14/7/43; Tinker 6/8/43; ret Bari 28/12/43; retUS; Civil Reg 60475; to Bolivia CB-79 cr 29/12/58.
41-24435 Ass 92BG Bangor 2/6/42; 340BS/97BG Polebrook 19/8/42; flew Operation 'Torch' commanders to Gibraltar 5/11/42; Maison Blanche 13/11/42; Tafaraoui 22/11/42; Biskra 25/12/42; Château-du-Rhumel 8/2/43; Pont-du-Fahs 1/8/43; Depienne 15/8/43; RAMBLIN' RECK; tran 429BS/2BG Massicault 14/11/43 re-named YANKEE DOO DIT; Bizerte 2/12/43; Amendola 9/12/43; MIA Villaorba, It. 18/3/44 w/Griffith, cr Trieste; MACR 3259.
41-24436 Del SAAD 9/7/42; Lowry 20/7/42; damaged Duncan Fd, Tex. 25/7/42, rep; landing accident Lowry 14/9/42, rep; New Castle 11/10/42; Middleton 2/1/43; Salina 25/1/43; Gowen 5/3/43; Wendover 29/5/43; Tinker 26/6/43; WO 18/10/44; Recl Comp 20/3/46.
41-24437 Ass 92BG Bangor 1/8/42; 341BS/97BG Polebrook 19/8/42; Maison Blanche 13/11/42; Tafaraoui 22/11/42; Biskra 25/12/42; Château-du-Rhumel 8/2/43; Pont-du-Fahs 1/8/43; Depienne 15/8/43; Cerignola 20/12/43; Amendola 16/1/44; sal 9/11/44 {100m}. THUNDERBIRD.
41-24438 Del MAD 9/7/42; Bangor 3/8/42; Colorado Springs 29/8/42; ass 15PRS/3PRG Membury, UK. 7/9/42; Steeple Morden, UK. 27/10/42; tran 12AF Tafaraoui 18/11/42; Algiers 25/12/42; Le Kroub, Alg. 5/6/43; La Marsa 28/6/43; Grottaglie 4/10/43; Bari 28/12/43; retUS Robins 3/8/44; Recl Comp 28/11/45.
41-24439 Ass 322BS/91BG [LG-Q] 6/9/42; Bassingbourn 29/9/42; b/d Romilly 20/12/42 w/Barton; c/l Fletchling, UK; badly damaged by flak and e/a attacks, just limped home across Channel. Sal. CHIEF SLY.
41-24440 Del SAAD 9/7/42; Lowry 26/7/42; ass 15PRS/3PRG Membury, UK 7/9/42; Steeple Morden 27/10/42; tran 12AF Le Senia, Alg. 6/12/42; Algiers 25/12/42; Le Kroub 5/6/43; La Marsa 28/6/43; Grottaglie 4/10/43; Bari 28/12/43; retUS Keesler 6/1/44; RFC Albuquerque 25/6/45. I GOT SPURS.
41-24441 Ass 326BS/92BG Bangor 31/7/42; 326BS/97BG Polebrook 12/8/42; MIA L'Orient 21/10/42 w/Schwartzenbeck. FRANCIS X.
41-24442 Ass 326BS/92BG Bangor 31/7/42; 342BS/97BG Polebrook 8/42; Maison Blanche 13/11/42; Tafaraoui 22/11/42; bombed on base by Luftwaffe 23/12/42; sal. LITTLE EVA.
41-24443 Ass 326BS/92BG Bangor 1/8/42; 414BS/97BG Polebrook 24/8/42; MIA L'Orient 21/10/44 w/Stenstrom. JOHNNY REB.
41-24444 Ass 92BG Bangor 2/8/42; 340BS/97BG Polebrook 24/8/42 THE RED GREMLIN; took Gen Eisenhower to Gibraltar (first B-17 to Gib) w/Paul Tibbets; Maison Blanche 13/11/42; Tafaraoui 22/11/42; Biskra 25/12/42; Château-du-Rhumel 8/2/43; Pont-du-Fahs 1/8/43; Depienne 15/8/43; Cerignola 20/12/43; Amendola 16/1/44; retUS 13/7/44; sal 19/6/46. SUPERMAN.
41-24445 Ass 326BS/92BG Bangor 12/8/42; 340BS/97BG Polebrook 8/42; MIA Meaulte 6/9/42 w/Lipsky, (first 8AF B-17 MIA), cr Flasselles. SOUTHERN BELLE.
41-24446 Del Cheyenne 10/7/42; ass 42BS &

431BS/11BG Hawaii but tran to New Caledonia en route; retUS 8/11/44.

41-24447 Ass 401BS/91BG [LL-H] Bangor 29/8/42; Bassingbourn 1/10/42; MIA {11m} Wilhelmshaven 26/2/44 w/Swais, cr Nth Sea, all killed. MACR 3575. KICKAPOO.

41-24448 Del Cheyenne 9/7/42; ass 5AF Sumac 1/9/42; s/d 7/1/43.

41-24449 Ass 401BS/91BG Bangor 31/8/42; Bassingbourn 1/10/42; MIA {3m} L'Orient w/Bloodgood 30/12/43, s/d all killed. MACR 3265. SHORT SNORTER.

41-24450 Del Cheyenne 9/7/42; Bolling 9/8/42; ass 72BS/5BG Hawaii 1/9/42; Guadalcanal 6/2/43; BD 9/2/43 over Nauru and ditched, 16 days in life raft to Buka, 50 more days. MY LOVIN' DOVE.

41-24451 Ass 401BS/91BG Bangor 29/8/42; en route Bassingbourn cr Mt Slievemorra, Cushendall, Co. Antrim, NI. 3/10/42; 8k 2inj (2 dead buried Madingley).

41-24452 Ass 401BS/91BG [LL-E] Bangor 29/8/42; Bassingbourn 1/10/42; MIA Romilly 20/12/42 w/English, cr Rouen 3k 7POW. MACR 16243.

41-24453 Ass 322BS/91BG [LG-O] Bangor 29/8/42; Bassingbourn 29/9/42; MIA {28m} Schweinfurt 17/8/43 w/Kenner, cr Mayen, nr Coblenz 5K 5POW. MACR 275. Names include MIZPAH - THE BEARDED LADY (ref THE BEARDED BEAUTY).

41-24454 Del Cheyenne 13/7/42; ass 28BS/19BG Hawaii 21/8/42; {109m} plus two subs, seven other vessels, 17 e/a and awarded seven Purple Hearts; tran 65BS/43BG; retUS 15/6/43. GEORGIA PEACH.

41-24455 Del Cheyenne 9/7/42; ass 5AF Sumac 21/8/42; retUS Rapid City 398BG (training) 12/11/43. WO 3/9/44. BALDY.

41-24456 Del Cheyenne 24/8/42; Salina 23/11; Cheyenne 30/1/43; Walla Walla 23/2/43; Geiger 30/4/43; Walla Walla 9/5/43; Spokane 25/6/43; Gt Falls 1/8/43; RFC Albuquerque 25/6/45.

41-24457 Del Cheyenne 13/7/42; Lowry 3/8/42; ass 26BS/11BG 21/8/42; tran 31BS/5BG; WO 30/4/45. AZTEC'S CURSE.

41-24458 Cheyenne 13/7/42; Lowry 3/8/42; ass 5AF Sumac 21/8/42; Brig Gen Ken Walker Medal of Honor 5/1/43; s/d 1/2/43. SAN ANTONIO ROSE.

41-24459 Ass 401BS/91BG [LL-B] Bangor 2/9/42; Bassingbourn 1/10/42; MIA Bremen 17/4/43 w/Wilson, cr Wundstorf, 5K 5POW; MACR 15520. HELLSAPOPPIN.

41-24460 Ass 423BS/306BG [RD-A] Westover 8/42; Thurleigh 13/10/42; wrecked 21/10/42 RAF Sutton Bridge, Cambs. w/Wilson, life raft latch broke loose and raft tangled round horizontal stabilizer, rep; tran 482BG Alconbury 22/8/43; 379BG Kimbolton 27/3/44; retUS 22/10/44; RFC Kingman 7/10/46.

41-24461 Ass 369BS/306BG Westover 22/8/42; Thurleigh 2/10/42; sal n/b/d 27/2/43.

41-24462 Ass 369BS/306BG Westover 21/8/42; not del; Boise 17/12/42; Tinker 7/4/43; Lewiston 23/4/43; Gore 19/5/43; Pocatello 2/6/43; Spokane 17/6/43; Moses Lake 20/9/43; RFC Albuquerque 25/6/45.

41-24463 Ass 423BS/306BG Westover 16/8/42; en route Thurleigh exploded over Atlantic and ditched off Greenland 5/9/42.

41-24464 Ass 367BS/306BG Westover 17/8/42; Thurleigh 13/10/42; tran 324BS/91BG [DF-J] Bassingbourn 20/2/43; MIA {2m} Hamm 4/3/43 w/Brill, s/d by Me 110, ditched Nth Sea, 3K 7 rescued by RN minesweeper. EXCALIBER.

41-24465 Ass 368BS/306BG Westover 17/8/42; Thurleigh 16/10/42; MIA 5/4/43 w/Seelos, cr Westkapelle, Bel. 3k 7POW; MACR 15533. MONTANA POWER.

41-24466 Ass 368BS/306BG Westover 19/7/42; Thurleigh 16/10/42; became trainer a/c 11/4/43; sal n/b/d 18/6/45.

41-24467 Del Ogden 21/7/42; damaged Cheyenne airport 7/9/42; brakes failed and a/c struck passenger DC-3 owned by Utd Air Lines, rep; ass 422BS/305BG Presque Is 19/10/42; Grafton Underwood 25/10/42; Chelveston 6/12/42; tran 368BS/306BG Thurleigh 20/1/43; MIA Bremen 17/4/43 w/Lally, cr Aurich, Ger. 2KIA 8POW. MACR 15525. THE GRIM REAPER (also BLASTED EVENT).

41-24468 Ass 3689BS/306BG Westover 20/8/42; Thurleigh 13/10/42; CCRC 26/3/43; sal n/b/d 31/5/45. WA-HOO!

41-24469 Ass 367BS/306BG Westover 16/8/42; Thurleigh 2/10/42; t/o from St Eval, Corn. for Thurleigh and disappeared 5/1/43.

41-24470 Ass 369BS/306BG Westover 22/8/42; Thurleigh 2/10/42; MIA St Nazaire 3/1/43 w/Cramer; ditched off Brest, w/Cramer. SONS OF FURY.

41-24471 Ass 369BS/306BG Westover 22/8/42; Thurleigh 2/10/42; MIA Lille 13/1/43 w/Johnston, coll w/41-24498 over France, cr Lille, 3K 7POW. MACR 15502. FOUR OF A KIND.

41-24472 Ass 369BS/306BG Westover 19/8/42; Thurleigh 2/10/42; MIA 13/1/43 w/Capt Adams, flak, cr Lille, 5KIA 4POW 1EVD.

41-24473 Ass 92BG Bangor 2/8/42; 414BS/97BG Polebrook 24/8/42; Maison Blanche 13/11/42; Tafaraoui 22/11/42; Biskra 25/12/42; Château-du-Rhumel 8/2/43; Pont-du-Fahs 1/8/43; De Pienn 15/8/43; Cerignola 20/12/43; Amendola 16/1/44. Sal 1/8/45. KISSY-ME-KOWBOY.

41-24474 Ass 367BS/306BG Westover 17/8/42; Thurleigh 17/9/42; MIA La Pallice 18/11/42 w/Gaston, s/d by AA, ditched Channel, 1K 9POW. FLOOZY.

41-24475 Ass 423BS/306BG Westover 16/8/42; Thurleigh 13/10/42; sal 5/12/43. OLD FAITHFUL.

41-24476 Ass 369BS/306BG [WW-D] Westover 16/8/42; Thurleigh 13/10/42; coll w/42-5251 1/3/43, sal n/b/d Chelveston 19/3/43. ADORABLE - UNBEARABLE.

41-24477 Ass 369BS/306BG [WW-H] Westover 16/8/42; Thurleigh 25/8/42 as JOAN OF ARC; tran 340BS/97BG Biskra 20/1/43; MIA Tunis 1/2/43 w/Coulter, coll w/FW190. MACR 3516. FLAMING MAYME.

41-24478 Ass 369BS/306BG Westover 19/8/42; Thurleigh 13/10/42; MIA St Nazaire 23/11/42 w/Isbell, cr St Nazaire, 7K 2POW.

41-24479 Ass 322BS/91BG [LG-R] 2/9/42; Bassingbourn 29/9/42; MIA {4m} La Pallice 18/11/42 w/Zienowicz (Sqd CO), coll w/41-24499, cr Youzil, 10K . MACR 16273. SAD SACK.

41-24480 Ass 324BS/91BG [DF-B] Bangor 31/8/42; Bassingbourn 26/9/42; 322BS [LG-A] 5/43 {16+m}; 403 AD 2/7/43; 8AF HQ Sqd 15/8/43 for VIP duties. Sal 19/10/44. Used as camera ship to film Wilder's *Memphis Belle*. THE BAD PENNY.

41-24481 Ass 322BS/91BG [LG-M] Bangor 2/9/42; Bassingbourn 26/9/42; MIA {10+m} Kiel 14/5/43 w/Broley, ditched Nth Sea, nr Amrum Is. (Frisians) 10K MACR 15498. HELL'S ANGELS.

41-24482 Ass 322BS/91BG [LG-S] Bangor 2/9/42; Bassingbourn 29/9/42; 4th mission to St Nazaire 27/2/43, badly damaged and salvaged. (crews claimed 6 e/a). HEAVYWEIGHT ANNIHILATORS.

41-24483 Ass 322BS/91BG [LG-U] Bangor 2/9/42; Bassingbourn 29/9/42; MIA Kiel 19/5/43 w/Baxley, cr fjord, 6POW 4K (inc British news man). MACR 15632. SPIRIT OF ALCOHOL.

41-24484 Ass 401BS/91BG [LL-C] Bangor 31/8/42; Bassingbourn 1/10/42; on return from Cognac {43+m} 31/12/43, diverted through weather to Gt Dunmow, then Andrews Field, but c/l hitting jeep and killing driver, Cpl Gillies. Badly damaged, taken to 2 SAD where front half joined 42-31229 and assigned 390BG. BAD EGG.

41-24485 Ass 324BS/91BG [DF-A] Bangor 31/8/42; Bassingbourn 26/10/42; one of first in group to 25m; retUS Columbia 25/6/43 for nationwide war bond tour; RFC Altus 1/8/45. Restored and on display at Mud Is. Memphis. MEMPHIS BELLE.

41-24486 Ass 367BS/306BG Westover 17/8/42; Thurleigh 13/10/42; MIA St Nazaire 9/11/42 w/Stewart, flak, cr Channel, 11KIA. MAN O' WAR.

41-24487 Ass 368BS/306BG [BO-Q] Westover 25/8/42; Thurleigh 13/10/42; AFSC 1/5/44; retUS Tinker 28/7/44; to Williamsport Technical Institute, Patterson Fd 20/6/45. EAGER BEAVER.

41-24488 Ass 369BS/306BG [WW-F] Westover 30/8/42; Thurleigh 13/10/42; tran 367BS [GY-F]; MIA Bremen 17/4/43 w/Casey, e/a, cr Greetsiel, Ger. 5K 5POW. MACR 15445. BANSHEE II.

41-24489 Ass 369BS/306BG Westover 17/8/42; Thurleigh 13/10/42; MIA Romilly 20/12/42 w/McKesson, e/a, cr?; TERRY AND THE PIRATES.

41-24490 Ass 324BS/91BG [DF-C] Bangor 31/8/42; Bassingbourn 26/9/42; MIA {27+m} Oschersleben 22/2/44 w/Considine, e/a, cr Münster. 1K 9POW. MACR 2640. JACK THE RIPPER.

41-24491 Ass 423BS/306BG Westover 15/8/42; Thurleigh 13/10/42; MIA St Nazaire 9/11/42 w/Felts, flak, cr Channel; 7KIA 3POW. MACR 6012. MAN O' WAR.

41-24492 Ass 367BS/306BG Westover 16/8/42; Thurleigh 5/9/42; c/l Spalding, UK w/Lt Ely on training flight 2/10/42, considered pilot error.

41-24493 Ass 368BS/306BG Westover 16/8/42; Thurleigh 13/10/42; tran to SBA trainer 11/4/43; retUS Seattle 2/6/44; Wright 27/6/44; Eglin 9/12/44; Ypsilanti 22/6/45; RFC Altus 29/10/45.

41-24494 Ass 367BS/306BG Westover 16/8/42; Thurleigh 13/10/42; c/l Portreath, UK 9/11/42; sal n/b/d 12/11/42.

41-24495 Ass 367BS/306BG Westover 17/8/42; Thurleigh 13/10/42; MIA 20/12/42 w/McKee, e/a, 1K 8POW 1EVD. ROSE O' DAY.

41-24496 Ass 423BS/306BG Westover 15/8/42; Thurleigh 8/9/42; f/l Exeter 17/11/42 with BD ex-St Nazaire. Sal. CHENNAULT'S PAPPY.

41-24497 Ass 322BS/91BG [LG-P] Westover 15/8/42; Bassingbourn 30/9/42; MIA {26m} Stuttgart 6/9/43 w/Cox, ditched Channel, all rescued. Possibly MIZPAH II one side and FRISCO JENNIE the other.

41-24498 Ass 369BS/306BG Westover 23/8/42; Thurleigh 30/10/42; MIA Lille 13/1/43 w/Spaulding, coll w/41-24471, cr Lille, 6KIA 4POW.

41-24499 Ass 322BS/91BG [LG-P] Bangor 2/9/42; Bassingbourn 29/9/42; {3m} La Pallice, coll w/41-24453 (91st) 18/11/42, c/l RAF Turweston; sal 26/11/42. FURY.

41-24500 Del Ogden 7/8/42; Scott 15/10/42; Presque Is 19/2/43; ass 535BS/381BG [MS-Y] Ridgewell, Ex. 27/5/43 ANNIE FREEZE; tran CCRC Bovingdon 18/7/43 as trainer; sal 29/11/45 FEA; re-ass 10HB SX Oberpfaffenhofen 30/4/47; Recl Comp, Germany 7/1/49.

41-24501 Ass 368BS/306BG Westover 28/8/42; Thurleigh 2/10/42; MIA St Nazaire 3/1/43 hit by AA, probably cr France.

41-24502 Ass 358BS/303BG Westover 27/8/42; tran

368BS/306BG [BO-E] Thurleigh 26/9/42; c/l BD Sudbourne, UK. AFSC sal 28/7/43.

41-24503 Ass 324BS/91BG [DF-E] Bangor 30/8/42; Bassingbourn 26/9/42; MIA {4m} St Nazaire 23/11/42 w/Jones & Smelser (401st CO), cr Channel, 11KIA. MACR 16162. PANDORA'S BOX.

41-24504 Ass 324BS/91BG [DF-D] Bangor 30/8/42; Bassingbourn 26/9/42; {42m} BAD Burtonwood 15/3/44; retUS for war bond tour. THE SAD SACK.

41-24505 Ass 324BS/91BG [DF-E] Bangor 30/8/42; Bassingbourn 26/9/42; {6m} St Nazaire 22/11/42 BD, in hangar for about a year, constantly raided for spares, before being restored to flying condition, and trans AFSC end of 1943 as trainer; retUS Tinker 14/6/44; RFC Arledge 22/11/44. QUITCHURBITCHIN.

41-24506 Ass 324BS/91BG [DF-G] Bangor 2/9/42; Bassingbourn 26/9/42; c/l Leavesden, UK 23/11/42; 5KIA, 5RTD. Sal. THE SHIFTLESS SKONK.

41-24507 Ass 368BS/306BG [BO-G] Westover 25/8/42; Thurleigh 17/9/42; tran SBA trainer 11/4/43; tran 546BS/384BG [BK-K] Grafton Underwood 23/8/43; tran 545BS [JD-B]; MIA Stuttgart 6/9/43 w/Armstrong; e/a, cr Etrepagny, Fr., 1KIA 6POW 3EVD. MACR 772. YANKEE RAIDER.

41-24508 Ass 423BS/306BG Westover 15/8/42; Thurleigh 5/9/42; f/l Graveley, UK, 27/10/42 on practice flight; sal 5/11/42.

41-24509 Ass 423BS/306BG Westover 15/8/42; MIA St Nazaire 9/11/42 w/Barnett, e/a, ditched Channel, 4KIA 6POW. MACR 16010. MISS SWOOSE.

41-24510 Ass 367BS/306BG Westover 16/8/42; Thurleigh 27/9/42; MIA Lille 9/10/42 w/Olsen, s/d by AA, cr Lille, 6KIA 2EVD 1POW. (first loss of group) MACR 6706. SNOOZY II.

41-24511 Ass 423BS/306BG [RD-W] Westover 15/8/42; Thurleigh 13/10/42; tran 322BS/91BG [LG-W] Bassingbourn 4/3/43; MIA Solingen {22+m} 1/12/43 w/Wennerberg, flak, cr Düsseldorf, 9POW 1KIA. MACR 1323. WHEEL 'N DEAL.

41-24512 Ass 322BS/91BG [LG-N] Bangor 1/9/42; Bassingbourn 29/9/42; MIA {7+m} Hamm 4/3/43 w/Felton, e/a, ditched Zuider Zee, 7K 3POW. ROSE O'DAY.

41-24513 Del Lowry 29/7/42; SAD 31/7/42; Hamilton 30/8/42; ass 5AF Sumac 20/9/42. Con WO 31/10/44.

41-24514 Ass 368BS/306BG Westover 24/8/42; Thurleigh 23/9/42; MIA Rennes 8/3/43 w/Buddenbaum, e/a, cr Colince, Fr, 8POW 1KIA 1EVD. MACR 6088.

41-24515 Ass 324BS/91BG [DF-H] Bangor 2/9/42; Bassingbourn 26/9/42; MIA {14m} Wilhelmshaven 21/5/43 w/Fischer, s/d?, cr Nth Sea, 10K. MACR 3458. JERSEY BOUNCE.

41-24516 Ass 368BS/306BG Westover 24/8/42; ditched Irish Sea en route Thurleigh 5/9/42; WO 31/10/44. MELTING POT.

41-24517 Ass 427BS/303BG [GN-O] Bangor 5/10/42; Molesworth 24/10/42; MIA St Nazaire 3/1/43 w/Gletz,MACR 6141. KALI.

41-24518 Del Lowry 29/7/42; Hamilton 31/8/42; ass 63BS/43BG Hawaii 9/9/42; BAD Mila 10/5/43. THE RECKLESS MOUNTAIN BOYS.

41-24519 Del Wright Fd 28/7/42; Patterson 29/7/42; Wright Mat Com 19/10/42; Tinker 25/4/43; Vandalia (glider testing) 16/8/43.

41-24520 Del Lowry 29/7/42; Hamilton 31/8/42; ass 19BG Sumac 1/9/42; tran 63BS/43BG s/d e/a 11/5/43. THE FIGHTING SWEDE.

41-24521 Del Lowry 29/7/42; Hamilton 31/8/42; ass 19BG Hawaii (possibly JOKERS WILD); tran 63BS/43BG; MIA Boga Boga, New Guinea 11/7/43; (found underwater 1986). BLACK JACK.

41-24522 Del Lowry 29/7/42; Hamilton 31/8/42; ass 5AF Sumac 1/9/42; WO 31/10/44.

41-24523 Ass 323BS/91BG [OR-N] Bangor 13/9/42; Bassingbourn 10/11/42; MIA {19m} Amiens 31/8/43 w/Rodman, coll w/29816, cr Channel, 10KIA. MACR 563. LI'L AUDREY, re-named SNOOKS.

41-24524 Ass 323BS/91BG [OR-O] Bangor 10/9/42; Bassingbourn 11/10/42; MIA {16m} Schweinfurt 17/8/43 w/Acaro, e/a, cr Harheim, Ger. 3KIA 5POW 2EVD. MACR 279. THE EAGLE'S WRATH.

41-24525 Ass 422BS/305BG [JJ-O] Presque Is 14/10/42; Grafton Underwood 25/9/42; tran 547BS/384BG [SO-Y] Grafton Underwood 22/9/43; MIA Ludwigshafen 7/1/44 w/Gamer. MACR 1608 WHAT'S COOKING DOC?

41-24526 Ass 358BS/303BG [VK-J] Bangor 19/9/42; Molesworth 16/10/42; MIA St Nazaire 3/1/43 w/Clark, e/a, cr Bay of Biscay, 10KIA; MACR 7650. LEAPIN' LIZ.

41-24527 Ass 401BS/91BG Bangor 6/9/42; Bassingbourn 1/10/42 GREAT SPECKLED BIRD; {1m} tran 324BS [DF-Y] re-named THE SKY WOLF; MIA {27+m} Schweinfurt 17/8/43 w/Munger, e/a, cr Waldeschaff, Ger. 10POW. MACR 274.

41-24528 Del Cheyenne 2/8/42; Sacramento 1/9/42; ass 5AF Sumac 4/9/42; WO 31/10/44.

41-24529 Ass 422BS/305BG [JJ-T] Syracuse 14/9/42; Grafton Underwood 25/10/42; tran 546BS/384BG Grafton Underwood [BK-E] 22/9/43; b/d Münster 10/10/43 w/?; c/l Eye, UK, sal.

41-24530 Ass 366BS/305BG Syracuse 14/9/42; en route Grafton Underwood, c/t/o Gander, Newfoundland 25/10/42. Sal.

41-24531 Del Cheyenne 2/8/42; Sacramento 1/9/42; ass 11BG Sumac 12/9/42; left 14/7/43; Homstead 14/6/45; (Ref: ditched Baga Is, Vella Lavella, all safe.)

41-24532 Ass 422BS/305BG Presque Is 19/10/42; Grafton Underwood 25/10/42; tran 414BS/97BG Polebrook 4/11/42; Maison Blanche 13/11/42; Tafaraoui. 22/11/42; Biskra 25/12/42; MIA Bizerte 26/12/42 w/Lawrence. A/c damaged by explosion of 41-24413, c/l no man's land, two baled, one rescued by British Army, the other POW. Rest landed with plane, 3WIA, all eventually returning to duty.

41-24533 Ass 365BS/305BG [XK-T] Presque Is 19/10/42; Grafton Underwood 25/10/42; MIA 22/6/43 w/Hall, e/a, cr Valburg, Holl. 4KIA 6POW. MACR 16205. CHERRY.

41-24534 Del Cheyenne 2/8/42; ass 403BS/43BG Hawaii 30/8/42; Mareeba, Aus. 5/9/42; tran 98BS/11BG New Caledonia; MIA 1/12/42 w/Jacobs, coll w/Jap fighter cut a/c in two, cr with TG Hartmann only survivor. OMAR KHAYYAM.

41-24535 Del Cheyenne 2/8/42; Hamilton 11/9/42; ass 5AF Sumac 19/9/42; retUS Hamilton 12/9/43; RFC Walnut Ridge 21/9/45.

41-24536 Del Cheyenne 3/8/42; Hamilton 6/10/42; ass 43BG 5AF Sumac 14/9/42; retUS 16/9/43; RFC Albuquerque 25/6/45.

41-24537 Del Cheyenne 4/8/42; Hamilton 4/10/42; ass 63BS/43BG Hawaii 10/9/42 TALISMAN; MacArthur aboard to watch parachute invasion of Nadzab, PNG 5/9/43; c/l Jackson Fd, Fla. 24/4/43, rep; when W/W used as hack by Maj/Gen Frink, Supply CO of SW Pacific, called USASOS WAR-HORSE. Sal 9/9/45.

41-24538 Del Cheyenne 3/8/42; Hamilton 4/10/42; ass 5AF Sumac 15/9/42; WO 31/10/44.

41-24539 Ass 358BS/303BG [VK-K] Kellogg Fd 15/9/42; Molesworth 16/9/42; CCRC Boving-don 27/3/43; 384BG Grafton Underwood 22/9/43; sal NBD 31/5/45. JERSEY BOUNCE.

41-24540 Del Cheyenne 2/8/42; Sacramento 1/9/42; Hamilton 11/9/42; ass 63BS/43BG 5AF Sumac 14/9/42; Bombed Dobodura, PNG. 18/1/43. Sal.

41-24541 Ass 358BS/303BG [VK-B] Kellogg Fd 14/9/42; Molesworth 16/9/42; MIA St Nazaire 16/2/43 w/Dunnica, e/a, ditched Channel, 6KIA 4POW. MACR 15476. SPOOK.

41-24542 Del Cheyenne 17/8/42; Westover 18/8/42; Syracuse 20/8/42; Rome 14/11/42; New Castle 9/12/42; West Palm Beach 15/1/43; ass 306BG 5/5/43; Patterson 5/8/43; WO Amarillo 24/10/45; Recl Comp 9/4/46.

41-24543 Del Cheyenne 2/8/42; Hamilton 16/9/42; ass 403BS-63BS/43BG Hawaii 18/9/42; MIA 2/7/43. PLUTO.

41-24544 Ass 323BS/91BG [OR-O] Bangor 10/9/42; Bassingbourn 26/10/42; MIA {7+m} Hamm 4/2/43 w/Bobrow, s/d by FW190, cr in Zuider Zee, 8KIA 2POW; MACR 3557 or 4635. PENNSYLVANIA POLKA.

41-24545 Ass 322BS/91BG [LG-T] Bangor 31/8/42; Bassingbourn 11/10/42; {16+m} Burned out on base, internal fire started by cigarette, 23/3/43; First a/c sal in ground accident. (possibly LUFTWAFFE'S WATERLOO or MARNITA) but better known as MOTSIE.

41-24546 Del Cheyenne 2/8/42; Hamilton 11/9/42; ass 403BS/43BG 5AF Sumac 17/9/42; WO 31/10/44.

41-24547 Ass 323BS/91BG [OR-P] Bangor 10/9/42; Bassingbourn 11/10/42; MIA {9+m} St Nazaire 1/5/43 w/Rand (& Major Rosener, 94BG sqd CO), e/a, ditched Channel, 5KIA 5POW. MACR 3573. VERTIGO.

41-24548 Del Cheyenne 3/8/42; Hamilton 4/9/42; ass 43BG Hawaii 14/9/42; tran 375TCG, 5AF; c/l Aitape, New Guinea 5/5/44. Sal.

41-24549 Ass 323BS/91BG [OR-Q] Bangor 10/9/42; Bassingbourn 11/10/42; MIA {14m} Hamm 4/3/43 w/McCarty, flak, cr Münster. 8KIA 2POW. MACR 15596. STUPEN TAKET.

41-24550 Del Lowry 6/8/42; Hamilton 15/9/42; ass 403BS/43BG Sumac 24/9/42; Con accident 18/12/42. Sal.

41-24551 Del Lowry 7/8/42; ass 403BS/43BG Sumac 18/9/42; bombed at base, Milne Bay, NG. 17/1/43. Sal. LISTEN HERE TOJO.

41-24552 Del Lowry 7/8/42; Hamilton 6/10/42; ass 403BS/43BG Sumac 5/11/42; ground accident 16/9/43. Sal.

41-24553 Ass 422BS/305BG Syracuse 16/9/42; Presque Is 19/10/42; Grafton Underwood 25/10/42; MIA Lille 6/12/42 w/Prentice, e/a, cr?; 9KIA 1POW. First group loss.

41-24554 Del Lowry 7/8/42; Hamilton 6/10/42; ass 63BS/43BG Hawaii 17/10/42; retUS Rapid City 2/12/43 (398BG training); RFC Albuquerque 25/6/45. THE MUSTANG.

41-24555 Del Lowry 9/8/42; Denver 12/8/42; Salina 11/11/42; ass 353BS/301BG St Donat 6/3/43; Oudna 6/8/43, Cerignola 7/12/43; Lucera 1/2/44; retUS Dalhart 13/5/44; WO Amarillo 17/12/44; Recl Comp 9/4/46.

41-24556 Del Lowry 9/8/42; Salina 16/11/42; Gore Fd 8/5/43; Ephrata 18/6/43; Kelly 5/1/44; RFC Kingman 7/1/46.

41-24557 Ass 423BS/306BG [RD-T] Denver 12/8/42; Thurleigh 18/11/42; tran 545BS/384BG [JD-O] Grafton Underwood 22/8/43 DAMN YANKEE (also FIREBALL MAIL); MIA Leverkusen 1/12/43 w/Sundlun, e/a, cr Ettingen, Ger. 5KIA 4POW 1EVD.

MACR 1334.

41-24558 Ass 358BS/303BG [VK-F] Bangor 14/10/42; Molesworth 16/10/42; MIA Vegasack 18/3/43 w/Austin (92BG crew), e/a, cr Bremerhafen. 5KIA 5POW. HUNGA-DUNGA.

41-24559 Ass 360BS/303BG [PU-C] Bangor 14/10/42; Molesworth 16/10/42; coll w/42-29573, cr Mears Ashby, UK 31/3/43; 8KIA, sal. OOLD SOLJER.

41-24560 Ass 368BS/306BG [BO-D] New Castle 4/10/42; Thurleigh 26/10/42; tran 369BS [WW-]; tran 544BS/384BG [SU-A] Grafton Underwood 5/9/43; 1 BAD Burtonwood 15/3/44; retUS Homestead 14/6/44; RFC Arledge Fd 23/11/44. LITTLE AUDREY.

41-24561 Ass 359BS/303BG [BN-T] Bangor 10/9/42; Molesworth 16/10/42; {59m} tran 1 BAD Burtonwood 7/7/44; retUS Altus 18/8/44; RFC Altus 14/8/45. (Posthumous MOH for Jack Mathis over Vegasack 18/3/43). THE DUCHESS.

41-24562 Ass 358BS/303BG [VK-A] Bangor 14/10/42; Molesworth 16/10/42; MIA Oschersleben 11/1/44 w/Emerson, cr nr target, 1KIA 9POW. MACR 1925. SKY WOLF.

41-24563 Ass 360BS/303BG Bangor 14/10/42; Molesworth 16/10/42; f/l Luton 11/11/43 hit RAF Anson EF939. Sal. GARBAGE.

41-24564 Ass 365BS/305BG [XK-W] Presque Is 19/10/42; Grafton Underwood 25/10/42; MIA Schweinfurt 17/8/43 w/Mutschler, e/a, cr Averbode, Bel. 3KIA 7POW. MACR 300. PATCHES.

41-24565 Ass 359BS/303BG [BN-P] Bangor 9/10/42; Molesworth 25/10/42 as IDAHO POTATO PEELER. MIA {28m} Gelsenkirchen 5/11/43 w/Grant, flak hit cr Rosenthal, Ger. 1KIA 9POW. MACR 1157.THE RAMBLIN' WRECK.

41-24566 Ass 359BS/303BG [BN-W] Bangor 3/10/42; Molesworth 25/10/42; MIA Romilly 20/12/42 w/Witt, cr Channel. 10KIA; MACR 15708. ZOMBIE.

41-24567 Ass 360BS/303BG [PU-U] Bangor 14/10/42; Molesworth 16/10/42; MIA Lorient 23/1/43 w/Christianson, flak, cr La Chez, Fr. 7KIA 3POW. MACR 15571. BEATS ME.

41-24568 Ass 359BS/303BG [BN-U] Bangor 9/10/42; Molesworth 25/10/42; MIA St Nazaire 23/11/42 w/Miller, e/a, ditched Bay of Biscay. (first group loss). LADY FAIRWEATHER.

41-24569 Ass 427BS/303BG [GN-W] Bangor 5/10/42; Molesworth 22/10/42; MIA Emden 4/2/43 w/Cole, e/a, cr Zwolle, Hol. MACR 15348. MEMPHIS TOT.

41-24570 Ass 323BS/91BG Bangor 10/9/42; Bassingbourn 11/10/42; first mission Abbeville 8/11/42; sal BD 27/11/43.

41-24571 Ass 323BS/91BG Bangor 14/9/42; West Palm Beach 24/11/42; tran MTO 97BG Biskra, Alg. 1/43; 49BS/2BG 14/11/3; Massicault 14/11/43; MIA Steyr, Aus. 24/2/44 w/Meyer, s/d no chutes seen. MACR 2619. INDIANAPOLIS WAR BIRD.

41-24572 Ass 364BS/305BG Presque Is 19/10/42; Grafton Underwood 22/10/42; tran 414BS/97BG Polebrook 4/11/42; Maison Blanche 13/11/42; Tafaraoui 22/11/42; Biskra 25/12/42; Château-du-Rhumel 8/2/43; 346BS/99BG Depienne 24/11/43; {20m}; depot 3/44; retUS Tinker 8/6/44; RFC Walnut Ridge 26/9/45.

41-24573 364BS/305BG [WF-S/N] Bangor 19/10/42; Grafton Underwood 29/10/42; MIA Kiel 19/5/43 w/MacCauley, e/a, ditched Nth Sea, 6KIA 4POW.

41-24574 Del Cheyenne 12/8/42; Hamilton 9/11/42; ass 63BS & 403BG/43BG Hawaii 14/11/42; retUS Rapid City 9/11/42 (398BG training); RFC Altus 30/8/45. TUFFY.

41-24575 Ass 365BS/305BG [XK-S] Presque Is 19/10/42; Grafton Underwood 25/10/42; tran 544BS/384BG [SU-J] Grafton Underwood 19/9/43; b/d Bremen 13/11/43 w/?; cr RAF Wargrave, UK; 9KIA. SUNRISE SERENADER.

41-24576 Ass 365BS/305BG Presque Is 19/10/42; Grafton Underwood 29/10/42; tran 341BS/97BG Polebrook 4/11/42; Maison Blanche 17/11/42; Tafaraoui 22/11/42; Biskra 25/12/42; Château-du-Rhumel 8/2/43; BD Messina 35/5/43, #3 engine fell off, bombardier KIA hit stabilizer baling out, c/l Tunis w/Allbright. Sal. MACR 16525.

41-24577 Ass 358BS/303BG [VK-D] Bangor 14/10/42; Molesworth 16/10/42; retUS Newark 10/2/44 for war bond tour (first a/c to complete 25m in UK). RFC Searcey Fd 7/8/45. HELL'S ANGELS.

41-24578 Ass 3675BS/305BG [XK-R/F] Presque Is 19/10/42; Grafton Underwood 25/10/42; tran 547BS/384BG [SU-U] Grafton Underwood 7/10/43; 1 BAD Burtonwood 15/3/44; retUS Amarillo 21/5/44; WO 28/11/44.(Ref: PROBLEM CHILD). OLD RELIABLE.

41-24579 Ass 360BS/303BG [PU-F] Bangor 14/10/42; Molesworth 16/10/42; cr Lulsgate Bottom, UK. 23/1/43, 1KIA. Sal 30/1/43. THUMPER.

41-24580 Ass 358BS/303BG [VK-C] Bangor 11/10/42; Molesworth 16/10/62; MIA Lorient 23/1/43 w/Byrom, cr Bay of Biscay, 10KIA. MACR 15473. HELL CAT.

41-24581 Ass 359BS/303BG [BN-O] Bangor 4/10/42; Molesworth 21/10/42; c/l Bovingdon 20/12/42. Sal 23/12/42. THE 8 BALL.

41-24582 Ass 358BS/303BG [VK-G] Bangor 11/10/42; Molesworth 16/10/42; MIA Rouen-Sotteville 12/12/42 w/Capt Frost. ONE O'CLOCK JUMP.

41-24583 Ass 379BG New Castle 6/10/42; Bovingdon 6/11/42; damaged on taxi accident w/Hennessy 11/8/43, rep; sal n/b/d 5/5/45.

41-24584 Ass 4127BS/303BG [GN-Q] Bangor 5/10/42; Molesworth 22/10/42; MIA Lorient 23/1/43 w/Kobley. MACR 15571. SUSFU.

41-24585 Ass 360BS/303BG [PU-B] Bangor 14/10/42; Molesworth 16/10/42; MIA Rouen-Sotteville 12/12/42 w/Flickinger, e/a, f/l Leeuwarden, Hol. First B-17 captured by Luftwaffe restored and used for affiliation duties. (WULF HUND) WOLF HOUND.

41-24586 Ass 365BS/305BG [XK-U/A] Presque Is 19/10/42; Grafton Underwood 26/10/42; 1 BAD Burtonwood 20/3/44; retUS Robins 1/8/44; Recl Comp 30/8/45. WHAM BAM.

41-24587 Ass 427BS/303BG [GN-P] Bangor 5/10/42; Molesworth 25/10/42; MIA Oschersleben 11/1/44 w/McClellan, e/a, cr Lienen, Ger, 4KIA 6POW, MACR 1922. BAD CHECK.

41-24588 Ass 364BS/305BG [WF-A] Presque Is 19/10/42; Grafton Underwood 25/10/42; MIA 8/3/43 w/Carter, e/a, cr Channel, 10KIA. MACR 15718. CARTER AND HIS LITTLE PILLS.

41-24589 Ass 323BS/91BG [OR-R] Bangor 15/9/42; wrecked 5/10/42 w/Ellis, while turning plane into take of position, tail wheel ran off runway causing tail section severed from rear bulkhead, rep; Bassingbourn 11/10/42; MIA {6+m} Emden 4/2/43 w/Ellis, e/a, cr Terschelling, Hol. 2KIA 8POW. MACR 15124. Sal Utrecht, Hol. TEXAS BRONCO.

41-24590 Ass 364BS/305BG [WF-B] Presque Is 19/10/43; Grafton Underwood 25/10/42; MIA Kiel 19/5/43 w/Kohler, 7KIA 3POW.

41-24591 Ass 366BS/305BG [KY-B] Presque Is 20/10/42; Grafton Underwood 29/10/42; MIA Stuttgart 6/9/43 w/Halliday, mech failure, cr Dieppe, 1KIA 6POW 3EVD. MACR 1344. RIGOR MORTIS.

41-24592 Ass 366BS/305BG [KY-C/G] Presque Is 19/10/42; Grafton Underwood 25/10/42; MIA Stuttgart 6/9/43 w/MacSpadden, no fuel, f/l Dubendorf, Switz. 10INT. MACR 1345. RetUS 15/9/45 (now Confederate AF as KY-D. MADAME BUTTERFLY.

41-24593 Ass 364BS/305BG [WF-G] Presque Is 19/10/42; Grafton Underwood 25/10/42; MIA Emden 4/2/43 w/Jenkins, flak hit caused mid-air coll., cr Emden, Ger. 5KIA 5POW. EL LOBO.

41-24594 Del Cheyenne 28/8/42; Wayne Co. 12/10/42; Gt Britain 14/11/42; RAF [FA-695] 218/206/519 Sqds; WO 31/7/47.

41-24595 Del Cheyenne 28/11/42; Wayne Co. 28/11/42; Gt Britain 2/2/43; RAF [FA-696] 206/519/251 Sqds. WO 15/2/46.

41-24596 Del Cheyenne 28/8/42; Wayne Co. 22/10/42; Gt Britain 28/10/42; RAF [FA-697] 220Sq, c/l Azores 19/12/43.

Below: B-17F-27-BO 41-24585 was the first aircraft of this block which introduced a strengthened landing gear drag strut. It was also the first of more than a dozen Fortresses captured little damaged by the *Luftwaffe*, repaired and flown for tactical evaluation and clandestine operations.

INDIVIDUAL B-17 HISTORIES

41-24597 Del Cheyenne 28/8/42; Wayne Co. 12/10/42; Gt Britain 14/11/42; RAF [FA-698] 59Sq cr Chivenor 26/3/43.

41-24598 Del Cheyenne 27/8/42; Wayne Co. 12/10/42; Gt Britain 27/11/42; RAF [FA-699] 206/220/519/251 Sqds. WO 29/12/45.

41-24599 Del Cheyenne 28/8/42; Wayne Co. 18/10/42; Gt Britain 11/2/43; RAF [FA-700] 206/220/519/251 Sqds. WO 22/12/45. (Ref: ass 303BG 11/2/43, FTR 29/5/43 or mid-air coll w/42-29573).

41-24600 Boeing 26/8/42; Cheyenne 29/11/42; Gt Falls 5/12/42; Geiger 12/4/43; Ephrata 24/3/43; Spokane 15/7/43; Ephrata 18/8/43. Recl Comp 9/2/45.

41-24601 Ass 365BS/305BG [XK-P] Presque Is 19/10/42; Grafton Underwood 25/10/42; MIA Lille 13/1/43 w/Hilbinger, e/a, cr LIlle, Fr. 10KIA. MACR 15639.

41-24602 Ass 360BS/303BG [PU-A] Bangor 14/10/42; Molesworth 16/10/42; MIA {25m} Nancy 25/5/44 w/Trojan, e/a, cr Provine, Fr. 2KIA 8POW. YARDBIRD. (II).

41-24603 Ass 359BS/303BG [BN-Y] Bangor 9/10/42; Molesworth 22/10/42; MIA Lorient 23/1/43 w/Sanderson. YEHUNDIE.

41-24604 Ass 366BS/305BG [KY-D] Presque Is 19/10/42; Grafton Underwood 25/10/42; MIA Wilhelmshaven 26/2/43 w/Tribbett, e/a, cr Tossens, Ger, 12KIA. MACR 15443. ARKIE.

41-24605 Ass 359BS/303BG [BN-R] Bangor 22/9/42; Molesworth 22/10/42; 1 BAD Burtonwood 5/6/44; RFC Searcey Rd, 19/7/45. First a/c to complete 50, then 75 missions. KNOCK-OUT DROPPER.

41-24606 Ass 358BG/303BG [VK-H] Bangor 14/9/42; Molesworth 16/10/42; {5m} c/l Dawlish, UK 13/1/43; sal 23/1/43; tran 401BS/91BG [LL-G] Bassingbourn 22/4/43; no missions 3 AAD Langford Lodge 11/6/43; 2 SAD Lt Staughton 14/6/43; CCRC Bovingdon; sal n/b/d 18/6/45. WEREWOLF.

41-24607 Ass 427BS/303BG [GN-W] Bangor 24/9/42; Molesworth 25/10/42; MIA 23/1/43 w/Byron, hit by AA, ditched Bay of Biscay.MACR 15473. JERRY JINX.

41-24608 Ass 359BS/303BG [BN-S] Bangor 3/10/42; Molesworth 12/10/42 (first to land); MIA 3/1/43; w/Saunders, e/a, ditched Bay of Biscay. GREEN HORNET.

41-24609 Ass 359BS/303BG [BN-Q] Bangor 3/10/42; Molesworth 22/10/42; MIA Paris 4/4/43 w/Eyster, e/a, Cr Rouen, Fr. 6KIA 4POW; MACR 15069. HOLY MACKEREL!

41-24610 Ass 427BS/303BG [GN-T] Bangor 5/10/42; Molesworth 25/10/42; MIA St Nazaire 1/5/43 w/Walsh, hit AA, cr St Nazaire. 7KIA 3POW. MACR 15727. JOE BTFSPLK.

41-24611 Ass 422BS/305BG [JJ-W] Presque Is 19/10/42; Grafton Underwood 25/10/42; flew Gen Eaker to Casablanca 15/1/43; MIA St Nazaire 16/2/43 w/Steenbarger, e/a, cr Malestroit, Fr. 1KIA 8POW 1EVD. MACR 16236. BOOMERANG.

41-24612 Ass 427BS/303BG [GN-R] Bangor 25/9/42; Molesworth 26/10/42; trans AFSC 25/5/43 for special gun tests; 1 CCRC Bovingdon /43; retUS 20/12/44; RFC Altus 9/11/45.

41-24613 Direct from Boeing to Moffatt 28/8/42 NACA (National Advisory Committee for Aeronautics); designated XB-17F for aerodynamic and performance testing; ASF (WO?) 4/5/46.

41-24614 Ass 364BS/305BG [JJ-R/A] Bangor 10/9/42; Grafton Underwood 25/10/42; tran 1 BAD Burtonwood 4/5/45; retUS La Junta 14/6/44; RFC Searcey Fd, 31/7/45. "WE THE PEOPLE".

41-24615 Ass 422BS/305BG [JJ-P/F] Presque Is 19/10/42; Grafton Underwood 25/10/42; tran 1 BAD Burtonwood 22/3/44; retUS Sheppard 2/5/44; RFC Walnut Ridge 25/10/45. TARGET FOR TONITE.

41-24616 Ass 422BS/305BG [JJ-U/K] Presque Is 19/10/42; Grafton Underwood 25/10/42; tran 2 SAD Warton 3/12/43; 1 BAD Burtonwood 21/3/44; retUS Keesler 4/5/44; RFC Stillwater 24/9/45. SAM'S LITTLE HELPER.

41-24617 Ass 364BS/305BG [WF-J] Presque Is 19/10/42; Grafton Underwood 25/10/42; cr Wickham Bishops, Ex. ex-Rotterdam 31/3/43; sal n/b/d 1/4/43. SOUTHERN COMFORT.

41-24618 Del Tulsa 30/8/42; New Castle 4/10/42; Syracuse 6/10/42; ass 352BS/301BG Chelveston 11/42; Tafaraoui 26/11/42; {60m} tran 49BS/2BG Massicault 14/11/43; Bizerte 2/12/43; Amendola, It. 9/12/43; MIA Steyr, Aus. 24/2/44 w/Durney, e/a, cr Kranj. MACR 2614. LIL JO.

41-24619 Ass 427BS/303BG [GN-S] Bangor 5/10/42; Molesworth 25/10/42; MIA Oschersleben 11/1/44 w/Simmons, e/a, cr Braunlage, Ger. 10POW. MACR 1923. S FOR SUGAR.

41-24620 Ass 360BS/303BG [PU-D] Bangor 14/9/42; Molesworth 16/10/42; MIA St Nazaire 3/1/43 w/Adams, hit flak, cr St Nazaire 7KIA 2POW 2EVD. MACR 15464. SNAP! CRACKLE! POP!

41-24621 Del Geiger 1/9/42; Blythe 11/12/42; Tinker 4/2/43; Wendover 26/2/43; Sioux City 25/4/43; Casper 4/5/43; McLelland 2/6/43; Tinker 12/7/43; Oklahoma City 2/8/43; Alexandria 8/8/43; WO 11/9/43.

41-24622 Del Geiger 1/9/42; Walla Walla 17/11/42; Blythe 9/12/42; Tinker 6/2/43; Glasgow 27/4/43; Gore 28/5/43; Moses Lake 10/6/43; WO 24/6/44. Recl Comp 9/12/46.

41-24623 Ass 365BS/305BG [XK-V] Presque Is 19/10/42; Grafton Underwood 25/10/42; MIA Wilhelmshaven 26/2/43 w/Stallman, flak, ditched Nth Sea, 5KIA 5POW.

41-24624 Ass 366BS/305BG [KY-J] Presque Is 22/9/42; Grafton Underwood 29/10/42; tran 422BS [JJ-J]; MIA Kiel 19/5/43 w/Clark, flak, ditched Nth Sea, 3KIA 7POW. MACR 15549.

41-24625 Del Geiger 1/9/42; Minneapolis 17/11/42; Boise 20/12/42; Biggs 31/1/43; Geiger 17/3/43; WO 15/10/43.

41-24626 Del Geiger 1/9/42; Casper 31/1/43; WO 18/12/42.

41-24627 Del Geiger 1/9/42; cr 10/9/42 on field; WO by 345 Sub Dep. Walla Walla 25/3/43.

41-24628 Del Cheyenne 1/9/42; Wayne Co. 2/11/42; West Palm Beach 15/12/42; ass Blot 12AF 12/1/43; WO 8/7/44.

41-24629 Ass 369BS/306BG [WW-O] Cheyenne 13/9/42; Thurleigh 23/1/43; tran 358BS/303BG Molesworth [VK-G] 25/9/43; MIA Duren 20/10/43 w/Hendry, e/a, cr St Nazaire, 7KIA 2POW 2EVD. MACR 1032.

41-24630 Del Geiger 21/9/42; Blyth 11/12/42; WO 27/1/43.

41-24631 Del Geiger 1/9/42; Walla Walla 3/1/43; Tinker 15/4/43; South Plains 4/5/43; cr 10/5/43 en route Glasgow, Mon. no fuel in stormy conditions w/Bashinger; did not burn and five passengers baled OK. WO 13/5/43.

41-24632 Del Geiger 2/9/42; Ephrata 6/10/42; Blythe 9/12/42; Tucson 17/1/43; Tinker 1/2/43; Rapid City 27/4/43; Moses Lake 2/8/43; WO 5/2/44.

41-24633 Del Geiger 2/9/42; Casper 29/10/42; Scotts Bluff 19/2/43; Casper 12/5/43; Sioux City 22/6/43; Kearney 3/8/43; RFC Walnut Ridge 26/9/45.

41-24634 Del Geiger 2/9/42; New Castle 13/11/42; Ephrata 2/12/42; Gt Falls 28/1/43; Pendleton 25/7/43; Geiger 8/8/43; RFC Altus 30/7/45.

41-24635 Ass 359BS/303BG [BN-O] New Castle 6/10/42; Molesworth 21/11/42; 1 BAD Burton- wood 7/4/44; retUS Patterson 6/7/44; RFC Albuquerque 2/8/45. (The 8 BALL MK III). EIGHT BALL.

41-24636 Del Geiger 3/9/42; Casper 29/10/42; Walla Walla 24/11/42; Ephrata 3/12/42; Tinker 3/2/43; Rapid City 13/4/43; Geiger 10/5/43; RFC Ontario 14/6/45.

41-24637 Ass 366BS/305BG [KY-F] New Castle 11/10/42; Grafton Underwood 24/10/42; MIA Wilhelmshaven 27/1/43 w/Beckham, e/a, cr Wilhelmshaven. 5KIA 5POW. MACR 15501.

41-24638 Del Geiger 3/9/42; Blythe 9/12/42; WO 24/2/43.

41-24639 Del Cheyenne 9/9/42; Boise 16/9/42; wrecked on landing with broken crankshaft, rep; Cheyenne 11/10/42; ass 323BS/91BG [OR-W] Bassingbourn 29/1/43; 2 SAD Lt Staughton 8/3/44; tran 7/5/44 {50+m} AFSC for Aphrodite operations; l/Mimoyecques 4/8/44. THE CAREFUL VIRGIN.

B-17F-DL

42-2964 Del Wright Fd, for test purposes 7/1/42, cr Frostburg, nr Cumberland, Md 21/11/43, crew baled OK. Caused by poor weather and shortage of gas.

42-2965 Del Wright Fd 20/7/42; landing accident Walla Walla, 5/8/42, rep; WO 9/9/44.

42-2966 Ass 427BS/303BG [GN-U] Bangor 16/9/42; Molesworth 28/10/42; 1 CCRC Bovingdon 4/7/43 as trainer.

42-2967 Ass 360BS/303BG [PU-G] Bangor 18/9/42; Molesworth 16/10/42; MIA St Nazaire 16/2/43 w/Breed, hit by AA, ditched Channel, 9KIA 1POW. MACR 15116. SHACK HACK.

42-2968 Del West Palm Beach 1/12/42; ass 342BS/97BG Tafaraoui 17/2/43; Biskra 25/12/42; Château-du-Rhumel 8/2/43; MIA Trapani 13/4/43 w/Blair.

42-2969 Ass 366BS/305BG Syracuse 17/9/42; Grafton Underwood 29/10/42; tran 341BS/97BG Polebrook 4/11/42; en route Maison Blanche 17/11/42, engine fire, a/c cr Bay of Biscay; all killed, inc Brig Gen Asa N. Duncan. MACR 15097.

42-2970 Ass 324BS/91BG [DF-E/C] New Castle 13/10/42; Bassingbourn 23/11/42; On return from Stuttgart {38m} 6/9/43 c/l Pett Level, Hastings, UK; crew OK, a/c sal. Completed 25m 17/5/43 and contender with Memphis Belle, Jersey Bounce and Delta Rebel II, for US war bond tour. CONNECTICUT YANKEE.

42-2971 MAD 20/8/42; New Castle 10/10/42; ass Wildflower (8AF) 30/10/42. RFC Arledge.

42-2972 Del Tulsa 23/8/42; Amarillo WO 17/12/44.

42-2973 Ass 360BS/303BG [PU-K] Presque Is 27/11/42; Molesworth 13/12/42; retUS 2/7/44; RFC Arledge 22/11/44. IZA VAILABLE.

42-2974 Del Geiger 2/9/42; Ephrata 31/1/43; Gt Falls 22/2/43; Dalhart 7/8/43; 4100 BU Patterson 21/8/43; 330 BU Dyersburg 1/3/44; 327 BU Drew 14/5/44; RFC Albuquerque 5/9/45.

42-2975 Ass 423BS/306BG Presque Is 17/11/42; Molesworth 25/11/42; MIA Lorient 30/12/42 w/Brady, e/a, e/a; cr Bay of Biscay, 10KIA.

42-2976 Del Tulsa 8/42; Lockbourn 18/10/42; 21 T/T Sq Felts Fd 29/10/42; Salina 16/12/42; Gowen 31/3/43; Sioux City 11/6/43; Geiger 13/7/43; 327 BU Drew 20/4/44; RFC Altus 1/8/45.

42-2977 Del Tulsa 11/9/42; 351 SD Pyote 10/10/42;

Grand Is 21/8/42; Wayne 5/11/42; Patterson 20/11/42; Wayne 16/12/42; 233 BU Davis Monthan 1/2/43; Romulus 1/3/43; New Castle 5/5/43; Smyrna 5/6/43; Roswell 11/6/43; 327 BU Drew 21/6/43; Hobbs 7/7/43; Kingman 13/1/45.

42-2978 Ass 369BS/303BG [WW-M] Wayne 2/11/42; Molesworth 7/2/43; tran 534BS/381BG Ridgewell, Ex. later 535BS [MS-V] 19/11/43; {5m} RetUS 1/5/44; Recl Comp 3/9/46. SIS.

42-2979 Ass 97BG Salina 29/11/42; tran Biskra 21/1/43; Château-du-Rhumel 8/2/43; Pont-du-Fahs, Tun. 1/8/43; Depienne 15/8/43; tran 49BS/2BG Massicault 14/11/43; Bizerte 2/12/43; Amendola 9/12/43; tran 346BS/99BG Tortorella 28/3/44; {1m} tran 815BS/483BG Tortorella 31/3/44; MIA Nis, Yugo 16/4/44 w/Warburton, flak, 4KIA. MACR 3908.

42-2980 Ass 352BS/301BG Salina 9/12/42; Biskra 22/12/42; Ain M'Lila 17/1/43; St Donat 6/3/43; Oudna, 6/8/43; {46m} tran 416BS/99BG Oudna 14/11/43; Tortorella 11/12/43; {19m} to depot 4/44; sal 29/6/44. SADIE HAWKINS.

42-2981 Del West Palm Beach 22/1/43; ass 414BS/97BG Château-du-Rhumel 30/1/43; Pont-du-Fahs, Tun. 1/8/43; Depienne 15/8/43; tran 348BS/99BG Oudna 14/11/43; Tortorella 11/12/43; {15m} WO 1/5/44, rep 30/9/44; sal 8/5/45. SNOOZIN' SUSAN.

42-2982 Del West Palm Beach 7/1/43; ass 342BS/97BG Château-du-Rhumel 3/43; Pont-du-Fahs 1/8/43; Depienne 15/9/43; Cerignola 20/12/43; Amendola 16/1/44; MIA 17/4/44. MACR 3684.

42-2983 Del Tulsa 8/1/43; Pyote 20/1/43; Pueblo 9/4/43; Geiger 8/5/43; Moses Lake 17/7/43; Williams 29/3/44; Albuquerque 10/8/44; RFC Kingman /45.

42-2984 Del Tulsa 20/10/42; New Castle 25/11/42; FAD 10/1/43 convert to F-9; Colorado Springs 6/4/43; Boise 23/4/43; Patterson 4/7/43; Tinker 9/6/43; Clovis 19/4/44; Lubbock 25/5/44; RFC Kingman 20/11/45.

42-2985 Del W Palm Beach 8/1/43; ass 414BS/97BG Biskra 28/1/43; Château-du-Rhumel 8/2/43; MIA Naples 1/8/43 w/Rast, flak, cr target. MACR 355.

42-2986 Del Tulsa 21/10/42; Sioux City 24/11/42; Gowen 30/4/43; Wendover 5/5/43; Casper 9/6/43; Smoky Hill 14/6/43; Sioux City 15/7/43; Tinker 5/8/43; Patterson 30/1/44; Lockburn 28/9/44; RFC Walnut Ridge 15/10/45.

42-2987 Del Tulsa 25/10/42; Boise 29/11/42; WO 14/4/43.

42-2988 Del Tulsa 29/10/42; Boise 17/11/42; Salina 3/1/43; Walla Walla 21/3/43; Madras, Or. 18/6/43; Ephrata 9/8/43; Gt Bend 26/8/43; Tinker 6/1/44; Patterson 14/2/44; RFC Altus 11/9/45.

42-2989 Del Geiger 4/11/42; Rapid City 30/12/42; Gore Fd 5/3/43; Sioux Falls 9/5/43; Moses Lake 6/6/43; San Marco 14/5/44; Recl Comp 13/2/46.

42-2990 Ass 322BS/91BG [LG-R] West Palm Beach 14/12/42; Bassingbourn 10/1/43; MIA {11+m} Schweinfurt 17/8/43 w/Hargis, e/a, cr Wannebecq, Bel, 4EVD, 2KIA, 4POW. MACR 277. DAME SATAN.

42-2991 Ass 95BG Geiger 1/12/42; Rapid City 17/12/42; c/l Pierre 24/12/42 w/Walker, rep; WO 26/8/43.

42-2992 Del Long Beach 10/11/42; Tulsa 20/12/42; Smyrna 23/1/43; Hobbs 3/2/43; Pueblo 6/4/43; Hobbs 25/4/43; Las Vegas 12/6/43; Roswell 23/9/43; Williams 9/12/43; La Junta 1/4/44; RFC Searcey Fd 31/7/45.

42-2993 Del Long Beach 10/11/42; Pueblo 27/1/43; Biggs 4/3/43; Blythe 14/6/43; Walla Walla 15/5/43; Redmond 15/6/43; Walla Walla 18/7/43; Ephrata 9/8/43; Pinecastle 10/6/44; McCook 18/6/44; Biggs 22/7/44; Syracuse 9/4/45; RFC Walnut Ridge 10/10/45.

42-2994 Ass 30BS/19BG Pyote 6/1/43; Syracuse 9/4/44; RFC Altus 7/1/46.

42-2995 Del Gowen 12/3/43; Pyote 27/7/43; Walker 11/6/443; Dalhart 19/9/44; WO 17/10/44. Recl Comp 7/6/46.

42-2996 Del Long Beach 12/11/42; Tulsa 24/12/42; Pueblo 27/1/43; Amarillo 8/2/43; Orlando 4/4/43; Geiger 2/5/43; Ephrata 1/8/43; RFC Walnut Ridge 14/2/46.

42-2997 Del Long Beach 11/11/42; Pueblo 27/1/43; Biggs 24/2/43; Blythe 15/4/43; Moses Lake 5/5/43; Robbins 26/7/43; Patterson 27/2/44; Drew 4/5/44; RFC Altus 29/2/46.

42-2998 Del Tulsa 30/12/42; Wendover 27/1/43; Sioux City 6/4/43; Casper 14/5/43; Moses Lake 8/6/43; cr 30 miles SW base, disintegrated in mid air. Pilot Lt Dranan and seven passengers all killed. Cause unknown.

42-2999 Del Tulsa 31/12/42; Pyote 26/1/43; Alexandria 11/7/43; Clovis 24/6/44; Tinker 28/8/44; Jackson 3/2/45; RFC Albuquerque 24/10/45.

42-3000 Del Long Beach 16/11/42; Tulsa 9/1/43; Pueblo 9/4/43; Geiger 25/5/43; Gt Falls 7/6/43; Gore 1/7/43; Rapid City 26/7/43; Fairport 29/6/44; Selfridge 26/8/44; Biggs 1/11/44; Jackson 24/2/45; Sioux City 29/8/45; RFC Altus 17/9/45.

42-3001 Del Long Beach 17/11/42; Tulsa 8/1/43 (962nd Bomb Trng Gp); Duncan Fd 12/2/43; Love Fd 30/3/43; c/l Kelly Fd, Tx, 1/4/43 w/Wiper, rep; Hobbs 15/5/43; Tinker 21/6/43; Hobbs 29/7/44.

42-3002 Del Pocatello 31/12/42; ass 359BS/303BG [BN-Z] Morrison 5/3/43; Molesworth 8/4/43; MIA 6/9/43 w/Hullar, no gas, ditched Nth Sea, all rescued. THE OLD SQUAW.

42-3003 Del Pocatello 30/12/42; Pyote 22/3/43; Harvard 11/6/43; Patterson 30/8/43; Eglin 16/2/44; RFC Walnut Ridge 19/12/45.

42-3004 Del Tulsa 3/12/42; Ainsworth 21/1/43; Pierre 9/2/43; Rapid City 28/4/43; Pendleton 8/7/43; WO 16/7/43.

42-3005 Del Tulsa 8/12/42; Biggs 19/1/43; damaged in landing w/Stewart 22/1/43, rep; Pueblo 27/3/43; Blythe 13/4/43; McClellan 16/5/43; Ephrata 19/6/43; Sioux City 24/6/43; WO 19/8/44; Recl Comp 3/1/46.

42-3006 Del Long Beach 23/11/42; Tulsa 15/12/42; Wendover 30/1/43; Sioux City 7/4/43; Smoky Hill 6/8/43; Alamogordo 2/8/44; Kelly 4/11/44.

42-3007 Del Long Beach 25/11/42; Tulsa 3/12/42; Ainsworth, Neb. 20/1/43; Rapid City 10/4/43; Geiger 22/6/43; Harvard 16/9/44; Davis-Monthan 21/10/44; Peterson 7/7/43; Lincoln 23/1/45; RFC Altus 9/10/45.

42-3008 Del Tulsa 3/12/42; Pocatello 31/12/42; Tinker 4/2/43; Pyote 10/2/43; Tinker 5/8/43; Dalhart 7/10/43; Dyersburg 14/2/44; WO 15/7/44.

42-3009 Del Long Beach 22/1/43; Blythe 23/1/43; Pueblo 14/4/43; Dyersburg 11/6/43; Dow Fd, Me. 15/6/43; Dyersburg 7/9/43; Gd Isle 26/6/44; Alliance 20/10/44; Souix City 22/1/45; RFC Albuquerque 25/6/45.

42-3010 Del Pyote 30/12/42; Biggs 9/2/43; Dalhart 18/3/43; Tinker 27/3/43; Dalhart 20/4/43; Tinker 7/8/43; Dalhart 19/9/43; Eglin 3/3/45; Pueblo 26/4/45; RFC Kingman 27/10/45.

42-3011 Del Tulsa 7/12/42; Salina 2/1/43; Tinker 17/4/43; Morrison 8/5/43; Topeka 2/6/43; Gd Island 29/7/43; McCook 30/6/44; WO 20/10/44.

42-3012 Del Pueblo 27/1/43; Gore 5/5/43; Ephrata 9/6/43; Orlando 3/7/43; Brooksville 1/8/43; Smoky Hill 2/7/44; Fairport 20/2/45; RFC Albuquerque 25/6/45.

42-3013 Del Tulsa 7/12/42; Del Monte 31/1/43; Sioux City 6/4/43; Gowen 19/4/43; WO 5/5/43.

42-3014 Del Cheyenne 8/12/42; Pyote 7/1/43; c/l 19/4/43 w/Thompson, loss of power. WO 27/4/43.

42-3015 Del Pocatello 27/12/42; Pyote 6/1/43; Pueblo 20/3/43; Ephrata 30/4/43; Gore Fd, 23/5/43; Walker 30/6/44; Alexandria 19/1/45; RFC Albuquerque 31/5/45.

42-3016 Del Pocatello 24/12/42; Pyote 22/1/43; Pratt 14/6/43; Dalhart 9/7/44; Memphis 2/12/44; Lincoln 6/1/45; 30BS/19BG Pyote 18/3/45; Mines 24/5/45; RFC Kingman 31/10/45.

42-3017 Del Blythe 26/1/43; Gulfport 16/3/43; McClellan 16/5/43; Ephrata 12/6/43; Biggs 29/7/44; WO 5/12/44.

42-3018 Ass 347BS/99BG Morrison 2/2/43 RED ASS; Navarin 23/2/43; Oudna 4/8/43; Tortorella 11/12/43; cargo/weather ac 9/44; retUS Bush Fd 18/5/45. SAD SACK.

42-3019 Del Pyote 26/1/43; Pueblo 10/4/43; Geiger 11/5/43; Ephrata 1/7/43; Alexandria 17/1/44; RFC Altus 19/9/44.

42-3020 Del Pyote 27/1/43; Love Fd 31/1/43; Ephrata 30/4/43; Geiger 13/5/43; Pratt 18/7/43; Smoky Hill 17/6/43; RFC Altus 30/1/46.

42-3021 Del Blythe 25/1/43; Geiger 29/3/43; Amarillo 17/11/44; Recl Comp 7/6/46.

42-3022 Del Pyote 26/1/43; Pueblo 6/4/43; Alamogordo 26/4/43; Pyote 15/5/43; WO 16/6/43.

42-3023 Ass 335BS/95BG [OE-V] Presque Is 18/5/43; Framlingham 12/5/43; tran 525BS/379BG Kimbolton 8/6/43; MIA Wangerooge Is, 25/6/43 w/Simones, e/a, cr Brahe; 5KIA 5POW; MACR 1365. BOOZENESS.

42-3024 Ass 544BS/384BG [SU-K] Morrison 13/3/43; Grafton Underwood 25/5/43; MIA Hamburg 25/7/43 w/Ward; flak, cr Hamburg, 7KIA 3POW. ROYAL FLUSH.

42-3025 Del Denver 15/1/43; Blythe 19/5/43; Gulfport, La. 8/8/43; Dalhart 17/9/43; WO 12/6/44; Recl Comp 16/12/44.

42-3026 Ass 346BS/99BG Morrison 21/4/43; Navarin 26/4/43; tran 483BG Tortorella 31/3/44; retUS Tinker 2/4/45; RFC Walnut Ridge 7/1/46. ROGER THE LODGER.

42-3027 Del Tulsa 17/1/43; Cheyenne 31/1/43; Salina 6/2/43; ass 12AF 4/3/43; Interned.

42-3028 Del Tulsa 11/1/43; Smyrna 1/2/43; Lincoln 21/4/43; Hobbs 7/5/43; Dow 30/5/43; Hobbs 11/6/43; Kelly 2/1/44; Stinson 21/3/44; Recl Comp 3/1/46.

42-3029 Del Tulsa 13/1/43; ass 358BS/303BG [VK-N] Homestead 5/3/43; Molesworth 8/4/43; MIA 14/1/44 w/Hungerford, flak, cr St Valery, Fr. 11POW. MACR 1965. WALLAROO.

42-3030 Del Cheyenne 18/1/43; Salina 2/2/43; Memphis 19/2/43; Glen 4/3/43. Con Invn 8/7/44.

42-3031 Del Cheyenne 20/1/43; ass 324BS/91BG [DF-F] Bassingbourn 19/4/43; MIA Hamburg 26/7/43 w/Randall, flak, cr Rottenburg, Ger. 4KIA 6POW; MACR 201. NITEMARE.

42-3032 Del Cheyenne 13/1/43; Salina 2/2/43; ass 20BS/2BG Morrison 3/3/43; Navarin, Alg. 4/43; Château-du-Rhumel 27/4/43; Ain M'Lila 17/6/43; Massicault 9/12/43; Bizerte 2/12/43; Amendola 9/12/43; tran 840BS/483BG Tortorella 31/3/44; RFC Walnut Ridge 14/12/45.

42-3033 Del Denver 26/1/43; ass 94BG Bury St Edmunds 26/6/43; tran 533BS/381BG [VP-U] Ridgewell, Ex. 7/43; {4+m} CCRC Bovingdon 9/1/44; retUS Grenier 25/12/44; RFC Bush Fd 24/6/45.

42-3034 Del Denver 26/1/43; ass 368BS/306BG Homestead 5/3/43; Thurleigh 12/3/43; MIA Bremen 17/4/43 w/Smiley, e/a, cr Channel; 10KIA. MACR 15518.

42-3035 Del Cheyenne 23/1/43; Gowen 13/2/43; Wendover 14/4/43; Rapid City 2/6/43; Ephrata 31/7/43; Recl Comp 9/2/45.

42-3036 Del Cheyenne 234/1/43; Gowen 13/2/43; Tinker 5/6/43; Dyersburg 17/7/43; WO 8/3/44.

42-3037 Del Cheyenne 25/1/43; ass 412BS/95BG Memphis 20/4/43; tran 366BS/305BG [KY-N] Grafton Underwood 1/8/43; 544BS/384BG [SU-Z] Grafton Underwood 20/9/43; c/l Corby, UK 12/10/43, sal. WINDY CITY AVENGER.

42-3038 Del Cheyenne 23/12/42; 4160 BU Albuquerque 3/2/43; RFC Albuquerque 3/8/45.

42-3039 Del Cheyenne 2/1/43; Gt Falls 14/2/43 (extn bomb racks fitted); Wendover 21/7/43; Pocatello 11/8/43; RFC Ontario 11/6/45.

42-3040 Del Denver 23/1/43; 303BG Molesworth 11/4/43; tran 369BS/306BG [WW-U] Thurleigh 17/7/43; tran 323BS/91BG [OR-Q] Bassingbourn 23/8/43 MISS OUACHITA; MIA {18m} Gutersloh 22/2/44 w/Osterberg, e/a, (Maj Heinz Baer), c/l Bexten, 2KIA 8POW. MACR 2457.

42-3041 Del Denver 23/1/43; Homestead 25/2/43; ass 303BG Molesworth 9/4/43; 369BS/306BG [WW-U] Thurleigh; 544BS/384BG [SU-H] Grafton Underwood; MIA Stuttgart 6/9/43 w/McMahon, no gas, cr Compeigne, Fr. 9POW 1EVD. MACR 772.

42-3042 Del Cheyenne 16/2/43; ass 337BS/96BG Andrews Fd, UK 24/4/43; MIA Emden 21/5/43 w/McMath, ditched Channel 7KIA 3POW; MACR 3984.

42-3043 Del Denver 29/1/43; ass 401BS/91BG [LL-B] Bassingbourn 22/4/43; MIA {16m} Schweinfurt 17/8/43 w/Lockhart, ditched Nth Sea, all rescued. HITLER'S GREMLIN.

42-3044 Del Denver 28/1/43; Memphis 9/3/43; ass 32BS/301BG St Donat 12/4/43; sal 30/4/44.

42-3045 Del Denver 1/2/43; Salina 20/2/43; Morrison 18/3/43; ass 978BG 17/4/43; Con Cr Duko 20/9/43.

42-3046 Del Cheyenne 1/2/43; ass 335BS/95BG [OE-V] Gulfport 7/4/43; Alconbury 15/4/43; tran 510BS/351BG [TU-X] Polebrook 17/6/43; c/l Woodbridge ELG, UK ex-Kassel 30/7/43 {6m}; sal. OLD JACKSON, THE FRISCO KID.

42-3047 Del Cheyenne 31/1/43; Gt Falls 18/2/43; Walla Walla 5/4/43; McChord 8/7/43; Peterson 30/7/43; Moses Lake 10/8/43; WO 22/11/44.

42-3048 Del Cheyenne 18/1/43; ass 366BS/305BG [KY-A] Morrison 5/3/43; Chelveston 26/4/43; tran 533BS/381BG [VP-U] Ridgewell 22/8/43; tran 524BS/379BG Kimbolton 26/8/43; {24m} RetUS Tinker 6/6/44; Patterson 15/2/45; RFC Altus 4/9/45.

42-3049 Del Tulsa 14/1/43; ass 422BS/305BG [JJ-W] New Castle 17/3/43; Chelveston 25/3/43; MIA Villacoublay 14/7/43 w/Perkins, e/a, cr Lieuesant, Fr. 7KIA 4POW; MACR 64. WINDY CITY CHALLENGER.

42-3050 Del Cheyenne 18/1/43; Salina 5/2/43; Morrison 10/3/43 Oklahoma City 8/4/43; WO 16/5/43.

42-3051 Del Cheyenne 18/1/43; ass 366BS/305BG [KY-M] Morrison 5/3/43; Chelveston 31/5/43; tran 546BS/384BG [BK-C] Grafton Underwood 19/9/43; retUS Tinker 8/7/44; RFC Altus 22/8/45. HELL'S ANGELS.

42-3052 Del Cheyenne 21/1/43; Salina 11/2/43; WO 20/9/43.

42-3053 Del Cheyenne 19/1/43; ass 324BS/91BG [DF-Z] Morrison 5/3/43; Bassingbourn 25/3/43; MIA Wilhelmshaven 21/5/43 w/Koll, e/a, cr nr target. 8KIA 2POW. MACR 4438. DESPERATE JOURNEY.

42-3054 Del Denver 17/1/43; Gore 31/3/43; Lewiston 14/4; Ephrata 29/6/43; Dyersburg 2/7/43; Felts Fd 15/8/43; RFC Ontario 22/5/45.

42-3055 Del Denver 19/1/43; Homestead 19/6/43; ass 97BG Cerignola 20/12/43; Amendola 16/1/44; trans 483BG Sterparone 7/45; sal 30/11/45.

42-3056 Del Denver 18/1/43; ass 527BS/379BG [FO-R] Presque Is 29/4/43; Kimbolton 26/6/43; MIA Anklam 14/10/43 w/Zack, e/a, cr Schweinfurt, 10KIA. MACR 955.

42-3057 Del Cheyenne 18/1/43; Nashville 27/2/43; ass 324BS/91BG [LG-N] 21/3/43; Bassingbourn 26/3/43; MIA Oschersleben {38+m} 11/1/44 w/Murdoch, cr Hornhausen, 2KIA 8POW, MACR 1918. PICADILLY COMMANDO later BLONDE BOMBER.

42-3058 Del Cheyenne 18/1/43; Morrison 23/2/43; ass 348BS/99BG Glen 9/3/43; Navarin 4/4/43; Oudna 4/8/43; Tortorella 11/12/43; b/d 18/12/43 by bombs from 347BS ship, c/l Naples; rep, ass ATC Europe as RB-17 30/4/47; sal 28/11/47.

42-3059 Del Cheyenne 28/1/43; Hobbs 30/3/43; Smoky Hill 3/6/43; Las Vegas 18/6/43; Roswell 23/9/43; Williams 9/12/43; Carlsbad 4/1/44; San Marco 27/9/44; RFC Kingman 20/12/45.

42-3060 Del Tulsa 14/1/43; 548BS/385BG Dow Fd 15/4/43; Gt Ashfield 26/6/43; tran 401BS/91BG [LL-G] Bassingbourn 3/9/43; MIA {4m} Solingen 1/12/43 w/Guinn; e/a, c/l Julich, Bel. 10POW, MACR 1319. Used for spares by Luftwaffe. HELL'S BELLE.

42-3061 Del Cheyenne 18/1/43; Mitchell 13/4/43; ass 335BS/95BG [OE-J] Alconbury 17/5/43 {4m}; tran 525BS/379BG [FO-L] Kimbolton 28/6/43; 91BG Bassingbourn 20/1/44; 306BG Thurleigh 2/5/44; 92BG Podington 6/11/44; 305BG Chelveston 16/2/45; 384BG Grafton Underwood 18/5/45; RFC Altus 17/9/45. 1AD radio relay ship. SKUNKFACE II.

42-3062 Del Cheyenne 15/1/43; Salina 2/2/43; Homestead 13/3/43; ass Glen 21/3/43; cr Hayle, Corn. 4/4/43. Sal.

42-3063 Del Long Beach 31/1/43; Tinker 12/3/43; ass 410BS/94BG Presque Is 7/4/43; Earls Colne, Ex. 12/5/43; MIA Kiel 13/6/43 w/Johnson, cr Channel. 9KIA 1POW. MACR 6142. OLE TOBE.

42-3064 Del Cheyenne 5/2/43; ass 353BS/301BG Morrison 25/3/43; tran 100BG Thorpe Abbotts /43; 358BS/303BG [VK-I] Molesworth 13/7/43; retUS Scott 15/4/44; RFC Albuquerque 27/7/45. STARDUST.

42-3065 Del Cheyenne 14/2/43; ass 353BS/301BG Morrison 7/6/43; Oudna 6/8/43; {24m} tran 429BS/2BG Massicault 14/11/43; Bizerte 2/12/43; MIA {9m} 19/12/43 Innsbruck w/Vogel, s/d by e/a. no chutes seen, MACR 1529.

42-3066 Del Denver 9/2/43; Tinker 10/3/43; ass 96BS/2BG Navarin 17/3/43; tran 353BS/301BG Oudna, Tun 10/43 {3m}; ret 429BS/2BG Massicault 16/11/43; Bizerte 2/12/43; Amendola 9/12/43; 348BS/99BG Tortorella, 28/3/44; {1m} 483BG Tortorella 31/3/44; retUS Homestead 3/7/44; RFC Altus 6/9/45. BETSY.

42-3067 Del Cheyenne 30/1/43; Walla Walla 5/3/43; cr Utica, Miss. 16/3/43 w/Moore. lost control, cp and two passengers baled safely, pilot killed attempting to bale. Sal.

42-3068 Del Cheyenne 30/1/43; Gt Falls 18/2/43; Lowry 23/2/43; Recl Comp 2/10/45.

42-3069 Del Cheyenne 30/1/43; ass 332BS/94BG [XM-A] Bangor 14/4/43; Rougham 6/43; tran 544BS/384BG [SU-F] Grafton Underwood 12/7/43; MIA St Lo 25/7/44 W/Hankinson, flak, cr nr Hamburg, 10POW. PASSES CANCELLED.

42-3070 Del Cheyenne 2/2/43; Pyote 18/2/43; Dalhart 7/5/43; Tinker 5/8/43; Patterson 27/10/43; McDill 3/2/44; Brookley 24/8/44; McDill 6/9/44; Recl Comp 13/11/45.

42-3071 Del Cheyenne 2/2/43; 331BS/94BG Presque Is 8/4/43; Bassingbourn 4/43; Earls Colne 12/5/43; Rougham 13/6/43; MIA Le Bourget 14/7/43 w/Watts, e/a, cr Le Bourget, 3KIA 2POW 5EVD. MACR 113.

42-3072 Del Cheyenne 5/2/43; ass 94BG Presque Is 4/43; tran 324BS/91BG [DF-B] Bassingbourn 15/9/43; 525BS/379BG Kimbolton 27/9/43; retUS 21/5/44; RFC Altus 24/1/45.

42-3073 Del Cheyenne 4/2/43; ass 410BS/94BG Bangor 13/4/43; 401BS/91BG [LL-A] Bassingbourn 22/4/43; MIA {23m} Leipzig 21/2/44 w/Simmons, e/a, cr Hergford, Ger. 10POW, MACR 2463. LIGHTNING STRIKES.

42-3074 Del Denver 7/2/43; ass 331BS/94BG [QE-U] Dow Fd 15/4/43; Rougham 13/6/43; tran 545BS/384BG Grafton Underwood 10/7/43; 367BG/306BG [GY-Y/T] Thurleigh 23/8/43; retUS Tinker 26/7/44; Clarke FEA 15/1/48. (Also named GOODTIME CHOLLY and KATHLEEN) LOMA LEE.

42-3075 Del Denver 1/2/43; Dow Fd 12/4/43; ass 332BS/94BG [XM-E] Bassingbourn 18/4/43; Earls Colne 12/5/43; tran 544BS/384BG Grafton Underwood 10/7/43; MIA Hamburg 25/7/43 W/Hegewald, flak, cr Wesel, Ger. 2KIA 8POW. LONGHORN.

42-3076 Del Denver 3/2/43; Morrison 12/3/43; ass 367BS/306BG [GY-H] Thurleigh 20/4/43; c/l n/b/d Hawkinge, UK 28/7/43; sal. WO 31/1/44.

42-3077 Del Denver 3/2/43; ass 419BS/301BG Oudna 7/4/43; Cerignola 7/12/43; Lucera 1/2/44; {23m} tran 816BS/483BG Sterparone 26/4/44; ret Cairo 28/11/44 w/Sperry, cr Buvo, It. burned out. 5K 4inj.

42-3078 Del Cheyenne 30/1/43; ass 334BS/95BG Dow Fd 24/4/43; tran 100BG /43; 534BS/381BG [GD-M] 15/6/43; MIA {12+m} Ludwigshafen 7/1/44 w/Wilson; flak, cr Saarbrücken, Ger. 2KIA 8POW. MACR 1873. WINSOME WINN.

42-3079 Del Cheyenne 1/2/43; ass 335BS/95BG [OE-O] 15/4/43; tran 323BS/91BG [OR-X] Bassingbourn 16/6/43; MIA Nantes 16/9/43 w/Smith, flak, cr St Nazaire, 1KIA 9POW, MACR 550.

42-3080 Del Cheyenne 1/2/43; Pyote 20/2/43; Tinker 27/7/43; Smoky Hill 26/7/44; Walker 19/12/44; Lincoln 13/1/45; Pratt 24/2/45; Orlando 13/3/45; RFC Kingman 20/10/45.

42-3081 Del Cheyenne 3/2/43; Pyote 18/2/43; McDill 20/1/44; Avon Park 27/2/44; Barks- dale 2/3/44; RFC Searcey Fd 25/6/45.

42-3082 Del Cheyenne 3/2/43; Presque Is 8/4/43; ass 333BS/94BG [TS-E] Rougham 10/6/43; c/l S England n/b/d 4/10/43 sal. DOUBLE TROUBLE.

42-3083 Del Denver 1/2/43; Brookley 15/3/43; ass 429BS/2BG 20/4/43; MIA Gerbini, It. 8/7/43. MISS CARRIAGE.

42-3084 Del Denver 26/1/43; ass 95BG 20/3/43; 367BS/306BG [GY-A] Thurleigh 10/4/43, 368BS [BO-A]; MIA Keil 29/7/43 w/Brown, e/a, cr Keil, 10KIA, MACR 121.

42-3085 Del Cheyenne 3/2/43; Dow Fd 12/4/43; ass 331BS/94BG [QE-N] Rougham 28/4/43; f/l Nth Weald, Ex. b/d Emden 21/5/43 sal 6/7/43 as Hangar Queen. HELNO GAL.

42-3086 Del Denver 5/2/43; Salina 25/2/43; f/l Rosedale, La. 17/3/43 w/Hendershot. WO.

42-3087 Del Denver 14/1/43; ass 95BG Alconbury 20/3/43; tran 367BS/306BG [GY-W] Thurleigh

11/4/43; 547BS/384BG [SO-O/A] Grafton Underwood 4/9/43; MIA Hamm 22/4/44 w/Kew, e/a, cr Wesel, Ger, 2KIA 8POW. MACR 2466.

42-3088 Del Cheyenne 6/2/43; ass 410BS/94BG Presque Is 9/4/43; Earls Colne 16/4/43; Rougham 15/6/43; tran 544BS/384BG [SU-G] Grafton Underwood 12/7/43; MIA Hamburg 25/7/43 w/Christman, e/a, cr Hamburg, 5KIA 5POW. SUGAR PUSS.

42-3089 Del Long Beach 31/1/43; ass 335BS/95BG Dow Fd 24/5/43; tran 338BS/96BG [BX-V] Andrews Fd /43; Snetterton 12/6/43; retUS Grenier 10/1/45; Eglin 3/4/45. CAPTAIN EDDIE.

42-3090 Del Cheyenne 6/2/43; ass 334BS/95BG [BG-C] Alconbury 17/4/43. f/l Clonakilty, N/Ireland 7/4/43; tran 510BS/351BG [YB-N] Polebrook 17/6/43; 2 BAD CCRC 10/11/43; sal 18/6/45 {13+m}. T'AINT A BIRD.

42-3091 Del Cheyenne 3/2/43; New Castle 18/4/43; ass 334BS/95BG [BG-K] Framlingham 12/5/43; tran 422BS/305BG [JJ-S/H] Chelveston 17/6/43; MIA Frankfurt 4/10/43 w/Seay, flak, cr Gross-Karben, Ger. 5KIA 5POW. MACR 785.

42-3092 Del Cheyenne 18/2/43; Dow Fd 23/5/43; ass 533BS/381BG [VP-T] Ridgewell 4/43; MIA {7m} Schweinfurt 17/8/43 w/Hudson; flak, cr Pesch, Ger. 1K 9POW. MACR 399. STRATO SAM.

42-3093 Del Denver 18/2/43; Presque Is 5/4/43; ass 338BS/96BG 4/43; tran 510BS/351BG [TU-K] Polebrook 11/7/43; 2 SAD {8m} sal 3/1/44. NOBODY'S DARLIN'.

42-3094 Del New Castle 16/2/43; Colorado Springs 29/3/43; ass 11AF Elmendorf 21/6/43; retUS Hunter 4/12/43; RFC Kingman 14/1/45.

42-3095 Del Pueblo 1/2/43; Dow Fd 10/6/43; ass 412BS/95BG [QW-Z] Horham 2/7/43; tran SAD 1/3/44; 2 BAD 19/6/44; retUS Tinker 26/7/44; RFC Bush Fd 23/5/45. PEGGY ANN.

42-3096 Del Denver 13/2/43; ass 96BS/2BG Morrison 12/3/43; Navarin 4/43 Château-du-Rhumel 27/4/43; Ain M'Lila 17/6/43; Massicault 31/7/43; {60m} tran 352BS/301BG; {4m} sal 23/1/45; RFC Bush Fd 9/5/45.

42-3097 Del Denver 11/2/43; Dow Fd 13/6/43; ass 335BS/95BG Horham 15/6/43; tran 549BS/385BG Gt Ashfield /43; MIA Ludwigshafen 30/12/43 w/Eckhart, flak, cr Fresnicourt. 2 EVD 2KIA 6POW. MACR 1898. THE GROUND HOG.

42-3098 Del Denver 5/2/43; Jackson 17/3/43; ass 429BS/2BG Navarin 9/4/43; Château-du-Rhumel 27/4/43; Ain M'Lila 17/6/43; Massicault 31/7/43; {55m} tran 353BS/301BG Oudna 13/11/43; {9m} MIA Piraeus 11/1/44, w/Goen, cr Patrai, Gr. 1EVD 9KIA. MACR 1832. SKIPPY.

42-3099 Del Denver 4/3/43; Dow Fd 19/6/43; ass 527BS/379BG [FO-R] Kimbolton 26/4/43; MIA Wilhelmshaven 11/6/43 w/Pinson, flak, cr Nth Sea, 9KIA 1POW. MACR 1368.

42-3100 Del Denver 11/2/43; Presque Is 27/4/43; ass 334BS/95BG Alconbury 1/5/43; tran 532BS/381BG [VE-A1] Ridgewell 20/7/43; MIA {1+m} Kassel 30/7/43 w/Post (Sq CO), e/a, cr Apeldoorn, Neth, 1KIA 9POW. MACR 129.

42-3101 Del Cheyenne 10/2/43; Presque Is 28/4/43; ass 334BS/95BG Alconbury 1/5/43; tran 533BS/381BG Ridgewell 21/7/43; MIA {3+m} Gilze Rijen w/Koenig, e/a, cr Rozenburg, Hol, 4KIA 6POW, MACR 662.

42-3102 Del Cheyenne 13/2/43; Morrison 30/4/43; ass 353BS/301BG St Donat 7/43; {8m} sal 8/7/44.

42-3103 Del Cheyenne 16/2/43; ass 334BS/95BG, c/l Kansas, Mo. 7/4/43; rep, but stayed USA. Recl Comp 17/7/45.

42-3104 Del Cheyenne 12/2/43; Dow Fd 16/4/43; ass 333BS/94BG Rougham 6/43 RAIDER; tran 547BS/384 (SO-A) Grafton Underwood 10/7/43; MIA Gelsenkirchen 12/8/43 w/Keck, e/a, cr Hennef, Ger. 6KIA 4POW; MACR 286.

42-3105 Del Denver 14/2/43; Presque Is 26/4/43; ass 96BG Grafton Underwood /43; tran 407BS/92BG [PY-N] Alconbury 5/43; 1 SAD Burtonwood 12/10/43; sal 2/6/45.

42-3106 Del Walker, Ks. 25/2/43; Dow Fd 16/4/43; ass 96BG Andrews Fd 19/4/43; tran 508BS/351BG [YB-M] Polebrook 28/5/43; c/t/o 13/8/43, sal.

42-3107 Del Denver 13/2/43; Presque Is 8/4/43; ass 337BS/96BG Grafton Underwood 17/4/43; MIA Keil 13/6/43 w/Webster, e/a, cr Doerphof, 8KIA 2POW. MACR 3687. MISS CARRIAGE.

42-3108 Del Denver 13/2/43; Kearney 12/3/43; c/l Bogalouse, La. w/Score, 25/3/43, WO.

42-3109 Del Cheyenne 16/2/43; Dow Fd 2/6/43; ass 92BG Podington 17/10/43; tran 332BSA/94BG [XM-E] Rougham /43; sal 22/6/45. STUD DUCK.

42-3110 Del Cheyenne 22/2/43; Morrison 24/3/43; ass 335BS/95BG [OE-D] Framlingham /43; MIA Emden 21/5/43 w/Schnebly, flak, cr Dreiborg, Hol. 4KIA 6POW. MACR 4907.

42-3111 Del Cheyennne 16/2/43; Gore Fd 7/3/43; ass 335BS/95BG [OE-T] Alconbury 5/43; THE BRASS RAIL {6m}; tran 324BS/91 [DF-A1] Bassingbourn 16/6/43; MIA {8m} Emden 27/9/43 w/Pegram, e/a, cr Geefsweer, Hol. 4KIA 6POW. MACR 667. LOCAL GIRL.

42-3112 Del Long Beach 13/2/43; Nashville 12/5/43; ass 352BS/301BG St Donat 5/43; Oudna 6/8/43; Cerignola 7/12/43; Lucera 1/2/44; {32m} RetUS Orlando 10/4/44; RFC Walnut Ridge 17/12/45.

42-3113 Del Cheyenne 4/3/43; Dow Fd 16/4/43; ass 94BG /43; tran 525BS/379BG [FR-F] Kimbolton 3/43; MIA St Nazaire 29/5/43 w/Hale, flak, cr Pontivy, Fr. 10POW, MACR 1292.

42-3114 Del Cheyenne 23/2/43; Dow Fd 18/4/43; ass 525BS/379BG [FR-T] Kimbolton 3/43; MIA Wilhelmshaven 11/6/43 w/Britten, e/a, ditched Nth Sea, 10POW. MACR 1295.

42-3115 Del Cheyenne 17/2/43; Kearney 28/3/43; ass 335BS/95BG Alconbury 4/43; MIA Antwerp 14/5/43 w/McKinley, e/a, cr Kats Is, Noord Beveland, Neth. 10KIA. MACR 4908.

42-3116 Del Cheyenne 26/2/43; Nashville 10/4/43; ass 96BG 26/4/43; tran 407BS/92BG [PY-U] Alconbury 5/43; MIA Kassel 28/7/43 W/Porter, e/a, cr c/Schelluinen, Hol. 2KIA 8POW, MACR 373.

42-3117 Del Long Beach 19/2/43; La Guardia 4/5/43; Scott Fd 17/8/43; ass 95BG (not to GB); WO 15/8/44; Recl Comp 3/1/46.

42-3118 Del Cheyenne 27/2/43; Presque Is 8/4/43; ass 339BS/96BG [QJ-A] Thurleigh 16/4/43 DAISY JUNE; tran 413BS SHACK RABBIT; tran 534BS/381BG [GD-N] Ridgewell 6/7/43; MIA {14m} Oschersleben 11/1/44 w/Larson, flak, cr Goslar, Ger. 1KIA 9POW. MACR 1875. THE GREEN HORNET.

42-3119 Del Cheyenne 18/2/43; Presque 28/4/43; ass 322BS/91BG [LG-M] Bassingbourn 4/6/43; MIA {5m} Hamburg 26/7/43 w/Hargis, ditched Nth Sea. All ten crew OK. Five flew off in RAF Walrus, but other five in second Walrus unable to take off and taxied back to port! (possibly FRISCO JENNY) Better known as DESTINY'S TOT.

42-3120 Del Denver 26/2/43; ass 509BS/351BG [RQ-O] Presque Is 8/4/43; Polebrook 15/4/43; {24m} tran 2 BAD 8/6/44; retUS Cincinnati 18/6/44; 613 BU Phillips Fd, 28/9/44. GREMLIN'S DELITE.

42-3121 Del Denver 12/2/43; ass 95BG Alconbury 3/43; sal 17/4/43.

42-3122 Del Denver 20/2/43; Presque Is 5/4/43; ass 413BS/96BG [MZ-Q] Thurleigh 17/4/43; tran 545BS/384BG [JD-N] Grafton Underwood 6/7/43; MIA Hamburg 25/7/43 W/Hall, e/a, cr Hamburg, 10POW. APRIL FOOL.

42-3123 Del Denver 18/2/43; Dow Fd 10/4/43; ass 339BS/96BG 4/43; WORRY WART; Snetterton 12/6/43; tran 535BS/381BG [MS-Z] Ridgewell 16/7/43; MIA {7m} Bremen 8/10/43 w/Kemp, e/a, cr Bremen, 10KIA. MACR 1396. RON CHEE.

42-3124 Del Denver 20/2/43; Presque Is 19/4/43; ass 427BS/303BG [GN-N] Molesworth 2/6/43; cr Bala, Wales 4/8/43; sal.

42-3125 Del Cheyenne 20/2/43; Blythe 4/3/43; McClellan 6/4/43; Pyote 30/5/43 (w/28BG and 19BG training); RFC Ontario 6/6/45.

42-3126 Del Cheyenne 20/2/43; Blythe 5/3/43; WO 27/4/43.

42-3127 Del Cheyenne 21/2/43; Morrison 20/3/43; ass 367BS/306BG [GY-M] Thurleigh 5/5/43; MIA Emden 21/5/43 (w/94BG crew?).

42-3128 Del Cheyenne 20/2/43; Dow Fd 15/4/43; cr Iceland 4/43. BOO HOO.

42-3129 Del Cheyenne 21/2/43; Palm Beach 30/3/43; ass 346BS/99BG Navarin 5/5/43; b/d Naples w/Ebbers 1/8/43, cr Djedeida; 10KIA. STARS AND STRIPES.

42-3130 Del Long Beach 18/2/43; Dow 12/6/43; ass 331BS/94BG [QE-O] Rougham 7/43; MIA Duren 20/12/43 w/Sharpe, flak, cr Luenen, Hol. 8KIA 2POW. MACR 902. NIP 'N TUCK.

42-3131 Del Cheyenne 20/2/43; 19/4/43; ass 427BS/303BG [GN-U] Molesworth 4/6/43; MIA Oschersleben 11/1/44 w/Carothers, e/a, cr Hamel, Ger. 7KIA 3POW; MACR 1966. WINNIE THE POOH then FLAK WOLF.

42-3132 Del Cheyenne 20/2/43; Smoky Hill 14/4/43; ass 526BS/379BG, cr in Atlantic 23/4/43.

42-3133 Del Cheyenne 6/3/43; Smoky Hill 21/3/43; ass 416BS/99BG Navarin 5/6/43; tran 353BS/301BG Lucera 3/44; {19m} 463BG weath/ship, Celone 25/4/44; sal 12/5/45. NOBODY'S BABY.

42-3134 Del Cheyenne 20/2/43; Presque Is 20/4/43; ass 407BS/92BG [PY-P] Alconbury 23/5/43; tran 1 BAD Burtonwood 8th FC 29/1/44; 381BG RR a/c Ridgewell 6/3/44; 838BS/487BG RR a/c Lavenham 17/7/44; sal 14/6/45.

42-3135 Del Long Beach 26/2/43; Presque Is 8/4/43; ass 332BS/94BG [XM-K] Bassingbourn 4/43 LARRUPPIN' LOU; tran 511BS/351BG Polebrook /43.

42-3136 Del Cheyenne 26/2/43; Presque Is 8/4/43; ass 511BS/351BG [DS-P] Polebrook 3/43 EIGHT BALL; MIA Amsterdam 22/2/44 w/Leclerc, flak, cr Amsterdam, 10POW, MACR 2772. NO BALLS AT ALL.

42-3137 Del Cheyenne 11/2/43; Morrison 29/4/43; ass 353BS/301BG St Donat 22/4/43; Oudna 6/8/43; Cerignola 7/12/43; MIA {38m} Athens 8/12/43 w/Scott, flak hit in ball turret and exploded; 3KIA 6POW, MACR 1481.

42-3138 Del Cheyenne 22/2/443; ass 527BS/379BG [FO-M] Dow Fd 13/4/43; Kimbolton 30/5/43; MIA Wilhelmshaven 11/6/43 w/Newman, e/a, cr Tossens, Ger. 8KIA 2POW, MACR 1357.

42-3139 Del Long Beach 22/2/43; Spokane 15/8/43; WO 10/5/44.

42-3140 Del Long Beach 23/2/43; Patterson 17/4/43; ass 509BS/351BG [RQ-P] Polebrook 23/4/43; MIA

INDIVIDUAL B-17 HISTORIES   91

{19m} Leverkusen 1/12/43 w/Harris, no gas, ditched Channel, 7KIA 3RTD; MACR 1550. PATTY ANN II.

42-3141 Del Long Beach 25/2/43; Presque Is 8/4/43; ass 508BS/351BG [YB-A/H] Polebrook 16/4/43; {15m} RetUS Eglin, 31/3/44; RFC Walnut Ridge 5/1/46. HITLER'S HEADACHE.

42-3142 Del Long Beach 27/2/43; Dow Fd 22/4/43; ass 368BS/306BG [BO-I] Thurleigh 18/5/43; cr Gt Haseley, ex-Bremen 13/11/43, 10KIA. BUTTERCUP.

42-3143 Del Cheyenne 23/2/43; ass 379BG Dow Fd 18/4/43; cr Bunderan, Ire. en route Kimbolton 9/5/43. Sal. WEREWOLF.

42-3144 Del Cheyenne 24/2/43; Salina 20/3/43; ass 2BG Navarin 4/43; Château-du-Rhumel 27/4/43; Ain M'Lila 17/6/43; Massicault 31/7/43; {26m} tran 32BS/301BG Oudna 14/11/43; Cerignola 7/12/43; Lucera 1/2/44; MIA {40m} Steyr, Aus. 2/4/44 w/Miller, e/a, cr Kleinrifling, 10KIA. MACR 4197.

42-3145 Del Cheyenne 24/2/43; Dow Fd 20/4/43; ass 527BS/379BG [FO-B/W] Kimbolton 30/5/43; MIA Stuttgart 6/9/43 w/Johnson, no gas, ditched Channel, 10 RTD. THE GREMLIN.

42-3146 Del Long Beach 20/2/43; Morrison 30/4/43; ass 20BS/2BG Château-du-Rhumel 1/6/43; Ain M'Lila 17/6/43; Massicault 31/7/43; Bizerte 2/12/43; Amendola 9/12/43; {15m} sal 23/1/45. MME DIABLO.

42-3147 Del Long Beach 27/2/43; Dow Fd 10/7/43; ass 49BS/2BG Ain M'Lila 18/7/43; Massicault 31/7/43; {26m} tran 341BS/97BG Depienne 14/11/43; MIA Istres, Fr. 16/11/43 w/Packard, cr target, 9KIA 1POW. MACR 1195. HOMESICK ANGEL.

42-3148 Del Denver 3/1/43; ass 527BS/379BG [FO-A] Patterson 17/4/43; then 526BS [LF-A] Kimbolton 30/5/43; MIA Wilhelmshaven 11/6/43 W/Brinkman, e/a, cr Marx, Ger. 8KIA 2POW. MACR 1369.

42-3149 Del Cheyenne 18/3/43; Orlando 6/3/43; 244 BU Harvard 19/8/43; 561 BU Rosencrans 13/1/44; RFA Albuquerque 25/5/45.

42-3150 Del Cheyenne 27/2/43; Presque Is 10/4/43; ass 511BS/351BG [DS-Q] Polebrook 25/4/43; MIA {11m} 6/9/43 w/Norris, no gas, ditched off Beachy Head, crew swam ashore and RTD. FOUL BALL.

42-3151 Del Denver 1/3/43; Morrison 9/5/43; ass 96BS/2BG Château-du-Rhumel 17/5/43; Ain M'Lila 17/6/43; Massicault 31/7/43; {7m} tran 352BS/301BG Oudna 14/11/43; 483BG Tortorella 4/44; Sterparone 22/4/44; sal {61m} 30/3/45.

42-3152 Del Denver 1/3/43; Presque Is 8/4/43; ass 508BS/351BG [YB-A] Polebrook 17/4/43; MIA {17m} Anklam 9/10/43 w/Warring; e/a, cr Schleswig, Ger. 10POW; MACR 876. SLEEPY LAGOON.

42-3153 Del Denver 1/4/43; Dow Fd 3/6/43; ass 339BS/96BG Snetterton 12/6/43; THE WORRY WART; tran 336BS/95BG [ET-A] 7/43; retUS Love Fd 9/4/44; RFC Ontario 13/10/45. THE DEVIL'S DAUGHTER.

42-3154 Del Denver 2/3/43; ass 526BS/379BG [LF-B] Dow Fd 19/4/43; Kimbolton 30/5/43; c/l Rougham b/d 12/8/43; sal 16/8/43.

42-3155 Del Denver 2/3/43; ass 333BS/94BG 5/43; Tinker 2/6/43; Galveston 4/8/43; WO 28/2/44.

42-3156 Del Cheyenne 3/3/43; ass 407BS/92BG [PY-Y]; tran Morrison 2/5/43; ass 49BS/2BG Château-du-Rhumel 2/6/43; Ain M'Lila 17/6/43; Massicault 31/7/43; {4m} c/t/o 9/11/43 w/Flournoy, no inj. Sal.

42-3157 Del Cheyenne 2/3/43; Morrison 10/6/43; ass 32BS/301BG St Donat 21/5/43; Oudna 6/8/43; Cerignola 7/12/43; Lucera 1/2/44; MIA Wiener Nuedorf 26/7/44 w/McDonald, e/a, cr Wiener Nuestadt, 3KIA 7POW, MACR 7138. LAURA.

42-3158 Del Denver 6/3/43; Morrison 31/3/43; ass 427BS/303BG [GN-Y] Molesworth 2/6/43; MIA Hanover 29/4/44 w/Fisher, e/a, cr target, 8KIA 2POW, MACR 4471. MAX.

42-3159 Del Denver 3/3/43; ass 94BG 27/5/43; Morrison 2/7/43; ass 96BS/2BG Massicault 25/8/43; {1m} tran 32BS/301BG Oudna 14/11/43; Cerignola 7/12/43; Lucera 1/2/44; {13m} to depot 4/6/44; sal 6/9/44.

42-3160 Del Denver 6/3/43; Tinker 16/12/43; tran to RCAF 168th Heavy Transport Squad, Rockcliffe, Ont. 16/12/43 as No. 9202, used for VIPs and mail; cr Münster 4/11/45 en route Poland, all killed. Sal.

42-3161 Del Cheyenne 5/3/43; Morrison 15/5/43; ass 20BS/2BG Château-du-Rhumel 4/6/43; Ain M'Lila 17/6/43; Massicault 31/7/43; {3m} tran 32BS/301BG Oudna 14/11/43; Cerignola 7/12/43; Lucera 1/2/44 {28m} retUS 13/9/45; RFC Altus 29/10/45.

42-3162 Del Cheyenne 5/3/43; Dow Fd 9/4/43; ass 332BS/94BG [XM-C] BLACK JACK Bassingbourn 18/4/43; then BLOOPY BLOOMERS; tran 401BS/91BG [LL-A] Bassingbourn 15/7/43; MIA {2+m} Gelsenkirchen 12/8/43 w/Wilson, coll w/42-29587 damaged tail, ditched Nth Sea, 10POW. MACR 259. BUCCANEER.

42-3163 Del Denver 4/3/43; Dalhart 6/6/43; c/l base 29/6/43 w/Witorel. Sal.

42-3164 Del Denver 6/3/43; Morrison 13/4/43; ass 347BS/99BG Navarin 4/6/43; Oudna 4/8/43; Tortorella 11/12/43; MIA Lake Albano, It, 17/2/44 w/Lombard, flak, ditched off Anzio, crew RTD 20/2/44.

42-3165 Del Cheyenne 6/3/43; Dow Fd 10/4/43; ass 327BS/92BG [UX-G/T] Alconbury 23/4/43; 325BS [NV-G]; 407BS [PY-T]; MIA Bremen 26/11/43 w/Dougherty, flak, cr Uphen, 7KIA 3POW. MACR 1385.

42-3166 Del Cheyenne 6/3/43; Morrison 24/5/43; ass 49BS/2BG Château-du-Rhumel 30/5/43; Ain M'Lila 17/6/43; Massicault 31/7/43; {4m} tran 32BS/301BG Oudna 14/11/43; Cerignola 7/12/43; MIA {42} Montpelier 27/1/44 w/Graves, 10KIA, MACR 2058.

42-3167 Del Cheyenne 6/3/43; Dow Fd 15/5/43; ass 423BS/306BG [RD-Z] Thurleigh 19/4/43; tran 527BS/379BG [FO-S/B] Kimbolton 17/6/43; 2 BAD Warton 4/4/44; retUS Homestead 16/4/44; RFC Altus 11/8/45. YE OLDE PUB.

42-3168 Del Cheyenne 8/3/43; Morrison 29/4/43; ass 97BG Château-du-Rhumel 24/5/43; tran 348BS/99BG Tortorella 3/5/44; to depot 9/5/44; retUS Rome 17/8/44; sal 23/11/44.

42-3169 Del Cheyenne 8/3/43; Memphis 8/4/43; ass 385BG Gt Ashfield 13/4/43; tran 369BS/306BG [WW-S] Thurleigh 18/6/43; tran RAF 214 sqd SR379 [BU-D] Sculthorpe 3/2/44; WO 11/47.

42-3170 Del Cheyenne 8/3/43; Morrison 19/5/43; ass 353BS/3201BG St Donat 21/5/43; MIA {2m} Foggia 27/7/43 w/Booker, ditched; 9KIA 1 surv; MACR 339.

42-3171 Del Cheyenne 11/3/43; Kearney 26/5/43; ass 334BS/95BG [BG-S] Horham 3/7/43; tran 326BS/92BG [JW-S] Alconbury 11/8/43; b/d cr Shiplake 14/10/43, sal.

42-3172 Del Cheyenne 10/3/43; Dow Fd 13/5/43; ass 423BS/306BG [RD-R] Thurleigh MISS PATRICIA 5/5/43; tran AFSC 27/6/43; 323BS/91BG [OR-R/X] Bassingbourn 25/9/43; {23m} RetUS Tinker 13/6/44; RFC Altus 9/10/45. CHENNAULT'S PAPPY.

42-3173 Del Cheyenne 18/3/43; Presque Is 8/4/43; ass 511BS/351BG [DS-R] Polebrook 19/4/43; MIA {1m} 15/5/43 w/Meli, hit by bombs from a/c above, ditched Nth Sea. MACR 15581. SPARE BALL.

42-3174 Del Cheyenne 10/3/43; Presque Is 8/4/43; ass 416BS/99BG Navarin 20/5/43; MIA Messina 25/5/43 w/Orance, flak, cr sea exploded, 10KIA. MACR 16451.

42-3175 Del Cheyenne 10/3/43; Dow Fd 15/4/43; ass 95BG 22/4/43; tran 524BS/379BG [WA-T] Kimbolton 4/43; MIA Hamburg 25/7/43 w/Hildebradt, e/a, cr target, 10POW. MACR 1766. THE HA.

42-3176 Del Cheyenne 10/3/43; Dow Fd 10/4/43; ass 336BS/95BG [ET-K] SPOOK II Framlingham 21/5/43; Horham 15/6/43; tran 527BS/379BG [FO-E] Kimbolton 22/6/43; 524BS [WA-E]; MIA Schweinfurt 14/10/43 w/Johnson, e/a, cr Dornheim, Ger. 6KIA 4POW. MACR 954. LADY ASTRID.

42-3177 Del Cheyenne 11/3/43; Dow Fd 15/4/43; ass 351BG Polebrook 26/4/43; tran 337BS/96BG [AW-K] HELLER'S ANGEL Andrews Field, then THE HELLION /43; 535BS/381BG [MS-O] Ridgewell 15/7/43; {28m} to RAF 214 Squad (SR376) Sculthorpe 25/1/44. WO 11/3/47.

42-3178 Del Cheyenne 11/3/43; Smoky Hill 24/3/43; ass 348BS/99BG Navarin 20/5/43; Oudna 4/8/43; Tortorella 11/12/43; tran 483BG Tortorella 31/3/44; 414BS/97BG Amendola 6/5/44; c/l Corsica 30/5/44. Sal.

42-3179 Del Cheyenne 10/3/43; Morrison 30/4/43; ass 347BS/99BG Navarin 3/5/43; Oudna 4/8/43; MIA Eleusis Afd, Athens 18/11/43 w/Carson, cr Ragusa, Sic. 10K.

42-3180 Del Cheyenne 11/3/43; Presque Is 2/5/43; ass 413BS/96BG Andrews Field KIPLING'S ERROR 3/5/43; tran 535BS/381BG [MS-Y] Ridgewell 16/7/43; MIA {12+m} Anklam 9/10/43 w/Carqueville, e/a, ditched Nth Sea, 9KIA 1POW. MACR 888. FORGET ME NOT II.

42-3181 Del Cheyenne 12/3/43; Dow Fd 6/5/43; ass 95BG /43 LIMITED SERVICE; tran 366BS/305BG [KY-L] Chelveston 1/8/43; 486BG Sudbury 16/7/44; sal 26/1/46.

42-3182 Del Cheyenne 12/3/43; Orlando 8/5/43; Yuma 12/12/43; WO 19/11/44.

42-3183 Del Cheyenne 13/3/43; Memphis 7/4/43; ass 413BS/96BG Snetterton /43; tran 327BS/92BG [UX-O] Alconbury 19/7/43; cr n/b/d Deeping St Nicholas 23/9/43. Sal.

42-3184 Del Cheyenne 12/3/43; Memphis 4/9/43; ass 407BS/92BG [PY-C/Q] Alconbury 24/4/43; MIA Osnabrück 22/12/43 w/Roeber, e/a, cr Bornetbroek, 1EVD 9POW. MACR 1711. USS ALIQUIPPA.

42-3185 Del Cheyenne 13/3/43; Bangor 21/5/43; ass 407BS/92BG [PY-Y] Alconbury 24/5/43; tran 2 BAD Warton 2/8/43; 333BS/94BG [TS-L] Rougham /43; MIA Ivry 26/11/3 w/Nienaber, e/a, cr Londinieres, Fr. 2EVD 6POW 2KIA. MACR 1125. QUEEN BEE.

42-3186 Del Cheyenne 12/3/43; Dow Fd 15/5/43; ass 407BS/92BG [PY-Y] Alconbury 23/5/43; MIA Bordeaux 31/12/43 w/Goldstein, flak, cr Niort, Fr. 6EVD 4POW. MACR 1959.

42-3187 Del Cheyenne 16/3/43; Dow Fd 24/5/43; ass 410BS/94BG Earls Colne 28/5/43; Rougham 13/6/43; MIA Kiel 13/6/43 w/Weldon, e/a, ditched Channel, 9KIA 1POW. BUCKSHOT.

42-3188 Del Cheyenne 13/3/43; Dow Fd 25/5/43; ass 544BS/384BG [SU-F] Grafton Underwood MISS CARRIAGE 9/6/43; MIA Villacoublay 26/6/43 w/Cuddeback, e/a, cr Mezidon, Fr. MACR 15568. FLAK ALLEY LIL'.

42-3189 Del Cheyenne 15/3/43; Sioux City 8/5/43; ass 347BS/99BG Navarin 6/6/43; Oudna 4/8/43; Tortorella 11/12/43; taxi acc. w/Russell 28/7/43; tran depot, WO. Sal 11/6/45. SUPERSTITIOUS ALOYSIUS.

42-3190 Del Cheyenne 15/3/43; Bangor 23/5/43; ass

333BS/94BG [TS-W] Rougham /43; MIA Le Bourget 14/11/43 w/Harrison, e/a, cr Evreux, Fr. (Luftwaffe restored) 6EVD 4POW. MACR 114. MR FIVE BY FIVE.

42-3191 Del Cheyenne 15/3/43; 3017 BU Hobbs 11/6/43; Recl Comp 13/11/45.

42-3192 Del Cheyenne 16/3/43; Dow Fd 16/4/43; ass 358BS/303BG [VK-G] Molesworth 16/5/43; MIA Gilze-Rijen 19/8/43 w/Nix, e/a, cr Roamsdankveer, Neth. 4KIA 6POW. MACR 284. CITY OF ALBUQUERQUE.

42-3193 Del Cheyenne 19/3/43, Hobbs 21/4/43; Sioux City 8/5/43; WO 11/7/43.

42-3194 Del Cheyenne 17/3/43; Dow Fd 11/6/43; ass 334BS/95BG [BG-A] Horham 19/6/43; MIA Schweinfurt 17/8/43 w/Hayden, flak, cr Santa Margherita, It. 4KIA 6POW; MACR 400.LITTLE HELL.

42-3195 Del Cheyenne 17/3/43; Presque Is 27/4/43; ass 366BS/305BG [KY-O] Chelveston 22/6/43; MIA 14/10/43 w/Fisher, e/a, cr Waldenrath, Ger. 4KIA 6POW. MACR 916.

42-3196 Del Cheyenne 17/3/43; Ft Sumner 16/4/43; Hobbs 30/5/43; RFC Altus 4/4/46.

42-3197 Del Cheyenne 17/3/43; Ft Sumner 21/4/43; Roswell 28/5/43; RFC Altus .

42-3198 Del Cheyenne 17/3/43; Memphis 16/4/43; ass 368BS/305BG [BO-Z] Thurleigh 5/5/43; tran 407BS/92BG Alconbury 25/7/43; c/l Wych Cross b/d 6/9/43; sal AFSC 7/9/43.

42-3199 Del Cheyenne 19/3/43; New Castle 19/4/43; ass 524BS/379BG [WA-S/Z] Kimbolton 22/6/43; MIA Gelsenkirchen 12/8/43 w/Paulin, flak, cr Lindler, 5KIA 6POW, (two 2AF crew)MACR 905. CALAMITY JANE.

42-3200 Del Cheyenne 19/3/43; Ft Sumner 21/4/43; Hobbs 30/5/43; 3036 BU Yuma 6/5/44; RFC Ontario 30/5/45.

42-3201 Del Cheyenne 18/3/43; 3017 BU Hobbs 2/4/43; RFC Altus 20/2/45.

42-3202 Del Cheyenne 19/3/43; Memphis 7/4/43; ass 92BG Alconbury 24/4/43; tran 334BS/95BG [BG-A] Framlingham 15/5/43; c/l Rackheath 13/6/43, 2WIA. BLONDIE.

42-3203 Del Cheyenne 19/3/43; 3017 BU Hobbs 24/4/43; RFC Altus 13/9/45.

42-3204 Del Cheyenne 20/3/43; 3017 BU Hobbs 2/4/43; Roswell 23/5/43; Lowry 20/6/43; WO 20/12/43.

42-3205 Del Cheyenne 20/3/43; 3017 BU Hobbs 3/4/43; Recl Comp 13/11/45.

42-3206 Del Cheyenne 22/3/43; Dow Fd 13/4/43; ass 412BS/95BG [QW-T] Alconbury 22/4/43; MIA Kiel 13/6/43 w/Peery, e/a, cr Kiel, 1KIA 9POW. MACR 4404.

42-3207 Del Cheyenne 22/3/43; Dow Fd 15/4/43; ass 94BG Bassingbourn 25/4/43; tran 422BS/305BG [JJ-Q/G] Chelveston 14/7/43; 486BG Sudbury 16/7/44; sal 26/6/45. MONKEY'S UNCLE.

42-3208 Del Cheyenne 22/3/43; Hobbs 5/6/43; WO 16/12/43.

42-3209 Del Cheyenne 23/3/43; Dow Fd 19/4/43; ass 367BS/306BG [GY-Q] Thurleigh 25/5/43; MIA Huls 22/6/43 w/Johnson, e/a, cr Ghent, 9POW. JANELL.

42-3210 Del Cheyenne 25/3/43; Dow Fd 13/4/43; ass 323BS/91BG Bassingbourn 18/5/43; flare caught fire in nose while taxying w/Kethley 3/6/43. Sal 6/7/43.

42-3211 Del Cheyenne 24/3/43; Dow Fd 21/5/43; ass 535BS/381BG [MS-O] Ridgewell 15/5/43; ret Amiens 14/7/43 coll w/FW 190 w/Manchester, c/l Manston. Sal {4+m}. T.S.

42-3212 Del Cheyenne 23/3/43; Dow Fd 19/4/43; ass 527BS/379BG [FO-H] Kimbolton 12/7/43; c/l Framlingham ex-Kassel 30/7/43. Sal.

42-3213 Del Cheyenne 25/3/43; La Guardia 10/4/43; ass 92BG Alconbury 24/4/43; tran 335BS/95BG [OE-W] Framlingham 19/5/43; {3m} 323BS/91BG [OR-M] Bassingbourn 16/6/43; MIA {7+m} Le Bourget 16/8/43 w/Smith, internal explosion, ditched Channel, 10RTD via Newhaven. ALL AMERICAN.

42-3214 Del Cheyenne 30/3/43; Sioux City 8/5/43; ass 423BS/306BG [RD-F] Thurleigh 5/5/43; MIA Wilhelmshaven 21/5/43 w/Judas, e/a, cr target, 3KIA 7POW. MACR 16173.

42-3215 Del Cheyenne 30/3/43; Presque Is 27/5/43; ass 533BS/381BG [VP-S] Ridgewell 28/4/43; MIA Berlin 6/3/44 w/Coyle, e/a, cr Magdeburg, 2KIA 8POW. MACR 3000. LINDA MARY.

42-3216 Del Cheyenne 1/4/43; Dow Fd 13/5/43; ass 545BS/384BG [JD-S] Grafton Underwood 29/5/43; MIA Schweinfurt 14/10/43 w/Kopf, e/a, cr Dilsen, Bel. 3EVD 7POW. MACR 841. THE JOKER.

42-3217 Del Cheyenne 30/3/43; Dow 23/5/43; ass 535BS/381BG [MS-T] Ridgewell 24/5/43; MIA {6m} Heroya 24/7/43 w/Jones, flak, f/l Vannacka, Swed. 10INT but later freed. MACR 132. (First US bomber to land in Sweden in WWII). GEORGIA REBEL.

42-3218 Del Cheyenne 1/4/43; Dow Fd 23/5/43; ass 545BS/384BG [JD-R] Grafton Underwood 29/5/43 DORIS MAE; tran 1 BAD Burtonwood 4/1/44; to RAF (SR389) 214 Squad BU-P; sal 4/4/45.

42-3219 Del Cheyenne 30/3/43; ass 534BS/381BG Dow Fd 4/43; tran 333BS/94BG [TS-N] Rougham 7/6/43; then 331BS; MIA convoy 17/7/43 w/Powledge, e/a, cr Heligoland, 10KIA, MACR 93. DEAR MOM.

42-3220 Del Cheyenne 1/4/43; Dow Fd 23/5/43; ass 535BS/381BG [MS-M] Ridgewell 28/5/43; MIA {9+m} Schweinfurt 17/8/43 w/Smith, e/a, cr Marksteinach, Ger. 10POW MACR 384. DAMFINO.

42-3221 Del Cheyenne 1/4/43; Dow 23/5/43; ass 384BG Grafton Underwood 29/5/43; tran 534BS/381BG [GD-E] Ridgewell 6/43; b/d Kiel {5+m} 4/8/43 w/Lishon, c/l Thetford, sal. WIIALETAIL.

42-3222 Del Cheyenne 1/4/43; Dow Fd 23/5/43; ass 545BS/384BG [JD-P] Grafton Underwood 28/5/43; MIA Schweinfurt 17/8/43 w/Mattes, e/a, cr Reichenbach, Ger, 2KIA 8POW. MACR 292. DUECES WILD.

42-3223 Del Cheyenne 14/4/43; Dow Fd 23/5/4 Ass 533BS/381BG [VP-R] Ridgewell 2/6/43; blew up over Rattlesden en route Amiens w/Hedin 14/7/43, 10K. RED HOT RIDING HOOD.

42-3224 Del Cheyenne 1/4/43; Fairfield 24/5/43; 16PMS/1PMG Bolling 7/7/43; Accra, Nth Africa 31/10/43; retUS McDill 2/10/44; Brazil mapping 1/6/46.

42-3225 Del Cheyenne 1/4/43; Dow Fd 23/5/43; ass 535BS/381BG [[MS-V] Ridgewell 6/6/43 WIDGET; MIA {11+m} Schweinfurt 17/8/43 w/Disbrow, e/a, cr Tongeren, Bel. 4EVD 6POW, MACR 378. CHUG-A-LUG LULU.

42-3226 Del Cheyenne 1/4/43; Dow Fd 23/5/43; ass 533BS/381BG [VP-S] Ridgewell 25/5/43; b/d {1m} Antwerp 22/6/43 w/Jobe, c/l Nth Foreland, UK. Sal 1/7/43. LITTLE CHUCK.

42-3227 Del Cheyenne 1/4/43; Presque Is 25/5/43; ass 534BS/381BG [GD-G] Ridgewell 26/5/43; MIA {9m} Schweinfurt 17/8/43 w/Forkner, e/a, cr Meerland, Hol; 4EVD 6POW, MACR 661.

42-3228 Del Cheyenne 1/4/43; Tinker 28/5/4; Dalhart 25/7/43; Clovis 23/12/43; 245 BU McCook 28/8/44; RFC Kingman 16/12/45.

42-3229 Del Cheyenne 2/4/43; Dow Fd 28/5/43; ass 349BS/100BG [XR-A] Thorpe Abbotts 30/5/43; MIA Münster 10/10/43 w/Justice, flak, cr Harskamp, Hol. IEVD 2KIA 7POW, MACR 1021. PASADENA NENA.

42-3230 Del Cheyenne 3/4/43; Dow Fd 23/5/43; ass 545BS/384BG [JD-U] MARY KATHLEEN Grafton Underwood 29/5/43; MIA Schweinfurt 17/8/43 w/Wofford, e/a, cr Weiler, Ger. 10POW, MACR 293. YANKEE POWERHOUSE II.

42-3231 Del Cheyenne 2/4/43; Dow Fd 25/5/43; ass 545BS/384BG [JD-M] Grafton Underwood 28/5/53; MIA Gelsenkirchen 12/8/43 w/Carrington, s/d/by e/a, cr Liblar, 4KIA 6POW, MACR 287. THE INFERNO.

42-3232 Del Cheyenne 5/4/43; Bangor 27/5/43; ass 350BS/100BG Thorpe Abbotts 9/6/43; MIA Schweinfurt 17/8/43 w/Hollenbeck, e/a, cr Ghedi, It. 1EVD 2KIA 7POW, MACR 676. FLAK HAPPY.

42-3233 Del Cheyenne 6/4/43; Dow Fd 28/5/43; ass 350BS/100BG Thorpe Abbotts 1/6/43; MIA Bremen 8/10/43 w/DeMarco, flak, cr Bremen, 11POW; MACR 950. OUR BABY.

42-3234 Del Cheyenne 6/4/43; Dow Fd 26/5/43; ass 351BS/100BG [EP-E] Thorpe Abbotts 31/5/43; b/d Münster 10/10/43, c/l Wattisham; sal 13/10/43. LITTLE MIKE.

42-3235 Del Cheyenne 7/4/43; ass 100BG Dow Fd 23/5/43; tran 545BS/384BG [JD-T] Grafton Underwood 23/6/43; MIA Le Mans 4/7/43 w/Meyer, e/a, cr Pipriac, Fr. 1EVD 9KIA; MACR 3035/4495. LAKANUKI.

42-3236 Del Cheyenne 1/4/43; Tinker 25/5/43; Barksdale 30/7/43; 223 BU Biggs 29/7/44; 225 BU Rapid City 6/12/44; RFC Ontario 22/8/46.

42-3237 Del Cheyenne 5/4/43; Dow Fd 30/5/43; ass 418BS/100BG [LD-R] Podington 31/5/43; Thorpe Abbotts 9/6/43; MIA Münster 10/10/43 w/Stephens, flak, cr Aalten, Ger. 10POW MACR 1030. STYMIE.

42-3238 Del Cheyenne 6/4/43; Ephrata 30/7/43; ass 100BG /43; tran 244 BU Harvard 28/7/44; 242 BU Alliance 21/10/44; 233 BU Davis-Monthan 1/2/45; RFC Ontario 15/6/45.

42-3239 Del Cheyenne 16/4/43; Lockburn 18/4/43; WO 28/4/44.

42-3240 Del Cheyenne 6/4/43; Gore 18/4/43; 249 BU Alliance 7/9/43; 224 BU Sioux City 6/3/44; 4160 BU Alamagordo 20/1/45; RFC Albuquerque 25/6/45.

42-3241 Del Cheyenne 6/4/43; Dyersburg 17/4/43; Gulfport 16/5/43; WO 1/6/43.

42-3242 Del Cheyenne 6/4/43; 2114 BU Lockburn 14/10/43; Recl Comp 1/6/45.

42-3243 Del Cheyenne 6/4/43; Tinker 30/5/43; Dalhart 5/6/43; Galveston 17/7/43; 298 VHGP Dalhart 2/9/43; 246 BU Pratt 15/9/43; WO 28/10/44; Recl Comp 3/1/46.

42-3244 Del Cheyenne 7/4/43; Morrison 16/5/43; ass 416BS/99BG Oudna 3/9/43; tran 414BS/97BG Depienne 14/11/43; Cerignola 20/12/43; Amendola 16/1/44; MIA Steyr, Aus. 2/4/44 w/Oleson, e/a, cr Ostario, MACR 3639. WIDOW MAKER.

42-3245 Del Cheyenne 8/4/43; Moses Lake 4/6/43; 327 BU Drew 5/8/43; 4104 BU Rome 7/12/43; Recl Comp 29/6/45.

42-3246 Del Cheyenne 7/4/43; Bolling 2/5/43; Spokane 3/5/43; Gt Falls 12/6/43; 225 BU Rapid City 29/4/44; RFC Ontario 27/8/45.

42-3247 Del Cheyenne 8/4/43; Moses Lake 4/6/43; WO 6/4/44.

42-3248 Del Cheyenne 7/4/43; Hobbs 8/6/43; WO 16/11/43.

42-3249 Del Denver 12/4/43; Presque Is 25/5/43; ass 413BS/96BG Andrews Fd 31/5/43; MIA Bremen 16/12/43 w/Greer, e/a, cr Zuider Zee (Ijselmeer), 10KIA, MACR 1569.

INDIVIDUAL B-17 HISTORIES 93

42-3250 Del Denver 8/4/43; Lockburn 18/4/43; 2137 BU Hendricks 16/7/43; RFC Walnut Ridge 24/9/45.

42-3251 Del Denver 13/4/43; Morrison 11/5/43; ass 348BS/99BG Navarin 16/6/43; Oudna 4/8/43; tran 342BS/97BG Depienne 14/11/43; Cerignola 20/12/43; MIA Piraeus 11/1/44 w/Mayo, coll w/42-29928, cr Kalami; MACR 2028.

42-3252 Del Denver 156/4/43; Morrison 16/5/43; ass 96BS/2BG Château-du-Rhumel 26/5/43; Ain M'Lila 17/6/43; Massicault 31/7/43; {8m} tran 353BS/301BG Oudna 14/11/43; Cerignola 7/12/44; Lucera 1/2/44; {61m} to weather ship 27/7/44; sal 16/5/45.

42-3253 Del Denver 12/4/43; 2137 BU Hendricks 18/7/43; RFC Walnut Ridge 19/12/45.

42-3254 Del Denver 13/4/43; Morrison 14/5/43; ass 97BG Château-du-Rhumel 17/5/43; trans 483BG Sterparone 8/44 as weather ship; sal 30/11/45.

42-3255 Del Cheyenne 14/4/43; Morrison 29/4/43; ass 12AF?; sal Duko 20/9/43.

42-3256 Del Cheyenne 13/4/43; Dyersburg 17/4/43; WO 24/8/43.

42-3257 Del Cheyenne 13/4/43; Tinker 5/11/43; WO 24/1/44.

42-3258 Del Cheyenne 13/4/43; Bangor 31/5/43; ass 527BS/379BG [FO-T] Kimbolton 11/6/43; MIA Bremen 8/10/43 w/Hinckley, flak, cr Bremen; 10POW MACR 959.

42-3259 Del Denver 13/4/43; Dow Fd 30/4/43; ass 332BS/94BG [XM-D] SNAFU Earls Colne 10/5/43; Rougham 13/6/43; tran 546BS/384BG [BK-N/K] Grafton Underwood 16/7/43; 545BS [JD-T] re-named ALABAMA WHIRLWIND; 2 SAD Lt Staughton 31/12/43; Shipdam Afd 1/3/44; retUS Tinker 5/8/44; Recl Comp 3/1/46.

42-3260 Del Denver 16/4/43; Dow Fd 30/5/43; ass 349BS/100BG Thorpe Abbotts 9/6/43; MIA convoy off Holland 25/6/43 w/Adams, e/a, cr Nth Sea, 9KIA 1POW. MACR 271. ANGEL'S TIT.

42-3261 Del Denver 16/4/43; Bangor 22/5/43; ass 413BS/96BG [MZ-Q] Grafton Underwood 18/4/43; Andrews Fd 13/5/43; Snetterton 12/6/43; MIA Hamburg 13/12/43 w/Parker, e/a, cr Pulverweg, 3KIA 7POW, MACR 1655. SHORT STRIDE IV.

42-3262 Del Denver 16/4/43; Dow Fd 12/6/43; ass 561BS/388BG Knettishall 23/6/43 SWEETHEART; retUS Tinker 7/7/44; RFC Kingman 28/11/45; also named JEANNIE and WILSON'S WILDCATS.

42-3263 Del Denver 15/4/43; Dow Fd 26/5/43; ass 335BS/95BG [OE-V] Horham 15/6/43; 412BS; SAD 21/6/44; retUS Patterson 7/7/44; RFC Kingman 28/11/45. SLIGHTLY DANGEROUS.

42-3264 Del Denver 16/4/43; Dow Fd 4/6/43; ass 335BS/95BG [OE-N] Horham 15/6/43; f/l Filton 4/7/43; MIA Hannover 26/7/43 w/Foutz, flak, cr Bremen, 10KIA; MACR 193.

42-3265 Del Denver 18/4/43; Dow Fd 28/5/43; ass 337BS/96BG [AW-Z] Andrews Fd 30/5/43; Snetterton 12/6/43; MIA Bremen 16/12/43 w/Leblanc, coll w/42-39860, cr Kimewerd, Hol; 9KIA 1POW; MACR 1568. HOLY MACKERAL.

42-3266 Del Denver 16/4/43; Dow Fd 2/6/43; ass 334BS/95BG [BG-T] Horham 17/6/43; MIA Romilly 15/9/43 w/Noyes, e/a, cr Channel, 10KIA; MACR 616. SITTING BULL.

42-3267 Del Denver 15/4/43; Dow Fd 28/5/43; ass 334BS/95BG [BG-A] Framlingham 28/5/43; Horham 15/6/43; MIA St Nazaire 28/6/43 w/Thomas, e/a, ditched; 10RTD.

42-3268 Del Denver 18/4/43; Dow Fd 1/6/43; ass 534BS/381BG Ridgewell MESSIE BESSIE 3/6/43; re-named CAROL JANE; {1+m} tran 413BS/96BG [MZ-Z] Snetterton 6/7/43; re-named BOOTS II; c/t/o Low Farm Laring, 10KIA, sal.

42-3269 Del Denver 15/4/43; ass 527BS/379BG [FO-U] Kimbolton 6/6/43; MIA Schweinfurt 14/10/43 w/Carnal, e/a, cr Schweinfurt, 2KIA 8POW, MACR 958. PICADILLY WILLY.

42-3270 Del Denver 18/4/43; ass 410BS/94BG [GL-Q] Rougham 13/6/43; retUS Lockburn 10/4/44; RFC Walnut Ridge 27/9/45. WACKY.

42-3271 Del Denver 17/4/43; Presque Is 27/5/43; ass 401BS/91BG [LL-U] Bassingbourn 7/6/43; tran 351BS/100BG [EP-L] Thorpe Abbotts 5/7/43; sal 7/3/44. NINE LITTLE YANKS AND A JERK.

42-3272 Del Denver 16/4/43; New Castle 29/4/43; La Guardia 30/8/43; ass 511BS/351BG [DS-M] Polebrook 28/5/43; MIA {10m} Hamburg 25/7/43 w/Bod, e/a, cr Hamburg, 4KIA 6POW; MACR 92. CAPTAIN BILL.

42-3273 Del Denver 18/4/43; ass 100BG Dow Fd 30/5/43; tran 412BS/95BG [QW-W] Horham 15/6/43; f/l St Eval ex-St Nazaire 28/6/43; c/l Gt Ashfield ex-La Pallice 16/9/43; c/l Potter Heigham w/Seager ex-Münster 22/12/43; 10RTD. Sal. IMPATIENT VIRGIN.

42-3274 Del Denver 13/4/43; Presque Is 15/5/43; ass 367BS/306BG [GY-L] Thurleigh 4/6/43; tran 323BS/91BG [OR-U] Bassingbourn 29/6/43; MIA Frankfurt 4/10/43 w/Schaper, cr Limburg, Bel. 1KIA 9POW, MACR 881.

42-3275 Del Denver 13/4/43; Dow Fd 2/6/43; ass 92BG Podington MARY B /43; tran 94BG Rougham /43; 339BS/96BG [QJ-O] Snetterton /43; retUS Morrison 2/8/43; sal 18/9/43; RFC Walnut Ridge 19/12/45. SACK TIME.

42-3276 Del Denver 19/4/43; Dow Fd 2/6/43; ass 8AF; sal 12/6/43.

42-3277 Del Denver 20/4/43; Dow Fd 25/5/43; ass 325BS/92BG Alconbury 15/6/43; tran 336BS/95BG [ET-G] Horham 95 16/6/43; MIA Hamburg 25/7/43 w/Mauldin, flak, cr?, 9KIA 1POW, MACR 194.

42-3278 Del Denver 20/4/43; Dow Fd 25/5/43; ass Occident 29/6/43; retUS 53 RNC Sq Grenier 24/10/43; Tinker 24/1/44; Grenier NOR ATC TSP 16/6/44.

42-3279 Del Denver 21/4/43; Dow Fd 21/5/43; ass 350BA/100BG Podington 2/6/43; Thorpe Abbotts 9/6/43; sal 29/5/44. BADGER BEAUTY.

42-3280 Del Denver 22/4/43; Presque Is 27/5/43; ass 333BS/94BG [TS-M] Earls Colne 12/5/43; Rougham 13/6/43; MIA Hannover 26/7/43 w/Smith, e/a, ditched Nth Sea, 10RTD, MACR 84.

42-3281 Del Denver 23/4/43; Dow Fd 27/5/43; ass 337BS/96BG Andrews Fd 30/5/43; Snetterton 12/6/43; MIA Hannover 26/7/43 w/Spino, e/a, cr Nindorf, Ger. 10POW MACR 96. THE MARY R.

42-3282 Del Denver 20/4/43; Dow Fd 21/5/43; ass 334BS/95BG [BG-J] Framlingham 25/5/43; Horham 15/6/43; MIA Oschersleben 28/7/43 w/Rivers, cr Hoenhn, 10POW, MACR 118.

42-3283 Del Denver 22/4/43; Dow Fd 6/6/43; ass 336BS/95BG [ET-E] Framlingham 25/5/43; Horham 15/6/43; c/l Earls Colne 4/10/43 w/O'Neal, ex-St Dizier, 7WIA 3RTD. Sal 30/1/44. YANKEE QUEEN.

42-3284 Del Denver 22/4/43; Bangor 31/5/43; ass 562BS/388BG; 413BS/96BG Snetterton 12/6/43 MIA Huls 22/6/43 w/Morrison, flak, cr?, 10POW. GUESS WHO?

42-3285 Del Denver 26/4/43; Dow Fd 20/6/43; ass 385BG Gt Ashfield 20/6/43; tran 562BS/388BG Knettishall 23/6/43; MIA Frankfurt 29/1/44 w/Hennessy, flak, cr Le Casray, 1EVD 5KIA 4POW, MACR 2349.

42-3286 Del Denver 25/4/43; Lincoln 20/5/43; ass 336BS/95BG [ET-E] Framlingham 12/5/43; MIA {1m} Kiel 13/6/43 w/Stone, cr Kiel, 10KIA MACR 2453.

42-3287 Del Denver 28/4/453; Dow Fd 24/5/43; ass 410BS/94BG [GL-O] Earls Colne DRIBBLE PUSS 6/43; Rougham 13/6/43 re-named SUGAR PUSS; sal n/b/d 4/8/43.

42-3288 Del Denver 24/4/43; Dow Fd 4/6/43; ass 338BS/96BG [BX-B] Snetterton 12/6/43; MIA Bremen 20/12/43 w/Budleski, flak, cr Nordeney, 6KIA 4POW, MACR 1704. GREEN FURY III - II.

42-3289 Del Denver 11/5/43; Bangor 15/6/43; ass 562BS/388BG Knettishall 23/6/43; MIA Stuttgart 6/9/43 w/Wick, flak, cr Stuttgart, 3KIA 7POW, MACR 3066. WOLF PACK.

42-3290 Del Denver 28/4/43; Bangor 15/6/43; ass 551BS/385BG Gt Ashfield 17/6/43; cr Bulphan, Ex. 26/9/43 ex-Rheims; sal b/d 28/9/43. RAUNCHY WOLF.

42-3291 Del Denver 30/4/43; Dow Fd 13/6/43; ass 561BS/388BG Knettishall 14/6/43; sal n/b/d 24/8/44. "MISS MAC".

42-3292 Del Denver 29/4/43; Bangor 19/6/43; ass 551BS/385BG Gt Ashfield 20/6/43; retUS San Bernardino 25/11/44; RFC Altus 9/10/45. MARY PAT.

42-3293 Del Denver 2/5/43; Dow Fd 15/6/43; ass 360BS/303BG Molesworth 12/8/43; tran 560BS/388BG Knettishall 8/43; MIA Stuttgart 6/9/43 w/Karnezis, e/a, cr Sarbonne, Fr. 5KIA 5POW, MACR 3113. SLIGHTLY DANGEROUS.

42-3294 Del Denver 20/4/43; Dow Fd 13/6/43; ass 550BS/385BG Gt Ashfield 16/6/43; MIA Merignac 5/12/43. SUZANNE.

42-3295 Del Cheyenne 27/4/43; Bangor 15/6/43; ass 562BS/388BG Knettishall 23/6/43 TECH SUPPLY; c/l base ex-Pas De Calais 24/12/43, sal 2/6/45. WAILUIKU MAID.

42-3296 Del Denver 23/4/43; Brooks Fd 3/6/43; 3017 BU Hobbs 8/11/43; 4124 BU Altus; RFC Altus 22/8/45.

42-3297 Del Cheyenne 29/4/43; Dow Fd 10/7/43; ass 571BS/390BG [FC-W] Framlingham 14/7/43; MIA Merignac 5/12/43 w/Palmer, no gas, ditched Nth Sea; MACR 1337. THE BAD PENNY.

42-3298 Del Cheyenne 30/4/43; Dow Fd 4/6/43; ass 412BS/95BG [QW-W] Horham 5/7/43; MIA Hannover 26/7/43 w/Massey, cr Hanover, 2KIA 8POW, MACR 195.

42-3299 Del Cheyenne 2/5/43; Dow Fd 10/7/43; ass 390BG Framlingham 14/7/43; sal b/d 16/8/43.

42-3300 Del Cheyenne 30/4/43; Dow Fd 30/5/43; ass 524BS/379BG [WA-F] Kimbolton 11/6/43; tran 526BS [LF-F]; MIA Evreux 3/9/43 w/Kraft, flak, cr Evreux, Fr. 3KIA 7POW, MACR 1349.

42-3301 Del Cheyenne 1/5/43; Wilmington 3/8/43; ass 367BS/306BG [GY-F] CAVALIER Thurleigh 5/43; re-named BOUNCIN' BABY; sal Shipdham 29/2/44.

42-3302 Del Cheyenne 1/5/43; Dow Fd 10/7/43; ass 571BS/390BG [FC-O] Framlingham 14/7/43; MIA Münster 10/10/43 w/Weldon, e/a, cr Diesothrup, 11POW, MACR 866. RICK-O-SHAY.

42-3303 Del Cheyenne 30/4/43; Roswell 25/5/43; c/l Hobbs 17/8/43 w/Pamperian; 3715 BU Burbank 27/8/43; RFC Kingman 18/5/45.

42-3304 Del Cheyenne 10/5/43; La Junta 6/7; WO 7/12/43.

42-3305 Del Cheyenne 7/5/43; Dow Fd 10/7/43; ass 568BS/390BG [BI-E] Framlingham 14/7/43 PRINCESS PAT; MIA Schweinfurt 17/8/43 w/Shaver, e/a, cr Hyeres, Fr. 1EVD 9POW, MACR 392. FERTILE MYRTLE.

42-3306 Del Cheyenne 23/5/43; Dow Fd 13/7/43; ass

569BS/390BG [CC-L] Framlingham 14/7/43; MIA Lille 15/8/43 w/Lawrence, mid-air coll, cr Calais, Fr. 4EVD 5KIA 1POW, MACR 258. PHOENIX.

42-3307 Del Cheyenne 27/5/43; Dow Fd 4/6/43; ass 351BS/100BG [EP-N] Thorpe Abbotts 9/6/43; c/t/o 24/1/44, 1KIA 9RTD. Sal 25/1/44. SKIPPER.

42-3308 Del Denver 27/5/43; Dow Fd 13/6/43; ass 548BS/385BG Gt Ashfield 26/6/43; MIA St Dizier 4/10/43 w/Dawurske, flak, ditched Nth Sea, 1ORTD.

42-3309 Del Cheyenne 12/5/43; Orland 1/6/43; Rapid City 3/7/43; Harvard 2/8/43; WO 24/8/43.

42-3310 Del Cheyenne 2/6/43; Dow Fd 11/7/43; ass 568BS/390BG Framlingham 14/7/43; MIA Schweinfurt 17/8/43 w/Sneed, flak, ditched Med Sea, 10RTD, MACR 396. BLOOD, GUTS AND RUST.

42-3311 Del Cheyenne 5/5/43; 3030 BU Roswell 24/5/43; 3010 BU Williams 9/12/43; 4120 BU San Bernardino 16/1/44; 3020 BU La Junta 29/3/44; RFC Walnut Ridge 31/7/45.

42-3312 Del Cheyenne 5/5/43; Dow Fd 13/7/43; ass 570BS/390BG [DI-K] Framlingham 14/7/43; MIA Huls 22/6/44 w/Bonner, flak, cr Dreux, Fr. 1KIA 9POW, MACR 5927. SEQUATCHIEE.

42-3313 Del Cheyenne 11/5/43; Roswell 23/5/43; 3036 BU Yuma 19/6/43; RFC Ontario 30/5/45.

42-3314 Del Cheyenne 11/5/43; 3030 BU Roswell 6/11/43; 3010 BU Williams 12/12/43; 3020 BU La Junta 25/4/44; RFC Searcey Fd 31/7/45.

42-3315 Del Cheyenne 11/5/43; 3030 BU Roswell 6/11/43; 3010 BU Williams 11/12/43; 4160 BU Alamogordo 10/8/44; RFC Ardmore 11/8/45.

42-3316 Del Denver 6/5/43; Kearney 29/5/43; ass 550BS/385BG Gt Ashfield 26/6/43 BIG STINKY; MIA Warnemünde 28/7/43 w/Storr, coll w/a/c, ditched Nth Sea, 10KIA, MACR 189B. BETTY BOOM.

42-3317 Del Denver 6/5/43; Dow Fd 30/5/43; ass 384BG Grafton Underwood 10/6/43; tran 412BS/95BG [QW-Y] Horham 28/6/43; MIA Solingen 30/11/43 w/Hensler, cr Solingen, Ger. 2KIA 8POW, MACR 195.

42-3318 Del Denver 6/5/43; Dow Fd 30/5/43; ass 545BS/384BG [JD-R] Grafton Underwood 2/6/43; tran 337BS/96BG [AW-V] Snetterton 6/43; MIA Kerlin 23/9/43 w/Wilcox, 10 KIA, MACR 670. SHACK RABBIT II.

42-3319 Del Denver 7/5/43; Presque Is 2/6/43; ass 333BS/94BG [XM-A2] Earls Colne 5/6/43 THIS END UP; re-named WACKEROO II, then SHACKEROO II; retUS Tinker 9/4/44; Wright Fd 26/11/44; Bolling 29/12/44; Drew 10/2/45; Wright 20/3/45; Drew 15/10/45; RFC Walnut Ridge 7/1/46.

42-3320 Del Denver 9/5/43; Gore Fd 14/5/43; WO 21/5/43.

42-3321 Del Denver 7/5/43; Dow Fd 2/6/43; ass 91BG Bassingbourn 5/6/43; tran 336BS/95BG [ET-K] Horham 16/6/43; MIA Stuttgart 6/9/43 w/Rothschild, ditched Nth Sea, 9RTD 1WIA. KATHY JANE II.

42-3322 Del Denver 10/5/43; Bangor 1/6/43; ass 339BS/96BG [QJ-J] Andrews Fd 2/6/43; Snetterton 12/6/43; MIA Sorau 11/4/44 w/Winslow, e/a, cr Baltic Sea, 4KIA 6POW, MACR 3819/3808. FULL HOUSE.

42-3323 Del Denver 7/5/43; Moses Lake 21/5/43; 325 BU Avon Park 9/4/44; RFC Walnut Ridge 17/9/45.

42-3324 Del Denver 8/5/43; Dow Fd 2/6/43; ass (F-9) 339BS/96BG [QJ-H] Andrews Fd 5/6/43 RIKKI TIKKI TAVI II; Snetterton 12/6/43; MIA Berlin 7/5/44 w/Behrens, cr Nedlitz, Ger. 8KIA 2POW, MACR 4565. GEORGIA PEACH.

42-3325 Del Denver 7/5/43; Dow Fd 30/5/43; ass 524BS/379BG [WA-Y] Kimbolton 1/6/43; MIA Brunswick 30/1/44 w/Davis, ditched Nth Sea, 10POW, MACR 2867. PADDY GREMLIN.

42-3326 Del Denver 10/5/43; Dow Fd 31/5/43; ass 413BS/96BG Andrews Fd 3/6/43; Snetterton 12/6/43; MIA Oschersleben 28/7/43 w/Moore, e/a, cr Nth Sea, 10KIA, MACR 137. MOORE-FIDITE II.

42-3327 Del Denver 10/5/43; Dow Fd 11/7/43; ass 569BS/390BG [CC-T] Framlingham 18/7/43; sal b/d 27/10/43. TET TMOTE.

42-3328 Del Denver 10/5/43; Tinker 22/7/43; ass 568BS/390BG [BI-D] Framlingham 15/7/43; MIA Münster 10/10/43 w/Sneed, e/a, cr Burgsteinfurt, Ger. 6KIA 4POW, MACR 861. MISS FORTUNE.

42-3329 Del Denver 14/5/43; Dow Fd 9/6/43; ass 570BS/390BG [DI-F] Framlingham 15/7/43; sal 8/2/44. SKIPPY.

42-3330 Del Denver 17/5/43; Dow Fd 11/6/43; ass 544BS/384BG [SU-N] Grafton Underwood 27/6/43; MIA 14/7/43 w/Munday.

42-3331 Del Denver 11/5/43; Dow Fd 2/6/43; ass 331BS/94BG [QE-Z] Earls Colne 5/6/43; Rougham 13/6/43 as "NATURALS"; MIA SOE Operation 'Cadillac' (Resistance supplies) 14/7/43 w/Purdy, coll e/a, cr Evreux, 2EVD 9KIA, MACR 116. SALTY'S NATURALS.

42-3332 Del Denver 15/5/43; 3030 BU Roswell 23/5/43; 3010 BU Williams 11/12/43; 3020 BU La Junta 29/3/44; RFC Searcey Fd 7/8/45.

Below: B-17F-45-DL 42-3328, serving with the 568th Bomb Squadron, sets out on a combat mission in morning sunshine, early September 1943. The aircraft is flying over Bloomville Hall, Hacheston, near its English base. The circular spot on the outer right wing section is one of the filler caps for the 'Tokyo tanks'. (USAAF)

Above: B-17F-50-DL 42-3352 with underwing racks and a 1,000lb HE bomb on each. The racks were rarely employed on high-altitude bombing missions as the extra weight and drag severely restricted range. (USAF)

42-3333 Del Denver 12/5/43; Dow Fd 12/7/43; ass 569BS/390BG [CC-O] Framlingham 14/7/43; MIA Schweinfurt 17/8/43 w/Becker, e/a, ditched Med Sea, 3KIA 7POW, MACR 389. PURGATORY PETE.

42-3334 Del Denver 15/5/43; 3030 BU Roswell 6/11/43; 3010 BU Williams 12/12/43; RFC Altus 7/11/45.

42-3335 Del Denver 17/5/43; Dow Fd 14/6/43; ass 549BS/385BG Gt Ashfield 14/6/43; sal 29/5/45. FICKLE FINGER OF FATE.

42-3336 Del Denver 17/5/43; Bangor 12/7/43; ass 549BS/385BG Gt Ashfield 26/6/43; sal 27/10/43; tran 97BG Amendola; sal 28/7/44.

42-3337 Del Denver 20/5/43; Dow Fd 8/7/43; ass 548BS/385BG Gt Ashfield 12/7/43; MIA Sorau 11/4/44 w/Mullins, e/a, cr Stettin, Ger. 10KIA, MACR 3819/4266.

42-3338 Del Denver 20/5/43; ass 385BG Dow Fd 29/6/43; tran 331BS/94BG [QE-P] Rougham 7/43; MIA Schweinfurt 14/10/43 w/Dodge, e/a, cr Essey-et-Maizeras, 5KIA 5POW, MACR 791.

42-3339 Del Denver 20/5/43; Dyersburg 14/7/43; Dalhart 14/8/43; 330 BU Dyersburg 1/3/44; 327 BU Drew 15/5/43; 4124 BU Altus 5/6/45; RFC Altus 9/10/45.

42-3340 Del Denver 15/5/43; Presque Is 27/6/43; ass 338BS/96BG [BX-U]; tran 20BG/2BG Ain M'Lila 28/6/43; Massicault 31/7/43; {22m} tran 340BS/97BG Depienne 14/11/43; Cerignola 20/12/43; Amendola 16/1/44; weather ship 15/7/44; cr base 14/5/45. Sal.

42-3341 Del Denver 15/5/43; Presque Is 27/6/43; ass 429BS/2BG Ain M'Lila 12/7/43; Massicault 31/7/43; MIA {7m} Weiner Nuestadt 2/11/43 w/Gillan, e/a, MACR 1142. LADY BE GOOD.

42-3342 Del Denver 15/5/43; Morrison 10/6/43; ass 429BS/2BG Château-du-Rhumel 11/6/43; Ain M'Lila 17/6/43; {4} c/t/o 6/7/43 10K.TUFF TIT.

42-3343 Del Denver 15/5/43; Presque Is 13/6/43; ass 32BS/301BG St Donat 14/6/43; Oudna 6/8/43; Cerignola 7/12/43; Lucera 1/2/44; {58m} became weather ship /44; depot 6/10/44; sal 11/7/45. SLICK CHICK.

42-3344 Del Denver 16/5/43; Presque Is 11/6/43; ass 346BS/99BG Navarin 29/6/43; Oudna 4/8/43; tran 97BG Depienne 14/11/43; Cerignola 20/12/43; Amendola 16/1/44; 353BS/301BG Lucera 2/4/44 ; MIA ({16}) Budapest 27/6/44 w/Lyon, e/a, cr Budapest 4KIA 6POW. MACR 6173.

42-3345 Del Denver 20/5/43; Dow Fd 26/6/43; ass 338BS/96BG Snetterton 31/6/43; MIA Oschersleben 28/7/43 w/Deshotels, e/a, cr Nth Sea, 10POW. MACR 128. PAPER DOLL.

42-3346 Del Denver 1/6/43; Dow Fd 25/6/43; ass 333BS/94BG [TS-C] Rougham 7/43; sal 10/12/43; retUS Patterson 2/3/45; RFC Cincinnati 30/7/45. TUFF TITTY.

42-3347 Del Denver 14/5/43; Dow Fd 25/6/43; ass 550BS/385BG 6/43; sal 14/10/43. CHARLENE.

42-3348 Del Denver 23/5/43; Dow Fd 26/6/43; ass337BS/96BG [AW-G] Snetterton 12/7/43; MIA Schweinfurt 14/10/43 w/Bye, s/d by e/a. cr Metz, Fr. 4EVD 6POW. MACR 833. DOTTIE J III.

42-3349 Del Denver 22/5/43; Dow Fd 27/6/43; ass 332BS/94BG [XM-E] Rougham 7/43 EL MANGAU; re-named EL DIABLO then LIBERTY; MIA Bordeaux 5/12/43 w/Perrine, e/a, cr Bordeaux, 10KIA, MACR 1175. EL LOBO.

42-3350 Del Denver 20/5/43; 10 STA Grenier 5/7/43; 110 BU Ft Dix 13/12/43; 121 RDC Bradley 20/12/43; 110 BU Mitchell 2/7/44; RFC Stillwater 23/8/45.

42-3351 Del Denver 18/5/43; Dow Fd 8/7/43; ass 407BS/92BG [PY-E/Z] Alconbury 24/7/43; c/l Winkfield 14/10/43, sal.

42-3352 Del Denver 15/5/43; Dow Fd 7/7/43; ass 410BS/94BG [GL-V] Rougham 7/43; MIA Solingen 29/11/43 w/Chyle, flak, cr Nth Sea, 9KIA 1POW, MACR 1186. VIRGIN'S DELIGHT.

42-3353 Del Denver 20/5/43; Dow Fd 7/7/43; ass 337BS/96BG [AW-L] Snetterton 13/7/43; MIA 9/9/43 w/Noordewier, flak, cr Paris. TAR FLY.

42-3354 Del Denver 20/5/43; Dow Fd 11/7/43; ass 353BS/301BG St Donat 13/7/43; Cerignola 7/12/43; Lucera 1/2/44; {21m} tran 97BG Amendola; depot 26/6/44; sal 30/11/45. BIG STOOP.

42-3355 Del Denver 22/5/43; Dow Fd 14/7/43; ass 550BS/385BG Gt Ashfield 18/7/43; sal 29/5/45. NAN B.

42-3356 Del Denver 23/5/43; Dow Fd 4/7/43; ass 548BS/385BG Gt Ashfield 9/7/43; retUS Bradley 3/7/44; RFC Altus 14/8/45. MAYFLY.

42-3357 Del Denver 21/5/43; Dow Fd 5/6/43; ass (H2S) 813BS/482BG [PC-S] Alconbury 1/7/43; MIA 8/2/44 w/Gold, e/a, cr Dreslincourt, Fr. MACR 2781.

42-3358 Del Denver 19/5/43; Presque Is 8/8/43; ass (H2S) 813BS/482BG Alconbury 28/8/43; tran MTO; retUS Morrison 14/11/44; RFC Walnut Ridge 3/11/45.

42-3359 Del Denver 25/5/43; Dow Fd 9/7/43; ass Soxo?; sal n/b/d 23/12/44.

42-3360 Del Denver 24/5/43; Orlando 10/6/43; 16 STA Grenier 8/7/43; 110 BU Bradley 5/1/44; 110 BU Mitchell 2/7/44; RFC 13/7/44. Civil Reg 67974; to Bolivia CB-70; cr La Paz 21/9/55.

42-3361 Del Denver 16/6/43; Presque Is 7/7/43; ass 340BS/2BG Ain M'Lila 13/7/43; Massicault 31/7/43; MIA w/Bryan, Capua 26/8/43; b/d ditched off Palermo, crew rescued.

42-3362 Del Denver 25/5/43; Dow Fd 5/7/43; ass 533BS/381BG Ridgewell 5/7/43; tran 2 BAD Lt Staughton 7/1/44; then MTO 340BS/97BG Château-du-Rhumel 13/7/43; Pont-du-Fahs 1/8/43; Depienne 15/8/43; Cerignola 20/12/43; Amendola 16/1/44; MIA Ponte Corvo 22/1/44 w/Oberly, cr Ponte Corvo, MACR 2032. CULTURED VULTURE.

42-3363 Del Denver 25/5/43; Presque Is 2/8/43; ass 367BS/306BG [GY-G] Thurleigh 14/8/43; MIA Osnabrück 22/12/43 w/Winter, e/a, cr Verwulde, 7KIA 3POW; MACR 1716. PUNCHY.

42-3364 Del Denver 25/5/43; Dyersburg 13/7/43; 202 BU Galveston 12/2/44; 268 BU Peterson 30/3/44; RFC Kingman 27/10/45.

Above: B-17F-50-DL 42-3389 saw three months of combat from North African bases before being lost in the Mediterranean. When photographed it was serving as *Rangy Lil* with the 347th Bomb Squadron (signified by the two vertical bars on the fin) of the 99th Bomb Group (identified by the diamond marking). The position of the ball turret guns indicates that the turret entry door is accessible from inside the fuselage. (USAF)

42-3365 Del Denver 26/5/43; 244 BU Harvard 2/8/43; Sioux City 6/3/44; 136 BU Tinker 30/4/44; Harvard 7/5/44; 4160 BU Albuquerque 20/6/44; RFC Albuquerque 19/6/45.

42-3366 Del Denver 24/5/43; Ephrata 15/7/43; 235 BU Biggs 17/1/44; 4202 BU Syracuse 19/2/44; RFC Walnut Ridge 20/12/45.

42-3367 Del Denver 27/5/43; ass 340BS/383BG Geiger 17/7/43; 542 BU Lackland 21/1/44; 222 BU Ardmore 24/3/44; 4120 BU Freeman 22/8/44; RFC Kingman 10/2/46.

42-3368 Del Denver 29/5/43; Dyersberg 14/7/43; 4136 BU Tinker 19/8/43; ass 505BG Harvard 16/9/43; 244 BU Alliance 16/12/43; 4160 BU Albuquerque 20/6/45.

42-3369 Del Denver 30/5/43; Dyersburg 15/7/43; Tinker 12/12/43; tran RCAF 168th Heavy Trans Sqd [9204] Rockcliffe, for VIPs & mail; c/l 17/9/44 Prestwick, sal.

42-3370 Del Denver 27/5/43; 223 BU Dyersburg 15/7/43; WO 27/9/44.

42-3371 Del Denver 1/6/43; Moses Lake 16/7/43; 4000 BU Patterson 23/7/43; 222 BU Ardmore 20/11/43; A F10 Brazil (Mapping) 8/6/44; 332 BU Ardmore 1/8/44; 581 BU Adams 18/9/44; Recl Comp 15/11/45.

42-3372 Del Denver 1/6/43; 247 BU Smoky Hill 28/6/43; 203 BU Dalhart 26/8/43; 242 BU Gd Isle 25/10/43; 4103 BU Tinker 18/2/44; 203 BU Jackson 11/3/44; A F10 Atkinson (Mapping) 1/9/44; RFC Walnut Ridge 14/2/45.

42-3373 Del Denver 17/5/43; ass 338BS/96BG Dow Fd 1/7/43 LADY MILLICENT III; 245 BU McCook 15/7/43; Peterson 26/7/43; 214 BU Alliance 14/9/43; 268 BU Peterson 28/3/44; Recl Comp 14/8/45.

42-3374 Del Denver 27/5/43; Gore 15/7/43; Dyersburg 13/11/43; WO 8/9/44. Restored as HOMESICK ANGEL, at Beale AFB 1988.

42-3375 Del Denver 13/5/43; Dyersburg 16/7/43; 3010 BU Williams 6/4/43; 3020 BU La Junta 10/2/45; RFC Love Fd 31/7/45.

42-3376 Del Denver 1/5/43; Moses Lake 16/7/43; 3701 BU Amarillo 26/1/44; RFC Walnut Ridge 9/10/45.

42-3377 Del Denver 1/6/43; Ephrata 16/7/43; Rapid City 1/10/43; 224 BU Sioux City 15/2/44; WO 28/11/44; Recl Comp 6/12/44.

42-3378 Del Denver 1/6/43; Dow Fd 7/7/43; ass 563BS/388BG Knettishall 9/7/43 SKY SHY; MIA 6/9/43 w/Roe, e/a, cr Stuttgart, 1KIA 9POW. MACR 3114. SILVER DOLLAR.

42-3379 Del Denver 1/6/43; Kearney 30/6/43; WO 3/7/43.

42-3380 Del Denver 31/5/43; Dow Fd 9/7/43; ass 32BS/301BG St Donat 13/7/43; Oudna 6/8/43; MIA {32m} Wiener Neustadt 2/11/43 w/Mason, e/a, cr Wiener Neustadt, 3KIA 7POW, MACR 1095.

42-3381 Del Denver 31/5/43; Dow Fd 9/7/43; ass 12AF 13/7/43; MIA 4/11/43, flak.

42-3382 Del Denver 1/6/43; Presque Is 7/8/43; ass 360BS/303BG Molesworth 12/8/43; tran 306BG Thurleigh 22/2/44; tran (Oboe) 813BS/482BG [PC-I] Alconbury 10/5/44; sal 9AAF Stansted /44.

42-3383 Del Denver 1/6/43; Dow Fd 9/7/43; ass 346BS/99BG Navarin 28/7/43; Oudna 4/8/43; tran 341BS/97BG Depienne 14/11/43; Cerignola 20/12/43; Amendola 16/1/44; MIA Focsani 11/6/44 w/Young, e/a, cr Bucharest, MACR 6425. SPIRIT OF McCOOK.

42-3384 Del Denver 1/6/43; Presque Is 6/8/43; ass 20BS/2BG Massicault 27/8/43; tran 353BS/301BG Oudna 14/11/43; Cerignola 7/12/43; Lucera 1/2/44; {53m} to depot 20/7/44; sal 14/9/44.

42-3385 Del Denver 1/6/43; Dow Fd 1/7/43; ass (Oboe) 407BS/92BG [PY-K] Alconbury 11/8/43; tran 813BS/482BG Alconbury 25/8/43; to 9AF Stansted 5/2/44.

42-3386 Del Denver 1/6/43; Presque Is 7/8/43; ass 351BS/100BG [EP-H] Thorpe Abbotts 23/8/43; MIA Bremen 8/10/43 w/Gormley, coll w/e/a, cr Bellingwolde; 10KIA, MACR 949. MARIE HELENA.

42-3387 Del Denver 1/6/43; Presque Is 4/8/43; ass 364BS/305BG [WF-O] Chelveston 20/8/43; MIA Bremen 26/11/43 w/Sartis, flak, cr Oldenburg, 10POW, MACR 1573.

42-3388 Del Denver 1/6/43; Dow Fd 13/7/43; ass 388BG Knettishall 3/8/43; tran 550BS/385BG Gt Ashfield /43; MIA Oberpfaffenhofen 24/4/44 w/Nesen, e/a, ditched Channel, 6KIA 1POW 3RTD; MACR 4452 SLEEPY TIME GIRL.

42-3389 Del Denver 1/6/43; Presque Is 31/7/43; ass 347BS/99BG Oudna 13/8/43; tran 340BS/97BG Depienne 14/11/43; MIA Toulon 22/11/43 w/Jones, ditched crew OK. RANGY LIL.

42-3390 Del Denver 1/6/43; 303 BU Roswell 6/11/43; 3010 BU Williams 11/1/44; 3020 BU La Junta 8/4/44; RFC Searcey Fd 31/7/45.

42-3391 Del Denver 1/6/43; Presque Is 1/8/43; ass 32BS/301BG St Donat 2/8/43; Oudna 6/8/43; MIA {32m} Wiener Neustadt 2/11/43 w/Veazey, e/a, cr Espang, 4KIA, MACR 1092. GEORGIA PEACH.

42-3392 Del Denver 4/6/43; Presque Is 31/7/43; ass 96BS/2BG Massicault 8/8/43; tran 353BS/301BG Cerignola; {89m} 97BG Amendola as weather ship /44; depot 11/10/44; RFC Bush Fd 10/5/45.

42-3393 Del Denver 1/6/43; Dow Fd 1/7/43; ass 418BS/100BG [LD-Y] Thorpe Abbotts 5/7/43 BLAKELY'S PROVISIONAL GROUP; b/d Bremen 8/10/43, c/l Ludham, sal 12/10/43. JUST-A-SNAPPIN'.

42-3394 Del Denver 2/6/43; 3030 BU Roswell 6/11/43; 3010 BU Williams 11/1/44; 4160 BU Albuquerque 10/8/44; RFC Albuquerque 13/8/45.

42-3395 Del Denver 4/6/43; Dow Fd 15/7/43; ass 561BS/388BG Knettishall 17/7/43; c/l Honington ex-Ludwigshafen 7/1/44. Sal. PASSIONATE WITCH II.

42-3396 Del Denver 5/6/43; Dow Fd 14/7/43; ass 337BS/96BG [AW-D] Snetterton 18/7/43; sal nbd 26/4/44.

42-3397 Del Denver 5/6/43; Dow Fd 14/7/43; ass 551BS/385BG Gt Ashfield 15/7/43; MIA Bordeaux 5/12/43 w/Kleuser, e/a, ditched Biscay, 7KIA 3POW, MACR 2164. FIGHTING COCK.

42-3398 Del Denver 5/6/43; Dow Fd 14/7/43; ass 12AF 16/7/43; retUS Tinker 24/7/43; 358BS/303BG 1/8/43; 813BS/482BG [PC-Q] 2/8/43; Ferry Comm 20/5/44; retUS Okmulgee 24/7/43; Eglin 18/2/45; RFC Walnut Ridge 28/1/46. MRS SATAN, THE QUEEN OF HELL.

42-3399 Del Dallas 7/6/43; Missing on flight to Geiger 29/6/43; WO 8/7/44.

42-3400 Del Dallas 7/6/43; Dow Fd 16/7/43; ass 334BS/95BG [BG-D] Horham 3/8/43; f/l Ford ex-Stuttgart 6/9/43; sal 21/6/45. THE GREMLIN'S SWEETHEART.

42-3401 Del Dallas 4/6/43; Sebring 30/6/43; 2137 BU Hendricks 4/10/43; Kansas City 9/12/43; Hendricks 5/9/44; RFC Walnut Ridge 9/11/45.

42-3402 Del Denver 10/6/43; Dow 15/7/43; ass Soxo?; MIA Stuttgart 6/9/43.

42-3403 Del Denver 9/6/43; Pyote 3/7/43; 221 BU Alexandria 3/8/43; RFC Altus 9/45.

42-3404 Del Denver 7/6/43; Hendricks 7/7/43; WO 16/3/44.

42-3405 Del Denver 3/6/43; 3030 BU Roswell 6/11/43; 3010 BU Williams 12/12/43; 3020 BU La Junta 29/3/44; RFC Kingman 31/7/45.

42-3406 Del Long Beach 9/6/43; Smoky Hill 9/7/43; ass 367BS/306BG [GY-V] Thurleigh 4/8/43; MIA Gelsenkirchen 12/8/43 w/Cunningham, flak, cr Hammerich, 8KIA 2POW, MACR 255. BIG OPERATOR.

42-3407 Del Long Beach 9/6/43; 2137 BU Hendricks 21/7/43; RFC Walnut Ridge 19/12/45.

42-3408 Del Long Beach 9/6/43; 2137 BU Hendricks 4/10/43; WO 1/12/44; Recl Comp 17/7/45.

42-3409 Del Long Beach 9/6/43; Hendricks 30/6/43; 2138 BU Tyndall 19/11/43; 2114 BU Lockburn 11/1/44; RFC Walnut Ridge 14/12/45.

42-3410 Del Long Beach 9/6/43; 2137 BU Hendricks 9/1/44; Sioux City 4/4/44; Hendricks 7/8/44; RFC Walnut Ridge 19/12/45.

INDIVIDUAL B-17 HISTORIES 97

42-3411 Del Dallas 1/6/43; Homestead 11/7/43; ass 532BS/381BG [VE-I] Ridgewell 21/9/43; {11+m} tran AFSC 19/5/44; retUS Tinker 12/7/44; RFC Bush Fd 10/5/45.

42-3412 Del Dallas 15/6/43; Presque Is 17/8/43; ass 365BS/305BG [XK-M] Chelveston 20/8/43; MIA 20/12/43 w/Nerdyke, flak, cr Beatstreck, 6KIA 4POW, MACR 1709.

42-3413 Del Dallas 10/6/43; Dow Fd 18/8/43; ass 350BS/100BG [LN-V] Thorpe Abbotts 20/8/43; MIA 14/8/44 w/Cielewich, flak, cr Falkengesass, 9POW, MACR 7899. HARD LUCK !

42-3414 Del Dallas 1/6/43; Dow Fd 14/8/43; ass 561BS/388BG Knettishall 18/7/43; MIA Schweinfurt 17/8/43 w/Parker, no gas, ditched Med Sea, 10RTD. PADDLEFOOT.

42-3415 Del Dallas 11/6/43; Topeka 21/7/43; ass 571BS/390BG [FC-Q] Framlingham 25/8/43; MIA Münster 10/10/43 w/Starnes, coll, cr Burgsteinfurt, 9KIA 1POW, MACR 859. MISS BEHAVIN'.

42-3416 Del Denver 10/6/43; 2126 BU Laredo 3/9/43; 1077 BU Bowman 7/7/44; Laredo 23/7/44; RFC Walnut Ridge 8/7/45.

42-3417 Del Denver 15/6/43; Chanute 16/8/43; c/l Patterson 9/10/43 w/Matthews,WO 22/10/43.

42-3418 Del Long Beach 13/6/43; Chanute 16/8/43; 2137 BU Hendricks 22/7/44; 2140 BU Sioux City 23/10/44; Hendricks 25/8/45; RFC Walnut Ridge 13/12/45.

42-3419 Del Long Beach 11/6/43; Pyote 3/7/44; 223 BU Dyersburg 15/8/43; F10 (mapping) Brazil 24/6/44; 330 BU Dyersburg 9/4/45; 327 BU Drew 14/5/45; RFC Altus 4/10/45.

42-3420 Del Denver 16/6/43; Hobbs 3/7/43; ATC HQ Hills 14/8/43; Inv Lst 30/11/45.

42-3421 Del Denver 4/6/43; Hobbs 3/7/43; c/l 5 miles SE base 19/10/43 w/Comstock, fire on board. WO. Pilot and one pass severe injuries, three passengers minor injuries.

42-3422 Del Denver 16/6/43; Dow Fd 20/7/43; ass 551BS/385BG Gt Ashfield 24/7/43; MIA Regensburg 25/2/44 w/Davis, flak, cr Regensburg, 1KIA 9POW, MACR 2775. WINNIE THE POOH.

42-3423 Del Tulsa 18/6/43; Alexandria 11/7/43; WO 18/11/43.

42-3424 Del Tulsa 16/6/43; Alexandria 11/7/43; WO 21/9/43.

42-3425 Del Denver 1/6/43; Dow Fd 14/7/43; ass 563BS/388BG Knettishall 18/7/43 SILVER DOLLAR II; MIA Stuttgart 6/9/43 w/Cunningham, e/a, cr Troyes, Fr, 2EVD 8POW, MACR 3115. IN GOD WE TRUST.

42-3426 Del Denver 6/6/43; Kearney 7/7/43; ass 571BS/390BG [FC-Y] Framlingham 25/7/43 SPIDER; re-named KEMY JR; MIA Münster 10/10/43 w/Smith, flak, cr Isendorf, 3KIA 7POW, MACR 864. KEMY II.

42-3427 Del Denver 16/6/43; Kearney 17/7/43; ass 568BS/390BG [BI-B] Framlingham 25/7/43 SIX NIGHTS IN TELERGMA (ARABIAN NUTS); sal 22/6/45. CANADIAN CLUB.

42-3428 Del Denver 17/6/43; Kearney 20/7/43; ass 407BS/92BG Alconbury 14/8/43; MIA Stuttgart 6/9/43 w/Carlson, e/a, ditched Channel, 10RTD.

42-3429 Del Denver 20/6/43; Kearney 20/7/43; ass 544BS/384BG [SU-F] Grafton Underwood 11/8/43; 1 BAD Burtonwood 8/6/44; retUS LU RTO A6F Phillips 29/11/44. FLAK HOUSE.

42-3430 Del Denver 1/6/43; Dow Fd 20/7/43; ass 338BS/96BG [BX-U] Snetterton 26/7/43; MIA Schweinfurt 14/10/43 w/Horton, e/a, cr Shambry, 2EVD 8POW, MACR 835. CAROLINA BOOMERANG.

42-3431 Del Denver 12/6/43; Hobbs 17/7/43; 93BG Pyote 9/10/43; 271 BU Kearney 15/9/43; 4136 BU Tinker 23/9/43; Kearney 12/10/43; 268 BU Peterson 1/12/43; 273 BU Lincoln 11/1/44; RFC Kingman 12/11/45.

42-3432 Del Denver 1/6/43; 19BG Pyote 2/7/43; 224 BU Sioux City 15/10/43; RFC Albuquerque 24/5/45.

42-3433 Del Denver 12/6/43; Dow Fd 14/7/43; ass 350BS/100BG [LN-W] Thorpe Abbotts 18/7/43; MIA Münster 10/10/43 w/Kramer, flak, cr Münster, 3KIA 7POW, MACR 1024. LENA.

42-3434 Del Denver 12/6/43; Dow Fd 20/7/43; ass 364BS/305BG [WF-E] Chelveston 12/8/43; MIA Stuttgart 6/9/43 w/ Glaiser, no gas, f/l Dubendorf, Switz. 10 INT, MACR 1342. Ret 12/10/45. SO WHAT?

42-3435 Del Denver 12/6/43; Dow Fd 20/7/43; ass 366BS/305BG [KY-F] Chelveston 26/7/43; tran 327BS/92BG Alconbury 12/8/42; MIA Schweinfurt 17/8/43 w/Sargent, e/a, cr St Huibrechts-Hern, Bel, 3EVD 7POW, MACR 654.

42-3436 Del Denver 15/6/43; Redmond 15/8/43; ass 96BG 16/8/43; tran 364BS/305BG [WF-R] Chelveston 18/9/43; MIA 14/10/43 w/McDarby, e/a, cr Eygelshofen, Holl. 5KIA 5POW, MACR 1034.

42-3437 Del Denver 18/6/43; Dow Fd 22/7/43; ass 339BS/96BG Snetterton 27/7/43; MIA 15/9/43 w/Richardson, flak, cr Paris, 9KIA 1EVD. MACR 726.

42-3438 Del Denver 23/6/43; Dow Fd 19/7/43; ass 337BS/96BG [AW-F] Snetterton 20/7/43; tran 36BS RCM Sculthorpe /44. MIA 30/10/44.

42-3439 Del Denver 21/6/43; Redmond 14/8/43; ass 413BS/96BG [MZ-V] Snetterton 15/8/43; MIA 20/10/43 w/Gerber, e/a, cr De Bilt, Hol, 1EVD 5KIA 4POW, MACR 1018.

42-3440 Del Denver 13/6/43; Dow Fd 29/7/43; ass 544BS/384BG [SU-B/P] Grafton Underwood 6/6/43; tran Aphrodite Knettishall 8/6/44; sal n/b/d 25/5/45. BROADWAY ROSE.

42-3441 Del Denver 14/6/43; Kearney 19/7/43; ass 547BS/384BG [SO-E] Grafton Underwood 9/8/43 THE SPOTTED COW; retUS Grenier 24/9/45; RFC Walnut Ridge 12/12/45. PATCHES II.

42-3442 Del Denver 23/6/43; Dow Fd 14/7/43; ass 338BS/96BG [BX-O] Snetterton 18/7/43 HELL'S CHARIOT; sal b/d 20/5/44. WACKY WOODY.

42-3443 Del Denver 23/6/43; Scott Fd 13/8/43; ass 8AF; MIA 22/10/43.

42-3444 Del Denver 23/6/43; ass 505BG Harvard 13/7/43; Tinker 19/9/43; 244 BU Harvard 23/9/44; 4121 BU Kelly 12/12/44, RFC Kingman 10/7/45.

42-3445 Del Denver 23/6/43; 383BG Geiger 26/7/43; 452BG Pendleton 28/10/43; 330 BU Dyersberg 1/3/44; 327 BU Drew 14/5/44; 4124 BU Altus 8/6/44; RFC Altus 9/10/45.

42-3446 Del Denver 18/6/43; Dow Fd 15/7/43; ass 331BS/94BG [QE-W] Rougham 9/43; sal 26/7/45. CHARLIE'S DELIGHT.

42-3447 Del Cheyenne 19/6/43; Geiger 19/7/43; ass 550BS/385BG Gt Ashfield 8/43; 6/2/44 plus; CHARLENE THE BAMA QUEEN.

42-3448 Del Cheyenne 13/6/43; Scott Fd 9/8/43; ass 359BS/303BG Molesworth 18/10/43; MIA Oschersleben 11/1/44 w/Eich, cr Brunswick, 1KIA 9POW, MACR 1924.

42-3449 Del Long Beach 24/6/43; Dow Fd 28/7/43; ass 369BS/306BG [WW-X] Thurleigh 14/8/43; c/l Wing, UK. 5/9/43, sal.

42-3450 Del Cheyenne 13/6/43; Roswell 19/7/43; WO 26/4/44.

42-3451 Del Cheyenne 24/6/43; 19BG Pyote 20/7/43; Galveston 2/2/44; 221 BU Alex- andria 22/2/44; 202 BU Alexandria 1/3/44; RFC Kingman 24/5/45.

42-3452 Del Cheyenne 24/6/43; Presque Is 17/8/43; ass 350BS/100BG [LN-Z] Thorpe Abbotts 20/8/43; MIA Paris 15/9/43 w/Vetter, flak, cr St Just, Fr. 7EVD 1KIA 2POW. MACR 645.

42-3453 Del Cheyenne 28/6/43; Presque Is 17/8/43; ass 331BS/94BG [TS-K] Rougham 17/8/43; MIA Schweinfurt 14/10/43 w/Nettles, e/a, cr Schweinfurt, 10POW, MACR 831.

42-3454 Del Cheyenne 26/6/43; 435BS/19BG Pyote 19/7/43; ass 333BS/94BG stayed US 25/6/43; WO 10/12/43.

42-3455 Del Cheyenne 21/6/43; Dow 28/7/43; ass 546BS/384BG [BK-M] Grafton Underwood 11/8/43; MIA Stuttgart 6/9/43 w/Faulkiner, no gas, cr Rheims, 2EVD 8POW, MACR 775. LUCKY THIRTEEN.

42-3456 Del Cheyenne 21/6/43; 19BG Pyote 20/7/43; Galena 5/12/43; WO 24/3/44.

42-3457 Del Cheyenne 25/6/43; 457BG Geiger 24/7/43; 224 BU Sioux City 6/3/44; 4160 BU Albuquerque 20/6/44; RFC Albuquerque 19/6/45.

42-3458 Del Cheyenne 26/6/43; Dalhart 25/7/43; WO 28/7/43.

42-3459 Del Cheyenne 26/6/43; Dow Fd 29/7/43; ass 546BS/384BG [BK-F] Grafton Underwood 9/8/43; MIA Rennes 23/9/43 w/Higdon, e/a, cr Pontivy, Fr. 3EVD 7POW, MACR 748.

42-3460 Del Cheyenne 30/6/43; Dalhart 20/7/43; ass 504BG McCook 19/8/43; 241 BU Fairmont 23/9/43; 2534 BU San Angelo 15/12/43; Recl Comp 17/12/45.

42-3461 Del Cheyenne 1/7/43; Dow Fd 29/7/43; ass 407BS/92BG [PY-S] Alconbury 23/8/43; tran Aphrodite Knettishall 17/6/44; l/Wizernes 4/8/44.

42-3462 Del Cheyenne 29/6/43; Dow 14/7/43; ass 336BS/95BG [ET-B] Horham 18/7/43; b/d by e/a Schweinfurt 14/10/43 w/Kerr, 3POW 7RTB w/a/c, MACR 856; MIA 21/2/44 w/Marks, e/a, cr ljselmeer, 8KIA 2POW, MACR 2424. SAN ANTONIO ROSE.

42-3463 Del Cheyenne 25/6/43; Moses Lake 3/8/43; 497BG Pratt 11/8/43; 225 ASC Rapid City 29/4/44; RFC Ontario 19/6/45.

42-3464 Del Denver 16/6/43; Dalhart 6/8/43; 327 BU Drew 21/7/44; WO 21/7/44.

42-3465 Del Denver 28/6/43; Presque Is 17/8/43; ass 412BS/95BG [QW-N] Horham 30/8/43; f/l RAF Friston 30/11/43 w/Conley 7RTD 3WIA. RetUS 3704 Keesler 10/4/44; RFC Altus 24/5/45.

42-3466 Del Denver 26/6/43; Ephrata 30/7/43; WO 5/11/43.

42-3467 Del Denver 24/6/43; 242 BU Gd Isle 18/6/44; 396BG Grand Is 8/7/44; 202 BU Galveston 5/10/44; RFC Walnut Ridge 13/12/45.

42-3468 Del Denver 4/7/43; 4501 BU Moses Lake 14/8/43; 327 BU Drew 20/8/43; 4100 BU Patterson 17/10/43; Drew 4/5/44; RFC Drew 11/8/45.

42-3469 Del Denver 3/7/43; 244 BU Harvard 13/9/43; 330 BU Dyersburg 1/3/44; 327 BU Drew 14/5/44; RFC Altus 28/7/45.

42-3470 Del Denver 3/7/43; 4100 BU Patterson 23/7/43; 326 BU McDill 26/9/43; RFC Bozeman 13/10/45. Civil Reg 66574, 9815-F; Nicaragua AN-AMI; Columbia HK-580, C-580; Peru OB-RAH-346; Bolivia CP-633 (last listed July '59).

42-3471 Del Denver 3/7/43; 327 BU Drew 15/9/43; 4124 BU Altus 2/7/43; RFC Altus 1/8/45.

42-3472 Del Denver 6/43; Scott 13/8/43; ass 568BS/390BG [BI-G/N/S] Framlingham 25/8/43 SHOOT A POUND; re-named THE VULTURE 4/44; retUS Altus 29/10/45. THE PAPER DOLL.

42-3473 Del Denver 6/43; 59 SD Lowry 19/11/43; 39 SD Buckingham 3/12/43; 2137 BU Hendricks 30/7/44; RFC Walnut Ridge 14/12/45.

42-3474 Del Denver 6/43; Gd Island 10/8/43; ass 351BG/100BG [EP-B] Thorpe Abbotts 1/9/43 QUEEN BEE; c/l base 27/12/43, sal 31/1/44. KING BEE.

42-3475 Del Denver 1/7/43; Moses Lake 21/7/43; 327 BU Drew 4/5/44; 4124 BU Altus 2/7/44; RFC Altus 1/8/45.

42-3476 Del Denver 4/7/43; Moses Lake 20/7/43; 327 BU Drew 4/8/44; 4124 BU Altus 2/7/44; RFC Altus 1/8/45.

42-3477 Del Denver 1/7/43; Moses Lake 24/7/43; 328 BU Gulfport 10/7/44; 4104 BU Rome 22/1/45; 2114 BU Lockburn 9/2/45; RFC Walnut Ridge 14/12/45.

42-3478 Del Denver 2/7/43; Moses Lake 19/7/43; 327 BU Drew 4/5/44; 4124 BU Altus 2/7/44; RFC Altus 1/8/45.

42-3479 Del Denver 2/7/43; Moses Lake 1/8/43; 2137 BU Hendricks 29/8/43; 327 BU Drew 16/9/43; 4124 BU Altus 2/7/44; RFC Altus 3/8/45.

42-3480 Del Denver 2/7/43; Smoky Hill 16/8/43; 4601 BU Lakeland 15/8/44; 325 BU Avon Park 17/8/44; RFC Walnut Ridge 15/8/45.

42-3481 Del Denver 6/7/43; Moses Lake 24/7/43; c/l base 1/8/43 w/Wong, rep; 352 BU Lakeland 27/8/43; 327 BU Drew 4/5/44; RFC Altus 22/8/45.

42-3482 Del Denver 6/7/43; Pendleton 8/8/43; 4117 BU Robins 13/7/44; 326 BU McDill 14/7/44; RFC Altus 25/6/45.

42-3483 Del Denver 20/6/43; Rome 7/8/43; ass 384BG Grafton Underwood 14/4/44; tran 401BG Deenethorpe 17/4/44; became radio-relay w/8th Fighter Command 22/7/44; retUS Bradley 12/7/45; RFC Kingman 30/12/45. CHOPSTICK A-ABLE.

42-3484 Del Denver 10/7/43; Grenier 12/8/43; ass 812BS/482BG [MI-B] Alconbury 27/9/43 (H2-X); retUS Bradley 11/7/45; RFC Kingman 21/12/45.

42-3485 Del Denver 11/7/43; Grenier 17/8/43; ass 812BS/482BG [MI-C] Alconbury 18/8/43 (H2-X); tran APII /44; sal n/b/d 29/5/45.

42-3486 Del Denver 10/7/43; Rome 24/7/43; ass 812BS/482BG [MI-D] Alconbury 22/9/43 (H2-X); MIA Oschersleben 11/1/44 w/McGinnis (first in group), e/a, cr Ijsselmeer, 10KIA, MACR 2522. (Found with bodies 3/68).

42-3487 Del Denver 10/7/43; Grenier 18/8/43; ass 812BS/482BG [MI-E] Alconbury 28/8/43 (H2-X); tran 349BS/100BG [XR-F] Thorpe Abbotts /43; sal n/b/d 31/1/44.

42-3488 Del Denver 13/7/43; Scott 15/8/43; ass 548BS/385BG Gt Ashfield 25/8/43; MIA Emden 11/12/43 w/Pollock, e/a, cr Offingerwier, Holl. 2KIA 8POW, MACR 1665.

42-3489 Del Denver 11/7/43; Grenier 18/8/43; ass 482BG; tran 1 EEL Bedford (TB-17-G) 20/7/44; 4148 BU Bedford 4/12/44; 4100 Patterson 8/3/45; RFC Walnut Ridge 12/7/45.

42-3490 Del Denver 11/7/43; Grenier 18/8/43; ass 812BS/482BG [MI-F] Alconbury 20/8/43 (H2-X); MIA 21/6/44, 10 interned Sweden; MACR 5919. Became liner SE-BAN; WO 1948.

42-3491 Del Denver 11/7/43; Grenier 18/8/43; ass 812BS/482BG [MI-G] Alconbury 20/8/43 (H2-X); MIA Berlin 6/3/44 w/Col Wilson. flak, cr Berlin, 6KIA 4POW, MACR 3362.

42-3492 Del Denver 11/7/43; Grenier 18/8/43; ass 305BG Chelveston 27/9/43; tran 812BS/482BG [MI-H] Alconbury 20/8/43 (H2-X); retUS Morrison 28/4/45; RFC Kingman 21/12/45. PAPER DOLL.

42-3493 Del Denver 14/7/43; Ogden 20/7/43; ass 325BS/92BG [NV-H] Podington 28/9/43; trans 1 BAD Burtonwood 7/6/44; sal 20/6/45.

42-3494 Del Denver 10/7/43; Presque Is 17/8/43; ass 325BS/92BG [NV-F] Podington 4/9/43; tran 407BS [PY-F]; MIA Kiel 4/1/44 w/Mancu, flak, cr Vinkwijk, Hol. 10KIA, MACR 1961.

42-3495 Del Denver 17/7/43; Rapid City 8/7/43; ass 510BS/351BG [TU-C] Polebrook 20/9/43; MIA {9m} Bordeaux 31/12/43 w/Saville, flak, cr Hourtin Vandice, Fr. 5EVD, 1KIA 4POW, MACR 1981.

42-3496 Del Denver 13/12/43; Presque Is 16/8/43; ass 327BS/92BG [UX-Z] Alconbury 4/9/43; c/l base 16/5/44, sal 2 SAD Lt Staughton. HARDSTAND HATTIE.

42-3497 Del Denver 12/7/43; Gore Fd 15/8/43; ass 335BS/95BG [OE-O] Horham 8/9/43; MIA Münster 10/10/43 w/Correia, e/a, cr Haaksbergen, Hol. 1KIA 9POW, MACR 943.

42-3498 Del Denver 12/7/43; Scott Fd 14/8/43; ass 571BS/390BG [FC-L] Framlingham 25/8/43 RED HEAD; MIA Berlin 8/5/44 w/Son, e/a, cr Ostenholz, Ger. 10KIA, MACR 4582. HAPS HAZARD.

42-3499 Del Del Denver 16/7/43; Harvard 9/8/43; Love Fd 9/10/43; Pyote 12/11/43; 246 BU Pratt 1/1/44; 4202 BU Syracuse 28/3/44; Charleston 28/10/44; RFC Altus 8/11/45.

42-3500 Del Long Beach 16/7/43; Rome 6/8/43; ass 812BS/482BG [MI-J] Alconbury 9/43 (H2-X); FTR 4/2/44 w/Bock, flak, cr Gladbach, MACR 3159.

42-3501 Del Hill 14/7/43; Gore 15/8/43; ass 413BS/96BG [MZ-K] Snetterton 9/9/43; c/l 5/2/44 Dymchurch b/d at Villacoublay, 10RTD; 1 inj and also killed British soldier on ground. KASCH'S KIDS.

42-3502 Del Denver 15/7/43; Rapid City 10/8/43; ass 331BS/94BG [QE-Q] Rougham 7/9/43; tran 550BS/385BG Gt Ashfield 9/43; cr Maldon, UK. 2/2/44, sal. SWINGING DOOR.

42-3503 Del Denver 14/3/43; Walla Walla 28/7/43; WO 14/8/43.

42-3504 Del Denver 16/7/43; Scott 11/8/43; ass 339BS/96BG [QJ-F] Snetterton 3/9/43; MIA Kiel 11/1/44 w/Ford, e/a, ditched Nth Sea, 10KIA, MACR 2376. First a/c with Bendix chin turret.

42-3505 Del Hill 14/7/43; Walla Walla 30/7/43; ass 562BS/388BG Knettishall 8/9/43; MIA Bremen 29/11/43 w/Maupin, mech fault, cr Nth Sea, 7KIA 3RTD, MACR 3153.

42-3506 Del Hill 12/7/43; Walla Walla 20/8/43; ass 401BS/91BG Bassingbourn 22/9/43 then 324BS [DF-B/H]; c/l Tannington, UK. no gas 10/10/43; 1 SAD Troston, rep & ret 19/2/44; MIA {4m} Waggum 29/3/44 w/Downing, e/a, ditched Hol, 10POW, MACR 3473. SIR BABOON McGOON.

42-3507 Del Tulsa 15/7/43; Scott 20/10/43; ass 613BS/401BG [IN-O] Deenethorpe 26/10/43; tran 838BS/487BG Lavenham 15/7/44; RFC South Plains 1/10/45. DUFFY'S TAVERN.

42-3508 Del Denver 13/7/43; Scott 15/8/43; ass 418BS/100BG [LD-P] Thorpe Abbotts 25/8/43; MIA Oberpfaffenhofen 18/3/44 w/Horn, e/a, cr Ulm, 10POW, MACR 3232. BASTARD'S BUNGALOW II.

42-3509 Del Denver 15/7/43; Redmond, Or, 15/8/43; ass 511BS/351BG [DS-Z] Polebrook 25/9/43; MIA {12m} Brunswick 30/1/44 w/Robertson, flak, cr Hengelo, 1KIA 9POW, MACR 2262. CRYSTAL BALL.

42-3510 Del Long Beach 15/7/43; Hill 20/8/43; ass 337BS/96BG [AW-P] Snetterton 9/9/43; MIA Schweinfurt 9/10/44 coll w/231053 or 337684, c/l nbd 13/10/44, 4KIA 1RTD, sal.

42-3511 Del Denver 15/7/43; Grenier 18/8/43; ass 812BS/482BG [MI-K] Alconbury 20/8/43; tran 535BS/381BG Ridgewell 22/4/44; MIA {1m} Metz 25/4/44 w/Claytor, flak, cr Pracy, Fr, 7EVD 2POW, MACR 4286.

42-3512 Del Long Beach 4/8/43; Tulsa 7/8/43; c/t/o 28/8/43 w/Christie, 3K, WO 8/10/43.

42-3513 Del Denver 19/7/43; Presque Is 17/8/43; ass 326BS/92BG [JW-T] Podington 2/9/43; MIA Berlin 29/4/44 w/Munson, flak, cr Millingen, Hol. 10POW, MACR 4260.

42-3514 Del Denver 13/7/43; Hill 20/8/43; ass 533BS/381BG [VP-V] Ridgewell 24/9/43 (DINAH MITE II?); MIA {18+m} Oschersleben 11/1/44 w/Chason, e/a, cr Minden, 10POW, MACR 1878. DOLL BABY.

42-3515 Del Denver 21/7/43; Hill 20/8/43; ass 423BS/306BG [RD-O] Thurleigh 21/9/43; tran 482BG Alconbury 30/3/44; retUS Bradley 4/6/44; RFC Kingman 19/11/45.

42-3516 Del Hill 17/7/43; Ephrata 4/8/43; ass 338BS/96BG [BX-S] Snetterton 9/9/43; MIA Münster 10/10/43 w/Williams e/a, cr?, 10POW, MACR 893.

42-3517 Del Denver 12/7/43; Rapid City 10/8/43; ass 508BS/351BG [YB-O] Polebrook 27/9/43; MIA {15m} 24/2/44 w/Caughman, flak, cr Ailly, Fr. 6EVD 1KIA 3POW, MACR 2773. HAPPY WARRIOR.

42-3518 Del Denver 15/7/43; Rapid City 10/8/43; ass 561BS/388BG Knettishall 9/9/43; tran RCM 803BS Sculthorpe /44; damaged by PB4Y explosion on APH mission; sal 14/11/44.

42-3519 Del Denver 20/7/43; Hill 17/8/43; ass 339BS/96BG [QJ-M] Snetterton 8/9/43; tran RAF 26/3/44, sal 12/9/45. PEE WEE II.

42-3520 Del Denver 20/7/43; Geiger 3/8/43; ass 368BS/306BG [BO-Y] Thurleigh 16/9/43; c/l Lt Staughton 29/11/43, sal.

42-3521 Del Denver 20/3/43; Lowry 17/8/43; ass 813BS/482BG [PC-L] Alconbury 8/9/43; tran 367BS/306BG [GY-A] Thurleigh 22/2/44; AFSC Stansted 12/5/44; retUS St Paul 12/6/44; tran USN [34106] Rome, NY 23/3/45; ret USAF 2/4/48.

42-3522 Del Hill 21/7/43; Ephrata 4/8/43; ass 482BG Alconbury 7/9/43; tran 337BS/96BG [AWJ] 7/9/43; 533BS/381BG [VP-L] Ridgewell 27/9/43; {16+m} RetUS Okmulgee 9/7/44; RFC Walnut Ridge 8/12/45. GREMLIN'S DELITE.

42-3523 Del Long Beach 22/7/43; Denver 16/8/43; ass 510BS/351BG [TU-M] Polebrook 24/9/43; MIA {11m} Oschersleben 11/1/44 w/Procak, e/a, cr Pillgrim, Ger. 2KIA 8POW; MACR 1940. APRIL GIRL.

42-3524 Del Denver 20/7/43; Lowry 17/8/43; ass 526BS/379BG [LF-G] Kimbolton 3/10/43; then 527BS [FO-G]; MIA Leipzig 20/7/44 w/Moore, flak, f/l Payerne, Switz, 9INT.MACR 7838 Ret GB 25/9/45. VONNIE GAL.

42-3525 Del Denver 20/7/43; Hill 17/8/43; ass 813BS/482BG [PC-D] Alconbury 8/9/43; tran 534BS/381BG [GD-C] Ridgewell 22/2/44; MIA {1+m} Eschwege 19/4/44 w/Bond, e/a, cr Frettenrode, 7KIA 2POW, MACR 4050.

42-3526 Del Denver 23/7/43; Rapid City 15/8/43; ass 568BS/390BG [BI-N] Framlingham; sal 20/10/43.

42-3527 Del Hill 22/7/43; Moses Lake 5/8/43; ass 813BS/482BG [PC-G] Alconbury 119//43; tran 306BG Thurleigh 22/2/44; AFSC 12/2/44; retUS Grenier 10/6/44; Rome, NY 30/10/45.

42-3528 Del Hill 26/7/43; Ephrata 4/8/43; ass 339BS/96BG Snetterton 9/9/43; MIA Schweinfurt 14/10/43 w/Barnhill, e/a, cr Barmsee, 1KIA 9POW, MACR 834.

42-3529 Del Hill 23/7/43; Ephrata 4/8/43; ass 336BS/95BG [ET-F] Horham 6/10/43; MIA Berlin

INDIVIDUAL B-17 HISTORIES 99

6/3/44 w/Frantz, e/a, cr Magdeburg, 1KIA 9POW, MACR 2979.

42-3530 Del Denver 20/7/43; Dyersburg 9/8/43; ass 332BS/94BG [XM-H] Rougham 9/43; MIA Oschersleben 11/1/44 w/Fairchild, e/a, cr Brunswick, MACR 1885.

42-3531 Del Denver 21/7/43; Dyersburg 7/8/43; ass 358BS/303BG [VK-N] Molesworth 9/9/43; tran 365BS/305BG [XK-N] Chelveston 17/9/43; MIA Bremen 26/11/43 w/Elliott, flak, cr Zuidbroek, Hol, 2KIA 8POW, MACR 1572.

42-3532 Del Denver 21/7/43; Dyersburg 8/8/43; ass 511BS/351BG [DS-O] Polebrook 21/9/43; {4m} b/d Gelsenkirchen 5/11/43; c/l Ipswich A/fd, UK, sal 7/11/43. LUCILLE BALL.

42-3533 Del Denver 24/7/43; Pyote 4/8/43; ass 368BS/306BG [BO-E] Thurleigh 21/9/43; MIA Wilhelmshaven 3/11/43 w/Wadley, coll w/230776, cr Nth Sea, 10KIA, MACR 1159.

42-3534 Del Denver 24/7/43; Dyersburg 31/8/43; ass 349BS/100BG [XR-L/N/R] Thorpe Abbotts 9/9/43; MIA Pas De Calais 27/4/44 w/Shaddix, flak, cr Ardoye, Fr, 1EVD 9POW, MACR 4268. OL' DAD.

42-3535 Del Denver 24/7/43; Dyersburg 8/8/43; ass 385BG Gt Ashfield 9/9/43; tran 339BS/96BG [QJ-L] Snetterton 9/9/43; MIA Sorau 11/4/44 w/Bethe, c/l St Hedingh, Den, 10EVD, MACR 4266.

42-3536 Del Denver 24/7/43; Dyersburg 15/8/43; ass 813BS/482BG Alconbury 9/9/43; tran 325BS/92BG Podington 20/2/44; cr base 9/3/44, sal.

42-3537 Del Denver 26/7/43; Dyersburg 8/8/43; ass 332BS/94BG [XM-B] Rougham 3/9/43; MIA Karlsruhe 27/5/44. MACR 5344 FRIDAY THE 13TH.

42-3538 Del Denver 26/7/43; Dyersburg 8/8/43; ass 333BS/94BG [TS-W] Rougham 1/9/43; MIA Hanau 4/10/43 w/Carlson, flak, cr Wesel, 6EVD 4POW, MACR 771. TEN KNIGHTS IN A BAR ROOM.

42-3539 Del Denver 26/7/43; Dyersburg 7/8/43; ass 550BS/385BG Gt Ashfield 3/9/43; MIA Münster 10/10/43 w/Whitlow, s/d by e/a. cr Holten, Hol, 3EVD 3KIA 4POW, MACR 826.

42-3540 Del Denver 26/7/43; Dyersbury 15/8/43; ass 535BS/381BG [MS-N] Ridgewell 20/9/43 LUCIFER JR II; MIA Leverkusen 1/12/43 w/Hess, flak, cr Huy, Bel. 2EVD 1KIA 7POW, MACR 1660. BACTA-TH'-SAC.

42-3541 Del Denver 26/7/43; Dyersburg 8/8/43; ass 339BS/96BG [QJ-N] Snetterton 9/9/43; MIA 5/1/44 w/Davison, e/a, ditched Biscay, 5KIA 5POW, MACR 2011. LITTLE GIRLS.

42-3542 Del Denver 27/7/43; Pendleton 15/8/43; ass 509BS/351BG [RQ-V] Polebrook 23/9/43; tran 487BG Lavenham 16/7/44; {24m} sal 21/5/45. SHADY LADY II (SEATTLE'S LUCKY LADY).

42-3543 Del Denver 27/7/43; Redmond 15/8/43; ass 338BS/96BG [BX-W] Snetterton 9/9/43; MIA Anklam 9/10/43 w/Greene, f/l Bulltofta, Swed, 10INT, MACR 946. Became liner SE-BAH, later as fire drill a/c 1946. SACK TIME SUZY.

42-3544 Del Denver 27/7/43; Grand Island 12/8/43; ass 550BS/385BG Gt Ashfield 9/43; c/l Badwell Ash, Sfk, b/d ex-Bordeaux, 7/11/44, 8KIA 1WIA, sal. STARS AND STRIPES.

42-3545 Del Denver 2/8/43; Grand Island 12/8/43; ass 334BS/95BG [BG-A] Horham 9/43; MIA Frankfurt 29/1/44 w/Rozentinsky, cr Brussels, 3EVD 5KIA 2POW, MACR 2257.

42-3546 Del Denver 28/7/43; Grand Island 7/8/43; ass 339BS/96BG [QJ-A] Snetterton 29/8/43 RAMBLIN' WRECK; MIA Bremen 29/11/43 w/Parks, e/a, cr Bremen, 10POW, MACR 1393. WILDFIRE.

42-3547 Del Denver 26/7/43; Scott 9/8/43; ass 549BS/385BG Gt Ashfield 25/8/43; sal 11/4/44. LATEST RUMOR.

42-3548 Del Denver 28/7/43; Scott 9/8/43; ass 563BS/385BG Gt Ashfield 25/8/43; MIA Brunswick 23/3/44 w/Davis, flak, cr Hullern, 2KIA 8POW, MACR 3593.

42-3549 Del Denver 28/7/43; Grand Island 9/8/43; ass 366BS/305BG [KY-H] Chelveston 1/10/43; MIA Schweinfurt 14/10/43 w/Willis, e/a, cr Hoorn, Hol, 4KIA 6POW, MACR 918.

42-3550 Del Denver 28/7/43; Grand Island 10/8/43; ass 365BS/305BG [XK-H] Chelveston 1/10/43; MIA Schweinfurt 14/10/43 w/Kincaid, cr Schweinfurt, 3KIA 7POW, MACR 921.

42-3551 Del Denver 29/7/43; Grand Island 9/8/43; ass 551BS/385BG Gt Ashfield 10/9/43; MIA Kiel 13/12/43 w/Fowles, e/a, cr Rendsburg, Ger, 1KIA 9POW, MACR 1667. SHACK BUNNY.

42-3552 Del Denver 29/7/43; Grand Island 10/8/43; ass 339BS/96BG [QJ-L] Snetterton 1/9/43; MIA Frankfurt 29/1/44 w/Parris, e/a, cr Frankfurt, 10POW, MACR 2379. FLYIN' GINNY.

42-3553 Del Denver 30/7/43; Grand Island 10/8/43; ass 339BS/96BG [QJ-H] Snetterton 29/8/43; c/t/o West Malling 8/11/43 10KIA, sal.

42-3554 Del Denver 29/7/43; Grand Island 10/8/43; ass 326BS/92BG [JW-B] Podington 16/9/43; tran 325BS [NV-B]; MIA Anklam 9/10/43 w/Whelan, e/a, ditched Nth Sea, 5KIA 5POW, MACR 746.

42-3555 Del Denver 30/7/43; Grand Island 10/8/43; ass 560BS/388BG Knettishall 9/43; MIA Bremen 26/11/43 w/Stickgras, flak, cr Münster, 9KIA 1POW, MACR 3116. TIGER GIRL.

42-3556 Del Denver 30/7/43; Grand Island 10/8/43; ass 338BS/96BG [BX-S/Z] Snetterton 9/9/43; c/l West Malling, ex-Pas De Calais, 13/2/44, sal. DEAR MOM.

42-3557 Del Denver 29/7/43; Grand Island 11/8/43; ass 570BS/390BG [DI-C] Framlingham 28/8/43; MIA Solingen 30/11/43 w/Leo, e/a, cr Golzheim, Ger, 2KIA 8POW, MACR 1401.

42-3558 Del Tulsa 30/7/43; Scott 28/9/43; ass 571BS/390BG [FC-T] Framlingham 29/9/43; sal 15/7/45. SHY ANN.

42-3559 Del Tulsa 30/7/43; Scott 28/9/43; ass 526BS/379BG [LF-K] Kimbolton 22/11/43; tran 525BS [FR-K]; MIA Leverkusen 1/12/43 w/Thomson, flak, cr Rotterdam, 4EVD 6KIA, MACR 1333. STARDUST.

42-3560 Del Tulsa 2/8/43; Scott 21/10/43; ass 401BG Deenethorpe 4/11/43; tran 508BS/351BG [YB-H] Polebrook 18/11/43; MIA {1m} Bremen 26/11/43 w/Blaisdell, mech, ditched Nth Sea, 10RTD. SALTY DOG.

42-3561 Del Tulsa 3/8/43; Pendleton 1/11/43; WO 6/1/44.

42-3562 Del Tulsa 2/8/43; Scott 22/10/43; ass 401BG Deenethorpe 10/43; tran 532BS/381BG [VE-N] Ridgewell 21/11/43; MIA {9m} Oschersleben 20/2/44 w/Cogswell, e/a, cr Leipzig, 1KIA 9POW, MACR 2929.

42-3563 Del Denver 10/8/43; Redmond 15/8/43; ass 535BS/381BG [MS-N] Ridgewell 10/43; MIA {1m} Bremen 20/12/43 w/Hollenkamp, e/a, cr Olenburg, Ger. 5KIA 5POW, MACR 1721.

B-17F-BO

42-5050 Del Cheyenne 9/9/42; West Palm Beach 8/1/43; ass 32BS/301BG Ain M'Lila 23/1/43; St Donat 6/3/43; Oudna 6/8/43; {65m} tran 96BS/2BG Massicault 14/11/43; Bizerte 1/12/43; MIA {10m} Piraeus w/Ward 14/12/43. MACR 1482.

42-5051 Del Cheyenne 9/9/42; Dow 11/6/43; ass 303BG Molesworth 1/11/42; tran 366BS/305BG [KY-M] Chelveston 2/11/42; tran 544BS/384BG [SU-M] Grafton Underwood 26/7/43; MIA 26/11/43 w/Gilmore, flak, cr Nth Sea, 3KIA 7RTD, MACR 1579. BARREL HOUSE BESSIE.

42-5052 Del Cheyenne 9/9/42; New Castle 13/10/42; ass 366BS/305BG [KY-A] Chelveston 2/11/42; tran 368BS/306BG [BO-E] Thurleigh 1/5/43; AFSC 19/4/43 - 9/6/43; 358BS/303BG Molesworth 25/9/43; MIA 22/2/44 w/Moffatt, e/a, cr Nordhausen, Ger, 5KIA 5POW, MACR 2646. MIZPAH.

42-5053 Del Cheyenne 9/9/42; Presque Is 28/10/42; ass 366BS/305BG [KY-L] Chelveston 14/11/42; MIA 4/7/43 w/Wetzel, flak, cr St Colunbin, Fr, 2EVD 2KIA, 6POW; MACR 14439. (Used in film *1000 Plane Raid*.)

42-5054 Del Cheyenne 9/9/42; New Castle 14/10/42; ass 306BG Thurleigh 7/8/43; tran 360BS/303BG [PU-I] Molesworth 25/9/43; retUS Miami 7/5/44; RFC Kingman 2/11/45. BELLE OF SAN JOAQUIN.

42-5055 Del Cheyenne 9/9/42; New Castle 10/10/42; ass 367BS/306BG [GY-H] Thurleigh 7/5/43; MIA Wilhelmshaven 15/5/43 w/Ritland, flak, ditched Nth Sea, 10POW.

42-5056 Del Cheyenne 9/9/42; Presque Is 19/10/42; ass 364BS/305BG [WF-C/L] Chelveston 30/10/42; MIA Wilhelmshaven 26/2/43 w/Benson, e/a, cr Nth Sea, 10KIA, MACR 15120. DEVIL'S PLAYMATE.

42-5057 Del Cheyenne 9/9/42; Presque Is 19/10/42; ass 422BS/305BG [JJ-M] Chelveston 30/10/42, then 364BS [WF-M]; MIA Stuttgart 6/9/43 w/Daghly, out of fuel, ditched English Channel, 2EVD 1KIA 7POW, MACR 15497. 4F.

42-5058 Del Cheyenne 9/9/42; Presque Is 19/10/42; ass 364BS/305BG [WF-H] Chelveston 30/10/42; MIA St Nazaire 16/2/43 w/Burman, e/a, cr Redon, Fr, 7KIA 3POW, MACR 15477/15497. HUN HUNTER.

42-5059 Del Cheyenne 6/9/42; Presque Is 19/10/42; Rome Fd 1/11/42; ditched off Nova Scotia 23/10/43. HELL'S ANGELS.

42-5060 Del Cheyenne 13/9/42; Houlton 22/10/42; ass 422BS/305BG [JJ-Q] Chelveston 12/11/42; MIA Emden 4/2/43 w/Davidson, ditched Waddenzee, Hol, 10KIA.

42-5061 Del Cheyenne 13/9/42; New Castle 12/10/42; ass 353BS/301BG Chelveston 1/11/42; Tarafaoui 26/11/42; Maison Blanche 5/12/42; Biskra 16/12/42; {71m} tran 346BS/99BG Navarin 8/1/43; Gen Doolittle aboard mission to Kiarouan Afd 9/2/43; Oudna 4/8/43; MIA Bolzano 10/11/43, w/Wickcliffe, cr Pavia; 1POW. MACR 1129.

42-5062 Del Cheyenne 13/9/42; Pocatello 14/11/42; Pyote 31/1/43; 241 BU Fairmont 7/7/43; 504BG Fairmont 22/7/43; 2534 BU San Angelo 15/12/43; Recl Comp 17/12/45.

42-5063 Del Cheyenne 13/9/42; Presque Is 29/10/42; ass 366BS/305BG [KY-K] Chelveston 14/11/42; MIA Lorient 17/5/43 w/Roney, flak, cr Lorient, 5KIA, 5POW, MACR 15238.

42-5064 Del Cheyenne 13/9/42; Walla Walla 30/11/42; Redmond 24/12/42; Walla Walla 31/1/43; Sioux City 8/4/43; Ephrata 9/8/43; c/l 18/6/43 w/Pearson, rep; WO 25/5/44.

42-5065 Del Cheyenne 8/9/42; Wayne Co 18/10/42; Gt Britain 3/11/42.

42-5066 Del Cheyenne 8/9/42; Wayne Co 18/10/42; Gt Britain 3/11/42.

42-5067 Del Cheyenne 8/9/42; Wayne Co 18/10/42; Gt Britain 1/11/42.

42-5068 Del Cheyenne 13/9/42; West Palm Beach 12/12/42; ass 353BS/301BG Biskra 31/12/42; Ain

M'Lila 17/1/43; Oudna 6/8/43; {48m} tran 20BS/2BG Massicault 14/11/43; Bizerte 2/12/43; 348BS/99BG Tortorella 28/3/44; 483BG Tortorella 31/3/44; retUS Homestead 18/7/44; RFC Altus 30/7/45. MISS ME.

42-5069 Del Cheyenne 13/9/42; New Castle 19/11/42; ass 324BS/91BG [DF-G] Bassing- bourn 23/11/42; MIA {20m} Schweinfurt 17/8/43 w/Wheeler (401BS), e/a, cr St Goar, Ger, 10POW, MACR 281. OUR GANG.

42-5070 Del Cheyenne 17/9/42; New Castle 11/10/42; ass 401BS/91BG [LL-A] Bassingbourn 14/12/42; MIA {18m} Bremen 17/4/43 w/O'Neill, flak, cr Nikolausdorf, Ger, 10POW; MACR 15519. INVASION 2nd.

42-5071 Del Tulsa 17/9/42; New Castle 10/10/42; ass 367BS/305BG Chelveston 1/11/42; MIA Romilly 20/12/43 w/Nygaard, e/a, 1EVD, 7KIA, 2POW.

42-5072 Del Tulsa 17/9/42; New Castle 7/10/42; ass 367BS/306BG Chelveston 19/11/42; MIA Antwerp 5/4/43 w/Parker, e/a, cr Dinteloord, Hol. 7KIA 3POW.

42-5073 Del Cheyenne 8/9/42; Wayne Co 9/11/42; Gt Britain RAF 9/11/42.

42-5074 Del Cheyenne 8/9/42; Wayne Co 18/10/42; Gt Britain 22/11/42.

42-5075 Del Cheyenne 7/9/42; Wayne Co 12/10/42; Gt Britain 23/10/42.

42-5076 Del Tulsa 15/9/42; W Palm Beach 7/1/43; ass 32BS/301BG Ain M'Lila 15/1/43; MIA {1m} Gabes 4/2/43 w/Broderick, s/d Gabes, 10POW. MACR 15358.

42-5077 Del Tulsa 15/9/42; Bangor 11/10/42; ass 323BS/91BG [OR-T] Bassingbourn 15/10/42; MIA {33m} Gelsenkirchen 12/8/43 w/Thompson, e/a, cr Brunninghausen, Ger, 4KIA, 6POW. MACR 261. (possibly completed 25 missions before Memphis Belle). DELTA REBEL No. 2.

42-5078 Del Tulsa 15/9/42; Presque Is 19/10/42; ass 366BS/305BG [KY-C] Chelveston 11/42; MIA 30/12/42 w/Love, e/a, cr Biscay, 10KIA.

42-5079 Del Tulsa 17/9/42; New Castle 8/10/42; ass 8AF 2114 BU Lockburn 17/8/43; Recl Comp 6/1/45.

42-5080 Del Geiger 26/9/42; Rapid City 3/11/42; ass 95BG, cr Huron, SD, 18/2/43; all killed. WO.

42-5081 Del Tulsa 17/9/42; West Palm Beach 17/1/43; ass 427BS/303BG [GN-V] Molesworth 15/2/43; tran 1 BAD Burtonwood 5/4/44; 419BS/301BG Lucera 7/7/44; {1m} RetUS 4136 BU Tinker 27/4/44; Recl Comp Eglin 3/1/46. LUSCIOUS LADY.

42-5082 Del Tulsa 17/9/42; New Castle 18/10/42; ass 419BS/301BG Tafaraoui 7/11/42 Maison Blanche 5/12/42; Biskra 16/12/42; Ain M'Lila 17/1/43; St Donat 6/3/43; Oudna 6/8/43; Cerignola 7/12/43; Lucera 1/2/44; {70m} sal 31/5/44.

42-5083 Del Tulsa 15/9/42; Presque Is 27/11/42; Ainsworth 1/3/43; Gore Fd 30/5/43; 77 S/Dep Geiger 21/7/43; 363BG Pendleton 13/9/43; 248 BU Walker 22/9/43; 3076 BU Sheppard 9/4/44; 4160 Albuquerque 20/6/44; RFC Albuquerque 25/6/45.

42-5084 Del Tulsa 16/9/42; New Castle 10/10/42; ass 323BS/91BG Bassingbourn 14/12/42; MIA St Nazaire 3/1/43 w/Anderson (his second so named a/c), flak, cr St Nazaire 9KIA 1POW. MACR 2286. PANHANDLE DOGIE.

42-5085 Del Denver 23/9/42; New Castle 7/10/42; ass 419BS/301BG Tafaraoui 7/11/42; Maison Blanche 5/12/42; Biskra 16/12/42; Ain M'Lila 17/1/43; St Donat 6/3/43; Oudna 6/8/43; Cerignola 7/12/43; Lucera 1/2/44; taxi acc {3m} sal 31/12/45.

42-5086 Del Tulsa 17/9/42; Presque Is 17/11/42; ass 369BS/306BG [WW-J] Thurleigh 25/11/42; tran 546BS/384BG [BK-B] Grafton Underwood 5/9/43; c/l Eye, Sfk, ex-Münster 10/10/43, crew baled Ipswich, sal. WAHOO II.

42-5087 Del Denver 23/9/42; Presque Is 15/10/42; ass 340BS/97BG Grafton Underwood 11/11/42; Maison Blanche 13/11/42; Tafaraoui 22/11/42; Biskra 25/12/42; Château-du-Rhumel 8/2/43; Pont-du-Fahs 1/8/43; Depienne 15/8/43; Cerignola 20/12/43; Amendola 16/1/44. Sal 2/3/45.

42-5088 Del Denver 23/9/42; New Castle 3/10/42; cr Greenland ice cap en route GB 23/12/42; WO.

42-5089 Del Denver 23/9/42; New Castle 31/1/43; Salina 5/3/43; 247 BU Smoky Hill 4/6/43.

42-5090 Del Denver 23/9/42; Presque Is 15/10/42; ass 414BS/97BG Grafton Underwood 11/11/42; MIA Gerbini 8/7/43 w/Bauman. MACR 69.

42-5091 Del Geiger 21/9/42; ass 379BG Sioux City 21/11/42; WO 3/4/43.

42-5092 Del Geiger 28/9/42; Redmond 23/12/42; Walla Walla 23/1/43; Kearney 3/8/43; 232 BU Dalhart 9/6/43; 241 BU (504BG) Fairmont 13/6/43; 249 BU Alliance 30/10/43; 222 BU Ardmore 15/3/44; RFC Ontario 14/6/45.

42-5093 Del Geiger 23/9/42; Blythe 13/12/42; Hobbs 11/5/43; 3701 BU Amarillo 10/8/43; Recl Comp 7/6/46.

42-5094 Del Geiger 21/9/42; Pierre 16/12/42; Rapid City 8/1/43; Geiger 8/4/43; Spokane 3/8/43; WO 4/1/44.

42-5095 Del Geiger 26/9/42; Pierre 16/12/42; Rapid City 15/1/43; Portland 13/6/43; McChord 8/7/43; 243 BU Gt Bend 20/6/44; 232 BU Dalhart 16/7/44; 273 BU Lincoln 9/1/45; 241 BU Fairmont 23/2/45; RFC Altus 9/10/45.

42-5096 Del Geiger 20/9/42; Redmond 24/12/42; Walla Walla 15/1/43 fire damage, rep; Tinker 10/4/43; Walla Walla 17/5/43; 4117 BU Robins 6/8/43; 325 BU Avon Park 16/12/43; Augusta 9/5/44; 4142 BU Altus 31/7/44. RFC Altus 4/9/45.

42-5097 Del Geiger 26/9/42; Redmond 26/12/42; Pueblo 7/2/43; Dalhart 16/5/43; 247 BU Smoky Hill 26/6/43; 4136 BU Tinker 27/6/43; 232 BU Dalhart 26/8/43; 244 BU Harvard 2/9/43; 249 BU Alliance 16/12/43; 519 BU Fort Worth; 244 BU Harvard 20/1/44; 202 BU Galveston 15/2/44; 237 BU Kirtland 25/5/44; RFC Kingman 27/10/45.

42-5098 Del Geiger 21/9/42; Walla Walla 31/1/43; 4117 BU Robins 13/7/43; 327 BU Drew 21/9/43; 366 BU Rayleigh 15/11/43; 2137 BU Hendricks 11/5/44; Drew 15/6/44; RFC Altus 28/8/45.

42-5099 Del Geiger 28/9/42; Ainsworth 16/12/42; Tinker 5/2/43; Rapid City 27/4/43; 540BS/383BG Geiger 8/7/43; 3701 BU Amarillo 26/1/44; Recl Comp 20/8/46.

42-5100 Del Geiger 24/9/42; Ephrata 3/12/42; WO 9/1/43.

42-5101 Del Geiger 25/9/42; 34BG Blythe 12/12/42; Pyote 8/2/43; Dyersburg 20/5/43; 326 BU McDill 22/6/43; 329 BU Columbia 21/10/43; 327 BU Drew 4/5/44; RFC Altus 29/8/45.

42-5102 Del Geiger 25/9/42; Casper 23/10/42; WO 16/2/43.

42-5103 Del Geiger 28/9/42; Casper 13/11/42; expoded mid-air over New Mexico 13/1/43 w/Lt George, all killed. Cause unknown.

42-5104 Del Geiger 26/9/42; Pendleton 9/11/42; Biggs 23/3/43; Orlando 28/4/43; 245 BU McCook 16/6/43; 9BG McCook 1/7/43; 202 BU Galveston 14/1/44; 4121 BU Kelly 6/12/43; 245 BU McCook 21/1/44; 4160 BU Albuquerque 20/7/44; RFC Walnut Ridge 27/5/45.

42-5105 Del Geiger 28/9/42; Casper 29/10/42; WO 1/2/43.

42-5106 Del Geiger 28/9/42; Casper 31/10/42; Biggs 2/1/43; 28BS/19BG Pyote 29/5/43; 202 BU Galveston 20/7/43; 282 BU Syracuse 25/7/43; 221 BU Alexandria 22/2/44; 4160 BU Albuquerque 20/6/43; RFC Albuquerque 25/6/45.

42-5107 Del Geiger 26/9/42; Casper 29/10/42; Tinker 30/3/43; Dalhart 8/7/43; cr after #1 engine fire 18/10/43, pilot Lt Walker killed, passengers baled OK. WO.

42-5108 Del Geiger 28/9/42; Walla Walla 30/11/42; Boise 7/1/43; Tinker 6/8/43; 3705 BU Lowry 3/3/44; Recl Comp 2/10/46.

42-5109 Del Geiger 28/9/42; Pierre 14/12/42; Tinker 5/2/43; Walla Walla 5/7/43; 504BG Harvard 10/6/43; 244 BU Harvard 27/7/43; 4100 BU Patterson 1/9/43; 53 Recon Sq Grenier 11/7/44; 3 WER Sqd McChord 24/5/45; RFC Kingman 23/1/46.

42-5110 Del Geiger 28/9/42; Blythe 12/12/42; Hobbs 12/3/43; WO 24/11/43.

42-5111 Del Geiger 28/9/42; Casper 29/10/42; Tinker 12/2/43; 221 BU Alexandria 25/7/43; 329 BU Alexandria 1/3/44; 4124 BU Altus 25/6/44; RFC Altus 9/10/45.

42-5112 Del Geiger 28/9/42; Ainsworth 15/12/42; Tinker 17/2/43; Rapid City 14/4/43; WO 28/5/43. DIXIE FLYER.

42-5113 Del Geiger 28/9/42; Salina 30/12/42; Ainsworth 1/3/43; 3701 BU Amarillo 23/7/43; RFC Walnut Ridge 2/1/46.

42-5114 Del Geiger 28/9/42; Biggs 3/1/43; Pyote 28/4/43; Tinker 30/7/43; WO 10/3/44.

42-5115 Del Geiger 28/9/42; Casper 31/10/42; Salina 5/2/43; 235 BU Biggs 13/9/43; 222 BU Ardmore 22/1/44; RFC Ontario 14/6/45.

42-5116 Del Geiger 28/9/42; Blythe 15/12/42; Hobbs 11/3/43; 3017 BU Hobbs 8/11/43; 3010 BU Williams 20/11/43; 3020 BU La Junta 23/4/44; RFC San Angelo 4/8/45.

42-5117 Del Geiger 28/9/42; Cutbank 14/3/43; 248 BU Walker 10/7/43; 4136 BU Tinker 5/8/53; 4100 BU Patterson 11/4/44; 325 BU Avon Park 22/4/44; RFC Altus 6/9/45.

42-5118 Del Geiger 28/9/42; Blythe 15/12/42; Hobbs 13/3/43; 3017 BU Hobbs 8/11/43; 4124 BU Altus 11/7/44; RFC Altus 27/8/45.

42-5119 Del Geiger 28/9/42; Casper 31/10/42; Scott 8/3/43; Ephrata 5/5/43; 327 BU Drew 14/7/43; 328 BU Gulfport 27/8/43; 221 BU Alexandria 24/11/43; 4204 BU Atlanta 1/1/44; 328 BU Gulfport 7/1/44; RFC Albuquerque 25/5/45.

42-5120 Del Geiger 28/9/42; Blythe 5/1/43; WO 2/3/43.

42-5121 Del Geiger 28/9/42; Ephrata 3/12/42; Spokane 10/4/43; 242 BU Grand Isle 23/6/43; 6BG Grand Isle 8/7/43; 202 BU Galveston 3/10/43; 327 BU Drew 5/4/44; Recl Comp 21/1/46.

42-5122 Del Geiger 28/9/42; Redmond 23/12/42; Walla Walla 18/1/43; Geiger 23/4/43; 328 BU Gulfport 20/7/43; RFC Albuquerque 25/6/45.

42-5123 Del Geiger 28/9/42; Great Falls 1/12/42; WO 1/1/43.

42-5124 Del Geiger 28/9/42; 379BG Sioux City 21/11/42; Rapid City 21/7/43; 3705 BU Lowry 1/5/44; RFC Altus 4/10/45.

42-5125 Del Denver 29/9/42; Houlton 13/11/42; ass 365BS/305BG [XK-Q] Chelveston 1/43; MIA Bremen 13/6/43 w/Higgs, flak, cr Vallburg, 8KIA 2POW, MACR 16205.

42-5126 Del Geiger 28/9/42; Gt Falls 15/12/42; 505BG Harvard 22/7/43; 244 BU Harvard 26/1/44; 558 BU Nashville 24/2/44; 244 BU 7/3/44; RFC

Kingman 27/10/45.

42-5127 Del Geiger 28/9/42; Glasgow 7/12/42; Gt Falls 3/2/43; Rapid City 17/7/43; 504BG Fairmont 5/8/43; 271 BU Kearney 2/9/43; 242 BU Grand Isle 10/12/43; 202 BU Galveston 15/2/44; 554 BU Memphis 2/3/44; 902 BU Orlando 5/6/44; 3020 BU La Junta 30/6/43; 242 BU Grand Isle 9/9/43; RFC Kingman 27/10/45.

42-5128 Del Geiger 28/9/42; Cutbank 7/12/42; Gt Falls 3/2/43; Orlando 28/4/43; Gt Falls 7/7/43; WO 3/9/43.

42-5129 Del Denver 29/9/42; New Castle 16/10/42; ass 368BS/306BG Thurleigh 1/1/43; MIA 4/3/43 w/Friend, e/a, cr Nth Sea, 9KIA. MACR 2749.

42-5130 Del Denver 29/9/42; Presque Is 20/11/42; ass 367BS/306BG Thurleigh 25/11/42; MIA Lorient 6/3/43 w/Ryan, flak, cr Bretagne, Fr, 1EVD, 1KIA, MACR 15568. SWEET PEA.

42-5131 Del Denver 29/9/42; New Castle 9/10/42; ass 32BS/301BG Chelveston 1/11/42; Tafaraoui 26/11/42; Maison Blanche 5/12/42; Biskra 16/12/42; Ain M'Lila 17/1/43; St Donat 6/3/43; Oudna 6/8/43; {50m} tran 429BS/2BG Bizerte 14/11/43; Amendola 9/12/43; 99BG Tortorella 28/3/44; {0m} RetUS South Plains 14/6/44; RFC Kingman 18/12/45. HUN PECKER.

42-5132 Del Denver 29/9/42; New Castle 15/10/42; ass 303BG Molesworth 21/12/42; tran 401BS/91BG [LL-E] Bassingbourn 18/1/43; MIA {23m} Huls 22/6/43 w/Fountain, e/a, cr Nth Sea, 9POW, (2 escaped, 1 being killed). ROYAL FLUSH!

42-5133 Del Denver 29/2/42; West Palm Beach 7/1/43; ass 342BS/97BG Biskra 15/1/43; Château-du-Rhumel 3/2/43; MIA Palermo 17/4/43 w/Schirmer, 10KIA. MACR 3684 & 16527.

42-5134 Del Cheyenne 1/10/42; West Palm Beach 15/12/42; ass 353BS/301BG Ain M'Lila 18/2/43; St Donat 6/3/43; Oudna 6/8/43; Cerignola 7/12/43; Lucera 1/2/44; {49m} sal 26/2/45.

42-5135 Del Cheyenne 4/10/42; West Palm Beach 11/12/43; ass 97BG Tafaraoui 22/12/42; Biskra 25/12/42; Château-du-Rhumel 3/2/43; Pont-du-Fahs 1/8/43; Depienne 15/8/43; tran 99BG Oudna 14/11/43; Tortorella 11/12/43; {29m} sal 26/2/45; retUS Homestead 23/6/45; RFC Altus 4/10/45. MUD HEN.

42-5136 Del Cheyenne 1/10/42; Boise 19/1/43; Wendover 28/5/43; Dyersburg 11/8/43; WO 16/12/43.

42-5137 Del Cheyenne 1/10/42; West Palm Beach 13/12/42; ass 32BS/301BG Biskra 22/12/42; Ain M'Lila 17/1/43; St Donat 6/3/43; Oudna 6/8/43; MIA {86m} Turin 30/10/43, w/Clowe, 9KIA. MACR 1060. CAROL JEAN IV.

42-5138 Del Cheyenne 2/10/42; Duncan 31/1/43; Topeka 2/6/43; 235 BU Biggs 28/7/43; 233 BU Davis-Monthan 28/3/44; 283 BU Galveston 29/8/44; RFC Walnut Ridge 11/12/45.

42-5139 Del Cheyenne 2/10/42; West Palm Beach 14/12/42; ass 322BS/91BG [LG-V] Bass- ingbourn 13/3/43; MIA Schweinfurt 17/8/43 w/Gatewood, e/a, cr Geisenheim, Ger, 6KIA, 4POW, MACR 276. CHIEF SLY II.

42-5140 Del Cheyenne 2/10/42; West Palm Beach 12/12/42; ass 97BG Amendola; {100m+} 463BG Celone; 483BG Sterparone; retUS Homestead 6/7/44; RFC Arledge Fd 22/11/44. YANKEE QUEEN.

42-5141 Del Cheyenne 2/10/42; Salina 26/11/42; Topeka 5/3/43; Geiger 22/6/43; 328 BU Gulfport 20/7/43; 902 BU Pincastle 4/9/43; 328 BU Gulfport 31/3/44; RFC Albuquerque 19/6/45.

42-5142 Del Cheyenne 2/10/42; Barksdale 16/11/42; West Palm Beach 11/12/42; ass MTO; WO 8/11/44.

42-5143 Del Cheyenne 2/10/42; West Palm Beach 11/12/42; ass 352BS/301BG Ain M'Lila 16/1/43; St Donat 6/3/43; c/l {52m} Sicily 16/7/43 w/Hammond; rep, tran 347BS/99BG Oudna 14/11/43; {25m} became weather a/c 6/8/44; tran 52FG Madna Fd, lt. 8/10/44; sal 2/11/44. DIRTY GERTIE.

42-5144 Del Cheyenne 4/10/42; 30BS/19BG Pyote 6/2/43; Tinker 13/8/43; 452BG Pendleton 1/11/43; WO 17/1/44.

42-5145 Del Cheyenne 4/10/42; West Palm Beach 7/1/43; ass 32BS/301BG Biskra 11/1/43; Ain M'Lila 17/1/43; St Donat 6/3/43; Oudna 6/8/43; {62m} tran 96BS/2BG Massicault 14/11/43; Bizerte 2/12/43; Amendola 9/12/43; MIA {40m} Padua 11/3/44 w/Peters, e/a, 6 baled. MACR 2836.

42-5146 Del Cheyenne 4/10/42; Presque Is 28/11/42; ass 422BS/305BG [JJ-S] Chelveston 7/12/42; MIA Paris 4/4/43 w/Ellis, e/a, cr Les Andelys, Fr, 2KIA 8POW, MACR 15543.

42-5147 Del Cheyenne 4/10/42; West Palm Beach 12/12/42; ass 414BS/97BG Biskra 22/12/42; Château-du-Rhumel 3/2/43; coll w/41-24415 Palermo w/Payne 7/43, nose sheared off but return base; Pont-du-Fahs 1/8/43; Depienne 15/8/43; MIA Frascati 8/9/43 w/Gueriniere, flak, 7KIA 3POW. MACR 720. OLD IRONSIDES.

42-5148 Del Cheyenne 4/10/42; Pueblo 3/2/43; 435BS/19BG Pyote 28/9/43; 556 BU Long Beach 21/6/44; 236 BU Pyote 28/7/43; RFC Kingman 31/10/45.

42-5149 Del Cheyenne 4/10/42; Wendover 8/12/42; Casper 11/1/43; Ephrata 14/6/43; Rapid City 6/8/43; 370 BU Lowry for US Navy 31/3/44; tran ASF 31/3/47.

42-5150 Del Cheyenne 4/10/42; Casper 30/5/43; Kearney 3/8/43; WO 20/2/44. VERA DE.

42-5151 Del Cheyenne 4/10/42; Wendover 8/12/42; Hamilton 10/1/43; Sioux City 5/4/43; 245 BU McCook 20/6/43; 3705 BU Lowry 16/10/43; WO 26/10/44.

42-5152 Del Cheyenne 2/20/42; Wendover 15/12/42; WO 12/1/43.

42-5153 Del Cheyenne 4/10/42; Pyote 12/1/43; Pueblo 6/4/43; Dyersburg 7/6/43; 4006 BU Miami 9/6/43; 3501 BU Boca Raton 2/9/43; 2137 BU Hendricks 17/10/44; RFC Walnut Ridge 3/1/46.

42-5154 Del Cheyenne 4/10/42; Pyote 8/1/43; Kelly 2/7/43; 4100 BU Patterson 9/6/44; 223 BU Dyersburg 8/9/44; 554 BU Memphis 5/12/44; 327 BU Drew 3/6/45; RFC Searcy Fd 11/8/45.

42-5155 Del Tulsa 4/10/42; West Palm Beach 11/12/42; ass 365BS/305BG [XK-T] Chelveston 21/3/43; MIA 19/5/43 w/Higgins, e/a, cr Kiel, 1EVD 3KIA 6POW, MACR 15488.

42-5156 Del Tulsa 4/10/42; Salina 19/1/43; ass 364BS/305BG [WF-D/B] Chelveston 1/2/43; tran AFSC 5/4-9/5/43 and 29/7-12/10/43; 2 BAD Lt Staughton 20/3/44; retUS 8/5/44; RFC Walnut Ridge 4/1/46.

42-5157 Del Tulsa 4/10/42; Biggs 11/2/43; 28BS/19BG Pyote 2/6/43; 504BG Fairmont 18/7/43; 241 BU Fairmont 23/8/43; 1103 BU Morrison 14/1/44; 233 BU Davis Monthan 1/3/44; RFC Ontario 22/5/45.

42-5158 Del Tulsa 4/10/42; 571BS/390BG Smyrna 14/11/42; Lockburn 3/1/43; 3501 BU Boca Raton 3/8/43; 4006 BU Miami 19/8/43; 3501 BU Boca Raton 8/9/43; Recl Comp 29/1/46.

42-5159 Del Tulsa 4/10/42; Salina 10/11/42; 3701 BU Amarillo 13/8/43; RFC Walnut Ridge 20/12/45.

42-5160 Del Tulsa 4/10/42; Smyrna 18/11/42; Fairfield 19/3/43; f/l Lockburn 1/7/43, rep; Patterson 14/7/43; WO 27/11/43.

42-5161 Del Tulsa 8/10/42; Smyrna 13/11/42; Lockburn 30/5/43; 2132 BU Maxwell 27/7/43; 2114 BU Lockburn 12/8/43; 4142 BU Dayton 17/4/44; 2114 BU Lockburn 24/8/44; RFC Walnut Ridge 14/12/45.

42-5162 Del Tulsa 4/10/42; Smyrna 13/11/42; Lockburn 28/4/43; WO 17/5/43.

42-5163 Del Tulsa 4/10/42; Smyrna 13/11/42; 2114 BU Lockburn 28/4/43; 4124 BU Altus 10/8/44; RFC Altus 9/10/45.

42-5164 Del Tulsa 5/10/42; Scott 6/1/43; Chicago 22/4/43; Lockburn 10/5/43; c/l Lockburn 23/10/43 w/Crupp; WO 1/11/43.

42-5165 Del Tulsa 5/10/42; Lockburn 28/4/43; La Junta 26/6/43; WO 1/1/44.

42-5166 Del Tulsa 5/10/42; Lockburn 28/4/43; 2112 BU Chanute 5/7/43; 2137 BU Hendricks 7/8/43; RFC Walnut Ridge 19/12/43.

42-5167 Del Tulsa 5/10/42; Smyrna 27/1/43; Lowry 7/6/43; 3017 BU Hobbs 2/10/43; 4124 BU Altus 12/7/44; RFC Altus 28/8/45.

42-5168 Del Tulsa 5/10/42; Smyrna 24/2/43; Lockburn 28/4/43; WO 6/9/43.

42-5169 Del Tulsa 5/10/42; Smyrna 14/11/42; Fairfield 20/3/43; Kearney 19/7/43; 2114 BU Lockburn 24/10/43; 4124 BU Altus 12/8/44; RFC Altus 9/10/45.

42-5170 Del Tulsa 5/10/42; West Palm Beach 15/12/42; ass 342BS/97BG Tafaraoui 7/12/42; Biskra 25/12/42; Château-du-Rhumel 8/2/43; Pont-du-Fahs 1/8/43; Depienne 15/8/43; {11m} tran 347BS/99BG Oudna 14/11/43; Tortorella 11/12/43; MIA {11m} Sofia 10/1/44 w/Shupe, e/a, cr Sofia, MACR 1819.

42-5171 Del Tulsa 5/10/42; Presque Is 27/11/42; ass 368BS/306BG Thurleigh 1/1/43; MIA Bremen 17/4/43 w/Gillogly, e/a, cr?, 10POW, MACR 15524.

42-5172 Del Tulsa 5/10/42; Salina 21/1/43; ass 401BS/91BG [LL-Z] Bassingbourn 26/3/43; MIA {4m} Bremen 17/4/43 w/Beasley, flak, cr Bruchhausen, Ger, 2KIA 8POW, MACR 15521. THUNDERBIRD.

42-5173 Del Tulsa 6/10/42; Pyote 31/12/42; Biggs 21/1/43; Pueblo 4/3/43; Geiger 3/5/43; Ephrata 1/8/43; WO 22/4/44.

42-5174 Del Tulsa 5/10/42; West Palm Beach 9/1/43; ass 340BS/97BG Château-du-Rhumel 17/4/43; Pont-du-Fahs 1/8/43; Depienne 15/8/43; Cerignola 20/12/43; Amendola 16/1/44; retUS Homstead 18/7/44; RFC Bush Fd 4/7/45.

42-5175 Del Denver 6/10/42; New Castle 4/11/42; ass 367BS/306BG Thurleigh 16/11/42; MIA St Nazaire 16/2/43; w/Downing, flak, cr Biscay, 2EVD 1KIA 7POW. MACR 15471.

42-5176 Del Denver 6/10/42; West Palm Beach 15/12/42; ass 97BG Biskra 12/1/43; Château-du-Rhumel 8/2/43; Pont-du-Fahs 1/8/43; Depienne 15/8/43; tran 416BS/99BG Oudna 14/11/43; Tortorella 11/12/43; dest when RAF Wellington exploded 30/12/43. Sal.

42-5177 Del Denver 6/10/42; New Castle 19/10/42; ass 359BS/303BG [BN-U] Molesworth 1/2/43; c/l Attlebridge 28/11/43, sal 13/12/43. FAST WORKER Mk II.

42-5178 Del Denver 6/10/42; New Castle 19/10/42; ass 303BG Molesworth 21/12/42; tran 322BS/91BG [LG-L] Bassingbourn 11/1/43; MIA {15m+} Anklam 9/10/43 w/Judy, e/a, cr Flemsburg (Kragstedt), 1KIA 9POW, MACR 898. OLD STAND BY.

42-5179 Del Denver 6/10/42; West Palm Beach

12/1/43; ass 352BS/301BG Ain M'Lila 22/2/43; St Donat 6/3/43; MIA {4m} Palermo 22/3/43 w/Hair, flak, exploded taking out Me-109, 3POW 6KIA. JUNIOR.

42-5180 Del Denver 5/10/42; Houlton 13/11/42; ass 423BS/306BG [RD-B] Thurleigh 24/11/42; MIA Bremen 25/6/43 w/Logan; flak, cr Bourtenge, Hol, 1KIA 9POW. DFC.

42-5181 Del Cheyenne 7/10/42; Geigerr 4/12/42; Pierre 25/2/43; Portland 13/6/43; 4115 BU Atlanta 27/6/43; 4117 BU Robins 17/7/43; 328 BU Gulfport 16/9/43; 221 BU Alexandria 3/12/43; 328 BU Gulfport 22/5/44; Recl Comp 3/8/45.

42-5182 Del Cheyenne 7/10/42; Blythe 22/3/43; Dyersburg 6/6/43; 504BG Fairmont 11/6/43; 4135 BU Hill 7/8/43; 241 BU Fairmont 11/8/43; 249 BU Alliance 2/2/44; 246 BU Pratt 9/2/44; 902 BU Orlando 24/3/44; 4160 BU Albuquerque 20/6/44; RFC Albuquerque 25/5/45.

42-5183 Del Cheyenne 7/10/42; Gowen 8/4/43; Pocatello 10/5/43; WO 27/5/44.

42-5184 Del Cheyenne 7/10/42; Pyote 9/1/43; Chico 13/3/43; Gowen 24/5/43; Geiger 22/6/43; 504BG Fairmont 19/7/43; WO 28/2/44; Recl Comp 3/1/46.

42-5185 Del Cheyenne 7/10/42; Pyote 12/1/43; Dalhart 6/5/43; Tinker 28/7/43; 504BG Fairmont 12/7/44; 241 BU Fairmont 9/8/44; 232 BU Dalhart 21/10/44; 273 BU Lincoln 21/11/44; 224 BU Sioux City 9/1/45; 235 BU Biggs 12/5/45; 233 BU Davis Monthan 21/5/45; RFC Kingman 30/10/45.

42-5186 Del Cheyenne 7/10/42; Geiger 18/12/42; Biggs 3/1/43; Redmond 18/6/43; Ephrata 8/8/43; 232 BU Dalhart 9/6/44; 4104 BU Rome 10/12/44; 4117 BU Robins 14/6/45; Recl Comp 2/3/46.

42-5187 Del Cheyenne 7/10/42; Biggs 9/12/42; Tucson 8/1/43; Moses Lake 2/5/43; 4006 BU Miami 16/6/44; 3501 BU Boca Raton 18/8/44; 4210 BU Lambert 2/9/44; 2137 BU Hendricks 17/10/45; RFC Walnut Ridge 3/1/46.

42-5188 Del Cheyenne 7/10/42; Gt Falls 10/12/43; Ladd Fd 30/12/42; Hendricks 27/3/43; 556 BU Long Beach 2/10/43; 2137 BU Hendricks 7/8/44; RFC Walnut Ridge 18/12/45.

42-5189 Del Cheyenne 6/10/42; Seattle 31/1/43; Sioux City 13/4/43; Grand Isle 3/5/43; 235 BU Biggs 28/7/44; 231 BU Alamogordo 10/12/44; 246 BU Pratt 15/1/45; RFC Kingman 29/10/45.

42-5190 Del Cheyenne 8/10/42; Biggs 11/12/42; f/l Biggs 18/12/42 w/Forsythe; WO 12/1/43.

42-5191 Del Cheyenne 8/10/42; West Palm Beach 15/12/42; ass 342BS/97BG Biskra 3/1/43; Château-du-Rhumel 3/2/43; Pont-du-Fahs 1/8/43; Depienne 15/8/43; MIA Levento 9/12/43, crew saved. PEGGY.

42-5192 Del Cheyenne 8/10/42; Biggs 3/1/43; Pueblo 31/3/43; Rapid City 16/5/43; Gt Falls 29/7/43; WO 26/10/43.

42-5193 Del Cheyenne 8/10/43; Pueblo 13/1/43; Gowen 9/5/43; Pocatello 13/7/43; 246 BU Pratt 4/6/44; 4136 BU Tinker 6/7/44; 4100 BU Patterson 15/2/45; 2114 BU Lockburn 24/4/45; 377 BU Grenier 5/7/45; 2114 BU Lockburn 28/9/45; RFC Walnut Ridge 19/12/45.

42-5194 Del Wright 8/10/42; Eglin 28/6/43; 3126 BU Tonopah 23/6/44; 433 BU Sacramento 31/7/44; 4127 BU McClellan 6/9/44; Tonopah 3/10/44, Wendover 11/12/44, Vandalia 17/12/44 - weapon carrier experiments; 4000 BU Wright 28/3/45; RFC Walnut Ridge 18/12/45.

42-5195 Del Cheyenne 8/10/42; Tucson 15/1/43; Pyote 10/3/43; Tinker 9/8/43; WO 2/3/44.

42-5196 Del Cheyenne 8/10/42; Pueblo 13/1/43; Pyote 6/2/43; Tinker 10/8/43; 222 BU Ardmore 22/1/44; RFC Ontario 14/6/45.

42-5197 Del Cheyenne 8/10/42; Pocatello 14/11/42; cr 10m S of Soda Springs, Id, 3/12/42; WO 7/12/42.

42-5198 Del Cheyenne 8/10/42; Ft Sumner 21/4/43; Hobbs 6/5/43; 3017 BU Hobbs 8/11/43; 4124 BU Long Beach 10/7/44; RFC Altus 22/8/45.

42-5199 Del Cheyenne 8/10/42; Biggs 31/1/43; Tinker 29/7/43; 504BG Fairmont 4/6/44; 4209 BU Des Moines 30/6/44; 241 BU Fairmont 9/8/44; 232 BU Dalhart 26/10/44; 273 BU Lincoln 29/11/44; 223 BU Dyersburg 14/2/45; 330 BU Dyersburg 9/4/45; 1098 BU Reading 21/5/45; RFC Stillwater 28/8/45.

42-5200 Del Cheyenne 8/10/42; Pyote 13/1/43; Gulfport 3/5/43; Pyote 29/7/43; 246 BU Pratt 6/6/44; 29BG Dalhart 5/9/44; 246 BU Pratt 16/9/44; 4134 BU Spokane 12/10/44; 3705 BU Lowry 20/10/44, WO.

42-5201 Del Cheyenne 8/10/42; Gt Falls 1/12/42; Pocatello 21/12/42; Pyote 12/1/43; Tinker 1/3/43; Dalhart 7/4/43; Tinker 4/8/43; 236 BU Pyote 24/6/44; 4136 BU Tinker 1/4/45; 266 BU Majors 4/4/45; 236 BU Love Fd 3/6/45; 236 BU Pyote 12/7/45; RFC Kingman 31/10/45.

42-5202 Del Cheyenne 8/10/42; Biggs 31/1/43; Dalhart 3/4/43; Amarillo 30/6/43; Barksdale 13/7/43; WO 22/7/43.

42-5203 Del Cheyenne 8/10/42; Salina 9/2/43; ass MTO 18/3/43; Con Inv 30/3/43.

42-5204 Del Cheyenne 8/10/42; Pierre 17/12/42; Rapid City 3/3/43; Moses lake 2/8/43; 4117 BU Robins 12/7/44; 328 BU Gulfport 2/9/44; 4160 BU Albuquerque 20/5/45; RFC Albuquerque 25/6/45.

42-5205 Del Cheyenne 8/10/42; Hobbs 2/12/42; Ft Sumner 21/4/43; Hobbs 6/5/43; 4136 BU Tinker 21/6/44; 3017 BU Hobbs 12/8/44; RFC Altus 29/6/45.

42-5206 Del Tulsa 15/10/42; West Palm Beach 14/11/42; ass 353BS/301BG Ain M'Lila 21/1/43; St Donat 6/3/43; b/d {9m} Bizerte 31/3/43 w/Evans, crew baled & EVD.

42-5207 Del Cheyenne 8/10/42; Rapid City 5/12/42; f/l Chamberlain Fd, Minn 7/1/43, w/Reed, superchargers ran away; WO 30/1/43.

42-5208 Del Cheyenne 8/10/42; Rapid City 21/12/42; Geiger 1/3/43; 30BS/19BG Pyote 28/5/43; 232 BU Dalhart 24/8/44; 241 BU Fairmont 12/9/44; 249 BU Alliance 14/10/44; 221 BU Alexandra 22/10/44; RFC Altus 29/10/45.

42-5209 Del Cheyenne 9/10/42; Morrison 7/3/43; Hobbs 24/4/43; Kelly 22/7/43; 4136 BU Tinker 21/6/44; 3017 BU Hobbs 29/7/44; WO 19/8/44.

42-5210 Del Cheyenne 9/10/42; Hobbs 22/11/42; 4136 BU Tinker 4/7/44; 3017 BU Hobbs 14/8/44; RFC Altus 29/8/45.

42-5211 Del Cheyenne 9/10/42; Smyrna 19/11/42; Ft Sumner 29/4/43; Hobbs 6/5/43; 3021 BU Las Vegas 18/6/44; 3030 BU Roswell 24/9/44; 3010 BU Williams 26/11/44; 3020 La Junta 23/4/45; RFC Searcey Fd 31/7/45.

42-5212 Del Cheyenne 9/10/42; Hobbs 22/11/42; Duncan Fd 9/4/43; Hobbs 18/5/43; 2112 BU Chanute 2/6/44; 338 BU Page 17/6/44; 2123 BU Harlingen 20/8/44; 2108 BU Harlingen 1/9/44; 2132 BU Maxwell 12/10/44; 2114 BU Lockburn 30/4/45; RFC Walnut Ridge 14/12/45.

42-5213 Del Cheyenne 9/10/42; Rapid City 23/12/42; Geiger 21/4/43; Moses Lake 4/6/43; 3501 BU Boca Raton 16/6/44; 4006 BU Miami 21/6/44; 4006 BU McDill 24/6/44; 3508 BU Truax 25/2/45.

42-5214 Del Cheyenne 9/10/42; Geiger 4/12/42; Ainsworth 20/3/43; Moses lake 7/8/43; 3701 BU Amarillo 12/11/44; 2114 BU Lockburn 16/3/45; RFC Walnut Ridge 14/12/45.

42-5215 Del Cheyenne 9/10/42; Geiger 4/12/42; Gowen 10/3/43; cr base 3/5/43 w/Arney, crew killed. WO 5/5/43.

42-5216 Del Cheyenne 9/10/42; 234 BU Clovis 15/7/44; 247 BU Smoky Hill 26/1/45; 203 BU Jackson 3/2/45; 203 BU Benning 28/6/45; RFC Albuquerque 2/8/45.

42-5217 Del Cheyenne 9/10/42; West Palm Beach 11/12/42; ass 352BS/301BG Biskra 12/1/43; Ain M'Lila 17/1/43; St Donat 6/3/43; MIA {11m} Bo Rizzo 10/5/43, w/Julienne, flak hit; plane exploded & blew bombardier Zahn out to be POW, rest KIA. MACR 15304. O'REILLY'S DAUGHTER.

42-5218 Del Tulsa 14/10/42; Salina 25/1/43; Morrison 14/2/43; ass 423BS/306BG [RD-J] 15/4/43; MIA 13/6/43 w/Marcotte, flak, 2KIA 7POW. SKY WOLF.

42-5219 Del Tulsa 14/10/42; Presque Is 26/11/42; West Palm Beach 15/1/43; ass 385BG Gt Ashfield 24/1/43; trans 366BS/305BG Chelveston 2/43; then 364BS [WF-K]; MIA Lorient 17/5/43 w/Indiere, e/a, 6KIA 4POW. MACR 15569.

42-5220 Del Tulsa 14/10/42; Salina 23/12/42; ass 366BS/305BG Chelveston (landed Rineanna, Ire, 21/3) 25/3/43; MIA Lorient 16/4/43 w/Leach, 5KIA 5POW.

42-5221 Del Tulsa 14/10/42; Salina 31/1/43; Morrison 4/3/43; ass 427BS/303BG [GN-Z] Molesworth 8/4/43; MIA Anklam 9/10/43 w/Clifford, e/a, cr Bad Doberan, Ger, 10KIA, MACR 874. SON.

42-5222 Del Tulsa 14/10/42; Lewiston 1/12/42; Gt Falls 8/1/43; Ephrata 17/2/43; Spokane 31/3/43; Felts Fd 13/7/43; Ephrata 6/8/43; 244 BU Harvard 19/9/44; 110 BU Mitchell 24/1/45; 244 BU Harvard 26/1/45; RFC Kingman 27/10/45.

42-5223 Del Tulsa 15/10/42; Salina 18/12/42; ass 414BS/97BG Biskra 15/1/43; Château-du-Rhumel 8/2/43; Pont-du-Fahs 1/8/43; Depienne 15/8/43; tran 346BS/99BG Oudna 14/11/43; Tortorella 11/12/43; MIA {11m/99} Innsbruck w/Simpson 19/12/43, ditched Adriatic, pilot drowned, 2POW 7RTD. MACR 1528.

42-5224 Del Tulsa 14/10/42; Ogden 28/10/42; WO 19/11/42.

42-5225 Del Tulsa 14/10/42; West Palm Beach 15/1/43; ass 323BS/91BG [OR-S] Bassingbourn 8/2/43 as STORMY WEATHER; c/l base 4/3/43, badly damaged, when repaired re-named V-PACKETTE; MIA Schweinfurt 17/8/43 w/Von Der Hyde, e/a, cr Baelen, Bel, 8KIA 1EVD (arrived day before) 1POW, MACR 280.

42-5226 Del Tulsa 14/10/42; Wendover 27/2/43; Casper 9/4/43; Tinker 13/6/43; Rapid City 14/7/43; WO 8/9/43.

42-5227 Del Tulsa 14/10/42; West Palm Beach 11/12/42; ass 97BG Biskra 31/12/42; on 3/1/43 w/Devers, crew baled over friendly territory, sal. BUCKET OF BOLTS.

42-5228 Del Denver 14/10/42; Bolling 1/1/43; Orlando 3/7/43; Montbrook 12/8/43; 4136 BU Tinker 28/9/44; survey Tinker 5/2/45; WO 1/8/45; Recl Comp 13/2/46.

42-5229 Del Denver 15/10/42; Brooksville 23/12/42; Eglin 3/2/43; Leesburg 22/6/43; WO 2/10/43.

42-5230 Del Denver 15/10/42; West Palm Beach 18/11/42; Morrison 31/1/43; ass 342BS/97BG Château-du-Rhumel 19/4/43; Pont-du-Fahs 1/8/43; Depienne 15/8/43; tran 347BS/99BG Oudna 14/11/43; Tortorella 11/12/43; {36m} 483BG Tortorella 31/3/44, retUS Tinker 3/7/45; sal Patterson 12/7/45; Recl Comp 27/11/45.

42-5231 Del Denver 15/10/42; Brooksville 21/12/42;

Eglin 3/2/43; Orlando 27/7/43; Brooksville 5/8/43; 2117 BU Buckingham 16/6/44; 2114 BU Lockburn 5/8/44; RFC Walnut Ridge 14/12/45.

42-5232 Del Tulsa 18/10/42; Presque Is 26/11/42; ass 364BS/305BG [WF-E] Chelveston 13/12/42; MIA Paris 4/4/43 w/Jones, e/a, cr Les Andelys, Fr, 1EVD 7POW 2KIA. MACR 15592. AVAILABLE JONES.

42-5233 Del Tulsa 18/18/42; Wayne Co 16/11/42; West Palm Beach 13/12/42; ass 32BS/301BG Tafaraoui 31/12/42; Maison Blanche 5/12/42; Biskra 16/12/42; Ain M'Lila 17/1/43; St Donat 6/3/43; Oudna 6/8/43; {95m} tran 96BS/2BG Massicault 14/11/43; Bizerte 2/12/43; Amendola 9/12/43; {6m} 346BS/99BG Tortorella 28/3/44; {0m} 817BS/483BG Tortorella 31/3/44; retUS Homestead 23/7/44; RFC Arledge Fd 23/11/44. RIGOR MORTIS.

42-5234 Del Cheyenne 23/10/42; Wayne Co 2/12/42; Gt Britain 11/12/42; RAF [FA707], 206Sq, 220Sq Cr Azores 26/7/44, sal.

42-5235 Del Cheyenne 23/10/42; Wayne Co 3/12/42; Gt Britain 13/12/42; RAF [FA708], 206Sq, 220Sq, cr Azores 7/11/44, sal.

42-5236 Del Cheyenne 18/10/42; Wayne Co 3/12/42; Gt Britain 8/12/42; RAF [FA709], 220Sq, 206Sq, WO 15/9/47.

42-5237 Del Cheyenne 18/10/42; Wayne Co 4/12/42; Gt Britain 22/2/43; RAF [FA710], 220Sq, 521Sq, WO 26/11/46.

42-5238 Del Cheyenne 18/10/42; Wayne Co 3/12/42; Gt Britain 2/1/43; RAF [FA711], 206Sq, WO 14/8/48.

42-5239 Del Cheyenne 18/10/42; Wayne Co 3/12/432; Gt Britain 2/1/43; RAF [FA712], 519Sq, 251Sq, WO 4/3/47.

42-5240 Del Cheyenne 23/10/42; Wayne Co 3/12/42; Gt Britain 3/2/43; RAF [FA713], 220Sq, 206Sq, WO 14/6/45.

42-5241 Del Tulsa 23/10/42; Lewiston 1/12/42; Gt Falls 4/2/43; Spokane 15/4/43; Ephrata 3/5/43; 901 BU Pincastle 16/6/44; 222 BU Ardmore 5/12/44; RFC Ontario 14/6/45.

42-5242 Del Tulsa 23/10/42; West Palm Beach 17/12/42; Salina 30/12/42; ass 342BS/97BG Biskra 21/1/43; Château-du-Rhumel 8/2/43; c/t/o 23/3/43 w/Peterson; sal. BUGS BUNNY.

42-5243 Del Tulsa 23/10/42; Wendover 5/12/42; ass 359BS/303BG Molesworth 29/1/43; MIA Kiel 4/5/43 w/Bales, s/d by e/a; ditched Nth Sea, 10KIA, MACR 15593. F.D.R.'s POTATO PEELER KIDS.

42-5244 Del Tulsa 22/10/42; West Palm Beach 9/1/43; ass Glen 12AF 27/1/43; WO 7/12/43.

42-5245 Del Tulsa 23/10/42; West Palm Beach 15/12/42; ass 414BS/97BG Biskra 12/1/43; Château-du-Rhumel 8/2/43; Pont-du-Fahs 1/8/43; Depienne 15/8/43; MIA Foggia w/Light 25/8/43, flak, ditched; MACR 482.

42-5246 Del Tulsa 23/10/42; Salina 9/2/43; Presque Is 30/4/43; Smoky Hill 6/6/43; Topeka 3/7/43; 243 BU Gt Bend 16/8/44; 581 BU Adams 1/9/44; RFC Albuquerque 25/6/45.

42-5247 Del Tulsa 23/10/42; Wendover 7/2/43; Tinker 27/5/43; Dyersburg 12/7/43; Dalhart 15/8/43; 4200 BU Chicago Mun. Apt 17/6/44; 504BG Fairmont 19/6/43; 241 BU Fairmont 6/8/44; 249 BU Alliance 11/10/44; 223 BU Dyersburg 10/2/45; 330 BU Dyersburg 1/3/45; 325 BU Avon Park 14/5/45; RFC Altus 28/7/45.

42-5248 Del Tulsa 23/10/42; Salina 16/12/42; ass 342BS/97BG Biskra 28/1/43; Château-du-Rhumel 8/2/43; MIA Trapani 13/4/43 w/Danish, flak, cr Med Sea, 10KIA. MACR 16526.

42-5249 Del Denver 23/10/42; Orlando 31/1/43; Eglin 5/3/43; Brooksville 25/6/43; 2114 BU Lockburn 2/9/43; 3017 BU Hobbs 24/1/44; 4124 BU Altus 11/7/44; RFC Altus 27/8/45.

42-5250 Del Denver 26/10/42; West Palm Beach 12/12/42; ass 97BG Biskra 9/1/43; Amendula 16/1/44. WO 11/5/45.

42-5251 Del Cheyenne 18/11/42; West Palm Beach 12/12/42; ass 368BS/306BG Thurleigh 1/1/43 PRIDE OF KARIANS; dam 1/3/43 coll w/42-24476; tran AFSC 3/3/43, ret 9/4/43; MIA Bremen 17/4/43 w/Jankowski, flak, cr Nth Sea, 3KIA 7POW. BODACIOUS CRITTER.

42-5252 Del Denver 26/10/42; West Palm Beach 4/12/42; Orlando 31/1/43; Eglin 5/3/43; Morris Fd 6/8/43; 3030 BU Roswell 29/6/44; 3010 BU Williams 2/12/44; 273 BU Lincoln 15/1/45; 3010 BU Williams 24/1/45; 3020 BU La Junta 4/5/45; RFC Searcey Fd 31/7/45.

42-5253 Del Denver 26/10/42; Homestead 18/12/42; ass 366BS/305BG [KY-C] Chelveston 2/3/43; MIA Rouen 4/4/43 w/O'Neill, e/a, cr Rouen, 1EVD 2KIA 7POW. MACR 15564.

42-5254 Del Denver 26/10/42; Brooksville 19/12/42; Orlando 31/1/43; Montbrook 13/8/43; 245 BU McCook 15/8/44; 9BG McCook 1/9/44; 249 BU Alliance 16/10/44; 224 BU Sioux City 25/1/45; RFC Searcey Fd 13/8/45.

42-5255 Del Geiger AF HQ 6/11/42; Pierre 4/3/43; Geiger 23/6/43; 556 BU Long Beach 10/7/44; 202 BU Galveston 20/7/44; 223 BU Dyersburg 23/2/45; 330 BU Dyersburg 1/3/45; 202 BU Syracuse 23/3/45; Rec Comp 3/1/46.

42-5256 Del Geiger AF HQ 9/11/42; Ainsworth 1/3/43; Rapid City 14/4/43; Geiger 22/6/43; Gt Falls 29/7/43; Lewiston 4/8/43; 248 BU Walker 9/6/44; 232 BU Dalhart 14/7/44; 3701 BU Amarillo 17/9/44; WO 20/10/44. Recl Comp 9/2/46.

42-5257 Del Denver 26/10/42; Salina 5/1/43; ass 359BS/303BG [BN-S] Molesworth 19/2/43; retUS Robins 29/4/44; Recl Comp 9/8/45. MISS BEA HAVEN.

42-5258 Del Denver 26/10/42; West Palm Beach 13/1/43; ass 8AF 15/1/43; cr Cardingham (?) UK, 10/2/43; sal 2/11/43.

42-5259 Del Denver 26/10/42; Brooksville 30/12/42; Orlando 29/5/43; Hobbs 26/11/43; Orlando 1/1/44; Dallas 9/1/44; 2117 BU Buckingham 29/6/44; 2114 BU Lockburn 11/8/44; RFC Walnut Ridge 14/12/45.

42-5260 Del Denver 26/10/42; Salina 15/12/42; ass 360BS/303BG [PU-A] Molesworth 29/1/43; MIA Emden 2/10/43 w/Tippet, e/a, cr Nth Sea, 11KIA. MACR 738. YARDBIRD.

42-5261 Del Geiger 5/11/42; Blythe 14/12/42; Hobbs 13/3/43; Roswell 24/5/43; 3108 BU Kingman 18/6/44; 4100 BU Patterson 21/9/44; 3010 BU Williams 31/1/45; 2114 BU Lockburn 16/7/45; RFC Albuquerque 9/8/45.

42-5262 Del Denver 27/10/42; Bury 6/12/42; ass 360BS/303BG Molesworth 29/1/43; MIA Lorient 6/3/43 w/Plocher, e/a, ditched Biscay, 2KIA, 8POW. MACR 15536.

42-5263 Del Denver 27/10/42; West Palm Beach 9/1/43; ass 340BS/97BG Biskra 21/1/43; Château-du-Rhumel 8/2/43; Pont-du-Fahs 1/8/43; Depiennne 15/8/43; tran 347BS/99BG Oudna 14/11/43; Tortorella 11/12/43; {13m 99th} RetUS Pope Fd 20/5/45; RFC Altus 29/10/45.

42-5264 Del Denver 2/11/42; Salina 15/12/42; ass

Below: B-17F-40-BO 42-5264, *Yankee Doodle Dandy*, photographed on 11 January 1944 at Watton, England, shortly after its return from an operation where it sustained heavy battle damage. Rocket and cannon shell fragments took the lives of the tail gunner and a waist gunner. Repaired, this Fortress was returned to the USA in April 1944 and served at a replacement crew training base. (USAAF)

358BS/303BG [VK-C/J/Q] Molesworth 1/2/43; tran 2AD Warton 11/1/44; retUS Amarillo 3/4/44; RFC Stillwater 24/9/45. YANKEE DOODLE DANDY.

42-5265 Del Geiger 1/11/42; Casper 17/1/43; Tinker 5/5/43; Dyersburg 15/7/43; 246 BU Pratt 23/6/44; 11 STA Morrison 29/7/44; 242 BU Grand Isle 16/9/44; 4103 BU Jackson 16/3/45; 246 BU Pratt 19/3/45; RFC Albuquerque 25/6/45.

42-5266 Del Geiger 1/11/42; Lewiston 2/12/42; Gt Falls 4/2/43; Gore 12/4/43; Ephrata 2/6/43; 4136 BU Tinker 19/6/43; 505BG Harvard 22/6/43; 244 BU Harvard 18/8/44; 3003 BU Luke 2/9/44; 244 BU Harvard 12/10/44; 203 BU Jackson 21/1/45; 232 BU Dalhart 20/9/45; RFC Kingman 27/10/46.

42-5267 Del Geiger 1/11/42; Glasgow 7/12/42; Gt Falls 4/2/43; Tinker 12/7/43; Dalhart 18/8/43; 2024 BU Walker 10/4/44; 4100 BU Patterson 8/6/44; 248 BU Walker 24/10/44; WO 24/10/44.

42-5268 Del Geiger 1/11/42; Lewiston 31/1/43; Ephrata 17/2/43; Gore 19/5/43; Ephrata 29/7/43; 4127 BU McClellan 18/6/44; 202 BU Galveston 20/6/44; 4136 BU Tinker 29/7/44; 202 BU Galveston 2/8/44; 268 BU Patterson 30/3/45; RFC Kingman 27/10/45.

42-5269 Del Geiger 5/11/42; Blythe 13/12/42; Hobbs 20/3/43; Ft Sumner 21/4/43; Hobbs 6/5/43; 3021 BU Las Vegas 18/6/44; 3030 BU Roswell 1/10/44; 3010 BU Williams 2/12/44; 3020 BU La Junta 2/5/45; RFC Searcey Fd 31/7/45.

42-5270 Del Geiger 1/11/42; 379BG Sioux City 8/1/43; Scribner 19/3/43; Dyersberg 13/4/43; Memphis 23/5/43; Dyersberg 2/6/43; 236 BU Pyote 10/9/44; 2543 BU Waco 13/1/45; 236 BU Pyote 29/1/45; 4202 BU Syracuse 26/3/45; Recl Comp 3/1/46.

42-5271 Del Geiger 5/11/42; 379BG Sioux City 3/1/43; Watertown 30/3/43; Gowen 25/4/43; 435BS/19BG Pyote 28/8/42; Tinker 18/11/43; 202 BU Galveston 14/6/44; 498BG Gt Bend 16/6/44; 901 BU Pinecastle 26/6/44; 243 BU Gt Bend 4/9/44; 3701 BU Amarillo 31/1/45; Recl Comp 9/4/46.

42-5272 Del Geiger 1/11/42; 379BG Sioux City 21/11/42; Wendover 14/3/43; Casper 14/5/43; Dalhart 14/6/43; 246 BU Walker 30/6/44; WO 15/9/44; Recl Comp 31/3/46.

42-5273 Del Geiger 1/11/42; Sioux City 21/11/32; Hammer Fd 9/3/43; Gowen 9/4/43; Dyersburg 1/6/43; 19BG Pyote 4/12/43; 326 BU McDill 20/1/44; 328 BU Gulfport 23/1/44; 4119 BU Brookley 1/2/44; 328 BU Gulfport 18/2/44; 4160 BU Albuquerque 20/6/44; RFC Albuquerque 25/6/45.

42-5274 Del Geiger 1/11/42; Casper 22/3/43; Tinker 26/5/43; Dyersburg 27/6/43; 246 BU Pratt 4/6/44; 233 BU Davis Monthan 24/2/45; RFC Ontario 29/6/45.

42-5275 Del Cheyenne 16/11/42; 379BG Sioux City 5/1/43; Tinker 18/3/43; Spokane 21/6/43; Ephrata 29/7/43; 331 BU Barksdale 25/8/44; 222 BU Ardmore 16/9/44; 3706 BU Sheppard 30/11/44; 222 BU Ardmore 21/12/44; RFC Ontario 14/6/45.

42-5276 Del Geiger 5/11/42; Blythe 18/12/42; Hobbs 18/3/43; Mather Fd 8/6/43; Hobbs 18/6/43; 3501 BU Boca Raton 3/8/44; 581 BU Adams 1/3/45; BU Truax 8/3/45; Recl Comp 7/6/45.

42-5277 Del Geiger 5/11/42; Rapid City 17/12/42; Spokane 14/4/43; Ephrata 17/7/43; 247 BU Smoky Hill 3/6/44; 232 BU Dalhart 9/7/44; 4104 BU Rome 10/12/44; 4108 BU Newark 11/6/45; RFC Bush Fd 18/6/45.

42-5278 Del Geiger 6/11/42; Redmond 23/12/42; Walla Walla 22/2/43; Ephrata 15/5/43; 3701 BU Amarillo 9/6/44; 497BG Pratt 11/7/44; 246 BU Pratt 16/7/44; 273 BU Lincoln 10/2/45; 271 BU Kearney 6/3/45; Recl Comp 22/10/45.

42-5279 Del Geiger 6/11/42; Amarillo 1/3/43; Gulfport 7/8/43; 497BG Pratt 9/6/44; 271 BU Kearney 20/6/44; 4136 BU Tinker 24/7/44; 246 BU Pratt 30/7/44; 29BG Dalhart 8/9/44; 4108 BU Newark 30/10/44; 246 BU Pratt 16/12/44; RFC Albuquerque 25/5/45.

42-5280 Del Geiger 9/11/42; Cutbank 19/12/42; Walla Walla 4/2/43; Spokane 1/8/43; 247 BU Smoky Hill 10/6/44; 4136 BU Tinker 30/7/44; 235 BU Biggs 27/9/44; 4202 BU Syracuse 14/11/44; Recl Comp 3/1/46.

42-5281 Del Geiger 5/11/42; 346BG Salina 18/11/42; Topeka 5/3/43; Rapid City 27/4/43; Geiger 28/6/43; Cutbank 30/7/43; 224 BU Sioux City 6/3/44; 4168 BU Albuquerque 20/6/44; RFC Albuquerque 25/6/45.

43-5282 Del Geiger 5/11/42; Walla Walla 3/1/43; Redmond 12/1/43; c/t/o 22/1/43, probably engine failure. WO

42-5283 Del Geiger 5/11/42; cr Sioux City 3/11/42 in snowstorm and burned out. WO

42-5284 Del Geiger 6/11/42; Elmendorf 11/5/43; 4100 BU Patterson 5/5/44; 1103 BU Morrison 8/6/44; 303 BU Gray 14/11/44; 613 BU Phillips 15/3/45; 1103 BU Morrison 31/5/45; 4112 BU Olmstead 27/10/45; 552 BU New Castle 24/12/45; 1100 BU West Palm Beach 15/2/46; 503 B/Depot Patterson 28/5/46.

42-5285 Del Geiger 6/11/42; Blythe 9/12/42; Tucson 7/1/43; Hobbs 17/3/43; 3701 BU Amarillo 1/11/43; RFC Stillwater 24/9/46.

42-5286 Del Geiger 5/11/42; 379BG Sioux City 21/11/42; Gowen 19/4/43; Tinker 8/6/43; Dalhart 8/7/43; Scott 18/8/43; 814 BU Stout 12/7/44; 498BG Gt Bend 31/7/44; 243 BU Gt Bend 20/8/44; 233 Davis Monthan 24/2/45; RFC Ontario 27/8/45.

42-5287 Del Geiger 5/11/42; Rapid City 18/2/42; Walla Walla 1/3/43; Gowen 10/3/43; WO 29/4/43.

42-5288 Del Geiger 5/11/42; Blythe 9/12/42; McLelland 6/4/43; Moses Lake 2/5/43; Spokane 3/6/43; Geiger 10/8/43; 4117 BU Robins 16/6/44; 327 BU Drew 18/8/44; RFC Altus 29/8/45.

42-5289 Del Geiger 5/11/42; Blythe 9/12/42; Tucson 3/1/43; Walla Walla 23/5/43; wrecked when u/c collapsed 26/5/43; WO 13/8/43.

42-5290 Del Geiger 5/11/42; 379BG Sioux City 8/1/43; Wendover 4/4/43; Tinker 26/6/43; Madras 29/6/43; Walla Walla 17/7/43; 244 BU Harvard 19/9/44; 272 BU Topeka 23/10/44; 224 BU Sioux City 1/12/45; RFC Albuquerque 25/5/45.

42-5291 Del Geiger 6/11/42; Hill Fd 31/1/43; Scribner 3/3/43; Sioux City 6/4/43; Casper 5/7/43; Dyersberg 3/8/43; 234 BU Clovis 24/6/44; 4200 BU Chicago Mun Apt 16/11/44; 245 BU McCook 1/3/45; 4202 BU Syracuse 6/4/45; RFC Altus 5/11/45.

42-5292 Del Geiger 6/11/42; Sioux City 3/1/43; Kearney 3/8/43; 2511 BU Bryan 2/11/44; 4124 BU Altus 18/10/45; RFC Walnut Ridge 21/12/45.

42-5293 Del Geiger 6/11/42; Pierre 25/2/43; Rapid City 29/4/43; Geiger 22/6/43; Spokane 13/8/43; 325 BU Avon Park 9/4/44; 801 BU Pope Fd 27/4/44; 325 BU Avon Park 25/5/44; RFC Altus 6/9/45.

42-5294 Del Geiger 9/11/42; Lowry 20/3/43; Pierre 1/4/43; Rapid City 24/4/43; WO 26/5/43.

42-5295 Del Geiger 6/11/42; Rapid City 21/12/42; Pierre 25/2/43; Lowry 20/3/43; c/l Rapid City 27/4/43 w/Katz, pilot & 5 pass slightly inj, 5 pass baled OK. WO 16/5/43.

42-5296 Del Geiger 6/11/42; Tinker 25/2/43; Casper 12/3/43; Wendover 14/4/43; Spokane 20/7/43; Moses Lake 8/8/43; 3701 BU Amarillo 17/11/43; Recl Comp 7/6/46.

42-5297 Del Geiger 6/11/42; Walla Walla 4/12/42; Redmond 21/2/43; Tinker 10/4/43; Spokane 12/8/43; 3701 BU Amarillo 17/11/44; 3706 BU Sheppard 13/3/45; 3701 BU Amarillo 7/4/45; RFC Walnut Ridge 20/12/45.

42-5298 Del Geiger 6/11/42; Ainsworth 16/12/42; Rapid City 31/1/43; Casper 12/4/43; Geiger 22/6/43; 29BG Dalhart 2/9/44; 29BG Pratt 9/9/44; 273 BU Lincoln 15/1/45; 246 BU Pratt 13/3/45; 902 BU Orlando 15/5/45; 246 BU Pratt 23/5/45; RFC Kingman 28/10/45.

42-5299 Del Tulsa 16/11/42; 379BG Sioux City 3/12/42; Biggs 20/3/43; Wendover 23/5/43; WO 25/6/43.

42-5300 Del Tulsa 16/11/42; Gt Falls 14/1/43; Gowen 10/3/43; Tinker 21/5/43; Spokane 1/7/43; Moses Lake 5/8/43; 4117 BU Robins 23/6/44; 327 BU Drew 7/8/44; WO 3/10/44; Recl Comp 4/45.

42-5301 Del Tulsa 16/11/42; Hobbs 22/12/42; 3017 BU Hobbs 8/11/44; 4124 BU Long Beach 16/7/45; RFC Altus 11/8/45.

42-5302 Del Tulsa 16/11/42; Gt Falls 9/12/42; Casper 6/1/43; Scotts Bluff 18/4/43; Tinker 13/6/43; Rapid City 16/7/43; 326 BU McDill 18/1/44; 331 BU Barksdale 20/1/44; 4160 BU Albuquerque 20/6/44; RFC Albuquerque 25/6/45.

42-5303 Del Geiger 6/11/42; Lewiston 8/12/42; Redmond 21/1/43; Blythe 14/3/43; Gowen 3/4/43; Tinker 26/5/43; Smoky Hill 30/7/43; 234 BU Clovis 23/6/44; 2525 BU Liberal 23/11/44; WO 24/11/44; Recl Comp 2/2/45.

42-5304 Del Tulsa 16/11/42; Sioux City 4/12/42; Rapid City 5/2/43; Ephrata 1/3/43; Spokane 28/4/43; Ephrata 14/5/43; 236 BU Pyote 10/9/44; 555 BU Love Fd 8/11/44; 236 BU Pyote 24/1/45; 224 BU Sioux City 6/3/45; RFC Albuquerque 25/6/45.

42-5305 Del Denver 11/11/42; Pyote 8/1/43; Pueblo 20/3/43; Gt Falls 21/4/43; Moses Lake 23/5/43; Tinker 7/6/43; Ephrata 29/7/43; WO 25/10/43.

42-5306 Del Tulsa 16/11/42; New Castle 9/12/43; ass 367BS/306BG [GY-P] Thurleigh 1/1/43; tran 359BS/303BG Molesworth 25/9/43; MIA Pas De Calais 28/2/44 w/Shoup, flak, cr Dieppe, 7KIA 3POW, MACR 2863.

42-5307 Del Cheyenne 16/11/42; Casper 3/12/42; Pyote 16/3/43; Dalhart 16/5/43; Tinker 4/8/43; 202 BU Galveston 20/7/44; 223 BU Dyersburg 23/2/45; 330 BU Dyersburg 1/3/45; 4202 BU Syracuse 25/3/45; Recl Comp 3/1/45.

42-5308 Del Denver 11/11/42; Ft Sumner 21/4/43; Roswell 21/5/43; Hobbs 12/7/43; 3014 BU Douglas 18/8/44; 3017 BU Hobbs 22/8/44; RFC Altus 30/8/45.

42-5309 Del Denver 11/11/42; Pyote 5/3/43; Pueblo 6/4/43; Gowen 15/5/43; Dalhart 27/6/43; 4136 BU Tinker 16/7/44; 235 BU Biggs 23/8/44; 4100 BU Patterson 25/1/45; 224 Sioux City 5/4/45; Recl Comp 22/5/45.

42-5310 Del Denver 11/11/42; Casper 5/1/43; Tinker 17/5/43; Pyote 5/6/43; 245 BU McCook 7/8/44; 225 BU Rapid City 5/10/44; 354 BU Rapid City 20/7/45; RFC Walnut Ridge 18/12/45.

42-5311 Del Denver 11/11/42; Pueblo 14/1/43; Biggs 24/2/43; Kirtland 20/3/43; Dyersburg 10/4/43; Pyote 8/5/43; Dyersburg 22/5/43; 4100 BU Patterson 8/6/44; 224 BU Sioux City 9/9/44; 224 BU Pueblo 27/5/45; 224 BU Sioux City 28/8/45; RFC Kingman 26/10/45.

42-5312 Del Denver 11/11/42; Blythe 26/1/43; Spokane 22/5/43; Moses Lake 10/6/43; Walla Walla 17/8/43; 326 BU McDill 4/7/44; 4204 BU Atlanta 21/6/45; RFC Altus 5/11/45.

42-5313 Del Cheyenne 26/11/42; Sioux City 6/12/42;

Rapid City 3/2/43; Ephrata 3/3/43; WO 30/3/43.
42-5314 Del Cheyenne 26/11/42; Casper 8/1/43; Tinker 20/5/43; Pyote 3/6/43; 556 BU Long Beach 23/6/44; 370 BU Lowry 26/6/44; 3701 BU Amarillo 23/7/44; RFC Walnut Ridge 9/10/45.
42-5315 Del Tulsa 12/11/42; Tinker 9/4/43; Spokane 8/5/43; Ephrata 7/8/43; 242 BU Gr Isle 23/6/44; 234 BU Clovis 10/10/44; 64 BU Andrews 16/10/45; 242 BU Gd Isle 23/10/45; RFC Kingman 8/10/46.
42-5316 Del Cheyenne 12/11/42; Geiger 1/12/42; Pueblo 22/1/43; Ainsworth 26/2/43; Cutbank 14/4/43; Gore 27/5/43; Ephrata 5/6/43; WO 16/6/43.
42-5317 Del Tulsa 12/11/42; Boise 2/12/42; Tinker 29/3/43; Walla Walla 12/4/43; WO 25/4/43.
42-5318 Del Tulsa 12/11/42; Wendover 27/12/42; Sioux City 1/3/43; Tinker 3/5/43; Casper 21/5/43; WO 31/5/43.
42-5319 Del Tulsa 12/11/42; Rapid City 16/12/42; Wendover 5/3/43; Pyote 5/6/43; Walla Walla 15/8/43; 4122 BU Hensley 15/6/44; 3701 BU Amarillo 19/6/44; 2114 BU Lockburn 16/3/45; RFC Walnut Ridge 14/12/45.
42-5320 Del Cheyenne 11/11/42; Casper 3/12/42; c/t/o Casper 8/5/43 w/Brown, burned out 6 killed. WO 19/5/43.
42-5321 Del Cheyenne 11/11/42; Casper 13/12/42; Amarillo 29/3/43; Scotts Bluff 8/4/43; Rapid City 15/8/43; 4136 BU Tinker 14/6/44; 224 BU Sioux City 14/8/44; 570 BU Bendix Fd 6/10/44; 235 BU Biggs 12/5/45; RFC Kingman 30/10/45.
42-5322 Del Cheyenne 11/11/42; Blythe 3/1/43; Pueblo 6/4/44; Lewiston 8/6/43; Gt Falls 5/8/43; 225 BU Rapid City 4/7/44; 4136 BU Tinker 5/7/44; RFC Ontario 9/6/45.
42-5323 Del Cheyenne 11/11/42; Ogden 10/1/43; Dalhart 25/2/43; Tinker 23/5/43; 222 BU Ardmore 18/6/44; 4200 BU Chicago Mun 22/7/44; 3508 BU Truax 18/9/44; 222 BU Ardmore 19/9/44; 552 BU New Castle 27/12/44; 4112 BU Olmstead 4/1/45; Recl Comp 9/2/45.
42-5324 Del Cheyenne 11/11/42; Blythe 11/12/42; Walla Walla 19/5/43; Felts Fd 11/7/43; Walla Walla 15/8/43; 325 BU Avon Park 29/7/44; 570 BU Bendix Fd 27/9/44; 353 BU Esler 9/2/45; 325 BU Avon Park 14/2/45; 331 BU Barksdale 2/3/45; RFC Albuquerque 25/6/45.
42-5325 Del Cheyenne 8/11/42; Wendover 29/12/42; Sioux City 6/4/43; Tinker 13/6/43; Scotts Bluff 11/8/43; 238 BU Dyersburg 25/1/44; Recl Comp 9/2/45.
42-5326 Del Cheyenne 8/11/42; Pyote 4/1/43; Pocatello 31/1/43; Biggs 14/2/43; WO 23/2/43.
42-5327 Del Cheyenne 8/11/42; Casper 12/1/43; Pueblo 13/3/43; Kearney 30/4/43; Madras 20/5/43; Scott Fd 17/8/43; 223 BU Dyersburg 22/8/44; 4209 BU Des Moines 18/12/44; 223 BU Dyersburg 23/12/44; 327 BU Drew 14/5/45; RFC Altus 26/7/45.
42-5328 Del Cheyenne 8/11/42; Tinker 1/5/43; Biggs 13/7/43; 460 BU Hamilton 29/6/44; 235 BU Biggs 30/6/44; 235 BU Hobbs 19/9/44; 235 BU Biggs 27/9/44; 233 BU Davis Monthan 5/10/44; RFC Walnut Ridge 14/12/45.
42-5329 Del Cheyenne 9/11/42; Pyote 9/1/43; Dalhart 6/5/43; Tinker 1/8/43; 4100 BU Patterson 9/6/44; 224 BU Sioux City 11/7/44; RFC Kingman 28/10/45.
42-5330 Del Cheyenne 8/11/42; Wendover 10/12/42; Biggs 20/3/43; Dyersburg 16/4/43; Memphis 21/5/43; Brookley 10/8/43; 4134 BU Spokane 13/6/44; 242 BU Gd Isle 16/6/44; 6BG Gr Isle 8/7/44; 224 BU Sioux City 5/1/45; 813 GAS Sedalia 21/3/45; Recl Comp 10/3/46.
42-5331 Del Cheyenne 10/11/42; Sioux City 4/12/42; Casper 2/1/43; Lincoln 5/2/43; Tinker 25/5/43; Dyersburg 1/7/43; 201 BU Peterson 9/7/44; 233 BU Davis Monthan 24/8/44; 200 BU Peterson 25/8/45; RFC Kingman 27/10/45.
42-5332 Del Cheyenne 11/10/42; Ainsworth 16/12/42; Rapid City 17/4/43; Geiger 22/6/43; Pendleton 25/7/43; Geiger 10/8/43; 230 BU Lambert 11/6/44; 201 BU Peterson 13/6/44; 4100 BU Patterson 16/6/44; 222 BU Ardmore 23/7/44; RFC Ontario 14/6/45.
42-5333 Del Tulsa 12/11/42; Casper 8/1/43; Scotts Bluff 28/3/43; Tinker 8/5/43; Ephrata 24/5/43; 246 BU Pratt 11/6/44; 497BG Pratt 23/6/44; 232 BU Dalhart 11/7/44; 223 BU Dyersburg 28/11/44; Recl Comp 24/2/45.
42-5334 Del Cheyenne 10/11/42; Rapid City 21/12/42; cr Ordway, Colo, 24/1/43, pilot and crew killed, a/c totally dest. WO 15/2/43.
42-5335 Del Tulsa 12/11/42; Casper 1/1/43; Tinker 26/5/43; Ephrata 10/6/43; Dalhart 1/7/43; 3705 BU Sioux Falls 20/6/44; 497BG Pratt 2/7/44; 29BG Dalhart 2/8/44; 246 BU Pratt 15/9/44; 273 BU Lincoln 7/12/44; 245 BU McCook 9/2/45; RFC Albuquerque 25/6/45.
42-5336 Del Cheyenne 11/11/42; Pierre 14/12/42; Rapid City 15/1/43; Tinker 9/4/43; Ephrata 22/7/43; 4136 BU Tinker 26/6/44; 505BG Harvard 21/6/44; 244 BU Harvard 22/9/44; 233 BU Davis Monthan 26/9/44; 241 BU Fairmont 7/1/45; RFC Kingman 2/11/45.
42-5337 Del Tulsa 12/11/42; West Palm Beach 12/12/42; ass 401BS/91BG [LL-J] Bassingbourn 8/1/43; MIA {10m} Bremen 17/4/43 w/Lindsey, e/a, ditched Nth Sea, 8KIA 2POW, MACR 16090. SHORT SNORTER III.
42-5338 Del Tulsa 10/11/42; West Palm Beach 11/12/42; ass 340BS/97BG Biskra 31/12/42; Château-du-Rhumel 8/2/43; Pont-du-Fahs 1/8/43; Depienne 15/8/43; tran 346BS/99BG Oudna 14/11/43; Tortorella 11/12/43; {22m/99} 483BG Tortorella 31/3/44; Sterparone 22/4/44; retUS Morrison 5/5/45; RFC Ontario 29/6/45. YE OLD BATTLE AXE.
42-5339 Del Denver 16/11/42; Sioux City 4/12/42; Casper 4/1/43; WO 16/2/43.
42-5340 Del Denver 16/11/42; West Palm Beach 11/12/42; ass 97BG Biskra 21/1/43; Château-du-Rhumel 8/2/43; Pont-du-Fahs 1/8/43; Depienne 15/8/43; tran 347BS/99BG Oudna 14/11/43; Tortorella 11/12/43; MIA Sofia 24/1/44 w/McDonnell, cr Trstenik, crew evades RTD, 6WIA. MACR 1991.
42-5341 Del Denver 16/12/42; West Palm Beach 9/1/43; ass 427BS/303BG [GH-Q] Molesworth 7/2/43; tran 1 BAD Burtonwood 7/4/44; retUS Tinker 6/1/45. RFC Altus 9/10/45. (SCARLOT HARLOT) VICIOUS VIRGIN.
42-5342 Del Denver 16/11/42; Pueblo 13/1/43; Tinker 24/3/43; Dalhart 2/4/43; cr 7/5/43 4m w of Dalhart, w/Leroy, 1 KAS..
42-5343 Del Cheyenne 16/11/42; Sioux City 10/1/43; Rapid City 3/2/43; Pierre 3/4/43; Geiger 22/6/43; 505BG Harvard 4/6/44; 558 BU Nashville 14/9/44; 244 BU Harvard 19/9/44; 3009 BU Carlsbad 21/11/44; 3010 BU Williams 8/2/45; 3020 BU La Junta 10/6/45; RFC Searcey Fd 31/7/45.
42-5344 Del Cheyenne 16/11/42; West Palm Beach 12/12/42; ass 419BS/301BG Biskra 20/12/42; Ain M'Lila 17/1/43; St Donat 6/3/43; Oudna 6/8/43; {76m} tran 429BS/2BG Massicault 14/11/43; Bizerte 2/12/43; Amendola 9/12/43; {20m} 346BS/99BG Tortorella 28/3/44; {0m} retUS Tinker 22/7/44; RFC Arledge Fd 22/11/44. BELCHING BUZZARD.
42-5345 Del Cheyenne 16/11/42; Wendover 3/12/42; Sioux City 3/1/43; Rapid City 4/2/43; Spokane 24/3/43; Ephrata 27/4/43; WO 10/11/43.
42-5346 Del Cheyenne 17/11/42; West Palm Beach 12/12/42; ass 414BS/97BG Biskra 31/12/42; Château-du-Rhumel 8/2/43; Pont-du-Fahs 11/8/43; Depienne 15/8/43; tran 347BS/99BG Oudna 14/11/43; Tortorella 11/12/43; 483BG Tortorella 31/3/44; Sterparone 22/4/44; retUS Tinker 8/7/44; Jackson 18/12/44; Patterson 12/1/45; RFC Altus 11/9/45. THE RELUCTANT DRAGON.
42-5347 Del Cheyenne 16/11/42; Pueblo 9/2/43; Dalhart 18/3/43; Gowen 19/4/43; Tinker 9/6/43; Dyersburg 16/7/43; WO 25/8/43.
42-5348 Del Cheyenne 20/11/42; Casper 1/1/43; Tinker 21/5/43; Moses Lake 12/6/43; 4117 BU Robins 21/6/44; 326 BU McDill 17/8/44; 331 BU Barksdale 20/1/45; RFC Albuquerque 25/6/45.
42-5349 Del Cheyenne 18/11/42; Sioux City 31/1/43; Rapid City 13/2/43; Walla Walla 3/3/43; Topeka 3/8/43; 4117 BU Robins 24/7/44; 238 BU Gulfport 22/9/44 for survey.
42-5350 Del Cheyenne 18/11/42; West Palm Beach 9/1/43; ass 32BS/301BG Biskra 21/1/43; Ain M'Lila 17/1/43; St Donat 6/3/43; Oudna 6/8/43; {67m} tran 429BS/2BG Massicault 14/11/43; Bizerte 2/12/43; Amendola 9/12/43; {1m} 347BS/99BG Tortorella 28/3/44; {2m} 816BS/483BG Tortorella 31/3/44; Sterparone 22/4/44; retUS Homestead 8/7/44; RFC Albuquerque 3/8/45. SKINHEAD.
42-5351 Del Cheyenne 18/11/42; Walla Walla 4/2/43; Redmond 21/2/43; Madras 19/6/43; Walla Walla 17/7/43; 370 BU Lowry 15/6/44; WO 3/11/44.
42-5352 Del Cheyenne 18/11/42; Sioux City 3/1/43; Rapid City 3/2/43; Tinker 1/5/43; Smoky Hill 6/8/43; 4006 BU Miami 14/6/44; 3501 BU Boca Raton 16/6/44; 120 BU Richmond 20/12/44; 3501 BU Boca Raton 4/2/45; 2114 BU Lockburn 2/5/45; RFC Walnut Ridge 14/12/45.
42-5353 Del Cheyenne 17/11/42; Colorado Springs 5/1/43; Lowry 6/4/43; Hill 16/5/43; Peterson 1/6/43; ass Mapping Group Bradley 1/9/43; 91PS/1PG (as F-9) Buckley 5/7/44; 3705 BU Lowry 14/5/45; trans US Navy 31/3/47.
42-5354 Del Cheyenne 18/11/42; 36BS/28BG Ladd Fd 15/1/43; retUS Gore Fd 6/6/43; Hendricks 18/9/43; Recl Comp 3/1/46.
42-5355 Del Denver 20/11/42; Casper 1/1/43; Pyote 24/5/43; 4200 BU Chicago Mun 13/6/44; 234 BU Clovis 14/6/44; 4100 BU Patterson 16/6/44; 2218 BU Alexandra 6/9/44; 329 BU Alexandra for survey 7/5/45.
42-5356 Del Denver 20/11/42; Walla Walla 1/3/43; Madras 19/6/43; Rapid City 29/7/43; Walla Walla 15/8/43; 331 BU Barksdale 9/11/44; RFC Albuquerque 25/6/45.
42-5357 Del Denver 20/11/42; West Palm Beach 11/12/42; ass 303BG Molesworth 1/1/43; trans AFSC 19/3/43; WO 27/8/44.
42-5358 Del Denver 20/11/42; Walla Walla 31/1/43; Seattle 5/3/43; Hill 28/5/43; Rapid City 2/6/43; Walla Walla 10/7/43; 357 BU Kellogg 18/9/44; 326 BU McDill 24/9/44; 4112 BU Olmstead 17/7/45; RFC Altus 9/10/45.
42-5359 Del Denver 20/11/42; Patterson 13/1/43; Geiger 2/3/43; Amarillo 27/4/43; Dyersburg 17/7/43; 248 BU Walker 17/6/44; 222 BU Ardmore 20/8/44; 332 BU Ardmore 30/1/45. Recl Comp 3/1/46.
42-5360 Del Tulsa 20/11/42; New Castle 13/12/42; ass 358BS/303BG Molesworth 8/1/43; MIA Oschersleben 11/1/44 w/Schwaebe, e/a, cr Goslar, Ger, 1KIA 9POW. MACR 1926. (WAR BRIDE) OLD

FAITHFUL.

42-5361 Del Tulsa 24/11/42; Glasgow 18/12/42; Walla Walla 4/2/43; Redmond 18/6/43; Spokane 31/7/43; 29BG Pratt 1/6/44; 460 BU Hamilton 5/6/44; 29BG Dalhart 2/9/44; 246 BU Pratt 18/9/44; 232 BU Dalhart 26/10/44; 273 BU Lincoln 21/11/44; 248 BU Walker 19/2/45; Recl Comp 16/3/45.

42-5362 Del Tulsa 24/11/42; Homestead 18/12/42; ass 401BS/91BG [LL-F] Bassingbourn 1/1/43; MIA {6+m} Wilhelmshaven 26/2/43 w/Smith, e/a, cr Nth Sea, 10KIA, MACR 15712. SHORT SNORTER II.

42-5363 Del Tulsa 24/11/42; Biggs 3/1/43; Blythe 18/3/43; Moses Lake 2/5/43; 231 BU Alamogordo 30/6/44; 202 BU Galveston 15/7/44; 120 BU Richmond 9/10/44; 222 BU Ardmore 23/2/45; 274 BU Herington 15/6/45; 4208 BU Mines 17/9/45; 486 BU Herington 9/10/45; RFC Kingman 14/11/45.

42-5364 Del Tulsa 24/11/42; Biggs 3/1/43; Pueblo 8/4/43; Gore 18/5/43; Felts 13/8/43; 4117 BU Robins 27/7/44; 328 BU Gulfport 16/12/44; Recl Comp 13/3/46.

42-5365 Del Tulsa 24/11/42; Biggs 3/1/43; Pueblo 31/3/43; Ephrata 28/4/43; Rapid City 29/7/43; Orlando 8/8/43; Westover 17/12/43; Wendover 9/1/44; 3701 BU Amarillo 17/11/44; RFC Stillwater 24/9/45.

42-5366 Del Tulsa 24/11/42; Wendover 14/12/42; Scotts Bluff 23/3/43; Casper 30/4/43; Tinker 28/6/43; Dalhart 35/7/43; WO 25/9/43; RFC Kingman 27/10/45.

42-5367 Del Tulsa 24/11/42; Gt Falls 26/12/42; 2BG Gore Fd 3/2/43; 88BG Walla Walla 6/2/43; WO 11/2/43.

42-5368 Del Tulsa 24/11/42; Wendover 7/12/42; Sioux City 3/1/43; Rapid City 2/2/43; Walla Walla 3/2/43; Redmond 18/6/43; Walla Walla 17/7/43; 3501 BU Boca Raton 26/11/44; 2114 BU Lockburn 13/6/45; RFC Walnut Ridge 14/12/45.

42-5369 Del Tulsa 24/11/42; Biggs 3/1/43; Dalhart 13/3/43; Luke 16/5/43; Dyersburg 24/6/43; Galveston 24/7/43; WO 21/1/44.

42-5370 Del Tulsa 24/11/42; Salina 2/1/43; Morrison 3/2/43; ass 324BS/91BG [DF-K] Bassingbourn 26/2/43; MIA Hamm 4/3/43 w/Henderson, e/a, cr Münster, 9KIA 1POW, MACR 16102.

42-5371 Del Tulsa 25/11/42; Wendover 27/12/42; Scribner 28/3/43; Dyersburg 13/4/43; 4100 BU Patterson 10/6/44; 268 BU Peterson 11/10/44; 274 BU Herington 18/10/44; 575 BU Pittsburg 11/12/44; 4135 BU Hill 22/12/44; 274 BU Herington 4/1/45; RFC Kingman 14/11/45.

42-5372 Del Tulsa 26/11/42; Blythe 28/12/42; Moses Lake 2/5/43; Geiger 2/8/43; 593BS/396BG Moses Lake 23/8/43; WO 1/5/44.

42-5373 Del Tulsa 25/11/42; Pocatello 17/12/42; Pyote 8/1/43; Tinker 31/1/43; Pyote 2/2/43; Tinker 1/8/43; 241 BU Fairmont 14/9/44; 249 BU Alliance 17/10/44; 243 BU Gt Bend 29/12/44; 902 BU Orlando 6/5/45; 243 BU Gt Bend 10/5/45; RFC Kingman 30/10/45.

42-5374 Del Tulsa 26/11/42; Blythe 5/1/43; Ephrata 24/5/43; 222 BU Ardmore 22/1/44; 3017 BU Hobbs 4/5/44; 222 BU Ardmore 17/5/44; RFC Ontario 14/6/45.

42-5375 Del Tulsa 25/11/42; Casper 14/1/43; Pyote 8/3/43; Sioux City 21/6/43; Casper 12/7/43; Kearney 3/8/43; 248 BU Patterson 2/9/44; 224 BU Sioux City 23/10/44; RFC Searcey Fd 13/8/45.

42-5376 Del Tulsa 25/11/42; Salina 4/1/43; Morrison 6/2/43; ass 422BS/305BG [JJ-X] Chelveston 1/3/43; coll w/Beaufighter (V8715) 31/8/43, cr Foulsham, Nfk. EAGER EAGLE.

42-5377 Del Tulsa 26/11/42; West Palmm Beach 9/1/43; ass 341BS/97BG Biskra 21/1/43; Château-du-Rhumel 8/2/43; MIA Grosseto A/fd 26/4/43, w/Charlton. AXIS AXES.

42-5378 Del Tulsa 26/11/42; New Castle 11/12/42; ass 367BS/306BG Thurleigh 1/1/43; MIA 6/3/43 w/Tunnell, e/a, 1EVD, 3KIA, 6POW.

42-5379 Del Tulsa 26/11/42; Salina 10/1/43; Morrison 4/2/43; ass 401BS/91BG [LL-D] Bassingbourn 15/3/43; {21+m inc some w/381BG}; tran 527BS/379BG [FO-W] Kimbolton 23/12/43; AFSC 8/4/44; retUS Tinker 14/9/44; 4136 BU Tinker 6/1/45; 4100 BU Patterson 11/2/45; 4000 BU Wright 3/8/45 convert to TB-17F (weather). YANKEE EAGLE.

42-5380 Del Tulsa 27/11/42; Hobbs 23/12/42; Lowry 25/7/43; Hobbs 3/8/43; 3017 BU Hobbs 8/11/44; 4124 BU Altus 13/7/45; RFC Altus 20/8/45.

42-5381 Del Denver 26/11/42; Wendover 12/12/42; Long Beach 9/3/43; WO 25/4/43.

42-5382 Del Denver 26/11/42; Berry 31/12/42; Morrison 6/2/43; ass 360BS/303BG Molesworth 25/2/43; MIA 25/6/43 w/Mack, s/d by e/a. THE WITCH'S TIT.

42-5383 Del Denver 28/11/42; Lewiston 18/12/42; Walla Walla 22/2/43; Redmond 28/7/43; Walla Walla 15/8/43; WO 4/4/44.

42-5384 Del Denver 28/11/42; Pocatello 20/12/42; Pyote 8/1/43; Tinker 14/2/43; 30BS/19BG Pyote 22/8/43; WO 8/9/43.

42-5385 Del Denver 28/11/42; Wendover 13/12/42; Biggs 20/3/43; Sioux City 11/6/43; Dalhart 23/7/43; 232 BU Dalhart 9/6/44; 242 BU Gr Isle 30/8/44; 223 BU Dyersburg 20/11/44; 330 BU Dyersburg 23/5/45; 327 BU Drew 1/6/45; RFC Altus 20/8/45.

42-5386 Del Cheyenne 26/11/42; Redmond 23/12/42; Sioux City 31/1/43; Gowen 10/3/43; Tinker 22/5/43; Dyersburg 12/6/43; WO 5/9/43.

42-5387 Del Cheyenne 27/11/42; Redmond 21/2/43; Dyersburg 13/6/43; Walla Walla 15/8/43; 3701 BU Amarillo 17/11/44; 2137 BU Hendricks 13/3/45; 2510 BU Enid 20/9/45; RFC Walnut Ridge 5/12/45.

42-5388 Del Cheyenne 28/11/42; Salina 4/1/43; Morrison 2/2/43; ass 348BS/99BG Navarin 11/5/43; Oudna 4/8/43; Tortorella 11/12/43; {90m} tran 817BS/483BG Tortorella 31/3/44; Sterparone 22/4/43; {14m} sal 30/11/45. {total-104m}. NEVER SATISFIED.

42-5389 Del Cheyenne 30/11/42; Wendover 14/12/42; WO 9/2/43.

42-5390 Del Cheyenne 30/11/42; Salina 20/1/43; ass 360BS/303BG [PU-L] Molesworth 26/3/43; MIA Wangerooge Is 25/6/43 w/Palmer, cr Bourgsweer, Hol. THE AVENGER.

42-5391 Del Tulsa 28/11/42; Homestead 14/2/43; ass 401BS/91BG [LL-D] Bassingbourn 25/3/43; MIA {1m} Bremen 17/4/43 w/Walker, e/a, cr Hilgenriederseil, 2KIA 8POW, MACR 15222/15522. RAIN OF TERROR.

42-5392 Del Tulsa 29/11/42; Salina 25/1/43; ass 427BS/303BG [GN-X] Molesworth 26/3/43; MIA Gilze-Rijen 19/8/43 w/Quillen, ditched Nth Sea, 6KIA 4POW, MACR 285. STRIC NINE.

42-5393 Del Tulsa 6/12/42; Morrison 6/2/43; ass 360BS/303BG [PU-G] Molesworth 25/2/43; tran 100BG ex-2SAD 4/3/44; retUS Tinker 18/6/44; RFC Altus 4/10/45. THUMPER AGAIN.

42-5394 Del Tulsa 29/11/42; Morrison 12/2/43; ass 367BS/306BG Thurleigh 2/3/43; MIA Bremen 17/4/43 w/Fortin, e/a, cr Benthullen, Ger, 4KIA 6POW, MACR 15516.

42-5395 Del Tulsa 30/11/42; New Castle 17/12/42; ass 353BS/301BG Biskra 3/1/43; Ain M'Lila 17/1/43; St Donat 6/3/43; MIA {43m} San Giovanni 16/7/43, w/Pearson, flak, MACR 209.

42-5396 Del Tulsa 4/12/42; Ainsworth 21/1/43; Tinker 25/2/43; Rapid City 24/4/43; Lowry 8/5/43; Pendleton 25/7/43; 505BG Harvard 2/6/44; 244 BU Harvard 27/7/44; 4100 BU Patterson 21/11/44; 610 BU Eglin 16/2/45; RFC Walnut Ridge 5/1/46.

42-5397 Del Cheyenne 2/12/42; New Castle 15/12/42; ass 352BS/301BG Biskra 9/1/43; Ain M'Lila 17/1/43; St Donat 6/3/43; Oudna 6/8/43; {61m} tran 2BG Massicault 14/11/43; MIA {1m} Athens 18/11/43 w/Flournoy. MACR 1200.

42-5398 Del Tulsa 4/12/42; Boise 15/1/43; Wendover 27/2/43; Gowen 19/4/43; Tinker 9/6/43; Dalhart 9/7/43; WO 23/10/43.

42-5399 Del Cheyenne 2/12/42; Ephrata 31/1/43; Spokane 15/6/43; Ephrata 9/7/43; 4136 BU Tinker 6/7/44; 4100 BU Patterson 15/2/45; 2114 BU Lockburn 3/5/45; 484 BU Topeka 14/8/45; 2114 BU Lockburn 22/8/45; RFC Walnut Ridge 14/12/45.

42-5400 Del Cheyenne 2/12/42; Boise 4/1/43; Gowen 18/3/43; Tinker 28/5/43; Dyersburg 26/6/43; Gulfport 11/7/43; Tinker 4/8/43; 498BG Gt Bend 4/8/44; 243 BU Gt Bend 20/9/44; 4100 BU Patterson 10/1/45; 225 BU Rapid City 11/4/45; 268 BU Peterson 6/7/45; 224 BU Sioux City 24/7/45; RFC Kingman 28/10/45.

42-5401 Del Cheyenne 2/12/42; Pyote 19/1/43; 93BS/19BG Pyote 21/8/43; 28BS/19BG Pyote 9/11/43; WO 27/3/44.

42-5402 Del Cheyenne 2/12/42; Homestead 27/12/42; ass 340BS/97BG Biskra 15/1/43; Château-du-Rhumel 8/2/43; Pont-du-Fahs 1/8/43; Depienne 15/8/43; c/l El Aouina beach, 4/10/43, w/Chaplick, sal. Crew safe.

42-5403 Del Cheyenne 2/12/42; New Castle 17/12/42; ass 352BS/301BG Biskra 14/1/43; Ain M'Lila 17/1/43; St Donat 6/3/43; Oudna 6/8/43; {72m} tran 20BS/2BG Massicault 10/11/43; Bizerte 2/12/43; Amendola 9/12/43; 347BS/99BG Tortorella 28/3/44; {2m} 816BS/483BG Tortorella 31/3/44; sal 30/3/45.

42-5404 Del Cheyenne 2/12/42; West Palm Beach 18/12/42; ass 369BS/306BG [WW-D] Thurleigh 1/2/43; tran 545BS/384BG [JD-M] Grafton Underwood 22/8/43; MIA 30/1/44 w/Writz, e/a, cr Himbergen, Ger, 7KIA 3POW, MACR 2264. GEEZIL.

42-5405 Del Denver 3/12/42; Geiger 1/1/43; rapid City 24/4/43; Geiger 11/5/43; Victorville 30/5/43; Peterson 13/6/43; HQ Sqd 2AF Peterson 29/11/43; 234 BU Clovis 24/6/44; 4100 BU Patterson 31/1/45; 611 BU Eglin 30/4/45; RFC Walnut Ridge 4/1/46.

42-5406 Del Denver 3/12/42; Morrison 17/3/43; ass 323BS/91BG Bassingbourn 19/4/43; MIA Meaulte 13/5/43 w/Biggs, 7KIA 3POW, MACR?.

42-5407 Del Denver 3/12/42; Morrison 5/2/43; ass 367BS/306BG [GY-L] Thurleigh 8/2/43; tran 323BS/91BG Bassingbourn 11/9/43; 526BS/379BG Kimbolton 27/9/43; MIA Anklam 9/10/43 w/Smith, e/a, cr Kiel, 1KIA 9POW, MACR 1354. FIGHTING PAPPY.

42-5408 Del Denver 3/12/42; Rapid City 31/1/43; Geiger 8/6/43; Gore 10/7/43; Walla Walla 8/8/43; 243 BU Gt Bend 19/9/44; 1 Continental AF Bolling 21/7/44; 243 BU Gt Bend 26/8/44; 237 BU Kirtland 22/10/44; RFC Kingman 31/10/45.

42-5409 Del Cheyenne 2/12/42; West Palm Beach 12/1/43; ass 419BS/301BG Ain M'Lila 3/3/43; St Donat 6/3/43; Oudna 6/8/43; {55m} tran 429BS/2BG Massicault 14/11/43; Bizerte 2/12/43; Amendola 9/12/43; MIA {8m} Innsbruck 19/12/43, w/Peterson, 6 chutes seen, MACR 1519. LYDIA PINKHAM.

42-5410 Del Cheyenne 2/12/42; Gt Falls 31/1/43; Ainsworth 21/2/43; Geiger 28/3/13; Gore 24/4/43;

INDIVIDUAL B-17 HISTORIES 107

Moses Lake 29/6/43; Tinker 29/11/43; 594BS/396BG Drew 3/12/43; 327 BU Drew 4/5/44; RFC Altus 6/9/45.

42-5411 Del Cheyenne 2/12/42; Homestead 25/12/42; ass 96BS/2BG Navarin 23/3/43; Château-du-Rhumel 27/4/43; Ain M'Lila 17/6/43; Massicault 31/7/43; Bizerte 2/12/43; Amendola 9/12/43; MIA {34m} Sofia 24/1/44, w/Lins. MACR 1988. SHADY LADY.

42-5412 Del Tulsa 5/12/42; Blythe 11/5/43; Pueblo 8/6/43; Alamogordo 10/7/43; Smoky Hill 3/8/43; 497BG Pratt 26/6/44; 246 BU Pratt 13/7/44; 3705 BU Lowry 16/10/44; WO 19/10/44; 3704 BU Keesler 29/1/45; Recl Comp 3/4/46.

42-5413 Del Tulsa 10/12/42; Morrison 31/1/43; ass 416BS/99BG Navarin 3/3/43; Oudna 4/8/43; MIA Foggia 25/8/43 w/Norris, 10POW, 2 escape & RTD. MACR 478. RAMBLIN RAIDER.

42-5414 Del Tulsa 5/12/42; Biggs 24/2/43; Dyersburg 18/3/43; Gulfport 23/6/43; Dyersburg 27/6/43; 245 BU McCook 1/6/44; 9BG McCook 16/8/44; 225 BU Rapid City 5/10/44; RFC Ontario 11/6/45.

42-5415 Del Tulsa 5/12/42; Blythe 31/1/43; Minden 6/2/43; Pueblo 12/3/43; Pyote 27/3/43; Tinker 8/10/43; 28BS/19BG Pyote 31/10/43; 248 BU Walker 4/6/44; 4100 BU Patterson 22/6/44; 248 BU Walker 30/7/44; 563 BU Homestead 13/2/45; 4160 BU Walker 1/10/45; RFC Altus 15/11/45.

42-5416 Del Tulsa 3/12/42; Ft Sumner 21/4/43; Hobbs 6/5/43; Roswell 23/5/43; 3018 BU Kingman 18/6/44; 3017 BU Hobbs 18/9/44; 4124 BU Altus 5/7/45; 3017 BU Hobbs 7/7/45; RFC Altus 29/8/45.

42-5417 Del Tulsa 4/12/42; Casper 13/1/43; Tinker 12/6/43; Dyersburg 12/7/43; Dalhart 13/8/43; Tinker 8/11/43; 411 BU Robins 29/7/44; 325 BU Avon Park 9/4/45; RFC Kingman 29/6/45.

42-5418 Del Tulsa 3/12/42; West Palm Beach 9/1/43; ass 97BG Biskra 20/1/43; Château-du-Rhumel 8/2/43; Pont-du-Fahs 1/8/43; Depienne 15/8/43; tran 346BG/99BG Oudna 14/11/43; {27m/99} 815BS/483BG Tortorella 31/3/44; MIA Milan 30/4/44 w/Landholt, flak & e/a. cr Vanette, 8POW 2 EVD to Switz., MACR 4612. CHIEF WAHOO.

42-5419 Del Tulsa 5/12/42; Morrison 2/2/43; ass 347BS/99BG Navarin 1/3/43; c/l base 3/5/43, WO. WHIZZER.

42-5420 Del Tulsa 3/12/42; ass 368BS/306BG LITTLE SAVAGE (not to UK); Blythe 27/1/43; Dalhart 23/5/43; Amarillo 29/6/43; Tinker 31/7/43; 232 BU Walker 6/6/44; 901 BU Pinecastle 10/6/44; 223 BU Dyersburg 14/6/44; 325 BU Avon Park 14/5/45; 326 BU McDill 15/5/45; 4124 BU Altus 5/6/45; RFC Searcey Fd 26/7/45.

42-5421 Del Cheyenne 6/12/42; Blythe 26/1/43; Geiger 5/3/43; Gt Falls 7/6/43; Lewiston 29/6/43; Rapid City 12/8/43; Tinker 18/11/43; 499BG Smoky Hill 23/8/44; 247 BU Smoky Hill 26/9/44; RFC Albuquerque 25/6/45.

42-5422 Del Denver 3/12/42; Salina 5/1/43; Morrison 6/2/43; ass 423BS/306BG Thurleigh 10/4/43; MIA 1/5/43 w/Popp, ditched Channel, 6KIA 4POW, MACR 15619.

42-5423 Del Tulsa 5/12/42; Pueblo 29/12/42; cr base 12/2/43 w/Esler & 1 pass killed, 6 injured (two major); A/c rolled into ravine at end of runway.

42-5424 Del Tulsa 6/12/42; Morrow 9/1/43; Blythe 15/1/43; Biggs 19/5/43; Alamogordo 7/6/43; Dalhart 22/7/43; Tinker 17/8/43; 499BG Smoky Hill 26/6/44; 232 BU Dalhart 10/7/44; 3701 BU Amarillo 14/10/44; WO 20/10/44; Recl Comp 9/4/46.

42-5425 Del Tulsa 6/12/42; Biggs 20/1/43; Dalhart 18/3/43; Tinker 21/5/43; Smoky Hill 16/8/43; 243 BU Gt Bend 3/6/44; 4100 BU Patterson 16/6/44; 221 BU Alexandra 24/7/44; 225 BU Rapid City 8/1/45; 4142 BU Patterson 1/11/45; RFC Kingman 18/1/46.

42-5426 Del Tulsa 6/12/42; Salina 7/1/43; ass 369BS/306BG [WW-X] Thurleigh 25/3/43; MIA Kiel 28/7/43 w/Winter, e/a, cr Kiel, 6KIA 4POW. MACR 123. FIGHTIN' BITIN'.

42-5427 Del Cheyenne 6/12/42; West Palm Beach 28/12/42; ass 20BS/2BG 14/1/43; MIA {62m} Innsbruck 19/12/43 w/Williams, e/a, 9 chutes seen. MACR 1530.

42-5428 Del Cheyenne 6/12/42; Wilmington 31/1/43; Salina 3/3/43; ass 368BS/306BG [BO-Z] 24/3/43; tran 322BS/91BG [LG-T] Bassingbourn 23/12/43; AFSC 8/4/44; retUS Tinker 21/6/44; RFC Bush Fd 2/7/45. BLACK MAGIC.

42-5429 Del Cheyenne 6/12/42; New Castle 17/12/42; ass 429BS/2BG Gt Falls 12/1/43; Navarin 4/3/43; Château-du-Rhumel 27/4/43; Ain M'Lila 17/6/43; Massicault 31/7/43; {2m} sal 8/11/43.

42-5430 Del Cheyenne 8/12/42; 54 Fry Gp Salina 4/1/43; Morrison 5/2/43; ass 359BS/303BG [BN-V] Molesworth 25/2/43; MIA Wilhelmshaven 11/6/43 w/Haines, coll w/FW190, cr Aschausen, 4KIA 6POW, MACR 15228. PAPPY.

42-5431 Del Cheyenne 8/12/42; Morrison 6/2/43; ass 368BS/306BG Thurleigh 8/2/43; MIA Antwerp 5/4/43 w/Fischer, e/a, cr Ghent, Bel, 10POW. LIL ABNER.

42-5432 Del Cheyenne 8/12/42; Morrison 6/2/43; ass 358BS/303BG [VK-B] Molesworth 25/2/43; MIA Huls 22/6/43 w/Jess, flak, cr Berg Bossendorf, 6KIA 4POW. MACR 3077. THE HUNTING CLUB.

42-5433 Del Cheyenne 8/12/42; Hamilton 11/1/43; Sioux City 6/4/43; Casper 14/5/43; Tinker 13/6/43; Rapid City 20/7/43; 4100 BU Patterson 6/6/44; 2AF HQ Peterson 2/7/44; 221 BU Alexandra 11/8/44; 2530 BU Selman 26/9/44; 4104 BU Rome 5/11/44; 4121 BU Kelly 7/8/45; RFC Kingman 5/12/46.

42-5434 Del Cheyenne 8/12/42; Morrison 6/2/43; ass 360BS/303BG [PU-J] Molesworth 6/3/43; c/l Winchester, UK, 26/9/43 w/Coggeswell. Sal 20/2/43. LADY LUCK.

42-5435 Del Cheyenne 8/12/42; Morrison 8/2/43; ass 303BG Molesworth 9/2/43; tran 366BS/306BG Thurleigh 2/43; MIA St Nazaire 1/5/43 w/Suomi, e/a, ditched Biscay, 10KIA, MACR 15721.

42-5436 Del Cheyenne 8/12/42; Pyote 5/1/43; Dyersburg 22/5/43; WO 26/6/43.

42-5437 Del Denver 8/12/42; Morrison 6/2/43; ass 401BS/91BG [LL-H] Bassingbourn 8/3/43; MIA {23m} Schweinfurt 17/8/43 w/Weiweneth, e/a, cr Hergarten, Ger, 9KIA 1POW. MACR 282. FRANK'S NIGHTMARE.

42-5438 Del Denver 8/12/42; Sioux City 3/1/43; Rapid City 3/2/43; Pierre 25/2/43; Rapid City 19/4/43; Geiger 22/6/43; 383BG Pendleton 27/7/43; 498BG Gt Bend 16/6/44; 243 BU Gt Bend 14/10/44; RFC Albuquerque 25/5/45.

42-5439 Del Cheyenne 8/12/42; Salina 5/1/43; Morrison 8/3/43; ass 437BS/99BG Navarin 10/3/43; Oudna 4/8/43; Tortorella 11/12/43; MIA Villaorba 18/3/44 w/Lombard, e/a, cr Udine, 1KIA (TG) 9 baled. MACR 3355.

42-5440 Del Cheyenne 8/12/42; New Castle 17/12/42; ass 97BG Biskra 22/1/43; Château-du-Rhumel 8/2/43; Pont-du-Fahs 1/8/43; Depienne 15/8/43; tran 20BS/2BG Massicault 14/11/43; Bizerte 2/12/43; Amendola 9/12/43; 347BS/99BG Tortorella 28/3/44; {0m/99th} 483BG Sterparone 31/3/44; sal 31/10/45. SAHARA SUE.

42-5441 Del Tulsa 8/12/42; Chico 13/3/43; Pyote 28/7/43; Tinker 16/10/43; 3701 BU Amarillo 18/11/43; Recl Comp 7/6/46.

42-5442 Del Tulsa 8/12/42; Casper 17/1/43; Salina 3/2/43; Dyersburg 14/4/43; Pyote 24/4/43; 28BS/19BG Pyote 28/10/43; 273 BU Lincoln 4/9/44; 504BG Fairmont 7/9/44; 241 BU Fairmont 23/9/44; 249 BU Alliance 14/10/44; 902 BU Orlando 16/3/45; RFC Altus 4/10/45.

42-5443 Del Tulsa 10/12/42; Ainsworth 21/1/43; Pierre 12/3/43; Rapid City 28/4/43; Gieger 22/6/43; 232 BU Dalhart 9/6/44; 242 BU Gr Isle 29/6/44; 6BG Gr Isle 8/7/44; 11 STA HQ Morrison 29/7/44; 242 BU Gr Isle 16/9/44; 232 BU Dalhart 21/10/44; 273 BU Lincoln 29/11/44; 245 BU McCook 9/2/45; RFC Albuquerque 25/6/45.

42-5444 Del Tulsa 10/12/42; Salina 7/1/43; ass 360BS/303BG [PU-C] Molesworth 2/6/43; 403AD Langford Lodge 5/7/43; 545BS/384BG [JD-N] Grafton Underwood 11/8/43; MIA 30/1/43 w/Ross, e/a, cr Minden, Ger, 7KIA 3POW, MACR 2466. WE DOOD IT!

42-5445 Del Cheyenne 10/12/42; Sioux City 8/1/43; Rapid City 2/2/43; Minneapolis 19/3/43; Ephrata 12/4/43; Spokane 3/5/43; 390BG Moses Lake 28/7/43; WO 20/8/43.

42-5446 Del Cheyenne 9/12/42; Wendover 28/12/42; Sioux City 10/5/43; Kearney 3/8/43; 225 BU Rapid City 27/6/44; RFC Ontario 14/6/45.

42-5447 Del Cheyenne 10/12/42; Sioux City 10/1/43; Wendover 31/1/43; Casper 5/5/43; McClellan 3/6/43; Sioux City 3/7/43; Kearney 3/8/43; Tinker 23/11/43; 232 BU Dalhart 9/6/44; 2AF HQ Peterson 20/6/44; 271 BU Kearney 11/9/44; 4136 BU Tinker 10/1/45; 271 BU Kearney 14/1/45; 485 BU Kearney 29/7/45; RFC Kingman 12/11/45.

42-5448 Del Cheyenne 10/12/42; Duncan 25/3/43; Hobbs 4/8/434; Ft Sumner 21/4/43; 3017 BU Hobbs 8/11/44; 3508 BU Truax 17/4/45; 3017 BU Hobbs 231/4/45; RFC Altus 28/8/45.

42-5449 Del Denver 11/11/12; Biggs 13/1/43; Wendover 31/1/43; Sioux City 7/4/43; Casper 29/5/43; Tinker 17/6/43; Gt Falls 1/8/43; 249 BU Alliance 13/9/44; 245 BU McCook 9/9/45; 237 BU Kirtland 22/10/45; RFC Kingman 7/11/45.

42-5450 Del Denver 14/12/42; Blythe 30/12/42; Denver 31/1/43; WO 18/3/43.

42-5451 Del Cheyenne 9/12/42; Wendover 27/12/42; Sioux City 8/4/43; Gowen 17/5/43; Casper 2/7/43; Kearney 3/8/43; WO 1/9/43.

42-5452 Del Cheyenne 10/12/42; Hobbs 22/12/42; 3017 BU Hobbs 8/11/44; 4100 BU Patterson 24/3/45; RFC Altus 29/10/45.

42-5453 Del Cheyenne 9/12/42; Sioux City 10/3/43; Gowen 28/4/43; Tinker 8/6/43; Dyersburg 11/7/43; 326 BU McDill 19/6/44; 4000 BU Patterson 23/7/44; 328 BU Gulfport 31/3/45; RFC Albuquerque 19/6/45.

42-5454 Del Cheyenne 10/12/42; 4 Eng Adv Fly Trng Smyrna 23/12/42; Hobbs 18/3/43; Alamogordo 23/6/43; Dalhart 21/7/43; 4136 BU Tinker 6/6/44; 3017 BU Hobbs 15/7/44; 4121 BU Kelly 8/12/44; 4168 BU Sth Plains 26/6/45; RFC Walnut Ridge 3/1/46.

42-5455 Del Cheyenne 10/12/42; Pocatello 28/12/42; Pyote 16/2/43; cr 5 mile S of base w/Folsom 6/6/43, WO 7/6/43.

42-5456 Del Cheyenne 10/12/42; New Castle 19/12/42; ass 419BS/301BG Biskra 3/1/43; Ain M'Lila 17/1/43; St Donat 6/3/43; Oudna 6/8/43; Cerignola 7/12/43; Lucera 1/2/44; {53m} sal 8/7/43.

42-5457 Del Denver 10/12/42; Wendover 3/2/43; Hammer Fd 7/3/43; Sioux City 6/4/43; Dalhart 15/4/43; 4136 BU Tinker 11/7/44; 4100 BU Patterson 6/1/45; 325 BU Avon Park 2/4/45; RFC Walnut Ridge 4/9/45.

42-5458 Del Denver 11/12/42; Pocatello 31/12/42; Pyote 11/1/43; WO 24/6/43.

42-5459 Del Denver 11/12/42; Pocatello 20/12/42; Pyote 13/1/43; Pocatello 31/1/43; cr Pyote 2/2/43; WO 3/2/43.

42-5460 Del Denver 11/12/42; Wendover 30/12/42; Sioux City 6/4/43; Dyersburg 13/4/43; Tinker 4/11/43; Smoky Hill 12/11/43; 235 BU Biggs 27/7/44; WO 18/8/44; Recl Comp 3/8/46.

42-5461 Del Tulsa 11/12/42; Pyote 2/1/43; Gowen 12/5/43; Alamogordo 21/6/43; Pueblo 16/8/43; 248 BU Walker 27/6/44; 500BG Walker 10/7/44; 2528 BU Midland 4/11/44; 2509 BU Big Spring 23/1/45; RFC Walnut Ridge 5/1/46.

42-5462 Del Cheyenne 10/12/42; Luke 22/1/43; Wendover 31/1/43; Tarrant 29/4/42; Orlando 11/5/43; Geiger 2/6/43; Gt Falls 7/7/43; Glasgow 28/7/43; 242 BU Gr Isle 1/6/44; 6BG Gr Isle 8/7/44; 247 BU Smoky Hill 21/3/45; 6138 BU Phillips 6/7/46.

42-5463 Del Denver 11/12/42; Pyote 30/12/42; Casper 21/2/43; Wendover 12/4/43; Sioux City 11/6/43; Dalhart 22/7/43; 505BG Harvard 2/6/44; 4100 BU Patterson 1/9/44; 3 WER Sq Grenier 29/4/45; McChord 24/5/45; 53 RCN Sq Grenier 14/7/45; RFC Kingman 6/3/46.

42-5464 Del Cheyenne 10/12/42; Pocatello 29/12/42; Pyote 16/2/43; Pueblo 3/3/43; Biggs 20/3/43; Tinker 30/7/43; cr 8/10/43 w/Schultz, engine exploded. WO 10/10/43.

42-5465 Del Cheyenne 10/12/42; Wendover 27/12/42; Casper 24/3/43; Tinker 4/6/43; Dyersburg 1/7/43; WO 26/9/43.

42-5466 Del Cheyenne 10/12/42; Dyersburg 13/5/43; Sheppard 3/11/43; 326 BU McDill 27/6/44; 325 BU Avon Park 23/1/45; 331 BU Barksdale 17/2/45; RFC Albuquerque 25/6/45.

42-5467 Del Cheyenne 10/12/42; Casper 13/1/43; Scotts Bluff 15/2/43; Casper 16/4/43; Sioux City 28/6/43; Dyersburg 4/8/43; 232 BU Dalhart 15/6/44; 201 BU Peterson 22/6/44; 233 BU Davis Monthan 23/8/44; 27 BU Lincoln 11/10/44; 200 BU Peterson 29/4/45; RFC Kingman 27/10/45.

42-5468 Del Denver 11/12/42; Salina 8/1/43; ass 360BS/303BG [PU-I] Molesworth 8/4/43; ditched Nth Sea 25/6/43 w/Stallings. (THE NASTY NINE) QUININE THE BITTER DOSE.

42-5469 Del Cheyenne 10/12/42; Blythe 29/12/42; Dyersburg 13/5/43; Orlando 29/6/43; Dyersburg 5/7/43; Tinker 6/8/43; MATCOM Wright Fd 16/6/44; 4200 BU Chicago Mun Apt 18/6/44; 202 BU Galveston 20/6/44; 223 BU Dyersburg 23/2/45; RFC Walnut Ridge 18/12/45.

42-5470 Del Cheyenne 4/12/42; Morrison 31/1/43; ass 346BS/99BG Navarin 3/3/43; Oudna 4/8/43; Tortorella 11/12/43; MIA Piraeus 11/1/44 w/Donahue, cr Kalavrya, 7KIA 3EVD & RTD. MACR 1820) RESTLESS BESS.

42-5471 Del Cheyenne 13/12/42; Biggs 24/2/43; Pueblo 4/3/43; Dalhart 16/3/43; Tinker 2/7/43; Dalhart 26/7/43; 231 BU Alamogordo 2/8/44; 235 BU Biggs 11/10/44; 4100 BU Patterson 5/3/45; 4202 BU Syracuse 8/4/45; Recl Comp 3/1/46.

42-5472 Del Denver 16/12/42; Blythe 1/1/43; Morrow 12/1/43; Dalhart 22/5/43; Tinker 13/6/43; Dalhart 2/7/43; WO 18/8/43; Tinker 27/8/43; 248 BU Walker 16/8/44; 221 BU Alexandra 18/8/44; Recl Comp 13/3/46.

42-5473 Del Denver 16/12/42; Salina 1/1/43; ass 353BS/301BG Ain M'Lila 28/1/43; St Donat 6/3/43; Oudna 6/8/43; {69m} tran 20BS/2BG Massicault 14/11/43; Bizerte 2/12/43; Amendola 9/12/43; 347BS/99BG Tortorella 28/3/44; {0m} 483BG Tortorella 31/3/44; Sterparone 22/4/44; retUS Morrison 25/3/45; RFC Altus 25/9/45. ERNT MERNT.

42-5474 Del Cheyenne 3/1/43; Lewiston 22/1/43; Walla Walla 4/2/43; Redmond 21/2/43; Dalhart 28/5/43; Walla Walla 21/7/43; WO 23/3/44.

42-5475 Del Cheyenne 14/12/42; Blyhte 29/12/42; Dyersburg 20/5/43; 505BG Harvard 19/6/44; 4136 BU Tinker 15/7/44; 235 BU Biggs 28/8/44; 4104 Rome 17/1/45; 235 BU Biggs 19/3/45; 4202 BU Syracuse 17/4/45; RFC Albuquerque 3/8/45.

42-5476 Del Cheyenne 13/12/42; Casper 11/1/43; Scotts Bluff 8/3/43; Sioux City 20/6/43; Casper 15/5/43; Scribner 19/7/43; Kearney 3/8/43; 4136 BU Tinker 14/8/43; 202 BU Galveston 21/6/44; 233 BU Davis Monthan 13/10/44; 225 BU Rapid City 23/2/45; 4202 BU Syracuse 27/3/45; RFC Altus 5/11/45.

42-5477 Del Cheyenne 13/12/42; Salina 1/1/43; Morrison 31/1/43; ass 346BS/99BG Navarin 3/3/43; Oudna 4/8/43; Tortorella 11/12/43; tran 483BG Tortorella 31/3/44; Sterparone 22/4/44; sal 30/3/45. ABLE MABLE.

42-5478 Del Cheyenne 15/12/42; Salina 1/1/43; De Ridder 31/1/43; Dyersburg 29/4/43; Alexandria 7/7/43; Galveston 13/8/43; 234 BU Clovis 24/6/44; RFC Walnut Ridge 14/12/45.

42-5479 Del Cheyenne 14/12/42; Pyote 2/1/43; Walker 10/3/43; Pueblo 7/4/43; Geiger 3/5/43; Gt Falls 7/6/43; Geiger 8/7/43; 390BG Gt Falls 15/9/43; 268 BU Peterson 25/8/44; RFC Altus 30/8/45.

42-5480 Del Cheyenne 14/12/42; Pyote 2/1/43; Tinker 26/10/43; 505BG Harvard 10/6/44; 4100 BU Patterson 30/8/44; 325 BU Avon Park 18/4/45; RFC Altus 31/8/45.

42-5481 Del Cheyenne 15/12/43; Wendover 5/1/43; Cheyenne 31/1/43; Scotts Bluff 31/3/43; Dalhart 10/4/43; Las Vegas 11/5/43; Dalhart 25/7/43; 241 BU Fairmont 24/6/44; 243 BU Gt Bend 20/7/44; 4136 BU Tinker 14/8/44; 504BG Fairmont 19/8/44; RFC Walnut Ridge 21/1/46.

42-5482 Del Cheyenne 15/12/43; Salina 10/1/43; Brookley 1/2/43; Homestead 14/2/43; ass 359BS/303BG [BN-W] Molesworth 6/3/43; c/l Riseley, UK ex-Schweinfurt 14/10/43, sal. CAT O'NINE TAILS.

42-5483 Del Cheyenne 16/12/42; Salina 8/1/43; 8/11/43; Homestead 17/2/43; ass 360BS/303BG [PU-F] Molesworth 7/3/43 RED ASS; tran 427BS; MIA Bremen 29/11/43 w/Brumbeloe, e/a, cr Quackenbrück, Ger, 3KIA 7POW, MACR 1656. THE DEVIL HIMSELF.

42-5484 Del Seattle 15/12/42; Eglin 4/3/43; McClellan 17/3/43; Seattle 8/5/43; Wright 23/6/43; Seattle 6/8/43; MATCOM Wright Fd 2/6/44; 110 BU Mitchell 19/9/44; Wright 27/9/44; RRD Nashville 3/8/45; 4020 BU Wendover 22/8/45; RFC Searcey Fd 11/9/45.

B-17F-VE

42-5705 Del Patterson 23/6/42; Biggs 22/4/43; WO 27/4/43.

42-5706 Del Geiger 14/10/42; Tinker 10/4/43; Geiger 11/5/43; Moses Lake 6/6/43; Portland 23/7/43; Moses Lake 16/8/43; 611 BU Eglin 4/6/44; 610 BU Bedford 1/7/44; 4119 BU Brookley 12/9/44; MATCOM Wright 13/10/44; Boca Raton 1/11/44; RFC Altus 14/6/45.

42-5707 Del Hendricks 12/8/42; Wayne 6/11/42; Salina 21/1/43; Gowen 4/3/43; Wendover 2/5/43; McDill 4/6/43; Atlanta 16/6/43; 4114 BU Lockburn 14/7/44; RFC Altus 9/10/45.

42-5708 Del Sebring 11/8/42; Wayne 6/11/42; Tinker 30/3/43; Scott 29/7/43; 234 BU Clovis 24/6/44; 202 BU Galveston 2/11/44; 2517 BU Ellington 7/11/44; 3704 BU Keesler 13/1/45; RFC Stillwater 19/9/45.

42-5709 Del Cheyenne 13/8/42; Wayne 6/11/42; Smoky Hill 29/3/43; 236 BU Pyote 13/7/44; 235 BU Biggs 16/8/44; 231 BU Alamogordo 13/12/44; 4202 BU Syracuse 28/3/45; RFC Walnut Ridge 10/10/45.

42-5710 Del Cheyenne 16/8/42; Wayne 6/11/42; Tinker 1/5/43; Dalhart 22/6/43; 500BG Walker 16/8/44; 222 BU Ardmore 6/10/44; 332 BU Ardmore 16/6/45; 327 BU Drew 21/8/45; RFC Walnut Ridge 14/12/45.

42-5711 Del Vega Mod Ctr 94BG 28/8/42; 3701 BU Amarillo 5/7/44; WO 30/9/44; Recl Comp 19/6/45.

42-5712 Del Cheyenne 20/8/42; Wayne 6/11/42; West Palm Beach 14/12/43; ass 322BS/91BG [LG-S] Bassingbourn 1/1/43 HEAVYWEIGHT ANNIHILATORS II; b/d 22/6/43, rep & tran 324BS; {17m} c/l Manston ret Schweinfurt 17/8/43 w/Judy, 2KIA 3POW 3RTD, sal. MY PRAYER.

42-5713 Del Cheyenne 27/8/42; Syracuse 5/10/42; Presque Is 19/10/42; ass 366BS/305BG Chelveston 29/10/42; tran MTO 342BS/97BG Depienne 4/11/43; Cerignola 20/12/43; Amendola 16/1/44; WO 31/10/44.

42-5714 Del?; ass 423BS/306BG [RD-S] Thurleigh 16/5/43 OLD FAITHFUL; tran 323BS/91BG Bassingbourn 11/9/43; tran 322BS [LL-S]; MIA Schweinfurt 14/10/43 w/Slane, e/a, cr Nancy, Fr, 1KIA 1EVD 8POW, MACR 899.

42-5715 Del Cheyenne 3/9/42; New Castle 4/10/42; ass 94BG 22/10/42; tran 342BS/97BG Depienne 11/42; c/l Bizerte b/d 18/12/42 w/Nichols, 4KIA 5EVD & RTD. SOONER II.

42-5716 Del Cheyenne 11/9/42; New Castle 14/10/42; Salina 31/1/43; Cheyenne 28/2/43; Gowen 26/3/43; Moses Lake 7/6/43; 3501 BU Boca Raton 28/11/44; 2114 BU Lockburn 13/6/45; RFC Walnut Ridge 19/12/45.

42-5717 Del Cheyenne 13/9/42; New Castle 11/10/42; ass 423BS/306BG [RD-F] Thurleigh 29/11/42; MIA St Nazaire 16/2/43 w/Warner, flak, cr Ploermel, Fr, 6KIA 2POW 2EVD. MACR 15472.

42-5718 Del 410BS/94BG Geiger 17/9/42 THE WIDOW MAKER; Wayne 2/11/42; Kearney 4/2/43; Sioux City 5/3/43; Hill 12/7/43; 452BG Pendleton 29/10/43; 244 BU Harvard 10/6/44; Patterson 30/8/44; West Palm Beach 12/3/45; Canal Zone 18/1/46; Panama 23/6/46; re-ass CAC06 (?) 30/4/47; Ftr Aff 27/7/48; Recl Comp.

42-5719 Del Tulsa 12/9/42; Smyrna 15/11/42; Hobbs 22/11/42; WO 11/5/43.

42-5720 Del Tulsa 23/9/42; Wayne 2/11/42; West Palm Beach 14/12/42; ass 367BS/306BG [GY-Y] Thurleigh SCARLET 2/2/43; then 368BS; tran 544BS/384BG [SU-A] Grafton Underwood 23/8/43; FTR Brussels 6/9/43 w/Aufmuth, no gas, cr Beauvais, Fr, 5EVD 5POW, MACR 776.

42-5721 Del Long Beach 24/9/42; Geiger 6/10/42; Boise 10/11/42; Hobbs 3/3/43; Pyote 1/4/43; Dyersburg 24/5/43; Tinker 7/8/43; Love Fd 7/12/43; Wendover 28/12/43; McDill 15/1/44; 3701 BU Amarillo 18/11/44; RFC Stillwater 24/9/45.

42-5722 Del Long Beach 27/9/42; Geiger 3/10/42; Ephrata 3/12/42; Ft Sumner 21/4/43; Hobbs 6/5/43; WO 6/1/44.

42-5723 Del Long Beach 30/9/42; Tulsa 4/10/42; Wayne 5/11/42; Salina 27/11/42; ass 360BS/303BG [PU-D] Molesworth 13/2/43; c/l base b/d 19/3/43, sal.

42-5724 Del Tulsa 9/10/42; Wayne 14/11/42; Salina 19/1/43; ass 322BS/91BG [LG-T] Bassingbourn

23/3/43; MIA {9m} St Nazaire 28/6/43 w/Brodnar, flak, ditched Channel, 2KIA 8RTD, MACR 15710. (possibly MARNITA earlier) THUNDERBIRD No. 2.
42-5725 Del Tulsa 6/10/42; Wayne 26/11/42; New Castle 24/12/42; Salina 9/1/43; West Palm Beach 17/1/43; ass 365BS/305BG [XK-P] Chelveston 1/2/43 FLAPPER; tran 532BS/381BG [VE-C] Ridgewell 22/8/43; retUS Homestead 13/7/44; Tinker 24/7/44; Patterson 26/8/44; Williams 19/3/45; La Junta 26/3/45; Searcey Fd 31/7/45. THIS IS IT!
42-5726 Del Tulsa 11/10/42; Blythe 28/12/42; Dalhart 16/5/43; Tinker 21/6/43; Dalhart 19/7/43; 242 BU Gr Isle 23/6/44; 6BG Gr Isle 29/8/44; 4100 BU Patterson 1/9/44; 232 BU Dalhart 4/9/44; RFC Ontario 7/6/45.
42-5727 Del Tulsa 13/10/42; Rapid City 11/11/42; Salina 17/12/42; West Palm Beach 9/1/43; ass 419BS/301BG Ain M'Lila 3/2/43; St Donat 6/3/43; MIA {37m} Messina 18/6/43 w/Flowers, c/l Constantine, sal.
42-5728 Del Tulsa 16/10/42; Ephrata 24/11/42; Gt Falls 1/12/42; Rapid City 9/3/43; Glasgow 14/4/43; Gore 18/5/43; Moses Lake 17/6/43; 328 BU Gulfport 25/7/44; 327 BU Drew 10/5/45; RFC Walnut Ridge 11/12/45.
42-5729 Del Tulsa 16/10/42; Wayne 14/11/42; Rome 9/12/42; Wilmington 1/2/43; ass 369BS/306BG [WW-G] Thurleigh PICCADILLY COMMANDO 27/2/43; tran 401BS/91BG [LL-E] Bassingbourn 8/9/43 {15+m}; retUS Eglin 15/3/44; RFC Walnut Ridge 19/12/45. BUCCANEER.
42-5730 Del Tulsa 18/10/42; Rapid City 25/11/42; Geiger 28/3/43; Walla Walla 18/7/43; WO 20/11/43.
42-5731 Del Cheyenne 20/10/42; Salina 4/12/42; ass 97BG Biskra 31/1/43; Château-du-Rhumel 8/2/43; Pont-du-Fahs 1/8/43; Depienne 15/8/43; Cerignola 20/12/43; Amendola 16/1/44; sal 27/8/44.
42-5732 (YB-40) Del Tulsa 29/10/42; Biggs 15/3/43; Orlando 29/4/43; Presque is 3/5/43; ass 327BS/92BG Alconbury, cr Isle of Lewis, UK 7/5/43; sal & taken to Stornaway; retUS 3036 BU Yuma 4/5/44; RFC Ontario 18/5/45.
42-5733 (YB-40) Del Tulsa 29/10/42; Biggs 18/3/43; Montbrook 31/3/43; Presque Is 30/4/43; ass 327BS/92BG [UX-F] Alconbury 3/5/43 PEORIA PROWLER; tran 322BS/91BG [LG-T] Bassingbourn 16/7/43; sal 20/3/44; retUS Yuma 5/9/44; Williams 26/9/44; RFC Ontario 18/5/45.
42-5734 (YB-40) Del Tulsa 29/10/42; Biggs 15/3/43; Presque Is 6/5/43; ass 327BS/92BG [UX-D] Alconbury SEYMOUR ANGEL 14/5/43; tran 323BS/91BG [OR-R] Bassingbourn RED BALLOON 16/7/43; retUS Eglin 4/9/44; Yuma 5/9/44; RFC Ontario 18/5/45. OLD IRONSIDES.
42-5735 (YB-40) Del Tulsa 30/10/42; Biggs 15/3/43; Montbrook 31/3/43; Presque Is 4/5/43; ass 327BS/92BG [UX-B] Alconbury 4/5/43; MIA 22/6/43 w/Bilek, e/a, only YB-40 lost in action; WANGO WANGO.
42-5736 (YB-40) Del Tulsa 5/11/42; Biggs 14/3/43; Orlando 5/4/43; Presque Is 3/5/43; ass 327BS/92BG [UX-C] Alconbury 14/5/43; tran 359BS/303BG [BN-Q] Molesworth 3/8/43; 524BS/379BG [WA-P] Kimbolton 28/8/43; 1 BAD Burtonwood 9/10/43; retUS 3010 BU Williams 26/9/44; 3036 BU Yuma 11/11/44; RFC Ontario 18/5/45. TAMPA TORNADO.
42-5737 (YB-40) Del Tulsa 4/11/42; Biggs 14/3/43; Orlando 30/4/43; Presque Is 3/5/43; ass 327BS/92BG [UX-K] Alconbury 11/5/43; tran 360BS/303BG [PU-D] Molesworth 16/7/43; AFSC 10/10/43; sal 6/1/46. DAKOTA DEMON.
42-5738 (YB-40) Del Tulsa 4/11/42; Biggs 18/3/43; Orlando 28/4/43; Presque is 1/5/43; ass 327BS/92BG [UX-G] Alconbury 4/5/43; retUS 2/11/43; Yuma 4/5/44; RFC Ontario 24/5/45. BOSTON TEA PARTY.
42-5739 (YB-40) Del Tulsa 6/11/42; Biggs 15/3/43; Montbrook 1/4/43; Presque Is 30/4/43; ass 327BS/92BG [UX-J] Alconbury 4/5/43; tran 427BS/303BG [GN-D] Molesworth 16/7/43; 545BS/384BG [JD-P] Grafton Underwood 28/8/43; 1 BAD Burtonwood 12/10/43; retUS 11/3/44; 3036 BU Yuma 4/5/44; RFC Ontario 18/5/45. LUFKIN RUFFIAN.
42-5740 (YB-40) Del Tulsa 7/11/42; Biggs 18/3/43; Montbrook 31/3/43; Presque Is 30/4/43; ass 327BS/92BG [UX-E] Alconbury 4/5/43; retUS Gander 2/11/43; 3010 BU Williams 26/9/44; 3036 BU Yuma 4/5/45; RFC Ontario 18/5/45. MONTICELLO.
42-5741 (YB-40) Del Tulsa 12/11/42; Biggs 17/3/43; Montbrook 31/3/43; Presque Is 30/4/43; ass 327BS/92BG [UX-H] Alconbury 7/5/43 CHICAGO; tran 401BS/91BG [LL-Y] Bassingbourn 22/7/43; retUS 2/11/43; 3036 BU Yuma 4/5/44; RFC Ontario 18/5/45. GUARDIAN ANGEL.
42-5742 (YB-40) Del Tulsa 15/11/42; Montbrook 31/3/43; Presque Is 30/4/43; ass 327BS/92BG [UX-L] Alconbury 13/5/43; 1 BAD Burtonwood 5/10/43; retUS 3/4/44; 3036 BU Yuma 4/5/44; RFC Ontario 18/5/45. PLAIN DEALING EXPRESS.
42-5743 (YB-40) Del Tulsa 15/11/42; Biggs 14/3/43; Orlando 28/4/43; Presque Is 3/5/43; ass 327BS/92BG [UX-M] Alconbury 11/5/43; tran Iceland 23/6/43; ret 25/7/43; 1 BAD Burtonwood 5/10/43; retUS 3036 BU Yuma 11/10/43; Recl Comp 8/11/44. WOOLAROC.
42-5744 (YB-40) Del Tulsa 18/11/42; Biggs 17/3/43; Montbrook 31/3/43; Orlando 27/4/43; Presque Is 5/5/43; ass 327BS/92BG [UX-A] Alconbury 11/5/43; 1 BAD Burtonwood 5/10/43; retUS 24/2/44; 3036 BU Yuma 4/5/44; RFC Ontario 18/5/45. DOLLIE MADISON.
42-5745 (YB-40) Del Tulsa 21/11/42; Homestead 18/12/42; ass 305BG Chelveston 18/3/43; tran 327BS/92BG [UX-H] Alconbury 20/4/43; 813BS/482BG Alconbury 25/8/43, ret 30/11/43; 322BS/91BG [LG-C] Bassingbourn 20/12/43; AFSC 27/4/44; retUS 3036 BU Yuma 4/5/44; RFC Albuquerque 19/6/45. THE FUHRER THE BETTER.
42-5746 Del Tulsa 24/11/42; Salina 10/1/43; Morrison 2/2/43; ass 347BS/99BG Navarin 2/3/43; Oudna 4/8/43; Tortorella 11/12/43; FTR Salon de Provence w/Coss 27/1/44, flak, cr Rognac, 8 baled. MACR 2039. STARDUST.
42-5747 Del Tulsa 25/11/42; New Castle 27/12/42; Salina 3/1/43; Mobile 20/1/43; ass 332BS/94BG /43 BUCKET OF BOLTS; tran 364BS/305BG [WF-F] Chelveston 5/3/43; tran 535BS/381BG [MS-0] Ridgewell 22/8/43; {2+m} 547BS/384BG [SO-M] Grafton Underwood 5/10/43; 1BAD Burtonwood 15/3/44; retUS Nashville 14/6/44; RFC Altus 18/8/45. HANGAR QUEEN.
42-5748 Del Tulsa 29/11/42; Pyote 2/1/43; Pueblo 28/3/43; Dalhart 25/5/43; Pyote 3/6/43; Gulfport 5/7/43; Dalhart 24/7/43; Tinker 30/10/43; 2511 BU Bryan 2/11/44; RFC Altus 20/12/45.
42-5749 Del Tulsa 30/11/42; Salina 9/1/43; De Ridder 31/1/43; Salina 5/3/43; Tinker 1/4/43; Smoky Hill 29/5/43; Scott Fd 19/7/43; 582BS/393BG Sioux City 11/8/43; 3701 BU Amarillo 18/11/44; RFC Stillwater 24/9/45.
42-5750 Del Tulsa 30/11/42; Wendover 3/1/43; Scribner 7/4/43; Sioux City 12/4/43; Gowen 5/5/43; Wendover 29/5/43; Sioux City 11/6/43; WO 15/6/43.
42-5751 Del Cheyenne 9/12/42; Blythe 30/12/42; Gowen 15/3/43; WO 27/4/43.
42-5752 Del Cheyenne 11/12/42; Pocatello 29/12/42; Pyote 18/1/43; Biggs 28/2/43; Dalhart 17/3/43; Tinker 30/7/43; Oklahoma City 22/10/43; 19BG Pyote 9/11/43; WO 7/2/44.
42-5753 Del Cheyenne 13/12/42; Pueblo 30/12/42; Biggs 24/2/43; Blythe 18/3/43; Walla Walla 20/5/43; Redmond 18/6/43; Walla Walla 15/8/43; Avon Park 23/11/43; 3701 BU Amarillo 18/11/44; (Converted to F-9 with cameras in nose, bomb bay and rear fuselage); Recl Comp 3/1/46.
42-5754 Del Cheyenne 16/12/42; Pyote 1/1/43; Pueblo 28/3/43; Ephrata 21/5/43; 2020 BU Galveston 6/8/44; 211 BU Oak Apt 18/1/45; 225 BU Rapid City 23/2/45; 202 BU Syracuse 30/3/45; RFC Walnut Ridge 14/12/45.
42-5755 Del Cheyenne 17/12/42; Gt Falls 14/1/43; Walla Walla 22/2/43; Madras 20/6/43; Walla Walla 15/8/43; Avon Park 23/11/43; 3705 BU Lowry 1/5/44; 3017 BU Hobbs 19/5/44; RFC Altus 5/11/45.
42-5756 Del Cheyenne 19/12/42; Kirtland 31/1/43; Cheyenne 27/2/43; Pueblo 18/3/43; Presque Is 7/4/43; ass 509BS/351BG [RQ-R] Polebrook 19/4/43; 1 BAD Burtonwood 9/3/44; retUS Robins 1/6/44; Amarillo 24/10/44; RFC Walnut Ridge 9/1/46. KAY L II.
42-5757 Del Cheyenne 25/12/42; Glasgow 22/1/43; Walla Walla 5/2/43; Dyersburg 18/5/43; Walla Walla 18/5/43; 2137 BU Robins 15/6/44; 326 BU McDill 29/7/44; 327 BU Drew 23/1/45; 231 BU Alamogordo 5/3/45; 331 BU Barksdale 15/4/45; 325 BU Avon Park 19/5/45; RFC Walnut Ridge 18/8/45.
42-5758 Del Cheyenne 23/12/42; Gt Falls 14/1/43; Presque Is 8/4/43; Rapid City 19/5/43; Harvard 21/9/43; Galveston 17/2/44; retUS 6/10/44; RFC Altus 9/10/45.
42-5759 Del Cheyenne 23/11/42; Long Beach 31/1/43; Colorado Spr 19/3/43; Peterson 21/4/43; Orlando 15/6/43; 1 Photo Gp Bolling 4/12/43; 499BG Smoky Hill 7/6/44; 11 Photo Gp McDill 14/6/44; 902 BU Orlando 29/7/44; 19 Photo Sq/11Gp McDill 5/8/44; 3701 BU Amarillo 10/8/44; RFC Walnut Ridge 21/1/46.
42-5760 Del Cheyenne 23/11/42; Casper 14/1/43; Moses Lake 8/6/43; 326 BU McDill 20/1/45; 327 BU Drew 23/2/45; 331 BU Barksdale 3/3/45; 325 BU Avon Park 19/5/45; RFC Walnut Ridge 17/9/45.
42-5761 Del Cheyenne 27/12/42; Boise 15/1/43; Orlando 24/3/43; Lowry 14/4/43; Wright Fd 14/6/43; Watertown 25/7/43; Hill Fd 6/8/43; 4136 BU Tinker 19/6/44; 244 BU Harvard 21/6/44; 505BG Harvard 20/7/44; 235 BU Biggs 16/8/44; WO 24/9/44.
42-5762 Del Cheyenne 23/12/42; Salina 6/1/43; Morrison 31/1/43; ass 346BS/99BG Navarin 23/2/43; tran Service Sq 28/6/43; b/d Messina 25/6/43; sal.
42-5763 Del Long Beach 29/12/42; Salina 7/1/43; Homestead 14/2/43; ass 401BS/91BG [LL-F] Bassingbourn 9/3/43; MIA {17m} Stuttgart 6/9/43 w/Arp, e/a, cr Laon, Fr, 4EVD 6POW. MACR 514. BOMB-BOOGIE.
42-5764 Del Cheyenne 28/12/42; Denver 2/1/43; Salina 10/1/43; Brookley 8/3/43; Morrison 13/4/43; ass 97BG Château-du-Rhumel 16/4/43; Pont-du-Fahs 1/8/43; Depienne 15/8/43; Cerignola 20/12/43; Amendola 16/1/44 tran 840BS/483BG Tortorella 31/3/44; Sterparone 22/4/44; sal 30/11/45.
42-5765 Del Long Beach 31/12/42; Denver 2/1/43; Morrison 31/1/43; ass 416BS/99BG (extn bomb racks fitted) Navarin 2/2/43; Oudna 4/8/43; Tortorella 11/12/43; b/d Innsbruck w/Scott 19/12/43, 3 WIA;

42-5766 Del Long Beach 31/12/42; Salina 8/1/43; Brookley 8/3/43; Morrison 10/4/43; ass 367BS/306BG [GY-G] Thurleigh 2/6/43; MIA Kiel 29/7/43 w/Brown, e/a, cr Kiel 2KIA 8POW, MACR 120.

42-5767 Del Long Beach 31/12/43; Salina 10/1/43; Tinker 3/3/43; Morrison 31/3/43; ass MTO?; retUS 18/3/44; RFC Altus 29/10/45.

42-5768 Del Long Beach 1/1/43; Salina 9/1/43; Morrison 5/3/43; ass 353BS/301BG St Donat 4/4/43; {6m} cr 27/6/43.

42-5769 Del Long Beach 2/1/43; Salina 8/1/43; Brookley 5/3/43; Morrison 15/4/43; ass 347BS/99BG Navarin 5/5/43; Oudna 4/8/43; b/d Turin 8/11/43 w/McDonnell, ditched off Corsica, 2KIA.

42-5770 Del Long Beach 2/1/43; Brookley 27/1/43; Morrison 7/2/43; cr mud-flats 25 miles off shore 14/2/43, w/Underwood, no gas. WO.

42-5771 Del Long Beach 2/1/42; Ainsworth 19/1/43; Rapid City 5/3/43; Ainsworth 23/5/43; Geiger 12/6/43; Hill Fd 1/7/43; Gore Fd 18/8/43; 452BG Pendleton 27/10/43; 235 BU Biggs 28/7/44; 4104 BU Rome 17/1/45; 4121 BU Kelly 30/5/45; 3028 BU Luke Fd 31/1/46; Ferry a/c for University of Dakota 20/5/46.

42-5772 Del Long Beach 2/1/43; Salina 21/1/43; Morrison 8/2/43; ass 352BS/301BG St Donat 19/3/43; Oudna 6/8/43; Cerignola 7/12/43; Lucera 1/2/44; {30m} tran 346BS/99BG Tortorella 28/3/44; {1m 99th} 483BG Tortorella 31/3/44; Sterparone 22/4/44; sal 14/6/45.

42-5773 Del Long Beach 18/1/43; Salina 27/1/43; Morrison 10/3/43; ass 96BS/2BG Massicault 14/8/43; Bizerte 2/12/43; Amendola 9/12/43; MIA Albano 10/2/44 w/Bosmans, Ditched in Med Sea. MACR 2206. SCRUBBY GOAT then IMPATIENT VIRGIN.

42-5774 Del Long Beach 12/1/43; Gt Falls 31/1/43; Hobbs 1/3/43; 3017 BU Hobbs 17/6/44; 3036 BU Yuma 24/6/44; 4160 BU Albuquerque 21/7/44; RFC Albuquerque 27/7/45.

42-5775 Del Long Beach 15/1/43; Salina 28/1/43; Kearney 13/3/43; Hammer Fd 29/7/43; Kearney 10/8/43; 6BG Gr Island 15/7/44; 260 BU Peterson 19/7/44; 201 BU Peterson 28/7/44; 271 BU Kearney 30/7/44; 273 BU Lincoln 23/11/44; 201 BU Peterson 6/12/44; 200 BU Peterson 25/8/45; RFC Kingman 27/10/45.

42-5776 Del Long Beach 17/1/43; Salina 27/1/43; Morrison 9/3/43; ass 96BS/2BG Navarin 8/4/43; Château-du-Rhumel 27/4/43; Ain M'Lila 17/6/43; Massicault 31/7/43; Bizerte 2/12/43; MIA {80m} Athens 20/12/43 w/Rohrig, flak, cr and exploded, no chutes seen; TG Horner baled 4,000' EVD & RTD 29/6/44; MACR 1518. EAGER BEAVER.

42-5777 Del Long Beach 16/1/43; Salina 29/1/43; ass 96BS/2BG Navarin 31/3/43; Château-du-Rhumel 27/4/43; Ain M'Lila 17/6/43; Massicault 31/7/43; Bizerte 2/12/43; Amendola 9/12/43; {83m} tran 416BS/99BG Tortorella 28/3/44; {2m} 840BS/483BG Tortorella 31/3/44; Sterparone 22/4/44; MIA Wiener Neustadt 23/4/44 w/Hucle, flak, cr Gromet, 10POW. MACR 4664. THE GIN MILL.

42-5778 Del Long Beach 15/1/43; Denver 31/1/43; Morrison 19/2/43; ass 20BS/2BG Navarin 22/4/43; Château-du-Rhumel 27/4/43; {3m} burned out being cleaned with gasoline 11/5/43. WO.

42-5779 Del Long Beach 17/1/43; Salina 28/1/43; Morrison 10/3/43; ass 96BS/2BG Ain M'Lila 5/7/43; Massicault 31/7/43; Bizerte 2/12/43; Amendola 9/12/43; MIA {72m} Anzio 2/3/44 w/Degan, ditched near Anzio, 2 MIA, 9 picked up by British after 4 hrs in dinghy. MACR 3216. LEAKIN' LENA.

42-5780 Del Long Beach 27/1/43; Denver 1/2/43; Salina 10/2/43; Morrison 5/3/43; ass 427BS/303BG Molesworth 8/4/43; MIA St Nazaire 1/5/43 w/Sterling, e/a, cr St Nazaire. MACR 15727.

42-5781 Del Long Beach 19/1/43; Salina 28/1/43; Morrison 8/3/43; ass 49BS/2BG Navarin 11/3/43; Château-du-Rhumel 27/4/43; Ain M'Lila 17/6/43; Massicault 31/7/43; {5m} tran 419BG/301BG Oudna 28/10/43; 2BG Massicault 31/7/43; Bizerte 2/12/43; Amendola 9/12/43; 346BS/99BG Tortorella 28/3/44; {2m} 483BG Tortorella 31/3/44; Sterparone 22/4/44; sal 3/6/44.

42-5782 Del Long Beach 20/1/43; Salina 28/1/43; Tinker 27/2/43; Morrison 31/3/43; ass 429BS/2BG Navarin 8/4/43; Château-du-Rhumel 27/4/43; Ain M'Lila 17/6/43; Massicault 31/7/43; Bizerte 2/12/43; Amendola 9/12/43; tran 483BG Tortorella 2/44; sal {24m} 21/7/45 at 5BW HQ. HIGH TENSION.

42-5783 Del Long Beach 20/1/43; Denver 27/1/43; Brooksville 3/2/43; Eglin 5/3/43; Orlando 27/5/43; Mitchell 9/8/43; 328 BU Gulfport 13/6/44; 2517 BU Ellington 16/1/45; 328 BU Gulfport 19/5/45; RFC Altus 28/7/45.

42-5784 Del Long Beach 25/1/43; Salina 1/2/43; New Castle 16/2/43; ass 423BS/306BG Thurleigh 12/3/43; tran 369BS [WW-R]; MIA St Nazaire 1/5/43 w/Wigginton, e/a, cr Channel, 10KIA, MACR 15635.

42-5785 Del Long Beach 25/1/43; Smyrna 1/2/43; Memphis 7/3/43; Hobbs 19/5/43; 3711 BU Seattle 25/6/44; 3017 BU Hobbs 10/4/45; RFC Altus 4/10/45.

42-5786 Del Long Beach 28/1/43; Denver 30/1/43; Memphis 20/3/43; Morrison 14/4/43; ass 347BSA/99BG Navarin 4/5/43; Oudna 4/8/43; damaged by fire 16/9/43, rep at depot; tran 840BS/483BG Tortorella 4/44; MIA Nis, Yugo. 15/4/44 w/Preston, flak, cr Nis, 10KIA. MACR 3909. WHIZZER II.

42-5787 Del Long Beach 19/1/43; Salina 2/2/43; Homestead 21/2/43; ass 323BS/91BG [OR-U] Bassingbourn 9/3/43; MIA {5+m} Gelsenkirchen 12/8/43 w/Kethley, e/a, cr Goch, Ger, 10POW, MACR 262. BILLIE K.

42-5788 Del Long Beach 24/1/43; Denver 23/1/43; Salina 12/2/43; ass 360BS/303BG [PU-H] Molesworth 8/4/43; MIA Bunde 22/2/44 w/Morris, e/a, cr Namur, Bel, 1EVD 6KIA 2POW. MACR 15727 or 2647. (PLUTO'S AVENGER). AOG, NOT IN STOCK.

42-5789 Del Long Beach 31/1/43; Denver 1/2/43; ass 322BG/91BG [LG-X] Bassingbourn 25/3/43; MIA {8m} Huls 22/6/43 w/Kahl; #3 & 4 engines out going down under control. GOLDEN BEAR.

42-5790 Del Long Beach 29/1/43; Gowen 13/2/43; Orlando 10/3/43; Gowen 16/3/43; Orlando 4/4/43; Wendover 16/4/43; McClellan 22/5/43; Sioux City 11/6/43; WO 15/6/43.

42-5791 Del Long Beach 31/1/43; Salina 14/2/43; Kearney 12/3/43; Brookley 27/3/43; ass 334BS/95BG [BG-E] Chelveston 19/4/43; AFSC 6/43; RUTHLESS.

42-5792 Del Long Beach 28/1/43; Salina 11/2/43; ass 358BS/303BG [VK-I] Molesworth 8/4/43; MIA 4/7/43 w/O'Connor. THE MUGGER.

42-5793 Del Long Beach 30/1/43; Salina 11/2/43; ass 332BS/94BG [XM-M] Bassingbourn 4/3/43; 325BS/92BG [NV-Y/M] Alconbury 20/4/43; tran 813BS/482BG [PC-M] Alconbury 5/8/43; c/l 10/11/43, sal. STINKY.

42-5794 Del Long Beach 3/2/43; Denver 15/2/43; Gowen 9/3/43; Orlando 4/4/43; Wendover 16/4/43; Sioux City 11/6/43; Kearney 10/8/43; Tinker 27/11/43; 242 BU Gr Island 23/6/44; 6BG Gr Isle 8/7/44; 242 BU Gr Isle 16/10/44; RFC Altus 29/10/45.

42-5795 Del Long Beach 31/1/43; Rapid City 16/2/43; Morrison 28/3/43; ass 334BS/95BG [BG-A] Alconbury 5/4/43; {1m} tran AFSC (92BG?) 8/4/43; 401BS/91BG [LL-B] Bassing-bourn 5/9/43; MIA {7m} Bremen 26/11/43 w/Tibbetts, e/a, ditched Nth Sea, all rescued 10RTD. SKOAL.

42-5796 Del Long Beach 31/1/43; Salina 25/2/43; Geiger 26/3/43; Casper 15/4/43; Colorado Sp 10/7/43; WO 19/8/44; Recl Comp 3/1/46.

42-5797 Del Long Beach 3/2/43; Rapid City 17/2/43; Brookley 28/3/43; Morrison 10/4/43; ass 335BS/95BG Alconbury 24/4/43; tran AFSC 5/43, then 546BS/384BG [BK-E] Grafton Underwood 7/8/43; MIA Gelsen-kirchen 16/8/43 w/Magowan, s/d/by e/a, cr Ramboville, Fr, 1KIA 3EVD 6POW. MACR 295.

42-5798 Del Long Beach 3/2/43; Rapid City 17/2/43; Brookley 12/3/43; Morrison 19/4/43; ass 92BG Alconbury 4/2/43; MIA Kassel 28/7/43 w/?.

42-5799 Del Long Beach 5/2/43; 29BG Gowen 22/2/43; Orlando 4/4/43; Sioux City 11/6/43; Kearney 15/8/43; 4136 BU Tinker 23/6/43; 234 BU Clovis 4/7/43; 3704 BU Keesler 15/1/44; 237 BU Kirtland 27/9/44; RFC Albuquerque 5/7/45.

42-5800 Del Long Beach 6/2/43; 88BG Walla Walla 17/2/43; Spokane 1/8/43; 325 BU Avon Park 20/5/44; WO 20/5/44.

42-5801 Del Long Beach 10/2/43; Salina 27/2/43; Smoky Hill 31/3/43; Presque Is 14/4/43; ass 410BS/94BG Earls Colne 22/4/43 FLAK HAPPY; 333BS Rougham 13/6/43; tran 327BS/92BG [UX-J] Alconbury 28/7/43; MIA 12/8/43 w/Casey, e/a, cr Phillipine, Holl, 2KIA 8POW. MACR 656.

42-5802 Del Long Beach 10/2/43; Pyote 21/3/43; 19BG Pyote 25/11/43; 236 BU Biggs 16/8/44; 4100 BU Patterson 26/2/45; 224 BU Sioux City 12/4/45; RFC Kingman 28/10/45.

42-5803 Del Long Beach 11/2/43; Tinker 12/3/43; Presque Is 8/4/43; ass 94BG Earls Colne 17/5/43; Rougham 13/6/43; sal 18/7/43.

42-5804 Del Long Beach 11/2/43; Walker 23/2/43; Nashville 9/4/43; ass 96BG Grafton Underwood 27/4/43; tran 423BS/306BG [RD-Z] Thurleigh 6/8/43; 323BS/91BG [OR-R] Bassingbourn 11/9/43; 322BS [LG-R]; damaged Oschersleben, c/l Hethel 11/1/44; sal 21/1/44. HELL'S HALO.

42-5805 Del Long Beach 17/1/43; Walker 28/2/43; Tinker 31/3/43; Smoky Hill 17/4/43; Thurleigh 27/4/43; sal 16/6/43.

42-5806 Del Long Beach 15/2/43; Smoky Hill 23/3/43; Tinker 24/5/43; Dow Fd 19/6/43; ass 545BS/384BG [JD-Y/Z] Grafton Underwood 3/7/43; 547BS [SO-Y/Z]; MIA 12/8/43 w/Swank, e/a, cr Bonn, 4KIA 6POW. MACR 288.

42-5807 Del Long Beach 16/2/43; Walker 27/2/43; Presque Is 8/4/43; ass 337BS/96BG [AW-Q] Thurleigh 17/4/43 RIKKI TIKKI TAVI; tran 511BS/351BG [DS-T] Polebrook 11/7/43; MIA {10m} Frankfurt 4/10/43 w/Nauman, e/a, cr Frankfurt, 10KIA. MACR 910. MINOR BALL.

42-5808 Del Long Beach 17/2/43; Gore Fd 26/2/43; Colorado Spr 7/4/43; Peterson 27/5/43; Colorado Spr 1/8/43; ass 1PCG Bolling 1/9/43; 3701 BU Amarillo 12/8/44; 206 BU Sheppard 23/4/45; 3701 BU Amarillo 17/5/45; RFC Walnut Ridge 27/10/45.

42-5809 Del Long Beach 20/2/43; Sioux City 20/3/43;

INDIVIDUAL B-17 HISTORIES 111

Dow Fd 16/4/43; ass 544BS/384BG [SU-A] Grafton Underwood /43; 546BS [BK-D]; 526BS/379BG [LF-D] Kimbolton 24/4/43; c/l RAF Coltishall 11/6/43; sal AFSC 17/6/43.

42-5810 Del Long Beach 20/2/43; Will Rogers 5/3/43; Smoky Hill 28/3/43; ass 306BG 8/6/43; tran 527BS/379BG [FO-S] Kimbolton 8/6/43; MIA Keil 29/7/43 w/Johnson, e/a, ditched Nth Sea, 1KIA 9POW. MACR 1363.

42-5811 Del Long Beach 19/2/43; Cheyenne 27/2/43; Salina 20/3/43; Smoky Hill 27/4/43; ass 353BS/301BG St Donat 17/5/43; Oudna 6/8/43; {19m} tran 20BS/2BG Bizerte 14/11/43; Amendola 9/12/43; MIA {20m} Sofia 10/1/44 w/Finch; e/a, no chutes seen; MACR 1824.

42-5812 Del Long Beach 26/2/43; Denver 1/3/43; Pueblo 13/3/43; Presque Is 8/4/43; ass 511BS/351BG [DS-O] Polebrook 24/4/43; MIA {9m} Schweinfurt 17/8/43 w/Pinkerton, e/a, cr Bad Emms, Ger, 10POW, MACR 302. CANNON BALL.

42-5813 Del Long Beach 25/2/43; Cheyenne 1/3/43; Sioux City 18/3/43; Kearney 8/4/43; Dow Fd 16/4/43; ass 306BG 22/4/43 JACKIE ELLEN; tran 525BS/379BG [FR-S/Z] Kimbolton 2/5/43; b/d Kassel c/l Alconbury 30/7/43, sal.

42-5814 Del Long Beach 25/2/43; Pueblo 12/3/43; Presque Is 8/4/43; ass 508BS/351BG [YB-B] Polebrook 17/4/43; MIA {1m} Bremen 13/6/43 w/Forrest, e/a, ditched Channel.

42-5815 Del Long Beach 25/2/43; Cheyenne 1/3/43; Gore Fd 14/3/43; Presque Is 8/4/43; ass 509BS/351BG [RQ-Q] Polebrook 17/4/43; MIA {1m} Bremen 13/6/43 w/Jackson, e/a, cr?.

42-5816 Del Long Beach 25/2/43; Cheyenne 3/3/43; Sioux City 16/3/43; Kearney 4/8/43; Dow Fd 19/4/43; ass 527BS/379BG [F0-Q] Kimbolton 23/4/43; 2 BAD Lt Staughton 4/4/44; retUS Homestead 25/7/44; Tinker 6/8/44; Patterson 27/1/45; RFC Altus 29/8/45. JUDY (also POLLY).

42-5817 Del Long Beach 26/2/43; Denver 3/3/43; Smoky Hill 25/3/43; Homestead 7/4/43; Morrison 12/4/43; ass 348BS/99BG Navarin 10/5/43; Oudna 4/8/43; tran 483BG Tortorella 31/3/44; retUS Hunter 17/8/45; RFC Altus 9/10/45.

42-5818 Del Long Beach 26/2/43; Smoky Hill 25/3/43; Morrison 12/4/43; ass 347BS/99BG Navarin 12/5/43; Oudna 4/8/43; tran 816BS/483BG Tortorella 31/3/44 as cargo a/c to 9/44; retUS Morrison 17/4/45; Rome 22/4/45; RFC Bush Fd 3/7/45. CRAPPY.

42-5819 Del Long Beach 26/2/43; Denver 4/3/43; Casper 13/3/43; Memphis 17/4/43; Presque 26/4/43; ass 92BG Alconbury 12/8/43; tran 813BS/482BG (H2S) [PC-R] Alconbury 25/8/43; retUS Gray 3/2/45; Patterson 18/2/45; RFC Walnut Ridge 27/11/45.

42-5820 Del Long Beach 27/2/43; Denver 4/3/43; Smoky Hill 7/4/43; Pueblo 21/4/43; Presque 26/4/43; ass 524BS/379BG [WA-C] Kimbolton 8/5/43; 526BS [LF-C]; MIA Gelsenkirchen 12/8/43 w/Freund, flak, cr Oberbruch, 3KIA 7POW, MACR 2340.

42-5821 Del Long Beach 27/2/43; Sioux City 18/3/43; Dow Fd 13/4/43; ass 527BS/379BG [F0-0] Kimbolton 22/4/43; MIA Gelsenkirchen 12/8/43 w/Rees, flak, cr Ahrweiler, Ger, 6KIA 4POW, MACR 1360. CINDY.

42-5822 Del Long Beach 27/2/43; Cheyenne 4/3/43; Gore Fd 18/3/43; Kearney 8/4/43; Dow Fd 16/4/43; ass 525BS/379BG [FR-G] Kimbolton 21/4/43; B/D 28/7/43 c/l Foulsham, sal.

42-5823 Del Long Beach 28/2/43; Pueblo 12/4/43; Presque 8/4/43; ass 508BS/351BG [YB-C] Polebrook 17/4/43; {29m} 2 BAD Lt Staughton 5/4/44; retUS Tinker 6/8/44; RFC Ontario 7/5/45. ROUND TRIP.

42-5824 Del Long Beach 28/2/43; Gore Fd 11/3/43; Presque 8/4/43; ass 511BS/351BG [DS-S] Polebrook 17/4/43; 1BAD Burtonwood 31/3/44; retUS Robins 1/6/44; Hendricks 10/8/44; RFC Walnut Ridge 18/12/45. SCREWBALL.

42-5825 Del Long Beach 28/2/43; Tinker 29/3/43; ass 49BS/2BG Navarin 9/4/43; Château-du-Rhumel 27/4/43; Ain M'Lila 17/8/43; Massicault 31/7/43; Bizerte 2/12/43; Amendola 9/12/43; tran 416BS/99BG Tortorella 28/3/44; 840BS/483BG Tortorella 31/3/44; Sterparone 22/4/44; sal 23/6/45.

42-5826 Del Long Beach 4/3/43; Walla Walla 29/3/43; Lowry 10/4/43; Presque Is 24/4/43; ass 369BS/306BG [WW-W] Thurleigh 7/5/43; MIA Kiel 29/7/43 w/Conley, e/a, cr Kiel 2KIA 8POW. MACR 122. JERAVAD 'UNE PETITE PEU'.

42-5827 Del Long Beach 1/3/43; Sioux City 16/3/43; Kearney 9/4/43; Dow Fd 21/4/43; ass 524BS/379BG Kimbolton 20/5/43; 526BS [LF-Y]; MIA 5/1/44 w/ Grisson, flak, c/l Slattarp, Swed, 2POW 8INT. MACR 1942. LAKANUKI.

42-5828 Del Long Beach 28/2/43; Sioux City 18/3/43; Kearney 8/4/43; Dow Fd 15/4/43; ass 524BS/379BG [WA-O/D] Kimbolton 22/4/43; MIA Bunde 22/2/44 w/Morse, flak, cr Cologne, 10POW. MACR 2868. SWEATER GIRL.

42-5829 Del Long Beach 2/3/43; Sioux City 19/3/43; Dow Fd 16/4/43; ass 332BS/94BG Bassingbourn 25/4/43 THE BETTER HALF; tran 525BS/379BG [FR-P/D] Kimbolton 18/5/43; 527BS [FO-D]; MIA Kassel 30/7/43, w/Hove-land, flak, cr Aachen, 4KIA 6POW, MACR 1361. FLYING JENNY.

42-5830 Del Long Beach 6/3/43; Sioux City 20/3/43; Kearney 9/4/43; Dow Fd 15/4/43; ass 524BS/379BG [WA-P] Kimbolton 20/5/43 AL JOLSON; tran 2 BAD Lt Staughton 4/4/44; retUS Homestead 26/7/44; Tinker 1/9/44; RFC Ontario 7/5/45. HAG OF HARDWYCK.

42-5831 Del Long Beach 8/3/43; Homestead 7/4/43; Morrison 15/4/43; ass 32BS/301BG St Donat 17/4/43; MIA {1m} Foggia 31/5/43, w/Lewin, ditched; 2KIA 8RTD. THE VIRGIN.

42-5832 Del Long Beach 8/3/43; Denver 13/3/43; Salina 28/3/43; ass 348BS/99BG Navarin 26/4/43; Oudna 4/8/43; Tortorella 11/12/43; MIA Innsbruck 19/12/43, w/Stidd, cr Innsbruck; 3KIA 7POW. MACR 1527. WAR BIRD II.

42-5833 Del Long Beach 11/3/43; Tulsa 15/6/43; Love Fd 12/7/43; Patterson 19/7/43; ass 92BG Alconbury 10/4/43 as YB-40 crew trainer; retUS Yuma 25/6/44; 3036 BU Yuma4/5/45; RFC Ontario 24/5/45.

42-5834 Del Long Beach 11/3/43; Tulsa 15/6/43; Wright Fd 12/7/43 as YB-40 crew trainer; 611 BU Eglin 8/6/44; 610 BU Eglin 12/11/44; 2137 BU Hendricks 14/11/44; RFC Ontario 19/12/45.

42-5835 Del Long Beach 11/3/43; Tinker 30/3/43; Nashville 10/4/43; Morrison 16/4/43; ass 353BS/301BG St Donat 27/4/43; Oudna 6/8/43; Cerignola 7/12/43; Lucera 1/2/44; {9m} sal 9/11/44.

42-5836 Del Long Beach 11/3/43; Denver 15/3/43; Tinker 30/3/43; Homestead 7/4/43; Morrison 15/4/43; ass 32BS/301BG St Donat 16/4/43; Oudna 6/8/43; Cerignola 7/12/43; {31m} tran 49BS/2BG Amendola 14/1/44; MIA Sofia 24/1/44 w/Grissom, hit by bombs from B-17 above, no chutes seen. MACR 1993.

42-5837 Del Long Beach 13/3/43; Smoky Hill 22/3/43; Tinker 7/4/43; Memphis 16/4/43; ass 20BS/2BG Château-du-Rhumel 29/4/43; Ain M'Lila 17/8/43; Massicault 31/7/43; MIA {21m} Foggia 19/8/43, w/Pasero; e/a, seven chutes seen. MACR 459. C-BATT.

42-5838 Del Long Beach 13/3/43; Denver 20/3/43; Sioux City 13/4/43; Kearney 2/5/43; ass 547BS/384BG [SO-P] Grafton Underwood 29/5/43; MIA Keil 4/1/44 w/Kaczaraba, e/a, cr Keil, 10POW, MACR 1483. MAD MONEY II.

42-5839 Del Long Beach 13/3/43; Smoky Hill 25/3/43; Dow Fd 10/4/43; ass 325BS/379BG [FR-X] Kimbolton 16/4/43; MIA Wangerooge Is 25/6/43 w/Quade, e/a, cr Munderloh, Ger, 9KIA 1POW. MACR 1367.

42-5840 Del Long Beach 15/3/43; Scotts Bluff 29/3/43; Salina 15/4/43; Presque 2/5/43; ass Davis Prov Gp, ditched Atlantic 7/5/43.

42-5841 Del Long Beach 15/3/43; Smoky Hill 26/3/43; Dow Fd 10/4/43; ass 423BS/306BG [RD-Y/I] Thurleigh 22/4/43; MIA Stuttgart 6/9/43 w/Andrews; f/l Magadino, Switz, 10INT. MACR 519. EST NULLA VIA IN VIA VIRTUTI.

42-5842 Del Long Beach 16/3/43; Morrison 27/4/43; ass 348BS/99BG Navarin 3/6/43; Oudna 4/8/43; Tortorella 11/12/43; tran 483BG Tortorella 31/3/44; Sterparone 22/4/44; 463BG Celone 9/44; sal 23/6/45. LETHAL LADY III.

42-5843 Del Long Beach 16/3/43; Sioux City 13/4/43; Kearney 4/5/43; Dow Fd 20/5/43; ass 547BS/384BG [SO-S] Grafton Underwood 29/5/43; MIA Stuttgart 6/9/43 w/Pulcipher; no gas, cr Beauvais, Fr. 4EVD 6POW. MACR 1455. BLACK GHOST.

42-5844 Del Long Beach 17/3/43; Gore Fd 31/3/43; Memphis 8/4/43; Morrison 15/4/43; ass 341BS/97BG Château-du-Rhumel 23/4/43; Pont-du-Fahs 1/8/43; Depienne 15/8/43; b/d Turin 8/11/43, w/Festel, 8 baled but ASR failed to locate, p & cp return to base. MACR 2098.

42-5845 Del Long Beach 17/3/43; Pueblo 10/4/43; Smoky Hill 7/5/43; Dow Fd 24/5/43; ass 534BS/381BG [GD-A] Ridgewell 25/5/43; MIA {13+m} Bremen 20/12/43 w/Canelake, flak, ditched Nth Sea, 10KIA, MACR 1724. WHALETAIL II.

42-5846 Del Long Beach 19/3/43; Pueblo 10/4/43; Smoky Hill 6/5/43; Presque Is 21/5/43; ass 535BS/381BG [MS-X] Ridgewell 26/5/43; MIA {19+m} Bremen 20/12/43 w/Lane, coll w/ e/a, cr Bremen, 7KIA 3POW. MACR 1723. (A/c shown in film shot in *Hers To Hold*, w/Deanna Durbin). TINKERTOY.

42-5847 Del Long Beach 17/3/43; Pueblo 10/4/43; Smoky Hill 6/5/43; Dow Fd 19/5/43; ass 532BS/381BG [VE-T] Ridgewell 26/5/43; MIA {1+m} Gelsenkirchen 12/8/43 w/Moon, flak, cr Maastricht, Hol, 10POW. MACR 660. MARGIE MAE.

42-5848 Del Long Beach 20/3/43; Sioux City 13/4/43; Kearney 4/5/43; Dow Fd 20/5/43; ass 547BS/384BG [SO-R] Grafton Underwood 24/5/43; b/d Kassel 30/7/43 w/?; c/l Boxted, UK; sal AFSC 6/8/43. PATCHES.

42-5849 Del Long Beach 20/3/43; Sioux City 13/4/43; Kearney 3/5/43; Dow Fd 20/5/43; ass 547BS/384BG [SO-N] Grafton Underwood 24/5/43; MIA Nantes 16/9/43 w/Butler, e/a, cr Rennes, Fr. 2EVD 3KIA 5POW. MACR 722. HELL'S BELLES II.

42-5850 Del Long Beach 20/3/43; Sioux City 13/4/43; Kearney 3/5/43; Dow Fd 20/5/43; ass 547BS/384BG [SO-M] Grafton Underwood 24/5/43; MIA Wangerooge Is 25/6/43 w/McMillin, e/a, cr Smallbroek, Hol, 1KIA 9POW. MACR 16357.

42-5851 Del Long Beach 20/3/43; Sioux City 13/4/43; Kearney 3/5/43; ass 384BG 4/43; cr Bangor, Me 19/5/43. WO.

42-5852 Del Long Beach 22/3/43; Sioux City 15/4/43; Kearney 4/5/43; Dow Fd 20/5/43; ass 547BS/384BG

[SO-T] Grafton Underwood 24/5/43; cr Chetwade, UK ret Schweinfurt 14/10/43; sal MRU 15/10/43. NATURAL.

42-5853 Del Long Beach 22/3/43; Sioux City 13/4/43; Kearney 4/5/43; Dow Fd 20/5/43; ass 547BS/384BG [SO-U] Grafton Underwood 24/5/43; MIA Antwerp 22/6/43 w/Disney, e/a, ditched Channel, 7KIA 3POW, MACR 14668. SALVAGE QUEEN.

42-5854 Del Long Beach 23/3/43; Kearney 15/4/43; Wendover 2/5/43; Dow Fd 27/5/43; ass 100B 30/5/43 Thorpe Abbotts; tran 360BS/303BG [PU-C] Molesworth 13/7/43; {28m} 1 BAD Burtonwood 5/4/44; retUS Tinker 6/6/44; Culver 15/7/44; Las Vegas 9/11/44; Kelley 10/6/45; Culver 1/9/45; Love Fd 8/10/45; RFC Kingman 14/12/45. ALLEY OOP.

42-5855 Del Long Beach 8/3/43; Denver 13/3/43; Memphis 8/4/43; Dow Fd 15/4/43; ass 95BG Alconbury 27/4/43; tran 545BS/384BG [JD-V] Grafton Underwood 28/6/43; 423BS/306BG [RD-T] Thurleigh 22/8/43; MIA Bremen 8/10/43 w/Rodman, flak, cr Golderstadt, Ger. 5KIA 5POW. MACR 869.

42-5856 Del Long Beach 27/3/43; Tarrant 25/4/43; Smoky Hill 11/6/43; Kearney 30/6/43; Dow Fd 9/7/43; ass 347BS/99BG Navarin 23/7/43; Oudna 4/8/43; MIA Augsburg 1/10/43 w/Cantwell, s/d by Swiss AF, cr Alvaneu, 5KIA 5INT. MACR 795. HUBBA HUBBA.

42-5857 Del Long Beach 27/3/43; Nashville 8/4/43; ass 324BS/91BG [DF-J] Bassingbourn 19/4/43; MIA Wilhelmshaven 21/5/43 w/Miller, 6KIA 4POW. MACR 16136.

42-5858 Del Long Beach 28/3/43; Smoky Hill 4/4/43; Morrison 5/5/43; Presque Is 13/5/43; ass 336BS/95BG [ET-L] Framlingham 19/5/43; MIA {1m} 29/5/43 w/Clark, coll w/42-29689 or 42-29709, 2EVD 3KIA 6POW. MACR 4894.

42-5859 Del Long Beach 28/3/43; Memphis 9/4/43; Romulus 14/4/43; ass 379BG Kimbolton 24/4/43; c/l 2 SAD Lt Staughton 1st mission; rep & tran 360BS/303BG [PU-M] Molesworth 2/10/43; c/l Bungay 30/11/43; n/b/d c/l Bozeat, UK, 20/2/44, sal.

42-5860 Del Long Beach 30/3/43; Denver 2/4/43; Wendover 2/5/43; Hill Fd 17/5/43; Dow Fd 29/5/43; ass 418BS/100BG Thorpe Abbotts 2/6/43; MIA Schweinfurt 17/8/43 w/Biddick, e/a, cr Schweinsberg, Ger. 4KIA 6POW. MACR 675. ESCAPE KIT.

42-5861 Del Long Beach 30/3/43; Kearney 15/4/43; Wendover 2/5/43; Kearney 22/5/43; Dow Fd 6/6/43; ass 349BS/379BG [XR-J] Kimbolton 8/6/43 STUD DUCK; MIA Ludwigshafen 30/12/43 w/Roane, e/a, cr Liry, 2EVD 8KIA. MACR 2020. LADEN MAIDEN.

42-5862 Del Long Beach 31/3/43; Denver 2/4/43; Kearney 15/4/43; Wendover 2/5/43; Hill Fd 13/5/43; Dow Fd 17/5/43; ass 350BS/100BG Thorpe Abbotts 30/5/43; MIA Keil 25/7/43 w/Carey, flak, cr Nth Sea, 6KIA 4POW. MACR 117. DURATION PLUS SIX.

42-5863 Del Long Beach 31/3/43; Kearney 15/4/43; Wendover 2/5/43; Dow Fd 30/5/43; ass 350BS/100BG Thorpe Abbotts 1/6/43; tran 568BS/390BG [BI-O] Framlingham /43. Sal Burtonwood 6/2/45. PADDLEFOOT'S PROXY.

42-5864 Del Long Beach 31/3/43; Keaqrney 15/4/43; Wendover 2/5/43; Dow Fd 30/5/43; ass 351BS/100BG Thorpe Abbotts 1/6/43; MIA Bremen 8/10/43 w/Murphy, flak, cr Bremen, 6KIA 5POW. MACR 948. PICCADILLY LILY.

42-5865 Del Long Beach 31/3/43; Kearney 15/4/43; Wendover 2/5/43; Dow Fd 28/5/43; ass 351BS/100BG Thorpe Abbotts 1/6/43; MIA Romilly 3/9/43 w/Feinup, flak, cr Evreux, Fr. 3EVD 2KIA 5POW. MACR 686. JANIE.

42-5866 Del Long Beach 31/3/43; Denver 3/4/43; Lockburn 18/4/43; cr base 2/9/43, cause unknown; WO.

42-5867 Del Long Beach 2/4/43; Kearney 15/4/43; Wendover 2/5/43; Dow Fd 27/6/43; ass 350BS/100BG [LN-O] Thorpe Abbotts 30/5/43; MIA Schweinfurt 17/8/43 w/Clayton, flak, cr Langerloo, Wangerooge, Hol, 5EVD 2KIA 3POW. MACR 678. ALICE FROM DALLAS.

42-5868 Del Long Beach 3/4/43; ass 100BG but trans Dyersburg 16/4/43; Tinker 13/12/43; 499BG Smoky Hill 9/8/44; 233 BU Davis Monthan 15/8/44; 235 BU Biggs 3/1/45; RFC Kingman 30/10/45.

42-5869 Del Long Beach 4/4/43; Ainsworth 17/4/43; Ephrata 11/5/43; 248 BU Walker 9/6/44; 4136 BU Tinker 25/6/44; 235 BU Biggs 19/8/43; 231 BU Alamogordo 12/1/45; 202 BU Galveston 28/1/45; 283 BU Galveston 30/3/45; 209 BU Galveston 15/6/45; RFC Walnut Ridge 21/12/45.

42-5870 Del Long Beach 3/4/43; Denver 12/4/43; Morrison 27/4/43; ass 49BS/2BG Château-du-Rhumel 1/5/43; Ain M'Lila 17/6/43; Massicault 31/7/43; {44m} tran 419BS/301BG Oudna 14/11/43; Cerignola 7/12/43; Lucera 1/2/44 {41m} weather a/c from 27/4/44; retUS Patterson 6/4/45; {85m} RFC Albuquerque 3/8/45.

42-5871 Del Long Beach 5/4/43; Tulsa as gunnery trainer YB-40 10/4/43; 3036 BU Yuma 4/5/44; RFC Ontario 18/5/45.

42-5872 Del Long Beach 5/4/43; Tulsa as crew trainer TB-40 13/4/43; 2137 BU Hendricks 13/10/44; RFC Walnut Ridge 19/12/45.

42-5873 Del Long Beach 5/4/43; Denver 12/4/43; Morrison 27/4/43; ass 96BG but tran 96BS/2BG Château-du-Rhumel 19/5/43; Ain M'Lila 17/6/43; Massicault 31/7/43; MIA {21m} Naples 4/8/43 w/Chrisom; 10 chutes, 7 in sea & 3 on Ischia Is. MACR 346. LITTLE TANNIE.

42-5874 Del Long Beach 10/4/43; Smoky Hill 20/4/43; Morrison 4/5/43; ass 353BS/301BG St Donat 1/6/43; Oudna 6/8/43; Cerignola 7/12/43; Lucera 1/2/44; MIA {21m} Breslau 4/3/44 w/Chamberlin (99BG crew); abort mech failurc. MACR 3523.

42-5875 Del Long Beach 10/4/43; Denver 14/4/43; Morrison 29/4/43; Patterson 3/5/43; ass 342BS/97BG Château-du-Rhumel 15/5/43; Pont-du-Fahs 1/8/43; Depienne 15/8/43; MIA Rimini 27/11/43 w/Elmore, cr Urbino. MACR 1304.

42-5876 Del Long Beach 12/4/43; Smoky Hill 21/4/43; Warner Robins 8/56/43; Morrison 16/5/43; ass 97BG Château-du-Rhumel 5/6/43; Pont-du-Fahs 1/8/43; Depienne 15/8/43; Cerignola 20/12/43; Amendola 16/1/43; weather a/c from 15/7/44. Sal 6/10/45.

42-5877 Del Long Beach 14/4/43; Smoky Hill 23/4/43; Dow Fd 28/5/43; ass 337BS/96BG Andrews Fd 1/6/43; Snetterton 12/6/43; MIA 22/6/43 w/Russell, flak hit & cr.

42-5878 Del Long Beach 14/4/43; Smoky Hill 22/4/43; Wendover 2/5/43; Salt Lake City 18/5/43; Dow Fd 27/5/43; ass 100BG Thorpe Abbotts 30/5/43 BADGER'S BEAUTY; tran 33BS/381BG [VP-Q] Ridgewell 18/9/43; MIA Oschersleben 11/1/44 w/Perot; coll w/e/a, cr Minden, Ger. 9KIA 1POW. MACR 1874. YANKEE EAGLE.

42-5879 Del Long Beach 14/4/43; Smoky Hill 23/4/43; Presque Is 10/5/43; ass 339BS/96BG Andrews Fd 13/5/43; tran 548BS/385BG Gt Ashfield /43; MIA 7/5/44 w/Hoffman, flak, cr Pechterfeld, Ger. 10POW. MACR 4562. DAISY JUNE II.

42-5880 Del Long Beach 17/4/43; New Castle 30/4/43; Presque Is 6/5/43; ass 333BS/94BG Earls Colne 14/5/43; Rougham 13/6/43; MIA Huls 22/6/43 w/Sabella, e/a, 10POW

42-5881 Del Long Beach 17/4/43; Smoky Hill 28/4/43; Tinker 6/5/43; Lincoln 18/5/43; Dow Fd 23/5/43; ass 332BS/94BG [XM-GH] Earls Colne 27/5/43; Rougham 13/6/43; retUS Grenier 23/12/44; Patterson 16/3/45; RFC Stillwater 4/10/45. THE HOUSE OF LORDS.

42-5882 Del Long Beach 20/4/43; Smoky Hill 27/4/43; Presque Is 27/5/43; ass 336BS/95BG [ET-D] Framlingham 4/6/43; Horham 15/6/43; MIA 28/7/43 w/Regan, e/a, cr Nth Sea, 10KIA. MACR 216. SPOOK III.

42-5883 Del Long Beach 20/4/43; New Castle 30/4/43; Presque Is 5/5/43; ass 413BS/96BG Andrews Fd 8/5/43 OLD PUSS II; Snetterton 12/6/43; tran 544BS/384BG [SU-D] Grafton Underwood 6/7/43 NO NAME JIVE; MIA 25/7/43 w/Estes, e/a, cr Nth Sea, 10RTD. WEARY WILLIE.

42-5884 Del Long Beach 24/4/43; Love Fd 28/4/43; Salina 2/6/43; Kearney 30/6/43; Eglin 8/7/43; Dow Fd 11/7/43; ass 20BS/2BG Ain M'Lila 20/7/43; Massicault 31/7/43; {12m} tran 97BG Cerignola 20/12/43; weather a/c from 3/7/44; retUS Morrison 29/3/45; Patterson 3/4/45; RFC Altus 9/10/45.

42-5885 Del Long Beach 20/4/43; Lowry 5/5/43; Smoky Hill 25/5/43; Dow Fd 2/6/43; ass 413BS/96BG [MZ-T] Snetterton 12/6/43; MIA Rostock 11/4/44 w/Johnson, e/a, cr Baltic Sea, 9KIA 1MIA. MACR 3809. KIPLING'S ERROR III.

42-5886 Del Long Beach 21/4/43; Denver 5/3/43; Kearney 30/5/43; ass 548BS/385BG Gt Ashfield 24/6/43; MIA Schweinfurt 17/8/43 w/Sommers; e/a, cr Woensdrecht, Bel. 1EVD 6KIA 3POW. MACR 387A. THE JOLLY ROGER.

42-5887 Del Long Beach Wendover 5/5/43; Smoky Hill 10/6/43; Dow Fd 15/6/43; ass 560BS/388BG Knettishall 23/6/43; retUS Grenier 19/2/45; RFC Walnut Ridge 19/12/45. SIOUX CITY SUE.

42-5888 Del Long Beach 22/4/43; Smoky Hill 28/4/43; Lincoln 22/5/43; Dow Fd 25/5/43; ass 331BS/94BG [QE-X] Earls Colne 27/5/43; Rougham 13/6/43; MIA Emden 7/9/43 w/Roberts, e/a, cr Norden, Ger. 10KIA 1POW. MACR 732. ELUSIVE ELCY.

42-5889 Del Long Beach 22/4/43; Lowry 5/5/43; Smoky Hill 26/5/43; Dow Fd 2/6/43; ass 544BS/384BG [SU-A] Grafton Underwood 23/6/43; tran 369BS/306BG [WW-W] Thurleigh 22/8/43; c/l Matlaske, Nfk, ex-Gdynia 9/10/43, sal. LIBERTY BELLE.

42-5890 Del Long Beach 22/4/43; Smoky Hill 2/5/43; Tinker 24/5/43; Dow Fd 2/6/43; ass 327BS/92BG Alconbury 7/8/43; MIA Stuttgart 6/9/43 w/Christenson, flak, cr Poissy, Fr. 4EVD 6POW, MACR 740.

42-5891 Del Long Beach 23/4/43; Dallas 29/4/43; Smoky Hill 4/5/43; Eglin 8/7/43; Dow Fd 11/7/43; ass 353BS/301BG Oudna 1/9/43; Cerignola 7/12/43; Lucera 1/2/44; {52m} weather a/c 27/7/44; sal 17/6/45.

42-5892 Del Long Beach 25/4/43; Gore Fd 1/5/43; Kearney 30/5/43; Dow Fd 17/5/43; ass 551BS/385BG Gt Ashfield 18/6/43; MIA Regensburg 17/8/43 w/Keeley, ditched Med Sea, 10RTD. PREGNANT PORTIA.

42-5893 Del Long Beach 24/4/43; Smoky Hill 29/4/43; Tinker 13/5/43; Dow Fd 21/5/43; ass 323BS/91BG [OR-M] Bassingbourn 24/5/43; tran 336BS/95BG [ET-F] Horham 16/6/43; MIA Hannover 26/7/43 w/Robichaud, flak, cr Diepholz, Ger. 2KIA 8POW. MACR 197.

42-5894 Del Long Beach 24/4/43; Salina 30/4/43; Tinker 13/5/43; Dow Fd 23/5/43; ass 8AF 9/6/43; sal n/b/d 16/6/45.

42-5895 Del Long Beach 24/4/43; Gt Falls 3/5/43; Kearney 30/5/43; ass 323BS/91BG [OR-M] Bassingbourn 4/6/43; tran 548BS/385BG Gt Ashfield 16/6/43; then 551BS; MIA Hannover 26/7/43 w/Harris, e/a, cr Nth Sea, 4KIA 6POW. MACR 191B. SOUSE FAMILY.

42-5896 Del Long Beach 27/4/43; Gt Falls 4/5/43; Kearney 30/5/43; Dow Fd 15/6/43; ass 385BG 18/5/43; lost en route UK 28/6/43.

42-5897 Del Long Beach 26/4/43; Gt Falls 4/5/43; Kearney 29/5/43; Denver 4/6/43; Dow Fd 17/6/43; ass 550BS/385BG Gt Ashfield 16/6/43; sal 29/5/45. ROUND TRIP JACK.

42-5898 Del Long Beach 27/4/43; Sioux City 4/5/43; Dow Fd 14/6/43; ass 562BS/388BG Knettishall 17/6/43; MIA Münster 10/10/43 w/Williams, flak, cr Nth Sea, 10POW. MACR 3117. LITTLE LASS.

42-5899 Del Long Beach 27/4/43; Sioux City 4/5/43; Smoky Hill 10/6/43; Dow Fd 15/6/43; ass 560BS/388BG Knettishall 17/6/43; sal 1/8/44. SIOUX CITY QUEEN.

42-5900 Del Long Beach 29/4/43; Sioux City 5/5/43; Smoky 9/6/43; Dow Fd 12/6/43; ass 561BS/388BG Knettishall 14/6/43; sal n/b/d 1/8/44. VIRGIN ON THE VERGE.

42-5901 Del Long Beach 28/4/43; Denver 2/5/43; Tinker 13/5/43; Dow Fd 21/5/43; ass 410BS/94BG [GL-T] Earls Colne 25/5/43; Rougham 13/6/43; MIA Schweinfurt 14/10/43 w/Reed, cr Landa, 1KIA 9POW. MACR 789. SUPERSTITOUS ALOYSIUS.

42-5902 Del Long Beach 30/4/43; Gore Fd 15/5/43; Kearney 29/5/43; Dow Fd 21/6/43; ass 550BS/385BG Gt Ashfield 30/6/43; sal BD 1/12/43. LADY LIZ.

42-5903 Del Long Beach 6/5/43; Geiger 23/6/43; Gt Falls 7/6/43; Dow Fd 10/7/43; ass 571BS/390BG [FC-R] Framlingham 14/7/43; cr Abergavenny, Wales, 24/9/43, sal. MACR 3720. ASCEND CHARLIE.

42-5904 Del Long Beach 29/4/43; Sioux City 4/5/43; Roswell 26/5/43; Smoky Hill 12/6/43; Dow Fd 19/6/43; ass 560BS/388BG Knettishall 18/6/43; BD c/l poor weather Simonsbath, UK 19/9/43; 5KIA 1RTD 4WIA. Sal. GREMLIN GUS.

42-5905 Del Long Beach 26/4/43; Sioux City 7/5/43; Smoky Hill 9/6/43; Dow Fd 30/6/43; ass 561BS/388BG Knettishall 3/7/43; c/l 30/11/43, sal. JUST AG.

42-5906 Del Long Beach 30/4/43; Sioux City 7/5/43; Dow Fd 15/6/43; ass 562BS/388BG Knettishall 16/6/43; BD cr RAF Shobden, UK in poor weather 16/9/43; 10KIA. Sal. MACR 3119. SONDRA KAY.

42-5907 Del Long Beach 29/4/43; Sioux City 19/5/43; Smoky Hill 3/6/43; Dow Fd 6/6/43; ass 563BS/388BG Knettishall 11/6/43; MIA Westrow 25/7/43 w/Fuller, ditched Nth Sea, 10KIA. MACR 3120. WING AND A PRAYER.

42-5908 Del Long Beach 30/4/43; Smoky Hill 6/5/43; Sioux City 19/5/43; Smoky Hill 10/6/43; Presque Is 14/6/43; ass 561BS/388BG Knettishall 16/6/43; MIA 29/7/43 w/Curlings, coll w/42-30370 (96BG), cr Nth Sea, 10KIA. MACR 3069.

42-5909 Del Long Beach 30/4/43; Smoky Hill 6/5/43; Dow Fd 3/6/43; ass 813BS/482BG (H2S) [PC-N] Alconbury 26/6/43; MIA Frankfurt 4/2/44 w/Collis. MACR 3361.

42-5910 Del Long Beach 5/5/43; Denver 11/5/43; Dow Fd 31/5/43; ass 326BS/92BG [JW-N] Alconbury 6/6/43 RUTHIE; tran 365BS/305BG [XK-N] Chelveston 10/6/43 HELL-CAT; then 422BS [JJ-Z/N]; 858BS/8AFCC Cheddington 26/6/44; c/l RAF Hawkinge ex-Romilly 15/9/43; sal 2 SAD Lt Staughton 16/9/43. HOMESICK ANGEL (RUBBER CHECK).

42-5911 Del Long Beach 30/4/43; Gore Fd 9/5/43; Dow Fd 13/6/43; ass 549BS/385BG Gt Ashfield 16/6/43; sal n/b/d 3/9/43. HESITATIN' HUSSY.

42-5912 Del Long Beach 5/5/43; Kearney 25/5/43; Dow Fd 15/6/43; ass 550BS/385BG Gt Ashfield 16/6/43 DIXIE FLYER; tran 94BG RetUS Sheppard 9/5/44; Amarillo 29/6/44; RFC Walnut Ridge 5/1/46. Also ref as LADY SUZIE II, LADY LIZ or THUNDERBIRD.

42-5913 Del Long Beach 5/5/43; Kearney 30/5/43; Dow Fd 19/6/43; ass 551BS/385BG Gt Ashfield 20/6/43; MIA Duren 20/10/43 w/Fryer, mech trouble, cr Namur, Bel, 10POW. MACR 828. SHACK BUNNY.

42-5914 Del Long Beach 5/5/43; Kearney 29/5/43; Dow Fd 16/6/43; ass 549BS/385BG Gt Ashfield 17/6/43; MIA Regensburg 17/8/43 w/Reichardt, e/a, cr Darmstadt, Ger, 10POW. MACR 387B. SACK TIME (ROGER WILCO).

42-5915 Del Long Beach 7/5/43; Geiger 26/5/43; Gt Falls 7/6/43; Dow Fd 13/7/43; ass 570BS/390BG [DI-J] Framlingham 15/7/43; MIA Münster 10/10/43 w/McGuire, e/a, Münster, 10POW. MACR 860. CASH & CARRIE.

42-5916 Del Long Beach 8/5/43; Smoky Hill 21/5/43; Presque Is 31/5/43; ass 325BS/92BG [NV-N] Alconbury 6/6/43; c/l RAF Portreath, UK 7/7/43, sal.

42-5917 Del Long Beach 5/5/43; Kearney 26/5/43; Dow Fd 2/6/43; ass 524BS/379BG [WA-Y] Kimbolton 21/6/43; 526BS [LF-Y]; MIA Hamburg 25/7/43 w/Mohr, e/a, cr Hamburg, 4KIA 6POW. MACR 1767.

42-5918 Del Long Beach 7/5/43; Denver 11/5/43; Smoky Hill 19/5/43; Dow Fd 4/6/43; ass 336BS/95BG [ET-J] Horham 15/6/43; MIA Oschersleben 11/1/44 w/Foley, e/a, cr Osnabrück, 1KIA 9POW. MACR 2010. HEAVENLY DAZE.

42-5919 YB-40 Del Long Beach 8/5/43; Romulus 16/6/43; Presque Is 23/6/43; ass 327BS/92BG [UX-N] Alconbury 28/6/43; tran Bovingdon 22/7/43; retUS Wright Fd MatCom 28/3/44; Dover 17/8/44; Wright 18/10/44; Patterson 21/10/44; Grenier 10/5/45; McChord 24/5/45; Grenier 12/7/45; RFC Kingman 24/1/46.

42-5920 Del Long Beach 2/5/43; YB-40 Tulsa 12/5/43; 2126 BU Buckingham 8/6/44; 2126 BU Laredo 11/6/44; RFC Walnut Ridge 19/12/45.

42-5921 Del Long Beach 2/5/43; YB-40 Tulsa 15/5/43; 333 BU Morris 1/6/44; 35FG Page Fd 5/6/43; 2118 BU Laredo 10/8/44; 2126 BU Laredo 8/9/44; 4121 BU Kelly 22/5/45; 2126 BU Laredo 11/6/45; RFC Walnut Ridge 19/12/45.

42-5922 Del Long Beach 16/5/43; YB-40 Tulsa 21/5/43; 2118 BU Buckingham 4/6/44; 610 BU Eglin 4/9/44; 2114 BU Lockburn 19/11/44; RFC Altus 8/10/45.

42-5923 Del Long Beach 11/5/43; YB-40 Tulsa 16/5/43; 2118 BU Laredo 10/8/44; 2126 BU Laredo 8/9/44; RFC Walnut Ridge 19/12/45.

42-5924 Del Long Beach 12/5/43; YB-40 Tulsa 21/5/43; 2126 BU Laredo 3/6/44; RFC Walnut Ridge 19/12/45.

42-5925 Del Long Beach 13/5/43; YB-40 Tulsa 16/5/43; 2118 BU Laredo 4/7/44; 2126 BU Laredo 8/9/44; RFC Walnut Ridge 19/12/45.

42-5926 Del Long Beach 13/5/43; YB-40 Tulsa 21/5/43; 2137 BU Hendricks 13/10/44; 2518 BU Enid 20/9/45; Recl Comp 13/2/46.

42-5927 Del Long Beach 14/5/43; YB-40 Tulsa 21/5/43; 2126 BU Laredo 11/6/44; 610 BU Eglin 11/7/44; 2118 BU Laredo 12/7/44; RFC Walnut Ridge 19/12/45.

42-5928 Del Long Beach 15/5/43; Roswell 26/5/43; 3030 BU Roswell 2/6/44; 3010 BU Williams 9/12/44; 3020 BU La Junta 27/3/45; RFC Searcey Fd 31/7/45.

42-5929 Del Long Beach 16/5/43; Roswell 25/5/43; Raton NM 5/6/43; Roswell 17/7/43; 30BG Pyote 12/10/43; 4209 BU Des Moines 4/6/44; 224 BU Sioux City 29/7/44; 235 BU Biggs 15/5/45; 556 BU Long Beach 30/8/45; 235 BU Biggs 16/9/45; RFC Kingman 30/10/45.

42-5930 Del Long Beach 16/5/43; Gore Fd 23/5/43; 3030 BU Roswell 2/6/44; 3010 BU Williams 14/12/44; 3020 BU La Junta 4/5/45; RFC Searcey Fd 312/7/45.

42-5931 Del Long Beach 16/5/43; Roswell 26/5/43; Long Beach 28/10/43; 236 BU Pyote 3/9/44; 4208 BU Mines Fd 13/9/44; 235 BU Biggs 16/9/44; 1103 BU Morrison 2/2/45; 203 BU Jackson 23/2/45; RFC Walnut Ridge 14/12/45.

42-5932 Del Long Beach 17/5/43; Roswell 15/5/43; Kelly 5/8/43; Roswell 13/8/43; 242 BU Gr Isle 11/9/44; 2028 BU Galveston 4/10/44; 268 BU Peterson 30/3/45; 1454 BU Minneapolis 7/5/45; 268 BU Peterson 25/5/45; RFC Searcey Fd 11/8/45.

42-5933 Del Long Beach 18/5/43; Roswell 26/5/43; 3030 BU Roswell 2/6/44; 3010 BU Williams 11/12/44; 3020 BU La Junta 26/3/45; RFC Searcey Fd 31/7/45.

42-5934 Del Long Beach 18/5/43; Gore Fd 8/6/43; Sioux City 22/11/43; WO 26/11/43.

42-5935 Del Long Beach 19/5/43; March Fd 10/6/43; Roswell 13/6/43; 246 BU Pratt 14/6/43; WO 14/6/44.

42-5936 Del Long Beach 19/5/43; Roswell 26/5/43; Gore Fd 2/6/43; 3030 BU Roswell 2/6/44; 3036 BU Yuma 19/6/44; 4160 BU Albuquerque 21/7/44; RFC Albuquerque 27/7/45.

42-5937 Del Long Beach 21/5/43; Denver 2/6/43; Morrison 7/6/43; ass 32BS/301BG St Donat 9/6/43; Oudna 6/8/43; Cerignola 7/12/43; Lucera 1/2/44; {32m} MIA Fischamend Markt 17/3/44 w/Turner, cr Zalaegerszeg, 1KIA, 9EVD & RTD. MACR 3200.

42-5938 Del Long Beach 20/5/43; Smoky Hill 29/5/43; Homestead 12/6/43; ass 416BS/99BG Navarin 15/6/43; Oudna 4/8/43; tran 414BS/97BG Depienne 14/11/43; Cerignola 20/12/43; Amendola 16/1/44 MIA Ploesti 5/4/44 w/Howard, flak, cr Zlot. MACR 3966.

42-5939 Del Long Beach 21/5/43; Smoky Hill 1/6/43; Eglin 3/7/43; Dow Fd 9/7/43; ass 342BS/97BG Château-du-Rhumel 19/7/43; Pont-du-Fahs 1/8/43; Depienne 15/8/43; Cerignola 20/12/43; Amendola 16/1/44; trans depot 26/6/44; retUS Morrison 25/6/45; RFC Altus 30/7/45.

42-5940 Del Long Beach 21/5/43; Denver 2/6/43; Morrison 8/6/43; ass 96BS/2BG Château-du-Rhumel 9/6/43; Ain M'Lila 17/6/43; Massicault 31/7/43; {6m} tran 352BS/301BG Oudna 14/11/43; Cerignola 7/12/43; Lucera 1/2/44; {43m w/301} to depot 3/44; cr 8/12/44.

42-5941 Del Long Beach 22/5/43; Smoky Hill 3/6/43; Memphis 20/6/43; Presque Is 2/7/43; ass 49BS/2BG Ain M'Lila 6/7/43; Massicault 31/7/43; {20m} tran 341BS/97BG Depienne 14/11/43; Cerignola 20/12/43; Amendola 16/1/44; cr 18/6/44, sal.

42-5942 Del Long Beach 26/5/43; Denver 4/6/43; Dow Fd 28/6/43; ass 563BS/388BG Knettishall SKY SHY 4/7/43; MIA Stuttgart 6/9/43 w/Bowen, flak, cr Stuttgart, 2KIA 8POW. MACR 3121. WENATCHEE SPECIAL.

42-5943 Del Long Beach 22/5/43; Smoky Hill 1/6/43;

Kearney 30/6/43; Dow Fd 8/7/43; ass 414BS/97BG Château-du-Rhumel 22/7/43; Pont-du-Fahs 1/8/43; Depienne 15/8/43; Cerignola 20/12/43; Amendola 16/1/44; MIA Wiener Nuestadt 23/4/44 w/Lewis; flak, cr near target, MACR 4393.

42-5944 Del Long Beach 28/5/43; Tinker 5/6/43; Presque Is 15/6/43; Orlando 9/7/43; Patterson 19/7/43; ass 419BS/301BG Cerignola 16/12/43; Lucera 1/2/44; {46m} MIA Blechhammer 30/6/44 w/Dodrill, ditched Vis Is, 10RTD.

42-5945 Del Long Beach 28/5/43; Gore Fd 10/6/43; Smoky Hill 23/6/43; Dow Fd 5/7/43; ass 96BS/2BG Massicault 4/8/43; {27m} tran 301BG Oudna 14/11/43; Cerignola 7/12/43; Lucera 1/2/44; sal 8/7/44. DINA-MITE.

42-5946 Del Long Beach 19/5/43; Cheyenne 4/6/43; Kearney 30/6/43; Dow Fd 12/7/43; ass 416BS/99BG Navarin 15/6/43; Oudna 4/8/43; Tortorella 11/12/43; tran 340BS/97BG Depienne 14/11/43; Cerignola 11/12/43; Amendola 16/1/44; MIA Brod 2/7/44 w/Ferro, e/a, cr Komarom. MACR 6617.

42-5947 Del Long Beach 30/5/43; Tinker 22/6/43; Memphis 1/7/43; Morrison 30/7/43; Presque Is 3/8/43; ass 342BS/97BG Pont-du-Fahs 12/8/43; tran 2BG Massicault; {21m w/2} 97BG Amendola as weather a/c 7/44; sal 1/9/43.

42-5948 Del Long Beach 28/5/43; Cheyenne 7/6/43; Gr Isle 29/6/43; Dow Fd 18/7/43; ass 99BG 9/8/43; tran 342BS/97BG Depienne 14/11/43; MIA Innsbruck 19/12/43 w/Dawson. e/a, #2 engine on fire, cr Linz, 4 chutes seen, pilot blown out of a/c, MACR 1520. THUNDERBOLT.

42-5949 Del Long Beach 28/5/43; Cheyenne 7/6/43; Gd Isle 29/6/43; Dow 18/7/43; ass 419BS/301BG Oudna 13/8/43; MIA {15m} Bolzano 25/9/43 w/Stapleton, 10KIA. MACR 767.

42-5950 Del Long Beach 28/5/43; Cheyenne 1/6/43; Dow 7/7/43; ass 410BS/94BG [GL-P] Rougham 12/7/43 MY DEVOTION; MIA Berlin 8/3/44 w/Babington, flak, dropped behind formation, cr Wieste, 10POW. MACR 2997. PETER'S PRIDE.

42-5951 Del Long Beach 30/5/43; Kearney 26/6/43; Dow Fd 14/7/43; ass 353BS/301BG Oudna 12/8/43; Cerignola 7/12/43; {17m} tran 341BS/97BG Depienne; l/Corsica 1/12/43 ex-Turin with 4 WIA; Cerignola 20/12/43; Amendola 16/1/44; MIA Ploesti 23/6/44 w/Symonds, e/a, cr Plovdiv; (cp Kingsley awarded MOH). MACR 6406. O PISSONYA

42-5952 Del Long Beach 30/5/43; Kearney 20/6/43; Dow Fd 14/7/43; ass 97BG Château-du-Rhumel 29/7/43; Pont-du-Fahs 12/8/43; Depienne 15/8/43; Cerignola 20/12/43; Amendola 16/1/44; cr 24/6/44, sal. STOP AND STARE.

42-5953 Del Long Beach 30/5/43; Kearney 10/6/43; Dow Fd 16/7/43; ass 338BS/96BG [BX-Q/G] Snetterton 20/7/43; MIA Keil 4/1/44 w/Davis, coll w/42-35018, cr Gronau, Ger, 4KIA 6POW. MACR 2017. SKIN & BONES.

42-5954 Del Long Beach 30/5/43; Kearney 10/6/43; Dow Fd 7/7/43; ass 562BS/388BG Knettishall 11/7/43; retUS 30/3/44. Sal 4/1/46. MR YANK II.

42-5955 Del Long Beach 30/5/43; Gore Fd 3/7/43; Walla Walla 23/7/43; Cutbank 4/8/43; WO 14/9/43.

42-5956 Del Long Beach 30/5/43; Sebring 30/6/43; Hendricks 20/7/43; 2137 BU Hendricks 3/10/44; RFC Walnut Ridge 18/12/45.

42-5957 Del Long Beach 31/5/43; Gore Fd 5/7/43; Dow Fd 20/7/43; ass 349BS/100BG Thorpe Abbotts 29/7/43; sal 9/5/44. HORNY II.

42-5958 Del Long Beach 31/5/43; Cheyenne 3/6/43; ass 549BS/385BG Gore Fd 8/7/43; Walla Walla 23/7/43; WO 19/4/44. MR SMITH.

42-5959 Del Long Beach 31/5/43; Gored Fd 1/7/43; Pyote 7/7/43; Walla Walla 24/7/43; Avon Park 23/11/43; 2117 BU Buckingham 20/11/44; 4100 BU Patterson 26/11/44; 327 BU Drew 31/3/45; 301 BU Drew 23/9/45; RFC Altus 29/10/45.

42-5960 Del Long Beach 31/5/43; Pyote 1/7/43; Kearney 19/7/43; Spokane 24/7/43; 328 BU Gulfport 11/7/44; 327 BU Drew 9/5/45; RFC Walnut Ridge 19/12/45.

42-5961 Del Long Beach 31/5/43; Cheyenne 3/6/43; Kearney 19/7/43; Walla Walla 26/7/43; 326 BU McDill 11/7/43; 331 BU Barksdale 15/11/43; 325 BU Avon Park 15/7/44; 348 BU Will Rogers 25/7/44; 4119 BU Brookley 11/11/44; 4100 BU Patterson 3/12/44; 331 BU Barksdale 20/2/45; 4200 BU Chicago Mun 31/3/45; 330 BU Dyersburg 26/6/45; 325 BU Avon Park 28/6/45; RFC Walnut Ridge 18/8/45.

42-5962 –

42-5963 Del Long Beach 31/5/43; Cheyenne 6/6/43; Dalhart 3/7/43; Love Fd 16/7/43; Walla Walla 7/10/43; 327 BU Drew 4/5/44; 301 BU Drew 25/9/45; RFC Altus 29/10/45.

42-5964 Del Long Beach 31/5/43; Cheyenne 3/6/43; Pyote 2/7/43; Walla Walla 23/7/43; 4117 BU Robins 3/8/44; 326 BU McDill 26/9/44; 327 BU Drew 29/4/45; 575 BU Pittsburg 2/7/45; 327 BU Drew 9/7/45; RFC Walnut Ridge 18/12/45.

42-5965 Del Long Beach 2/6/43; Walla Walla 5/7/43; Hammer Fd 1/8/43; 3705 BU Lowry 12/6/44; 3701 BU Amarillo 23/7/44; 3706 BU Sheppard 2/5/45; 3701 BU Amarillo 12/9/45; RFC Walnut Ridge 9/10/45.

42-5966 Del Long Beach 1/6/43; Gore 1/7/43; Walla Walla 23/7/43; WO 2/9/43.

42-5967 Del Long Beach 2/6/43; Gore 1/7/43; Walla Walla 23/7/43; Newark 9/10/43; Romulus 20/10/43; Avon Park 4/2/44; Hendricks 10/5/44; Avon Park 23/5/44; RFC Walnut Ridge 18/5/45.

42-5968 Del Long Beach 3/6/43; Rapid City 1/7/43; Walla Walla 23/7/43; 4100 BU Patterson 1/6/44; 225 BU Rapid City 3/6/43; 242 BU Gd Isle 30/8/44; 272 BU Topeka 26/3/45; 225 BU Rapid City 29/4/45; RFC Altus 8/8/45.

42-5969 Del Long Beach 5/6/43; Walla Walla 24/7/43; 4100 BU Patterson 25/1/44; 325 BU Avon Park 1/4/44; RFC Walnut Ridge 20/8/45.

42-5970 Del Long Beach 3/6/43; Gore 3/7/43; Dow Fd 20/7/43; ass 813BS/482BG [PC-T] Alconbury 29/7/43; c/l Eye, Sfk 13/12/43, sal. Re-ass 369BS/306BG [WW-K] Thurleigh 21/4/44; MIA 16/7/44.

42-5971 Long Beach 4/6/43; Dalhart 3/7/43; Walla Walla 16/7/43; 327 BU Drew 8/6/43; 3701 BU Amarillo 17/7/43; 3708 BU Sheppard 20/7/43; 3701 BU Amarillo 8/4/43; RFC Walnut Ridge 9/10/45.

42-5972 Del Long Beach 4/6/43; Gore Fd 3/7/43; Walla Walla 24/7/43; 325 BU Avon Park 9/4/44; RFC Walnut Ridge 20/8/45.

42-5973 Del Long Beach 4/6/43; Gore Fd 28/6/43; Sebring 6/7/43; 2137 BU Hendricks 5/10/44; 2156 BU Enid 20/9/45; RFC Walnut Ridge 27/11/45.

42-5974 Del Long Beach 4/6/43; Gore 28/6/43; Hendricks 9/7/43; 3017 BU Hobbs 15/9/44; 4124 BU Altus 5/7/45; RFC Altus 6/9/45.

42-5975 Del Long Beach 5/6/43; Gore 3/7/43; Walla Walla 23/7/43; 4100 BU Patterson 1/9/44; 327 BU Drew 8/11/44; 301 BU Drew 22/10/45; RFC Altus 5/11/45.

42-5976 Del Long Beach 5/6/43; Gore 6/7/43; Pendleton 24/7/43; Geiger 10/8/43; 457BG Ephrata 5/11/43; 3701 BU Amarillo 17/7/44; 2137 BU Hendricks 13/3/45; RFC Walnut Ridge 14/12/45.

42-5977 Del Long Beach 6/6/43; Roswell 22/6/43; Palm Springs 18/7/43; Pendleton 25/7/43; Kearney 10/8/43; 540BS/383BG Geiger, cr 2/9/43; WO 10/12/43.

42-5978 Del Long Beach 10/6/43; Walla Walla 8/7/43; Pendleton 25/7/43; Kearney 15/9/43; Geiger 20/10/43; Pendleton 2/11/43; 4100 BU Patterson 9/7/44; 497BG Pratt 10/7/44; 233 BU Davis Monthan 12/8/44; 246 BU Pratt 13/9/44; 2132 BU Maxwell 16/3/45; 246 BU Pratt 22/3/45; RFC Altus 9/10/45.

42-5979 Del Long Beach 7/6/43; Gore 5/7/43; Pendleton 24/7/43; Geiger 10/8/43; 540BS/383BG Geiger 27/10/43; 225 BU Rapid City 15/8/44; WO 15/8/44; Recl Comp 2/8/46.

42-5980 Del Long Beach 10/6/43; Denver 16/6/43; Dalhart 2/8/43; 505BG Harvard 16/7/44; 244 BU Harvard 16/9/44; 202 BU Galveston 19/10/44; 268 BU Peterson 30/3/45; RFC Searcey Fd 7/8/45.

42-5981 Del Long Beach 10/6/43; Dalhart 30/7/43; WO 25/9/43.

42-5982 Del Long Beach 10/6/43; Gore 11/7/43; Brooksville 15/7/43; Orlando 20/11/43; 2117 BU Buckingham 23/6/44; 3501 BU Boca Raton 14/7/44; 3539 BU Langley 28/12/44; Recl Comp 6/7/45.

42-5983 Del Long Beach 10/6/43; Gore 6/7/43; Pendleton 24/7/43; Gt Falls 12/8/43; 328 BU Gulfport 15/3/44; Recl Comp 22/3/45.

42-5984 Del Long Beach 11/6/43; Gore Fd 7/7/43; Dow Fd 18/7/43; ass 568BS/390BG [BI-F] Framlingham 20/7/43 RUSTY LODE; sal 10/10/43; re-named BUCKSHOT ANNIE; RFC Altus 9/10/45. BUCKSHOT BLUES.

42-5985 Del Long Beach 11/6/43; Gore 7/7/43; Dow Fd 19/7/43; ass 549BS/385BG Gt Ashfield 20/7/43; MIA Hamburg 20/6/44 w/Montgomery, 1KIA 9POW. MACR 5899.

42-5986 Del Long Beach 15/6/43; Kearney 15/7/43; Dow Fd 20/7/43; ass 334BS/95BG [BG-J] Horham 26/7/43; MIA Münster 10/10/43 w/Riggs, e/a, cr Münster, 3KIA 7POW. MACR 994. BROWN'S MULE.

42-5987 Del Long Beach 7/6/43; Cheyenne 5/7/43; Orlando 17/7/43; Yuma 3/1/44; 231 BU Alamogordo 2/8/44; 4202 BU Syracuse 14/5/45.

42-5988 Del Long Beach 12/6/43; Gore Fd 8/7/43; Brooksville 14/7/43; Orlando 30/11/43; 2114 BU Lockburn 24/10/44; RFC Walnut Ridge 18/12/45.

42-5989 Del Long Beach 14/6/43; Gore Fd 8/7/43; Dow Fd 19/7/43; ass 331BS/94BG [QE-S] Rougham 20/7/43; MIA Emden 27/9/43 w/Haskins, e/a, cr Aurich, Ger, 10KIA. MACR 5674. MARGE H.

42-5990 Del Long Beach 12/6/43; Kearney 15/7/43; 541BS/383BG Pendleton 24/7/43; 3507 BU Sioux Falls 2/8/44; 225 BU Rapid City 10/8/44; 249 BU Alliance 29/12/44; 225 BU Rapid City 7/1/45; RFC Altus 29/8/45.

42-5991 Del Long Beach 15/6/43; New Orleans 14/7/43; Orlando 15/12/43; 331 BU Barksdale 24/6/44; 3036 BU Yuma 5/7/44; 331 BU Barksdale 15/7/44; 2137 BU Hendricks 27/7/44; RFC Walnut Ridge 9/10/45.

42-5992 Del Long Beach 15/6/43; Orlando 12/7/43; Mont Brook 15/8/43; Orlando 28/11/43; 3017 BU Hobbs 6/11/43; RFC Altus 22/8/45.

42-5993 Del Long Beach 15/6/43; Palm Springs 24/7/43; Dyersburg 29/7/43; WO 22/3/44.

42-5994 Del Long Beach 15/6/43; Kearney 15/7/43; Geiger 541BS/383BG 17/8/43; Kearney 10/9/43; 236 BU Pyote 10/9/44; 203 BU Jackson 23/2/45; Cincinnati 23/9/45; RFC Walnut Ridge 14/12/45.

42-5995 Del Long Beach 16/6/43; Kearney 15/7/43;

541BS/383BG Geiger 17/8/43; 243 BU Gt Bend 6/6/44; 4210 BU Lambert 9/6/44; 221 BU Alexandra 24/7/44; 331 BU Barksdale 10/10/44; 223 BU Dyersburg 2/12/44; 330 BU Dyersburg 9/4/45; 325 BU Avon Park 21/6/45; RFC Walnut Ridge 19/8/45.

42-5996 Del Long Beach 17/6/43; Moses lake 25/7/43; 244 BU Harvard 10/6/44; 505BG Harvard 18/6/44; 272 BU Topeka 15/10/44; 330 BU Dyersburg 23/5/45; 325 BU Avon Park 21/6/45; RFC Walnut Ridge 18/8/45.

42-5997 Del Long Beach 16/6/43; Smoky Hill 12/7/43; Dow Fd 16/7/43; ass 351BS/100BG [EP-F/L] Thorpe Abbotts 17/7/43; MIA 30/12/43 w/Smith, e/a, cr Les Rosiers, Fr (?), 8EVD 2POW. MACR 2019. HEAVEN CAN WAIT.

42-5998 Del Long Beach 16/6/43; Love Fd 1/8/43; Las Vegas 8/6/43; Tinker 20/12/43; 2137 BU Hendricks 11/11/44; 200 BU Chicago Mun 24/6/45; 2137 BU Hendricks 25/8/45; RFC Walnut Ridge 18/12/45.

42-5999 Del Long Beach 15/6/43; Las Vegas 1/8/43; Tinker 20/12/43; 3017 BU Hobbs 15/9/44; 3010 BU Williams 5/1/45; 3020 BU La Junta 18/4/45; RFC Searcey Fd 31/7/45.

42-6000 Del Long Beach 17/6/43; Dallas 24/6/43; Kingman 2/8/43; 2117 BU Buckingham 23/6/43; 3501 BU Boca Raton 16/7/44; 3017 BU Hobbs 30/5/45; 3000 BU Orange 8/6/45; 3010 BU Williams 21/7/45; RFC Ontario 21/8/45.

42-6001 Del Long Beach 16/6/43; Gt falls 12/8/43; 4117 BU Robins 9/7/44; WO 21/4/45.

42-6002 Del Long Beach 17/6/43; Love Fd 30/7/43; Las Vegas 7/8/43; Oklahoma City 10/12/43; 2117 BU Buckingham 8/6/44; WO 12/6/44.

42-6003 Del Long Beach 18/6/43; Kingman 2/8/43; 234 BU Clovis 26/6/43; 249 BU Alliance 15/10/44; 460 BU Hamilton 15/7/45; 233 BU Davis Monthan 19/7/43; 1077 BU Bowman 21/10/45; Recl Comp 5/6/46.

42-6004 Del Long Beach 18/6/43; Kingman 1/8/43; 231 BU Alamogordo 2/8/44; 370 BU Keesler 5/2/45; RFC Altus 29/10/45.

42-6005 Del Long Beach 15/6/43; Las Vegas 5/8/43; Tinker 2/12/43; 3030 BU Roswell 16/9/44; 3010 BU Williams 24/11/44; 3020 BU La Junta 18/4/45; RFC Searcey Fd 4/8/45.

42-6006 Del Long Beach 18/6/43; Las Vegas 31/7/43; 231 BU Alamogordo 2/8/44; 4121 BU Kelly 2/11/44; WO 29/11/44; RFC Kingman 24/11/46.

42-6007 Del Long Beach 18/6/43; Las Vegas 31/7/43; Tinker 2/12/43; 2114 BU Lockburn 2/9/44; Vandalia 27/9/44; 4100 BU Patterson 16/1/45; 4142 BU Dayton 20/6/45; Recl Comp 5/6/46.

42-6008 Del Long Beach 19/6/43; Gr Isle 20/7/43; 303BG Pendleton 24/7/43; 457BG Geiger 18/11/43; 4117 BU Robins 27/6/44; 326 BU McDill 6/8/44; 329 BU Alexandra 19/4/45; 325 BU Avon Park 22/6/45; RFC Walnut Ridge 18/8/45.

42-6009 Del Long Beach 19/6/43; Alexandra 25/7/43; 242 BU Gr Isle 8/6/44; 6BG Gr Isle 8/7/44; 249 BU Alliance 12/10/44; 224 BU Sioux City 21/10/44; 235 BU Biggs 12/5/45; 233 BU Davis Monthan 23/10/45; RFC Kingman 30/10/45.

42-6010 Del Long Beach 19/6/43; Pemdleton 24/7/43; Gt Falls 12/8/43; Walla Walla 21/10/43; 505BG Harvard 18/6/44; 146 BU Selfridge 14/8/44; 244 BU Harvard 20/8/44; 232 BU Dalhart 23/8/44; 203 BU Jackson 8/3/45; Recl Comp 2/4/45.

42-6011 Del Long Beach 20/6/43; Walla Walla 26/7/43; Pendleton 2/11/43; 236 BU Pyote 10/9/44; 244 BU Harvard 10/1/45; 202 BU Galveston 15/2/45; 244 BU Harvard 20/2/45; 4006 BU Miami 14/4/45; 244 BU Harvard 28/4/45; RFC Altus 9/10/45.

42-6012 Del Long Beach 21/6/43; Alexandra 26/7/43; cr 4 mls E Rocklands, Tex, w/Flaherty (381BG) 13/8/43; fire in 3 engines, all baled OK. WO.

42-6013 Del Long Beach 20/6/43; Dallas 25/6/43; Lewiston 10/8/43; WO 4/1/44.

42-6014 Del Long Beach 20/6/43; Dallas 25/6/43; Kingman 9/8/43; Yuma 30/3/44; 231 BU Alamogordo 2/8/44; 4202 BU Syracuse 14/5/45; RFC Walnut Ridge 19/12/45.

42-6015 Del Long Beach 22/6/43; Kingman 8/8/43; 2117 BU Buckingham 16/6/44; 2114 BU Lockburn 5/8/44; RFC Walnut Ridge 14/12/45.

42-6016 Del Long Beach 24/6/43; Kingman 8/8/43; 231 BU Alamogordo 2/8/44; 203 BU Jackson 31/1/45; RFC Walnut Ridge 14/12/45.

42-6017 Del Long Beach 23/6/43; Gt Falls 16/8/43; WO 14/1/44.

42-6018 Del Long Beach 24/6/43; Cheyenne 21/7/43; Alexandra 26/7/43; WO 18/10/43.

42-6019 Del Long Beach 24/6/43; Walla Walla 25/7/43; Redmond 15/8/43; WO 20/8/43.

42-6020 Del Long Beach 24/6/43; Walla Walla 25/7/43; Redmond 15/8/43; 4104 BU Rome 21/10/44; 611 BU Eglin 9/6/45; 621 BU Pinecastle 1/8/44; 611 BU Eglin 19/9/45; 2137 BU Hendricks 25/11/45; RFC Walnut Ridge 5/1/46.

42-6021 Del Long Beach 24/6/43; Alexandra 27/7/43; Brookley 12/8/43; Pyote 25/10/43; 245 BU McCook 9/6/44; 3705 BU Lowry 20/8/44; 9BG McCook 1/9/44; 232 BU Dalhart 7/10/44; 248 BU Walker 21/1/45; 4208 BU Mines Fd 10/2/45; 2132 BU Maxwell 10/3/45; 248 BU Walker 11/6/45; 3505 BU Scott 24/6/45; 4180 BU Walker 1/10/45; RFC Walnut Ridge 13/12/45.

42-6022 Del Long Beach 24/6/43; Alexandria 25/7/43; 241 BU Fairmont 6/9/44; 504BG Fairmont 10/9/44; 273 BU Lincoln 25/1/45; 241 BU Fairmont 16/3/45; RFC Altus 28/7/45.

42-6023 Del Long Beach 25/6/43; Walla Walla 26/7/43; Pendleton 28/10/43; 245 BU McCook 4/6/44; 9BG McCook 28/8/44; 3705 BU Lowry 16/10/44; WO 6/11/44; 3704 BU Keesler 20/3/45; Recl Comp 3/4/46.

42-6024 Del Long Beach 25/6/43; Walla Walla 25/7/43; Redmond 15/8/43; 328 BU Gulfport 14/11/44; 4119 BU Brookley 21/11/44; 2116 BU Napier 16/1/45; 328 BU Gulfport 15/2/45; 327 BU Drew 9/5/45; RFC Walnut Ridge 18/12/45.

42-6025 Del Long Beach 25/6/43; Walla Walla 22/7/43; Lewiston 2/8/43; c/l 8 m NE Roy, Mont, w/Bill Pridmore 7/9/43; 6 pass, 5 minor injs, 5 chutes OK; WO 21/9/43.

42-6026 Del Long Beach 26/6/43; Walla Walla 22/7/43; 328 BU Gulfport 8/3/44; WO 2/9/44.

42-6027 Del Long Beach 24/6/43; Cheyenne 5/7/43; Redmond 10/12/43; McDill 14/1/44; 4000 BU Patterson 23/7/44; 326 BU McDill 13/11/44; 327 BU Drew 14/4/45; RFC Walnut Ridge 7/12/45.

42-6028 Del Long Beach 26/6/43; Cheyenne 25/7/43; Alexandria 7/8/43; 236 BU Pyote 10/9/43; 203 BU Jackson 23/2/45; RFC Walnut Ridge 14/12/45.

42-6029 Del Long Beach 26/6/43; Walla Walla 24/7/43; 452BG Pendleton 26/10/43; 236 BU Pyote 10/9/44; 3010 BU Williams 29/11/44; 236 BU Pyote 21/12/44; Recl Comp 17/4/45.

42-6030 Del Long Beach 28/6/43; Cheyenne 2/7/43; Lowry 28/7/43; Dalhart 10/11/43; 244BU Harvard 10/6/44; 505BG Harvard 16/6/44; 232 BU Dalhart 23/8/44; 203 BU Jackson 21/1/45; RFC Walnut Ridge 14/12/45.

42-6031 Del Long Beach 29/6/43; Palm Springs 1/7/43; Alexandria 30/7/43; WO 11/9/43.

42-6032 Del Long Beach 29/6/43; Cheyenne 11/7/43; Burbank 6/8/43; Lewiston 14/8/43; 505BG Harvard 2/6/44; 244 BU Harvard 7/8/44; 4100 BU Patterson 10/8/44; 223 BU Dyersburg 5/11/44; WO 13/11/44.

42-6033 Del Long Beach 29/6/43; Amarillo 8/7/43; Dallas 10/8/43; Sioux City 11/11/43; 504BG Fairmont 14/8/44; 241 BU Fairmont 19/9/44; 2512 BU Childress 10/11/44; Recl Comp 7/8/46.

42-6034 Del Long Beach 30/6/43; Amarillo 3/7/43; Love Fd 9/8/43; 4117 BU Robins 3/7/44; 328 BU Gulfport 27/8/44; 325 BU Avon Park 9/5/45; RFC Walnut Ridge 18/8/45.

42-6035 Del Long Beach 29/6/43; Amarillo 11/7/43; Dallas 10/8/43; 242 BU Gr Isle 23/6/44; 6BG Gd Isle 8/7/44; 9AF Spec Project 18/8/44; 244 BU Harvard 10/10/44; 242 BU Gd Isle 16/10/44; 268 BU Peterson 18/10/44; 2116 BU Napier 19/1/45; RFC Altus 28/7/45.

42-6036 Del Long Beach 30/6/43; Amarillo 7/7/43; Dallas 9/8/43; 4100 BU Patterson 27/1/44; modified to XC-108 as taxi for Gen Frank Hackett 10AF Bengal, India; retUS 4/2/45; RFC Augusta 25/11/46; ass ATC Europe 30/4/47, probably at Oberpfaffenhofen, Germany.

42-6037 Del Long Beach 30/6/43; Amarillo 3/7/43; Love Fd 9/8/43; Dallas 10/8/43; ass 331BS/94BG [QE-P] Rougham 9/10/43; MIA Cognac 31/12/43, e/a, MACR 1755.

42-6038 Del Long Beach 29/6/43; Palm Springs 6/7/43; Dallas 9/8/43; Scott 25/9/43; McDill 15/12/43; Chanute 7/1/44; 326 BU McDill 22/10/44; 325 BU Avon Park 5/5/45; RFC Walnut Ridge 17/9/45.

42-6039 Del Long Beach 30/6/43; Amarillo 18/7/43; Dallas 9/8/43; ass 334BS/95BG [BG-H] Horham 14/10/43; MIA 29/11/43 w/Palmer, s/d by e/a cr/Cloppenburg, Ger, IKIA 9POW. MACR 1560.

42-6040 Del Long Beach 30/6/43; Amarillo 3/7/43; Dallas 8/8/43; 4154 BU Spokane 4/6/44; 9BG McCook 18/6/44; 235 BU Biggs 22/7/44; RFC Altus 5/11/45.

42-6041 Del Long Beach 30/6/43; Amarillo 3/7/43; Dallas 9/8/43; 441 BU Glendale 4/6/44; 497BG Pratt 7/6/44; 246 BU Pratt 29/6/44; 232 BU Dalhart 9/7/44; 202 BU Galveston 7/12/44; 222 BU Ardmore 28/3/45; 3505 BU Scott 6/4/45; 4202 BU Syracuse 24/4/45; RFC Walnut Ridge 18/12/45.

42-6042 Del Burbank 2/7/43; Dallas 8/8/43; cr 18/10/43 w/Creamer, hit mountain nr Rapid City, SD. WO 21/10/43.

42-6043 Del Long Beach 4/7/43; Geiger 29/7/43; Gt Falls 5/8/43; Kearney 5/10/43; 245 BU McCook 3/6/44; 9BG McCook 11/9/44; 3705 BU Lowry 16/10/44; WO 6/11/44; RFC Altus 24/9/45.

42-6044 Del Long Beach 2/7/43; Dalhart 20/7/43; 4115 BU Atlanta 16/6/44; 6BG Gd Isle 8/7/44; 242 BU Gd Isle 16/9/44; 202 BU Galveston 3/10/44; 902 BU Orlando WO 27/10/44; 446 BU Orlando 31/10/46; Recl Comp 29/5/47.

42-6045 Del Long Beach 4/7/43; Pendleton 26/7/43; Lewiston 4/8/43; 541BS/383BG Geiger 22/10/43; WO 17/11/43.

42-6046 Del Long Beach 2/7/43; Pendleton 24/7/43; Geiger 17/8/43; Kearney 15/9/43; Geiger 23/9/43; 326 BU McDill 18/1/45; 331 BU Barksdale 19/1/45; 325 BU Avon Park 19/5/45; RFC Walnut Ridge 17/9/45.

42-6047 Del Long Beach 5/7/43; Pendleton 24/7/43; Geiger 17/8/43; 500BG Walker 8/8/44; 248 BU Walker 30/9/44; 2132 BU Maxwell 8/10/44; 248 BU Walker 8/11/44; 552 BU Pinecastle 10/11/44; 2528 BU Midland 23/1/45; 2509 BU Big Spring 3/2/45; RFC Walnut Ridge 10/1/46.

42-6048 Del Long Beach 4/7/43; Pendleton 26/7/43; Kearney 4/10/43; Geiger 18/11/43; 241 BU Fairmont 27/12/44; 2113 BU Columbus 19/3/45; 241 BU Fairmont 1/5/45; RFC Altus 28/7/45.

42-6049 Del Long Beach 7/7/43; Burbank 6/8/43; Gt Falls 15/8/43; WO 19/5/44.

42-6050 Del Long Beach 6/7/43; Orlando 24/12/43; El Paso 2/1/44; 2117 BU Buckingham 16/7/44; 2114 BU Lockburn 10/8/44; 1077 BU Bowman 26/2/45; 2114 BU Lockburn 14/8/45; RFC Walnut Ridge 28/12/45.

42-6051 Del Long Beach 6/7/43; Dalhart 20/7/43; 241 BU Fairmont 14/9/44; 249 BU Alliance 17/10/44; 299 BU Smoky Hill 29/1/45; 203 BU Jackson 3/2/45; 902 BU Orlando 14/2/45; Special Project 22/7/45; 290 BU Sioux City 5/8/45; WO 5/46.

42-6052 Del Long Beach 6/7/43; Pendleton 24/7/43; Geiger 11/8/43; Walla Walla 18/11/43; 497BG Pratt 8/8/44; 232 BU Dalhart 24/8/44; 331 BU Barksdale 29/10/44; 247 BU Smoky Hill 5/4/45; RFC Altus 30/7/45.

42-6053 Del Long Beach 6/7/43; Pendleton 25/7/43; Sioux City 30/11/43; WO 25/3/44.

42-6054 Del Long Beach 7/7/43; Dalhart 20/7/43; 3007 BU Kirtland 28/7/44; 231 BU Alamogordo 7/8/44; 3009 BU Carlsbad 25/11/44; 3010 BU Williams 3/2/45; 3020 BU La Junta 20/4/45; RFC Stillwater 24/8/45.

42-6055 Del Long Beach 7/7/43; Walla Walla 24/7/43; 4100 BU Patterson 26/10/44; 328 BU Gulfport 31/3/45; 2137 BU Hendricks 10/5/45; 325 BU Avon Park 23/5/45; RFC Walnut Ridge 19/7/45.

42-6056 Del Long Beach 7/7/43; Alexandria 25/7/43; 2509 BU Big Spring 19/7/43; 236 BU Pyote 25/7/44; 235 BU Biggs 30/7/44; 4202 BU Syracuse 8/4/45; RFC Altus 5/11/45.

42-6057 Del Long Beach 9/7/43; Patterson 24/7/43; 4000 BU Patterson 2/8/44; 4100 BU Patterson 19/9/44; 4121 BU Kelly 10/10/44; 4006 BU Miami 25/11/44; 4000 BU Patterson 4/2/45; RFC Walnut Ridge 5/12/45.

42-6058 Del Long Beach 8/7/43; Cheyenne 12/7/43; Walla Walla 23/7/43; WO 3/1/44.

42-6059 Del Long Beach 8/7/43; Gr Isle 20/7/43; Pendleton 25/7/43; Geiger 10/8/43; WO 28/2/44.

42-6060 Del Long Beach 8/7/43; Cheyenne 12/7/43; Tinker 12/10/43; 2114 BU Lockburn 14/8/44; RFC Walnut Ridge 19/12/45.

42-6061 Del Long Beach 8/7/43; Walla Walla 25/7/43; WO 13/9/43.

42-6062 Del Long Beach 8/7/43; Walla Walla 20/7/43; Lewiston 4/8/43; WO 21/9/43.

42-6063 Del Long Beach 10/7/43; Cheyenne 12/7/43; Tinker 12/10/43; 2114 BU Lockburn 14/8/44; RFC Walnut Ridge 14/12/45.

42-6064 Del Long Beach 9/7/43; Dalhart 23/7/43; Albuquerque 12/10/43; WO 30/11/43.

42-6065 Del Long Beach 10/7/43; Cheyenne 24/7/43; 2AF HQ Peterson 29/11/43; 500BG Pinecastle 26/6/44; 901 BU Pinecastle 28/6/44; 500BG Walker 29/6/44; 271 BU Kearney 7/9/44; 275 BU Lincoln 10/10/44; 223 BU Dyersburg 24/11/44; 330 BU Dyersburg 1/3/45; 325 BU Avon Park 21/6/45; RFC Walnut Ridge 19/7/45.

42-6066 Del Long Beach 9/7/43; Ephrata 1/8/43; 3701 BU Amarillo 23/7/44; 3706 BU Sheppard 20/10/44; 3701 BU Amarillo 2/5/45; RFC Walnut Ridge 21/1/46.

42-6067 Del Long Beach 10/7/43; Alexandria 25/7/43; 235 BU Biggs 28/7/44; WO 18/9/44; 369 BU Biggs 1/9/45; Recl Comp 3/8/46.

42-6068 Del Long Beach 13/7/43; Cheyenne 15/7/43; 9BG McCook 9/6/44; 245 BU McCook 16/9/44; 4100 BU Patterson 13/12/44; 233 BU Davis Monthan 16/3/45; RFC Altus 18/9/45.

42-6069 Del Long Beach 13/7/43; 393BG Sioux City 11/11/43; 326 BU McDill 18/1/45; 331 BU Barksdale 20/1/45; 325 BU Avon Park 19/5/45; RFC Walnut Ridge 19/8/45.

42-6070 Del Long Beach 13/7/43; Cheyenne 17/7/43; 303 BU Roswell 2/6/44; 3021 BU Las Vegas 28/11/44; 3010 BU Williams 11/12/44; 4160 BU Lockburn 2/8/45; RFC Albuquerque 2/8/45.

42-6071 Del Long Beach 13/7/43; Cheyenne 18/7/43; 245 BU McCook 9/6/44; 9BG McCook 17/6/44; 4210 BU Lambert 13/1/45; 245 BU McCook 27/1/45; Recl Comp 2/4/45.

42-6072 Del Long Beach 13/7/43; Cheyenne 18/7/43; 3014 DU Douglas 17/6/44; 236 BU Pyote 24/6/44; 245 BU McCook 16/1/45; RFC Altus 9/10/45.

42-6073 Del Long Beach 13/7/43; Cheyenne 17/7/43; 248 BU Walker 4/6/44; 232 BU Dalhart 11/7/44; 248 BU Walker 25/1/45; 4112 BU Olmstead 23/7/45; 248 BU Walker 5/8/45; RFC Santa Maria 22/9/45. US Civil S/No.7942 A; cr Trinidad, Bolivia 4/11/65 (CP-686).

42-6074 Del Long Beach 13/7/43; Cheyenne 16/7/43; Tinker 14/12/43; 3017 BU Hobbs 14/9/44; RFC Altus 28/8/45.

42-6075 Del Long Beach 14/7/43; 232 BU Dalhart 9/6/44; 3505 BU Scott 17/8/44; 3017 BU Hobbs 25/9/44; 4124 BU Long Beach 10/7/45; RFC Altus 24/8/45.

42-6076 Del Long Beach 14/7/43; Cheyenne 17/7/43; 3030 BU Roswell 2/6/44; 3010 BU Williams 11/12/44; 3020 BU La Junta 18/4/45; RFC Searcey Fd 4/8/45.

42-6077 Del Long Beach 16/7/43; Cheyenne 18/7/43; 330 BU Dyersburg 1/3/44; 325 BU Avon Park 21/6/44; RFC Walnut Ridge 17/9/45.

42-6078 Del Long Beach 15/7/43; Cheyenne 17/7/43; 9BG McCook 9/6/44; 4136 BU Tinker 25/8/44; 245 BU McCook 2/9/44; RFC Kingman 16/10/45.

42-6079 Del Long Beach 16/7/43; Cheyenne 12/8/43; Ft Myers 14/11/43; 3036 BU Yuma 1/10/44; RFC Albuquerque 27/7/45.

42-6080 Del Long Beach 15/7/43; Cheyenne 18/7/43; (Fitted with Sperry gyroscope); ass 336BS/95BG [ET-P] Horham 3/9/43; tran 36BS Alconbury (RCM) as Aphrodite a/c 23/3/44; also Harrington for Carpetbagger ops; retUS Bolling 11/2/45; RFC Kingman 19/2/46. MARY RUTH - THE WE WA SPECIAL.

42-6081 Del Long Beach 16/7/43; Cheyenne 20/7/43; Ft Myers 14/11/43; 2137 BU Hendricks 23/11/44; RFC Walnut Ridge 19/12/45.

42-6082 Del Long Beach 16/7/43; c/l 6mls NE Gulfport 26/8/43; WO 7/9/43.

42-6083 Del Long Beach 17/7/43; Cheyenne 20/7/43; Ft Myers 14/11/43; 9BG McCook 7/6/44; 2121 BU Keesler 9/6/44; Mat Com Lockheed Burbank 24/6/44; 3704 BU Keesler 1/8/45; Recl Comp 3/8/45.

42-6084 Del Long Beach 16/7/43; Cheyenne 19/7/43; Tinker 2/12/43; 3501 BU Boca Raton 16/7/44; 2137 BU Hendricks 17/10/44; RFC Walnut Ridge 11/1/46.

42-6085 Del Long Beach 16/7/43; Cheyenne 20/7/43; WO 24/2/44.

42-6086 Del Long Beach 16/7/43; Cheyenne 20/7/43; 94 Sub Dep Scott 30/9/44; ass 323BS/91BG [OR-P] Bassingbourn 21/10/43; tran 401BS [LL-P]; MIA Leverkusen 1/12/43 w/Weiby, flak, cr Leutesdorf, Ger, 10KIA. MACR 1322.

42-6087 Del Long Beach 18/7/43; Cheyenne 19/7/43; ass 418BS/100BG [LD-Z] Thorpe Abbotts 5/9/43; flak hit Mulhouse 11/8/44 w/Aske, c/l Mendon (?), 4KIA 5POW. MACR 8074. ROYAL FLUSH.

42-6088 Del Long Beach 18/7/43; Cheyenne 20/7/43; Sioux City 13/12/43; 244 BU Harvard 9/6/44; 505BG Harvard 17/6/44; 235 BU Biggs 22/7/44; 299 BU Smoky Hill 29/1/45; 203 BU Jackson 24/2/45; 290 BU Sioux City 29/4/45; RFC Walnut Ridge 5/9/45.

42-6089 Del Long Beach 17/7/43; Cheyenne 21/7/43; 242 Gd Isle 17/10/44; 224 BU Sioux City 28/10/44; 235 BU Biggs 15/5/45; 441 BU Metropolitan 31/8/45; Recl Comp 25/10/45.

42-6090 Del Long Beach 18/7/43; Cheyenne 20/7/43; WO 14/10/43.

42-6091 Del Long Beach 18/7/43; Cheyenne 22/7/43; 247 BU Smoky Hill 9/6/44; 273 BU Lincoln 12/8/44; 247 BU Smoky Hill 30/8/44; 235 BU Biggs 6/10/44; 4202 BU Syracuse 3/4/45; 593 BU Charleston 28/10/45; RFC Altus 7/11/45.

42-6092 Del Long Beach 20/7/43; Cheyenne 22/7/43; Dyersburg 1/9/43; 4100 BU Patterson 3/8/44; 326 BU McDill 29/10/44; 327 BU Drew 18/5/45; RFC Walnut Ridge 18/12/45.

42-6093 Del Long Beach 20/7/43; Cheyenne 23/7/43; 202 BU Galveston 18/6/44; 4200 Chicago Mun 6/8/44; Fairfax 21/8/44; 202 BU Galveston 10/10/44; 222 BU Ardmore 23/2/45; 4202 BU Syracuse 1/4/45; RFC Walnut Ridge 12/12/45.

42-6094 Del Long Beach 20/7/43; Cheyenne 23/7/43; Dalhart 17/8/43; Eglin 10/10/43; ass 418BS/100BG [LD-Q] Thorpe Abbotts 6/9/43; c/l base 27/12/43 non-ops; sal 31/1/44.

42-6095 Del Long Beach 21/7/43; Cheyenne 23/7/43; 248 BU Walker 2/6/44; 4136 BU Tinker 28/6/44; 232 BU Dalhart 4/9/44; 241 BU Fairmont 21/10/44; 203 BU Jackson 21/1/45; RFC Walnut Ridge 19/12/45.

42-6096 Del Long Beach 21/7/43; Cheyenne 23/7/43; Gr Island 3/9/43; ass 511BS/351BG [DS-W] Polebrook 22/9/43; MIA Schweinfurt 14/10/43 w/Crimson, e/a, cr Schweinfurt, 1KIA 9POW. MACR 1036. ONDA BALL.

42-6097 Del Long Beach 21/7/43; Cheyenne 23/7/43; ass 339BS/96BG [QJ-O] Snetterton 12/9/43; used as 3AD trainer; retUS Bradley 9/7/44; RFC Albuquerque 13/8/45. THE BAD PENNY (RED HOT RIDING HOOD).

42-6098 Del Long Beach 22/7/43; Cheyenne 25/7/43; Gr Island 3/9/43; ass 335BS/95BG [OE-R] Horham; MIA Keil 4/1/44 w/Milward; ditched off Bawdsey, Sfk. 10RTD. SUPERSTITIOUS ALOYSIUS

42-6099 Del Long Beach 22/7/43; Palm Springs 23/7/43; Cheyenne 25/7/43; Dalhart 15/8/43; ass 337BS/96BG Snetterton 9/9/43 RUTH L; tran 339BS [QJ-R]; MIA Oranienburg 22/3/44 w/Young; hit by bomb from a/c above, cr Falkenhoehe, 6KIA 4POW. MACR 3420. WINNIE C.

42-6100 Del Long Beach 22/7/43; Amarillo 24/7/43; Dallas 10/8/43; 497BG Pratt 8/8/44; 246 BU Pratt 6/9/44; 222 BU Ardmore 6/10/44; 332 BU Ardmore 16/5/45; RFC Walnut Ridge 20/8/45.

42-6101 Del Long Beach 22/7/43; Amarillo 25/7/43; Dallas 10/8/43; Sioux City 26/11/43; Tinker 6/12/43; ass RCAF (as No. 9203) 168th Heavy Trans Sq, Rockcliffe, Ont. mail and VIPs to Prestwick, UK. MIA Rabat, Alg, en route Azores 25/12/43.

42-6102 Del Long Beach 21/7/43; Amarillo 24/7/43; Dallas 10/8/43; 505BG Harvard 2/6/44; 244 BU Harvard 5/8/44; 249 BU Alliance 20/9/44; 4119 BU Brookley 17/1/45; 243 Gr Bend 23/1/45; 4126 BU San Bernadino 1/3/45; 243 BU Gr Bend 9/8/45; RFC Kingman 27/10/45.

42-6103 Del Long Beach 22/7/43; Amarillo 24/7/43;

Dallas 9/8/43; WO 14/5/44.

42-6104 Del Long Beach 22/7/43; Amarillo 28/7/43; Dallas 9/8/43; 202 BU Galveston 9/6/44; 498BG Gr Bend 10/6/44; 232 BU Dalhart 20/7/44; 4104 BU Rome 10/12/44; 4168 Sth Plains 27/6/45; RFC Kingman 3/11/45.

42-6105 Del Long Beach 28/7/43; Dallas 9/8/43; 901 BU Pinecastle 10/6/44; 9BG McCook 5/7/44; 245 BU McCook 16/9/44; 233 BU Davis Monthan 27/2/45; RFC Altus 4/10/45.

42-6106 –

42-6107 Del Long Beach 24/7/43; Denver 17/8/43; Dalhart 25/10/43; 202 BU Galveston 20/7/44; 554 BU Memphis 15/11/44; 222 BU Ardmore 23/2/45; 4202 BU Syracuse 30/3/45; RFC Altus 7/11/45. Fitted with Rolls-Royce turbo-prop engines as US civil N 1340 N; used as tanker, cr/Dubois, Wyo 18/8/70.

42-6108 Del Long Beach 27/7/43; Denver 16/8/43; WO 15/4/44.

42-6109 Del Long Beach 24/7/43; Denver 17/8/43; 202 BU Galveston 2/8/44; 225 BU Rapid City 23/2/45; 4202 BU Syracuse 29/3/45; RFC Altus 29/10/45.

42-6110 Del Long Beach 28/7/43; Denver 16/8/43; 242 BU Gr Isle 2/6/44; 6BG Gr Isle 8/7/44; 202 BU Galveston 3/10/44; 4100 BU Patterson 11/1/45; 202 BU Galveston 22/3/45; 268 BU Peterson 30/3/45; RFC Searcey Fd 7/8/45.

42-6111 Del Long Beach 24/7/43; Denver 16/8/43; 246 BU Pratt 4/6/44; 232 BU Dalhart 9/7/44; WO 24/10/44; 3701 BU Amarillo 24/12/44; Recl Comp 7/6/46.

42-6112 Del Long Beach 25/7/43; Amarillo 30/7/43; Denver 17/8/43; 499BG Smoky Hill 9/6/44; WO 16/6/44.

42-6113 Del Long Beach 30/7/43; Dallas 1/8/43; 242 BU Gr Isle 23/6/44; 6BG Gr isle 7/8/44; 202 BU Galveston 4/10/44; 224 BU Sioux City 23/2/45; 4202 BU Syracuse 27/4/45; RFC Altus 29/10/45.

42-6114 Del Long Beach 25/7/43; Dallas 31/7/43; 3108 BU Kingman 18/6/44; 4100 BU Patterson 21/9/44; 3017 BU Hobbs 30/11/44; 4210 BU Lambert 29/1/45; 3017 BU Hobbs 10/2/45; RFC Altus 11/9/45.

42-6115 Del Long Beach 27/7/43; Dallas 30/7/43; 3017 BU Hobbs 8/11/44; RFC Altus 28/8/45.

42-6116 Del Long Beach 28/7/43; Dallas 31/7/43; 4119 BU Brookley 23/10/44; 223 BU Dyersburg 9/12/44; 330 BU Dyersburg 1/3/45; 325 BU Avon Park 21/6/45; RFC Walnut Ridge 18/8/45.

42-6117 Del Long Beach 27/7/43; Dallas 31/7/43; WO 15/4/44.

42-6118 Del Long Beach 28/7/43; Dallas 1/8/43; WO 9/7/44.

42-6119 Del Long Beach 28/7/43; Dallas 31/7/43; 2117 BU Buckingham 30/6/44; 3017 BU Hobbs 14/9/44; 3010 BU Williams 5/1/45; 3020 BU La Junta 20/4/45; RFC Searcey Fd 4/8/45.

42-6120 Del Long Beach 28/7/43; Dallas 1/8/43; 234 BU Clovis 24/6/44; 268 BU Peterson 27/12/44; 234 BU Clovis 3/2/45; 4202 BU Syracuse 1/4/45; 268 BU Peterson 30/4/45; RFC Walnut Ridge 9/1/46.

42-6121 Del Long Beach 29/7/43; Dallas 312/7/43; 242 BU Gr Isle 23/6/44; 6BG gr Isle 12/7/44; 421 BU Muroc 2/10/44; 242 BU Gr Isle 24/10/44; RFC Altus 30/7/45.

42-6122 Del Long Beach 28/7/43; Dallas 3/8/43; WO 28/3/44.

42-6123 Del Long Beach 29/7/43; Dallas 1/8/43; 393BG Sioux City 21/12/43; 242 BU Gr Isle 23/6/44; 6BG Gr Isle 8/7/44; 272 BU Topeka 2/8/44; 9BG Gr Isle 6/8/44; 4119 BU Brookley 6/11/44; 242 BU Gr Isle 15/11/44; RFC Kingman 28/10/45.

42-6124 Del Long Beach 29/7/43; Dallas 3/8/43; 242 BU Gr Isle 23/6/44; 9BG Gr Isle 8/7/44; 563 BU Homestead 10/2/45; 242 BU Gr Isle 9/9/45; RFC Kingman 29/10/45.

42-6125 Del Long Beach 30/7/43; Dallas 2/8/43; 3501 BU Boca Raton 16/7/44; 3704 BU Keesler 11/4/45; 3501 BU Boca Raton 20/9/45; 2137 BU Hendricks 17/10/45; RFC Walnut Ridge 4/1/46.

42-6126 Del Long Beach 30/7/43; Dallas 2/8/43; 4119 BU Brookley 21/6/44; 223 BU Dyersburg 16/1/45; Recl Comp 29/1/45.

42-6127 Del Long Beach 30/7/43; Dallas 4/8/43; Dyersburg 4/10/43; Dalhart 19/10/43; 247 BU Smoky Hill 3/6/44; 232 BU Dalhart 10/7/44; 4121 BU Kelly 2/11/44; 224 BU Sioux City 1/12/44; 235 BU Biggs 12/5/45; 555 BU Love Fd 3/10/45; RFC Biggs 1/4/46.

42-6128 Del Long Beach 30/7/43; Denver 17/8/43; 498BG Gr Bend 1/7/44; 243 BU Gr Bend 20/9/44; 3701 BU Amarillo 24/1/45; Recl Comp 7/6/46.

42-6129 Del Long Beach 31/7/43; Denver 16/8/43; (F-9) Ass Min Map Asia 1/4/44; WO 1/6/46.

42-6130 Del Long Beach 1/8/43; Denver 17/8/43; 498BG Smoky Hill 9/8/44; 247 BU Smoky Hill 19/9/44; RFC Altus 9/10/45.

42-6131 Del Long Beach 1/8/43; Denver 16/8/43; 221 BU Alexandria, WO 24/9/44.

42-6132 Del Long Beach 30/7/43; Dallas 8/8/43; 247 BU Smoky Hill 12/7/44; 4119 BU Brookley 2/2/45; 247 BU Smoky Hill 14/3/45; Recl Comp 20/11/45.

42-6133 Del Long Beach 1/8/43; Denver 3/8/43; 19BG Pyote 9/11/43; 2519 BU Fort Worth 19/9/44; 236 BU Pyote 4/10/44; 3704 BU Keesler 12/1/45; 235 BU Biggs 3/4/45; 4117 BU Robins 11/4/45; Recl Comp 20/4/45. **42-6134** Del Long Beach 3/8/43; Denver 4/8/43; (F-9) Ass Min Map Asia 1/4/44; retUS Bradley 13/6/44; RFC Altus 4/10/45.

42-6135 Del Long Beach 3/8/43; 3705 BU Lowry /44; Recl Comp 18/9/47.

42-6136 Del Long Beach 1/8/43; Denver 4/8/43; 225 BU Rapid City 24/4/44; RFC Altus 29/8/45.

42-6137 Del Long Beach 3/8/43; Denver 5/8/43; 242 BU Gr Isle 6/9/44; 235 BU Biggs 7/10/44; 233 BU Davis Monthan 28/3/45; 283 BU Galveston 14/6/45; RFC Kingman 31/10/45.

42-6138 Del Long Beach 3/8/43; Denver 6/8/43; (F-9) Ass Accra, Gold Coast (Jogo) Mapping Mission 29/2/44; retUS 4100 BU Patterson 12/5/44; 19 Photo Gp McDill 12/8/44; sal French-Holland coast (Wipe) 18/11/46.

42-6139 Del Long Beach 3/8/43; Denver 6/8/43; 498BG Gr Bend 4/8/44; 110 BU Mitchell 12/9/44; 243 BU Gr Bend 20/9/44; WO 5/10/44; Recl Comp 2/1/45.

42-6140 Del Long Beach 4/8/43; Denver 6/8/43; 1 Photo Gp McDill 9/10/43; 4104 BU Rome 27/10/43; 9 Photo Gp Buckley 18/12/43; Malta and Africa; retUS 9/10/44; sal Canal Zone (Bade) 12/6/45.

42-6141 Del Long Beach 7/8/43; Cheyenne 12/8/43; Ft Myers 28/9/43; 86 Sub Dep Tyndall 30/11/43; 3017 BU Hobbs 5/10/44; RFC Altus 30/8/45.

42-6142 Del Long Beach 3/8/43; Denver 6/8/43; 234 BU Clovis 24/6/44; 4200 BU Chicago Mun 18/12/44; 234 BU Clovis 22/12/44; 420 BU March 24/4/45; 234 BU Clovis 9/6/45; RFC Walnut Ridge 14/12/45.

42-6143 Del Long Beach 5/8/43; Denver 7/8/43; 221 BU Alexandria 17/1/45; 327 BU Drew 29/6/45; RFC Walnut Ridge 18/12/45.

42-6144 Del Long Beach 5/8/43; Denver 8/8/43; Sioux City 11/8/43; 243 BU Gr Bend 5/8/44; 2132 BU Maxwell 21/4/45; 902 BU Orlando 5/5/45; 234 BU Gr Bend 26/8/45; RFC Kingman 2/11/45.

42-6145 Del Long Beach 5/8/43; Denver 8/8/43; WO 26/2/44.

42-6146 Del Long Beach 4/8/43; Denver 6/8/43; 398BG Rapid City 9/9/43; Wendover 13/12/43; 329 BU Columbus 21/6/44; 326 BU McDill 23/10/44; 325 BU Avon Park 20/6/45; RFC Walnut Ridge 19/8/45.

42-6147 Del Long Beach 4/8/43; Denver 7/8/43; WO 16/1/44.

42-6148 Del Long Beach 5/8/43; Dallas 8/8/43; 3017 BU Hobbs 8/10/44; 3007 BU Kirtland 21/12/44; 3017 BU Hobbs 3/1/45; RFC Altus 27/8/45.

42-6149 Del Long Beach 5/8/43; Cheyenne 9/8/43; 424 Sub Gp Gr Island 3/9/43 fitted with Sperry Gyroscope; ass 413BS/96BG [MZ-X] Snetterton 10/9/43; sal 29/9/43.

42-6150 Del Long Beach 6/8/43; Cheyenne 10/8/43; 202 BU Galveston 9/6/44; 497BG Pratt 18/6/44; 29BG Dalhart 2/9/44; 246 BU Pratt 16/9/44; 347 BU Key Fd 22/3/45; 246 BU Pratt 9/6/45; RFC Altus 9/10/45.

42-6151 Del Long Beach 6/8/43; Cheyenne 9/8/43; 424 Sub Gp Gr Island 3/9/43; ass 508BS/351BG [YB-J/M] Polebrook 24/9/43; tran 486BG Sudbury 17/7/44; 490BG Eye 8/44; sal n/b/d 11/6/45. ROUND TRIP.

42-6152 Del Long Beach 6/8/43; Cheyenne 9/8/43; 4100 BU Patterson 18/6/44; 500BG Walker 23/6/44; 500BG Victoria 29/6/44; 232 BU Dalhart 4/9/44; 241 BU Fairmont 13/9/44; 902 BU Orlando 27/2/45; 241 BU Fairmont 1/5/45; RFC Altus 26/7/45.

42-6153 Del Long Beach 7/8/43; Pyote 8/8/43; 232 BU Dalhart 26/8/44; 235 BU Biggs 31/10/44; 2318 BU Alamogordo 8/1/45; 235 BU Biggs 10/1/45; RFC Kingman 30/10/45.

42-6154 Del Long Beach 6/8/43; Cheyenne 12/8/43; 3017 BU Hobbs 8/11/44; RFC Altus 18/9/45.

42-6155 Del Long Beach 11/8/43; Cheyenne 15/8/43; 424 Suv Dep Gr Island for Sperry turret 7/9/43; ass 549BS/385BG Gt Ashfield 15/9/43; MIA Münster 10/10/43 w/Pettenger, e/a, cr Münster, 10POW; MACR 827.

42-6156 Del Long Beach 10/8/43; Denver 12/8/43; 2542 BU Lackland 10/12/44; 221 BU Alexandria 31/12/44; 329 BU Alexandria 1/3/45; 327 BU Drew 23/6/45; RFC Walnut Ridge 7/12/45.

42-6157 Del Long Beach 7/8/43; Cheyenne 10/8/43; Tinker 14/12/43; 2135 BU Tyndall 16/9/44; 3017 BU Hobbs 18/9/44; RFC Altus 27/8/45.

42-6158 Del Long Beach 10/8/43; Cheyenne 12/8/43; Tinker 12/12/43; 3501 BU Boca Raton 14/7/44; 2137 BU Hendricks 17/10/45; RFC Walnut Ridge 16/10/45.

42-6159 Del Long Beach 7/8/43; (F-9) Min Mapping Asia 1/4/44; sal n/b/d Soxo (Europe) 28/8/45.

42-6160 Del Long Beach 7/8/43; Colorado Springs 11/8/43; 241 BU Fairmont 22/6/44; 504BG Fairmont 24/6/44; 232 BU Dalhart 22/8/44; 244 BU Harvard 1/10/44; 203 BU Jackson 12/2/45; 224 BU Sioux City 25/8/45; RFC Kingman 28/10/45.

42-6161 Del Long Beach 7/8/43; Colorado Springs 11/8/43; 351 Sub Dep Pyote 9/11/43; 2136 BU Tinker 24/6/44; 235 BU Biggs 27/7/44; WO 13/12/44; Recl Comp 17/1/45.

42-6162 Del Long Beach 11/8/43; Denver 15/8/43; 28BG Pyote 2/10/43; 19BG Pyote 9/11/43; 235 BU Biggs 27/8/44; 4202 BU Syracuse 3/4/45; RFC Walnut Ridge 8/1/46.

42-6163 Del Long Beach 10/8/43; Denver 12/8/43; 221 BU Alexandria 17/1/45; 329 BU Alexandria 1/3/45; 327 BU Drew 1/8/45; RFC Walnut Ridge

19/12/45.

42-6164 Del Long Beach 10/8/43; Denver 15/8/43; ass Min Mapping Asia 1/4/44; sal Cairo (Ache) 8/9/45.

42-6165 Del Long Beach 10/8/43; Denver 15/8/43; 221 BU Alexandria 17/1/45; 329 BU Alexandria 1/3/45; 327 BU Drew 23/6/45; RFC Walnut Ridge 11/12/45.

42-6166 Del Long Beach 14/8/43; Cheyenne 16/8/43; Dalhart 17/10/43; 248 BU Walker 9/6/44; RFC Altus 1/8/45.

42-6167 Del Long Beach 13/8/43; Cheyenne 16/8/43; Tinker 14/12/43; 2114 BU Lockburn 10/8/44; RFC Walnut Ridge 14/12/45.

42-6168 Del Long Beach 12/8/43; Denver 15/8/43; WO 12/4/44.

42-6169 Del Long Beach 11/8/43; Denver 15/8/43; 4103 BU Jackson 5/10/44; 221 BU Alexandria 6/10/44; 329 BU Alexandria 1/3/45; 327 BU Drew 22/6/44; RFC Walnut Ridge 18/12/45.

42-6170 Del Long Beach 11/8/43; Cheyenne 15/8/43; WO 26/1/44.

42-6171 Del Long Beach 12/8/43; Cheyenne 15/12/43; Ft Myers 30/11/43; 3030 BU Roswell 19/9/44; 3010 BU Williams 21/11/44; 3020 BU La Junta 1/4/45; RFC Searcey Fd 4/8/45.

42-6172 Del Long Beach 13/8/43; Cheyenne 15/8/43; 3010 BU Williams 28/11/44; 225 BU Rapid City 29/4/45; RFC Altus 8/8/45.

42-6173 Del Long Beach 13/8/43; Cheyenne 15/8/43; Tinker 13/12/43; 2137 BU Hendricks 11/11/44; Recl Comp 27/7/45.

42-6174 Del Long Beach 13/8/43; Cheyenne 15/8/43; ass 422BS/305BG [JJ-K] Chelveston 7/11/43 HOMESICK ANGEL; 858BS/492BG Alconbury (Carpetbagger Ops) 26/6/44. STRIPPED FOR ACTION.

42-6175 Del Long Beach 13/8/43; Palm Springs 15/8/43; Tinker 6/12/43; WO 15/3/44.

42-6176 Del Long Beach 13/8/43; Palm Springs 15/8/43; 4126 BU San Bernadino 6/10/44; 223 BU Dyersburg 26/11/44; 330 BU Dyersburg 26/11/44; 325 BU Avon Park 21/6/45; RFC Walnut Ridge 18/8/45.

42-6177 Del Long Beach 13/8/43; Cheyenne 17/8/43; 223 BU Dyersburg 25/1/45; Recl Comp 9/2/45.

42-6178 Del Long Beach 13/8/43; Cheyenne 15/8/43; 4119 BU Brookley 23/10/44; 223 BU Dyersburg 13/12/44; 330 BU Dyersburg 1/3/45; 325 BU Avon Park 21/6/45; RFC Walnut Ridge 19/8/45.

42-6179 Del Long Beach 14/8/43; Cheyenne 17/8/43; 2114 BU Lockburn 6/9/44; RFC Walnut Ridge 14/12/45.

42-6180 Del Long Beach 15/8/43; Cheyenne 16/8/43; Mat Com Patterson 2/6/44; Minneapolis 15/6/44; Mat Com Wright 10/7/44; 554 BU Memphis 28/7/44; 110 BU Mitchell 30/8/44; RFA Albuquerque 25/6/45.

42-6181 Del Long Beach 14/8/43; Cheyenne 17/8/43; 30BS/19BG Pyote 16/9/43; Tinker 11/10/43; 222 BU Ardmore 19/9/44; 332 BU Ardmore 16/5/45; 215 BU Pueblo 20/6/45; 4210 BU Lambert 12/7/45; 215 BU Pueblo 19/9/45; RFC Kingman 29/10/45.

42-6182 Del Long Beach 15/8/43; Cheyenne 18/8/43; Tinker 14/12/43; 7AB Dow Fd 30/5/44; 2114 BU Lockburn 16/8/44; WO 22/11/44.

42-6183 Del Long Beach 16/8/43; Cheyenne 17/8/43; (F-9) Ass Min Mapping Asia 1/4/44; retUS Independence 13/9/44; RFC Kingman 13/11/45.

42-6184 Del Long Beach 17/8/43; Cheyenne 18/8/43; (F-9) Ass Mapping Dakar (Senegal), 29/2/44; retUS McDill 11/8/44; Robins 16/8/44; RFC Bush Fd 30/7/45.

42-6185 Del Long Beach 16/8/43; Cheyenne 18/8/43; (F-9) Ass 4143 BU Gander 10/2/44; 4168 BU Sth Plains 31/1/46; 4112 BU Olmstead 6/6/46; 16 Photo Gp McDill 17/7/46; 4104 BU Rome 2/10/46; 16 Photo Gp McDill 13/10/46; Recl Comp 14/11/47.

42-6186 Del Long Beach 17/8/43; Cheyenne 18/8/43; (F-9B) Algiers (Elms) 11/9/44; retUS Walnut Ridge 29/12/44; RFC Walnut Ridge 29/12/46.

42-6187 Del Long Beach 17/8/43; Cheyenne 18/8/43; (F-9B) Ass 1 Photo Gp McDill 26/4/44; 410 BU Rome 21/10/44; 91 Photo Sq Buckley 23/12/44; Accra, W Africa 22/1/45; Trinidad Mapping 14/6/46. THE GOLDEN HIND

42-6188 Del Long Beach 17/8/43; Cheyenne 18/8/43; 2117 BU Buckingham 16/6/44; 3501 Boca Raton 16/17/44; 2114 BU Lockburn 4/7/45; RFC Altus 9/10/45.

42-6189 Del Long Beach 17/8/43; Cheyenne 18/8/43; WO 1/1/44.

42-6190 Del Long Beach 17/8/43; 356 Sub Dep Dalhart 17/10/43; 232 BU Dalhart 9/6/44; 421 BU Muroc 15/7/44; 232 BU Dalhart 3/12/44; 357 BU Kellogg 29/12/44; 246 BU Pratt 23/1/45; 902 BU Orlando 17/5/45; RFC Altus 9/10/45.

42-6191 Del Long Beach 17/8/43; Cheyenne 18/8/43; 2114 BU Lockburn 10/8/44; 357 BU Kellogg 13/11/44; 2114 BU Lockburn 10/12/44; RFC Walnut Ridge 18/12/45.

42-6192 Del Long Beach 17/8/43; Cheyenne 18/8/43; 3036 BU Yuma 12/10/44; 4126 BU San Bernardino 7/11/44; 3036 BU Yuma 21/11/44; RFC Albuquerque 27/7/45.

42-6193 Del Long Beach 20/8/43; Cheyenne 21/8/43; 2114 BU Lockburn 31/7/45; RFC Altus 9/10/45.

42-6194 Del Long Beach 18/8/43; Yuma 19/8/43; 231 BU Alamogordo 26/3/45; 4202 BU Syracuse 29/3/45; RFC Altus 5/11/45.

42-6195 Del Long Beach 18/8/43; RAAF Gunnery Sch Las Vegas 4/9/43; Love Fd 12/12/43; Ft Myers 6/1/44; 2114 BU Lockburn 10/8/44; 575 BU Pittsburgh 3/10/44; 2114 BU Lockburn 7/11/44; RFC Walnut Ridge 14/12/45.

42-6196 Del Long Beach 18/8/43; Yuma 23/3/44; 231 BU Alamogordo 2/8/44; RFC Searcey Fd 7/8/45.

42-6197 Del Long Beach 18/8/43; 327 BU McDill, WO 18/12/44.

42-6198 Del Long Beach 21/8/43; Alexandria 22/9/43; WO 17/2/44.

42-6199 Del Long Beach 21/8/43; 4136 BU Tinker 1/6/44; 497BG Pratt 7/6/44; 4100 BU Patterson 11/6/44; 246 BU Pratt 26/6/44; 222 BU Ardmore 7/8/44; 332 BU Ardmore 16/6/45; RFC Walnut Ridge 13/11/45.

42-6200 Del Long Beach 21/8/43; (F-9B) Ass Min Mapping Asia 1/4/44; retUS 121 BU Bradley 28/8/44; RFC Altus 11/10/45.

42-6201 Del Long Beach 21/8/43; (F-9B) Ass Min Mapping Asia 1/4/44; retUS 1377 BU Yuma 21/9/45; 4132 BU Garden City 25/9/45; 4168 BU Sth Plains 5/6/46; 4112 BU Olmstead 9/6/46; 16 Photo Gp McDill 24/9/46; 307 BU McDill 7/12/46; Recl Comp 12/2/47.

42-6202 Del Long Beach 21/8/43; Alexandria 21/9/43; 221 BU Alexandria 17/1/45; 329 BU Alexandria 1/3/45; 327 BU Drew 22/6/45; RFC Walnut Ridge 11/12/45.

42-6203 Del Long Beach 21/8/43; Lockburn 7/9/43; 2114 BU Lockburn 24/10/43; RFC Walnut Ridge 14/12/45.

42-6204 Del Long Beach 21/8/43; Tinker 6/12/43; 3501 BU Boca Raton 22/7/44; 2137 BU Hendricks 17/10/44; RFC Walnut Ridge 29/12/45.

B-17F-BO

42-29467 Del Cheyenne 20/12/42; Salina 2/1/43, cheek guns and astrodome fitted; Morrison 2/2/43; ass 348BS/99BG Navarin 26/2/43; Oudna 4/8/43; condemned 11/8/43, but rep. for weather a/c; Tortorella 11/12/43; tran 52FG Madna, It. 10/10/44; Piagiolino 21/4/45; Lesina 8/7/45; retUS Drew 25/8/45; WO 14/7/46. FLAK DODGER.

42-29468 Del Denver 20/12/42; Salina 1/1/43; West Palm Beach 31/1/43; ass 346BS/99BG Navarin 26/2/43; b/d Messina 25/6/43 w/Hunter, c/l Bizerte, sal. 2KIA, first in Sq. OUR FAVORITE BITCH.

42-29469 Del Denver 20/12/42; Salina 1/1/43; Morrison 2/2/43; ass 348BS/99BG Navarin 26/2/43; {11m} cr Bizerte 3/5/43 w/McLaughlin. WO.

42-29470 Del Denver 20/12/42; Salina 30/12/42; West Palm Beach 4/1/43; ass 8AF 5/4/43; cr 16/7/43. WO 8/7/44.

42-29471 Del Denver 18/12/42; Pueblo 29/12/42; Biggs 24/2/43; Blythe 19/3/43; damaged when groundlooped 5/5/43 w/Schroeder, rep; c/t/o 19/5/43, WO 31/5/43.

42-29472 Del Denver 22/12/42; Salina 3/1/43; West Palm Beach 31/3/43; ass 416BS/99BG Navarin 3/3/43; Oudna 4/8/43; Tortorella 11/12/43; {111m} became weather a/c; retUS Morrison 23/9/45; RFC Walnut Ridge 26/9/45. SWEATER GIRL.

42-29473 Del Denver 20/12/42; Salina 3/1/43; DeRidder 31/1/43; Morrison 2/2/43; ass 347BS/99BG Navarin 2/2/43; Oudna 4/8/43; tran 483BG Tortorella 31/3/44; Sterparone 22/4/44; 342BS/97BG Amendola as weather a/c 6/44; sal 9/3/46. YANKEE DOODLE.

42-29474 Del Denver 20/12/42; Salina 3/1/43; DeRidder 31/1/43; Brookley 1/2/43; ass 347BS/99BG Navarin 2/2/43; Oudna 4/8/43; Tortorella 11/12/43; {96m} became weather a/c; 650 hrs w/original engines, sal 3/11/45. WARRIOR.

42-29475 Del Denver 28/12/42; Salina 3/1/43; Homestead 14/2/43; ass 323BS/91BG [OR-R] Bassingbourn 7/3/43; {3+m} MIA Villacoublay 10/7/43 w/Forsblad, mech ex, cr Channel nr Caen,8KIA 2POW. MACR 34. STRIC NINE.

42-29476 Del Denver 31/12/42; Pueblo 19/2/43; Gulfport 18/3/43; Presque is 10/4/43; ass 8AF 22/4/43; MIA Soxo 29/5/43.

42-29477 Del Cheyenne 3/1/43; Salina 11/1/43; Morrison 5/2/43; ass 369BS/306BG [WW-H] Thurleigh 17/4/43 LITTLE AUDREY; tran 358BS/303BG [VK-B] Molesworth 25/9/43; MIA Schweinfurt 14/10/43 w/Sanders, e/a, cr Bamberg, Ger. 2KIA 9POW. MACR 907. JOAN OF ARK.

42-29478 Del Cheyenne 20/12/42; Salina 4/1/43; Morrison 2/2/43; ass 348BS/99BG Navarin 26/4/43; cr base ex Bizerte 3/5/43; w/Davis & crew baled safely. Sal. WAR BIRD.

42-29479 Del Cheyenne 20/12/42; Casper 14/1/43; Scotts Bluff 15/2/43; Casper 27/6/43; Dalhart 28/7/43; 247 BU Smoky Hill 9/8/44; 235 BU Biggs 6/10/44; 4202 BU Syracuse 5/4/45; RFC Ontario 4/6/45.

42-29480 Del Cheyenne 20/12/42; Salina 3/1/43; DeRidder 31/1/43; Morrison 2/2/43; ass 347BS/99BG Navarin 20/2/43; Oudna 4/8/43; Tortorella 11/12/43; tran 483BG Tortorella 31/3/44; Sterparone 22/4/44; ret 99BG Tortorella 17/5/45; sal 28/9/45. COTTON EYED JOE.

42-29481 Del Cheyenne 20/12/42; Salina 7/2/43; Denver 27/2/43; Morrison 9/3/43; ass 427BS/303BG Molesworth 6/4/43; MIA Wilhelmshaven 15/5/43 w/Jacques, e/a, cr Nth Sea, 10KIA. MACR 15515.

42-29482 Del Cheyenne 20/12/42; Salina 3/1/43;

Morrison 31/1/43; ass 416BS/99BG Navarin 2/2/43 ROBERT E. LEE; retUS Sth Plains 9/5/45; RFC Cincinnati 28/6/45. BALSANAL.

42-29483 Del Cheyenne 22/12/42; Salina 4/1/43; DeRidder 31/1/43; Morrison 4/2/43; ass 348BS/99BG Navarin 20/2/43; MIA Gerbini 5/7/43 w/Davis; 4KIA 6POW (Perry escapes, ret 9/6/44, Terssel escapes, ret 27/6/43); 2WIA Huckabee & Fleming, rescued by US Army. MACR 240/386.

42-29484 Del Cheyenne 22/12/42; Salina 3/1/43; Morrison 31/1/43; ass 346BS/99BG Navarin 2/2/43; cr 3/5/43 ex-Bizerte w/Ebbers, sal. STARS AND STRIPES.

42-29485 Del Cheyenne 20/12/42; Salina 3/1/43; West Palm Beach 31/1/43; ass 416BS/99BG Navarin 20/2/43; Oudna 4/8/43; Tortorella 11/12/43; tran 483BG Tortorella 31/3/44; 7 more missions, Sterparone 22/4/44; WO 31/7/44, rep to 463BG Celone as weather a/c 4/45; sal 5/10/45. MISS FURY.

42-29486 Del Cheyenne 22/12/42; Salina 5/1/43; Morrison 3/2/32; ass 348BS/99BG Navarin 2/3/43; MIA Gerbini 5/7/43 w/Devane; 5KIA 5POW. MACR 988/1133.

42-29487 Del Cheyenne 22/12/42; Salina 2/2/43; Duncan 23/2/43; ass 324BS/91BG [DF-K] Bassingbourn 9/3/43; {48m} MIA Oschersleben 11/1/44 w/Hedglin; e/a, cr Wennigsen, Ger, 5KIA 5POW. MACR 1915. (bombardier's chute failed). RITZY BLITZ.

42-29488 Del Cheyenne 22/12/42; Salina 4/1/43; Morrison 31/1/43; ass 416BS/99BG Navarin 20/2/43; cr 3/5/43 ex-Bizerte, w/Buck & crew OK, sal. LADY LUCK.

42-29489 Del Cheyenne 23/12/42; Salina 4/1/43; DeRidder 31/1/43; Morrison 2/2/43; ass 347BS/99BG Navarin 2/2/43; b/d Messina 25/5/43 w/Bankhead, 2WIA; a/c rep, Oudna 4/8/43; 11/12/43 Tortorella; sal 30/10/45. PERSUADER.

42-29490 Del Cheyenne 22/12/42; Salina 7/1/43; DeRidder 31/1/43; Morrison 4/2/43; ass 347BS/99BG Navarin 20/2/43; b/d Terni 14/10/43 w/Wardwell; 8 baled, p & cp bring a/c home {64m}; Oudna 4/8/43; c/l Sardinia 8/11/43 ex-Turin w/Carson; p & cp land a/c, 8 baled OK, all return 10/11/43. WO. AXIS ASS-ACHE.

42-29491 Del Great Falls 23/12/42; Denver 27/2/43; Pueblo 18/3/43; Presque Is 10/4/43; ass 509BS/351BG Polebrook 18/4/43; mid air coll on practice op w/42-29865, all killed.

42-29492 Del Denver 23/12/42; Salina 5/1/43; Morrison 3/2/43; ass 346BS/99BG Navarin 20/2/43; MIA Gerbini 5/7/43 w/Graham; 7KIA 3POW. MACR 98A/1132. RAMBLIN' WRECK.

42-29493 Del Gt Falls 23/12/42; Cheyenne 13/1/43; Hobbs 28/1/43; Ft Sumner 21/4/43; Hobbs 6/5/43; Chicago Mun 16/5/43; Hobbs 24/6/43; New Orleans 3/8/43; 3017 BU Hobbs 8/11/44; 4121 BU Kelly 20/2/45; 4505 BU Kelly 28/3/45; 4160 BU Ardmore 20/7/45; RFC Albuquerque 27/7/45.

42-29494 Del Denver 23/12/42; Salina 4/1/43; ass 348BS/99BG Navarin 23/2/43; Oudna 4/8/43; b/d Foggia 25/8/43 w/Whitmore; {50m} c/l nr base, crew baled OK but 5 WIA. MAVERICK.

42-29495 Del Denver 23/12/42; Salina 5/1/43; DeRidder 31/1/43; Morrison 2/2/43; ass 348BS/99BG Navarin 23/2/43; c/l 3/5/43 ex-Bizerte, WO 2/9/43; rep but sal 2/12/43.

42-29496 Del Denver 23/12/42; Salina 5/1/43; Morrison 2/2/43; ass 346BS/99BG Navarin 20/2/43; MIA Bizerte 3/5/43 w/Rainey, ditched Med Sea, 4 survived 6 drowned. MACR 16175.

42-29497 Del Cheyenne 26/12/42; Boise 16/1/43; Gowen 22/5/43; Moses Lake 17/6/43; Spokane 14/8/43; WO 30/4/44.

42-29498 Del Cheyenne 26/12/42; Salina 11/1/43; Morrison 14/2/43; ass 368BS/306BG [BO-L] Thurleigh 2/3/43; tran 360BS/303BG [PU-D] Molesworth 25/9/43; MIA Bremen 29/11/43 w/Fyler, e/a, cr Dreiangel, 2KIA 8POW. MACR 1657. DARK HORSE.

42-29499 Del Cheyenne 26/12/42; Salina 9/1/43; Morrison 12/2/43; ass 422BS/305BG [JJ-Q] Chelveston 7/3/43; MIA Hamburg 25/6/43 w/Wilcox, e/a, ditched Nth Sea (cr Oude Rekela, Hol). MA MA CHANG.

42-29500 Del Cheyenne 24/12/42; Rapid City 16/1/43; Geiger 10/3/43; Ephrata 18/3/43; WO 20/7/43.

42-29501 Del Cheyenne 26/12/42; Casper 14/1/43; Rapid City 31/1/43; Casper 2/2/43; Ephrata 28/4/43; WO 17/5/43.

42-29502 Del Cheyenne 26/12/42; Salina 11/1/43; Morrison 31/1/43; ass 416BS/99BG Navarin 20/2/43; Oudna 4/8/43; MIA Toulon 24/11/43 w/Adams, mech failure, cr Med Sea, 8 chutes seen and life-rafts dropped. MACR 1308. BIG TIME OPERATOR.

42-29503 Del Cheyenne 28/12/42; Rapid City 15/1/43; Ainsworth 27/2/43; Sioux Falls 4/3/43; Rapid City 7/4/43; Hill Fd 16/5/43; Geiger 24/6/43; 383BG Geiger 22/10/43; 4136 BU Tinker 14/6/44; 234 BU Clovis 5/7/44; 202 BU Galveston 25/10/44; 234 BU Clovis 2/11/44; 3704 BU Keesler 14/1/45; 2519 BU Ft Worth 3/7/45; RFC Altus 20/8/45.

42-29504 Del Cheyenne 28/12/42; Gt Falls 14/1/43; Rapid City 31/1/43; Ainsworth 22/3/43; Rapid City 5/5/43; Geiger 22/6/43; WO 17/2/44.

42-29505 Del Cheyenne 31/12/42; Salina 10/1/43; Brookley 8/3/43; Morrison 19/3/43; ass 368BS/306BG; o/s St Eval Afd, cr Foel Cwm, Wales 11/4/43, sal.

42-29506 Del Cheyenne 28/12/42; Salina 9/1/43; Morrison 12/2/43; Homestead 18/2/43; ass 365BS/305BG [XK-V] Chelveston 2/3/43 YE WHITE SWAN; tran 532BS/381BG [VE-A] Ridgewell 22/8/43; MIA Leverkusen 1/12/43 w/Duncan; e/a, cr Kassel, 6KIA 4POW. MACR 1578. FULL BOOST!

42-29507 Del Denver 28/12/42; Salina 6/1/43; Morrison 31/1/43; ass 416BS/99BG Navarin 20/2/43; Oudna 4/8/43; Tortorella 11/12/43; tran 840BS/483BG Tortorella 31/3/44; 419BS/301BG Lucera 17/5/44 as training a/c; 463BG Celone 9/44; retUS Morrison 20/3/45; RFC Bush Fd 7/7/45. LADY LUCK.

42-29508 Del Denver 28/12/42; Salina 5/1/43; ass 364BS/305BG [WF-D] Chelveston 6/4/43; dest in base fire 26/8/43, sal. SOUTHERN COMFORT Jr.

42-29509 Del Denver 28/12/42; Salina 5/1/43; Morrison 31/1/43; ass 416BS/99BG Navarin 20/2/43; Oudna 4/8/43; Tortorella 11/12/43; {114m} tran 840BS/483BG Torto-rella 31/3/44; Sterparone 22/4/44; {12m} RetUS Altus 7/3/45; {126m} RFC Altus 10/8/45. BAD PENNY.

42-29510 Del Denver 28/12/42; Wendover 6/1/43; Denver 31/1/43; Casper 22/3/43; Sioux City 19/6/43; Dalhart 22/7/43; 232 BU Dalhart 9/6/44; 245 BU McCook 22/6/44; 9BG McCook 18/7/44; 3705 BU Lowry 16/10/44; WO 28/10/44; 2530 BU Selman 14/5/45; RFC Walnut Ridge 17/9/45.

42-29511 Del Denver 3/1/43; Salina 11/1/43; Morrison 5/3/43; ass 407BS/92BG [PY-W] Alconbury 19/5/43; tran 525BS/379BG [FR-W] Kimbolton 4/9/43; MIA Schweinfurt 14/10/43 w/Martin, e/a, cr Schweinfurt, 10POW. MACR 957. THE IRON MAIDEN.

42-29512 Del Cheyenne 28/12/42; Salina 10/1/43; DeRidder 31/1/43; Morrison 3/2/43; ass 346BS/99BG Navarin 23/2/43; b/d Messina 16/7/43 w/Larkin, c/l Sicily, 3WIA. WO. CORRINE ANN.

42-29513 Del Cheyenne 31/12/42; Salina 10/1/43; DeRidder 31/1/43; Morrison 1/2/43; ass 346BS/99BG Navarin 23/2/43; Oudna 4/8/43; Tortorella 11/12/43; {114m} tran weather a/c 304BW Cerignola 28/10/44; sal 23/8/45. El DIABLO.

42-29514 Del Cheyenne 31/12/42; Gt Falls 14/1/43; Rapid City 31/1/43; Pueblo 1/2/43; Rapid City 9/2/43; Walla Walla 4/3/43; a/c missing 31/3/43; WO 19/5/43.

42-29515 Del Cheyenne 28/12/42; Salina 10/1/43; Morrison 5/3/43; ass 429BS/2BG Navarin 13/4/43; Château-du-Rhumel 27/4/43; Ain M'Lila 17/6/43; Massicault 31/7/43; Bizerte 2/12/43; Amendola 9/12/43; MIA {11m} Sofia 24/1/44 w/Willis, ditched off Bari, crew rescued by British ship. WOLF PACK.

42-29516 Del Cheyenne 3/1/43; Gt Falls 14/1/43; Rapid City 31/1/43; Walla Walla 23/4/43; Spokane 1/5/43; Gt Falls 31/7/43; Glasgow 3/8/43; ass 540BS/383BG Geiger 15/10/43; 4117 BU Robins 12/7/44; 327 BU Drew 24/8/44; 4100 BU Patterson 18/2/45; 1077 BU Bowman 20/5/45; RFC Walnut Ridge 5/1/46.

42-29517 Del Cheyenne 4/1/43; Sioux City 15/1/43; Casper 5/5/43; Lowry 11/5/43; Sioux City 28/6/43; Kearney 3/8/43; Tinker 18/11/43; 4136 BU Tinker 17/7/44; 224 BU Sioux City 28/8/44; 4160 BU Albuquerque 27/5/45; RFC Albuquerque 25/6/45.

42-29518 Del Cheyenne 4/1/43; Sioux City 19/1/43; Cheyenne 31/1/43; Rapid City 14/3/43; Casper 5/5/43; Sioux City 28/6/43; Kearney 6/8/43; Tinker 30/10/43; 224 BU Sioux City 6/3/44; 4160 BU Albuquerque 20/6/44; RFC Albuquerque 25/6/45.

42-29519 Del Cheyenne 31/12/42; Gt falls 14/1/43; Ephrata 4/2/43; Geiger 5/3/43; 222 BU Ardmore 22/1/45; RFC Ontario 6/6/45.

42-29520 Del Cheyenne 31/12/42; Salina 9/1/43; Morrison 12/2/43; Homestead 17/2/43; ass 427BS/303BG [GN-O] Molesworth 6/3/43; tran 323BS/91BG [OR-S] Bassingbourn 7/9/43; MIA Bremen 8/10/43 w/Kamp; e/a, cr Prenss-Srechen, 3KIA 7POW. MACR 909.

42-29521 Del Cheyenne 31/12/42; Pueblo 27/1/43; Biggs 24/2/43; Blythe 18/3/43; Walla Walla 17/5/43; Redmond 18/6/43; Madras 21/6/43; Walla Walla 15/8/43; 4117 BU Robins 27/4/43; 328 BU Gulfport 31/3/45; RFC Albuquerque 23/6/45.

42-29522 Del Denver 31/12/42; Cheyenne 13/1/43; Ainsworth 19/1/43; Rapid City 8/3/43; Lowry 29/4/43; Rapid City 5/5/43; Portland 15/6/43; Geiger 12/11/43; 247 BU Smoky Hill 10/6/44; 4136 BU Tinker 26/7/44; 235 BU Biggs 17/1/45; 4202 BU Syracuse 18/4/45; Recl Comp 3/1/46.

42-29523 Del Denver 31/12/42; Ogden 1/1/43; Salina 29/1/43; Kearney 6/2/43; ass 20BS/2BG Navarin 23/3/43; Château-du-Rhumel 27/4/43; Ain M'Lila 17/6/43; Massicault 31/7/43; MIA {39m} Foggia 19/8/43 w/Thomas e/a, cr sea, 7 chutes seen. MACR 457.

42-29524 Del Denver 31/12/42; Salina 7/1/43; Morrison 2/12/43; Homestead 14/2/43; ass 423BS/306BG [RD-D] Thurleigh 2/3/43; tran 358BS/303BG [VK-K] Molesworth 30/7/43; MIA Oschersleben 26/1/44 w/Watson, e/a, cr Ijsselmeer, Hol. MEAT HOUND.

42-29525 Del Cheyenne 4/1/43; Boise 16/1/43; Gowen 7/6/43; Dalhart 6/7/43; 232 BU Dalhart 9/6/44; 201 BU Peterson 11/7/44; 222 BU Ardmore 9/8/44; 4103 BU Jackson 21/10/44; 268 BU Peterson 9/11/44; 233 BU Davis Monthan 22/11/44;

202 BU Galveston 6/1/45; 207 BU Deming 22/2/45; 202 BU Galveston 23/2/45; 268 BU Peterson 30/3/45; 4208 BU Mines Fd 2/7/45; 268 BU Peterson 7/7/45; RFC Kingman 6/11/45.

42-29526 Del Cheyenne 31/12/42; Salina 11/1/43; DeRidder 31/1/43; Morrison 1/2/43; ass 346BS/99BG Navarin 3/2/43; Oudna 4/8/43; Tortorella 11/12/43; {100+m} tran 483BG Tortorella 31/3/44; 429BS/2BG Amendola 4/44; sal 2/8/45. BUGS.

42-29527 Del Cheyenne 31/12/42; Salina 10/1/43; Morrison 5/3/43; Brookley 8/3/43; Morrison 10/4/43; ass 416BS/99BG Navarin 5/6/43; Oudna 4/8/43; b/d Messina 6/8/43 w/Barton, l/Comiso, 2 engines out & 3 WIA, a/c rep 12/8/43; Tortorella 11/12/43; tran 483BG Tortorella 31/3/44; sal 2/8/45. JIG-JIG.

42-29528 Del Cheyenne 31/12/42; Biggs 20/1/43; Gt Falls 31/1/43; WO 27/2/43.

42-29529 Del Cheyenne 31/12/42; Salina 10/1/43; Morrison 5/3/43; Brookley 8/3/43; ass 369BS/306BG Thurleigh 24/3/43; tran 422BS/305BG [JJ-L] Chelveston 10/4/43; 545BS/384BG [JD-U] Grafton Underwood 6/11/43; c/l base 13/12/43, sal. NORA II.

42-29530 Del Cheyenne 31/12/42; Salina 10/2/43; Morrison 5/3/43; Brookley 8/3/43; ass 365BS/305BG [XK-Y] MOONBEAM McSWAIN Chelveston 8/4/43; MIA Watten 27/8/43 w/Moore, flak, cr Watten, 4KIA 6POW. MACR 394. BOOM TOWN JR.

42-29531 Del Cheyenne 3/1/43; Salina 11/1/43; Morrison 8/3/43; ass 422BS/305BG [JJ-Z] Chelveston 8/4/43; MIA St Nazaire 29/5/43 w/Peterson, flak, cr St Nazaire, 1KIA 9POW.

42-29532 Del Cheyenne 31/12/42; Salina 11/1/43; cr Smoky Hill 11/3/43. WO.

42-29533 Del Cheyenne 4/1/43; Pyote 20/1/43; Pueblo 6/4/43; Cutbank 21/4/43; Gore Fd 19/5/43; Moses Lake 27/5/43; 4100 BU Patterson 14/6/44; 235 BU Biggs 26/8/44; 233 BU Davis Monthan 18/3/45; 209 BU Galveston 6/6/45; RFC Walnut Ridge 7/12/45.

42-29534 Del Cheyenne 3/1/43; Rapid City 17/1/43; Walla Walla 4/3/43; Avon Park 20/11/43; 4117 BU Robins 13/7/44; 328 BU Gulfport 26/8/44; RFC Albuquerque 19/6/45.

42-29535 Del Cheyenne 3/1/43; Gt Falls 14/1/43; Geiger 14/2/43; cr nr Spokane 3/2/43 w/Brown; crew baled OK, one minor injury, a/c WO.

42-29536 Del Cheyenne 4/1/43; Salina 11/1/43; Brookley 8/3/43; Morrison 25/3/43; ass 401BS/91BG [LL-A] Bassingbourn 19/4/43; MIA {7m} Huls 22/6/43 w/Brown; e/a, cr 2KIA 8POW. MARY RUTH - MEMORIES OF MOBILE.

42-29537 Del Denver 3/1/43; Salina 9/1/43; Lake Charles 31/1/43; Morrison 12/2/43; Homestead 17/2/43; ass 324BS/91BG [DF-L] Bassingbourn 7/3/43; MIA Rouen-Sotteville 28/3/43 w/Coe, s/d by e/a. ditched Channel, 10KIA. MACR 16086.

42-29538 Del Denver 3/1/43; Pueblo 18/1/43; Biggs 24/2/43; Blythe 13/3/43; Walla Walla 24/5/43; Tinker 3/12/43; WO 1/3/44.

42-29539 Del Denver 3/1/43; Orlando 10/1/43; Brooksville 13/1/43; Eglin 5/3/43; Wright Fd 7/5/434; Brooksville 8/6/43; Orlando 7/12/43; 3705 BU Lowry 20/4/44; 234 BU Clovis 4/7/44; 3017 BU Hobbs 8/11/44; RFC Altus 18/9/45.

42-29540 Del Denver 3/1/43; Salina 20/1/43; Morrison 6/2/43; ass 427BS/303BG [GN-O] Molesworth 25/2/43; tran 323BS/91BG [OR-O] Bassingbourn 1/6/43; MIA Stuttgart 6/9/43 w/Schaper; no gas, cr Channel, 4KIA 6TRD. MACR 515. SHOOTING STAR.

42-29541 Del Cheyenne 3/1/43; Pueblo 19/1/43; WO 30/4/43.

42-29542 Del Cheyenne 3/1/43; Casper 14/1/43; Ephrata 24/2/43; Geiger 24/3/43; Gt Falls 15/4/43; Moses Lake 21/5/43; Tinker 20/11/43; 4100 BU Patterson 3/2/45; 327 BU Drew 21/4/45; 4108 BU Newark 30/4/45; 327 BU Drew 2/5/45; RFC Searcey Fd 11/8/45.

42-29543 Del Cheyenne 3/1/43; Blythe 25/1/43; Geiger 27/2/43; Orlando 13/3/43; Moses Lake 17/8/43; 4117 BU Robins 29/7/44; 326 BU McDill 22/10/44; 327 BU Drew 21/11/44; RFC Searcey Fd 7/8/45.

42-29544 Del Cheyenne 3/1/43; Pueblo 19/1/43; Tucson 31/1/43; Pueblo 13/2/43; Biggs 30/3/43; Pyote 1/4/43; Tinker 14/12/43; 4100 BU Patterson 8/6/44; 235 BU Biggs 21/8/44; Recl Comp 17/1/45.

42-29545 Del Cheyenne 4/1/43; Sioux City 15/1/43; Kearney 4/5/43; Casper 14/5/43; WO 1/7/43.

42-29546 Del Cheyenne 4/1/43; Pueblo 19/1/43; Pyote 9/3/43; Dalhart 6/5/43; Pyote 24/5/43; 383BG Geiger 27/10/43; 3705 BU Lowry 8/6/44; Recl Comp 23/10/45.

42-29547 Del Cheyenne 3/1/43; Biggs 20/1/43; Gt Falls 11/3/43; Blythe 18/3/43; Pyote 30/5/43; Tinker 23/10/43; Pyote 9/11/43; WO 1/4/44.

42-29548 Del Cheyenne 4/1/43; Ogden 25/1/43; Gowen 15/2/43; Wendover 3/6/43; Sioux City 11/6/43; Kearney 3/8/43; WO 21/7/44.

42-29549 Del Cheyenne 4/1/43; Biggs 20/1/43; Blythe 18/3/43; Moses Lake 2/5/43; Geiger 2/8/43; Sioux City 15/12/43; 224 BU Sioux City 6/3/44; 4160 BU Albuquerque 20/6/44; RFC Albuquerque 19/6/45.

42-29550 Del Cheyenne 4/1/43; Sioux City 19/1/43; Casper 5/3/43; Rapid City 7/6/43; Geiger 8/6/43; Gore Fd 8/7/43; Hill Fd 9/8/43; WO 11/8/43.

42-29551 Del Cheyenne 4/1/43; Smyrna 21/1/43; Gt Falls 31/1/43; Smyrna 13/2/43; Hobbs 17/3/43; Roswell 30/3/43; Hobbs 6/4/43; Kelly 27/7/43; 3017 BU Hobbs 15/8/44; RFC Altus 27/8/45.

42-29552 Del Cheyenne 4/1/43; Blythe 25/1/43; Orlando 10/4/43; Ephrata 29/4/43; Geiger 5/5/43; Rapid City 21/6/43; 325 BU Avon Park, WO 10/11/44; Recl Comp 3/1/46.

42-29553 Del Denver 3/1/43; Salina 9/1/43; Homestead 18/2/43; ass 366BS/305BG [KY-D] Chelveston 4/3/43; MIA Gelsenkirchen 12/8/43 w/Gerke, flak, cr Gelsenkirchen, 8KIA 2POW. MACR 252. ARKY.

42-29554 Del Denver 3/1/43; Salina 8/1/43; ass 367BS/306BG [GY-X] Thurleigh 25/3/43; tran 545BS/384BG [JD-Y] Grafton Underwood 21/8/43; RAF Farnborough (ER Flt) 19/2/44; BAD 1 Burtonwood 11/4/44, retUS Tinker 4/5/44; 2167 BU Birmingham 13/7/44; 4136 BU Tinker 6/8/44; 4117 BU Robins 20/12/44; 4100 BU Patterson 2/3/45; RFC Bush Fd 17/5/45. MARYLAND, MY MARYLAND.

42-29555 Del Denver 3/1/43; Salina 9/1/43; Tinker 26/2/43; ass 422BS/305BG [JJ-Y/D] Chelveston 6/4/43; MIA Hannover 28/9/43 w/Rodgers, s/s by e/a, cr Hannover, 7KIA 3POW. MACR 730/906. (First B-17 lost on night mission). CENTAUR.

42-29556 Del Denver 4/1/43; Boise 23/1/43; Geiger 8/5/43; Tinker 26/5/43; Ephrata 1/7/43; Rapid City 29/7/43; Orlando 8/8/43; 500BG Walker 7/6/44; 248 BU Walker 9/6/44; 232 BU Dalhart 15/7/44; WO 21/10/44; 3701 BU Amarillo 21/3/45; Recl Comp 7/6/46.

42-29557 Del Denver 4/1/43; Salina 12/1/43; Homestead 1/2/43; Morrison 9/2/43; ass 366BS/305BG [KY-O] Chelveston 10/2/43; tran 547BS/384BG [SO-S] Grafton Underwood 20/9/43; c/l Desford, hit hangar 10/10/43. Sal 29/10/43. YANKEE GAL.

42-29558 Del Denver 4/1/43; Casper 15/1/43; Lowry 22/2/43; Ephrata 27/2/43; Felts Fd 8/4/43; Ephrata 29/4/43; Spokane 1/6/43; Rapid City 2/8/43; WO 15/12/43.

42-29559 Del Denver 4/1/43; Salina 13/1/43; Homestead 1/2/43; Morrison 6/2/43; ass 323BS/91BG [OR-Q] Bassingbourn 25/2/43; MIA {13m} Schweinfurt 17/8/43 w/Bennett, s/d by e/a. cr Langdorf, 3EVD (inc P) 3KIA 4POW (2WIA). MACR 278. STUPNTAKIT.

42-29560 Del Denver 5/1/43; Pueblo 19/1/43; Pyote 14/3/43; Dalhart 6/5/43; Pyote 21/5/43; Tinker 13/8/43; 325 BU Avon Park 23/8/44; 331 BU Barksdale 24/2/45; 325 BU Avon Park 27/2/45; RFC Albuquerque 25/6/45.

42-29561 Del Cheyenne 5/1/43; Salina 28/1/43; Morrison 10/4/43; ass 96BS/2BG Navarin 8/4/43; Château-du-Rhumel 22/4/43; Ain M'Lila 17/6/43; Massicault 31/7/43; Bizerte 2/12/43; Amendola 9/12/43; {53m} last Bologna 5/10/43; used as hack?; sal 14/1/46.

42-29562 Del Cheyenne 5/1/43; Wendover 20/1/43; Dover 31/1/43; Wendover 8/2/; 43; Pocatello 7/5/43; WO 5/1/44.

42-29563 Del Cheyenne 5/1/43; Hobbs 24/1/43; Gt Falls 31/1/43; Hobbs 20/3/43; WO 4/12/43.

42-29564 Del Cheyenne 5/1/43; Wendover 23/1/43; Tinker 15/5/43; Casper 18/5/43; Scribner 25/7/43; Kearney 3/8/43; WO 3/11/43.

42-29565 Del Cheyenne 5/1/43; Smyrna 28/1/43; Lockburn 7/2/43; a/c missing 10/3/43.

42-29566 Del Cheyenne 6/1/43; Blythe 26/1/43; Geiger 8/5/43; Pendleton 25/7/43; Geiger 2/9/43; 273 BU Lincoln 23/6/44; 243 BU Gt Bend 25/6/44; 498BG Gt Bend 8/8/44; 271 BU Kearney 10/8/44; 243 BU Gt Bend 22/9/44; Recl Comp 3/8/45.

42-29567 Del Cheyenne 5/1/43; Blythe 29/1/43; Gowen 16/3/43; Tinker 2/5/43; Casper 16/5/43; WO 27/7/43.

42-29568 Del Denver 5/1/43; Salina 30/1/43; Kearney, WO 20/2/43.

42-29569 Del Denver 5/1/43; Gt Falls 9/1/43; Denver 31/1/43; Gowen 15/2/43; Sioux City 24/2/43; Casper 5/3/43; Moses Lake 14/6/43; WO 1/10/43.

42-29570 Del Denver 5/1/43; Gt Falls 31/1/43; Denver 2/2/43; Salina 11/2/43; ass 360BS/303BG [PU-D] Molesworth 21/3/43; tran BAD 1 Burtonwood 22/5/43; 532BS/381BG [VE-D] Ridgewell 7/9/43; {6+m} RetUS 26/4/44; sal 5/5/44. BIG TIME OPERATOR II.

42-29571 Del Denver 6/1/43; Salina 12/1/43; Mobile 23/1/43; Salina 31/1/43; Homestead 4/2/43; Morrison 8/2/43; ass 358BS/303BG [VK-L] Molesworth 6/4/43; MIA Duren 20/10/43 w/Hartigan, s/d by e/a; cr Cambrai, Fr, 3EVD 2KIA 6POW. MACR 1033. CHARLIE HORSE.

42-29572 Del Denver 6/1/43; Pueblo 19/1/43; Salina 31/1/43; Pyote 10/3/43; Drew 16/5/43; Pyote 21/5/43; Tinker 15/8/43; 224 BU Sioux City 6/3/45; RFC Albuquerque 22/5/45.

42-29573 Del Denver 6/1/43; Salina 12/1/43; Morrison 12/2/43; Homestead 15/2/43; ass 358BS/303BG Molesworth 6/3/43; MIA Rotterdam 31/3/43; col w/41-24559 (303) cr Mears Ashby, nr Wellingboro, UK, 15KIA. TWO BEAUTS.

42-29574 Del Denver 6/1/43; Salina 12/1/43; Homestead 4/2/43; ass 401BS/91BG [LL-G] Bassingbourn 25/2/43; MIA {8m} Bremen 17/4/43 w/Stoffel (92BG crew); cr Fiebing, Ger, 5KIA 5POW. MACR 6574. THE SKY WOLF II.

42-29575 Del Denver 6/1/43; Gore Fd 30/6/43; Lockburn 1/7/43; 3010 BU Williams 21/9/44; 3020 BU La Junta 27/3/45; RFC Searcey Fd 31/7/45.

42-29576 Del Cheyenne 6/1/43; Smyrna 24/1/43; Hobbs 6/5/43; Oklahoma Cy 23/6/43; Hobbs 26/6/43; San Antonio 11/7/43; 4511 BU Kelly 10/9/44; 4121 BU Kelly 27/11/44; RFC Kingman 2/12/45.

42-29577 Del Cheyenne 6/1/43; Smyrna 23/1/43; Lockburn 7/2/43; Kansas 29/5/43; Lockburn 2/6/43; 2114 BU Lockburn 1/10/44; Recl Comp 23/10/44.

42-29578 Del Cheyenne 13/1/43; Hobbs 23/1/43; Gt Falls 31/1/43; Hobbs 19/3/43; 3017 BU Hobbs 8/11/44; 4124 BU Altus 12/7/45; RFC Altus 4/10/45.

42-29579 Del Cheyenne 19/1/43; Salina 27/1/43; Morrison 30/3/43; ass 429BS/2BG Navarin 14/3/43; Château-du-Rhumel 27/4/43; Ain M'Lila 17/6/43; Massicault 31/7/43; Bizerte 2/12/43; Amendola 9/12/43; MIA Verona 22/3/44 w/Cravath, ditched Adriatic, crew rescued by British.

42-29580 Del Cheyenne 15/1/43; Salina 28/1/43; Morrison 9/3/43; ass 429BS/2BG Navarin 11/3/43; FTR {2m} Bizerte 3/5/43 w/Bentley, c/l sth of Constantine, crew safe, a/c WO.

42-29581 Del Cheyenne 15/1/43; Salina 31/1/43; Kearney 6/2/43; Morrison 10/3/43; ass 429BS/2BG Navarin 31/3/43; Château-du-Rhumel 27/4/43; Ain M'Lila 17/6.43; Massicault 31/7/43; MIA {53m} Terni 14/10/43 w/McCarty; 4 chutes landed in water, MACR 968. SUGARPUSS.

42-29582 Del Denver 17/1/43; Salina 29/1/43; Kearney 20/2/43; c/l Bryner, Mo. 18/3/43 w/Spinning, WO.

42-29583 Del Denver 17/1/43; Cheyenne 26/1/43; Slaina 31/1/43; Morrison 9/3/43; ass 429BS/2BG Navarin 19/3/43; Château-du-Rhumel 27/4/43; Ain M'Lila 17/6/43; MIA {33m} Messina 14/7/43 w/McIntyre; flak hit in radio room, cr into sea, 9 chutes seen. MACR 968. 60-50.

42-29584 Del Cheyenne 15/1/43; Salina 23/1/43; Morrison 10/3/43; ass 429BS/2BG Navarin 19/3/43; MIA Villaorba 18/3/44 w/Magnuson (inc 4 463rd crew), gas leak #2 tank, cr Nova Mesto. MACR 3253. SAD SACK.

42-29585 Del Cheyenne 13/1/43; Blythe 26/1/43; Geiger 27/2/43; Gt Falls 7/6/43; Lewiston 26/6/43; Gore Fd 1/7/43; Cutbank 1/8/43; 245 BU McCook 1/6/44; 3705 BU Lowry 16/10/44; WO 28/10/44; RFC Albuquerque 9/8/45.

42-29586 Del Cheyenne 12/1/43; Blythe 27/1/43; WO 6/3/43.

42-29587 Del Cheyenne 13/1/43; Salina 2/2/43; Nashville 30/3/43; Homestead 7/4/43; ass 401BS/91BG [LL-J] Bassingbourn 19/4/43; MIA {9m} Gelsenkirchen 12/8/43 w/Heller; coll w/42-3162, cr Sevenum, Hol, 1KIA 9POW, MACR 260. JOLLY ROGER.

42-29588 Del Cheyenne 12/1/43; Blythe 27/1/43; Cheyenne 31/1/43; Gowen 17/3/43; Sioux City 4/7/43; WO 31/7/43.

42-29589 Del Cheyenne 15/1/43; Salina 31/1/43; Brooksville 2/2/43; Eglin 5/3/43; Brooksville 16/3/43; Orlando 8/6/43; Mitchell 7/7/43; two landing accidents both at Olmstead, Pa; w/Berryman 27/10/43, w/Sherman 12/11/43. WO 27/2/44.

42-29590 Del Cheyenne 15/1/43; Pueblo 27/1/43; Cheyenne 31/1/43; Pyote 9/3/43; WO 26/5/43.

42-29591 Del Cheyenne 12/1/43; Rapid City 21/2/43; Kearney 12/3/43; Salina 31/3/43; Memphis 8/4/43; Dow Fd 16/4/43; ass 336BS/95BG [ET-K] Alconbury 22/4/43; tran 401BS/91BG [LL-Z] Bassingbourn 16/6/43; AFSC 15/4/44; retUS 4135 BU Hill Fd 22/6/44; 617 BU Tooele 1/3/45; RFC Kingman 13/11/45. THE SHAMROCK SPECIAL.

42-29592 Del Cheyenne 13/1/43; Blythe 29/1/43; March 26/2/43; Moses Lake 2/5/43; Minneapolis 15/5/43; Moses Lake 24/5/43; 3701 BU Amarillo 18/11/44; 3706 BU Sheppard 5/7/45; 3701 BU Amarillo 27/7/45; RFC Walnut Ridge 29/12/45.

42-29593 Del Cheyenne 13/1/43; Wendover 28/1/43; Delmonte 31/1/43; Wendover 20/2/43; Geiger 12/5/43; Moses Lake 13/6/43; WO 25/3/44.

42-29594 Del Cheyenne 13/1/43; Salina 29/1/43; Morrison 10/3/43; Brookley 15/3/43; ass 429BS/2BG Navarin 13/4/43; Château-du-Rhumel 27/4/43; Ain M'Lila 17/6/43; Massicault 31/7/43; MIA {29m} Naples 4/8/43 w/Mayer; 7 chutes seen. MACR 371. LITTLE BUTCH.

42-29595 Del Denver 15/1/43; Salina 29/1/43; Kearney 4/2/43; ass 20BS/2BG Navarin 19/3/43; Château-du-Rhumel 27/4/43; Ain M'Lila 17/6/43; Massicault 31/7/43; Bizerte 2/12/43; c/t/o 10/12/43 w/Rice as group moved to Amendola {62m}; crew safe, a/c WO.

42-29596 Del Denver 15/1/43; Blythe 26/1/43; Lowry 29/5/43; Salina 22/6/43; Blythe 20/7/43; 241 BU Fairmont 22/6/44; 504BG Fairmont 26/6/44; 241 BU Fairmont 19/9/44; 1103 BU Morrison 12/1/45; 2132 BU Maxwell 21/4/45; 241 BU Fairmont 24/4/45; RFC Altus 9/10/45.

42-29597 Del Denver 15/1/43; Pueblo 26/1/43; Pyote 14/3/43; 3701 BU Amarillo 5/7/43; WO 11/8/43.

42-29598 Del Denver 15/1/43; Blythe 26/1/43; Rapid City 29/5/43; Sioux City 18/6/43; Geiger 24/6/43; 77 Sub Group Geiger 20/10/43; 225 BU Rapid City 29/4/45; RFC Ontario 19/6/45.

42-29599 Del Denver 15/1/43; Hobbs 25/1/43; Wayne Co 15/2/43; Hobbs 17/3/43; cr Lake Cormorant, Ms, w/Ulmsted, exploded in mid air, undetermined. 10 killed.

42-29600 Del Cheyenne 15/1/43; Blythe 26/1/43; Dyersburg 5/6/43; Lake Charles 16/6/43; Alexandria 28/6/43; Orlando 5/7/43; 231 BU Alamagordo 2/8/44; RFC Albuquerque 26/5/45.

42-29601 Del Cheyenne 15/1/43; Wendover 2/2/43; 384BG Wendover 20/2/43; Sioux City 6/4/43; Casper 15/5/43; McClellan 31/5/43; Tinker 18/6/43; Walla Walla 21/7/43; 325 BU Avon Park 17/7/44; RFC Walnut Ridge 14/12/45.

42-29602 Del Cheyenne 15/1/43; Salina 23/1/43; Kearney 26/2/43; Morrison 9/3/43; ass 20BS/2BG Navarin 4/4/43; Château-du-Rhumel 27/4/43; Ain M'Lila 17/6/43; Massi-cault 31/7/43; Bizerte 2/12/43; Amendola 9/12/43; MIA Porto Civitanova 21/1/44 w/Watkins, ditched off Bari, crew rescued by two small Italian boats.

42-29603 Del Cheyenne 16/1/43; Salina 9/2/43; Brookley 12/3/43; Morrison 31/3/43; ass 511BS/351BG [DS-R] Polebrook 18/4/43; MIA {15m} Anklam 9/10/43 w/Maser; e/a, cr Flemsburg, Ger, 1KIA 9POW. MACR 875. SPIT BALL.

42-29604 Del Cheyenne 16/1/43; Salina 27/1/43; Kearney 6/2/43; Lincoln 4/3/43; Morrison 10/3/43; ass 20BS/2BG Navarin 19/3/43; Château-du-Rhumel 27/4/43; Ain M'Lila 17/6/43; Massicault 31/7/43; Bizerte 2/12/43; Amendola 9/12/43; tran 99BG Tortorella 28/3/44; 483BG Tortorella 31/3/43; 463BG Celone 4/44 as weather a/c; sal 10/10/44. THUNDERMUG.

42-29605 Del Cheyenne 17/1/43; Salina 31/1/43; Kearney 7/2/43; Morrison 9/3/43; ass 429BS/2BG Navarin 17/4/43; Château-du-Rhumel 27/4/43; Ain M'Lila 16/6/43; MIA {15m} Naples 21/6/43 w/Bentley; coll w/ME 109; MACR 313. HONEY BUN.

42-29606 Del Cheyenne 18/1/43; Salina 9/2/43; Morrison 10/3/43; ass 360BS/303BG [PU-W] Molesworth 6/4/43; MIA Hamburg 25/7/43 w/Van Wie, flak, cr Hamburg, 4KIA 6POW. MACR 91. TOOTS - BUTCH.

42-29607 Del Cheyenne 17/1/43; Salina 28/1/43; Kearney 4/2/43; Morrison 8/3/43; ass 20BS/2BG Navarin 19/3/43; Château-du-Rhumel 27/4/43; Ain M'Lila 17/6/43; MIA {27m} Catania 4/7/43 w/Laich; hit by bomb from above a/c and exploded; six chutes seen. MACR 88.

42-29608 Del Cheyenne 17/1/43; Salina 28/1/43; Morrison 9/3/43; ass 96BS/2BG Navarin 17/4/43; Château-du-Rhumel 27/4/43; Ain M'Lila 17/6/43; Massicault 31/7/43; Bizerte 2/12/43; Amendola 9/12/43; MIA Udine 31/1/44 w/Kolstad, flak, 10 chutes seen. MACR 2063.

42-29609 Del Cheyenne 17/1/43; Salina 28/1/43; Kearney 4/2/43; Morrison 10/3/43; ass 20BS/2BG Navarin 17/4/43; Château-du-Rhumel 27/4/43; Ain M'Lila 17/6/43; Massicault 31/7/43; MIA {66m} Bolzano 10/11/43 w/Wika; e/a, 2 chutes seen. MACR 1120.

42-29610 Del Cheyenne 17/1/43; Wright Fd 20/1/43; Denver 26/1/43; Smyrna 31/1/43; Tinker 28/2/43; Hobbs 29/4/43; 3017 BU Hobbs 8/11/44; RFC Altus 11/9/45.

42-29611 Del Denver 17/1/43; Cheyenne 26/1/43; Kearney 4/2/43; ass 8 Weather Region, Grenier 25/3/43; 1380 BU Presue Is 3/10/43; tran 49BS/2BG Bizerte 30/11/43; Amendola 9/12/43; {52m} RetUS Azores 9/8/44; RFC Kingman 7/10/46. A-MERRY-CAN.

42-29612 Del Denver 17/1/43; Salina 26/1/43; Kearney 4/2/43; Orlando 11/3/43; Nashville 10/4/43; Dow Fd 12/4/43; ass 325BS/92BG [JW-J] (& 325BS) Alconbury 25/4/43; MIA Hannover 26/7/43 w/Belongia; e/a, ditched off Sheringham, UK.

42-29613 Del Cheyenne 17/1/43; Salina 31/1/43; Morrison 9/3/43; ass 20BS/2BG Navarin 17/4/43; Château-du-Rhumel 27/4/43; Ain M'Lila 17/6/43; Massicault 31/7/43; Bizerte 2/12/43; Amendola 9/12/43; tran 99BG Tortorella 28/3/44; 840BS/483BG Tortorella 31/3/45; retUS Morrison 27/2/45; RFC Bush Fd 3/7/45.

42-29614 Del Cheyenne 17/1/43; Salina 31/1/43; Morrison 9/3/43; ass 20BS/2BG Navarin 17/4/43; MIA {3m} La Goulette 9/5/43 w/Thompson; ditched Med Sea. MACR 2817 & 2824 (sqd's first loss).

42-29615 Del Cheyenne 17/1/43; Salina 31/1/43; Kearney 4/2/43; Morrison 9/3/43; ass 49BS/2BG Navarin 17/4/43; Château-du-Rhumel 27/4/43; Ain M'Lila 17/6/43; MIA {23m} Messina 25/6/43 w/Hinsey, coll w/ME 109 (tore of wing & #4 engine); one chute seen; MACR 46.

42-29616 Del Wright Fd 17/1/43; Gore Fd 19/3/43; Memphis 31/3/43; Wright 5/5/43; Eglin 16/6/43; Mat Com Wright 2/6/44; 611 BU Eglin 8/6/44; 4117 BU Robins 22/8/44; 610 BU Eglin 13/10/44; ATS Wright 31/10/44; 4100 BU Patterson 14/11/44; 611 BU Eglin 1/4/45; 4032 BU Ypsilanti 20/6/45; RFC Altus 29/10/45.

42-29617 Del Cheyenne 17/1/43; Salina 31/1/43; Kearney 6/2/43; ass 49BS/2BG Navarin 17/4/43; Château-du-Rhumel 27/4/43; Ain M'Lila 17/6/43; Massicault 31/7/43; Bizerte 2/12/43; Amendola 9/12/43; {40m}, c/l Palermo (non op) 10/12/43 w/Taylor, one killed.

42-29618 Del Cheyenne 17/1/43; Denver 20/1/43; Pueblo 25/1/43; Blythe 18/3/43; Biggs 7/4/43; Clovis 28/4/43; Biggs 5/5/43; Lowry 17/5/43; Salina (Cal) 4/6/43; Blythe 20/7/43; Davis Monthan 11/8/43; 241

BU Fairmont 22/6/44; 504BG Fairmont 4/7/44; 232 BU Dalhart 24/8/44; 2038 BU Jackson 4/4/45; RFC Albuquerque 2/8/45.

42-29619 Del Cheyenne 17/1/43; Salina 31/1/43; Kearney 7/2/43; Morrison 10/3/43; ass 301BG St Donat 19/3/43; tran 96BS/2BG Navarin 17/4/43; Château-du-Rhumel 27/4/43; Ain M'Lila 17/6/43; Massicault 31/7/43; Bizerte 2/12/43; Amendola 9/12/43; 99BG Tortorella 28/3/43; 483BG Tortorella 31/3/43; 463BG 9/44; retUS Morrison 26/4/45; RFC Bush Fd 18/6/43.

42-29620 Del Cheyenne 24/1/43; Salina 9/2/43; ass 303BG Molesworth 15/4/43; tran 367BS/206BG Thurleigh 17/4/43; MIA St Nazaire 1/5/43 w/Luby, e/a, ditched Channel, 10KIA, MACR 15715.

42-29621 Del Denver 18/1/43; Pueblo 26/1/43; Denver 31/1/43; Pyote 9/3/43; Tinker 8/11/43; WO 12/1/44.

42-29622 Del Denver 17/1/43; Blythe 26/1/43; Dyersburg 13/5/43; 9BG McCook 8/6/44; 245 BU McCook 16/9/44; 120 BU Richmond 28/9/44; 245 BU McCook 6/1/45; RFC Albuquerque 27/6/45.

42-29623 Del Cheyenne 17/1/43; Salina 30/1/43; Morrison 10/3/43; ass 49BS/2BG Navarin 17/4/43; Château-du-Rhumel 27/4/43; Ain M'Lila 17/6/43; Massicault 31/7/43; Bizerte 2/12/43; Amendola 9/12/43; coll w/42-29909in taxi acc. 3/2/44, WO. BOYS.

42-29624 Del Cheyenne 24/1/43; Salina 9/2/43; Morrison 9/3/43; ass 359BS/303BG Molesworth 6/4/43; tran 326BS/92BG Alconbury 27/7/43; 527BS/379BG [FO-N] Kimbolton 13/9/43; 2 BAD Lt Staughton 5/4/44, sal. PAPPY.

42-29625 Del Cheyenne 26/1/43; Salina 9/2/43; ass 369BS/306BG [WW-B] Thurleigh 12/3/43; MIA Bremen 17/4/43 w/Harwood, flak, cr Bremen, 3KIA 7POW. MACR 15517.

42-29626 Del Cheyenne 23/1/43; Gt Falls 31/1/43; Cheyenne 18/2/43; Gore Fd 28/2/43; Brooksville 6/3/43; Hendricks 30/3/43; New York PE 20/5/43; Orlando 3/12/43; 234 BU Clovis 24/6/44; 249 BU Alliance 15/10/44; 243 BU Gt Bend 15/1/45; 902 BU Orlando 16/4/43; 241 BU Fairmont 8/7/45; 243 BU Gt Bend 12/7/45; RFC Kingman 27/10/45.

42-29627 Del Cheyenne 29/1/43; Pueblo 19/2/43; Salina 25/2/43; Tinker 20/3/43; Smoky Hill 29/3/43; Presque Is 6/4/43; ass 410BS/94BG Bassingbourn 25/4/43; Earls Colne 12/5/43; MIA Lorient 17/5/43 w/ Spevak, flak, cr Lorient, 4EVD 1KIA 5POW. (First group loss) MIDNIGHT.

42-29628 Del Cheyenne 18/1/43; Salina 28/1/43; Kearney 4/2/43; Memphis 9/3/43; ass 49BS/2BG Navarin 17/4/43; Château-du-Rhumel 27/4/43; Ain M'Lila 17/6/43; Massicault 31/7/43; Bizerte 2/12/43; Amendola 9/12/43; {80m} tran 99BG Tortorella 28/3/44; 840BS/483BG Tortorella 31/3/44; retUS Morrison 14/5/44; RFC Bush Fd 23/5/45. MEL'S MESS.

42-29629 Del Cheyenne 18/1/43; Salina 1/2/43; Homestead 17/2/43; New Castle 25/2/43; ass 369BS/306BG [WW-A] Thurleigh 12/3/43; tran 358BS/303BG Molesworth 25/9/43; retUS 560 BU Palm Springs 25/4/44; 4100 BU Patterson 23/2/45; RFC Bush Fd 7/7/45. CONNECTICUT YANKEE.

42-29630 Del Cheyenne 23/1/43; Salina 9/2/43; ass 508BS/351BG [YB-S] Polebrook 27/5/43; then 509BS [RQ-S]; MIA {30m} Bordeaux 31/12/43 w/Smith, flak, cr Cognac, 10POW. MACR 1985. PICCADILLY COMMANDO.

42-29631 Del Cheyenne 18/1/43; Salina 3/2/43; Morrison 25/2/43; ass 423BS/306BG Thurleigh 25/3/43; MIA Bremen 17/4/43 w/George; e/a, cr Wiesens, Ger, 2KIA 8POW. MACR 15444. UNMENTIONABLE.

42-29632 Del Cheyenne 23/1/43; Salina 5/3/43; Smoky Hill 14/3/43; Nashville 8/4/43; ass 422BS/305BG [JJ-N] Chelveston 23/6/43; tran 545BS/384BG [JD-K] Grafton Underwood 8/10/43; 2 BAD Lt Staughton 4/4/44; retUS Rome 20/8/44; Williams 15/11/44; La Junta 1/4/45; RFC Searcey Fd 4/8/45. CASED ACE.

42-29633 Del Cheyenne 26/1/43; Salina 12/2/43; ass 364BS/305BG [WF-H/J/N/D] Chelveston 4/3/43; tran 381BG Ridgewell 11/9/43 {1m}; 526BS/379BG [LF-U] Kimbolton 26/9/43; then 525BS [FR-C]; MIA Frankfurt 8/2/44 w/Beam; e/a, cr Amiens, 4EVD 1KIA 5POW. MACR 2869.

42-29634 Del Cheyenne 26/1/43; Salina 31/1/43; Salina 9/2/43; ass 364BS/305BG [WF-A] Chelveston 21/3/43; became training a/c 3/6/43; tran CCRC Bovingdon as trainer 30/6/43; sal 18/6/45.

42-29635 Del Cheyenne 24/1/43; Salina 7/2/43; ass 358BS/303BG [VK-M] Molesworth 26/3/43; MIA Amiens-Glisy 31/8/43 w/Monahan, e/a, cr Abbeville, 3EVD 1KIA 6POW. MACR 470. AUGERHEAD.

42-29636 Del Cheyenne 23/1/43; Gt Falls 31/1/43; Salina 3/2/43; Nashville 23/2/43; ass 364BS/305BG [WF-G] Chelveston VANISHING VIRGIN 24/3/43; tran 546BS/384BG [BK-F] Grafton Underwood 30/9/43; 1 BAD Burtonwood 15/3/44; retUS Lockburn 3/8/44; RFC Walnut Ridge 18/12/45. X-VIRGIN.

42-29637 Del Denver 24/1/43; Salina 31/1/43; Tinker 14/4/43; Spokane 31/5/43; Ephrata 8/6/43; ground-looped and burned out 8/7/43 w/Voellneck. Sal.

42-29638 Del Denver 24/1/43; Salina 29/1/43; Morrison 10/3/43; ass 49BS/2BG Navarin 17/4/43; Château-du-Rhumel 27/4/43; Ain M'Lila 17/6/43; Massicault 31/7/43; Bizerte 2/12/43; Amendola 9/12/43; MIA Steyr 24/2/44 w/Glass; e/a, cr Fuehl. MACR 2618.

42-29639 Del Denver 28/1/43; Salina 31/1/43; Morrison 10/3/43; ass 96BS/2BG Navarin 17/4/43; Château-du-Rhumel 27/4/43; Ain M'Lila 17/6/43; Massicault 31/7/43; Bizerte 2/12/43; Amendola 9/12/43; MIA {85m} Steyr 24/2/44 w/ Byrne; e/a, cr Kaisergut, 4 chutes seen. MACR 2702.

42-29640 Del Cheyenne 23/1/43; Salina 7/2/43; ass 359BS/303BG [BN-X] Molesworth 26/3/43; MIA Gelsenkirchen 12/8/43 w/Pentz; e/a, cr Linnich, nr Wuppertal; 1KIA 9POW. MACR 256. OL' IRONSIDES.

42-29641 Del Cheyenne 26/1/43; Salina 9/2/43; ass 422BS/305BG [JJ-V] Chelveston 21/3/43; MIA Nantes 4/7/43 w/Scott, flak, cr Biscay, 10KIA; MACR 4483. BLACK SWAN.

42-29642 Del Cheyenne 22/1/43; Salina 3/2/43; ass 323BS/91BG [OR-L] Bassingbourn 16/3/43; MIA {6m} Meaulte 13/5/43 w/Starke, e/a, exploded cr Abbeville 8KIA 3POW. (extra man - photographer).VULGAR VIRGIN.

42-29643 Del Cheyenne 18/1/43; Salina 6/2/43; Duncan 19/2/43; Homestead 28/2/43; ass 367BS/306BG Thurleigh 13/3/43; MIA Bremen 17/4/43 w/Miller; flak, cr Bremen, 10POW. MACR 15523.

42-29644 Del Denver 23/1/43; Wright Fd 1/2/43; Boca Raton 29/3/43; Smoky Hill 16/4/43; ass Glen 23/4/43; retUS Mitchel 7/12/43; Scott Fd 13/1/44; 2114 BU Lockburn 24/9/44; RFC Walnut Ridge 14/12/45.

42-29645 Del Denver 23/1/43; Salina 29/1/43; Morrison 8/3/43; ass 49BS/2BG Navarin 17/4/43; Château-du-Rhumel 27/4/43; Ain M'Lila 17/6/43; Massicault 31/7/43; Bizerte 2/12/43; Amendola 9/12/43; MIA Sofia 24/1/44 w/McCrary; ditched off Civitanova, nr Bari; crew rescued. WILEY WITCH.

42-29646 Del Denver 26/1/43; Salina 31/1/43; Kearney 6/2/43; ass 49BS/2BG Navarin 17/4/43; Château-du-Rhumel 27/4/43; Ain M'Lila 17/6/43; Massicault 31/7/43; MIA {64m} Bolzano 10/11/43 w/Spinning, 2 engines on fire, ditched Adriatic. MACR 1144.

42-29647 Del Cheyenne 26/1/43; Salina 9/2/43; ass 365BS/305BG Chelveston 8/4/43; damaged in coll w/Halifax at RAF St Eval 29/3/43; MIA Meaulte 13/5/43 w/Pierce; e/a, cr nr target, 10KIA. MACR 16542.

42-29648 Del Denver 30/1/43; Gt falls 19/2/43; Pyote 22/2/43; Alexandria 11/7/43; 234 BU Clovis 24/6/44; 4100 BU Patterson 13/1/45; 2038 BU Jackson 17/4/45; 215 BU Pueblo 16/9/45; RFC Kingman 27/10/45.

42-29649 Del Denver 29/1/43; Gt Falls 31/1/43; Salina 13/2/43; ass 423BS/306BG Thurleigh 24/3/43; b/d St Nazaire 1/5/43; f/l Predannack, UK, sal 5/3/43. (MOH for Sgt Maynard 'Snuffy' Smith.)

42-29650 Del Cheyenne 29/1/43; Gt falls 31/1/43; Gowen 13/2/43; Geiger 9/6/43; Rapid City 20/6/43; Tinker 18/11/43; 328 BU Gulfport 12/11/44; 4100 BU Patterson 25/1/45; 325 BU Avon Park 9/4/45; RFC Walnut Ridge 29/8/45.

42-29651 Del Cheyenne 26/1/43; Salina 9/2/43; Brookley 3/3/43; Morrison 9/3/43; ass 544BS/384BG [SU-I] Grafton Underwood 27/6/43; then [SU-K/G]; on arrival in UK f/l in field at Lytchett Minster, stripped to lighten and flew out OK; tran 2 BAD Lt Staughton 4/4/44; retUS Tinker 3/7/44; Homestead 8/7/44; Patterson 15/2/45; RFC Altus 17/8/45. STELLA.

42-29652 Del Cheyenne 29/1/43; Gt Falls 31/1/43; Salina 18/2/43; Smoky Hill 8/4/43; Tinker 19/4/43; Memphis 7/5/43; Olmstead 16/5/43; Morrison 20/5/43; ass 353BS/301BG St Donat 28/5/43; Oudna 6/8/43; {27m} tran 20BS/2BG Massicault 14/11/43; Bizerte 2/12/43; Amendola 9/2/43; 347BS/99BG Tortorella 28/3/44 {2m}; 483BG Tortorella 31/3/44; retUS Morrison 13/4/45; Rome 24/4/45; RFC Bush Fd 3/7/45.

42-29653 Del Cheyenne 30/1/43; Salina 11/2/43; Morrison 28/2/43; {Secret mission 19/5/43}; ass 96BG Dow Fd 4/6/43; tran 327BS/92BG Alconbury 19/7/43; 525BS/379BG [FR-D] Kimbolton 4/9/43; MIA Schweinfurt 14/10/43 w/Jones, e/a, cr Schweinfurt, 4KIA 6POW. MACR 956. BAD NEWS.

42-29654 Del Cheyenne 28/1/43; Walker 23/2/43; Smoky Hill 28/3/43; Presque Is 5/4/43; ass 337BS/96BG Grafton Underwood 18/4/43; tran 508BS/351BG [YB-B] Polebrook 11/7/43; then 509BS [RQ-B]; 1 BAD Burtonwood 31/3/44; retUS Tinker 3/7/44; Homestead 8/7/44; Patterson 22/2/45; RFC Altus 29/10/45. DOTTIE J.

42-29655 Del Denver 2/2/43; Gt Falls 17/2/43; Walla Walla 23/2/43; Madras 19/6/43; Walla Walla 17/7/43; McChord 10/8/43; 4117 BU Robins 26/7/44; 325 BU Avon Park 27/7/44; 2137 BU Hendricks 10/5/45; 325 BU Avon Park 23/5/45; RFC Altus 22/8/45.

42-29656 Del Denver 2/2/43; Salina 9/2/43; ass 358BS/303BG [VK-F] Molesworth 21/3/43 THE TERRIBLE TEN; tran 322BS/91BG [LG-S] Bassingbourn 5/7/43; MIA {19m} Aschersleben w/Kidd 20/2/44; e/a, cr Malmedy, Bel; 2KIA 8POW. MACR 2460. SKUNKFACE.

42-29657 Del Cheyenne 30/1/43; Salina 12/2/43; ass 323BS/91BG [OR-X] Bassingbourn 26/3/43; MIA Wilhemshafen 21/5/43 w/Retchin; s/d by e/a.

42-29658 Del Cheyenne 29/1/43; Salina 11/2/43; ass 367BS/306BG Thurleigh 16/3/43; then 369BS; MIA

Bremen 17/4/43 w/Watson; flak, cr Stotel; 5KIA 5POW; MACR 15446.
42-29659 Del Denver 28/1/43; Salina 9/2/43; ass 324BS/91BG Bassingbourn 15/3/43; MIA {1m} Wilhelmshaven 22/3/43 w/McClellan (w/92BG crew); s/d by e/a; cr Nth Sea, 11KIA, (hit by bomb from ME 109 above). MACR 16291. LIBERTY BELL.
42-29660 Del Denver 29/1/43; Salina 9/2/43; ass 367BS/306BG Thurleigh 22/3/43; MIA Antwerp 5/4/43 w/Ross; e/a, cr Antwerp; 2KIA 7POW; L'LL ABNER.
42-29661 Del Denver 29/1/43; Gt Falls 31/1/43; Gowen 15/2/43; Tinker 12/5/43; Dyersburg 26/5/43; 498BG Gt Bend 23/7/44; 233 BU Davis Monthan 14/8/44; 243 BU Gt Bend 30/9/44; 902 BU Orlando 22/4/45; 243 BU Gt Bend 20/5/45; RFC Albuquerque 25/6/45.
42-29662 Del Denver 29/1/43; Patterson 12/2/43; Wright 1/3/43; Colorado Springs 14/3/43; Kirtland 9/6/43; San Antonio 13/6/43; Peterson 21/6/43; Will Rogers 3/12/43; 326 BU McDill 11/8/44; 328 BU Gulfport 25/1/45; RFC Albuquerque 25/6/45.
42-29663 Del Denver 29/1/43; Salina 3/2/43; Homestead 19/2/43; ass 364BS/305BG [WF-H] Chelveston 2/3/43; MIA Lorient 17/5/43 w/Tuttle; e/a, cr Lorient, 1EVD 4KIA 6POW. MACR 15555.
42-29664 Del Denver 30/1/43; Salina 12/2/43; Morrison 28/2/43; ass 358BS/303BG [VK-C] Molesworth 21/3/43; MIA Bremen 20/12/43 w/Henderson; flak, ditched Channel, 10RTD. (MOH Sgt Forrest Vosler). JERSEY BOUNCE Jr.
42-29665 Del Cheyenne 29/1/43; Gowen 16/2/43; Tinker 12/5/43; Dyersburg 27/5/43; 504BG Fairmont 14/6/44; 241 BU Fairmont 16/9/44; 249 BU Alliance 11/10/44; 221 BU Alexandra 20/10/44; 329 BU Alexandra 1/3/45; RFC Altus 9/10/45.
42-29666 Del Cheyenne 30/1/43; Salina 14/2/43; Barksdale 22/2/43; Morrison 5/3/43; ass 423BS/306BG [RD-O] Thurleigh 25/3/43; MIA Wilhelmshaven 21/5/43 w/Smith; e/a, ditched Nth Sea, 9RTD. DEARLY BELOVED.
42-29667 Del Cheyenne 30/1/43; Gowen 13/2/43; Moses Lake 15/6/43; WO 11/7/43.
42-29668 Del Cheyenne 31/1/43; Gowen 13/2/43; Sioux City 25/2/43; Casper 25/3/43; Sioux City 30/6/43; Tinker 9/7/43; Dalhart 30/7/43; WO 26/9/43.
42-29669 Del Cheyenne 31/1/43; Gowen 13/2/43; Sioux City 25/2/43; Gowen 9/4/43; Moses Lake 9/6/43; Spokane 21/7/43; Moses Lake 8/8/43; 3705 BU Lowry 1/5/45; 3017 BU Hobbs 4/7/45; RFC Albuquerque 2/8/45.
42-29670 Del Cheyenne 31/1/43; Pueblo 18/2/43; Salina 15/2/43; Brookley 19/3/43; Smoky Hill 23/3/43; Dow Fd 18/4/43; ass 333BS/94BG Bassingbourn 22/4/43; tran 544BS/384BG [SU-K] Grafton Underwood 16/7/43; MIA Hamburg 25/7/43 w/Hall, flak, cr Hamburg; 2KIA 8POW. THUNDERMUG.
42-29671 Del Cheyenne 31/1/43; Gowen 13/2/43; Tinker 22/5/43; Dalhart 13/6/43; Smoky Hill 16/8/43; 29BG Geiger 27/10/43; Avon Park 23/11/43; 4100 BU Patterson 22/10/44; 331 BU Barksdale 12/2/45; 4104 BU Rome 10/4/45; 331 BU Barksdale 5/5/45; RFC Altus 4/10/45.
42-29672 Del Cheyenne 31/1/43; Gowen 13/2/43; Sioux City 25/2/43; Smoky Hill 29/3/43; Gowen 10/5/43; Casper 20/7/43; 222 BU Ardmore 14/8/44, WO.
42-29673 Del Cheyenne 31/1/43; Gt Falls 8/2/43; Morrison 5/3/43; ass 365BS/305BG [XK-S] Chelveston 6/4/43; then 422BS; b/d Wangerooge 15/5/43, sal 16/5/43. OLD BILL.

42-29674 Del Cheyenne 31/1/43; Gt Falls 14/2/43; Gowen 19/2/43; Sioux City 25/2/43; Watertown 3/3/43; Sioux City 6/3/43; Walla Walla 12/4/43; 325 BU Avon Park 5/7/44, 4104 BU Rome 2/11/44; Wright Air. Corp, Caldwell, NJ 30/3/45; Patterson 28/8/45; RFC Walnut Ridge 8/10/45. CINCINNATI QUEEN.
42-29675 Del Cheyenne 4/2/43; Rapid City 22/2/43; Kearney 12/3/43; Morrison 24/4/43; ass 336BS/95BG Alconbury 5/4/43; MIA Keil 13/6/43 w/Adams; e/a, cr Lindholm, Den; 10KIA MACR 2169.
42-29676 Del Denver 2/2/43; Gt Falls 15/1/43; Fairfield 23/2/43; Romulus 8/3/43; Colorado Springs 14/3/43; Peterson 11/6/43; 902 BU Orlando 2/6/44; RFC Walnut Ridge 21/1/46.
42-29677 Del Cheyenne 2/2/43; Walker 27/2/43; Salina 10/3/43; Presque Is 8/4/43; Stephenville, Nfd, 12/4/43; ass 96BG Grafton Underwood 18/4/43; tran 367BS/306BG Thurleigh 20/4/43; MIA Heligoland 15/5/43 w/Mann, e/a, ditched Nth Sea, 7KIA 3POW. MACR 16060. BATTLIN' B.
42-29678 Del Cheyenne 2/2/43; Gowen 19/2/43; Tinker 25/5/43; Dyersburg 22/6/43; Tinker 30/7/43; 328 BU Gulfport 12/6/44; 3705 BU Lowry 18/6/44; 3701 BU Amarillo 23/7/44; 3706 BU Sheppard 27/2/45; 3701 BU Amarillo 19/8/45; RFC Walnut Ridge 5/1/46.
42-29679 Del Cheyenne 3/2/43; Salina 17/2/43; Rapid City 20/2/43; Kearney 12/3/43; Morrison 28/3/43; ass 336BS/95BG [ET-F] 29/3/43; {4m} tran 401BS/91BG [LL-A1] (then M) Bassingbourn 13/6/43; {24m} ASFSC 30/4/44; retUS Lockburn 4/8/45; RFC Altus 4/9/45. RAMBLIN'. WRECK.
42-29680 Del Denver 2/2/43; Salina 14/2/43; Rapid City 16/2/43; Kearney 12/3/43; Morrison 25/3/43; ass 335BS/95BG [OE-R] Alconbury 24/4/43; MIA Kiel 13/6/43 w/Nunes, e/a, cr Tonder, Den, 10KIA MACR 2751.
42-29681 Del Cheyenne 29/1/43; Orlando 25/12/43; El Paso 31/12/43; 2117 BU Buckingham 11/7/44; 2114 BU Lockburn 10/9/44; RFC Walnut Ridge 18/12/45.
42-29682 Del Cheyenne 4/2/43; Pueblo 18/2/43; Salina 25/2/43; Brookley 19/3/43; Smoky Hill 23/3/43; Syracuse 14/4/43; Dow Fd 19/4/43; ass 410BS/94BG Earls Colne 25/4/43; MIA Emden 21/5/43 W/Wieand; e/a, ditched Nth Sea; 10KIA. EASY ACES.
42-29683 Del Cheyenne 2/2/43; Gt Falls 17/2/43; 381BG Pyote 24/2/43; Tinker 9/8/43; Walla Walla 11/10/43; 4104 BU Rome 31/10/44; RFC Walnut Ridge 14/12/45.
42-29684 Del Cheyenne 2/2/43; Gore 17/3/43; Presque Is 8/4/43; ass 509BS/351BG [RQ-T] Polebrook 17/4/43; MIA Stuttgart 6/9/43 w/Hatheway, no gas, ditched Channel; 10RTD. EAGER EAGLE.
42-29685 Del Cheyenne 2/2/43; Salina 17/2/43; Rapid City 20/2/43; Kearney 12/3/43; Presque Is 8/4/43; ass 334BS/95BG Alconbury 30/3/43; blew up on base 27/5/43, sal (along with 3 other a/c, 5 severe damage & 6 minor damage).
42-29686 Del Denver 2/2/43; 94BG Pueblo 18/2/43; Salina 25/2/43; Brookley 19/3/43; Smoky Hill 23/3/43; Gulfport 10/4/43; ass 331BS/94BG [QE-R] Earls Colne 12/5/43; tran 547BS/384BG [SO-B] Grafton Underwood 12/7/43; MIA Bonn 12/8/43 w/Bigelow; e/a, cr Heisterbacherrott, Ger; 2KIA 8POW, MACR 290. PIE-EYED PIPER.
42-29687 Del Denver 3/2/43; Gowen 12/2/43; Geiger 11/5/43; Moses Lake 3/6/43; Spokane 13/8/43; 3701 BU Amarillo 12/6/44; 2114 BU Lockburn 16/3/45;

RFC Altus 9/10/45.
42-29688 Del Denver 3/2/43; Salina 10/2/43; ass 365BS/305BG [XK-X] Chelveston 17/3/43; tran 546BS/384BG [BK-X] Grafton Underwood 26/8/43; then 547BS [SO-S]; 2 BAD Lt Staughton 4/4/44; retUS Brookley 11/8/44; Homestead 17/7/45; Patterson 22/7/45; WO Mobile 31/9/45. KAYO.
42-29689 Del Denver 3/2/43; Salina 14/2/43; Rapid City 16/2/43; Kearney 12/3/43; ass 334BS/95BG [BG-H] Alconbury 29/3/43; MIA Rennes 29/5/43 w/Watson; coll w/e/a, cr Rennes; 5EVD 5POW. MACR 4895.
42-29690 Del Cheyenne 4/2/43; Pueblo 19/2/43; Salina 27/2/43; Syracuse 15/4/43; Dow Fd 18/4/43; ass 331BS/94BG [QE-S] Earls Colne 12/5/43; tran 366BS/305BG [KY-L] Chelveston 14/7/43; b/d Warnemünde, c/l Oulton 29/7/43, sal AFSC. OLD FAITHFUL.
42-29691 Del Cheyenne 4/2/43; 19BG & 381BG Pyote 19/2/43; Dyersburg 22/5/43; WO 3/9/43.
42-29692 Del Cheyenne 4/2/43; Pueblo 18/2/43; Salina 25/2/43; Smoky Hill 18/3/43; ass 410BS/94BG Earls Colne 12/5/43; MIA Rennes 29/5/43 w/Brown; e/a, cr Rennes 8KIA 1POW.
42-29693 Del Cheyenne 4/2/43; Rapid City 20/2/43; Kearney 12/3/43; ass 412BS/95BG [QW-O] Alconbury 29/3/43; MIA Cuxhaven 11/6/43 w/MacKinnon; e/a, cr Nth Sea, 10KIA. MACR 2807. LONESOME POLECAT.
42-29694 Del Denver 5/2/43; Salina 12/2/43; Rapid City 16/2/43; Kearney 12/3/43; Morrison 29/3/43; ass 412BS/95BG Alconbury 5/4/43; tran 407BS/92BG [PY-V] Alconbury 7/7/43; 527BS/379BG [FO-X] Kimbolton 4/9/43; MIA Bremen 26/11/43 w/Malarin; flak, cr Bremen; 6KIA 4POW. MACR 1577. SOUTHERN BELLE.
42-29695 Del Denver 5/2/43; Gowen 12/2/43; Lowry 12/3/43; Oklahoma City 12/5/43; Pyote 30/5/43; Tinker 16/10/43; Pyote 9/11/43; 329 BU Alexandra 24/8/43; 3701 BU Amarillo 20/11/43; WO 27/12/43; Recl Comp 9/4/46.
42-29696 Del Denver 5/2/43; Gore 18/3/43; Tinker 29/3/43; New castle 4/4/43; Homestead 12/4/43; Morrison 24/4/43; ass 416BS/99BG Navarin 11/5/43; Oudna 4/8/43; Tortorella 11/12/43; tran 840BG/483BG Tortorella 31/3/44; {131m} WW 15/10/44, sal. FORT ALAMO II.
42-29697 Del Denver 5/2/43; Gowen 12/2/43; Gt Falls 17/2/43; Gowen 20/5/43; Tinker 22/5/43; Walker 25/6/43; New castle 17/6/43; Dalhart 17/7/43; c/l Amarillo 17/8/43 w/Bob Deering (later 381BG); WO 18/8/43.
42-29698 Del Cheyenne 5/2/43; 94BG Pueblo 18/2/43; Salina 27/2/43; Selman 17/3/43; Brookley 25/3/43; Dow Fd 16/4/43; ass 331BS/94BG [QE-T] Earls Colne 12/5/43; Rougham 13/6/43; tran 326BS/92BG Alconbury 3/8/43 HELL'S ANGEL; then 407BS; c/l Alconbury 27/8/43; sal 29/8/43. WILD ANGEL.
42-29699 Del Cheyenne 5/2/43; 94BG Pueblo 18/2/43; Salina 27/2/43; Brookley 19/3/43; Smoky Hill 23/3/43; Presque Is 9/4/43; ass 332BS/94BG [XM-F] Earls Colne 12/5/43 FIFI; Rougham 13/6/43; tran 547BS/384BG Grafton Underwood [SO-D] 16/7/43; MIA Nantes 16/9/43 w/Price; s/d by e/d, ditched Nth Sea, 10RTD. OLD BATTLE AXE.
42-29700 Del Cheyenne 6/2/43; 94BG Pueblo 18/2/43; Salina 25/2/43; Presque Is 8/4/43; ass 331BS/94BG [QE-O] Bassingbourn 17/4/43; Earls Colne 12/5/43; Rougham 13/6/43; tran 384BG Grafton Underwood 12/7/43; MIA T/Os w/Roberts 29/7/43. JIMMIE BOY.
42-29701 Del Denver 3/1/43; Pueblo 12/3/43; Presque

Is 8/4/43; ass 510BS/351BG [TU-B] Polebrook 17/4/43; MIA {1m} Kiel 19/5/43 w/Mansfield; flak hit ditched Baltic; 2EVD 3KIA 5POW. MACR 15719. IN THE MOOD.

42-29702 Del Cheyenne 7/2/43; Rapid City 20/2/43; Kearney 12/3/43; Brookley 27/3/43; Morrison 9/4/43; ass 336BS/95BG [ET-H] Alconbury 13/4/43; Framlingham 12/5/43; MIA Kiel 13/6/43 w/Renaud; s/d by ea, cr Lindholm, Den. 10KIA. MACR 4896. RAT KILLER.

42-29703 Del Cheyenne 7/2/43; Rapid City 22/2/43; Kearney 12/3/43; ass 336BS/95BG [ET-A] Alconbury 8/4/43; Framlingham 12/5/43; tran 544BS/384BG [SU-E] Grafton Underwood 10/7/43; 2 BAD Lt Staughton 5/4/44; retUS Tinker 6/6/44; Recl Comp 9/2/45. KATHY JANE.

42-29704 Del Cheyenne 6/2/43; Rapid City 20/2/43; Kearney 12/3/43; ass 336BS/95BG [ET-J] Alconbury 29/3/43; Framlingham 12/5/43; b/d Lorient, c/l RAF Exeter 17/5/43 w/Bender. 10RTD. SPOOK.

42-29705 Del Cheyenne 7/2/43; Rapid City 22/2/43; Kearney 12/3/43; ass 336BS/95BG Alconbury 30/3/43; tran 524BS/379BG [WA-G] Kimbolton 5/43; 2 SAD Lt Staughton 28/11/43; sal 22/6/45. SWEET 17.

42-29706 Del Cheyenne 7/2/43; Rapid City 22/2/43; Kearney 12/3/43; Morrison 14/4/43; Dow Fd 21/4/43; ass 412BS/95BG [QW-W] Alconbury 25/4/43; Framlingham 12/5/43; WO after another a/c exploded on base 27/5/43, sal. PASSION FLOWER.

42-29707 Del Cheyenne 7/2/43; Gt Falls 17/2/43; Pyote 22/2/43; Amarillo 21/7/43; 505BG Harvard 2/6/44; 244 BU Harvard 23/8/44; 4209 BU Des Moines 8/4/45; 244 BU Harvard 18/4/45; RFC Albuquerque 25/6/45.

42-29708 Del Cheyenne 7/2/43; Pueblo 19/2/43; Salina 25/2/43; Brookley 19/3/43; Smoky Hill 23/3/43; Brookley 9/4/43; ass 336BS/95BG Alconbury 27/4/43; tran 333BS/94BG Earls Colne 12/5/43; then 322BS; Rougham 13/6/43; MIA Kiel 13/6/43 w/Thorup; e/a, ditched Nth Sea, 10RTD. SHACKEROO !

42-29709 Del Cheyenne 7/2/43; Rapid City 20/2/43; Kearney 12/3/43; ass 335BS/95BG [OE-C] Alconbury 30/3/43; Framlingham 12/5/43; MIA Rennes 29/5/43 w/Hermance; coll w/42-5858 (ret); MACR 190. YO' BROTHER.

42-29710 Del Cheyenne 8/2/43; 94BG Pueblo 18/2/43; Salina 25/2/43; Laurel 18/3/43; Smoky Hill 25/3/43; Syracuse 10/4/43; Dow Fd 15/4/43; ass 410BS/94BG Bassingbourn 20/4/43; Earls Colne 12/5/43; MIA Rennes 29/5/43 w/Hecox; e/a, ditched Channel; 9KIA 2POW. MACR 15139. HELL BELOW.

42-29711 Del Cheyenne 7/2/43; 94BG Pueblo 18/2/43; Salina 25/2/43; Gulfport 18/3/43; Brookley 28/3/43; Presque Is 10/4/43; ass 331BS/94BG [QE-Q] Bassingbourn 17/4/43; Earls Colne 12/5/43; Rougham 13/6/43; tran 322BS/91BG [LG-V] Bassingbourn 29/8/43; MIA Anklam 9/10/43 w/Pinning; s/d by e/a cr Baltic; 10KIA, MACR 894. (SALTY'S) NATURALS.

42-29712 Del Cheyenne 7/2/43; Rapid City 22/2/43; Kearney 12/3/43; Morrison 24/3/43; ass 412BS/95BG Alconbury 5/4/43 MISS CARRIAGE; tran 325BS/92BG [NV-R] Alconbury 17/6/43; then 326BS; 546BS/384BG [BK-O] Grafton Underwood 14/9/43; MIA Anklam 9/10/43 w/Calhoun; e/a, cr Schel-swig; 2KIA 8POW. MACR 873. PHILLY-BROOKLYN.

42-29713 Del Cheyenne 8/2/43; Pueblo 19/2/43; Salina 27/2/43; Brookley 19/3/43; Smoky Hill 23/3/43; Syracuse 7/4/43; ass 333BS/94BG Bassingbourn 18/4/43; Earls Colne 12/5/43; Rougham 13/6/43; tran 407BS/92BG [PY-K] Alconbury 26/7/43; 525BS/379BG [FR-X] Kimbolton 5/9/43; MIA Frankfurt 4/10/43 w/ Ondo; e/a, cr Paris. 10POW. MACR 960. BAD PENNY.

42-29714 Del Cheyenne 8/2/43; Rapid City 5/3/43; Geiger 22/6/43; Rapid City 30/6/43; Geiger 27/10/43; 327 BU Drew 27/7/44; 324 BU Chatham 11/9/44; RFC Kingman 2/12/45.

42-29715 Del Cheyenne 8/2/43; 94BG Pueblo 18/2/43; Salina 25/2/43; Brookley 18/3/43; Smoky Hill 23/3/43; Presque Is 7/4/43; ass 410BS/94BG Bassingbourn 17/4/43; Earls Colne 12/5/43; Rougham 13/6/43; MIA Kiel 13/6/43 w/Herbert; e/a, ditched Nth Sea; 9KIA 1POW. MACR 15162. KLO KAY.

42-29716 Del Cheyenne 11/2/43; Rapid City 22/2/43; ass 334BS/95BG Alconbury 8/4/43; Framlingham 12/5/43; Horham 15/6/43; tran 508BS/351BG [YB-A] Polebrook 12/7/43; MIA Watten 27/8/43 w/Suit; flak, cr St Omer. MACR 469. FAST WOMAN.

42-29717 Del Cheyenne 9/2/43; 94BG Pueblo 18/2/43; Salina 25/2/43; Brookley 19/3/43; Smoky Hill 23/3/43; Syracuse 8/4/43; ass 332BS/94BG [XM-Z] Bassingbourn 17/4/43; Earls Colne 12/5/43; Rougham 13/6/43; tran 326BS/92BG Alconbury 1/8/43; 544BS/384BG [SU-H/M] Grafton Underwood 13/8/43; MIA Stuttgart 25/2/44 w/Larsen; mech, c/l Bruchsal, Ger, 10POW. MACR 2774. MR FIVE BY FIVE.

42-29718 Del Cheyenne 9/2/43; 94BG Pueblo 18/2/43; Salina 25/2/43; Gulfport 18/3/43; Brookley 28/3/43; Presque Is 8/4/43; ass 333BS/94BG Bassingbourn 7/4/43; then 410BS; tran 327BS/92BG [UX-H] Alconbury 23/7/43; 524BS/379BG [WA-C] Kimbolton 4/9/43; then 526BS [LF-C]; AFSC 7/4/44; retUS Tinker 6/8/44; Lockburn 28/9/44; RFC Walnut Ridge 19/12/45. THE WIDOW MAKER (FATSO).

42-29719 Del Denver 7/2/43; Gt Falls 15/2/43; Patterson 17/2/43; Amarillo 10/3/43; Colorado Springs 17/3/43; Orlando 11/6/43; Eglin 2/6/44; Brookley 4/12/44; RFC Walnut Ridge 6/12/45.

42-29720 Del Denver 7/2/43; Gt Falls 20/2/43; Walla Walla 24/2/43; Madras 19/6/43; Walla Walla 17/7/43; Spokane 6/8/43; 325 BU Avon Park 26/7/44; 4139 BU Birmingham 8/11/44; 325 BU Avon Park 2/12/44; RFC Altus 25/9/45.

42-29721 Del Denver 9/2/43; Gt Falls 17/2/43; 381BG Pyote 22/2/43; Tinker 10/8/43; Alexandria 21/9/43; 3701 BU Amarillo 18/11/44; RFC Walnut Ridge 9/1/46.

42-29722 Del Denver 9/2/43; Gt Falls 22/2/43; 88BG Walla Walla 24/2/43; Geiger 3/3/43; Rapid 26/3/43; Geiger 15/8/43; 325 BU Avon Park 12/6/44; 4117 BU Robins 20/6/44; 215 BU Avon Park 3/8/44; 2137 BU Hendricks 10/5/45; 325 BU Avon Park 23/5/45; RFC Walnut Ridge 4/9/45. (Acc- ording to Bowes' Winged Majesty - used as demo a/c named BESSIE).

42-29723 Del Cheyenne 9/2/43; Pueblo 24/2/43; Tinker 14/3/43; Smoky Hill 29/3/43; Presque Is 10/4/43; ass 94BG Bassingbourn 20/4/43; tran AFSC 14/5/43; 546BS/384BG [BK-B] Grafton Underwood 16/10/43; 2 BAD Lt Staughton 5/4/44; retUS Hendricks 29/6/44; RFC Walnut Ridge 14/12/45. WOLF PACK.

42-29724 Del Cheyenne 9/2/43; Pueblo 19/2/43; Salina 24/2/43; Brookley 19/3/43; Smoky Hill 23/3/43; Dow Fd 15/4/43; ass 332BS/94BG [XM-B] Bassingbourn 20/4/43; Earls Colne 12/5/43; Rougham 13/6/43; tran 327BS/92BG [UX-K] Alconbury 3/8/43; 524BS/379BG [WA-H] Kimbolton 4/9/43; then 526BS [LF-H]; MIA Osnabrück 22/12/43 w/Mueller; ditched Nth Sea, 9KIA 1POW. MACR 1718. LITTLE MINNIE.

42-29725 Del Cheyenne 9/2/43; 94BG Pueblo 18/2/43; Salina 25/2/43; Brookley 19/3/43; Smoky Hill 23/3/43; Dow Fd 18/4/43; ass 332BS/94BG [XM-G] Bassingbourn 10/4/43; Earls Colne 12/5/43; Rougham 13/6/43; tran 407BS/92BG [PY-U] Alconbury 30/7/43; MIA St Andre de L'Uere 3/9/43 w/Evans; e/a, cr Touran, Fr; 6EVD 4POW; MACR 659. HI-LO JACK.

42-29726 Del Cheyenne 9/2/43; Walker 23/2/43; Smoky Hill 25/3/43; Presque Is 8/4/43; ass 337BS/96BG Grafton Underwood 20/4/44 THE DALLAS REBEL; Andrews Fd 13/5/43; Snetterton 12/6/43; tran 509BS/351BG [RQ-Q] Polebrook 11/7/43; b/d Kassel 30/7/43 c/l Leiston {3m}; sal 2/8/43. POISONALITY.

42-29727 Del Cheyenne 9/2/43; 94BG Pueblo 18/2/43; Salina 25/2/43; Tinker 20/5/43; Smoky Hill 29/3/43; Presque Is 8/4/43; ass 331BS/94BG [QE-M] Bassingbourn 18/4/43; Earls Colne 21/5/43; MIA Emden 21/5/43 w/Wetzel; e/a, cr Vleegtwedde, Hol; 8KIA 2POW. IN DER FUEHRER'S FACE.

42-29728 Del Cheyenne 9/2/43; Pueblo 19/2/43; Salina 25/2/43; Casper 1/4/43; Dow Fd 15/4/43; ass 332BS/94BG [XM-H] Bassingbourn 20/4/43; Earls Colne 12/5/43; Rougham 13/6/43; tran 544BS/384BG [SU-K/L] Grafton Underwood 12/7/43; b/d Schweinfurt, c/l base 17/8/43, sal. EL RAUNCHO.

42-29729 Del Cheyenne 9/2/43; Wright Fd 12/2/43; Eglin (w/Boeing, using B-32 nose turret) 2/11/43; Wright 2/6/44; 4012 Oakland 18/7/44; 610 BU Eglin 14/9/44; 110 BU Mitchell 7/12/44; 553 BU Romulus 12/12/44; 110 BU Eglin 11/1/45; 4000 BU Wright 27/4/45; 591 BU Stockton 3/10/45; RFC Walnut Ridge 14/12/45.

42-29730 Del Denver 11/2/43; Gt Falls 17/2/43; Redmond 18/6/43; Madras 22/6/43; Walla Walla 31/12/43; Gt Falls 17/1/44; Bismarck 19/1/44; Atlanta 23/1/44; 328 BU Gulfport 13/7/44, WO.

42-29731 Del Denver 12/2/43; Walker 23/2/43; Smoky Hill 28/3/43; Presque 8/4/43; ass 413BS/96BG Grafton Underwood 18/4/43 MOOR-FIDITE; Andrews Fd 13/5/43; Snetterton 12/6/43; tran 532BS/381BG [VE-E] Ridgewell 16/7/43; MIA Schweinfurt 17/8/43 w/Jarvis; e/a, cr Ebrach, Ger; 10POW, MACR 663. OL' SWAYBACK.

42-29732 Del Denver 11/2/43; 19BG Pyote 19/12/43; Tinker 9/11/43; 505BG Harvard 2/6/44; 3033 BU Stockton 7/9/44; 244 BU Harvard 16/9/44; 224 Sioux City 16/10/44; RFC Albuquerque 22/5/45.

42-29733 Del Denver 11/2/43; Pueblo 19/2/43; Salina 25/2/43; Golfport 18/3/43; Brookley 28/3/43; Presque Is 8/4/43; ass 331BS/94BG [QE-P] Bassingbourn 17/4/43 HEAVY DATE; Earls Colne 12/5/43; Rougham 13/6/43; tran 422BS/305BG [JJ-V/L] Chelveston 14/7/43; 544BS/384BG Grafton Underwood 6/11/43; o/s RAF Coltishall 19/12/43, rep; b/d Kiel c/l base 4/1/44, sal. LOUISIANA PURCHASE.

42-29734 Del Denver 12/2/43; Walker 23/2/43; Smoky Hill 28/3/43; Presque 8/4/43; ass 337BS/96BG Grafton Underwood 22/4/43; Andrews Fd 13/5/43; MIA Emden 21/5/43 w/Stephenson; e/a, cr Nth Sea, 10KIA. MACR 3685.

42-29735 Del Cheyenne 12/2/43; Walker 26/2/43; Smoky Hill 29/3/43; Presque Is 5/4/43; ass 337BS/96BG Grafton Underwood 18/4/43 RUM BOOGIE; Andrews Fd 13/6/43; Snetterton 12/6/43;

tran 532BS/381BG Ridgewell 16/7/43; MIA {2m} Schweinfurt 17/8/43 w/Darrow; ditched Nth Sea, 10RTD.

42-29736 Del Cheyenne 11/2/43; Gt Falls 17/2/43; Salina 5/3/43; Morrison 28/3/43; ass 96BS/2BG Navarin 22/4/43; Château-du-Rhumel 27/4/43; Ain M'Lila 17/6/43; Massicault 31/7/43; Bizerte 2/12/43; Amendola 9/12/43; MIA {41m} Athens 20/12/43 w/Doughty. MACR 1517. 60-50 II.

42-29737 Del Cheyenne 11/2/43; Rapid City 22/2/43; Salina 4/3/43; Kearney 12/3/43; ass 92BG Alconbury 9/4/43; tran 412BS/95BG [QW-N] Framlingham 12/5/43; MIA Kiel 13/6/43 w/Morisette; e/a, cr Nth Sea, 10POW. MACR 4898. LOUISE.

42-29738 Del Cheyenne 11/2/43; Walker 23/2/43; Smoky 28/3/43; Kearney 25/4/43; Wendover 2/5/43; Kearney 21/5/43; Dow Fd 27/5/43; ass 100BG Podington 1/6/43; Thorpe Abbotts 9/6/43; tran 303BG Molesworth 13/7/43; MIA Kassel 30/7/43 w/Coggeswell; s/d & ditched Nth Sea.

42-29739 Del Cheyenne 11/2/43; Rapid City 22/2/43; Kearney 12/3/43; ass 412BS/95BG [QW-P] Alconbury 15/4/43; Framlingham 12/5/43; Horham 15/6/43; {2m} tran 369BS/306BG [WW-F] Thurleigh 4/8/43 WOLF PACK; 323BS/91BG [OR-M] Bassingbourn 11/9/43 THE VILLAGE FLIRT; {30m} AFSC 5/4/44; retUS 1105 BU Miami 6/9/44; 4104 BU Rome 21/12/44; 4149 BU Ft Dix 2/2/45; 110 BU Mitchell 20/2/45; 4112 BU Olmstead 1/5/45; 4149 BU Ft Dix 11/5/45; 4000 BU Wright 8/11/45; 4100 BU Patterson 17/1/46; 4150 BU Boca Raton (US Navy) 1/4/46; then to FAA for instr. landing training, and found by former 91BG pilot Phil Mack at Weir Cook Apt. Indianapolis, 3/6/46.

42-29740 Del Cheyenne 11/2/43; Rapid City 22/2/43; Kearney 12/3/43; ass 337BS/96BG [AW-G] Grafton Underwood 14/4/43; Andrews Fd 13/5/43; Snetterton 12/6/43; {4m} tran 323BS/91BG [OR-P] Bassingbourn 12/9/43; MIA {4m} Anklam 9/10/43 w/Guttu; e/a cr Flensbury, Ger. 5KIA 5POW. MACR 896. TONDELAYO.

42-29741 Del Cheyenne 11/2/43; Gt Falls 17/2/43; Salina 5/3/43; ass 303BG Molesworth 15/4/43; tran 368BS/306BG [BO-V] Thurleigh 17/4/43; 324BS/91BG [DF-F/D/P] Bassingbourn 11/9/43; then 401BS [LL-D]; AFSC 6/4/44; retUS Tinker 29/4/44; Winston Salem 5/22/44; RFC Bush Fd 15/5/45. CORN STATE TERROR.

42-29742 Del Cheyenne 11/2/43; Salina, Ks 5/3/43; Salina, Cal 9/3/43; ass MTO but tran 366BS/305BG [KY-M] Chelveston 8/4/43; MIA St Nazaire 29/5/43 w/Stevenson; flak, ditched off Start Point, Dev. 1KIA 9RTD.

42-29743 Del Denver 11/2/43; Gt Falls 16/2/43; Walla Walla 22/2/43; Redmond 15/8/43; Tinker 18/11/43; 327 BU Drew 21/11/44; RFC Altus 4/9/45.

42-29744 Del Cheyenne 18/2/43; Salina 2/3/43; ass 367BS/306BG Thurleigh 20/4/43; MIA Wangerooge 15/5/43 w/Clemons; s/d by e/a cr Nth Sea; 6KIA 4POW. MACR 15512. BATTLING B.

42-29745 Del Denver 12/2/43; Salina 2/3/43; ass 364BS/305BG [WF-M] Chelveston 16/4/43; MIA Lorient 17/5/43 w/Cline; s/d by e/a cr Channel, 7KIA 3RTD. MACR 15545.

42-29746 Del Denver 12/2/43; Gt Falls 23/2/43; Walker 27/2/43; Salina, Cal 10/3/43; Presque Is 8/4/43; ass 339BS/96BG Grafton Underwood 18/4/43; Andrews Fd 13/5/43; Snetterton 12/6/43; tran 524BS/379BG Kimbolton 12/7/43; MIA Kassel 30/7/43 w/Kain; flak, cr Angeran, Hol; 6KIA 4POW, MACR 1355. EXCALIBER.

42-29747 Del Denver 12/2/43; Walker 27/2/43; Smoky Hill 13/3/43; Presque Is 8/4/43; ass 339BS/96BG Grafton Underwood 18/4/43; Andrews Fd 13/5/43; Snetterton 12/6/43; tran 526BS/379BG [LF-D] Kimbolton 12/7/43; cr Catworth, UK, assembling for Kiel 5/1/44 w/?; col w/42-31441 (303BG); 10KIA. Sal. RIKKI-TIKKI-TAVI II.

42-29748 Del Denver 12/2/43; Walker 27/2/43; Salina 10/3/43; Presque Is 5/4/43; ass 338BS/96BG Grafton Underwood 27/4/43; Andrews Fd 13/5/43; Snetterton 12/6/43; MIA Kiel 13/6/43 w/Rossman, s/d by e/a cr Kiel. 8KIA 2POW. MACR 15631. PARADISE LOST.

42-29749 Del Cheyenne 15/2/43; Salina 5/3/43; ass 511BS/351BG [DS-Y] Polebrook 28/5/43; then 509BS [RQ-Z]; 2 SAD Lt Staughton 5/4/44; retUS Tinker 6/7/44; RFC Stillwater 2/10/45. BELLE OF THE BAYOUS.

42-29750 Del Cheyenne 12/2/43; Walker 26/2/43; Smoky Hill 19/3/43; Presque Is 8/4/43; ass 96BG Grafton Underwood 16/4/43; Andrews Fd 13/5/43; Snetterton 12/6/43; tran 323BS/91BG [OR-L] Bassingbourn 24/8/43 REBEL'S REVENGE; MIA {4m} Emden 27/9/43 w/Perritt; s/d by e/a cr Emden; 9KIA 1POW. MACR 668/906. RAMBLIN' REBEL.

42-29751 Del Cheyenne 12/2/43; Walker 23/2/43; Smoky Hill 28/3/43; Presque Is 5/4/43; Dow Fd 12/4/43; ass 96BG Grafton Underwood 19/4/43; tran 534BS/381BG [GD-D] Ridgewell 7/12/43 MISS ABORTION; {21m} c/l base 31/3/43 test flt, all 6k. Sal. STUFF.

42-29752 Del Cheyenne 12/2/43; Walker 26/2/43; Salina 10/3/43; Presque Is 8/4/43; ass 338BS/96BG Grafton Underwood 17/4/43; cr Wash en route St Omer 13/5/43 w/Rogers; 1KIA 9RTD. (1st group loss).

42-29753 Del Cheyenne 12/2/43; Fairfield 1/3/43; Gt Falls 28/3/43; Colorado Springs 6/4/43; Peterson 8/6/43; c/l Romulus Fd 9/6/43; WO 17/6/43.

42-29754 Del Cheyenne 12/2/43; Rapid City 22/2/43; Kearney 12/3/43; ass 336BS/95BG [ET-B] Alconbury 15/4/43 MASON'S MORONS; Framlingham 12/5/43; Horham 15/6/43; tran 360BS/303BG [PU-B] Molesworth 17/6/43; MIA Watten 27/8/43 w/Crockatt; flak hit cr St Omer; 3KIA 7POW. MACR 405. SHANGRI-LA LIL.

42-29755 Del Cheyenne 12/2/43; Walker 27/2/43; Salina 11/3/43; Gulfport 28/3/43; Dow Fd 8/4/43; ass 338BS/96BG Grafton Underwood 20/4/43 LITTLE CAESER, VINI VIDI VICI; tran 533BS/381BG [VP-Y] Ridgewell 14/7/43 GREMLINS DELITE; AFSC 5/4/44; retUS Homestead 18/6/44; 4136 BU Tinker 1/9/44; Keesler 10/1/45; RFC Altus 9/10/45. LAST STRAW.

42-29756 Del Cheyenne 12/2/43; Walker 26/2/43; Salina 10/3/43; Mitchell 8/4/43; ass 339BS/96BG Grafton Underwood 20/4/43; MIA Kiel 13/6/43 w/McKell; s/d by e/a ditched Channel, 5KIA 5POW. MACR 16142. BIG CHIEF II.

42-29757 Del Denver 17/4/43; Walla Walla 5/3/43; Madras 19/6/43; Walla Walla 17/7/43; 325 BU Avon Park 10/11/44; WO 11/11/44.

42-29758 Del Denver 17/2/43; Gore Fd 28/2/43; Patterson 2/3/43; Colorado Springs 29/3/43; Bolling 21/6/43; Gore Fd 25/6/43; Elmendorf 23/6/43; retUS 22/12/43; Gulfport 6/8/44; Brookley 9/8/44; McDill 7/3/44; Newark 3/8/44; McDill 31/10/44; RFC Altus 5/11/43.

42-29759 Del Denver 15/2/43; Walker 26/2/43; Salina 10/3/43; Presque Is 8/4/43; ass 338BS/96BG Grafton Underwood 27/4/43; Andrews Fd 13/5/43; Snetterton 12/6/43; tran 525BS/379BG [FR-K] Kimbolton 12/7/43; b/d Schweinfurt c/l RAF Biggin Hill 14/10/43; 2 SAD Lt Staughton 15/10/43; 323BS/91BG [OR-V] Bassingbourn 21/12/43; AFSC 6/4/44; retUS Homestead 11/6/44; Hobbs 22/8/44; RFC Altus 18/9/45. GAY CABALLEROS.

42-29760 Del Denver 15/2/43; Salina 2/3/43; Morrison 29/3/43; ass 49BS/2BG Navarin 22/4/43; Château-du-Rhumel 27/4/43; Ain M'Lila 17/6/43; Massicault 31/7/43; MIA {24m} Foggia 19/8/43 w/Carter; e/a, cr in sea; 2 chutes seen. MACR 456.

42-29761 Del Denver 15/2/43; Walker 27/2/43; Salina 10/3/43; Presque Is 8/4/43; ass 338BS/96BG Grafton Underwood 17/4/43 RUTH L II (re-named LUCKY LADY); tran 533BS/381BG [VP-W] Ridgewell 14/7/43; MIA {28m} Brunswick w/Steele; flak, cr Deurne, Hol; 4KIA 6POW. MACR 2244. MARTHA II.

42-29762 Del Cheyenne 15/2/43; Walker 27/2/43; Salina 10/3/43; Smoky Hill 20/3/43; Presque Is 8/4/43; ass 338BS/96BG Grafton Underwood 18/4/43; Andrews Fd 13/5/43; Snetterton 12/6/43; tran 510BS/351BG [TU-D] Polebrook 11/7/43; {41m} 2 BAD Warton 5/4/44; retUS Tinker 2/6/44; Hendricks 27/7/45; RFC Walnut Ridge 19/12/45. COUP DE GRACE.

42-29763 Del Cheyenne 15/2/43; Casper 13/3/43; Smoky Hill 10/4/43; Presque Is 5/5/43; ass 335BS/95BG Framlingham 12/5/43; MIA {2m} Kiel 13/6/43 w/Rubin; coll w/42-29765 or 42-30118, cr Lindholm, Den; 10KIA. MACR 4899.

42-29764 Del Cheyenne 15/2/43; Gore 1/3/43; Blythe 6/5/43; Dalhart 2/6/43; WO 7/6/43.

42-29765 Del Cheyenne 15/2/43; Walker 27/2/43; Salina 10/3/43; Presque 5/4/43; ass 338BS/96BG Grafton Underwood 18/4/43; Andrews Fd 13/5/43; Snetterton 12/6/43; tran 533BS/381BG [VP-R] Ridgewell 14/7/43; MIA {17m} Bremen 8/10/43 w/Hartje; e/a, cr Bremen; 3KIA 7POW. MACR 883. NIP AND TUCK.

42-29766 Del Cheyenne 15/2/43; Walker 27/2/43; Salina 11/3/43; Dow Fd 15/4/43; ass 339BS/96BG Grafton Underwood 20/4/43; Andrews Fd 13/5/43; Snetterton 12/6/43; n/b/d 13/6/43; sal 19/6/43. BLACK HEART.

42-29767 Del Cheyenne 15/2/43; Walker 27/2/43; Salina 10/3/43; ass 338BS/96BG Grafton Underwood 17/4/43; Andrews Fd 13/5/43; MIA L'Orient 17/5/43 w/Halton; flak, cr Spizet, Fr; 6EVD 1KIA 3POW. MACR 15546. BOOT HILL.

42-29768 Del Cheyenne 17/2/43; Walker 27/2/43; Salina 5/3/43; Gulfport 31/3/43; ass 334BS/96BG [BG-G] Alconbury 9/4/43 WINSOME WINN; Framlingham 12/5/43; b/d L'Orient 17/5/43 w/Thomas; c/l Sth UK, 1ORTD; a/c rep and tran 547BS/384BG [SO-X] Grafton Underwood 28/6/43; MIA Solingen 1/12/43 w/Nelson; e/a, cr Solingen; 2EVD 8POW. MACR 1336. WINSOME WINN II.

42-29769 Del Cheyenne 17/2/43; Patterson 28/2/43; Colorado Springs 24/3/43; Peterson 15/6/43; Orlando 16/10/43; Bolling 13/11/43; 611 BU Eglin 2/6/44; 610 BU Eglin 25/8/44; sal 29/1/45.

42-29770 Del Denver 17/2/43; Blythe 7/4/43; Dyersburg 6/6/43; Lincoln 8/8/43; 231 BU Alamogordo 2/8/44; WO 8/10/44.

42-29771 Del Denver 17/2/43; Long Beach 6/3/43; Blythe 7/5/43; Geiger 28/5/43; Redmond 18/6/43; Walla Walla 15/8/43; 325 BU Avon Park 9/4/44; 327 BU Drew 16/8/44; 301 BU Drew 19/9/44; RFC Altus 5/11/43.

42-29772 Del Denver 17/2/43; Sioux City 14/3/43; Kearney 9/4/43; Dow Fd 15/4/43; ass 524BS/379BG [WA-R] Kimbolton 2/5/43; AFSC 7/4/44; retUS Rome 1/9/44; Williams 20/3/45; La Junta 29/3/45;

RFC Searcey Fd 4/8/45.

42-29773 Del Denver 17/2/43; Sioux City 14/3/43; Kearney 9/4/43; Dow Fd 14/4/43; ass 526BS/379BG [LF-F] Kimbolton 22/4/43; MIA St Nazaire 29/5/43 w/Hall, flak, cr Vannes, Fr; 6KIA 4POW. MACR 1370.

42-29774 Del Denver 17/2/43; Long Beach 4/3/43; Blythe 6/3/43; Biggs 28/4/43; Dalhart 9/8/43; Pyote 22/9/43; Tinker 6/12/43; Clovis 23/12/43; 4117 BU Robins 13/6/44; 242 BU Gr Isle 14/6/44; 273 BU Lincoln 24/6/44; 242 BU Gr Isle 23/8/44; 4112 BU Olmstead 10/11/44; 268 BU Peterson 28/11/44; 224 BU Sioux City 25/2/45; 247 BU Smoky Hill 16/3/45; 554 BU Memphis 26/8/45; 224 BU Sioux City 9/9/45; RFC Kingman 29/10/45.

42-29775 Del Denver 18/2/43; Gt Falls 20/2/43; Salina 18/3/43; Morrison 29/3/43; ass 341BS/97BG Château-du-Rhumel 16/4/43; Pont-du-Fahs 1/8/43; Depienne 15/8/43; tran 346BS/99BG Oudna 14/11/43; Tortorella 11/12/43; 483BG Tortorella 31/3/44; Sterparone 22/4/44; retUS 1103 BU Morrison 22/6/44; RFC Altus 9/10/45. WONGO.

42-29776 Del Cheyenne 19/2/43; Gore 2/3/43; Tinker 5/4/43; Romulus 12/4/43; Presque Is 26/4/43; ass 305BG Chelveston 19/7/43; tran 326BS/92BG Alconbury 21/7/43; 524BS/379BG [WA-F] Kimbolton 4/9/43; MIA Schweinfurt 14/10/43 w/Gaffield; coll w/e/a, cr Grettstadt, Ger; 9KIA 1POW. MACR 1353.

42-29777 Del Denver 17/2/43; Casper 13/3/43; Tinker 10/4/43; Long Beach 14/4/43; ass 423BS/306BG [RD-H] Thurleigh 19/5/43; MIA Kassel 28/7/43 w/Peck; flak, cr Diepholz, Ger; 10POW. MACR 125. PECK'S BAD BOYS.

42-29778 Del Denver 18/2/43; Salina 10/3/43; Smoky Hill 15/4/43; Dow Fd 18/4/43; ass 338BS/96BG Grafton Underwood 25/4/43 GREEN FURY; tran 322BS/91BG [LG-M] Bassingbourn 24/8/43; MIA Anklam 9/10/43 w/Stewart; e/a, cr Neu Brandenburg, Ger; 6KIA 4POW. MACR 897.

42-29779 Del Cheyenne 18/2/43; Salina 8/3/43; Romulus 10/4/43; Wayne Co 13/4/43; Presque Is 27/4/43; o/s Meeks Fd, Iceland 1/5/43, rep; New York PE 20/5/43; ass 423BS/306BG [RD-A] Thurleigh 4/6/43; MIA Kassel 28/7/43 w/Harris; flak, cr Wolftun?; 6KIA 4POW. MACR 124. BAB'S BEST.

42-29780 Del Denver 17/2/43; Gore 8/3/43; Gulfport 31/3/43; ass 334BS/95BG [BG-P] Alconbury 5/4/43; tran 92BG Alconbury 12/6/43 but switched to 3BD HQ as hack for Curtis Le May; retUS Grenier 26/12/44; Patterson 28/4/45; RFC Walnut Ridge 5/1/46. (first NMF a/c in 8AF) SILVER QUEEN.

42-29781 Del Denver 17/2/43; Gore 28/2/43; Patterson 2/3/43; Colorado Springs 30/3/43; Romulus 10/4/43; Esler 7/5/43; Peterson 11/5/43; ass 1st Photo Gp, Bolling 1/9/43; 499BG Smoky Hill 8/6/44; 11 Ph Gp McDill 15/6/44; 19 Ph Gp McDill 2/8/44; 3701 BU Amarillo 10/8/44; RFC Walnut Ridge 28/12/45.

42-29782 Del Cheyenne 17/2/43; Blythe 4/3/43; McClellan 16/5/43; Moses Lake 15/6/43; c/l 20/9/43 w/Reid, main wheel came off, rep; ass 8AF; retUS Drew 2/4/44; RFC Altus 5/11/45. Used as crop sprayer N17W Yakima; took part in films *Memphis Belle* & *Tora! Tora! Tora!*; now in Museum of Flight, Seattle (GREAT WHITE BIRD).

42-29783 Del Cheyenne 16/2/43; Patterson 2/3/43; Colorado Springs 18/3/43; Patterson 30/4/43; McClellan 9/6/43; ass 1st Photo Gp Bradley 1/9/43; 1st Ph Sq McDill 21/12/43; sal 5/12/45.

42-29784 Del Cheyenne 18/2/43; Salina 2/3/43; ass 366BS/305BG [KY-K] Chelveston 18/5/43; tran 534BS/381BG [GD-E/F] Ridgewell 11/9/43; 545BS/384BG [JD-V] Grafton Underwood 4/10/43; b/d Schweinfurt 14/10/43 c/l Blayden, Glos; sal 18/10/43. SMILIN-THRU.

42-29785 Del Cheyenne 18/2/43; Orlando 4/4/43; Brooksville 28/4/43; Lowry 30/4/43; Geiger 3/5/43; Rapid City 21/6/43; while on bombing range 13/8/43 #2 engine caught fire and fell off; crew baled, one injured, but pilot Lt Highfill rode it down alone and c/l base; sal 14/8/43.

42-29786 Del Cheyenne 18/2/43; Salina 5/3/43; Gore 8/3/43; Tinker 19/3/43; Morrison 31/3/43; ass 96BG Grafton Under-wood 2/4/43; tran 368BS/306BG [BO-N] Thurleigh 20/4/43; cr Dunsby, UK, on training mission 20/5/43; sal 21/5/43.

42-29787 Del Cheyenne 18/2/43; Salina 5/3/43; Gulfport 31/3/43; ass 334BS/95BG [BG-F] Alconbury 15/4/43; Framlingham 12/5/43; Horham 15/6/43; tran 326BS/92BG Alconbury 6/8/43; 525BS/379BG [FR-E] Kimbolton 4/9/43; MIA Bremen 29/11/43 w/Lefevre; flak, ditched Nth Sea, 9KIA 1POW. MACR 1332. WILDER NELL.

42-29788 Del Cheyenne 18/2/43; Will Rogers 5/3/43; ass 49BS/2BG Navarin 17/4/43; Château-du-Rhumel 27/4/43; Ain M'Lila 16/7/43; Massicault 31/7/43; Bizerte 2/12/43; Amendola 9/12/43; tran 346BS/99BG Tortorella 28/3/44; {3m w/99} 483BG Tortorella 31/3/44; ret 8AF 2/4/44; retUS Morrison 20/4/45; Rome 9/5/45; RFC Bush Fd 21/6/45.

42-29789 Del Cheyenne 18/2/43; Salina 8/3/43; Pueblo 8/4/43; Smoky Hill 6/5/43; Dow Fd 19/5/43; Presque Is 21/5/43; ass 535BS/381BG [MS-O] Ridgewell 25/5/43; MIA {4m} Romilly 3/9/43 w/Zum; s/d by e/a cr Provine, Fr; 3EVD 1KIA 6POW. MACR 473. BIG TIME OPERATOR.

42-29790 Del Cheyenne 19/2/43; Salina 8/3/43; Smoky Hill 12/3/43; ass 348BS/99BG Navarin 6/6/43; Oudna 4/8/43; Tortorella 12/11/43; sal 5/1/45. QUEENIE.

42-29791 Del Cheyenne 21/2/43; Gore 7/3/43; ass 334BS/95BG [BG-Q] Alconbury 19/4/43 LITTLE JIMMIE; Framlingham 12/5/43; Horham 15/6/43; tran 358BS/303BC [VK-B] Molesworth 17/6/43, MIA Villacoublay 14/7/43 w/Swaffer; ditched Nth Sea, 10RTD.

42-29792 Del Cheyenne 18/2/43; Salina 2/3/43; ass 366BS/305BG [KY-G] Chelveston 8/4/43; MIA St Nazaire 29/5/43 w/Perry; flak, cr St Nazaire; 8KIA 2POW.

42-29793 Del Cheyenne 19/2/43; Salina 5/3/43; Tinker 19/3/43; Morrison 31/3/43; ass 368BS/306BG [BO-P] Thurleigh 20/4/43; {15m} tran 401BS/91BG [LL-F] Bassingbourn 11/9/43; b/d {5m} Frankfurt 1 SAD Troston 4/10/43; sal 8/10/43. RetUS 28/4/44. SHEILA B. CUMMIN.

42-29794 Del Cheyenne 21/2/43; Salina 8/3/43; Nashville 8/4/43; ass 367BS/306BG [GY-K] Thurleigh 16/4/43; tran 322BS/91BG [LG-O] Bassingbourn 11/9/43; MIA Leverkusen 1/12/43 w/Anderson; flak, cr Nth Sea, 10KIA, MACR 1321.

42-29795 Del Cheyenne 19/2/43; Will Rogers 5/3/43; ass 368BS/306BG Thurleigh 20/4/43; tran 427BS/303BG [GN-O] Molesworth 25/9/43; 1 BAD Burtonwood 5/9/44; retUS 29/5/44; RFC Stillwater 4/10/45. THE FLYING BITCH.

42-29796 Del Cheyenne 19/2/43; Will Rogers 5/3/43; ass 527BS/379BG [FO-M] Kimbolton 20/6/43; MIA Kassel 28/7/43 w/Taylor; flak, cr Vreis, Hol. MACR 1761.

42-29797 Del Cheyenne 19/2/43; Will Rogers 5/3/43; ass 401BS/91BG [LL-Y] Bassingbourn 18/5/43; MIA {2m} Huls 22/6/43 w/Peck; flak, ditched Nth Sea, 1KIA 9RTD. OLD IRONSIDES.

42-29798 Del Cheyenne 19/2/43; Salina 8/3/43; Dow Fd 19/4/43; ass 326BS/92BG [JW-L] Alconbury 25/4/43; then 325BS; MIA Kassel 28/7/43 w/Smotherman; e/a, cr Wageningen, Hol. 10POW. MACR 657.

42-29799 Del Cheyenne 20/2/43; Salina 5/3/43; ass 353BS/301BG St Donat 17/6/43; MIA {7m} San Giovanni 16/7/43 w/Fonner; cr Reggio de Calabria. MACR 209.

42-29800 Del Cheyenne 20/2/43; Gore 7/3/43; Smoky Hill 14/3/43; Morrison 9/4/43; ass 335BS/95BG [OE-L] Alconbury 17/5/43; tran 422BS/305BG [JJ-E/J] Chelveston 17/6/43; 546BS/384BG Grafton Underwood 7/10/43; MIA Schweinfurt 14/10/43 w/Harry; e/a, cr Soissons, Fr. 1EVD 2KIA 7POW. MACR 840. ME AND MY GAL.

42-29801 Del Denver 20/2/43; Patterson 28/2/43; Colorado Springs 29/3/43; Kirtland 9/5/43; Peterson 12/5/43; Geiger 23/7/43; ass 1 Photo Gp Bolling 1/9/43; 19 Ph Gp McDill 2/8/44; 902 BU Orlando 5/8/44; 19 Ph Gp McDill 14/10/44; 247 BU Smoky Hill 31/10/44; 234 BU Clovis 1/3/45; RFC Kingman 9/11/45.

42-29802 Del Denver 20/2/43; Tinker 10/3/43; Duncan 31/3/43; ass 326BS/92BG [JW-C] Alconbury 3/4/43; Podington 11/9/43; tran 527BS/379BG [FO-C] Kimbolton 19/9/43; AFSC 7/4/44; retUS 27/4/44; Spokane 6/12/44; RFC Altus 30/7/45. (John Morgan won MOH 26/7/43 Hamburg). RUTHIE II.

42-29803 Del Denver 22/2/43; Gore 8/3/43; ass 334BS/95BG [BG-D] Alconbury 8/4/43; Framlingham 12/5/43; Horham 15/6/43; tran 365BS/305BG [XK-Q/E] Chelveston 17/6/43 FLAT FOOT FLOOGIE; 534BS/381BG [GD-P] Ridgewell 11/9/43; MIA {6m 381} Schwein- furt 14/10/43 w/Yorba; e/a, cr Schweinfurt; 4KIA 6POW. MACR 1037.

42-29804 Del Denver 20/2/43; Gore 28/2/43; Colorado Springs 27/3/43; Dallas 17/5/43; Colorado Springs 25/6/43; Peterson 13/8/43; 325 BU Avon Park 10/11/44; RFC Altus 4/9/45.

42-29805 Del Denver 20/2/43; Gore 28/2/43; Colorado Springs 19/3/43; Peterson 8/6/43; Bolling 22/7/43; Bradley 14/8/43; ass 1 Photo Gp Bolling 1/9/43; McDill 10/10/43; Smoky Hill 28/10/43; Patterson 14/12/43; Clovis 28/3/44; Patterson 18/8/44; Clovis 14/11/44; RFC Kingman 9/11/45.

42-29806 Del Cheyenne 21/2/43; Gore 7/3/43; New Castle 6/4/43; Dow Fd 12/4/43; ass 368BS/306BG [BO-T] Thurleigh 19/5/43; MIA Wilhelmshaven 21/5/43 w/Fields; flak, ditched Nth Sea. 5KIA 5POW (rescued by German seaplane). MACR 16018.

42-29807 Del Cheyenne 21/2/43; Gore 7/3/43; New Castle 6/4/43; Dow Fd 12/4/43; ass 334BS/95BG [BG-B] Alconbury 15/4/43 PATSY ANN; Framlingham 12/5/43; Horham 15/6/43; tran 364BS/305BG [WF-O] Chelveston 17/6/43; MIA Gilze Rijen 19/8/43 w/Miller; flak, cr Westerschelde, Hol; 8KIA 2POW. MACR 304. LADY LIBERTY.

42-29808 Del Cheyenne 21/2/43; Stillwater 8/3/43; ass 412BS/95BG [QW-C] Alconbury 15/4/43; Framlingham 12/5/43; sal after bomb loading accident w/42-29685 14/6/43.

42-29809 Del Cheyenne 22/2/43; Gore 9/3/43; Presque Is 8/4/43; Stephenville, Nfd 12/4/43; ass 368BS/306BG [BO-T] Thurleigh 20/4/43; then 423BS [RD-B]; tran 545BS/384BG [JD-X] Grafton Underwood 4/9/43 QUEEN JEANIE; 2 SAD Lt Staughton 12/9/43; retUS 12/11/44; RFC Arledge 23/11/44. DAMN YANKEE II (DINAH MITE).

42-29810 Del Cheyenne 21/2/43; Salina 5/3/43; Gore 8/3/43; Palm Beach 30/3/43; Tinker 5/5/43; Long Beach 3/7/43; Presque Is 7/7/43; ass 8AF HQ but trans MTO 24/7/43; sal Italy 16/6/44.

42-29811 Del Cheyenne 21/2/43; Gore 7/3/43; Gulfport 31/3/43; ass 336BS/95BG [ET-U] Alconbury 15/4/43; Framlingham 12/5/43; Horham 15/6/43; b/d St Dizier 4/10/43, sal. CHATTANOOGA CHOO CHOO.

42-29812 Del Cheyenne 22/2/43; Casper 13/3/43; Smoky Hill 4/3/43; ass 509BS/351BG [RQ-U] Polebrook 28/5/43; 1BAD Burtonwood 31/3/44; retUS Tinker 1/9/44; Banks Fd 29/3/45; LeMoore 12/6/45; Santa Maria 11/7/45; March 18/12/45; RFC Kingman 22/1/46. LUCIFER JR.

42-29813 Del Cheyenne 22/2/43; Gowen Fd 26/2/43; Cheyenne 23/3/43; Smoky Hill 4/4/43; Dow Fd 15/4/43; ass 336BS/95BG [ET-G] Alconbury 20/4/43; Framlingham 12/5/43; Horham 15/6/43; tran 324BS/91BG [DF-B1] Bassingbourn 16/6/43; MIA Hamburg 25/7/43 w/Pilert; flak, cr Emden, 1KIA 9POW. MACR 94.

42-29814 Del Cheyenne 22/2/43; Salina 2/3/43; Gulfport 23/3/43; ass 544BS/384BG [SU-D] Grafton Underwood 26/7/43; MIA 9/10/43 Anklam w/Ingles; e/a, ditched Nth Sea; 10KIA. MACR 872. DALLAS REBEL.

42-29815 Del Denver 22/2/43; Gore 9/3/43; Duncan 31/3/43; ass 367BS/306BG [GY-N] Thurleigh 20/4/43; tran 322BS/91BG [LG-P] Bassingbourn 11/9/43; AFSC 7/4/44; retUS Amarillo 16/4/44; RFC Walnut Ridge 9/1/46; MIAMI CLIPPER.

42-29816 Del Denver 22/2/43; Salina 3/3/43; ass 401BS/91BG [LL-K] Bassingbourn 19/4/43; MIA Amiens Glisy 31/8/43 w/Peek; coll w/41-24523 (91st), cr Channel; 9KIA 1RTD. MACR 671. EAGER BEAVER.

42-29817 Del Cheyenne 22/2/43; Pueblo 12/3/43; Presque Is 8/4/43; ass 508BS/351BG [YB-D] Polebrook 20/4/43; MIA {7m} St Nazaire 28/6/43 w/King; e/a, ditched Biscay; MACR 15511/15130. ARGONAUT II.

42-29818 Del Denver 22/2/43; Hobbs 7/4/43; Ft Sumner 21/4/43; Hobbs 6/5/43; Mather 18/6/43; 3017 BU Hobbs 26/6/43; RF Altus 18/9/45.

42-29819 Del Cheyenne 23/2/43; Gore 8/3/43; Morrison 19/3/43; ass 305BG 16/4/43; 1 BAD Burtonwood 3/5/43; AFSC 18/5/43; WO 31/10/44.

42-29820 Del Cheyenne 22/2/43; Memphis 8/4/43; ass 407BS/92BG [PY-V] Alconbury 24/4/43; MIA Wangerooge 15/5/43 w/Washer; flak, ditched Nth Sea; 5KIA 5POW. MACR 16060.

42-29821 Del Cheyenne 22/2/43; Wichita 20/3/43; Bangor 8/4/43; ass 508BS/351BG [YB-F] Polebrook 17/4/43; b/d Ludwigshafen 7/1/44 {21m} c/l Lutham Bridge, UK; sal. ARGONAUT (VOX POP).

42-29822 Del Cheyenne 22/2/43; Salina 8/3/43; Presque Is 10/4/43; ass 331BS/94BG Bassingbourn 17/4/43; Earls Colne 12/5/43; MIA Kiel 13/6/43 w/Hendershot; e/a, cr Channel; 10KIA. VISITING FIREMAN.

42-29823 Del Cheyenne 22/2/43; Salina 8/3/43; Dow Fd 10/4/43; ass 368BS/306BG [BO-Y] Thurleigh 19/4/43; tran 427BS/303BG [GN-X] Molesworth 26/9/43; 1 BAD Burtonwood 5/4/44; retUS Tinker 4/6/44; Long Beach 5/6/44; RFC Ontario 45/6/45.

42-29824 Del Cheyenne 22/2/43; Gore 9/3/43; Memphis 27/3/43; Dow Fd 15/4/43; ass 369BS/306BG [WW-B] Thurleigh 24/4/43; tran 526BS/379BG [LF-G] Kimbolton 3/10/43; b/d Bremen 29/11/43 c/l Leiston; 2 SAD Lt Staughton 1/12/43; RG 14/1/44; AFSC 7/4/44; retUS Miami 1/9/44; Tinker 24/9/44; RFC Walnut Ridge 28/1/46. FEARLESS FOSDYKE.

42-29825 Del Cheyenne 22/2/43; Stillwater 8/3/43; Dow Fd 15/4/43; ass 511BS/351BG [DS-Z] Polebrook 25/4/43 MAJOR BALL; n/b/d {9m} Nantes 16/9/43 w/Stewart, c/l Lutton, Nthts; sal. MEAT BALL.

42-29826 Del Cheyenne 22/2/43; Casper 13/3/43; Smoky Hill 3/4/43; ass 508BS/351BG [YB-H] Polebrook 17/5/43; MIA {3m} Huls 22/6/43 w/Turgeon; e/a, cr Huls; 10POW.

42-29827 Del Denver 23/2/43; Gore 24/3/43; Stillwater 8/3/43; Gulfport 31/3/43; ass 365BS/305BG [XK-O] Chelveston 8/4/43; tran 335BS/95BG [OE-V] Alconbury 13/5/43; MIA Kiel 13/6/43 w/Mason; e/a, cr Bredstedt, Ger; 6KIA 4POW. MACR 4901.

42-29828 Del Denver 23/2/43; Stillwater 8/4/43; Presque Is 8/4/43; ass 413BS/96BG Grafton Underwood 17/4/43 SHORT STRIDE; tran 545BS/384BG [JD-Q] Grafton Underwood 14/7/43; retUS 5/6/44; Tinker 26/6/44; RFC Walnut Ridge 18/12/45.

42-29829 Del Denver 23/2/43; Sioux City 16/3/43; Kearney 8/4/43; Dow Fd 16/4/43; ass 527BS/379BG [FO-F/P] Kimbolton 18/5/43; MIA Bernburg 22/2/44 w/Haston; e/a, cr Gottingen, Ger; 5KIA 5POW. MACR 2870. SONS O' SATAN.

42-29830 Del Denver 23/2/43; Sioux City 20/3/43; Kearney 8/4/43; Dow Fd 15/4/43; ass 525BS/379BG [FR-A] Kimbolton; then 524BS [WA-T]; MIA Schweinfurt 17/8/43 w/Wagner; e/a, cr Dorrebach, Ger; 10KIA; MACR 1350. PETER WABBIT.

42-29831 Del Denver 23/2/43; Salina 9/3/43; New Castle 6/4/43; Kansas City 14/4/43; ass 510BS/351BG [TU-H] Polebrook 17/5/43; {40m} 1 BAD Burtonwood 31/3/44; retUS Tinker 16/6/44; Fairfax 24/6/44; Eglin 17/8/44; Wright 26/11/44; RFC Kingman 1/11/45. THE INVADER.

42-29832 Del Cheyenne 24/2/43; Casper 13/3/43; Smoky Hill 3/4/43; ass 364BS/305BG [WF-H] Chelveston 18/5/43 SPIRIT OF A NATION; tran 534BS/381BG [GD-H] Ridgewell 22/8/43; AFSC 5/4/44; retUS Tinker 16/6/44; Memphis 13/7/44; Tinker 14/9/44; RFC Arledge Fd 23/11/44. OUR MOM.

42-29833 Del Cheyenne 24/2/43; Casper 13/3/43; Morrison 13/4/43; Presque Is 6/5/43; ass 92BG Alconbury 8/5/43; sal n/b/d 14/6/43.

42-29834 Del Cheyenne 24/2/43; Casper 13/3/43; Smoky Hill 3/4/43; ass 332BS/94BG Bassingbourn 25/4/43; then 333BS; Earls Colne 12/5/43; MIA Emden 21/5/43 w/Ecklund; s/d by e/a; cr Emden 5KIA 5POW. BOOMERANG.

42-29835 Del Cheyenne 24/2/43; Casper 13/3/43; Smoky Hill 3/4/43; ass 336BS/95BG [ET-J] Alconbury 11/6/43; tran 511BS/351BG [DS-Y] Polebrook 17/6/43; {35m} 2 BAD Warton 5/4/44; retUS Amarillo 18/7/44; Hendricks 1/8/44; Smyrna 9/11/44; Rome 29/1/45; Recl Comp 9/2/45. PISTOL BALL.

42-29836 Del Cheyenne 24/2/43; Dayton 14/4/43; Moses Lake 16/5/43; Walla Walla 30/5/43; Orlando 1/6/43; Brooksville 21/6/43; Rapid City 4/7/43; Harvard 2/8/43; 224 BU Sioux City 6/3/44; RFC Albuquerque 22/5/45.

42-29837 Del Cheyenne 24/2/43; Gore 9/3/43; Duncan 31/3/43; ass 324BS/91BG [DF-A] Bassingbourn 7/6/43; AFSC 6/4/44 then MTO (Italy & N. Africa); retUS Tinker 11/6/44; Patterson 23/2/45; RFC Searcey Fd 27/7/45. LADY LUCK.

42-29838 Del Cheyenne 24/2/43; Pueblo 12/3/43; Presque Is 8/4/43; ass 509BS/351BG [RQ-U] Polebrook 17/4/43; MIA {4m} St Nazaire 29/5/43 w/Lt Col Russell; flak, cr St Nazaire. THE CONCHO CLIPPER.

42-29839 Del Cheyenne 26/2/43; Pueblo 16/3/43; Presque Is 8/4/43; ass MIA {13m} Schweinfurt 17/8/43 w/Hansen; e/a, cr Koblenz; 1KIA 9POW; MACR 303. CHEROKEE GIRL.

42-29840 Del Denver 24/2/43; Gore 31/3/43; Ephrata 2/4/43; Orlando 28/4/43; Geiger 2/6/43; Gt Falls 7/7/43; Pendleton 17/7/43; WO 19/8/43.

42-29841 Del Denver 24/2/43; Gore 13/3/43; Presque Is 10/4/43; ass 509BS/351BG [RQ-V] Polebrook 17/4/43; b/d {15m} T/O 6/9/43, c/l New Romney, Kent; sal 11/10/43. SHADY LADY.

42-29842 Del Denver 24/2/43; Eglin 10/3/43; 611 BU Eglin 2/6/43; 610 BU Eglin 4/9/44; 611 BU Eglin 1/4/44; 2137 BU Hendricks 25/11/44; RFC Walnut Ridge 5/1/46.

42-29843 Del Denver 24/2/43; Pueblo 13/3/43; Kearney 2/4/43; Patterson 13/4/43; Presque Is 17/4/43; ass 510BS/351BG [TU-D] Polebrook 24/4/43; MIA {7m} St Nazaire 28/6/43 w/Moss; flak, cr Biscay; 6KIA 4POW; MACR 15130.

42-29844 Del Denver 24/2/43; Eglin 9/3/43; Englewood 12/3/43; Eglin 14/4/43; Midland 21/6/43; Eglin 24/6/43; 2137 BU Hendricks 1/10/44; RFC Walnut Ridge 19/12/45.

42-29845 Del Cheyenne 25/2/43; Tinker 10/3/43; ass 419BS/301BG St Donat 14/7/43; Oudna 6/8/43; {41m} tran 429BS/2BG Massicault 14/11/43; Bizerte 2/12/43; Amendola 9/12/43; 99BG Tortorella 28/3/44; {2m 99} 816BS/483BG Tortorella 31/3/44; sal 31/3/45; RFC Bush Fd 3/7/45. NUTCRACKER II.

42-29846 Del Cheyenne 25/2/43; Gore 9/3/43; Duncan 31/3/43; Dow Fd 10/4/43; ass 359BS/303BG [BN-P] Molesworth 16/5/43; MIA Frankfurt 4/10/43 w/Loughman; mech problem, cr St Vith, Bel; 10POW; MACR 780.

42-29847 Del Cheyenne 26/2/43; Pueblo 12/3/43; Presque Is 8/4/43; ass 511BS/351BG [DS-T] Polebrook 27/4/43; MIA {4m} St Nazaire 28/6/43 w/Adams, cr St Nazaire, 2EVD 4KIA 4POW. HIGH BALL.

42-29848 Del Cheyenne 25/2/43; Pueblo 12/3/43; Presque Is 8/4/43; ass 510BS/351BG [TU-E/F] Polebrook 26/4/43; {27m} 1 BAD Burtonwood 19/3/44; retUS Tinker 28/5/44; Amarillo 7/7/44; RFC Walnut Ridge 21/1/46. AMATOL.

42-29849 Del Cheyenne 26/2/43; Pueblo 12/3/43; Presque Is 8/4/43; ass 511BS/351BG [DS-U] Polebrook 22/4/43; {34m} RetUS Homestead 11/6/44; Maxwell 20/6/44; Tinker 14/9/44; Patterson 18/2/45; RFC Altus 9/10/45. LINDA BALL.

42-29850 Del Cheyenne 25/2/43; Pueblo 12/3/43; Presque 8/4/43; ass 510BS/351BG [TU-G] Polebrook 22/4/43; {28m} RetUS Tinker 15/7/44; Amarillo 17/7/43; RFC Walnut Ridge 29/12/45. GREMLIN CASTLE.

42-29851 Del Cheyenne 25/2/43; Casper 13/3/43; Smoky Hill 3/4/43; ass 508BS/351BG [YB-J] Polebrook 16/5/43; b/d {28m} Münster 10/10/43 w/Argiropulos; ditched Nth Sea, 10RTD. ARGONAUT III.

42-29852 Del Cheyenne 26/2/43; Pueblo 12/3/43; Presque Is 9/4/43; ass 511BS/351BG [DS-V] Polebrook 16/4/43; MIA {18m} Wilhelmshaven 3/11/43 w/Nardi; e/a, cr Wilhelmshaven; 4KIA 6POW; MACR 1160. FIREBALL.

42-29853 Del Denver 26/2/43; Gore 9/3/43; Duncan 31/3/43; ass 412BS/95BG [QW-P] Framlingham 13/6/43; tran 327BS/92BG [UX-S/U] Alconbury 17/6/43; MIA Schweinfurt 17/8/43 w/Stewart; e/a, cr Eifel, Ger; 10POW. MACR 653.

42-29854 Del Denver 26/2/43; Casper 13/3/43; Tinker 10/4/43; Memphis 17/4/43; Presque 27/4/43; ass

532BS/381BG [VE-B] Ridgewell 4/5/43; MIA {1+m} Bremen 8/10/43 w/Sample; e/a, cr Diepholz, Ger; 8KIA 2POW; MACR 1395. 'OLE FLAK SACK.'

42-29855 Del Denver 27/2/43; Hobbs 3/4/43; Roswell 28/4/43; Hobbs 12/5/43; WO 12/9/44.

42-29856 Del Denver 27/2/43; Smoky Hill 22/3/43; Tinker 9/4/43; Nashville 13/4/43; Morrison 18/4/43; ass 346BS/99BG Navarin 5/5/43; Oudna 4/8/43; Tortorella 11/12/43; tran 815BS/483BG Tortorella 31/3/44; MIA Weiner Neustadt 10/5/44 w/Scranton; flak hit cr Wiener Neustadt; 2KIA 8POW; MACR 4846. PATCHES.

42-29857 Del Denver 28/2/43; Tinker 31/3/43; Morrison 10/4/43; ass 510BS/351BG [TU-J] Polebrook 17/4/43; tran 12AF 23/4/43; 348BS/99BG Navarin 10/5/43; Oudna 4/8/43; Tortorella 11/12/43; tran 483BG Tortorella 31/3/44; 12AF 30/9/44; declared excess 10/6/45; rep & re-ass 9AF as RB-17F at Oberpfaffenhofen, Ger, 11/4/46; sal 7/1/49.

42-29858 Del Denver 28/2/43; Smoky Hill 22/3/43; ass 508BS/351BG [YB-G] Polebrook 17/5/43 MURDER INCORPORATED {29m}; c/t/o Barnwell, UK 21/2/44; 2 SAD Lt Staughton 22/2/44, sal {2m}. CENSORED.

42-29859 Del Cheyenne 28/2/43; Gore 12/3/43; Presque Is 8/4/43; ass 510BS/351BG [TU-H] Polebrook 16/4/43; MIA {1m} Courtrai 14/5/43 w/Forsythe, cr Courtrai, Bel. THE ANNIHILATOR.

42-29860 Del Cheyenne 27/2/43; Denver 1/3/43; Gore 12/3/43; Presque Is 8/4/43; ass 509BS/351BG [RQ-W] Polebrook 17/4/43; b/d Bordeaux 31/12/43 {37m}, c/l Sywell, Notts; 1 BAD Burtonwood; retUS Rome 21/7/44; Roswell 5/9/44; RFC Altus 4/10/45. SNOOZIN' SUSAN.

42-29861 Del Cheyenne 27/2/43; Denver 1/3/43; Pueblo 12/3/43; Presque Is 8/4/43; ass 509BS/351BG [RQ-X] Polebrook 16/4/43; MIA {31m} Oschersleben 11/1/44 w/Cannon; e/a, cr Oschersleben; 10POW; MACR 1936. BUCK-SHOT.

42-29862 Del Cheyenne 26/2/43; Pueblo 12/3/43; Presque Is 12/4/43; ass 508BS/351BG [YB-H] Polebrook 16/4/43; MIA {1m} Courtrai 14/5/43 w/McCoy; cr Courtrai, Bel. MACR 15557.

42-29863 Del Cheyenne 27/2/43; Denver 1/3/43; Gore 12/3/43; Presque Is 8/4/43; ass 509BS/351BG [RQ-Y] Polebrook 16/4/43 AINT IT GRUESOME; MIA {43m} Frankfurt w/Carson; flak, cr Dieppe, Fr; 4EVD 1KIA 5POW; MACR 2528. KENTUCKY BABE.

42-29864 Del Cheyenne 28/2/43; Gore 4/3/43; Sioux City 16/3/43; Kearney 8/4/43; Dow Fd 16/4/43; Bangor 28/4/43; ass 525BS/379BG [FR-E] Kimbolton 3/5/43; MIA Wangerooge 25/6/43 w/Browne; e/a, cr Oldenburg; 8KIA 2POW; MACR 1759.

42-29865 Del Cheyenne 27/2/43; Pueblo 28/3/43; Presque Is 7/4/43; ass 508BS/351BG [YB-X] Polebrook 16/4/43; coll w/42-29491 (351st) on training op 7/5/43, sal; crew killed.

42-29866 Del Denver 27/2/43; Sioux City 16/3/43; Kearney 8/4/43; Dow Fd 15/4/43; ass 524BS/379BG [WA-L] Kimbolton 21/4/43; MIA Le Bourget 16/8/43 w/Biglar; flak, cr Le Bourget, 4EVD 1KIA 5POW. MACR 1352. JUDY B.

42-29867 Del Denver 28/2/43; Casper 13/3/43; Metropolitan 13/4/43; Dow Fd 30/4/43; ass 364BS/305BG [WF-A] Chelveston 12/7/43; tran 535BS/381BG [MS-T] Ridgewell 22/8/43 LUCIFER II; {4+m} 544BS/384BG [SU-C] Grafton Underwood 4/10/43; MIA Schweinfurt 14/10/43 w/Williams; cr Metz, Fr; 10POW. MACR 838.

42-29868 Del Denver 27/2/43; Pueblo 13/3/43; Presque Is 8/4/43; ass 508BS/351BG [YB-K] Polebrook 17/4/43 FLAP RAISER; MIA {23m} Anklam 9/10/43 w/Turley; e/a, ditched Nth Sea; 8KIA 2POW; MACR 877. THE VENUS.

42-29869 Del Denver 1/3/43; Sioux City 14/3/43; Kearney 9/4/43; Dow Fd 15/4/43; ass 525BS/379BG [FR-J] Kimbolton 29/4/43; AFSC 7/4/44; retUS Tinker 18/6/44; Jacksonville 13/7/44; Biggs 7/11/43; Kirtland 8/3/45; RFC Walnut Ridge 7/12/45. DAMNDIFINO !

42-29870 Del Denver 28/2/43; Casper 13/3/43; Metropolitan 13/4/43; Presque Is 30/4/43; Dow Fd 1/5/43; ass 379BG Kimbolton 2/5/43; tran 365BS/305BG [XK-T/H] Chelveston 23/6/43; 545BS/384BG [JD-U] Grafton Underwood 29/9/43; MIA Schweinfurt 14/10/43 w/Kauffman; cr Brückenau?; 10POW; MACR 1038. BIG MOOSE.

42-29871 Del Cheyenne 28/2/43; Colorado Springs 19/3/43; Patterson 24/3/43; Colorado Springs 6/4/43; Esler Fd 8/5/43; Peterson 4/6/43; Cheyenne 21/7/43; Peterson 29/7/43; ass 1st Photo Gp Bolling 1/9/43; Mexico 9/11 - 27/12/43; retUS Smoky Hill 6/6/44; McDill 22/6/44; Amarillo 10/8/44; RFC Walnut Ridge 2/1/46.

42-29872 Del Cheyenne 28/2/43; Pueblo 13/3/43; Presque Is 8/4/43; ass 511BS/351BG [DS-W] Polebrook 16/4/43; MIA {6m} T/Ops 17/7/43 w/Petus; flak, ditched Channel. SNOW BALL.

42-29873 Del Cheyenne 28/2/43; Denver 1/3/43; Colorado Springs 29/3/43; Patterson 1/4/43; Colorado Springs 15/4/43; Peterson 17/4/43; ass 1st Photo Gr Bolling 1/9/43; 19 Ph Sq/11PMG McDill 2/8/44; 91 Ph Gp Buckley 22/11/44; Bolling 30/11/44; 91 Ph Gp Buckley 30/12/44; 234 BU Clovis 14/1/45; RFC Kingman 9/11/45.

42-29874 Del Cheyenne 2/3/43; Pueblo 14/3/43; Presque Is 8/4/43; ass 510BS/351BG [TU-J] Polebrook 16/4/43; b/d Bochum {10m} 12/8/43; c/l Leiston, Sfk; sal 16/8/43. EL CONQUISTADOR.

42-29875 Del Cheyenne 28/2/43; Sioux City 16/3/43; Kearney 8/4/43; Dow Fd 19/4/43; ass 525BS/379BG [FO-L] Kimbolton 2/5/43; MIA Wilhelmshaven 11/6/43 w/Hamrick; e/a, cr Grossheide, Ger; 9KIA 1POW; MACR 1358.

42-29876 Del Cheyenne 28/2/43; Gore 4/3/43; Siouix City 18/3/43; Kearney 9/4/43; Dow Fd 15/4/43; ass 525BS/379BG [FR-B/E] Kimbolton 23/4/43; MIA Nantes 16/9/43 w/Hoyt; flak, cr Redon, Fr; 8EVD 2KIA; MACR 978. BATTLIN' BOBBIE.

42-29877 Del Cheyenne 1/3/43; Pueblo 14/3/43; Presque Is 10/4/43; ass 511BS/351BG [DS-X] Polebrook 16/4/43; MIA {24m} Bordeaux 31/12/43 w/Jones; e/a, ditched off Guernsey; MACR 1982. SPEED BALL.

42-29878 Del Cheyenne 3/3/43; Sioux City 18/3/43; Kearney 9/4/43; Dow Fd 13/4/43; ass 526BS/379BG [LF-G] Kimbolton 9/5/43; MIA St Nazaire 29/5/43 w/Peterson; flak, cr Channel; 2EVD 8POW; MACR 1293. LADY GODIVA.

42-29879 Del Denver 28/2/43; ass 379BG Sioux City 18/3/43; sal Kearney 9/4/43; 499BG Smoky Hill 9/8/44; 247 BU Smoky Hill 19/9/44; 232 BU Dalhart 14/10/44; 273 BU Lincoln 29/11/44; 246 BU Pratt 10/1/45; RFC Albuquerque 25/6/45.

42-29880 Del Denver 3/3/43; Geiger 31/3/43; Minneapolis 17/4/43; Gt Falls 21/4/43; Gore 1/6/43; Ephrata 8/6/43; Rapid City 26/6/43; Orlando 8/7/43; Rapid City 2/8/43; Wall; a Walla 18/11/43; 499BG Gt Bend 6/6/44; 243 BU Gt Bend 10/6/44; 19BG Gt Bend 9/9/44; 232 BU Dalhart 7/10/44; 202 BU Galveston 11/10/44; 4121 BU Kelly 31/12/44; 224 BU Sioux City 23/2/45; 4202 BU Syracuse 24/4/45; RFC Altus 22/8/45.

42-29881 Del Denver 3/3/43; Eglin 19/3/43; Patterson 2/5/43; Wright 7/5/43; Boca Raton 15/5/43; Eglin 27/5/43; Smoky Hill 11/6/43; Boca Raton 14/6/43; Homestead 19/6/43; 398BG Rapid City 4/2/44; 225 BU Rapid City 29/4/44; RFC Ontario 20/6/45.

42-29882 Del Denver 3/3/43; Pueblo 12/3/43; Presque Is 8/4/43; ass 94BG Bassingbourn 17/4/43; tran 508BS/351BG [YB-L] Polebrook 18/4/43; 2 BAD Warton 5/4/44; retUS Amarillo 18/7/44; RFC Walnut Ridge 29/12/45. SHARON ANN.

42-29883 Del Denver 4/3/43; Salina, Cal 18/3/43; Tinker 31/3/43; Memphis 8/4/43; Morrison 15/4/43; ass 416BS/99BG Navarin 10/5/43; Oudna 4/8/43; Tortorella 11/12/43; tran 840BS/483BG Tortorella 31/3/44; Sterparone 22/4/44; 463BG Celone 9/44 to 6/45 as weather a/c; sal 28/7/45.

42-29884 Del Denver 4/3/43; Patterson 8/4/43; Eglin 16/4/43; Dow Fd 19/4/43; ass 325BS/92BG [NV-D] Alconbury 23/5/43; then 326BG; MIA Gelsenkirchen 12/8/43 w/Johnson; flak, cr Haltern, Ger; 10POW. MACR 374.

42-29885 Del Denver 5/3/43; Hobbs 3/4/43; Mather 12/5/43; New Castle 2/6/43; Hobbs 21/7/43; Tinker 6/6/44; Hobbs 15/7/44; RFC Altus 14/9/45.

42-29886 Del Denver 3/3/43; Sioux City 16/3/43; Kearney 8/4/43; Selfridge 16/4/43; Dow Fd 19/4/43; ass 525BS/379BG [FR-H] Kimbolton 23/4/43; MIA Frankfurt 24/1/44 w/Moses; e/a, cr Blankenheim, Ger; 5KIA 5POW; MACR 2871. SCHEHERAZADE.

42-29887 Del Denver 3/3/43; Gore 12/3/43; Presque Is 8/4/43; ass 510BS/351BG [TU-K] Polebrook 17/4/43; MIA {7m} Tricqueville 28/6/43 w/Copeland; flak, cr St Nazaire; 3KIA 7POW. MEHITABEL.

42-29888 Del Denver 5/3/43; Gore 6/3/43; Denver 20/3/43; Pueblo 10/4/43; Smoky Hill 5/5/43; Dow Fd 21/5/43; ass 532BS/381BG [VE-H] Ridgewell 6/4/43; {20+m} AFSC 11/5/44; retUS Tinker 6/8/44; RFC Arledge Fd 22/11/44. THE JOKER.

42-29889 Del Denver 4/3/43; Sioux City 20/3/43; Kearney 9/4/43; Dow Fd 13/4/43; ass 526BS/379BG [LF-H] Kimbolton 22/4/43; then 525BS [FR-N]; burnt out base 23/2/44, sal 2 SAD Lt Staughton 24/2/44. ROCKY.

42-29890 Del Denver 4/3/43; Sioux City 20/3/43; Kearney 9/4/43; Bangor 14/4/43; ass 525BS/379BG [FR-E] Kimbolton 22/4/43 STUPIFIER; then 526BS [LF-J]; b/d Anklam 9/10/43, c/l base; sal 2 SAD Lt Staughton 10/10/43. MADAME PISONYER.

42-29891 Del Denver 4/3/43; Sioux City 20/3/43; Kearney 8/4/43; Dow Fd 15/4/43; ass 524BS/379BG [WA-N] Kimbolton 22/4/43; b/d Osnabrück 22/12/43 c/l Lesfield, UK; sal 24/12/43. DANGEROUS DAN.

42-29892 Del Denver 6/3/43; Sioux City 18/3/43; Kearney 8/4/43; Bangor 14/4/43; ass 527BS/379BG [FO-N] Kimbolton 22/4/43; MIA Bochum 25/6/43 w/Groom; e/a, cr Neu Arenberg, Ger; 5KIA 5POW; MACR 1758.

42-29893 Del Cheyenne 4/3/43; Sioux City 16/3/43; Kearney 8/4/43; Dow Fd 22/4/43; ass 524BS/379BG [WA-Q] Kimbolton 24/4/43; MIA Nantes 16/9/43 w/Jamerson; flak, cr Nantes; 2EVD 2KIA 6POW; MACR 1346.

42-29894 Del Cheyenne 5/3/43; Gore 6/3/43; Cheyenne 24/3/43; Romulus 16/4/43; ass 367BS/306BG [GY-D] Thurleigh 18/5/43; tran 359BS/303BG Molesworth 25/9/43; MIA Oschersleben 11/1/44 w/Pursell; e/a, cr Hamelin, Ger; 10KIA; MACR 1928. BALTIMORE BOUNCE.

42-29895 Del Cheyenne 4/3/43; Scott Fd 28/3/43; Scotts Bluff 7/4/43; Smoky Hill 16/4/43; Presque Is 2/5/43; ass 324BS/91BG [DF-H] Bassingbourn 23/5/43; MIA {20+M} Bordeaux 31/12/43 w/Mendelsohn; flak, cr Lorient; 2EVD 2KIA 6POW;

MACR 1975. THE BLACK SWAN.

42-29896 Del Cheyenne 5/3/43; Sioux City 20/3/43; Tinker 28/3/43; Kearney 8/4/43; Dow Fd 16/4/43; ass 527BS/379BG [FO-Y/V] Kimbolton 2/5/43; MIA T/Ops 6/9/43 w/Fawkes; ditched, 10RTD. TONDELAYO.

42-29897 Del Cheyenne 5/3/43; Gore 28/3/43; Metropolitan 13/4/43; Dow Fd 30/4/43; ass 325BS/92BG [NV-B] Alconbury 26/5/43; tran 524BS/379BG [WA-A] Kimbolton 4/9/43; retUS 30/4/44; Hendricks 29/7/44; Maxwell 9/10/44; Hendricks 31/10/44; RFC Walnut Ridge 14/1/46. CENSORED (FOREQUETOO).

42-29898 Del Cheyenne 4/3/43; Sioux City 19/3/43; Kearney 8/4/43; Bangor 13/4/43; ass 524BS/379BG [WA-K/I] Kimbolton 22/4/43; MIA Bochum 12/8/43 w/Osborne; flak, cr Metternich, Ger; 6KIA 4POW; MACR 1762.

42-29899 Del Cheyenne 5/3/43; Colorado Springs 18/3/43; Patterson 2/4/43; Colorado Springs 15/4/43; Esler Fd 22/5/43; Peterson 25/5/43; ass 1st Photo Gp 1/9/43; 499BG Smoky Hill 6/6/44; 11 Ph Map Gp McDill 28/7/44; 19 Ph Sq McDill 2/8/44; 4117 BU Robins 8/11/44; 91 Photo Gp Buckley 12/11/44; RFC Ontario 24/5/45.

42-29900 Del Cheyenne 5/3/43; Walla Walla 28/3/43; Metropolitan 13/4/43; Presque Is 29/4/43; ass 423BS/306BG [RD-J/D] Thurleigh 23/5/43; MIA Hanover 26/7/43 w/Armbrust; flak, cr Diepholz, Ger; 1KIA 9POW; MACR 126. UNBEARABLE II.

42-29901 Del Cheyenne 5/3/43; Sioux City 18/3/43; Kearney 9/4/43; Dow Fd 13/4/43; ass 526BS/379BG [LF-K] Kimbolton 22/4/43; MIA Nantes 16/9/43 w/Euwer; hit by bomb from above, cr Redon, Fr; 4EVD 6KIA; MACR 1347.

42-29902 Del Cheyenne 8/3/43; Colorado Springs 18/3/43; Patterson 23/3/43; Colorado Springs 7/4/43; San Bernadino 22/5/43; Peterson 28/5/43; ass 1st Photo Gp Colorado Springs 1/9/43; WO 8/1/44.

42-29903 Del Denver 9/3/43; Tinker 31/3/43; New Castle 10/4/43; Morrison 16/4/43; ass 429BS/2BG Navarin 22/4/43; Château-du-Rhumel 27/4/43; Ain M'Lila 17/6/43; Massicault 31/7/43; Bizerte 2/12/43; Amendola 9/12/43; MIA Toulon 4/2/44 w/Bingham; 6 chutes seen, #2 engine on fire; MACR 2301. HIGH TENSION II.

42-29904 Del Cheyenne 6/3/43; Colorado Springs 18/3/43; Patterson 24/3/43; Colorado Springs 10/4/43; ass 1st Photo Gp Colorado Springs 1/9/43; Mexico 9/11/43 - 27/12/43; Smoky Hill 6/6/44; McDill 13/6/44; Robins 30/10/44; Buckley 14/11/44; RFC Bush Fd 26/6/45.

42-29905 Del Denver 6/3/43; New Castle 6/4/43; Metropolitan 15/4/43; New Castle 21/4/43; ass 526BS/379BG [LF-K/Z] Kimbolton 21/5/43; AFSC 7/4/44; retUS Rome 29/8/44; Hobbs 11/9/44; Kirtland 7/1/44; RFC Altus 14/9/45. 4-Q-2.

42-29906 Del Denver 6/3/43; Salina 18/3/43; Tinker 31/3/43; Morrison 12/4/43; Homstead 21/4/43; ass 12AF 11/5/43; Independence 24/10/43; RFC Altus 7/11/45.

42-29907 Del Denver 6/3/43; Salina 18/3/43; Tinker 31/3/43; Homestead 21/4/43; ass 49BS/2BG Château-du-Rhumel 30/4/43; Ain M'Lila 17/6/43; Massicault 31/7/43; MIA {29m} Bologna 5/10/43 w/Fitzpatrick; e/a, 10 chutes seen; MACR 933.

42-29908 Del Denver 6/3/43; Tinker 29/3/43; Hobbs 4/4/43; Ft Sumner 23/4/43; Hobbs 14/6/43; 3017 BU Hobbs 8/11/43; RFC Altus 31/8/45.

42-29909 Del Denver 6/3/43; Gore 20/3/43; Birmingham 31/3/43; Nashville 10/4/43; Morrison 14/4/43; ass 20BS/2BG Navarin 22/4/43; Château-du-Rhumel 27/4/43; Ain M'Lila 17/6/43; Massicault 31/7/43; Bizerte 2/12/43; Amendola 9/12/43; taxi accident w/42-29623 3/2/44, sal.

42-29910 Del Cheyenne 6/3/43; Colorado Springs 20/2/43; Wright Fd 8/4/43; Colorado Springs 13/4/43; Peterson 23/4/43; Kirtland 20/5/43; Peterson 28/5/43; Kirtland 1/6/43; Peterson 15/6/43; ass 1st Photo Gp Colorado Springs 12/9/43; WO 15/1/44.

42-29911 Del Cheyenne 8/3/43; Colorado Springs 18/3/43; Patterson 2/4/43; Colorado Springs 16/4/43; Patterson 19/6/43; ass 1st Photo Gp Colorado Springs 1/9/43; Mexico 9/11/43 - 23/12/43; Smoky Hill 6/6/44; McClellan 7/8/44; Patterson 14/12/44; Clovis 10/3/45; RFC Kingman 9/11/45.

42-29912 Del Cheyenne 8/3/43; Colorado Springs 18/3/43; Patterson 24/3/43; Colorado Springs 10/4/43; Peterson 19/5/43; Hill Fd 12/8/43; ass 1st Photo Gp Ogden 1/9/43; Will Rogers 14/11/43; McDill 24/11/43; 499BG Smoky Hill 6/6/44; 11 Photo Gp McDill 13/6/44; 19 Ph Sq McDill 2/8/44; 3701 BU Amarillo 12/8/44; 3706 BU Sheppard 28/6/45; 3701 BU Amarillo 20/7/45; RFC Walnut Ridge 29/12/45.

42-29913 Del Cheyenne 8/3/43; Colorado Springs 18/3/43; Patterson 24/3/43; Colorado Springs 7/4/43; Esler 10/5/43; Barksdale 21/5/43; Peterson 26/5/43; ass 1st Photo Gp Colorado Springs 1/9/43; 499BG Smoky Hill 6/6/44; 11 Ph Sq McDill 29/7/44; 19 Ph Gp McDill 2/8/44; 4117 BU Robins 29/10/44; 19 Ph GP McDill 12/11/44; RFC Ontario 24/5/45.

42-29914 Del Cheyenne 8/3/43; Smoky Hill 26/3/43; Baer Fd 10/4/43; Smoky Hill 13/4/43; Dow Fd 18/4/43; ass 339BS/96BG Grafton Underwood 24/4/43 MISCHIEF MAKER; Andrews Fd 13/5/43; Snetterton 12/6/43; tran 546BS/384BG Grafton Underwood 14/8/43; MIA Evreux 3/9/43 w/Jones; e/a, ditched Channel; 10POW; MACR 743.

42-29915 Del Cheyenne 8/3/43; Gore 31/3/43; Bangor 14/4/43; ass 524BS/379BG [WA-U] Kimbolton 22/4/43; MIA Wilhelmshaven 11/6/43 w/Zucker; e/a, cr Nth Sea; 10KIA; MACR 1760. THUNDER GOD.

42-29916 Del Cheyenne 20/3/43; Walla Walla 31/3/43; Tinker 10/4/43; Memphis 17/4/43; Presque Is 10/5/43; ass 323BS/91BG [OR-L] Bassingbourn 7/6/43; MIA {6+m} Kassel 30/7/43 w/Miles; e/a, cr Zoetemeer, Hol; 2KIA 8POW; MACR 147. YANKEE DANDY.

42-29917 Del Cheyenne 9/3/43; Colorado Springs 8/3/43; Patterson 2/4/43; Peterson 21/4/43; Presque Is 6/5/43; Peterson 28/5/43; ass 1st Photo Gp, Riverside, Cal 1/9/43; Mexico 9/11/43 - 27/12/43; Smoky Hill 6/6/44; McDill 30/6/43; Robins 2/11/43; Buckley 22/11/43; Peterson 1/8/45; RFC Altus 8/10/45.

42-29918 Del Denver 9/3/43; Gore 20/3/43; Tinker 30/3/43; Homestead 7/4/43; Morrison 12/4/43; ass 346BS/99BG Navarin 12/5/43; Oudna 4/8/43; b/d Messina 16/8/43, 1KIA; tran 342BS/97BG Depienne 14/11/43; Cerignola 20/12/43; MIA Piraeus w/Easterling 11/1/44; coll w/42-3251, cr Kalami; MACR 2027. WEBFOOT.

42-29919 Del Cheyenne 9/3/43; Memphis 8/4/43; Presque Is 1/5/43; ass 412BS/95BG [QW-Z] Framlingham 11/6/43; sal 13/6/43 (possibly b/d Kiel or transfer from Alconbury?). CARBONDALE SPECIAL.

42-29920 Del Denver 9/3/43; Hobbs 3/4/43; Ft Sumner 21/4/43; Hobbs 6/5/43; 3017 BU Hobbs 8/11/44; 553 BU Romulus 13/11/44; 3017 BU Hobbs 12/6/45; 4124 BU Long Beach 10/7/45; RFC Altus 20/8/45.

42-29921 Del Denver 13/3/43; New Castle 6/4/43; ass 324BS/91BG [DF-Z] Bassingbourn 23/5/43; MIA {29+m} Cognac 31/12/43 w/Dudley; e/a, cr Parentis-en-Born, Fr; 1EVD(wg) 5KIA 4POW; MACR 1976. OKLAHOMA OKIE.

42-29922 Del Cheyenne 9/3/43; Colorado Springs 18/3/43; Patterson 24/3/43; Colorado Springs 7/4/43; Peterson 24/5/43; Scott Fd 4/7/43; Peterson 11/7/43; Cheyenne 9/8/43; Peterson 14/8/43; ass 1st Photo Gp Colorado Springs 1/9/43; 499BG Smoky Hill 6/6/44; 3705 BU Lowry 1/7/44; 3rd Ph Sq Smoky Hill 5/7/44; 554 BU Memphis 1/8/44; 331 BU Barksdale 6/9/44; 3rd Ph Sq Smoky Hill 14/9/44; 19 Ph Gp McDill 1/10/44; 247 BU Smoky Hill 31/10/44; 4100 BU Patterson 23/1/45; 234 BU Clovis 24/10/45; RFC Kingman 9/11/45.

42-29923 Del Cheyenne 13/3/43; Casper 28/3/43; Tinker 10/4/43; ass 364BS/305BG [WF-K] Chelveston 18/5/43 PAPPY'S HELLIONS III; tran 532BS/381BG [VE-K] Ridgewell 11/9/43; b/d {2m} Keil 4/1/44 w/Evans, c/l Cawston, Nfk; 2 SAD Lt Staughton 5/1/44; sal 7/1/44. LUCKY STRIKE.

42-29924 Del Cheyenne 13/3/43; Gowen 17/3/43; Brooksville 10/4/43; Montbrook 12/8/43; Orlando 30/11/43; 3017 BU Hobbs 25/10/44; WO, Recl Comp 2/11/44.

42-29925 Del Cheyenne 17/3/43; Pueblo 28/3/43; Presque Is 9/4/43; ass 510BS/351BG [TU-L] Polebrook 17/5/43; 2 BAD Warton 5/4/44; retUS Tinker 7/6/44; Hendricks 9/8/44; Rapid City 12/9/44; RFC Walnut Ridge 14/12/45. THE DUCHESS.

42-29926 Del Cheyenne 17/3/43; Colorado Springs 24/3/43; Patterson 2/4/43; Colorado Springs 15/4/43; Peterson 17/5/43; Kirtland 9/5/43; Peterson 30/5/43; ass 1st Photo Gp Colorado Springs 1/9/43; 499BG Smoky Hill 6/6/44; 11 Ph Sq McDill 13/6/44; 19 Ph Gp McDill 2/8/44; 3701 BU Amarillo 11/8/44; 3706 BU Sheppard 12/3/45; 3701 BU Amarillo 3/4/45; 4135 BU Hill 22/10/45; 3701 BU Amarillo 26/11/45; RFC Walnut Ridge 5/1/46.

42-29927 Del Cheyenne 13/3/43; Smoky Hill 26/3/43; Presque Is 10/4/43; ass 413BS/96BG Grafton Underwood 17/4/43 WABBIT TWACKS; Andrews Fd 13/5/43; Snetterton 12/6/43; tran 546BS/384BG [BK-B] 6/7/43; then 547BS [SO-R]; 2 BAD Warton 5/4/44; retUS Tinker 4/6/44; Hendricks 2/8/44; Redford 24/4/45; Biggs 9/9/45; Hendricks 2/10/45; RFC Walnut Ridge 13/12/45. HOMESICK GAL.

42-29928 Del Cheyenne 12/3/43; Walla Walla 25/3/43; Metropolitan 13/4/43; Presque Is 29/4/43; ass 533BS/381BG [VP-W] Ridgewell 23/6/43; MIA {2m} Le Mans 4/7/43 w/Ballinger; e/a, cr Tours, Fr; 3EVD 4KIA 3POW; MACR 161.

42-29929 Del Cheyenne 13/3/43; Sioux City 14/4/43; Wendover 23/5/43; Sioux City 11/6/43; Kearney 3/8/43; Gore 13/8/43; 582BS/393BG Sioux City 12/11/43; 247 BU Smoky Hill 20/6/44; 222 BU Ardmore 26/6/44; RFC Ontario 14/6/45.

42-29930 Del Cheyenne 13/3/43; Casper 29/3/43; Smoky Hill 14/4/43; Walla Walla 5/7/43; Tinker 21/5/43; Dow Fd 3/6/43; ass 423BS/306BG [RD-J] Thurleigh 17/6/43; tran 360BS/303BG [PU-I] Molesworth 25/9/43 MISS PATRICIA; c/t/o at Keyston 23/10/43, sal. QUI-NINE THE BITTER DOSE.

42-29931 Del Cheyenne 13/3/43; Casper 28/3/43; Tinker 10/4/43; Memphis 16/4/43; ass 100BG Thorpe Abbotts 9/6/43 JAYBIRD; tran 360BS/303BG [PU-L] Molesworth 13/7/43; MIA Bernburg 22/2/44 w/Underwood; e/a, cr Channel; 10KIA, MACR 2564. SATAN'S WORKSHOP.

42-29932 En route from Boeing 13/3/43 w/civilian pilot

Elliot A/Merrill. On test flight suffered structural failure while in dive. Pilot and five passengers baled safely. A/c cr Port Orchard, Wash. WO 12/4/43.

42-29933 Del Cheyenne 14/3/43; Gore 31/3/43; Presque Is 8/4/43; ass 338BS/96BG 17/4/43 GREEN FURY II; re-named LUCKY LADY; tran 524BS/379BG [WA-M] Kimbolton 12/7/43; b/d Gelsenkirchen 12/8/43; 1 BAD Burtonwood 15/8/43; AFMSC 4/2/44. PANAMA HATTIE.

42-29934 Del Denver 15/3/43; Cheyenne 17/3/43; Walla Walla 2/4/43; Metropolitan 13/4/43; Selfridge 27/4/43; Dow Fd 30/4/43; ass 526BS/379BG [LF-G] Kimbolton 6/6/43; MIA Nantes 16/9/43 w/Murray; hit by bomb from above, cr Nantes, 10KIA; MACR 1348.

42-29935 Del Cheyenne 15/3/43; Smoky Hill 26/3/43; Dow Fd 10/4/43; ass 413BS/96BG Grafton Underwood 27/4/43 THE CAT'S SASS; Andrews Fd 13/5/43; Snetterton 12/6/43; tran 546BS/384BG [BK-K] Grafton Underwood 14/8/43; MIA Bremen 20/12/43 w/Carnes (crew's 1st mission); no gas ditched Channel; 1KIA 9POW; MACR 1725.

42-29936 Del Cheyenne 17/3/43; Gore 27/3/43; Metropolitan 13/4/43; Presque Is 29/4/43; ass Ugly 1/5/43; Con 31/7/43.

42-29937 Del Cheyenne 15/3/43; Walla Walla 28/3/43; Metropolitan 13/4/43; Presque Is 29/4/43; ass 306BS/306BG [BO-N] Thurleigh 23/5/43; tran 525BS/379BG [FR-C] Kimbolton 27/6/43; MIA Rennes 23/9/43 w/Braidenthal; e/a, cr Rennes; 3EVD 7POW; MACR 1051.

42-29938 Del Cheyenne 15/3/43; Smoky Hill 20/6/43; Presque Is 8/4/43; ass 337BS/96BG Grafton Underwood 27/4/43; Andrews Fd 13/5/43; Snetterton 12/6/43; c/l base 26/5/43; sal. TARFU.

42-29939 Del Cheyenne 15/3/43; Walla Walla 28/3/43; Metropolitan 13/4/43; Presque Is 29/4/43; ass 338BS/96BG [BX-X] Grafton Underwood 15/5/43 THE DUCHESS; MIA Stettin 11/4/44 w/Young; flak, cr Baltic; 9KIA 1POW; MACR 3810. WABASH CANNONBALL.

42-29940 Del Cheyenne 15/3/43; Casper 29/3/43; Smoky Hill 10/4/43; Dow Fd 30/4/43; ass 332BS/94BG Bassingbourn 8/5/43; Earls Colne 12/5/43; MIA Kiel 13/6/43 w/Loog; e/a, ditched Channel, 9KIA 1POW; MACR 16200.

42-29941 Del Cheyenne 15/3/43; Smoky Hill 26/3/43; Dow Fd 12/4/43; ass 337BS/96BG Grafton Underwood 18/4/43 TARFU; Andrews Fd 13/5/43; Snetterton 12/6/43; tran 535BS/381BG [MS-R] Ridgewell 15/7/43 TS TARFU; MIA {15m} Bremen 8/10/43 w/Manchester; flak, cr Talge, Ger; 6KIA 4POW; MACR 884. TS TOO.

42-29942 Del Cheyenne 15/3/43; Sioux City 29/3/43; Bangor 16/4/43; Dow Fd 20/4/43; ass 527BS/379BG Kimbolton but c/l Prestwick 1/5/43, sal.

42-29943 Del Cheyenne 15/3/43; Smoky Hill 26/3/43; Dow Fd 31/5/43; ass 305BG Chelveston 15/6/43; tran 334BS/95BG [BG-K] Alconbury 16/6/43; Framlingham 12/5/43; Horham 15/6/43; MIA Oldenburg 6/3/44 w/Mailman; exploded, cr Barnsdorf, Ger; 5KIA 5POW; MACR 2890. SITUATION NORMAL.

42-29944 Del Cheyenne 17/3/43; Gore 28/3/43; Metropolitan 13/4/43; Presque Is 29/4/43; ass 427BS/303BG [GN-E] Molesworth 9/6/43 BUZZIN' BRONCO; secret mission to Nth Africa 16/8/43 ret 23/8/43; b/d T/Ops 6/9/43; c/l West Malling, UK; sal 7/9/43. WINNING RUN.

42-29945 Del Cheyenne 13/3/43; Walla Walla 28/3/43; Smoky Hill 13/3/43; Dow Fd 30/4/43; ass 339BS/96BG Grafton Underwood 2/5/43 DAISY JUNE II; Andrews Fd 13/5/43; Snetterton 12/6/43; tran 326BS/92BG Alconbury 23/7/43; MIA Recklinghausen 12/8/43 w/Davis; flak, cr Nth Sea; 10POW; MACR 658.

42-29946 Del Cheyenne 15/3/43; Gore 16/3/43; Cheyenne 22/3/43; Walla Walla 2/4/43; Metropolitan 13/4/43; ass 525BS/379BG Kimbolton 4/5/43; MIA Huls 22/6/43 w/Dollarhyde; flak, cr Huls; 6KIA 4POW; MACR 1294.

42-29947 Del Cheyenne 17/3/43; Walla Walla 28/3/43; Smoky Hill 13/4/43; Selfridge 4/5/43; Dow Fd 6/5/43; ass 100BG Podington 8/5/43; Thorpe Abbotts 9/6/43; tran 322BS/91BG Bassingbourn 6/7/43; {60+m} 303BG (as HQ hack) Molesworth 27/7/43; retUS Bradley Fd 12/7/45; RFC Cincinnati 16/7/45. WABASH CANNONBALL.

42-29948 Del Cheyenne 17/3/43; Walla Walla 28/3/43; Metropolitan 13/4/43; Dow Fd 30/4/43; ass 510BS/351BG [TU-B] Polebrook 28/5/43; MIA Cognac 31/12/43 w/Wells; flak, cr Cognac; 10POW; MACR 1979. JENNIE.

42-29949 Del Cheyenne 17/3/43; Casper 31/3/43; Smoky Hill 10/4/43; Dow Fd 30/4/43; ass 332BS/94BG Earls Colne 3/6/43; MIA Kiel 13/6/43 w/Tower; e/a, ditched Channel; 1KIA 9POW. SICK CALL.

42-29950 Del Cheyenne 3/4/43; Pueblo 30/4/43; Smoky Hill 11/5/43; Dow Fd 23/5/43; ass 535BS/381BG [MS-N] Ridgewell 29/5/43; MIA {12m} Gelsenkirchen 12/8/43 w/Evans; e/a, cr Rheudt, Ger; 5KIA 5POW, MACR 385. FORGET ME NOT.

42-29951 Del Denver 15/3/43; Patterson 27/3/43; Cheyenne 8/4/43; Tinker 24/4/43; Mines Fd 4/5/43; Hobbs 14/5/43; Wright Fd 29/5/43; Eglin 10/6/43; Wright 8/7/43; Zanesville 9/7/43; Eglin 15/7/43; Orlando 6/8/43; 610 BU Eglin 2/6/44; RFC Kingman 23/10/45.

42-29952 Del Denver 17/3/43; Smoky Hill 5/4/43; Selfridge 21/4/43; ass 96BG Grafton Underwood 25/4/43; Andrews Fd 13/5/43; tran 364BS/305BG [WF-J] Chelveston 31/5/43; MIA Schweinfurt 14/10/43 w/Murdock; e/a, cr Maastricht, Hol; 5KIA 5POW; MACR 917. SIZZLE.

42-29953 Del Denver 17/3/43; Pueblo 8/4/43; Smoky Hill 14/5/43; Dow Fd 21/5/43; ass 535BS/381BG [MS-Q] Ridgewell 25/5/43 MAN O' WAR; {10m} tran 364BS/305BG [WF-H/F] Chelveston 22/8/43; FTR training op. 25/11/43 coll w/42-30666, ditched Nth Sea; all killed. MACR 1402. WOLFESS.

42-29954 Del Denver 17/3/43; Pueblo 8/4/43; Smoky Hill 7/5/43; Dow Fd 25/5/43; ass 534BS/381BG [GD-D] Ridgewell 25/5/43; MIA Gelsenkirchen 12/8/43 w/Wroblicka, flak, cr Cologne; 5KIA 5POW; MACR 383. DEVIL'S ANGEL.

42-29955 Del Denver 17/3/43; Smoky Hill 5/4/43; Presque Is 29/4/43; ass 427BS/305BG [GN-I] Chelveston 16/5/43; MIA Bremen 26/11/43 w/Cote; mech fault, cr Den Helder, Hol; 1EVD 9KIA; MACR 1324. MR FIVE BY FIVE.

42-29956 Del Denver 17/3/43; Cheyenne 6/4/43; Sioux City 14/4/43; Kearney 4/5/43; Dow Fd 24/5/43; ass 544BS/384BG [SU-B] Grafton Underwood 29/5/43; MIA Schweinfurt 17/8/43 w/Hausenfluck; e/a, cr St Goarshausen, Ger, 2KIA 8POW; MACR 296. VERTICAL SHAFT.

42-29957 Del Denver 17/3/43; Romulus 10/4/43; ass 410BS/94BG Bassingbourn 22/4/43; Earls Colne 12/5/43; MIA Kiel 13/6/43 w/Roemke; e/a, ditched Channel; 6KIA 4POW. HELNO GAL II.

42-29958 Del Denver 17/3/43; Pueblo 8/4/43; Smoky Hill 7/5/43; Dow Fd 21/5/43; ass 534BS/381BG [GD-J] Ridgewell 24/5/43; MIA Anklam 9/10/43 w/Loftin; e/a, cr Schonberg, Ger; 2KIA 8POW; MACR 886. BATTLIN' BOMBSPRAYER.

42-29959 Del Denver 17/3/43; Gore 20/3/43; New Castle 13/4/43; Dow Fd 21/4/43; ass 367BS/306BG [GY-M] Thurleigh 23/5/43; then 423BS; MIA Bremen 8/10/43 w/Kooima; flak, cr Fischerhude, Ger; 6KIA 4POW; MACR 867.

42-29960 Del Denver 18/3/43; Sioux City 14/4/43; Kearney 3/5/43; Dow Fd 24/5/43; ass 545BS/384BG [JD-Y] Grafton Underwood 31/5/43; MIA Le Mans 4/7/43 w/Erikson; mid air collision. NYMOKYMI.

42-29961 Del Cheyenne 18/3/43; Casper 28/3/43; Smoky Hill 16/4/43; Tinker 16/5/43; Lincoln 17/5/43; Dow Fd 24/5/43; ass 333BS/94BG [QE-V] Earls Colne 29/5/43; Rougham 13/6/43; MIA Brunswick 11/1/44 w/Butler; e/a, cr Pott-Holtensen, Ger; 1KIA 9POW; MACR 1882. PASSIONATE WITCH.

42-29962 Del Cheyenne 18/3/43; Walla Walla 28/3/43; Metropolitan 13/4/43; Selfridge 29/4/43; Presque Is 4/5/43; ass 339BS/96BG Andrews Fd 13/5/43; Snetterton 12/6/43 RUM BOOGIE II; tran 326BS/92BG [JW-E] Alconbury 26/7/43; Bovingdon 16/10/43; 2 SAD Lt Staughton 8/11/43.

42-29963 Del Cheyenne 18/3/43; Walla Walla 28/3/43; Metropolitan 13/4/43; Dow Fd 30/4/43; ass 527BS/379BG [FO-I] Kimbolton 11/6/43; MIA Ludwigshafen 30/12/43 w/Camp; flak, cr Noailles, Fr; 2EVD 4KIA 2POW; MACR 1977.

42-29964 Del Smoky Hill 13/4/43; Boeing Seattle 21/5/43; 505BG Harvard 4/6/44; 244 BU Harvard 9/6/44; 504BG Fairmont 8/9/44; 244 BU Harvard 22/9/44; 249 BU Alliance 2/2/45; RFC Altus 28/7/45.

42-29965 Del Cheyenne 18/3/43; Gore 28/3/43; Presque Is 5/5/43; ass 333BS/94BG Earls Colne 12/5/43; Rougham 13/6/43; tran 407BS/92BG [PY-L] Alconbury 26/7/43; MIA Cognac 16/9/43 w/Prasse; flak, ditched Channel; 10RTD.

42-29966 Del Cheyenne 19/3/43; Gore 19/3/43; Dyersburg 30/3/43; Amarillo 9/4/43; Albuquerque 16/4/43; Amarillo 19/4/43; Gr Island 6/9/43; Tinker 18/11/43; 273 BU Lincoln 23/6/43; 236 BU Pyote 30/7/44; 221 BU Alexandra 4/10/44; 329 BU Alexandra 1/3/45; RFC Altus 29/10/45.

42-26667 Del Cheyenne 18/3/43; Gore 19/3/43; Walla Walla 30/3/43; Metropolitan 13/4/43; ass 412BS/95BG [QW-Q] Framlingham 12/5/43; Horham 15/6/43; tran 407BS/92BG Alconbury 17/6/43; MIA Nantes 4/7/43 w/Campbell.

42-29968 Del Cheyenne 20/3/43; Hobbs 2/4/43; Ft Sumner 21/4/43; Hobbs 30/4/43; 4136 BU Tinker 6/6/44; 3017 BU Hobbs 7/6/44; 4121 BU Kelly 1/12/44; RFC Albuqueque 13/8/45.

42-29969 Del Cheyenne 22/3/43; Hobbs 3/4/43; Ft Sumner 21/4/43; Hobbs 6/5/43; Eglin 29/6/43; Hobbs 5/7/43; 3017 BU Hobbs 8/11/44; RFC Altus 14/9/45.

42-29970 Del Cheyenne 18/3/43; Scotts Bluff 28/3/43; Smoky Hill 16/4/43; Dow Fd 6/5/43; ass 333BS/94BG Bassingbourn 9/5/43; Earls Colne 12/5/43; Rougham 13/6/43; tran 364BS/305BG Chelveston 14/7/43; MIA Kassel 28/7/43 w/Dragasavac; flak, cr Seigen, Ger; 10POW; MACR 192.

42-29971 Del Cheyenne 18/3/43; Walla Walla 29/3/43; Metropolitan 13/4/43; Dow Fd 30/4/43; ass 423BS/305BG [RD-F] Chelveston 23/5/43; MIA Schweinfurt 14/10/43 w/Cole; e/a, cr Beek, Hol; 4KIA 6POW; MACR 819.

42-29972 Del Cheyenne 20/3/43; Hobbs 1/4/43; Dow Fd 16/4/43; Hobbs 18/4/43; 3017 BU Hobbs 8/11/44; 4124 BU Altus 25/7/45; RFC Altus 30/8/45.

42-29973 Del Cheyenne 20/3/43; Tinker 10/4/43;

Memphis 17/4/43; ass 322BS/91BG [LG-Q] Bassingbourn 11/6/43; b/d Amiens 31/8/43 w/Rogers; dam by debris from a/cs collision above and flak over target; c/l Polegate, UK, all killed. PATTY GREMLIN JR.

42-29974 Del Denver 20/3/43; Romulus 10/4/43; ass 367BS/306BG [GY-V] Thurleigh 19/4/43; b/d Kassel 28/7/43, coll w/42-30302 c/l Framlingham, sal.

42-29975 Del Cheyenne 23/3/43; Smoky Hill 3/4/43; Memphis 12/4/43; Dow Fd 16/4/43; ass 337BS/96BG Grafton Underwood 21/4/43 RUM BOOGIE 3rd; Andrews Fd 13/5/43; Snetterton 12/6/43; tran 326BS/92BG [JW-F] Alconbury 23/7/43; 1 BAD Burtonwood 13/6/44; retUS Homestead 26/7/44; Tinker 6/8/44; RFC Stillwater 4/10/45.

42-29976 Del Denver 20/3/43; Pueblo 8/4/43; Smoky Hill 6/5/43; Dow Fd 19/5/43; ass 532BS/381BG [VE-Q] Ridgewell 25/5/43; MIA {2+m} Hamburg 25/7/43 w/Owen; flak, cr Hamburg; 10POW; MACR 128. SAD SACK.

42-29977 Del Denver 20/3/43; Hobbs 31/3/43; Ft Sumner 21/4/43; Hobbs 6/5/43; Roswell 24/5/43; Hobbs 27/5/43; 3017 BU Hobbs 8/11/44; RFC Altus 11/9/45.

42-29978 Del Denver 20/3/43; Pueblo 8/4/43; Smoky Hill 7/5/43; Dow Fd 24/5/43; ass 534BS/381BG [GD-F] Ridgewell 31/5/43; MIA {3m} Schweinfurt 17/8/43 w/King; e/a, cr Bad Schwalbach; 10POW; MACR 382. HELL'S ANGEL.

42-29979 Del Cheyenne 23/3/43; Hobbs 3/4/43; Romulus 15/4/43; Ft Sumner 21/4/43; Hobbs 28/5/43; 3017 BU Hobbs 8/11/44; 3034 BU Gardner 13/11/44; RFC Altus 18/9/45.

42-29980 Del Cheyenne 20/3/43; Hobbs 2/4/43; Ft Sumner 21/4/43; Hobbs 6/5/43; 3017 BU Hobbs 8/11/44; RFC Altus 14/9/45.

42-29981 Del Cheyenne 20/3/43; Gore 31/3/43; Presque Is 8/4/43; Dow Fd 11/4/43; ass 338BS/96BG Grafton Underwood 27/4/43 HELL-LENA; Andrews Fd 13/5/43; Snetterton 12/6/43; tran 326BS/92BG Alconbury 23/7/43; MIA Hanover 26/7/43 w/Casey; e/a, ditched Nth Sea.

42-29982 Del Cheyenne 20/3/43; Hobbs 31/3/43; Long Beach 16/11/43; 3017 BU Hobbs 8/11/44; RFC Altus 14/9/45.

42-29983 Del Cheyenne 20/3/43; Dyersburg 31/3/43; Presque Is 10/4/43; Dow Fd 12/4/43; ass 338BS/96BG [BX-K] Grafton Underwood 24/4/43 GLORIA ANN; Andrews Fd 13/5/43; Snetterton 12/6/43; tran 533BS/381BG [VP-X] Ridgewell 17/6/43; MIA {6m} Schweinfurt 17/8/43 w/Atkinson; flak, cr Kesseling, Ger; 2KIA 8POW; MACR 398. IRIS.

42-29984 Del Denver 22/3/43; Cheyenne 31/3/43; Oklahoma City 6/4/43; Romulus 12/4/43; ass 533BS/381BG Ridgewell 16/6/43; b/d {1m} Antwerp 22/6/43 w/Shenk; c/l North Foreland, Kent; sal. LITTLE CHUCK.

42-29985 Del Denver 22/3/43; Cheyenne 31/3/43; Smoky Hill 5/4/43; Dow Fd 15/4/43; ass 545BS/384BG [JD-Y] Grafton Underwood 28/6/43 KATHLEEN; tran 367BS/306BG Thurleigh 22/8/43; MIA Bremen 8/10/43 w/Ledgerwood; e/a, cr Bremen; 1KIA 9POW; MACR 868. BARREL HOUSE BESSIE.

42-29986 Del Denver 22/3/43; Cheyenne 7/4/43; Kearney 16/4/43; Wendover 2/5/43; Kearney 22/5/43; Baer Fd 27/5/43; Dow Fd 3/6/43; ass 349BS/100BG [XR-Q] Thorpe Abbotts 5/6/43; MIA Juist Is (convoy) 25/6/43 w/Petrick; ditched Nth Sea,

10KIA; MACR 269.

42-29987 Del Denver 22/3/43; Cheyenne 31/3/43; Romulus 10/4/43; ass 366BS/305BG [KY-F] Chelveston 18/5/43; tran 547BS/384BG [SO-Q] Grafton Underwood 19/9/43; MIA Bremen 26/11/43 w/Amundsen; e/a, cr Duners-Woude, Hol; 8EVD 2POW; MACR 1662.

42-29988 Del Denver 22/3/43; Pueblo 8/4/43; Smoky Hill 11/5/43; Dow Fd 21/5/43; ass 535BS/381BG [MS-S] Ridgewell 24/5/43 LUCIFER JR.; {7m} tran 364BS/305BG [WF-A] Chelveston 22/8/43; MIA Schweinfurt 14/10/43 w/Holt; e/a, cr Puffendorf, Ger; 6KIA 4POW; MACR 914.

42-29989 Del Cheyenne 22/3/43; Gore 23/3/43; Hobbs 3/4/43; Lowry 9/8/43; Hobbs 13/8/43; 3017 BU Hobbs 8/11/44; 3505 BU Scott 1/4/45; 3017 BU Hobbs 21/4/45; RFC Altus 14/9/45.

42-29990 Del Cheyenne 22/3/43; Hobbs 2/4/43; Ft Sumner 21/4/43; Hobbs 6/5/43; Roswell 23/5/43; Hobbs 30/5/43; WO 9/9/43.

42-29991 Del Cheyenne 25/3/43; Dallas 2/4/43; Dow Fd 12/4/43; Love Fd 13/5/43; Geiger 26/5/43; Gt Falls 7/6/43; Smoky Hill 29/6/43; Dow Fd 11/7/43; ass 571BS/390BG [FC-T] Framlingham 14/7/43 PATCHES; MIA Schweinfurt 14/10/43 w/McEwin; e/a, cr Karlsruhe, Ger; 10POW, MACR 858. WE'LL NEVER KNOW.

42-29992 Del Denver 1/4/43; Pueblo 8/4/43; Smoky Hill 6/5/43; Dow Fd 23/5/43; ass 533BS/381BG [VP-J] Ridgewell 29/5/43; n/b/d 23/6/43, base explosion {1m} loading up for Bernay St Martin, sal. CONNIE.

42-29993 Del Cheyenne 24/3/43; Dow Fd 10/4/43; ass 369BS/306BG [WW-K] Thurleigh 19/4/43; MIA Oschersleben 11/1/44 w/Tattershall; flak, cr Diepenvean, Hol; 9KIA 1POW; MACR 1935.

42-29994 Del Cheyenne 23/3/43; Smoky Hill 3/4/43; Dow Fd 15/4/43; ass 325BS/92BG [NV-K] Alconbury 25/4/43; tran 812BS/482BG [MI-K] Alconbury 25/8/43; 360BS/303BG Moles-worth 15/1/44; sal 25/5/45.

42-29995 Del Cheyenne 23/3/43; Hobbs 3/4/43; Roswell 23/5/43; Hobbs 30/5/43; 3017 BU Hobbs 8/11/44; 4100 BU Patterson 24/3/45; RFC Altus 9/10/45.

42-29996 Del Cheyenne 23/3/43; Dow Fd 10/4/43; ass 407BS/92BG [PY-R] Alconbury 24/4/43; MIA Knaben 16/11/43 w/Thornton; e/a, cr Mandal, Nor; 1EVD 9POW; MACR 1384. FLAGSHIP.

42-29997 Del Cheyenne 23/3/43; Smoky Hill 3/4/43; Brookley 12/4/43; Smoky Hill 16/4/43; Dow Fd 19/4/43; ass 94BG Bassingbourn 24/4/43; Earls Colne 12/5/43; tran 527BS/379BG [FO-A] Kimbolton 20/5/43; then 526BS [LF-A]; AFSC 7/4/44; retUS Tinker 7/6/44; Recl Comp 9/2/45. SACK.

42-29998 Del Cheyenne 25/3/43; Memphis 8/4/43; Dow Fd 18/4/43; ass 324BS/91BG [DF-J] Bassingbourn 7/6/43; MIA Huls 22/6/43 w/Slattery; s/d vy e/a, cr Bungern; 8KIA 2POW; MACR 15576.

42-29999 Del Cheyenne 25/3/43; Smoky Hill 3/4/43; Presque Is 2/5/43; ass 96BG Grafton Underwood 8/5/43 GENIE; Andrews Fd 13/5/43; Snetterton 12/6/43; tran 533BS/381BG [VP-Z] Ridgewell 16/7/43; MIA {18m} Oschersleben 11/1/44 w/McEvoy; e/a, cr Eickholz, Ger; 10POW, MACR 1880. FERTILE MYRTLE.

42-30000 Del Cheyenne 25/3/43; Smoky Hill 3/4/43; Dow Fd 15/4/43; ass 96BG Grafton Underwood 22/4/43; tran 325BS/92BG [NV-C] Alconbury 24/4/43; then 327BG [UX-D]; MIA T/Ops 6/9/43 w/Bogard; e/a, cr Nancy, Fr; 7EVD 3POW; MACR 741.

42-30001 Del Cheyenne 25/3/43; Smoky Hill 3/4/43;

Dow Fd 15/4/43; ass 526BS/379BG [LF-E] Kimbolton 23/6/43; MIA Le Bourget 16/8/43 w/Bidwell; e/a, cr Plessis Chenet, Fr; 1EVD 4KIA 5POW; MACR 1297. MARY ANN.

42-30002 Del Cheyenne 1/4/43; Kearney 15/4/43; Gore 17/4/43; Hamilton 28/4/43; Wendover 2/5/43; Hill 12/5/43; Wendover 19/5/43; Kearney 22/5/43; Dow Fd 31/5/43; ass 349BS/100BG Thorpe Abbotts 9/6/43 THE WAAC HUNTER; MIA Schweinfurt 17/8/43 w/Shotland; e/a, cr Roxheim, Ger; 1KIA 9POW; MACR 680. DAMIFINO.

42-30003 Del Cheyenne 28/3/43; Smoky Hill 4/4/43; Dow Fd 12/4/43; ass 407BS/92BG [PY-S] Alconbury 25/4/43; MIA Kiel 14/5/43 w/Walker; e/a, cr Rendsburg, Ger; 9POW; MACR 16055. WAR EAGLE.

42-30004 Del Denver 2/4/43; Smoky Hill 22/4/43; Dow Fd 24/5/43; ass 534BS/381BG [GD-B] Ridgewell 15/6/43 JANICE; tran 305BG Chelveston 22/8/43; MIA T/Ops 6/9/43 w/Kenyon; no gas, ditched Channel; 10RTD.

42-30005 Del Denver 1/4/43; Sioux City 13/4/43; Kearney 2/5/43; Syracuse 22/5/43; Dow Fd 24/5/43; McCook 31/5/43; ass 546BS/384BG [BK-A] Grafton Underwood 13/6/43; b/d Solingen 1/12/43, c/l Leiston, UK; AFSC sal 9/12/43; 1 BAD Burtonwood 1/5/44. SALVAGE QUEEN.

42-30006 Del Denver 28/3/43; Cheyenne 31/3/43; Smoky Hill 4/4/43; Dow Fd 15/4/43; ass 325BS/92BG [NV-A] Alconbury 25/4/43; tran 812BS/482BG [MI-A] Alconbury 25/8/43; sal 16/3/44.

42-30007 Del Denver 25/3/43; Cheyenne 30/3/43; Smoky Hill 4/4/43; Dow Fd 12/4/43; ass 325BS/92BG [NV-E] Alconbury 25/4/43l; then 327BS [UX-B]; MIA T/Ops 6/9/43 w/Booker; flak, ditched Channel; 10RTD.

42-30008 Del Denver 28/3/43; Cheyenne 30/3/43; Smoky Hill 4/4/43; Dow Fd 12/4/43; Presque Is 16/4/43; ass 407BS/92BG [PY-T] Alconbury 25/4/43; MIA Ludwigshafen 30/1/44 w/Larsen; mid air coll, cr Braunschweig, Ger; 6KIA 4POW; MACR 2255. READY TEDDY.

42-30009 Del Cheyenne 25/3/43; Pueblo 8/4/43; Hobbs 6/5/43; Presque Is 21/5/43; Dow Fd 23/5/43; ass 532BS/381BG [VE-G] Ridgewell 25/5/43; MIA {5m} Bremen 8/10/43 w/Pry; e/a, cr Diepholz, Ger; 2KIA 8POW; MACR 1397. FEATHER MERCHANT.

42-30010 Del Cheyenne 28/3/43; Smoky Hill 4/4/43; ass 407BS/92BG [PY-X] Alconbury 25/4/43; MIA T/Ops 6/9/43 w/Asher; flak, ditched Channel; 2EVD 6KIA 2POW; MACR 739.

42-30011 Del Cheyenne 1/4/43; Pueblo 8/4/43; Smoky Hill 11/5/43; Dow Fd 23/5/43; ass 535BS/381BG [MS-R] Ridgewell 6/4/43; MIA {3m} Amiens-Glisy 4/7/43 w/Holdom; e/a, cr Amiens; MACR 133. WIDGET.

42-30012 Del Cheyenne 1/4/43; Smoky Hill 7/5/43; Dow Fd 23/5/43; ass 533NS/381BG [VP-K] Ridgewell 4/6/43; MIA {10m} Anklam 9/10/43 w/Maj Hendricks (CO); e/a, cr Nth Sea; 10KIA; MACR 887.

42-30013 Del Cheyenne 1/4/43; Pueblo 8/4/43; Smoky Hill 6/5/43; Dow Fd 19/5/43; ass 532BS/381BG [VE-E] Ridgewell 22/5/43; MIA {1m} Hamburg 24/7/43 w/Moore; flak, cr Hamburg; 4KIA 6POW; MACR 130. LETHAL LADY.

42-30014 Del Cheyenne 1/4/43; Pueblo 8/4/43; Smoky Hill 6/5/43; Dow Fd 25/5/43; ass 533BS/381BG [VP-B] Ridgewell 4/6/43; damaged in base explosion 23/6/43; {26m} tran RAF 214 Sq (SR377) [BU-M] 29/1/44; WO 11/3/47.

42-30015 Del Cheyenne 1/4/43; Pueblo 8/4/43; Smoky Hill 6/5/43; Dow Fd 21/5/43; ass

533BS/381BG [VP-O] Ridgewell 6/4/43 FLYING HOBO; {12m} tran 368BS/305BG [BO-A] Chelveston 22/8/43; the 366BS [KY-A]; MIA Bremen 26/11/43 w/Jones; flak, cr Oldenburg; 9KI1 1POW; MACR 1571.

42-30016 Del Cheyenne 1/4/43; Pueblo 8/4/43; Smoky Hill 6/5/43; Dow Fd 19/5/43; ass 532BS/381BG [VE-M] Ridgewell 6/4/44; MIA {2m} Antwerp 22/6/43 w/Horr; flak, cr Terneuzen, Hol; 2KIA 8POW; MACR 134. IRONGUT GERT.

42-30017 Del Dallas 2/4/43; Geiger 23/5/43; Gt Falls 7/6/43; Smoky Hill 30/6/43; Dow Fd 10/7/43; ass 535BS/381BG [MS-W] Ridgewell 10/7/43; tran Mildenhall 17/7/43, then 568BS/390BG Framlingham 14/7/43; MIA Scheweinfurt 17/8/43 w/Tyson; e/a, cr Bingen, Ger, 10POW; MACR 388. ALL SHOT TO HELL.

42-30018 Del Cheyenne 1/4/43; Pueblo 8/4/43; Smoky Hill 6/5/43; Dow Fd 19/5/43; ass 423BS/381BG [VE-L] Ridgewell 24/5/43; {14m} tran 365BS/305BG [XK-J] Chelveston 22/8/43; 2 BAD Warton 20/3/44; retUS Tinker 23/6/44; Amarillo 7/7/44; Keesler 6/11/44; Sheppard 24/3/45; Amarillo 4/11/45; RFC Walnut Ridge 28/12/45. OLD COFFINS.

42-30019 Del Cheyenne 10/4/43; Gore 18/4/43; Lockburn 23/4/43; 2114 BU Lockburn 24/10/44; Recl Comp 17/2/45.

42-30020 Del Denver 1/4/43; Pueblo 8/4/43; Smoky Hill 6/5/43; Dow Fd 23/5/43; ass 532BS/381BG [VE-N] Ridgewell 25/5/43; c/l base n/b/d 10/6/43; sal AFSC 16/6/43 (first in group). SWEET ELOISE.

42-30021 Del Denver 1/4/43; Pueblo 8/4/43; Smoky Hill 17/4/43; Pueblo 27/4/43; Smoky Hill 6/5/43; Dow Fd 23/5/43; ass 533BS/381BG [VP-L] Ridgewell 29/5/43; MIA Antwerp 22/6/43 (first group loss) w/Martin; flak, cr Westerscheldte, Hol; 9KIA 1POW; MACR 160.

42-30022 Del Denver 2/4/43; Gore 3/4/43; Smoky Hill 21/4/43; Walla Walla 7/5/434; Gt Falls 7/6/43; Gr Isle 17/6/43; 1 BAS Bolling 15/6/44; 270 BU Topeka 16/6/44; 272 BU Topeka 9/4/45; 482 BU Merced 10/10/45; RFC Kingman 14/11/45.

42-30023 Del Denver 2/4/43; Smoky Hill 27/4/43; Dow Fd 19/5/43; Presque Is 20/5/43; Geiger 26/5/43; Presque Is 28/5/43; ass 349BS/100BG [XR-M] Thorpe Abbotts 5/6/43 HORNY; MIA Münster 10/10/43 w/Stork; flak, cr Münster; 2KIA 8POW; MACR 1022. FOREVER YOURS.

42-30024 Del Cheyenne 1/4/43; Smoky Hill 10/4/43; Pueblo 26/4/43; Smoky Hill 6/5/43; Dow Fd 23/5/43; ass 533BS/381BG [VP-A] Ridgewell 25/5/43; dest in base explosion 23/6/43 & damaged several others (23 men killed, inc civilian). Carried Br Gen Hunter CO 8AF FC as observer on first mission previous day. CAROLINE?

42-30025 Del Cheyenne 1/4/43; Pueblo 8/4/43; Smoky Hill 7/5/43; Selfridge 21/5/43; ass 532BS/381BG LUCKY LADY but not to UK; tran 234 BU Gt Bend 3/6/44; 19BG Gt Bend 9/9/44; 1103 BU Morrison 22/1/45; 243 BU Gt Bend 30/1/45; RFC Ontario 19/6/45.

42-30026 Del Cheyenne 1/4/43; Sioux City 13/4/43; Kearney 4/5/43; Bangor 20/4/43; ass 534BS/381BG as BATTLE WAGON but not to UK; tran 546BS/384BG [BK-J] 29/5/43; retUS 13/7/43; 4100 BU Patterson 31/7/43; 4000 BU Patterson 5/12/43; 326 BU McDill 15/5/44; 4006 BU Miami 28/6/44; 4000 BU Wright 9/9/44; 4117 BU Robins 12/9/45; ass 6AF Caribbean 27/9/45; Recl Comp 7/3/48.

42-30027 Del Cheyenne 1/4/43; Pueblo 8/4/43; Smoky Hill 6/5/43; Dow Fd 21/5/43; ass 533BS/381BG [VP-E] Ridgewell 25/5/43; MIA {1m} Hamburg 25/6/43 w/Schrader, flak, cr Bengerseil, Ger; 10KIA; MACR 162.

42-30028 Del Cheyenne 1/4/43; Pueblo 10/4/43; Smoky Hill 7/5/43; Dow Fd 23/5/43; ass 534BS/381BG [GD-H] Ridgewell 26/5/43; MIA {5m} Schweinfurt 17/8/43 w/Wright; e/a, cr Duren, Ger; 10POW, MACR180. SWEET IS LANI.

42-30029 Del Cheyenne 1/4/43; Pueblo 8/4/43; Smoky Hill 11/5/43; Dow Fd 21/5/43; ass 535BS/381BG [MS-P] Ridgewell 26/5/43; MIA {28m} Oschersleben 30/1/44 w/Baer; e/a, ditched Nth Sea, 10KIA; MACR 2495. (Last original lost). CHAP'S FLYING CIRCUS.

42-30030 Del Cheyenne 2/4/43; Sioux City 13/4/43; Kearney 4/5/43; Bangor 23/5/43; ass 544BS/384BG [BK-E/F] Grafton Underwood 29/5/43; tran 2 SAD Lt Staughton 31/7/43 then 560BS/388BG; MIA La Rochelle 16/9/43 w/Nagorka; no gas, ditched Nth Sea; 2KIA 8RTD. OLD IRONSIDES.

42-30031 Del Cheyenne 2/4/43; Sioux City 14/4/43; Kearney 4/5/43; Bangor 24/5/43; ass 544BS/384BG [SU-D] Grafton Underwood 9/6/43; MIA Villacoublay 26/6/43 w/Burgoon.

42-30032 Del Cheyenne 2/4/43; Sioux City 13/4/43; Kearney 4/5/43; Bangor 20/5/43; ass 532BS/381BG Ridgewell 6/6/43; tran 546BS/384BG [BK-D] Grafton Underwood 9/6/43; MIA Kassel 28/7/43 w/Dietzel; e/a, cr Kortwoude, Hol; 8KIA 2POW; MACR 15165. SKY QUEEN.

42-30033 Del Cheyenne 2/4/43; Sioux City 13/4/43; Kearney 4/5/43; Bangor 20/5/43; ass 547BS/384BG [S0-G] Grafton Underwood 24/5/43; MIA Leverkusen 1/12/43 w/Dillingham; mech problems, cr Prum, Ger; 1EVD 9POW; MACR 1335. LITTLE AMERICA.

42-30034 Del Cheyenne 2/4/43; Pueblo 12/4/43; Smoky Hill 6/5/43; Presque Is 17/5/43; ass 532BS/381BG [VE-K] Ridgewell 19/5/43 NOBODY'S BABY (taken by CO Col Leber to UK as no pilot wanted it); {4m} tran 365BS/305BG [XK-D] Chelveston 22/8/43; RAF 100 Gp 28/12/43, RG 13/1/44; training a/c 20/3/44 to 27/5/45; sal 26/7/45.

42-30035 Del Cheyenne 3/4/43; Kearney 15/4/43; Wendover 4/5/43; Hill 11/5/43; Wendover 16/5/43; Kearney 22/5/43; Dow Fd 30/5/43; ass 333BS/94BG 3/43; tran 349BS/100BG Thorpe Abbotts 2/6/43 TORCHY; MIA Paris 3/9/43 w/Winkleman; mid air coll, cr France; 7EVD 1KIA 2POW. PASADENA NENA.

42-30036 Del Cheyenne 2/4/43; Sioux City 13/4/43; Kearney 2/5/43; Dow Fd 30/5/43; ass 384BG Grafton Underwood 1/6/43; c/l base, mid air coll, training op 9/6/43; sal 12/6/43.

42-30037 Del Cheyenne 2/4/43; Casper 4/4/43; Sioux City 13/4/43; Kearney 2/5/43; Dow Fd 24/5/43; ass 546BS/384BG [BK-F] Grafton Underwood 29/5/43; MIA Villacoublay 26/6/43 w/Henderson.

42-30038 Del Cheyenne 2/4/43; Kearney 15/4/43; Wendover 4/5/43; Hill 12/5/43; Wendover 16/5/43; Kearney 22/5/43; Dow Fd 27/5/43; ass 349BS/100BG Thorpe Abbotts 30/5/43; MIA Convoy 25/6/43 w/Schmalenbach; s/d by e/a, ditched NTH sea; 6KIA 4POW; MACR 270.

42-30039 Del Cheyenne 2/4/43; Sioux City 14/4/43; Kearney 3/5/43; Dow Fd 24/5/43; ass 337BS/96BG [AW-Q] in US; tran 544BS/384BG [SU-H] Grafton Underwood 29/5/43; 2 SAD Lt Staughton 14/8/43; then Aphrodite 803BS RCM Knettishall 1/44; MIA Heligoland 15/8/44. LIBERTY BELLE.

42-30040 Del Cheyenne 2/4/43; Sioux City 14/4/43; Kearney 3/5/43; Dow Fd 20/5/43; ass 546BS/384BG [BK-B] Grafton Underwood 22/5/43 PICCADILLY COMMANDO; tran 337BS/96BG [AW-A] Snetterton 6/7/43; MIA Schweinfurt 14/10/43 w/Harmeson; e/a, cr Avincourt, Fr; 4EVD 1KIA 5POW; MACR 837. WABBIT-TWACKS III.

42-30041 Del Cheyenne 2/4/43; Sioux City 14/4/43; Kearney 3/5/43; Dow Fd 23/5/43; ass 544BS/384BG, ditched off Greenland en route Grafton Underwood 27/5/43.

42-30042 Del Cheyenne 2/4/43; Kearney 15/4/43; Wendover 2/5/43; Hill 12/5/43; Wendover 19/5/43; Kearney 22/5/43; Patterson 29/5/43; Detroit 3/6/43; Dow Fd 6/6/43; ass 349BS/100BG Thorpe Abbotts 9/6/43; MIA Regensburg 17/8/43 w/Van Noy, mech problem, ditched Med Sea; 10POW, MACR 682. OH NAUSEA.

42-30043 Del Cheyenne 3/4/43; Sioux City 14/4/43; Kearney 4/5/43; Bangor 23/5/43; ass 547BS/384BG [SO-V] Grafton Underwood 29/5/43; MIA Frankfurt 4/10/43 w/Kauffman; ditched Nth Sea, 10RTD. RUTHLESS.

42-30044 Del Cheyenne 3/4/43; Kearney 15/4/43; Hamilton 24/4/43; Long Beach 29/5/43; Gr Isle 3/6/43; Pendleton 2/11/43; 248 BU Walker 9/6/44; 3502 BU Chanute 3/9/44; 248 BU Walker 5/9/44; RFC Albuquerque 25/6/45.

42-30045 Del Cheyenne 3/4/43; Sioux City 14/4/43; Kearney 3/5/43; Bangor 23/5/43; ass 545BS/384BG Grafton Underwood 29/5/43; tran 334BS/95BG [BG-M] Horham 28/6/43 SHE'S MY GAL; MIA Saarlautern 4/10/43 w/Crowder; e/a, ditched of Bayeux, Fr; 1KIA 9POW. MACR 744. FIGHT'N 'N BIT'N.

42-30046 Del Cheyenne 3/4/43; Sioux City 14/4/43; Kearney 4/5/43; Bangor 20/5/43; ass 546BS/384BG [BK-H/K] Grafton Underwood 24/5/43; MIA Recklinghausen 12/8/43 w/Sierens; flak, cr Gelsenkirchen; 8KIA 2POW; MACR 289. MERRIE HELL.

42-30047 Del Cheyenne 3/4/43; Kearney 15/4/43; Hill 5/5/43; Wendover 10/5/43; Kearney 21/5/43; Dow Fd 28/5/43; ass 350BS/100BG [LN-Q] Thorpe Abbotts 2/6/43; MIA Münster 10/10/43 w/Λtchinson; mid air coll, cr Ostbereh, Ger; 4KIA 6POW; MACR 1031. SWEATER GIRL.

42-30048 Del Cheyenne 3/4/43; Sioux City 14/4/43; Kearney 3/5/43; Dow Fd 24/5/43; ass 544BS/384BG [SU-K] Grafton Underwood 12/6/43 FLAK DANCER; MIA Villacoublay 26/6/43 w/Wheat; cr Laon, Fr. FLAK DODGER.

42-30049 Del Cheyenne 3/4/43; Sioux City 14/4/43; Kearney 4/5/43; Dow Fd 24/5/43; ass 544BS/384BG [SU-F/G] Grafton Underwood 30/5/43; MIA Wangerooge 25/6/43 w/Way; e/a, ditched Nth Sea; 2KIA 8POW; MACR 16349. MISS DEAL.

42-30050 Del Cheyenne 3/4/43; Kearney 15/4/43; Hamilton 28/4/43; Wendover 2/5/43; Hill 13/5/43; Wendover 17/2/43; Kearney 21/5/43; Dow Fd 27/2/43; ass 350BS/100BG Thorpe Abbotts 29/5/43; MIA Le Bourget 10/7/43 w/Chiesl; flak, cr Dieppe; 2EVD 8POW; MACR 268. JUDY D.

42-30051 Del Cheyenne 3/4/43; Kearney 15/4/43; Wendover 2/5/43; Hill 15/5/43; Wendover 18/5/43; Kearney 23/5/43; Dow Fd 28/5/43; ass 351BS/100BG Thorpe Abbotts 1/6/43; MIA La Pallice 4/7/43 w/Pearson; mech problem, cr Isle D'Oleran, Fr; 1EVD 9POW; MACR 685.

42-30052 Del Denver 3/4/43; Gore 16/4/43; Walla Walla 18/4/43; Redmond 15/8/43; 4135 BU Hill 11/8/44; 3705 BU Lowry 23/8/44; trans US Navy 23/2/47.

42-30053 Del Denver 3/4/43; Smoky Hill 29/4/43; Morrison 5/5/43; Warner Robins 8/5/43; Morrison

16/5/43; ass 352BS/301BG St Donat 24/5/43; Oudna 6/8/43; MIA {26} Augsburg 1/10/43 w/Zimmer; 4KIA 6POW; MACR 760.
42-30054 Del Denver 7/4/43; Gore 18/4/43; Lockburn 20/4/43; 2000 BU Ft Worth 23/10/44; 2114 BU Lockburn 21/12/44; 2003 BU Ft Worth 8/1/45; 273 BU Lincoln 16/3/45; 2003 BU Ft Worth 10/4/45; RFC Walnut Ridge 21/12/45.
42-30055 Del Denver 5/4/43; Dyersburg 16/4/43; Gulfport 16/5/43; Tinker 9/11/43; 3007 BU Kirtland 20/6/44; 271 BU Kearney 30/6/44; 499BG Smoky Hill 12/7/44; 3705 BU Lowry 1/8/44; WO 1/8/44.
42-30056 Del Denver 5/4/43; Morrison 29/4/43; ass 342BS/97BG Château-du-Rhumel 24/5/43; Pont-du-Fahs 1/8/43; Depienne 15/8/43; Cerignola 20/12/43; Amendola 16/1/43; MIA Brod, Yugo 2/7/44 w/Schuchardt; e/a, cr Komaron; 3KIA 7POW; MACR 6338.
42-30057 Del Cheyenne 5/4/43; Kearney 15/4/43; Wendover 2/5/43; Hill 15/5/43; Wendover 21/5/43; Dow Fd 28/5/43; ass 351BS/100BG [EP-D] Thorpe Abbbotts 9/6/43; MIA Stuttgart 6/9/43 w/Turner; e/a, ditched Lake Constance, Switz; 1KIA 9INT. MACR 689. RAUNCHY.
42-30058 Del Cheyenne 5/4/43; Newcastle 29/4/43; Presque Is 6/5/43; ass 546BS/384BG [BK-M] Grafton Underwood 17/6/43; MIA Villacoublay 26/6/43 w/Rosio.
42-30059 Del Cheyenne 5/4/43; Kearney 16/4/43; Wendover 2/5/43; Hill 16/5/43; Wendover 21/5/43; Dow Fd 28/5/43; ass 351BS/100BG [EP-G] Thorpe Abbotts 9/6/43; MIA Paris 3/9/43 w/Floyd; e/a, cr Beaumont, Fr; 8KIA 2POW; MACR 685. BARKER'S BURDEN.
42-30060 Del Cheyenne 6/4/43; Colorado Springs 16/4/43; Patterson 18/4/43; Peterson 5/5/43; Dow Fd 30/5/43; ass 1 Photo GP Buckley 1/6/44; 2 Ph GP Buckley 2/8/44; 91 Ph Map Gp Buckley 12/9/44; 311 Ph Wing Buckley 6/2/45; 4100 BU Patterson 26/5/45; 3 WER Grenier 5/6/45; 3 WER McChord 19/6/45; 53 RCN McChord 21/7/45; 1 WER Grenier 14/8/45; 53 RCN Grenier 23/8/45; RFC Kingman 24/1/46.
42-30061 Del Cheyenne 6/4/43; Kearney 15/4/43; Wendover 2/5/43; Kearney 22/5/434; Dow Fd 30/5/43; ass 418BS/100BG [LD-Q/T] Thorpe Abbotts 9/6/43 WOLF PACK; retUS Homestead 12/7/44; 1 BU Wright 17/7/44; 328 BU Gulfport 26/1/45; 4119 BU Brookley 31/3/45; Recl Comp 17/4/45. JUST-A-SNAPPIN'.
42-30062 Del Cheyenne 6/4/43; Gore 14/4/43; Kearney 16/4/43; Wendover 2/5/43; Hill 18/5/43; Kearney 22/5/54; Dow Fd 30/5/43; ass 418BS/100BG [LD-O] Thorpe Abbotts 9/6/43 BASTARD'S BUNGALOW, re-named TERRY 'N TEN; MIA Brunswick 10/2/44 w/Scoggins; e/a, cr Hannover; 1KIA 9POW; MACR 2383. REILLY'S RACEHORSE.
42-30063 Del Cheyenne 5/4/43; Kearney 15/4/43; Wendover 2/5/43; Kearney 22/5/43; Dow Fd 29/5/43; ass 561BS/388BG Knettishall 2/6/43 PADDLEFOOT; tran 418BS/100BG Thorpe Abbotts 9/6/43; MIA Schweinfurt 17/8/43 w/Knox; e/a, Schmalgraf, Ger; 6KIA 4POW; MACR 677. PICKLEPUSS.
42-30064 Del Cheyenne 5/4/43; Kearney 15/4/43; Wendover 2/5/43; Hill 22/5/43; Dow Fd 30/5/43; ass 418BS/100BG [LD-T] Thorpe Abbotts 9/6/43; MIA La Rochelle 16/9/43 w/Wolff; flak, cr Surgeres, Fr; 1KIA 9POW; MACR 647. WILD CARGO.
42-30065 Del Cheyenne 5/4/43; Sioux City 14/4/43; Kearney 4/5/43; Bangor 20/5/43; ass 547BS/384BG [SO-O] Grafton Underwood 24/5/43; tran 369BS/306BG [WW-U] Thurleigh 22/8/43; c/l New Romney, UK. 10/9/43; sal 16/9/43.
42-30066 Del Cheyenne 6/4/43; Gore 14/4/43; Kearney 16/4/43; Wendover 2/5/43; Hill 16/5/43; Kearney 22/5/43; Dow Fd 30/5/43; ass 413BS/96BG [MZ-X] Andrews Fd 2/6/43; RUM BOOGIE II; tran 418BS/100BG [LD-X] Thorpe Abbotts 9/6/43; to Aphrodite project Knettishall, MIA 30/10/44. MUGWUMP.
42-30067 Del Cheyenne 6/4/43; Geiger 16/4/43; Peterson 5/6/43; Bolling 27/7/43; Peterson 6/8/43; Rapid City 13/8/43; Colorado Springs 7/10/43; 246 BU Pratt 8/6/44; 244 BU Harvard 24/6/44; 4136 BU Tinker 15/7/44; 235 BU Biggs 17/1/45; 233 BU Davis Monthan 18/3/45; 209 BU Galveston 14/6/45; RFC Kingman 8/11/45.
42-30068 Del Cheyenne 5/4/43; Gore 10/4/43; Kearney 15/4/43; Wendover 2/5/43; Hill 13/5/43; Kearney 23/5/43; Dow Fd 27/5/43; ass 350BS/100BG Podington 29/5/43 PHARTZAC; Thorpe Abbotts 6/6/43; tran 561BS/388BG Knettishall 6/4/43; MIA Woensdrecht 19/8/43 w/Howe; flak, cr Haamstede, Hol; 8KIA 2POW.
42-30069 Del Cheyenne 6/4/43; Denver 16/4/43; Patterson 18/4/43; Peterson 5/5/43; WO 20/5/43.
42-30070 Del Cheyenne 6/4/43; Kearney 15/4/43; Hamilton 2/5/43; Kearney 21/5/43; Dow Fd 22/5/43; ass 350BS/100BG Thorpe Abbotts 9/6/43; MIA Regensburg 17/8/43 w/Braley; flak, cr Pfullingen, Ger; 1KIA 9POW; MACR 679. TWEEDLE-O-TWILL.
42-30071 Del Cheyenne 6/4/43; Kearney 15/4/43; Wendover 2/5/43; Hill 8/5/43; Kearney 22/5/43; Dow Fd 30/5/43; ass 413BS/96BG [QJ-B] Andrews Fd 2/6/43; then 339BS [MZ-B] Snetterton 12/6/43; c/l Honington, n/b/d 18/4/44, sal.
42-30072 Del Cheyenne 7/4/43; Denver 10/4/43; Gore 18/4/43; Tinker 21/4/43; Morrison 29/4/43; ass 342BS/97BG Château-du-Rhumel 10/5/43; Pont-du-Fahs 1/8/43; Depienne 15/8/43; Cerignola 20/12/43; Amendola 16/1/44; MIA Ploesti 5/5/44 w/Weil; cr Ploesti; MACR 4607. VIRGINIA LEE.
42-30073 Del Denver 6/4/43; Sioux City 14/4/43; Kearney 4/5/43; Dow Fd 25/5/43; ass 384BG Grafton Underwood 29/5/43; tran 413BS/96BG [MZ-U] Andrews Fd 6/7/43; Snetterton 12/6/43; c/l East Wretham, UK, 17/4/44, sal. OLE PUSS II.
42-30074 Del Denver 6/4/43; Sioux City 14/4/43; ass 384BG; c/l base u/c collapsed 1/9/43 w/McMillin, sal; rep tran Hill 10/6/43; Rapid City 20/7/43; 222 BU Ardmore 22/1/45; 332 BU Ardmore 16/6/45; RFC Walnut Ridge 11/12/45.
42-30075 Del Denver 7/4/43; Cheyenne 13/4/43; Geiger 17/4/43; Gt Falls 7/6/43; Cutbank 16/6/43; Gore 2/7/43; Gt Falls 13/7/43; Tinker 10/12/43; 247 BU Smoky Hill 3/6/44; 4100 BU Patterson 17/6/43; 247 BU Smoky Hill 21/7/43; 233 BU Davis Monthan 11/11/44; 268 BU Peterson 11/2/45; 233 BU Davis Monthan 26/2/45; RFC Kingman 27/10/45.
42-30076 Del Denver 6/4/43; Sioux City 14/4/43; Kearney 4/5/43; Bangor 23/5/43; ass 545BS/384BG [JD-V] Grafton Underwood 4/6/43; MIA {1} Huls 22/6/43 w/Oblinski; e/a, cr Wilhelminadoorp, Hol; MACR 2165.
42-30077 Del Cheyenne 7/4/43; Hobbs 19/4/43; Ft Sumner 21/4/43; Hobbs 6/5/43; Roswell 23/5/43; Hobbs 30/5/43; 3017 BU Hobbs 8/11/43; 4124 BU Altus 21/7/45; RFC Altus 14/9/45.
42-30078 Del Cheyenne 7/4/43; Hobbs 19/4/43; 2114 BU Lockburn 23/8/44; 3017 BU Hobbs 25/8/44; 3030 BU Roswell 23/11/44; 3017 BU Hobbs 2/1/45; RFC Altus 18/9/45.
42-30079 Del Cheyenne 7/4/43; Lewiston 16/4/43; Geiger 4/6/43; Gore 21/6/43; Walla Walla 17/7/43; Rapid City 22/7/43; Hill 25/7/43; Walla Walla 29/8/43; 325 BU Avon Park 6/12/44; Recl Comp 6/1/45.
42-30080 Del Cheyenne 7/4/43; Kearney 16/4/43; Westover 3/5/43; Wendover 16/5/43; Kearney 23/5/43; Dow Fd 22/5/43; ass 351BS/100BG [EP-F] Thorpe Abbotts 9/6/43; MIA Regensburg 17/8/43 w/Oakes; e/a, c/l Dubendorf, Switz (1st US a/c); 10INT; MACR 683. HIGH LIFE (PEG O' MY HEART).
42-30081 Del Cheyenne 7/4/43; New Castle 29/4/43; Presque Is 3/5/43; ass 407BS/92BG [PY-O] Alconbury 23/5/43; MIA Gelsenkirchen 12/8/43 w/Wiley; flak hit cr Gelsenkirchen; 11POW, MACR 655. USS ALIQUIPPA.
42-30082 Del Cheyenne 8/4/43; Smoky Hill 22/4/43; Morrison 5/5/43; Warner Robbins 11/5/43; Morrison 16/5/43; ass 20BS/2BG Château-du-Rhumel 28/5/43; Ain M'Lila 17/6/43; {36m} tran 419BS/301BG Oudna 14/11/43; Cerignola 7/12/43; Lucera 1/2/44; {0m} RetUS Grenier 14/9/45; RFC Altus 29/10/45.
42-30083 Del Cheyenne 8/4/43; Gore 16/4/43; Patterson 18/4/43; Peterson 5/5/43; Long Beach 6/7/43; Colorado Springs 15/7/43; Peterson 21/7/43; ass mapping Accra, E.Africa, retUS 9/10/44; Kirtland 29/11/44; Buckley 9/12/44; Kirtland 31/12/44. RFC Albuquerque 7/2/46.
42-30084 Del Cheyenne 6/4/43; Colorado Springs 16/4/43; Patterson 18/4/43; Peterson 2/5/43; Patterson 2/7/43; Barksdale 6/8/43; 3701 BU Amarillo 10/8/44; 3706 BU Sheppard 15/7/44; 3701 BU Amarillo 7/8/44; RFC Walnut Ridge 20/12/45.
42-30085 Del Cheyenne 7/4/43; Gt Falls 8/4/43; Cheyenne 16/4/43; Walla Walla 15/5/43; Gt Falls 18/5/43; Moses Lake 23/5/43; 4136 BU Tinker 23/7/44; 4100 BU Patterson 24/10/44; RFC Altus 17/8/45.
42-30086 Del Cheyenne 8/4/43; Kearney 16/4/43; Wendover 2/5/43; Hill 16/5/43; Kearney 23/5/43; Dow Fd 26/5/43; ass 351BS/100BG [EP-B] Thorpe Abbotts 9/6/43 BLACK JACK; b/d Regensburg 17/8/43; sal 23/9/43. BILLY JACK.
42-30087 Del Cheyenne 8/4/43; Gore 14/4/43; Kearney 16/4/43; Hamilton 23/5/43; Wendover 2/5/43; Kearney 23/5/43; Dow Fd 31/5/43; ass 351BS/100BG [EP-M] Thorpe Abbotts 11/6/43; MIA Münster 10/10/43 w/Beatty; flak, cr Münster; 8KIA 2POW; MACR 1020. SHACKRAT.
42-30088 Del Cheyenne 8/4/43; Kearney 16/4/43; Wendover 2/5/43; Hill 12/5/43; Wendover 18/5/43; Kearney 22/5/43; Dow Fd 27/5/43; ass 349BS/100BG [XR-E] Thorpe Abbotts 9/6/43; retUS 17/5/44; Hendricks 8/6/44; RFC Walnut Ridge 13/12/45. First a/c in group to 50 missions. SQUAWKIN' HAWK II.
42-30089 Del Cheyenne 9/4/43; Gore 13/4/43; Kearney 22/4/43; Denver 30/4/43; Wendover 2/5/43; Hill 15/5/43; Dow Fd 28/5/43; ass 351BS/100BG [EP-J] Thorpe Abbotts 9/6/43; MIA Paris 3/9/43 w/King; flak, cr Beaumont, Fr; 1EVD 6KIA 3POW; MACR 684. SUNNY.
42-30090 Del Cheyenne 8/4/43; Kearney 16/4/43; Wendover 2/5/43; Hill 12/5/43; Wendover 16/5/43; Kearney 22/5/43; Dow Fd 28/5/43; ass 385BG Gt Ashfield 2/6/43; tran 349BS/100BG [XR-B] Thorpe Abbotts 9/6/43; MIA Münster 10/10/43 w/Beddow; flak, cr Ostberven, Ger; 10POW; MACR 1027. EL P'SSTOFO.
42-30091 Del Denver 9/4/43; Gore 10/4/43; Denver

27/4/43; Tinker 1/5/43; Gt Falls 25/5/43; Kearney 29/5/43; Dow Fd 16/6/43; ass 418BS/100BG [LD-S] Thorpe Abbotts 17/6/43; c/l Eye, UK, 21/4/44, non ops, 10KIA; sal 5/5/44. BLIVIT.

42-30092 Del Cheyenne 9/4/43; Gore 10/4/43; Cheyenne 13/4/43; Columbus 19/4/43; Lockburn 15/8/43; Chanute 16/8/43; c/l base 1/9/43 w/Case, #1 engine on fire. WO 22/10/43.

42-30093 Del Denver 10/4/43; Tinker 19/4/43; Memphis 25/4/43; Homestead 30/4/43; Macon 16/5/43; Memphis 22/5/43; Homestead 1/6/43; ass 419BS/301BG St Donat 17/6/43; Oudna 6/8/43; {2m} c/l 11/8/43; sal 19/8/43.

42-30094 Del Denver 13/4/43; Gore 14/4/43; St Joseph 29/4/43; Denver 8/5/43; Gt Falls 10/5/43; Kearney 30/5/43; Dow Fd 15/6/43; ass 551BS/385BG Gt Ashfield 26/6/43; sal 6/9/45. BELLE OF THE BLUE.

42-30095 Del Denver 9/4/43; Gore 10/4/43; Tinker 21/4/43; Morrison 29/4/43; ass 346BS/99BG Navarin 1/6/43; tran 353BS/301BG St Donat 24/6/43; Oudna 6/8/43; Cerignola 7/12/43; Lucera 1/2/44; b/d flak Regensburg 25/2/44 w/Snyder; 6 baled but rest flew a/c home; sal 14/1/46.

42-30096 Del Denver 9/4/43; Gore 10/4/43; Denver 29/4/43; Glasgow 3/5/43; Kearney 29/5/43; Dow Fd 15/6/43; ass 549BS/385BG Gt Ashfield 26/6/43; MIA Solingen 30/11/43 w/Smith; mech problem, ditched Nth Sea; 4KIA 6RTD; MACR 4403. LIBERTY BELLE.

42-30097 Del Cheyenne 9/4/43; Gore 10/4/43; Cheyenne 13/4/43; Columbus 19/4/43; Lockbourne 23/3/43; c/l base 22/9/43 w/Scoggins, one passenger minor injury; WO 1/10/43.

42-30098 Del Cheyenne 9/4/43; Gore 10/4/43; Cheyenne 13/4/43; Hobbs 19/4/43; 4136 BU Tinker 4/7/44; 3017 BU Hobbs 8/11/44; RFC Altus 11/9/45.

42-30099 Del Cheyenne 12/4/43; Denver 14/4/43; 3030 BU Roswell 7/10/44; 3010 BU Williams 16/11/44; 3020 BU La Junta 26/3/45; RFC Stillwater 4/8/45.

42-30100 Del Cheyenne 9/4/43; Gore Fd 10/4/43; Cheyenne 13/4/43; Gore 21/4/43; Lockbourne 25/4/43; Morrison 14/5/43; ass Glen 17/5/43; taxi accident 24/6/43; sal 14/1/46.

42-30101 Del Cheyenne 10/4/43; Hobbs 19/4/43; Smoky Hill 22/4/43; Hobbs 6/5/43; Ellington 2/8/43; Hobbs 16/8/43; WO 21/8/43.

42-30102 Del Cheyenne 10/4/43; Smoky Hill 29/5/43; Morrison 8/6/43; ass 97BG Château-du-Rhumel 16/6/43; Pont-du-Fahs 1/8/43; Depienne 14/11/43; Cerignola 20/12/43; Amendola 16/1/44; weather ship from 15/7/44; sal 30/3/45.

42-30103 Del Cheyenne 10/4/43; Hobbs 19/4/43; Ft Sumner 21/4/43; Hobbs 6/5/43; 3017 BU Hobbs 8/11/44; Recl Comp 22/3/45.

42-30104 Del Cheyenne 10/4/43; Hobbs 19/4/43; Ft Sumner 21/4/43; Hobbs 6/5/43; Mather 18/6/43; Hobbs 11/7/43; 3017 BU Hobbs 8/11/44; RFC Altus 4/9/45.

42-30105 Del Cheyenne 13/4/43; Tinker 12/5/43; Lincoln 20/5/43; Bangor 23/5/43; ass 412BS/95BG [QW-R] Framlingham 6/6/43 EXTERMINATOR; Horham 12/6/43; MIA Le Bourget 10/7/43 w/Sarchet; e/a, cr Elbent, Fr; 2EVD 6KIA 2POW; MACR 4902. SLIGHTLY DANGEROUS.

42-30106 Del Cheyenne 10/4/43; Smoky Hill 22/4/43; Morrison 5/5/43; ass 353BS/301BG St Donat 4/6/43; Oudna 6/8/43; Cerignola 7/12/43; Lucera 1/2/44; MIA {86m} Budapest 27/6/44 w/McGee; flak, cr Budapest; 10POW. MACR 6175. WILLY.

42-30107 Del Cheyenne 10/4/43; Pendleton 12/4/43; Smoky Hill 5/5/43; Dow Fd 25/5/43; ass 526BS/379BG Kimbolton 20/6/43; MIA Wangerooge 25/6/43 w/Homes; e/a, cr Gross Bergen, Hol; 2KIA 8POW; MACR 1366.

42-30108 Del Cheyenne 13/4/43; Morrison 5/5/43; Warner Robins 11/5/43; Morrison 17/5/43; ass 352BS/301BG St Donat 5/6/43; Oudna 6/8/43; Cerignola 7/12/43; Lucera 1/2/44; depot 15/5/44; {67m} RetUS Patterson 10/8/44; RFC Albuquerque 25/6/45.

42-30109 Del Cheyenne 13/4/43; Smoky Hill 22/4/43; Morrison 5/5/43; Warner Robins 10/5/43; Morrison 20/5/43; ass 49BS/2BG Château-du-Rhumel 30/5/43; Ain M'Lila 17/6/43; Massicault 31/7/43; MIA {31m} Bologna 25/9/43; ditched off Bizerte w/Abel; 4WIA, all rescued.

42-30110 Del Cheyenne 10/4/43; Gore Fd 14/4/43; Smoky Hill 22/4/43; Morrison 9/5/43; Warner Robins 10/5/43; Morrison 20/5/43; ass 32BS/301BG St Donat 1/6/43; Oudna 6/8/43; Cerignola 7/12/43; Lucera 1/2/44; {7m} sal 8/7/44.

42-30111 Del Cheyenne 13/4/43; Gore 14/4/43; Cheyenne 17/4/43; Smoky Hill 22/4/43; Morrison 5/5/43; Warner Robins 10/5/43; Morrison 19/5/43; ass 32BS/301BG St Donat 24/6/43; Oudna 6/8/43; Cerignola 7/12/43; Lucera 1/2/44; MIA {27m} Wiener Neustadt 2/11/43 w/Gibson; e/a, cr Wiener Neustadt; 10KIA; MACR 1093.

42-30112 Del Cheyenne 12/4/43; Gore 21/4/43; Smoky Hill 25/4/43; Walla Walla 30/4/43; Smoky Hill 10/5/43; Dow Fd 29/5/43; ass 410BS/94BG [GL-Z] Rougham 13/6/43; MIA Merignac 5/1/44 w/Powell; e/a, cr Bordeaux; 2EVD 7KIA 1POW; MACR 1891. LIL BUTCH.

42-30113 Del Cheyenne 13/4/43; Dow Fd 5/5/43; ass 333BS/94BG Earls Colne 8/5/43; MIA Kiel 13/6/43 w/Dauth; e/a, cr Renesburg, Ger; 10POW. WOLFPACK.

42-30114 Del Cheyenne 13/4/43; Smoky Hill 22/4/43; Presque Is 3/5/43; ass 381BG Ridgewell 8/5/43; MU 19/8/43; tran 335BS/95BG [BG-L] Horham 13/9/43; MIA Duren 20/10/43 w/Ronstad; e/a, ditched Nth Sea; 10RTD.

42-30115 Del Cheyenne 12/4/43; Smoky Hill 22/4/43; Morrison 5/5/43; ass 419BS/301BG St Donat 27/6/43; Oudna 6/8/43; Cerignola 7/12/43; Lucera 1/2/44; MIA {47m} Istres le Tube 10/11/44 w/Dodge; e/a, ditched Med Sea.

42-30116 Del Cheyenne 12/4/43; Ft Sumner 21/4/43; Hobbs 30/4/43; Roswell 24/5/43; Hobbs 27/5/43; 3017 BU Hobbs 20/6/44; WO 27/6/44.

42-30117 Del Cheyenne 13/4/43; Gore 21/4/43; Smoky Hill 22/4/43; Morrison 4/5/43; ass 12AF 31/5/43; retUS Bradley 4/7/44; RFC Altus 9/10/45.

42-30118 Del Cheyenne 13/4/43; Smoky Hill 22/4/43; Presque Is 16/5/43; ass 335BS/95BG [OE-N] Framlingham 29/5/43; MIA Kiel 13/6/43 w/Cornett; b/d cr Nth Sea, 10KIA. MACR 4738.

42-30119 Del Cheyenne 14/4/43; Smoky Hill 22/4/43; Morrison 5/5/43; Warner Robins 10/5/43; Morrison 18/5/43; ass 346BS/99BG Navarin 14/6/43; Oudna 4/8/43; Tortorella 11/12/43; MIA Foggia 22/7/43 w/Hunter; 8KIA 2POW. MACR 464. HUNTER'S ANSWER.

42-30120 Del Cheyenne 14/4/43; Smoky Hill 25/4/43; Tinker 23/5/43; Dow Fd 2/6/43; ass 91BG Bassingbourn 15/6/43; tran 334BS/95BG [BG-D] Horham 16/6/43; sal 6/1/45. PATCHES.

42-30121 Del Cheyenne 14/4/43; Smoky Hill 22/4/43; Morrison 5/5/43; Warner Robins 11/5/43; ass 414BS/97BG Château-du-Rhumel 29/5/43; c/t/o 6/7/43, hit oil drums and burned. All killed.

42-30122 Del Cheyenne 14/4/43; Smoky Hill 21/5/43; Morrison 4/5/43; ass 32BS/301BG St Donat 29/5/43; Oudna 6/8/43; Cerignola 7/12/43; Lucera 1/2/44; {29m} sal 31/7/45.

42-30123 Del Cheyenne 15/4/43; Gore 21/4/43; Smoky Hill 26/4/43; Walla Walla 30/4/43; Smoky Hill 10/5/43; Dow Fd 27/5/43; ass 338BS/96BG [BX-W] Andrews Fd 29/5/43 BIG DICK; Snetterton 12/6/43; MIA Regensburg 25/2/44 w/Jarrett (and his 452BG crew); e/a, cr Regensburg; 5EVD 5POW; MACR 2859. THE IRONBIRD BIG DICK.

42-30124 Del Cheyenne 15/4/43; Ft Sumner 21/4/43; Hobbs 6/5/43; 3017 BU Hobbs 8/11/44; RFC Altus 9/10/45.

42-30125 Del Cheyenne 14/4/43; Smoky Hill 22/4/43; Morrison 5/5/43; Middleton 10/5/43; Morrison 19/5/43; ass 419BS/301BG St Donat 15/7/43; Oudna 6/8/43; Cerignola 7/12/43; c/t/o 14/12/43 w/Moseley, rep; Lucera 1/2/44; {30m} sal 2/3/44.

42-30126 Del Cheyenne 14/4/43; Smoky Hill 22/4/43; Morrison 5/5/43; Warner Robins 10/5/43; Morrison 21/5/43; ass 416BS/99BG Navarin 24/6/43; Oudna 4/8/43; MIA Augsburg 1/10/43 w/English; s/d by Swiss AF, c/l Landquart, Switz; 7KIA 3INT. MACR 796. SUGARFOOT.

42-30127 Del Cheyenne 15/4/43; Gore 21/4/43; Smoky Hill 22/4/43; Morrison 20/5/43; ass 32BS/301BG St Donat 25/5/43; Oudna 6/8/43; MIA {24m} Wiener Neustadt 2/11/43 w/Pattison; e/a, cr Wiener Neustadt; 10KIA. MACR 1094.

42-30128 Del Cheyenne 15/4/43; Smoky Hill 21/4/43; Morrison 21/5/43; ass 12AF 2/6/43; sal 8/7/44.

42-30129 Del Cheyenne 15/4/43; Morrison 4/5/43; Warner Robins 10/5/43; Morrison 19/5/43; ass 346BS/99BG Navarin 30/5/43; Oudna 4/8/43; tran 97BG Depienne 14/11/43; Cerignola 20/12/43; Amendola 16/1/44; sal 8/7/44. CREW NO. 1.

42-30130 Del Cheyenne 15/4/43; Smoky Hill 24/4/43; Presque Is 16/5/43; ass 337BS/96BG [AW-J] Andrews Fd 25/5/43 THE KLAP-TRAP II; Snetterton 12/6/43 then 413BS; MIA Ludwigshafen 7/1/44 w/Peterson; flak, cr Thionville, Fr; 8KIA 2POW; MACR 2018. ALIA BUBBLE TROUBLE.

42-30131 Del Cheyenne 15/4/43; Gore 25/4/43; Sioux City 30/4/43; Kearney 4/5/43; Bangor 20/5/43; ass 547BS/384BG [SO-Q] Grafton Underwood 9/6/43; 2 SAD Lt Staughton 17/7/43.

42-30132 Del Cheyenne 14/4/43; Gore 21/4/43; Smoky Hill 25/4/43; Morrison 4/5/43; Warner Robins 10/5/43; Memphis 3/8/43; Geiger 6/8/43; Pendleton 12/8/43; 245 BU McCook 9/6/44; 9BG McCook 4/7/44; 245 BU McCook 2/9/44; 4119 BU Brookley 16/10/44; 245 BU McCook 23/10/44; RFC Kingman 29/10/45.

42-30133 Del Cheyenne 17/4/43; Smoky Hill 23/4/43; Morrison 5/5/43; Warner Robins 8/5/43; Morrison 18/5/43; ass 429BS/2BG Château-du-Rhumel 4/6/43; Ain M'Lila 17/6/43; Massicault 31/7/43; MIA {41m} Wiener Neustadt 1/12/43 w/Eggers; s/d by e/a. MACR 1112. RAGGEDY ANN.

42-30134 Del Cheyenne 15/4/43; Gore 21/4/43; Smoky Hill 22/4/43; Morrison 5/5/43; ass 429BS/2BG Ain M'Lila 20/6/43; Massicault 31/7/43; {26m} tran 429BS/301BG Oudna 14/11/43; Cerignola 7/12/43; MIA {10m} Bolzano 25/12/43 w/Col Byerly, Gp CO; flak, cr Bolzano; 6KIA 4POW inc Byerly; MACR 1589.

42-30135 Del Cheyenne 15/4/43; Smoky Hill 22/4/43; Presque Is 10/5/43; ass 511BS/351BG [DS-N] Polebrook 26/5/43; tran 334BS/95BG [BG-H] Horham 16/6/43; MIA Schweinfurt 14/10/43 w/McPherson; cr Schweinfurt, 10POW. MACR 855.

TROUBLE SHOOTER.

42-30136 Del Cheyenne 15/4/43; Smoky Hill 21/4/43; Morrison 4/5/43; Warner Robins 10/5/43; Morrison 18/5/43; ass 353BS/301BG St Donat 4/6/43; Oudna 6/8/43; Cerignola 7/12/43; Lucera 1/2/44; {62m} then weather ship 27/7/44; sal 25/10/44. LADIES DELIGHT.

42-30137 Del Cheyenne 15/4/43; Smoky Hill 21/4/43; Warner Robins 12/5/43; Morrison 18/5/43; ass 341BS/97BG Château-du-Rhumel 8/6/43; Pont-du-Fahs 1/8/43; MIA Bologna 25/9/43 w/Hansen; ditched of Cape Comino, Sardinia; 10RTD two days later.

42-30138 Del Cheyenne 16/4/43; Smoky Hill 21/4/43; Morrison 4/5/43; Meridian 9/5/43; Kearney 6/1/44; 2218 BU Alexandra 17/1/45; 329 BU Alexandra 1/3/45; RFC Altus 9/10/45.

42-30139 Del Cheyenne 15/4/43; Smoky Hill 25/4/43; Sioux City 30/4/43; Kearney 6/5/43; Tinker 22/5/43; Kearney 26/5/43; Dow Fd 29/5/43; ass 545BS/384BG [JD-O] Grafton Underwood 14/6/43; MIA Schweinfurt 17/8/43 w/Sweningsen; flak, cr Stangenroth, Ger; MACR 294. SNUFFY.

42-30140 Del Cheyenne 15/4/43; Smoky Hill 25/4/43; Walla Walla 2/5/43; Smoky Hill 10/5/43; Dow Fd 26/5/43; ass 532BS/381BG [VE-V] Ridgewell 23/6/43; MIA {6m} Schweinfurt 17/8/43 w/Painter; e/a, cr Esch, Lux; 2EVD 1KIA 7POW; MACR 379. KING MALFUNCTION II.

42-30141 Del Cheyenne 16/4/43; Smoky Hill 25/4/43; Walla Walla 30/4/43; Smoky Hill 10/5/43; Dow Fd 28/5/43; ass 337BS/96BG [AW-B] Andrews Fd 1/6/43; Snetterton 12/6/43; MIA Oschersleben 28/7/43 w/Fulton; e/a, cr Nth Sea; 10KIA 1POW; MACR 140. LIBERTY BELLE.

42-30142 Del Cheyenne 15/4/43; Sioux City 30/4/43; Kearney 4/5/43; Bangor 22/5/43; ass 544BS/384BG [SU-L] Grafton Underwood 29/9/43; trans 560BS/388BG Knettishall /43; MIA {35m} Gelsenkirchen 5/11/43 w/Walker; flak, cr Biervliet, Hol; 1EVD 4KIA 5POW; MACR 3123. PISTOL PACKIN' MAMA.

42-30143 Del Cheyenne 16/4/43; Smoky Hill 25/4/43; Sioux City 30/4/43; Kearney 5/5/43; Bangor 23/5/43; ass 545BS/384BG [JD-Q] Grafton Underwood; MIA Wangerooge 25/6/43 w/Riches; flak, cr Oldenburg. MACR 16378. YANKEE POWERHOUSE.

42-30144 Del Cheyenne 16/4/43; Smoky Hill 25/4/43; Lowry 6/5/43; Smoky Hilly 26/5/43; Dow Fd 2/6/43; ass 335BS/95BG [OE-R] Horham 15/6/43; tran 306BG Thurleigh 6/43; sal Italy 15/2/44.

42-30145 Del Cheyenne 21/4/43; Tinker 27/4/43; Memphis 30/4/43; Presque Is 5/5/43; ass 333BS/94BG Earls Colne 12/5/43; Rougham 13/6/43; tran 384BG Grafton Underwood 12/7/43; 368BS/306BG [BO-G] Thurleigh 22/8/43; RAF 100 Gp 7/1/44, ret 13/3/44; sal 11/10/45.

42-30146 Del Cheyenne 17/4/43; Smoky Hill 25/4/43; Presque Is 15/5/43; ass 333BS/94BG [TS-A] Earls Colne 24/5/43 DOWN AND GO!; Rougham 13/6/43; MIA Warnemünde 29/7/43 w/Palmer; flak hit; 1KIA 9POW; MACR 202. CHEROKEE.

42-30147 Del Cheyenne 16/4/43; Smoky Hill 25/4/43; Presque Is 15/5/43; ass 544BS/384BG [SU-O] Grafton Underwood 28/6/43 M'HONEY; MIA Schweinfurt 17/8/43 w/Wilson; e/a, cr Rheims, Fr; 4EVD 6POW; MACR 291. FLAK DANCER.

42-30148 Del Cheyenne 17/4/43; Smoky Hill 24/4/43; Walla Walla 30/4/43; Smoky Hill 21/5/43; Dow Fd 2/6/43; ass 8AF .... sal n/b/d 14/7/43.

42-30149 Del Cheyenne 17/4/43; Smoky Hill 24/4/43; Walla Walla 30/4/43; Smoky Hill 10/5/43; Dow Fd 25/5/43; ass 333BS/94BG [XM-A2] Earls Colne 27/5/43; Rougham 12/6/43; MIA Schweinfurt 14/10/43 w/Mullinax; e/a, cr Bamberg, Ger; 10POW; MACR 790. SPARE PARTS.

42-30150 Del Cheyenne 17/4/43; Smoky Hill 24/4/43; Walla Walla 30/4/43; Rapid City 9/5/43; Dow Fd 24/5/43; ass 412BS/95BG [QW-S] Horham 27/6/43; MIA Oschersleben 28/7/43 w/Hodges; e/a, cr Lathen, Ger; 10 POW; MACR 214. EXTERMINATOR.

42-30151 Del Cheyenne 21/4/43; Tinker 27/4/43; New Castle 30/4/43; Presque Is 5/5/43; ass 532BS/381BG [VE-J] Ridgewell 15/5/43; MIA {6m} Cologne 4/3/44 w/Keyes; mech fault, cr St Omer, Fr; 10POW; MACR 2910. SPARE PARTS.

42-30152 Del Cheyenne 17/4/43; Smoky Hill 24/4/43; Walla Walla 30/4/43; Smoky Hill 20/5/43; Dow Fd 28/5/43; ass 96BG Andrews Fd 1/6/43; Snetterton 12/6/43; tran 381BG Ridgewell 16/7/43; 418BS/100BG [LD-X] Thorpe Abbotts 7/43; sal 28/4/45. MESSIE BESSIE.

42-30153 Del Cheyenne 17/4/43; Smoky Hill 24/4/43; Dow Fd 6/5/43; ass 339BS/96BG Andrews Fd 9/5/43 WORRY WART; Snetterton 12/6/43; tran 532BS/381BG Ridgewell 16/7/43; MIA {1m} Hamburg (Heide) 25/7/43 w/Alexander; flak, cr Hamburg area; 10POW; MACR 131.

42-30154 Del Cheyenne 17/4/43; Smoky Hill 24/4/43; Dow Fd 19/5/43; Presque Is 21/5/43; ass 92BG Alconbury 13/6/43; tran 334BS/95BG [BG-Z] Alconbury 16/6/43; 349BS/100BG [XR-H] Thorpe Abbotts 6/43; MIA Bremen 8/10/43 w/Becktoft; flak, cr Bremen; 1KIA 9POW; MACR 953. WAR EAGLE.

42-30155 Del Cheyenne 21/4/43; Tinker 27/4/43; Memphis 30/4/43; Presque Is 6/5/43; ass 366BS/305BG [KY-C/E] Chelveston 31/5/43; f/l RAF St Eval 4/7/43, ret 12/8/43; MIA Kiel 5/1/44 w/Hoag; e/a, cr Simonsberg, Ger; 10POW. MACR 1684.

42-30156 Del Cheyenne 17/4/43; Smoky Hill 24/4/43; Presque Is 16/5/43; ass 423BS/306BG [RD-Z] Thurleigh 22/6/43; MIA Hanover 26/7/43 w/Courson; flak, cr Vriescheloo, Hol; 3KIA 7POW; MACR 127.

42-30157 Del Cheyenne 21/4/43; Tinker 27/4/43; Smoky Hill 5/5/43; Tinker 24/5/43; Smoky Hill 29/5/43; Dow Fd 1/6/43; ass 323BS/91BG [OR-P] Bassingbourn 10/6/43 DIRTY GERTIE {1m}; c/l base 30/7/43 w/Van der Heyde; sal 25/8/43. HELLS BELLS {2m}.

42-30158 Del Cheyenne 20/4/43; Tinker 28/4/43; New Castle 29/4/43; ass 525BS/379BG [FR-X] Kimbolton 23/5/43; MIA Schweinfurt 17/8/43 w/Koeppen; e/a, cr Abenheim, Ger; 2KIA 8POW; MACR 1764. MARY JANE II.

42-30159 Del Cheyenne 21/4/43; Tinker 27/4/43; New Castle 2/5/43; Presque Is 6/5/43; ass 366BS/305BG [KY-H] Chelveston 24/5/43; MIA Schweinfurt 17/8/43 w/McKeegan; flak, cr Bilstain, Bel; 2KIA 8POW; MACR 301. SETTING BULL.

42-30160 Del Cheyenne 20/4/43; Smoky Hill 24/4/43; Dow Fd 28/5/43; ass 339BS/96BG [QJ-E] Andrews Fd 27/5/43; Snetterton 12/6/43; c/l base 13/12/43, 4KIA 6WIA; sal 15/12/43. DOTTIE J II.

42-30161 Del Cheyenne 23/4/43; Smoky Hill 28/4/43; Walla Walla 5/7/43; Smoky Hill 28/5/43; Tinker 23/5/43; Dow Fd 2/6/43; ass 303BG Molesworth 16/6/43; tran 336BS/95BG [ET-B] Horham 18/6/43; then 335BS [OE-B]; MIA Stuttgart 6/9/43 w/Cabeen; cr Stuttgart, 10POW, MACR 547. CUDDLE CAT.

42-30162 Del Cheyenne 20/4/43; Smoky Hill 29/4/43; Walla Walla 7/5/43; Smoky Hill 21/5/43; Dow Fd 24/5/43; ass 410BS/94BG [GL-X] Rougham 13/6/43; MIA Kiel 4/1/44 w/Hudgens; e/a, ditched Nth Sea; 10KIA 1POW; MACR 1756. THE PICCADILLY VIRGIN.

42-30163 Del Cheyenne 21/4/43; Tinker 27/4/43; Memphis 30/4/43; Presque Is 20/5/43; ass 368BS/306BG [BO-D] Thurleigh 23/5/43; MIA Stuttgart 6/9/43 w/Peterson; no gas, c/L Rouen, Fr; 4EVD 1KIA 5POW. MACR 518.

42-30164 Del Cheyenne 21/4/43; Tinker 27/4/43; Memphis 30/4/43; Presque Is 5/5/43; ass 334BS/95BG [BG-E] Framlingham 12/5/43; MIA Kiel 13/6/43 w/Stirwalt; col w/e/a, cr Kiel; 11KIA 2POW; Brig Gen Forrest as observer. MACRS 1371 and 8960.

42-30165 Del Cheyenne 21/4/43; Tinker 28/4/43; Smoky Hill 4/5/43; Lowry 6/5/43; Walla Walla 15/5/43; Tinker 21/5/43; Smoky Hill 25/5/43; Dow Fd 2/6/43; ass 100BG Thorpe Abbotts 5/6/43; tran 524BS/379BG Kimbolton 21/6/43; MIA {1m} Wangerooge 25/6/43 w/Hartman; e/a, cr Wiestel Sogel, Ger; 2KIA 8POW; MACR 1356.

42-30166 Del Cheyenne 21/4/43; Tinker 27/4/43; Memphis 30/4/43; Presque Is 8/5/43; ass 332BS/94BG [XM-L] Earls Colne 15/5/43; Rougham 13/6/43 BLACK JACK III; MIA Gelsenkirchen 5/11/43 w/Killien; flak, ditched Nth Sea off Belgium; 8KIA 2POW; MACR 1043. YOU CAWN'T MISS IT.

42-30167 Del Cheyenne 21/4/43; Tinker 27/4/43; Smoky Hill 5/5/43; Tinker 12/5/43; Lincoln 20/5/43; Bangor 23/5/43; ass 336BS/95BG [ET-H] Framlingham; Horham 15/6/43 ANGEL PUMPKIN; tran 457BG Glatton 3/44; 2 BAD Warton 17/3/44; retUS Homestead 18/7/44; Tinker 24/7/44; Patterson 19/8/44; Eglin 14/12/44; Recl Comp 31/10/45. DESTINY'S TOT.

42-30168 Del Cheyenne 22/4/43; Gt Falls 6/5/43; Kearney 29/5/43; Dow Fd 18/6/43; ass 550BS/385BG Gt Ashfield 26/6/43; MIA Emden 11/12/43 w/Jennings; ditched Nth Sea, 7KIA 3POW; MACR 1666. SLO-JO.

42-30169 Del Cheyenne 22/4/43; Tinker 24/5/43; Smoky Hill 29/5/43; Chicago 1/6/43; Smoky Hill 16/6/43; Tinker 19/6/43; Kearney 26/6/43; Eglin 7/7/43; Dow Fd 12/7/43; ass 414BS/97BG Château-du-Rhumel 14/7/43; Pont-du-Fahs 1/8/43; Depienne 15/8/43; Cerignola 20/12/43; Amendola 16/1/44; MIA Atzerdorf 24/5/44 w/Close; e/a, cr St Marien; MACR 5070. LADY LUCK.

42-30170 Del Cheyenne 21/4/43; Tinker 27/4/43; Smoky Hill 5/5/43; Kearney 28/5/43; Dow Fd 7/6/43; ass 349BS/100BG [XR-G] Thorpe Abbotts 10/6/43 TORCHY 2; HOT SPIT; MISS CARRIAGE; MIA Verden 6/3/44 w/Montgomery; e/a, cr Cologne; 1KIA 9POW; MACR 3015. OH NAUSEA.

42-30171 Del Cheyenne 24/4/43; Kearney 30/5/43; Dow Fd 18/6/43; ass 548BS/385BG Gt Ashfield 26/6/43; sal 2/11/43. WAR CRY.

42-30172 Del Cheyenne 22/4/43; Smoky Hill 28/4/43; Walla Walla 7/5/43; Smoky Hill 21/5/43; Dow Fd 6/6/43; ass 339BS/96BG [QJ-F] Snettisham 12/6/43; c/l Wolferton, Nfk; 19/8/43 w/Attaway; 10RTD (2 minor and 1 major injury); sal 21/8/44. BLACK HEART JR.

42-30173 Del Cheyenne 22/4/43; Smoky Hill 29/4/43; Tinker 12/5/43; Lincoln 21/5/43; Dow Fd 25/5/43; ass 410BS/94BG Earls Colne 28/5/43 GORGEOUS HUSSY; tran 412BS/95BG [QW-O] Framlingham 6/6/43 CIRCE; Horham 12/6/43; MIA Brunswick 10/2/44 w/Pearson; cr Sreimbeke, Ger; 3KIA 7POW; MACR 2544. ALL AMERICAN.

42-30174 Del Cheyenne 22/4/43; Smoky Hill 29/4/43; Tinker 13/5/43; Lincoln 17/5/43; Dow Fd 21/5/43; ass 332BS/94BG [XM-S] Earls Colne 25/5/43 LADY

LUCK II; Rougham 13/6/43; MIA Hanover 26/7/43 w/Tessier; e/a, cr Bremen; 1KIA 9POW; MACR 90. CHEROKEE MAID.

42-30175 Del Cheyenne 22/4/43; Smoky Hill 28/4/43; Walla Walla 7/5/43; Smoky Hill 21/5/43; Dow Fd 2/6/43; ass 367BS/306BG [GY-B] Thurleigh 18/6/43; MIA Schweinfurt 14/10/43 w/Butler; e/a, cr Schweinfurt; 10POW; MACR 822. THE HAMMER OF HELL.

42-30176 Del Cheyenne 22/4/43; Smoky Hill 28/4/43; Walla Walla 7/5/43; Smoky Hill 25/5/43; Presque Is 6/6/43; ass 335BS/95BG [OE-P] Framlingham 5/6/43; Horham 15/6/43; MIA Schweinfurt 17/8/43 w/Sundberg; e/a, cr Oostmalle, Bel; 4EVD 1KIA 5POW; MACR 401. ASSASSIN.

42-30177 Del Cheyenne 24/4/43; Gore Fd 27/4/43; Cheyenne 2/5/43; Sioux City 13/5/43; Smoky Hill 11/6/43; Dow Fd 16/6/43; ass 562BS/388BG Knettishall 23/6/43; {15m} tran RCM 803BS Sculthorpe 19/1/44; Oulton 16/5/44; 36BS Cheddington 14/8/44; Alconbury 3/45; CHARLENE. Given by Ike to French Gen Koenig 17/12/45; renamed BIR-HACKEIM and had tail shot up during Cold War en route to Berlin; 1953 sold to IGN at Creil until 1960s.

42-30178 Del Cheyenne 24/4/43; Smoky Hill 5/5/43; Presque Is 24/5/43; ass 335BS/95BG [OE-S] Framlingham 29/5/43; Horham 15/6/43; DARLIN' DOLLY; tran 388BG APH Knettishall 4/44; 803BS RCM Oulton 16/5/44; MIA Oldenburg 1/1/45.

42-30179 Del Cheyenne 24/4/43; Gt Falls 8/5/43; Kearney 29/5/43; Dow Fd 15/6/43; ass 550BS/385BG Gt Ashfield 16/6/43 GRIM REAPER; MIA Oschersleben 28/7/43 w/Gurgel; cr Oschersleben, 4KIA 6POW; MACR 189A. MURDER INC.

42-30180 Del Cheyenne 24/4/43; Smoky Hill 5/5/43; Presque Is 30/5/43; ass 384BG Grafton Underwood 10/6/43; tran 337BS/96BG [AW-H] Andrews Fd 6/7/43 GUZZLERS; Snetterton 12/6/43, BLACK HAWK; 388BG APH Knettishall /43; MIA (as drone) Heligoland, pilot killed baling out, 11/9/44.

42-30181 Del Cheyenne 24/4/43; Smoky Hill 5/5/43; Kearney 29/5/43; Atlanta 2/6/43; Dow Fd 16/6/43; ass 335BS/95BG [OE-X] Framlingham 19/6/43 HERKY JERKY II; Horham 15/6/43; MIA Eschweiler 24/1/44 w/Burnett; cr Brussels, 4KIA 6POW; MACR 2258. LOVER BOY.

42-30182 Del Cheyenne 22/4/43; Smoky Hill 28/4/43; Walla Walla 5/7/43; Tinker 28/5/43; Smoky Hill 1/6/43; Dow Fd 6/6/43; ass 412BS/95BG [QW-E] Horham 15/6/43; MIA Emden 11/12/43 w/Moore; ditched off Dantumadeel, Hol, 10KIA; MACR 1562. BLONDIE II.

42-30183 Del Cheyenne 28/4/43; Tinker 15/5/43; Lincoln 22/5/43; Dow Fd 24/5/43; ass 338BS/96BG Andrews Fd 27/5/43; Snetterton 12/6/43; MIA Kassel 30/7/43 w/Miracle; e/a, cr Nth Sea, 10RTD. DRY RUN II.

42-30184 Del Cheyenne 24/4/43; Smoky Hill 5/5/43; Dow Fd 9/6/43; ass 349BS/100BG Thorpe Abbotts 10/6/43; sal 5/8/44."MUGGS."

42-30185 Del Cheyenne 24/4/43; Smoky Hill 5/5/43; Dow Fd 25/5/43; ass 412BS/95BG [QW-H] Horham 15/6/43; b/d Schweinfurt 17/8/43; sal 24/8/43. WEE BONNIE.

42-30186 Del Cheyenne 24/4/43; Gt Falls 6/5/43; Kearney 29/5/43; Dow Fd 13/6/43; ass 549BS/385BG Gt Ashfield 17/6/43; n/b/d 3/11/43; b/d Brunswick 29/2/44; sal 2/5/45.

42-30187 Del Cheyenne 24/4/43; Gore 6/5/43; Kearney 30/5/43; Dow Fd 15/6/43; ass 551BS/385BG Gt Ashfield 16/6/43; MIA Evreux 24/8/43 w/Maj Piper; e/a, cr Nth Sea; 4KIA 6RTD; MACR 961. LULU BELLE.

42-30188 Del Cheyenne 25/4/43; Smoky Hill 6/5/43; Tinker 25/5/43; Dow Fd 1/6/43; ass 413BS/96BG [MS-Z] Snetterton 12/6/43 KATS SASS II; b/d Frankfurt 4/2/44, c/l East Shropham, UK; 10RTD. TEMPTATION.

42-30189 Del Cheyenne 27/4/43; Sioux City 8/5/43; Smoky Hill 12/6/43; Dow Fd 16/6/43; ass 563BS/388BG Knettishall 23/6/43; MIA Hanover 26/7/43 w/Gunn; flak, cr Nth Sea; 2KIA 8POW; MACR 3067. LA CHIQUITA.

42-30190 Del Wright Fd 24/4/43; Gore 27/4/43; Boeing 29/5/43; Blythe 23/6/43; Wright 29/7/43; Pendleton 21/9/43; 1105 BU Miami 12/10/43; converted to XC-108B fuel tanker for CBI theater; retUS 25/9/44; 4100 BU Patterson 28/3/45; 4202 BU Syracuse 29/5/43; RFC Bush Fd 26/5/45.

42-30191 Del Cheyenne 24/4/43; Smoky Hill 14/5/43; Tinker 24/5/43; Smoky Hill 29/5/43; Dow Fd 1/6/43; ass 525BS/379BG [FR-C] Kimbolton 6/6/43; MIA Schweinfurt 17/8/43 w/Merchant; flak, cr Elfershausen, Ger; 1KIA 9POW; MACR 1765. THE BOLEVICH.

42-30192 Del Cheyenne 24/4/43; Smoky Hill 5/5/43; Dow Fd 5/6/43; ass 379 Kimbolton 5/6/43; tran 335BS/95BG [OE-Y] Horham 27/6/43; MIA Kassel 30/7/43 w/Jutzi; flak, cr Channel; 2KIA 3POW 2WIA 3RTD; MACR 217.

42-30193 Del Cheyenne 24/4/43; Sioux City 8/5/43; Smoky Hill 9/6/43; Dow Fd 14/6/43; ass 561BS/388BG Knettishall 15/6/43; c/t/o for Schweinfurt 14/10/43 w/Swift; 10RTD, sal.

Below: B-17F-130-BO 42-30177 was one of very few combat-employed Fortresses to survive for post-war service. After fifteen missions with the 388th Bomb Group came assignment to the Eighth Air Force's Radio Countermeasures Squadron. In December 1945 it was given to the French and for several years served as a VIP transport carrying the name *Bir-Hackeim*. (H. Perrin)

HARDLUCK.

42-30194 Del Cheyenne 24/4/43; Gore Fd 25/4/43; Smoky Hill 12/5/43; Tinker 25/5/43; Smoky Hill 29/5/43; Dow Fd 1/6/43; ass 91BG Bassingbourn 15/6/43; tran 335BS/95BG [OE-O] Horham 16/6/43; MIA Bonn 12/8/43 w/Hamilton; cr Kattenbusch, Bel; 1EVD 5KIA 4POW; MACR 253. WE AIN'T SCARED.

42-30195 Del Cheyenne 29/4/43; Sioux City 11/5/43; Smoky Hill 10/6/43; Dow Fd 15/6/43; ass 560BS/388BG Knettishall 16/6/43; c/t/o Walpole, Nfk 7/10/44; 9RTD, sal. (first in group to 75 missions); BLIND DATE.

42-30196 Del Cheyenne 26/4/43; Smoky Hill 6/5/43; Tinker 25/5/43; Smoky Hill 30/5/43; Dow Fd 6/6/43; ass 546BS/384BG [BK-Y] Grafton Underwood 23/6/43; MIA Schweinfurt 14/10/43 w/Keller; e/a, cr Wursburg, Ger; 6KIA 4POW; MACR 839. SAD SACK.

42-30197 Del Cheyenne 27/4/43; Gt Falls 6/5/43; Kearney 29/5/43; Dow Fd 13/6/43; ass 549BS/385BG Gt Ashfield 14/6/43; MIA Rostock 11/4/44 w/Pangle; flak, c/l Kristianopel, Swed; crew interned. MACR 3822. MISSION BELLE.

42-30198 Del Cheyenne 26/4/43; Smoky Hill 5/5/43; Cheyenne 14/5/43; Tinker 21/5/43; Kearney 27/5/43; Dow Fd 2/6/43; ass 339BS/96BG [QJ-L] Andrews Fd 5/6/43; Snetterton 12/6/43; tran 563BS/388BG Knettishall /43; MIA Hanover 26/7/43 w/Bobbitt; e/a, cr Holtland, Ger; 5KIA 5POW. MACR 3142. GUZZLERS.

42-30199 Del Cheyenne 26/4/43; Smoky Hill 6/5/43; Westover 9/6/43; Dow Fd 10/6/43; Presque Is 13/6/43; Rome Fd 15/6/43; Patterson 27/6/43; Bolling 4/7/43; Louisville 8/8/43; ass 369BS/306BG [WW-R] Thurleigh 24/8/43; MIA Schweinfurt 14/10/43 w/Bettinger; e/a, cr Frankfurt; 1EVD 1KIA 8POW; MACR 821. THE WICKED WAAC.

42-30200 Del Cheyenne 27/4/43; Smoky Hill 6/5/43; Tinker 21/5/43; Dow Fd 25/5/43; ass 410BS/94BG [GL-R] Earls Colne 5/6/43; Rougham 13/6/43; MIA Bordeaux 5/1/44 w/Born; e/a, cr Boubriac, Fr; 7EVD 1KIA 2POW; MACR 1892. (The pilot's brother, an infantry Sgt, arranged to meet at base on return from mission). SLO-TIME SALLY.

42-30201 Del Cheyenne 29/4/43; Gore 7/5/43; Sioux City 11/5/43; Smoky Hill 10/6/43; Dow Fd 19/6/43; ass 560BS/388BG Knettishall 20/6/43 SHEDONWANNA?; MIA Stuttgart 6/9/43 w/Melville; e/a, cr Chartres, Fr; 4KIA 6POW; MACR 3124. TIGER GIRL.

42-30202 Del Cheyenne 29/4/43; Sioux City 11/5/43; Dow Fd 18/6/43; ass 563BS/388BG Knettishall; MIA Kassel 30/7/43 w/Pickard; flak, cr Lier(ge), Bel; 1EVD 9POW; MACR 3125.

42-30203 Del Cheyenne 29/4/43; Gore 9/5/43; Sioux City 10/5/43; Smoky Hill 10/5/43; Dow Fd 23/6/43; ass 560BS/388BG Knettishall 17/6/43; MIA Stuttgart 6/9/43 w/Mohr; e/a, cr Goudray, Fr; 4KIA 6POW; MACR 3126. SHACK-UP.

42-30204 Del Cheyenne 26/5/43; Gore 6/5/43; Gt Falls 8/5/43; Kearney 30/5/43; Dow Fd 15/6/43; ass 94BG Rougham 17/6/43; tran 548BS/385BG Gt Ashfield 14/8/43; MIA Bremen 29/11/43 w/Yoder; flak, cr Vesenfeld, Ger; 5KIA 5POW; MACR 1581. GREMLIN'S BUGGY.

42-30205 Del Cheyenne 29/4/43; Sioux City 11/5/43; Smoky Hill 9/6/43; Dow Fd 12/6/43; ass 563BS/388BG Knettishall 14/6/43; sal n/b/d 30/1/44. "BATTLIN' BETSY".

42-30206 Del Cheyenne 29/4/43; Smoky Hill 6/5/43; Tinker 21/5/43; Kearney 28/5/43; Dow Fd 2/6/43; ass 410BS/94BG Rougham 13/6/43; MIA Warnemünde 25/7/43 w/Keelan; flak, ditched Nth Sea; 1KIA 9RTD; MACR 89. HAPPY DAZE.

42-30207 Del Cheyenne 29/4/43; Smoky Hill 9/6/43; Dow Fd 12/6/43; ass 561BS/388BG Knettishall 14/6/43; MIA Bordeaux 27/3/44 w/Lenderman; flak, cr Aicenay, Fr; 2EVD 5KIA 3POW; MACR 3540. BIG RED.

42-30208 Del Cheyenne 29/4/43; Gore 8/5/43; Sioux City 10/5/43; Dow Fd 16/6/43; ass 563BS/388BG Knettishall 17/6/43; MIA Hanover 26/7/43 w/?; cr Nth Sea; 10KIA; MACR 3142.

42-30209 Del Cheyenne 29/4/43; Gore 8/5/43; Sioux City 10/5/43; Smoky Hill 9/6/43; Dow Fd 12/6/43; ass 561BS/388BG Knettishall 14/6/43; MIA Hanover 26/7/43 w/Porter; ditched Nth Sea, 3EVD 7POW. WEE BONNIE.

42-30210 Del Cheyenne 29/4/43; Gore 8/5/43; Sioux City 10/5/43; Smoky Hill 9/6/43; Dow Fd 12/6/43; ass 561BS/388BG Knettishall 15/6/43; MIA Kassel 30/7/43 w/Penn; flak, cr Kassel; 3KIA 7POW; MACR 3264.

42-30211 Del Cheyenne 27/4/43; Smoky Hill 6/5/43; Tinker 15/5/43; Lincoln 21/5/43; Dow Fd 24/5/43; ass 95BG Alconbury 13/6/43; tran 335BS/95BG [OE-T] Horham 16/6/43; MIA Huls 22/6/43 w/Bunch, cr Gelsenkirchen; 2KIA 8POW; MACR 4903.

42-30212 Del Cheyenne 29/4/43; Sioux City 14/5/43; Smoky Hill 11/6/43; Dow Fd 16/6/43; ass 562BS/388BG Knettishall 17/6/43; tran APH, MIA Watten 6/8/44. QUARTERBACK.

42-30213 Del Cheyenne 29/4/43; Gore 9/5/43; Sioux City 10/5/43; Smoky Hill 11/6/43; Dow Fd 15/6/43; ass 562BS/388BG Knettishall 16/6/43; c/t/o for Bremen 13/11/43, c/l East Wretham, Nfk; 10RTD, sal. LI'L ONE.

42-30214 Del Cheyenne 29/4/43; Sioux City 8/5/43; Smoky Hill 10/6/43; Dow Fd 15/6/43; ass 560BS/388BG Knettishall 16/6/43; MIA Gdynia 9/10/43 w/Nagorka; e/a, cr Nth Sea; 4KIA 6POW; MACR 3141. IZA ANGEL II.

42-30215 Del Cheyenne 29/4/43; Gore 8/5/43; Sioux City 10/5/43; Smoky Hill 10/6/43; Dow Fd 15/6/43; ass 560BS/388BG Knettishall 17/6/43; MIA Osnabrück 11/1/44 w/Carpentier; mech problem, cr Hameln, Ger; 9POW; MACR 3127. SLIGHTLY DANGEROUS II.

42-30216 Del Cheyenne 29/4/43; Gore 9/5/43; Sioux City 10/5/43; Dow Fd 12/6/43; ass 563BS/388BG Knettishall 18/6/43; MIA Oschersleben 28/7/43 w/Swanson; e/a, cr Minden, Ger; 10POW, MACR 3128. JOHNNIE.

42-30217 Del Cheyenne 29/4/43; Sioux City 13/5/43; Smoky Hill 15/6/43; Dow Fd 15/6/43; ass 560BS/388BG Knettishall 16/6/43 IZA BLUE; b/d Duren 20/10/43, sal. IMPATIENT VIRGIN.

42-30218 Del Cheyenne 30/4/43; Smoky Hill 14/5/43; Tinker 25/5/43; Smoky Hill 29/5/43; Dow Fd 6/6/43; ass 335BS/95BG [OE-W] Horham 15/6/43; MIA Emden 11/12/43 w/Beatty; cr Ferwerd, Hol; 6KIA 4POW; MACR 1561. HEAVENLY DAZE.

42-30219 Del Cheyenne 30/4/43; Smoky Hill 12/5/43; Bangor 6/6/43; ass 334BS/95BG [BG-J] Horham 15/6/43; b/d Kassel 28/7/43 w/Thomas 3POW; c/l Framlingham, 7RTD, sal 13/8/43; MACR 215.

42-30220 Del Cheyenne 30/4/43; Gore 10/5/43; Peterson 20/5/43; Patterson 13/6/43; ass 1st Map Gp Bolling 4/7/43; Bradley 27/7/43; Accra, Gold Coast 31/12/43; retUS 1st Photo Gp McDill 3/4/44; 4100 BU Patterson 20/10/44; 91 Photo Gp Buckley 13/12/44; 1103 BU Morrison 26/1/45; sal Patterson 19/6/46.

42-30221 Del Cheyenne 30/4/43; Gore 14/5/43; Smoky Hill 21/5/43; Kearney 26/5/43; Dow Fd 2/6/43; ass 423BS/306BG [RD-G] Thurleigh 18/6/43; MIA Pas De Calais 27/12/43 w/Manning; s/d by Spitfires and coll w/42-30841, cr Nth Sea.

42-30222 Del Cheyenne 30/4/43; Sioux City 11/5/43; Smoky Hill 12/5/43; Dow Fd 19/6/43; ass 563BS/388BG Knettishall 10/6/43; MIA Stuttgart 6/9/43 w/Kramer; e/a, cr Troyes, Fr; 7EVD 2KIA 1POW; MACR 3129. LONE WOLF.

42-30223 Del Cheyenne 30/4/43; Gore 22/5/43; Spokane 24/5/43; Gore 11/6/43; Smoky Hill 29/6/43; Dow Fd 11/7/43; ass 571BS/390BG [FC-S] Framlingham 11/7/43 NORMA J; MIA Emden 11/12/43 w/Ryon; e/a, cr Westerstede, Ger; 8KIA 2POW; MACR 1582. RICK-O-SHAY.

42-30224 Del Cheyenne 30/4/43; Sioux City 12/5/43; Patterson 20/5/43; Smoky Hill 10/6/43; Dow Fd 15/6/43; ass 560BS/388BG Knettishall 17/6/43; MIA Hanvover 26/7/43 w/Horn; flak, cr Deskbergsh?; 3KIA 7POW; MACR 3130.

42-30225 Del Cheyenne 30/4/43; Sioux City 11/5/43; Smoky Hill 11/6/43; Dow Fd 2/7/43; ass 562BS/388BG Knettishall 1/7/43; MIA Hanover 27/7/43 w/Denton; flak, cr Aurich, Ger, 6KIA 4POW; MACR 3131. MR YANK.

42-30226 Del Cheyenne 30/4/43; Gore 14/5/43; Kearney 27/5/43; Tinker 1/6/43; Dow Fd 6/6/43; ass 336BS/95BG [ET-L] Horham 15/6/43; MIA Frankfurt 29/1/44 w/Higgins; cr Ziegfeld?; 5KIA 5POW; MACR 2256. SPOOK #5.

42-30227 Del Cheyenne 1/5/43; Smoky Hill 17/5/43; Dow Fd 30/5/43; ass 413BS/96BG [MZ-R] Snetterton 12/6/43 WABBIT TWACKS III; tran 401BG Deenethorpe 13/12/43; 1 BAD Burtonwood 17/3/44; retUS Tinker 3/6/44; Gore Air Trans Com 7/6/44; Kirtland 21/11/45; Long Beach 18/5/45; RFC Ontario 4/6/45. BOOTS III.

42-30228 Del Cheyenne 30/4/43; Sioux City 11/5/43; ass 388BG, c/l Casper 10/6/43; WO 16/6/43; sal 19/11/44; Recl Comp 17/9/46.

42-30229 Del Cheyenne 30/4/43; Sioux City 11/5/43; Smoky Hill 12/6/43; Dow Fd 18/6/43; ass 563BS/388BG, l/Atlantic en route UK 20/6/43. MACR 4.

42-30230 Del Cheyenne 30/4/43; sioux City 13/5/43; Smoky Hill 11/6/43; Dow Fd 15/6/43; ass 562BS/388BG Knettishall 17/6/43; b/d Bordeaux 24/8/43; no gas, c/l Stanton, Sfk, 10RTD; sal 31/8/43. HOMESICK ANGEL.

42-30231 Del Cheyenne 1/5/43; Smoky Hill 12/5/43; Dow Fd 29/5/43; ass 325BS/95BG [NV-Z] Alconbury 6/6/43; tran 326BS [JW-O]; MIA Schweinfurt 14/10/43 w/Clough; e/a, cr St Goar, Ger; 10POW, MACR 844.

42-30232 Del Cheyenne 3/5/43; ass 100BG Gore 18/5/43; Peterson 20/5/43; Patterson 13/6/43; tran 1st Map Gp Bolling 4/7/43; Bradley 17/8/43; ass Accra, Gold Coast 21/12/43; retUS 1st Ph Gp MacDill 2/4/44; 4100 BU Patterson 20/4/44; 1103 BU Morrison 2/2/45; 91st Ph Sq Buckley 5/2/45; Mapping Trinidad 1/6/46; WO 24/6/46.

42-30233 Del Cheyenne 3/5/43; Gore 24/5/43; Smoky Hill 25/5/43; Kearney 27/5/43; Dow Fd 2/6/43; ass 412BS/95BG [QW-X] Alconbury 16/6/43; MIA Augsburg 13/4/44 w/Johnson; f/l Altenheim, Switz; 2INT 8POW; MACR 3765; retUS Morrison 22/10/45; RFC Walnut Ridge 8/1/46. RHAPSODY IN FLAK.

42-30234 Del Cheyenne 1/5/43; Sioux City 13/5/43; Smoky Hill 12/6/43; Dow Fd 18/6/43; ass 563BS/388BG Knettishall 19/6/43; MIA Stuttgart 6/9/43 w/Miller; e/a, cr Mesnil, (Merzig?) Ger; 7KIA

3POW; MACR 3132.

42-30235 Del Cheyenne 3/5/43; Gore 16/5/43; Smoky Hill 17/5/43; Dow Fd 30/5/43; ass 401BS/91BG [LL-L/Z] Bassingbourn 6/6/43; tran 412BS/95BG [QW-U] Horham 16/6/43 LONESOME POLECAT; RFC Altus 9/10/45. THE ZOOT SUITERS.

42-30236 Del Cheyenne 1/5/43; Smoky Hill 12/5/43; Kearney 26/5/43; Dow Fd 2/6/43; WO 16/6/43.

42-30237 Del Cheyenne 1/5/43; Gore 13/5/43; Smoky Hill 14/5/43; Dow Fd 30/5/43; ass 524BS/379BG [WA-V] Kimbolton 1/6/43; tran 1 BAD Burtonwood 4/8/44; APH Knettishall, MIA Oldenburg 1/1/45. STUMP JUMPER.

42-30238 Del Cheyenne 1/5/43; Sioux City 13/5/43; Casper 12/6/43; Smoky Hill 13/6/43; Dow Fd 15/6/43; ass 563BS/388BG Knettishall 24/6/43 CLASSY CHASSY; MIA Kassel 30/7/43 w/Kelly; flak, cr Lichtenau, Ger; 10POW; MACR 315(3)3. WING AND A PRAYER.

42-30239 Del Cheyenne 1/5/43; Moses Lake 20/5/43; Walla Walla 30/5/43; Dow Fd 31/5/43; Hill Fd 3/6/43; Tinker 4/6/43; Orlando 6/6/43; Brooksville 21/6/43; Rapid City 3/7/43; Harvard 2/8/43; WO 30/8/43; RFC Altus 1/8/45.

42-30240 Del Cheyenne 1/5/43; Smoky Hill 12/5/43; Kearney 26/5/43; Dow Fd 2/6/43; ass 410BS/94BG Earls Colne 7/6/43; Rougham 13/6/43; MIA Huls 22/6/43 w/McFarland; 3KIA 7POW. BLACK KITTEN.

42-30241 Del Cheyenne 1/5/43; Rapid City 15/7/43; ass 388BG Knettishall 26/10/43 WORRY WART; tran RAF 214 Sq [BU-D] Feltwell (SR 378) 21/1/44; WO 11/3/47.

42-30242 Del Cheyenne 2/5/43; Gore 13/5/43; Smoky Hill 14/5/43; Dow Fd 30/5/43; ass 364BS/305BG [WF-N] Chelveston 10/6/43; MIA Schweinfurt 14/10/43 w/Kenyon; e/a, cr Schweinfurt; 1KIA 9POW; MACR 911. LALLAH-V III.

42-30243 Del Cheyenne 2/5/43; Gore 13/5/43; Smoky Hill 14/5/43; Kearney 27/5/43; Dow Fd 2/6/43; ass 331BS/94BG [QE-Z2] Rougham 15/6/43 NIP 'N TUCK; MIA Le Bourget 14/7/43 w/Frank; e/a, crc Evreux, 2EVD 8POW; MACR 115. GOOD TIME CHOLLY II.

42-30244 Del Cheyenne 1/5/43; Smoky Hill 14/5/43; Tinker 24/5/43; Smoky Hill 29/5/43; Dow Fd 31/5/43; ass 351BG Polebrook 9/6/43; tran 388BG Knettishall 17/6/43; 334BS/95BG [BG-M] Horham 18/6/43; MIA Eberfeld 5/1/44 w/Williams; ditched Channel, 1EVD 9POW; MACR 1687. HOLY TERROR.

42-30245 Del Cheyenne 2/5/43; Smoky Hill 17/5/43; Dow Fd 21/5/43; ass 534BS/381BG [GD-L] Ridgewell 15/6/43; MIA {5m} Schweinfurt 17/8/43 w/Simpson; e/a, cr Oostmalle, Bel; 1EVD 1KIA 8POW; MACR 381. LADY LUCK.

42-30246 Del Cheyenne 3/5/43; Gore 22/5/43; Spokane 24/5/43; Geiger 26/5/43; Smoky Hill 2/7/43; Dow Fd 13/7/43; ass 570BS/390BG [DI-H] Framlingham 14/7/43; MIA Rostock 20/2/44 w/Gallard; no gas, cr Tierstrup, Ger; 10POW; MACR 2436. SPOT REMOVER.

42-30247 Del Cheyenne 3/5/43; Gore 20/5/43; Moses Lake 21/5/43; 328 BU Gulfport 23/10/43; WO 23/10/43; Recl Comp 27/10/44.

42-30248 Del Cheyenne 3/5/43; Smoky Hill 14/5/43; Tinker 24/5/43; Smoky Hill 29/5/43; Dow Fd 31/5/43; ass 410BS/94BG [GL-X] Earls Colne 2/6/43 THE SOUTHERN QUEEN; Rougham 13/6/43 tran 333BS THE BUZZARD; MIA Brunswick 11/1/44 w/Randall; e/a, cr Uiezen, Ger; 2KIA 8POW; MACR 1889.

42-30249 Del Cheyenne 3/5/43; Gore 13/5/43; Smoky Hill 14/5/43; Gt Falls 24/5/43; Kearney 30/5/43; Dow Fd 4/6/43; ass 551BS/385BG Gt Ashfield 26/6/43; MIA Ludwigshafen 30/12/43 w/Frye; flak, cr Ligay; 3EVD 1KIA 6POW; MACR 1899. EL SABO.

42-30250 Del Cheyenne 3/5/43; Smoky Hill 14/5/43; Gt Falls 24/5/43; Kearney 30/5/43; Dow Fd 15/6/43; Peterson 18/6/43; ass 548BS/385BG Gt Ashfield 17/6/43; sal n/b/d 30/1/44. YANK.

42-30251 Del Cheyenne 6/5/43; Denver 8/5/43; Gt Falls 13/5/43; Kearney 29/5/43; Dow Fd 13/6/43; ass 549BS/385BG Gt Ashfield 14/6/43; MIA Frankfurt 29/1/44 w/Notestein; e/a, cr Kaiserlautern, Ger; 6KIA 4POW; MACR 2267. PICCADILLY QUEEN.

42-30252 Del Cheyenne 4/5/43; Gore 17/5/43; Patterson 20/5/43; Peterson 19/6/43; ass 1st Map Gp Bolling 7/7/43; Bradley 12/7/43; Bolling 1/8/43; Accra, Gold Coast 23/11/43; Recl Comp 20/11/44.

42-30253 Del Cheyenne 4/5/43; Patterson 20/5/43; ass 1st Map Gp Bolling 4/7/43; Bradley 16/7/43; Accra, Gold Coast 1/4/44; retUS 1st Ph Sq McDill 12/10/44; 91st Ph Sq Buckley 30/12/44; 4100 BU Patterson 29/12/44; 91st Ph Sq Buckley 1/2/45; WO 24/6/46.

42-30254 Del Cheyenne 6/5/43; Denver 8/5/43; Gore 12/5/43; Kearney 29/5/43; Dow Fd 16/6/43; ass 385BG, l/Atlantic en route UK 22/6/43. MACR 3.

42-30255 Del Cheyenne 4/5/43; Smoky Hill 14/5/43; Tinker 25/5/43; Smoky Hill 29/5/43; Dow Fd 31/5/43; ass 351BG Polebrook 10/6/43; tran 412BS/95BG [QW-V] Horham 16/6/43; MIA Bremen 16/12/43 w/Delbern; cr Texel Is, Hol; 4KIA 6POW; MACR 1558. LONESOME POLECAT II.

42-30256 Del Cheyenne 4/5/43; Gore 18/5/43; Peterson 20/5/43; Smoky Hill 26/5/43; Gt Falls 7/6/43; Patterson 13/6/43; Wright Fd 1/7/43; ass 1st Map Gp Bolling 9/7/43; Bradley 13/7/43; Bolling 25/7/43; Accra, Gold Coast 31/12/43; retUS Rome 29/9/44; WO 18/7/45; Recl Comp 14/8/45.

42-30257 Del Cheyenne 4/5/43; Smoky Hill 14/5/43; Gt Falls 24/5/43; Kearney 29/5/43; Tinker 13/6/43; Dow Fd 16/6/43; ass 100BG Thorpe Abbotts 16/6/43; tran 548BS/385BG Gt Ashfield 17/6/43; MIA Oschersleben 28/7/43 w/Robbins; flak, ditched Nth Sea; 8KIA 2POW; MACR 189C.

42-30258 Del Cheyenne 6/5/43; Gore 7/5/43; Roswell 24/5/43; Peterson 18/6/43; 3030 BU Roswell 2/6/44; 3010 BU Williams 21/9/44; 3020 BU La Junta 30/4/45; RFC Stillwater 31/7/45.

42-30259 Del Cheyenne 8/5/43; Smoky Hill 25/4/43; Kearney 27/5/43; Dow Fd 7/6/43; ass 349BS/100BG Thorpe Abbotts 10/6/43; FTR 24/9/43, ditched Nth Sea; 5KIA 5RTD, MACR 778. DAMIFINO II.

42-30260 Del Cheyenne 6/5/43; Denver 8/5/43; Gore 12/5/43; cr 6 mls SW Yellowstone, Mon, 23/5/43; burned out. Sal 27/5/43.

42-30261 Del Cheyenne 8/5/43; Kearney 26/5/43; Atlanta 3/6/43; Robins 24/6/43; Memphis 8/8/43; Gd Island 9/8/43; ass 325BS/92BG [NV-C] Podington 27/9/43; {50m} c/l base 28/5/44; sal 2SAD Lt Staughton 29/5/44.

42-30262 Del Cheyenne 8/5/43; Geiger 28/5/43; Gt Falls 7/6/43; Gore 12/5/43; Gt Falls 16/5/43; Smoky Hill 30/6/43; Dow Fd 12/7/43; ass 561BS/388BG Knettishall 13/7/43; tran 568BS/390BG [BI-K] Framlingham 8/43; MIA Münster 10/10/43 w/Winant; e/a, cr Ladbergen, Ger; 4KIA 6POW; MACR 862. TECH SUPPLY.

42-30263 Del Cheyenne 6/5/43; Denver 8/5/43; Gore 12/5/43; Kearney 30/5/43; Dow Fd 18/6/43; ass 551BS/385BG Gt Ashfield 19/6/43 PREGNANT PORTIA; c/l Docking, Nfk 30/10/43; sal 2/11/43. PORTIA'S REVENGE.

42-30264 Del Denver 8/5/43; Gore 9/5/43; Kearney 10/4/43; Dow Fd 15/5/43; ass 551BS/385BG Ashfield 17/6/43; coll w/385BG a/c, cr West Horndon, Ex. 26/9/43 10KIA; sal 28/9/43. DORSAL QUEEN.

42-30265 Del Denver 10/5/43; Gore 21/5/43; Geiger 22/5/43; Gt Falls 7/6/43; Gore 11/6/43; Smoky Hill 10/7/43; Dow Fd 14/7/43; ass 571BS/390BG [FC-V] Framlingham 18/7/43; MIA Münster 10/10/43 w/Ward; e/a, cr Buurse, Hol; 1EVD 1KIA 8POW; MACR 865. PINKY.

42-30266 Del Cheyenne 8/5/43; Gore 9/5/43; Moses Lake 22/5/43; Geiger 25/5/43; Smoky Hill 26/5/43; Gt Falls 7/6/43; Smoky Hill 1/7/43; Dow Fd 11/7/43; ass 569BS/390BG [CC-W] Framlingham 1/8/43 WILD CHILDREN; b/d Zeitz 16/8/44 c/l base; sal 17/8/44. LUCKY STRIKE.

42-30267 Del Cheyenne 18/5/43; Smoky Hill 30/5/43; Tinker 8/6/43; Smoky Hill 17/6/43; Casper 28/6/43; Kearney 30/6/43; Eglin 4/7/43; Dow 9/7/43; ass 96BS/2BG Ain M'Lila 27/7/43; Massicault 31/7/43; {19m} tran 341BS/97BG Depienne 14/11/43; Cerignola 20/12/43; Amendola 16/1/44; MIA Ploesti 23/6/44 w/Fleener; e/a, cr Bucharest; MACR 6951. HUSTLIN' HUZZY.

42-30268 Del Cheyenne 6/5/43; Gore 7/5/43; Patterson 23/5/43; Peterson 15/6/43; ass 1st Map Gp Bolling 2/11/43; 11 STA Morrison 11/6/44; 1st Ph Gp Peterson 18/6/44; Buckley 4/7/44; 8 STA Homestead 1/8/44; 326 BU McDill 19/8/44; Buckley 4/10/44; 1st Ph Gp McDill 12/10/44; Atkinson 14/11/44; RFC Ontario 20/5/45.

42-30269 Del Cheyenne 6/5/43; Gore 7/5/43; Roswell 24/6/43; Hobbs 7/7/43; Roswell 4/8/43; 3701 BU Amarillo 2/11/44; 3030 BU Roswell 6/11/44; 3010 BU Williams 10/12/44; 3020 BU La Junta 4/5/45; RFC Stillwater 4/8/45.

42-30270 Del Cheyenne 5/5/43; Denver 8/5/43; Gore 12/5/43; Kearney 30/5/43; ass 551BS/385BG Gt Ashfield 19/6/43; MIA Warnemünde 29/7/43. THE OLD SHILLELAGH.

42-30271 Del Cheyenne 7/5/43; Gore 8/5/43; Smoky Hill 17/5/43; Dow Fd 30/5/43; ass 379BG Kimbolton 6/6/43; tran 335BS/95BG [OE-R] Horham 28/6/43; MIA Stuttgart 6/9/43 w/Ransom; e/a, cr Pancy (?Nancy); 5EVD 1KIA 4POW; MACR 545. BOMB BOOGIE.

42-30272 Del Cheyenne 7/5/43; Gore 8/5/43; Smoky Hill 17/5/43; Dow Fd 30/5/43; ass 335BS/95BG [OE-U] Horham 15/6/43; MIA Münster 10/10/43 w/Broman; cr Haaksbergen, Hol; 1KIA 10POW; MACR 1118. FRITZ BLITZ.

42-30273 Del Cheyenne 7/5/43; Gore 8/5/43; Cheyenne 20/5/43; Smoky Hill 25/5/43; Kearney 27/5/43; Dow Fd 2/6/43; ass 303BG Molesworth 16/6/43; tran 334BS/95BG [BG-F] Horham 17/6/43; MIA Münster 10/10/43 w/Buckley; cr Lingen, Ger; 5KIA 5POW; MACR 942. PATSY ANN III.

42-30274 Del Cheyenne 8/5/43; Gore 9/5/43; Smoky Hill 17/5/43; Dow Fd 5/6/43; ass 334BS/95BG [BG-Q] Horham 15/6/43; MIA Schweinfurt 17/8/43 w/Baker; cr Mol, Bel; 3EVD 7POW; MACR 402. OUR BAY-BEE.

42-30275 Del Cheyenne 7/5/43; Gore 8/5/43; Kearney 30/5/43; Dow Fd 16/6/43; ass 548BS/385BG G Ashfield 17/6/43; MIA Bremen 8/10/43 w/Jensen; flak, cr Quackenbrück, Ger; 10POW; MACR 825. THE VIBRANT VIRGIN.

42-30276 Del Cheyenne 13/5/43; Roswell 27/5/43; Smoky Hill 29/5/43; Dow Fd 2/6/43; ass 336BS/95BG Horham 15/6/43; MIA La Pallice 16/9/43 w/Jutzi; cr Ile d'Yeu, Fr; 10POW; MACR 615. TERRY AND THE PIRATES.

42-30277 Del Cheyenne 11/5/43; Roswell 24/5/43;

3030 BU Roswell 2/6/44; 4124 BU Altus 17/7/44; RFC Altus 4/10/45.

42-30278 Del Denver 8/5/43; Gore 9/5/43; Kearney 29/5/43; Dow Fd 19/6/43; ass 550BS/385BG Gt Ashfield 20/6/43 SLY FOX; tran 418BS/100BG [LD-R] Thorpe Abbotts /43; MIA Berlin 6/3/44 w/Kendall; e/a, cr Haseluene, Ger; 10POW; MACR 3016.

42-30279 Del Denver 8/5/43; Kearney 29/5/43; Dow Fd 13/6/43; ass 549BS/385BG Gt Ashfield 14/6/43; tran 551BS; MIA Wesermünde 26/7/43 w/Daniel; e/a, cr Alte Mellum, Hol?; 7KIA 3POW; MACR 191C. BLACK JACKER.

42-30280 Del Boeing (by land) 17/6/43 (H2X); Wright Fd 5/7/43; Rome 21/7/43; Patterson 3/8/43; Kansas Cy 8/8/43; Gd Island 22/9/43; ass 812BS/482BG [MI-L] Alconbury 30/9/43; MIA 21/2/44 w/Holcombe; mech problem, ditched; MACR 2470. Recovered August 1970.

42-30281 Del Denver 8/5/43; Gore 9/5/43; Kearney 30/5/43; Dow Fd 15/6/43; ass 548BS/385BG Gt Ashfield 16/6/43; MIA Wesermünde 26/7/43 w/Duncan; e/a, ditched Nth Sea; 10KIA; MACR 191A.

42-30282 Del Denver 9/5/43; Gore 10/5/43; Smoky Hill 17/5/43; Dow Fd 30/5/43; ass 366BS/305BG [KY-N] Chelveston 10/6/43; MIA Hanover 26/7/43 w/Kuhlnan; e/a, ditched Nth Sea; 2KIA 8POW; MACR 95.

42-30283 Del Denver 9/5/43; Gore 17/5/43; Smoky Hill 19/5/43; Dow Fd 30/5/43; ass 324BS/91BG Bassingbourn 10/6/43; tran 334BS/95BG [BG-B] Horham 16/6/43; then 336BS; MIA Regensburg 17/8/43 w/Mason; cr Darmstadt, Ger; 10POW; MACR 403. MASON'S MORONS.

42-30284 Del Denver 10/5/43; Gore 20/5/43; Smoky Hill 21/5/43; Dow Fd 30/5/43; ass 334BS/95BG [BG-B] Horham 15/6/43; MIA St Nazaire 28/6/43 w/Smith; ditched Channel, 2WIA 8RTD.

42-30285 Del Denver 10/5/43; Gt Falls 16/5/43; Kearney 29/5/43; Dow Fd 15/6/43; ass 388BG Knettishall 30/9/43; tran 550BS/385BG Gt Ashfield 1/10/43; then 549BS; MIA Oschersleben 28/7/43 w/Noel; mid air coll, ditched Nth Sea; 8KIA 2POW; MACR 1890. ROUNDTRIP TICKET.

42-30286 Del Cheyenne 17/5/43; Gore 24/5/43; Smoky Hill 25/5/43; Kearney 27/5/43; Dow Fd 2/6/43; ass 336BS/95BG [ET-M] Horham 15/6/43; MIA St Nazaire 28/6/43 w/Bender; no gas, ditched Channel; 10RTD. SPOOK IV.

42-30287 Del Cheyenne 11/5/43; Gore 23/5/43; Roswell 21/6/43; 3030 BU Roswell 2/6/44; WO 16/10/44; Recl Comp 25/10/44.

42-30288 Del Cheyenne 9/5/43; Smoky Hill 17/5/43; Dow Fd 30/5/43; ass 412BS/95BG [QW-T] Horham 14/6/43; b/d Marienberg 9/10/43 w/Caspers; c/l Rackheath A/fd, 10RTD; sal 26/10/43. LOUISE II.

42-30289 Del Cheyenne 9/5/43; Gore 18/5/43; Geiger 25/5/43; Gt Falls 7/6/43; Smoky Hill 30/5/43; Dow Fd 12/7/43; ass 568BS/390BG [BI-H] Framlingham 13/7/43 THE DOUCHE BAG; MIA Keil 4/1/44 w/Prophett; e/a, cr Husum, Ger; 4KIA 6POW; MACR 2021. THE DULL TOOL.

42-30290 Del Cheyenne 11/5/43; Gore 24/5/43; Smoky Hill 25/5/43; Kearney 27/5/43; Dow Fd 2/6/43; ass 338BS/96BG Snetterton 12/6/43; MIA Kassel 30/7/43 w/Pelusi; e/a, cr Aalst, Fr; 5KIA 5POW; MACR 145. LUCKY LADY II.

42-30291 Del Cheyenne 10/5/43; Geiger 21/5/43; Ephrata 28/5/43; Walla Walla 30/5/43; Hill 31/5/43; Orlando 1/6/43; Brooksville 21/6/43; Rapid City 3/7/43; Harvard 2/8/43; 2531 BU Pampa 4/12/44; 224 BU Sioux City 10/12/44; RFC Albuquerque 22/5/45.

42-30292 Del Cheyenne 9/5/43; Gore 10/5/43; Moses Lake 22/5/43; Geiger 25/5/43; Smoky Hill 1/7/43; Dow Fd 11/7/43; ass 551BS/385BG Gt Ashfield 12/7/43; tran 569BS/390BG [CC-Q] Framlingham 13/7/43; MIA Bremen 8/10/43 w/Sheperd; e/a, cr Quelkhorn, Ger; 6KIA 4POW; MACR 783. PULSATIN' POLLY.

42-30293 Del Cheyenne 11/5/43; Roswell 24/5/43; 3030 BU Roswell 2/6/44; 3010 BU Williams 9/12/44; 3010 BU La Junta 23/4/45; RFC Stillwater 4/8/45.

42-30294 Del Cheyenne 11/5/43; Roswell 24/5/43; ass 385BG SUZANNE, then RAUNCHY WOLF; WO 29/7/43.

42-30295 Del Cheyenne 11/5/43; Gore 23/5/43; Roswell 24/5/43; 3030 BU Roswell 2/6/44; 3010 BU Williams 9/12/44; 3010 BU La Junta 26/3/45; RFC Stillwater 4/8/45.

42-30296 Del Cheyenne 11/5/43; Roswell 24/5/43; Dow Fd 2/6/43; Raton 5/6/43; Roswell 15/6/43; 3030 BU Roswell 2/6/44; 3010 BU Williams 10/12/44; 3020 BU La Junta 4/6/45; RFC Stillwater 4/8/45.

42-30297 Del Cheyenne 11/5/43; Gore 23/5/43; Roswell 25/5/43; 3030 BU Roswell 2/6/44; 3010 BU Williams 12/12/44; 3010 BU La Junta 23/4/45; RFC Stillwater 7/8/45.

42-30298 Del Cheyenne 11/5/43; Gore 24/5/43; Smoky Hill 29/5/43; Dow Fd 3/6/43; ass 525BS/379BG [FR-M] Kimbolton 13/6/43 TENDER TIT TILLIE, then RAGIN' RED II; tran 837BS/487BG [4F] Lavenham 15/7/44; 78TH Fighter Wing 24/10/44; sal 29/5/45.

42-30299 Del Cheyenne 11/5/43; Gore 18/5/43; Fairfield 23/5/43; Peterson 15/6/43; ass 1st Map Gp Bolling 6/7/43; Bradley 18/7/43; Accra, Gold Coast 31/12/43; retUS 1st Ph Gp McDill 9/10/44; 4100 BU Patterson 22/10/44; 91 Ph Sq Buckley 30/12/44; sal 5/2/45.

42-30300 Del Cheyenne 11/5/43; Gore 24/5/43; Smoky Hill 25/5/43; Kearney 27/5/43; Dow Fd 2/6/43; ass 303BG Molesworth 16/6/43; tran 334BS/95BG [BG-C] Horham 17/6/43; MIA Stuttgart 6/9/43 w/Tyler; e/a. cr Stuttgart; 10POW; MACR 546. HELL-N-BACK.

42-30301 Del Cheyenne 11/5/43; Smoky Hill 25/5/43; Kearney 26/5/43; Dow Fd 2/6/43; ass 332BS/94BG [XM-B2] Earls Colne 5/6/43; Rougham 13/6/43 MISSY G; then IDIOT'S DELIGHT; tran 710BS/447BG Rattlesden 4/44; MIA Pas de Calais 19/6/44 w/Milton; flak, ditched Channel; 9KIA 1POW; MACR 5901.

42-30302 Del Cheyenne 11/5/43; Gore 21/5/43; Geiger 22/5/43; Gt Falls 7/6/43; Smoky Hill 30/5/43; Dow Fd 10/7/43; ass 568BS/390BG [BI-O] Framlingham 11/7/43; MIA Kassel 28/7/43; coll w/306BG a/c, c/l and sal as hangar queen. CALAMITY JANE.

42-30303 Del Cheyenne 11/5/43; Smoky Hill 25/5/43; Kearney 26/5/43; Dow Fd 2/6/43; ass 333BS/94BG [TS-M2] Rougham 13/6/43; MIA Duren 20/10/43 w/Loblein; mech problem, cr Nth Sea; 10KIA; MACR 903. RAIDER.

42-30304 Del Cheyenne 10/5/43; Gore 24/5/43; Smoky Hill 25/5/43; Kearney 26/5/43; Dow Fd 2/6/43; ass 334BS/95BG [BG-B] Horham 15/6/43; MIA Hanover 26/7/43 w/Quirk; cr Lavenstein, Ger; 4KIA 6POW; MACR 196.

42-30305 Del Cheyenne 11/5/43; Gore 24/5/43; Smoky Hill 25/5/43; Kearney 26/5/43; Presque Is 3/6/43; ass 305BG Chelveston 24/6/43; tran 100BG Thorpe Abbotts 30/6/43; b/d Le Bourget 10/7/43; c/l Dickleburgh, UK; 7KIA 3RTD; sal 16/7/43. FLAK SHACK.

42-30306 Del Cheyenne 10/5/43; Morrison 8/6/43; ass 306BG 9/6/43; tran 99BG Navarin 8/7/43; Oudna 4/8/43; tran Service Sq 16/8/43; 390BG Framlingham 4/1/44; sal 26/3/44.

42-30307 Del Cheyenne 11/5/43; Smoky Hill 25/5/43; Morrison 9/6/43; ass 419BS/301BG St Donat 1/7/43; Oudna 6/8/43; MIA {14m} Terni, It. 11/8/43 w/Fensel; shot down by German P-38; cr Med Sea, 6KIA 3RTD. BONNIE SUE.

42-30308 Del Cheyenne 11/5/43; Geiger 28/5/43; Gt Falls 7/6/43; Smoky Hill 30/6/43; Dow Fd 10/7/43; ass 568BS/390BG [BI-A] Framlingham 13/7/43; MIA Evreux 24/8/43 w/Daugherty; mech proble, ditched Channel; 1KIA 9RTD; MACR 393. HOT ROCKS.

42-30309 Del Cheyenne 10/5/43; Smoky Hill 23/5/43; Kearney 26/5/43; Dow Fd 2/6/43; ass 525BS/379BG [FR-P] Kimbolton 21/6/43; MIA Schweinfurt 17/8/43 w/Sexton; e/a, cr Niederwetz, Ger; 1KIA 9POW; MACR 1763. RAGING RED.

42-30310 Del Cheyenne 14/5/43; Smoky Hill 29/5/43; Morrison 9/6/43; ass 419BS/301BG St Donat 12/6/43; Oudna 6/8/43; Cerignola 7/12/43; Lucera 1/2/44; MIA {31m} Regensburg 25/2/44 w/Koch; e/a, cr Seebach; 1KIA 9POW; MACR 2597.

42-30311 Del Dallas 14/5/43; Gore 15/5/43; Love 15/5/43; Rapid City 19/6/43; Geiger 22/6/43; Gd Isle 30/6/43; Dallas 7/7/43; Kearney 23/7/43; Dow Fd 26/7/43; ass 350BS/100BG Thorpe Abbotts 26/7/43; MIA Regensburg 17/8/43 w/Hummel; e/a, cr Schorsheim, Ger; 2KIA 8POW; MACR 681.

42-30312 Del Boeing 10/5/43; Mat Com Seattle 2/6/44; ATS Boeing 20/11/44; 4134 BU Spokane 22/1/45; 4168 BU South Plains 28/1/45; RFC La Mesa 6/3/46.

42-30313 Del Cheyenne 13/5/43; Smoky Hill 31/5/43; Morrison 8/6/43; ass 346BS/99BG Navarin 24/6/43; Oudna 4/8/43; tran 97BG Depienne 15/11/43; cr on delivery; sal.

42-30314 Del Cheyenne 13/5/43; Smoky HIll 30/5/43; Morrison 8/6/43; ass 353BS/301BG St Donat 16/6/43; Oudna 6/8/43; MIA {10m} Istres le Tube 17/8/43 w/Cunningham; 7KIA 3RTD; MACR 407. BEAUTIFUL BABY.

42-30315 Del Cheyenne 13/5/43; Geiger 26/5/43; Gt Falls 7/6/43; Smoky Hill 1/7/43; Dow Fd 11/7/43; ass 569BS/390BG [CC-S] Framlingham 12/7/43; MIA Regensbury 17/8/43 w/Rapport; flak, cr Utzendorf, Switz; 10INT; MACR 391. BATTLE QUEEN 'PEG OF MY HEART'.

42-30316 Del Cheyenne 15/5/43; Gore 17/5/43; Cheyenne 20/5/43; Geiger 27/5/43; Gt Falls 7/6/43; Smoky Hill 30/6/43; Dow Fd 10/7/43; ass 568BS/390BG [BI-J] Framlingham 11/7/43; MIA Conches 24/8/43 w/Regan; e/a, cr Bellheim, Ger; 1KIA 9POW; MACR 390. MAUDIE.

42-30317 Del Cheyenne 13/5/43; Smoky Hill 30/5/43; Dow Fd 15/6/43; ass 562BS/388BG Knettishall 17/6/43; MIA Bremen 26/11/43 w/McGowan; coll w/401BG 42-37838, cr Bremen, 10KIA; MACR 3075. SECOND CHANCE.

42-30318 Del Cheyenne 15/5/43; Gore 17/5/43; Cheyenne 18/5/43; Spokane 26/5/43; Gt Falls 7/6/43; Smoky Hill 2/7/43; Dow Fd 13/7/43; ass 570BG/390BG [DI-G] Framlingham 15/7/43; MIA Bremen 8/10/43 w/Rennels; flak, cr Bremen; 1KIA 9POW; MACR 781. DEVIL'S DAUGHTER.

42-30319 Del Cheyenne 13/5/43; Gore 26/5/43; Smoky Hill 29/5/43; Morrison 8/6/43; ass 419BS/301BG St Donat 6/7/43; Oudna 6/8/43; tran 49BS/2BG Massicault 7/10/43; {9m} 419BS/301BG Oudna 14/11/43; {44m} 414BS/97BG Amendola

10/5/44; MIA Debrecen 2/6/44 w/Bond; flak & exploded, cr Debrecen; MACR 6310.

42-30320 Del Cheyenne 14/5/43; Gore 15/5/43; Cheyenne 20/5/43; Geiger 28/5/43; Gt Falls 7/6/43; Langley 25/6/43; Cutbank 27/6/43; Smoky Hill 1/7/43; Dow Fd 11/7/43; ass 569BS/390BG [CC-S] Framlingham 11/7/43; MIA Kiel 4/1/44 w/Patterson; e/a, cr Husum, Ger; 10POW; MACR 2022. COY DE COY.

42-30321 Del Cheyenne 14/5/43; Smoky Hill 29/5/43; Tinker 18/6/43; Dow Fd 27/6/43; Eglin 21/7/43; ass 419BS/301BG St Donat 6/8/43; Oudna 6/8/43; MIA {5m} Ciampino A/Fd 29/11/43 w/Hubel; mech problem, cr Villaputzu; 4RTD 6KIA; MACR 1404.

42-30322 Del Cheyenne 14/5/43; Kearney 30/5/43; Dow Fd 2/6/43; ass 412BS/95BG [QW-P] Horham 15/6/43 LIBERTY BELLE; then PATCHES; tran 2SAD Lt Staughton 18/5/44; sal n/b/d 23/6/44.

42-30323 Del Dallas 15/5/43; Gore 20/5/43; Love 16/6/43; Roswell 2/6/43; Dallas 17/7/43; Love 28/7/43; Roswell 29/7/43; 3030 BU Roswell 2/6/44; 3010 BU Williams 9/12/44; 3020 BU La Junta 20/4/45; RFC Stillwater 4/8/45.

42-30324 Del Dallas 14/5/43; Love 16/6/43; Roswell 22/6/43; Dallas 17/7/43; Roswell 29/7/43; 435BS/19BG Pyote 9/11/43; 2114 BU Lockburn 4/6/44; WO 13/6/44.

42-30325 Del Cheyenne 18/5/43; Spokane 20/5/43; Portland 4/6/43; Gt Falls 7/6/43; Smoky Hill 2/7/43; Dow Fd 13/7/43; ass 570BS/390BG [DI-D] Framlingham 18/7/43; sal 2/5/45. MISS CARRY.

42-30326 Del Dallas 15/5/43; Gore 17/5/43; Geiger 26/5/43; Love 20/6/43; Rapid City 27/6/43; Geiger 21/7/43; Pendleton 25/7/43; WO 4/8/43.

42-30327 Del Dallas 15/5/43; Gore 17/5/43; Dallas 19/5/43; Roswell 27/5/43; WO 27/2/44.

42-30328 Del Cheyenne 17/5/43; Gore 18/5/43; Gr Isle 4/6/43; Cheyenne 9/6/43; Smoky Hill 12/6/43; Dow Fd 27/6/43; ass 92BG Alconbury 8/43; tran 813BS/482BG [PC-B] Alconbury 25/8/43; later used by Royal Aircraft Establishment 22/2/45; sal 23/5/46.

42-30329 Del Cheyenne 15/5/43; Gore 17/5/43; Cheyenne 20/5/43; Smoky Hill 30/5/43; Morrison 7/6/43; ass 352BS/301BG St Donat 9/6/43; Oudna 6/8/43; Cerignola 7/12/43; Lucera 1/2/44; MIA {60m} Regensburg w/Van Nortwick; e/a, cr Trebon, Czech; 10POW; MACR 2595.

42-30330 Del Cheyenne 15/5/43; Gore 28/5/43; Smoky Hill 29/5/43; Dyersburg 27/6/43; Gr Isle 22/7/43; Presque Is 2/8/43; ass 568BS/390BG [BI-A] Framlingham 4/8/43; MIA Bremen 8/10/43 w/Peterson; flak, cr Bremen; 4KIA 6POW; MACR 784. BLOOD, GUTS & RUST II.

42-30331 Del Cheyenne 15/5/43; Gore 28/5/43; Smoky Hill 29/5/43; Tinker 19/6/43; Casper 28/6/43; Kearney 30/6/43; Eglin 6/7/43; Dow Fd 9/7/43; ass 12AF 10/7/43; Con Inv 8/7/44.

42-30332 Del Cheyenne 15/5/43; Gore 17/5/43; Cheyenne 20/5/43; Geiger 28/5/43; Walla Walla 3/6/43; Gt Falls 7/6/43; Smoky Hill 30/6/43; Dow Fd 10/7/43; ass 571BS/390BG [FC-N] Framlingham 12/7/43 SHORT STUFF; then SPIRIT OF '76; MIA Brandenburg 18/4/44 w/Procopio; flak, f/l Bulltofta, Swed; MACR 4012. (left Sweden 16/6/45). SHORT STUFF.

42-30333 Del Cheyenne 14/5/43; Gore 17/5/43; Cheyenne 20/5/43; Smoky Hill 30/5/43; Tinker 19/5/43; Casper 28/5/43; Kearney 30/6/43; Greenville 7/7/43; Eglin 10/7/43; Dow Fd 12/7/43; ass 32BS/301BG St Donat 8/43; Oudna 6/8/43; Cerignola 7/12/43; Lucera 1/2/44; {18m} tran 341BS/97BG Amendola, then weath a/c 15/7/44; sal 14/10/44. SANDMAN.

42-30334 Del Cheyenne 15/5/43; Geiger 28/5/43; Gt Falls 7/6/43; Chanute 22/6/43; Lewiston 23/6/43; Smoky Hill 2/7/43; Dow Fd 13/7/43; ass 570BS/390BG [DI-E] Framlingham 15/7/43 EIGHT BALL; MIA Frankfurt 29/1/44 w/Harding; mid air coll, cr Hamlin, Ger; 10POW; MACR 2271. VIRGIN STURGEON.

42-30335 Del Cheyenne 18/5/43; Gore 1/6/43; Smoky Hill 2/6/43; Gr Isle 3/6/43; Dow Fd 2/7/43; ass 350BS/100BG [LN-U] Thorpe Abbotts 4/7/43; MIA Stuttgart 6/9/43 w/Grenier; flak, cr Colmar, FR; 1KIA 9POW; MACR 687. SANS FINIS.

42-30336 Del Cheyenne 17/5/43; Gore 1/6/43; Smoky Hill 2/6/43; Gr Isle 4/6/43; Dow Fd 27/6/43; ass 548BS/385BG Gt Ashfield 27/6/43; MIA Anklam 9/10/43 w/Bell; mech prob, f/l Denmark; 1EVD 10POW; MACR 824. MISS NONALEE II.

42-30337 Del Cheyenne 18/5/43; Gore 20/5/43; Geiger 28/5/43; Gt Falls 7/6/43; Smoky Hill 2/7/43; Dow Fd 13/7/43; ass 570BS/390BG [DI-B] Framlingham 13/7/43 EIGHTBALL; tran 571BS [FC-D]; MIA Brunswick 10/2/44 w/Dover; c/l Streipe, Ger; 7KIA 3POW; MACR 2503. 8 BALL - FLAK HACK.

42-30338 Del Cheyenne 21/5/43; Geiger 28/5/43; Gt Falls 7/6/43; Gore 12/6/43; Smoky Hill 29/6/43; Dow Fd 10/7/43; ass 571BS/390BG [FC-P] Framlingham 11/7/43 CABIN IN THE SKY; re-named ROUGH GROUP then DOROTHY DEE; retUS Bradley 4/7/45; RFC Altus 14/8/45. Reverted to CABIN IN THE SKY.

42-30339 Del Cheyenne 17/5/43; Gore 19/5/43; Smoky Hill 29/5/43; Tinker 13/6/43; Casper 28/6/43; Kearney 13/6/43; Eglin 4/7/43; Dow Fd 7/7/43; ass 347BS/99BG Navarin 29/7/43; Oudna 4/8/43; tran 340BS/97BG Depienne 14/11/43; Cerignola 20/12/43; Amendola 16/1/44; retUS 1103 BU Morrison 21/6/44; 302 BU Hunter 29/6/44; RFC Altus 1/8/45.

42-30340 Del Cheyenne 18/5/43; Gr Isle 4/6/43; Dow Fd 25/6/43; ass 563BS/388BG Knettishall 26/6/43; MIA Berlin 8/3/44 w/Amman; e/a, cr Magdeburg, Ger; 9KIA 1POW; MACR 3079. SCREAMIN' RED ASS.

42-30341 Del Cheyenne 18/5/43; Smoky Hill 25/5/43; Morrison 8/6/43; ass 49BS/301BG St Donat 1/7/43; {2m} tran 429BS/2BG Massicault 2/8/43; {14m} 49BS/301BG Oudna 14/11/43; Cerignola 7/12/43; MIA {64m} Piraeus 11/1/44 w/Cherrington; mid air coll, cr Kalavatra, Gr; 7KIA 3RTD; MACR 1834.

42-30342 Del Cheyenne 18/5/43; Gore 20/6/43; Smoky Hill 30/5/43; Wright 30/6/43; Smoky Hill 20/7/43; Kearney 22/7/43; Dow Fd 25/7/43; ass 334BS/95BG [BG-B] Horham 28/7/43 TAINT A BIRD; tran APH Knettishall; MIA Watten 4/8/44.

42-30343 Del Cheyenne 19/5/43; Gore 20/5/43; Smoky Hill 30/5/43; Dow Fd 3/6/43; Tinker 13/6/43; Smoky Hill 22/6/43; Casper 28/6/43; Kearney 30/6/43; Eglin 4/7/43; Kearney 11/7/43; Dow Fd 12/7/43; ass 346BS/99BG Navarin 30/7/43; Oudna 4/8/43; tran 342BS/97BG Depienne 14/11/43; Cerignola 20/12/43; Amendola 16/1/44; MIA Steyr 2/4/44 w/King; e/a, cr Neustift, Aus; MACR 3586.

42-30344 Del Cheyenne 19/5/43; Gore 20/5/43; Smoky Hill 31/5/43; Morrison 8/6/43; ass 32BS/301BG St Donat 20/6/43; Oudna 6/8/43; MIA {13m} Capua, It. 4/9/43 w/Crouch; MACR 513. THE LADY EVELYN.

42-30345 Del Cheyenne 20/5/43; Smoky Hill 31/5/43; Tinker 13/6/43; Casper 28/6/43; Kearney 30/6/43; Eglin 7/7/43; Dow Fd 9/7/43; ass 352BS/301BG 15/7/43; b/d {23m} Bolzano 10/11/43 w/Lyndsly; c/l Calvi, Corsica; sal.

42-30346 Del Cheyenne 19/5/43; Smoky Hill 31/5/43; Dyersburg 27/6/43; Gr Isle 22/7/43; Presque Is 31/7/43; ass 419BS/301BG St Donat 3/7/43; Oudna 6/8/43; Cerignola 7/12/43; Lucera 1/2/44; {15m} sal 31/3/44.

42-30347 Del Cheyenne 19/5/43; Gore 20/5/43; Smoky Hill 30/5/43; Morrison 9/6/43; ass 419BS/301BG St Donat 3/7/43; Oudna 6/8/43; Cerignola 7/12/43; Lucera 1/2/44; MIA {98m} Wollersdorf 29/5/44 w/Phillips; mech problem, cr Vebelbach; 10POW; MACR 5445.

42-30348 Del Cheyenne 18/5/43; Geiger 27/5/43; Gt Falls 7/6/43; Smoky Hill 9/7/43; Dow Fd 14/7/43; ass 569BS/390BG [CC-N] Framlingham 13/7/43; MIA Bremen 16/12/43 w/Gill; e/a, cr Oldenburg, Ger; 10POW; MACR 1728. ROYAL FLUSH.

42-30349 Del Cheyenne 21/5/43; Smoky Hill 2/6/43; Gr Isle 4/6/43; Dow Fd 27/6/43; ass 563BS/388BG Knettishall 1/7/43; MIA Stuttgart 6/9/43 w/Wilken; e/a, cr Montgeux (?targis, Fr); 2EVD 8KIA; MACR 2409.

42-30350 Del Cheyenne 20/5/43; Spokane 21/5/43; Gore 1/6/43; Smoky Hill 2/6/43; Gr Isle 4/6/43; Dow Fd 27/6/43; ass 563BS/388BG Knettishall 27/6/43; MIA Bordeaux 5/12/43 w/Moyers; ditched Nth Sea; 10RTD.

42-30351 Del Cheyenne 23/5/43; Gore 25/5/43; Gr Isle 3/6/43; Dow Fd 1/7/43; ass 339BS/96BG Snetterton 12/7/43 ALCOHOL ANNIE; MIA Oschersleben 28/7/43 w/Wilcox; e/a, ditched Nth Sea; 5KIA 5RTD. MACR 142. EXCALIBER.

42-30352 Del Cheyenne 20/5/43; Smoky Hill 1/6/43; Gr Isle 4/6/43; Dow Fd 6/7/43; ass 333BS/94BG [TS-G] Rougham 27/6/43 THUNDERMUG II; 410BS [GL-G]; sal n/b/d 2/5/45; POLLY JO.

42-30353 Del Cheyenne 23/5/43; Gr Isle 3/6/43; Dow Fd 27/6/43; ass 95BG Horham 27/6/43 TEN KNIGHTS IN A BAR ROOM; tran 388BG APH Knettishall; 803BS RCM Sculthorpe; MIA Berlin 5/12/44; cr Herford, Ger.

42-30354 Del Cheyenne 23/5/43; Smoky Hill 2/6/43; Gr Isle 3/6/43; Dow Fd 20/6/43; ass 549BS/385BG Gt Ashfield 1/7/43 SWEET 17; MIA Frankfurt 29/1/44 w/Palmer; e/a, cr Charleroi, Bel; 7EVD 1KIA 2POW; MACR 2268. HUSTLIN' HUSSY.

42-30355 Del Cheyenne 23/5/43; Gr Isle 4/6/43; Dow Fd 1/7/43; ass 337BS/96BG Snetterton 4/7/43; MIA Warnemünde 28/7/43 w/Nance; e/a, cr Nth Sea; 4KIA 6POW; MACR 141. DALLAS REBEL.

42-30356 Del Cheyenne 23/5/43; Smoky Hill 2/6/43; Gr Isle 5/6/43; Dow Fd 20/6/43; ass 337BS/96BG [AW-B] 3/7/43; c/l Lt Snoring A/fd n/b/d 27/7/43, sal. TARFU II.

42-30357 Del Cheyenne 20/5/43; Smoky Hill 31/5/43; Morrison 9/6/43; ass 353BS/301BG St Donat 18/6/43; Oudna 6/8/43; Cerignola 7/12/43; MIA {46m} Piraeus 11/1/44 w/Williams; mid air coll, cr Poretson, Gr (?); 7KIA 3SURV; MACR 1831.

42-30358 Del Cheyenne 23/5/43; Gr Isle 3/6/43; Dow Fd 27/6/43; ass 350BS/100BG [LN-X] Thorpe Abbotts 4/7/43; MIA Bremen 8/10/43 w/Meadows; flak, cr Bremen; 8KIA 2POW; MACR 947. PHARTZAC.

42-30359 Del Cheyenne 21/5/43; Gore 1/6/43; Smoky Hill 2/6/43; Gr Isle 3/6/43; Dow Fd 25/6/43; ass 339BS/96BG [QJ-D] Snetterton 27/6/43; MIA Bremen 29/11/43 w/Langley; e/a, cr Oldenburg, Ger; 8KIA 2POW; MACR 1392.

42-30360 Del Cheyenne 23/5/43; Gore 1/6/43; Smoky Hill 2/6/43; Gr Isle 4/6/43; Dow Fd 28/6/43; ass 338BS/96BG [BX-P] Snetterton 1/7/43 CHINOOK;

MIA Quackenbrück 8/4/43 w/Stinnett; e/a, cr Azewijen, Hol; 2EVD 8POW; MACR 3649 LADY MILLICENT.

42-30361 Del Cheyenne 20/5/43; Smoky Hill 31/5/43; Morrison 9/6/43; ass 341BS/97BG Château-du-Rhumel 18/6/43; Pont-du-Fahs 1/8/43; Depienne 15/8/43; Cerignola 20/12/43; Amendola 16/1/44; weath a/c 9/7/44; retUS Sth Plains 4/5/45; RFC Ontario 27/6/45.

42-30362 Del Cheyenne 23/5/43; Gore 25/5/43; Kearney 5/6/43; Dow Fd 1/7/43; ass 561BS/388BG Knettishall 7/7/43; MIA Beaumont Sur Oise 9/9/43 w/Porter; flak, cr Houilles, Fr; 5EVD 6POW; MACR 3134. WEE BONNIE II.

42-30363 Del Cheyenne 21/5/43; Smoky Hill 1/6/43; Gr Isle 5/6/43; Dow Fd 1/7/43; ass 338BS/96BG Snetterton 4/7/43 RUTH L III; tran 388BG APH Knettishall; MIA Hemmingstadt 14/9/44.

42-30364 Del Cheyenne 21/5/43; Smoky Hill 1/6/43; Gr Isle 4/6/43; Dow Fd 29/6/43; ass 551BS/385BG Gt Ashfield 26/6/43; MIA Bordeaux 24/8/43 w/Grodi; e/a, cr Toulouse, Fr; 6EVD 3KIA; MACR 395.

42-30365 Del Cheyenne 20/5/43; Smoky Hill 31/5/43; Dow Fd 11/7/43; ass 337BS/96BG [AW-B] Snetterton 13/7/43; Duren mission aborted 17/10/43 w/Stoneburner; caught fire, cr Nth Sea; 10KIA; MACR 1019. RUM BOOGIE III.

42-30366 Del Cheyenne 24/5/43; Gore 1/6/43; Smoky Hill 2/6/43; Gr Isle 4/6/43; Dow Fd 25/6/43; ass 338BS/96BG [BX-A] Snetterton 26/6/43; n/b/d, cr Silver Fox Farm, Taverham, UK; 16/12/43; 10RTD; sal 31/1/44. FERTILE MYRTLE 3rd.

42-30367 Del Cheyenne 23/5/43; Gore 1/6/43; Smoky Hill 2/6/43; Gr Isle 4/6/43; Dow Fd 27/6/43; ass 337BS/96BG [AW-Y] Snetterton 1/7/43; MIA Bremen 8/10/43 w/Bolstad; e/a, cr Bremen; 7KIA 3POW; MACR 852. FLAK HAPPY.

42-30368 Del Cheyenne 23/5/43; Gore 1/6/43; Smoky Hill 2/6/43; Gr Isle 4/6/43; Dow Fd 7/6/43; ass 338BS/96BG [BX-R] Snetterton 26/6/43; MIA Bremen 20/12/43 w/Fuller; flak, cr Bremen; 10POW; MACR 1703. GIL.

42-30369 Del Cheyenne 23/5/43; Gr Isle 4/6/43; Dow Fd 28/6/43; ass 339BS/96BG [QJ-K] Snetterton 1/7/43; MIA Augsburg 16/3/44 w/Hanish; e/a, cr Balingen, Ger; 3KIA 7POW; MACR 3421. DAISY JUNE IV - BOMB-BOOGIE.

42-30370 Del Cheyenne 23/5/43; Gr Isle 4/6/43; Dow Fd 27/6/43; ass 338BS/96BG Snetterton 4/7/43 LITTLE CAESER; then 337BS; MIA Warnemünde 29/7/43 w/Walters; mid air coll w/42-5908 (388BG); cr Nth Sea, 10KIA; MACR 144. VENI VEDI VICI.

42-30371 Del Cheyenne 23/5/43; Gr Isle 6/4/43; Dow Fd 25/6/43; ass 560BS/388BG Knettishall 26/6/43; MIA Gdynia 9/10/43 w/?; 2KIA 8POW. IZA ANGEL II.

42-30372 Del Cheyenne 24/5/43; Gore 25/5/43; Gr Isle 4/6/43; Dow Fd 27/6/43; ass 413BS/96BG [MZ-P] Snetterton 26/6/43; MIA Duren 10/10/43 w/Grimes; e/a, cr Venray, Bel; 2EVD 4KIA 4POW; MACR 1017. SHACK RABBIT III.

42-30373 Del Cheyenne 24/5/43; Gore 25/5/53; Gr Isle 4/6/43; Dow Fd 1/7/43; ass 338BS/96BG [BX-T] Snetterton 4/7/43; MIA Bremen 8/10/43 w/Jones; flak, cr Weingarten, Ger; 5KIA 6POW; MACR 854. LUCKY LADY III.

42-30374 Del Cheyenne 24/5/43; Gore 25/5/43; Gr Isle 3/6/43; Dow Fd 27/6/43; ass 332BS/94BG [XM-A] Rougham 27/6/43; b/d Duren 20/10/43; sal 21/10/43. LITTLE SIR ECHO.

42-30375 Del Cheyenne 24/5/43; Gore 25/5/43; Kearney 5/6/43; Dalhart 27/6/43; Gr isle 26/7/43; Patterson 8/8/43; Gr Isle 11/8/43; Presque Is 16/8/43; ass 365BS/305BG [XK-B] Chelveston 3/9/43; tran 1 BAD Burtonwood 20/5/44; retUS 8STA Homestead 24/7/44; 4136 BU Tinker 25/7/44; Recl Comp 17/7/45. MISS DONNA MAE.

42-30376 Del Cheyenne 23/5/43; Gore 1/6/43; Smoky Hill 2/6/43; Gr Isle 3/6/43; Dow Fd 25/6/43; ass 333BS/94BG Rougham 26/6/43 BOUNCING BITCH; tran 331BS; MIA Bordeaux 5/12/43 w/Fant; e/a, ditched Channel; 10RTD. SOUTHERN BELLE.

42-30377 Del Cheyenne 24/5/43; Gore 25/5/43; Gr Isla 4/6/43; Dow Fd 27/6/43; ass 412BS/95BG [QW-R] Horham 12/7/43; MIA Marienburg 9/10/43 w/Eherts; exploded mid air, cr Nth Sea; 10KIA; MACR 854. ROGER THE LODGER II.

42-30378 Del Cheyenne 25/5/43; Kearney 5/6/43; Dow Fd 4/7/43; ass 331BS/94BG [QE-A] Rougham 4/7/43 WOLF PACK; MIA Brunswick 10/2/44 w/Anderson; e/a, cr Biemelten, Ger (?); 10POW; MACR 2386. GOOD TIME CHOLLY III.

42-30379 Del Cheyenne 24/5/43; Gore 25/5/43; Kearney 4/6/43; Dyersburg 27/6/43; Gr Isle 22/7/43; Presque Is 31/7/43; ass 12AF 7/8/43; MIA Tunis 25/1/44; MACR 2059.

42-30380 Del Cheyenne 24/5/43; Gore 25/5/43; Kearney 9/6/43; Dow 27/6/43; ass 350BS/100BG [LN-W] Thorpe Abbotts 1/7/43; retUS 8STA Homestead 21/6/44; 4136 BU Tinker 30/6/44; RFC Bush Fd 19/5/45.

42-30381 Del Cheyenne 25/5/43; Tinker 7/6/43; Smoky Hill 18/6/43; Casper 28/6/43; Kearney 30/6/43; Eglin 7/7/43; Kearney 9/6/43; Dow Fd 10/7/43; ass 419BS/301BG St Donat 26/7/43; Oudna 6/8/43; Cerignola 7/12/43; Lucera 1/2/44; {17m} tran 341BS/97BG Amendola? ; MIA Budapest 3/4/44 w/Daniels; flak, cr Sarajevo, Yugo; MACR 3581. LITTLE RED HEAD.

42-30382 Del Cheyenne 25/5/43; Kearney 5/6/43; Bangor 6 4/7/43; ass 331BS/94BG [QE-Z2] Rougham 8/7/43; sal 23/6/43; retUS 1377 BU Grenier 16/10/43; 4104 BU Rome 17/1/43; 4168 BU Sth Plains 13/7/44; RFC Kingman 3/11/45. HORRIBLE HANKS.

42-30383 Del Cheyenne 25/5/43; Kearney 5/6/43; Dow Fd 7/7/43; ass 332BS/94BG [XM-D2] Rougham 8/7/43; MIA Schweinfurt 14/10/43 w/Brennan; e/a, ditched Nth Sea; 10RTD. BRENNAN'S CIRCUS.

42-30384 Del Cheyenne 25/5/43; Tinker 6/6/43; Memphis 8/6/43; ass 347BS/99BG Navarin 29/6/43; Oudna 4/8/43; b/d Bolzano 10/11/43, c/l Calvi, Corsica; tran 340BS/97BG Depienne 14/11/43; Cerignola 20/12/43; Amendola 16/1/44; retUS 1103 BU Morrison 17/4/44; 4104 BU Rome 27/4/44; RFC Albuquerque 27/7/45. SIROCCO.

42-30385 Del Cheyenne 25/5/43; Kearney 5/6/43; Dow Fd 11/7/43; ass 353BS/301BG St Donat 18/7/43; Oudna 6/8/43; Cerignola 7/12/43; Lucera 1/2/44; MIA {87m} Wiener Nuedorf 26/7/44 w/Kerr; e/a, cr Baden; 9KIA 1POW; MACR 7000.

42-30386 Del Cheyenne 27/5/43; Smoky Hill 11/6/43; Dyersburg 27/6/43; Smoky Hill 28/6/43; Gr Isle 22/7/43; Presque Is 2/8/43; ass 364BS/305BG [WF-E] Chelveston 6/9/43; MIA Ludwigshafen 7/1/44 w/Lathrop; flak, ditched off Calais; 2EVD 2KIA 6POW; MACR 1963.

42-30387 Del Cheyenne 25/5/43; Kearney 5/6/43; Gore 7/6/43; Tinker 9/6/43; Dalhart 15/6/43; Gr Isle 27/6/43; Presque Is 3/8/43; ass 326BS/92BG [JW-A] Alconbury 21/8/43; MIA Schweinfurt 14/10/43 w/Maj Ott; e/a, cr Kastellerweg, Ger?; 1KIA 9POW; MACR 849.

42-30388 Del Cheyenne 26/5/43; Smoky Hill 11/6/43; Gr Isle 20/6/43; Geiger 22/6/43; smoky Hill 23/6/43; Dow Fd 5/7/43; ass 249BS/2BG Ain M'Lila 13/7/43; Massicault 31/7/43; MIA {7m} Istres le Tube 17/8/43 w/Fisher; #4 engine fire, eight chutes seen; MACR 406. SUNNY BOY.

42-30389 Del Cheyenne 26/5/43; Gore 27/5/43; Cheyenne 2/6/43; Smoky Hill 12/6/43; Geiger 22/6/43; Smoky Hill 23/6/43; Dow Fd 5/7/43; ass 331BS/94BG [QE-Z] Rougham 7/7/43; MIA Regensburg 17/8/43 w/Nayovitz; e/a, cr Lummen, Bel; 2EVD 6KIA 2POW; MACR 323. DEAR MOM.

42-30390 Del Cheyenne 26/5/43; Smoky Hill 10/6/43; 2345 BU Clovis 24/6/44; 247 BU Smoky Hill 26/1/45; 2038 BU Jackson 3/2/45; 232 BU Dalhart 22/10/45; RFC Kingman 27/10/45.

42-30391 Del Cheyenne 29/5/43; Kearney 9/6/43; Dyersburg 27/6/43; Gr Isle 22/7/43; Presque Is 2/8/43; ass 97BG Pont-du-Fahs 12/8/43; Depienne 15/8/43; Cerignola 20/12/43; Amendola 16/1/44; tran 301BG Cerignola, from Cairo 25/11/44; used as weather a/c; sal 1/5/45.

42-30392 Del Cheyenne 29/5/43; Kearney 9/6/43; Dyersburg 27/6/43; Gr Isle 22/7/43; Presque Is 2/8/43; ass 414BS/97BG Depienne 26/8/43; Cerignola 20/12/43; Amendola 16/1/44; blew up while being re-fuelled 21/4/44; sal.

42-30393 Del Cheyenne 28/5/43; Gore 7/6/43; Tinker 8/6/43; Memphis 24/6/43; Presque Is 2/7/43; ass 348BS/99BG Navarin 11/7/43; Oudna 4/8/43; tran 340BS/97BG Depienne 14/11/43; Cerignola 20/12/43; cr 31/12/43; sal. LUCKY LADY.

42-30394 Del Cheyenne 26/5/43; Kearney 5/6/43; Dow Fd 27/6/43; ass 339BS/96BG Snetterton 27/6/43; MIA Oschersleben 28/7/43 w/Covert; e/a, ditched Nth Sea; 4KIA 6POW; MACR 143.

42-30395 Del Cheyenne 27/5/43; Roswell 7/6/43; 3030 BU Roswell 2/6/44; RFC Albuquerque 3/8/45.

42-30396 Del Cheyenne 26/5/43; Gore 27/5/43; Tinker 9/6/43; Presque Is 27/6/43; ass 348BS/99BG Navarin 11/7/43; Oudna 4/8/43; MIA Bologna 2/9/43 w/Caraberis; 2EVD 8POW; MACR 565.

42-30397 Del Cheyenne 27/5/43; Roswell 7/6/43; 3030 BU Roswell 2/6/44; 3508 BU Truax 23/10/43; 3030 BU Roswell 27/10/43; 4126 BU San Bernadino 13/1/45; 3030 BU Roswell 1/5/45; RFC Albuquerque 3/8/45.

42-30398 Del Cheyenne 27/5/43; Tinker 6/6/43; Memphis 8/6/43; ass 429BS/2BG 19/6/43; MIA {37m} Genoa 29/10/43 w/Howell; flak, exploded; five chutes seen; MACR 1111. PATCHES.

42-30399 Del Cheyenne 27/5/43; Roswell 7/6/43; 225 BU Rapid City 3/8/44; WO 3/8/44.

42-30400 Del Cheyenne 28/5/43; Roswell 9/6/43; Dyersburg 7/6/43; 3030 BU Roswell 2/6/44; 4124 BU Altus 20/7/45; RFC Altus 9/10/45.

42-30401 Del Cheyenne 28/5/43; Kearney 9/6/43; Dow Fd 27/6/43; ass 338BS/96BG Snetterton 26/6/43; MIA Oschersleben 28/7/43 w/Hettrick; e/a, cr Nth Sea; 10KIA; MACR 139.

42-30402 Del Cheyenne 28/5/43; Kearney 9/6/43; Dow Fd 27/6/43; ass 418BS/100BG Thorpe Abbotts 25/6/43; MIA Stuttgart 6/9/43 w/?; to Switzerland; 1INT 9POW; MACR 688. THE POONTANG.

42-30403 Del Cheyenne 29/5/43; Smoky Hill 6/10/43; Rapid City 20/6/43; Geiger 23/6/43; Dow Fd 5/7/43; ass 20BS/2BG Ain M'Lila 23/7/43; Massicault 31/7/43; {33m} tran 419BS/301BG Oudna 14/11/43; Cerignola 7/12/43; Lucera 1/2/44; {62m} sal {total 95m} 5/11/45.

42-30404 Del Cheyenne 27/5/43; Roswell 9/6/43; 3030 BU Roswell 2/6/44; 3017 BU Hobbs 28/4/45; RFC Altus 14/9/45.

42-30405 Del Cheyenne 27/5/43; Tinker 8/6/43;

Nashville 20/6/43; Presque Is 2/6/43; ass 346BS/99BG Navarin 11/7/43; Oudna 4/8/43; c/l 12/10/43 w/Donahue, rep; tran 414BS/97BG Depienne 14/11/43; Cerignola 20/12/43; Amendola 16/1/43; MIA Steyr 24/3/44 w/Monthei; mid air coll, tail cut off; cr Bosawski; 3KIA 7RTD; MACR 2392.

42-30406 Del Cheyenne 27/5/43; Roswell 9/6/43; Hobbs 7/7/43; Roswell 6/8/43; 3030 BU Roswell 2/6/44; 3010 BU Williams 10/12/44; 3020 BU La Junta 29/3/45; RFC Searcey Fd 4/8/45.

42-30407 Del Cheyenne 27/5/43; Gore 7/6/43; Tinker 10/6/43; Memphis 20/6/43; Eglin 27/6/43; Kearney 6/7/43; Presque Is 9/7/43; ass 414BS/97BG Château-du-Rhumel 19/7/43; Pont-du-Fahs 1/8/43; Depienne 15/8/43; Cerignola 20/12/43; Amendola 16/1/44; 100th mission Ferrara 14/5/44; retUS Morrison 15/4/45; Rome 28/6/45; RFC Bush Fd 4/7/45. WAR PAPPY.

42-30408 Del Cheyenne 28/5/43; Gore 9/6/43; Dalhart 27/6/43; Tinker 7/7/43; Gr Isle 28/7/43; Presque Is 4/8/43; ass 327BS/92BG [UX-Q] Alconbury 14/8/43; blew up Helmdon, UK, (Heilbronn, Ger.?) after recall 30/11/43 w/Woodward; MACR 688; sal 13/12/43.

42-30409 Del Cheyenne 28/5/43; Gore 8/6/43; Roswell 12/6/43; slated for 94BG but WO 30/7/44.

42-30410 Del Cheyenne 30/5/43; Dallas 12/6/43; Love 20/7/43; Ephrata 23/7/43; Ardmore 27/10/43; 222 BU Ardmore 22/1/44; RFC Ontario 6/6/45.

42-30411 Del Cheyenne 26/5/43; Kearney 9/6/43; Dalhart 27/6/43; Gr Isle 26/7/43; Presque Is 3/8/43; ass 568BS/390BG [BI-J] 6/8/43 ROSE MARIE; MIA Emden 11/12/43 w/Lashly; flak, cr Norden, Ger; 2KIA 8POW; MACR 1727. HOT ROCKS.

42-30412 Del Cheyenne 28/5/43; Roswell 9/6/43; Kearney 10/6/43; Dow Fd 2/7/43; ass 339BS/96BG [QJ-B] Snetterton 3/7/43; MIA {15m} Berlin 4/3/44 w/Herring; e/a, cr Vegenstedt, Ger; 6EVD 5POW; MACR 3425. MISCHIEF-MAKER II.

42-30413 Del Cheyenne 28/5/43; Roswell 9/6/43; 3030 BU Roswell 2/6/44; 2509 BU Big Spring 31/7/44; 3705 BU Lowry 1/11/44; 3030 BU Roswell 8/12/44; RFC Altus 9/10/45.

42-30414 Del Cheyenne 28/5/43; Kearney 9/6/43; Dow Fd 7/7/43; ass 385BG Gt Ashfield 8/7/43; sal 31/1/44. ROUNDTRIP TICKET II.

42-30415 Del Cheyenne 28/5/43; Kearney 9/6/43; Dow Fd 5/7/43; ass 410BS/94BG [GL-P] Rougham 7/7/43 SUGAR PUSS III; MIA Emden 11/12/43 w/Berwalt; e/a, cr Orvelte, Hol; 1KIA 10POW; MACR 1257. LUCKY LADY,

42-30416 Del Cheyenne 25/5/43; Gore 12/6/43; Smoky Hill 14/6/43; Rapid City 20/6/43; Geiger 22/6/43; Smoky Hill 23/6/43; Dow Fd 5/7/43; ass 346BS/99BG Navarin 30/7/43; Oudna 4/8/43; b/d Mestre 6/10/43 w/Crooks; c/l Foggia and WO; but repaired at depot and tran 340BS/97BG Cerignola; Amendola 16/1/44; MIA Padua 11/3/44 w/Taylor; e/a, ditched Adriatic; MACR 2835. LIL' JOAN.

42-30417 Del Cheyenne 29/5/43; Gore 31/5/43; Cheyenne 4/6/43; Smoky Hill 11/6/43; Gr Isle 14/6/43; WO 1/7/43.

42-30418 Del Cheyenne 29/5/43; Gore 31/5/43; Smoky Hill 10/6/43; Gr Isle 14/6/43; Dow Fd 27/6/43; ass 94BG Rougham 27/6/43; tran 334BS/95BG [BG-L] Horham 7/43; MIA Bonn 12/8/43 w/Lemke; c/l Mutnenich, Ger; 10POW; MACR 254. PICADILLY COMMANDO.

42-30419 Del Cheyenne 30/5/43; Gore 10/6/43; Smoky Hill 13/6/43; Rapid City 19/6/43; Geiger 22/6/43; Smoky Hill 23/6/43; Dow Fd 5/7/43; ass 419BS/301BG St Donat 15/8/43; Oudna 6/8/43; MIA {35m} Istres le Tube 16/11/43 w/Westbrook; e/a, cr Med Sea; 10KIA; MACR 1127.

42-30420 Del Cheyenne 30/5/43; Gore 1/6/43; Rapid City 10/6/43; Geiger 22/6/43; Gr Isle 28/6/43; Laurel 1/7/43; Gr Isle 18/7/43; Dow Fd 20/7/43; ass 340BS/97BG Pont-du-Fahs 1/8/43; Depienne 15/8/43; Cerignola 20/12/43; Amendola 16/1/44; weather a/c from 9/7/44; retUS 1103 BU Morrison 13/3/45; 4100 BU Patterson 23/5/45; 2137 BU Hendricks 28/4/45; RFC Altus 6/9/45. HER DID.

42-30421 Del Cheyenne 29/5/43; Kearney 14/6/43; Dow Fd 29/6/43; ass 561BS/388BG Knettishall 5/7/43; MIA Emden 2/10/43 w/Felece; flak, cr Emden; 10KIA; MACR 3135.

42-30422 Del Cheyenne 30/5/43; Gore 10/6/43; Smoky Hill 13/6/43; Rapid City 19/6/43; Geiger 22/6/43; Smoky Hill 23/6/43; Tinker 30/6/43; Smoky Hill 4/7/43; Dow Fd 16/7/43; ass 422BS/305BG [JJ-B] Chelveston 12/8/43; tran 1 BAD Burtonwood 20/5/44; retUS 8ATS Homestead 23/7/44; 4136 BU Tinker 6/8/44; Recl Comp 17/5/45. ANY TIME ANNIE.

42-30423 Del Cheyenne 29/5/43; Gore 31/5/43; Rapid City 16/6/43; Dow Fd 5/7/43; ass 407BS/92BG [PY-P] Alconbury 7/8/43; MIA Frankfurt 4/2/44 w/Cook; flak, cr Kurzell, Ger; 2EVD 8POW; MACR 2237.

42-30424 Del Cheyenne 29/5/43; Rapid City 18/6/43; Geiger 22/6/43; Gr Isle 29/6/43; Dow Fd 20/7/43; ass 419BS/301BG Oudna 12/8/43; Cerignola 7/12/43; MIA {31m} Innsbruck 15/12/43; sal. THE SKY HAG.

42-30425 Del Cheyenne 30/5/43; Smoky Hill 12/6/43; Rapid City 19/6/43; Geiger 22/6/43; Dow Fd 5/7/43; ass 333BS/94BG [TS-J] Rougham 9/7/43; MIA Oschersleben 11/1/44 w/Lemly; e/a, cr Abensen, ; 12POW; MACR 1888. ROGER DODG'-HER.

42-30426 Del Cheyenne 29/5/43; Gore 31/5/43; Dallas 11/6/43; Smoky Hill 14/6/43; Love 17/7/43; Moses Lake 20/7/43; 325 BU Avon Park 9/4/44; RFC Altus 6/9/45.

42-30427 Del Cheyenne 30/5/43; Rapid City 19/6/43; Dow Fd 29/6/43; ass 410BS/94BG [GL-W] Rougham 9/7/43; LIL' OPERATOR.

42-30428 Del Cheyenne 30/5/43; ass 429BS/2BG Massicault 6/8/43; {24m} tran 32BS/301BG Oudna 14/11/43; Cerignola 7/12/43; Lucera 1/2/44; MIA {29m} Regensburg 25/2/44 w/Epps; e/a, cr Krakaudorf, Ger; MACR 2591. TOUCHY GOOSE.

42-30429 Del Cheyenne 30/5/43; Gore 1/6/43; Geiger 22/6/43; Gr Isle 29/6/43; Dow Fd 20/7/43; slated for 94BG, but ass 340BS/97BG Château-du-Rhumel 29/7/43; Pont-du-Fahs 1/8/43; Depienne 15/8/43; Cerignola 20/12/43; Amendola 16/1/44; MIA Steyr 2/4/44 w/Braun; e/a, cr Grossramming, Aus; MACR 3583.

42-30430 Del Cheyenne 30/5/43; Gore 2/6/43; Cheyenne 16/6/43; Roswell 21/6/43; Gore 25/6/43; 3030 BU Roswell 2/6/44; RRD Kansas City 12/8/44; 3030 BU Roswell 6/11/44; 3017 BU Hobbs 29/4/45; RFC Altus 31/8/45.

42-30431 Del Cheyenne 30/5/43; Gore 25/6/43; Lowry 27/6/43; Gore 1/7/43; Denver 13/7/43; Lowry 15/7/43; Wright 10/9/43; Scott 8/10/43; ass 423BS/306BG [RD-F] Thurleigh 19/10/43; retUS Bradley 21/6/44; Ypsilanti 22/6/44; RFC Altus 29/10/45. KWITCHURBITCHIN.

42-30432 Del Cheyenne 30/5/43; Gore 13/6/43; Rapid City 19/6/43; Geiger 22/6/43; Smoky Hill 23/6/43; Dow Fd 5/7/43; ass 342BS/97BG Château-du-Rhumel 13/7/43; Pont-du-Fahs 1/8/43; Depienne 15/8/43; c/t/o 20/12/43, (lost two engines) w/Mayo; 10RTD; sal. PISTOL PACKIN' MAMA.

42-30433 Del Cheyenne 1/6/43; Gore 2/6/43; Smoky Hill 12/6/43; Rapid City 19/6/43; Geiger 22/6/43; Smoky Hill 23/6/43; Dow Fd 5/7/43; ass 410BS/94BG [GL-U] Rougham 5/7/43 JIMMY BOY; MIA Posnan 11/4/44 w/Vaughn; flak, f/l Sweden; 10INT; MACR 4437. MISS DONNA MAE.

42-30434 Del Cheyenne 31/5/43; Smoky Hill 12/6/43; Rapid City 19/6/43; Geiger 22/6/43; Smoky Hill 23/6/43; Dow Fd 13/7/43; ass 570BS/390BG [DI-A] Framlingham 18/7/43; MIA Regensburg 25/2/44 w/Bowman; flak, cr Laon, Fr; 2KIA 8POW; MACR 2659. BETTY BOOP - THE PISTOL PACKIN' MAMA.

42-30435 Del Cheyenne 31/5/43; Gore 16/6/43; Smoky Hill 17/6/43; Rapid City 19/6/43; Geiger 22/6/43; Dow Fd 5/7/43; ass 342BS/97BG Château-du-Rhumel 13/7/43; Pont-du-Fahs 1/8/43; Depienne 15/8/43; Cerignola 20/12/43; Amendola 16/1/44; weather a/c from 15/7/44; retUS 1103 BU Morrison 19/3/45; 4100 BU Patterson 27/3/45; RFC Altus 28/8/45.

42-30436 Del Cheyenne 31/5/43; Smoky Hill 13/6/43; Rapid City 19/6/43; Geiger 22/6/43; Smoky Hill 23/6/43; Dow Fd 5/7/43; ass 414BS/97BG Château-du-Rhumel 13/7/43; Pont-du-Fahs 1/8/43; Depienne 15/8/43; Cerignola 20/12/43; Amendola 16/1/44; MIA Budapest 3/4/44 w/Harris; e/a, cr Budapest; MACR 3962.

42-30437 Del Cheyenne 31/5/43; Gore 18/6/43; Rapid City 19/6/43; Geiger 22/6/43; Gr Isle 29/6/43; Dow Fd 24/7/43; ass 97BG Château-du-Rhumel 24/7/43; Pont-du-Fahs 1/8/43; Depienne 15/8/43; Cerignola 20/12/43; Amendola 16/1/44; retUS 302 BU Hunter 13/11/44; 4100 BU Patterson 22/11/44; 611 BU Eglin 30/4/45; 75 BU Ashville 26/6/45; 123 BU Seymour Johnson 14/8/45; 76 BU Langley 3/9/46.

42-30438 Del Cheyenne 31/5/43; Gore 18/6/43; Rapid City 20/6/43; Geiger 23/6/43; Gr Isle 29/6/43; Dow Fd 23/7/43; ass 414BS/97BG Pont-du-Fahs 1/8/43; Depienne 15/8/43; MIA Ancona, It. 14/10/43 w/Walker; cr in sea; MACR 973.

42-30439 Del Cheyenne 1/6/43; Gore 2/6/43; Dow Fd 8/7/43; ass 410BS/94BG [GL-S] Rougham 9/7/43; sal 31/5/45. DONNA LOU II.

42-30440 Del Cheyenne 1/6/43; Smoky Hill 11/6/43; Dyersburg 27/6/43; Gr Isle 22/7/43; Presque Is 3/8/43; ass 340BS/97BG Pont-du-Fahs 8/8/43; Depienne 15/8/43; Cerignola 20/12/43; Amendola 16/1/44; coll w/gas truck 22/1/44, sal.

42-30441 Del Cheyenne 1/6/43; Roswell 20/6/43; 3030 BU Roswell 2/6/44; 3010 BU Williams 9/12/44; 3020 BU La Junta 29/3/45; RFC Searcey Fd 4/8/45.

42-30442 Del Cheyenne 1/6/43; Gore 12/6/43; Rapid City 19/6/43; Geiger 22/6/43; Dow Fd 5/7/43; ass 414BS/97BG Château-du-Rhumel 21/7/43; Pont-du-Fahs 1/8/43; Depienne 15/8/43; blew up while loading for Sulmona, It. mission 27/8/43; 6KIA 6INJ

42-30443 Del Cheyenne 1/6/43; Gore 12/6/43; Smoky Hill 14/6/43; Rapid City 19/6/43; Geiger 22/6/43; Smoky Hill 23/6/43; Dow Fd 5/7/43; ass 352BS/301BG St Donat 13/7/43; Oudna 6/8/43; f/l Calvi, Cors 31/11/43; 10RTD; rep as weather a/c from 27/7/44; tran depot 8/10/44; retUS 1103 BU Morrison 29/3/45; 4100 BU Patterson 3/4/45; RFC Bush Fd 7/7/45.

42-30444 Del Cheyenne 1/6/43; Gore 14/6/43; Kearney 15/6/43; Dow Fd 8/7/43; ass 332BS/94BG [XM-C2] Rougham 8/7/43 RAMROD RAMSBOTTOM; MIA Bordeaux 5/1/44 w/Lockwood (Adcock?); e/a, ditched Biscay; 1KIA 4POW 5RTD; MACR 1893. BLACK JACK IV.

42-30445 Del Cheyenne 1/6/43; Smoky Hill 11/6/43; mid air explosion near Rapid City 20/6/43 w/Owens;

a/c disintegrated when falling; 10KIA and 1 chute failed. Sal.

42-30446 Del Cheyenne 1/6/43; Gore 12/6/43; Smoky Hill 14/6/43; Tinker 22/6/43; Kearney 26/6/43; Eglin 7/7/43; Dow Fd 9/7/43; ass 348BS/99BG Navarin 29/7/43; Oudna 4/8/43; MIA Athens 10/10/43 w/Gilmore; 5 chutes seen, 1EVD; MACRs 924 & 6615.

42-30447 Del Cheyenne 1/6/43; Smoky Hill 11/6/43; Gore 22/6/43; Kearney 15/7/43; Dow Fd 20/7/43; ass 92BG Alconbury 21/7/43; b/d Schweinfurt 17/8/43; sal.

42-30448 Del Cheyenne 1/6/43; Gore 16/6/43; WO 21/6/43.

42-30449 Del Cheyenne 1/6/43; Rapid City 20/6/43; Geiger 22/6/43; Gr Isle 28/6/43; Dow Fd 18/7/43; ass 96BS/2BG Massicault 6/8/43; b/d {17m} Battaglia 15/9/43 w/Train; c/l 15 mls from base; WO. JULIE A.

42-30450 Del Cheyenne 1/6/43; Gore 14/6/43; Kearney 15/6/43; Eglin 7/7/43; Dow Fd 8/7/43; ass 332BS/94BG Rougham 8/7/43; trans 410BS; MIA Wilhelmshaven (T/O) 26/7/43 w/Alsop; GR, cr Nth Sea; 9KIA 1POW; MACR 84. RAMSBITCH.

42-30451 Del Cheyenne 1/6/43; Rapid 15/6/43; Gore 24/6/43; Portland 11/7/43; Gr Isle 21/7/43; Presque Is 7/8/43; ass 368BS/306BG [BO-N] Thurleigh 3/9/43; sal n/b/d 5/7/44. V-MAIL GETS THERE FASTEST.

42-30452 Del Cheyenne 3/6/43; Kearney 16/6/32; Dow Fd 29/6/43; ass 331BS/94BG Rougham 1/7/43; sal 6/8/43.

42-30453 Del Cheyenne 3/6/43; Rapid City 15/6/43; Geiger 22/6/43; Gr Isle 28/6/43; Dow Fd 14/7/43; ass 333BS/94BG [TS-K] Rougham 13/7/43; MIA Regensburg 17/8/43 w/Davison; flak, cr Saverne, Fr; 3EVD 1KIA 6POW; MACR 831. THUNDERBIRD.

42-30454 Del Cheyenne 3/6/43; Smoky Hill 14/6/43; Rapid City 19/6/43; Geiger 22/6/43; Smoky Hill 23/6/43; Dow Fd 5/7/43; ass 333BS/94BG [TS-B] Rougham 7/7/43; MIA Emden 9/9/43 w/Thalman; e/a, ditched Nth Dea; 1KIA 9POW; MACR 733. RELUCTANT DRAGON.

42-30455 Del Cheyenne 3/6/43; Kearney 14/6/43; Dalhart 27/6/43; Gr Isle 26/7/43; ass 569BS/390BG [CC-R] Framlingham 6/8/43; MIA Knaben 16/11/43 w/Becker; e/a, cr Nth Sea; 10KIA; MACR 1400. SCHIFLISS SKUNK.

42-30456 Del Cheyenne 4/6/43; Rapid City 16/6/43; Geiger 22/6/43; Gr Isle 28/6/43; Dow Fd 18/7/43; ass 96BS/2BG Massicault 6/8/43; MIA {7m} Sulmona, It. 27/8/43 w/Koch; flak, two chutes seen; MACR 481. CACTUS CLIPPER.

42-30457 Del Cheyenne 4/6/43; Gore 16/6/43; Kearney 18/6/43; Dow Fd 8/7/43; ass 331BS/94BG Rougham 9/7/43; MIA Schweinfurt 14/10/43 w/Beal; e/a, cr?; 6EVD 1KIA 3POW; MACR 792. JIMMY BOY II.

42-30458 Del Cheyenne 4/6/43; Gore 16/6/43; Kearney 18/6/43; Dow Fd 1/7/43; 1377 BU Grenier 23/12/43; 3WER Grenier 3/1/44; 4100 BU Patterson 8/4/44; 3WER Grenier 27/3/45; Ex Inv 10/12/45.

42-30459 Del Cheyenne 4/6/43; Rapid City 15/6/43; Geiger 22/6/43; Gr Isle 28/6/43; Dow Fd 20/7/43; ass 416BS/99BG Oudna 7/8/43; tran 341BS/97BG Depienne 14/11/43; Cerignola 20/12/43; Amendola 16/1/44; MIA Regensburg 22/2/44 w/Ciscoe; e/a, cr Klagenfurt; MACR 2491. LITTLE CHUM.

42-30460 Del Cheyenne 4/6/43; Rapid City 15/6/43; WO 21/6/43.

42-30461 Del Cheyenne 4/6/43; Gore 22/6/43; Roswell 24/6/43; WO 19/3/44.

42-30462 Del Cheyenne 4/6/43; Rapid City 15/6/43; Geiger 22/6/43; Gr Isle 29/6/43; Dow Fd 17/7/43; ass 347BS/99BG Oudna 7/8/43; tran 414BS/97BG Depienne 14/11/43; Cerignola 20/12/43; Amendola 16/1/44; MIA Udine 18/3/44 w/Loving; e/a, cr nr Udine; MACR 3521.

42-30463 Del Dallas 8/6/43; Gore 9/6/43; Dallas 19/6/43; New Orleans 26/6/43; Buckingham 27/7/43; Ft Myers 29/9/43; 2137 BU Hendricks 3/12/43; RFC Walnut Ridge 13/12/45.

42-30464 Del Cheyenne 4/6/43; Kearney 15/6/43; Dow Fd 7/7/43; ass 332BS/94BG [XM-A2] Rougham 5/7/43; sal 24/8/43. LITTLE MINNIE II.

42-30465 Del Cheyenne 5/6/43; Rapid City 16/6/43; Geiger 22/6/43; Gr Isle 28/6/43; Dow Fd 18/7/43; ass 429BS/2BG Masssicault 6/8/43; {27m} tran 419BS/301BG Oudna 14/11/43; Cerignola 7/12/43; Lucera 1/2/44; MIA {36m} Sofia 30/3/44 w/Miller; mech fault, cr Uleine (?) {73m in total}; 10POW; MACR 3714. VAGABOND.

42-30466 Del Cheyenne 5/6/43; Rapid City 19/6/43; Geiger 22/6/43; Gr Isle 30/6/43; Dow Fd 18/7/43; ass 49BS/2BG Ain M'Lila 29/7/43; Massicault 31/7/43; {27m} tran 419BS/301BG Oudna 14/11/43; Cerignola 7/12/43; MIA {12m} Piraeus 11/1/44 w/Ready; dam by explosion of another a/c, cr Patrai, Gr; 8KIA 2SURV; MACR 1830.

42-30467 Del Cheyenne 5/6/43; Rapid City 19/6/43; Geiger 22/6/43; Gr Isle 28/6/43; Dow Fd 21/7/43; ass 20BS/2BG Massicault 24/7/43; MIA {3m} Foggia 19/8/43 w/Rozelle; e/a, cr sea; five chutes seen; MACR 458.

42-30468 Del Cheyenne 5/6/43; Rapid City 18/6/43; Geiger 22/6/43; Gr Isle 29/6/43; Tinker 21/7/43; Presque Is 1/8/43; ass 12AF 3/8/43; c/l Italy 5/8/43.

42-30469 Del Dallas 8/6/43; Love 4/7/43; Peterson (F-9B) 7/7/43; ass 6AF (poss 91 Rec Sq) 20/1/44; Asencion Is 29/2/44; Asia 1/4/44.

42-30470 Del Cheyenne 5/6/43; Rapid City 19/6/43; Gore 22/6/43; Geiger 25/6/43; Gr Isle 29/6/43; Dow Fd 14/7/43; ass 416BS/99BG Navarin 29/7/43; Oudna 4/8/43; tran 342BS/97BG Depienne 14/11/43; Cerignola 20/12/43; Amendola 16/1/44; weather a/c from 15/7/44; burned out when washed by gasoline 30/7/44. WOLF PACK.

42-30471 Del Cheyenne 5/6/43; Rapid City 19/6/43; Geiger 22/6/43; Gr Isle 30/6/43; Dow Fd 18/7/43; ass 416BS/99BG Oudna 6/9/43; tran 97BG Depienne 14/11/43; Cerignola 20/12/43; Amendola 16/1/44; MIA Cassino 15/2/44 w/Paul; ditched Med Sea; 10RTD.

42-30472 Del Cheyenne 5/6/43; Rapid City 18/6/43; Geiger 22/6/43; Gr Isle 29/6/43; Dow Fd 14/7/43; ass 353BS/301BG St Donat 19/7/43; Oudna 6/8/43; Cerignola 7/12/43; MIA {51m} Salon de Provence, Fr. 21/1/44 w/Ryan; e/a, cr Med Sea; 10KIA; MACR 1952.

42-30473 Del Dallas 8/6/43; Gore 9/6/43; Patterson 8/7/43; Ephrata 1/8/43; Peterson 17/8/43; Drew 19/10/43; 617 BU Tooele 2/6/44; 4135 BU Hill Fd 26/8/44; 6-17 BU Tooele 18/9/45; RFC Walnut Ridge 14/12/45.

42-30474 Del Dallas 8/6/43; Gore 9/6/43; Dallas 19/6/43; Geiger 28/6/43; Gr Isle 28/6/43; Dow Fd 14/7/43; ass 346BS/99BG 1/8/43; MIA Mestre, It. 6/10/43 w/Lee; 1KIA 3POW 5EVD 1RTD; MACR 929. BUM'S RUSH.

42-30475 Del Dallas 8/6/43; Patterson 9/7/43; 328 BU Gulfport 31/3/45; RFC Albuquerque 25/6/45.

42-30476 Del Dallas 8/6/43; Smoky Hill 8/7/43; Dow Fd 15/7/43; ass 568BS/390BG [BI-L] Framlingham 16/7/43; MIA Bremen 20/12/43 w/Reeve; flak, cr Bremen; 10KIA; MACR 1731. ROVIN' ROMONA.

42-30477 Del Dallas 8/6/43; Gore 9/6/43; Dallas 11/6/43; Love 5/7/43; Dalhart 7/7/43; c/l 9/8/43, WO.

42-30478 Del Dallas 9/6/43; Smoky Hill 10/7/43; Dow Fd 15/7/43; ass 560BS/388BG Knettishall 18/7/43; MIA Stuttgart 6/9/43 w/Beecham; e/a, f/l Dubendorf, Switz; 10INT; MACR 3136. (Rep and used by Swiss AF); retUS Grenier 23/10/45; RFC Walnut Ridge 20/10/45. IMPATIENT VIRGIN II.

42-30479 Del Dallas 8/6/43; Love 19/7/43; Ephrata 20/7/43; Rapid City 2/8/43; 225 BU Rapid City 23/3/45; RFC Ontario 19/6/45.

42-30480 Del Dallas 6/8/43; Love 14/7/43; Ephrata 15/7/43; Ardmore 27/10/43; 222 BU Ardmore 22/1/45; RFC Ontario 20/6/45.

42-30481 Del Dallas 9/6/43; Ephrata 15/7/43; Ardmore 12/2/44; WO 13/2/44.

42-30482 Del Dallas 8/6/43; Love 5/7/43; Dow Fd 6/7/43; Dalhart 7/7/43; 326 BU McDill 6/7/44; 4117 BU Robins 27/7/44; 327 BU Drew 8/10/44; 2137 BU Hendricks 11/5/45; 327 BU Drew 24/5/45; RFC Searcey FD 11/8/45.

42-30483 Del Dallas 8/6/43; Gore 9/6/43; Love 14/7/43; Ephrata 15/7/43; Rapid City 27/7/43; Orlando 8/8/43; WO 22/11/43.

42-30484 Del Dallas 9/6/43; Gore 10/6/43; Dallas 12/6/43; Ephrata 18/7/43; WO 9/2/44.

42-30485 Del Dallas 9/6/43; Gore 10/6/43; Dallas 12/6/43; Ephrata 18/7/43; Rapid City 2/8/43; WO 23/11/43.

42-30486 Del Dallas 6/8/43; (F-9) Peterson 8/7/43; ass MTO 20/1/44; Alps 29/2/44; Asia Minor 1/4/44; 4185 BU Independence 11/9/44; RFC Kingman 16/1/46.

42-30487 Del Dallas 9/6/43; Gore 11/6/43; Love 28/7/43; Scott 11/8/43; Presque Is 17/8/43; ass 349BS/100BG [XR-F] Thorpe Abbotts 20/8/43 LADEN MAIDEN; MIA Regensburg 25/2/44 w/?; ditched Channel; 10RTD. TORCHY III.

42-30488 Del Dallas 10/6/43; Gore 11/6/43; Ephrata 18/7/43; WO 20/7/43.

42-30489 Del Dallas 10/6/43; Ephrata 19/7/43; Love 3/8/43; Ephrata 4/8/43; 221 BU Alexandra 5/10/44; 329 BU Alexandra 1/3/45; RFC Altus 27/8/45.

42-30490 Del Dallas 10/6/43; Smoky Hill 11/7/43; Dow Fd 20/7/43; ass 352BS/301BG St Donat 1/8/43; Oudna 6/8/43; Cerignola 7/12/43; MIA {55m} Sofia 24/1/44 w/Romans; flak, cr Mitrovica; 10EVD & RTD 31/5/44; MACR 1992.

42-30491 Del Cheyenne 11/6/43; Rapid City 19/6/43; Geiger 22/6/43; Gr Isle 30/6/43; Dow Fd 20/7/43; ass 346BS/99BG Oudna 8/8/43; c/l Sardinia 1/10/43 w/Crooks; 10RTD (1WIA); sal. HOT FOR THE BODY.

42-30492 Del Dallas 11/6/43; Gore 13/6/43; Dallas 18/6/43; Ft Wayne 25/7/43; Buckingham 27/7/43; Ft Myers 4/8/43; Buckingham 7/8/43; 3030 BU Roswell 7/10/44; 3010 BU Williams 6/11/44; 3020 BU La Junta 4/5/45; RFC Searcey Fd 31/7/45.

42-30493 Del Dallas 10/6/43; Smoky Hill 11/7/43; Dow Fd 15/7/43; ass 94BG Rougham 18/7/43 DOUBLE DOO; tran 339BS/96BG Snetterton 8/43; MIA Paris 15/9/43 w/Reed; e/a, cr Paris; 9KIA 1POW; MACR 727.

42-30494 Del Cheyenne 10/6/43; Gore 24/6/43; Roswell 26/6/43; 3030 BU Roswell 2/6/44; RFC Altus 4/10/45.

42-30495 Del Dallas 10/6/43; Gowen 27/3/43; Ephrata 24/7/43; Tinker 7/12/43; 332 BU Lake Charles 21/6/44; 499BG Smoky Hill 25/6/44; 1108 BU Mitchell 25/9/44; 247 BU Smoky Hill 3/11/44; RFC Kingman 11/1/46.

42-30496 Del Dallas 10/6/43; Ft Myers 23/6/43; Love 25/6/43; Buckingham 27/6/43; 2114 BU Lockburn 24/10/44; RFC Walnut Ridge 19/12/45.

42-30497 Del Cheyenne 10/6/43; Rapid City 19/6/43; Geiger 22/6/43; Gr Isle 29/6/43; Dow Fd 18/7/43; ass 352BS/301BG St Donat 29/7/43; Oudna 6/8/43; Cerignola 7/12/43; Lucera 1/2/44; {94m} tran depot 20/7/44; sal 19/4/45.

42-30498 Del Cheyenne 14/6/43; Roswell 25/6/43; Kelly 3/8/43; Roswell 15/8/43; 3030 BU Roswell 2/6/44; 3010 BU Williams 9/12/44; 3020 BU La Junta 27/3/45; RFC Searcey Fd 4/8/45.

42-30499 Del Cheyenne 10/6/43; Rapid City 18/6/43; Geiger 22/6/43; Gr Isle 30/6/43; Tinker 16/7/43; Gr Isle 23/7/43; Kearney 8/8/43; Topeka 14/8/43; ass 509BS/351BG [RQ-Q] Polebrook 27/9/43; {46m} b/d sal 1/8/44. MY PRINCESS.

42-30500 Del Cheyenne 11/6/43; Gore 13/6/43; Rapid City 20/6/43; Geiger 22/6/43; Gr Isle 30/6/43; Dow Fd 18/7/43; ass 20BS/2BG Massicault 17/8/43; Bizerte 1/12/43; {13m} tran 885BS (TD at Maison Blanche, Alg); MIA secret mission 10/9/44 w/Meyers. MACR 9578. MISS CHARLOTTE.

42-30501 Del Boeing 12/6/43; Fairfield 2/7/43; Gore 10/7/43; Wright 3/8/43; Clinton 12/8/43; 810 BU Laurnburg (Glider training) 17/6/43; MAC HQ Wright 6/7/43; Mat Flt Muroc 31/8/43; Wright 31/10/43; 4100 BU Patterson 17/1/45; 4000 BU Wright 25/3/45; 4117 BU Robins 22/4/45; AMC Wright 30/6/46; 4000 BU Patterson 31/3/47; Recl Comp 1/12/47.

42-30502 Del Cheyenne 11/6/43; Rapid City 19/6/43; Geiger 22/6/43; Gr Isle 1/7/43; ass 20BS/2BG Ain M'Lila 16/7/43; Massicault 31/7/43; MIA {3m} Foggia 19/8/43 w/Bradley; e/a, four chutes seen; MACR 429.

42-30503 Del Cheyenne 11/6/43; Roswell 22/6/43; Patterson 11/8/43; Tinker 12/8/43; 3030 BU Roswell 2/6/44; 3010 BU Williams 10/12/44; 3020 BU La Junta 3/4/45; RFC Altus 14/8/45.

42-30504 Del Cheyenne 11/6/43; Rapid City 19/6/43; Gr Isle 29/6/43; Dow Fd 18/7/43; ass 348BS/99BG Oudna 3/9/43; tran 419BS/301BG Oudan 14/11/43; Cerignola 7/12/43; Lucera 1/2/44; {40m} RetUS 1103 BU Morrison 2/4/45; 4104 BU Rome 30/4/45; 4108 BU Newark 11/6/45; RFC Bush Fd 20/6/45.

42-30505 Del Cheyenne 15/6/43; Roswell 21/6/43; 3030 BU Roswell 2/6/44; RFC Altus 9/10/45.

42-30506 Del Cheyenne 12/6/43; Gore 14/6/43; Roswell 19/6/43; 3030 BU Roswell 2/6/44; 554 BU Memphis 23/4/45; 3030 BU Roswell 1/6/45; RFC Altus 9/10/45.

42-30507 Del Cheyenne 12/6/43; Gore 14/6/43; Roswell 19/6/43; Hobbs 8/7/43; Roswell 4/8/43; 93BS/19BG Pyote 13/9/43; 232 BU Dalhart 9/6/44; 19BG Dalhart 19/7/44; 268 BU Peterson 13/12/44; 225 BU Rapid City 2/3/45; RFC Ontario 19/6/45.

42-30508 Del Cheyenne 12/6/43; Gore 14/6/43; Roswell 23/6/43; 3030 BU Roswell 2/6/44; RFC Altus 9/10/45.

42-30509 Del Cheyenne 14/6/43; Roswell 26/6/43; 3030 BU Roswell 2/6/44; WO 18/7/44.

42-30510 Del Cheyenne 18/6/43; Roswell 23/6/43; 232 BU Dalhart 8/7/44; 242 BU Gr Isle 19/7/44; 4100 BU Patterson 23/8/44; 242 BU Gr Isle 12/1/45; 224 BU Sioux City 17/4/45; 211 BU Sioux Falls 3/9/45; RFC Kingman 28/10/45.

42-30511 Del Cheyenne 14/6/43; Roswell 22/6/43; 3030 BU Roswell 2/6/44; 3010 BU Williams 10/12/44; 3020 BU La Junta 23/7/45; RFC Altus 4/8/45.

42-30512 Del Cheyenne 14/6/43; Roswell 21/6/43; c/l 14/9/43 w/Carson, rep; 3030 BU Roswell 2/6/44; 110 BU Mitchell 26/7/44; 3030 BU Roswell 6/11/44; 3010 BU Williams 9/12/44; 3020 BU La Junta 1/4/45; RFC Altus 4/8/45.

42-30513 Del Cheyenne 15/6/43; Roswell 23/6/43; 3030 BU Roswell 2/6/44; 2509 BU Big Spring 6/10/43; 3030 BU Roswell 6/11/44; 3017 BU Hobbs 28/4/45; RFC Altus 24/9/45.

42-30514 Del Boeing 17/6/43; Seattle 25/6/43; Mat Spl Tonopah 2/6/44; 4126 BU San Bernardino 8/6/44; Mat Spl Tonopah 29/6/44; 4127 BU McClellan 8/7/44; 216 BU Wendover 18/10/44; 4135 BU Hill 16/3/45; 216 BU Wendover 24/4/45; 4135 BU Hill 6/8/46; 613 BU Phillips 7/1/47; 4145 BU Wendover 8/1/47.

42-30515 Del Boeing 17/6/43; Seattle 25/6/43; 3715 BU Burbank 24/9/44; 3701 BU Amarillo 7/9/54; 3706 BU Sheppard 8/3/45; 3701 BU Amarillo 29/3/45; RFC Walnut Ridge 25/10/45.

42-30516 Del Boeing 17/6/43; Seattle 25/6/43; slated 96BG, tran 3715 BU Burbank 10/8/44; 499BG Smoky Hill 23/8/44; 3715 BU Burbank 28/9/44; RFC Ontario 16/6/45.

42-30517 Del Boeing 17/6/43; Seattle 25/6/43; 3715 BU Burbank 15/7/44; Mat Lockheed Burbank 28/7/44; 3710 BU Amarillo 20/9/44; 3706 BU Sheppard 8/3/45; 3701 BU Amarillo 24/3/45; RFC Walnut Ridge 20/12/45.

42-30518 Del Boeing 18/6/43; Gore 29/6/43; Cheyenne 30/6/43; Kearney 14/7/43; Dow Fd 21/7/43; ass 413BS/96BG [MZ-Y] Snetterton 26/7/43; MIA Kiel 4/1/44 w/McLean; mid air coll w/42-5953, cr Lingen, Ger; 7KIA 3POW; MACR 2016. SHORT STRIDE IV.

42-30519 Del Cheyenne 15/6/43; Roswell 24/6/43; 3030 BU Roswell 2/6/44; 3010 BU Williams 10/12/44; Recl Comp 10/3/45.

42-30520 Del Cheyenne 15/6/43; Roswell 22/6/43; 3030 BU Roswell 2/6/44; 3017 BU Hobbs 28/4/45; RFC Altus 30/8/45.

42-30521 Del Cheyenne 15/6/43; Roswell 24/6/43; 3030 BU Roswell 2/6/44; RFC Altus 29/10/45.

42-30522 Del Cheyenne 15/6/43; Roswell 24/6/43; 3030 BU Roswell 2/6/44; 3010 BU Williams 9/12/44; 3020 BU La Junta 4/5/45; RFC Altus 1/8/45.

42-30523 Del Cheyenne 15/6/43; Roswell 24/6/43; 3030 BU Roswell 2/6/44; 3010 BU Williams 10/12/44; 3009 BU Carlsbad 12/1/45; 2619 BU Carlsbad 1/3/45; 2536 BU San Marcos 27/9/45; 2532 BU Randolph 29/11/45; RFC Kingman 20/12/45.

42-30524 Del Cheyenne 15/6/43; Roswell 23/6/43; 3030 BU Roswell 2/6/44; 3010 BU Williams 11/12/44; RFC Albuquerque 9/8/45.

42-30525 Del Cheyenne 15/6/43; Roswell 24/6/43; 3030 BU Roswell 2/6/44; 3017 BU Hobbs 28/4/45; RFC Altus 11/9/45.

42-30526 Del Cheyenne 15/6/43; Roswell 23/6/43; 3030 BU Roswell 2/6/44; ATS 4208 BU Mines Fd 25/3/45; 3030 BU Roswell 30/3/45; RFC Albuquerque 9/8/45.

42-30527 Del Cheyenne 16/6/43; Gore 19/6/43; Geiger 4/7/43; Bolling 15/7/43; New Castle 7/8/43; Geiger 9/8/43; 393BG Sioux City 1/12/43; WO 25/3/44.

42-30528 Del Cheyenne 17/6/43; Gore 28/6/43; Hendricks 3/7/43; 3505 BU Scott 25/8/44; 2137 BU Hendricks 20/9/44; Recl Comp 29/1/46.

42-30529 Del Cheyenne 18/6/43; Gore 27/6/43; Hendricks 29/6/43; 2137 BU Hendricks 4/10/44; WO 17/11/44.

42-30530 Del Cheyenne 18/6/43; Gore 29/6/43; Siouix City 30/6/43; Watertown 17/7/43; Kearney 3/8/43; WO 26/9/43.

42-30531 Del Cheyenne 15/6/43; Gore 2/7/43; Dyersburg 3/7/43; Alexandria 11/7/43; 3505 BU Scott 29/6/44; 4117 BU Robins 1/11/44; RFC Bush Fd 13/6/45.

42-30532 Del Cheyenne 18/6/43; Roswell 25/6/43; 3030 BU Roswell 2/6/44; RFC Altus 29/10/45.

42-30533 Del Cheyenne 21/6/43; Gore 2/7/43; Geiger 4/7/43; Pendleton 25/7/43; Rapid City 30/7/43; Harvard 2/8/43; 225 BU Rapid City 24/3/45; RFC Ontario 19/6/45.

42-30534 Del Cheyenne 17/6/43; Sioux City 30/6/43; 248 BU Walker 27/10/44; 274 BU Herington 5/1/45; 248 BU Walker 11/1/45; 4104 BU Rome 21/1/45; RFC Altus 27/8/45.

42-30535 Del Cheyenne 17/6/43; Gore 28/6/43; Sebring 30/6/43; Hendricks 3/7/43; WO 10/2/44.

42-30536 Del Cheyenne 17/6/43; Gore 28/6/43; Sebring 30/6/43; Hendricks 3/7/43; 3502 BU Chanute 22/6/44; 2140 BU Smyrna 22/8/44; 3505 BU Scott 27/8/43; 3502 BU Chanute 17/1/45; 3539 BU Langley 6/4/45; Recl Comp 2/3/46.

42-30537 Del Cheyenne 18/6/43; Hendricks 26/6/43; 2137 BU Hendricks 14/7/44; Recl Comp 6/1/45.

42-30538 Del Cheyenne 18/6/43; Gore 27/6/43; Sebring 29/6/43; Hendricks 3/7/43; 2137 BU Hendricks 4/10/44; RFC Walnut Ridge 19/12/45.

42-30539 Del Boeing 29/6/43; Ladd Fd (Winter test) 16/10/43; Mat Com Wright 2/6/44; Ladd Fd 7/4/44; 4104 BU Rome 25/8/44; ATS HA Hartford 6/9/43; 4136 BU Tinker 2/11/44; ATS Wright 14/11/44; ATS HA Hartford 16/11/44; ATS Wright 28/11/44; RFC Walnut Ridge 27/3/46.

42-30540 Del Cheyenne 18/6/43; Gore 27/6/43; WO 15/1/44.

42-30541 Del Cheyenne 18/6/43; Roswell 25/6/43; WO 31/1/44.

42-30542 Del Cheyenne 18/6/43; Sioux City 29/6/43; Scribner 17/7/43; Kearney 3/8/43; WO 18/8/43.

42-30543 Del Cheyenne 17/6/43; Roswell 24/6/43; 3030 BU Roswell 2/6/44; 4121 BU Kelly 3/11/44; 3030 BU Roswell 7/11/44; RFC Albuquerque 9/8/45.

42-30544 Del Cheyenne 18/6/43; Roswell 25/6/43; 3030 BU Roswell 2/7/44; RFC Altus 29/10/45.

42-30545 Del Cheyenne 18/6/43; Gore 2/7/43; Dyersburg 3/7/43; Alexandria 11/7/43; 221 BU Alexandria 17/1/45; 329 BU Alexandria 1/3/45; RFC Altus 9/10/45.

42-30546 Del Cheyenne 18/6/43; Roswell 25/6/43; Hobbs 7/7/43; Roswell 3/8/43; 3030 BU Roswell 2/6/44; 3017 BU Hobbs 28/4/45; RFC Altus 30/8/45.

42-30547 Del Cheyenne 18/6/43; Gore 20/6/43; Sioux City 1/7/43; Watertown 17/7/43; Kearney 3/8/43; 580BS/393BG Sioux City 11/11/43; 326 BU McDill 18/1/45; 331 BU Barksdale 20/1/45; RFC Walnut Ridge 14/12/45.

42-30548 Del Cheyenne 19/6/43; Alexandria 13/7/43; 221 BU Alexandria 20/8/44; 329 BU Alexandria 1/3/45; 331 BU Barksdale 2/4/45; 326 BU McDill 2/5/45; 331 BU Barksdale 9/9/45; RFC Walnut Ridge 14/12/45.

42-30549 Del Cheyenne 18/6/43; Gore 28/6/43; Sebring 30/6/43; 2137 BU Hendricks 1/10/44; RFC Walnut Ridge 18/12/45.

42-30550 Del Cheyenne 19/6/43; Gore 7/7/43; Dalhart 8/7/43; 444BG Dalhart 10/10/43; 902 BU Orlando 6/7/44; 243 BU Gt Bend 14/7/44; 19BG Dalhart 1/9/44; 556 BU Long Beach 28/11/44; 243 BU Gt Bend 13/1/45; 902 BU Orlando 27/3/45; 243 BU Gt Bend 2/5/45; RFC Altus 9/10/45.

42-30551 Del Cheyenne 19/6/43; Ephrata 11/7/43;

INDIVIDUAL B-17 HISTORIES

332 BU Ardmore 13/7/44; 347 BU Key Fd 6/8/44; RFC Altus 29/10/45.
42-30552 Del Cheyenne 19/6/43; Gore 2/7/43; Dyersburg 3/7/43; Alexandria 11/7/43; 221 BU Alexandria 7/11/44; 329 BU Alexandria 1/3/45; RFC Altus 9/10/45.
42-30553 Del Cheyenne 19/6/43; Walla Walla 7/7/43; Redmond 15/7/43; Walla Walla 15/8/43; 325 BU Avon Park 4/2/45; RFC Walnut Ridge 29/8/45.
42-30554 Del Cheyenne 19/6/43; Gore 30/6/43; Sioux City 1/7/43; Mitchell 17/7/43; Kearney 3/8/43; WO 21/4/44.
42-30555 Del Cheyenne 19/6/43; Walla Walla 7/7/43; Madras 15/7/43; Redmond 16/7/43; Walla Walla 15/8/43; WO 25/5/44.
42-30556 Del Cheyenne 21/6/43; Spokane 2/7/43; 393BG Geiger 4/7/43; Pendleton 25/7/43; Geiger 10/8/43; 4117 BU Robins 13/7/44; 327 BU Drew 22/9/44; 2137 BU Hendricks 11/5/44; 327 BU Drew 24/5/44; RFC Altus 14/9/45.
42-30557 Del Cheyenne 19/6/43; Gore 4/7/43; Rapid City 5/7/43; 225 BU Rapid City 23/3/45; 400 BU Hamilton 25/4/45; 225 BU Rapid City 2/5/45; 237 BU Kirtland 24/5/45; RFC Altus 9/10/45.
42-30558 Del Cheyenne 21/6/43; Gore 2/7/43; Dyersburg 3/7/43; Alexandria 11/7/43; WO 21/3/44.
42-30559 Del Cheyenne 22/6/43; Rapid City 4/7/43; Galveston 28/9/43; 4119 BU Brookley 21/10/44; 328 BU Gulfport 15/12/44; 4119 BU Brookley 19/12/44; 328 BU Gulfport 3/3/45; 327 BU Drew 15/6/45; RFC Albuquerque 25/6/45.
42-30560 Del Cheyenne 21/6/43; Gore 2/7/43; Dyersburg 3/7/43; Gulfport 8/8/43; galveston 12/8/43; Dalhart 15/8/43; 223 BU Dyersburg 15/8/44; 330 BU Dyersburg 1/3/45; 327 BU Drew 3/6/45; RFC Searcey Fd 7/8/45.
42-30561 Del Cheyenne 21/6/43; Biggs 3/7/43; Dalhart 17/7/43; WO 20/8/43.
42-30562 Del Cheyenne 21/6/43; Dalhart 3/7/43; Gulfport 11/7/43; Dalhart 3/8/43; 4135 BU Hill 30/5/45; 468BG Smoky Hill 30/9/45; 468BG Salina 5/12/45.
42-30563 Del Cheyenne 22/6/43; Ephrata 2/7/43; Gore 4/7/43; Ephrata 26/7/43; Rapid City 28/7/43; Orlando 7/8/43; ass 13AF New Caledonia, PTO 14/2/44; 224 BU Sioux City 19/11/44; RFC Albuquerque 19/6/45.
42-30564 Del Cheyenne 21/6/43; Gore 2/7/43; Rapid City 4/7/43; 4136 BU Tinker 9/7/44; 222 BU Ardmore 14/7/44; 332 BU Ardmore 16/6/45; RFC Walnut Ridge 18/12/45.
42-30565 Del Cheyenne 22/6/43; Gore 2/7/43; 540BS/385BG Geiger 4/7/43; Pendleton 15/8/43; 326 BU McDill 11/8/44; 357 BU Kellogg 20/9/45; Recl Comp 9/2/45. CAREFUL VIRGIN.
42-30566 Del Cheyenne 22/6/43; Gore 2/7/43; 540BS/383 BG Geiger 4/7/43; Rapid City 29/7/43; Harvard 2/8/43; 4117 BU Robins 13/7/44; 328 BU Gulfport 16/7/44; RFC Albuquerque 25/6/45.
42-30567 Del Cheyenne 22/6/43; Moses Lake 3/7/43; Geiger 2/8/43; Gt Falls 12/8/43; Geiger 28/10/43; 224 BU Sioux City 6/3/45; RFC Albuquerque 19/6/45.
42-30568 Del Cheyenne 23/6/43; Gore 4/7/43; 435BS/19BG Pyote 5/7/43; 274 BU Herington 8/6/44; 499BG Smoky Hill 9/6/44; 2517 BU Ellington 25/6/44; 499BG Smoky Hill 7/7/44; 233 BU Davis Monthan 15/8/44; 235 BU Biggs 28/9/44; 4202 BU Syracuse 5/4/45; RFC Walnut Ridge 11/9/45.
42-30569 Del Cheyenne 23/6/43; Rapid City 4/7/43; 4119 BU Brookley 11/11/44; 4100 BU Patterson 28/11/44; 331 BU Barksdale 21/2/45; 326 BU McDill 11/4/45; 331 BU Barksdale 15/5/45; RFC Walnut Ridge 14/12/45.
42-30570 Del Cheyenne 22/6/43; Dalhart 3/7/43; Tinker 11/7/43; Dalhart 18/7/43; 232 BU Dalhart 9/6/44; 4200 BU Chicago Mun 2/9/44; 232 BU Dalhart 15/9/43; 610 BU Eglin 27/10/44; 232 BU Dalhart 6/11/44; 4108 BU Newark 11/11/44; 245 BU McCook 22/12/44; 237 BU Kirtland 7/3/45; 4136 BU Tinker 15/5/45; Recl Comp 19/6/45.
42-30571 Del Cheyenne 22/6/43; Dalhart 3/7/43; WO 21/7/43.
42-30572 Del Cheyenne 23/6/43; Gore 2/7/43; Geiger 4/7/43; 452BG Pendleton 25/7/43; 498BG Gt Bend 23/7/44; 243 BU Gt Bend 20/8/44; 232 BU Dalhart 27/9/44; ass Puerto Rico 9/11/44; sal 21/6/46.
42-30573 Del Cheyenne 23/6/43; Gore 4/7/43; 19BG Pyote 5/7/43; 221 BU Alexandria 17/1/45; 329 BU Alexandria 1/3/45; 331 BU Barksdale 3/4/45; RFC Albuquerque 25/6/45.
42-30574 Del Cheyenne 23/6/43; Pyote 4/7/43; Alexandria 7/7/43; 202 BU Galveston 13/7/44; 221 BU Alexandria 21/7/43; WO 21/7/44.
42-30575 Del Cheyenne 23/6/43; Gore 2/7/43; Pendleton 25/7/43; 452BG Geiger 31/7/43; 500BG Walker 8/6/44; 901 BU Pinecastle 8/7/44; 902 BU Orlando 2/8/43; 248 BU Walker 16/8/44; 232 BU Dalhart 4/9/44; 241 BU Fairmont 12/9/44; RFC Altus 9/10/45.
42-30576 Del Amarillo 1/7/43; Cheyenne 27/7/43; Geiger 1/8/43; Rapid City 10/8/43; Pendleton 12/8/43; WO 19/1/44.
42-30577 Del Cheyenne 23/6/43; Kearney 26/7/43; WO 9/8/43.
42-30578 Del Cheyenne 23/6/43; Gore 4/7/43; 28BS/19BG Pyote 5/7/43; WO 24/3/44.
42-30579 Del Cheyenne 23/6/43; Gore 5/7/43; 19BG Pyote 6/7/43; 554 BU Memphis 7/8/44; 222 BU Ardmore 30/8/44; 332 BU Ardmore 16/6/45; RFC Walnut Ridge 18/12/45.
42-30580 Del Cheyenne 27/6/43; Smoky 10/7/43; Dow Fd 15/7/43; ass 326BS/92BG [JW-N] Alconbury 14/8/43; sal n/b/d 6/1/44 following ground collision w/42-31377. EQUIPOISE.
42-30581 Del Cheyenne 24/6/43; Gore 5/7/43; Gt Falls 7/7/43; Glasgow 28/7/43; Sioux City 19/12/43; 232 BU Dalhart 9/6/44; 268 BU Peterson 30/9/44; 232 BU Dalhart 11/10/44; 253 BU Selman 6/12/44; RFC Kingman 17/10/45.
42-30582 Del Cheyenne 24/6/43; Walla Walla 5/7/43; Redmond 15/7/43; Walla Walla 15/8/43; WO 29/2/44.
42-30583 Del Cheyenne 24/6/43; Gore 16/7/43; 29BS/19BG Pyote 17/7/43; WO 5/10/43.
42-30584 Del Cheyenne 24/6/43; Gore 4/7/43; Gt Falls 7/7/43; Gore 29/7/43; Lewiston 30/7/43; Sioux City 9/12/43; 221 BU Alexandria 7/11/44; 329 BU Alexandria 1/3/45; RFC Altus 29/10/45.
42-30585 Del Cheyenne 24/6/43; Rapid City 6/7/43; Geiger 18/11/43; 4119 BU Brookley 14/11/44; 4100 BU Patterson 28/11/44; RFC Bush Fd 4/7/45.
42-30586 Del Cheyenne 24/6/43; Gr Isle 16/7/43; Kearney 20/7/43; ass 368BS/306BG [BO-A] Thurleigh 8/8/43; MIA Erding 24/4/44 w/MacDowell; e/a, cr Heinnhausen, Ger; 1KIA 9POW; MACR 4239.
42-30587 Del Cheyenne 27/6/43; Gore 9/7/43; Dalhart 10/7/43; 232 BU Dalhart 9/6/44; HQ Peterson 14/7/44; 558 BU Nashville 1/8/44; HQ Peterson 11/9/44; 3033 BU Stockton 25/9/44; 271 BU Kearney 15/3/45; 485 BU Kearney 3/10/45; RFC Walnut Ridge 10/1/46.
42-30588 Del Cheyenne 24/6/43; Walla Walla 7/7/43; Madras 15/7/43; Redmond 17/7/43; WO 20/7/43.
42-30589 Del Cheyenne 25/6/43; Dalhart 8/7/43; slated 92BG, WO 27/8/43.
42-30590 Del Cheyenne 22/6/43; Gore 8/7/43; Dalhart 9/7/43; Tinker 25/7/43; Dalhart 9/8/43; 232 BU Dalhart 9/6/44; 271 BU Kearney 8/10/44; 232 BU Dalhart 19/10/44; 110 BU Mitchell 6/11/44; 232 BU Dalhart 10/11/44; 272 BU Topeka 2/12/44; 232 BU Dalhart 8/12/44; 244 BU Harvard 5/1/45; RFC Kingman 2/11/45.
42-30591 Del Cheyenne 25/6/43; Dalhart 8/7/43; 202 BU Galveston 8/8/44; 224 BU Sioux City 23/2/45; 4202 BU Syracuse 24/4/45.
42-30592 Del Cheyenne 25/6/43; Dalhart 9/7/43; WO 24/4/44.
42-30593 Del Cheyenne 25/6/43; Gore 7/7/43; Dalhart 9/7/43; 468BG Dalhart 10/10/43; 4100 BU Patterson 28/6/44; 497BG Pratt 29/6/44; 247 BU Smoky Hill 19/7/44; 246 BU Pratt 25/7/44; 247 BU Smoky Hill 2/8/44; ATC 1103 BU Morrison 21/2/45; 902 BU TAC Orlando 15/4/45; 247 BU Smoky Hill 1/5/45; RFC Albuquerque 25/6/45.
42-30594 Del Cheyenne 25/6/43; Gore 17/7/43; 19BG Pyote 9/11/43; Chicago 21/6/44; 222 BU Ardmore 22/1/45; RFC Ontario 19/5/45.
42-30595 Del Cheyenne 26/6/43; Smoky Hill 13/7/43; Kearney 16/7/43; Dow Fd 19/7/43; ass 560BS/388BG Knettishall 20/7/43; tran APH as OLIN'S 69'ERS; when W/W fuselage cut down and vehicle windshield fitted before open cockpit. Sal 24/6/46. GREMLIN GUS II.
42-30596 Del Cheyenne 25/6/43; 542BS/383BG Geiger 12/7/43; Pendleton 25/7/43; Rapid City 30/7/43; Harvard 2/8/43; WO 1/1/44.
42-30597 Del Cheyenne 25/6/43; Dalhart 10/7/43; 4117 BU Robins 21/6/44; 242 BU Gr Isle 23/6/44; 6BG Gr Isle 8/7/44; 4209 BU Des Moines 10/8/44; 68BG Gr Isle 28/9/44; 242 BU Gr Isle 16/9/43; 249 BU Alliance 19/10/44; 223 BU Dyersburg 15/2/45; 327 BU Drew 3/6/45; RFC Searcey Fd 7/8/45.
42-30598 Del Cheyenne 26/6/43; Smoky Hill 12/7/43; Dow Fd 16/7/43; ass 549BS/385BG Gt Ashfield 16/7/43; MIA Lille 15/8/43 w/Stone; flak, cr Channel; 10KIA; MACR 267.
42-30599 Del Cheyenne 26/6/43; Ephrata 11/7/43; 273 BU Lincoln 16/6/44; 272 BU Topeka 22/7/44; CAF 484 BU Topeka 9/10/44; RFC Kingman 14/11/45.
42-30600 Del Cheyenne 26/6/43; Ephrata 11/7/43; 452BG Pendleton 2/11/43; Walla Walla 17/11/43; WO 18/12/43.
42-30601 Del Cheyenne 26/6/43; Kearney 12/7/43; Dow Fd 16/7/43; ass 550BS/385BG Gt Ashfield 21/7/43; b/d Bordeaux 16/9/43, c/l Rickinghall, Sfk; sal 19/9/43. MARY ELLEN II.
42-30602 Del Cheyenne 26/6/43; Kearney 12/7/43; Dow Fd 16/7/43; ass 338BS/96BG [BX-X] Snetterton 16/7/43; MIA Hamburg 13/12/43 w/Chesmore; flak, ditched Nth Sea; 10POW; MACR 1654. DRY RUN IV.
42-30603 Del Cheyenne 26/6/43; Gore 11/7/43; Kearney 16/7/43; Dow Fd 18/7/43; ass 423BS/306BG [RD-H] Thurleigh 8/8/43; MIA Bremen 26/11/43 w/Jeffries; flak, cr St Nicolaas, Bel; 4KIA 6POW; MACR 1329. LAS VEGAS AVENGER.
42-30604 Del Cheyenne 26/6/43; Gore 29/6/43; Gr Isle 22/6/43; Walla Walla 1/8/43; Scott 8/8/43; Presque Is 17/8/43; ass 306BG Thurleigh 10/8/43; tran 350BS/100BG [LN-T] Thorpe Abbotts 20/8/43; MIA St Dizier 4/10/43 w/Helstrom; flak, c/l Caen, Fr; 4EVD 6POW; MACR 843. Sal and survived at Boeing Museum. BADGER'S BEAUTY V.

42-30605 Del Cheyenne 29/6/43; English Fd 16/7/43; Pyote 17/7/43; 19BG Pyote 9/11/43; MAT Kansas City 19/8/44; 224 BU Sioux City 29/8/43; 225 BU Rapid City 22/9/43; 224 BU Sioux City 6/10/44; RFC Albuquerque 19/6/45.

42-30606 Del Cheyenne 28/6/43; Kearney 14/7/43; Dow Fd 18/7/43; ass 367BS/306BG [GY-U] Thurleigh 4/8/43; MIA Kiel 4/1/44 w/Tucker; flak, ditched Nth Sea; 10POW; MACR 1681. EL DIABLO.

42-30607 Del Cheyenne 28/6/43; Kearney 14/7/43; Dow Fd 18/7/43; ass 337BS/96BG Snetterton 18/7/43; MIA Paris 15/9/43 w/Murphy; flak, cr Paris; 10KIA 1POW; MACR 728. PAT HAND.

42-30608 Del Cheyenne 29/6/43; Gr Isle 15/7/43; Patterson 19/7/43; Scott 15/8/43; ass 326BS/92BG [JW-G] Alconbury; MIA Bremen 9/10/43 w/Shannon; flak, cr Nth Sea; 10KIA; MACR 1386.

42-30609 Del Cheyenne 29/6/43; Gr Isle 15/7/43; Dalhart 20/7/43; Rome 7/8/43; Presque Is 16/8/43; ass 335BS/95BG [OE-N] Horham 20/8/43; MIA Brunswick 10/2/44 w/Balman; cr Wiethmarschen, Ger; 1KIA 9POW; MACR 2542. PISTOL PACKIN' MAMA.

42-30610 Del Cheyenne 29/6/43; Gr Isle 15/7/43; Dalhart 20/7/43; Gr Isle 26/7/43; Presque Is 3/8/43; ass 568BS/390BG [BI-M] Framlingham 6/8/43; b/d Schweinfurt 14/10/43; Sa; 17/10/43. RED ASS.

42-30611 Del Cheyenne 28/6/43; Seattle 30/6/43; Kearney 14/7/43; Dow Fd 18/7/43; ass 100BG Thorpe Abbotts 20/7/43; MIA Paris 3/9/43 w/Henington; flak, ditched Channel.

42-30612 Del Cheyenne 29/6/43; Gore 30/9/43; Dow Fd 18/7/43; ass 333BS/94BG [TS-D] Rougham 29/7/43; sal 20/3/44. (HOT FOOT II) FREESTRIDER.

42-30613 Del Cheyenne 29/6/43; Gore 30/6/43; Gr Isle 16/7/43; Dalhart 20/7/43; Gr Isle 26/7/43; ass 813BS/482BG [PC-J] Alconbury; tran 535BS/381BG [MS-S] Ridgewell 28/2/44; 2 SAD Lt Staughton 9/4/44; sal 12/4/44.

42-30614 Del Cheyenne 29/6/43; Gore 30/6/43; Rapid City 18/7/43; 247 BU Smoky Hill 3/6/44; 4136 BU Tinker 10/7/44; 4100 BU Patterson 24/1/45; 4127 BU McClellan 27/3/45; Recl Comp 3/1/46.

42-30615 Del Cheyenne 29/6/43; Gore 30/6/43; Rapid City 8/8/43; 242 BU Gr Isle 19/6/44; WO 24/6/44.

42-30616 Del Amarillo 2/7/43; Cheyenne 26/7/43; Geiger 4/8/43; Kearney 8/8/43; 271 BU Kearney 4/7/44; 247 BU Smoky Hill 26/7/44; 499BG Smoky Hill 2/8/44; 4103 BU Jackson 17/4/45; 247 BU Smoky Hill 22/5/45; 237 BU Kirtland 2/8/45; 247 BU Smoky Hill 7/8/45; RFC Kingman 28/10/45.

42-30617 Del Cheyenne 29/6/43; Gore 30/6/43; Gr Isle 16/7/43; Dalhart 20/7/43; Gr Isle 26/7/43; Presque Is 2/8/43; ass 92BG Alconbury 21/8/43; MIA Watten 27/8/43 w/Tucker; ditched Channel off Sheppey, 10RTD.

42-30618 Del Amarillo 1/7/43; Ephrata 18/7/43; Dallas 19/7/43; Cheyenne 31/7/43; Love 3/8/43; 3036 BU Yuma 6/10/44; RFC Albuquerque 27/7/45.

42-30619 Del Cheyenne 29/6/43; Gore 20/7/43; Rapid City 21/7/43; 242 BU Gr Isle 10/6/44; 6BG Gr Isle 8/7/44; 242 BU Gr Isle 16/9/44; RFC Albuquerque 25/6/45.

42-30620 Del Cheyenne 30/6/43; English Fd 16/7/43; Pyote 17/7/43; 19BG Pyote 9/11/43; 500BG Walker 8/8/44; 233 BU Davis Monthan 18/8/44; 242 BU Gr Isle 17/12/44; 202 BU Galveston 18/12/44; 242 BU Gr Isle 21/12/44; TAC 902 BU Orlando 20/3/45; 242 BU Gr Isle 14/5/45; 120 BU Richmond 17/7/45; 242 BU Gr Isle 9/9/45; 4136 BU Tinker 9/10/45; CAF 242 BU Gr Isle 29/10/45; RFC Kingman 8/10/46.

42-30621 Del Cheyenne 30/6/43; Moses Lake 29/7/43; 497BG Pratt 8/7/44; ASC 4136 BU Tinker 15/7/44; 246 BU Pratt 6/8/44; 29BG Pratt 10/9/44; 4136 BU Tinker 3/10/44; 233 BU Davis Monthan 23/2/45; RFC Kingman 23/11/45.

42-30622 Del Cheyenne 30/6/43; Gore 1/7/43; Cheyenne 2/7/43; 435BS/19BG Pyote 18/7/43; 110 BU Mitchell 1/8/44; 248 BU Walker 20/8/44; 233 BU Davis Monthan 6/9/44; 223 BU Dyersburg 2/11/44; 330 BU Dyersburg 1/3/45; 325 BU Avon Park 14/5/45; 326 BU McDill 15/5/45; 325 BU Avon Park 16/5/45; 335 BU Del Marbry 13/6/45; RFC Altus 4/10/45.

42-30623 Del Amarillo 1/7/434; Cheyenne 27/7/43; Gore 7/8/43; Dyersburg 8/8/43; ass 326BS/92BG [JW-L] Podington 16/9/43; MIA Augsburg 25/2/44 w/Nashold; flak, cr Saarbrücken; 1EVD 2KIA 7POW; MACR 2754.

42-30624 Del Amarillo 1/7/43; Cheyenne 26/7/43; Dyersburg 7/8/43; ass 322BS/91BG [LG-Q] Bassingbourn 23/9/43; MIA Emden 27/9/43 w/Struble; e/a, cr Emden; 5KIA 5POW; MACR 669. Sal 30/9/46. QUEEN BEE.

42-30625 Del Amarillo 1/7/43; Love 4/7/43; Dallas 19/7/43; Kingman 6/8/43; Geiger 8/8/43; Pendleton 12/8/43; ass 563BS/388BG Knettishall 3/9/43; sal n/b/d 15/7/45. JOHO'S JOKERS.

42-30626 Del Amarillo 1/7/43; Ephrata 18/7/43; Love 1/8/43; Kingman 2/8/43; 231 BU Alamogordo 22/7/44; 203 BU Jackson 2/2/45; 243 BU Gt Bend 6/9/45; RFC Kingman 27/10/45.

42-30627 Del Amarillo 1/7/43; Dallas 19/7/43; Kingman 4/8/43; 3030 BU Roswell 5/10/44; 3010 BU Williams 11/1/45; 3020 BU La Junta 20/4/45; RFC Altus 4/8/45.

42-30628 Del Amarillo 1/7/43; Ephrata 18/7/43; Las Vegas 1/8/43; Tinker 14/12/43; 3017 BU Hobbs 5/10/44; 3010 BU Williams 6/1/45; RFC Albuquerque 9/8/45.

42-30629 Del Amarillo 2/7/43; Ephrata 18/7/43; Love 1/8/43; Kingman 2/8/43; 2528 BU Midland 22/12/44; 231 BU Alamogordo 17/1/45; 4202 BU Syracuse 28/3/45; RFC Walnut Ridge 7/10/45.

42-30630 Del Amarillo 1/7/43; Ephrata 18/7/43; Kingman 1/8/43; Love 3/8/43; WO 29/8/43.

42-30631 Del Boeing 31/7/43; Seattle 12/8/43; Mat Com Eglin armament testing 7/10/43; ass 8AF; retUS 121 BU Bradley 11/8/45; RFC Altus 9/10/45. SHERRY GAL.

42-30632 Del Amarillo 2/7/43; Cheyenne 25/7/43; Ephrata 1/8/43; 242 BU Gr Isle 29/8/44; 504BG Fairmont 3/9/44; 241 BU Fairmont 16/9/44; 235 BU Biggs 3/11/44; 4202 BU Syracuse 3/4/45; Recl Comp 3/1/46.

42-30633 Del Amarillo 1/7/43; Ephrata 18/7/43; Kingman 1/8/43; Love 3/8/43; 359BS HQ Alamogordo 30/3/45; 203 BU Jackson 31/1/45; Recl Comp 2/4/45.

42-30634 Del Amarillo 2/7/43; Gr Isle 22/7/43; Walla Walla 1/8/43; Scott 9/8/43; Presque Is 17/8/43; ass 412BS/95BG [QW-O] Horham 20/8/43; MIA Brunswick 21/2/44 w/McGuigan; cr Zuider Zee; 6KIA 4POW; MACR 2423. LIBERTY BELLE.

42-30635 Del Amarillo 2/7/43; Dallas 19/7/43; Kingman 5/8/53; 2117 BU Buckingham 24/6/44; 2137 BU Hendricks 3/8/43; RFC Walnut Ridge 2/10/45.

42-30636 Del Amarillo 2/7/43; Presque Is 17/8/43; ass 327BS/92BG [UX-Y] Alconbury 31/8/43; MIA Frankfurt 2/3/44 w/Swart; e/a, cr Moerdijk, Hol; 10KIA. MACR 2853.

42-30637 Del Cheyenne 3/7/43; Gr Isle 22/7/43; Presque Is 30/7/43; ass MTO 6/8/43; Con Invm 7/8/44.

42-30638 Del Cheyenne 3/7/43; Gr Isle 22/7/43; Walla Walla 1/8/43; Scott 9/8/43; Presque Is 17/8/43; ass 327BS/92BG [UX-Y] Alconbury 30/8/43; Podington 16/9/43; tran 351BG Polebrook 16/11/43; 2 SAD Lt Staughton 17/11/43; sal n/b/d 29/5/45.

42-30639 Del Cheyenne 3/7/43; Dow Fd 27/7/43; ass 569BS/390BG [CC-U] Framlingham 6/8/43 COY-DE-COY II; tran RAF No 214Sq [BU-S] as SR380 21/4/44; WO 20/11/44.

42-30640 Del Cheyenne 3/7/43; Gr Isle 22/7/43; Walla Walla 1/8/43; Scott 9/8/43; Presque Is 17/8/43; ass 560BS/388BG Knettishall 20/8/43; sal n/b/d 3/1/44.

42-30641 Del Boeing 30/6/43; Mat Com Wright 2/6/44; MAT IRE Minneapolis 3/8/44; 510 BU New York City 1/9/44; 1454 BU Minneapolis 6/9/44; ATS Wright 31/10/44; ATC IRE Minneapolis 5/11/44; 1454 BU Minneapolis 10/11/44; 4000 BU Wright 23/7/45; RFC Altus 9/10/45.

42-30642 Del Cheyenne 3/7/43; Gore 4/7/43; Cheyenne 26/7/43; Dow Fd 27/7/43; ass 568BS/390BG [BI-O] Framlingham 6/8/43; tran 569BS [CC-O]; MIA Schweinfurt 19/7/44 w/Smith; flak, cr Malmedy, Bel; 10KIA; MACR 7555. GERONIMO.

42-30643 Del Cheyenne 3/7/43; Gr Isle 22/7/43; Walla Walla 1/8/43; Scott 9/8/43; ass 364BS/305BG [WF-P] Chelveston 2/9/43; u/c collapsed taxying for Brunswick mission; sal n/b/d 30/1/44.

42-30644 Del Cheyenne 5/7/43; Gr Isle 26/7/43; Walla Walla 1/8/43; Scott 11/8/43; Presque Is 16/8/43; ass 327BS/92BG [UX-V] Alconbury 7/9/43; Podington 11/9/43; MIA Merseburg 12/5/44 w/Marshall; flak, cr Koblenz; 3KIA 7POW; MACR 4851.

42-30645 Del Cheyenne 3/7/43; Kearney 24/7/43; Dow Fd 28/7/43; ass 364BS/305BG [WF-E] Chelveston 22/8/43; MIA Bremen 26/11/43 w/Jackman; flak, cr Oldenburg, Ger; 1KIA 9POW; MACR 1327.

42-30646 Del Cheyenne 5/7/43; Kearney 28/7/43; Topeka 12/8/43; ass 326BS/92BG [JW-O] Alconbury 2/9/43; MIA Schweinfurt 14/10/43 w/Fleming; e/a, cr Gerolstein, Ger; 2KIA 8POW; MACR 745.

42-30647 Del Cheyenne 5/7/43; Dow Fd 27/7/43; ass 366BS/305BG [KY-H] Chelveston 17/8/43; c/l base 23/9/43; sal. POLLY ANN.

42-30648 Del Cheyenne 5/7/43; Kearney 26/7/43; Topeka 14/8/43; ass 327BS/92BG [UX-U] Alconbury; MIA Bremen 20/12/43 w/Cole; e/a, cr Oldenburg, Ger; 8KIA 2POW; MACR 1710. WOOLAROC.

42-30649 Del Cheyenne 5/7/43; Kearney 26/7/43; Topeka 14/8/43; ass 327BS/92BG [UX-X] Alconbury 31/8/43; Podington 11/9/43; MIA Sorau 11/4/44 w/Harris; e/a, cr Martinsbuettel, Ger; 10KIA; MACR 3668.

42-30650 Del Cheyenne 7/7/43; Kearney 25/7/43; Dow Fd 28/7/43; ass 366BS/305BG [KY-D] Chelveston 12/8/43; 2 BAD Lt Staughton 20/3/44; retUS 20/4/44; 4136 BU Tinker 4/6/44; 556 BU Long Beach 5/8/44; 450 BU Hammer 17/8/44; 556 BU Long Beach 25/11/44; 4136 BU Tinker 17/3/45; 4100 BU Patterson 19/3/45; RFC Altus 20/8/45.

42-30651 Del Amarillo 3/7/45; Dallas 2/8/43; Gr Isle 13/8/43; ass 551BS/385BG Gt Ashfield 3/9/43; sal 6/4/44. PAT PENDING.

42-30652 Del Amarillo 3/7/43; Love 20/7/43; Dallas 21/7/43; Geiger 8/8/43; Love 10/8/43; ass 364BS/305BG [WF-J] Chelveston 15/9/43; 2 BAD Warton 20/3/44; retUS 611 BU Eglin 15/7/44; 610 BU Eglin 6/11/44; 4119 BU Brookley 4/12/44; 610 BU Eglin 17/1/45; RFC Walnut Ridge 5/1/46.

42-30653 Del Amarillo 3/7/43; Cheyenne 25/7/43; Geiger 5/8/43; Rapid City 10/8/43; Redmond 15/8/43; 325 BU Avon Park 9/7/44; 4117 BU Robins 11/9/44; 325 BU Avon Park 28/9/44; 331 BU Barksdale 1/3/45; RFC Walnut Ridge 26/9/45.

42-30654 Del Amarillo 5/7/43; Dallas 19/7/43; Geiger 8/8/43; Pendleton 14/8/43; ass 327BS/92BG [UX-W] Podington 16/9/43; MIA Schweinfurt 14/10/43 w/Brown; coll with e/a, cr Schweinfurt; 7KIA 3POW; MACR 848.

42-30655 Del Amarillo 5/7/43; Cheyenne 25/7/43; Gore 2/8/43; Geiger 3/8/43; Pendleton 12/8/43; WO 17/8/43.

42-30656 Del Amarillo 8/7/43; Dallas 21/7/43; Geiger 8/8/43; Walla Walla 12/8/43; Redmond 15/8/43; Gr Isle 3/9/43; ass 422BS/305BG NLS [JJ-D] Chelveston 6/9/43; tran 858BS SOP Cheddington 24/6/44; retUS 121 BU Bradley 12/7/44; RFC Altus 4/10/45. MISS MICKY FINN.

42-30657 Del Amarillo 5/7/43; slated 339BS/96BG [QJ-S]; Cheyenne 25/7/43; Pyote 1/8/43; 30BS/19BG Pyote 9/11/43; 247 BU Smoky Hill 4/6/44; 505 BU Scott 5/7/44; 247 BU Smoky Hill 2/8/44; 248 BU Walker 6/1/45; 247 BU Smoky Hill 8/1/45; 902 BU Orlando 12/3/45; 247 BU Smoky Hill 18/3/45; RFC Albuquerque 25/6/45.

42-30658 Del Amarillo 5/7/43; Cheyenne 25/7/43; Geiger 1/8/43; Pendleton 15/8/43; 225 BU Rapid City 7/6/44; 901 BU Pinecastle 10/6/44; 4136 BU Tinker 22/6/44; 9BG McCook 8/7/44; 245 BU McCook 16/9/43; 705 BU Lowry 16/10/44; 517 BU Elington 1/5/45; 705 BU Lowry 27/4/45; RFC Albuquerque 2/8/45.

42-30659 Del Amarillo 7/7/43; Dallas 19/7/434; ass 337BS/96BG [AW-K] Snetterton 3/9/43; sal n/b/d 29/5/45.

42-30660 Del Amarillo 7/7/43; Cheyenne 25/7/43; Geiger 3/8/43; 393BG Sioux City 22/12/43; 224 BU Sioux City 6/3/45; RFC Albuquerque 19/6/45.

42-30661 Del Amarillo 7/7/43; Dallas 19/7/43; Geiger 8/8/43; Pendleton 12/8/43; ass 562BS/388BG Knettishall 3/9/43; MIA Rostock 24/2/44 w/Montgomery; mechanical problem, f/l Rinkaby, Swed; 10INT; MACR 3080. VENI, VIDI, VICI. Became Swedish air liner SE-BAK, WO 12/46.

42-30662 Del Amarillo 7/7/43; Dallas 19/7/43; Geiger 8/8/43; Pendleton 12/8/43; ass 550BS/385BG Gt Ashfield 8/43; MIA Rostock 24/2/44 w/Terrace; e/a, cr Demmin, Ger; 1KIA 9POW; MACR 2778. CLARISSA JEAN.

42-30663 Del Cheyenne 8/7/43; Geiger 26/7/43; Walla Walla 8/8/43; 332 BU Lake Charles 13/7/44; 221 BU Alexandria 3/8/44; 329 BU Alexandria 1/3/45; 326 BU McDill 18/4/45; 331 BU Barksdale 15/5/45; RFC Walnut Ridge 26/9/45.

42-30664 Del Cheyenne 7/7/43; Gr Isle 26/7/43; Gore 28/7/43; Pendleton 30/7/43; Felts Fd 9/8/43; WO 29/9/43.

42-30665 Del Boeing 7/7/43; Gore 17/7/43; Dallas 8/8/43; Palm Springs 9/8/43; Geiger 10/8/43; Pendleton 12/8/43; ass 339BS/96BG [QJ-E] Snetterton 1/9/43; MIA Bordeaux 5/1/44 w/ Cole; flak, cr Bordeaux; 5EVD 1KIA 4POW; MACR 2814/2014. HUNYAK.

42-30666 Del Cheyenne 2/7/43; Kearney 25/7/43; Topeka 14/8/43; Scott 17/8/43; ass 364BS/305BG [WF-M] Chelveston 18/9/43; FTR from training flight 25/11/43; coll w/42-29953, 10KIA. WOLFESS.

42-30667 Del Cheyenne 8/7/43; Kearney 24/7/43; Topeka 13/8/43; Scott 14/8/43; ass 569BS/390BG [CC-V] Framlingham 25/8/43; MIA Emden 11/12/43 w/Gerald; flak, cr Harkstede, Hol; 10POW; MACR 1584. WILD CHILDREN.

42-30668 Del Cheyenne 8/7/43; Kearney 24/7/43; Dow Fd 28/7/43; ass 327BS/92BG Alconbury 15/8/43; Podington 16/9/43; MIA Stuttgart 6/9/43 w/Belongia; ditched Channel, 10RTD.

42-30669 Del Cheyenne 10/7/43; Spokane 25/7/43; Westover 26/12/43; Wendover 1/2/44; Cheyenne 24/2/44; Denver 8/3/44; Tampa 9/3/43; 328 BU Gulfport 26/7/44; RFC Albuquerque 25/6/45.

42-30670 Del Cheyenne 9/7/43; Orlando 11/7/43; Geiger 28/7/43; 383BG Pendleton 29/7/43; 393BG Geiger 27/11/43; 224 BU Sioux City 14/10/44; RFC Albuquerque 19/6/45.

42-30671 Del Cheyenne 9/7/43; 383BG Geiger 28/7/43; Pendleton 29/7/43; 224 BU Sioux City 6/3/45; RFC Albuquerque 25/6/45.

42-30672 Del Cheyenne 9/7/43; Dyersburg 27/7/43; Galveston 12/8/43; Dalhart 13/8/43; 9BG McCook 6/6/44; Mat NC Kansas City 31/8/44; 245 BU McCook 16/9/43; 100 BU Patterson 25/2/45; 244 BU Harvard 26/2/45; RFC Kingman 27/10/45.

42-30673 Del Cheyenne 10/7/43; Orlando 11/7/43; Dalhart 29/7/43; 232 BU Dalhart 9/6/44; 3034 BU Gardner 19/8/44; 4200 BU Chicago Mun 11/9/44; 232 BU Dalhart 26/9/44; 247 BU Smoky Hill 17/1/45; RFC Albuquerque 25/6/45.

42-30674 Del Dallas 10/7/43; Gr Isle 28/7/43; ass 336BS/95BG [ET-C] Horham 3/9/43 DESTINY'S TOT; then CINCINNATI QUEEN; MIA Ludwigshafen 30/12/43 w/Smith; cr St Justin?; 7EVD 3POW; MACR 2024. KATHY JANE III.

42-30675 Del Dallas 9/7/43; Kearney 28/7/43; Topeka 12/8/43; ass 8AF 11/9/43.

42-30676 Del Dallas 9/7/43; Kearney 29/7/43; Love 1/8/43; Topeka 12/8/43; ass 482BG Alconbury 24/8/43; tran 532BS/381BG [VE-E] Ridgewell 19/9/43; MIA Tours 5/1/44 w/Zeman; e/a, cr La Suze, Fr; 3EVD 1KIA 6POW; MACR 1962. BABY DUMPLING.

42-30677 Del Dallas 10/7/43; Kearney 29/7/43; Gulfport 8/8/43; Topeka 12/8/43; ass 326BS/92BG JW-K] Alconbury 30/8/43; MIA Bremen 16/12/43 w/Walsh; cr Weener, Ger; 2EVD 6KIA 2POW; MACR 1586.

42-30678 Del Dallas 10/7/43; Dow Fd 28/7/43; Kearney 6/8/43; Topeka 12/8/43; Scott 17/8/43; ass 366BS/305BG [KY-B] Chelveston 6/9/43; MIA Augsburg 25/2/44 w/Safranek; flak, cr Neresheim, Ger; 3KIA 7POW; MACR 2765.

42-30679 Del Dallas 10/7/43; Las Vegas 3/8/43; 2137 BU Hendricks 23/11/44; RFC Walnut Ridge 27/9/45.

42-30680 Del Cheyenne 12/7/43; Moses Lake 29/7/43; 4100 BU Patterson 19/2/45; 327 BU Drew 22/4/45; 301 BU Drew 23/9/45; RFC Altus 29/10/45.

42-30681 Del Boeing 8/7/43; 11AF Ladd Fd, Alaska, cold weather testing 9/9/43.

42-30682 Del Dallas 10/7/43; Love 1/8/43; Las Vegas 3/8/43; 2137 BU Hendricks 30/7/44; RFC Walnut Ridge 27/9/45.

42-30683 Del Dallas 12/7/43; Las Vegas 1/8/43; Tinker 14/12/43; 2137 BU Hendricks 11/11/44; Recl Comp 3/1/46.

42-30684 Del Dallas 10/7/43; Love 1/8/43; Las Vegas 2/8/43; Tinker 20/12/43; 3030 BU Roswell 16/9/44; 3010 BU Williams 2/12/44; 3020 BU La Junta 10/6/45; RFC Altus 3/8/45.

42-30685 Del Cheyenne 12/7/43; Geiger 26/7/43; Gt Falls 2/8/43; Glasgow 8/8/43; 543BS/388BG Geiger 16/9/43; Wendover 22/1/44; McDill 4/2/44; 328 BU Gulfport 8/7/44; RFC Albuquerque 19/6/45.

42-30686 Del Cheyenne 12/7/43; Dyersburg 27/7/43; c/l base, u/c collapsed 31/7/43 w/Adams, rep; WO 25/9/43.

42-30687 Del Cheyenne 12/7/43; Toppenish 27/7/43; Pendleton 30/7/43; Geiger 10/8/43; 542BS/383BG Geiger 23/10/43; 330 BU Dyersburg 1/3/45; 325 BU Avon Park 14/5/45; RFC Albuquerque 2/6/45.

42-30688 Del Cheyenne 3/7/43; Walla Walla 30/7/43; Redmond 15/8/43; 335 BU Del Marbry 9/11/44; 325 BU Avon Park 12/11/44; 2137 BU Hendricks 10/5/45; 325 BU Avon Park 23/5/45; RFC Altus 24/8/45.

42-30689 Del Cheyenne 13/7/43; Gr Isle 22/7/43; Presque Is 1/8/43; ass 416BS/99BG Navarin 28/8/43; Oudna 4/8/43; tran 97BG Depienne 14/11/43; Cerignola 20/12/43; Amendola 16/1/44; WO 31/3/44; rep, re-ass 885BS/68RG Blida, Alg; for secret mission into occupied territory; sal 24/5/45.

42-30690 Del Cheyenne 12/7/43; Dyersburg 27/7/43; WO 30/9/43.

42-30691 Del Cheyenne 12/7/43; Dalhart 28/7/43; 243 BU Gt Bend 19/9/44; 3502 BU Chanute 13/2/45; Recl Comp 20/8/46.

42-30692 Del Cheyenne 13/7/43; Pyote 1/8/43; 19BG Pyote 9/11/43; 500BG Walker 25/7/44; 248 BU Walker 20/8/44; 3505 BU Scott 16/10/44; 248 BU Walker 22/11/44; 2132 BU Maxwell 11/4/45; 4180 BU Walker 1/10/45; RFC Walnut Ridge 7/10/45.

42-30693 Del Cheyenne 10/7/43; Gt Falls 28/7/43; Spokane 4/8/43; Walla Walla, radar mod; 8/12/43; Denver 5/1/44; Mat Lockheed Burbank 24/6/44; 3701 BU Amarillo 23/7/44; 3706 BU Sheppard 12/5/44; 3701 BU Amarillo 1/11/45; RFC Walnut Ridge 5/1/46.

42-30694 Del Cheyenne 13/7/43; Gore 28/7/43; Geiger 29/7/43; Cutbank 2/8/43; WO 24/1/44.

42-30695 Del Cheyenne 14/7/43; Toppenish 27/7/43; Geiger 28/7/43; Pendleton 29/7/43; Geiger 10/8/43; 541BS/383BG Geiger 27/10/43; 245 BU McCook 1/6/44; 221 BU Alexandra 7/11/44; 329 BU Alexandra 1/3/45; RFC Altus 9/10/45.

42-30696 Del Cheyenne 14/7/43; Dyersburg 29/7/43; Galveston 12/8/43; Dalhart 13/8/43; 9BG McCook 6/6/44; 245 BU McCook 16/9/44; 3705 BU Lowry 16/10/44; WO 6/11/44; 3098 BU Burbank 28/2/45; Recl Comp 13/2/46.

42-30697 Del Cheyenne 13/7/43; Gore 14/7/43; Dyersburg 30/7/43; a/c fell from high altitude, exploded and burned at McKenzie, Tenn, 10/8/43 w/Moles; all eight killed.

42-30698 Del Cheyenne 13/7/43; Moses Lake 29/7/43; 327 BU Drew 15/7/44; RFC Altus 17/8/45.

42-30699 Del Cheyenne 14/7/43; Dyersburg 28/7/43; WO 21/4/44.

42-30700 Del Cheyenne 15/7/43; Moses Lake 29/7/43; 245 BU McCook 3/6/44; 224 BU Sioux City 6/3/45; RFC Albuquerque 25/6/45.

42-30701 Del Cheyenne 14/7/43; Moses Lake 29/7/43; 327 BU Drew 4/5/45; RFC Searcey Fd 11/8/45.

42-30702 Del Cheyenne 14/7/43; Moses Lake 29/7/43; 2142 BU Shaw Fd 29/10/44; 327 BU Drew 11/11/44; RFC Searcey Fd 7/8/45.

42-30703 Del Cheyenne 15/7/43; Pyote 1/8/43; 19BG Pyote 11/11/43; 235 BU Biggs 16/8/44; 233 BU Davis Monthan 12/11/44; 235 BU Biggs 14/11/44; 202 BU Galveston 28/1/45; 283 BU Galveston 30/3/45; 209 BU Galveston 28/4/45; RFC Searcey Fd 11/8/45.

42-30704 Del Dallas 15/7/43; Geiger 10/8/43; Pendleton 12/8/43; ass 422BS/305BG [JJ-M] Chelveston 18/9/43; 2 SAD Lt Staughton 17/5/44, sal n/b/d. DINAH MITE.

42-30705 Del Denver 15/7/43; Colorado Springs

16/7/43; Kearney 6/8/43; Topeka 12/8/43; Scott 17/8/43; ass 347BS/99BG Oudna 31/8/43; tran 414BS/97BG Depienne 14/11/43; MIA Rimini 27/11/43 w/Stedman; e/a, cr Rimini; MACR 1303.

42-30706 Del Denver 15/7/43; Gr Isle 23/7/43; Kearney 8/8/43; Topeka 13/8/43; Presque Is 17/8/43; ass 367BS/306BG [GY-W] Thurleigh 25/8/43; MIA Bremen 20/12/43 w/Ryther; e/a, cr off Frischenmoor?; 4KIA 6POW; MACR 1701.

42-30707 Del Denver 15/7/43; Gr Isle 27/7/43; Kearney 8/8/43; Topeka 13/8/43; Scott 17/8/43; ass 369BS/306BG [WW-B] Chelveston 25/8/43; MIA Schweinfurt 14/10/43 w/Holstrom; e/a, cr Hanau, Ger; 1EVD 3KIA 6POW; MACR 816. PICCADILLY COMMANDO.

42-30708 Del Denver 15/7/43; Gore 16/7/43; Kearney 8/8/43; Topeka 14/8/43; Scott 17/8/43; ass 407BS/92BG [PY-L] Alconbury 31/8/43; MIA Schweinfurt 14/10/43 w/Byrne; e/a, cr Schweinfurt; 3KIA 7POW; MACR 845.

42-30709 Del Denver 15/7/43; Gore 16/7/43; Gr Isle 24/7/43; Walla Walla 1/8/43; Scott 11/8/43; Presque 16/8/43; ass 388BG Knettishall 20/8/43; tran 96BG Snetterton 21/8/43; MIA Schweinfurt 14/10/43 w/Goodner; e/a, cr Metz, Fr; 10POW; MACR 836.

42-30710 Del Denver 15/7/43; Gr Isle 25/7/43; Walla Walla 1/8/43; Scott 9/8/43; Presque Is 17/8/43; ass 423BS/306BG [RD-I] Thurleigh 6/9/43; MIA Schweinfurt 14/10/43 w/Jackson; flak, cr Schweinfurt; 4KIA 6POW; MACR 818.

42-30711 Del Denver 16/7/43; Gore 28/7/43; Watertown 31/7/43; Kearney 3/8/43; Topeka 12/8/43; Scott 13/8/43; ass 407BS/92BG [PY-H] Alconbury 31/8/43; MIA Frankfurt 29/1/44 w/Holdren; mid air coll, cr Westende, Bel; 8KIA 2POW; MACR 2253. FERTILE TURTLE MYRTLE.

42-30712 Del Denver 16/7/43; Gore 7/8/43; Geiger 9/8/43; Walla Walla 12/8/43; Redmond 15/8/43; ass 323BS/91BG [OR-O/R] Bassingbourn 27/9/43; MIA {23m} Achmer 21/2/44 w/Ward; e/a, cr Luechtreigen, Ger?; 4KIA 6POW; MACR 2461. MISS MINOOKIE.

42-30713 Del Denver 17/7/43; Scott 10/8/43; ass 568BS/390BG [BI-G] Framlingham 25/8/43; MIA Berlin 6/3/44 w/Quakenbush; e/a, cr Werben, Ger; 10POW; MACR 2987. PHYLLIS MARIE. Sal by Luftwaffe and found OK in Bavaria in 1945.

42-30714 Del Denver 16/7/43; Gr Isle 8/8/43; ass 423BS/306BG [RD-A] Thurleigh 25/8/43; c/l Lasham, UK 1/12/43; sal n/b/d. HUSTLING SUE.

42-30715 Del Denver 17/7/43; Geiger 8/8/43; Walla Walla 28/8/43; Redmond 15/8/43; ass 569BS/390BG [CC-Y] Framlingham 12/9/43 CINCINNATI QUEEN; MIA Berlin 21/6/44. BLUES IN THE NIGHT.

42-30716 Del Denver 16/7/43; Gore 26/7/43; Gr Isle 27/7/43; Kearney 9/8/43; Topeka 13/8/43; Scott 17/8/43; ass 407BS/92BG [PY-G] Alconbury 2/9/43; c/l Barford St John, UK, 28/1/44; crew OK; sal n/b/d 30/1/44.

42-30717 Del Denver 16/7/43; Kearney 27/7/43; Scott 14/8/43; ass 548BS/385BG Gt Ashfield 25/8/43; MIA Bremen 13/11/43 w/Dawurake; mid air coll, cr Bissel, Ger; 4KIA 6POW; MACR 1402. MAN O' WAR.

42-30718 Del Denver 16/7/43; Sioux City 30/7/43; Kearney 3/8/43; Topeka 14/8/43; Scott 17/8/43; ass 8AF 2/9/43; sal n/b/d Prestwick 7/9/43.

42-30719 Del Denver 17/7/43; Kearney 27/7/43; Scott 14/8/43; ass 569BS/390BG [CC-P] Framlingham 25/8/43; MIA Duren 20/10/43 w/Schyler; e/a, cr Hertgenbosch, Ger; 1EVD 2KIA 7POW; MACR 1039. SHATZI.

42-30720 Del Dallas 17/7/43; Gore 18/7/43; Dallas 21/7/43; Geiger 8/8/43; Gr Isle 10/8/43; ass 367BS/306BG Thurleigh; tran 526BS/379BG [LF-O] Kimbolton 19/10/43; tran 15AF 2/5/44; Ret UK AFSC 7/6/44; retUS 4136 BU 3/7/44; 610 BU Eglin 23/2/45; RFC Walnut Ridge 5/1/46. NINE YANKS AND A REBEL.

42-30721 Del Dallas 19/7/43; Gr Isle 11/8/43; ass 482BG Alconbury 31/8/43; tran 533BS/381BG [VP-T] Ridgewell 20/9/43; {28m} 8AF Fight Com as radio relay a/c 25/4/44; 610BS/398BG [3O] Nuthampstead 15/11/44; retUS 121 BU Bradley 12/7/45; RFC Altus 4/10/45. SWEET AND LOVELY.

42-30722 Del Dallas 19/7/43; Gr Isle 16/8/43; ass 482BG Alconbury 31/8/43; tran 534BS/381BG [GD-G] Ridgewell 20/9/43; MIA {1m} Bremen 8/10/43 w/Lishon; e/a, cr Bremen; 10POW; MACR 1398. BOBBY T.

42-30723 Del Dallas 17/7/43; Geiger 8/8/43; Pendleton 22/8/43; ass 351BS/100BG [EP-D] Thorpe Abbotts 31/8/43 HOLY TERROR; MIA Münster 10/10/43 w/MacCarter; flak, cr Xanten, Ger; 6KIA 4POW; MACR 1026. SEXY SUZY, MOTHER OF TEN.

42-30724 Del Dallas 17/7/43; Scott 8/8/43; Presque Is 17/8/43; ass 368BS/306BG Thurleigh 20/8/43; tran 364BS/305BG [WF-D] Chelveston 31/8/43; MIA Kiel 5/1/44 w/Barker; e/a, cr Cuxhaven, Ger; 1KIA 9POW; MACR 1685.

42-30725 Del Dallas 17/7/43; Love 7/8/43; Geiger 8/8/43; Pendleton 12/8/43; ass 359BS/100BG [LN-D] Thorpe Abbotts 3/9/43; MIA Münster 10/10/43 w/Cruikshank; flak, cr Lienen, Ger; 2KIA 8POW; MACR 1028. AW-R-GO.

42-30726 Del Dallas 19/7/43; Dalhart 17/8/43; ass 407BS/92BG [PY-X] Alconbury 16/9/43; MIA Schweinfurt 14/10/43 w/Webb; e/a, cr Duren, Ger; 6KIA 4P0W; MACR 846.

42-30727 Del Dallas 19/7/43; Scott 10/8/43; ass 367BS/306BG [GY-Z] Thurleigh 2/9/43; MIA Schweinfurt 14/10/43 w/Bisson; flak, cr Mannheim, Ger; 5KIA 5POW; MACR 817. FIGHTIN' BITIN'.

42-30728 Del Dallas 19/7/43; Gr Isle 11/8/43; ass 367BS/306BG [GY-S] Thurleigh; MIA Augsburg 25/2/44 w/Gay; e/a, cr St Aignan, Fr; 5KIA 5POW; MACR 2769.

42-30729 Del Dallas 20/7/43; GR Isle 15/8/43; ass 813BS/482BG [PC-V] Alconbury 5/9/43; tran 306BG Thurleigh 2/5/44; sal 29/6/45.

42-30730 Del Denver 19/7/43; Geiger 9/8/32; Walla Walla 11/8/43; Redmond 15/8/43; ass 369BS/306BG [WW-B] Thurleigh 20/9/43; MIA Erding 24/4/44 w/Ramsey; e/a, cr Augsburg, Ger; 10POW; MACR 4278. DEARLY BELOVED.

42-30731 Del Denver 20/7/43; Gore 21/7/43; Gr Isle 14/8/43; ass 388BG Knettishall 4/9/43; tran 813BS/482BG [PC-U] Alconbury 5/9/43; MIA 7/7/44. MACR 8195.

42-30732 Del Denver 21/7/43; Geiger 6/8/43; Pendleton 7/8/43; ass 534BS/381BG [GD-B] Ridgewell 26/9/43; {7m} c/l Alconbury on non-op diverted from Lt Staughton 3/2/44; sal n/b/d. PISTOL PACKIN' MAMA.

42-30733 Del Denver 20/7/43; Gore 8/8/43; Dyersburg 10/8/43; ass 326BS/92BG Alconbury 16/9/43; MIA Bordeaux 31/12/43 w/Grumbler; flak, cr Chet Bettone, Fr; 2EVD 1KIA 7POW; MACR 1958.

42-30734 Del Denver 20/7/43; long Beach 8/8/43; Geiger 10/8/43; Walla Walla 12/8/43; Redmond 15/8/43; ass 351BS/100BG [EP-G] Thorpe Abbotts 5/9/43; MIA Münster 10/10/43 w/Thompson; e/a, cr Hohenhalte, Ger?; 3KIA 7POW; MACR 1025. SLIGHTLY DANGEROUS.

42-30735 Del Denver 20/7/43; Geiger 8/8/43; Gore 13/8/43; Redmond 15/8/43; ass 327BS/92BG [UX-P] Alconbury 26/9/43; MIA Bordeaux 31/12/43 w/Stroff; flak, cr La Rochelle; 3EVD 7POW; MACR 1957.

42-30736 Del Denver 20/7/43; Geiger 8/8/43; Walla Walla 11/8/43; Redmond 15/8/43; ass 413BS/96BG [MZ-A] Snetterton 13/9/43; sal 20/10/43; retUS 121 BU Bradley 31/7/44. PAPER DOLL.

42-30737 Del Denver 21/7/43; Love 23/7/43; Dyersburg 9/8/43; ass 549BS/385BG Gt Ashfield 3/9/43; MIA Augsburg 16/3/44 w/Krause; e/a, cr St Quentin, Fr; 2KIA 8POW; MACR 3245. OHIO AIR FORCE.

42-30738 Del Denver 21/7/43; Walla Walla 30/7/43; 325 BU Avon Park 9/4/45; Recl Comp 9/6/45.

42-30739 Del Denver 21/7/43; Gore 30/7/43; Walla Walla 31/7/43; 110 Mitchell 8/6/44; WO 12/8/44.

42-30740 Del Cheyenne 21/7/43; Dalhart 29/7/43; 232 BU Dalhart 9/6/44; Mat Lockheed Burbank 15/6/44; 4208 BU Mines Fd 11/9/44; 232 BU Dalhart 19/9/44; 4200 Chicago Mun 10/11/44; 232 BU Dalhart 21/11/44; 246 BU Pratt 13/12/44; 232 BU Dalhart 10/1/45; 248 BU Walker 1/2/45; RFC Albuquerque 25/6/45.

42-30741 Del Cheyenne 22/7/43; Moses Lake 30/7/43; 225 BU Rapid City 29/4/45; RFC Ontario 27/8/45.

42-30742 Del Cheyenne 21/7/43; Walla Walla 29/7/43; WO 19/9/43.

42-30743 Del Cheyenne 22/7/43; Ephrata 1/8/43; 504BG Fairmont 8/9/44; 241 BU Fairmont 16/9/44; 1103 BU Morrison 12/1/45; 241 BU Fairmont 19/1/45; 233 BU Davis Monthan 4/3/45; RFC Ontario 29/6/45.

42-30744 Del Cheyenne 21/7/43; Walla Walla 30/7/43; Redmond 15/8/43; WO 20/8/43.

42-30745 Del Cheyenne 21/7/43; Walla Walla 30/7/43; Gt Falls 2/8/43; c/l 4/8/43 w/Garland, u/c collapsed, rep; 225 BU Rapid City 29/4/45; RFC Ontario 29/6/45.

42-30746 Del Cheyenne 22/7/43; Walla Walla 30/7/43; Gt Falls 2/8/43; Cutbank 4/8/43; WO 5/5/44.

42-30747 Del Cheyenne 24/7/43; Geiger 3/8/43; Pendleton 15/8/43; 225 BU Rapid City 10/10/44, WO; Recl Comp 2/11/44.

42-30748 Del Cheyenne 23/7/43; Geiger 6/8/43; Pendleton 15/8/43; 457BG Geiger 6/11/43; 234 BU Clovis 24/6/44; 249 BU Alliance 25/10/44; 2168 BU Wendover 22/1/45; RFC Kingman 30/10/45.

42-30749 Del Cheyenne 22/7/43; Walla Walla 30/7/43; Cheyenne 4/8/43; WO 2/10/43.

42-30750 Del Cheyenne 23/7/43; Geiger 3/8/43; 542BS/383BG Geiger 23/10/43; WO 7/1/44.

42-30751 Del Cheyenne 23/7/43; Ephrata 1/8/43; 222 BU Ardmore 22/1/45; 332 BU Ardmore 19/8/45; RFC Walnut Ridge 14/9/45.

42-30752 Del Cheyenne 23/7/43; Geiger 6/8/43; Pendleton 12/8/43; 236 BU Pyote 9/11/44; 222 BU Ardmore 28/11/44; 332 BU Ardmore 16/6/45; RFC Walnut Ridge 26/9/45.

42-30753 Del Cheyenne 24/7/43; Geiger 4/8/43; Rapid City 10/8/43; Geiger 14/8/43; 543BS/383BG Geiger 22/9/43; 4115 BU Atlanta 5/10/44; 4204 BU Atlanta 11/10/44; 325 BU Avon Park 27/10/44; 4100 BU Patterson 19/2/45; 4108 BU Newark 5/6/45; 4100 BU Patterson 6/6/45; 4114 BU Oak Apt 29/6/45; 4127 BU McClellan 23/9/45; RFC Kingman 27/12/45.

42-30754 Del Cheyenne 23/7/43; Ephrata 1/8/43; Felts Fd 14/8/43; 222 BU Peterson 15/9/43; 2533 BU Goodfellow 25/10/44; 268 BU Peterson 14/2/45;

201 BU Peterson 16/2/45; 200 BU Peterson 25/8/45; RFC Kingman 27/10/45.

42-30755 Del Cheyenne 23/7/43; slated 325BS/92BG [NV-R]; tran 542BS/383BG Geiger 3/8/43; 452BG Pendleton 23/10/43; 202 BU Galveston 8/8/44; 268 BU Peterson 30/3/45; RFC Altus 9/10/45.

42-30756 Del Cheyenne 24/7/43; Gore 1/8/43; Geiger 3/8/43; Pendleton 12/8/43; 452BG Geiger 19/10/43; 330 BU Dyersburg 1/3/45; 325 BU Avon Park 3/6/45; RFC Altus 22/8/45.

42-30757 Del Cheyenne 24/7/43; Gore 1/8/43; Geiger 3/8/43; 245 BU McCook 13/6/44; 9BG McCook 20/6/44; 245 BU McCook 16/9/44; 202 BU Galveston 22/11/44; 245 BU McCook 27/11/44; RFC Albuquerque 25/6/45.

42-30758 Del Cheyenne 24/7/43; Dyersburg 7/8/43; Dalhart 15/8/43; ass 418BS/100BG [LD-W] Thorpe Abbotts 31/8/43; MIA Frankfurt 4/2/44 w/McPhee; flak, cr Weisbaden, Ger; 10POW; MACR 2344. ROSIE'S RIVETERS.

42-30759 Del Cheyenne 24/7/43; Gore 1/8/43; Spokane 4/8/43; Geiger 5/8/43; Kearney 9/8/43; WO 8/9/43.

42-30760 Del Cheyenne 24/7/43; Pyote 1/8/43; 435BS/19BG Pyote 9/11/43; 222 BU Ardmore 22/1/45; RFC 20/6/45.

42-30761 Del Cheyenne 24/7/43; Geiger 6/8/43; Pendleton 12/8/43; 202 BU Galveston 13/8/44; 222 BU Ardmore 19/8/44; 332 BU Ardmore 16/6/45; RFC Walnut Ridge 13/11/45.

42-30762 Del Cheyenne 25/7/43; Geiger 4/8/43; Rapid City 11/8/43; 383BG Geiger 10/11/43; WO 20/4/44.

42-30763 Del Cheyenne 24/7/43; Pendleton 7/8/43; Geiger 15/8/43; 88BG Walla Walla 18/8/43; 2137 BU Hendricks 10/5/45; 325 BU Avon Park 23/5/45; RFC Altus 9/10/45.

42-30764 Del Cheyenne 27/7/43; 3701 BU Amarillo 23/7/44; 3706 BU Sheppard 29/3/45; 3701 BU Amarillo 23/4/45; RFC Walnut Ridge 26/10/45.

42-30765 Del Cheyenne 25/7/43; Dyersburg 8/8/43; ass 535BS/381BG [MS-U] Ridgewell 20/9/43; {9m} f/l Warminster, UK, 29/12/43 w/Ridley; sal n/b/d 2/1/44. CHUG-A-LUG IV.

42-30766 Del Cheyenne 25/7/43; Geiger 3/8/43; 398BG Geiger 18/8/43; 242 BU Gr Isle 19/6/44; 6BG Gr isle 8/7/44; 268 BU Peterson 18/9/44; 242 BU Gr Isle 25/9/44; 249 BU Alliance 14/10/44; 245 BU McCook 9/1/45; RFC Albuquerque 25/6/45.

42-30767 Del Cheyenne 27/7/43; Gore 28/7/43; Cheyenne 4/8/43; Scott 9/8/43; ass 367BS/306BG [GY-Y] Thurleigh 21/9/43; c/l Sharnbrook, UK 5/1/44; 8KIA; sal n/b/d.

42-30768 Del Cheyenne 25/7/43; Geiger 5/8/43; Omaha 8/8/43; Kearney 10/8/43; WO 2/3/44.

42-30769 Del Cheyenne 25/7/43; Geiger 6/8/43; Omaha 8/8/43; Kearney 9/8/43; 224 BU Sioux City 6/3/45; RFC Albuquerque 19/6/45.

42-30770 Del Cheyenne 25/7/43; Spokane 4/8/43; Geiger 5/8/43; Omaha 8/8/43; Kearney 10/8/43; 224 BU Sioux City 6/3/45; RFC Albuquerque 19/6/45.

42-30771 Del Cheyenne 27/7/43; Geiger 4/8/43; Rapid City 18/8/43; Pendleton 12/8/43; 225 BU Rapid City 29/4/45; RFC Ontario 10/6/45.

42-30772 Del Cheyenne 27/7/43; Dyersburg 8/8/43; ass 524BS/379BG [WA-R] Kimbolton 31/8/43; tran 323BS/91BG [OR-V] Bassingbourn 23/9/43; MIA Anklam 9/10/43 w/Walsh; e/a, cr Baltic Sea; 8KIA 2POW; MACR 895.

42-30773 Del Cheyenne 27/7/43; Gore 7/8/43; Dyersburg 8/8/43; ass 324BS/91BG [DF-B/J] Bassingbourn 26/9/43; tran RAF No 214Sq (SR381) [BU-F] Sculthorpe 19/1/44; hit by JU88 31/7/44.

42-30774 Del Cheyenne 26/7/43; Geiger 6/8/43; Pendleton 12/8/43; Harvard 19/8/43; WO 31/8/43.

42-30775 Del Cheyenne 26/7/43; Geiger 5/8/43; Pendleton 12/8/43; ass 422NLS/305BG [JJ-P] Chelveston 18/9/43; tran 858BS Cheddington 24/6/44; sal n/b/d 6/1/45.

42-30776 Del Cheyenne 26/7/43; Dyersburg 7/8/43; ass 368BS/306BG [BO-F] Thurleigh 20/9/43; MIA Wilhelmshaven 3/11/43 w/Goris; mid air col w/42-3533, cr Nth Sea; 10KIA; MACR 158.

42-30777 Del Cheyenne 26/7/43; 444BG Gt Bend 27/8/43; 331 BU Barksdale 18/7/44; 500BG Walker 27/7/43; 558 BU Nashville 27/8/43; 500BG Walker 3/10/43; 4200 Chicago Mun 15/10/43; 248 BU Harvard 17/10/44; 248 BU Walker 28/10/44; RFC Albuquerque 25/6/45.

42-30778 Del Cheyenne 28/7/43; Gore 6/8/43; Pendleton 12/8/43; Reno 14/8/43; Pierre 16/8/43; ass 561BS/388BG Knettishall 3/9/43; c/t/o 13/8/44; 9RTD; sal. LADY MARGARET.

42-30779 Del Cheyenne 28/7/43; Dyersburg 8/8/43; ass 369BS/306BG [WW-U] Thurleigh 18/9/43; MIA Schweinfurt 14/10/43 w/Lockyear; e/a, cr Hammerstein, Ger; 3KIA 7POW; MACR 815.

42-30780 Del Cheyenne 27/7/43; Geiger 9/8/43; Pendleton 12/8/43; ass 509BS/351BG [RQ-H/T] Polebrook 21/9/43; MIA {10m} Oschersleben 11/1/44 w/Myers; e/a, cr Oschersleben; 7KIA 3POW; MACR 1938. EAGER EAGLE II.

42-30781 Del Cheyenne 27/7/43; Dyersburg 7/8/43; ass 413BS/96BG [MZ-M] Snetterton 1/9/43; MIA Anklam 9/10/43 w/Hunt; e/a, cr Denmark; 10KIA, MACR 945.

42-30782 Del Cheyenne 29/7/43; Gr Isle 8/8/43; ass 368BS/306BG [BO-O] Thurleigh; tran 369BS; MIA Oschersleben 11/1/44 w/Reed; flak, cr Nijverdal, Hol; 5KIA 5POW; MACR 1931.

42-30783 Del Cheyenne 28/7/43; Scott 9/8/43; ass 388BG Knettishall 24/8/43; tran 570BS/390BG [DI-M] 25/8/43 STORK'S CLUB; MIA Augsburg 16/3/44 w/DeMayo; e/a, cr Lautern?; 8KIA 2POW; MACR 3180. THE STORK CLUB.

42-30784 Del Cheyenne 28/7/43; Dyersburg 7/8/43; ass 325BS/92BG [NV-G] Alconbury 27/9/43; sal n/b/d 6/1/44.

42-30785 Del Cheyenne 29/7/43; Dyersburg 8/8/43; ass 508BS/351BG [YB-H] Polebrook 23/9/43; MIA {1m} Frankfurt 4/10/43 w/Reed; e/a, cr Frankfurt; 3KIA 7POW; MACR 908.

42-30786 Del Cheyenne 30/7/43; WO 22/11/43.

42-30787 Del Cheyenne 29/7/43; Gore 30/7/43; Cheyenne 31/7/43; 223 BU Dyersburg 27/9/44; WO 27/9/44.

42-30788 Del Cheyenne 28/7/43; Dyersburg 8/8/43; Denver 9/8/43; Lowry 12/8/43; Dyersburg 14/8/43; ass 350BS/100BG [LN-R] Thorpe Abbotts 5/9/43; MIA Regensburg 25/2/44 w/McLain; flak, cr Channel; 8KIA 2POW; MACR 2760. MISMALOVIN'.

42-30789 Del Cheyenne 28/7/43; Dyersburg 7/8/43; ass 563BS/388BG Knettishall 3/9/43; MIA Gelsenkirchen 5/11/43 w/Bramwell; flak, cr Lokeren, Bel; 3EVD 2KIA 5POW; MACR 3137. FLAK SUIT.

42-30790 Del Cheyenne 28/7/43; Gore 29/7/43; Cheyenne 4/8/43; Dalhart 15/8/43; ass 511BS/351BG [DS-Q] Polebrook 22/9/43; MIA {2m} Anklam 9/10/43 w/Capt Morse; e/a, cr Anklam; 11POW; MACR 878. CUE BALL.

42-30791 Del Cheyenne 29/7/43; Dyersburg 8/8/43; ass 422NLS/305BG JJ-J] Chelveston 1/10/43; tran 858BS Cheddington 24/6/44; then 406BS Cheddington 11/8/44; sal 4/12/44. PISTOL PACKIN' MAMA.

42-30792 Del Cheyenne 29/7/43; Dyersburg 8/8/43; Galveston 15/8/43; Dyersburg 17/8/43; ass 339BS/96BG [QJ-E] Snetterton 5/9/43; MIA Emden 27/9/43 w/Drabnis; flak, cr Emden; 2KIA 8POW; MACR 756.

42-30793 Del Cheyenne 29/7/43; Dyersburg 8/8/43; ass 562BS/388BG Knettishall 3/9/43; sal 11/4/44. TOM PAINE.

42-30794 Del Cheyenne 29/7/43; Dyersburg 8/8/43; ass 369BS/306BG [WW-V/P] Thurleigh 25/8/43; MIA Kiel 5/1/44 w/ Wolfe; e/a, cr Kiel; 8KIA 2POW; MACR 1683.

42-30795 Del Cheyenne 29/7/43; Dyersburg 8/8/43; ass 548BS/385BG Gt Ashfield 2/9/43; MIA Münster 11/11/43 w/McGowan; flak, cr Druner?; 1EVD 1KIA 8POW; MACR 1161. THE WILD HARE.

42-30796 Del Cheyenne 29/7/43; Gr Isle 9/8/43; ass 351BS/100BG [EP-K] Thorpe Abbotts 28/8/43; c/l Harleston, UK 30/12/43; sal 2/1/44. SUNNY II.

42-30797 Del Eglin 29/7/43; Gore 30/7/43; Eglin 8/8/43; WO 26/9/43.

42-30798 Del Cheyenne 29/7/43; 611 BU Eglin 2/6/44; 610 BU Eglin 4/9/44; 216 BU Wendover 19/9/44; RFC Walnut Ridge 11/12/45.

42-30799 Del Cheyenne 29/7/43; Gore 9/8/43; Scott 10/8/43; Presque Is 16/8/43; ass 349BS/100BG [XR-L] Thorpe Abbotts 20/8/43; MIA Berlin 6/3/44 w/Murray; e/a, cr Haseluene, Ger; 3KIA 7POW. MACR 3017. BIG ASS BIRD II.

42-30800 Del Cheyenne 30/7/43; Gr Isle 9/8/43; ass 563BS/388BG Knettishall 3/9/43; MIA Brunswick 29/2/44 w/Colvin (and 730BS/452BG crew); 4KIA 6POW; MACR 2893. COCK O' THE WALK.

42-30801 Del Cheyenne 30/7/43; Gr Isle 8/8/43; ass 8AF 1/9/43; MIA 10/9/43.

42-30802 Del Dallas 30/7/43; Gr Isle 14/8/43; ass 560BS/388BG Knettishall 5/9/43; MIA Anklam 9/10/43 w/Kinney; e/a, ditched Nth Sea; 1KIA 9POW; MACR 3138. GYNIDA.

42-30803 Del Dallas 30/7/43; Gore 31/7/43; Dallas 3/8/43; ass 325BS/92BG [NV-O] Podington 27/9/43; MIA Leverkusen 1/12/43 w/Hale; flak, cr Montjoie, Fr; 9KIA 1POW; MACR 1387.

42-30804 Del Dallas 30/7/43; Gore 31/7/43; Dallas 2/8/43; Redmond 17/8/43; ass 365BS/305BG [XK-G] Chelveston 18/9/43; MIA Schweinfurt 14/10/43 w/Maxwell; e/a, cr Schweinfurt; 7KIA 3POW; MACR 922.

42-30805 Del Dallas 30/7/43; Love 16/8/43; Redmond 17/8/43; ass 401BS/91BG [LL-H] Bassingbourn 24/9/43; MIA {2m} Wilhelmshaven 3/11/43 w/Pitts; e/a, cr Wilhelmshaven; 7KIA 3POW; MACR 1155. BOMB BOOGIE'S REVENGE.

42-30806 Del Dallas 30/7/43; Love 16/8/43; Redmond 17/8/43; ass 339BS/96BG [QJ-G] Snetterton 9/9/43; MIA Schweinfurt 14/10/43 w/Scarborough; e/a, cr Rheims, Fr; 10POW; MACR 832. V-PACKET.

42-30807 Del Dallas 30/7/43; Dyersburg 8/8/43; Galveston 17/8/43; ass 364BS/305BG [WF-K] Chelveston 18/9/43; MIA Schweinfurt 14/10/43 w/Eakle; e/a, cr Elsden?; 1EVD 1KIA 8POW; MACR 912.

42-30808 Del Cheyenne 30/7/43; Dyersburg 8/8/43; ass 563BS/388 Knettishall 4/9/43; MIA Münster 23/3/44 w/Filler; e/a, cr Walle, Ger; 5KIA 5POW; MACR 3541.

42-30809 Del Cheyenne 4/8/43; Gr Isle 10/8/43; ass 366BS/305BG [KY-G] Chelveston 6/9/43; tran RAF No214Sq (SR382) [BU-B] 22/1/44 Sculthorpe, Nfk.

42-30810 Del Cheyenne 4/8/43; Gr Isle 11/8/43; ass 338BS/96BG [BX-Y] Snetterton 11/9/43; MIA Munich

18/3/44 w/Muirhead; e/a, cr Freiburg, Ger; 3KIA 7POW; MACR 3422.

42-30811 Del Cheyenne 4/8/43; Gr Isle 12/8/43; ass 369BS/306BG [WW-D] Thurleigh 2/9/43; MIA Schweinfurt 14/10/43 w/Peters; e/a, cr Schweinfurt; 10POW; MACR 814.

42-30812 Del Cheyenne 4/8/43; Gr Isle 12/8/43; ass 423BS/306BG [RD-Q] Thurleigh 4/9/43; tran RAF No214Sq (SR383) [BU-F] Sculthorpe, Nfk, 29/1/44; 223Sq [6G-X]; 1699Flt [4Z-Z]; BDU RAF 1483 Flt Newmarket; WO 1/8/45.

42-30813 Del Cheyenne 31/7/43; Seattle 1/8/43; Cheyenne 2/8/43; Scott 10/8/43; ass 423BS/306BG [RD-L] Thurleigh 2/9/43; MIA Schweinfurt 14/10/43 w/McCallum; e/a, cr Dornes, Fr; 5KIA 5POW; MACR 820. QUEEN JEANNIE.

42-30814 Del Cheyenne 30/7/43; Dyersburg 8/8/43; ass 96BG Snetterton 7/9/43; tran 366BS/305BG [KY-F] Chelveston 21/9/43; MIA Schweinfurt 14/10/43 w/Skerry; e/a, cr Adendorf, Ger; 2KIA 8POW; MACR 919.

42-30815 Del Cheyenne 4/8/43; 498BG Kansas City 3/6/43; 243 BU Gt Bend 12/6/44; 554 BU Memphis 19/8/44; 243 BU Gt Bend 29/6/44; 2519 BU Fort Worth 11/9/44; 19BG Gt Bend 12/9/44; 243 BU Gt Bend 13/10/44; 241 BU Fairmont 12/2/45; 243 BU Gt Bend 18/2/45; 902 BU Orlando 16/4/45; 243 BU Gt Bend 26/4/45; RFC Albuquerque 25/5/45.

42-30816 Del Cheyenne 31/7/43; Gr Isle 9/8/43; ass 551BS/385BG Gt Ashfield 25/8/43; MIA Emden 11/12/43 w/Poore; e/a, cr Warfhuizen, Hol; 2KIA 8POW; MACR 1664. MARY ELLEN III.

42-30817 Del Cheyenne 4/8/43; Gr Isle 11/8/43; ass 334BS/95BG [BG-G] Horham 15/6/43; MIA Münster 10/10/43 w/Adams; cr?; 10POW; MACR 1044. MISS FLOWER III.

42-30818 Del Cheyenne 4/8/43; Gr Isle 11/8/43; ass 350BS/100BG [LN-S] Thorpe Abbotts 25/8/43; MIA Bremen 8/10/43 w/Capt McDonald; flak, cr Wijn Jeterp, Hol; 1EVD 1KIA 8POW; MACR 952. SALVO SAL.

42-30819 Del Cheyenne 4/8/43; Gr Isle 12/8/43; ass 551BS/385BG Gt Ashfield 25/8/43 SHACK BUNNY; sal n/b/d 29/5/45 LULU BELLE.

42-30820 Del Cheyenne 4/8/43; 234 BU Clovis 24/6/44; 3701 BU Amarillo 23/7/44; 234 BU Clovis 29/7/43; 4202 BU Syracuse 29/4/45; RFC Altus 29/10/45.

42-30821 Del Cheyenne 31/7/43; Gr Isle 9/8/43; ass 407BS/92BG Podington 16/9/43; c/l Chipping Warden RAF 13/11/43; sal AFSC 12/11/43.

42-30822 Del Dallas 4/8/43; Denver 16/8/43; Dalhart 17/8/43; ass 551BS/385BG Gt Ashfield 8/9/43 THE DORSAL QUEEN; MIA Regensburg 25/2/44 w/Gray; flak, cr Regensburg; 7KIA 3POW; MACR 2776. FOOLISH VIRGIN.

42-30823 Del Dallas 4/8/43; Gore 5/8/43; Dallas 8/8/43; ass 350BS/100BG [LN-F] Thorpe Abbotts 6/9/43 INVADIN' MAIDEN; MIA Münster w/Brady; e/a, cr Münster; 5KIA 5POW; MACR 1029. THE GNOMO.

42-30824 Del Dallas 4/8/43; Gore 5/8/43; Dallas 8/8/43; Dalhart 17/8/43; ass 327BS/92BG [UX-R] Podington 26/9/43; MIA Schweinfurt 14/10/43 w/Talbot; e/a, cr Villingen, Ger; 5KIA 5POW; MACR 847.

42-30825 Del Dallas 4/8/43; Gore 5/8/43; Dallas 8/8/43; 19BG Pyote 9/11/43; 235 BU Biggs 19.8.43; 231 BU Alamogordo 18/10/44; 235 BU Biggs 9/11/44; 233 Davis Monthan 18/3/45; 290 BU Pueblo 27/5/43; 224 mBU Sioux City 12/6/45; 237 BU Drew 7/7/45; 2113 BU Columbus 10/9/45; 610 BU Eglin 5/12/45; sal Eglin 29/1/46.

42-30826 Del Dallas 4/8/43; Gore 5/8/43; Dallas 8/8/43; Dalhart 17/8/43; Gr Isle 3/9/43; ass 571BS/390BG [FC-R] Framlingham 10/9/43; MIA Münster 10/10/43 w/Capt Short; e/a, cr Ost Bevern, Ger; 2KIA 9POW; MACR 863. SHORT STUFF.

42-30827 Del Cheyenne 4/8/43; Gr Isle 13/8/43; ass 549BS/385BG Gt Ashfield 25/8/43; tran 17th Airborne Div; sal n/b/d 12/6/45. ROUND TRIP TICKET III.

42-30828 Del Cheyenne 4/8/43; 241 BU Fairmont 27/12/44; Recl Comp 7/6/46.

42-30829 Del Cheyenne 4/8/43; Gr Isle 13/8/43; ass 563BS/388BG Knettishall 5/9/43; MIA Berlin 8/3/44 w/ Moran; e/a, cr Noepke?; 1KIA 9POW; MACR 3081. THE PRINCESS PAT.

42-30830 Del Cheyenne 4/8/43; Gr Isle 14/8/43; ass 418BS/100BG [LD-U] Thorpe Abbotts 28/8/43; MIA Münster 10/10/43 w/Walts; e/a, cr Münster; 1KIA 10POW; MACR 1023. M'LLE ZIG ZAG.

42-30831 Del Cheyenne 4/8/43; Gr Isle 14/8/43; ass 364BS/305BG [WF-H] Polebrook 15/9/43; MIA Schweinfurt 14/10/43 w/ Dienhart; e/a, c/l Reinach Asch, Switz; 9INT 1KIA(nav); MACR 913. Lazy Baby.

42-30832 Del Cheyenne 4/8/43; Gr Isle 14/8/43; ass 368BS/306BG Thurleigh 18/9/43; MIA Bremen 26/11/43 w/Hoey; e/a, cr Schwerninsdorf, Ger; 10POW; MACR 1328.

42-30833 Del Cheyenne 5/8/43; Peterson 17/8/43; 201 BU Peterson 20/6/44; 200 BU Peterson 25/8/45; RFC Kingman 27/10/45.

42-30834 Del Cheyenne 3/8/43; Geiger 15/8/43; ass 534BS/381BG [GD-E] Ridgewell 23/9/43; {9m} c/l base 4/2/44 w/Kuhl; sal n/b/d 7/2/44. MICKEY FINN.

42-30835 Del Cheyenne 5/8/43; Peterson 17/8/43; 435BS/19BG Pyote 9/11/43; 242 BU Gr Isle 1/6/44; 9BG Gr Isle 8/7/44; 232 BU Dalhart 15/7/44; 6BG Gr Isle 19/7/43; 242BU Gr Isle 5/9/44; 202 BU Galveston 8/10/44; 268 BU Peterson 30/3/45; RFC Altus 9/10/45.

42-30836 Del Cheyenne 5/8/43; Geiger 13/8/43; ass 551BS/385 Gt Ashfield 12/9/43; MIA Pas de Calais 13/2/44 w/Herron; flak, ditched Channel; 4KIA 6RTD; MACR 2345. DRAGON LADY.

42-30837 Del Cheyenne 5/8/43; Gr Isle 14/8/43; ass 561BS/388BG Knettishall 5/9/43; MIA Bordeaux 5/12/43 w/Todd; flak, cr Cognac, Fr; 1EVD 7KIA 2POW; MACR 5022 & 7325. OLE BASSAR.

42-30838 Del Cheyenne 5/8/43; Redmond 15/8/43; ass 422NLS/305BG [JJ-O] Chelveston 1/10/43; Tran 858BS 24/6/44 Harrington. PAPER DOLL.

42-30839 Del Cheyenne 5/8/43; Gore 13/8/43; ass 562BS/388BG Knettishall 21/9/43; c/l Strathaven, Scot. 1/9/43 w/Warrin; sal. STRATO EXPRESS.

42-30840 Del Cheyenne 5/8/43; Gr Isle 13/8/43; ass 350BS/100BG [LN-O] Thorpe Abbotts 25/8/43; MIA Bremen 8/10/43 w/Nash; flak, cr Damme, Ger; 5KIA 5POW; MACR 951.

42-30841 Del Cheyenne 5/8/43; Gore 15/8/43; Redmond 16/8/43; ass 423BS/306BG [RD-R] Thurleigh 19/9/43; coll mid air w/42-30221 27/12/43; sal 28/12/43.

42-30842 Del Dallas 5/8/43; Gore 6/8/43; Dallas 10/8/43; 19BG Pyote 9/11/43; 271 BU Kearney 15/6/44; 4136 BU Tinker 22/9/44; 271 BU Kearney 9/1/45; 2519 BU Fort Worth 8/6/45; 271 BU Kearney 22/7/45; 485 BU Kearney 29/7/45; RFC Kingman 16/11/45.

42-30843 Del Dallas 6/8/43; Gore 7/8/43; Dallas 10/8/43; 19BG Pyote 9/11/43; 221 BU Pierre 20/6/44; 504BG Fairmont 26/8/44; 241 BU Fairmont 17/12/44; 249 BU Alliance 19/10/44; 268 BU Peterson 1/3/45; 4134 BU Spokane 8/6/45; 268 BU Peterson 12/6/45; RFC Walnut Ridge 29/12/45.

42-30844 Del Dallas 6/8/434; Gore 7/8/43; Dallas 12/8/43; 435BS/19BG Pyote 21/8/43; 9BG McCook 6/6/44; 245 BU McCook 16/9/44; 245 BU Brookley 16/10/44; 245 BU McCook 9/12/44; 4100 BU Patterson 11/12/44; 237 BU Kirtland 3/3/45; RFC Altus 26/11/45.

42-30845 Del Dallas 6/8/43; Gore 7/8/43; Dallas 10/8/43; 93BS/19BG Pyote 21/8/43; 4006 BU Miami 5/8/44; 4200 BU Chicago Mun 1/1/45; 236 BU Pyote 2/1/45; 4104 BU Rome 18/1/45; WO Recl Comp 14/8/45.

42-30846 Del Dallas 6/8/43; Gore 7/8/43; Dallas 10/8/43; Tinker 20/12/43; 3501 BU Boca Raton 16/7/43; 4006 BU Miami 19/8/44; 3501 BU Boca Raton 24/8/44; 3539 BU Langley 7/1/45; RFC Walnut Ridge 20/12/45.

42-30847 Del Cheyenne 7/8/43; Dalhart 17/8/43; ass 413BS/96BG [MZ-N] Snetterton 8/9/43; MIA Berlin 8/3/44 w/Kasch; e/a, cr Vechta, Ger; 2KIA 8POW; MACR 1389/3423. PEGASUS.

42-30848 Del Cheyenne 7/8/43; 225 BU Rapid City 14/6/44; 2517 BU Elington 15/5/45; 225 BU Rapid City 11/6/45; RFC Ontario 12/6/45.

42-30849 Del Cheyenne 6/8/43; Redmond 15/8/43; ass 325BS/92BG [NV-F] Podington 27/9/43; b/d Crossbow V-Sites, c/l Hawkinge, UK 1/5/44; sal MRU 20/5/44. FART SACK.

42-30850 Del Cheyenne 7/8/43; 224 BU Sioux City 6/3/45; RFC Altus 14/9/45.

42-30851 Del Cheyenne 7/8/43; Dalhart 17/8/43; ass 560BS/388BG Knettishall 8/9/43; mid air coll w/B17, cr Thurston, UK 19/7/44; 8KIA 2RTD. LITTLE BOY BLUE.

42-30852 Del Cheyenne 7/8/43; Memphis 10/8/43; Dalhart 16/8/43; ass 535BS/381BG [MS-Y] Ridgewell 24/9/43 HOT TODDY; MIA {3m} Gelsenkirchen 5/11/43 w/Hopp; cr Dieppe, Fr; 7KIA 3POW; MACR 1399. (Recovered Oct 1969). BLOWIN' BESSIE.

42-30853 Del Cheyenne 9/8/43; 30BS/19BG Pyote 9/11/43; 246 BU Pratt 4/6/44; 271 BU Kearney 18/6/43; 246 BU Pratt 19/7/44; 232 BU Dalhart 23/8/44; 244 BU Harvard 4/10/44; 203 BU Jackson 21/1/45; 215 BU Pueblo 16/9/45; RFC Kingman 30/11/45.

42-30854 Del Cheyenne 7/8/43; Dalhart 17/8/43; ass 339BS/96BG [QJ-E] Snetterton 4/9/43; MIA Bremen 26/11/43 w/Phelps; flak, cr Oldenburg, Ger; 10KIA; MACR 1389. BLACK HEART III.

42-30855 Del Cheyenne 10/8/43; Gr Isle 3/9/43; ass 613BS/401BG [IN-N] Deenethorpe 3/1/44; MIA Berlin 8/5/44 w/Lenkelt; e/a, cr Balkum, Ger/Den?; 7KIA 3POW; MACR 4586. OL' MASA.

42-30856 Del Cheyenne 9/8/43; Love 10/8/43; Cheyenne 11/8/43; 223 BU Dyersburg 6/6/44; 901 BU Pinecastle 10/6/44; 223 BU Dyersburg 16/6/44; 554 BU Memphis 6/11/44; 223 BU Dyersburg 16/11/44; 3451 BY Waycross 1/3/45; 244 BU Harvard 4/3/45; 223 BU Dyersburg 10/5/45; 325 BU Avon Park 3/6/45; RFC Altus 22/8/45.

42-30857 Del Cheyenne 10/8/43; Cheyenne 11/8/43; ass 510BS/351BG [TU-J] Polebrook 22/9/43 MY DEVOTION; tran 837BS/487BG [4F] Lavenham 16/7/44; retUS 377 BU Grenier 17/12/44; RFC Altus 6/8/45.

42-30858 Del Cheyenne 9/8/43; Love 10/8/43; Cheyenne 11/8/43; 19BG Pyote 9/11/43; 4100 BU Patterson 12/6/44; 268 BU Peterson 6/9/44; Minneapolis 4/12/44; 268 BU Peterson 8/12/44; 4108 BU Newark 10/7/45; 268 BU Peterson 26/8/45;

RFC Kingman 27/10/45.
42-30859 Del Cheyenne 10/8/43; Gr Isle 31/8/43; ass 413BS/96BG [MZ-O] Snetterton 5/9/43; MIA Frankfurt 29/1/44 w/Kandl; mid air collision w/ME109, cr Frankfurt; 8KIA 2POW; MACR 2377. SKYLARK.
42-30860 Del Cheyenne 11/8/43; Gr Isle 31/8/43; ass 337BS/96BG [AW-L] Snetterton 13/9/43; MIA Bremen 16/12/43 w/Schroeder; mid air coll w/42-3265, cr Bremen; 10KIA; MACR 1563.
42-30861 Del Cheyenne 9/8/43; Gore 10/8/43; Cheyenne 11/8/43; 248 BU Walker 11/6/44; 225 BU Rapid City 14/8/44; WO 15/8/44; Recl Comp 2/8/46.
42-30862 Del Cheyenne 10/8/43; 248 BU Walker 4/6/44; 4136 BU Tinker 13/7/44; 4100 BU Patterson 11/1/45; 6 BU Winston Salem 20/5/45; RFC Walnut Ridge 21/2/46.
42-30863 Del Cheyenne 11/8/43; Gr Isle 31/8/43; ass 563BS/388BG Knettishall 6/9/43; b/d Gelsenkirchen 5/11/43; c/l Elmham St Cross, UK; 10RTD; sal. MY DEVOTION.
42-30864 Del Cheyenne 11/8/43; Gore 13/8/43; Cheyenne 14/8/43; Gr Isle 31/8/43; ass 535BS/381BG [MS-T] Ridgewell 19/9/43; MIA {2m} Bremen 8/10/43 w/Cormany; flak, cr Haupstedt, Ger; 1KIA 9POW; MACR 885.
42-30865 Del Cheyenne 11/8/43; Gr Isle 31/8/43; ass 358BS/303BG Molesworth 18/10/43; MIA Oschersleben 11/1/44 w/Campbell; e/a, cr Oschersleben; 6KIA 4POW; MACR 1927.
42-30866 Del Cheyenne 10/8/43; Scott 24/10/43; ass 401BG Deenethorpe 30/10/43; landed Bassingbourn 9/11/43 tran 563BS/388BG Knettishall YANKEE BELLE; 508BS/351BG [YB-S/X] Polebrook 21/11/43; MIA {5m} Achmer 21/2/44 w/Kogelman; e/a, ditched Nth Sea; 5KIA 5POW; MACR 6063. PISTOL PACKIN' MAMA.
42-30867 Del Cheyenne 11/8/43; ass 510BS/351BG [TU-N] Polebrook 27/9/43; MIA {2m} Anklam 9/10/43 w/Christman; e/a, cr Hallig Hooge?; 3KIA 7POW; MACR 1035.
42-30868 Del Cheyenne 11/8/43; 2114 BU Lockburn 27/10/44; RFC Walnut Ridge 14/12/45.
42-30869 Del Cheyenne 12/8/43; 93BS/19BG Pyote 1/10/43; 236 BU Pyote 10/9/44; 4202 BU Syracuse 26/3/45; Recl Comp 3/1/46.
42-30870 Del Cheyenne 12/8/43; 40BG Pratt 27/8/43; WO 29/2/44.
42-30871 Del Cheyenne 13/8/43; Buckingham 24/11/43; 231 BU Alamogordo 2/8/44; 202 BU Galveston 7/12/44; 268 BU Peterson 30/3/45; RFC Walnut Ridge 14/12/45.
42-30872 Del Cheyenne 11/8/43; Gr Isle 31/8/43; ass 337BS/96BG [AW-R] Snetterton 9/9/43; MIA Bremen 16/12/43 w/Kerrick; mid air coll w/42-31133, cr Nth Sea; 10KIA; MACR 1565. OLE PUSS.
42-30873 Del Cheyenne 12/8/43; 242 BU Gr Isle 10/6/44; 6BG Gr Isle 8/7/44; 242 BU Gr Isle 16/9/44; 221 BU Alexandra 24/10/44; 329 BU Alexandra 1/3/45; RFC Altus 9/10/45.
42-30874 Del Cheyenne 12/8/43; 435BS/19BG Pyote 9/11/43; 201 BU Peterson 20/6/44; 260 BU Peterson 28/7/44; 4121 BU Kelly 2/2/45; 201 BU Peterson 24/2/45; 260 BU Peterson 17/3/45; RFC Kingman 3/12/45.
42-30875 Del Cheyenne 12/8/43; 40BG Pratt 27/8/43; 556 BU Long Beach 19/6/44; 497BG Pratt 26/6/44; 246 BU Pratt 7/7/44; 232 BU Brownsville 24/8/44; 232 BU Dalhart 1/9/44; 244 BU Harvard 17/9/44; 249 BU Alliance 16/12/44; 244 BU Harvard 28/12/44.
42-30876 Del Dallas 25/8/43; Tinker 18/11/43; 2137 BU Hendricks 30/7/44; RFC Walnut Ridge 27/9/45.

42-30877 Del Cheyenne 12/8/43; Gore 13/8/43; Fort Myers 29/9/43; 2135 BU Tyndall 15/9/44; 3017 BU Hobbs 27/9/44; RFC Altus 18/9/45.
42-30878 Del Cheyenne 12/8/43; Gore 13/8/43; Cheyenne 14/8/43; WO 21/9/43.
42-30879 Del Cheyenne 12/8/43; 460 BU Rapid City 10/10/44; 225 BU Rapid City 6/11/44; 354 BU Rapid City 20/7/44; 4142 BU Patterson 1/11/44; 4100 BU Patterson 20/1/45; RFC Kingman 1/3/46.
42-30880 Del Cheyenne 12/8/43; 40BG Pratt 27/8/43; 3007 BU Kirtland 23/7/43; 497BG Pratt 26/7/43; 29BG Dalhart 2/9/44; 29BG Pratt 9/9/44; 246 BU Pratt 15/9/44; 4100 BU Patterson 20/4/45; 2114 BU Lockburn 24/4/45; RFC Walnut Ridge 14/12/45.
42-30881 Del Cheyenne 13/8/43; 19BG Pyote 27/8/43; 505BG Harvard 2/6/44; 441 BU Glendale 31/7/44; 244 BU Harvard 6/8/44; 232 BU Dalhart 21/8/44; 241 BU Fairmont 28/9/44; 2512 BU Childress 7/12/44; Recl Comp 7/6/46.
42-30882 Del Cheyenne 13/8/43; Gore 15/8/43; Cheyenne 17/8/43; Pyote 27/8/43; 19BG Pyote 9/11/43; 236 BU Pyote 10/9/44; 581 BU Adams 23/10/44; 236 BU Pyote 4/1/45; 223 BU Dyersburg 1/3/45; 330 BU Dyersburg 9/4/45; 325 BU Avon Park 15/5/45; RFC Altus 9/10/45.
42-30883 Del Dallas 13/8/43; 444BG Gt Bend 27/8/43; 234 BU Clovis 24/6/44; 807 BU Bergstrom 21/10/44; 3704 BU Keesler 7/1/45; Recl Comp 3/8/45.
42-30884 Del Dallas 13/8/43; 444BG Gt Bend 27/8/43; 243 BU Gt Bend 24/6/44; 232 BU Dalhart 16/7/44; 246 BU Pratt 9/12/44; 2132 BU Maxwell 15/3/45; 246 BU Pratt 21/3/45; 237 BU Kirtland 22/10/45; RFC Kingman 6/11/45.
42-30885 Del Dallas 13/8/43; Gore 14/8/32; Dallas 17/8/43; 225 BU Rapid City 29/4/45; RFC Ontario 12/6/45.
42-30886 Del Cheyenne 13/8/43; 28BS/19BG Pyote 9/11/43; 234 BU Clovis 24/6/44; 4100 BU Patterson 13/1/45; 225 BU Rapid City 29/3/45; RFC Ontario 13/6/45.
42-30887 Del Cheyenne 14/8/43; 498BG Gt Bend 4/8/44; 19BG Dalhart 1/9/44; 243 BU Gt Bend 10/9/44; 19BG Dalhart 12/9/44; 271 BU Kearney 5/3/45; 2158 BU Pueblo 20/6/45; 232 BU Dalhart 17/7/45; RFC Kingman 19/11/45.
42-30888 Del Cheyenne 14/8/43; 146 BU Selfridge 4/8/44; 2137 BU Hendricks 20/8/44; RFC Walnut Ridge 18/12/45.
42-30889 Del Cheyenne 13/8/43; cr nr Dyersburg 21/12/43; WO 23/12/43.
42-30890 Del Cheyenne 13/8/43; Pyote 27/8/43; 435BS/19BG Pyote 9/11/43; 222 BU Ardmore 22/1/45; RFC Ontario 20/6/45.
42-30891 Del Cheyenne 14/8/43; 225 BU Rapid City 15/6/44, went missing WO.
42-30892 Del Dallas 14/8/43; Gore 16/8/43; 330 BU Dyersburg 1/3/45; 327 BU Drew 14/5/45; RFC Altus 9/10/45.
42-30893 Del Dallas 14/8/43; Gore 16/8/43; Dallas 17/8/43; 221 BU Alexandra 17/1/45; 329 BU Alexandra 1/3/45; Recl Comp 10/3/45.
42-30894 Del Dallas 14/8/43; 444BG Gt Bend 27/8/43; 498BG Gt Bend 8/8/44; 243 BU Gt Bend 19/9/44; 902 BU Orlando 2/4/44; 243 BU Gt Bend 18/4/45; RFC Altus 20/6/45.
42-30895 Del Dallas 14/8/43; Gore 16/8/43; Dallas 17/8/43; 330 BU Dyersburg 1/3/45; 325 BU Avon Park 3/6/45; RFC Altus 25/9/45.
42-30896 Del Dallas 14/8/43; Gore 17/8/43; WO 15/10/43.
42-30897 Del Dallas 23/8/43; 2100 BU Maxwell

3/6/44; 281 BU Pierre 31/10/43; 2137 BU Hendricks 20/3/45; 2100 BU Maxwell 14/7/47; cr McKenzie, Tenn, 8/9/45 w/Moles; fell from high altitude, cr and burned; 8KIA; RFC Walnut Ridge 10/1/46.
42-30898 Del Dallas 14/8/43; Gore 16/8/43; 202 BU Galveston 20/7/44; 1108 BU Mitchell 26/1/45; 202 BU Galveston 1/2/45; 268 BU Peterson 30/3/45; RFC Altus 9/10/45.
42-30899 Del Dallas 16/8/43; Gore 17/8/43; 9BG McCook 6/6/44; 245 BU McCook 16/9/44; 249 BU Alliance 16/10/44; 235 BU Biggs 28/12/44; RFC Kingman 29/10/45.
42-30900 Del Dallas 16/8/43; Gore 17/8/43; 221 BU Alexandra 1/8/44; 329 BU Alexandra 1/3/45; RFC Altus 9/10/45.
42-30901 Del Dalls 16/8/43; Gore 17/8/43; 498BG Gt Bend 8/8/44; 232 BU Dalhart 27/8/44; 241 BU Fairmont 13/9/44; 1103 BU Morrison 12/1/45; 241 BU Fairmont 19/1/45; 902 BU Orlando 6/7/45; 241 BU Fairmont 13/7/45; RFC Walnut Ridge 12/12/45.
42-30902 Del Dallas 16/8/43; Gore 17/8/43; 4119 BU Brookley 18/9/44; 2135 BU Tyndall 26/9/44; 3017 BU Hobbs 29/9/44; RFC Altus 18/9/45.
42-30903 Del Cheyenne 16/8/43; Gore 17/8/43; Dyersburg 1/9/43; 805 BU George 4/1/45; Recl Comp 27/11/43.
42-30904 Del Cheyenne 19/8/43; Tinker 14/12/43; 2117 BU Buckingham 10/8/43; 2114 BU Lockburn 2/9/44; 4112 BU Olmstead 14/12/44; 2114 BU Lockburn 24/8/45; RFC Walnut Ridge 14/12/45.
42-30905 Del Cheyenne 16/8/43; Gore 17/8/43; WO 23/9/43.
42-30906 Del Cheyenne 19/8/43; 2137 BU Hendricks 5/7/44; RFC Walnut Ridge 13/12/45.
42-30907 Del Cheyenne 19/8/43; 3017 BU Hobbs 2/10/44; RFC Altus 4/10/45.
42-30908 Del Cheyenne 19/8/43; 2137 BU Hendricks 4/10/44; RFC Walnut Ridge 18/12/45.
42-30909 Del Cheyenne 19/8/43; 246 BU Pratt 3/7/44; 11STA Morrison 29/7/44; 246 BU Pratt 19/9/44; RFC Kingman 28/10/45.
42-30910 Del Cheyenne 19/8/43; coll w/42-3311 in taxi acc Santa Ana, Cal 14/10/43 w/Drodelbis; a/c rep; 3030 BU Roswell 2/6/44; 3017 BU Hobbs 28/4/45; RFC Altus 11/9/45.
42-30911 Del Cheyenne 19/8/43; Tinker 13/12/43; 3501 BU Boca Raton 14/7/44; 3502 BU Chanute 23/4/45; RFC Walnut Ridge 7/1/46.
42-30912 Del Cheyenne 19/8/43; Tinker 20/12/43; 2137 BU Hendricks 3/8/44; RFC Walnut Ridge 18/12/45.
42-30913 Del Dallas 19/8/43; 2117 BU Buckingham 3/7/44; 3501 BU Boca Raton 14/7/44; 2539 BU Langley 4/1/45; Recl Comp 5/7/45.
42-30914 Del Dallas 19/8/43; 497BG Pratt 11/8/44; 225 BU Rapid City 12/8/44; RFC Ontario 19/6/45.
42-30915 Del Dallas 19/8/43; 327 BU Drew 14/9/44; 325 BU Avon Park 21/9/44; RFC Walnut Ridge 4/9/45.
42-30916 Del Dallas 19/8/43; Kingman 10/9/43; WO 10/10/43.
42-30917 Del Dallas 19/8/43; Tinker 27/12/43; 2137 BU Hendricks 31/10/44; RFC Walnut Ridge 14/12/45.
42-30918 Del Cheyenne 19/8/43; Tinker 20/12/43; 3030 BU Roswell 1/10/44; 2135 BU Tyndall 2/10/44; 3010 BU Williams 12/12/44; 3020 BU La Junta 19/4/45; RFC Altus 1/8/45.
42-30919 Del Cheyenne 19/8/43; Tinker 6/12/43; 3501 BU Boca Raton 14/7/44; 3704 BU Keesler 2/4/45; 3501 BU Boca Raton 20/5/45; Recl Comp 29/1/46.
42-30920 Del Cheyenne 19/8/43; Tinker 13/12/43;

WO 29/12/43.

42-30921 Del Wright Fd 19/8/43; Mat Spl Tonopah 9/6/44; 4127 BU McClellan 28/7/44; Tonopah 16/8/44; 4127 BU McClellan 6/10/44; 216 BU Wendover 7/11/44; 4135 BU Hill Fd 2/4/45; 216 BU Wendover 20/4/45; 554 BU Memphis 7/5/45; 4145 BU Wendover 30/4/46; 594 BU Minneapolis 31/5/46; 554 BU Memphis 31/5/46; RFC 31/5/46.

42-30922 Del Newark 20/8/43; 4000 BU Wright Fd 2/6/44; 4100 BU Patterson 14/1/45; 4000 BU Wright 7/3/45; 611 BU Eglin 25/4/45; Re-assigned 31/3/47; 609 BU Eglin 17/4/47; 611 BU Eglin 17/7/47; 4000 BU Patterson 15/5/47; Recl Comp 25/11/49.

42-30923 Del Cheyenne 19/8/43; Panama City 20/3/44; 231 BU Alamogordo 2/8/44; 450 BU Hammer 2/11/44; 450 BU Fresno 17/12/44; 4127 BU McClellan 22/1/45; RFC Kingman 17/11/45.

42-30924 Del Cheyenne 23/8/43; 2117 BU Buckingham 3/7/44; 35601 BU Boca Raton 16/7/44; 3505 BU Scott 20/1/45; 3539 BU Langley 28/12/45; RFC Walnut Ridge 3/1/46.

42-30925 Del Cheyenne 23/8/43; 2137 BU Hendricks 3/8/44; 4108 BU Newark 14/5/45; 2137 BU Hendricks 18/5/45; 237BU Kirtland 8/8/45; 2137 BU Hendricks 18/8/45; RFC Walnut Ridge 18/12/45.

42-30926 Del Wright Fd 23/8/43; MAT COM Wright 2/6/44; ARL Dover 1/10/44; 237 BU Kirtland 27/11/44; ARL Dover 17/1/45; RFC Walnut Ridge 28/3/46.

42-30927 Del Cheyenne 23/8/43; 2117 BU Buckingham 18/6/44; 3017 BU Hobbs 7/10/44; 244 BU Harvard 8/12/44; 3017 BU Hobbs 11/12/44; RFC Altus 29/8/45.

42-30928 Del Cheyenne 23/8/43; 30BS/19BG Pyote 16/9/44; 242 BU Gr Isle 27/7/44; 268 Peterson 2/5/45; RFC Kingman 27/10/45.

42-30929 Del Cheyenne 23/8/43; 3030 BU Roswell 1/10/44; 3010 BU Williams 21/11/44; 3020 BU La Junta 23/4/45; RFC Altus 1/8/45.

42-30930 Del Cheyenne 23/8/43; 2517 BU Elington 2/10/44; 2135 BU Tyndall 10/10/44; 2137 BU Hendricks 23/12/44; RFC Walnut Ridge 14/12/45.

42-30931 Del Dallas 23/8/43; Tinker 22/12/43; 3017 BU 2/10/44; RFC Altus 30/8/45.

42-30932 Del Dallas 23/8/43; WO 28/12/43.

42-30933 Del Dallas 23/8/43; WO 9/2/44.

42-30934 Del from Boeing delayed through damage on take off 20/8/43; Mat Boeing Seattle 2/6/44; RFC Seattle 14/11/45.

42-30935 Del Dallas 23/8/43; Tinker 14/12/43; 2137 BU Hendricks 30/7/44; RFC Walnut Ridge 14/12/45.

42-30936 Del Cheyenne 23/8/43; 2126 BU Laredo 3/9/44; 3018 BU Kingman 9/10/44; 2126 BU Laredo 12/10/44; Recl Comp 13/11/45.

42-30937 Del Cheyenne 23/8/43; 3030 BU Roswell 18/9/44; 3010 BU Williams 11/12/44; 3020 BU La Junta 29/3/45; RFC Altus 1/8/45.

42-30938 Del Cheyenne 23/8/43; Kingman 5/9/43; 203 BU Jackson 31/1/45; 261 BU Abilene 17/2/45; 203 BU Jackson 22/2/45; 3505 BU Scott 9/8/45; RFC Walnut Ridge 5/1/46.

42-30939 Del Cheyenne 23/8/43; Scott 25/9/43; ass 369BS/306BG [WW-A] Thurleigh 21/10/43; tran 493BG Debach 8/4/44; n/b/d nosed over 17/8/44; sal.

42-30940 Del Cheyenne 23/8/43; 504BG Mines Fd 14/8/44; 504BG Fairmont 18/8/44; WO 27/8/44.

42-30941 Del Dallas 23/8/43; 4100 BU Patterson 21/6/44; 202 BU Galveston 22/6/44; 268 BU Peterson 30/3/45; RFC Altus 1/8/45.

42-30942 Del Dallas 23/8/43; 247 BU Smoky Hill 3/6/44; 4100 BU Patterson 6/6/44; 247 BU Smoky Hill 6/8/44; 902 BU Orlando 7/3/45; 247 BU Smoky Hill 21/6/45; Recl Comp 27/7/45.

42-30943 Del Dallas 23/8/43; 325 BU Avon Park 15/6/44; 4200 BU Chicago Mun 10/11/44; 203 BU Jackson 22/3/45; 325 BU Avon Park 9/4/45; 2137 BU Hendricks 10/5/45; 325 BU Avon Park 23/5/45; RFC Altus 14/8/45.

42-30944 Del Dallas 23/8/43; 224 BU Sioux City 23/7/44; WO 13/7/44.

42-30945 Del Dallas 24/8/43; 2126 BU Laredo 3/9/44; RFC Walnut Ridge 7/1/46.

42-30946 Del Cheyenne 23/8/43; 2137 BU Hendricks 1/10/44; RFC Walnut Ridge 14/12/45.

42-30947 Del Cheyenne 23/8/43; 2137 BU Hendricks 31/10/44; RFC Walnut Ridge 14/12/45.

42-30948 Del Cheyenne 24/8/43; 2114 BU Lockburn 24/10/44; RFC Altus 9/10/45.

42-30949 Del Cheyenne 24/8/43; Tinker 9/12/43; 3501 BU Boca Raton 14/7/44; 4208 BU Mines 17/7/44; 504BG Fairmont 29/8/44; 3501 BU Boca Raton 4/9/44; 2532 BU Randolph 11/4/45; RFC Walnut Ridge 20/12/45.

42-30950 Del Cheyenne 25/8/43; 223 BU Dyersburg 16/11/44; WO 16/11/44; Recl Comp 17/1/45.

42-30951 Del Cheyenne 24/8/43; 2114 BU Lockburn 24/10/44; RFC Altus 4/10/45.

42-30952 Del Cheyenne 25/8/43; Tinker 18/11/43; 2137 BU Hendricks 30/7/44; RFC Walnut Ridge 19/12/45.

42-30953 Del Cheyenne 24/8/43; Tinker 9/12/43; 2137 BU Hendricks 3/8/44; RFC Walnut Ridge 14/12/45.

42-30954 Del Cheyenne 25/8/43; 3030 BU Roswell 16/9/44; 3010 BU Williams 9/12/44; 3020 BU La Junta 18/4/45; RFC Altus 3/8/45.

42-30955 Del Cheyenne 25/8/43; Tinker 22/11/43; 2114 BU Lockburn 5/8/44; RFC Walnut Ridge 14/12/45.

42-30956 Del Cheyenne 26/8/43; 234 BU Clovis 24/6/44; 2534 BU San Angelo 5/10/44; WO 5/10/44.

42-30957 Del Cheyenne 25/8/43; 2114 BU Lockburn 24/10/44; 2530 BU Selman 8/6/45; 2114 BU Lockburn 18/6/45; 4124 BU Altus 13/8/45; 2114 BU Lockburn 23/8/45; RFC Altus 9/10/45.

42-30958 Del Cheyenne 25/8/43; Harvard 12/9/43; WO 20/4/44.

42-30959 Del Cheyenne 27/8/43; slated 385BG 8/43; 3030 BU Roswell 2/6/44; 3017 BU Hobbs 22/4/45; RFC Altus 30/8/45.

42-30960 Del Cheyenne 25/8/43; 2114 BU Lockburn 24/10/44; RFC Walnut Ridge 14/12/45.

42-30961 Del Cheyenne 25/6/44; 202 BU Galveston 8/8/44; 4104 BU Rome 18/1/45; RFC Altus 14/9/45.

42-30962 Del Cheyenne 25/8/43; 2135 BU Tyndall 5/10/44; 3030 BU Roswell 5/10/44; 3010 BU Williams 26/11/44; 3020 BU La Junta 1/4/45; RFC Altus 4/8/45.

42-30963 Del Cheyenne 26/8/43; 4122 BU Hensley 12/9/44; 3030 BU Roswell 13/9/44; 3010 BU Williams 12/12/44; RFC Albuquerque 9/8/45.

42-30964 Del Cheyenne 26/8/43; Dyersburg 4/10/43; Dalhart 17/10/43; 2530 BU Selman 15/8/44; 221 BU Alexandra 18/8/44; 221 BU Alexandra 28/9/44; 329 BU Alexandra 8/4/45; RFC Altus 29/10/45.

42-30965 Del Cheyenne 28/8/43; 3017 BU Hobbs 15/9/44; Recl Comp 29/1/45.

42-30966 Del Cheyenne 26/8/43; 3017 BU Hobbs 15/9/44; RFC Altus 29/8/45.

42-30967 Del Cheyenne 27/8/43; 3030 BU Roswell 11/9/44; 3010 BU Williams 9/12/44; 3020 BU La Junta 27/3/45; RFC Altus 1/8/45.

42-30968 Del Cheyenne 27/8/43; 3017 BU Hobbs 8/11/44; RFC Altus 30/8/45.

42-30969 Del Cheyenne 27/8/43; Damaged Yucca Fd 20/11/43 w/Lawson, rep; 3018 BU Kingman 5/7/44; Recl Comp 19/6/45.

42-30970 Del Cheyenne 27/8/43; Gr Isle 23/9/43; ass 549BS/385BG Gt Ashfield 26/10/43; tran RAF No 214Sq (SR384) [BU-A] Sculthorpe 21/1/44; MIA Antwerp 25/5/44.

42-30971 Del Dallas 27/8/43; Tinker 16/11/43; 4115 BU Atlanta 6/8/44; 2114 BU Lockburn 2/9/44; RFC Walnut Ridge 14/12/45.

42-30972 Del Dallas 27/8/43; Tinker 16/11/43; 2137 BU Hendricks 25/8/44; RFC Walnut Ridge 14/12/45.

42-30973 Del Dallas 27/8/43; Tinker 20/11/43; 3501 BU Boca Raton 14/7/44; 2132 BU Maxwell 10/4/45; 2137 BU Hendricks 3/7/45; 2132 BU Maxwell 22/7/45; RFC Walnut Ridge 14/1/46.

42-30974 Del Dallas 28/8/43; 221 BU Alexandra 17/1/45; 329 BU Alexandra 28/4/45; RFC Altus 29/10/45.

42-30975 Del Dallas 27/8/43; 221 BU Alexandra 17/1/45; 329 BU Alexandra 20/5/45; RFC Altus 9/10/45.

42-30976 Del Cheyenne 28/8/43; Kingman 28/3/44; Alamogordo 30/3/44; 4115 BU Atlanta 29/8/44; 203 BU Jackson 31/1/45; 4103 BU Jackson 23/6/45; 203 BU Jackson 25/7/45; 232 BU Dalhart 20/9/45; RFC Kingman 27/10/45.

42-30977 Del Cheyenne 28/8/43; 2117 BU Buckingham 25/5/44; 2137 BU Hendricks 1/10/44; RFC Walnut Ridge 19/12/45.

42-30978 Del Cheyenne 28/8/43; 3017 BU Hobbs 2/11/44; RFC Altus 14/9/45.

42-30979 Del Cheyenne 28/8/43; Roswell 19/9/43; WO 26/4/44.

42-30980 Del Cheyenne 28/8/43; 345 BU Waycross 1/3/45; 330 BU Dyersburg 9/4/45; 325 BU Avon Park 3/6/45; RFC Altus 14/8/45.

42-30981 Del Wright Fd 28/8/43; Winter Test Ladd Fd, Alaska 5/11/43; retUS Mat HQ Wright 2/6/44; 4000 Wright 19/9/44; 902 BU Orlando 13/7/44; 613 BU Phillips 14/7/45; 4000 BU Wright 31/7/45. SHUTTERBUG.

42-30982 Del Cheyenne 30/8/43; 2137 BU Hendricks 11/11/44; RFC Walnut Ridge 14/12/45.

42-30983 Del Cheyenne 28/8/43; Yuma 30/3/44; Alamogordo 3/4/44; 4200 BU Chicago Mun 7/8/44; 233 BU Davis Monthan 29/12/44; 231 BU Alamogordo 20/3/45; 465 BU Paine 3/4/45; 231 BU Alamogordo 27/4/45; 4208 BU Mines 7/10/45; 231 BU Alamogordo 15/10/45; RFC Kingman 30/10/45.

42-30984 Del Cheyenne 30/8/43; 2114 BU Lockburn 5/8/44; RFC Walnut Ridge 26/9/45.

42-30985 Del Cheyenne 30/8/43; 2114 BU Lockburn 25/6/44; Mat Com Vandalia 24/7/44; 2114 BU Lockburn 25/7/44; RFC Altus 9/10/45.

42-30986 Del Cheyenne 30/8/43; Gr Isle 27/9/43; ass 562BS/388BG Knettishall 7/10/43; tran RAF No 214Sq (SR385) [BU-E] Sculthorpe 6/10/44; WO 11/3/47.

42-30987 Del Dallas 30/8/43; Alexandra 21/9/43; 221 BU Alexandra 7/11/44; 329 BU Alexandra 1/3/45; RFC Altus 29/10/45.

42-30988 Del Dallas 30/8/43; 2114 BU Lockburn 30/7/44; RFC Altus 9/10/45.

42-30989 Del Dallas 30/8/43; 2530 BU Selman 5/11/44; 328 BU Gulfport 23/11/44; 4100 BU Patterson 25/2/45; 330 BU Dyersburg 7/5/45; 325 BU Avon Park 3/6/45; RFC Altus 11/8/45.

42-30990 Del Dallas 31/8/43; Las Vegas 23/9/43; Tinker 19/12/43; 2137 BU Hendricks 3/12/44; RFC Walnut Ridge 27/9/45.

42-30991 Del Cheyenne 30/8/43; 3017 BU Hobbs 8/11/44; RFC Altus 11/9/45.

42-30992 Del Cheyenne 30/8/43; 3030 BU Roswell 2/6/44; RFC Albuquerque 9/8/45.
42-30993 Del Cheyenne 30/8/43; 3030 BU Roswell 2/6/44; 3017 BU Hobbs 28/4/45; RFC Altus 31/8/45.
42-30994 Del Cheyenne 30/8/43; Gt Falls 9/10/43; Scott 28/10/43; ass 401BG 30/10/43; tran 508BS/351BG [YB-T] Polebrook 21/11/43 VOX POP II then OLE DAD; 486BG Sudbury 15/7/44; {27m} sal 29/5/45.
42-30995 Del Cheyenne 31/8/43; 2114 BU Lockburn 21/10/44; 2003 BU Fort Worth 8/1/45; 2114 BU Lockburn 21/9/45; 2100 BU Maxwell 28/9/45; RFC Walnut Ridge 7/1/46.
42-30996 Del Cheyenne 30/8/43; Tinker 18/11/43; 2137 BU Hendricks 3/8/44; RFC Walnut Ridge 19/12/45.
42-30997 Del Cheyenne 30/8/43; Kingman 7/9/43; Yuma 30/3/44; 231 BU Alamagordo 9/7/44; 4136 BU Tinker 13/1/45; 231 BU Alamagordo 25/1/45; 4210 BU Lambert 9/5/45; 4136 BU Tinker 24/7/45; 4208 BU Mines 27/8/45; RFC Walnut Ridge 11/1/46.
42-30998 Del Cheyenne 31/8/43; Tinker 18/11/43; 2114 BU Lockburn 5/8/44; RFC Walnut Ridge 14/12/45.
42-30999 Del Cheyenne 2/9/43; Lockburn 20/9/43; WO 26/5/44.
42-31000 Del Cheyenne 2/9/43; 3030 BU Roswell 2/6/44; 3010 BU Williams 9/12/44; 3020 BU La Junta 1/4/45; RFC Altus 1/8/45.
42-31001 Del Dallas 31/8/43; Alexandra 21/9/43; 221 BU Alexandra 17/1/45; 329 BU Alexandra 1/3/45; RFC Altus 29/10/45.
42-31002 Del Dallas 31/8/43; Slated 94BG 28/8/43; Kearney 19/9/43; 328 BU Gulfport 31/3/45; RFC Albuquerque 25/6/45.
42-31003 Del Dallas 31/8/43; Las Vegas 27/9/43; WO 5/1/44.
42-31004 Del Dallas 2/9/43; Las Vegas 23/9/43; Tinker 14/12/43; 2137 BU Hendricks 31/10/44; Recl Comp 17/7/45.
42-31005 Del Dallas 2/9/43; Las Vegas 22/9/43; WO 23/1/44.
42-31006 Del Cheyenne 3/9/43; WO 11/5/44.
42-31007 Del Cheyenne 3/9/43; Gr Isle 27/9/43; ass 369BS/306BG [WW-F] Thurleigh 13/10/43; MIA Frankfurt 4/2/44 w/Berry; flak, cr Cologne; 7KIA 3POW; MACR 2239.
42-31008 Del Cheyenne 3/9/43; Tinker 20/10/43; 2114 BU Lockburn 10/8/44; RFC Walnut Ridge 14/12/45.
42-31009 Del Cheyenne 3/9/43; Eglin 1/10/43; 611 BU Eglin 2/6/44; 617 BU Tooele 12/8/44; 4135 BU Hill 16/8/44; 617 BU Tooele 26/8/43; 216 BU Wendover 26/9/44; 617 BU Tooele 4/10/44; RFC Kingman 13/11/45.
42-31010 Del Cheyenne 30/8/43; Buffalo 3/9/43; Rapid City 7/10/43; Cheyenne 8/2/44; 1EEL Bedford 20/7/44; 4140 BU Bedford 4/12/44; 4100 BU Patterson 3/4/45; 4148 BU Bedford 1/5/45; 4147 BU Bedford 18/9/43; RFC Walnut Ridge 5/1/46.
42-31011 Del Cheyenne 3/9/43; Las Vegas 23/9/43; 2137 BU Hendricks 30/7/44; RFC Walnut Ridge 19/12/45.
42-31012 Del Cheyenne 3/9/43; Gr Isle 27/9/43; ass 331BS/94BG Rougham 6/10/43; sal 6/10/44. GRAND DUCHESS.
42-31013 Del Cheyenne 3/9/43; Gr Isle 28/9/43; ass 332BS/94BG [XM-L] Rougham 10/10/43 OLE CASEY JONES; MIA Regensburg 21/7/44 w/Gregg; flak, cr Gilze Rijen, Hol; 10KIA; MACR 7836. MYASAM DRAGON.
42-31014 Del Cheyenne 3/9/43; Gr Isle 27/9/43; ass 337BS/96BG [AW-A] Snetterton 28/10/43; MIA Brux 12/5/44 w/Kinman; e/a, cr?; 1MIA 9POW; MACR 5093. SMOKY STOVER JR.
42-31015 Del Cheyenne 3/9/43; Tinker 20/11/43; 2137 BU Hendricks 30/7/44; 4200 BU Chicago Mun 19/9/44; 2137 BU Hendricks 14/10/44; RFC Walnut Ridge 14/12/45.
42-31016 Del Cheyenne 3/9/43; Scott 1/10/43; ass 326BS/92BG Podington 17/10/43; MIA Keil 4/1/44 w/Hughes; flak, cr Sadden?; 1EVD 1KIA 8POW; MACR 1754. SWEET SIXTEEN.
42-31017 Del Dallas 3/9/43; Las Vegas 27/9/43; Tinker 14/12/43; 3030 BU Roswell 21/9/43; 3010 BU Williams 16/11/44; 3020 BU La Junta 26/3/456/; RFC Altus 1/8/45.
42-31018 Del Dallas 3/9/43; Yuma 24/9/43; 3030 BU Roswell 23/9/44; 3010 BU Williams 21/11/44; 3020 BU La Junta 20/4/45; RFC Altus 1/8/45.
42-31019 Del Dallas 3/9/43; Scott 25/9/43; ass 366BS/305BG [KY-F] Chelveston 18/10/43; tran 2 BAD Warton 20/3/44; retUS 4136 BU Tinker 1/9/44; RFC Walnut Ridge 8/1/46.
42-31020 Del Dallas 3/9/43; Scott 25/9/43; ass 560BS/388BG Knettishall 13/10/43; MIA Emden 11/12/43 w/Hughes; e/a, cr Finsterwalde, Hol; 4KIA 6POW; MACR 3122.
42-31021 Del Dallas 4/9/43; Scott 25/9/43; ass 524BS/379BG [WA-K] Kimbolton 22/11/43; c/l Ash, UK; sal 3/2/44.
42-31022 Del Cheyenne 3/9/43; Scott 25/9/43; ass 407BS/92BG Podington 23/11/43; MIA Augsburg 16/3/44 w/Starks; e/a, cr Rheims, Fr; 6EVD 4POW; MACR 3225.
42-31023 Del Cheyenne 3/9/43; Scott 27/9/43; ass 339BS/96BG [QJ-Q] Snetterton 15/10/43; c/l RAF Honington 29/1/44; sal 18/4/44. SKYBALL.
42-31024 Del Cheyenne 3/9/43; 3030 BU Roswell 2/6/44; RFC Albuquerque 9/8/45.
42-31025 Del Cheyenne 4/9/43; Gr Isle 25/9/43; ass 367BS/306BG [GY-B] Thurleigh 19/10/43; sal 2BAD Warton 6/3/44.
42-31026 Del Cheyenne 3/9/43; Roswell 27/9/43; 2114 BU Lockburn 24/10/44; RFC Altus 4/10/45.
42-31027 Del Cheyenne 4/9/43; Gr Isle 3/10/43; ass 569BS/390BG [CC-R] Framlingham 7/10/43 MISS LACE, then PINKY III; to HONEY CHILE, tran RAF No 214Sq (SR387) [BU-G] Sculthorpe 21/1/44; No1699 FLT [4Z-Z]; WO 13/11/46.
42-31028 Del Cheyenne 4/9/43; Gr Isle 7/10/43; ass 524BS/379BG [WA-C] Kimbolton 19/11/43; MIA Aschersleben 22/2/44 w/Capt Simons; flak, cr Mulheim, Ger; 7KIA 3POW; MACR 2872. MOJO.
42-31029 Del Cheyenne 4/9/43; Scott 7/10/43; u/c collapsed waiting taxi instructions at Prestwick 10/10/43 w/Charholtzer, rep; ass 388BG Knettishall 9/10/43; sal n/b/d 31/1/44.
42-31030 Del Cheyenne 4/9/43; Gr Isle 7/10/43; ass 571BS/390BG [FC-A] Framlingham 7/10/43; MIA Gelsenkirchen 5/11/43 w/Hoyt; mech fault, cr Nth Sea; 10KIA; MACR 1162. SHY ANN. (Last B-17F assigned USAAF Combat Theater).
42-31031 Del Boeing (by hand!) 4/9/43; Gr Isle 11/10/43; ass Soxo 24/10/43; tran RAF No 214Sq (SR388) [BU-H] Sculthorpe 21/1/44; No 1699 FLT [4Z-Z]; WO 26/7/45. (Last B-17F).

B-17G-BO

42-31032 Del Boeing Material Command (by hand!) 4/9/43; Grand Island 20/10/43; ass 422NLS/305BG Chelveston 25/11/43; sal b/d 2 SAD Lt Staughton 29/12/44.
42-31033 Del Cheyenne 7/9/43; Scott 11/10/43; ass 613BS/401BG [IN-B] Deenethorpe 26/11/43; MIA Oschersleben 28/5/44 w/Nasen; e/a, cr Duderstadt, Ger; 2KIA 8POW; MACR 2507. PEE TAY KUN.
42-31034 Del Dallas 8/9/43; Scott 20/10/43; ass 612BS/401BG [SC-G] Deenethorpe 8/11/43; MIA Cologne 28/5/44 w/West; flak, cr Leipzig; 3KIA 7POW; MACR 5309. BONNIE DONNIE.
42-31035 Del Dallas 7/9/43; Scott 5/10/43; ass 351BS/100BG [EP-E] Thorpe Abbotts 8/10/43; b/d Bremen, c/l Dickleburgh, UK 26/11/43; sal 29/11/43. HANG THE EXPENSE.
42-31036 Del Dallas 7/9/43; Scott 24/10/43; ass 303BG Molesworth 25/10/43, 1 BAD Burtonwood; tran 614BS/401BG [IW-X] Deenethorpe 8/11/43; MIA Frankfurt 4/2/44 w/Zitkovic; flak, cr Mulheim, Ger; 10KIA; MACR 2285. NOBODY'S BABY.
42-31037 Del Dallas 8/9/43; ass 613BS/401BG [IN-F] Deenethorpe 30/10/43; MIA Leipzig 20/7/44 w/Murgatroyd; flak, cr Liebstedt, Ger; MACR 7545. PISTOL PACKIN' MAMA.
42-31038 Del Dallas 10/9/43; Scott 9/10/43; ass 367BS/306BG [GY-N] Thurleigh 19/10/43; c/l Princes Risborough, UK 13/11/43; sal.
42-31039 Del Cheyenne 8/9/43; Gr Island 19/10/43; ass 560BS/388BG Knettishall 25/10/43; MIA Osnabrück 29/9/44 w/Burkheimer; ditched Channel, 10RTD. MISS FORTUNE.
42-31040 Del Cheyenne 13/9/43; Scott 21/9/43; ass 527BS/379BG [FO-A] Kimbolton 27/9/43; MIA Frankfurt 29/1/44 w/Capt Hoverkamp; e/a, cr Prum, Ger; 9EVD 1POW; MACR 2873. DUFFY'S TAVERN.
42-31041 Del Cheyenne 9/9/43; ass 571BS/390BG [FC-B] Framlingham 29/9/43; b/d Montdidier 30/6/44, sal. CABIN ION THE SKY.
42-31042 Del Cheyenne 9/9/43; ass 385BG Gt Ashfield 10/10/43; tran 303BG Molesworth 19/10/43, then 1 BAD Burtonwood 23/10/43; 544BS/384BG [SU-L] Grafton Underwood 2/11/43; MIA Bremen 26/11/43 w/Holland; e/a, cr Hagen, Ger; 1KIA 9POW; MACR 1663.
42-31043 Del Cheyenne 10/9/43; Ass 381BG Ridgewell 19/10/43; tran 526BS/379BG [LF-L] Kimbolton 3/3/44; landing gear collapsed 12/9/44; sal 2 SAD Lt Staughton 14/9/44. ELSIE MAE.
42-31044 Del Cheyenne 10/9/43; ass 350BS/100BG Thorpe Abbotts 24/9/43; tran 340BS/97BG Depienne 5/10/43; Cerignola 20/12/43; Amendola 16/1/44; MIA Verona, It. 14/2/44 w/Chaplick; e/a, ditched 100 yds offshore at Calvi, Corsica; 3KIA, 7RTD, crew inc 1 WIA swam ashore; MACR 2395.
42-31045 Del Cheyenne 10/9/43; Gd Island 1/11/43; ass 305BG Chelveston 11/11/43; tran 546BS/384BG [BK-M] Grafton Underwood 29/11/43; b/d Frankfurt 8/2/44, c/l 2 SAD Lt Staughton; sal 17/2/44.
42-31046 Del Cheyenne 10/9/43; Scott 29/9/43; ass 365BS/305BG [XK-E] Chelveston 18/10/43; MIA Bremen 26/11/43 w/Reid; flak, cr Emden; 10POW; MACR 1326.
42-31047 Del Cheyenne 11/9/43; Scott 28/9/43; ass 535BS/381BG Ridgewell 20/10/43 WOLVERINE; MIA {19m} Brunswick 30/1/44 w/Deering; e/a, cr Ottbergen, Ger; 8KIA 2POW; MACR 2243. LITTLE DUCHESS.
42-31048 Del Cheyenne 11/9/43; North Platte 19/9/43; ass 545BS/384BG [JD-L] Grafton Underwood 1/3/44; MIA Schweinfurt 12/4/44 w/Miller; e/a, cr Mannheim; 8KIA 2POW; MACR 3866.
42-31049 Del Cheyenne 10/9/43; Gr Island 23/9/43; ass 350BS/100BG [LN-U] Thorpe Abbotts 5/10/43; retUS 12/1/45; RFC Altus 18/9/45. SUPERSTITIOUS ALOYSIUS.
42-31050 Del Cheyenne 11/9/43; Gr Island 3/10/43; ass 525BS/379BG [FR-R] Kimbolton 19/10/43; tran

527BS; MIA Frankfurt 29/1/44 w/Rhyner; e/a, cr Dannemarie, Fr; MACR 2874.

42-31051 Del Cheyenne 11/9/43; Gr Island 21/9/43; ass 349BS/100BG [XR-R] Thorpe Abbotts 3/11/43; then 351BS [EP-K]; MIA Oranienburg w/Koper 6/3/44; e/a, cr Jump?; 7KIA 3POW; MACR 3018. GOIN' JESSIES.

42-31052 Del Cheyenne 11/9/43; Scott 24/9/43; ass 360BS/303BG Molesworth 11/10/43; tran 447BG Rattlesden /43; b/d Berlin 8/3/44; sal 2 SAD Abbotts Ripton 17/3/44.

42-31053 Del Cheyenne 12/9/43; ass 338BS/96BG [BX-W] Snetterton 29/9/43; damaged in mid air coll w/B-17, 9/11/44, 7KIA; sal 11/10/44. STINGY. (named by M/Gen Fred Anderson, CO of 8thBC, for his son).

42-31054 Del Cheyenne 13/9/43; ass 412BS/95BG [QW-Q] Horham 7/10/43; MIA Brunswick 10/2/44 w/Huddleston; cr Lengerich, Ger; 1KIA 9POW; MACR 2545. IRISH LUCK.

42-31055 Del Cheyenne 11/9/43; Scott 19/9/43; ass 360BS/303BG [PU-J] Molesworth 18/10/43; b/d Berlin 6/3/44; 2 SAD Lt Staughton, ret 9/4/44; dec war weary 9/4/45; sal Alconbury 1/6/45. ALOHA.

42-31056 Del Cheyenne 15/9/43; Scott 30/9/43; ass 369BS/306BG [WW-U] Thurleigh 19/10/43; MIA Wilhelmshaven 3/2/44 w/Wong; flak, cr Hausleiten; 3KIA 7POW; MACR 2494.

42-31057 Del Cheyenne 13/9/43; ass 334BS/95BG [BG-G] Horham 29/9/43; sal n/b/d 6/10/44. DEVIL'S DAUGHTER II.

42-31058 Del Cheyenne 13/9/43; Gr Island 27/9/43; ass 546BS/384BG [BK-T] Grafton Underwood 18/10/43; MIA Pas de Calais 28/2/44 w/Rinne; cr Forges-les-Laux, Fr; 1EVD 1KIA 8POW; MACR 2937. LIBERTY RUN.

42-31059 Del Cheyenne 13/9/43; ass 547BS/384BG Grafton Underwood 2/10/43; MIA Schweinfurt 14/10/43 w/Ogilvie (first group loss); cr Soissons, Fr; 7EVD 1KIA 2POW; MACR 842.

42-31060 Del Cheyenne 11/9/43; ass 427BS/303BG [GN-N] Molesworth 18/10/43; FTR Lutzkendorf, l/Continent 9/2/45; MACR 12245. Sal n/b/d. POGUE-MA-HONE.

42-31061 Del Cheyenne 14/9/43; ass 331BS/94BG [QE-T] Rougham 30/10/43; retUS Bradley 10/7/45; Independence 30/11/45; RFC Kingman 18/12/45. GOOD TIME CHOLLY III.

42-31062 Del Cheyenne 14/9/43; Gr Island 28/9/43; ass 351BS/100BG [EP-D] Thorpe Abbotts 28/9/43; b/d Pas de Calais, c/l Detling, UK. 21/1/44; sal 31/1/44. HOLY TERROR.

42-31063 Del Cheyenne 14/9/43; ass 335BS/95BG [OE-T] Horham 29/9/43 SPOOK SIX; tran 457BG Glatton 6/44; 384BG Grafton Underwood 22/3/45; RFC Kingman 18/12/45.

42-31064 Del Cheyenne 15/9/43; ass 614BS/401BG [IW-H] Deenethorpe 30/10/43; MIA Kiel 31/12/43 w/Lawry; flak, cr sea off Isle of Wight, UK; 10KIA; MACR 1872. HEY LOU.

42-31065 Del Cheyenne 13/9/43; Scott 28/9/43; ass 367BS/306BG [GY-Z] Thurleigh 19/10/43; MIA Brux 12/9/44 w/Bailey; flak, cr Kasserolhof, Ger; 1KIA 8POW; MACR 8827.

42-31066 Del Cheyenne 14/9/43; Scott 29/9/43; ass 351BS/100BG [EP-H] Thorpe Abbotts 4/10/43 DIXIE BABY; MIA Hamburg 31/12/44 w/Henderson; flak, cr Radegast, Ger; 6KIA 3POW; MACR 11366. FOOLS RUSH IN.

42-31067 Del Cheyenne 15/9/43; ass 534BS/381BG Ridgewell 20/10/43 BLACK WIDOW; tran 535BS [MS-T/Q]; {67m} RetUS 121 BU Bradley 8/6/45; 4168 BU Sth Plains 15/6/45; RFC Kingman 13/12/45. PHYLLIS.

42-31068 Del Cheyenne 14/9/43; Scott 22/10/43; ass 612BS/401BG [SC-D] Deenethorpe 8/11/43; c/l Ware, UK, 31/12/43, sal. FOOL'S LUCK.

42-31069 Del Cheyenne 15/9/43; Scott 20/10/43; ass 615BS/401BG [IY-K] Deenethorpe 11/11/43; MIA Kassel 28/9/44 w/Daves; flak, cr Helmstedt, Ger; 9POW; MACR 9415. LITTLE MOE.

42-31070 Del Cheyenne 15/9/43; ass 322BS/91BG [LG-M] Bassingbourn 14/12/43; retUS SSTA Homestead 16/7/44; 4100 BU Patterson 24/7/44; 610 BU Eglin 20/10/44; Wright Fd 24/10/44; 610 BU Eglin 19/12/44; RFC Walnut Ridge 5/12/45. DAME SATAN II.

42-31071 Del Cheyenne 14/9/43; Scott 28/9/43; ass 418BS/100BG [LD-U] Thorpe Abbotts 4/10/43; MIA Münster 22/12/43 w/Goupill; flak, cr Nth Sea; 9KIA; MACR 1705. DORHELCIA.

42-31072 Del Cheyenne 15/9/43; Scott 20/10/43; ass 613BS/401BG [IN-K] Deenethorpe 26/10/43; TDY Polebrook 16/6/44, ret 6/7/44; TDY Egypt 6/8/44, ret 29/8/44; f/l Continent 3/3/45; RetUS 121 BU Bradley 7/6/45; 4168 BU Sth Plains 13/6/45; RFC Kingman 17/12/45. BETTY J.

42-31073 Del Cheyenne 15/9/43; Scott 29/9/43; ass 547BS/384BG Grafton Underwood 18/10/43; c/l Whittlesey, UK. 31/12/43; sal n/b/d 2 BAD Lt Staughton 5/1/44.

42-31074 Del Cheyenne 15/9/43; Scott 28/9/43; ass 350BS/100BG [LN-Q] Thorpe Abbotts 4/10/43; MIA Munich 13/7/44 w/Waters; flak, f/l Emmen, Switz; 10INT; MACR 7501. CAHEPIT.

42-31075 Del Cheyenne 15/9/43; Scott 4/10/43; ass 535BS/381BG [MS-S] Ridgewell 19/10/43; MIA Bremen 20/12/43 w/Crosson; e/a, cr Albstadt, Ger; 3KIA 7POW; MACR 1722. THE REBEL.

42-31076 Del Cheyenne 16/9/43; Gr island 3/10/43; ass 323BS/91BG [OR-L] Bassingbourn 16/10/43; tran 323BS [OR-L]; MIA {18m} Oschersleben 11/1/44 w/Page; e/a, cr Scheude, Dummer Lake, Ger; 2KIA 8POW; MACR 1919. CHIEF SLY'S SON.

42-31077 Del Cheyenne 16/9/43; Scott 21/10/43; ass 612BS/401BG [SC-A] Deenethorpe 26/10/43; tran 615BS [IY-A]; MIA Münster 30/9/44 w/Davis; flak, cr Burgsteinfurt, Ger; 9POW; MACR 9416. PAKAWALUP II.

42-31078 Del Cheyenne 15/9/43; Gr Island 1/10/43; ass 369BS/306BG [WW-R] Thurleigh 19/10/43; MIA Emden 11/12/43 w/Bailey; flak, cr Emden; 1KIA 9POW; MACR 1574. (No cheek guns).

42-31079 Del Cheyenne 15/9/43; Scott 23/10/43; ass 401BG Deenethorpe 14/11/43; tran 401BS/91BG [LL-J/F] Bassingbourn 20/11/43; MIA Erkner 6/3/44 w/Coleman; e/a, cr Gardelegen, Ger; 4KIA 6POW; MACR 2897.

42-31080 Del Cheyenne 16/9/43; Gr Island 3/10/43; ass 331BS/94BG Rougham 10/10/43; MIA Brunswick 10/2/44 w/MacWilliams; e/a, cr Lauingen, Ger; 5KIA 5POW; MACR 2371. HEY MOITLE.

42-31081 Del Cheyenne 16/9/43; ass 613BS/401BG [IN-C] Deenethorpe 4/11/43; MIA Zwickau 7/10/44 w/Hill; flak, cr Politz, Ger; 9KIA; MACR 9757. SON OF A BLITZ.

42-31082 Del Cheyenne 20/9/43; Harvard 4/10/43; ass 710BS/447BG Rattlesden 25/11/43; MIA Oschersleben 11/1/44 w/Hickey; e/a, cr Diepholz, Ger; 2KIA 8POW; MACR 2512.

42-31083 Del Cheyenne 15/9/43; ass 525BS/379BG [FR-A] Kimbolton 19/10/43; b/d Sorau 11/4/44; c/l Stow Bardolph, UK. Sal 18/4/44. TENNY BELLE.

42-31084 Del Cheyenne 16/9/43; ass 561BS/388BG Knettishall 9/10/43; MIA Bremen 20/12/43 w/Eccleston; flak, cr Vegasack, Ger; 10KIA; MACR 3154.

42-31085 Del Cheyenne 16/9/43; Gr Island 1/10/43; ass 524BS/379BG [WA-D] Kimbolton 6/10/43; tran 525BS [FR-D]; MIA Leipzig 7/7/44 w/Riedman; flak, cr Altenroda, Ger; 3KIS 6POW; MACR 7357. ANITA MARIE.

42-31086 Del Cheyenne 16/9/43; Gr Island 27/9/43; ass 337BS/96BG [AW-O] Snetterton 11/10/43; MIA Bremen 16/12/43 w/Smith; e/a, cr Poppengweiler, Ger; 10KIA; MACR 1567.

42-31087 Del Cheyenne 17/9/43; Gt Falls 28/9/43; ass 612BS/401BG [SC-K] Deenethorpe 26/10/43; MIA Politz 7/10/44 w/?; flak, f/l Bredakara, Swe; 9INT; MACR 9758. BOCHE BUSTER. Left Sweden 13/5/45.

42-31088 Del Cheyenne 20/9/43; Scott 25/10/43; ass 447BG Rattlesden 19/11/43; b/d sal 13/4/44.

42-31089 Del Cheyenne 20/9/43; Gt Falls 4/10/43; Scott 28/10/43; ass 612BS/401BG [SC-M] Deenethorpe 16/11/43; MIA Kiel 4/1/44 w/Capt Garland; mechan fault, ditched Nth Sea; 2KIA 8RTD; MACR 6468. CAROLYNE.

42-31090 Del Cheyenne 20/9/43; Scott 3/10/43; ass 613BS/401BG [IN-L] Deenethorpe 4/11/43; b/d Pas de Calais 14/1/44; c/l Matlaske, UK; sal 21/1/44. NASTY HABIT.

42-31091 Del Cheyenne 20/9/43; Gt Falls 2/10/43; Scott 21/10/43; ass 615BS/401BG [IY-O] Deenethorpe 4/11/43; MIA Merseburg 11/9/44 w/Wingard; flak, cr Merseburg; MACR 8920. MAGGIE.

42-31092 Del Cheyenne 17/9/43; Gr Island 3/10/43; ass 401BG Deenethorpe 19/11/43; tran 447BG Rattlesden /43; sal 20/4/45. BUTCH II.

42-31093 Del Cheyenne 20/9/43; Scott 1/10/43; ass 525BS/379BG [FR-L] Kimbolton 9/10/43; MIA Kiel 5/1/44 w/Eaton; e/a, cr Kiel; 8KIA 2POW; MACR 1944. DEACON'S SINNERS.

42-31094 Del Cheyenne 20/9/43; WO Kearney 14/12/44.

42-31095 Del Cheyenne 20/9/43; Harvard 4/10/43; ass 708BS/447BG Rattlesden 19/11/43; MIA Hamm 29/11/44. THE GROUND POUNDER.

42-31096 Del Cheyenne 20/9/43; Harvard 4/10/43; ass 94BG Rougham 29/11/43; tran 711BS/447BG Rattlesden /44; MIA Brunswick 10/2/44 w/Jellison; e/a, cr Evenkamp?; 10POW; MACR 2534. THE SQUIRMING SQUAW.

42-31097 Del Cheyenne 20/9/43; Gt Falls 12/10/43; Scott 18/11/43; ass 401BG Deenethorpe 19/11/43; tran 535BS/381BG Ridgewell 21/11/43; MIA {1m} Leverkusen 1/12/43 w/Sunde; flak, cr Niew Lekkarland, Hol; 3KIA 7POW; MACR 1661. MISSION BELLE.

42-31098 Del Cheyenne 20/9/43; Gt Falls 2/10/32; Scott 25/10/43; ass 614BS/401BG [IW-B] Deenethorpe 30/10/43; MIA 29/5/44. MACR 8717 PENNY'S THUNDERHEAD.

42-31099 Del Cheyenne 20/9/32; Gt Falls 2/10/43; Scott 22/10/43; ass 401BG Deenethorpe 8/11/43; tran 532BS/381BG [VE-G] Ridgewell 21/11/43; MIA {8m} Frankfurt 11/2/44 w/Laux; flak, cr Amiens, Fr; 7EVD 3POW; MACR 2431. TENABUV.

42-31100 Del Cheyenne 20/9/43; Harvard 4/10/43; ass 709BS/447BG Rattlesden 25/11/43; b/d Dollenbergen, c/l base 1/1/45; THE GIMP.

42-31101 Del Cheyenne 20/9/43; Gr Island 7/10/43; Wilmington 10/10/43; ass 332BS/94BG Rougham 15/10/43; MIA Wilhelmshaven 3/11/43 w/Brunson; flak, cr Wilhelmshaven; 8KIA 2POW; MACR 1012.

MARGIE.

42-31102 Del Cheyenne 21/9/43; Gr Island 6/10/43; Wilmington 13/10/43; ass 550BS/385BG Gt Ashfield 26/10/43; MIA Brunswick 23/3/44 w/Salvards; flak, cr Dortmund; 10POW; MACR 3316.

42-31103 Del Cheyenne 20/9/43; Gr Island 5/10/43; ass 563BS/388BG Knettishall 26/10/43; MIA Brunswick 23/3/44 w/Wilson; col with e/a, cr Steyerberg, Ger; 7KIA 3POW; MACR 3594. PEGASUS, TOO.

42-31104 Del Cheyenne 20/9/43; Harvard 5/10/43; ass 708BS/447BG Rattlesden 19/11/43; b/d Nantes 7/6/44, sal.

42-31105 Del Cheyenne 20/9/43; Gr Island 5/10/43; ass 548BS/385BG Gt Ashfield 26/10/43; sal 18/4/44.

42-31106 Del Cheyenne 20/9/43; Gr Island 5/10/43; Wilmington 10/10/43; ass 338BS/96BG [BX-C] Snetterton 17/10/43 GEORING'S NIGHTMARE; tran 390BG Framlingham /44; 486BG Sudbury /44; c/l base 23/7/44, sal.

42-31107 Del Cheyenne 20/9/43; Harvard 5/10/43; ass 708BS/447BG Rattlesden 29/11/43; MIA Halbestadt 11/1/44 w/Jarrell; e/a, cr Hildersheim, Ger; 8KIA 2POW; MACR 2513.

42-31108 Del Cheyenne 20/9/43; Harvard 4/10/43; ass 709BS/447BG Rattlesden 21/11/43; MIA Frankfurt 29/1/44 w/Allen; e/a, cr Hunsrueck, Ger; 10KIA; MACR 2879. THE DEVIL'S MATE.

42-31109 Del Dallas 20/9/43; Scott 4/10/43; Wilmington 9/10/43; ass 332BS/94BG [XM-H] Rougham 10/10/43; tran 327BS/92BG Alconbury 17/10/43; MIA Frankfurt 4/2/44 w/Walther; mech fault, cr Peruwelz, Bel; 5EVD 1KIA 4POW; MACR 2236. DOLLIE MADISON.

42-31110 Del Dallas 20/9/43; Gr Island 12/10/43; Wilmington 15/10/43; ass 331BS/94BG [QE-M] Rougham 23/10/43; MIA Cognac 31/12/43 w/Sullivan; flak, cr Cognac, Fr; 6EVD 4POW; MACR 1672. PACIFIC'S DREAM.

42-31111 Del Dallas 20/9/43; Scott 4/10/43; Wilmington 7/10/43; ass 535BS/381BG [MS-R] Ridgewell 19/10/43; MIA Leverkusen 1/12/43 w/Nixon; flak, cr Cologne; 10KIA; MACR 1659. FOUR ACES - PAT HAND.

42-31112 Del Dallas 21/9/43; Harvard 5/10/43; ass 94BG Rougham 27/11/43; tran 710BS/447BG Rattlesden 30/11/43; MIA Wilhelmshaven 3/3/44 w/Graham; mid air coll, cr Wesermünde; 10KIA; MACR 2887.

42-31113 Del Dallas 21/9/43; Scott 3/10/43; Wilmington 7/10/43; ass 339BS/96BG Snetterton 15/10/43; MIA Bremen 16/12/43; mid air coll w/42-30872, cr Nth Sea; 10KIA; MACR 1564. ZILCH.

42-31114 Del Cheyenne 21/9/43; Gr Island 6/10/43; ass 568BS/390BG [BI-G] Framlingham 25/10/43; MIA Orleans 8/6/44 w/Sechrist; flak, cr Maissemy, Fr; 8EVD 1KIA 1POW; MACR 5479. PROWLIN' TOM.

42-31115 Del Cheyenne 21/9/43; Gr Island 6/10/43; ass 562BS/388BG Knettishall 25/10/43; MIA Brunswick 10/2/44 w/Feeney; flak, cr Uitgeest, Hol; 4KIA 7POW; MACR 2348. HELL'S BELLS.

42-31116 Del Cheyenne 21/9/43; Gt Falls 14/10/43; Bowman 28/10/43; ass 614BS/401BG [IW-O] Deenethorpe 30/10/43; MIA Berlin 29/4/44 w/Singleton; flak, cr Liers, Bel; 5EVD 5KIA; MACR 4344. CAWN'T MISS.

42-31117 Del Cheyenne 21/9/43; Gr Island 22/10/43; ass 551BS/385BG Gt Ashfield 9/11/43; sal FEA 2/8/46; Re-Ass ET 30/4/47; Recl Comp 1/11/47. DAISY MAE.

42-31118 Del Cheyenne 22/9/43; Gr Island 7/10/43; Wilmington 10/10/43; ass 338BS/96BG [BX-U] Snetterton 14/10/43; sal 13/1/44; LADY MILLICENT II.

42-31119 Del Cheyenne 21/9/43; Gr Island 6/10/43; ass 524BS/379BG [WA-L] Kimbolton 22/11/43; c/l base on training flight 28/12/43; sal.

42-31120 Del Cheyenne 21/9/43; Gr Island 5/10/43; Wilmington 13/10/43; ass 410BS/94BG [GL-U] Rougham 23/10/43; MIA Brunswick 23/3/44 w/Johnson; e/a, ditched Channel, crew missing after rescue launch caught fire and sank; MACR 3534.

42-31121 Del Cheyenne 22/9/43; Gr Island 6/10/43; Wilmington 10/10/32; ass 338BS/96BG [BX-E] Snetterton 14/10/43; MIA Bordeaux 31/12/43 w/Woodward; flak, cr Paris, Fr; 10KIA; MACR 1673.

42-31122 Del Cheyenne 22/9/43; Gr Island 6/10/43; Wilmington 10/10/43; ass 568BS/390BG [BI-A] Framlingham 14/10/43; MIA Emden 11/12/43 w/Maj Hansell; flak, cr Nth Sea; 8KIA 3POW; MACR 1583. SIX NIGHTS IN TELERGMA (ARABIAN NUTS).

42-31123 Del Cheyenne 22/9/43; Gr Island 7/10/43; Wilmington 10/10/43; ass 334BS/95BG [BG-J] Horham 14/10/43; c/t/o 19/11/43 w/Rongstad, at Redlingfield, UK; 10KIA.

42-31124 Del Cheyenne 23/9/43; Harvard 11/10/43; ass 711BS/447BG Rattlesden 19/11/43; MIA Berlin 29/4/44 w/Davidson; e/a, cr Eickendorf, Ger; 1KIA 9POW; MACR 4246.

42-31125 Del Dallas 23/9/43; Harvard 10/10/43; ass 711BS/447BG Rattlesden 19/11/43; MIA Bordeaux 31/12/43 w/Moore; flak, cr Cognac, Fr; 1EVD 3KIA 6POW; MACR 1789. NO REGRETS.

42-31126 Del Dallas 22/9/43; Harvard 9/10/43; Wilmington 12/10/43; ass 401BG Deenethorpe 23/12/43; tran 560BS/388BG Knettishall /44; MIA Lutzkendorf 20/2/44 w/Reed; e/a, cr Bellinge, Den; 2KIA 8POW; MACR 2433.

42-31127 Del Dallas 22/9/43; Harvard 8/10/43; ass 94BG Rougham 19/11/43; tran 447BG Rattlesden /44; sal b/d Brussels 20/5/44.

42-31128 Del Dallas 23/9/43; Harvard 8/10/43; ass 94BG Rougham 19/11/43; tran 709BS/447BG Rattlesden /44; MIA Lutzkendorf 20/7/44 w/Miller; flak, cr Teutleben, Ger; 3KIA 6POW; MACR 1769/7547.

42-31129 Del Dallas 23/9/43; Gr Island 9/10/43; Wilmington 12/10/43; slated 381BG 23/10/43; tran 32BS/301BG Oudna 1/11/43; Cerignola 7/12/43; Lucera 1/2/44; b/d {27m} Regensburg 25/2/44 w/Welsh; cr Trigno, It; 1KIA 2WIA, rest OK.

42-31130 Del Dallas 23/9/43; Gr Island 11/10/43; Wilmington 13/10/43; ass 8AF 16/10/43; 652BS/25BG. RetUS 4000 BU Patterson 16/4/46; 4185 BU Independence 29/10/46; 4000 BU Patterson 30/10/46; re-ass USN (CB-17) 31/3/47; 4141 BU Pyote 16/10/47; Recl Comp 7/6/48.

42-31131 Del Dallas 24/9/43; Gr Island 9/10/43; Wilmington 14/10/43; ass 563BS/388BG Knettishall 26/10/43; MIA Ludwigshafen 30/12/43 w/Carlson; coll w/42-31176, cr Heppenheim, Ger; 6KIA 4POW; MACR 3041. SATAN'S SISTER.

42-31132 Del Dallas 24/9/43; Gr Island 9/10/43; Wilmington 12/10/43; ass 388BG Knettishall 15/10/43; sal n/b/d 21/1/44.

42-31133 Del Dallas 23/9/43; Gr Island 9/10/43; Romulus 1/11/43; ass 551BS/385BG Gt Ashfield 2/11/43; MIA Berlin 29/4/44 w/Garza; e/a, cr Ruhen, Ger; 10POW; MACR 4453.

42-31134 Del Cheyenne 24/9/43; Gr Island 7/10/43; Wilmington 10/10/43; ass 569BS/390BG [CC-G] Framlingham 13/10/43; MIA Nuremberg 10/9/44 w/McIntosh; flak, cr Nuremberg; 6KIA 3POW; MACR 8910. GUNG HO.

42-31135 Del Cheyenne 25/9/43; Gr Isle 8/10/43; Romulus 12/10/43; ass 562BS/388BG Knettishall 14/10/43; MIA Berlin 6/3/44 w/Givens; e/a, cr Emmen, Hol; 1KIA 9POW; MACR 3082. SUSIE SAG TITS.

42-31136 Del Cheyenne 24/9/43; Gr Island 9/10/43; ass 369BS/306BG Thurleigh 19/10/43; c/l Andrews Fd, UK. 12/1/44, sal 2 SAD Lt Staughton.

42-31137 Del Cheyenne 24/9/43; Gr Island 7/10/43; Romulus 10/10/43; ass 563BS/388BG Knettishall 14/10/43; MIA Warnemünde 9/4/44 w/Abramowitz; flak, f/l Kalmar, Swed; 10INT; MACR 3654. RetUS 121 BU Bradley 16/8/45; 4185 BU Independence 19/8/45; RFC Kingman 17/12/45. CLASSY CHASSY.

42-31138 Del Cheyenne 24/9/43; Gr Island 7/10/43; Romulus 10/10/43; ass 560BS/388BG Knettishall 15/10/43; MIA Augsburg 13/4/44 w/Nelson; e/a, cr Speyerdorf, Ger; 1KIA 9POW; MACR 3773. WINGED FURY.

42-31139 Del Cheyenne 24/9/43; Gr Island 7/10/43; Romulus 10/10/43; ass 388BG Knettishall 14/10/43; tran 423BS/306BG [RD-L] Thurleigh 19/10/43; MIA Brunswick 24/2/44 w/Garrett; e/a, cr Talge, Ger; 2KIA 8POW; MACR 2771.

42-31140 Del Cheyenne 24/9/43; Gr Island 7/10/43; Romulus 10/10/43; ass 339BS/96BG [QJ-T] Snetterton 17/10/43; sal 7/6/45.

42-31141 Del Cheyenne 23/9/43; Gr Island 8/10/43; ass 332BS/94BG [XM-N] Rougham 15/10/43; MIA Berlin 8/3/44 w/Scott; e/a, ditched Channel; 1KIA 9POW; MACR 2976.

42-31142 Del Cheyenne 24/9/43; Gr Island 7/10/43; Romulus 10/10/43; ass 339BS/96BG [QJ-U] Snetterton 14/10/43; MIA Regensburg 25/2/44 w/Lindstrom; e/a, cr St Martin, Bel; 2EVD 8POW; MACR 2860.

42-31143 Del Cheyenne 24/9/43; Gr Island 8/10/43; Memphis 10/10/43; ass 369BS/306BG [WW-R] Thurleigh 19/10/43; tran 381BG Ridgewell 5/45; retUS 121 BU Bradley 12/6/45; RFC Kingman 5/12/45. SATAN'S LADY.

42-31144 Del Dallas 25/9/43; Harvard 6/10/43; ass 708BS/447BG Rattlesden 21/11/43; MIA Berlin 29/4/44 w/Hughes; e/a, cr Destedt, Ger?; 9KIA 1POW; MACR 4247.

42-31145 Del Dallas 25/9/43; Harvard 6/10/43; ass 423BS/306BG [RD-N] Thurleigh 19/11/43; tran 708BS/447BG Rattlesden /44; MIA Evreux 6/2/44 w/ Reed; flak, cr Evreux; 4KIA 6POW; MACR 2353. OLD MAN.

42-31146 Del Dallas 25/9/43; Harvard 14/10/43; ass 708BS/447BG Rattlesden 19/11/43; MIA Brunswick 30/1/44 w/ Putnam; mech fault, cr Gladbach, Ger; 2KIA 8POW; MACR 2277.

42-31147 Del Dallas 24/9/43; Romulus 17/4/43; 357 BU Kellogg 14/6/44; 553 BU Romulus 31/7/44; 552 BU New Castle 14/10/44; 593 BU Charleston 28/10/45; RFC Walnut Ridge 3/1/46.

42-31148 Del Dallas 25/9/43; Harvard 7/10/43; ass 710BS/447BG Rattlesden 21/11/43; MIA Wilhelmshaven 3/3/44 w/Ralston; mech fault, ditched Nth Sea; 7KIA 3RTD; MACR 4436.

42-31149 Del Cheyenne 25/9/43; Gr Island 9/10/43; Love Fd 12/10/43; ass 560BS/388BG Knettishall 15/10/43; MIA Ludwigshafen 30/12/43 w/Comelia; flak, ditched Channel; 6KIA 4RTD; MACR 3139. MY DAY.

42-31150 Del Cheyenne 25/9/43; Gr Island 8/10/43; Love Fd 12/10/43; ass 332BS/94BG [XM-Q] Rougham 15/10/43; c/l Debach AF, UK. 22/2/44; sal b/d. WONGA WONGA.

42-31151 Del Cheyenne 25/9/43; Gr Island 9/10/43; Long Beach 13/10/43; ass 337BS/96BG [AW-S] Snetterton 15/10/43; MIA Frankfurt 29/1/44 w/Sisler; mid air coll w/42-31436, cr Frankfurt; 6KIA 4POW; MACR 2381.

42-31152 Del Cheyenne 25/9/43; Gr Island 8/10/43; Nashville 12/10/43; ass 339BS/96BG [QJ-E] Snetterton 14/10/43; MIA Pas de Calais 1/5/44 w/Dingledine; flak, cr Chivres, Bel; 1EVD 1KIA 8POW; MACR 4237.

42-31153 Del Cheyenne 25/9/43; Gr Island 9/10/43; Romulus 12/10/43; ass 562BS/388BG Knettishall 26/10/43 BOOMERANG; MIA Frankfurt 20/3/33 w/Patterson; flak, cr Wernincourt, Fr; 3KIA 7POW; MACR 3542. CAPTAIN JOE.

42-31154 Del Dallas 25/9/43; Harvard 7/10/43; ass 708BS/447BG Rattlesden 19/10/43; MIA Merseburg 25/11/43 w/Wiggin; flak, cr Merseburg; 7KIA 2POW; MACR 10755. SHACK HAPPY.

42-31155 Del Dallas 25/9/43; Harvard 6/10/43; ass 447BG Rattlesden 18/11/43; Berlin 9/3/44; sal.

42-31156 Del Cheyenne 26/9/43; Gr Island 13/10/43; ass 708BS/447BG Rattlesden 19/11/43; MIA Rostock 11/4/44 w/Pauling; flak, c/l Bornholm Is, Den; 6EVD 4POW; MACR 3824. BIG STOOP.

42-31157 Del Dallas 25/9/43; Gr Island 14/10/43; ass 709BS/447BG Rattlesden 23/11/43; MIA Pas de Calais 13/2/44 w/McDonald; flak, cr Fraincourt, Fr; 10POW; MACR 2533. RED ASS, possibly (DONKEY).

42-31158 Del Dallas 26/9/43; Luke Fd 7/10/43; Memphis 15/11/43; ass 368BS/306BG [BO-J] Thurleigh 12/12/43; b/d, sal 2 SAD Lt Staughton 27/7/44.

42-31159 Del Cheyenne 27/9/43; Gr Island 10/10/43; Wilmington 13/10/43; ass 333BS/94BG Rougham 23/10/43; MIA Munich 18/3/44 w/Croft; e/a, cr Villingen, Ger; 3KIA 7POW; MACR 3419.

42-31160 Del Cheyenne 26/9/43; Harvard 10/10/43; ass 710BS/447BG Rattlesden 25/11/43; MIA Pas de Calais 13/2/44 w/Kayfun; flak, cr Channel; 9KIA 1POW; MACR 2532.

42-31161 Del Dallas 25/9/43; Harvard 6/10/43; ass 711BS/447BG Rattlesden 25/11/43; MIA Berlin 29/4/44 w/Peper; e/a, c/l Magdeburg; 10POW; MACR 4248.

42-31162 Del Cheyenne 26/9/43; Gr Island 10/10/43; Memphis 14/10/43; ass 508BS/351BG [YB-V] Polebrook 7/11/43; tran 511BS [DS-V]; MIA {8m} Ludwigshafen 30/12/43 w/Parsons; flak, cr St Pol-de-Leon, Fr; 5KIA 5POW; MACR 1757. VICTORY BALL.

42-31163 Del Cheyenne 27/9/43; Gr Island 9/10/43; Nashville 12/10/43; ass 562BS/388BG Knettishall 14/10/43; MIA Berlin 6/3/44 w/Wallace; b/d, f/l Rinkaby, Swed; 10INT; MACR 3083. A GOOD SHIP AND A HAPPY SHIP. (Used by Swedish air line ABA as SE-BAM, crashed Dec/45, WO.) TOM.

42-31164 Del Cheyenne 26/9/43; Gr Island 9/10/43; Nashville 12/10/43; ass 337BS/96BG [AW-T] Snetterton 14/10/43; MIA Kiel 5/1/44 w/Stakes; e/a, cr St Ceir, Fr; 6EVD 1KIA 3POW; MACR 2012. LUCKY LADY.

42-31165 Del Cheyenne 27/9/43; Harvard 13/10/43; 708BS/447BG Rattlesden 21/11/43; MIA Bonn 4/3/44 w/Geyer; flak, cr St Pierre, BEL; 1EVD 9POW; MACR 2888.

42-31166 Del Cheyenne 27/9/43; MAT COM Wright Fd 10/10/43; Langley 6/12/43; ass 813BS/482BG [PC-K] Alconbury 22/11/43; tran 545BS/384BG [JD-Z] Grafton Underwood 5/2/44; c/l Nuthampstead 24/3/44; SAL 2 SAD Lt Staughton. MISS BILLIE JR.

42-31167 Del Cheyenne 27/9/43; Harvard 13/10/43; ass 710BS/447BG Rattlesden 21/11/43; MIA Brunswick 10/2/44 w/Finfinger; e/a, cr Barver, Ger; 5KIA 5POW; MACR 2535.

42-31168 Del Cheyenne 27/9/43; Harvard 14/10/43; ass 447BG Rattlesden; RetUS 121 BU Bradley 28/6/45; 4168 BU Sth Plains 6/7/45; RFC Kingman 8/12/45.

42-31169 Del Cheyenne 28/9/43; Harvard 14/10/43; ass 331BS/94BG Rougham 23/11/43; MIA Berlin 4/3/44 w/Pollock; flak, cr Calais, Fr; 1EVD 6KIA 3POW; MACR 2998. WOLVERINE II.

42-31170 Del Cheyenne 28/9/43; Harvard 13/10/43; Memphis 18/10/43; ass 8AF; 652BS/25BG; sal n/b/d 18/4/45.

42-31171 Del Cheyenne 27/9/43; Gr Island 9/10/43; ass 551BS/385BG Gt Ashfield 21/10/43; b/d French tactical targets 17/7/44, c/l Woodbridge ELG, UK; sal 19/7/44.

42-31172 Del Cheyenne 27/9/43; Harvard 13/10/43; ass 367BS/306BG [GY-B] Thurleigh 26/11/43; MIA Oberpfaffenhofen 24/4/44 w/Schwedock; f/l Dubendorf, Switz; 10INT; MACR 4279; (old B-17F top turret installed). MISS PATRICIA.

42-31173 Del Cheyenne 27/9/43; Harvard 13/10/43; ass 711BS/447BG Rattlesden 24/11/43; MIA Ludwigshafen 30/12/43 w/Schrero; e/a, cr Beauvais, Fr; 1EVD 4KIA 5POW; MACR 1770.

42-31174 Del Dallas 27/9/43; Gr Island 19/10/43; Long Beach 28/11/43; ass 551BS/385BG Gt Ashfield 5/12/43; MIA Berlin 29/4/44 w/Hart; e/a, cr Magdeburg, Ger; 1KIA 9POW; MACR 4454.

42-31175 Del Denver 29/9/43; Gr Island 21/10/43; Memphis 15/11/43; ass 326BS/92BG Podington 2/12/43; MIA Oschersleben 11/1/44 w/Lock; e/a, cr Heerde, Hol; 3EVD 2KIA 5POW; MACR 1920. TRUDY.

42-31176 Del Dallas 27/9/43; Gr Island 17/10/43; Wilmington 24/10/43; ass 560BS/388BG Knettishall 26/11/43; MIA Berlin 24/4/44 w/Gwin; flak, ditched Channel; 10POW; MACR 4288.

42-31177 Del Denver 28/9/43; Gr Island 18/10/43; Memphis 24/10/43; ass 359BS/303BG [BN-L] Molesworth 18/11/43; MIA Brux 12/9/43; e/a, cr Berlin; 4KIA 5POW; MACR 8823. LONESOME POLECAT.

42-31178 Del Denver 28/9/43; Gr Island 18/10/43; Romulus 16/11/43; ass 324BS/91BG Bassingbourn 20/12/43; c/l Old Windsor, UK. Sal 1 SAD 1/1/44.

42-31179 Del Denver 29/9/43; Gr Island 22/10/43; Wilmington 31/10/43; ass 511BS/351BG [DS-B] Polebrook 23/12/43; MIA {2m} Bordeaux 31/12/43 w/Putnam; e/a, cr Cognac, Fr; 1EVD 4KIA 5POW; MACR 1980. STINKY WEATHER.

42-31180 Del Denver 28/9/43; Gr Island 18/10/43; Nashville 24/10/43; ass 407BS/92BG Podington 23/11/43; MIA Schweinfurt 24/2/44 w/Clayton; e/a, cr Zwolle, Hol; 8KIA 2POW; MACR 2854.

42-31181 Del Denver 29/9/43; Casper 7/10/43; ass 549BS/385BG Gt Ashfield 2/11/43; MIA Brunswick 30/1/44 w/Lojinger; e/a, cr Wolfenbuettel, Ger; 10POW; MACR 2266.

42-31182 Del Boeing Mat Com 7/10/43; Gr Island 12/11/43; Memphis 20/11/43; ass 419BS/301BG Cerignola 17/12/43; Lucera 1/2/44 MIA {17m} Ploesti 5/4/44 w/Coppedge; e/a, cr Plovdiv, Bul; 10POW; 3882.

42-31183 Del Denver 28/9/43; Gr Island 21/10/43; Wilmington 28/10/43; ass 358BS/303BG [VK-Y] Molesworth 18/11/43; tran 359BS [BN-J]; MIA Cologne 15/8/44 w/Goss; e/a, cr Wittlich, Ger; 2KIA 7POW; MACR 8170. BAD PENNY.

42-31184 Del Cheyenne 29/9/43; Harvard 14/10/43; ass 388BG Gt Ashfield 18/11/43; tran 711BS/447BG Rattlesden 1/44; MIA Schweinfurt 13/4/44 w/Kruezer; flak, cr Sieben, Switz; crew baled; MACR 4295. OLD CROW.

42-31185 Del Cheyenne 29/9/43; Harvard 13/10/43; ass 708BS/447BG Rattlesden 19/11/43; c/l 4/9/44, sal.

42-31186 Del Cheyenne 28/9/43; Harvard 13/10/43; ass 709BS/447BG Rattlesden 21/11/43; MIA Pas de Calais 28/2/44 w/Harris; flak, cr Hiricourt, Fr; 1EVD 9POW; MACR 2889.

42-31187 Del Cheyenne 30/9/43; Gt Falls 14/10/43; Bowman 18/10/43; ass 401BG Deenethorpe 16/11/43; tran 401BS/91BG [LL-F] Bassingbourn 20/11/43; b/d Oschersleben {10m} 11/1/44, f/l Deopham Green, UK. rep; c/l Newmarket en route to base, 4/3/44, sal. BUCKEYE BOOMERANG.

42-31188 Del Cheyenne 30/9/43; Harvard 16/10/43; ass 709BS/447BG Rattlesden 21/11/43; MIA Pirna 19/4/45 w/Glazner; jet e/a, cr Dresden; 1KIA 9POW; MACR 14180. DEAD MAN'S HAND.

42-31189 (GH) Del Cheyenne 29/9/43; Gr Island 22/10/43; Memphis 4/11/43; ass 525BS/379BG Kimbolton 22/11/43; MIA Leipzig 7/7/44 w/Harrah; flak, cr Noordoospolder, Hol; 4EVD 1KIA 4POW; MACR 7358.

42-31190 Del Cheyenne 29/9/43; Harvard 15/10/43; WO 23/12/44.

42-31191 Del Cheyenne 29/9/43; Harvard 16/10/43; ass 710BS/447BG Rattlesden 25/11/43; MIA Bordeaux 27/3/44 w/Gaskell; e/a, cr Merignac, Fr; 2EVD 8POW; MACR 3546. VIRGINIA LEE.

42-31192 Del Cheyenne 30/9/43; Scott Fd 24/10/43; Presque Is 1/11/43; ass 612BS/401BG Deenethorpe 2/11/43; tran 509BS/351BG [RQ-R] Polebrook 3/12/43; 508BS [YB-R]; MIA {41m} Politz 7/10/44 w/Peterson; flak, c/l Farabol, Swed; 2INT 7KIA; MACR 9566.

42-31193 Del Cheyenne 29/9/43; Gt Falls 14/10/43; Scott 21/10/43; ass 615BS/401BG [IY-B] Deenethorpe 4/11/43; MIA Frankfurt 29/1/44 w/Capt Beers; e/a, cr Worms, Ger; 5KIA 5POW; MACR 2274. LITTLE BOOTS.

42-31194 Del Denver 30/9/43; Gr Island 19/10/43; Memphis 26/10/43; ass 562BS/388BG Knettishall 1/11/43; MIA Berlin 6/3/44 w/Grindley; e/a, cr Schoeningsdorf, Ger; 3KIA 7POW; MACR 3084. DUCHESS OF DIXIE.

42-31195 Del Denver 30/9/43; Las Vegas 27/10/43; 3021 BU Las Vegas 16/6/44; 2126 BU Laredo 4/5/45; 331 BU Barksdale 22/10/45; 2126 BU Laredo 7/11/45; RFC Walnut Ridge 10/1/46.

42-31196 Del Cheyenne 4/10/43; Gr Island 2/11/43; Memphis 10/11/43; ass 369BS/306BG [BO-O] Thurleigh 14/12/43; b/d Stuttgart 9/12/44, f/l Continent; sal 20/1/45. EXTRA JOKER.

42-31197 Del Denver 30/9/43; Gr Island 1/11/43; Romulus 6/11/43; ass 533BS/381BG [VP-Q] Ridgewell 13/1/44; {28m} RetUS Homestead 12/7/44; 4136 BU Tinker 6/8/44; 4100 BU Patterson 5/2/45; 4210 BU Lambert 16/4/45; 4000 BU Wright Fd 26/6/45; 611 BU Eglin 2/4/46; 4117 BU Robins 27/12/46; Re-ass AMCWR 31/3/47; Recl Comp 14/9/48. SHACK RABBIT.

42-31198 Del Denver 30/9/43; Gr Island 1/11/43; Memphis 6/11/43; ass 612BS/401BG [SC-N] Deenethorpe 24/12/43; b/d Bordeaux 31/12/43, c/l Kimbolton; sal 4/1/44. FANCY NANCY II.

42-31199 Del Denver 30/9/43; Gr Island 31/10/43; Wilmington 9/11/43; ass 571BS/390BG [FC-F] Framlingham 15/11/43; sal 16/4/44. ROSIE

WRECKTUM.

42-31200 Del Denver 2/10/43; Gr Island 31/10/43; Long Beach 25/11/43; ass 427BS/303BG [GN-V] Molesworth 1/1/44 OLD CROW; MIA Paris 28/6/44 w/Wardowski; flak, cr Chievres, Bel; 3KIA 6POW; MACR 6740. THE BAD PENNY.

42-31201 Del Denver 3/10/43; Gr Island 31/10/43; Memphis 20/11/43; ass 414BS/97BG Depienne 30/11/43; Cerignola 20/12/43; Amendola 16/1/44; MIA Ploesti, Rom. 24/4/44 w/White; e/a, cr Topoloveni, Bul; MACR 4519.

42-31202 Del Denver 3/10/43; Gr Island 31/3/43; Wilmington 9/11/43; ass 613BS/401BG [IN-D] Deenethorpe 12/12/43; b/d Brunswick 29/3/44; sal.

42-31203 Del Denver 1/10/43; Gr Island 1/11/43; Gt Falls 6/11/43; ass 548BS/385BG Gt Ashfield 29/11/43; MIA Pas de Calais 28/2/44.

42-31204 Del Cheyenne 1/10/43; Harvard 14/10/43; ass 711BS/447BS Rattlesden 19/11/43; MIA Brunswick 28/2/44 w/Foutts; flak, cr Croisette, Fr; 7KIA 3POW; MACR 2890.

42-31205 Del Cheyenne 5/10/43; Gr Island 17/10/43; Gt Falls 20/10/43; ass 336BS/95BG [ET-E] Horham 2/11/43; MIA Augsburg 16/3/44 w/McAllister; cr Nellingen, Ger; 10POW; MACR 3228.

42-31206 Del Cheyenne 1/10/43; Harvard 14/10/43; ass 709BS/447BG Rattlesden 18/11/43; retUS Bradley 4/7/45; Sth Plains 7/7/45; RFC Kingman 26/11/45.

42-31207 Del Cheyenne 1/10/43; Harvard 14/10/43; ass 447BG Rattlesden 19/11/43; b/d Berlin 6/3/44; sal 7/3/44.

42-31208 Del Cheyenne 1/10/43; Harvard 14/10/43; ass 447BG Rattlesden 21/11/43; MIA Berlin 9/3/44.

42-31209 Del Cheyenne 5/10/43; Gr Island 17/10/43; Long Beach 23/11/43; ass 561BS/388BG Knettishall 26/11/43; MIA Brunswick 30/1/44 w/Bianchi; flak, cr Stemahorn, Ger; 4KIA 6POW; MACR 2884. JANIE BB.

42-31210 Del Denver 4/10/43; Harvard 15/10/43; ass 447BG Rattlesden 25/11/43; MIA Berlin 9/3/43 w/?; flak, ditched Channel.

42-31211 Del Cheyenne 5/10/43; Gr Island 17/10/43; Romulus 24/10/43; ass 544BS/384BG [SU-H] Grafton Underwood 23/11/43; MIA Berlin 8/5/44 w/Allison; flak, cr Sottevast, Fr; 2EVD 5KIA 3POW; MACR 4560.

42-31212 Del Denver 4/10/43; Gr Island 17/10/43; Memphis 24/10/43; ass 331BS/94BG [QE-K] Rougham 1/11/43; MIA Bordeaux 5/1/44 w/Johnson; e/a, cr Kergrist?; 7EVD (6 escaped) 3KIA; MACR 1890.

42-31213 (GH) Del Denver 4/10/43; Gr Island 19/10/43; Romulus 26/10/43; ass 359BS/303BG [BN-Z] Molesworth 18/11/43; MIA Dessau 30/5/44 w/Van; mech fault, cr Nordhausen, Ger; 4KIA 5POW; MACR 5341. PISTOL PACKIN' MAMA.

42-31214 Del Denver 4/10/43; Harvard 16/10/43; Wilmington 19/10/43; ass 560BS/388BG Knettishall 26/10/43; MIA Bremen 8/3/44 w/Pou; e/a, cr Solingen, Ger; 2KIA 8POW; MACR 3085. RETURN ENGAGEMENT.

42-31215 Del Denver 4/10/43; Gr Isle 15/10/43; Wilmington 19/10/43; ass 349BS/100BG [XR-H] Thorpe Abbotts 26/11/43; MIA Bremen 26/11/43 w/Ford; e/a, cr Laneuville, Fr; 3EVD 2KIA 5POW; MACR 1394.

42-31216 Del Denver 4/10/43; Gr Isle 16/10/43; Wilmington 19/10/43; ass 331BS/94BG [QE-L] Rougham 26/10/43; MIA Brunswick 11/1/44 w/Rubin; e/a, cr Lingen, Ger; 1KIA 9POW; MACR 1884.

42-31217 Del Denver 4/10/43; Harvard 15/10/43; ass 710BS/447BG Rattlesden 21/11/43; MIA Berlin 29/4/44 w/Paris; e/a, cr Eggenstedt, Ger; 10POW; MACR 4249.

42-31218 Del Cheyenne 5/10/43; Gr Island 16/10/43; Wilmington 1/11/43; ass 571BS/390BG [FC-E] Framlingham 15/11/43; MIA Brunswick 10/2/44 w/Burke; e/a, cr Baarlo, Hol; 4EVD 1KIA 5POW; MACR 2504. ETO-ITIS.

42-31219 Del Denver 4/10/43; Harvard 14/10/43; ass 8AF 22/11/43.

42-31220 Del Denver 4/10/43; Gr Island 16/10/43; Wilmington 21/10/43; ass 350BS/100BG [LN-P] Thorpe Abbotts 5/11/43 FLETCHER'S CASTORIA II; c/t/o 4/12/43, rep; tran 390BG Framlingham /44; retUS Rome 27/4/45; Recl Comp 2/10/45.

42-31221 Del Cheyenne 6/10/43; Las Vegas 24/10/43; 3022 BU Indian Springs 5/2/45; 3021 BU Las Vegas 10/3/45; 3036 BU Yuma 20/3/45; 3017 BU Hobbs 4/6/45; 3028 BU Luke 5/8/45; 3017 BU Hobbs 24/8/45; RFC Walnut Ridge 11/1/46.

42-31222 Del Denver 4/10/43; Gr Island 17/10/43; Memphis 24/10/43; ass 545BS/384BG [JD-D] Grafton Underwood 23/11/43; MIA Berlin 28/9/44 w/Brodie; flak, cr Erxleben, Ger; 6KIA 3POW; MACR 9366. LAZY DAISY.

42-31223 Del Denver 4/10/43; Harvard 15/10/43; ass 711BS/447BG Rattlesden 25/11/43; b/d sal 21/3/44.

42-31224 (GH) Del Boeing 7/10/43; Wright Fd Mat Com 19/10/43; Memphis 28/11/43; ass 358BS/303BG [VK-F] Molesworth 13/1/44; MIA Weisbaden 15/8/44 w/Smithy; e/a, cr Wittlich, Ger; 3KIA 6POW; MACR 8169. HELEN HEAVEN.

42-31225 Del Denver 4/10/43; Harvard 15/10/43; ass 709BS/447BG Rattlesden 21/11/43; retUS 121 BU Bradley 4/7/45; 4168 BU Sth Plains 8/7/45; RFC Kingman 10/11/45. SCHEHERAZADE.

42-31226 Del Denver 4/10/43; Gr Island 16/10/43; Memphis 19/10/43; ass 613BS/401BG [IN-G] Deenethorpe 22/12/43; MIA Berlin 29/4/44 w/Butterfoss; flak, cr Arnhem, Hol; 1EVD 9POW; MACR 4345.

42-31227 Del Denver 4/10/43; Harvard 15/10/43; ass 94BG Rougham; tran 447BG Rattlesden /44; b/d Berlin 6/3/44 1KIA, MACR 2278. Sal 7/3/44. DOTTIE JANE.

42-31228 Del Denver 4/10/43; Gr Island 17/10/43; Romulus 24/10/43; ass 525BS/379BG [FR-G] Kimbolton 22/11/43; c/t/o into base quarters, 4 CREW & 5 EM killed 23/1/45; sal 2 SAD Lt Staughton 25/1/45. LONDON AVENGER.

42-31229 Del Cheyenne 8/10/43; Gr Island 26/10/43; Romulus 1/11/43; ass 570BS/390BG [DI-S] Framlingham 11/11/43; MIA Düsseldorf 9/9/44, f/l on continental A/Fd; repaired by modifying to F model by 458 St/Sqd; sal 14/11/44. BAD EGG.

42-31230 Del Denver 4/10/43; Gr Island 20/10/43; Memphis 26/10/43; ass 324BS/91BG [DF-A1] Bassingbourn 22/12/43; MIA {3+m} Oschersleben 11/1/44 w/Uskala; e/a, cr Schoepenstedt, Ger; 6KIA 4POW; MACR 1916. LITTLE JEAN.

42-31231 Del Cheyenne 7/10/43; Gr Island 19/10/43; Romulus 28/10/43; ass 326BS/92BG Podington 23/11/43; MIA Brunswick 23/3/44 w/Wall; e/a, cr Scheidingen, Ger; 3KIA 7POW; MACR 3413.

42-31232 Del Boeing Mat Com 22/10/43; 2511 BU Bryan 9/6/44; 571 BU Greensboro 7/11/45; 2511 BU Bryan 9/12/45; 4121 BU Kelly 12/12/45; 2621 BU Barksdale 31/12/45; 613 BU Phillips 24/6/46; 554 BU Memphis 13/8/46.

42-31233 Del Cheyenne 6/10/43; Gr Island 26/10/43; Wilmington 28/10/43; ass 427BS/303BG Molesworth 18/11/43; MIA Bremen 20/12/43 w/Leve; e/a, cr Bremen; 8KIA 2POW; MACR 1707.

42-31234 Del Cheyenne 6/10/43; Gr Island 17/10/43; Wilmingtonn 245/10/43; ass 332BS/94BG Rougham 27/10/43 JOHNNIE WALKER III; MIA Ludwigshafen 7/1/44 w/Barber; e/a, cr Arlon, Bel; 3KIA 7POW; MACR 1894. THE BARBER SHOP.

42-31235 Del Cheyenne 6/10/43; Gr Island 16/10/43; Nashville 26/11/43; ass 544BS/384BG [SU-C] Grafton Underwodd 6/1/44; MIA Berlin 7/5/44 w/ Goller; flak, cr Brunswick; 10POW; MACR 4811. GOIN' DOG.

42-31236 Del Cheyenne 8/10/43; Gr Island 11/11/43; Wilmington 17/11/43; ass 367BS/306BG [GY-F] Thurleigh 21/12/43; MIA Oschersleben 11/1/44 w/Campert; e/a, cr Realte, Hol; 10KIA; MACR 1933. ARCH BISHOP.

42-31237 Del Cheyenne 7/10/43; Gr Island 16/10/43; Wilmington 19/10/43; ass 551BS/385BG Gt Ashfield 26/10/43; b/d Pas de Calais 1/5/44, c/l Mendlesham, UK.; 2RTD 8 baled over France; sal 2/5/44. ALEXANDERS'S RAGTIME BAND.

42-31238 Del Cheyenne 7/10/43; Gr Island 21/10/43; Nashville 27/10/43; ass 511BS/351BG [DS-A] Polebrook 23/12/43; b/d {64m} Mannheim 8/9/44, c/l Market Deeping, UK; sal 2 SAD Lt Staughton 9/9/44. DEVIL'S BALL.

42-31239 Del Cheyenne 7/10/43; Gr Island 21/10/43; Nashville 29/10/43; ass 358BS/303BG [VK-N] Molesworth 18/11/43; MIA Schweinfurt 24/2/44 w/Smith; e/a, cr Schweinfurt; 7KIA 3POW; MACR 2763.

42-31240 Del Cheyenne 7/10/43; Gr Island 21/10/43; ass 561BS/388BG Knettishall 2/11/43; MIA Berlin 6/3/44 w/McLaughlin; e/a, cr Soltau, Ger; 10POW; MACR 3086. SHACK JOB.

42-31241 Del Cheyenne 7/10/43; Gr Island 21/10/43; Wilmington 29/10/43; ass 427BS/303BG [GN-W] Molesworth 18/11/43 SPIRIT OF WANNETTE; MIA Berlin 29/4/44 w/Bohle; flak, cr Berlin; 1EVD 5KIA 4POW; MACR 4463. CITY OF WANNETTE.

42-31242 Del Cheyenne 7/10/43; Gr Island 17/10/43; Gt Falls 23/10/43; ass 563BS/388BG Knettishall 9/11/43; mid air coll w/452BG a/c 19/5/44 w/Salles; c/l Old Buckenham, UK; 1ORTD; sal 25/7/46. PATTY JO.

42-31243 Del Cheyenne 8/10/43; Gr Island 19/10/43; Wilmington 27/10/43; Slated 94BG, ass 427BS/303BG Molesworth 18/11/43; MIA Leverkusen 1/12/43 w/Eckhart; no gas, ditched Pegwell Bay, UK; 10RTD.

42-31244 Del Cheyenne 11/10/43; Gr Island 25/10/43; Wilmington 1/11/43; ass 334BS/95BG [BG-O] Horham 15/11/43; sal n/b/d 9/2/44.

42-31245 Del Cheyenne 7/10/43; Gr Island 1/11/43; Dallas 6/11/43; ass 368BS/306BG Thurleigh 14/12/43; MIA Augsburg 25/2/44 w/Coleman; e/a, cr Charleville, Fr; 1EVD 9POW; MACR 2768. TOP HAT.

42-31246 Del Cheyenne 8/10/43; Gr Island 21/10/43; Nashville 28/10/43; ass tran 547BS/384BG [SO-A] Grafton Underwood 27/11/43; 545BS [JD-A]; MIA Pas de Calais 14/1/44 w/Britt; flak, cr St Valery, Fr; 1EVD 9POW; MACR 2497.

42-31247 Del Cheyenne 12/10/43; Las Vegas 25/10/43; 3021 BU Las Vegas 16/9/44; 2126 BU Laredo 23/5/45; RFC Walnut Ridge 3/1/46.

42-31248 Del Cheyenne 13/10/43; Gr Island 25/10/43; Wilmington 2/11/43; ass 325BS/92BG Podington 30/11/43; MIA Sorau 11/4/44 w/Fortson; e/a, cr Bohnsdorf, Ger; 6KIA 4POW; MACR 2669.

42-31249 Del Cheyenne 8/10/43; Gr Island 22/10/43; Memphis 28/10/43; ass 349BS/100BG [XR-L]

Thorpe Abbotts 2/11/43; c/l base after aborted mission 10/5/44; sal 20/5/44.

42-31250 Del Cheyenne 8/10/43; Gr Island 19/10/43; Wilmington 29/10/43; ass 327BS/92BG [UX-B] Podington 2/12/43; MIA Sth Germany oil 13/9/43 w/Eck; e/a, cr Neustadt; 8KIA 1POW; MACR 8882. MAG THE HAG II.

42-31251 Del Cheyenne 12/10/43; Gr Island 22/10/43; Wilmington 1/11/43; ass 334BS/95BG [BG-P] Horham 11/11/43; MIA Berlin 6/3/43 w/Keasbey; e/a, cr Bremen; 10POW; MACR 2981.

42-31252 Del Cheyenne 8/10/43; Gr Island 17/10/43; Wilmington 24/10/43; ass 331BS/94BG [QE-N] Rougham 30/10/43; MIA Berlin 24/5/44 w/Whorton; flak, ditched Nth Sea; 10RTD. SWEATY BETTY.

42-31253 Del Cheyenne 12/10/43; Gr Isle 22/10/43; Romulus 28/10/43; ass 562BS/388BG Knettishall 2/11/43; MIA Freeidrichshafen 24/4/44 w/McWhite; flak, cr Oshsenhausen, Ger; 10POW; MACR 4289.

42-31254 Del Cheyenne 12/10/43; Las Vegas 25/10/43; 3022 BU Indian Springs 5/2/45; 3021 BU Las Vegas 22/2/45; 3018 BU Kingman 28/2/45; 3702 BU Buckley 8/6/45; Recl Comp 20/3/46.

42-31255 Del Cheyenne 12/10/43; Gr Island 20/10/43; Memphis 28/10/43; ass 365BS/305BG [XK-O] Chelveston 4/12/43 LIBERTY BELLE; b/d Saarbrücken 3/8/44, c/l Wymington, UK. 5KIA; sal 10/8/44. FLAK MAGNET.

42-31256 Del Cheyenne 12/10/43; Gr Island 20/10/43; Memphis 6/11/43; ass 350BS/100BG [LN-B] Thorpe Abbotts 11/11/43; 351BS [EP-S]; c/l training flight /7/44, sal 13/7/44. KING BEE II.

42-31257 Del Cheyenne 12/10/43; Las Vegas 23/10/43; WO 5/1/44.

42-31258 Del Cheyenne 12/10/43; Gr Island 24/10/43; Wilmington 4/11/43; ass 334BS/95BG [BG-J] Horham 11/11/43; MIA Brussels 10/4/44 w/Thompson; mid air explosion, cr Ercis, Bel; 2EVD 4KIA 4POW; MACR 3648.

42-31259 Del Cheyenne 12/10/43; Las Vegas 25/10/43; Salt Lake City 1/4/44; Dalhart 2/4/44; 241 BU Fairmont 26/7/44; 504BG Fairmont 16/9/44; 225 BU Rapid City 28/12/44; 2137 BU Hendricks 18/8/45; RFC Kingman 9/11/45.

42-31260 Del Cheyenne 13/10/43; Las Vegas 24/10/43; 3022 BU Indian Springs 5/2/44; 3021 BU Las Vegas 7/3/44; 3036 BU Yuma 16/3/44; 3017 BU Hobbs 5/6/44; 4160 BU Hobbs 5/11/44; RFC Kingman 1/12/45.

42-31261 Del Cheyenne 12/10/43; Las Vegas 24/10/43; 3022 BU Indian Springs 5/2/45; 3021 BU Las Vegas 22/2/44; 3018 BU Kingman 10/3/44; 3017 BU Hobbs 9/6/44; 4135 BU Hill Fd 13/8/44; 3017 BU Hobbs 1/9/44; RFC Walnut Ridge 11/1/46.

42-31262 Del Cheyenne 13/10/43; Gr Island 26/10/43; Wilmington 11/11/43; ass 568BS/390BG Framlingham 12/1/43 ALE SMOKE; MIA Augsburg 16/3/44 w/Jenkins; e/a, cr Himmlingen, Ger; 1KIA 9POW; MACR 3181. OLE SMOKE.

42-31263 Del Cheyenne 12/10/43; Las Vegas 22/10/43; 3021 BU Las Vegas 2/9/44; 2126 BU Laredo 19/4/45; RFC Walnut Ridge 29/12/45.

42-31264 Del Cheyenne 12/10/43; Las Vegas 25/10/43; 3021 BU Las Vegas 9/2/45; 2126 BU Laredo 19/4/45; RFC Walnut Ridge 11/1/46.

42-31265 Del Cheyenne 12/10/43; Gr Island 22/10/43; Wilmington 3/12/43; ass 349BS/100BG Thorpe Abbotts 14/12/43; MIA Brunswick 10/2/44 w/Croft; e/a, cr Hanover, Ger; 1KIA 9POW; MACR 2382.

42-31266 Del Cheyenne 13/10/43; Las Vegas 26/10/43; 3021 BU Las Vegas 9/2/44; Recl Comp 9/5/45.

42-31267 Del Cheyenne 13/10/43; Las Vegas 24/10/43; WO 4/12/43.

42-31268 Del Cheyenne 13/10/43; Wilmington 1/11/43; ass 8AF 10/11/43; sal n/b/d 16/12/43.

42-31269 Del Cheyenne 13/10/43; Las Vegas 26/10/43; 3021 BU Las Vegas 2/6/44; 2126 BU Laredo 24/4/45; RFC Walnut Ridge 5/1/45.

42-31270 Del Cheyenne 13/10/43; Las Vegas 24/10/43; 3021 BU Las Vegas 22/2/44; 3018 BU Kingman 28/2/44; 3017 BU Hobbs 9/6/44; RFC Walnut Ridge 4/1/46.

42-31271 Del Cheyenne 13/10/43; Las Vegas 24/10/43; 3021 BU Las Vegas 10/3/44; 3036 BU Yuma 20/3/44; 3017 BU Hobbs 4/6/44; 4160 BU Hobbs 5/11/44; RFC Kingman 6/12/45.

42-31272 Del Cheyenne 13/10/43; Las Vegas 25/10/43; WO 18/1/44.

42-31273 Del Cheyenne 13/10/43; Las Vegas 26/10/43; Salt Lake City 1/4/44; Dalhart 2/4/44; 224 BU Sioux City 6/3/45; 225 BU Rapid City 16/6/45; 2038 BU Jackson 4/7/45; 242 BU Gr Island 25/9/45; 348 BU Will Rogers 7/11/45; RFC Altus 14/12/45.

42-31274 Del Cheyenne 13/10/43; Romulus 3/11/43; ass 544BS/384BG Grafton Underwood 22/11/43; MIA Ludwigshafen 30/12/43 w/Jacobs; mech fault, ditched Channel; 1KIA 8RTD; MACR 1768. SEA HAG.

42-31275 Del Cheyenne 13/10/43; Gr Island 25/10/43; Romulus 1/11/43; ass 570BS/390BG [DI-A] Framlingham 10/11/43; retUS 4168 BU Sth Plains 11/7/45; RFC Kingman 13/11/45. GI WONDER.

42-31276 Del Cheyenne 13/10/43; Las Vegas 25/10/43; 4126 BU San Bernadino 16/8/44; 3022 BU Indian Springs 14/9/44; 3021 BU Las Vegas 23/3/45; 2126 BU Laredo 10/4/45; RFC Walnut Ridge 9/1/46.

42-31277 Del Cheyenne 14/10/43; Las Vegas 29/10/43; Wilmington 4/11/43; ass 327BS/92BG [UX-P] Podington 21/1/44; MIA Berlin 8/5/44 w/Fishburn; flak, c/l Glemminge, Swed; 10INT; MACR 4577.

42-31278 Del Cheyenne 14/10/43; Gr Island 29/10/43; Memphis 5/11/43; ass 532BS/381BG [VE-A] Ridgewell 20/12/43; c/t/o {2m} Kiel 4/1/44 w/Clore; at Sible Hedingham, UK. 10KIA. Sal n/b/d.

42-31279 Del Cheyenne 16/10/43; Las Vegas 26/10/43; 2114 BU Lockburn 3/9/44; 4152 BU Lockburn 1/10/44; 2114 BU Lockburn 29/9/45; RFC Walnut Ridge 7/1/46.

42-31280 Del Cheyenne 14/10/43; Las Vegas 26/10/43; 3018 BU Kingman 28/11/43; WO 28/11/43; Recl Comp 5/12/44.

42-31281 Del Cheyenne 14/10/43; Las Vegas 25/10/43; 3021 BU Las Vegas 2/6/44; 2126 BU Laredo 19/4/45; RFC Walnut Ridge 8/1/46.

42-31282 Del Cheyenne 15/10/43; Las Vegas 27/10/43; Kingman 30/3/44; Dalhart 1/4/44; MHR Minneapolis 5/10/44; 224 BU Sioux City 6/3/45; 222 BU Ardmore 13/6/45; 332 BU Ardmore 16/6/45; RFC Walnut Ridge 7/12/45.

42-31283 Del Cheyenne 14/10/43; Las Vegas 25/10/43; Dalhart 2/4/44; 224 BU Sioux City 17/10/44; WO 4/4/45.

42-31284 Del Cheyenne 14/10/43; Las Vegas 26/10/43; 3018 BU Kingman 23/3/45; 3017 BU Hobbs 22/9/45; RFC Walnut Ridge 20/12/45.

42-31285 Del Cheyenne 14/10/43; Las Vegas 26/10/43; 3022 BU Indian Springs 5/2/45; 3021 BU Las Vegas 24/2/45; 3036 BU Yuma 12/3/45; 3017 BU Hobbs 22/9/45; RFC Walnut Ridge 10/1/46.

42-31286 Del Cheyenne 14/10/43; Las Vegas 26/10/43; 3018 BU Kingman 23/3/45; 3017 BU Hobbs 25/6/45; 3028 BU Luke 7/8/45; 3017 BU Hobbs 13/8/45; 3036 BU Yuma 3/9/45; 3017 BU Hobbs 31/10/45; RFC Walnut Ridge 7/1/46.

42-31287 Del Cheyenne 16/10/43; Las Vegas 26/10/43; 3018 BU Kingman 23/3/45; 3017 BU Hobbs 2/6/45; RFC Walnut Ridge 18/10/45.

42-31288 Del Cheyenne 18/10/43; Las Vegas 27/10/43; 3021 BU Las Vegas 2/6/45; 2126 BU Laredo 21/4/45; 3017 BU Hobbs 4/6/45; 2126 BU Laredo 4/10/45; RFC Walnut Ridge 14/11/46.

42-31289 Del Cheyenne 16/10/43; Gr Island 28/10/43; Memphis 1/11/43; ass 410BS/94BG Rougham 11/11/43; sal 6/10/44. BELLE OF MARYLAND.

42-31290 Del Cheyenne 16/10/43; Las Vegas 26/10/43; 3018 BU Kingman 23/3/45; 3017 BU Hobbs 11/6/45; RFC Walnut Ridge 4/1/46.

42-31291 Del Cheyenne 16/10/43; Gr Island 26/10/43; Palm Springs 8/11/43; ass 533BS/381BG [VP-F] Ridgewell 11/12/43; MIA {14m} Berlin 24/5/44 w/Gardon; mid air coll, cr Wilmersdorf, Ger; 2KIA 7POW; MACR 5176. AVENGRESS.

42-31292 Del Cheyenne 16/10/43; Gr Island 30/10/43; Wilmington 6/11/43; ass 569BS/390BG [CC-F] Framlingham 11/11/43; MIA Frankfurt 4/2/44 w/Strait; flak, cr Lekkerkerk, Bel?; 10POW; MACR 2352.

42-31293 Del Cheyenne 16/10/43; Las Vegas 24/10/43; 3021 BU Las Vegas 22/2/45; 3018 BU Kingman 8/3/45; 3017 BU Hobbs 9/6/45; RFC Walnut Ridge 2/1/46.

42-31294 Del Wright Fd Mat Com 19/10/43; ATC Kansas City 28/8/44; 4152 BU Clinton 5/5/46; ATC Kansas City 29/5/46; 4152 BU Clinton 3/7/46; Recl Comp 17/12/46.

42-31295 Del Cheyenne 16/10/43; Gr Island 31/10/43; Dallas 11/11/43; ass 548BS/385BG Gt Ashfield 18/11/43; MIA Frankfurt 4/2/44 w/Horstman; e/a, cr Aachen, Ger; 3EVD 7POW; MACR 2200.

42-31296 Del Cheyenne 16/10/43; Las Vegas 26/10/43; 3018 BU Kingman 3/11/43; WO 3/11/43; Recl Comp 28/11/44.

42-31297 Del Cheyenne 16/10/43; Las Vegas 28/10/43; 3018 BU Kingman 23/3/45; 3017 BU Hobbs 9/6/45; RFC Walnut Ridge 7/1/46.

42-31298 Del Cheyenne 16/10/43; Las Vegas 17/10/43; 3021 BU Las Vegas 2/6/45; 3017 BU Hobbs 22/9/44; RFC Kingman 1/12/45.

42-31299 Del Cheyenne 16/10/43; Gr Island 29/10/43; Memphis 5/11/43; ass 334BS/95BG [BG-M] Horham 12/11/43 JUNIOR; MIA Berlin 6/3/44 w/Lloyd; e/a, cr Beilen, Hol; 1EVD 9POW; MACR 2999. SHE'S MY GAL II.

42-31300 Del Cheyenne 16/10/43; Las Vegas 28/10/43; 110 BU Mitchell 15/8/44; 2137 BU Hendricks 18/11/44; RFC Kingman 1/11/45.

42-31301 Del Cheyenne 18/10/43; Las Vegas 26/10/43; 3021 BU Las Vegas 2/6/45; 2126 BU Laredo 9/4/45; RFC Walnut Ridge 2/1/46.

42-31302 Del Cheyenne 18/10/43; Las Vegas 27/10/43; 3021 BU Las Vegas 19/4/45; RFC Walnut Ridge 7/1/46.

42-31303 Del Cheyenne 18/10/43; Las Vegas 24/10/43; 3018 BU Kingman 3/12/44; 4126 BU San Bernadino 22/1/45; 3018 BU Kingman 23/3/45; 3017 BU Hobbs 12/6/45; RFC Walnut Ridge 2/1/46.

42-31304 Del Wright Fd Mat Com 18/10/43; Winter Test Ladd Fd 25/11/43; 619 BU Waterton 8/7/44; sal accident Adak 30/4/45.

42-31305 Del Cheyenne 19/10/43; Gr Island 1/11/43; Wilmington 5/11/43; ass 335BS/95BG [OE-M] Horham 11/11/43; MIA Bremen 20/12/43 w/Kelley; e/a, cr Osterholz, Ger; 7KIA 3POW; MACR 1557.

42-31306 Del Cheyenne 20/10/43; Gr Island 3/11/43; Romulus 10/11/43; ass 351BS/100BG [EP-V] Thorpe Abbotts 15/11/43; MIA Berlin 24/5/44 w/Siewart; e/a, cr Wittstock, Ger; 3KIA 7POW; MACR 5165. NELSON KING.

42-31307 Del Cheyenne 19/10/43; Las Vegas 27/10/43; 3018 BU Kingman 20/8/44; WO 20/8/44.

42-31308 Del Cheyenne 18/10/43; Gr Island 29/10/43; Wilmington 4/11/43; ass 364BS/305BG Chelveston 23/11/43; MIA Schweinfurt 24/2/44 w/Patterson; flak, cr Geisselhardt, Ger; 6KIA 4POW; MACR 2766.

42-31309 Del Cheyenne 18/10/43; Las Vegas 27/10/43; 3021 BU Las Vegas 2/6/44; 2126 BU Laredo 19/4/45; 554 BU Adams 5/12/45; RFC Walnut Ridge 11/2/46.

42-31310 Del Cheyenne 18/10/43; Las Vegas 28/10/43; 3021 BU Las Vegas 14/7/44; 3017 BU Hobbs 21/7/44; RFC Kingman 7/12/45.

42-31311 Del Cheyenne 20/10/43; Las Vegas 27/10/43; 3021 BU Las Vegas 16/6/44; 2126 BU Laredo 10/4/45; RFC Walnut Ridge 3/1/46.

42-31312 Del Cheyenne 18/10/43; Las Vegas 27/10/43; 2126 BU Laredo 10/4/45; RFC Walnut Ridge 7/1/46.

42-31313 Del Cheyenne 18/10/43; Las Vegas 27/10/43; 3021 BU Las Vegas 10/9/44; 2126 BU Laredo 9/4/45; RFC Walnut Ridge 10/1/46.

42-31314 Del Cheyenne 19/10/43; Gr Island 1/11/43; Memphis 2/11/43; ass 359BS/303BG [BN-E] Molesworth 18/11/43; ex-Frankfurt, o/s Shoreham Afd, UK. 11/2/44; 10RTD; sal n/b/d 13/2/44. SCORCHY.

42-31315 Del Cheyenne 19/10/43; Gr Island 1/11/43; Romulus 18/11/43; ass 614BS/401BG [IW-C] Deenethorpe 23/12/43; MIA Bordeaux 19/6/44 w/File; flak, c/l Spain; 9INT 1KIA; MACR 5999. LIBERTY RUN.

42-31316 Del Cheyenne 19/10/43; Las Vegas 27/10/43; 3021 BU Las Vegas 2/6/44; 2126 BU Laredo 9/4/45; RFC Walnut Ridge 3/1/46.

42-31317 Del Cheyenne 19/10/43; Las Vegas 27/10/43; 3021 BU Las Vegas 16/6/44; 2126 BU Laredo 10/4/45; 807 BU Bergstrom 11/9/45; 2126 BU Laredo 19/9/45; RFC Walnut Ridge 10/1/46.

42-31318 Del Cheyenne 20/10/43; Walla Walla 6/11/43; ass 731BS/452BG Deopham Green 6/1/44; MIA Brunswick 10/2/44 w/Turner; mid air coll w/42-39961, cr Diepholz, Ger; 2KIA 8POW; MACR 2536.

42-31319 Del Cheyenne 20/10/43; Walla Walla 7/11/43; ass 452BG Deopham Green 6/1/44; c/t/o 26/4/44; sal n/b/d.

42-31320 Del Cheyenne 20/10/43; Gr Island 2/11/43; Dallas 6/11/43; ass 412BS/95BG Horham 12/11/43; MIA Berlin 29/4/44 w/Leaser; flak, cr Hamstede, Ger?; 10POW; MACR 4469. I'LL BE AROUND.

42-31321 Del Vandalia 26/10/43; ass 569BS/390BG [CC-M] Framlingham 23/12/43; MIA Pas de Calais 21/6/44 w/Ratliffe; ditched Channel.

42-31322 Del Cheyenne 16/10/43; Vandalia 26/10/43; Des Moines 1/12/43; Denver 2/12/43; Cheyenne 11/12/43; Kearney 22/12/43; Prestwick 16/1/44; ass 452BG Deopham Green 17/1/44; tran 364BS/305BG Chelveston 30/1/44; ex-Aschersleben 23/2/44 w/Kreighauser, cr Sheffield, UK, 10KIA; sal 25/2/44 2 SAD Lt Staughton. MI AMIGO.

42-31323 Del Cheyenne 20/10/43; Las Vegas 27/10/43; 3021 BU Las Vegas 2/6/44; 2126 BU Laredo 24/4/45; RFC Walnut Ridge 4/1/46.

42-31324 Del Cheyenne 20/10/43; Las Vegas 28/10/43; WO 27/2/44.

42-31325 Del Cheyenne 20/10/43; Walla Walla 6/11/43; ass 730BS/452BG Deopham Green 12/1/44; MIA Frankfurt 8/2/44 w/Lorenzi; no gas, cr Montdidier, Fr; 4EVD 1KIA 5POW; MACR 2801.

42-31326 Del Cheyenne 20/10/43; Gr Island 2/11/43; Romulus 10/11/43; ass 327BS/92BG [UX-W] Podington 30/11/43; b/d Mannheim 22/9/44, f/l Continent; sal 14/11/44.

42-31327 Del Cheyenne 20/10/43; Gr Island 1/11/43; Romulus 6/11/43; ass 367BS/306BG Thurleigh 12/12/43; c/l Cromer, UK. 31/12/43, ex-Bordeaux; 10RTD; sal AFSC 1/1/44.

42-31328 Del Cheyenne 22/10/43; Gr Island 3/11/43; Memphis 10/11/43; ass 366BS/305BG Chelveston 22/12/43; MIA Augsburg 25/2/44 w/Czarnecki; e/a, cr Zweibruecken, Ger; 4KIA 6POW; MACR 2764.

42-31329 Del Cheyenne 22/10/43; Gr Island 3/11/43; Memphis 10/11/43; ass 334BS/95BG [BG-H] Horham 15/11/43; MIA Augsburg 16/3/44 w/Reed; c/l Kriessen, Switz; 5INT 5POW (baled over Germany); MACR 3229.

42-31330 Del Cheyenne 22/10/43; Walla Walla 9/11/43; ass 728BS/452BG Deopham Green 3/1/44; MIA Bordeaux 19/6/44 w/Graham; mech fault, f/l Spain; 10INT; MACR 5931. DOG BREATH.

42-31331 Del Cheyenne 25/10/43; Walla Walla 6/11/43; ass 731BS/452BG Deopham Green 3/1/44; TINA TANGERINE; MIA Berlin w/Butterworth 4/3/44, e/a, cr Nienburg; 1KIA 9POW; MACR 3190. MON TETE ROUGE.

42-31332 Del Cheyenne 19/10/43; Gt Falls 1/11/43; Denver 20/11/43; Prestwick 8/1/44; ass 730BS/452BG Deopham Green 9/1/44; f/l mid air w/42-102660 24/2/44; sal 28/12/44; retUS 121 BU Bradley 4/7/45; 4168 BU Sth Plains 10/7/45; RFC Kingman 13/12/45. FRIVOLOUS SAL.

42-31333 Del Cheyenne 22/10/43; Gr Island 3/11/43; Memphis 9/11/43; ass 322BS/91BG [LG-W] Bassingbourn 20/12/43; MIA {128m} Stendahl 8/4/45 w/Fuller; flak took of wing, cr Stendahl; 9KIA; MACR 13881; (oldest G in group) WEE WILLIE.

42-31334 Del Vandalia 21/10/43; Bunker Hill 10/11/43; Denver 20/11/43; Gt Falls 10/12/43; Nutts Corner (Belfast) 5/1/44; ass 730BS/452BG Deopham Green 6/1/44; MIA Leipzig 12/4/44 w/Evers; mech fault, ditched Nth Sea; 4EVD 6KIA; MACR 3933. THREE CADS AND A LAD.

42-31335 Del Cheyenne 22/10/43; Gr Island 30/10/43; Wilmington 13/11/43; ass 548BS/385BG Gt Ashfield 19/11/43; sal 15/3/45. HONKY TONK GAL.

42-31336 Del Vandalia 26/10/43; ass 561BS/388BG Knettishall 14/12/43; MIA Frankfurt 10/2/44 w/Tolles; e/a, cr Nth Sea; 10KIA; MACR 2347.

42-31337 Del Cheyenne 22/10/43; Walla Walla 9/11/43; ass 731BS/452BG Deopham Green 1/1/44; MIA Berlin 6/3/44 w/Sweeny; flak, cr Fassburg, Ger; 1KIA 9POW; MACR 2914. HELL'S CARGO.

42-31338 Del Cheyenne 22/10/43; Walla Walla 10/11/43; ass 728BS/452BF Deopham Green 1/1/44; MIA Brunswick 10/2/44 w/Smith; e/a, cr Kemmel, Bel; 3KIA 7POW; MACR 2540.

42-31339 Del Cheyenne 22/10/43; Gr Island 28/10/43; Wilmington 4/11/43; ass 568BS/390BG [BI-M] Framlingham 10/11/43; b/d Berlin 22/3/44, sal. SHIFTLESS SKUNK.

42-31340 Del Cheyenne 23/10/43; Gr Island 3/11/43; Romulus 12/11/43; ass 360BS/303BG [PU-D] Molesworth 27/12/43; MIA Brux 12/9/44 w/Mosel; e/a, f/l on Continent. MISS LIBERTY.

42-31341 Del Cheyenne 23/10/43; Gr Island 6/11/43; ass 730BS/452BG Deopham Green 3/12/43; MIA Berlin 4/3/44 w/Mittman; flak, cr Staaken, Ger; 2KIA 8POW; MACR 2915. BREAKS OF THE GAME.

42-31342 Del Cheyenne 23/10/43; Gr Island 3/11/43; Wilmington 9/11/43; ass 365BS/305BG [XK-L] Chelveston 3/12/43; MIA Pirmasens, Sth Germany 9/8/44 w/Canon; e/a, cr Unzhurst, Ger; 7KIA 2POW;

MACR 8071. BOEING'S BEST.

42-31343 Del Cheyenne 23/10/43; Gr Island 3/11/43; Memphis 28/11/43; ass 338BS/96BG [BX-E] Snetterton 5/12/43; MIA Brux 12/5/43 w/Lewis; e/a, cr Mershausen, Ger; 6KIA 4POW; MACR 4855.

42-31344 Del Cheyenne 25/10/43; Pendleton 26/10/43; WO 29/1/44.

42-31345 Del Cheyenne 23/10/43; Walla Walla 6/11/43; ass 100 Thorpe Abbotts 7/1/44; tran 728BS/452BG Deopham Green 8/1/44 KICKAPOO JOY JUICE; MIA Brux 12/5/44 w/Eastman; e/a, ditched Channel; 1KIA 9RTD; MACR 5021. LADY STARDUST II.

42-31346 Del Cheyenne 23/10/43; Gr Island 31/10/43; Wilmington 27/11/43; ass 544BS/384BG [SU-Q] Grafton Underwood 20/1/44; MIA Berlin 24/4/44 w/Harvey; flak, cr Paris; 4EVD 6POW; MACR 4355. SHACK RABBIT.

42-31347 Del Cheyenne 23/10/43; Gr Island 3/11/43; Romulus 12/11/43; 349BS/100BG [XR-K] Thorpe Abbotts 12/1/44; retUS 121 BU Bradley 12/7/45; 4185 BU Independence 14/7/45; RFC Kingman 13/12/45. BILLY BOY.

42-31348 Del Cheyenne 26/10/43; Walla Walla 7/11/43; ass 728BS/452BG Deopham Green 6/1/44; 729BS; MIA Misburg 31/12/44 w/Ferguson; e/a, cr Rhade, Ger; 4KIA 5POW; MACR 11230. SWING SHIFT BABY.

42-31349 Del Cheyenne 23/10/43; Gr Island 8/11/43; Memphis 14/11/43; ass 388BG Knettishall 27/11/43; tran 550BS/385BG Gt Ashfield 28/11/43; MIA Rostock 24/2/44 w/Capt McIveen; 2KIA 8POW; MACR 2777.

42-31350 Del Cheyenne 23/10/43; Walla Walla 6/11/43; ass 452BG Deopham Green 4/1/44; sal 11/4/44.

42-31351 Del Cheyenne 23/10/43; Gr Island 11/11/43; Dallas 21/11/43; ass 341BS/97BG Depienne 27/11/43; Cerignola 20/12/43; Amendola 16/1/44; MIA Ploesti 23/6/44 w/Parr; e/a, cr Bucharest; MACR 6407.

42-31352 Del Cheyenne 23/10/43; Walla Walla 7/11/43; ass 728BS/452BG Deopham Green 6/1/44 LEADING LADY; MIA Warnemünde 9/4/44 w/Mayek; e/a, cr Baltic Sea; 10KIA; MACR 3661. IRON BIRD.

42-31353 Del Cheyenne 25/10/43; Gr Island 3/11/43; Romulus 12/11/43; ass 322BS/91BG [LG-Q] Bassingbourn 20/12/43; 323BS [OR-Q]; MIA {18+m} Berlin 29/4/44 w/Purdy; flak, cr Berlin; 5KIA 5POW; MACR 4236. QUEENIE.

42-31354 Del Cheyenne 26/10/43; Walla Walla 10/11/43; ass 385BG Gt Ashfield 5/1/44 LOUNGE LIZARD; tran 731BS/452BG Deopham Green 6/1/44; MIA Berlin 8/3/44 w/Sorensen; e/a, cr Zerbst, Ger; 3KIA 7POW; MACR 3191.

42-31355 Del Cheyenne 23/10/43; Gr Island 3/11/43; Memphis 12/11/43; ass 548BS/385BG Gt Ashfield 21/11/43; MIA Frankfurt 4/2/44 w/McAdams; e/a, cr Arbonne, Fr; 10POW; MACR 2198.

42-31356 Del Cheyenne 25/10/43; ass 341BS/97BG Depienne 7/12/43; Cerignola 20/12/43; Amendola 16/1/44; MIA Verona, It; 22/3/44 w/Taylor; mech fault, ditched Adriatic; MACR 3697.

42-31357 Del Cheyenne 25/10/43; Gr Island 3/11/43; Romulus 12/11/43; ass 535BS/381BG [MS-N] Ridgewell 11/12/43; MIA {10m} Schweinfurt 13/4/44 w/Mullane; flak, cr Hunsrueck, Ger; 9POW; MACR 3865. OUR DESIRE.

42-31358 Del Cheyenne 25/10/43; Walla Walla 9/11/43; ass 729BS/452BG Deopham Green 3/1/44; MIA Leipzig 29/5/43 w/Parvin; flak, cr Goddula, Ger; 2KIA 8POW; MACR 5229. BIG NOSIE.

42-31359 Del Cheyenne 25/10/43; Walla Walla 9/11/43; ass 731BS/452BG Deopham Green 3/1/44; MIA Berlin 21/6/43 w/Lerum; mid air coll w/42-102662, cr Rheinberg, Ger; 6KIA 4POW; MACR 6238.

42-31360 Del Cheyenne 25/10/43; Walla Walla 9/11/43; ass 452BG Deopham Green 5/1/44; MIA Merseburg 28/9/44 b/d, f/l on Continent; sal 14/11/44.

42-31361 Del Cheyenne 25/10/43; Walla Walla 9/11/43; ass 729BS/452BG Deopham Green 3/1/44; MIA Berlin 19/5/44 w/Arey; flak, ditched Nth Sea; 1KIA 8POW; MACR 7710. THE PUNCHED FOWL.

42-31362 Del Cheyenne 26/10/43; Gr Island 12/11/43; Dallas 18/11/43; ass 326BS/92BG [JW-R] Podington 30/12/43; MIA Rostock 11/4/44 w/Donaher; f/l Rinkaby, Swed; 10INT; MACR 3670; retUS 121 BU Bradley 24/7/45; 4185 BU Independence 26/7/45; RFC Kingman 14/12/45. ALCOHOL ANNIE.

42-31363 Del Cheyenne 25/6/43; Gr Island 7/11/43; Nashville 13/11/43; ass 368BS/306BG [BO-G] Thurleigh 19/12/43; MIA Tours 27/3/44 w/Fix; flak, cr Biscay; 10POW; MACR 3479. VAPOR TRAIL.

42-31364 Del Cheyenne 25/10/43; Gr Island 13/11/43; Wilmington 26/11/43; ass 544BS/384BG [SU-D] Grafton Underwood 10/1/44; MIA Berlin 24/5/44 w/Seamon; flak, cr Berlin; 2KIA 7POW; MACR 5268. NUTTAL'S NUT HOUSE.

42-31365 Del Cheyenne 25/10/43; Gr Island 13/11/43; Wilmington 26/11/43; ass 305BG Chelveston 1/1/44; f/l Continent 30/11/44 ex-Merseburg, rep, ret 3/2/45; f/l cont 14/2/45 ex-Dresden; rep, ret 27/3/45; tran 401BG Deenethorpe 25/5/45; retUS 121 BU Bradley 4/6/45; Columbus 9/6/45; Tulsa 11/6/45; 4168 BU Sth Plains 21/7/45; 237 BU Kirtland 18/12/45; RFC Albuquerque 7/2/46.

42-31366 Del Cheyenne 25/10/43; Walla Walla 9/11/43; ass 731BS/452BG Deopham Green 3/1/44 SNAKE EYE; MIA Kaltenkirchen 7/4/45 w/Owens; mid air coll, cr Stadthagen,Ger; 9KIA; MACR 13886. OLD OUTHOUSE - NEVER A DRY RUN.

42-31367 Del Cheyenne 25/10/43; ass 322BS/91BG [LG-R] Bassingbourn 25/1/44; MIA {50+m} Caen 8/8/44 w/Thompson; flak, blew in half, cr Gelnannes, Fr; 9KIA; MACR 8079. CHOW-HOUND.

42-31368 Del Cheyenne 26/10/43; Walla Walla 9/11/43; ass 452BG Deopham Green 6/1/44; sal Scotland 26/12/44.

42-31369 Del Cheyenne 26/10/43; Gr Island 13/11/43; Romulus 25/11/43; ass 614BS/401BG [IW-K] Deenethorpe 14/1/44; MIA Brandenburg 6/8/44 w/Sauerwald; flak, cr Warnemünde; 9POW; MACR 7887. ROUND TRIPPER.

42-31370 Del Cheyenne 26/10/43; Gr Island 9/11/43; Nashville 11/11/43; ass 550BS/385BG Gt Ashfield 24/11/43; mid air coll w/B-17 ex-Deipholz, Ger; c/l Reedham, UK 21/2/44; sal b/d 26/2/44.

42-31371 Del Cheyenne 26/10/43; Walla Walla 9/11/43; ass 728BS/452BG Deopham Green 4/1/44; MIA Brunswick 23/3/44 w/Stephens; e/a, cr Varneson, (Vaassen, Hol?) 6KIA 4POW; MACR 3342. HAIRLESS JOE.

42-31372 Del Cheyenne 26/10/43; Gr Island 11/11/43; Romulus 18/11/43; ass 323BS/91BG [OR-P] Bassingbourn 20/12/43 HARASS DRAGON; MIA {5m} Oschersleben 11/1/44 w/Reid; e/a, cr Bad Muender, Ger; 7KIA 3POW; MACR 1917. MALAYAN LADY.

42-31373 Del Cheyenne 26/10/43; Walla Walla 9/11/43; ass 731BS/452BG Deopham Green 3/1/44; MIA Berlin 6/3/43 w/Wagner; e/a, cr Staphorst, Hol; 5EVD 4KIA 1POW; MACR 2916. FLAKSTOP.

42-31374 Del Cheyenne 27/10/43; ass 613BS/401BG [IN-B] Deenethorpe 14/1/44; MIA Poix, Fr. 13/3/44 w/Hellmuth; flak, cr St Quentin; 5KIA 5POW; MACR 3185.

42-31375 Del Cheyenne 27/10/43; ass 546BS/384BG [BK-S] Grafton Underwood 21/1/44; MIA Stettin 11/4/44 w/Rich; flak, cr Brunswick; 2KIA 8POW; MACR 3820.

42-31376 Del Cheyenne 27/10/43; ass 336BS/95BG [ET-U] Horham 26/12/43; MIA Gdynia 6/8/44 w/?; f/l Russia, sal & rep 12/11/44; tran 463BG Celone, It. 20/12/44; retUS Hunter 25/6/45; 4168 BU Sth Plains 27/6/45; RFC Kingman 14/12/45.

42-31377 Del Cheyenne 27/10/43; Gr Island 9/11/43; Nashville 17/11/43; ass 327BS/95BG Horham 27/12/43; MIA Aschersleben 22/2/44 w/Lavies; e/a, cr Hoerdum (Herborn?, Ger; 1KIA 9POW; MACR 2750.

42-31378 Del Cheyenne 27/10/43; Gr Island 12/11/43; Memphis 18/11/43; ass 550BS/385BG Gt Ashfield 1/12/43; sal n/b/d 30/5/45. RUM DUM.

42-31379 Del Cheyenne 29/10/43; ass 341BS/97BG Depienne 6/12/43; Cerignola 20/12/43; Amendola 16/1/44; MIA Bucharest 7/5/44 w/Galloway; ditched Adriatic, off Bari; 10RTD.

42-31380 Del Cheyenne 28/10/43; Gr Island 9/11/43; Nashville 11/11/43; ass 548BS/385BG Gt Ashfield 21/11/43; MIA Frankfurt 8/2/44 w/Pabich; no gas, cr Le Havre, Fr; 7EVD 3POW; MACR 2498.

42-31381 Del Cheyenne 29/10/43; ass 535BS/381BG [MS-O] Ridgewell 22/1/44; MIA Oschersleben 11/1/44 w/McIntosh; flak, ditched Channel; 10POW; MACR 3315. JAYNEE B.

42-31382 Del Cheyenne 28/10/43; ass 729BS/452BG Deopham Green 5/1/44; sal n/b/d 19/7/44.

42-31383 Del Cheyenne 29/10/43; Denver 18/11/43; Kearney 16/12/43; Patterson 8/3/44; New Castle 26/4/44; Grenier 5/5/44; ass 751BS/457BG Glatton 31/5/44; MIA Brux 12/9/44 w/Selling; e/a, cr Biesenthal, Ger; 8KIA 1POW; MACR 10207. AMERICAN EAGLE.

42-31384 Del Cheyenne 20/10/43; Gr Island 12/11/43; Romulus 4/12/43; ass 509BS/351BG [RQ-T] Polebrook 20/1/44; MIA {107m} Paderborn 17/1/45 w/Della-Cieppe; flak, cr Nienburg, Ger; 9POW; MACR 12000. BUCKEYE BABE.

42-31385 Del Cheyenne 28/10/43; Gr Island 13/11/43; Romulus 25/11/43; ass 369BS/306BG [WW-U] Thurleigh 4/1/44; MIA Stettin 11/4/44 w/Capt Opdyke; e/a, cr Eldena, Ger; 1KIA 9POW; MACR 3676.

42-31386 Del Cheyenne 28/10/43; ass 359BS/303BG [BN-W] Molesworth 18/1/44; MIA Berlin 19/5/44 w/Wilson; flak, cr Berlin; 6KIA 4POW; MACR 4949. SKY DUSTER.

42-31387 Del Cheyenne 28/10/43; Gr Island 12/11/43; Wilmington 26/11/43; ass 326BS/92BG Podington 4/1/44; MIA Frankfurt 8/2/44 w/McMurray; e/a, cr Chatreux, Fr; 4KIA 6POW; MACR 2365.

42-31388 Del Cheyenne 28/10/43; Gr Island 12/11/43; Memphis 18/11/43; ass 423BS/306BG [RD-A] Thurleigh 21/12/43; MIA Frankfurt 11/2/44 w/Betta; flak & e/a, cr Inval?; 6EVD 1KIA 3POW; MACR 2527.

42-31389 Del Cheyenne 28/10/43; Gr Island 13/11/43; Wilmington 26/11/43; slated 447BG; ass 351BS/100BG [EP-J] Thorpe Abbotts 1/1/44; 350BS [LN-J]; MIA Kiel 28/5/44 w/Lacy; e/a, cr Barleben, Ger; 3KIA 7POW; MACR 5382. LUCIOUS LUCY.

42-31390 Del Cheyenne 29/10/43; ass 96BS/2BG Amendola 7/1/44; MIA Steyr, Aus. 24/4/44 w/Mayfield; e/a, cr Kranj, Aus; 4 chutes seen; MACR 2708.

42-31391 Del Cheyenne 27/10/43; ass 419BS/301BG Cerignola 9/1/44; Lucera 1/2/44; MIA {14m} Regensburg 25/2/44 w/Thomas; ditched Med Sea; 10RTD; MACR 2616. SCREAMING EAGLE II.

42-31392 Del Cheyenne 28/10/43; Gr Island 12/11/43; Dallas 18/11/43; ass 341BS/97BG Depienne 27/11/43; Cerignola 20/12/43; Amendola 16/1/44; MIA Ploesti, Rum. 24/5/44 w/Clem; e/a, cr Sisak, Yugo; MACR 5197.

42-31393 Del Cheyenne 28/10/43; ass 560BS/388BG Knettishall 14/12/43; MIA Berlin 29/4/44 w/Walker; flak, cr Parsau, Fr; 1EVD 1KIA 8POW; MACR 4243. SNAFU.

42-31394 Del Cheyenne 28/10/43; ass 526BS/379BG [LF-D] Kimbolton 20/1/44; tran AFSC Aphrodite (388BG) Knettishall 7/6/44; MIA Watten, Fr; 6/8/44.

42-31395 Del Cheyenne 29/10/43; ass 549BS/385BG Gt Ashfield 1/1/44; sal n/b/d 6/5/45. RAGGEDY ANN.

42-31396 Del Cheyenne 1/11/43; ass 353BS/301BG Cerignola 8/12/43; MIA {4m} Piraeus 11/1/44 w/Dunbar; mid air coll, cr Patri, Gr; 10KIA; MACR 1833.

42-31397 Del Cheyenne 29/10/43; ass 353BS/301BG Cerignola 15/12/43; Lucera 1/2/44; MIA {18m} Regensburg 25/2/44 w/Hurley; e/a, cr Winden, Ger; 6KIA 4POW; MACR 2722.

42-31398 Del Cheyenne 29/10/43; ass 353BS/301BG Cerignola 7/12/43; Lucera 1/2/44; MIA {32m} Verona 22/3/44 w/Moore; ditched Adriatic; 9RTD.

42-31399 Del Cheyenne 29/10/43; Gr Island 12/11/43; Memphis 18/11/43; ass 360BS/303BG Molesworth 27/12/43; MIA Berburg 22/2/44 w/Crook; e/a, cr Wijk Bij Duurstede, Hol; 4EVD 6POW; MACR 2645.

42-31400 Del Cheyenne 29/10/43; Gr Island 12/11/43; Memphis 20/11/43; ass 352BS/301BG Cerignola 19/12/43; Lucera 1/2/44; MIA {23m} Ploesti 15/4/44 w/Simon; flak, #3 engines drops in sea, ditched Ortona; crew rescued by Italian fishing boats.

42-31401 Del Cheyenne 29/10/43; Kearney 15/11/43; ass 331BS/94BG [QE-D] Rougham 1/1/44; MIA Berlin 18/4/44 w/Gordon; e/a, cr Friesach, Aus; 4KIA 6POW; MACR 4151; OLD HICKORY.

42-31402 Del Cheyenne 29/10/43; Gr Island 13/11/43; Nashville 29/11/43; ass 365BS/305BG Chelveston 22/12/43; MIA Liége 11/5/44 w/Thomaiden; flak, cr Charleville, Fr; 7KIA 3POW; MACR 4869.

42-31403 Del Cheyenne 29/10/43; Gr Island 13/11/43; Nashville 27/11/43; ass 413BS/96BG [MZ-Y] Snetterton 23/12/43; MIA Berlin 8/3/43 w/Ross; e/a, cr Hohlbeck, Ger; 2KIA 8POW; MACR 3424.

42-31404 Del Cheyenne 29/10/43; Gr Island 13/11/43; Memphis 27/11/43; ass 350BS/100BG [LN-V/T] Thorpe Abbotts 23/12/43; sal n/b/d 2/7/44.

42-31405 Del Cheyenne 30/10/43; Gr Island 13/11/43; Romulus 26/11/43; ass 359BS/303BG [BN-X] Molesworth 14/1/44; f/l Weston, UK 7/8/44; sal 2 SAD Lt Staughton 12/8/44. WALLEROO MARK II.

42-31406 Del Cheyenne 31/10/43; Kearney 13/11/43; ass 368BS/306BG [BO-O] Thurleigh 21/1/44; MIA Aschersleben 22/2/44 w/Symons; e/a, cr Deenbach, Ger; 5KIA 5POW; MACR 2650.

42-31407 Del Cheyenne 30/10/43; Gr Island 13/11/43; Romulus 26/11/43; ass 331BS/94BG [QE-V] Rougham 23/12/43; MIA Brandeburg 18/4/44 w/Craig; e/a, cr Gnoien, Ger; 10POW; MACR 4152. CHIEF CHILLETACAUX.

42-31408 Del Cheyenne 31/10/43; Gr Island 12/11/43; Nashville 19/11/43; ass 407BS/92BG [PY-Z] Podington 27/12/43; MIA Merkville 3/8/44 w/Curtiss; e/a, cr Bruelingen?; 1KIA 9POW; MACR 7698.

INDIVIDUAL B-17 HISTORIES **161**

42-31409 Del Cheyenne 31/10/43; Kearney 13/11/43; ass 364BS/305BG Chelveston 22/1/44; MIA Aschersleben 22/2/44 w/Barnes; e/a, cr Nth Sea; 10KIA; MACR 2648.

42-31410 Del Cheyenne 31/10/43; Kearney 13/11/43; ass 336BS/95BG [ET-G] Horham 1/1/44 I DOOD IT; flak damage Berlin 6/10/44 w/Lennox; 8POW 2RTD; MACR 9352; sal b/d base; rep, retUS 121 BU Bradley 26/6/45; Love Fd 27/6/45; 4168 BU Sth Plains 28/8/45; RFC Kingman 10/11/45. BERLIN BESSIE.

42-31411 Del Cheyenne 31/10/43; Gr Island 11/11/43; Nashville 18/11/43; ass 327BS/92BG Podington 2/12/43; MIA Achmer 21/2/44 w/McEvoy; e/a, cr Bad Driburg, Ger; 8KIA 2POW; MACR 2757.

42-31412 Del Cheyenne 31/10/43; Gr Island 12/11/43; Long Beach 19/11/43; ass 351BS/100BG [EP-G] Thorpe Abbotts 27/11/43; sal WW /45; retUS 121 BU Bradley 30/6/45; Greenboro 1/7/45; Tinker 2/7/45; 4168 BU Sth Plains 21/10/45; RFC Kingman 19/12/45. MASON AND DIXON.

42-31413 Del Cheyenne 31/10/43; Gr Island 12/11/43; Nashville 21/11/43; ass 350BS/100BG [LN-V] Thorpe Abbotts 26/11/43; sal 15/5/44.

42-31414 Del Cheyenne 1/11/43; Kearney 16/11/43; ass 615BS/401BG [IY-J] Deenethorpe 14/1/44; c/l base, u/c up 27/1/44; sal n/b/d 2 SAD Lt Staughton 30/1/44.

42-31415 Del Cheyenne 1/11/43; Gr Island 13/11/43; Dallas 28/11/43; ass 545BS/384BG Grafton Underwood 8/1/44; c/l base 30/1/44; sal 2 SAD Lt Staughton 17/2/44. HAM-ON-RYE.

42-31416 Del Cheyenne 1/11/43; ass 20BS/2BG Amendola 10/12/43; MIA Regensburg 25/2/44 w/Withers; e/a, cr Moosdorf, Ger; MACR 2576.

42-31417 Del Cheyenne 1/11/43; Kearney 9/11/43; Nashville 11/11/43; ass 533BS/381BG [VP-R] Ridgewell 11/12/43 BIG TIME OPERATOR II; MIA {7m} Oshersleben 11/11/44 w/Klein; e/a, cr Minden, Ger; 2KIA 8POW; MACR 1879. PATCHES.

42-31418 Del Cheyenne 1/11/43; Kearney 15/11/43; ass 423BS/306BG [RD-J] Thurleigh 1/1/44; tran 381BG Ridgewell 5/45; 91BG Bassingbourn 30/5/45; retUS 121 BU Bradley 11/6/45; Romulus 13/6/45; Memphis 14/6/45; 4168 BU Sth Plains 15/6/45; RFC Kingman 9/12/45. JACK-O.

42-31419 Del Cheyenne 3/11/43; ass 49BS/2BG Amendola 7/12/43; MIA Steyr, Aus. 24/2/44 w/Vandy; e/a, cr Wels, Aus; MACR 2632.

42-31420 Del Cheyenne 2/11/43; Kearney 16/11/43; ass 8AF 3/12/43. c/l Ireland 11/12/43.

42-31421 Del Cheyenne 5/11/43; Gt Falls 10/1/44; Kingman 18/1/44; 3018 BU Kingman 23/3/45; 3017 BU Hobbs 25/6/45; RFC Walnut Ridge 8/1/46.

42-31422 Del Cheyenne 1/11/43; ass 20BS/2BG Amendola 9/12/43; MIA Lake Albano 10/2/44 w/Licence; flak, a/c exploded; MACR 2299.

42-31423 Del Cheyenne 2/11/43; ass 427BS/303BG [GN-M] Molesworth 14/1/44; MIA Cologne 15/8/44 w/Clark; e/a, cr Malberg?; 6KIA 3POW; MACR 8168. JIGGER ROUCHE – KRAUT KILLER.

42-31424 Del Cheyenne 4/11/43; ass 353BS/301BG Cerignola 30/12/43; MIA {13m} Villaorba, It. 30/1/44 w/Perkins; flak, cr Udine; MACR 2062.

42-31425 Del Cheyenne 2/11/43; ass 20BS/2BG Amendola 9/12/43; MIA Steyr, Aus. 24/2/44 w/Smith; e/a, cr in mountains, no chutes seen; MACR 2709.

42-31426 Del Cheyenne 2/11/43; ass 352BS/301BG 8/12/43; MIA {24m} Cagliari, Sic. 26/3/44 w/Gianacovo; mid air col w/42-30405 97BG); 2KIA when ditched off Ancona, 3 rescued by RAF Walrus, 4MIA. MACR 3644.

42-31427 Del Cheyenne 2/11/43; ass 305BG Chelveston 21/12/43; MIA Sorau 11/4/44 w/Vance; f/l Switz, 10INT; MACR 4010.

42-31428 Del Cheyenne 2/11/43; ass 367BS/306BG Thurleigh 21/1/44; MIA Aschersleben 22/2/44 w/Oliver; e/a, cr Maastricht, Hol; 9KIA 1POW; MACR 2655.

42-31429 Del Cheyenne 2/11/43; ass 97BG Cerignola 23/12/43; tran 429BS/2BG Amendola; MIA Padua 11/3/44 w/Senta; e/a, control shot out, f/l Sibonik, Yugo; 10RTD 15/3/44; MACR 2827.

42-31430 Del Cheyenne 4/11/43; ass 366BS/305BG Chelveston 6/1/44; MIA Leipzig 20/2/44 w/Stahl; flak, cr Liége, Bel; 7EVD 3POW; MACR 2428.

42-31431 Del Cheyenne 4/11/43; ass 710BS/447BG Rattlesden 23/12/43; MIA Regensburg 25/2/44 w/Chardi; flak, cr Ottweiler, Ger; 10POW; MACR 2891.

42-31432 Del Cheyenne 2/11/43; ass 360BS/303BG Molesworth 18/1/44; MIA NW France A/Fds 22/6/44 w/Fisher; flak, cr Tressen, Fr; 1EVD 8KIA; MACR 6541. OLD GLORY.

42-31433 Del Cheyenne 3/11/43; Kearney 15/11/43; ass 547BS/384BG [SO-V] Grafton Underwood 8/1/44; MIA Schweinfurt 13/4/44 w/Stearns; e/a, cr Wurzburg, Ger; 1KIA 9POW; MACR 3867. RUM POT.

42-31434 Del Cheyenne 2/11/43; Kingman 15/11/43; 3018 BU Kingman 23/3/45; 3017 BU Hobbs 25/6/45; RFC Walnut Ridge 5/1/46.

42-31435 Del Cheyenne 31/10/43; Gt Falls 2/11/43; Kansas City 7/12/43; Eglin 17/12/43; Wright Fd 11/1/44 for a special six-gun nose to be fitted; Kearney 14/1/44; Oklahoma City 26/1/44; Grenier 18/2/44; ass 544BS/384BG [SU-S] Grafton Underwood 2/3/44; sal b/d AFSC 7/7/44. WEST'S END.

42-31436 Del Cheyenne 2/11/43; Kearney 16/11/43; ass 413BS/96BG Snetterton 1/1/44; MIA Frankfurt 29/1/44 w/Hammond; mid air coll w/42-31151; cr Montherme, Fr; 1KIA 9POW; MACR 2378.

42-31437 Del Cheyenne 3/11/43; ass 352BS/301BG Cerignola 7/12/43; Lucera 1/2/44; MIA {31m} Steyr, Aus. 24/2/44 w/Abramson; e/a, cr Enns, Aus; MACR 2636.

42-31438 Del Cheyenne 3/11/43; Kingman 16/11/43; 3018 BU Kingman 23/3/45; 3017 BU Hobbs 25/6/45; RFC Walnut Ridge 29/12/45.

42-31439 Del Cheyenne 3/11/43; ass Soxo 8/12/43 via Goose Bay and Valley; c/l Thrusmore Mt, Sligo, Ireland 9/12/43; MACR 1190.

42-31440 Del Cheyenne 3/11/43; Kearney 16/11/43; ass 367BS/306BG [GY-M] Thurleigh 4/1/44; MIA Frankfurt 4/2/44 w/Ware; flak, cr Calais, Fr; 10POW; MACR 2240. ROUND TRIP TICKET.

42-31441 Del Cheyenne 3/11/43; Kearney 16/11/43; ass 360BS/303BG Molesworth 1/4/44; MIA Keil 5/1/44; coll w/379BG aircraft when forming up; cr Catworth, UK; sal 2 SAD Lt Staughton.

42-31442 Del Cheyenne 31/10/43; Portland 4/11/43; Billings 7/11/43; Cheyenne 15/11/43; El Paso 16/11/43; Yuma 3/12/43; 4126 BU San Bernardino 4/8/45; 303 BU Yuma 25/8/45; 3017 BU Hobbs 22/9/45; RFC Walnut Ridge 5/1/46.

42-31443 Del Cheyenne 5/11/43; Gt falls 6/11/43; Billings 7/11/43; Cheyenne 16/11/43; Kearney 17/11/43; Topeka 29/11/43; Romulus 30/11/43; Syracuse 3/12/43; Bangor 4/12/43; ass 532BS/381BG [VE-M] Ridgewell 6/1/44; MIA {7m} Oshersleben 22/2/44 w/Flaherty; e/a, cr Kraks-Senne?; 6KIA 4POW; MACR 2930. FRIDAY THE 13TH.

42-31444 Del Cheyenne 2/11/43; Gt Falls 6/11/43; Kearney 16/11/43; ass 423BS/306BG [RD-Y] Thurleigh 18/1/44; tran RAF 8/1/45; ret 5/3/45; sal n/b/d 15/3/45. PAPER DOLL.

42-31445 Del Cheyenne 2/11/43; Gt Falls 5/11/43; Kearney 17/11/43; Romulus 2/12/43; Syracuse 5/12/43; Bangor 6/12/43; ass 367BS/306BG [GY-G] Thurleigh 21/1/44; MIA Erding 24/4/44 w/Peterson; flak, cr St Saens, Fr; 6KIA 4POW; MACR 4280.

42-31446 Del Cheyenne 9/11/43; Gt Falls 27/11/43; ass 429BS/2BG Amendola 9/12/43; MIA Klagenfurt 19/3/44 w/Marshall; e/a, cr mountains; (5 crew from 463BG) MACR 3289. LIL PETE.

42-31447 Del Denver 18/11/43; Kearney 2/12/43; Romulus 9/12/43; Syracuse 10/12/43; Presque Is 14/12/43; ass 338BS/96BG [BX-D] Snetterton 21/12/43; MIA Rostock 11/4/44 w/Splan; e/a, cr Baltic; 10KIA; MACR 3811. COOKIE.

42-31448 Del Cheyenne 2/11/43; Portland 4/11/43; Gt Falls 6/11/43; Cheyenne 17/11/43; Kearney 19/11/43; St Angelo (N. Ireland) 9/12/43; ass 532BS/381BG [VE-A] Ridgewell 6/1/44; MIA {4m} Berlin 6/3/44 w/Fastrup; e/a, cr Etzweiler, Ger; 10POW; MACR 3001. HALF BREED.

42-31449 Del Cheyenne 2/11/43; Portland 4/11/43; Cheyenne 13/11/43; Kearney 16/11/43; ass 332BS/94BG [XM-A] Rougham 20/12/43; 333BS [TS-B]; retUS 121 BU Bradley 26/6/45; Patterson 27/6/45; 4168 BU Sth Plains 21/10/45; RFC Kingman 22/11/45. TEXAS MAULER.

42-31450 Del Cheyenne 2/11/43; Portland 5/11/43; Salt Lake 6/11/43; Cheyenne 9/11/43; Yuma 17/11/43; 3017 BU Hobbs 4/6/45; RFC Walnut Ridge 3/1/46.

42-31451 Del Cheyenne 2/11/43; Gt Falls 6/11/43; Billings 7/11/43; Cheyenne 12/11/43; Kearney 15/11/43; ass 369BS/306BG Thurleigh 21/12/43; 367BS [GY-G]; MIA Oschersleben 11/1/44 w/McCollum; mid air coll w/e/a, Epe, Hol; 9KIA 1POW; MACR 1934.

42-31452 Del Cheyenne 2/11/43; Denver 7/11/43; Cheyenne 20/11/43; Gr Island 25/11/43; ass 20BS/2BG Amendola 25/12/43; MIA Ploesti 22/7/44 w/Austin; flak, #3 out, cr Zimicea, Rum; MACR 6949. FIFTY PACKIN MAMA.

42-31453 Del Cheyenne 2/11/43; Rock Springs 7/11/43; Yuma 18/11/43; 3021 BU Las Vegas 2/6/44; 3022 BU Indian Springs 16/6/44; 3021 BU Las Vegas 15/3/45; 3017 BU Hobbs 22/5/45; 574 BU Winslow 3/10/45; 3017 BU Hobbs 28/10/45; RFC Walnut Ridge 5/1/46.

42-31454 Del Cheyenne 2/11/43; Gt Falls 6/11/43; Kearney 19/11/43; Romulus 2/12/43; Bangor 4/12/43; ass 368BS/306BG [BO-B] Thurleigh 30/12/43; secret mission 4/11/44, ret gp 9/11/44; tran 29TAC 24/5/45; sal 31/1/46. ST ANTHONY.

42-31455 Del Cheyenne 5/11/43; Kearney 15/11/43; ass 326BS/92BG Podington 23/1/44; MIA Münster 23/3/44 w/Robbins; e/a, cr Nateln?; 3KIA 7POW; MACR 3414.

42-31456 Del Cheyenne 5/11/43; Yuma 17/11/43; 3018 BU Kingman 24/8/44; 4126 BU San Bernardino 20/12/43; 3018 BU Kingman 30/12/43; 3017 BU Hobbs 22/9/45; RFC Walnut Ridge 9/1/46.

42-31457 Del Cheyenne 2/11/43; Albuquerque 18/11/43; Yuma 19/11/43; 3017 BU Hobbs 4/6/44; RFC Walnut Ridge 4/1/46.

42-31458 Del Cheyenne 5/11/43; Spokane 6/11/43; Gt Falls 8/11/43; Cheyenne 23/11/43; ass 96BS/2BG Amendola 25/12/43; {73m} RetUS 1103 BU Morrison 2/2/45; 4104 BU Rome 4/2/45; 4100 BU Patterson 24/3/45; Recl Comp 2/5/46.

42-31459 Del Cheyenne 2/11/43; Gt Falls 6/11/43; Gr Island 25/11/43; ass 96BS/2BG Amendola 7/1/44; MIA {20m} Steyr 24/2/44 w/Lyons; e/a, cr Letten, Aus; 8 chutes seen; MACR 2622. LYON'S DEN.

42-31460 Del Cheyenne 5/11/43; Kingman 17/11/43; 3018 BU Kingman 23/3/45; 3017 BU Hobbs 25/6/45; RFC Walnut Ridge 7/1/46.

42-31461 Del Cheyenne 3/11/43; Kearney 26/11/43; ass 365BS/305BG Chelveston 28/12/43; MIA Brunswick 30/1/44 w/Scott; e/a, cr Hameln, Ger; 2KIA 8POW; MACR 2861.

42-31462 Del Cheyenne 5/11/43; Kearney 17/11/43; ass 335BS/95BG [OE-R] Horham 13/12/43; MIA Strasburg 20/1/45 w/Capt Beard; flak, cr Eutsheim, Ger; 2POW 7RTD; MACR 12320. ROARIN' BILL.

42-31463 Del Cheyenne 3/11/43; Gr Island 27/11/43; ass 96BS/2BG Amendola 1/1/44; MIA {14m} Sofia 24/1/44 w/Brockman; ditched 55 miles NE Bari, rescued by British ship taken to Brindisi, 10RTD next day.

42-31464 Del Cheyenne 3/11/43; Gr Island 25/11/43; ass 342BS/301BG Cerignola 18/12/43; Lucera 1/2/44; sal 28/7/44.

42-31465 Del Cheyenne 8/11/43; Gr Island 25/11/43; ass 49BS/2BG Amendola 18/12/43; MIA Budapest 3/4/44 w/Carlson; e/a, 2 engines out, cr Pancevo, Yugo; MACR 3713.

42-31466 Del Cheyenne 8/11/43; Gr Island 24/11/43; New Castle 4/12/43; Bangor 9/12/43; ass 569BS/390BG [CC-A] Framlingham 5/1/44; MIA Leipzig 29/5/44 w/Shymanski; e/a, cr Rochefort, Fr; MACR 5314. SITTING PRETTY.

42-31467 Del Cheyenne 4/11/43; Kearney 1/12/43; Romulus 9/12/43; Grenier 10/12/43; Presque Is 14/12/43; ass 613BS/401BG [IN-J] Deenethorpe 6/1/44; MIA Frankfurt 2/3/44 w/Sheahan; e/a, exploded mid air; 3KIA 7POW; MACR 2742. SAC HOUND.

42-31468 Del Cheyenne 4/11/43; Gt Falls 8/11/43; ass 8AF 17/11/43; Con lost 9/12/43.

42-31469 Del Cheyenne 4/11/43; Gt Falls 8/11/43; Gr Island 18/11/43; Romulus 26/11/43; Presque Is 27/11/43; Prestwick 1/12/43; ass 367BS/306BG [GY-K] Thurleigh 2/12/43; c/t/o for Brunswick 26/4/44, near base, sal.

42-31470 Del Cheyenne 4/11/43; Gr Island 27/11/43; ass 348BS/99BG Tortorella 29/12/43; {23m} tran 429BS/2BG Amendola 28/3/44; MIA Blechammer, Ger. 7/7/44 w/Horton; 2 engines feath. cr St Micheil?; MACR 6564. OLD SHEP.

42-31471 Del Cheyenne 5/11/43; Kearney 20/11/43; Prestwick 7/12/43; ass 360BS/306BG Thurleigh 1/1/44; MIA Berlin 8/3/44 w/McGarth; flak, cr Brandenburg; 10POW; MACR 2908. DOOLITTLE'S DESTROYERS.

42-31472 Del Cheyenne 5/11/43; Gt Falls 9/11/43; Kearney 26/11/43; Kansas City 28/11/43; Wright Fd 30/11/43; Kearney 1/12/43; ass 414BS/97BG Amendola 7/12/43; MIA Udine 18/3/44 w/Munson; e/a, cr Fiume, It; 10 baled RTD; MACR 3359.

42-31473 Del Cheyenne 6/11/43; Gt Falls 11/11/43; Gr Island 26/11/43; ass 347BS/99BG Tortorella 31/12/43 (first G in sqd); {29m} tran 20BS/2BG Amendola 28/3/44; MIA Moravska Ostrova, Czech. 29/8/44 w/McCloskey; e/a, cr Bohmen, Czech; MACR 8109. MY BABY.

42-31474 Del Cheyenne 5/11/43; Gr Island 21/11/43; Romulus 27/11/43; Syracuse 28/11/43; Presque Is 1/12/43; ass 368BS/306BG [BO-V] Thurleigh 23/9/44; sal 17/4/45. ELIZABETH.

42-31475 Cheyenne 5/11/43; Gr Island 21/11/43; Detroit 26/11/43; Presque Is 30/11/43; ass 364BS/305BG Chelveston 28/12/43; MIA Sorau 29/5/44 w/Wilkinson; e/a, cr Prittisch, Ger; 1KIA 9POW; MACR 5319.

42-31476 Del Cheyenne 5/11/43; Gt Falls 12/11/43; Gr Island 27/11/43; ass 342BS/97BG Cerignola 20/12/43; Amendola 16/1/44; MIA Regensburg 22/2/44 w/Kovacs; e/a, cr Regensburg; 9 chutes seen; MACR 2490.

42-31477 Del Cheyenne 10/11/43; Kearney 1/12/43; Romulus 9/12/43; Presque Is 11/12/43; ass 709BS/447BG Rattlesden 3/3/44; MIA Pas de Calais 27/4/44 w/Hofsess; flak, cr Hesle-Hodeng, Fr; 1EVD 2KIA 7POW. MACR 4294.

42-31478 Del Cheyenne 9/11/43; Gt Falls 27/11/43; ass 32BS/301BG Cerignola 10/12/43; Lucera 1/2/44; MIA {18m} Steyr, Aus. 24/2/44 w/Robertson; e/a, ditched Adriatic. MACR 2633.

42-31479 Del Cheyenne 6/11/43; Gt Falls 9/11/43; Gr Island 27/11/43; Kearney 18/12/43; ass 346BS/99BG Tortorella 19/12/43; {32m} tran 49BS/2BG Amendola 28/3/44; cr base 8/5/44; sal.

42-31480 Del Cheyenne 10/11/43; Kearney 28/11/43; Gr Island 4/12/43; Romulus 5/12/43; Presque Is 10/12/43; ass 365BS/305BG Chelveston 27/12/43; tran 401BG Deenethorpe 20/5/45; retUS 121 BU Bradley 7/6/45; 4168 BU Sth Plains 9/6/45; RFC Kingman 8/12/45. REICH'S RUIN.

42-31481 Del Cheyenne 6/11/43; Gr Island 21/11/43; Wilmington 30/11/43; Presque Is 1/12/43; Prestwick 7/12/43; ass 510BS/351BG [TU-B] Polebrook 2/1/44; MIA {1m} Oschersleben 11/1/44 w/Case; e/a, cr Gottingen, Ger; 1KIA 9POW; MACR 1941.

42-31482 Del Cheyenne 10/11/43; Gr Island 27/11/43; ass 32BS/301BG Cerignola 29/12/43; Lucera 1/2/44; MIA {66m} Vienna 26/6/44 w/Phillips; e/a & flak, cr Gyor, Hung; 5KIA 5POW. MACR 6328.

42-31483 Del Cheyenne 10/11/43; Kearney 28/11/43; Bangor 5/12/43; ass 359BS/303BG [BN-P] Molesworth 1/1/44; MIA Stuttgart 5/9/44; f/l on Continent; sal 12/9/44. BONNIE 'B'.

42-31484 Del Cheyenne 11/11/43; Kearney 10/12/43; Presque Is 14/12/43; ass 545BS/384BG [JD-F] Grafton Underwood 20/1/44; 546BS [BK-F]; b/d Gerolstein 27/12/44, c/l Manston; 9KIA; sal 28/12/44.

42-31485 Del Cheyenne 11/10/43; Gr Island 21/11/43; La Guardia 29/11/43; New York 1/12/43; Presque Is 2/12/43; ass 615BS/401BG Deenethorpe 6/1/44; RAF Stornaway 5/4/44, ret grp 6/4/44; retUS 121 BU Bradley 9/6/45; Syracuse 10/6/45; 4168 BU Sth Plains 13/6/45; Recl Comp 7/6/46. OLD IRONSIDES.

42-31486 Del Cheyenne 12/11/43; Kearney 27/11/43; Prestwick 6/12/43; ass 612BS/401BG [SC-Y] Deenethorpe 14/1/44; MIA Frankfurt 29/1/44 w/Tannahill; e/a, cr Oberndorf, Ger; 8KIA 2POW; MACR 2272.

42-31487 Del Cheyenne 11/11/43; slated 401BG, cr Gt Falls 6/12/43; WO.

42-31488 Del Cheyenne 8/11/43; Gt Falls 11/11/43; Kearney 28/11/43; Romulus 4/12/43; Bangor 5/12/43; ass 614BS/401BG [IW-D] Deenethorpe 2/1/44; MIA Berlin 8/3/44 w/Peterson; e/a, cr Lingen, Ger; 10POW; MACR 2911. SHADE RUFF.

42-31489 Del Cheyenne 11/11/43; Kearney 26/11/43; Kansas City 28/11/43; Memphis 29/11/43; Kearney 3/12/43; ass 414BS/97BG Cerignola 20/12/43; Amendola 16/1/44; MIA Cechina, It. 10/2/44 w/Brennan; flak, cr Littori; 2 picked up by US army patrol, 2 landed in sea rescued by USN, 6POW; MACR 2305.

42-31490 Del Cheyenne 11/11/43; Gt Falls 12/11/43; Kearney 28/11/43; Gr Island 3/12/43; Bangor 5/12/43; ass 532BS/381BG [VE-K] Ridgewell 10/1/44; MIA {5m} Frankfurt 24/3/44 w/Rickerson; mid air coll w/42-40008; cr Nuestedt, Ger; 4EVD 6POW; MACR 3538.

42-31491 Del Cheyenne 8/11/43; Kearney 27/11/43; Cleveland 4/12/43; unassigned, cr nr Langford Lodge, Nth. Ireland 7/12/43; sal.

42-31492 Del Cheyenne 12/11/43; Kearney 27/11/43; ass 413BS/96BG Snetterton 16/12/43; MIA Brunswick 10/2/44 w/Magilavy; flak, cr Liebenau, Ger; 1KIA 9POW; MACR 2374. DISCOVEREE.

42-31493 Del Cheyenne 11/11/43; Kearney 27/11/43; ass 332BS/94BG Rougham 20/12/43; 410BG [GL-G] DOUBLE DOO; MIA Munich 12/7/44 w/Handskemager; flak, cr Grenaa, Den; 2KIA 8POW; MACR 7509. DOODLEE DOO.

42-31494 Del Cheyenne 11/11/43; Kearney 27/11/43; Prestwick 6/12/43; ass 407BS/92BG Podington 31/12/43; engine failure c/l Matching, UK. 5KIA 4/2/44; sal AFSC 6/2/44.

42-31495 Del Cheyenne 11/11/43; Kearney 1/12/43; Romulus 9/12/43; Presque Is 16/12/43; ass 544BS/384BG [SU-R] Grafton Underwood 21/1/44; MIA Berlin 8/5/44 w/Foster; flak, cr Sottevast, Fr; 1EVD 10KIA; MACR 4561. WABBIT TWACKS.

42-31496 Del Cheyenne 12/11/43; Kearney 27/11/43; ass 612BS/401BG [SC-Q] Deenethorpe 1/2/44; MIA Berlin 21/6/44 w/ Atherton; flak, cr Gruenewald, Ger; 10POW; MACR 6000.

42-31497 Del Cheyenne 11/11/43; Kearney 1/12/43; Wilmington 13/12/43; Westover 16/12/43; Presque Is 17/12/43; ass 534BS/381BG [GD-N] Ridgewell 22/1/44; MIA Cottbus 11/4/44 w/Hesse; flak, cr Altteich, Ger; 9POW; MACR 3821. ROUND TRIP JEANNIE.

42-31498 Del Cheyenne 12/11/43; Kearney 1/12/43; Wilmington 9/12/43; Presque Is 12/12/43; ass 331BS/94BG [QE-X] Rougham 16/12/43; MIA Berlin 29/4/44 w/Chism; flak, cr Hassenberg, Ger?; 1KIA 9POW; MACR 4467. PASSIONATE WITCH.

42-31499 Del Cheyenne 13/11/43; Kearney 1/12/43; Romulus 11/12/43; Grenier 12/12/43; Presque Is 14/12/43; ass 369BS/306BG Thurleigh 21/1/44; MIA Frankfurt 8/2/44 w/Snyder; e/a, cr Macquenoise, Bel; 2EVD 6KIA 2POW; MACR 2493.

42-31500 Del Cheyenne 12/11/43; Kearney 28/11/43; Des Moines 4/12/43; Romulus 6/12/43; Presque Is 9/12/43; ass 367BS/306BG [GY-L] Thurleigh 4/1/44; MIA Oschersleben 22/2/44 w/Macomber; e/a, cr Gran-Hallet, Fr?; 10KIA; MACR 2653. THE DUCHESS.

42-31501 Del Cheyenne 12/11/43; Billings 15/11/43; Kearney 28/11/43; Presque Is 10/12/43; ass 366BS/305BG [KY-R] Chelveston 12/12/43 'OLE' MISS DESTRY; {138m} tran 401BG Deenethorpe 20/5/45; retUS 121 BU Bradley 8/6/45; 4168 BU Sth Plains 12/6/45; RFC Kingman 8/12/45. SON OF A BLITZ.

42-31502 Del Cheyenne 16/11/43; Kearney 3/12/43; Grenier 11/12/43; Presque Is 14/12/43; ass 350BS/100BG [LN-S] Thorpe Abbotts 9/12/43; c/t/o Diss, UK. for Frankfurt 29/1/44; 7KIA 3WIA; sal. TERRY 'N TEN.

42-31503 Del Cheyenne 12/11/43; Kearney 28/11/43; Romulus 4/12/43; Presque Is 8/12/43; ass 325BS/92BG Podington 30/12/43; MIA Berlin 6/3/44 w/Krizan; e/a, cr Brachwitz, Ger; 10POW; MACR 2903.

42-31504 Del Cheyenne 13/11/43; Kearney 28/11/43; Romulus 5/12/43; Presque Is 8/12/43; ass 418BS/100BG [LD-Q] Thorpe Abbotts 16/12/43; 350BS [LN-Q]; MIA Brux 12/5/44 w/Kinder; flak, cr

Goarhausen, Ger?; 10POW; MACR 4865. ROSIE'S RIVETERS.

42-31505 Del Denver 16/11/43; Gt Falls 25/11/43; Denver 9/12/43; Wendover 11/12/43; Grenier 19/1/44; ass 751BS/457BG Glatton 26/1/44; MIA Merseburg 30/11/44 w/?; flak, c/l France; MACR 11151. MISS CUE.

42-31506 Del Denver 15/11/43; Gr Island 27/11/43; ass 348BS/99BG Tortorella 18/12/43; {27m} tran 96BS/2BG Amendola 28/3/44; MIA {8m} Gyor, Hung. 13/4/44 w/Applegate; e/a, cr Papa, Hung; 6 chutes seen; MACR 3913.

42-31507 Del Denver 15/11/43; Kearney 27/11/43; ass 401BG Deenethorpe 6/12/43; sal n/b/d 6/6/44.

42-31508 Del Denver 12/11/43; Kearney 27/11/43; RAF Valley 7/12/43; ass 613BS/401BG [IN-Q] Deenethorpe 21/1/44; MIA Schweinfurt 13/4/44 w/Vokaty; e/a, cr Kaiburg, Ger?; 2KIA 8POW; MACR 3938. COMMAND PERFORMANCE.

42-31509 Del Denver 16/11/43; Spokane 19/11/43; Gt Falls 25/11/43; Kearney 14/12/43; Romulus 19/12/43; Grenier 22/12/43; Presque Is 31/12/43; ass 508BS/351BG [YB-V] Polebrook 14/1/44; 510BS [TU-V]; MIA {41m} Brandenburg 6/8/44 w/Petty; flak, f/l Sovde, Swed; 9INT; MACR 7589; retUS 121 BU Bradley 20/7/45; 4185 BU Independence 30/11/45; RFC Kingman 21/12/45. TWINKLE TOES.

42-31510 Del Denver 16/11/43; Gt Falls 25/11/43; Kearney 14/12/43; Romulus 26/12/43; Presque Is 30/12/43; ass 524BS/379BG [WA-D] Kimbolton 4/1/44; MIA Oschersleben 22/2/44 w/McCall; e/a, cr Afferden, Hol; 6EVD 4POW. MACR 2875.

42-31511 Del Denver 16/11/43; Kearney 3/12/43; Presque Is 9/12/43; ass 612BS/401BG [SC-D] Deenethorpe 1/1/44; MIA Evere A/fd 10/4/44 w/Fox; e/a, cr Calais, Fr; 4KIA 6POW; MACR 3939. FOOLS LUCK III.

42-31512 Del Denver 13/11/43; Gt Falls 15/11/43; Denver 22/11/43; Kearney 27/11/43; Presque Is 25/12/43; ass 569BS/390BG [CC-H] Framlingham 2/1/44; sal n/b/d 4/6/44. ICE COLD KATIE (BUCKSHOT ANNIE).

42-31513 Del Denver 15/11/43; Ogden 18/11/43; Gr Island 10/12/43; ass 401BS/91BG [LL-S] Bassingbourn 24/2/44; c/l base 6/4/44; sal n/b/d 2SAD Lt Staughton.

42-31514 Del Denver 15/11/43; Gr Island 3/12/43; Presque Is 9/12/43; ass 336BS/95BG [ET-K] Horham 17/12/43; MIA Zeitz 16/8/44 w/Severson; cr Mohlau, Ger; 9POW. MACR 8178. FULL HOUSE.

42-31515 Del Denver 16/11/43; Rock Springs 26/11/43; Kearney 14/12/43; Romulus 17/12/43; Syracuse 19/12/43; Presque Is 22/12/43; ass 324BS/91BG [DF-J/N] Bassingbourn 21/1/44; 401BS [LL-M] 29/4/44; MIA {25m} Altenbeken 26/11/44 w/Flint; e/a, exploded cr Grossenging, Ger; 5KIA 4POW; MACR 10836. THE WILD HARE.

42-31516 Del Denver 16/11/43; Spokane 19/11/43; Missoula 24/11/43; Kearney 17/12/43; Romulus 6/1/44; Presque Is 7/1/44; ass 546BS/384BG Grafton Underwood 18/2/44; forming up for Oschersleben 22/2/44 coll w/42-38041 (303BG), cr Irthlingborough, UK; 18KIA. Sal AFSC 23/2/44.

42-31517 Del Denver 16/11/43; Pendleton 24/11/43; Salt Lake 12/12/43; Wendover 14/12/43; ass 748BS/457BG Glatton 15/12/43; MIA Augsburg 25/2/44 w/Chinn; e/a. cr Mont St Martin, Fr; 1EVD 7KIA 2POW; MACR 3003.

42-31518 Del Denver 17/11/43; Kearney 3/12/43; Cincinnati 9/12/43; Rome 11/12/43; Presque Is 14/12/43; ass 615BS/401BG [IY-M] Deenethorpe 1/2/44; MIA Leipzig 20/2/44 w/Gardner; e/a, cr Pockau, Ger; 3KIA 7POW; MACR 2437. DOOLITTLE'S DOUGHBOYS.

42-31519 Del Denver 16/11/43; Boise 24/11/43; Kearney 17/12/43; Chicago 8/1/44; Romulus 9/1/44; Presque Is 11/1/44; ass 447BG Rattlesden 18/1/44; MIA Berlin 29/4/44 w/?; ditched Channel.

42-31520 Del Denver 16/11/43; Spokane 19/11/43; Gr Island 24/11/43; Wendover 12/11/43; Rapid City 10/4/43; ass 751BS/457BG Glatton 26/1/44; MIA Cologne 28/5/44 w/Knipfer; e/a, cr Doellbach, Ger?; 9POW; MACR 5300.

42-31521 Del Denver 16/11/43; Gt Falls 25/11/43; Kearney 17/12/43; Romulus 9/1/44; Presque Is 13/1/44; ass 615BS/401BG [IY-M] Deenethorpe 1/2/44; MIA Berlin 29/4/44 w/Capt Gould; flak, cr Celle, Ger; 10POW; MACR 4346. BADLAND BAT.

42-31522 Del Denver 16/11/43; Kearney 25/11/43; ass 416BS/99BG Tortorella 18/12/43; MIA {16m} Regensburg w/Perry; ditched off Pula, Yugo; 10POW; MACR 2391. SPOOFER.

42-31523 Del Denver 12/11/43; Gt Falls 16/11/43; Kearney 25/11/43; ass 419BS/301BG Cerignola 11/1/44; Lucera 1/2/44; MIA Wiener Nuedorf 26/7/44 w/Starling; e/a, cr St Katherin; 5KIA 5POW; MACR 7127. BAR FLY.

42-31524 Del Denver 16/11/43; Boise 17/11/43; Kearney 30/11/43; Gr Island 4/12/43; Romulus 6/12/43; Dorvel (Canada) 7/12/43; Presque Is 9/12/43; ass 423BS/306BG [RD-G] Thurleigh 21/1/44; b/d Berlin 22/3/44, 5 baled; c/l Horsey?; (Hornsea, UK?); 5RTD; MACR 3434. ABLE MABEL.

42-31525 Del Denver 16/11/43; Pendleton 18/11/43; Gr Island 10/12/43; ass 730BS/452BG Deopham Green 4/1/44; retUS 121 BU Bradley 28/6/45; 4168 BU Sth Plains 21/10/45; RFC Kingman 24/11/45. THE REINCARNATION.

42-31526 Del Denver 17/11/43; Kearney 1/12/43; Presque Is 10/12/43; ass 427BS/303BG Molesworth 1/1/44 LIL' BUTCH; MIA Keil 4/1/44 w/Humphreys; flak, cr Keil; 10POW; MACR 1682. SWEET ANNA.

42-31527 Del Denver 16/11/43; Kearney 28/11/43; ass 429BS/2BG Amendola 29/12/43; MIA Budapest 14/6/44 w/Britton; e/a, exploded, cr Banja Luka, Yugo; 10 chutes seen; MACR 6015. BROWN NOSE.

42-31528 Del Denver 16/11/43; Kearney 2/12/43; New York 8/12/43; Presque Is 9/12/43; ass 305BG Chelveston 28/12/43; c/l Oxford 31/12/43; sal 2 SAD Lt Staughton 3/1/44.

42-31529 Del Denver 19/11/43; Gt Falls 20/11/43; Kearney 12/12/43; Romulus 8/1/44; New Castle 9/1/44; Presque Is 10/1/44; ass 407BS/92BG Podington 23/1/44; MIA Erding 24/4/44 w/Howard; e/a, cr Weissbach, Ger; 10POW; MACR 4146.

42-31530 Del Denver 19/11/43; Spokane 22/11/43; Kearney 12/12/43; Prestwick 16/1/44; ass 100BG Thorpe Abbotts 17/1/44; sal 31/5/45. QUITTIN' TIME.

42-31531 Del Denver 20/11/43; Gt Falls 22/11/43; Wendover 11/12/43; ass 332BS/94BG Rougham 25/1/44; tran 749BS/457BG Glatton 26/1/44; MIA Brunswick 29/3/44 w/Lennartson; e/a, cr 5Riestedt, Ger; 2KIA 8POW; MACR 3487.

42-31532 Del Denver 18/11/43; Gt Falls 6/12/43; New Castle 14/12/43; Presque Is 16/12/43; ass 326BS/92BG Podington 4/1/44; MIA Brunswick 23/3/44 w/Murdeck; e/a, cr Coesfeld, Ger; 3KIA 7POW; MACR 3415.

42-31533 Del Denver 18/11/43; Gt Falls 4/12/43; New Castle 13/12/43; Presque Is 15/12/43; ass 535BS/381BG [MS-U] Ridgewell 5/1/44; MIA {4m} Oschersleben 22/2/44 w/Downey; e/a, cr Wiedenbrück, Ger; 7KIA 3POW; MACR 2931.

42-31534 Del Denver 19/11/43; Kearney 5/12/43; Grenier 18/12/43; Presque Is 20/12/43; ass 350BS/100BG [LN-N] Thorpe Abbotts 26/12/43 POWERHOUSE; 349BS [XR-N]; MIA Berlin 24/5/44 w/Malooly; e/a, exploded cr Goericke, Ger?; 10POW; MACR 5166. SHILAYEE.

42-31535 Del Cheyenne 19/11/43; Kearney 2/12/43; Syracuse 8/12/43; Presque Is 11/12/43; ass 527BS/379BG Kimbolton 24/1/44; MIA Brunswick 30/1/44 w/Adams; flak, cr Minden, Ger; 1KIA 9POW; MACR 2876.

42-31536 Del Cheyenne 19/11/43; Kearney 1/12/43; Grenier 9/12/43; Presque Is 11/12/43; ass 388BG Knettishall 20/12/43; tran 326BS/92BG [JW-O] Podington 27/1/44; b/d Cologne 28/1/45, f/l Continent; sal 2/2/45. IRENE - JEAN B.

42-31537 Del Cheyenne 19/11/43; Kearney 2/12/43; Presque Is 10/12/43; ass 332BS/94BG [XM-B] Rougham 23/12/43 FRIDAY THE 13TH; tran 350BS/100BG [LN-S] Thorpe Abbotts 24/12/43 BUFFALO GAL; 349BS; MIA Merseburg 29/7/44 w/Fitzroy; e/a, cr Pauschrau, Ger?; 4KIA 5POW; MACR 7809. RANDY LOU.

42-31538 Del Cheyenne 19/11/43; Kearney 6/12/43; Grenier 20/12/43; Presque Is 22/12/43; ass 368BS/306BG Thurleigh 21/1/44; 367BS [GY-V]; MIA Oschersleben 11/1/44 w/Cavos; e/a, cr Realte, Hol; 10KIA; MACR 1932.

42-31539 Del Cheyenne 20/11/43; Gr Island 5/12/43; Romulus 16/12/43; Presque Is 19/12/43; ass 423BS/306BG [RD-O] Thurleigh 4/1/44; MIA Erding 24/4/44 w/Ebert; e/a, c/l Neftenbach, Switz; 10INT; MACR 4821.

42-31540 Del Cheyenne 16/11/43; Kearney 3/12/43; Cleveland 9/12/43; Syracuse 11/12/43; Presque Is 15/12/43; Prestwick 19/12/43; ass 331BS/94BG [QE-B] Rougham 20/12/43; MIA Berlin 19/5/44 w/Reid; hit by bombs from aircraft above; cr Berlin; 11KIA; MACR 4946. MISS DONNA MAE.

42-31541 Del Cheyenne 19/11/43; Spokane 20/11/43; Gt Falls 25/11/43; Wendover 8/12/43; ass 457BG but W/O in US 24/12/43.

42-31542 Del Cheyenne 19/11/43; Spokane 22/11/43; Gt Falls 25/11/43; Wendover 7/12/43; ass 748BS/457BG Glatton 27/1/44 BUNKY; tran 92BG Podington 11/3/44; 323BS/91BG [OR-T] Bassingbourn 12/3/44; MIA {45m} Lechfeld 19/7/44 w/Burwick; mid air coll w/42-107075 (91BG); tail broke off, cr Hughlfing, Ger; 9KIA; MACR 7417. "BUNKY."

42-31543 Del Cheyenne 20/11/43; Gr Island 5/12/43; Presque Is 14/12/43; RAF Valley 20/12/43; ass 332BS/94BG [XM-D] Rougham 21/12/43; MIA Augsburg 13/4/44 w/McDowell; flak #1, and runaway prop #1, cr Channel. NINE YANKS AND A JERK.

42-31544 Del Cheyenne 21/11/43; Seattle 23/11/43; Gr Island 4/12/43; Romulus 14/12/43; Presque Is 17/12/43; ass 366BS/305BG Chelveston 21/1/44; MIA Frankfurt 24/3/44 w/Cornell; flak, cr Winkel, Ger; 1KIA 9POW; MACR 3537.

42-31545 Del Cheyenne 20/11/43; Boise 23/11/43; Wendover 7/12/43; Grenier 20/1/44; ass 749BS/457BG Glatton 26/1/44; sal b/d 2 SAD Lt Staughton 18/6/44. BAD TIME INC.

42-31546 Del Cheyenne 21/11/43; Kearney 1/12/43; Bangor 9/12/43; ass 332BS/94BG [XM-C] Rougham 2/1/44; MIA Augsburg 16/3/44 w/Kocher; flak, cr Fuessin, Ger?; 2KIS 8POW; MACR 3227. THE OLD SARGE.

42-31547 Del Denver 20/11/43; Wendover 15/12/43;

ass 457BG in US but W/O 5/1/44.

42-31548 Del Denver 20/11/43; Midford 22/11/43; Salt Lake 24/11/43; Wendover 12/12/43; ass 749BS/457BG Glatton 29/1/44; tran 325BS/92BG [NV-D] Podington 11/3/44; MIA Stettin 11/4/44 w/Shufeldt; f/l Rinkaby, Swed; 10INT. MACR 3671. Left 20/6/45; retUS 121 BU Bradley 1/8/45; 4185 BU Independence 30/11/45; RFC Kingman 21/12/45. SHU SHU BABY (MIRANDY).

42-31549 Del Denver 21/11/43; Gr Island 7/12/43; New Castle 16/12/43; Presque Is 19/12/43; ass 561BS/388BG Knettishall 1/1/44; MIA Brux 12/5/44 w/Loslo; e/a, cr Stammheim, Ger; 10POW; MACR 4881. JEANNIE.

42-31550 Del Denver 21/11/43; Kearney 14/12/43; La Guardia 21/12/43; Presque Is 23/12/43; ass 534BS/381BG [GD-G] Ridgewell 13/1/44; MIA {55M} Cologne 17/10/44 w/Rice; flak, f/l Belgium, some crew baled, 2WIA but all OK; sal 21/11/44. GREEN HORNET 2ND.

42-31551 Del Denver 20/11/43; Seattle 23/11/43; Wendover 12/12/43; ass 750BS/457BG Glatton 29/1/44; retUS 121 BU Bradley 9/6/45; 4168 BU Sth Plains 21/10/45; RFC Kingman 29/11/45. ELIZABETH ANN.

42-31552 Del Denver 21/11/43; Gt Falls 25/11/43; Wendover 12/12/43; ass 748BS/457BG Glatton 26/1/44; MIA Munich 12/7/44 w/Kerr; flak, f/l Pratigau, Switz; 1INT 4KIA 4POW; MACR 6926.

42-31553 Del Denver 21/11/43; Kearney 16/12/43; Oklahoma City 24/12/43; New Castle 8/1/44; Presque Is 9/1/44; ass 534BS/381BG [[GD-B] Ridgewell 19/2/44; MIA {4m} Berlin 6/3/44 w/Haushalter; e/a, cr Wernsdorf, Ger; 5KIA 5POW; MACR 3241. MYER'S FLAW.

42-31554 Del Denver 21/11/43; Kearney 5/12/43; Romulus 18/12/44; Presque Is 20/12/43; ass 551BS/385BG Gt Ashfield 30/12/43; sal n/b/d 24/5/44.

42-31555 Del Denver 21/11/43; Kearney 17/12/43; Oklahoma City 24/12/43; Kearney 8/1/44; Presque Is 17/1/44; ass 527BS/379BG Kimbolton 31/1/44; MIA Berlin 6/3/44 w/Hendrickson; e/a, cr Ochawnmoor, (?); 1KIA 9POW; MACR 2909.

42-31556 Del Denver 21/11/43; Gr Island 3/12/43; Kearney 8/12/43; Presque Is 10/12/43; ass 368BS/306BG [BO-D] Thurleigh 4/1/44; MIA Berlin 29/4/44 w/Lutz; flak, cr Hecklingen, Ger; 8KIA 2POW; MACR 4240.

42-31557 Del Denver 21/11/43; Kearney 5/12/43; Presque Is 20/12/43; ass 613BS/401BG [IN-R] Deenethorpe 21/1/44; MIA Cologne 28/5/44 w/Keith; flak, cr Belzig, Ger; 4KIA 6POW; MACR 5308.

42-31558 Del Denver 21/11/43; Kearney 14/12/43; Chicago 18/12/43; Syracuse 19/12/43; Presque Is 21/12/43; ass 369BS/306BG [WW-M] Thurleigh 21/1/44; MIA Erding 24/4/44 w/James; e/a, cr Hoerburg, Ger?; 10POW; MACR 4282.

42-31559 Del Denver 21/11/43; Kearney 6/12/43; Presque Is 20/12/43; ass 337BS/96BG [AW-J] Snetterton 26/12/43; MIA Frankfurt 20/3/44 w/Denissen; ditched Channel; 10RTD.

42-31560 Del Denver 21/11/43; Gr Island 10/12/43; ass 510BS/351BG [TU-A] Polebrook 25/2/44; MIA Ludwigshafen 8/9/44 w/Shera; flak, cr Thionville, Fr; 1EVD 3KIA 5POW; MACR 10534.

42-31561 Del Denver 24/11/43; Kearney 11/12/43; Romulus 17/12/43; Presque Is 20/12/43; ass 335BS/95BG [OE-Z] Horham 24/12/43; MIA Rostock 24/2/44 w/Costales; flak, cr Luegumkloster, Ger?; 2KIA 8POW; MACR 2644.

42-31562 Del Denver 24/11/43; Kearney 11/12/43; Romulus 19/12/43; Presque Is 20/12/43; ass 358BS/303BG [VK-A] Molesworth 13/1/44; MIA Schweinfurt 24/2/44 w/Henderson; e/a, cr Boppard, Ger; 10POW; MACR 2762.

42-31563 Del Denver 24/11/43; Kearney 7/12/43; Romulus 17/12/43; Presque Is 20/12/43; ass 710BS/447BG Rattlesden 26/12/43; MIA Regensburg 25/2/44 w/Kautt; e/a, cr Kaiserlautern, Ger; 1KIA 9POW; MACR 2892.

42-31564 Del Denver 23/11/43; Gt Falls 25/11/43; Kearney 5/12/43; Presque Is 13/12/43; ass 325BS/92BG [NV-O] Podington 30/12/43; MIA Berlin 9/3/44 w/Floyd; flak, f/l Bredakra, Swed; 10INT. MACR 3064. Sal 29/6/45.

42-31565 Del Denver 21/11/43; Gr Island 7/12/43; Selfridge 14/12/43; Presque Is 15/12/43; ass 335BS/95BG [OE-U] Horham 26/12/43; MIA Berlin 4/3/44 w/Roehm; cr Berlin; 3EVD 1KIA 6POW; MACR 2795.

42-31566 Del Denver 21/11/43; Gr Island 5/12/43; Romulus 13/12/43; Presque 15/12/43; ass 339BS/96BG Snetterton 20/12/43; MIA Brunswick 10/2/44 w/Thompson; flak, cr Brunswick; 10KIA; MACR 2375.

42-31567 Del Denver 21/11/43; Tacoma 22/11/43; Gt Falls 25/11/43; Kearney 17/12/43; Kansas City 28/12/43; New Castle 8/1/44; Presque Is 9/1/44; RAF Valley 15/1/44; ass 337BS/96BG [AW-R] Snetterton 16/1/44; MIA Berlin 8/3/44.

42-31568 Del Denver 21/11/43; Billings 25/11/43; Wendover 12/12/43; Grenier 20/1/44; ass 750BS/457BG Glatton 8/2/44; 748BS; mia French A/fds 14/6/44 w/Rogers; flak, cr Iverni, Fr; 7EVD 2POW; MACR 5904.

42-31569 Del Denver 23/11/43; Gt Falls 25/11/43; Cheyenne 11/12/43; Kearney 21/12/43; Romulus 6/1/44; Grenier 9/1/44; Presque Is 10/1/44; ass 534BS/381BG [GD-E] Ridgewell 19/2/44; MIA {4m} Ludwigshafen 3/9/44 w/Fulton; b/d f/l Continent; 1EVD 8POW; sal 5/5/45. SWEET PATTOOTIE.

42-31570 Del Denver 24/11/43; Kearney 11/12/43; Romulus 18/12/43; Presque Is 20/12/43; ass 533BS/381BG [VP-W] Ridgewell 2/2/44; MIA {65m} Frankfurt 25/9/44 w/Gills; mech fault, cr St Goar, Ger; 9POW; MACR 10203. LUCKY ME!

42-31571 Del Denver 20/11/43; Gt Falls 28/11/43; Cheyenne 12/12/43; Kearney 19/12/43; Morrison 3/1/44; ass 342BS/97BG Tortorella 12/1/44; MIA Piombino, It. 28/4/44 w/Curlin; flak, cr San Angelo; MACR 4527.

42-31572 Del Denver 24/11/43; Gt Falls 25/11/43; Billings 26/11/43; Kearney 12/12/43; New Castle 18/12/43; Presque Is 19/12/43; ass 457BG Glatton 27/12/43; tran 401BS/91BG [LL-Y] Bassingbourn 23/1/44 MY BELOVED ALSO; MIA {1m} Achmer 21/2/44 w/Piacentini; e/a, cr Herford, Ger; 3KIA 7POW; MACR 2462. MY BELOVED TOO.

42-31573 Del Boeing 2/12/43; Mat Com (crash testing, no u/c) Seattle 2/6/44; 4100 BU Patterson 18/3/45; 2114 BU Lockburn 8/6/45; 2137 BU Hendricks 22/9/45; RFC Walnut Ridge 7/1/46.

42-31574 Del Denver 20/11/43; Gt Falls 24/11/43; Kearney 16/12/43; Ft Wayne 25/12/43; Wilmington 27/12/43; Presque Is 29/12/43; ass 358BS/303BG [VK-G] Molesworth 13/1/44; MIA Merzhausen 24/12/44. MACR 11112 OLE GEORGE.

42-31575 Del Denver 24/11/43; Kearney 17/12/43; Oklahoma City 7/1/44; Kearney 15/1/44; ass 532BS/381BG [VE-P] Ridgewell 20/2/44; {61+m} RetUS 121 BU Bradley 27/5/45; 4168 BU Sth Plains 21/10/45; RFC Kingman 23/11/45. MIZPAH.

42-31576 Del Denver 20/11/43; Gt Falls 25/11/43; Kearney 22/12/43; Romulus 31/12/43; Presque Is 2/1/44; ass 339BS/96BG [QJ-G] Snetterton 16/1/44; MIA Erkner 8/3/44 w/Lemanski; e/a, cr Helmstedt, Ger; 10POW; MACR 3426.

42-31577 Del Cheyenne 25/11/43; Gr Island 8/12/43; Romulus 14/12/43; Mitchell 17/12/43; Syracuse 26/12/43; Grenier 31/12/43; Presque Is 2/1/44; ass 560BS/388BG Knettishall 9/1/44; l/Poltava, Russia 21/4/44; dest on ground by Luftwaffe; sal. AQUILA.

42-31578 Del Cheyenne 25/11/43; Gr Island 5/12/43; Romulus 15/12/43; Presque Is 17/12/43; ass 401BS/91BG [LL-L] Bassingbourn 29/12/43; MIA {11m} Berlin 6/3/44 w/Tibbetts; mid air coll w/FW190, cr Magdeburg, Ger; 8KIA 2POW; MACR 2898. MY DARLING ALSO.

42-31579 Del Cheyenne 23/11/43; Gr Island 5/12/43; Milwaukee 14/12/43; Presque Is 17/12/43; ass 324BS/91BG [DF-N] Bassingbourn 1/2/44 BETTY LOU'S BUGGY; 323BS [OR-D]; c/l RAF Chilbolton 27/4/44, rep 2 SAD Lt Staughton, ret 23/5/44; n/b/d in taxi accident 14/9/44; sal 30/9/44. {67m} declared W/W, tran SAD Watton. BETTY LOU'S BLOCK BUSTER.

42-31580 Del Cheyenne 26/11/43; Paine Fd 27/11/43; Portland 3/12/43; Cheyenne 5/12/43; Kearney 12/12/43; Sth Bend 3/1/44; Grenier 8/1/44; Presque Is 12/1/44; Prestwick 15/1/44; ass 323BS/91BG [OR-A] Bassingbourn 29/1/44; MIA Berlin 7/5/44 w/Kovachevich; flak #3, cr Heidenau, Ger; 2KIA 7POW; MACR 4579. MERRY WIDOW.

42-31581 Del Cheyenne 26/11/43; Paine Fd 28/11/43; Portland 2/12/43; Gt Falls 5/12/43; Kearney 16/12/43; Chicago 21/12/43; La Guardia 22/12/43; Grenier 24/12/43; Presque Is 30/12/43; ass 8AF 1/1/44; sal n/b/d 2/10/44.

42-31582 Del Cheyenne 26/11/43; Paine Fd 28/11/43; Toledo 1/12/43; Felts Fd 4/12/43; Gt falls 5/12/43; Cheyenne 7/12/43; Kearney 19/12/43; Detroit 8/1/44; Montreal 10/1/44; Presque 12/1/44; ass 711BS/447BG Rattlesden 23/1/44; MIA Holzwickede 23/3/45 w/?; b/d f/l Continent, MACR 13617; sal 8/4/45. OL' SCRAPIRON.

42-31583 Del Cheyenne 26/11/43; Kearney 16/12/43; Chicago 21/12/43; New York 23/12/43; Presque Is 25/12/43; ass 358BS/303BG [VK-V] Molesworth 13/1/44; MIA Augsburg 19/7/44 w/Botce; e/a, cr Tutzing, Ger?; 4KIA 5OPOW; MACR 7415. CLOVER LEAF.

42-31584 Del Cheyenne 25/11/43; Spokane 26/11/43; Gt Falls 5/12/43; Cheyenne 11/12/43; Kearney 24/12/43; Memphis 29/12/43; Morrison 3/1/44; ass 32BS/301BG Lucera 14/1/44; {12m} tran depot 2/44; sal 17/4/45.

42-31585 Del Cheyenne 26/11/43; Paine 28/11/43; Gt Falls 5/12/43; Cheyenne 7/12/43; Kearney 16/12/43; Oklahoma City 7/1/44; Kearney 12/1/44; Romulus 17/1/44; Grenier 18/1/44; ass 323BS/91BG [OR-B] Bassingbourne 1/2/44; MIA Augsburg 16/3/44 w/Bradford; mech fault, f/l Dubendorf, Switz; 10INT. MACR 3221. Ret Burtonwood, UK. Sal 8/10/45. MOUNT 'N RIDE.

42-31586 Del Cheyenne 29/11/43; Kearney 20/12/43; Oklahoma City 28/12/43; Morrison 17/1/44; ass 457BG, sal 11/12/43; rep, tran 414BS/97BG Tortorella 18/1/44; {111m} Vienna 3/11/44; tran depot 3/1/45; retUS 1103 BU Morrison 26/4/45; 4104 BU Rome 28/4/45; Recl Comp 2/10/45. PISTOL PACKIN' MAMA.

42-31587 Del Cheyenne 26/11/43; Wendover 7/12/43; ass 457BG Glatton 8/12/43; tran 100BG Thorpe Abbotts 22/1/44; 325BS/92BG Podington 11/3/44; MIA Stettin 11/4/44 w/Mikesell; e/a, cr Kathendorf,

Ger; 5KIA 5POW; MACR 3672.

42-31588 Del Cheyenne 26/11/43; Wendover 7/12/43; ass 748BS/457BG Glatton 26/1/44; b/d Augsburg 25/2/44; sal 2 SAD Lt Staughton 23/8/44.

42-31589 Del Cheyenne 25/11/43; Gt Falls 1/12/43; Kearney 17/12/43; Romulus 6/1/44; Grenier 9/1/44; Presque Is 12/1/44; ass 334BS/95BG [BG-O] Horham 23/1/44; MIA Zeitz 16/8/44n w/Price; flak, cr Altenburg, Ger; 3KIA 6POW; MACR 8177.

42-31590 Del Cheyenne 27/11/43; Gt Falls 30/11/43; Kearney 21/12/43; Oklahoma City 4/1/44; Lincoln 12/1/44; Kearney 16/1/44; Memphis 18/1/44; McDill 21/1/44; Homestead 23/1/44; ass 49BS/2BG Amendola 25/2/44; {29m}; retUS 1103 BU Morrison 20/2/45; 4100 BU Patterson 27/7/45; Recl Comp 24/5/46.

42-31591 Del Cheyenne 26/11/43; Wendover 9/12/43; Grenier 20/1/44; ass 457BG Glatton 25/1/44; tran 613BS/401BG [IN-J] Deenethorpe 11/3/44; MIA Pas de Calais 19/3/44, f/l Continent; sal 1 SAD Troston 22/4/44. HOMESICK ANGEL.

42-31592 Del Cheyenne 27/11/43; Wendover 10/12/43; Presque Is 19/1/44; ass 457BG Glatton 22/1/44; tran 525BS/379BG [FR-R] Kimbolton 18/3/44; c/t/o 23/1/45 (stalled), sal.

42-31593 Del Cheyenne 25/11/43; Spokane 26/11/43; Geiger 2/12/43; Gt Falls 5/12/43; Kearney 16/12/43; Madison, WI 3/1/44; Rome 4/1/44; Presque Is 8/1/44; ass 613BS/401BG [IN-L] Deenethorpe 1/2/44; MIA Pas de Calais 20/4/44 w/Daugherty; flak, cr Abbeville, Fr; 8KIA 2POW; MACR 4054.

42-31594 Del Cheyenne 26/11/43; Wendover 9/12/43; ass 751BS/457BG Glatton 25/1/44; MIA Ludwigshafen 27/5/44 w/Whitlow; e/a Bergheim, Ger; 1EVD 2KIA 6POW; MACR 5299.

42-31595 Del Cheyenne 27/11/43; Gt Falls 30/11/43; Wendover 9/12/43; ass 750BS/457BG Glatton 25/1/44; MIA Berlin 6/3/44; w/Whalen; mid air coll w/ME410 after wreckage from above fell, 42-31627; cr Berlin; 10KIA; MACR 3197.

42-31596 Del Cheyenne 27/11/43; Billings 29/11/43; Wendover 9/12/43; ass 750BS/457BG Glatton 26/12/44; MIA Achmer 21/2/44 w/Bredeson (first in grp); e/a, Lengerich, Ger; 1KIA 9POW; MACR 3004.

42-31597 Del Denver 27/11/43; Salt Lake 28/11/43; Cheyenne 17/12/43; Kearney 20/12/43; Romulus 6/1/44; Grenier 9/1/44; Presque Is 12/1/44; Prestwick 15/1/44; ass 527BS/379BG [FO-C] Kimbolton 30/1/44; MIA Zeitz 30/11/44 w/Conroy; flak, cr Doelzig, Ger; 3KIA 6POW; MACR 11127.

42-31598 Del Denver 28/11/43; Kearney 19/12/43; Wilmington 31/12/43; Presque Is 2/1/44; ass 551BS/385BG Gt Ashfield 18/1/44; MIA Paris 2/8/44 w/Newcomer; flak, cr Paris; 5EVD 4POW; MACR 8161.

42-31599 Del Denver 25/11/43; Kearney 12/12/43; Romulus 17/12/43; Grenier 21/12/43; Presque Is 23/12/43; Newtownards 24/12/43; ass 410BS/ 94BG [GL-O] Rougham 30/12/43 FIFI, then BOOTS & HER BUDDIES; MIA Berlin 6/10/44 w/Brasher; e/a, cr ; 9POW; MACR 9349. THE FILTHY HAG.

42-31600 Del Denver 28/11/43; Kearney 15/12/43; San Bernardino 20/12/43; Grenier 21/12/43; Presque Is 23/12/32; ass 334BS/95BG [BG-T] Horham 2/1/44 PRIDE OF NEW MEXICO; 335BS [OE-M]; MIA Osnabrück 21/11/44 w/Schoaf; b/d cr St Vithan, Bel?; 10POW; MACR 11195. SPIRIT OF NEW MEXICO.

42-31601 Del Denver 27/11/43; Cheyenne 12/12/43; Kearney 22/12/43; Memphis 29/12/43; Morrison 3/1/44; ass 352BS/301BG Cerignola 14/1/44; Lucera 1/2/44; cr base non-operational 12/8/44, sal.

42-31602 Del Denver 28/11/43; Cheyenne 20/12/43; Gr Island 24/12/43; Romulus 20/1/44; Grenier 29/1/44; Presque Is 5/2/44; ass 364BS/305BG Chelveston 22/2/44; MIA Pas de Calais 23/3/44 w/Forrest; e/a, cr Zelham, Hol; 2EVD 8POW; MACR 3431.

42-31603 Del Denver 28/11/43; Kearney 16/12/43; Wilmington 31/12/43; Presque Is 2/1/44; ass 569BS/390BG [CC-N] Framlingham 16/1/44; MIA Berlin 8/5/44 w/Miller; flak, cr Breuville, Fr?; 7KIA 2POW; MACR 4583. BELLE OF THE BRAWL.

42-31604 Del Denver 28/11/43; Cheyenne 12/12/43; Kearney 22/12/43; Meeks Fd 4/1/44; ass 8AF as replacement a/c to Nutts Corner, N. Ireland; abandoned over Fort William, Scotland, cr Lake Quioch; sal RAF 28/2/44.

42-31605 Del Denver 29/11/43; Cheyenne 14/12/43; Kearney 20/12/43; Morrison 3/1/44; ass 352BS/301BG Cerignola 6/1/44; Lucera 1/2/44; MIA {38m} Lyon 25/5/44 w/McCarthy; mid air coll w/42-31853; cr, 9KIA; MACR?

42-31606 Del Cheyenne 27/11/43; Gr Island 10/12/43; Bangor 14/12/43; ass 547BS/384BG [SO-O] Grafton Underwood 6/1/44; MIA Bonn 4/3/44 w/Lawson; flak, cr Bonn, Ger; 3EVD 7POW; MACR 2739.

42-31607 Del Cheyenne 27/11/43; Wendover 12/10/43; Presque Is 19/1/44; ass 748BS/457BG Glatton 23/2/44; MIA Merseburg 12/5/44 w/Akers; e/a, cr Naunheim, Ger; 10POW; MACR 4800.

42-31608 Del Denver 28/11/43; Cheyenne 12/12/43; Kearney 20/12/43; Nashville 26/12/43; Morrison 3/1/44; ass 352BS/301BG Cerignola 6/1/44; Lucera 1/2/44; re-ass weather ship 12/10/44; depot 22/2/45; retUS Grenier 21/9/45; 4185 BU Independence 30/11/45; RFC Walnut Ridge 7/1/46.

42-31609 Del Denver 29/11/43; ass Soxo 15/1/44; retUS 4136 BU Tinker 4/7/44; 3017 BU Hobbs 14/8/44; 3021 BU Las Vegas 26/9/44; 3022 BU Indian Springs 2/10/44; 3021 BU Las Vegas 19/3/45; 2126 BU Laredo 29/3/45; RFC Walnut Ridge 11/1/46.

42-31610 Del Denver 29/11/43; Cheyenne 10/12/43; Kearney 21/12/43; Romulus 6/1/44; Presque Is 9/1/44; Nutts Corner; 15/1/44; ass 322BS/91BG [LG-M] Bassingbourn 1/2/44; MIA Munich 16/7/44 w/DeLisle; flak, knocked out engine; ditched Channel; 9RTD (1WIA). THE LIBERTY BELLE.

42-31611 Del Denver 28/11/43; Kearney 23/12/43; Romulus 9/1/44; Presque Is 10/1/44; ass 366BS/305BG Chelveston 29/1/44; MIA Saarbrücken 11/5/44 w/Holbrook; flak, cr Saarbrücken, Ger; 10KIA 1POW; MACR 4870.

42-31612 Del Denver 28/11/43; Kearney 17/12/43; Syracuse 2/1/44; Presque Is 4/1/44; ass 510BS/351BG [TU-B] Polebrook 30/1/44; MIA {8m} Oschersleben 22/2/44 w/Ritzema; flak, cr Muthagen, Ger; 1KIA 9POW; MACR 2657.

42-31613 Del Cheyenne 28/11/43; Billings 29/11/43; Wendover 10/12/43; ass 749BS/457BG Glatton 27/1/44; tran 325BS/92BG [NV-N] Horham 11/3/44; c/l 20/4/44; sal.

42-31614 Del Cheyenne 27/11/43; Seattle 29/11/43; Portland 2/12/43; Felts Fd 4/12/43; Cheyenne 6/12/43; Kearney 16/12/43; Cleveland 20/12/43; Syracuse 21/12/43; Presque Is 3/1/44; ass 533BS/381BG [VP-L] Ridgewell 21/1/44; MIA Merseburg Ger; 29/11/44 w/Nelson; f/l Continent; sal 27/1/45. MINNIE THE MERMAID.

42-31615 Del Cheyenne 27/11/43; Portland 28/11/43; Wendover 9/12/43; Presque Is 26/1/44; ass 748BS/457BG Glatton 5/2/44; MIA Hamburg 20/6/44 w/Bomer; flak, cr Hamburg; 3KIA 6POW; MACR 6003. SNAFUSK SHAMROCK.

42-31616 Del Cheyenne 27/11/43; Gr Island 5/12/43; Presque Is 17/12/43; ass 427BS/303BG Molesworth 14/1/44 THE SPIRIT OF FLAK WOLF; c/t/o Winwick, UK 9/4/44; sal 11/4/44. THE SPIRIT OF WANETTE.

42-31617 Del Cheyenne 27/11/43; Kansas City 7/12/43; Scott Fd 8/12/43; Dayton 9/12/43; Wright Fd 15/12/43; Kearney 19/12/43; Oklahoma City 10/1/44; Kearney 15/1/44; ass 413BS/96BG Snetterton 29/1/44; MIA Brunswick 10/2/44 w/Scott; e/a, cr Emsdetten, Ger; 10POW; MACR 2373.

42-31618 Del Cheyenne 28/11/43; Rock Springs 8/12/43; Wendover 9/12/43; Grenier 20/1/44; ass 750BS/457BG Glatton 27/1/44; 748BS; MIA Florennes 14/6/44 w/LaPaze; flak, ditched Channel; 5KIA 4RTD; MACR 5905.

42-31619 Del Cheyenne 1/12/43; Gt Falls 5/12/43; Kearney 19/12/43; Romulus 18/1/44; Presque Is 20/1/44; ass 615BS/401BG [IY-L] Deenethorpe 31/1/44; MIA Stettin 24/5/44 w/Whiteman; flak, cr Bornholm, Den; 10INT; MACR 4957. BTO IN THE ETO.

42-31620 Del Cheyenne 27/11/43; Wendover 11/12/43; ass 750BS/457BG Glatton 26/1/44; f/l no hydraulics, sal 22/6/44. SKUNK HOLLOW.

42-31621 Del Denver 28/11/43; Kearney 19/12/43; Oklahoma City 8/1/44; ass 338BS/96BG [BX-L] Snetterton 5/2/44; MIA Brux 12/5/44 w/Filer; e/a, cr Eisenbach, Ger; 5KIA 5POW; MACR 4856. STORMY WEATHER.

42-31622 Del Denver 29/11/43; Kearney 23/12/43; Oklahoma City 30/12/43; Scott 8/1/44; Memphis 9/1/44; Morrison 10/1/44; ass 414BS/97BG Amendola 22/1/44; mid air coll w/42-30405 on Steyr mission 24/3/44; takes tail of 405, but returns base; rep, but re-ass cargo ship from 9/10/44; sal 30/5/45.

42-31623 Del Denver 29/11/43; Gt Falls 3/12/43; Hobbs 19/12/43; 3021 BU Las Vegas 28/9/44; 3022 BU Indian Springs 9/10/44; 3021 BU Las Vegas 15/3/45; 2126 BU Laredo 28/3/45; RFC Walnut Ridge 5/1/46.

42-31624 Del Cheyenne 28/11/43; Gt Falls 1/12/43; Kearney 19/12/43; Romulus 31/12/43; Presque Is 5/1/44; ass 338BS/96BG [BX-X] Snetterton 12/1/44; MIA Brunswick 23/3/44 w/Taylor; flak, cr Schayk, Hol; 10POW; MACR 3427. JOKER.

42-31625 Del Denver 28/11/43; Paine Fd 2/12/43; Geiger 5/12/43; Denver 10/12/43; Cheyenne 16/12/43; Savannah 20/12/43; ass 419BS/301BG Lucera 13/2/44; MIA Wiener Neudorf 26/7/44 w/Lilligren; e/a, cr Rattern, Aus; 6KIA 4POW; MACR 7135.

42-31626 Del Denver 29/11/43; Paine 30/11/43; Geiger 2/12/43; Chanute 18/12/43; 3036 BU Yuma 6/7/44; 4136 BU Tinker 7/7/44; 3036 BU Yuma 9/7/44; 3021 BU Las Vegas 27/8/44; 3022 BU Indian Springs 30/8/44; WO 28/11/44; Recl Comp 16/12/44.

42-31627 Del Cheyenne 27/11/43; Gt Falls 1/12/43; Cheyenne 3/12/43; Wendover 11/12/43; ass 748BS/457BG Glatton 26/1/44; MIA Berlin 6/3/44 w/Graves; mid air coll w/42-31595, cr Truenbrietzen, Ger; 9KIA 1POW; MACR 3198.

42-31628 Del Cheyenne 30/11/43; Paine 2/12/43; Portland 5/12/43; Gowen 6/12/43; Gt Falls 7/12/43; Cheyenne 10/12/43; Atlanta 19/12/43; Savannah 20/12/43; ass 353BS/301BG Lucera 22/1/44; MIA {9m} Regensburg 25/2/44 w/Pierce; e/a, cr Bodenkirchen, Ger; 2KIA 6POW; MACR 2724. MISS CARRIAGE.

42-31629 Del Cheyenne 30/11/43; Wendover

12/12/43; Presque Is 19/1/44; ass 749BS/457BG Glatton 26/1/44; MIA Warnemünde 9/4/44 w/Parks; e/a, cr Gdynia, Pol; 7KIA 3POW; MACR 3664.

42-31630 Del Cheyenne 30/11/43; Wendover 8/12/43; ass 751BS/457BG Glatton 29/1/44; b/d Nuremberg, c/l Grafton Underwood 20/2/45; sal. PAKAWALUP.

42-31631 Del Denver 30/11/43; Gt Falls 7/12/43; Kearney 23/12/43; ass 818BS/483BG Tortorella 6/1/44; Sterparone 22/4/44; b/d Budapest 22/6/44 w/Owens; 5 baled, RTD; rest return to base; retUS Hunter 26/6/45; 4168 BU Sth Plains 27/6/45; RFC Kingman 30/11/45.

42-31632 Del Denver 14/12/43; Gt Falls 27/12/43; Denver 9/1/44; Kearney 20/1/44; ass 335BS/95BG [OE-Z] Podington 21/2/44; MIA Oberpfaffenhofen w/Wilson; mech fault, f/l Dubendorf, Switz; 10INT; MACR 4264.

42-31633 Del Cheyenne 30/11/43; Wendover 9/12/43; ass 749BS/457BG Glatton 29/1/44; MIA Hamm 25/11/44; f/l France; sal 18/3/45.

42-31634 Del Cheyenne 1/12/43; Portland 3/12/43; Boise 5/12/43; Kearney 16/12/43; Ft Wayne 25/12/43; Grenier 27/12/43; Presque Is 3/1/44; ass 322BS/91BG [LG-O] Bassingbourn 23/1/44; MIA {50m} Halle 16/8/44 w/Sherrill; e/a, exploded and cr Kichenberg, Ger; 5KIA 4POW; MACR 8184. TEXAS CHUBBY - THE J'VILLE JOLTER.

42-31635 Del Cheyenne 30/11/43; Wendover 8/12/43; Grenier 19/1/44; ass 457BG Glatton 26/1/44; tran 327BS/92BG [UX-Y] Podington 11/3/44; MIA Berlin 24/5/44 w/Reuther; e/a, cr Schmabek, Ger?; 10POW; MACR 5159.

42-31636 Del Cheyenne 30/11/43; Wendover 11/12/43; ass 457BG Glatton 26/1/44; tran 323NS/91BG [OR-N] Bassingbourn 12/3/44; {139m} RetUS 121 BU Bradley 26/5/45; 4168 BU Sth Plains 11/6/45; RFC Kingman 30/11/45, but scrapped until 1963. (first heavy bomber attacked by German jet a/c.) OUTHOUSE MOUSE.

42-31637 Del Cheyenne 30/11/43; Paine 2/12/43; Kearney 11/12/43; Romulus 18/12/43; Presque Is 19/12/43; ass 333BS/94BG Rougham 27/12/43; MIA Berlin 22/3/44 w/Carlson; flak, cr Grunewald, Ger; MACR 3535. ATHENIAN ADVENTURER.

42-31638 Del Cheyenne 30/11/43; Paine 4/12/43; Kearney 11/12/43; Romulus 20/12/43; Presque Is 21/12/43; ass 548BS/385BG Gt Ashfield 30/12/43; MIA Magdeburg 12/4/44 w/Newman; e/a, cr Ruppershutten, Ger; 4KIA 5POW. MACR 8907. BIG GAS BIRD.

42-31639 Del Denver 30/11/43; Paine 2/12/43; Gt Falls 5/12/43; Kearney 23/12/43; Atlanta 30/12/43; Morrison 6/1/44; ass 419BS/301BG Cerignola 16/1/44; Lucera 1/2/44; MIA {21m} Steyr, Aus. 2/4/44 w/Zuidema; e/a, cr Grossening, Aus; 3KIA 7POW. MACR 3707.

42-31640 Del Denver 30/11/43; Paine 2/12/43; Kearney 23/12/43; Dallas 3/1/44; Morrison 5/1/44; ass 96BS/2BG Amendola 7/1/44; MIA {11m} Steyr 24/2/44 w/McCord; e/a and flak, cr Wegesheid, Aus; 4 chutes seen; MACR 2686.

42-31641 Del Denver 1/12/43; Paine 4/12/43; Billings 7/12/43; Denver 10/12/43; Tulsa 20/1/44; Sebring 21/1/44; 3502 BU Chanute 17/11/44; 2137 BU Hendricks 18/11/44; 119 BU Morris 12/2/45; 2137 BU Hendricks 24/2/45; RFC Kingman 9/11/45.

42-31642 Del Denver 1/12/43; Paine 4/12/43; Kearney 26/12/43; Memphis 1/1/44; Morrison 3/1/44; ass 347BS/99BG Tortorella 10/1/44; 2WIA and 2MIA after baling out 17/2/44 en route Lake Albano, It, w/Norton; MIA Regensburg 25/2/44 w/Laino; cr Walchsee, Aus; MACR 2704.

42-31643 Del Denver 1/12/43; Paine 4/12/43; Denver 5/12/43; Kearney 23/12/43; Prestwick 15/1/44; ass 527BS/379BG [FO-X] Kimbolton 24/1/44; MIA Brunswick 30/1/44 w/Winter; e/a, cr Bergen Aan See, Hol; 10KIA; MACR 2877.

42-31644 Del Denver 1/12/43; Kearney 28/12/43; Memphis 4/1/44; Jacksonville 5/1/44; Morrison 6/1/44; Casablanca 11/1/44; ass 414BS/97BG Amendola 16/1/44; MIA Udine 18/3/44 w/Adams; e/a, cr Fiume, It; MACR 3290. (part 463BG crew).

42-31645 Del Denver 1/12/43; Paine 2/12/43; Gowen 6/12/43; Boise 9/12/43; Denver 10/12/43; Kearney 23/12/43; Memphis 1/1/44; Morrison 4/1/44; ass 341BS/97BG Amendola 16/1/44; MIA Pardubice, Czech. 24/8/44 w/Boone; flak, cr Marburg; MACR 7981. BABE.

42-31646 Del Denver 1/12/43; Gt Falls 5/12/43; Denver 6/12/43; Roswell 11/12/43; slated Soxo; tran 3030 BU Roswell 2/6/44; 3021 BU Las Vegas 24/9/44; 3022 BU Indian Springs 5/10/44; 3021 BU Las Vegas 23/3/45; 2126 BU Laredo 28/3/45; RFC Walnut Ridge 10/1/46.

42-31647 Del Denver 1/12/43; Kansas City 18/12/43; Lockburb 20/12/43; slated Soxo; tran 2114 BU Lockburn 2/9/44; 2137 BU Hendricks 18/8/45; RFC Kingman 16/12/45.

42-31648 Del Cheyenne 1/12/43; Gt Falls 5/12/43; Cheyenne 7/12/43; Kearney 19/12/43; Grenier 31/12/43; Presque Is 3/1/44; ass 526BS/379BG [LF-H] Kimbolton 17/2/44; MIA Noball Site 16/6/44 w/McHugh; flak, cr Eidelstedt (?), Fr; 2EVD 2KIA 5POW; MACR 5988.

42-31649 Del Cheyenne 1/12/43; Kearney 17/12/43; Grenier 26/1/43; ass 569BS/390BG Framlingham 2/2/44 OLD SOLDIER; b/d Karlsruhe, sal 27/5/44. SHATZI III.

42-31650 Del Cheyenne 1/12/43; Gowen 5/12/43; Salt Lake 6/12/43; Rock Springs 7/12/43; Laramie 9/12/43; Cheyenne 10/12/43; Kearney 17/12/43; Presque Is 2/1/44; ass 410BS/94BG [GL-Z] Rougham 6/1/44; MIA Brandeburg 18/4/44 w/McMeekin; e/a, cr Loboefsund, Ger; 8KIA 2POW; MACR 4153. IMPATIENT VIRGIN.

42-31651 Del Cheyenne 1/12/43; Gowen 5/12/43; Salt Lake 6/12/43; Rock Springs 7/12/43; Laramie 9/12/43; Cheyenne 10/12/43; Kearney 17/12/43; Romulus 6/1/44; Presque Is 9/1/44; ass 571BS/390BG [FC-G] Framlingham 18/1/44; MIA Koenigsburg 28/5/44 w/Strate; e/a, cr Magdeburg, Ger; 7KIA 3POW; MACR 5259. DECATUR DEB.

42-31652 Del Cheyenne 1/12/43; Gowen 6/12/43; Rocks Springs 9/12/43; Cheyenne 10/12/43; Atlanta 20/12/43; Savannah 22/12/43; ass 353BS/301BG Cerignola 13/1/44; Lucera 1/2/44; MIA Wiener Neudorf 26/7/44 w/Rinderknecht; e/a, cr Guens, Aus; 3KIA 6POW; MACR 7136.

42-31653 Del Cheyenne 2/12/43; Helena 4/12/43; Gt Falls 5/12/43; Cheyenne 6/12/43; Kearney 12/12/43; New Castle 17/12/43; Presque Is 19/12/43; ass 410BS/94BG [GL-V] Rougham 26/12/43 ERIE FERRY; MIA Bohlen 11/9/44 w/Green; mid air coll w/42-97153, cr Gelnhausen, Ger; 2KIA 7POW; MACR 8840. KAC'S FLAK SHAK.

42-31654 Del Cheyenne 1/12/43; Kearney 16/12/43; W/O 18/12/43.

42-31655 Del Cheyenne 1/12/43; Gowen 5/12/43; Rock Springs 7/12/43; Laramie 9/12/43; Cheyenne 10/12/43; Savannah 17/12/43; ass 429BS/2BG Amendola 20/1/44; MIA {15m} Fredrichshafen 3/8/44 w/Heintz; mech failure, f/l Dubendorf, Switz; 10INT; MACR 7205. WANITA.

42-31656 Del Cheyenne 20/12/43; Topeka 3/1/44; Oklahoma City 5/1/44; Kearney 17/1/43; Gr Island 22/1/44; Grenier 26/1/44; ass 751BS/457BG Glatton 3/2/44; 749BS; MIA Berlin 21/6/44 w/Wilson; flak, cr Nauen, Ger; 5KIA 5POW; MACR 6004.

42-31657 Del Cheyenne 6/12/43; Kearney 12/12/43; Romulus 17/12/43; Presque Is 19/12/43; ass 339BS/96BG [QJ-S] Snetterton 26/12/43; MIA Saarbrücken 23/5/44 w/DeBrades; flak, ditched Channel; 10RTD. WILDFIRE II.

42-31658 Del Cheyenne 6/12/43; Kearney 12/12/43; Romulus 17/12/43; Presque Is 19/12/43; ass 334BS/95BG [BG-G] Horham 26/12/43; MIA Brunswick 10/2/44 w/Kelly; cr Quackenbrück, Ger; 4KIA 6POW; MACR 2546.

42-31659 Del Denver 2/12/43; Felts Fd 4/12/43; Denver 8/12/43; Love Fd 20/12/43; Sebring 21/12/43; 2137 BU Hendricks 18/11/44; RFC Kingman 29/10/45.

42-31660 Del Denver 3/12/43; Gt Falls 5/12/43; Cheyenne 16/12/43; Jackson 20/12/43; Savannah 21/12/43; Homestead 3/3/44; ass 353BS/301BG Lucera 4/3/44; MIA {4m} Verona 22/3/44 w/Lawrence; exloded over target, cr Verona, It; 4KIA 6POW; MACR 3285.

42-31661 Del Denver 2/12/43; Roswell 18/12/43; 3030 BU Roswell 2/6/44; 3010 BU Williams 20/1/45; 3020 BU La Junta 19/4/45; 2114 BU Lockburn 25/6/45; 2137 BU Hendricks 18/8/45; RFC Kingman 1/11/45.

42-31662 Del Denver 2/12/43; Kearney 17/12/43; Romulus 6/1/44; Kearney 7/1/44; Memphis 9/1/44; Presque Is 10/1/44; ass 612BS/401BG [SC-B] Deenethorpe 31/1/44; {134m} c/l Polebrook 22/4/44, sal 1 SAD Troston. FANCY NANCY IV.

42-31663 Del Denver 3/12/43; Boise 5/12/43; Denver 6/12/43; Kearney 17/12/43; Romulus 2/1/44; Grenier 8/1/44; Presque Is 10/1/44; ass 526BS/379BG [LF-G] Kimbolton 2/2/44; MIS Merseburg 8/11/44 w/Duffy; flak, cr Merseburg; 1KIA 8POW; MACR 10354. TAG0-A-LONG.

42-31664 Del Denver 2/12/43; Felts Fd 4/12/43; Gt Falls 5/12/43; Denver 17/12/43; Savannah 22/12/43; ass 32BS/301BG Lucera 5/2/44; MIA {5m} Regensburg 25/2/44 w/Paxton; e/a, cr Bodenkirchen, Ger; 7KIA 3POW; MACR 2593.

42-31665 Del Denver 6/12/43; Lockburn 16/12/43; Lincoln 17/12/43; Cleveland 18/12/43; 3036 BU Yuma 28/6/44; 3018 BU Kingman 24/8/44; 3017 BU Hobbs 11/6/45; RFC Walnut Ridge 5/1/46.

42-31666 Del Denver 2/12/43; Kearney 23/12/43; Memphis 1/1/44; New Castle 6/1/44; Morrison 10/1/44; ass 96BS/2BG Amendola 12/1/44; MIA {10m} Steyr, Aus. 24/2/44 w/Thalken; e/a, ditched Med Sea; MACR 2579.

42-31667 Del Denver 3/12/43; Gt Falls 5/12/43; Denver 6/12/43; Houston 22/12/43; Jackson 28/12/43; Savannah 29/12/43; ass 341BS/97BG Amendola 13/1/44; MIA Toulon, Fr. 4/2/44 w/Myer; mid air coll w/FW190, exploded; MACR 2064.

42-31668 Del Denver 3/12/43; Robins 19/12/43; Sebring 20/12/43; 2114 BU Lockburn 2/9/44; 120 BU Richmond 11/12/44; 2114 BU Lockburn 17/1/45; 2137 BU Hendricks 24/9/45; RFC Walnut Ridge 8/1/46.

42-31669 Del Cheyenne 6/12/43; Gt Falls 8/12/43; Kearney 22/12/43; Romulus 8/1/44; Presque Is 10/1/44; ass 358BS/303BG [VK-J] Molesworth 15/2/44; MIA Erding 24/4/44 w/Hoffman; flak, f/l Dubendorf, Switz; 10INT; MACR 4270. Sal 12/10/45. SHOO SHOO 'BABY'.

42-31670 Del Cheyenne 3/12/43; Gowen 5/12/43; Kearney 16/12/43; Westover 21/12/43; Presque Is 23/12/43; ass 367BS/306BG Thurleigh 14/1/44; MIA

Oschersleben 22/2/44 w/Rector; e/a, cr Nieder Rieferath, Ger; 4KIA 6POW; MACR 2654.
42-31671 Del Cheyenne 6/12/43; Hill Fd 9/12/43; Atlanta 19/12/43; Savannah 20/12/43; ass 353BS/301BG Cerignola 11/1/44; Lucera 1/2/44; MIA {12m} Steyr 24/2/44 w/LaForge; e/a, cr Lambach, Aus; 9POW; MACR 2634.
42-31672 Del Cheyenne 6/12/43; Kearney 16/12/43; Presque Is 2/1/44; ass 401BS/91BG Bassingbourn 23/1/44; MIA {6m} Stuttgart 20/3/44 w/Turk; flak and e/a, cr Bacqueville, Fr; 1KIA 1EVD 8POW; MACR 3411. BUCKEYE BOOMERANG II.
42-31673 Del Cheyenne 6/12/43; Kearney 17/12/43; harrisburg 8/1/44; New Castle 9/1/43; Presque Is 11/1/44; Prestwick 16/1/44; ass 96BG Snetterton 16/1/44; tran 322BS/91BG [LG-B] Bassingbourn 27/1/44; MIA {76M} Halle 16/8/44 w/Figier; e/a, cr Deiderode, Ger; 4KIA 5POW; MACR 8183. (one of six a/c lost in about 30 secs). LASSIE COME HOME.
42-31674 Del Cheyenne 6/12/43; Kearney 8/1/44; Detroit 26/1/44; Grenier 30/1/44; ass 8AF 7/2/44; 652BS/25BG; sal n/b/d 29/5/45.
42-31675 Del Cheyenne 6/12/43; Kearney 12/12/43; Romulus 17/12/43; Grenier 19/12/43; Presque Is 22/12/43; ass 412BS/95BG [QW-W] Horham 26/12/43; MIA Ludwigshafen 27/9/44; f/l France, sal 29/11/44. BERLIN BESSIE.
42-31676 Del Denver 6/12/43; Lincoln 17/12/43; Chanute 18/12/43; 2112 BU Chanute 7/7/44; 3036 BU Yuma 9/7/44; 3017 BU Hobbs 4/6/45; RFC Walnut Ridge 28/12/45.
42-31677 Del Cheyenne 6/12/43; New Castle 7/1/44; Presque Is 8/1/44; RAF Valley 16/1/44; ass 548BS/385BG Gt Ashfield 17/1/44; sal n/b/d 14/6/45. THOROBRED.
42-31678 Del Cheyenne 6/12/43; Kearney 19/12/43; Presque Is 9/1/44; RAF Nutts Corner 18/1/44; ass 324BS/91BG [DF-L] Bassingbourn 27/1/44; 401BS [LL-L]; {100+m} RetUS 121 BU Bradley 11/6/45; Romulus 12/6/45; Topeka 13/6/45; 4168 BU Sth Plains 12/9/45; RFC Kingman 7/12/45. LITTLE PATCHES.
42-31679 Del Cheyenne 6/12/43; Maxwell 19/12/43; Savannah 20/12/43; ass 49BS/2BG Amendola 11/1/44; MIA Regensburg 25/2/44 w/Storm; mid air coll w/42-38070, cr Landshut, Ger; five chutes seen. MACR 2615.
42-31680 Del Denver 6/12/43; Kearney 10/12/43; Presque Is 26/1/44; ass 407BS/92BG Podington 7/2/44; MIA Berlin 6/3/44 w/Cooper; e/a, cr Plantlunne, Ger; 1KIA 9POW; MACR 2904.
42-31681 Del Denver 6/12/43; Kearney 17/12/43; New Castle 8/1/44; Presque Is 9/1/44; ass 412BS/95BG [QW-G] Horham 24/1/44; MIA Berlin 14/6/44 w/Wells; cr Nth Sea off Felixstowe, UK; 10KIA; MACR 5794.
42-31682 Del Denver 6/12/43; Atlanta 26/12/43; Savannah 27/12/43; ass 96BS/2BG Amendola 1/2/44; {59m} c/t/o for Yugo targets 6/12/44 w/Sachrison; burnt out, 10KIA. JOCKO.
42-31683 Del Denver 6/12/43; Casper 13/12/43; Cheyenne 31/12/43; Houston 21/1/44; Lakeland 6/1/44; Morrison 25/2/44; ass 346BS/99BG Tortorella 26/2/44; {16m} tran 20BS/2BG Amendola 28/3/44; MIA {1m} Sofia 30/3/44 w/Rigney; mid air coll w/42-31851, cr Trun, Bul; MACR 3364.
42-31684 Del Denver 6/12/43; Kearney 24/12/43; Memphis 2/1/44; Drew Fd 4/1/44; Morrison 8/1/44; ass 774BS/463BG Celone 9/3/44; MIA Bleckhammer 7/7/44 w/Doran; e/a, cr Vicany, Ger; MACR 6864. THE JOKER.
42-31685 Del Denver 8/12/43; Kingman 21/12/43; Denver 6/1/44; Jackson 11/1/44; Atlanta 12/1/44; Lakeland 13/1/44; ass 775BS/463BG Celone 9/3/44; MIA Wiener Neustadt 10/5/44 w/Dwyer; flak, cr Lichtenwearth; MACR 4723. PETE'S PLAYHOUSE.
42-31686 Del Denver 6/12/43; Hobbs 18/12/43; 3017 BU Hobbs 6/7/44; 30128 BU Kingman 18/9/44; 3030 BU Roswell 8/6/45; 4210 BU Lambert 29/8/45; 3030 BU Roswell 30/8/45; RFC Walnut Ridge 8/1/46.
42-31687 Del Denver 6/12/43; Kearney 17/12/43; New Castle 8/1/44; Presque Is 10/1/44; Prestwick 18/1/44; ass 407BS/92BG [PY-M] Podington 28/1/44; MIA Merseburg 11/9/44 w/Andrew; e/a, cr Froeunstedt, Ger; 4KIA 5POW; MACR 8883. WABBITT.
42-31688 Del Denver 6/12/43; Roswell 17/12/43; W/O 24/12/43.
42-31689 Del Cheyenne 6/12/43; McChord 8/12/43; Gt Falls 10/12/43; Cheyenne 13/12/43; Kingman 27/12/43; 3018 BU Kingman 23/3/45; 3017 BU Hobbs 27/6/45; RFC Walnut Ridge 5/1/46.
42-31690 Del Cheyenne 8/12/43; Kearney 22/12/43; Prestwick 16/1/44; ass 368BS/306BG [BO-W] Thurleigh 18/1/44; MIA Ruhrland 12/9/44 w/Maj Farwell; flak, cr Berlin; 1KIA 9POW; MACR 8828/3984. BELLE OF THE BRAWL.
42-31691 Del Cheyenne 6/12/43; Kearney 16/12/43; Gt Falls 1/1/44; Presque Is 3/1/44; ass 571BS/390BG [FC-O] Framlingham 16/1/44; MIA Augsburg 13/4/44 w/Cooper; flak, cr Oberglatt, Ger; MACR 3948. LASSIE.
42-31692 Del Cheyenne 6/12/43; Kearney 17/12/43; Gt Falls 1/1/44; Presque Is 3/1/44; ass 526BS/379BG Kimbolton 24/1/44; MIA Brunswick 30/1/44 w/Upson; e/a, cr Hjolsen, Ger/Den?; 8KIA 2POW; MACR 2878.
42-31693 Del Cheyenne 6/12/43; Atlanta 19/12/43; Savannah 20/12/43; ass 419BS/301BG Cerignola 12/1/44; Lucera 2/1/44; {16m} cr Foggia on practice flight 8/5/44 w/Gilbert; 1KIA other four survive.
42-31694 Del Cheyenne 6/12/43; Kearney 17/12/43; Gt Falls 1/1/44; Presque Is 3/1/44; ass 511BS/351BG [DS-V] Polebrook 30/1/44; c/l RAF Rochford, UK. 12/2/44; sal n/b/d 2 SAD Lt Staughton 13/2/44.
42-31695 Del Cheyenne 6/12/43; Kearney 17/12/43; New Castle 31/12/43; Presque Is 2/1/44; ass 369BS/306BG [WW-D] Thurleigh 29/1/44; MIA Oschersleben 22/2/44 w/Quaintance; e/a, cr Kirchen, Ger?; 9KIA 1POW; MACR 2652.
42-31696 Del Cheyenne 6/12/43; Kearney 17/12/43; New Castle 30/12/43; Presque Is 7/1/44; ass 535BS/381BG Ridgewell 20/2/44; MIA {1m} Oschersleben 22/2/44 w/Hustedt; e/a, cr Detmold, Ger; 2KIA 8POW; MACR 2932.
42-31697 Del Cheyenne 6/12/43; Gt Falls 8/12/43; Cheyenne 11/12/43; Kearney 21/12/43; Kansas City 31/12/43; Morrison 3/1/44; Casablanca 8/1/44; ass 353BS/301BG Cerignola 9/1/44; Lucera 1/2/44; MIA Bleckhammer 7/8/44 w/Pryde; flak, cr Brun, Aus; 9POW. MACR 7468.
42-31698 Del Denver 7/12/43; Gt Falls 8/12/43; Cheyenne 28/12/43; Gr Island 28/12/43; ass 533BS/381BG [VP-N] Ridgewell 23/2/44; MIA {30+m} Berlin 24/5/44 w/Wainwright; mid air coll w/a/c, cr Melchow, Ger; 7KIA 2POW; MACR 5319.
42-31699 Del Denver 6/12/43; Sebring 26/12/43; 2118 BU Laredo 24/8/44; 2126 BU Laredo 1/2/45; RFC Walnut Ridge 4/1/46.
42-31700 Del Denver 7/12/43; Kearney 28/12/43; RAF Nutts Corner 15/1/44; ass 368BS/306BG Thurleigh 29/1/44; b/d Pas de Calais, c/l base 26/3/44; sal MU 27/3/44.
42-31701 Del Denver 7/12/43; Savannah 21/12/43; ass 32/301BG Cerignola 15/1/44; Lucera 1/2/44; MIA {54m} Vienna 26/6/44 w/Gourley; flak, cr Ugarn, Aus; 10POW. MACR 6353.
42-31702 Del Denver 9/12/43; Keraney 28/12/43; ass 508BS/351BG [YB-A] Polebrook 30/1/44; MIA Delitzsch, Ger. 16/8/44 w/Cartwright; flak, cr Burgwerben, Ger; 3KIA 6POW; MACR 7902.
42-31703 Del Denver 7/12/43; Kearney 22/12/43; New Castle 30/12/43; Morrison 1/1/44; ass 353BS/301BG Cerignola 14/1/44; Lucera 1/2/44; MIA {18m} Regensburg 25/2/44 w/Rose; e/a, cr Kranj; 9POW; MACR 2721.
42-31704 Del Denver 11/12/43; Kearney 6/1/44; ass 331BS/94BG [QE-P] Rougham 24/1/44; MIA Zwickau 12/5/44 w/Walker; e/a, cr Bad Orb, Ger; 2KIA 8POW; MACR 4826.
42-31705 Del Denver 9/12/43; Phoenix 29/12/43; Kingman 30/12/43; W/O 15/2/44.
42-31706 Del Denver 7/12/43; Cheyenne 19/12/43; Kearney 22/12/43; ass 749BS/457BG Glatton 14/2/44; tran 1 SAD Burtonwood 24/3/45 modified for airborne lifeboat; retUS 121 BU Bradley 30/6/45; Jackson 1/7/45; 4168 BU Sth Plains 4/7/45; RFC Kingman 9/11/45. SLOW BUT SURE.
42-31707 Del Denver 8/12/43; Kearney 24/12/43; Long Beach 2/1/44; Presque Is 5/1/44; Prestwick 15/1/44; ass 561BS/388BG Knettishall 17/1/44; MIA Kiel 22/5/44 w/Glantz; flak, cr Hollstein, Ger; 10POW. MACR 4955. JAKE'S JERKS.
42-31708 Del Cheyenne 9/12/43; Kearney 20/12/43; Prestwick 15/1/44; ass 351BS/100BG [EP-N/R] Thorpe Abbotts 17/1/44; retUS 121 BU Bradley 5/7/45; Love Fd 6/7/45; 4168 BU Sth Plains 7/7/45; RFC Kingman 6/12/45. SKIPPER II.
42-31709 Del Denver 9/12/43; Maxwell 19/12/43; Savannah 20/12/43; ass 341BS/97BG Amendola 21/1/44; MIA Pilsen 23/10/44 w/Cooning; flak, cr Doltech, Czech; MACR 9513.
42-31710 Del Denver 9/12/43; Kearney 24/12/43; Romulus 7/1/44; Presque Is 9/1/44; ass 349BS/100BG [XR-P/F] Thorpe Abbotts 20/1/44; MIA La Glacerie 8/5/44 w/Riggle; e/a, cr Holingen, Fr?; 2KIA 8POW; MACR 4578. THE SAVAGE.
42-31711 Del Cheyenne 9/12/43; Kearney 22/12/43; Prestwick 16/1/44; ass 508BS/351BG [YB-F] Polebrook 30/1/44; {87m} 1 BAD Burtonwood 28/5/44; retUS 121 BU Bradley 19/6/44; 4168 BU Sth Plains 21/6/44; RFC Kingman 6/12/45.
42-31712 Del Cheyenne 9/12/43; Kingman 25/12/43; Dyersburg 27/3/44; WO 30/5/44.
42-31713 Del Cheyenne 10/12/43; Missoula 13/12/43; Cheyenne 15/12/43; Gr Island 27/12/43; Detroit 25/1/44; Grenier 26/1/44; ass 327BS/92BG [UX-T] Podington 11/2/44; flak, b/d Merseburg 24/8/44, f/l RAF Woodbridge; sal 2 SAD Lt Staughton 25/8/44. SNAKE HIPS.
42-31714 Del Cheyenne 9/12/43; Kearney 24/12/43; ass 511BS/351BG [DS-R] Polebrook 29/1/44; 510BS [TU-R]; {60m} ass war weary 21/2/45; caught fire, sal 18/5/45. SKY BALL.
42-31715 Del Cheyenne 9/12/43; Kearney 16/1/44; RAF Nutts Corner 15/1/44; ass 306BG 29/1/44, but c/t/o Drem, UK, 4/2/44; sal n/b/d. (Roskovitch killed, first EM to complete tour of 25 missions.)
42-31716 Del Cheyenne 10/12/43; Gt Falls 25/12/43; Cheyenne 10/1/44; Kearney 18/1/44; Grenier Fd 26/1/44; ass 413BS/96BG [MZ-P] Snetterton 3/2/44; MIA Berlin 8/3/44 w/Swendenman; e/a, cr Burg, Ger; 2KIA 8POW; MACR 3428.
42-31717 Del Cheyenne 9/12/43; Kearney 24/12/43; Prestwick 15/1/44; ass 568BS/390BG [BI-A]

Framlingham 17/1/44; MIA Berlin 8/3/44 w/Quillin; e/a, cr Koerbelitz, Ger; 1KIA 9POW; MACR 2988. HELLS BELLS.

42-31718 Del Denver 10/12/43; Kearney 24/12/43; ass 337BS/96BG [AW-T] Snetterton 9/1/44; MIA Brux 12/5/44 w/Musser; e/a, cr Hartmannshein, Ger; 2KIA 8POW; MACR 4857.

42-31719 Del Denver 11/12/43; Kearney 24/12/43; ass 711BS/447BG Rattlesden 16/1/44; c/l base n/b/d 14/4/44; sal. BLUE HEN'S CHICKS.

42-31720 Del Denver 10/12/43; Kearney 24/12/43; Prestwick 15/1/44; ass 524BS/379BG [WA-H/M] Kimbolton 27/1/44; MIA Ludwigshafen 8/9/44 w/Ellingson; flak, cr Mannheim, Ger; 4KIA 5POW; MACR 8844. THE BLUE BLAZING BLIZZARD.

42-31721 Del Denver 10/12/43; Kearney 24/12/43; ass 510BS/351BG [TU-S] Polebrook 29/1/44; MIA {35m} Posen 28/5/44 w/McClelland; e/a, cr Hanau, Ger; 1KIA 9POW; MACR 5334. BLACK MAGIC.

42-31722 Del Denver 10/12/43; Colorado Springs 22/12/43; Kingman 23/12/43; 3018 BU Kingman 22/4/44; 3017 BU Hobbs 24/6/45; RFC Walnut Ridge 2/1/46.

42-31723 Del Denver 12/12/43; Kearney 31/12/43; ass 349BS/100BG [XR-R] Thorpe Abbotts 15/2/44; MIA Merseburg 29/7/44 w/Phelps; e/a, cr Bad Kosen, Ger; 8KIA 1POW; MACR 7810. SPARKY.

42-31724 Del Denver 10/12/43; Kearney 29/12/43; Oklahoma City 11/1/44; Kearney 16/1/44; ass 708BS/447BG Rattlesden 18/1/44; MIA Hamm 22/4/44 w/Gilleran; flak, cr Werl, Ger; 10POW; MACR 4174.

42-31725 Del Denver 10/12/43; Kearney 23/12/43; Romulus 7/1/43; Presque Is 9/1/44; ass 509BS/351BG [RQ-L] Polebrook 31/1/44 LIL' GINNY; MIA Halberstadt 30/5/44 w/Hicks; e/a. cr Tweelbacke, Ger?; 1KIA 9POW; MACR 5236. CASA DE EMBRIAGOS.

42-31726 Del Denver 12/12/43; Kearney 30/12/43; Prestwick 15/1/44; ass 367BS/306BG [GY-O] Thurleigh 10/2/44; MIA German oil ints 13/9/44 w/Nallier; flak, c Ammendorf, Ger; 3KIA 6POW; MACR 8829. DURATION-PLUS.

42-31727 Del Denver 11/12/43; Kingman 1/1/44; 3018 BU Kingman 23/3/45; 3017 BU Hobbs 24/6/45; RFC Walnut Ridge 4/1/46.

42-31728 Del Denver 11/12/43; Kearney 30/12/43; RAF Nutts Corner 14/1/44; ass 570BS/390BG [DI-B] Framlingham 17/1/44; retUS 121 BU Bradley 3/7/45; 4168 BU Sth Plains 5/7/45; RFC Kingman 9/12/45. SWEETHEART OF PAS DE CALAIS.

42-31729 Del Cheyenne 11/12/43; Salt Lake City 26/12/43; Kingman 27/12/43; 3018 BU Kingman 23/3/45; 3017 BU Hobbs 22/9/45; RFC Walnut Ridge 18/1/46.

42-31730 Del Cheyenne 10/12/43; Kearney 27/12/43; RAF Nutts Corner 15/1/44; ass 615BS/401BG [IY-A/C/B] Deenethorpe 31/1/44; 613BS [IN-O]; retUS 121 BU Bradley 7/6/45; 4168 BU Sth Plains 9/6/45; 4100 BU Patterson 9/10/45; 4100 BU Rome Recl Comp 29/1/46. MORNING STAR.

42-31731 Del Cheyenne 11/12/43; Gr Island 24/12/43; Romulus 24/1/44; Grenier 26/1/44; Presque Is 30/1/44; ass 349BS/100BG [XR-M] Thorpe Abbotts 4/2/44; MIA Berlin 6/3/44 w/Amiero; e/a, cr Quackenbrück, Ger; 9KIA 1POW; MACR 3019.

42-31732 Del Cheyenne 11/12/43; Kearney 26/12/43; Prestwick 15/1/44; ass 568BS/390BG [BI-D] Framlingham 17/1/44; MIA Pas de Calais w/Crouch; flak, cr Maison le Fitte, Fr; 7KIA 3POW; MACR 5231. PAPER DOLL.

42-31733 Del Cheyenne 11/12/43; Independence 26/12/43; Bowman Fd 30/12/43; Orlando 1/1/44; 330 BU Dyersburg 1/3/45; RFC Walnut Ridge 14/12/45.

42-31734 Del Cheyenne 11/12/43; Gr Island 29/12/43; Detroit 25/1/44; Grenier 2/2/44; Presque Is 4/2/44; ass 412BS/95BG [QW-H] Horham 15/2/44; MIA Berlin 4/3/44 w/Worthy; cr Ramstadt, Ger; 10POW; MACR 2796.

42-31735 Del Cheyenne 11/12/43; Kearney 30/12/43; RAF Nutts Corner 15/1/44; ass 351BS/100BG [EP-B] Thorpe Abbotts 17/1/44; MIA Berlin 6/3/44 w/Brannan; e/a, cr Haustette, Ger?; 2KIA 8POW; MACR 3020. LUCKY LEE.

42-31736 Del Cheyenne 11/12/43; Gr Island 24/12/43; Detroit 25/1/44; Presque Is 30/1/44; ass 652BS/25BG Watton 5/2/44; cr t/o 8/9/44. 5 KIA.

42-31737 Del Cheyenne 11/12/43; Gr Island 24/12/43; Romulus 25/1/44; Presque Is 5/2/44; ass 423BS/306BG [RD-U] Thurleigh 28/2/44; MIA Peenemünde 18/7/44 w/Parks; flak, f/l Bulltofta, Swed; 9INT; MACR 7416.

42-31738 Del Cheyenne 11/12/43; Kansas City 28/1/44; Orlando 31/12/43; 901 BU Pinecastle 2/6/44; 441 BU Glendale 24/6/44; 901 BU Pinecastle 29/6/44; 903 BU Pinecastle 10/9/44; 902 BU Orlando 20/12/44; 903 BU Pinecastle 12/6/45; 621 BU Pinecastle 6/9/45; 6138 BU Phillips 19/6/46.

42-31739 Del Denver 11/12/43; Gr Island 27/12/43; Presque Is 29/1/44; ass 358BS/303BG [VK-P] Molesworth 15/2/44; MIA Koblenz 11/10/44 w/Price; flak, cr Wesseling, Ger; 9POW; MACR 9563. PUGNACIOUS PETER.

42-31740 Del Denver 11/12/43; Kearney 27/12/43; Oklahoma City 12/1/44; Kearney 16/1/44; ass 546BS/384BG [BK-T] Grafton Underwood 1/3/44; MIA Marienburg 9/4/44 w/Schock; flak, cr Kiel; 2EVD 1KIA 7POW; MACR 3653.

42-31741 Del Denver 11/12/43; Kearney 30/12/43; RAF Nutts Corner 14/1/44; ass 562BS/388BG Knettishall 17/1/44; MIA French A/fds 25/5/44 w/Capt Zengerle; flak, cr Gubersmil, Fr; 1EVD 2KIA 8POW; MACR 5264. THUNDERBOLT.

42-31742 Del Denver 12/12/43; Kearney 30/12/43; RAF Cluntoe 14/1/44; ass 548BS/385BG Gt Ashfield 17/1/44; MIA Berlin 24/5/44 w/King; flak, cr Midwolde, Hol; 10POW; MACR 5267.

42-31743 Del Denver 11/12/43; Rosencrans 29/12/43; Orlando 2/1/44; W/O 11/5/44.

42-31744 Del Denver 12/12/43; Kearney 5/1/44; ass 568BS/390BG Framlingham 5/2/44; MIA Derben, Ger. 14/1/45 w/Wiegnad; e/a, cr Goerne, Ger?; 4KIA 5POW; MACR 11720. LITTLE BUTCH II.

42-31745 Del Denver 12/12/43; Kearney 30/12/43; RAF Nutts Corner 14/1/44; ass 563BS/388BG Knettishall 17/1/44; MIA Brunswick 23/3/44 w/McFall; e/a, cr Wilderhausen, Ger; 10POW; MACR 3595. HEAVEN CAN WAIT.

42-31746 Del Denver 12/12/43; Ellensburg 14/12/43; Gt Falls 20/12/43; Kearney 31/12/43; RAF Nutts Corner 14/1/44; ass 385BG Gt Ashfield 17/1/44; c/l Honington A/fd 24/2/44; sal n/b/d 21/3/44.

42-31747 Del Denver 12/12/43; Kearney 31/12/43; Oklahoma City 15/1/44; Kearney 26/1/44; ass 332BS/94BG [XM-Q] Rougham 17/2/44; MIA Augsburg 13/4/44 w/Gault; flak, f/l Dubendorf, Switz; 10INT; MACR 4006. LASSIE COME HOME.

42-31748 Del Denver 12/12/43; Kearney 31/12/43; Oklahoma City 16/1/44; Tinker 1/2/44; ass 511BS/351BG [DS-V] Polebrook 19/2/44; MIA {41m} Creil 13/7/44 w/Aldridge; flak, cr Neuffen, Ger; 1KIA 8POW; MACR 7504.

42-31749 Del Cheyenne 10/12/43; Gt Falls 20/12/43; Oklahoma City 6/1/44; Love Fd 15/1/44; Maxwell 16/1/44; Savannah 18/1/44; Homestead 28/1/44; ass 20BS/2BG Amendola 28/1/44; MIA Villaorba 18/3/44 w/Butler; JU88 shot off tail with rocket; one chute seen, cr Cres Is; MACR 3257.

42-31750 Del Cheyenne 12/12/43; Kingman 25/12/43; 3018 BU Kingman 23/3/45; 3017 BU Hobbs 25/6/45; RFC Walnut Ridge 11/1/46.

42-31751 Del Cheyenne 12/12/43; Gr Island 27/12/43; Detroit 26/1/44; Grenier 28/1/44; ass 549BS/385BG Gt Ashfield 1/23/44; MIA Pas de Calais 28/2/44 w/Clark; flak, cr Boulougne, Fr; 8KIA 2POW; MACR 2883.

42-31752 Del Cheyenne 11/12/43; Dallas 4/1/44; Lakeland 6/1/44; Morrison 17/2/44; ass 773BS/463BG Celone 20/2/44; MIA Odertal, Ger. 22/8/44 w/Buterac; flak, cr Slatina; MACR 8108. THE SIMP.

42-31753 Del Cheyenne 13/12/43; Romulus 24/12/43; Middleton 28/12/43; Orlando 30/12/43; 9030 BU Pinecastle 2/6/44; 902 BU Orlando 7/12/44; 903 BU Pinecastle 1/1/45; 621 BU Pinecastle 2/7/45; 4000 BU Wright Fd 15/7/45; RFC Walnut Ridge 14/1/46.

42-31754 Del Cheyenne 11/12/43; Gt Falls 24/12/43; Grenier 6/2/44; ass 427BS/303BG [GN-L] Molesworth 28/2/44; c/l RAF Sculthorpe 9/4/44; sal 10/4/44.

42-31755 Del Cheyenne 11/12/43; Gr Island 23/12/43; Des Moines 24/12/43; Indianapolis 25/12/43; Nashville 31/12/43; Orlando 1/1/44; 225 BU Rapid City 1/5/45; 203 BU Jackson 3/6/45; 245 BU McCook 27/9/45; RFC Kingman 20/11/45.

42-31756 Del Cheyenne 11/12/43; Gr Island 27/12/43; ass 360BS/303BG [PU-M] Molesworth 11/2/44; n/b/d 12/3/44, u/c collapsed; sal 13/3/44.

42-31757 Del Cheyenne 11/12/43; Gr Island 21/12/43; ass 508BS/351BG [YB-G] Polebrook 25/2/44; MIA {23m} Ruhrland Oil 28/5/44 w/Condon; e/a, cr Waldau, Ger?; 6KIA 3POW; MACR 5333.

42-31758 Del Cheyenne 11/12/43; Billings 17/12/43; Gr Island 27/12/43; Presque Is 20/2/44; ass 367BS/306BG [GY-F] Thurleigh 3/3/44; MIA Oberpfaffenhofen 24/4/44 w/Capt Stoltz; b/d f/l Dubendorf, Switz; 10INT. MACR 4357.

42-31759 Del Denver 11/12/43; Spokane 17/12/43; Gt Falls 20/12/43; Denver 27/12/43; Lincoln 5/1/44; Mobile 6/1/44; Lakeland 7/1/44; Morrison 22/2/44; ass 774BS/463BG Celone 24/2/44; MIA Ploesti, Rom. 24/4/44 w/Namiotka; e/a, exploded and 5 chutes seen with ME109 circling, ship cr Tirgoviste, Rom; MACR 4611. HUSTLIN' GAL.

42-31760 Del Denver 11/12/43; Gt Falls 17/12/43; Danver 20/12/43; Kearney 31/12/43; Presque Is 24/1/44; ass 334BS/95BG [BG-D] Horham 4/2/44; MIA night practice mission 6/11/44 w/McVay; mech fault, cr?; 1EVD 6POW; MACR 10418. IKKI POO.

42-31761 Del Denver 11/12/43; Gt Falls 17/12/43; Denver 20/12/43; Kearney 30/12/43; RAF Nutts Corner 14/1/44; ass 533BS/381BG [VP-O] Ridgewell; {73m+} RetUS 121 BU Bradley 9/6/45; 4168 BU Sth Plains 13/6/45; RFC Kingman 28/11/45. ROTHERHITHE'S REVENGE.

42-31762 Del Denver 12/12/43; Gt Falls 16/12/43; Denver 20/12/43; Kearney 29/12/43; RAF Nutts Corner 15/1/44; ass 551BS/385BG Gt Ashfield 17/1/44; MIA French A/fds 12/6/44 w/Jackson; flak, cr Boulounge, Fr; 8KIA 2POW; MACR 2883/5628.

42-31763 Del Denver 12/12/43; Gt Falls 16/12/43; Denver 21/12/43; Kearney 1/1/44; RAF Nutts Corner 14/1/44; ass 510BS/351BG [TU-A] Polebrook 30/1/44; {6m} b/d Leipzig 20/2/44 c/p KIA; Lt Walter Truemper and Sgt Archie Mathies earned

posthumous Medal of Honor for attempting to land aircraft with wounded man aboard after others baled. They crashed nearby on fourth attempt to land at base. TEN HORSEPOWER.
42-31764 Del Denver 12/12/43; Gt Falls 17/12/43; Denver 19/12/43; Kearney 31/12/43; Presque Is 24/1/44; ass 549BS/385BG Gt Ashfield 22/4/44; 551BS; c/l Easton UK. 10/11/44, 1KIA 3WIA; sal 11/11/44.
42-31765 Del Denver 12/12/43; Gt Falls 25/12/43; Denver 2/1/44; Gr Island 4/2/44; Grenier 10/2/44; ass 407BS/92BG [PY-L] Podington 2/3/44; sal 11/10/45.
42-31766 Del Denver 12/12/43; Gt Falls 16/12/43; Romulus 24/1/44; Grenier 28/1/44; ass 8AF 6/2/44; sal CU 31/3/46.
42-31767 Del Denver 12/12/43; Kearney 31/12/43; RAF Nutts Corner 16/1/44; ass 351BS/100BG [EP-E] Thorpe Abbotts 17/1/44; tran 482BG Alconbury 20/5/45; retUS 121 BU Bradley 31/5/45; 4168 BU Sth Plains 3/6/45; RFC Kingman 8/11/45. OUR GAL SAL.
42-31768 Del Denver 12/12/43; Kearney 8/1/44; Prestwick 15/1/44; ass 369BS/306BG [WW-Y] Thurleigh 17/1/44; MIA Erding 24/4/44 w/Biggs; e/a, cr Mainburg, Ger; 10POW. MACR 4283. MISS CARRIAGE.
42-31769 Del Cheyenne 12/12/43; Gr Island 22/12/43; ass 563BS/388BG Knettishall 19/2/44; tran 2BG Amendola 6/9/44; sal 6/11/45.
42-31770 Del Cheyenne 12/12/43; Gt Falls 17/12/43; Cheyenne 23/12/43; Dallas 8/1/44; Lakeland 10/1/44; Morrison 13/2/44; ass 777BS/463BG Celone 15/2/44; MIA Munich 13/6/44 w/Davies; flak, cr Brod?; MACR 6094.
42-31771 Del Cheyenne 12/12/43; Gr Island 23/12/43; Grenier 16/1/44; ass 407BS/92BG [PY-R] Podington 28/1/44; MIA Merseburg 24/8/44 w/Nagy; e/a, cr Lindelthal, Ger; 5KIA 4POW; MACR 8213. AVAILABLE – EXCITEABLE.
42-31772 Del Cheyenne 12/12/43; Gr Island 30/12/43; Grenier 28/1/44; ass 407BS/92BG Podington 1/2/44; MIA Berlin 9/3/44 w/Patrick; flak, cr Templin, Ger; 10POW; MACR 2995.
42-31773 Del Cheyenne 12/12/43; Gt Falls 20/12/43; Kearney 30/12/43; Presque Is 20/2/44; ass 548BS/385BG Gt Ashfield 25/2/44; MIA Berlin 29/4/44 w/Johnston; e/a, cr Gleidingen, Ger; 1KIA 9POW; MACR 4456.
42-31774 Del Cheyenne 12/12/43; Kearney 31/12/43; ass 338BS/96BG [BX-L] Snetterton 8/2/44; MIA Augsburg 13/4/4 w/Bevers; e/a, cr Mettendorf, Ger; 9POW 1MIA; MACR 3766. VERA MAE.
42-31775 Del Cheyenne 13/12/43; Portland 19/12/43; Gt Falls 20/12/43; Cheyenne 21/12/43; Kansas City 5/1/44; Memphis 6/1/44; Lakeland 7/1/44; Morrison 18/2/44; ass 773BS/463BG Celone 20/2/44; MIA Bleckhammer 7/7/44 w/Sorensen; e/a, cr Gyor, Hung; MACR 6566.
42-31776 Del Cheyenne 13/12/43; Gt Falls 20/12/43; Cheyenne 21/12/43; Kearney 2/1/44; Grenier 26/1/44; Presque Is 2/2/44; ass 508BS/351BG [YB-H] Polebrook 25/2/44; MIA {1m} Frankfurt 2/3/44 w/Seaman; e/a, cr Aachen, Ger; 1EVD 9POW; MACR 2865. MAGGIE'S DRAWERS.
42-31777 Del Cheyenne 13/12/43; Gt Falls 18/12/43; Cheyenne 20/12/43; Kearney 27/12/43; ass 709BS/447BG Rattlesden 10/2/44; b/d Paris area, c/l 4/8/44, sal.
42-31778 Del Cheyenne 13/12/43; Salina 28/12/43; Kearney 4/1/44; Presque Is 24/1/44; ass 548BS/385BG Gt Ashfield 2/2/44; retUS 121 BU Bradley 29/6/45; 4168 BU Sth Plains 26/6/45; RFC Kingman 10/12/45. WELLS CARGO.
42-31779 Del Denver 13/12/43; Cheyenne 18/12/43; Kearney 30/12/43; ass 524BS/379BG [WA-J] Kimbolton 6/2/44; b/d Esbjerg, c/l 27/8/44; sal 28/8/44. THIS IS IT.
42-31780 Del Denver 13/12/43; Kearney 31/12/43; ass 731BS/452BG Deopham Green 9/2/44; MIA Frankfurt 5/11/44 w/Leith; flak, cr Keschnich, Ger; 2KIA 7POW; MACR 10346. WINDY LOU.
42-31781 Del Denver 13/12/43; Portland 19/12/43; Gt Falls 20/12/43; Denver 21/12/43; Kearney 31/12/43; ass 563BS/388BG Knettishall 29/1/44; MIA Frankfurt 4/2/44 w/DeJan; flak, cr Frankfurt; 8KIA 2POW; MACR 2350. COCK OF THE WALK.
42-31782 Del Denver 18/12/43; Billings 19/12/43; Kearney 30/12/43; Presque Is 24/1/44; ass 337BS/96BG [AW-Z] Snetterton 2/2/44; MIA Rostock w/Capt Firestone; e/a, cr Keisby, Ger; 4KIA 6POW; MACR 3812.
42-31783 Del Denver 19/12/43; Kearney 31/12/43; ass 407BS/92BG [PY-T] Podington 5/2/44; MIA Misburg 9/9/44 w/?; f/l France; sal 29/11/44. READY TEDDY II.
42-31784 Del Denver 19/12/43; Kearney 31/12/43; Oklahoma City 17/1/44; Kearney 1/2/44; ass 729BS/452BG Deopham Green 4/2/44; MIA Berlin 29/4/44 w/?; ditched Nth Sea, 10RTD.
42-31785 Del Denver 14/12/43; Gt Falls 20/12/43; Denver 22/12/43; Kearney 1/1/44; ass 335BS/95BG [OE-N] Horham 4/2/44; MIA Berlin 4/3/44 w/Dunham; cr Roteburg, Ger; 2KIA 8POW; MACR 2797. SLIGHTLY DANGEROUS.
42-31786 Del Denver 14/12/43; Gt Falls 20/12/43; Kearney 1/1/44; Grenier 21/1/44; ass 548BS/385BG Gt Ashfield 2/2/44; MIA Berlin 8/5/44 w/Drobysh; e/a, cr Druen, Ger?; 10POW; MACR 4563.
42-31787 Del Denver 14/12/43; Gt falls 20/12/43; Denver 26/12/43; Kearney 2/1/44; Presque Is 24/1/44; Grenier 29/1/44; Ass 548BS/385BG Gt Ashfield 4/2/44; MIA Brux 12/5/44 w/Worster; mid air coll w/e/a, cr Langerhein, Ger; 9KIA 1POW; MACR 4879.
42-31788 Del Cheyenne 14/12/43; Kearney 26/1/44; ass 332BS/94BG Rougham 8/2/44; f/l Continent 10/11/44, sal 18/11/44. JANIE.
42-31789 Del Cheyenne 14/12/43; Gt Falls 21/12/43; Oklahoma City 3/1/44; Love Fd 18/1/44; Savannah 20/1/44; Homestead 28/1/44; 20BS/2BG Amendola 31/1/44; MIA Brux 21/7/44 w/MacKenzie; e/a, tail blown off, cr mountains near Neukirchen, Ger; MACR 6685.
42-31790 Del Cheyenne 22/12/43; Dallas 5/1/44; Dale Marbry 10/1/44; Lakeland 18/1/44; Morrison 19/1/44; ass 774BS/463BG Celone 21/2/44; MIA Zagreb 6/4/44 w/Little; flak knocked out #3, e/a attacked and ship exploded; 9 chutes opened but one caught on tail, cr Wittmansberg, Ger?; MACR 3881.
42-31791 Del Cheyenne 22/12/43; Dallas 5/1/44; Lakeland 11/1/44; Morrison 16/2/44; ass 773BS/463BG Celone 19/2/44; MIA Ploesti 18/5/44 w/Bollei; e/a, cr Gaeti, Rom; MACR 5834.
42-31792 Del Cheyenne 20/12/43; Hobbs 20/1/44; 3017 BU Hobbs 27/6/44; W/O 27/6/44.
42-31793 Del Cheyenne 22/12/43; Scott Fd 9/1/44; Lakeland 11/1/44; Morrison 21/1/44; ass 774BS/463BG Celone 22/2/44; MIA Ploesti 5/5/44 w/Mellinger (KIA); flak, cr Ploesti; MACR 4623. LAVERN'S BAD PENNY.
42-31794 Del Cheyenne 22/12/43; Kearney 18/1/44; ass 365BS/305BG Chelveston 22/2/44; tran 401BG Deenethorpe 20/5/45; retUS 121 BU Bradley 7/6/45; Tulsa 10/6/45; 4168 BU Sth Plains 13/6/45; RFC Kingman 29/11/45. BETSY.
42-31795 Del Cheyenne 20/12/43; Gt Falls 21/12/43; Cheyenne 7/1/44; Lakeland 9/1/44; Morrison 23/2/44; ass 774BS/463BG Celone 25/2/44; MIA Budapest 14/7/44 w/Parks; flak, cr Budapest. MACR 6858.
42-31796 Del Cheyenne 24/12/43; Scott Fd 6/1/44; Hunter 10/1/44; Lakeland 11/1/44; Morrison 13/2/44; ass 774BS/463BG Celone 15/2/44; MIA Ploesti 5/5/44 w/Smith; flak, cr Ploesti, Rom; MACR 4616.
42-31797 Del Cheyenne 24/12/43; Lowry 12/1/44; Savannah 13/1/44; Morrison 24/1/44; ass 346BS/99BG Tortorella 25/1/44; MIA {6m} Regensburg 25/2/44 w/Mahan; e/a, cr Rottenburg, Ger; 2KIA 8POW; MACR 2705.
42-31798 Del Denver 21/12/43; Kearney 31/12/43; ass 412BS/95BG [QW-J] Horham 3/2/44; MIA Rostock 11/4/44 w/Maddox; e/a, cr Mecklenburg, Ger; 7KIA 3POW; MACR 3801.
42-31799 Del Denver 20/12/43; Kearney 31/12/43; Presque Is 2/1/44; ass 524BS/379BG [WA-C] Kimbolton 7/2/44; 527BS [FR-C], then 527BS [FO-X]; MIA Frankfurt 2/3/44 w/Heath; flak, cr Fumay, Fr; 3EVD 7POW; MACR 2736.
42-31800 Del Denver 16/12/43; Gt Falls 21/12/43; Kearney 2/1/44; Presque Is 29/1/44; ass 418BS/100BG [LD-U] Thorpe Abbotts 29/1/44; MIA Berlin 6/3/44 w/Barton; e/a, cr Oldenburg, Ger; 10POW; MACR 3021.
42-31801 Del Denver 16/12/43; Gt Falls 28/12/43; Langley 24/1/44; Mitchell 2/2/44; ass 482BG (H2S) Alconbury 11/2/44; tran 422BS/305BG [JJ-R] Chelveston 20/3/44; 327BG/92BG [UX-Q] Podington 2/8/44; MIA Misburg 26/11/44 w/?; b/d f/l Continent; sal 13/12/44.
42-31802 Del Denver 22/12/43; Gr Island 45/2/44; Presque Is 28/2/44; Grenier 9/3/44; ass 561BS/388BG Knettishall 12/3/44; MIA Pas de Calais 8/7/44 w/Fisher; flak, cr St Maclou, Fr; 1EVD 7KI1 2POW; MACR 7361. GYNIDA.
42-31803 Del Denver 16/12/43; Gt Falls 24/12/43; Billings 26/12/43; Denver 3/1/44; Barksdale 14/1/44; Lakeland 16/1/44; Morrison 21/2/44; ass 774BS/463BG Celone 22/2/44; MIA Ploesti 18/5/44 w/Kelley; e/a, cr Gaeti, Rom; MACR 5832.
42-31804 Del Denver 22/12/43; St Joseph 6/1/43; Kansas City 7/1/44; St Louis 9/1/44; Lakeland 10/1/44; Morrison 14/2/44; ass 775BS/463BG Celone 16/2/44; MIA Weiner Neustadt, Aus. 10/5/44 w/Gowen; flak, cr Foestenhof, Aus; MACR 4660. THE IRISH ORPHANS.
42-31805 Del Denver 16/12/43; Salt Lake City 26/12/43; Denver 28/12/43; Lincoln 8/1/43; Lakeland 9/1/44; Morrison 21/2/44; ass 773BS/463BG Celone 23/2/44; MIA Varese, It. 30/4/44 w/Donner; flak, ditched Adriatic; five rescued by RAF Walrus, 4POW; MACRS 4606/6689.
42-31806 Del Denver 24/12/43; Oklahoma City 8/1/44; Savannah 19/1/44; Morrison 20/1/44; ass 348BS/99BG Tortorella 1/2/44; {5m} tran 429BS/2BG Amendola 28/3/44; sal 4/9/44. KRAUT CHASER.
42-31807 Del Denver 22/12/43; Oklahoma City 4/1/44; Hunter 14/1/44; Savannah 19/1/44; Homestead 3/2/44; ass 15AF 6/3/44; MIA Vienna 8/7/44.
42-31808 Del Cheyenne 22/12/43; Roanoke 6/1/44; Lakeland 7/1/44; Morrison 21/2/44; ass 772BS/463BG Celone 23/2/44; tran 341BS/97BG Amendola 1/7/44; {100m on 31/1/45 Vienna}; sal 25/7/45.
42-31809 Del Cheyenne 28/12/43; Lakeland 3/1/44;

Morrison 16/2/44; ass 775BS/463BG Celone 18/2/44; MIA Vienna 21/6/44 w/Heres; no gas, cr Dutica, It; MACR 11396. NAMELESS!

42-31810 Del Cheyenne 24/12/43; Gr Island 18/1/44; ass 729BS/452BG Deopham Green 10/2/44; MIA Magdeburg 21/6/44 w/Anderson; flak, c/l Sovde, Swed; 10INT. MACR 5932.

42-31811 Del Cheyenne 22/12/43; Gt Falls 26/12/43; Cheyenne 28/12/43; Yuma 17/1/44; Alamogordo 22/2/44 (request crew); 206 BU Alamogordo 5/10/44; 231 BU Alamogordo 22/10/44; 235 BU Biggs 13/12/44; 225 BU Rapid City 5/3/45; 2114 BU Lockburn 14/7/45; 554 BU Memphis 29/8/45; 2137 BU Hendricks 20/9/45; RFC Kingman 9/11/45.

42-31812 Del Cheyenne 24/12/43; Kearney 7/1/44; Grenier 24/1/44; ass 401BS/91BG [LL-H] Bassingbourn 20/2/44; (completed first 44 missions on original engines for which crew chief Jack Gaffney awarded Bronze Star); MIA {53m} Leipzig 20/7/44 w/Van Ausdall; e/a, cr Glauehau, Ger; 4KIA 5POW. MACR 7281. DESTINY'S CHILD.

42-31813 Del Cheyenne 25/12/43; Dallas 8/1/44; Lakeland 10/1/44; ass 774BS/463BG Celone 3/3/44; MIA Vienna 8/7/44 w/Dunker(KIA); flak, cr Varazdin, Yugo; MACR 6866.

42-31814 Del Cheyenne 24/12/43; Gt Falls 26/12/43; Cheyenne 7/1/44; Omaha 9/1/44; Lakeland 11/1/44; Morrison 19/2/44; ass 463BG Celone 21/2/44; retUS 25/11/44; 4006 BU Miami 7/3/45; 4117 BU Robins 22/11/45; US Navy as CB-17 in 1946; re-ass Air Force 30/4/47; 6AF (Carib) Albrook 18/1/48; Panama 30/9/49; Olmstead 18/10/49.

42-31815 Del Cheyenne 25/12/43; Savannah 10/1/44; ass 346BS/99BG Tortorella 25/1/44; {14m} tran 49BS/2BG Amendola 28/3/44; retUS 301 BU Drew 25/11/45; 326 BU McDill 20/2/46; Recl Comp 30/10/46.

42-31816 Del Cheyenne 10/1/44; Gt Falls 14/1/44; Kearney 28/1/44; ass 366BS/305BG Chelveston (GH ship) 15/2/44; MIA Freidrichshafen 24/4/44 w/Capt Lincoln; e/a, cr Leuze, Bel; 8EVD 2KIA; MACR 4275.

42-31817 Del Cheyenne 24/12/43; Gt Falls 26/12/43; Des Moines 8/1/44; Maxwell 9/1/44; Lakeland 10/1/44; Morrison 17/2/44; ass 772BS/463BG Celone 21/2/44; MIA Pioppi, It. 5/6/44 w/Newcomb; flak, cr with bombs and exploded Bologna, 5 chutes seen. MACR 5843. HAIRLESS JOE.

42-31818 Del Denver 26/12/43; Lincoln 8/1/44; Louisville 9/1/44; Jacksonville 12/1/44; Lakeland 13/1/44; Morrison 25/2/44; ass 774BS/463BG Celone 27/2/44; MIA Weiner Neustadt 10/5/44 w/Nagel; e/a, cr Puschberg, Aus; MACR 5069.

42-31819 Del Denver 25/12/43; Lakeland 16/1/44; Morrison 21/2/44; ass 774BS/463BG Celone 22/2/44; sal 16/11/44.

42-31820 Del Denver 29/12/43; Kearney 13/1/44; Presque Is 24/1/44; ass 364BS/305BG [WF-E] Chelveston 15/2/44; MIA Augsburg 25/2/44 w/Perry; e/a, cr Rouocort, Fr?; 1EVD 4KIA 5POW; MACR 2541.

42-31821 Del Denver 24/12/43; Lakeland 8/1/44; Morrison 16/2/44; ass 775BS/463BG Celone 28/2/44; MIA Linz, Aus. 25/7/44 w/Sayers; flak damage, on return ditched Adriatic. MACR 12530. MARY LOU.

42-31822 Del Denver 26/12/43; Dallas 6/1/44; Dale Marbry 10/1/44; Maxwell 11/1/44; Morrison 13/2/44; crew to 775BS/463BG Celone via ATC, but a/c tran 379BG Kimbolton 24/5/44; MIA Toulouse 25/6/44?

42-31823 Del Denver 25/12/43; Tulsa 9/1/44; Maxwell 14/1/44; Lakeland 16/1/44; Morrison 14/2/44; ass 772BS/463BG Celone 15/2/44; MIA 19/3/44 training mission w/Burgess; mid air coll w/42-38143 (2BG); tail cut off, cr Adriatic; 10KIA. MACR 3286 (of 2BG).

42-31824 Del Denver 24/12/43; Barksdale 9/1/44; Savannah 10/1/44; Lakeland 11/1/44; Morrison 14/2/44; ass 772BS/463BG Celone 16/2/44; MIA Ploesti 19/8/44 w/Gomolac; mech fault, f/l Turkey; 10INT. MACR 12531.

42-31825 Del Denver 24/12/43; Chicago 13/1/44; Nashville 15/1/44; Lakeland 18/1/44; Morrison 14/2/44; ass 775BS/463BG Celone 21/2/44; MIA Ploesti 18/5/44 w/Menge; e/a, cr Corabia, Rom; MACR 5791.

42-31826 Del Denver 25/12/43; Dallas 5/1/44; Lakeland 6/1/44; Morrison 20/2/44; ass 774BS/463BG Celone 22/2/44; MIA Weiner Neustadt 10/5/44 w/McLaughlin; flak & e/a, cr Graz, Aus; MACR 5065.

42-31827 Del Denver 24/12/43; Dallas 5/1/44; Dale Marbry 6/1/44; Lakeland 9/1/44; Morrison 16/2/44; ass 772BS/463BG Celone 18/2/44; MIA Ploesti 31/7/44 w/Spencer; flak, cr Ploesti; MACR 7154.

42-31828 Del Cheyenne 29/12/43; Gr Island 15/1/44; Presque Is 20/2/44; ass 407BS/92BG [PY-Q] Podington 2/3/44; MIA Merseburg 11/9/44 w/Kannapinn; e/a, cr Schwittersdorf, Ger; 4KIA 5POW; MACR 8884. JUNKERS JOY.

42-31829 Del Cheyenne 24/12/43; Scott 10/1/44; Lakeland 12/1/44; Morrison 12/2/44; ass 772BS/463BG Celone 14/2/44; MIA Ploesti 18/5/44 w/Nosal; e/a, cr Bucharest; 2KIA; MACR 5434.

42-31830 Del Cheyenne 24/12/43; Billings 27/12/43; Cheyenne 3/1/44; Kearney 7/1/44; Grenier 22/1/44; ass 359BS/303BG [BN-N] Molesworth 20/2/44; MIA Cologne 10/11/44 w/Boulter; flak, cr Cologne; 2KIA 7POW; MACR 10355. MARIE.

42-31831 Del Cheyenne 24/12/43; Houston 9/1/44; Lakeland 10/1/44; Morrison 16/2/44; ass 775BS/463BG Celone 18/2/44; MIA Zagreb 6/4/44 w/Wistock. MACR 4098. BANSHEE.

42-31832 Del Cheyenne 24/12/43; Des Moines 12/1/44; Jackson 14/1/44; Lakeland 16/1/44; Morrison 21/2/44; ass 773BS/463BG Celone 25/2/44; {99m} c/l 27/2/45. THE BIGGEST BIRD.

42-31833 Del Cheyenne 28/12/43; Gr Island 18/1/44; ass 548BS/385BG Gt Ashfield 19/2/44; sal 12/3/45; retUS 121 BU Bradley 24/6/45; 4168 BU Sth Plains 28/6/45; RFC Kingman 28/12/45.

42-31834 Del Cheyenne 25/12/43; Gt Falls 29/12/43; Cheyenne 7/1/44; Nth Platte 9/1/44; Chicago 10/1/44; Albany 11/1/44; Lakeland 12/2/44; Morrison 18/2/44; ass 773BS/463BG Celone 20/2/44; MIA Brux 23/9/44 w/Kaub; no gas, l/Dubendorf, Switz; 10INT. MACR 9878. HOLEY JOE.

42-31835 Del Cheyenne 24/12/43; Kearney 12/1/44; Slated 388BG, tran 334BS/95BG [BG-A] Horham 3/2/44; MIA Rostock 11/4/44 w/Miles; cr Warnemünde, Ger; 10POW; MACR 3802.

42-31836 Del Cheyenne 25/12/43; New Orleans 9/1/44; Lakeland 10/1/44; Morrison 12/2/44; ass 773BS/463BG Celone 14/2/44; retUS 23/2/45; 1103 BU Morrison 13/3/45; 4100 BU Patterson 19/3/45; Recl Comp 24/5/46.

42-31837 Del Denver 25/12/43; Savannah 10/1/44; Morrison 21/1/44; ass 20BS/2BG Amendola 26/1/44; MIA Gyor, Hung. 13/4/44 w/German; e/a, cr Papa, Hung; MACR 3916.

42-31838 Del Denver 28/12/43; Kearney 12/1/44; ass 333BS/94BG Rougham 29/1/44; MIA Brunswick 10/2/44 w/Grengold; e/a, cr Levern, Ger; 2KIA 8POW; MACR 2370. SACK TIME CHARLIE.

42-31839 Del Denver 25/12/43; Charlotte 11/1/44; Savannah 12/1/44; Morrison 24/1/44; ass 352BS/301BG Cerignola 26/1/44; Lucera 1/2/44; b/d Milan 30/4/44; re-ass weather ship 12/10/44; tran depot 3/4/45; sal 14/6/45.

42-31840 Del Denver 22/12/43; Tulsa 9/1/44; Brookley 10/1/44; Lakeland 11/1/44; Morrison 28/2/44; ass 774BS/463BG Celone 1/3/44; MIA Treviso 7/4/44 w/Florsheim; ditched Adriatic, all crew rescued by RAF Walrus which could not take off so taxied 30 miles to safe territory.

42-31841 Del Denver 26/12/43; Omaha 6/1/44; Atlanta 10/1/44; Lakeland 16/1/44; Morrison 13/2/44; ass 775BS/463BG Celone 15/2/44; MIA Atzgersdorf, Aus. 24/5/44 w/Orf; e/a, cr Schonstein, Aus; MACR 5195.

42-31842 Del Denver 20/12/43; Lincoln 5/1/44; Lakeland 10/1/44; ass 773BS/463BG Celone 23/2/44; MIA Vienna, Aus. 16/6/44 w/Klentzman; flak, cr Dijon, Fr; MACR 6020.

42-31843 Del Denver 25/12/43; Scott 8/1/44; Lakeland 13/1/44; Morrison 20/1/44; slated 303BG, ass 774BS/463BG Celone 22/2/44; MIA Valence, Fr. 15/8/44 w/Swain; flak, 8 chutes seen as a/c went straight in with bombs on board, cr near Valence; MACR 7673.

42-31844 Del Denver 25/12/43; Gt Falls 27/12/43; Denver 30/12/43; Lakeland 20/1/44; ass 772BS/463BG Celone 28/3/44; sal 16/5/45. THE SWOOSE 1944 MODEL. IT FLYS?

42-31845 Del Denver 25/12/43; Oklahoma 6/1/44; Brookley 16/1/44; Lakeland 18/1/44; Morrison 16/2/44; ass 775BS/463BG Celone 18/2/44; MIA Budapest 14/6/44 w/Wacker; mid air coll w/42-38105; cr near Budapest. MACR 6102.

42-31846 Del Denver 26/12/43; Lincoln 8/1/44; Oklahoma City 9/1/44; Jacksonville 10/1/44; Lakeland 18/1/44; Morrison 12/2/44; ass 772BS/463BG Celone 14/3/44; sal 6/11/45. BOOMERANG BABY.

42-31847 Del Denver 25/12/43; Dallas 14/1/44; Lakeland 16/1/44; Morrison 2/2/44; ass 772BS/463BG Celone 14/2/44; MIA Oradea, Rom. 2/6/44 w/Hanson; mech fault, cr Taravice, Rom; MACR 5827.

42-31848 Del Cheyenne 21/12/43; Oklahoma City 12/1/44; Birmingham 14/1/44; Savannah 16/1/44; Morrison 26/1/44; ass 347BS/99BG Tortorella 1/2/44; {14m} tran 429BS/2BG Amendola 28/3/44; MIA Parma 6/7/44 w/Runyan; e/a, ship exploded, 3 chutes seen, one burning, cr Rovigo, It; MACR 6376.

42-31849 Del Cheyenne 26/12/43; Hobbs 20/1/44; 3021 BU Las Vegas 26/9/44; 3022 BU Indian Springs 9/10/44; 3021 BU Las Vegas 22/2/45; 3018 BU Kingman 8/3/45; 3017 BU Hobbs 9/6/45; RFC Walnut Ridge 14/1/46.

42-31850 Del Cheyenne 25/12/43; Hobbs 20/1/44; 3018 BU Kingman 18/9/44; 3017 BU Hobbs 9/6/45; RFC Walnut Ridge 21/1/46.

42-31851 Del Cheyenne 24/12/43; Oklahoma 12/1/44; Savannah 16/1/44; Morrison 24/1/44; ass 348BS/99BG Tortorella 2/3/44; {10m} tran 20BS/2BG Amendola 28/3/44; MIA Sofia, Bulg. 30/3/44 w/Wickham (loaned by 483BG); mid air coll w/42-31683, cr Trun. MACR 3370.

42-31852 Del Cheyenne 24/12/43; Lakeland 16/1/44; Morrison 20/2/44; ass 773BS/463BG Celone 22/2/44; MIA Vienna 8/7/44 w/Welter; flak, cr Gyor, Hung; MACR 6974.

42-31853 Del Cheyenne 28/12/43; Kearney 10/1/44; Savannah 12/1/44; Morrison 20/1/44; ass 33BS/301BG Cerignola 27/1/44; Lucera 1/2/44; MIA {27m} Lyon 25/5/44 w/Bogar; mid air coll w/42-

31605, cr mountains, 10KIA. MACR?

42-31854 Del Cheyenne 24/12/43; Kearney 30/1/44; Grenier 18/2/44; ass 570BS/390BG [DI-L] Framlingham 26/2/44; MIA Düsseldorf 9/9/44 w/Hilsenhoff; flak, cr Hubbelrath, Ger; 7KIA 2POW; MACR 8911. BABY BUGGY.

42-31855 Del Cheyenne 27/12/43; Oklahoma City 12/1/44; Savannah 16/1/44; Morrison 22/1/44; ass 342BS/97BG Amendola 26/1/44; re-ass cargo/weather ship from 10/10/44; sal 18/6/45.

42-31856 Del Cheyenne 29/12/43; Kearney 23/1/43; ass 331BS/94BG [QE-Y] Rougham 9/2/44; MIA Handorf, Ger. 8/4/44 w/Burnette; flak, cr Westerode, Ger; 2KIA 8POW; MACR 3798. LUSCIOUS DUCHESS.

42-31857 Del Cheyenne 26/12/43; Lincoln 10/1/44; Savannah 13/1/44; Morrison 26/1/44; ass 340BS/97BG Amendola 28/1/44; MIA Wollersdorf A/fd, Aus. 29/5/44 w/Rosenberg; flak, cr Ransdorf, Aus; MACR 5437.

42-31858 Del Denver 28/12/43; Gr Island 10/1/44; Scott 11/1/44; Savannah 13/1/44; Morrison 24/1/44; ass 346BS/99BG Tortorella 26/1/44; MIA {4m} Regensburg 25/2/44 w/Tomlin; e/a, cr Straubing, Ger; MACR 2706.

42-31859 Del Denver 28/12/43; Kansas City 12/1/44; Savannah 16/1/44; Morrison 26/1/44; ass 49BS/2BG Amendola 27/1/44; MIA Steyr, Aus. 24/2/44 w/Verbruggen; e/a, cr Wels, Aus; MACR 2620.

42-31860 Del Denver 28/12/43; Kearney 14/1/44; Presque Is 29/1/44; ass 407BS/92BG Podington 5/2/44; MIA Achmer 21/2/44 w/Skoubo; e/a, cr Ostend, Bel; 1KIA 9POW; MACR 2855.

42-31861 Del Denver 28/12/43; Columbus 16/1/44; Lakeland 18/1/44; Morrison 18/2/44; ass 773BS/463BG Celone 20/2/44; flak damage Bleckhammer, Ger. 13/9/44; sal.

42-31862 Del Denver 28/12/43; Lakeland 16/1/44; Morrison 15/2/44; ass 773BS/463BG Celone 21/2/44; b/d Bleckhammer, Ger 7/7/44 w/Thompson; c/l base, sal 11/7/44.

42-31863 Del Denver 27/12/43; Gt Falls 29/12/43; Kearney 12/1/44; Presque Is 26/1/44; ass 614BS/401BG [IW-X] Deenethorpe 6/2/44; b/d Cologne 6/1/45; sal 2 SAD Lt Staughton 19/2/45. MISS 'B' HAVEN.

42-31864 Del Denver 30/12/43; Kearney 14/1/44; Morrison 31/1/44; ass 549BS/385BG Gt Ashfield 21/2/44; MIA Venlo, Ger 15/8/44 w/Harrington; flak, cr Deurkheim, Ger?; 1EVD 8POW; MACR 7907.

42-31865 Del Denver 29/12/43; Scott 14/1/44; Atlanta 16/1/44; Lakeland 18/1/44; Morrison 14/2/44; ass 775BS/463BG Celone 29/2/44; MIA Munich 13/6/44 w/Weaver; mech failure, f/l Magadino, Switz; 10INT; MACR 6408. RetUS 1377 BU Grenier 26/11/45; RFC Walnut Ridge 27/11/45. OLE IRONSIDES.

42-31866 Del Denver 28/12/43; Kearney 18/1/44; Morrison 31/1/44; ass 550BS/385BG Gt Ashfield 15/2/44; MIA Schweinfurt 13/4/44 w/Downs; flak, f/l Dubendorf, Switz; 10INT; MACR 3771.

42-31867 Del Denver 29/12/43; Kearney 12/1/44; Morrison 31/1/44; Memphis 19/4/44; Kansas City 20/4/44; Kearney 24/4/44; Presque Is 28/4/44; Grenier 30/4/44; ass 335BS/95BG [OE-P] Podington 2/5/44; b/d Frankfurt 5/1/45, f/l France; retUS 121 BU Bradley 21/6/45; 4168 BU Sth Plains 24/6/45; RFC Kingman 19/12/45.

42-31868 Del Cheyenne 29/12/43; Omaha 10/1/44; Savannah 12/1/44; ass 342BS/97BG Amendola 26/1/44; tran depot 18/10/44; sal 10/11/44.

42-31869 Del Cheyenne 29/12/43; Kearney 12/1/44; ass 401BS/91BG [LL-Y] Bassingbourn 25/2/44; MIA {2m} Berlin 6/3/44 Mason; e/a, #3 exploded, cr Trebbin, Ger; 2KIA 8POW; MACR 2899. HELL AND HIGH WATER.

42-31870 Del Cheyenne 29/12/43; Atlanta 11/1/44; Savannah 12/1/44; ass 49BS/2BG Amendola 20/1/44; MIA Steyr, Aus. 24/2/44 w/Moyer; e/a, cr Wels, Aus; MACR 2589.

42-31871 Del Cheyenne 29/12/43; Kearney 23/1/44; ass 547BS/384BG [SO-T] Grafton Underwood 21/2/44; MIA Oberpfaffenhofen 18/3/44 w/LeDeur; flak, lost 2 engines, f/l Dubendorf, Switz; 10INT; MACR 3485.

42-31872 Del Cheyenne 30/12/43; Savannah 11/1/44; Morrison 24/1/44; ass 352BS/301BG Cerignola 26/1/44; Lucera 1/2/44; MIA {5m} Regensburg 25/2/44 w/Simon; e/a, cr Carano, It?; 3KIA 6POW; MACR 2596.

42-31873 Del Cheyenne 30/12/43; Savannah 13/1/44; Morrison 24/1/44; ass 49BS/2BG Amendola 27/1/44; MIA Steyr, Aus. 24/2/44 w/Pausha; e/a, cr?; MACR 2710.

42-31874 Del Cheyenne 30/12/43; Gr Island 31/1/44; ass 331BS/94BG Rougham 2/3/44; MIA Berlin 18/4/44 w/Williams; e/a, cr Neuruppin, Ger; 11POW; MACR 4154.

42-31875 Del Cheyenne 31/12/43; Kearney 12/1/44; ass 511BS/351BG [DS-P] Polebrook 25/2/44; {26m} b/d Merseburg 29/7/44; c/l base; sal 30/7/44.

42-31876 Del Cheyenne 30/12/43; Gt falls 3/1/44; Cheyenne 5/1/44; Kearney 13/1/44; ass 412BS/95BG [QW-Q] Horham 17/2/44; aborted after take off for Düsseldorf, on return to base o/s runway, hit cement mixer; 10RTD (5 minor inj); sal 10/9/44. FIRE BALL RED.

42-31877 Del Cheyenne 30/12/43; Kearney 10/1/44; Atlanta 12/1/44; Savannah 13/1/44; ass 416BS/99BG Tortorella 25/1/44; {10m} tran 20BS/2BG Amendola 28/3/44; sal 25/7/45. FLAK HOLES.

42-31878 Del Cheyenne 30/12/43; Kearney 18/1/44; ass 535BS/381BG [MS-Z] Ridgewell 20/2/44; MIA {5+m} Berlin 24/5/44 w/Higgins; e/a, cr Gratze, Ger; 6KIA 4POW; MACR 5177. SPAMCAN.

42-31879 Del Denver 24/12/43; Gt Falls 29/12/43; Kearney 13/1/44; ass 508BS/351BG [YB-Q] Polebrook 22/2/44; {53m} sal 2 SAD Lt Staughton 4/10/44; retUS 9/44. THE SHARK.

42-31880 Del Denver 30/12/43; Kearney 12/1/44; Morrison 31/1/44; Barksdale 15/4/44; Memphis 19/4/44; Kearney 24/4/44; Grenier 29/4/44; ass 366BS/305BG Chelveston /44; MIA Ludwigshafen 27/5/44 w/Gilbert; flak, cr Deurkheim, Ger; 2KIA 8POW; MACR 5338.

42-31881 Del Denver 30/12/43; Memphis 12/1/44; Savannah 16/1/44; Hunter 19/1/44; Jacksonville 30/1/44; Homestead 2/2/44; ass 332BS/94BG [XM-G], tran 352BS/301BG Lucera 15/2/44; MIA Ploesti 22/7/44 w/Hebert; flak, cr Ploesti; MACR 7033.

42-31882 Del Denver 30/12/43; Kearney 12/1/44; ass 511BS/351BG [DS-F] Polebrook 17/2/44; MIA {3m} Oschersleben 22/2/44 w/Mears; ditched Nth Sea off Cromer; 10RTD.

42-31883 Del Denver 30/12/43; Casper 4/1/44; Denver 4/2/44; Kearney 12/2/44; ass 401BS/91BG [LL-Y] Bassingbourn 29/2/44; MIA {69m} Merseburg 2/11/44 w/Chouinard; flak, #3 exploded and nose blew off, cr Leipzig; 7KIA 2POW; MACR 10304. THE JUB JUB BIRD.

42-31884 Del Denver 30/12/43; Pueblo 12/1/44; Savannah 13/1/44; Morrison 20/1/44; ass 340BS/97BG Amendola 26/1/44; 100th mission, Regensburg 9/12/44; sal 30/11/45. MISS MAYWOOD.

42-31885 Del Denver 30/12/43; Scott Fd 10/1/44; Savannah 12/1/44; ass 347BS/99BG Tortorella 25/1/44; {14m} tran 20BS/2BG Amendola 28/3/44; MIA Moravska Ostrova, Czech. 29/8/44 w/Prentice; e/a, cr Vsetin, Czech. MACR 8099. LOVELY LADIES.

42-31886 Del Denver 30/12/43; Des Moines 12/1/44; Charleston 17/1/44; Savannah 18/1/44; Homestead 1/2/44; slated 709BS/446BG; tran 32BS/301BG Lucera 5/2/44; MIA Bleckhammer 7/8/44 w/Bauer; e/a & flak, cr Aus; 10POW; MACR 11976. AMAZING MAZIE.

42-31887 Del Denver 31/12/43; Kearney 15/1/44; ass 412BS/95BG [QW-K] Horham 15/2/44; 336BS [ET-K], 335BS [OE-F]; MIA Frankfurt 17/2/45 w/Schaad; cr Tillowitz, Ger?; 9P0W; MACR 12378. BIG CASINO.

42-31888 Del Cheyenne 30/12/43; Kearney 13/1/44; ass 326BS/92BG Podington 19/2/44; MIA Münster 23/3/44 w/Larrivce; e/a, cr Utrup, Ger?; 8KIA 2POW; MACR 3416.

42-31889 Del Cheyenne 30/12/43; Barksdale 11/1/44; Savannah 16/1/44; Morrison 18/1/44; ass 416BS/99BG Tortorella 28/1/44; {6m} tran 429BS/2BG Amendola 28/3/44; MIA Memmingen, Ger; 18/7/44 w/Pedigo; c/l Dubendorf, Switz; MACR 6863. MAMMY YOKUM.

42-31890 Del Cheyenne 30/12/43; Kearney 12/1/44; ass 94BG Rougham 5/2/44; Con sal 28/2/44.

42-31891 Del Cheyenne 31/12/43; Kearney 12/1/44; ass 612BS/401BG [SC-P] Deenethorpe 15/2/44; retUS 121 BU Bradley 1/6/45; 4168 BU Sth Plains 8/6/45; RFC Kingman 10/12/45.

42-31892 Del Cheyenne 31/12/43; Kearney 12/1/44; ass 570BS/390BG [DI-H] Framlingham 19/2/44; b/d D-Day Beach Head 6/6/44; sal 5/7/44. I'LL BE AROUND.

42-31893 Del Cheyenne 30/12/43; Savannah 16/1/44; Morrison 27/1/44; ass 419BS/301BG Lucera 1/2/44; MIA first mission, Pontadera 14/2/44 w/Bond; rammed by e/a, cr Foggia; 1KIA 1WIA 8RTD. MACR 2303.

42-31894 Del Cheyenne 31/12/43; Kearney 14/1/44; ass 306BG Thurleigh 28/2/44; c/l base 26/3/44; sal MU 27/3/44.

42-31895 Del Cheyenne 3/1/44; Kearney 14/1/44; Presque Is 3/2/44; Grenier 11/2/44; ass 418BS/100BG [LD-Y] Thorpe Abbotts 16/2/44; MIA Misburg 31/12/44 w/Carroll; e/a, cr Wesermünde, Ger; 9POW; MACR 11365.

42-31896 Del Cheyenne 31/12/43; Kearney 13/1/44; ass 339BS/96BG [QJ-M] Snetterton 8/2/44; MIA Rostock 11/4/44 w/Fleming; e/a, cr Vadersdorf Is, Lubeck, Ger; 1KIA 9POW; MACR 3813.

42-31897 Del Cheyenne 31/12/43; Kearney 19/1/44; ass 423BS/306BG [RD-S] Thurleigh 6/2/44; MIA Merseburg 20/7/44 w/McNaught; flak, cr Vielau, Ger; 9POW; MACR 7277.

42-31898 Del Denver 1/1/44; Kearney 13/1/44; ass 326BS/92BG [JW-A] Podington 2/3/44; sal n/b/d 15/7/44. IRENE A.

42-31899 Del Cheyenne 3/1/44; Kearney 13/1/44; ass 510BS/351BG [TU-B] Polebrook 29/2/44; MIA {18m} Ludwigshafen 27/5/44 w/Peters; f/l Dubendorf, Switz; 10INT. MACR 5332. CHATTERBOX.

42-31900 Del Denver 1/1/44; Kearney 15/1/44; ass 333BS/94BG [TS-N] Rougham 14/2/44; 331BS [QE-O], 332BS [XM-T]; MIA Geissen, Ger. 11/12/44 w/Shankland; lost #1 and #2, 5 baled and RTD; 4 MIA; MACR 11105. SALLY.

42-31901 Del Denver 1/1/44; Kearney 13/1/44; ass

369BS/306BG [WW-Y] Thurleigh 25/2/44; MIA Erding 24/4/44 w/Tarr; e/a, cr Straubing, Ger; 11POW; MACR 4284.

42-31902 Del Denver 31/12/43; Kearney 18/1/44; ass 710BS/447BG Rattlesden 6/2/44; sal 9/8/44.

42-31903 Del Denver 3/1/44; Kearney 30/1/44; Grenier 18/2/44; ass 350BS/100BG [LN-T] Thorpe Abbotts 23/2/44; MIA Merseburg 29/7/44 w/Jones; e/a, cr Wuelfingerode, Ger; 5KIA 4POW; MACR 7811.

42-31904 Del Denver 31/12/43; Gt Falls 2/1/44; Casper 4/1/44; Kearney 13/1/44; W/O 10/2/44.

42-31905 Del Denver 3/1/44; Hendricks 21/1/44; 2137 BU Hendricks 4/10/44; 4108 BU Newark 5/6/45; 2137 BU Hendricks 28/9/45; RFC Kingman 1/11/45.

42-31906 Del Denver 31/12/43; Kearney 13/1/44; ass 410BS/94BG Rougham 21/2/44; 331BS [QE-J]; MIA Munich 31/7/44 w/Johnson; flak, cr Guezenhausen, Ger; 6KIA 3POW; MACR 7739.

42-31907 Del Denver 3/1/44; Kearney 14/1/44; ass 326BS/92BG [JW-J] Podington 19/2/44; MIA Merseburg 11/9/44. J FOR JOHNNY, then HOMESICK ANGEL.

42-31908 Del Cheyenne 5/1/44; Kearney 14/1/44; Wilmington 24/1/44; Grenier 26/1/44; ass 337BS/96BG [AW-L] Snetterton 3/2/44; sal 4/5/44.

42-31909 Del Cheyenne 4/1/44; Kearney 12/1/44; Romulus 24/1/44; Grenier 29/1/44; ass 323BS/91BG [OR-R] Bassingbourn 24/2/44; retUS 1321 BU Bradley 11/6/45; 4168 BU Sth Plains 18/6/45; RFC Kingman 7/12/45. NINE O NINE. (8AF record for no aborts 140 missions).

42-31910 Del Cheyenne 3/1/44; Kearney 13/1/44; Romulus 24/1/44; Grenier 25/1/44; ass 336BS/95BG [ET-P] Horham 2/2/44; MIA Berlin 4/3/44 w/Brownlow; cr Marienburg, Ger; 3KIA 7POW; MACR 2798.

42-31911 Del Cheyenne 3/1/44; Gr Island 16/4/44; ass 323BS/91BG [OR-Q] Bassingbourn 24/2/44; MIA Berlin 6/3/44 w/Harding; e/a, cr Ramstadt, Ger; 10POW. MACR 2900.

42-31912 Del Cheyenne 4/1/44; Kearney 14/1/44; Romulus 24/1/44; Grenier 25/1/44; ass 337BS/96BG [AW-L] Snetterton 3/2/44; MIA Berlin 8/3/44 w/Capt Thomas; e/a, cr Dummer Lake, Ger; 1KIA 9POW. MACR 3429. MYASAM DRAGON.

42-31913 Del Cheyenne 4/1/44; Kearney 13/1/44; Grenier 25/1/44; ass 571BS/390BG Framlingham 3/2/44 ETO-ITIS; MIA Berlin 8/5/44 w/Hammond; e/a, cr Hadensdorft, Ger?; 1EVD 5KIA 4POW. MACR 4584. SHY ANN.

42-31914 Del Cheyenne 4/1/44; Kearney 17/1/44; Grenier 25/1/44; ass 326BS/92BG [JW-S] Podington 11/2/44; MIA Erding 24/4/44 w/Rosenfeld; e/a, c/l Dubendorf, Switz; 10INT; MACR 4147. BUTCH.

42-31915 Del Cheyenne 4/1/44; Kearney 14/1/44; Romulus 20/1/44; Grenier 26/1/44; ass 527BS/379BG Kimbolton 6/2/44; MIA Hamm 19/9/44 w/Walker; flak, cr Duppach, Ger; 1EVD 8POW. MACR 9374. MARY JO.

42-31916 Del Cheyenne 6/1/44; Kingman 19/1/44; 3018 BU Kingman 23/3/45; 3030 BU Roswell 28/6/45; RFC Walnut Ridge 4/1/46.

42-31917 Del Cheyenne 4/1/44; Kearney 13/1/44; Grenier 26/1/44; ass 551BS/385BG Gt Ashfield 2/2/44; MIA Munich 12/7/44 w/Capt White; mid air coll, cr Perl, AGer; 9KIA 1POW; MACR 7507. OFF SPRING.

42-31918 Del Denver 4/1/44; Kearney 12/1/44; Chicago 24/1/44; Grenier 25/1/44; ass 447BG Rattlesden 2/2/44; sal n/b/d 17/4/44. LITTLE ROCK BLOND.

42-31919 Del Denver 4/1/44; Kearney 13/1/44; Grenier 25/1/44; ass 452BG Deopham Green 4/2/44; b/d Berlin 6/3/44; sal 8/3/44.

42-31920 Del Denver 3/1/44; Kearney 28/1/44; ass 447BG Rattlesden 9/2/44; tran 334BS/95BG [BG-G] Horham; sal n/b/d 9/11/44. ABLE MABEL.

42-31921 Del Denver 6/1/44; Kearney 14/1/44; Grenier 26/1/44; ass 407BS/92BG Podington 5/2/44; MIA Erding 24/4/44 w/King; e/a, cr Munich; 10KIA; MACR 4148. LIL BRAT.

42-31922 Del Denver 6/1/44; Kearney 14/1/44; Grenier 31/1/44; ass 550BS/385BG Gt Ashfield 15/2/44; f/l Hoesch A/fd, Hol. 15/3/45; sal & RetUS 121 BU Bradley 24/6/45; 4168 BU Sth Plains 26/6/45; RFC Kingman 28/11/45.

42-31923 Del Denver 7/1/44; Kearney 14/1/44; Grenier 26/1/44; Presque Is 7/3/44; ass 750BS/457BG Glatton 23/6/44; MIA Merseburg 2/11/44. PROP WASH.

42-31924 Del Denver 5/1/44; Kearney 15/1/44; Presque Is 29/1/44; ass 334BS/95BG [BG-Q] Horham 2/2/44; MIA Leipzig 29/5/44 w/Ulrich; e/a, cr Packenbusch, Ger; 10POW; MACR 5343. OL' DOG.

42-31925 Del Denver 5/1/44; Kearney 14/1/44; ass 331BS/94BG Rougham 7/2/44; MIA Bohlen 7/10/44 w/Levy; e/a blew tail off, cr Ostramonda, Ger; 8KIA 1POW; MACR 9550. GOON GIRL.

42-31926 Del Denver 6/1/44; Kearney 14/1/44; Homestead 27/1/44; ass 545BS/384BG [JD-G] Grafton Underwood 19/2/44; MIA Watten V-site 19/3/44 w/Brookings; flak, cr Waurens, Bel?; 6KIA 4POW; MACR 3242. LOVELL'S HOVEL.

42-31927 Del Denver 6/1/44; Kearney 15/1/44; ass 526BS/379BG [LF-F] Kimbolton 8/2/44; MIA Oranienburg 13/8/44 w/Felgar; flak, cr Falaise, Fr; 2KIA 7POW; MACR 7905.

42-31928 Del Cheyenne 7/1/44; Kearney 15/1/44; ass 551BS/385BG Gt Ashfield 6/2/44; dest on base by Luftwaffe 23/5/44, possibly the only B-17 lost this way. POWERFUL KATRINKA.

42-31929 Del Cheyenne 7/1/44; Gr Island 15/1/44; Presque Is 21/2/44; ass 427BS/303BG Molesworth 1/3/44; MIA Pas de Calais 26/3/44 w/Mass; flak, cr Frevent, Fr; 1KIA 9POW; MACR 3475.

42-31930 Del Cheyenne 6/1/44; Kearney 14/1/44; New Castle 24/1/44; ass 613BS/401BG [IN-M] Deenethorpe 7/2/44; MIA Oschersleben 22/2/44 w/Shanks; e/a, cr Waldkappel, Ger; 1KIA 9POW; MACR 2660.

42-31931 Del from Boeing 10/2/44 (experimental with no top turret glazing); McChord 23/7/44; Spokane 25/7/44; Nashville 30/8/44; 1EEL Bedford 1/12/44; 902 BU Orlando 19/1/45; 903 BU Pinecastle 23/1/45; 4000 BU Wright Fd 30/6/45; 4148 BU Hensley 2/8/45; 4000 BU Wright Fd 7/8/45; RFC Kingman 5/12/45.

42-31932 Del Cheyenne 27/1/44; Gr Island 1/2/44; Grenier 23/2/44; ass 571BS/390BG [FC-H] Framlingham 23/2/44 RICK-O-SHAY then PURDY BABY; retUS 121 BU Bradley 6/7/45; 4168 BU Sth Plains 8/7/45; RFC Kingman 18/12/45. SISTER KATE.

42-31933 Del Cheyenne 10/1/44; Yuma 19/1/44; 3017 BU Hobbs 5/6/44; RFC Kingman 1/12/45.

42-31934 Del Cheyenne 6/1/44; Gr Island 15/1/44; ass 731BS/452BG Deopham Green 9/2/44; retUS 121 BU Bradley 5/7/45; 4168 BU Sth Plains 25/8/45; RFC Kingman 17/11/45.

42-31935 Del Cheyenne 7/1/44; Kearney 28/1/44; ass 571BS/390BG Framlingham 10/2/44; MIA Berlin 6/3/44 w/Starks; e/a, cr Hemmelte, Ger; 3KIA 7POW; MACR 2989. STARK'S ARK.

42-31936 Del Cheyenne 10/1/44; Scott 20/1/44; 2114 BU Lockburn 2/9/44; 4152 BU Lockburn 1/10/44; 2114 BU Lockburn 29/9/45; 4152 BU Lockburn 9/10/45; RFC Walnut Ridge 7/1/46.

42-31937 Del Cheyenne 10/1/44; Slated 100BG, tran Lockburn 21/1/44; 2118 BU Laredo 28/6/44; 2126 BU Laredo 1/2/45; RFC Walnut Ridge 8/1/46.

42-31938 Del Cheyenne 7/1/44; Gr Island 16/1/44; WO 31/1/44.

42-31939 Del Denver 6/1/44; Kearney 15/1/44; Romulus 23/1/44; Grenier 25/1/44; ass 336BS/95BG [ET-J] Horham 2/2/44; retUS 121 BU Bradley 21/6/44; 4168 BU Sth Plains 23/6/45; RFC Kingman 24/11/45.

42-31940 Del Cheyenne 8/1/44; Yuma 19/1/44; 233 BU Davis Monthan 3/6/44; 3036 BU Yuma 9/6/45; 3017 BU Hobbs 11/6/45; Recl Comp 8/45.

42-31941 Del Cheyenne 7/1/44; Gr Island 15/1/44; Presque Is 28/2/44; ass 350BS/100BG [LN-W] Thorpe Abbotts 3/3/44; MIA Berlin 24/5/44 w/Wiliamson; e/a, cr & exploded Bueckwitzer, Ger; 2KIA 8POW; MACR 5167.

42-31942 Del Cheyenne 10/1/44; Yuma 17/1/44; 3017 BU Hobbs 4/6/44; Recl Comp 5/7/45.

42-31943 Del Cheyenne 10/1/44; Yuma 19/1/44; Alamogordo 20/3/44; 206 BU Alamogordo 8/9/44; 203 BU Jackson 22/4/45; 243 BU Gt Bend 20/9/45; RFC Altus 7/11/45.

42-31944 Del Cheyenne 9/1/44; Yuma 19/1/44; 3017 BU Hobbs 4/6/44; RFC Walnut Ridge 7/1/46.

42-31945 Del Alamogordo 10/2/44; 4208 BU Mines Fd 3/10/44; 231 BU Alamogordo 6/10/44; 235 BU Biggs 10/12/44; 224 BU Sioux City 27/2/45; 225 BU Rapid City 15/6/45; 203 BU Jackson 28/6/45; 234 BU Clovis 23/9/45; RFC Walnut Ridge 16/2/46.

42-31946 Del Cheyenne 10/1/44; Gt Bend 19/1/44; ass 333BS/94BG Rougham 9/2/44; MIA Pas de Calais 20/4/44 w/Swanson; flak in right wheel well and ball turret door fell off; 8 chutes seen; cr France?; 1EVD 9POW; MACR 4156. ESKY.

42-31947 Del Cheyenne 9/1/44; Lockburn 21/1/44; 3036 BU Yuma 5/7/44; 3017 BU Hobbs 22/9/44; 4160 BU Hobbs 5/11/44; RFC Kingman 8/12/45.

42-31948 Del Cheyenne 9/1/44; Kingman 19/1/44; Albuquerque 26/3/44; 2543 BU Waco 28/11/44; 2218 BU Alexandra 10/12/44; 3290 BU Alexandra 1/3/45; WO Alexandra 7/5/45.

42-31949 Del Cheyenne 10/1/44; Yuma 19/1/44; 3017 BU Hobbs 4/6/44; RFC Walnut Ridge 20/12/45.

42-31950 Del Cheyenne 9/1/44; Chanute 20/1/44; 3501 BU Boca Raton 28/11/44; RFC Kingman 22/2/46.

42-31951 Del Cheyenne 9/1/44; Yuma 21/1/44; 3017 BU Hobbs 5/6/44; RFC Walnut Ridge 3/1/46.

42-31952 Del Cheyenne 9/1/44; Hobbs 28/1/44; 3021 BU Las Vegas 28/9/44; 3022 BU Indian Springs 7/10/44; 2126 BU Laredo 9/4/45; RFC Walnut Ridge 4/1/46.

42-31953 Del Cheyenne 10/1/44; Yuma 21/1/44; 3017 BU Hobbs 4/8/44; 4160 BU Hobbs 3/11/44; RFC Kingman 2/12/45.

42-31954 Del Cheyenne 10/1/44; Lockburn 19/1/44; 2137 BU Hendricks 17/11/44; 1377 BU Grenier 10/1/45; 4136 BU Tinker 30/1/45; 2137 BU Hendricks 11/7/45; Recl Comp 17/7/45.

42-31955 Del Cheyenne 9/1/44; Savannah 24/1/44; ass 508BS/351BG [YB-K] Polebrook 29/2/44; MIA {14m} Oranienburg 18/4/44 w/Apperson; flak, cr Oranienburg; 9KIA 1POW; MACR 4049.

42-31956 Del Cheyenne 9/1/44; Montezuma 17/1/44; Lockburn 21/1/44; 3501 Boca Raton 28/11/44; 4136 BU Tinker 17/9/45; 3501 BU Boca Raton 23/9/45;

RFC Kingman 22/2/46.
42-31957 Del Denver 9/1/44; Las Vegas 18/1/44; 2137 BU Hendricks 18/11/44; RFC Kingman 14/11/45.
42-31958 Del Denver 9/1/44; Kingman 19/1/44; 1377 BU Grenier 10/1/45; 3018 BU Kingman 23/3/45; 3017 BU Hobbs 9/6/45; RFC Walnut Ridge 4/1/46.
42-31959 Del Denver 9/1/44; Las Vegas 18/1/44; 3021 BU Las Vegas 2/6/44; 3022 BU Indian Springs 16/6/44; 3021 BU Las Vegas 23/3/45; 2126 BU Laredo 31/3/45; RFC Walnut Ridge 5/1/46.
42-31960 Del Denver 9/1/44; Albuquerque 24/1/44; Kingman 26/1/44; Pyote 26/3/44; WO 30/5/44.
42-31961 Del Denver 10/1/44; Yuma 22/1/44; 3021 BU Las Vegas 2/6/44; 3022 BU Indian Springs 14/7/44; 3021 BU Las vegas 15/3/45; 2126 BU Laredo 31/3/45; RFC Walnut Ridge 20/12/45.
42-31962 Del Denver 9/1/44; Kingman 19/1/44; Albuquerque 30/3/44; 222 BU Ardmore 22/1/45; 332 BU Ardmore 16/6/45; RFC Walnut Ridge 11/12/45.
42-31963 Del Denver 9/1/44; Kingman 19/1/44; 3018 BU Kingman 23/3/45; 3017 BU Hobbs 29/12/45.
42-31964 Del Denver 9/1/44; Kingman 19/1/44; Pyote 30/3/44; 235 BU Biggs 28/7/44; Mat HQ Wright Fd 14/8/44; 235 BU Biggs 16/8/44; 224 BU Sioux City 27/2/45; 222 BU Ardmore 14/6/45; 332 BU Ardmore 16/6/45; RFC Walnut Ridge 26/9/45.
42-31965 Del Denver 9/1/44; Spokane 10/1/44; Palm Springs 19/1/44; 3036 BU Yuma 29/9/44; Recl Comp 29/1/45.
42-31966 Del Denver 13/1/44; Gt Falls 14/1/44; Gr Island 24/1/44; ass 511BS/351BG [DS-X] Polebrook 29/2/44; MIA {5m} Oberpfaffenhofen 18/3/44 w/Martin; flak, cr Uttenweiler, Ger; 9KIA 1POW; MACR 3236.
42-31967 Del Cheyenne 11/1/44; Roswell 26/1/44; 347 BU Key Fd 24/1/45; 330 BU Dyersburg 1/3/45; RFC Walnut Ridge 19/12/45.
42-31968 Del Cheyenne 11/1/44; Savannah 21/1/44; Morrison 2/2/44; ass 350BS/100BG [LN-D] Thorpe Abbotts 3/2/44; b/d flak, Mimoyecques, Fr. f/l Raydon A/fd, UK. 19/3/44; 1KIA 9RTD. Sal. MISS IRISH.
42-31969 Del Cheyenne 8/1/44; Billings 14/1/44; Savannah 24/1/44; ass 381BG Ridgewell 6/2/44; tran 369BS/306BG [WW-F] Thurleigh 22/2/44; MIA Berlin 8/5/44 w/Schlect; mid air coll, cr Hallenbeck, Ger?; 9KIA 1POW; MACR 4553.
42-31970 Del Cheyenne 10/1/44; Savannah 22/1/44; ass 349BS/100BG Thorpe Abbotts 3/2/44; MIA Wilhelmshaven 3/3/44 w/Capt Lohof; mid air coll, cr Itzehoe, Ger; 10POW; MACR 3022.
42-31971 Del Cheyenne 2/1/44; Gt Falls 12/1/44; Kearney 23/1/44; (f/l Rineanna, Eire from Labrador to UK 8/2/44); ass 570BS/390BG [DI-E] Framlingham 9/2/44; MIA Saarbrücken 11/5/44 w/Cockrean; flak, cr Dongen, Hol; 2KIA 8POW; MACR 4787. TWENTY-ONE OR BUST (BAD PENNY).
42-31972 Del Cheyenne 11/1/44; Savannah 21/1/44; ass 526BS/379BG [LF-F] Kimbolton 22/2/44; MIA Osnabrück 13/5/44 w/Wilde; e/a, cr Beldringe, Ger?; 9POW; MACR 4876. GAME COCK.
42-31973 Del Cheyenne 12/1/44; Savannah 24/1/44; ass 562BS/388BG Knettishall 5/2/44; dest by Luftwaffe on ground Poltava, Russia 21/6/44; sal 2/7/44.
42-31974 Del Cheyenne 11/1/44; Memphis 23/1/44; Savannah 24/1/44; ass 570BS/390BG [DI-G] Framlingham 5/2/44; retUS 121 BU Bradley 3/7/45; 4168 BU Sth Plains 6/7/45; RFC Kingman 30/11/45. BOMBOOGIE.

42-31975 Del Cheyenne 11/1/44; Sth Bend 23/1/44; Savannah 24/1/44; ass 510BS/351BG [TU-O] Polebrook 22/2/44; MIA {28m} Ludwigshafen 27/5/44 w/Hopkins; e/a, cr Clefoy, Fr?; 1EVD 8KIA; MACR 5331. QUEEN OF THE AIR.
42-31976 Del Cheyenne 12/1/44; Roswell 20/1/44; 3030 BU Roswell 26/12/44; 3010 BU Williams 20/1/45; 3020 BU La Junta 23/4/45; 2114 BU Lockburn 25/6/45; 2137 BU Hendricks 18/8/45; RFC Kingman 9/11/45.
42-31977 Del Cheyenne 12/1/44; Savannah 26/1/44; ass 332BS/94BG [XM-Q] Rougham 5/2/44; MIA Augsburg 13/4/44 w/Wiren; flak, f/l Dubendorf, Switz; 10INT. MACR 4007. FLAK QUEEN.
42-31978 Del Cheyenne 11/1/44; Savannah 22/1/44; Morrison 13/2/44; ass 325BS/92BG [NV-Q] Podington 2/3/44; MIA Munich 16/7/44 w/Herrington; e/a, cr Ebersbach, Ger; 1KIA 8POW; MACR 7571. DOTTIE G 2nd.
42-31979 Del Cheyenne 11/1/44; Savannah 23/1/44; ass 368BS/306BG [BO-U] Thurleigh 22/2/44; MIA {1m} Augsburg 25/2/44 w/Bayless; flak, cr Landau, Ger; 1KIA 9POW; MACR 2767. (First NMF a/c lost in 1st Air Div).
42-31980 Del Cheyenne 12/1/44; Savannah 23/1/44; ass 532BS/381BG [VE-J] Ridgewell 26/5/44; MIA {4m} Berlin 21/6/44 w/Dassault; e/a, cr Prenzlau, Ger; 2KIA 7POW; MACR 5990.
42-31981 Del Cheyenne 12/1/44; Savannah 25/1/44; ass 350BS/100BG [LN-E] Thorpe Abbotts 6/2/44; c/l Honington A/fd 15/5/44; sal.
42-31982 Del Cheyenne 12/1/44; Savannah 21/1/44; ass 322BS/91BG [LG-S] Bassingbourn 24/2/44; MIA {11m} Leipzig 20/7/44 w/Deshaw; e/a, wing broke off between #3 & #4, cr Ruppertagruen, Ger?; 3KIA (one killed by German civilians) 6POW; MACR 7282. SUPERSTITUOUS ALOYSIUS.
42-31983 Del Cheyenne 13/1/44; Kearney 28/1/44; Presque Is 18/2/44; Grenier 2/3/44; ass 615BS/401BG [IY-Y] Deenethorpe 7/3/44; 613BS [IN-G]; retUS 121 BU Bradley 6/6/45; 4168 BU Sth Plains 9/6/45; RFC Kingman 7/11/45. MARY ALICE. (Replica a/c Duxford War Museum, UK.)
42-31984 Del Cheyenne 13/1/44; Kearney 18/1/44; Grenier 1/2/44; ass 407BS/92BG [PY-U] Podington 2/3/44; MIA Dessau 20/7/44 w/Stein; flak, cr Leopold, Bel; 5EVD 4POW; MACR 7408. BERLIN SPECIAL.
42-31985 Del Cheyenne 13/1/44; Kearney 28/1/44; Grenier 20/2/44; ass 570BS/390BG [DI-P] Framlingham 27/2/44; MIA Konigsberg 28/5/44 w/Ingram; e/a, cr Ebendorf, Ger; 7KIA 3POW; MACR 5258. DEVIL'S ACES.
42-31986 Del Cheyenne 134/1/44; Kearney 22/1/44; Presque Is 16/1/44; ass 349BS/100BG [XR-M/B] Thorpe Abbotts 27/2/44; b/d Saarbrücken 9/11/44, f/l Continent; sal 8/12/44. ONCE IN A WHILE.
42-31987 Del Cheyenne 13/1/44; Kewarney 22/1/44; Romulus 23/2/44; Grenier 28/2/44; ass 350BS/100BG [LN-A] Thorpe Abbotts 10/3/44 THE LITTLE SKIPPER; 418BS [LD-D]; MIA Misburg 31/12/44 w/Rojohn; mis air coll, cr Rustringen, Ger; 3KIA 6POW; MACR 8174/11550. SHILAYLEE (FOOLS RUSH IN).
42-31988 Del Cheyenne 11/1/44; Savannah 26/1/44; ass 510BS/351BG [TU-C] Polebrook 30/3/44; {3m} c/t/o 23/4/44; sal 2 SAD Lt Staughton 24/4/44. THE BLONDE BOMBER.
42-31989 Del Cheyenne 13/1/44; Kearney 22/1/44; Grenier 25/2/44; ass 334BS/95BG [BG-M] Horham 27/2/44; 336BS [ET-B]; MIA Munich 25/2/45 w/Havlik; c/l Emmersen, Switz. 10INT. BLACK MAGIC (not painted on a/c).
42-31990 Del Cheyenne 10/1/44; ass 535BS/381BG [MS-R] Ridgewell 6/4/44; {113m} RetUS 5/45; RFC Kingman 26/2/46. STAGE DOOR CANTEEN.
42-31991 Del Cheyenne 13/1/44; Kearney 31/1/44; Grenier 22/2/44; ass 351BS/100BG [EP-D] Polebrook 1/3/44 FEVER BEAVER; {122m} taxi accident 14/5/45; sal 30/7/45. MISS-CHIEF.
42-31992 Del Cheyenne 13/1/44; Dalhart 29/1/44; Presque Is 29/2/44; ass 92BG, tran 334BS/95BG [BG-P] Horham 1/3/44; MIA Politz 25/8/44 w/Bussen; c/l Sovde, Swed; 9INT; MACR 8280. Left 30/6/45; sal 12/10/45. MIRANDY.
42-31993 Del Cheyenne 13/1/44; Dalhart 28/1/44; Presque Is 29/2/44; ass 334BS/95BG [BG-F] Horham 3/3/44; MIA Freidrichshafen 24/4/44 w/Cunningham; f/l Dubendorf, Switz; 1KIA 9INT; MACR 4265. Sal 12/10/45. "GEN'RIL OOP."
42-31994 Del Training Command Seattle 13/1/44; 3715 BU Burbank 13/8/44; 3701 BU Amarillo 7/9/45; RFC Kingman 28/12/45.
42-31995 Del Cheyenne 13/1/44; Kearney 28/1/44; ass 327BS/92BG [UX-M] Podington 23/3/44; MIA Stuttgart 13/9/44 w/Stallings; f/l Dubendorf, Switz; 9INT; MACR 8885; retUS 1377 BU Grenier 28/9/45; RFC Walnut Ridge 2/1/46. HEAVEN'S ABOVE.
42-31996 Del Cheyenne 11/1/44; Gt Falls 14/1/44; Kearney 29/1/44; ass 561BS/388BG Knettishall 8/2/44 LADY LILLIAN; MIA Kassel 18/10/44 w/?; flak, cr Gosselies A/fd, Bel; 9RTD; sal 6/11/44. WAR WEARY.
42-31997 Del Cheyenne 12/1/44; Lt Rock 23/1/44; Savannah 25/1/44; ass 360BS/303BG Molesworth 22/2/44; MIA Hamburg 20/6/44 w/Parker; flak, cr Nordholz, Ger; 9POW; MACR 5985.
42-31998 Del Cheyenne 13/1/44; Omaha 1/2/44; Scott 4/2/44; Morrison 8/3/44; ass 815BS/483BG Tortorella 28/3/44; tran 347BS/97BG Amendola 31/3/44; MIA {35m} Vinkovci, Yugo 2/7/44 w/Pate; mech fault, cr Sarajevo; MACR 6444. BARAZ TWINS.
42-31999 Del Cheyenne 14/1/44; Dalhart 28/1/44; Kearney 22/2/44; Grenier 25/2/44; ass 412BS/95BG [QW-X] Horham 27/2/44 CHICKEN SHIP PICKWICKIAN; MIA {35m} Gdynia 6/8/44, f/l Russia; rep, tran 815BS/483BG 20/12/44 KING SALVO; sal 7/2/45; re-ass Eastern Command 30/4/47; Recl Comp 1/12/47.
42-32000 Del Cheyenne 14/1/44; Dalhart 26/1/44; Kearney 22/2/44; Grenier 24/2/44; ass 524BS/379BG [WA-P] Kimbolton 27/2/44; c/l Felpham, UK. 4/7/44; sal 2 SAD Lt Staughton 10/7/44. TWENTIETH CENTURY.
42-32001 Del Cheyenne 14/1/44; Dalhart 28/1/44; Kearney 22/2/44; Wilmington 25/2/44; Drew 9/4/44; ass 92BG Podington 23/4/44; c/l and burned 20/5/44, sal.
42-32002 Del Cheyenne 14/1/44; Gr Island 30/1/44; ass 335BS/95BG [OE-X] Horham 11/2/44; MIA Berlin 6/3/44 w/Barksdale; cr Barnsdorf, Ger; 10POW; MACR 2982. BERLIN FIRST.
42-32003 Del Cheyenne 14/1/44; Dalhart 26/1/44; Kearney 22/2/44; Presque Is 24/2/44; ass 385BG, but tran 561BS/388BG Knettishall 3/4/44; MIA Rostock 11/4/44 w/Knowles; e/a, cr Rostock; 9KIA 1POW; MACR 3774. SHOO SHOO BABY.
42-32004 Del Cheyenne 14/1/44; Kearney 23/1/44; ass 560BS/388BG Knettishall 9/2/44; MIA Magdeburg 20/6/44 w/Patrick; flak, ditched Channel; 3KIA 7POW; MACR 5921. PRIDE OF THE YANKS.
42-32005 Del Denver 12/1/44; Kearney 28/1/44; ass 613BS/401BG [IN-M] Deenethorpe 7/3/44; MIA St

Lo 24/7/44 w/Coleman; ditched Channel. MACR? ANNE.

42-32006 Del Denver 14/1/44; Kearney 28/1/44; Presque Is 25/2/44; ass 339BS/96BG [QJ-V] Snetterton 3/3/44; MIA Nuremberg 3/10/44 w/?; f/l France?; sal 15/11/45. DURATION PLUS.

42-32007 Del Denver 15/1/44; Kearney 28/1/44; ass 533BS/381BG Ridgewell 21/2/44; tran 545BS/384BG Grafton Underwood 1/3/44; MIA Bonn 4/3/44 w/Cosentino; flak, cr Ransart, Bel; 2EVD 7POW; MACR 2740.

42-32008 Del Denver 15/1/44; Kearney 29/1/44; ass 551BS/385BG Gt Ashfield 21/2/44; retUS 121 BU Bradley 24/6/45; 4168 BU Sth Plains 5/7/45; 237 BU Kirtland 10/12/45; RFC Albuquerque 7/2/46. LIL AUDREY.

42-32009 Del Denver 15/1/44; Gr Island 29/1/44; ass 350BS/100BG [LN-X] Thorpe Abbotts 14/2/44; MIA Brussels 28/7/44 w/?; mid air coll w/42-97621; 9KIA; MACR 8174. BUFFALO GAL.

42-32010 Del Cheyenne 15/1/44; McDill 30/1/44; Morrison 9/3/44; ass 840BS/483BG Tortorella 11/3/44; Sterparone 22/4/44; MIA Budapest 30/7/44 w/Weston; flak, cr Budapest; 10POW; MACR 7107.

42-32011 Del Denver 15/1/44; Kearney 28/1/44; ass 427BS/303BG [GN-A] Molesworth 3/3/44 SWEET ADELINE; tran 562BS/388BG Knettishall 4/3/44; MIA Berlin 8/5/44 w/Heving; flak, cr Cherbourg, Fr; 5KIA 5POW; MACR 4599. PEG OF MY HEART.

42-32012 Del Denver 15/1/44; Kearney 28/1/44; ass 614BS/401BG [IW-P] Deenethorpe 5/3/44; retUS 121 BU Bradley 8/6/45; 4168 BU Sth Plains 13/6/45; RFC Kingman 5/12/45. SHARK TOOTH.

42-32013 Del Denver 15/1/44; Omaha 1/2/44; McDill 5/2/44; Morrison 11/3/44; ass 813BS/483BG Tortorella 30/3/44; tran 347BS/99BG Tortorella 31/3/44; MIA {1m} Steyr, Aus. 2/4/44 w/Koehne; e/a, cr Spanheim, no chutes seen; MACR 3887. OLE MOSE.

42-32014 Del Denver 15/1/44; McDill 4/2/44; Morrison 8/3/44; ass 817BS/483BG Tortorella 30/3/44; tran 347BS/97BG Tortorella 31/3/44; MIA {14m} Varese 30/4/44 w/Klein; e/a, cr Bologna, 10 chutes seen; MACR 4610. PAPPY YOKUM.

42-32015 Del Denver 16/1/44; McDill 3/2/44; Morrison 9/3/44; ass 815BS/483BG Tortorella 30/3/44; tran 416BS/99BG Tortorella 31/3/44; {108m} RetUS 121 BU Bradley 18/6/45; 4168 BU Sth Plains 21/6/45; RFC Kingman 28/11/45. ACTION PREFERRED.

42-32016 Del Denver 15/1/44; McDill 5/2/44; Morrison 12/3/44; ass 817BS/483BG Tortorella 30/3/44; tran 347BS/99BG Tortorella 31/3/44; MIA {87m} Brux 25/12/44 w/Brandon; flak, cr Oslip, Czech?; MACR 10704. SWAMP GAL.

42-32017 Del Cheyenne 15/1/44; Barksdale 4/2/44; Homestead 14/3/44; ass 815BS/483BG Tortorella 28/3/44; Sterparone 22/4/44; MIA {144m} Almasfuzito, Hung. 14/3/45 w/Mitchell; mech fault, cr Koprivnica, Hung; 10POW. MACR 12822. SWEET 17.

42-32018 Del Cheyenne 15/1/44; Gr Island 28/1/44; ass 351BS/100BG [EP-L] Thorpe Abbotts 11/2/44; dest on ground by Luftwaffe at Poltava, Russia, 21/6/44; sal 25/11/45.

42-32019 Del Cheyenne 15/1/44; Gr Island 28/1/44; ass 336BS/95BG [ET-R] Horham 9/2/44; MIA Rostock 11/4/44 w/Francis; e/a, cr Laendorf, Ger; 1KIA 9POW; MACR 3803.

42-32020 Del Cheyenne 18/1/44; Gr Island 31/1/44; Presque Is 7/4/44; ass 331BS/94BG [QE-U] Rougham 6/4/44; MIA Bohlen 7/10/44 w/Golden; e/a, cr Garnbach, Ger?; 6KIA 3POW; MACR 9551. BELLE OF THE BRAWL II.

42-32021 Del Cheyenne 16/1/44; St Joseph 1/2/44; McDill 5/2/44; Morrison 9/3/44; ass 840BS/483BG Tortorella 13/3/44; tran 346BS/99BG Tortorella 31/3/44; {30m} c/l 21/6/44; sal.

42-32022 Del Cheyenne 15/1/44; McDill 30/1/44; Morrison 5/3/44; ass 483BG Tortorella 15/3/44; tran 96BS/2BG Amendola 31/3/44; MIA {10m} Brasov 6/5/44 w/Weiss; #3 & #4 engines out and 10 chutes seen; 7EVD 3POW; MACR 4793. LONESOME POLECAT.

42-32023 Del Cheyenne 14/1/44; Kansas City 1/2/44; McDill 5/2/44; Morrison 9/3/44; ass 815BS/483BG Tortorella 12/3/44; tran 416BS/99BG Tortorella 31/3/44; {87m} RetUS 121 BU Bradley 6/6/45; 4104 BU Rome 28/6/45; Chanute 12/10/45; 4168 BU Sth Plains 17/12/45; 4136 BU Tinker 8/12/46; 4104 BU Rome 31/12/46; Recl Comp 19/6/47. FLAK HAPPY.

42-32024 Del Cheyenne 15/1/44; Gr Island 30/1/44; ass 524BS/379BG [WA-L] Kimbolton 20/2/44; first 8AF 100m, 1/11/44; tran Alconbury 1/6/45; retUS 121 BU Bradley 12/7/45; 4185 BU Independence 14/7/45; 4136 BU Tinker 16/12/45; RFC Kingman 29/12/45. SWAMP FIRE.

42-32025 Del Cheyenne 15/1/44; Gr Island 30/1/44; ass 533BS/381BG [VP-P] Ridgewell 25/2/44 (first NMF a/c in group); {73+m} RetUS 121 BU Bradley 23/6/45; 4168 BU Sth Plains 21/10/45; RFC Kingman 20/12/45. DREAMBABY.

42-32026 Del Cheyenne 18/1/44; Gr Island 30/1/44; ass 568BS/390BG Framlingham 10/2/44; MIA Kassel 30/12/44 w/Sweeney; flak, cr Nth Sea; 9KIA; MACR 11247. TIS A MYSTERY.

42-32027 Del Cheyenne 18/1/44; Gr Island 31/1/44; ass 427BS/303BG [GN-E] Molesworth 1/3/44; MIA Gera Oil Inst 19/9/44 w/?; MACR 8824. BETTY JANE.

42-32028 Del Denver 18/1/44; McDill 2/2/44; Morrison 9/3/44; ass 840BS/483BG Tortorella 13/3/44; tran 346BS/99BG Tortorella 31/3/44; MIA {43m} Ploesti 22/7/44 w/Carr; flak, cr Bucharest; 2KIA 8POW; MACR 6948.

42-32029 Del Denver 16/1/44; Gt Falls 19/1/44; Scott 2/2/44; McDill 4/2/44; Homestead 21/3/44; ass 815BS/483BG Tortorella 22/3/44; c/l base ex-Salzburg 11/11/44 w/Nueman; two engines out, bomb hung, burned and exploded; crew safe. MISS TREATED.

42-32030 Del Cheyenne 17/1/44; Gr Island 4/2/44; ass 561BS/388BG Knettishall 11/2/44; MIA Munich 31/7/44 w/Castrup; flak, exploded Schleisheim, Ger; 8KIA 1POW; MACR 7744. DEVIL'S LUCK.

42-32031 Del Denver 19/1/44; Dallas 4/2/44; McDill 5/2/44; Morrison 10/3/44; ass 817BS/483BG Tortorella 13/3/44; tran 429BS/2BG Amendola 31/3/44; sal 14/1/46. MAMMY YOKUM.

42-32032 Del Cheyenne 16/1/44; Lincoln 1/2/44; McDill 4/2/44; Morrison 12/3/44; ass 840BS/483BG Tortorella 14/3/44; tran 346BS/99BG Tortorella 31/3/44; {74m} taxi accident 19/12/44; sal. BATTLIN' BOBBY.

42-32033 Del Cheyenne 16/1/44; Gt Falls 19/1/44; Scott 31/1/44; McDill 4/2/44; Morrison 2/3/44; ass 816BS/483BG Tortorella 11/3/44; tran 347BS/99BG Tortorella 31/3/44; MIA {57m} Bleckhammer 13/10/44 w/Shafer; mech fault, cr Nordungau, Ger; MACR 9327. RITA ANN.

42-32034 Del Cheyenne 17/1/44; Gr Island 30/1/44; ass 407BS/92BG Podington 20/2/44; MIA Erding 24/4/44 w/Rapp; e/a, f/l Sweden; 3KIA 7INT; MACR 2579.

42-32035 Del Cheyenne 16/1/44; Kansas City 1/2/44; McDill 5/2/44; Morrison 9/3/44; ass 815BS/483BG Tortorella 13/3/44; tran 416BS/99BG Tortorella 31/3/44; MIA {10m} Ploesti 24/4/44 w/Schmaltz; mech fault, cr Ploesti; MACR 4390.

42-32036 Del Cheyenne 15/1/44; McDill 5/2/44; Morrison 8/3/44; Ass 816BS/483BG Tortorella 11/3/44; tran 348BS/99BG Tortorella 31/3/44; mid air coll w/42-106997 on 7/7/44; sheared tail off 997, landed Amendola (2BG); to depot 11/12/44; {74m} RetUS 4100 BU Patterson 27/7/45; Recl Comp 2/5/46.

42-32037 Del Cheyenne 15/1/44; Gr Island 20/1/44; ass 358BS/303BG [VK-N] Molesworth 28/2/44; MIA Berlin 21/6/44 w/Way; flak, cr Berlin; 5KIA 5POW; MACR 6540.

42-32038 Del Cheyenne 15/1/44; Gt Falls 18/1/44; Gr Island 30/1/44; Grenier 15/2/44; Presque Is 25/2/44; cr Iceland 10/3/44 en route UK. MACR 2732.

42-32039 Del Cheyenne 18/1/44; McDill 5/2/44; Morrison 10/3/44; ass 561BS/388BG 13/3/44 SHOO SHOO BABY; tran 815BS/483BG Tortorella 14/3/44; 416BS/99BG Tortorella 31/3/44; {70m} to depot 26/11/44; retUS 1103 BU Morrison 2/4/45; RFC Walnut Ridge 14/12/45. RABID RABBIT.

42-32040 Del Cheyenne 17/1/44; McDill 2/2/44; Morrison 7/3/44; ass 817BS/483BG Tortorella 14/3/44; tran 416BS/99BG Tortorella 31/3/44; {66m} to depot 26/11/44; sal 12/3/46. TURNIP TERMITE.

42-32041 Del Cheyenne 17/1/44; McDill 2/2/44; Morrison 7/3/44; ass 817BS/483BG Tortorella 14/3/44; tran 348BS/99BG Tortorella 31/3/44; MIA {38m} Vinkovci, Yugo. 2/7/44 w/Reuse; flak & e/a, cr Plattensee?; MACR 6518.

42-32042 Del Cheyenne 15/1/44; Gr Island 30/1/44; WO 31/1/44.

42-32043 Del Denver 18/1/44; Cheyenne 23/1/44; McDill 6/2/44; Morrison 8/3/44; ass 815BS/483BG Tortorella 13/3/44; one of two a/c conducted secret mission to Czechoslovakia on 17/9/44, with supplies to resistance and returning with US evadees; sal 30/4/45. PAPER DOLL.

42-32044 Del Denver 18/1/44; McDill 4/2/44; Morrison 9/3/44; ass 815BS/483BG Tortorella 13/3/44; retUS Cincinnati 20/9/45; RFC Walnut Ridge 17/12/45. GOOD DEAL.

42-32045 Del Denver 19/1/44; Cheyenne 25/1/44; Omaha 3/2/44; Hunter 15/2/44; Grenier 13/3/44; ass 339BS/96BGB [QJ-R] Snetterton 21/3/44; MIA Schweinfurt 19/7/44 w/Quinby; flak, cr Koblenz; 10POW; MACR 7411. SILVER SLIPPER.

42-32046 Del Denver 18/1/44; McDill 2/2/44; Morrison 9/3/44; ass (first NMF a/c issued) 817BS/483BG Tortorella 13/3/44; tran 347BS/99BG Tortorella 31/3/44; (had 20mm cannon fitted in tail turret); {63m} became weather a/c; retUS 1103 BU Morrison 19/9/45; RFC Walnut Ridge 18/12/45. LIL ABNER.

42-32047 Del Cheyenne 17/1/44; McDill 4/2/44; Morrison 9/3/44; ass 840BS/483BG Tortorella 13/3/44; tran 346BS/99BG Tortorella 31/3/44; one mission then taxi collision w/42-32115 on take off 4/4/44; sal.

42-32048 Del Cheyenne 17/1/44; Billings 20/1/44; Amarillo 4/2/44; McDill 4/2/44; Morrison 9/3/44; slated 96BG, but ass 840BS/483BG Tortorella 14/3/44; tran 20BS/2BG Amendola 31/3/44; MIA Moravska Ostrova, Czech. 2/8/44 w/Weiler; e/a cr Wiseham; MACR 8098. QUEEN.

42-32049 Del Denver 16/1/44; Cheyenne 22/1/44; Gr Island 17/2/44; Grenier 20/3/44; ass 534BS/381BG [GD-D] Ridgewell 6/4/44; MIA {20+m} Mulhouse 3/8/44 w/Wilcock; flak, one engine out, cr Nth Sea off Hol; 9KIA (pilot's body washed up Orfordness, UK). MACR 7883. YANKEE REBEL.

42-32050 Del Cheyenne 19/1/44; Sheppard 2/2/44; McDill 4/2/44; cr & burned 18/2/44; WO.

42-32051 Del Cheyenne 18/1/44; Gr Island 31/1/44; Grenier 4/2/44; ass 749BS/457BG Glatton 27/2/44; tran 56FG Boxted 12/6/44, ret 21/6/44; sal 1/11/44. LADY LUCK.

42-32052 Del Cheyenne 19/1/44; Amarillo 2/2/44; MsDill 6/2/44; Morrison 12/3/44; ass 840BS/493BG Tortorella 31/3/44; tran 416BS/99BG Tortorella 31/3/44; {91m} RetUS 121 BU Bradley 6/6/45; 4104 BU Rome 4/7/45; Recl Comp 13/11/45.

42-32053 Del Cheyenne 19/1/44; St Louis 2/2/44; McDill 5/2/44; Morrison 9/3/44; ass 816BS/483BG Tortorella 14/1/44; tran 49BS/2BG Amendola 31/3/44; MIA {27m} Budapest 27/6/44 w/Korb; flak & e/a, cr Budapest, five chutes seen; MACR 6428.

42-32054 Del Cheyenne 23/1/44; Gr Island 9/2/44; Presque Is 21/2/44; ass 407BS/92BG [PY-R] Podington 2/4/44; MIA Cologne 28/1/45 w/Flood; flak, cr Palmersheim, Ger?; 1KIA 8POW; MACR 12014. FLAK SHAK.

42-32055 Del Cheyenne 19/1/44; McDill 4/2/44; Homestead 17/3/44; ass 840BS/483BG Tortorella 21/3/44; tran 346BS/99BG Tortorella 31/3/44; b/d {99m} Bleckhammer, Ger. 26/12/44; three engines out, f/l Vis Is, Yugo; 1WIA; sal 11/2/45. DINAH MIGHT.

42-32056 Del Cheyenne 20/1/44; McDill 6/2/44; Morrison 9/3/44; ass 815BS/483BG Tortorella 13/3/44; tran 416BS/99BG Tortorella 31/3/44; MIA {1m} Steyr 2/4/44 w/Klansnic; e/a, five chutes seen, cr Steyr, Aus; MACR 3888.

42-32057 Del Cheyenne 19/1/44; Lubbock 3/2/44; McDill 5/2/44; Morrison 6/3/44; ass 816BS/483BG Tortorella 11/3/44; tran 348BS/99BG Tortorella 31/3/44; MIA {38m} Vienna 8/7/44 w/Gibson; flak, a/c exploded, chutes seen, cr Novi Marov, Yugo; MACR 6368.

42-32058 Del Denver 19/1/44; Cheyenne 22/1/44; McDill 5/2/44; Morrison 9/3/44; ass 840BS/483BG Tortorella 13/3/44; tran 96BS/2BG Amendola 31/3/44; MIA {9m} Gyor, Hung. 13/4/44 w/Reeves; e/a, #3 on fire, a/c exploded. MACR 3917.

42-32059 Del Denver 21/1/44; Cheyenne 25/1/44; Gr Island 17/2/44; Grenier 10/3/44; ass 550BS/385BG Gt Ashfield 12/3/44; MIA Merseburg 27/8/44 w/Quick; ditched Channel. POLTERGEIST.

42-32060 Del Denver 20/1/44; Cheyenne 23/1/44; Kearney 18/2/44; Presque Is 19/2/44; ass 535BS/381BG [MS-V] Ridgewell 6/4/44; MIA {48+m} Stuttgart 9/12/44 w/Clarke; 5WIA, f/l with two engines out at Nancy, Fr; sal 22/12/44. BOULDER BUF.

42-32061 Del Denver 20/1/44; Amarillo 2/2/44; McDill 5/2/44; Morrison 8/3/44; ass 816BS/483BG Tortorella 11/3/44; tran 348BS/99BG Tortorella 31/3/44; {94m} RetUS 1103 BU Morrison 3/4/45; 4104 BU Rome 2/7/45; Recl Comp 13/11/45. LUSCIOUS LOUISE.

42-32062 Del Denver 18/1/44; Cheyenne 21/1/44; McDill 5/2/44; Morrison 9/3/44; ass 815BS/483BG Tortorella 13/3/44; tran 416BS/99BG Tortorella 31/3/44; MIA {1m} Steyr, Aus. 2/4/44 w/Moffitt; e/a, two engines out, c/l Oglin, Yugo; 3EVD ret 2/5/44; MACR 4909.

42-32063 Del Cheyenne 20/1/44; McDill 4/2/44; Morrison 7/3/44; ass 817BS/483BG Tortorella 11/3/44; tran 347BS/99BG Tortorella 31/3/44; {14m} Varese, It. 30/4/44 w/Maslow; c/l Tertoli and burned out; crew safe.

42-32064 Del Cheyenne 20/1/44; Ft Bragg 4/2/44; McDill 5/2/44; Morrison 9/3/44; ass 840BS/483BG Tortorella 15/3/44; tran 346BS/99BG Tortorella 31/3/44; {64m} became cargo a/c from 14/11/44; retUS, RFC Walnut Ridge 20/12/45. GOING.

42-32065 Del Cheyenne 20/1/44; McDill 5/2/44; Morrison 12/3/44; ass 346BS/483BG Tortorella 14/3/44; tran 346BS/99BG Tortorella 31/3/44; MIA {7m} Belgrade 16/4/44 w/Headrick; flak, cr Belgrade; 8KIA 2POW; MACR 4076. EL DIABLO.

42-32066 Del Cheyenne 20/1/44; Gr Island 11/2/44; Presque Is 11/2/44; ass 412BS/95BG [QW-D] Horham 3/3/44; b/d Stuttgart 16/12/44; sal 17/12/44. SILVER SLIPPER.

42-32067 Del Cheyenne 20/1/44; McDill 4/2/44; slated 483BG c/l 20/2/44, rep; 901 BU Pinecastle 2/6/44; 327 BU Drew 14/6/44; RFC Altus 5/11/45.

42-32068 Del Cheyenne 20/1/44; McDill 3/2/44; Morrison 9/3/44; ass 840BS/483BG Tortorella 13/3/44; tran 346BS/99BG Tortorella 31/3/44; MIA {46m} Ploesti 28/7/44 w/Conner; flak, cr Sienisa, Yugo?; MACR 7122. HEAVEN CAN WAIT.

42-32069 Del Cheyenne 20/1/44; McDill 4/2/44; Morrison 8/3/44; ass 816BS/483BG Tortorella 11/3/44; tran 348BS/99BG Tortorella 31/3/44; {81m} RetUS 4100 BU Patterson 3/3/45; Recl Comp 24/5/46.

42-32070 Del Cheyenne 21/1/44; Gr Island 14/2/44; Presque Is 13/3/44; ass 729BS/452BG Deopham Green 13/3/44; MIA Warnemünde 9/4/44 w/Patterson; e/a, cr Soilested, Ger?; 4EVD 6POW; MACR 4363.

42-32071 Del Cheyenne 21/1/44; McDill 4/2/44; Morrison 7/3/44; ass 817BS/483BG Tortorella 11/3/44; tran 416BS/99BG Tortorella 31/3/44 MOONBEAM McSWINE; re-named NINE WOLVES & POPPA; MIA {93m} Graz, Aus. 8/2/45 w/Schuld; mid air coll w/44-6691, cr Kapsovar; 9KIA 2POW (TG who rode tail down). MACR 12082. FREDDY-H.

42-32072 Del Cheyenne 21/1/44; Kearney 17/2/44; Grenier 24/2/44; ass 401BS/91BG [LL-L] Bassingbourn 31/3/44; MIA {9m} La Glacerie 27/4/44 w/Tilton; flak, #3 afire cr Bricquebec, Fr; 1KIA (radio op) 9POW (nav WIA); MACR 4258. MARY.

42-32073 Del Cheyenne 23/1/44; Billings 27/1/44; Gr Island 21/2/44; Presque Is 12/3/44; ass 339BS/96BG [QJ-D] Snetterton 13/2/44; MIA Augsburg 13/4/44 w/Potter; e/a, f/l Dubendorf, Switz; 9INT 1KIA; MACR 3767. (used by Swiss AF) RetUS 1377 BU Grenier 9/10/45; RFC Walnut Ridge 7/1/46.

42-32074 Del Denver 21/1/44; Cheyenne 23/1/44; Amarillo 2/2/44; McDill 4/2/44; Morrison 9/3/44; ass 815BS/483BG Tortorella 13/3/44; tran 416BS/99BG Tortorella 31/3/44; {82m} RetUS 4100 BU Patterson 14/3/45; 1103 BU Morrison 26/3/45; Recl Comp 24/5/46. OH JOSIE.

42-32075 Del Denver 21/1/44; McDill 7/2/44; Morrison 8/3/44; ass 817BS/483BG Tortorella 11/3/44; tran 347BS/99BG Tortorella 31/3/44; {63m} c/t/o, exploded 5/10/44; sal. FEARLESS FOSDICK.

42-32076 Del Denver 24/1/44; Cheyenne 28/1/44; Gr Island 6/2/44; Presque Is 29/2/44; ass 401BS/91BG [LL-E] Bassingbourn 23/3/44; MIA {23m} Posnan 29/5/44 w/Guenther; flak, three engines out, f/l Bulltofta, Swed; 9INT; MACR 5354. Used as Swedish airliner SE-BAP, the sold to Denmark for $1 and called STIG VIKING, later to STORE BJORN on African routes; bought by FNGI for geographical work before retiring at Creuil, Fr; sold to USAF for 20 cents and re-stored at Wright-Patterson in over 60,000 man hours, now in AF Museum as SHOO SHOO SHOO BABY.

42-32077 Del Denver 21/1/44; Cheyenne 24/1/44; McDill 5/2/44; Homestead 11/2/44; ass 815BS/483BG Tortorella 14/3/44; MIA Vienna 13/10/44 w/Houghtelin; flak, cr Baja, Hung; 10EVD ret 17/10/44; MACR 9142.

42-32078 Del Cheyenne 21/1/44; Gr Island 17/2/44; Presque Is 4/3/44; ass 550BS/385BG Gt Ashfield 6/3/44; retUS 121 BU Bradley 26/6/45; 4168 BU Sth Plains 21/10/44; RFC Kingman 3/12/45. BARBARA B.

42-32079 Del Cheyenne 21/1/44; Kearney 15/2/44; Grenier 25/3/44; Presque Is 28/3/44; ass 749BS/457BG Glatton 9/6/44 JAYHAWK; MIA Bremen 26/9/44 w/Gooch; flak, cr Lisse, Hol; 4EVD 2KIA 3POW. MACR 9419. DELAYED LADY II.

42-32080 Del Cheyenne 21/1/44; Gr Island 17/2/44; Presque Is 2/3/44; ass 708BS/447BG Rattlesden 17/3/44; caught fire on training flight 2/5/45, sal. STINKY.

42-32081 Del Cheyenne 23/1/44; Gr Island 6/2/44; Presque Is 4/3/44; ass 708BS/447BG Rattlesden 6/3/44; MIA Hamburg 4/11/44 w/Adams; flak, cr Channel, 9KIA; MACR 10162. YELLOW CAB.

42-32082 Del Cheyenne 22/1/44; Billings 25/1/44; Cheyenne 30/1/44; Kearney 11/2/44; Presque Is 28/2/44; ass 728BS/452BG Deopham Green 3/3/43; MIA Berlin 28/3/44 w/Cook; flak, cr Châteaudun, Fr; 7KIA 3POW; MACR 3488.

42-32083 Del Cheyenne 21/1/44; Kearney 19/2/44; Grenier 1/3/43; Presque Is 10/3/44; ass 731BS/452BG Deopham Green 12/3/44; MIA Berlin 26/2/45 w/Marksian; flak, cr Zossen, Ger; 9RTD; MACR 12772. FLATBUSH FLOOZIE.

42-32084 Del Cheyenne 22/1/44; Kearney 7/2/44; Presque Is 18/2/44; ass 750BS/457BG Glatton 3/3/44; b/d Bremen 24/6/44, sal. LI'L SATAN.

42-32085 Del Cheyenne 24/1/44; WO Gt Falls 28/1/44, but rep; Cheyenne 20/5/44; Kearney 3/6/44; Bangor 13/6/44; ass 324BS/91BG [DF-H] Bassingbourn 10/7/44; tran 322BS; MIA {51m} Tempelhof 3/2/45 w/Miller; flak, lost # 3 &4; under control, c/l Altentreptow, Ger; 9POW; MACR 12233. YANKEE BELLE.

42-32086 Del Cheyenne 22/1/44; Kearney 7/2/44; Presque Is 18/2/44; ass 401BG Deenethorpe 3/3/44; tran 749BS/457BG Glatton 5/3/44; b/d Gaggenau, f/l France 10/9/44, ret 11/9/44; sal 15/2/45. YOU NEVER KNOW.

42-32087 Del Cheyenne 23/1/44; Gr Island 17/2/44; Presque Is 12/3/44; ass 728BS/452BG Deopham Green 13/3/44; MIA Gdynia 6/8/44 w/Graber; flak, f/l Resmo, Swed; 9INT; MACR 7387. Left 28/5/45.

42-32088 Del Cheyenne 23/1/44; Gr Island 6/2/44; Grenier 10/2/44; ass 532BS/381BG [VE-M] Ridgewell 6/4/44; MIA {1+m} Berlin 19/5/44 w/Blog; 9POW; MACR 5030. DRY GULCHER.

42-32089 Del Cheyenne 28/1/44; Gr Island 11/2/44; Presque Is 21/2/44; ass 570BS/390BG Framlingham 22/2/44; MIA Magdeburg 28/5/44 w/Mathias; e/a, cr Holzhausen, Ger; 10POW; MACR 5257.

42-32090 Del Cheyenne 23/1/44; Gr Island 7/2/44; Grenier 22/2/44; Presque Is 28/2/44; ass 350BS/100BG [LN-R] Thorpe Abbotts 3/3/44; taxi accident 19/4/45; sal 21/4/45; {102m} RetUS 3505 BU Scott 19/9/45; re-ass 8AF Dutch-Belgian coast 26/12/46; Recl Comp 19/11/47. SILVER DOLLAR.

42-32091 Del Cheyenne 26/1/44; Gr Island 7/2/44; Presque Is 11/3/44; ass 524BS/379BG [WA-K] Kimbolton 30/3/44; b/d Saarbrücken 23/5/44; sal 26/5/44.

42-32092 Del Cheyenne 24/1/44; McDill 5/2/44; Morrison 12/3/44; ass 817BS/483BG Tortorella

14/3/44; tran 347BS/99BG Tortorella 31/3/44; {80m} RetUS 121 BU Bradley 6/6/45; 4104 BU Rome 28/6/45; Recl Comp 13/11/45. MISS NATURAL.

42-32093 Del Cheyenne 23/1/44; Gr Island 3/2/44; Grenier 1/3/44; Presque Is 12/3/44; ass 527BS/379BG Kimbolton 11/3/44; MIA Ulm 9/8/44 w/Jones; flak, cr Walheim, Ger; 3KIA 6POW; MACR 7392. BIG BARN SMELL.

42-32094 Del Cheyenne 23/1/44; McDill 7/2/44; Morrison 9/3/44; ass 840BS/483BG Tortorella 14/3/44; tran 416BS/99BG Tortorella 31/3/44; {88m} RetUS 1103 BU Morrison 11/5/45; 4168 BU Sth Plains 9/6/45; RFC Kingman 14/12/45.

42-32095 Del Cheyenne 28/1/44; Kearney 11/2/44; Presque Is 25/2/44; ass 457BG Glatton 14/3/44; tran 322BS/91BG [LG-L] Bassingbourn 16/3/44; {143m inc group's last 25/4/45} RetUS 121 BU Bradley 11/6/45; 4168 BU Sth Plains 16/6/45; RFC Kingman 13/12/45. ACK-ACK ANNIE.

42-32096 Del Cheyenne 23/1/44; Kearney 5/2/44; Presque Is 18/2/44; ass 711BS/477BG Rattlesden 22/2/44; MIA Augsburg 16/3/44 w/Huckins; e/a, cr Orconte, Fr?; 2EVD 2KIA 6POW; MACR 3187.

42-32097 Del Cheyenne 24/1/44; McDill 5/2/44; Morrison 9/3/44; ass 817BS/483BG Tortorella 13/3/44 SADIE HAWKINS; tran 347BS/99BG Tortorella 31/3/44; MIA {90m} Odertal, Ger. 18/12/44 w/Buster; cr Bruenn, Ger; MACR 10635. SLIPSTREAM.

42-32098 Del Cheyenne 24/1/44; Gr Island 7/2/44; Presque Is 21/2/44; ass 388BG Knettishall 25/2/44; tran 750BS/457BG Glatton 4/3/44; b/d Cologne 2/10/44, f/l France; sal 14/11/44. GI VIRGIN II.

42-32099 Del Cheyenne 23/1/44; Seattle 26/1/44; Gr Island 7/2/44; Presque Is 21/2/44; ass 390BG Framlingham 23/2/44; tran 457BG Glatton 4/3/44; 367BS/306BG [GY-S] Thurleigh 12/3/44; MIA Berlin 5/12/44 w/Manning; flak, cr Nth Sea; 9KIA; MACR 11039. FIGHTIN' CARBARN HAMMERSLAW.

42-32100 Del Cheyenne 23/1/44; Billings 26/1/44; Orlando 6/2/44, modified for Azon bombing; Morrison 28/3/44; ass 419BS/301BG Lucera 19/4/44; MIA Vienna 1/2/45 w/Owens; hit by flak; 9POW 1MIA; MACR 12077.

42-32101 Del Cheyenne 24/1/44; Kearney 5/2/44; ass 748BS/457BG Glatton 6/3/44; b/d {113m} Hannover 14/3/45, f/l Continent; sal. EL LOBO II.

42-32102 Del Cheyenne 24/1/44; Kearney 14/2/44; Grenier 25/2/44; Presque Is 28/2/44; ass 535BNS/381BG [MS-O] Ridgewell 3/5/44 MALE CALL; b/d {55m} Mannheim 1/2/45, c/l base; sal 2 SAD Lt Staughton 2/2/45. JULIE LINDA.

42-32103 Del Cheyenne 24/1/44; Billings 28/1/44; Gr Island 3/2/44; Orlando 8/2/44, modified for Azon bombing; Morrison 28/3/44; ass 419BS/301BG Lucera 19/4/44; MIA Szolnok, Hung. 2/7/44 w/Olivarri; ditched, 1KIA 8RTD.

42-32104 Del Cheyenne 24/1/44; Billings 29/1/44; Dallas 6/2/44; Orlando 13/2/44, modified for Azon bombing; Morrison 28/3/44; ass 419BS/301BG Lucera 19/4/44; MIA Bleckhammer 17/12/44 w/Kearns; 1KIA 1EVD 8POW; MACR 10670. ST FRANCIS.

42-32105 Del Cheyenne 23/1/44; Orlando 8/2/44, modified for Azon bombing; Morrison 30/3/44; ass 419BS/301BG Lucera 19/4/44; sal 2/8/45.

42-32106 Del Cheyenne 24/1/44; Gr Island 11/2/44; Presque Is 11/3/44; ass 711BS/447BG Rattlesden 13/3/44; tran 545BS/384BG [JD-R] Grafton Underwood 24/3/44; {100+m} sal 31/10/45. SNUFFY.

42-32107 Del Cheyenne 24/1/44; Orlando 8/2/44, modified for Azon bombing; Morrison 26/3/44; ass 419BS/301BG Lucera 19/4/44; MIA Weiner Neudorf 26/7/44 w/McManaman; e/a, cr Weinder Neustadt; 1KIA, 9POW; MACR 7129.

42-32108 Del Cheyenne 24/1/44; Orlando 7/2/44, modified for Azon bombing; Morrison 28/3/44; ass 419BS/301BG Lucera 19/4/44; sal 20/4/45.

42-32109 Del Cheyenne 24/1/44; McDill 5/2/44; Morrison 9/3/44; ass 840BS/483BG Tortorella 13/3/44; MIA Budapest 14/7/44 w/Swanson; flak, nose blown off, cr Solt; 2KIA 8POW; MACR 6901. MIZPAH.

42-32110 Del Cheyenne 24/1/44; McDill 5/2/44; slated 91BG, tran 457BG, but switched Morrison 9/3/44; ass 840BS/483BG Tortorella 14/3/44; tran 416BS/99BG Tortorella 31/3/44; MIA {72m} Odertal, Ger. 18/12/44 w/Clark; flak, cr Kaposvar, Hung; 1KIA 9EVD,RTD; MACR 10633.

42-32111 Del Cheyenne 24/1/44; McDill 7/2/44; Morrison 9/3/44; ass 816BS/483BG Tortorella 13/3/44; b/d Budapest 14/7/44 w/Goesling; f/l Foggia w/300 flak holes; sal 15/7/45.

42-32112 Del Cheyenne 26/1/44; Hunter 22/2/44; Presque Is 1/3/44; ass 337BS/96BG [AW-F] Snetterton 6/3/44; cr during assembly at Beachamwell, UK 2/1/45; 9KIA.

42-32113 Del Cheyenne 24/1/44; Gr Island 6/2/44; Grenier 23/2/44; ass 368BS/306BG [BO-G] Thurleigh 12/3/44; MIA Berlin 24/5/44 w/Ehrler; flak, cr Berlin; 4KIA 5POW; MACR 4952.

42-32114 Del Cheyenne 24/1/44; Kearney 5/2/44; ass 447BG Rattlesden 13/2/44; sal 6/4/44.

42-32115 Del Cheyenne 26/1/44; slated 457BG; McDill 7/2/44; Morrison 9/3/44; ass 840BS/483BG Tortorella 13/3/44; tran 346BS/99BG Tortorella 31/3/44; {2m} taxi accident w/42-32047; WO sal 4/4/44.

42-32116 Del Cheyenne 26/1/44; Presque Is 1/3/44; ass 452BG Deopham Green 3/3/44; tran 457BG Glatton 11/3/44; 323BS/91BG [OR-B] Bassingbourn 16/3/44 HEIGH HO SILVER; 322BS [LG-A] the 401BS [LL-B]; {130m} RetUS, RFC Kingman 27/5/45. HI-HO SILVER.

B-17G-DL

42-37714 Del Long Beach 6/8/43; Scott 20/10/43; slated 401BG, ass 510BS/351BG [TU-T] Polebrook 11/11/43; MIA Berlin 7/5/44 w/Presley; flak, ditched Nth Sea; 10POW; MACR 4953. RONCHI.

42-37715 Del Long Beach 6/8/43; Gr Island 20/9/43; ass 351BS/100BG [EP-G] Thorpe Abbotts 25/9/43; MIA Emden 11/12/43 w/Haddox; e/a, cr Nth Sea; 9KIA 1POW; MACR 1570. SUGAR FOOT.

42-37716 Del Tulsa 10/8/43; Scott 9/10/43; ass 338BS/96BG [BX-P] Snetterton 14/10/43; tran 95BG Horham 15/10/43; retUS 121 BU Bradley 12/7/45; 4185 BU Independence 10/10/45; RFC Kingman 20/12/45.

42-37717 Del Long Beach 6/8/43; Scott 8/10/43; ass 422BS/305BG [JJ-B] Chelveston 20/12/32; 858BS Cheddington 20/6/44; ASR Halesworth /45; retUS 121 BU Bradley 29/6/45; 4168 BU Sth Plains 21/10/45; RFC Kingman 18/11/45. CHANNEL FEVER BABY.

42-37718 Del Long Beach 7/8/43; Redmond 15/8/43; ass 92BG Podington 10/9/43; tran 368BS/306BG [BO-H] Thurleigh 19/9/43; MIA Anklam 9/10/43 w/Ranck; e/a, cr Samsoe Is, Hol; 1KIA 9POW; MACR 870.

42-37719 Del Long Beach 6/8/43; Walla Walla 15/8/43; ass 533BS/381BG [VP-X] Ridgewell 8/10/43; MIA (12m) Oschersleben 11/1/44 w/Nason; flak, ditched Zuider Zee, Hol; 9KIA 1POW (John Lantz returned when a/c recovered from Ijsselmeer in Feb 1975, after found in June 1966); MACR 1881. HELLCAT.

42-37720 Del Long Beach 6/8/43; Denver 14/8/43; ass 367BS/306BG [GY-N] Thurleigh 18/9/43; MIA Schweinfurt 14/10/43 w/White; e/a, cr Schweinfurt; 9KIA 1POW; MACR 823.

42-37721 Del Denver 10/8/43; Redmond 15/8/43; ass 534BS/381BG [GD-L] Ridgewell 1/10/43; b/d Berlin 19/5/44; sal 2/6/45. SUGAR.

42-37722 Del Denver 10/8/43; Redmond 15/8/43; Walla walla 21/10/43; Gr Island 15/11/43; ass 401BG Deenethorpe 21/1/44; c/f on base 28/1/44; sal 2 SAD 30/1/44; as SB-17G AMC to REC 2/5/49.

42-37723 Del Denver 10/8/43; Redmond 15/8/43; ass 569BS/390BG [CC-D] Framlingham 9/9/43 PAYDOLA; retUS 121 BU Bradley 16/7/45; 4168 BU Sth Plains 12/9/45; RFC Kingman 14/11/45. JOHNNY WALKER.

42-37724 Del Denver 10/8/43; Walla Walla 15/8/43; ass 368BS/306BG [BO-Z] Thurleigh 20/9/43; AFSC 2/5/44; retUS 4136 BU Tinker 14/8/44; 3022 BU Indian Springs 2/9/44; 3021 Las Vegas 23/3/45; 2126 BU Laredo 10/4/45; 233 BU Davis Monthan 14/4/45; 2126 BU Laredo 17/4/45; RFC Walnut Ridge 5/1/46.

42-37725 Del Denver 10/8/43; Gr Island 20/10/43; ass 546BS/384BG Grafton Underwood 19/12/43; MIA Bordeaux 31/12/43 w/Rich; ditched Nth Sea; 10RTD.

42-37726 Del Denver 10/8/43; Redmond 15/8/43; ass 366BS/305BG [KY-N] Chelveston 1/10/43; 422BS [JJ-L]; tran 856BS Cheddington 26/6/44; sal 18/7/45. SHADY LADY.

42-37727 Del Denver 11/8/43; Scott 16/9/43; ass 303BG Molesworth 10/10/43; 1 BAD 23/10/43; tran 545BS/384BG [JD-Z] Grafton Underwood 2/11/43; MIA Brunswick 30/1/44 w/Penney; e/a, cr Ban Muender, Ger; 3KIA 7POW; MACR 2265.

42-37728 Del Denver 10/8/43; Redmond 15/8/43; ass 525BS/379BG Kimbolton 3/10/43; MIA Anklam 9/10/43 w/Lash; flak, cr Odense, Den; 10POW; MACR 1045.

42-37729 Del Denver 10/8/43; 3701 BU Love Fd, WO 15/12/43.

42-37730 Del Denver 10/8/43; Gr Island 3/9/43; ass 533BS/381BG [VP-U] Ridgewell 20/9/43; MIA {15+m} Oschersleben 11/1/44 w/Crozier; flak, cr Mekkelenberg, Hol; 1KIA 9POW; MACR 1887.

42-37731 Del Denver 10/8/43; Dalhart 17/8/43; ass 510BS/351BG [TU-A] Polebrook 22/9/43; 508BS [YB-A]; MIA {12m} Bordeaux 31/12/43 w/Maj Blalock; flak & e/a, cr Cognac; 2KIA 9POW (inc group CO, Col Hatcher); MACR 1984.

42-37732 Del Denver 10/8/43; Dalhart 17/8/43; Gr Island 5/9/43; ass 526BS/379BG [LF-R] Kimbolton 19/10/43; MIA Augsburg 25/2/44 w/Bochna; flak, cr Saarbrücken; MACR 2879. THE CELESTIAL SIREN.

42-37733 Del Denver 10/8/43; Gr Island 3/9/43; Buffalo, NY 4/9/44 where navigator killed when he stepped from a/c into still spinning prop; ass 813BS/482BG [PC-W] Alconbury 12/9/43; tran 535BS/381BG [MS-J] Ridgewell 22/2/44; MIA Oranienburg 18/4/44 w/Soeder; flak, cr Kidenz, Ger?; 9POW; MACR 4051. PATCHES N' PRAYERS.

42-37734 Del Denver 10/8/43; Gr Island 3/9/43; ass 336BS/95BG [ET-G] Horham 8/9/43; MIA Kiel 5/1/44 w/Currence; cr Biesmore, Ger?; 2EVD 1KIA 7POW; MACR 4886. CUDDLE CAT.

42-37735 Del Denver 10/8/43; Long Beach 13/8/43;

ass 813BS/482BG [PC-X] Alconbury 8/9/43; tran 326BS/92BG [JW-X] Podington 20/2/44; retUS 121 BU Bradley 13/7/45; 4185 BU Independence 27/7/45; RFC Kingman 18/12/45.

42-37736 Del Denver 11/8/43; Gr Island 5/9/43; ass 324BS/91BG [DF-G] Bassingbourn 24/9/43; ass radio relay a/c; {29m} sal 6/11/45. DUKE OF PADUCAH.

42-37737 Del Denver 10/8/43; Long Beach 13/8/43; ass 401BS/91BG [LL-K] Bassingbourn 26/9/43; MIA {1m} Munster 10/10/43 w/Verril; mech fault, cr Brockland, Hol; 1EVD 1KIA 8POW; MACR 1941. TENNESSEE TODDY.

42-37738 Del Denver 11/8/43; Gr Island 3/9/43; ass 322BS/91BG [LG-T] Bassingbourn 24/9/43; MIA Osnabrück 22/12/43 w/Steel; e/a, cr Ijmuiden, Hol; 1KIA 9POW; MACR 1715.

42-37739 Del Denver 10/8/43; Gr Island 3/9/43; ass 337BS/96BG [AW-N] Snetterton 8/9/44; MIA Bremen 16/12/43 w/Freemole; e/a, cr Poppengweiler, Ger; 10KIA; MACR 1566.

42-37740 Del Denver 12/8/43; ass 365BS/305BG [XK-E] Chelveston 15/9/43; MIA Schweinfurt 14/10/43 w/Bullock; e/a, cr Schweinfurt; 2EVD 1KIA 7POW; MACR 920.

42-37741 Del Denver 14/8/43; ass 366BS/305BG Chelveston 18/9/43; MIA Frankfurt 4/10/43 w/Bailey; flak, cr Brussels; 3KIA 7POW; MACR 779.

42-37742 Del Denver 13/8/43; Gr Island 3/9/43; ass 401BS/91BG [LL-J] Bassingbourn 22/9/43; MIA {5m} Wilhelmshafen 3/11/43 w/McAdams; e/a, cr Nth Sea; 10KIA; MACR 1154. VAGABOND LADY.

42-37743 Del Tulsa 16/8/43; Long Beach 17/8/43; ass 333BS/94BG [TS-M] Rougham 11/9/43; tran 803BS RCM Sculthorpe 1/44; APH Knettishall; MIA Heligoland 15/10/44. YANKEE DOODLE DANDY.

42-37744 Del Denver 13/8/43; Tulsa 17/8/43; Scott 1/10/43; ass 8AF Bovingdon 10/6/43; cr t/o 10KAS 10/12/43.

42-37745 Del Tulsa 16/8/43; Gr Island 25/9/43; ass 812BS/482BG [MI-M] Alconbury 28/9/43; sal 22/6/45.

42-37746 Del Tulsa 14/9/43; Denver 15/8/43; Scott 25/10/43; ass 401BG Deenethorpe 1/11/43; tran 323BS/91BG [OR-T] Bassingbourn 20/11/43; MIA {18m} Oschersleben 22/2/43 w/Kolts; e/a, cr Detmold, Ger; 3KIA 7POW; MACR 2643. PAPER DOLLY.

42-37747 Del Tulsa 14/9/43; Denver 15/8/43; Scott 26/9/43; ass 332BS/94BG [XM-A] Rougham 30/9/43; MIA Bordeaux 5/12/43 w/Devine; e/a, cr Callac, Fr; 10KIA; MACR 1174. BUCKET OF BOLTS.

42-37748 Del Tulsa 16/8/43; Gr Island 24/9/43; ass 418BS/100BG [LD-V] Thorpe Abbotts 27/9/43; MIA Gelsenkirchen 5/11/43 w/Martin; flak, ditched Channel; 2EVD 8KIA; MACR 1156.

42-37749 Del Denver 16/8/43; ass 337BS/96BG [AW-O] Snetterton 11/9/43; MIA Duren 20/10/43.

42-37750 Del Denver 16/8/43; Long Beach 17/8/43; ass 366BS/305BG [KY-M] Chelveston 16/9/43; MIA Schweinfurt 14/10/43 w/Lang; e/a, cr Floverish, Ger?; MACR 779.

42-37751 Del Denver 7/8/43; ass 365BS/305BG [XK-P] Chelveston 16/9/43; MIA Bremen 8/10/43 w/Emmert; flak, cr Noordospolder, Hol; 1EVD 9POW MACR 871.

42-37752 Del Denver 17/8/43; ass 339BS/96BG [QJ-A] Snetterton 8/9/43; MIA Bremen 8/10/43 w/Flahive; e/a, cr Bremen; 10POW; MACR 853.

42-37753 Del Denver 17/8/43; ass 813BS/482BG [PC-O] Alconbury (Oboe a/c) 19/9/43; tran 326BS/92BG [JW-Q] Podington 21/2/44; sal 13/10/45. MORTIMER.

42-37754 Del Denver 17/8/43; ass 534BS/381BG [GD-K] Ridgewell 20/9/43; {9m} b/d Rheims 28/3/44 w/Henry; 3KIA 6RTD (baled over base, before pilot dumped at sea); WHO DAT - DINGBAT?

42-37755 Del Denver 17/8/43; ass 325BS/92BG [NV-A] Podington 16/9/43; MIA {11m} Stuttgart 25/2/44 w/Beach; flak, f/l Dubendorf, Switz; 10INT; MACR 2755. DOTTY G.

42-37756 Del Denver 17/8/43; ass 335BS/95BG [OE-O] Horham 6/9/43; MIA Eschweiler 24/1/44 w/Mowers; cr Waterloo, Bel; 3EVD 1KIA 6POW; MACR 2259. ROARIN' BULL.

42-37757 Del Denver 19/8/43; Scott 16/9/43; ass 360BS/303BG [PU-N] Molesworth 18/10/43; c/l Lt Staughton 10/12/43; sal 2 SAD 11/12/43.

42-37758 Del Denver 20/8/43; Gr Island 18/8/43; ass 545BS/384BG [JD-W] Grafton Underwood 3/10/43; sal 10/12/44; retUS 1377 BU Grenier 12/1/45; 4124 BU Altus 16/8/45; RFC Altus 9/10/45. KENTUCKY KERNEL.

42-37759 Del Denver 19/8/43; ass 367BS/306BG [GY-V] Thurleigh 19/9/43; b/d Anklam 9/10/43; c/l base hit 42-30730, MACR 2755.

42-37760 Del Denver 19/8/43; ass 532BS/381BG [VE-F] Ridgewell 20/9/43; {6m} tran AFSC, 487BG Lavenham; APH & Azon duties Knettishall /44. AVENGER

42-37761 Del Denver 21/8/43; ass 323BS/91BG [OR-L] Bassingbourn 4/10/43; c/l Steeple Morden, UK 6/3/44; sal 2 SAD 7/3/44. BLUE DREAMS.

42-37762 Del Denver 20/8/43; Scott 16/9/43; ass 303BG Molesworth 22/10/43; tran 545BS/384BG Grafton Underwood 1/11/43; MIA Bremen 26/11/43 w/Zituik; e/a, cr Zwischenahn, Ger; 1KIA 9POW; MACR 1580. CHAPLAIN'S OFFICE.

42-37763 Del Denver 20/8/43; Scott 29/9/43; ass 571BS/390BG Framlingham 5/11/43; MIA Bremen 20/12/43 w/Riley; e/a, cr Bremen; 1KIA 9POW; MACR 1730.

42-37764 Del Denver 21/8/43; Gr Island 18/9/43; ass 526BS/379BG [LF-P] Kimbolton 21/10/43; b/d Berlin 6/3/44; sal 2 SAD 8/3/44.

42-37765 Del Denver 20/8/43; Scott 8/11/43; ass 457BG Glatton 18/11/43; tran 369BS/306BG [WW-D] Thurleigh 14/12/43; AFSC 12/5/44; retUS 8ETA Tinker 13/7/45; 4136 BU Tinker 19/7/45; re-ass 31/3/47; 4141 BU Pyote 20/5/47; Recl Comp 1/6/49.

42-37766 Del Denver 25/8/43; Scott 30/9/43; ass 334BS/95BG [BG-F] Horham 13/10/43; MIA Munster 22/12/43 w/Mangis; cr Zuidwolde, Hol; 1EVD 4KIA 5POW; MACR 1702.

42-37767 Del Denver 24/8/43; Scott 29/9/43; ass 332BS/94BG Rougham 4/10/43; tran 401BS/91BG [LL-D] Bassingbourn 5/11/43; c/l Cambridge A/fd, UK 20/12/43; sal 2 SAD 23/12/43. MACR 1886. VOX POP.

42-37768 Del Denver 23/8/43; Gr Island 18/9/43; ass 526BS/379BG [LF-J] Kimbolton 19/10/43; MIA Oschersleben 11/1/44 w/Waggoner; e/a, cr Haeingen, Ger?; 2KIA 8POW; MACR 1943.

42-37769 Del Denver 23/8/43; WO 24/9/43.

42-37770 Del Denver 23/8/43; Scott 23/10/43; ass 614BS/401BG [IW-A] Deenethorpe 1/11/43; MIA Bordeaux 31/12/43 w/McDanal; e/a, cr Morceux, Fr; 3EVD 5KIA 2POW; MACR 1871. FLAK RAT.

42-37771 Del Denver 23/8/43; Scott 30/9/43; ass 422BS/305BG [JJ-Q] Chelveston 18/10/43; tran 858BS Watton 24/6/44; retUS 121 BU Bradley 3/7/45; 4168 BU Sth Plains 21/9/45; RFC Kingman 19/12/45.

42-37772 Del Denver 24/8/43; Gr Island 21/9/43; ass 350BS/100BG [LN-S] Thorpe Abbotts 27/9/43; non-op landing acc, 27/12/43; sal. FLYIN' JENNY.

42-37773 Del Denver 23/8/43; ass 94BG Rougham 10/10/43; tran 563BS/388BG Knettishall 11/10/43; MIA Munster 22/12/43 w/Bull; mech fault, ditched Ijsselmeer, Hol; 8KIA 2POW; MACR 3148. FULL HOUSE.

42-37774 Del Denver 24/8/43; ass 401BG Deenethorpe 27/10/43; tran 508BS/351BG [YB-N] Polebrook 21/11/43; {6m} b/d Bordeaux 31/12/43, cr Whitwell, UK; sal 1/1/44.

42-37775 Del Denver 25/8/43; Scott 29/9/43; ass 410BS/94BG Rougham 8/10/43; b/d Noball 3/7/44, sal.

42-37776 Del Denver 25/8/43; Gr Island 19/9/43; ass 303BG Molesworth 18/10/43; 1 BAD 23/10/43; tran 546BS/384BG [BK-R] Grafton Underwood 2/11/43; 486BG Sudbury 16/7/44; retUS 21/3/45; 1103 BU Morrison 16/4/45; RFC Kingman 14/1/46. LADY DREW.

42-37777 Del Denver 25/8/43; Albuquerque 19/1/43; 222 BU Ardmore 22/1/44; 332 BU Ardmore 16/8/44; RFC Walnut Ridge 17/9/45.

42-37778 Del Denver 25/8/43; Scott 30/9/43; ass 366BS/305BG Chelveston 20/11/43; MIA Stettin 13/5/44 w/Schultz; flak, f/l Sweden; 10INT; MACR 4871; retUS 121 BU Bradley 2/8/45; 4185 BU Independence 12/8/45; Kingman 16/12/45.

42-37779 Del Denver 25/8/43; Scott 23/10/43; ass 401BG Deenethorpe 14/11/43; tran 324BS/91BG [DF-B] Bassingbourn 20/11/43; AFSC 3/5/44; retUS 8STA Homestead 11/6/45; 4136 BU Tinker 14/8/45; 3017 BU Hobbs 1/9/45; RFC Walnut Ridge 3/1/46.

42-37780 Del Denver 26/8/43; Scott 20/10/43; ass 401BG Deenethorpe 27/10/43; tran 511BS/351BG [DS-G] Polebrook 18/11/43; {26m} 836BS/487BG [2G] Lavenham 14/7/44; sal b/d 16/7/44. GOLDEN BALL.

42-37781 Del Denver 26/8/43; Gr Island 18/9/43; ass 303BG Molesworth 19/10/43; 1 BAD 23/10/43; tran 546BS/384BG [BK-U] Grafton Underwood 2/11/43; 544BS, 545BS; MIA Berlin 9/3/44 w/ Reed; hit by bomb from above, cr Berlin; 8KIA 2POW; MACR 3005. SILVER DOLLAR.

42-37782 Del Denver 27/8/43; ass Mat Com Seattle survey 7/7/44; sal 5/8/44.

42-37783 Del Denver 27/8/43; Scott 29/9/43; ass 384BG Grafton Underwood 2/11/43; tran 349BS/100BG [XR-B] Thorpe Abbotts 3/11/43; MIA Hamm 22/4/44 w/Harte; e/a, cr Obershelden, Ger; 3KIA 7POW; MACR 4166. DOBIE.

42-37784 Del Denver 27/8/43; Scott 29/9/43; ass 525BS/379BG [FR-P] Kimbolton 19/10/43; MIA Berlin 24/5/44 w/Gease; coll w/e/a; cr Melchow, Ger; 8KIA 1POW; MACR 5322. THE OLD FOX.

42-37785 Del Denver 27/8/43; ass 303BS Molesworth 18/10/43; 1 BAD 23/10/43; tran 544BS/384BG [SU-N] Grafton Underwood 2/11/43; re-ass 9th AF 21/3/45. LITTLE BARNEY.

42-37786 Del Denver 27/8/43; ass 401BG Deenethorpe 2/11/43; tran 532BS/381BG [VE-B] Ridgewell 21/11/43; MIA Augsburg 25/2/43 w/Henderson; mech fault, cr Willmandingen, Ger; 6KIA 4POW; MACR 2933.

42-37787 Del Denver 27/8/43; ass 303BG Molesworth 19/10/43; 1 BAD 23/10/43; 544BS/384BG Grafton Underwood 2/11/43; 526BS/379BG [LF-C] Kimbolton 11/11/43; MIA Bremen 26/11/43 w/Bender; flak, cr Borgen Hol; 10POW; MACR 1330.

42-37788 Del Denver 28/8/43; Scott 16/9/43; ass 544BS/384BG Grafton Underwood 7/11/43; 547BG

[SO-N]; retUS Bradley 14/7/45; 4185 BU Independence 17/7/45; RFC Kingman 18/12/45. HELL'S MESSENGER.

42-37789 Del Denver 29/8/43; Scott 16/9/43; ass 303BG Molesworth 18/3/43; 1 BAD 23/10/43; tran 544BS/384BG [SU-H] Grafton Underwood 2/11/43; b/d Hamm 22/4/44; sal 25/4/44.

42-37790 Del Denver 29/8/43; ass 418BS/100BG [LD-Y] Thorpe Abbotts 28/9/43; MIA Rostock 20/2/44 w/Smith; flak, cr Harslau, Ger; 1EVD 9POW; MACR 2426. AIN'T MIS BEHAVIN'.

42-37791 Del Denver 30/8/43; Scott 27/9/43; ass 303BG Molesworth 19/3/43; 1 BAD 23/10/43; tran 546BS/384BG Grafton Underwood 2/11/43; 526BS/379BG Kimbolton 7/11/43; MIA Berlin 7/5/44 w/Smith; flak, cr Wittenburg, Ger; 8KIA 1POW; MACR 4558. BLUES IN THE NIGHT.

42-37792 Del Denver 29/8/43; ass 545BS/384BG [JD-B] Grafton Underwood 2/11/43; tran 836BS/487BG Lavenham 16/7/44; retUS Bradley 24/6/45; 4168 BU Sth Plains 12/9/45; RFC Kingman 14/12/45. BERMONDSEY.

42-37793 Del Denver 30/8/43; Scott 17/9/43; ass 547BS/384BG [SO-X] Grafton Underwood 2/11/43; MIA Oberpfaffenhofen 18/3/44 w/Smith; flak, c/l Altenrhein, Switz; 10INT. MACR 3843. WINSOME WINN II.

42-37794 Del Denver 28/8/43; Gr Island 27/9/43; ass 388BG Knettishall 30/9/43; sal 18/4/45. ANN HOWE TOO.

42-37795 Del Denver 1/9/43; Gr Island 22/9/43; ass 388BG Knettishall 24/9/43; retUS 121 BU Bradley 6/6/45; 4185 BU Independence 6/8/45; RFC Kingman 20/12/45.

42-37796 Del Denver 3/9/43; Gr Island 27/9/43; ass 350BS/100BG [LN-T] Thorpe Abbotts 28/9/43; MIA Brunswick 21/2/44 w/Fletcher; mech fault, cr Spaarndam, Hol; 10POW; MACR 2761. FLETCHER'S CASTORIA II.

42-37797 Del Denver 1/9/43; Gr Island 23/9/43; ass 410BS/94BG Rougham 29/9/43; MIA Berlin 18/4/44 w/Brinkmier; 2KIA 8POW; MACR 1883. WOLVERINE.

42-37798 Del Denver 1/9/43; Gr Island 22/9/43; ass 331BS/94BG [QE-X] Rougham 27/9/43; MIA Brunswick 11/11/44 w/Service; e/a, cr Rahden, Ger; MACR 3243. BIG STOOP.

42-37799 Del Denver 1/9/43; Gr Island 1/10/43; ass 326BS/92BG Podington 21/9/43; c/l base non-op flight 15/2/44; sal 17/2/44.

42-37800 Del Denver 1/9/43; ass 351BS/100BG [EP-A] Thorpe Abbotts 24/9/43; {39m} c/t/o 27/6/44, sal. PICCADILLY LILY II.

42-37801 Del Denver 2/9/43; Gr Island 1/10/43; ass 547BS/384BG [SO-G] Grafton Underwood 25/11/43; MIA Augsburg 16/3/44 w/Ledbetter; e/a, cr Augsburg; 2KIA 8POW; MACR 3243. DYNAMITE EXPRESS (THE DUCHESS).

42-37802 Del Denver 2/9/43; ass 338BS/96BG Snetterton 30/9/43; MIA Bremen 29/11/43 w/Hendrickson; 10KIA; MACR 1390.

42-37803 Del Denver 3/9/43; Gr Island 20/9/43; ass 390BG Framlingham 3/10/43; sal 30/10/43.

42-37804 Del Long Beach 6/9/43; Gr Island 15/10/43; ass 333BS/94BG [TS-P] Rougham 26/10/43; MIA Laon 9/5/44 w/Bond; shot by friendly fire by B-17; cr Dieppe, 7EVD 3POW; MACR 4853. PRIDE OF THE YANKS.

42-37805 Del Long Beach 6/9/43; Gr Island 23/9/43; ass 525BS/379BG [FR-R] Kimbolton 2/12/43; retUS Bradley 12/6/45; 4168 BU Sth Plains 15/6/45; RFC Kingman 5/12/45. CAROL DAWN.

42-37806 Del Long Beach 6/9/43; Gr Island 27/9/43; ass 571BS/390BG [FC-Z] Framlingham 15/10/43; MIA Magdeburg 28/5/44 w/Holmes; e/a, cr Walternienburg, Ger; 1EVD 1KIA 8POW; MACR 5256. STARK'S ARK.

42-37807 Del Long Beach 7/9/43; ass 350BS/100BG [LN-O] Thorpe Abbotts 28/9/43; MIA Berlin 19/5/44 w/?; ditched Nth Sea; 10RTD. SUPERSTITUOUS ALOYSIUS.

42-37808 Del Long Beach 5/9/43; Gr Island 21/9/43; ass 339BS/96BG [QJ-S] Snetterton 7/10/43; MIA Bordeaux 5/1/44 w/Rueff; flak, cr Lesparre, Fr; 4EVD 6POW; MACR 2015.

42-37809 Del Long Beach 6/9/43; Scott 22/10/43; ass 615BS/401BG [IY-G] Deenethorpe 26/10/43; MIA Oschersleben 11/1/44 w/Chapman; e/a, cr Oschersleben; 4KIA 6POW; MACR 2506. CAROLINE QUEEN.

42-37810 Del Long Beach 5/9/43; Gr Island 12/10/43; ass 560BS/388BG Knettishall 15/10/43; sal 18/4/44.

42-37811 Del Long Beach 7/9/43; Gr Island 3/10/43; ass 338BS/96BG Snetterton 8/10/43; MIA Hamm 29/11/43 w/Meuli; e/a, cr Bremen; 10KIA; MACR 1391.

42-37812 Del Long Beach 7/9/43; Gr Island 1/10/43; ass 570BS/390BG [DI-O] Framlingham 26/10/43; MIA Berlin 8/3/44 w/Branum; e/a, cr Bitterfeld, Ger; 1KIA 9POW; MACR 2990. HEAVENLY BODY.

42-37813 Del Long Beach 10/9/43; Denver 2/11/43; Savannah 21/12/43; Morrison 5/1/44; ass 32BS/301BG Cerignola 4/1/44; Lucera 1/2/44; MIA {64m} Ploesti 23/6/44 w/Muirhead; e/a, cr Ploesti; 3KIA 7POW; MACR 16203.

42-37814 Del Long Beach 5/10/43; Las Vegas 25/10/43; 4126 BU San Bernardino 13/1/45; 3018 BU Kingman 23/1/45; 3030 BU Roswell 22/6/45; RFC Walnut Ridge 2/1/46.

42-37815 Del Long Beach 7/9/43; Gr Island 27/9/43; ass 333BS/94BG Rougham 9/10/43; MIA Hamm 26/11/43 w/Porter; e/a, cr Belleville, Fr; 2EVD 5KIA 3POW; MACR 1124. MISS LACE.

42-37816 Del Long Beach 10/9/43; Gr Island 27/9/43; ass 545BS/384BG [JD-D] Grafton Underwood 18/10/43; MIA Schweinfurt 13/4/44 w/Heffley; e/a, cr; 4EVD 6POW; MACR 3868. BIG STUPE V.

42-37817 Del Long Beach 10/9/43; Scott 28/9/43; ass 510BS/351BG [TU-A] Polebrook 24/10/43; MIA {2m} Bremen 26/11/43 w/Castle; flak, cr Bremen; 3KIA 7POW; MACR 1576. ARISTOCRAP.

42-37818 Del Long Beach 10/9/43; Gr Island 30/9/43; ass 568BS/390BG [BI-D] Framlingham 7/10/43 DINAH MIGHT; MIA Pas de Calais 21/1/44 w/Baugher; flak, cr Hueringham?; 1KIA 9POW; MACR 2270. PUB PETE.

42-37819 Del Long Beach 10/9/43; Scott 7/10/43; ass 560BS/388BG Knettishall 25/10/43; MIA Berlin 8/3/44 w/Tobias; e/a, cr Hannover; 3KIA 7POW; MACR 3087.

42-37820 Del Long Beach 9/9/43; Gr Island 17/10/43; ass 331BS/94BG [QE-R] Rougham 26/10/43; 333BS [TS-F]; MIA Bordeaux 31/12/43 w/Wainwright; flak, cr La Chisse, Fr; 7KIA 4POW; MACR 1755. PACIFIC STREAM.

42-37821 Del Long Beach 10/9/43; Gr Island 13/10/43; ass 410BS/94BG Rougham 26/10/43; MIA Bremen 26/11/43 w/Pyles; mid air coll w/e/a; cr Chevry-Cossigny, Fr; 1EVD 9KIA; MACR 1126.

42-37822 Del Long Beach 9/9/43; Gr Island 17/10/43; ass 544BS/384BG [SU-C] Grafton Underwood 12/5/44; landing accident RAF Ringway, UK 16/3/45, u/c coll; sal AFSC 19/3/45.

42-37823 Del Long Beach 9/9/43; Gr Island 6/10/43; ass 569BS/390BG Framlingham 26/10/43; MIA Emden 11/12/43 w/Fish; flak, cr Barkholt, Ger?; 8KIA 2POW; MACR 1726.

42-37824 Del Denver 11/9/43; ass 447BG Rattlesden 21/10/43; MIA Oschersleben 11/1/44 w/?; ditched Nth Sea.

42-37825 Del Denver 11/9/43; Scott 23/9/43; ass 379BG Kimbolton 7/10/43; tran 511BS/351BG [DS-Q] Polebrook 21/10/43; MIA Lechfeld 18/3/44 w/Mears; flak, f/l Dubendorf, Switz; 10INT; MACR 3237. SUPER BALL.

42-37826 Del Denver 13/9/43; Scott 28/9/43; ass 335BS/95BG [OE-O] Horham 30/9/43; MIA Brunswick 10/2/44 w/Cole; cr Engden, Ger?; 3KIA 7POW; MACR 2543. NO EXCUSE.

42-37827 Del Denver 11/9/43; Gr Island 29/9/43; ass 509BS/351BG [RQ-J] Polebrook 27/10/43; 508BS [YB-J]; MIA Schweinfurt 13/4/44 w/Whitechurch; 1KIA 9POW; MACR 3863.

42-37828 Del Denver 15/9/43; Scott 29/9/43; ass 544BS/384BG Grafton Underwood 18/10/43; 547BS; damaged by truck and sal 3/1/44.

42-37829 Del Denver 13/9/43; Scott 30/9/43; ass 332BS/94BG [XM-F] Rougham 11/10/43; sal 18/10/44. THE BETTER HALF.

42-37830 Del Denver 16/9/43; Scott 29/9/43; ass 410BS/94BG [GL-N] Rougham 8/10/43; 332BS [XM-F]; tran 413BS/96BG [MZ-V] Snetterton /10/43; MIA Bremen 13/11/43 w/Marks; mid air coll w/B17; cr Ommen, Hol; 7KIA 3POW; MACR 1388.

42-37831 Denver 16/9/43; Scott 25/9/43; ass 94BG Rougham 7/10/43; sal 13/11/43.

42-37832 Denver 19/9/43; Scott 2/10/43; ass 509BS/351BG [RQ-N] Polebrook 24/10/43; MIA {15m} Oberpfaffenhofen 18/3/44 w/Illies; flak, cr Eristetten, Ger?; 6KIA 4POW; MACR 3238. CASA DE EMBRIAGOS.

42-37833 Denver 17/9/43; Gt Falls 25/9/43; ass 615BS/401BG [IY-F] Deenethorpe 4/11/43; MIA Pas de Calais 26/3/44 w/Capt Rumsey; e/a, cr Pouquermai, Fr; 8KIA 2POW; MACR 3599. OMAR THE DENT MAKER.

42-37834 Long Beach 17/9/43; Scott 28/9/43; ass 8AF 7/10/43; sal 31/10/45 9AF in Germany.

42-37835 Long Beach 16/9/43; Gt Falls 21/9/43; Scott 24/10/43; ass 612BS/401BG [SC-J] Deenethorpe 5/11/43; cr Walsingley, UK 22/12/43; sal 2 SAD. CHANNEL EXPRESS.

42-37836 Long Beach 16/9/43; Scott 23/10/43; ass 368BS/306BG Thurleigh 30/12/43; MIA Merseburg 11/9/44 w/Machosky; flak, cr Koenigswald, Ger?; 9POW; MACR 8830. RAIN CHECK.

42-37837 Long Beach 21/9/43; Scott 30/9/43; ass 401BG Deenethorpe 4/10/43; tran 413BS/96BG [MZ-P] Snetterton 5/10/43; sal 23/3/44.

42-37838 Long Beach 21/9/43; Gt Falls 25/9/43; ass 612BS/401BG [SC-F] Deenethorpe 26/10/43; {1m} mid air coll w/388BG B17, 26/11/43; c/l RAF Detling, UK; sal 2 SAD 9/12/43. FANCY NANCY.

42-37839 Tulsa 20/9/43; Gr Island 14/10/43; ass 563BS/388BG Knettishall 26/10/43; MIA Berlin 9/3/43 w/Dopko; flak, cr Proetze, Ger?; 10POW; MACR 3088. LITTLE WILLIE.

42-37840 Long Beach 21/9/43; Gt Falls 13/10/43; ass 457BG Glatton 20/2/44; tran 367BS/306BG [GY-Y] Thurleigh 12/3/44; cr Glen Chase, Isle of Man, UK 15/4/45; 11KIA inc nurse; sal. COMBINED OPERATIONS.

42-37841 Del Long Beach 21/9/43; Gr Island 22/10/43; ass 360BS/303BG [PU-P] Molesworth 18/11/43; c/l Badingham, UK 27/8/44; sal 2 SAD 30/8/44. BANSHEE.

Above: B-17G-15-DL 42-37843 landing with bomb-bay doors still extended owing to battle damage. The doors were operated by an electrically driven screw mechanism, which could be hand-cranked in an emergency. In this case damage to the screw rods prevented closure. Named *Dry Run*, the aircraft served with the 615th Bomb Squadron, 401st Bomb Group. (USAAF)

42-37842 Del Long Beach 19/9/43; Gr Island 13/10/43; ass 711BS/447BG Rattlesden 26/11/43; MIA Achmer 8/4/44 w/Anderson; flak, cr Welbregen, Ger?; 10POW; MACR 3658.

42-37843 Del Long Beach 19/9/43; Gt Falls 25/9/43; Scott 21/10/43; ass 615BS/401BG [IY-H] Deenethorpe 2/11/43; MIA French A/fds 14/6/44 w/Schroeder; e/a, cr Charly, Fr; 1KIA 9RTD; MACR 5801. DRY RUN.

42-37844 Del Long Beach 19/9/43; Scott 26/9/43; ass 561BS/388BG Knettishall 10/10/43; des on ground by e/a at Poltava, Rus. 21/7/44; sal 2/7/44.

42-37845 Del Long Beach 19/9/43; Scott 26/9/43; ass 509BS/351BG [RQ-F] Polebrook 25/11/43; MIA {55m} 12/6/44 W/Guthery; flak, ditched Channel; 3EVD 6POW. WILDFIRE.

42-37846 Del Denver 20/9/43; Gr Island 6/10/43; ass 331BS/94BG [QE-S] Rougham 9/10/43; sal 2/6/45. LUCKY 13.

42-37847 Del Denver 19/9/43; Scott 26/9/43; ass 511BS/351BG [DS-R] Polebrook 24/10/43; MIA {3m} Solingen 1/12/43 w/Plant; e/a, cr Solingen, Ger; 2KIA 8POW; MACR 1658.

42-37848 Del Denver 20/9/43; Gr Island 30/9/43; ass 447BG Rattlesden 8/10/43; tran 546BS/384BG [BK-E] Grafton Underwood 18/10/43; MIA Augsburg 16/3/44 w/Steir; e/a, cr Selestat, Ger; 10POW; MACR 3244. SISSY.

42-37849 Del Denver 20/9/43; Gr Island 30/9/43; ass 560BS/388BG Knettishall 11/10/43; sal 31/5/45. MISS FORTUNE.

42-37850 Del Denver 20/9/43; Gr Island 30/9/43; ass 413BS/96BG [MZ-V] Snetterton 9/10/43; tran MTO /44; Ret 9AF RTG to USR 24/1/47. BOOTS IV.

42-37851 Del Denver 20/9/43; Scott 12/10/43; ass 527BS/379BG [FO-C] Kimbolton 13/12/43; MIA Bremen 20/12/43 w/Reicheld; e/a, cr Osterholz-Scharmbeck, Ger; 7KIA 3POW; MACR 1719.

42-37852 Del Denver 20/9/43; Gr Island 3/10/43; ass 410BS/94BG [GL-T] Rougham 9/10/43 GRAND OLD LADY; MIA Berlin 18/4/44 w/Dillard; e/a, cr Freisach, Aus; 1KIA 9POW; MACR 4157. THE PAYOFF.

42-37853 Del Denver 21/9/43; Gr Island 10/10/43; ass 452BG Deopham Green 14/10/43; sal n/b/d 18/4/44. LEADING LADY.

42-37854 Del Denver 23/9/43; Harvard 9/10/43; ass 708BS/447BG Rattlesden 19/11/43; sal 6/1/45.

42-37855 Del Denver 21/9/43; Harvard 10/10/43; ass 92BG Podington 18/11/43; tran 447BG Rattlesden /1/44; sal 2/3/44.

42-37856 Del Denver 21/9/43; Scott 7/10/43; ass 612BS/401BG [SC-B] Deenethorpe 23/12/43; MIA Brunswick 30/1/44 w/Rohner; e/a, cr Helmstedt, Ger; 5KIA 5POW; MACR 2876. FANCY NANCY III.

42-37857 Del Denver 22/9/43; Scott 7/10/43; ass 336BS/95BG [ET-P] Horham 15/11/43; sal 3/4/44.

42-37858 Del Tulsa 23/9/43; Las Vegas 21/10/43; 3021 BU Las Vegas 2/6/44; 237 BU Kirtland 4/6/45; 3017 BU Hobbs 10/7/45; 4200 BU Mines 29/9/45; 3017 BU Hobbs 18/10/45; RFC Walnut Ridge 10/1/46.

42-37859 Del Tulsa 24/9/43; Gr Island 2/10/43; ass 332BS/94BG [XM-P] Rougham 19/2/44; MIA Emden 11/12/43 w/?; e/a, ditched Nth Sea; MACR 1258.

42-37860 Del Tulsa 23/9/43; Las Vegas 20/10/43; 3021 BU Las Vegas 28/10/44; 2126 BU Laredo 4/10/45; RFC Walnut Ridge 5/1/46.

42-37861 Del Tulsa 23/9/43; Las Vegas 20/10/43; 225 BU Rapid City 1/5/45; 2158 BU Pueblo 7/9/45; RFC Altus 21/11/45.

42-37862 Del Long Beach 23/9/43; Amarillo 20/10/43; 3701 BU Amarillo 10/12/44; RFC Kingman 17/10/45.

42-37863 Del Denver 27/9/43; Las Vegas 25/10/43; WO 20/8/44.

42-37864 Del Denver 25/10/43; Harvard 19/10/43; ass 709BS/447BG Rattlesden 21/11/43; MIA Brussels 20/5/44 w/Mitchell; flak, cr Neerbeck, Hol?; 7EVD 3POW; MACR 4938.

42-37865 Del Denver 24/9/43; Gr Island 21/10/43; ass 447BG, lost Atlantic en route UK, 27/11/43. MACR 1119.

42-37866 Del Denver 25/9/43; Harvard 17/10/43; ass 708BS/447BG Rattlesden 19/11/43; MIA Berlin 29/4/44 w/Donahue; e/a, cr Abbenrode, Ger; 2KIA 8POW; MACR 4250.

42-37867 Del Denver 24/9/43; Gr Island 7/10/43; ass 561BS/388BG Knettishall 15/10/43; MIA Oschersleben 11/1/44 w/Hoehn; flak, cr Zwolle, Hol; 4KIA 6POW; MACR 3140. BERLIN AMBASSADOR.

42-37868 Del Denver 25/9/43; Harvard 15/10/43; ass 708BS/447BG Rattlesden 19/11/43; MIA Friedrichshafen 29/4/44 w/Blom; e/a, cr Parsan, Ger?; 4KIA 6POW; MACR 4251.

42-37869 Del Denver 25/9/43; Gr Island 7/10/43; ass 20FG, 8TH Weather Flight 25/10/43; n/b/d cr Oakhampton, UK 21/1/44; sal.

42-37870 Del Denver 25/9/43; Gr Island 16/10/43; ass 447BG Rattlesden 2/11/43; tran 333BS/94BG [TS-R] Rougham 3/11/43; 364BS/305BG [WF-F] Chelveston 23/11/43; MIA Kiel 22/5/44 w/Rippstein; flak, cr Kiel; 7KIA 3POW; MACR 4950; PALMA II.

42-37871 Del Denver 25/9/43; Harvard 13/10/43; ass 711BS/447BG Rattlesden 25/11/43; RFC Kingman 8/11/45.

42-37872 Del Denver 27/9/43; Harvard 13/10/43; ass 708BS/447BG Rattlesden 21/11/43; MIA Bordeaux 5/1/44 w/Huff; e/a, cr Biscay; 7KIA 3POW; MACR 1688.

42-37873 Del Denver 28/9/43; Gr Island 21/10/43; ass 710BS/447BG Rattlesden 25/11/43; 709BS; MIA

Munich 11/7/44 w/Jacobs; flak; f/l Dubendorf, Switz; 10INT; MACR 7223. RetUS 1377 BU Grenier 13/9/45; 4185 BU Independence 30/11/45; RFC Kingman 12/12/45.

42-37874 Del Denver 1/10/43; Gr Island 21/10/43; ass 709BS/447BG Rattlesden 2/11/43; tran 548BS/385BG Gt Ashfield 2/11/43; MIA Bremen 29/11/43 w/Swope; no gas, cr Tessel Is; Hol; 10KIA; MACR 1532. WHO DAT DING BAT.

42-37875 Del Denver 29/9/43; Gr Island 20/10/43; ass 427BS/303BG [GN-A] Molesworth 18/11/43 EMPRESS OF D STREET; sal n/b/d 2 SAD 16/8/44; FLYING BISON.

42-37876 Del Denver 28/9/43; Gr Island 21/10/43; ass 412BS/95BG [QW-S] Horham 3/11/43; MIA Rostock 11/4/44 w/Schiapacasse; cr Baltic, 10KIA; MACR 3804. MISS RAPS-O-DEE.

42-37877 Del Denver 28/9/43; Gr Island 20/10/43; ass 325BS/92BG [NV-K] Podington 20/10/43; MIA Posen 29/5/44 w/Avery; e/a, cr Choszczno, Pol; 3KIA 6POW. MACR 5357. POPCORN FORT.

42-37878 Del Denver 28/9/43; Gr Island 20/10/43; ass 560BS/388BG Knettishall 2/11/43; MIA Ludwigshafen 28/9/44 w/Frawley; flak, cr Saalfeld, Ger; 9POW; MACR 9376. MILLIE K.

42-37879 Del Denver 29/9/43; Gr Island 22/10/43; ass 334BS/95BG [BG-U] Horham 11/11/43; MIA Zeitz 16/8/44 w/Williams; mid air coll w/42-97797; cr Rohmdorf, Ger; 4KIA 5POW; MACR 8176. WRINKLED BELLY BABY.

42-37880 Del Denver 29/9/43; Gr Island 22/10/43; ass 570BS/390BG [DI-T] Framlingham 11/11/43; MIA Regensburg 25/2/44 w/Rains; e/a, cr Poix Terron, Fr; 6KIA 4POW; MACXR 2658. LIBERTY BELL-E.

42-37881 Del Denver 2/10/43; Gr Island 22/10/43; ass 365BS/305BG [XK-K] Chelveston 23/11/43; MIA Ulm 9/8/44 w/Hegendeffer; e/a, cr Sinzheim, Ger; 5KIA 5POW; MACR 8069. LEAP YEAR LADY.

42-37882 Del Denver 4/10/43; Gr Island 22/10/43; ass 412BS/95BG [QW-T] Horham 18/11/43; f/l Merville, Bel. 15/4/45 w/Grant; sal, 9RTD. A GOOD BET.

42-37883 Del Denver 1/10/43; Gr Island 22/10/43; ass 569BS/390BG Framlingham 10/11/43; MIA Bremen 20/12/43 w/Hoffman; flak, cr Bremen; 1KIA 9POW; MACR 1729.

42-37884 Del Denver 1/10/43; Gr Island 22/10/43; ass 534BS/381BG [GD-J] Ridgewell 20/12/43; MIA {3m} Frankfurt 29/1/44 w/Mickow; e/a, cr Mannheim; 5KIA 5POW; MACR 2241.

42-37885 Del Denver 2/10/43; Gr Island 22/10/43; ass 544BS/384BG [SU-L] Grafton Underwood 22/11/43 MRS F.D.R.; 545BS [JD-D]; MIA Erding 24/4/44 w/Broyhill; f/l Dubendorf, Switz; 10INT; MACR 4287. FROSTIE.

42-37886 Del Denver 2/10/43; Gr Island 21/10/43; ass 562BS/388BG Knettishall 25/10/43; MIA Berlin 6/3/44 w/Watts; e/a, coll w/42-40054; cr Zwartemeer, Hol; 4KIA 6POW; MACR 3089. BLITZING BETTY.

42-37887 Del Denver 1/10/43; Gr Island 24/10/43; ass 527BS/379BG [FO-S] Kimbolton 22/11/43; mid air coll w/42-31441 (303); cr Covington, UK. Sal.

42-37888 Del Denver 4/10/43; Gr Island 28/10/43; ass 527BS/379BG [FO-J] Kimbolton 21/11/43; sal b/d 5/7/44.

42-37889 Del Denver 2/10/43; Gr Island 22/10/43; ass 336BS/95BG [ET-L] Horham 11/11/43; MIA Bohlen 29/6/44 w/Cook; cr Vroomshoop, Hol; 2EVD 8POW; MACR 6741. PRIDE OF VHELHALIS.

42-37890 Del Denver 4/10/43; Gr Island 24/10/43; ass 568BS/390BG [BI-R] Framlingham 8/11/43 ROVIN' ROMONA II; MIA Pas de Calais 20/4/44 w/Mann;

Above: B-17G-15-DL 42-37882 landing at Denver, Colorado, after the delivery flight from the Long Beach factory, 4 October 1943. The following month the aircraft was assigned to the 95th Bomb Group in England, flying a total of 98 missions before force-landing in Belgium in April 1945. (W. T. Larkins)

flak, cr Valognes, Fr; 9KIA 1POW; MACR 4169. BIG FRIEND.

42-37891 Del Denver 4/10/43; Gr Island 22/10/43; ass 568BS/390BG [BI-Q] Framlingham 11/11/43. Sal 4/3/44. MINNIE-SO-TAN;

42-37892 Del Denver 4/10/43; Las Vegas 26/10/43; 225 BU Rapid City 1/5/45; 2114 BU Lockburn 22/6/45; 2137 BU Hendricks 14/5/45; RFC Walnut Ridge 4/1/46.

42-37893 Del Denver 5/10/43; Gr Island 20/10/43; ass 358BS/303BG [VK-O] Molesworth 18/11/43; b/d French A/fds, c/l UK. MACR 2505. Sal 2 SAD 11/6/44. BAM BAM.

42-37894 Del Denver 29/9/43; Gr Island 23/10/43; ass 334BS/95BG [BG-L] Horham 11/11/43; c/l Bovingdon A/fd, UK 10/6/44; sal 12/6/44. PEGASUS IV.

42-37895 Del Denver 8/10/43; Las Vegas 30/10/43; ass 91BG, but c/l Cliffory, N. Ireland, en route UK 9/12/43; WO 20/5/44.

42-37896 Del Denver 7/10/43; Gr Island 29/10/43; ass 360BS/303BG Molesworth 27/12/43; MIA Oschersleben 11/1/44 w/Hallden; e/a, cr Rheine, Ger; 2KIA 8POW; MACR 9554.

42-37897 Del Denver 6/10/43; Las Vegas 26/10/43; 3021 BU Las Vegas 1/12/44; 3017 BU Hobbs 28/6/45; RFC Walnut Ridge 11/1/46.

42-37898 Del Denver 7/10/43; Las Vegas 24/10/43; 3021 BU Las Vegas 8/10/44; 2126 BU Laredo 31/3/45; 4136 BU Tinker 26/8/45; 2126 BU Laredo 1/9/45; RFC Walnut Ridge 4/1/46.

42-37899 Del Denver 7/10/43; Las Vegas 27/10/43; 3021 BU Las Vegas 8/10/44; 4134 BU Spokane 16/9/44; 3017 BU Hobbs 31/1/45; 3021 BU Las Vegas 3/2/45; 2126 BU Laredo 24/4/45; RFC Walnut Ridge 5/1/46.

42-37900 Del Denver 8/10/43; Las Vegas 25/10/43; 3021 BU Las Vegas 9/10/44; 3018 BU Kingman 26/2/45; 3702 BU Buckley 4/10/45; RFC Kingman 8/11/45.

42-37901 Del Denver 7/10/43; Las Vegas 23/10/43; 3021 BU Las Vegas 9/10/44; Recl Comp 2/1/45.

42-37902 Del Denver 8/10/43; Gr Island 27/10/43; ass 568BS/390BG [BI-K] Framlingham 8/11/43 HELL'S BELLS; MIA Oranienburg 18/4/44 w/Harrison; flak, cr Berge, Ger; 10POW; MACR 4013. SURE THING.

42-37903 Del Denver 9/10/43; Las Vegas 29/10/43; WO 16/4/44.

42-37904 Del Denver 8/10/43; Las Vegas 24/10/43; WO 16/2/44.

42-37905 Del Denver 9/10/43; Las Vegas 26/10/43; 3021 BU Las Vegas 23/3/45; 2126 BU Laredo 21/4/45; RFC Walnut Ridge 11/1/46.

42-37906 Del Denver 8/10/43; Gr Island 24/10/43; ass 568BS/390BG [BI-V] Framlingham 11/11/43 WILD CHILDREN III; MIA Paris 2/8/44 w/Perry; flak, ditched Channel; 9POW; MACR 7749. ANGEL IN DISGUISE.

42-37907 Del Denver 11/10/43; Las Vegas 26/10/43; WO 19/12/43.

42-37908 Del Denver 11/10/43; Las Vegas 1/11/43; 3021 BU Las Vegas 23/3/45; 2126 BU Laredo 16/4/45; RFC Walnut Ridge 7/1/46.

42-37909 Del Denver 9/10/43; Las Vegas 25/10/43; 3021 BU Las Vegas 9/10/44; 3018 BU Kingman 20/6/45; 3017 BU Hobbs 26/6/45; RFC Walnut Ridge 4/1/46.

42-37910 Del Denver 12/10/43; Gr Island 27/10/43; ass 339BS/96BG Snetterton 15/12/43; MIA Augsburg 13/4/44 w/Tate; e/a, cr Eglingen, Ger; 10POW; MACR 3768.

42-37911 Del Denver 11/10/43; Gr Island 28/10/43; ass 401BS/91BG [LL-C] Bassingbourn 10/1/44; {92m} b/d Kassel 1/1/45; c/l Steeple Morden A/fd, UK; 10KIA. Sal 2 SAD 2/1/45. THE "HEATS ON".

42-37912 Del Long Beach 1/11/43; Las Vegas 4/11/43; 225 BU Rapid City 1/5/45; 2114 BU Lockburn 6/7/45; RFC Walnut Ridge 14/1/46.

42-37913 Del Denver 13/10/43; Gr Island 29/10/43; ass 418BS/100BG [LD-W] Thorpe Abbotts 18/11/43; MIA Oberpfaffenhofen 18/3/44 w/Stuke; mid air coll w/42-39830; cr Harderwjik, Hol; 1EVD 8KIA 1POW; MACR 3233.

42-37914 Del Denver 13/10/43; Las Vegas 27/10/43; 3021 BU Las Vegas 9/10/44; 3017 BU Hobbs 25/3/45; RFC Walnut Ridge 5/1/46.

42-37915 Del Denver 13/10/43; Las Vegas 28/10/43; 3021 BU Las Vegas 9/10/44; 3018 BU Kingman 20/2/45; 3702 BU Buckley 2/6/45; 3706 BU Sheppard 7/11/45; Recl Comp 20/3/46.

42-37916 Del Long Beach 13/10/43; Las Vegas 27/10/43; 225 BU Rapid City 1/5/45; 2114 BU Lockburn 27/6/45; RFC Walnut Ridge 4/1/46.

42-37917 Del Denver 15/10/43; Las Vegas 29/10/43; 3021 BU Las Vegas 2/6/44; 3017 BU Hobbs 29/5; 45; RFC Walnut Ridge 4/1/46.

42-37918 Del Denver 14/10/43; Gr Island 26/10/43; ass 333BS/94BG [TS-R] Rougham 14/12/43; MIA Poznan 11/4/44 w/Churchwell; flak, cr Nemitz, Ger?; 10POW; MACR 3861. DOG TIRED.

42-37919 Del Denver 14/10/43; Las Vegas 26/10/43; 3021 BU Las Vegas 9/10/44; 3018 BU Kingman 22/2/45; 3017 BU Hobbs 25/6/45; RFC Walnut Ridge 8/1/46.

42-37920 Del Denver 15/10/43; Gr Island 27/10/43; ass 338BS/96BG [BX-N] Snetterton 4/12/43; MIA Rostock 11/4/44 w/Beckman; e/a, cr Baltic Sea; 8KIA 2POW; MACR 3814.

42-37921 Del Denver 14/10/43; Las Vegas 27/10/43; 3021 BU Las Vegas 15/3/45; 2126 BU Laredo 1/4/45; RFC Walnut Ridge 11/1/46.

42-37922 Del Denver 16/10/43; Gr Island 3/11/43; ass 331BS/94BG [QE-M] Rougham 18/11/43; b/d Geissen 7/4/45; f/l Continent, sal. SKINNY.

42-37923 Del Denver 15/10/43; Las Vegas 26/10/43; 225 BU Rapid City 1/5/45; 2144 BU Lockburn 17/7/45; 2137 BU Hendricks 10/9/45; RFC Walnut Ridge 3/1/46.

42-37924 Del Denver 15/10/43; Gr Island 29/10/43; ass 547BS/384BG Grafton Underwood 2/12/43; c/l Lt Staughton on training flight 9/1/44; sal 2 SAD 16/1/44.

42-37925 Del Denver 15/10/43; Gr Island 1/11/43; ass 571BS/390BG [FC-M] Framlingham 16/11/43; MIA Munich 18/3/44 w/Biesecker; e/a, cr Wallburg, Ger?; 7KIA 3POW; MACR 3182. RICK-O-SHAY III.

42-37926 Del Ogden 15/10/43; Tooele 1/11/43; 3021 BU Las Vegas 9/10/44; 3017 BU Hobbs 22/5/45; RFC Walnut Ridge 4/1/46.

42-37927 Del Denver 16/10/43; Gr Island 27/10/43; ass 358BS/303BG Molesworth 18/11/43; MIA Wilhelmshafen 3/2/44 w/Capt White; flak, cr Nth Sea; 10KIA; MACR 2238.

42-37928 Del Denver 19/10/43; Gr Island 31/10/43; ass 407BS/92BG Podington 1/12/43; sal 6/1/44 after earlier damage.

42-37929 Del Denver 19/10/43; Gr Island 6/11/43; Presque Is 11/11/43; ass 335BS/95BG [OE-Y] Horham 15/11/43; MIA Berlin 8/3/44 w/Fagan; cr Brandenburg; 10POW; MACR 2983. DIANA.

42-37930 Del Denver 19/10/43; Gr Island 1/11/43; ass 388BG Knettishall 11/11/43; tran 365BS/305BG Chelveston 3/12/43; MIA Bremen 20/12/43 w/Hunter; flak, cr Breskens, Hol; 1KIA 9POW; MACR 1708.

42-37931 Del Denver 13/10/43; Gr Island 5/11/43; Bangor 7/11/43; ass 364BS/305BG [WF-D] Chelveston 5/1/44; c/l base 12/4/44; sal 2 SAD 13/4/44. BERTIE LEE.

42-37932 Del Denver 15/10/43; Gr Island 1/11/43; ass 570BS/390BG [DI-P] Framlingham 12/11/43; MIA Frankfurt 2/3/44 w/Ferguson; flak, cr Abbeville, Fr; 1EVD 5KIA 4POW; MACR 2886. OLE BASSER.

42-37933 Del Denver 19/10/43; Gr Island 1/11/43; ass 535BS/381BG [MS-R] Ridgewell 1/1/44; b/d Rheims 28/3/44 w/Evans; c/l Lympne, UK; 2KIA 2WIA; sal 2 SAD 29/3/44. SUPERSTITUOUS ALOYSIUS.

42-37934 Del Denver 19/10/43; Gr Island 1/11/43; Presque Is 8/11/43; ass 325BS/92BG [NV-E] Podington 30/11/43; c/l base 20/5/44, caught fire, sal.

42-37935 Del Denver 20/10/43; Gr Island 2/11/43; ass 336BS/95BG [ET-K] Horham 25/11/43; MIA Rostock 11/4/44 w/Westmyer; cr Bad Dorkran, Ger?; 7KIA 3POW; MACR 3805.

42-37936 Del Denver 19/10/43; Gr Island 5/11/43; Presque Is 7/11/43; ass 351BS/100BG [EP-M] Thorpe Abbotts 11/11/43; MIA {98m} Cologne 10/1/45 w/Dodrill; flak, cr Gladbach; 9KIA; MACR 11744. THE ALL AMERICAN GIRL.

42-37937 Del Denver 19/10/43; Gr Island 1/11/43; 8AF 10/11/43; sal n/b/d 3/1/44.

42-37938 Del Denver 21/10/43; Gr Island 4/11/43; 323BS/91BG [OR-E] Bassingbourn 30/3/44; 324BS [DF-E] retUS Bradley 12/6/45; 4168 BU Sth Plains 21/10/45; RFC Kingman 4/12/45. BETTY LOU'S BUGGY.

42-37939 Del Denver 21/10/43; Gr Island 9/11/43; ass 323BS/91BG Bassingbourn 20/12/43; MIA {15m} Oschersleben 22/2/44 w/Maziarz; ditched Nth Sea, 10RTD. SUGAR BLUES.

42-37940 Del Denver 21/10/43; Gr Island 5/11/43; ass 323BS/91BG Bassingbourn 13/12/43; {6m} c/l Deopham Green A/fd 11/1/44; sal 2 SAD 16/1/44. SPIRIT OF '44.

42-37941 Del Denver 22/10/43; Walla Walla 9/11/43; ass 728BS/452BG Deopham Green 16/11/43; MIA Warnemunde 9/4/44 w/Bodet; e/a, cr Linnau, Ger?; 3KIA 7POW; MACR 3784. LUCKY LADY.

42-37942 Del Denver 21/10/43; Gr Island 5/11/43; ass 367BS/306BG [GY-A] Thurleigh 19/12/43; MIA Berlin 8/5/44 w/Jacobs; mid air coll, cr Schmolde,Ger; 10KIA; MACR 4554. FOUR LEAF CLOVER.

42-37943 Del Denver 21/10/43; Gr Island 4/11/43; ass 368BS/306BG [BO-L] Thurleigh 12/12/43; taxi acc 17/9/44, sal. WEARY BONES.

42-37944 Del Denver 21/10/43; Gr Island 5/11/43; ass 365BS/305BG [XK-P] Chelveston 12/12/43; MIA Stettin 13/5/44 w/Capt Davey; flak, f/l Echernforde, Swed; 11INT; MACR 4572; retUS Bradley 24/7/45; 4168 BU Independence 18/10/45; RFC Kingman 15/12/45.

42-37945 Del Denver 21/10/43; Gr Island 5/11/43; ass 305BG Chelveston 21/12/43; taxi acc 18/11/44; sal 2 SAD 20/11/44.

42-37946 Del Denver 23/10/43; Walla Walla 7/11/43; ass 729BS/452BG Deopham Green 3/1/44; MIA Frankfurt 8/2/44 w/Treux; mech fault, cr St Goar, Ger; 1EVD 9POW; MACR 4520. THE WORRY BIRD.

42-37947 Del Denver 23/10/43; Walla Walla 9/11/43; ass 730BS/452BG Deopham Green 4/1/44; MIA Brux 12/5/44 w/Davis; e/a, cr Dachsberg, Ger; 10POW; MACR 4816. PRINCESS PAT.

42-37948 Del Denver 22/10/43; Kingman 16/11/43; 330 BU Dyersburg 1/3/45; 347 BU Drew 28/8/45; 330 BU Dyersburg 11/9/45; RFC Walnut Ridge 14/2/45.

42-37949 Del Denver 23/10/43; Walla Walla 9/11/43; ass 730BS/452BG Deopham Green 4/1/44; MIA Pas de Calais 1/5/44 w/?; MACR 4492. SUNRISE SERENADE.

42-37950 Del Denver 23/10/43; Walla Walla 9/11/43; ass 731BS/452BG Deopham Green 4/1/44; MIA {1m} Frankfurt 10/2/44 w/Sharpless; e/a, cr Leuarden, Hol?; 1KIA 9POW; MACR 2538. DINAH MITE.

42-37951 Del Denver 25/10/43; Walla Walla 7/11/43; ass 728BS/452BG Deopham Green 6/1/44; MIA Rostock 20/2/44 w/Huffman; e/a, cr Nakskov, Den; 2EVD 8KIA; MACR 2779.

42-37952 Del Denver 25/10/43; Walla Walla 7/11/43; ass 551BS/385BG Gt Ashfield 12/3/44; retUS 121 BU Bradley 5/7/45; 4168 BU Sth Plains 21/10/45; RFC Kingman 17/12/45. BABE.

42-37953 Del Denver 28/10/43; Gr Island 9/11/43; ass 369BS/306BG [WW-L] Thurleigh 4/1/44; MIA Brunswick 29/3/44 w/Schuering; e/a, cr Winzlar, Ger?; 10POW; MACR 3480.

42-37954 Del Denver 25/10/43; Walla Walla 9/11/43; ass 729BS/452BG Deopham Green 3/1/44; MIA Berlin 8/3/44 w/Wilson; e/a, cr Toeppel, Ger; 2KIA 8POW; MACR 3192. PAPER DOLL.

42-37955 Del Santa Monica 3/11/43; Mat Com Seattle 1/12/43; Topeka 28/12/43; Kansas City 5/1/44; Warner Robins 8/1/44; Hunter 18/3/44; Love Fd 13/5/44; Long Beach 14/5/44.

42-37956 Del Denver 26/10/43; Walla Walla 9/11/43; ass 729BS/452BG Deopham Green 3/1/44; MIA Pas de Calais 20/4/44 w/Thomas; flak, ditched Channel; 4KIA 6RTD; MACR 4179.

42-37957 Del Denver 26/10/43; Gr Island 12/11/43; ass 366BS/305BG Chelveston 12/12/43; MIA Berlin 22/3/44 w/Wipple; flak, cr Pfarlhausen, Ger?; 5KIA 5POW; MACR 3432.

42-37958 Del Denver 27/10/43; Gr Island 11/11/43; ass 401BS/91BG [LL-G] Bassingbourn 20/12/43; {36m} c/l Wincanton, UK 26/4/44 w/Mikonis; 9KIA; sal 2 SAD. OLD FAITHFULL.

42-37959 Del Denver 25/10/43; Gr Island 12/11/43; ass 550BS/385BG Gt Ashfield 5/12/43; MIA Munster 23/3/44 w/Stubler; e/a, cr Oerrel, Ger; 6KIA 4POW. MACR 3317. ESKY.

42-37960 Del Denver 27/10/43; Walla Walla 7/11/43; ass 728BS/452BG Deopham Green 4/1/44; MIA Brunswick 10/2/44 w/Noell; e/a, cr Dankem, Ger?; 3KIA 7POW; MACR 2539. DELTA GIRL.

42-37961 Del Denver 26/10/43; Gr Island 12/11/43; ass 327BS/92BG Podington 30/12/43; c/l Lt Staughton on ferry flight 23/1/44; sal AFSC 25/1/44.

42-37962 Del Denver 26/10/43; Gr Island 11/11/43; ass 532BS/381BG [VE-L] Ridgewell 20/12/43; MIA {4m} Oschersleben 11/1/44 w/Saur; flak, cr Gellenbeck, Ger; 8KIA 2POW; MACR 1876. BETTY LOU.

42-37963 Del Denver 26/10/43; Gr Island 10/11/43; ass 549BS/385BG Gt Ashfield 24/11/43; c/l Reedham, UK 21/2/44, sal.

42-37964 Del Denver 29/10/43; Gr Island 11/11/43; ass 419BS/301BG Cerignola 5/12/43; Lucera 1/2/44; c/t/o {76m} 11/6/44 w/Hall; exploded, crew safe.

42-37965 Del Denver 28/10/43; Gr Island 9/11/43; ass 323BS/91BG [OR-U] Bassingbourn 20/12/43; MIA {13m} Wilhelmshaven 3/3/44 w/Pickard; flak, cr Nth Sea; 5KIA 5POW; MACR 3222. MY DESIRE.

42-37966 Del Denver 29/10/43; Gr Island 9/11/43; ass 8AF 18/11/43; sal b/d 10/7/44.

42-37967 Del Denver 29/10/43; Gr Island 12/11/43; ass 353BS/301BG Cerignola 1/44; {7m} tran 2BG Amendola; sal 8/7/44.

42-37968 Del Denver 28/10/43; Kearney 13/11/43; ass 410BS/94BG [GL-X] Rougham 9/12/43; MIA Munich 18/3/44 w/O'Neill; flak, cr Munich; 3KIA 7POW; MACR 3418. LITTLE AUDREY.

42-37969 Del Denver 29/10/43; Gr Island 13/11/43; ass 532BS/381BG [VE-L] Ridgewell 23/12/43; sal {54m} n/b/d 2 SAD 31/5/45. OLD IRON GUT.

42-37970 Del Denver 1/11/43; Gr Island 11/11/43; ass 20BS/2BG Amendola 21/12/43; MIA Steyr, Aus 24/2/44 w/Foust; e/a, cr Obernau; 7 chutes seen, MACR 2621.

42-37971 Del Denver 1/11/43; Gr Island 12/11/43; ass 335BS/95BG [OE-W] Horham 1/12/43; MIA Brunswick 10/2/44 w/Tuberose; cr Rheine, Ger; 1KIA 9POW; MACR 2526.

42-37972 Del Denver 1/11/43; Gr Island 12/11/43; ass 349BS/100BG [XR-F] Thorpe Abbotts 27/11/43; {100m} tran 482BG Alconbury 20/5/45; retUS Bradley 1/6/45; 4168 BU Sth Plains 5/6/45; RFC Kingman 17/12/45. GOLD BRICK.

42-37973 Del Denver 1/11/43; Bolling 16/11/43; 610 BU Eglin 30/10/44; ass 305BG Chelveston 1/12/43; retUS 553 BU Romulus 15/7/44; 611 BU Eglin 26/8/44; ATS Wright 3/10/44; 1454 BU Minneapolis 25/1/45; 4000 BU Wright 3/9/45; 611 BU Eglin 21/12/45; WO Eglin 31/10/46.

42-37974 Del Denver 2/11/43; Kearney 14/11/43; ass

547BS/384BG [SO-O] Grafton Underwood 21/1/44; 545BS [JD-O], 533BS [SU-M]; MIA German oil inst 20/7/44 w/Grant; e/a, cr Zetteritz, Ger; 2KIA 7POW; MACR 7278. SECTION 8.

42-37975 Del Denver 2/11/43; Gr Island 12/11/43; ass 418BS/100BG [LD-U] Thorpe Abbotts 1/12/43; MIA Frankfurt 4/2/44 W/Green; flak, cr Walcheren Is, Hol; 10KIA; MACR 2343.

42-37976 Del Denver 2/11/43; Gr Island 21/11/43; ass 407BS/92BG [PY-Y] Podington 8/1/44; MIA {45m} Munich 11/7/44 w/Seilheimer; flak, two engines out; also attacked by Swiss flak (took off 4ft of wing) and a/c on approach f/l Switzerland ; 9INT; MACR 7508. MANCHESTER LEADER.

42-37977 Del Denver 3/11/43; Kearney 13/11/43; ass 549BS/385BG Gt Ashfield 1/12/43; MIA Stettin 11/4/44 w/Bailey; flak, cr Dargen, Ger?; 10POW; MACR 3823. BLUE CHAMPAGNE.

42-37978 Del Denver 2/11/43; Gr Island 12/11/43; ass 365BS/305BG Chelveston 5/1/44; MIA Stettin 13/5/44 w/Bailey; no gas, f/l Sweden; 10INT; MACR 4870; left 25/5/45; sal 21/6/45.

42-37979 Del Denver 2/11/43; Gr Island 11/11/43; ass 364BS/305BG Chelveston 5/1/44; MIA Kiel 22/5/44 w/Gerber; flak, cr Kiel; 10KIA; MACR 4951.

42-37980 Del Denver 3/11/43; Kearney 14/11/43; ass 562BS/388BG Knettishall 1/12/43; MIA Berlin 29/4/44 w/Coynes; flak, cr Ypern, Hol; 10POW; MACR 4244.

42-37981 Del Denver 3/11/43; Gr Island 12/11/43; ass 615BS/401BG [IY-P] Deenethorpe 3/12/43; retUS 27/5/44; ret 401BG 27/5/44; MIA Leipzig 7/7/44 w/Neill; mech fault, cr Buckhorst, Ger?; 2KIA 7POW; MACR 7222. BELLE OF THE BARBARY COAST.

42-37982 Del Denver 3/11/43; Gr Island 12/11/43; ass 544BS/384BG [SU-K] Grafton Underwood 21/1/44; MIA Hamm 19/9/44 w/Carnes; MACR?. TREMBLIN' GREMLIN.

42-37983 Del Denver 4/11/43; Kearney 14/11/43; Presque Is 9/12/43; ass 532BS/381BG [VE-N] Ridgewell 22/1/44; b/d Berlin 6/3/44 w/Cahill; c/l beach Nth Foreland, UK.

42-37984 Del Denver 4/11/43; Kearney 12/11/43; ass 326BS/92BG Podington 6/1/44; MIA Frankfurt 8/2/44 w/Shevchik; e/a, cr Amiens, Fr; 9EVD 1POW; MACR 2364.

42-37985 Del Denver 4/11/43; Kearney 13/11/43; ass 338BS/96BG [BX-V] Snetterton 3/12/43; MIA Warnemunde 9/4/44 w/Williamson; flak, f/l Bulltofta, Swed; 10INT; MACR 3650; left 25/5/45; sal 31/5/45. THE SAINT.

42-37986 Del Denver 5/11/43; Kearney 14/11/43; ass 534BS/381BG [GD-K] Ridgewell 15/1/44; MIA {2m} Wilhelmshafen 3/3/44 w/Rogers; mid air coll, cr Baflo, Hol; 10POW; MACR 4737.

42-37987 Del Denver 4/11/43; Kearney 15/11/43; ass 322BS/91BG Bassingbourn 21/12/43; b/d Frankfurt (1st m) 29/1/44; c/l Bredgar, UK; sal 2 SAD 2/2/44. MAN O' WAR HORSEPOWER LTD.

42-37988 Del Denver 5/11/43; Kearney 14/11/43; ass 336BS/95BG [ET-M] Horham 3/12/43; MIA Berlin 29/4/44 w/Vilberg; cr Nendorf, Ger; 1EVD 9POW; MACR 4470. FLAGSHIP.

42-37989 Del Denver 5/11/43; Orlando 21/11/43; 901 BU Pinecastle 2/6/44; 902 BU Orlando 29/7/44; 903 BU Pinecastle 10/9/44; ATSC Wright 7/7/45; 4000 BU Wright 13/8/45; RFC Walnut Ridge 5/1/46.

42-37990 Del Denver 5/11/43; Orlando 20/11/43; 906 BU Pinecastle 3/6/44; 903 BU Pinecastle 10/9/44; 902 BU Orlando 6/1/45; 903 BU Pinecastle 30/3/45; 2137 BU Hendricks 30/7/45; RFC Altus 21/11/45.

42-37991 Del Denver 7/11/43; Orlando 21/11/43; 225 BU Rapid City 1/6/44; 211 BU Lockburn 22/6/45; RFC Walnut Ridge 5/1/46.

42-37992 Del Denver 7/11/43; Orlando 20/11/43; 224 BU Sioux City 15/9/44; WO 18/9/44.

42-37993 Del Denver 7/11/43; Orlando 26/11/43; 903 BU Pinecastle 10/9/44; 902 BU Orlando 24/11/44; 621 BU Pinecastle 9/7/45; 613 BU Phillips 17/12/45.

42-37994 Del Denver 8/11/43; Orlando 22/11/43; 224 BU Sioux City 6/3/45; 332 BU Ardmore 20/4/45; RFC Walnut Ridge 25/9/45.

42-37995 Del Denver 8/11/43; Orlando 22/11/43; 903 BU Pinecastle 10/9/44; 621 BU 9/7/45; 4000 BU Wright 13/8/45; RFC Walnut Ridge 4/1/46.

42-37996 Del Denver 10/11/43; Orlando 21/11/43; 901 BU Pinecastle 10/9/44; 902 BU Orlando 16/1/45; 903 BU Pinecastle 30/1/45; 902 BU Orlando 29/3/45; 621 BU Pinecastle 9/7/45; RFC Walnut Ridge 18/1/46.

42-37997 Del Denver 9/11/43; Long Beach 19/12/43; Cheyenne 27/12/43; Lakeland 10/1/44; ass 775BS/463BG Celone 9/3/44; MIA Mestre, It 10/6/44 w/Smith; flak, cr Adriatic; MACR 5846.

42-37998 Del Denver 9/11/43; Kingman 21/11/43; 3018 BU Kingman 23/3/45; 3017 BU Hobbs 22/6/45; RFC Walnut Ridge 18/1/46.

42-37999 Del Denver 9/11/43; Presque Is 29/11/43; Prestwick, UK 1/12/43; ass 482BG Alconbury 2/12/43; tran 422BS/305BG [JJ-E] Chelveston 10/12/43; b/d Berlin 6/3/44; sal 2 SAD

42-38000 Del Denver 9/11/43; Orlando 21/11/43; 224 BU Sioux City 24/10/44; WO 28/10/44.

42-38001 Del Denver 11/11/43; Romulus 10/12/43; Presque Is 14/12/43; ass 338BS/96BG Snetterton 17/12/43; MIA Frankfurt 29/1/44 w/Anthony; e/a, cr Frankfurt; 10KIA; MACR 2380.

42-38002 Del Denver 9/11/43; Grenier 4/12/43; ass 614BS/401BG [IW-Q] Deenethorpe 21/1/44; MIA Aschersleben 22/2/44 w/Arneson; e/a, cr Brunswick; 2KIA 8POW; MACR 2661.

42-38003 Del Long Beach 11/11/43; Denver 16/11/43; Orlando 29/11/43; 241 BU Fairmont 7/7/44; 225 BU Rapid City 28/12/44; 2114 BU Lockburn 6/7/45; 2317 BU Hendricks 18/8/45; RFC Kingman 15/10/45.

42-38004 Del Denver 10/11/43; Presque Is 30/11/43; Prestwick, UK 7/12/43; ass 534BS/381BG [GD-A] Ridgewell 6/1/44; MIA {6+m} Eschwege 19/4/44 w/Rayburn; e/a, cr Rosenburg; 3KIA 6POW; MACR 4052. OL' MAN TUCKER.

42-38005 Del Denver 10/11/43; Kearney 21/11/43; Prestwick, UK 7/12/43; ass 509BS/351BG [RQ-G] Polebrook 4/1/44; 511BS [DS-G]; MIA {24m} Berlin 24/5/44 w/Capt Clay; mech fault, cr Sose Odde, Den?; 10POW; MACR 5175. STORMY WEATHER.

42-38006 Del Cheyenne 11/11/43; Gr Island 1/12/43; Presque Is 17/12/43; ass 324BS/91BG [DF-H] Bassingbourn 8/1/44; MIA {21m} Kassel 19/4/44 w/Swensum; e/a, cr Eschwege, Ger; 2KIA 8POW; MACR 4046. HOOSIER HOT SHOT.

42-38007 Del Cheyenne 11/11/43; Gr Island 3/12/43; Presque Is 14/12/43; Nutts Corner, UK 20/12/43; ass 332BS/94BG [XM-F] Rougham 21/12/43; MIA Munich 31/7/43 w/Ellis; flak, ditched Channel; 10RTD. HELLO MR MAIER.

42-38008 Del Cheyenne 11/11/43; New Castle 7/12/43; Nutts Corner, UK 20/12/43; ass 367BS/306BG Thurleigh 21/12/43; 369BS; MIA Berlin 8/5/44 w/Matichka; flak, f/l off Vallo, Swed; 10INT; MACR 4669.

42-38009 Del Cheyenne 11/11/43; Gr Island 1/12/43; Presque Is 13/12/43; ass 534BS/381BG [GD-N] Ridgewell 8/1/44; MIA {12+m} Bordeaux 15/6/44 w/Kelley; flak, cr Bazas, Fr; 9EVD; MACR 5799.

42-38010 Del Cheyenne 12/11/43; Kearney 3/12/43; Presque Is 13/12/43; ass 532BS/381BG [VE-J] Ridgewell 13/1/44; MIA {1+m} Berlin 24/5/44 w/Ezzell; e/a, cr Berlin; 2KIA 7POW; MACR 5178.

42-38011 Del Cheyenne 12/11/43; New Castle 7/12/43; Presque Is 11/12/43; ass 351BS/100BG [EP-P] Thorpe Abbotts 17/12/43; MIA Berlin 6/3/44 w/Handorf; e/a, cr Diepholz, Ger; 8KIA 2POW; MACR 3023. KINDA RUFF.

42-38012 Del Cheyenne 12/11/43; Romulus 2/12/43; Presque Is 4/12/43; ass 615BS/401BG [IY-M] Deenethorpe 21/1/44; MIA Frankfurt 29/1/44 w/Van Sycle; e/a, cr Bremen; 2KIA 8POW; MACR 2275.

42-38013 Del Cheyenne 26/11/43; New Castle 10/12/43; Presque Is 15/12/43; ass 547BS/384BG [SO-C] Grafton Underwood 21/1/44; sal b/d 27/4/44. NEVADA AVENGER.

42-38014 Del Cheyenne 14/11/43; Kearney 3/12/43; Presque Is 9/12/43; ass 546BS/384BG [BK-G] Grafton Underwood 6/1/44; b/d Kassel 2/1/45, c/l base hitting hut; sal AFSC 3/1/45.

42-38015 Del Cheyenne 14/11/43; Syracuse 9/12/43; Presque Is 11/12/43; ass 338BS/96BG Snetterton 16/12/43; MIA Evreux 6/2/44 w/Kurfzberg; e/a, cr Pisseleux, Fr; 9KIA 1POW; MACR 2342.

42-38016 Del Cheyenne 14/11/43; Kearney 8/12/43; Presque Is 9/12/43; ass 350BS/100BG [LN-B] Thorpe Abbotts 16/12/43; MIA Berlin 6/3/44 w/Seaton; e/a, cr Berlin; 1KIA 9POW; MACR 3024. SEATON'S SAD SACK.

42-38017 Del Cheyenne 15/11/43; Syracuse 7/12/43; Presque Is 15/12/43; ass 349BS/100BG [XR-O] Thorpe Abbotts 28/12/43; MIA Schwelswig A/fd 3/3/44 w/Gossage; e/a, cr Schwelswig; 10POW; MACR 3025. (Assgd KG200 by Luftwaffe)

42-38018 Del Cheyenne 15/11/43; Presque Is 6/12/43; Nutts Corner, UK 27/12/43; ass 349BS/100BG [XR-J] Thorpe Abbotts 22/12/43; sal b/d 25/4/44. WATICARE.

42-38019 Del Cheyenne 15/11/43; Grenier 12/12/43; Presque is 14/12/43; ass 369BS/306BC Thurleigh 21/1/44; MIA Stettin 11/4/44 w/Ahlstrom; e/a, cr Brunswick; 10POW; MACR 3677.

42-38020 Del Cheyenne 15/11/43; Syracuse 17/12/43; Valley, UK 22/12/43; ass 427BS/303BG [GN-V] Molesworth 20/1/44; b/d Avord 25/4/44, c/l RAF Halton, UK; sal 29/4/44. V-PACKET.

42-38021 Del Cheyenne 16/11/43; Wendover 7/12/43; ass 384BG Grafton Underwood 10/12/43; tran 748BS/457BG Glatton 26/1/44; 751BS; dec W/W tran 5 SAD, then ASR 24/3/45; retUS 121 BU Bradley 11/7/44; 4185 BU Independence 13/7/44; RFC Kingman 19/12/45.

42-38022 Del Cheyenne 16/11/43; Gr Island 4/12/43; Presque Is 10/12/43; ass 410BS/94BG [GL-M] Rougham 16/1/44; MIA Berlin 6/3/44 w/Johnston; e/a, cr Paintluene, Ger; 2KIA 8POW; MACR 2977. JEANNE.

42-38023 Del Cheyenne 17/11/43; Romulus 9/12/43; Presque Is 14/12/43; Prestwick, UK 19/12/43; ass 508BS/351BG [YB-H] Polebrook 1/1/44; {10m} c/l Framlingham 22/2/44, sal. YANKEE REBEL.

42-38024 Del Cheyenne 17/11/43; Kearney 7/12/43; Presque Is 8/12/43; ass 336BS/95BG [ET-Q] Horham 16/12/43; MIA Berlin 6/3/44 w/Russell; cr Colnrode, Ger; 1KIA 9POW; MACR 2984.

42-38025 Del Cheyenne 17/11/43; Gr Island 8/12/43; Presque Is 12/12/43; ass 327BS/92BG [UX-Q] Podington 4/1/44; MIA Munich 16/7/44 w/Johnson; mech fault, cr Mittenwald, Ger; 9POW; MACR 7565. FLAK HAPPY.

42-38026 Del Cheyenne 18/11/43; Kearney 5/12/43; Presque Is 22/12/43; ass 612BS/401BG [SC-N] Deenethorpe 2/2/44; MIA Kiel 19/5/44 w/Hagen; flak, cr Kiel; 9KIA 1POW; MACR 4815. MY DAY (SAD SACK).

42-38027 Del Cheyenne 18/11/43; Kearney 4/12/43; Presque Is 15/12/43; ass 322BS/91BG [LG-A] Bassingbourn 10/1/44; MIA {31+m} Leipzig 20/7/44 w/Strong; e/a, cr Lichtenstein, Ger; 5KIA 4POW; MACR 7285. HEAVENLY BODY.

42-38028 Del Cheyenne 18/11/43; Romulus 9/12/43; Presque Is 11/12/43; ass 510BS/351BG [TU-Q] Polebrook 1/1/44; MIA {36m} Munich 12/7/44 w/Irwin; flak, cr Munich; 5KIA 4POW; MACR 7505. PAPPY'S PRIDE.

42-38029 Del Cheyenne 18/11/43; Syracuse 10/12/43; Presque Is 15/12/43; ass 532BS/381BG [VE-M] Ridgewell 1/3/44; MIA {1m} Berlin 8/3/44 w/Pirtle; e/a, cr Lettele, Hol; 10POW; MACR 3002.

42-38030 Del Cheyenne 18/11/43; Kearney 3/12/43; ass 337BS/96BG Snetterton 6/12/43; MIA Frankfurt 4/2/44 w/Fabian; flak, cr Frankfurt; 10POW; MACR 2195. THE MERRY WIDOW.

42-38031 Del Cheyenne 19/11/43; Kearney 9/12/43; Presque Is 12/12/43; ass 548BS/385BG Gt Ashfield 16/12/43; retUS Bradley 19/6/45; 4168 BU Sth Plains 12/9/45; RFC Kingman 20/11/45. HIT PARADE JR.

42-38032 Del Cheyenne 22/11/43; Kearney 5/12/43; Presque Is 23/12/43; ass 509BS/351BG [RQ-X] Polebrook 27/12/43; MIA Oberpfaffenhoffen 18/3/44 w/Neuburg; flak, cr Heiligkruestal, Ger?; 6KIA 4POW; MACR 3239.

42-38033 Del Cheyenne 19/11/43; Gr Island 15/12/43; Presque Is 21/12/43; ass 612BS/401BG [SC-M] Deenethorpe 6/1/44; MIA Frankfurt 20/3/44 w/Dunaway; e/a, cr Brueil, Fr; 3EVD 3KIA 4POW; MACR 3332.

42-38034 Del Cheyenne 20/11/43; Kearney 4/12/43; Presque Is 19/12/43; ass 332BS/94BG [XM-E] Rougham 16/12/43; MIA Munich 31/7/44 w/Lewis; flak, f/l Dubendorf, Switz; 9INT; MACR 7740. TWAT'S IT TO YOU.

42-38035 Del Cheyenne 21/11/43; Kearney 7/12/43; Presque Is 12/12/43; ass 550BS/385BG Gt Ashfield 16/12/43; b/d Ulm 1/3/45 w/Armbruster; coll w/B-17, (tail cut off with TG Joe Jones, who floated down and survived); c/l Ostend, Bel. MR LUCKY.

42-38036 Del Cheyenne 21/11/43; Romulus 10/12/43; Presque Is 13/12/43; ass 525BS/379BG [FR-T] Kimbolton 21/1/44; c/l base on practice flight 2/2/44; sal 2 SAD 4/2/44.

42-38037 Del Cheyenne 21/11/43; Romulus 20/12/43; Presque Is 20/12/43; slated 351BG, ass 422BS/305BG [JJ-M] Chelveston 22/1/44; retUS Bradley 13/6/45; 4168 BU Sth Plains 12/9/43; RFC Kingman 8/12/45. LIBERTY RUN.

42-38038 Del Cheyenne 21/11/43; Gr Island 4/12/43; Presque Is 15/12/43; ass 510BS/351BG [TU-P] Polebrook 14/1/44; retUS Bradley 13/6/45; 4168 BU Sth Plains 12/9/45; RFC Kingman 26/11/45. APRIL GIRL II.

42-38039 Del Cheyenne 18/11/43; Syracuse 10/12/43; Presque Is 15/12/43; slated 447BG, ass 561BS/388BG Knettishall 20/12/43; MIA Warnemunde 9/4/44 w/Trubia; flak, cr Berkel, Hol; 1KIA 9POW; MACR 3655.

42-38040 Del Cheyenne 22/11/43; Kearney 5/12/43; Presque Is 23/12/43; Prestwick, UK 4/1/44; ass 568BS/390BG Framlingham 12/1/44 LITTLE BUTCH; b/d 20/11/44, cr Ossogne-Florinchamps, Bel; sal 28/11/44. EL LOBO.

42-38041 Del Cheyenne 22/11/43; La Guardia 21/12/43; Presque Is 23/12/43; slated 379BG, ass 358BS/303BG [VK-D] Molesworth 18/1/44; mid air coll w/42-31516 22/4/44; c/l Irthlingborough, UK; sal 24/2/44. HELL'S ANGELS II.

42-38042 Del Cheyenne 23/11/43; Wilmington 17/12/43; Presque Is 25/12/43; ass 367BS/306BG [GY-P] Thurleigh 9/1/44; MIA Ruhland, Ger. 12/9/44 w/White; flak & e/a, cr Lichterfelde, Ger; 1KIA 9POW; MACR 8831. LADY LUCK.

42-38043 Del Cheyenne 23/11/43; Gr Island 4/12/43; Presque Is 10/12/43; Prestwick, UK 17/12/43; ass 413BS/96BG Snetterton 18/12/43; MIA Stuttgart 25/2/44 w/Smiley; cr Stuttgart; 2KIA 8POW; MACR 2861.

42-38044 Del Cheyenne 24/11/43; Romulus 16/12/43; Presque Is 24/12/43; ass 351BS/100BG [EP-R] Thorpe Abbotts 27/12/43; MIA Berlin 6/3/44 w/Rish; e/a, cr Quackenbrück, Ger; 4KIA 6POW; MACR 3026. SPIRIT OF '44.

42-38045 Del Cheyenne 24/11/43; Presque Is 11/12/43; Nutts Corner, UK 21/12/43; ass 534BS/381BG [GD-C] Ridgewell 22/1/44; MIA {2+m} Brunswick 29/1/44 w/Monacky; e/a, cr Frankfurt; 5KIA 5POW; MACR 2242.

42-38046 Del Cheyenne 24/11/43; Romulus 16/12/43; Presque Is 19/12/43; Valley, UK 24/12/43; ass 339BS/96BG Snetterton 26/12/43; 413BS [MZ-M]; MIA Brunswick 23/3/44 w/Seeman; ditched Channel, 10RTD.

42-38047 Del Cheyenne 25/11/43; Kearney 6/12/43; Grenier 19/12/43; Presque Is 3/1/44; ass 351BS/100BG [EP-O] Thorpe Abbotts 9/1/44; retUS Independence 21/7/45; 4168 BU Independence 10/11/45; RFC Kingman 21/12/45. FEVER BEAVER.

42-38048 Del Cheyenne 25/11/43; Syracuse 17/12/43; Presque Is 24/12/43; ass 571BS/390BG [FC-D] Framlingham 2/2/44 BOMB BAY ANN; retUS Bradley 3/7/45; 4168 BU Sth Plains 12/9/45; RFC Kingman 18/12/45. DOROTHY DEE.

42-38049 Del Cheyenne 25/11/43; Gr Island 6/12/43; Presque Is 21/12/43; ass 549BS/385BG Gt Ashfield 16/2/44; retUS Morrison 15/6/45; 4168 BU Sth Plains 21/10/45; RFC Kingman 5/12/45.

42-38050 Del Cheyenne 25/11/43; Syracuse 18/12/43; Presque Is 22/12/43; ass 359BS/303BG [BN-U] Molesworth 18/1/44; tran 384BG Grafton Underwood 23/3/45; 303BG Molesworth 14/4/45; 388BG 30/4/45; retUS Bradley 11/7/45; 4185 BU Independence 12/7/45; RFC Kingman 21/12/45. THUNDER BIRD. (Preserved after restoration at Duxford, UK)

42-38051 Del Cheyenne 25/11/43; Romulus 15/12/43; Presque Is 18/12/43; ass 427BS/303BG [GN-P] Molesworth 13/1/44; MIA Leipzig 29/6/44 w/Roy; flak, cr Zettweil, Ger; 8KIA 1POW; MACR 6739. MY YORKSHIRE DREAM.

42-38052 Del Cheyenne 25/12/43; Presque Is 25/12/43; ass 379BG Kimbolton 25/12/43; retUS Bradley 9/7/45; 4168 BU Sth Plains 12/9/45; RFC Kingman 8/11/45.

42-38053 Del Cheyenne 25/11/43; Wendover 20/12/43; ass 457BG Glatton 10/2/44; tran 349BS/100BG [XR-G] Thorpe Abbotts 21/1/44; col during assembly 7/5/44, cr Herringfleet, UK; 5KIA 5RTD; sal 8/5/44.

42-38054 Del Cheyenne 26/11/43; Presque Is 23/12/43; ass 334BS/95BG [BG-V] Horham 30/12/43 HAMAWA; 412BS [QW-V]; MIA Politz 25/8/44 w/Peery; cr West Hofen, Ger; 9POW; MACR 8282. HOLY MATRIMONY.

42-38055 Del Cheyenne 26/11/43; Wendover 11/12/43; Grenier 2/1/44; ass 748BS/457BG Glatton 23/1/44; MIA Ludwigshafen 27/5/44 w/Birkman; e/a, cr Overslag, Hol; 5EVD 5POW; MACR 5298.

42-38056 Del Cheyenne 28/11/43; Wendover 11/12/43; ass 751BS/457BG Glatton 7/4/44; sal 22/6/44. QUEEN BEA.

42-38057 Del Cheyenne 28/11/43; Wendover 11/12/43; ass 457BG Glatton 26/1/44; tran 526BS/379BG [LF-K] Kimbolton 18/3/44; sal 2 SAD 10/11/44.

42-38058 Del Cheyenne 28/11/43; Albuquerque 3/12/43; Wendover 3/1/44; ass 457BG Glatton 22/1/44; tran 526BS/379BG [LF-C] Kimbolton 18/3/44; retUS Bradley 9/7/45; 4168 BU Sth Plains 12/9/45; RFC Kingman 8/11/45. THE WISHBONE.

42-38059 Del Cheyenne 29/11/43; Kearney 11/12/43; Presque Is 19/12/43; ass 457BG Glatton 26/1/44; tran 418BS/100BG [LD-A] Thorpe Abbotts 25/12/43; MIA Berlin 6/3/44 w/Capt Miner; e/a, cr Quackenbrück; 4KIA 6POW; MACR 3027.

42-38060 Del Cheyenne 29/11/43; Wendover 12/12/43; Grenier 2/1/44; ass 750BS/457BG Glatton 29/1/44; MIA Rostock 24/2/44 w/Morrow; flak, cr Ostsrand, Ger?; 2KIA 8POW; MACR 2917.

42-38061 Del Cheyenne 29/11/43; Kearney 17/12/43; Presque Is 2/1/44; ass 535BS/381BG [MS-P] Ridgewell 2/2/44; MIA {5+m} St Avord 28/4/44 W/Jones; flak, cr St Avord; 7KIA 3POW; MACR 4241. GEORGIA REBEL II.

42-38062 Del Cheyenne 29/11/43; Kearney 12/12/43; Presque Is 19/12/43; ass 338BS/96BG [BX-U] Snetterton 25/12/43; MIA Berlin 8/5/44 w/King; e/a, c/l Ostenholz, Ger; 1KIA 9POW; MACR 4566. LAURA JANE.

42-38063 Del Cheyenne 1/12/43; Wendover 12/12/43; ass 749BS/457BG Glatton 26/1/44; MIA Munich 12/7/44 w/?; ditched Channel. THE G.I. VIRGIN.

42-38064 Del Cheyenne 1/12/43; Wendover 11/12/43; Grenier 10/1/44; ass 749BS/457BG Glatton 26/1/44; MIA Merseburg 8/11/44 w/?; mid air coll, cr Channel; 9KIA; MACR 10344. HALF 'N HALF.

42-38065 Del Cheyenne 1/12/43; Wendover 12/12/43; slated 457BG, 223 BU Gt Bend 3/8/44; 232 BU Dalhart 27/8/44; 242 BU Gr Island 14/9/44; 249 BU Alliance 12/2/45; 202 BU Galveston 15/2/45; 268 BU Peterson 30/3/45; 252 BU Lubbock 23/6/45; 253 BU Randolph 13/1/46; RFC Walnut Ridge 9/3/46.

42-38066 Del Denver 1/12/43; Dallas 21/12/43; Savannah 30/12/43; ass 20BS/2BG Amendola 29/1/44; tran 32BS/301BG Lucera 2/45; sal 1/8/45. MARISHKA.

42-38067 Del Denver 2/12/43; Chanute 21/12/43; Savannah 29/12/43; ass 49BS/2BG Amendola 9/1/44; MIA Stazi de Campoleone 17/2/44 w/Cooper; flak, cr Anzio; MACR 2387.

42-38068 Del Denver 2/12/43; Dallas 17/12/43; Savannah 22/12/43; ass 20BS/2BG Amendola 3/1/44; sal 24/1/45. MARISHKA.

42-38069 Del Denver 2/12/43; Memphis 20/12/43; Savannah 5/1/44; ass 96BS/2BG Amendola 26/1/44; MIA {68m} Odertal, Ger 22/8/44 w/Duncan; e/a, cr Sarvar, Ger?; three chutes seen; MACR 11270. BIG WIDGET.

42-38070 Del Cheyenne 2/12/43; Savannah 27/12/43; ass 20BS/2BG Amendola 7/2/44; MIA Regensburg 25/2/44 w/O'Shea; mid air coll w/42-31679; five chutes seen, cr Ergolding; MACR 2829.

42-38071 Del Cheyenne 2/12/43; Savannah 21/12/43; ass 342BS/97BG Cerignola 10/1/44; Amendola 16/1/44; completed 100 missions 19/1/45 to Brod, Yugo; sal 2/8/45. MAGNETIC MAGGIE.

42-38072 Del Cheyenne 2/12/43; Salt Lake City

24/12/43; 3018 BU Kingman 23/3/45; Recl Comp 11/1/45.

42-38073 Del Cheyenne 16/12/43; Gr Island 27/12/43; ass 750BS/457BG Glatton 3/2/44; tran 1 SAD Troston 16/8/44. LUCK OF JUDITH ANN.

42-38074 Del Cheyenne 2/12/43; Kearney 17/12/43; Presque Is 10/1/44; Prestwick, UK 14/1/44; ass 367BS/306BG [GY-Q] Thurleigh 16/1/44; MIA Schweinfurt 24/2/44 w/Page; e/a, cr Herdake, Ger?; 6KIA 4POW; MACR 2770.

42-38075 Del Cheyenne 3/12/43; Kearney 14/12/43; ass 331BS/94BG [QE-Q] Rougham 7/1/44; MIA Berlin 3/3/44 w/Ahlwardt; mid air coll, cr Itzeho, Ger; 10KIA; MACR 3476.

42-38076 Del Denver 3/12/43; Lincoln 19/12/43; Savannah 22/12/43; ass 32BS/301BG Cerignola 8/1/44; MIA {11m} Regensburg 25/2/44 w/Berner; e/a, cr Mittnitz, Ger; 7KIA 3POW; MACR 2594.

42-38077 Del Denver 3/12/43; Savannah 21/12/43; ass 353BS/301BG Lucera 4/1/44; MIA {13m} Verona 22/3/44 w/Campbell; flak, exploded, cr Verona; 1KIA 9POW; MACR 3303.

42-38078 Del Denver 6/12/43; Savannah 23/12/43; ass 347BS/99BG Tortorella 7/1/44; {14m} tran 429BS/2BG Amendola 28/3/44; b/d Debreczen 21/9/44 w/Miller; 3KIA 1WIA 6RTD; c/l base and broke in half; repaired and c/l Bari 1/6/45 w/Morton; dest by fire. SWEET PEA.

42-38079 Del Denver 6/12/43; Langley 12/1/44; ass 532BS/381BG [VE-R] Ridgewell 20/2/44; {46m} sal 16/5/45. CARNIVAL QUEEN.

42-38080 Del Denver 7/12/43; Chicago 24/12/43; Savannah 31/12/43; ass 341BS/97BG Cerignola 4/1/44; Amendola 16/1/44; MIA Munich 22/9/44 w/Bezold; flak, cr Munich; MACR 9026.

42-38081 Del Cheyenne 6/12/43; Savannah 20/12/43; ass 341BS/97BG Amendola 16/1/44; MIA Rome 20/1/44 w/Byrd; nine chutes seen; MACR 1953.

42-38082 Del Cheyenne 6/12/43; Kearney 26/12/43; Nutts Corner, UK 14/1/44; ass 525BS/379BG [FR-L] Kimbolton 29/1/44; MIA Berlin 24/5/44 w/Capt Shumake; coll w/e/a, cr Melchow, Ger; 9KIA; MACR 5321.

42-38083 Del Cheyenne 6/12/43; Kearney 24/12/43; Nutts Corner, UK 14/1/44; ass 322BS/91BG [LG-V] Bassingbourn 1/2/44; MIA {77m} Merseburg 2/11/44 w/Hare; e/a, cr Gnotsch, Ger?; 5KIA 4POW; MACR 10144. MAN 'O WAR II HORSEPOWER LTD.

42-38084 Del Cheyenne 6/12/43; Romulus 29/12/43; ass 348BS/99BG Tortorella 1/1/44; {17m} tran 429BS/2BG Amendola 28/3/44; c/l base on training flight 18/10/44 w/Ball, sal 100 MISSION.

42-38085 Del Cheyenne 6/12/43; Kearney 24/12/43; Presque Is 8/1/44; Prestwick, UK 17/1/44; ass 447BG Rattlesden 14/1/44; sal 3/4/44.

42-38086 Del Denver 7/12/43; Kearney 23/12/43; Morrison 30/12/43; ass 346BS/99BG Tortorella 3/1/44; {15m} c/l Lucera (301BG) 10/2/44 w/Connors; rep, tran 840BS/483BG Sterparone; c/t/o 17/1/44 w/Nance, two engines fail, crew OK; sal 18/11/44.

42-38087 Del Denver 8/12/43; Dallas 30/12/43; Savannah 10/1/44; ass 49BS/2BG Amendola 2/2/44 (20m cannon in tail); retUS BU Spokane 12/7/45; Recl Comp 2/5/46. TAIL CRAZY.

42-38088 Del Denver 8/12/43; Barksdale 29/12/43; Morrison 31/12/43; ass 348BS/99BG Tortorella 3/1/44; {15m} tran 20BS/2BG Amendola 28/3/44; b/d Belgrade 17/4/44 w/Atwill, c/l base; sal 18/4/44.

42-38089 Del Denver 8/12/43; Kearney 3/1/44; Savannah 17/1/44; ass 301BG Lucera 18/1/44; tran 49BS/2BG Amendola 28/3/44; MIA Vienna 16/6/44 w/Vaughn; two engines out, no chutes, cr Djurdjevac, Yugo?; MACR 6032.

42-38090 Del Denver 9/12/43; Romulus 29/12/43; Morrison 30/12/43; ass 340BS/97BG Cerignola 3/1/44; Amendola 16/1/44; (20m cannon in tail); ass cargo ship 10/10/44; sal 27/2/45. MISS WINDY CITY.

42-38091 Del Cheyenne 9/12/43; Tulsa 21/12/43; Orlando 31/12/43; 901 BU Pinecastle 2/6/44; 903 BU Pinecastle 10/9/44; 621 BU Pinecastle 9/7/45; 6138 BU Phillips 19/6/46.

42-38092 Del Cheyenne 9/12/43; Orlando 31/12/43; 901 BU Pinecastle 2/6/44; 902 BU Orlando 19/6/44; 901 BU Pinecastle 13/7/44; 903 BU Pinecastle 10/9/44; 610 BU Eglin 27/8/45; RFC Walnut Ridge 7/1/46.

42-38093 Del Cheyenne 13/12/43; Kearney 10/1/44; Grenier 16/1/44; ass 368BS/306BG [BO-V] Thurleigh 28/2/44; c/l 11/9/44; sal 2 SAD 13/9/44.

42-38094 Del Cheyenne 9/12/43; Wichita Falls 26/12/43; Orlando 30/12/43; WO 31/1/44.

42-38095 Del Cheyenne 12/12/43; Omaha 24/12/43; Orlando 30/12/43; 225 BU Rapid City 26/3/45; 2137 BU Hendricks 24/6/45; RFC Walnut Ridge 28/1/46.

42-38096 Del Denver 10/12/43; Memphis 4/1/44; Morrison 6/1/44; ass 347BS/99BG Tortorella 9/1/44; {7m} tran 20BS/2BG Amendola 28/3/44; MIA Moravska Ostrova 29/8/44 w/Thomas; e/a, cr Vsetin, Czech; MACR 8110. BIG TIME.

42-38097 Del Denver 13/12/43 Kearney 31/12/43; Nutts Corner, UK 17/1/44; ass 447BG Rattlesden 18/1/44; sal 18/4/44.

42-38098 Del Denver 13/12/43; Kearney 23/12/43; ass 366BS/305BG [KY-E] Chelveston 22/2/44; retUS Bradley 13/6/45; 4168 BU Sth Plains 12/9/45; RFC Kingman 27/11/43.

42-38099 Del Denver 13/12/43; Kearney 23/12/43; Morrison 4/1/44; ass 352BS/301BG Cerignola 8/1/44; Lucera 1/2/44; {11m} c/l near Foggia 12/2/44 w/Simon; sal.

42-38100 Del Denver 13/12/43; Love Fd 31/12/43; Morrison 4/1/44; ass 96BS/2BG Amendola 5/1/44; MIA {8m} Klagenfurt 19/3/44 w/Southern; flak, cr Klagenfurt; MACR 3258.

42-38101 Del Cheyenne 13/12/43; Kearney 30/12/43; Romulus 21/1/44; Grenier 2/2/44; ass 327/92BG [UX-D] Podington 20/2/44; sal 24/12/44. HURBERT.

42-38102 Del Cheyenne 13/12/43; Gr Island 27/12/43; Presque Is 10/1/44; ass 457BG Glatton 26/1/44; tran 532BS/381BG [VE-A] Ridgewell 11/3/44; c/t/o {1m} for Frankfurt at Birdbrook, UK 24/3/44 w/Bailey; sal.

42-38103 Del Cheyenne 13/12/43; Gr Island 29/12/43; Presque Is 25/1/44; ass 457BG Glatton 26/1/44; tran 532BS/381BG [VE-B] Ridgewell 11/3/44; b/d {44m} Oberpfaffenhofen 9/4/44; c/l, sal. OUR BOARDING HOUSE.

42-38104 Del Cheyenne 14/12/43; Gr Island 27/12/43; Presque Is 26/1/44; ass 457BG Glatton 17/2/44; tran 325BS/92BG Podington 11/3/44; MIA Munster 23/3/44 w/MacDonald; e/a, cr Durnai, Bel; 10POW; MACR 3417.

42-38105 Del Cheyenne 14/12/43; Lakeland 7/1/44; ass 775BS/463BG Celone 9/3/44; MIA Budapest 14/6/44 w/Fridley; col w/42-31845; MACR 6093. THE CLUB 105.

42-38106 Del Cheyenne 14/12/43; Mitchell 7/1/44; ass 366BS/305BG Chelveston 11/2/44; MIA Brunswick 29/3/44 w/Wayenberg; e/a, cr Laufwedel, Ger; 9KIA 1POW; MACR 3476.

42-38107 Del Cheyenne 15/12/43; Kearney 31/12/43; ass 331BS/94BG Rougham 5/1/44; MIA Brunswick 10/2/44 w/Repas; e/a, cr Gross Hehlen, Ger; 10POW; MACR 2372.

42-38108 Del Denver 15/12/43; Mitchell 18/1/44; Nutts Corner, UK 29/1/44; ass 366BS/305BG Chelveston 16/2/44; MIA Brunswick 29/3/44 w/Capt Taylor; e/a, cr Huxahl, Ger?; 4KIA 6POW; MACR 3477. BARBARA II.

42-38109 Del Denver 15/12/43; Mitchell 20/1/44; ass 364BS/305BG Chelveston 10/2/44; b/d 20/2/44; sal 2 SAD 23/2/44.

42-38110 Del Denver 15/12/43; Gr Island 29/12/43; Presque Is 21/1/44; ass 457BS Glatton 26/1/44; tran 407BS/92BG [PY-H] Podington 11/3/44; c/l Little Rissington,. UK 8/9/44; sal 10/9/44.

42-38111 Del Denver 16/12/43; Kearney 27/12/43; Presque Is 9/1/44; Nutts Corner, UK 21/1/44; ass 525BS/379BG [FR-H] Kimbolton 12/2/44; b/d, sal 2 SAD 9/7/44.

42-38112 Del Denver 18/12/43; Kearney 31/12/43; Presque Is 20/1/44; Nutts Corner, UK 27/1/44; ass 545BS/384BG [JD-J] Grafton Underwood 10/2/44; MIA Schweinfurt 13/4/44 w/Fioretti; e/a, cr Elmahausen, Ger; 4KIA 6POW; MACR 3869.

42-38113 Del Cheyenne 16/12/43; Gr Island 29/12/43; Presque Is 21/1/44; ass 749BS/457BG Glatton 23/1/44; 750BS; MIA Rheine 21/3/44 w/Creason; flak, cr Bremen; 1POW 8RTD; MACR 13895. (1000th Douglas B17). RENE III.

42-38114 Del Cheyenne 16/12/43; Lakeland 7/1/44; Morrison 21/1/44; ass 772BS/463BG Celone 9/3/44; MIA Belgrade 6/6/44 w/Barrett; flak, two engines out, cr Udize, Yugo; MACR 5847.

42-38115 Del Cheyenne 18/12/43; Lakeland 6/1/44; Morrison 20/1/44; ass 773BS/463BG Celone 9/3/44; b/d Toulon 29/4/44, c/l base; sal 1/5/44.

42-38116 Del Cheyenne 18/12/43; Lakeland 8/1/44; Morrison 16/1/44; ass 772BS463BG Celone 9/3/44; retUS 4100 BU Patterson 27/3/45; Recl Comp 24/5/46.

42-38117 Del Denver 18/12/43; Kearney 31/12/43; ass 535BS/381BG [MS-T] Ridgewell 26/2/44; MIA {4+m} Tours 4/7/44 w/Bobrof; mech fault, cr Persac, Fr; 2EVD 7KIA; MACR 6779. (Dug up by French archeological group in Feb '87). TOUCH THE BUTTON NELL II.

42-38118 Del Denver 18/12/43; Kearney 31/12/43; Nutts Corner, UK 8/1/44; ass 323BS/91BG [OR-N] Bassingbourn 25/2/44; MIA Erkner 6/3/44 w/Fourmy; flak, cr Quackenbrück, Ger; 2KIA 8POW; MACR 2901.

42-38119 Del Denver 18/12/43; Kearney 31/12/43; WO 4/2/44.

42-38120 Del Cheyenne 19/12/43; Columbus 23/1/44; ass 561BS/388BG Knettishall 5/2/44; MIA Brunswick 23/3/44 w/Gerstenhaber; flak, cr Wesendorf, Ger; 1KIA 9POW; MACR 3543.

42-38121 Del Denver 19/12/43; Phoenix 2/1/44; Kearney 3/1/44; ass 551BS/385BG Gt Ashfield 28/1/44; MIA Pas de Calais 28/2/44 w/Kemmann; flak, cr Boulogne, Fr; 8KIA 2POW. MACR 2882.

42-38122 Del Cheyenne 19/12/43; St Joseph 4/1/44; Lakeland 10/1/44; ass 772BS/463BG Celone 9/3/44; sal 7/7/44.

42-38123 Del Cheyenne 19/12/43; Gr Island 1/1/44; ass 334BS/95BG [BG-E] Horham 8/2/44; MIA Pas de Calais 23/6/44 w/Mangan; cr Mauberge, Fr; 5EVD 2KIA 3POW; MACR 5915. TO HELL OR GLORY.

42-38124 Del Cheyenne 20/12/43; Gr Island 6/1/44; ass 452BG Deopham Green 14/2/44; sal 27/3/44.

42-38125 Del Denver 20/12/43; Kearney 16/1/44; ass 332BS/94BG Rougham 16/2/44; retUS Bradley 30/6/45; 4168 BU Sth Plains 12/9/45; RFC Kingman

16/11/45.

42-38126 Del Denver 20/12/43; Salt Lake City 27/12/43; Palm Springs 22/1/44; 3018 BU Kingman 23/3/45; 3017 BU Hobbs 24/6/45; RFC Walnut Ridge 3/1/46.

42-38127 Del Denver 21/12/43; Gr Island 24/1/44; ass 336BS/95BG [ET-F] Horham 6/2/44; ditched on ASR mission 24/4/44 w/Huie; 2KIA 8POW. MACR 4/2/63. LIBERTY SHIP.

42-38128 Del Denver 21/12/43; Las Vegas 26/12/43; Kearney 12/1/44; ass 324BS/91BG [DF-Z] Bassingbourn 25/2/44 CUTTY SARK {36m}; renamed RED ALERT (21m); MIA {26m} Altenbeken 26/11/44 w/Miller; e/a, cr Furstenau, Ger; 1KIA 8POW; MACR 10838. DEAR BECKY.

42-38129 Del Denver 21/12/43; Kearney 12/1/44; ass 369BS/306BG [WW-L] Thurleigh 25/2/44; tran 29 TAC 14/5/45; 398BG Nuthampstead 24/5/45; retUS Bradley 1/6/45; 4168 BU Sth Plains 12/9/45; RFC Kingman 28/12/45.

42-38130 Del Cheyenne 22/12/43; Kearney 24/1/44; ass 570BS/390BG Framlingham 8/2/44; MIA Hamm 22/4/44 w/Reich; e/a, cr Alsbach, Ger; 2KIA 8POW. MACR 4170.

42-38131 Del Cheyenne 22/12/43; Rosewell 2/1/44; ass 364BS/305BG Chelveston 8/2/44; MIA Cottbus-Sorau 5/4/44 w/?; MACR 4170 recovered July '71. BERTIE LEE.

42-38132 Del Cheyenne 22/12/43; Hobbs 21/1/44; 3021 BU Las Vegas 26/9/44; 3022 BU Indian Springs 3/10/44; 3021 BU Las Vegas 15/3/45; 3017 BU Hobbs 25/6/45; RFC Walnut Ridge 5/1/46.

42-38133 Del Cheyenne 23/12/43; Kearney 7/1/44; ass 337BS/96BG [AW-O] Snetterton 15/1/44; sal 24/10/44; MIA 5/12/44; MACR 4567.

42-38134 Del Cheyenne 23/12/43; Lincoln 10/1/44; Savannah 8/2/44; ass 429BS/2BG Amendola 14/2/44; MIA Olching, Ger. 22/2/44 w/Melzer; mech fault, ditched Adriatic; MACR 2631. BLOW IT OUT YOUR .....!

42-38135 Del Denver 23/12/43; Kearney 15/1/44; ass 549BS/385BG Gt Ashfield 9/2/44; MIA Berlin 21/6/44 w/Lohmeyer; e/a, f/l Dorrod, Sweden; 7INT 3KIA. MACR 5920.

42-38136 Del Denver 23/12/43; Gr Island 14/1/44; ass 615BS/401BG [IY-G] Deenethorpe 23/2/44; MIA Berlin 6/3/44 w/ Kolb; flak & e/a, cr Biesow, Ger?; 10POW. MACR 2743.

42-38137 Del Denver 23/1/43; Gr Island 28/12/43; Boca Raton 20/1/44; 3501 BU Boca Raton 28/11/44; 3704 BU Keesler 15/1/45; 3704 BU Boca Raton 1/8/45; RFC Kingman 8/12/45.

42-38138 Del Denver 24/12/43; Gr Island 16/1/44; ass 560BS/388BG Knettishall 8/2/44; MIA Berlin 8/3/44 w/Lentz; mid air coll w/e/a; cr Nienburg, Ger; 5KIA 5POW; MACR 3090.

42-38139 Del Cheyenne 23/12/43; Gr Island 12/1/44; ass 410BS/94BG [GL-N] Rougham 8/2/44; MIA Berlin 18/4/44 w/Pomeranz; e/a, cr Barnewitz, Ger; 10POW; MACR 4158. THE PAYOFF.

42-38140 Del Cheyenne 26/12/43; Kearney 12/1/44; ass 8AF RetUS Bradley 26/6/45; 4168 BU Sth Plains 12/9/45; RFC Kingman 12/11/45.

42-38141 Del Cheyenne 26/12/43; Kearney 12/1/44; ass 525BS/379BG [FR-D] Kimbolton 28/2/44; 524BS [WA-D]; MIA French A/fds 9/7/44 w/Frye; flak, ditched Nth Sea; MACR 7359. PANSY YOKUM.

42-38142 Del Cheyenne 26/12/43; Long Beach 29/12/43; Witchita 10/1/44; Lakeland 17/1/44; WO 13/2/44; sal 326 BU McDill 20/4/44.

42-38143 Del Cheyenne 26/12/43; Savannah 17/1/44; ass 775BS/463BG Celone 9/3/44; loaned 49BS/2BG Amendola; MIA 19/3/44 on familiarisation mission w/Chambers; mid air coll w/42-31823 (463BG); ditched Adriatic. MACR 3286.

42-38144 Del Cheyenne 26/12/43; El Paso 4/1/44; Kearney 14/1/44; ass 401BS/91BG [LL-O] Bassingbourn 28/2/44; b/d 14/2/45, f/l Continent; sal 13/3/45. JEZEBEL.

42-38145 Del Denver 27/12/43; Gr Island 14/1/44; ass 730BS/452BG Deopham Green 6/2/44; coll w/B-17(388BG) c/l Old Buckenham 19/5/44, 2KIA; sal 20/5/44. ROSALIE ANN.

42-38146 Del Denver 27/12/43; Gr Island 6/1/44; ass 508BS/351BG [YB-D] Polebrook 29/2/44; MIA Merseburg 29/7/44 w/Morton; flak, cr Beendorf, Ger; 9KIA MACR 7323.

42-38147 Del Denver 27/12/43; Boca Raton 21/1/44; 123 BU Seymour Johnson 29/8/44; 3501 BU Boca Raton 16/9/44; 3704 BU Keesler 16/1/45; 554 BU Memphis 10/6/45; Recl Comp 31/7/46.

42-38148 Del Denver 27/12/43; Gr Island 12/1/44; ass 368BS/306BG [BO-K] Thurleigh 9/4/44; tran 381BG Ridgewell 5/45; retUS Bradley 7/6/45; 4168 BU Sth Plains 12/9/45; RFC Kingman 3/12/45. MAMU.

42-38149 Del Denver 27/12/43; Gr Island 16/1/44; ass 364BS/305BG Chelveston 22/2/44; MIA Stettin 11/4/44 w/Cooke; e/a, cr Paplitz, Ger; 1KIA 9POW; MACR 4011.

42-38150 Del Cheyenne 29/12/43; Roswell 28/1/44; 3030 BU Roswell 2/6/44; 3021 BU Las Vegas 22/9/44; 3022 BU Indian Springs 6/10/44; 3017 BU Hobbs 22/5/45; 3028 BU Luke Fd 30/9/45; 3017 BU Hobbs 10/10/45; RFC Walnut Ridge 7/1/46.

42-38151 Del Cheyenne 29/12/43; Kearney 12/1/43; ass 336BS/95BG [ET-L] Horham 6/2/44; MIA Berlin 16/3/44 w/Norred; cr Leipheim, Ger; 10POW; MACR 3230.

42-38152 Del Cheyenne 29/12/43; Albuquerque 5/1/44; Yuma 17/1/44; 3017 BU Hobbs 4/6/44; 4160 BU Hobbs 6/11/44; RFC Kingman 7/12/45.

42-38153 Del Cheyenne 29/12/43; Long Beach 2/1/44; Grenier 4/2/44; ass 511BS/351BG [DS-F] Polebrook 25/2/44; MIA {51m} Hamm 19/9/44 w/Butler; flak, ditched Channel; 2EVD 8POW. BEDLAM BALL.

42-38154 Del Cheyenne 29/12/43; Kearney 12/1/44; ass 358BS/303BG Molesworth 18/2/44; sal 25/6/44.

42-38155 Del Denver 31/12/43; Phoenix 2/1/44; ass 368BS/306BG [BO-J] Thurleigh 25/2/44; tran 2 BAD Warton 21/3/45; ATC 29/3/45; retUS 4100 BU Patterson 30/4/45; 4126 BU San Bernardino 16/5/45; 4119 BU Brookley 13/9/45; 4112 BU Olmstead 16/12/45; RFC Walnut Ridge 8/4/46; later to US Navy as CB-17.

42-38156 Del Denver 31/12/43; Presque Is 7/1/44; ass 326BS/92BG [JW-E] Podington 23/3/44; sal 9AF on Continent 31/10/45. MARY B.

42-38157 Del Denver 1/1/44; Grenier 16/1/44; ass 452BG Deopham Green 24/2/44; dest on ground by Luftwaffe at Poltava, Rus. 2/7/44; sal 2/7/44.

42-38158 Del Denver 1/1/44; Gr Island 13/1/44; ass 547BS/384BG [SO-L] Grafton Underwood 1/3/44; MIA Erding 24/4/44 w/McKichan; 8KIA 2POW;

Below: B-17G-30-DL 42-38133, *Reluctant Dragon* of the 337th Bomb Squadron, 96th Bomb Group, was one of the first Fortresses modified with fully enclosed waist windows and a Cheyenne tail gun installation to arrive in the UK. (USAAF)

42-38159 Del Denver 2/1/44; Gr Island 14/1/44; ass 534BS/381BG [GD-J] Ridgewell 21/2/44; b/d Aschaffenberg 21/1/45, f/l Continent; rep & ret 30/1/45; tran 91BG Bassingbourn 30/5/45. RetUS 8/6/45. COLONEL BUB.

42-38160 Del Cheyenne 3/1/44; Kearney 14/1/44; ass 550BS/385BG Gt Ashfield 6/2/44 LITTLE CHUB; MIA Augsburg 16/3/44 w/Meyer; e/a, ditched Lake Zug, Switz; 9INT 1KIA; MACR 3246. Recovered from lake and displayed at St Moritz, 1970, sal 1973. LONESOME POLECAT.

42-38161 Del Cheyenne 3/1/44; Kearney 14/1/44; ass 525BS/379BG [FR-O] Kimbolton 19/2/44; MIA Berlin 9/7/44 w/Darnell; flak, cr Nijelmeer, Hol; MACR 4559. SARAH JANE.

42-38162 Del Cheyenne 3/1/44; Gr Island 16/1/44; ass 614BS/401BG [IW-R] Deenethorpe 22/3/44; MIA Marienburg 9/4/44 w/Dawes; e/a, cr Baltic Sea; 10KIA; MACR 3940.

42-38163 Del Cheyenne 3/1/44; Kearney 14/1/44; ass 379BG Kimbolton 6/2/44; tran 367BS/306BG [GY-N] Thurleigh 29/2/44; MIA French A/fds 17/6/44 w/Pedersen; flak, cr Le Mans, Fr; 5EVD 1KIA 3POW; MACR 5896.

42-38164 Del Cheyenne 3/1/44; Gr Island 16/1/44; ass 709BS/447BG Rattlesden 6/2/44; MIA Brux 12/5/44 w/Capt Larson; e/a, cr Angolsheim, Ger; 10POW; MACR 4767.

42-38165 Del Denver 3/1/44; Long Beach 5/1/44; Albuquerque 20/1/44; 224 BU Sioux City 6/3/45; 225 BU Rapid City 14/3/45; 203 BU Jackson 4/7/45; 215 BU Pueblo 9/9/45; 422 BU Tonopah 27/9/45; 215 BU Pueblo 9/10/45; 224 BU Sioux City 7/12/45; RFC Kingman 20/12/45.

42-38166 Del Denver 3/1/44; Kingman 18/1/44; 225 BU Rapid City 1/5/45; 237 BU Kirtland 9/7/45; RFC Altus 7/11/45.

42-38167 Del Cheyenne 4/1/44; Gr Island 16/1/44; ass 422NLS/305BG [JJ-L] Chelveston 22/2/44; tran 858BS as ASR 25/6/44; sal 11/10/45.

42-38168 Del Cheyenne 4/1/44; Savannah 21/1/44; Morrison 2/2/44; ass 359BS/303BG Molesworth 22/2/44; sal 2 SAD 22/4/44. DEAR MOM.

42-38169 Del Cheyenne 4/1/44; Kearney 14/1/44; ass 331BS/94BG Rougham 5/2/44; 410BS [GL-B]; MIA Berlin 4/3/44 w/?. MACR 2998.

42-38170 Del Denver 3/1/44; Kingman 14/1/44; 3018 BU Kingman 23/3/45; 3017 BU Hobbs 24/6/45; RFC Kingman 4/12/45.

42-38171 Del Denver 3/1/44; 3501 BU Boca Raton 28/11/44; RFC Kingman 22/2/46.

42-38172 Del Denver 5/1/44; Mat Com Burbank 22/6/44; 3715 BU Burbank 25/6/44; 3715 BU Amarillo 31/8/45; RFC Kingman 27/11/45.

42-38173 Del Denver 5/1/44; Boca Raton 19/1/44; 3501 BU Boca Raton 26/11/45; RFC Kingman 22/2/46.

42-38174 Del Denver 5/1/44; 3705 BU Lowry 2/9/44; RFC Kingman 31/1/46.

42-38175 Del Cheyenne 5/1/44; Savannah 22/1/44; ass 418BS/100BG [LD-O] Thorpe Abbotts 15/2/44; sal 2/11/45.

42-38176 Del Cheyenne 5/1/44; Gr Island 16/1/44; ass 3466BS/305BG [KY-W] Chelveston 16/2/44; MIA Cottbus 29/5/44 w/Kass; e/a, cr Ransow, Ger?; 8KIA 2POW; MACR 5337.

42-38177 Del Cheyenne 6/1/44; Gr Island 10/1/44; Grenier 24/1/44; ass 561BS/388BG Knettishall 14/2/44; MIA Berlin 6/3/44 w/Christiani; e/a, cr Zwolle, Hol; 5KIA 5POW; MACR 3091. SHACK RABBITS.

42-38178 Del Cheyenne 6/1/44; Gr Island 16/1/44; ass 334BS/95BG [BG-K] Horham 11/2/44; MIA Schweinfurt 19/7/44 w/Hamlik; cr Vielbrunn, Ger?; 10POW; MACR 7409.

42-38179 Del Cheyenne 6/1/44; Mobile 24/1/44; 611 BU Eglin 8/6/44; 610 BU Eglin 4/9/44; 4119 BU Galeville 10/11/44; 611 BU Eglin 1/4/45; 2137 BU Hendricks 13/8/45; RFC Kingman 16/11/45.

42-38180 Del Denver 6/1/44; Albuquerque 8/1/44; 3705 BU Lowry 10/9/45; RFC Kingman 9/12/46.

42-38181 Del Denver 7/1/44; Las Vegas 12/1/44; 3021 BU Las Vegas 23/3/45; 3017 BU Hobbs 22/5/45; 2114 BU Lockburn 25/6/45; 3017 BU Hobbs 23/8/45; RFC Walnut Ridge 4/1/46.

42-38182 Del Denver 9/1/44; Mat Com Burbank 22/6/44; 3715 BU Burbank 25/6/44; 3701 BU Amarillo 21/10/44; RFC Kingman 2/1/46.

42-38183 Del Denver 8/1/44; Albuquerque 12/1/44; ass 525BS/379BG [FR-C] Kimbolton 10/2/44; flak b/d, cr Magdeburg 28/9/44 w/Bailey; MACR 9363; rep & ret; sal 1/6/45. THE LOST ANGEL.

42-38184 Del Cheyenne 9/1/44; Las Vegas 17/1/44; 3021 BU Las Vegas 16/3/45; 3017 BU Hobbs 22/5/45; RFC Walnut Ridge 9/1/46. 42-38185 Del Cheyenne 9/1/44; Morrison 4/2/44; ass 526BS/379BG [LF-J] Kimbolton 22/2/44; sal 2 SAD 14/6/44.

42-38186 Del Cheyenne 9/1/44; Roswell 22/1/44; 3030 BU Roswell 28/12/44; 3010 BU Williams 20/1/45; 3020 BU La Junta 20/4/45; 2114 BU Lockburn 25/6/45; 4152 BU Lockburn 1/10/45; RFC Walnut Ridge 8/1/46.

42-38187 Del Cheyenne 9/1/44; Gr Island 21/1/44; ass 560BS/388BG Knettishall 9/2/44; damaged at Poltava by Luftwaffe 21/4/44; rep & ret; retUS 4100 BU Patterson 23/3/45; Recl Comp 2/5/46.

42-38188 Del Cheyenne 10/1/44; Gr Island 23/1/44; ass 533BS/381BG [VP-K] Ridgewell 6/4/44; MIA {21m} Dessau 30/5/44 w/Monahan; e/a, cr Koethen, Ger?; 4KIA 5POW; MACR 5234.

42-38189 Del Cheyenne 10/1/44; Kingman 19/1/44; 2120 BU Greenville 4/7/44; 221 BU Alexandra 7/7/44; 3290 BU Alexandra 1/3/45; 330 BU Dyersburg 25/6/45; 327 BU Drew 30/8/45; 330 BU Dyersburg 4/9/45; RFC Walnut Ridge 14/12/45.

42-38190 Del Denver 10/1/44; Kearney 20/1/44; ass 339BS/96BG [QJ-K] Snetterton 27/2/44; MIA Berlin 8/5/44 w/Fitzpatrick; e/a & exploded, cr Lindhorst, Ger; 9KIA 1POW; MACR 4568.

42-38191 Del Denver 10/1/44; Gr Island 28/1/44; ass 418BS/100BG [LD-W] Thorpe Abbotts 2/3/44; MIA Berlin 19/5/44 w/Ruppert; e/a, cr Roedbyhavn, Den?; 9KIA 1POW; MACR 4947.

42-38192 Del Denver 12/1/44; Gr Island 28/1/44; ass 524BS/379BG [WA-C] Kimbolton 1/3/44; MIA Munich 12/7/44 w/Hutchins; flak, cr Stuebenwasen, Ger; 8KIA 1POW; MACR 7506.

42-38193 Del Denver 11/1/44; Kearney 2/2/44; ass 338BS/96BG [BX-J] Snetterton 13/3/44; c/l Honington A/fd, UK 13/4/44; 10RTD; retUS Bradley 2/7/45; 4168 BU Sth Plains 13/10/45; RFC Kingman 10/12/45.

42-38194 Del Denver 11/1/44; Presque Is 11/2/44; ass 533BS/381BG [VP-V] Ridgewell 25/3/44; MIA {28m} Berlin 21/6/44 w/Bailey; e/a, f/l Rinkaby, Swed; 7INT 2POW; MACR 5992; rep & ret /45; retUS Bradley 22/8/45; 4185 BU Independence 30/11/45; RFC Kingman 14/12/45. BABOON McGOON.

42-38195 Del Cheyenne 12/1/44; Kearney 26/1/44; ass 549BS/385BG Gt Ashfield 8/2/44; MIA Augsburg 16/3/44 w/McLaughlin; e/a, f/l Wildhaus, Switz; 8INT 1KIA; MACR 3247.

42-38196 Del Cheyenne 12/1/44; Gr Island 21/1/44; ass 550BS/385BG Gt Ashfield 9/2/44; MIA Schweinfurt 13/4/44 w/Jorgensen; flak, f/l Dubendorf, Switz; 10INT; MACR 3772.

42-38197 Del Cheyenne 12/1/44; Gr Island 27/1/44; ass 350BS/100BG [LN-T] Thorpe Abbotts 10/2/44; MIA Berlin 6/3/44 w/Lautenschlager; e/a, cr Haltern, Ger; 1KIA 9POW; MACR 3028. HALF AND HALF.

42-38198 Del Cheyenne 12/1/44; Kearney 25/1/44; ass 369BS/306BG [WW-D] Thurleigh 6/4/44; tran 92BG Podington; sal 1 BAD Burtonwood 9/5/45.

42-38199 Del Cheyenne 12/1/44; Kearney 24/1/44; ass 548BS/385BG Gt Ashfield 8/2/44; MIA Hamburg 4/8/44 w/Masterson; flak & e/a, cr Midlam, Ger?; 9POW; MACR 7743. HAIRS BREATH.

42-38200 Del Cheyenne 15/1/44; Gr Island 20/1/44; ass 551BS/385BG Gt Ashfield 27/2/44; MIA Hamm 22/4/44 w/Cornwall; e/a & flak, cr Hillbeck, Ger?; 10POW; MACR 4167.

42-38201 Del Denver 13/1/44; Lakeland 1/2/44; Morrison 9/2/44; ass 815BS/483BG Tortorella 30/3/44; tran 346BS/99BG Tortorella 31/3/44; 429BS; {41m} c/t/o 24/8/44; sal. 2ND PATCHES.

42-38202 Del Denver 15/1/44; Gr Island 21/1/44; ass 729BS/452BG Deopham Green 10/2/44; MIA Ruhland 21/6/44 w/Hernandez; e/a, cr Swory, Ger?; 7EVD 3POW; MACR 10282. BTO IN THE ETO.

42-38203 Del Denver 15/1/44; Gr Island 19/1/44; WO 26/2/44.

42-38204 Del Denver 14/1/44; Gr Island 31/1/44; ass 358BS/303BG [VK-H] Molesworth 29/2/44; 360BS; MIA Oberpfaffenhofen 24/4/44 w/McClure; e/a & flak; c/l Geneva, Switz; MACR 4271.

42-38205 Del Denver 14/1/44; Morrison 6/2/44; Savannah 14/2/44; ass 364BS/385BG [WF-K] Gt Ashfield 10/2/44 THUNDERMUG; tran 816BS/483BG Tortorella 30/3/44; tran 49BS/2BG Amendola 31/3/44; MIA Vienna 16/7/44 w/O'Brien; flak, wing fire, cr Goetzendorf; one chute seen; MACR 6906. WINGED FURY.

42-38206 Del Cheyenne 14/1/44; Gr Island 26/1/44; ass 305BG Chelveston 1/3/44; MIA Merseburg 12/12/44 w/?; f/l Continent.

42-38207 Del Cheyenne 14/1/44; McDill 6/2/44; ass 94BG Rougham 16/3/44; tran 815BS/483BG Tortorella 30/3/44; 346BS/99BG Tortorella 31/3/44; MIA {1m} Ploesti 5/4/44 w/Currie; flak, cr Caracal, Rom?; ten chutes seen; MACR 3695.

42-38208 Del Cheyenne 16/1/44; Gr Island 6/2/44; ass 331BS/94BG [QE-X] Rougham 10/2/44 GEORGIA'S PEACHES; tran 547BS/384BG [SO-A] Grafton Underwood 4/4/44; 398BG Nuthampstead 27/5/45; retUS Bradley 7/6/45; 4168 BU Sth Plains 21/10/45; RFC Kingman 1/12/45. LILLY BELLE.

42-38209 Del Cheyenne 16/1/44; McDill 4/2/44; ass 817BS/483BG Tortorella 30/3/44; tran 347BS/99BG Tortorella 31/3/44; {58m} RetUS 4100 BU Patterson 1/8/45; Recl Comp 2/5/46. EARTHQUAKE McGOON.

42-38210 Del Denver 16/1/44; McDill 6/2/44; ass 840BS/483BG Tortorella 30/3/44; tran 346BS/99BG Tortorella 31/3/44; MIA {6m} Fischamend Markt, Aus. 12/4/44 w/Hrostowsky; flak, cr Zwolfaxing; 6KIA 4POW; MACR 3955.

42-38211 Del Denver 16/1/44; Presque Is 1/2/44; 731BS/452BG Deopham Green 9/2/44; MIA Berlin 8/3/44 w/MacDonald; e/a, cr Nienburg, Ger; 1KIA 9POW; MACR 3193. SLEEPY TIME GAL.

42-38212 Del Denver 17/1/44; Morrison 1/3/44; ass 817BS/483BG Tortorella 30/3/44; tran 49BS/2BG Amendola 31/3/44; sal 1/10/46.

42-38213 Del Denver 17/1/44; McDill 6/2/44; ass

815BS/483BG Tortorella 30/3/44; tran 20BS/2BG Amendola 31/3/44; MIA Bleckhammer 7/7/44 w/Nabinger; flak, blew off nose to cockpit; cr Friedernau; three chutes seen; MACR 6519.

B-17G-VE

42-39758 Del Long Beach 24/8/43; ass 325BS/92BG Podington 2/12/43; MIA Oschersleben 11/1/44 w/Trynes; e/a, cr Almelo, Hol; 10POW; MACR 1921.

42-39759 Del Long Beach 24/8/43; Scott 2/10/43; ass 571BS/390BG [FC-C] Framlingham 7/10/43 PICKLE DROPPER; MIA Kassel 30/12/43 w/Brigman; e/a, cr Wimy?; 8EVD 2POW; MACR 1675. SARAH JANE.

42-39760 Del Long Beach 24/8/43; Scott 18/11/43; ass 401BG Deenethorpe 11/11/43; tran 509BS/351BG [RQ-M] Polebrook 25/11/43; {30m} tran 487BG Lavenham 16/7/44; sal 27/7/44.

42-39761 Del Long Beach 25/8/43; Scott 22/10/43; ass 401BG Deenethorpe 26/10/43; tran 511BS/351BG [DS-D] Polebrook 25/11/43; MIA {14m} Oschersleben 11/1/44 w/White; e/a, cr Zweelop, Hol; 3EVD 7POW; MACR 1939. FIRE BALL II.

42-39762 Del Long Beach 25/8/43; Scott 16/9/43; ass 526BS/379BG Kimbolton 21/10/43; f/l Rattlesden 31/12/43; sal 8/1/44.

42-39763 Del Long Beach 25/8/43; Cheyenne 11/9/43; Mat Com Wright 2/6/44 (propeller feathering test a/c); 4100 BU Patterson 15/2/45; 234 BU Clovis 19/2/45; 400 BU Wright 4/3/45; 4145 BU Wendover 18/4/45; 4135 BU Hill Fd 6/4/46; 4145 BU Alamogordo 31/3/47; 4136 BU 23/12/47; 4146 BU Holloman 29/4/48; 2754 ABGp Holloman 5/4/49; 2753 ASTGp Pyote 13/4/49; Recl Comp Pyote 4/4/50.

42-39764 Del Long Beach 25/8/43; Scott 16/9/43; ass 427BS/303BG Molesworth 18/10/43; MIA Bremen 20/12/43 w/Alex; e/a, cr Bremen; 1KIA 9POW; MACR 1706. SANTA ANA.

42-39765 Del Long Beach 26/8/43; Scott 25/10/43; ass 359BS/303BG Molesworth 11/10/43 MISSMANOOKI; tran 612BS/401BG [SC-A] Deenethorpe 14/11/43; 1 BAD Burtonwood 8/4/44; retUS 4186 BU Tinker 24/7/45; 4100 BU Patterson 1/9/45; 3704 BU Keesler 10/1/46; RFC Kingman 7/5/46. BABY LU III.

42-39766 Del Long Beach 25/8/43; ass 482BG Alconbury 8/10/43; tran 422BS/305BG Chelveston 23/3/44; 482BG Alconbury 6/7/44; sal 6/12/44.

42-39767 Del Long Beach 27/8/43; Scott 5/10/43; ass 332BS/94BG Rougham 11/10/43; MIA Oschersleben 11/1/44 w/Cota; e/a, cr Brunswick; 2KIA 8POW; MACR 1886.

42-39768 Del Long Beach 26/8/43; ass 367BS/306BG [GY-A] Thurleigh 9/10/43; MIA Bremen 13/12/43 w/Brinkley; 7KIA 3POW; MACR 1575.

42-39769 Del Long Beach 25/8/43; Scott 19/9/43; ass 359BS/303BG Molesworth 13/10/43; c/l base on practice flight, sal 19/12/43.

42-39770 Del Long Beach 26/8/43; ass 326BS/92BG Podington 25/12/43; MIA Leipzig 20/2/44 w/Jessen; flak, cr Eisenach, Ger; 1KIA 9POW; MACR 2756.

42-39771 Del Long Beach 26/8/43; Gt Falls 13/10/43; Scott 25/10/43; ass 401BG Deenethorpe 4/11/43; tran 401BS/91BG [LL-H] Bassingbourn 20/11/43; MIA Frankfurt 4/2/44 w/Lutz; flak, cr Eindhoven, Hol; 2EVD 8POW; MACR 2234. JEANNIE MARIE.

42-39772 Del Long Beach 26/8/43; Gr Island 5/10/43; ass 332BS/94BG [XM-R] Rougham 13/10/43; MIA Frankfurt 4/2/44 w/Eisner; flak, cr Frankfurt; 10POW; MACR 2194. GRIN 'N BEAR IT.

42-39773 Del Long Beach 26/8/43; Gr Island 4/10/43; ass 548BS/385BG Gt Ashfield 10/10/43; MIA Hamm 22/4/44 w/McDavitt; flak, cr Bislich, Ger; 10POW; MACR 4168. WAR CRY II.

42-39774 Del Long Beach 27/8/43; ass 323BS/91BG [OR-R] Bassingbourn 18/10/43; {26m} tran AFSC 3/5/44; DEMO DARLING.

42-39775 Del Long Beach 27/8/43; ass 333BS/94BG [TS-K] Rougham 13/10/43; sal 3/11/44. FRENESI.

42-39776 Del Long Beach 28/8/43; Scott 8/10/43; ass 423BS/306BG Thurleigh 13/10/43; MIA Erding 24/4/44 w/Coughlin; e/a, cr Sainbach, Ger?; 5POW 5KIA; MACR 4285.

42-39777 Del Long Beach 28/8/43; Scott 29/9/43; ass Soxo 7/10/43 but re-assigned from Lt Staughton as weather ship; sal 17/9/44. STUMBLE BULL.

42-39778 Del Long Beach 30/8/43; Scott 20/10/43; ass 401BG Deenethorpe 5/10/43; tran 511BS/351BG [DS-A] Polebrook 18/11/43; MIA {17m} Osnabrück 22/12/43 w/Maginn; flak, ditched Nth Sea; 5KIA 5POW; MACR 1717. LUCKY BALL.

42-39779 Del Long Beach 28/8/43; Scott 16/9/43; ass 526BS/379BG Kimbolton 21/10/43; MIA Bremen 29/11/43 w/Planalp; e/a, cr Grossenging, Ger?; 2KIA 8POW; MACR 1331.

42-39780 Del Long Beach 29/8/43; Scott 22/10/43; ass 401BG Deenethorpe 26/10/43; tran 510BS/351BG [TU-S] Polebrook 18/11/43; {4m} c/l Hawkinge, UK 30/12/43; sal SAD 2/1/44; LITTLE TWINKLE.

42-39781 Del Long Beach 29/8/43; Scott 19/9/43; ass 360BS/303BG Molesworth 18/10/43; MIA Solingen 1/12/43 w/Luke; flak, cr Aachen, Ger; 1EVD 9POW; MACR 1325.

42-39782 Del Long Beach 29/8/43; Scott 19/9/43; ass 527BS/379BG [FO-M] Kimbolton 21/10/43; 526BS [LF-M]; MIA Frankfurt 8/2/44 w/Rossberg; e/a, cr Schlebusen, Ger; 1EVD 3KIA 6POW; MACR 2880. PISTOL PACKIN' MAMA.

42-39783 Del Long Beach 30/8/43; Scott 17/9/43; ass 360BS/303BG Molesworth 19/10/43; tran 545BS/384BG Grafton Underwood 2/11/43; 526BS/379BG [LF-B] Kimbolton 11/11/43; MIA Berlin 19/5/44 w/?; flak, cr Kletkamp, Ger; 1KIA 8POW; MACR 4929. BLUES IN THE KNIGHT.

42-39784 Del Long Beach 30/8/43; Scott 17/9/43; ass 303BG Molesworth 18/10/43; tran 1 BAD Burtonwood 23/10/43; 544BS/384BG [SU-J] Grafton Underwood 2/11/43; MIA Frankfurt 8/2/44 w/Covington; flak, cr Rethel, Fr; 2EVD 8POW; MACR 2496. CABIN IN THE SKY.

42-39785 Del Long Beach 31/8/43; Scott 18/9/43; ass 358BS/303BG [VK-H] Molesworth 18/10/43; MIA Hamm 22/4/44 w/Larson; flak, cr Werl, Ger; 4KIA 6POW; MACR 4272. THRU HEL'EN HIWATER.

42-39786 Del Long Beach 30/8/43; ass 427BS/303BG [GN-R] Molesworth 18/10/43; MIA Frankfurt 29/1/44 w/Fowlerl e/a, cr Barbencon, Farl; 4EVD 1KIA 5POW; MACR 2260. G.I. SHEETS.

42-39787 Del Long Beach 31/8/43; Scott 19/9/43; ass 358BS/303BG Molesworth 18/10/43; tran training 12/2/44; Ferry Command 20/5/45; retUS Lubbock 10/6/45; 2532 BU Randolph 15/1/46; RFC Walnut Ridge 13/4/46. WANTON WOMAN.

42-39788 Del Long Beach 2/9/43; Gr Island 4/10/43; ass 331BS/94BG [QE-O] Rougham 7/10/43 HARD TO GET; 332BS [XM-M]; c/t/o 10/4/44, sal. HOUSE OF LORDS.

42-39789 Del Long Beach 31/8/43; Scott 19/9/43; ass 527BS/379BG Kimbolton 19/10/43; 526BS [LF-W]; tran 487BG Lavenham 15/7/44; retUS 1103 BU Morrison 31/1/45; RFC Altus 4/10/45. LITTLE SKUNKFACE.

42-39790 Del Long Beach 2/9/43; Gr Island 23/9/43; ass 365BS/305BGB [XK-F] Chelveston 18/10/43; tran 422NLS 23/5/44; ASR 858BS 26/6/44; retUS 1103BU Morrison 2/11/45; RFC Walnut Ridge 9/1/46. RetUS 1103 BU Morrison 2/11/45; RFC Walnut Ridge 9/1/46.

42-39791 Del Long Beach 2/9/43; Gr Island 21/9/43; ass 350BS/100BG [LN-X] Thorpe Abbotts 27/9/43; c/t/o non op 3/12/43; sal 10/12/43. FLETCHER'S CASTORIA.

42-39792 Del Long Beach 2/9/43; ass 350BS/100BG [LN-X] Thorpe Abbotts 29/9/43; MIA Rostock 20/2/44 w/Harris; e/a, cr Tofthogs, Swed; 10INT; MACR 2427. HALF & HALF.

42-39793 Del Long Beach 2/9/43; Scott 29/9/43; ass 412BS/95BG [QW-V] Horham 8/10/43; MIA Berlin 6/3/44 w/Read; cr Quackenbrück, Ger; 10POW; MACR 2985.

42-39794 Del Long Beach 3/9/43; ass 358BS/303BG Molesworth 18/10/43; MIA Oschersleben 11/1/44 w/DaShiell; e/a, cr Oschersleben; 10KIA; MACR 1929.

42-39795 Del Long Beach 2/9/43; ass 360BS/303BG Molesworth 18/10/43; MIA Ludwigshafen 30/12/43 w/Osborn; e/a, cr Sedan, Fr; 2EVD 3KIA 5POW; MACR 1674. WOMEN'S HOME COMPANION.

42-39796 Del Long Beach 3/9/43; Scott 21/9/43; ass 303BG Molesworth 21/10/43; tran 1 BAD Burtonwood 23/10/43; 546BS/384BG Grafton Underwood 2/11/43; MIA Leverkusen 1/12/43 w/Martin; e/a, ditched Nth Sea; 1ORTD. MACR 1334.

42-39797 Del Long Beach 4/9/43; Scott 19/9/43; ass 547BS/384BG Grafton Underwood 2/11/43; tran 535BS/381BG Ridgewell 21/1/44; {3m} sal 12/2/44. NANCY M.

42-39798 Del Long Beach 4/9/43; ass 535BS/381BG [MS-L] Ridgewell 23/1/44; tran 837BS/487BG [4F] Lavenham 17/7/44; 828BS [2C]; retUS1377 BU Grenier 24/9/45; RFC Walnut Ridge 14/12/45. BUCKET 'O BOLTS.

42-39799 Del Long Beach 3/9/43; ass 349BS/100BG [XR-M] Thorpe Abbotts 29/9/43; MIA Frankfurt 4/2/44 w/Brown; flak, cr Casterlee?; 2EVD 8POW; MACR 2564. DOBIE.

42-39800 Del Long Beach 4/9/43; ass 303bg Molesworth 18/10/43; tran 1 BAD Burtonwood 23/10/43; 547BS/384BG Grafton Underwood 2/11/43; 526BS/379BG [LF-T] Kimbolton 7/11/43; f/l Wilton, UK 2/12/44; sal 2 SAD 5/12/44. PATCHES.

42-39801 Del Long Beach 4/9/43; Gr Island 22/9/43; ass 332BS/94BG [XM-B] Rougham 27/9/43; MIA Berlin 6/3/44 w/Blake; flak, cr Werwigo, Ger; 1EVD 1KIA 8POW; MACR 2978. NORTHERN QUEEN.

42-39802 Del Long Beach 5/9/43; Gr Island 24/9/43; ass 401BS/91BG [LL-D] Bassingbourn 7/10/43; MIA Wilhelmshafen 3/11/43 w/Rutledge; e/a, cr Nth Sea; 7KIA 3POW; MACR 1153.

42-39803 Del Long Beach 4/9/43; ass 324BS/91BG [DF-Y] Bassingbourn 7/10/43; MIA {16m} Frankfurt 4/2/44 w/McGee; flak, cr Wehrmaspiere?; 2KIA 8POW; MACR 2235. THE WOLF.

42-39804 Del Long Beach 4/9/43; ass 561BS/388BG Knettishall 9/10/43; MIA Brunswick 10/2/44 w/Evans; e/a, cr NOrdlehne, Ger?; 7KIA 3POW; MACR 2346. BAD PENNY.

42-39805 Del Long Beach 5/9/43; Gr Island 22/9/43; ass 96BG 27/9/43; lost Atlantic en route UK 30/9/44; MACR 664.

42-39806 Del Long Beach 5/9/43; Gr Island 4/10/43; ass 8AF 14/10/43; sal 11/11/43.

42-39807 Del Long Beach 9/9/43; ass 358BS/303BG

Molesworth 19/11/43; MIA Hamm 22/4/44 w/Seddon; mech fault, cr Hamm; 2EVD 8POW; MACR 4273. NERO.

42-39808 Del Long Beach 7/9/43; Scott 29/9/43; ass 534BS/381BG [GD-F] Ridgewell 19/10/43; MIA {4+m} Leverkusen 1/12/43 w/Hytinen; b/d & 3WIA, cr Allhallows, UK; sal 2 SAD 2/12/43.

42-39809 Del Long Beach 7/9/43; ass 547BS/384BG [SO-M] Grafton Underwood 6/1/44; MIA Oschersleben 22/2/44 w/MacDonald; e/a, cr Wesel, Ger; 3KIA 7POW; MACR 2467.

42-39810 Del Long Beach 7/9/43; ass 358BS/303BG [VK-E] Molesworth 18/10/43; cr West Mallin A/fd, UK 11/2/44; sal 14/2/44. BIG 'A' BIRD.

42-39811 Del Long Beach 8/9/43; ass 365BS/305BG [XK-C] Chelveston 17/10/43; 422NLS [JJ-E] 23/5/44; MIA France 6/7/44. MACR 6988.

42-39812 Del Long Beach 8/9/43; Gr Island 3/10/43; ass 332BS/94BG [XM-N] Rougham 8/10/43; tran 838BS/487BG Lavenham; MIA Munster 11/11/43 w/Ralls; flak, cr Tilburg, Hol; 9KIA 1POW; MACR 1066.

42-39813 Del Long Beach 7/9/43; Gr Island 28/9/43; ass 568BS/390BG [BI-N] Framlingham 4/10/43; sal 17/11/43. YANKEE REBEL.

42-39814 Del Long Beach 8/9/43; ass 337BS/96BG [AW-T] Snetterton 29/9/43; MIA Brunswick 21/2/44 w/Smith; e/a, cr Salzgitter, Ger; 5KIA 5POW; MACR 2425.

42-39815 Del Long Beach 10/9/43; ass 323BS/91BG [OR-N] Bassingbourn 16/10/43; MIA Oschersleben 22/2/44 w/Sutherland; e/a, cr Munster; 7KIA 3POW; MACR 2641. EMEIGH.

42-39816 Del Long Beach 8/9/43; Scott 29/9/43; ass 339BS/96BG [QJ-H] Snetterton 14/10/43; MIA Bordeaux 5/1/44 w/Pierce; e/a, cr Biscay; 9KIA 1POW; MACR 2013.

42-39817 Del Long Beach 9/9/43; ass 349BS/100BG [XR-A] Thorpe Abbotts 27/9/43; MIA Wilhelmshafen 3/3/44 w/Vollmer; mid ait coll, cr Iztehoe, Ger; 5KIA 5POW; MACR 3029. MURDERER'S ROW.

42-39818 Del Long Beach 9/9/43; Scott 29/9/43; ass 364BS/305BG [WF-H] Chelveston 19/10/43; b/d Erding 24/4/44; sal 2 SAD 28/4/44.

42-39819 Del Long Beach 10/9/43; Scott 28/9/43; ass 568BS/390BG [BI-F] Framlingham 7/10/43; MIA Augsburg 13/4/44 w/Swavel; flak, f/l Switz; 10INT; MACR 3947. ANOXIA QUEEN.

42-39820 Del Long Beach 9/9/43; Scott 28/9/43; ass 614BS/401BG [IW-J] Deenethorpe 14/11/44; MIA Stettin 11/4/44 w/Wilson; flak, cr Steinhagen, Ger; 2EVD 8POW; MACR 4015. ALSO RAN - STILL RUNNING.

42-39821 Del Long Beach 10/9/43; ass 570BS/390BG [DI-J] Framlingham 13/10/43; MIA Rostock 11/4/44 w/Zallers; flak, cr Augsburg; 1KIA 9POW; MACR 3946. HEY MOITLE.

42-39822 Del Long Beach 11/9/43; Scott 29/9/43; ass 333BS/94BG Rougham 8/10/43; MIA Brunswick 11/1/44 w/Sharps; e/a, cr Rheine, Ger; 2KIA 8POW; MACR 1887.

42-39823 Del Long Beach 11/9/43; Gr Island 10/10/43; Scott 30/10/43; ass 401BG Deenethorpe 4/11/43; tran 510BS/351BG [TU-O] Polebrook 18/11/43; MIA Bordeaux 31/12/43 w/Bender; flak, cr Cognac, Fr; 2EVD 8POW; MACR 1983. IRON ASS.

42-39824 Del Long Beach 11/9/43; Scott 27/9/43; ass 388BG Knettishall 4/11/43; APH, c/t/o for Herford, Ger. 5/12/44; sal.

42-39825 Del Long Beach 12/9/43; Scott 21/9/43; ass 613BS/401BG [IN-M] Deenethorpe 26/10/43; c/t/o 5/12/43; sal. ZENOBIA - EL ELEPHANTA.

42-39826 Del Long Beach 11/9/43; Scott 23/10/43; ass 612BS/401BG [SC-H] Deenethorpe 31/10/43; MIA Ludwigshafen 30/12/43 w/Neag; hit by bomb from above, cr Zierolshofen, Ger; 1KIA 9POW; MACR 1678. STUBBORN JEAN.

42-39827 Del Long Beach 13/9/43; Gr Island 1/10/43; ass 369BS/306BG [WW-G] Thurleigh 24/11/43; tran AFSC 1/5/44; APH, l/Hemmingstadt 14/8/44.

42-39828 Del Long Beach 12/9/43; Gr Island 1/10/43; ass 524BS/379BG [WA-B] Kimbolton 19/11/43; MIA Berlin 24/5/44 w/Kunda; e/a, cr Eberswalde, Ger; 3KIA 6POW; MACR 5320.

42-39829 Del Long Beach 11/9/43; Scott 30/9/43; ass 366BS/305BG Chelveston 19/10/43; MIA Nancy 27/4/44 w/Capt Copley; flak, cr Chalon, Fr; 1EVD 1KIA 9POW; MACR 4276.

42-39830 Del Long Beach 14/9/43; Gr Island 3/10/43; ass 350BS/100BG [LN-Y] Thorpe Abbotts 8/10/43; MIA Munich 18/3/44 w/Martin; mid air coll w/42-37913; cr Les Defends, Fr; 9KIA 1POW; MACR 3234. BERLIN PLAYBOY.

42-39831 Del Long Beach 14/9/43; Gr Island 5/10/43; ass 327BS/92BG Podington 21/10/43; MIA Gelsenkirchen 5/11/43 w/Capt Booker; e/a, cr Wesel, Ger; 1EVD 9POW; MACR 1383.

42-39832 Del Long Beach 13/9/43; Gr Island 3/10/43; ass 364BS/305BG [WF-A] Chelveston 18/10/43; c/l base 18/4/44; sal 19/4/44. HITLER'S HEADACHE.

42-39833 Del Long Beach 14/9/43; Gr Island 3/10/43; Scott 22/10/43; ass 333BS/94BG [TS-E] Rougham 7/10/43; retUS Bradley 3/7/45; 4168 BU Sth Plains 21/10/45; RFC Kingman 17/12/45. SHACKEROO II.

42-39834 Del Long Beach 14/9/43; Scott 21/10/43; ass 401BG Deenethorpe 16/11/43; tran 511BS/351BG [DS-F] Polebrook 18/11/43; {14m} c/l base 30/1/44; sal 5/2/44. CANNON BALL.

42-39835 Del Long Beach 14/9/43; Scott 21/10/43; ass 401BG Deenethorpe 26/10/43; tran 510BS/351BG TU-N] Polebrook 18/11/43; 1 BAD Burtonwood 8/6/44; APH Knettishall 7/44; {15m} MIA Siracourt, Fr 4/8/44. WANTTA SPA?

42-39836 Del Long Beach 14/9/43; Scott 26/10/43; ass 401BG Deenethorpe 2/11/43; tran 332BS/91BG [LG-M] Bassingbourn 20/11/43; MIA Leverkusen 1/12/43 w/Early; e/a, cr Koblenz, Ger; 2KIA 8POW; MACR 1320.

42-39837 Del Long Beach 14/9/43; Scott 24/10/43; ass 612BS/401BG [SC-L] Deenethorpe 9/11/43; MIA Dessau 28/5/44 w/? RED'S ROGUES.

42-39838 Del Long Beach 15/9/43; Scott 22/10/43; ass 335BS/95BG [OE-Z] Horham 29/10/43; c/l nr Stradbroke, UK 7/1/44; sal 8/1/44.

42-39839 Del Long Beach 16/9/43; Scott 18/10/43; ass 401BG Deenethorpe 14/10/43; tran 511BS/351BG [DS-D] Polebrook 18/11/43; {1m} c/l Marham, UK 26/11/43; sal 2 SAD 28/11/43 for use by 8AF HQ; retUS 4104 BU Rome 30/3/47.

42-39840 Del Long Beach 17/9/43; Scott 3/10/43; ass 613BS/401BG [IN-A] Deenethorpe 13/10/43; tran AFSC 6/6/44 as development and test a/c; retUS and used by US Navy from 20/11/45; 4148 BU Bedford 30/1/46; 4136 BU Tinker 24/7/46; 4104 BU Rome 30/1/47; re-ass 31/3/47. THE LOPIN' LOBO.

42-39841 Del Long Beach 16/9/43; ass 337BS/96BG [AW-G] Snetterton 9/10/43; MIA Regensburg 8/4/44 w/Gecks; e/a, cr Saarbrücken; 5EVD 5POW; MACR 2862. WACKY WOODY.

42-39842 Del Long Beach 17/9/43; Scott 21/9/43; ass 388BG Knettishall 26/10/43; sal 9AF Germany 19/9/45.

42-39843 Del Long Beach 18/9/43; Scott 9/10/43; ass 364BS/305BG [WF-G] Chelveston 11/10/43; 406NLS [JJ-G] 23/5/44; 858BS 24/6/44; sal 11/12/44. DALEY'S MALE.

42-39844 Del Long Beach 17/9/43; ass 410BS/94BG [GL-L] Rougham 13/10/43; sal 21/4/44.

42-39845 Del Long Beach 18/9/43; ass 563BS/388BG Knettishall 7/10/43; MIA Dessau 28/5/44 w/Fjelsted; flak, cr Weira, Ger; 2EVD 8POW; MACR 5317. HULTCHER'S VULTURES.

42-39846 Del Long Beach 18/9/43; Scott 27/10/43; ass 614BS/401BG [IW-M] Deenethorpe 3/11/43; tran 487BG Lavenham 15/7/44; 493BG Debach, sal 16/8/44. WIDDLE TWINKLE.

42-39847 Del Long Beach 18/9/43; Scott 24/10/43; ass 614BS/401BG [IW-G] Deenethorpe 2/11/43; MIA Stettin 11/4/44 w/Shaw; flak, cr Blumenthal, Ger; MACR 4016. BATTLIN' BETTY.

42-39848 Del Long Beach 18/9/43; Scott 22/10/43; ass 401BG Deenethorpe 4/11/43; tran 511BS/351BG [DS-C] Polebrook 18/11/43; {27m} 487BG Lavenham 16/7/44; sal 27/7/44; ARCHI BALL.

42-39849 Del Long Beach 18/9/43; Scott 19/9/43; ass 401BG Deenethorpe 27/10/43; tran 508BS/351BG [YB-K] Polebrook 18/11/43; MIA Berlin 22/3/44 w/Slosson; flak, cr Altlandsberg, Ger; 2KIA 8POW; MACR 3314.

42-39850 Del Long Beach 19/9/43; ass 423BS/306BG [RD-B] Thurleigh 7/10/43; retUS 4168 Sth Plains 7/6/45; RFC Kingman 18/12/45.

42-39851 Del Long Beach 23/9/43; Gr Island 31/10/43; ass 325BS/92BG [NV-J] Podington 2/12/43; tran 486BG Sudbury 16/7/44; sal 12/10/44.

42-39852 Del Long Beach 20/9/43; Scott 7/10/43; ass 568BS/390BG [BI-Z] Framlingham 10/10/43; retUS 121 BU Bradley 4/7/45; 4168 BU Sth Plains 9/7/45; RFC Kingman 16/11/45. SHATZI II.

42-39853 Del Long Beach 21/9/43; Scott 21/10/43; ass 401BG Deenethorpe 4/11/43; tran 510BS/351BG [TU-P] Polebrook 18/11/43; MIA {23m} Dessau 29/5/44 w/Neal; flak, ditched Channel; 10POW. PAPA'S PASSION.

42-39854 Del Long Beach 21/9/43; Scott 2/10/43; ass Soxo, tran Las Vegas as TB-17G 24/10/43; 2126 BU Laredo 26/4/44; 3021 BU Las Vegas 21/10/44; RFC Walnut Ridge 9/1/46.

42-39855 Del Long Beach 22/9/43; Scott 1/10/43; ass 331BS/94BG [QE-N] Rougham 8/10/43; MIA Oberlanstein 11/11/43 w/Kane; e/a, cr Fijnaart, Hol; 3KIA 7POW; MACR 1068. OLE BASSER.

42-39856 Del Long Beach 22/9/43; Gr Falls 6/10/43; Scott 22/10/43; ass 337BS/96BG [AW-G] Snetterton 9/10/43 WACKY WOODY; MIA Achmer 8/4/44 w/Gecks; flak, ditched Noordvost Polder, Hol; 5EVD 4POW; MACR 3651. LANE TECH OF CHICAGO.

42-39857 Del Long Beach 23/9/43; Walla Walla 9/11/43; ass 401BG Deenethorpe 26/10/43; tran 511BS/351BG [DS-H] Polebrook 18/11/43; MIA {16m} Aschersleben 22/2/44 w/Pugh; flak, cr Bernburg, Ger; 10POW; MACR 2656. BELLE OF THE BALL.

42-39858 Del Long Beach 23/9/43; Gr Island 6/10/43; ass 452BG Deopham Green 6/1/44; sal 25/3/44.

42-39859 Del Long Beach 23/9/43; Gr Island 15/10/43; ass 332BS/94BG [XM-P] Rougham 26/10/43; MIA Emden 11/12/43 w/Capehart; e/a, cr Nth Sea; 4KIA 6POW; MACR 1258. MISS MARY.

42-39860 Del Long Beach 23/9/43; Gr Island 6/10/43; ass 548BS/385BG Gt Ashfield 23/10/43; MIA Bremen 13/11/43 w/?; mid air coll, ditched Nth Sea; 1KIA 9RTD; MACR 1403.

42-39861 Del Long Beach 23/9/43; Gr Island 13/10/43; ass 561BS/388BG Knettishall 26/10/43;

sal 31/5/45.
42-39862 Del Long Beach 23/9/43; Harvard 8/10/43; ass 100BG Thorpe Abbotts 10/10/43; W/O 29/3/44.
42-39863 Del Long Beach 23/9/43; Gr Island 26/10/43; ass 401BS/91BG Bassingbourn 22/12/43; c/l Steeple Morden A/fd, UK 30/12/43; sal 2 SAD 31/12/43.
42-39864 Del Long Beach 23/9/43; Harvard 6/10/43; ass 447BG Rattlesden 21/11/43; exploded base 21/4/44, sal.
42-39865 Del Long Beach 23/9/43; Harvard 14/10/43; ass 710BS/447BG Rattlesden 27/11/43; MIA Laon, Fr 9/5/44 w/Owens; flak, cr Channel; 8KIA 2POW; MACR 4588.
42-39866 Del Long Beach 23/9/43; Gr Island 6/10/43; Presque Is 14/10/43; ass 563BS/388BG Knettishall 14/10/43; MIA Merseburg 29/7/44 w/Boyce; e/a, cr Rottendorf, Ger; 7KIA 2POW; MACR 7820.
42-39867 Del Long Beach 24/9/43; Gr Island 6/11/43; ass 349BS/100BG [XR-Z] Thorpe Abbotts 11/11/43 BOEING BELLE; 351BS [EP-Z]; retUS 121 BU Bradley 19/6/45; 4168 BU Sth Plains 22/6/45; RFC Kingman 11/12/45. HANG THE EXPENSE III.
42-39868 Del Long Beach 23/9/43; Gr Island 6/10/43; ass 331BS/94BG [QE-K] Rougham 27/11/43; MIA Munster 11/11/43 w/O'Hara; flak, cr Numansdorp, Ger; 7KIA 3POW; MACR 1067.
42-39869 Del Long Beach 25/9/43; Gr Island 6/10/43; ass 412BS/95BG [QW-R] Horham 15/10/43; MIA Rostock 11/4/44 w/Bannerman; e/a, cr Bandelsdorf, Ger; 10KIA; MACR 3806. HEAVEN CAN WAIT.
42-39870 Del Long Beach 25/9/43; Gr Island 7/10/43; ass 410BS/94BG [GL-J] Rougham 14/10/43; MIA Pas de Calais 14/2/44.
42-39871 Del Long Beach 25/9/43; Gr Island 7/10/43; ass 8AF 25/10/43; 8WS(P); 652BS/25BG Watton 22/4/44; WW 21/2/45.
42-39872 Del Long Beach 24/9/43; Gr Island 24/10/43; ass 350BS/100BG [LN-A] Thorpe Abbotts 19/11/43; MIA Berlin 6/3/44 w/Granack; flak, cr Ostpriegnnitz, Ger; 2KIA 8POW; MACR 3030. RUBBER CHECK.
42-39873 Del Long Beach 26/9/43; Harvard 8/10/43; Scott 22/10/43; ass 615BS/401BG [IY-Q] Deenethorpe 26/10/43; MIA Orleans 1/8/44 w/Melofchick; flak & mid air coll, cr Chartres, Fr; MACR 7824. STORMY WEATHER.
42-39874 Del Long Beach 27/9/43; Harvard 10/10/43; ass 447BG Rattlesden 31/10/43; MIA Pas de Calais 22/6/44; f/l French beach head; sal.
42-39875 Del Long Beach 26/9/43; Gr Island 26/10/43; ass 358BS/303BG Molesworth 14/1/44; sal b/d 6/2/45. BUZZ BLONDE.
42-39876 Del Denver 27/9/43; Gr Island 15/10/43; ass 569BS/390BG [CC-E] Framlingham 21/10/43; b/d Berlin 6/3/44; sal 8/3/44. GLORIA ANN.
42-39877 Del Long Beach 29/9/43; Las Vegas 29/10/43; 3021 BU Las Vegas 2/6/44; 2126 BU Laredo 24/5/45; RFC Walnut Ridge 4/1/46.
42-39878 Del Long Beach 28/9/43; Gr Island 26/10/43; ass 365BS/305BG Chelveston 3/1/44; MIA Zwickau 28/5/44 w/Herrick; mech fault, cr Zerf, Ger; 2EVD 8POW; MACR 5336.
42-39879 Del Long Beach 28/9/43; Gr Island 29/10/43; ass 569BS/390BG [CC-A] Framlingham 23/11/43; MIA Oschersleben 11/1/44 w/Sanders; e/a, cr Lingen, Ger; 1KIA 9POW; MACR 2023.
42-39880 Del Long Beach 29/9/43; Gr Island 29/10/43; ass 812BS/482BG [MI-O] Alconbury 14/12/43; HSX scanner fitted in ball turret; retUS 4168 BU Sth Plains 3/6/45; Love Fd 28/11/45; 3501 BU Boca Raton 16/12/45; RFC Walnut Ridge 21/2/46.
42-39881 Del Long Beach 28/9/43; Gr Island 12/10/43; ass 614BS/401BG [IW-F] Deenethorpe 13/12/43; MIA Stettin 11/4/44 w/Stine; flak, cr Hannover; 8KIA 2POW; MACR 4017. GLORIA J.
42-39882 Del Long Beach 28/9/43; Harvard 14/10/43; ass 711BS/447BG Rattlesden 1/11/43; retUS Bradley 10/7/45; 4168 BU Sth Plains 13/7/45; RFC Kingman 19/12/45.
42-39883 Del Long Beach 29/9/43; Gr Island 22/10/43; ass 336BS/95BG [ET-O] Horham 11/11/43; c/l base 22/12/43 w/Foley, 1ORTD; sal 8/1/44.
42-39884 Del Long Beach 29/9/43; Gr Island 21/10/43; ass 96BG, tran 336BS/95BG [ET-N] Horham 5/11/43; MIA Zwickau 12/5/44 w/Yablonski; 8KIA 2POW; MACR 4854.
42-39885 Del Long Beach 30/9/43; Gr Island 21/10/43; ass 427BS/303BG [GN-Z] Molesworth 30/12/43; tran 750BS/457BG Glatton 22/5/45; 351BG Polebrook 29/5/45; retUS Bradley 13/6/45; 4168 BU Sth Plains 18/6/45; RFC Kingman 8/12/45.
42-39886 Del Long Beach 30/9/43; Harvard 14/10/43; ass 388BG Knettishall 22/11/43; tran 447BG Rattlesden 23/11/43; c/l base 29/6/44; sal.
42-39887 Del Long Beach 24/9/43; Gr Island 24/10/43; ass 571BS/390BG [FC-J] Framlingham 2/11/43; MIA Pas de Calais 5/6/44 w/Pickell; flak, cr Channel, 9KIA; MACR 5480. PICKLE DROPPER IV.
42-39888 Del Long Beach 29/9/43; Gr Island 19/10/43; ass 544BS/384BG [SU-B] Grafton Underwood 23/11/43; tran 1 BAD Burtonwood 2/5/45; retUS 121 BU Bradley 4/7/45; 2114 BU Lockburn 13/7/45; 4168 BU Sth Plains 21/10/45; RFC Kingman 23/11/45.
42-39889 Del Long Beach 30/9/43; Gr Island 20/10/43; ass 527BS/379BG [FO-K] Kimbolton 22/11/43; sal 30/12/44.
42-39890 Del Long Beach 30/9/43; Gr Island 3/11/43; ass 535BS/381BG [MS-Y] Ridgewell 22/12/43; MIA {17m} Berlin 24/5/44 w/Dasso; e/a, cr Melchow, Ger; 5KIA 4POW; MACR 5179. RETURN TICKET.
42-39891 Del Long Beach 30/9/43; Gr Island 29/10/43; ass 533BS/381BG [VP-V] Ridgewell 13/1/44; MIA {3m} Frankfurt 2/3/44 w/Schultz; flak, cr Arlon, Bel; 1EVD 9POW; MACR 2378.
42-39892 Del Long Beach 1/10/43; Gr Island 29/10/43; ass 401BS/91BG [LL-B] Bassingbourn 13/12/43; MIA Berlin 8/3/44 w/Williams; e/a, cr Einwinkel, Ger; 4KIA 6POW; MACR 3223.
42-39893 Del Long Beach 30/9/43; Gr Island 1/11/43; ass 615BS/401BG [IY-J] Deenethorpe 2/1/44; MIA Oschersleben 11/1/44 w/Sprecher; e/a, cr Oschersleben; 3KIA 7POW; MACR 2505.
42-39894 Del Long Beach 1/10/43; Gr Island 18/10/43; ass 561BS/388BG Knettishall 2/11/43; MIA Rostock 20/2/44 w/Payne; mech fault, cr Assen, Hol; 9KIA 1POW; MACR 2432. BARBARA.
42-39895 Del Long Beach 1/10/43; Gr Island 1/11/43; ass 535BS/381BG [MS-S] Ridgewell 22/12/43; MIA {12+m} Bunde 22/2/44 w/Smith; e/a, cr Hiddesen, Ger?; 10KIA; MACR 2935. BERMONDSEY BATTLER.
42-39896 Del Long Beach 1/10/43; Gr Island 30/10/43; ass 331BS/94BG [QE-L] Rougham 11/11/43; 410BS [GL-H]; MIA Bohlen 7/10/44 w/Williams; cr Wiehe, Ger; 8KIA 1POW; MACR 9954.
42-39897 Del Long Beach 1/10/43; Gr Island 31/10/43; ass 336BS/95BG [ET-O] Horham 1/12/43; MIA Evreux, Fr 6/2/44 w/Hamby; exploded, cr Arbonne, Fr; 1KIA 9POW; MACR 2199.
42-39898 Del Long Beach 1/10/43; Gr Island 3/11/43; ass 323BS/91BG Bassingbourn 13/12/43; 322BS [LG-L]; MIA {14m} Oschersleben 22/2/44 w/Wood; e/a, cr Freckenhorst, Ger; MACR 2642. BOSTON BOMBSHELL (not painted).
42-39899 Del Long Beach 2/10/43; Las Vegas 29/10/43; W/O 15/1/44.
42-39900 Del Long Beach 2/10/43; Gr Island 31/10/43; W/O 3/11/43.
42-39901 Del Long Beach 3/10/43; Gr Island 31/10/43; ass 551BS/385BG Gt Ashfield 24/11/43; b/d Pas de Calais 15/2/44; 1WIA; c/l Detling, UK; sal 15/2/44. STAR DUST.
42-39902 Del Long Beach 8/10/43; Walla Walla 7/11/43; ass 730BS/452BG Deopham Green 5/1/44; sal b/d 21/9/44; retUS Bradley 5/7/45; 4168 BU Sth Plains 23/10/45; 237 BU Kirtland 29/11/45; RFC Albuquerque 7/2/46. BIG NOISE.
42-39903 Del Long Beach 2/10/43; Walla Walla 7/11/43; ass 729BS/452BG Deopham Green 9/2/44; MIA French rail jcts 8/7/44 w/Hale; flak, cr Ymare, Fr; 5EVD 5POW; MACR 7225. MARJORIE ANN.
42-39904 Del Long Beach 4/10/43; Gr Island 2/11/43; ass 615BS/401BG [IY-C] Deenethorpe 19/12/43; MIA Stettin 13/5/44 w/Tonti; mech fault, f/l Bulltofta, Swed; 10INT; MACR 4785. (left 11/6/45) BAD PENNY.
42-39905 Del Long Beach 5/10/43; Gr Island 31/10/43; ass 508BS/351BG [YB-C] Polebrook 2/1/44; MIA {2m} Oschersleben 11/1/44 w/Garner; e/a, cr Oschersleben; 2KIA 8POW; MACR 1937.
42-39906 Del Long Beach 5/10/43; Gr Island 31/10/43; ass 535BS/381BG [MS-X] Ridgewell 20/12/43; {9m} taxi acc 15/4/44; sal 2 SAD 17/4/44. SQUAT 'N DROPPIT.
42-39907 Del Long Beach 5/10/43; ass 560BS/388BG Knettishall 25/12/43; MIA Berlin 8/5/44 w/Pittman; e/a, cr Hustedt, Ger; 4KIA 6POW; MACR 4580. NASTY NELLIE.
42-39908 Del Long Beach 5/10/43; Gr Island 31/10/43; ass 550BS/385BG Gt Ashfield 30/11/43; MIA Brunswick 23/3/44 w/Fulton; e/a, cr Schijndel, Hol; 1EVD 8KIA 1POW; MACR 3321.
42-39909 Del Long Beach 6/10/43; Walla Walla 9/11/43; ass 8AF 2/1/44; retUS Bradley 28/6/45; 4168 BU Sth Plains 8/7/45; RFC Kingman 18/12/45.
42-39910 Del Long Beach 6/10/43; Gr Island 2/11/43; ass 384BG, tran 535BS/381BG Ridgewell 20/12/43; MIA {1m} Bordeaux 31/12/43 w/Duarte; e/a, cr Toulouse, Fr; 2EVD 8POW; MACR 1978.
42-39911 Del Long Beach 5/10/43; Gr Island 17/11/43; ass 570BS/390BG [DI-N] Framlingham 18/11/43; MIA Berlin 8/5/44 w/Simmons; e/a, cr Suedstedt, Ger; 2KIA 8POW; MACR 4585. MARY LOU.
42-39912 Del Long Beach 5/10/43; Gr Island 31/10/43; ass 548BS/385BG Gt Ashfield 23/11/43; c/l Capel, UK 16/7/44; sal 19/7/44. SKY CHIEF.
42-39913 Del Long Beach 6/10/43; Gr Island 4/11/43; ass 8AF 23/11/43; AFMSC 20/3/44.
42-39914 Del Long Beach 7/10/43; Gr Island 5/11/43; ass 509BS/351BG [RQ-S] Polebrook 21/1/44 LUCKY STRIKE; {51m} RetUS Bradley 13/6/45; Memphis 16/6/45; 4168 BU Sth Plains 21/10/45; RFC Kingman 9/11/45. THE BLACK BITCH.
42-39915 Del Long Beach 6/10/43; Gr Island 3/11/43; ass 482BG Alconbury 15/11/43; sal 9AF 26/9/45 Germany.
42-39916 Del Long Beach 7/10/43; Walla Walla 7/11/43; ass 731BS/452BG Deopham Green 31/12/43; MIA Augsburg 16/3/44 w/Callow; e/a, cr Le Titre, Fr; 1KIA 9POW; MACR 3194 (?).
42-39917 Del Long Beach 8/10/43; Walla Walla

9/11/43; ass 728BS/452BG Deopham Green 4/1/44; MIA Rostock 24/2/44 w/Holland; e/a, cr Scherwin, Ger?; 1KIA 9POW; MACR 2894 LADY SATAN.

42-39918 Del Long Beach 8/10/43; Gr Island 8/11/43; ass 550BS/385BG Gt Ashfield 18/11/43; MIA Pas de Calais 2/6/44 w/Schock; flak, cr Elbeuf, Fr; 3EVD 1KIA 6POW; MACR 5232.

42-39919 Del Long Beach 8/10/43; Walla Walla 8/11/43; W/O 23/11/43.

42-39920 Del Long Beach 8/10/43; Walla Walla 9/11/43; ass 729BS/452BG Deopham Green 6/1/44; MIA Berlin 29/4/44 w/Nelson; flak, cr Rurrio, Ger?; 5EVD 2KIA 3POW; MACR 4449.

42-39921 Del Long Beach 8/10/43; Walla Walla 9/11/43; W/O 4/12/43.

42-39922 Del Long Beach 8/10/43; Hobbs 22/10/43; 4126 BU San Bernardino 30/12/44; 3018 BU Kingman 12/1/45; 3017 BU Hobbs 25/6/45; RFC Walnut Ridge 3/1/46.

42-39923 Del Long Beach 9/10/43; Las Vegas 26/10/43; 3021 BU Las Vegas 2/6/44; 3025 BU Marfa 22/4/45; 2126 BU Laredo 26/4/45; RFC Walnut Ridge 10/1/46.

42-39924 Del Long Beach 9/10/43; Gr Island 22/10/43; ass 334BS/95BG [BG-N] Horham 12/11/43; MIA Berlin 24/5/44 w/Sheehan; e/a, cr Oranienburg; 8KIA 2POW; MACR 5160. TORNADO.

42-39925 Del Long Beach 9/10/43; Gr Island 22/10/43; ass 550BS/385BG Gt Ashfield 19/11/43; MIA Berlin 4/3/44.

42-39926 Del Long Beach 9/10/43; Gr Island 22/10/43; Lubbock 28/10/43; ass 569BS/390BG [CC-B] Framlingham 10/11/43 HOLEY JOE; retUS Bradley 9/7/45; 4168 BU Sth Plains 12/9/45; RFC Kingman 18/12/45. GENERAL SHERMAN.

42-39927 Del Long Beach 9/10/43; Gr Island 24/10/43; ass 570BS/390BG [DI-R/C] Framlingham 11/11/43; retUS Bradley 5/7/45; 4168 BU Sth Plains 12/9/45; RFC Kingman 16/11/45. THE SKILLET.

42-39928 Del Long Beach 8/10/43; Hobbs 24/10/43; 4126 BU San Bernardino 23/1/45; 3018 BU Kingman 23/3/45; 3017 BU Hobbs 27/6/45; RFC Walnut Ridge 2/1/46.

42-39929 Del Long Beach 10/10/43; Gr Island 22/10/43; ass 401BS/91BG [LL-K] Bassingbourn 20/12/43; 322BS; MIA {11m} Stettin 11/4/44 w/Ammann; e/a, f/l Vollsjo, Swed; 10INT (but secretly released seven months later); MACR 3667. LACKIN' SHACKIN'.

42-39930 Del Long Beach 11/10/43; Las Vegas 25/10/43; 3021 BU Las Vegas 23/3/45; 3017 BU Hobbs 16/7/45; RFC Walnut Ridge 5/1/46.

42-39931 Del Long Beach 9/10/43; Hobbs 22/10/43; 3018 BU Kingman 8/1/45; Recl Comp 17/1/45.

42-39932 Del Long Beach 12/10/43; Gr Island 5/11/43; ass 613BS/401BG [IN-H] Deenethorpe 2/1/44; sal 2 SAD 17/7/44. SWEAT'ER OUT.

42-39933 Del Long Beach 12/10/43; Walla Walla 9/11/43; ass 381BG Ridgewell 20/12/43; tran 728BS/452BG Deopham Green /44; MIA Brunswick 23/3/44 w/Young; e/a, cr Roedenbeck, Ger; 7KIA 3POW; MACR 3343. SUPERSTITIOUS ALOYSIUS.

42-39934 Del Long Beach 11/10/43; Gr Island 31/10/43; ass 452BG, tran 350BS/100BG [LN-Z] Thorpe Abbotts 21/11/43; MIA Brunswick 15/3/44 w/Devore; flak, cr Watenbuel, Ger; 7KIA 3POW; MACR 3915. MYACHINBACK.

42-39935 Del Long Beach 11/10/43; Gr Island 2/11/43; ass 369BS/306BG Thurleigh 22/10/43; MIA Aschersleben 22/2/44 w/Horst; e/a, cr Bonn; 10KIA; MACR 2651.

42-39936 Del Long Beach 12/10/43; Walla Walla 11/10/43; ass 728BS/452BG Deopham Green 31/12/43; MIA Warnemunde 9/4/44 w/Boyd; e/a, cr Boetoe, Ger?; 6KIA 4POW; MACR 3662.

42-39937 Del Long Beach 12/10/43; Walla Walla 11/11/43; ass 728BS/452BG Deopham Green 3/1/44; MIA Brux 12/5/44 w/?; MACR 4815.

42-39938 Del Long Beach 13/10/43; Gr Island 31/10/43; ass 548BS/385BG Gt Ashfield 21/11/43; MIA Wilhelmshafen 3/2/44 w/Heuser; mid air cool, cr Nettersheim, Ger; 10KIA; MACR 2197.

42-39939 Del Long Beach 13/10/43; Gr Island 8/11/43; ass 730BS/452BG Deopham Green 27/11/43; MIA Brux 12/5/44 w/Homer; e/a, cr Rudersdorf, Ger; 5KIA 5POW; MACR 4818. DUCHESS.

42-39940 Del Long Beach 12/10/43; Walla Walla 9/11/43; ass 731BS/452BG Deopham Green 4/1/44; MIA Frankfurt 8/2/44 w/Jameson; no gas, cr Krueznach, Ger; 2EVD 1KIA 6POW; MACR 2521.

42-39941 Del Long Beach 14/10/43; Walla Walla 9/11/43; ass 731BS/452BG Deopham Green 11/2/44; MIA Brux 12/5/44 w/Noble; flak, cr Liége, Bel; 2EVD 1KIA 7POW; MACR 4819. LUCKY LADY.

42-39942 Del Long Beach 13/10/43; Walla Walla 7/11/43; ass 305BG Chelveston 3/1/44; sal 25/1/44.

42-39943 Del Long Beach 13/10/43; Gr Island 31/10/43; ass 612BS/401BG [SC-F] Deenethorpe 2/1/44; MIA Berlin 7/5/44 w/Grimmett; flak, cr Hohnebostel, Ger; 9KIA 1POW; MACR 4587. LASSIE COME HOME.

42-39944 Del Long Beach 14/10/43; Gr Island 2/11/43; ass 366BS/305BG Chelveston 3/12/43; MIA Frankfurt 2/3/44 w/Keysar; e/a, cr Kamberg, Ger; 10POW; MACR 2866.

42-39945 Del Long Beach 13/10/43; Gr Island 8/11/43; ass 423BS/306BG [RD-S] Thurleigh 12/12/43; MIA Aschersleben 22/2/44 w/Tooms; e/a, cr Herfun, Ger?; 7KIA 3POW; MACR 2649. HOLY HELLCAT.

42-39946 Del Long Beach 14/10/43; Gr Island 12/11/43; ass 533BS/381BG Ridgewell 22/1/44; MIA {7m} Aschersleben 22/2/44 w/Roling; e/a, cr Leopoldshohe, Ger; 5KIA 5POW; MACR 2936.

42-39947 Del Long Beach 15/10/43; Gr Island 2/11/43; ass 364BS/305BG Chelveston 12/12/43; MIA Berlin 5/12/43 w/Todd; flak, cr Preikin, Ger?; 9KIA; MACR 11040. CHIQUITA.

42-39948 Del Long Beach 14/10/43; Gr Island 31/10/43; ass 364BS/305BG [WF-M] Chelveston 15/11/43; (first in group to 100 missions) tran 401BG Deenethorpe 20/5/45; retUS 121 BU Bradley 7/6/45; Romulus 8/6/45; 4168 BU Sth Plains 12/9/45; RFC Kingman 8/11/45. LEADING LADY.

42-39949 Del Long Beach 14/10/43; ass 365BS/305BG Chelveston 30/11/43; MIA Berlin 24/5/44 w/Brown; e/a, cr Hamburg; 10POW; MACR 5174.

42-39950 Del Long Beach 16/10/43; Gr Island 8/11/43; ass 423BS/306BG [RD-K] Thurleigh 18/12/43; MIA Brunswick 29/3/44 w/Hardin; e/a, cr Ouderkerk, Hol; 10POW; MACR 3481. WAMPUS CAT.

42-39951 Del Long Beach 18/10/43; Gr Island 10/11/43; ass 551BS/385BG Gt Ashfield 27/11/43; MIA Saarbrücken 23/5/44 w/?;

42-39952 Del Long Beach 15/10/43; Gr Island 31/10/43; ass 551BS/385BG Gt Ashfield 27/11/43; MIA Wilhelmshafen 3/2/44 w/Morse; mid air coll, cr Nth Sea; 10KIA; MACR 2196.

42-39953 Del Long Beach 15/10/43; Gr Island 1/11/43; ass 569BS/390BG [CC-D] Framlingham 18/11/43 DUTCH CLEANSER; MIA Leipzig 29/5/44 w/Nesbitt; flak, cr Leipzig; 4KIA 6POW; MACR 5313. YANKEE DOODLE DANDY.

42-39954 Del Long Beach 18/10/43; Walla Walla 10/11/43; ass 728BS/452BG Deopham Green 3/1/44; MIA Saarbrücken 23/3/44 w/Yates; e/a, cr Oppenwehe, Ger; 5KIA 5POW; MACR 3344.

42-39955 Del Long Beach 18/10/43; Walla Walla 10/11/43; ass 452BG Deopham Green 12/1/44; sal 12/2/44.

42-39956 Del Long Beach 18/10/43; Walla Walla 11/11/43; 3501 BU Boca Raton 28/11/44; RFC Kingman 22/2/46.

42-39957 Del Long Beach 19/10/43; Gr Island 2/11/43; ass 364BS/305BG [WF-O] Chelveston 12/12/43; b/d Oschersleben 11/1/44; sal 2 SAD 16/1/44.

42-39958 Del Long Beach 19/10/43; Gr Island 2/11/43; ass 326BS/92BG [JW-X] Podington 27/12/43; MIA Merseburg 11/9/44 w/?; f/l Continent; sal 14/11/44.

42-39959 Del Long Beach 19/10/43; Gr Island 10/11/43; ass 385BG Gt Ashfield 9/12/43; trans 652BS Watton. Sal 22/6/45.

42-39960 Del Long Beach 19/10/43; ass 325BS/92BG Podington 23/1/44; MIA Frankfurt 2/3/44 w/Chesmore; e/a, cr Brussels, Bel; 3EVD 2KIA 5POW; MACR 2856.

42-39961 Del Long Beach 20/10/43; Walla Walla 10/11/434; ass 730BS/452BG Deopham Green 6/1/44; MIA Brunswick 10/2/44 w/Triska; mid air coll w/42-31318, cr Hemsloher, Ger?; 7KIA 3POW; MACR 2537.

42-39962 Del Long Beach 20/10/43; ass 547BS/384BG Grafton Underwood 21/1/44; MIA Frankfurt 11/2/44 w/Widner; hit by prop wash, cr St Vaast, Hol?; 1KIA 9POW; MACR 2529.

42-39963 Del Long Beach 20/10/43; ass 423BS/306BG Thurleigh 30/12/43; MIA Berlin 5/12/44 w/Stetler; flak, cr Schoenfliesis, Ger?; 6KIA 3POW; MACR 11038. LITTLE LULU.

42-39964 Del Long Beach 20/10/43; Walla Walla 12/11/43; 235 BU Biggs 18/8/44; 4127 BU McClellan 24/9/44; W/O 25/9/44; Recl Comp 14/9/45.

42-39965 Del Long Beach 20/10/43; Gr Island 13/11/43; ass 369BS/306BG [WW-W] Thurleigh 19/12/43; MIA Brunswick 29/3/44 w/Haywood; e/a, cr Ahnebeck, Ger?; 6KIA 4POW; MACR 3482.

42-39966 Del Long Beach 20/10/43; ass 366BS/305BG Chelveston 5/1/44; MIA Merkville 3/8/44 w/Buttrey; flak, cr Baden-Baden; 9POW; MACR 7702. SWINGING DOOR.

42-39967 Del Long Beach 21/10/43; ass 324BS/91BG [DF-K] Bassingbourn 25/1/44; MIA {15m} Oberpfaffenhofen 18/3/44 w/Theophilus; e/a, cr Lake Brengenz, Switz?; 2KIA 8POW; MACR 3224. MARY KAY.

42-39968 Del Long Beach 21/10/43; ass 562BS/388BG Knettishall 15/12/43; tran 303BG Molesworth 9/4/44; 535BS/379BG [FR-A] Kimbolton 3/2/45; retUS 121 BU Bradley 4/7/45; 4168 BU Sth Plains 7/7/45; 237 BU Kirtland 19/12/45; RFC Albuquerque 7/2/46.

42-39969 Del Long Beach 21/10/43; ass 614BS/401BG [IW-K] Deenethorpe 2/1/44; MIA Oschersleben 11/1/44 w/Capt Foster; e/a, c/l Osterode, Ger; 10POW; MACR 2508; recovered & re-ass TB-17G 27/4/48.

42-39970 Del Long Beach 22/10/43; Walla Walla 11/11/43; ass 730BS/452BG Deopham Green 3/11/43; retUS Bradley 28/6/45; 4168 BU Sth Plains 12/9/45; RFC Kingman 28/11/45. 'E-RAT-ICATOR'.

42-39971 Del Long Beach 23/10/43; Walla Walla

Above: B-17G-10-VE 42-39973, named *Inside Curve*, heading for Berlin with a 730th Bomb Squadron crew on 9 March 1944. The aircraft displays the revised Plexiglas nosepiece which was slightly shorter than the earlier moulding and had a steeper forward upturn on the underside. The change was primarily to prevent blast damage from chin turret guns when these were fired at maximum elevation. (USAF)

9/11/43; ass 729BS/452BG Deopham Green 18/11/43; c/l Horham A/fd, UK; 6KIA 4WIA; sal 24/4/44. LITTLE CHUM.

42-39972 Del Long Beach 23/10/43; Walla Walla 9/11/43; ass 728BS/452BG Deopham Green 18/1/44; 730BS; MIA Misburg, Ger 31/12/43 w/Money; e/a, cr Rotenburg, Ger; 5KIA 4POW; MACR 11233. OUR BUDDY.

42-39973 Del Long Beach 22/10/43; Walla Walla 9/11/43; ass 730BS/452BG Deopham Green 4/1/44; explosion 12/10/44; sal 18/10/44. INSIDE CURVE.

42-39974 Del Long Beach 23/10/43; Walla Walla 9/11/43; ass 731BS/452BG Deopham Green 12/1/44; MIA Warnemunde 9/4/44 w/Roener; e/a, cr Vaerlose, Den?, 10POW; MACR 3785.

42-39975 Del Long Beach 22/10/43; ass 326BS/92BG Podington 5/12/43; tran 324BG/91BG [DF-Z] Bassingbourn 10/1/44; 323BS; MIA {40m} Dessau 30/5/44 w/Collier; flak, cr Dessau; 7KIA 2POW; MACR 5355. JUST PLAIN LONESOME.

42-39976 Del Long Beach 23/10/43; Walla Walla 9/11/43; ass 731BS/452BG Deopham Green 31/12/43; MIA Brux 12/5/44 w/Martin; mech fault, cr Koengen, Ger?; 10POW; MACR 4820. MY ACHIN' BACK.

42-39977 Del Long Beach 25/10/43; Walla Walla 9/11/43; ass 729BS/452BG Deopham Green 30/11/43; c/l/o 9/2/44, cr Wymondham, UK; 10KIA; sal 10/2/44. HARD TO GET.

42-39978 Del Long Beach 23/10/43; Walla Walla 10/11/43; ass 452BG Deopham Green 5/1/44; sal 7/3/44.

42-39979 Del Long Beach 23/10/43; Gr Island 13/11/43; ass 612BS/401BG [SC-H] Deenethorpe 2/1/44; MIA Stettin 11/4/44 w/Kuhl; flak, cr Oythe,?; 1KIA 9POW; MACR 4018.

42-39980 Del Long Beach 26/10/43; ass 526BS/379BG [LF-C] Kimbolton 14/1/44; MIA Poix, Fr 13/4/44 w/Soso; flak, cr Boulougne, Fr; 5KIA 5POW; MACR 3240. JUST SO.

42-39981 Del Long Beach 24/10/43; Walla Walla 11/11/43; ass 728BS/452BG Deopham Green 9/11/43; MIA Berlin 29/4/44 w/Haskenson; e/a, cr Lieren, Hol; 10POW; MACR 4450. SECTION EIGHT.

42-39982 Del Long Beach 20/10/43; Gr Island 12/11/43; ass 32BS/301BG Oudna 23/11/43; Cerignola 7/12/43; Lucera 1/2/44; MIA {22m} Regensburg 25/2/44 w/Walker; e/a, cr Spittal, Ger?; 1KIA 8POW; MACR 2592.

42-39983 Del Long Beach 26/10/43; ass 351BS/100BG [EP-F] Thorpe Abbotts 4/12/43; MIA German rail juncts 11/5/44 w/Hunter; flak, cr Ougree, Fr; 7KIA 3POW; MACR 4866. KATIE.

42-39984 Del Long Beach 26/10/43; Gr Island 13/11/43; ass 331BS/94BG Rougham 10/12/43; MIA Brunswick 10/2/44 w/Barker; e/a, cr Liebenau, Ger; 4KIA 6POW; MACR 2369.

42-39985 Del Long Beach 26/10/43; Walla Walla 10/11/43; ass 730BS/452BG Deopham Green 3/1/44; MIA Brunswick 23/3/44 w/Brannon; e/a, cr Rengershausen, Ger; 2KIA 8POW; MACR 3531.

42-39986 Del Long Beach 27/10/43; Gr Island 12/11/43; ass 352BS/301BG Oudna 27/11/43; Cerignola 7/12/43; Lucera 1/2/44; MIA {49m} Budapest 3/4/44 w/Ross; e/a, cr Mostar, Hung; 2KIA 7MIA; MACR 1401.

42-39987 Del Long Beach 27/10/43; ass 511BS/351BG [DS-D] Polebrook 30/1/44; MIA German oil insts 28/5/44 w/Probasco; e/a, cr Alt-Loennewitz, Ger?; 4KIA 6POW; MACR 5328. PIN BALL.

42-39988 Del Long Beach 27/10/43; ass 339BS/96BG [QJ-A] Snetterton 4/12/43 LACE'S ACES; MIA Berlin 8/3/44 w/Pond; e/a, cr Berlin; 10POW; MACR 3430. THE IRON ASS.

42-39989 Del Long Beach 27/10/43; Gr Island 13/11/43; ass 334BS/95BG Horham 15/12/43; MIA Augsburg 16/3/44 w/Herman; cr Schieighausen, Ger; 10POW; MACR 4904 & 3231.

42-39990 Del Long Beach 27/10/43; Walla Walla 10/11/43; ass 730BS/452BG Deopham Green 3/1/44; MIA Berlin 19/5/44 w/Gaal; flak, cr Althyltendorf, Ger; 10POW; MACR 4958. JUNIOR.

42-39991 Del Long Beach 28/10/43; Kearney 13/11/43; ass 544BS/384BG [SU-V] Grafton Underwood 8/1/44; MIA Bonn 4/3/44 w/Carpenter; flak, cr Lahr, Ger; 1EVD 2KIA 7POW; MACR 2741.

42-39992 Del Long Beach 26/10/43; ass 305BG Chelveston 21/1/44; tran 401BG Deenethorpe 20/5/45; retUS Bradley 9/6/45; 4168 BU Sth Plains 12/9/45; RFC Kingman 29/11/45. YOU'VE HAD IT.

42-39993 Del Long Beach 28/10/43; ass 612BS/401BG [SC-C] Deenethorpe 1/1/44; {93m} landing acc 4/5/45; sal 2 SAD 8/5/45. HELL'S ANGELS OUT OF CHUTE 13.

42-39994 Del Long Beach 29/10/43; ass 418BS/100BG Thorpe Abbotts 16/12/43; MIA Berlin 6/3/44 w/Barrick; e/a, f/l Bulltofta, Swed; 10INT; MACR 3031. 222 BARRICK'S BAG. RetUS 121 BU Bradley 20/7/45; 4185 BU Independence 24/7/45; 237 BU Kirtland 16/12/45; RFC Albuquerque 7/2/46.

42-39995 Del Long Beach 29/10/43; Gr Island 13/11/43; ass 731BS/452BG Deopham Green 9/12/43; MIA Rostock 11/4/44 w/Schimmel; mech fault, f/l Angeltofta, Swed; 10INT; MACR 3826. RetUS 121 BU Bradley 16/7/45; 4185 BU Independence 22/7/45; RFC Kingman 22/12/45. COW TOWN BOOGIE.

42-39996 Del Long Beach 29/10/43; ass 322BS/91BG [LG-N] Bassingbourn 14/1/44; MIA {46m} Halle 16/8/44 w/Dunlap; e/a, cr Marshausen, Ger; 7KIA 2POW; MACR 8179. BOSTON BOMBSHELL.

42-39997 Del Long Beach 29/10/43; ass 533BS/381BG [VP-R] Ridgewell 13/1/44 BIG MIKE; severe b/d 2/5/44, but repaired by volunteers over weeks using F model wing; {95+m} RetUS Bradley 30/5/45; 4168 BU Sth Plains 21/10/45; RFC Kingman 28/11/45. FRENCHY'S FOLLY.

42-39998 Del Long Beach 29/10/43; Kearney 16/11/43; ass 337BS/96BG [AW-V] Snetterton 30/11/43; MIA Berlin 8/5/44 w/Capt Shoesmith; e/a, cr Rosthausen, Ger; 11POW; MACR 4569.

42-39999 Del Long Beach 1/11/43; Kearney 30/11/43; ass 49BS/2BG Amendola 9/12/43; MIA St Brux 20/10/44 w/Reilly; no gas, ditched Adriatic, crew picked up by Catalina; MACR 5831. BATAAN AVENGER.

42-40000 Del Long Beach 29/10/43; Gr Island 12/11/43; ass 324BS/91BG [DF-F] 4/1/44 QUAD ZERO; MIA {22m} Hamm 22/4/44 w/Capt Heese; flak, cr Delecke, Ger?; 10POW; MACR 4259. JUST NOTHING.

42-40001 Del Long Beach 9/10/43; ass 614BS/401BG [IW-L] Deenethorpe 5/1/44; ATC 30/5/45; retUS 4168 BU Sth Plains 11/6/45; RFC Kingman 19/11/45. PARIS EXPRESS

42-40002 Del Long Beach 1/11/43; Cheyenne 16/11/43; Kearney 19/11/43; ass 615BS/401BG [IY-D] Deenethorpe 29/12/43; MIA Bordeaux 9/6/44 w/Trimble; mech fault, cr Lesparre, Fr; 10EVD; MACR 6001. BREEZING HOME.

42-40003 Del Long Beach 1/11/43; Denver 27/11/43; Presque Is 11/12/43; ass 524BS/379BG [WA-H] Kimbolton 21/1/44 TOPPER; tran 490BG Eye /45; 157 missions was top a/c in 8AF, only one abort; retUS Bradley 28/6/45; 4168 BU Sth Plains 12/9/45; RFC Kingman 10/11/45. OL' GAPPY.

42-40004 Del Long Beach 1/11/43; Denver 18/11/43; Kearney 24/11/43; ass 548BS/385BG Gt Ashfield 9/12/43; cr Mutford, UK 20/2/44; sal 22/2/44.

42-40005 Del Long Beach 2/11/43; Gr Island 13/11/43; ass 546BS/384BG [BK-A] Grafton Underwood 6/1/44; MIA Frankfurt 11/2/44 w/Moore; e/a, cr Frankfurt; 4EVD 1KIA 5POW; MACR 2330. SALVAGE QUEEN.

42-40006 Del Long Beach 1/11/43; Gr Island 13/11/43; ass 368BS/306BG [BO-H] Thurleigh 18/1/44; MIA Berlin 6/3/44 w/Smith; flak, c/l Mastermyr, Swed; 10INT; MACR 2735. LIBERTY LADY.

42-40007 Del Long Beach 1/11/43; Kearney 13/11/43; ass 535BS/381BG [MS-W] Ridgewell 22/1/44; 533BS [VP-M]; b/d Brux 12/9/44 w/Hill, c/l France 1KIA 3WIA 6RTD; {75m} b/d Mannheim 25/11/44 w/Riza; f/l Bel; sal 13/12/44. HONEY.

42-40008 Del Long Beach 1/11/43; Gr Island 12/11/43; ass 532BS/381BG [VE-E] Ridgewell 8/1/44; MIA {1+m} Frankfurt 24/3/44 w/Thompson; mid air coll w/42-31490; cr Neustadt, Ger; 9KIA 1POW; MACR 3539. BAR FLY.

42-40009 Del Long Beach 2/11/43; Kearney 14/11/43;

Above: B-17G-10-VE 42-40043 carrying two GB-4 guided bombs on the underwing racks. This specially equipped aircraft, photographed here on its first combat mission in August 1944, was assigned to the secret Batty Project unit at Fersfield, England. (USAAF)

ass 324BS/91BG [DF-K] Bassingbourn 21/1/44; c/l Ickleton Abbey, UK 24/1/44 W/DeMara; 3KIA 6RTD; sal 2 SAD 26/1/44.

42-40010 Del Long Beach 3/11/43; Las Vegas 16/11/43; 3021 BU Las Vegas 2/6/44; 3502 BU Chanute 31/3/45; RFC Walnut Ridge 5/1/46.

42-40011 Del Long Beach 3/11/43; Kearney 14/11/43; ass 534BS/381BG [GD-O] Ridgewell 22/1/44; mid air coll w/42-97511 over field returning from Aschaffenburg 21/1/45 w/Smith; cr base area, 9KIA. SCHNOZZLE.

42-40012 Del Long Beach 2/11/43; Kearney 14/11/43; ass 8AF 30/11/43; lost Atlantic 18/12/43 en route UK; MACR 1318.

42-40013 Del Long Beach 2/11/43; Las Vegas 15/11/43; 4126 BU San Bernardino 8/1/45; 3018 BU Kingman 14/1/45; 3017 BU Hobbs 22/9/45; RFC Kingman 4/12/45.

42-40014 Del Long Beach 2/11/43; Kearney 13/11/43; ass 325BS/92BG Podington 6/1/44; MIA Wilhelmshafen 3/3/44 w/Lansford; flak, cr Hamburg; 10KIA; MACR 2857.

42-40015 Del Long Beach 4/11/43; Denver 7/11/43; Las Vegas 16/11/43; W/O 13/2/44.

42-40016 Del Long Beach 3/11/43; Kearney 14/11/43; ass 339BS/96BG [QJ-H] Snetterton 30/11/44; MIA Augsburg 13/4/44 w/Daniel; flak, cr Augsburg; 6KIA 4POW; MACR 4267/4577. THE CHARACTER.

42-40017 Del Long Beach 3/11/43; Kearney 15/11/43; ass 533BS/381BG [VP-W] Ridgewell 5/1/44 ASSEND, then MIASSES DRAGON; 535BS [MS-W]; b/d {55m} Brux 14/2/45 w/Wulf; 6 baled; MACR 5385; sal 14/3/45; ME AND MY GAL.

42-40018 Del Denver 3/11/43; Des Moines 10/1/44; Mitchell 23/1/44; ass 482BG (H2X) Alconbury 10/12/43; tran 422NLS/305BG [JJ-U] Chelveston 11/2/44; 384BG Grafton Underwood 1/8/44; 379BG Kimbolton 4/8/44; f/l Continent 15/1/45; sal 21/1/45.

42-40019 Del Long Beach 4/11/43; Las Vegas 16/11/43; 3018 BU Kingman 23/3/45; 3017 BU Hobbs 27/6/45; RFC Kingman 4/12/45.

42-40020 Del Long Beach 5/11/43; Kearney 15/11/43; ass 364BS/305BG Chelveston 22/1/44; MIA Frankfurt 8/2/44 w/Stuckey; e/a, cr Macquenoise, Bel; 4EVD 5KIA 1POW; MACR 2492.

42-40021 Del Long Beach 4/11/43; Las Vegas 15/11/43; 3018 BU Kingman W/O 9/11/44

42-40022 Del Long Beach 5/11/43; Las Vegas 17/11/43; 2137 BU Hendricks 17/11/44; RFC Kingman 1/11/45.

42-40023 Del Long Beach 5/11/43; Las Vegas 16/11/43; 3018 BU Kingman 23/3/45; 3017 BU Hobbs 9/6/45; RFC Kingman 4/12/45.

42-40024 Del Long Beach 5/11/43; Las Vegas 15/11/43; W/O 6/1/44.

42-40025 Del Long Beach 6/11/43; Denver 22/11/43; Kearney 24/11/43; Valley, UK 14/12/43; ass 535BS/381BG Ridgewell 6/1/44; b/d Nancy 6/2/44 w/Putek; c/l Dunkeswell, UK; sal 2 SAD 7/2/44. TOUCH THE BUTTON NELL.

42-40026 Del Long Beach 8/11/43; Las Vegas 18/11/43; 3018 BU Kingman W/O 12/7/44.

42-40027 Del Long Beach 8/11/43; Kingman 18/11/43; 225 BU Rapid City 1/5/45; 2114 BU Lockburn 27/6/45; 2137 BU Hendricks 22/9/45; RFC Walnut Ridge 4/1/46.

42-40028 Del Long Beach 5/11/43; Las Vegas 17/11/43; 3018 BU Kingman 23/3/45; 3017 BU Hobbs 9/6/45; RFC Kingman 5/12/45.

42-40029 Del Long Beach 5/11/43; Las Vegas 16/11/43; 3021 BU Las Vegas 2/6/44; Recl Comp 1/1/45.

42-40030 Del Long Beach 8/11/43; Denver 15/11/43; Kingman 20/11/43; 3018 BU Kingman 23/3/45; 3017 BU Hobbs 9/6/45; 3028 BU Luke 16/8/45; 3017 BU Hobbs 18/8/45; RFC Kingman 5/12/45.

42-40031 Del Long Beach 9/11/43; Kingman 20/11/434; 3018 BU Kingman 23/3/45; 3017 BU Hobbs 22/9/45; RFC Kingman 5/12/45.

42-40032 Del Long Beach 8/11/43; Kearney 24/11/43; ass 327BS/92BG Podington 27/1/44; MIA Erkner 8/2/44 w/Lehner; e/a, cr Vailly, Fr; 1EVD 6KIA 3POW; MACR 2363.

42-40033 Del Long Beach 8/11/43; Kingman 18/11/43; Denver 23/3/44; 224 BU Sioux City 6/3/45; 222 BU Ardmore 15/6/45; 332 BU Ardmore 19/6/45; RFC Walnut Ridge 25/9/45.

42-40034 Del Long Beach 9/11/43; Denver 15/11/43; 3018 BU Kingman W/O 9/10/44; Recl Comp 2/11/44.

42-40035 Del Long Beach 9/11/43; Kingman 18/11/43; 3018 BU Kingman 23/3/45; 3017 BU Hobbs 25/6/45; RFC Walnut Ridge 14/1/46.

42-40036 Del Long Beach 9/11/43; Las Vegas 18/11/43; 3018 BU Kingman 23/3/45; 3017 BU Hobbs 9/6/45; RFC Walnut Ridge 7/1/46.

42-40037 Del Long Beach 10/11/43; Orlando 28/11/43; 235 BU Biggs 16/8/44; 224 BU Sioux City 28/3/45; 225 BU Rapid City 15/6/45; 237 BU Kirtland 20/7/45; RFC Altus 7/11/45.

42-40038 Del Long Beach 10/11/43; Orlando 29/11/43; W/O 14/1/44.

42-40039 Del Long Beach 10/11/43; Yuma 19/11/43; 3021 BU Las Vegas 2/6/44; 3018 BU Kingman 22/2/45; 3017 BU Hobbs 24/6/45; RFC Kingman 5/12/45.

42-40040 Del Long Beach 11/11/43; Las Vegas 20/11/43; 3018 BU Kingman W/O 7/7/44.

42-40041 Del Long Beach 11/11/43; Yuma 19/11/43; 3017 BU Hobbs 4/6/44; RFC Walnut Ridge 28/12/45.

42-40042 Del Long Beach 11/11/43; Orlando 22/11/43; 901 BU BU Pinecastle 2/6/44; 903 BU Pinecastle 10/9/44; 902 BU Orlando 3/10/44; 903 BU Pinecastle 25/11/44; 621 BU Pinecastle 9/7/46. 42-40043 Del Long Beach 11/11/43; 4185 BU Independence 30/11/45; RFC Kingman 20/12/45.

42-40043 Del 11/11/43; Independence 30/11/43; to 8AF Batty Project summer 1944; Kingman 20/12/45.

42-40044 Del Denver 10/11/43; Yuma 20/11/43; 3018 BU Kingman 27/8/45; 3036 BU Yuma 28/8/45; 3008 BU Minter 27/9/45; RFC Ontario 18/1/46.

42-40045 Del Long Beach 11/11/43; Orlando 21/11/43; 4115 BU Atlanta 11/6/44; 2530 BU Selman 22/6/44; 223 BU Dyersburg 26/6/44; 2530 BU Selman 2/7/44; 223 BU Dyersburg 13/7/44; W/O 1/8/44.

42-40046 Del Long Beach 11/11/43; Gr Island 24/11/43; Presque Is 30/11/43; Prestwick, UK 6/12/43; ass 551BS/385BG Gt Ashfield 4/12/43; MIA Kiel 4/1/44 w/Bean; mech fault, cr Luetjennhelm?; 10POW; MACR 1897.

42-40047 Del Long Beach 11/11/43; Kearney 24/11/43; Prestwick, UK 7/12/43; ass 407BS/92BG Podington 31/12/43; MIA Schweinfurt 24/2/44 w/Scarborough; e/a, cr Zwolle, Hol; 1KIA 9POW; MACR 2753.

42-40048 Del Long Beach 11/11/43; Las Vegas 20/11/43; 560 BU Palm Springs 16/9/44; 3018 BU Kingman 8/10/44; 3017 BU Hobbs 24/6/45; RFC Kingman 6/12/45.

42-40049 Del Long Beach 12/11/43; Yuma 19/11/43; 3017 BU Hobbs 2/9/45; 4208 BU Mines Fd 16/10/45; 3017 BU Hobbs 5/11/45; RFC Kingman 6/12/45.

42-40050 Del Long Beach 16/11/43; Gr Island 4/12/43; Presque Is 11/12/43; Prestwick, UK 15/12/43; ass 612BS/401BG [SC-J] Deenethorpe 1/1/44; MIA Bordeaux 19/6/44 w/Massey; mech fault, cr Jouldes, Fr?; 3EVD 7KIA; MACR 6002. CHANNEL EXPRESS III.

42-40051 Del Long Beach 13/11/43; Gr Island 21/11/43; Presque Is 2/12/43; Prestwick, UK 6/12/43; ass 339BS/96BG [QJ-F] Snetterton 4/12/43; MIA Warnemünde 9/4/44 w/Massey; e/a, cr Hystead, Hol?; 10KIA; MACR 3652.

42-40052 Del Long Beach 13/11/43; Gr Island 21/11/43; Bangor 4/12/43; ass 407BS/92BG Podington 30/12/43; MIA Berlin 6/3/44 w/Upson; flak, cr Hengelo, Hol; 4EVD 1KIA 5POW; MACR 2905.

42-40053 Del Long Beach 13/11/43; Kearney 21/11/43; ass 367BS/306BG Thurleigh 13/4/44; sal 2 SAD 5/10/44. PATCHES AND PRAYERS.

42-40054 Del Long Beach 16/11/43; Kearney 24/11/43; ass 562BS/388BG Knettishall 8/12/43; MIA Berlin 6/3/44 w/Capt Brown; mid air coll w/42-37886; cr Schoonberkerveld, Hol; 5KIA 6POW; MACR 3092.

42-40055 Del Long Beach 16/11/43; Gr Island 27/11/43; ass 347BS/99BG Tortorella 21/12/43; MIA {25m} Regensburg 25/2/44 w/Kirkpatrick; cr Murau; MACR 2707.

42-40056 Del Long Beach 16/11/43; Kearney 24/11/43; ass 351BS/100BG [EP-D] Thorpe Abbotts 9/12/43 KATIE'S BOYS; MIA Berlin 8/3/44 w/Chapman; e/a, cr Hohengoersdorf, Ger?; 10POW; MACR 3032. HOLY TERROR III.

42-40057 Del Long Beach 16/11/43; Kearney 24/11/43; Prestwick, UK 7/12/43; ass 615BS/401BG [IY-N] Deenethorpe 5/1/44; MIA Frankfurt 29/1/44 w/Nickawsky; e/a, cr Entenphuhl, Ger?; 1KIA 9POW; MACR 2273.

B-17G-BO

42-97058 Del Cheyenne 24/1/44; Gr Island 11/2/44; Presque Is 27/2/44; ass 359BS/303BG [BN-V] Molesworth 27/3/44; MIA Aschaffenburg 21/1/45 w/Tasker; mid air coll, cr Rottweil, Ger; 9KIA 1POW; MACR 11760. SCORCHY.

42-97059 Del Cheyenne 24/1/44; Gr Island 6/2/44; ass 457BG Glatton 12/2/44; tran 533BS/381BG Ridgewell 15/3/44; {48m} b/d Cologne 12/12/44 w/Ruf; coll en route w/43-38986, sheared rudder off, f/l Belgium; sal 5/1/45. MARSHA SUE.

42-97060 Del Cheyenne 24/1/44; Grenier 23/2/44; ass 749BS/457BG Glatton 4/3/44; MIA Nienburg 5/8/44. CALAMITY JANE II.

42-97061 Del Cheyenne 24/1/44; Grenier 23/2/44; ass 457BG Glatton 13/3/44; tran 323BS/91BG [OR-U] Bassingbourn 16/3/44; 401BS [LL-B]; retUS Bradley 13/6/45; 4168 BU Sth Plains 21/10/45. GENERAL IKE.

42-97062 Del Cheyenne 24/1/44; Kearney 20/2/44; Presque Is 2/3/44; ass 94BG Rougham 3/3/44; tran 749BS/457BG Glatton 15/3/44; MIA Le Bourget 14/6/44 w/Johnson; flak, cr Champdueil, Fr; 6KIA 4POW; MACR 5906.

42-97063 Del Cheyenne 24/1/44; Gr Island 6/2/44; ass 351BG Polebrook 11/2/44; tran 750BS/457BG Glatton 1/3/44; MIA Augsburg 16/3/44 w/Lenartson; ditched Channel. MISS YU III.

42-97064 Del Cheyenne 24/1/44; Kearney 11/2/44; Grenier 25/2/44; Presque Is 2/3/44; ass 711BS/447BG Rattlesden 16/3/44; MIA Augsburg 13/4/44 w/Capt Keller; flak, f/l Dubendorf, Switz; 10INT. MACR 4296.

42-97065 Del Cheyenne 24/1/44; Gr Island 2/3/44; Presque Is 22/3/44; ass 418BS/100BG [LD-P] Thorpe Abbotts 7/3/44; MIA Bremen 24/6/44 w/Roth; flak, cr Longuail, Fr; 3EVD 2KIA 5POW; MACR 6343. RETURN TICKET.

42-97066 Del Cheyenne 24/1/44; Gr Island 8/2/44; Presque Is 21/1/44; ass 508BS/351BG [YB-O] Polebrook 26/3/44; MIA {22m} Le Bourget 14/6/44 w/Dixey; flak, cr Abbeville, Fr; 2EVD 1KIA 7POW; MACR 5796.

42-97067 Del Cheyenne 24/1/44; Gr Island 3/2/44; Presque Is 21/2/44; ass 94BG Rougham 22/2/44; tran 748BS/457BG Glatton 4/4/44 BLACK PUFF POLLY; MIA Ruhland 28/5/44 w/Stohl; e/a, cr Osterholz, Ger; 1KIA 9POW; MACR 5297. GEORGIA PEACH.

42-97068 Del Cheyenne 24/1/44; Gr Island 9/2/44; Presque Is 21/2/44; ass 336BS/95BG [ET-H] Horham 26/2/44; MIA Hannover 18/6/44 w/Bullard; cr Nth Sea, 10KIA; MACR 5956.

42-97069 Del Cheyenne 24/1/44; Gr Island 11/2/44; Presque Is 23/2/44; ass 401BS/91BG [LL-N] Bassingbourn 11/3/44; tran 731BS/452BG Deopham Green 12/3/44; MIA Kassel 4/12/44 w/Downy; flak, cr Bitburg, Ger; 3KIA 6POW; MACR 11050. MON TETE ROUGE II.

42-97070 Del Cheyenne 24/1/44; Kearney 16/2/44; Presque Is 2/3/44; ass 750BS/457BG Glatton 15/3/44; MIA Metz 25/4/44 w/Capt Bender; mech fault, cr St Germaine, Fr. 5EVD 6POW; MACR 4306.

42-97071 Del Cheyenne 24/1/44; Kearney 11/2/44; Presque Is 28/2/44; ass 418BS/100BG [LD-P] Thorpe Abbotts 4/3/44; MIA Parchim, Ger. 7/4/45 w/Calder; rammed by 109, exploded cr Hannover; 9KIA; MACR 13718. CANDY'S DANDY.

42-97072 Del Cheyenne 24/1/44; Kearney 15/2/44; Presque Is 28/2/44; ass 547BS/384BG [SO-H] Grafton Underwood 24/3/44; 544BS [SU-A]; c/l France 1/8/44, sal. MACR 7807.

42-97073 Del Cheyenne 24/1/44; Alexandra 12/2/44; Presque Is 4/3/44; ass 615BS/401BG [IY-N] Deenethorpe 23/3/44; MIA Ruhland 28/5/44 w/Kaminski; e/a, cr Steinburg, Ger; 8KIA 2POW; MACR 5311.

42-97074 Del Cheyenne 24/1/44; Kearney 16/2/44; Grenier 25/2/44; ass 8AF, WO 26/2/44.

42-97075 Del Cheyenne 24/1/44; Gr Island 9/2/44; ass 750BS/457BG Glatton 7/3/44; dec War Weary 26/3/45; tran 351BG Polebrook 21/4/45; ret 457BG Glatton 11/5/45; retUS Bradley 8/6/45; 4124 BU Altus 13/9/45; RFC Altus 9/10/45. FLAK DODGER.

42-97076 Del Cheyenne 24/1/44; Gr Island 8/2/43; tran 534BS/381BG [GD-K] Ridgewell 15/3/44; {63m} RetUS Bradley 9/6/45; 4168 BU Sth Plains 13/6/45; RFC Kingman 25/11/45. DEE MARIE.

42-97077 Del Cheyenne 25/1/44; Gr Island 20/2/44; Grenier 13/3/44; ass 366BS/305BG [KY-D] Chelveston 31/3/44; MIA Saarbrücken 11/5/44 w/Capt Thomas; flak, cr Saarbrücken; 2EVD 9POW; MACR 4875.

42-97078 Del Cheyenne 25/1/44; Lincoln 20/2/44; Presque Is 21/2/44; ass 550BS/385BG Gt Ashfield 7/3/44; MIA Berlin 29/4/44 w/Henry; e/a, cr Hermeskeil, Ger; 2KIA 8POW; MACR 4457.

42-97079 Del Cheyenne 26/1/44; Kearney 18/2/44; ass 548BS/385BG Gt Ashfield 3/3/44; MIA Berlin 6/10/44 w/Isaacson; e/a, cr Brandenburg; 5KIA 4POW; MACR 9521. DOZY DOATS.

42-97080 Del Cheyenne 25/1/44; Kearney 17/2/44; Grenier 3/3/44; ass 333BS/94BG Rougham 12/3/44; 410BS [GL-H]; MIA Warnemunde 9/4/44 w/Branson; flak, ditched Nth Sea; 7KIA 3POW; MACR 3800.

42-97081 Del Cheyenne 25/1/44; Kearney 11/2/44; Presque Is 23/2/44; ass 457BG Glatton 2/3/44; tran 547BS/384BG [SO-K] Grafton Underwood 12/3/44; 546BS [BK-K]; MIA Berlin 8/5/44 w/Brown; flak, cr Channel; 8KIA 2POW; MACR 4812.

42-97082 Del Cheyenne 25/1/44; Gr Island 20/2/44; Presque is 12/3/44; ass 333BS/94BG Rougham 16/3/44; 410BS; c/t/o for Kaiserlauten 6/1/45 w/Collins; lost engine on take off and ploughed into woods at Moreton Hall; 5KIA 4WIA plus three civilians injured; exploding bombs damaged several homes; sal. MISSION MISTRESS.

42-97083 Del Cheyenne 25/1/44; Gr Island 20/2/44; Grenier 11/3/44; ass 728BS/452BG Deopham Green 16/3/44; MIA Poznan 11/4/44 w/Gardner; flak, cr Jadebuesen, Ger; 10POW; MACR 3932. FLATBUSH FLOOGIE.

42-97084 Del Cheyenne 25/1/44; Gr Island 20/2/44; Presque Is 28/2/44; ass 534BS/381BG [GD-H] Ridgewell 6/4/44; cr continent 22/6/44 w/Peak; 8KIA 1POW; MACR 5918. SPARE CHARLIE.

42-97085 Del Cheyenne 25/1/44; Gr Island 11/2/44; Grenier 22/2/44; ass 305BG Chelveston 6/5/44; tran 358BS/303BG [VK-S] Molesworth 6/5/44; MIA Cologne 15/8/44 w/Charnick; e/a, cr Wittlich, Ger; 2KIA 7POW; MACR 8439.

42-97086 Del Cheyenne 25/1/44; Hunter 22/2/44; Grenier 8/3/44; ass 332BS/94BG [XM-K] Rougham 13/3/44; MIA Poznan 11/4/44 w/Totoshek; flak, cr Osterby, Ger; 4KIA 6POW; MACR 4008. AMERICAN MAID.

42-97087 Del Cheyenne 25/1/44; Gr Island 11/2/44; Presque Is 21/2/44; ass 379BG Kimbolton 1/3/44; tran 748BS/457BG Glatton 2/3/44; MIA Munich 31/7/44 w/Schiffman; flak, cr Perlach, Ger; 7KIA 3POW; MACR 7829. TUJUNGA.

42-97088 Del Cheyenne 26/1/44; Kearney 11/2/44; Presque Is 28/2/44; ass 748BS/457BG Glatton 9/3/44; sal 2 SAD 11/7/44.

42-97089 Del Cheyenne 26/1/44; Gr Island 6/2/44; Kearney 15/2/44; ass 338BS/96BG Snetterton 3/3/44; MIA Rostock 11/4/44 w/Swanlund; e/a, cr Baltic Sea; 10KIA; MACR 3815.

42-97090 Del Cheyenne 26/1/44; Alexandra 18/2/44; Grenier 10/3/44; ass 418BS/100BG [LD-D] Thorpe Abbotts 12/3/44; c/l Framlingham A/fd 29/6/44; sal 10/7/44.

42-97091 Del Cheyenne 26/1/44; Alexandra 12/2/44; Presque Is 4/3/44; ass 561BS/388BG Knettishall 6/3/44; MIA Kiel 22/5/44 w/Mergenthaler; flak, cr Nettlesse, Ger; 1KIA 9POW. MACR 4956. DEAR MOM.

42-97092 Del Cheyenne 26/1/44; Alexandra 12/2/44; Presque Is 10/3/44; ass 708BS/447BG Rattlesden 11/3/44; 710BS; sal 2/11/44; retUS Bradley 5/7/45; 1103 BU Morrison 8/10/45; 4168 BU Sth Plains 21/10/45; RFC Kingman 29/11/45. HEEL DER FUHRER.

42-97093 Del Cheyenne 28/1/44; Kearney 14/2/44;

Presque Is 20/2/44; ass 568BS/390BG [BI-S] Framlingham 3/3/44 DOC'S FLYING CIRCUS, then GIRL OF MY DREAMS; retUS Bradley 29/6/45; 4168 BU Sth Plains 12/9/45; RFC Kingman 15/12/45. I'LL GET BY.

42-97094 Del Cheyenne 27/1/44; Alexandra 12/2/44; Presque Is 12/3/44; ass 728BS/452BG Deopham Green 13/3/44; MIA Brux 12/5/44 w/Ward; ditched Channel; 10RTD. WHY WORRY.

42-97095 Del Cheyenne 27/1/44; Alexandra 15/2/44; Presque Is 3/3/44; ass 350BS/100BG [LN-Y] Thorpe Abbotts 6/3/44; MIA Berlin 24/5/44 w/Pearson; e/a, cr Friesack, Ger; 1KIA 9POW; MACR 5168.

42-97096 Del Cheyenne 27/1/44; Alexandra 22/2/44; Grenier 20/3/44; ass 427BS/303BG [GN-T] Molesworth 8/4/44; MIA Berlin 21/6/44 w/Allen; flak, cr Schweilowsee, Ger; 1KIA 9POW; MACR 5986.

42-97097 Del Cheyenne 27/1/44; Alexandra 12/2/44; Presque Is 18/3/44; ass 366BS/305BG Chelveston 31/3/44; MIA Nancy 27/4/44 w/Knight; flak, cr Mailley le Camp, Fr; 6KIA 4POW; MACR 4277.

42-97098 Del Dorval (Montreal) 7/2/44; ass RAF [HB-761]; tran 561BS/388BG Knettishall 1/7/44; MIA Berlin 6/8/48 w/Kluth; flak, cr Zehlendorf, Ger; 9POW; MACR 7705. FORTRESS NINE.

42-97099 Del Bismark 26/2/44; Dorval 3/3/44; ass RAF [HB-762] 51MU; A & AEE; Struck Off Charge 11/8/47.

42-97100 Del Bismark 2/2/44; Dorval 3/2/44; ass RAF [HB-763] 214 Sq [BU-T]; MIA Russelheim 26/8/44.

42-97101 Del Gt Falls 6/2/44; Dorval 9/2/44; ass RAF [HB-764]; tran 8 AFSC 7/4/44; 388BG Knettishall 1/7/44; f/l Fouches, Lux? 9/11/44; sal 28/11/44.

42-97102 Del Dorval 1/2/44; ass RAF [HB-765] 214Sq [BU-B]; tran 562BS/388BG Knettishall /4/44; f/l Fouches, Lux? 9/11/44; 2KIA 7RTD; sal 24/10/45. CICERO KID.

42-97103 Del Romulus 3/2/44; Dorval 4/2/44; ass RAF [HB-766] tran 8 AFSC 30/5/44; retUS 121 BU Bradley 2/6/45; 4100 BU Patterson 6/6/45; 4168 BU Sth Plains 30/8/45; RFC Kingman 20/12/45; US Navy CB-17 1946.

42-97104 Del Dorval 2/2/44; ass RAF [HB-767] 214 Sq [BU-A]; MIA Frankfurt 13/9/44.

42-97105 Del Selfridge Fld 3/2/44; Dorval 4/3/44; ass RAF [HB-768]; tran 561BS/388BG Knettishall 13/3/44; MIA Parchim 7/4/45 w/Hickman; mid air coll w/Bf109; cr Luneburg, Ger; 4KIA 5POW. MACR 13724.

42-97106 Del Gt Falls 7/2/44; Dorval 11/2/44; ass RAF [HB-769]; sal 24/6/44.

42-97107 Del Bismark 2/2/44; Dorval 4/2/44; ass RAF [HB-770]; tran 562BS/388BG Knettishall 1/7/44; MIA French RR juncts 8/7/44 w/Gill; flak, cr Abbeville, Fr; 3EVD 8POW; MACR 7362.

42-97108 Del Tacoma 1/2/44; Dorval 14/2/44; ass RAF [HB-771] To USAAF as CB-108. RetUS 24/1/45; RFC Walnut Ridge 19/12/45.

42-97109 Del Gt Falls 1/2/44; Dorval 3/2/44; ass RAF [HB-772] 214Sq [BU-Q]; SOC 11/3/47.

42-97110 Del Gt Falls 1/2/44; Dorval 4/2/44; ass RAF [HB-773]; retUS 1 BU Bolling 20/8/45; 610 BU Eglin 13/12/45; sal 29/1/46.

42-97111 Del Gt Falls 2/2/44; Dorval 20/2/44; ass RAF [HB-774] 214Sq [BU-G]; SOC 11/3/47.

42-97112 Del Dorval 12/2/44; ass RAF [HB-775]; tran 561BS/388BG Knettishall 18/3/44; b/d Frankfurt 5/1/45 w/Edelman; flak, f/l Zweibrücken; 3POW 6RTD; MACR 11562; sal 21/1/45. LITTLE JOE JR.

42-97113 Del Gt Falls 1/2/44; Dorval 2/2/44; ass RAF [HB-776] 1674HCU; SOC 11/3/47.

42-97114 Del Gt Falls 2/2/44; Dorval 3/2/44; ass RAF [HB-777]; tran 560BS/388BG Knettishall 1/7/44; MIA Ruhland 17/3/45 w/Brown; flak, cr Halle, Ger; 6KIA 3POW; MACR 13112. BORROWED TIME.

42-97115 Del Gt Falls 8/2/44; Dorval 21/2/44; ass RAF [HB-778]; tran 333BS/94BG [TS-C] Rougham 24/2/44; 388BG Knettishall /4/44; (?Swedish airliner, [SE-BAO]; W/O 1948, sal 31/12/49?). TED.

42-97116 Del Gt Falls 2/2/44; Dorval 8/2/44; ass RAF [HB-779] 214Sq [BU-L]; SOC 11/3/47.

42-97117 Del Gt Falls 2/2/44; Dorval 4/2/44; ass RAF [HB-780] 214Sq [BU-C]; SOC 11/3/47.

42-97118 Del Bismark 2/2/44; Dorval 9/2/44; ass RAF [HB-781] RetUS Bradley 1/8/45; 4185 BU Independence 30/11/45; 237 BU Kirtland 9/12/45; RFC Albuquerque 7/2/46.

42-97119 Del Gt Falls 6/2/44; Dorval 10/2/44; ass RAF [HB-782]; sal 2/11/44.

42-97120 Del Cheyenne 29/1/44; Gr Island 15/2/44; Kearney 29/2/44; ass 336BS/95BG [ET-E] Horham 3/3/44; MIA Regensburg 21/7/44 w/Laird; cr Eitelbrück, Lux; 6EVD 4POW; MACR 7410.

42-97121 Del Cheyenne 29/1/44; Alexandra 12/2/44; Grenier 6/4/44; ass 326BS/92BG [JW-G] Podington 25/4/44; MIA Peenemunde 25/8/44 w/Lindstrom; flak, c/l Sovde, Swed; 9INT; MACR 8276; retUS Bradley 13/7/45; 4185 BU Independence 30/11/45; RFC Kingman 14/12/45. CALAMITY JANE.

42-97122 Del Cheyenne 29/1/44; Kearney 4/2/44; Grenier 25/2/44; ass 751BS/457BG Glatton 17/3/44; sal 12/5/44.

42-97123 Del Cheyenne 29/1/44; Kearney 6/2/44; Presque Is 25/2/44; ass 751BS/457BG Glatton 8/3/44; retUS Bradley 9/6/44; 4168 BU Sth Plains 14/6/45; RFC Kingman 14/12/45. IPANA SMILE.

42-97124 Del Cheyenne 29/1/44; Kearney 20/2/44; Presque Is 27/2/44; ass 457BG Glatton 11/3/44; tran 545BS/384BG [JD-M] Grafton Underwood 12/3/44; MIA Augsburg 16/3/44 w/Swanson; e/a, cr Laroche, Fr; 6EVD 1KIA 3POW; MACR 3870.

42-97125 Del Cheyenne 29/1/44; Kearney 16/2/44; Grenier 26/2/44; ass 457BG Glatton 13/3/44; tran 401BS/91G Bassingbourn 16/3/44; MIA Berlin 22/3/44 w/Capt Phillips; flak, cr Behlicke, Ger?; 10POW; MACR 3312.

42-97126 Del Cheyenne 29/1/44; Alexandra 12/2/44; Presque Is 4/3/44; ass 351BS/100BG [EP-D] Thorpe Abbotts 6/3/44 THE LATEST RUMOR; sal 24/5/45; SILVER DOLLAR.

42-97127 Del Cheyenne 29/1/44; Kearney 14/2/44; Grenier 25/2/44; ass 535BS/381BG [MS-P] Ridgewell 6/3/44; tran 349BS/100BG [XR-J] Thorpe Abbotts 7/3/44; MIA Brux 12/5/44 w/Moore; flak, cr Georgendorf, Ger; 1KIA 9POW; MACR 4867.

42-97128 Del Cheyenne 29/1/44; Alexandra 15/2/44; Presque Is 4/3/44; ass 457BG Glatton 6/3/44; tran 384BG Grafton Underwood 12/3/44; 527BS/379BG [FO-M] Kimbolton 28/12/44; MIA Ingolstadt 5/4/45 w/Hourtal; cr Bellhiem, Ger; SCREWBALL EXPRESS.

42-97129 Del Cheyenne 29/1/44; Kearney 12/2/44; Grenier 25/2/44; Presque 10/3/44; ass 367BS/306BG Thurleigh 12/3/44 SKIPPER; tran 337BS/96BG [AW-B] Snetterton 13/3/44; MIA Rostock 11/4/44 w/Van Hixon; e/a, cr Grummark, Den; 10POW; MACR 3816.

42-97130 Del Cheyenne 29/1/44; Tucson 20/2/44; Grenier 4/3/44; Slated 731BS/452BG, ass 570BS/390BG [DI-Q] Framlingham 7/3/44 AVENGER II; MIA Mannheim 9/9/44 w/Latci; flak, cr Luedenscheid, Ger; 9POW; MACR 8913. THE AVENGER III.

42-97131 Del Cheyenne 29/1/44; Kearney 15/2/44; Presque Is 25/2/44; ass 751BS/457BG Glatton 8/3/44; MIA Brandenburg 6/8/44 w/Frost; flak, cr Michelsmoor, Ger?; 4KIA 5POW; MACR 7889. HOME JAMES!

42-97132 Del Cheyenne 29/1/44; Kearney 16/2/44; Grenier 1/3/44; ass 562BS/388BG Knettishall 6/3/44; sal 9/6/44.

42-97133 Del Cheyenne 29/1/44; Kearney 12/2/44; Presque Is 2/3/44; ass 367BS/306BG Thurleigh 26/3/44; tran 91BG 30/5/45; retUS Bradley 11/6/45; 4168 BU Sth Plains 21/10/45; RFC Kingman 8/12/45. PRETTY BABY.

42-97134 Del Cheyenne 29/1/44; Gt Falls 7/2/44; Savannah 23/2/44; Homestead 15/3/44; ass 353BS/301BG Lucera 17/3/44; weather ship from 9/10/44; retUS 593 BU Charleston 28/10/45; RFC Walnut Ridge 8/1/46.

42-97135 Del Cheyenne 29/1/44; Kearney 16/2/44; Presque 27/2/44; ass 306BG Thurleigh 2/3/44; tran 710BS/447BG Rattlesden 3/3/44; MIA Berlin 29/4/44 w/Marcy; e/a, cr Oranienburg; 10POW; MACR 4252.

42-97136 Del Cheyenne 30/1/44; Hunter 22/2/44; ass 457BG Glatton 11/3/44; tran 544BS/384BG [SU-J] Grafton Underwood 12/3/44; MIA Pas de Calais 27/4/44 w/Small; flak, cr Sottevast, Fr; 10KIA; MACR 4350.

42-97137 Del Cheyenne 30/1/44; Kearney 16/2/44; Presque Is 28/2/44; ass 751BS/457BG Glatton 9/3/44; MIA Pas de Calais 20/4/44 w/Milner; flak, cr Bailleul, Fr; 8KIA 2POW; MACR 4058. SILVER QUEEN.

42-97138 Del Cheyenne 30/1/44; Kearney 27/2/44; Grenier 5/3/44; ass 332BS/94BG [XM-C] Rougham 12/3/44; MIA Freidrichshafen 24/4/44 w/McCullum; flak, f/l Dubendorf, Switz; 10INT; MACR 4262. RetUS 1377 BU Grenier 14/9/45; Independence 16/9/45; RFC Kingman 4/11/45.

42-97139 Del Cheyenne 30/1/44; Kearney 16/2/44; Presque Is 28/2/44; ass 457BG Glatton 11/3/44; tran 546BS/384BG [BK-M] Grafton Underwood 12/3/44; 547BS; sal 18/6/44.

42-97140 Del Cheyenne 30/1/44; Kearney 16/2/44; Presque Is 21/2/44; ass 338BS/96BG [BX-Y] Snetterton 3/3/44; MIA Regensburg 21/7/44 w/Forciea; flak, cr Heubach, Ger; 9POW; MACR 7413.

42-97141 Del Cheyenne 30/1/44; Gr Island 15/2/44; Grenier 1/3/44; ass 325BS/92BG [NV-A] Podington 22/3/44; b/d Soest 28/1/45, f/l continent; sal 9/3/45. MARY JANE.

42-97142 Del Cheyenne 2/2/44; Kearney 18/2/44; ass 457BG Glatton 11/3/44; tran 546BS/384BG [BK-N] Grafton Underwood 12/3/44; MIA Magdeburg 12/9/44 w/Hanlon; e/a, cr Fulda, Ger; 6KIA 3POW; MACR 8901. DANIEL WEBSTER.

42-97143 Del Cheyenne 2/2/44; Gr Island 16/2/44; Presque Is 11/3/44; ass 729BS/452BG Deopham Green 16/3/44; MIA Merseburg 12/5/44 w/Stogsdill; e/a, cr Wicher, Ger; 8KIA 2POW; MACR 4776. YOU'VE HAD IT.

42-97144 Del Cheyenne 2/2/44; Gr Island 20/2/44; Presque Is 11/3/44; ass 509BS/351BG [RQ-R] Polebrook 26/3/44; MIA {30m} Berlin 21/6/44 w/Walters; mech fault, f/l Bulltofta, Swed; 10INT; MACR 6536.

42-97145 Del Cheyenne 2/2/44; Gr Island 15/2/44; Presque Is 12/3/44; ass 327BS/92BG [UX-K] Podington 1/4/44; c/l base 14/7/44; sal. PATRICIA.

42-97146 Del Cheyenne 3/2/44; Gr Island 15/2/44; Presque Is 5/3/44; ass 423BS/306BG [RD-W] Thurleigh 24/3/44; sal 2 SAD 2/5/44.

42-97147 Del Cheyenne 2/2/44; Kearney 19/2/44;

Grenier 1/3/44; ass 711BS/447BG Rattlesden 12/3/44; c/l base 7/7/44; sal.

42-97148 Del Cheyenne 3/2/44; Kearney 15/2/44; Grenier 25/2/44; ass 711BS/447BG Rattlesden 7/3/44; MIA Hannover 18/6/44 w/Schreiner; flak, cr Hildesheim, Ger; 10POW; MACR 5903.

42-97149 Del Cheyenne 3/2/44; Gr Island 23/2/44; Presque Is 13/3/44; ass 509BS/351BG [RQ-X] Polebrook 26/3/44; MIA {13m} Mannheim 27/5/44 w/Myers; e/a, cr Hessenheim, Ger?; 10POW; MACR 5327.

42-97150 Del Cheyenne 3/2/44; Kearney 16/2/44; Presque Is 26/2/44; ass 547BS/384BG [SO-F] Grafton Underwood 12/3/44; 544BS [SU-F]; f/l continent 10/1/45; sal. SILVER QUEEN.

42-97151 Del Cheyenne 3/2/44; Gr Island 16/2/44; Presque Is 2/3/44; ass 323BS/91BG [OR-L] Bassingbourn 22/3/44; {14+m} b/d Troyes 3/5/44, c/l base; sal 2 SAD. SHERIFF'S POSSE.

42-97152 Del Cheyenne 3/2/44; Hunter 22//2/44; Morrison 4/3/44; ass 20BS/2BG Amendola 6/3/44; MIA Turin 29/3/44 w/Wronkoski; e/a, cr Bormida de Dego, It; eight chutes seen; MACR 3514.

42-97153 Del Cheyenne 3/2/44; Gr Island 7/2/44; Kearney 24/2/44; ass 333BS/94BG [TS-E] Rougham 3/3/44 DARLING DORIS; 410BS [GL-X], 331BS; b/d Bohlen 11/9/44 w/Duda; mid air coll w/42-31653, cr Audigast, Ger; 9KIA; MACR 8841. DARING DORIS.

42-97154 Del Cheyenne 4/2/44; Gr Island 18/2/44; Presque Is 4/3/44; ass 350BS/100BG [LN-A] Thorpe Abbotts 6/3/44; MIA Bohlen 11/9/44 w/Carlton; e/a, cr Ober Weisenthal, Ger; 7KIA 2POW; MACR 8817.

42-97155 Del Cheyenne 4/2/44; Gr Island 7/2/44; Kearney 18/2/44; ass 333BS/94BG [TS-C] Rougham 3/3/44; MIA Poznan 11/4/44 w/Johnson; f/l Bulltofta, Swed; 10INT; MACR 3862. Later used as Swedish air liner, scrapped 1948.

42-97156 Del Cheyenne 3/2/44; Gr Island 16/2/44; Presque Is 12/3/44; ass 410BS/94BG [GL-R] Rougham 12/3/44 MY IDEAL; 333BS [TS-D]; b/d Berlin 26/2/45; f/l Luxembourg; sal 20/3/45. YOU IS MY IDEAL.

42-97157 Del Cheyenne 3/2/44; Kearney 23/2/44; Presque Is 12/3/44; ass 508BS/351BG [YB-N] Polebrook 24/3/44; MIA {30m} Ludwigshafen 27/5/44 w/Sengstock; cr Epinal, Fr; 2KIA 7POW; MACR 5330.

42-97158 Del Cheyenne 3/2/44; Gr Island 18/2/44; Dow Fd 1/4/44; ass 337BS/96BG [BX-D] Snetterton 7/4/44; b/d Berlin 5/1/45, c/l Remagne, Bel; sal 31/1/45.

42-97159 Del Cheyenne 4/2/44; Savannah 22/2/44; Homstead 17/3/44; ass 20BS/2BG Amendola 17/3/44; MIA Moravska Ostrova, Czech 29/8/44 w/Tune; e/a, cr Boikowitz, Czech?; MACR 8763. TAIL END CHARLIE.

42-97160 Del Cheyenne 4/2/44; Kearney 16/2/44; Presque Is 25/2/44; ass 568BS/390BG [BI-M] Framlingham 3/3/44; MIA French bridges 2/8/44 w/Seaborn; flak, cr Roeselaere, Fr; 1EVD 8POW; MACR 7750. SOUTHERN COMFORT.

42-97161 Del Cheyenne 4/2/44; Savannah 22/2/44; Morrison 5/3/44; ass 96BS/2BG Amendola 15/3/44; b/d Maribor 7/11/44 w/Reynolds; two engines out, no hydraulics then ground looped, rep; {99m} RetUS, RFC Walnut Ridge 20/12/45.

42-97162 Del Cheyenne 4/2/44; Kearney 16/2/44; ass 748BS/457BG Glatton 8/3/44; sal 27/4/44.

42-97163 Del Cheyenne 4/2/44; Kearney 16/2/44; Presque Is 28/3/44; ass 527BS/379BG [FO-R] Kimbolton 9/4/44; b/d Altenberg 13/9/44; f/l continent; MACR 8899. Sal 6/2/45. SNOW WHITE.

42-97164 Del Cheyenne 4/2/44; Kearney 15/2/44; Presque Is 23/2/44; ass 751BS/457BG Glatton 15/3/44 REBEL QUEEN; 749BS; MIA Cologne 28/1/45 w/Boyes; mech fault, cr Koblenz; 1EVD 2KIA 6POW; MACR 11987. MISS YU II.

42-97165 Del Cheyenne 4/2/44; Nashville 19/2/44; Morrison 5/3/44; Homestead 17/3/44; ass 353BS/301BG Lucera 16/3/44; MIA Munich 19/7/44 w/McGill; mech fault, cr Lesach, Ger?; 10POW. MACR 6910. SLEEPY TIME GAL.

42-97166 Del Cheyenne 4/2/44; Kearney 15/2/44; Grenier 25/2/44; ass 337BS/96BG Snetterton 7/3/44; b/d Ruhland 24/8/44 w/Bauman; ditched Channel; 9RTD. MACR 3591. OLD GATEMOUTH.

42-97167 Del Cheyenne 7/2/44; Hunter 23/2/44; Grenier 4/3/44; ass 339BS/96BG [QJ-N] Snetterton 7/3/44; MIA Brux 12/5/44 w/Capt Link; e/a, cr Hahsatten, Ger; 9KIA 1POW; MACR 4858.

42-97168 Del Cheyenne 5/2/44; Kearney 16/2/44; Grenier 25/2/44; ass 336BS/95BG [ET-C] Horham 3/3/44; b/d Achmer 8/4/44 w/McCall; c/l RAF Beccles, UK; 10RTD; sal 12/4/44.

42-97169 Del Cheyenne 5/2/44; Gr Island 16/2/44; Presque Is 11/3/44; ass 509BS/351BG [RQ-N] Polebrook 24/3/44; {109m} RetUS Bradley 14/6/45; 4168 BU Sth Plains 21/10/45; RFC Kingman 2/12/45. MY GAL SAL II.

42-97170 Del Cheyenne 5/2/44; Kearney 13/2/44; ass 527BS/379BG [FO-A] Kimbolton 30/3/44; MIA Stuttgart 9/12/44 w/?; mid air coll w/42-97833; cr Echterdingen, Ger; sal 16/12/44. JULIE MAY.

42-97171 Del Cheyenne 3/2/44; Kearney 24/2/44; Grenier 8/3/44; ass 563BS/388BG Knettishall 12/3/44; MIA Paris 2/8/44 w/?; flak, cr Pierrelay, Fr; 1EVD 1KIA 7POW; MACR 7745. 4TH TERM.

42-97172 Del Cheyenne 5/2/44; Gr Island 19/2/44; Presque Is 12/3/44; ass 561BS/388BG Knettishall 12/4/44; MIA Poltava 21/6/44; sal Russia; retUS 1103 BU Morrison 1/10/45; RFC Walnut Ridge 20/12/45.

42-97173 Del Cheyenne 15/2/44; Rapid City 5/3/44; Dow Fd 21/4/44; ass 398BG Nuthampstead 25/4/44; tran 323BS/91BG Bassingbourn 9/5/44; MIA {12m} Etaples 8/7/44 w/Fore; flak, cr Chartres, Fr; 1KIA 7POW 1RTD; MACR 8323. TAKE IT EASY.

42-97174 Del Cheyenne 3/2/44; Nashville 19/2/44; Hunter 23/2/44; Grenier 17/3/44; ass 534BS/381BG [GD-P] Ridgewell 7/4/44; MIA {12+m} Berlin 21/6/44 w/Pendergist; flak, cr Wagnitzer, Ger; 2KIA 7POW; MACR 5993. JOANNE.

42-97175 Del Cheyenne 5/2/44; Hunter 24/2/44; Presque Is 13/3/44; Slated 447BG, ass 728BS/452BG Deopham Green 14/3/44; MIA {85m} Strasbourg 6/2/45 w/Bayless; flak, cr Strasbourg; 1KIA 8POW; MACR 12240. LADY SATAN.

42-97176 Del Cheyenne 7/2/44; Gr Island 15/2/44; Presque Is 4/3/44; ass 710BS/447BG Rattlesden 4/3/44; MIA Brussels 20/5/44 w/Kesterke; shot down by B-17, cr Channel; 8KIA 2RTD. MACR 4939.

42-97177 Del Cheyenne 3/2/44 (F-9); Gt Falls 8/2/44; 11 Ph Gp Bolling 19/6/44; 311 Ph Gp Buckley 10/7/44; 610 BU Eglin 20/8/44; 326 BU McDill 27/3/45; 16 Ph Gp McDill 17/4/45; 343 RVM McDill 17/5/45; 307 MSU McDill 18/7/45; US Coast Guard Sep/48; 3902 AB Gp Offutt 14/4/49; re-ass USN as PB-1R Apr/50, then scrapped.

42-97178 Del Cheyenne 7/2/44; Gr Island 17/2/44; Grenier 13/3/44; ass 96BG Snetterton 15/3/44; tran 545BS/384BG [JD-N] Grafton Underwood 16/3/44; MIA Augsburg 19/7/44 w/Heim; e/a, cr Perchting, Ger; 7KIA 2POW; MACR 7279.

42-97179 Del Cheyenne 4/2/44; Gr Island 27/2/44; Grenier 10/3/44; ass 711BS/447BG Rattlesden 22/3/44; MIA Brux 12/5/44 w/Pettus; e/a, cr Friedberg, Ger; 10POW; MACR 4768.

42-97180 Del Cheyenne 4/2/44; Gr Island 22/2/44; Grenier 23/3/44; ass 423BS/306BG [RD-K] Thurleigh 2/4/44; MIA Brux 12/9/44 w/Freeman; e/a, cr Berlin; 6KIA 3POW; MACR 8832.

42-97181 Del Cheyenne 6/2/44; Hunter 22/2/44; Morrison 5/3/44; Dow Fd 8/4/44; ass 327BS/92BG [UX-X] Podington 9/4/44; tran 369BS/306BG [WW-B] Thurleigh 25/4/44; 92BG Podington 9/5/45; sal 31/10/45. STEADY HEDY.

42-97182 Del Cheyenne 6/2/44; Kearney 24/2/44; Grenier 13/3/44; ass 568BS/390BG [BI-P] Framlingham 16/3/44; b/d Brest gun batteries 26/8/44 w/?; mid air coll w/42-102936, cr Weston, UK (14 crew killed plus two civilians); sal 27/8/44. DING DONG DADDY.

42-97183 Del Cheyenne 8/2/44; Nashville 20/2/44; Morrison 5/3/44; Homestead 15/3/44; ass 96BS/2BG Amendola 18/3/44; MIA {41m} Bleckhammer 7/7/44 w/Corpening; e/a, cr Senica, It?. MACR 6568.

42-97184 Del Cheyenne 4/2/44; Gr Island 19/2/44; Presque Is 12/3/44; ass 562BS/388BG Knettishall 11/3/44; c/l base 26/8/44; sal 30/10/44. LADY GODIVA.

42-97185 Del Cheyenne 4/2/44; Wright 23/2/44; Gr Island 28/2/44; Grenier 13/3/44; ass 96BG Snetterton 20/3/44; tran 369BS/306BG [WW-J] Thurleigh 31/3/44; MIA Dresden 14/2/45 w/Capt Lewis; e/a, cr Bad Belohrad, Ger?; 1KIA 8POW; MACR 12333.

42-97186 Del Cheyenne 6/2/44; Savannah 24/2/44; Morrison 4/3/44; ass 353BS/301BG Lucera 8/3/44; MIA {3m} Budapest 14/6/44 w/Stone; exploded soon after take off; 3KIA 7RTD.

42-97187 Del Cheyenne 4/2/44; Gr Island 23/2/44; Presque is 11/3/44; slated 447BG, ass 360BS/303BG [PU-I] Molesworth 26/3/44; MIA Magdeburg 28/9/44 w/Miller; e/a, cr Witmar, Ger; 6KIA 3POW; MACR 9410. MISS UMBRIAGO.

42-97188 Del Cheyenne 8/2/44; Gr Island 20/2/44; Grenier 22/3/44; ass 544BS/384BG [SU-A] Grafton Underwood 6/4/44; MIA Le Bourget 14/6/44 w/Summerville; e/a, cr Châteaudun, Fr; 3EVD 3KIA 3POW; MACR 5800.

42-97189 Del Cheyenne 4/2/44; Hunter 23/2/44; Savannah 1/3/44; Morrison 9/3/44; ass 32BS/301BG Lucera 14/3/44; MIA {32m} Ploesti 23/6/44 w/Cooke; e/a, cr target area; 1KIA 9POW; MACR 5080.

42-97190 Del Cheyenne 5/2/44; Gr Island 18/2/44; Grenier 10/3/44; ass 748BS/457BG Glatton 24/3/44; 749BS; f/l Florennes, Bel a/fd 17/9/44; rep & ret 7/12/44; retUS Bradley 7/6/45; 4168 BU Sth Plains 21/10/45; RFC Kingman 5/12/45. HITLER'S MILKMAN.

42-97191 Del Cheyenne 5/2/44; Memphis 21/2/44; Presque Is 1/3/44; ass 303BG Molesworth 6/3/44; tran 511BS/351BG [DS-X] Polebrook 25/3/44; MIA {16m} Ruhland 28/5/44 w/Miller; e/a, cr Flur Medlitz, Ger?; 5EVD 4KIA; MACR 5326. SILVER BALL.

42-97192 Del Cheyenne 5/2/44; Gr Island 18/2/44; Grenier 10/3/44; ass 562BS/388BG Knettishall 12/3/44; MIA Rostock 11/4/44 w/Thomas; e/a, c/l Gardsanga, Swed; 9INT 1KIA; MACR 3775. BOTTLED IN BOND.

42-97193 Del Cheyenne 5/2/44; Kearney 24/2/44; Grenier 8/3/44; ass 509BS/351BG [RQ-P] Polebrook 24/3/44; {81m} RetUS Bradley 14/6/45; 4168 BU Sth Plains 21/10/44; RFC Kingman 4/12/45. STAR DUSTER.

42-97194 Del Cheyenne 5/2/44; Kearney 24/2/44; Presque Is 11/3/44; ass 336BS/95BG [ET-O] Horham 11/3/44; retUS Bradley 25/6/45; 4168 BU Sth Plains 21/10/45; RFC Kingman 8/12/45.

42-97195 Del Cheyenne 5/2/44; Kearney 24/2/44; Presque Is 11/3/44; Slated 452BG, ass 337BS/96BG [AW-Q] Snetterton 13/3/44; MIA Magdeburg 4/8/44 w/Wynne; flak, cr Wittstadt, Ger; 6KIA 3POW; MACR 7741. MISS MINNEAPOLIS.

42-97196 Del Cheyenne 5/2/44; Hunter 15/2/44; Presque Is 10/3/44; ass 510BS/351BG [TU-M] Polebrook 24/3/44; MIA Politz 7/10/44 w/Evans; flak, f/l Kykoping-Skavsta, Swed; 9INT; MACR 9568; left 23/5/45; retUS Bradley 29/6/45; 4168 BU Sth Plains 21/10/45; RFC Kingman 27/11/45. BOBBIE ANNE.

42-97197 Del Cheyenne 5/2/44; Hunter 22/2/44; Morrison 5/3/44; slated 711BS/447BG, ass 419BS/301BG Lucera 17/3/44; {8m} crashed and burned on practice mission 8/4/44 w/Griffin; 7KIA plus three army officers, one English.

42-97198 Del Cheyenne 5/2/44; Nashville 20/2/44; Savannah 14/3/44; ass 2BG Amendola 17/3/44, confirmed 22/3/44.

42-97199 Del Cheyenne 7/2/44; Gr Island 22/2/44; Grenier 21/2/44; ass 324BS/91BG Bassingbourn 7/4/44; MIA St Avord 28/4/44 w/Cater; flak, cr St Avord, Fr; 3RVD 7POW; MACR 4235.

42-97200 Del Cheyenne 5/2/44; Gr Island 20/2/44; Presque Is 12/3/44; ass 728BS/452BG Deopham Green 12/3/44; MIA Châteaudun 28/3/44 w/Robinson; flak, cr Châteaudun, Fr; MACR 3489. KICKAPOO JOY JUICE.

42-97201 Del Cheyenne 6/2/44; Kearney 27/2/44; Grenier 20/3/44; ass 547BS/384BG [SO-J] Grafton Underwood 31/3/44; sal 24/7/44. JAMAICA MARY.

42-97202 Del Cheyenne 6/2/44; Gr Island 23/2/44; Presque Is 12/3/44; ass 509BS/351BG [RQ-Z] Polebrook 6/4/44; MIA French a/fds 22/6/44 w/Watkins; flak, cr Rouen; 2EVD 1KIA 5POW; MACR 6535.

42-97203 Del Cheyenne 6/2/44; Kearney 25/2/44; Presque Is 5/3/44; ass 407BS/92BG [PY-P] Podington 22/3/44; MIA Oberpfaffenhofen 24/4/44 w/Parramore; e/a, f/l Altenrhein, Switz; 10INT; MACR 4149.

42-97204 Del Cheyenne 6/2/44; Gr Island 23/2/44; Grenier 13/3/44; ass 547BS/384BG [SO-K] Grafton Underwod 30/3/44; MIA Gelsenkirchen 26/8/44 w/Rainey; flak, cr Wezep, Hol; 1EVD 1KIA 8POW; MACR 8466. SKY LARK.

42-97205 Del Cheyenne 6/2/44; Gr Island 22/2/44; Presque Is 12/3/44; ass 336BS/95BG [ET-L] Horham 14/3/44; b/d Merseburg 28/7/44 w/Snowden; 10RTD. Sal 29/7/44.

42-97206 Del Cheyenne 6/2/44; Gr Island 25/2/44; Presque Is 10/3/44; ass 452BG Deopham Green 16/3/44; b/d Rechlin, Ger 25/8/44 w/?; f/l continent; sal 14/11/44.

42-97207 Del Cheyenne 6/2/44; Gr Island 22/2/44; Grenier 13/3/44; ass 549BS/385BG Gt Ashfield 16/3/44; b/d Brux 12/5/44 w/?; sal 15/5/44. MACR 4880.

42-97208 Del Cheyenne 6/2/44; Kearney 24/2/44; Grenier 8/3/44; Presque Is 10/3/44; slated 305BG; W/O 13/3/44.

42-97209 Del Cheyenne 6/2/44; Kearney 23/2/44; Presque Is 11/3/44; ass 728BS/452BG Deopham Green 11/3/44; MIA Brux 12/5/44 w/Hochstetter; e/a, cr Frankfurt; 10POW; MACR 4777.

42-97210 Del Cheyenne 6/2/44; Kearney 27/2/44; Grenier 9/3/44; ass 563BS/388BG Knettishall 22/3/44; retUS Bradley 28/6/45; 4168 BU Sth Plains 21/10/45; RFC Kingman 10/12/45. JAMAICAN GINGER II.

42-97211 Del Cheyenne 10/2/44; Gr Island 22/2/44; Grenier 13/3/44; ass 548BS/385BG Gt Ashfield 16/3/44; MIA Munich 11/7/44 w/Henderson; flak, cr Augsburg; 10POW; MACR 7360.

42-97212 Del Cheyenne 10/2/44; Gr Island 22/2/44; Presque Is 12/3/44; ass 339BS/96BG [QJ-G] Snetterton 16/3/44; MIA Rostock 11/4/44 w/Gillespie; e/a, f/l Bulltofta, Swed; 10INT; MACR 3817. RetUS Hunter 1/8/45; 4185 BU Independence 30/11/45; RFC Kingman 16/12/45.

42-97213 Del Cheyenne 9/2/44; Gt Falls 10/3/44; Des Moines 19/3/44; 330 BU Dyersburg 1/3/45; RFC Walnut Ridge 14/12/45.

42-97214 Del Cheyenne 8/2/44; Kearney 27/2/44; Grenier 8/3/44; ass 534BS/381BG [GD-B] Ridgewell 25/3/44; MIA {2m} Berlin 8/5/44 w/Wardencki; mid air coll, cr Gratze, Ger; 9KIA; MACR 5181. CAROLINA QUEEN.

42-97215 Del Cheyenne 8/2/44; Kearney 24/2/44; Presque Is 12/3/44; ass 334BS/95BG [BG-J] Horham 12/3/44; MIA Hamburg 31/12/44 w/Reed; cr Wesermunde, Ger; 3KIA 1MIA 5POW; MACR 11368.

42-97216 Del Cheyenne 8/2/44; Gr Island 4/3/44; Grenier 2/4/44; ass 509BS/351BG [RQ-U] Polebrook 12/4/44; 510BS [TU-U]; {79m} burned on base 8/5/45; sal 2 SAD 11/5/45. 2 AND 6.

42-97217 Del Cheyenne 8/2/44; Kearney 27/2/44; Presque Is 6/3/44; ass 326BS/92BG [JW-L] Podington 23/3/44; b/d Ludwigshafen 5/9/44 w/Anthony; f/l France. MACR 4852. PUNKIN.

42-97218 Del Cheyenne 8/2/44; Kearney 23/2/44; Grenier 8/3/44; ass 326BS/92BG Podington 24/3/44; MIA Erding 24/4/44 w/Anthony; e/a, cr Ruback, Ger?; 2EVD 8POW; MACR 4150. TOONERVILLE TROLLEY.

42-97219 Del Cheyenne 8/2/44; Kearney 24/2/44; Grenier 12/3/44; ass 560BS/388BG Knettishall 12/3/44; MIA Merseburg 28/9/44 w/Olson; flak, cr Merseburg; 1KIA 8POW; MACR 9378. REVEL'S REVENGE.

42-97220 Del Cheyenne 8/2/44; Gr Island 23/2/44; Grenier 13/3/44; ass 730BS/385BG Gt Ashfield 15/3/44; tran 728BS/452BG Deopham Green 16/3/44; MIA Berlin 8/5/44 w/Morehouse; cr Salzdahlen, Ger; 10POW; MACR 4589. KICKAPOO JOY JUICE.

42-97221 Del Cheyenne 8/2/44; Kearney 25/2/44; Dow Fd 4/4/44; Langford Lodge, UK 3/4/44; ass 92BG Podington 24/3/44; tran 384BG Grafton Underwood 15/4/44; MIA Augsburg 24/4/44 w/Brouillard; e/a, cr Augsburg; 10POW; MACR 4351.

42-97222 Del Cheyenne 8/2/44; Gr Island 19/2/44; Presque Is 11/3/44; ass 728BS/452BG Deopham Green 13/3/44; b/d Chemnitz, Ger 6/2/45 w/?; f/l continent; sal 20/5/45. DUECES WILD.

42-97223 Del Cheyenne 8/2/44; Kearney 27/2/44; Presque Is 10/3/44; ass 412BS/95BG [QW-H] Horham 13/3/44; MIA Rostock 11/4/44 w/Powell; e/a, ditched Baltic; 1KIA 9POW; MACR 3807.

42-97224 Del Cheyenne 8/2/44; Kearney 21/2/44; crashed and W/O 8/3/44.

42-97225 Del Cheyenne 9/2/44; Kearney 27/2/44; Grenier 2/4/44; ass 325BS/92BG [NV-D] Podington 15/4/44; 326BS; MIA Munich 16/7/44 w/Huettel; e/a, cr Nuremburg; 2KIA 7POW; MACR 7566. BATTLE BABY.

42-97226 Del Cheyenne 9/2/44; Kearney 24/2/44; Presque Is 10/3/44; ass 551BS/385BG Gt Ashfield 11/3/44; MIA Berlin 29/4/44 W/Huntingdon; e/a, cr Magdeburg; 2KIA 8POW; MACR 4458.

42-97227 Del Cheyenne 9/2/44; Kearney 23/2/44; Grenier 10/3/44; ass 326BS/92BG [JW-P] Podington 27/3/44; c/t/o Kassel 2/10/44; sal 4/10/44. COOKIN' WITH GAS.

42-97228 Del Cheyenne 9/2/44; Gr Island 23/2/44; Presque Is 12/3/44; ass 988BG Nuthampstead 16/3/44; tran 545BS/384BG [JD-G] Grafton Underwood 31/3/44; MIA Schweinfurt 13/4/44 w/Poole; e/a, cr Messbach, Ger?; 1KIA 9POW; MACR 3871. G.I. JIVE.

42-97229 Del Cheyenne 9/12/44; Kearney 21/2/44; Presque Is 6/3/44; ass 524BS/379BG [WA-Q] Kimbolton 23/3/44; b/d Ruhland 12/9/44 w/?; prop off, hit nose; sal 2 SAD 14/9/44. HI HO SILVER.

42-97230 Del Cheyenne 9/2/44; Rapid City 26/2/44; Dow Fd 18/4/44; ass 398BG Nuthampstead 28/4/44; tran 418BS/100BG [LD-Q] Thorpe Abbotts 29/4/44; b/d Nurnburg, Ger 20/2/45 w/?; f/l continent; sal. LAY OR BUST.

42-97231 Del Cheyenne 9/2/44; Kearney 27/2/44; Grenier 5/3/44; ass 547BS/384BG [SO-D] Grafton Underwood 24/3/44; MIA Schweinfurt 13/4/44 w/Tollisen; e/a, cr Wittlich, Ger?; 4KIA 6POW; MACR 3872.

42-97232 Del Cheyenne 9/2/44; Kearney 24/2/44; Grenier 8/3/44; ass 412BS/95BG [QW-O] Horham 12/3/44 GOVERNMENT PROPERTY; MIA Stuttgart 16/12/44 w/Coffman; cr off Zodutelande, Hol; 9KIA; MACR 11259. G.I. ISSUE.

42-97233 Del Cheyenne 9/2/44; Dalhart 2/3/44; Presque Is 25/3/44; ass 545BS/384BG [JD-K] Grafton Underwood 9/4/44; MIA Schweinfurt 13/4/44 w/Briley; e/a, cr target area; 1KIA 9POW; MACR 3874.

42-97234 Del Cheyenne 9/2/44; Gr Island 27/2/44; Grenier 20/3/44; ass 322BS/91BG [LG-M] Bassingbourn 7/4/44; MIA {30+m} Merseburg 2/11/44 w/Sparkman; e/a, cr Barby, Ger; 6KIA 3POW; MACR 10360. BOMBER DEAR.

42-97235 Del Cheyenne 9/2/44; Kearney 27/2/44; Grenier 13/3/44; ass 729BS/452BG Deopham Green 16/3/44; MIA Brux 12/5/44 W/Naylor; e/a, cr Tanus, Ger?; 5KIA 5POW; MACR 4778.

42-97236 Del Cheyenne 10/2/44; Kearney 4/3/44; Presque Is 11/3/44; ass 748BS/452BG Deopham Green 31/3/44; c/l base, sal 23/4/45.

42-97237 Del Cheyenne 10/2/44; Kearney 24/2/44; Grenier 8/3/44; ass 547BS/384BG [SO-G] Grafton Underwood 24/3/44; MIA Freidrichshafen 19/7/44 w/Mount; e/a, f/l Dubendorf, Switz; 8INT 1KIA; MACR 7280. ROYAL FLUSH II.

42-97238 Del Cheyenne 10/2/44; Kearney 25/2/44; Presque Is 22/3/44; ass 534BS/381BG [GD-I] Ridgewell 6/4/44; MIA {3m} Kerlin-Bastard, Fr 8/6/44 w/Martyniak; ditched Channel, 10RTD. OUR CAPTAIN.

42-97239 Del Cheyenne 10/2/44; Gr Island 27/2/44; McDill 22/3/44; ass 369BS/306BG [WW-L] Thurleigh 2/4/44; MIA Berlin 8/5/44 w/Lambert; mid air coll, cr Warnsdorf, Ger; 7KIA 3POW; MACR 4555.

42-97240 Del Cheyenne 10/2/44; Kearney 24/2/44; Presque Is 12/3/44; ass 325BS/92BG [JW-P] Podington 1/4/44; MIA Rostock 11/4/44 w/Rasmussen; e/a, cr Buchholz, Ger; 1EVD 9KIA; MACR 3673.

42-97241 Del Cheyenne 10/2/44; Gr Island 4/3/44; Grenier 20/3/44; ass 563BS/388BG Knettishall 22/3/44; MIA Rostock 11/4/44 w/Ely; e/a, cr Mecklenburg, Ger; 4KIA 6POW; MACR 3776.

42-97242 Del Cheyenne 10/2/44; Kearney 27/2/44; Grenier 12/3/44; ass 568BS/390BG Framlingham 13/3/44; MIA Brandenburg 18/4/44 w/Wassel; flak, cr Germendorf, Ger; 10KIA; MACR 4014.

42-97243 Del Cheyenne 10/2/44; Kearney 27/2/44; Presque Is 10/3/44; ass 325BS/92BG [JW-O] Podington 23/3/44; MIA Rostock 11/4/44 w/Easley; e/a, cr Stargard?; 10POW; MACR 3674.

42-97244 Del Cheyenne 10/2/44; Kearney 27/2/44; Dow Fd 9/4/44; ass 407BS/92BG [PY-N] Podington 25/4/44; landing acc 19/5/44; sal 2 SAD 21/5/44.

42-97245 Del Cheyenne 11/2/44; Dallas 2/3/44; Kearney 1/4/44; Dow Fd 7/4/44; ass 407BS/92BG Podington 25/4/44; MIA Hamburg 20/6/44 w/Wareham; flak, cr Wangerooge, Hol; 8KIA 1POW; MACR 5984.

42-97246 Del Cheyenne 11/2/44; Kearney 27/2/44; Presque Is 11/3/44; ass 401BS/91BG Bassingbourn 25/3/44; MIA Brunswick 29/3/44 w/Anderson; e/a, cr Nuenkirchen, Ger; 5KIA 5POW; MACR 3474.

42-97247 Del Cheyenne 11/2/44; Rapid City 2/3/44; Grenier 20/4/44; ass 452BG Deopham Green 22/4/44; b/d Poltava 21/6/44 w/?; sal 7/7/44.

42-97248 Del Cheyenne 11/2/44; Kearney 27/2/44; Presque Is 16/3/44; ass 332BS/94BG [XM-U] Rougham 13/3/44; 410BS [GL-U]; b/d Merseburg 25/11/44 w/?; f/l continent, sal 13/12/44.

42-97249 Del Cheyenne 11/2/44; Kearney 2/3/44; Dow Fd 6/4/44; ass 600BS/398BG [N8-P] Nuthampstead 26/4/44; 603BS; retUS Bradley 6/6/45; Sth Plains 11/6/45; RFC Kingman 20/12/45. HOW WAS IT? WELL?

42-97250 Del Cheyenne 11/2/44; Gr Island 4/3/44; Grenier 23/3/44; ass 423BS/306BG Thurleigh 6/4/44; MIA Hamburg 20/6/44 w/Latham; flak, cr Hamburg; 5KIA 4POW; MACR 5987.

42-97251 Del Cheyenne 11/2/44; Gr Island 27/2/44; Grenier 13/3/44; ass 546BS/384BG [BK-O] Grafton Underwood 24/3/44; b/d Aschaffenburg 21/1/45 w/?; c/l and exploded, sal

42-97252 Del Cheyenne 11/2/44; Rapid City 5/3/44; Dow Fd 28/4/44; ass 398BG Nuthampstead 6/5/44; tran 510BS/351BG [TU-K] Polebrook 24/5/44; {92m} RetUS Bradley 11/6/45; 4168 BU Sth Plains 21/10/45; RFC Kingman 4/12/45. DEVIL'S MISTRESS.

42-97253 Del Cheyenne 12/2/44; Kearney 27/2/44; Grenier 26/3/44; ass 332BS/94BG [XM-T] Rougham 6/4/44; 410BS [GL-T]; MIA Hamburg 31/12/44 w/Rosenzweig; flak, cr Twirlstringen, Ger; 9POW; MACR 11370. MORGAN'S RAIDERS.

42-97254 Del Cheyenne 11/2/44; Kearney 27/2/44; Presque Is 11/3/44; ass 360BS/303BG [PU-K] Molesworth 26/3/44; sal b/d 8/5/44. IZA VAILABLE TOO.

42-97255 Del Cheyenne 11/2/44; Kearney 4/3/44; Grenier 10/3/44; ass 563BS/388BG Knettishall 12/3/44; MIA Rostock 11/4/44 w/Osterkamp; e/a, cr Rostock; 1OKIA; MACR 3777.

42-97256 Del Cheyenne 11/2/44; Kearney 27/2/44; Presque Is 10/3/44; ass 452BG Deopham Green 16/3/44; dest by e/a at Poltava 21/6/44; sal Russia 2/7/44. BIG TIME OPERATOR.

42-97257 Del Cheyenne 11/2/44; Dalhart 3/3/44; Grenier 26/3/44; ass 412BS/95BG [QW-L] Horham 28/3/44; retUS Bradley 26/6/45; 4168 BU Sth Plains 28/6/45; RFC Kingman 8/11/45. KNOCK-OUT BABY.

42-97258 Del Cheyenne 11/2/44; Kearney 27/2/44; Grenier 8/3/44; ass 508BS/351BG [YB-P] Polebrook 24/4/44; {84m} RetUS Bradley 31/5/44; 4168 BU Sth Plains 21/10/45; RFC Kingman 13/12/45. SILVER METEOR.

42-97259 Del Cheyenne 12/2/44; Gr Island 4/3/44; Grenier 22/3/44; ass 423BS/306BG Thurleigh 6/4/44; MIA Berlin 8/5/44 w/Smith; flak, cr Havelte, Hol; 10KIA; MACR 4556.

42-97260 Del Cheyenne 12/2/44; Kearney 4/3/44; Presque Is 11/3/44; ass 360BS/303BG [PU-Q] Molesworth 26/3/44; MIA Saarbrücken 11/5/44 w/Long; flak, cr Saarbrücken, Ger; 8KIA 3POW; MACR 4868. BOW-ER-NECK-STEVENS.

42-97261 Del Cheyenne 12/2/44; Kearney 26/3/44; ass 527BS/379BG [FO-P] Kimbolton 8/4/44; MIA Hamburg 20/6/44 w/Wheat; flak, ditched Channel; 9RTD.

42-97262 Del Cheyenne 12/2/44; Kearney 12/3/44; Grenier 2/4/44; ass 413BS/96BG [MZ-F] Snetterton 6/4/44; MIAMerseburg 29/7/44 w/Colflesh; flak, cr Boebber, Ger; 9KIA; MACR 7808. SILVER SLIPPER.

42-97263 Del Cheyenne 12/2/44; Dalhart 2/3/44; Kearney 1/4/44; Grenier 6/4/44; ass 547BS/384BG [SO-D] Grafton Underwood 15/4/44; c/t/o 10/1/45, sal.

42-97264 Del Cheyenne 12/2/44; Kearney 27/2/44; Grenier 2/3/44; slated 447BG, ass 334BS/95BG [BG-H] Horham 10/3/44; MIA Merseburg 7/10/44 w/Neal; cr Jena-Leebstedt, Ger; 1KIA 9POW; MACR 9560. SHOO SHOO BABY.

42-97265 Del Cheyenne 12/2/44; Rapid City 5/3/44; Gr Island 13/4/44; Dow Fd 14/4/44; ass 398BG Nuthampstead 24/4/44; tran 535BS/381BG [MS-P] Ridgewell 27/4/44; retUS Bradley 10/6/45; Sth Plains 12/6/45; RFC Kingman 28/11/45. HELL'S ANGEL.

42-97266 Del Cheyenne 12/2/44; Kearney 29/9/44; Presque Is 12/3/44; ass 388BG Knettishall 12/3/44; tran 602BS/398BG [K8-G] Nuthampstead 12/1/45; MIA Pilsen 25/4/45 w/Ferguson; flak, cr Pilsen, Czech; 6KIA 2POW; MACR 14224. GODFATHER'S INC.

42-97267 Del Cheyenne 12/2/44; Rapid City 5/3/44; Dow Fd 14/4/44; ass 398BG Nuthampstead 22/4/44; tran 535BS/381BG [MS-X] Ridgewell 27/4/44; caught fire and exploded base 25/4/45; sal 26/4/45. THE TOMAHAWK WARRIOR.

42-97268 Del Cheyenne 12/2/44; Rapid City 5/3/44; Dow Fd 14/4/44; ass 410BS/94BG [GL-Z] Rougham 6/4/44; tran 34BG Mendlesham /45; retUS Bradley 4/8/45; 4185 BU Independence 30/11/45; RFC Kingman 27/12/45. MILLION DOLLAR BABY.

42-97269 Del Cheyenne 12/2/44; Dalhart 2/3/44; Grenier 2/4/44; ass 398BG Nuthampstead 22/4/44; tran 337BS/96BG [AW-U] Snetterton 28/4/44; MIA Karlsruhe 27/5/44 w/Zeigler; mid air coll w/42-102515; cr Vily, Fr; 10KIA; MACR 5161.

42-97270 Del Cheyenne 12/2/44; Rapid City 5/3/44; Grenier 14/4/44; ass 398BG Nuthampstead 24/4/44; tran 527BS/379BG [FO-H] Kimbolton 29/4/44; 838BS/487BG [2C] Lavenham 22/5/45; retUS Bradley 13/7/45; 4185 BU Independence 10/11/45; RFC Kingman 15/12/45.

42-97271 Del Cheyenne 15/2/44; Dalhart 29/2/44; Dow Fd 3/4/44; ass 545BS/384BG [JD-A] Grafton Underwood 25/4/44; MIA Hamburg 30/3/45 w/Hicks; flak, cr Ramhausen, Ger; 1KIA 8POW; MACR 13565. BOSS LADY.

42-97272 Del Cheyenne 13/2/44; Dalhart 2/3/44; Grenier 26/3/44; ass 359BS/303BG [BN-T] Molesworth 9/4/44; sal 2 SAD 7/7/44. DUCHESS' DAUGHTER.

42-97273 Del Cheyenne 15/2/44; Dalhart 1/3/44; Grenier 26/3/44; ass 546BS/384BG [BK-F] Grafton Underwood 9/4/44; MIA Munich 12/7/44 w/Roseborough; flak, cr Munich; 4KIA 5POW; MACR 7568. ACES & EIGHTS.

42-97274 Del Cheyenne 15/2/44; Gr Island 29/2/44; Grenier 22/3/44; ass 547BS/384BG [SO-M] Grafton Underwood 6/4/44; MIA Schweinfurt 13/4/44 w/Lavin; flak, cr Brussels; 3EVD 6KIA 3POW; MACR 3873.

42-97275 Del Cheyenne 15/2/44; Rapid City 5/3/44; Gr Island 27/4/44; ass 398BG Nuthampstead 3/5/44; tran 549BS/385BG Gt Ashfield 4/5/44 REBEL; 551BS; MIA Munich 6/10/44 w/Leverett; e/a, cr Vehlgast, Ger?; 1KIA 9POW; MACR 9522. ROGER THE DODGER.

42-97276 Del Cheyenne 15/2/44; Gr Island 4/3/44; Grenier 10/3/44; ass 323BS/91BG [OR-S/B] Bassingbourn 7/3/44; {83+m} RetUS Bradley 6/6/45; Sth Plains 11/6/45; RFC Kingman 1/12/45. SWEET 17 THE SPIRIT OF ST LOUIS.

42-97277 Del Cheyenne 12/2/44; Wright Fd 6/3/44; Lowry 16/3/44; W/O 16/3/44.

42-97278 Del Cheyenne 12/2/44; Rapid City 4/3/44; Gr Island 19/4/44; Dow Fd 21/4/44; ass 398BG Nuthampstead 25/4/44; tran 367BS/306BG [GY-K] Thurleigh 12/5/44; MIA Ruhland 12/9/44 w/Wagener; e/a, cr Uedersee, Ger; 2KIA 7POW; MACR 8833. UMBRIAGO.

42-97279 Del Cheyenne 16/2/44; Kearney 4/3/44; Grenier 10/3/44; ass Soxo 26/2/44; con 13/3/44.

42-97280 Del Cheyenne 15/2/44; Rapid City 4/3/44; Dow Fd 28/4/44; ass 398BG Nuthampstead 3/5/44; tran 550BS/385BG Gt Ashfield 6/5/44; {105m} c/l Valley, UK 19/6/45; sal 26/6/45. "HAY BAG" ANNIE.

42-97281 Del Cheyenne 12/2/44; Dalhart 2/3/44; Kearney 25/3/44; Grenier 26/3/44; ass 427BU/303BG [GN-Q] Molesworth 12/4/44; b/d Berlin 28/3/45 w/?; c/l Rye, UK; sal 2 SAD 31/3/45. QUEENY.

42-97282 Del Cheyenne 13/2/44; Kearney 25/3/44; Presque Is 26/3/44; ass 544BS/384BG [SU-H] Grafton Underwood 27/4/44; MIA Hamburg 8/11/44 w/Drake; flak, cr Neirstein, Ger; 1KIA 8POW; MACR 10352. REBEL.

42-97283 Del Cheyenne 13/2/44; Rapid City 3/3/44; Dow Fd 28/4/44; ass 398BG Nuthampstead 1/5/44; tran 452BG Deopham Green 2/5/44; dest by e/a Poltava 21/6/44; sal Russia 2/7/44.

42-97284 Del Cheyenne 15/2/44; Dalhart 2/3/44; Grenier 26/3/44; ass 359BS/303BG [BN-C] Molesworth 9/4/44; tran 15AF Galera, Italy 16/7/44; re-ass 301BG Lucera 14/3/45; retUS Bradley 16/6/44; 4168 BU Sth Plains 21/10/45; RFC Kingman 7/12/45. AIN'T MISS BEA HAVEN.

42-97285 Del Cheyenne 15/2/44; Rapid City 5/3/44; Dow Fd 29/4/44; ass 398BG Nuthampstead 6/5/44; tran 534BS/381BG Ridgewell [GD-C] 21/5/44; {87+m} RetUS Bradley 10/6/45; Sth Plains 2/7/45; RFC Kingman 1/12/45. PATSY ANN.

42-97286 Del Cheyenne 15/2/44; Kearney 4/3/44; Grenier 15/3/44; ass 398BG Nuthampstead 12/3/44; tran 560BS/388BG Knettishall 13/3/44; c/l Isle of Arran, UK 11/2/45 w/Littlejohn; sal 15/3/45. SKIPPER 'N THE KIDS.

42-97287 Del Cheyenne 15/2/44; Dalhart 2/3/44; Grenier 6/4/44; ass 447BG Rattlesden 6/4/44; sal 22/4/44.

42-97288 Del Cheyenne 13/2/44; Rapid City 4/3/44; Gr Island 19/4/44; Dow Fd 21/4/44; ass 398BG Nuthampstead 24/4/44; tran 325BS/92BG [NV-U] Podington 7/5/44; MIA Berlin 18/3/45 w/Culver; flak, f/l Bulltofta, Swed; 9INT; MACR 13150. ret group /45; retUS Bradley 1/8/45; 4185 BU Independence 30/11/45; RFC Kingman 19/12/45. FLAGSHIP.

42-97289 Del Cheyenne 15/2/44; Rapid City 5/3/44; Dow Fd 14/4/44; ass 388BG Knettishall 20/4/44; sal

30/7/44;

42-97290 Del Cheyenne 15/2/44; Kearney 27/2/44; Presque Is 11/3/44; ass 398BG Nuthampstead 22/4/44; tran 334BS/95BG [BG-H] Horham 28/4/44; MIA Berlin 19/5/44 w/Capt Waltman; c/l Akesholm, Swed; 10INT; MACR 4928. SMILIN' SANDY SANCHEZ.

42-97291 Del Cheyenne 15/2/44; Rapid City 5/3/44; Grenier 14/4/44; ass 398BG Nuthampstead 17/4/44; 527BS/379BG [FO-S] Kimbolton 18/4/44; tran 359BS/303BG [BN-W] Molesworth 21/5/44; MIA Merseburg 24/8/44 w/Hillary; flak, cr Merseburg; 7KIA 2POW; MACR 8212. ASSENDRAGON.

42-97292 Del Cheyenne 16/2/44; Gr Island 2/3/44; Grenier 22/3/44; ass 322BS/91BG [LG-C] Bassingbourn 7/4/44; MIA {3+m} Toulouse 25/6/44 w/Goodrich; flak, f/l Spain; 9INT. MACR 6545. BACHELOR'S BRIDE.

42-97293 Del Cheyenne 16/2/44; Rapid City 6/3/44; Dow Fd 28/4/44; ass 398BG Nuthampstead 3/5/44; tran 326BS/92BG [JW-B] Podington 7/5/44; MIA Merkwille 3/8/44 w/Henrickson; e/a, cr Lesch, Ger; 3KIA 6POW; MACR 7699.

42-97294 Del Cheyenne 16/2/44; Gt Falls 19/2/44; Lowry 21/2/44; slated 398BG, ass 4CB Bowman 7/10/44; 3705 BU Lowry 15/7/45; RFC Kingman 9/12/46.

42-97295 Del Cheyenne 16/2/44; Rapid City 4/3/44; Dow Fd 28/4/44; ass 571BS/390BG Framlingham 29/4/44; MIA Karlsruhe 27/5/44 w/Schoenig; flak, cr St Omer, Fr; 5KIA 5POW; MACR 5255.

42-97296 Del Cheyenne 16/2/44; Rapid City 4/3/44; Dow Fd 28/4/44; ass 551BS/385BG Gt Ashfield 29/4/44; tran 711BS/447BG Rattlesden 30/4/44; non op taxi acc 20/4/45, sal.

42-97297 Del Cheyenne 16/2/44; Rapid City 3/3/44; Grenier 14/4/44; ass 398BG Nuthampstead 20/4/44; tran 369BS/306BG [WW-N] Thurleigh 26/4/44; 92BG Podington 9/5/45; sal 9AF Germany 31/10/45. HOW SOON?

42-97298 Del Cheyenne 16/2/44; Rapid City 4/3/44; Grenier 14/4/44; ass 398BG Nuthampstead 22/4/44; tran 96BG Snetterton 22/4/44; 358BS/303BG [VK-H] Molesworth 6/5/44; {100+m} c/l base 28/12/44; sal 2 SAD. THE FLOOSE.

42-97299 Del Cheyenne 16/2/44; Rapid City 5/3/44; Dow Fd 17/4/44; ass 398BG Nuthampstead 20/4/44; tran 326BS/92BG [JW-R] Podington 28/4/44; sal 9AF Germany 31/10/45. DEVIL MAY CARE.

42-97300 Del Cheyenne 16/2/44; Memphis 6/3/44; Grenier 7/4/44; ass 339BS/96BG [QJ-X] Snetterton 9/4/44; sal 21/6/44.

42-97301 Del Cheyenne 16/2/44; Rapid City 5/3/44; Grenier 20/3/44; ass 398BG Nuthampstead 25/4/44; tran 369BS/306BG [WW-U] Thurleigh 12/5/44; 92BG Podington 9/5/45; sal 9AF Germany 31/10/45. BOUNCING BABY.

42-97302 Del Cheyenne 16/2/44; Gr Island 4/3/44; Grenier 20/3/44; ass 525BS/379BG [FR-B] Kimbolton 9/4/44; b/d Nordstern 16/2/45 w/?; c/l base, sal.

42-97303 Del Cheyenne 16/2/44; Rapid City 3/3/44; Grenier 14/4/44; ass 398BG Nuthampstead 22/4/44; tran 369BS/306BG [WW-Q] Thurleigh 7/5/44; MIA Saarbrücken 11/5/44 w/Wills; flak, cr Hunkirch, Ger?; 1KIA 9POW; MACR 4557.

42-97304 Del Cheyenne 16/2/44; Gr Island 5/3/44; Grenier 20/3/44; ass 323BS/91BG [OR-C] Bassingbourn 1/4/44; MIA {50m} Munich 31/7/44 w/Supchak; flak, cr Newstift, Ger?; 9POW; MACR 7806. PRIORITY GAL.

42-97305 Del Cheyenne 17/2/44; Gr Island 4/3/44; Grenier 22/3/44; ass 511BS/351BG [DS-L] Polebrook 6/4/44; 508BS [YB-L]; MIA {5m} Metz 24/4/44 w/Evans; flak, ditched Channel; 10RTD.

42-97306 Del Cheyenne 17/2/44; Rapid City 5/3/44; Grenier 14/4/44; ass 398BG Nuthampstead 22/4/44; tran 729BS/452BG Deopham Green 23/4/44; b/d at Poltava 21/4/44; rep Russia; sal 17/8/45. LADY JANET. (Only ship to have two MOH awarded).

42-97307 Del Cheyenne 17/2/44; Rapid City 5/3/44; Dow Fd 28/4/44; ass 398BG Nuthampstead 3/5/44; tran 385BG Gt Ashfield 4/5/44; b/d Brux 12/9/44 w/?; f/l France; sal 3/1/45.

42-97308 Del Cheyenne 17/2/44; Rapid City 5/3/44; Dow Fd 14/4/44; ass 398BG Nuthampstead 25/4/44; tran 728BS/452BG Deopham Green 26/4/44; 730BS; MIA Bremen 31/3/45 w/Moore; flak, cr Zeitz; 5KIA 5POW; MACR 13733. HAIRLESS JOE.

42-97309 Del Cheyenne 17/2/44; Gr Island 4/3/44; Grenier 20/3/44; ass 545BS/384BG [JD-C] Grafton Underwood 6/4/44; sal 9AF Germany 31/10/45.

42-97310 Del Cheyenne 17/2/44; Rapid City 4/3/44; Dow Fd 28/4/44; ass 398BG Nuthampstead 3/5/44; tran 333BS/94BG Rougham 7/5/44; retUS Bradley 25/6/45; 4168 BU Sth Plains 21/10/45; RFC Kingman 19/12/45.

42-97311 Del Cheyenne 17/2/44; Rapid City 5/3/44; Dow Fd 28/4/44; ass 398BG Nuthampstead 1/5/44; tran 427BS/303BG [GN-O] Molesworth 13/5/44; 457BG Glatton 22/4/45; 351BG Polebrook 29/5/45; retUS Bradley 13/6/45; 4168 BU Sth Plains 21/10/45; RFC Kingman 27/11/45. SHOO SHOO "BABY".

42-97312 Del Cheyenne 17/2/44; Rapid City 4/3/44; Dow Fd 15/4/44; ass 398BG Nuthampstead 22/4/44; tran 367BS/306BG [GY-T] Thurleigh 12/5/44; MIA French A/fds 17/6/44 w/Dingham; flak, cr Bacqueville, Fr; 2EVD 7POW; MACR 5898.

42-97313 Del Cheyenne 17/2/44; Rapid City 10/3/44; Dow Fd 21/4/44; ass 398BG Nuthampstead 24/4/44; tran 535BS/381BG [MS-N] Ridgewell 5/5/44; b/d {51m} Cologne 14/1/45 w/Roebuck; two baled, f/l continent; MACR 11763. THE COLUMBUS MISS.

42-97314 Del Cheyenne 17/2/44; Rapid City 4/3/44; Dow Fd 14/4/44; ass 398BG Nuthampstead 26/4/44, LITTLE MAX; tran 327BS/92BG [UX-J] Podington 7/5/44; MIA Posen 29/5/44 w/Trost; e/a, c/l Bulltofta, Swed; 10INT. MACR 5345. POP.

42-97315 Del Cheyenne 17/2/44; Gr Island 5/3/44; Grenier 20/3/44; ass 532BS/381BG [VE-N] Ridgwell 6/4/44; mech test, c/l and burned Halstead, Ex. 5/5/44; No injuries; sal 2 SAD.

42-97316 Del Cheyenne 17/2/44; Gr Island 8/3/44; Grenier 22/3/44; ass 331BS/94BG Rougham 9/4/44; MIA Bohlen 7/10/44 w/Warren; e/a, cr Furstenburg, Ger; 9POW; MACR 9555. TOMMY.

42-97317 Del Cheyenne 18/2/44; Gr Island 9/3/44; Grenier 14/4/44; ass 603BS/398BG [N7-P] Nuthampstead 28/4/44; retUS Bradley 26/8/45; 4185 BU Independence 30/11/45; RFC Kingman 4/1/46.

42-97318 Del Cheyenne 18/2/44; Gr Island 8/3/44; Grenier 20/3/44; ass 511BS/351BG [DS-S] Polebrook 7/4/44; MIA {48m} Brux 12/9/44 w/Lopert; e/a, cr Stakken, Ger?; 2KIA 7POW; MACR 8898. DINA MITE.

42-97319 Del Cheyenne 18/2/44; Hunter 9/3/44; Grenier 7/4/44; ass 326BS/92BG Podington 23/4/44; MIA Berlin 29/4/44 w/Langfeldt; flak, cr Lille, Fr; 7EVD 3POW; MACR 4261.

42-97320 Del Cheyenne 18/2/44; Gr Island 6/3/44; Grenier 20/3/44; ass 544BS/384BG [SU-G] Grafton Underwood 7/4/44; f/l continent 10/1/45; sal.

42-97321 Del Cheyenne 18/2/44; Gr Island 6/3/44; Grenier 20/3/44; ass 366BS/305BG [KY-A] Chelveston 31/3/44; b/d Merseburg w/? 12/5/44; sal 2 SAD. HITLER'S HEADACHE.

42-97322 Del Cheyenne 18/2/44; Dow Fd 7/3/44; ass 398BG Nuthampstead 1/5/44; tran 614BS/401BG [IW-D] Deenethorpe 21/5/44; retUS Bradley 5/7/45; 4168 BU Sth Plains 21/10/45; RFC Kingman 8/12/45.

42-97323 Del Cheyenne 18/2/44; Gr Island 3/3/44; Grenier 21/3/44; ass 368BS/306BG [BO-M] Thurleigh 2/4/44; tran 534BS/381BG Ridgewell 5/45; retUS Bradley 11/6/45; 4168 BU Sth Plains 14/6/45; RFC Kingman 6/12/45. BEGIN THE BEGUINE - SHE DOOD IT.

42-97324 Del Cheyenne 18/2/44; Hunter 8/3/44; Homestead 16/4/44; ass Soxo, but tran 341BS/97BG Amendola 18/10/44; MIA Ruhland 22/3/45 w/Wetzloff; MACR 13265. SILVER SHEEN.

42-97325 Del Cheyenne 18/2/44; Gr Island 5/3/44; Grenier 20/3/44; ass 508BS/351BG [YB-H] Polebrook 7/4/44; {17m} c/l Hoxne, UK 24/5/44; 6KIA 3WIA; sal.

42-97326 Del Cheyenne 18/2/44; Hunter 9/3/44; Dow Fd 4/4/44; ass 407BS/92BG [PY-V] Podington 7/5/44; MIA Merseburg 11/9/44 w/Potter; e/a, cr Leuttenhendorf, Ger; 4KIA 5POW; MACR 8890. LITTLE LAMSEY DIVEY.

42-97327 Del Cheyenne 18/2/44; Gr Island 4/3/44; Grenier 22/3/44; ass 368BS/306BG [BO-U] Thurleigh 1/4/44; sal 1/7/44.

42-97328 Del Cheyenne 20/2/44; Gr Island 5/3/44; Grenier 22/3/44; ass 561BS/388BG Knettishall 23/3/44; retUS Bradley 29/6/45; 4168 BU Sth Plains 2/7/45; RFC Kingman 17/12/45. HEAVEN'S ABOVE.

42-97329 Del Cheyenne 19/2/44; Hunter 12/3/44; Grenier 3/4/44; ass 360BS/303BG [PU-L/H] Molesworth 22/4/44; MIA Magdeburg 28/9/44 w/Michaelis; e/a, cr Bad Grund, Ger; 8KIA 1POW; MACR 9411. FLAK HACK.

42-97330 Del Cheyenne 19/2/44; Hunter 9/3/44; Grenier 7/4/44; ass 535BS/381BG [MS-S] Ridgewell 24/4/44; MIA {33+m} Hamburg 6/11/44 w/Levitoff; flak, cr Rotenburg, Ger; 2KIA 7POW. MACR 10154. CHUG-A-LUG (IV).

42-97331 Del Cheyenne 19/2/44; Hunter 9/3/44; Grenier 7/4/44; ass 8AF; l/Atlantic en route UK 9/4/44; MACR 3682.

42-97332 Del Cheyenne 19/2/44; Hunter 5/3/44; Homestead 12/3/44; ass 419BS/301BG Lucera 2/4/44; {46m} b/d Munich 19/7/44; c/l base & collided with bulldozer; sal.

42-97333 Del Cheyenne 19/2/44; Hunter 9/3/44; Grenier 7/4/44; ass 333BS/94BG Rougham 9/4/44; MIA Bohlen 7/10/44 w/Loesing; e/a, cr Sibbersdorf, Ger; 1KIA 8POW; MACR 9556. DUCHESS.

42-97334 Del Cheyenne 19/2/44; Gr Island 4/3/44; Dow Fd 4/4/44; ass 336BS/95BG [ET-S] Horham 4/4/44; MIA Brux 11/9/44 w/Mooring; cr Brux; 9POW; MACR 8892. HARD LUCK.

42-97335 Del Cheyenne 19/2/44; Hunter 9/3/44; Dow Fd 9/4/44; ass 407BS/92BG [PY-J] Podington 13/11/44; secret mission 1/6/45; sal 9AF Germany 31/10/45. GRINNIN BEARIT.

42-97336 Del Cheyenne 19/2/44; Gr Island 9/3/44; Dow Fd 4/4/44; ass 325BS/92BG [NV-A] Podington 10/4/44; tran 401BG Deenethorpe 20/5/45; retUS Columbus 9/6/45; 4168 BU Sth Plains 13/6/44; RFC Kingman 1/12/45.

42-97337 Del Cheyenne 19/2/44; Hunter 20/3/44; Grenier 7/4/44; ass 94BG Rougham 9/4/44; tran 602BS/398BG [K8-R] Nuthampstead 26/4/44; base accident, sal 12/11/44.

42-97338 Del Cheyenne 19/2/44; Hunter 9/3/44; Grenier 7/4/44; ass 601BS/398BG [30-C] Nuthampstead 24/4/44; 600BS [N8-C]; sal 12/3/45. UGLY DUCKLING.

42-97339 Del Cheyenne 19/2/44; Hunter 9/3/44; Dow Fd 10/4/44; ass 600BS/398BG [N8-H] Nuthampstead 5/5/44; MIA Berlin 19/5/44 w/O'Neil; flak, cr Ruednitz, Ger?; 8KIA 2POW; MACR 4937.

42-97340 Del Cheyenne 20/2/44; Alexandra 12/3/44; 332 BU Lake Charles 2/8/44; 221 BU Alexandra 17/9/44; 329 BU Alexandra 1/3/45; 330 BU Dyersburg 24/6/45; 327 BU Drew 28/8/45; 330 BU Dyersburg 4/9/45; RFC Walnut Ridge 19/12/45.

42-97341 Del Cheyenne 20/2/44; Sioux City 17/3/44; 224 BU Sioux City 11/10/44; 332 BU Ardmore 17/6/45; RFC Walnut Ridge 19/8/45.

42-97342 Del Cheyenne 20/2/44; Hunter 4/3/44; Grenier 7/4/44; ass 332BS/94BG [XM-H] Rougham 9/4/44; MIA Ingolstadt 21/4/45 w/Kirk; hit by prop wash, cr Halle, Ger; 7KIA 1RTD. MACR 14167. STRUGGLE BUNNY.

42-97343 Del Cheyenne 20/2/44; Dyersburg 14/3/44; 814 BU 1TC Stout 10/9/44; 223 BU Dyersburg 16/9/44; 330 BU Dyersburg 1/3/45; RFC Walnut Ridge 14/12/45.

42-97344 Del Cheyenne 20/2/44; Tinker 4/3/44; Hunter 6/3/44; Grenier 7/4/44; ass 613BS/401BG [IN-P] Deenethorpe 28/4/44; MIA Merseburg 24/8/44 w/Cain; e/a, cr Dreilingen, Ger?; 2KIA 7POW; MACR 8203.

42-97345 Del Cheyenne 20/2/44; Rapid City 9/3/44; Grenier 13/4/44; ass 398BG Nuthampstead 22/4/44; tran 728BS/452BS Deopham Green 3/5/44; retUS Bradley 3/7/45; 4168 BU Sth Plains 5/7/45; RFC Kingman 8/12/45. RAMBLIN' WRECK.

42-97346 Del Cheyenne 21/2/44; Hunter 10/3/44; ass 20BS/2BG Amendola 3/4/44; MIA Gyor 13/4/44 w/Martin; e/a, cr Bjelovan, Hung; ten chutes seen; MACR 3911.

42-97347 Del Cheyenne 21/2/44; Hunter 8/3/44; Homestead 16/3/44; ass 32BS/301BG Lucera 2/4/44; MIA {29m} Vado, It 5/6/44 w/Baldree; cr Rimini; 6POW 4EVD; MACR 5837.

42-97348 Del Cheyenne 21/2/44; Hunter 6/3/44; Grenier 7/4/44; ass 603BS/398BG [N7-R] Nuthampstead 25/4/44; MIA Munich 13/7/44 w/Foster; flak, cr Wesenbeck, Ger; 9KIA; MACR 7498.

42-97349 Del Cheyenne 22/2/44; Homestead 19/3/44; Dow Fd 8/4/44; ass 398BG Nuthampstead 28/4/44; tran 508BS/351BG [YB-B] Polebrook 7/5/44; {121m} RetUS Bradley 31/5/45; 4168 BU Sth Plains 21/10/45; RFC Kingman 17/12/45. SILVER DOLLAR.

42-97350 Del Cheyenne 20/2/44; Rapid City 8/3/44; Grenier 30/4/44; ass 601BS/398BG Nuthampstead 6/5/44 STRICTLY FROM HUNGER; tran 365BS/305BG Chelveston 7/5/44; MIA Mannheim 21/7/44 w/Kornblau; flak, cr Epfenhofen, Ger; 5KIA 4POW; MACR 7276.

42-97351 Del Cheyenne 21/2/44; Hunter 5/3/44; Homestead 16/3/44; ass 20BS/2BG Amendola 4/3/44; MIA Bleckhammer 7/7/44 w/Tomlinson; cr Pressburg; one chute seen; MACR 6565.

42-97352 Del Cheyenne 20/2/44; Kearney 16/3/44; Dow Fd 5/4/44; ass 560BS/388BG Knettishall 7/4/44; sal 20/5/44.

42-97353 Del Cheyenne 22/2/44; Rapid City 8/3/44; Grenier 21/4/44; ass 398BG Nuthampstead 25/4/44; tran 366BS/305BG Chelveston 1/5/44; MIA battle area support 13/8/44 w/Terry; flak, cr Flers, Fr; 1KIA 2POW 6RTD; MACR 10709.

42-97354 Del Cheyenne 22/2/44; Scott 14/3/44; Dyersburg 15/3/44; 2132 BU Maxwell 25/6/44; 223 BU Dyersburg 11/7/44; 2122 BU Greenwood 14/9/44; 223 BU Dyersburg 16/9/44; 2113 BU Columbus 2/2/45; 330 BU Dyersburg 1/3/45; RFC Walnut Ridge 19/12/45.

42-97355 Del Cheyenne 22/2/44; Amarillo 20/3/44; Alexandra 27/3/44; 332 BU Lake Charles 5/10/44; 221 BU Alexandra 6/10/44; 329 BU Alexandra 1/3/45; 302 BU Hunter 30/3/45; 329 BU Alexandra 13/6/45; 330 BU Dyersburg 24/6/45; RFC Walnut Ridge 189/12/45.

42-97356 Del Cheyenne 22/2/44; Gt Falls 27/3/44; Cheyenne 2/3/44; Kansas City 13/3/44; Dyersburg 16/3/44; 555 BU Love Fd 21/12/44; 223 BU Dyersburg 2/1/45; 330 BU Dyersburg 1/3/45; 327 BU Drew 28/8/45; 330 BU Dyersburg 4/9/45; RFC Walnut Ridge 14/12/45.

42-97357 Del Cheyenne 22/2/44; Rapid City 5/3/44; Dow Fd 28/4/44; ass 398BG Nuthampstead 3/5/44; tran 533BS/381BG [VP-Z] Ridgewell 19/5/44; {57m} b/d Germersheim w/Fawcett 13/1/45; f/l continent, sal. THE RAILROADER.

42-97358 Del Cheyenne 22/2/44; Kearney 18/3/44; Grenier 2/4/44; ass 332BS/94BG [XM-D] Rougham 6/4/44; retUS Bradley 28/6/45; 4168 BU Sth Plains 2/7/45; RFC Kingman 8/11/45. ORDNANCE EXPRESS.

42-97359 Del Cheyenne 23/2/44; Tinker 11/3/44; Alexandra 13/3/44; 263 BU Harding 29/6/44; 221 BU Alexandra 1/7/44; 4119 BU Brookley 25/11/44; 221 BU Alexandra 15/12/44; 329 BU Alexandra 1/3/45; 327 BU Drew 20/7/45; 203 BU Jackson 4/9/45; 268 BU Peterson 9/10/45; RFC Altus 7/11/45.

42-97360 Del Cheyenne 23/2/44; Tulsa 11/3/44; Alexandra 12/3/44; slated 338BG/96BG [BX-S], ass 331 BU Barksdale 27/10/44; 221 BU Alexandra 6/11/44; 329 BU Alexandra 1/3/45; 3030 BU Roswell 24/6/45; 330 BU Dyersburg 11/9/45; RFC Walnut Ridge 14/12/45.

42-97361 Del Cheyenne 22/2/44; Kearney 16/3/44; Grenier 2/4/44; ass 728BS/452BG Deopham Green 6/4/44; MIA Brux 12/5/44 w/Halbleib; e/a, cr Ohren, Ger; 4KIA 6POW; MACR 4821. THE PUNCHED FOWL.

42-97362 Del Cheyenne 22/2/44; Gt Falls 26/2/44; Cheyenne 28/2/44; W/O 11/5/44.

42-97363 Del Cheyenne 23/2/44; Rapid City 10/3/44; Grenier 21/4/44; ass 398BG Nuthampstead 21/4/44; tran 91BG Bassingbourn 4/5/44; 413BS/96BG Snetterton 6/5/44; MIA Fallersleben 20/6/44 w/Hunt; e/a, cr Celle, Ger; 1KIA 9POW; MACR 5894.

42-97364 Del Cheyenne 23/2/44; Alexandra 8/3/44; Oklahoma City 16/3/44; 221 BU Alexandra 17/1/45; 329 BU Alexandra 1/3/45; 327 BU Drew 7/6/45; 326 BU McDill 12/12/45; 300 BU McDill 20/3/46; 73 WVG McDill 27/3/46; 326 BU McDill 31/5/46; Recl Comp 30/10/46.

42-97365 Del Cheyenne 23/2/44; Rapid City 8/3/44; Dow Fd 21/4/44; ass 398BG Nuthampstead 25/4/44; tran 369BS/306BG [WW-Z] Thurleigh 2/6/44; MIA Halle 16/8/44 w/Newsom; flak, cr Rotenkirchen, Ger; 1KIA 8POW; MACR 7901. ZAMRO.

42-97366 Del Cheyenne 23/2/44; Oklahoma City 6/3/44; Dow Fd 28/4/44; ass 398BG Nuthampstead 1/5/44; tran 413BS/96BG [MZ-D] Snetterton 3/5/44; MIA Fallersleben 20/6/44 w/Seefurth; flak, cr Letzlingen Forest, Ger; 6KIA 4POW; MACR 5895.

42-97367 Del Cheyenne 23/2/44; Kearney 12/3/44; Dow Fd 4/4/44; ass 547BS/384BG [SO-T] Grafton Underwood 11/4/44; sal 18/7/44. UMBRIAGO.

42-97368 Del Cheyenne 23/2/44; Rapid City 10/3/44; Grenier 14/4/44; ass 398BG Nuthampstead 25/4/44; tran 368BS/306BG [BO-O] Thurleigh 6/6/44; MIA Dutch AA 12/9/44 w/Sasser; flak, cr Feyensein, Hol?; 5KIA 4POW; MACR 8834. TAILWIND.

42-97369 Del Cheyenne 23/2/44; Dyersburg 5/3/44; 223 BU Dyersburg 1/3/45; 330 BU Dyersburg 9/4/45; RFC Walnut Ridge 14/12/45.

42-97370 Del Cheyenne 23/2/44; Rapid City 15/3/44; Dow Fd 14/4/44; ass 398BG Nuthampstead 24/4/44; tran 527BS/379BG [FO-G] Kimbolton 6/5/44; 526BS [LF-G]; retUS Bradley 3/7/45; 4168 BU Sth Plains 21/10/45; RFC Kingman 22/11/45. THE HELLION.

42-97371 Del Cheyenne 23/2/44; Kearney 17/3/44; Dow Fd 4/4/44; ass 728BS/452BG Deopham Green 5/4/44; MIA Brux 12/5/44 w/Atkinson; e/a, cr Buedlingen, Ger; 10POW; MACR 4822. HAIRLESS JOE.

42-97372 Del Cheyenne 23/2/44; Kearney 12/3/44; Grenier 2/4/44; ass 547BS/384BG [SO-P] Grafton Underwood 15/4/44; MIA Erding 24/4/44 w/Haley; flak, cr Fussen, Ger; 10POW; MACR 4349. BOOBY TRAP.

42-97373 Del Cheyenne 23/2/44; Gt Falls 26/2/44; Cheyenne 2/3/44; 222 BU Ardmore 30/8/44; 332 BU Ardmore 16/6/45; 370 BU Sheppard 19/6/45; 332 BU Ardmore 26/6/45; RFC Walnut Ridge 24/8/45.

42-97374 Del Cheyenne 23/2/44; Kearney 17/3/44; Grenier 5/4/44; ass 602BS/398BG [K8-X] Nuthampstead 7/4/44; c/l 24/12/44, sal.

42-97375 Del Cheyenne 24/2/44; Gt Falls 26/2/44; Cheyenne 2/3/44; slated 452BG, 330 BU Dyersburg 1/3/45; 347 BU Key Fd 3/5/45; 330 BU Dyersburg 9/5/45; RFC Walnut Ridge 14/12/45.

42-97376 Del Cheyenne 24/2/44; Kearney 10/3/44; Grenier 2/4/44; ass 412BS/95BG [QW-J] Horham 7/4/44 AUNT CALLIE'S BABY; 335BS [OE-H]; aban Goose Bay, Lab. due to engine failure 26/6/45; retUS Bradley 5/7/45; 4168 BU Sth Plains 7/7/45; RFC Kingman 20/12/45. LUCKY LADY.

42-97377 Del Cheyenne 24/2/44; Gt Falls 26/2/44; Cheyenne 2/3/44; 222 BU Ardmore 22/1/45; 332 BU Ardmore 16/6/45; RFC Walnut Ridge 20/8/45.

42-97378 Del Cheyenne 24/2/44; Kearney 16/3/44; Grenier 2/4/44; ass 410BS/94BG [GL-P] Rougham 7/4/44; retUS Bradley 6/7/45; 4168 BU Sth Plains 21/10/45; RFC Kingman 23/11/45. MISS GLORIA II.

42-97379 Del Cheyenne 23/2/44; Gt Falls 27/2/44; Cheyenne 2/3/44; 222 BU Ardmore 20/8/44; 332 BU Ardmore 16/6/45; RFC Walnut Ridge 17/9/45.

42-97380 Del Cheyenne 24/2/44; Kearney 17/3/44; Dow Fd 5/4/44; ass 600BS/398BG [N8-R] Nuthampstead 3/5/44; c/l 8/7/44, sal 2 SAD.

42-97381 Del Cheyenne 24/2/44; Kearney 17/3/44; Grenier 6/4/44; ass 511BS/351BG [DS-U] Polebrook 12/4/44; cr t/o 10/1/45; rep 18/4/45; {66m} RetUS Bradley 31/5/45; 4168 BU Sth Plains 21/10/45; RFC Kingman 14/12/45. LINDA BALL II.

42-97382 Del Cheyenne 24/2/44; Gr Island 26/3/44; Grenier 6/4/44; ass 398BG Nuthampstead 7/4/44; tran 337BS/96BG [AW-K] Snetterton 8/4/44; MIA Brux 12/5/44 w/Hon; mid air coll w/42-102452, cr Wehrheime, Ger; 7KIA 3POW; MACR 4859.

42-97383 Del Cheyenne 24/2/44; Kearney 14/3/44; Grenier 2/4/44; ass 398BG Nuthampstead 20/4/44; tran 334BS/95BG [BG-F] Horham 1/5/44; 336BS [ET-F]; MIA Merseburg 30/11/44 w/Payne; cr Merseburg; 2KIA 7POW; MACR 10839.

42-97384 Del Cheyenne 24/2/44; Billings 1/3/44; Cheyenne 3/3/44; 222 BU Ardmore 22/1/45; 273 BU Lincoln 27/1/45; 222 BU Ardmore 10/5/45; 332 BU Ardmore 16/6/45; RFC Walnut Ridge 21/8/45.

42-97385 Del Cheyenne 24/2/44; Sheridan 12/3/44;

Grenier 14/4/44; ass 601BS/398BG [3O-X] Nuthampstead 22/4/44; MIA Ludwigshafen 8/9/44 w/Wade; mech fault, f/l Rechicourt, Fr; 2EVD 3KIA 4POW; sal 29/3/45. MACR 8605. SHADY LADY.

42-97386 Del Cheyenne 24/2/44; Gr Island 26/2/44; Cheyenne 2/3/44; 202 BU Galveston 1/12/44; 222 BU Ardmore 11/12/44; 332 BU Ardmore 16/6/45; RFC Walnut Ridge 20/8/45.

42-97387 Del Cheyenne 27/2/44; Kearney 16/3/44; Dow Fd 6/4/44; ass 602BS/398BG [K8-H] Nuthampstead 28/4/44; MIA Berlin 3/2/45 w/McCormick; mid air coll w/43-38697, cr Gardelegen, Ger; 7KIA 2POW; MACR 12214. MAUDE AN' MARIA.

42-97388 Del Cheyenne 25/2/44; Gt Falls 27/2/44; Cheyenne 3/3/44; Ardmore 12/3/44; 202 BU Galveston 10/8/44; 222 BU Ardmore 20/8/44; 555 BU Love Fd 6/4/45; 222 BU Ardmore 15/4/45; 332 BU Ardmore 16/6/45; RFC Walnut Ridge 18/8./45.

42-97389 Del Cheyenne 25/2/44; Sioux City 16/3/44; 224 BU Sioux City 6/3/45; 225 BU Rapid City 16/6/45; 203 BU Jackson 13/7/45; 247 BU Smoky Hill 24/9/45; RFC Altus 7/11/45.

42-97390 Del Cheyenne 25/2/44; Gt Falls 2/3/44; Kearney 17/3/44; Dow Fd 7/4/44; ass 731BS/452BG Deopham Green 8/4/44; 730BS; dest on ground Poltava 21/6/44; sal Russia 2/7/44.

42-97391 Del Cheyenne 28/2/44; Billings 2/3/44; Kearney 12/3/44; Dow Fd 5/7/44; ass 427BS/303BG [GN-R] Molesworth 22/4/44; b/d Lepizig 29/6/44 w/?; c/l Woodbridge, UK; sal 2SAD 1/7/44.

42-97392 Del Cheyenne 28/2/44; Kearney 16/3/44; Dow Fd 5/4/44; ass 711BS/447BG Rattlesden 11/4/44; retUS Bradley 9/7/45; 4168 BU Sth Plains 21/10/45; RFC Kingman 20/12/45.

42-97393 Del Cheyenne 2/3/44; Billings 2/3/44; Dow Fd 28/4/44; ass 398BG Nuthampstead 30/4/44; tran 349BS/100BG [XR-G] Thorpe Abbotts 3/5/44; c/l base 28/7/44, sal. PRIDE OF THE CENTURY.

42-97394 Del Cheyenne 25/2/44; Kearney 16/3/44; Dow Fd 5/4/44; ass 601BS/398BG [3O-P] Nuthampstead 28/4/44; MIA Cauvincourt 8/8/44 w/Blackwell; flak, cr Falaise, Fr; 2MIA 7RTD; MACR 8065. KENTUCKY COLONEL.

42-97395 Del Cheyenne 25/2/44; Kearney 17/3/44; Grenier 6/4/44; ass614BG/401BG [IW-F] Deenethorpe 16/4/44; sal 2 SAD 25/3/45. CHUTE THE WORKS.

42-97396 Del Cheyenne 25/2/44; Kearney 16/3/44; Dow Fd 5/4/44; ass 369BS/306BG [WW-M] Thurleigh 25/4/44; base explosion 6/8/44, sal 2 SAD. FORTUNATE YOUTH.

42-97397 Del Cheyenne 25/2/44; Kearney 16/3/44; Dow Fd 5/4/44; ass 423BS/306BG Thurleigh 25/4/44; tran 381BG Ridgewell /5/44; retUS Bradley 10/6/45; 4168 BU Sth Plains 21/10/45; RFC Kingman 20/12/45. UNAVAILABLE MABEL.

42-97398 Del Cheyenne 25/2/44; Kearney 16/3/44; Dow Fd 3/4/44; ass 401BS/91BG [LL-C] Bassingbourn 7/4/44; tran 836BS/487BG [2G] Lavenham 8/4/44; MIA Misburg 31/12/44 w/Gatlin; flak, cr Nth Sea; 9KIA; MACR 11352.

42-97399 Del Cheyenne 26/2/44; Kearney 17/3/44; Dow Fd 5/4/44; ass 600BS/398BG [N8-H] Nuthampstead 28/4/44; MIA Cauvincourt 8/8/44 w/Capt Baker; flak, cr Falaise, Fr; 7KIA 2POW; MACR 7383.

42-97400 Del Cheyenne 26/2/44; Kearney 12/3/44; Dow Fd 5/4/44; ass 708BS/447BG Rattlesden 7/4/44; MIA Misburg 30/12/44 w/Leverett; mid air coll, cr Wenings, Ger?; 7KIA 2POW; MACR 11228. FUDDY DUDDY.

42-97401 Del Cheyenne 26/2/44; Kearney 14/3/44; Grenier 2/4/44; ass 601BS/398BG [3O-T] Nuthampstead 28/4/44; sal 29/11/44.

42-97402 Del Cheyenne 26/2/44; Kearney 16/3/44; Grenier 2/4/44; ass 325BS/92BG [NV-L] Podington 15/4/44; b/d Ludwigshafen 5/9/44, f/l Manston, UK; sal 7/9/44.

42-97403 Del Cheyenne 26/2/44; Kearney 16/3/44; Grenier 2/4/44; ass 337BS/96BG [AW-U] Snetterton 8/4/44; MIA Berlin 8/5/44 w/Fancher; e/a, cr Hiddesdorf, Ger; 7KIA 3POW. MACR 4570.

42-97404 Del Cheyenne 26/2/44; Kearney 16/3/44; Grenier 26/3/44; ass 544BS/384BG [SU-L] Grafton Underwood 27/3/44; MIA Stettin 13/5/44 w/Francis; e/a, cr Friedland, Ger; 1KIA 9POW; MACR 4813.

42-97405 Del Cheyenne 26/2/44; Kearney 16/3/44; Grenier 2/4/44; ass 94BG Rougham 27/4/44; tran 360BS/303BG [PU-H] Molesworth 30/4/44; MIA French A/fds 22/6/44 w/Erickson; flak, ditched Channel; 5KIA 5RTD. MACR 7131. MARY CARY.

42-97406 Del Cheyenne 26/2/44; Gr Island 17/3/44; Grenier 2/4/44; ass 413BS/96BG Snetterton 7/4/44; tran 401BS/91BG [LL-D] Bassingbourn 12/4/44; MIA Kassel 19/4/44 w/La Fontin; e/a, cr Roehrig, Ger; 3KIA 6POW; MACR 4047.

42-97407 Del Cheyenne 26/2/44; Kearney 12/3/44; Grenier 2/4/44; ass 412BS/95BG [QW-N] Horham 7/4/44; SAD 10/6/44; tran 570BS/390BG [DI-V] Framlingham 11/4/44 ASTE-RISK; MIA Merseburg 30/11/44 w/Peterson; mid air coll, cr Flur Oberklobikau, Ger?; 6KIA 3POW; MACR 11136..

B-17G-VE

42-97436 Del Denver 15/11/43; Kearney 1/12/43; ass 346BS/99BG Tortorella 1/44; {79m} sal 9/2/45. SILVER METEOR.

42-97437 Del Denver 16/11/43; Kearney 28/11/43; ass 342BS/97BG Cerignola 5/12/43; Amendola 16/1/44; MIA Vienna 10/9/44 w/Boyce; flak, cr Karlovacs; MACR 8365.

42-97438 Del Denver 16/11/43; Kearney 27/11/43; ass 416BS/99BG Tortorella 1/44; {29m} tran 96BS/2BG Amendola 28/3/44; {66m} RetUS 121 BU Bradley 6/6/45; 4104 BU Rome 28/6/45; 4124 BU Altus 16/10/45; RFC Altus 5/11/45.

42-97439 Del Denver 16/11/43; Kearney 27/11/43; ass 416BS/99BG Tortorella 1/44; {17m} MIA Regensburg 22/2/44 w/McGee; e/a, cr Pereshausen, Ger; three baled, MACR 2390.

42-97440 Del Denver 16/11/43; Kearney 1/12/43; Presque Is 11/12/43; ass 614BS/401BG [IW-A] Deenethorpe 1/1/44; MIA Halberstadt 30/5/44 w/Wilson; e/a, cr Bookholzberg, Ger?; 3KIA 7POW; MACR 5310. FLAK RAT II.

42-97441 Del Denver 17/11/43; Kearney 30/11/43; Bangor 13/12/43; ass 407BS/92BG Podington 10/1/44; MIA Brunswick 30/1/44 w/Russell; mid air coll w/42-30008, cr Brunswick; 8KIA 2POW; MACR 2254.

42-97442 Del Denver 17/11/43; Kearney 20/12/43; New Castle 2/1/44; Westover 7/1/44; Presque Is 12/1/44; ass 533BS/381BG [VP-Q] Ridgewell 21/2/44; {35m} damaged on practice mission 1/10/44; sal 2 SAD 3/10/44.

42-97443 Del Denver 19/11/43; Rock Springs 11/12/43; Wendover 12/12/43; ass 749BS/457BG Glatton; cr en route UK 22/1/44, Belmullet, Ireland; sal 24/1/44.

42-97444 Del Denver 18/11/43; Kearney 27/11/43; ass 340BS/97BG Cerignola 14/12/43; Amendola 16/1/44; MIA Anzio 17/2/44 w/Csupak; flak, cr Anzio; MACR 2392.

42-97445 Del Burbank 10/4/44; Ardmore 9/5/44; 222 BU Ardmore 22/1/45; 332 BU Ardmore 16/6/45; RFC Walnut Ridge 13/11/45.

42-97446 Del Denver 17/11/43; Kearney 19/12/43; ass 419BS/301BG Cerignola 29/1243; Lucera 1/22/44; {69m} tran 463BG Celone 8/44; sal 25/7/45.

42-97447 Del Denver 17/11/43; Kearney 2/12/43; Bangor 9/12/43; ass 334BS/95BG [BG-E] Horham 15/12/43; MIA Brunswick 10/2/44 w/Wilson; e/a, cr Brandlecht, Ger; 7KIA 3POW; MACR 2547.

42-97448 Del Denver 18/11/43; Gr Island 4/12/43; Presque Is 10/12/43; ass 614BS/401BG [IW-H] Deenethorpe 1/1/44; MIA Pas de Calais 20/4/44 w/Ksiewiewicz; flak, cr Menoval, Fr; 3EVD 1KIA 6POW; MACR 4055.

42-97449 Del Denver 18/11/43; Kearney 1/12/43; Presque Is 15/12/43; ass 547BS/384BG [SO-B] Grafton Underwood 21/1/44; MIA Augsburg 19/7/44 w/Bodker; e/a, cr Mils Inntal, Ger?; 9POW; MACR 7261. CHALLENGER.

42-97450 Del Denver 19/11/43; Wendover 11/12/43; Presque Is 28/1/44; ass 457BG Glatton 11/2/44; tran 546BS/384BG Grafton Underwood 20/2/44; MIA Aschersleben {1m} 22/2/44 w/Markow; e/a, cr Wesel, Ger; 10POW; MACR 2464.

42-97451 Del Denver 19/11/43; Wendover 11/12/43; Grenier 16/1/44; ass 751BS/457BG Glatton 3/2/44; mid air coll 10/9/44; sal 2 SAD 11/9/44. NANCY K.

42-97452 Del Denver 19/11/43; Wendover 11/12/43; ass 751BS/457BG Glatton 29/1/44; 750BS; MIA Cologne 28/5/44 w/Hauf; e/a, cr Channel; 9KIA; MACR 5296.

42-97453 Del Denver 19/11/43; Kearney 2/12/43; Presque Is 15/12/43; Prestwick, UK 21/12/43; ass 388BG Knettishall 27/12/43; sal 11/4/44.

42-97454 Del Denver 19/11/43; Gr Island 1/12/43; Presque Is 10/12/43; ass 533BS/381BG [VP-U] Ridgewell 13/1/44; MIA {29m} Berlin 19/5/44 w/Sharp; flak, cr Adlig-Reetz, Ger?; 1KIA 8POW; MACR 4932.

42-97455 Del Denver 21/11/43; Wendover 12/12/43; Grenier 16/1/44; ass 457BG Glatton 19/2/44; tran 401BS/91BG [LL-J] Bassingbourn 11/3/44; MIA Berlin 19/5/44 w/Reid; flak, cr Berlin; 8KIA 1POW; MACR 4829. THE KEYSTONE MAMA.

42-97456 Del Cheyenne 21/11/43; Salt Lake City 8/12/43; Wendover 11/12/43; ass 751BS/457BG Glatton 26/1/44; f/l continent 10/9/44, sal. MIGHTY LITTLE JOHN.

42-97457 Del Denver 19/11/43; Albuquerque 25/11/43; Wendover 11/12/43; ass 749BS/457BG Glatton 29/1/44; MIA Augsburg 25/2/44 w/Bower; e/a, cr Birkweiler, Ger; 5KIA 5POW; MACR 2918.

42-97458 Del Cheyenne 21/11/43; Wendover 7/12/43; ass 457BG Glatton 27/1/44; c/l RAF Detling 27/2/44; rep & ret 29/2/44; f/l continent 10/9/44, sal.

42-97459 Del Cheyenne 21/11/43; Wendover 6/12/43; Nutts Corner, UK 23/1/44; ass 457BG Glatton 3/2/44; sal 20/5/44.

42-97460 Del Cheyenne 22/11/43; Wendover 7/12/43; Grenier 6/1/44; ass 749BS/457BG Glatton 17/2/44; MIA Ludwigshafen 27/5/44 w/Dee; e/a, cr Saarlautern, Ger; 1KIA 9POW; MACR 5295. DE LAYED LADY.

42-97461 Del Cheyenne 22/11/43; Denver 25/1/44; Kearney 11/2/44; Grenier 10/3/44; ass 447BG Rattlesden 24/3/44; f/l continent 7/10/44; sal 14/11/44. SKYLARK.

42-97462 Del Denver 22/11/43; Kearney 14/12/43; Presque Is 20/12/43; ass 527BS/379BG [FO-C] Kimbolton 9/1/44; f/l continent 8/9/44; sal 14/11/44.

42-97463 Del Denver 22/11/43; Kearney 16/12/43;

Presque Is 8/1/44; Nutts Corner, UK 15/1/44; ass 423BS/306BG Thurleigh 27/1/44; MIA Leipzig 20/2/44 w/Richard; flak & e/a, cr Efurt, Ger; 2KIA 8POW; MACR 2430.

42-97464 Del Denver 23/11/43; Wendover 9/12/43; ass 749BS/457BG Glatton 19/1/44; tran 614BS/401BG [IW-D] Deenethorpe 11/3/44 WHAT NEXT?; MIA Schweinfurt 13/4/44 w/Stimson; e/a, cr Rohrbrunn, Ger; 2KIA 8POW; MACR 3941.

42-97465 Del Denver 23/11/43; Wendover 10/12/43; ass 751BS/457BG Glatton 9/2/44; MIA Marienburg 9/4/44 w/Walker; e/a, cr Ossecken, Ger?; 1EVD 3KIA 6POW; MACR 3665.

42-97466 Del Denver 23/11/43; Kearney 16/12/43; New Castle 1/1/44; Presque Is 8/1/44; Nutts Corner, UK 17/1/44; ass 457BG Glatton 12/1/44; tran 366BS/305BG Chelveston 8/2/44; MIA Brunswick 29/3/44 w/Engel; e/a, cr Celle, Ger; 1KIA 9POW; MACR 3478.

42-97467 Del Denver 24/11/43; Wendover 9/12/43; ass 748BS/457BG Glatton 2/2/44; tran 401BS/91BG [LL-F] Bassingbourn 11/3/44; MIA Peenemunde 18/7/44 w/Bare; mech fault, f/l Bulltofta, Swed; 9INT; MACR 7418. (Left 1/6/45).

42-97468 Del Denver 24/11/43; Wendover 12/12/43; ass 750BS/457BG Glatton 27/1/44; sal 10/8/44. TUJUNGA III.

42-97469 Del Denver 24/11/43; Wendover 8/12/43; ass 401BG Deenethorpe 26/2/44; 457BG Glatton 12/3/44; 527BS/379BG [FO-I] Kimbolton 18/3/44; w/w 11/1/45; 34BG Mendlesham /45; 1 BAD Burtonwood 22/4/45; retUS Bradley 20/6/45; 4168 BU Sth Plains 21/10/45; RFC Kingman 3/12/45.

42-97470 Del Cheyenne 25/11/43; Wendover 10/12/43; ass 748BS/457BG Glatton 26/1/44; MIA Osnabrück 26/9/44 w/Ellsworth; e/a, cr Scheinbeck, Ger?; 9POW; MACR 9771. OH KAY!

42-97471 Del Cheyenne 25/11/43; Wendover 11/12/43; ass 457BG Glatton 27/1/44; tran 532BS/381BG [VE-N] Ridgewell 11/3/44; {1m} c/l base ex-Frankfurt 20/3/44 w/Winter (u/c coll); sal 2 SAD 21/3/44.

42-97472 Del Denver 25/11/43; Kearney 18/12/43; New Castle 2/1/44; Presque Is 8/1/44; ass 510BS/351BG [TU-H] Polebrook 25/2/44; 511BS [DS-H] MIA {23m} Ruhland oil 28/5/44 w/Anderson; e/a, cr Aschersleben; 3KIA 7POW; MACR 5329.

42-97473 Del Denver 26/11/43; Kearney 14/12/43; Presque Is 19/12/43; ass 457BG Glatton 23/12/43; tran 571BS/390BG [FC-O] Framlingham 23/12/43 HAP'S HAZARD; MIA Pas de Calais 5/6/44 w/Armstrong; flak, cr Dargniers, Fr; 1KIA 8POW; MACR 5481. BERLIN EXPRESS.

42-97474 Del Denver 26/11/43; Kearney 14/12/43; Presque Is 22/12/43; ass 533BS/381BG [VP-Z] Ridgewell 15/1/44; MIA Oschersleben 22/2/44 w/Fridgen; e/a, cr Opherdicke, Ger; 2EVD 4KIA 4POW; MACR 2934. HOMING PIGEON.

42-97475 Del Denver 26/11/43; South Bend 21/12/43; ass 1st SAG Langley Fd 1/1/44; Mitchell 9/1/44; Morrison 12/1/44; ass 482BG Alconbury 15/1/44; 305BG Chelveston 11/2/44; c/t/o 3/12/44, sal.

42-97476 Del Denver 27/11/43; Kearney 15/12/43; Presque Is 22/1/44; ass 333BS/94BG [TS-K] Rougham 24/12/43; MIA Brunswick 23/3/44 w/Reno; e/a, cr Lobmargetersen, Ger?; 7KIA 3POW; MACR 3536.

42-97477 Del Cheyenne 28/11/43; Kearney 17/12/43; Presque 2/1/44; ass 457BG Glatton 4/1/44; tran 545BS/384BG [JD-A] Grafton Underwood 20/1/44; MIA Erding 24/4/44 w/Capt Edwards; e/a, cr Oberpfaffenhofen; 10POW; MACR 4348. PORKY'S PIG.

42-97478 Del Cheyenne 28/11/43; Wendover 12/12/43; Nutts Corner, UK 20/1/44; ass 748BS/457BG Glatton 9/1/44; 749BS; tran 614BS/401BG [IW-Q] Deenethorpe 11/3/44; retUS Bradley 7/6/45; 4168 BU Sth Plains 13/6/45; RFC Kingman 6/12/45. SHADE RUFF #2.

42-97479 Del Cheyenne 28/11/43; Kearney 12/12/43; Cleveland 26/12/43; Presque Is 30/12/43; ass 327BS/92BG [UX-L] Podington 27/1/44; b/d Kaiserlautern 12/10/44 w?; c/l base, burned and sal. BELLE OF LIBERTY.

42-97480 Del Cheyenne 28/11/43; Kearney 11/12/43; Presque Is 19/12/43; ass 337BS/96BG [AW-B] Snetterton 23/12/43; MIA Augsburg 13/4/44 w/Brandau; e/a, cr Augsburg; 4MIA 6POW; MACR 3769.

42-97481 Del Cheyenne 28/11/43; Wendover 12/12/43; ass 92BG Podington 20/1/44 POCAHONTAS; 751BS/457BG Glatton 26/1/44; MIA Berlin 19/5/44 w/Birong; e/a, cr Koenighorst, Ger; 1KIA 9POW; MACR 4941. LIBERTY RUN.

42-97482 Del Denver 29/11/43; Kearney 16/12/43; Romulus 2/1/44; Westover 10/1/44; Presque Is 14/1/44; ass 418BS/100BG [LD-W] Thorpe Abbotts 16/1/44; MIA Berlin 6/3/44 w/Terry; e/a, cr Quackenbrück, Ger; 7KIA 3POW; MACR 3033. TERRY AND THE PIRATES.

42-97483 Del Denver 29/11/43; Kearney 30/12/43; ass 322BS/91BG [LG-L] Bassingbourn 24/2/44; MIA Berlin 6/3/44 w/Evertson; e/a, cr Wilmersdorf, Ger; 10POW; MACR 2902.

42-97484 Del Denver 29/11/43; Kearney 15/12/43; Presque Is 23/12/43; ass 710BS/447BG Rattlesden 4/1/44; MIA Münster 11/3/44 w/Overdord; flak, cr Haamstede, Hol; 9KIA 1POW; MACR 3188.

42-97485 Del Denver 29/11/43; Kearney 28/12/43; Presque Is 8/1/44; Prestwick, UK 18/1/44; ass 526BS/379BG Kimbolton 29/1/44; MIA Pas de Calais 26/3/44 w/Bielawski; flak, cr Marie-Capelin, Fr; 10POW; MACR 3592. TALETHA ANN.

42-97486 Del Denver 29/11/43; Pyote 14/3/44; 233 BU Davis Monthan 28/7/44; 236 BU Pyote 29/8/44; 235 BU Biggs 17/8/44; 224 BU Sioux City 28/3/45; 222 BU Ardmore 15/6/45; 332 BU Ardmore 16/6/45; RFC Walnut Ridge 21/8/45.

42-97487 Del Denver 30/11/43; Kearney 16/12/43; Presque Is 19/12/43; ass 612BS/401BG [SC-O] Deenethorpe 11/1/44; c/l base 3/10/44, sal 2 SAD. HANGOVER HAVEN.

42-97488 Del Cheyenne 30/11/43; Wendover 9/12/43; Kearney 15/1/44; ass 96BG Snetterton 8/2/44; tran 457BG Glatton 9/2/44; 457BG/384BG Grafton Underwood 19/2/44; MIA Oschersleben 22/2/44 w/DeFrees; e/a, cr Wesel, Ger; 10POW; MACR 2465.

42-97489 Del Cheyenne 30/11/43; Kearney 11/12/43; Presque Is 22/12/43; ass 326BS/92BG [JW-F] Podington 23/1/44; c/l base, burned 20/5/44, sal.

42-97490 Del Cheyenne 30/11/43; Kearney 20/12/43; Witchita 1/1/44; Morrison 10/1/44; ass 429BS/2BG Amendola 3/2/44; MIA Bleckhammer 13/9/44 w/Stuckey; cr Verebely, one hour from target; MACR 8363.

42-97491 Del Cheyenne 30/11/43; Kearney 16/12/43; Romulus 31/12/43; ass 418BS/100BG [LD-B] Thorpe Abbotts 6/1/44; MIA Berlin 6/3/44 w/Radtke; e/a, cr Twirstringen, Ger; 1KIA 9POW; MACR 3043. RONNIE R.

42-97492 Del Cheyenne 1/12/43; Kearney 16/12/43; Presque Is 30/12/43; ass 511BS/351BG [DS-B] Polebrook 14/1/44; MIA Saarbrücken 3/8/44 W/Brackens; flak, cr Saarbrücken; 9POW; MACR 7704. SLOW BALL.

42-97493 Del Denver 1/12/43; Kearney 15/12/43; Presque Is 21/12/43; ass 8AF 4/1/44.

42-97494 Del Denver 1/12/43; Kearney 16/12/43; Presque Is 24/12/43; ass 325BS/92BG Podington 20/1/44; MIA Oschersleben 22/2/44 w/Wolf; mech fault, cr Nth Sea; 10KIA; MACR 2758. HOT ROCK.

42-97495 Del Denver 1/12/43; Kearney 16/12/43; Presque Is 23/12/43; ass 336BS/95BG [ET-C] Horham 24/12/43; MIA Berlin 6/3/44 w/Conley; cr Haseleunne, Ger; 10POW; MACR 2986.

42-97496 Del Denver 2/12/43; Kearney 16/12/43; Presque Is 24/12/43; ass 615BS/401BG [IY-J] Deenethorpe 31/1/44; MIA Marienburg 9/4/44 w/Byrd; e/a, f/l Bulltofta, Swed; 10INT; MACR 3942. (left 25/5/45).

42-97497 Del Cheyenne 2/12/43; Kearney 16/12/43; Presque Is 23/12/43; ass 711BS/447BG Rattlesden 27/12/43; MIA Bremen 12/10/44 w/Unger; flak, cr Osnabrück; 1KIA 8POW; MACR 9573. TUXEDO TOMMY.

42-97498 Del Cheyenne 2/12/43; Kearney 12/12/43; Presque Is 22/12/43; ass 358BS/303BG Molesworth 14/1/44; MIA Caen 6/2/44 w/Bass; flak, cr Vendome, Fr; 2KIA 8POW; MACR 2384. PADDED CELL.

42-97499 Del Cheyenne 3/12/43; Salt Lake City 9/12/43; Savannah 20/12/43; ass 340BS/97BG Amendola 10/1/44; MIA Ploesti 15/4/44 w/McConkey; MACR 3977.

42-97500 Del Cheyenne 2/12/43; Kearney 16/12/43; Presque Is 25/12/43; ass 364BS/305BG Chelveston 22/1/44; MIA Leipzig 20/2/44 w/Lingley; flak, cr Merseburg; 6KIA 4POW; MACR 2429.

42-97501 Del Cheyenne 3/12/43; Kearney 16/12/43; Presque Is 4/1/44; ass 711BS/447BG Rattlesden 5/1/44; MIA Berlin 29/4/44 w/Johnson; e/a, cr Burg, Ger; 9KIA 1POW; MACR 4853. GUM CHUM!

42-97502 Del Denver 4/12/43; Kearney 24/12/43; ass 527BS/379BG [FO-D] Kimbolton 18/2/44; MIA Stettin 13/5/44 w/Marinello; e/a, cr Demmin, Ger; 6KIA 3POW; MACR 4930.

42-97503 Del Denver 4/12/43; Kearney 16/12/43; Presque Is 23/12/43; ass 533BS/381BG [VP-X] Ridgewell 13/1/44; c/l base, burned 26/3/45; sal 2 SAD. PRINCESS PAT.

42-97504 Del Denver 4/12/43; Kearney 16/12/43; Presque Is 2/1/44; ass 323BS/91BG [OR-P] Bassingbourn 23/1/44; {70m} b/d Frieberg 14/10/44 w/?; c/l base, sal 2 SAD. MARY LOU.

42-97505 Del Denver 4/12/43; Kearney 23/12/43; Prestwick, UK 16/1/44; ass 423BS/306BG Thurleigh 12/1/44; tran 381BG Ridgewell 5/45; retUS Bradley 10/6/45; 4168 BU Sth Plains 21/10/45; RFC Kingman 5/12/45. THE DINGLEBURY KIDS.

42-97506 Del Denver 4/12/43; Kearney 16/12/43; Presque Is 23/12/43; ass 550BS/385BG Gt Ashfield 25/1/44; MIA Frankfurt 29/1/44 w/Bostwick; e/a, cr Simmern, Ger; 10POW; MACR 2269.

42-97507 Del Cheyenne 6/12/43; Gr Island 28/12/43; Grenier 25/1/44; ass 549BS/385BG Gt Ashfield 24/1/44; ct fire 6/6/45, sal. JERRY BOY.

42-97508 Del Cheyenne 6/12/43; Savannah 30/12/43; ass 416BS/99BG Tortorella 1/44; {19m} tran 96BS/2BG Amendola 28/3/44; {63m} RetUS 2137 BU Hendricks 22/9/45; RFC Walnut Ridge 9/1/46. JUANITA.

42-97509 Del Cheyenne 7/12/43; Kearney 30/12/43; Presque Is 17/2/44; ass 358BS/303BG Molesworth 28/2/44; MIA Frankfurt 2/3/44 w/Elder; flak, cr Kettenbach, Ger; 2KIA 8POW; MACR 2864. OLD HICKORY.

42-97510 Del Cheyenne 7/12/43; Kearney 25/12/43; ass 546BS/384BG [BK-A] Grafton Underwood 18/2/44; tran 398BG Nuthampstead 27/5/45; retUS Bradley 7/6/45; 4168 BU Sth Plains 13/6/45; RFC Kingman 9/12/45. SATAN'S PLAYMATE.

42-97511 Del Cheyenne 7/12/43; Albuquerque 15/12/43; Kearney 4/1/44; ass 535BS/381BG [MS-K] Ridgewell 22/2/44; mid air coll w/42-40011 ex Aschaffenburg 2/1/45 w/Tauro; cr nr base, 10KIA. Sal 2 SAD. EGG HAID.

42-97512 Del Cheyenne 7/12/43; Kingman 24/12/43; slated 447BG, 3018 BU Kingman 23/3/45; 3017 BU Hobbs 11/6/45; RFC Walnut Ridge 4/1/46.

42-97513 Del Denver 7/12/43; Kearney 23/12/43; ass 341BS/97BG Amendola 18/12/43; tran depot 13/12/44; sal 20/12/44.

42-97514 Del Denver 7/12/43; Cincinnati 12/1/44; Morrison 26/1/44; ass 482BG Alconbury 29/1/44; tran 422BS/305BG [JJ-H] Chelveston 20/3/44; 482BG Alconbury 6/7/44; retUS 1103 BU Morrison 14/10/45; RFC Walnut Ridge 5/1/46.

42-97515 Del Denver 7/12/43; Kearney 13/12/43; ass 96BG Snetterton 12/1/44; tran 325BS/92BG [NV-P] Podington 28/1/44; MIA Oberpfaffenhofen 18/3/44 w/Capps; flak, lost two engines; f/l Dubendorf, Switz; 10INT; (TG escaped, later German POW), MACR 3226. LITTLE RUNT.

42-97516 Del Denver 8/12/43; Kearney 24/12/43; Morrison 4/1/44; ass 341BS/97BG Amendola 21/12/43; MIA Linz 25/7/44 w/Webster; flak, cr Klagenfurt; MACR 7126.

42-97517 Del Cheyenne 8/12/43; Memphis 24/12/43; Orlando 1/1/44; 236 BU Pyote 8/6/44; 235 BU Biggs 16/8/44; 222 BU Ardmore 1/5/45; 332 BU Ardmore 16/6/45; RFC Walnut Ridge 20/8/45.

42-97518 Del Cheyenne 8/12/43; Kansas City 27/12/43; Orlando 1/1/44; 902 BU Orlando 2/6/44; Mat Spl Tonopah 23/6/44; Mat Com Wright Fd 28/6/44; Grenier 28/6/44; Prestwick, UK 30/6/44; ass Soxo 2/7/44.

42-97519 Del Cheyenne 8/12/43; Kearney 30/12/43; ass 401BS/91BG [LL-A] Bassingbourn 12/2/44; MIA {19m} Kassel 19/4/44 w/Evans; e/a, cr Kassel; 4KIA 6POW; MACR 4048. SPIRIT OF BILLY MITCHELL.

42-97520 Del Cheyenne 9/12/43; Gr Island 30/12/43; Presque Is 20/1/44; ass 525BS/379BG Kimbolton 29/1/44; MIA Oschersleben 22/2/44 w/Sloane; flak, cr Koblenz; 9KIA 1POW; MACR 2881.

42-97521 Del Cheyenne 9/12/43; Kearney 31/12/43; Presque Is 27/1/44; ass 545BS/384BG [JD-H] Grafton Underwood 10/2/44; f/l continent 28/1/45; sal. THE SAINT.

42-97522 Del Cheyenne 9/12/43; Denver 15/12/43; Langley 12/1/44; Mitchell 31/1/44; ass 482BG Alconbury 5/2/44; tran 305BG Chelveston 4/4/44; sal 2 SAD 1/5/44.

42-97523 Del Denver 9/12/43; Sth Bend 11/1/44; Langley 14/1/44; ass 482BG (H2X) Alconbury 28/1/44; tran 422BS/305BG Chelveston 20/3/44; MIA Berlin 22/3/44 w/Burnett; flak, cr Amendorf, Ger; 1KIA 9POW; MACR 3433.

42-97524 Del Denver 11/12/43; Kearney 28/12/43; ass 413BS/96BG [MZ-S] Snetterton 25/1/44; MIA Pas de Calais 22/6/44 w/Martin; flak, cr Joinville, Fr; 9KIA 1POW; MACR 5916.

42-97525 Del Denver 11/12/43; Kearney 31/12/43; ass 96BG Snetterton 22/2/44; tran 730BS/452BG Deopham Green 23/2/44; MIA Berlin 8/3/44 w/Stephens; e/a, cr Rothensee, Ger; 1KIA 9POW; MACR 3195. INVICTUS.

42-97526 Del Denver 11/12/43; Kearney 24/12/43; New Orleans 3/1/44; Morrison 5/1/44; ass 353BS/301BG Tortorella 21/12/43; MIA {19m} Regensburg 25/2/44 w/Kisselburgh; e/a, cr Kranj; 4KIA 6POW; MACR 2723.

42-97527 Del Cheyenne 11/12/43; Kearney 31/12/43; Grenier 6/1/44; ass 327BS/92BG Podington 5/2/44; MIA Berlin 6/3/44 w/Townsend; flak, cr Vechta, Ger; 9KIA 1POW; MACR 2996.

42-97528 Del Cheyenne 13/12/43; Kearney 30/12/43; Grenier 29/1/44; ass 563BS/388BG Knettishall 9/2/44; b/d Frankfurt 5/1/45 w/?; c/l RAF Hawkinge, UK; 4KIA 5WIA; sal 6/1/45. MARY'S SISTER.

42-97529 Del Cheyenne 13/12/43; Kearney 31/12/43; Presque Is 31/1/44; ass 728BS/452BG Deopham Green 27/1/44; MIA Warnemunde 9/4/44 W/Roy; e/a, cr Todendorf, Ger; 2KIA 7POW; MACR 3663. DINAH MIGHT II.

42-97530 Del Cheyenne 13/12/43; Kearney 28/12/43; Presque Is 21/1/44; ass 548BS/385BG Gt Ashfield 25/1/44; retUS Bradley 26/6/45; 4168 BU Sth Plains 21/10/45; RFC Kingman 1/12/45.

42-97531 Del Cheyenne 13/12/43; Lakeland 6/1/44; Morrison 14/1/44; ass 772BS/463BG Celone 16/2/44; tran 414BS/97BG Amendola 3/7/44; MIA Brux 21/7/44 w/Cunningham; flak, cr Teplitz-Schonau; MACR 6950.

42-97532 Del Denver 13/12/43; Columbus 11/1/44; Langley 12/1/44; ass 482BG (H2X) Alconbury 25/1/44; tran 422BS/305BG [JJ-V] Chelveston 26/3/44; sal 2 SAD 26/4/44.

42-97533 Del Denver 13/12/43; Langley 14/1/44; Presque Is 11/2/44; ass 482BG Alconbury 19/2/44; tran 364BS/305BG [WF-E] Chelveston 20/3/44; 422NLS /44; MIA Merseburg 24/8/44 w/Lt Col Chas Normand; 10POW; MACR 8208.

42-97534 Del Denver 14/12/43; Newark 11/1/44; Langley 12/1/44; ass 482BG (H2X) Alconbury 25/1/44; tran 413BS/96BG [MZ-A] Snetterton 25/1/44 PEE WEE; 728BS/452BG Deopham Green 26/1/44; MIA Merseburg 25/11/44 w/Cohen; flak, cr Schweinfurt; 7KIA 2POW; MACR 11049. PATCHES.

42-97535 Del Denver 14/12/43; Kearney 28/12/43; Grenier 16/1/44; ass 384BG Grafton Underwood 10/2/44; tran 750BS/457BG Glatton 19/2/44; retUS Bradley 28/5/45; 4168 BU Sth Plains 21/10/45; RFC Kingman 1/12/45. BNOUNCING BETTY II.

42-97536 Del Denver 15/12/43; Phoenix 22/12/43; Tulsa 9/1/44; Lakeland 11/1/44; Morrison 18/1/44; ass 773BS/463BG Celone 20/2/44; MIA Budapest 27/6/44 w/East; flak, cr Budapest; MACR 6414.

42-97537 Del Cheyenne 15/12/43; Kearney 17/1/44; Presque Is 14/1/44; ass 749BS/457BG Glatton 25/2/44; 748BS; MIA Marienburg 9/4/44 w/Shephard; e/a, cr?; 10POW; MACR 3666.

42-97538 Del Cheyenne 15/12/43; Gr Island 16/1/44; ass 447BG Rattlesden 9/2/44; f/l continent, Eppegham 21/11/44; sal.

42-97539 Del Cheyenne 15/12/43; Lakeland 6/1/44; Morrison 15/1/44; ass 447BG Rattlesden 16/2/44; tran 775BS/463BG Celone 22/5/44; sal 22/10/45.

42-97540 Del Cheyenne 16/12/43; Lakeland 6/1/44; Morrison 21/2/44; ass 323BS/91BG [OR-Z]

Below: B-17G-15-VE 42-97532 suffered tail wheel loss during landing, the ground impact causing the fuselage to buckle near station No 6. Many B-17s were written off due to damage in this area when a wheels-up landing forced the ball turret supports through the top of the fuselage and distorted formers. This aircraft is an early Pathfinder conversion, having an H2X radome in the ball turret well. The gap in the fin leading edge is where a lifting ring was located. (USAAF)

Bassingbourn 2/4/44; tran 775BS/463BG Celone 19/2/44; MIA Ploesti 18/5/44 w/Tucker; flak, cr Budapest; MACR 5061.

42-97541 Del Cheyenne 16/12/43; Lakeland 5/1/44; Morrison 21/2/44; ass 773BS/463BG Celone 23/2/44; retUS 1103 BU Morrison 12/3/45; 4100 BU Patterson 23/3/45; Recl Comp 24/5/46.

42-97542 Del Denver 16/12/43; Rochester 11/1/44; Langley 13/1/44; ass 482BG (H2X) Alconbury 25/1/44; tran 413BS/96BG [MZ-B] Snetterton 26/1/44; 563BS/388BG Knettishall 27/1/44; MIA Chemnitz 5/3/45 w/Kittle; flak, cr Kraslice, Czech; 1EVD 1KIA 7POW; MACR 12926. CITY OF SAVANNAH.

42-97543 Del Denver 17/12/43; Langley 10/1/44; Mitchell 23/1/44; ass 482BG (H2X) Alconbury 29/1/44; tran 413BS/96BG Snetterton 30/1/44; 422BS/305BG Chelveston 20/3/44; MIA St Lo 25/7/44.

42-97544 Del Denver 17/12/43; Lakeland 11/1/44; Morrison 18/1/44; slated 360BS/303BG [PU-K] Molesworth, ass 773BS/463BG Celone 20/2/44; MIA Nis, Yugo 17/8/44 w/Birnberg; mech fault, cr Bachina; MACR 7458.

42-97545 Del Denver 17/12/43; Albuquerque 21/12/43; Langley 14/1/44; ass 482BG (H2X) Alconbury 29/1/44; tran 413BS/96BG [MZ-D] Snetterton 30/1/44; 33BS/94BG Rougham 3/44; MIA Brandenburg 18/4/44 w/Rieder; e/a, cr Nauen, Ger; 3KIA 7POW; MACR 4160.

42-97546 Del Denver 17/12/43; Kearney 2/1/44; ass 92BG Podington 11/2/44; tran 457BG Glatton 24/2/44; 360BS/303BG [PU-E] Molesworth 13/3/44; retUS Bradley 7/6/45; 4168 BU Sth Plains 12/6/45; RFC Kingman 1/12/45. IDALIZA.

42-97547 Del Cheyenne 17/12/43; Albuquerque 24/12/43; Dallas 10/1/44; Lakeland 12/1/44; ass 772BS/463BG Celone 18/2/44; MIA Weiner Neustadt 10/5/44 w/Smithwick; flak, cr Popovac; MACR 4748. PRINCESS ELIZABETH.

42-97548 Del Cheyenne 17/12/43; Lakeland 10/1/44; ass 774BS/463BG Celone 23/2/44; sal 5/11/44.

42-97549 Del Cheyenne 17/12/43; Gr Island 16/1/44; Grenier 24/2/44; ass 728BS/452BG Deopham Green 15/2/44; MIA Leipzig 29/5/44 w/Brogan; flak, cr Rocquigny, Fr?; 6EVD 4POW; MACR 5228. ROUND TRIPPER.

42-97550 Del Cheyenne 17/12/43; Lincoln 8/1/44; Lakeland 11/1/44; Morrison 13/2/44; ass 772BS/463BG Celone 15/2/44; dest 11/10/44. LASSIE AND HER LADS.

42-97551 Del Cheyenne 18/12/43; Lakeland 8/1/44; Morrison 17/2/44; ass 772BS/463BG Celone 23/2/44; MIA Weiner Neustadt 10/5/44 w/Kort; flak, cr Otterhal; MACR 4747.

42-97552 Del Denver 19/12/43; Kearney 5/1/44; ass 351BG Polebrook 25/2/44; tran 457BG Glatton 1/3/44; 303BG Molesworth 11/3/44; MIA Oranienburg 18/4/44 w/?; MACR 4009.

42-97553 Del Denver 21/12/43; Kearney 7/1/44; Presque Is 24/1/44; ass 8AF 6/2/44.

42-97554 Del Denver 19/12/43; Salt Lake City 27/1/44; 1SAG Langley 15/1/44; Mitchell 1/2/44; ass 482BG (H2X) Alconbury ; tran 337BS/96BG [AW-E] Snetterton 4/2/44; 413BS [MZ-Z]; taxi acc w/447BG a/c 6/4/44; sal 9/4/44.

42-97555 Del Denver 19/12/43; Langley 12/1/44; Mitchell 28/1/44; ass 413BS/96BG [MZ-F] Snetterton 29/1/44; tran 95BG Horham 30/1/44; 350BS/100BG [LN-F] Thorpe Abbotts 31/1/44; MIA Merseburg 28/7/44 w/Capt Mason; flak, cr Offlin?; 2KIA 9POW; MACR 7880. ISLAND F FOR FOX.

42-97556 Del Denver 20/12/43; 1SAG Langley 12/1/44; Mitchell 1/2/44; ass 413BS/96BG [MZ-G] Snetterton 4/2/44; b/d Rostock 11/4/44; hit by bomb from above; cr Gt Glemham, UK; 1KIA 7RTD 2WIA; sal 13/4/44.

42-97557 Del Denver 20/12/43; 1SAG Langley 12/1/44; Mitchell 15/1/44; ass 482BG (H2X) Alconbury 5/2/44; tran 422NLS/305BG [JJ-S] Chelveston 20/3/44; 544BS/384BG [SU-X] Grafton Underwood 4/8/44; retUS Bradley 7/6/45; 4168 BU Sth Plains 13/6/45; RFC Kingman 1/12/45. MERCY'S MADHOUSE.

42-97558 Del Cheyenne 20/12/43; Kearney 10/1/44; Grenier 16/1/44; ass 748BS/457BG Glatton 15/2/44; MIA Merseburg 24/8/44 w/Shaw; e/a, cr Burg, Ger; 9KIA; MACR 8200. TIS ME SUGAR.

42-97559 Del Cheyenne 20/12/43; Dalhart 16/1/44; Kearney 23/2/44; Presque Is 4/3/44; ass 549BS/385BG Gt Ashfield 5/3/44; MIA Berlin 29/4/44 w/Barney; e/a, cr Helmstedt, Ger; 1KIA 9POW; MACR 4459.

42-97560 Del Denver 21/12/43; Lincoln 18/1/44; Mitchell 31/1/44; ass 100BG Thorpe Abbotts 3/2/44; tran 413BS/96BG [MZ-H] Snetterton 4/2/44; sal 19/5/55. HANG THE EXPENSE IV.

42-97561 Del Denver 21/12/43; 1SAG Langley 12/1/44; Scott 18/1/44; Langley 21/1/44; ass 413BS/96BG Snetterton 3/2/44; tran 100BG Thorpe Abbotts 4/2/44; caught fire, cr Felixstowe, UK 7/11/44 w/Dyatt; 3KIA 6RTD. BACHELOR'S HEAVEN.

42-97562 Del Denver 17/12/43; 1SAG Langley 12/1/44; Mitchell 1/2/44; ass 457BG Glatton 2/2/44; tran 324BS/91BG [DF-D] Bassingbourn 27/2/44; 306BG Thurleigh 5/45 for VIP's; sal 9AF Germany 23/5/46. EVENIN' FOLKS! HOW Y'ALL?

42-97563 Del Cheyenne 22/12/43; Dalhart 16/1/44; Kearney 22/2/44; Grenier 24/2/44; ass 457BG Glatton 13/3/44; tran 323BS/91BG [OR-U] Bassingbourn 16/3/44; MIA {68m} Merseburg 2/11/44 w/Snow; e/a, cr Nichaln, Ger?; 1KIA 8POW; MACR 10147. WINGED VICTORY.

42-97564 Del Denver 22/12/43; 1SAG Langley 17/1/44; ass 413BS/96BG [MZ-J] Snetterton (H2X) 4/2/44; tran 418BS/100BG Thorpe Abbotts 2/44; MIA Merseburg 20/7/44 w/Maj Magee; flak, cr Louvain, Bel; 6EVD 6POW; MACR 7414. PATHFINDERS.

42-97565 Del Denver 22/12/43; 1SAG Langley 14/1/44; ass 413BS/96BG [MZ-K] Snetterton (H2X) 29/1/44; tran 95BG Horham 6/44; sal 17/10/44.

42-97566 Del Denver 22/12/43; 1SAG Langley 21/1/44; Mitchell 1/2/44; Presque Is 29/2/44; ass 111 BU Langley 16/9/44; 3539 BU Langley 18/9/44; Recl Comp 2/10/44; W/O 18/10/44.

42-97567 Del Denver 22/12/43; Langley 12/1/44; Chicago 18/1/44; Langley 19/1/44; Presque Is 19/2/44; ass 413BS/96BG [MZ-K] Snetterton 1/2/44; MIA Brux 12/5/44 w/Moore; e/a, cr Weisbaden, Ger; 7KIA 4POW; MACR 4860.

42-97568 Del Denver 23/12/43; Palm Springs 30/12/43; Langley 10/2/44; ass 49BS/2BG Amendola 2/3/44; tran 816BS/483BG Tortorella 28/3/44; Sterparone 22/4/44; MIA Linz 15/11/44 w/Eder; flak, cr Zeltweg; MACR 9900.

42-97569 Del Denver 23/12/43; Salt Lake City 27/12/43; 1SAG Langley 12/1/44; ass 94BG Rougham 3/2/44; tran 413BS/96BG [MZ-M] Snetterton 4/2/44; MIA Brandenburg 18/4/44 w/Capt Hogan; hit by bomb from a/c above; cr Bluethen, Ger; 1KIA 9POW; MACR 4161.

42-97570 Del Cheyenne 23/12/43; McDill 3/2/44; Morrison 10/3/44; ass 815BS/483BG Tortorella 13/3/44; tran 346BS/99BG Tortorella 31/3/44; MIA {59m} Bleckhammer 27/8/44 w/Humbrecht; flak, cr Loebschutz; six chutes seen; MACR 7991. ACHTUNG.

42-97571 Del Cheyenne 23/12/43; Salt Lake City 29/12/43; Kearney 18/1/44; ass 750BS/457BG Glatton 24/2/44; MIA Merseburg 24/8/44 w/Pugh; e/a, cr Hartmansdorf, Ger; 5KIA 4POW; MACR 8201.

42-97572 Del Cheyenne 24/12/43; Dalhart 16/1/44; Kearney 22/2/44; ass 457BG Glatton 2/3/44; tran 711BS/447BG Rattlesden 3/3/44; 709BS; sal 23/6/44. FEATHER MERCHANT.

42-97573 Del Cheyenne 24/12/43; Dalhart 24/1/44; Kearney 23/2/44; Omaha 2/3/44; Patterson 12/3/44; Grenier 14/3/44; ass 545BS/384BG [JD-Q] Grafton Underwood 15/4/44; MIA Krzesinski 29/5/44 w/Moore; flak, cr Stralsund; 9POW; MACR 5318.

42-97574 Del Denver 26/12/43; Long Beach 29/12/43; 1SAG Langley 29/1/44; ass 482BG (H2X) Alconbury 9/2/44; tran 422BS/305BG [JJ-A] Chelveston 20/3/44; 423BS/306BG Thurleigh 2/8/44; MIA Merseburg 21/11/44 w/Schoenbachler; flak, cr Osnabrück; 10POW; MACR 10414. CASA DE UMBRIAGO.

42-97575 Del Denver 28/12/43; Atlanta 21/1/44; 1SAG Langley 30/1/44; ass 49BS/2BG Amendola 24/3/44; tran 774BS/463BG Celone /44; (loaned 347BS/99BG for one mission); MIA Linz 27/12/44 w/Demos; flak, cr Linz; MACR 10747.

42-97576 Del Denver 26/12/43; Omaha 31/1/44; 1SAG Langley 1/2/44; Slated 447BG, ass (PFF) 49BS/2BG Amendola 3/3/44; tran 772BS/463BG Celone 3/44; (loaned 347BS/99BG for one mission); MIA Weiner Neustadt 10/5/44 w/Lackey; flak, cr Karlstadt; MACR 4839.

42-97577 Del Denver 29/12/43; 1SAG Langley 24/1/44; ass 413BS/96BG [MZ-N] Snetterton 9/2/44; tran 569BS/390BG Framlingham 2/44; MIA Gaggenau 10/9/44 w/Markward; flak, cr Nurnberg, Ger; 7KIA 2POW; MACR 8914.

42-97578 Del Denver 28/12/43; 1SAG Langley 24/1/44; ass H2S 482BG Alconbury 5/2/44; tran 422BS/305BG Chelveston 20/3/44; c/t/o for Schweinfurt 24/3/44, skidded across road and hit bungalow, killing two children; sal.

42-97579 Del Cheyenne 28/12/43; Kearney 14/1/44; Presque Is 24/1/44; ass 749BS/457BG Glatton 23/2/44; 750BS; MIA Le Bourget 14/6/44 w/Allen; flak, cr Combles, Fr; 9EVD 1KIA; MACR 5804. LOCAL MISSION.

42-97580 Del Cheyenne 28/12/43; Oklahoma City 12/1/44; Homestead 24/1/44; Slated 390BG, then 381BG, ass 353BS/301BG Lucera 3/2/44; MIA {28m} Wollersdorf 29/5/44 w/DeDomizio; mech fault, cr Kimmith; 3EVD 7POW; MACR 5444.

42-97581 Del Cheyenne 28/12/43; Dallas 12/1/44; Morrison 16/1/44; ass 96BS/2BG Amendola 12/2/44; MIA {8m} Brasov 16/4/44 w/Voss; flak, cr Niksic; 9EVD & ret; MACR 4023.

42-97582 Del Denver 28/12/43; Long Beach 2/1/44; 1SAG Langley 20/1/44; ass 429BS/2BG Amendola 9/3/44; caught fire on training mission w/James 18/2/45; sal 2/3/45.

42-97583 Del Denver 29/12/43; 1SAG Langley 11/1/44; ass 49BS/2BG Amendola 2/3/44; tran 32BS/301BG Lucera 9/4/44; 774BS/463BG 4/44; MIA Ploesti 5/5/44 w/Fontaneau; flak, cr Moreni; 9KIA (inc group bombardier Haas); MACR 4712.

42-97584 Del Denver 29/12/43; 1SAG Langley 18/1/44; ass 49BS/2BG Amendola 2/3/44; (loaned to

346BS/99BG for three missions); tran 816BS/483BG Sterparone 22/4/44; MIA Memmingen 18/7/44 w/Hommel; e/a, cr Gerats; 5KIA 6POW (inc Intel Off Fitzgibbon); MACR 6981.

42-97585 Del Denver 29/12/43; 1SAG Langley 21/1/44; ass (PFF) 457BG Glatton 15/2/44; tran 49BS/2BG Amendola 2/3/44; tran 301BG Lucera 14/5/44; 840BS/483BG Sterparone 20/7/44; MIA Brux 25/12/44 w/Chapman; flak, cr Laibach; 10POW; MACR 10730.

42-97586 Del Denver 29/12/43; 1SAG Langley 21/1/44; Presque Is 24/2/44; ass 413BS/96BG Snetterton 2/2/44; tran 335BS/95BG [OE-D] Horham 3/3/44; sal 8/6/45.

42-97587 Del Cheyenne 30/12/43; Kearney 12/1/44; Grenier 26/1/44; ass 751BS/457BG Glatoon 2/2/44; retUS Bradley 8/6/45; 4168 BU Sth Plains 14/6/45; RFC Kingman 5/12/45. DISCIPLINARY ACTION.

42-97588 Del Cheyenne 30/12/43; Phoenix 2/1/44; Kearney 14/1/44; ass 457BG Glatton 7/3/44; tran 306BG Thurleigh 12/3/44; c/l RNAF Ford, UK 23/5/44, sal.

42-97589 Del Cheyenne 30/12/43; Kearney 12/1/44; ass 533BS/381BG [VP-Y] Ridgewell 8/2/44; b/d Cologne 26/3/45 w/Schein; c/l base, sal 28/3/45.

42-97590 Del Cheyenne 30/12/43; Kearney 14/1/44; ass 457BG Glatton 22/2/44; tran 360BS/303BG Molesworth 13/3/44; b/d French a/fd 10/6/44; c/l Gt Gidding, UK; 6KIA; MACR 4009; sal 2 SAD 13/6/44. VIRGIN MARY.

42-97591 Del Cheyenne 30/12/43; Kearney 14/1/44; ass 482BG Alconbury 9/2/44; tran 748BS/457BG Glatton 2/3/44; b/d German oil inst 16/2/45; f/l continent; sal 22/2/45.

42-97592 Del Denver 31/12/43; 1SAG Langley 13/1/44; ass 544BS/384BG [SU-Y] Grafton Underwood 1/3/44; tran 457BG Glatton 9/5/45; 422BS/305BG [JJ-T] Chelveston 23/5/45; sal 9AF Germany 3/4/46.

42-97593 Del Denver 31/12/43; 1SAG Langley 22/1/44; Presque Is 17/2/44; ass 333BS/94BG [TS-H] Rougham 18/2/44; 332BS [XM-J]; tran 550BS/385BG Gt Ashfield 3/4/44; retUS Bradley 8/7/45; 4168 BU Sth Plains 11/7/45; RFC Kingman 30/11/45. DIMPLES DARLING.

42-97594 Del Denver 31/12/43; Salt Lake City 4/1/44; 1SAG Langley 25/1/44; Presque Is 27/2/44; ass 324BS/91BG Bassingbourn 27/4/44; tran 532BS/381BG [VE-B] Ridgewell 5/7/44; c/t/o for Peenemunde, at Shalford, Ex. UK 4/8/44 w/Cuppernall; 9RTD, TG Norris killed; sal 5/8/44. DRY GULCHER.

42-97595 Del Denver 31/12/43; 1SAG Langley 23/1/44; Grenier 5/2/44; ass 8AF 19/2/44; sal b/d 18/3/44.

42-97596 Del Denver 2/1/44; 1SAG Langley 16/1/44; ass 447BG Rattlesden 2/3/44; tran 333BS/94BG Rougham 3/3/44; sal 9AF Germany 10/5/46.

42-97597 Del Denver 2/1/44; 1SAG Langley 25/1/44; Presque Is 23/2/44; ass 413BS/96BG Snetterton 25/2/44; tran 710BS/447BG Rattlesden 26/2/44; MIA Oranienburg 18/4/44 w/Capt Esterline; hit by bomb from a/c above, cr?; 10POW; MACR 4175.

42-97598 Del Denver 3/1/44; Hendricks 23/1/44; slated 482BG but sal 18/3/44; 3501 BU Boca Raton 28/11/44; 3704 BU Keesler 17/1/45; 4119 BU Brookley 13/3/45; 3704 BU Keesler 2/4/45; 613 BU Phillips 24/6/46.

42-97599 Del Denver 2/1/44; 1SAG Langley 23/1/44; Grenier 24/2/44; ass 335BS/95BG [OE-T] Horham 28/2/44; MIA Ludwigshafen 25/9/44 w/96BG; sal 14/11/44.

42-97600 Del Denver 3/1/44; Langley 26/1/44; Grenier 25/2/44; ass 91BG Bassingbourn 27/4/44; tran 351BG Polebrook 14/6/44; 614BS/401BG [IW-Y] Deenethorpe 20/8/44; 613BS [IN-Y]; MIA Merseburg 21/11/44 w/Rundell; flak, cr Merseburg; 9POW; MACR 10410.

42-97601 Del Denver 3/1/44; 1SAG Langley 4/2/44; 13/3/44; ass 91BG Bassingbourn 27/4/44; tran 351BG Polebrook 14/6/44; 751BS/457BG Glatton 15/6/44; MIA Augsburg 19/7/44 w/Cunefare; e/a, cr Telfts, Aus; 4KIA 5POWP; MACR 7548. GYPSY GAL.

42-97602 Del Denver 3/1/44; El Paso 6/1/44; Hendricks 21/1/44; 2116 BU Laredo 25/8/44; 2126 BU Laredo 1/2/45; RFC Walnut Ridge 11/1/46.

42-97603 Del Denver 3/1/44; Scott 10/2/44; Langley 13/2/44; Presque Is 11/3/44; ass (H2X) 333BS/94BG Rougham 12/3/44; tran 385BG Gt Ashfield 12/3/44; MIA Karlsruhe 27/5/44 w/Capt Richards (94BG); Capt Radin (radar crew, later escaped); flak hit #2; bellied in Knutwil, Switz; set on fire to destroy radar equip; 10INT; MACR 5266. GREMLIN BUGGY II.

42-97604 Del Denver 4/1/44; Hendricks 20/1/44; 2137 BU Hendricks 17/11/44; 4209 BU Des Moines 10/4/45; 2137 BU Hendricks 18/4/45; RFC Walnut Ridge 29/10/45.

42-97605 Del Denver 4/1/44; Del Marbry 20/1/44; 2137 BU Hendricks 17/11/44; RFC Kingman 9/11/45.

42-97606 Del Denver 4/1/44; Albuquerque 23/1/44; 3017 BU Hobbs 4/6/44; RFC Walnut Ridge 3/1/46.

42-97607 Del Denver 4/1/44; Savannah 23/1/44; ass 349BS/100BG [XR-H] Thorpe Abbotts 7/2/44; MIA Berlin 19/5/45 w/Horne; e/a, ditched Baltic; 10POW; MACR 4948.

42-97608 Del Denver 5/1/44; Lockburn 21/1/44; 3501 BU Boca Raton 28/11/44; RFC Kingman 29/11/45.

42-97609 Del Denver 5/1/44; Hendricks 21/1/44; 3501 BU Boca Raton 28/11/44; RFC Kingman 22/2/46.

42-97610 Del Denver 5/1/44; 1 Ph Gp Bolling 23/1/44; Cheyenne 7/9/44; Washington 2/11/44; 613 BU Phillips 6/11/44; re-ass AAF 25/1/46.

42-97611 Del Denver 5/1/44; Hendricks 23/1/44; 3501 BU Boca Raton 28/11/44; 3508 BU Truax 9/8/45; 3501 BU Boca Raton 12/8/45; RFC Kingman 20/12/45.

42-97612 Del Denver 6/1/44; Yuma 21/1/44; 3017 BU Hobbs 4/6/44; RFC Walnut Ridge 28/12/45.

42-97613 Del Denver 6/1/44; Lockburn 19/1/44; 303 BU Yuma 13/7/44; 3017 BU Hobbs 4/6/45; RFC Walnut Ridge 7/1/46.

42-97614 Del Denver 6/1/44; 1SAG Langley 4/2/44; Grenier 4/3/44; ass 326BS/92BG [JW-H] Podington 7/3/44 PINUP GIRL; tran 333BS/94BG Rougham 7/3/44; MIA Berlin 21/6/44 w/Nichols; flak, cr Leibenwalde, Ger; 10KIA; MACR 5914. NICK'S PLACE.

42-97615 Del San Diego 6/1/44; Denver 13/1/44; 1SAG Langley 14/2/44; Morrison 25/3/44; ass (PFF) 49BS/2BG Amendola 26/3/44; 96BG {36m}; (often loaned to 99BG Tortorella); retUS Hunter 5/7/45; 4168 BU Sth Plains 21/10/45; RFC Kingman 9/11/45.

42-97616 Del Denver 7/1/44; Salt Lake City 12/1/44; 1SAG Langley 4/2/44; Dow Fd 4/4/44; ass 413BS/96BG Snetterton 5/4/44; MIA Merseburg 28/7/44 w/Franklin (+ 452BG crew); mid air coll, cr Merseburg; 6KIA 3POW; MACR 7827. HI-BLOWER.

42-97617 Del Denver 7/1/44; Savannah 21/1/44; ass 358BS/303BG Molesworth 23/2/44; MIA Schweinfurt 13/4/44 w/Viets; e/a, cr Kirn, Ger; 1EVD 9POW; MACR 3770.

42-97618 Del Denver 7/1/44; 419 Base HQ Dyersburg 22/3/44; Albuquerque 6/2/44; 330 BU Dyersburg 1/3/45; 327 BU Drew 28/8/45; 330 BU Dyersburg 4/9/45; RFC Walnut Ridge 19/12/45.

42-97619 Del Denver 7/1/44; Yuma 23/1/44; 3036 BU Yuma, W/O 29/6/44.

42-97620 Del Denver 9/1/44; 1SAG Langley 4/2/44; Grenier 4/3/44; ass 413BS/96BG Snetterton 7/3/44; MIA Friedrichshafen 24/4/44 w/Lt Col Francis Tiller; flak, cr Kaiserlautern; 11POW; MACR 4164.

42-97621 Del Denver 9/1/44; 1SAG Langley 22/1/44; Hendricks 26/2/44; Presque Is 28/2/44; ass 350BS/100BG [LN-A] Thorpe Abbotts 3/3/44; MIA Merseburg 28/7/44 w/Spear; mid air coll w/42-32009; cr Channel; 9KIA 1POW; MACR 8173.

42-97622 Del Denver 9/1/44; Savannah 29/1/44; ass 457BG Glatton 10/2/44; tran 358BS/303BG [VK-K] Molesworth 23/2/44; b/d Creil 23/7/44 w/?; f/l Greenham Common A/fd, UK; sal 2 SAD 25/7/44. PAPER DOLLIE.

42-97623 Del Denver 9/1/44; 1SAG Langley 4/2/44; Grenier 16/3/44; ass (H2X) 482BG Alconbury 23/3/44; tran 413BS/96BG Snetterton 24/3/44; sal 9AF Germany 28/3/46.

42-97624 Del Denver 10/1/44; Gr Island 23/1/44; ass 457BG Glatton 22/2/44; tran 709BS/447BG Rattlesden 23/2/44; MIA Lutzkendorf 9/2/45 w/DeDiemar; mech fault, cr Ohrdruf, Ger; 9POW; MACR 12241. DEVIL'S MATE II.

42-97625 Del Denver 10/1/44; 1SAG Langley 31/1/44; Grenier 14/3/44; ass (H2X) 535BS/381BG [MS-I] Ridgewell 22/3/44; loaned to 324BS/91BG [DF-K] Bassingbourn 27/4/44 {13m}; ret 381BG 5/7/44; {50m} c/l base 8/3/45, sal. SUNKIST SPECIAL.

42-97626 Del Denver 10/1/44; 1SAG Langley 13/2/44; Presque Is 11/3/44; ass 322BS/91BG [LG-M] Bassingbourn 27/4/44; 324BG; tran 601BS/398BG [3O-Q] Nuthampstead 6/44; MIA Hamburg 18/6/44 w/Hatter; flak, cr Fleestedt, Ger; 6KIA 4POW; MACR 5996.

42-97627 Del Denver 10/1/44; 1SAC Langley 31/1/44; Grenier 23/2/44; ass 413BS/96BG [MZ-T] Snetterton 3/3/44; retUS Bradley 21/7/45; 4185 BU Independence 30/11/44; RFC Kingman 22/12/45.

42-97628 Del Denver 11/1/44; 1SAG Langley 4/2/44; Grenier 7/3/44; slated 452BG Deopham Green, ass 413BS/96BG [MZ-U] Snetterton 11/3/44; dest at Poltava, Russia 21/6/44; sal 2/7/44.

42-97629 Del Denver 11/1/44; 1SAG Langley 6/2/44; Grenier 2/4/44; ass (H2X) 482BG Alconbury 9/4/44; sal 9AF Germany 4/6/46.

42-97630 Del Denver 11/1/44; 1SAG Langley 6/2/44; Presque Is 10/3/44; ass 324BS/91BG [DF-H] Bassingbourn 27/4/44 PEG O' MY HEART; 323BS [OR-T]; {41+m} tran 306BG Thurleigh 21/5/45; sal 9AF Germany 28/3/46. GERALDINE.

42-97631 Del Denver 11/1/44; 1SAG Langley 4/2/44; Presque Is 15/3/44; ass 413BS/96BG Snetterton 14/3/44; MIA Berlin 8/5/44 w/White; e/a, cr Kirchlinteln, Ger; 3KIA 8POW; MACR 4571.

42-97632 Del Denver 12/1/44; 1SAG Langley 6/2/44; Grenier 14/3/44; ass 324BS/91BG [DF-R] Bassingbourn 27/4/44; MIA Berlin 3/2/45 w/Adams; flak, cr Berlin; 10KIA; MACR 12232.

42-97633 Del Denver 12/1/44; 1SAG Langley 6/2/44; Grenier 29/3/44; ass 333BS/94BG Rougham 23/3/44; tran 457BG Glatton 3/4/44; retUS, RFC Walnut Ridge 7/1/46.

42-97634 Del Denver 12/1/44; 1SAG Langley 4/2/44; Grenier 17/3/44; ass 333BS/94BG Rougham 24/3/44; tran 711BS/447BG Rattlesden 3/4/44; MIA Merseburg 2/11/44 w/Capt Reynolds; 5KIA 5POW;

MACR 10164.

42-97635 Del Denver 12/1/44; 1SAG Langley 4/2/44; W/O 3/3/44.

42-97636 Del Denver 13/1/44; 1SAG Langley 4/2/44; Presque Is 13/3/44; ass 324BS/91BG [DF-P] Bassingbourn 27/4/44; tran 351BG Polebrook 14/6/44; 615BS/401BG Deenethorpe 26/8/44; 305BG Chelveston 8/44; sal 9AF Germany 3/4/46.

42-97637 Del Denver 13/1/44; 1SAG Langley 4/2/44; Grenier 4/3/44; ass 422BS/305BG Chelveston; b/d Saarbrücken 23/5/44 w/Capt Fullilove; c/l continent; sal.

42-97638 Del Denver 14/1/44; 1SAG Langley 4/2/44; Grenier 16/3/44; ass 305BG Chelveston 20/3/44; tran 91BG Bassingbourn 27/4/44; 351BG Polebrook 14/6/44; 748BS/457BG Glatton 7/8/44; 749BS; MIA Politz, Ger 7/10/44 w/Flannery; flak, cr Politz; 5KIA 5POW; MACR 9773.

42-97639 Del Denver 13/1/44; 1SAG Langley 6/2/44; 3501 BU Boca Raton 28/11/44; W/O 29/11/44.

42-97640 Del Denver 13/1/44; 1SAG Langley 13/2/44; ass (PFF) 49BS/2BG Amendola 2/3/44; tran 301BG Lucera 14/5/44; MIA Worgl, Aus. 23/2/45 w/Douglas; mech fault, cr Gussing; 10POW; MACR 12470.

42-97641 Del Denver 13/1/44; 1SAG Langley 22/2/44; Morrison 22/3/44; ass (PFF) 49BS/2BG Amendola 23/3/44; tran 414BS/97BG Amendola 4/44; 301BG Lucera /44; retUS 1103 BU Morrison 20/2/45; 4100 BU Patterson 23/2/45; Recl Comp 2/5/46.

42-97642 Del Denver 14/1/44; 1SAG Langley 13/2/44; ass 49BS/2BG Amendola 2/3/44; 301BG Lucera 15/5/44; 97BG Amendola /44; sal 25/7/45.

42-97643 Del Denver 14/1/44; 1SAG Langley 11/2/44; Grenier 20/3/44; ass 333BS/94BG Rougham 24/3/44; retUS Bradley 25/6/45; 4168 BU Sth Plains 27/6/45; RFC Kingman 8/12/45.

42-97644 Del Denver 16/1/44; 1SAG Langley 13/2/44; Boca Raton 11/3/45; 420 BU March 21/8/45; 3539 BU Langley 3/10/45; RFC Walnut Ridge 9/1/46.

42-97645 Del Denver 16/1/44; 1SAG Langley 25/2/44; Dow Fd 8/4/44; ass (H2X) 482BG Alconbury 10/4/44; tran 349BS/100BG [XR-P] Thorpe Abbotts 5/45; retUS, RFC Walnut Ridge 7/1/46.

42-97646 Del Denver 16/1/44; 1SAG Langley 1/3/44; Presque Is 3/4/44; ass 333BS/94BG [TS-B] Rougham 4/4/44; tran 447BG Rattlesden 4/44; c/l Rougham 25/8/44, sal & rep; retUS Bradley 13/7/45; 4185 BU Independence 15/7/45; RFC Kingman 12/1/46.

42-97647 Del Denver 17/1/44; 1SAG Langley 27/2/44; Grenier 1/4/44; ass 482BG Alconbury 4/44; tran 366BS/305BG [KY-A] Chelveston 16/5/44; MIA Hamburg 18/6/44 w/Col Ernest Lawson; 10KIA 1POW; MACR 5939.

42-97648 Del Denver 17/1/44; 1SAG Langley 14/2/44; Morrison 23/3/44; ass (PFF) 49BS/2BG Amendola 26/3/44; tran 348BS/99BG Tortorella {2m}; 340BS/97BG Amendola 4/44; MIA Bleckhammer 13/9/44 w/Waters; cr Gross Strehiltz; MACR 8729.

42-97649 Del Denver 17/1/44; 1SAG Langley 7/2/44; Grenier 14/3/44; ass 91BG Bassingbourn 27/4/44; tran 351BG Polebrook 14/6/44; 748BS/457BG Glatton 28/8/44; 305BG Chelveston 23/5/45; sal 9AF Germany 4/4/46.

42-97650 Del Denver 17/1/44; 1SAG Langley 15/2/44; Morrison 25/3/44; ass 49BS/2BG Amendola 29/3/44; tran 346BS/99BG Tortorella 22/5/44; {46m} depot 29/1/45; retUS Hunter 25/6/45; 4168 BU Sth Plains 27/6/45; RFC Kingman 8/12/45.

42-97651 Del Denver 18/1/44; 1ASG Langley 7/2/44; Grenier 19/3/44; ass 91BG Bassingbourn 27/4/44; tran 510BS/351BG [TU-Y] Polebrook 14/6/44; 511BS [DS-Y]; 305BG Chelveston 5/45; sal 9AF Germany 3/4/46.

42-97652 Del Denver 18/1/44; 1SAG Langley 10/2/44; Morrison 22/3/44; ass 49BS/2BG Amendola 23/3/44; 20BS; MIA Salzburg 7/12/44 w/Pederson; flak, cr Agram; MACR 10223.

42-97653 Del Denver 18/1/44; 1SAG Langley 13/2/44; Slated 381BG, ass 49BS/2BG Amendola 2/3/44; tran 840BS/483BG Sterparone; MIA Nis, Yugo 15/7/44 w/Kilpatrick; flak, hit #1 & 2, cr Nis; 10EVD, ret 26/8/44; MACR 6826.

42-97654 Del Denver 18/1/44; 1SAG Langley 14/2/44; Presque Is 13/3/44; ass 413BS/96BG [MZ-J] Snetterton 14/4/44; MIA Brux 12/5/44 w/Capt Knupp; e/a, cr Kamberg, Ger; 8KIA 2POW; MACR 4861.

42-97655 Del Denver 18/1/44; 1SAG Langley 13/2/44; ass 49BS/2BG Amendola 2/3/44; tran 414BS/97BG Amendola; MIA Weiner Neustadt 10/5/44 w/Col Jacob Smart (Gp CO); flak, cr Stinkenbrunn; MACR 4722.

42-97656 Del Mat Com Wright Fd 19/1/44; 4CBC Bowman 8/10/44; Mat HQ Wright 24/8/45; 4126 BU San Bernardino 29/11/45; 4119 BU Brookley 11/12/45; 610 BU Eglin 14/2/46; 613 BU Phillips 28/3/46; 620 BU Muroc 29/3/46; Recl Comp 1/11/46.

42-97657 Del Denver 19/1/44; 1SAG Langley 13/2/44; slated 15AF, MatVN Nashville 28/8/44; 3018 BU Kingman 16/3/45; 4100 BU Patterson 18/3/45; Recl Comp 2/5/46.

42-97658 Del Denver 19/1/44; 1SAG Langley 1/2/44; Grenier 2/4/44; ass 367BS/306NG [GY-S] Thurleigh 8/4/44; MIA Berlin 3/2/35 w/Lissner; flak, f/l Bulltofta, Swed; 9INT; MACR 12495; (Left 5/6/45). THE JONES FAMILY.

42-97659 Del Denver 19/1/44; 1SAG Langley 1/2/44; Dow Fd 3/4/44; ass 482BG Alconbury 11/4/44; retUS Morrison 18/10/45; RFC Walnut Ridge 20/12/45.

42-97660 Del Denver 21/1/44; 1SAG Langley 1/2/44; Grenier 2/4/44; ass 305BG Chelveston 19/5/44; tran 326BS/92BG [JW-X] Podington 4/8/44; sal 9AF Germany 23/8/46. LADY KATHRYN.

42-97661 Del Denver 21/1/44; 1SAG Langley 1/2/44; Dow Fd 7/4/44; ass 482BG Alconbury 8/4/44; tran 534BS/381BG [GD-L] Ridgewell 9/4/44; sal 9AF Germany 31/5/46.

42-97662 Del Denver 21/1/44; 1SAG Langley 9/2/44; Dow Fd 2/4/44; ass 748BS/457BG Glatton 3/3/44; f/l continent 30/11/44; sal 23/1/45.

42-97663 Del Denver 21/1/44; Gr Island 6/2/44; Grenier 23/2/44; ass 452BG Deopham Green 22/2/44; tran 457BG Glatton 4/3/44; 369BS/306BG [WW-V] Thurleigh 12/3/44; MIA Pas de Calais 26/3/44 w/Price; flak, cr Godincihum, Fr; 10POW; MACR 3483.

42-97664 Del Denver 21/1/44; Gr Island 6/2/44; Presque Is 21/3/44; ass 615BS/401BG [IY-F] Deenethorpe 17/4/44; 612BS [SC-X]; f/l continent 10/5/45; sal 2 SAD. AW COME ON.

42-97665 Del Denver 21/1/44; Las Vegas 26/1/44; Pyote 17/3/44; 235 BU Biggs 16/8/44; 3028 BU Luke Fd 1/12/44; 235 BU Biggs 23/12/44; 222 BU Ardmore 4/3/45; 332 BU Ardmore 16/6/45; RFC Walnut Ridge 7/12/45.

42-97666 Del Denver 21/1/44; 1SAG Langley 3/3/44; Grenier 6/4/44; ass 96BG Snetterton 7/4/44; tran 728BS/452BG Deopham Green 8/4/44; MIA Hamburg 31/12/44 w/Kostuck; e/a, cr Rotenburg, Ger; 1KIA 8POW; MACR 11234.

42-97667 Del Denver 22/1/44; 1SAG Langley 3/3/44; Dow Fd 4/4/44; ass (H2X) 482BG Alconbury 5/4/44; tran 418BS/100BG [LD-A] Thorpe Abbotts 5/45; retUS, RFC Walnut Ridge 8/1/46.

42-97668 Del Denver 21/1/44; 1SAG Langley 1/2/44; Grenier 2/4/44; ass 333BS/94BG [TS-N] Rougham 7/4/44; tran 306BG Thurleigh 8/4/44; retUS Bradley 24/6/45; 4168 BU Sth Plains 29/6/45; RFC Kingman 29/11/45. LEADING LADY.

42-97669 Del Denver 23/1/44; Albuquerque 16/2/44; Pyote 17/3/44; 235 BU Biggs 16/8/44; 222 BU Ardmore 4/3/45; 332 BU Ardmore 16/6/45; RFC Walnut Ridge 19/8/45.

42-97670 Del Denver 23/1/44; Las Vegas 29/1/44; Denver 2/2/44; Pyote 14/3/44; 235 BU Biggs 17/8/44; 207 BU Minneapolis 14/12/44; 1454 BU Minneapolis 17/12/44; 235 BU Biggs 20/12/44; 222 BU Ardmore 8/3/45; 332 BU Ardmore 16/6/45; RFC Walnut Ridge 21/8/45.

42-97671 Del Denver 24/1/44; Hunter 15/3/44; Morrison 3/5/44; ass 816BS/483BG Sterparone 5/5/44; MIA Memmingen 18/7/44 w/Gussarson; e/a, cr Kempten, Ger? 10KIA 1POW; MACR 6976.

42-97672 Del Denver 23/1/44; Pyote 14/3/44; 235 BU Biggs 16/8/44; 3009 BU Carlsbad 22/9/44; 235 BU Biggs 13/10/44; 225 BU Rapid City 23/3/45; 426 BU Mt Home 25/8/45; 237 BU Kirtland 2/10/45; RFC Altus 7/11/45.

42-97673 Del Denver 23/1/44; Hunter 13/3/44; Grenier 29/4/44; ass 350BS/100BG Thorpe Abbotts 4/5/44; retUS Bradley 20/6/45; 4168 BU Sth Plains 22/6/45; RFC Kingman 10/12/45.

42-97674 Del Denver 24/1/44; Hunter 15/3/44; Dow Fd 19/4/44; ass 364BS/305BG [WF-A] Chelveston 30/4/44; MIA Brandenburg 6/8/44 w/Farmer; flak, cr Wittmundehafe, Ger; 9POW; MACR 7881.

42-97675 Del Denver 24/1/44; Pyote 14/3/44; 4136 BU Tinker 28/7/44; 224 BU Sioux City 2/11/44; 225 BU Rapid City 16/6/45; 246 BU Pratt 30/9/45; RFC Altus 7/11/45.

42-97676 Del Denver 24/1/44; 1SAG Langley 11/3/44; Greenboro 14/5/44; 330 BU Dyersburg 1/3/45; RFC Walnut Ridge 19/12/45.

42-97677 Del Denver 23/1/44; 1SAG Langley 12/3/44; Rapid City 16/3/44; 225 BU Rapid City 1/5/45; 283 BU Galveston 19/7/45; RFC Kingman 15/12/45.

42-97678 Del Denver 25/1/44; Kearney 15/3/44; Grenier 2/4/44; ass 526BS/379BG [LF-J] Kimbolton 11/4/44; 525BS; MIA Chemnitz 3/2/35 w/Webber; flak, cr Ilvenstadt; MACR 12217. {128m} THE BIRMINGHAM JEWEL.

42-97679 Del Denver 25/1/44; 1SAG Langley 9/3/44; Greenboro 13/5/44; Dyersburg 1/3/45; RFC Walnut Ridge 19/12/45.

42-97680 Del Denver 25/1/44; 1SAG Langley 7/3/44; Dow Fd 5/4/44; ass 413BS/96BG [MZ-G] Snetterton 7/4/44; retUS Bradley 5/7/45; 4168 BU Sth Plains 7/7/45; RFC Kingman 15/11/45.

42-97681 Del Denver 27/1/44; 1SAG Langley 12/3/44; Dow Fd 5/4/44; ass 333BS/94BG Rougham 7/4/44; 331BS [XM-T]; b/d Frankfurt 9/3/45, sal (rear half used on 44-6890); THE BIG WHEEL.

42-97682 Del Denver 26/1/44; 1SAG Langley 13/3/44; Grenier 27/4/44; ass (H2X) 482BG Alconbury 31/4/44; tran 418BS/100BG [LD-V] Thorpe Abbotts 5/45; retUS, RFC Walnut Ridge 2/1/46.

42-97683 Del Denver 26/1/44; 1SAG Langley 7/3/44; Grenier 7/4/44; Slated 95BG, ass (PFF) 335BS/95BG [OE-M] Horham 8/4/44; MIA Warsaw (Op Frantic IV) 18/9/44 w/Miller; flak, f/l Russia; 4POW 5RTD; sal & rep; MACR 10201; tran 352BS/301BG Lucera 28/10/44; MIA Ruhland 15/3/45 w/Thornton; 1KIA 9POW; MACR 12824.

42-97684 Del Denver 27/1/44; 1SAG Langley 7/3/44; Morrison 20/4/44; ass (PFF) 49BS/2BG Amendola 21/4/44; tran 416BS/99BG Tortorella 25/4/44; {76m};

sal 9AF Germany 19/5/46.

42-97685 Del Denver 27/1/44; 1SAG Langley 11/4/44; Morrison 28/4/44; ass (PFF) 49BS/2BG Amendola 30/4/44; tran 353BS/301BG Lucera 15/5/44; MIA Linz, Aus 25/11/44 w/Govatsos; mech fault, cr Cili?; 2POW 8EVD and ret; MACR 10108. STARDUST.

42-97686 Del Denver 27/1/44; 1SAG Langley 6/3/44; Dow Fd 23/4/44; ass 398BG Nuthampstead 24/4/44; tran 324BS/91BG Bassingbourn 23/5/44; MIA Berlin 21/6/44 w/? (part 398BG crew); MACR 5997.

42-97687 Del Denver 27/1/44; 1SAG Langley 8/3/44; Grenier 7/4/44; ass 323BS/91BG [OR-Y] Bassingbourn 23/5/44; tran 508BS/351BG [YB-Z] Polebrook 14/6/44; 511BS [DS-Z]; 305BG Chelveston 23/5/45; sal 9AF Germany 10/5/46.

42-97688 Del Denver 27/1/44; 1SAG Langley 10/3/44; Dow Fd 12/4/44; ass (H2X) 482BG Alconbury 11/4/44; sal 2/4/45.

42-97689 Del Denver 28/1/44; 1SAG Langley 11/3/44; Grenier 6/4/44; ass (H2X) 482BG Alconbury 10/4/44; retUS 1103 BU Morrison 18/10/45; RFC Walnut Ridge 2/1/46.

42-97690 Del Denver 28/1/44; 1SAG Langley 12/3/44; Dow Fd 21/4/44; ass (H2X) 482BG Alconbury 22/4/44; retUS 1103 BU Morrison 29/10/45; RFC Walnut Ridge 5/1/46.

42-97691 Del Denver 28/1/44; 1SAG Langley 11/3/44; Dow Fd 17/5/44; ass 803BS/305BG RCM Chelveston 19/5/44; tran 384BG Grafton Underwood 1/8/44; tran 427BS/303BG [GN-Y] Molesworth 4/8/44; MIA Misburg 26/11/44 w/?; f/l continent, sal 29/12/44; MACR 11193.

42-97692 Del Denver 28/1/44; 1SAG Langley 6/3/44; ass (H2X) 482BG Alconbury 5/4/44; tran 418BS/100BG [LD-O] Thorpe Abbotts 5/45; re-ass 108BS Oberpfaffenhofen 30/4/47; Recl Comp 1/7/49.

42-97693 Del Denver 31/1/44; 1SAG Langley 18/2/44; Dow Fd 21/4/44; ass 413BS/96BG Snetterton 22/4/44; lost on practice mission 11/6/44 w/Wilcox; a/c stalled, cr Channel; 11KIA 1POW; MACR 5624.

42-97694 Del Denver 31/1/44; 1SAG Langley 5/3/44; Dow Fd 8/4/44; ass (H2X) 482BG Alconbury 11/4/44; sal 9AF Germany 29/3/46.

42-97695 Del Denver 31/1/44; 1SAG Langley 15/3/44; Grenier 7/4/44; ass 96BG Snetterton 8/4/44; b/d 13/7/44, rep; sal 9AF Germany 30/4/47; Recl Comp 19/11/47.

42-97696 Del Denver 31/1/44; Langley 13/3/44; Dow Fd 7/4/44; ass 95BG Horham 8/4/44; tran 349BS/100BG [XR-W] Thorpe Abbotts 5/45; retUS 1103 BU Morrison 14/10/45; RFC Walnut Ridge 7/1/46.

42-97697 Del Denver 31/1/44; 1SAG Langley 7/3/44; Dow Fd 5/4/44; ass 728BS/452BG Deopham Green 7/4/44; 729BS; MIA Kassel 2/10/44 w/Hankins; flak, cr Kassel; 1KIA 9POW; MACR 9526.

42-97698 Del Denver 31/1/44; Langley 13/3/44; Dow Fd 7/4/44; ass 413BS/96BG [MZ-L] Snetterton 8/4/44; damaged by e/a at Poltava 21/6/44; rep but c/l Algiers 12/7/44, sal.

42-97699 Del Denver 31/1/44; 1SAG Langley 11/3/44; Dow Fd 21/4/44; ass (H2X) 482BG Alconbury 22/4/44; tran 305BG Chelveston 16/5/44; 384BG Grafton Underwood 1/8/44; 303BG Molesworth 4/8/44; 2 SAD 25/9/44; 67FW Troston (radio relay?); 351BG Polebrook 7/11/44; retUS Bradley 8/8/45; 4185 BU Independence 25/10/45; RFC Kingman 7/1/46.

42-97700 Del Denver 1/2/44; Albuquerque 17/3/44; 1SAG Langley 30/5/44; Dow Fd 24/6/44; ass 729BS/452BG Deopham Green 28/6/44; tran 96BG Snetterton 29/6/44; retUS Bradley 28/6/45; 4168 BU Sth Plains 21/10/45; RFC Kingman 11/12/45.

42-97701 Del Denver 1/2/44; 1SAG Langley 21/3/44; ass 509BS/351BG [RQ-B] Polebrook 6/7/44; 511BS [DS-B] JULIE LINDA; {42m} tran 305BG Chelveston 5/45; sal 9AF Germany 4/4/46. NADINE L.

42-97702 Del Denver 1/2/44; 1SAG Langley 11/4/44; Grenier 3/5/44; ass (H2X) 482BG Alconbury 8/5/44; tran 339BS/96BG [QJ-D] Snetterton 9/5/44; retUS, 1103 BU Morrison 22/10/45; RFC Walnut Ridge 27/12/45.

42-97703 Del Denver 1/2/44; 1SAG Langley 11/4/44; Grenier 24/4/44; ass (H2X) 482BG Alconbury 26/4/44; sal 9AF Germany 23/5/46.

42-97704 Del Denver 2/2/44; 1SAG Langley 11/3/44; Grenier 3/5/44; ass (H2X) 482BG Alconbury 9/5/44; re-ass AAF 30/4/47; Recl Comp 19/11/47.

42-97705 Del Denver 2/2/44; 1SAG Langley 1/4/44; Morrison 30/4/44; ass 49BS/2BG Amendola 2/5/44; tran 32BS/301BG Lucera; MIA Bleckhammer 26/12/44 w/Ewing; flak, cr Milice; 10EVD, ret from Russia. MACR 10745. DEDE.

42-97706 Del Denver 4/2/44; 1SAG Langley 20/3/44; Grenier 5/5/44; ass (H2X) 482BG Alconbury 13/5/44; tran 349BS/100BG [XR-G] Thorpe Abbotts 5/45; retUS, RFC Walnut Ridge 3/1/46.

42-97707 Del Denver 2/2/44; 1SAG Langley 21/3/44; ass (H2X) 482BG Alconbury 7/5/44; retUS 1103 BU Morrison 29/10/45; RFC Walnut Ridge 8/1/46.

42-97708 Del Denver 3/2/44; 1SAG Langley 1/3/44; Grenier 30/4/44; ass (H2X) 482BG Alconbury 3/5/44; retUS 1103 BU Morrison 29/10/45; RFC Walnut Ridge 29/12/45.

42-97709 Del Denver 3/2/44; 1SAG Langley 1/3/44; Dow Fd 24/5/44; ass (H2X) 482BG Alconbury 25/5/44; sal 9AF Germany 23/5/46.

42-97710 Del Denver 3/2/44; 1SAG Langley 21/3/44; ass (H2X) 482BG Alconbury 8/5/44; sal 9AF Germany 23/5/46.

42-97711 Del Denver 3/2/44; 1SAG Langley 11/4/44; Morrison 30/4/44; ass 2BG (PFF) Amendola 2/5/44; tran 772BS/463BG Celone 5/44; sal 11/5/44.

42-97712 Del Denver 4/2/44; 1SAG Langley 1/4/44; Dow Fd 23/4/44; ass (H2X) 482BG Alconbury 26/4/44; tran 351BS/100BG [EP-T] Thorpe Abbotts 5/45; retUS, RFC Walnut Ridge 5/1/46. FRANCIS, MARK & PHIL.

42-97713 Del Denver 4/2/44; 1SAG Langley 29/3/44; Dow Fd 24/4/44; ass (H2X) 482BG Alconbury 25/4/44; retUS 1103 BU Morrison 20/10/45; Charleston 28/10/45; RFC Walnut Ridge 14/1/46.

42-97714 Del Denver 4/2/44; 1SAG Langley 7/3/44; Dow Fd 24/4/44; ass (H2X) 482BG Alconbury 25/4/44; tran 381BG Ridgewell 26/5/44; 350BS/100BG [LN-F] Thorpe Abbotts 5/45; re-ass 108 BU Oberpfaffenhofen 30/4/47; Recl Comp 27/5/48.

42-97715 Del Denver 4/2/44; 1SAG Langley 6/4/44; Morrison 24/5/44; ass (PFF) 49BS/2BG Amendola 31/5/44; tran 96BS; MIA Bleckhammer 26/12/44 w/Redden; flak, f/l Russia; 1WIA (cp McHood) 9RTD, via Russia, Teheran and Cairo 11/1/45; MACR 10732. FRANKIE.

42-97716 Del Denver 4/2/44; 1SAG Langley 24/3/44; Grenier 24/4/44; ass (H2X) 482BG Alconbury 26/4/44; sal 6/7/45.

42-97717 Del Denver 6/2/44; 1SAG Langley 21/3/44; Grenier 24/4/44; ass (H2X) 482BG Alconbury 25/4/44; sal 9AF Germany 11/5/46.

42-97718 Del Denver 6/2/44; 1SAG Langley 24/3/44; ass (H2X) 482BG Alconbury 7/5/44; tran 349BS/100BG [XR-N] Thorpe Abbotts 5/45; retUS, RFC Walnut Ridge 8/1/46.

42-97719 Del Denver 6/2/44; 1SAG Langley 1/4/44; Morrison 7/5/44; ass (PFF) 49BS/2BG Amendola 8/5/44; tran 774BS/463BG Celone; b/d Valence, Fr 15/8/44 w/Florsheim; two engines shot out, another damaged, equipment jettisoned and a/c returned; retUS 4100 BU Patterson 1/3/45; Recl Comp 2/5/46. GODDESS ON A FORTRESS.

42-97720 Del Denver 6/2/44; Langley 4/5/44; Grenier 5/5/44; ass (H2X) 482BG Alconbury 10/5/44; re-ass 108 BU Ober-pfaffenhofen 30/4/47; Recl Comp 7/1/49.

42-97721 Del Denver 5/2/44; 1SAG Langley 1/4/44; Salina, Ks 11/4/44; 233 BU Davis Monthan 25/6/44; 204 BU Smoky Hill 1/7/44; 420 BU March 29/9/44; 3539 BU Langley 3/10/44; 4117 BU Robins 26/7/45; 3539 BU Langley 1/8/45; RFC Walnut Ridge 20/12/45.

42-97722 Del Denver 5/2/44; 1SAG Langley 15/3/44; ass 482BG Alconbury 7/5/44; retUS, RFC Walnut Ridge 20/12/45.

42-97723 Del Denver 5/2/44; 1SAG Langley 29/2/44; ass 482BG (H2X) Alconbury 7/5/44; tran 349BG/100BG [XR-J] Thorpe Abbotts 5/45; retUS, RFC Walnut Ridge 3/1/46.

42-97724 Del Denver 5/2/44; 1SAG Langley 1/4/44; Morrison 7/5/44; ass (PFF) 49BS/2BG Amendola 8/5/44; tran 772BS/463BG Celone 5/44; MIA Munich 9/6/44 w/Russell; flak, ditched Adriatic; four baled; MACR 5852.

42-97725 Del Denver 5/2/44; 1SAG Langley 1/4/44; Morrison 7/5/44; ass (PFF) 49BS/2BG Amendola 9/5/44; tran 414BS/97BG Amendola 14/6/44; MIA Ploesti 22/7/44 w/Cofer; flak, cr Turgu?; MACR 6854.

42-97726 Del Denver 5/2/44; 1SAG Langley 1/4/44; Morrison 29/4/44; ass (PFF) 49BS/2BG Amendola 1/5/44; tran 772BS/463BG Celone 5/44; MIA Ploesti 18/5/44 w/Marek; e/a, cr Turgu?; MACR 4916.

42-97727 Del Denver 5/2/44; 1SAG Langley 1/4/44; Morrison 29/4/44; ass (PFF) 49BS/2BG Amendola 1/5/44; sal 9AF Germany 10/5/46.

42-97728 Del Denver 8/2/44; 1SAG Langley 7/4/44; Morrison 2/5/44; ass (PFF) 49BS/2BG Amendola 4/5/44; tran 352BS/301BG Lucera 15/5/44; MIA Linz 15/11/44 w/Mitchko; cr Salzburg; 8KIA 2POW; MACR 10081.

42-97729 Del Denver 10/2/44; 1SAG Langley 4/4/44; Morrison 1/5/44; ass (PFF) 49BS/2BG Amendola 3/5/44; 416BS/99BG Tortorella 22/5/44; {48m} sal 9AF Germany 10/5/46.

42-97730 Del Denver 10/2/44; Salina, Ks 11/4/44; 204 BU Smoky Hill 8/5/44; 420 BU March 21/8/44; 2FG Wilmington 15/3/45; 3539 BU Langley 24/9/45; RFC Walnut Ridge 4/1/46.

42-97731 Del Denver 10/2/44; 1SAG Langley 4/4/44; Morrison 28/4/44; ass (PFF) 49BS/2BG Amendola 6/5/44; tran 97BG Cerignola 30/5/44; flak damage, to depot and sal 20/7/44.

42-97732 Del Denver 10/2/44; 1SAG Langley 11/4/44; Dow Fd 1/5/44; ass 482BG Alconbury 4/5/44; tran 338BS/96BG Snetterton 5/5/44; sal 9AF Germany 31/5/46.

42-97733 Del Denver 10/2/44; 1SAG Langley 11/4/44; Morrison 27/4/44; ass (PFF) 49BS/2BG Amendola 11/5/44; 346BS/99BG Tortorella 22/5/44; {54m} to depot 2/2/45; retUS Bradley 21/6/45; 4168 BU Sth Plains 23/6/45; RFC Kingman 2/12/45.

42-97734 Del Denver 10/2/44; 1SAG Langley 6/4/44; Morrison 28/4/44; ass (PFF) 49BS/2BG Amendola 9/5/44; 346BS/99BG Tortorella 22/5/44; MIA {37m} Innsbruck 29/12/44 w/McClanahan; flak, cr

42-97735 Del Denver 10/2/44; 1EEL Bedford 28/4/44; 4148 BU Bedford 4/12/44; 4104 BU Rome 21/5/45; 4147 BU Bedford 11/8/45; 4149 BU Ft Dix 27/2/46; 4112 BU Olmstead 14/3/46; 4150 BU Boca Raton 30/9/46; 4149 BU Olmstead 8/4/47; 313 EEU Griffin 3/9/48; Recl Comp 31/3/49.

42-97736 Del Denver 10/2/44; 1SAG Langley 6/4/44; Morrison 27/4/44; ass (PFF) 49BS/2BG Amendola 11/5/44; 419BS/301BG Lucera 15/5/44; MIA Bleckhammer 1/2/45 w/Muskus; flak, cr Stockerau; 4KIA 1EVD (bdr Baer returned) 5POW; MACR 12078.

42-97737 Del Denver 10/2/44; 1SAG Langley 4/4/44; Morrison 26/4/44; ass (PFF) 49BS/2BG Amendola 8/5/44; 774BS/463BG Celone 5/44; cr 29/11/44 w/Atchison; 7KIA 3WIA (survived); MACR 10627.

42-97738 Del Denver 11/2/44; 1SAG Langley 11/4/44; Morrison 26/4/44; ass (PFF) 49BS/2BG Amendola 7/5/44; 352BS/301BG Lucera 15/5/44; MIA Bleckhammer (night op) 13/11/44 w/Wendt; bad weather, cr Krauthenn; 6KIA 4POW; MACR 9863.

42-97739 Del Denver 11/2/44; 1SAG Langley 8/4/44; Morrison 26/4/44; ass (PFF) 49BS/2BG Amendola 7/5/44; tran to 20BS; MIA Regensburg 9/12/44 w/Warren; flak, cr Linz; MACR 10131.

42-97740 Del Denver 12/2/44; 1SAG Langley 12/3/44; Dow Fd 29/5/44; ass 91BG Bassingbourn 18/6/44; tran 600BS/398BG [N8-Q] Nuthampstead 29/6/44; 602BS [K8-Q]; MIA Misburg 26/11/44 w/Capt Douglas; flak, cr Detmold; 10POW; MACR 11146.

42-97741 Del Denver 12/2/44; 1SAG Langley 21/4/44; 902 BU Orlando 16/6/44; Mat Com Wright 19/6/44; 4100 BU Patterson 21/6/44; 111 BU Langley 26/6/44; 3539 BU Langley 16/9/44; RFC Walnut Ridge 20/12/45.

42-97742 Del Denver 12/2/44; 1SAG Langley 2/4/44; Morrison 29/4/44; ass (PFF) 49BS/2BG Amendola 2/5/44; tran 775BS/463BG Celone; SAl 9AF Germany 31/5/46.

42-97743 Del Denver 12/2/44; 1SAG Langley 11/4/44; Dow Fd 1/5/44; ass (H2X) 482BG Alconbury 4/5/44; sal 9AF Germany 31/5/46.

42-97744 Del Denver 12/2/44; 1SAG Langley 11/4/44; Morrison 30/4/44; ass (PFF) 49BS/2BG Amendola 2/5/44; tran 347BS/99BG Tortorella 23/5/44; {49m} to depot 9/1/45; sal 16/5/45.

42-97745 Del Denver 4/2/44; 1SAG Langley 21/4/44; 234 BU Clovis 24/6/44; 3026 BU Luke Fd 16/8/44; 234 BU Clovis 27/8/44; 3502 BU Chanute 4/5/45; RFC Walnut Ridge 8/1/46.

42-97746 Del Denver 14/2/44; 1SAG Langley 12/3/44; Dow Fd 29/5/44; ass 602BS/398BG [K8-T] Nuthampstead 29/6/44; 601BS [3O-C]; 603BS [N7-T]; c/l base 15/10/44, sal 2 SAD.

42-97747 Del Denver 14/2/44; 1SAG Langley 11/4/44; Grenier 12/5/44; ass 8AF 12/5/44.

42-97748 Del Denver 14/2/44; 1SAG Langley 16/3/44; Grenier 9/6/44; ass 305BG Chelveston 11/6/44; sal 9AF Germany 23/5/46.

42-97749 Del Denver 15/2/44; 1SAG Langley 12/4/44; Dow Fd 17/5/44; ass (PFF) 482BG Alconbury 19/5/44; caught fire non-op 20/1/45, sal.

42-97750 Del Denver 15/2/44; 1SAG Langley 21/4/44; 420 BU March 21/8/44; 3539 BU Langley 3/10/44; RFC Walnut Ridge 4/1/46.

42-97751 Del Denver 15/2/44; 1SAG Langley 23/4/44; 3539 BU Langley 14/1/45; 3502 BU Chanute 17/3/45; RFC Kingman 12/1/46.

42-97752 Del Denver 15/2/44; 1SAG Langley 21/4/44; 247 BU Smoky Hill 6/6/44; 204 BU Smoky Hill 8/6/44; 233 BU Davis Monthan 25/6/44; 204 BU Smoky Hill 3/7/44; 420 BU March 21/8/44; 3539 BU Langley 3/10/44; RFC Walnut Ridge 11/1/46.

42-97753 Del Denver 16/2/44; 1SAG Langley 21/4/44; 204 BU Smoky Hill 18/6/44; 420 BU March 21/8/44; 3539 BU Langley 3/10/44; 4112 BU Olmstead 21/12/44; Recl Comp 1/1/45.

42-97754 Del Denver 16/2/44; 1SAG Langley 4/6/44; Dow Fd 27/6/44; ass 401BS/91BG [LL-M] Bassingbourn 28/6/44; re-ass AF 30/4/47; 108 BSX Oberpfaffenhofen 18/1/48; Recl Comp 7/1/49.

42-97755 Del Denver 16/2/44; 1SAG Langley 11/4/44; 420 BU March 21/8/44; 3539 BU Langley 8/10/44; 119 BU Morris 12/3/45; 3539 BU Langley 30/3/45; RFC Walnut Ridge 27/12/45.

42-97756 Del Denver 17/2/44; 1SAG Langley 12/4/44; Dow Fd 1/5/44; ass 384BG Grafton Underwood 4/5/44; tran 364BS/305BG [WF-G] Chelveston 30/1/45; sal 9AF 10/5/46.

42-97757 Del Denver 17/2/44; 1SAG Langley 17/4/44; 3501 BU Boca Raton 2/6/44; 3539 BU Langley 14/10/44; RFC Walnut Ridge 7/1/46.

42-97758 Del Denver 17/2/44; 1SAG Langley 17/4/44; Dow Fd 24/5/44; ass (H2X) 482BG Alconbury 27/4/44; 338BS/96BG Snetterton 28/4/44; RFC Walnut Ridge 9/1/46.

42-97759 Del Denver 17/2/44; 1SAG Langley 21/4/44; 420 BU March 14/8/44; W/O 15/8/44.

42-97760 Del Denver 16/2/44; 1SAG Langley 12/3/44; Dow Fd 29/5/44; ass 562BS/388BG Knettishall 31/5/44; sal 9AF Germany 11/1/46.

42-97761 Del Denver 15/2/44; 1SAG Langley 11/4/44; Dow Fd 11/5/44; ass (H2X) 482BG Alconbury 19/5/44; sal 9AF Germany 18/5/46.

42-97762 Del Denver 16/2/44; 1SAG Langley 17/4/44; 3539 BU Langley 11/10/44; 76 BU Langley 3/12/44; Recl Comp 22/3/46.

42-97763 Del Denver 15/2/44; 1SAG Langley 23/4/44; Dow Fd 19/5/44; ass (H2X) 482BG Alconbury 27/5/44; tran 338BS/96BG Snetterton 28/5/44; sal 9AF Germany 31/5/46.

42-97764 Del Cheyenne 17/2/44; Denver 2/3/44; 1SAG Langley 30/5/44; Grenier 19/6/44; ass 413BS/96BG Snetterton 29/6/44; MIA Merseburg 28/7/44 w/Capt Boyer (+ 452BG crew); mid air coll, cr Merseburg; 8KIA 3POW; MACE 7828.

42-97765 Del Cheyenne 9/2/44; Denver 2/3/44; 1SAG Langley 15/3/44; Dow Fd 24/5/44; ass (H2X) 482BG Alconbury 27/5/44; 350BS/100BG [LN-S] Thorpe Abbotts 5/45; retUS 1103 BU Morrison 29/10/45; RFC Walnut Ridge 5/1/46.

42-97766 Del Cheyenne 11/2/44; Denver 2/3/44; 1SAG Langley 22/4/44; Dow Fd 20/5/44; ass (H2X) 482BG Alconbury 21/5/44; c/l 20/1/45, sal.

42-97767 Del Cheyenne 20/2/44; Denver 2/3/44; 1SAG Langley 3/6/44; Grenier 28/6/44; ass 305BG Chelveston 22/7/44; tran 306BG Thurleigh 2/8/44; b/d Merseburg 11/9/44 w/?; f/l continent, sal 14/11/44.

42-97768 Del Cheyenne 24/2/44; Denver 2/3/44; 1SAG Langley 2/6/44; Grenier 28/6/45; ass 333BS/94BG Rougham 1/7/44; retUS, RFC Walnut Ridge 28/10/45. MAINLINER II.

42-97769 Del Cheyenne 24/2/44; Denver 2/3/44; 1SAG Langley 3/6/44; Grenier 27/6/44; ass 447BG Rattlesden 19/5/44; tran 333BS/94BG [TS-Q] Rougham 1/7/44; retUS, RFC Kingman 16/12/45.

42-97770 Del Cheyenne 24/2/44; Denver 2/3/44; 1SAG Langley 2/6/44; Dow Fd 20/5/44; ass 95BG Horham 1/7/44; b/d Magdeburg 11/9/44 w/?BG; sal 12/11/44.

42-97771 Del Cheyenne 25/2/44; Denver 3/3/44; 1SAG Langley 3/6/44; Dow Fd 20/5/44; ass 91BG Bassingbourn 11/6/44; tran 533BS/381BG Ridgewell 5/7/44; MIA {6+m} Nienburg 5/8/44 w/Melomo; flak, cr Jadebusen, Ger; 5KIA 5POW; MACR 7884.

42-97772 Del Cheyenne 24/2/44; Denver 2/3/44; 1SAG Langley 4/6/44; Dow Fd 20/5/44; ass 8AF.

42-97773 Del Cheyenne 23/2/44; Denver 2/3/44; 1SAG Langley 21/4/44; Atlanta 7/5/44; 112 BU Westover 9/3/45; 3539 BU Langley 16/9/44; RFC Walnut Ridge 20/12/45.

42-97774 Del Cheyenne 23/2/44; Denver 2/3/44; 1SAG Langley 20/4/44; 3539 BU Langley 16/9/44; RFC Walnut Ridge 8/1/46.

42-97775 Del Cheyenne 22/2/44; Denver 3/3/44; 1SAG Langley 1/6/44; Dow Fd 24/6/44; ass 413BS/96BG [MZ-L] Snetterton 29/6/44; c/l 14/1/45, sal 15/1/45.

42-97776 Del Cheyenne 24/2/44; Denver 2/3/44; 1SAG Langley 3/6/44; Dow Fd 27/6/44; ass 548BS/385BG Gt Ashfield 28/6/44; tran 333BS/94BG Rougham 29/6/44; retUS Bradley 27/6/44; 4168 BU Sth Plains 1/7/45; RFC Kingman 22/11/45.

42-97777 Del Cheyenne 24/2/44; Denver 2/3/44; 1SAG Langley 21/5/44; Grenier 23/6/44; ass 305BG Chelveston 27/7/44; tran 384BG Grafton Underwood 30/7/44; 524BS/379BG [WA-F] Kimbolton 4/8/44; cr Grafton Underwood 9/8/44; sal 2 SAD 25/8/44.

42-97778 Del Cheyenne 24/2/44; Denver 2/3/44; 1SAG Langley 1/6/44; Dow Fd 24/6/44; ass 379BG Kimbolton 15/7/44; tran 305BG Chelveston 16/7/44; 327BS/92BG [UX-R] Podington 1/8/44; 407BS; 91BG Bassingbourn 7/5/45; sal 9AF 18/5/46; re-ass AF 30/4/47; Recl Comp 19/11/47.

42-97779 Del Cheyenne 24/2/44; Denver 2/3/44; 1SAG Langley 26/4/44; 3539 BU Langley 16/9/44; RFC Walnut Ridge 7/1/46.

42-97780 Del Cheyenne 24/2/44; Denver 2/3/44; Kearney 1/4/44; Grenier 14/4/44; ass 452BG Deopham Green 19/4/44 NOW GO!; tran 614BS/401BG [IW-R] Deenethorpe 28/4/44; retUS Bradley 6/6/45; 4168 BU Sth Plains 21/10/45; RFC Kingman 9/12/45. BLUE BOMB EXPRESS.

42-97781 Del Cheyenne 24/2/44; Denver 3/3/44; Gr Island 312/3/44; Dow Fd 28/4/44; ass 359BS/303BG [BN-O] Molesworth 12/5/44; MIA Sterkrade, Ger 2/11/44 w/Davis; flak, cr Sterkrade; 1KIA 9POW; MACR 10151. EIGHT BALL III.

42-97782 Del Cheyenne 24/2/44; Denver 2/3/44; Kearney 4/4/44; Dow Fd 14/4/44; ass 337BS/96BG Snetterton 22/4/44; MIA Berlin 8/5/44 w/Niswonger; mid air col w/e/a, cr Daverden, Ger; 3KIA 7POW; MACR 4572.

42-97783 Del Cheyenne 25/2/44; Denver 1/3/44; Alexandra 20/3/44; 221 BU Alexandra 17/1/45; 329 BU Alexandra 1/3/45; 326 BU McDill 8/6/45; RFC Altus 29/10/45.

42-97784 Del Cheyenne 25/2/44; Denver 6/3/44; Alexandra 18/3/44; 221 BU Alexandra 17/1/45; 329 BU Alexandra 1/3/45; 325 BU Avon Park 13/8/45; RFC Walnut Ridge 18/12/45.

42-97785 Del Cheyenne 25/2/44; Denver 6/3/44; Alexandra 21/3/44; 215 BU Pueblo 27/8/44; 221 BU Alexandra 8/11/44; 329 BU Alexandra 1/3/45; 326 BU McDill 8/6/45; 324 BU Chatham 16/6/45; 326 BU McDill 28/6/45; 327 BU Drew 3/7/45; 326 BU McDill 9/7/45; RFC Altus 19/10/45.

42-97786 Del Cheyenne 28/2/44; Denver 26/3/44; Kearney 4/4/44; Dow Fd 14/4/44; ass 729BS/452BG Deopham Green 22/4/44; MIA Brux 12/5/44 w/Thomas; e/a, cr Koblenz; 4KIA 6POW; MACR 4823. THE HARDWAY.

42-97787 Del Denver 26/2/44; Hunter 15/3/44; Grenier

7/4/44; ass 358BS/303BG [VK-M] Molesworth 22/4/44; MIA Berlin 24/5/44 w/Worthy; flak, cr Nth Sea; 9KIA 1POW; MACR 5173.

42-97788 Del Denver 27/2/44; Alexandra 17/3/44; 335 BU Del Marbry 12/10/44; 221 BU Alexandra 28/10/44; 329 BU Alexandra 1/3/45; 325 BU Avon Park 13/8/45; 3704 BU Keesler 14/8/45; re-ass TB-17G 31/7/46; Recl Comp 6/10/47.

42-97789 Del Denver 27/2/44; Kearney 22/3/44; Dow Fd 6/4/44; ass 603BS/398BG [N7-H] Nuthampstead 26/4/44; 602BS [K8-H]; f/l RAF Graveley 17/12/44; sal 19/12/44.

42-97790 Del Denver 28/2/44; Kearney 4/4/44; Dow Fd 21/4/44; ass 549BS/385BG Gt Ashfield 22/4/44; sal 12/8/44. RAGGED BUT RIGHT.

42-97791 Del Denver 28/2/44; 1SAG Langley 17/3/44; Grenier 5/4/44; ass 332BS/94BG [XM-O] Rougham 10/4/44; retUS Bradley 21/7/45; 4185 BU Independence 30/11/45; 237 BU Kirtland 25/12/45; RFC Albuquerque 7/2/46. TRUDY.

42-97792 Del Denver 28/2/44; Hunter 23/3/44; Morrison 8/4/44; slated 413BS/96BG [MZ-N] 11/4/44; ass 840BS/483BG Sterparone 17/4/44; retUS 1103 BU Morrison 29/10/45; 5938 BU Charleston 30/10/45; RFC Walnut Ridge 2/1/46. YVONNE.

42-97793 Del Denver 28/2/44; Alexandra 16/3/44; 221 BU Alexandra 17/1/45; 329 BU Alexandra 1/3/45; RFC Altus 29/10/45.

42-97794 Del Denver 28/2/44; Kearney 1/4/44; Dow Fd 14/4/44; ass 709BS/447BG Rattlesden 20/4/44; MIA Berlin 12/5/44 w/Moses; flak, ditched Channel; 1EVD 2KIA 3POW 4RTD; MACR 4769.

42-97795 Del Denver 28/2/44; Alexandra 17/3/44; 221 BU Alexandra 17/1/45; 329 BU Alexandra 1/3/45; Recl Comp 20/4/45.

42-97796 Del Denver 28/2/44; Kearney 1/4/44; Dow Fd 19/4/44; ass 368BS/306BG [BO-D] Thurleigh 5/6/44; landing accident 19/9/44, sal. LADY ELAINE.

42-97797 Del Denver 28/2/44; Kearney 18/3/44; Dow Fd 7/4/44; ass 412BS/95BG [QW-H] Horham 8/4/44; MIA Brandenburg 16/8/44 w/Hannum; mid air w/42-37879; cr Rondorf,Gr. 6KIA, 4POW. MACR 8175. FULL HOUSE.

42-97798 Del Denver 28/2/44; Hunter 7/4/44; Dow Fd 21/4/44; ass 510BS/351BG [TU-H] Polebrook 24/5/44; MIA {10m} Le Bourget 14/6/44 w/Williamson; flak, ditched Channel; 10POW; MACR 5797.

42-97799 Del Denver 29/2/44; Alexandra 17/3/44; slated 339BS/96BG [QJ-W]; 224 BU Sioux City 6/3/45; RRD Cheyenne 25/5/45; 332 BU Ardmore 17/6/45; RFC Walnut Ridge 7/12/45.

42-97800 Del Denver 1/3/44; Roswell 26/4/44; 3030 BU Roswell 2/6/44; 3018 BU Kingman 1/10/44; 4126 BU San Bernardino 12/1/45; 3018 BU Kingman 18/1/45; 3030 BU Roswell 8/6/45; RFC Walnut Ridge 3/1/46.

42-97801 Del Denver 1/3/44; Hunter 2/4/44; Dow Fd 24/4/44; ass 447BG Rattlesden 4/5/44; sal 10/12/44; retUS, RFC Walnut Ridge 10/9/45.

42-97802 Del Denver 1/3/44; Slated 92BG, Hendricks 2/5/44; 2137 BU Hendricks 9/5/44; Recl Comp 25/10/45.

42-97803 Del Denver 1/3/44; Kearney 4/4/44; Dow Fd 14/4/44; ass 447BG Rattlesden 22/4/44; retUS Bradley 9/7/45; 4168 BU Sth Plains 13/7/45; RFC Kingman 19/11/45.

42-97804 Del Denver 2/3/44; Hunter 7/4/44; Dow Fd 29/4/44; ass 711BS/447BG Rattlesden 1/5/44; retUS Bradley 11/9/45; RFC Kingman 12/11/45.

42-97805 Del Denver 2/3/44; Kearney 9/4/44; Grenier 21/4/44; ass 527BS/379BG [FO-B] Kimbolton 5/5/44; tran 360BS/303BG [PU-Q] Molesworth 12/5/44; MIA Magdeburg 28/9/44 w/Hahn; e/a, cr Halcten?; 6KIA 3POW; MACR 9412.

42-97806 Del Denver 3/3/44; Hunter 16/4/44; Grenier 3/5/44; ass 349BS/100BG [XR-D] Thorpe Abbotts 4/5/44; MIA Bohlen 11/9/44 w/Baker; e/a, cr Liepnitzen, Ger; 6KIA 3POW; MACR 8818.

42-97807 Del Denver 3/3/44; Gr Island 11/4/44; Grenier 29/4/44; ass 568BS/390BG [BI-O] Framlingham 4/5/55; tran 100BG Thorpe Abbotts 5/45; retUS Bradley 5/7/45; 4168 BU Sth Plains 7/7/45; RFC Kingman 13/12/45. LITTLE BUTCH III.

42-97808 Del Denver 3/3/44; Kearney 11/4/44; Grenier 14/4/44; ass 729BS/452BG Deopham Green 22/5/44; MIA Liepzig 29/5/44 w/Lowell; flak, cr Grand-Leez, Bel; 10POW; MACR 5227.

42-97809 Del Denver 3/3/44; Hendricks 2/5/44; 2137 BU Hendricks 18/11/44; RFC Kingman 1/11/45.

42-97810 Del Denver 4/3/44; Hunter 7/4/44; Dow Fd 21/4/44; ass 602BS/398BG [K8-S] Nuthampstead 3/5/44; MIA Kassel 9/3/45 w/Jacobs; flak, cr Fritzlar, Ger; 1EVD 1KIA 7POW; MACR 12962.

42-97811 Del Denver 4/3/44; Hunter 7/4/44; Grenier 30/4/44; ass 612BS/401BG [SC-N] Deenethorpe 21/5/44; MIA Toulouse 25/6/44 w/Myrtrus; flak, cr Vaubecourt, Fr; 3KIA 7POW; MACR 6230. SLICK CHICK.

42-97812 Del Denver 5/3/44; Gulfport 20/4/44; slated 3451BS/100BG [EP-P] Lt Rock 24/4/44; 4204 BU Atlanta 12/11/44; 328 BU Gulfport 31/3/45; 324 BU Chatham 9/5/45; 326 BU McDill 24/7/45; RFC Walnut Ridge 8/1/46.

42-97813 Del Denver 5/3/44; 88BG Avon Park 21/4/44; Tulsa 25/4/44; 325 BU Avon Park, W/O 10/11/44.

42-97814 Del Denver 6/3/44; 88BG Avon Park 21/4/44; Atlanta 30/4/44; 325 BU Avon Park 9/4/45; RFC Walnut Ridge 7/12/45.

42-97815 Del Denver 5/3/44; Hunter 5/4/44; Dow Fd 21/4/44; ass 710BS/447BG Rattlesden 22/4/44; MIA Berlin 12/5/44 w/Capt Van Every; e/a, cr Frieberg, Ger; 3EVD 7POW; MACR 4770.

42-97816 Del Denver 6/3/44; Hunter 16/4/44; Grenier 15/5/44; ass 775BS/463BG Celone 24/5/44; MIA Munich 19/7/44 w/Wynn; flak, cr Kufstein, Ger; MACR 7321.

42-97817 Del Denver 6/3/44; Gulfport 19/4/44; 328 BU Gulfport 30/3/45; 329 BU Alexandra 6/4/45; 330 BU Dyersburg 24/6/44; 327 BU Drew 28/8/45; 330 BU Dyersburg 4/9/45; RFC Walnut Ridge 19/12/45.

42-97818 Del Denver 6/3/44; Hunter 16/4/44; Grenier 9/5/44; ass 551BS/385BG Gt Ashfield 10/5/44; sal 15/6/44.

42-97819 Del Denver 7/3/44; Kearney 14/4/44; Dow Fd 28/4/44; ass 710BS/447BG Rattlesden 30/4/44; taxi accident 21/2/45, sal.

42-97820 Del Denver 7/3/44; Kearney 14/4/44; Grenier 27/4/44; ass 560BS/388BG Knettishall 1/5/44; MIA Fallersleben 20/6/44 w/?; mid air coll w/42-97873; ditched Nth Sea; 11RTD.

42-97821 Del Denver 7/3/44; Hunter 16/4/44; Grenier 5/5/44; ass 571BS/390BG [FC-M] Framlingham 8/5/44; MIA Kassel 8/9/44 w/Handley; flak, cr Idstein, Ger; 7KIA 2POW; MACR 8602.

42-97822 Del Denver 7/3/44; 488BG McDill 22/4/44; 326 BU McDill 2/2/45; 329 BU Alexandra 9/3/45; 330 BU Dyersburg 25/6/45; RFC Walnut Ridge 19/12/45.

42-97823 Del Denver 7/3/44; Gulfport 20/4/44; 4119 BU Brookley 30/8/44; 328 BU Gulfport 9/9/45; 3704 BU Keesler 2/4/45; 138 BU Lake Charles 16/10/45; 3704 BU Keesler 13/11/45; 554 BU Memphis 7/6/46; 4168 BU Sth Plains 8/7/46; 3704 BU Keesler 30/8/46; 4168 BU Sth Plains 30/9/46; Recl Comp 29/5/47.

42-97824 Del Denver 8/3/44; Hunter 16/4/44; Grenier 3/5/44; ass 544BS/384BG [SU-U] Grafton Underwood 10/5/44; tran 401BG Deenethorpe 24/5/44; sal 9AF Germany 10/12/45.

42-97825 Del Denver 8/4/44; Cheyenne 1/5/44; Hunter 16/5/44; Grenier 6/6/44; ass 379BG Kimbolton 28/6/44; retUS Bradley 29/6/45; 4168 BU Sth Plains 5/9/45; RFC Kingman 2/12/45.

42-97826 Del Denver 8/3/44; Kearney 13/4/44; Grenier 28/4/44; ass 710BS/447BG Rattlesden 30/4/44; hit by debris from another a/c 21/2/45, sal.

42-97827 Del Denver 8/3/44; Kearney 13/4/44; Grenier 30/4/44; ass 751BS/457BG Glatton 1/5/44; retUS Bradley 8/6/45; 4168 BU Sth Plains 14/6/45; RFC Kingman 7/12/45. MY MARY MYRTLE.

42-97828 Del Denver 8/3/44; Kearney 15/4/44; Grenier 29/4/44; ass 535BS/381BG [MS-Q] Ridgewell 28/5/44; {35+m} b/d Arnsberg 9/2/45 w/Williamson; f/l continent, sal 4/3/45. QUEENIE.

42-97829 Del Denver 9/3/44; Hunter 16/4/44; Dow Fd 30/4/44; ass 350BS/100BG [LN-O] Thorpe Abbotts 4/5/44; MIA Merseburg 29/7/44 w/Steussy; flak, cr Mannstedt, Ger; 9POW; MACR 7813.

42-97830 Del Denver 9/3/44; Kearney 13/4/44; Grenier 29/4/44; ass 390BG Framlingham 1/5/44; MIA Bohlen 29/6/44 w/Moody; ditched Channel 2KIA 8RTD; MACR 15326.

42-97831 Del Denver 9/3/44; Gulfport 20/4/44; Presque Is 15/6/44; 568 BU Greenwood 19/3/45; 328 BU Gulfport 19/6/45; 325 BU Avon Park 3/7/45; 3508 BU Truax 17/8/45; RFC Kingman 8/12/45.

42-97832 Del Denver 9/3/44; Kearney 13/4/44; Grenier 29/4/44; ass 563BS/388BG Knettishall 1/5/44; dest by e/a on ground Poltava, Russia 21/6/44, sal. FAIRMAN WILLIE.

42-97833 Del Denver 10/3/44; Kearney 14/4/44; Grenier 13/4/44; ass 525BS/379BG [FR-L] Kimbolton 26/5/44; mid air coll w/42-97170 9/12/44; rep & ret 29/3/45; retUS Bradley 6/7/45; 4168 BU Sth Plains 8/7/45; RFC Kingman 28/11/45. SILVER DOLLAR.

42-97834 Del Denver 10/3/44; Hunter 16/4/44; Grenier 29/4/44; ass 349BS/100BG [XR-J] Thorpe Abbotts 4/5/44; MIA Chemnitz 11/9/44 w/Everitt; e/a, cr Schuiedeberg, Ger?; 7KIA 2POW; MACR 8819.

42-97835 Del Denver 10/3/44; 88BG Avon Park 31/4/44; 325 BU Avon Park 9/4/45; RFC Walnut Ridge 12/11/45.

42-97836 Del Denver 10/3/44; Kearney 13/4/44; Grenier 29/4/44; ass 709BS/447BG Rattlesden 1/5/44; MIA Oranienburg 15/3/45 w/Putnam; flak, cr Osted, Den; 9POW; MACR 13043. BUGS BUNNY JR.

42-97837 Del Denver 12/3/44; Gulfport 19/4/44; 328 BU Gulfport 31/3/45; 330 BU Dyersburg 18/7/45; 327 BU Drew 28/8/45; 330 BU Dyersburg 4/9/45; RFC Walnut Ridge 12/11/45.

42-97838 Del Tulsa 12/3/44; Roswell 29/4/44; 3030 BU Roswell 2/6/44; slated 379BG, 3010 BU Williams 20/1/45; 3020 BU La Junta 30/4/45; 2114 BU Lockburn 25/6/45; RFC Walnut Ridge 7/1/46.

42-97839 Del Tulsa 13/3/44; Hendricks 20/4/44; 3518 BU Minneapolis 6/7/44; 3505 BU Scott 17/3/45; 3518 BU Minneapolis 20/3/45; 3502 BU Chanute 19/7/45; 4141 BU Pyote 13/4/47; Recl Comp 31/3/49.

42-97840 Del Tulsa 13/3/44; Roswell 29/4/44; 3030 BU Roswell 2/6/44; 3018 BU Kingman 1/10/44; 3017 BU Hobbs 9/6/45; RFC Walnut Ridge 10/1/46.

42-97841 Del Tulsa 13/3/44; 396BG Drew 15/4/44; 4117 BU Robins 12/12/44; 327 BU Drew 5/1/45; 3505 BU Scott 18/9/45; 301 BU Drew 29/10/45; RFC Altus 5/11/45.

42-97842 Del Tulsa 13/3/44; slated 385BG, Lockburn 9/4/44; St Louis 5/5/44; 2114 BU Lockburn 9/5/45; 2137 BU Hendricks 24/9/45; RFC Walnut Ridge 4/1/46.

42-97843 Del Tulsa 13/3/44; Hunter 4/5/44; Grenier 21/5/44; ass 508BS/351BG [YB-C] Polebrook 22/5/44; {57m} RetUS Bradley 28/5/44; 4168 BU Sth Plains 1/6/45; Recl Comp 7/6/46.

42-97844 Del Denver 14/3/44; Dow Fd 29/4/44; ass 336BS/95BG [ET-R] Horham 20/4/44; MIA Frankfurt 9/3/45 w/Ourant; cr Castl, Ger; 10POW; MACR 12948.

42-97845 Del Denver 14/3/44; Hunter 7/4/44; Dow Fd 29/4/44; ass 350BS/100BG Thorpe Abbotts 1/5/44; MIA Berlin 24/5/44 w/Maj Fitzgerald; e/a, cr Parchim, Ger; 10POW; MACR 5151.

42-97846 Del Denver 14/3/44; Hunter 16/4/44; Dow Fd 30/4/44; ass 569BS/390BG [CC-F] Framlingham 4/5/44; b/d Bad Kreuznach, Ger 2/1/45 w/Drinkwater; flak, cr Pfalz; 9POW; MACR 11244; sal 6/4/45. BELLE OF THE BRAWL.

42-97847 Del Denver 14/3/44; Kearney 8/4/44; Dow Fd 14/4/44; ass 549BS/385BG Gt Ashfield 22/4/44; MIA Magdeburg 28/5/44 w/Hunter; flak, cr Albrechtshain, Ger?; 10POW; MACR 5265.

42-97848 Del Denver 14/3/44; Kearney 8/4/44; Grenier 14/4/44; ass 327BS/92BG [UX-M] Podington 4/5/44; 325BS [JW-M]; MIA Altenburg, Ger 13/9/44 w/Peck; e/a, cr Altenburg; 7KIA 2RTD; MACR 10286. SILVER WINGS.

42-97849 Del Tulsa 15/3/44; Kearney 9/5/44; Grenier 26/5/44; ass 570BS/390BG [DI-O] Framlingham 27/5/44; f/l continent 14/2/45; sal 18/2/45. LIBERTY BELL.

42-97850 Del Tulsa 15/3/44; Roswell 19/4/44; 3030 BU Roswell 2/6/44; 3018 BU Kingman 1/10/44; 3017 BU Hobbs 9/6/45; RFC Walnut Ridge 3/1/46.

42-97851 Del Tulsa 15/3/44; Kearney 4/5/44; Grenier 26/5/44; ass 401BS/91BG [LL-K] Bassingbourn 3/6/44; {72m} b/d Cologne 14/1/45 w/?; f/l France, sal 28/1/45. QUALIFIED QUAIL.

42-97852 Del Tulsa 15/3/44; Hunter 4/5/44; Grenier 21/5/44; ass 728BS/452BG Deopham Green 22/5/44; MIA Mannheim 14/8/44 w/Stuiles; flak, cr Strasbourg, Fr; 3EVD 1KIA 5POW; MACR 8425.

42-97853 Del Tulsa 15/3/44; Kearney 13/5/44; Grenier 26/5/44; ass 360BS/303BG [PU-O] Molesworth 4/6/44; c/l 18/9/44, sal 21/9/44. LUCKY LINDA.

42-97854 Del Denver 15/3/44; Gr Island 31/3/44; Grenier 6/4/44; ass 390BG Framlingham but cr Greenland en route UK, 9/4/44; MACR 3637.

42-97855 Del Denver 15/3/44; Kearney 4/4/44; Grenier 21/4/44; ass 601BS/398BG [3O-A] Nuthampstead 8/5/44; b/d French A/fds 9/7/44 w/Capt Petersen; c/l Sandwich, UK; sal 2 SAD 10/7/44.

42-97856 Del Denver 16/3/44; Hunter 7/4/44; Dow Fd 29/4/44; ass 335BS/95BG [OE-W] Horham 1/5/44; 336BS [ET-R]; MIA Munich 12/7/44 w/Redin; cr Neubiburg, Ger; 10KIA; MACR 7500.

42-97857 Del Denver 17/3/44; Kearney 7/4/44; Grenier 29/4/44; ass 339BS/96BG [QJ-N] Snetterton 1/5/44; c/l base 20/5/44; sal 21/5/44.

42-97858 Del Denver 17/3/44; Kearney 2/4/44; Grenier 29/4/44; ass 100BG Thorpe Abbotts 30/4/44 LADY FORTUNE; tran 412BS/95BG [QW-Y] 1/5/44; MIA Cologne 10/1/45 w/Rand; cr Okoven?; 6KIA 3POW; MACR 11743. CARMEN'S FOLLY.

42-97859 Del Tulsa 17/3/44; Kearney 11/5/44; Grenier 26/5/44; ass 418BS/100BG Thorpe Abbotts 27/5/44; MIA on supply drop on Operation 'Zebra' 25/6/44 w/Houghton; flak, cr Chartres, Fr; 4EVD 1KIA 4POW; MACR 6542.

42-97860 Del Tulsa 17/3/44; Kearney 15/5/44; Grenier 25/5/44; ass 360BS/303BG [PU-L] Molesworth 4/6/44; retUS Bradley 9/6/45; 4168 BU Sth Plains 13/6/45; RFC Kingman 28/11/45.

42-97861 Del Tulsa 19/3/44; Kearney 15/5/44; Grenier 26/5/44; ass 360BS/303BG [PU-C] Molesworth 31/5/44; f/l continent 15/1/45, sal. IZA VAILABLE.

42-97862 Del Tulsa 21/3/44; 88BG Hunter 18/5/44; Dow Fd 29/5/44; slated 401BG, cr Cave Hill, Belfast en route UK 3/6/44; sal Nutts Corner, UK 6/8/44.

42-97863 Del Tulsa 20/3/44; Kearney 15/5/44; Grenier 26/5/44; ass 568BS/390BG [BI-S] Framlingham 27/5/44; MIA Merseburg 29/7/44 w/Norby; flak, cr Bad Bibra, Ger; 1KIA 8POW; MACR 7821. SHACK RAT.

42-97864 Del Tulsa 20/3/44; Kearney 1/4/44; Dow Fd 8/4/44; ass 728BS/452BG Deopham Green 11/4/44; MIA Brux 12/5/44 w/Capt Patrick; e/a, cr Mershausen, Ger; 10POW; MACR 4779.

42-97865 Del Denver 20/3/44; Yuma 26/4/44; Palm Springs 1/5/44; 3036 Yuma 3/2/45; Recl Comp 1/3/45.

42-97866 Del Denver 20/3/44; Yuma 26/4/44; 3017 BU Hobbs 4/6/45; RFC Walnut Ridge 4/1/46.

42-97867 Del Denver 21/3/44; Yuma 26/4/44; 3017 BU Hobbs 5/6/45; RFC Walnut Ridge 7/1/46.

42-97868 Del Denver 20/3/44; Gulfport 20/4/44; 3018 BU Kingman 4/5/44; 3017 BU Hobbs 27/6/45; 3008 BU Minter 13/7/45; RFC Ontario 12/1/46.

42-97869 Del Tulsa 21/3/44; 88BG Hunter 19/5/44; Dow Fd 29/5/44; ass 614BS/401BG [IW-H] Deenethorpe 8/6/44 MAID TO ORDER; 615BS [IY-H]; MIA Münster 16/2/45 w/Hansen; flak, cr Hardenborg, Hol; 2KIA 7POW. MACR 12444. HULA GIRL.

42-97870 Del Tulsa 21/3/44; Kearney 11/5/44; Grenier 27/5/44; ass 327BS/92BG [UX-Y] Podington 2/6/44; no gas Darmstadt, Ger, cr near Rougham A/fd, UK, 7KIA 3RTD; sal 24/12/44.

42-97871 Del Tulsa 21/3/44; Hunter 12/5/44; Dow Fd 26/5/44; ass 570BS/390BG [DI-P] Framlingham 27/5/44; MIA Dusseldorf 9/9/44 w/Hobbs; flak, cr Hubbelrath, Ger; 9KIA; MACR 8915. BUNDLES OF TROUBLE.

42-97872 Del Tulsa 22/3/44; Hunter 16/5/44; Dow Fd 25/5/44; ass 614BS/401BG [IW-A] Deenethorpe 1/6/44; c/t/o Dutch flak inst. 17/9/44, sal. ROSIE'S SWEAT BOX.

42-97873 Del Tulsa 22/5/44; Hunter 16/5/44; Grenier 29/5/44; ass 563BS/388BG Knettishall 1/6/44; c/t/o Munich 24/2/45, 10RTD, sal 25/2/45. SACK HAPPY.

42-97874 Del Denver 22/3/44; 88BG Avon Park 24/4/44; Des Moines 29/4/44; 325 BU Avon Park 9/4/45; RFC Walnut Ridge 22/8/45.

42-97875 Del Denver 22/3/44; Sioux City 26/4/44; 2140 BU Smyrna 9/10/44; 224 BU Sioux City 14/10/44; W/O 3/12/44; Recl Comp 16/12/44.

42-97876 Del Denver 22/3/44; Sioux City 26/4/44; 224 BU Sioux City, W/O 11/10/44; Recl Comp 2/11/44.

42-97877 Del Denver 23/3/44; Lockheed, Dallas as mock-up 17/4/44; Kearney 31/5/44; Grenier 28/6/44; ass 835BS/486BG Sudbury 29/6/44; b/d Hamburg 4/8/44 w/?; sal 9/8/44.

42-97878 Del Denver 23/3/44; Rapid City 26/4/44; 225 BU Rapid City 1/5/45; 238 BU Mt Home 8/7/45; 426 BU Mt Home 25/8/45; 231 BU Alamogordo 3/9/45; RFC Altus 15/11/45.

42-97879 Del Tulsa 23/3/44; 88BG Hunter 18/5/44; Grenier 6/6/44; ass 324BS/91BG [DF-E] Bassingbourn 15/6/44; MIA Chartres A/fd 1/8/44 w/Stevens; flak, cr Chartres, Fr; 8KIA 1POW; MACR 5981.

42-97880 Del Tulsa 23/3/44; 88BG Hunter 18/5/44; Dow Fd 29/5/44; ass 324BS/91BG [DF-F] Bassingbourn 15/6/44; {50+m} lost engine en route Fassberg A/fd 4/4/45; on return c/l base when u/c coll; rep & tran 306BG 5/45. LITTLE MISS MISCHIEF.

42-97881 Del Tulsa 24/3/44; Kearney 22/5/44; Grenier 29/5/44; ass 339BS/96BG [QJ-N] Snetterton 7/6/44; dest by e/a at Poltava 21/6/44; sal 2/7/44.

42-97882 Del Tulsa 23/3/44; Kearney 20/5/44; Grenier 27/5/44; ass 533BS/381BG [VP-K] Ridgewell 4/6/44; {81+m} sal 14/6/45.

42-97883 Del Tulsa 24/3/44; Kearney 22/5/44; Grenier 29/5/44; ass 349BS/100BG Thorpe Abbotts 1/6/44; MIA French A/fds 12/6/44 w/McKeague; flak, ditched off Calais, Fr; 7KIA 3RTD; MACR 6521. MISS LOLLIPOP.

42-97884 Del Denver 24/3/44; Tyndall 27/4/44; Tinker 30/4/44; Tyndall 4/5/44; 2114 BU Lockburn 2/9/44; 2137 BU Hendricks 22/9/45; RFC Walnut Ridge 4/1/46.

42-97885 Del Denver 24/3/44; Ft Myers 27/4/44; Dallas 5/5/44; Ft Myers 7/5/44; 2118 BU Buckingham 2/6/44; 2539 BU Foster 6/6/44; 2117 BU Buckingham 9/6/44; 2118 BU Laredo 11/8/44; 2126 BU Laredo 1/2/45; RFC Walnut Ridge 5/1/46.

42-97886 Del Denver 26/3/44; Hendricks 27/4/44; Pueblo 2/5/44; 2137 BU Hendricks 18/11/44; 4112 BU Olmstead 21/7/45; 2137 BU Hendricks 26/7/45; RFC Kingman 29/1/46.

42-97887 Del Denver 26/3/44; Hendricks 27/4/44; Slated 457BG, 2137 BU Hendricks 17/11/44; 2518 BU Enid 20/9/45; RFC Kingman 6/12/45.

42-97888 Del Denver 26/3/44; Kingman 26/4/44; 3018 BU Kingman 4/5/44; 3017 BU Hobbs 24/6/45; RFC Kingman 6/12/45.

42-97889 Del Tulsa 27/3/44; Kearney 22/5/44; Grenier 29/5/44; ass 748BS/457BG Glatton 30/5/44; 750BS; MIA Hamburg 25/10/44 w/Angier; cr Brake, Ger; 3KIA 6POW; MACR 10178. FISH 'N CHIPS.

42-97890 Del Tulsa 27/3/44; Kearney 22/5/44; Grenier 29/5/44; ass 524BS/379BG Kimbolton 12/6/44 QUEEN OF HEARTS; MIA Magdeburg 28/9/44 w/Rutledge; flak, cr Niederdodelbau, Ger?; 2KIA 7POW; MACR 4364. LIL SATAN.

42-97891 Del Tulsa 27/3/44; Kearney 22/5/44; Grenier 29/5/44; ass 401BS/91BG [LL-M] Bassingbourn 17/6/44; MIA Berlin 21/6/44 w/Follett; e/a, cr Anklam, Ger; 9POW; MACR 5981.

42-97892 Del Tulsa 27/3/44; Kearney 26/5/44; Dow Fd 6/6/44; ass 324BS/91BG Bassingbourn 15/6/44/ MIA Hamburg 20/6/44 w/Capt Burch; flak, cr Hamburg; 8KIA 1POW; MACR 5982.

42-97893 Del Tulsa 27/3/44; Kearney 23/5/44; Dow Fd 30/5/44; ass 360BS/303BG [PU-M] Molesworth 12/6/44; 427BS; MIA Magdeburg 28/9/44 w/Matheson; e/a, cr Schladen, Ger; 5KIA 4POW; MACR 9413. MINNIE THE MOUCHER.

42-97894 Del Denver 28/3/44; Rapid City 26/4/44; 225 BU Rapid City 1/5/44; Recl Comp 8/45.

42-97895 Del Denver 28/3/44; 88BG Avon Park 24/4/44; Tulsa 30/4/44; 325 BU Avon Park 9/4/45; 1108 BU Mitchell 6/8/45; 325 BU Avon Park 11/8/45; RFC Walnut Ridge 7/12/45.

42-97896 Del Tulsa 27/3/44; Kearney 27/5/44; Dow Fd 1/6/44; ass 369BS/306BG [WW-X] Thurleigh 10/6/44; tran 92BG Podington 9/5/45; sal 9AF

Germany 10/12/45. MISS AMERICA.

42-97897 Del Denver 28/3/44; Ft Myers 27/4/44; Jacksonville 6/5/44; 328 BU Gulfport, W/O 26/5/44.

42-97898 Del Tulsa 27/3/44; Kearney 24/5/44; Dow Fd 12/6/44; ass 338BS/96BG [BX-Z] Snetterton 3/6/44; retUS Bradley 3/7/45; 4168 BU Sth Plains 21/10/45; RFC Kingman 19/11/45.

42-97899 Del Tulsa 29/3/44; Kearney 27/5/44; Dow Fd 6/6/44; ass 748BS/457BG Glatton 7/6/44; MIA Münster 28/10/44. MACR 10178.

42-97900 Del Tulsa 27/3/44; Kearney 28/5/44; Dow Fd 6/6/44; ass 711BS/447BG Rattlesden 7/6/44; retUS Bradley 9/7/45; 4168 BU Sth Plains 12/9/45; RFC Kingman 7/11/45.

42-97901 Del Tulsa 30/3/44; Kearney 28/5/44; Dow Fd 6/6/44; ass 729BS/452BG Deopham Green 7/6/44; MIA Varrelbusch A/fd 19/3/45 w/?; f/l Radomsk, Pol; sal 28/3/45.

42-97902 Del Tulsa 30/3/44; 88BG Hunter 13/6/44; Morrison 24/6/44; Dow Fd 28/6/44; ass 419BS/301BG Lucera 6/7/44; MIA Brux 9/3/45 w/O'Callaghan; baled over friendly territory and all returned.

42-97903 Del Tulsa 30/3/44; Kearney 28/5/44; Grenier 6/6/44; ass 96BG Snetterton 11/6/44; dest by e/a at Poltava, Russia 21/6/44; sal 1/7/44.

42-97904 Del Tulsa 31/3/44; Kearney 29/5/44; Dow Fd 6/6/44; ass 729BS/452BG Deopham Green 7/6/44 WHY WORRY; MIA Saarbrücken 9/11/44 w/Gott; flak, cr Saarbrücken; sal 18/11/44. LADY JANET.

42-97905 Del Tulsa 31/3/44; Kearney 30/5/44; Grenier 7/6/44; ass 360BS/303BG [PU-R] Molesworth 19/6/44; MIA Munich 13/7/44 w/Long; flak, f/l Dubendorf, Switz; 9INT. MACR 7503.

42-97906 Del Tulsa 31/3/44; 88BG Hunter 9/6/44; Dow Fd 24/6/44; ass 32BS/301BG Lucera 4/7/44; sal 25/4/45.

42-97907 Del Tulsa 31/3/44; 88BG Hunter 12/6/44; Morrison 21/6/44; Dow Fd 28/6/44; ass 775BS/463BG Celone 2/7/44; retUS Bradley 13/7/45; 4185 BU Independence 25/7/45; RFC Kingman 16/12/45.

42-97908 Del Tulsa 3/4/44; Kearney 30/5/44; Grenier 6/6/44; 4104 BU Rome 17/7/44; 4100 BU Patterson 4/8/44; 1377 BU Grenier 23/10/44; 3WER Grenier 30/12/44; 311 Ph Gp Buckley 15/2/45; 53WRS Grenier 9/9/45; 503 BU Gray Pt 31/3/46; 53WRS McChord 11/4/46; 53WRS Grenier 21/4/46.

42-97909 Del Tulsa 3/4/44; Hunter 14/6/44; Dow Fd 28/6/44; ass 348BS/99BG Tortorella 13/7/44; MIA first mission, Vienna, Aus 16/7/44 w/George; mech fault, made SOS call, c/l Koprivnica, Yugo; 10RTD; MACR 6857.

42-97910 Del Tulsa 3/4/44; Hunter 15/6/44; Grenier 28/6/44; ass 353BS/301BG Lucera 4/7/44; mid air coll w/44-6549 Winterhofen, Aus; (6549 ditched); 910 returns and sal.

42-97911 Del Tulsa 3/4/44; Kearney 29/6/44; Grenier 12/7/44; ass 817BS/483BG Sterparone 13/7/44; ret from Moosbeirbaum, Aus 31/1/45 w/Carenbauer; 500lb bomb exploded on landing, when concussion killed WG Cesarz.

42-97912 Del Tulsa 3/4/44; Hunter 15/6/44; Dow Fd 28/6/44; ass 775BS/463BG Celone 4/7/44; b/d Wiener Neustadt 26/3/45, sal.

42-97913 Del Tulsa 3/4/44; Hunter 16/6/44; Dow Fd 28/6/44; ass 815BS/483BG Sterparone 3/7/44; MIA Moosbeirbaum, Aus 28/8/44 w/Blank; flak, cr Karlstadt; 7POW 3RTD 10/9/44; MACR 11278.

42-97914 Del Tulsa 3/4/44; Hunter 16/6/44; Dow Fd 28/6/44; ass 352BS/301BG Lucera 4/7/44; sal 9AF Germany 14/7/45; sal Belgian/Dutch coast 11/2/47.

42-97915 Del Tulsa 3/4/44; Hunter 15/6/44; Dow Fd 2/7/44; ass 429BS/2BG Amendola 4/7/44; MIA Moravaska Ostrova 19/8/44 w/Fitzpatrick; hit by e/a; MACR 7950.

42-97916 Del Tulsa 4/4/44; Hunter 20/6/44; Dow Fd 30/6/44; ass 342BS/97BG Amendola 29/7/44; MIA Vienna 15/1/45 w/Murphy; cr Hungary?; 11RTD.

42-97917 Del Tulsa 4/4/44; 36 St Aprt Miami, fuel consumption test for Ferry Command 20/6/44; Hunter 18/7/44; Dow Fd 4/8/44; ass 483BG Sterparone 2/8/44; 108BU Oberpfaffenhofen 18/1/46; re-ass AF 30/4/47; Recl Comp overseas 9/1/49.

42-97918 Del Tulsa 4/4/44; Hunter 20/6/44; Dow Fd 30/6/44; ass 352BS/301BG Lucera 9/7/44; MIA Vienna 12/3/45 w/Gulley; mech fault, cr Kezethely, Hung; 10POW. MACR 12992.

42-97919 Del Tulsa 4/4/44; Hunter 26/6/44; Dow Fd 9/7/44; ass 840BS/483BG Sterparone 10/7/44; c/t/o for Bleckhammer 17/10/44 w/Bush; 6WIA, a/c sal.

42-97920 Del Tulsa 4/4/44; Kearney 29/6/44; Grenier 16/7/44; ass 49BS/2BG Amendola 11/7/44; b/d Debrecen, Hun 21/9/44 w/Williams; two engines out, c/l base, sal.

42-97921 Del Tulsa 5/4/44; Hunter 20/6/44; Grenier 28/6/44; ass 340BS/97BG Amendola 3/7/44; MIA Brux 20/10/44 w/Wilson; flak, cr Otrokowitz; MACR 9591.

42-97922 Del Denver 5/4/44; Kingman 16/4/44; 3018 BU Kingman 4/5/44; 3017 BU Hobbs 30/9/45; RFC Walnut Ridge 2/1/46.

42-97923 Del Denver 5/4/44; Hendricks 2/5/44; 2137 BU Hendricks 4/10/44; 1108 BU Mitchell 16/2/45; 2137 BU Hendricks 7/3/45; 4200 BU Chicago Mun 30/5/45; 2137 BU Hendricks 4/6/45; RFC Kingman 9/11/45.

42-97924 Del Denver 5/4/44; Cheyenne 1/5/44; Hunter 21/5/44; Grenier 29/5/44; ass 350BS/100BG [LN-H] Thorpe Abbotts 30/5/44; MIA Brest 3/9/44 w/David; flak, ditched Channel; 6KIA 3RTD; MACR 8843. PARTY TONIGHT.

42-97925 Del Denver 6/4/44; Yuma 26/4/44; 3036 BU Yuma 24/4/45; Recl Comp 2/7/45.

42-97926 Del Denver 6/4/44; Hunter 5/5/44; Grenier 21/5/44; ass 509BS/351BG [RQ-X] Polebrook 31/5/44; b/d {48m} Magdeburg 28/9/44 w/?; c/l Ypres, Bel; sal. FAST BABY.

42-97927 Del Denver 6/4/44; Hendricks 2/5/44; Selman 6/5/44; 2137 BU Hendricks 17/11/44; RFC Kingman 23/11/45.

42-97928 Del Denver 6/4/44; Ft Myers 27/4/44; 2117 BU Buckingham 15/6/44; 3036 BU Yuma 24/4/45; 3017 BU Hobbs 4/6/45; RFC Walnut Ridge 10/1/46.

42-97929 Del Denver 6/4/44; Kingman 16/4/44; 3018 BU Kingman 23/3/45; 3030 BU Rosewell 8/6/45; RFC Walnut Ridge 3/1/46.

42-97930 Del Denver 6/4/44; Hendricks 2/5/44; 3036 BU Yuma 20/6/44; 3017 BU Hobbs 4/6/45; RFC Walnut Ridge 4/1/46.

42-97931 Del Denver 8/4/44; Kearney 4/5/44; Dow Fd 21/5/44; ass 613BS/401BG [IN-Q] Deenethorpe 1/6/44; 614BS [IW-A]; retUS Bradley 8/6/45; 4168 BU Sth Plains 10/6/45; RFC Kingman 4/12/45. MADAME QUEEN.

42-97932 Del Denver 6/4/44; Kearney 3/5/44; Grenier 21/5/44; ass 708BS/447BG Rattlesden 23/5/44; MIA Berlin 21/6/44 w/Carter; flak, cr Berlin; 1KIA 9POW; MACR 5930.

42-97933 Del Denver 8/4/44; Kearney 3/5/44; Grenier 21/5/44; ass 526BS/379BG [LF-X] Kimbolton 6/6/44; MIA Frankfurt 19/9/44 w/?; flak, cr Saargemund, Ger. GILDED ORION.

42-97934 Del Denver 8/4/44; Kearney 9/5/44; Dow Fd 21/5/44; ass 750BS/457BG Glatton 23/5/44; tran 547BS/384BG [SO-F] Grafton Underwood 9/5/45; sal 9AF Germany 29/12/45. RENE V.

42-97935 Del Denver 9/4/44; Kearney 3/5/44; Grenier 21/5/44; ass 447BG Rattlesden 23/5/44; tran 452BG Deopham Green 24/5/44; dest by e/a at Poltava 21/6/44; sal 2/7/44.

42-97936 Del Denver 9/4/44; 1SAG Langley 18/5/44; Grenier 19/6/44; Dow Fd 27/6/44; ass 94BG Rougham 27/6/44; tran 708BS/447BG Rattlesden 28/6/44; tran MTO 29/5/45; sal 9AF Italy 14/1/46.

42-97937 Del Denver 10/4/44; Cheyenne 1/5/44; Kearney 26/5/44; Dow Fd 6/6/44; ass 561BS/388BG Knettishall 7/6/44; dest by e/a at Poltava 21/6/44. Sal.

42-97938 Del Denver 10/4/44; Kearney 9/5/44; Dow Fd 21/5/44; ass 612BS/401BG [SC-S] Deenethorpe 6/6/44; sal 2 SAD 30/11/44. TWAN-N-G-G-G.

42-97939 Del Denver 10/4/44; Cheyenne 1/5/44; Kearney 26/5/44; Dow Fd 6/6/44; ass 339BS/96BG [QJ-B] Snetterton 7/6/44; retUS Bradley 9/7/45; 4168 BU Sth Plains 11/7/45; RFC Kingman 19/12/45.

42-97940 Del Denver 10/4/44; Cheyenne 1/5/44; Hunter 14/5/44; Dow Fd 4/6/44; ass 548BS/385BG Gt Ashfield 7/6/44; c/l Kentford, UK 13/9/44; sal (rep with rear end of DOZY DOATS) HALF AND HALF.

42-97941 Del Denver 11/4/44; Hunter 5/5/44; Dow Fd 24/5/44; ass 545BS/384BG [JD-D] Grafton Underwood 4/6/44; taxi accident 17/11/44; sal AFSC 18/11/44. MARION

42-97942 Del Denver 11/4/44; Kearney 4/5/44; Dow Fd 23/5/44; ass 525BS/379BG Kimbolton 24/5/44; mid air coll w/44-6133 19/6/44 w/Burns; cr River Thames, UK 3KIA 6RTD. MACR 6983.

42-97943 Del Denver 11/4/44; 1SAG Langley 18/5/44; Dow Fd 5/7/44; ass 560BS/388BG Knettishall 6/7/44; retUS Bradley 27/6/45; 4168 BU Sth Plains 2/7/45; RFC Kingman 9/12/45.

42-97944 Del Denver 11/4/44; Cheyenne 1/5/44; Kearney 12/5/44; Grenier 27/5/44; ass 384BG Grafton Underwood 30/5/44; tran 359BS/303BG [BN-I] Molewsworth 2/6/44; retUS Bradley 6/6/45; 4168 BU Sth Plains 8/6/45; RFC Kingman 13/12/45. DADDY'S DELIGHT.

42-97945 Del Denver 12/4/44; 1SAG Langley 18/5/44; Dow Fd 9/6/44; ass 335BS/95BG [OE-E] Horham 11/6/44; retUS Bradley 1/7/45; 4168 BU Sth Plains 4/7/45; RFC Kingman 18/11/45. LUCK OF THE IRISH.

42-97946 Del Denver 12/4/44; Cheyenne 1/5/44; Kearney 16/5/44; Dow Fd 2/6/44; ass 368BS/306BG Thurleigh 14/6/44; MIA Gelsenkirchen 26/8/44 w/Allen; flak, cr Budberg, Ger; 4KIA 5POW; MACR 8464. HARD TO GET.

42-97947 Del Denver 12/4/44; 1SAG Langley 16/6/44; Grenier 6/7/44; ass 351BG Polebrook 8/7/44; tran 612BS/401BG [SC-U] Deenethorpe 7/8/44; 613BS; tran 305BG Chelveston 20/8/44; sal 9AF Germany 10/5/46.

42-97948 Del Denver 12/4/44; Cheyenne 1/5/44; Hunter 14/5/44; Dow Fd 24/6/44; ass 326BS/92BG [JW-M] Podington 28/5/44; tran 546BS/384BG [BK-U] Grafton Underwood 10/6/44; MIA Wesseling, Ger 11/10/44 w/Peterson; flak, cr Mayen, Ger; 10POW; MACR 9479. HELL ON WINGS.

42-97949 Del Denver 13/4/44; Cheyenne 1/5/44; Hunter 14/5/44; Dow Fd 23/4/44; ass 568BS/390BG [BI-B] Framlingham 11/6/44; PROBLEM CHILD; tran 358BS/303BG [VK-O] Molesworth 19/6/44; retUS Bradley 10/7/45; 4185 BU Independence 12/7/45;

RFC Kingman 17/12/45.
42-97950 Del Denver 13/4/44; Albuquerqe 17/4/44; Cheyenne 1/5/44; Lowry Fd 5/5/44; W/O 7/5/44.
42-97951 Del Denver 13/4/44; 1SAG Langley 5/6/44; Grenier 28/6/44; ass 351BG Polebrook 22/7/44; tran 748BS/457BG Glatton 28/8/44; 750BS; MIA Dutch flak inst. 17/9/44 w/Grantham; flak, cr Maastricht; 1EVD 10POW; MACR 10208.
42-97952 Del Denver 13/4/44; Cheyenne 1/5/44; Hunter 14/5/44; Dow Fd 27/5/44; ass 339BS/96BG Snetterton 1/6/44; retUS Bradley 5/7/45; 4168 BU Sth Plains 7/7/45; RFC Kingman 19/11/45.
42-97953 Del Denver 15/4/44; Cheyenne 1/5/44; Hunter 14/5/44; Dow Fd 26/5/44; ass 385BG Gt Ashfield 30/5/44; tran 615BS/401BG [IY-N] Deenethorpe 5/6/44; MIA Munich 13/7/44 w/Otton; e/a, cr Benfeld, Fr; 1EVD 8POW; MACR 7499.
42-97954 Del Denver 15/4/44; Cheyenne 1/5/44; Hunter 14/5/44; Dow Fd 22/5/44; ass 401BS/91BG [LL-Z] Bassingbourn 2/6/44; MIA {19m} Liepzig 20/7/44 w/Knapp; e/a, cr Zwickau, Ger; 4KIA 5POW. MACR 7272. WINNIE FRANK JOE.
42-97955 Del Denver 15/4/44; Cheyenne 1/5/44; Kearney 12/5/44; Grenier 27/5/44; ass 748BS/457BG Glatton 30/5/44; b/d Magdeburg 28/9/44 w/?; f/l Moelsbrook A/fd, Bel, sal 14/11/44.
42-97956 Del Denver 13/4/44; Cheyenne 1/5/44; Hunter 14/5/44; Dow Fd 24/5/44; ass 323BS/91BG [OR-L] Bassingbourn 3/6/44; MIA {38m} Merseburg 2/11/44 w/Rustland; cr Libehna, Ger?; 6KIA 3POW; MACR 10148. "PARD".
42-97957 Del Denver 16/4/44; Cheyenne 1/5/44; Hunter 14/5/44; Dow Fd 29/5/44; ass 570BS/390BG [DI-H] Framlingham 30/5/44; pitch problems on #1 & #4, left formation and landed Payerne, Switz w/O'Hare; 10INT; MACR 7493. Sal 9AF Germany 10/12/45. HELL'S BELLE.
42-97958 Del Denver 16/4/44; Cheyenne 1/5/44; Hunter 14/5/44; Dow Fd 2/6/44; ass 401BS/91BG [LL-G] Bassingbourn 7/6/44; tran 407BS/92BG [PY-G] Podington 15/6/44; MIA Peenemunde 25/8/44 w/Tiche; flak, cr Baltic; 9KIA; MACR 8277.
42-97959 Del Denver 16/4/44; Cheyenne 1/5/44; Kearney 27/5/44; Dow Fd 6/6/44; ass 324BS/91BG [DF-Y] Bassingbourn 15/6/44; {90+m} RetUS Bradley 29/5/45; 4168 BU Sth Plains 31/5/45; RFC Kingman 28/11/45. RHAPSODY IN RED.
42-97960 Del Denver 16/4/44; Cheyenne 1/5/44; Hunter 14/5/44; Dow Fd 26/5/44; ass 547BS/384BG [SO-M] Grafton Underwood 3/6/44; MIA Berlin 3/2/45 w/Molder; flak, cr Neustadt, Ger; 9POW. MACR 12153.
42-97961 Del Denver 16/4/44; 1SAG Langley 5/6/44; Grenier 28/6/44; ass 336BS/95BG [ET-K] Horham 29/6/44; MIA Mannheim 21/1/45 w/Savage; lost to weather conditions, c/l Nancy A/fd, Fr; 9RTD; sal 20/3/45.
42-97962 Del Denver 16/4/44; Cheyenne 1/5/44; Kearney 12/5/44; Grenier 27/5/44; ass 612BS/401BG [SC-G] Deenethorpe 5/6/44; MIA Mannheim 9/9/44 w/Loughlin; flak, cr Mannheim; 7KIA 2POW; MACR 8607. CASEY'S STRAWBERRY BLONDE.
42-97963 Del Denver Denver 16/4/44; Cheyenne 1/5/44; Langley 9/6/44; Grenier 28/6/44; ass 8AF 5/7/44; retUS 1103 BU Morrison 19/10/45; RFC Walnut Ridge 5/12/45.
42-97964 Del Denver 17/4/44; 1SAG Langley 1/6/44; W/O 15/6/44.
42-97965 Del Denver 17/4/44; 1SAG Langley 3/6/44; Dow Fd 24/6/44; ass 510BS/351BG [TU-Z] Polebrook 29/6/44; 508BS[YB-Z]; {14m} b/d Cologne 15/10/44 w/?; f/l Belgium; sal 22/11/44.
42-97966 Del Denver 17/4/44; 1SAG Langley 30/5/44; Dow Fd 28/6/44; ass 338BS/96BG [BX-S] Snetterton 29/6/44; retUS, RFC Walnut Ridge 4/1/46.
42-97967 Del Dallas 17/4/44; Hunter 30/5/44; Grenier 12/6/44; ass 379BG Kimbolton 15/7/44; b/d Frieberg, Ger 15/1/45 w/?; f/l continent; sal 6/3/45. HUN RUNNER.
42-97968 Del Dallas 18/4/44; Kearney 2/6/44; Dow Fd 27/6/44; ass 835BS/486BG [H8-V] Sudbury 28/6/44; b/d Frankfurt 8/1/45 w/?; f/l continent; sal 30/1/45. MACR 11352.
42-97969 Del Dallas 19/4/44; Hunter 30/5/44; Dow Fd 27/6/44; ass 839BS/487BG Lavenham 27/7/44; 836BS; retUS Bradley 11/7/45; 4168 BU Sth Plains 16/7/45; RFC Kingman 8/12/45.
42-97970 Del Dallas 19/4/44; Kearney 2/6/44; Dow Fd 27/6/44; ass 837BS/487BG [4F-H] Lavenham 28/6/44; retUS Bradley 11/7/45; 4185 BU Independence 30/11/45; RFC Kingman 21/12/45.
42-97971 Del Dallas 19/4/44; Hunter 30/5/44; Grenier 18/6/44; ass (H2X) 482BG Alconbury 19/6/44; tran 339BS/96BG [QJ-X] Snetterton 20/6/44; retUS Bradley 2/6/45; 4168 BU Sth Plains 8/6/45; RFC Kingman 14/12/45.
42-97972 Del Dallas 19/4/44; Hunter 30/5/44; Grenier 15/6/44; ass 358BS/303BG [VK-N] Molesworth 6/7/44; MIA Misburg 26/11/44 w/Jameson; e/a, cr Bielefeld; 9POW; MACR 11200.
42-97973 Del Dallas 20/4/44; Hunter 30/5/44; Grenier 14/6/44; ass 339BS/96BG Snetterton 16/6/44; b/d Munich 13/7/44 w/?; c/l Hersheim, Ger; sal 3/1/45.
42-97974 Del Dallas 20/4/44; Hunter 30/5/44; Grenier 15/6/44; ass 331BS/94BG [QE-S] Rougham 16/6/44; MIA Berlin 6/8/44 w/Hicks; flak, ditched Nth Sea; 1EVD 1KIA 7POW; MACR 8076.
42-97975 Del Dallas 20/4/44; Langley 11/6/44; Dow Fd 2/7/44; ass (H2X) 401BG Deenethorpe 4/7/44; tran 602BS/398BG [K8-U/P] Nuthampstead 22/7/44; 601BS [3O-P], 603BG [N7-P]; sal 9AF Germany 31/5/46.
42-97976 Del Dallas 21/4/44; Hunter 30/5/44; Grenier 14/6/44; ass 709BS/447BG Rattlesden 19/6/44; retUS Bradley 5/7/45; 4168 BU Sth Plains 7/7/45; RFC Kingman 9/11/45. A BIT O' LACE.
42-97977 Del Dallas 21/4/44; Hunter 30/5/44; Grenier 10/6/44; ass 730BS/452BG Deopham Green 11/6/44; MIA Hardorf, Ger 21/3/45 w/Rosholt; flak, cr Münster; 1EVD 2KIA 6POW; MACR 13533.
42-97978 Del Dallas 21/4/44; Hunter 30/5/44; Grenier 12/6/44; ass 338BS/96BG [BX-B] Snetterton 16/6/44; b/d Merseburg 29/7/44 w/?; c/l base, 3KIA 1WIA 5RTD; sal 30/7/44. GIN RICKEY.
42-97979 Del Dallas 21/4/44; Langley 15/6/44; Grenier 6/7/44; ass 550BS/385BG Gt Ashfield 8/7/44; MIA Dresden 2/3/45 w/Vaadi; e/a, cr Ruhland; 9POW; MACR 12855. LEADING LADY.
42-97980 Del Dallas 23/4/44; Langley 12/6/44; Dow Fd 2/7/44; slated 96BG, ass 305BG Chelveston 4/7/44; tran 384BG Grafton Underwood 29/7/44; tran 526BS/379BG [LF-X] Kimbolton 4/8/44; MIA Dresden 14/2/45 w/?; f/l continent; sal 13/3/45.
42-97981 Del Dallas 23/4/44; Kearney 2/6/44; Grenier 17/6/44; ass 337BS/96BG [AW-K] Snetterton 19/6/44; MIA Osnabrück 21/11/44 w/?; mech fault, c/l Vden, Hol; 2KIA 7RTD; sal 1/3/45. ALL AMERICAN GIRL.
42-97982 Del Dallas 23/4/44; Kearney 2/6/44; Dow Fd 27/6/44; ass 615BS/401BG [IY-P] Deenethorpe 10/7/44; MIA Munich 16/7/44 w/Johnson; flak, cr Neuried, Ger; 9POW; MACR 7558.
42-97983 Del Dallas 23/4/44; Kearney 2/6/44; Grenier 17/6/44; ass 570BS/390BG Framlingham 20/6/44; MIA Leipzig 7/7/44 w/Cribbs; mid air coll w/42-107070; cr Hoorn, Hol; 5KIA 5POW; MACR 7367.
42-97984 Del Dallas 23/4/44; Hunter 8/6/44; Presque Is 28/6/44; ass 401BS/91BG [LL-G] Bassingbourn 29/6/44; 323BS; MIA {21+m} Merseburg 2/11/44 w/Faris; e/a, cr Koethen, Ger?; 3KIA 6POW; MACR 10149. SHERRY'S CHERRIES.
42-97985 Del Dallas 24/4/44; Kearney 2/6/44; Dow Fd 27/6/44; ass 332BS/94BG [XM-Q] Rougham 28/6/44; mid air coll w/44-8177 in assembly 30/11/44; c/l base & burnt, 9KIA; sal.
42-97986 Del Dallas 24/4/44; Langley 15/6/44; Dow Fd 7/7/44; ass 305BG Chelveston 8/7/44; tran 547BS/384BG [SO-Z] Grafton Underwood 29/7/44; 544BS [SU-Z], 545BS [JD-A]; nosed over in landing 16/5/45, sal.
42-97987 Del Dallas 24/4/44; Hunter 30/5/44; Grenier 15/6/44; ass 730BS/452BG Deopham Green 17/7/44; retUS Bradley 28/6/45; 4168 BU Sth Plains 2/7/45; RFC Kingman 22/11/45.
42-97988 Del Dallas 24/4/44; Langley 13/6/44; Dow Fd 5/7/44; ass 94BG Rougham 6/7/44; sal 21/8/44. FLAGSHIP.
42-97989 Del Dallas 25/4/44; Langley 17/6/44; Dow Fd 7/7/44; ass 96BG Snetterton 8/7/44; tran 335BS/95BG [OE-Y] Horham 9/7/44; MIA Warsaw (Operation 'Frantic VII') 18/9/44 w/?; f/l Russia; sal 24/11/44; rep & ass 15AF, 301BG Lucera 9/1/45.
42-97990 Del Dallas 25/4/44; Langley 19/6/44; Grenier 9/7/44; ass (PFF) 532BS/381BG [VE-F] Ridgewell 6/8/44; {24+m} sal 6/3/45; re-ass AF 30/4/47; 108 BU Oberpfaffenhofen 18/1/48; Recl Comp 7/1/49.
42-97991 Del Dallas 26/4/44; Langley 26/6/44; Grenier 13/7/44; ass 366BS/305BG Chelveston 9/8/44; MIA Merseburg 24/8/44 w/Maj Von Turgeln; flak, cr Merseburg; 2KIA 9POW; MACR 8207.
42-97992 Del Dallas 26/4/44; Langley 24/6/44; Dow Fd 15/7/44; ass 336BS/95BG [ET-Q] Horham 16/7/44 HAP HAZARD; 336BS [OE-G]; retUS Bradley 24/6/45; 4168 BU Sth Plains 26/6/45; RFC Kingman 29/11/45. TROUBLE BUGGY.
42-97993 Del Dallas 26/4/44; Langley 17/6/44; Dow Fd 9/7/44; ass 413BS/96BG Snetterton 15/7/44; b/d Stuttgart 10/9/44 w/Maj Mulholland; flak, f/l Saargermund, Ger; 10POW; MACR 8842. Sal 9/5/45.
42-97994 Del Dallas 26/4/44; Langley 16/6/44; Dow Fd 7/7/44; ass 305BG Chelveston 8/7/44; tran 384BG Grafton Underwood 29/7/44; 359BS/303BG Molesworth 4/8/44; MIA Merseburg 24/8/44 w/Eldridge; flak, cr Merseburg; 10POW; MACR 8211.
42-97995 Del Dallas 26/4/44; Hunter 5/6/44; Grenier 18/6/44; ass 305BG Chelveston 28/6/44; tran 351BG Polebrook 23/5/45; retUS Bradley 12/6/45; 4168 BU Sth Plains 15/6/45; RFC Kingman 14/12/45.
42-97996 Del Dallas 27/4/44; Kearney 7/6/44; Grenier 28/6/44; ass 487BG Lavenham 30/6/44; b/d Ruhland 17/3/45 w/?; c/l Rudnicke, Pol; sal 28/3/45.
42-97997 Del Dallas 27/4/44; Kearney 2/6/44; Hunter 8/6/44; Kearney 19/6/44; Grenier 30/6/44; ass 838BS/487BG [2C-J] Lavenham 4/7/44; c/l UK? 25/11/44, sal.
42-97998 Del Dallas 27/4/44; Hunter 6/6/44; Dow Fd 2/7/44; ass 834BS/486BG [2S-F] Sudbury 6/7/44; b/d Mannheim 21/1/45 w/?; f/l continent; sal 6/4/45. MISS IRISH.
42-97999 Del Dallas 27/4/44; Kearney 6/6/44; Dow Fd 27/6/44; ass 324BS/91BG Bassingbourn 10/7/44; MIA Leipzig 20/7/44 w/Capt Holmes; flak, cr Karden,

Above: B-17G-40-VE 42-98026 became Fortress B.III serial HB796/G in RAF service. It was fitted with Piperack, a device for jamming the radar of enemy night fighters, the antenna of which was carried in the under-nose shield and around the tail gun position. (Crown)

Ger?; 9POW; MACR 7273.

42-98000 Del Dallas 27/4/44; Hunter 7/6/44; Dow Fd 27/6/44; ass 544BS/384BG [SU-J] Grafton Underwood 15/7/44; MIA Kyllburg, Ger 8/1/45 w/DeFrancesso; flak, cr Rochefort, Fr; 1KIA 8POW; MACR 11579. FIGHTIN' HEBE.

42-98001 Del Dallas 27/4/44; Hunter 5/6/44; Grenier 19/6/44; 111 BU Langley 12/7/44; Grenier 16/7/44; ass 834BS/486BG [2S-S] Sudbury 17/7/44; tran 838BS/487BG Lavenham 10/4/45; retUS Bradley 7/7/45; 4168 BU Sth Plains 9/7/45; RFC Kingman 9/12/45.

42-98002 Del Dallas 28/4/44; Kearney 7/6/44; Dow Fd 27/6/44; ass 8AF 9/7/44; retUS Bradley 11/7/44; 4185 BU Independence 12/7/45; RFC Kingman 10/12/45.

42-98003 Del Dallas 28/4/44; Kearney 6/6/44; Presque Is 28/6/44; ass 850BS/490BG Eye 29/6/44; retUS Bradley 9/7/45; 4168 BU Sth Plains 11/7/45; RFC Kingman 28/11/45.

42-98004 Del Dallas 28/4/44; Hunter 9/6/44; Dow Fd 24/6/44; ass 508BS/351BG [YB-H] Polebrook 17/4/44; {25m} sal 2 SAD 27/9/44.

42-98005 Del Dallas 30/4/44; Kearney 13/6/44; Grenier 29/6/44; ass 326BS/92BG [JW-A] Podington 3/7/44; b/d Ludwigshafen 5/9/44 w/?; sal 8/9/44.

42-98006 Del Dallas 30/4/44; Kearney 13/6/44; Grenier 30/6/44; ass 832BS/486BG [3R-F] Sudbury 3/7/44; ret POWs from Linz 11/7/45; retUS Bradley 13/7/45; 4185 BU Independence 7/11/45; RFC Kingman 19/12/45. THE OLD YARD DOG.

42-98007 Del Dallas 30/4/44; Kearney 15/6/44; Dow Fd 30/6/44; ass 833BS/486BG [4N-D] Sudbury 4/7/44; retUS Bradley 7/7/45; 4168 BU Sth Plains 28/8/45; RFC Kingman 11/12/45. SLEEPY TIME GAL.

42-98008 Del Dallas 30/4/44; Kearney 14/6/44; Presque Is 5/7/44; ass 834BS/486BG [2S-G] Sudbury 7/7/44; tran 92BG Podington 17/7/44; retUS Bradley 8/7/45; 4168 BU Sth Plains 11/7/45; RFC Kingman 23/11/45. AMERICAN BEAUTY.

42-98009 Del Dallas 1/5/44; Long Beach 11/6/44; Hunter 18/7/44; Grenier 3/8/44; ass 861BS/493BG Debach 4/7/44; Lt Walden 1/3/45; retUS Bradley 3/7/45; 4168 BU Sth Plains 7/7/45; RFC Kingman 29/11/45.

42-98010 Del Dallas 1/5/44; Long Beach 12/6/44; Hunter 18/7/44; Dow Fd 3/8/44; ass 551BS/385BG Gt Ashfield 4/8/44; MIA Berlin (Spandau) 6/10/44 w/Taylor; e/a, cr Liepe, Ger; 8KIA 1POW; MACR 9523.

42-98011 Del Dallas 1/5/44; Kearney 15/6/44; Grenier 28/6/44; ass 838BS/487BG Lavenham 3/7/44; retUS Bradley 13/7/44; 4185 BU Independence 25/10/45; RFC Kingman 10/1/46.

42-98012 Del Dallas 1/5/44; Kearney 9/6/44; Grenier 28/6/44; ass 322BS/91BG Bassingbourn 31/7/44; MIA {12m} Merseburg 2/11/44 w/Hamilton; e/a, cr Haideburger, Ger; 4KIA 5POW; MACR 10150. CANNON BALL TOO.

42-98013 Del Dallas 2/5/44; Hunter 8/6/44; Presque Is 28/6/44; ass 838BS/487BG Lavenham 30/6/44; 839BS [R5-E]; MIA Magdeburg 14/1/45 w/Kochczynski; mid air coll w/43-37933; cr Ventschow, Ger; 4KIA 5POW; MACR 11734.

42-98014 Del Dallas 2/5/44; Hunter 10/6/44; Dow Fd 28/6/44; ass 836BS/487BG [2G-K] Lavenham 2/7/44; MIA Berlin 3/2/45 w/?.

42-98015 Del Dallas 2/5/44; Kearney 14/6/44; Grenier 28/6/44; ass 349BS/100BG [XR-N] Thorpe Abbotts 8/4/44; tran 482BG Alconbury 20/5/45; retUS Bradley 31/5/45; 4168 BU Sth Plains 3/6/45; RFC Kingman 17/11/45. HUNDRED PROOF.

42-98016 Del Dallas 2/5/44; Kearney 16/6/44; Grenier 30/6/44; ass 548BS/385BG Gt Ashfield 2/8/44; MIA Berlin (Spandau) 6/10/43 w/Funk; e/a, cr Friesack, Ger; 8KIA 1POW; MACR 9524.

42-98017 Del Dallas 2/5/44; Kearney 16/6/44; Grenier 30/6/44; ass 849BS/490BG Eye 2/8/44; retUS Bradley 12/7/45; 4185 BU Independence 25/10/45; RFC Kingman 9/12/45. ALL'ER NOTHIN'.

42-98018 Del Dallas 2/5/44; Kearney 16/6/44; Grenier 31/6/44; ass 750BS/457BG Glatton 2/8/44; MIA Peenemunde 25/8/44 w/Goss; flak, f/l Ljungbyhed, Swed; 9INT; MACR 8294. LADY KATHERINE.

42-98019 Del Dallas 3/5/44; Langley 26/6/44; Dow Fd 20/7/44; ass 838BS/487BG [2C-L] Lavenham 2/8/44; MIA Merzehausen, Ger 24/12/44 w/?; f/l continent. MUTZIE 'B'.

42-98020 Del Dallas 3/5/44; Kearney 17/6/44; Grenier 29/6/44; ass 487BG Lavenham 2/8/44; sal 31/8/44.

42-98021 Del Denver 3/5/44; Dorval (Montreal) 6/6/44; ass RAF [HB791] 220Sq Azores (ZZ-T); 251Sq Iceland; SOC 11/3/47. POTS & PANS.

42-98022 Del Denver 3/5/44; Dorval 1/6/44; ass RAF [HB792] 220Sq Azores (ZZ-U); 251Sq Iceland; SOC 11/3/47.

42-98023 Del Denver 3/5/44; Dorval 14/5/44; ass RAF [HB793] 214Sq RCM Oulton (BU-S); 223Sq (6G-O); 1699 Flt (4Z-B); SOC 11/3/47.

42-98024 Del Denver 3/5/44; Dorval 8/6/44; ass RAF [HB794]; tran 8AF 750BS/457BG Glatton 2/8/44; 749BS; 305BG Chelveston 23/5/45. Sal 9AF Germany 31/5/46. QUE UP.

42-98025 Del Denver 3/5/44; Dorval 14/5/44; ass RAF [HB795] 214Sq RCM Oulton (BU-S); 51MU; SOC 11/3/47.

42-98026 Del Denver 4/5/44; Dorval 16/5/44; ass RAF [HB796] 214Sq RCM Oulton (BU-T); MIA window patrol 9/2/45.

42-98027 Del Denver 4/5/44; Dorval 4/6/44; ass RAF [HB797]; tran 8AF 351BG Polebrook 2/8/44; 544BS/384BG [SU-Z] Grafton Underwood 11/12/44; 547BS [SO-Z]; 305BG Polebrook 9/5/45; sal 9AF Germany 23/5/46. SWAMP ANGEL.

42-98028 Del Denver 5/5/44; Dorval 22/6/44; ass RAF [HB798]; tran 8AF 457BG Glatton 2/8/44; 305BG Chelveston 23/5/45; sal 9AF Germany 10/5/46.

42-98029 Del Denver 6/5/44; Dorval 15/6/44; ass RAF [HB799] 214Sq RCM Oulton (BU-K); SOC 11/3/47.

42-98030 Del Denver 6/5/44; Dorval 15/6/44; ass RAF [HB800] 214Sq RCM Oulton (BU-V); b/d 31/10/44; c/l Ford; sal 12/2/45.

42-98031 Del Denver 6/5/44; Dorval 16/5/44; ass RAF [HB801] 214Sq RCM Oulton (BU-T); SOC 11/3/47.

42-98032 Del Denver 6/5/44; Dorval 17/5/44; ass RAF [HB802] 214Sq RCM Oulton (BU-O); MIA Lutzkendorf 15/3/45.

42-98033 Del Denver 7/5/44; Dorval 16/5/44; ass RAF [HB803] 214Sq RCM Oulton (BU-L); MIA Ludwigshafen 22/3/45.

42-98034 Del Denver 7/5/44; Dorval 6/6/44; ass RAF [HB804]; tran 526BS/379BG [LF-Y] Kimbolton 4/10/44; retUS Bradley 28/6/45; Roumulus 29/6/45; 4168 BU Sth Plains 26/10/45; RFC Kingman 7/12/45.

42-98035 Del Denver 7/5/44; Dorval 17/5/44; ass RAF [HB805] 214Sq RCM Oulton (BU-C); MIA window patrol 25/2/45.

B-17G-BO

42-102379 Del Gt Falls 1/3/44; first a/c with staggered waist guns; 224 BU Sioux City 6/3/44; 222 BU Ardmore 13/6/44; 332 BU Ardmore 16/6/44; RFC Walnut Ridge 20/8/45.

42-102380 Del Cheyenne 1/3/44; Kearney 27/3/44; ass 331BS/94BG [QE-Y] Rougham 4/4/44; MIA Merseburg 7/10/44 w/Kennedy; e/a, cr Sonneberg, Ger; sal 15/4/45. RENO - VATION.

42-102381 Del Cheyenne 2/3/44; 225 BU Rapid City 28/3/44; 236 BU Pyote 20/7/44; 325 BU Biggs 18/1/45; 305 BU Biggs 18/11/45; RFC Walnut Ridge 2/4/46.

42-102382 Del Cheyenne 17/2/44; Lincoln 25/3/44; Morrison 4/4/44; ass 817BS/483BG Sterparone 21/4/44; MIA Memmingen 18/7/44 w/Smith; e/a, cr Leutkirch, Ger?; MACR 6977. VIRGIL'S VIRGIN.

42-102383 Del Cheyenne 27/2/44; 225 BU Rapid City 1/5/44; 232 BU Dalhart 28/7/44; RFC Altus 15/11/45.

42-102384 Del Cheyenne 27/2/44; 225 BU Rapid City 1/5/44; 354 BU Rapid City 20/7/44; 125 BU Pueblo 29/7/44; RFC Kingman 4/1/46.

42-102385 Del Cheyenne 27/2/44; Dyersburg 20/3/44; W/O 23/3/44.

42-102386 Del Cheyenne 27/2/44; 225 BU Rapid City 1/5/44; 2114 BU Lockburn 19/7/44; 2137 BU Hendricks 14/10/44; RFC Walnut Ridge 8/1/46.

42-102387 Del Cheyenne 27/2/44; Gt Falls 2/3/44; 225 BU Rapid City 4/4/45; 239 BU March 19/7/45; 237 BU Kirtland 23/7/45; 420 BU March 7/10/45; 321 BU March 28/4/46; 4135 BU Hill 6/6/46; 556 BU Long Beach 7/6/46; 4135 BU Hill 2/7/46; Recl Comp 2/10/46.

42-102388 Del Cheyenne 27/2/44; Gt Falls 2/3/44; Morrison 19/4/44; ass 815BS/483BG Sterparone 30/4/44; MIA Fornova de Taro 22/6/44 w/Schild; flak, right wing shot off, cr Bologna; 3EVD 4KIA 3POW; MACR 11543.

42-102389 Del Cheyenne 27/2/44; Gt Falls 1/3/44; Rapid City 18/3/44; 225 BU Rapid City 1/3/45; 2114 BU Lockburn 19/7/45; 2137 BU Hendricks 18/8/45; RFC Kingman 1/11/45.

42-102390 Del Cheyenne 27/2/44; Hunter 15/3/44; Dow Fd 8/4/44; ass 547BS/384BG [SO-M] Grafton Underwood 11/4/44; tran 600BS/398BG [N8-X/S] Nuthampstead 26/4/44; 603BS; sal 9AF Germany 10/12/45.

42-102391 Del Cheyenne 27/2/44; Gt Falls 2/3/44; Hunter 15/3/44; Grenier 9/4/44; ass 601BS/398BG [3O-B] Nuthampstead 26/4/44; MIA Hamburg 18/6/44 w/Hadjes; flak, cr Bavendorf, Ger; 9POW; MACR 5998.

42-102392 Del Cheyenne 27/2/44; Gt Falls 2/3/44; Hunter 14/3/44; Grenier 7/4/44; ass 401BS/91BG Bassingbourn 22/4/44; MIA {7m} Troyes 1/5/44 w/McCarile; flak hit cockpit, cr Bavereyde, Fr; 8KIA 2POW; MACR 4465. COOL PAPA.

42-102393 Del Cheyenne 27/2/44; Hunter 22/3/44; Grenier 2/4/44; ass 612BS/401BG [SC-A] Deenethorpe 16/4/44; retUS Bradley 8/6/45; 4168 BU Sth Plains 12/6/45; RFC Kingman 27/11/45. DIANE QUEEN OF THE CHASE.

42-102394 Del Cheyenne 27/2/44; Kearney 15/3/44; Dow Fd 4/4/44; ass 614BS/401BG [IW-C] Deenethorpe 16/4/44; MIA Merseburg 24/8/44 w/Finney; e/a, cr Brockhoefe, Ger; 3KIA 6POW; MACR 8202. DOWN 'N GO.

42-102395 Del Cheyenne 27/2/44; Gr Island 15/3/44; Grenier 2/4/44; ass 711BS/447BG Rattlesden 8/4/44; MIA Brux 12/5/44 w/Mandrell; e/a, cr Giessen, Ger; 10POW; MACR 4771.

42-102396 Del Cheyenne 27/2/44; Gr Island 18/3/44; Presque Is 5/4/44; ass 325BS/92BG Podington 14/4/44; MIA Cologne 10/1/45 w/?; f/l Continent; sal 23/1/45.

42-102397 Del Cheyenne 27/2/44; Hunter 15/3/44; Dow Fd 10/4/44; ass 730BS/452BG Deopham Green 20/4/44 MUGWUMP; 729BS; MIA Hamburg 17/1/45 w/Skoglund; 9POW; MACR 11794. C'EST LA GUERRE.

42-102398 Del Cheyenne 29/2/44; Gr Island 22/3/44; Grenier 20/4/44; ass 612BS/401BG [SC-H] Deenethorpe 13/5/44; retUS Bradley 6/6/45; 4168 BU Sth Plains 8/6/45; RFC Kingman 17/12/45.

42-102399 Del Cheyenne 29/2/44; Pyote 5/3/44; 235 BU Biggs 17/8/44; W/O 23/11/44; Recl Comp 16/12/44.

42-102400 Del Cheyenne 29/2/44; Gt Falls 6/3/44; 222 BU Ardmore 22/1/45; 3017 BU Hobbs 17/6/45; 327 BU Drew 21/6/45; 332 BU Ardmore 20/7/45; RFC Walnut Ridge 18/8/45.

42-102401 Cheyenne 29/2/44; Gt Falls 5/3/44; Ardmore 21/3/44; 222 BU Ardmore 22/1/45; 332 BU Ardmore 16/6/45; RFC Walnut Ridge 18/9/45.

42-102402 Cheyenne 29/2/44; Gr Island 11/3/44; Bangor 2/4/44; ass 547BS/384BG [SO-L] Grafton Underwood 4/4/44; MIA Kiel 22/5/44 w/Castleman; mech fault, cr Neumünster, Ger; 1KIA 8POW; MACR 4954.

42-102403 Cheyenne 29/2/44; Hunter 22/3/44; Morrison 9/4/44; ass 816BS/483BG Sterparone 9/4/44; MIA Friedrichshafen 3/8/44 w/Mullins; ditched Adriatic; 10RTD.

42-102404 Cheyenne 29/2/44; Pyote 11/3/44; 235 BU Biggs 17/8/44; 4505 BU Kelly 20/9/44; 203 BU Jackson 28/3/45; 253 BU St Angelo 25/7/45; 203 BU Jackson 15/8/45; 235 BU Biggs 9/9/45; 230 BU Biggs 25/11/45; 268 BU Peterson 11/12/45l; RFC Kingman 7/1/46.

42-102405 Cheyenne 4/3/44; Kearney 22/3/44; Grenier 7/4/44; ass 332BS/94BG Rougham 8/4/44; c/l Lawshall, UK on training mission 23/4/44 w/?; 9KIA 2RTD; sal 24/4/44.

42-102406 Cheyenne 2/3/44; Hunter 22/3/44; Morrison 8/4/44; ass 817BS/483BG Sterparone 15/4/44; MIA Belgrade 7/5/44 w/Lanford; 6KIA 4POW; MACR 4924.

42-102407 Cheyenne 1/3/44; Des Moines 17/3/44; Ardmore 27/3/44; 202 BU Galveston 10/8/44; 222 BU Ardmore 22/1/45; 332 BU Ardmore 16/6/45; RFC Walnut Ridge 18/8/45.

42-102408 Cheyenne 1/3/44; Dyersburg 21/3/44; 554 BU Memphis 12/10/44; 4119 BU Brookley 7/11/44; 330 BU Dyersburg 2/1/45; RFC Walnut Ridge 19/12/45.

42-102409 Cheyenne 1/3/44; Ardmore 21/3/44; 268 BU Peterson 2/1/45; 222 BU Ardmore 22/1/45; 332 BU Ardmore 16/6/45; 327 BU Drew 21/6/45; 332 BU Ardmore 3/7/45; Recl Comp 3/1/46.

42-102410 Cheyenne 1/3/44; Ardmore 20/3/44; 222 BU Ardmore W/O 23/9/44.

42-102411 Cheyenne 1/3/44; Hunter 21/3/44; Grenier 10/4/44; ass 427BS/303BG [GN-Y/P] Molesworth 30/4/44; b/d Berlin 18/3/45 w/?; f/l Warsaw, Pol.; sal 28/3/45. MISS LACE.

42-102412 Cheyenne 1/3/44; Pyote 19/3/44; 235 BU Biggs 18/8/44; 4505 BU Kelly 1/9/44; 235 BU Biggs 17/1/45; 224 BU Sioux City 8/3/45; 332 BU Ardmore 19/6/45; RFC Walnut Ridge 19/8/45.

42-102413 Cheyenne 1/3/44; Dyersburg 22/3/44; 330 BU Dyersburg 1/3/45; 327 BU Drew 28/8/45; 330 BU Dyersburg 4/9/45; RFC Walnut Ridge 14/12/45.

42-102414 Cheyenne 2/3/44; Hunter 21/3/44; Grenier 10/4/44; ass 8AF 19/4/44.

42-102415 Cheyenne 1/3/44; Ardmore 17/3/44; 222 BU Ardmore 8/9/44; 2517 BU Elington 21/9/44; 222 BU Ardmore 22/1/45; 332 BU Ardmore 16/6/45; RFC Walnut Ridge 10/9/45.

42-102416 Cheyenne 1/3/44; Hunter 14/3/44; Grenier 11/4/44; ass 349BS/100BG [XR-H] Thorpe Abbotts 19/4/44; MIA St Lo, Fr 25/7/44 w/Townsend; flak, cr Paris; 3EVD 6POW; MACR 7837. LADY LUCK.

42-102417 Cheyenne 1/3/44; Des Moines 21/3/44; 222 BU Ardmore 22/1/45; 332 BU Ardmore 16/6/45; RFC Walnut Ridge 18/8/45.

42-102418 Cheyenne 3/3/44; Hunter 12/3/44; Dow Fd 9/4/44; ass 600BS/398BG [N8-M] Nuthampstead 24/4/44; 601BS; b/d Germersheim, Ger 13/1/45 w/?; c/l base; sal 14/1/45.

42-102419 Cheyenne 2/3/44; Hunter 16/3/44; Nashville 23/3/44; Dow Fd 12/4/44; ass 709BS/447BG Rattlesden 20/4/44; c/l Woolpit, UK 28/6/44, sal.

42-102420 Cheyenne 2/3/44; Lincoln 19/3/44; 330 BU Dyersburg 3/1/45; RFC Walnut Ridge 19/12/45.

42-102421 Del Cheyenne 2/3/44; Gr Island 18/3/44; Presque Is 2/4/44; ass 709BS/447BG Rattlesden 6/4/44; MIA Berlin 29/4/44 w/Dowler; e/a, cr Weferlingen, Ger; 9KIA 1POW; MACR 4254.

42-102422 Del Cheyenne 2/3/44; Hunter 15/3/44; Morrison 7/4/44; ass 816BS/483BG Sterparone 17/4/44; MIA Memmingen 18/7/44 w/Gunn; e/a, cr Schwarserd, Ger; 9KIA 1POW (wg Jaski); MACR 7098.

42-102423 Del Cheyenne 2/3/44; Kearney 14/4/44; Grenier 29/4/44; ass 533BS/381BG [VP-Q] Ridgewell 21/5/44; MIA {2+m} Munich 31/7/44 w/Pearson; flak, cr Stafflangen, Ger; 9POW; MACR 7742. MY DEVOTION.

42-102424 Del Cheyenne 2/3/44; Gr Island 10/3/44; Grenier 6/4/44; ass 325BS/92BG [NV-B] Podington 7/4/44; MIA Cologne 5/10/44 w/Richards; mech fault, ditched Channel; 3KIA 6RTD; MACR 9347. EL LOBO.

42-102425 Del Cheyenne 2/3/44; Gt Falls 6/3/44; Ardmore 20/3/44; 222 BU Ardmore 24/8/44; 2509 BU Big Spring 25/8/44; 222 BU Ardmore 30/8/44; 332 BU Ardmore 16/6/45; RFC Walnut Ridge 21/8/45.

42-102426 Del Cheyenne 2/3/44; Hunter 13/3/44; Dow Fd 9/4/44; ass 407BS/92BG [PY-W] Podington 7/5/44; MIA Merseburg 11/9/44 w/McIlonie; e/a, cr Hlefta, Ger?; 8KIA 1POW; MACR 8891. KIDLEY DIVEY.

42-102427 Del Cheyenne 2/3/44; Kearney 25/3/44; Grenier 2/4/44; ass 336BS/95BG [ET-C] Horham 7/4/44; b/d Mainz 9/10/44 w/Taylor; f/l France, 9RTD; sal 14/11/44.

42-102428 Del Cheyenne 2/3/44; Kansas City 14/3/44; Dyersburg 20/3/44; W/O 22/4/44.

42-102429 Del Cheyenne 2/3/44; Hunter 18/3/44; Morrison 2/4/44; ass 840BS/483BG Sterparone 17/4/44; MIA Ploesti 15/7/44 w/Vlahovich; flak, cr on mountain; 10KIA. MACR 6955.

42-102430 Del Cheyenne 2/3/44; Gr Island 13/3/44; Grenier 2/4/44; ass 545BS/384BG [JD-O] Grafton Underwood 15/4/44; tran 403 AD Langford Lodge training 4/3/45; sal 9AF Germany 10/12/45. SPAM-O-LINER.

42-102431 Del Cheyenne 4/3/44; Kearney 6/4/44; Dow Fd 21/4/44; ass 447BG Rattlesden 22/4/44; tran 550BS/385BG Gt Ashfield 23/4/44; b/d

Mannheim 21/1/45 w/?; c/l Bradwell, UK, sal. SLICK CHICK.

42-102432 Del Cheyenne 5/3/44; Kearney 22/3/44; Presque Is 4/4/44; ass 427BS/303BG [GN-U] Molesworth 12/4/44; MIA Handorf, Ger 15/8/44 w/Cook; e/a, cr Bitburg, Ger; 3KIA 6POW; MACR 8438.

42-102433 Del Cheyenne 3/3/44; Gr Island 22/3/44; Grenier 6/4/44; ass 562BS/388BG Knettishall 7/4/44; c/l RAF Ludham, UK, 22/5/44; 2KIA 8RTD; sal 24/5/44.

42-102434 Del Cheyenne 3/3/44; Dorval (Montreal) 10/3/44; ass RAF [HB783]; tran 561BS/388BG Knettishall 22/3/44 REVEL'S REVENGE; b/d Merseburg 28/9/44 w/? c/l Lesvillette, Bel; 9RTD.

42-102435 Del Cheyenne 3/3/44; Dorval 10/3/44; ass RAF [HB784]; tran 562BS/388BG Knettishall 1/7/44; MIA Munich 31/7/44 w/Crider; flak, cr Legea?: 8POW; MACR 7746.

42-102436 Del Cheyenne 3/3/44; Dorval 10/3/44; ass RAF [HB785] 214Sq RCM Oulton (BU-A); MIA 21/3/45.

42-102437 Del Cheyenne 3/3/44; Dorval 10/3/44; ass RAF [HB786] 220Sq, 521 Met Sq, 51MU; SOC 21/6/47.

42-102438 Del Cheyenne 3/3/44; Dorval 10/3/44; ass RAF [HB787] 214Sq RCM Oulton (BU-J); cr Foulsham 16/11/44, sal.

42-102439 Del Cheyenne 3/3/44; Dorval 10/3/44; ass RAF [HB788] 214Sq RCM Oulton (BU-B); MIA Gravenhorst 7/11/44.

42-102440 Del Cheyenne 3/3/44; Kearney 22/3/44; Dow Fd 4/4/44; ass 568BS/390BG [BI-K] Framlingham 5/4/44; MIA Magdeburg 28/5/44 w/Weigle; e/a, cr Burg, Ger; 10POW; MACR 5254. SILVER SLIPPER.

42-102441 Del Cheyenne 3/3/44; Gr Island 13/3/44; Dow Fd 7/4/44; ass 711BS/447BG Rattlesden 8/4/44; MIA Merseburg 7/10/44 w/Harwood; flak, cr Merseburg; 2KIA 7POW; MACR 9764. TNT KATIE.

42-102442 Del Cheyenne 3/3/44; Kearney 15/3/44; Dow Fd 4/4/44; ass 545BS/384BG [JD-J] Grafton Underwood 15/4/44; during assembly for Leipzig, mid air coll w/B17 7/7/44; cr Withersfield, UK, 14KIA; sal 8/7/44.

42-102443 Del Cheyenne 3/3/44; Sioux City 20/3/44; W/O 21/3/44.

42-102444 Del Cheyenne 3/3/44; Gr Island 30/3/44; Dow Fd 6/4/44; ass 339BS/96BG Snetterton 7/4/44; MIA Berlin 8/5/44 w/Green; e/a, cr Bremen; 10POW; MACR 4573. SMILIN' THRU.

42-102445 Del Cheyenne 3/3/44; Kearney 22/3/44; Dow Fd 5/4/44; ass 601BS/398BG [3O-B] Nuthampstead 26/4/44; MIA Noball V-1 sites 8/7/44 w/Fisher; flak, cr Money Cayeux, Fr; 2EVD 1KIA 7POW; MACR 7217.

42-102446 Del Cheyenne 4/3/44; Gr Island 21/3/44; Presque Is 6/4/44; Langford Lodge 7/4/44; ass 545BS/384BG [JD-M] Grafton Underwood 15/4/44; MIA Oberpfaffenhofen 24/4/44 w/Bailey; flak damage the shot down by Swiss AF, cr Lake Greifensee, Switz; 9KIA; MACR 4347. (a/c recovered from lake in 1950s, then later scrapped.) LITTLE CHUB.

42-102447 Del Cheyenne 4/3/44; Kearney 24/3/44; Dow Fd 4/4/44; ass 334BS/95BG [BG-A] Horham 6/4/44; retUS Bradley 21/6/45; 4168 BU Sth Plains 23/6/45; RFC Kingman 25/11/45. EL'S BELLES.

42-102448 Del Cheyenne 4/3/44; Kearney 24/3/44; Grenier 2/4/44; ass 545BS/384BG [JD-P] Grafton Underwood 15/4/44; MIA Berlin 29/4/44 w/Bouvier; e/a, cr Berlin; 2KIA 8POW; MACR 4242.

42-102449 Del Cheyenne 4/3/44; Gr Island 22/3/44; Grenier 2/4/44; ass 547BS/384BG [SO-R] Grafton Underwood 16/4/44; b/d Cologne 10/11/44 w/?; f/l Continent; sal; retUS Bradley 4/6/45; 4168 BU Sth Plains 8/6/45; RFC Kingman 18/12/45.

42-102450 Del Cheyenne 4/3/44; Kearney 22/3/44; Dow Fd 7/4/44; ass 96BG Snetterton 7/4/44; tran 336BS/95BG Horham 8/4/44; MIA Chemnitz 3/3/45 w/Duncan; mid air coll w/42-97376, cr Schonbeck, Ger; 9KIA; MACR 12889. PAISANO.

42-102451 Del Cheyenne 4/3/44; Gr Island 22/3/44; Grenier 6/4/44; slated 385BG, ass 338BS/96BG [BX-T] Snetterton 7/4/44; MIA Berlin 8/5/44 w/Sturler; e/a, cr Sehlau, Ger?; 8KIA 2POW; MACR 4574.

42-102452 Del Cheyenne 4/3/44; Kearney 22/3/44; Grenier 5/4/44; ass 337BS/96BG [AW-R] Snetterton 7/4/44; MIA Brux 12/5/44 w/Moore; mid air coll w/42-97382, ct Wehrheim, Ger; 2KIA 8POW; MACR 4862.

42-102453 Del Cheyenne 4/3/44; Kearney 22/3/44; Grenier 6/4/44; ass 358BS/303BG [VK-J] Molesworth 30/4/44; sal 2SAD 26/7/44. "PRINCESS PAT".

42-102454 Del Cheyenne 4/3/44; Gr Island 24/3/44; Dow Fd 5/4/44; ass 413BS/96BG [MZ-T] Snetterton 6/4/44; MIA Merseburg 7/10/44 w/Anglen; e/a, cr West Klosterholz, Ger; 9POW; MACR 9353. MARZI DOATS.

42-102455 Del Cheyenne 4/3/44; Gt Falls 6/3/44; Cheyenne 4/4/44; Hunter 18/4/44; Grenier 5/5/44; ass 335BS/95BG [OE-Z] Horham 8/5/44 LUCKY LADY; tran 351BG Polebrook 21/5/45; sal 31/5/45. SCREAMING EAGLE.

42-102456 Del Cheyenne 4/3/44; Gr Island 22/3/44; Dow Fd 7/4/44; ass 333BS/94BG Rougham 8/4/44; 331BS [QE-T]; sal 11/10/44. SHADY LADY.

42-102457 Del Cheyenne 5/3/44; Kearney 22/3/44; Dow Fd 4/4/44; ass 410BS/94BG [GL-R] Rougham 6/4/44 FILTHY HAG; MIA Munich 12/7/44 w/Scott; mech fault, f/l Dubendorf, Switz; 10INT; MACR 7510; retUS 1103 BU Morrison 7/10/45; RFC Walnut Ridge 14/1/46. GLORIA.

42-102458 Del Cheyenne 5/3/44; Kearney 6/4/44; Grenier 29/4/44; ass 457BG Glatton 1/5/44; sal b/d SAD 27/6/44.

42-102459 Del Cheyenne 5/3/44; Kearney 5/4/44; Grenier 22/4/44; ass 544BS/384BG [SU-O] Grafton Underwood 3/5/44; sal 9AF Germany 10/12/45. LITTLE KENNY.

42-102460 Del Cheyenne 5/3/44; Gr Island 22/3/44; Rapid City 1/4/44; 225 BU Rapid City 22/1/45; Recl Comp 1/3/45.

42-102461 Del Cheyenne 5/3/44; Alexandra 3/4/44; 221 BU Alexandra 17/1/45; 329 BU Alexandra 1/3/45; 330 BU Dyersburg 24/6/45; 237 BU Drew 28/8/45; 330 BU Dyersburg 4/9/45; RFC Walnut Ridge 18/12/45.

42-102462 Del Cheyenne 5/3/44; Alexandra 24/3/44; 221 BU Alexandra 17/1/45; 329 BU Alexandra 1/3/45; 330 BU Dyersburg 24/6/45; 237 BU Drew 30/8/45; 330 BU Dyersburg 4/9/45; RFC Walnut Ridge 17/12/45.

42-102463 Del Cheyenne 5/3/44; Kearney 5/4/44; Dow Fd 19/4/44; ass 602BS/398BG [K8-Z] Nuthampstead 28/4/44; 601BS [3O-Z]; MIA Toulouse 25/6/44 w/Godwin; flak, cr Comebarrion, Fr; 2KIA 7POW; MACR 6220.

42-102464 Del Cheyenne 5/3/44; Kearney 5/4/44; Dow Fd 6/5/44; ass 750BS/457BG Glatton 7/5/44; MIA French A/fds 14/6/44 w/Blackwell; flak, cr Bleckmar, Fr?; 4EVD 5POW; MACR 5805.

42-102465 Del Cheyenne 5/3/44; Kearney 5/4/44; Dow Fd 14/4/44; ass 551BS/385BG Gt Ashfield 20/4/44; MIA Berlin 6/10/44 w/Jens; e/a, cr Liepe, Ger; 9KIA; MACR 9525. WEE WILLIE WILBUR.

42-102466 Del Cheyenne 5/3/44; Rapid City 24/3/44; 225 BU Rapid City, W/O 17/6/44.

42-102467 Del Cheyenne 5/3/44; Gr Island 27/3/44; Grenier 7/4/44; ass 600BS/398BG [N8-J] Nuthampstead 27/4/44; MIA Brandenburg 6/8/44 w/Alhadeff; flak, cr Stade, Ger; 9POW; MACR 7886. AGONY WAGON III.

42-102468 Del Cheyenne 5/3/44; Hunter 7/4/44; Dow Fd 29/4/44; ass 615BS/401BG Deenethorpe 3/5/44; 614BS [IW-S]; retUS Bradley 7/6/45; 4168 BU Sth Plains 14/6/45; RFC Kingman 5/12/45.

42-102469 Del Cheyenne 5/3/44; Kearney 6/4/44; Grenier 21/4/44; ass 603BS/398BG [N7-Q] Nuthampstead 3/5/44; f/l Continent 7/8/44; sal 28/1/45.

42-102470 Del Cheyenne 11/3/44; Gr Island 1/4/44; Grenier 6/4/44; ass 508BS/351BG [YB-J] Polebrook 29/4/44; MIA {9m} Ludwigshafen 27/5/44 w/Johnson; e/a, cr Durlach, Ger; 9POW; MACR 5325.

42-102471 Del Cheyenne 7/3/44; Kearney 6/4/44; Dow Fd 14/4/44; ass 710BS/447BG Rattlesden 22/4/44; MIA Chemnitz 11/9/44 w/Hyder; flak, cr Zeitz, Ger; 1KIA 8POW; MACR 8924.

42-102472 Del Cheyenne 7/3/44; Hunter 15/3/44; Morrison 7/4/44; ass 816BS/483BG Steparone 17/4/44; b/d Fornovo di Taro, It 22/6/44 w/Johnston; u/c collapsed on landing, 10RTD. Sal. SHOO SHOO BABY.

42-102473 Del Cheyenne 7/3/44; Avon Park 4/4/44; 325 BU Avon Park 9/4/45; 1103 BU Morrison 23/4/45; 325 BU Avon Park 13/8/45; RFC Walnut Ridge 13/11/45.

42-102474 Del Cheyenne 7/3/44; Gr Island 30/3/44; 326 BU McDill 24/12/44; 4117 BU Robins 3/1/45; 120 BU Richmond 18/1/45; 4140 BU Rome 22/1/45; Hunter 29/4/45; 3704 BU Keesler 3/5/45; 6138 BU Phillips 4/7/46; 3704 BU Keesler 30/6/48.

42-102475 Del Cheyenne 7/3/44; Hunter 9/4/44; Dow Fd 29/4/44; ass 338BS/96BG Snetterton 1/5/44; MIA Karlsruhe 27/5/44 w/Brean; mid air coll w/42-102561; cr Ortenburg, Ger; 7KIA 3POW; MACR 5162.

42-102476 Del Cheyenne 7/3/44; Kearney 5/4/44; Dow Fd 14/4/44; ass 603BS/398BG [N7-B] Nuthampstead 28/4/44; MIA Munich 16/7/44 w/Gallagher; e/a, cr Hinter-Henbach, Ger; 2KIA 7POW; MACR 7242.

42-102477 Del Cheyenne 7/3/44; Gr Island 30/3/44; 224 BU Sioux City, W/O 9/8/44.

42-102478 Del Cheyenne 7/3/44; Kearney 2/5/44; Grenier 14/5/44; ass 510BS/351BG [TU-O] Polebrook 16/5/44; MIA {3m} French A/fds 14/6/44 w/Cessarini; flak, ditched Channel; 1EVD 2KIA 7POW; MACR 5798.

42-102479 Del Cheyenne 7/3/44; Gr Island 29/3/44; Dow Fd 7/4/44; ass 708BS/447BG Rattlesden 8/4/44; MIA Berlin 29/4/44 w/Farrell; flak, cr Eickendorf, Ger; 4KIA 6POW; MACR 4255.

42-102480 Del Cheyenne 7/3/44; Kearney 22/3/44; Dow Fd 1/5/44; ass 337BS/96BG Snetterton 2/4/44; sal 5/5/44.

42-102481 Del Cheyenne 7/3/44; Kearney 4/5/44; Grenier 19/4/44; ass 550BS/385BG Gt Ashfield 20/4/44; MIA Berlin 18/3/45 w/Cocke; flak, cr Grodzisk, Rus; 1KIA 8RTD; MACR 13141. KENTUCKY WINNER.

42-102482 Del Cheyenne 7/3/44; Gr Island 29/3/44; Dow Fd 7/4/44; ass 339BS/96BG [QJ-A] Snetterton 8/4/44; MIA Berlin 8/5/44 w/Eye; e/a, cr Wolfenbuettel, Ger; 3KIA 7POW; MACR 4575.

42-102483 Del Cheyenne 8/3/44; McDill 29/3/44; 325 BU Avon Park 20/12/44; RFC Walnut Ridge 20/8/45.

42-102484 Del Cheyenne 8/3/44; Gr Island 11/4/44; Grenier 6/4/44; ass 359BS/303BG [BN-S] Molesworth 23/4/44; MIA Merseburg 21/11/44 w/Chance; flak, cr Leipzig; 3KIA 6POW; MACR 11201. HELLER'S ANGEL.

42-102485 Del Cheyenne 8/3/44; Gr Island 2/4/44; Dow Fd 28/4/44; ass 562BS/388BG Knettishall 12/5/44; MIA Dessau, Ger; 28/5/44 w/Codding; flak, cr Groeneken, Hol; 3KIA 7POW; MACR 5316. BARE ESSENTIAL.

42-102486 Del Cheyenne 8/3/44; Kearney 27/3/44; Grenier 20/4/44; ass 548BS/385BG Gt Ashfield 22/4/44; f/l Continent 2/1/45; sal 18/1/45.

42-102487 Del Cheyenne 8/3/44; Gr Island 29/3/44; Grenier 6/4/44; ass 600BS/398BG [N8-F] Nuthampstead 26/4/44; tran ATC 21/5/45; retUS Bradley 25/5/45; 4168 BU Sth Plains 29/5/45; RFC Kingman 4/12/45.

42-102488 Del Cheyenne 8/3/44; Kearney 29/3/44; Dow Fd 6/4/44; ass 561BS/388BG Knettishall; lost over Atlantic en route UK 9/4/44; MACR 3634.

42-102489 Del Cheyenne 8/3/44; McDill 8/4/44; 326 BU McDill 5/2/45; 327 BU Drew 17/2/45; RFC Altus 5/11/45.

42-102490 Del Cheyenne 8/3/44; Gr Island 29/3/44; Grenier 6/4/44; ass 323BS/91BG [OR-V] Bassingbourn 22/4/44; MIA {70m} Nuremberg 20/2/45 w/McKnight; flak, cr Nuremberg; 6KIA 3POW; MACR 12556. WICKED WITCH.

42-102491 Del Cheyenne 8/3/44; Hunter 21/3/44; Homestead 15/4/44; ass 817BS/483BG Sterparone 19/4/44; {92m} RetUS Bradley 12/7/44; 4185 BU Independence 15/7/45; RFC Kingman 21/12/45. JANIE.

42-102492 Del Cheyenne 8/3/44; Ardmore 21/3/44; 222 BU Ardmore 20/7/44; 202 BU Galveston 13/8/44; 222 BU Ardmore 16/8/44; 332 BU Ardmore 16/6/45; RFC Walnut Ridge 11/12/45.

42-102493 Del Cheyenne 8/3/44; Gr Island 21/3/44; Kearney 10/5/44; Bangor 25/5/44; ass 561BS/388BG Knettishall 26/5/44; b/d en route Poltava 21/6/44 w/?; f/l France; re-ass 49BS/2BG Amendola, It; taxi acc w/RAF a/c 5/2/45 w/Edelen; sal 6/2/45.

42-102494 Del Cheyenne 8/3/44; Kearney 5/4/44; Dow Fd 19/4/44; ass 708BS/447BG Rattlesden 20/4/44; MIA Berlin 24/5/44 w/Simon; hit by prop wash from another B-17, cr Nth Sea; 10KIA; MACR 5249.

42-102495 Del Cheyenne 8/3/44; Gr Island 21/3/44; Grenier 6/4/44; ass 325BS/92BG [NV-R] Podington 23/4/44; tran 2 SAD Lt Staughton 24/3/45; sal 9AF Germany 2/1/46. SHORT STRAW. PICCADILLY SPECIAL.

42-102496 Del Cheyenne 9/3/44; Gr Island 2/4/44; Grenier 21/4/44; ass 359BS/303BG [BN-M] Molesworth 30/4/44; c/l 18/9/44, sal. SPECIAL DELIVERY.

42-102497 Del Cheyenne 9/3/44; Hunter 10/4/44; Dow Fd 29/4/44; ass 836BS/487BG [2G-A] Lavenham 1/5/44; MIA Darmstadt 24/12/44 w/Curtiss; e/a, f/l Hods, Bel; 3KIA 6RTD; MACR 12177.

42-102498 Del Cheyenne 9/3/44; Gr Island 29/3/44; Grenier 20/4/44; ass 600BS/398BG [N8-W] Nuthampstead 5/5/44; MIA Halberstadt, Ger 30/5/44 w/Thompson; flak, cr Aken, Ger; 3KIA 6POW; MACR 5312.

42-102499 Del Cheyenne 9/3/44; Gr Island 29/3/44; Dow Fd 4/4/44; ass 728BS/452BG Deopham Green 5/4/44; dest by e/a at Poltava, 21/6/44; sal 2/7/44.

42-102500 Del Cheyenne 9/3/44; Hunter 7/4/44; Grenier 20/4/44; ass 546BS/384BG [BK-L] Grafton Underwood 3/5/44; b/d Gerolstein, Ger; 2/1/45 w/?; AFSC, sal 18/1/45.

42-102501 Del Cheyenne 9/3/44; Gr Island 11/4/44; Dowe Fd 28/4/44; ass 546BS/384BG [BK-H] Grafton Underwood 12/5/44; MIA Berlin 3/2/45 w/Long; flak, ditched Nth Sea; 3KIA 6RTD. THE CHALLENGER.

42-102502 Del Cheyenne 9/3/44; Gr Island 29/3/44; Dow Fd 7/4/44; ass 100BG Thorpe Abbotts 7/4/44; tran 339BS/96BG [QJ-G] Snetterton 8/4/44; MIA Politz 25/8/44 w/Jennings; flak, cr Hagen, Ger; 7KIA 2POW; MACR 8283. CHATTERBOX!

42-102503 Del Cheyenne 9/3/44; Hunter 7/4/44; Dow Fd 29/4/44; slated 96BG, ass 398BG Nuthampstead 1/5/44; 423BS/306BG [RD-R/W] Thurleigh 18/5/44; MIA Brux 12/9/44 w/Gates; e/a, cr Elsenhau, Ger; 1KIA 9POW; MACR 8835. BELLE OF THE BLUE.

42-102504 Del Cheyenne 9/3/44; Gr Island 31/3/44; Grenier 6/4/44; ass 401BS/91BG [LL-D] Bassingbourn 11/5/44; MIA {107m} Stendahl 8/4/45 w/Pastras; flak, exploded in mid air; 7KIA 2POW; MACR 14295. TIMES A-WASTIN'.

42-102505 Del Cheyenne 9/3/44; Gr Island 29/3/44; Grenier 1/4/44; slated 398BG, ass 336BS/95BG [ET-A] Horham 8/4/44; tran 571BS/390BG [FC-X] Framlingham 1/6/44 ODD BALL; retUS Bradley 3/7/45; 4168 BU Sth Plains 5/7/45; RFC Kingman 10/12/45. DOUBLE IN BRASS.

42-102506 Del Cheyenne 9/3/44; McDill 28/3/44; Grenier 20/4/44; ass 602BS/398BG [K8-L] Nuthampstead 8/4/44; MIA Plauen, Ger 23/2/45 w/?; f/l Continent, sal.

42-102507 Del Cheyenne 9/3/44; Gr Island 29/3/44; Dow Fd 6/4/44; ass 600BS/398BG [N8-I] Nuthampstead 28/4/44; 601BS [3O-I]; retUS Bradley 4/6/45; 4168 BU Sth Plains 9/6/45; RFC Kingman 14/12/45.

42-102508 Del Cheyenne 9/3/44; Gr Island 29/3/44; Grenier 6/4/44; ass 603BS/398BG [N7-J] Nuthampstead 24/4/44; MIA Leipzig 7/7/44 w/Nisewonger; flak, cr Liebschwitz, Ger; 2KIA 7POW; MACR 7219.

42-102509 Del Cheyenne 10/3/44; Gr Island 29/3/44; Dow Fd 6/4/44; ass 401BS/91BG [LL-A] Bassingbourn 22/4/44; MIA Leipzig 20/7/44 w/Hultin; flak, cr Lauterbach, Ger; 10POW; MACR 7274. THE LIBERTY RUN.

42-102510 Del Cheyenne 10/3/44; Gr Island 29/3/44; Dow Fd 6/4/44; ass 398BG Nuthampstead 27/5/44; retUS, 3704 BU Keesler 4/7/46; 554 BU Memphis 7/7/46; Recl Comp Keesler 28/1/47.

42-102511 Del Cheyenne 10/3/44; Gr Island 27/3/44; Dow Fd 6/4/44; ass 602BS/398BG [K8-P] Nuthampstead 27/4/44; MIA Lechfeld 19/7/44 w/Hawkins; flak, cr Weil, Ger; 9KIA; MACR 7544.

42-102512 Del Cheyenne 10/3/44; Gr Island 31/3/44; Dow Fd 21/4/44; ass 368BS/306BG [BO-A] Thurleigh 5/5/44; tran 534BS/381BG Ridgewell 5/45; retUS Bradley 10/6/45; 4168 BU Sth Plains 17/6/45; RFC Kingman 4/12/45. SHE HAS TO.

42-102513 Del Cheyenne 10/3/44; Gr Island 29/3/44; Grenier 6/4/44; ass 731BS/452BG Deopham Green 10/4/44; b/d Ludwigshafen 25/9/44 w/?; f/l Mondorff, Ger?; sal 22/12/44. SWING SHIFT BABY.

42-102514 Del Cheyenne 10/3/44; Gr Island 30/3/44; Dow Fd 8/4/44; ass 452BS/Deopham Green 11/4/44; dest by e/a at Poltava, Rus 21/6/44; sal 2/7/44.

42-102515 Del Cheyenne 10/3/44; Gr Island 29/3/44; Grenier 7/4/44; ass 338BS/96BG [BX-J] Snetterton 8/4/44; MIA Magdeburg 27/5/45 w/Borkowski; mid air coll w/42-97269; cr Vily, Fr; 7KIA 3POW; MACR 5163.

42-102516 Del Cheyenne 10/3/44; Kearney 6/4/44; Dow Fd 14/4/44; ass 601BS/398BG [3O-H] Nuthampstead 28/4/44; MIA battle support area 13/8/44 w/Weekley; flak, cr Bosville, Fr; 7EVD 2POW; MACR 7910. BRONX BOMBER II.

42-102517 Del Cheyenne 10/3/44; McDill 5/4/44; 301 BU Pinecastle 2/6/44; 326 BU McDill 24/12/44; 4117 BU Robins 3/1/45; 4104 BU Rome 17/1/45; Hunter 22/3/45; 3704 BU Keesler 30/4/46; 554 BU Memphis 11/5/46; 4168 BU Sth Plains 3/6/46; 4136 BU Tinker 8/12/46; 4104 BU Rome 31/12/46; re-ass AMC 31/3/47; Recl Comp 19/6/47.

42-102518 Del Cheyenne 10/3/44; Gr Island 31/3/44; Grenier 8/4/44; ass 545BS/384BG Grafton Underwood 15/4/44; sal 9AF Germany 10/12/45. DAMN YANKEE.

42-102519 Del Cheyenne 10/3/44; Kearney 6/4/44; Grenier 11/4/44; ass 600BS/398BG [N8-A] Nuthampstead 6/5/44; 601BS; retUS Bradley 6/6/45; 4168 BU Sth Plains 13/6/45; RFC Kingman 28/11/45.

42-102520 Del Cheyenne 10/3/44; Gr Island 31/3/44; Grenier 7/4/44; ass 333BS/94BG Rougham 8/4/44; 332BS; MIA Berlin 29/4/44 w/McClurkin; flak, cr Texel, Hol; 9KIA 1POW; MACR 4468.

42-102521 Del Cheyenne 10/3/44; Hunter 16/4/44; Dow Fd 29/4/44; ass 8AF 30/4/45; 652BS/25BG Watton; Ret US ,4100 BU Patterson 14/2/45; 1103 BU Morrison 27/2/45; Recl Comp 2/5/46.

42-102522 Del Cheyenne 14/3/44; Gr Island 31/3/44; McDill 3/4/44; 327 BU Drew 4/5/45; 3704 BU Keesler 19/8/45; 327 BU Drew 28/8/45; 301 BU Drew 22/10/45; RFC Altus 5/11/45.

42-102523 Del Cheyenne 14/3/44; Kearney 27/3/44; Dow Fd 7/4/44; ass 333BS/94BG [TS-H] Rougham 8/4/44; 331BS [QE-H]; tran 34BG Mendlesham 5/45; retUS Bradley 21/6/45; 4168 BU Sth Plains 23/6/45; RFC Kingman 16/11/45.

42-102524 Del Cheyenne 11/3/44; McDill 29/3/44; Avon Park 2/4/44; 4109 BU Reading 20/8/44; 325 BU Avon Park 9/4/45; RFC Walnut Ridge 20/8/45.

42-102525 Del Cheyenne 11/3/44; Gr Island 21/3/44; Grenier 6/4/44; ass 427BS/303BG Molesworth 9/4/44; tran 338BS/96BG [BX-R] Snetterton 10/4/44; MIA Berlin 8/5/44 w/Birdsey; e/a, cr Holtorf, Ger; MACR 3576.

42-102526 Del Cheyenne 11/3/44; Kearney 29/3/44; Dow Fd 4/4/44; ass 96BG Snetterton 8/4/44; tran 571BS/390BG Framlingham 9/4/44; MIA Freidrichafaen 29/4/44 w/Rayburn; flak, cr Geitsche, Ger; 10POW; MACR 4245.

42-102527 Del Cheyenne 11/3/44; Gr Island 21/3/44; Dow Fd 6/4/44; ass 322BS/91BG [LG-A/P/H] Bassingbourn 22/4/44; MIA {14+m} Berlin 21/6/44 w/Abbott; e/a, cr Ruehlow, Ger?; 6KIA 4POW; MACR 5983. SLEEPYTIME GAL.

42-102528 Del Cheyenne 11/3/44; Hunter 7/4/44; Dow Fd 29/4/44; ass 92BG Podington 30/4/44; tran 350BS/100BG Thorpe Abbotts 1/5/44; MIA Berlin 24/5/44 w/Jespersen; e/a, cr Ratzeburg, Ger; 5POW; MACR 5169. TIMES A-WASTIN'.

42-102529 Del Cheyenne 11/3/44; McDill 31/3/44; 327 BU Drew 4/5/45; 301 BU Drew 22/10/45; RFC Altus 5/11/45.

42-102530 Del Cheyenne 11/3/44; Gr Island 29/3/44; Dow Fd 7/4/44; ass 410BS/94BG [GL-N] Rougham 8/4/44; b/d Karlsruhe 10/1/45 w/?; f/l Continent, sal 21/1/45.

42-102531 Del Cheyenne 11/3/44; McDill 29/3/44; Bangor 7/4/44; slated 94BG, ass 390BG

Framlingham 4/4/44; tran 338BS/96BG [BX-A] Snetterton 5/4/44; MIA Weisbaden 10/11/44 w/Bordsky; flak, cr Weisbaden; 9KIA; MACR 10358. TANGERINE II.

42-102532 Del Cheyenne 11/3/44; Kearney 31/3/44; Dow Fd 8/4/44; ass 570BS/390BG Framlingham 11/4/44; MIA Berlin 19/5/44 w/Tannehill; e/a, cr Ostermoor, Ger?; 1KIA 9POW; MACR 4935.

42-102533 Del Cheyenne 11/3/44; Gr Island 29/3/44; Dow Fd 7/4/44; ass 568BS/390BG Framlingham 8/4/44; MIA Munich 13/7/44 w/Spann; flak, cr Motzing, Ger; 10POW; MACR 7494.

42-102534 Del Cheyenne 11/3/44; McDill 31/3/44; 326 BU McDill 15/2/45; 329 BU Alexandra 3/3/45; 4168 BU Sth Plains 20/6/45; RFC Walnut Ridge 18/12/45.

42-102535 Del Cheyenne 12/3/44; Gr Island 29/3/44; Dow Fd 4/4/44; ass 729BS/452BG Deopham Green 8/4/44; MIA Munich 31/7/44 w/Williams; flak, cr Munich; 7KIA 2POW; MACR 7751. LOVELY LADY.

42-102536 Del Cheyenne 12/3/44; Gr Island 31/3/44; Grenier 6/4/44; ass 600BS/398BG [N8-C] Nuthampstead 26/4/44; c/t/o Merzehausen, Ger 24/12/44; sal 25/12/44.

42-102537 Del Cheyenne 12/3/44; McDill 30/3/44; 326 BU McDill 21/2/45; 325 BU Avon Park 8/3/45; 326 BU McDill 8/3/45; RFC Walnut Ridge 7/12/45.

42-102538 Del Cheyenne 12/3/44; McDill 30/3/44; 327 BU Drew 4/5/45; 326 BU McDill 16/8/45; 2621 BU Barksdale 23/7/46; 326 BU McDill 28/7/46; 4168 BU Sth Plains 6/10/46; Re-ass AMCOKL 31/3/47; 4141 BU Pyote 15/6/47. Recl Comp 10/1/48.

42-102539 Del Cheyenne 12/3/44; McDill 29/3/44; 326 BU McDill 14/2/45; 330 BU Dyersburg 5/3/45; 328 BU Gulfport 19/5/45; 3704 BU Keesler 23/5/45; 330 BU Dyersburg 11/9/45; RFC Walnut Ridge 19/12/45.

42-102540 Del Cheyenne 12/3/44; McDill 30/3/44; Avon Park 2/4/44; 325 BU Avon Park 9/4/45; RFC Walnut Ridge 12/12/45.

42-102541 Del Cheyenne 12/3/44; Gr Island 2/4/44; Grenier 29/4/44; ass 452BG Deopham Green 3/5/44; on return from Bordeaux A/fds c/l Wattisham & burned 19/6/44; sal 21/6/44. AIN'T MISS BEHAVIN'.

42-102542 Del Cheyenne 12/3/44; McDill 29/3/44; Daytona 1/4/44; McDill 2/4/44; 327 BU Drew 4/5/45; 301 BU Drew 22/10/45; RFC Altus 8/11/45. Ass US Civil N5845, cr Philadelphia 1958.

42-102543 Del Cheyenne 12/3/44; Kearney 31/3/44; Grenier 19/4/44; ass 602BS/398BG [K8-B] Nuthampstead 20/4/44; MIA Münster 28/10/44 w/Farmer; flak, cr Uelson, Ger; 2KIA 7POW; MACR 10176.

42-102544 Del Cheyenne 12/3/44; Gr Island 7/4/44; Dow Fd 28/4/44; ass 427BS/303BG [GN-K] Molesworth 12/5/44; MIA Dresden 17/4/45 w/Thomas; flak, cr Dresden; 2KIA 6POW; MACR 14168. SACK TIME.

42-102545 Del Cheyenne 12/3/44; McDill 30/3/44; slated 94BG, trans 4108 BU Newark 22/11/44; 325 BU Avon Park 9/4/45; RFC Walnut Ridge 22/8/45.

42-102546 Del Cheyenne 12/3/44; McDill 30/3/44; Avon Park 4/2/44; 325 BU Avon Park 9/4/45; RFC Walnut Ridge 12/12/45.

42-102547 Del Cheyenne 12/3/44; Gr Island 22/3/44; Dow Fd 3/4/44; ass 401BG Deenethorpe 2/5/44; tran 367BS/306BG [GY-F] Thurleigh 5/5/44; MIA {63M} Berlin 3/2/45 w/Daley; flak, cr Channel; 10KIA; MACR 12283. ROSE OF YORK.

42-102548 Del Cheyenne 12/3/44; Kearney 5/4/44; Dow Fd 14/4/44; ass 544BS/384BG [SU-M] Grafton Underwood 20/4/44; 547BS [SO-M]; MIA Stettin 13/5/44 w/Baker; e/a, cr Friedland, Ger; 34KIA 7POW; MACR 4814.

42-102549 Del Cheyenne 12/3/44; Kearney 30/3/44; Dow Fd 7/4/44; ass 569BS/390BG [CC-L] Framlingham 8/4/44; MIA Merseburg 29/7/44 w/Stewart; e/a, cr Hassenhausen, Ger; 2KIA 7POW; MACR 7822. LADY SATAN.

42-102550 Del Cheyenne 12/3/44; Gr Island 16/3/44; 326 BU McDill 7/4/44; 333 BU Morris 29/11/44; W/O 1/12/44; Recl Comp 1/2/45.

42-102551 Del Cheyenne 12/3/44; Kearney 5/4/44; Grenier 14/4/44; ass 550BS/385BG Gt Ashfield 20/4/44; b/d Merseburg 25/11/44 w/?; f/l Renoixe, Fr?; sal 23/1/45.

42-102552 Del Cheyenne 12/3/44; Gr Island 31/3/44; Dow Fd 21/4/44; ass 339BS/96BG [QJ-J] Snetterton 22/4/44; MIA Nucourt, Fr 22/6/44 w/Horn; flak, cr Paris; 10KIA; MACR 5917.

42-102553 Del Cheyenne 12/3/44; Kearney 31/3/44; Dow Fd 6/4/44; ass 603BS/398BG [N7-K] Nuthampstead 26/4/44; tran AFSC 29/7/44.

42-102554 Del Cheyenne 14/3/44; Kearney 30/6/44; Grenier 12/7/44; ass 338BS/96BG [BX-G] Snetterton 14/7/44; MIA Osnabrück 21/11/44 w/Warden; flak, cr Nieuw-Milligen, Hol; 4EVD 5POW; MACR 10416. JEAN O.

42-102555 Del Cheyenne 14/3/44; Gr Island 6/4/44; Dow Fd 28/4/44; ass 366BS/305BG [KY-F] Chelveston 14/5/44; MIA Bohlen 3/2/45 w/?.

42-102556 Del Cheyenne 14/3/44; McDill 31/3/44; 329 BU Columbia 21/10/44; 326 BU McDill 23/10/44; 4100 BU Patterson 30/12/44; Rome 19/4/45; Hunter 28/4/45; Keesler 5/8/45; 3704 BU Keesler 2/4/46; 615 BU Phillips 7/7/46; 554 BU Memphis 26/7/46.

42-102557 Del Cheyenne 14/3/44; Gr Island 30/3/44; Grenier 6/4/44; ass 369BS/306BG [WW-Y] Thurleigh 25/4/44; b/d Ueskirchen, Ger 10/1/45 w/?; c/l Hombeck, Bel; sal 28/1/45. ICE COLD KATIE.

42-102558 Del Cheyenne 14/3/44; Gr Island 30/3/44; Dow Fd 28/4/44; ass 369BS/306BG [WW-W] Thurleigh 13/5/44; c/t/o for Cologne 15/8/44 w/?; 5KIA, sal. SILVER STREAK.

42-102559 Del Cheyenne 14/3/44; Gr Island 1/4/44; Grenier 6/4/44; ass 561BS/388BG Knettishall 8/4/44 STAR DUST; b/d Berlin 26/2/45 w/?; f/l Thionville A/fd, Fr; sal 9/3/45. MY TRUE LOVE.

42-102560 Del Cheyenne 14/3/44; Gr Island 1/4/44; Dow Fd 8/4/44; ass 334BS/95BG [BG-X] Horham 11/4/44; MIA Merseburg 30/11/44 w/Wicker; flak, cr Merseburg; 5KIA 4POW; MACR 10840. THE THOMPER.

42-102561 Del Cheyenne 14/3/44; Gr Island 2/4/44; Dow Fd 21/4/44; slated 385BG, ass 337BS/96BG [AW-D] Snetterton 22/4/44; MIA Karlsruhe 27/5/44 w/Irving; mis air coll w/42-102457; cr Woessingen, Ger; 6KIA 4POW; MACR 5164.

42-102562 Del Cheyenne 15/3/44; Gr Island 1/4/44; Grenier 6/4/44; ass 603BS/398BG [N7-C] Nuthampstead 26/4/44; MIA Merseburg 2/11/44 w/Newman; flak, cr Polleben, Ger; 5KIA 4POW; MACR 10157. KNOCK OUT.

42-102563 Del Cheyenne 15/3/44; Hunter 16/4/44; Dow Fd 24/4/44; ass 364BS/305BG Chelveston 22/5/44; MIA Metz 9/11/44 w/?; MACR 11653.

42-102564 Del Cheyenne 15/3/44; McDill 31/3/44; W/O 10/5/44.

42-102565 Del Cheyenne 15/3/44; Kearney 31/3/44; Dow Fd 8/4/44; ass 601BS/398BG [3O-M/H] Nuthampstead 27/4/44; MIA Misburg 26/11/44 w/Rolfe; flak, cr Zwolle, Hol; 9KIA; MACR 11147. THE UGLY DUCKLING.

42-102566 Del Cheyenne 15/3/44; Gr Island 1/4/44; Grenier 20/4/44; ass 545BS/384BG [JD-M] Grafton Underwood 4/5/44; u/c coll on landing 22/11/44; sal AFSC.

42-102567 Del Cheyenne 15/3/44; Gr Island 1/4/44; Dow Fd 24/4/44; ass 709BS/447BG Rattlesden 3/5/44; c/l 1/1/45, sal.

42-102568 Del Cheyenne 15/3/44; Kearney 5/4/44; Grenier 15/4/44; ass 603BS/398BG [N7-N] Nuthampstead 28/4/44; 602BS [K8-N]; b/d Münster 28/10/44 w/?; sal 2 SAD 29/10/44.

42-102569 Del Cheyenne 15/3/44; Kearney 31/3/44; Dow Fd 4/4/44; ass 94BG Rougham 8/4/44; tran 427BS/303BG [GN-X] Molesworth 22/4/44; b/d Kyllburg, Ger 8/1/45 w/?; c/l base, sal 2 SAD 9/1/45. MISS LACE.

42-102570 Del Cheyenne 15/3/44; Kearney 31/3/44; Dow Fd 2/4/44; ass 603BS/398BG [N7-F] Nuthampstead 26/4/44; c/l 23/10/44; sal.

42-102571 Del Cheyenne 15/3/44; Gr Island 1/4/44; Grenier 5/4/44; ass 339BS/96BG [QJ-U] Snetterton 8/4/44; MIA Brux 12/5/44 w/Laurie; e/a, cr Kamberg, Ger; 8KIA 2POW; MACR 4863.

42-102572 Del Cheyenne 15/3/44; Gr Island 1/4/44; Dow Fd 28/4/44; ass 728BS/452BG Deopham Green 30/4/44; MIA Karlsruhe 27/5/44 w/Ward; mech fault, cr Avoudrey, Fr; 4EVD 6KIA; MACR 5301.

42-102573 Del Cheyenne 15/3/44; Gr Island 1/4/44; Dow Fd 28/4/44; ass 338BS/96BG [BX-T] Snetterton 30/4/44; dest by e/a at Poltava 21/6/44; sal.

42-102574 Del Cheyenne 16/3/44; Gr Island 31/3/44; Grenier 7/4/44; ass 332BS/94BG [XM-N] Rougham 8/4/44; MIA Conches, Fr 8/7/44 w/Skelton; flak, ditched Channel; 10RTD. FLORENCIA.

42-102575 Del Cheyenne 16/3/44; Gr Island 1/4/44; Grenier 7/4/44; ass 731BS/452BG Deopham Green 10/4/44; b/d Rechlin 25/8/44 w/?; o/s runway; sal 26/8/44.

42-102576 Del Cheyenne 16/3/44; Kearney 1/4/44; Grenier 14/4/44; ass 510BS/351BG [TU-C] Polebrook 29/4/44; {63m} c/l base 10/12/44 w/?; sal 2 SAD. EASTER BUNNY.

42-102577 Del Cheyenne 16/3/44; Kearney 1/4/44; Grenier 1/4/44; ass 331BS/94BG [QE-O] Rougham 10/4/44; MIA Merseburg 2/11/44 w/Peterson; flak & e/a, cr Merseburg; 6KIA 3POW; MACR 10307. BOUNCIN' ANNIE.

42-102578 Del Cheyenne 16/3/44; Hunter 8/4/44; Dow Fd 29/4/44; ass 398BG Nuthampstead 30/4/44; tran 367BS/306BG [GY-D] Thurleigh 18/5/44; 532BS/381BG Ridgewell 5/45; retUS Bradley 10/6/45; 4168 BU Sth Plains 14/6/45; Recl Comp 7/6/46. WE PROMISED.

42-102579 Del Cheyenne 16/3/44; Gr Island 1/4/44; Grenier 6/4/44; ass 603BS/398BG [N7-C] Nuthampstead 27/4/44; MIA Merseburg 28/7/44 w/Dwyer; flak, cr Charleroi, Bel; 2EVD 7POW; MACR 7823. STINKER.

42-102580 Del Cheyenne 16/3/44; Gr Island 1/4/44; Dow Fd 8/4/44; ass 613BS/401BG [IN-Q] Deenethorpe 3/5/45; MIA Dessau 28/5/44 w/?; flak, cr Aken, Ger; MACR 5307.

42-102581 Del Cheyenne 16/3/44; Kearney 1/4/44; Grenier 14/4/44; ass 613BS/401BG [IN-L] Deenethorpe 29/4/44; MIA Dessau 28/5/44 w/Scharff; flak, cr Dessau; 4KIA 6POW; MACR 56306. LONESOME POLECAT.

42-102582 Del Cheyenne 16/3/44; Kearney 5/4/44; Grenier 21/4/44; ass 326BS/92BG [JW-D] Podington 7/5/44; b/d Pirmasens 9/8/44 w/?; sal 2 SAD 12/8/44. CANVAS BACK III.

42-102583 Del Cheyenne 16/3/44; Kearney 1/4/44; Dow Fd 8/4/44; ass 332BS/94BG [XM-C] Rougham

10/4/44; {102m} RetUS Bradley 21/6/45; 4168 BU Sth Plains 25/6/45; RFC Kingman 9/12/45. FORTRESS McHENRY.
42-102584 Del Cheyenne 16/3/44; Gr Island 1/4/44; Grenier 7/4/44; ass 332BS/94BG Rougham 8/4/44; MIA Brux 12/5/44 w/Williams; e/a, cr?; 10POW. BOTTLED IN BOND.
42-102585 Del Cheyenne 16/3/44; Kearney 1/4/44; Dow Fd 8/4/44; ass 534BS/381BG [GD-A] Ridgewell 24/4/44; MIA {12m} Tours 24/6/44 w/Romasco; flak, cr Tours; 1EVD 4KIA 4POW; MACR 6534. THE BETTY L.
42-102586 Del Cheyenne 16/3/44; Hunter 14/4/44; Dow Fd 26/4/44; ass 339BS/96BG [QJ-Z] Snetterton 1/5/44; sal 31/5/45. LITTLE JOE.
42-102587 Del Cheyenne 16/3/44; Hunter 9/4/44; Dow Fd 29/4/44; ass 452BG Deopham Green 30/4/44; dest by e/a at Poltava 21/6/44; sal 2/7/44.
42-102588 Del Cheyenne 17/3/44; Gr Island 6/4/44; Dow Fd 28/4/44; ass 8AF 29/4/44. Became ASR SB-17G in 1953.
42-102589 Del Cheyenne 17/3/44; Gr Island 6/4/44; Dow Fd 28/4/44; ass 561BS/388BG Knettishall 30/4/44; MIA Munich 11/7/44 w/?; flak, cr Rtrange, Fr; sal 26/2/45.
42-102590 Del Cheyenne 17/3/44; Gr Island 10/4/44; Dow Fd 29/4/44; ass 535BS/381BG [MS-M] Ridgewell 22/5/44; MIA {91m} Bremen 30/3/45 w/Bennett; flak, cr Syke, Ger; 3KIA 7POW; MACR 13542. IN LIKE ERROL.
42-102591 Del Cheyenne 17/3/44; Kearney 1/4/44; Dow Fd 14/4/44; ass 447BG Rattlesden 22/4/44; c/l base 6/6/44, sal. CACTUS PETE.
42-102592 Del Cheyenne 17/3/44; Kearney 5/4/44; Grenier 14/4/44; ass 600BS/398BG [N8-G] Nuthampstead 28/4/44; sal 8/2/45.
42-102593 Del Cheyenne 17/3/44; Kearney 1/4/44; Dow Fd 6/4/44; ass 602BS/398BG [K8-C] Nuthampstead 3/5/44; retUS Bradley 7/6/45; 4168 BU Sth Plains 9/6/45; RFC Kingman 5/12/45.
42-102594 Del Cheyenne 17/3/44; Kearney 5/4/44; Grenier 14/4/44; ass 570BS/390BG Framlingham 20/4/44; MIA Düsseldorf 9/9/44 w/Gallagher; flak, cr Ennepe Dam, Ger?; 4KIA 5POW; MACR 8916.
42-102595 Del Cheyenne 17/3/44; Hunter 9/4/44; Grenier 1/5/44; ass 427BS/303BG [GN-L] Molesworth 6/6/44; b/d Metz 14/8/44 w/?; sal 15/8/44. LITTLE FLUSH.
42-102596 Del Cheyenne 17/3/44; Kearney 1/4/44; Grenier 14/4/44; ass 601BS/398BG [3O-N] Nuthampstead 28/4/44; retUS Bradley 4/6/45; 4168 BU Sth Plains 14/6/45; RFC Kingman 29/11/45.
42-102597 Del Cheyenne 17/3/44; Kearney 5/4/44; Grenier 14/4/44; slated 303BG, ass 602BS/398BG [K8-V] Nuthampstead 3/5/44; MIA Ruhland, Ger 12/9/44 w/Fields; flak, cr Trelleborg, Swed; 8KIA 1POW; MACR 8907. STINKER.
42-102598 Del Cheyenne 17/3/44; Hunter 10/4/44; Dow Fd 29/4/44; ass 351BS/100BG [EP-F] Thorpe Abbotts 30/4/44; c/l base 28/7/44; sal 30/7/44. SUPER RABBIT.
42-102599 Del Cheyenne 17/3/44; Hunter 17/4/44; Grenier 1/5/44; ass 600BS/398BG Nuthampstead 4/5/44; MIA Munich 16/7/44 w/Lovelace; flak, cr Achenkirchen, Ger; 2KIA 7POW; MACR 7564.
42-102600 Del Cheyenne 17/3/44; Kearney 5/4/44; Dow Fd 14/4/44; ass 603BS/398BG [N7-Z] Nuthampstead 4/5/44; MIA Merseburg 21/11/44 w/Wisner; flak, cr Gotha, Ger; 1KIA 8POW; MACR 11212. ZOOMERIAGO.
42-102601 Del Cheyenne 18/3/44; Hunter 18/4/44; Grenier 5/5/44; ass 546BS/384BG [BK-K] Grafton Underwood 24/5/44; b/d Mannheim 9/9/44; sal.
42-102602 Del Cheyenne 18/3/44; Hunter 31/3/44; Dow Fd 18/4/44; ass 366BS/305BG Chelveston 1/5/44; MIA Merseburg 24/78/44 w/Mockett; flak, c/l Hagen, Ger; 1KIA 8POW; MACR 8206.
42-102603 Del Cheyenne 18/3/44; Hunter 8/4/44; Dow Fd 29/4/44; ass 339BS/96BG [QJ-B] Snetterton 1/5/44; damaged by e/a at Poltava 21/6/44; sal, retUS Bradley 11/7/45; 4185 BU Independence 10/11/45; RFC Kingman 23/12/45.
42-102604 Del Cheyenne 18/3/44; Hunter 13/4/44; Presque Is 19/5/44; ass 710BS/447BG Rattlesden 22/4/44; f/l Continent 10/1/45; sal 11/1/45.
42-102605 Del Cheyenne 18/3/44; Hunter 14/4/44; Dow Fd 29/4/44; ass 331BS/94BG [QE-X] Rougham 1/5/44; MIA battle support area, Fr 13/8/44 w/Griffith; flak, cr St Andre, Fr; 2EVD 1KIA 6POW; MACR 8362. KISMET.
42-102606 Del Cheyenne 18/3/44; Kearney 2/4/44; Dow Fd 14/2/44; ass 550BS/385BG Gt Ashfield 20/4/44; MIA Munich 12/7/44 w/McDonald; mid air coll, cr Arlon, Bel; 9KIA 1POW; MACR 7489.
42-102607 Del Cheyenne 18/3/44; Kearney 2/4/44; Grenier 4/4/44; ass 601BS/398BG [3O-F] Nuthampstead 20/4/44; MIA Magdeburg 28/9/44 w/Conrow; flak, cr Helmstedt, Ger; 10POW; MACR 9382. LODIAN.
42-102608 Del Cheyenne 18/3/44; Hunter 8/4/44; Dow Fd 28/4/44; ass 364BS/305BG [WF-R] Chelveston 25/5/44; tran 379BG Kimbolton 21/1/45; 401BG Deenethorpe 25/5/45; retUS Bradley 7/6/45; 4168 BU Sth Plains 9/6/45; RFC Kingman 6/11/45.
42-102609 Del Cheyenne 18/3/44; Hunter 9/4/44; Dow Fd 29/4/44; ass 365BS/305BG [XK-B] Chelveston 30/4/44; b/d Delitzsch, Ger 16/8/44 w/?; MACR 8435. Sal 2 SAD 17/8/44.
42-102610 Del Cheyenne 18/3/44; Gr Island 6/4/44; Dow Fd 19/4/44; ass 602BS/398BG [K8-Y/L] Nuthampstead 5/5/44; MIA Bischoffsheim, Ger 30/12/44 w/Doerr; flak, cr off Beachy Head, UK; 9KIA; MACR 11243. BOOMERANG.
42-102611 Del Cheyenne 18/3/44; Gr Island 2/4/44; Dow Fd 19/4/44; ass 350BS/100BG [LN-E] Thorpe Abbotts 22/4/44; MIA practice mission 27/6/44; cr Nth Sea; 10killed; MACR 6993.
42-102612 Del Cheyenne 18/3/44; Hunter 11/4/44; Grenier 18/5/44; ass 339BS/96BG [QJ-U] Snetterton 21/5/44; MIA Magdeburg 20/6/44 w/DeBrandes; e/a, cr Magdeburg; 1KIA 1MIA 8POW; MACR 5897.
42-102613 Del Cheyenne 18/3/44; Kearney 3/4/44; Grenier 14/4/44; ass 508BS/351BG [YB-C] Polebrook 29/4/44; MIA {9m} Ludwigshafen 27/5/44 w/Evans; e/a, f/l Switz; 6KIA 3POW; MACR 5324.
42-102614 Del Cheyenne 18/3/44; Oklahoma City 7/6/44; Cheyenne 27/7/44; Kearney 10/8/44; Manchester, NH 19/8/44; ass 551BS/385BG Gt Ashfield; {119m} RetUS Bradley 26/6/45; 4168 BU Sth Plains 28/6/45; RFC Kingman 1/12/45.
42-102615 Del Cheyenne 18/3/44; Kearney 13/4/44; Dow Fd 29/4/44; ass 728BS/452BG Deopham Green 30/4/44; 729BS; b/d Frankfurt 17/2/45 w/?; overshot runway, sal 23/2/45. FORBIDDEN FRUIT II.
42-102616 Del Cheyenne 18/3/44; Kearney 5/4/44; Grenier 30/4/44; ass 410BS/94BG [GL-K] Rougham 3/5/44; MIA Bohlen 7/10/44 w/Wheeler; e/a, cr Langenroda, Ger?; 7KIA 2POW; MACR 9558. SPIRIT OF VALLEY FORGE.
42-102617 Del Cheyenne 18/3/44; Kearney 5/4/44; Dow Fd 14/4/44; ass 544BS/384BG [SU-T] Grafton Underwood 7/5/44; b/d Merkwille 3/8/44 w/?; sal 2 SAD 5/8/44.
42-102618 Del Cheyenne 18/3/44; 11th Photo Gp McDill 18/4/44; 327 BU Drew 27/9/44; 301 BU Drew 22/10/45; RFC Altus 5/11/45.
42-102619 Del Cheyenne 18/3/44; Hunter 16/4/44; Grenier 1/5/44; ass 368BS/306BG [BO-G] Thurleigh 25/5/44; sal 2 SAD 9/8/44. REPORT TO THE NATION.
42-102620 Del Cheyenne 18/3/44; Kearney 5/4/44; Grenier 14/4/44; ass 545BS/384BG [JD-P] Grafton Underwood 7/5/44; 546BS [BK-P], 544BS [SU-F]; taxi acc 14/5/45; nosed over, sal 15/5/45.
42-102621 Del Cheyenne 19/3/44; Hunter 9/4/44; Dow Fd 27/4/44; ass 350BS/100BG [LN-A] Thorpe Abbotts 1/5/44; sal 8/8/44.
42-102622 Del Cheyenne 19/3/44; Hunter 9/4/44; Dow Fd 29/4/44; ass 452BG Deopham Green 1/5/44; dest by e/a at Poltava 21/6/44; sal 2/7/44.
42-102623 Del Cheyenne 19/3/44; Gt Falls 25/3/44; McDill 1/4/44; 325 BU Avon Park 9/4/45; 3017 BU Hobbs 21/8/45; 4160 BU Hobbs 20/11/45; RFC Kingman 8/1/46.
42-102624 Del Cheyenne 19/3/44; Hunter 9/4/44; Dow Fd 29/4/44; ass 349BS/100BG Thorpe Abbotts 1/5/44; MIA Berlin 24/5/44 w/Johnson; e/a, cr Rothenhaln, Ger?; 7KIA 3POW; MACR 5170.
42-102625 Del Cheyenne 19/3/44; Hunter 9/4/44; Dow Fd 29/4/44; ass 338BS/96BG Snetterton 1/5/55; 337BS [AW-B]; dest by e/a at Poltava 21/6/44; sal 1/7/44. ALL AMERICAN GIRL.
42-102626 Del Cheyenne 19/3/44; Hunter 17/4/44; Grenier 26/4/44; ass 561BS/388BG Knettishall 3/5/44 THE WORRY BIRD; retUS Bradley 24/6/45; 4168 BU Sth Plains 27/6/45; b/d Bischofsheim, Ger 13/1/45 w/?; f/l Continent; sal 12/3/45. RFC Kingman 29/11/45. OL' FAITHFUL.
42-102627 Del Cheyenne 19/3/44; Kearney 13/4/44; Grenier 29/4/44; ass 527BS/379BG Kimbolton 19/5/44; tran 91BG Bassingbourn 25/5/45; retUS Bradley 11/6/45; 4168 BU Sth Plains 20/6/45; RFC Kingman 6/12/45. QUEENIE.
42-102628 Del Cheyenne 19/3/44; Kearney 14/4/44; Grenier 28/4/44; ass 526BS/379BG [LF-P] Kimbolton 13/5/44; MIA Hamburg 18/6/44 w/King; flak, cr Hamburg; 4KIA 5POW; MACR 5989. G.I. JANE.
42-102629 Del Cheyenne 19/3/44; Kearney 14/4/44; McDill 1/4/44; 327 BU Drew 4/5/45; 301 BU Drew 22/10/45; RFC Altus 5/11/45.
42-102630 Del Cheyenne 19/3/44; McDill 1/4/44; 325 BU Avon Park 22/9/44; 335 BU Del Marbry 2/10/44; 325 BU Avon Park 7/10/44; RFC Walnut Ridge 22/8/45.
42-102631 Del Cheyenne 19/3/44; Kearney 15/4/44; Grenier 29/4/44; ass 729BS/452BG Deopham Green 1/5/44; b/d St Vith 9/8/44 w/?; c/l base, sal 10/8/44.
42-102632 Del Cheyenne 19/3/44; Hunter 1/4/44; Dow Fd 18/4/44; ass 708BS/447BG Rattlesden 22/4/44; MIA Ausum A/Fd, Ger 27/8/44 w/Bowers; flak, cr Nth Sea; 9KIA; MACR 8458. DUE BACK.
42-102633 Del Cheyenne 19/3/44; Hunter 13/4/44; Dow Fd 29/4/44; ass 413BS/96BG [MZ-F] Snetterton 3/5/44; retUS Bradley 3/7/45; 4168 BU Sth Plains 6/7/45; RFC Kingman 8/11/45. LOVELY LADY.
42-102634 Del Cheyenne 20/3/44; Gr Island 12/4/44; Dow Fd 28/4/44; ass 570BS/390BG [DI-B] Framlingham 3/5/44 MARY JANE; MIST'ER COMPLETELY; b/d Saarbrücken 9/11/44 w/?; f/l Continent; sal 29/11/44. MAIRZEY DOATS.
42-102635 Del Cheyenne 20/3/44; Kearney 15/4/44; Grenier 29/4/44; ass 349BS/100BG Thorpe Abbotts 1/5/44; MIA Berlin 24/5/44 w/Hoskinson; e/a, cr

Rothenhaln, Ger?; 10KIA. MACR 5171.
42-102636 Del Cheyenne 20/3/44; Kearney 2/4/44; Dow Fd 14/4/44; ass 550BS/385BG Gt Ashfield 22/4/44; retUS Bradley 30/6/45; 4168 BU Sth Plains 4/7/45; RFC Kingman 27/11/45. SLEEPYTIME GAL.
42-102637 Del Cheyenne 20/3/44; Gt Falls 25/3/44; McDill 15/4/44; 327 BU Drew 4/5/45; 301 BU Drew 22/10/45; RFC Altus 5/11/45.
42-102638 Del Cheyenne 20/3/44; Kearney 5/4/44; Grenier 14/4/44; ass 711BS/447BG Rattlesden 20/4/44; MIA Osnabrück 13/5/44 w/McClintock; flak, cr Greffern, Ger; 1KIA 9POW; MACR 4772.
42-102639 Del Cheyenne 20/3/44; Gt Falls 25/3/44; Billings 27/3/44; McDill 2/4/44; 326 BU McDill 2/4/45; 4124 BU Altus 1/10/45; RFC Altus 29/10/45.
42-102640 Del Cheyenne 20/3/44; Billings 27/3/44; Jackson 31/3/44; McDill 1/4/44; 327 BU Drew 4/5/45; 301 BU Drew 22/10/45; RFC Altus 5/11/45.
42-102641 Del Cheyenne 22/3/44; Hunter 7/4/44; Dow Fd 20/4/44; ass 339BS/96BG [QJ-K] Snetterton 22/4/44; dest by e/a at Poltava 21/6/44; sal 1/7/44.
42-102642 Del Cheyenne 22/3/44; Hunter 7/4/44; Dow Fd 18/4/44; ass 8AF 22/4/44; sal 9AF Germany 8/11/45.
42-102643 Del Cheyenne 22/3/44; Hunter 7/4/44; Grenier 24/4/44; ass 326BS/92BG [JW-C] Podington 7/5/44; MIA Noball site 8/7/44 w/Sabin; flak, cr St Saire, Fr; 4EVD 5KIA; MACR 7356.
42-102644 Del Cheyenne 22/3/44; Buckley 31/3/44; Cheyenne 4/4/44; Hunter 22/4/44; W/O 27/4/44.
42-102645 Del Cheyenne 22/3/44; Kearney 14/4/44; Grenier 29/4/44; ass 365BS/305BG Chelveston 14/5/44; MIA Karlsruhe 9/8/44 w/Child; e/a, cr Segelsen, Ger?; 4EVD 4KIA 1POW; MACR 8067.
42-102646 Del Cheyenne 22/3/44; Hunter 17/4/44; Grenier 30/4/44; ass 337BS/96BG [AW-A] Snetterton 3/5/44; MIA Osnabrück 21/11/44 w/Sullivan; hit by prop wash, cr Lamspringe, Ger; 9KIA; MACR 10415.
42-102647 Del Cheyenne 23/3/44; Hunter 9//4/44; Dow Fd 29/4/44; ass 613BS/401BG [IN-G] Deenethorpe 24/5/44; 615DS [IY-M]; MIA Ruhland 28/5/44 w/Windham; flak & e/a, cr Niemeck, Ger?; 5KIA 5POW; MACR 5305. BTO IN THE ETO.
42-102648 Del Cheyenne 23/3/44; Kearney 13/4/44; Grenier 28/4/44; Slated 447BG, ass 349BS/100BG Thorpe Abbotts 21/4/44; MIA Berlin 24/5/44 w/Roeder; e/a, cr Itstedt, Ger?; 6KIA 4POW; MACR 5172.
42-102649 Del Cheyenne 23/3/44; Hunter 9/4/44; Grenier 30/4/44; ass 452BG Deopham Green 3/4/44; tran 350BS/100BG [LN-S] Thorpe Abbotts 4/4/44; tran 482BG Alconbury 20/5/45; {75m} RetUS Bradley 1/6/45; 4168 BU Sth Plains 4/6/45; RFC Kingman 18/12/45. LADY GERALDINE.
42-102650 Del Cheyenne 23/3/44; Gr Island 12/4/44; Dow Fd 28/4/44; ass 452BG Deopham Green 30/4/44; dest by e/a at Poltava 21/6/44; sal 2/7/44.
42-102651 Del Cheyenne 23/3/44; Hunter 16/4/44; Grenier 30/4/44; ass 710BS/447BG Rattlesden 3/5/44; MIA Munich 11/7/44 w/Altman; flak, f/l Dubendorf, Switz; 10INT; MACR 6937. RetUS 1377 BU Grenier 24/10/45; RFC Walnut Ridge 21/12/45. PICCADILLY ANN II.
42-102652 Del Cheyenne 23/3/44; Kearney 14/4/44; Dow Fd 29/4/44; ass 708BS/447BG Rattlesden 30/4/44; MIA Bohlen 29/6/44 w/Leitch; flak, cr Genthin, Ger; 10POW; MACR 6729.
42-102653 Del Cheyenne 23/3/44; Kearney 14/4/44; Grenier 27/4/44; ass 339BS/96BG [QJ-A] Snetterton 1/5/44; dest by e/a at Poltava 21/6/44; sal 1/7/44.
42-102654 Del Cheyenne 23/3/44; McDill 18/4/44; 326 BU McDill 2/2/45; 325 BU Avon Park 15/2/45; RFC Walnut Ridge 11/12/45.
42-102655 Del Cheyenne 23/3/44; Gulfport 19/4/44; 367 BU Hatisburg 14/10/44; 328 BU Gulfport 22/10/44; 330 BU Dyersburg 11/9/45; RFC Walnut Ridge 17/12/45.
42-102656 Del Cheyenne 23/3/44; Hunter 17/4/44; Grenier 30/4/44; ass 534BS/381BG [GD-L] Ridgewell 21/5/44; {70+m} tran 92BG Podington 10/5/45; sal 9AF Germany 10/12/45. CAROL LEIGH.
42-102657 Del Cheyenne 23/3/44; Gr Island 12/4/44; Dow Fd 11/5/44; ass 350BS/100BG [LN-Y] Thorpe Abbotts 14/5/44; MIA Fulda 11/9/44 w/Trommer; e/a, cr Schuiederberg, Hol?; 5KIA 4POW; MACR 8820.
42-102658 Del Cheyenne 23/3/44; Gr Island 12/45/44; Dow Fd 28/4/44; ass 708BS/447BG Rattlesden 30/4/44; MIA Merseburg 6/12/44 w/DeMallie; flak, cr Ronduite, Hol; 1EVD 1KIA 7POW; MACR 11052. BLANC DIABLO.
42-102659 Del Cheyenne 23/3/44; Kearney 13/4/44; Grenier 15/5/44; ass 447BG Rattlesden 16/5/44; tran 614BS/401BG [IW-J] Deenethorpe 30/5/44; sal 10/1/45. HARD LUCK.
42-102660 Del Cheyenne 23/3/44; Kearney 12/4/44; Grenier 29/4/44; ass 728BS/452BG Deopham Green 3/5/44 LOVELY LADY; taxi acc 28/12/44; struck 43-38822; sal 29/12/44. SACK TIME SIOUX.
42-102661 Del Cheyenne 23/3/44; Hunter 9/4/44; Dow Fd 29/4/44; ass 544BS/384BG [SU-C] Grafton Underwood 1/5/44; sal 9AF Germany 29/12/45. BIG DOG.
42-102662 Del Cheyenne 24/3/44; Hunter 16/4/44; Grenier 25/4/44; ass 728BS/452BG Deopham Green 3/5/44; MIA Berlin 21/6/44 w/Arum; mid air coll w/42-31359; cr East Priegnitz, Ger?; 9KIA 1POW. MACR 6239.
42-102663 Del Cheyenne 24/3/44; Kearney 15/4/44; Grenier 29/4/44; ass 533BS/381BG [VP-U] Ridgewell 21/5/44; MIA {23m} Peenemünde w/O'Black; flak, f/l Bulltofta, Swed; 9INT; MACR 7552, left 4/6/45; retUS Bradley 13/7/45; RFC Independence 16/7/45; RFC Kingman 13/12/45. YARDBIRD.
42-102664 Del Cheyenne 24/3/44; Kearney 14/4/44; Dow Fd 29/4/44; ass 532BS/381BG [VE-F] Ridgewell 19/5/44; MIA {8m} Munich 16/7/43 w/McGregor; ditched Nth Sea off Clacton; 9RTD; HAPPY BOTTOM.
42-102665 Del Cheyenne 24/3/44; Hunter 19/4/44; Dow Fd 29/4/44; ass 730BS/452BG Deopham Green 1/5/44; dest by e/a at Poltava 21/6/44; sal 16/7/44.
42-102666 Del Cheyenne 24/3/44; Kearney 12/4/44; Grenier 28/4/44; ass 563BS/388BG Knettishall 30/4/44; dest by e/a at Poltava 21/6/44; sal 2/7/44. WIZARD OF OZ.
42-102667 Del Cheyenne 24/3/44; Hunter 16/4/44; Grenier 28/4/44; ass 334BS/95BG [BG-C] Horham 3/5/44; tran 351BS/100BG [EP-J] Thorpe Abbotts 8/6/44; MIA Merseburg 29/7/44 w/Schomp; flak, cr Klein Ebersdorf, Ger?; 9POW; MACR 7814.
42-102668 Del Cheyenne 24/3/44; Kearney 11/4/44; Dow Fd 29/4/44; ass 710BS/447BG Rattlesden 4/5/44; retUS Bradley 6/7/45; 4168 BU Sth Plains 11/7/45; RFC Kingman 29/11/45.
42-102669 Del Cheyenne 24/3/44; Kearney 15/4/44; Grenier 29/4/44; ass 369BS/306BG [WW-G] Thurleigh 24/5/44; MIA Cauvincourt, Fr 8/8/44 w/Kata; flak, cr Caen, Fr; 4POW; 6RTD; MACR 8434. DAMYANKEE.
42-102670 Del Cheyenne 24/3/44; Hunter 11/4/44; Grenier 29/4/44; ass 338BS/96BG [BX-Q] Snetterton 3/5/44; dest by e/a at Poltava 21/6/44; sal 1/7/44.
42-102671 Del Cheyenne 24/3/44; Dyersburg 29/4/44; 330 BU Dyersburg 1/3/45; RFC Walnut Ridge 19/12/45.
42-102672 Del Cheyenne 24/3/44; Hunter 9/4/44; Dow Fd 29/4/44; ass 533BS/381BG Ridgewell 21/5/44; MIA Dessau 30/5/44 w/Burton; e/a, cr Piethen, Ger?; 4KIA 5POW; MACR 5233. OL' SWAYBACK.
42-102673 Del Cheyenne 24/3/44; Hunter 16/4/44; Dow Fd 2/5/44; ass 571BS/390BG [FC-L/B] Framlingham 4/5/44 PREFERRED RISK; MIA Derben, Ger 14/1/45 w/Lewis; e/a, cr Goerne, Ger?; 5KIA 4POW; MACR 11724. GOOD OLD YANK.
42-102674 Del Cheyenne 25/3/44; Kearney 12/4/44; Grenier 29/4/44; ass 94BG Rougham 1/5/44; tran 615BS/401BG [IY-M] Deenethorpe 19/5/44; b/d Frankfurt 5/11/44 w/?; f/l Dunmow, UK A/fd; sal 2 SAD 8/11/44.
42-102675 Del Cheyenne 25/3/44; Kearney 13/4/44; Grenier 27/4/44; ass 525BS/379BG Kimbolton 19/5/44; MIA Merseburg 11/9/44 w/Smithdeal; flak, cr Aeltrebruegge?; 3EVD 6POW; MACR 8900.
42-102676 Del Cheyenne 25/3/44; Kearney 23/4/44; Grenier 29/4/44; ass 511BS/351BG [DS-P] Polebrook 21/9/44; 510BS [TU-P]; retUS Bradley 23/5/45; 4168 BU Sth Plains 26/5/45; {29m} RFC Kingman 3/12/45. 17 AND MISS LEDD.
42-102677 Del Cheyenne 25/3/44; Billings 3/5/44; Kearney 12/5/44; Grenier 26/5/44; ass 568BS/390BG [BI-R] Framlingham 27/5/44 MISSISSIPPI MISSION; MIA Derben, Ger 14/1/45 w/Johnson; e/a, cr Garlitz, Ger; 5KIA 5POW; MACR 11725. BOB TAIL BATTLER.
42-102678 Del Cheyenne 25/3/44; Hunter 16/4/44; Grenier 29/4/44; ass 334BS/95BG [BG-R] Horham 3/5/44; MIA Merseburg 2/11/44 w/Pozolo; cr Gottingen, Ger; 1KIA 8POW; MACR 10309. OLE WORRYBIRD.
42-102679 Del Cheyenne 25/3/44; Hunter 10/4/44; Grenier 29/4/44; ass 385BG Gt Ashfield 3/5/44; retUS Bradley 24/6/45; 330 BU Dyersburg 11/9/45; 4168 BU Sth Plains 21/10/45; RFC Kingman 19/11/45.
42-102680 Del Cheyenne 25/3/44; Gt Falls 23/4/44; Kearney 11/5/44; Grenier 26/5/44; ass 358BS/303BG [VK-I] Molesworth 2/6/44; MIA Cologne 15/8/44 w/Cathey; e/a, cr Wittlich, Ger; 3EVD 1KIA 6POW; MACR 8437.
42-102681 Del Cheyenne 25/3/44; ass 331BS/94BG [QE-T] but re-ass Drew 18/4/44; Oklahoma City 23/4/44; 327 BU Drew 25/8/44; 301 BU Drew 22/10/45; RFC Altus 5/11/45.
42-102682 Del Cheyenne 25/3/44; Gulfport 19/4/44; Amarillo 21/4/44; Gulfport 24/4/44; 328 BU Gulfport 7/10/44; Recl Comp 9/2/45.
42-102683 Del Cheyenne 25/3/44; Kearney 13/4/44; Grenier 29/4/44; ass 423BS/306BG Thurleigh 25/5/44; MIA Dessau 20/7/44 w/Frazee; flak, ditched Channel; 9RTD.
42-102684 Del Cheyenne 25/3/44; Hunter 9/4/44; Grenier 29/4/44; ass 549BS/385BG Gt Ashfield 4/5/44; 551BS; retUS Bradley 24/6/45 4168 BU Sth Plains 27/6/45; RFC Kingman 13/12/45. SWEET CHARIOT.
42-102685 Del Cheyenne 25/3/44; Kearney 14/3/44; cr & W/O 26/4/44.
42-102686 Del Cheyenne 26/3/44; Kearney 13/4/44; Grenier 29/4/44; ass 339BS/96BG [QJ-M] Snetterton 3/5/44; dest by e/a at Poltava 21/6/44; sal 1/7/44.
42-102687 Del Cheyenne 26/3/44; Gulfport 19/4/44; 326 BU Gulfport 31/3/45; 4124 BU Altus 1/10/45;

RFC Altus 29/10/45.
42-102688 Del Cheyenne 26/3/44; Kearney 13/4/44; Grenier 29/4/44; ass 305BG Chelveston 23/5/44; b/d Dresden 14/2/45 w/?; f/l Continent.
42-102689 Del Cheyenne 26/3/44; Kearney 15/4/44; Grenier 7/5/44; ass 379BG Kimbolton 10/5/44; retUS Bradley 12/7/45; 4185 BU Independence 7/11/45; RFC Kingman 16/12/45.
42-102690 Del Cheyenne 26/3/44; Kearney 13/4/44; Grenier 29/4/44; ass 526BS/379BG [LF-Q] Kimbolton 18/5/44; MIA Cauvincourt, Fr 8/8/44 w/Greenough; 9RTD.
42-102691 Del Cheyenne 26/3/44; Kearney 13/4/44; Grenier 29/4/44; ass 452BG Deopham Green 3/5/44; dam by e/a at Poltava 21/6/44; rep & re-ass 15AF Italy 29/9/44; ass 346BS/99BG Tortorella 11/12/44; {18m} to depot 4/45; retUS 1103 BU Morrison 28/9/45; RFC Walnut Ridge 4/1/46. BIG BARN SMELL.
42-102692 Del Cheyenne 26/3/44; Kearney 14/4/44; Grenier 29/4/44; ass 457BG Glatton 3/5/44; b/d Berlin 24/5/44 w/?; sal 14/11/44.
42-102693 Del Cheyenne 26/3/44; Gulfport 19/4/44; 328 BU Gulfport 31/3/45; 324 BU Chatham 12/5/45; RFC Altus 29/10/45.
42-102694 Del Cheyenne 26/3/44; Kearney 15/4/44; Grenier 29/4/44; ass 332BS/94BG [XM-K] Rougham 3/5/44; 333BS [TS-K]; retUS Bradley 9/7/45; 4168 BU Sth Plains 12/7/45; RFC Kingman 18/11/45. ATHENIAN AVENGER II.
42-102695 Del Cheyenne 26/3/44; Kearney 15/4/44; Grenier 29/4/44; ass 350BS/100BG [LN-F] Thorpe Abbotts 1/5/44; MIA Chemnitz 11/9/44 w/Holladay; e/a, cr Obersiesenthal, Ger; 5KIA 4POW; MACR 8821.
42-102696 Del Cheyenne 26/3/44; Hunter 16/4/44; Dow Fd 2/5/44; ass 560BS/388BG Knettishall 8/5/44; used on Aphrodite training project; retUS Bradley 3/7/45; 4168 BU Sth Plains 18/7/45; RFC Kingman 17/11/45. MIDGE.
42-102697 Del Cheyenne 26/3/44; Gulfport 19/4/44; 328 BU Gulfport 31/3/45; RFC Walnut Ridge 18/12/45.
42-102698 Del Cheyenne 26/3/44; Drew 18/4/44; 327 BU 4/5/45; 301 BU Drew 22/10/45; RFC Altus 5/11/45.
42-102699 Del Cheyenne 26/3/44; Hunter 16/4/44; Grenier 29/4/44; ass379BG Kimbolton 23/5/44; tran 365BS/305BG Chelveston 25/5/44; MIA Cottbus 29/5/44 w/Hanson; e/a, cr Messerik, Ger?; 10POW; MACR 5335.
42-102700 Del Cheyenne 26/3/44; Hunter 16/4/44; Dow Fd 3/5/44; ass 412BS/95BG [QW-Z] Horham 4/5/44; MIA Paris 2/8/44 w/Capt Baber; cr Lisieux, Fr; 7KIA 3POW; MACR 7701. I'LL GET BY.
42-102701 Del Cheyenne 26/3/44; Hunter 16/4/44; Grenier 21/5/44; ass 338BS/96BG [BX-M] Snetterton 22/5/44; dest by e/a at Poltava 21/6/44; sal 1/7/44; ANGEL PUSS.
42-102702 Del Cheyenne 26/3/44; Gulfport 19/4/44; 328 BU Gulfport 31/3/45; 3704 BU Keesler 21/4/45; RFC Kingman 16/3/46.
42-102703 Del Cheyenne 26/3/44; Kearney 14/4/44; Grenier 29/4/44; ass 532BS/381BG [VE-M] Ridgewell 22/5/44; {30+m} flak b/d Cologne 16/10/44 w/Reseigh; 2WIA & TTG Nushy ext fire; sal 2 SAD 16/10/44. PELLA TULIP.
42-102704 Del Cheyenne 26/3/44; Gulfport 19/4/44; 328 BU Gulfport 31/3/45; 330 BU Dyersburg 17/5/45; 327 BU Drew 28/8/45; 330 BU Dyersburg 4/9/45; RFC Walnut Ridge 18/12/45.
42-102705 Del Cheyenne 26/3/44; Gulfport 19/4/44;

4103 BU Jackson 24/10/44; 328 BU Gulfport W/O 13/11/44; Recl Comp 28/11/44.
42-102706 Del Cheyenne 26/3/44; Hunter 19/4/44; Morrison 3/5/44; ass 817BS/483BG Sterparone 5/5/44; MIA Hall, Aus 16/2/45 w/Solowitz; hit by bomb from B-24, severing tail; cr Innsbruck; 9KIA; MACRs 12145 & 14764.
42-102707 Del Cheyenne 26/3/44; Gulfport 19/4/44; 328 BU Gulfport 31/3/45; Recl Comp 11/4/45.
42-102708 Del Cheyenne 26/3/44; Gulfport 19/4/44; 347 BU Key Fd 2/10/44; 328 BU Gulfport 9/10/44; 324 BU Chatham 12/5/45; 324 BU Stewart 14/7/45; RFC Kingman 12/10/45.
42-102709 Del McDill 31/3/44; 325 BU Avon Park 15/10/44; 3539 BU Langley 4/9/45; 3502 BU Chanute 18/10/45; Recl Comp 3/1/46.
42-102710 Del McDill 31/3/44; Avon Park 4/4/44; 442 BU New Castle 17/12/44; 325 BU Avon Park 20/2/45; RFC Walnut Ridge 22/8/45.
42-102711 Del McDill 31/3/44; Grenada 2/4/44; W/O 4/4/44.
42-102712 Del McDill 31/3/44; 325 BU Avon Park 25/11/44; Recl Comp 2/4/45.
42-102713 Del McDill 31/3/44; 3501 BU Boca Raton 2/2/45; 326 BU McDill 9/2/45; 324 BU Chatham 18/8/45; RFC Altus 29/10/45.
42-102714 Del McDill 31/3/44; 325 BU Avon Park, W/O 2/8/44.
42-102715 Del McDill 31/3/44; 327 BU Drew 4/5/45; 301 BU Drew 22/10/45; RFC Altus 5/11/45.
42-102716 Del McDill 31/3/44; 327 BU Drew 4/5/45; 301 BU Drew 22/10/45; RFC Altus 5/11/45.
42-102717 Del McDill 31/3/44; 325 BU Avon Park 9/4/45; RFC Walnut Ridge 22/8/45.
42-102718 Del McDill 31/3/44; 326 BU McDill 28/2/45; 330 BU Dyersburg 23/3/45; 327 BU Drew 28/8/45; 330 BU Dyersburg 4/9/45; RFC Walnut Ridge 18/12/45.
42-102719 Del McDill 31/3/44; 327 BU Drew 4/5/45; 301 BU Drew 22/10/45; RFC Altus 5/11/45.
42-102720 Del McDill 31/3/44; 326 BU McDill 24/12/44; 4117 BU Robins 4140 BU Rome 18/1/45; Hunter 26/4/45; 3704 BU Keesler 2/4/46; 554 BU Memphis 5/6/46; 4136 BU Tinker 23/6/46; 4112 BU Olmstead 3/9/46; 62 BU Andrews 29/12/46; 5 RES Pope 16/6/47; 316 BU Shaw 18/8/47; 5 RES Pope 1/4/48; Recl Comp 1/2/49.
42-102721 Del McDill 31/3/44; 327 BU Drew 4/5/45; Recl Comp 4/8/45.
42-102722 Del McDill 31/3/44; Houston 7/4/44; McDill 11/4/44; 327 BU Drew 4/5/45; 301 BU Drew 22/10/45; RFC Altus 15/11/45.
42-102723 Del McDill 31/3/44; 327 BU Drew 4/5/45; 62 BU Morrison 13/1/46; 62 BU McDill 3/9/46; 5 ERS Morrison 10/12/46; 4141 BU Pyote 11/2/47; Recl Comp 31/3/49.
42-102724 Del McDill 31/3/44; 325 BU Avon Park 9/12/44; Recl Comp 9/2/45.
42-102725 Del McDill 31/3/44; 4103 BU Jackson 29/11/44; 327 BU Drew 4/5/45; 301 BU Drew 22/11/45; RFC Kingman 28/11/45.
42-102726 Del McDill 31/3/44; 326 BU McDill, W/O 7/9/44; Recl Comp 21/8/45.
42-102727 Del McDill 31/3/44; Del Marbry 11/4/44; McDill 13/4/44; 335 BU Del Marbry 10/11/44; 326 BU McDill 16/11/44; 325 BU Avon Park 15/2/45; RFC Kingman 22/8/45.
42-102728 Del McDill 31/3/44; 327 BU Drew 4/5/45; 301 BU Drew 22/10/45; RFC Altus 5/11/45.
42-102729 Del McDill 31/3/44; 327 BU Drew 4/5/45; 301 BU Drew 22/10/45; RFC Altus 5/11/45.
42-102730 Del McDill 31/3/44; 326 BU McDill 17/2/45;

327 BU Drew 1/3/45; 610 BU Eglin, sal 29/1/46.
42-102731 Del McDill 31/3/44; 4108 BU Newark 22/11/44; 325 BU Avon Park 9/4/45; RFC Walnut Ridge 24/8/45.
42-102732 Del McDill 31/3/44; 325 BU Avon Park 23/12/44; 4117 BU Robins 3/1/45; 4104 BU Rome 18/1/45; 3704 BU Keesler 6/6/45; 4168 BU Sth Plains 5/6/46; 4136 BU Tinker 8/12/46; 4104 BU Rome 22/1/47; Recl 10/4/47.
42-102733 Del McDill 31/3/44; 325 BU Avon Park 9/4/45; RFC Walnut Ridge 21/8/45.
42-102734 Del McDill 31/3/44; 4204 BU Atlanta 10/1/45; 326 BU McDill 4/2/45; 329 BU Alexandra 23/3/45; 327 BU Drew 20/7/45; 203 BU Jackson 21/8/45; 268 BU Peterson 30/10/45; RFC Altus 7/11/45.
42-102735 Del McDill 31/3/44; Bismarck 5/4/44; McDill 10/4/44; 4050 BU Daniel 6/11/44; 325 BU Avon Park 22/11/44; 554 BU Memphis 5/6/45; RFC Walnut Ridge 12/12/45.
42-102736 Del McDill 31/3/44; 326 BU McDill 7/2/45; 330 BU Dyersburg 3/3/45; RFC Walnut Ridge 19/12/45.
42-102737 Del McDill 31/3/44; 326 BU McDill 13/2/45; 325 BU Avon Park 23/2/45; 3704 BU Keesler 14/8/45; 338 OT Keesler 28/8/45.
42-102738 Del McDill 31/3/44; 325 BU Avon Park 28/12/44; RFC Walnut Ridge 12/12/45.
42-102739 Del McDill 31/3/44; 325 BU Avon Park 17/2/45; RFC Walnut Ridge 20/8/45.
42-102740 Del McDill 31/3/44; 326 BU McDill, W/O 27/6/44.
42-102741 Del McDill 31/3/44; 327 BU Drew 4/5/45; 301 BU Drew 22/11/45; RFC Kingman 28/11/45.
42-102742 Del McDill 31/3/44; 325 BU Avon Park 9/4/45; RFC Walnut Ridge 22/8/45.
42-102743 Del McDill 31/3/44; 325 BU Avon Park 9/4/45; RFC Walnut Ridge 22/8/45.
42-102744 Del McDill 31/3/44; 326 BU McDill 2/4/45; 4124 BU Altus 1/10/45; RFC Altus 29/10/45.
42-102745 Del McDill 31/3/44; 311 BU Lawson 5/9/45; 327 BU Drew 17/9/45; 301 BU Drew 22/11/45; RFC Kingman 4/12/45.
42-102746 Del McDill 31/3/44; 325 BU Avon Park 1/8/44; W/O 7/8/44.
42-102747 Del McDill 31/3/44; 325 BU Avon Park 9/4/45; 2114 BU Lockburn 17/8/45; RFC Walnut Ridge 21/1/46.
42-102748 Del McDill 31/3/44; 327 BU Drew 4/5/45; 301 BUN Drew 22/10/45; RFC Altus 5/11/45.
42-102749 Del McDill 31/3/44; 326 BU McDill 8/2/45; 325 BU Avon Park 9/4/45; RFC Walnut Ridge 22/8/45.
42-102750 Del McDill 31/3/44; 327 BU Drew, W/O 24/10/44.
42-102751 Del McDill 31/3/44; 4005 BU Robins 29/11/44; 326 BU McDill 18/12/44; 329 BU Alexandra 3/3/45; 325 BU Avon Park 29/6/45; RFC Walnut Ridge 11/12/45.
42-102752 Del McDill 31/3/44; 301 BU Pinecastle 10/6/44; 326 BU McDill 24/6/44; 329 BU Alexandra 24/3/45; 327 BU Drew 20/8/45; 200 BU Peterson 26/2/46; RFC Walnut Ridge 27/2/46.
42-102753 Del McDill 31/3/44; 327 BU Drew 4/5/45; 326 BU McDill 22/11/45; 62 BU Morrison 5/1/46; 519 BU Lawson 13/2/47; 5 ERS Morrison 17/3/47; 4141 BU Pyote 29/5/47; Recl Comp 14/1/49.
42-102754 Del McDill 31/3/44; 225 BU Rapid City 10/4/45; Recl Comp 19/6/45.
42-102755 Del McDill 31/3/44; 225 BU Rapid City 1/5/45; 234 BU Clovis 15/7/45; RFC Walnut Ridge 18/10/45.

42-102756 Del Rapid City 1/4/44; 225 BU Rapid City 1/5/45; 2114 BU Lockburn 19/7/45; 2137 BU Hendricks 25/10/45; RFC Walnut Ridge 7/1/46.

42-102757 Del Rapid City 1/4/44; 225 BU Rapid City 1/5/45; 268 BU Peterson 14/7/45; 232 BU Dalhart 19/7/45; 201 BU Peterson 3/2/46; RFC Walnut Ridge 15/2/46.

42-102758 Del Rapid City 1/4/44; 2325 BU Rapid City 6/12/44; 2114 BU Lockburn 27/6/45; 2137 BU Hendricks 11/12/45; RFC Walnut Ridge 8/1/46.

42-102759 Del Rapid City 1/4/44; 225 BU Rapid City 1/5/45; 354 BU Rapid City 20/9/45; RFC Walnut Ridge 14/12/45.

42-102760 Del Rapid City 1/4/44; 231 BU Pierre 5/1/45; 224 BU Sioux City 10/1/45; 222 BU Ardmore 13/6/45; 332 BU Ardmore 16/6/45; RFC Walnut Ridge 19/8/45.

42-102762 Del Sioux City 1/4/44; 224 BU Sioux City 6/3/45; 225 BU Rapid City 21/6/45; 203 BU Jackson 30/6/45; 420 BU March 27/9/45; RFC Kingman 16/1/46.

42-102763 Del Sioux City 1/4/44; 224 BU Sioux City, W/O 9/8/44.

42-102764 Del Sioux City 1/4/44; 224 BU Sioux City 6/3/45; 222 BU Ardmore 14/6/45; 554 BU Memphis 18/7/45; 332 BU Ardmore 23/7/45; RFC Walnut Ridge 19/8/45.

42-102765 Del Sioux City 1/4/44; 224 BU Sioux City 24/12/44; 209 BU Des Moines 26/12/44; 224 BU Sioux City 6/3/45; 225 BU Rapid City 17/6/45; 203 BU Jackson 6/7/45; 239 BU March 27/9/45; 420 BU March 7/10/45; RFC Walnut Ridge 17/2/46.

42-102766 Del Alexandra 2/4/44; Bismarck 7/4/44; 254 BU San Angelo 14/8/44; 221 BU Alexandra 17/1/45; 329 BU Alexandra 1/3/45; 330 BU Dyersburg 25/6/45; 327 BU Drew 28/8/45; 330 BU Dyersburg 11/9/45; RFC Walnut Ridge 18/12/45.

42-102767 Del Alexandra 2/4/44; 120 BU Greenville 27/7/44; 221 BU Alexandra 28/7/44; 329 BU Alexandra 1/3/45; 503 Gray Pt 14/6/45; 329 BU Alexandra 21/6/45; 327 BU Drew 1/8/45; 203 BU Jackson 18/8/45; 268 BU Peterson 9/10/45; RFC Altus 7/11/45.

42-102768 Del Alexandra 2/4/44; 120 BU Greenville 27/6/44; 221 BU Alexandra 17/1/45; 329 BU Alexandra 1/3/45; 325 BU Avon Park 28/6/45; RFC Walnut Ridge 13/11/45.

42-102769 Del Alexandra 2/4/44; Omaha 17/4/44; Alexandra 21/4/44; 353 BU Keesler 11/8/44; 221 BU Alexandra 17/1/45; 329 BU Alexandra 1/3/45; 327 BU Drew 8/7/45; 203 BU Jackson 27/8/45; 268 BU Peterson 7/10/45; RFC Altus 7/11/45.

42-102770 Del Alexandra 2/4/44; Oklahoma City 17/4/44; 221 BU Alexandra, W/O 1/2/45.

42-102771 Del Alexandra 2/4/44; 221 BU Alexandra 17/1/45; 329 BU Alexandra 1/3/45; 325 BU Avon Park 29/6/45; RFC Walnut Ridge 21/8/45.

42-102772 Del Dyersburg 2/4/44; 120 BU Greenville 12/6/44; 330 BU Dyersburg 1/3/45; RFC Walnut Ridge 17/12/45.

42-102773 Del Dyersburg 2/4/44; 330 BU Dyersburg 1/3/45; RFC Walnut Ridge 18/12/45.

42-102774 Del Dyersburg 2/4/44; 330 BU Dyersburg 1/3/45; RFC Walnut Ridge 17/12/45.

42-102775 Del Dyersburg 2/4/44; 347 BU Key Fd 27/8/44; 223 BU Dyersburg 3/9/44; 3390 BU Dyersburg 9/4/45; RFC Walnut Ridge 18/12/45.

42-102776 Del Dyersburg 2/4/44; 223 BU Dyersburg 8/1/45; 330 BU Dyersburg 1/3/45; RFC Walnut Ridge 17/12/45.

42-102777 Del Dyersburg 2/4/44; Bismarck 14/4/44; Minneapolis 22/10/44; 223 BU Dyersburg 24/10/44; 330 BU Dyersburg 1/3/45; RFC Walnut Ridge 19/12/45.

42-102778 Del Pyote 2/4/44; 235 Biggs 16/8/44; 202 BU Galveston 21/1/45; 268 BU Peterson 30/3/45; 2114 BU Lockburn 27/6/45; Recl Comp 19/10/45.

42-102779 Del Pyote 2/4/44; 235 BU Biggs 17/8/44; 206 BU Alamogordo 11/10/44; 235 BU Biggs 24/10/44; 225 BU Rapid City 22/3/45; 2114 BU Lockburn 27/6/45; RFC Golden 10/12/45.

42-102780 Del Pyote 2/4/44; 4104 BU Pyote 24/4/44; 235 BU Biggs 16/8/44; 224 BU Sioux City 27/2/45; 222 BU Ardmore 13/6/45; 332 BU Ardmore 16/6/45; RFC Walnut Ridge 19/8/45.

42-102781 Del Pyote 2/4/44; 235 BU Biggs 16/8/44; 202 BU Galveston 21/1/45; 268 BU Peterson 30/3/45; 2114 BU Lockburn 25/6/45; RFC Walnut Ridge 18/1/46.

42-102782 Del Pyote 4/4/44; 235 BU Biggs 18/8/44; 231 BU Alamogordo 21/10/44; 235 BU Biggs 17/1/45; 225 BU Rapid City 22/3/45; 2114 BU Lockburn 27/6/45; RFC Walnut Ridge 8/1/46.

42-102783 Del Pyote 4/4/44; 263 BU Pyote 25/7/44; 555 BU Love 1/8/44; 235 BU Biggs 16/8/44; 202 BU Galveston 21/1/45; 268 BU Peterson 30/3/45; 2114 BU Lockburn 23/6/45; 200 BU Chicago Mun 21/8/45; 2137 BU Hendricks 8/10/45; RFC Walnut Ridge 7/1/46.

42-102784 Del Ardmore 4/4/44; 4136 BU Tinker 15/10/44; 222 BU Ardmore 22/1/45; 332 BU Ardmore 16/6/45; RFC Walnut Ridge 18/8/45.

42-102785 Del Ardmore 4/4/44; Gt Falls 13/4/44; 222 BU Ardmore 19/9/44; 348 BU Will Rogers 11/3/45; 332 BU Ardmore 16/6/45; RFC Walnut Ridge 18/8/45.

42-102786 Del Ardmore 5/4/44; Bismarck 11/4/44; Ardmore, W/O 25/4/44.

42-102787 Del Ardmore 5/4/44; Gt Falls 11/4/44; 222 BU Ardmore 22/1/45; 332 BU Ardmore 16/6/45; RFC Walnut Ridge 20/8/45.

42-102788 Del Ardmore 5/4/44; Gt Falls 11/4/44; 222 BU Ardmore 22/1/45; 332 BU Ardmore 16/6/45; RFC Walnut Ridge 22//8/45.

42-102789 Del Ardmore 6/4/44; Gt Falls 12/4/44; 202 BU Galveston 13/7/44; 222 BU Ardmore 15/7/44; 332 BU Ardmore 16/6/45; RFC Walnut Ridge 13/11/45.

42-102790 Del Ardmore 6/4/44; Gt Falls 9/4/44; 202 BU Galveston 20/9/44; 2114 BU Lockburn 27/6/45; 2137 BU Hendricks 18/8/45; RFC Kingman 9/11/45.

42-102791 Del Galveston 5/4/44; Gt Falls 8/4/44; 202 BU Galveston 20/9/45; 268 BU Peterson 28/11/44; 202 BU Galveston 29/11/44; 460 BU Hamilton 3/12/44; 202 BU Galveston 18/1/45; 464 BU McChord 20/1/45; 268 BU Peterson 30/3/45; 2114 BU Lockburn 27/6/45; 2137 BU Hendricks 9/10/45; 64 BU Andrews 10/10/45; RFC Kingman 5/1/46.

42-102792 Del Alamogordo 5/4/44; Cheyenne 11/4/44; Gulfport 24/4/44; 328 BU Gulfport 31/3/45; 4124 BU Altus 1/10/45; RFC Altus 29/10/45.

42-102793 Del Cheyenne 6/4/44; Gulfport 20/4/44; 103 BU Jackson 24/10/44; 328 BU Gulfport 31/3/45; 331 BU Barksdale 18/5/45; RFC Altus 14/12/45.

42-102794 Del Cheyenne 6/4/44; Gulfport 20/4/44; 328 BU Gulfport 14/1/45; 324 BU Chatham 11/8/45; RFC Altus 29/10/45.

42-102795 Del Cheyenne 6/4/44; Gulfort 27/4/44; 328 BU Gulfport 31/3/45; 326 BU McDill 12/5/45; 328 BU Gulfport 6/7/45; RFC Altus 29/10/45.

42-102796 Del Cheyenne 5/4/44; Gulfport 19/4/44; 326 BU Gulfport, W/O 29/8/44.

42-102797 Del Cheyenne 5/4/44; Gulfport 14/4/44; 328 BU Gulfport 31/3/45; 331 BU Barksdale 16/5/45; RFC Kingman 16/10/45.

42-102798 Del Cheyenne 6/4/44; Eglin 23/4/44; Pyote 28/4/44; 235 BU Biggs 16/8/44; 202 BU Galveston 24/1/45; 268 BU Peterson 30/3/45; 2114 BU Lockburn 11/7/45; 2137 BU Hendricks 14/10/45; RFC Walnut Ridge 4/1/46.

42-102799 Del Cheyenne 6/4/44; Gulfport 14/4/44; 202 BU Galveston 24/1/45; 3704 BU Keesler 4/7/46; 554 BU Memphis 7/7/46; 4168 BU Sth Plains 30/9/46; Recl Comp 29/5/47.

42-102800 Del Cheyenne 5/4/44; Gulfport 20/4/44; 347 BU Key Fd 19/3/45; 328 BU Gulfport 28/3/45; 4200 BU Chicago Mun 24/8/45; 328 BU Gulfport 31/8/45; RFC Altus 29/10/45.

42-102801 Del Cheyenne 6/4/44; Gulfport 20/4/44; 328 BU Gulfport 31/3/45; 324 BU Chatham 11/5/45; RFC Altus 29/10/45.

42-102802 Del Cheyenne 6/4/44; Gulfport 20/4/44; 116 BU Ft Dix 11/12/44; 328 BU Gulfport 20/12/44; 331 BU Barksdale 18/5/45; 330 BU Dyersburg 24/5/45; RFC Walnut Ridge 17/12/45.

42-102803 Del Cheyenne 6/4/44; Gulfport 20/4/44; 4119 BU Brookley 22/11/44; 328 BU Gulfport 24/11/44; 4117 BU Robins 4/1/45; 4104 BU Rome 18/1/45; 3704 BU Keesler 21/6/45.

42-102804 Del Cheyenne 6/4/44; Gulfport 20/4/44; 328 BU Gulfport 24/11/44; 233 BU Ft Worth 3/2/45; 3018 BU Kingman 7/12/45; RFC Walnut Ridge 14/2/46.

42-102805 Del Cheyenne 6/4/44; Gulfport 21/4/44; Barksdale 28/4/44; 328 BU Gulfport 30/11/44; 347 BU Key Fd 20/12/44; 328 BU Gulfport 31/12/44; 324 BU Chatham 9/5/45; RFC Altus 29/10/45.

42-102806 Del Cheyenne 6/4/44; Gulfport 21/4/44; 328 BU Gulfport 31/3/45; 326 BU McDill 21/7/45; RFC Walnut Ridge 12/10/45.

42-102807 Del Cheyenne 6/4/44; Gulfport 21/4/44; 328 BU Gulfport 31/3/45; 330 BU Dyersburg 17/5/45; 327 BU Drew 28/8/45; 330 BU Dyersburg 11/9/45; RFC Walnut Ridge 17/12/45.

42-102808 Del Cheyenne 7/4/44; Gulfport 21/4/44; 4119 BU Brookley 5/10/44; 328 BU Gulfport 18/10/44; 331 BU Barksdale 18/5/45; RFC Walnut Ridge 18/12/45.

42-102809 Del Cheyenne 7/4/44; Gulfport 21/4/44; 328 BU Gulfport 31/3/45; 330 BU Dyersburg 17/5/45; RFC Walnut Ridge 19/12/45.

42-102810 Del Cheyenne 7/4/44; Gulfport 21/4/44; 328 BU Gulfport 30/3/45; 329 BU Alexandra 4/4/45; 330 BU Dyersburg 5/9/45; RFC Walnut Ridge 18/12/45.

42-102811 Del Cheyenne 7/4/44; Gulfport 20/4/44; 4119 BU Brookley 12/10/44; 328 BU Gulfport 31/10/44; 330 BU Dyersburg 17/5/45; RFC Walnut Ridge 18/12/45.

42-102812 Del Cheyenne 7/4/44; 488BG McDill 21/4/44; 326 BU McDill 2/2/45; 327 BU Drew 17/2/45; 301 BU Drew 2/11/45; RFC Kingman 28/11/45.

42-102813 Del Cheyenne 7/4/44; 488BG McDill 23/4/44; Drew, WO 20/5/44.

42-102814 Del Cheyenne 7/4/44; 488BG McDill 21/4/44; 327 BU Drew 4/5/45; 301 BU Drew 22/10/45; RFC Altus 5/11/45.

42-102815 Del Cheyenne 7/4/44; 488BG McDill 21/4/44; 326 BU McDill 24/12/44; 4117 BU Robins 4/1/45; Rome 18/4/45; Hunter 24/4/45; 3704 BU Keesler 2/4/46; 554 BU Memphis 7/7/46; 613 BU Phillips 10/7/46; 554 BU Memphis 11/7/46.

42-102816 Del Cheyenne 8/4/44; 488BG McDill 23/4/44; 330 BU Greenville 3/7/44; 326 BU McDill 22/7/44; 330 BU Dyersburg 16/3/45; RFC Walnut

Above: B-17G-60-BO 42-102803 never went to war, spending its time with replacement training units and eventually being abandoned at Kessler Field. The post-WW2 high-visibility code BA 803 was intended to deter unauthorised low flying, BA being the prefix for all B-17s. (Crown)

Ridge 18/12/45.

42-102817 Del Cheyenne 7/4/44; 396BG Drew 24/4/44; 901 BU Pinecastle 10/6/44; 4006 BU Robins 10/10/44; 327 BU Drew 21/11/44; 4104 BU Rome 18/1/45; 302 BU Hunter 22/3/45; 3704 BU Keesler 8/8/45; 613 BU Phillips 7/7/46.

42-102818 Del Cheyenne 7/4/44; 488BG McDill 23/4/44; 325 BU Avon Park 21/2/45; RFC Walnut Ridge 25/9/45.

42-102819 Del Cheyenne 7/4/44; 488BG McDill 21/4/44; 327 BU Drew 23/2/45; 6110 BU Eglin 15/12/45; sal Eglin 29/1/46.

42-102820 Del Cheyenne 7/4/44; 488BG McDill 21/4/44; 326 BU McDill 5/2/45; 325 BU Avon Park 17/2/45; RFC Walnut Ridge 21/8/45.

42-102821 Del Cheyenne 8/4/44; 88BG Avon Park 21/4/44; 325 BU Avon Park 9/4/45; RFC Walnut Ridge 24/8/45.

42-102822 Del Cheyenne 8/4/44; 488BG McDill 23/4/44; 326 BU McDill 28/2/45; 329 BU Alexandra 23/3/45; 325 BU Avon Park 29/6/45; RFC Walnut Ridge 24/8/45.

42-102823 Del Cheyenne 8/4/44; 88BG Avon Park 21/4/44; 325 BU Avon Park 9/4/45; RFC Walnut Ridge 12/12/45.

42-102824 Del Cheyenne 8/4/44; 488BG McDill 23/4/44; 326 BU McDill 28/2/45; 330 BU Dyersburg 16/3/45; RFC Walnut Ridge 17/12/45.

42-102825 Del Cheyenne 8/4/44; Ft Myers 26/4/44; 2124 BU Buckingham 19/10/44; 2126 BU Laredo 1/2/45; RFC Walnut Ridge 7/1/46.

42-102826 Del Cheyenne 8/4/44; 488BG McDill 23/4/44; 328 BU Gulfport 31/3/45; 330 BU Dyersburg 17/5/45; RFC Walnut Ridge 18/12/45.

42-102827 Del Cheyenne 8/4/44; 346BG Drew 24/4/44; 327 BU Drew 4/5/45; 326 BU McDill 12/11/45; 300 BU McDill 17/1/46; 62 BU McDill 5/4/46; 62 BU Morrison 18/7/46; 5ERS Morrison 30/1/47; 1103 BU Morrison 14/7/47; Recl Comp 25/9/47.

42-102828 Del Cheyenne 8/4/44; 488BG McDill 23/4/44; 326 BU McDill, W/O 9/8/44.

42-102829 Del Cheyenne 9/4/44; 396BG Drew 24/4/44; 326 BU McDill 7/11/44; 327 BU Drew 13/11/45; 301 BU Drew 22/10/45; RFC Altus 5/11/45.

42-102830 Del Cheyenne 9/4/44; Hunter 25/4/44; Dow Fd 15/5/44; ass 49BS/2BG Amendola 22/5/44; {49m} sal 2/12/44.

42-102831 Del Cheyenne 9/4/44; 488BG McDill 25/4/44; 326 BU McDill, W/O 29/9/44.

42-102832 Del Cheyenne 9/4/44; 488BG McDill 23/4/44; 326 BU McDill 24/2/45; 327 BU Drew 5/3/45; 554 BU Memphis 20/8/45; 327 BU Drew 3/9/45; RFC Kingman 28/11/45.

42-102833 Del Cheyenne 9/4/44; 488BG McDill 23/4/44; 325 BU Avon Park 9/4/45; RFC Walnut Ridge 24/8/45.

42-102834 Del Cheyenne 9/4/44; 346BG Drew 24/4/44; 327 BU Drew 24/10/44; 326 BU McDill 30/12/44; 62 BU McDill 9/4/45; 554 BU Memphis 31/7/46.

42-102835 Del Cheyenne 9/4/44; slated 379BG 10/4/44 PHYLLIS; 488BG McDill 23/4/44; 325 BU Avon Park 2/8/44; Recl Comp 22/11/44.

42-102836 Del Cheyenne 9/4/44; Hunter 24/4/44; Morrison 9/5/44; ass 816BS/483BG Sterparone 7/5/44; MIA Maribor, Yugo 1/4/45 w/Moore; flak, cr Bihac; 7KIA 4EVD, ret 5/4/45; MACR 13471. LYLA LUE.

42-102837 Del Cheyenne 9/4/44; 346BG Drew 24/4/44; 327 BU Drew 4/5/45; 301 BU Drew 22/10/45; RFC Altus 5/11/45.

42-102838 Del Cheyenne 9/4/44; 346BG Drew 24/4/44; 327 BU Drew 4/5/45; 301 BU Drew 22/10/45; RFC Altus 5/11/45.

42-102839 Del Cheyenne 9/4/44; 346BG Drew 24/4/44; 222 BU Ardmore 22/1/45; 332 BU Ardmore 16/6/45; RFC Walnut Ridge 11/12/45.

42-102840 Del Cheyenne 9/4/44; Roswell 1/5/44; 3030 BU Roswell 2/6/44; 3010 BU Williams 20/1/45; 3020 BU La Junta 19/4/45; 2114 BU Lockburn 25/6/45; 2137 BU Hendricks 4/10/45; RFC Walnut Ridge 14/1/46.

42-102841 Del Cheyenne 9/4/44; Dyersburg 25/4/44; Hunter 30/4/44; ass 840BS/483BG Sterparone 8/5/44; MIA Pilsen 23/10/44 w/Dallman; flak, cr Doeltech, Czech; 10POW. MACR 9319. SHADRACK.

42-102842 Del Cheyenne 9/4/44; 396BG Drew 24/4/44; 327 BU Drew 4/5/45; 203 BU Jackson 24/8/45; 268 BU Peterson 9/10/45; RFC Kingman 21/12/45.

42-102843 Del Cheyenne 9/4/44; 396BG Drew 24/4/44; 327 BU Drew 4/5/45; 326 BU McDill 22/11/45; 301 BU Drew 2/12/45; RFC Kingman 29/11/45.

42-102844 Del Cheyenne 9/4/44; Gulfport 24/4/44; Amarillo 29/4/44; 328 BU Gulfport 15/2/45; 2116 BU Napier 16/2/45; 328 BU Gulfport 31/3/45; 330 BU Dyersburg 17/5/45; 327 BU Drew 28/8/45; 330 BU Dyersburg 4/9/45; RFC Walnut Ridge 17/12/45.

42-102845 Del Cheyenne 10/4/44; 396BG Drew 24/4/44; 327 BU Drew 4/5/45; 301 BU Drew 22/10/45; RFC Altus 5/11/45.

42-102846 Del Cheyenne 10/4/44; Alexandra 25/4/44; 221 BU Alexandra 17/1/45; 329 BU Alexandra 1/3/45; 330 BU Dyersburg 4/9/45; RFC Walnut Ridge 17/12/45.

42-102847 Del Cheyenne 10/4/44; Alexandra 25/4/44; 221 BU Alexandra 17/1/45; 329 BU Alexandra 1/3/45; 330 BU Dyersburg 4/9/45; RFC Walnut Ridge 17/12/45.

42-102848 Del Cheyenne 10/4/44; Tyndall 26/4/44; 2114 BU Lockburn 2/9/45; 2137 BU Hendricks 22/9/45; RFC Walnut Ridge 8/1/46.

42-102849 Del Cheyenne 10/4/44; Hunter 27/4/44; Dow Fd 11/5/44; ass 840BS/483BG Sterparone 10/5/44; MIA Odertal 18/12/44 w/Dunn; e/a, c/l Biograd, Yugo; 3WIA, but except nav return 21/12/44 (nav ret 1/45); JOANNE.

42-102850 Del Cheyenne 10/4/44; 396BG Drew 24/4/44; 327 BU Drew, W/O 9/7/44; Recl Comp 6/7/45.

42-102851 Del Cheyenne 10/4/44; Hunter 24/4/44; Dow Fd 11/5/44; ass 346BS/99BG Tortorella 19/5/44; MIA {18m} Brasov, Rom 4/7/44 w/Elliott; mech fault, one engine out, 10 chutes seen; MACR 6397.

42-102852 Del Cheyenne 10/4/44; Hunter 24/4/44; Grenier 11/5/44; ass 817BS/483BG Sterparone 15/5/44; {97m - no aborts} RetUS Morrison 26/9/45; RFC Walnut Ridge 14/12/45. MARY ALICE.

42-102853 Del Cheyenne 10/4/44; Dyersburg 25/4/44; 330 BU Dyersburg 1/3/45; RFC Walnut Ridge 17/12/45.

42-102854 Del Cheyenne 10/4/44; Ardmore 25/4/44; 222 BU Ardmore 22/1/45; 332 BU Ardmore 16/6/45; RFC Walnut Ridge 24/8/45.

42-102855 Del Cheyenne 10/4/44; Hunter 27/4/44;

Dow Fd 10/5/44; ass 346BS/99BG Tortorella 19/5/44; {97m} sal 26/4/45; WEARY WILLIE.

42-102856 Del Cheyenne 10/4/44; Hunter 27/4/44; Dow Fd 12/5/44; ass 816BS/483BG Sterparone 16/5/44; MIA Odertal 26/12/44 w/Brown; pilot KIA when ditching; 8RTD.

42-102857 Del Cheyenne 10/4/44; Pyote 25/4/44; 235 BU Biggs 16/8/44; 202 BU Galveston 21/1/45; 268 BU Peterson 30/3/45; 4108 BU Newark 3/6/45; 268 BU Peterson 5/6/45; 2114 BU Lockburn 2/7/45; 2137 BU Hendricks 14/10/45; RFC Walnut Ridge 9/1/46.

42-102858 Del Cheyenne 10/4/44; Hunter 27/4/44; Grenier 15/5/44; ass 429BS/2BG Amendola 27/5/44; c/t/o for training flight 12/9/44; sal.

42-102859 Del Cheyenne 11/4/44; Hunter 27/4/44; Morrison 7/5/44; ass 483BG Sterparone 11/5/44; tran 342BS/97BG Amendola 12/7/44; retUS Bradley 4185 BU Independence 7/11/45; RFC Kingman 7/1/46. BABY.

42-102860 Del Cheyenne 11/4/44; Pyote 25/4/44; 235 BU Biggs 18/8/44; 222 BU Ardmore 7/3/45; 4210 BU Lambert 7/5/45; 222 BU Ardmore 19/5/45; 332 BU Ardmore 16/6/45; RFC Walnut Ridge 11/12/45.

42-102861 Del Cheyenne 13/4/44; Pyote 25/4/44; 235 BU Biggs 16/8/44; 3013 BU Deming 26/1/44; Recl Comp 2/11/44.

42-102862 Del Cheyenne 13/4/44; Hunter 27/4/44; Morrison 5/5/44; ass 817BS/483BG Sterparone 10/5/44; MIA Memmingen 18/7/44 w/Maclin; e/a, cr Kempten; 5KIA 5POW; MACR 6954.

42-102863 Del Cheyenne 13/4/44; Lockburn 26/4/44; 2114 BU Lockburn 2/9/44; RFC Walnut Ridge 7/1/46.

42-102864 Del Hendricks 13/4/44; 3036 BU Yuma 20/6/44; W/O 31/10/44; Recl Comp 20/11/44.

42-102865 Del Hendricks 13/4/44; Denver 18/4/44; 2137 BU Hendricks 17/11/44; RFC Kingman 1/11/45.

42-102866 Del Hendricks 13/4/44; Denver 18/4/44; Hendricks 25/4/44; 3036 BU Yuma 14/6/44; 3017 BU Hobbs 5/6/45; RFC Walnut Ridge 4/1/46.

42-102867 Del Ft Myers 13/4/44; Bismarck 18/4/44; 2126 BU Laredo 11/6/44; RFC Walnut Ridge 5/1/46.

42-102868 Del Ft Myers 13/4/44; Bismarck 5/5/44; 2118 BU Buckingham 11/5/44l 2126 BU Laredo 1/2/45; RFC Walnut Ridge 27/11/45.

42-102869 Del Cheyenne 14/4/44; Hunter 27/4/44; Morrison 7/5/44; ass 815BS/483BG Sterparone 11/5/44; MIA Brux 20/10/44 w/Potter; flak, two engines out, cr Budapest; 10EVD, ret 21/10/44; MACR 9203.

42-102870 Del Cheyenne 14/4/44; Hunter 27/4/44; Dow Fd 11/5/44; ass 560BS/388BG Knettishall 12/5/44; dest by e/a at Poltava 21/6/44; sal 24/7/44. CHISTLIN DADDIES.

42-102871 Del Cheyenne 14/4/44; Lockburn 26/4/44; 2114 BU Lockburn 2/9/44; 4152 BU Lockburn 1/10/44; RFC Walnut Ridge 7/1/46.

42-102872 Del Cheyenne 14/4/44; Lockburn 26/4/44; 2114 BU Lockburn 2/9/44; 2137 BU Hendricks 11/10/45; RFC Walnut Ridge 14/1/46.

42-102873 Del Cheyenne 14/4/44; Hunter 27/4/44; Grenier 11/5/44; ass 532BS/381BG [VE-H] Ridgewell 22/5/44; MIA {51+m} Bremen 3/2/45 w/Anderson; flak, cr Jagen, Ger?; 1KIA 8POW; MACR 12096. THE JOKER II.

42-102874 Del Ft Myers 14/4/44; Buckingham 15/6/45; 3036 BU Yuma 16/6/45; 3017 BU Hobbs 24/6/45; RFC Walnut Ridge 8/1/46.

42-102875 Del Ft Myers 14/4/44; 3036 BU Yuma 29/6/44; 3017 BU Hobbs 4/6/45; 591 BU Stockton 25/7/45; 3017 BU Hobbs 15/10/45; RFC Walnut Ridge 11/1/46.

42-102876 Del Ft Myers 14/4/44; Bismarck 20/4/44; Ft Myers 23/4/44; 2118 BU Buckingham 8/7/44; 2116 BU Laredo 8/9/44; RFC Walnut Ridge 5/1/46.

42-102877 Del Ft Myers 14/4/44; Gt Falls 18/4/44; 2118 BU Buckingham 21/6/44; 2126 BU Laredo 1/2/45; Recl Comp 3/1/46.

42-102878 Del Ft Myers 14/4/44; Dallas 21/4/44; RFC Walnut Ridge 5/1/46.

42-102879 Del Cheyenne 14/4/44; Hunter 28/4/44; Grenier 11/5/44; ass 347BS/99BG Tortorella 19/5/44; {100m} to depot 17/3/45; sal 2/8/45.

42-102880 Del Cheyenne 14/4/44; Lockburn 26/4/44; 2114 BU Lockburn 2/9/45; 4152 BU Lockburn 1/10/45; RFC Walnut Ridge 7/1/46.

42-102881 Del Cheyenne 14/4/44; Hendricks 26/4/44; 2137 BU Hendricks 17/11/44; 381 BU Marianna 21/1/45; 2137 BU Hendricks 31/1/45; 4139 BU Birmingham 5/2/45; 2137 BU Hendricks 8/2/45; RFC Kingman 9/11/45.

42-102882 Del Cheyenne 15/4/44; Gt Falls 23/4/44; 3030 BU Roswell 2/6/44; 3010 BU Williams 20/1/45; 4209 BU Des Moines 8/3/45; 3010 BU Williams 15/3/45; 3020 BU La Junta 20/4/45; 3508 BU Truax 4/6/45; 3017 BU Hobbs 1/8/45; RFC Walnur Ridge 3/1/46.

42-102883 Del Cheyenne 15/4/44; Hendricks 27/4/44; Oklahoma City 30/4/44; 2137 BU Hendricks 18/11/44; RFC Kingman 3/10/45.

42-102884 Del Ft Myers 15/4/44; Gt Falls 18/4/44; Ft Myers 24/4/44; 2126 BU Laredo 3/6/45; RFC Walnut Ridge 3/1/46.

42-102885 Del Ft Myers 15/4/44; Gt Falls 18/4/44; Ft Myers 22/4/44; 2126 BU Laredo 11/6/44; 4136 BU Tinker 4/5/45; 2126 BU Laredo 8/5/45; RFC Walnut Ridge 11/1/46.

42-102886 Del Ft Myers 15/4/44; Memphis 19/4/44; Buckingham 26/4/44; 3036 BU Yuma 20/6/44; 3017 BU Hobbs 8/6/45; RFC Walnut Ridge 29/12/45.

42-102887 Del Hobbs 15/4/44; Hunter 29/4/44; Dow Fd 15/5/44; ass 772DS/463BC Celone 20/5/44; MIA Ploesti 31/7/44 w/Martin; flak, cr Lubinca; MACR 7206.

42-102888 Del Hobbs 15/4/44; Gt Falls 18/4/44; Hobbs 20/4/44; 3017 BU Hobbs 16/1/45; Recl Comp 4/9/45.

42-102889 Del Cheyenne 15/4/44; Hunter 27/4/44; Dow Fd 15/5/44; ass 774BS/463BG Celone 20/5/44; MIA Bleckhammer 7/7/44 w/Lindbloom; cr Bradisch; MACR 6862.

42-102890 Del Cheyenne 15/4/44; Hobbs 27/4/44; 3017 BU Hobbs 25/6/44; 3000 BU Orange 3/4/45; 3017 BU Hobbs 4/5/45; 4202 BU Syracuse 21/5/45; 3017 BU Hobbs 25/5/45; 420 BU March 7/10/45; 3017 BU Hobbs 14/10/45; 3036 BU Yuma 15/10/46; 4160 BU Hobbs 5/1/46; RFC Walnut Ridge 7/1/46.

42-102891 Del Cheyenne 15/4/44; Hunter 27/4/44; Grenier 11/5/44; ass 340BS/97BG Amendola 28/5/44; MIA Vienna 7/2/45 w/Bauer; mech fault, cr Pettau; MACR 12141.

42-102892 Del Cheyenne 15/4/44; Hunter 25/4/44; Dow Fd 11/5/44; ass 775BS/463BG Celone 15/5/44; retUS 1103 BU Morrison 19/10/45; RFC Walnut Ridge 9/1/46.

42-102893 Del Cheyenne 16/4/44; slated 832BS/486BG [3R-H], Kingman 28/4/44; 4126 BU San Bernardino 30/12/44; 3018 BU Kingman 7/1/45; 3017 BU Hobbs 24/6/45; 1504 BU Fairfield 29/10/45; RFC Walnut Ridge 8/1/46.

42-102894 Del Hobbs 16/4/44; Lowry 24/4/44; Hobbs 29/4/44; 4136 BU Tinker 21/6/44; 3017 BU Hobbs 23/6/44; 3028 BU Luke 30/7/45; 3017 BU Hobbs 7/8/45; RFC Walnut Ridge 4/1/46.

42-102895 Del Hobbs 16/4/44; Gr Island 21/4/44; 3017 BU Hobbs, W/O 3/8/44.

42-102896 Del Roswell 16/4/44; slated 306BG CAP'N and HIS KIDS 17/4/44; 3018 BU Kingman 1/10/44; 4126 BU San Bernardino 17/1/45; 3018 BU Kingman 26/1/45; 3030 BU Roswell 22/6/45; 3541 BU Lincoln 23/8/45; 3030 BU Roswell 28/8/45; RFC Walnut Ridge 20/12/45.

42-102897 Del Roswell 16/4/44; Gt Falls 20/4/44; Roswell 24/4/44; 3030 BU Roswell 11/9/44; 555 BU Love Fd 13/9/44; 3030 BU Roswell 16/9/44; 3010 BU Williams 20/1/45; 3020 BU La Junta 21/4/45; 21124 BU Lockburn 25/6/45; 2137 BU Hendricks 14/10/45; RFC Walnut Ridge 8/1/46.

42-102898 Del Roswell 16/4/44; Gt Falls 25/4/44; 3030 BU Roswell 2/6/44; 3018 BU Kingman 1/10/44; 3017 BU Hobbs 27/6/45; RFC Walnut Ridge 2/1/46.

42-102899 Del Cheyenne 16/4/44; Kingman 28/4/44; 3018 BU Kingman, W/O 19/9/44; Recl Comp 16/10/44.

42-102900 Del Cheyenne 16/4/44; Hobbs 27/4/44; 3017 BU Hobbs 17/12/44; 3701 BU Amarillo 31/10/45; RFC Kingman 21/11/45.

42-102901 Del Cheyenne 16/4/44; Yuma 28/4/44; 2519 BU Ft Worth 15/9/45; 3017 BU Hobbs 7/10/45; 3701 BU Amarillo 31/10/45; RFC Kingman 21/11/45.

42-102902 Del Cheyenne 16/4/44; Yuma 28/4/44; 3017 BU Hobbs 4/6/45; 3701 BU Amarillo 4/10/45; RFC Kingman 28/12/45.

42-102903 Del Cheyenne 16/4/44; Lockburn 24/4/44; 2114 BU Lockburn 2/9/44; 4142 BU Daytona 6/4/45; Recl Comp 27/11/45.

42-102904 Del Cheyenne 16/4/44; Kingman 27/4/44; 3018 BU Kingman 23/3/45; 3017 BU Hobbs 25/6/45; 3701 BU Amarillo 7/10/45; RFC Kingman 27/11/45.

42-102905 Del Cheyenne 16/4/44; Kearney 7/5/44; Grenier 15/5/44; ass 748BS/457BG Glatton 16/5/44; MIA Politz 7/10/44 w/Jennings; flak, cr Jonkoping, Swed; 10INT; MACR 9774.

42-102906 Del Cheyenne 16/4/44; Hunter 29/4/44; Grenier 11/5/44; ass 416BS/99BG Tortorella 15/5/44; {68m} weather ship; taxi acc 23/4/45; sal.

42-102907 Del Cheyenne 16/4/44; Lockburn 29/4/44; 602 BU Stewart 24/8/45; 2114 BU Lockburn 26/8/45; 4102 BU Newark 8/11/45; 814 BU Stout 9/1/46; Recl Comp 9/4/46.

42-102908 Del Cheyenne 17/4/44; Hunter 28/4/44; Grenier 15/5/44; ass 96BS/2BG Amendola 23/5/44; MIA {33m} Oswiecim, Pol 20/8/44 w/Lambert; e/a, cr Balassog; MACR 11699.

42-102909 Del Cheyenne 17/4/44; Hunter 28/4/44; Grenier 13/5/44; ass 775BS/463BG Celone 20/5/44; MIA Ruhland 23/3/44 w/Sander; flak, f/l Russia; crew ret.

42-102910 Del Cheyenne 17/4/44; Lockburn 24/4/44; 3017 BU Hobbs 2/6/45; 3036 BU Yuma 15/7/45; 3026 BU Luke 22/8/45; 3017 BU Hobbs 16/10/45; 34701 BU Amarillo 21/10/45; RFC Kingman 6/12/45.

42-102911 Del Cheyenne 17/4/44; Kearney 2/5/44; Grenier 15/5/44; ass 613BS/401BG [IN-L] Deenethorpe 30/5/44; sal 2 SAD 3/7/44.

42-102912 Del Cheyenne 17/4/44; Hobbs 27/4/44; 3017 BU Hobbs 16/1/45; 3010 BU Williams 22/3/45; 3017 BU Hobbs 30/3/45; 3701 BU Amarillo 7/10/45; RFC Kingman 21/11/45.

42-102913 Del Cheyenne 17/4/44; Hunter 29/4/44; Grenier 15/5/44; ass 32BS/301BG Lucera 25/5/44; MIA Wiener Neudorf 26/7/44 w/Sullivan; e/a, cr Wiener Neustadt; MACR 7124.

42-102914 Del Cheyenne 17/4/44; Hunter 28/4/44;

INDIVIDUAL B-17 HISTORIES **223**

Grenier 14/5/44; ass 340BS/97BG Amendola 23/5/44; MIA Ploesti 10/8/44 w/Abrams; flak, cr Ploesti; MACR 7194.
42-102915 Del Cheyenne 17/4/44; Hunter 1/5/44; Dow Fd 10/5/44; ass 419BS/301BG Lucera 26/5/44; MIA Wiener Neudorf 26/7/44 w/Martin; e/a, cr Langewung; 7KIA 3POW; MACR 7123.
42-102916 Del Cheyenne 17/4/44; Hunter 29/4/44; Grenier 11/5/44; ass 774BS/463BG Celone 17/5/44; MIA Munich 8/7/44 w/Bodine; flak, cr Witselsdorf; MACR 7320.
42-102917 Del Cheyenne 17/4/44; Kearney 5/2/44; Grenier 21/5/44; ass 612BS/401BG [SC-E] Deenethorpe 30/5/44; MIA Dessau 20/7/44 w/Frederick; flak, cr Numansdorp, Hol; 9POW; MACR 7546.
42-102918 Del Cheyenne 17/4/44; Hunter 29/4/44; Grenier 14/5/44; ass 342BS/97BG Amendola 26/5/44; first 15AF a/c to land in Russia on shuttle mission 2/6/44; MIA Munich 19/7/44 w/Williams; flak, fire and tail broke off, cr Ascheim; MACR 6688; IDIOT'S DELIGHT.
42-102919 Del Cheyenne 17/4/44; Gt Falls 22/4/44; 3030 BU Roswell 2/6/44; 3010 BU Williams 20/1/45; 3020 BU La Junta 30/4/45; 2114 BU Lockburn 25/6/45; 2137 BU Hendricks 14/10/45; RFC Walnut Ridge 5/1/46.
42-102920 Del Cheyenne 17/4/44; Lockburn 29/4/44; Scott 4/5/44; Lockburn 10/5/44; 2114 BU Lockburn 23/1/45 for survey work.
42-102921 Del Cheyenne 18/4/44; Hunter 10/5/44; Dow Fd 30/5/44; ass 325BS/92BG [NV-K] Podington 8/6/44; sal 9AF Germany 25/10/45. THE DUCHESS.
42-102922 Del Cheyenne 18/4/44; Hunter 1/5/44; Dow Fd 11/5/44; ass 817BS/483BG Sterparone 27/5/44; retUS 1103 BU Morrison 19/9/45; RFC Walnut Ridge 18/12/45.
42-102923 Del Cheyenne 18/4/44; Hunter 28/4/44; Dow Fd 17/5/44; ass 817BS/483BG Sterparone 28/5/44; MIA Memmingen, Ger 18/7/44 w/Rickey; e/a, cr Kempten; 5KIA 5POW: MACR 6979. BARAZ TWINS II.
42-102924 Del Cheyenne 18/4/44; Hunter 29/4/44; Dow Fd 14/5/44; ass 774BS/463BS Celone 17/5/44; MIA Novi Sad, Yugo 30/8/44 w/Green; flak, left wing afire, eight chutes seen, cr Mostar, Yugo; MACR 8731.
42-102925 Del Cheyenne 18/4/44; Hunter 2/5/44; Dow Fd 17/5/44; ass 347BS/99BG Tortorella 20/5/44; b/d {57m} Ploesti 9/7/44 w/Henry; one engine out, seven baled; P and rest of crew put out fire and fly home; sal 23/9/44; from repair 4/10/44; c/t/o 9/12/44 and destroyed.
42-102926 Del Cheyenne 18/4/44; Hendricks 1/5/44; Hondo 2/5/44; Hendricks 5/5/44; 225 BU Rapid City 12/9/44; 2137 BU Hendricks 13/9/44; RFC Kingman 22/10/45.
42-102927 Del Cheyenne 19/4/44; Hunter 27/4/44; Grenier 11/5/44; ass 815BS/483BG Sterparone 17/5/44; MIA Memmingen, Ger 18/7/44 w/Vandendries; e/a, cr Ravensburg; 4KIA 6POW: MACR 6980. BUNKY.
42-102928 Del Cheyenne 19/4/44; Hobbs 1/5/44; 3017 BU Hobbs 16/1/45; 3701 BU Amarillo 7/10/45; RFC Kingman 27/11/45.
42-102929 Del Cheyenne 19/4/44; Hunter 27/4/44; Grenier 15/5/44; ass 352BS/301BG Lucera 26/5/44; MIA Wiener Neudorf 26/7/44 w/Howell; e/a, cr Wiener Neustadt; 8KIA 2POW; MACR 7143.
42-102930 Del Cheyenne 19/4/44; Hunter 27/4/44; Grenier 12/5/44; 4121 BU Kelly 17/3/45; 4117 BU Robins 17/5/45; 1 BU Bolling 27/8/45; 4104 BU Rome 1/10/45; RFC Altus 5/11/45.
42-102931 Del Cheyenne 19/4/44; Hunter 4/5/44; Dow Fd 16/5/44; ass 731BS/452BG Deopham Green 20/5/44; MIA Saarbrücken 9/11/44 w/Meyers; flak, cr Channel; 9KIA; MACR 10345. FIKLEBITCH.
42-102932 Del Cheyenne 19/4/44; Hunter 30/4/44; Grenier 12/5/44; ass 96BS/2BG Amendola 23/5/44; MIA {24m} Vienna 16/7/44 w/Harrington; flak hit nose & #3, cr Strasshof; three chutes seen; MACR 6904.
42-102933 Del Cheyenne 19/4/44; Kearney 22/5/44; Grenier 27/5/44; ass 546BS/384BG [BK-Q] Grafton Underwood 8/6/44; b/d Merseburg 12/12/44 w/?; c/l Continent; MACR 11340. QUEENIE.
42-102934 Del Cheyenne 19/4/44; Kearney 2/5/44; Grenier 15/5/44; ass 350BS/100BG [LN-W] Thorpe Abbotts 16/5/44; sal 13/7/44.
42-102935 Del Cheyenne 19/4/44; Hunter 4/5/44; Grenier 15/5/44; ass 331BS/94BG [QE-L] Rougham 20/5/44; retUS Bradley 21/7/45; Romulus 30/7/45; 4185 BU Independence 11/10/45; RFC Kingman 14/12/45.
42-102936 Del Cheyenne 20/4/44; Kearney 16/5/44; Grenier 27/5/44; ass 92BG Podington 30/5/44; tran 390BG Framlingham 1/6/44; b/d Ausum, Ger 28/8/44 w/?; mid air coll w/42-97182; sal 27/8/44.
42-102937 Del Cheyenne 20/4/44; Kearney 16/5/44; Grenier 27/5/44; ass 412BS/95BG [QW-E] Horham 30/5/44; non operation crash Duxford A/fd, UK 19/7/44 w/Sasser; 14KIA 2WIA; sal 21/7/44. READY FREDDIE.
42-102938 Del Cheyenne 20/4/44; Hunter 2/5/44; Grenier 20/5/44; ass 340BS/97BG Tortorella 24/5/44; hit by w/44-9406 in landing accident 2/1/45; both sal.
42-102939 Del Cheyenne 20/4/44; Hunter 1/5/44; Dow Fd 15/5/44; ass 483BS Sterparone 20/5/44; tran 340BS/97BG Tortorella 17/7/44; MIA Vienna 16/3/44 w/Kelley; coll w/44-6757, ditched Adriatic; 7KIA 3RTD; MACR 10353.
42-102940 Del Gt Falls 26/4/44; Dorval (Canada) 28/4/44; ass RAF {HB789} 214Sq [BU-Q]; SOC 11/3/47.
42-102941 Del Gt Falls 27/4/44; Dorval (Canada) 29/4/44; ass RAF {HB790} 214Sq [BU-B]; c/l Woodbridge A/fd, UK 15/1/45; SOC 11/3/47.
42-102942 Del Bolling 21/4/44; Minneapolis 20/4/44; Bolling 28/4/44; 4136 BU Tinker 1/11/44; 1502 BU Mather 25/11/44; 4112 BU Olmstead 17/1/45; 1 BU Bolling 19/7/45; 64 BU Andrews 20/6/45; 326 BU McDill 10/7/45; Pacific 24/2/46; Rio de Janiero 7/4/48; Panama 20/4/48; Recl Comp 29/12/48.
42-102943 Del Cheyenne 21/4/44; Hunter 1/5/44; Grenier 19/5/44; ass 352BS/301BG Lucera 26/5/44; MIA Memmingen 18/7/44 w/Wilson; e/a, cr Bozen; 1KIA 9POW; MACR 7310.
42-102944 Del Cheyenne 21/4/44; Hunter 4/5/44; Grenier 16/5/44; ass 414BS/97BG Amendola 24/5/44; MIA Bleckhammer 26/4/44 w/?; MACR 8934. THE OLD LADY.
42-102945 Del Cheyenne 21/4/44; Kearney 3/5/44; Grenier 27/5/44; ass 358BS/303BG [VK-M] Molesworth 2/6/44; f/l Continent 8/1/45 w/?; sal 10/2/45. SWEET PEA.
42-102946 Del Cheyenne 21/4/44; Kearney 2/5/44; Grenier 21/5/44; ass 562BS/388BG Knettishall 23/5/44; MIA Krzesinki 29/5/44 w/Callahan; flak, cr Eilenburg, Ger; 10POW; MACR 5315.
42-102947 Del Cheyenne 21/4/44; Kearney 2/5/44; Grenier 26/5/44; ass 613BS/401BG [IN-S] 27/5/44; retUS Bradley 8/6/45; 4168 BU Sth Plains 12/6/45; RFC Kingman 26/11/45.
42-102948 Del Cheyenne 21/4/44; Kearney 2/5/44; Grenier 21/5/44; ass 749BS/457BG Glatton 23/5/44; MIA Magdeburg 28/9/44 w/Clarke; e/a, cr Buckau, Ger; 2KIA 7POW; MACR 9775. THE DENVER BANDIT.
42-102949 Del Cheyenne 21/4/44; Kearney 2/5/44; Grenier 15/5/44; ass 457BG Glatton 30/6/44; tran 509BS/351BG [RQ-G] Polebrook 1/7/44; 510BS; MIA {19m} Augsburg 19/7/44 w/Konecbeck; e/a, cr Stossberg, Ger?; 7KIA 2POW; MACR 7557.
42-102950 Del Cheyenne 21/4/44; Hunter 4/5/44; Dow Fd 17/5/44; ass 339BS/96BG [QJ-S] Snetterton 19/5/44; dest by e/a ar Poltava 21/6/44; sal 1/7/44.
42-102951 Del Cheyenne 21/4/44; Kearney 6/5/44; Grenier 27/5/44; ass 334BS/95BG [BG-Q] Horham 30/5/44; MIA Berlin 3/2/45 w/Morris; b/d, cr Den Berg Texel, Hol; 7KIA 1POW 1MIA; MACR 12048.
42-102952 Del Cheyenne 22/4/44; Kearney 7/5/44; Grenier 24/5/44; ass 511BS/351BG [DS-H] Polebrook 31/5/44; MIA {29m} Merseburg 28/7/44 w/Long; e/a, cr Frankfurt; 3KIA 6POW; MACR 7817.
42-102953 Del Cheyenne 22/4/44; Kearney 2/5/44; Grenier 13/5/44; ass 563BS/388BG Knettishall 16/5/44; MIA Magdeburg 28/9/44 w/Lord; mid air coll w/43-38404, cr Merseburg; 7KIA 2POW; MACR 9380. SHY ANN.
42-102954 Del Cheyenne 22/4/44; Kearney 3/5/44; Dow Fd 1/6/44; ass 748BS/457BG Glatton 13/6/44; b/d Cologne 3/1/45 w/?; f/l Continent, sal 9/2/45.
42-102955 Del Cheyenne 22/4/44; Kearney 2/5/44; Dow Fd 20/5/44; ass 510BS/351BG [TU-P] Polebrook 23/5/44; 509BS [RQ-L]; b/d Plauen 19/3/45 w/?; f/l Continent, sal; {66m} RetUS Bradley 29/5/45; 4168 BU Sth Plains 1/6/45; RFC Kingman 19/12/45. CHATTERBOX II.
42-102956 Del Cheyenne 22/4/44; Kearney 7/5/44; Grenier 21/5/44; ass 568BS/390BG Framlingham 23/5/44 GIRL OF MY DREAMS; MIA Cologne 14/1/45 w/Goodrich; e/a, cr Vietnitz, Ger; 2KIA 7POW; MACR 11726. DOC'S FLYING CIRCUS.
42-102957 Del Cheyenne 22/4/44; Kearney 3/5/44; Grenier 21/5/44; ass 358BS/303BG Molesworth 23/4/44; tran 612BS/401BG [SC-F] Deenethorpe 1/6/44; c/l Leicester A/fd 12/9/44; sal. FEARLESS FOSDICK.
42-102958 Del Cheyenne 22/4/44; Kearney 6/5/44; Dow Fd 21/5/44; ass 350BS/100BG [LN-Z] Thorpe Abbotts 23/4/44; MIA Berlin 3/2/45 w/Beck; flak, cr Berlin; 7KIA 2POW; MACR 12047.
42-102959 Del Cheyenne 22/4/44; Kearney 7/5/44; Grenier 25/7/44; ass 544BS/384BG [SU-D] Grafton Underwood 4/6/44; c/l Ford RN A/fd, UK 7/8/44; sal AFSC 18/8/44.
42-102960 Del Cheyenne 22/4/44; Kearney 7/5/44; Grenier 21/5/44; ass 359BS/303BG Molesworth 6/6/44; MIA Creil, Fr 23/7/44 w/Morgan; ditched Channel; 10RTD.
42-102961 Del Cheyenne 22/4/44; Kearney 7/5/44; Dow Fd 6/6/44; ass 526BS/379BG Kimbolton 28/6/44; MIA French Noball site 17/7/44 w/Barish; flak, cr Channel; 9KIA; MACR 7839.
42-102962 Del Cheyenne 22/4/44; Kearney 3/5/44; Grenier 1/5/44; ass 365BS/305BG Chelveston 23/4/44; MIA Karlsruhe 9/8/44 w/Bowling; e/a, cr Unzhurst, Ger; 4KIA 5POW; MACR 8066.
42-102963 Del Cheyenne 23/4/44; Kearney 7/5/44; Grenier 21/5/44; ass 452BG Deopham Green 23/5/44; dest by e/a at Poltava 21/6/44; sal 2/7/44.
42-102964 Del Cheyenne 23/4/44; Kearney 6/5/44; Grenier 21/5/44; ass 366BS/305BG [KY-M] Chelveston 2/6/44; tran 351BG Polebrook 23/4/45; retUS Bradley 13/6/45; 4168 BU Sth Plains 18/6/45; RFC Kingman 4/12/45. MISS YVONNE.

42-102965 Del Cheyenne 23/4/44; Kearney 6/5/44; Dow Fd 23/5/44; ass 457BG Glatton 24/5/44; MIA Berlin 24/5/44 w/Stafford; flak, ditched Nth Sea; 10 RTD.

42-102966 Del Cheyenne 23/4/44; Kearney 7/5/44; Dow Fd 21/5/44; ass 534BS/381BG [GD-F] Ridgewell 23/5/44; {102m} RetUS Bradley 9/6/45; 4168 BU Sth Plains 14/6/45; RFC Kingman 18/12/45. AVENGRESS II.

42-102967 Del Cheyenne 23/4/44; Kearney 9/5/44; Dow Fd 21/5/44; ass 569BS/390BG [CC-A] Framlingham 25/5/44; b/d Chemnitz 6/2/45 w/?; f/l Sth France; sal 11/3/45. DIPLOMAT.

42-102968 Del Cheyenne 23/4/44; Hunter 4/5/44; Grenier 18/5/44; ass 534BS/381BG [GD-N] Ridgewell 27/5/44; {60m} b/d Cologne 10/11/44 w/Schilling; f/l Brussels; sal & re-ass 67 Tac Rec Gp; VIA PANOLA EXPRESS.

42-102969 Del Cheyenne 24/4/44; Kearney 6/5/44; Grenier 24/5/44; ass 367BS/306BG [GY-X] Thurleigh 5/6/44; MIA Brux 12/9/44 w/Barr; e/a, cr Brodowin?; 1KIA 8POW; MACR 8836. METHUSELAH 989 YEARS.

42-102970 Del Cheyenne 24/4/44; Kearney 6/5/44; Dow Fd 21/5/44; ass 561BS/388BG Knettishall 23/5/44; retUS Cincinnati 4/11/45; RFC Walnut Ridge 4/1/46. GROUPE AND HOPE.

42-102971 Del Cheyenne 24/4/44; Hunter 4/5/44; Grenier 19/5/44; ass 508BS/351BG [YB-J] Polebrook 29/5/44; MIA {25m} Brandenburg 6/8/44 w/Pattison; flak & e/a, cr Werder, Ger; 3KIA 6POW; MACR 7586.

42-102972 Del Cheyenne 24/4/44; Kearney 6/5/44; Dow Fd 21/5/44; ass 571BS/390BG [FC-F] Framlingham 26/5/44 HEAVENLY CENT; MIA Hannover 14/3/45 w/Creaseman; mid air coll w/43-37831, cr Alfeld, Ger; 9KIA; MACR 13025. BOSTON BLACKIE.

42-102973 Del Cheyenne 24/4/44; Kearney 6/5/44; Grenier 13/5/44; ass 457BG Glatton 16/5/44; b/d sal 2 SAD 26/6/44.

42-102974 Del Cheyenne 24/4/44; Hunter 4/5/44; Dow Fd 17/5/44; ass 338BS/96BG Snetterton 19/6/44; tran 379BG Kimbolton 26/5/44; retUS Bradley 3/7/45; 4168 BU Sth Plains 28/8/45; RFC Kingman 7/11/45. HELLCAT AGNES.

42-102975 Del Cheyenne 25/4/44; Kearney 3/5/44; Grenier 21/5/44; ass 369BS/306BG [WW-F] Thurleigh 6/6/44; MIA Dresden 14/2/45 w/Hanley; flak, cr Nachtsheim, Ger; 9POW; MACR 12324. VERNA E.

42-102976 Del Cheyenne 25/4/44; Hunter 4/5/44; Grenier 29/6/44; ass 365BS/305BG Chelveston 6/8/44; MIA Merseburg 24/8/44 w/Buck; flak, cr Wessmar, Ger?; 7KIA 2POW; MACR 8205.

42-102977 Del Cheyenne 25/4/44; Kearney 7/5/44; Dow Fd 21/5/44; ass 349BS/100BG [XR-L] Thorpe Abbotts 23/5/44; b/d French Noball site 17/7/44 w/?; c/l Friston; sal 19/7/44.

42-102978 Del Cheyenne 25/4/44; Kearney 4/6/44; Grenier 17/6/44; ass 413BS/96BG [MZ-D] Snetterton 21/6/44; sal 7/9/44; retUS Bradley 3/7/45; 4168 BU Sth Plains 6/7/45; RFC Kingman 14/12/45.

B-17G-DL

42-106984 Del Denver 17/1/44; McDill 30/1/44; ass 816BS/483BG Sterparone 12/3/44; tran 346BS/99BG Tortorella 31/3/44; {71m} 5th BW HQ 8/10/44 as hack for Gen Charles Lawrence; retUS 902 BU Orlando 4/5/45; 64 BU Andrews 13/6/45; 1377 BU Grenier 5/7/45; 2114 BU Lockburn 17/7/45; Recl Comp 9/4/46. GLITTERING GAL.

42-106985 Del Denver 17/1/44; McDill 7/2/44; Grenier 15/2/44; ass 379BG Kimbolton 18/2/44; tran 749BS/457BG Glatton 2/3/44; sal 27/4/44. LA LEGENDE.

42-106986 Del Denver 18/1/44; McDill 23/1/44; Grenier 5/2/44; ass 418BS/100BG [LD-B] Thorpe Abbotts 28/2/44; MIA Weisbaden 10/11/44 w/Lundquist; flak, cr Weisbaden; 1KIA 8POW; MACR 10356.

42-106987 Del Denver 18/1/44; McDill 5/2/44; Grenier 5/2/44; ass 816BS/483BG Sterparone 9/3/44; tran 348BS/99BG Tortorella 31/3/44; {82m} sal 30/11/45.

42-106988 Del Denver 18/1/44; McDill 24/1/44; Morrison 6/2/44; ass 816BS/483BG Sterparone 9/3/44; tran 347BS/99BG Tortorella 31/3/44; MIA {11m} Wiener Neustedt 10/5/44 w/Waltermire; e/a, #4 knocked out, then two morer e/a, cr Allhau; 9-10 chutes seen; MACR 4729.

42-106989 Del Cheyenne 19/1/44; McDill 14/2/44; Grenier 24/2/44; ass 563BS/388BG Knettishall 28/2/44; retUS Bradley 3/7/45; 4168 BU Sth Plains 16/8/45; Recl Comp 6/5/46. MISS ADVENTURE.

42-106990 Del Denver 19/1/44; McDill 29/1/44; Grenier 10/2/44; ass 816BS/483BG Sterparone, but ditched Atlantic en route 15/3/44 w/Coombs.

42-106991 Del Denver 19/1/44; McDill 29/1/44; Morrison 1/3/44; ass 817BS/483BG Sterparone 12/3/44; tran 347BS/99BG Tortorella 31/3/44; MIA {22m} Ploesti 18/5/44 w/McClain; flak, cr Mostar; MACR 5066.

42-106992 Del Denver 19/1/44; Dalhart 4/2/44; Presque 23/3/44; ass 612BS/401BG [SC-D] Deenethorpe 16/4/44; f/l Continent 19/4/45; sal; retUS Bradley 11/7/45; 4185 BU Independence 12/7/45; RFC Kingman 25/12/45. "BABY LU".

42-106993 Del Cheyenne 21/1/44; Kearney 22/1/44; Grenier 25/2/44; ass 336BS/95BG [ET-P] Horham 13/3/44; retUS Bradley 26/6/45; 4168 BU Sth Plains 2/7/45; RFC Kingman 25/12/45. PRETTY BABY.

42-106994 Del Cheyenne 21/1/44; Gr Island 18/2/44; Grenier 22/2/44; ass 532BS/381BG [VE-K] Ridgewell 3/4/44; MIA {37+m} Altenbeken 26/11/44 w/Smith; flak, cr Apeldoorn, Hol; 3KIA 6POW; MACR 11205. LITTLE GUY.

42-106995 Del Cheyenne 21/1/44; McDill 3/2/44; Morrison 1/3/44; ass 816BS/483BG Sterparone 10/3/44; tran 348BS/99BG Tortorella 31/3/44; MIA {27m} Ploesti 23/6/44 w/Brazier; e/a, cr Balsh; MACR 6076. ANTHONY J.

42-106996 Del Cheyenne 21/1/44; McDill 29/1/44; Morrison 5/3/44; ass 483BG Sterparone 13/3/44; tran 348BS/99BG Tortorella 31/3/44; {62m} weather/cargo ship from 11/10/44; retUS 1103 BU Morrison 20/10/45; RFC Walnut Ridge 2/1/46.

42-106997 Del Cheyenne 21/1/44; Gr Island 3/2/44; Morrison 9/3/44; ass 816BS/483BG Sterparone 13/3/44; tran 348BS/99BG Tortorella 31/3/44; MIA {33m} Bleckhammer 7/7/44 w/Hackney; mid air coll w/42-32036, shearing off '997 tail, cr near Manfredonia; 10KIA. BLONDIE.

42-106998 Del Cheyenne 21/1/44; Gr Island 29/1/44; ass 379BG Kimbolton 28/2/44; tran 751BS/457BG Glatton 2/3/44; MIA Merseburg 2/11/44 w/Bow; e/a, cr Annarode, Ger; 5KIA 4POW; MACR 10322. PAPER DOLL.

42-106999 Del Cheyenne 21/1/44; Gr Island 2/2/44; Morrison 1/3/44; ass 840BS/483BG Sterparone 9/3/44; mid air coll w/44-6288 4/2/45; landed but sal. PECK'S BAD BOYS.

42-107000 Del Cheyenne 21/1/44; Gr Island 10/2/44; Morrison 6/3/44; ass 817BS/483BG Sterparone 9/3/44; tran 347BS/99BG Tortorella 31/3/44; MIA {7m} Ploesti 3/12/44 w/Petrovkovich; e/a, cr Titu, six chutes seen, one on fire; MACR 3972. PRINCESS NO NO.

42-107001 Del Tulsa 23/1/44; Dow Fd 5/2/44; Grenier 26/2/44; ass 751BS/457BG Glatton 2/3/44; sal 2 SAD 15/6/44.

42-107002 Del Tulsa 23/1/44; Kearney 16/2/44; ass 358BS/303BG [VK-A] Molesworth 24/3/44; MIA Berlin 21/6/44 w/Morningstar; flak, cr Techin, Ger?; 9POW; MACR 6538. MAIRZY DOATS.

42-107003 Del Tulsa 23/1/44; Kearney 16/2/44; Grenier 17/2/44; ass 710BS/447BG Rattlesden 12/3/44; hit by debris from another a/c on non op flight 21/2/45, sal. BOUNCING BABY.

42-107004 Del Tulsa 23/1/44; Kearney 14/2/44; ass 525BS/379BG [FR-S] Kimbolton 23/3/44; b/d Frankfurt 5/11/44 w/?; sal 2 SAD 7/11/44.

42-107005 Del Tulsa 23/1/44; Kearney 14/2/44; Grenier 12/2/44; ass 511BS/351BG [DS-Q] Polebrook 24/3/44; caught fire on hardstand 12/8/44; {26m} sal 2 SAD 14/8/44. LUCILLE BALL II.

42-107006 Del Cheyenne 24/1/44; McDill 18/2/44; Morrison 6/3/44; ass 815BS/483BG Sterparone 16/3/44; tran 96BS/2BG Amendola 31/3/44; MIA {{3m} Bleckhammer 17/10/44 w/Peart; mid air coll w/44-6379, cr Malacky; nine chutes seen; MACR 9208. OLD BIRD.

42-107007 Del Cheyenne 24/1/44; Kearney 15/2/44; Presque Is 2/3/44; ass 351BS/100BG [EP-B] Thorpe Abbotts 6/3/44; MIA Merseburg 29/7/44 w/Greiner; e/a, ditched Nth Sea; 1KIA 8POW; MACR 7815. SHE-HAS TA.

42-107008 Del Cheyenne 24/1/44; McDill 14/2/44; Morrison 7/3/44; ass 816BS/483BG Sterparone 10/3/44; MIA Memmingen 18/7/44 w/Maj Hildreth; e/a, cr Kempten; 10POW; MACR 6953. FLAK OFF LIMITS.

42-107009 Del Cheyenne 25/1/44; Kearney 16/2/44; Grenier 10/3/44; ass 613BS/401BG [IN-F] Deenethorpe; MIA Hamburg 6/11/44 w/Hillestad; flak, cr Enschede, Hol; 9POW; MACR 10349. LADY JANE.

42-107010 Del Tulsa 25/1/44; Kearney 2/3/44; ass 385BG Gt Ashfield 3/3/44; tran 569BS/390BG [CC-E] Framlingham 8/3/44 GLORIA ANN II; c/t/o at Parham, UK for Fulda 27/12/44; 9KIA; sal. CLOSE CROP.

42-107011 Del Tulsa 25/1/44; Kearney 16/2/44; ass 418BS/100BG [LD-T] Thorpe Abbotts 7/3/44; bomb from above a/c killed one crew 8/5/44, rest RTD; MIA Politiz 29/5/44 w/Williams; e/a, cr Torgau, Ger; 4KIA 6POW; MACR 5237 & 4214.

42-107012 Del Tulsa 26/1/44; Kearney 1/3/44; ass 407BS/92BG Podington 22/3/44; MIA Lyon-Bron A/fd 30/4/44 w/Campbell; e/a, cr Lyon; 1EVD 6KIA 3POW; MACR 4466.

42-107013 Del Tulsa 26/1/44; Grenier 2/3/44; ass 612BS/401BG [SC-O] Deenethorpe 7/3/44; tran 423BS/306BG Thurleigh 14/3/44; c/l base and sal 28/3/44.

42-107014 Del Cheyenne 26/1/44; Kearney 15/2/44; ass 527BS/379BG [FO-K] Kimbolton 30/3/44; MIA Zeitz 30/11/44 w/ Puckett; flak, cr Zeitz; 9POW; MACR 11057. LUCY.

42-107015 Del Cheyenne 26/1/44; Presque Is 3/2/44; ass 750BS/457BG Glatton 3/3/44; MIA Berlin 21/6/44 w/Krumm; mech fault, c/l Rinkaby, Swed; 9INT; MACR 6005 (left 29/6/45). RetUS Bradley 14/7/45; 4185 BU Independence 25/10/45; RFC Kingman 14/12/45.

42-107016 Del Cheyenne 26/1/44; McDill 2/2/44;

Above: B-17G-35-BO 42-107006, assigned to the 96th Bomb Squadron, 2nd Bomb Group, was destroyed in a mid-air collision with another B-17G. (USAAF)

Morrison 7/3/44; slated 385BG, ass 816BS/483BG Sterparone 10/3/44; tran 348BS/99BG Tortorella 31/3/44; MIA {41m} Turin 24/7/44 w/Ernst; flak, cr Saluzzo; 4EVD, ret 10/44; MACR 7032.

42-107017 Del Cheyenne 27/1/44; Kearney 1/2/44; Presque Is 5/3/44; ass 560BS/388BG Knettishall 6/3/44; MIA Brussels 25/5/44 w/Warren; flak, cr Poix, Fr; 2EVD 2KIA 6POW; MACR 5262.

42-107018 Del Cheyenne 27/1/44; Kearney 17/2/44; Presque Is 5/3/44; ass 535BS/381BG [MS-U] Ridgewell 25/3/44; retUS Bradley 9/6/45; 4168 BU Sth Plains 14/6/45; {72+m} RFC Kingman 7/12/45. LOS ANGELES CITY LIMITS.

42-107019 Del Cheyenne 27/1/44; Kearney 13/2/44; Presque Is 29/2/44; ass 333BS/94BG Rougham 12/3/44; MIA Berlin 18/4/44 w/Schommer; e/a, cr Freisach, Aus; 2KIA 8POW; MACR 4163. WABBIT...WHAT'S UP DOC?

42-107020 Del Cheyenne 27/1/44; Kearney 14/2/44; Grenier 7/3/44; ass 398BG Nuthampstead 11/3/44; tran 708BS/447BG Rattlesden 12/3/44; MIA Brux 12/5/44 w/Wright; e/a, cr Ailingen, Ger; 9KIA 1POW; MACR 4773.

42-107021 Del Tulsa 31/1/44; Kearney 5/2/44; ass 710BS/447BG Rattlesden 3/3/44; MIA Augsburg 13/4/44 w/Thornbury; flak, cr Weilheim, Ger; MACR 4297.

42-107022 Del Tulsa 31/1/44; Kearney 3/2/44; Presque Is 17/2/44; ass 338BS/96BG [BX-F] Snetterton 14/3/44; MIA Münster 5/10/44 w/Berve; flak, cr Roxel, Ger?; 5KIA 4POW; MACR 9514.

42-107023 Del Tulsa 31/1/44; Kearney 10/2/44; Grenier 6/3/44; ass 532BS/381BG Ridgewell 25/3/44; MIA {2+m} Ludwigshafen 27/5/44 w/Stuart; e/a, cr Champfleury, Fr; 3EVD 1KIA 5POW; MACR 5182.

42-107024 Del Tulsa 31/1/44; Gr Island 25/2/44; Presque Is 2/3/44; ass 350BS/100BG [LN-B] Thorpe Abbotts 6/3/44; MIA Sottevast 28/4/44 w/Col Rob Kelly; flak, cr Croix Jacob, Fr; 6KIA 5POW; MACR 4234.

42-107025 Del Tulsa 31/1/44; Grenier 5/3/44; ass 711BS/447BG Rattlesden 7/3/44; 710BS; c/l 29/1/45; sal 1/2/45.

42-107026 Del Tulsa 1/2/44; Presque Is 21/2/44; ass 751BS/457BG Glatton 4/3/44; b/d Zeitz 30/11/44 w/?; f/l France; MACR 11150. HAM TRAMACK MAMA.

42-107027 Del Tulsa 1/2/44; Grenier 27/2/44; ass 401BS/91BG Bassingbourn 7/4/44 ANNE, then BLOODY BUCKET; 322BS [LG-Y/X]; 324BS [DF-Y]; b/d Dresden 14/2/45 w/Fuller (WIA); f/l Denain, Fr 20/2/45; (first B-17 repaired on Continent & ret to group); after VE-Day tran Istres, S. France w/384BG and carried POWs and displaced persons from N.Africa, adorned with airline type strips on fuselage; {125+m} sal 9AF 31/12/45. HIKIN' FOR HOME.

42-107028 Del Tulsa 1/2/44; Grenier 10/2/44; ass 338BS/96BG [BX-F] Snetterton 24/3/44; tran 358BS/303BG [VK-I] Molesworth 8/4/44; MIA Ruhland oil 28/5/44 w/Determan; e/a, cr Leipzig; 7KIA 3POW; MACR 5340.

42-107029 Del Tulsa 1/2/44; Kearney 7/2/44; ass 710BS/447BG Rattlesden 3/3/44; 708BG; MIA Merseburg 2/11/44 w/Johnson; e/a, cr Gross Himmlage, Ger; 1KIA 8POW; MACR 10313. TAILWIND.

42-107030 Del Tulsa 2/2/44; Grenier 5/3/44; ass 322BS/91BG [LG-T] Bassingbourn 25/3/44; MIA {54m} Le Manoir RR bridge, Fr 13/8/44 w/Smith; flak, cr Epreville, Fr; 5EVD 1KIA 3POW; MACR 7898. FIFINELLA.

42-107031 Del Tulsa 2/2/44; Grenier 5/3/44; ass 96BG Snetterton 13/3/44; 550BS/385BG Gt Ashfield 12/3/44; MIA Munich 13/7/44 w/Turner; flak, f/l Dubendorf, Switz; 10INT; MACR 7490. RetUS 1103 BU Morrison 22/8/45; RFC Walnut Ridge 18/12/45.

42-107032 Del Tulsa 2/2/44; Gr Island 13/4/44; Dow Fd 17/4/44; ass 398BG Nuthampstead 22/4/44; tran 367BS/306BG Thurleigh 12/5/44; MIA Stettin 13/5/44 w/Hanson; flak, ditched Nth Sea; 10RTD. ANY TIME ANNIE.

42-107033 Del Tulsa 2/2/44; Grenier 7/3/44; ass 324BS/91BG [DF-Z/D] Bassingbourn 24/3/44; 322BS [LG-D]; MIA {58m} Ludwigshafen 5/9/44 w/Kelley; mech fault (#3 out), cr nr Bazailles, Fr; 1KIA 1POW 7RTD; MACR 8595. MY BABY. (Years later Kelley returned to France when ship was dug up.)

42-107034 Del Tulsa 3/2/44; Dow Fd 18/4/44; ass 398BG Nuthampstead 1/5/44; 749BS/457BG Glatton 3/5/44; b/d Stuttgart 9/12/44 w/?; c/l Continent, sal 2 SAD. RAMPANT PANSY.

42-107035 Del Tulsa 3/2/44; Dow Fd 24/4/44; ass 398BG Nuthampstead 30/4/44; tran 548BS/385BG Gt Ashfield 6/5/44; MIA Bremen 26/9/44 w/Lundsberg; flak, cr Wesermünde, Ger; MACR 10204.

42-107036 Del Tulsa 3/2/44; Dow Fd 15/4/44; ass 398BG Nuthampstead 3/5/44; tran 730BS/452BG Deopham Green 6/5/44; MIA Berlin 21/6/44 w/Sorensen; flak, f/l Rinkaby, Swed; 10INT; MACR 6237; retUS Bradley 30/7/45; 4185 BU Independence 4/8/45; RFC Kingman 22/12/45. BIG NOISE II.

42-107037 Del Tulsa 3/2/44; Dow Fd 16/3/44; ass 385BG Gt Ashfield 13/3/44; tran 452BG Deopham Green 14/3/44; sal 11/4/44.

42-107038 Del Tulsa 3/2/44; Presque Is 6/3/44; ass 710BS/447BG Rattlesden 9/3/44; MIA Berlin 22/3/44 w/Stull; flak, cr Amsterdam, Hol; 10POW; MACR 3338.

42-107039 Del Tulsa 3/2/44; Grenier 27/2/44; ass 612BS/401BG [SC-M] Deenethorpe 23/3/44; retUS Bradley 7/6/45; 4168 BU Sth Plains 13/6/45; RFC Kingman 28/11/45. ICE COLD KATY.

42-107040 Del Tulsa 3/2/44; Grenier 17/2/44; ass 323BS/91BG [OR-K] Bassingbourn 1/4/44; 324BS [DF-D]; {98+m} RetUS Bradley 11/6/45; 4168 BU Sth Plains 15/6/45; RFC Kingman 14/12/45. SHIRLEY JEAN.

42-107041 Del Tulsa 3/2/44; Presque Is 3/3/44; ass 570BS/390BG [DI-M] Framlingham 6/3/44 MISS BEHAVIN'; MIA Merseburg 30/11/44 w/Meigide; flak, cr Rommerode, Ger?; 5KIA 4POW; MACR 11137. AIN'T MISBEHAVIN'.

42-107042 Del Tulsa 3/2/44; Grenier 2/3/44; ass 401BS/91BG [LL-Z] Bassingbourn 5/3/44; MIA {15m} Ludwigshafen 27/5/44 w/Pressey; flak, f/l Payerne, Switz; 9INT; MACR 5356; sal 9AF Germany 10/12/45. LIBERTY RUN.

42-107043 Del Tulsa 3/2/44; Grenier 2/3/44; ass 613BS/401BG [IN-B] Deenethorpe 23/3/44; b/d Pas de Calais 3/6/44 w/?; sal 2 SAD 14/6/44. FITCH'S BANDWAGON.

42-107044 Del Tulsa 4/2/44; Presque Is 6/3/44; ass 325BS/92BG Podington 25/3/44; MIA Sorau, Ger 11/4/44 w/Weaver; e/a, cr Altteich, Ger?; 2KIA 8POW; MACR 3675.

42-107045 Del Tulsa 6/2/44; Grenier 28/2/44; ass 550BS/385BG Gt Ashfield 3/3/44; MIA Berlin 29/4/44 w/Sexton; e/a, cr Schleibnitz, Ger; 10POW; MACR 4460.

42-107046 Del Tulsa 6/2/44; Grenier 27/2/44; ass 511BS/351BG [DS-Z] Polebrook 26/3/44; MIA {20m} Brandenburg 6/8/44 w/Boyd; flak, cr Wust, Ger; 4KIA 5POW; MACR 7584. SCREW BALL.

42-107047 Del Tulsa 6/2/44; Grenier 3/3/44; ass 334BS/95BG [BG-M] Horham 17/3/44; b/d Berlin 3/2/45 w/?; f/l Charleroi, Bel; rep & ret; retUS Bradley 26/6/45; 4168 BU Sth Plains 27/6/45; RFC Kingman 8/12/45. THE DOODLE BUG.

42-107048 Del Tulsa 6/2/44; Gr Island 27/2/44; ass 452BG Deopham Green 5/3/44 TANGERINE; tran 360BS/303BG [PU-M] Molesworth 23/3/44; MIA French A/fds 12/6/44 w/Eisele; flak, cr Cambrai, Fr; 9KIA 1POW; MACR 5626.

42-107049 Del Tulsa 6/2/44; Dow Fd 18/4/44; ass 398BG Nuthampstead 1/5/44; tran 452BG Deopham Green 30/4/44; dest by e/a at Poltava 21/6/44; sal 2/7/44.

42-107050 Del Tulsa 7/2/44; Dow Fd 28/4/44; ass 398BG Nuthampstead 1/5/44; tran 334BS/95BG [BG-O] Horham 4/5/44 TORNADO JR; MIA Merseburg 7/10/44 w/Farrar; e/a, cr Sommerda, Ger; 9POW; MACR 9561. DELTRESS.

42-107051 Del Tulsa 7/2/44; Rapid City 1/3/44; Dow Fd 21/4/44; ass 398BG Nuthampstead 25/4/44; tran

525BS/379BG [FR-A] Kimbolton 9/5/44; MIA Saarbrücken 11/5/44 w/Romberger; flak, cr Trier, Ger; 7KIA 2POW; MACR 4877.

42-107052 Del Tulsa 7/2/44; Grenier 3/3/44; ass 710BS/447BG Rattlesden 10/3/44; MIA Leipzig 29/5/44 w/Moran; flak, cr Seegeritz, Ger?; 5KIA 5POW; MACR 5303.

42-107053 Del Tulsa 7/2/44; Hunter 4/3/44; Grenier 7/4/44; ass 603BS/398BG [N7-M] Nuthampstead 11/4/44; 602BS [K8-M]; MIA Merseburg 2/11/44 w/Reed; flak, cr Leipzig; 9POW; MACR 10158. ESQUIRE.

42-107054 Del Tulsa 8/2/44; Rapid City 2/3/44; Grenier 14/4/44; ass 398BG Nuthampstead 24/4/44; retUS Bradley 26/6/45; 4168 BU Sth Plains 29/6/45; RFC Kingman 20/11/45. VAT 69.

42-107055 Del Tulsa 8/2/44; Hunter 14/2/44; Presque Is 6/3/44; ass 423BS/306BG [RD-M] Thurleigh 1/4/44; b/d Koblenz 28/12/44 w/?; c/l St Albans, UK; sal 1/1/45.

42-107056 Del Tulsa 8/2/44; Hunter 17/2/44; Grenier 5/3/44; ass 349BS/100BG [XR-O] Thorpe Abbotts 10/3/44; MIA Pas de Calais 28/4/44 w/McGuire; flak, cr Tamerville, Fr; 6KIA 4POW; MACR 4238.

42-107057 Del Tulsa 8/2/44; Gr Island 19/2/44; Presque Is 5/3/44; ass 546BS/384BG [BK-T] Grafton Underwood 11/4/44; MIA Frankfurt 25/9/44 w/Plowman; flak, cr Wiesbaden, Ger; MACR 9414. SPIRIT OF '96.

42-107058 Del Tulsa 8/2/44; Gr Island 19/2/44; Grenier 29/2/44; ass 545BS/384BG Grafton Underwood 24/4/44; 546BS [BK-C]; MIA Merseburg 11/9/44 w/Chadwick; flak, cr Halle, Ger; 7KIA 2POW; MACR 8903 & 7885. WHITE ANGEL.

42-107059 Del Tulsa 9/2/44; Gr Island 19/2/44; Grenier 28/2/44; ass 410BS/94BG [GL-Q] Rougham 24/4/44; retUS Bradley 24/6/45; 4168 BU Sth Plains 27/6/45; RFC Kingman 6/12/45.

42-107060 Del Tulsa 9/2/44; Hunter 17/2/44; Grenier 2/3/44; ass 711BS/447BG Rattlesden 7/3/44; c/l non op flight 3/12/44; sal.

42-107061 Del Tulsa 9/2/44; Gr Island 18/2/44; ass 561BS/388BG Knettishall 13/3/44 LITTLE JOE JR; MIA Laon 8/5/44 w/Pickett; e/a, cr Bremen; 5KIA 5POW; MACR 4581. PEG OF MY HEART.

42-107062 Del Denver 9/2/44; Rapid City 2/3/44; Dow Fd 3/4/44; ass 398BG Nuthampstead 25/4/44; tran 562BS/388BG Knettishall 29/4/44 WORRY BIRD; retUS Bradley 8/6/45; 4168 BU Sth Plains 29/11/45; RFC Kingman 29/11/45. MISS BEA HAVEN.

42-107063 Del Denver 9/2/44; Rapid City 2/3/44; Dow Fd 28/4/44; ass 398BG Nuthampstead 1/5/44; tran 367BS/306BG [GY-A] Thurleigh 18/5/44; b/d Merseburg 3/12/44 w/?; c/l sal.

42-107064 Del Denver 9/2/44; Hunter 3/3/44; Dow Fd 21/4/44; ass 398BG Nuthampstead 22/4/44; tran 547BS/384BG [SO-S] Grafton Underwood 30/4/44; MIA Munich 16/7/44 w/Capt Coleman; flak, cr Neuried, Ger; 4KIA 5POW; MACR 7553. MISS FIT.

42-107065 Del Denver 9/2/44; Hunter 3/3/44; Homestead 16/3/44; slated 398BG, ass 817BS/483BG Sterparone 17/3/44; tran 97BG Amendola 15/4/44; b/d Atzgerdorf, Aus 24/5/44 w/?; BTG Wasnuk shot out of turret, a/c landed Foggia; MIA Salzburg 17/11/44 w/Laser; MACR 9877. RIGOR MORTIS II.

42-107066 Del Denver 10/2/44; Hunter 3/3/44; Homestead 17/3/44; ass 429BS/2BG Amendola 18/3/44; MIA {87m} Munich 16/11/44 w/?; mech fault, landed Eisi?; crew ret in another a/c; sal 6/11/45. MERCURY.

42-107067 Del Denver 10/2/44; Gr Island 20/2/44; Grenier 6/3/44; ass 709BS/447BG Rattlesden 24/3/44; MIA Berlin 11/4/44 w/Jurnecka; flak, f/l Bulltofta, Swed; 10INT; MACR 3895. Rep by Swedish airline as SE-BAR; sold to AFA Denmark as OY-DFA; W/O 30/1/46.

42-107068 Del Tulsa 10/2/44; Gr Island 15/2/44; Grenier 5/3/44; ass 525BS/379BG [WA-O] Kimbolton 11/4/44; MIA Toulouse 25/6/44 w/Butcher; f/l Spain; 10INT; MACR 6737. POWERFUL KATRINKA.

42-107069 Del Tulsa 11/2/44; Gr Island 15/2/44; Grenier 5/3/44; ass 401BS/91BG [LL-M/N/W] Bassingbourn 1/4/44; b/d {70m} Altenbeken 26/11/44 w/Smith; w/#2 on fire c/l Halesworth A/fd, UK. hit two trucks and concrete mixer and burnt out; sal 2 SAD 28/11/44; ROUND TRIP TOPSY.

42-107070 Del Tulsa 11/2/44; Gr Island 13/2/44; Grenier 4/3/44; ass 571BS/390BG [FC-A] Framlingham 17/3/44; MIA Leipzig 7/7/44 w/Gregor; mid air coll w/42-97983; cr Hoorn, Hol; 8KIA 2POW; MACR 7218/7368. NORTH STAR.

42-107071 Del Tulsa 11/2/44; Kearney 25/2/44; Grenier 3/4/44; ass 325BS/92BG [NV-P] Podington 23/4/44; 327BS; b/d Dresden 14/2/45 w/?; f/l Continent, sal. MACR 8596.

42-107072 Del Tulsa 12/2/44; Kearney 25/2/44; Grenier 4/4/44; ass 710BS/447BG Rattlesden 12/3/44; MIA Brux 12/5/44 w/Capt Johnson; e/a, cr Lustzellinden, Ger?; MACR 4774.

42-107073 Del Tulsa 13/2/44; Kearney 21/2/44; Presque Is 4/4/44; ass 730BS/452BG Deopham Green 14/3/44; retUS Bradley 6/7/45; 4168 BU Sth Plains 7/7/45; RFC Kingman 8/11/45.

42-107074 Del Tulsa 13/2/44; Kearney 21/2/44; Presque Is 6/4/44; ass 546BS/384BG [BK-P] Grafton Underwood 15/4/44; b/d Berlin 2/5/44 w/?; sal 8/5/44.

42-107075 Del Tulsa 14/2/44; Kearney 22/2/44; Presque Is 6/4/44; ass 323BS/91BG [OR-Q] Bassingbourn 22/3/44 FANCY PANTS; MIA {45m} Lechfeld 19/7/44 w/Braund; mid air coll w/42-31542 (BUNKY, cut in half); cr Obersaxen, Switz; 9INT (baled out); MACR 7407. CHAMPAGNE GIRL.

42-107076 Del Tulsa 14/2/44; Presque Is 6/3/44; ass 563BS/388BG Knettishall 9/4/44; MIA Warnemünde 9/4/44 w/Sundstrom; flak, cr Tastrup, Denm; 10KIA; MACR 3656.

42-107077 Del Denver 14/2/44; Gr Island 3/3/44; Grenier 23/3/44; ass 510BS/351BG [TU-D] Polebrook 11/4/44; MIA {75m} 19/7/44 w/Chapman; e/a, cr Guezenberg, Switz; 4KIA 5POW; MACR 7556. SHOO SHOO BABY.

42-107078 Del Denver 14/2/44; Rapid City 17/2/44; Dow Fd 4/4/44; ass 603BS/398BG [N7-U] Nuthampstead 25/4/44; b/d Merseburg 21/11/44 w/?; f/l Belgium, sal 28/11/44. OLE BLOOD-N-GUTS.

42-107079 Del Denver 14/2/44; Hunter 3/3/44; Grenier 3/4/44; ass 708BS/447BG Rattlesden 11/4/44; sal 23/6/44.

42-107080 Del Denver 15/2/44; Hunter 3/3/44; Grenier 7/4/44; ass 601BS/398BG [3O-S] Nuthampstead 25/4/44; 602BS [K8-S]; b/d Kassel 4/12/44 w/?; f/l Belgium, sal 5/1/45. "OXO".

42-107081 Del Denver 15/2/44; Hunter 3/3/44; Morrison 19/3/44; ass 815BS/483BG Sterparone 18/4/44; one of two squadron a/c (the other 42-32043) used on SOE missions to Czechoslovakia, with supplies to Resistance, and returning with US evadees; sal 6/12/44. CRAZY HOUSE.

42-107082 Del Tulsa 15/2/44; Presque Is 26/2/44; ass 526BS/379BG [LF-N] Kimbolton 23/3/44; MIA Stettin 13/5/44 w/Dunn; e/a, cr St Heddinge, (nr school?) Den; 9POW; MACR 4931. LASSIE-COME-HOME.

42-107083 Del Tulsa 15/2/44; Grenier 11/3/44; ass 547BS/384BG [SO-B] Grafton Underwood 6/4/44; 546BS [BK-B]; MIA Koblenz 27/12/44 w/Nelson; flak, cr Prum; 7KIA 2POW; MACR 11248.

42-107084 Del Tulsa 16/2/44; Kearney 22/3/44; Grenier 3/4/44; ass 614BS/401BG [IW-G] Deenethorpe 16/4/44; MIA Politz, Ger 7/10/44 w/Harasym; flak, cr Politz; 2KIA 7POW; MACR 9760. BETTY'S REVENGE.

42-107085 Del Tulsa 16/2/44; Kearney 24/2/44; Presque Is 10/3/44; ass 562BS/388BG Knettishall 13/3/44; MIA Magdeburg 12/9/44 w/Creagh; flak, cr Helmstedt, Ger; 1KIA 9POW; MACR 8908. LITTLE CHUM.

42-107086 Del Tulsa 16/2/44; Rapid City 2/3/44; Grenier 14/4/44; ass 603BS/398BG [N7-L] Nuthampstead 24/4/44; tran 369BS/306BG [WW-Q] Thurleigh 13/5/44; c/f & exp base 7/8/44; sal 2 SAD 8/8/44. FICKLE FINGER.

42-107087 Del Tulsa 16/2/44; Kearney 23/2/44; Presque Is 2/3/44; ass 92BG Podington 12/3/44; tran 728BS/452BG Deopham Green 13/3/44; MIA Ulm 9/8/44 w/Gilbert; flak, ditched Channel; 9RTD. BIG BARN SMELL.

42-107088 Del Tulsa 16/2/44; Kearney 24/2/44; Presque Is 4/3/44; ass 532BS/381BG [VE-V] Ridgewell 25/3/44; MIA Bordeaux 19/6/44 w/Doyle; flak, cr Tartyfume, Fr?; 7KIA 2POW; MACR 5994.

42-107089 Del Tulsa 17/2/44; Gr Island 27/2/44; Grenier 6/3/44; ass 728BS/452BG Deopham Green 13/3/44; MIA Brux 12/5/44 w/Slanin; e/a, cr Buedesheim, Ger; 3KIA 7POW; MACR 4780.

42-107090 Del Tulsa 17/2/44; Rapid City 2/3/44; Grenier 20/4/44; ass 398BG Nuthampstead 24/4/44; tran 325BS/92BG [NV-T] Podington 7/5/44; MIA Pirmasens, Ger 9/8/44 w/Schramm; flak, cr Echterdingen, Ger; 9POW; MACR 5793.

42-107091 Del Tulsa 17/2/44; Grenier 7/3/44; ass 728BS/452BG Deopham Green 12/3/44; b/d Leige & Brussels 20/5/44 w/?; sal. FORBIDDEN FRUIT.

42-107092 Del Tulsa 17/2/44; Kearney 22/2/44; Grenier 6/3/44; ass 710BS/447BG Rattlesden 13/3/44; tran 615BS/401BG [IY-E] Deenethorpe 23/3/44 FRECKLES!; MIA Munich 31/7/44 w/Ossiander; flak, f/l Dubendorf, Switz; 9INT; MACR 7825. UMBRIAGO!

42-107093 Del Tulsa 18/2/44; Rapid City 6/3/44; Dow Fd 18/4/44; ass 602BS/398BG [K8-C] Nuthampstead 1/5/44; tran 452BG Deopham Green 3/5/44; dest by e/a at Poltava 21/6/44; sal 2/7/44.

42-107094 Del Tulsa 18/2/44; Rapid City 7/3/44; Grenier 14/4/44; ass 602BS/398BG [K8-M] Nuthampstead 26/4/44; b/d Cologne 5/10/44 w/?; c/l RAF Manston, sal 11/10/44.

42-107095 Del Tulsa 18/2/44; Gr Island 2/3/44; Grenier 3/4/44; ass 349BS/100BG [XR-F] Thorpe Abbotts 7/4/44; MIA French A/Fds 5/6/44 w/Wilson; flak, mid air coll w/43-37591; cr Boulougne, Fr; 3KIA 7POW; MACR 5384.

42-107096 Del Tulsa 18/2/44; Grenier 1/4/44; ass 601BS/398BG [3O-K] Nuthampstead 10/4/44; MIA French noball sites 8/7/44 w/Capt Berry; flak, ditched Channel; 7KIA 2RTD; MACR 7220.

42-107097 Del Tulsa 18/2/44; Dow Fd 14/4/44; ass 398BG Nuthampstead 22/4/44; tran 360BS/303BG Molesworth 12/5/44; b/d French A/fds 11/6/44 w/?; c/l Honington A/fd, UK; sal 13/6/44. SWEET MELODY.

42-107098 Del Tulsa 18/2/44; Rapid City 2/3/44; Dow Fd 9/4/44; ass 601BG/398BG [3O-Y] Nuthampstead 24/4/44; MIA Peenemünde 4/8/44 w/Carter; flak, cr

Koitenhage, Ger?; 9POW; MACR 7707.
42-107099 Del Tulsa 21/2/44; Gr Island 3/3/44; Grenier 23/3/44; ass 427BS/303BG [GN-W] Molesworth 30/4/44; MIA Germersheim 13/1/45 w/Capt McGinnis; flak, cr Bobenheim, Ger; 3KIA 6POW; MACR 11577. OLD '99'.
42-107100 Del Tulsa 21/2/44; Gr Island 3/3/44; Grenier 24/3/44; ass 532BS/381BG [VE-O/D] Ridgewell 6/4/44; {47+m} RetUS Bradley 28/5/45; 4168 BU Sth Plains 31/5/45; RFC Kingman 28/11/45. CENTURY NOTE.
42-107101 Del Tulsa 21/2/44; Hunter 1/3/44; Homestead 6/3/44; ass 96BS/2BG Amendola 15/3/44; MIA Brux 21/7/44 w/Wagner; e/a, #3 on fire, three chutes seen, cr Reid, Ger?; MACR 6684.
42-107102 Del Tulsa 21/2/44; Gr Island 3/3/44; Grenier 7/4/44; ass 338BS/96BG [BX-N] Snetterton 5/4/44; sal 20/1/45.
42-107103 Del Tulsa 21/2/44; Gr Island 5/3/44; Grenier 18/4/44; ass 602BS/398BG [K8-A] Nuthampstead 5/5/44; MIA Gaggennau, Ger 10/9/44 w/Wright; flak, cr Bautzen, Ger; 5KIA 4POW; MACR 8918. MARIE NOTRE DAME.
42-107104 Del Tulsa 22/2/44; Denver 2/3/44; Grenier 14/4/44; ass 398BG Nuthampstead 25/4/44; tran 339BS/96BG [QJ-D] Snetterton 1/5/44; MIA Osnabrück 31/5/44 w/Ciembronowicz; flak, cr Winnen, Ger; 10POW; MACR 5342.
42-107105 Del Tulsa 22/4/44; Rapid City 2/3/44; Dow Fd 18/4/44; ass 398BG Nuthampstead 6/5/44; tran 366BS/305BG Chelveston 22/5/44; MIA Anklam 4/8/44 w/Littlefield; flak, cr Baltic; 8KIA 1POW; MACR 7703.
42-107106 Del Tulsa 22/2/44; Hunter 4/3/44; Dow Fd 24/6/44; ass 341BS/97BG Amendola 2/7/44; MIA Regensburg 28/12/44 w/Neider; mech fault, cr Peelton; MACR 10876.
42-107107 Del Tulsa 22/2/44; Hunter 26/3/44; Morrison 13/4/44; ass 483BG Sterparone 25/4/44?
42-107108 Del Tulsa 23/2/44; slated 398BG, Amarillo 2/3/44; 252 BU Lubbock 3/7/44; 236 BU Pyote 8/7/44; 235 BU Biggs 16/8/44; 202 BU Galveston 24/1/45; 2114 BU Lockburn 6/7/45; 2137 BU Hendricks 9/10/45; 112 BU Westover 29/10/45; RFC Walnut Ridge 17/1/46.
42-107109 Del Tulsa 23/2/44; Gr Island 3/3/44; Grenier 25/3/44; ass 550BS/385BG Gt Ashfield 27/3/44; c/l Thames Estuary UK 10/5/44 w/?; sal 12/5/44. STORK CLUB.
42-107110 Del Tulsa 23/2/44; Hunter 4/3/44; Homestead 6/4/44; ass 398BG Nuthampstead 22/4/44; tran 32BS/301BG Lucera 19/8/44; cr non-op flight 11/1/45; sal.
42-107111 Del Tulsa 24/2/44; 222 BU Ardmore 20/12/44; 332 BU Ardmore 16/6/45; RFC Walnut Ridge 12/12/45.
42-107112 Del Tulsa 24/2/44; Gr Island 3/3/44; Grenier 24/3/44; ass 532BS/381BG [VE-O] Ridgewell 6/4/44; {47+m} RetUS Bradley 29/5/45; RFC Kingman 18/11/45. SLEEPY TIME GAL.
42-107113 Del Tulsa 24/2/44; Gr Island 7/3/44; Grenier 5/4/44; ass 615BS/401BG [IY-J] Deenethorpe 2/5/44; 612BS [SC-O]; retUS Bradley 6/6/45; 4168 BU Sth Plains 21/6/45; RFC Kingman 4/12/45. MISS ALDAFLAK.
42-107114 Del Tulsa 25/2/44; Gr Island 3/3/44; Grenier 22/3/44; ass 600BS/398BG [N8-L/A] Nuthampstead 24/4/44; b/d Dreux 4/7/44 w/?; c/l Truleigh Sands, UK; 9TRD; sal.
42-107115 Del Tulsa 25/2/44; Hunter 4/3/44; Homestead 10/3/44; ass 482BG Alconbury 19/3/44; tran 353BS/301BG Lucera 27/3/44; cargo ship from 11/11/44; c/l 28/6/45; sal.
42-107116 Del Tulsa 26/2/44; Rapid City 2/3/44; Dow Fd 14/4/44; ass 398BG Nuthampstead 24/4/44; tran 338BS/96BG [BX-B] Snetterton 2/5/44; dest by e/a at Poltava; sal 1/7/44. GYPSY GIRL.
42-107117 Del Tulsa 27/2/44; Rapid City 2/3/44; Grenier 27/3/44; ass 398BG Nuthampstead 6/5/44; tran 710BS/447BG Rattlesden 3/2/45; hit by debris from other a/c on non-op flight 21/2/45; sal.
42-107118 Del Tulsa 27/2/44; Hunter 4/3/44; Homestead 8/3/44; ass 20BS/2BG Amendola 17/3/44; MIA Moravska Ostrova 29/8/44 w/Garland; e/a, cr Fritschendorf; MACR 7987. SNAFUPERMAN.
42-107119 Del Tulsa 27/2/44; Long Beach 2/3/44; 235 BU Biggs 17/8/44; 202 BU Galveston 24/1/45; 268 BU Peterson 30/3/45; 2114 BU Lockburn 6/7/45; 2137 BU Hendricks 14/10/45; RFC Walnut Ridge 9/1/46.
42-107120 Del Tulsa 27/2/44; Long Beach 2/3/44; 235 BU Biggs 17/8/44; 224 BU Sioux City 8/3/45; 225 BU Rapid City 17/6/45; 268 BU Peterson 14/7/45; 232 BU Dalhart 17/7/45; 241 BU Fairmont 11/8/45; 268 BU Peterson 18/8/45; Phillips 12/2/46; Aberdeen Proving Grd 28/2/46.
42-107121 Del Tulsa 1//3/44; Gr Island 21/3/44; Dow Fd 14/4/44; ass 398BG Nuthampstead 24/4/44; tran 546BS/384BG [BK-J] Grafton Underwood 5/5/44; landing acc 7/12/44; sal AFSC. KENTUCKY COLONEL.
42-107122 Del Tulsa 2/3/44; 333 BU Morris 6/6/44; 224 BU Sioux City 7/3/45; 2132 BU Maxwell 21/5/45; 225 BU Rapid City 15/6/45; 224 BU Sioux City 15/7/45; Recl Comp 15/10/45.
42-107123 Del Tulsa 2/3/44; Kansas City 7/3/44; Grenier 21/4/44; ass 398BG Nuthampstead 25/4/44; tran 339BS/96BG Horham 28/4/44; MIA Brux 12/5/44 w/Tucker; e/a, cr Mershausen, Ger; 5KIA 5POW; MACR 5359.
42-107124 Del Tulsa 2/3/44; Rapid City 6/3/44; Grenier 20/4/44; ass 398BG Nuthampstead 25/4/44; tran 510BS/351BG [TU-F] Polebrook 29/4/44; {75m} RetUS Bradley 11/6/45; 4168 BU Sth Plains 19/6/45; RFC Kingman 6/12/45. MOLLIE MULE.
42-107125 Del Tulsa 1/3/44; Rapid City 5/3/44; Dow Fd 21/4/44; ass 603BS/398BG Nuthampstead 25/4/44; 600BS [N8-G]; tran 545BS/384BG [JD-G] Grafton Underwood 7/12/44; sal 9AF Germany 10/12/45.
42-107126 Del Tulsa 1/3/44; Gr Island 7/3/44; 224 BU Sioux City 1/8/44; 561 BU Rosencrans 4/8/44; 224 BU Sioux City 28/9/44; 2509 Big Spring 20/12/44; 2515 BU Dodge City 21/12/44; 2509 BU Big Spring 26/12/44; 224 BU Sioux City 27/12/44; 619 BU Waterton 1/5/45; 224 BU Sioux City 2/5/45; 225 BU Rapid City 15/6/45; 203 BU Jackson 27/6/45; 239 BU March 27/9/45; 420 BU March 7/10/45; RFC Kingman 16/1/46.
42-107127 Del Tulsa 2/3/44; Dalhart 13/3/44; 554 BU Memphis 10/10/44; 223 BU Dyersburg 14/10/44; 4119 BU Brookley 31/10/44; 223 BU Dyersburg 29/11/44; Recl Comp 19/1/45.
42-107128 Del Tulsa 1/3/44; Dalhart 10/3/44; 221 BU Alexandra, W/O 20/7/44.
42-107129 Del Tulsa 1/3/44; Dalhart 12/3/44; 225 BU Rapid City 1/5/45; 203 BU Jackson 3/6/45; 233 BU Davis Monthan 27/9/45; RFC Kingman 3/12/45.
42-107130 Del Tulsa 1/3/44; Dalhart 12/3/44; 224 BU Sioux City 3/6/45; Recl Comp 22/5/45.
42-107131 Del Tulsa 1/3/44; Pyote 6/3/44; 556 BU Long Beach 10/7/44; 236 BU Pyote 14/7/44; 235 BU Biggs 16/8/44; 224 BU Sioux City 28/1/45; 225 BU Rapid City 15/6/45; 354 BU Rapid City 20/7/45; 209 BU Galveston 25/7/45; 2621 BU Barksdale 30/11/45; 331 BU Barksdale 2/12/45; 554 BU Memphis 6/2/46; 62 BU Memphis 20/5/46; 62 BU Morrison 30/9/46; 4141 BU Pyote 30/1/47; Recl Comp 22/12/48.
42-107132 Del Denver 2/3/44; Kearney 22/3/44; Dow Fd 14/4/44; ass 601BS/398BG [3O-V] Nuthampstead 4/5/44; MIA Berlin 24/5/44 w/Ingram; flak, cr Biesenthal, Ger; 9KIA 1POW; MACR 5253.
42-107133 Del Denver 2/3/44; Rapid City 12/5/44; W/O 19/5/44.
42-107134 Del Denver 2/3/44; Kearney 12/5/44; Presque Is 5/4/44; ass 563BS/388BG Knettishall 6/4/44; dest by e/a at Poltava 21/6/44; sal 2/7/44. ROUND TRIP.
42-107135 Del Denver 2/3/44; Kearney 22/3/44; Grenier 21/4/44; ass 549BS/385BG Gt Ashfield 24/4/44; MIA Handorf 15/8/44 w/Rosner; flak, cr Ijsselmeer, Hol; 10POW; MACR 7908. HOMESICK ANGEL.
42-107136 Del Denver 2/3/44; Kearney 22/3/44; Dow Fd 14/4/44; ass 305BG Chelveston 30/4/44; b/d Merseburg 24/8/44 w/?; c/l base; sal 2 SAD 26/8/44.
42-107137 Del Denver 2/3/44; Kearney 22/3/44; Grenier 27/4/44; ass 349BS/100BG [XR-O] Thorpe Abbotts 3/5/44; MIA Munich 13/7/44 w/Harding; flak hit after dropping bombs, lost #3; f/l Payerne, Switz; 10INT; MACR 7502; rep 7 ret group, the last to leave Switz for Burtonwood, UK; sal 9AF Germany 2/1/46.
42-107138 Del Tulsa 3/3/44; Rapid City 12/3/44; Dow Fd 14/4/44; ass 603BS/398BG [N7-T] Nuthampstead 22/4/44; MIA Merseburg 21/11/44 w/Rich; flak, cr Hilburghausen, Ger; 7KIA 2POW; MACR 11213. WITKA TANKA TON.
42-107139 Del Tulsa 4/3/44; Rapid City 13/3/44; Dow Fd 28/4/44; ass 398BG Nuthampstead 1/5/44; tran 305BG Chelveston 8/5/44; sal 2 SAD 4/7/44; 388BG Knettishall 5/44; sal 14/7/44.
42-107140 Del Tulsa 3/3/44; Dalhart 12/3/44; 224 BU Sioux City 6/3/45; 222 BU Ardmore 14/6/45; 332 BU Ardmore 16/6/45; RFC Walnut Ridge 20/8/45.
42-107141 Del Tulsa 3/3/44; Rapid City 6/3/44; 225 BU Rapid City 19/4/45; 2114 BU Lockburn 27/6/45; 2137 BU Hendricks 15/10/45; RFC Walnut Ridge 8/1/46.
42-107142 Del Tulsa 5/3/44; Rapid City 9/3/44; 225 BU Rapid City 1/5/45; 283 BU Galveston 19/7/45; RFC Kingman 21/12/45.
42-107143 Del Tulsa 5/3/44; Hunter 12/3/44; Morrison 11/4/44; ass 840BS/483BG Sterparone 23/4/44; retUS Hunter 23/6/45; 4168 BU Sth Plains 25/6/45; RFC Kingman 18/12/45.
42-107144 Del Tulsa 5/3/44; Dalhart 12/3/44; 224 BU Sioux City, W/O 6/8/44.
42-107145 Del Tulsa 6/3/44; Dalhart 15/3/44; 1701 BU Amarillo 23/12/44; 224 BU Sioux City 3/1/45; 4100 BU Patterson 7/3/45; 224 BU Sioux City 12/3/45; 225 BU Rapid City 17/6/45; 268 BU Peterson 14/7/45; 232 BU Dalhart 17/7/45; 201 BU Peterson 3/2/46; 427 BU Roswell 12/2/46; 509 BU Roswell 17/2/46; 234 BU Clovis 27/2/46; 427 BU Roswell 20/3/46; 613 BU Phillips 20/4/46; 427 BU Roswell 30/4/46.
42-107146 Del Tulsa 6/3/44; Gr Island 12/3/44; Dow Fd 14/4/44; ass 527BS/379BG [FO-G] Kimbolton 11/4/44; MIA Gelsenkirchen 26/8/44 w/Spencer; flak, ditched Channel; 7KIA 2RTD; MACR 8465. MAIRZY DOATS.
42-107147 Del Tulsa 6/3/44; Hunter 12/3/44; Grenier 1/4/44; ass 360BS/303BG [PU-C] Molesworth 22/4/44; b/d Liége 11/5/44 w/?; c/l RAF Rochford, UK; SaL 14/5/44. SWEET MELODY.

42-107148 Del Tulsa 6/3/44; Hunter 15/3/44; Dow Fd 8/4/44; ass 545BS/384BG [JD-G/P] Grafton Underwood 29/4/44; MIA Bohlen 17/3/45 w/Schauer; flak, ditched Channel; 1KIA0 8POW; MACR 13114. DARK ANGEL.

42-107149 Del Tulsa 6/3/44; Sioux City 20/3/44; 3507 Sioux City 2/12/44; 224 BU Sioux City 8/12/44; 273 BU Lincoln 24/12/44; 224 BU Sioux City 5/1/45; 332 BU Ardmore 19/6/45; RFC Walnut Ridge 24/8/45.

42-107150 Del Tulsa 7/3/44; Hunter 15/3/44; Grenier 7/4/44; ass 602BS/398BG [K8-J/V] Nuthampstead 26/4/44; b/d Cologne 5/10/44 w/?; f/l Continent; sal 14/11/44.

42-107151 Del Tulsa 7/3/44; Kearney 22/3/44; Grenier 7/4/44; ass 614BS/401BG [IW-B] Deenethorpe 15/4/44; retUS Bradley 8/6/45; 4168 BU Sth Plains 12/6/45; RFC Kingman 30/11/45. COVER GIRL.

42-107152 Del Tulsa 7/3/44; Sioux City 17/3/44, W/O 27/5/44.

42-107153 Del Tulsa 7/3/44; Sioux City 17/3/44; Grenier 5/4/44; ass 369BS/306BG [WW-V] Thurleigh 25/4/44; MIA Munich 16/7/44 w/Jones; flak, cr Leninges, Bel?; 9EVD; MACR 7567.

42-107154 Del Tulsa 7/3/44; Hunter 15/3/44; Grenier 5/4/44; ass 334BS/95BG [BG-F] Horham 10/4/44; retUS Bradley 24/6/45; 4168 BU Sth Plains 28/6/45; RFC Kingman 12/11/45. PUDDLES.

42-107155 Del Tulsa 7/3/44; Sioux City 16/3/44; 224 BU Sioux City 6/3/45; 225 BU Rapid City 15/6/45; 234 BU Clovis 15/7/45; RFC Altus 7/11/45.

42-107156 Del Tulsa 8/3/44; McDill 30/3/44; Morrison 8/4/44; ass 817BS/483BG Sterparone 29/4/44; MIA Ruhland 22/3/45 w/Robinson; flak & hit by jet e/a, shot off most of tail, cr Breslau; cp Craig killed by German sniper, 3WIA (r/op Chupa died in Russian hospital); 6EVD & ret; MACR 13244. THE GREAT SPECKLED BIRD.

42-107157 Del Tulsa 8/3/44; Sioux Cith 20/3/44; 224 BU Sioux City, W/O 6/8/44.

42-107158 Del Tulsa 8/3/44; Sioux City 17/3/44; 224 BU Sioux City 28/7/44; Recl Comp 11/10/44.

42-107159 Del Tulsa 8/3/44; Sioux City 13/3/44; 224 BU Sioux City, W/O 8/9/44.

42-107160 Del Tulsa 9/3/44; Kearney 22/3/44; Grenier 6/4/44; ass 562BS/388BG Knettishall 20/4/44; MIA Berlin 19/5/44 w/White; ditched Channel; 10RTD; LITTLE JOE.

42-107161 Del Tulsa 9/3/44; McDill 20/3/44; Hunter 29/3/44; Morrison 11/4/44; ass 483BG Sterparone 19/4/44; sal 20/4/45.

42-107162 Del Tulsa 9/3/44; McDill 27/3/44; Hunter 29/3/44; Homestead 24/4/44; ass 49BS/2BG Amendola 27/4/44; MIA Arad, Rom. 3/7/44 w/Twibell; ditched Adriatic; 10RTD.

42-107163 Del Tulsa 9/3/44; Kearney 22/3/44; Grenier 6/4/44; ass 407BS/92BG Podington 4/5/44; MIA Le Bourget 14/6/44 w/Long; flak, cr Villiers-sur-Orge, Fr; 3EVD 6POW; MACR 5793.

42-107164 Del Tulsa 9/3/44; Kearney 22/3/44; Grenier 3/4/44; ass 339BS/96BG Snetterton 7/4/44; MIA Pas de Calais 20/4/44 w/Liles; flak, cr Halines, Fr; 9KIA 1POW; MACR 4165.

42-107165 Del Tulsa 9/3/44; Kearney 22/3/44; Dow Fd 4/4/44; ass 563BS/388BG Knettishall 8/4/44; sal 30/5/44. PAULA SUE.

42-107166 Del Tulsa 9/3/44; McDill 23/3/44; Hunter 29/3/44; Morrison 11/4/44; ass 815BS/483BG Sterparone 20/4/44; MIA Ploesti 9/7/44 w/Berger; flak, cr Toca, Rom?; 8EVD & ret 10/8/44; 2POW; MACR 6817.

42-107167 Del Tulsa 12/3/44; Hunter 29/3/44; Presque Is 10/5/44; W/O 13/5/44.

42-107168 Del Tulsa 12/3/44; Kearney 27/3/44; Grenier 5/4/44; ass 325BS/92BG [NV-D] Podington 14/4/44; b/d Cauvincourt 16/8/44 w/?; sal 18/8/44.

42-107169 Del Tulsa 12/3/44; Kearney 22/3/44; Dow Fd 4/4/44; ass 401BG Deenethorpe 24/6/44; tran 527BS/379BG [FO-T] Kimbolton 12/7/77; b/d Hannover 5/8/44 w/?; c/l, sal 2 SAD.

42-107170 Del Tulsa 12/3/44; McDill 20/3/44; Hunter 29/3/44; Homestead 12/4/44; ass 817BS/483BG Sterparone 14/4/44; MIA Memmingen 18/7/44 w/Haley; e/a, cr Kempten; 1KIA 9POW; MACR 6978.

42-107171 Del Tulsa 13/3/44; McDill 24/3/44; Hunter 29/3/44; Homestead 14/4/44; ass 15AF 15/4/44; retUS Bradley 10/6/45; Romulus 16/7/45; 4185 BU Independence 18/7/45; 8 BU Winston Salem 2/9/45; RFC Walnut Ridge 11/3/46.

42-107172 Del Tulsa 13/3/44; McDill 22/3/44; Hunter 27/3/44; Morrison 4/4/44; ass 816BS/483BG Sterparone 19/4/44; MIA Memmingen 18/7/44 w/Combs; e/a, cr Memmingen; 8KIA 2POW; MACR 7153.

42-107173 Del Tulsa 13/3/44; Kearney 24/3/44; Dow FD 4/4/44; ass 571BS/390BG [FC-F] Framlingham 8/4/44; b/d Brux 12/5/44 w/?; sal. LAMZY DIVY.

42-107174 Del Tulsa 14/3/44; Gr Island 27/3/44; Dow Fd 3/4/44; ass 730BS/452BG Deopham Green 11/4/44; 731BS; damaged at Poltava 21/6/44, rep & ret 2/7/44; b/d Frankfurt 5/1/45 w/?; c/l Saarbrücken, crew safe; sal 23/1/45. PANTING STORK II.

42-107175 Del Tulsa 14/3/44; Gr Island 23/3/44; Dow Fd 2/4/44; ass 525BS/379BG [FR-Z] Kimbolton 11/4/44; 526BS; MIA Battle support area 13/8/44 w/Miller; flak, cr Pont le Beck, Fr; 1EVD 7KIA 1POW; MACR 7906.

42-107176 Del Tulsa 14/3/44; Kearney 2/4/44; Grenier 6/4/44; ass 568BS/390BG [BI-C] Framlingham 10/4/44 THE MISSIONAIRES; MIA Mannheim 21/1/45 w/Spragins; mech fault, cr Channel; 9KIA; MACR 11801. THE UNINVITED.

42-107177 Del Tulsa 14/3/44; Gr Island 29/3/44; Crenicr 4/4/44; ass 569BS/390BG Framlingham 8/4/44; MIA Friedrichshafen 24/4/44 w/Newell; flak, cr Kluftern, Ger; 10KIA; MACR 4291.

42-107178 Del Tulsa 14/3/44; McDill 23/3/44; Dow Fd 6/4/44; ass 401BS/91BG [LL-K] Bassingbourn 22/4/44; MIA Berlin 24/5/44 w/Nee; flak, f/l Switz; 3INT 3KIA 3POW; MACR 5358.

42-107179 Del Tulsa 14/3/44; Hunteer 29/3/44; Morrison 9/4/44; ass 816BS/483BG Sterparone 22/4/44; MIA Memmingen 18/7/44 w/Smithers; e/a, cr Kempten; 1KIA 9POW: MACR 6856.

42-107180 Del Tulsa 15/3/44; Kearney 29/3/44; Dow Fd 6/4/44; ass 410BS/94BG [GL-K] Rougham 11/4/44 LUCKY REBEL; sal 9AF Germany 29/12/45. THE EAGLE'S WRATH.

42-107181 Del Tulsa 15/3/44; Gr Island 29/3/44; Grenier 14/4/44; ass 326BS/92BG [JW-H] Podington 7/5/44; tran 306BG Thurleigh 6/5/45; retUS Bradley 15/6/45; 4168 BU Sth Plains 17/6/45; RFC Kingman 8/12/45.

42-107182 Del Tulsa 15/3/44; McDill 30/3/44; 327 BU Drew 4/5/45; 301 BU Drew 22/10/45; RFC Altus 5/11/45.

42-107183 Del Tulsa 15/3/44; Kearney 29/3/44; Dow Fd 4/4/44; ass 602BS/398BG [K8-J/V] Nuthampstead 26/4/44; b/d Cologne 5/10/44 w/?; f/l Continent, sal 14/11/44.

42-107184 Del Tulsa 16/3/44; Kearney 29/3/44; Dow Fd 4/4/44; ass 568BS/390BG [BI-L] Framlingham 8/4/44 THE WALRUS; non-op taxi accident 23/3/45; sal. SILVER METEOR.

42-107185 Del Tulsa 16/3/44; Kearney 29/3/44; Dow Fd 4/4/44; ass 331BS/94BG [QE-V] Rougham 8/4/44; MIA Berlin 6/8/44 w/Spenst; flak, ditched Nth Sea; 2KIA 7POW; MACR 8075.

42-107186 Del Tulsa 16/3/44; Gr Island 29/3/44; Grenier 6/4/44; ass 603BS/398BG [N7-L] Nuthampstead 27/4/44; MIA Peenemünde 4/8/44 w/McArthur; flak, cr Fresendorf, Ger; 9KIA; MACR 7708.

42-107187 Del Tulsa 17/3/44; McDill 31/3/44; 325 BU Avon Park, W/O 29/9/44; Recl Comp 28/11/44.

42-107188 Del Tulsa 18/3/44; Kearney 29/3/44; Dow Fd 6/4/44; ass 602BS/398BG [K8-G] Nuthampstead 5/5/44; MIA Bingen, Ger 29/12/44 w/Erickson; flak, cr Luxembourg; 3EVD 6POW; MACR 10374. RAMP ROOSTER.

42-107189 Del Tulsa 18/3/44; Kearney 29/3/44; Dow Fd 6/4/44; ass 339BS/96BG [QJ-M] Snetterton 11/4/44; MIA Brux 12/5/44 w/Simons; e/a, cr Dauborn, Ger; 9KIA 1POW; MACR 4864. 7TH SON.

42-107190 Del Tulsa 18/3/44; Kearney 4/4/44; Grenier 7/4/44; ass 601BS/398BG [3O-L] Nuthampstead; 600BS [N8-L]; retUS Bradley 4/6/44; 4168 BU Sth Plains 28/8/45; RFC Kingman 14/12/45. MAXINE.

42-107191 Del Tulsa 18/3/44; Kearney 29/9/44; Grenier 6/4/44; ass 600BS/398BG [N8-K] Nuthampstead 9/4/44; c/l Bovingdon A/fd 12/8/44; sal 14/8/44. THE TOMAHAWK WARRIOR.

42-107192 Del Tulsa 17/3/44; McDill 30/3/44; Avon Park 4/4/44; 325 BU Avon Park 9/4/45; RFC Walnut Ridge 12/12/45.

42-107193 Del Tulsa 17/3/44; McDill 30/3/44; Avon Park 4//4/44; 325 BU Avon Park 23/12/44; 4117 BU Warner Robins 23/1/44; cr mountains nr Chattanooga in poor weather, killing all three crew 15/1/45; Recl Comp 24/1/45.

42-107194 Del Tulsa 17/3/44; McDill 31/3/44; Avon Park 4/4/44; 120 BU Richmond 30/1/45; 325 BU Avon Park 24/2/45; Recl Comp 22/5/45.

42-107195 Del Tulsa 20/3/44; McDill 31/3/44; 327 BU Drew 7/12/44; Recl Comp 1/1/45.

42-107196 Del Tulsa 20/3/44; Kearney 31/3/44; Dow Fd 4/4/44; ass 360BS/303BG [PU-D] Molesworth 22/4/44; MIA Ruhland 12/9/44 w/Mehlhoff; e/a, cr Jachymov, Czech; 1KIA 8POW; MACR 8825.

42-107197 Del Tulsa 20/3/44; Kearney 31/3/44; Dow Fd 4/4/44; ass 710BS/447BG Rattlesden 11/4/44; MIA Pas de Calais 27/4/44 w/Gwynn; flak, cr Ostend, Bel; 3KIA 7POW; MACR 4299.

42-107198 Del Tulsa 20/3/44; Kearney 31/3/44; Dow Fd 6/4/44; slated 303BG, ass 562BS/388BG Knettishall 8/4/44; dest by e/a at Poltava 21/6/44; sal 2/7/44.

42-107199 Del Tulsa 20/3/44; Kearney 31/3/44; Dow Fd 4/4/44; ass 570BS/390BG [DI-J] Framlingham 8/4/44; MIA French A/fds 11/6/44 w/Gavin; flak, cr Channel; 10KIA; MACR 5629. POWERFUL KATRINKA.

42-107200 Del Tulsa 20/3/44; Kearney 312/3/44; Grenier 6/4/44; ass 358BS/303BG Molesworth 23/4/44; MIA Friedrichshafen 24/4/44 w/Stewart; flak, f/l Switz; 7KIA 3POW; MACR 4274.

42-107201 Del Tulsa 20/3/44; Kearney 29/3/44; Dow Fd 6/4/44; ass 334BS/95BG [BG-J] Horham 8/4/44; retUS Bradley 2/6/45; 4168 BU Sth Plains 23/6/45; RFC Kingman 1/12/45. WORRY BIRD.

42-107202 Del Tulsa 20/3/44; Kearney 31/3/44; Dow Fd 7/4/44; ass 563BS/388BG Knettishall 8/4/44; MIA Ruhland 24/8/44 w/Edwards; flak, cr Prague, Czech; 5KIA 4POW; MACR 8287. BELLE OF THE BRAWL.

42-107203 Del Tulsa 20/3/44; Kearney 3/4/44; Grenier 7/4/44; ass 96BG Snetterton 12/4/44; tran

601BS/398BG [3O-Z] Nuthampstead 26/4/44; sal 4/4/45.

42-107204 Del Tulsa 20/3/44; Kearney 2/4/44; Grenier 21/4/44; ass 412BS/95BG [QW-B] Horham 22/4/44 STAND BY; b/d Leipzig 6/4/45 w/Davis; cr Continent; 9KIA; MACR ?; GOIN' MY WAY.

42-107205 Del Tulsa 20/3/44; Kearney 2/4/44; Grenier 6/4/44; ass 602BS/398BG [K8-F] Nuthampstead 9/4/44; 600BS [N8-F]; tran 324BS/91BG [DF-O] Bassingbourn 9/8/44; MIA {3+m} Neumünster 13/4/45 w/?; damaged when two other B17s exploded in mid air, but f/l on French US A/fd (1KIA); sal 17/4/45. THE RUPTURED DUCK.

42-107206 Del Tulsa 21/3/44; Kearney 2/4/44; Dow Fd 8/4/44; ass 359BS/303BG [BN-R] Molesworth 23/4/44; b/d Pilsen 25/4/45 w/?; f/l Continent, sal 26/5/45. OLD BLACK MAGIC.

42-107207 Del Tulsa 21/3/44; Kearney 2/4/44; Grenier 14/4/44; ass 614BS/401BG [IW-D] Deenethorpe 2/5/44; MIA Dessau 30/5/44 w/Kilmer; e/a, cr Everingen, Ger; 3KIA 7POW; MACR 5304.

42-107208 Del Tulsa 21/3/44; Kearney 2/4/44; Dow Fd 21/4/44; ass 338BS/96BG [BX-U] Snetterton 25/4/44; b/d Berlin 3/2/45 w/?; c/l Javac, Pol; 9RTD; MACR 8810; sal. WHY NOT?

42-107209 Del Tulsa 21/3/44; Kearney 4/4/44; Grenier 14/4/44; ass 305BG Chelveston 9/8/44; b/d Pilsen 25/4/45 w/?; f/l Continent, sal. THE WHEEL'S WAGON.

42-107210 Del Tulsa 21/3/44; Kearney 4/4/44; Grenier 10/4/44; ass 614BS/401BG [IW-N] Deenethorpe 29/4/44; damaged by bomb from above, exploded Evereux, Fr 12/6/44 w/?; sal 2 SAD 14/6/44; MACR 8925. BE COMING BACK.

42-107211 Del Tulsa 21/3/44; Kearney 4/4/44; Grenier 14/4/44; ass 349BS/100BG [XR-N] Thorpe Abbotts 20/4/44; MIA Merseburg 29/7/44 w/Gustafson; e/a, cr Mannstedt, Ger; 8KIA 1POW; MACR 7816/8795.

42-107212 Del Tulsa 21/3/44; Kearney 5/4/44; Grenier 14/4/44; ass 423BS/306BG [RD-Z] Thurleigh 6/5/44; MIA Nantes, Fr 15/6/44 w/O'Brien; flak, cr Nantes; 1EVD 8POW; MACR 5795.

42-107213 Del Tulsa 21/3/44; Kearney 4/4/44; Grenier 14/4/44; ass 524BS/379BG [WA-H/F] Kimbolton 20/4/44; c/t/o for Neuss, Ger 23/1/45; hit base quarters, 4 crew KIA & 5 e/m killed; sal 2 SAD.

42-107214 Del Tulsa 21/3/44; Kearney 5/4/44; Grenier 21/4/44; ass 600BS/398BG [N8-V] Nuthampstead 5/5/44; b/d Merseburg 25/11/44 w/?; c/l Barkway, UK, sal. LADY ELLA.

42-107215 Del Tulsa 21/3/44; Kearney 4/4/44; Dow Fd 14/4/44; ass 709BS/447BG Rattlesden 25/4/44; retUS Bradley 5/7/45; 4168 BU Sth Plains 21/10/45; Recl Comp 7/6/46. L'IL EIGHT BALL.

42-107216 Del Tulsa 27/3/44; Kearney 6/4/44; Dow Fd 14/4/44; ass 511BS/351BG [DS-Y] Polebrook 7/5/44; MIA (35m) Ulm 9/8/44 w/Myl; flak, ditched Bradwell Bay, Ex; 2KIA 7RTD; MACR 7391. THUNDER BALL.

42-107217 Del Tulsa 27/3/44; Kearney 4/4/44; Grenier 14/4/44; ass 601BS/398BG [3O-U] Nuthampstead 5/5/44; sal 22/6/44.

42-107218 Del Tulsa 27/3/44; Kearney 5/4/44; Grenier 21/4/44; ass 600BS/398BG [N8-T] Nuthampstead 3/5/44; MIA Leipzig 7/7/44 w/Folger; flak, cr Dueben, Ger?; 1KIA 8POW; MACR 7221.

42-107219 Del Tulsa 27/3/44; Kearney 13/4/44; Grenier 29/4/44; ass 711BS/447BG Rattlesden 3/5/44; sal 2/8/44.

42-107220 Del Tulsa 27/3/44; Kearney 6/4/44; Dow Fd 14/4/44; ass 708BS/447BG Rattlesden 22/4/44; c/l non-op flight 24/5/45; sal. SWANEE PRIDE.

42-107221 Del Tulsa 28/3/44; Hunter 7/4/44; Grenier 17/4/44; ass 544BS/384BG [SU-J] Grafton Underwood 2/5/44; MIA Berlin 21/6/44 w/Finch; flak, f/l Bulltofta, Swed; 9INT; MACR 5995; retUS Bradley 7/7/45; 4168 BU Sth Plains 10/7/45; RFC Kingman 14/1/46.

42-107222 Del Tulsa 28/3/44; Kearney 7/4/44; Grenier 14/4/44; ass 325BS/92BG [NV-S] Podington 4/5/44; c/l base & burned 3/8/44; sal. MOUNTAINEER.

42-107223 Del Tulsa 28/3/44; Kearney 7/4/44; Grenier 14/4/44; ass 603BS/398BG [N7-S] Nuthampstead 5/5/44; MIA Cauvincourt, Fr 8/8/44 w/?; MACR 7384.

42-107224 Del Tulsa 28/3/44; Kearney 4/5/44; Grenier 21/5/44; ass 544BS/384BG [SU-Q] Grafton Underwood 6/5/44; b/d Lille, Fr 4/8/44 w/?; c/l, sal.

42-107225 Del Tulsa 28/3/44; Kearney 6/4/44; Dow Fd 14/4/44; ass 731BS/452BG Deopham Green 22/4/44; MIA Eindhoven, Hol 9/8/44 w/Bradshaw; flak, cr Eindhoven; 1EVD 1KIA 7POW; MACR 7388.

42-107226 Del Tulsa 28/3/44; Kearney 13/4/44; Dow Fd 21/4/44; ass 385BG Gt Ashfield 22/4/44; landing acc, hit P-51 at Honington A/fd 30/7/44.

42-107227 Del Tulsa 28/3/44; Kearney 13/4/44; Dow Fd 29/4/44; ass 337BS/96BG [AW-E] Snetterton 1/5/44; dest by e/a at Poltava 21/6/44; sal 1/7/44. CABIN IN THE SKY.

42-107228 Del Tulsa 28/3/44; Hunter 11/4/44; W/O 22/4/44.

42-107229 Del Tulsa 28/3/44; Kearney 11/4/44; Grenier 28/4/44; ass 710BS/447BG Rattlesden 1/5/44; MIA Rechlin 25/8/44 w/Henningson; ditched Channel; 9RTD. ROWDY REBEL.

42-107230 Del Tulsa 28/3/44; Kearney 6/4/44; Dow Fd 14/4/44; ass 349BS/100BG [XR-B] Thorpe Abbotts 22/4/44; b/d Mainz 4/12/44 w/?; sal 5/12/44.

42-107231 Del Tulsa 24/3/44; Hunter 11/4/44; Grenier 21/4/44; ass 603BS/398BG [N7-A] Nuthampstead 3/5/44; MIA Berlin 24/5/44 w/Maj Gray; flak, cr Berlin; 9KIA 2POW; MACR 5252.

42-107232 Del Tulsa 24/3/44; Kearney 15/4/44; Grenier 29/4/44; ass 385BG Gt Ashfield 8/5/44; sal 16/6/44.

42-107233 Del Tulsa 24/3/44; Kearney 13/4/44; Grenier 29/4/44; ass 351BS/100BG [EP-W] Thorpe Abbotts 3/5/44; MIA Misburg 31/12/44 w/Wilson; e/a, cr Tauenbrueck, Ger?; 9POW; MACR 11356.

B-17G-BO

43-37509 Del Cheyenne 25/4/44; Kearney 9/5/44; Grenier 21/5/44; ass 601BS/398BG [3O-B/J] Nuthampstead 23/5/44; b/d Mannheim 1/2/45 w/?; c/l Hollesley Bay, UK; sal 2 SAD 2/2/45.

43-37510 Del Cheyenne 25/4/44; Kearney 10/5/44; Grenier 24/5/44; ass 612BS/401BG [SC-T] Deenethorpe 10/6/44; MIA Cauvincourt 8/8/44 w/Capt Ball; flak, cr St Lo, Fr; 4KIA 5RTD.

43-37511 Del Cheyenne 26/4/44; Kearney 5/5/44; Grenier 21/5/44; ass 613BS/401BG [IN-G] Deenethorpe 23/5/44; 614BS [IW-Y], 615BS [IY-L]; MIA Merseburg 24/8/44 w/Fish; e/a, cr Little Tondorf, Ger?; 3KIA 6POW; MACR 8204. JILL'S JALOPY.

43-37512 Del Cheyenne 25/4/44; Kearney 7/5/44; Grenier 24/5/44; ass 510BS/351BG [TU-S] Polebrook 4/6/44; {115m} RetUS Bradley 25/5/45; 4168 BU Sth Plains 25/8/45; RFC Walnut Ridge 11/12/45. TRADE WINDS.

43-37513 Del Cheyenne 25/4/44; Hunter 4/5/44; Dow Fd 17/5/44; ass 569BS/390BG [CC-D] Framlingham 19/5/44; b/d Cologne 15/10/44 w/?; f/l St Trond A/fd, Bel; MACR 9483; sal 14/11/44. ANNA.

43-37514 Del Cheyenne 25/4/44; Hunter 5/5/44; Dow Fd 17/5/44; ass 534BS/381BG [GD-B] Ridgewell 12/8/44; {72+m} RetUS Bradley 6/6/45; 4168 BU Sth Plains 26/6/45; RFC Kingman 4/11/45. MY SON BOB.

43-37515 Del Cheyenne 25/4/44; Hunter 4/5/44; Grenier 19/5/44; ass 510BS/351BG [TU-L] Polebrook 27/5/44; {91m} RetUS Bradley 11/6/44; 4168 BU Sth Plains 14/6/45; RFC Kingman 4/12/45. JOHN SILVER.

43-37516 Del Cheyenne 25/4/44; Hunter 4/5/44; Dow Fd 25/5/44; ass 422BS/305BG [JJ-T] Chelveston 4/6/44; tran 858BS Cheddington 26/6/44; on NLS mission shot down by intruder off Clacton, UK 4/3/45; MACR 13535; sal 5/3/45. TONDELAYO.

43-37517 Del Cheyenne 25/4/44; Kearney 7/5/44; Grenier 25/5/44; ass 350BS/100BG [LN-T] Thorpe Abbotts 28/5/44; c/l base & exp 29/1/45; sal 31/1/45. HEAVEN CAN WAIT.

43-37518 Del Cheyenne 25/4/44; Kearney 9/5/44; Grenier 24/5/44; ass 751BS/457BG Glatton 27/5/44; 749BS; MIA Merseburg 28/9/44 w/Gay; e/a, cr Dorstadt, Ger; 9KIA; MACR 9768. GINI.

43-37519 Del Cheyenne 25/4/44; Kearney 9/5/44; Dow Fd 21/5/44; ass 571BS/390BG [] Framlingham 25/5/44; MIA Zeitz, Ger 30/11/44 w/Booth; flak, cr Zwickau; 1EVD 4KIA 4POW; MACR 11133. JOKER.

43-37520 Del Cheyenne 25/4/44; Kearney 9/5/44; Grenier 24/5/44; ass 560BS/388BG Knettishall 27/5/44; MIA Merseburg 28/9/44 w/Michael; flak, cr Alken, Ger; 9POW; MACR 9375. G.I. JANE.

43-37521 Del Cheyenne 25/4/44; Kearney 6/5/44; Grenier 25/5/44; ass 351BS/100BG [EP-K] Thorpe Abbotts 30/5/44; MIA Berlin 18/3/44 w/King; jet e/a, cr Tangermünde, Ger; 3KIA 6POW; MACR 13143. SKYWAY CHARIOT.

43-37522 Del Chamberlain Fd, Minn 26/4/44; Gt Falls 29/4/44; Minneapolis 1/5/44; McDill 7/7/44; 328 BU Gulfport 13/12/44; Recl Comp 11/1/45.

43-37523 Del Cheyenne 26/4/44; Hunter 4/5/44; Dow Fd 22/5/44; ass 560BS/388BG Knettishall 27/5/44; retUS Bradley 29/6/45; 4168 BU Sth Plains 1/7/45; RFC Kingman 9/12/45.

43-37524 Del Cheyenne 26/4/44; Kearney 9/5/44; Dow Fd 21/5/44; ass 511BS/351BG [DS-D] Polebrook 23/5/44; {65m} b/d Stuttgart 9/12/44 w/?; f/l Continent; MACR 7903; sal 10/12/45. QUEEN OF THE BALL.

43-37525 Del Cheyenne 26/4/44; Kearney 9/5/44; Dow Fd 21/5/44; ass 338BS/96BG [BX-J] Snetterton 23/5/44; b/d Cauvincourt 8/8/44 w/?; sal.

43-37526 Del Cheyenne 26/4/44; Hunter 4/5/44; Grenier 21/5/44; ass 816BS/483BG Sterparone 26/5/44; Pisa 4/9/45; retUS 1103 BU Morrison 19/9/45; RFC Walnut Ridge 19/12/45.

43-37527 Del Cheyenne 26/4/44; Kearney 9/5/44; Grenier 25/5/44; ass 398BG Nuthampstead 13/6/44; b/d Metz 12/8/44 w/?; sal.

43-37528 Del Cheyenne 26/4/44; Kearney 9/5/44; Dow Fd 21/5/44; ass 549BS/385BG Gt Ashfield 23/5/44; b/d Berlin 6/8/44 w/?; cr Thelnetham, UK; crew baled, 3WIA; sal 9/8/44.

43-37529 Del Cheyenne 26/4/44; Hunter 4/5/44; Dow Fd 21/5/44; ass 305BG Chelveston 2/6/44; b/d Hamm, Ger 19/9/44 w/?; MACR 8070; sal 21/9/44.

43-37530 Del Cheyenne 26/4/44; Kearney 11/5/44; Grenier 24/5/44; ass 96BG Snetteron 27/5/44; tran 422BS/305BG [JJ-A] Chelveston 4/6/44; tran 858BS Cheddington 26/6/44; c/l base 10/7/44; sal 4/1/45.

43-37531 Del Cheyenne 26/4/44; Kearney 10/5/44; Grenier 24/5/44; ass 708BS/447BG Rattlesden 8/5/44; MIA Merseburg 2/11/44 w/Wing; flak, cr Nordhausen, Ger; 4KIA 5POW; MACR 10163. QUIEN SABE?

43-37532 Del Cheyenne 26/4/44; Kearney 9/5/44; Grenier 21/5/44; ass 751BS/457BG Glatton 23/5/44; MIA Merseburg 2/11/44 w/Corriher; e/a, cr Leimbach, Ger; 7KIA 2POW; MACR 10316. PATCHES & PRAYERS.

43-37533 Del Cheyenne 26/4/44; Lowry 10/5/44; Cheyenne 16/6/44; Kearney 27/6/44; Dow Fd 7/7/44; ass 511BS/351BG [DS-G] Polebrook 17/7/44; MIA {3m} Brandenburg 6/8/44 w/Strange; flak, cr Berlin; 3KIA 6POW; MACR 7587.

43-37534 Del Cheyenne 26/4/44; Kearney 7/5/44; Grenier 24/6/44; ass 508BS.351BG [YB-L] Polebrook 31/5/44; {13m} b/d Leipzig 7/7/44 w/?; c/l base, sal 2 SAD 8/7/44.

43-37535 Del Cheyenne 26/4/44; Kearney 11/5/44; Grenier 24/5/44; ass 326BS/92BG [JW-F] Podington 4/6/44; MIA Kassel 22/9/44 w/Sample; flak, cr Trier, Ger; IKIA 8POW; MACR 9371. BABY BUTTON.

43-37536 Del Cheyenne 26/4/44; Kearney 7/5/44; Grenier 20/5/44; ass 532BS/381BG [VE-C] Ridgewell 12/6/44; {40+m} RetUS Bradley 18/6/45; 4168 BU Sth Plains 21/6/45; Recl Comp 7/6/46. FRENCH DRESSING.

43-37537 Del Cheyenne 27/4/44; Kearney 22/5/44; Grenier 27/5/44; ass 350BS/100BG [LN-T] Thorpe Abbotts 30/5/44; tran 359BS/303BG [BN-Q/X] Molesworth 7/6/44; retUS Walnut Ridge 10/1/46. QUEEN OF HEARTS.

43-37538 Del Cheyenne 27/4/44; Kearney 11/5/44; Grenier 20/5/44; ass 535BS/381BG [MS-Z] Ridgewell 29/8/44; {24+m} RetUS Bradley 10/6/45; 4168 BU Sth Plains 14/6/45; RFC Kingman 5/12/45. WILD BILL.

43-37539 Del Cheyenne 27/4/44; Kearney 7/5/44; Grenier 20/5/44; ass 447BG Rattlesden 26/5/44; sal 24/6/44.

43-37540 Del Cheyenne 27/4/44; Kearney 13/5/44; Grenier 24/5/44; ass 323BS/91BG [OR-B/Z] Bassingbourn 2/6/44; took part in POW return trips; {100+m} RetUS Bradley 11/7/45; 4185 BU Independence 12/7/45; RFC Kingman 16/12/45. RAMBLIN' REBEL.

43-37541 Del Cheyenne 27/4/44; Kearney 7/5/44; Grenier 25/5/44; ass 710BS/447BG Rattlesden 30/5/44; MIA Ruhland 11/9/44 w/Martenson; flak, cr Oberatsteinach, Ger; 9POW; MACR 8923. DOWN AND GO (MAH IDEEL).

43-37542 Del Cheyenne 27/4/44; Kearney 11/5/44; Grenier 24/5/44; ass 385BG Gt Ashfield 30/5/44; tran 730BS/452BG Deopham Green 30/5/44 SMOKEY LIZ II; 729BS; MIA Zwickau 19/3/45 w/Caldwell; e/a, cr Zwickau; MACR 13561. FRIVOLOUS SAL.

43-37543 Del Cheyenne 27/4/44; Kearney 7/5/44; Grenier 26/5/44; ass 532BS/381BG [VE-I] Ridgewell 4/6/44; tran 452BG Deopham Green 24/5/45; retUS Bradley 28/5/45; 4168 BU Sth Plains 31/5/45; RFC Kingman 17/12/45. LIBERTY BELLE.

43-37544 Del Cheyenne 27/4/44; Kearney 11/5/44; Grenier 24/5/44; ass 710BS/447BG Rattlesden 2/5/44; retUS Bradley 7/7/45; 4168 BU Sth Plains 15/8/45; RFC Kingman 8/11/45. D-DAY DOLL.

43-37545 Del Cheyenne 28/4/44; Kearney 7/5/44; Dow Fd 4/6/44; ass 728BS/452BG Deopham Green 1/5/44; tran 306BG Thurleigh 7/6/44; retUS Bradley 3/7/45; 4168 BU Sth Plains 6/7/45; RFC Kingman 16/12/45.

43-37546 Del Cheyenne 28/4/44; Kearney 24/5/44; Dow Fd 29/5/44; ass 407BS/92BG [PY-X] Podington 3/6/44 RAMBLIN' REBEL; MIA Merseburg 11/9/44 w/Smith; e/a, cr Helfta, Ger; 5KIA 4POW; MACR 8886. ROWDY REBEL.

43-37547 Del Cheyenne 28/4/44; Kearney 12/5/44; Grenier 25/5/44; ass 325BS/92BG [NV-F] Podington 3/6/44; MIA Peenemünde 25/8/44 w/Boye; flak, cr Baltic; 9KIA; MACR 8274.

43-37548 Del Cheyenne 28/4/44; Kearney 10/5/44; Grenier 25/5/44; ass 92BG Podington 12/6/44; tran 548BS/385BG Gt Ashfield 28/6/44; MIA Berlin 6/10/44 w/Kaplan; e/a, cr Liepe, Ger; 3KIA 6POW; MACR 9517.

43-37549 Del Cheyenne 28/4/44; Kearney 10/5/44; Grenier 26/5/44; ass 423BS/306BG Thurleigh 13/6/44; tran 534BS/381BG Ridgewell 5/45; retUS Bradley 11/6/45; 4168 BU Sth Plains 14/6/45; RFC Kingman 20/12/45. SWEAT'ER GIRL.

43-37550 Del Cheyenne 28/4/44; Kearney 11/5/44; Grenier 21/5/44; ass 96BS Snetterton 23/5/44; dest by e/a at Poltava 21/6/44; sal 1/7/44, rep & ret group; retUS 4117 BU Robins 28/8/45; 4160 BU Hobbs 5/11/45; RFC Knoxville 21/1/46.

43-37551 Del Cheyenne 28/4/44; Kearney 11/5/44; Grenier 26/5/44; ass 614BS/401BG [IW-L] Deenethorpe 1/6/44; MIA Berlin 28/3/45 w/McCullough; flak, cr Zobbenitz, Ger; 4KIA 6POW; MACR 13544.

43-37552 Del Cheyenne 28/4/44; Kearney 11/5/44; Grenier 25/5/44; ass 401BS/91BG [LL-E] Bassingbourn 2/6/44; {84m} c/l Baldock, UK on test flight 12/4/45 w/?; all 6KIA; sal 13/4/45. THE PEACEMAKER.

43-37553 Del Cheyenne 28/4/44; Kearney 11/5/44; Grenier 21/5/44; ass 535BS/381BG [MS-Y] Ridgewell 27/5/44; b/d {51m} Kassel 1/1/45 w/Peters; f/l France, crew flew home in C-47; sal. FEATHER MERCHANT II.

43-37554 Del Cheyenne 28/4/44; Kearney 10/5/44; Grenier 27/5/44; ass 525BS/379BG [FR-V] Kimbolton 8/6/44; sal 2 SAD 15/6/44.

43-37555 Del Cheyenne 28/4/44; Kearney 10/5/44; Grenier 25/5/44; ass 570BS/390BG [DI-G] Framlingham 28/5/44; 571BS [FC-G]; b/d Frankfurt 5/1/45 w/?; f/l Sedan A/fd, Fr; sal 30/1/45. THE JEANNIE BEE.

43-37556 Del Cheyenne 28/4/44; Kearney 12/5/44; Grenier 24/5/44; ass 751BS/457BG Glatton 27/5/44; MIA Merseburg 2/11/44 w/Dawson; e/a, cr Emseloh, Ger?; 1KIA 9POW; MACR 10317.

43-37557 Del Cheyenne 28/4/44; Kearney 11/5/44; Grenier 21/5/44; ass 511BS/351BG [DS-K] Polebrook 23/5/44; MIA {30m} Brandenburg 6/8/44 w/Barieau; flak, cr Potsdam, Ger; 1KIA 8POW; MACR 7588. HUBBA HUBBA.

43-37558 Del Cheyenne 28/4/44; Kearney 10/5/44; Grenier 25/5/44; ass 452BG Deopham Green 28/5/44; dest by e/a at Poltava 21/6/44; sal 2/7/44.

43-37559 Del Cheyenne 28/4/44; Hunter 17/5/44; Grenier 1/6/44; 16 STA Grenier 3/6/44; ass 325BS/92BG [NV-N] Podington 12/6/44; 327BS; sal 9AF Germany 10/12/45. I'LL GET BY.

43-37560 Del Cheyenne 28/4/44; Kearney 13/5/44; Grenier 27/5/44; ass 533BS/381BG [VP-R] Ridgewell 3/6/44; {66+m} RetUS Bradley 26/5/45; 4168 BU Sth Plains 31/5/45; RFC Kingman 9/11/45.

43-37561 Del Cheyenne 28/4/44; Hunter 16/5/44; Grenier 27/5/44; ass 533BS/381BG [VP-J] Ridgewell 12/6/44; b/d {53+m} Oranienburg 15/3/45 w/Carpenter; c/l Woodbridge ELG, UK; 1KIA 2WIA 6RTD; sal.

43-37562 Del Cheyenne 28/4/44; Kearney 11/5/44; Dow Fd 30/5/44; ass 751BS/457BG Glatton 1/6/44; MIA Leipzig 29/6/44 w/Gumulauskas; e/a, cr Gross Muehlingen, Ger; 9POW; MACR 6724.

43-37563 Del Cheyenne 29/4/44; Kearney 10/5/44; Grenier 25/5/44; ass 728BS/452BG Deopham Green 27/5/44 PANTING STORK II; 729BS; b/d Frankfurt 5/1/45 w/?; f/l Continent; sal 21/1/45; b/d, sal 6/3/45.

43-37564 Del Cheyenne 29/4/44; Kearney 10/5/44; Grenier 26/5/44; ass 571BS/390BG 27/5/44 Framlingham 27/5/44; MIA Berlin 18/3/45 w/Freeman; flak, cr Dreilingen, Ger?; 9POW; MACR 13139. LITTLE MORON.

43-37565 Del Cheyenne 29/4/44; Kearney 10/5/44; Grenier 25/5/44; ass 571BS/390BG [FC-N] Framlingham 27/5/44; b/d Hannover 28/3/45 w/?; f/l Chievres A/fd, Bel; rep & ret group 7/45; retUS Bradley 5/7/45; 4168 BU Sth Plains 7/7/45; RFC Kingman 12/12/45. SONGOON.

43-37566 Del Cheyenne 30/4/44; Gt Falls 3/5/44; Kearney 29/5/44; 16 STA Grenier 6/6/44; ass 331BS/94BG [QE-O] Rougham 7/6/44 A LITTLE BEHIND; MIA Bohlen 7/10/44 w/Waldorf; 9POW; MACR 9552. FORTRESS JOKER.

43-37567 Del Cheyenne 30/4/44; Gt Falls 3/5/44; Kearney 3/6/44; Grenier 18/6/44; ass 750BS/457BG Glatton 29/6/44; MIA Merseburg 12/12/44 w/Higgins; flak, cr Sensweiler, Ger; 1KIA 9POW; MACR 11334. WILLIE III.

43-37568 Del Cheyenne 30/4/44; Kearney 11/5/44; Grenier 24/5/44; ass 327BS/92BG [UX-Z] Podington 2/6/44; c/l 14/8/44; sal 2 SAD 16/8/44. BIG ASCAR (D-DAY).

43-37569 Del Cheyenne 30/4/44; Kearney 11/5/44; Grenier 27/5/44; ass 836BS/487BG [2G-P] Lavenham 30/5/44; 839BS [R5-P]; MIA Darmstadt 24/12/44 w/Ball; e/a, cr Hods, Bel; 6KIA 3RTD. MACR 11599.

43-37570 Del Cheyenne 30/4/44; Kearney 11/5/44; Grenier 27/5/44; ass 379BG Kimbolton 4/6/44; retUS Bradley 10/7/45; 4168 BU Sth Plains 6/10/45; RFC Kingman 9/11/45. MISS LIBERTY.

43-37571 Del Cheyenne 30/4/44; Kearney 11/5/44; Grenier 25/5/44; ass 511BS/351BG [DS-X] Polebrook 4/6/44; MIA {57m} Misburg 26/11/44 w/Boetcher; flak, cr Koeln, Ger; 2KIA 7POW; MACR 11203.

43-37572 Del Cheyenne 30/4/44; Kearney 11/5/44; Grenier 27/5/44; ass 349BS/100BG [XR-S] Thorpe Abbotts 30/5/44; MIA Halberstadt 5/8/44 w/Gallagher; flak, cr Magdeburg; 9KIA; MACR 7878.

43-37573 Del Cheyenne 30/4/44; Kearney 11/5/44; Grenier 25/5/44; ass 339BS/96BG [QJ-H] Snetterton 28/5/44; MIA Regensburg 21/7/44 w/Beaudry; e/a, cr Russenhoffen, Ger; 3KIA 6POW; MACR 7412.

43-37574 Del Cheyenne 30/4/44; Kearney 11/5/44; Grenier 25/5/44; ass 749BS/457BG Glatton 28/5/44; retUS Bradley 9/6/45; Cleveland 11/6/45; Scott 26/6/45; 4168 BU Sth Plains 22/7/45; RFC Kingman 8/12/45. BUTCH.

43-37575 Del Cheyenne 2/5/44; Kearney 11/5/44; Grenier 27/5/44; ass 368BS/306BG [BO-X] Thurleigh 6/6/44; tran 398BG Nuthampstead 27/5/45; retUS Bradley 14/6/45; 4168 BU Sth Plains 18/6/45; RFC Kingman 4/12/45.

43-37576 Del Alexandra 2/5/44; 4103 BU Jackson 3/10/44; 221 BU Alexandra 4/10/44; 329 BU Alexandra 2/1/45; 327 BU Drew 20/7/45; 268 BU Peterson 7/10/45; RFC Kingman 7/1/46.

43-37577 Del Ardmore 2/5/44; 222 BU Ardmore 22/1/45; 332 BU Ardmore 16/6/45; RFC Walnut Ridge 17/9/45.

43-37578 Del Ardmore 2/5/44; 4136 BU Tinker 9/7/44; 235 BU Biggs 25/8/44; 222 BU Ardmore 18/3/45; 332 BU Ardmore 1/8/45; RFC Walnut Ridge 10/9/45.

43-37579 Del Ardmore 2/5/44; 222 BU Ardmore

22/1/45; 332 BU Ardmore 1/8/45; RFC Walnut Ridge 26/9/45.

43-37580 Del Ardmore 2/5/44; 222 BU Ardmore 22/1/45; 332 BU Ardmore 16/6/45; RFC Walnut Ridge 25/9/45.

43-37581 Del Ardmore 2/5/44; 222 BU Ardmore 22/1/45; 332 BU Ardmore 16/6/45; RFC Walnut Ridge 17/9/45.

43-37582 Del Dyersburg 2/5/44; 4103 BU Jackson 7/10/44; 330 BU Dyersburg 1/3/45; 327 BU Drew 28/8/45; 330 BU Dyersburg 4/9/45; RFC Walnut Ridge 17/10/45.

43-37583 Del Dyersburg 2/5/44; 347 BU Key Fd 23/8/44; 223 BU Dyersburg 30/8/44; 263 BU Harding 5/9/44; 223 BU Dyersburg 15/9/44; 330 BU Dyersburg 1/3/45; 327 BU Drew 28/8/45; 330 BU Dyersburg 4/9/45; RFC Walnut Ridge 19/12/45.

43-37584 Del Dyersburg 2/5/44; 330 BU Dyersburg 1/3/45; RFC Walnut Ridge 18/12/45.

43-37585 Del Dyersburg 2/5/44; 379 BU Coffeyville 13/2/45; 330 BU Dyersburg 9/3/45; 327 BU Drew 28/8/45; 330 BU Dyersburg 4/9/45; RFC Walnut Ridge 18/12/45.

43-37586 Del Dyersburg 2/5/44; 330 BU Dyersburg 9/4/45; RFC Walnut Ridge 18/12/45.

43-37587 Del Dyersburg 2/5/44; 330 BU Dyersburg 9/4/45; RFC Walnut Ridge 18/12/45.

43-37588 Del Hobbs 2/5/44; 3017 BU 10/5/44; 3508 BU Truax 13/2/45; 3017 BU Hobbs 22/9/45; 3701 BU Amarillo 7/10/45; RFC Kingman 21/11/45.

43-37589 Del Cheyenne 2/5/44; Slated 379BG, Hunter 16/5/44; Tulsa 20/5/44; 3701 BU Amarillo 5/7/44; W/O 15/11/44.

43-37590 Del Cheyenne 2/5/44; Hunter 15/5/44; Dow Fd 29/5/44; ass 358BS/303BG [VK-Q] Molesworth 7/6/44; tran 457BG Glatton 22/5/45; 351BG Polebrook 29/5/45; retUS Bradley 13/6/45; 4168 BU Sth Plains 18/6/45; RFC Kingman 27/11/45. NEVA - THE SILVER LADY.

43-37591 Del Cheyenne 2/5/44; Hunter 2/5/44; Dow Fd 24/5/44; ass 349BS/100BG Thorpe Abbotts 27/5/44; MIA Pas de Calais 5/6/44 w/Peterson; mid air coll w/42-107095; cr Boulogne, Fr; 9KIA 1POW; MACR 5383.

43-37592 Del Cheyenne 2/5/44; Kearney 12/5/44; Grenier 26/5/44; ass 305BG Chelveston 29/5/44; tran 562BS/388BG Knettishall 30/5/44; dest by e/a at Poltava 21/6/44; sal 2/7/44.

43-37593 Del Cheyenne 2/5/44; Hunter 16/5/44; Grenier 3/6/44; ass 388BG Knettishall 3/6/44; tran 364BS/305BG Chelveston 12/6/44; MIA Merseburg 24/8/44 w/Graham; flak, cr Barnstedt, Ger; 7KIA 2POW; MACR 8210.

43-37594 Del Cheyenne 2/5/44; Hunter 15/5/44; Dow Fd 30/5/44; ass 323BS/91BG [OR-O] Bassingbourn 10/6/44; MIA {31m} Ludwigshafen 9/9/44 w/Jensen; flak & #4 exploded, cr Karlsruhe; 5KIA 4POW; MACR 8806. STRICTLY G.I.

43-37595 Del Cheyenne 2/5/44; Kearney 12/5/44; Grenier 27/5/44; ass 509BS/351BG [RQ-O] Polebrook 10/6/44; {73m} coll during assembly w/43-38080 6/2/45 w/?; sal 2 SAD 7/2/45. VERGEN'S VIRGINS.

43-37596 Del Cheyenne 2/5/44; Hunter 16/5/44; Dow Fd 28/5/44; ass 327BS/92BG [UX-J] Podington 8/6/44; MIA Peenemünde 25/8/44 w/Holcomb; flak, f/l Sovde, Swed; 9INT; rep & ret group /45; retUS Bradley 14/7/45; 4185 BU Independence 17/7/45; RFC Kingman 21/12/45.

43-37597 Del Cheyenne 2/5/44; Hunter 16/5/44; Dow Fd 29/5/44; ass 427BS/303BG [GN-G/I] Molesworth 7/7/44; MIA Dresden 17/4/45 w/Kahler; flak, cr Brux, Czech; 4EVD 2KIA 2POW; MACR 14169. EARTHQUAKE McGOON.

43-37598 Del Cheyenne 3/5/44; Hunter 16/5/44; Grenier 26/5/44; ass 323BS/306BG [RD-X] Thurleigh 9/6/44; tran 381BG Ridgewell 5/45; retUS Bradley 10/6/45; 4168 BU Sth Plains 15/6/45; RFC Kingman 6/12/45. TOGGLE TESSY.

43-37599 Del Cheyenne 3/5/44; Hunter 18/5/44; Dow Fd 4/6/44; ass 562BS/388BG Knettishall 9/6/44; MIA Stuttgart 5/9/44 w/Paaske; flak, cr Rottweil, Ger; 4EVD 1KIA 4POW; MACR 8454. MOONLIGHT SERENADE.

43-37600 Del Cheyenne 3/5/44; Hunter 17/5/44; Grenier 3/6/44; ass 367BS/306BG [GY-Q] Thurleigh 12/6/44; tran 92BG Podington 9/5/45; sal 9AF Germany 2/1/46. IMPATIENT VIRGIN.

43-37601 Del Cheyenne 3/5/44; Hunter 17/5/44; Dow Fd 30/5/44; ass 349BS/100BG Thorpe Abbotts 1/6/44; MIA French A/fds 12/6/44 w/Ryan; flak, cr Dunkerque, Fr; 9KIA 1POW; MACR 5625.

43-37602 Del Cheyenne 3/5/44; Hunter 17/5/44; Dow Fd 29/5/44; ass 602BS/401 BG [IW-O] Deenethorpe 10/6/44; retUS Bradley 6/6/45; 4168 BU Sth Plains 14/6/45; RFC Kingman 24/11/45. LADY VIVIAN.

43-37603 Del Cheyenne 3/5/44; Hunter 16/5/44; Grenier 3/6/44; ass 338BS/96BG [BX-R] Snetterton 3/6/44; MIA Nuremberg 10/9/44 w/Williamson; flak, cr Schirmeck, Ger; 9POW; MACR 8809. I'LL BE AROUND.

43-37604 Del Cheyenne 3/5/44; 1 SAG Langley 17/5/44; 3539 BU Langley 16/9/44; RFC Walnut Ridge 4/1/46.

43-37605 Del Cheyenne 3/5/44; 1 SAG Langley 17/5/44; 111 BU Langley 23/5/44; 3539 BU Langley 16/9/44; 110 BU Mitchell 28/8/45; 76 BU Langley 3/12/45; 110 BU Mitchell 2/3/46; Recl Comp 2/5/46.

43-37606 Del Cheyenne 4/5/44; Hunter 17/5/44; Dow Fd 4/6/44; ass 750BS/457BG Glatton 7/6/44; MIA Misburg 17/10/44 w/Chapman; flak, cr Prum, Ger; 2KIA 7POW; MACR 9634. B.T.O. (BIG TIME OPERATOR II).

43-37607 Del Cheyenne 4/5/44; 1 SAG Langley 17/5/44; 111 BU Langley 23/5/44; 3539 BU Langley 16/9/44; RFC Walnut Ridge 4/1/46.

43-37608 Del Cheyenne 4/5/44; Hunter 16/5/44; Grenier 3/6/44; ass 337BS/96BG [AW-W] Snetterton 3/6/44; MIA Cologne 18/10/44 w/Rubadue; flak, c/l Sprang-Chapelle, Hol; 9POW; MACR 10260. "CHUTE THE WORKS".

43-37609 Del Cheyenne 4/5/44; Orlando 17/5/44; 901 BU Pinecastle 3/6/44; 902 BU Orlando 5/6/44; 903 BU Pinecastle 10/9/44; 621 BU Pinecastle 9/7/45; 4152 BU Clinton 22/5/46; 4121 BU Kelly 9/6/46; 621 BU Pinecastle 25/7/46; 613 BU Phillips 25/7/46.

43-37610 Del Cheyenne 4/5/44; Hunter 17/5/44; Dow Fd 27/5/44; ass 401BS/91BG [LL-A] Bassingbourn 10/6/44; b/d Frankfurt 11/12/44 w/Melton; f/l Continent; rep & ret group 4/3/45; retUS Bradley 11/6/45; 4168 BU Sth Plains 16/6/45; RFC Kingman 4/12/45. ZOOTIE CUTIE.

43-37611 Del Cheyenne 4/5/44; Hunter 18/5/44; Dow Fd 30/5/44; ass 367BS/306BG [GY-G] Thurleigh 12/6/44; tran 381BG Ridgewell 5/45; retUS Bradley 11/6/45; 4168 BU Sth Plains 13//6/45; RFC Kingman 12/12/45. FUDDLES FOLLY.

43-37612 Del Cheyenne 4/5/44; Hunter 17/5/44; Grenier 31/5/44; ass 533BS/381BG Ridgewell 18/6/44; MIA {1+m} Hamburg 20/6/44 w/Dunkel; flak, cr Hamburg; 6KIA 3POW; MACR 5991. OLD IRON GUT.

43-37613 Del Cheyenne 4/5/44; Hunter 18/5/44; Grenier 3/6/44; ass 324BS/91BG [DF-A] Bassingbourn 15/6/44; b/d Delitzsch 16/8/44 w/Marpil; c/l Halesworth A/fd, UK; 1KIA 1POW 7RTD; MACR 8182; sal 2 SAD 17/8/44.

43-37614 Del Cheyenne 4/5/44; Hunter 18/5/44; Grenier 6/6/44; ass 92BG Podington 15/6/44; c/t/o Osnabrück 26/9/44; ct fire, sal.

43-37615 Del Cheyenne 4/5/44; Hunter 18/5/44; Grenier 31/5/44; ass 306BG Thurleigh 12/6/44; sal 2 SAD 27/7/44. ELIZABETH'S OWN.

43-37616 Del Cheyenne 5/5/44; Hunter 18/5/44; Dow Fd 4/6/44; ass 423BS/306BG [RD-X] Thurleigh 10/6/44; {30+m} tran 381BG Ridgewell 5/45; 91BG Bassingbourn 30/5/45; retUS Bradley 11/6/45; 4168 BU Sth Plains 14/6/45; RFC Kingman 10/12/45. SOLID SENDER.

43-37617 Del Cheyenne 4/5/44; Hunter 19/5/44; Grenier 6/6/44; ass 562BS/388BG Knettishall 7/6/44; b/d Cologne 17/10/44 w/?; f/l Le Culot A/fd, Bel; 1KIA 1MIA 7POW; sal 14/11/44. BETTY ANN.

43-37618 Del Cheyenne 4/5/44; Kearney 17/6/44; Grenier 2/7/44; ass 848BS/490BG Eye 3/7/44; mid air coll w/42-38051 13/8/44 w/?; c/l Thelveton, UK; 7KIA; sal 14/8/44.

43-37619 Del Cheyenne 4/5/44; Hunter 18/5/44; Grenier 3/6/44; ass 369BS/306BG [WW-S] Thurleigh 12/6/44; MIA Oranienburg 10/4/45 w/Babin; flak, cr Hannover; 4EVD 1KIA 4POW; MACR 13878. FLACK SHACK.

43-37620 Del Cheyenne 4/5/44; Hunter 18/5/44; Grenier 3/6/44; ass 365BS/305BG Chelveston 28/6/44; MIA Cologne 10/1/45 w/Leuthesser; flak, cr Fischbach, Ger; 7KIA 2POW; MACR 11745.

43-37621 Del Cheyenne 5/5/44; Patterson 21/5/44; Kearney 2/6/44; Dow Fd 10/7/44; ass 337BS/96BG [AW-A] Snetterton 14/7/44; b/d Merseburg 25/11/44 w/?; f/l Continent; sal 8/12/44.

43-37622 Del Cheyenne 5/5/44; Patterson 21/5/44; Kearney 5/6/44; Dow Fd 27/6/44; ass 379BG Kimbolton 8/7/44; b/d Hannover 5/8/44 w/?; c/l, sal 2 SAD 6/8/44.

43-37623 Del Cheyenne 5/5/44; Hunter 18/5/44; Dow Fd 29/5/44; ass 413BS/96BG [MZ-B] Snetterton 1/6/44; retUS Bradley 5/7/45; 4168 BU Sth Plains 8/7/45; RFC Kingman 17/12/45.

43-37624 Del Cheyenne 5/5/44; Hunter 19/5/44; Dow Fd 4/6/44; ass 401BS/91BG [LL-P] Bassingbourn 10/6/44 VICTORY QUEEN; MIA {17m} Leipzig 20/7/44 w/Fusco; e/a, cr Zwickau; 1KIA (p) 8POW; MACR 7283. LIBERTY QUEEN.

43-37625 Del Cheyenne 5/5/44; Hunter 19/5/44; Dow Fd 29/5/44; ass 323BS/91BG [OR-Q/W] Bassingbourn 11/6/44; MIA {42m} Merseburg 2/11/44 w/Harris; e/a, cr Ottersleben, Ger; 2KIA 7POW; MACR 10361. CHERI.

43-37626 Del Cheyenne 5/5/44; Hunter 19/5/44; Dow Fd 4/6/44; ass 322BS/91BG [LG-M] Bassingbourn 10/6/44; MIA Berlin 21/6/44 w/Pakvan; e/a, cr Prenzlau, Ger; 3KIA 6POW; MACR 5929.

43-37627 Del Cheyenne 5/5/44; Kearney 25/5/44; Grenier 6/6/44; ass 327BS/92BG [UX-H] Podington 15/6/44; f/l Continent three times, last at Istres-le-Tube, Fr 22/6/45; sal 9AF 31/12/45.

43-37628 Del Cheyenne 5/5/44; Hunter 18/5/44; Dow Fd 30/5/44; ass 614BS/401BG [IW-O] Deenethorpe 10/6/44; retUS Bradley 7/6/45; 4168 BU Sth Plains 12/6/45; RFC Kingman 10/11/45. HEAVENLY BODY.

43-37629 Del Cheyenne 5/5/44; Hunter 20/5/44; Grenier 1/6/44; ass 360BS/303BG [PU-A] Molesworth 27/6/44; MIA Esbjerg, Den 27/8/44 w/Yarnall; flak, cr Esbjerg; MACR 8575.

43-37630 Del Cheyenne 5/5/44; Hunter 19/5/44; Dow Fd 5/6/44; ass 410BS/94BG [GL-N] Rougham

6/6/44 SASSY SUZY; MIA Bohlen 6/10/44 w/Fausnaugh; e/a, seen peeling off, cr?; 6KIA 4POW; MACR 9350. OUR BABY.

43-37631 Del Cheyenne 5/5/44; Hunter 20/5/44; Dow Fd 4/6/44; ass 8AF 8/6/44; sal n/b/d 12/7/44.

43-37632 Del Cheyenne 6/5/44; Hunter 21/5/44; Dow Fd 4/6/44; ass 612BS/401BG [SC-L] Deenethorpe 10/6/44; MIA Münster 30/9/44 w/Nagel; flak, cr Burgsteinfurt; 9POW; MACR 9417. I.P.

43-37633 Del Cheyenne 6/5/44; Hunter 21/5/44; Dow Fd 4/6/44; ass 368BS/306BG [BO-Z] Thurleigh 10/6/44; mid air coll w/43-38019 over Greenham Common, UK 15/12/44 w/?; 16 killed; sal.

43-37634 Del Cheyenne 6/5/44; Kearney 24/5/44; Dow Fd 5/6/44; ass 332BS/94BG Rougham 8/6/44; tran 96BG Snetterton 9/6/44; 731BS/452BG Deopham Green 6/44; retUS Bradley 5/7/45; 4168 BU Sth Plains 16/10/45; RFC Kingman 22/11/45.

43-37635 Del Cheyenne 6/5/44; Kearney 24/5/44; Dow Fd 1/6/44; ass 560BS/388BG Knettishall 3/6/44; MIA Holzwickede, Ger 23/3/45 w/Dennis; flak, cr Düsseldorf; 1KIA 8POW; MACR 13612.

43-37636 Del Cheyenne 6/5/44; Kearney 20/5/44; Grenier 17/6/44; ass 418BS/100BG [LD-W] Thorpe Abbotts 20/6/44; MIA Nuremberg 5/4/45 w/Estes; flak, cr Liége, Bel; 9KIA; MACR 13849.

43-37637 Del Cheyenne 6/5/44; Hunter 21/5/44; Grenier 6/6/44; ass 332BS/94BG [XM-U] Rougham (Azon a/c) 7/6/44; b/d Nuremberg 21/2/45 w/?; f/l Continent, sal; tran 34BG Mendlesham 9/6/45; retUS Bradley 26/6/45; 4168 BU Sth Plains 29/6/45; RFC Kingman 30/11/45.

43-37638 Del Dyersburg 6/5/44; 223 BU Dyersburg 15/5/44; 330 BU Dyersburg 1/3/45; 327 BU Drew 28/8/45; 330 BU Dyersburg 4/9/45; RFC Walnut Ridge 17/12/45.

43-37639 Del Dyersburg 6/5/44; 330 BU Dyersburg 2/3/45; 327 BU Drew 28/8/45; 330 BU Dyersburg 4/9/45; RFC Walnut Ridge 19/12/45.

43-37640 Del Dyersburg 6/5/44; 330 BU Dyersburg 1/3/45; 327 BU Drew 28/8/45; 330 BU Dyersburg 4/9/45; RFC Walnut Ridge 18/12/45.

43-37641 Del Pyote 6/5/44; Cheyenne 13/5/44; Pyote 18/5/44; 235 BU Biggs 23/7/44; 222 BU Ardmore 4/3/45; 332 BU Ardmore 16/6/45; RFC Walnut Ridge 26/9/45.

43-37642 Del Pyote 6/5/44; 236 BU Pyote 15/5/44; 235 BU Biggs 19/8/44; 225 BU Rapid City 22/3/45; 4003 BU Philadelphia 29/3/45; 225 BU Rapid City 28/4/45; 2114 BU Lockburn 19/7/45; 2137 BU Hendricks 29/9/45; RFC Walnut Ridge 8/1/46.

43-37643 Del Cheyenne 8/5/44; Patterson 21/5/44; Kearney 26/6/44; Grenier 6/7/44; ass 339BS/96BG [QJ-R] Snetterton 8/7/44; retUS Bradley 3/7/45; 4168 BU Sth Plains 6/7/45; RFC Kingman 7/12/45.

43-37644 Del Cheyenne 8/5/44; Hunter 21/5/44; Dow Fd 4/6/44; ass 728BS/452BG Deopham Green 7/6/44; 729BS; MIA Misburg, Ger 31/12/44 w/Segers; e/a, cr Hamburg; 2KIA 7POW; MACR 11231. FEATHER MERCHANT.

43-37645 Del Cheyenne 8/5/44; Hunter 21/5/44; Grenier 6/6/44; ass 452BG Deopham Green 8/6/44; tran 413BS/96BG Snetterton 11/6/44; MIA Steenwjik, Hol 24/3/45 w/Birch; mech fault, cr Channel, 9KIA; MACR 13603.

43-37646 Del Cheyenne 8/5/44; Kearney 29/5/44; Presque Is 28/6/44; ass 833BS/486BG Sudbury 29/6/44; MIA Osnabrück 21/11/44 w/Glashoff; mech fault, cr Halle; 1KIA 8POW; MACR 10405. LOW PRESSURE LULU.

43-37647 Del Cheyenne 8/5/44; Hunter 21/5/44; Dow Fd 9/6/44; ass 339BS/96BG [QJ-F] Snetterton 12/6/44; retUS Bradley 29/6/45; 4168 BU Sth Plains 2/7/45; RFC Kingman 18/12/45. PILGRIM'S PROGRESS.

43-37648 Del Pyote 8/5/44; Gt Falls 11/5/44; Pyote 16/5/44; 235 BU Biggs 16/8/44; 225 BU Rapid City 24/3/45; 2114 BU Lockburn 19/7/45; 2137 BU Hendricks 24/9/45; RFC Walnut Ridge 4/1/46.

43-37649 Del Pyote 8/5/44; Gt Falls 11/5/44; Pyote 14/5/44; 235 BU Biggs 16/8/44; 225 BU Rapid City 30/4/45; 2114 BU Lockburn 19/7/45; 2137 BU Hendricks 24/9/45; RFC Walnut Ridge 14/1/46.

43-37650 Del Pyote 8/5/44; Gt Falls 11/5/44; Pyote 14/5/44; 235 BU Biggs 19/8/44; 225 BU Rapid City 22/3/45; 232 BU Dalhart 15/7/45; 4136 BU Tinker 9/9/45; 232 BU Dalhart 15/9/45; 244 BU Harvard 29/10/45; RFC Altus 7/11/45. (Served California Airways 1952; Bolivia BC-97 Civil No. 66570).

43-37651 Del Rapid City 8/5/44; Gt Falls 11/5/44; Rapid City 12/5/44; 239 BU March 21/7/45; 420 BU March 15/10/45; RFC Walnut Ridge 25/2/46.

43-37652 Del Rapid City 8/5/44; Galveston 7/45; Barksdale 12/45; Memphis 10/46; mod to TB-17G 62 BU McDill; McChord 3/46; ass US Coast Guard 5/47 as PB-1R; Bolling for the US Sec/Treasury trip to Europe; McChord 6/51; 4 ERS Hamilton 6/51; mod to QB-17G at Brookley; as drone target blown up over Holloman, NM 7/54.

43-37653 Del Cheyenne 8/5/44; Hunter 22/5/44; Grenier 6/6/44; ass 8AF 9/6/44.

43-37654 Del Cheyenne 9/5/44; Kearney 29/5/44; Grenier 7/6/44; ass 360BS/303BG Molesworth 19/6/44; MIA Bremen 24/6/44 w/Farthing; mech fault, cr Hamburg; 9POW; MACR 6539.

43-37655 Del Cheyenne 9/5/44; Kearney 29/5/44; Dow Fd 17/6/44; ass 349BS/100BG Thorpe Abbotts 28/6/44; MIA Merseburg 29/7/44 w/Clark; e/a, cr Punschrau, Ger; 5KIA 4POW; MACR 7812.

43-37656 Del Cheyenne 9/5/44; Hunter 21/5/44; Dow Fd 4/6/44; ass 338BS/96BG [BX-O] Snetterton 11/6/44; ct fire & sal 21/1/45; retUS Bradley 3/7/45; 4168 BU Sth Plains 6/7/45; RFC Kingman 7/12/45. Re-ass USAAF, but finally W/O 21/7/47.

43-37657 Del Cheyenne 9/5/44; Hunter 22/5/44; Dow Fd 4/6/44; ass 534BS/381BG [GD-I] Ridgewell 10/6/44; b/d Brux 14/2/45 w/Anderson; 4POW 6RTD (inc p); sal 4/3/45. THE FOX.

43-37658 Del Rapid City 9/5/44; 4136 BU Tinker 5/9/44; 225 BU Rapid City 9/9/44; 2114 BU Lockburn 18/7/45; 2137 BU Hendricks 24/9/45; RFC Walnut Ridge 14/1/46.

43-37659 Del Rapid City 9/5/44; Gt Falls 12/5/44; Rapid City 15/5/44; 225 BU Rapid City 1/5/45; 246 BU Pratt 30/9/45; 3505 BU Scott 21/10/45; 246 BU Pratt 22/10/45; RFC Altus 3/1/46.

43-37660 Del Sioux City 9/5/44; Gt Falls 12/5/44; Sioux City 14/5/44; 224 BU Sioux City 6/3/45; 222 BU Ardmore 14/6/45; 332 BU Ardmore 16/6/45; 330 BU Dyersburg 12/9/45; RFC Walnut Ridge 11/12/45.

43-37661 Del Sioux City 9/5/44; 224 BU Sioux City 13/12/44; Recl Comp 1/1/45.

43-37662 Del Sioux City 9/5/44; 224 BU Sioux City 29/10/44; 225 BU Rapid City 16/6/45; 203 BU Jackson 30/6/45; 215 BU Pueblo 9/9/45; RFC Kingman 4/1/46.

43-37663 Del Cheyenne 9/5/44; Hunter 21/5/44; Grenier 1/6/44; ass 551BS/385BG Gt Ashfield 7/6/44; MIA Merseburg 29/7/44 w/Benefield; flak, cr Bloesien,?; 8KIA 1POW; MACR 7819.

43-37664 Del Cheyenne 9/5/44; Hunter 22/5/44; Grenier 6/6/44; ass 8AF 8/6/44; sal b/d 14/7/44.

43-37665 Del Cheyenne 10/5/44; Kearney 22/5/44; Dow Fd 30/5/44; ass 551BS/385BG Gt Ashfield 1/6/44; tran 510BS/351BG [TU-N] Polebrook 10/6/44; c/f & expl on base 25/3/45 {82m}; sal 2 SAD. LASSIE COME HOME.

43-37666 Del Cheyenne 10/5/44; Kearney 29/5/44; Dow Fd 17/6/44; ass 427BS/303BG [GN-T] Molesworth 10/7/44; mid air coll w/43-38057 during assembly 9/11/44; 17KIA; sal 2 SAD 10/11/44. FULL HOUSE.

43-37667 Del Cheyenne 10/5/44; Kearney 29/5/44; Grenier 17/6/44; ass 709BS/447BG Rattlesden 20/6/44; training mission, cr Meltham Moor, UK 6/4/45; sal 7/4/45.

43-37668 Del Sioux City 14/5/44; Gt Falls 13/5/44; Sioux City 16/5/44; 224 BU Sioux City 7/11/44; 273 BU Lincoln 11/11/44; 224 BU Sioux City 6/3/45; 222 BU Ardmore 15/6/45; 332 BU Ardmore 16/6/45; RFC Walnut Ridge 7/12/45.

43-37669 Del Sioux City 10/5/44; Gt Falls 13/5/44; Sioux City 15/5/44; 224 BU Sioux City 6/3/45; 222 BU Ardmore 14/6/45; 332 BU Ardmore 16/6/45; RFC Walnut Ridge 21/8/45.

43-37670 Del 488BG Avon Park 10/5/44; 330 BU Greenville 25/10/44; 325 BU Avon Park 29/10/44; RFC Walnut Ridge 7/12/45.

43-37671 Del 488BG Avon Park 10/5/44; Gt Falls 13/5/44; 325 BU Avon Park 13/8/45; RFC Walnut Ridge 13/11/45.

43-37672 Del 488BG Avon Park 10/5/44; Gt Falls 13/5/44; Avon Park 18/5/44; 325 BU Avon Park 9/4/45; RFC Walnut Ridge 18/12/45.

43-37673 Del Cheyenne 10/5/44; Hunter 21/5/44; Dow Fd 4/6/44; ass 728BS/452BG Deopham Green 7/6/44; MIA Misburg 31/12/44 w/Traynelis; e/a, cr Tauenbrueck, Ger?; 1KIA 8POW; MACR 11232.

43-37674 Del Cheyenne 10/5/44; Hunter 21/5/44; Dow Fd 4/6/44; ass 509BS/351BG [RQ-F] Polebrook 28/6/44; MIA {32m} Politz 7/10/44 w/McGuire; flak, f/l Bredakra, Swed; 9INT; MACR 9356. rep & ret group 6/45; retUS Bradley 9/7/45; 4168 BU Sth Plains 11/7/45; RFC Kingman 15/11/45.

43-37675 Del Cheyenne 10/5/44; Kearney 22/5/44; Dow Fd 29/5/44; ass 532BS/381BG [VE-N] Ridgewell 10/6/44 PATCHES; {55+m} b/d Neckarsulm 1/3/45 w/Price; last sighted St Pol sur Ternoise, Fr, f/l France?; rep & ret group; MACR 12810. RetUS Bradley 28/5/45; 4168 BU Sth Plains 6/6/45; RFC Kingman 17/12/45. FLAK MAGNET.

43-37676 Del Cheyenne 11/5/44; Kearney 25/5/44; Dow Fd 31/5/44; ass 509BS/351BG [RQ-L] Polebrook 8/6/44; b/d {57m} Merseburg 12/12/44 w/?; flak, f/l St Trond, Bel; sal 4/1/45.

43-37677 Del Cheyenne 12/5/44; Kearney 24/5/44; Dow Fd 6/6/44; ass 351BG Polebrook 6/6/44; tran 524BS/379BG [WA-A] Kimbolton 7/6/44; retUS Bradley 9/7/45; 4168 BU Sth Plains 12/7/45; RFC Kingman 13/12/45.

43-37678 Del 488BG Avon Park 11/5/44; McDill 23/5/44; 326 BU McDill 28/2/45; 330 BU Dyersburg 20/3/45; RFC Walnut Ridge 18/12/45.

43-37679 Del 488BG Avon Park 11/5/44; 325 BU Avon Park 9/4/45; RFC Walnut Ridge 7/12/45.

43-37680 Del 488BG Avon Park 11/5/44; 325 BU Avon Park 27/1/45; Recl Comp 11/4/45.

43-37681 Del 488BG Avon Park 11/5/44; McDill 24/5/44; 327 BU Drew 3/8/44; W/O 3/8/44; Recl Comp 6/7/45.

43-37682 Del 488BG Avon Park 11/5/44; Gt Falls 15/11/44; Avon Park 19/5/44; 901 BU Pinecastle 2/6/44; 903 BU Orlando 2/6/44; 325 BU Avon Park 15/6/44; RFC Walnut Ridge 21/8/45.

43-37683 Del Cheyenne 11/5/44; Kearney 22/5/44; Grenier 1/6/44; ass 339BS/96BG [QJ-J] Snetterton

3/6/44; retUS Bradley 28/6/45; 4168 BU Sth Plains 1/7/45; RFC Kingman 26/11/45. ROUND TRIP TICKET.

43-37684 Del Cheyenne 11/5/44; Patterson 25/5/44; Kearney 26/6/44; Grenier 9/7/44; ass 337BS/96BG [AW-E] Snetterton 11/7/44; b/d Mannheim 19/10/44 w/?; mid air coll w/42-3510; sal 23/10/44.

43-37685 Del Cheyenne 11/56/44; Kearney 24/5/44; Dow Fd 6/6/44; ass 563BS/388BG Knettishall 7/6/44; b/d Frankfurt 9/3/45 w/?; f/l Belgium; 9RTD; sal 1/4/45; retUS Bradley 30/6/45; 4168 BU Sth Plains 4/7/45; RFC Kingman 25/11/45. SLAVE'S DREAM.

43-37686 Del Cheyenne 11/5/44; Kearney 25/5/44; Dow Fd 30/5/44; ass 350BS/100BG [LN-G] Thorpe Abbotts 1/6/44; taxi acc w/44-6010 21/6/44, sal. JOSEPHINE.

43-37687 Del Cheyenne 12/5/44; Patterson 23/5/44; Kearney 27/6/44; Dow Fd 9/7/44; ass 385BG Gt Ashfield 11/7/44; tran 338BS/96BG [BX-Y] Snetterton 12/7/44; MIA Cottbus 15/2/45 w/?; flak, f/l Stachow, Pol; sal 17/2/45 & ret Group; retUS Bradley 13/7/45; 4185 BU Independence 15/7/45; RFC Kingman 17/12/45.

43-37688 Del 488BG Avon Park 12/5/44; 325 BU Avon Park 13/8/45; 2114 BU Lockburn 17/8/45; 4152 BU Lockburn 19/11/45; RFC Walnut Ridge 6/1/46.

43-37689 Del 488BG Avon Park 12/5/44; McDill 23/5/44; Cheyenne 5/10/44; 311 Ph Gp Buckley 3/11/44; 7 GEO Buckley 30/4/46; 7 GEO McDill 10/6/46; 3203 MSU Eglin 1/9/49; Recl Comp 12/49.

43-37690 Del 488BG Avon Park 12/5/44; Gt Falls 15/5/44; Avon Park 19/5/44; 328 BU Gulfport 31/3/45; 324 BU Chatham 11/5/45; RFC Altus 29/10/45.

43-37691 Del 488BG Avon Park 12/5/44; 4108 BU Newark 15/12/44; 325 BU Avon Park 18/12/44; RFC Walnut Ridge 12/12/45.

43-37692 Del 488BG Avon Park 12/5/44; 901 BU Pinecastle 2/6/44; 325 BU Avon Park 15/6/44; RFC Walnut Ridge 12/12/45.

43-37693 Del Cheyenne 12/5/44; Kearney 24/5/44; Dow Fd 1/6/44; ass 369BS/306BG [WW-L] Thurleigh 13/6/44; MIA Delitzsch 16/8/44 w/Ralstin; flak, cr Obermolbitz, Ger; 2KIA 7POW; MACR 7900.

43-37694 Del Cheyenne 12/5/44; Kearney 24/5/44; Dow Fd 4/6/44; ass 750BS/457BG Glatton 5/6/44; retUS Bradley 9/6/45; 4168 BU Sth Plains 13/6/45; RFC Kingman 30/11/45. PATTY ANN.

43-37695 Del Cheyenne 12/5/44; Patterson 23/5/44; Kearney 6/6/44; Grenier 17/6/44; ass 731BS/452BG Deopham Green 28/6/44; b/d Chemnitz 6/2/44 w/?; f/l Assigny, Fr; sal 25/2/45.

43-37696 Del Cheyenne 12/5/44; Kearney 23/5/44; Dow Fd 1/6/44; ass 509BS/351BG [RQ-Z] Polebrook 28/6/44; 510BS [TO-Z]; retUS Bradley 25/5/45; 4168 BU Sth Plains 28/5/45; {105m} RFC Kingman 27/11/45. TRANSIT BELLE.

43-37697 Del Cheyenne 12/5/44; Kearney 23/5/44; Dow Fd 30/5/44; ass 326BS/92BG [JW-N] Podington 7/6/44; sal 9AF Germany 10/12/45. LIBERTY RUN II.

43-37698 Del 88BG McDill 12/5/44; 4501 BU Lakeland 13/8/44; 326 BU McDill 30/8/44; 330 BU Dyersburg 16/3/45; RFC Walnut Ridge 19/12/45.

43-37699 Del 88BG McDill 12/5/44; 326 BU McDill 28/2/45; 330 BU Dyersburg 20/3/45; 555 BU Love Fd 18/8/45; 330 BU Dyersburg 20/8/45; 327 BU Drew 28/8/45; 330 BU Dyersburg 4/9/45; RFC Walnut Ridge 19/12/45.

43-37700 Del 88BG McDill 12/5/44; 326 BU McDill 21/5/44; 325 BU Avon Park 19/2/45; Recl Comp 20/3/46.

43-37701 Del 88BG McDill 12/5/44; 326 BU McDill 24/2/45; 327 BU Drew 2/3/45; 203 BU Jackson 3/9/45; 268 BU Peterson 11/10/45; RFC Kingman 27/10/45.

43-37702 Del 88BG McDill 13/5/44; 326 BU McDill 26/2/45; 329 BU Alexandra 12/3/45; 330 BU Dyersburg 25/6/45; RFC Walnut Ridge 17/12/45.

42-37703 Del Cheyenne 13/5/44; Kearney 23/5/44; Dow Fd 31/5/44; ass 544BS/384BG [SU-P] Grafton Underwood 8/6/44; MIA Sterkrade, Ger 22/1/45 w/Birder; flak, cr Düsseldorf; 9POW; MACR 11764. TREMBLIN' GREMLIN.

43-37704 Del Cheyenne 13/5/44; Kearney 24/5/44; Dow Fd 6/6/44; ass 535BS/381BG [MS-J] Ridgewell 16/6/44; b/d {17m} Cauvincourt 8/8/44 w/Beackley; a/c abandoned nr Caen, 9RTD. BUTTON NOSE.

43-37705 Del Cheyenne 13/5/44; Kearney 23/5/44; Dow Fd 30/5/44; ass 510BS/351BG [TU-V/T] Polebrook 1/6/44; 511BS [DS-F]; retUS Bradley 31/5/45; 4168 BU Sth Plains 4/6/45; RFC Kingman 17/12/45. THE LITTLE ONE.

43-37706 Del Cheyenne 13/5/44; Kearney 24/5/44; Dow Fd 1/6/44; ass 613BS/401BG [IN-U] Deenethorpe 12/6/44; retUS Bradley 7/6/45; 4168 BU Sth Plains 9/6/45; RFC Kingman 2/12/45.

43-37707 Del Cheyenne 13/5/44; Kearney 25/5/44; Dow Fd 1/6/44; ass 322BS/91BG [LG-M] Bassingbourn 28/6/44; 324BS [DF-M]; b/d Stendahl 8/4/45 w/Hanst; f/l Continent, sal. MADAME SHOO SHOO.

43-37708 Del 88BG McDill 13/5/44; 326 BU McDill 23/5/44; 3501 BU Boca Raton 9/2/45; 326 BU McDill 20/2/45; 4210 BU Lambert 6/4/45; 326 BU McDill 10/4/45; 575 BU Pittsburg 27/7/45; 326 BU McDill 19/9/45; 554 BU Memphis 31/5/46; 4000 BU Patterson 5/6/46; 554 BU Memphis 6/6/46; 4000 BU Wright 2/7/46.

43-37709 Del 483BG McDill 13/5/44; McDill 22/5/44; 351 BU Myrtle 7/9/44; 4139 BU Birmingham 6/11/44; 326 BU McDill 10/2/45; 325 BU Avon Park 19/2/45; RFC Walnut Ridge 21/8/45.

43-37710 Del 88BG McDill 13/5/44; 327 BU Drew 25/5/44; W/O 11/12/44.

43-37711 Del 88BG McDill 13/5/44; 19 Ph Gp McDill 25/4/44; 19 Ph Gp Buckley 29/11/44; ass 9AF Britain 24/5/44; sal 30/10/46.

43-37712 Del 88BG McDill 13/5/44; 4115 BU Atlanta 20/9/44; 326 BU McDill 4/10/44; 329 Alexandra 18/3/45; 327 BU Drew 8/7/45; 203 BU Jackson 31/8/45; 268 BU Peterson 7/10/45; RFC Kingman 27/10/45.

43-37713 Del Cheyenne 13/5/44; Kearney 24/5/44; Dow Fd 1/6/44; ass 546BS/384BG [BK-S] Grafton Underwood 3/6/44; MIA Zeitz 30/11/44 w/Evans; flak, cr Zeitz; 4KIA 5POW; MACR 11129.

43-37714 Del Cheyenne 15/5/44; Kearney 24/5/44; Dow Fd 1/6/44; ass 708BS/447BG Rattlesden 3/6/44; MIA Hannover 18/6/44 w/Golden; flak, cr Ohlum, Gr?; 1KIA 9POW; MACR 5902.

43-37715 Del Cheyenne 15/5/44; Kearney 25/5/44; Dow Fd 1/6/44; ass 367BS/306BG [V] Thurleigh 13/6/44; sal 8/1/45. LASSIE COME HOME.

43-37716 Del Cheyenne 15/5/44; Kearney 30/5/44; Dow Fd 13/7/44; ass 338BS/96BG [BX-H] Snetterton 14/7/44; tran 388BG 5/45; retUS Bradley 14/7/45; 4168 BU Sth Plains 29/7/45; {78m} RFC Kingman 22/11/45. (so named as 5,000th B-17 off Boeing production line and signed by all workers) 5 GRAND.

43-37717 Del Cheyenne 15/5/44; Kearney 25/5/44; Dow Fd 1/6/44; ass 545BS/384BG [JD-S] Grafton Underwood 3/6/44; b/d Koblenz 5/1/45 w/?; f/l Continent; rep & ret group 22/3/45; sal 9AF Germany 18/2/46. PRO-KID.

43-37718 Del 88BG McDill 15/5/44; Gt Falls 19/5/44; McDill 24/5/44; 327 BU Drew 25/5/45; 301 BU Drew 22/10/45; RFC Altus 5/11/45.

43-37719 Del 88BG McDill 15/5/44; 326 BU McDill 22/5/44; 330 BU Dyersburg 5/3/45; RFC Walnut Ridge 9/12/45.

43-37720 Del 88BG McDill 15/5/44; 575 BU Pittsburg 9/11/44; 326 BU McDill 6/12/44; 335 BU Del Marbry 14/6/45; 326 BU McDill 18/6/45; 4000 BU Patterson 9/8/46; 4000 BU Wright 14/8/46.

43-37721 Del 396BG Drew 15/5/44; 327 BU Drew 4/5/45; 326 BU McDill 6/11/45; RFC Walnut Ridge 21/2/46.

43-37722 Del 396BG Drew 15/5/44; 327 BU Drew 4/5/45; 326 BU McDill 13/10/45; 62 BU McDill 13/10/46; 62 BU Morrison 12/2/47; 4141 BU Pyote 13/3/47; re-ass 31/3/47; 4141 BU Pyote 11/5/48.

43-37723 Del Cheyenne 15/5/44; Kearney 7/6/44; Grenier 12/7/44; ass 337BS/96BG [AW-H] Snetterton 14/7/44; b/d Fulda 3/1/45 w/?; f/l Continent; sal 28/6/45.

43-37724 Del Cheyenne 15/5/44; Kearney 25/5/44; Dow Fd 6/6/44; ass 561BS/388BG Knettishall 7/6/44 OLD SILVER; b/d Kassel 30/12/44 w/?; f/l Lille, Fr; sal 28/1/45; retUS Bradley 29/6/45; 4168 BU Sth Plains 2/7/45; RFC Kingman 18/12/45. SOLVANG REVENGER.

43-37725 Del Cheyenne 15/5/44; Fairfield 28/5/44; Kearney 26/6/44; Grenier 9/7/44; ass 338BS/96BG [BX-K] Snetterton 12/7/44; retUS Bradley 2/7/45; 4168 BU Sth Plains 8/7/45; RFC Kingman 27/11/45.

43-37726 Del Cheyenne 15/5/44; Hunter 26/5/44; Grenier 6/6/44; ass 731BS/452BG Deopham Green 7/6/44; b/d Darmstadt, Ger 24/12/44 w/?; f/l Moelsbroek A/fd, Bel; sal 2/1/45.

43-37727 Del Cheyenne 16/5/44; Kearney 25/5/44; Dow Fd 1/6/44; ass 508BS/351BG [YB-N] Polebrook 9/6/44; MIA {48m} Merseburg 21/11/44 w/Loehndorf; flak, cr Merseburg; MACR 11204.

43-37728 Del 396BG Drew 16/5/44; 327 BU Drew 14/2/45; Recl Comp 1/3/45.

43-37729 Del 396BG Drew 16/5/44; Gt Falls 19/5/44; Drew 24/5/44; 328 BU Gulfport 31/3/45; 330 BU Dyersburg 17/5/45; 327 BU Drew 28/8/45; 330 BU Dyersburg 18/9/45; RFC Walnut Ridge 18/12/45.

43-37730 Del 396BG Drew 16/5/44; 327 BU Drew 26/5/44; 203 BU Jackson 12/9/45; 268 BU Peterson 11/10/45; RFC Kingman 7/11/45.

43-37731 Del 396BG Drew 16/5/44; 327 BU Drew 25/5/44; 110 BU Mitchell 6/3/45; 327 BU Drew 4/6/45; 110 BU Mitchell 9/1/46; 326 BU McDill 16/1/46; RFC Walnut Ridge 21/2/46.

43-37732 Del 396BG Drew 16/5/44; 327 BU Drew 26/5/44; 203 BU Jackson 4/9/45; 268 BU Peterson 9/10/45; RFC Kingman 27/10/45.

43-37733 Del Cheyenne 16/5/44; Kearney 26/5/44; Dow Fd 6/6/44; ass 749BS/457BG Glatton 7/6/44; retUS Bradley 22/5/45; 4168 BU Sth Plains 24/5/45; RFC Kingman 14/12/45. ACE OF HEARTS.

43-37734 Del Cheyenne 16/5/44; Kearney 25/5/44; Dow Fd 1/6/44; ass 338BS/96BG [BX-X] Snetterton 3/6/44; b/d Hamburg 4/8/44 w/?; c/l Hardwick A/fd, UK; sal 7/8/44.

43-37735 Del Cheyenne 16/5/44; Kearney 29/5/44; Grenier 28/6/44; ass 837BS/487BG [4F-Q] Lavenham 7/6/44; tran 457BG Glatton 29/6/44; sal 9AF Germany 10/12/45. MY GAL ELLEN.

43-37736 Del Cheyenne 16/5/44; Kearney 24/5/44;

Dow Fd 1/6/44; ass 613BS/401BG [IN-T] Deenethorpe 10/6/44 LITTLE PIECES; b/d Merseburg 8/11/44 w/?; rep & ret group; sal 9AF Germany 18/2/46. LITTLE PEDRO!

43-37737 Del Cheyenne 16/5/44; Kearney 25/5/44; Dow Fd 1/6/44; ass 533BS/381BG Ridgewell 10/6/44; sal 2 SAD 24/6/44. SECOND YEAR.

43-37738 Del 396BG Drew 17/5/44; 327 BU Drew 4/5/45; 203 BU Jackson 9/9/45; 268 BU Peterson 15/10/45; RFC Altus 7/11/45.

43-37739 Del 396BG Drew 17/5/44; 327 BU Drew 1/8/44; 326 BU McDill 12/12/44; 300 BU McDill 20/3/45; 73 WG McDill 31/3/45; 326 BU McDill 31/5/45; Recl Comp 30/1/46.

43-37740 Del 396BG Drew 17/5/44; Gt Falls 20/5/44; Drew 25/5/44; 328 BU Gulfport 3/6/44; 326 BU McDill 10/5/45; 325 BU Avon Park 30/5/45; 326 BU McDill 6/6/45; 4200 BU Davis Monthan 17/9/45; 326 BU McDill 19/9/45; 427 BU Roswell 31/7/46; sal 29/8/46.

43-37741 Del 396BG Drew 17/5/44; 4200 BU Chicago Mun 25/5/44; 2185 BU Nashville 7/7/44; 328 BU Gulfport 31/3/45; 330 BU Dyersburg 17/5/45; 327 BU Drew 26/8/45; 330 BU Dyersburg 4/9/45; RFC Walnut Ridge 18/12/45.

43-37742 Del 396BG Drew 17/5/44; Gt Falls 22/5/44; Drew 26/5/44; 328 BU Gulfport 31/3/45; 330 BU Dyersburg 17/5/45; RFC Walnut Ridge 17/12/45.

43-37743 Del Cheyenne 17/5/44; Kearney 27/5/44; Grenier 7/6/44; ass 379BG Kimbolton 19/6/44; retUS Bradley 29/6/45; 4168 BU Sth Plains 2/7/45; RFC Kingman 5/12/45.

43-37744 Del Cheyenne 17/12/44; Kearney 29/5/44; Grenier 17/6/44; ass 731BS/452BG Deopham Green 20/6/44; MIA Münster 5/10/44 w/Green; flak, cr Wesel, Ger; 10POW; MACR 9765. FINAL APPROACH.

43-37745 Del Cheyenne 17/5/44; Kearney 29/5/44; Grenier 17/6/44; ass 731BS/452BG Deopham Green 19/6/44; MIA Hamburg 17/1/45 w/Betts; flak, f/l Kalamar, Swed; 9INT; MACR 11729. RetUS Bradley 1/8/45; 4185 BU Independence 3/8/45; RFC Kingman 7/10/46. LACKA SACKY.

43-37746 –

43-37747 Del Cheyenne 17/5/44; Kearney 26/5/44; Dow Fd 4/6/44; ass 729BS/452BG Deopham Green 7/6/44; MIA French Noball sites 8/7/44 w/Hansen; flak, cr Boubrers, Fr; 9KIA 1POW; MACR 7224.

43-37748 Del Lockburn 17/5/44; Gt Falls 20/5/44; Columbus 24/5/44; 2114 BU Lockburn 25/5/44; RFC Walnut Ridge 8/1/46.

43-37749 Del Lockburn 17/5/44; Columbus 24/5/44; 2114 Lockburn 25/5/45; 2137 BU Hendricks 22/9/45; RFC Walnut Ridge 21/1/46.

43-37750 Del Hendricks 18/5/44; 2137 BU Hendricks 28/8/44; 3715 BU Burbank 29/8/44; 3701 BU Amarillo 24/5/45; 3017 BU Hobbs 25/5/45; RFC Altus 3/1/46.

43-37751 Del Hendricks 18/5/44; 2137 BU Hendricks 12/11/44; RFC Kingman 1/11/45.

43-37752 Del Hendricks 18/5/44; 271 BU Kearney 7/7/44; 2002 BU Stewart 19/8/44; 2114 BU Lockburn 1/9/44; 4104 BU Rome 2/10/44; 1 BU Bolling 21/12/44; 2002 BU Stewart 4/1/45; 2137 BU Hendricks 13/2/45; 237 BU Kirtland 28/6/45; 2137 BU Hendricks 30/8/45; 235 BU Biggs 8/11/45; 305 BU Biggs 28/11/45; RFC Kingman 4/12/45.

43-37753 Del Cheyenne 18/5/44; Kearney 27/5/44; Grenier 5/6/44; ass 729BS/452BG Deopham Green 11/6/44; retUS Bradley 29/6/45; 4168 BU Sth Plains 1/7/45; RFC Kingman 27/11/45.

43-37754 Del Cheyenne 18/5/44; Kearney 27/5/44; Grenier 4/6/44; ass 385BG Gt Ashfield 7/6/44; b/d French Noball sites 8/7/44 w/?; f/l Continent; sal 14/11/44, rep & ret group; retUS, RFC Kingman 27/11/45. MICKEY II.

43-37755 Del Cheyenne 18/5/44; Kearney 29/5/44; Grenier 4/6/44; ass 526BS/379BG [LF-Z] Kimbolton 28/6/44; b/d Merseburg 13/9/44 w/?; c/l Belgium, 9RTD; sal 13/2/45. EVERYBODY'S BABY.

43-37756 Del Cheyenne 18/5/44; Kearney 27/5/44; Dow Fd 8/6/44; ass 708BS/447BG Rattlesden 9/6/44; completed 129 missions with no abort; retUS Bradley 9/7/45; 4168 BU Sth Plains 13/7/45; RFC Kingman 21/11/45. MILK WAGON.

43-37757 Del Cheyenne 18/5/44; Kearney 28/5/44; Grenier 4/6/44; ass 561BS/388BG Knettishall 7/6/44; c/l RAF Manston, UK 17/6/44; sal. PANHANDLE.

43-37758 Del Hobbs 18/5/44; 2519 BU Ft Worth 5/12/44; 3017 BU Hobbs 8/12/44; 3701 BU Amarillo 7/10/45; RFC Kingman 21/11/45.

43-37759 Del Hobbs 18/5/44; 3017 BU Hobbs 16/1/45; 3701 BU Amarillo 27/9/45; RFC Kingman 28/12/45.

43-37760 Del Roswell 18/5/44; 3030 BU Roswell 2/6/44; RFC Walnut Ridge 7/1/46.

43-37761 Del Roswell 18/5/44; Denver 26/5/44; 3030 BU Roswell 2/6/44; W/O 17/11/44.

43-37762 Del Ft Myers 19/5/44; 3036 BU Yuma 24/6/44; 3017 BU Hobbs 4/6/45; 3701 BU Amarillo 27/9/45; RFC Kingman 23/11/45.

43-37763 Del Cheyenne 19/5/44; Kearney 2/6/44; Grenier 18/6/44; ass 422BS/305BG Chelveston 28/6/44; MIA Wurzberg 21/7/44 w/Toftness; flak, cr Nth Sea; 8KIA 1RTD; MACR 8233.

43-37764 Del Cheyenne 19/5/44; Patterson 20/5/44; Kearney 26/6/44; Grenier 6/7/44; ass 337BS/96BG [AW-B] Snetterton 8/7/44 - 7 UP 'N CIDER; c/t/o Osnabrück 21/11/44 w/?; c/l Quidenham, UK; 9WIA; sal 22/11/44. BOYD'S BOIDS.

43-37765 Del Cheyenne 19/5/44; Kearney 1/6/44; Grenier 18/6/44; ass 413BS/96BG [MZ-K] Snetterton 18/6/44 THE DUCHESS; tran 457BG Glatton 19/6/44; 8 ERS Halesworth 24/3/45; sal 9AF Germany 10/12/45. DONNA J II.

43-37766 Del Cheyenne 19/5/44; Hunter 2/6/44; Grenier 14/6/44; ass 751BS/457BG Glatton 17/6/44; MIA Merseburg 2/11/44 w/Morrow; e/a, cr Volkstedt, Ger; 3KIA 6POW; 10318. DELORES.

43-37767 Del Cheyenne 19/5/44; Patterson 26/5/44; Kearney 26/6/44; Grenier 6/7/44; ass 339BS/96BG [QJ-H] Snetterton 8/7/44; MIA Brunswick 2/3/45 w/Gatch; mid air coll w/44-8697; cr Channel; 9KIA; MACR 12846. MY IDEA - MY IDEAL.

43-37768 Del Ft Myers 19/5/44; 2117 BU Buckingham 30/5/44; 3036 BU Yuma 16/6/44; 3017 BU Hobbs 4/6/45; 3701 BU Amarillo 14/10/45; RFC Kingman 6/12/45.

43-37769 Del Kingman 19/5/44; 3018 BU Kingman 29/5/44; 3017 BU Hobbs 27/6/45; 3701 BU Amarillo 4/10/45; RFC Kingman 27/11/45.

43-37770 No early details, but in service as VB-17G with Air Training Command, Chanute AFB 1956.

43-37771 Del Las Vegas 19/5/44; 3021 BU Las Vegas 2/6/44; 3022 BU Indian Springs 16/6/44; 4126 BU San Bernardino 13/12/45; 3022 BU Indian Springs 20/12/44; 3021 BU Las Vegas 15/3/45; 3006 BU Las Vegas 3/4/45; 3000 BU Orange 28/7/45; RFC Walnut Ridge 2/1/46.

43-37772 Del Las Vegas 19/5/44; 3021 BU Las Vegas 2/6/44; 3022 BU Indian Springs 16/6/44; 4126 BU San Bernardino 23/12/45; 3022 BU Indian Springs 2/1/45; 3021 BU Las Vegas 19/3/45; 2137 BU Hendricks 14/10/45; RFC Kingman 1/11/45.

43-37773 Del Cheyenne 19/5/44; Hunter 2/6/44; Grenier 12/6/44; ass 410BS/94BG [GL-W] Rougham 16/6/44; b/d Wetzlar 21/11/44 w/Ullrey; f/l Antwerp A/fd, Bel; sal 22/12/44. THE UNINVITED.

43-37774 Del Cheyenne 20/5/44; Kearney 1/6/44; Grenier 16/6/44; ass 708BS/447BG Rattlesden 20/6/44; retUS Bradley 5/7/45; 4168 BU Sth Plains 7/7/45; RFC Kingman 17/12/45.

43-37775 Del Cheyenne 20/5/44; Kearney 1/6/44; Grenier 18/6/44; ass 339BS/96BG [QJ-E] Snetterton 19/6/44 HELL'S CHARIOT; retUS Bradley 9/7/45; 4168 BU Sth Plains 8/8/45; RFC Kingman 21/12/45. OH! HARD LUCK.

43-37776 Del Cheyenne 20/5/44; Kearney 31/5/44; Grenier 7/6/44; ass 490BG Eye 11/6/44; sal b/d 3/10/44; tran 15AF MTO, Exc Inv 30/11/45.

43-37777 Del Cheyenne 20/5/44; Kearney 29/5/44; Grenier 7/6/44; ass 525BS/379BG Kimbolton 19/6/44; 527BS; sal 18/6/45. FOUR OF A KIND.

43-37778 Del Yuma 20/5/44; 3017 BU Hobbs 4/6/45; 425 BU Gowen 13/8/45; 3017 BU Hobbs 1/9/45; 3701 BU Amarillo 14/10/45; RFC Kingman 6/12/45.

43-37779 Del Yuma 20/5/44; 3017 BU Hobbs 4/6/45; 3701 BU Amarillo 7/10/45; RFC Kingman 28/12/45.

43-37780 Del Cheyenne 20/5/44; Kearney 29/5/44; Grenier 4/6/44; ass 508BS/351BG [YB-O] Polebrook 9/6/44; {5m} b/d Munich 12/7/44 w/?; c/l base, sal 15/7/44.

43-37781 Del Cheyenne 20/5/44; Kearney 29/5/44; Grenier 7/6/44; ass 337BS/96BG [AW-R] Snetterton 11/6/44; dest by e/a at Poltava 21/6/44; sal 1/7/44.

43-37782 Del Cheyenne 20/5/44; Kearney 3/8/44; Grenier 15/8/44; ass 750BS/457BG Glatton 16/8/44 LADY MARGARET; MIA Merseburg 2/11/44 w/Murdock; e/a, cr Emseloh, Ger; 3KIA 6POW; MACR 10319. LADY KATHERINE.

43-37783 Del Cheyenne 20/5/44; Hunter 17/8/44; Grenier 7/9/44; ass 412BS/95BG [QW-F] Horham 8/9/44 TEMPTATION; 335BS [OE-R]; b/d Frankfurt 5/1/45 w/?; f/l Laon A/fd, Fr; retUS Bradley 6/7/45; 4168 BU Sth Plains 8/7/45; RFC Kingman 23/11/45. LUCKY SHERRY.

43-37784 Del Cheyenne 20/5/44; Kearney 31/5/44; Presque Is 28/6/44; ass 569BS/390BG [CC-S] Framlingham 28/6/44; tran 407BS/92BG [PY-O] Podington 18/7/44; b/d Cologne 28/1/45 w/?; f/l St Trond, Bel; sal 2/2/45. BIG CHIEF.

43-37785 Del Cheyenne 21/5/44; Hunter 1/6/44; Grenier 13/6/44; ass 748BS/457BG Glatton 17/6/44; retUS Bradley 8/6/45; 4168 BU Sth Plains 11/6/45; RFC Kingman 29/11/45. TARFU.

43-37786 Del Cheyenne 21/5/44; Hunter 2/6/44; Grenier 14/6/44; ass 551BS/385BG Gt Ashfield 16/6/44; retUS Bradley 26/6/45; 4168 BU Sth Plains 28/6/45; RFC Kingman 23/11/45. MADAM SHOO SHOO.

43-37787 Del Cheyenne 21/5/44; Kearney 5/6/44; Grenier 17/6/44; ass 413BS/96BG Snetterton 19/6/44; tran 560BS/388BG Knettishall 20/6/44; b/d Berlin 5/12/44 w/?; f/l Knocke, Bel; 9RTD; sal. HOLY SMOKES.

43-37788 Del Cheyenne 21/5/44; Hunter 3/6/44; Grenier 15/6/44; ass 709BS/447BG Rattlesden 17/6/44; MIA Munich 13/7/44 w/Hilding; flak, cr Vendrest?; 8EVD 2POW; MACR 6938. Sal 13/10/44.

43-37789 Del Cheyenne 21/5/44; Patterson 30/5/44; Kearney 30/6/44; Dow Fd 13/7/44; ass 413BS/96BG Snetterton 14/7/44; MIA Frankfurt 9/3/45 w/Fox; flak, cr Langen, Ger; 1KIA 8POW; sal 14/4/45; MACR 12958.

43-37790 Del Cheyenne 21/5/44; Kearney 30/5/44;

Grenier 17/6/44; ass 612BS/401BG [SC-J] Deenethorpe 10/7/44; b/d 28/3/45 w/?; c/l Belgium, 9RTD; sal. LADY LUCK.

43-37791 Del Cheyenne 21/5/44; Kearney 29/5/44; Grenier 18/6/44; ass 533BS/381BG [VP-V] Ridgewell 28/6/44; b/d Cologne 18/12/44 w/Pearce; f/l Continent; sal 5/1/45.

43-37792 Del Cheyenne 22/5/44; Kearney 30/5/44; Grenier 7/6/44; ass 413BS/96BG [MZ-N] Snetterton 11/6/44; MIA Osnabrück 21/11/44 w/Chrisman; flak, cr Poye, Ger; 8KIA 1MIA; MACR 10417.

43-37793 Del Cheyenne 22/5/44; Hunter 1/6/44; Grenier 17/6/44; ass APH/388BG Knettishall 6/44; retUS Bradley 5/7/45; 4168 BU Sth Plains 10/7/45; RFC Kingman 9/12/45.

43-37794 Del Cheyenne 22/5/44; Hunter 1/6/44; Grenier 9/6/44; ass 447BG Rattlesden 11/6/44; tran 337BS/96BG [AW-T] Snetterton 12/6/44; MIA Weisbaden 19/9/44 w/Bauman; flak, cr Weisbaden; 9POW; MACR 10202.

43-37795 Del Cheyenne 22/5/44; Hunter 1/6/44; Grenier 14/6/44; ass 709BS/447BG Rattlesden 16/6/44; c/l 8/5/45; sal, rep & ret group 6/45; retUS 121 BU Bradley 5/7/45; 4168 BU Sth Plains 7/7/45; RFC Kingman 19/12/45.

43-37796 Del Cheyenne 23/5/44; Kearney 1/6/44; Dow Fd 27/6/44; ass 423BS/306BG Thurleigh 8/11/44; MIA Brunswick 22/10/44 w/Capt Mathis; mid air coll w/306BG, cr sea off Clacton, UK; 9KIA; MACR 9656.

43-37797 Del Cheyenne 23/5/44; Hunter 1/6/44; Grenier 14/6/44; ass 708BS/447BG Rattlesden 16/6/44; sal 8/5/45; retUS Bradley 5/7/45; 4168 BU Sth Plains 7/7/45; RFC Kingman 14/12/45. AMERICAN BEAUTY.

43-37798 Del Cheyenne 23/5/44; Kearney 1/6/44; Grenier 16/6/44; ass 339BS/96BG [QJ-Q] Snetterton 20/6/44; retUS Bradley 29/6/45; 4168 BU Sth Plains 2/7/45; RFC Kingman 22/11/45.

43-37799 Del Cheyenne 23/5/44; Hunter 1/6/44; Grenier 14/6/44; ass 447BS Rattlesden 16/6/44; tran 339BS/96BG [QJ-W] Snetterton 17/6/44; b/d French Noball sites 8/7/44 w/?; c/l RAF Sutton Bridge, UK; sal 10/7/44.

43-37800 Del Cheyenne 23/5/44; Hunter 2/6/44; Grenier 11/6/44; ass 401BG Deenethorpe 28/6/44; tran 835BS/486BG [H8-S] Sudbury 29/6/44; retUS Bradley 7/7/45; 4168 BU Sth Plains 9/7/45; RFC Kingman 8/12/45.

43-37801 Del Cheyenne 23/5/44; Hunter 3/6/44; Grenier 14/6/44; ass 336BS/95BG [ET-P] Horham 17/6/44; MIA Merseburg 28/9/44 w/Heath; cr Heinzil, Ger; 9POW; MACR 9372.

43-37802 Del Cheyenne 23/5/44; Hunter 3/6/44; Grenier 15/6/44; ass 728BS/452BG Deopham Green 19/6/44; retUS Bradley 5/7/45; 4168 BU Sth Plains 8/7/45; RFC Kingman 13/12/45. MY-ASSIS-DRAGON.

43-37803 Del Cheyenne 23/5/44; Kearney 2/6/44; Grenier 17/6/44; ass 549BS/385BG Gt Ashfield 20/6/44; retUS Bradley 26/6/45; 4168 BU Sth Plains 28/6/45; RFC Kingman 24/11/45. HELLS BELLE.

43-37804 Del Cheyenne 23/5/44; Kearney 1/6/44; Dow Fd 27/6/44; ass 570BS/390BG Framlingham 28/6/44; MIA Düsseldorf 9/9/44 w/Harris; flak, cr Landsberg, Ger; 9POW; MACR 8912.

43-37805 Del Cheyenne 23/5/44; Hunter 3/6/44; Dow Fd 27/6/44; ass 837BS/487BG Lavenham 28/6/44; MIA Berlin 6/8/44 w/Hatfield; flak, cr Germany; 1KIA 8POW; MACR 7892.

43-37806 Del Cheyenne 24/5/44; Kearney 2/6/44; Grenier 16/6/44; ass 486BG Sudbury 18/6/44; tran 561BS/388BG Knettishall 19/6/44; during assembly for Chemnitz 6/2/45 w/?, mid air coll w/490BG a/c, cr Wicken, UK, two civilians killed; cp killed when chute failed; 9RTD; sal. MISS FORTUNE.

43-37807 Del Cheyenne 24/5/44; Kearney 2/6/44; Grenier 17/6/44; ass 731BS/452BG Deopham Green 20/6/44; retUS Bradley 6/7/45; 4168 BU Sth Plains 9/7/45; RFC Kingman 8/12/45.

43-37808 Del Cheyenne 24/5/44; Hunter 3/6/44; Grenier 14/6/44; ass 350BS/100BG [LN-U] Thorpe Abbotts 16/6/44; b/d Cologne 10/1/45 w/?; f/l Belgium. MILK RUN MABEL.

43-37809 Del Cheyenne 24/5/44; Kearney 2/6/44; Grenier 16/6/44; ass 305BG Chelveston 28/6/44; tran 351BG Polebrook 23/5/45; retUS Bradley 11/6/45; 4168 BU Sth Plains 14/6/45; RFC Kingman 5/12/45.

43-37810 Del Cheyenne 24/5/44; Hunter 3/6/44; Grenier 14/6/44; 41204 BU Rome 17/9/44; 1308 BU Presque Is 9/11/44; 4104 BU Rome 5/12/44; 3704 BU Keesler 8/1/45; 1377 BU Grenier 20/1/45; ass 401BG Deenethorpe 16/6/44; c/l Grenier 1/8/44; sal 1377 BU Grenier 31/8/44.

43-37811 Del Cheyenne 24/5/44; Hunter 3/6/44; Grenier 15/6/44; ass 401BG Deenethorpe 16/6/44; tran 350BS/100BG [LN-D] Thorpe Abbotts 17/6/44; b/d Brandenburg 10/4/45 w/?; c/l Leiston A/fd, sal 12/4/45.

43-37812 Del Cheyenne 24/5/44; Hunter 3/6/44; Grenier 14/6/44; ass 351BS/100BG [EP-P] Thorpe Abbotts 16/6/44; MIA Marburg 23/3/45 w/Guardino; flak, cr Montabaur, Ger; 9KIA; MACR 13604.

43-37813 Del Cheyenne 25/5/44; Hunter 3/6/44; Grenier 15/6/44; ass 422BS/305BG Chelveston 28/6/44; MIA Mannheim 9/9/44 w/Keeney; flak, cr Viernheim, Ger; 9KIA; MACR 8598. SCOOTERINI.

43-37814 Del Cheyenne 25/5/44; Hunter 3/6/44; Grenier 17/6/44; ass 729BS/452BG Deopham Green 20/6/44; returning Nuremberg nosed over on landing 5/4/45; sal 6/4/45. RICHTER'S WRECKERS.

43-37815 Del Cheyenne 25/5/44; Kearney 5/6/44; Dow Fd 27/6/44; ass 351BS/100BG [EP-L] Thorpe Abbotts 28/6/44; tran 482BG Alconbury 20/5/45; retUS Bradley 2/6/45; 4168 BU Sth Plains 13/6/45; RFC Kingman 28/11/45. HUMPTY DUMPTY.

43-37816 Del Cheyenne 25/5/44; Kearney 4/6/44; Grenier 16/6/44; ass 305BG Chelveston 28/6/44; b/d Montbartier, Fr fuel dumps 7/8/44 w/?; c/l France.

43-37817 Del Cheyenne 26/5/44; Kearney 4/6/44; Grenier 17/6/44; ass 452BG 20/6/44; sal 14/7/44. MOLLITA.

43-37818 Del Cheyenne 26/5/44; Hunter 5/6/44; Dow Fd 17/6/44; ass 709BS/447BG Rattlesden 28/6/44; MIA Ludwigshafen 26/9/44 w/Calef; flak, cr Oldenburg; 7KIA 2POW; MACR 9401. HURRY HOME.

43-37819 Del Cheyenne 26/5/44; Kearney 4/6/44; Grenier 17/6/44; ass 322BS/91BG Bassingbourn 19/7/44; MIA Leipzig 20/7/44 w/Walby; e/a, cr Silbestr, Ger?; 2KIA 7POW; MACR 7284.

43-37820 Del Cheyenne 26/5/44; Kearney 7/6/44; Grenier 17/6/44; ass 832BS/486BG [3R-T] Sudbury 28/6/44; MIA Brandenburg 10/4/45 w/Thaler; flak, cr Ziesar, Ger; 10POW; MACR 13910.

43-37821 Del Cheyenne 25/5/44; Kearney 4/6/44; Grenier 17/6/44; ass 711BS/447BG Rattlesden 20/6/44; 710BG; MIA Berlin 6/8/44 w/Mateyka; e/a, ditched Nth Sea; 9POW; MACR 9779. RED HOT MAMA.

43-37822 Del Cheyenne 25/5/44; Kearney 8/6/44; Grenier 28/6/44; ass 544BS/384BG [SU-N] Grafton Underwood 29/6/44; MIA Magdeburg 28/9/44 w/Broadie; flak, cr Ingersleben, 8KIA 1POW; MACR 9753.

43-37823 Del Cheyenne 25/5/44; Hunter 5/6/44; Grenier 15/6/44; ass 349BS/100BG [XR-V] Thorpe Abbotts 17/6/44; b/d Bohlen 11/9/44 w/?; c/l Isle of Sheppey, UK; sal 12/9/44. NOW AN' THEN.

43-37824 Del Cheyenne 25/5/44; Hunter 5/6/44; Grenier 15/6/44; ass 731BS/452BG Deopham Green 19/6/44; 729BS; retUS Bradley 3/7/45; 4168 BU Sth Plains 5/7/45; RFC Kingman 10/12/45.

43-37825 Del Cheyenne 25/5/44; Kearney 4/6/44; Grenier 19/6/44; ass 603BS/398BG [N7-J] Nuthampstead 18/7/44; MIA Vlotho, Ger; 14/3/45 w/Ellis; flak, cr Bielefeld; 5KIA 4POW; MACR 10391.

43-37826 Del Cheyenne 26/5/44; Kearney 4/6/44; Presque Is 28/6/44; ass 748BS/457BG Glatton 19/6/44; retUS Bradley 25/5/45; 4168 BU Sth Plains 26/5/45; RFC Kingman 28/11/45.

43-37827 Del Cheyenne 26/5/44; Kearney 6/6/44; Grenier 18/6/44; ass 422BS/305BG Chelveston 28/6/44; MIA Berlin 5/12/44 w/Pounds; flak, cr Wedesbuettel, Ger; 1KIA 8POW; MACR 11043. WALLY'S WHEELS.

43-37828 Del Cheyenne 26/5/44; Kearney 4/6/44; Grenier 17/6/44; ass 749BS/457BG Glatton 30/6/44 REMEMBER ME; retUS Bradley 8/6/45; 4168 BU Sth Plains 12/6/45; RFC Kingman 1/12/45. GEORGIA PEACH.

43-37829 Del Cheyenne 26/5/44; Kearney 7/6/44; Grenier 29/6/44; ass 729BS/452BG Deopham Green 28/6/44; b/d Merseburg 28/9/44 w/?; f/l Continent, sal 19/12/44.

43-37830 Del Cheyenne 26/5/44; Hunter 6/6/44; Dow Fd 27/6/44; ass 94BG Rougham 19/6/44; tran 708BS/447BG Rattlesden 20/6/44; b/d Soest, Ger 10/3/45 w/?; f/l Continent; sal 14/3/45. LADY JANE.

43-37831 Del Cheyenne 26/5/44; Hunter 5/6/44; Grenier 15/6/44; ass 571BS/390BG [FC-C] Framlingham 17/6/44; MIA Hannover 14/3/45 w/Cast; mid air coll w/42-102972, cr Alfeld, Ger; 9KIA 1POW; MACR 13024. LADY VELMA.

43-37832 Del Cheyenne 26/5/44; Hunter 5/6/44; Grenier 15/6/44; 302 BU Hunter 23/6/44; ass 525BS/379BG [FR-K] Kimbolton 8/7/44; c/l 19/7/44, sal.

43-37833 Del Cheyenne 26/5/44; Kearney 4/6/44; Dow Fd 27/6/44; ass 729BS/452BG Deopham Green 28/6/44; MIA Saarbrücken 9/11/44 w/Bickford; flak, cr Korscheid, Ger; 1EVD 8POW; MACR 10347. THE UNINVITED.

43-37834 Del Cheyenne 26/5/44; Kearney 6/6/44; Dow Fd 27/6/44; Slated 100BG, ass 730BS/452BG Deopham Green 28/6/44; tran 748BS/457BG Glatton 29/6/44; MIA Magdeburg 28/9/44 w/Lockwald; e/a, cr Wetzleben, Ger; 2KIA 7POW; MACR 9769.

43-37835 Del Cheyenne 27/5/44; Hunter 6/6/44; Presque Is 28/6/44; ass 833BS/486BG [4N-B] Sudbury 2/7/44; retUS Bradley 8/7/45; 4168 BU Sth Plains 10/7/45; RFC Kingman 8/11/45.

43-37836 Del Cheyenne 12/6/44; Kearney 26/6/44; Grenier 30/6/44; ass 570BS/390BG [DI-J] Framlingham 20/6/44; retUS Bradley 8/7/45; 4168 BU Sth Plains 10/7/45; RFC Kingman 8/11/45. MERRY MAX.

43-37837 Del Cheyenne 27/5/44; Kearney 6/6/44; Grenier 17/6/44; ass 422BS/305BG Chelveston 28/6/44; MIA Magdeburg 1/1/45 w/Wadhams; e/a, cr Croechern, Ger?; 6KIA 4POW; MACR 11354. STAG PARTY.

43-37838 Del Cheyenne 27/5/44; Hunter 6/6/44;

Grenier 15/6/44; ass 358BS/303BG [VK-A] Molesworth 27/6/44; MIA Weisbaden 15/8/44 w/Capt Litman; e/a, cr Wittlich, Ger; 8EVD 1KIA; MACR 8440. FEARLESS FOSDICK.

43-37839 Del Cheyenne 27/5/44; Kearney 7/6/44; Grenier 18/6/44; ass 349BS/100BG [XR-L] Thorpe Abbotts 3/7/44; MIA Magdeburg 5/8/44 w/Scott; flak, cr Magdeburg; 2KIA 7POW; MACR 7879.

43-37840 Del Cheyenne 27/5/44; Kearney 6/6/44; Grenier 26/6/44; ass 486BG Sudbury 30/6/44; sal 21/7/44.

43-37841 Del Cheyenne 27/5/44; Kearney 6/6/44; Grenier 16/6/44; ass 339BS/96BG [QJ-P] Snetterton 20/6/44; retUS Bradley 6/7/45; 4168 BU Sth Plains 8/7/45; RFC Kingman 18/12/45.

43-37842 Del Cheyenne 27/5/44; Hunter 6/6/44; Dow Fd 17/6/44; ass 548BS/385BG Gt Ashfield 1/7/44; retUS Bradley 26/6/45; 4168 BU Sth Plains 28/6/45; RFC Kingman 27/11/45.

43-37843 Del Cheyenne 27/5/44; Kearney 6/6/44; Dow Fd 27/6/44; ass 547BS/384BG [SO-B] Grafton Underwood 21/7/44; collision damage Ingoldstadt 5/4/45 w/?; f/l Continent, sal. RECALL.

43-37844 Del Cheyenne 27/5/44; Hunter 7/6/44; Dow Fd 27/6/44; ass 324BS/91BG [DF-K] Bassingbourn 10/7/44; {71m} RetUS Bradley 31/5/45; 4168 BU Sth Plains 3/6/45; RFC Kingman 14/12/45. YANKEE GAL.

43-37845 Del Cheyenne 27/5/44; Hunter 7/6/44; Dow Fd 3/7/44; ass 305BG Chelveston 4/7/44; b/d Gelsenkirchen 26/8/44 w/?; sal 2 SAD.

43-37846 Del Cheyenne 27/5/44; Hunter 7/6/44; Dow Fd 28/6/44; ass 600BS/398BG [N8-T] Nuthampstead 18/7/44; MIA Misburg 26/11/44 w/Pope; flak, cr Velswijk, Hol; 9POW; MACR 11144. PHONEY EXPRESS.

43-37847 Del Cheyenne 26/6/44; Hunter 7/6/44; Grenier 26/6/44; ass 326BS/92BG [JW-C] Podington 17/7/44 HI HO SILVER; b/d Dresden 17/4/45 w/?; f/l Continent, sal 20/4/45. SILVER.

43-37848 Del Cheyenne 29/5/44; Kearney 8/6/44; Dow Fd 27/6/44; ass 326BS/92BG [JW-S] Podington 19/7/44; MIA Battle support area 13/8/44 w/Brechbill; flak, cr Evreux, Fr; 8KIA 1POW; MACR 8078. SCRAPPY MIKE.

43-37849 Del Cheyenne 29/5/44; Hunter 7/6/44; Presque Is 28/6/44; ass 490BG Eye 29/6/44; retUS Bradley 10/7/45; 4185 BU Independence 11/7/45; RFC Kingman 21/12/45.

43-37850 Del Cheyenne 29/5/44; Kearney 8/6/44; Grenier 6/7/44; ass 508BS/351BG [YB-G] Polebrook 21/7/44; MIA {26m} Ruhland 12/9/44 w/Brown; e/a, cr Werneuchen, Ger; 5KIA 4POW; MACR 8894. UMBRIAGO.

43-37851 Del Cheyenne 29/5/44; Kearney 8/6/44; Grenier 28/6/44; ass 525BS/379BG Kimbolton 18/7/44; MIA Oranienburg 10/4/45 w/McFadden; jet e/a, cr?. MACR 13874.

43-37852 Del Cheyenne 29/5/44; Hunter 7/6/44; Grenier 19/6/44; ass 534BS/381BG [GD-A] Ridgewell 17/7/44; {22+m} RetUS Bradley 9/6/45; 4168 BU Sth Plains 12/6/45; RFC Kingman 28/11/45.

43-37853 Del Cheyenne 29/5/44; Hunter 7/6/44; Dow Fd 27/6/44; ass 560BS/388BG Knettishall 27/6/44; tran 729BS/452BG Deopham Green 28/6/44; retUS Bradley 3/7/45; 4168 BU Sth Plains 6/7/45; RFC Kingman 18/11/45.

43-37854 Del Cheyenne 29/5/44; Hunter 7/6/44; Grenier 28/6/44; ass 509BS/351BG [RQ-V] Polebrook 17/7/44; MIA {57m} Dresden 15/2/45 w/Alplanalp; flak, c/l Ermensee, Switz; 8INT 1KIA (pilot); MACR 12728. TOUCHY TESS.

43-37855 Del Cheyenne 29/5/44; Hunter 7/6/44; Grenier 19/8/44; ass 524BS/379BG [WA-T] Kimbolton 18/7/44; MIA Berlin 18/3/45 w/Mohr; flak, cr Verden, Ger; 8RTD; MACR 13567.

43-37856 Del Cheyenne 29/5/44; Hunter 7/6/44; Presque Is 28/6/44; ass 100BG Thorpe Abbotts 28/6/44; tran 834BS/486BG [2S-R] Sudbury 29/6/44; b/d Oranienburg 20/4/45 w/?; f/l Continent, sal. LADY V.

43-37857 Del Cheyenne 29/5/44; Hunter 9/6/44; Dow Fd 28/6/44; ass 548BS/385BG Gt Ashfield 1/7/44; MIA Mannheim 21/1/45 w/Capt McErlane; flak, cr Joehlingen, Ger?; 1KIA 8POW; MACR 11765. HONEY-CHILE.

43-37858 Del Cheyenne 30/5/44; Kearney 18/6/44; Grenier 30/6/44; ass 836BS/487BG Lavenham 2/7/44; MIA Ludwigshafen 5/11/44 W/Schwarzin; flask, cr Wittlich, Ger; 9POW; MACR 10324.

43-37859 Del Cheyenne 30/5/44; Kearney 8/6/44; Grenier 17/6/44; ass 615BS/401BG [IY-D] Deenethorpe 10/7/44; MIA Orleans 1/8/44 w/Sproul; mid air coll, cr Harderwijk, Hol; 9KIA; MACR 9189. JEANNE.

43-37860 Del Cheyenne 30/5/44; Hunter 9/6/44; Grenier 28/6/44; ass 549BS/385BG Gt Ashfield 4/7/44; MIA Münster 5/10/44 w/Selmeier; flak, cr Herne, Ger; 9POW; MACR 9518.

43-37861 Del Cheyenne 30/5/44; Hunter 10/6/44; Grenier 29/6/44; ass 490BG Eye 2/7/44; retUS Bradley 13/7/45; 4185 BU Independence 16/7/45; RFC Kingman 18/12/45.

43-37862 Del Cheyenne 30/5/44; Kearney 8/6/44; Grenier 1/7/44; ass 510BS/351BG [TU-G] Polebrook 17/7/44; {80m} RetUS Bradley 9/6/45; 4168 BU Sth Plains 18/6/45; RFC Kingman 1/12/45. FEARLESS FOSDICK.

43-37863 Del Cheyenne 30/5/44; Hunter 8/6/44; Grenier 30/6/44; ass 350BS/100BG Thorpe Abbotts 1/7/44; MIA Bohlen 11/9/44 w/Capt Giles; e/a, cr Berlin; 9POW; MACR 8812.

43-37864 Del Cheyenne 30/5/44; Long Beach 12/6/44; Kearney 13/7/44; Dow Fd 3/8/44; ass 391BS/34BG Mendlesham 4/8/44; retUS Bradley 21/6/45; 4168 BU Sth Plains 24/6/45; RFC Kingman 5/12/45. PENNY JIVE.

43-37865 Del Cheyenne 30/5/44; Hunter 9/6/44; Dow Fd 30/6/44; ass 349BS/100BG [XR-P] Thorpe Abbotts 10/7/44; MIA Cauvincourt 8/8/44 w/Keys; flak, cr St Sylvain, Fr; 8KIA 1POW; MACR 8073.

43-37866 Del Cheyenne 30/5/44; Hunter 8/6/44; Dow Fd 24/6/44; ass 571BS/390BG [FC-B] Framlingham 29/6/44; MIA Stuttgart 5/9/44 w/Gallagher; flak, f/l Dubendorf, Switz; 9INT; MACR 8456. BLUES IN THE NIGHT. RetUS 1103 BU Morrison 7/10/45; RFC Walnut Ridge 8/1/46.

43-37867 Del Cheyenne 30/5/44; Hunter 8/6/44; Grenier 26/6/44; ass 836BS/487BG Lavenham 29/6/44; retUS Bradley 8/7/45; 4168 BU Sth Plains 10/7/45; RFC Kingman 6/12/45.

43-37868 Del Cheyenne 30/5/44; Kearney 9/6/44; Grenier 28/6/44; ass 571BS/390BG [FC-Y] Framlingham 29/6/44; retUS Bradley 5/7/45; 4168 BU Sth Plains 6/7/45; RFC Kingman 1/12/45. GENTLEMAN JIM.

43-37869 Del Cheyenne 31/5/44; Kearney 9/6/44; Grenier 28/6/44; ass 710BS/447BG Rattlesden 29/6/44; MIA Merseburg 25/11/44 w/Blair; flak, cr Plauen, Ger; 3KIA 6POW; MACR 10756. BLONDE BOMBER.

43-37870 Del Cheyenne 31/5/44; Kearney 9/6/44; Presque Is 28/6/44; ass 710BS/447BG Rattlesden 28/6/44; tran 547BS/384BG [SO-H] Grafton Underwood 17/7/44; MIA Merseburg 29/7/44 w/Sweeney; e/a, cr Bad Bibra, Gerl 2KIA 8POW; MACR 7818.

43-37871 Del Cheyenne 31/5/44; Kearney 9/6/44; Grenier 30/6/44; ass 551BS/385BG Gt Ashfield 2/7/44; MIA Dresden 2/4/45 w/Krahn; e/a, cr Dresden; 1EVD 8POW; MACR 12857. SLICK CHICK.

43-37872 Del Cheyenne 31/5/44; Kearney 9/6/44; Grenier 28/6/44; ass 100BG Thorpe Abbotts 29/6/44; tran 407BS/92BG [PY-S] Podington 10/7/44; b/d Kyllburg 8/1/45 w/?; cr Rheims, crew baled; sal 21/1/45.

43-37873 Del Cheyenne 31/5/44; Long Beach 12/6/44; Kearney 13/7/44; Dow Fd 3/8/44; ass 447BG Rattlesden 4/8/44; retUS Bradley 7/7/45; 4168 BU Sth Plains 8/10/45; RFC Kingman 19/12/45.

43-37874 Del Cheyenne 31/5/44; Kearney 9/6/44; Grenier 28/6/44; ass 601BS/398BG [3O-N] Nuthampstead 15/7/44; landed on Continent four times, rep & ret group; retUS Bradley 6/6/45; 4168 BU Sth Plains 22/6/45; RFC Kingman 13/12/45.

43-37875 Del Cheyenne 31/5/44; Kearney 9/6/44; Grenier 28/6/44; ass 835BS/486BG Sudbury 30/6/44; MIA Stuttgart 5/9/44 w/Crawford; mid air coll w/486BG, cr Brest, Fr; 1EVD 7KIA 1POW; MACR 8459.

43-37876 Del Cheyenne 31/5/44; Hunter 10/6/44; Grenier 26/6/44; ass 570BS/390BG [DI-D] Framlingham 29/6/44; MIA Tours, Fr 1/8/44 w/Forte; flak, cr Tours; 3EVD 2KIA 4POW; MACR 7748. SEQUATCHIEE.

43-37877 Del Cheyenne 31/5/44; Hunter 12/6/44; Dow Fd 3/7/44; ass 379BG Kimbolton 19/6/44; tran 837BS/487BG Lavenham 4/7/44; 836BS [2G-E]; MIA Zeitz 30/11/44 w/Kersten; flak, cr Halle; 7KIA 2POW; MACR 11154.

43-37878 Del Cheyenne 31/5/44; Kearney 16/6/44; Grenier 30/6/44; ass 730BS/452BG Deopham Green 2/7/44; MIA Münster 4/10/44 w/?.

43-37879 Del Cheyenne 31/5/44; Kearney 9/6/44; Grenier 26/6/44; ass 711BS/447BG Rattlesden 29/6/44; b/d Aachen 9/8/44 w/?; c/l, sal 12/8/44.

43-37880 Del Cheyenne 31/5/44; Kearney 9/6/44; Grenier 26/6/44; ass 350BS/100BG Thorpe Abbotts 29/6/44; MIA Chemnitz 11/9/44 w/Corley; e/a, cr Littnitz, Ger; 9POW; MACR 8813.

43-37881 -

43-37882 Del Cheyenne 1/6/44; Kearney 16/6/44; Grenier 30/6/44; ass 350BS/100BG Thorpe Abbotts 29/6/44; MIA Berlin 6/10/44 w/Reed; flak, cr Spandau, Ger; 8KIA 1POW; MACR 9509.

43-37883 Del Cheyenne 1/6/44; Hunter 10/6/44; Dow Fd 28/6/44; ass 834BS/486BG Sudbury 2/7/44; MIA Merseburg 2/11/44 w/Paris; flak, cr Merseburg; 9KIA; MACR 10168. BLUE STREAK.

43-37884 Del Cheyenne 1/6/44; Hunter 10/6/44; Dow Fd 30/6/44; ass 848BS/490BG Eye 1/7/44; MIA Ludwigshafen 5/11/44 w/Bridwell; mid air coll, cr Neustadt; 8KIA 1POW; MACR 10325. PENNS-BELLE.

43-37885 Del Wright Fd 1/6/44; 4126 BU San Bernardino 20/11/44; Wright Mat Com ATS 8/12/44; 4119 BU Brookley 14/12/44; 610 BU Eglin 10/2/45; 613 BU Phillips 28/3/45; 620 BU Muroc 17/4/45; 613 BU Phillips as TB-17G 9/7/46; 620 BU Muroc 9/7/46.

43-37886 Del Cheyenne 9/6/44; Kearney 18/6/44; Grenier 22/8/44; ass 848BS/490BG Eye 24/8/44; MIA Merseburg 25/11/44 w/Delmerico; flak, cr Apolda, Ger; 1KIA 9POW: MACR 10759. PENNSY-

BELLE.

43-37887 Del Cheyenne 1/6/44; Hunter 10/6/44; Dow Fd 30/6/44; ass 323BS/91BG [OR-T] Bassingbourn 31/7/44; 401BG [LL-J]; after 22 missions switched to Carpet Jammer Ops; retUS Bradley 15/6/45; 4168 BU Sth Plains 28/6/45; RFC Kingman 1/12/45. (nose art painted by pilot Dave Hettema) OLD BATTLE AXE.

43-37888 Del Cheyenne 1/6/44; Hunter 10/6/44; Presque Is 28/6/44; ass 551BS/385BG Gt Ashfield 1/7/44; MIA Merseburg 2/11/44 w/Keeler; flak, cr Detmold, Ger; MACR 10155.

43-37889 Del Cheyenne 1/6/44; Hunter 10/6/44; Grenier 30/6/44; ass 601BS/398BG [3O-B] Nuthampstead 16/7/44; MIA Mannheim 20/1/45 w/Mitchell; flak, cr Bechtersheim, Ger; 2KIA 67POW; MACR 11797.

43-37890 Del Cheyenne 1/6/44; Hunter 10/6/44; Dow Fd 28/6/44; ass 324BS/91BG Bassingbourn 29/6/44; MIA {43m} Merseburg 21/11/44 w/Whitesell; flak #3, cr Dobitschen, Ger; 4KIA 5POW (inc TG blown out when ship exploded in mid air); MACR 10420. FEARLESS FOSDICK.

43-37891 Del Cheyenne 1/6/44; Hunter 10/6/44; Grenier 28/6/44; ass 835BS/486BG [H8-J] Sudbury 2/7/44; sal 20/5/45. OLD MAN'S FOLLY.

43-37892 Del Cheyenne 1/6/44; Kearney 15/6/44; Grenier 28/6/44; ass 603BS/398BG Nuthampstead 15/7/44; b/d Orleans 1/8/44 w/?; c/l RAF Merston, UK; sal 2 SAD 4/8/44.

43-37893 Del Cheyenne 2/6/44; Hunter 13/6/44; Dow Fd 27/6/44; ass 551BS/385BG Gt Ashfield 28/6/44; mid air coll w/43-38233 24/12/44; ret base & rep; retUS Bradley 24/6/45; 4168 BU Sth Plains 27/6/45; RFC Kingman 13/12/45.

43-37894 Del Cheyenne 2/6/44; Kearney 13/6/44; Grenier 28/6/44; ass 849BS/490BG Eye 1/7/44; on assembly for Chemnitz 6/2/45 mid air coll w/43-37806; cr Prickwillow, UK; crews baled, 1K and two civilians; sal. BIG POISON.

43-37895 Del Cheyenne 2/6/44; Kearney 12/6/44; Grenier 30/6/44; ass 385BG Gt Ashfield 2/7/44; tran 571BS/390BG [FC-R] Framlingham 3/7/44; c/l 5/4/45, sal 25/6/45. TAKE IT EASY.

43-37896 Del Cheyenne 2/6/44; Kearney 12/6/44; Grenier 2/7/44; ass 563BS/388BG Knettishall 3/7/44; ct fire en route Bordeaux 14/4/45 w/?; f/l Lyon, Fr; 9RTD. FOREVER AMBER.

43-37897 Del Cheyenne 2/6/44; Kearney 12/6/44; Grenier 28/6/44; ass 838BS/487BG [2G-C] Lavenham 29/6/44; b/d Dresden 2/3/45 w/?; f/l Russia.

43-37898 Del Cheyenne 2/6/44; Kearney 13/6/44; Dow Fd 3/7/44; ass 535BS/381BG Ridgewell 3/7/44; tran 412BS/95BG [QW-A] Horham 4/7/44; MIA Rechlin 25/8/44 w/Shepherd; flak, cr Tutow, Ger; 9POW; MACR 8281. BELLE IN THE KEYHOLE.

43-37899 Del Cheyenne 2/6/44; Kearney 13/6/44; Grenier 1/7/44; ass 835BS/486BG [H8-T] Sudbury 2/7/44; c/l base 6/2/45; rep & tran 601BS/398BG [3O-B] Nuthampstead; retUS Bradley 7/7/45; 4168 BU Sth Plains 10/7/45; RFC Kingman 24/11/45. RACK AND RUIN.

43-37900 Del Cheyenne 2/6/44; Kearney 12/6/44; Grenier 9/7/44; ass 508BS/351BG [YB-H] Polebrook 26/7/44; b/d {84m} Bremen 30/3/45; f/l Continent; sal 20/5/45.

43-37901 Del Cheyenne 2/6/44; Kearney 14/6/44; Grenier 28/6/44; ass 837BS/487BG [4F-B] Lavenham 29/6/44; retUS Bradley 10/7/45; 4185 BU Independence 12/7/45; RFC Kingman 6/1/46. MISS BEA HAVEN.

43-37902 Del Cheyenne 2/6/44; Hunter 12/6/44; Grenier 28/6/44; ass 8AF 5/7/44; retUS Bradley 9/7/45; 4168 BU Sth Plains 11/7/45; RFC Kingman 28/11/45.

43-37903 Del Cheyenne 2/6/44; Hunter 13/6/44; Dow Fd 24/6/44; ass 385BG Gt Ashfield 29/6/44; tran 525BS/379BG Kimbolton 8/7/44; MIA Merseburg 24/8/44 w/Connell; flak, cr Leeuwarden, Hol; 9KIA; MACR 8285.

43-37904 Del Cheyenne 2/6/44; Hunter 13/6/44; Dow Fd 24/6/44; ass 569BS/390BG [CC-L] Framlingham 29/6/44; retUS Bradley 3/7/45; 4168 BU Sth Plains 4/7/45; RFC Kingman 30/11/45. PRINCESS PAT.

43-37905 Del Cheyenne 3/6/44; Hunter 13/6/44; Dow Fd 27/6/44; ass 729BS/452BG Deopham Green 28/6/44; tran 524BS/379BG [WA-B] Kimbolton 8/7/44; retUS Bradley 3/7/45; 4168 BU Sth Plains 6/7/45; RFC Kingman 10/11/45.

43-37906 Del Cheyenne 3/6/44; Kearney 15/6/44; Grenier 28/6/44; ass 730BS/452BG Deopham Green 29/6/44; on assembly for Hannover 26/10/44 mid air coll w/43-38696 w/?; cr Caston, UK; 8KIA. Sal 27/10/44.

43-37907 Del Cheyenne 3/6/44; Kearney 17/6/44; Grenier 30/6/44; ass 851BS/490BG Eye 2/7/44; retUS Bradley 9/7/45; 4168 BU Sth Plains 12/7/45; RFC Kingman 5/12/45. CAROLINA MOON.

43-37908 Del Cheyenne 3/6/44; Kearney 20/6/44; Grenier 30/6/44; ass 835BS/486BG [H8-H] Sudbury 2/7/44; MIA Weisbaden 10/11/44 w/Dimel; flak, cr Ixel, Bel; sal 22/11/44. WOLFEL BEAR.

43-37909 Del Cheyenne 3/6/44; Kearney 16/6/44; Grenier 30/6/44; ass 832BS/486BG [3R-C] Sudbury 3/7/44; MIA Hamburg 4/8/44 w/Walthall; flak & mid air coll, cr Rotenburg, Ger; 7KIA 2POW; MACR 7711.

43-37910 Del Cheyenne 3/6/44; Kearney 17/6/44; Grenier 30/6/44; ass 832BS/486BG [3R-C] Sudbury 2/7/44; c/t/o at Cornard, UK, for Misburg 31/12/44 w/?; crew safe; sal 3/1/45.

43-37911 Del Cheyenne 3/6/44; Kearney 13/6/44; Grenier 28/6/44; ass 836BS/487BG Lavenham 29/6/44; retUS Bradley 11/7/45; 4185 BU Independence 12/7/45; RFC Kingman 22/12/45.

43-37912 Del Cheyenne 3/6/44; Kearney 15/6/44; Grenier 28/6/44; ass 407BS/92BG [PY-Y] Podington 30/6/44; b/d Mannheim 11/12/44 w/?; f/l France; sal 8/2/45.

43-37913 Del Cheyenne 3/6/44; Hunter 13/6/44; Presque Is 28/6/44; ass 323BS/91BG [OR-T] Bassingbourn 29/6/44; MIA {25m} Altenbeken 26/11/44 w/Stevens; e/a, exploded & cr Haulerwijk, Hol; 6EVD 3POW; MACR 10837. SEATTLE SLEEPER.

43-37914 Del Cheyenne 3/4/44, mod to prototype F-9C; 11 Ph Gp McDill 12/8/44; chin turret replaced by three cameras, three in radio comp; heaters fitted in camera bays. Sal 6/11/46.

43-47915 Del Cheyenne 3/6/44; Gt Falls 13/7/44; Hunter 20/7/44; Grenier 1/8/44; ass 452 Deopham Green 11/8/44; tran 100BG Thorpe Abbotts 12/8/44; b/d Operation 'Frantic VII' (Warsaw supply drop) 18/9/44 w/?; f/l Russia; sal 18/5/45.

43-37916 Del Cheyenne 5/6/44; Kearney 18/6/44; Grenier 3/7/44; ass 486BG Sudbury 4/7/44; sal 19/11/44.

43-37917 Del Cheyenne 5/6/44; Kearney 18/6/44; Grenier 30/6/44; ass 545BS/384BG [JD-B] Grafton Underwood 17/7/44; sal 31/12/45. PAULINE.

43-37918 Del Cheyenne 5/6/44; Kearney 19/6/44; Grenier 30/6/44; ass 839BS/487BG [R5-Q] Lavenham 2/7/44; retUS Bradley 12/7/45; 4185 BU Independence 13/7/45; RFC Kingman 9/12/45.

43-37919 Del Cheyenne 5/6/44; Kearney 19/6/44; Grenier 30/6/44; ass 550BS/385BG Gt Ashfield 2/7/44; b/d Merseburg 25/11/44 w/?; f/l Aermee, Ger?; sal 16/12/44.

43-37920 Del Cheyenne 5/6/44; Kearney 19/6/44; Grenier 30/6/44; ass 511BS/351BG [DS-L] Polebrook 17/7/44; MIA {8m} Brandenburg 6/8/44 w/Uttley; flak & e/a, cr Wilhelmshorst, Ger; 6KIA 3POW; MACR 7585.

43-37921 Del Cheyenne 5/6/44; Kearney 16/6/44; Grenier 30/6/44; ass 325BS/92BG [NV-K] Podington 18/7/44; b/d 13/9/44 w/?; crew aban, cr?; sal 14/11/44.

43-37922 Del Cheyenne 5/6/44; Kearney 16/6/44; Grenier 30/6/44; ass 305BG Chelveston 23/7/44; sal 2SAD 15/2/45.

43-37923 Del Cheyenne 5/6/44; Kearney 16/6/44; Grenier 2/7/44; ass 837BS/487BG [4F-P] Lavenham 3/7/44; retUS Bradley 11/7/45; 4185 BU Independence 13/7/45; RFC Kingman 9/12/45.

43-37924 Del Cheyenne 5/6/44; Kearney 18/6/44; Grenier 1/7/44; ass 325BS/92BG [NV-C] Podington 18/7/44; sal 22/11/44.

43-37925 Del Cheyenne 5/6/44; Kearney 16/6/44; Grenier 1/7/44; ass 490BS Eye 2/7/44; retUS Bradley 12/7/45; 4185 BU Independence 13/7/45; RFC Kingman 7/1/46.

43-37926 Del Cheyenne 6/6/44; Kearney 18/6/44; Grenier 6/7/44; ass 490BG Eye 2/7/44; tran 100BG Thorpe Abbotts 7/7/44; retUS Bradley 13/7/45; 4185 BU Independence 16/7/45; RFC Kingman 16/12/45. LOTTA STERN.

43-37927 Del Cheyenne 6/6/44; Kearney 16/6/44; Grenier 30/6/44; ass 833BS/486BG Sudbury 2/7/44; MIA Merseburg 6/12/44 w/Alexander; flak, cr Ijmuiden, Hol; 9KIA; MACR 11048.

43-37928 Del Cheyenne 6/6/44; Kearney 19/6/44; Grenier 1/7/44; ass 490BS Eye 2/7/44; retUS Bradley 12/8/45; 4185 BU Independence 16/8/45; RFC Kingman 17/12/45.

43-37929 Del Cheyenne 6/6/44; Kearney 18/6/44; Grenier 1/7/44; ass 835BS/486BG Sudbury 2/7/44; MIA Hamburg 4/8/44 w/Adler; flak, cr Wesermünde, Ger; 9POW; MACR 7712.

43-37930 Del Cheyenne 5/6/44; Kearney 18/6/44; Grenier 3/7/44; ass 360BS/303BG [PU-F] Molesworth 4/7/44; MIA Kassel 28/9/44 w/Howard; e/a, cr Dorstadt, Ger; 1KIA 8POW; MACR 9406.

43-37931 Del Cheyenne 6/6/44; Kearney 16/6/44; Grenier 1/7/44; ass 832BS/486BG [3R-H] Sudbury 2/7/44; 834BS; MIA Dresden 17/4/45 w/Bartl; flak, cr Dresden; 9KIA; MACR 14186. PURSUIT OF HAPPINESS.

43-37932 Del Cheyenne 6/6/44; Kearney 18/6/44; Grenier 29/6/44; ass 525BS/379BG Kimbolton 16/7/44; MIA Frankfurt 5/11/44 w/Anderson; flak, cr Frankfurt; 1KIA 8POW; MACR 10353. SPRATT-O-LINER.

43-37933 Del Cheyenne 6/6/44; Kearney 18/6/44; Grenier 1/7/44; ass 838BS/487BG Lavenham 2/7/44; MIA Derben, Ger 14/1/45 w/Nyland; mid air coll w/42-98013; cr Redefin, Ger; 1KIA 8POW; MACR 11732. YANKEE MAID.

43-37934 Del Cheyenne 6/6/44; Kearney 16/6/44; Grenier 1/7/44; ass 379BG Kimbolton 15/7/44; retUS Bradley 28/6/45; 4168 BU Sth Plains 30/6/45; RFC Kingman 8/12/45. HUNDRED MILLION DOLLAR BABY.

43-37935 Del Cheyenne 7/6/44; Kearney 19/6/44; Grenier 1/7/44; ass 418BS/100BG [LD-V] Thorpe Abbotts 2/7/44; taxi acc 1/9/44; sal 3/9/44.

43-37936 Del Cheyenne 7/6/44; Kearney 16/6/44; Grenier 30/6/44; ass 711BS/447BG Rattlesden 2/7/44; MIA Merseburg 2/11/44 w/Tetrault; ditched Channel; 9RTD.

43-37937 Del Cheyenne 7/6/44; Kearney 26/6/44; Dow Fd 10/7/44; ass 832BS/486BG [3R-K] Sudbury 15/7/44; c/l on practice op 17/3/45 w/?; sal 21/3/45. THE PROWLER.

43-37938 Del Cheyenne 7/6/44; Kearney 18/6/44; Grenier 30/6/44; ass 710BS/447BG Rattlesden 2/7/44; 708BS; MIA Frankfurt 8/1/45 w/Weeks; flak, cr Frankfurt; 5KIA 4POW; MACR 11582. LITTLE ROCK BLONDE.

43-37939 Del Cheyenne 7/6/44; Kearney 18/6/44; Dow Fd 7/7/44; ass 832BS/486BG [3R-E] Sudbury 9/7/44; MIA Bingen 27/11/44 w/?; f/l Vilvorbe, Ger?; sal 1/12/44.

43-37940 Del Cheyenne 7/6/44; Kearney 18/6/44; Grenier 30/6/44; ass 8AF 5/7/44; retUS Bradley 14/7/45; 4185 BU Independence 18/7/45; RFC Kingman 16/12/45.

43-37941 Del Cheyenne 7/6/44; Kearney 20/6/44; Grenier 1/7/44; ass 849BS/490BG Eye 2/7/44; b/d Hallach 1/9/44 w/?; f/l France; sal 1/4/45. MACR 8854. MISS ANA BORTION.

43-37942 Del Cheyenne 8/6/44; Kearney 19/6/44; Grenier 1/7/44; ass 832BS/486BG [3R-J] Sudbury 2/7/44; MIA Grafenwohr 8/4/45 w/Wood; flak, cr Rehau, Ger; 2KIA 7POW; MACR 13739. BLUE FAIRY.

43-37943 Del Cheyenne 8/6/44; Kearney 19/6/44; Grenier 30/6/44; ass 833BS/486BG [4N-G] Sudbury 2/7/44; b/d Leipzig 27/2/45 w/?; fg/l Bernstadtgram, Ger; sal 1/4/45. MACR 12782.

43-37944 Del Cheyenne 8/6/44; Kearney 20/6/44; Dow Fd 9/7/44; ass 834BS/486BG [2S-R] Sudbury 11/7/44; MIA Merseburg 6/12/44 w/Miller; flak, cr Uuddorp, Ger?; 9POW; MACR 11047. MR TACOMA.

43-37945 Del Cheyenne 8/6/44; Kearney 24/6/44; Grenier 30/6/44; ass 834BS/486BG [2S-K] Sudbury 2/7/44; taxi acc 21/5/45, sal.

43-37946 Del Cheyenne 8/6/44; Kearney 21/6/44; Dow Fd 9/7/44; ass APH/388BG Knettishall 10/7/44; used for navigation ; retUS Bradley 9/6/45; 4168 BU Sth Plains 13/6/45; RFC Kingman 28/11/45.

43-37947 Del Cheyenne 8/6/44; Kearney 21/6/44; Dow Fd 7/7/44; ass 364BS/305BG [WF-S] Chelveston 8/7/44; b/d Cologne 10/1/45 w/?; f/l Continent; sal 22/1/45.

43-37948 Del Cheyenne 8/6/44; Kearney 21/6/44; Dow Fd 7/7/44; ass 837BS/487BG Lavenham 9/7/44; tran 832BS/486BG Sudbury 27/10/44; MIA Merseburg 30/11/44 w/Cornelison; mech fault, cr Stolzenbach, Ger; 1KIA 8POW: MACR 11153.

43-37949 Del Cheyenne 8/6/44; Kearney 21/6/44; Grenier 1/7/44; ass 835BS/486BG Sudbury 2/7/44; MIA Stuttgart 5/9/44 w/Eacham; mid air coll, cr Brest; 8KIA 1POW; MACR 8450. NOBODY GETSZIT.

43-37950 Del Cheyenne 8/6/44; Kearney 20/6/44; Grenier 6/7/44; ass 527BS/379BG [FO-G] Kimbolton 20/7/44; 525BS [FR-G]; retUS Bradley 9/7/45; 4168 BU Sth Plains 11/7/45; RFC Kingman 23/11/45. GRAVEL GERTIE.

43-37951 Del Cheyenne 8/6/44; Kearney 18/6/44; Grenier 1/7/44; ass 527BS/379BG Kimbolton 15/7/44; MIA Permasens, Ger 9/8/44 w/Hamilton; flak, cr Antwerp; 9EVD; MACR 7393. RED DRAGON.

43-37952 Del Cheyenne 8/6/44; Kearney 20/6/44; Grenier 30/6/44; ass 835BS/486BG [H8-F] Sudbury 2/7/44; retUS Bradley 7/7/45; 4168 BU Sth Plains 9/7/45; RFC Kingman 9/12/45.

43-37953 Del Cheyenne 8/6/44; Kearney 21/6/44; Dow Fd 9/7/44; ass APH/388BG Knettishall 10/7/44; drone control ship on APH and Castor missions fitted w/special radio antenna; retUS Bradley 6/6/45; 4168 BU Sth Plains 9/6/45; RFC Kingman 29/11/45.

43-37954 Del Cheyenne 9/6/44; Kearney 27/6/44; Dow Fd 7/7/44; ass 835BS/486BG [H8-C] Sudbury 8/7/44; retUS Bradley 7/7/45; 4168 BU Sth Plains 10/7/45; RFC Albuquerque 6/2/46. GOIN' JESSIE.

43-37955 Del Cheyenne 9/6/44; Kearney 20/6/44; Grenier 6/7/44; ass 365BS/305BG Chelveston 8/7/44; MIA Misburg 26/11/44 w/Schmid; flak, ditched off Diepenveen, Hol; 2EVD 7POW; MACR 11202.

43-37956 Del Cheyenne 9/6/44; Hunter 13/7/44; Grenier 24/7/44; ass 508BS/351BG [YB-L] Polebrook 10/8/44; {79m} RetUS Bradley 29/5/45; 4168 BU Sth Plains 1/6/45; RFC Kingman 28/11/45.

43-37957 Del Cheyenne 9/6/44; Kearney 27/6/44; Dow Fd 6/7/44; ass 510BS/351BG [TU-D] Polebrook 21/7/44; 508BS [YB-M]; retUS Bradley 11/6/45; 4168 BU Sth Plains 14/6/45; RFC Kingman 8/12/45.

43-37958 Del Cheyenne 9/6/44; Kearney 21/6/44; Dow Fd 11/7/44; ass 834BS/486BG [2S-H] Sudbury 14/7/44; retUS Bradley 9/7/45; 4168 BU Sth Plains 10/7/45; RFC Kingman 22/11/45.

43-37959 Del Cheyenne 9/6/44; Kearney 20/6/44; Dow Fd 7/7/44; ass 834BS/486BG [2S-K] Sudbury 8/7/44; b/d Koblenz 19/9/44 w/?; f/l Belgium; sal 14/11/44.

43-37960 Del Cheyenne 9/6/44; Kearney 21/6/44; Grenier 9/7/44; ass 34BG Mendlesham 12/7/44; retUS Bradley 21/6/45; 4168 BU Sth Plains 22/6/45; RFC Kingman 19/12/45.

43-37961 Del Cheyenne 13/6/44; Kearney 21/6/44; Dow Fd 7/7/44; ass 305BG Chelveston 2/8/44; b/d Cologne 10/1/45 w/?; f/l Continent; MACR 11564. Sal 23/1/45.

43-37962 Del Cheyenne 9/6/44; Kearney 21/6/44; Grenier 6/7/44; ass 305BG Chelveston 8/7/44; tran APH/388BG Knettishall 10/7/44; retUS Bradley 4/6/45; 4168 BU Sth Plains 7/6/45; RFC Kingman 19/12/45.

43-37963 Del Cheyenne 9/6/44; Kearney 20/6/44; Grenier 6/7/44; ass 834BS/486BG [2S-J] Sudbury 8/7/44; retUS 1103 BU Morrison 3/11/45; RFC Walnut Ridge 4/1/46. DIRTY DUECE.

43-37964 Del Cheyenne 14/6/44; Kearney 21/6/44; Dow Fd 7/7/44; ass 401BG Deenethorpe 8/7/44; tran 509BS/351BG [RQ-M] Polebrook 22/7/44; b/d {89m} Oberpfaffenhofen 9/4/45 w/?; f/l Continent, sal. Rep & ret UK; retUS Bradley 7/6/45; 4168 BU Sth Plains 13/6/45; RFC Kingman 28/11/45. DOZEY DOATS.

43-37965 Del Cheyenne 14/6/44; Kearney 23/6/44; Grenier 6/7/44; ass 365BS/305BG Chelveston 8/7/44; MIA Karlsruhe 9/8/44 w/Wood; e/a, cr Beinheim, Ger; 5KIA 4POW; MACR 8068.

43-37966 Del Cheyenne 14/6/44; Kearney 21/6/44; Grenier 6/7/44; ass 835BS/486BG [H8-G] Sudbury 8/7/44; b/d Frankfurt 5/1/45 w/?; f/l Continent, sal.

43-37967 Del Cheyenne 14/6/44; Kearney 25/6/44; Grenier 6/7/44; ass 423BS/306BG [RD-B] Thurleigh 20/7/44; b/d 28/9/44 w/?; f/l Continent; sal 1/12/44. DONALD DUCK WITH BOMBS.

43-37968 Del Cheyenne 14/6/44; Kearney 25/6/44; Grenier 6/7/44; ass 837BS/487BG Lavenham 8/7/44; tran 486BG Sudbury 27/10/44; retUS Bradley 7/7/45; 4168 BU Sth Plains 10/7/45; RFC Kingman 12/7/45.

43-37969 Del Cheyenne 14/6/44; Kearney 27/6/44; Dow Fd 9/7/44; ass 836BS/487BG [2G-N] Lavenham 11/7/44; b/d Jena 19/3/45 w/?; mid air coll w/43-38083, cr Couvron, Fr; sal 21/3/45.

43-37970 Del Cheyenne 14/6/44; Kearney 27/6/44; Dow Fd 9/7/44; ass 838BS/487BG Lavenham 11/7/44; retUS Bradley 7/7/45; 4168 BU Sth Plains 12/7/45; RFC Kingman 28/11/45.

43-37971 Del Cheyenne 14/6/44; Kearney 21/6/44; Grenier 12/7/44; ass 545BS/384BG [JD-T] Grafton Underwood 17/7/44; c/l Guernsey 12/6/45, sal.

43-37972 Del Cheyenne 14/6/44; Kearney 22/6/44; Dow Fd 7/7/44; ass 349BS/100BG [XR-F] Thorpe Abbotts 8/7/44; tran 833BS/486BG Sudbury 9/7/44; MIA Münster 5/10/44 w/Coy; flak, cr Zutphen, Hol; 9POW; MACR 9528. ULA LUME.

43-37973 Del Cheyenne 14/6/44; Kearney 28/6/44; Grenier 9/7/44; ass 447BG Rattlesden 11/7/44; tran 834BS/486BG [2S-N] Sudbury 12/7/44; returned POWs from Austria 5/45; retUS Bradley 13/7/45; 4185 BU Independence 17/7/44; RFC Kingman 9/12/45. THE WORRY BIRD.

43-37974 Del Cheyenne 12/6/44; Kearney 25/6/44; Grenier 13/7/44; ass 487BG Lavenham 14/7/44; retUS Bradley 12/7/45; 4185 BU Independence 13/7/45; RFC Kingman 18/12/45.

43-37975 Del Cheyenne 12/6/44; Kearney 25/6/44; Grenier 6/7/44; ass 839BS/487BG [R5-A] Lavenham 8/7/44; retUS Bradley 12/7/45; 4185 BU Independence 13/7/45; RFC Kingman 27/12/45.

43-37976 Del Cheyenne 12/6/44; Kearney 22/6/44; Dow Fd 7/7/44; ass 379BG Kimbolton 7/7/44; tran 305BG Chelveston 8/7/44; MIA Merseburg 24/8/44 w/?; ditched Nth Sea; MACR 9656. LILI MARLENE.

43-37977 Del Cheyenne 12/6/44; Kearney 22/6/44; Dow Fd 7/7/44; ass 603BS/398BG [N7-R] Nuthampstead 20/7/44; 602BS [K8-R]; retUS Bradley 10/7/45; 4185 BU Independence 12/7/45; RFC Kingman 17/12/45. MISS X.

43-37978 Del Cheyenne 12/6/44; Hunter 7/7/44; Dow Fd 25/7/44; ass 508BS/351BG [YB-L/J] Polebrook 7/8/44; {52m} RetUS Bradley 12/6/45; 4168 BU Sth Plains 15/6/45; RFC Kingman 18/12/45.

43-37979 Del Cheyenne 12/6/44; Kearney 25/6/44; Dow Fd 9/7/44; ass 838BS/487BG [2C-B] Lavenham 11/7/44; b/d en route Darmstadt 24/12/44 w/?; f/l Le Culot A/fd, Bel.

43-37980 Del Cheyenne 12/6/44; Kearney 27/6/44; Dow Fd 7/7/44; ass 839BS/487BG Lavenham 8/7/44; MIA Politz 25/8/44 w/Duncan; flak, cr Lake Mueritz?; 9KIA 2POW; MACR 8470.

43-37981 Del Cheyenne 12/6/44; Kearney 23/6/44; Grenier 6/7/44; ass 838BS/487BG [2C-B] Lavenham 8/7/44; retUS Bradley 11/7/45; 4185 BU Independence 18/7/45; RFC Kingman 14/12/45.

43-37982 Del Cheyenne 12/6/44; Kearney 23/6/44; Grenier 7/7/44; ass 603BS/398BG [N7-K] Nuthampstead 31/7/44; retUS Bradley 31/5/45; 4168 BU Sth Plains 1/6/45; RFC Kingman 13/12/45. BEBE.

43-37983 Del Cheyenne 12/6/44; Kearney 25/6/44; Dow Fd 9/7/44; ass 835BS/486BG [H8-M] Sudbury 11/7/44; retUS Bradley 7/7/45; 4168 BU Sth Plains 10/7/45; RFC Kingman 29/11/45. UMBRIAGO.

43-37984 Del Cheyenne 13/6/44; Kearney 22/6/44; Grenier 6/7/44; ass 390BG Framlingham 8/7/44; tran 839BS/487BG [R5-H] Lavenham 9/7/44; f/l Melsbroek, Bel 19/12/44; sal 3/1/45.

43-37985 Del Cheyenne 13/6/44; Kearney 23/6/44; Dow Fd 9/7/44; ass 834BS/486BG Sudbury 16/7/44; MIA Duren 16/11/44 w/?; f/l Nivelles?; sal 17/11/44. Re-ass 67 Tac Recon Gp.

Above: B-17G-75-BO 43-37981 served with the 838th Bomb Squadron, 487th Bomb Group and survived hostilities. (USAAF)

43-37986 Del Cheyenne 13/6/44; Kearney 27/6/44; Grenier 6/7/44; ass 511BS/351BG [DS-H] Polebrook 31/7/44; MIA {10m} Brux 12/9/44 w/Schoenian; e/a, cr Proetzel, Ger?; 3KIA 6POW; MACR 8895.
43-37987 Del Cheyenne 13/6/44; Kearney 25/6/44; Dow Fd 10/7/44; ass 838BS/487BG [R5-J] Lavenham 15/7/44; MIA Brandenburg 10/4/45 w/Althouse; flak, cr Havelberg, Ger; 2KIA 8POW; MACR 13883. MEAN WIDDLE KID.
43-37988 Del Cheyenne 13/6/44; Kearney 25/6/44; Grenier 13/7/44; ass 835BS/486BG [H8-F] Sudbury 14/7/44; tran 324BS/91BG [DF-C] Bassingbourn 22/7/44; MIA Cologne 10/1/45 w/Martin; f/l Evere A/fd, Bel, coll w/C-47; 3KIA 6RTD; sal 18/1/45. THE B.T.O.
43-37989 Del Cheyenne 13/6/44; Kearney 23/6/44; Dow Fd 9/7/44; ass 837BS/487BG Lavenham 11/7/44; b/d Rechlen 25/8/44 w/?; sal 27/8/44.
43-37990 Del Cheyenne 13/6/44; Kearney 25/6/44; Grenier 6/7/44; ass 547BS/384BG [SO-G] Grafton Underwood 23/7/44; b/d Nürnberg 3/10/44 w/?; f/l Belgium, sal 14/11/44.
43-37991 Del Cheyenne 13/6/44; Kearney 25/6/44; Dow Fd 9/7/44; ass 487BG Lavenham 8/7/44; retUS Bradley 11/7/45; 4185 BU Independence 12/7/45; RFC Kingman 15/1/46.
43-37992 Del Cheyenne 13/6/44; Kearney 25/6/44; Dow Fd 9/7/44; ass 832BS/486BG [3R-P] Sudbury 11/7/44; b/d Chemnitz 6/2/45 w/?; c/l Upper Beeding, UK, sal.
43-37993 Del Cheyenne 13/6/44; Kearney 23/6/44; Dow Fd 9/7/44; ass 401BS/91BG [LL-U] Bassingbourn 23/7/44; 324BS [DF-N]; {72m} RetUS Bradley 11/6/45; 4168 BU Sth Plains 15/6/45; RFC Kingman 19/12/45. MAH IDEEL.
43-37994 Del Cheyenne 14/6/44; Kearney 23/6/44; Dow Fd 9/7/44; ass 418BS/100BG [LD-D] Thorpe Abbotts 11/7/44; tran 482BG Alconbury 20/5/45; retUS Bradley 2/6/45; 4168 BU Sth Plains 6/6/45; RFC Kingman 25/11/45.
43-37995 Del Cheyenne 14/6/44; Kearney 25/6/44; Grenier 9/7/44; ass 849BS/490BG Eye 12/7/44; c/l Sutton Valence, UK 9/12/44 w/?; sal; 11/12/44.
43-37996 Del Cheyenne 14/6/44; Kearney 25/6/44; Grenier 6/7/44; ass 835BS/486BG [4N-A] Sudbury 8/7/44; retUS Bradley 7/7/45; 4168 BU Sth Plains 10/7/45; RFC Kingman 18/12/45. HOCK SHOP.
43-37997 Del Cheyenne 14/6/44; Kearney 27/6/44; Grenier 6/7/44; ass 837BS/487BG [4F-E] Lavenham 8/7/44; retUS Bradley 12/7/45; 4185 BU Independence 13/7/45; RFC Kingman 16/1/46.

43-37998 Del Cheyenne 14/6/44; Kearney 26/6/44; Dow Fd 9/7/44; ass 835BS/486BG [4N-E] Sudbury 11/7/44; retUS Bradley 9/7/45; 4168 BU Sth Plains 11/7/45; RFC Kingman 4/12/45. ROANOKE MAGICAN.
43-37999 Del Cheyenne 14/6/44; Kearney 25/6/44; Dow Fd 13/7/44; ass 837BS/487BG [4F-M] Lavenham 14/7/44; b/d Brandenburg 14/4/45 w/?; f/l Continent, sal.
43-38000 Del Cheyenne 14/6/44; Kearney 28/6/44; Dow Fd 9/7/44; ass 324BS/91BG [DF-E] Bassingbourn 23/7/44; MIA Halle 16/8/44 w/Lindsay; e/a & exploded, cr Lehna, Ger; 8KIA 1POW; MACR 8181.
43-38001 Del Cheyenne 14/6/44; Kearney 25/6/44; Dow Fd 9/7/44; ass 836BS/487BG Lavenham 10/7/44; tran 835BS/486BG [H8-B] Sudbury 27/10/44; MIA Dresden 17/4/45 w/Allbright; flak, cr Dresden, 9POW; MACR 14197. OLD MISS AGNES.
43-38002 Del Cheyenne 14/6/44; Kearney 25/6/44; Dow Fd 9/7/44; ass 838BS/487BG Lavenham 11/7/44; MIA Derben, Ger 14/1/45 w/Moser; flak, cr Rhoden, Ger; 9POW; MACR 11733. OUR BABY.
43-38003 Del Cheyenne 14/6/44; Kearney 23/6/44; Dow Fd 9/7/44; ass 839BS/487BG [R5-D] Lavenham 11/7/44; MIA Hannover 15/12/44 w/?; ditched off Southwold, UK; crew RTD.
43-38004 Del Cheyenne 15/6/44; Kearney 27/6/44; Dow Fd 9/7/44; ass 850BS/490BG Eye 11/7/44; mission to Koblenz 2/12/44 w/? aban thru poor weather; f/l Belgium, sal 6/12/44.
43-38005 Del Cheyenne 15/6/44; Kearney 26/6/44; Dow Fd 9/7/44; ass 486BG Sudbury 11/7/44; during assembly for Ludwigshafen 27/9/44 w/?; mid air coll w/43-37942; crew baled, a/c cr sea off Suffolk coast.
43-38006 Del Cheyenne 15/6/44; Kearney 25/6/44; Dow Fd 9/7/44; ass APH/388BG Knettishall 10/7/44; retUS Bradley 11/6/45; 4168 BU Sth Plains 13/6/44; RFC Kingman 17/12/45.
43-38007 Del Cheyenne 15/6/44; Kearney 29/6/44; Dow Fd 9/7/44; ass 838BS/487BG Lavenham 11/7/44; MIA Magdeburg 5/8/44 w/Deusche; flak, cr Lossau, Ger; 8KIA 2POW; MACR 7893.
43-38008 Del Cheyenne 15/6/44; Kearney 27/6/44; Dow Fd 9/7/44; ass 839BS/487BG Lavenham 11/7/44; 838BS; MIA Cologne 15/10/44 w/Warner; flak, cr Mayen, Ger; 9POW; MACR 9492.
43-38009 Del Cheyenne 3/7/44; Kearney 12/7/44; Dow Fd 20/7/44; ass 850BS/490BG Eye 21/7/44; MIA Stuttgart 13/9/44 w/Davis; flak, cr Hochheim, Ger; 7KIA 2 POW; MACR 8855.

43-38010 Del Cheyenne 15/6/44; Kearney 27/6/44; Dow Fd 13/7/44; ass 490BG Eye 16/7/44; retUS Bradley 7/7/45; 4168 BU Sth Plains 9/7/45; RFC Kingman 11/12/45.
43-38011 Del Cheyenne 15/6/44; Kearney 27/6/44; Dow Fd 8/7/44; ass 349BS/100BG [XR-H] Thorpe Abbotts 12/7/44; b/d Merseburg 30/11/44 w/?; sal 1/12/44. THE RELUCTANT DRAGON.
43-38012 Del Cheyenne 15/6/44; Kearney 27/6/44; Dow Fd 9/7/44; ass 324BS/91BG [DF-L] Bassingbourn 23/7/44; MIA Halle 16/8/44 w/Fonks; e/a, cr Witzenhausen, Ger; 1KIA 8POW; MACR 8424.
43-38013 Del Cheyenne 15/6/44; Kearney 25/6/44; Dow Fd 9/7/44; ass 487BG Lavenham 11/7/44; retUS Bradley 13/7/44; 4185 BU Independence 16/7/45; RFC Kingman 2/1/46.
43-38014 Del Cheyenne 15/6/44; Kearney 29/6/44; Grenier 9/7/44; ass 422BS/305BG Chelveston 12/7/44; b/d Berlin 18/3/45 w/McCaldin; flak, cr Berlin; 2KIA 7RTD; MACR 13146. Sal 4/4/45. THE NAUGHTY VIRGIN.
43-38015 Del Cheyenne 16/6/44; Kearney 28/6/44; Dow Fd 13/7/44; ass 838BS/487BG [2C-H] Lavenham 14/7/44; b/d Cottbus 15/2/45 w/?; f/l Continent; sal 5 SAD 18/2/45.
43-38016 Del Cheyenne 16/6/44; Kearney 27/6/44; Grenier 9/7/44; ass 544BS/384BG [SU-R] Grafton Underwood 23/7/44; sal 9AF Germany 6/11/45. LORRAINE.
43-38017 Del Cheyenne 16/6/44; Kearney 27/6/44; Grenier 9/7/44; ass 423BS/306BG Thurleigh 23/7/44; MIA Pirmasens 9/8/44 w/?; mid air coll, sal.
43-38018 Del Cheyenne 16/6/44; Kearney 27/6/44; Grenier 9/7/44; ass 851BS/490BG Eye 12/7/44; retUS Bradley 12/7/45; 4185 BU Independence 13/7/45; RFC Kingman 30/12/45.
43-38019 Del Cheyenne 16/6/44; Kearney 27/6/44; Grenier 9/7/44; ass 423BS/306BG [RD-T] Thurleigh 23/7/44; during assembly for Kassel 15/12/44 w/?; mid air coll w/43-37633; cr Greenham Common, UK; 16 killed, sal. MILK RUN SPECIAL.
43-38020 Del Cheyenne 16/6/44; Kearney 27/6/44; Grenier 9/7/44; ass 834BS/486BG [2S-T] Sudbury 13/7/44; MIA Grafenwohr 8/4/45 w/Sauler; flak, cr Rehau, Ger; 1KIA 8POW; MACR 13887. MISS ANTHRACITE.
43-38021 Del Cheyenne 16/6/44; Hunter 14/7/44; Grenier 21/7/44; ass 490BG Eye 25/7/44; b/d Chemnitz 6/2/45 w/?; f/l Melsbroek A/fd, Bel; sal 5 SAD.
43-38022 Del Cheyenne 16/6/44; Kearney 27/6/44; Grenier 8/7/44; ass 486BG Sudbury 11/7/44; tran 836BS/487BG [2G-D] Lavenham 12/7/44; taxi acc 22/1/45; sal 23/1/45.
43-38023 Del Cheyenne 16/6/44; Kearney 27/6/44; c/l Dow Fd 15/7/44, WO.
43-38024 Del Cheyenne 16/6/44; Kearney 27/6/44; Grenier 9/7/44; ass 490BG Eye 12/7/44; b/d Frankfurt 9/3/45 w/?; f/l Continent; sal 24/3/45.
43-38025 Del Cheyenne 17/6/44; Kearney 28/6/44; Dow Fd 13/6/44; ass 364BS/305BG Chelveston 29/7/44; b/d Berlin 3/2/45 w/Creson; f/l Continent, rep & ret 16/2/45; tran 545BS/384BG [JD-P] Grafton Underwood 9/5/45; sal 9AF Germany 10/12/45.
43-38026 Del Cheyenne 17/6/44; Kearney 26/6/44; Grenier 9/7/44; ass 748BS/457BG Glatton 2/7/44; MIA Magdeburg 28/9/44 w/Schultz; e/a, cr Hornburg, Ger; 8KIA 1POW; MACR 9770.
43-38027 Del Cheyenne 17/6/44; Kearney 27/6/44; Grenier 15/7/44; ass 832BS/486BG [3R-R] Sudbury 16/7/44; retUS Bradley 9/7/45; 4168 BU Sth Plains

11/7/45; RFC Kingman 25/11/45. BATCHELOR'S DELIGHT.

43-38028 Del Cheyenne 17/6/44; Kearney 29/6/44; Presque Is 12/7/44; ass 838BS/487BG [2C-O] Lavenham 14/7/44; MIA Oranienburg 15/3/45 w/?; f/l Bomst, Pol; sal 28/3/45. HIGH TAILED LADY.

43-38029 Del Cheyenne 17/6/44; Kearney 28/6/44; Grenier 13/7/44; ass 835BS/486BG [H8-B] Sudbury 16/7/44; b/d Cologne 14/10/44 w/?; f/l Continent; sal 14/11/44.

43-38030 Del Cheyenne 17/6/44; Kearney 28/6/44; Dow Fd 13/7/44; ass 422BS/305BG [JJ-E] Chelveston 14/7/44; mid air coll w/43-38133, cr Thurleigh 22/10/44; 9KIA. MY ACHIN' B.

43-38031 Del Cheyenne 17/6/44; Kearney 29/6/44; Grenier 15/7/44; ass 835BS/486BG [H8-M] Sudbury 17/7/44; 833BS [4N-M]; b/d Berlin 3/2/45 w/?; c/l Raydon, UK; 5KIA; sal 4/2/45. BLUE GRASS GIRL.

43-38032 Del Cheyenne 17/6/44; Hunter 18/7/44; Dow Fd 25/7/44; ass 849BS/490BG Eye 28/7/44; retUS Bradley 13/7/45; 4185 BU Independence 17/7/45; RFC Kingman 2/1/46.

43-38033 Del Cheyenne 17/6/44; Kearney 28/6/44; Dow Fd 16/7/44; ass 838BS/487BG [2C-G] Lavenham 5/7/44; b/d Weimar 9/2/45 w/?; f/l Rennes, Fr; sal 13/3/45.

43-38034 Del Cheyenne 17/6/44; Kearney 28/6/44; Dow Fd 11/7/44; ass 834BS/486BG [4N-V] Sudbury 12/7/44; retUS Bradley 10/7/45; 4168 BU Sth Plains 12/7/45; RFC Kingman 7/11/45.

43-38035 Del Cheyenne 19/6/44; Kearney 29/6/44; Dow Fd 11/7/44; ass 385BG Gt Ashfield 13/7/44; tran 401BS/91BG [LL-F] Bassingbourn 14/7/44; {70+m} RetUS Bradley 11/6/45; 4168 BU Sth Plains 14/6/45; RFC Kingman 5/12/45. ANXIOUS ANGEL.

43-38036 Del Cheyenne 19/6/44; Kearney 28/6/44; Dow Fd 13/7/44; ass 322BS/91BG [LG-D] Bassingbourn 22/7/44; 401BS [LL-H]; {18+m} also used on Carpet Jamming duties; retUS Bradley 11/6/45; 4168 BU Sth Plains 14/6/45; RFC Kingman 8/12/45. HEY DADDY.

43-38037 Del Cheyenne 19/6/44; Kearney 28/6/44; Dow Fd 11/7/44; ass 836BS/487BG Lavenham 13/7/44; MIA Bielefeld 30/9/44 w/Jackson; mid air coll w/43-38154; cr Kentrup, Ger?; 7KIA 2POW. MACR 9422.

43-38038 Del Cheyenne 19/6/44; Kearney 28/6/44; Grenier 9/7/44; ass 838BS/487BG Lavenham 12/7/44; b/d Jena 19/3/45 w/?; mid air coll w/43-37969; cr Allied terr?; sal 21/3/45.

43-38039 Del Cheyenne 19/6/44; Kearney 29/6/44; Dow Fd 14/7/44; ass 487BG Lavenham 16/7/44; retUS Bradley 13/7/45; 4185 BU Independence 17/7/45; RFC Kingman 22/12/45. BASHFUL BESSIE.

43-38040 Del Cheyenne 19/6/44; Kearney 29/6/44; Dow Fd 13/7/44; ass 832BS/486BG [3R-L] Sudbury 14/7/44; tran 390BG 28/7/44; retUS Bradley 9/7/45; 4168 BU Sth Plains 11/7/45; RFC Kingman 19/12/45.

43-38041 Del Cheyenne 19/6/44; Kearney 29/6/44; Dow Fd 11/7/44; ass 835BS/486BG [H8-L] Sudbury 28/7/44; retUS Bradley 7/7/45; 4168 BU Sth Plains 12/7/45; RFC Kingman 19/11/45.

43-38042 Del Cheyenne 19/6/44; Kearney 29/6/44; Dow Fd 13/7/44; ass 487BG Lavenham 14/7/44; retUS Bradley 12/7/45; 4185 BU Independence 13/7/45; RFC Kingman 27/12/45.

43-38043 Del Cheyenne 19/6/44; Kearney 28/6/44; Grenier 15/7/44; ass 350BS/100BG Thorpe Abbotts 17/7/44; MIA Bohlen 11/9/44 w/Schulte; e/a, cr Machern, Ger; 3KIA 6POW; MACR 8814.

43-38044 Del Cheyenne 19/6/44; Kearney 29/6/44; Dow Fd 13/7/44; ass 323BS/91BG [OR-L] Bassingbourn 13/7/44; tran 837BS/487BG [4F-D] Lavenham 14/7/44; MIA Chemnitz 6/2/45 w/Parker; flak, cr Tripitz, Ger; 1KIA 8POW; MACR 12239. PICCADILLY LILY.

43-38045 Del Cheyenne 20/6/44; Kearney 29/6/44; Dow Fd 13/7/44; ass 839BS/487BG [R5-O] Lavenham 14/7/44; retUS Bradley 12/7/45; 4185 BU Independence 14/7/45; RFC Kingman 16/12/45.

43-38046 Del Cheyenne 20/6/44; Hunter 3/7/44; Grenier 24/7/44; ass 849BS/490BG Eye 26/7/44; MIA Ruhland 17/3/45 w/Stein; mid air cool, cr Kamberg, Ger; 9KIA; MACR 13080.

43-38047 Del Cheyenne 20/6/44; Hunter 16/7/44; Dow Fd 26/7/44; ass 350BS/100BG [LN-O] Thorpe Abbotts 2/8/44; MIA Bohlen 11/9/44 w/Baine; e/a, cr Gottesgab, Ger?; 5KIA 4POW; MACR 8815.

43-38048 Del Cheyenne 20/6/44; Hunter 13/7/44; Grenier 24/7/44; ass 849BS/490BG Eye 26/7/44; MIA Karlsbad 19/4/45 w/Stovall; jet e/a, cr Dresden; 1EVD 1KIA 8POW; MACR 14195.

43-38049 Del Cheyenne 20/6/44; Hunter 15/7/44; Grenier 22/7/44; ass 385BG Gt Ashfield 24/7/44; tran 379BG Kimbolton 14/8/44; retUS Bradley 28/6/45; 4168 BU Sth Plains 2/7/45; RFC Kingman 6/12/45.

43-38050 Del Cheyenne 20/6/44; Hunter 13/7/44; Dow Fd 23/7/44; ass 849BS/490BG Eye 26/7/44; during assembly for Frankfurt 5/1/45, w/Aldeman; mid air coll w/43-38111; c/l Rougham A/fd, UK; 7KIA 3WIA; sal.

43-38051 Del Cheyenne 20/6/44; Hunter 16/7/44; Dow Fd 26/7/44; ass 848BS/490BG Eye 28/7/44; mid air coll w/42-37618, c/l Roydon, Nfk, UK; 4KIA; sal 14/8/44.

43-38052 Del Cheyenne 20/6/44; Hunter 16/7/44; Dow Fd 23/7/44; ass 366BS/305BG Chelveston 6/8/44; MIA Cologne 17/10/44 w/Potucek; flak, cr Cologne; 7KIA 2POW; MACR 9473.

43-38053 Del Cheyenne 20/6/44; Hunter 16/7/44; Grenier 24/7/44; ass 569BS/390BG Framlingham 28/7/44; MIA Zeitz 30/11/44 w/Torrance; flak, cr Grosskanya, Ger; 4KIA 5POW; MACR 11134.

43-38054 Del Cheyenne 20/6/44; Hunter 13/7/44; Grenier 24/7/44; ass 851BS/490BG Eye 26/7/44; b/d Chemnitz 6/2/45 w/?; c/l Darsham, UK; crew injured; sal. LIL EDIE.

43-38055 Del Cheyenne 20/6/44; Hunter 18/7/44; Dow Fd 25/7/44; ass 490BG Eye 27/7/44; retUS Reading 20/7/45; 4185 BU Independence 24/7/45; RFC Kingman 10/12/45.

43-38056 Del Cheyenne 20/6/44; Hunter 16/7/44; Grenier 24/7/44; ass 490BG Eye 28/7/44; retUS Bradley 13/7/45; 4185 BU Independence 15/7/45; RFC Kingman 22/12/45.

43-38057 Del Cheyenne 21/6/44; Hunter 21/7/44; Presque Is 1/8/44; ass 427BS/303BG [GN-L] Molesworth 15/8/44; b/d Schweinfurt 9/10/44 w/?; mid air coll w/43-37666; sal 10/11/44. MISS UMBRIAGO.

43-38058 Del Cheyenne 21/6/44; Hunter 16/7/44; Grenier 24/7/44; ass 850BS/490BG Eye 26/7/44; b/d Parchim 7/4/45 w/Cagle; mid air coll w/Me109 (by Sonderkommando Elbe rammer); ret allied territory safely despite two engines out; retUS, RFC Kingman 17/12/45.

43-38059 Del Cheyenne 21/6/44; Lincoln 14/7/44; Grenier 11/8/44; ass 391BS/34BG Mendlesham 12/7/44; MIA Merseburg 30/11/44 w/Capt Nanson; flak, cr Sommerda, Ger; 1EVD 4KIA 4POW; MACR 10841.

43-38060 Del Cheyenne 21/6/44; Kearney 16/7/44; Grenier 1/8/44; ass 548BS/385BG Gt Ashfield 2/8/44; MIA Berlin 6/10/44 w/Courcelle; e/a, cr Pessin, Ger; 8KIA 1POW; MACR 9508. TEXAS BLUEBONNET.

43-38061 Del Cheyenne 21/6/44; Hunyer 4/7/44; Grenier 24/7/44; ass 410BS/94BG Rougham 26/7/44 ERIE FERRY; 332BS [XM-E]; b/d Mainz 18/12/44 w/Ogren; three engines out, c/l Dinant, Fr; 8RTD 1MIA (pilot); sal 18/1/45. ROBIN HOOD.

43-38062 Del Cheyenne 21/6/44; Hunter 20/7/44; Grenier 27/7/44; ass 544BS/384BG [SU-A] Grafton Underwood 11/8/44; sal 9AF Germany 10/12/45. PLEASURE BENT.

43-38063 Del Cheyenne 21/6/44; Kearney 13/7/44; Dow Fd 20/7/44; ass 850BS/490BG Eye 21/7/44; retUS Reading 20/7/45; 4185 BU Independence 21/7/45; RFC Kingman 17/12/45.

43-38064 Del Cheyenne 21/6/44; Hunter 17/7/44; Grenier 27/7/44; ass 601BS; 398BG [3O-H] Nuthampstead 15/8/44; retUS Bradley 6/6/45; 4168 BU Sth Plains 7/6/45; RFC Kingman 8/11/45.

43-38065 Del Cheyenne 21/6/44; Kearney 28/6/44; Dow Fd 13/7/44; ass 358BS/303BG [VK-J] Molesworth 28/7/44; b/d Dresden 14/2/45 w/?; c/l RAF Lakenheath, UK; sal 17/2/45. PRINCESS PAT 2.

43-38066 Del Cheyenne 21/6/44; Kearney 28/6/44; Grenier 24/7/44; ass 365BS/305BG Chelveston 12/8/44; MIA Cologne 14/10/44 w/Nichols; mid air coll, cr Elsenhorn, Bel; 8KIA 1POW; MACR 9474.

43-38067 Del Cheyenne 21/6/44; Kearney 16/7/44; Dow Fd 3/8/44; ass 412BS/95BG [QW-E] Horham 4/8/44 JOY RIDE; f/l b/d twice, Melsbroek, Bel and St Trond, Bel; retUS Bradley 27/6/45; 4168 BU Sth Plains 1/7/45; RFC Kingman 20/11/45. BIG CHIEF ILLINIWEK.

43-38068 Del Cheyenne 21/6/44; Kearney 5/7/44; Grenier 19/7/44; ass 850BS/490BG Eye 22/7/44; MIA Frankfurt 9/3/45 w/Faust; flak, cr Mulheim; 2KIA 7POW; MACR 12947. MAGNIFICENT OBSESSION.

43-38069 Del Cheyenne 21/6/44; Hunter 13/7/44; Grenier 21/7/44; ass 327BS/92BG [UX-U] Podington 27/8/44; 407BS; secret mission 1/6/45; Re-ass USAF 31/7/46; 108 BU Oberpfaffenhofen 22/9/48; Recl Comp 7/1/49.

43-38070 Del Cheyenne 21/6/44; Hunter 13/7/44; Dow Fd 25/7/44; ass 511BS/351BG [DS-G] Polebrook 7/8/44; 509BS [RQ-V]; {41m} RetUS Bradley 29/5/45; 4168 BU Sth Plains 31/5/45; RFC Kingman 5/11/45.

43-38071 Del Cheyenne 22/6/44; Hunter 14/7/44; Grenier 24/7/44; ass 490BG Eye 26/7/44; b/d Ruhland 17/3/45 w/?; f/l St Trond A/fd, Bel; sal 23/3/45.

43-38072 Del Cheyenne 22/6/44; Hunter 13/7/44; Grenier 24/7/44; ass 848BS/490BG Eye 27/7/44; 850BS; MIA Plauen 21/3/45 w/Schultz; jet e/a, cr Falkenberg, Swed; 8KIA 1POW; MACR 13556.

43-38073 Del Cheyenne 22/6/44; Hunter 14/7/44; Grenier 24/7/44; ass 349BS/100BG [XR-L] Thorpe Abbotts 27/7/44; b/d Zeitz 30/11/44 w/?; f/l Cambrai A/fd, Fr; sal 14/2/45.

43-38074 Del Cheyenne 22/6/44; Hunter 14/7/44; Dow Fd 25/7/44; ass 366BS/305BG Chelveston 6/8/44; MIA Berlin 5/12/44 w/Funkhouser; flak, cr Berlin; 1KIA 8POW; MACR 11041.

43-38075 Del Cheyenne 22/6/44; Kearney 13/7/44; Grenier 21/7/44; ass 603BS/398BG [N7-A] Nuthampstead 9/8/44; ground acc 7/11/44; sal 9/11/44.

43-38076 Del Cheyenne 22/6/44; Hunter 21/7/44; Grenier 29/7/44; ass 350BS/100BG Thorpe Abbotts 2/8/44; MIA Saarbrücken 11/9/44 w/Taylor; e/a, cr Brux, Cz; 8KIA 1POW; MACR 8816.

43-38077 Del Cheyenne 22/6/44; Hunter 14/7/44; Grenier 24/7/44; ass 615BS/401BG [IY-Q] Deenethorpe 5/8/44 DUKE'S MIXTURE; 614BS [IW-H]; retUS Bradley 6//6/45; 4169 BU Sth Plains 8/6/45; RFC Kingman 26/11/45. TAG A LONG.

43-38078 Del Cheyenne 22/6/44; Kearney 13/7/44; Grenier 20/7/44; ass 849BS/490BG Eye 22/7/44; 850BS; MIA Pirna 19/4/45 w/Norvell; jet e/a, cr Schonau, Ger; 6KIA 3POW; MACR 14194.

43-38079 Del Cheyenne 22/6/44; Kearney 13/7/44; Grenier 24/7/44; ass 490BG Eye 26/7/43; retUS Bradley 13/7/44; 4185 BU Independence 17/7/45; RFC Albuquerque 7/2/46.

43-38080 Del Cheyenne 22/6/44; Hunter 13/7/44; Grenier 22/7/44; ass 511BS/351BG [DS-Q] Polebrook 14/8/44; {41m} on 6/2/45 w/?, mid air coll w/43-37595 approaching base on return from target; 19KIA. Sal 8/2/45.

43-38081 Del Wright Fd 23/6/44; Cheyenne 13/7/44; Grenier 16/7/44; ass APH/388BG Knettishall 17/7/44; retUS Bradley 2/6/45; 4168 BU Sth Plains 7/6/45; RFC Kingman 30/1/46.

43-38082 Del Cheyenne 23/6/44; Hunter 14/7/44; Grenier 16/7/44; ass 850BS/490BG Eye 30/7/44; MIA Kaltenkirchen 7/4/45 w/?; MACR 14294. LADY HELENE.

43-38083 Del Cheyenne 24/6/44; Hunter 14/7/44; Dow Fd 23/7/44; ass 323BS/91BG [OR-V] Bassingbourn 11/8/44; {48m} b/d Aschaffenburg 22/1/45 w/?; c/l Metfield A/fd; sal 23/1/45. HAPPY VALLEY EXPRESS.

43-38084 Del Cheyenne 26/6/44; Kearney 13/7/44; Dow Fd 20/7/44; ass 490BG Eye 22/7/44; retUS Bradley 14/7/45; 4185 BU Independence 16/7/45; RFC Kingman 9/12/45.

43-38085 Del Cheyenne 24/6/44; Hunter 17/6/44; Dow Fd 23/7/44; ass 366BS/305BG [KY-L] Chelveston 11/8/44; MIA Dresden 17/4/45 w/Harris; mid air coll w/jet a/c, cr Brux, Cz; 8KIA MACR 14172. TOWERING TITAN.

43-38086 Del Cheyenne 24/6/44; Kearney 13/7/44; Grenier 20/7/44; ass 603BS/398BG [N7-C] Nuthampstead 11/8/44; retUS Bradley 6/6/45; 4168 BU Sth Plains 8/6/45; RFC Kingman 3/12/45. BAD PENNY.

43-38087 Del Cheyenne 24/6/44; Hunter 16/7/44; Grenier 22/7/44; ass 849BS/490BG Eye 25/7/44; MIA Ludwigshafen 5/11/44 w/?; MACR 10326.

43-38088 Del Cheyenne 24/6/44; Hunter 14/7/44; Grenier 24/7/44; ass 322BS/91BG [LG-R] Bassingbourn 11/8/44; {60m} RetUS Bradley 12/6/45; 4168 BU Sth Plains 15/6/45; RFC Kingman 12/8/45. REDWING (FIGHTIN' SWEDE).

43-38089 Del Cheyenne 24/6/44; Kearney 13/7/44; Grenier 20/7/44; ass 511BS/351BG [DS-P] Polebrook 8/8/44; MIA Brux 12/9/44 w/Adams; e/a, cr Weser; 9POW; MACR 8896. WILD OATS.

43-38090 Del Cheyenne 24/6/44; Hunter 13/7/44; Dow Fd 23/7/44; ass 490BG Eye 26/7/44; retUS Bradley 12/7/45; 4185 BU Independence 14/7/45; RFC Kingman 21/12/45.

43-38091 Del Cheyenne 24/6/44; Kearney 13/7/44; Grenier 20/7/44; ass 603BS/398BG [N7-L] Nuthampstead 10/8/44; sal 3/12/44.

43-38092 Del Cheyenne 24/6/44; Hunter 14/7/44; Grenier 22/7/44; ass 527BS/379BG [FO-G] Kimbolton 14/8/44; MIA Mannheim 9/9/44 w/Butler; flak, cr Luwigshafen; 7KIA 2POW; MACR 8845.

43-38093 Del Cheyenne 25/6/44; Kearney 13/7/44; Dow Fd 20/7/44; ass 728BS/452BG Deopham Green 21/7/44; retUS Bradley 11/7/45; 4168 BU Sth Plains 12/7/45; RFC Kingman 10/12/45.

43-38094 Del Cheyenne 25/6/44; Kearney 14/7/44; Grenier 20/7/44; ass 849BS/490BG Eye 22/7/44; c/t/o for Ahrweiler 25/12/44 w/?; sal 27/12/44.

43-38095 Del Cheyenne 25/6/44; Kearney 13/7/44; Grenier 20/7/44; ass 418BS/100BG [LD-X] Thorpe Abbotts 22/7/44; sal 2/12/44. WEATHERSHIP.

43-38096 Del Cheyenne 25/6/44; Kearney 13/7/44; Grenier 23/7/44; ass 490BG Eye 26/7/44; retUS Bradley 7/7/45; 4168 BU Sth Plains 11/7/45; RFC Kingman 18/11/45.

43-38097 Del Cheyenne 25/6/44; Lincoln 14/7/44; Grenier 20/8/44; ass 562BS/388BG Knettishall 22/8/44; retUS Bradley 7/7/45; 4168 BU Sth Plains 10/7/45; RFC Kingman 8/11/45.

43-38098 Del Cheyenne 25/6/44; Kearney 16/7/44; Grenier 3/8/44; ass 863BS/493BG Debach 4/8/44; MIA Magdeburg 12/9/44 w/Kittleson; e/a, cr Nadueralebau, Ger?; 5KIA 4POW; MACR 8863.

43-38099 Del Cheyenne 26/6/44; Kearney 14/7/44; Grenier 20/7/44; ass 333BS/94BG Rougham 22/7/44; bomb rack fault en route Fulda 3/1/45 w/Miller; c/l base on ret; sal 4/1/45. DOROTHY V.

43-38100 Del Cheyenne 26/6/44; Kearney 15/7/44; Grenier 20/7/44; ass 850BS/490BG Eye 22/7/44; retUS Bradley 14/7/45; 4185 BU Independence 16/7/45; 237 BU Kirtland 25/12/45; RFC Albuquerque 6/2/46.

43-38101 Del Cheyenne 26/6/44; Hunter 15/7/44; Dow Fd 26/7/44; ass 490BG Eye 29/7/44; tran 327BS/92BG [UX-O] Podington 30/7/44; retUS Bradley 7/7/45; 4168 BU Sth Plains 8/7/45; RFC Kingman 19/12/45.

43-38102 Del Cheyenne 26/6/44; Hunter 13/7/44; Grenier 23/7/44; ass 366BS/305BG Chelveston 6/8/44; MIA Chemnitz 2/3/45 w/Gordon; flak, cr Trier, Ger; 1KIA 8POW; MACR 12852.

43-38103 Del Cheyenne 26/6/44; Hunter 15/7/44; Grenier 24/7/44; ass 848BS/490BG Eye 26/7/44; MIA Nuremberg 5/4/45 w/Bates; flak, cr Frisian Is, Hol; 7KIA 3POW; MACR 13855.

43-38104 Del Cheyenne 26/6/44; Orlando 6/7/44; 902 BU Orlando 10/7/44; 903 BU Pinecastle 10/9/44; 621 BU Pinecastle 9/7/45; 4152 BU Clinton 22/5/46; 1 EGMP Eglin 3/9/46; 4104 BU Rome 5/9/46; 609 BU Eglin 6/4/47; 605 BU Eglin 3/5/48; 3203 MS Eglin 9/7/48; Recl Comp 3/11/48.

43-38105 Del Cheyenne 26/6/44; Kearney 13/7/44; Dow Fd 20/7/44; ass 490BG Eye 26/7/44; retUS Bradley 15/7/45; 4185 BU Independence 17/7/45; RFC Kingman 30/12/45.

43-38106 Del Cheyenne 26/6/44; Hunter 15/7/44; Grenier 23/7/44; ass 336BS/95BG [ET-E] Horham 25/7/44; retUS Bradley 24/7/45; 4168 BU Sth Plains 27/6/45; RFC Kingman 21/11//45.

43-38107 Del Cheyenne 26/6/44; Hunter 21/7/44; Dow Fd 3/8/44; ass 861BS/493BG Debach 4/8/44; MIA Osnabrück 21/11/44 w/Baxter; flak, cr Enschede, Hol; 1KIA 8POW; MACR 10404.

43-38108 Del Cheyenne 26/6/44; Hunter 15/7/44; Dow Fd 23/7/44; ass 365BS/305BG Chelveston 11/8/44; MIA Cologne 14/10/44 w/Gustafson; mid air coll, cr Elsenborn, Bel; 9KIA; MACR 9475.

43-38109 Del Cheyenne 27/6/44; Hunter 15/7/44; Grenier 22/7/44; ass 305BG Chelveston 1/8/44; f/l Fritzlar A/fd, Ger twice and Kassel A/fd, Ger; tran 401BG Deenethorpe 28/5/45; retUS Bradley 8/6/45; 4168 BU Sth Plains 12/6/45; RFC Kingman 29/11/45.

43-38110 Del Cheyenne 27/6/44; Kearney 8/7/44; Grenier 15/7/44; ass 835BS/486BG Sudbury 19/7/44; MIA Mersdeburg 28/9/44 w/Oltman; flak, cr Merseburg; 9KIA 1POW; MACR 9420. MARGE.

43-38111 Del Cheyenne 27/6/44; Hunter 13/7/44; Grenier 22/7/44; ass 849BS/490BG Eye 25/7/44; lost on training flight 5/1/45 w/Wood; mid air coll w/43-38050; cr Rougham A/fd, UK; all killed; sal 17/1/45.

43-38112 Del Cheyenne 27/6/44; Hunter 13/7/44; Grenier 22/7/44; ass 851BS/490BG Eye 25/7/44; sal n/b/d 15/11/44.

43-38113 Del Cheyenne 28/6/44; Lincoln 14/7/44; Grenier 15/8/44; ass 7BS/34BG Mendlesham 16/8/44; retUS Bradley 20/6/45; 4168 BU Sth Plains 23/6/45; RFC Kingman 17/2/46. WEE WILLIE'S WOLVES.

43-38114 Del Cheyenne 28/6/44; Hunter 15/7/44; Dow Fd 26/7/44; ass 534BS/381BG [GD-N] Ridgewell 6/8/44; MIA {2+m} Hamburg 6/11/44 w/Brummett; flak, cr Wittmundhafen, Ger?; 9KIA; MACR 10153. NO COMMENT NEEDED.

43-38115 Del Cheyenne 28/6/44; Lincoln 14/7/44; Grenier 11/8/44; ass 860BS/493BG Debach 13/8/44; MIA Bielefeld, Ger 30/9/44 w/Treece; hit by bomb from a/c above, cr Bielefeld; 8KIA 1POW; MACR 9429. RELUCTANT LASSIE.

43-38116 Del Cheyenne 28/6/44; Hunter 16/7/44; Grenier 23/7/44; ass 509BS/351BG [RQ-Q] Polebrook 15/8/44; b/d Chemnitz 2/3/45 w/?; c/l base, sal 4/3/45. CLASSY CHASSIS.

43-38117 Del Cheyenne 28/6/44; Hunter 13/7/44; Grenier 22/7/44; ass 305BG Chelveston 14/8/44; c/l 7/4/45, sal.

43-38118 Del Cheyenne 28/6/44; Hunter 15/7/44; Grenier 24/7/44; ass 549BS/385BG Gt Ashfield 2/8/44; retUS Bradley 26/6/45; 4168 BU Sth Plains 28/6/45; RFC Kingman 22/11/45. MISS FORTUNE.

43-38119 Del Cheyenne 28/6/44; Hunter 13/7/44; Grenier 22/7/44; ass 729BS/452BG Deopham Green 25/7/44; MIA Brest, Fr. 3/9/44 w/Parmely; flak, cr Channel Is, UK; 10KIA; MACR 8609.

43-38120 Del Cheyenne 28/6/44; Kearney 13/7/44; Grenier 20/7/44; ass 407BS/92BG [PY-N] Podington 22/7/44; tran 305BG Chelveston 12/8/44; 351BG Polebrook 23/5/45; retUS Bradley 9/6/45; 4168 BU Sth Plains 18/6/45; RFC Kingman 6/12/45.

43-38121 Del Cheyenne 28/6/44; Hunter 14/7/44; Grenier 20/7/44; ass 601BS/398BG [3O-Q] Nuthampstead 11/8/44; MIA Neumünster 13/4/45 w/Traeder; cr & burned Paderborn A/fd.

43-38122 Del Cheyenne 28/6/44; Hunter 13/7/44; Grenier 24/7/44; ass 8AF 24/7/44; retUS Bradley 15/7/45; 4185 BU Independence 19/7/45; RFC Kingman 7/1/46.

43-38123 Del Cheyenne 28/6/44; Hunter 11/7/44; Grenier 22/7/44; ass 510BS/351BG [TU-V] Polebrook 14/8/44; MIA {8m} Brux 12/9/44 w/Hennigan; e/a, cr Werneuchen, Ger; 1KIA 8POW; MACR 8897. BABY BUTCH.

43-38124 Del Cheyenne 28/6/44; Kearney 13/7/44; Dow Fd 20/7/44; ass 351BS/100BG [EP-S] Thorpe Abbotts 21/7/44; MIA Hamburg 31/12/44 w/Williams; mid air coll, cr Hamburg; 6KIA 3POW; MACR 11363.

43-38125 Del Cheyenne 28/6/44; Hunter 13/7/44; Dow Fd 26/7/44; ass 615BS/401BG [IY-D] Deenethorpe 5/8/44; during assembly for Sterkrade 22/1/45 w/?, cr RAF Saltby, UK; sal; 24/1/45.

43-38126 Del Cheyenne 28/6/44; Kearney 13/7/44; Grenier 20/7/44; ass 600BS/398BG [N8-J] Nuthampstead 10/8/44; retUS Bradley 31/5/45; 4168 BU Sth Plains 3/6/45; RFC Kingman 18/12/45.

43-38127 Del Cheyenne 28/6/44; Hunter 15/7/44; Dow Fd 23/7/44; ass 535BS/381BG [MS-Q] Ridgewell 28/7/44; {67m} RetUS Bradley 9/6/45; 41678 BU Sth Plains 15/6/45; RFC Kingman 18/12/45. PAIR OF QUEENS GEE AND BEE.

43-38128 Del Cheyenne 28/6/44; Lincoln 14/7/44; Grenier 11/8/44; ass 849BS/490BG Eye 22/8/44; MIA Stuttgart 13/9/44 w/Funk; flak, cr Fuerth, Ger; 4KIA 5POW; MACR 8856. BOMBO.

43-38129 Del Cheyenne 29/6/44; Hunter 13/7/44; Grenier 24/7/44; ass 601BS/398BG [3O-A] Nuthampstead 10/8/44; sal 25/9/44.

43-38130 Del Cheyenne 29/6/44; Hunter 15/7/44; Dow Fd 24/7/44; ass 508BS/351BG [YB-K] Polebrook 10/8/44; retUS 121 BU Bradley 30/6/45; 4168 BU Sth Plains 3/7/45; RFC Kingman 14/12/45. TEXAS BELLE.

43-38131 Del Cheyenne 29/6/44; Kearney 13/7/44; Grenier 23/7/44; ass 851BS/490BG Eye 6/8/44; 850BS; b/d Nuremberg 5/4/45 w/?; c/l Outdorp, Hol; MACR 13854. MISS MO.

43-38132 Del Cheyenne 29/6/44; Kearney 13/7/44; Dow Fd 20/7/44; ass 849BS/490BG Eye 21/7/44; MIA Cologne 10/1/45 w/McGarth; flak, cr Julich, Ger?; 5KIA 4POW; MACR 11585. OLD PATCH.

43-38133 Del Cheyenne 29/6/44; Kearney 13/7/44; Grenier 23/7/44; ass 364BS/305BG [WF-N] Chelveston 25/8/44; mid air coll w/43-38030, cr Thurleigh 22/10/44.10KIA

43-38134 Del Cheyenne 29/6/44; Kearney 8/7/44; Grenier 15/7/44; ass 849BS/490BG Eye 25/7/44; returning from Darmstadt, hit by landing 43-38838 12/12/44; sal 13/12/44.

43-38135 Del Cheyenne 29/6/44; Kearney 8/7/44; Grenier 16/7/44; ass 849BS/490BG Eye 17/7/44; MIA Pirna 19/4/45 w/McCallister; jet e/a, cr Marienburg; 7KIA 2POW; MACR 14193.

43-38136 Del Cheyenne 29/6/44; Kearney 13/7/44; Grenier 15/7/44; ass 835BS/486BG [H8-R] Sudbury 17/7/44; MIA Cologne 15/10/44 w/List; flak, cr Overath, Ger; 7KIA 2POW; MACR 9491. SNOW WHITE.

43-38137 Del Cheyenne 29/6/44; Kearney 8/7/44; Grenier 16/7/44; ass 835BS/486BG [H8-N] Sudbury 17/7/44; c/t/o for Cologne 15/10/44 w/? at Woodhall Farm, Sudbury, UK; 8KIA plus a civilian; sal.

43-38138 Del Cheyenne 29/6/44; Lincoln 14/7/44; Grenier 11/8/44; ass 4BS/34BG Mendlesham 13/8/44; tran 490BG Eye 14/8/44; retUS Bradley 20/6/45; 4168 BU Sth Plains 23/6/45; RFC Kingman 17/12/45. OLE-TIMER.

43-38139 Del Cheyenne 29/6/44; Kearney 13/7/44; Grenier 17/7/44; ass 5608BS/351BG [YB-D] Polebrook 31/7/44; MIA {12m} Ludwigshafen 5/9/44 w/Wright; flak, cr Viernheim, Ger; MACR 8452; rep & ret group 30/11/44; sal 8/12/44.

43-38140 Del Cheyenne 29/6/44; Kearney 11/7/44; Grenier 16/7/44; ass 832BS/486BG Sudbury 17/7/44; MIA Merseburg 2/11/44 w/Pierce; flak, cr Sommerda, Ger; 4KIA 5POW; MACR 10167.

43-38141 Del Cheyenne 29/6/44; Kearney 11/7/44; Grenier 16/7/44; ass 838BS/487BG Lavenham 17/7/44; 839BS [R5-V]; MIA Hamm 26/11/44 w/Davidson; flak, cr Osnabrück; 9POW; MACR 10758.

43-38142 Del Cheyenne 29/6/44; Kearney 11/7/44; Grenier 18/7/44; ass 835BS/486BG [H8-P] Sudbury 19/7/44 RODNEY THE ROCKS; MIA Hamburg 30/3/45 w/Veal; flak, cr Pinneberg, Ger; 7KIA 2POW; MACR 13550. LIL' BUTCH.

43-38143 Del Cheyenne 30/6/44; Kearney 11/7/44; Grenier 16/7/44; ass 385BG Gt Ashfield 17/7/44; retUS Bradley 10/7/45; 4185 BU Independence 12/7/45; Recl Comp 15/5/47.

43-38144 Del Cheyenne 30/6/44; Kearney 11/7/44; Dow Fd 20/7/44; ass 364BS/305BG Chelveston 14/8/44; MIA Ludwigshafen 3/9/44 w/Wreyford; flak, cr Neuburg, Ger; 9POW; MACR 8451.

43-38145 Del Cheyenne 30/6/44; Kearney 11/7/44; Grenier 17/7/44; ass 832BS/486BG Sudbury 18/7/44; MIA Hamburg 4/8/44 w/Harper; mid air coll, cr Quelkhorn, Ger; 7KIA 2POW; MACR 7713.

43-38146 Del Cheyenne 30/6/44; Kearney 11/7/44; Dow Fd 20/7/44; ass 366BS/305BG Chelveston 10/8/44; MIA Merseburg 24/8/44 w/Dabeny; e/a, cr Leipzig; 9POW; MACR 8209.

43-38147 Del Cheyenne 30/6/44; Kearney 11/7/44; Grenier 17/7/44; ass 603BS/398BG [N7-L] Nuthampstead 9/8/44; 600BS [N8-L]; MIA Osnabrück 21/11/44 w/Howell; e/a, cr Efurt, Ger; 7KIA 3POW; MACR 11210. FUDDY DUDDY.

43-38148 Del Cheyenne 30/6/44; Kearney 11/7/44; Grenier 1/8/44; ass 549BS/385BG Gt Ashfield 3/8/44; MIA Dresden 2/3/45 w/Tripp; e/a, cr Jueldorf, Ger?; 7KIA 2POW; MACR 12856.

43-38149 Del Cheyenne 30/6/44; Kearney 11/7/44; Grenier 16/7/44; ass 834BS/487BG [2S-M] Lavenham 17/7/44; retUS Bradley 7/7/45; 4168 BU Sth Plains 12/7/45; RFC Kingman 14/11/45. WINGED VIRGIN.

43-38150 Del Cheyenne 30/6/44; Kearney 11/7/44; Dow Fd 20/7/44; ass 490BG Eye 21/7/44; b/d Berlin 3/2/45 w/?; f/l Russia, sal 23/3/45. MACR 12238.

43-38151 Del Cheyenne 30/6/44; Kearney 11/7/44; Dow Fd 19/7/44; ass 365BS/305BG Chelveston 10/8/44; MIA Politz, Ger 7/10/44 w/Bailey; flak, cr Koerde, Ger?; 8KIA 2POW; MACR 9355.

43-38152 Del Cheyenne 30/6/44; Kearney 11/7/44; Grenier 16/7/44; ass 849BS/490BG Eye 17/7/44; retUS Bradley 9/7/45; 4168 BU Sth Plains 11/7/45; RFC Kingman 8/11/45.

43-38153 Del Cheyenne 30/6/44; Kearney 11/7/44; Dow Fd 20/7/44; ass 423BS/306BG [RD-G] Thurleigh 21/7/44; tran 381BG Ridgewell 5/45; retUS Bradley 10/6/45; 4168 BU Sth Plains 13/6/45; RFC Kingman 9/12/45. SWINGING ON A STAR.

43-38154 Del Cheyenne 30/6/44; Kearney 11/7/44; Grenier 15/7/44; ass 836BS/487BG Lavenham 18/7/44; MIA Beilefeld, Ger 30/9/44 w/Oesch; mid air coll w/43-38037, cr Halle; 8KIA 1POW; MACR 9423.

43-38155 Del Cheyenne 1/7/44; Gt Falls 6/7/44; McDill 30/8/44 mod as F-9; 19 Ph Gp McDill 5/9/44; sal 9AF 6/12/45.

43-38156 Del Cheyenne 1/7/44; Kearney 11/7/44; Grenier 15/7/44; ass 551BS/385BG Gt Ashfield 18/7/44; MIA Eindhoven 9/8/44 w/Bristol; flak, cr Baumholder, Ger; 3KIA 6POW; MACR 7389.

43-38157 Del Cheyenne 1/7/44; Kearney 12/7/44; Dow Fd 20/7/44; ass 490BG Eye 21/7/44; b/d Cologne 10/1/45 w/?; f/l Continent, 3KIA; sal 28/1/45. MACR 11548.

43-38158 Del Cheyenne 1/7/44; Kearney 11/7/44; Dow Fd 20/7/44; ass 534BS/381BG [GD-D] Ridgewell 26/7/44; b/d {27m} Aschaffenburg 21/1/45 w/Bradley; f/l Sauverne, Fr; sal 28/2/45. SMASHING TIME!

43-38159 Del Cheyenne 1/7/44; Kearney 11/7/44; Dow Fd 20/7/44; ass 615BS/401BG [IY-N] Deenethorpe 11/8/44; MIA Merseburg 2/11/44 w/Oas; flak, cr Merseburg; 8KIA 1POW; MACR 10159. WOLF PACK.

43-38160 Del Cheyenne 1/7/44; Kearney 12/7/44; Dow Fd 20/7/44; ass 613BS/401BG [IN-C] Deenethorpe 11/8/44; 615BS [IY-A]; retUS Bradley 8/6/45; 4168 BU Sth Plains 12/6/45; RFC Kingman 29/11/45. BUDD'S DUDDS.

43-38161 Del Cheyenne 1/7/44; Kearney 11/7/44; Dow Fd 20/7/44; ass 349BS/100BG [XR-O] Thorpe Abbotts 21/7/44; b/d Chemnitz 11/9/44 w/Heironimus; f/l France; 9RTD. MACR 11980.

43-38162 Del Cheyenne 1/7/44; slated 100BG, Gt Falls 5/7/44; McDill 2/9/44 mod as F-9C; 19 Ph Gp McDill 10/9/44; 311 Ph Gp Buckley 18/12/44; 311 Ph Gp McDill 2/5/46; 16 Ph Gp McDill 15/5/46; 326 BU McDill 8/7/46; 16 Ph Gp McDill 12/8/46; Recl Comp 30/10/46.

43-38163 Del Cheyenne 1/7/44; Kearney 11/7/44; Dow Fd 17/7/44; ass 838BS/487BG Lavenham 18/7/44; retUS Bradley 7/7/45; 4168 BU Sth Plains 9/7/45; Recl Comp 7/6/46.

43-38164 Del Cheyenne 1/7/44; Kearney 12/7/44; Grenier 21/7/44; ass 600BS/398BG [N8-H] Nuthampstead 15/8/44; 602BG; b/d Koblenz 5/1/45 w/?; c/l Continent; sal 10/2/45.

43-38165 Del Cheyenne 3/7/44; Kearney 10/7/44; Dow Fd 20/7/44; ass 332BS/94BG [XM-B] Rougham 22/7/44 CAROLYN SUE; MIA Hamburg 4/11/44 w/Hummel; flak, cr Channel; 9KIA; MACR 10305. ST CHRISTOPHER KIDS.

43-38166 Del Cheyenne 3/7/44; Kearney 11/7/44; Dow Fd 20/7/44; ass 365BS/305BG Chelveston 10/8/44; MIA Merseburg 11/9/44 w/Hogaboam; e/a, cr Irlich, Ger; 9POW; MACR 8826.

43-38167 Del Cheyenne 3/7/44; Kearney 12/7/44; Grenier 20/7/44; ass 490BG Eye 22/7/44; during assembly for Chemnitz 6/2/45 w/?, mid air coll w/43-38699; cr Prickwillow, UK; crews baled, but one man killed plus two civilians; MACR 12371; sal 2/3/45.

43-38168 Del Cheyenne 3/7/44; Gt Falls 6/7/44; Cheyenne 8/7/44 mod as F-9C; McDill 2/9/44; 19 Gp McDill 10/9/44; 91 Rec Sq Buckley 11/11/44; 1103 BU Morrison 5/6/45; 91 Rec Sq Buckley 11/6/45; 4200 BU Chicago Mun 15/4/46; 91 Rec Sq Buckley 17/4/46; 91 Rec Sq McDill 2/5/46; 1103 BU Morrison 23/5/46; 91 Rec Sq McDill 4/6/46; re-ass 6AF Panama 30/4/47, 91 Rec Sq Howard; 91 Rec Sq Waller 5/4/49; retUS, 91 RLP Sq McGuire 9/2/49; 91 RLP Sq Barksdale 30/9/49; 91 SRC Gp Maguire 11/10/49; Olmstead 12/10/49; Recl Comp 8/11/49.

43-38169 Del Cheyenne 3/7/44; Kearney 11/7/44; Grenier 17/7/44; ass 838BS/487BG Lavenham 18/7/44; 836BG [2G-J]; MIA Frankfurt 29/12/44 w/Perrot; flak, cr Bitburg Eifel, Ger; 3EVD 7POW; MACR 11374.

43-38170 Del Cheyenne 3/7/44; Kearney 12/7/44; Dow Fd 1/8/44; ass 860BS/493BG Debach 4/8/44; b/d Mannheim 21/1/45 w/?; f/l Continent; sal 4/4/45.

43-38171 Del Cheyenne 3/7/44; Kearney 12/7/44; Grenier 21/7/44; ass 511BS/351BG [DS-Y] Polebrook 9/8/44; MIA {21m} Politz 7/10/44 w/Merril; flak, c/l Sweden; 9POW; MACR 9357.

43-38172 Del Cheyenne 3/7/44; Kearney 12/7/44; Dow Fd 20/7/44; ass 601BS/398BG [3O-P] Nuthampstead 13/8/44; b/d Cologne 15/10/44 w/?; sal.

43-38173 Del Cheyenne 3/7/44; Kearney 11/7/44; Dow Fd 20/7/44; ass 569BS/390BG Framlingham 21/7/44; MIA Darmstadt 24/12/44 w/Herring; flak, cr Weisbaden; 3KIA 6POW; MACR 11116.

43-38174 Del Cheyenne 4/7/44; Kearney 13/7/44; Dow Fd 20/7/44; ass 401BG Deenethorpe 21/7/44; retUS Bradley 8/6/45; 4168 BU Sth Plains 12/6/45; RFC Kingman 4/12/45.

43-38175 Del Cheyenne 4/7/44; Kearney 13/7/44; Grenier 20/7/44; ass 563BS/388BG Knettishall 22/7/44; tran 568BS/390BG Framlingham 23/7/44

'TIL WE MEET AGAIN; MIA Frantic IV supply drop 18/9/44 w/Akins; flak, cr Warsaw; 1EVD 1POW 8KIA; MACR 10205. I'LL BE SEEING YOU.

43-38176 Del Cheyenne 4/7/44; Kearney 13/7/44; Dow Fd 20/7/44; ass 358BS/303BG [VK-B] Molesworth 20/7/44; MIA 28/9/44 w/Mayer, e/a, cr Luxembourg; 1KIA, 8RTD; MACR 10586. BOUNCING BETTY.

43-38177 Del Cheyenne 4/7/44; Kearney 13/7/44; Dow Fd 22/7/44; ass 8AF 25/7/44; sal n/b/d 27/7/44.

43-38178 Del Cheyenne 4/7/44; Kearney 13/7/44; Dow Fd 20/7/44; ass 525BS/379BG [FR-P] Kimbolton 14/8/44; b/d Pilsen 25/4/45 w/Evans; mid air coll w/43-38272; c/l Allied territory, 9KIA. SEATTLE SUE.

43-38179 Del Cheyenne 4/7/44; Kearney 13/7/44; Grenier 20/7/44; ass 390BG Framlingham 20/7/44; sal b/d 21/3/45. POWERFUL KATRINKA..

43-38180 Del Cheyenne 4/7/44; Kearney 13/7/44; Grenier 20/7/44; ass 848BS/490BG Eye 22/7/44; MIA Berlin 6/10/44 w/McLennan; flak, cr Spandau; 5KIA 4POW; MACR 9529.

43-38181 Del Cheyenne 4/7/44; Kearney 13/7/44; Grenier 20/7/44; ass 751BS/457BG Glatton 22/7/44; 749BS, 748BS; MIA Magdeburg 28/9/44 w/Sikkenga; e/a, cr Gehoelz, Ger?; 6KIA 3POW; MACR 9772.

43-38182 Del Cheyenne 4/7/44; Kearney 14/7/44; Grenier 20/7/44; ass 8AF 31/7/44; retUS Bolling Fd 27/6/45; 4185 BU Independence 31/7/45; RFC Kingman 9/12/45.

43-38183 Del Cheyenne 4/7/44; Kearney 14/7/44; Grenier 20/7/44; ass 332BS/94BG [XM-J] Rougham 22/7/44 ICE COLD KATIE; tran 379BG Kimbolton 23/7/44; 457BG Glatton 24/4/45; retUS Bradley 1/7/45; 4168 BU Sth Plains 11/7/45; RFC Kingman 25/11/45.

43-38184 Del Cheyenne 5/7/44; Kearney 13/7/44; Grenier 20/7/44; ass 849BS/490BG Eye 22/7/44; b/d Ludwigshafen 1/9/44 w/?; mission recalled thru weather; mid air coll w/B-17, f/l Querqueville A/fd, Fr; MACR 8857; sal 1/4/45.

43-38185 Del Cheyenne 5/7/44; Kearney 14/7/44; Dow Fd 1/8/44; ass 729BS/452BG Deopham Green 4/8/44; b/d Mainz 4/12/44 w/?; f/l Continent; sal 16/12/44. LACKA SACKY.

43-38186 Del Cheyenne 5/7/44; Kearney 16/7/44; Dow Fd 1/8/44; ass 358BS/303BG [VK-I] Molesworth 16/8/44; MIA Magdeburg 28/9/44 w/Gillespie; e/a, cr Linden, Ger; 9KIA; MACR 9407.

43-38187 Del Cheyenne 5/7/44; Kearney 14/7/44; Dow Fd 3/8/44; ass 613BS/401BG [IN-C] Deenethorpe 27/8/44; MIA Minster Stein 16/2/45 w/Donaldson; flak, cr Imuiden, Hol?; 9POW; MACR 12246. CARRIE B. II.

43-38188 Del Cheyenne 5/7/44; Kearney 23/7/44; Grenier 3/8/44; ass 7BS/34BG Mendlesham 4/8/44; MIA Merseburg 7/10/44 w/Heiby; flak, f/l Zutphen, Hol?; 2KIA 7POW; sal. MACR 9549.

43-38189 Del Cheyenne 5/7/44; Kearney 14/7/44; Dow Fd 3/8/44; ass 710BS/447BG Rattlesden 3/8/44; tran 568BS/390BG Framlingham 4/8/44; MIA Kassel 18/10/44 w/Coletti; flak, cr Cochem, Ger; 5KIA 4POW; MACR 9484. BUGS BUNNY.

43-38190 Del Cheyenne 5/7/44; Kearney 16/7/44; Dow Fd 3/8/44; ass 863BS/493BG Debach 4/8/44; b/d Nuremberg 25/2/45 w/?; f/l Nancy A/fd, Fr; MACR 1253; rep & ret gp; retUS Bradley 1/7/45; 4168 BU Sth Plains 4/7/45; RFC Kingman 26/11/45. SWEET SUE.

43-38191 Del Cheyenne 6/7/44; Kearney 16/7/44; Grenier 1/8/44; ass 358BS/303BG [VK-A] Molesworth 16/8/44; retUS Bradley 13/7/45; 4185 BU Independence 16/7/45; RFC Kingman 27/12/45. SHASTA.

43-38192 Del Cheyenne 6/7/44; Kearney 16/7/44; Grenier 2/8/44; ass 364BS/305BG Chelveston 26/8/44; tran 351BG Polebrook 23/5/45; retUS Bradley 11/6/45; 4168 BU Sth Plains 14/6/45; RFC Kingman 8/12/45. HALF PINT.

43-38193 Del Cheyenne 6/7/44; Kearney 15/12/44; Grenier 4/8/44; ass 730BS/452BG Deopham Green 5/8/44; retUS Bradley 28/6/45; 4268 BU Sth Plains 6/7/45; RFC Kingman 13/12/45.

43-38194 Del Cheyenne 6/7/44; Kearney 16/7/44; Dow Fd 3/8/44; ass 832BS/486BG [3R-N] Sudbury 4/8/44; retUS Bradley 7/7/45; 4168 BU Sth Plains 5/8/45; RFC Kingman 13/12/45.

43-38195 Del Cheyenne 6/7/44; Kearney 18/7/44; Dow Fd 3/8/44; ass 863BS/493BG Debach 4/8/44; retUS Bradley 3/7/45; 4168 BU Sth Plains 6/7/45; RFC Kingman 26/11/45.

43-38196 Del Cheyenne 6/7/44; Kearney 15/7/44; Grenier 7/8/44; ass 570BS/390BG [DI-A] Framlingham 9/8/44; n/b/d, c/l 17/5/45 w/?; sal.

43-38197 Del Cheyenne 6/7/44; Kearney 16/7/44; Dow Fd 3/8/44; ass 427BS/303BG [GN-U] Molesworth 16/8/44; taxi acc 9/12/44; sal.

43-38198 Del Cheyenne 6/7/44; Kearney 16/7/44; Dow Fd 3/8/44; ass 860BS/493BG Debach 4/8/44; 863BS; retUS Bradley 7/7/45; 4168 BU Sth Plains 8/7/45; RFC Kingman 19/12/45. $1.98.

43-38199 Del Cheyenne 6/7/44; Hunter 22/7/44; Dow Fd 2/8/44; ass 336BS/95BG [ET-Z] Horham 3/8/44; b/d Cottbus 15/2/45 w/?; f/l Deblin, Pol; sal.

43-38200 Del Cheyenne 6/7/44; Kearney 16/7/44; Dow Fd 3/8/44; ass 358BS/303BG [VK-E] Molesworth 16/8/44; MIA Wesseling, Ger 11/10/44 w/Lord; flak, cr Wesseling; 6KIA 3POW; MACR 9564. Sal 25/2/45.

43-38201 Del Cheyenne 7/7/44; Kearney 18/7/44; Dow Fd 4/8/44; ass 452BG Deopham Green 5/8/44; b/d Beilefeld 30/9/44 w/?; sal 1/10/44.

43-38202 Del Cheyenne 7/7/44; Kearney 16/7/44; Dow Fd 3/8/44; ass 322BS/91BG [LG-T] Bassingbourn 18/4/44; MIA {20m} Merseburg 2/11/44 w/Brant; e/a, cr Marbitz, Ger; 2KIA (inc pilot shot on ground) 7POW; MACR 10145. MISS SLIPSTREAM.

43-38203 Del Cheyenne 7/7/44; Kearney 16/7/44; Dow Fd 3/8/44; ass 749BS/457BG Glatton 4/8/44; 748BS; MIA Berlin 18/3/45 w/Schwickert; jet e/a, cr Berlin; 9POW; MACR 13558.

43-38204 Del Cheyenne 7/7/44; Kearney 16/7/44; Dow Fd 4/8/44; ass 410BS/94BG [GL-Y] Rougham 4/8/44; retUS Bradley 28/6/45; 4168 BU Sth Plains 30/6/45; RFC Kingman 15/11/45.

43-48205 Del Cheyenne 7/7/44; Kearney 16/7/44; Dow Fd 4/8/44; ass 452BG Deopham Green 5/8/44; b/d Jena, Ger 19/3/45 w/?; f/l Maastricht A/fd, Bel; sal 28/3/45.

43-38206 Del Cheyenne 7/7/44; Kearney 18/7/44; Grenier 4/8/44; ass 358BS/303BG [VK-F] Molesworth 16/8/44; MIA Magdeburg 28/9/44 w/Lay; flak, cr Heiningen, Ger; 8KIA 1POW; MACR 9408. SILVER FOX.

43-38207 Del Cheyenne 7/7/44; Kearney 16/7/44; Grenier 3/8/44; ass 333BS/94BG Rougham 4/8/44; MIA Berlin 6/10/44 w/Davis; e/a, cr Channel; 10KIA; MACR 9351.

43-38208 Del Cheyenne 7/7/44; Kearney 16/7/44; Grenier 4/8/44; ass 333BS/94BG Rougham 5/8/44; MIA Merseburg 7/10/44 w/Davies; e/a, cr Wiehe, Ger; 7KIA 3POW; MACR 9553.

43-38209 Del Cheyenne 7/7/44; Kearney 18/7/44; Grenier 3/8/44; ass 860BS/493BG Debach 3/4/44; MIA Hamm 19/9/44 w/Laberman; flak, cr Oberstein, Ger; 8KIA 1POW; MACR 10212.

43-38210 Del Cheyenne 7/7/44; Kearney 16/7/44; Dow Fd 3/8/44; ass 549BS/385BG Gt Ashfield 4/8/44; MIA Kiel 4/4/45 w/Ritchie; mid air coll w/B-17, cr Nth Sea; 9KIA; MACR 13720.

43-38211 Del Cheyenne 8/7/44; Kearney 18/7/44; Grenier 3/8/44; ass 349BS/100BG [XR-R] Thorpe Abbotts 4/8/44; MIA Merseburg 30/11/44 w/Anderson; e/a, cr Merseburg; 6KIA 3POW; MACR 10831.

43-38212 Del Cheyenne 8/7/44; Kearney 17/7/44; Grenier 3/8/44; Presque Is 7/8/44; ass 322BS/91BG [LG-P] Bassingbourn 18/8/44; MIA {11m} Merseburg 2/11/44 w/Burne; e/a, cr Gross Oesingen, Ger; 5KIA 4POW; MACR 10146. GAL O' MY DREAMS.

43-38213 Del Cheyenne 8/7/44; Kearney 17/7/44; Dow Fd 5/8/44; ass 544BS/384BG [SU-D] Grafton Underwood 16/8/44; MIA Merseburg 13/9/44 w/White; flak, cr Saalfeld, Ger; 4KIA 5POW; MACR 8902.

43-38214 Del Cheyenne 8/7/44; Kearney 16/7/44; Grenier 3/8/44; Dow Fd 5/8/44; ass 861BS/493BG Debach 4/8/44; 860BS; MIA Magdeburg 12/9/44 w/Goodman; e/a, cr Stapelburg, Ger; 2KIA 6POW; MACR 8864.

43-38215 Del Cheyenne 8/7/44; Kearney 18/7/44; Dow Fd 5/8/44; ass 418BS/100BG [LD-P] Thorpe Abbotts 6/8/44; MIA Hamburg 31/12/44 w/Blackman; flak & e/a, cr Wesseloh, Ger; 4KIA 5POW; MACR 11364.

43-38216 Del Cheyenne 8/7/44; Kearney 18/7/44; Dow Fd 3/8/44; ass 862BS/493BG Debach 4/8/44; tran 18BS/34BG Mendlesham /45; retUS Bradley 26/6/45; 4168 BU Sth Plains 28/6/45; RFC Kingman 24/11/45. 'TEMPEST TURNER.'

43-38217 Del Cheyenne 8/7/44; Hunter 20/7/44; Grenier 1/8/44; ass 551BS/385BG Gt Ashfield 2/8/44; MIA Berlin 6/10/44 w/Tuley; e/a, cr Barnewitz, Ger; 6KIA 3POW; MACR 9519.

43-38218 Del Cheyenne 8/7/44; Kearney 19/7/44; Dow FD 12/8/44; ass 863BS/493BG Debach 13/8/44; retUS Bradley 3/7/45; 4168 BU Sth Plains 7/7/45; RFC Kingman 13/12/45.

43-38219 Del Cheyenne 8/7/44; Kearney 18/7/44; Grenier 4/8/44; ass 862BS/493BG Debach 5/8/44; aborted Darmstadt mission, c/l & exploded 12/12/44; sal. DEVIL'S OWN.

43-38220 Del Cheyenne 8/7/44; Kearney 19/7/44; Dow Fd 4/8/44; ass 324BS/91BG [DF-L] Bassingbourn 18/8/44; {71m} RetUS Bradley 31/5/45; 4168 Sth Plains 12/6/45; RFC Kingman 1/12/45. LADY LOIS.

43-38221 Del Vandalia Mat Wea Exp 21/7/44; Ladd Fd 6/12/44; 4143 BU Clinton 1/4/45; 4148 BU Bedford 24/6/45; 4147 BU Bedford 11/8/45; 4119 BU Brookley 25/8/45; RFC Kingman 23/10/45.

43-38222 Del Cheyenne 10/7/44; Kearney 18/7/44; Grenier 4/8/44; ass 391BS/34BG Mendlesham 5/8/44; landing collision ex-Darmstadt 24/12/44 w/?; sal.

43-38223 Del Cheyenne 10/7/44; Kearney 18/7/44; Grenier 7/8/44; ass 862BS/493BG Debach 9/8/44; tran 410BS/94BG [GL-H] Rougham 10/8/44; retUS Bradley 10/7/45; 4185 BU Independence 12/7/45; RFC Kingman 24/10/45. DAY'S PAY.

43-38224 Del Cheyenne 10/7/44; Kearney 19/7/44; Dow Fd 3/8/44; ass 863BS/493BG Debach 5/8/44; 861BS; b/d Cologne 10/1/45 w/?; f/l Continent; sal 18/1/45.

43-38225 Del Cheyenne 10/7/44; Kearney 19/7/44; Dow Fd 5/8/44; ass 861BS/493BG Debach 7/8/44; MIA Stuttgart 13/9/44 w/Vanderbill; flak, cr Boerstadt, Ger?; 9POW; MACR 8865.

43-38226 Del Cheyenne 10/7/44; Kearney 19/7/44; Grenier 7/8/44; ass 562BS/388BG Knettishal 8/8/44; tran 862BS/493BG Debach 9/8/44; retUS Bradley 5/7/45; 4168 BU Sth Plains 6/7/45; 237 Kirtland 31/12/45; RFC Albuquerque 7/2/46.

43-38227 Del Cheyenne 10/7/44; Kearney 19/7/44; Dow Fd 3/8/44; ass 861BS/493BG Debach 5/8/44; b/d Magdeburg 12/9/44 w/?; sal.

43-38228 Del Cheyenne 10/7/44; Kearney 19/7/44; Grenier 3/8/44; ass 493BG Debach 5/8/44; b/d Darmstadt 12/12/44 w/?; f/l Melsbroek A/fd, Bel; sal 2/1/45.

43-38229 Del Cheyenne 10/7/44; Kearney 19/7/44; Dow Fd 3/8/44; ass 862BS/493BG Debach 4/8/44; retUS Bradley 24/6/45; 4168 BU Sth Plains 27/6/45; RFC Kingman 9/12/45.

43-38230 Del Cheyenne 10/7/44; Kearney 19/7/44; Grenier 3/8/44; ass 708BS/447BG Rattlesden 4/8/44; 709BG; retUS Bradley 5/7/45; 4168 BU Sth Plains 7/7/45; RFC Kingman 14/12/45. WOLF WAGON.

43-38231 Del Cheyenne 10/7/44; Hunter 20/7/44; Dow Fd 2/8/44; ass 452BG Deopham Green 3/8/44; b/d Jena 19/3/45 w/?; f/l Poland, crew safe; sal 28/3/45. TRY'N GETIT.

43-38232 Del Cheyenne 11/7/44; Hunter 20/7/44; Grenier 1/8/44; ass 861BS/493BG Debach 3/8/44; 8612BS; MIA Merseburg 25/11/44 w/Miller; flak, cr Merseburg; 7KIA 2POW; MACR 10769. PROUD PAPPY.

43-38233 Del Cheyenne 11/7/44; Kearney 19/7/44; Dow Fd 1/8/44; ass 549BS/385BG Gt Ashfield 5/8/44; MIA Darmstadt 24/12/44 w/Vogt; flak, mid air coll w/43-37893; cr Namur, Bel; 8KIA 1POW; MACR 11113.

43-38234 Del Cheyenne 11/7/44; Kearney 19/7/44; Dow Fd 3/8/44; ass 322BS/91BG [LG-E] Bassingbourn 18/8/44; MIA {27m} Berlin 5/12/44 w/Freer; flak hit #3, cr Templin, Ger; 1KIA 8POW; MACR 11036. EASY DOES IT.

43-38235 Del Cheyenne 11/7/44; Hunter 20/7/44; Grenier 2/8/44; ass 862BS/493BG Debach 3/8/44; retUS Bradley 1/7/45; 4168 BU Sth Plains 4/7/44; RFC Kingman 24/11/45. SKIPPER.

43-38236 Del Cheyenne 11/7/44; Kearney 21/7/44; Dow Fd 3/8/44; ass 614BS/401BG [IW-M] Deenethorpe 25/8/44; b/d Frankfurt 5/11/44 w/?; c/l Dunmow A/fd, UK; sal 8/11/44.

43-38237 Del Cheyenne 11/7/44; Hunter 20/7/44; Lowry 22/7/44; Hunter 24/9/44; Grenier 2/10/44; ass 527BS/379BG Kimbolton 5/11/44; MIA Cologne 10/1/45 w/Maj Davis; mid air coll w/43-38955, cr Koblenz; 7KIA 2POW; MACR 11762. DALLAS DOLL.

43-38238 Del Cheyenne 11/7/44; Kearney 23/7/44; Grenier 9/8/44; ass 358BS/303BG [VK-L] Molesworth 16/8/44; b/d Essen 8/3/45 w/?; c/l, sal 9/3/45.

43-38239 Del Cheyenne 11/7/44; Hunter 22/7/44; Dow Fd 7/8/44; ass 861BS/493BG Debach 9/8/44; retUS Bradley 9/7/45; 4168 BU Sth Plains 11/7/45; RFC Kingman 20/11/45.

43-38240 Del Cheyenne 11/7/44; Hunter 22/7/44; Grenier 3/8/44; ass 337BS/96BG [AW-G] Snetterton 4/8/44; tran 751BS/457BG Glatton 5/8/44; retUS Bradley 23/5/45; 4168 BU Sth Plains 26/5/45; RFC Kingman 7/12/45.

43-38241 Del Cheyenne 11/7/44; Kearney 21/7/44; Grenier 3/8/44; ass 863BS/493BG Debach 5/8/44; retUS Bradley 7/7/45; 4168 BU Sth Plains 11/7/45; RFC Kingman 16/11/45. ULPY.

43-38242 Del Cheyenne 12/7/44; Hunter 20/7/44; Dow Fd 2/8/44; ass 863BS/493BG Debach 4/8/44; MIA Berlin 3/2/45 w/Sherman; flak, cr Julianadorf, Hol; 9POW; MACR 12157.

43-38243 Del Cheyenne 12/7/44; Kearney 21/7/44; Grenier 7/8/44; ass 860BS/493BG Debach 9/8/44; retUS Bradley 7/7/45; 4168 BU Sth Plains 11/7/45; RFC Kingman 2/12/45.

43-38244 Del Cheyenne 12/7/44; Kearney 21/7/44; Grenier 7/8/44; ass 861BS/493BG Debach 9/8/44; retUS Bradley 5/7/45; 4185 BU Independence 4/8/44; RFC Kingman 2/1/46.

43-38245 Del Cheyenne 12/7/44; Hunter 20/7/44; Presque Is 31/7/44; ass 447BG Rattlesden 2/8/44; during assembly for Kassel 2/10/44 w/?; mid air coll w/44-6460; cr Hitcham, UK; 18 killed; sal.

43-38246 Del Cheyenne 12/7/44; Hunter 20/7/44; Presque Is 31/7/44; ass 835BS/486BG [H8-D] Sudbury 2/8/44; retUS Bradley 11/7/45; 4185 BU Independence 13/7/45; RFC Kingman 12/12/45. VERMONT MAID.

43-38247 Del Cheyenne 12/7/44; Kearney 23/7/44; Grenier 8/8/44; ass 569BS/390BG Framlingham 10/8/44; MIA Hamburg 31/12/44 w/Monit; flak, cr Maschen, Ger; 5KIA 4POW; MACR 11246.

43-38248 Del Cheyenne 12/7/44; Kearney 21/7/44; Dow Fd 3/8/44; ass 427BS/303BG [GN-M] Molesworth 16/8/44; MIA Berlin 28/3/45 w/Frederickson; flak, ditched Channel; 1KIA 7RTD; MACR 13541. JIGGER ROUCHE II.

43-38249 Del Cheyenne 12/7/44; Kearney 24/7/44; Grenier 7/8/44; ass 862BS/493BG Debach 9/8/44; tran 836BS/487BG [2G-E] Lavenham 10/8/44; sal 5/10/44.

43-38250 Del Cheyenne 12/7/44; Kearney 21/7/44; Grenier 15/8/44; ass 368BS/306BG Thurleigh 18/9/44; b/d Cologne 10/1/45 w/?; f/l Hombeck, Bel; sal 18/1/45. MACR 11761. DEBBIE.

43-38251 Del Cheyenne 12/7/44; Kearney 21/7/44; Grenier 5/8/44; ass 8AF 7/8/44; sal n/b/d 10/9/44.

43-38252 Del Cheyenne 12/7/44; Hunter 22/7/44; Dow Fd 2/8/44; ass 364BS/305BG Chelveston 27/8/44; MIA Magdeburg 1/1/45 w/Mann; e/a, cr Windberg, Ger; 5KIA 5POW; MACR 11353.

43-38253 Del Cheyenne 13/7/44; Kearney 21/7/44; Grenier 7/8/44; ass 861BS/493BG Debach 9/8/44; 863BS; sal b/d 3/3/45. OLE RAMBLER.

43-38254 Del Cheyenne 13/7/44; Kearney 21/7/44; Grenier 7/8/44; ass 838BS/487BG [2C-Q] Lavenham 12/8/44; retUS Bradley 14/7/45; 4185 BU Independence 16/7/45; RFC Kingman 21/12/45.

43-38255 Del Cheyenne 13/7/44; Hunter 22/7/44; Dow Fd 4/8/44; ass 335BS/95BG [OE-A] Horham 5/8/44; 334BS [BG-C]; caught fire en route Hamm 28/10/44 w/Braund; ret safely, 9RTD; MACR 10259. RetUS 4168 BU Sth Plains 28/6/45; RFC Kingman 23/12/45.

43-38256 Del Cheyenne 13/7/44; Hunter 22/7/44; Dow Fd 2/8/44; ass 524BS/379BG [WA-C] Kimbolton 15/8/44; MIA Ludwigshafen 8/9/44 w/Jones; flak, cr Ludwigshafen; 9POW; MACR 8846. OUR BABY.

43-38257 Del Cheyenne 13/7/44; Kearney 21/7/44; Grenier 7/8/44; ass 391BS/34BG Mendlesham 10/8/44; retUS Bradley 20/6/45; 4168 BU Sth Plains 23/6/45; RFC Kingman 1/12/45. TYSON'S TRAMPS.

43-38258 Del Cheyenne 13/7/44; Hunter 22/7/44; Presque Is 31/7/44; ass 358BS/303BG [VK-L] Molesworth 15/8/44; 359BS [BN-H]; tran 749BS/457BG Glatton 8/44; retUS Bradley 9/6/45; 4168 BU Sth Plains 14/6/45; RFC Kingman 5/12/45. FORGET ME NOT OLLY.

43-38259 Del Cheyenne 13/7/44; Kearney 21/7/44; Dow Fd 4/8/44; ass 549BS/385BG Gt Ashfield 5/8/44; b/d Münster 5/10/44 w/Stevenson; f/l Continent; 8KIA 1POW; sal 2/12/44. MACR?

43-38260 Del Cheyenne 13/7/44; Kearney 23/7/44; Grenier 7/8/44; ass 837BS/487BG Lavenham 9/8/44; MIA Kassel 22/9/44 w/Smith; flak, cr Weisbaden; 1KIA 8POW; MACR 10210. FIME SIENTZ.

43-38261 Del Cheyenne 13/7/44; Kearney 24/7/44; Grenier 6/8/44; ass 863BS/493BG Debach 8/8/44; MIA Magdeburg 12/9/44 w/Tucker; e/a, cr Germany; 8KIA 1POW; MACR 8866.

43-38262 Del Cheyenne 13/7/44; Hunter 25/7/44; Dow Fd 7/8/44; Rome 31/8/44; Dow Fd 7/9/44; ass 547BS/384BG [SO-K] Grafton Underwood 29/9/44; left wing caught fire 1/1/45; sal.

43-38263 Del Cheyenne 13/7/44; Hunter 22/7/44; Presque Is 31/7/44; ass 7BS/34BG Mendlesham 2/8/44; retUS Bradley 21/6/45; 4168 BU Sth Plains 23/6/45; RFC Kingman 17/12/45. DIES IRAE.

43-38264 Del Cheyenne 14/7/44; Hunter 22/7/44; Dow Fd 3/8/44; ass 863BS/493BG Debach 4/8/44; MIA Ludwigshafen 5/11/44 w/Kolberg; flak, cr Ludwigshafen; 5KIA 4POW; MACR 10327.

43-38265 Del Cheyenne 14/7/44; Kearney 24/7/44; Grenier 7/8/44; ass 7BS/34BG Mendlesham 13/8/44; MIA Kassel 2/10/44 w/McCage; flak, cr Muenchenhof, Ger?; 9KIA; MACR 9369.

43-38266 Del Cheyenne 14/7/44; Kearney 24/7/44; Grenier 7/8/44; ass 863BS/493BG Debach 9/8/44; retUS Bradley 5/7/45; 4168 BU Sth Plains 8/7/45; 237 BU Kirtland 26/11/45; RFC Kingman 13/12/45. BABY ME.

43-38267 Del Cheyenne 14/7/44; Hunter 25/7/44; Dow Fd 7/8/44; ass 613BS/401BG [IN-M] Deenethorpe 25/8/44; sal 30/11/44. MAXIMUM EFFORT.

43-38268 Del Cheyenne 14/7/44; Kearney 24/7/44; Grenier 7/8/44; ass 18BS/34BG Mendlesham 9/8/44; c/t/o 15/10/44; sal 16/10/44.

43-38269 Del Cheyenne 14/7/44; Kearney 25/7/44; Grenier 7/8/44; ass 410BS/94BG [GL-N] Rougham 9/8/44; 331BS [QE-N]; retUS Bradley 7/7/45; 4168 BU Sth Plains 10/7/45; RFC Kingman 8/1/45.

43-38270 Del Cheyenne 14/7/44; Hunter 22/7/44; Dow Fd 4/8/44; ass 390BG Framlingham 4/8/44; tran 549BS/385BG Gt Ashfield 5/8/44; MIA Osnabrück 21/11/44 w/Webb; mid air coll w/43-37566; cr Pyremont, Fr?; 9KIA; MACR 10413.

43-38271 Del Cheyenne 14/7/44; Hunter 25/7/44; Dow Fd 7/8/44; ass 863BS/493BG Debach 8/8/44; MIA Mainz 13/1/45 w/Lamoreaux; flak, cr Bauscheim, Ger; 6KIA 3POW; MACR 11736. BIG BUSTER.

43-38272 Del Cheyenne 14/7/44; Kearney 24/7/44; Grenier 8/8/44; ass 379BG Kimbolton 27/8/44; b/d Pilsen 25/4/45 w/Blain; mid air coll w/43-38178; cr Allied territory; 9KIA.

43-38273 Del Cheyenne 15/7/44; Kearney 24/7/44; Grenier 8/8/44; ass 550BS/385BG Gt Ashfield 13/8/44; b/d Ulm 1/3/45 w/?; mid air coll w/B-17, cr Ostend, Bel; 16KIA; sal 20/3/45.

43-38274 Del Cheyenne 15/7/44; Kearney 25/7/44; Grenier 8/8/44; ass 569BS/390BG [CC-M] Framlingham 10/8/44; GALLOPIN GREMLIN; MIA Darmstadt 24/12/44 w/Fackelman; flak, cr Weisbaden; 5KIA 4POW; MACR 11117. GREMLIN.

43-38275 Del Cheyenne 15/7/44; Hunter 25/7/44; Dow Fd 1/8/44; ass 527BS/379BG Kimbolton 8/9/44; MIA Zeitz 30/11/44 w/Sullivan; flak, cr Zeitz; 9POW; MACR 11059. TAKE-ME-HOME.

43-38276 Del Cheyenne 15/7/44; Hunter 25/7/44; Dow Fd 7/8/44; ass 862BS/493BG Debach 8/8/44; retUS Bradley 5/7/45; 4168 BU Sth Plains 8/7/45; RFC Kingman 26/11/45.

43-38277 Del Cheyenne 15/7/44; Hunter 16/7/44; Dow Fd 9/8/44; ass 508BS/351BG [YB-O] Polebrook 21/8/44; 509BS [RQ-O]; {60m} RetUS Bradley 12/6/45; 4168 BU Sth Plains 15/6/45; RFC Kingman 17/12/45.

43-38278 Del Cheyenne 15/7/44; Kearney 25/7/44; Grenier 7/8/44; ass 838BS/487BG Lavenham 9/8/44; tran 8861BS/490BG Debach 10/8/44; retUS Bradley 12/7/45; 4185 BU Independence 13/7/45; RFC Kingman 9/12/45.

43-38279 Del Cheyenne 15/7/44; Kearney 25/7/44; Grenier 8/8/44; ass 326BS/92BG [JW-N] Podington 27/8/44; sal 29/1/46.

43-38280 Del Cheyenne 15/7/44; Kearney 26/7/44; Grenier 9/8/44; ass 4BS/34BG Mendlesham 12/8/44; retUS Bradley 24/6/45; 4168 BU Sth Plains 26/6/45; RFC Kingman 13/12/45. MISBEHAVIN RAVEN.

43-38281 Del Cheyenne 17/7/44; Kearney 25/7/44; Grenier 9/8/44; ass 326BS/92BG [JW-A] Podington 10/8/44; tran 412BS/95BG [QW-Z] Horham 11/8/44; retUS Bradley 21/6/45; 4168 BU Sth Plains 24/6/45; RFC Kingman 6/12/45. KIMMIE KAR FOR 9.

43-38282 Del Cheyenne 17/7/44; Hunter 25/7/44; Dow Fd 7/8/44; ass 862BS/493BG Debach 8/8/44; tran 338BS/96BG [BX-G] Snetterton 9/8/44; retUS Bradley 6/7/45; 4168 BU Sth Plains 7/7/45; RFC Kingman 13/12/45. SWEENY'S BRATS.

43-38283 Del Cheyenne 17/7/44; Kearney 25/7/44; Grenier 7/8/44; ass 334BS/95BG [BG-A] Horham 13/8/44; 336BS [ET-A]; MIA Ruhland 17/3/45 w/Vermillion; mech fault, cr Neustadt, Ger; MACR 13111.

43-38284 Del Cheyenne 17/7/44; Kearney 26/7/44; Grenier 15/8/44; ass 863BS/493BG Debach 22/8/44 STRAIGHTEN UP AND FLY RIGHT; MIA Merseburg 2/11/44 w/Prochwit; flak, cr Rijn Saterwoude, Hol; 1POW 8RTD; MACR 10170. LEVEL UP AND FLY RIGHT - THE ROCK.

43-38285 Del Cheyenne 17/7/44; Kearney 26/7/44; Grenier 8/8/44; ass 860BS/493BG Debach 10/8/44; retUS Bradley 3/7/45; 4168 BU Sth Plains 8/7/45; RFC Kingman 8/12/45. BOMBBAY OF BLUES.

43-38286 Del Cheyenne 17/7/44; Kearney 28/7/44; Grenier 6/8/44; ass 7BS/34BG Mendlesham 16/8/44; retUS Bradley 21/6/45; 4168 BU Sth Plains 23/6/45; RFC Kingman 9/12/45. FLYING DUTCHMAN.

43-38287 Del Cheyenne 17/7/44; Kearney 27/7/44; Grenier 8/8/44; ass 369BS/306BG [WW-V] Thurleigh 22/8/44; tran 92BG Podington 9/5/45; special mission Port Lyautey, Mor. 20/6/45; f/l Istres, Fr 25/6/45; sal 9AF 31/10/45.

43-38288 Del Cheyenne 17/7/44; Hunter 26/7/44; Dow Fd 7/8/44; ass 490BG Eye 7/8/44; tran 412BS/95BG [QW-V] Horham 8/8/44 V FOR VICTORY; aborted Osnabrück 19/3/45 w/Ristine; c/l base, 9RTD; retUS Bradley 22/6/45; 4168 BU Sth Plains 24/6/45; RFC Kingman 26/11/45. GOIN' MY WAY.

43-38289 Del Cheyenne 17/7/44; Kearney 27/7/44; Grenier 7/8/44; ass 359BS/303BG [BN-J] Molesworth 31/8/44; tran 457BG Glatton 22/5/45; 351BG Polebrook 29/5/45; retUS Bradley 14/6/45; 4168 BU Sth Plains 19/6/45; RFC Kingman 27/11/45. LA-RHONDA.

43-38290 Del Cheyenne 17/7/44; Hunter 26/7/44; Dow Fd 12/8/44; ass 326BS/92BG [JW-B] Podington 24/8/44; MIA Merseburg 11/9/44 w/Glasco; e/a, cr Groet, Hol; 3KIA 6POW; MACR 8887. CANVAS BACK IV.

43-38291 Del Cheyenne 17/7/44; Kearney 26/7/44; Grenier 8/8/44; ass 305BG Chelveston 27/8/44; c/t/o for Dresden 15/2/45 w/?; 7KIA; sal.

43-38292 Del Cheyenne 18/7/44; Hunter 26/7/44; Dow Fd 7/8/44; ass 338BS/96BG [BX-D] Snetterton 7/8/44 CONGA BABE; tran 4BS/34BG Mendlesham 8/8/44; MIA Bad Kreuznach, Ger 2/1/45 w/Hoffman; flak, cr Eggenstedt, Ger; 10KIA; MACR 11566.

43-38293 Del Cheyenne 18/7/44; Kearney 26/7/44; Grenier 7/8/44; ass 861BS/493BG Debach 9/8/44; retUS Bradley 5/7/45; 4168 BU Sth Plains 8/7/45; RFC Kingman 28/11/45. MISS GREEN BAY.

43-38294 Del Cheyenne 18/7/44; Kearney 26/7/44; Grenier 7/8/44; ass 7BS/34BG Mendlesham 9/8/44; MIA Kassel 22/9/44 w/Whited; mid air coll, cr Buren, Ger; 4KIA 5POW; MACR 10199.

43-38295 Del Cheyenne 18/7/44; Kearney 27/7/44; Grenier 8/8/44; ass 861BS/493BG Debach 10/8/44; MIA Magdeburg 12/9/44 w/Spencer; e/a, cr Oschersleben; 4KIA 5POW; MACR 8867.

43-38296 Del Cheyenne 18/7/44; Kearney 27/7/44; Grenier 7/8/44; ass 369BS/306BG Thurleigh 22/8/44; MIA Cologne 15/10/44 w/Ritter; flak, cr Cologne; 3KIA 6POW; MACR 9476.

43-38297 Del Cheyenne 18/7/44; Kearney 27/7/44; Grenier 7/8/44; ass 860BS/493BG Debach 10/8/44; MIA Brunswick 3/3/45 w/White; e/a, cr Apelern, Ger?; 9POW; MACR 12887.

43-38298 Del Cheyenne 18/7/44; Kearney 28/7/44; Grenier 8/8/44; ass 863BS/493BG Debach 10/8/44; MIA Koblenz 19/9/44 w/Capt Holman; flak, cr Prum, Ger; 1EVD 6POW 2RTD; MACR 9494.

43-38299 Del Cheyenne 18/7/44; Kearney 27/7/44; Grenier 10/8/44; ass 391BS/34BG Mendlesham 16/8/44; retUS Bradley 21/6/45; 4168 BU Sth Plains 23/6/45; RFC Kingman 8/12/45. ROGER'S DODGERS.

43-38300 Del Cheyenne 18/7/44; Kearney 27/7/44; Grenier 8/8/44; ass 391BS/34BG Mendlesham 10/8/44; MIA Mannheim 19/10/44 w/Halbert; flak, cr Ludwigshafen; 9KIA 1POW; MACR 9467.

43-38301 Del Cheyenne 18/7/44; Kearney 28/7/44; Grenier 8/8/44; ass 751BS/457BG Glatton 10/8/44; retUS Bradley 9/6/45; 4168 BU Sth Plains 14/6/45; RFC Kingman 10/12/45.

43-38302 Del Cheyenne 18/7/44; Kearney 27/7/44; Grenier 15/8/44; ass 367BS/306BG [GY-Z] Thurleigh 23/9/44; secret mission 3/11/44, ret 17/12/44; MIA Kassel 9/3/45 w/?; MACR 12961. HELLCAT HATTIE.

43-38303 Del Cheyenne 19/7/44; Kearney 27/7/44; Grenier 15/8/44; ass 388BG Knettishall 22/8/44; b/d Nuremberg 3/10/44 w/?; c/l; sal 14/11/44.

43-38304 Del Cheyenne 19/7/44; Kearney 28/7/44; Grenier 8/8/44; ass 860BS/493BG Debach 9/8/44; tran 18BS/34BG Mendlesham 10/8/44; c/l 5/1/45 w/?; sal.

43-38305 Del Cheyenne 19/7/44; Kearney 29/7/44; Grenier 9/8/44; ass 860BS/493BG Debach 11/8/44; c/fire 11/3/45, sal.

43-38306 Del Cheyenne 19/7/44; Kearney 28/7/44; Grenier 9/8/44; ass 322BS/91BG [LG-B] Bassingbourn 18/8/44; b/d Pilsen 25/4/45 w/Marlow; f/l Continent; sal AFSC. THE BIGGEST BIRD.

43-38307 Del Cheyenne 19/7/44; Kearney 28/7/44; Grenier 8/8/44; ass 861BS/493BG Debach 10/8/44; retUS Bradley 1/7/45; 4168 BU Sth Plains 4/7/45; RFC Kingman 3/12/45.

43-38308 Del Cheyenne 19/7/44; Kearney 29/7/44; Grenier 9/8/44; ass 860BS/493BG Debach 11/8/44; MIA Magdeburg 12/9/44 w/Capt Carter; flak, cr Oschersleben 5KIA 5POW; MACR 8868.

43-38309 Del Cheyenne 19/7/44; Kearney 28/7/44; Grenier 15/8/44; ass 750BS/457BG Glatton 18/8/44; MIA Merseburg 2/11/44 w/Guptill; e/a, cr Dedensen, Ger; 9POW; MACR 10320.

43-38310 Del Cheyenne 19/7/44; Kearney 27/7/44; Grenier 7/8/44; ass 860BS/493BG Debach 9/8/44; retUS Bradley 5/7/45; 4168 BU Sth Plains 6/7/45; RFC Kingman 21/11/45.

43-38311 Del Cheyenne 19/7/44; Kearney 28/7/44; Grenier 8/8/44; ass 862BS/493BG Debach 10/8/44; MIA Hamburg 30/3/45 w/Hoagland; flak, cr Buchholz, Ger; 1KIA 9POW; MACR 13553.

43-38312 Del Cheyenne 20/7/44; Kearney 28/7/44; Grenier 8/8/44; ass 860BS/493BG Debach 10/8/44; sal 6/1/45.

43-38313 Del Cheyenne 20/7/44; Kearney 29/7/44; Grenier 9/8/44; ass 349BS/100BG [XR-S] Thorpe Abbotts 11/8/44; tran 482BG Alconbury 20/5/45; retUS Bradley 5/7/45; 4168 BU Sth Plains 6/7/45; 237 BU Kirtland 31/12/45; RFC Albuquerque 7/2/46.

43-38314 Del Cheyenne 20/7/44; Kearney 29/7/44; Grenier 9/8/44; ass 100BG Thorpe Abbotts 9/8/44; tran 862BS/493BG Debach 10/8/44; 482BG Alconbury 30/5/45; retUS Bradley 2/6/45; 4168 BU Sth Plains 6/6/45; RFC Kingman 18/12/45. LITTLE DINAH.

43-38315 Del Cheyenne 20/7/44; Kearney 3/8/44; Grenier 9/8/44; ass **8AF** 10/8/44; retUS Morrison 11/2/45; RFC Walnut Ridge 7/1/46.

43-38316 Del Cheyenne 20/7/44; Kearney 28/7/44; Grenier 9/8/44; ass 860BS/493BG Debach 11/8/44; retUS Bradley 7/7/45; 4168 BU Sth Plains 9/7/45; RFC Kingman 9/12/45. HANK'S BOTTLE.

43-38317 Del Cheyenne 20/7/44; Kearney 20/9/44; Grenier 9/8/44; ass 334BS/95BG [BG-K] Horham 12/8/44; retUS Bradley 21/6/45; Ypsilanti 23/6/45; 4168 BU Sth Plains 21/10/45; RFC Kingman 25/11/45. FLAK EVADER.

43-38318 Del Cheyenne 20/7/44; Kearney 29/7/44; Grenier 8/8/44; ass 731BS/452BG Deopham Green 10/8/44; retUS Bradley 6/7/45; 4168 BU Sth Plains 8/7/45; RFC Kingman 17/12/45.

43-38319 Del Cheyenne 20/7/44; Kearney 29/7/44; Grenier 8/8/44; ass 860BS/493BG Debach 12/8/44; MIA Magdeburg 12/9/44 w/Bisaro; flak & expl, cr Pechau, Ger; 8KIA 1POW; MACR 8869.

43-38320 Del Cheyenne 20/7/44; Kearney 30/7/44; Grenier 8/8/44; ass 549BS/385BG Gt Ashfield 11/8/44; b/d Darmstadt 12/12/44 w/?; f/l Antwerp A/fd, Bel; sal 10/2/45.

43-38321 Del Cheyenne 20/7/44; Gt Falls 25/7/44; Spokane 24/8/44; 432 BU Port 1/1/45; 4134 BU Spokane 8/1/45; RFC Walnut Ridge 9/3/46.

43-38322 Del Wright Fd 20/7/44; Gt Falls 23/7/44; Mat Com Wright 27/7/44; ATS Dayton 11/1/45; Clinton 30/1/45; Wright 5/3/45; 4142 BU Dayton 19/3/45; 4000 BU Wright 20/4/45; RFC Claremore 18/1/46; to CAA as NC-66568; La Paz, Bol. as civil CP-936 and CB-80; W/O 12/2/72.

43-38323 Del Cheyenne 21/7/44; Kearney 30/7/44; Grenier 9/8/44; ass 427BS/303BG [GN-P] Molesworth 16/8/44; MIA Mannheim 9/9/44 w/Newton; flak, cr Ludwigshafen; 7KIA 1POW; MACR 8597.

43-38324 Del Cheyenne 21/7/44; Kearney 30/7/44; Grenier 9/8/44; ass 851BS/490BG Eye 12/8/44; MIA Mannheim 9/9/44 w/Beach; flak, cr Zweieichen, Ger; 3KIA 6POW; MACR 8929.

43-38325 Del Cheyenne 21/7/44; Kearney 29/7/44; Grenier 15/8/44; ass 4BS/34BG Mendlesham

22/8/44; retUS Bradley 21/6/45; 4168 BU Sth Plains 23/6/45; RFC Kingman 7/12/45.

43-38326 Del Cheyenne 21/7/44; Kearney 30/7/44; Grenier 15/8/44; ass 18BS/34BG Mendlesham 22/8/44; retUS Bradley 23/6/45; 4168 BU Sth Plains 25/6/45; RFC Kingman 14/12/45. BOTTOMS UP.

43-38327 Del Cheyenne 21/7/44; Kearney 31/7/44; Grenier 9/8/44; ass 849BS/490BG Eye 11/8/44; retUS Bradley 9/7/45; 4168 BU Sth Plains 13/7/45; RFC Kingman 19/11/45.

43-38328 Del Cheyenne 21/7/44; Kearney 31/7/44; Grenier 9/8/44; ass 358BS/303BG [VK-I] Molesworth 12/8/44; tran 95BG Horham 14/8/44; 569BS/390BG [CC-J] 14/9/44; retUS Bradley 3/7/45; 4168 BU Sth Plains 6/7/45; RFC Kingman 17/12/45.

43-38329 Del Cheyenne 21/7/44; Kearney 29/7/44; Grenier 9/8/44; ass 862BS/493BG Debach 12/8/44; sal b/d 12/9/44.

43-38330 Del Cheyenne 21/7/44; Kearney 31/7/44; Grenier 9/8/44; ass 614BS/401BG [IW-Z] Deenethorpe 21/8/44; retUS Bradley 2/6/45; 4168 BU Sth Plains 7/6/45; RFC Kingman 15/11/45. GAMBLER'S CHOICE.

43-38331 Del Cheyenne 21/7/44; Hunter 1/8/44; Grenier 13/8/44; ass 18BS/34BG Mendlesham 15/8/44; retUS Bradley 21/6/45; 4168 BU Sth Plains 23/6/45; RFC Kingman 3/11/45.

43-38332 Del Cheyenne 22/7/44; Hunter 1/8/44; Dow Fd 14/8/44; ass 391BS/34BG Mendlesham 15/8/44 QUEENIE; 18BS; c/t/o for Sterkrade w/? at Gipping, UK, 2KIA; 20/1/45; sal. GALLOPIN' GHOST.

43-38333 Del Cheyenne 22/7/44; Kearney 31/7/44; Grenier 9/8/44; ass 336BS/95BG [ET-H] Horham 12/8/44; c/l base, non op 6/5/45; sal 26/5/45. HEAVY DATE.

43-38334 Del Cheyenne 22/7/44; Hunter 1/8/44; Grenier 13/8/44; ass 4BS/34BG Mendlesham 15/8/44; retUS Bradley 21/6/45; 4168 BU Sth Plains 23/6/45; Recl Comp 19/6/47.

43-38335 Del Cheyenne 22/7/44; Hunter 1/8/44; Grenier 14/8/44; ass 325BS/92BG [NV-Q] Podington 27/8/44; MIA Merseburg 11/9/44 w/Wallace; e/a, cr Neushausen, Ger; 4KIA 5POW; MACR 8888.

43-38336 Del Cheyenne 22/7/44; Kearney 30/7/44; Grenier 9/8/44; ass 551BS/385BG Gt Ashfield 11/8/44; c/l 25/5/45; sal.

43-38337 Del Cheyenne 22/7/44; Hunter 1/8/44; Grenier 30/8/44; ass 568BS/390BG [BI-N] Framlingham 2/9/44; MIA Derben, Ger 14/1/45 w/Richter; e/a, cr Dreezt, Ger; 6KIA 3POW; MACR 11721. CLOUD HOPPER.

43-38338 Del Cheyenne 22/7/44; Hunter 1/8/44; Grenier 13/8/44; ass 92BG Podington 15/8/44; tran 18BS/34BG Mendlesham 16/8/44; b/d Ingolstadt 4/3/45 w/?; cr France; sal. MACR 12923.

43-38339 Del Cheyenne 22/7/44; Hunter 31/7/44; Grenier 13/8/44; ass 305BG Chelveston 25/8/44; b/d Hamm 19/9/44 w/?; f/l Continent on return; sal 13/12/44.

43-38340 Del Cheyenne 22/7/44; Hunter 1/8/44; Dow Fd 7/8/44; ass 493BS Debach 13/8/44; MIA Mannheim 21/1/45 w/Lindsay; mech fault, cr Georgefeld, Ger; 9POW; MACR 12236. MILK RUN.

43-38341 Del Cheyenne 22/7/44; Hunter 1/8/44; Grenier 2/8/44; ass 848BS/490BG Eye 22/8/44; retUS Bradley 11/7/45; 4168 BU Sth Plains 12/7/45; RFC Kingman 23/11/45.

43-38342 Del Cheyenne 23/7/44; Kearney 2/8/44; Grenier 13/8/44; ass 4BS/34BG Mendlesham 15/8/44; c/fire 6/10/44, sal.

43-38343 Del Cheyenne 23/7/44; Hunter 4/8/44; Dow Fd 15/8/44; ass 391BS/34BG Mendlesham 17/8/44; retUS Bradley 20/6/45; 4168 BU Sth Plains 22/6/45; RFC Kingman 13/12/45.

43-38344 Del Cheyenne 23/7/44; Kearney 2/8/44; Grenier 9/8/44; ass 305BG Chelveston 22/8/44; b/d Bohlen 17/3/45 w/?; c/l Radom, Poland; sal 30/3/45; MACR 13113.

43-38345 Del Cheyenne 23/7/44; Kearney 2/8/44; Grenier 9/8/44; ass 571BS/390BG [FC-V] Framlingham 11/8/44; b/d Merseburg 30/11/44 w/?; f/l Melsbroek, Bel; sal 6/12/44. SLEEPY TIME GAL.

43-38346 Del Cheyenne 23/7/44; Kearney 2/8/44; Grenier 9/8/44; ass 334BS/95BG [BG-E] Horham 11/8/44 KURCHOW; 335BS [OE-X]; retUS Bradley 21/6/45; 4168 BU Sth Plains 23/6/45; RFC Kingman 14/12/45. EXCELSIOR.

43-38347 Del Cheyenne 23/7/44; Kearney 2/8/44; Grenier 9/8/44; ass 493BG Debach 11/8/44; sal 26/8/44.

43-38348 Del Cheyenne 23/7/44; Kearney 2/8/44; Grenier 9/8/44; ass 322BS/91BG [LG-O] Bassingbourn 18/8/44; MIA {5m} Ludwigshafen 8/9/44 w/McCarty; flak hit#3, wing blew off, cr Oggersheim, Ger; 7KIA 2POW (b & n); MACR 8807. ROXY'S SPECIAL.

43-38349 Del Cheyenne 23/7/44; Kearney 3/8/44; Dow Fd 12/8/44; ass 863BS/493BG Debach 13/8/44; retUS Bradley 7/7/45; 4168 BU Sth Plains 10/7/45; RFC Kingman 30/11/45.

43-38350 Del Cheyenne 23/7/44; Kearney 2/8/44; Dow Fd 12/8/44; ass 325BS/92BG [NV-J] Podington 19/8/44; sal 9AF Germany 31/10/45.

43-38351 Del Cheyenne 23/7/44; Kearney 2/8/44; Grenier 16/8/44; ass 391BS/34BG Mendlesham 23/8/44; b/d Merseburg 25/11/44 w/?; f/l St Trond A/fd, Bel; sal 1/12/44.

43-38352 Del Cheyenne 24/7/44; Kearney 3/8/44; Dow Fd 12/8/44; ass 863BS/493BG Debach MIA Magdeburg 12/9/44 w/Cockerham; e/a, cr Hillrose?; 1KIA 8POW; MACR 8870.

43-38353 Del Cheyenne 24/7/44; Hunter 4/8/44; Grenier 14/8/44; ass 7BS/34BG Mendlesham 19/8/44; MIA Cologne 17/10/44 w/Capt McAllister; flak, cr Ahrweiler, Ger; 1KIA 9POW; MACR 9468.

43-38354 Del Cheyenne 24/7/44; Kearney 2/8/44; Grenier 9/8/44; ass 305BG Chelveston 25/8/44; c/t/o for Cologne 10/1/45 w/?; sal 11/1/45.

43-38355 Del Cheyenne 24/7/44; Kearney 3/8/44; Grenier 12/8/44; ass 863BS/493BG Debach 13/8/44; MIA Magdeburg 12/9/44 w/Owen; e/a, cr Britz, Ger; 4KIA 5POW; MACR 8871.

43-38356 Del Cheyenne 24/7/44; Kearney 2/8/44; Grenier 9/8/44; ass 730BS/452BG Deopham Green 11/8/44 SILENTHE JE VAHR; b/d Landsberg, Ger 21/4/45 w/?; c/l Continent, 8KIA; ; sal 26/4/45; MACR 14114. QUIVERING QUEENIE.

43-38357 Del Cheyenne 25/7/44; Kearney 3/8/44; Mitchell 6/8/44; Lincoln 23/8/44; Grenier 8/9/44; ass 2BG Amendola 24/9/44; retUS 1103 BU Morrison 20/10/45; 593 BU Charleston 28/10/45; RFC Walnut Ridge 7/1/46.

43-38358 Del Cheyenne 25/7/44; Kearney 3/8/44; Grenier 9/8/44; ass 730BS/452BG Deopham Green 11/8/44 SLIGHTLY DANGEROUS; b/d Berlin 3/2/45 w/Fry; f/l Rinkaby, Swed; 9INT; MACR 12496; Ret UK 27/6/45; retUS Bradley 13/8/45; 4185 BU Independence 21/8/45; RFC Kingman 9/12/45. BIG NOISE II.

43-38359 Del Cheyenne 25/7/44; Kearney 3/8/44; Dow Fd 12/8/44; ass 861BS/493BG Debach 13/8/44; MIA Ludwigshafen 5/11/44 w/Capt Johnson; flak, cr Viernheim, Ger; 6KIA 5POW; MACR 10340.

43-38360 Del Cheyenne 25/7/44; Hunter 3/8/44; Dow Fd 30/8/44; ass 322BS/91BG [LG-D] Bassingbourn 9/9/44; MIA {28m} Berlin 5/12/44 w/Blanton; flak #1, cr Spandau; 9POW; MACR 11045. BRIDE OF MARS.

43-38361 Del Cheyenne 25/7/44; Kearney 3/8/44; Dow Fd 12/8/44; ass 549BS/385BG Gt Ashfield 13/8/44; retUS Bradley 28/6/45; 4168 BU Sth Plains 30/6/45; RFC Kingman 16/11/45. HOT CHOCOLATE.

43-38362 Del Cheyenne 25/7/44; Kearney 3/8/44; Dow Fd 10/8/44; ass 369BS/306BG [WW-K] Thurleigh 22/8/44; MIA Stuttgart 9/12/44 w/Brown; flak, cr Wolfach, Ger; 1KIA 8POW; MACR 11342. SLEEPY TIME GAL.

43-38363 Del Cheyenne 26/7/44; Kearney 5/8/44; Grenier 15/8/44; ass 7BS/34BG Mendlesham 16/8/44; MIA Ludwigshafen 5/11/44 w/Alleman; flak, cr Ludwigshafen; 10KIA; MACR 10303.

43-38364 Del Cheyenne 26/7/44; Hunter 4/8/44; Grenier 30/8/44; ass 391BS/34BG Mendlesham 1/9/44; tran 325BS/92BG [NV-L] Podington 9/9/44; MIA Berlin 3/2/45 w/Morrow; flak, cr Neu Hardenburg, Ger; 9POW; MACR 12031. DEMOBILIZER.

43-38365 Del Cheyenne 26/7/44; Hunter 4/8/44; Grenier 13/8/44; ass 391BS/34BG Mendlesham 15/8/44; sal 3/4/45. SUGAR. (later US Civil 3702 G).

43-38366 Del Cheyenne 26/7/44; Kearney 3/8/44; Dow Fd 10/8/44; ass 863BS/493BG Debach 13/8/44; retUS Bradley 6/7/45; 4168 BU Sth Plains 7/7/45; RFC Kingman 14/12/45. FLAK FLIRTER.

43-38367 Del Cheyenne 26/7/44; Kearney 5/8/44; Grenier 15/8/44; ass 4BS/34BG Mendlesham 16/8/44; retUS Bradley 24/6/45; 4168 BU Sth Plains 28/5/45; RFC Kingman 18/12/45. GOTTA HAVER.

43-38368 Del Cheyenne 26/7/44; Hunter 4/8/44; Grenier 14/8/44; ass 730BS/452BG Deopham Green 15/8/44; 729BS; MIA Zwickau, Ger 19/3/45 w/Ettredge; e/a, cr Zwickau; 10POW; MACR 13562. DAISY MAE.

43-38369 Del Cheyenne 26/7/44; Kearney 4/8/44; Dow Fd 10/8/44; ass 327BS/92BG [UX-D] Podington 21/8/44; 325BS; MIA Pilsen, Cz. 25/4/45 w/Fisher; flak, cr Pilsen; 6KIA 2POW; MACR 14222. CHECKERBOARD FORT.

43-38370 Del Cheyenne 26/7/44; Kearney 3/8/44; Dow Fd 10/8/44; ass 860BS/493BG Debach 13/8/44; retUS Bradley 3/7/45; Oklahoma City 5/7/45; RFC Altus 5/11/45. THE TRIBE.

43-38371 Del Cheyenne 26/7/44; Kearney 4/8/44; Dow Fd 15/8/44; ass 863BS/493BG Debach 13/8/44; c/l 19/1/45; sal 20/1/45.

43-38372 Del Cheyenne 27/7/44; Lincoln 5/8/44; Grenier 15/8/44; ass 391BS/34BG Mendlesham 15/8/44; tran 96BG Snetterton 16/8/44; retUS Bradley 22/6/45; 4168 Bu Sth Plains 24/6/45; RFC Kingman 9/12/45. RAINBOW.

43-38373 Del Cheyenne 27/7/44; Hunter 4/8/44; Dow Fd 14/8/44; ass 7BS/34BG Mendlesham 17/8/44; retUS Bradley 21/6/45; 4168 BU Sth Plains 23/6/45; RFC Kingman 17/12/45.

43-38374 Del Cheyenne 27/7/44; Hunter 4/8/44; Dow Fd 14/8/44; ass 18BS/34BG Mendlesham 16/8/44; sal 17/1/45.

43-38375 Del Cheyenne 27/7/44; Kearney 4/8/44; Grenier 15/8/44; ass 390BG Framlingham 18/8/44; retUS Bradley 3/7/45; 4168 BU Sth Plains 16/7/45; RFC Kingman 18/11/45. THE HELLION.

43-38376 Del Cheyenne 27/7/44; Hunter 5/8/44; Grenier 7/9/44; ass 423BS/306BG [RD-F] Thurleigh 24/10/44; tran 381BG Ridgewell 5/45; retUS Bradley 9/6/45; 4168 BU Sth Plains 14/6/45; RFC Kingman

9/12/45.

43-38377 Del Cheyenne 27/7/44; Kearney 4/8/44; Dow Fd 10/8/44; ass 493BG Debach 13/8/44; retUS Bradley 3/7/45; 4168 BU Sth Plains 7/7/45; RFC Kingman 17/12/45.

43-38378 Del Cheyenne 27/7/44; Hunter 5/8/44; Dow Fd 15/8/44; ass 568BS/390BG Framlingham 17/8/44 HOTTER 'N HELL; tran 391BS/34BG Mendlesham 18/8/44; retUS Bradley 21/6/45; 4168 BU Sth Plains 24/6/45; RFC Kingman 29/11/45. LITTLE KING.

43-38379 Del Cheyenne 27/7/44; Hunter 5/8/44; Dow Fd 20/8/44; ass 571BS/390BG Framlingham 2/9/44; tran 323BS/91BG [OR-O] Bassingbourn 10/9/44; retUS Bradley 21/5/45; 4168 BU Sth Plains 3/6/45; RFC Kingman 18/12/45. MARGIE.

43-38380 Del Cheyenne 27/7/44; Kearney 6/8/44; Grenier 15/8/44; ass 391BS/34BG Mendlesham 16/8/44; retUS Bradley 21/6/45; 4168 BU Sth Plains 24/6/45; RFC Kingman 30/11/45. TONI-7TH.

43-38381 Del Cheyenne 27/7/44; Kearney 4/8/44; Grenier 20/8/44; ass 418BS/100BG [LD-Z] Thorpe Abbotts 23/8/44; MIA Hamburg 31/12/44 w/Mayo; flak, cr Jever, Ger; 9KIA MACR 11362.

43-38382 Del Cheyenne 27/7/44; Kearney 4/8/44; Grenier 15/8/44; ass 391BS/34BG Mendlesham 17/8/44; retUS Bradley 20/6/45; 4168 BU Sth Plains 22/6/45; RFC Kingman 19/12/45.

43-38383 Del Cheyenne 27/7/44; Hunter 5/8/44; Dow Fd 30/8/44; ass 482BG Alconbury 1/9/44; tran 532BS/381BG Ridgewell 2/9/44; tran 350BS/100BG [LN-F] Thorpe Abbotts 3/9/44; retUS Bradley 1/6/45; 4168 BU Sth Plains 5/6/45; RFC Kingman 13/12/45.

43-38384 Del Cheyenne 28/7/44; Hunter 8/8/44; Grenier 20/8/44; ass 368BS/306BG [BO-G] Thurleigh 21/9/44; b/d Mannheim 20/1/45 w/?; f/l Continent; sal 14/2/45.

43-38385 Del Cheyenne 28/7/44; Hunter 5/8/44; Dow Fd 18/8/44; ass 563BS/388BG Knettishall 22/8/44; retUS Bradley 21/6/45; 4168 BU Sth Plains 30/6/45; RFC Kingman 8/12/45. CRUISIN' CRADLE.

43-38386 Del Cheyenne 28/7/44; Kearney 4/8/44; Grenier 14/8/44; ass 4BS/34BS Mendlesham 15/8/44; b/d Hamburg 20/3/45 w/?; c/l Eye A/fd, UK; sal 21/3/45.

43-38387 Del Cheyenne 28/7/44; Hunter 9/8/44; Dow Fd 30/8/44; ass 527BS/379BG [FO-P] Kimbolton 10/9/44; b/d Frankfurt 25/9/44 w/?; f/l Continent; sal 14/11/44.

43-38388 Del Cheyenne 28/7/44; Kearney 6/8/44; Grenier 2/9/44; ass 379BG Kimbolton 10/9/44; retUS Bradley 25/6/45; 4168 BU Sth Plains 27/6/45; RFC Kingman 24/11/45.

43-38389 Del Cheyenne 28/7/44; Kearney 6/8/44; Grenier 15/8/44; ass 327BS/92BG Podington 27/8/44; MIA Merseburg 13/9/44 w/Donlon; e/a, cr Brandis, Ger; 8KIA 2POW; MACR 8889. U'V 'AD IT.

43-38390 Del Cheyenne 28/7/44; Hunter 5/8/44; Grenier 30/8/44; ass 569BS/390BG [CC-X] Framlingham 2/9/44; retUS Bradley 30/6/45; 4168 BU Sth Plains 3/7/45; RFC Kingman 18/12/45.

43-38391 Del Cheyenne 28/7/44; Hunter 5/8/44; Grenier 14/8/44; ass 7BS/34BG Mendlesham 15/8/44; retUS Bradley 21/6/45; 4168 BU Sth Plains 27/6/45; RFC Kingman 20/11/45. HIT AND RUN.

43-38392 Del Cheyenne 28/7/44; Kearney 6/8/44; Dow Fd 17/8/44; ass 18BS/34BG Mendlesham 18/8/44; during assembly for Dessau w/? 16/1/45; c/l Ampton, UK; 1KIA; sal. OLD CROW.

43-38393 Del Cheyenne 28/7/44; Hunter 8/8/44; Dow Fd 30/8/44; ass 569BS/390BG [CC-V] Framlingham 2/9/44; retUS Bradley 30/6/45; 4168 BU Sth Plains 6/7/45; RFC Kingman 28/11/45.

43-38394 Del Cheyenne 28/7/44; Kearney 6/8/44; Grenier 15/8/44; ass 748BS/457BG Glatton 17/8/44; retUS Bradley 7/6/45; 4168 BU Sth Plains 12/6/45; RFC Kingman 30/11/45.

43-38395 Del Cheyenne 28/7/44; Hunter 7/8/44; Dow FD 30/8/44; ass 863BS/493BG Debach 2/9/44; 862BG; retUS Bradley 1/7/45; 4168 BU Sth Plains 6/7/45; RFC Kingman 24/11/45.

43-38396 Del Cheyenne 28/7/44; Hunter 5/8/44; Dow Fd 17/8/44; ass 327BS/92BG [UX-J] Podington 26/8/44; MIA Nuremberg 3/10/44 w/Dornburgh; mid air coll, cr Giessen, Ger; 7KIA 2POW; MACR 9344. INSOMNIA.

43-38397 Del Cheyenne 28/7/44; Hunter 8/8/44; Dow Fd 30/8/44; ass 493BG Debach 1/9/44; tran 100BG Thorpe Abbotts 2/9/44; b/d Chemnitz 6/2/45 w/?; f/l Chagny, Fr?; sal 13/3/45.

43-38398 Del Cheyenne 28/7/44; Hunter 7//8/44; Dow Fd 1/9/44; ass 322BS/91BG [LG-O] Bassingbourn 10/9/44; sal 25/10/44.

43-38399 Del Cheyenne 28/7/44; Lincoln 11/8/44; Grenier 22/8/44; ass 7BS/34BG Mendlesham 24/8/44; MIA Kassel 22/9/44 w/Durratt; mid air coll, cr Buren, Ger; 9KIA; MACR 10200.

43-38400 Del Cheyenne 28/7/44; Hunter 8/8/44; Grenier 3/9/44; ass 851BS/490BG Eye 12/8/44; retUS Bradley 16/7/45; 4185 BU Independence 18/7/45; RFC Kingman 15/12/45. ALICE BLUE GOWN.

43-38401 Del Cheyenne 29/7/44; Hunter 8/8/44; Dow Fd 30/8/44; ass 325BS/92BG [NV-E] Podington 24/9/44; sal 9AF Germany 29/10/45. ROUND TRIP TICKET II.

43-38402 Del Cheyenne 29/7/44; Kearney 9/8/44; Grenier 16/8/44; ass 391BS/34BG Mendlesham 18/8/44; during assembly for Plauen 26/3/44 w/?; mid air coll w/452BG B17; cr Framsden and Crettingham, UK; all killed; sal.

43-38403 Del Cheyenne 29/7/44; Kearney 9/8/44; Grenier 16/8/44; ass 4BS/34BG Mendlesham 23/8/44; b/d Berlin 26/2/45 w/?; c/l Lodz, Pol.; sal 1/3/45. MACR 12768.

43-38404 Del Cheyenne 29/7/44; Hunter 7/8/44; Dow Fd 30/8/44; ass 563BS/388BG Knettishall 2/9/44; MIA Merseburg 28/9/44 w/Maring; mid air coll w/42-102953, cr Merseburg; 5KIA 1MIA 3POW; MACR 9377.

43-38405 Del Cheyenne 29/7/44; Hunter 7/8/44; Dow Fd 30/8/44; ass 508BS/351BG [YB-D] Polebrook 10/9/44; MIA Dresden 14/2/45 w/Ash; flak, cr Wormvervear, Hol; 1KIA 8POW; MACR 12334.

43-38406 Del Cheyenne 29/7/44; Hunter 7/8/44; Dow Fd 22/8/44; ass 391BS/34BG Mendlesham 23/8/44; b/d Hannover 15/12/44 w/?; f/l Melsbroek A/fd, Bel; sal 2/1/45.

43-38407 Del Cheyenne 29/7/44; Hunter 8/8/44; Dow Fd 30/8/44; ass 94BG Rougham 2/9/44; tran 367BS/306BG [GY-P] Thurleigh 15/9/44; b/d Berlin 3/2/45 w/Luckett; flak, cr Berlin; 7KIA 2POW; sal 29/3/45; MACR 12218.

43-38408 Del Cheyenne 29/7/44; Hunter 8/8/44; Dow Fd 30/8/44; ass 350BS/100BG Thorpe Abbotts 2/9/44; MIA Hamburg 31/12/44 w/Ross; e/a, cr Bartelsdorf, Ger; 9POW; MACR 11360. FAITHFUL FOREVER.

43-38409 Del Cheyenne 29/7/44; Kearney 10/8/44; Grenier 16/8/44; ass 18BS/34BG Mendlesham 18/8/44; retUS Bradley 21/6/45; 4168 BU Sth Plains 28/6/45; RFC Kingman 26/11/45. BETTY.

43-38410 Del Cheyenne 31/7/44; Hunter 8/8/44; Grenier 16/8/44; ass 18BS/34BG Mendlesham 18/8/44; retUS Bradley 21/6/45; 4168 BU Sth Plains 23/6/45; RFC Kingman 25/11/45. THE SEX MANIACS.

43-38411 Del Cheyenne 31/7/44; Kearney 12/8/44; Grenier 22/9/44; ass 348BS/99BG Tortorella 17/10/44; {55m} tran 301BG Lucera 5/45; retUS Bradley 3/7/45; 4168 BU Sth Plains 4/7/45; RFC Kingman 26/11/45.

43-38412 Del Cheyenne 31/7/44; Hunter 9/8/44; Dow Fd 30/8/44; ass 367BS/306BG [GY-T] Thurleigh 16/9/44; tran 381BG Ridgewell 5/45; retUS Bradley 9/6/45; 4168 BU Sth Plains 14/6/45; RFC Kingman 5/12/45.

43-38413 Del Cheyenne 31/7/44; Hunter 8/8/44; Dow Fd 30/8/44; ass 561BS/388BG Knettishall 2/9/44; MIA Ludwigshafen 5/11/44 w/McRee; flak, cr Mannheim; 7KIA 3POW; MACR 10311.

43-38414 Del Cheyenne 31/7/44; Hunter 8/8/44; Grenier 30/8/44; ass 482BG Alconbury 2/9/44; tran 350BS/100BG [LN-Y] Thorpe Abbotts 2/9/44; retUS Bradley 2/6/45; 4168 BU Sth Plains 6/6/45; RFC Kingman 18/11/45. "HEAVEN SENT."

43-38415 Del Cheyenne 31/7/44; Kearney 10/8/44; Grenier 22/8/44; ass 391BS/34BG Mendlesham 24/8/44; retUS Bradley 23/6/45; 4168 BU Sth Plains 25/6/45; RFC Kingman 19/12/45. SMOKEY JOE.

43-38416 Del Cheyenne 31/7/44; Lincoln 11/8/44; Grenier 21/8/44; ass 7BS/34BG Mendlesham 23/8/44; retUS Bradley 28/6/45; 4168 Bu Sth Plains 2/7/45; 237 BU Kirtland 18/11/45; RFC Albuquerque 6/2/46. NO GUM CHUM.

43-38417 Del Cheyenne 31/7/44; Kearney 12/8/44; Grenier 26/9/44; ass 551BS/385BG Gt Ashfield 30/9/44; f/l Nivelles A/fd, Bel 28/3/45; rep & ret gp; retUS Bradley 27/6/45; 4168 BU Sth Plains 3/7/45; RFC Kingman 24/11/45. LADY B GOOD.

43-38418 Del Cheyenne 31/7/44; Kearney 10/8/44; Grenier 9/9/44; ass 348BS/99BG Tortorella 10/10/44; MIA {36m} Korneunerg, Aus 20/3/45 w/Urban; flak, cr Kriszevci; MACR 13054. GLITTERING GAL.

43-38419 Del Cheyenne 1/8/44; Lincoln 11/8/44; Grenier 22/8/44; ass 7BS/34BG Mendlesham 23/8/44; MIA Derben, Ger 14/1/45 w/Raver; flak, cr Eggenstedt, Ger; 7KIA 2POW; MACR 11567.

43-38420 Del Cheyenne 1/8/44; Lincoln 11/8/44; Grenier 2/9/44; ass 526BS/379BG [LF-J] Kimbolton 10/9/44; b/d Berlin 18/3/45 w/?; c/l Bydgoszcz, Pol.; sal 30/3/45. YVONNE.

43-38421 Del Cheyenne 1/8/44; Lincoln 12/8/44; Grenier 28/8/44; ass 731BS/452BG Deopham Green 23/8/44; 730BG; retUS Bradley 11/7/45; 4168 BU Sth Plains 12/7/45; RFC Kingman 1/12/45.

43-38422 Del Cheyenne 1/8/44; Kearney 12/8/44; Grenier 22/8/44; ass 391BS/34BG Mendlesham 24/8/44; returning Darmstadt, coll w/B-17s on landing 24/12/44; sal.

43-38423 Del Cheyenne 1/8/44; Kearney 12/8/44; Grenier 22/8/44; ass 96BG Snetterton 27/8/44; tran 391BS/34BG Mendlesham 28/8/44; MIA Hamburg 31/12/44 w/Sproul; flak, cr Tossener Dike, Hol?; 3KIA 6POW; MACR 11372.

43-38424 Del Cheyenne 1/8/44; Lincoln 12/8/44; Grenier 22/8/44; ass 561BS/388BG Knettishall 23/9/44; b/d Darmsadt 24/12/44 w/?; f/l Melsbroek, Bel; sal.

43-38425 Del Cheyenne 19/8/44; Lincoln 27/8/44; Grenier 22/9/44; ass 615BS/401BG [IY-K] Deenethorpe 7/10/44; retUS Bradley 2/6/45; 4168 BU Sth Plains 6/6/45; RFC Kingman 16/11/45. NET RESULT.

43-38426 Del Cheyenne 1/8/44; Lincoln 12/8/44; Grenier 6/9/44; ass 511BS/351BG [DS-B] Polebrook

21/9/44; MIA {7m} Zwickau 7/10/44 w/Fisher; flak; f/l Jonkopping, Swed; 9INT; MACR 9367; ret gp 25/5/45; retUS Bradley 28/6/45; 4168 BU Sth Plains 2/7/45; RFC Kingman 14/2/46.

43-38427 Del Cheyenne 1/8/44; Kearney 12/8/44; Grenier 18/9/44; ass 96BG Snetterton 19/9/44; sal 16/3/45.

43-38428 Del Cheyenne 1/8/44; Hunter 12/8/44; Grenier 2/9/44; ass 511BS/351BG [DS-A] Polebrook 10/9/44; 509BS [RQ-A]; {76m} RetUS Bradley 9/6/45; 4168 BU Sth Plains 14/6/45; RFC Kingman 17/12/45.

43-38429 Del Cheyenne 2/8/44; Hunter 12/8/44; Grenier 30/8/44; ass 368BS/306BG [BO-W] Thurleigh 15/9/44; retUS Bradley 7/6/45; ATC Columbus 10/6/45; 4168 BU Sth Plains 6/7/45; Recl Comp 7/6/46. NICOTINE NELLY.

43-38430 Del Cheyenne 2/8/44; Hunter 12/8/44; Grenier 2/9/44; ass 548BS/385BG Gt Ashfield 8/9/44; MIA Berlin 6/10/44 w/Andreas; e/a, cr Koenigshorst, Ger; 4KIA 5POW; MACR 9520.

43-38431 Del Cheyenne 2/8/44; Hunter 12/8/44; Dow Fd 30/8/44; ass 527BS/379BG [FO-J] Kimbolton 10/9/44; flak damage by friendly fire, cr Knodishall, UK 2/11/44; sal.

43-38432 Del Cheyenne 2/8/44; Lincoln 16/8/44; Grenier 2/9/44; ass 511BS/351BG [DS-P] Polebrook 10/9/44; MIA Berlin 5/12/44 w/Capt Williamson; flak, cr Berlin; MACR 11037.

43-38433 Del Cheyenne 2/8/44; Kearney 12/8/44; Grenier 22/8/44; ass 18BS/34BG Mendlesham 30/8/44; c/l 14/4/45; sal.

43-38434 Del Cheyenne 2/8/44; Hunter 12/8/44; Grenier 2/9/44; ass 327BS/92BG Podington 13/9/44; MIA Zwickau 7/10/44 w/Kerr; flak, cr Emmerich; 5KIA 5POW; MACR 9345.

43-38435 Del Cheyenne 2/8/44; Hunter 12/8/44; Dow Fd 30/8/44; ass 511BS/351BG [DS-H] Polebrook 21/9/44; 510BS [TU-O]; {65m} ground col w/43-37665, sal 25/3/45. GLORY BOUND.

43-38436 Del Cheyenne 2/8/44; Hunter 12/8/44; Grenier 2/9/44; ass 350BS/100BG Thorpe Abbotts 5/9/44; MIA Hamburg 31/12/44 w/Webster; e/a, cr Osenhorst, Ger; 4KIA 5POW; MACR 11361.

43-38437 Del Cheyenne 6/8/44; Hunter 12/8/44; Grenier 30/8/44; ass 350BS/100BG [LN-S] 2/9/44; b/d Chemnitz 6/2/45 w/?; cr Rochester A/fd, UK; 1WIA; sal 11/2/45.

43-38438 Del Cheyenne 7/8/44; Hunter 14/8/44; Dow Fd 9/9/44; ass 368BS/306BG [BO-U] Thurleigh 1/10/44; sal 8/1/45.

43-38439 Del Patterson 3/8/44; Ft Dix 4/9/44; 116 BU Ft Dix 1/1/45; 129 BU Columbia 17/5/45; 139 BU Shaw 25/11/45; 2528 BU Midland 26/12/45; 2622 BU Mather 10/3/46; 613 BU Phillips 4/6/46; 556 BU Long Beach 31/5/47.

43-38440 Del Cheyenne 3/8/44; Hunter 12/8/44; Grenier 4/9/44; ass 407BS/92BG [PY-E] Podington 5/9/44; b/d Lutzkendorf 9/2/45 w/?; f/l Continent; sal 16/3/45.

43-38441 Del Cheyenne 7/8/44; Hunter 13/8/44; Grenier 7/9/44; ass 412BS/95BG [QW-P] Horham 11/9/44; retUS Bradley 24/6/45; 4168 BU Sth Plains 30/6/45; RFC Kingman 23/11/45.

43-38442 Del Cheyenne 3/8/44; Lincoln 16/8/44; Dow Fd 31/8/44; ass 358BS/303BG [VK-F] Molesworth 2/9/44; b/d Cologne 10/11/44 w/?; f/l Continent; sal 28/11/44.

43-38443 Del Cheyenne 5/8/44; Hunter 12/8/44; Dow Fd 7/9/44; ass 385BG Gt Ashfield 11/9/44; retUS Bradley 28/6/45; 4168 BU Sth Plains 30/6/45; RFC Kingman 30/11/45.

43-38444 Del Cheyenne 5/8/44; Hunter 16/8/44; Grenier 2/9/44; ass 92BG Podington 13/9/44; b/d Mainz 21/9/44 w/?; f/l France, sal.

43-38445 Del Cheyenne 3/8/44; Hunter 12/8/44; Grenier 2/9/44; ass 325BS/92BG Podington 9/9/44; MIA Nuremberg 3/10/44 w/Nielsen; mid air coll, cr Neuhof, Ger; 8KIA 1POW; MACR 9346.

43-38446 Del Cheyenne 3/8/44; Hunter 12/8/44; Grenier 4/9/44; ass 407BS/92BG [PY-F] Podington 5/9/44; 327BS; sal 9AF Germany 22/11/45; re-ass AF Oberpfaffenhofen 30/4/47; Recl Comp 5/8/48.

43-38447 Del Cheyenne 3/8/44; Hunter 12/8/44; Grenier 7/9/44; ass 326BS/92BG [JW-Z] Podington 9/9/44; retUS Bradley 28/6/45; 4168 BU Sth Plains 30/6/45; RFC Kingman 10/12/45.

43-38448 Del Cheyenne 3/8/44; Hunter 12/8/44; Grenier 3/9/44; ass 413BS/96BG Snetterton 8/9/44; retUS Bradley 5/7/45; 4168 BU Sth Plains 6/7/45; RFC Kingman 14/12/45.

43-38449 Del Cheyenne 4/8/44; Hunter 14/8/44; Grenier 4/9/44; ass 326BS/92BG [JW-Z] Podington 5/9/44; retUS Bradley 11/7/45; 4185 BU Independence 12/7/45; RFC Kingman 21/12/45.

43-38450 Del Cheyenne 4/8/44; Hunter 12/8/44; Grenier 4/9/44; ass 710BS/447 BG Rattlesden 4/9/44; retUS Bradley 5/7/45; 4168 BU Sth Plains 6/7/45; RFC Kingman 1/12/45. LITTLE HERBIE.

43-38451 Del Cheyenne 4/8/44; Hunter 14/8/44; Grenier 7/9/44; ass 360BS/303BG [PU-D] Molesworth 28/9/44; ret Berlin 28/3/45 w/?; no gas, c/l Camber Sands, Rye, UK; crew OK; sal 30/3/45.

43-38452 Del Cheyenne 4/8/44; Hunter 12/8/44; Grenier 4/9/44; ass 614BS/401BG [IW-D] Deenethorpe 23/9/44; b/d Politz 7/10/44 w/James; flak, f/l Backs Torvmosse, Swed; 9INT; MACR 9759. UNDECIDED.

43-38453 Del Cheyenne 4/8/44; Hunter 14/8/44; Grenier 4/9/44; ass 326BS/92BG [JW-F] Podington 27/9/44; secret mission 28/5/45, ret 29/5/45; sal 9AF Germany 10/12/45. SOLDIER'S VOTE.

43-38454 Del Cheyenne 4/8/44; Hunter 14/8/44; Grenier 2/9/44; ass 326BS/92BG [JW-B] Podington 21/9/44; mission to Port Lyautey, Morr 16/6/45, ret 17/6/45; sal 9AF Germany 10/12/45.

43-38455 Del Cheyenne 4/8/44; Lincoln 15/8/44; Grenier 3/9/44; ass 407BS/92BG [PY-K] Podington 4/9/44; c/t/o Kassel 15/12/44 w/?; a/c expl, crew safe; sal.

43-38456 Del Cheyenne 4/8/44; Hunter 14/8/44; Grenier 2/9/44; ass 569BS/390BG Framlingham 5/9/44; MIA Merseburg 30/11/44 w/Philip; flak, cr Zeitz; 9KIA; MACR 11135.

43-38457 Del Cheyenne 4/8/44; Hunter 14/8/44; Grenier 2/9/44; ass 350BS/100BG Thorpe Abbotts 3/9/44; MIA Hamburg 31/12/44 w/McNab; mid air coll w/42-31981, cr Rustringen, Ger; 5KIA 4POW; MACR 11359.

43-38458 Del Cheyenne 4/8/44; Lincoln 15/8/44; Grenier 3/9/44; ass 398BG Nuthampstead 10/9/44; tran 613BS/401BG [IN-D] Deenethorpe 12/9/44; 615BS [IY-P]; retUS Bradley 6/6/45; 4168 BU Sth Plains 12/6/45; RFC Kingman 6/12/45. BOTTLE BABY.

43-38459 Del Cheyenne 6/8/44; Lincoln 16/8/44; Grenier 2/9/44; ass 418BS/100BG [LD-V] Thorpe Abbotts 3/9/44; MIA Hamburg 31/12/44 w/Marin; e/a, cr Westerhusen, Ger?; 1KIA 8POW; MACR 11358.

43-38460 Del Cheyenne 6/8/44; Hunter 15/8/44; Dow Fd 8/9/44; ass 336BS/95BG [ET-V] Horham 10/9/44; b/d Merseburg 28/9/44 w/Miller; f/l Continent, sal.

43-38461 Del Cheyenne 6/8/44; Hunter 15/8/44; Dow Fd 4/9/44; ass 510BS/351BG [TU-T] Polebrook 25/9/44; {48m} b/d Berlin 26/2/45 w/?; c/l Continent; sal 3/3/45.

43-38462 Del Cheyenne 6/8/44; Hunter 14/8/44; Dow Fd 6/9/44; ass 358BS/303BG [VK-I] Molesworth 29/8/44; tran 457BG Glatton 22/5/45; 351BG Polebrook 29/5/45; retUS Bradley 13/6/45; 4168 BU Sth Plains 18/6/44; RFC Kingman 8/12/45.

43-38463 Del Cheyenne 6/8/44; Lincoln 17/8/44; Grenier 3/9/44; ass 390BG Framlingham 4/9/44; tran 600BS/398BG [N8-X] Nuthampstead 5/9/44; 601BS; MIA Zeitz 30/11/44 w/Weum; flak, cr Grossloebichau, Ger; 1EVD 6KIA 2POW; MACR 11315.

43-38464 Del Cheyenne 6/8/44; Hunter 15/8/44; Grenier 3/9/44; ass 549BS/385BG Gt Ashfield 11/9/44; retUS Bradley 25/6/45; 4168 BU Sth Plains 25/6/45; RFC Kingman 7/12/45. HARES BREATH.

43-38465 Del Cheyenne 6/8/44; Hunter 15/8/44; Grenier 2/9/44; ass 510BS/351BG [TU-A] Polebrook 10/9/44; {78m} RetUS Bradley 12/6/45; 4168 BU Sth Plains 15/6/45; RFC Kingman 10/12/45. FAVORITE LADY.

43-38466 Del Cheyenne 6/8/44; Lincoln 15/8/44; Grenier 3/9/44; ass 447BS Rattlesden 5/9/44; tran 524BS/379BG [WA-D] Kimbolton 25/9/44; loaned 15AF 12/11 - 12/12/44; retUS Bradley 6/7/45; 4168 BU Sth Plains 7/7/45; RFC Kingman 17/12/45.

43-38467 Del Cheyenne 6/8/44; Lincoln 18/8/44; Grenier 2/9/44; ass 423BS/306BG Thurleigh 4/9/44; b/d Merseburg 30/11/44 w/?; c/l Continent; sal 14/2/45.

43-38468 Del Cheyenne 6/8/44; Lincoln 18/8/44; Grenier 2/9/44; ass 407BS/92BG [PY-G] Podington 5/9/44; special mission Port Lyautey, Morr 14/6/45, ret 15/6/45; sal 9AF Germany 30/12/45.

43-38469 Del Cheyenne 6/8/44; Lincoln 17/8/44; Grenier 2/9/44; ass 336BS/95BG [ET-U] Horham 5/9/44; retUS Bradley 24/6/45; 4168 BU Sth Plains 26/6/45; RFC Kingman 10/12/45.

43-38470 Del Cheyenne 7/8/44; Lincoln 15/8/44; Grenier 2/9/44; ass 571BS/390BG [FC-K] Framlingham 5/9/44; retUS Bradley 3/7/45; 4168 BU Sth Plains 6/7/45; RFC Kingman 14/12/45. RAIN CHECK.

43-38471 Del Cheyenne 7/8/44; Hunter 15/8/44; Grenier 4/9/44; ass 8AF 7/9/44.

43-38472 Del Cheyenne 7/8/44; Lincoln 18/8/44; Grenier 2/9/44; ass 570BS/390BG [DI-F] Framlingham 5/9/44; retUS Bradley 3/7/45; 4168 BU Sth Plains 6/7/45; RFC Kingman 26/11/45. BABY BUGGY II.

43-38473 Del Cheyenne 7/8/44; Lincoln 17/8/44; Grenier 2/9/44; ass 708BS/447BG Rattlesden 8/9/44; (first a/c fitted with Cheyenne turret); MIA Kassel 30/12/44 w/Bates; mid air coll, cr Wenings, Ger?; 9KIA; MACR 11240.

43-38474 Del Cheyenne 7/8/44; Lincoln 18/8/44; Grenier 6/9/44; ass 815BS/483BG Sterparone 9/9/44; (radio compt gun fitted); sal 10/10/44.

43-38475 Del Cheyenne 7/8/44; Lincoln 17/8/44; Grenier 7/9/44; ass 493BG Debach 9/9/44; retUS Bradley 3/7/45; 4168 BU Sth Plains 6/7/45; RFC Olmstead 28/2/46.

43-38476 Del Cheyenne 7/8/44; Lincoln 18/8/44; Grenier 6/9/44; ass 100BG Thorpe Abbotts 13/9/44; tran 482BG Alconbury 20/5/45; retUS Bradley 2/6/45; 4168 BU Sth Plains 6/6/45; RFC Kingman 8/11/45.

43-38477 Del Cheyenne 7/8/44; Lincoln 18/8/44; Grenier 1/9/44; ass 327BS/92BG [UX-R] Podington 3/9/44; sal 9AF Germany 10/12/45.

43-38478 Del Cheyenne 7/8/44; Lincoln 18/8/44; Grenier 3/9/44; ass 570BS/390BG [DI-S] Framlingham 4/9/44; retUS Bradley 3/7/45; 4168 BU Sth Plains 6/7/45; RFC Kingman 25/11/45. HOTTER 'N HELL.

43-38479 Del Cheyenne 8/8/44; Lincoln 18/8/44; Grenier 2/9/44; ass 748BS/457BG Glatton 8/9/44; retUS Bradley 7/6/45; 4168 BU Sth Plains 12/6/45; RFC Kingman 27/11/45. THY WILL BE DONE.

43-38480 Del Cheyenne 8/8/44; Lincoln 18/8/44; Grenier 2/9/44; ass 860BS/493BG Debach 13/9/44; MIA Bielefeld 30/9/44 w/LaFlame; hit by debris from 43-38115, cr Bielefeld; 8KIA 1POW; MACR 9430.

43-38481 Del Cheyenne 8/8/44; Lincoln 18/8/44; Grenier 3/9/44; ass 407BS/92BG [PY-B] Podington 4/9/44; sal 9AF Germany 2/1/46. LORD LEMON.

43-38482 Del Cheyenne 8/8/44; Lincoln 19/8/44; Grenier 9/9/44; ass 773BS/463BS Celone 12/9/44; MIA Vienna 13/10/44 w/Kirby; flak, cr Aspern; 4POW 6KIA. MACR 9054.

43-38483 Del Cheyenne 8/8/44; Lincoln 18/8/44; Grenier 9/9/44; ass 301BG Lucera 17/9/44; {0m} tran 96BS/2BG Amendola 7/10/44; retUS Hunter 19/6/45; 4168 BU Sth Plains 21/6/45; RFC Kingman 17/12/45.

43-38484 Del Cheyenne 8/8/44; Hunter 18/8/44; Dow Fd 1/9/44; ass 32BS/301BG Lucera 7/10/44; retUS Hunter 17/6/45; 4168 BU Sth Plains 19/6/45; RFC Kingman 26/11/45.

43-38485 Del Cheyenne 8/8/44; Lincoln 19/8/44; Grenier 8/9/44; ass 49BS/2BG Amendola 24/9/44; retUS, RFC Walnut Ridge 14/12/45.

43-38486 Del Cheyenne 8/8/44; Lincoln 19/8/44; Grenier 9/9/44; ass 483BG Sterparone; retUS, RFC Walnut Ridge 19/12/45.

43-38487 Del Cheyenne 8/8/44; Hunter 19/8/44; Dow Fd 30/8/44; ass 352BS/301BG Lucera 17/9/44; retUS Hunter 14/7/45; 4185 BU Independence 15/7/44; RFC Kingman 9/12/45.

43-38488 Del Cheyenne 8/8/44; Lincoln 19/8/44; Grenier 11/9/44; ass 773BS/463BG Celone 12/9/44; MIA Linz 25/2/45 w/Bissonette; mech fault, cr Tettning; MACR 12468.

43-38489 Del Cheyenne 9/8/44; Lincoln 19/8/44; Grenier 7/9/44; ass 97BG Amendola 11/10/44; retUS Bradley 12/7/45; 4185 BU Independence 13/7/45; RFC Kingman 10/12/45.

43-38490 Del Cheyenne 9/8/44; Kearney 19/8/44; Grenier 9/9/44; ass 772BS/463BG Celone 4/10/44; retUS 1103 BU Morrison 28/9/44; RFC Walnut Ridge 11/12/45.

43-38491 Del Cheyenne 9/8/44; Lincoln 19/8/44; Grenier 9/9/44; ass 341BS/97BG Amendola 10/10/44; retUS Bradley 14/6/45; 4168 BU Sth Plains 18/6/45; RFC Kingman 2/12/45.

43-38492 Del Cheyenne 9/8/44; Lincoln 19/8/44; Grenier 6/9/44; ass 353BS/301BG Lucera 12/10/44; retUS Hunter 10/7/45; 4168 BU Sth Plains 12/7/45; RFC Kingman 13/11/45. VENUS RAMEY.

43-38493 Del Cheyenne 9/8/44; Lincoln 19/8/44; Grenier 6/9/44; ass 463BG Celone 3/10/44; tran 49BS/2BG Amendola 12/4/45; c/l 30/4/45.

43-38494 Del Cheyenne 9/8/44; Kearney 19/8/44; Grenier 9/9/44; ass 850BS/409BG Eye 11/9/44; b/d Mannheim 21/1/45 w/?; c/l Continent; sal 28/1/45.

43-38495 Del Cheyenne 9/8/44; Kearney 19/8/44; Dow Fd 9/9/44; ass 352BS/301BG Lucera 12/9/44; sal.

43-38496 Del Cheyenne 9/8/44; Kearney 19/8/44; Dow Fd 18/9/44; ass 772BS/463BG Celone 19/9/44; MIA Vienna 21/2/45 w/Bandi; prop wash & coll, cr Vienna; MACR 12702.

43-38497 Del Cheyenne 9/8/44; Lincoln 21/8/44; Grenier 18/9/44; ass 532BS/381BG [VE-Q] Ridgewell 20/9/44; retUS Bradley 28/5/45; 4168 BU Sth Plains 30/5/45; Recl Comp 7/6/46. THE JOKER III.

43-38498 Del Santa Monica 9/8/44; 2316 BU Santa Monica 9/10/44; 4145 BU Wendover 10/10/44; 4135 BU Hill Fd 11/7/46; 4145 BU Wendover 12/8/46; 4185 BU Independence 24/10/46; Recl Comp 13/2/47.

43-38499 Del Cheyenne 9/8/44; Kearney 17/8/44; Grenier 9/9/44; ass 463BG Celone 10/44; coll 11/1/45; sal.

43-38500 Del Cheyenne 10/8/44; Lincoln 21/8/44; Grenier 9/9/44; ass 353BS/301BG Lucera 12/10/44; tran depot 22/11/45; Re-ass AF Obepfaffenhofen 30/4/47; Recl Comp 6/12/48.

43-38501 Del Cheyenne 10/8/44; Kearney 21/8/44; Grenier 7/9/44; ass 546BS/384BG [BK-C] Grafton Underwood 23/9/44; MIA Pilsen, Cz 25/4/45 w/Lovett; flak, cr Pilsen; 3EVD 5POW; MACR 14317. SWEET CHARIOT.

43-38502 Del Cheyenne 10/8/44; Kearney 22/8/44; Grenier 9/9/44; ass 340BS/97BG Amendola 14/10/44; MIA Brux 21/10/44 w/?; sal.

43-38503 Del Cheyenne 10/8/44; Kearney 18/8/44; Grenier 9/9/44; ass 817BS/483BG Sterparone 28/9/44; MIA Vienna 7/2/45 w/Borders; flak, c/l Papa; 9RTD 14/3/45; MACR 12128.

43-38504 Del Cheyenne 10/8/44; Kearney 22/8/44; Grenier 9/9/44; ass 562BS/388BG Knettishall 11/9/44; during assembly for Hamm 16/2/45 w/Beatty; mech fault, ditched Nth Sea; 9RTD.

43-38505 Del Cheyenne 10/8/44; Kearney 20/8/44; Grenier 11/9/44; ass 49BS/2BG Amendola 4/10/44; tran 352BS/301BG Lucera 29/10/44; MIA Linz, Aus 25/2/45 w/Stueve; flak, cr Linz; 3POW 7KIA; MACR 12474.

43-38506 Del Cheyenne 10/8/44; Kearney 22/8/44; Grenier 18/9/44; ass 748BS/457BG Glatton 20/9/44; retUS Bradley 8/6/45; 4168 BU Sth Plains 14/6/45; RFC Kingman 17/12/45.

43-38507 Del Cheyenne 10/8/44; Lincoln 27/8/44; Grenier 18/9/44; ass 305BG Chelveston 4/12/44; b/d Zwickau 19/3/45 w/?; c/l base, sal.

43-38508 Del Cheyenne 10/8/44; Lincoln 20/8/44; damaged in training, to Lowry for repair 19/10/44; Grenier 7/11/44; ass 384BG Grafton Underwood 10/11/44 EILEEN'S KINDERGARDEN; tran 447BG Rattlesden 11/11/44; b/d Mannheim 21/1/45 w/?; f/l Yerhavcourt, Fr?; sal 7/3/45.

43-38509 Del Cheyenne 11/8/44; Lincoln 21/8/44; Grenier 7/9/44; ass 815BS/483BG Sterparone 24/9/44; MIA Vienna 20/2/45 w/Neuman; three engines out, crew baled nr Russian lines, a/c cr Csaloy; 1KIA 1POW, 1WIA along with rest of crew evade, ret March 1945; MACR 12451.

43-38510 Del Cheyenne 11/8/44; Lincoln 21/8/44; Grenier 8/9/44; ass 327BS/92BG [UX-V] Podington 24/9/44; ground acc 15/12/44; sal 16/12/44.

43-38511 Del Cheyenne 11/8/44; Lincoln 20/8/44; Grenier 7/9/44; ass 773BS/463BG Celone 24/9/44; MIA Linz, Aus 25/4/45 w/Wilson; flak, cr Pebneurchin; 2POW 8KIA; MACR 14059.

43-38512 Del Cheyenne 11/8/44; Lincoln 21/8/44; Grenier 6/9/44; ass 570BS/390BG [DI-K] Framlingham 10/9/44; tran 463BG Celone 24/9/44; retUS, RFC Walnut Ridge 11/12/45. OLD BLOOD AND GUTS.

43-38513 Del Cheyenne 11/8/44; Lincoln 22/8/44; Grenier 12/9/44; slated 482BG Alconbury, ass 452BG Deopham Green 16/9/44; tran 339BS/96BG [QJ-M] Snetterton 17/9/44; retUS Bradley 1/6/45; 4168 BU Sth Plains 4/6/45; RFC Kingman 17/12/45. NEVER HAD IT SO GOOD.

43-38514 Del Cheyenne 11/8/44; Hunter 23/8/44; Dow Fd 8/9/44; ass 349BS/100BG [XR-J] Thorpe Abbotts 8/9/44; 351BS [EP-J]; tran 482BG Alconbury 20/5/45; retUS Bradley 2/6/45; 4168 BU Sth Plains 6/6/45; RFC Kingman 17/12/45.

43-38515 Del Cheyenne 11/8/44; Lincoln 20/8/44; Grenier 10/9/44; ass 571BS/390BG [FC-K] Framlingham 13/9/44; b/d Frankfurt 5/1/45 w/?; cr France, 9KIA; sal 21/1/45. MISS YOU.

43-38516 Del Cheyenne 11/8/44; Lincoln 22/8/44; slated 303BG, tran Cheyenne 9/9/44; Waterton 20/10/44; 619 BU Waterton 25/3/45; Ladd Fd (Cold Weather Test) 2/11/44; 3704 BU Keesler 2/4/45; 554 BU Memphis 11/6/46.

43-38517 Del Cheyenne 11/8/44; Hunter 22/8/44; Grenier 8/9/44; ass 327BS/92BG [UX-T] Podington 23/9/44; sal 12/5/45.

43-38518 Del Cheyenne 11/8/44; Hunter 22/8/44; Grenier 6/9/44; ass 511BS/351BG [DS-N] Polebrook 21/9/44; MIA {4m} Nurnberg 3/10/44 w/Cregar; flak, cr Stellnau, Ger?; 1KIA 8POW; MACR 9358.

43-38519 Del Cheyenne 13/8/44; Lincoln 22/8/44; Grenier 9/9/44; ass 483BG Sterparone 4/10/44; retUS 1103 BU Morrison 8/10/44; RFC Walnut Ridge 4/1/46.

43-38520 Del Cheyenne 13/8/44; Lincoln 23/8/44; Grenier 9/9/44; ass 327BS/92BG [UX-B] Podington 21/9/44; MIA 4/4/45 w/Marozas; flak, cr Nienburg; 8RTD.

43-38521 Del Cheyenne 13/8/44; Hunter 22/8/44; Grenier 4/9/44; ass 92BG Podington 5/9/44; tran 570BS/390BG [DI-K] Framlingham 6/9/44; 836BS/487BG Lavenham 21/11/45; retUS Bradley 3/7/45; 4185 BU Independence 15/7/45; RFC Kingman 20/12/45.

43-38522 Del Cheyenne 12/8/44; Gt Falls 17/8/44; Cheyenne 23/8/44; Hunter 28/8/44; 53 WRS Presque Is 31/8/44 (special comm equip fitted); 53 WRS Grenier 9/11/44; 53 WRS Buckley 11/3/45; Guam 11/3/46; ret 53 WRS Grenier 9/5/46; 53 WRS Morrison 30/6/46; re-ass AF, 373 RV Kindley 18/1/47; 2016 WA Weisbaden 18/8/48; 7165 CMP Erbenheim 19/3/49; Recl Comp 20/5/49.

43-38523 Del Cheyenne 12/8/44; Hunter 22/8/44; Grenier 7/9/44; ass 351BS/100BG [EP-F] Thorpe Abbotts 11/9/44; b/d Hamburg 31/12/44 w/?; c/l & burned; sal 1/1/45.

43-38524 Del Cheyenne 12/8/44; Lincoln 22/8/44; Grenier 7/9/44; ass 710BS/447BG Rattlesden 17/9/44; retUS Bradley 6/7/45; 4168 BU Sth Plains 7/7/45; RFC Kingman 21/12/45. BLONDE BOMBER II.

43-38525 Del Cheyenne 12/8/44; Hunter 22/8/44; Dow Fd 7/9/44; ass 482BG Alconbury 8/9/44; tran 418BS/100BG [LD-A] Thorpe Abbotts 9/9/44; retUS Bradley 2/6/45; 4168 BU Sth Plains 11/6/45; 237 BU Kirtland 30/11/45; RFC Albuquerque 5/2/46. MISS CON DUCT.

43-38526 Del Cheyenne 12/8/44; Hunter 23/8/44; Grenier 4/9/44; ass 568BS/390BG [B-IZ] Framlingham 8/9/44 BIG GAS BIRD; MIA Derben 14/1/45 w/Niebergall; e/a, cr Friesack, Ger; 4KIA 6POW; MACR 11722. STAR DUSTER.

43-38527 Del Cheyenne 12/8/44; Hunter 23/8/44; Grenier 9/10/44; ass 511BS/351BG [DS-C] Polebrook 25/9/44; MIA {3m} Politz 7/10/44 w/Dargue; flak, cr Stettin, Ger; 1KIA 9POW; MACR 9359.

43-38528 Del Cheyenne 12/8/44; Hunter 23/8/44;

Grenier 7/9/44; ass 750BS/457BG Glatton 8/9/44; RetUS Bradley 28/5/45; 4168 BU Sth Plains 31/5/45; RFC Kingman 9/12/45. THAT'S MY BABY.

43-38529 Del Cheyenne 14/8/44; Hunter 23/8/44; Dow Fd 7/9/44; ass 457BG Glatton 8/9/44; b/d Politz 7/10/44 w/Salzer; ditched Nth Sea; 10RTD.

43-38530 Del Cheyenne 14/8/44; Hunter 23/5/44; Grenier 4/9/44; ass 358BS/303BG [VK-G] Molesworth 28/10/44; MIA Sterkrade 22/1/45 w/Woodson; flak, cr Sterkrade, Ger; 7KIA 2POW; MACR 11758.

43-38531 Del Cheyenne 14/8/44; Hunter 23/8/44; Dow Fd 8/9/44; ass 350BS/100BG Thorpe Abbotts 8/9/44; MIA Merseburg 7/10/44 w/Grigg; flak, cr Bielefeld; 2KIA 7POW; MACR 9562. SAD FLAK.

43-38532 Del Cheyenne 14/8/44; Lincoln 24/8/44; Grenier 10/9/44; ass 360BS/303BG [PU-G] Molesworth 17/9/44; b/d Merzhausen 24/12/44 w/St Julien; c/l Snetterton A/fd, UK; rep & ret; retUS Bradley 7/6/45; 4168 BU Sth Plains 12/6/45; RFC Kingman 1/12/45.

43-38533 Del Cheyenne 14/8/44; Lincoln 24/8/44; Grenier 18/9/44; ass 729BS/452BG Deopham Green 19/9/44; MIA Hamburg 17/1/45 w/Halik; flak, cr Sittensen, Ger; 9POW; MACR 11795.

43-38534 Del Cheyenne 14/8/44; Lincoln 24/8/44; Grenier 18/9/44; ass 749BS/457BG Glatton 19/9/44; 750BS; retUS Bradley 10/6/45; 4168 BU Sth Plains 15/6/45; RFC Kingman 1/12/45. THE WOLF PACK.

43-38535 Del Cheyenne 14/8/44; Hunter 23/8/44; Grenier 6/9/44; ass 350BS/100BG Thorpe Abbotts 8/9/44; MIA Hamburg 31/12/43 w/Whitcomb; e/a, cr Rothenburg, Ger; 5KIA 4POW; MACR 11357.

43-38536 Del Cheyenne 14/8/44; Lincoln 24/8/44; Grenier 18/9/44; slated 34BG, tran 554 BU Memphis 12/3/45; Ret 14/3/46. QUIVERING QUEENIE.

43-38537 Del Cheyenne 14/8/44; Lincoln 26/8/44; Grenier 11/9/44; ass 749BS/457BG Glatton 14/9/44; 384BG Grafton Underwood 23/5/45; sal 9AF Germany 10/12/45.

43-38538 Del Cheyenne 14/8/44; Lincoln 24/8/44; Grenier 11/9/44; ass 750BS/457BG Glatton 13/9/44; 751BS; MIA Münster 30/9/44 w/Millea; flak, cr Lunen, Ger; 10KIA; MACR 9527/10320.

43-38539 Del Cheyenne 16/8/44; Lincoln 24/8/44; Grenier 10/9/44; ass 379BG Kimbolton 22/9/44; b/d Cologne 10/1/45 w/?; coll w/B-17; c/l Continent; sal 26/1/45.

43-38540 Del Cheyenne 16/8/44; Lincoln 24/8/44; Grenier 11/9/44; ass 748BS/457BG Glatton 13/9/44 MYSTERIOUS WITCH; 749BS; retUS Bradley 9/6/45; 4168 BU Sth Plains 14/6/45; RFC Kingman 25/11/45. MURDEROUS WITCH.

43-38541 Del Cheyenne 16/8/44; Lincoln 24/8/44; Grenier 18/9/44; ass 612BS/401BG [SC-F] Deenethorpe 17/10/44; retUS Bradley 6/6/45; 4168 BU Sth Plains 8/6/45; RFC Kingman 10/12/45. DIABOLICAL ANGEL.

43-38542 Del Cheyenne 16/8/44; Lincoln 24/8/44; Grenier 10/9/44; ass 547BS/384BG [SO-J] Grafton Underwood 23/9/44; c/l 20/1/45, sal.

43-38543 Del Cheyenne 16/8/44; Lincoln 24/8/44; Grenier 10/9/44; ass 337BS/96BG [AW-A] Snetterton 13/9/44 LAIDEN MAIDEN; tran 412BS/95BG [QW-A] Horham 14/9/44; hit by incoming aircraft 16/12/44; sal 17/12/44; retUS Bradley 26/6/45; 4168 BU Sth Plains 29/6/45; RFC Kingman 25/11/45.

43-38544 Del Cheyenne 16/8/44; Lincoln 24/8/44; Grenier 12/9/44; ass 548BS/385BG Gt Ashfield 13/9/44; retUS Bradley 26/6/45; 4168 BU Sth Plains 29/6/45; RFC Kingman 25/11/45. SHACK 'N LADY.

43-38545 Del Cheyenne 16/8/44; Topeka 25/8/44; Grenier 17/9/44; ass 401BS/91BG [LL-J] Bassingbourn 4/11/44; 324BS; b/d Merseburg 21/11/44 w/DeBolt; c/l Belgium; 9RTD; sal 28/11/44.

43-38546 Del Cheyenne 16/8/44; Lincoln 25/8/44; Grenier 10/9/44; ass 457BG Glatton 12/9/44; tran 860BS/493BG Debach 13/9/44; 861BS; MIA Münster 5/10/44 w/Bisaro; flak, cr Ludenscheid, Ger; 2POW 7RTD; MACR 9576.

43-38547 Del Cheyenne 16/8/44; Lincoln 25/8/44; Grenier 10/9/44; ass 388BG Knettishall 13/9/44; tran 569BS/390BG Framlingham 14/9/44; MIA Hamburg 25/10/44 w/Bivins; flak, cr Münster; 6KIA 3POW; MACR 10261.

43-38548 Del Cheyenne 16/8/44; Lincoln 25/8/44; Grenier 12/9/44; ass 385BG Gt Ashfield 18/9/44; tran 546BS/384BG [BK-M] Grafton Underwood 27/9/44; sal 9AF Germany 10/12/45.

43-38549 Del Cheyenne 16/8/44; Lincoln 24/8/44; Grenier 12/9/44; ass 8AF 16/9/44; retUS Bradley 24/6/45; 4168 BU Sth Plains 27/6/45; RFC Kingman 24/11/45.

43-38550 Del Cheyenne 16/8/44; Lincoln 25/8/44; Grenier 11/9/44; ass 532BS/381BG [VE-A] Ridgewell 19/9/44; {27+m} RetUS Bradley 9/6/45; 4168 BU Sth Plains 14/6/45; RFC Kingman 3/1/46. DAISY MAE.

43-38551 Del Cheyenne 16/8/44; Lincoln 24/8/44; Grenier 11/9/44; ass 334BS/95BG [BG-L] Horham 13/9/44; MIA Cologne 7/1/45 w/Klein; mid air coll w/96BG B-17; cr Erfelfront, Ger?; 9KIA; MACR 11569.

43-38552 Del Cheyenne 16/8/44; Lincoln 26/8/44; Grenier 18/9/44; ass 561BS/388BG Knettishall 20/9/44; retUS Bradley 27/6/45; 4168 BU Sth Plains 2/7/45; RFC Kingman 29/11/45.

43-38553 Del Cheyenne 16/8/44; Topeka 28/8/44; Grenier 18/9/44; ass 548BS/385BG Gt Ashfield 20/9/44; retUS Bradley 25/6/45; 4168 BU Sth Plains 27/6/45; RFC Kingman 9/12/45.

43-38554 Del Cheyenne 16/8/44; Lincoln 26/8/44; Grenier 18/9/44; ass 358BS/303BG [VK-B] Molesworth 23/11/44; retUS Bradley 8/6/45; 4168 BU Sth Plains 12/6/45; RFC Kingman 20/12/45. BOUNCING BETTY III.

43-38555 Del Cheyenne 16/8/44; Lincoln 25/8/44; Grenier 18/9/44; ass 652REC/25BG Watton 24/9/44; sal 23/12/44.

43-38556 Del Cheyenne 17/8/44; Gt Falls 21/8/44; Wright Fd 31/8/44; ATS Wright 12/10/44; 4000 BU Wright 20/4/45; 4100 BU Newark 16/5/45; 4000 BU Wright 12/6/46; Recl Comp 2/8/46.

43-38557 Del Cheyenne 17/8/44; Lincoln 26/8/44; Grenier 18/9/44; ass 9AF HQ Sunninghill Park, Berks, UK 19/9/44; retUS 1103 BU Morrison 26/12/45; RFC Walnut Ridge 3/1/46.

43-38558 Del Cheyenne 17/8/44; Lincoln 27/8/44; Grenier 18/9/44; ass 561BS/388BG Knettishall 19/9/44; MIA Munich 25/2/45 w/Farley; flak, cr Nuremburg; 5KIA 4POW; MACR 12718.

43-38559 Del Cheyenne 17/8/44; Lincoln 26/8/44; Grenier 21/9/44; ass 8AF 25/9/44; retUS Bradley 24/6/45; 4168 BU Sth Plains 28/6/45; RFC Kingman 30/11/45.

43-38560 Del Cheyenne 17/8/44; Lincoln 6/9/44; Grenier 18/9/44; ass 15AF Italy 19/9/44; retUS Bradley 24/6/45; 4168 BU Sth Plains 27/6/45; RFC Kingman 20/12/45.

43-38561 Del Cheyenne 17/8/44; Lincoln 26/8/44; Grenier 18/9/44; ass 749BS/457BG Glatton 19/9/44; MIA Merseburg 2/11/44 w/Harrison; e/a, cr Nebra, Gwer; 2KIA 7POW; MACR 10321.

43-38562 Del Cheyenne 17/8/44; Lincoln 25/8/44; Grenier 18/9/44; ass 9AF HQ 19/9/44 Sunninghill, UK 24/9/44; tran 603BS/398BG [N7-L] Nuthampstead 17/1/45; MIA Oranienburg 15/3/45 w/Thomas; flak, cr Oranienburg; 1EVD 6KIA 2POW; MACR 13090. KITTY KAY - KATY.

43-38563 Del Cheyenne 18/8/44; Lincoln 27/8/44; Grenier 18/9/44; ass 360BS/303BG [PU-H] Molesworth 20/9/44; retUS Bradley 8/6/45; 4168 BU Sth Plains 14/6/45; RFC Kingman 14/12/45.

43-38564 Del Cheyenne 18/8/44; Topeka 30/8/44; Lincoln 6/9/44; Grenier 18/9/44; ass 600BS/398BG [N8-X] Nuthampstead 23/11/44; tran 457BG Glatton 26/5/45; retUS Bradley 7/6/45; 4168 BU Sth Plains 12/6/45; RFC Kingman 28/11/45.

43-38565 Del Cheyenne 18/8/44; Lincoln 6/9/44; Dow Fd 21/9/44; ass 614BS/401BG [IW-X] Deenethorpe 5/10/44; retUS Bradley 2/6/45; 4168 BU Sth Plains 6/6/45; RFC Kingman 20/12/45. MISS GEE EYEWANTA (GO HOME).

43-38566 Del Cheyenne 18/8/44; Lincoln 6/9/44; Grenier 24/9/44; ass 550BS/385BG Gt Ashfield 25/9/44; retUS Bradley 26/6/45; 4168 BU Sth Plains 28/6/45; RFC Kingman 5/12/45.

43-38567 Del Cheyenne 18/8/44; Lincoln 7/9/44; Grenier 18/9/44; ass 413BS/96BG [MZ-Q] Snetterton 25/9/44; tran 508BS/351BG [YB-G] Polebrook 6/10/44; b/d {26m} Koblenz 28/12/44 w/?; f/l Belgium; sal 5/1/45.

43-38568 Del Cheyenne 18/8/44; Hunter 27/8/44; Grenier 8/9/44; ass 860BS/493BG Debach 11/9/44; c/t/o for Nurnberg 20/2/45 w/?; cr River Deben at Ramsholt, UK; 8KIA 2RTD; sal. LITTLE DAVEY II.

43-38569 Del Cheyenne 18/8/44; Hunter 27/8/44; Dow Fd 10/9/44; ass 861BS/493BG Debach 13/9/44; b/d Cologne 15/10/44 w/?; f/l Continent; sal 31/10/44.

43-38570 Del Cheyenne 18/8/44; Hunter 25/8/44; Grenier 7/9/44; ass 407BS/92BG [PY-H] Podington 23/9/44; mission to Port Lyautey, Morr 7/6/45; ret 9/6/45; sal 9AF Germany 10/12/45.

43-38571 Del Cheyenne 18/8/44; Hunter 27/8/44; Grenier 6/9/44; ass 305BG Chelveston 7/12/44; sal 4/4/45.

43-38572 Del Cheyenne 18/8/44; Hunter 27/8/44; Grenier 6/9/44; ass 360BS/303BG Molesworth 26/9/44; MIA Magdeburg 28/9/44 w/Railing; e/a, cr Hornburg, Ger; 9KIA; MACR 9409.

43-38573 Del Cheyenne 18/8/44; Hunter 27/8/44; Grenier 7/9/44; ass 652BS/25BG Watton 24/9/44; retUS 1103 BU Morrison 29/10/45; RFC Walnut Ridge 7/1/46.

43-38574 Del Cheyenne 18/8/44; Hunter 27/8/44; Grenier 8/9/44; ass 407BS/92BG [PY-P] Podington 24/9/44; 326BS [JW-P]; sal 9AF Germany 31/5/46. RUSSIAN LULLABY.

43-38575 Del Cheyenne 20/8/44; Lincoln 7/9/44; Grenier 18/9/44; ass 850BS/490BG Eye 19/9/44; MIA Plauen, Ger 21/3/45 w/Bailard; jet e/a, cr Elsterwerda, Ger; 8KIA 1POW; MACR 13557.

43-38576 Del Cheyenne 20/8/44; Lincoln 7/9/44; Grenier 18/9/44; ass 413BS/96BG [MZ-Q] Snetterton 19/9/44; mid air coll w/43-38930; sal.

43-38577 Del Cheyenne 20/8/44; Hunter 27/8/44; Grenier 6/9/44; ass 338BS/96BG Snetterton 11/9/44; tran 379BG Kimbolton 23/9/44; retUS Bradley 3/7/45; 4168 BU Sth Plains 7/7/45; RFC Kingman 14/12/45.

43-38578 Del Cheyenne 20/8/44; Lincoln 7/9/44; Grenier 18/9/44; ass 561BS/388BG Knettishall 1/10/44; MIA Cologne 17/10/44 w/Resch; flak, cr Koblenz; 1KIA 8POW; MACR 9480.

43-38579 Del Cheyenne 20/8/44; Lincoln 1/9/44;

Grenier 11/9/44; ass 545BS/384BG [JD-F] Grafton Underwood 13/9/44; MIA Cologne 5/10/44 w/Birckhead; flak, cr München-Gladbach; 4KIA 5POW; MACR 9754. LITTLE REBEL.

43-38580 Del Cheyenne 20/8/44; Hunter 27/8/44; Grenier 7/9/44; ass 749BS/457BG Glatton 11/9/44; 748BS; b/d Cologne 15/10/44 w/?; sal. FLORY.

43-38581 Del Cheyenne 20/8/44; Lincoln 7/9/44; Grenier 18/9/44; ass 96BG Snetterton 19/9/44; b/d Ijmuiden, Hol 6/2/45 w/?; (first Disney op, using RN rocket bombs). Sal 10/2/45.

43-38582 Del Cheyenne 22/8/44; Lincoln 7/9/44; Grenier 19/9/44; ass 751BS/457BG Glatton 20/9/44; retUS Bradley 9/6/45; Memphis 20/9/45; Recl Comp 26/10/45. FLEDIA FAY.

43-38583 Del Cheyenne 22/8/44; Lincoln 7/9/44; Grenier 18/9/44; ass 360BS/303BG [PU-H] Molesworth 20/9/44; 748BS/457BG Glatton 21/9/44; MIA Sterkrade 22/1/45 w/Jellinek; flak, cr Westladbergen, Ger?; 9POW; MACR 11828. JACKIE.

43-38584 Del Cheyenne 22/8/44; Lincoln 1/9/44; Grenier 18/9/44; ass 336BS/95BG [ET-H] Horham 25/9/44; retUS Bradley 24/6/45; 4168 BU Sth Plains 26/6/45; RFC Kingman 30/11/45.

43-38585 Del Cheyenne 22/8/44; Lincoln 2/9/44; Grenier 8/9/44; ass 511BS/351BG [DS-K] Polebrook 21/9/44; b/d {32m} Neuss 31/12/44 w/?; c/l base; sal.

43-38586 Del Cheyenne 22/8/44; Gt Falls 25/8/44; Cheyenne 26/8/44; Watertown 20/10/44; CWT Watertown 5/11/44; 2137 BU Hendricks 18/8/45; RFC Altus 21/11/45.

43-38587 Del Cheyenne 22/8/44; Lincoln 2/9/44; Grenier 11/9/44; ass 457BG Glatton 12/9/44; b/d Operation 'Varsity' 25/3/45 w/?; sal.

43-38588 Del Cheyenne 22/8/44; Lincoln 1/9/44; Grenier 11/9/44; ass 545BS/384BG [JD-F] Grafton Underwood 1/10/44; 546BS [BK-D]; sal 9AF Germany 10/12/45.

43-38589 Del Cheyenne 22/10/44; Topeka 1/9/44; Grenier 26/9/44; ass 838BS/487BG [2C-E] Lavenham 28/9/44; retUS Bradley 11/7/45; 4185 BU Independence 12/7/45; RFC Kingman 20/12/45.

43-38590 Del Cheyenne 22/8/44; Lincoln 1/9/44; Grenier 11/9/44; ass 410BS/94BG Rougham 17/9/44; tran 34BG Mendlesham 5/45; retUS Bradley 22/6/45; 4168 BU Sth Plains 24/6/44; RFC Kingman 19/12/45. HEAVENLY COMRADE.

43-38591 Del Cheyenne 22/8/44; Hunter 31/9/44; Grenier 15/9/44; ass 509BS/351BG [RQ-U] Polebrook 28/9/44; {52m} tran 384BG Grafton Underwood 23/5/45; sal 9AF Germany 10/12/45. MYASSIS DRAGGIN.

43-38592 Del Cheyenne 22/8/44; Lincoln 7/9/44; Grenier 17/9/44; ass 303BG Molesworth 20/9/44; tran 511BS/351BG [DS-N] Polebrook 18/10/44; 509BS [RQ-B]; {77m} RetUS Bradley 23/5/45; 4168 BU Sth Plains 26/5/45; RFC Kingman 27/11/45.

43-38593 Del Cheyenne 22/8/44; Lincoln 2/9/44; Grenier 7/9/44; ass 861BS/493BG Debach 8/9/44; b/d Chemnitz 6/2/45 w/?; f/l Oppeln, Ger; sal 21/2/45; MACR 12235.

43-38594 Del Cheyenne 22/8/44; Lincoln 7/9/44; Grenier 18/9/44; ass 749BS/457BG Glatton 19/9/44; retUS Bradley 10/6/45; 4168 BU Sth Plains 12/6/45; RFC Kingman 26/11/45. LADY B GOOD.

43-38595 Del Cheyenne 22/8/44; Lincoln 1/9/44; Grenier 11/9/44; ass 334BS/95BG [BG-B] Horham 13/9/44; MIA Cologne 17/10/44 w/McCulley; flak, cr Cologne; 1KIA 8POW; MACR 9471.

43-38596 Del Cheyenne 22/8/44; Lincoln 8/9/44; Grenier 22/9/44; ass 837BS/487BG Lavenham 6/10/44; 836BS [2G-G]; MIA Nurnberg 20/2/45 w/McCullough; flak, cr Rosthenbach, Ger; 5KIA 5POW; MACR 12550.

43-38597 Del Cheyenne 22/8/44; Lincoln 8/9/44; Grenier 18/9/44; ass 549BS/385BG Gt Ashfield 20/9/44; c/l ex-Chemnitz 6/2/45; sal; retUS Bradley 25/6/45; 4168 BU Sth Plains 27/6/45; RFC Kingman 5/12/45.

43-38598 Del Cheyenne 22/8/44; Hunter 31/8/44; Dow Fd 20/9/44; ass 839BS/487BG [R5-U] Lavenham 6/10/44; retUS Bradley 12/7/45; 4185 BU Independence 14/7/45; RFC Kingman 18/12/45.

43-38599 Del Cheyenne 22/8/44; Hunter 31/8/44; Dow Fd 10/9/44; ass 860BS/493BG Debach 13/9/44; caught fire 22/4/45; sal 25/4/45.

43-38600 Del Cheyenne 23/8/44; Lincoln 2/9/44; Grenier 6/9/44; ass 568BS/390BG [BI-S] Framlingham 8/9/44; b/d Berlin 18/3/45 w/Berryman; flak, cr Grodzisk, Russian territory; 4KIA 1POW 4TRD; sal 30/3/45; MACR 13138. NO NAME JIVE.

43-38601 Del Cheyenne 23/8/44; Hunter 3/9/44; Grenier 15/9/44; ass 94BG Rougham 25/9/44; tran 325BS/92BG [NV-O] Horham 4/10/44; sal 9AF Germany 10/12/45.

43-38602 Del Cheyenne 23/8/44; Lincoln 1/9/44; Grenier 11/9/44; ass 482BG Alconbury 13/9/44; tran 349BS/100BG [XR-P] Thorpe Abbotts 14/9/44; retUS Bradley 2/6/45; 4168 BU Sth Plains 12/6/45; RFC Kingman 29/11/45. GRUMBLIN' GREMLIN II.

43-38603 Del Cheyenne 23/8/44; Hunter 6/9/44; Grenier 28/9/44; ass 850BS/490BG Eye 13/10/44; retUS Bradley 13/7/45; 4185 BU Independence 17/7/45; RFC Kingman 25/12/45.

43-38604 Del Cheyenne 23/8/44; Lincoln 3/9/44; Grenier 11/9/44; ass 359BS/303BG [BN-H] Molesworth 24/9/44; MIA Cologne 15/10/44 w/Gaines; flak, cr Cologne; 6KIA 3POW; MACR 9472.

43-38605 Del Cheyenne 23/8/44; Hunter 2/9/44; Dow Fd 10/9/44; ass 388BG Knettishall 13/9/44; retUS Bradley 5/7/45; 4168 BU Sth Plains 8/7/45; RFC Kingman 26/11/45.

43-38606 Del Cheyenne 23/8/44; Lincoln 4/9/44; Grenier 17/9/44; ass 748BS/457BG Glatton 18/9/44; MIA Oranienburg 10/4/45 w/Thompson; jet e/a, cr Genthin, Ger; 4KIA 5POW; MACR 13912. MOONLIGHT MISSION.

43-38607 Del Cheyenne 23/8/44; Hunter 7/9/44; Dow Fd 18/9/44; ass 613BS/401BG [IN-H] Deenethorpe 5/10/44; MIA Berlin 18/3/45 w/Vermeer; jet e/a, cr Berlin; 4KIA 5POW; MACR 13137. Lady JANE.

43-38608 Del Cheyenne 23/8/44; Lincoln 2/9/44; Grenier 6/9/44; ass 94BG Rougham 8/9/44; tran 359BS/303BG [BN-E] Molesworth 23/10/44; 360BS [PU-C]; 457BG Glatton 26/5/45; retUS Bradley 9/6/45; 4168 BU Sth Plains 12/6/45; RFC Kingman 30/11/45. LUCILLE.

43-38609 Del Cheyenne 23/8/44; Hunter 2/9/44; Dow Fd 10/9/44; ass 359BS/303BG [BN-F] Molesworth 13/9/44; retUS Bradley 7/6/45; 4168 BU Sth Plains 10/7/45; RFC Kingman 19/11/45.

43-38610 Del Cheyenne 23/8/44; Hunter 7/9/44; Grenier 16/9/44; ass 351BS/100BG [EP-T] Thorpe Abbotts 17/9/44; damaged by debris from exploding 43-37517 on base 31/1/45; sal 2/2/45.

43-38611 Del Cheyenne 24/8/44; Lincoln 3/9/44; Grenier 12/9/44; ass 326BS/95BG [JW-J] Horham 21/9/44; MIA Merseburg 30/11/44 w/Smith; flak, cr Merseburg; 2KIA 7POW; MACR 11042. UMBRIAGO.

43-38612 Del Cheyenne 24/8/44; Gt Falls 29/8/44; Hunter 7/9/44; Grenier 15/9/44; ass 549BS/385BG Gt Ashfield 19/9/44; MIA Merseburg 6/12/44 w/Hufford; flak, cr Nordoellen, Hol?; 9POW; MACR 11056. LIL-LU.

43-38613 Del Cheyenne 24/8/44; Hunter 3/9/44; Grenier 12/9/44; ass 569BS/390BG [CC-H] Framlingham 13/9/44; tran 493BG Debach 14/9/44; 360BS/303BG [PU-A] Molesworth 15/9/44; retUS Bradley 3/7/45; 4168 BU Sth Plains 5/7/45; RFC Kingman 18/12/45. YARDBIRD.

43-38614 Del Cheyenne 24/8/44; Hunter 4/9/44; Grenier 15/9/44; ass 730BS/452BG Deopham Green 19/9/44; retUS Bradley 28/6/45; 4168 BU Sth Plains 30/6/45; RFC Kingman 8/12/45. UTAH GAL.

43-38615 Del Cheyenne 24/8/44; Hunter 3/9/44; Dow Fd 12/9/44; ass 547BS/384BG [SO-D] Grafton Underwood 23/9/44; 544BS [SU-D]; sal 14/11/44.

43-38616 Del Cheyenne 24/8/44; Hunter 4/9/44; Grenier 15/9/44; ass 546BS/384BG [BK-K] Grafton Underwood 27/9/44; c/t/o for Cologne 10/1/45 w/?; sal.

43-38617 Del Cheyenne 24/8/44; Hunter 7/9/44; Dow Fd 18/9/44; ass 336BS/95BG [ET-Q] Horham 19/9/44; retUS Bradley 24/6/45; 4168 BU Sth Plains 28/6/45; RFC Kingman 24/11/45.

43-38618 Del Cheyenne 24/8/44; Patterson 11/9/44; Hunter 28/9/44; Grenier 2/10/44; ass 493BG Debach 6/10/44; retUS Bradley 6/7/45; 4168 BU Sth Plains 8/7/45; RFC Kingman 26/11/45.

43-38619 Del Cheyenne 25/8/44; Patterson 10/9/44; Hunter 29/9/44; Dow Fd 9/10/44; ass 338BS/96BG [BX-L] Snetterton 14/10/44; tran 359BS/303BG [BN-A] Molesworth 15/10/44; b/d Dresden 14/2/45 w/?; f/l Continent; sal 13/3/45.

43-38620 Del Cheyenne 25/8/44; Hunter 3/9/44; Dow Fd 10/9/44; ass 601BS/398BG [3O-F] Nuthampstead 17/10/44; retUS Bradley 7/6/45; 4168 BU Sth Plains 14/6/45; RFC Kingman 2/12/45.

43-38621 Del Cheyenne 25/8/44; Patterson 8/9/44; Hunter 16/9/44; Grenier 25/9/44; ass 427BS/303BG [GN-E] Molesworth 3/10/44; tran 457BG Glatton 22/5/45; 351BG Polebrook 29/5/45; retUS Bradley 13/6/45; 4168 BU Sth Plains 18/6/45; RFC Kingman 21/11/45. SO RAGGED.

43-38622 Del Cheyenne 25/8/44; Hunter 4/9/44; Grenier 15/9/44; ass 710BS/447BG Rattlesden 17/9/44; retUS Bradley 5/7/45; 4168 BU Sth Plains 7/7/45; RFC Kingman 21/11/45.

43-38623 Del Cheyenne 25/8/44; Patterson 7/9/44; Hunter 15/9/44; Grenier 23/9/44; ass 561BS/388BG Knettishall 20/10/44; MIA Frankfurt 17/2/45 w/Taylor; flak, cr Wiesbaden; 10KIA; MACR 12432. EASY DOES IT.

43-38624 Del Cheyenne 25/8/44; Hunter 17/9/44; Dow Fd 25/9/44; ass 327BS/92BG [UX-W] Podington 6/10/44; secret mission 1/6/45, ret 2/6/45; sal 9AF Germany 31/5/46.

43-38625 Del Cheyenne 25/8/44; Hunter 20/9/44; Grenier 26/9/44; ass 551BS/385BG Gt Ashfield 29/9/44; retUS Bradley 27/6/45; 4168 BU Sth Plains 29/6/45; RFC Kingman 14/12/45. OLE DOODLE BUG!

43-38626 Del Cheyenne 25/8/44; Hunter 20/9/44; Grenier 27/9/44; ass 482BG Alconbury 1/10/44; retUS, RFC Walnut Ridge 8/1/46.

43-38627 Del Cheyenne 25/8/44; Hunter 20/9/44; Dow Fd 25/9/44; ass 602BS/398BG [K8-Z] Nuthampstead 17/10/44; retUS Bradley 7/6/45; 4168 BU Sth Plains 10/6/45; RFC Kingman 10/12/45.

43-38628 Del Cheyenne 25/8/44; Hunter 15/9/44; Dow Fd 15/10/44; ass 339BS/96BG [QJ-A] Snetterton 17/10/44; tran 401BG Deenethorpe 8/1/45; b/d

Plauen 19/3/45 w/?; f/l Continent, sal; retUS Bradley 21/5/45; 4168 BU Sth Plains 2/6/45; RFC Kingman 18/12/45.

43-38629 Del Cheyenne 27/8/44; Patterson 8/9/44; Hunter 18/9/44; Dow Fd 25/9/44; ass 860BS/493BG Debach 28/9/44; retUS Bradley 5/7/45; 4168 BU Sth Plains 7/7/45; RFC Kingman 24/11/45.

43-38630 Del Cheyenne 27/8/44; Hunter 17/9/44; Grenier 27/8/44; ass 547BS/384BG [SO-G] Grafton Underwood 7/10/44; sal 13/6/45.

43-38631 Del Cheyenne 27/8/44; Patterson 10/9/44; Lincoln 13/9/44; Grenier 27/9/44; ass 603BS/398BG [N7-T] Nuthampstead 23/11/44; retUS Bradley 31/5/45; 4168 BU Sth Plains 6/6/45; RFC Kingman 19/12/45. TONDELAYO.

43-38632 Del Cheyenne 27/8/44; Hunter 7/9/44; Grenier 15/9/44; ass 568BS/390BG [BI-T] Framlingham 17/9/44; MIA Hamburg 31/12/44 w/Nash; flak, cr Neuendorf, Ger; KIA 7POW; MACR 11245. FREE DELIVERY.

43-38633 Del Cheyenne 27/8/44; Hunter 17/9/44; Dow Fd 25/9/44; ass 527BS/379BG [FO-F] Kimbolton 2/1/45; b/d Cologne 28/1/45 w/?; c/l Woodbridge ALG, UK w/pilot only, rest of crew baled over enemy territory; sal.

43-38634 Del Cheyenne 27/8/44; Patterson 10/9/44; Hunter 30/9/44; Grenier 8/10/44; ass 490BG Eye 14/10/44; retUS Bradley 9/7/45; 4168 BU Sth Plains 11/7/45; RFC Kingman 7/12/45.

43-38635 Del Cheyenne 27/8/44; Hunter 19/9/44; Grenier 26/9/44; ass?; restored as VIRGIN'S DELITE at Castle AF Museum, Cal 1989 to at least 1995.

43-38636 Del Cheyenne 27/8/44; Hunter 19/9/44; Grenier 26/9/44; ass 410BS/94BG [GL-J] Rougham 1/10/44; b/d Cologne 10/1/45 w/?; f/l Continent; sal 18/1/45.

43-38637 Del Cheyenne 27/8/44; Hunter 16/9/44; Grenier 24/9/44; ass 612BS/401BG [SC-L] Deenethorpe 5/10/44; retUS Bradley 7/6/45; 4168 BU Sth Plains 13/6/45; RFC Kingman 30/11/45.

43-38638 Del Cheyenne 27/8/44; Patterson 10/9/44; Hunter 30/9/44; Dow Fd 15/10/44; ass 305BG Chelveston 5/12/44; tran 351BG Polebrook 23/5/45; retUS Bradley 12/6/45; 4168 BU Sth Plains 18/6/45; RFC Kingman 25/11/45.

43-38639 Del Cheyenne 28/8/44; Patterson 8/9/44; Hunter 20/9/44; Grenier 26/9/44; ass 548BS/385BG Gt Ashfield 1/10/44; MIA Kiel 4/4/45 w/Capt Crimmins; mid air coll w/385BG B-17, cr Nth Sea; 9KIA; MACR 13722.

43-38640 Del Cheyenne 28/8/44; Lincoln 13/9/44; Grenier 30/9/44; ass 509BS/351BG [RQ-C] Polebrook 16/10/44; {70m} RetUS Bradley 3/7/45; 4168 BU Sth Plains 5/7/45; RFC Kingman 9/12/45. ANNIE MARIE.

43-38641 Del Cheyenne 28/8/44; Hunter 17/9/44; Dow Fd 25/9/44; ass 96BG Snetterton 27/9/44; retUS Bradley 28/6/45; 4168 BU Sth Plains 30/6/45; RFC Kingman 27/11/45.

43-38642 Del Cheyenne 28/8/44; Patterson 19/9/44; Hunter 29/9/44; Dow Fd 7/10/44; ass 323BS/91BG Bassingbourn 4/11/44; b/d flak {15m} Wittlich 29/12/44 w/Shambaugh; pilot f/l Nazons, Fr; crew baled OK; sal 21/1/45. SUPER MOUSE.

43-38643 Del Cheyenne 28/8/44; Patterson 8/9/44; Hunter 20/9/44; Grenier 26/9/44; ass 569BS/390BG [CC-K] Framlingham 28/9/44; retUS Bradley 30/8/45; 4185 BU Independence 3/9/45; RFC Kingman 27/12/45.

43-38644 Del Cheyenne 30/8/44; Hunter 15/9/44; Grenier 22/9/44; ass 338BS/96BG [BX-A] Snetterton 23/9/44; MIA Berlin 5/12/44 w/David; flak, cr Parchim, Ger; 10POW; MACR 11343. GREEN WEENIE.

43-38645 Del Cheyenne 30/8/44; Patterson 11/9/44; Hunter 30/9/44; Grenier 8/10/44; ass 359BS/303BG [BN-B] Molesworth 22/11/44; retUS Bradley 7/6/45; 4168 BU Sth Plains 12/6/45; RFC Kingman 1/12/45.

43-38646 Del Cheyenne 30/8/44; Hunter 19/9/44; Dow Fd 25/9/44; ass 614BS/401BG [IW-Y] Deenethorpe 7/10/44; MIA Rosenheim 18/4/45 w/Viehman; flak, cr Krallsheim, Ger; 10POW; MACR 14175.

43-38647 Del Cheyenne 30/8/44; Patterson 7/9/44; Hunter 27/9/44; Grenier 8/10/44; ass 547BS/384BG [SO-D] Grafton Underwood 19/1/45; sal 9AF Germany 10/12/45.

43-38648 Del Cheyenne 29/8/44; Patterson 11/9/44; Hunter 29/9/44; Grenier 7/10/44; ass 835BS/486BG [H8-H] Sudbury 14/10/44; MIA Bremen 25/2/45 w/Wiley; flak, cr Sonthofen, Ger; 9POW; MACR 12578.

43-38649 Del Cheyenne 29/8/44; Gt Falls 1/9/44; Cheyenne 3/9/44 mod as F-9C; 91 Ph Gp Buckley 26/10/44; 19 Ph Sq Buckley 29/11/44; 91 RLP Howard 18/1/45; 91 RLP Waller 18/7/45; 91 RLP McGuire 9/2/49; 91 SRG Gp Barksdale 30/9/49; 91 SRG Gp McGuire 11/10/49; Recl Comp 8/11/49.

43-38650 Del Cheyenne 29/8/44; Patterson 10/9/44; Hunter 20/9/44; Grenier 30/9/44; ass 511BS/351BG [DS-M] Polebrook 7/10/44; b/d {38m} Dresden 14/2/45 w/?; f/l France; sal 20/2/45. MERRIE CHRISTIE.

43-38651 Del Cheyenne 29/8/44; Gt Falls 2/9/44; Cheyenne 3/9/44 mod as F-9C; 91 Ph Gp Buckley 29/10/44; Dallas 16/5/45; Bangor 3/6/45; 108 BS Oberpfaffenhofen as RB-17G 18/1/46; 7290 Oberpfaffenhofen 18/10/46; Recl Comp 3/8/49.

43-38652 Del Cheyenne 29/8/44; Hunter 10/9/44; Grenier 25/9/44; ass 602BS/398BG [K8-V] Nuthampstead 4/10/44; MIA Pilsen 25/4/45 w/Colville; 1KIA 7RTD; MACR 14220. STINKY jR.

43-38653 Del Cheyenne 29/8/44; Gt Falls 2/9/44; Chcyonno 3/9/44 mod as F-9C; 91 Ph Gp Buckley 30/10/44; Dallas 16/5/45; Bangor 1/6/45; 108 BS Oberpfaffenhofen 18/1/46; 7290 Oberpfaffenhofen 18/7/46; Recl Comp 11/2/49.

43-38654 Del Cheyenne 30/8/44; Lincoln 3/9/44; Grenier 12/9/44; ass 379BG Kimbolton 26/9/44; tran 836BS/487BG Lavenham 22/5/45; retUS Bradley 11/7/45; 4185 BU Independence 12/7/45; RFC Kingman 21/12/45.

43-38655 Del Lincoln 30/8/44; Gt Falls 1/9/44; Lincoln 3/9/44; Grenier 11/9/44; ass 561BS/388BG Knettishall 13/9/44; retUS Bradley 27/6/45; 4168 BU Sth Plains 1/7/45; RFC Kingman 13/12/45.

43-38656 Del Lincoln 30/8/44; Grenier 11/9/44; ass 8AF 24/9/44; RFC Walnut Ridge 9/1/46.

43-38657 Del Cheyenne 30/8/44; Lincoln 4/9/44; Grenier 18/9/44; ass 412BS/95BG [QW-V] Horham 19/9/44; retUS Bradley 21/6/45; 4168 BU Sth Plains 23/6/45; RFC Kingman 19/12/45. EVASIVE ACTION.

43-38658 Del Cheyenne 30/8/44; Lincoln 6/9/44; Grenier 18/9/44; ass 601BS/398BG [3O-A] Nuthampstead 3/10/44; b/d Neumünster 13/4/45 w/?; f/l Continent, sal.

43-38659 Del Cheyenne 30/8/44; Lincoln 4/9/44; Grenier 18/9/44; ass 338BS/96BG [BX-N] Snetterton 19/9/44; MIA Mannheim 21/4/45 w/Oelker; flak, cr Hockenheim, Ger; 7KIA 2MIA; MACR 11757. MAMMY YOKUM.

43-38660 Del Cheyenne 30/8/44; Lincoln 4/9/44; Grenier 18/9/44; ass 334BS/95BG [BG-W] Horham 19/9/44; 335BS [OE-W]; MIA Mannheim 20/1/45 w/Conover; cr Hirtzfeldon, Ger; 4KIA 6POW; MACR 11755.

43-38661 Del Cheyenne 30/8/44; Lincoln 4/9/44; Grenier 11/9/44; ass 601BS/398BG [3O-P] Nuthampstead 18/10/44; retUS Bradley 7/6/45; 4168 BU Sth Plains 12/6/45; RFC Kingman 13/12/45.

43-38662 Del Cheyenne 30/8/44; Lincoln 4/9/44; Grenier 18/9/44; ass 332BS/94BG Rougham 19/9/44; MIA Oranienburg 15/3/45 w/Thorndyke; flak, cr Gransee, Ger; 4KIA 6POW; MACR 13028.

43-38663 Del Cheyenne 30/8/44; Lincoln 4/9/44; Grenier 18/9/44; ass 569BS/390BG [CC-M] Framlingham 19/9/44; retUS Bradley 30/6/45; 4168 BU Sth Plains 4/7/45; RFC Kingman 8/12/45. THE GREAT McGINTY.

43-38664 Del Cheyenne 30/8/44; Lincoln 4/9/44; Grenier 18/9/44; ass 602BS/398BG [K8-P] Nuthampstead 18/10/44; MIA Frieham 11/4/45 w/Shirk; mech fault, cr Muhldorf, Ger; 3KIA 7POW; MACR 13868.

43-38665 Del Cheyenne 30/8/44; Hunter 4/9/44; Grenier 15/9/44; ass 571BS/390BG Framlingham 19/9/44; MIA Derben 14/1/45 w/Hanneke; e/a, cr Bartschendorf, Ger; 9KIA 1POW; MACR 11723.

43-38666 Del Cheyenne 30/8/44; Hunter 9/9/44; Dow Fd 20/9/44; ass 385BG Gt Ashfield 25/9/44; tran 509BS/351BS [RQ-T] Polebrook 6/10/44; 508BS [YB-H]; {48m} RetUS Bradley 12/6/45; 4168 BU Sth Plains 18/6/45; RFC Kingman 26/11/45.

43-38667 Del Cheyenne 30/8/44; Hunter 18/9/44; Grenier 27/9/44; ass 551BS/385BG Gt Ashfield 1/10/44; 335BS/95BG [OE-L] Horham 1/10/44; retUS Bradley 24/6/45; 4168 BU Sth Plains 28/6/45; RFC Kingman 13/12/45.

43-38668 Del Cheyenne 31/8/44; Hunter 5/9/44; Grenier 15/9/44; ass 568BS/390BG Framlingham 25/9/44; MIA Cologne 10/1/45 w/Skinner; flak, cr Düsseldorf; 5KIA 4POW; MACR 11580.

43-38669 Del Cheyenne 31/8/44; Hunter 3/9/44; Dow Fd 18/9/44; ass 603BS/398BG [N7-G] Nuthampstead 23/11/44; retUS Bradley 8/6/45; 4168 BU Sth Plains 7/7/45; RFC Kingman 18/12/45.

43-38670 Del Cheyenne 31/8/44; Hunter 5/9/44; Grenier 15/9/44; ass 601BS/398BG [3O-W] Nuthampstead 28/9/44; MIA Merseburg 2/11/44 w/Campbell; e/a, cr Merseburg; 1KIA 8POW; MACR 10156.

43-38671 Del Cheyenne 31/8/44; Hunter 4/9/44; Grenier 15/9/44; ass 603BS/398BG [N7-P] Nuthampstead 4/11/44; MIA Merseburg 21/11/44 w/Lehmer; e/a, cr Zimmernsupra, Ger?; 4KIA 5POW; MACR 11211.

43-38672 Del Cheyenne 31/8/44; Hunter 7/9/44; Grenier 15/9/44; ass 94BG Rougham 17/9/44; tran 360BS/303BG [PU-I] Molesworth 28/9/44; retUS Bradley 7/6/45; 4168 BU Sth Plains 12/6/45; RFC Kingman 26/11/45.

43-38673 Del Cheyenne 31/8/44; Hunter 5/9/44; Grenier 15/9/44; ass 545BS/384BG [JD-L] Grafton Underwood 28/10/44; sal 4/10/45.

43-38674 Del Cheyenne 31/8/44; Hunter 7/9/44; Dow Fd 20/9/44; ass 423BS/306BG Thurleigh 3/10/44; MIA Lutzkendorf 9/2/45 w/?.

43-38675 Del Cheyenne 1/9/44; Hunter 19/9/44; Grenier 24/9/44; ass 92BG Podington 1/10/44; mid air col w/44-6584 3/3/45 w/?; cr nr Brussels, Bel. 9KIA; sal 9/3/45.

43-38676 Del Cheyenne 1/9/44; Hunter 20/9/44; Dow Fd 25/9/44; ass 336BS/95BG [ET-V] Horham 28/9/44; retUS Bradley 21/6/45; 4168 BU Sth Plains 23/6/45; RFC Kingman 19/12/45.

Above: B-17G-90-BO 43-38663, illustrating the survivability of the Fortress. A main fuel cell was ignited by enemy fire, the flames trailing back to burn the elevator fabric. Despite this severe damage weakening the wing structure, the fire was extinguished and the aircraft landed safely. At the time of this incident, January 1945, radio compartment guns were no longer installed. (USAAF)

43-38677 Del Cheyenne 1/9/44; Hunter 20/9/44; Grenier 28/9/44; ass 614BS/401BG [IW-K] Deenethorpe 11/10/44; retUS Bradley 7/6/45; 4168 BU Sth Plains 13/6/45; 237 BU Kirtland 31/12/45; RFC Albuquerque 6/2/46.

43-38678 Del Cheyenne 1/9/44; Hunter 20/9/44; Grenier 28/9/44; ass 92BG Podington 1/10/44; tran 545BS/384BG [JD-F] Grafton Underwood 7/10/44; b/d Bordeaux 14/4/45 w/?; f/l Continent; sal.

43-38679 Del Cheyenne 1/9/44; Hunter 19/9/44; Dow Fd 25/9/44; ass 379BG Kimbolton 28/10/44; retUS Bradley 13/7/45; 4185 BU Independence 19/7/45; 4136 BU Tinker 31/12/45; RFC Kingman 11/1/46.

43-38680 Del Cheyenne 1/9/44; Hunter 28/9/44; Grenier 3/10/44; ass 612BS/401BG [SC-S] Deenethorpe 7/11/44; retUS Bradley 4/6/45; 4168 BU Sth Plains 8/6/45; RFC Kingman 6/11/45. HONEY PIE.

43-38681 Del Cheyenne 1/9/44; Hunter 8/9/44; Grenier 23/9/44; ass 349BS/100BG [XR-V] Thorpe Abbotts 26/9/44; c/l 14/5/45, sal.

43-38682 Del Cheyenne 1/9/44; Gt Falls 6/9/44; Hunter 29/9/44; ass 359BS/303BG [BN-K] Molesworth 22/11/44; tran 457BG Glatton 22/5/45; retUS Bradley 8/6/45; 4168 BU Sth Plains 14/6/45; RFC Kingman 5/12/45.

43-38683 Del Cheyenne 3/9/44; Hunter 16/9/44; Grenier 25/9/44; ass 367BS/306BG [GY-Q] Thurleigh 3/10/44; tran 381BG Ridgewell 5/45; retUS Bradley 9/6/45; 4168 BU Sth Plains 12/6/45; RFC Kingman 28/11/45.

43-38684 Del Fairfield 3/9/44; Hunter 19/9/44; Grenier 25/9/44; ass 326BS/92BG [JW-L] Podington 4/10/44; tran 384BG Grafton Underwood 1/6/45; sal 9AF Germany 29/12/45.

43-38685 Del Cheyenne 3/9/44; Hunter 17/9/44; Grenier 25/9/44; ass 526BS/379BG [LF-O] Kimbolton 4/10/44; MIA Rheine A/fds on Operation 'Varsity' 24/3/45 w/?; MACR 14112.

43-38686 Del Cheyenne 3/9/44; Hunter 28/9/44; Grenier 9/10/44; ass 482BG Alconbury 10/10/44; tran 338BS/96BG [BX-P] Snetterton 11/10/44; retUS Bradley 12/6/45; 4168 BU Sth Plains 15/6/45; RFC Kingman 19/12/45.

43-38687 Del Cheyenne 3/9/44; Hunter 17/9/44; Grenier 25/9/44; ass 848BS/490BG Eye 27/9/44; b/d Darmstadt 24/12/44 w/?; f/l Lewines, Fr?; sal 23/1/45.

43-38688 Del Patterson 3/9/44; Hunter 20/9/44; Dow Fd 25/9/44; ass 332BS/94BG [XM-E] Rougham 29/9/44; MIA Munich 8/4/45 w/Rogers; flak, cr Hof, Ger; 2KIA 6POW; MACR 13880.

43-38689 Del Fairfield 4/9/44; Hunter 25/9/44; Grenier 3/10/44; ass 601BS/398BG Nuthampstead 11/10/44; tran 427BS/303BG [GN-A] Molesworth 28/10/44; MIA Germersheim 13/1/45 w/Eisenhart; flak, cr Roxheim, Ger; 9KIA; MACR 11574.

43-38690 Del Patterson 5/9/44; Lincoln 12/9/44; Dow Fd 2/10/44; ass 369BS/306BG Thurleigh 6/11/44; 368BS [BO-M]; MIA Kassel 1/1/45 w/Stewart; flak, cr Nth Sea; 9KIA; MACR 11249.

43-38691 Del Patterson 5/9/44; Hunter 20/9/44; Grenier 28/9/44; ass 303BG Molesworth 1/10/44; tran 511BS/351BG [DS-B] Polebrook 9/10/44; 509BS [RQ-M]; {27m} RetUS Bradley 9/6/45; 4168 BU Sth Plains 14/6/45; RFC Kingman 7/12/45.

43-38692 Del Patterson 5/9/44; Lincoln 12/9/44; Grenier 18/9/44; ass 560BS/388BG Knettishall 25/9/44; retUS Bradley 30/6/45; 4168 BU Sth Plains 3/7/45; RFC Kingman 18/12/45.

43-38693 Del Patterson 4/9/44; Hunter 15/9/44; Grenier 23/9/44; ass 322BS/91BG [LG-C] Bassingbourn 4/11/44; MIA Berlin 5/12/44 w/Mitchell; flak, cr Talge-Wilsten, Ger; 4KIA 5POW; MACR 11333.

43-38694 Del Patterson 4/9/44; Hunter 19/9/44; Grenier 30/9/44; ass 511BS/351BG [DS-C] Polebrook 9/10/44; 510BS [TU-D]; {53m} RetUS Bradley 12/6/45; 4168 BU Sth Plains 15/6/45; RFC Kingman 4/12/45. BIGAS BIRD.

43-38695 Del Patterson 5/9/44; Hunter 29/9/44; Grenier 7/10/44; ass 524BS/379BG [WA-Q] Kimbolton 13/11/44; retUS Bradley 3/7/45; 4168 BU Sth Plains 6/7/45; RFC Kingman 20/12/45.

43-38696 Del Patterson 5/9/44; Hunter 20/9/44; Grenier 28/9/44; ass 447BG Rattlesden 30/9/44; tran 730BS/452BG Deopham Green 1/10/44; during assembly for Hannover w/? 26/10/44, mid air coll w/43-37906; cr Caston, UK; 8KIA 1WIA; sal.

43-38697 Del Patterson 5/9/44; Hunter 19/9/44; Dow Fd 25/9/44; ass 603BS/398BG [N7-M] Nuthampstead 4/11/44; MIA Berlin 3/2/45 w/Powell; mid air coll w/42-97387; cr Gardelegen, Ger; 8KIA 1POW; MACR 12215.

43-38698 Del Patterson 5/9/44; Lincoln 12/9/44; Grenier 18/9/44; ass 731BS/452BG Deopham Green 20/9/44; MIA Hamm 16/2/45 w/Payne; flak, cr Sundern, Ger; 9POW; MACR 12447.

43-38699 Del Patterson 5/9/44; Hunter 29/9/44; Dow Fd 7/10/44; ass 490BG Eye 14/10/44; MIA Chemnitz 6/2/45 w/?; mid air coll w/43-38167; cr Continent; sal 2/3/45; MACR 12426.

43-38700 Del Patterson 5/9/44; Hunter 20/9/44; Dow Fd 25/9/44; ass 549BS/385BG Gt Ashfield 28/9/44; retUS Bradley 26/6/45; 4168 BU Sth Plains 29/6/45; RFC Kingman 19/11/45.

43-38701 Del Gt Falls 9/9/44; Hunter 29/9/44; Dow Fd 15/10/44; ass 850BS/490BG Eye 19/10/44; MIA Pirna, Ger 19/4/45 w/Snyder; jet e/a, cr Schonau, Ger; 10KIA; MACR 14192.

43-38702 Del Gt Falls 9/9/44; Hunter 15/9/44; Grenier 23/9/44; ass 728BS/452BG Deopham Green 25/9/44; retUS Bradley 3/7/45; 4168 BU Sth Plains 6/7/45; RFC Kingman 7/12/45.

43-38703 Del Gt Falls 6/9/44; Hunter 29/9/44; Grenier 16/10/44; ass 482BG Alconbury 17/10/44; retUS Bradley 30/5/45; 4168 BU Sth Plains 31/5/45; RFC Kingman 18/11/45.

43-38704 Del Gt Falls 6/9/44; Hunter 18/9/44; Grenier 25/9/44; ass 379BG Kimbolton 4/10/44; tran 836BS/487BG Lavenham 22/5/45; retUS Bradley 16/7/45; 4185 BU Independence 26/7/45; RFC Kingman 9/12/45.

43-38705 Del Gt Falls 6/9/44; Lincoln 13/9/44; Grenier 19/9/44; ass 360BS/303BG [PU-B] Molesworth 20/9/44; MIA Merseburg 21/11/44 w/Cureton; flak, cr Leipzig; 9KIA; MACR 11199.

43-38706 Del Gt Falls 9/9/44; Hunter 29/9/44; Dow Fd 15/10/44; ass 603BS/398BG [N7-V] Nuthampstead 9/2/45; b/d Zossen Army HQ 15/3/45 w/?; f/l Continent; sal 22/3/45.

43-38707 Del Gt Falls 7/9/44; Hunter 15/9/44; Grenier 27/9/44; ass 493BG Debach 28/9/44; tran 751BS/457BG Glatton 30/9/44; 750BS; retUS Bradley 9/6/45; 4168 BU Sth Plains 13/6/45; RFC Kingman 28/11/45.

43-38708 Del Gt Falls 7/9/44; Hunter 28/9/44; Grenier 7/10/44; ass 836BS/487BG [2G-T] Lavenham 17/10/44; tran 601BS/398BG [3O-T] Nuthampstead 4/11/44; MIA Nuemünster 13/4/45 w/?; f/l Continent.

43-38709 Del Gt Falls 7/9/44; Hunter 18/9/44; Grenier 27/9/44; ass 652BS/25BG Watton 27/9/44; retUS 1103 BU Morrison 29/10/45; RFC Walnut Ridge 8/1/46.

43-38710 Del Gt Falls 7/9/44; Hunter 4/10/44; Grenier 11/10/44; ass 570BS/390BG Framlingham 13/10/44; MIA Alhorn, Ger 22/3/45 w/Flotron; mech fault, cr Struschlingen, Ger; 1KIA 8POW; MACR 13614.

43-38711 Del Gt Falls 7/9/44; Hunter 28/9/44; Grenier 5/10/44; ass 368BS/306BG [BO-D] Thurleigh 17/10/44; tran 381BG Ridgewell 5/45; retUS Bradley 10/6/45; 4168 BU Sth Plains 14/6/45; RFC Kingman 28/11/45.

43-38712 Del Gt Falls 7/9/44; Hunter 18/9/44; Grenier

26/9/44; ass 710BS/447BG Rattlesden 28/9/44; retUS Bradley 5/7/45; 4168 BU Sth Plains 8/7/45; RFC Kingman 17/12/45. BUDDY BUDDY.

43-38713 Del Lincoln 8/9/44; Gt Falls 11/9/44; Lincoln 13/9/44; Dow Fd 25/9/44; ass 369BS/306BG [WW-K] Thurleigh 3/1/45; tran 92BG Podington 9/5/45; sal 9AF Germany 31/5/46.

43-38714 Del Lincoln 8/9/44; Dow Fd 7/10/44; ass 332BS/94BG [XM-G] Rougham 19/10/44; retUS Bradley 20/6/45; 4168 BU Sth Plains 23/6/45; RFC Kingman 4/12/45.

43-38715 Del Lincoln 8/9/44; Grenier 26/9/44; ass 563BS/388BG Knettishall 28/9/44; re-ass AF Oberpfaffenhofen 18/1/46; Recl Comp 7/1/49.

43-38716 Del Lincoln 8/9/44; Dow Fd 25/9/44; ass 96BG Snetterton 28/9/44; sal 9AF Germany 4/3/46; re-ass AF photos. Dutch-Belgian coast 16/12/47; 10 HBS Oberpfaffenhofen 18/1/48; Recl Comp 9/6/48.

43-38717 Del Lincoln 8/9/44; Grenier 26/9/44; ass 551BS/385BG Gt Ashfield 28/9/44; retUS Bradley 28/6/45; 4168 BU Sth Plains 30/6/45; RFC Kingman 10/12/45.

43-38718 Del Lincoln 8/9/44; Grenier 27/9/44; ass 8AF 30/9/44; retUS Bradley 9/7/45; 4168 BU Sth Plains 11/7/45; RFC Kingman 21/11/45.

43-38719 Del Lincoln 8/9/44; Dow Fd 25/9/44; ass 709BS/447BG Rattlesden 28/9/44; retUS Bradley 6/7/45; 4168 BU Sth Plains 8/7/45; RFC Kingman 17/12/45. THE BLUE HEN CHICK.

43-38720 Del Lincoln 10/12/44; Dow Fd 25/9/44; ass 385BG Gt Ashfield 1/10/44; tran 326BS/92BG [JW-K] Podington 11/10/44; secret mission 1/6/45, ret 2/6/45; sal 9/1/46. BUNNEY.

43-38721 Del Lincoln 12/9/44; Grenier 27/9/44; ass 545BS/384BG [JD-J] Grafton Underwood 28/10/44; taxi acc 24/1/45, sal.

43-38722 Del Lincoln 12/9/44; Grenier 26/9/44; ass 527BS/379BG [FO-M] Kimbolton 14/10/44; retUS Bradley 3/7/45; 4168 BU Sth Plains 6/7/45; RFC Kingman 8/12/45.

43-38723 Del Spokane 13/9/44; Lincoln 16/9/44; Grenier 27/9/44; ass 305BG Chelveston 17/10/44; tran 401BG Deenethorpe 20/5/45; retUS Bradley 7/6/45; 4168 BU Sth Plains 11/6/45; RFC Kingman 30/11/45.

43-38724 Del Lincoln 12/9/44; Dow Fd 25/9/44; ass 568BS/390BG [BI-Q] Framlingham 25/9/44; retUS Bradley 11/7/45; 4168 BU Sth Plains 12/7/45; RFC Kingman 19/11/45. "TARFU".

43-38725 Del Lincoln 12/9/44; Dow Fd 25/9/44; ass 708BS/447BG Rattlesden 28/9/44; MIA Merseburg 30/11/44 w/Buthe; flak, cr Leipzig; 6KIA 3POW; MACR 11149.

43-38726 Del Lincoln 13/9/44; Grenier 27/9/44; ass 8AF 30/9/44; retUS Bradley 8/7/45; 4168 BU Sth Plains 10/7/45; 237 BU Kirtland 25/12/45; RFC Albuquerque 7/2/46.

43-38727 Del Lincoln 13/9/44; Grenier 26/9/44; ass 410BS/94BG [GL-N] Rougham 28/9/44; MIA Ludwigshafen 5/11/44 w/Capt Haller; flak hit #2, cr Hameln, Ger; 4KIA (BTG chute failed) 5POW (3 died later); MACR 10306. THE CHARACTERS.

43-38728 Del Lincoln 21/9/44; Dow Fd 15/10/44; ass 851BS/490BG Eye 19/10/44; retUS Bradley 9/7/45; 4168 BU Sth Plains 11/7/45; RFC Kingman 9/11/45. £5 WITH BREAKFAST.

43-38729 Del Lincoln 13/9/44; Grenier 26/9/44; ass 490BG Eye 1/10/44; retUS Bradley 9/7/45; 4168 BU Sth Plains 12/7/45; RFC Kingman 23/11/45.

43-38730 Del Spokane 13/9/44; Lincoln 18/9/44; Grenier 27/9/44; ass 601BS/398BG [3O-R] Nuthampstead 10/10/44; rctUS Bradley 25/5/45;

4168 BU Sth Plains 30/5/45; RFC Kingman 24/11/45.

43-38731 Del Lincoln 13/9/44; Grenier 27/9/44; ass 711BS/447BG Rattlesden 1/10/44; MIA Oranienburg 15/3/45 w/Jesse; flak, cr Schonhausen, Ger; 8KIA 2POW; MACR 13044. BLYTHE SPIRIT.

43-38732 Del Lincoln 14/9/44; Grenier 27/9/44; ass 482BG Alconbury 1/10/44; 339BS/96BG [QJ-O] Snetterton 2/10/44; retUS Bradley 10/6/45; 4168 BU Sth Plains 13/6/45; RFC Kingman 28/11/45.

43-38733 Del Lincoln 13/9/44; Grenier 27/9/44; ass 612BS/401BG [SC-K] Deenethorpe 11/10/44; b/d on Operation 'Varsity' 25/3/45 w/?; sal. I'LL BE SEEING YOU.

43-38734 Del Lincoln 14/9/44; Dow Fd 6/10/44; ass 427BS/303BG [GN-C] Molesworth 22/11/44; tran 457BG Glatton 26/5/45; retUS Bradley 8/6/45; 4168 BU Sth Plains 12/6/45; RFC Kingman 30/11/45. CHESHIRE CAT.

43-38735 Del Lincoln 13/9/44; Grenier 26/9/44; ass 407BS/92BG [PY-K/D] Podington 11/10/44; MIA Dresden 14/2/45 w/Kelly; flak, cr Conderque, Bel; 8KIA 1POW; MACR 12354. FLAT TOP.

43-38736 Del Lincoln 14/9/44; Grenier 27/9/44; ass 548BS/385BG Gt Ashfield 1/10/44 MAIDEN AMERICA; retUS Bradley 24/6/45; 4168 BU Sth Plains 26/6/45; RFC Kingman 28/11/45. AMERICAN MAID.

43-38737 Del Lincoln 14/9/44; Grenier 26/9/44; ass 305BG Chelveston 17/10/44; retUS Bradley 7/6/45; 4168 BU Sth Plains 12/6/45; RFC Kingman 10/1/46.

43-38738 Del Spokane 13/9/44; Lincoln 18/9/44; Grenier 27/9/44; ass 614BS/401BG [IW-N] Deenethorpe 11/11/44; retUS Bradley 4/6/45; 4168 BU Sth Plains 7/6/45; RFC Kingman 13/12/45. BECOMING BACK.

43-38739 Del Lincoln 14/9/44; Grenier 27/9/44; ass 493BG Debach 1/10/44; b/d Merseburg 30/11/44 w/?; sal 22/12/44.

43-38740 Del Lincoln 14/9/44; Grenier 22/9/44; ass 390BG Framlingham 23/9/44; tran 338BS/96BG [BX-W] Snetterton 24/9/44; retUS Bradley 1/6/45; 4168 BU Sth Plains 10/6/45; RFC Kingman 8/12/45. RAIN CHECK.

43-38741 Del Lincoln 13/9/44; Grenier 27/9/44; ass 332BS/94BG Rougham 1/10/44; 331BS [QE-G]; retUS Bradley 28/6/45; 4168 BU Sth Plains 30/6/45; RFC Kingman 5/12/45.

43-38742 Del Lincoln 14/9/44; Dow Fd 6/10/44; ass 324BS/91BG Bassingbourn 4/11/44; 322BG; MIA Zeitz 30/11/44 w/Stolz; flak, cr Zeitz; 8KIA 1POW; MACR 11044.

43-38743 Del Lincoln 16/9/44; Grenier 27/9/44; ass 550BS/385BG Gt Ashfield 1/10/44; retUS Bradley 25/6/45; 4168 BU Sth Plains 27/6/45; RFC Kingman 16/11/45.

43-38744 Del Lincoln 16/9/44; Grenier 30/9/44; ass 413BS/96BG [MZ-R] Snetterton 2/10/44; b/d Merseburg 30/11/44 w/?; c/l Eschweiler, Ger; sal 22/1/45.

43-38745 Del Lincoln 16/9/44; Grenier 27/9/44; ass 379BG Kimbolton 14/10/44; b/d Plauen 23/2/45 w/?; c/l Continent; sal.

43-38746 Del Lincoln 16/9/44; Dow Fd 30/9/44; ass 338BS/96BG [BX-G] Snetterton 13/10/44; during assembly for Kassel 29/1/45 w/?, mid air coll w/44-6137; cr Nth Lopham, UK; 9KIA; sal.

43-38747 Del Lincoln 16/9/44; Grenier 27/9/44; ass 546BS/384BG [BK-N] Grafton Underwood 15/10/44; sal 9AF Germany 10/12/45.

43-38748 Del Lincoln 18/9/44; Grenier 27/9/44; ass 339BS/96BG [QJ-V] Snetterton 1/10/44; b/d

Merseburg 25/11/44 w/?; cr Westleton, UK; sal 28/11/44.

43-38749 Del Lincoln 16/9/44; Grenier 27/9/44; ass 751BS/457BG Glatton 1/10/44; retUS Bradley 29/5/45; 4168 BU Sth Plains 25/6/45; RFC Kingman 17/12/45.

43-38750 Del Lincoln 16/9/44; Grenier 27/9/44; ass 544BS/384BG [SU-D] Grafton Underwood 16/10/44; c/t/o for Kassel 4/12/44 w/?; cr nr Deenethorpe, UK; sal. TU YUNG TU.

43-38751 Del Lincoln 16/9/44; Grenier 27/9/44; Dow Fd 2/10/44; ass 457BG Glatton 14/10/44; sal 10/2/45.

43-38752 Del Lincoln 16/9/44; Grenier 27/9/44; ass 547BS/384BG [SO-O] Grafton Underwood 16/10/44; sal 9AF Germany 10/12/45.

43-38753 Del Lincoln 16/9/44; Grenier 27/9/44; ass 508BS/351BG [YB-C] Polebrook 9/10/44; {70m} RetUS Bradley 4/6/45; 4168 BU Sth Plains 12/6/45; RFC Kingman 28/11/45. LUCKY JEWELL.

43-38754 Del Lincoln 16/9/44; Grenier 30/9/44; ass 602BS/398BG [K8-A] Nuthampstead 23/11/44; retUS Bradley 9/6/45; 4168 BU Sth Plains 13/6/45; RFC Kingman 17/12/45.

43-38755 Del Lincoln 7/10/44; Grenier 16/10/44; ass 322BS/91BG [LG-A] Bassingbourn 2/12/44; {16m} (en route home with 20 passengers a/c recalled by Burtonwood 3 hours out with reports of sustaining puncture on t/o from RAF Valley, which later proved incorrect!) RetUS Bradley 14/6/45; 4168 BU Sth Plains 17/6/45; RFC Kingman 5/12/45. LEWD ANGEL.

43-38756 Del Lincoln 16/9/44; Dow Fd 2/10/44; ass 493BG Debach 13/10/44; retUS Bradley 3/7/45; 4168 BU Sth Plains 6/7/45; RFC Kingman 6/12/45.

43-38757 Del Lincoln 16/9/44; Grenier 30/9/44; ass 547BS/384BG [SO-L] Grafton Underwood 6/10/44; retUS Bradley 12/7/45; 4185 BU Independence 12/7/45; 4136 BU Tinker 19/12/45; RFC Kingman 12/1/46. PEASELY'S PAYOFF.

43-38758 Del Lincoln 16/9/44; Grenier 22/10/44; ass 615BS/401BG [IY-P] Deenethorpe 5/12/44; 613BS [IN-P]; retUS Bradley 5/6/45; 4168 BU Sth Plains 6/6/45; RFC Kingman 19/11/45.

43-38759 Del Lincoln 18/9/44; Grenier 30/9/44; ass 527BS/379BG Kimbolton 14/10/44; MIA Zeitz 30/11/44 w/Alderman; flak, cr Zeitz; 1KIA 8POW; MACR 11058. DIMPLES.

43-38760 Del Lincoln 16/9/44; Grenier 30/9/44; ass 335BS/95BG [OE-X] Horham 11/10/44; b/d Darmstadt 24/12/44 w/Purdy; c/l France, 10RTD; sal 21/1/45. LUCKY LADY (not painted on).

43-38761 Del Lincoln 18/9/44; Dow Fd 2/10/44; ass 322BS/91BG [LG-A] Bassingbourn 4/11/44; retUS Bradley 11/6/45; 4168 BU Sth Plains 14/6/45; RFC Kingman 5/12/45.

43-38762 Del Lincoln 18/9/44; Dow Fd 2/10/44; ass 8AF 18/10/44; retUS Bradley 9/7/45; 4168 BU Sth Plains 1/7/45; RFC Kingman 29/1/46.

43-38763 Del Lincoln 18/9/44; Grenier 11/10/44; ass 427BS/303BG [GN-B] Molesworth 31/10/44; retUS Bradley 16/8/45; 4185 BU Independence 17/8/45; RFC Kingman 21/12/45.

43-38764 Del Lincoln 18/9/44; Grenier 30/9/44; ass 359BS/303BG [BN-C] Molesworth 28/10/44; b/d Lutzkendorf 9/2/45 w/Bailey; e/a, c/l St Trond?, Bel; 7POW 2RTD; sal 17/3/45; MACR 12230.

43-38765 Del Lincoln 19/9/44; Grenier 11/10/44; ass 306BG Thurleigh 10/2/45; tran 407BS/92BG [PY-K] Podington 9/5/45; sal 9AF 23/10/46. MILK RUN SPECIAL II.

43-38766 Del Lincoln 18/9/44; Grenier 30/9/44; ass

410BS/94BG [GL-F] Rougham 2/10/44; tran 546BS/384BG [BK-R] Grafton Underwood 16/10/44; sal 9AF Germany 10/12/45.

43-38767 Del Lincoln 18/9/44; Dow Fd 2/10/44; ass 332BS/94BG Rougham 4/10/44 VOX POP; tran 359BS/303BG [BN-L] Molesworth 23/11/44; MIA Hamburg 20/3/45 w/Moors; e/a, cr Neuengoehrs, Ger?; 5KIA 3POW; MACR 13570.

43-38768 Del Lincoln 19/9/44; Grenier 10/10/44; ass 8AF 16/10/44; retUS Bradley 5/7/45; 4168 BU Sth Plains 7/7/45; RFC Kingman 13/12/45.

43-38769 Del Lincoln 19/9/44; Grenier 16/10/44; ass 571BS/390BG [FC-Q] Framlingham 17/10/44; retUS Bradley 5/7/45; 4168 BU Sth Plains 7/7/45; RFC Kingman 12/1/46.

43-38770 Del Lincoln 19/9/44; Grenier 11/10/44; ass 351BS/100BG Thorpe Abbotts 13/10/44; b/d by debris from another a/c 31/1/45 w/?; sal 2/2/45.

43-38771 Del Lincoln 19/9/44; Grenier 11/10/44; ass 534BS/381BG [GD-E] Ridgewell 6/11/44; {25m} RetUS Bradley 9/6/45; 4168 BU Sth Plains 14/6/45; RFC Kingman 3/12/45.

43-38772 Del Lincoln 19/9/44; Grenier 22/10/44; ass 94BG Rougham 29/10/44 VOX POP; tran 324BS/91BG [DF-P] Bassingbourn 2/12/44; {47+m} RetUS Bradley 31/5/45; 4168 BU Sth Plains 3/6/45; 237 BU Kirtland 25/12/45; RFC Albuquerque 7/2/46. SWEET FREDA.

43-38773 Del Lincoln 19/9/44; Dow Fd 6/10/44; Grenier 16/10/44; ass 482BG Alconbury 17/10/44; retUS Bradley 30/5/45; 4168 BU Sth Plains 1/6/45; RFC Kingman 8/2/46.

43-38774 Del Lincoln 19/9/44; Grenier 6/10/44; ass 412BS/95BG [QW-B] Horham 16/10/44; 335BS [OE-B]; retUS Bradley 24/6/45; 4168 BU Sth Plains 28/6/45; RFC Kingman 29/11/45. DER FUEHRER'S NIGHTMARE.

43-38775 Del Lincoln 20/9/44; Dow Fd 15/10/44; ass 602BS/398BG [K8-H] Nuthampstead 9/2/45; retUS Bradley 7/6/45; 4168 BU Sth Plains 13/6/45; RFC Kingman 6/12/45.

43-38776 Del Lincoln 20/9/44; Grenier 11/10/44; ass 334BS/95BG [BG-B] Horham 13/10/44; retUS Bradley 26/6/45; 4168 BU Sth Plains 28/6/45; RFC Kingman 29/11/45.

43-38777 Del Lincoln 20/9/44; Grenier 6/10/44; ass 482BG Alconbury 11/10/44; tran 338BS/96BG [BX-W] Snetterton 12/10/44; retUS Bradley 1/6/45; 4168 BU Sth Plains 3/6/45; RFC Kingman 17/12/45. PEDER'S PARADE.

43-38778 Del Lincoln 20/9/44; Grenier 11/10/44; ass 358BS/303BG [VK-C] Molesworth 17/10/44; tran 457BG Glatton 22/5/45; retUS Bradley 9/6/45; 4168 BU Sth Plains 15/6/45; RFC Kingman 2/12/45.

43-38779 Del Lincoln 20/9/44; Grenier 11/10/44; ass 615BS/401BG [IY-O] Deenethorpe 7/11/44; b/d Minster Stein 16/2/45 w/?; abandoned over RAF Bardney, UK; sal 22/2/45. ROUGH BUT RIGHT.

43-38780 Del Lincoln 21/9/44; Grenier 7/10/44; ass 532BS/381BG [VE-J] Ridgewell 14/11/44; MIA {12m} Mannheim 11/12/44 w/Belskis; flak, cr Mannheim; 7KIA 2POW; MACR 11341.

43-38781 Del Lincoln 21/9/44; slated 100BG, Dow Fd 6/10/44; 1377 BU Grenier 16/10/44; 3 WER Grenier 16/3/45; 53 RCN Sq Grenier 26/7/45; 53 RCN Sq Buckley 11/3/46; 53 RCN Sq Morrison 12/5/46; 53 RCN Sq McChord 23/5/46; 59 RCN McChord 31/5/46; 59 RCN Castle 9/9/46; 53 RCN Morrison 14/1/47 Atlantic duties; re-ass TB-17G 31/3/47; 48 SR Borinquen, PR 9/1/48; Recl Comp 4/4/48.

43-38782 Del Lincoln 20/9/44; Grenier 7/10/44; ass 561BS/388BG Knettishall 17/10/44; retUS Bradley 24/6/45; 4168 BU Sth Plains 27/6/45; RFC Kingman 8/11/45. READY MAID.

43-38783 Del Lincoln 20/9/44; Grenier 7/10/44; ass 390BG Framlingham 17/10/44; tran 379BG Kimbolton 13/11/44; retUS Bradley 30/6/45; 4168 BU Sth Plains 4/7/45; RFC Kingman 17/12/45. THE MERRY MAX.

43-38784 Del Lincoln 20/9/44; Grenier 11/10/44; ass 569BS/390BG [CC-S] Framlingham 13/10/44; retUS Bradley 5/7/45; 4168 BU Sth Plains 7/7/45; RFC Kingman 10/12/45.

43-38785 Del Lincoln 21/9/44; Dow 7/10/44; ass 8AF 18/10/44; retUS Bradley 25/6/45; 4168 BU Sth Plains 28/6/45; RFC Kingman 8/11/45.

43-38786 Del Lincoln 21/9/44; Dow Fd 6/10/44; ass 8AF 18/10/44; retUS Bradley 12/7/45; 4185 BU Independence 13/7/45; RFC Kingman 30/12/45.

43-38787 Del Lincoln 21/9/44; Grenier 11/10/44; ass 8AF 16/10/44; retUS Bradley 11/7/45; 4168 BU Sth Plains 12/7/45; RFC Kingman 18/11/45.

43-38788 Del Lincoln 21/9/44; Grenier 11/10/44; ass 612BS/401BG [SC-T] Deenethorpe 7/11/44; b/d Oranienburg 10/4/45 w/Spence; flak, cr Wilsnack, Ger; 2EVD 7POW; sal 16/5/45; MACR 13913. HEAVY DATE.

43-38789 Del Lincoln 21/9/44; Dow Fd 6/10/44; ass 303BG Molesworth 28/9/44; tran 391BS/34BG Mendlesham 29/9/44; retUS Bradley 20/6/45; 4168 BU Sth Plains 23/6/45; RFC Kingman 18/12/45. FAST COMPANY.

43-38790 Del Lincoln 21/9/44; Dow Fd 15/10/44; ass 322BS/91BG [LG-O] Bassingbourn 7/12/44; {47m} (also completed 3 POW trips and 2 Rubbernecks) RetUS Bradley 11/6/45; 4168 BU Sth Plains 14/6/45; RFC Kingman 4/12/45. OH HAPPY DAY.

43-38791 Del Lincoln 21/9/44; Dow Fd 15/10/44; ass 18BS/34BG Mendlesham 19/10/44; MIA Holswickede, Ger 23/3/45 w/Bolser; flak & mid air coll, cr Hamm; 9KIA; MACR 13598.

43-38792 Del Lincoln 21/9/44; Dow Fd 15/10/44; ass 8AF 18/10/44; sal 9AF Germany 1/7/46.

43-38793 Del Lincoln 21/9/44; Grenier 7/10/44; ass 837BS/487BG Lavenham 30/11/44; retUS Bradley 10/7/45; 4185 BU Independence 14/7/45; RFC Kingman 17/12/45.

43-38794 Del Hunter 21/9/44; Grenier 2/10/44; ass 601BS/398BG [3O-J] Nuthampstead 16/10/44; 602BS; retUS Bradley 6/6/45; 4168 BU Sth Plains 9/6/45; RFC Kingman 14/12/45.

43-38795 Del Hunter 21/9/44; Grenier 2/10/44; ass 751BS/457BG Glatton 21/10/44; MIA Cologne 14/1/45 w/Popham; flak, cr Karlsruhe; 9KIA; MACR 11586.

43-38796 Del Hunter 21/9/44; Dow Fd 2/10/44; ass 410BS/94BG [GL-O] Rougham 15/10/44; MIA Bremen 24/2/45 w/Tejan; flak, cr Bremen; 2KIA 7POW; MACR 12614. THE LAD.

43-38797 Del Hunter 21/9/44; Dow Fd 13/10/44; ass 602BS/398BG Nuthampstead 15/10/44; retUS Bradley 29/6/45; 4168 BU Sth Plains 4/7/45; RFC Kingman 26/11/45.

43-38798 Del Hunter 21/9/44; Grenier 1/10/44; ass 385BG Gt Ashfield 13/10/44; tran 332BS/94BG [XM-M] Rougham 14/10/44; retUS Bradley 24/6/45; 4168 BU Sth Plains 27/6/45; RFC Kingman 29/11/45.

43-38799 Del Hunter 21/9/44; Grenier 2/10/44; ass 508BS/351BG [YB-Q] Polebrook 16/10/44; {61m} RetUS Bradley 23/5/45; 4168 BU Sth Plains 26/5/45; RFC Kingman 8/12/45. HEAVEN CAN WAIT.

43-38800 Del Hunter 24/9/44; Grenier 2/10/44; ass 547BS/384BG [SO-K] Grafton Underwood 6/10/44; b/d Zeitz 30/11/44 w/?; abandoned over Continent, 4KIA; sal 9AF Germany 31/1/45. MACR 11111. BUSY BUZZARD.

43-38801 Del Hunter 21/9/44; Grenier 2/10/44; ass 544BS/384BG [SU-M] Grafton Underwood 28/10/44; MIA Leipzig 6/4/45 w/Hastings; mid air coll, cr Leipzig; 7KIA 1POW; MACR 13851. RUTH.

43-38802 Del Hunter 21/9/44; Grenier 2/10/44; ass 306BG Thurleigh 31/10/44; tran 381BG Ridgewell 5/45; retUS Bradley 10/6/45; 4168 BU Sth Plains 13/6/45; RFC Kingman 4/12/45. KONDITORI BABY.

43-38803 Del Lincoln 23/9/44; Grenier 7/10/44; ass 368BS/306BG [BO-O] Thurleigh 17/10/44; tran 305BG Chelveston 4/12/44; MIA Oranienburg 10/4/45 w/Laubach; mid air coll, cr Wilsnack, Ger; 9KIA; MACR 13877.

43-38804 Del Lincoln 24/9/44; Dow Fd 6/10/44; ass 8AF 16/10/44; retUS Bradley 24/6/45; 4168 BU Sth Plains 26/6/45; RFC Kingman 7/12/45.

43-38805 Del Lincoln 24/9/44; Grenier 7/10/44; ass 600BS/398BG [N8-Z] Nuthampstead 23/11/44; retUS Bradley 25/5/45; 4168 BU Sth Plains 30/5/45; RFC Kingman 27/11/45.

43-38806 Del Lincoln 24/9/44; Dow Fd 15/10/44; ass 323BS/91BG [OR-D] Bassingbourn 4/11/44; b/d Feldhausen 22/3/45 w/?; c/l Melsbroek A/fd, Bel; sal 25/3/45.

43-38807 Del Lincoln 24/9/44; Grenier 7/10/44; ass 848BS/490BG Eye 17/10/44; b/d Mannheim 21/1/45 w/?; c/l Continent; sal 4/2/45; MACR 11770.

43-38808 Del Lincoln 25/9/44; Grenier 7/10/44; ass 839BS/487BG. MIA 15/10/44 9POW. Mayen, Gr.MACR 9492. Rep; retUS Bradley 9/7/45; 4168 BU Sth Plains 12/7/45; RFC Kingman 16/11/45.

43-38809 Del Lincoln 25/9/44; Dow Fd 15/10/44; ass 836BS/487BG Lavenham 19/2/45; retUS Bradley 12/7/45; 4185 BU Independence 13/7/45; RFC Kingman 10/12/45.

43-38810 Del Lincoln 25/9/44; Grenier 11/10/44; ass 615BS/401BG [IY-N] Deenethorpe 7/11/44; 612BS [SC-V]; retUS Bradley 7/6/45; 4168 BU Sth Plains 10/6/45; RFC Kingman 1/12/45. MRS KNOBBY.

43-38811 Del Lincoln 25/9/44; Grenier 11/10/44; ass 602BS/398BG [K8-R] Nuthampstead 23/11/44; retUS Bradley 29/5/45; 4168 BU Sth Plains 1/6/45; RFC Kingman 17/12/45.

43-38812 Del Lincoln 25/9/44; Grenier 11/10/44; ass 749BS/457BG Glatton 17/10/44; sal 26/12/44.

43-38813 Del Lincoln 25/9/44; Dow Fd 15/10/44; ass 508BS/351BG [YB-M] Polebrook 20/2/45; {39m} RetUS Bradley 23/5/45; 4168 BU Sth Plains 26/5/45; RFC Kingman 28/11/45.

43-38814 Del Lincoln 25/9/44; Grenier 11/10/44; ass 336BS/95BG [ET-S] Horham 11/10/44 NO NO NANNETTE; b/d Ludwigshafen 5/11/44 w/Wright; flak, f/l Miracourt, Fr; 1KIA 6POW 2RTD; MIA {39m} Kiel 4/4/45 w/Tuss; flak, f/l Bulltofta, Swed; 10INT; MACR 13848; ret group in UK 27/6/45; retUS Bradley 24/7/45; 4185 BU Independence 26/7/45; 3030 BU Roswell 8/10/45; 4185 BU Independence 30/11/45; RFC Kingman 17/12/45. CADET NURSE THE 2ND.

43-38815 Del Lincoln 25/9/44; Grenier 7/10/44; ass 1OOBG Thorpe Abbotts 11/10/44; tran 860BS/493BG Debach 12/10/44; b/d Kassel 28/2/45 w/?; f/l Continent, sal; retUS Bradley 6/7/45; 4168 BU Sth Plains 8/7/45; RFC Kingman 17/12/45.

43-38816 Del Lincoln 25/9/44; Grenier 7/10/44; ass 305BG Chelveston 10/10/44; tran 487BG Lavenham 12/10/44; b/d Frankfurt 12/1/45 w/?; f/l Continent; sal 21/1/45.

43-38817 Del Lincoln 25/9/44; Grenier 7/10/44; ass 305BG Chelveston 18/10/44; tran 384BG Grafton

Underwood 9/5/45; sal 9AF Germany 2/1/46.
43-38818 Del Lincoln 25/9/44; Grenier 7/10/44; ass 524BS/379BG Kimbolton 11/10/44; MIA Hopsten, Ger 24/3/45 w/Howell; flak, cr Hopsten, Ger; 8KIA; MACR 13605.
43-38819 Del Lincoln 25/9/44; Grenier 7/10/44; ass 303BG Molesworth 22/11/44; tran 750BS/457BG Glatton 23/11/44; c/to for Merzhausen 24/12/44 w/?; cr Holme, UK, 1KIA; sal.
43-38820 Del Lincoln 26/9/44; Grenier 7/10/44; ass 331BS/94BG [QE-R] Rougham 11/10/44; 333BS [TS-R]; tran 34BG Mendlesham /44; retUS Bradley 21/6/45; 4168 BU Sth Plains 23/6/45; RFC Kingman 1/12/45. ROLL ME OVER.
43-38821 Del Lincoln 25/9/44; Grenier 7/10/44; ass 100BG Thorpe Abbotts 10/10/44; tran 482BG Alconbury 20/5/45; retUS Bradley 6/6/45; 4168 BU Sth Plains 8/6/45; RFC Kingman 29/11/45.
43-38822 Del Lincoln 26/9/44; Grenier 16/10/44; ass 452BG Deopham Green 20/10/44; taxi acc, struck 42-102660 28/12/44; sal 29/12/44.
43-38823 Del Lincoln 26/9/44; Grenier 7/10/44; ass 545BS/384BG [JD-H] Grafton Underwood 23/10/44; MIA Berlin 26/2/45 w/Barnett; flak, cr Berlin; 9RTD; MACR 12760.
43-38824 Del Lincoln 26/9/44; Grenier 7/10/44; ass 410BS/94BG Rougham 11/10/44; b/d Weisbaden 9/11/44 w/?; f/l Continent; sal 10/11/44; ret UK re-ass 303BG Molesworth; tran 457BG Glatton 23/5/45; retUS 4/6/45.
43-38825 Del Lincoln 26/9/44; Grenier 11/10/44; ass 94BG Rougham 17/10/44; (chin turret removed & .50 cal m/gun fitted as F model); tran 34BG Mendlesham /44; retUS Bradley 20/6/45; 4168 BU Sth Plains 28/6/45; RFC Kingman 4/12/45.
43-38826 Del Lincoln 26/9/44; Grenier 7/10/44; ass 412BS/95BG [QW-J] Horham 13/10/44; f/l twice on Continent, Laon, Fr & Melsbroek, Bel; retUS Bradley 21/6/45; 4168 BU Sth Plains 23/6/45; RFC Kingman 7/12/45.
43-38827 Del Lincoln 26/9/44; Dow Fd 15/10/44; ass 562BS/388BG Knettishall 19/10/44; RFC Walnut Ridge 2/1/46.
43-38828 Del Lincoln 26/9/44; Grenier 15/10/44; ass 332BS/94BG [XM-T] Rougham 17/10/44; 333BS [TS-T]; tran 413BS/96BG Snetterton 19/10/44; MIA Dresden 2/3/45 w/Hemphill; flak, cr Benterode, Ger; 9POW; MACR 12859.
43-38829 Del Lincoln 26/9/44; Grenier 7/10/44; ass 493BG Debach 11/10/44; retUS Bradley 7/7/45; 4168 BU Sth Plains 11/7/45; RFC Kingman 10/12/45.
43-38830 Del Lincoln 26/9/44; Grenier 7/10/44; ass 332BS/94BG [XM-F] Rougham 11/10/44; retUS Bradley 7/7/45; 4168 BU Sth Plains 12/7/45; RFC Kingman 10/12/45.
43-38831 Del Lincoln 26/9/44; Grenier 7/10/44; ass 749BS/457BG Glatton 11/10/44; help operation? 13/5/44 w/?; f/l Continent; sal n/b/d 24/5/45. SCREAMING EAGLE.
43-38832 Del Lincoln 27/9/44; Grenier 11/10/44; ass 306BG Thurleigh 19/2/45; (Disney bomb carrier); tran 92BG Podington 9/5/45; secret missions on 28/5/45 & 1/6/45, each ret next day; to Port Lyautey, Morr 24/6/45, ret 25/6/45; sal 9AF Germany 12/9/45; re-ass AF 30/4/47; Recl Comp 19/11/47. IRENE (BRONX EXPRESS; LITTLE LADY).
43-38833 Del Lincoln 27/9/44; Grenier 11/10/44; ass 652REC/25BG Watton 16/10/44; retUS 613 BU Phillips 26/3/46.
43-38834 Del Lincoln 27/9/44; Dow Fd 15/10/44; ass 332BS/94BG [XM-N] Rougham 19/10/44 TUTORWOLF; retUS Bradley 21/6/45; 4168 BU Sth Plains 25/6/45; RFC Kingman 15/12/45. FRENESI II.
43-38835 Del Lincoln 27/9/44; Grenier 11/10/44; ass 527BS/379BG [FO-X] Kimbolton 17/10/44; tran 836BS/487BG Lavenham 22/5/45; 94BG Rougham 23/5/45; retUS 1103 BU Morrison 25/10/45; RFC Walnut Ridge 28/12/45.
43-38836 Del Lincoln 27/9/44; Grenier 11/10/44; ass 332BS/94BG [XM-R] Rougham 11/10/44; tran 709BS/447BG Rattlesden 12/10/44; 602BS/398BG [K8-T] Nuthampstead 18/10/44; sal 9AF Germany 10/2/45.
43-38837 Del Lincoln 27/9/44; Dow Fd 12/10/44; ass 569BS/390BG [CC-D] Framlingham 17/10/44; retUS Bradley 3/7/45; 4168 BU Sth Plains 6/7/45; RFC Kingman 24/11/45.
43-38838 Del Lincoln 27/9/44; Grenier 11/10/44; ass 849BS/490BG Eye 17/10/44; taxi acc, hit 43-38134 12/12/44; sal 13/12/44.
43-38839 Del Lincoln 27/9/44; Grenier 12/10/44; ass 545BS/384BG [JD-H] Grafton Underwood 12/4/45; sal 9AF Germany 23/8/46.
43-38840 Del Lincoln 27/9/44; Gt Falls 29/9/44; Lincoln 1/10/44; Grenier 11/10/44; ass 349BS/100BG [XR-H] Thorpe Abbotts 13/10/44; MIA Brandenburg 10/4/45 w/Reeve; jet e/a, cr Zobbenitz, Gerl; 1EVD 8KIA; MACR 14171. LITTLE REBEL.
43-38841 Del Lincoln 27/9/44; Grenier 12/10/44; ass 323BS/91BG [OR-L] Bassingbourn 4/11/44; {45m} RetUS Bradley 31/5/45; Columbus 9/6/45; Memphis 12/6/45; 4168 BU Sth Plains 5/8/45; RFC Kingman 20/12/45. JUDY'S LITTLE ASS.
43-38842 Del Lincoln 27/9/44; Grenier 7/10/44; ass 360BS/303BG [PU-N] Molesworth 28/10/44; retUS Bradley 7/6/45; 4168 BU Sth Plains 12/6/45; RFC Kingman 27/11/45.
43-38843 Del Lincoln 27/9/44; Dow Fd 15/10/44; ass 323BS/91BG [OR-L] Bassingbourn 4/11/44; 401BS [LL-L]; sal 9AF Germany 2/1/46.
43-38844 Del Lincoln 28/9/44; Bismarck 3/10/44; Grenier 15/10/44; ass 748BS/457BG Glatton 17/10/44; tran 92BG Podington 10/5/45; secret mission 28/5/45, ret 29/5/45; retUS Bradley 22/5/45; 4168 BU Sth Plains 24/5/45; RFC Kingman 28/11/45.
43-38845 Del Lincoln 28/9/44; Grenier 11/10/44; ass 561BS/388BG Knettishall 17/10/44; MIA Hamburg 31/12/44 w/Senter; flak, cr Delfzijl, Hol; 5KIA 4POW; MACR 11242.
43-38846 Del Lincoln 28/9/44; Grenier 22/10/44; ass 8AF 23/10/44; retUS 1103 BU Morrison 26/12/45; RFC Walnut Ridge 9/1/46.
43-38847 Del Lincoln 28/9/44; Grenier 11/10/44; ass 8AF 12/10/44; sal n/b/d 30/11/44.
43-38848 Del Lincoln 28/9/44; Grenier 11/10/44; ass 8AF 16/10/44; retUS Bradley 28/6/45; 4168 BU Sth Plains 4/8/45; RFC Kingman 23/11/45.
43-38849 Del Lincoln 28/9/44; Bismarck 2/10/44; Grenier 12/10/44; ass 711BS/447BG Rattlesden 17/10/44; MIA Oranienburg 15/3/45 w/Karst; flak, cr Salzwedel, Ger; 2KIA 7POW; MACR 13030.
43-38850 Del Lincoln 28/9/44; Bismarck 2/10/44; Grenier 12/10/44; ass 544BS/384BG [SU-D] Grafton Underwood 8/12/44; MIA Sterkrade, Ger 22/1/45 w/Van Popering; flak, cr Düsseldorf; 2EVD 2KIA 5POW; MACR 11994.
43-38851 Del Lincoln 29/9/44; Bismarck 3/10/44; Dow Fd 15/10/44; ass 331BS/94BG [QE-K] Rougham 19/10/44; retUS Bradley 29/6/45; 4168 BU Sth Plains 2/7/45; RFC Kingman 25/11/45.
43-38852 Del Lincoln 29/9/44; Bismarck 4/10/44; Grenier 12/10/44; ass 482BG Alconbury 17/10/44; tran 569BS/390BG [CC-A] Framlingham 18/10/44; tran 351BS/100BG [EP-N] Thorpe Abbotts 30/5/45; retUS Bradley 2/6/45; 4168 BU Sth Plains 9/6/45; RFC Kingman 19/12/45.
42-38853 Del Lincoln 29/9/44; Bismarck 4/10/44; Grenier 12/10/44; ass 600BS/398BG [N8-L] Nuthampstead 23/11/44; MIA Oranienburg 10/4/45 w/McAfee; flak, cr Berlin; MACR 13867.
43-38854 Del Lincoln 29/9/44; Grenier 12/10/44; ass 751BS/457BG Glatton 19/10/44; MIA Achmer 24/3/44 w/Williams; flak, cr Greven, Ger; 6KIA 3POW; MACR 123616. TENNESSEE TODDY.
43-38855 Del Lincoln 29/9/44; Dow Fd 15/10/44; ass 750BS/457BG Glatton 19/10/44; 749BS; retUS Bradley 28/5/45; 4168 BU Sth Plains 31/5/45; RFC Kingman 28/12/45.
43-38856 Del Lincoln 30/9/44; Dow Fd 15/10/44; ass 534BS/381BG [GD-M] Ridgewell 19/10/44; {7m} cr Isle of Man, UK w/Ackerman on furlough flight 23/4/45; all 31 killed (inc groundcrew) when a/c hit Nth Barrule Mt en route Belfast for President Roosevelt's memorial service; sal.
43-38857 Del Lincoln 30/9/44; Gt Falls 1/10/44; Grenier 12/10/44; ass 750BS/457BG Glatton 19/10/44; retUS Bradley 28/5/45; 4168 BU Sth Plains 30/5/45; RFC Kingman 28/11/45.
43-38858 Del Lincoln 30/9/44; Grenier 12/10/44; ass 327BS/92BG [UX-J] Podington 30/12/44; b/d Chemnitz 2/3/45 w/?; f/l Continent, sal 17/3/45.
43-38859 Del Lincoln 30/9/44; Dow Fd 12/10/44; ass 385BG Gt Ashfield 14/10/44; retUS Bradley 7/7/45; 4168 BU Sth Plains 10/7/45; RFC Kingman 28/11/45.
43-38860 Del Lincoln 30/9/44; Dow Fd 15/10/44; ass 323BS/91BG [OR-M] Bassingbourn 9/2/45; b/d Dresden 14/2/45 w/?; f/l Continent, sal 22/2/45.
43-38861 Del Hunter 30/9/44; Grenier 11/10/44; ass 351BS/100BG Thorpe Abbotts 13/10/44; MIA Berlin 18/3/45 w/Gwin; jet e/a, cr Gage, Ger?; 4KIA 6POW; MACR 13144. SWEET NANCY II.
43-38862 Del Hunter 30/9/44; Dow Fd 11/10/44; ass 613BS/401BG [IN-N] Deenethorpe 23/11/44; retUS Bradley 4/6/45; 4168 BU Sth Plains 10/6/44; RFC Kingman 19/12/45.
43-38863 Del Hunter 30/9/44; Dow Fd 15/10/44; ass 92BG Podington 19/10/44 MORALE; tran 750BS/457BG Glatton 6/11/44; retUS Bradley 9/6/45; 4168 BU Sth Plains 12/6/45; RFC Kingman 20/12/45.
43-38864 Del Hunter 30/9/44; Grenier 16/10/44; ass 600BS/398BG [N8-F] Nuthampstead 23/11/44; tran 34BG; c/t/o 15/1/45.
43-38865 Del Hunter 30/9/44; Grenier 11/10/44; ass 100BG Thorpe Abbotts 13/10/44; retUS Bradley 9/7/45; 4168 BU Sth Plains 10/7/45; RFC Kingman 20/12/45.
43-38866 Del Hunter 30/9/44; Grenier 13/10/44; ass 493BG Debach 17/10/44; b/d Cottbus, Ger 15/2/45 w/?; f/l Continent, sal 19/2/45.
43-38867 Del Hunter 30/9/44; Dow Fd 15/10/44; ass 652REC/25BG Watton 17/10/44; RFC Walnut Ridge 5/1/46.
43-38868 Del Hunter 30/9/45; Grenier 11/10/44; ass 728BS/452BG Deopham Green 13/10/44; MIA Parchim, Ger 7/4/45 w/Richardson; rammed by Sonderkommando Elbe Me109, cr Hamburg; 8KIA 2POW; MACR 13888.
43-38869 Del Hunter 30/9/44; Dow Fd 11/10/44; ass 563BS/388BG Knettishall 17/10/44; MIA Parchim, Ger 7/4/45 w/Bars; e/a & hit by debris from a/c above; cr Steinhuden Meeres, Ger; 10KIA; PAULA SUE.

43-38870 Del Hunter 30/9/44; Dow Fd 12/10/44; ass 303BG Molesworth 9/2/45; tran 457BG Glatton 23/5/45; retUS Bradley 9/6/45; 4168 BU Sth Plains 12/6/45; RFC Kingman 29/11/45.

43-38871 Del Hunter 2/10/44; Grenier 10/10/44; ass 339BS/96BG [QJ-V] Snetterton 17/10/44; MIA Kiel 3/4/45 w/McFarland; flak, f/l Bulltofta, Swed, 10INT; RetUK 27/6/45; retUS Bradley 2/8/45; 4185 BU Independence 4/8/45; RFC Kingman 15/1/46. RACTUP.

43-38872 Del Hunter 2/10/44; Dow Fd 15/10/44; ass 511BS/351BG [DS-G] Polebrook 20/2/45; {10m} tran 544BS/384BG [SU-M] Grafton Underwood 9/5/45; re-ass duties Morocco 7/12/45 and Dutch-Belgian coast 30/11/46; sal 5/1/47.

43-38873 Del Hunter 2/10/44; Dow Fd 23/10/44; ass 385BG Gt Ashfield 25/10/44; tran 561BS/388BG Knettishall 26/10/44; RFC Walnut Ridge 7/1/46.

43-38874 Del Hunter 2/10/44; Dow Fd 11/10/44; ass 524BS/379BG [WA-U] Kimbolton 13/11/44; retUS Bradley 5/7/45; 4168 BU Sth Plains 6/7/45; RFC Kingman 23/11/45. PIPE DREAM.

43-38875 Del Hunter 2/10/44; Dow Fd 12/10/44; ass 303BG Molesworth 9/2/45; tran 457BG Glatton 23/5/45; retUS Bradley 8/6/45; 4168 BU Sth Plains 13/6/45; 1103 BU Morrison 3/11/45; RFC Kingman 28/11/45.

43-38876 Del Hunter 2/10/44; Grenier 11/10/44; ass 452BG Deopham Green 17/10/44; during assembly for Plauen 26/3/45 w/?; mid air coll with 43-38402; cr Crettingham, UK; all killed; sal 28/3/45.

43-38877 Del Hunter 2/10/44; Dow Fd 12/10/44; ass 325BS/92BG [NV-G] Podington 9/2/45; sal 9AF Germany 29/12/45. EL LOBO'S CUB; ELIZABETH.

43-38878 Del Hunter 2/10/44; Grenier 11/10/44; ass 359BS/303BG [BN-D] Molesworth 28/10/44; tran 457BG Glatton 23/5/45; retUS Bradley 8/6/45; 4168 BU Sth Plains 14/6/44; RFC Kingman 30/11/45.

43-38879 Del Hunter 2/10/44; Dow Fd 15/10/44; ass 728BS/452BG Deopham Green 19/10/44; ex-Berlin w/Bishop 18/3/45; mid air coll with 43-38982, cr Nth Sea off Holland; 9KIA; MACR 13560.

43-38880 Del Lincoln 3/10/44; Grenier 15/10/44; ass 544BS/384BG [SU-K] Grafton Underwood 24/10/44; 547BS [SO-K]; tran 324BS/91BG [DF-R] Bassingbourn 9/2/45; retUS Bradley 30/5/45; 4168 BU Sth Plains 1/6/45; RFC Kingman 17/12/45.

43-38881 Del Lincoln 3/10/44; Grenier 15/10/44; ass 750BS/457BG Glatton 4/11/44; sal 13/5/45. RUTH ANNE.

43-38882 Del Cheyenne 3/10/44; Wright 9/12/44; Hunter 28/2/45; San Francisco 6/4/45; Oahu (Haw) 5/8/45; lost at sea 31/7/45.

43-38883 Del Cheyenne 3/10/44; Hunter 7/11/44; Grenier 14/11/44; ass 359BS/303BG [BN-A] Molesworth 17/2/45; tran 457BG Glatton 22/5/45; retUS Bradley 8/6/45; 4168 BU Sth Plains 13/6/45; RFC Kingman 17/12/45. LADY BETH.

43-38884 Del Cheyenne 3/10/44; Hunter 7/11/44; Grenier 12/11/44; ass 8AF ; retUS Bradley 7/7/45; 4168 BU Sth Plains 9/7/45; RFC Kingman 8/11/45.

43-38885 Del Lincoln 4/10/44; Gt Falls 7/7/45; Grenier 15/10/44; ass 751BS/457BG Glatton 17/11/44; 749BS; retUS Bradley 28/5/45; 4168 BU Sth Plains 31/5/45; RFC Kingman 26/11/45. RUTHANNE.

43-38886 Del Lincoln 4/10/44; Grenier 15/10/44; ass 8AF 16/10/44; retUS Bradley 9/7/45; 4168 BU Sth Plains 11/7/45; RFC Kingman 9/12/45.

43-38887 Del Lincoln 4/10/44; Grenier 17/10/44; ass 751BS/457BG Glatton 19/10/44; retUS Bradley 28/5/45; 4168 BU Sth Plains 31/5/45; RFC Kingman 19/11/45. PERPETUAL HELL.

43-38888 Del Lincoln 5/10/44; Grenier 16/10/44; ass 839BS/487BG Lavenham 30/11/44; MIA Hamburg 11/3/45 w/Sugerman; flak, cr Harburg; 9KIA 1POW; MACR 12979.

43-38889 Del Lincoln 5/10/44; Grenier 16/10/44; ass 324BS/91BG [DF-M] Bassingbourn 4/11/44; {50+m} RetUS Bradley 11/6/45; 4168 BU Sth Plains 14/6/45; RFC Kingman 19/11/45. CHIPPEWA - THE MILWAUKEE ROAD.

43-38890 Del Lincoln 7/10/44; Grenier 16/10/44; ass 34BG Mendlesham 19/10/44; retUS Bradley 21/6/45; 4168 BU Sth Plains 24/6/45; RFC Kingman 8/12/45.

43-38891 Del Lincoln 6/10/44; Grenier 15/10/44; ass 359BS/303BG [BN-H] Molesworth 19/10/44; b/d Halberstadt 8/4/45 w/?; sal 25/4/45. BLUES IN THE NIGHT.

43-38892 Del Lincoln 6/10/44; Grenier 15/10/44; ass 836BS/487BG Lavenham 22/1/45; retUS Bradley 12/7/45; 4185 BU Independence 13/7/45; RFC Kingman 10/12/45.

43-38893 Del Lincoln 6/10/44; Grenier 15/10/44; ass 836BS/487BG [2G-R] Lavenham 5/1/45; retUS Bradley 12/7/45; 4185 BU Independence 13/7/45; RFC Kingman 14/10/45.

43-38894 Del Lincoln 6/10/44; Grenier 15/10/44; ass 8AF 19/10/44; retUS Bradley 9/7/45; 4168 BU Sth Plains 12/7/45; RFC Kingman 9/12/45.

43-38895 Del Lincoln 5/10/44; Grenier 15/10/44; ass 603BS/398BG [N7-V] Nuthampstead 23/11/44; ex-Kassel 1/1/45 w/Pinner; mech fault, ditched Channel; 3KIA 6RTD; MACR 11581.

43-38896 Del Lincoln 5/10/44; Grenier 22/10/44; ass 8AF 23/10/44; Re-ass AF 30/4/47; 19HBS Oberpfaffenhofen 19/1/48; Recl Comp 7/1/49.

43-38897 Del Lincoln 6/10/44; Grenier 16/10/44; ass 410BS/94BG [GL-R] Rougham 17/10/44; 331BS [QE-Q]; tran 34BG Mendlesham /44; retUS Bradley 20/6/45; 4168 BU Sth Plains 25/6/45; RFC Kingman 17/12/45.

43-38898 Del Lincoln 6/10/44; Grenier 15/10/44; ass 534BS/381BG [GD-G] Ridgewell 14/11/44 HITLER'S HO DO; MIA Berlin 3/2/45 w/Pucylowski; flak, cr Tutow, Ger; 1KIA 8POW; MACR 12295. BLIND DATE.

43-38899 Del Lincoln 6/10/44; Grenier 15/10/44; ass 336BS/95BG [ET-N] Horham 17/10/44; MIA Berlin 3/2/45 w/Taylor; flak, crWerneuchen, Ger; 9POW; MACR 12156.

43-38900 Del Lincoln 7/10/44; Grenier 15/10/44; ass 8AF 17/10/44; retUS Bradley 5/7/45; 4168 BU Sth Plains 7/7/45; RFC Kingman 17/12/45.

43-38901 Del Hunter 7/10/44; Dow 15/10/44; ass 322BS/91BG [LG-T] Bassingbourn 18/10/44; {47m} three POW trips & two Rubbernecks; retUS Bradley 20/6/45; 4168 BU Sth Plains 23/6/45; RFC Kingman 30/11/45. STAR DUST.

43-38902 Del Hunter 7/10/44; Dow Fd 16/10/44; ass 384BG Grafton Underwood 19/10/44; tran 748BS/457BG Glatton /45; f/l Jasienki, Pol., 18/3/45; retUS Bradley 8/6/45; 4168 BU Sth Plains 12/6/45; RFC Kingman 10/12/45. LADY BE GOOD.

43-38903 Del Hunter 7/10/44; Dow Fd 24/10/44; ass 8AF 25/10/44; retUS Bradley 5/7/45; Ft Riley 8/7/45; 4185 BU Independence 14/7/45; RFC Kingman 17/12/45.

43-38904 Del Hunter 7/10/44; Dow Fd 16/10/44; ass 751BS/457BG Glatton 19/10/44; MIA Hamburg 6/11/44 w/McGoarty; flak, cr Rotenburg, Ger; 8KIA 1POW; MACR 10343.

43-38905 Del Hunter 7/10/44; Dow Fd 22/10/44; ass 8AF 24/10/44; retUS Bradley 5/7/45; 4168 BU Sth Plains 6/7/45; RFC Kingman 16/12/45.

43-38906 Del Lincoln 9/10/44; Grenier 18/10/44; ass 8AF 19/10/44; sal 9AF Germany 10/5/46.

43-38907 Del Lincoln 9/10/44; Grenier 16/10/44; ass 534BS/381BG [GD-I] Ridgewell 20/10/44; {26m} tran 401BG Deenethorpe /45; retUS Bradley 7/6/45; 4168 BU Sth Plains 12/6/45; RFC Kingman 29/11/45.

43-38908 Del Lincoln 9/10/44; Grenier 16/10/44; ass 535BS/381BG [MS-L] Ridgewell 18/10/44; retUS Bradley 28/5/45; 4168 BU Sth Plains 30/5/45; RFC Kingman 5/12/45.

43-38909 Del Lincoln 9/10/44; Grenier 17/10/44; ass 748BS/457BG Glatton 21/10/44; b/d Dresden 14/2/45 w/?; f/l Continent; sal 28/2/45. KRAUT KRUSHER.

43-38910 Del Lincoln 9/10/44; Grenier 16/10/44; ass 423BS/306BG [RD-B] Thurleigh 19/2/45 SALVOIN' SACHEM; tran 535BS/381BG Ridgewell 21/2/45; retUS Bradley 10/6/45; 4168 BU Sth Plains 17/6/45; RFC Kingman 9/12/45.

43-38911 Del Lincoln 9/10/44; Grenier 16/10/44; ass 323BS/91BG Bassingbourn 5/11/44; b/d {18m} Cologne 14/1/45 w/Meyer; flak, cr Wengerrohr, Ger; 8KIA 1POW; MACR 11772; sal 6/3/45. BULL SESSION.

43-38912 Del Lincoln 9/10/44; Grenier 17/10/44; ass 7BS/34BG Mendlesham 20/10/44; 18BS; b/d Berlin 18/3/45 w/?; f/l Melaszewicze, Pol.; sal. OLD TIMES.

43-38913 Del Lincoln 9/10/44; Grenier 17/10/44; ass 367BS/306BG [GY-P] Thurleigh 21/10/44; tran 532BS/381BS Ridgewell 5/45; retUS Bradley 9/6/45; 4168 BU Sth Plains 14/6/45; RFC Kingman 6/12/45.

43-38914 Del Lincoln 9/10/44; Grenier 17/10/44; ass 368BS/306BG [BO-B] Thurleigh 10/2/45; tran 534BS/381BG Ridgewell 14/5/45; retUS Bradley 9/6/45; 4168 BU Sth Plains 13/6/45; RFC Kingman 30/11/45.

43-38915 Del Lincoln 11/10/44; Grenier 22/10/44; ass 860BS/493BG Debach 24/10/44; retUS Bradley 3/7/44; 4168 BU Sth Plains 5/7/45; RFC Kingman 29/11/45.

43-38916 Del Lincoln 10/10/44; Grenier 17/10/44; ass 368BS/306BG [BO-B] Thurleigh 8/2/45; tran 533BS/381BG Ridgewell 5/45; retUS Bradley 9/6/45; Columbus 11/6/45; 4168 BU Sth Plains 29/6/45; RFC Kingman 9/12/45.

43-38917 Del Lincoln 10/10/44; Grenier 17/10/44; ass 731BS/452BG Deopham Green 20/10/44; retUS Bradley 3/7/45; 4168 BU Sth Plains 7/7/45; RFC Kingman 23/11/45. NOT TODAY CLEO.

43-38918 Del Lincoln 10/10/44; Dow Fd 22/10/44; ass 96BG Snetterton 25/10/44; b/d Mannheim 21/1/45 w/?; sal 8/2/45.

43-38919 Del Lincoln 11/10/44; Grenier 22/10/44; ass 337BS/96BG [AW-L] Snetterton 1/11/44; tran 388BG Knettishall 2/11/44; c/t/o 31/5/45, 9KIA; sal.

43-38920 Del Lincoln 10/10/44; Grenier 18/10/44; ass 92BG Podington 20/10/44 CANVAS BACK IV; tran 509BS/351BG [RQ-O] Polebrook 9/2/45; {32m} RetUS Bradley 23/5/45; 4168 BU Sth Plains 28/5/45; RFC Kingman 28/11/45. MORT'S ORPHAN.

43-38921 Del Lincoln 10/10/44; Grenier 17/10/44; ass 729BS/452BG Deopham Green 24/10/44; MIA Bad Krueznach, Ger 2/1/45 w/Capt Jones; flak, cr Bitburg, Ger; 8KIA 1POW; MACR 11225.

43-38922 Del Lincoln 11/10/44; Grenier 22/10/44; ass 412BS/95BG [QW-D] Horham 24/10/44; b/d Nurnberg 20/2/45 w/?; f/l Charleroi, Bel; sal 7/3/45.

43-38923 Del experimental dept Seattle 10/10/44; 4142 BU Dayton 25/5/45; 4000 BU Patterson

17/1/46; 4168 BU Sth Plains 31/1/46; 4000 BU Patterson 30/9/46; 4141 BU 12/6/47; Recl Comp 31/3/49.

43-38924 Del Lincoln 11/10/44; Grenier 22/10/44; ass 364BS/305BG [WF-E] Chelveston 5/12/44; tran 401BG Deenethorpe 20/5/45; retUS Bradley 7/6/45; 4168 BU Sth Plains 14/6/45; RFC Kingman 1/12/45.

43-38925 Del Lincoln 12/10/44; Dow Fd 24/10/44; ass 833BS/486BG Sudbury 25/10/44; MIA Mannheim 21/1/45 w/Heldefer; flak, cr Ingstettin, Ger; 9POW; MACR 11798.

43-38926 Del Lincoln 12/10/44; Grenier 22/10/44; ass 836BS/487BG Lavenham 2/12/44; MIA Darmstadt 24/12/44 w/?; mid air coll w/FW 190 en route target; cr Belgium; MACR 11675.

43-38927 Del Lincoln 12/10/44; Grenier 22/10/44; ass 544BS/384BG [SU-H] Grafton Underwood 8/12/44; tran 303BG Molesworth, but c/l 1/2/45; sal 4/2/45.

43-38928 Del Lincoln 12/10/44; Dow Fd 24/10/44; ass 8AF 24/10/44; retUS Bradley 9/7/45; 4168 BU Sth Plains 12/7/45; RFC Kingman 28/11/45.

43-38929 Del Lincoln 12/10/44; Grenier 22/10/44; ass 337BS/96BG Snetterton 1/11/44; b/d Zwickau, Ger 19/3/45 w/?; f/l Poznan, Pol, crew OK; sal 17/4/45.

43-38930 Del Lincoln 12/10/44; Grenier 27/10/44; ass 413BS/96BG [MZ-N] Snetterton 29/10/44; b/d Koblenz 28/12/44 w/?; mid air coll w/43-38576; sal.

43-38931 Del Lincoln 14/10/44; Grenier 27/10/44; ass 560BS/388BG Knettishall 2/11/44; retUS Bradley 26/6/45; 4168 BU Sth Plains 28/6/45; RFC Kingman 23/11/45.

43-38932 Del Lincoln 14/10/44; Cheyenne 26/10/44; Grenier 7/11/44; ass 407BS/92BG [PY-T] Podington 30/12/44; MIA Kassel 1/1/45 w/Rollins; flak, cr Stendahl; 9KIA; MACR 11371.

43-38933 Del Lincoln 14/10/44; Dow Fd 26/10/44; ass 561BS/388BG Knettishall 29/10/44 DEAR MOM II; c/l Lands End, UK 31/5/45; 6KIA; sal; retUS Bradley 24/6/45; 4168 BU Sth Plains 27/6/45; RFC Kingman 20/11/45. WEARY WOLF.

43-38934 Del Lincoln 14/10/44; Dow Fd 26/10/44; ass 8AF 28/10/44; retUS Bradley 9/7/45; 4168 BU Sth Plains 11/7/45; RFC Kingman 24/11/45.

43-38935 Del Lincoln 14/10/44; Dow Fd 26/10/44; ass 413BS/96BG [MZ-A] Snetterton 29/10/44; MIA Brandenburg 31/3/45 w/Murphy; flak, c/l Fulda A/fd, Ger; 8KIA 1POW; MACR 13715.

43-38936 Del Hunter 14/10/44; Dow Fd 26/10/44; ass 324BS/91BG Bassingbourn 29/11/44; retUS Bradley 31/5/45; 4168 BU Sth Plains 3/6/45; RFC Kingman 15/12/45.

43-38937 Del Hunter 19/10/44; Grenier 28/10/44; ass 8AF, trans 4152 BU Lockburn 8/11/44; 4152 BU Clinton 5/5/46; 4143 BU Lockburn 13/6/46; Recl Comp 17/12/46.

43-38938 Del Hunter 15/10/44; Dow Fd 27/10/44; ass 482BG Alconbury 29/10/44; tran 339BS/96BG [QJ-S] Snetterton 30/10/44; retUS Bradley 1/6/45; 4168 BU Sth Plains 3/6/45; 237 BU Kirtland 8/1/46; RFC Albuquerque 7/2/46.

43-38939 Del Hunter 19/10/44; Dow Fd 27/10/44; ass 323BS/91BG [OR-A] Bassingbourn 2/12/44; (took nav Capt Wellings on honeymoon trip to Devon 22/3/44!); {37m} b/d Coesfeld 11/4/45 w/?; f/l Continent; sal 9AF Germany 10/12/45. PEACE OR BUST.

43-38940 Del Hunter 20/10/44; Dow Fd 27/10/44; ass 8AF 29/10/44; retUS Bradley 5/7/45; 4168 BU Sth Plains 7/7/45; RFC Kingman 13/12/45.

43-38941 Del Hunter 20/10/44; Dow Fd 27/10/44; ass 613BS/401BG [IN-L] Deenethorpe 6/12/44; 612BS [SC-K], 615BS [IY-L]; sal 12/5/45.

43-38942 Del Hunter 20/10/44; Dow Fd 28/10/44; ass 360BS/303BG [PU-N] Molesworth 1/11/44; tran 335BS/95BG [OE-Y] Horham 2/11/44; retUS Bradley 20/6/45; 4168 BU Sth Plains 23/6/45; RFC Kingman 22/11/45. BELLIGERENT LADY.

43-38943 Del Hunter 20/10/44; Dow Fd 27/10/44; ass 729BS/452BG Deopham Green 29/10/44; MIA Cologne 10/1/45 w/Larson; flak, cr Mannheim; 9KIA; MACR 11585.

43-38944 Del Hunter 23/10/44; Dow Fd 31/10/44; ass 748BS/457BG Glatton 10/11/44; non-op flight, cr Birchenhough Hill, UK 31/1/45; sal 1/2/45.

43-38945 Del Hunter 20/10/44; Dow Fd 28/10/44; ass 351BS/100BG [EP-F] Thorpe Abbotts 2/11/44 DUFFY'S TUFFYS; tran 568BS/390BG [BI-N] Framlingham 3/11/44; retUS Bradley 30/6/45; 4168 BU Sth Plains 2/7/45; RFC Kingman 6/12/45. THIS IS IT.

43-38946 Del Hunter 20/10/44; Dow Fd 28/10/44; ass 324BS/91BG [DF-H] Bassingbourn 12/12/44; c/t/o for Merzhausen 24/12/44 w/?; c/l Foxton, UK; crew OK; sal 26/12/44.

43-38947 Del Hunter 20/10/44; Dow Fd 29/10/44; ass 751BS/457BG Glatton 2/11/44; retUS Bradley 28/5/45; 4168 BU Sth Plains 31/5/45; RFC Kingman 13/12/45.

43-38948 Del Hunter 20/10/44; Dow Fd 28/10/44; ass 561BS/388BG Knettishall 2/11/44; retUS Bradley 28/5/45; 4168 BU Sth Plains 30/5/45; RFC Kingman 23/11/45.

43-38949 Del Topeka 21/10/44; Lincoln 23/10/44; Grenier 27/10/44; ass 482BG Alconbury 29/10/44; tran 338BS/96BG [BX-A] 30/10/44; retUS Bradley 2/6/45; 4168 BU Sth Plains 7/6/45; RFC Kingman 5/11/45.

43-38950 Del Topeka 14/10/44; Lincoln 20/10/44; Grenier 7/11/44; ass 708BS/447BG Rattlesden 10/11/44; retUS Bradley 5/7/45; 4168 BU Sth Plains 6/7/45; RFC Kingman 9/12/45.

43-38951 Del Lincoln 20/10/44; Grenier 27/10/44; ass 603BS/398BG [N7-B] Nuthampstead 3/1/45; retUS Bradley 7/6/45; 4168 BU Sth Plains 13/6/45; RFC Kingman 28/11/45.

43-38952 Del Lincoln 30/10/44; Grenier 9/11/44; ass 839BS/487BG Lavenham 30/12/44; retUS Bradley 15/7/45; 4185 BU Independence 18/7/45; RFC Kingman 16/12/45.

43-38953 Del Lincoln 21/10/44; Grenier 27/10/44; ass 18BS/34BG Mendlesham 1/11/44; retUS Bradley 21/6/45; 4168 BU Sth Plains 23/6/45; RFC Kingman 18/12/45.

43-38954 Del Lincoln 21/10/44; Grenier 27/10/44; ass 305BG Chelveston 29/10/44; tran 508BS/351BG [YB-H] Polebrook 2/1/45; {56m} RetUS Bradley 11/6/45; 4168 BU Sth Plains 15/6/45; RFC Kingman 9/12/45.

43-38955 Del Lincoln 21/10/44; Grenier 27/10/44; ass 527BS/379BG Kimbolton 7/12/44; MIA Euskirchen, Ger 10/1/45 w/Jordan; mid air coll w/43-38237; cr Koblenz; 2KIA 7POW; MACR 11737.

43-38956 Del Lincoln 21/10/44; Grenier 27/10/44; ass 487BG Lavenham 28/10/44; sal n/b/d 30/1/45.

43-38957 Del Lincoln 23/10/44; Dow Fd 2/11/44; ass 8AF 9/11/44; 10HBS Oberpfaffenhofen 30/4/47; Recl Comp 1/10/48.

43-38958 Del Hunter 23/10/44; Dow Fd 1/11/44; ass 427BS/303BG [GN-H] Molesworth 2/11/44; MIA Leipzig 6/4/45 w/Alderman; mid air coll w/303BG a/c, cr Teplitz, Ger; 8KIA; MACR 13719. GREEN HILL BELLE.

43-38959 Del Hunter 23/10/44; Dow Fd 30/10/44; ass 4BS/34BG Mendlesham 1/11/44; retUS Bradley 21/6/45; 4168 BU Sth Plains 23/6/45; RFC Kingman 28/11/45. SHORT AND SWEET.

43-38960 Del Hunter 22/10/44; Dow Fd 30/10/44; ass 482BG Alconbury 1/11/44; tran 337BS/96BG [AW-A] Snetterton 1/11/44; sal 17/1/45; retUS Bradley 1/6/45; 4168 BU Sth Plains 3/6/45; RFC Kingman 17/12/45. SCATTER FLAK.

43-38961 Del Hunter 21/10/44; Dow Fd 31/10/44; ass 305BG Chelveston 2/11/44; retUS Bradley 3/7/45; 4168 BU Sth Plains 6/7/45; RFC Kingman 21/11/45. SHE'S A HONEY.

43-38962 Del Hunter 21/10/44; Dow Fd 29/10/44; ass 8AF 1/11/44; retUS Bradley 9/7/45; 4168 BU Sth Plains 11/7/45; RFC Kingman 8/12/45.

43-38963 Del Hunter 21/10/44; Grenier 1/11/44; ass 351BS/100BG [EP-E] Thorpe Abbotts 3/11/44; b/d Brandenburg 10/4/45 w/Bazin; jet e/a, cr Jemmeritz, Ger?; 1EVD 5KIA 4POW; sal 20/4/45; MACR 14170.

43-38964 Del Hunter 21/10/44; Dow Fd 30/10/44; ass 305BG Chelveston 3/1/45; tran 401BG Deenethorpe 1/6/45; retUS Bradley 7/6/45; 4168 BU Sth Plains 11/6/45; RFC Kingman 30/11/45.

43-38965 Del Hunter 23/10/44; Dow Fd 31/10/44; ass 349BS/100BG [XR-Q] Thorpe Abbotts 2/11/44; tran 560BS/388BG Knettishall 3/11/44; ct fire en route Nurnberg 21/2/45 w/?; c/l Belgium; 9RTD; sal 5/3/45. OH KAY.

43-38966 Del Hunter 24/10/44; Tulsa 27/10/44; Grenier 5/11/44; ass 493BG Debach 10/11/44; retUS Bradley 12/7/45; 4185 BU Independence 13/7/45; RFC Kingman 18/12/45. HUN BUMP.

43-38967 Del Hunter 23/10/44; Dow Fd 30/10/44; ass 533BS/381BG [VP-L] Ridgewell 19/12/44; retUS Bradley 28/5/45; 4168 BU Sth Plains 31/5/45; RFC Kingman 18/11/45.

43-38968 Del Hunter 23/10/44; Grenier 1/11/44; ass 338BS/96BG Snetterton 4/11/44; MIA Cologne 7/1/45 w/Yenton; mid air coll w/95BG a/c; cr Hintermulin, Ger; 7KIA 3POW; MACR 11571.

43-38969 Del Hunter 26/10/44; Fairfield 5/11/44; ass 836BS/487BG [2G-N] Lavenham 19/11/44; tran 327BS/92BG [UX-M] Podington 30/12/44; sal 13/5/45; re-ass 10 HBS Oberpfaffenhofen 30/4/47; Recl Comp 5/8/48. BABY STEVE.

43-38970 Del Hunter 24/20/44; Dow Fd 30/10/44; ass 603BS/398BG [N7-A] Nuthampstead 3/1/45; retUS Bradley 7/6/45; 4168 BU Sth Plains 11/6/45; RFC Kingman 30/11/45.

43-38971 Del Hunter 24/10/44; Dow Fd 9/11/44; ass 7BS/34BG Mendlesham 10/11/44; 18BS; b/d Ahlhorn, Ger 22/3/45 w/?; c/l Continent; sal 23/3/45; MACR 13598.

43-38972 Del Hunter 27/10/44; Dow Fd 7/11/44; ass 391BS/34BG Mendlesham 10/11/44 DUKE THE SPOOK; retUS Bradley 20/6/45; 4168 BU Sth Plains 24/6/44; RFC Kingman 8/11/45. LUCIE.

43-38973 Del Hunter 24/10/44; Dow Fd 1/11/44; ass 305BG Chelveston 5/12/44; ex-Kassel 15/12/44 w/?; hit radio mast in poor visibilty, cr Norton, UK; 9KIA; sal.

43-38974 Del Hunter 26/10/44; Dow Fd 3/11/44; ass 544BS/384BG [SU-H] Grafton Underwood 7/2/45; sal 9AF Germany 10/12/45.

43-38975 Del Hunter 26/10/44; Dow Fd 9/11/44; ass 350BS/100BG [LN-Z] Thorpe Abbotts 10/11/44; retUS Bradley 26/6/45; 4168 BU Sth Plains 29/6/45; RFC Kingman 30/11/45.

43-38976 Del Hunter 27/10/44; Grenier 21/11/44; ass 96BG Snetterton 27/11/44; tran 305BG Chelveston 28/11/44; 544BS/384BG [SU-A] Grafton Underwood 9/5/45; sal 9AF Germany 31/5/46.

43-38977 Del Hunter 27/10/44; Dow Fd 7/11/44; ass 532BS/381BG [VE-H] Ridgewell 8/2/45; {1+m} RetUS Bradley 27/5/45; 4168 BU Sth Plains 30/5/45; RFC Kingman 20/11/45. FRENCH DRESSING.

43-38978 Slated 305BG, but tran Eglin Fd 23/10/44; Gt Falls 27/10/44; 610 BU Eglin 31/10/44; 611 BU Eglin 1/4/45; 2137 BU Hendricks 12/8/45; RFC Altus 21/11/45. (survived as Civil N4960V and broken up Oregon in late 1950s).

43-38979 Del Hunter 27/10/44; Grenier 5/11/44; ass 524BS/379BG [WA-E] Kimbolton 20/2/45; retUS Bradley 3/7/45; 4168 BU Sth Plains 4/7/45; RFC Kingman 24/11/45.

43-38980 Del Hunter 28/10/44; Dow Fd 7/11/44; ass 8AF? 11/44; retUS Bradley 29/6/45; 4168 BU Sth Plains 3/7/45; RFC Kingman 26/11/45.

43-38981 Del Hunter 28/10/44; Cheyenne 3/11/44; Lowry 20/11/44; Dow Fd 19/1/45; ass 407BS/92BG [PY-L] Podington 20/3/45; b/d Pilsen 25/4/45 w/?; c/l Continent; sal 8/5/45.

43-38982 Del Hunter 29/10/44; Dow Fd 7/11/44; ass 452BG Deopham Green 10/11/44; retUS Bradley 29/6/45; 4168 BU Sth Plains 2/7/45; RFC Kingman 23/11/45.

43-38983 Del Hunter 29/10/44; Dow Fd 9/11/44; ass 351BS/100BG Thorpe Abbotts 19/11/44; tran 533BS/381BG [VP-S] Ridgewell 19/12/44; retUS Bradley 28/5/45; 4168 BU Sth Plains 30/5/45; RFC Kingman 30/11/45. FORT LANSING EMANCIPATOR.

43-38984 Del Lincoln 28/10/44; Dow Fd 2/11/44; ass 8AF 9/11/44; retUS Bradley 15/7/45; 4185 BU Independence 19/7/45; RFC Kingman 14/12/45.

43-38985 Del Lincoln 29/10/44; Grenier 7/11/44; ass 305BG Chelveston 2/1/45; tran 351BG Polebrook 5/45; retUS Bradley 13/6/45; 4168 BU Sth Plains 17/6/45; RFC Kingman 2/12/45.

43-38986 Del Lincoln 29/10/44; Dow Fd 2/11/44; ass 533BS/381BG [VP-M] Ridgewell 8/12/44; b/d Ludwigsdorf 12/12/44 w/Orcutt; slight mid air coll, c/l Continent, crew OK; sal 2/1/45.

43-38987 Del Lincoln 29/10/44; Grenier 12/11/44; ass 7BS/34BG Mendlesham 19/11/44; retUS Bradley 21/6/45; 4168 BU Sth Plains 23/6/45; RFC Kingman 25/11/45.

43-38988 Del Lincoln 29/10/44; Dow Fd 12/11/44; ass 839BS/487BG Lavenham 2/1/45; MIA Weimar 9/2/45 w/Shepard; flak, cr Heringen, Ger; 9POW; MACR 12372.

43-38989 Del Lincoln 28/10/44; Grenier 2/11/44; ass 407BS/92BG Podington 3/12/44; retUS Bradley 3/7/45; 4168 BU Sth Plains 8/7/45; RFC Kingman 16/12/45.

43-38990 Del Lincoln 28/10/44; Grenier 2/11/44; ass 334BS/95BG [BG-X] Horham 3/11/44; retUS Bradley 20/6/45; 4168 BU Sth Plains 23/6/45; RFC Kingman 15/12/45.

43-38991 Del Lincoln 30/10/44; Dow Fd 12/11/44; ass 7BS/34BG Mendlesham 19/11/44; retUS Bradley 20/6/45; Greenville 27/6/45; 4168 BU Sth Plains 16/7/45; RFC Kingman 22/11/45. START SWIMMING.

43-38992 Del Lincoln 1/11/44; Grenier 12/11/44; ass 351BS/100BG [EP-S] Thorpe Abbotts 19/11/44; b/d Kiel 3/4/45 w/Baldwin; flak, cr Texel Is, Hol; 8KIA 2POW; MACR 13717.

43-38993 Del Lincoln 31/10/44; Dow Fd 12/11/44; ass 600BS/398BG [N8-Y] Nuthampstead 3/1/45; sal 19/6/45.

43-38994 Del Lincoln 31/10/44; Grenier 12/11/44; ass 546BS/384BG [BK-Q] Grafton Underwood 17/12/44; sal 9AF Germany 29/12/45. DEVASTATING LADY.

43-38995 Del Lincoln 31/10/44; Grenier 12/11/44; ass 710BS/447BG Rattlesden 11/11/44; hit by debris from exploding B-17 during morning preparation 21/2/45, sal; two other a/c dest and six men injured.

43-38996 Del Lincoln 1/11/44; Grenier 12/11/44; ass 334BS/95BG [BG-T] Horham 19/11/44; retUS Bradley 22/5/45; 4168 BU Sth Plains 24/5/45; RFC Kingman 17/12/45.

43-38997 –

43-38998 Del Lincoln 1/11/44; Dow Fd 12/11/44; ass 535BS/381BG [MS-S] Ridgewell 19/12/44; retUS Bradley 11/6/45; 4168 BU Sth Plains 16/6/45; RFC Kingman 20/12/45. CRACK-A-DAWN.

43-38999 Del Lincoln 1/11/44; Grenier 12/11/44; ass 493BG Debach 14/11/44; tran 358BS/303BG [VK-F] Molesworth 17/12/44; 457BG Glatton 22/5/45; retUS Bradley 10/6/45; 4168 BU Sth Plains 15/6/45; RFC Kingman 25/11/45. EMMA.

43-39000 Del Lincoln 3/11/44; Grenier 12/11/44; ass 322BS/91BG [LG-E] Bassingbourn 11/12/44; {38m} RetUS Bradley 12/6/45; 4168 BU Sth Plains 15/6/45; RFC Kingman 4/12/45. EXTRA SPECIAL.

43-39001 Del Lincoln 3/11/44; Dow Fd 12/11/44; ass 510BS/351BG [TU-M] Polebrook 11/11/44; {64m} RetUS Bradley 11/6/45; 4168 BU Sth Plains 14/6/45; RFC Kingman 5/12/45. COUPE DE GRACE II.

43-39002 Del Lincoln 3/11/44; Grenier 12/11/44; ass 8AF? 20/11/44; retUS Bradley 7/7/45; 4168 BU Sth Plains 10/7/45; RFC Kingman 22/11/45.

43-39003 Del Lincoln 3/11/44; Dow Fd 12/11/44; ass 524BS/379BG [WA-G] Kimbolton 2/1/45; MIA Oranienburg 10/4/45 w/Howard; jet e/a, cr Berlin; 3KIA 5POW; MACR 13879.

43-39004 Del Lincoln 3/11/44; Grenier 15/11/44; ass 8AF 31/12/44; sal 9AF Germany 10/5/46.

43-39005 Del Lincoln 4/11/44; Dow Fd 15/11/44; ass 418BS/100BG [LD-Y] Thorpe Abbotts 4/12/44; tran 571BS/390BG [FC-J] 5/12/44; retUS Bradley 3/7/45; 4168 BU Sth Plains 8/7/45; RFC Kingman 18/12/45. LUCKY LASSIE.

43-39006 Del Lincoln 6/11/44; Grenier 3/12/44; ass 8AF 4/12/44; retUS Bradley 10/7/45; 4168 BU Sth Plains 12/7/45; RFC Kingman 25/11/45.

43-39007 Del Lincoln 6/11/44; Dow Fd 26/11/44; ass 338BS/96BG [BX-Z] Snetterton 29/11/44; tran 731BS/452BG Deopham Green 30/11/44; retUS 1103 BU Morrison 25/12/45; 594 BU Topeka 14/1/46; RFC Walnut Ridge 21/1/46.

43-39008 Del Lincoln 6/11/44; Dow Fd 26/11/44; ass 563BS/388BG Knettishall 27/11/44; retUS Bradley 28/6/45; 4168 BU Sth Plains 30/6/45; RFC Kingman 8/12/45. IRRESISTABLE YOU.

43-39009 Del Hunter 6/11/44; Grenier 17/11/44; ass 493BS Debach 19/11/44; retUS Bradley 9/7/45; 4168 BU Sth Plains 11/7/45; RFC Kingman 24/11/45.

43-39010 Del Hunter 6/11/44; Grenier 17/11/44; ass 335BS/95BG [OE-X] Horham 19/11/44; b/d Frankfurt 5/1/45 w/?; f/l France; sal 21/1/45.

43-39011 Del Hunter 6/11/44; Grenier 17/11/44; ass 427BS/303BG [GN-A] Molesworth 28/1/45; b/d Plauen, Ger 19/3/45 w/?; f/l Soviet territory; sal 1/4/45.

43-39012 Del Hunter 6/11/44; Grenier 14/11/44; ass 532BS/381BG [VE-J] Ridgewell 8/2/45; MIA {1+m} Kassel 9/3/45 w/Schermann; flak, cr Fritzlar, Ger; 7KIA 2POW; MACR 12960. MISS FORTUNE.

43-39013 Del Hunter 6/11/44; Grenier 14/11/44; ass 568BS/390BG [BI-H] Framlingham 19/11/44; retUS Bradley 30/6/45; 4168 BU Sth Plains 3/7/45; RFC Kingman 10/12/45. SMILING JACK.

43-39014 Del Hunter 6/11/44; Grenier 14/11/44; ass 401BS/91BG [LL-C] Bassingbourn 9/1/45; (flew two POW trips) {26m} RetUS Bradley 12/7/45; 4185 BU Independence 13/7/45; RFC Kingman 9/12/45. HOT SHOT CHARLIE.

43-39015 Del Lincoln 6/11/44; Grenier 2/12/44; ass 8AF 4/12/44; retUS 1103 BU Morrison 22/10/45; 593 BU Charleston 28/10/45; RFC Walnut Ridge 8/1/46.

43-39016 Del Lincoln 9/11/44; Grenier 3/12/44; ass 525BS/379BG [FR-A] Kimbolton 6/12/44; retUS Bradley 11/7/45; 4168 BU Sth Plains 12/7/45; RFC Kingman 17/11/45.

43-39017 Del Lincoln 9/11/44; Dow Fd 26/11/44; ass 338BS/96BG Snetterton 1/1/45; retUS Bradley 5/7/45; 4168 BU Sth Plains 6/7/45; RFC Kingman 6/11/45.

43-39018 Del Lincoln 9/11/44; Grenier 2/12/44; ass 379BG Kimbolton 6/12/44; tran 337BS/96BG [AW-P] Snetterton 10/12/44; MIA Regensburg 25/2/45 w/Proctor; flak, f/l Deipoldsau, Switz; 7INT 1KIA 1WIA. DINAH MITE.

43-39019 Del Lincoln 9/11/44; Dow Fd 3/12/44; ass 545BS/384BG [JD-A] Grafton Underwood 8/12/44; tran 401BG Deenethorpe 8/5/45; 305BG Chelveston 20/5/45; sal 9AF Germany 23/5/46.

43-39020 Del Hunter 24/11/44; Grenier 16/12/44; ass 510BS/351BG [TU-C] Polebrook 20/2/45; {38m} RetUS Bradley 28/5/45; 4168 BU Sth Plains 30/5/45; RFC Kingman 23/11/45. WAR HAWK.

43-39021 Del –

43-39022 Del Lincoln 9/11/44; Grenier 16/12/44; ass 8AF 18/12/44; sal 9AF Germany 31/5/46.

43-39023 Del Lincoln 10/11/44; Grenier 2/12/44; ass 563BS/388BG Knettishall 15/12/44; tran 568BS/390BG [BI-K] Framlingham 1/1/45 MAIDEN PRAYER; retUS Bradley 30/6/45; 4168 BU Sth Plains 2/7/45; RFC Kingman 25/11/45. MY BONNIE.

43-39024 Del Lincoln 10/11/44; Dow Fd 16/12/44; ass 568BS/390BG [BI-X] Framlingham 17/12/44; 570BS [DI-X]; retUS Bradley 3/7/45; 4168 BU Sth Plains 6/7/45; RFC Kingman 5/11/45. LADY FAITHFUL.

43-39025 Del Lincoln 10/11/44; Dow Fd 3/12/44; ass 535BS/381BG [MS-W] Ridgewell 17/2/45; {38+m} (one POW trip); retUS Bradley 10/6/45; 4168 BU Sth Plains 14/6/45; RFC Kingman 6/12/45. BUCKEYE.

43-39026 Del Hunter 10/11/44; Grenier 20/11/44; ass 327BS/92BG [UX-L] Podington 2/1/45; MIA Munich 25/2/45 w/Chase; flak, cr Karolsheim, Ger; 9POW; MACR 12719. REBA JANE.

43-39027 Del Hunter 11/11/44; ATS Wright Fd 15/11/44; 116 BU Ft Dix 24/11/45; 610 BU Eglin 6/4/45; 4000 BU Wright 14/6/45; 4000 BU Patterson 12/9/45; RFC Walnut Ridge 7/1/46.

43-39028 Del Hunter 11/11/44; Grenier 19/11/44; ass 368BS/306BG [BO-O] Thurleigh 17/12/44; retUS Bradley 7/6/45; 4168 BU Sth Plains 16/6/45; RFC Kingman 5/12/45.

43-39029 Del Hunter 11/11/44; Grenier 19/11/44; ass 708BS/447BG Rattlesden 21/11/44; 710BS; tran 388BG Knettishall 28/11/44; retUS Bradley 20/8/45; 4185 BU Independence 28/8/45; RFC Kingman 25/12/45.

43-39030 Del Hunter 11/11/44; Grenier 23/11/44; ass 8AF 26/11/44; re-ass 10HBS Oberpfaffenhofen 30/4/47; Recl Comp 7/1/49.

43-39031 Del Hunter 11/11/44; Grenier 25/11/44; ass 368BS/306BG Thurleigh 17/12/44; MIA bingen, Ger 29/12/44 w/Woellner; flak, cr Bingen; 4KIA 5POW; MACR 11254.

43-39032 Del Lincoln 13/11/44; Grenier 3/12/44; ass 571BS/390BG [FC-B] Framlingham 6/12/44; retUS Bradley 3//7/45; 4168 BU Sth Plains 6/7/45; RFC Kingman 21/11/45. THE DEACON.

43-39033 Del Lincoln 11/11/44; Grenier 3/12/44; ass

366BS/305BG [KY-S] Chelveston 3/1/45; sal 9AF Germany 22/6/45; retUS Bradley 23/6/45; 4168 BU Sth Plains 18/6/45; RFC Kingman 4/12/45.

43-39034 Del Lincoln 11/11/44; Dow Fd 3/12/44; ass 838BS/487BG Lavenham 2/1/45; retUS Bradley 13/7/45; 4185 BU Independence 16/7/45; RFC Kingman 14/12/45.

43-39035 Del Lincoln 11/11/44; Dow Fd 3/12/44; ass 547BS/384BG [SO-F] Grafton Underwood 1/1/45; b/d Plauen, Ger 19/3/45 w/?; cr Reigate, UK; 9KIA; sal.

43-39036 Del Lincoln 11/11/44; Grenier 3/12/44; ass 8AF 6/12/44; retUS Bradley 28/6/45; 4168 BU Sth Plains 1/7/45; RFC Kingman 26/11/45.

43-39037 Del Lincoln 13/11/44; Dow Fd 3/12/44; ass 336BS/95BG [ET-T] Horham 12/12/44; retUS Bradley 21/6/45; 4168 BU Sth Plains 24/6/45; RFC Kingman 14/12/45.

43-39038 Del Lincoln 13/11/44; Grenier 15/12/44; ass 384BG Grafton Underwood 4/2/45; tran 603BS/398BG [N7-Q] Nuthampstead 4/3/45; retUS Bradley 7/6/45; 4168 BU Sth Plains 13/6/45; RFC Kingman 30/11/45.

43-39039 Del Lincoln 13/11/44; Grenier 15/12/44; ass 407BS/92BG [PY-P] Podington 28/3/45; sal 9AF Germany 29/12/45. LUCKY ROZZIE.

43-39040 Del Cleveland 14/11/44; 2114 BU Lockburn 3/1/45; 610 BU Eglin 5/1/45; 611 BU Eglin 1/11/45; 609 BU Eglin 3/2/47; 611 BU Eglin 20/2/47; Recl Comp 8/5/47.

43-39041 Del Lincoln 12/11/44; Dow Fd 3/12/44; ass 570BS/390BG [DI-U] Framlingham 12/12/44; retUS Bradley 7/7/45; 4168 BU Sth Plains 9/7/45; 237 BU Kirtland 12/12/45; RFC Albuquerque 7/2/46.

43-39042 Del Milwaukee 16/11/44; 2114 BU Lockburn 23/11/44; Columbus 6/1/45; 121 BU Bradley 28/6/45; 4168 BU Sth Plains 1/7/45; 613 BU Phillips 28/2/46; Aberdeen 6/3/46.

43-39043 –

43-39044 Del Lincoln 18/11/44; Dow Fd 19/12/44; ass 8AF 4/12/44; retUS Bradley 12/7/45; 4185 BU Independence 13/7/45; RFC Kingman 21/12/45.

43-39045 Del Lincoln 19/11/44; Dow Fd 3/12/44; ass 838BS/487BG Lavenham 2/1/45; retUS Bradley 14/7/45; 4185 BU Independence 17/7/45; RFC Kingman 8/12/45. CARRY ME BACK.

43-39046 Del Lincoln 19/11/44; Dow Fd 3/12/44; ass 407BS/92BG [PY-D] Podington 2/1/45; sal 9AF Germany 31/7/46. CON GIRL.

43-39047 Del Lincoln 19/11/44; Dow Fd 3/12/44; ass 8AF 5/12/44; retUS Bradley 28/5/45; 4168 BU Sth Plains 30/5/45; 613 BU Phillips 13/3/46.

43-39048 Del Lincoln 19/11/44; Dow Fd 28/11/44; ass 407BS/92BG [PY-J] Podington 2/1/45; secret mission 1/6/45, ret 2/6/45; sal 9AF Germany 29/12/45.

43-39049 Del Hunter 19/11/44; Grenier 4/12/44; ass 839BS/487BG Lavenham 13/4/45; retUS Bradley 12/7/45; 4185 BU Independence 16/7/45; RFC Kingman 14/12/45.

43-39050 Del Hunter 19/11/44; Dow Fd 2/12/44; ass 863BS/493BG Debach 4/12/44; MIA Brunswick 3/3/45 w/Graff; e/a, cr Hildesheim, Ger; 3KIA 6POW; MACR 12886.

43-39051 Del Hunter 19/11/44; Grenier 4/12/44; ass 8AF 7/12/44; retUS Bradley 7/7/45; 4168 BU Sth Plains 9/7/45; Recl Comp 7/6/46.

43-39052 Del Hunter 19/11/44; Grenier 2/12/44; ass 335BS/95BG [OE-S] Horham 4/12/44; retUS Bradley 25/6/45; 4168 BU Sth Plains 28/6/45; RFC Kingman 1/12/45.

43-39053 Del Hunter 19/7/44; Dow Fd 29/11/44; ass 546BS/384BG [BK-D] Grafton Underwood 7/1/45; MIA Coesfeld 23/3/45 w/Conner; flak, cr Duisburg; 4KIA 6POW; MACR 13611. HEAVENLY BODY.

43-39054 Del Hunter 19/11/44; Dow Fd 28/11/44; ass 388BG Knettishall 30/11/44; tran 710BS/447BG Rattlesden 1/12/44; n/b/d 24/3/45; sal 28/3/45.

43-39055 Del Hunter 29/11/44; Grenier 10/12/44; ass 335BS/95BG [OE-R] Horham 12/12/44; b/d Hohenbudberg, Ger 28/1/45 w/Mercer; f/l France; 1KIA 8RTD; sal.

43-39056 Del Hunter 20/11/44; Grenier 2/12/44; ass 8AF 3/12/44; sal n/b/d 6/9/45.

43-39057 Del Hunter 19/11/44; Dow Fd 29/11/44; ass 708BS/447BG Rattlesden 4/12/44; retUS Bradley 5/7/45; 4168 BU Sth Plains 7/7/45; RFC Kingman 17/11/45.

43-39058 Del Hunter 19/11/44; Grenier 2/12/44; ass 570BS/390BG [DI-N] Framlingham 4/12/44; MIA Dresden 2/3/45 w/Alberts; flak, cr Leitmeritz, Ger; 9RTD; MACR 12847.

43-39059 Del Hunter 19/11/44; Grenier 2/12/44; ass 532BS/381BG Ridgewell 6/12/44; retUS Bradley 11/7/45; 4168 BU Sth Plains 12/7/45; RFC Kingman 21/11/45.

43-39060 Del Hunter 19/11/44; Dow Fd 6/12/44; ass 487BG Lavenham 12/12/44; tran 546BS/384BG [BK-F] Grafton Underwood 7/1/45; sal 9AF Germany 23/8/46.

43-39061 Del Hunter 20/11/44; Grenier 3/12/44; ass 427BS/303BG Molesworth 5/12/44; MIA Minster Stein 16/2/45 w/Wertz; flak, cr Kleve, Ger; 3KIA 6POW; MACR 12439.

43-39062 Del Hunter 20/11/44; Grenier 3/12/44; ass 8AF 4/12/44; sal 9AF Germany 10/5/46.

43-39063 Del Lincoln 22/11/44; Grenier 3/12/44; ass 326BS/92BG [JW-J] Podington 2/1/45; sal b/d 11/4/45.

43-39064 Del Lincoln 19/11/44; Grenier 3/12/44; ass 569BS/390BG [CC-E] Framlingham 6/12/44; retUS Bradley 3/7/45; 4168 BU Sth Plains 6/7/45; RFC Kingman 8/12/45. SKY QUEEN.

43-39065 Del Lincoln 20/11/44; Grenier 3/12/44; ass 8AF 4/12/44; re-ass ATC (Europe) 31/7/46; retUS 4141 BU Pyote 23/11/47; 4112 BU Olmstead 30/11/47; 4141 BU Pyote 18/1/48; Recl Comp 27/7/48.

43-39066 Del Lincoln 22/11/44; Dow Fd 3/12/44; ass 493BG Debach 6/12/44; retUS Bradley 5/7/45; 4168 BU Sth Plains 7/7/45; RFC Kingman 17/12/45.

43-39067 Del Lincoln 23/11/44; Grenier 15/12/44; ass 8AF 17/12/44; retUS Bradley 29/6/45; 4168 BU Sth Plains 1/7/45; RFC Kingman 26/2/46.

43-39068 Del Lincoln 20/11/44; Dow Fd 3/12/44; ass 838BS/487BG [2C-C] Lavenham 6/12/44; b/d Frankfurt 8/1/45 w/?; c/l St Margaret's, UK; crew OK, sal 11/1/45.

43-39069 Del Lincoln 20/11/44; Grenier 3/12/44; ass 561BS/388 Knettishall 6/12/44 MY LIL BABY; retUS Bradley 24/6/45; 4168 BU Sth Plains 27/6/45; RFC Kingman 7/11/45. SWEET LORRAINE.

43-39070 Del Lincoln 23/11/44; Grenier 15/12/44; ass 860BS/493BG Debach 19/12/44; MIA Kaltenkirchen 7/4/45 w/Whitson; e/a, cr Warin, Ger; 10POW; MACR 13890.

43-39071 Del Lincoln 23/11/44; Grenier 15/12/44; ass 18BS/34BG Mendlesham 19/12/44; b/d Ulm 4/3/45 w/?; cr France; 9KIA; sal 4/4/45.

43-39072 Del Lincoln 26/11/44; Dow Fd 15/12/44; ass 748BS/457BG Glatton 3/45; retUS Bradley 22/5/45; 4168 BU Sth Plains 25/5/45; RFC Kingman 27/11/45.

43-39073 Del ATS Seattle 21/11/44; 4000 BU Wright 13/9/45; 4117 BU Robins 17/9/45; 4000 BU Wright 13/11/45; Recl Comp 2/8/46.

43-39074 Del Hunter 24/11/44; Dow Fd 8/12/44; slated 8AF 11/12/44; tran 4121 BU Kelly 17/1/45; re-ass 2ER Kadena, Japan 18/1/45; 3168 VB Kanoya 18/6/45; 13 AR Tachikawa 3/6/48; 3168 VB Kadena 5/6/48; 13 AR Jama 13/7/48; 13 AR Itami 8/10/48; Recl Comp 2/3/49.

43-39075 Del Hunter 24/11/44; Dow Fd 21/12/44; ass 337BS/96BG Snetterton 23/12/44; b/d Plauen 26/3/44 w/?; cr?; sal 27/3/45.

43-39076 Del Hunter 24/11/44; Dow Fd 3/12/44; ass 527BS/379BG [FO-N] Kimbolton 19/1/45; retUS Bradley 5/7/45; 4168 BU Sth Plains 7/7/45; RFC Kingman 22/11/45.

43-39077 Del Hunter 25/11/44; Grenier 4/12/44; ass 8AF 7/12/44; retUS Bradley 6/7/45; 4168 BU Sth Plains 9/7/45; 613 BU Phillips 24/3/46.

43-39078 Del Hunter 24/11/44; Grenier 16/12/44; ass 863BS/493BG Debach 19/12/44; b/d Hamburg 30/3/45 w/?; cr Bartlow, UK, 6KIA; sal 26/4/45.

43-39079 Del Hunter 25/11/44; Grenier 7/12/44; ass 569BS/390BG Framlingham 12/12/44; MIA Chemnitz 14/2/45 w/Gaik; flak, cr Weisbaden; 7KIA 2POW; MACR 12350.

43-39080 Del Hunter 25/11/44; Dow Fd 8/12/44; ass 749BS/457BG Glatton 4/2/45; retUS Bradley 9/6/45; 4168 BU Sth Plains 14/6/45; RFC Kingman 4/12/45.

43-39081 Del Lincoln 25/11/44; Grenier 15/12/44; ass 427BS/303BG [GN-G] Molesworth 28/1/45; MIA Minster Stein 16/2/45 w/?.

43-39082 Del Lincoln 25/11/44; Grenier 15/12/44; ass 8AF 16/12/44; retUS Bradley 15/8/45; 4168 BU Sth Plains 26/11/45; 613 BU Phillips 17/4/46.

43-39083 Del Lincoln 26/11/44; Grenier 15/12/44; ass 8AF 18/12/44; re-ass 10HBS Oberpfaffenhofen 30/4/47; Recl Comp 11/2/49.

43-39084 Del Lincoln 26/11/44; Grenier 15/12/44; ass 560BS/388BG Knettishall 19/12/44; retUS Bradley 24/6/45; 4168 BU Sth Plains 28/6/45; RFC Kingman 30/11/45.

43-39085 Del Lincoln 29/11/44; Grenier 15/12/44; ass 8AF 29/12/44; burned out, sal 3/1/45.

43-39086 Del Lincoln 29/11/44; Grenier 20/12/44; ass 8AF 23/12/44; re-ass 10HBS Oberpfaffenhofen 30/4/47; Recl Comp 1/10/48.

43-39087 Del Lincoln 29/11/44; Grenier 15/12/44; ass 749BS/457BG Glatton 23/12/44; 751BS; retUS Bradley 22/5/45; 4168 BU Sth Plains 24/5/45; RFC Kingman 5/12/45. BETTER, QUICKER & CHEAPER.

43-39088 Del Lincoln 29/11/44; Grenier 15/12/44; ass 550BS/385BG Gt Ashfield 17/12/44; retUS Bradley 26/6/45; 4168 BU Sth Plains 28/6/44; RFC Kingman 29/11/45. GYPSY PRINCESS.

43-39089 Del Lincoln 29/11/44; Grenier 15/12/44; ass 452BG Deopham Green 19/12/44; retUS Bradley 29/6/45; 4168 BU Sth Plains 1/7/45; RFC Kingman 1/12/45.

43-39090 Del Lincoln 29/11/44; Grenier 15/12/44; ass 8AF 18/12/44; sal 9AF Germany 10/5/46.

43-39091 Del Lincoln 29/11/44; Dow Fd 11/12/44; ass 832BS/486BG [3R-D] Sudbury 19/12/44; retUS Bradley 11/7/45; 4168 BU Sth Plains 13/7/45; RFC Kingman 24/11/45. CALIFORNIA'S GOLDEN BARE.

43-39092 Del Lincoln 30/11/44; Grenier 15/12/44; ass 748BS/457BG Glatton 21/3/45; retUS Bradley 4/6/45; 4168 BU Sth Plains 6/6/45; RFC Kingman 17/12/45.

43-39093 Del Lincoln 30/11/44; Grenier 23/12/44; ass 562BS/388BG Knettishall 1/1/45; retUS Bradley 27/6/45; 4168 BU Sth Plains 2/7/45; RFC Kingman

3/12/45. PUNCHIN' JUDY.
43-39094 Del Lincoln 30/11/44; Dow Fd 18/12/44; ass 379BG Kimbolton 11/4/45; retUS Bradley 30/6/45; 4168 BU Sth Plains 4/7/45; RFC Kingman 28/11/45.
43-39095 Del Lincoln 30/11/44; Grenier 15/12/44; ass 8AF 19/12/44; retUS Bradley 30//6/45; 4168 BU Sth Plains 2/7/45; RFC Kingman 26/2/46.
43-39096 Del Lincoln 30/11/44; Grenier 15/12/44; ass 410BS/94BG [GL-K] Rougham 17/12/44 MIGHTY MIKE; tran 358BS/303BG [VK-M] Molesworth 28/1/45; {30+m} RetUS, RFC Walnut Ridge 4/1/46.
43-39097 Del Lincoln 30/11/44; Grenier 15/12/44; ass 8AF 18/12/44; retUS Bradley 17/6/45; 4168 BU Sth Plains 21/6/45; RFC Kingman 26/2/46.
43-39098 Del Lincoln 3/12/44; Grenier 15/12/44; ass 601BS/398BG [3O-C] Nuthampstead 17/1/45; b/d Chemnitz 6/2/45 w/?; f/l Continent, sal.
43-39099 Del Hunter 30/11/44; Grenier 9/12/44; ass 838BS/487BG Lavenham 13/4/45; retUS Bradley 11/7/45; 4168 BU Sth Plains 12/7/45; RFC Kingman 10/12/45.
43-39100 Del Hunter 1/12/44; Grenier 13/12/44; ass 410BS/94BG [GL-J] Rougham 16/12/44; retUS Bradley 5/7/45; 4168 BU Sth Plains 6/7/45; RFC Kingman 7/12/45.
43-39101 Del Lincoln 2/12/44; Grenier 15/10/44; ass 603BS/398BG [N7-C] Nuthampstead 4/3/45; retUS Bradley 29/5/45; 4168 BU Sth Plains 31/5/45; RFC Kingman 18/11/45.
43-39102 Del Lincoln 2/12/44; Grenier 15/12/44; ass 600BS/398BG [N8-V] Nuthampstead 27/2/45; retUS Bradley 25/5/45; 4168 BU Sth Plains 29/5/45; RFC Kingman 27/11/45.
43-39103 Del Lincoln 8/12/44; Grenier 21/12/44; ass 350BS/100BG Thorpe Abbotts 23/12/44; tran 34BG Mendlesham 24/12/44; retUS Bradley 20/6/45; 4168 BU Sth Plains 23/6/45; RFC Kingman 14/12/45.
43-39104 Del Lincoln 2/12/44; Grenier 15/12/44; ass 8AF 16/12/44; sal 9AF Germany 23/5/46.
43-39105 Del Lincoln 3/12/44; Grenier 15/12/44; ass 337BS/96BG [AW-Q] 17/12/44; MIA Zeitz 31/3/45 w/?; flak, f/l Fulda, Ger; 2KIA 8RTD; sal 14/4/45.
43-39106 Del Hunter 7/12/44; Dow Fd 17/12/44; ass 327BS/92BG [UX-D] Podington 4/3/45; 407BG; mission to Port Lyautey, Morr 12/6/45; ret 13/6/45; sal 9AF Germany 10/12/45. POP'S FLOP SHOP.
43-39107 Del Hunter 7/12/44; Dow Fd 21/12/44; ass 96BG Snetterton 23/12/44; tran 560BS/388BG Knettishall 24/12/44; retUS Bradley 24/6/45; 4168 BU Sth Plains 27/6/45; RFC Kingman 3/11/45. SNAFU II.
43-39108 Del Lincoln 6/12/44; Grenier 15/12/44; ass 839BS/487BG Lavenham 19/12/44; MIA Brunswick 3/3/45 w/Webb; e/a, cr Cologne; 4EVD 5POW; MACR 12888.
43-39109 Del Hunter 7/12/44; Dow Fd 19/12/44; ass 561BS/388BG Knettishall 1/1/45; tran 401BG Deenethorpe 28/5/45; retUS Bradley 5/7/45; 4168 BU Sth Plains 6/7/45; 613 BU Phillips 28/3/46. IKKY POO.
43-39110 Del Hunter 7/12/44; Dow Fd 21/12/44; ass 327BS/92BG [UX-E] Podington 4/3/45; MIA Dresden 17/4/45 w/Paul; mid air coll w/44-8903; cr Dresden; 6KIA 2POW; MACR 14053.
43-39111 Del Lincoln 7/12/44; Grenier 15/12/44; ass 527BS/379BG [FO-K] Kimbolton 19/1/45; MIA Nurnberg 20/2/45 w/Palmer; flak, cr Nurnberg; 9KIA; MACR 12541.
43-39112 Del Lincoln 7/12/44; Grenier 15/12/44; ass 8AF 18/12/44; used as ASR/Radar a/c from Weisbaden, Ger, at end of war.
43-39113 Del Lincoln 7/12/44; Grenier 15/12/44; ass 379BG Kimbolton 9/2/45; retUS Bradley 6/7/45; 4168 BU Sth Plains 8/7/45; RFC Kingman 5/12/45.
43-39114 Del Lincoln 7/12/44; Grenier 15/12/44; ass 8AF 18/12/44; sal 9AF Germany 31/5/46.
43-39115 Del Lincoln 7/12/44; Grenier 15/12/44; ass 8AF 16/12/44; re-ass 10HBS Oberpfaffenhofen 30/4/47; Recl Comp 11/2/49.
43-39116 Del Hunter 7/12/44; Grenier 16/12/44; ass 423BS/306BG [T] 23/2/45; tran 544BS/384BG [SU-G] Grafton Underwood 9/5/45; sal 9AF Germany 23/8/46. NAUGHTY NANCY.
43-39117 Del Hunter 8/12/44; Dow Fd 21/12/44; ass 548BS/385BG Gt Ashfield 22/12/44; retUS Bradley 24/6/45; 4168 BU Sth Plains 26/6/45; RFC Kingman 8/12/45.
43-39118 Del Lincoln 8/12/44; Dow Fd 17/12/44; ass 8AF 19/12/44; retUS Bradley 11/6/45; 4168 BU Sth Plains 14/6/45; 613 BU Phillips 13/3/46.
43-39119 Del Wright Fd 8/12/44 for rocket launch tests to combat V-1s; Romulus 12/12/44; ATS Wright 15/12/44; 4119 BU Brookley 29/1/45; 610 BU Eglin 22/2/45; 4000 BU Wright 22/4/45; SPW Wendover 4/8/45; 4000 BU Wright 7/8/45; RFC Walnut Ridge 18/11/46.
43-39120 Del Lincoln 8/12/44; Dow Fd 17/12/44; ass 8AF 18/12/44; retUS Bradley 1103 BU Morrison 24/6/46; 554 BU Memphis 11/8/46; 613 BU Phillips 8/9/46.
43-39121 Del Lincoln 8/12/44; Dow Fd 17/12/44; ass 8AF 23/12/44; retUS Bradley 28/6/45; 4168 BU Sth Plains 30/6/45; 613 BU Phillips 20/3/46.
43-39122 Del Lincoln 8/12/44; Dow Fd 17/12/44; ass 8AF 20/12/44; retUS Bradley 7/6/45; 4168 BU Sth Plains 13/6/45; RFC Kingman 2/12/45.
43-39123 Del Lincoln 10/12/44; Dow Fd 17/12/44; ass 551BS/385BG Gt Ashfield 19/12/44; 550BS; retUS, Kingman 30/11/45. POSSIBLE STRAIGHT.
43-39124 Del Lincoln 9/12/44; Grenier 15/12/44; ass 568BS/390BG [BI-E] Framlingham 17/12/44; c/l, sal n/b/d 17/5/45. CHAPEL IN THE SKY.
43-39125 Del Lincoln 9/12/44; Grenier 21/12/44; ass 613BS/401BG [IN-M] Deenethorpe 8/3/45 DER GROSSARSSCHVOGEL; MIA Brandenburg 20/4/45 w/Bradlet; flak, cr Brandenburg; 5KIA 4POW; MACR 14174. YOU ALL RIGHT.
43-39126 Del Hunter 8/12/44; Dow Fd 21/12/44; ass 838BS/487BG Lavenham 7/3/45; retUS Bradley 13/7/45; 4185 BU Independence 15/7/45; RFC Kingman 3/1/46.
43-39127 Del Hunter 9/12/44; Dow Fd 27/12/44; ass 359BS/303BG [BN-K] Molesworth 28/1/45; 360BS; retUS Bradley 7/6/45; 4168 BU Sth Plains 10/6/45; RFC Kingman 1/12/45.
43-39128 Del Lincoln 9/12/44; Dow Fd 17/12/44; ass 600BS/398BG [N8-M] Nuthampstead 13/2/45; MIA Wittenberg, Ger 22/2/45 w/Beatty; jet e/a, cr Wolfsburg; 3KIA 6POW; MACR 12650. BEATTY'S 8-BALLS.
43-39129 Del Lincoln 10/12/44; Dow Fd 17/12/44; ass 8AF 23/12/44; retUS Bradley 3/7/45; 4168 BU Sth Plains 9/7/45; RFC Kingman 22/11/45.
43-39130 Del Lincoln 10/12/44; Dow Fd 17/12/44; ass 848BS/490BG Eye 19/12/44; MIA Plauen 21/3/45 w/Audette; jet e/a, cr Strehia, Ger?; 6KIA 3POW; MACR 13555.
43-39131 Del Lincoln 9/12/44; Grenier 21/12/44; ass 546BS/384BG [BK-B] Grafton Underwood 17/1/45; sal 9AF Germany 18/9/46; re-ass AF 10 HBS Oberpfaffenhofen 30/4/47; Recl Comp 19/11/47. PRIMO'S GIN MILL.
43-39132 Del Lincoln 9/12/44; Dow Fd 17/12/44; ass 8AF 19/12/44; retUS Bradley 5/7/45; 4168 BU Sth Plains 7/7/45; 613 BU Phillips 6/3/46.
43-39133 Del Hunter 12/12/44; Dow Fd 21/12/44; ass 8AF 1/1/45; re-ass AF 10 HBS Oberpfaffenhofen 30/4/47; Recl Comp 1/10/48.
43-39134 Del Hunter 10/12/44; Dow Fd 21/12/44; ass 571BS/390BG [FC-L] Framlingham 23/12/44; retUS Bradley 3/7/45; 4168 BU Sth Plains 6/7/45; RFC Kingman 29/11/45.
43-39135 Del Hunter 10/12/44; Dow Fd 22/12/44; ass 8AF 24/12/44; sal 9AF Germany 10/5/46.
43-39136 Del Lincoln 11/12/44; Dow Fd 17/12/44; ass 8AF 23/12/44; W/O 9/7/45.
43-39137 Del Lincoln 10/12/44; Dow Fd 18/12/44; ass 600BS/398BG [N8-H] Nuthampstead 29/1/45; retUS Bradley 7/6/45; 4168 BU Sth Plains 10/6/45; 613 BU Phillips 4/7/45.
43-39138 Del Lincoln 13/12/44; Grenier 29/12/44; ass 568BS/390BG [BI-A] Framlingham 31/12/44; tran 544BS/384BG [SU-G] Grafton Underwood 3/2/45; sal 27/4/45.
43-39139 Del Lincoln 13/12/44; Grenier 21/12/44; ass 568BS/390BG [BI-A] Framlingham 22/12/44; retUS Bradley 30/6/45; 4168 BU Sth Plains 4/7/45; RFC Kingman 17/12/45.
43-39140 Del Hunter 13/12/44; Dow Fd 27/12/44; ass 8AF 31/12/44; re-ass AF 10 HBS Oberpfaffenhofen 30/4/47; Recl Comp 18/11/48.
43-39141 Del Lincoln 13/12/44; Grenier 21/12/44; ass 305BG Chelveston 4/3/45; tran 401BG Deenethorpe 25/5/45; retUS Bradley 7/6/45; 4168 BU Sth Plains 12/6/45; RFC Kingman 28/11/45.
43-39142 Del Lincoln 13/12/44; Grenier 21/12/44; ass 8AF 23/12/44; retUS Bradley 9/6/45; 4168 BU Sth Plains 14/6/45; 613 BU Phillips 6/3/46.
43-39143 Del Lincoln 13/12/44; Dow Fd 22/12/44; ass 731BS/452BG Deopham Green 4/1/45; retUS Bradley 6/7/45; 4168 BU Sth Plains 8/7/45; Recl Comp 7/6/46.
43-39144 Del Lincoln 13/12/44; Grenier 21/12/44; ass 305BG Chelveston 10/2/45; tran 351BG Polebrook 23/5/45; retUS Bradley 14/6/45; 4168 BU Sth Plains 15/6/45; RFC Kingman 2/12/45.
43-39145 Del Lincoln 14/12/44; Grenier 21/12/44; ass 8AF 23/12/44; retUS Bradley 29/5/45; 4168 BU Sth Plains 31/5/45; RFC Kingman 22/2/46.
43-39146 Del Hunter 14/12/44; Dow Fd 27/12/44; ass 603BS/398BG [N7-N] Nuthampstead 3/2/45; retUS Bradley 31/5/45; 4168 BU Sth Plains 6/6/45; RFC Kingman 17/12/45.
43-39147 Del Hunter 15/12/44; Dow Fd 3/1/45; ass 527BS/379BG Kimbolton 1/2/45; MIA Dresden 14/2/45 w/Cebuhar; flak, cr Elsenborn, Bel; 2KIA 7POW; MACR 12338.
43-39148 Del Lincoln 21/12/44; Grenier 3/1/45; ass 614BS/401BG [IY-Q] Deenethorpe 21/3/45; retUS Bradley 2/6/45; 4168 BU Sth Plains 9/6/45; RFC Kingman 29/11/45.
43-39149 Del Lincoln 21/12/44; Dow Fd 3/1/45; ass 303BG Molesworth 3/2/45; MIA Lutzkendorf 9/2/45 w/?; mid air coll w/B-17 over Allied territory, 5KIA. MACR 12229.
43-39150 Del Hunter 21/12/44; Grenier 6/1/45; ass 8AF 12/1/45; retUS Bradley 13/7/45; 4185 BU Independence 15/7/45; RFC Kingman 19/12/45.
43-39151 Del Hunter 22/12/44; Dow Fd 12/1/45; ass 8AF 21/12/44; retUS Bradley 29/6/45; 4168 BU Sth Plains 1/7/45; 613 BU Phillips 6/3/46.
43-39152 Del Lincoln 21/12/44; Grenier 6/1/45; ass 344BS/95BG [BG-P] Horham 7/1/45; retUS Bradley 21/6/45; 4168 BU Sth Plains 23/6/45; RFC Kingman 25/11/45.
43-39153 Del Hunter 22/12/44; Grenier 3/1/45; ass 324BS/91BG [DF-H] Bassingbourn 5/2/45; retUS

Bradley 30/5/45; 4168 BU Sth Plains 1/6/45; RFC Kingman 14/12/45.

43-39154 Del Hunter 22/12/44; Grenier 10/1/45; ass 751BS/457BG Glatton 6/2/45; retUS Bradley 9/6/45; 4168 BU Sth Plains 12/6/45; RFC Kingman 28/11/45.

43-39155 Operated as DB-17P drone a/c with black belly, possibly in US after war.

43-39156 Del Hunter 22/12/44; Dow Fd 13/1/45; ass 381BG Ridgewell 21/1/45; tran 510BS/351BG [TU-T] Polebrook 22/1/45; {32m} RetUS Bradley 28/5/45; 4168 BU Sth Plains 31/5/45; RFC Kingman 18/11/45.

43-39157 Del Hunter 22/12/44; Grenier 6/1/45; ass 8AF 21/1/45; retUS Bradley 6/7/45; 4168 BU Sth Plains 8/7/45; RFC Kingman 9/12/45.

43-39158 Del Hunter 28/12/44; Grenier 10/1/45; ass 493BG Debach 12/1/45; b/d Dresden 15/2/45 w/?; f/l Continent; sal 18/2/45.

43-39159 Del Hunter 22/12/44; Grenier 4/1/45; ass 602BS/398BG [K8-C] Nuthampstead 7/2/45; b/d Berlin 26/2/45 w/?; sal 28/2/45.

43-39160 Del Lincoln 23/12/44; Grenier 3/1/44; ass 358BS/303BG [VK-G] Molesworth 4/2/45; MIA Hamburg 20/3/45 w/Taub; e/a, cr Westerade, Ger?; 3KIA 7POW; MACR 13569.

43-39161 Del Hunter 22/12/44; Grenier 3/1/45; ass 534BS/381BG [GD-G] Ridgewell 5/2/45; {27m} RetUS Bradley 10/6/45; 4168 BU Sth Plains 15/6/45; RFC Kingman 4/12/45. SHOOT LUKE.

43-39162 Del Lincoln 22/12/44; Dow Fd 3/1/45; ass 418BS/100BG [LD-U] Thorpe Abbotts 7/1/45; retUS Bradley 24/6/45; 4168 BU Sth Plains 26/6/45; RFC Kingman 10/12/45.

43-39163 Del Lincoln 22/12/44; Grenier 3/1/45; ass 835BS/486BG [H8-S] Sudbury 7/1/45; MIA Parchim 7/4/45 w/Center; hit by bombs from above a/c; cr Parchim; 4KIA 6POW; MACR 13889. HAPPY WARRIOR.

43-39164 Del Lincoln 23/12/44; Grenier 3/1/45; ass 544BS/384BG [SU-F] Grafton Underwood 1/2/45; MIA Leipzig 6/4/45 w/Gray; mid air coll, cr Leipzig; 5KIA 3POW; MACR 13850.

43-39165 Del Lincoln 22/12/44; Grenier 3/1/45; ass 527BS/379BG [FO-C] Kimbolton 7/1/45; tran 836BS/487BG Lavenham 22/5/45; retUS Bradley 13/7/45; 4185 BU Independence 16/7/45; RFC Kingman 2/1/46.

43-39166 Del Lincoln 23/12/44; Grenier 3/1/45; ass 418BS/100BG [LD-R] Thorpe Abbotts 7/1/45; retUS Bradley 24/6/45; 4168 BU Sth Plains 26/6/45; RFC Kingman 7/12/45.

43-39167 Del Lincoln 23/12/44; Grenier 3/1/45; ass 534BS/381BG [GD-D] Ridgewell 5/2/45; retUS Bradley 9/6/45; 4168 BU Sth Plains 14/6/45; RFC Kingman 7/12/45.

43-39168 Del Lincoln 23/12/44; Dow Fd 3/1/45; ass 8AF 6/1/45; re-ass AF 10 HBS Oberpfaffenhofen 30/4/47; Recl Comp 6/12/48.

43-39169 Del Lincoln 26/12/44; Dow Fd 10/1/45; ass 379BG Kimbolton 12/4/45; sal 9AF Germany 23/5/46.

43-39170 Del Lincoln 23/12//44; Grenier 1/3/45; ass 535BS/381BG [MS-V] Ridgewell 21/2/45; retUS Bradley 9/6/45; 4168 BU Sth Plains 13/6/45; RFC Kingman 29/11/45.

43-39171 Del Lincoln 23/12/44; Dow Fd 25/1/45; ass 8AF 1/2/45; retUS Bradley 3/7/45; 4168 BU Sth Plains 7/7/45; 613 BU Phillips 7/3/46.

43-39172 Del Hunter 23/12/44; Grenier 2/1/45; ass 532BS/381BG [VE-K] Ridgewell 5/2/45; retUS Bradley 28/5/45; 4168 BU Sth Plains 31/5/45; RFC Kingman 25/11/45. LITTLE LULU.

43-39173 Del Hunter 23/12/44; Dow Fd 10/1/45; ass 838BS/487BG Lavenham 19/2/45; MIA Ruhland 17/3/45 w/Kohr; flak, c/l Kamenz, Ger; 9RTD; MACR 13110. LEACHEROUS LOU.

43-39174 Del Hunter 23/12/44; Dow Fd 13/1/45; ass 367BS/306BG Thurleigh 21/2/45; tran 533BS/381BG Ridgewell 5/45; retUS Bradley 10/6/45; 4168 BU Sth Plains 13/6/45; RFC Kingman 30/11/45. LITTLE JOE.

43-39175 Del Hunter 23/12/44; Dow Fd 3/1/45; ass 334BS/95BG [BG-L] Horham 7/1/45; retUS Bradley 21/6/45; 4168 BU Sth Plains 25/6/45; RFC Kingman 10/12/45.

43-39176 Del Lincoln 23/12/44; Dow Fd 10/1/45; ass 8AF 21/1/45; retUS Bradley 29/6/45; 4168 BU Sth Plains 4/7/45; RFC Kingman 25/11/45.

43-39177 Del Lincoln 23/12/44; Dow Fd 3/1/45; ass 412BS/95BG [QW-Y] Horham 7/1/45; retUS Bradley 28/6/45; 4168 BU Sth Plains 30/6/45; RFC Kingman 7/12/45. THE BLESSED EVENT.

43-39178 Del Lincoln 23/12/44; Grenier 3/1/45; ass 8AF 6/1/45; retUS Bradley 12/7/45; 4185 BU Independence 13/7/45; RFC Kingman 5/1/46.

43-39179 Del Lincoln 23/12/44; Dow Fd 3/1/45; ass 7BS/34BG Mendlesham 7/1/45; retUS Bradley 1/7/45; 4168 BU Sth Plains 3/7/45; RFC Kingman 17/12/45. SHAKY.

43-39180 Del Lincoln 26/12/44; Dow Fd 10/1/45; ass 600BS/398BG [N8-G] Nuthampstead 7/2/45; retUS Bradley 25/5/45; 4168 BU Sth Plains 30/5/45; RFC Kingman 25/11/45. HITLER'S HEADACHE.

43-39181 Del Lincoln 26/12/44; Dow Fd 10/1/45; ass 385BG Gt Ashfield 22/1/45; retUS Bradley 6/7/45; 418 BU Sth Plains 7/7/45; 613 BU Phillips 3/3/46.

43-39182 Del Lincoln 26/12/44; Grenier 3/1/45; ass 8AF 6/1/45; sal 9AF Germany 31/5/46.

43-39183 Del Lincoln 28/12/44; Dow Fd 10/1/45; ass 18BS/34BG Mendlesham 21/1/45; retUS Bradley 20/6/45; 4168 BU Sth Plains 23/6/45; RFC Kingman 10/12/45.

43-39184 Del Lincoln 30/12/44; Dow Fd 10/1/45; ass 601BS/398BG [3O-U] Nuthampstead 27/2/45; MIA Neumünster 13/4/45 w/Martineck; exploded, cr Garbeck, Ger; 2KIA 6POW; MACR 14176.

43-39185 Del Lincoln 30/12/44; Dow Fd 10/1/45; ass 8AF 15/1/45; retUS Bradley 28/6/45; 4168 BU Sth Plains 30/6/45; RFC Kingman 28/12/45.

43-39186 Del Lincoln 31/12/44; Grenier 25/1/45; ass 8AF 5/2/45; retUS Bradley 11/7/45; 4185 BU Independence 12/7/45; RFC Kingman 18/12/45.

43-39187 Del Hunter 30/12/44; Dow Fd 13/1/45; ass 8AF 4/2/45; retUS Bradley 18/6/45; 4168 BU Sth Plains 21/6/45; RFC Kingman 23/1/46.

43-39188 Del Hunter 30/12/44; Dow Fd 13/1/45; ass 839BS/487BG Lavenham 3/3/45; retUS Bradley 13/7/45; 4185 BU Independence 17/7/45; RFC Kingman 27/12/45.

43-39189 Del Hunter 29/12/44; Dow Fd 13/1/45; ass 8AF 21/1/45; retUS Bradley 6/7/45; 4168 BU Sth Plains 8/7/45; RFC Kingman 17/12/45.

43-39190 Del Hunter 30/12/44; Dow Fd 13/1/45; ass 8AF 22/1/45; retUS Bradley 12/6/45; 4168 BU Sth Plains 19/6/45; RFC Kingman 30/11/45.

43-39191 Del Hunter 30/12/44; Dow Fd 10/1/45; ass 305BG Chelveston 4/3/45; tran 401BG Deenethorpe 20/5/45; retUS Bradley 7/6/45; 4168 BU Sth Plains 13/6/45; RFC Kingman 10/12/45.

43-39192 Del Lincoln 30/12/44; Grenier 6/2/45; ass 8AF 17/2/45; re-ass 10 HBS Oberpfaffenhofen 30/4/47; Recl Comp 1/10/48.

43-39193 Del Lincoln 30/12/44; Dow Fd 25/1/45; ass 366BS/305BG Chelveston 13/2/45; re-ass 10HBS Oberpfaffenhofen 30/4/47; Recl Comp 19/11/47. 'CHALK UP.'

43-39194 Del Lincoln 30/12/44; Dow Fd 10/1/45; ass 8AF 22/1/45; retUS Bradley 5/7/45; 4168 BU Sth Plains 6/7/45; RFC Kingman 10/12/45.

43-39195 Del Lincoln 2/1/45; Dow Fd 25/1/45; ass 750BS/457BG Glatton 26/2/45; retUS Bradley 28/5/45; 4168 BU Sth Plains 31/5/45; RFC Kingman 28/11/45.

43-39196 Del Lincoln 30/12/44; Dow Fd 25/1/45; ass 8AF 31/1/45; re-ass 10 HBS Oberpfaffenhofen 30/4/47; Recl Comp 19/11/47.

43-39197 Del Lincoln 31/12/44; Grenier 25/1/45; ass 546BS/384BG [BK-K] Grafton Underwood 20/2/45; b/d Pilsen 25/4/45 w/?; sal 2/1/46. SCHOOL MARM.

43-39198 Del Hunter 31/12/44; Dow Fd 13/1/45; ass 493BG Debach 21/1/45; retUS Bradley 6/7/45; 4168 BU Sth Plains 7/7/45; RFC Kingman 17/12/45.

43-39199 Del Hunter 31/12/44; Dow Fd 18/1/45; ass 549BS/385BG Gt Ashfield 30/1/45; MIA Zwickau 19/3/45 w/Lowry; flak, cr Frankfurt; 1KIA 10POW; MACR 13148. HAIRS BREATH.

43-39200 Del Hunter 3/1/45; Grenier 15/1/45; ass 749BS/457BG Glatton 18/2/45; retUS Bradley 22/5/45; 4168 BU Sth Plains 24/5/45; RFC Kingman 9/12/45. RATTLESNAKE DADDY.

43-39201 Del Lincoln 3/1/45; Dow Fd 6/2/45; ass 8AF 8/2/45; sal 9AF German 31/5/46.

43-39202 Del Lincoln 3/1/45; Dow Fd 25/1/45; ass 482BG Alconbury 1/2/45; retUS Bradley 1/6/45; 4168 BU Sth Plains 4/6/45; RFC Kingman 17/12/45.

43-39203 Del Lincoln 3/1/45; Dow Fd 13/1/45; ass 546BS/384BG [BK-L] Grafton Underwood 20/2/45; sal 9AF Germany 18/9/46; re-ass 10 HBS Oberpfaffenhofen 30/4/47; Recl Comp 19/11/47.

43-39204 Del Hunter 4/1/45; Grenier 15/1/45; ass 8AF 3/2/45; re-ass 10 HBS Oberpfaffenhofen 30/4/47; Recl Comp 1/10/48.

43-39205 Del Lincoln 6/1/45; Grenier 25/1/45; ass 8AF 4/2/45; re-ass 10 HBS Oberpfaffenhofen 30/4/47; Recl Comp 1/10/48.

43-39206 Del Lincoln 6/1/45; Grenier 25/1/45; ass 8AF 13/2/45; (radio comp gun removed); sal 9AF Germany 6/11/46.

43-39207 Del Lincoln 6/1/45; Dow Fd 25/1/45; ass 305BG Chelveston 21/2/45; retUS Bradley 13/6/45; 4168 BU Sth Plains 15/6/45; RFC Kingman 18/12/45.

43-39208 Del Lincoln 7/1/45; Grenier 25/1/45; ass 379BG Kimbolton 11/4/45; tran 837BS/487BG Lavenham 22/5/45; retUS Bradley 13/7/45; 4185 BU Independence 13/7/45; RFC Kingman 10/12/45.

43-39209 Del Hunter 7/1/45; Grenier 19/1/45; ass 860BS/493BG Debach 22/1/45; retUS Bradley 5/7/45; 4168 BU Sth Plains 6/7/45; RFC Kingman 10/12/45.

43-39210 Del Hunter 9/1/45; Grenier 19/1/45; ass 96BG Snetterton 22/1/45; b/d Ansbach 23/2/45 w/?; f/l Continent; sal.

43-39211 Del Hunter 10/1/45; Grenier 2/2/45; ass 750BS/457BG Glatton 18/2/45; retUS Bradley 8/6/45; 4168 BU Sth Plains 12/6/45; RFC Kingman 28/11/45. McGUIRE'S CHOP HOUSE.

43-39212 Del Hunter 10/1/45; Dow Fd 19/1/45; ass 525BS/379BG [FR-F] Kimbolton 1/2/45; retUS Bradley 9/7/45; 4168 BU Sth Plains 11/7/45; RFC Kingman 19/11/45.

43-39213 Del Hunter 9/1/45; Grenier 19/1/45; ass 601BS/398BG [3O-C] Nuthampstead 7/2/45; tran 306BG Thurleigh 2/5/45; sal 9AF Germany 12/9/46; re-ass 10 HBS Oberpfaffenhofen 30/4/47; Recl

INDIVIDUAL B-17 HISTORIES

Comp 19/11/47.
43-39214 Del Hunter 9/1/45; Dow Fd 24/1/45; ass 8AF 14/2/45; sal 9AF Germany 12/9/46; re-ass 10 HBS Oberpfaffenhofen 30/4/47; Recl Comp 19/11/47.
43-39215 Del Hunter 9/1/45; Grenier 24/1/45; ass 8AF 3/2/45; re-ass 10 HBS Oberpfaffenhofen 30/4/47; Recl Comp 1/10/48.
43-39216 Del Hunter 9/1/45; Dow Fd 19/1/45; ass 8AF 1/2/45; retUS Bradley 28/6/45; 4168 BU Sth Plains 29/6/45; RFC Kingman 30/1/46.
43-39217 Del Hunter 9/1/45; Dow Fd 19/1/45; ass 401BG/91BG [LL-O] Bassingbourn 23/2/45 MERRY ANN; {18+m} RetUS Bradley 11/6/45; 4168 BU Sth Plains 14/6/45; RFC Kingman 25/11/45. PEG OF MY HEART.
43-39218 Del Hunter 11/1/45; Grenier 22/1/45; ass 8AF 3/2/45; re-ass 10 HBS Oberpfaffenhofen 30/4/47; Recl Comp 6/12/48.
43-39219 Del Hunter 10/1/45; Grenier 24/1/45; ass 8AF 3/2/45; re-ass 10 HBS Oberpfaffenhofen 30/4/47; Recl Comp 30/8/48.
43-39220 Del Hunter 10/1/45; Dow Fd 25/1/45; ass 427BS/303BG [GN-G] Molesworth 20/2/45; b/d Oranienburg 15/3/45 w/?; f/l Continent; sal 20/3/45.
43-39221 Del Hunter 10/1/44; Dow Fd 19/1/45; ass 563BS/388BG Knettishall 4/2/45; retUS Bradley 28/6/45; 4168 BU Sth Plains 30/6/45; RFC Kingman 29/11/45.
43-39222 Del Hunter 11/1/45; Grenier 24/1/45; ass 305BG Chelveston 4/3/45; tran 384BG Grafton Underwood 9/5/45; sal 9AF Germany 18/9/46; re-ass 10 HBS Oberpfaffenhofen 30/4/47; Recl Comp 19/11/47.
43-39223 Del Hunter 11/1/45; Grenier 31/1/45; ass 305BG Chelveston 21/2/45; tran 384BG Grafton Underwood 9/5/45; retUS Bradley 7/6/45; 4168 BU Sth Plains 13/6/45; RFC Kingman 10/12/45.
43-39224 Del Hunter 11/1/45; Grenier 24/1/45; ass 601BS/398BG [3O-W] 3/2/45 Nuthampstead 3/2/45; retUS Bradley 25/5/45; 4168 BU St Plains 29/5/45; RFC Kingman 2/3/46.
43-39225 Del Hunter 12/1/45; Grenier 28/1/45; ass 323BS/91BG [OR-V] Bassingbourn 23/2/45; retUS Bradley 29/5/45; 4168 BU Sth Plains 4/6/45; RFC Kingman 3/11/45.
43-39226 Del Hunter 10/1/45; Grenier 24/1/45; ass 861BS/493BG Debach 3/2/45; MIA Hamburg 30/3/45 w/Dwyer; flak, cr Pinneberg; 1KIA 9POW; MACR 13506.
43-39227 Del Hunter 11/1/45; Grenier 24/1/45; ass 601BS/398BG [3O-S] Nuthampstead 25/2/45; retUS Bradley 25/5/45; 4168 BU Sth Plains 8/11/45; RFC Kingman 8/11/45.
43-39228 Del Hunter 11/1/45; Grenier 22/1/45; ass 8AF 3/2/45; sal 9AF Germany 10/5/46.
43-39229 Del Hunter 11/1/45; Grenier 22/1/45; ass 379BG Kimbolton 12/4/45; tran 401BG Deenethorpe 5/45; retUS Bradley 30/6/45; 4168 BU Sth Plains 3/7/45; RFC Kingman 19/11/45.
43-39230 Del Hunter 11/1/45; Grenier 24/1/45; ass 709BS/447BG Rattlesden 3/2/45; sal 9AF Germany 31/5/46.
43-39231 Del Hunter 12/1/45; Grenier 26/1/45; ass 8AF 8/2/45; sal 9AF Germany 31/5/46; re-ass 10 HBS Oberpfafffenhofen 30/4/47; Recl Comp 16/12/48.
43-39232 Del Hunter 12/1/45; Dow Fd 28/1/45; ass 482BG Alconbury 1/2/45; retUS Bradley 31/5/45; 4168 BU Sth Plains 11/6/45; RFC Kingman 1/12/45.
43-39233 Del Hunter 11/1/45; Grenier 31/1/45; ass 303BG Molesworth 10/4/45; tran 457BG Glatton 23/5/45; retUS Bradley 10/6/45; 4168 BU Sth Plains 13/6/45; RFC Kingman 25/11/45.
43-39234 Del Hunter 12/1/45; Grenier 3/2/45; ass 838BS/487BG Lavenham 3/3/45; retUS Bradley 14/7/45; 4185 BU Independence 20/7/45; RFC Kingman 21/12/45.
43-39235 Del Hunter 13/1/45; Grenier 31/1/45; ass 8AF 6/2/45; retUS 4000 Patterson 17/4/45; 4168 BU Sth Plains 30/6/46; re-ass AF 31/3/47; 4141 BU Pyote 25/6/47; Recl Comp 16/9/48.
43-39236 Del Hunter 13/1/45; Dow Fd 1/2/45; ass 547BS/384BG [SO-A] Grafton Underwood 20/2/45; sal 9AF Germany 4/3/46.
43-39237 Del Hunter 16/1/45; Grenier 6/2/45; ass 8AF 13/2/45; re-ass 10 HBS Oberpfaffenhofen 30/4/47; Recl Comp 18/5/48.
43-39238 Del Hunter 13/1/45; Grenier 31/1/45; ass 8AF 7/2/45; retUS Bradley 7/7/45; 4168 BU Sth Plains 9/7/45; 613 BU Phillips 6/3/46.
43-39239 Del Hunter 16/1/45; Grenier 2/2/45; ass 562BS/388BG Knettishall 8/2/45; retUS Bradley 3/7/45; 4168 BU Sth Plains 7/7/45; RFC Kingman 21/12/45.
43-39240 Del Hunter 15/1/45; Grenier 31/1/45; ass 490BG Eye 7/2/45; retUS, RFC Walnut Ridge 9/1/46.
43-39241 Del Hunter 17/1/45; Dow Fd 26/1/45; ass 8AF 3/2/45; retUS Bradley 9/7/45; 4168 BU Sth Plains 12/7/45; RFC Kingman 24/11/45.
43-38242 Del Hunter 15/1/45; Grenier 31/1/45; ass 603BS/398BG [N7-F] Nuthampstead 4/3/45; retUS Bradley 7/6/45; 4168 BU Sth Plains 13/6/45; RFC Kingman 27/11/45.
43-39243 Del Hunter 17/1/45; Dow Fd 1/2/45; ass 8AF 5/2/45; retUS Bradley 16/6/45; 4168 BU Sth Plains 18/6/45; RFC Kingman 15/2/46.
43-39244 Del Hunter 15/1/45; Dow Fd 28/1/45; ass 447BG Rattlesden 1/2/45; retUS Bradley 6/7/45; 4168 BU Sth Plains 7/7/45; RFC Kingman 14/2/46.
43-39245 Del Hunter 15/1/45; Grenier 31/1/45; ass 8AF 12/2/45; re-ass 10 HBS Oberpfaffenhofen 30/4/47; Recl Comp 7/1/49.
43-39246 Del -
43-39247 Del Hunter 16/1/45; Grenier 31/1/45; ass 8AF 12/2/45; re-ass 10 HBS Oberpfaffenhofen 30/4/47; Recl Comp 6/12/48.
43-39248 Del Hunter 15/1/45; Grenier 31/1/45; ass 563BS/388BG Knettishall 8/2/45; retUS Bradley 11/6/45; 4168 BU Sth Plains 14/6/45; RFC Kingman 31/1/46.
43-39249 Del Hunter 17/1/45; Grenier 30/1/45; ass 836BS/487BG [2G-E] Lavenham 12/4/45; retUS Bradley 11/7/45; 4168 BU Sth Plains 12/7/45; RFC Kingman 10/11/45.
43-39250 Del Hunter 17/1/45; Grenier 31/1/45; ass 8AF 8/2/45; retUS Bradley 3/7/45; 4168 BU Sth Plains 6/7/45; RFC Kingman 25/11/45.
43-39251 Del Hunter 18/1/45; Dow Fd 2/2/45; ass 490BG Eye 5/2/45; Sat 9AF Germany 23/5/46.
43-39252 Del Hunter 18/1/45; Grenier 31/1/45; ass 8AF 13/2/45; sal 9AF Germany 23/5/46.
43-39253 Del Hunter 18/1/45; Dow Fd 15/2/45; ass 8AF 12/3/45; sal 9AF Germany 18/9/46; re-ass 10 HBS Oberpfaffenhofen 30/4/47; Recl Comp 19/11/47.
43-39254 Del Hunter 19/1/45; Dow Fd 4/2/45; ass 482BG Alconbury 5/2/45; retUS Bradley 30/5/45; 4168 BU Sth Plains 31/5/45; RFC Kingman 11/12/45.
43-39255 Del Lincoln 19/1/45; Dow Fd 6/2/45; ass 8AF 14/2/45; re-ass 10 HBS Oberpfaffenhofen 30/4/47; Recl Comp 30/8/48.
43-39256 Del Lincoln 18/1/45; Dow Fd 6/2/45; ass 8AF 14/2/45; sal 9AF Germany 23/5/46.
43-39257 Del Lincoln 19/1/45; Grenier 6/2/45; ass 837BS/487BG Lavenham 12/4/45; retUS Bradley 11/7/45; 4185 BU Independence 13/11/45; RFC Kingman 9/12/45.
43-39258 Del Lincoln 19/1/45; Grenier 6/2/45; ass 8AF 15/2/45; retUS Bradley 5/7/45; 4168 BU Sth Plains 6/7/45; RFC Kingman 29/11/45.
43-39259 Del Lincoln 19/1/45; Grenier 6/2/45; ass 8AF 14/2/45; retUS Bradley 11/6/45; 4168 BU Sth Plains 14/6/45; RFC Kingman 1/2/46.
43-39260 Del Lincoln 19/1/45; Grenier 17/2/45; ass 8AF 26/2/45; retUS Bradley 26/2/45; 4168 BU Sth Plains 6/7/45; RFC Kingman 28/11/45.
43-39261 Del Cheyenne 22/1/45; Hunter 22/3/45; Tulsa 28/3/45; San Francisco 2/4/45; ass 20 HBS Harmon 18/6/45; 24 HBS Harmon 17/7/48; Recl Comp 6/6/49.
43-39262 Del Cheyenne 22/1/45; Dallas 28/2/45; Hunter 1/3/45; San Francisco 6/4/45; ass DUVA WCW ; sal 23/1/46.
43-39263 Del Cheyenne 22/1/45; Hunter 26/2/45; San Francisco 9/3/45; ass 13 ASR Clark Fd, Phill. 5/2/48; 358 SR Clark 9/4/48; 6 SR Clark 9/7/48; Recl Comp 1/10/48.
43-39264 Del Cheyenne 22/1/45; Hunter 26/2/45; San Francisco 10/3/45; ass 3 ERS Itami 18/1/46; 3 ERS Ashiya 26/4/49; 347 MSU Ashiya 9/11/49; sal 3/5/50.
43-39265 Del Cheyenne 22/1/45; Hunter 28/3/45; San Francisco 2/4/45; ass ATC 5/4/45; 338 RV Momote 18/1/46; 5RVP Gp Clark Fd 18/4/46; retUS 24/5/49; 9SRG Gp Fairmont 27/9/49; Hill 9/12/49; Recl Comp 19/5/50.
43-39266 Del Cheyenne 25/1/45; Hunter 28/2/45; ATC San Francisco 9/3/45; ass 3ERS/5RG Okinawa 7/45; Recl Comp 15/1/48. PRETTY BABY.
43-39267 Del Cheyenne 26/1/45; Hunter 26/2/45; ATC San Francisco 1/3/45; ass WCW Manila 31/12/45; sal 11/10/46.
43-39268 Del Cheyenne 25/1/45; Hunter 26/2/45; ATC San Francisco 3/4/45; ass WCW Manila 27/7/47; 13 AR Clark Fd 5/2/48; Recl Comp 15/1/49.
43-39269 Del Cheyenne 25/1/45; Hunter 23/2/45; ATC San Francisco 9/3/45; ass Manila 14/5/46.
43-39270 Del Cheyenne 27/1/45; Hunter 23/2/45; ATC San Francisco 9/3/45; ass 358 SR Clark Fd 15/1/48; 6 SR Clark 26/6/48; 18 MSU Clark 1/12/48; Recl Comp 2/3/49.
43-39271 Del Cheyenne 27/1/45; Hunter 1/3/45; ATC San Francisco 4/4/45; 338 RVP Momote 18/1/46; 5 RVP Clark 18/4/46; 567 MAT Clark 13/7/47; retUS 24/5/49; re-ass 9 SRC Gp Fairmont 4/9/49; Hill Fd 28/11/49; Recl Comp 18/1/50.
43-39272 Del Cheyenne 27/1/45; Hunter 26/2/45; ATC San Francisco 9/3/45; 2 RES Kadena 31/1/48; Recl Comp 8/3/49.
43-39273 Del Cheyenne 27/1/45; Hunter 21/2/45; Witchita 3/3/45; Recl Comp 27/3/45.
43-39274 Del Cheyenne 28/1/45; Hunter 23/2/45; ATC San Francisco 9/3/45; ass 358 SR Clark 1/4/48; 6 SR Clark 13/7/48; 18 MSU Clark 14/8/48; Recl Comp 2/3/49.
43-39275 Del Lincoln 28/1/45; Grenier 20/2/45; ass 8AF 26/2/45; re-ass ATC 30/4/47; 1414 BAS Dharan 28/1/48; Recl Comp 16/12/48.
43-39276 Del Lincoln 27/1/45; Grenier 18/2/45; ass 8AF 19/2/45; retUS Bradley 18/6/45; 4168 BU Sth Plains 20/6/45; RFC Kingman 30/1/46.
43-39277 Del Lincoln 27/1/45; Grenier 12/2/45; ass 8AF 16/2/45; retUS Bradley 29/6/45; 4168 BU Sth Plains 3/7/45; RFC Kingman 26/11/45.

43-39278 Del Lincoln 27/1/45; Grenier 12/2/45; ass 8AF 18/2/45; sal 9AF Germany 31/5/46.
43-39279 Del Lincoln 27/1/45; Grenier 12/2/45; ass 8AF 14/2/45; retUS Bradley 11/7/45; 4185 BU Independence 12/7/45; RFC Kingman 15/12/45.
43-39280 Del Lincoln 27/1/45; Dow Fd 12/2/45; ass 8AF 14/2/45; sal 9AF Germany 10/5/46.
43-39281 Del Lincoln 27/1/45; Dow Fd 13/2/45; ass 8AF 15/2/45; re-ass AMC 3/6/47; 4112 BAS Olmstead 9/1/48; Recl Comp 21/3/48. (US Civil serial N7043C).
43-39282 Del Lincoln 28/1/45; Dow Fd 15/2/45; ass 563BS/388BG Knettishall 18/2/45; retUS Bradley 29/6/45; 4168 BU Sth Plains 2/7/45; 613 BU Phillips 13/3/46. SWEENY'S BRATS.
43-39283 Del Lincoln 28/1/45; Dow Fd 12/2/45; ass 8AF 14/2/45; re-ass 10 HBS Oberpfaffenhofen 30/4/47; Recl Comp 18/11/48.
43-39284 Del Hunter 28/1/45; Grenier 11/2/45; ass 8AF 15/2/45; re-ass 10 HBS Oberpfaffenhofen 30/4/47; Recl Comp 7/1/49.
43-39285 Del Hunter 28/1/45; Grenier 11/2/45; ass 358BS/303BG [VK-E] Molesworth 11/4/45; tran 457BG Glatton 23/5/45; retUS Bradley 8/6/45; 4168 BU Sth Plains 12/6/45; RFC Kingman 1/12/45.
43-39286 Del Hunter 29/1/45; Grenier 11/2/45; ass 8AF 13/2/45; sal 9AF Germany 10/5/46.
43-39287 Del Hunter 28/1/45; Dow Fd 11/2/45; ass 8AF 14/2/45; retUS Bradley 28/6/45; 4168 BU Sth Plains 1/7/45; RFC Kingman 1/2/46.
43-39288 Del Hunter 28/1/45; Dow Fd 13/2/45; ass 8AF 15/2/45; retUS Bradley 13/7/45; 4185 BU Independence 17/7/45; RFC Kingman 14/12/45.
43-39289 Del Hunter 28/1/45; Grenier 11/2/45; ass 327BS/92BG [UX-F] Podington 4/3/45; mission to Port Lyautey 9/6/45, ret 10/6/45; sal 9AF Germany 23/8/45.
43-39290 Del Hunter 31/1/45; Dow Fd 15/2/45; ass 8AF 17/2/45; re-ass 10 HBS Oberpfaffenhofen 30/4/47; Recl Comp 3/8/49.
43-39291 Del Hunter 30/1/45; Dow Fd 13/2/45; ass 8AF 16/2/45; sal 9AF Germany 31/5/46.
43-39292 Del Hunter 29/1/45; Dow Fd 13/2/45; ass 8AF 17/2/45; re-ass 10 HBS Oberpfaffenhofen 30/4/47; Recl Comp 7/1/49.
43-39293 Del Hunter 30/1/45; Grenier 11//2/45; ass 603BS/398BG [N7-J] Nuthampstead 29/3/45; retUS Bradley 8/6/45; 4168 BU Sth Plains 18/6/45; RFC Kingman 5/12/45.
43-39294 Del Hunter 31/1/45; Dow Fd 15/2/45; ass 8AF 17/2/45; re-ass 10 HBS Oberpfaffenhofen 30/4/47; Recl Comp 30/8/48.
43-39295 Del Lincoln 1/2/45; Dow Fd 12/2/45; ass 8AF 13/2/45; re-ass 10 HBS Oberpfaffenhofen 30/4/47; 501 SR Weisbaden 18/1/48; 7169 AB Oberpfaffenhofen 18/7/47; 7290 AB Oberp. 1/2/49; MTC 20/4/49; 1414 AB Dhahran 6/5/49; 85 Mat GP Erding 14/11/49; Recl Comp 3/5/50.
43-39296 Del Lincoln 31/1/45; Grenier 25/2/45; ass 8AF 26/2/45; retUS Bradley 11/6/45; 4168 BU Sth Plains 17/6/45; RFC Kingman 5/2/46.
43-39297 Del Lincoln 31/1/45; Dow Fd 13/2/45; ass 490BG Eye 16/2/45; b/d Nurnberg 5/4/45 w/?; f/l Continent; sal 10/4/45; MACR 13741.
43-39298 Del Lincoln 1/2/45; Grenier 12/2/45; ass 8AF 18/2/45; retUS Bradley 5/7/45; 4168 BU Sth Plains 6/7/45; RFC Kingman 5/2/46.
43-39299 Del Lincoln 2/2/45; Dow Fd 12/2/45; ass 391BS/34BG Mendlesham 18/2/45; sal 9AF Germany 23/5/46.
43-39300 Del Lincoln 2/2/45; Dow Fd 12/2/45; ass 533BS/381BG [VP-X] Ridgewell 12/4/45; {4+m} RetUS Bradley 29/5/45; 4168 BU Sth Plains 31/5/45; RFC Kingman 14/11/45.
43-39301 Del Lincoln 3/2/45; Grenier 17/2/45; ass 8AF 2/3/45; retUS Bradley 14/5/45; 4168 BU Sth Plains 18/5/45; RFC Kingman 6/2/46.
43-39302 Del Lincoln 29/1/45; Grenier 12/2/45; ass 379BG Kimbolton 21/2/45; sal 9AF Germany 23/5/46.
43-39303 Del Lincoln 3/2/45; Grenier 17/2/45; ass 8AF 18/2/45; landing accident Rumania 2/11/46; ret 24/12/46, re-ass 10 HBS Oberpfaffenhofen 30/4/47; 7290 AB Oberp. 18/4/47; 59 HBS Burtonwood 1/12/48; 7520 AB Burtonwood 31/8/49; 59 AB Burtonwood 8/9/49; Recl Comp 18/4/50.
43-39304 Del Lincoln 6/2/45; Grenier 17/2/45; ass 8AF 19/2/45; retUS, RFC Walnut Ridge 29/3/46. US Civil N9407H 12/12/49; tran to IGN France as F-BDAT; cr Niamey, Nigeria 12/12/50.
43-39305 Del Lincoln 6/2/45; Grenier 19/2/45; ass 8AF 20/2/45; re-ass 10 HBS Oberpfaffenhofen 30/4/47; 89 BAS Weisbaden 18/1/48; retUS MTC Langley 1/7/48; 71 AC Hickam 8/9/48; 1810 AC Hickam 1/10/48; 811 AC Kadena 21/9/49; 1500 MSU Hickam 23/9/49; Recl Comp 3/5/50.
43-39306 Del Lincoln 3/2/45; Grenier 17/2/45; ass 8AF 25/2/45; sal 9AF Germany 10/5/46.
43-39307 Del –; still in USAF in 1953 as BA-307, possibly as a hack.
43-39308 Del Lincoln 7/2/45; Grenier 17/2/45; ass 8AF 20/2/45; retUS Bradley 27/6/45; 4168 BU Sth Plains 30/6/45; RFC Kingman 30/1/46.
43-39309 Del Lincoln 5/2/45; Grenier 17/2/45; ass 561BS/388BG Knettishall 19/2/45; retUS Bradley 24/6/45; 4168 BU Sth Plains 26/6/45; RFC Kingman 9/11/45.
43-39310 Del Lincoln 5/2/45; Grenier 17/2/45; ass 8AF 6/3/45; retUS Bradley 20/6/45; 4168 BU Sth Plains 23/6/45; RFC Kingman 28/1/46.
43-39311 Del Lincoln 7/2/45; Grenier 19/2/45; ass 8AF 20/2/45; sal 9AF Germany 10/5/46.
43-39312 Del Lincoln 6/2/45; Grenier 17/2/45; ass 8AF 19/2/45; sal 9AF Germany 31/5/46.
43-39313 Del Lincoln 6/2/45; Grenier 17/2/45; ass 8AF 18/2/45; re-ass 10 HBS Oberpfaffenhofen 30/4/47; Recl Comp 17/1/49.
43-39314 Del Lincoln 7/2/45; Grenier 17/2/45; ass 8AF 18/2/45; retUS, 613 BU Phillips 7/8/46.
43-39315 Del Lincoln 7/2/45; Grenier 17/2/45; ass 8AF 18/2/45; re-ass 10 HBS Oberpfaffenhofen 30/4/47; Recl Comp 7/1/49.
43-39316 Del Lincoln 7/2/45; Grenier 17/2/45; ass 8AF 19/2/45; retUS Bradley 5/7/45; 4168 BU Sth Plains 9/7/45; RFC Kingman 26/11/45.
43-39317 Del Lincoln 10/2/45; Grenier 17/2/45; ass 8AF 19/2/45; retUS Bradley 9/6/45; 4168 BU Sth Plains 18/6/45; RFC Kingman 31/1/46.
43-39318 Del Lincoln 8/2/45; Grenier 19/2/45; ass 603BS/398BG [N7-P] Nuthampstead 29/3/45; retUS Bradley 7/6/45; 4168 BU Sth Plains 9/6/45; RFC Kingman 1/12/45.
43-39319 Del Lincoln 8/2/45; Grenier 19/2/45; ass 8AF 26/2/45; retUS Bradley 9/7/45; 4168 BU Sth Plains 11/7/45; RFC Kingman 19/2/46.
43-39320 Del Lincoln 8/2/45; Grenier 17/2/45; ass 8AF 19/2/45; re-ass 10 HBS Oberpfaffenhofen 30/4/47; Recl Comp 7/1/49.
43-39321 Del Hunter 10/2/45; Grenier 19/2/45; ass 486BG RetUS Bradley 11/7/45; 4185 BU Independence 16/7/45; RFC Kingman 18/12/45.
43-39322 Del Hunter 10/2/45; Grenier 24/2/45; ass 8AF 25/2/45; re-ass 10 HBS Oberpfaffenhofen 30/4/47; Recl Comp 7/1/49.

43-39323 Del Lincoln 10/2/45; Grenier 19/2/45; ass 8AF 20/2/45; re-ass 10 HBS Oberpfaffenhofen 30/4/47; Recl Comp 7/1/49.
43-39324 Del Lincoln 12/2/45; Grenier 25/2/45; ass 390BG RetUS Bradley 20/6/45; 4168 BU Sth Plains 23/6/45; RFC Kingman 5/2/46.
43-39325 Del Wright Fd 10/2/45; 4000 BU Wright 8/3/45; 327 BU Drew 14/3/45; 4000 BU Wright 29/3/45; 327 BU Drew 1/8/45; 610 BU Eglin 27/9/45; RFC Walnut Ridge 18/1/46.
43-39326 Del Lincoln 12/2/45; Bangor 1/3/45; ass 728BS/452BG RetUS Bradley 29/6/45; 4168 BU Sth Plains 2/7/45; RFC Kingman 29/11/45. FLAK-SHY LADY.
43-39327 Del Hunter 12/2/45; Grenier 24/2/45; ass 8AF 26/2/45; retUS Bradley 3/7/45; 4168 BU Sth Plains 7/7/45; RFC Kingman 19/12/45.
43-39328 Del Hunter 12/2/45; Grenier 23/2/45; ass 8AF 26/2/45; retUS 1103 BU Morrison 2/3/46; 613 BU Phillips 1/4/47.
43-39329 Del Lincoln 12/2/45; Bangor 1/3/45; ass 8AF 6/3/45; sal 9AF Germany 31/5/46.
43-39330 Del Hunter 12/2/45; Grenier 24/2/45; ass 8AF 26/2/45; re-ass 10 HBS Oberpfaffenhofen 30/4/47; Recl Comp 7/1/49.
43-39331 Del Hunter 12/2/45; Grenier 25/2/45; ass 8AF 2/3/45; sal 9AF Germany 23/5/46.
43-39332 Del Hunter 12/2/45; Grenier 15/2/45; ass 8AF 27/2/45; retUS Bradley 12/7/45; 4185 BU Independence 13/7/45; RFC Kingman 14/12/45.
43-39333 Del Lincoln 14/2/45; Grenier 1/3/45; ass 8AF 3/3/45; re-ass 10 HBS Oberpfaffenhofen 30/3/47; Recl Comp 5/8/48.
43-39334 Del Lincoln 14/2/45; Grenier 3/3/45; ass 8AF 4/3/45; retUS Bradley 7/6/45; 4168 BU Sth Plains 13/6/45; RFC Kingman 7/2/46.
43-39335 Del –. VIP a/c USAFE 2/48.
43-39336 Del Hunter 9/2/45; 3711 BU Seattle (Training Command) 26/2/45; 3098 BU Burbank 31/1/46; Recl Comp 25/10/45.
43-39337 Del Hunter 16/2/45; Grenier 25/2/45; ass 8AF 2/3/45; sal 9AF Germany 18/9/46; re-ass 10 HBS Oberpfaffenhofen 30/4/47; Recl Comp 19/11/47.
43-39338 Del Hunter 15/2/45; Grenier 18/3/45; ass 8AF 26/3/45; re-ass Holland 31/12/46; tran 10 HBS Oberpfaffenhofen 30/4/47; Recl Comp 9/4/48.
43-39339 Del Hunter 15/2/45; Grenier 25/2/45; ass 8AF 27/2/45; retUS 112 BU Wendover 9/10/45; RFC Walnut Ridge 8/1/46.
43-39340 Del –; ass 8AF; retUS, as QB-17N Drone in Day-Glo red with wing tip cameras installed in 1950s.
43-39341 Del Hunter 16/2/45; Grenier 25/2/45; ass 8AF 10/3/45; retUS Bradley 18/6/45; 4168 BU Sth Plains 20/6/45; RFC Kingman 2/2/46.
43-39342 Del Hunter 15/2/45; Grenier 25/2/45; ass 8AF 26/2/45; re-ass 10 HBS Oberpfaffenhofen 30/4/47; Recl Comp 7/1/49.
43-39343 Del Hunter 15/2/45; Grenier 25/2/45; ass 8AF 26/2/45; re-ass 10 HBS Oberpfaffenhofen 30/4/47; Recl Comp 7/1/49.
43-39344 Del Hunter 16/2/45; Grenier 1/3/45; ass 8AF 11/2/45; retUS Bradley 13/6/45; 4168 BU Sth Plains 18/6/45; RFC Kingman 22/1/46.
43-39345 Del Hunter 17/2/45; Grenier 1/3/45; ass 563BS/388BG Knettishall 6/3/45; retUS Bradley 28/6/45; 4168 BU Sth Plains 30/6/45; RFC Kingman 17/12/45.
43-39346 Del Lincoln 16/2/45; Grenier 8/3/45; ass 8AF 18/3/45; retUS Bradley 22/5/45; 4168 BU Sth Plains 24/5/45; RFC Kingman 2/2/46.
43-39347 Del Lincoln 17/2/45; Grenier 1/3/45; ass

8AF 4/3/45; retUS Bradley 12/7/45; 4185 BU Independence 13/7/45; RFC Kingman 21/12/45.
43-39348 Del Lincoln 16/2/45; Grenier 1/3/45; ass 8AF 6/3/45; re-ass 10 HBS Oberpfaffenhofen 30/4/47; Recl Comp 18/11/48.
43-39349 Del Lincoln 17/2/45; Grenier 1/3/45; ass 332BS/94BG Rougham 4/3/45; sal 9AF Germany 23/5/46.
43-39350 Del Lincoln 17/2/45; Grenier 1/3/45; ass 8AF 11/2/45; retUS Bradley 7/7/45; 4168 BU Sth Plains 10/7/45; RFC Kingman 20/11/45.
43-39351 Del Lincoln 19/2/45; Grenier 4/3/45; ass 8AF 6/3/45; sal 9AF Germany 18/9/46; Recl Comp 19/11/47.
43-39352 Del Hunter 23/2/45; Grenier 5/3/45; ass 8AF 8/3/45; retUS Bradley 7/7/45; 4168 BU Sth Plains 10/7/45; RFC Kingman 9/2/46.
43-39353 Del Hunter 19/2/45; Grenier 2/3/45; ass 8AF 6/3/45; retUS Bradley 5/7/45; 4168 BU Sth Plains 6/7/45; RFC Kingman 7/2/46.
43-39354 Del Hunter 20/2/45; Grenier 9/3/45; ass 8AF 13/3/45; sal 9AF Germany 31/5/46.
43-39355 Del Hunter 27/2/45; Grenier 12/3/45; ass 413BS/96BG Snetterton 15/3/45; tran 452BG Deopham Green 16/3/45; retUS Bradley 30/5/45; 4168 BU Sth Plains 1/6/45; RFC Kingman 17/12/45.
43-39356 Del –. Ass 8th Air Division as VIP taxi (VB-17), Castle AB 1956.
43-39357 Del Lincoln 20/2/45; Grenier 8/3/45; ass 34BG Mendlesham 13/3/45; retUS Bradley 30/6/45; 4168 BU Sth Plains 3/7/45; RFC Kingman 31/1/46.
43-39358 Del Lincoln 22/2/45; Grenier 4/3/45; ass 452BG 6/3/45; retUS Bradley 20/6/45; 4168 BU Sth Plains 23/6/45; RFC Kingman 6/12/45. Eventually was used as VIP liner extensively re-furbished, and took part in Boeing flypast 30/7/56.
43-39359 Del –. Used in Korea as one of last armed B-17s.
43-39360 Del Rome 23/2/45; Cheyenne 12/3/45; Hunter 13/4/45; Bangor 5/5/45; ass 5AF Karachi 8/5/45; re-ass FEA 30/4/47.
43-39361 Del Rome 22/2/45; Hunter 28/3/45; ass 5AF 30/4/47; 3 ER Itami 18/1/48; 3 RES Chitose 18/5/48; 13 AR Jama 22/6/48; 3 RES Chitose 23/7/48; 3 RES Misawa 12/7/49; retUS, AMC Hill 29/8/50; Recl Comp 5/12/50.
43-39362 Del –.
43-39363 Del Rome 23/2/45; Hunter 12/4/45; ATC San Francisco 22/4/45; ass 5AF, 385 SR Chitose 11/3/48; 385 SR Misawa 23/7/48; 49 MSS Misawa 7/9/48; Recl Comp 7/1/49.
43-39364 Del Rome 24/2/45; Cheyenne 10/3/45; Hunter 13/4/45; ATC San Francisco 26/4/45; ass 5AF, 3 ER Yokota 18/1/48; 18 ARE Jama 18/3/49.
43-39365 Del Rome 24/2/45; Hunter 26/3/45; ATC San Francisco 14/4/45; ass 5AF, 3 ER Yokota 18/1/48; Recl Comp 8/6/49; 3 BL Johnson 4/5/50; 6122 AB Ashiya 8/11/50; Recl Comp 5/12/50.
43-39366 Del –.
43-39367 Del –. As CP-625 sal 17/11/59, San Lorenzo, Bolivia.
43-39368 Del –.
43-39369 Del –.
43-39370 Del –.
43-39371 Del Hunter 24/2/45; Grenier 9/3/45; ass Soxo 18/3/45; sal 9AF Germany 23/5/46.
43-39372 Del Hunter 26/2/45; Grenier 11/3/45; ass Soxo 13/3/45; retUS Bradley 13/6/45; 4168 BU Sth Plains 15/6/45; RFC Kingman 5/2/46.
43-39373 Del Lincoln 26/2/45; Grenier 8/3/45; ass 8AF 10/3/45; retUS Bradley 7/6/45; 4168 BU Sth Plains 12/6/45; 428 BU Kirtland 6/2/46; RFC Albuquerque 19/3/46.
43-39374 Del –.
43-39375 Del Rome 26/2/45; Cheyenne 12/3/45; Hunter 13/4/45; ATC San Francisco 17/5/45; sal 31/7/46.
43-39376 Del Rome 26/2/45; Cheyenne 12/3/45; Hunter 13/4/45; ATC San Francisco 30/4/45; ass 8AF then trans 5AF, 2 ER Clark Fd 18/1/48; 358 SR Clark 19/5/48; 567 MAT Clark 1/7/48; 18 MSU Clark 8/12/48; Recl Comp 10/5/49.
43-39377 Del Lincoln 26/2/45; Grenier 8/3/45; ass 8AF 10/3/45; retUS Bradley 7/6/45; 4168 BU Sth Plains 9/6/45; RFC Kingman 7/2/46.
43-39378 Del Lincoln 26/2/45; Grenier 13/3/45; ass 8AF 15/3/45; re-ass 10 HBS Oberpfaffenhofen 30/4/47; Recl Comp 1/10/48.
43-39379 Del Lincoln 28/2/45; Grenier 12/3/45; ass 8AF 15/3/45; retUS Bradley 24/5/45; 4168 BU Sth Plains 24/5/45; RFC Kingman 5/2/46.
43-39380 Del Lincoln 27/2/45; Grenier 8/3/45; ass 8AF 10/3/45; re-ass 10 HBS Oberpfaffenhofen 30/4/47; Recl Comp 7/6/49.
43-39381 Del Lincoln 28/2/45; Grenier 12/3/45; ass 8AF 17/3/45; retUS Bradley 30/5/45; 4168 BU Sth Plains 31/5/45; RFC Kingman 5/2/46.
43-39382 Del Hunter 27/2/45; Grenier 8/3/45; ass 8AF 10/3/45; retUS Bradley 3/7/45; 4168 BU Sth Plains 7/7/45; 613 BU Phillips 6/3/46.
43-39383 Del Hunter 27/3/45; Grenier 16/3/45; ass 8AF 20/3/45; retUS Bradley 25/5/45; RFC Kingman 8/2/46.
43-39384 Del Hunter 28/2/45; Grenier 10/3/45; ass 8AF 13/3/45; re-ass 10 HBS Oberpfaffenhofen 30/4/47; Recl Comp 16/12/48.
43-39385 Del Lincoln 28/2/45; Grenier 12/3/45; ass 8AF 15/3/45; retUS Bradley 22/6/45; 4168 BU Sth Plains 23/6/45; RFC Kingman 5/2/46.
43-39386 Del Lincoln 1/3/45; Grenier 12/3/45; ass 8AF 15/3/45; sal 9AF Germany 10/5/46.
43-39387 Del Hunter 1/3/45; Grenier 11/3/45; ass 8AF 13/3/45; re-ass 10 HBS Oberpfaffenhofen 30/4/47; Recl Comp 7/1/49.
43-39388 Del Hunter 1/3/45; Grenier 10/3/45; ass 8AF 17/3/45; re-ass ATC Europe 30/4/47; Recl Comp 16/3/48.
43-39389 Del Hunter 1/3/45; Grenier 10/3/45; ass 8AF 13/3/45; sal 9AF Germany 16/5/46.
43-39390 Del Hunter 1/3/45; Grenier 11/3/45; ass 8AF 13/3/45; retUS Bradley 12/6/45; 4168 BU Sth Plains 15/6/45; RFC Kingman 22/2/46.
43-39391 Del Hunter 1/3/45; Grenier 16/3/45; ass 8AF 20/3/45; re-ass 10 HBS Oberpfaffenhofen 30/4/47; Recl Comp 18/11/48.
43-39392 Del Hunter 1/3/45; Grenier 20/3/45; ass 8AF 25/3/45; retUS Bradley 3/7/45; 4168 BU Sth Plains 6/7/45; RFC Kingman 22/1/46.
43-39393 Del Hunter 2/3/45; Grenier 9/3/45; ass 8AF 20/3/45; sal 9AF Germany 23/5/46.
43-39394 Del Hunter 1/3/45; Grenier 16/3/45; ass 8AF 20/3/45; sal 9AF Germany 23/5/45.
43-39395 Del Hunter 1/3/45; Grenier 16/3/45; ass 8AF 20/3/45; retUS Bradley 23/5/45; 4168 BU Sth Plains 25/5/45; RFC Kingman 8/2/46.
43-39396 Del Hunter 1/3/45; Grenier 12/3/45; ass 8AF 15/3/45; sal 9AF Germany 5/11/46; re-ass 10 HBS Oberpfaffenhofen 30/4/47; Recl Comp 6/12/48.
43-39397 Del Hunter 2/3/45; Grenier 16/3/45; ass 8AF 25/3/45; retUS Bradley 27/6/45; 4168 BU Sth Plains 30/6/45; RFC Kingman 22/1/46.
43-39398 Del Hunter 2/3/45; Grenier 17/3/45; ass 8AF 20/3/45; retUS Bradley 3/7/45; 4168 BU Sth Plains 5/7/45; RFC Kingman 9/12/45.
43-39399 Del Hunter 2/3/45; Grenier 16/3/45; ass 8AF 20/3/45; sal 9AF Germany 31/5/46.
43-39400 Del Hunter 3/3/45; Grenier 17/3/45; ass 8AF 20/3/45; retUS 1103 BU Morrison 13/12/45; RFC Walnut Ridge 3/1/46.
43-39401 Del Hunter 5/3/45; Grenier 23/3/45; ass 563BS/388BG Knettishall 26/3/45; retUS Bradley 24/6/45; 4168 BU Sth Plains 27/6/45; RFC Kingman 5/12/45.
43-39402 Del Hunter 5/3/45; Grenier 13/3/45; ass 8AF 17/3/45; re-ass 10 HBS Oberpfaffenhofen 30/4/47; Recl Comp 18/11/48.
43-39403 Del Hunter 5/3/45; Grenier 29/3/45; ass 8AF 1/4/45; retUS Bradley 28/6/45; 4168 BU Sth Plains 3/7/45; RFC Kingman 25/11/45.
43-39404 Del Hunter 7/3/45; Grenier 17/3/45; ass 8AF 20/3/45; re-ass 10 HBS Oberpfaffenhofen 30/4/47; Recl Comp 7/1/49.
43-39405 Del Hunter 7/3/45; Grenier 24/3/45; ass 8AF 26/3/45; retUS Bradley 6/6/45; 4168 BU Sth Plains 12/6/45; 613 BU Phillips 28/2/46; Sth Plains 19/3/46.
43-39406 Del Hunter 7/3/45; Grenier 17/3/45; ass 8AF 20/3/45; sal 9AF Germany 23/5/46.
43-39407 Del Hunter 7/3/45; Grenier 18/3/45; ass 8AF 20/3/45; sal 9AF Germany 10/5/46.
43-39408 Del Hunter 7/3/45; Grenier 18/3/45; ass 8AF 20/3/45; sal 9AF Germany 23/5/46.
43-39409 Del Hunter 7/3/45; Grenier 17/3/45; ass 8AF 29/3/45; retUS Bradley 23/5/45; 4168 BU Sth Plains 25/5/45; RFC Kingman 13/2/46.
43-39410 Del Hunter 7/3/45; Grenier 19/3/45; ass 8AF 20/3/45; retUS 1 BU Bolling 28/8/45; 716 BU Grenier 14/1/46; 90 BU Ft Totten 17/3/46; 4121 BU Kelly 29/8/46; 90 BU Mitchell 15/9/46; re-ass 10 HBS Oberpfaffenhofen 30/4/47; retUS, 2621 BU Barksdale 9/7/47; 4117 BU Robins 4/3/48; Recl Comp 4/11/48.
43-39411 Del Hunter 8/3/45; Grenier 17/3/45; ass 8AF 20/3/45; sal 9AF Germany 31/5/45.
43-39412 Del Hunter 9/3/45; Grenier 18/3/45; ass 8AF 26/3/45; retUS Bradley 8/6/45; Sth Plains 14/6/45; RFC Kingman 28/1/46.
43-39413 Del Hunter 9/3/45; Grenier 18/3/45; ass 8AF 20/3/45; retUS Bradley 6/6/45; Sth Plains 12/6/45; RFC Kingman 6/12/46.
43-39414 Del Hunter 9/3/45; Grenier 18/3/45; ass 8AF 20/3/45; sal 9AF Germany 23/5/46.
43-39415 Del Hunter 9/3/45; Grenier 18/3/45; ass 8AF 26/3/45; re-ass 10 HBS Oberpfaffenhofen 30/4/47; Recl Comp 7/1/49.
43-39416 Del Hunter 9/3/45; Grenier 30/3/45; ass 8AF 25/3/45; retUS Bradley 6/6/45; 4168 BU Sth Plains 10/6/45; RFC Kingman 15/2/46.
43-39417 Del Hunter 10/3/45; Grenier 20/3/45; ass 8AF 26/3/45; retUS Bradley 2/6/45; Sth Plains 7/6/45; RFC Kingman 14/2/46.
43-39418 Del Hunter 10/3/45; Grenier 23/3/45; ass 8AF 26/3/45; sal 9AF Germany 10/5/46.
43-39419 Del Hunter 10/3/45; Grenier 20/3/45; ass 8AF 29/3/45; retUS Bradley 28/5/45; Sth Plains 31/5/45; RFC Kingman 8/2/46.
43-39420 Del Hunter 10/3/45; Grenier 20/3/45; ass 8AF 25/3/45; retUS Bradley 20/6/45; Sth Plains 23/6/45; RFC Kingman 5/2/46.
43-39421 Del Hunter 10/3/45; Grenier 20/3/45; ass 8AF 1/4/45; retUS Bradley 28/6/45; Sth Plains 2/7/45; RFC Kingman 5/12/45.
43-39422 Del Hunter 16/3/45; Grenier 20/3/45; ass 8AF 27/3/45; sal 9AF Germany 31/5/45.
43-39423 Del Hunter 13/3/45; Grenier 23/3/45; ass 8AF 26/3/45; retUS Bradley 22/5/45; Sth Plains 24/5/45; RFC Kingman 21/2/46.

43-39424 Del Hunter 12/3/45; Grenier 25/3/45; ass 100BG 1/4/45; retUS Bradley 24/6/45; 4168 BU Sth Plains 26/6/45; RFC Kingman 9/12/45.

43-39425 Del Hunter 12/3/45; Grenier 23/3/45; ass 8AF 26/3/45; sal 9AF Germany 10/5/46.

43-39426 Del Hunter 12/3/45; Grenier 20/3/45; ass 8AF 25/3/45; retUS Bradley 29/6/45; Sth Plains 1/7/45; RFC Kingman 14/2/46.

43-39427 Del Hunter 12/3/45; Grenier 30/3/45; ass 8AF 25/3/45; sal 9AF Germany 22/6/45; retUS 1103 BU Morrison 26/2/46; 613 BU Phillips 22/4/46.

43-39428 Del Hunter 13/3/45; Grenier 25/3/45; ass 563BS/388BG Knettishall 1/4/45; retUS Bradley 3/7/45; Sth Plains 6/7/45; RFC Kingman 14/12/45.

43-39429 Del Hunter 13/3/45; Grenier 24/3/45; ass 8AF 27/3/45; retUS Bradley 6/7/45; Sth Plains 8/7/45; RFC Kingman 7/2/46.

43-39430 Del Hunter 13/3/45; Grenier 23/3/45; ass 8AF 26/3/45; retUS Bradley 24/6/45; 4168 BU Sth Plains 28/6/45; RFC Kingman 27/11/45.

43-39431 Del Hunter 13/3/45; Grenier 17/3/45; ass 8AF 26/3/45; retUS Bradley 2/8/45; 4185 BU Independence 3/8/45; RFC Kingman 9/12/45.

43-39432 Del Hunter 14/3/45; Grenier 27/3/45; ass 8AF 27/3/45; retUS Bradley 11/6/45; Sth Plains 14/6/45; RFC Kingman 11/2/46.

43-39433 Del Hunter 14/3/45; Grenier 24/3/45; ass 8AF 26/3/45; sal 9AF Germany 23/5/46.

43-39434 Del Hunter 14/3/45; Grenier 23/3/45; ass 8AF 26/3/45; retUS Bradley 4/6/45; Sth Plains 7/6/45; RFC Kingman 28/1/46.

43-39435 Del Hunter 15/3/45; Grenier 23/3/45; ass 8AF 26/3/45; retUS Bradley 10/6/45; Sth Plains 13/6/45; RFC Kingman 11/2/46.

43-39436 Del Hunter 16/3/45; Grenier 24/3/45; ass 8AF 26/3/45; retUS Bradley 31/5/45; Sth Plains 3/6/45; RFC Kingman 11/2/45.

43-39437 Del Hunter 16/3/45; Grenier 28/3/45; ass 8AF 1/4/45; retUS Bradley 31/5/45; Sth Plains 3/6/45; RFC Kingman 26/2/45.

43-39438 Del Hunter 20/3/45; Grenier 30/3/45; ass 306BG Thurleigh 1/4/45; sal 9AF Germany 10/5/46.

43-39439 Del Hunter 16/3/45; Grenier 28/3/45; ass 728BS/452BG Deopham Green 29/3/45 CYANIDE FOR HITLER; retUS Bradley 28/6/45; Sth Plains 2/7/45; RFC Kingman 20/11/45. JEANNIE WITH LIGHT BROWN HAIR.

43-39440 Del Hunter 19/3/45; Grenier 28/3/45; tran 327 BU Drew 1/8/45; 326 BU McDill 12/12/45; 110 BU Mitchell 7/3/46; 100 BU Mitchell 27/3/46; 104 BU Mitchell 4/6/46; 35 BU Bolling 7/11/46; US Navy as CB-17; re-ass USAF 30/4/47; 16 SAM Bolling 10/3/48; 1100 BU Bolling 3/1/50; Recl Comp 9/11/50.

43-39441 Del Hunter 17/3/45; Grenier 24/3/45; ass 8AF 26/3/45; retUS Bradley 4/6/45; Sth Plains 7/6/45; RFC Kingman 7/2/46.

43-39442 Del Hunter 19/3/45; Grenier 29/3/45; ass 8AF 1/4/45; retUS Bradley 1/6/45; Sth Plains 3/6/45; RFC Kingman 5/2/46.

43-39443 Del Hunter 19/3/45; Grenier 28/3/45; ass 8AF 1/4/45; retUS Bradley 23/5/45; Sth Plains 25/5/45; RFC Kingman 7/2/45.

43-39444 Del Hunter 19/3/45; Grenier 28/3/45; ass 544BS/384BG [SU-J] Grafton Underwood 10/4/45; sal 9AF Germany 18/9/46; re-ass 10 HBS Oberpfaffenhofen 30/4/47; Recl Comp 19/11/47.

43-39445 Del Topeka 19/3/45; Grenier 1/4/45; ass 8AF 5/4/45; retUS Bradley 31/5/45; Sth Plains 3/6/45; RFC Kingman 7/2/45.

43-39446 Del Topeka 19/3/45; Grenier 1/4/45; ass 8AF 5/4/45; retUS Bradley 28/5/45; Sth Plains 30/5/45; RFC Kingman 8/2/45.

43-39447 Del Hunter 20/3/45; Grenier 29/3/45; ass 8AF 1/4/45; retUS Bradley 4/6/45; Sth Plains 8/6/45; RFC Kingman 21/2/46.

43-39448 Del Hunter 27/3/45; Sth Plains 16/4/45; 3017 BU Hobbs 1/10/45; 3028 BU Luke 18/10/45; 3017 BU Hobbs 29/10/45; 2137 BU Hendricks 27/11/45; 2140 BU Smyrna 19/12/45; Recl Comp 17/9/46.

43-39449 Del Hunter 24/3/45; Grenier 1/4/45; ass 381BG Ridgewell 12/5/45; retUS Bradley 28/5/45; Sth Plains 31/5/45; RFC Kingman 21/2/46.

43-39450 Del Hunter 22/3/45; Grenier 30/3/45; ass 303BG Molesworth 10/4/45; tran 457BG Glatton 22/5/45; retUS Bradley 8/6/45; 4168 BU Sth Plains 12/6/45; 613 BU Phillips 6/3/46.

43-39451 Del Hunter 22/3/45; Grenier 29/3/45; ass 8AF 29/3/45; retUS Bradley 20/6/45; Sth Plains 22/6/45; RFC Kingman 14/2/46.

43-39452 Del Hunter 24/3/45; Grenier 30/3/45; ass 533BS/381BG [VP-Y] Ridgewell 11/4/45; {1m} RetUS Bradley 28/5/45; Sth Plains 31/5/45; RFC Kingman 26/11/45.

43-39453 Del Hunter 23/3/45; Grenier 30/3/45; ass 303BG Molesworth 10/4/45; tran 457BG Glatton 22/5/45; retUS Bradley 9/6/45; Sth Plains 12/6/45; RFC Kingman 9/12/45.

43-39454 Del Hunter 26/3/45; ass 8AF, tran Sth Plains 14/4/45; Hobbs 1/10/45; 2140 BU Smyrna 14/2/46; 342 BU Smyrna 21/4/46; Recl Comp 15/7/46.

43-39455 Del Hunter 29/3/45; ass 8AF, tran Sth Plains 14/4/45; 3017 BU Hobbs 1/10/45; 2137 BU Hendricks 28/10/45; 2140 BU Smyrna 19/12/45; 342 BU Smyrna 5/5/46; 594 BU Topeka 26/6/46.

43-39456 Del Topeka 29/3/45; ass 8AF, tran Sth Plains 15/4/45; RFC Kingman 7/2/46.

43-39457 Del Topeka 29/3/45; ass 100BG Thorpe Abbotts 3/45; retUS, tran as SB-17G, 10 ERS Alaska 1949.

43-39458 Del Topeka 30/3/45; ass 8AF, tran Sth Plains 16/4/45; 2137 BU Hendricks 5/11/45; 2140 BU Smyrna 19/12/45; 613 BU Phillips 20/6/46; 594 BU Topeka 7/7/46; 613 BU Phillips 20/8/46.

43-39459 Del Topeka 27/3/45; ass 8AF, tran Sth Plains 17/4/45; 593 BU Charleston 2/1/46; RFC Walnut Ridge 16/1/46.

43-39460 Del Hunter 28/3/45; ass 8AF, tran Sth Plains 20/4/45; 2140 BU Smyrna 6/11/45; 554 BU Memphis 17/6/46; 613 BU Phillips 23/6/46.

43-39461 Del Topeka 28/3/45; ass 8AF, tran Sth Plains 15/4/45; 3017 BU Hobbs 11/10/45; 2137 BU Hendricks 29/10/45; 2140 BU Smyrna 19/12/45; 342 BU Smyrna 6/4/46; 613 BU Phillips 10/6/46.

43-39462 Del Topeka 29/3/45; ass 8AF, tran Sth Plains 15/4/45; RFC Walnut Ridge 5/12/45.

43-39463 Del Topeka 29/3/45; ass 8AF, tran Sth Plains 15/4/45; RFC Kingman 15/2/46.

43-39464 Del Hunter 30/3/45; ass 8AF, tran Sth Plains 15/4/45; RFC Walnut Ridge 5/12/45.

43-39465 Del Hunter 30/3/45; ass 8AF, tran Sth Plains 7/4/45; Rome 23/8/45; 1 BAS Bolling 26/5/46; 4112 BU Olmstead 16/6/46; re-ass 5AF Tacloban (Ph Is), 30/4/47; Recl Comp 29/4/48.

43-39466 Del Topeka 31/3/45; ass 8AF, tran Sth Plains 17/4/45; RFC Kingman 8/2/46.

43-39467 Del Topeka 30/3/45; ass 8AF, tran Sth Plains 18/4/45; 3017 BU Hobbs 11/10/45; 2137 BU Hendricks 28/10/45; 2140 BU Smyrna 19/12/45; 342 BU Smyrna 5/5/46; 554 BU Memphis 13/6/46.

43-39468 Del Topeka 31/3/45; ass 8AF, tran Sth Plains 15/4/45; 3017 BU Hobbs 12/10/45; 2137 BU Hendricks 28/10/45; 2140 BU Smyrna 19/12/45; 342 BU Smyrna 5/5/46; 554 BU Memphis 31/7/46.

43-39469 Del Hunter 31/3/45; ass 8AF, tran Sth Plains 15/4/45; RFC Walnut Ridge 5/1/46.

43-39470 Del Hunter 31/3/45; ass 8AF, tran Sth Plains 6/4/45; RFC Walnut Ridge 5/12/45.

43-39471 Del Hunter 3/4/45; ass 8AF, tran Sth Plains 16/4/45; 3017 BU Hobbs 2/10/45; 2137 BU Hendricks 29/10/45; 2140 BU Smyrna 19/12/45; 342 BU Smyrna 5/5/46; 594 BU Topeka 26/6/46.

43-39472 Del Hunter 3/4/45; ass 8AF, tran Sth Plains 16/4/45; 3017 BU Hobbs 2/10/45; 2137 BU Hendricks 27/11/45; 2140 BU Smyrna 26/12/45; 342 BU Smyrna 5/5/46; 554 BU Memphis 12/6/46.

43-39473 Del Hunter 4/4/45; ass 8AF, tran Sth Plains 16/4/45; 2519 BU Ft Worth 18/10/45; 3017 BU Hobbs 21/10/45; 2140 BU Smyrna 19/12/45; 342 BU Smyrna 30/4/46; 594 BU Topeka 12/6/46; 4104 BU Rome 18/6/46; sal 5/8/47.

43-39474 Del Hunter 4/4/45; ass 8AF, tran Sth Plains 16/4/45; RFC Walnut Ridge 5/1/46.

43-39475 Del Hunter 4/4/45; ass 8AF, tran Sth Plains 14/4/45; 2621 BU Barksdale 3/12/45; 613 BU Phillips 24/6/46; 554 BU Memphis 13/8/46.

43-39476 Del Sth Plains 4/4/45; 2140 BU Smyrna 14/11/45; 342 BU Smyrna 5/5/46; 594 BU Topeka 26/6/46.

43-39477 Del Sth Plains 4/4/45; Gore Fd 10/4/45; RFC Walnut Ridge 5/1/46.

43-39478 Del Cheyenne 10/4/45; Hunter 7/5/45; San Francisco 22/5/45; ass 5AF, Biak Is 30/5/45; 4 ER Guam 18/1/46; re-ass 30/4/47; 4 RCU Sq 31/7/47; 2 RCU Sq Anderson 14/4/50; Recl Comp 12/10/50.

43-39479 Del Sth Plains 7/4/45; 2003 BU Ft Worth 19/9/45; 2137 BU Hendricks 5/11/45; 2140 BU Smyrna 19/12/45; 342 BU Smyrna 30/4/46; 554 BU Memphis 19/6/46; 613 BU Phillips 23/6/46.

43-39480 Del Sth Plains 7/4/45; 3017 BU Hobbs 5/10/45; 2137 BU Hendricks 29/10/45; 2140 BU Smyrna 19/12/45; 594 BU Topeka 12/6/46; 4104 BU Rome 18/6/46; 4136 BU Tinker 29/1/47; 4141 BU Pyote 3/2/47; Recl Comp 18/4/50.

43-39481 Del Sth Plains 9/4/45; 484 BU Topeka 8/10/45; 482 BU Merced 24/1/46; ATC San Francisco 4/4/46; ass 5AF, 91 BU Tokyo 30/4/47; 7 AC Tokyo 18/6/47; Hickam 19/7/48; 108 AC Tokyo 11/1/50; Recl Comp 3/10/50.

43-39482 Del Sth Plains 7/4/45; 3017 BU Hobbs 2/10/45; 2137 BU Hendricks 29/10/45; 2140 BU Smyrna 19/12/45; 342 BU Smyrna 5/5/46; 594 BU Topeka 26/6/46.

43-39483 Del Sth Plains 11/4/45; Lincoln 15/4/45; RFC Walnut Ridge 5/1/46.

43-39484 Del Sth Plains 9/4/45; 3017 BU Hobbs 1/10/45; 2140 BU Smyrna 31/1/46; 342 BU Smyrna 30/4/46; 594 BU Topeka 26/6/46.

43-39485 Del Sth Plains 9/4/45; 3017 BU Hobbs 11/10/45; 2137 BU Hendricks 28/10/46; 2140 BU Smyrna 19/12/45; 342 BU Smyrna 5/5/46; 554 BU Memphis 31/7/46.

43-39486 Del Cheyenne 11/4/45; Hunter 8/5/45; ATC San Francisco 22/5/45; ass 5AF, Biok Is 27/5/45; sal Manila 11/10/46.

43-39487 Del Cheyenne 12/4/44; Hunter 7/5/45; ATC San Francisco 12/6/45; ass 5AF, Oahu 30/4/47; 23 Ph Rec Momote 18/1/48; 23 Ph Rec Clark Fd 11/1/48; 5 RVP Clark 1/4/48; retUS 9 SAC Gp Fairfield 26/4/49; 56 MSU Selfridge 31/7/49.

43-39488 Del Cheyenne 12/4/45; Hunter 8/5/45; ATC San Francisco 20/5/45; sal Manila 19/9/45.

43-39489 Del Cheyenne 11/4/45; Hunter 8/5/45; ATC Long Beach 21/5/45; ass 5AF, Biok Is 30/4/47; 23 Ph Rec Momote 18/1/48; 5 RVP Clark Fd 18/4/45; 18 MSU Clark 1/4/49; retUS 9 SRC Gp Fairfield

2/6/49; Hill 9/12/49; Recl Comp 19/5/50.
43-39490 Del Cheyenne 12/4/45; Hunter 7/5/45; ATC San Francisco 23/5/45; ass 5AF, Biok Is 30/4/47; sal Manila 8/12/47.
43-39491 Del Cheyenne 11/4/45; Hunter 3/5/45; ATC San Francisco 20/5/45; ass 5AF, Brisbane 30/4/47; 4 RES Guam 18/1/48; 2 RCU Sq Anderson 14/4/50; Recl Comp 12/10/50.
43-39492 Del –. Became QB-17L radio controlled Drone target a/c for missiles, live ammunition etc. The last was shot down in 1960.
43-39493 Del Cheyenne 12/4/45; Hunter 15/5/45; ATC San Francisco 31/5/45; ass 5AF 1/2/47; Recl Comp 15/1/48.
43-39494 Del Cheyenne 12/4/45; Hunter 16/5/45; ATC San Francisco 31/5/45; ass 5AF 30/4/47; Recl Comp 29/4/48.
43-39495 Del Cheyenne 12/4/45; Hunter 10/5/45; ATC San Francisco 27/5/45; ass 5AF, Manila 14/11/46; Recl Comp 29/4/48.
43-39496 Del Cheyenne 12/4/45; Hunter 4/5/45; ATC Long Beach 31/5/45; ass 5AF; sal Taclobon 2/8/46.
43-39497 Del Cheyenne 12/4/45; Hunter 10/5/45; ATC Long Beach 21/5/45; ass 5AF, Biak Is 30/5/45; sal Manila 23/7/46.
43-39498 Del Cheyenne 12/4/45; Hunter 7/5/45; ATC San Francisco 30/5/45; ass 5AF, 31 Ph Rec Momote 18/1/48; 31 Ph Rec Clark 11/1/48; 6 SR Clark 4/2/48; 5 RVP Clark 1/4/48; 358 SR Clark 6/4/48; 567 MAT Clark 24/6/48; 18 MSU Clark 16/2/49; retUS 9 SRC Fairfield 2/6/49; Recl Comp 24/1/50.
43-39499 Del –.
43-39500 Del Cheyenne 13/4/45; Hunter 12/5/45; ATC San Francisco 31/5/45; ass 5AF, 23 Ph Rec Momote 18/1/48; 5 RVP Gp Clark 1/4/48; Hickam 17/4/49; 5 RVP Gp Clark 15/5/49; retUS 9 SRG Gp Fairfield 2/6/49; Recl Comp 13/1/50.
43-39501 Del Cheyenne 12/4/45; Hunter 2/5/45; Grenier 15/5/45; ass 5AF, 358 SHR Clark 31/1/48; 13 AR Clark 18/4/48; 328 SR Clark 19/5/48; 6 SR Clark 26/6/48; 18 MSU Clark 18/12/48; Recl Comp 2/3/49.
43-39502 Del Cheyenne 12/4/45; Hunter 14/5/45; ATC San Francisco 31/5/45; ass 5AF, 4 ER Guam 18/1/48; 13 ARE Jama 8/7/49; Recl Comp 29/7/49. ONE MORE TIME.
43-39503 Del –. ASR (5AF?).
43-39504 Del Cheyenne 13/4/45; Hunter 3/5/45; ATC San Francisco 19/5/45; ass 5AF, 2 ER Kadena 18/1/48; 2 RCU Sq Kadena 31/7/49; 6332 AB Kadena 18/4/50; 2 RCU Sq Clark 24/5/50; 6332 AB Kadena 22/6/50; Recl Comp 12/10/50.
43-39505 Del Cheyenne 14/4/45; Hunter 15/5/45; ATC San Francisco 2/6/45; ass ASR 11AF Shemya 1945; tran 5AF, Okinawa; Recl Comp 28/5/46; 2 WW Furstenfelde, Ger 1955.
43-39506 Del Cheyenne 14/4/45; Hunter 15/5/45; ATC San Francisco 2/6/45; ass 5AF, Okinawa 12/12/46; Recl Comp 1/10/48.
43-39507 Del –.
43-39508 Del –. Last Seattle built a/c, Bu No 6981. On the ceremonial roll out on 9/4/45 it was covered with card cut-outs of every target a B-17 attacked.

B-17G-DL
44-6001 Del Tulsa 2/4/44; Kearney 13/4/44; Grenier 29/4/44; ass 728BS/452BG Deopham Green 3/5/44; dest by e/a at Poltava 21/6/44; sal 2/7/44.
44-6002 Del Tulsa 2/4/44; Hunter 8/4/44; Grenier 30/4/44; ass 305BG Chelveston 22/5/44; retUS Bradley 7/6/45; Sth Plains 10/6/45; RFC Kingman 1/12/45.
44-6003 Del Tulsa 2/4/44; Hunter 8/4/44; Dow Fd 25/4/44; ass 709BS/447BG Rattlesden 21/4/44; retUS Bradley 19/6/45; Sth Plains 24/6/45; RFC Kingman 8/11/45.
44-6004 Del Tulsa 2/4/44; Kearney 15/4/44; Grenier 18/4/44; ass 527BS/379BG [FO-D] Kimbolton 23/5/44; MIA Merseburg 24/8/44 w/Burns; flak, cr Merseburg; 2KIA 7POW; MACR 8284. RONNY BOY.
44-6005 Del Tulsa 2/4/44; Kearney 15/4/44; Grenier 29/4/44; ass 422BS/305BG [JJ-O] Chelveston 22/5/44; cr Craig Cwm Llwdd, UK 8/6/45 w/?; 20 killed.
44-6006 Del Tulsa 2/4/44; Hunter 8/4/44; Dow Fd 25/4/44; ass 358BS/303BG [VK-D] Molesworth 30/4/44; tran 457BG Glatton 22/5/44; 351BG Polebrook 29/5/45; retUS Bradley 13/6/45; Sth Plains 15/6/45; RFC Kingman 8/12/45.
44-6007 Del Tulsa 2/4/44; Hunter 17/4/44; Dow Fd 30/4/44; ass 571BS/390BG [FC-M] Framlingham 4/5/44; retUS Bradley 3/7/45; Sth Plains 5/7/45; RFC Kingman 19/12/45. LUCKY.
44-6008 Del Tulsa 3/4/44; Hunter 17/4/44; Grenier 30/4/44; ass 548BS/385BG Gt Ashfield 7/5/44; b/d Bremen 26/9/44 w/Lamont; flak, ditched Channel.
44-6009 Del Tulsa 3/4/44; Hunter 15/4/44; Grenier 1/5/44; ass 364BS/305BG [WF-J] Chelveston 17/5/44; {28+m} tran 351BG Polebrook 23/5/45; retUS Bradley 13/6/45; Sth Plains 18/6/45; RFC Kingman 1/12/45. FLAK EATER.
44-6010 Del Tulsa 3/4/44; Kearney 15/4/44; Grenier 29/4/45; ass 447BG Rattlesden 3/5/44; tran 418BS/100BG [LD-W] Thorpe Abbotts 4/5/44; taxi acc w/43-37686 21/6/44; sal.
44-6011 Del Tulsa 3/4/44; Hunter 15/4/44; Grenier 29/4/44; ass 452BG Deopham Green 3/5/44; dest by e/a at Poltava 21/6/44; sal 2/7/44.
44-6012 Del Tulsa 3/4/44; Hunter 15/4/44; Grenier 29/4/44; ass 423BS/306BG [RD-A] Thurleigh 24/5/44; tran 381BG Ridgewell 5/45; 91BG Bassingbourn 30/5/45; retUS Bradley 6/7/45; Sth Plains 9/7/45; RFC Kingman 19/12/45. SPARE PARTS.
44-6013 Del Tulsa 4/4/44; Hunter 15/4/44; Grenier 29/4/44; ass 336BS/96BG [ET-A] Snetterton 3/5/44; MIA Brux 24/8/44 w/Schmidt; cr Tennenheide, Ger?; 9POW; MACR 8278.
44-6014 Del Tulsa 5/4/44; ass 88BG Avon Park 26/4/44; 3026 BU McDill 28/2/45; 329 BU Alexandra 21/3/45; 330 BU Dyersburg 5/9/45; RFC Walnut Ridge 20/9/45.
44-6015 Del Tulsa 5/4/44; Hunter 17/4/44; Dow Fd 29/4/44; ass 305BG Chelveston 17/5/44; tran 401BG Deenethorpe 30/5/44; retUS Bradley 7/6/45; Sth Plains 12/6/45; RFC Kingman 17/12/45. DEAR MOM.
44-6016 Del Tulsa 5/4/44; Hunter 15/4/44; Grenier 30/4/44; ass 486BG Sudbury 4/5/44; tran 711BS/447BG Rattlesden 5/5/44; MIA Oranienburg 15/3/45 w/Chandler; flak, cr Wilsnack, Ger; 6KIA 3POW; MACR 13045. TNT KATIE.
44-6017 Del Tulsa 4/4/44; Hunter 17/4/44; Dow Fd 30/4/44; ass 327BS/92BG [UX-P] Podington 24/5/44; b/d Merzhausen 24/12/44 w/?; f/l Continent; sal 10/1/45.
44-6018 Del Tulsa 6/4/44; Gulfport 19/4/44; Jackson 21/4/44; 328 BU Gulfport 31/3/45; 3704 BU Keesler 11/4/45; RFC Kingman 16/3/46.
44-6019 Del Tulsa 5/4/44; Hunter 15/4/44; Grenier 30/4/44; ass 367BS/306BG [GY-V] Thurleigh 21/5/44; MIA French a/fds 12/6/44 w/Magner; flak, cr Antwerp, Bel; 3KIA 6POW; MACR 5627.
44-6020 Del Tulsa 6/4/44; Hunter 17/4/44; Dow Fd 8/5/44; ass 532BS/381BG [VE-A] Ridgewell 28/5/44; MIA Brandenburg 6/8/44 w/Webb; flak, ditched Baltic; 1KIA 8POW; MACR 7882. UNDERGROUND FARMER.
44-6021 Del Tulsa 6/4/44; Gulfport 19/4/44; Hammond 21/4/44; 328 BU Gulfport 31/3/45; 3704 BU Keesler 3/4/45; Recl Comp 7/6/46.
44-6022 Del Tulsa 6/4/44; Hunter 17/4/44; Dow Fd 27/4/44; ass 379BG Kimbolton 18/5/44; c/l base? 2/10/44, sal.
44-6023 Del Tulsa 6/4/44; Gulfport 19/4/44; Love Fd 21/4/44; 328 BU Gulfport 31/3/45; 3704 BU Keesler 3/4/45; RFC Kingman 11/2/46.
44-6024 Del Tulsa 7/4/44; ass 396BG Drew Fd 18/4/44; Recl Comp 2/1/45; WO 8/4/45.
44-6025 Del Tulsa 9/4/44; Hunter 17/4/44; Dow Fd 29/4/44; ass 532BS/381BG [VE-I] Ridgewell 19/5/44; {1+m} MIA Dessau 30/5/44 w/Zapinski; e/a, cr Magdeburg; 9POW; MACR 5235. SO WHAT?
44-6026 Del Tulsa 9/4/44; Gulfport 19/4/44; Key Fd 21/4/44; 328 BU Gulfport 31/3/45; 324 BU Chatham 11/5/45; RFC Altus 29/10/44.
44-6027 Del Tulsa 9/4/44; Hunter 17/4/44; Dow Fd 29/4/44; ass 709BS/447BG Rattlesden 1/5/44; MIA Bohlen 29/6/44 w/Hoyer; flak, cr Jahnsheim, Ger; 8KIA 2POW; MACR 6730.
44-6028 Del Tulsa 9/4/44; Barksdale 20/4/44; 328 BU Gulfport 31/3/45; 330 BU Dyersburg 17/5/45; RFC Walnut Ridge 19/9/45.
44-6029 Del Tulsa 9/4/44; 396BG Drew 18/4/44; 327 BU Drew 4/5/45; 203 BU Jackson 19/9/45; 268 BU Peterson 11/10/45; RFC Kingman 7/1/46.
44-6030 Del Tulsa 11/4/44; 88BG Avon Park 23/4/44; 325 BU Avon Park 23/12/44; 4117 BU Robins 4/1/45; Rome 14/3/45; 3704 BU Keesler 5/8/45; Recl Comp 28/12/45.
44-6031 Del Tulsa 10/4/44; 488BG McDill 23/4/44; 326 BU McDill 27/2/45; 329 BU Alexandra 12/3/45; 330 BU Dyersburg 25/6/45; RFC Walnut Ridge 20/9/45.
44-6032 Del Tulsa 11/4/44; 88BG Avon Park 23/4/44; 325 BU Avon Park 9/4/45; RFC Walnut Ridge 26/9/45.
44-6033 Del Tulsa 11/4/44; 88BG Avon Park 23/4/44; 325 BU Avon Park, WO 10/11/44; Recl Comp 24/11/44.
44-6034 Del Tulsa 11/4/44; 88BG Avon Park 23/4/44; 325 BU Avon Park 9/4/45; RFC Walnut Ridge 26/9/45.
44-6035 Del Tulsa 11/4/44; 488BG McDill 23/4/44; 325 BU Avon Park, WO 14/9/44; Recl Comp 26/10/44.
44-6036 Del Tulsa 13/4/44; Love Fd 28/4/44; Dyersburg 2/5/44; 330 BU Dyersburg 1/3/45; RFC Walnut Ridge 20/9/45.
44-6037 Del Tulsa 12/4/44; Alexandra 25/4/44; 221 BU Alexandra 17/1/45; 329 BU Alexandra 1/3/45; 330 BU Dyersburg 25/6/45; RFC Walnut Ridge 21/9/45.
44-6038 Del Tulsa 11/4/44; 88BG Avon Park 23/4/44; Buckingham 8/6/45; 325 BU Avon Park 17/8/45; RFC Walnut Ridge 26/9/45.
44-6039 Del Tulsa 12/4/44; 88BG Avon Park 23/4/44; 325 BU Avon Park, WO 8/11/44; Recl Comp 6/1/45.
44-6040 Del Tulsa 12/4/44; 88BG Avon Park 23/4/44; 325 BU Avon Park 9/4/45; RFC Walnut Ridge 26/9/45.
44-6041 Del Tulsa 12/4/44; Alexandra 25/4/44; 221 BU Alexandra 17/1/45; 329 BU Alexandra 1/3/45; 330 BU Dyersburg 24/6/45; 327 BU Drew 28/8/45; 330 BU Dyersburg 4/9/45; RFC Walnut Ridge 20/9/45.

44-6042 Del Tulsa 13/4/44; Ardmore 25/4/44; 222 BU Ardmore 17/12/44; 332 BU Ardmore 16/6/45; RFC Walnut Ridge 17/9/45.

44-6043 Del Tulsa 13/4/44; 223 BU Dyersburg 13/10/44; 554 BU Memphis, WO 20/10/44; Recl Comp 23/10/44.

44-6044 Del Tulsa 15/4/44; Ft Myers 27/4/44; 2118 BU Buckingham 2/6/44; 2126 BU Laredo 1/2/45; RFC Walnut Ridge 12/10/45.

44-6045 Del Tulsa 14/4/44; Alexandra 25/4/44; 221 BU Alexandra 17/1/45; 329 BU Alexandra 1/3/45; 330 BU Dyersburg 5/9/45; RFC Walnut Ridge 20/9/45.

44-6046 Del Tulsa 13/4/44; Hobbs 25/4/44; 3000 BU Orange 23/8/44; 3017 BU Hobbs 24/8/44; 3021 BU Las Vegas 28/9/44; 3022 BU Indian Springs 10/10/44; 3021 BU Las Vegas 15/3/45; 3017 BU Hobbs 16/7/45; RFC Kingman 27/11/45.

44-6047 Del Tulsa 14/4/44; Ft Myers 27/4/44; 2118 BU Buckingham 2/6/44; 2126 BU Laredo 1/2/45; 4208 BU Mines Fd 28/8/45; 2126 BU Laredo 6/9/45; RFC Walnut Ridge 7/11/45.

44-6048 Del Tulsa 15/4/44; Alexandra 25/4/44; 221 BU Alexandra, WO 19/9/44; Recl Comp 26/10/44.

44-6049 Del Tulsa 14/4/44; Alexandra 23/4/44; 221 BU Alexandra 17/1/45; 329 BU Alexandra 1/3/45; 325 BU Avon Park 29/6/45; RFC Walnut Ridge 26/9/45.

44-6050 Del Tulsa 14/4/44; Ft Myers 27/4/44; 2118 BU Buckingham 2/6/44; 2118 BU Laredo 28/6/44; WO 11/8/44.

44-6051 Del Tulsa 14/4/44; Ft Myers 27/4/44; 2118 BU Buckingham 2/6/44; 2118 BU Laredo 23/6/44; 2126 BU Laredo 1/2/45; RFC Walnut Ridge 10/1/46.

44-6052 Del Tulsa 15/4/44; Ft Myers 27/4/44; 2118 BU Buckingham 2/6/44; 2126 BU Laredo 1/2/45; 2137 BU Hendricks 1/10/45; 2126 BU Laredo 4/10/45; RFC Walnut Ridge 12/10/45.

44-6053 Del Tulsa 15/4/44; Lockburn 29/4/44; 2114 BU Lockburn 2/9/44; 2137 BU Hendricks 14/9/44; RFC Walnut Ridge 13/10/45.

44-6054 Del Tulsa 17/4/44; Roswell 28/4/44; 3030 BU Roswell 2/6/44; 3021 BU Las Vegas 6/10/44; 3022 BU Indian Springs 10/10/44; 3021 BU Las Vegas 15/3/45; 2137 BU Hendricks 16/10/45; RFC Kingman 17/10/45.

44-6055 Del Tulsa 15/5/44; Dyersburg 27/4/44; 333 BU Morris 2/10/44; Recl Comp 13/10/44; WO 24/10/44.

44-6056 Del –.

44-6057 Del Tulsa 17/4/44; Hendricks 29/4/44; 2137 BU Hendricks 17/11/44; RFC Kingman 29/10/45.

44-6058 Del Tulsa 17/4/44; Hendricks 29/4/44; 2137 BU Hendricks 18/11/44; RFC Kingman 1/11/45.

44-6059 Del Tulsa 18/4/44; Roswell 28/4/44; 3030 BU Roswell 2/6/44; 3018 BU Kingman 8/10/44; 3028 BU Luke Fd 11/8/45; 3017 BU Hobbs 22/8/45; 3701 BU Amarillo 4/10/45; RFC Kingman 28/12/45.

44-6060 Del Tulsa 18/4/44; Roswell 28/4/44; 3030 BU Roswell 2/6/44; 3018 BU Kingman 3/10/44; 3017 BU Hobbs 24/6/45; 3701 BU Amarillo 7/10/45; RFC Kingman 23/11/45.

44-6061 Del Tulsa 18/4/44; Lockburn 29/4/44; 2114 BU Lockburn 2/9/44; 2137 BU Hendricks 26/9/44; RFC Walnut Ridge 13/10/45.

44-6062 Del Tulsa 18/4/44; Lockburn 24/4/44; 2114 BU Lockburn 2/9/44; 2132 BU Maxwell 14/11/44; 2114 BU Lockburn 23/11/44; 2137 BU Hendricks 18/8/45; RFC Kingman 29/10/45.

44-6063 Del Tulsa 18/4/44; Lockburn 30/4/44; 2114 BU Lockburn 2/9/44; 2137 BU Hendricks 24/9/44; RFC Walnut Ridge 20/9/45.

44-6064 Del Tulsa 19/4/44; Hendricks 27/4/44; 2137 BU Hendricks 17/11/44; 4147 BU Bedford 2/7/45; 2137 BU Hendricks 6/7/45; RFC Kingman 29/10/45.

44-6065 Del Tulsa 19/4/44; Hobbs 29/4/44; 3017 BU Hobbs 16/1/45; 3701 BU Amarillo 7/10/45; RFC Kingman 28/12/45.

44-6066 Del Tulsa 18/4/44; Hobbs 29/4/44; 3017 BU Hobbs, WO 22/6/44.

44-6067 Del Tulsa 19/4/44; Hendricks 29/4/44; 2137 BU Hendricks 7/5/44; 2517 BU Elington 14/7/45; 2137 BU Hendricks 12/8/45; RFC Kingman 9/11/45.

44-6068 Del Tulsa 20/4/44; Hobbs 29/4/44; 3017 BU Hobbs 16/1/45; Recl Comp 20/3/46.

44-6069 Del Tulsa 21/4/44; Hendricks 30/4/44; 2137 BU Hendricks 18/11/44; 4108 BU Newark 22/5/45; 2137 BU Hendricks 29/6/45; RFC Kingman 9/11/45.

44-6070 Del Tulsa 20/4/44; Hobbs 29/4/44; 3017 BU Hobbs 16/1/45; 3701 BU Amarillo 27/9/45; RFC Kingman 28/12/45.

44-6071 Del Tulsa 21/4/44; Hendricks 30/4/44; 2137 BU Hendricks 18/11/44; RFC Kingman 9/11/45.

44-6072 Del Tulsa 21/4/44; Hendricks 30/4/44; 2137 BU Hendricks 17/11/44; RFC Kingman 29/10/45.

44-6073 Del Tulsa 21/4/44; Roswell 29/4/44; 3030 BU Roswell 2/6/44; 3010 BU Williams 20/1/45; 3020 BU La Junta 30/4/45; 2114 BU Lockburn 25/6/45; 2137 BU Hendricks 22/9/45; 4108 BU Newark 9/10/45; 2137 BU Hendricks 14/10/45; RFC Walnut Ridge 4/1/46.

44-6074 Del Tulsa 21/4/44; Hendricks 30/4/44; 2137 BU Hendricks, WO 21/11/44; Recl Comp 2/1/45.

44-6075 Del Tulsa 22/4/44; Hendricks 30/4/44; 2137 BU Hendricks 9/7/44; 4109 BU Reading 11/9/44; 2137 BU Hendricks 27/10/44; 2518 BU Enid 20/9/45; 2137 BU Hendricks 3/11/45; RFC Kingman 16/11/45.

44-6076 Del Tulsa 23/4/44; Hunter 5/5/44; Grenier 21/5/44; ass 359BS/303BG [BN-Y] Molesworth 28/5/44; MIA Merseburg 13/9/44 w/Walker; flak, cr Merseburg; 3KIA 6POW; MACR 8822. LIBERTY RUN.

44-6077 Del Tulsa 24/4/44; Kearney 2/5/44; Grenier 15/5/44; ass 511BS/351BG [DS-W] Polebrook 29/5/44; 509BS [RQ-W]; {27m} MIA Ulm 9/8/44 w/Zotollo; flak, cr Antwerp; 3EVD 9POW; MACR 7394.

44-6078 Del Tulsa 24/4/44; Kearney 2/5/44; Grenier 15/5/45; ass 509BS/351BG [RQ-G] Polebrook 27/5/44; {58m} MIA Sterkrade 22/1/45 w/Goldsborough; flak, cr Aachen; 1KIA 8POW; MACR 12011. HARD HEARTED MAMA.

44-6079 Del Tulsa 24/4/44; Kearney 4/5/44; Dow Fd 22/5/44; ass 305BG Chelveston 2/6/44; retUS Bradley 7/6/45; Sth Plains 12/6/45; RFC Kingman 8/12/45.

44-6080 Del Tulsa 24/4/44; Kearney 2/5/44; Grenier 15/5/44; ass 547BS/384BG [SO-L] Grafton Underwood 27/5/44; taxi acc 28/9/44; sal.

44-6081 Del Tulsa 25/4/44; Kearney 3/5/44; Grenier 14/5/44; ass 338BS/96BG [BX-K] Snetterton 16/5/44; dest by e/a at Poltava 21/6/44; sal 1/7/44.

44-6082 Del Tulsa 25/4/44; Kearney 2/5/44; Grenier 15/5/44; ass 510BS/351BG [TU-B] Polebrook 30/5/44; 508BS [YB-D]; {90m} RetUS Bradley 11/6/45; Sth Plains 15/6/45; RFC Kingman 5/12/45. WISCONSIN BEAUTY.

44-6083 Del Tulsa 16/4/44; Kearney 10/5/44; Grenier 21/5/44; ass 603BS/398BG [N7-V] Nuthampstead 26/5/44; b/d Cologne 17/10/44 w/?; f/l Berlare, Bel; sal 19/10/44. BETSY ROSS.

44-6084 Del Tulsa 27/4/44; Kearney 4/5/44; Grenier 21/5/44; ass 560BS/388BG Knettishall 23/5/44 BUCKET OF BOLTS; tran 326BS/92BG Podington 27/5/44 DEMOBILIZER; 327BS [UX-V]; MIA Chemnitz 11/9/44 w/Cook; e/a, cr Helfta, Ger; 2KIS 7POW; MACR 8880. DERUMBELIZER.

44-6085 Del Tulsa 27/4/44; Kearney 7/5/44; Dow Fd 21/5/44; ass 335BS/95BG Horham 23/5/44; 334BS [BG-H]; MIA Rechlin 25/8/44 w/Powell; cr Schwabach, Ger; 3KIA 7POW; MACR 8279.

44-6086 Del Tulsa 27/4/44; Kearney 9/5/44; Grenier 21/5/44; ass 358BS/303BG [VK-L] Molesworth 27/5/44; MIA Cologne 15/8/44 w/Larson; e/a, cr Wittlich, Ger; 1KIA 8POW; MACR 8172. MY BLONDE BABY.

44-6087 Del Tulsa 25/4/44; Kearney 7/5/44; Grenier 21/5/44; ass 368BS/306BG [BO-F] Thurleigh 27/5/44; MIA Cologne 15/10/44 w/Moroz; flak, cr Cologne; 9POW; MACR 8074.

44-6088 Del Tulsa 28/4/44; Kearney 10/5/44; Grenier 24/5/44; ass 749BS/457BG Glatton 23/5/44; f/l Continent; sal 11/1/45. RATTLESNAKE DADDY II.

44-6089 Del Tulsa 28/4/44; Kearney 4/5/44; Grenier 21/5/44; ass 350BS/100BG [LN-B] Thorpe Abbotts 23/5/44; MIA Bohlen 11/9/44 w/Riegal; e/a, cr Schuiedeberg, Ger?; 6KIA 3POW; MACR 8811.

44-6090 Del Tulsa 28/4/44; Kearney 4/5/44; Grenier 21/5/44; ass 365BS/305BG Chelveston 2/6/44; MIA Karlsruhe 9/8/44 w/Finney; e/a, cr Bundeltal, Ger?; 1KIA 8POW; MACR 8072.

44-6091 Del Tulsa 29/4/44; Kearney 10/5/44; Grenier 21/5/44; ass 561BS/388BG Knettishall 26/5/44; mech fault, Kassel 8/9/44 w/?; c/r France; 9RTD. LOTTA BULL.

44-6092 Del Tulsa 29/4/44; Hunter 5/5/44; Grenier 19/5/44; ass 350BS/100BG [LN-F] Thorpe Abbotts 22/5/44; MIA Berlin 3/2/45 w/Oldham; e/a, cr Eichholz, Ger; 9POW; MACR 12044.

44-6093 Del Tulsa 29/4/44; Hunter 5/5/44; Grenier 19/5/44; ass 401BS/91BG [LL-J] Bassingbourn 27/5/44; {47m} MIA Merseburg 2/11/44 w/Atkins; e/a, cr Clappenburg, Ger; 1KIA 8POW; MACR 10141. U.S.A. THE HARD WAY.

44-6094 Del Tulsa 29/4/44; Kearney 10/5/44; Grenier 25/5/44; ass 379BG Kimbolton 4/6/44; b/d Cologne 15/10/44 w/?; f/l Continent; sal 14/11/44.

44-6095 Del Tulsa 29/4/44; Kearney 4/5/44; Dow Fd 21/5/44; ass 533BS/381BG [VP-N] Ridgewell 26/5/44; {30m} MIA Gaggenau 10/9/44 w/Germano; flak, cr Neibsheim, Ger; 1KIA 8POW; MACR 8906. FORT WORTH GAL.

44-6096 Del Tulsa 1/5/44; Kearney 10/5/44; Grenier 24/5/44; ass 560BS/388BG Knettishall 27/6/44; c/l base 29/7/44; 9RTD; sal. LADY COURAGEOUS.

44-6097 Del Tulsa 1/5/44; Kearney 10/5/44; Grenier 21/5/44; ass 570BS/390BG [DI-D] Framlingham 23/5/44; sal 6/8/44; retUS Bradley 5/7/45; Sth Plains 7/7/45; RFC Kingman 17/12/45. COCAINE BILL.

44-6098 Del Tulsa 2/5/44; Kearney 10/5/44; Grenier 27/5/44; ass 336BS/95BG [ET-N] Horham 30/5/44; b/d Hamburg 4/8/44 w/Hamilton; flak, ditched Channel; 1KIA 8POW; MACR 7700.

44-6099 Del Tulsa 1/5/44; Kearney 10/5/44; Grenier 24/5/44; ass 569BS/390BG [CC-H] Framlingham 25/5/44; sal 4/8/44.

44-6100 Del Tulsa 1/5/44; Kearney 10/5/44; Grenier 24/5/44; ass 549BS/385BG Gt Ashfield 27/5/44; {1m} MIA Cologne 9/1/45 w/?. MACR 11718. MISS 'D' DAY.

44-6101 Del Tulsa 3/5/44; Kearney 10/5/44; Grenier 27/5/44; ass 325BS/92BG [NV-E] Podington 2/6/44; b/d Hagenau 14/8/44 w/?; sal 16/8/44. SATAN'S LADY.

44-6102 Del Tulsa 4/5/44; Kearney 10/5/44; Grenier

24/5/44; ass 563BS/388BG Knettishall 27/5/44; retUS Bradley 3/7/45; Sth Plains 6/7/45; RFC Kingman 8/12/45. CICERO KID.

44-6103 Del Tulsa 3/5/44; Kearney 10/5/44; Grenier 24/5/44; ass 748BS/457BG Glatton 6/6/44; MIA Schweinfurt 21/7/44 w/Gerber; flak, cr Schweinfurt; 2KIA 7POW; MACR 6925/7254.

44-6104 Del Tulsa 4/5/44; Kearney 11/5/44; Grenier 26/5/44; ass 613BS/401BG [IN-N] Deenethorpe 1/6/44; MIA Merseburg 21/11/44 w/Keck; flak & e/a, cr Zeitz; 2KIA 7POW; MACR 10411. HOMING PIGEON.

44-6105 Del Tulsa 5/5/44; Hunter 16/5/44; Dow Fd 24/5/44; ass 547BS/384BG [SO-P] Grafton Underwood 4/6/44; MIA Cologne 28/1/45 w/Jackson; flak, cr Ossenzijl, Holl; 7EVD 2KIA; MACR 11990. SLEEPY LAGOON.

44-6106 Del Tulsa 2/5/44; Kearney 11/5/44; Grenier 25/5/44; ass 363BS/388BG Knettishall 28/5/44; retUS Bradley 30/6/45; Sth Plains 3/7/45; RFC Kingman 18/11/45. GREMLIN'S HIDEOUT.

44-6107 Del Tulsa 5/5/44; Hunter 16/5/44; Dow Fd 24/5/44; ass 526BS/379BG [LF-S] Kimbolton 2/6/44; MIA Cologne 28/9/44 w/Arnold; e/a, cr Anderton?; 9POW; MACR 9361.

44-6108 Del Tulsa 6/5/44; Kearney 10/5/44; Grenier 24/6/44; ass 385BG Gt Ashfield 27/5/44; tran 509BS/351BG [RQ-Y] Polebrook 2/6/44; 508BS [YB-Y]; {93m} RetUS Bradley 11/6/45; Sth Plains 16/6/45; RFC Kingman 17/12/45.

44-6109 Del Tulsa 4/5/44; Kearney 11/5/44; Grenier 26/5/44; ass 545BS/384BG [JD-Q] Grafton Underwood 7/6/44; b/d Plauen 26/3/45 w/?; c/l Cranbrook, UK; 1KIA; sal 27/3/45.

44-6110 Del Tulsa 4/5/44; Hunter 21/6/44; Dow Fd 1/7/44; ass 774BS/463BG Celone 7/7/44; MIA Regensburg 20/12/44 w/Saum; cr Wels, Ger?; MACR 10731. HELL ON WINGS.

44-6111 Del Tulsa 3/5/44; Kearney 10/5/44; Grenier 24/5/44; ass 749BS/457BG Glatton 5/6/44; MIA Munich 12/7/44 w/Kozel; flak, f/l Payerne, Switz; 9INT; MACR 6925. HELL'S BELLE.

44-6112 Del Tulsa 4/5/44; Kearney 11/5/44; Grenier 26/5/44; ass 96BG Snetterton 26/5/44; tran 550BS/385BG Gt Ashfield 27/5/44; MIA Stuttgart 16/7/44 w/Robbins; flak & mech fault; f/l Dubendorf, Switz; 10INT; MACR 7569. RetUS, RFC Walnut Ridge 14/12/45.

44-6113 Del Tulsa 6/5/44; Hunter 14/5/44; Dow Fd 23/5/44; ass 613BS/401BG [IN-R] Deenethorpe 2/6/44; b/d Ingoldstadt 5/4/45 w/?; f/l Continent, sal.

44-6114 Del Tulsa 4/5/44; Kearney 11/5/44; Grenier 25/5/44; ass 838BS/487BG Lavenham 27/5/44; tran 332BS/94BG Rougham 28/5/44; sal 12/8/44;

44-6115 Del Tulsa 6/5/44; Hunter 17/5/44; Dow Fd 27/5/44; ass 534BS/381BG [GD-Q] Ridgewell 10/6/44; {56+m} RetUS Bradley 15/6/45; Sth Plains 19/6/45; RFC Kingman 29/11/45. ICE COL' KATY.

44-6116 Del Tulsa 6/5/44; Hunter 28/6/44; Grenier 11/7/44; ass 96BS/2BG Amendola 16/7/44; {64m} RetUS 1103 BU Morrison 18/9/45; RFC Walnut Ridge 19/12/45.

44-6117 Del Tulsa 6/5/44; Hunter 17/5/44; Dow Fd 24/5/44; ass 322BS/91BG [LG-Q] Bassingbourn 27/5/44; MIA Berlin 21/6/44 w/O'Hannon; e/a, cr Rothenklempenow, Ger; 1KIA 8POW; MACR 5980.

44-6118 Del Tulsa 8/5/44; Hunter 18/5/44; Dow Fd 29/5/44; ass 457BG Glatton 15/6/44; c/l 28/8/44, sal.

44-6119 Del Tulsa 6/5/44; Hunter 15/5/44; Grenier 25/5/44; ass 526BS/379BG [LF-A] Kimbolton 4/6/44; MIA Lutzkendorf 9/2/45 w/Pearlman; flak, cr Gierath, Ger; 10POW; MACR 12337. WHITE LIGHTNING.

44-6120 Del Tulsa 6/5/44; Hunter 12/5/44; Dow Fd 23/5/44; ass 407BS/92BG Podington 24/5/44; b/d Merseburg 13/9/44 w/Norris; f/l Continent; sal 14/11/44.

44-6121 Del Tulsa 6/5/44; Hunter 17/5/44; Grenier 26/5/44; ass 569BS/390BG Framlingham 28/5/44; retUS Bradley 20/6/45; Sth Plains 3/7/45; RFC Kingman 27/11/45.

44-6122 Del Tulsa 6/5/44; Hunter 13/5/44; Dow Fd 23/5/44; ass 305BG Chelveston 2/6/44; sal 18/7/44.

44-6123 Del Tulsa 6/5/44; Hunter 13/5/44; Dow Fd 22/5/44; ass 561BS/388BG Knettishall 28/5/44; MIA Delitzsch, Ger 16/8/44 w/Sarten; mid air coll w/42-97328; cr Wurzen, Ger; 2KIA 8MIA; MACR 8433.

44-6124 Del Tulsa 8/5/44; Hunter 17/5/44; Dow Fd 30/5/44; ass 360BS/303BG [PU-A] Molesworth 19/6/44; MIA Osnabrück 26/9/44 w/Bennett; flak, cr Osnabrück; 3KIA 6POW; MACR 9403.

44-6125 Del Tulsa 8/5/44; Boca Raton 18/7/44; 3035 BU Victorville 20/11/44; RFC Kingman 25/10/45.

44-6126 Del Tulsa 8/5/44; Hunter 18/5/44; Grenier 10/6/44; ass 324BS/91BG [OR-P] Bassingbourn 10/7/44; 324BS [DF-P], 322BS; MIA Halle 16/8/44 w/Leslie; e/a, cr Chartres, Fr; 6KIA 3POW; MACR 8185.

44-6127 Del Tulsa 9/5/44; Hunter 19/5/44; Grenier 29/5/44; ass 337BS/96BG [AW-R] Snetterton 1/6/44; sal n/b/d 14/6/44.

44-6128 Del Tulsa 8/5/44; Hunter 19/5/44; Dow Fd 29/5/44; ass 547BS/384BG [SO-O] Grafton Underwood 7/6/44; b/d Montdidier A/fd 30/6/44 w/?; sal 10/7/44.

44-6129 Del Tulsa 10/5/44; Hunter 19/5/44; Dow Fd 29/5/44; ass 613BS/401BG [IN-A] Deenethorpe 7/6/44; MIA Augsburg 19/7/44 w/McKeon; flak, cr Corne, Fr; 1KIA 8POW; MACR 8157.

44-6130 Del Tulsa 9/5/44; Hunter 17/5/44; Ft Dix 2/6/44; Middletown 7/6/44; Hunter 3/7/44; Grenier 12/7/44; ass 366BS/305BG Thurleigh 28/7/44; MIA Mulhouse 3/8/44; w/Alford; flak, cr Miesenbach, Aus; 8KIA 1POW; MACR 7845.

44-6131 Del Tulsa 10/5/44; Hunter 21/5/44; Grenier 31/5/44; ass 413BS/96BG [MZ-J] Snetterton 3/6/44; b/d Hamm 7/1/45 w/?; c/l, sal. FEARLESS FOSDICK.

44-6132 Del Tulsa 9/5/44; Hunter 19/5/44; Dow Fd 29/5/44; ass 613BS/401BG [IN-B] Deenethorpe 8/6/44; retUS Bradley 6/6/45; Sth Plains 13/6/45; RFC Kingman 1/12/45.

44-6133 Del Tulsa 10/5/44; Hunter 19/5/44; Dow Fd 29/5/44; ass 525BS/379BG [FR-Y] Kimbolton 8/6/44; mid air coll w/42-97942 19/6/44 w/? en route Bordeaux; cr Canvey Is, UK; 8KIA; sal.

44-6134 Del Tulsa 9/5/44; Hunter 18/5/44; Grenier 25/5/44; ass 568BS/390BG [BI-D] Framlingham 28/5/44 GUNG HO, then PANDORA; sal 22/1/45; retUS Bradley 24/6/45; Sth Plains 26/6/45; RFC Kingman 17/12/45. DOTSY.

44-6135 Del Tulsa 10/5/44; Kearney 23/5/44; Dow Fd 30/5/44; ass 545BS/384BG [JD-J] Grafton Underwood 10/6/44; 547BS [SO-H], 546BS [BK-B]; b/d Cologne 10/1/45 w/?; f/l Continent; sal 22/1/45.

44-6136 Del Tulsa 12/5/44; Kearney 22/5/44; Grenier 29/5/44; ass 550BS/385BG Gt Ashfield 30/5/44; retUS Bradley 24/6/45; Sth Plains 28/6/45; RFC Kingman 28/11/45. ARCHER'S STORK CLUB.

44-6137 Del Tulsa 12/5/44; Kearney 24/5/44; Dow Fd 1/6/44; ass 452BG Deopham Green 2/6/44; tran 337BS/96BG [AW-J] Snetterton 3/6/44; mid air coll w/43-38746 on return from Kassel w/? 29/1/45; cr N/Lopham, UK; 9KIA; sal 30/1/45.

44-6138 Del Tulsa 12/5/44; Hunter 21/5/44; Dow Fd 29/5/44; ass 331BS/94BG [QE-P] Rougham 1/6/44; MIA Münster 5/10/44 w/Messersmith; flak, ditched Channel; 9POW; MACR 9510.

44-6139 Del Tulsa 12/5/44; Hunter 21/5/44; Dow Fd 29/5/44; ass 509BS/351BG [DS-K] Polebrook 8/6/44; {32m} b/d Brux 12/9/44 w/?; f/l Continent; sal 14/11/45.

44-6140 Del Tulsa 14/5/44; Kearney 24/5/44; Dow Fd 1/6/44; ass 327BS/379BG Kimbolton 10/6/44; MIA Zeitz 30/11/44 w/Schlesinger; flak, cr Zeitz; 8KIA 1POW; MACR 11126. MISS LACE.

44-6141 Del Tulsa 13/5/44; Kearney 25/5/44; Dow Fd 1/6/44; ass 544BS/384BG [SU-F] Grafton Underwood 10/6/44; b/d Merseburg 30/11/44 w/?; f/l Continent, sal.

44-6142 Del Tulsa 12/5/44; Hunter 21/5/44; Grenier 1/6/44; ass 337BS/96BG [AW-N] Snetterton 4/6/44; retUS Bradley 5/7/45; Sth Plains 6/7/45; RFC Kingman 16/11/45. THE STORK.

44-6143 Del Tulsa 14/5/44; Kearney 24/5/44; Dow Fd 1/6/44; ass 527BS/379BG Kimbolton 10/6/44; MIA Stralsund 6/10/44 w/Doherty; flak, cr Stralsund; 9POW; MACR 9362. MISS BEHAVEN.

44-6144 Del Tulsa 13/5/44; Hunter 21/5/44; Grenier 1/6/44; ass 398BG Nuthampstead 3/6/44; tran 326BS/92BG [NV-V] Podington 12/6/44; sal 9AF Germany 10/12/45. LORRIE MAE.

44-6145 Del Tulsa 12/5/44; Kearney 22/5/44; Grenier 29/5/44; ass 614BS/401BG [IW-S] Deenethorpe 12/6/44; MIA Politz 7/10/44 w/Silverstein; flak, cr Kienwerder, Ger; 8KIA 1POW; MACR 9756. COVER GIRL.

44-6146 Del Tulsa 14/5/44; Kearney 24/5/44; Dow Fd 1/6/44; ass 615BS/401BG [IY-R] Deenethorpe 10/6/44; 613BS [IN-R]; retUS Bradley 7/6/45; Sth Plains 9/6/45; RFC Kingman 14/12/45.

44-6147 Del Tulsa 14/5/44; Kearney 24/5/44; Dow Fd 1/6/44; ass 545BS/384BG [JD-U] Grafton Underwood 10/6/44; during assembly for Leipzig, mid air coll w/384; cr Withersfield, UK; 14KIA; sal 8/7/44.

44-6148 Del Tulsa 14/5/44; Kearney 24/5/44; Dow Fd 1/6/44; ass 534BS/381BG [GD-M] Ridgewell 16/6/44; {11+m} c/t/o for Munich 13/7/44 w/Houston, at Gt Yeldham, UK; (lost two engines during assembly) 7KIA 2WIA; sal. SMASHING THRU.

44-6149 Del Tulsa 14/5/44; Kearney 26/5/44; Dow Fd 1/6/44; ass 547BS/384BG [SO-U] Grafton Underwood 12/6/44; MIA Koblenz 11/10/44 w/Levine; flak, cr Mayen, Ger; 4KIA 5POW; MACR 9478. HOT AFTER IT.

44-6150 Del Tulsa 19/5/44; Kearney 30/5/44; Dow Fd 6/6/44; ass 332BS/94BG [XM-L] Rougham 7/6/44; 333BS [TS-L]; retUS Bradley 24/6/45; Sth Plains 28/6/45; RFC Kingman 30/11/45. VIE'S GUYS.

44-6151 Del Tulsa 16/5/44; Kearney 27/5/44; Dow Fd 6/6/44; ass 324BS/91BG [DF-J/Q] Bassingbourn 7/6/44; {71m} RetUS Bradley 31/5/45; Sth Plains 3/6/45; RFC Kingman 19/12/45. SHURE SHOT.

44-6152 Del Tulsa 18/5/44; Kearney 26/5/44; Dow Fd 6/6/44; ass 728BS/452BG Deopham Green 7/6/44; land acc 5/3/45; sal n/b/d 7/3/45.

44-6153 Del Tulsa 16/5/44; Kearney 27/5/44; Grenier 7/6/44; ass 452BG Deopham Green 10/6/44; tran 337BS/96BG [AW-S] Snetterton 11/6/44; retUS Bradley 2/6/45; Sth Plains 11/6/45; RFC Kingman 30/11/45.

44-6154 Del Tulsa 16/5/44; Kearney 26/5/44; Dow Fd 4/6/44; ass 560BS/388BG Knettishall 7/6/44 b/d Zeitz 16/8/44; mid air coll w/42-97328; c/l Ger; 2KIA 8MIA. SHOOT THE WORKS.

44-6155 Del Tulsa 16/5/44; Kearney 25/5/44; Dow Fd

6/6/44; ass 751BS/457BG Glatton 16/6/44; MIA Kassel 2/11/44 w/Schimel; e/a, cr Ziegelrode, Ger; 3KIA 6POW; MACR 10314.

44-6156 Del Tulsa 18/5/44; Kearney 29/5/44; Dow Fd 6/6/44; ass 509BS/351BG [RQ-R] Polebrook 28/6/44; {93m} RetUS Bradley 30/5/45; Sth Plains 1/6/45; RFC Kingman 15/12/45. LITTLE CHAPEL.

44-6157 Del Tulsa 19/5/44; Kearney 29/5/44; Dow Fd 9/6/44; ass 600BS/398BG [N8-W] Nuthampstead 19/6/44; tran 92BG Podington 7/5/45; 398BG Nuthampstead 12/5/45; retUS Bradley 6/6/44; Sth Plains 26/6/45; RFC Kingman 9/12/45.

44-6158 Del Tulsa 16/5/44; Kearney 29/5/44; Grenier 29/6/44; ass 327BS/92BG [UX-U] Podington 17/7/44; MIA Merseburg 13/9/44 w/Henrickson; e/a, cr Altenburg, Ger?; MACR 8881. SKY MONSTER.

44-6159 Del Tulsa 18/5/44; Kearney 29/5/44; Grenier 7/6/44; ass 551BS/385BG Gt Ashfield 11/6/44; MIA Berlin 6/10/44 w/Noiseau; e/a, cr Brandenburg; 7KIA 2POW; MACR 9515. WEST VIRGINIAN.

44-6160 Del Tulsa 16/5/44; Kearney 27/5/44; Dow Fd 6/6/44; ass 337BS/96BG [AW-L] Snetterton 7/6/44; retUS Bradley 5/7/45; Herington 9/7/45; Recl Comp 23/7/45.

44-6161 Del Tulsa 18/5/44; Kearney 29/5/44; Grenier 5/6/44; ass 749BS/457BG Glatton 19/6/44; retUS Bradley 9/6/45; Sth Plains 12/6/45; RFC Kingman 28/11/45.

44-6162 Del Tulsa 18/5/44; Kearney 25/5/44; Grenier 7/6/44; ass 364BS/305BG Chelveston 28/6/44; sal 18/7/44; tran 401BG Deenethorpe 7/44; retUS Bradley 7/6/45; Sth Plains 12/6/45; RFC Kingman 29/11/45.

44-6163 Del Tulsa 19/5/44; Kearney 29/5/44; Grenier 7/6/44; ass 534BS/381BG [GD-P] Ridgewell 28/6/44; {71+m} RetUS Bradley 8/6/45; Sth Plains 12/6/45; RFC Kingman 28/11/45. PASSAIC WARRIOR.

44-6164 Del Tulsa 19/5/44; Hunter 9/6/44; Morrison 18/6/44; ass 96BS/2BG Amendola 29/6/44; tran 353BS/301BG Lucera 18/11/44; b/d Bleckhammer 17/4/45 w/?; sal.

44-6165 Del Tulsa 19/5/44; Kearney 30/5/44; Grenier 7/6/44; ass 730BS/452BG Deopham Green 11/6/44; tran 96BG Snetterton 12/6/44; c/l 12/12/44; sal; retUS Bradley 28/6/45; Sth Plains 3/7/45; RFC Kingman 13/12/45.

44-6166 Del Tulsa 19/5/44; Kearney 29/5/44; Grenier 5/6/44; ass 327BS/303BG [GN-V] Molesworth 5/7/44; MIA Germersheim 13/1/45 w/Rose; flak, cr Pirmasens, Ger; 10POW; MACR 11572. RED – THE RED.

44-6167 Del Tulsa 19/5/44; Kearney 29/5/44; Grenier 4/6/44; ass 750BS/457BG Glatton 15/6/44; retUS Bradley 9/6/45; Sth Plains 11/6/45; RFC Kingman 18/12/45.

44-6168 Del Tulsa 20/5/44; Kearney 30/5/44; Hunter 7/6/44; Morrison 19/6/44; ass 352BS/301BG Lucera 30/6/44; MIA Wiener Neudorf 26/7/44 w/Delenney; e/a, cr Mariazell; 8KIA 2POW; MACR 7142.

44-6169 Del Tulsa 20/5/44; Kearney 30/5/44; Grenier 6/6/44; slated 94BG, tran 1377 BU Grenier 13/9/44; 4185 BU Independence 30/11/44; RFC Kingman 18/12/45.

44-6170 Del Tulsa 19/5/44; Kearney 29/5/44; Grenier 4/6/44; ass 94BG Rougham 7/6/44; tran 413BS/96BG [MZ-M] Snetterton 8/6/44; 337BS; MIA Berlin 3/2/45 w/Wyman; flak, cr Berlin; 3KIA 6POW; MACR 12155. SITTIN' PRETTY.

44-6171 Del Tulsa 19/5/44; Kearney 29/5/44; Grenier 5/6/44; ass 561BS/388BG Knettishall 11/6/44; MIA Peenemünde 25/8/44 w/Sutton; flak, cr Stettin; 3KIA 6POW: MACR 8286. CUTIE ON DUTY.

44-6172 Del Tulsa 19/5/44; Kearney 19/5/44; Dow Fd 4/6/44; ass 379BG Kimbolton 19/6/44; sal 13/3/45.

44-6173 Del Tulsa 19/5/44; Kearney 30/5/44; Grenier 7/6/44; ass 534BS/381BG [GD-H] Ridgewell 28/6/44; MIA Stendahl 8/4/45 w/Adelmeyer; flak, cr Gottingen, Ger; 6KIA 2RTD; MACR 13873. (last group a/c lost in action) MISS FLORALA.

44-6174 Del Tulsa 20/5/44; Hunter 9/6/44; Morrison 21/6/44; ass 816BS/483BG Sterparone 3/7/44; MIA Memmingen 18/7/44 w/Jackson; e/a, cr Memmingen; 9KIA 1POW; MACR 6975.

44-6175 Del Tulsa 19/5/44; Hunter 23/6/44; Grenier 7/7/44; ass 341BS/97BG Amendola 16/7/44; retUS 21/6/45; RFC Kingman 12/6/45. MISS FITS.

44-6176 Del Tulsa 20/5/44; Hunter 14/6/44; Grenier 23/6/44; Presque Is 28/6/44; ass 49BS/2BG Amendola 4/7/44; MIA Bleckhammer 7/8/44 w/Hastings; flak hit #2, cr Mechnitz; MACR 7470.

44-6177 Del Tulsa 20/5/44; Kearney 30/5/44; Hunter 7/6/44; Morrison 17/6/44; ass 815BS/483BG Sterparone 7/7/44; MIA Memmingen 18/7/44 w/Ward; e/a, cr Ravensburg; 1KIA 9POW; MACR 7099. DRY RUN.

44-6178 Del Tulsa 24/5/44; Hunter 13/6/44; Dow Fd 24/6/44; ass 352BS/301BG Lucera 3/7/44; MIA Regensburg 13/3/45 w/Berry; mech fault, cr Traunstein; MACR 12943.

44-6179 Del Tulsa 24/5/44; Hunter 15/6/44; Dow Fd 28/6/44; ass 775BS/463BG Celone 2/7/44; c/l base 18/4/45 w/Cragg, from mission to bomb troops in Charlie area; burned out.

44-6180 Del Tulsa 24/5/44; Hunter 13/6/44; Morrison 21/6/44; Dow Fd 28/6/44; ass 32BS/301BG Lucera 4/7/44; MIA Lechfeld 12/9/44 w/Allen; flak, cr Karwendelhaus; 10POW; MACR 8623.

44-6181 Del Tulsa 24/5/44; Hunter 15/6/44; Dow Fd 24/6/44; ass 341BS/97BG Amendola 2/7/44; flak damage, to depot 18/3/45.

44-6182 Del Tulsa 25/5/44; Hunter 13/6/44; Dow Fd 28/6/44; ass 346BS/99BG Tortorella 5/7/44; MIA {51m} Bleckhammer 2/12/44 w/Webb; flak, cr Ratibor; no witnesses, radio call to lead ship at 12.45hrs; MACR 10030.

44-6183 Del Tulsa 24/5/44; Hunter 13/6/44; Dow Fd 24/6/44; ass 342BS/97BG Amendola 4/7/44; b/d Linz tank works 25/7/44 w/Murphy; cr base; MACR 7125.

44-6184 Del Tulsa 26/5/44; Hunter 20/6/44; Grenier 28/6/44; ass 815BS/483BG Sterparone 3/7/44; c/t/o for St Tropez 15/8/44 w/Teasley; 9KIA.

44-6185 Del Tulsa 26/5/44; Hunter 15/6/44; Dow Fd 24/6/44; ass 419BS/301BG Lucera 3/7/44; sal 5/5/45.

44-6186 Del Tulsa 26/5/44; Hunter 14/6/44; Dow Fd 24/6/44; ass 419BS/301BG Lucera 3/7/44; MIA Bleckhammer 2/12/44 w/Tillotson; mech failure, ditched Adriatic; 6KIA 4RTD; MACR 10790.

44-6187 Del Tulsa 25/4/44; Hunter 15/6/44; Dow Fd 24/6/44; ass 342BS/97BG Amendola 6/7/44; MIA Vienna 16/7/44 w/Howard; flak, cr Vienna; MACR 6825.

44-6188 Del Tulsa 26/5/44; Hunter 14/6/44; Dow Fd 24/6/44; ass 342BS/97BG Amendola 2/7/44; MIA Munich 19/7/44 w/Haas; flak, cr Forsten; MACR 6745.

44-6189 Del Tulsa 25/5/44; Hunter 20/6/44; Dow Fd 30/6/44; ass 32BS/301BG Lucera 9/7/44; MIA Wiener Neudorf 26/7/44 w/Luebke; e/a, cr Perin; 3KIA 7POW; MACR 7141.

44-6190 Del Tulsa 27/5/44; Hunter 23/6/44; Dow Fd 1/7/44; ass 775BS/463BG Celone 3/7/44; MIA Bleckhammer 10/12/44 w/Freschi; cr?; 10KIA. MACR 10689.

44-6191 Del Tulsa 29/5/44; Hunter 20/6/44; Grenier 29/6/44; ass 97BG Amendola 4/7/44; cr base 10/8/44 w/Tomovich; 3WIA.

44-6192 Del Tulsa 26/5/44; Hunter 17/6/44; Grenier 27/6/44; ass 774BS/463BG Celone 2/7/44; b/d Odertal 18/12/44 w/?; depot for repair; retUS Bradley 14/7/45; Independence 19/7/45; RFC Kingman 22/12/45.

44-6193 Del Tulsa 26/5/44; Hunter 17/6/44; Grenier 27/6/44; ass 773BS/463BG Celone 4/7/44; retUS Morrison 7/10/45; RFC Walnut Ridge 10/12/45.

44-6194 Del Tulsa 27/5/44; Hunter 21/6/44; Dow Fd 2/7/44; ass 772BS/463BG Celone 12/7/44; MIA Ploesti 19/8/44 w/Heap; flak, cr Ploesti; 4KIA 6POW; MACR 9717. BERLIN SLEEPER III.

44-6195 Del Tulsa 29/5/44; Hunter 23/6/44; Dow Fd 9/7/44; ass 341BS/97BG Amendola 10/7/44; caught fire, sal 12/3/45.

44-6196 Del Tulsa 27/5/44; Hunter 14/6/44; Grenier 23/6/44; ass 347BS/99BG Tortorella 4/7/44; {96m} RetUS Bradley 30/6/45; Sth Plains 2/7/45; RFC Kingman 21/11/45.

44-6197 Del Tulsa 27/5/44; Hunter 21/6/44; Dow Fd 1/7/44; ass 414BS/97BG Amendola 9/7/44; MIA Ploesti 22/7/44 w/Glascoe; flak, cr Ploesti; MACR 6855.

44-6198 Del Tulsa 28/5/44; Hunter 23/6/44; Dow Fd 3/7/44; ass 429BS/2BG Amendola 4/7/44; MIA Vienna 21/2/45 w/Trowbridge; flak, cr nr Papa; MACR 12461. DOLLAR 98.

44-6199 Del Tulsa 2/6/44; Hunter 25/6/44; Dow Fd 9/7/44; ass 816BS/483BG Sterparone 14/7/44; MIA Vienna 21/1/45 w/Prescott; mech failure, cr Kiskumajsa; 10EVD, ret 13/2/45. MACR 11539.

44-6200 Del Tulsa 29/5/44; Hunter 23/6/44; Dow Fd 3/7/44; ass 20BS/2BG Amendola 12/7/44; retUS Bradley 25/6/45; Sth Plains 27/6/45; RFC Kingman 27/11/45.

44-6201 Del Tulsa 29/5/44; Hunter 23/6/44; Dow Fd 10/7/44; ass 817BS/483BG Sterparone 17/7/44; MIA Budapest 30/7/44 w/Nivens; flak, cr Sziget Szent; 5KIA 5POW; MACR 7105.

44-6202 Del Tulsa 30/5/44; ass 486BG as THE BABY SHOE III; tran Boca Raton 29/8/44; 3501 BU Boca Raton 2/9/44; 4119 BU Brookley 19/9/45; 3501 BU Boca Raton 7/10/45; RFC Kingman 20/12/45.

44-6203 Del Tulsa 30/5/44; Boca Raton 7/8/44; ATC Tulsa 8/8/44; 3501 BU Boca Raton 13/8/44; 4119 BU Brookley 19/9/45; 3501 BU Boca Raton 1/11/45; RFC Kingman 22/1/46.

44-6204 Del Tulsa 30/5/44; Boca Raton 5/9/44; 3501 BU Boca Raton 10/9/44; 3035 BU Victorville 5/2/45; RFC Kingman 25/10/45.

44-6205 Del Tulsa 30/5/44; Nashville 6/9/44; 3501 BU Boca Raton 10/9/44; 3035 BU Victorville 5/2/45; RFC Kingman 25/10/45.

44-6206 Del Tulsa 30/5/44; Boca Raton 21/8/44; 3035 BU Victorville 19/11/44; Recl Comp 21/8/45.

44-6207 Del Tulsa 2/6/44; 3501 BU Boca Raton 8/9/44; 120 BU Richmond 9/10/44; 3501 BU Boca Raton 16/10/44; 326 BU McDill 30/10/44; 4203 BU Jackson 21/1/45; 3501 BU Boca Raton 27/1/45; 4141 BU Pyote 31/7/46; Recl Comp 6/6/49.

44-6208 Del Tulsa 30/5/44; 3501 BU Boca Raton 28/8/44; 3705 BU Lowry 13/12/44; 2621 BU Barksdale 18/1/46; 4117 BU Robins 4/3/48; Recl Comp 30/11/48.

44-6209 Del Tulsa 30/5/44; Jackson 29/8/44; 3501 BU Boca Raton 20/9/44; RFC Kingman 19/12/45.

44-6210 Del Tulsa 30/5/44; Boca Raton 2/9/44; 3035

BU Victorville 5/2/45; RFC Kingman 25/10/45.
44-6211 Del Tulsa 31/5/44; 3501 BU Boca Raton 31/8/44; 3705 BU Lowry 13/12/44; 4141 BU Pyote 13/3/47; Recl Comp 14/1/49.
44-6212 Del Tulsa 2/6/44; 3501 BU Boca Raton 19/9/44; 2621 BU Barksdale 16/6/47; 4117 BU Robins 18/3/48; Recl Comp 30/11/48.
44-6213 Del Tulsa 31/5/44; 3501 BU Boca Raton 30/9/44; 3705 BU Lowry 13/12/44; 2621 BU Barksdale 8/8/47; 4117 BU Robins 4/3/48; Recl Comp 4/11/48.
44-6214 Del Tulsa 5/6/44; 3501 BU Boca Raton 8/9/44; 2621 BU Barksdale 19/5/47; Recl Comp 30/11/48.
44-6215 Del Tulsa 31/5/44; 3501 BU Boca Raton 3/9/44; 347 BU Key Fd 28/11/44; 3501 BU Boca Raton 30/11/44; 4105 BU Davis Monthan 17/12/44; 3501 BU Boca Raton 30/1/45; 3505 BU Scott 18/4/45; 3501 BU Boca Raton 27/5/46; 4141 BU Pyote 7/5/47; Recl Comp 2/3/49.
44-6216 Del Tulsa 2/6/44; 3501 BU Boca Raton 21/9/44; 2621 BU Barksdale 5/8/47; 4117 BU Robins 4/3/48; Recl Comp 11/2/49.
44-6217 Del Tulsa 2/6/44; 3501 BU Boca Raton 8/9/44; WO 19/9/44.
44-6218 Del Tulsa 2/6/44; Boca Raton 7/9/44; 613 BU (Training Command) Phillips 22/1/46.
44-6219 Del Tulsa 2/6/44; 3501 BU Boca Raton 8/9/44; Recl Comp 4/12/45.
44-6220 Del Tulsa 2/6/44; 3501 BU Boca Raton 12/9/44; RFC Kingman 9/12/45.
44-6221 Del Tulsa 2/6/44; 3501 BU Boca Raton 10/10/44; 4141 BU Pyote 7/5/47; Recl Comp 2/5/49.
44-6222 Del Tulsa 2/6/44; 582 BU Boca Raton 26/9/44; 4136 BU Tinker 17/9/45; 3501 BU Boca Raton 23/9/45; RFC Kingman 8/12/45.
44-6223 Del Tulsa 2/6/44; 3501 BU Boca Raton 18/9/44; RFC Kingman 20/12/45.
44-6224 Del Tulsa 5/6/44; 3501 BU Boca Raton 23/10/44; RFC Kingman 20/12/45.
44-6225 Del Tulsa 3/6/44; 3501 BU Boca Raton 29/10/44; Recl Comp 17/3/47.
44-6226 Del Tulsa 3/6/44; Harvard 21/9/44; MAT Tulsa 22/9/44; 244 BU Harvard 30/10/44; 233 BU Davis Monthan 29/3/45; 237 BU Kirtland 25/5/45; 233 BU Davis Monthan 28/5/45; 4105 BU Davis Monthan 20/11/45; RFC Kingman 1/12/45.
44-6227 Del Tulsa 3/6/44; 3501 BU Boca Raton 14/10/44; Recl Comp 5/8/46.
44-6228 Del Tulsa 3/6/44; 3501 BU Boca Raton 4/10/44; 2519 BU Ft Worth 23/9/45; 3501 BU Boca Raton 16/10/45; 1103 BU Morrison 29/1/46; 3501 BU Boca Raton 3/2/46; 4141 BU Pyote 7/5/47; Recl Comp 2/3/49.
44-6229 Del Tulsa 4/6/44; 241 BU Fairmont 24/9/44; 234 BU Clovis 25/9/44; 241 BU Fairmont 6/10/44; 902 BU Orlando 19/11/44; 326 BU McDill 1/2/45; RFC Kingman 17/10/45.
44-6230 Del Tulsa 5/6/44; 3501 BU Boca Raton 29/10/44; 4136 BU Tinker 17/9/45; ATC West Palm Beach 10/12/44; 3501 BU Boca Raton 30/4/46; 1103 BU Morrison 26/2/47; Recl Comp 19/6/47.
44-6231 Del Tulsa 5/6/44; 3501 BU Boca Raton 1/11/44; 4141 BU Pyote 7/5/47; Recl Comp 22/12/48.
44-6232 Del Tulsa 6/6/44; slated 96BG FELLOWSHIP 16/6/44; tran 3501 BU Boca Raton 1/8/44; RFC Kingman 20/12/45.
44-6233 Del Tulsa 6/6/44; 3501 BU Boca Raton 30/10/44; Recl Comp 1/3/45.
44-6234 Del Tulsa 6/6/44; 3501 BU Boca Raton 27/9/44; RFC Kingman 20/12/45.

44-6235 Del Tulsa 7/6/44; Boca Raton 2/10/44; 234 BU Clovis 13/11/44l; 379 BU Coffeyville 14/2/45; Recl Comp 16/3/45.
44-6236 Del Tulsa 6/6/44; 3501 BU Boca Raton 1/11/44; W/O 9/9/45.
44-6237 Del Tulsa 6/6/44; 3501 BU Boca Raton 29/9/44; 242 BU Gr Island 14/11/44; 233 BU Davis Monthan 21/4/45; 268 BU Peterson 9/6/45; 247 BU Smoky Hill 7/11/45; RFC Walnut Ridge 3/11/46.
44-6238 Del Tulsa 7/6/44; 3501 BU Boca Raton 7/10/44; 4141 BU Pyote 7/5/47; Recl Comp 2/5/49.
44-6239 Del Tulsa 7/6/44; 3501 BU Boca Raton 1/10/44; 236 BU Tinker 17/9/45; 3501 BU Boca Raton 2/10/45; RFC Kingman 20/12/45.
44-6240 Del Tulsa 9/6/44; 231 BU Alamogordo 11/10/44; 268 BU Peterson 31/10/44; 427 BU Roswell 22/1/45; 234 BU Clovis 27/2/45; 613 BU Phillips, W/O 22/4/46.
44-6241 Del Tulsa 9/6/44; 3501 BU Boca Raton 6/10/44; 4141 BU Pyote 7/5/47; Recl Comp 2/3/49.
44-6242 Del Tulsa 9/6/44; 245 BU McCook 7/10/44; 235 BU Biggs 6/4/45; 268 BU Peterson 12/6/45; 427 BU Roswell 2/12/45; 4134 BU Spokane 28/4/46; 427 BU Roswell 5/8/46; 4168 BU Sth Plains 11/8/46; 594 BU Topeka 14/8/46; 427 BU Roswell 30/8/46; 4141 BU Pyote 23/6/47; Recl Comp 2/3/49.
44-6243 Del Tulsa 9/6/44; Salina 11/10/44; 247 BU Smoky Hill 14/10/44; 234 BU Clovis 6/4/45; 268 BU Peterson 3/6/45; RFC Kingman 18/1/46.
44-6244 Del Tulsa 9/6/44; 248 BU Walker 14/10/44; 235 BU Biggs 6/4/45; 268 BU Peterson 12/6/45; 231 BU Alamogordo 29/10/45; RFC Kingman 29/2/46.
44-6245 Del Tulsa 9/6/44; 3501 BU Boca Raton 7/10/44; RFC Kingman 19/12/45.
44-6246 Del Tulsa 10/6/44; 243 BU Gt Bend 14/10/44; 3705 BU Lowry 7/4/45; RFC Kingman 29/1/46.
44-6247 Del Tulsa 10/6/44; 234 BU Clovis 10/10/44; 3501 BU Boca Raton 14/11/44; 234 BU Clovis 10/10/44; 555 BU Love Fd 20/12/44; 3505 BU Scott 12/1/45; 3501 BU Boca Raton 27/5/46; RFC Kingman 8/12/45.
44-6248 Del Tulsa 10/6/44; 242 BU Gr Island 6/10/44; 3501 BU Boca Raton 13/11/44; 347 BU Key Fd 19/9/45; 3501 BU Boca Raton 30/9/45; 4141 BU Pyote 7/5/47; Recl Comp 22/12/48.
44-6249 Del Tulsa 10/6/44; 236 BU Pyote 25/10/44; 234 BU Clovis 25/2/45; Recl Comp 24/5/46.
44-6250 Del Tulsa 10/6/44; 246 BU Pratt 24/10/44; 237 BU Kirtland 8/4/45; 268 BU Peterson 6/6/45; 216 BU Wendover 29/10/45; 4208 BU Mines 9/11/45; 4126 BU Mines 8/4/46; Recl Comp 28/5/46.
44-6251 Del Hunter 15/6/44; Dow Fd 28/6/44; ass 772BS/463BG Celone 3/7/44; cr 3/2/45, sal.
44-6252 Del Hunter 15/6/44; Dow Fd 28/6/44; ass 96BG Snetterton 6/44; tran 813BS/482BG [PC-A] Alconbury 4/2/45; retUS, Recl Comp Pyote 14/1/49.
44-6253 Del Hunter 15/6/44; Dow Fd 25/6/44; ass 353BS/301BG Lucera 3/7/44; MIA Padua 11/4/45 w/Haaser; flak, cr Morbegno; 10INT Switz; MACR 13978.
44-6254 Del Hunter 15/6/44; Dow Fd 26/6/44; ass 348BS/99BG Tortorella 9/7/44; nav Allen died of anoxia on Sopron, Yugo mission 4/3/45 w/Goad; tran depot 12/4/45; sal 14/1/46.
44-6255 Del Hunter 16/6/44; Dow Fd 24/6/44; ass 342BS/97BG Amendola 3/7/44; retUS Bradley 15/6/45; Sth Plains 21/10/45; RFC Kingman 7/12/45.
44-6256 Del Hunter 16/6/44; Grenier 26/6/44; ass 340BS/97BG Amendola 3/7/44; MIA Budapest 20/9/44 w/Furcht; flak, cr Brod; MACR 9738.
44-6257 Del Hunter 17/6/44; Dow Fd 28/6/44; ass 840BS/483BG Sterparone 4/7/44; sal 29/9/45.

DEVIL'S BOUQUET.
44-6258 Del Hunter 16/6/44; Presque Is 28/6/44; ass 341BS/97BG Amendola 3/7/44; MIA Vienna 16/7/44 w/Fetty; flak, cr Orth; MACR 6686.
44-6259 Del Hunter 16/6/44; Dow Fd 28/6/44; ass 419BS/301BG Lucera 4/7/44; retUS Bradley 15/6/45; Sth Plains 20/6/45; RFC Kingman 25/11/45.
44-6260 Del Hunter 18/6/44; Presque Is 28/6/44; ass 414BS/97BG Amendola 3/7/44; MIA Ploesti 22/7/44 w/Call; flak, exploded cr Ploesti; MACR 7094.
44-6261 Del Hunter 17/6/44; Grenier 26/6/44; ass 773BS/463BG Celone 12/7/44; MIA Vienna 13/10/44 w/Patterson; flak, cr Csurga; 10POW; MACR 9204. NEVER SATISFIED.
44-6262 Del Hunter 17/6/44; Presque Is 28/6/44; ass 772BS/463BG Celone 3/7/44; retUS 1103 BU Morrison 28/9/45; RFC Walnut Ridge 20/12/45.
44-6263 Del Hunter 21/6/44; Dow Fd 3/7/44; ass 353BS/301BG Lucera 10/7/44; MIA Vienna 7/11/44 w/Kulp; flak, cr Rehitsch; 3POW 7EVD & ret; MACR 9667.
44-6264 Del Hunter 20/6/44; Dow Fd 30/6/44; ass 49BS/2BG Amendola 3/7/44; hit by RAF a/c in parking accident 5/11/44; sal.
44-6265 Del Hunter 19/6/44; Grenier 28/6/44; ass 340BS/97BG Amendola 3/7/44; MIA Bleckhammer 13/9/44 w/Reardon; flak, cr Bleckhammer; MACR 8730.
44-6266 Del Hunter 22/6/44; Dow Fd 30/6/44; ass 32BS/301BG Lucera 8/7/44; b/d Linz 2/3/45 w/?; c/l base, sal.
44-6267 Del Hunter 19/6/44; Dow Fd 1/7/44; ass 817BS/483BG Sterparone 7/7/44; MIA Memmingen 18/7/44 w/Clark; e/a, cr Kempten; 1KIA 10POW (inc pass); MACR 7097.
44-6268 Del Hunter 20/6/44; Grenier 28/6/44; ass 348BS/99BG Tortorella 3/7/44; MIA {56m} Regensburg 20/1/45 w/Sunderlin; e/a, cr Beluno; MACR 11276.
44-6269 Del Kearney 20/6/44; Grenier 30/6/44; ass 97BG Amendola 7/7/44; to depot 23/11/44; retUS Hunter 25/6/45; Sth Plains 20/10/45; RFC Kingman 15/12/45.
44-6270 Del Kearney 22/6/44; Presque Is 7/7/44; ass 414BS/97BG Amendola 13/7/44; MIA Vienna 16/7/44 w/Haase; flak, cr Wiener Neustadt; MACR 6961.
44-6271 Del Kearney 20/6/44; Grenier 30/6/44; ass 772BS/463BG Celone 3/7/44; MIA Fortezza 20/4/45 w/Cunningham; flak, cr Cassal Maggiore; MACR 14019. MAGNIFICENT MALFUNCTION.
44-6272 Del Kearney 22/6/44; Grenier 30/6/44; ass 774BS/463BG Celone 6/7/44; MIA Odertal 22/8/44 w/Daker; flak, cr Erenforst; MACR 7990.
44-6273 Del Kearney 22/6/44; Presque Is 7/7/44; ass 414BS/97BG Amendola 17/7/44; burned out 26/2/45; sal.
44-6274 Del Kearney 21/6/44; Presque Is 7/7/44; ass 342BS/97BG Amendola 14/7/44; MIA Bleckhammer 13/9/44 w/Shelton; flak, cr Gross Strelite; MACR 8954.
44-6275 Del Kearney 22/6/44; Dow Fd 7/7/44; ass 20BS/2BG Amendola 8/7/44; MIA Ploesti 18/8/44 w/Rogers; #3 fire, cr sea; 3KIA 7RTD; MACR 7683.
44-6276 Del Kearney 21/6/44; Presque Is 7/7/44; ass 772BS/463BG Celone 8/7/44; MIA Linz 25/7/44 w/Carroll; flak, cr Linz; MACR 7001.
44-6277 Del Kearney 19/6/44; Dow Fd 4/8/44; ass 863BS/493BG Debach 4/8/44; MIA Bohlen 12/9/44 w/Oates; e/a, cr Germany; MACR 8862.
44-6278 Del Kearney 19/6/44; Grenier 4/8/44; ass 861BS/493BG Debach 3/8/44; b/d Cologne 10/1/45

w/?; f/l Continent, sal.

44-6279 Del Kearney 22/6/44; Presque Is 8/7/44; ass 773BS/463BG Celone 8/7/44; sal 6/5/45.

44-6280 Del Kearney 22/6/44; Presque Is 7/7/44; ass 774BS/463BG Celone 12/7/44; MIA Ploesti 28/7/44 w/Grinnell; ditched off Turkey; MACR 7128.

44-6281 Del Kearney 22/6/44; Presque Is 6/7/44; ass 429BS/2BG Amendola 12/7/44; retUS Bradley 24/7/45; Independence 27/7/45; RFC Kingman 9/12/45.

44-6282 Del Kearney 24/6/44; Grenier 6/7/44; ass 347BS/97BG Amendola 12/7/44; b/d Vienna 22/8/44 w/Christianson; 10 baled near Zagreb, ret 29/8/44; pilot returns on two engines; MACR 7989; {42m} tran depot 9/1/45; retUS 4100 Patterson 22/8/45; 4104 BU Rome 3/9/45; RFC Walnut Ridge 8/1/46. To USN as CB-17 in 1946.

44-6283 Del Kearney 22/6/44; Grenier 6/7/44; ass 773BS/463BG Celone 8/7/44; MIA Berlin 24/3/45 w/Tubman; jet e/a, cr Luckenwalde; MACR 13278. BETTY LOU.

44-6284 Del Kearney 24/6/44; Presque Is 7/7/44; ass 352BS/301BG Lucera 8/7/44; MIA Friedrichshafen 3/8/44 w/Simon; flak, cr Sterzing; 1KIA 9POW; MACR 7316.

44-6285 Del Kearney 24/6/44; Grenier 6/7/44; ass 774BS/463BG Celone 12/7/44; retUS, RFC Walnut Ridge 18/1/46. HERSHEY WOLVES II.

44-6286 Del Kearney 24/6/44; Dow Fd 7/7/44; ass 346BS/99BG Tortorella 18/7/44; {80m} RetUS Bradley 30/6/45; Sth Plains 4/7/45; RFC Kingman 13/12/45.

44-6287 Del Kearney 24/6/44; Dow Fd 7/7/44; ass 772BS/463BG Celone 11/7/44; MIA Valence 15/8/44 w/Gault; flak, cr Montmeyran; MACR 7461.

44-6288 Del Kearney 27/6/44; Grenier 9/7/44; ass 840BS/483BG Sterparone 14/7/44; taxi coll w/42-106999 2/2/45; sal.

44-6289 Del Kearney 24/6/44; Presque Is 7/7/44; ass 96BS/2BG Amendola 11/7/44; MIA {25m} Belgrade 3/9/44 w/Kwiatkowski; c/l Vis.

44-6290 Del Kearney 26/6/44; Grenier 6/7/44; ass 836BS/487BG [2G-D] Lavenham 8/7/44; MIA Saarbrücken 9/11/44 w/Herring; flak, cr Saverne, Fr; 2KIA 7POW; MACR 10341.

44-6291 Del Kearney 27/6/44; Grenier 6/7/44; ass 358BS/303BG [VK-F] Molesworth 26/7/44; MIA Cologne 15/8/44 w/Smith; e/a, cr Wittlich, Ger; MACR 8171.

44-6292 Del Kearney 27/6/44; Grenier 6/7/44; ass 833BS/486BG [4N-V] Sudbury 8/7/44; b/d Düsseldorf 9/9/44 w/?; f/l Continent, sal 14/11/44. MACR 8612.

44-6293 Del Kearney 26/6/44; Dow Fd 9/7/44; ass 401BS/91BG [LL-A] Bassingbourn 22/7/44 PEGGY {20+m}; retUS Bradley 12/6/45; Sth Plains 14/6/45; RFC Kingman 5/12/45. {2m} SUNKIST SUE.

44-6294 Del Kearney 27/6/44; Grenier 6/7/44; ass 545BS/384BG [JD-N] Grafton Underwood 21/7/44; MIA Ruhland 7/10/44 w/Capt Mandelbaum; flak, cr Ruhland; 2KIA 7POW; MACR 9365. SCOTTY.

44-6295 Del Kearney 27/6/44; Grenier 8/7/44; ass 100BG Thorpe Abbotts 11/7/44; b/d Berlin 18/3/45 w/?; f/l Kakoneiwicz, Pol; sal 26/3/45; tran 91BG Bassingbourn 7/5/45.

44-6296 Del Kearney 29/6/44; Dow Fd 14/7/44; ass 4BS/34BG Mendlesham 16/7/44; c/l 6/4/45; sal 8/4/45.

44-6297 Del Kearney 28/6/44; Dow Fd 13/7/44; ass 350BS/100BG [LN-X] Thorpe Abbotts 14/7/44; tran 482BG Alconbury 20/5/45; RetUS Bradley 2/6/45; Sth Plains 8/6/45; RFC Kingman 14/12/45.

44-6298 Del Kearney 28/6/44; Grenier 9/7/44; ass 322BS/91BG [LG-A] Bassingbourn 22/7/44 WHITE CARGO; MIA {32m} Merseburg 2/11/44 w/Brown; e/a, cr Neugattersleben, Ger; 6KIA 3POW; MACR 10142; HEAVENLY BODY.

44-6299 Del Kearney 28/6/44; Dow Fd 13/7/44; ass 836BS/487BG [2G-Q] Lavenham 14/8/44; MIA Chemnitz 6/2/45 w/?.

44-6300 Del Kearney 28/6/44; Grenier 9/7/44; ass 366BS/305BG [KY-K] Chelveston 12/8/44; MIA Pilsen 25/4/45 w/Hodges; flak, cr Czech?; 8KIA 1POW.

44-6301 Del Kearney 28/6/44; Dow Fd 13/7/44; ass 8AF 16/7/44, trans 4100 BU Patterson 11/10/44; extn tail cone and extra windows installed; (single star forward of entry door indicated aircraft used by Brig Gen?); 4168 BU Sth Plains 3/5/45; 494 BU Topeka 6/45; 4136 BU Tinker 13/7/47; 4141 BU Pyote 7/8/47; Recl Comp 4/11/48. HORIZON.

44-6302 Del Kearney 28/6/44; Dow Fd 9/7/44; ass 839BS/487BG Lavenham 12/7/44; tran 486BS Sudbury 27/10/44; b/d Merseburg 30/11/44 w/?; f/l Melsbroek, Bel; sal 21/12/44.

44-6303 Del Kearney 28/6/44; Grenier 9/7/44; ass 850BS/490BG Eye 11/7/44; 851BS; MIA Schlessheim, Ger 9/4/45 w/Schoenfeld; flak, cr Schlessheim; 2KIA 7POW; MACR 13909. THE LUCKY STRIKE.

44-6304 Del Kearney 27/8/44; Grenier 9/7/44; ass 422BS/305BG Chelveston 12/7/44; MIA Delitzsch 16/8/44 w/Betz; flak, cr Volradisroda, Ger?; MACR 8436.

44-6305 Del Kearney 27/6/44; Grenier 9/7/44; ass 838BS/487BG Lavenham 12/7/44; MIA Ruhland 12/9/44 w/Preston; mech fault, cr Pruen, Ger; 6EVD 1KIA 2POW; MACR 10209.

44-6306 Del Kearney 28/6/44; Grenier 9/7/44; ass 349BS/100BG [XR-G] Thorpe Abbotts 12/7/44; MIA Merseburg 28/9/44 w/Harney; e/a, cr Schwickershausen, Ger; 6KIA 3POW; MACR 9373.

44-6307 Del Kearney 29/6/44; Dow Fd 13/7/44; ass 837BS/487BG [4F-K] Lavenham 14/7/44; MIA Merseburg 25/11/44 w/Shields; flak, cr Apolda, Ger; 9POW; MACR 10757. BLONDE BOMBER.

44-6308 Del Kearney 28/6/44; Grenier 9/7/44; ass 322BS/91BG [LG-S] Bassingbourn 22/7/44 MUNCHIN' KID; 323BS; {72m} RetUS Bradley 13/6/45; Sth Plains 15/6/45; RFC Kingman 1/12/45. STINKY (BUTCHER SHOP).

44-6309 Del Kearney 28/6/44; Grenier 12/7/44; ass 359BS/303BG [BN-T] Molesworth 26/7/44; retUS Bradley 30/7/45; Independence 2/8/45; RFC Kingman 18/12/45. DUCHESS' GRAND DAUGHTER.

44-6310 Del Kearney 29/6/44; Dow Fd 11/7/44; ass 615BS/401BG [IY-P] Deenethorpe 23/7/44; MIA Gaggenau 10/9/44 w/Woodward; flak, cr Heinerdingen, Ger; 2KIA 7POW; MACR 8606. ROCKY LOIS.

44-6311 Del Kearney 30/6/44; Dow Fd 11/7/44; ass 8AF 19/7/44; retUS Chanute 8/7/45; Sth Plains 24/10/45; Recl Comp 7/6/46.

44-6312 Del Kearney 29/6/44; Grenier 12/7/44; ass 8AF 14/7/44; retUS Badley 8/7/45; Sth Plains 10/7/45; RFC Kingman 7/12/45.

44-6313 Del Kearney 29/6/44; Grenier 12/7/44; ass 613BS/401BG [IN-F] Deenethorpe 23/7/44; retUS Bradley 6/6/45; Sth Plains 8/6/45; RFC Kingman 19/12/45. BUDD'S DUDDS.

44-6314 Del Kearney 29/6/44; Grenier 12/7/44; ass 8AF 13/7/44; retUS Bradley 8/7/45; Sth Plains 11/7/44; RFC Kingman 19/11/45.

44-6315 Del Kearney 29/6/44; Grenier 12/7/44; ass 837BS/487BG [4F-L] Lavenham 14/7/44; retUS Bradley 10/7/45; Independence 12/7/45; RFC Kingman 16/12/45. FEARLESS F.

44-6316 Del Kearney 29/6/44; Grenier 12/7/44; ass 358BS/303BG [VK-C] Molesworth 18/7/44; b/d Berlin 26/2/45 w/?; sal.

44-6317 Del Kearney 1/7/44; Grenier 13/7/44; ass 840BS/483BG Sterparone 18/7/44; MIA Regensburg 13/3/45 w/Parrish; flak, cr Ljubijana; 10POW; MACR 12945.

44-6318 Del Kearney 3/7/44; Grenier 12/7/44; ass 816BS/483BG Sterparone 17/7/44; W/O 8/7/45, sal.

44-6319 Del Kearney 3/7/44; Grenier 12/7/44; ass 816BS/483BG Sterparone 18/7/44; engine fire causing early return from Ploesti 10/8/44 w/Brown; crew baled and Brown c/l at base; rep; retUS Bradley 12/7/45; Independence 13/7/45; RFC Albuquerque 7/2/46.

44-6320 Del Kearney 3/7/44; Grenier 12/7/44; ass 816BS/483BG Sterparone 17/7/44; retUS 1103 BU Morrison 29/4/45; 4104 BU Rome 2/5/45; RFC Altus 5/11/45. THE NORTHERN GALE.

44-6321 Del Kearney 1/7/44; Grenier 13/7/44; ass 342BS/97BG Amendola 18/7/44; retUS Bradley 15/6/45; Sth Plains 17/6/45; Recl Comp 7/6/46.

44-6322 Del Kearney 4/7/44; Grenier 12/7/44; ass 816BS/483BG Sterparone 15/7/44; retUS Bradley 14/6/45; Sth Plains 18/6/45; RFC Kingman 6/12/45.

44-6323 Del Kearney 5/7/44; Grenier 13/7/44; ass 815BS/483BG Sterparone 18/7/44; retUS Bradley 7/7/45; Sth Plains 10/7/45; RFC Kingman 9/12/45.

44-6324 Del Kearney 4/7/44; Grenier 15/7/44; ass 816BS/483BG Sterparone 19/7/44; cr 25/6/45, sal.

44-6325 Del Kearney 4/7/44; Grenier 16/7/44; ass 816BS/483BG Sterparone 17/7/44; MIA Vienna 16/3/45 w/Anderson; flak, cr Igol; 10EVD, ret 30/3/45; MACR 13059.

44-6326 Del Kearney 12/7/44; Grenier 12/7/44; ass 816BS/483BG Sterparone 14/7/44; retUS Bradley 12/7/45; Independence 22/7/45; RFC Kingman 31/12/45. PICK UP.

44-6327 Del Kearney 5/6/44; Grenier 12/7/44; ass 816BS/483BG Steparone 17/7/44; MIA Linz 25/4/45 w/Sinton; flak, cr Amstettin; 4KIA 6POW: MACR 14060.

44-6328 Del Kearney 6/7/44; Grenier 13/7/44; ass 342BS/97BG Amendola 21/7/44; MIA Fortezza 20/4/45 w/Sullivan; MACR 13818.

44-6329 Del Kearney 5/7/44; Grenier 12/7/44; ass 817BS/483BG Sterparone 17/7/44; retUS 1103 BU Morrison 18/9/45; RFC Walnut Ridge 18/12/45.

44-6330 Del Kearney 6/7/44; Grenier 15/7/44; ass 348BS/99BG Tortorella 19/7/44; {88m} RetUS Bradley 14/6/45; Sth Plains 18/6/45; RFC Kingman 19/12/45.

44-6331 Del Hunter 6/7/44; Grenier 15/7/44; ass 341BS/97BG Amendola 19/7/44; retUS Bradley 15/6/45; Sth Plains 20/6/45; RFC Kingman 5/12/45.

44-6332 Del Hunter 6/7/44; Grenier 15/7/44; ass 817BS/483BG Sterparone 19/7/44; MIA Vienna 10/9/44 w/Simons; flak, cr Vienna; 5KIA 4POW; MACR 10645.

44-6333 Del Hunter 5/7/44; Grenier 15/7/44; ass 815BS/483BG Sterparone 19/7/44; MIA Linz 27/12/44 w/Sampson; flak, cr Wolz; 4KIA 6POW: MACR 10645.

44-6334 Del Hunter 6/7/44; Dow Fd 17/7/44; ass 349BS/100BG [XR-B] Thorpe Abbotts 19/7/44; MIA Kaltenkirchen 7/4/45 w/Howard; e/a, cr Hannover; 3KIA 6POW; MACR 13716.

44-6335 Del Hunter 6/7/44; Grenier 15/7/44; ass 2BG Amendola 31/7/44; Recl Comp 5/12/44.

44-6336 Del Hunter 7/7/44; Dow Fd 16/7/44; ass 775BS/463BG Celone 24/7/44; MIA Graz 9/3/45 w/Hanley; cr Graz; MACR 12914. JANIE.

44-6337 Del Hunter 10/7/44; Dow Fd 20/7/44; ass 352BS/301BG Lucera 27/7/44; MIA Bleckhammer 26/12/44 w/Filer; flak, cr Krakow; 10POW; MACR 10746. KANDY.

44-6338 Del Hunter 10/7/44; Dow Fd 17/7/44; ass 414BS/97BG Amendola 23/7/44; MIA Salzburg 11/11/44 w/Faith; mech fault, cr Fruli; MACR 9862.

44-6339 Del Hunter 8/7/44; Presque Is 26/7/44; ass 342BS/97BG Amendola 30/7/44; retUS Hunter 18/6/45; Sth Plains 20/6/45; RFC Kingman 4/12/45.

44-6340 Del Hunter 8/7/44; Grenier 17/7/44; ass 414BS/97BG Amendola 23/7/44; MIA Ploesti 18/8/44 w/Lloyd; no gas, cr Paramithia; MACR 7970. REMEMBER ME.

44-6341 Del Hunter 8/7/44; Grenier 15/7/44; ass 414BS/97BG Amendola 19/7/44; retUS Hunter 18/6/45; Sth Plains 20/6/45; RFC Kingman 4/12/45.

44-6342 Del Hunter 10/7/44; Dow Fd 22/7/44; ass 32BS/301BG Lucera 9/8/44; to depot 10/3/45; ditched 21/5/45.

44-6343 Del Hunter 10/7/44; Grenier 24/7/44; ass 32BS/301BG Lucera 31/7/44; to depot 20/4/45; sal 26/4/45.

44-6344 Del Hunter 16/7/44; Grenier 27/7/44; ass 2BG Amendola 31/7/44; sal 4/8/44.

44-6345 Del Hunter 10/7/44; Dow Fd 17/7/44; ass 342BS/97BG Amendola 23/7/44; MIA Vienna 20/2/45 w/Essor; mech fault, cr Gospic; MACR 12478.

44-6346 Del Hunter 10/7/44; Dow Fd 20/7/44; ass 419BS/301BG Lucera 27/7/44; depot 3/4/45.

44-6347 Del Hunter 11/7/44; Dow Fd 20/7/44; ass 32BS/301BG Lucera 29/7/44; MIA Vipiteno 20/4/45 w/Adams; flak, #1 & 4 feathered; f/l Dubendorf, Switz; 10INT; MACR 14030 (last US crew to land Switz); Ret Burtonwood, UK 1/9/45; RFC Walnut Ridge 18/12/45. PRINCESS O'ROURKE.

44-6348 Del Hunter 11/7/44; Dow Fd 3/8/44; ass 342BS/97BG Amendola 11/8/44; tran 32BS/301BG Lucera 14/8/44; MIA Vienna 10/9/44 w/Wisner; flak, cr Scnorja; 10POW; MACR 8622.

44-6349 Del Hunter 11/7/44; Dow Fd 26/7/44; ass 840BS/483BG Sterparone 2/8/44; MIA Bleckhammer 13/9/44 w/Condraski; mech fault, cr Heydebreck; 9KIA 1POW; MACR 8448.

44-6350 Del Hunter 14/7/44; Presque Is 22/7/44; ass 429BS/2BG Amendola 30/7/44; MIA Bleckhammer 17/12/44 w/Waldman; f/l Yugoslavia, where crew flew home on C-47 except p & cp Stemwedel; they attempted to fly from Belgrade to Bari 10/1/45, but cr Pristina; MACR 11286. HELEN BELLE.

44-6351 Del Hunter 12/7/44; Presque Is 26/7/44; ass 352BS/301BG Lucera 6/8/44; MIA Brux 4/3/45 w/Bedzyk; flak, cr Waidhofen; MACR 12903.

44-6352 Del Hunter 14/7/44; Presque Is 26/7/44; ass 772BS/463BG Celone 9/8/44; MIA Valence 15/8/44 w/Ciccone; flak, cr Valence; 4KIA; MACR 7459.

44-6353 Del Kearney 14/7/44; Presque Is 26/7/44; ass 32BS/301BG Lucera 8/8/44; MIA Vienna 10/9/44 w/Stubbs; flak, cr Vienna; 7KIA 3POW; MACR 8261.

44-6354 Del Kearney 14/7/44; Dow Fd 20/7/44; ass 301BG Lucera 12/8/44; tran 97BG Amendola 14/8/44; MIA Bleckhammer 13/9/44 w/Tomavich; MACR 8953.

44-6355 Del Kearney 14/7/44; Presque Is 26/7/44; ass 419BS/301BG Lucera 30/7/44; retUS Hunter 16/6/45; Sth Plains 19/6/45; RFC Kingman 1/12/45.

44-6356 Del Kearney 14/7/44; Dow Fd 20/7/44; ass 353BS/301BG Lucera 29/7/44; depot 20/4/45; sal 26/4/45.

44-6357 Del Kearney 12/7/44; Dow Fd 20/7/44; ass 32BS/301BG Lucera 29/7/44; sal 23/4/45.

44-6358 Del Hunter 14/7/44; Grenier 29/7/44; ass 352BS/301BG Lucera 9/8/44; retUS 1103 BU Morrison 16/10/45; 593 BU Charleston 28/10/45; RFC Walnut Ridge 9/1/46.

44-6359 Del Hunter 14/7/44; Grenier 27/7/44; ass 20BS/2BG Amendola 18/8/44; MIA Moravska Ostrova 29/8/44 w/Bullock; e/a, cr Ziln; MACR 8083.

44-6360 Del Hunter 14/7/44; Dow Fd 25/7/44; ass 419BS/301BG Lucera 9/8/44; sal 5/5/45.

44-6361 Del Hunter 14/7/44; Grenier 27/7/44; ass 352BS/301BG Lucera 15/8/44.

44-6362 Del Hunter 16/7/44; Grenier 27/7/44; ass 483BG Sterparone 26/7/44; retUS Bradley 14/6/45; Sth Plains 21/6/45; RFC Kingman 13/12/45.

44-6363 Del Hunter 16/7/44; Presque Is 26/7/44; ass 353BS/301BG Lucera 9/8/44.

44-6364 Del Hunter 14/7/44; Presque Is 4/8/44; ass 419BS/301BG Lucera 13/8/44.

44-6365 Del Hunter 14/7/44; Dow Fd 5/8/44; ass 20BS/2BG Amendola 13/8/44; sal 2/8/45.

44-6366 Del Hunter 17/7/44; Dow Fd 4/8/44; ass 341BS/97BG Amendola 13/8/44; MIA Salzburg 11/11/44 w/Miller; coll w/44-6486; cr Castelfranco; MACR 9860.

44-6367 Del Hunter 16/7/44; Grenier 26/7/44; ass 49BS/2BG Amendola 31/7/44; retUS Bradley 10/7/45; Independence 12/7/45; RFC Kingman 2/1/46.

44-6368 Del Hunter 20/7/44; Dow Fd 4/8/44; ass 352BS/301BG Lucera 13/8/44; tran 20BS/2BG Amendola 14/8/44; sal 5/5/45.

44-6369 Del Hunter 17/7/44; Dow Fd 4/8/44; ass 49BS/2BG Amendola 11/8/44; MIA Moravska Ostrova 29/8/44 w/Seaman; e/a, cr Settini; MACR 8084.

44-6370 Del Hunter 18/7/44; Grenier 27/7/44; ass 419BS/301BG Lucera 12/8/44; retUS Bradley 3/7/45; Sth Plains 28/8/45; RFC Kingman 17/12/45.

44-6371 Del Hunter 20/7/44; Dow Fd 3/8/44; ass 840BS/483BG Sterparone 11/8/44; cr 13/4/45, sal. EVA DEE.

44-6372 Del Hunter 18/7/44; Dow Fd 4/8/44; ass 346BS/99BG Tortorella 13/8/44; {60m} RetUS Hunter 27/7/45; Independence 30/7/45; RFC Kingman 21/12/45.

44-6373 Del Hunter 17/7/44; Dow Fd 3/8/44; ass 346BS/99BG Tortorella 14/8/44; {81m} RetUS Hunter 7/7/45; Sth Plains 7/7/45; RFC Kingman 20/2/46.

44-6374 Del Hunter 20/7/44; Dow Fd 3/8/44; ass 49BS/2BG Amendola 11/8/44; MIA Vipiteno 20/4/45 w/Baer; flak KO'd two engines, wing blown off and cr Rica; MACR 13815. TUFF TITTY.

44-6375 Del Hunter 20/7/44; Dow Fd 3/8/44; ass 774BS/463BG Celone 11/8/44; retUS, RFC Walnut Ridge 9/1/46.

44-6376 Del Hunter 21/7/44; Presque Is 4/8/44; ass 348BS/99BG Tortorella 13/8/44; {68m} RetUS Bradley 18/7/45; Sth Plains 21/6/45; RFC Kingman 17/12/45.

44-6377 Del Hunter 20/7/44; Presque Is 6/8/44; ass 772BS/463BG Celone 13/8/44; MIA Vienna 20/3/45 w/Lincoln; mech fault, cr Koeuje; MACR 13050. PRETTY BABY'S BOYS.

44-6378 Del Hunter 20/7/44; Grenier 2/10/44; ass 20BS/2BG Amendola 5/10/44; retUS Hunter 18/8/45; Sth Plains 20/8/45; RFC Kingman 26/11/45.

44-6379 Del Hunter 22/7/44; Presque Is 4/8/44; ass 96BS/2BG Amendola 13/8/44; MIA {28m} Bleckhammer 17/10/44 w/Kwiatkoski; coll w/42-107006, broke in half, no chutes seen; cr Bleckhammer; MACR 9149.

44-6380 Del Hunter 20/7/44; Dow Fd 3/8/44; ass 416BS/99BG Tortorella 11/8/44; {79m} RetUS Hunter 25/6/45; Sth Plains 27/6/45; RFC Kingman 28/11/45.

44-6381 Del Hunter 20/7/44; Dow Fd 3/8/44; ass 775BS/463BG Celone 11/8/44; cr 4/4/45.

44-6382 Del Hunter 21/7/44; Dow Fd 3/8/44; ass 352BS/301BG Lucera 13/8/44; retUS Bradley 30/6/45; Sth Plains 4/7/45; RFC Kingman 28/11/45.

44-6383 Del Hunter 20/7/44; Dow Fd 3/8/44; ass 32BS/301BG Lucera 13/8/44; retUS Hunter 18/6/45; Sth Plains 20/6/45; RFC Kingman 28/11/45.

44-6384 Del Hunter 20/7/44; Presque Is 4/8/44; ass 353BS/301BG Lucera 15/8/44; depot 20/4/45; sal 26/4/45.

44-6385 Del Hunter 20/7/44; Dow Fd 3/8/44; ass 348BS/99BG Tortorella 26/8/44; {58m} RetUS Hunter 23/6/45; Sth Plains 25/6/45; RFC Kingman 17/12/45.

44-6386 Del Hunter 21/7/44; Dow Fd 3/8/44; ass 429BS/2BG Amendola 11/8/44; b/d Bleckhammer 19/12/44 w/Grossman; c/l Vis, sal.

44-6387 Del Hunter 22/7/44; Presque Is 4/8/44; ass 20BS/2BG Amendola 13/8/44; tran 815BS/483BG Sterparone 14/8/44; MIA Ruhland 22/3/45 w/Davis; flak & jet e/a, cr Ruhland; 2KIA 8POW; MACR 13247.

44-6388 Del Tulsa 21/7/44; 903 BU Pinecastle 29/9/44; 609 BU Eglin 24/3/47; Recl Comp 19/7/48.

44-6389 Del Tulsa 22/7/44; Orlando 25/9/44; 903 BU Pinecastle 29/9/44; 902 BU Orlando 2/2/45; 621 BU Pinecastle 4/7/45; 613 BU Phillips 25/7/46.

44-6390 Del Kearney 21/7/44; Grenier 8/8/44; ass 816BS/483BG Sterparone 15/8/44; ret Bologna 12/10/44 w/Howe; 8 baled over friendly territory; 2KIA 8RTD following day.

44-6391 Del Kearney 25/7/44; Grenier 8/8/44; ass 773BS/463BG Celone 15/8/44; retUS 3/10/45; RFC Walnut Ridge 10/1/46.

44-6392 Del Kearney 25/7/44; Grenier 8/8/44; ass 817BS/483BG Sterparone 19/8/44; b/d Moosebierbaum 1/3/45 w/Hoskins; flak hit in radio room, 2WIA; a/c returns, but sal 2/3/45.

44-6393 Del Kearney 22/7/44; Grenier 8/8/44; ass 97BG Amendola 20/8/44; depot 20/8/44; sal; retUS Bolling 5/45; 4112 BU Olmstead 3/46; used by Gen Ira Eaker as STARDUSTER from Bolling 3/48; 18 MSG Clark Fd, Philippines 9/48; 1130 SAG Nanking, China; US Embassy in Canada 11/49; 3510 FTW Randolph 2/53; Davis-Monthan 9/55; Aero Boliviano as CP-627 6/56; cr La Paz, Bolivia, but rep; retUS 1980, restored now in 15AF Museum as 2ND PATCHES.

44-6394 Del Kearney 25/7/44; Grenier 8/8/44; ass 774BS/463BG Celone 15/8/44; MIA Udine 5/4/45 w/Wetzel; flak, ditched Adriatic; MACR 13640. OH, MY ACHING BACK.

44-6395 Del Kearney 25/7/44; Grenier 8/8/44; ass 96BS/2BG Amendola 16/8/44; {62m} RetUS Bradley 14/7/45; Independence 17/7/45; RFC Albuquerque 7/2/46.

44-6396 Del Kearney 25/7/44; Grenier 8/8/44; ass 352BS/301BG Lucera 16/8/44; sal n/b/d 27/3/45.

44-6397 Del Kearney 25/7/44; Grenier 8/8/44; ass 416BS/99BG Tortorella 17/8/44; MIA {38m} Ruhland 23/3/45 w/Lea; flak, cr Hoyerswerde; cp Korupp POW, 9 to Russian lines; MACR 13255.

44-6398 Del Kearney 25/7/44; Grenier 8/8/44; ass 775BS/463BG Celone 16/8/44; retUS 1103 BU Morrison 28/9/45; RFC Walnut Ridge 18/12/45. BUCKET BUNNY.

44-6399 Del Kearney 25/7/44; Grenier 8/8/44; ass 20BS/2BG Amendola 16/8/44; Missing on practice op 2/11/44 w/Reilly and four crew; MACR 9683.

44-6400 Del Kearney 25/7/44; Grenier 8/8/44; ass 347BS/99BG Tortorella 17/8/44; [25m] c/t/o for Vienna 13/10/44 w/Wileman; #4 broke off ko'd #3 engine, c/l with bomb load; sal.

44-6401 Del Kearney 25/7/44; Grenier 7/8/44; ass 774BS/463BG Celone 13/8/44; retUS 1103 BU Morrison 27/9/45; RFC Walnut Ridge 14/12/45.

44-6402 Del Kearney 27/7/44; Grenier 8/8/44; ass 775BS/463BG Celone 16/8/44; retUS 1103 BU Morrison 22/9/45; RFC Walnut Ridge 5/1/46.

44-6403 Del Kearney 27/7/44; Grenier 8/8/44; ass 32BS/301BG Lucera 17/8/44; tran 340BS/97BG Amendola 18/8/44; retUS Hunter 17/6/45; Sth Plains 19/6/45; RFC Kingman 5/12/45.

44-6404 Del Kearney 25/7/44; Grenier 8/8/44; ass 775BS/463BG Celone 15/8/44; retUS Bradley 24/7/45; Independence 26/7/45; RFC Kingman 19/12/45.

44-6405 Del Kearney 27/7/44; Grenier 8/8/44; ass 840BS/483BG Sterparone 17/8/44; used for ASR at Pisa; retUS Sth Plains 23/6/45; RFC Walnut Ridge 28/12/45. BIG YANK.

44-6406 Del Kearney 27/7/44; Grenier 8/8/44; ass 772BS/463BG Celone 15/8/44; sal 23/11/44.

44-6407 Del Kearney 27/7/44; Grenier 8/8/44; ass 32BS/301BG Lucera 17/8/44; b/d Bleckhammer 14/3/45 w/Podasek; aban over Biala Podlaska, Pol; 10 RTD from Russia. MISS BELLA.

44-6408 Del Kearney 27/4/44; Grenier 8/8/44; ass 346BS/99BG Tortorella 16/8/44; MIA {12m} Maribor 7/11/44 w/Delp; flak, cr Marburg, 10 chutes seen; 4EVD, ret 8/1/45; MACR 9668. HAMMER HEAD.

44-6409 Del Kearney 27/7/44; Grenier 8/8/44; ass 340BS/97BG Amendola 22/8/44; tran 463BG Celone; retUS Hunter 25/6/45; Sth Plains 27/6/45; RFC Kingman 10/12/45.

44-6410 Del Hunter 27/7/44; Dow Fd 14/8/44; ass 774BS/463BG Celone 26/8/44; retUS 593 BU Charleston 11/1/45; RFC Walnut Ridge 4/1/46.

44-6411 Del Hunter 31/7/44; Dow Fd 14/8/44; ass 20BS/2BG Amendola 27/8/44; retUS Bradley 3/7/45; Sth Plains 6/7/45; RFC Kingman 8/12/45.

44-6412 Del Hunter 28/7/44; Dow Fd 7/8/44; ass 817BS/483BG Sterparone 13/8/44; MIA Bleckhammer 13/9/44 w/Robson; b/d by bomb beneath formation; 5POW 5EVD, ret 23/3/45; MACR 8620.

44-6413 Del Hunter 27/7/44; Dow Fd 8/8/44; ass 348BS/99BG Tortorella 14/8/44; b/d {46m} Vienna 21/2/45 w/Hartnett; flak hit in bomb bay where two crewmen dislodged bombs; 1WIA; sal 22/2/45.

44-6414 Del Hunter 31/7/44; Dow Fd 14/8/44; ass 96BS/2BG Amendola 25/8/44; {51m} RetUS Bradley 30/6/45; Sth Plains 3/7/45; RFC Kingman 28/11/45.

44-6415 Del Hunter 28/7/44; Dow Fd 9/8/44; ass 97BG Amendola 18/8/44; retUS Bradley 10/7/45; Independence 12/7/45; RFC Kingman 10/12/45.

44-6416 Del Hunter 31/7/44; Dow Fd 9/8/44; ass 49BS/2BG Amendola 15/8/44; two engines out, emergency landing Iesi Fd w/Marsh; tire came off and a/c crashed into ditch; sal.

44-6417 Del Hunter 28/7/44; Grenier 14/8/44; ass 774BS/463BG Celone 29/8/44; MIA Lechfeld 12/9/44 w/Milner; flak, cr Munich; MACR 8360.

44-6418 Del Hunter 31/7/44; Dow Fd 10/8/44; ass 775BS/463BG Celone 19/8/44; MIA Fortezza 20/4/45 w/Turner; flak, cr Merano; 1KIA; MACR 14020. MARY LOU II.

44-6419 Del Hunter 28/7/44; Dow Fd 7/8/44; ass 772BS/463BG Celone 16/8/44; MIA Bleckhammer 17/10/44 w/McCoy; no gas, cr Ornis; MACR 9210.

44-6420 Del Kearney 31/7/44; Grenier 9/8/44; ass 346BS/99BG Tortorella 21/8/44; {53m} to Rome depot 15/4/45; retUS Bradley 24/7/45; Independence 4/8/45; RFC Kingman 18/12/45.

44-6421 Del Kearney 1/8/44; Grenier 9/8/44; ass 773BS/463BG Celone 16/8/44; MIA Vienna 20/3/45 w/Ark; flak, cr Vienna; 4KIA 6POW; MACR 13052.

44-6422 Del Kearney 1/8/44; Dow Fd 10/8/44; ass 816BS/483BG Sterparone 19/8/44; MIA Vienna 20/3/45 w/Kessler; flak, cr Somboy; 11EVD, ret; MACR 13048.

44-6423 Del Kearney 3/8/44; Grenier 10/8/44; ass 840BS/483BG Sterparone 16/8/44; MIA Vienna 21/1/45 w/Grossman; severe flak damage; 10EVD, ret 30/3/45; MACR 11273.

44-6424 Del Kearney 3/8/44; Dow Fd 10/8/44; ass 97BG Amendola 18/8/44; b/d Berlin 24/3/45 w/?; ret but sal.

44-6425 Del Kearney 3/8/44; Grenier 9/8/44; ass 97BG Amendola 22/8/44; retUS Hunter 25/6/45; Sth Plains 25/6/45; RFC Kingman 6/12/45.

44-6426 Del Kearney 1/8/44; Grenier 14/8/44; ass 340BS/97BG Amendola 2/9/44; retUS Bradley 14/6/45; Sth Plains 25/6/45; RFC Kingman 7/12/45.

44-6427 Del Lincoln 31/7/44; Grenier 11/8/44; ass 341BS/97BG Amendola 26/8/44; retUS Hunter 16/6/45; Sth Plains 19/6/45; RFC Kingman 8/12/45.

44-6428 Del Lincoln 31/7/44; Dow Fd 17/8/44; ass 20BS/2BG Amendola 28/8/44; MIA Szony oil ref. 14/3/45 w/Reid; flak hit #2, a/c on fire; 4 chutes seen one ablaze; a/c exploded, cr Tata; MACR 12823.

44-6429 Del Lincoln 31/7/44; Grenier 21/8/44; ass 353BS/301BG Lucera 7/9/44; retUS Bradley 30/6/45; Sth Plains 3/7/45; RFC Kingman 28/11/45.

44-6430 Del Hunter 3/8/44; Grenier 14/8/44; ass 347BS/99BG Tortorella 26/8/44; MIA {15m} Maribor 7/11/44 w/Niketh; flak, cr Marburg; 7 chutes seen, 3EVD and ret; MACR 9666.

44-6431 Del Hunter 3/8/44; Dow Fd 15/8/44; ass 346BS/99BG Tortorella 11/9/44; MIA {51m} Linz 25/4/45 w/Schwarz; flak hit #2 ct fire, cr Linz; 9 chutes seen; MACR 13988. OLD FOLKS.

44-6432 Del Hunter 5/8/44; Dow Fd 22/8/44; ass 816BS/483BG Sterparone 14/9/44; retUS Bradley 31/7/45; Independence 11/8/45; RFC Kingman 19/12/45. SKY WOLF.

44-6433 Del Hunter 3/8/44; Dow Fd 30/8/44; ass 817BS/483BG Sterparone 15/9/44; MIA Munich 22/11/44 w/Bartusch; mech fault, cr Sanskimost; 1KIA 5POW 3RTD; MACR 9950.

44-6434 Del Hunter 3/8/44; Dow Fd 16/8/44; ass 414BS/97BG Amendola 3/9/44; retUS Bradley 12/7/45; Independence 16/7/45; RFC Kingman 2/1/46.

44-6435 Del Hunter 4/8/44; Grenier 14/8/44; ass 346BS/99BG Tortorella 29/8/44; {75m} RetUS Bradley 14/6/45; Sth Plains 18/6/45; RFC Kingman 3/12/45.

44-6436 Del Hunter 4/8/44; Grenier 11/9/44; ass 414BS/97BG Amendola 3/10/44; MIA Bleckhammer 3/10/44 w/DeHaas; ditched Adriatic; 2KIA 8RTD.

44-6437 Del Hunter 5/8/44; Grenier 26/8/44; ass 817BS/483BG Sterparone 16/8/44; MIA Graz 9/3/45 w/Logan; 10EVD, ret 13/3/45.

44-6438 Del Hunter 4/8/44; Dow Fd 16/8/44; ass 483BG Sterparone 9/9/44; retUS Bradley 30/6/45; Sth Plains 5/7/45; RFC Kingman 29/11/45.

44-6439 Del Hunter 5/8/44; Dow Fd 14/8/44; ass 20BS/2BG Amendola 28/8/44; sal 2/8/45.

44-6440 Del Kearney 7/8/44; Grenier 15/8/44; ass 20BS/2BG Amendola 28/8/44; MIA Ruhrland 22/4/45 w/Williams; jet e/a, broke in half, cr Berlin; MACR 13249.

44-6441 Del Kearney 7/8/44; Grenier 15/8/44; ass 352BS/301BG Lucera 9/9/44; cr 20/4/45. MARY ROSE.

44-6442 Del Kearney 5/8/44; Grenier 24/8/44; 273 BU Lincoln 4/9/44; ass 340BS/97BG Amendola 15/9/44; MIA Kalmaki A/fd, Greece 21/1/45 w/Potkalitsky; ditched, 3WIA, rest OK.

44-6443 Del Kearney 7/8/44; Grenier 11/8/44; 273 BU Lincoln 13/8/44; ass 96BS/2BG Amendola 25/8/44; b/d {64m} Kolin 15/3/45 w/Collens; attacked by Me 262, f/l Lodz, Pol., ret; MACR 13000. RetUS Bradley 13/7/45; Independence 22/7/45; RFC Kingman 11/12/45.

44-6444 Del Hunter 7/8/44; Dow Fd 8/9/44; ass 97BG Amendola 17/9/44; sal 25/9/45.

44-6445 Del Hunter 10/8/44; Grenier 3/9/44; ass 419BS/301BG Lucera 17/9/45; MIA Vienna 16/3/45 w/Neidemire; flak, cr Karlobad; 1EVD (p) ret, 9POW; MACR 13055.

44-6446 Del Hunter 7/8/44; Grenier 19/8/44; ass 97BG Amendola 15/9/44; retUS Bradley 10/7/45; Independence 12/7/45; RFC Kingman 2/1/46.

44-6447 Del Kearney 8/8/44; Dow Fd 15/8/44; ass 486BG Sudbury 16/8/44; tran 20BS/2BG Amendola 28/8/44; sal 25/7/45.

44-6448 Del Hunter 8/8/44; Grenier 3/9/44; ass 96BS/2BG Amendola 25/8/44; {42m} RetUS Bradley 30/6/45; Sth Plains 2/7/45; RFC Kingman 14/12/45. HUBBA HUBBA "BIG NOSE".

44-6449 Del Kearney 8/8/44; Grenier 27/8/44; ass 419BS/301BG Lucera 9/9/44; retUS Bradley 10/7/45; Independence 23/7/45; RFC Kingman 6/12/45.

44-6450 Del Kearney 10/8/44; Grenier 2/9/44; ass 346BS/99BG Tortorella 2/10/44; {51m} RetUS Bradley 29/6/45, Sth Plains 3/7/45; RFC Kingman 28/11/45. BU BU DOC'S BUGS BUDDY.

44-6451 Del Kearney 10/8/44; Grenier 22/8/44; ass 419BS/301BG Lucera 17/9/44; retUS Bradley 12/7/45; Independence 13/7/45; RFC Kingman 6/12/45.

44-6452 Del Kearney 8/8/44; Grenier 15/8/44; ass 20BS/2BG Amendola 22/8/44; MIA Ruhrland 23/3/45 w/Ferkin; 2 engines out, bellied in Kety, Pol; crew OK; MACR 13276. BIG STUFF.

44-6453 Del Kearney 13/8/44; Grenier 18/8/44; ass 97BS Amendola 28/8/44; cr 29/12/44.

44-6454 Del Kearney 10/8/44; Grenier 20/8/44; ass 816BS/483BG Sterparone; MIA Vienna 21/1/45 w/Cunningham; flak, cr Gyor; 11EVD (inc photographer) & ret; MACR 11387.

44-6455 Del Kearney 10/8/44; Grenier 18/8/44; ass 429BS/2BG Amendola 28/8/44; retUS Bradley 3/7/45; Sth Plains 7/7/45; RFC Kingman 26/11/45.

44-6456 Del Kearney 10/8/44; Grenier 15/8/44; ass 20BS/2BG Amendola 28/8/44; b/d Bleckhammer 2/12/44 w/Hickey; flak hit #4; c/l Russian lines where equipment was dest; sal; 10RTD. THE GREAT SPECKLED BIRD.

44-6457 Del Kearney 10/8/44; Grenier 15/8/44; ass 97BG Amendola 28/8/44; retUS Hunter 24/6/45; Sth Plains 27/6/45; RFC Kingman 28/11/45.

44-6458 Del Kearney 10/8/44; Grenier 1/9/44; ass 326BS/92BG [NV-S] Podington 7/9/44; sal 9AF Germany 10/12/45.

44-6459 Del Kearney 10/8/44; Grenier 23/8/44; ass 525BS/379BG [FR-G] Kimbolton 30/8/44; dam in collision w/truck when landing 24/3/45, rep & ret 3/5/45; retUS Bradley 30/6/45; Sth Plains 3/7/45; RFC Kingman 29/11/45.

44-6460 Del Kearney 11/8/44; Grenier 20/8/44; ass 447BG Rattlesden 26/8/44; mid air coll w/43-38245 on assembly for Kassel 2/10/44; cr Treacles Farm, Kettlebaston, UK; sal.

44-6461 Del Kearney 10/8/44; Grenier 16/8/44; ass 326BS/92BG [JW-G] Podington 27/8/44; MIA Berlin 26/2/45 w/Mason; mech fault, cr Hoejrup, Ger?; 2EVD 7POW; MACR 12771. SWEET CHICK WITH A HOT LICK.

44-6462 Del Kearney 11/8/44; Grenier 22/8/44; ass 710BS/447BG Rattlesden 27/8/44; 709BS; retUS Bradley 7/7/45; Sth Plains 9/7/45; RFC Kingman 3/12/45. SANDUSKY JO-ANN.

44-6463 Del Kearney 11/8/44; Grenier 22/8/44; ass 839BS/487BG Lavenham 5/10/44; MIA Merseburg 28/9/44 w/Lamason; flak, cr Neustadt; 10POW; MACR 9421.

44-6464 Del Kearney 15/8/44; Grenier 6/9/44; ass 614BS/401BG [IW-H] Deenethorpe 23/9/44; on take off for Ulm w/?, caught fire, c/l RAF Bitteswell 4/3/45; sal 5/3/45. PROP WASH.

44-6465 Del Kearney 12/8/44; Grenier 21/8/44; Presque Is 1/9/44; ass 7BS/34BG Mendlesham 23/8/44; retUS Bradley 24/7/45; Sth Plains 27/6/45; RFC Kingman 10/12/45. FANCY NANCY.

44-6466 Del Kearney 12/8/44; Grenier 2/9/44; ass 368BS/306BG Thurleigh 18/9/44; c/l 28/3/45; sal 29/3/45.

44-6467 Del Lincoln 11/8/44; Albuquerque 15/8/44; Grenier 3/9/44; ass 863BS/493BG Debach 4/9/44; retUS Bradley 3/7/45; Sth Plains 7/7/45; RFC Kingman 20/12/45.

44-6468 Del Lincoln 17/8/44; Grenier 2/9/44; ass 838BS/487BG [2C-R] Lavenham 27/9/44; retUS Bradley 12/7/45; Independence 13/7/45; RFC Kingman 4/1/46.

44-6469 Del Lincoln 14/8/44; Grenier 10/9/44; ass 748BS/457BG Glatton 29/9/44; MIA Politz 7/10/44 w/Moland; flak, cr Stettin; 9POW; MACR 9766.

44-6470 Del Kearney 12/8/44; Grenier 22/8/44; ass 349BS/100BG Thorpe Abbotts 23/8/44; MIA Zeitz 31/3/45 w/Larsen; flak, cr Altenburg; 8KIA 1POW; MACR 13714.

44-6471 Del Hunter 14/8/44; Dow Fd 3/9/44; ass 326BS/92BG [JW-M] Podington 24/9/44; sal 9AF Germany 10/12/45. ELMER'S TUNE.

44-6472 Del Kearney 15/8/44; Presque Is 4/9/44; ass 563BS/388BG Knettishall 8/9/44; MIA Merseburg 25/11/44 w/Wilson; flak, cr Arenrath, Ger; 6KIA 3POW; sal 24/3/45. MACR 11206.

44-6473 Del Kearney 17/8/44; Grenier 7/9/44; ass 326BS/92BG [JW-K] Podington 26/9/44; b/d Politz 7/10/44 w/?; f/l Continent, sal 14/11/44.

44-6474 Del Kearney 16/8/44; Grenier 4/9/44; ass 305BG Chelveston 27/9/44; 401BG Deenethorpe 28/9/44; retUS Bradley 7/6/45; Sth Plains 10/6/45; RFC Kingman 1/12/45.

44-6475 Del Kearney 15/8/44; Dow Fd 4/9/44; ass 336BS/95BG [ET-T] Horham 8/9/44; 335BS [OE-T]; retUS Bradley 20/6/45; Sth Plains 23/6/45; RFC Kingman 26/11/45.

44-6476 Del Kearney 17/8/44; Dow Fd 3/9/44; ass 546BS/384BG [BK-G] Grafton Underwood 23/9/44; 544BS [SU-L]; sal 9AF Germany 2/1/46.

44-6477 Del Kearney 17/8/44; Dow Fd 3/9/44; ass 862BS/493BG Debach 8/9/44; tran 486BG Sudbury, used to return POWs fron Linz, Aus; retUS Bradley 8/7/45; Sth Plains 11/7/45; RFC Kingman 22/11/45.

44-6478 Del Kearney 16/8/44; Grenier 3/9/44; ass 533BS/381BG [VP-W] Ridgewell 29/9/44; MIA {43+m} Vechtal 24/3/45 w/Jankowiak; flak, cr Greven; 4KIA 5POW; MACR 13606.

44-6479 Del Hunter 17/8/44; Grenier 3/9/44; ass 327BS/92BG [UX-K] Podington 21/9/44; sal 9AF Germany 10/12/45.

44-6480 Del Hunter 15/8/44; Grenier 4/9/44; ass 568BS/390BG Framlingham 5/9/44; MIA Derben 14/1/45 w/Thumlert; e/a, cr Ketzin, Ger; 7KIA 2POW; MACR 11826.

44-6481 Del Hunter 17/8/44; Dow Fd 3/9/44; ass 8AF 11/9/44; sal n/b/d 20/12/44.

44-6482 Del Hunter 18/8/44; Dow Fd 3/9/44; ass 336BS/95BG [ET-X] Horham 8/9/44; MIA Politz 7/10/44 w/Capt Waltman; flak, cr Willingsdorf; 5KIA 4POW; MACR 9559.

44-6483 Del Hunter 17/8/44; Grenier 4/9/44; ass 550BS/385BG Gt Ashfield 8/9/44; retUS Bradley 26/6/45; Sth Plains 28/6/45; RFC Kingman 5/11/45. RUBY'S RAIDERS.

44-6484 Del Hunter 18/8/44; Dow Fd 4/9/44; ass 568BS/390BG [BI-X] Framlingham 8/9/44 POWERFUL KATRINKA II; retUS Bradley 29/6/45; Sth Plains 3/7/45; RFC Kingman 23/11/45. DISORGANISED CONFUSION (LADY FAITHFUL).

44-6485 Del Hunter 19/8/44; Dow Fd 3/9/44; ass 401BG Deenethorpe 23/9/44; during acceptance check ground crew in bomb bay created spark which ignited oxygen and a/c caught fire; sal 25/9/44.

44-6486 Del Lincoln 18/8/44; Grenier 9/9/44; ass 342BS/97BG Amendola 28/9/44; MIA Salzburg 11/11/44 w/Bohonek; mid air coll w/44-6366, cr Treviso; MACR 9861.

44-6487 Del Lincoln 18/8/44; Grenier 6/9/44; ass 429BS/2BG Amendola 13/9/44; MIA Munich 22/11/44 w/Joyce; ditched and attacked by Me 109s and German patrols boats which were driven off by RAF Spitfires; a/c floated for 55 minutes before crew rescued by RAF Walrus.

44-6488 Del Lincoln 17/8/44; Grenier 18/9/44; ass 816BS/483BG Sterparone 21/9/44; retUS Bradley 30/7/45; Independence 3/8/45; RFC Kingman 30/12/45. THE LITTLE ONE.

44-6489 Del Lincoln 21/8/44; W/O 30/8/44.

44-6490 Del Lincoln 21/8/44; Grenier 13/9/44; ass 490BG Eye 17/9/44; tran 100BG Thorpe Abbotts 18/9/44; retUS Bradley 15/7/45; Independence 15/7/45; RFC Kingman 6/1/46.

44-6491 Del Lincoln 22/8/44; Grenier 8/9/44; ass 568BS/390BG [BI-T] Framlingham 17/9/44; MIA Hamm 26/11/44 w/Meyer; flak, cr Dortmund; 9POW; MACR 11209. I'LL BE AROUND.

44-6492 Del Lincoln 21/8/44; Grenier 9/9/44; ass 416BS/99BG Tortorella 2/10/44; retUS Hunter 18/6/45; Sth Plains 20/6/45; RFC Kingman 7/12/45.

44-6493 Del Lincoln 19/8/44, left US 29/8/44?

44-6494 Del Lincoln 23/8/44; Dow Fd 7/9/44; ass 97BG Amendola 28/9/44; retUS Bradley 5/7/45; Sth Plains 8/7/45; RFC Kingman 12/1/46.

44-6495 Del Lincoln 22/8/44; Grenier 18/9/44; ass 483BG Sterparone 4/10/44; retUS Cincinnati 30/10/45; RFC Walnut Ridge 4/1/46.

44-6496 Del Lincoln 22/8/44; Grenier 9/9/44; ass 860BS/493BG Debach 11/9/44; c/l 3/12/44; sal 6/12/44.

44-6497 Del Lincoln 21/8/44; Grenier 25/9/44; ass 840BS/483BG Sterparone 12/10/44; b/d Regensburg 28/12/44 w/Keen; nine baled, but pilot and engineer (Dobbie?) fly a/c to Ancona; retUS 1103 BU Morrison 19/10/45; RFC Walnut Ridge 4/1/46.

44-6498 Del Lincoln 22/8/44; Grenier 7/9/44; ass 349BS/100BG [XR-G] Thorpe Abbotts 11/9/44; sal 4/11/44.

44-6499 Del Lincoln 22/8/44; Grenier 18/9/44; ass 352BS/301BG Lucera 7/10/44; sal 5/5/45.

44-6500 Del Lincoln 25/8/44; Grenier 8/9/44; ass 350BS/100BG Thorpe Abbotts 11/9/44; MIA Berlin 3/2/45 w/Cotner; flak, cr Berlin; 9KIA; MACR 12045.

44-6501 Del Lincoln 25/8/44; Grenier 9/9/44; ass 429BS/2BG Amendola 13/9/44; b/d Brux 9/12/44 w/Pierce; flak, ditched but all crew rescued.

44-6502 Del Lincoln 23/8/44; Grenier 9/9/45; ass 359BS/303BG [BN-G] Molesworth 24/9/44; b/d Cologne 10/1/45 w/?; f/l Continent, sal.

44-6503 Del Lincoln 25/8/44; Grenier 18/9/44; ass 358BS/303BG [VK-P] Molesworth 17/10/44; MIA Merseburg 21/11/44 w/Glass; flak, cr Leipzig; 9POW; MACR 11197. LADY ALTA.

44-6504 Del Lincoln 24/8/44; Grenier 10/9/45; ass 360BS/303BG [PU-M] Molesworth 29/9/44; on assembly for Stuttgart, cr Braydon Crag, UK 16/12/44 w/?; all killed; sal 19/12/44.

44-6505 Del Lincoln 25/8/44; Grenier 10/9/45; ass 350BS/100BG [LN-V] Thorpe Abbotts 13/9/44; retUS Bradley 2/6/45; Sth Plains 7/6/45; RFC Kingman 8/11/45. SPIRIT OF PITWOOD.

44-6506 Del Lincoln 24/8/44; Grenier 10/9/44; ass 615BS/401BG [SC-N] Deenethorpe 12/9/44; retUS Bradley 4/6/45; Sth Plains 6/8/45; RFC Kingman 8/11/45.

44-6507 Del Lincoln 24/8/44; Grenier 9/9/44; ass 837BS/487BG Lavenham 13/9/44; tran 527BS/379BG [FO-K] Kimbolton 24/9/44; u/c coll on landing 3/5/45; sal 6/5/45. LUCKY PATCH.

44-6508 Del Lincoln 24/8/44; Grenier 9/9/44; ass 614BS/401BG [IW-A] Deenethorpe 23/9/44; 613BS [IN-A]; b/d Berlin 3/2/45 w/?; f/l Continent, rep & ret UK; retUS Bradley 6/6/45; Sth Plains 18/6/45; RFC Kingman 27/11/45. MAIDEN U.S.A.

44-6509 Del Lincoln 28/8/44; Grenier 15/9/44; ass 748BS/457BG Glatton 30/9/44; retUS Bradley 8/6/45; Sth Plains 13/6/45; RFC Kingman 25/11/45.

44-6510 Del Lincoln 24/8/44; Grenier 10/9/44; ass 8AF 22/9/44; retUS, RFC Walnut Ridge 3/1/46.

44-6511 Del Hunter 26/8/44; Grenier 6/9/44; ass 708BS/447BG Rattlesden 16/9/44; b/d Merseburg 2/11/44 w/?; f/l Volzel A/fd, Holl; sal 14/11/44.

44-6512 Del Lincoln 29/8/44; Grenier 9/9/44; ass 544BS/384BG [SU-K] Grafton Underwood 1/11/44; b/d Eschweiler 16/11/44 w/?; mid air coll, c/l Belgium; sal. MACR 10448.

44-6513 Del Lincoln 26/8/44; Grenier 11/9/44; ass 860BS/493BG Debach 13/9/44; MIA Munich 9/4/45 w/Silverman; flak, cr Munich; 10KIA; MACR 13908. BOISE BELL.

44-6514 Del Lincoln 25/8/44; Grenier 17/9/44; ass 547BS/384BG [SO-Q] Grafton Underwood 21/9/44; sal 9AF Germany 10/12/45.

44-6515 Del Lincoln 26/8/44; Grenier 11/9/44; ass 357BS/306BG Thurleigh 23/9/44; tran 29 TAC 381BG Ridgewell 14/5/45; 398BG Nuthampstead 27/5/45; retUS Bradley 7/6/45; Sth Plains 12/6/45; RFC Kingman 1/12/45.

44-6516 Del Lincoln 26/8/44; Grenier 18/9/44; ass 360BS/303BG [PU-Q] Molesworth 22/9/44; retUS Bradley 7/6/45; Sth Plains 9/6/45; RFC Kingman 8/12/45. MY DARLING.

44-6517 Del Lincoln 28/8/44; Grenier 18/9/44; ass 360BS/303BG [PU-F] Molesworth 3/10/44; retUS Bradley 7/8/45; Sth Plains 13/6/45; RFC Kingman 28/11/45.

44-6518 Del Lincoln 29/8/44; Grenier 17/9/44; ass 749BS/457BG Glatton 17/10/44; sal 13/5/45.

44-6519 Del Lincoln 29/8/44; Grenier 18/9/44; ass 602BS/398BG [K8-F] Nuthampstead 3/10/44; MIA Münster 28/10/44 w/Connelly; flak, cr Altena, Ger; 8KIA 1POW; MACR 10175.

44-6520 Del Hunter 28/9/44; Grenier 12/9/44; ass 351BS/100BG Thorpe Abbotts 13/9/44; MIA Ludwigshafen 5/11/44 w/Hopkins; e/a, cr Cochem, Ger; 9POW; MACR 10357. TANGERINE II.

44-6521 Del Hunter 30/8/44; Grenier 15/9/44; ass 8AF 20/9/44; retUS Bradley 24/6/45; Sth Plains 27/6/45; RFC Kingman 28/11/45.

44-6522 Del Hunter 29/8/44; Grenier 15/9/44; ass 412BS/95BG [QW-H] Horham 17/9/44 HARD LUCK; (also named DIRTY DUCHESS, SNAFU, SWEET JOE); retUS Bradley 24/6/45; Sth Plains 28/6/45; RFC Kingman 9/11/45. IT FLIES.

44-6523 Del Hunter 28/8/44; Grenier 6/9/44; ass 360BS/303BG [PU-A] Molesworth 29/9/44; tran 351BG Polebrook 5/45; retUS Bradley 13/6/45; Sth Plains 15/6/45; RFC Kingman 3/12/45.

44-6524 Del Hunter 28/8/44; Grenier 15/9/44; ass 562BS/388BG Knettishall 20/9/44; retUS Bradley 29/6/45; Sth Plains 2/7/45; RFC Kingman 22/11/45.

44-6525 Del Hunter 30/8/44; Grenier 12/9/44; ass 527BS/379BG [FO-T] Kimbolton 13/9/44; tran 305BG Chelveston 27/9/44; tran 384BG Grafton Underwood 9/5/45; sal 9AF Germany 10/12/45.

44-6526 Del Hunter 30/8/44; Dow Fd 20/9/44; ass 333BS/94BG [TS-G] Rougham 25/9/44 LEAVE US FACE IT; 410BS [GL-S]; retUS Bradley 28/6/45; Sth Plains 30/6/45; RFC Kingman 11/12/45. OUR QUEEN MARTHA.

44-6527 Del Hunter 30/8/44; Grenier 15/9/44; ass 305BG Chelveston 16/9/44; tran 548BS/385BG Gt Ashfield 17/9/44; MIA Neuburg, Ger 9/4/45 w/Williams; flak, cr Neuburg; 9POW; MACR 13872.

44-6528 Del Lincoln 1/9/44; Grenier 18/9/44; ass 334BS/95BG [BG-P] Horham 25/9/44; MIA Hamburg 31/12/44 w/O'Reilly; e/a, cr Weertzlen, Hol?; 4KIA 5POW; MACR 11369. QUEEN MARY.

44-6529 Del Hunter 1/9/44; Dow Fd 17/9/44; ass 32BS/301BG Lucera 4/10/44; b/d Vienna 11/12/44 w/Morris; f/l Debrecen, Hung; crew ret.

44-6530 Del Hunter 1/9/44; Dow Fd 17/9/44; ass 49BS/2BG Amendola 3/10/44; f/l Okecie, Pol.; retUS Bradley 10/7/45; Independence 12/7/45; RFC Kingman 13/12/45.

44-6531 Del Hunter 1/9/44; Grenier 13/9/44; ass 416BS/99BG Tortorella 22/9/44; {63m} sal 25/4/45.

44-6532 Del Hunter 1/9/44; Dow Fd 18/9/44; ass 20BS/2BG Amendola 27/9/44; MIA Bleckhammer 19/12/44 w/Johnson; flak, cr Bia Mare; crew ret 14/1/45. MACR 10638.

44-6533 Del Hunter 1/9/44; Dow Fd 18/9/44; ass 414BS/97BG Amendola 17/10/44; retUS Hunter 18/6/45; Sth Plains 30/6/45; RFC Kingman 5/12/45.

44-6534 Del Hunter 1/9/44; Dow Fd 18/9/44; ass 416BS/99BG Tortorella 10/10/44; MIA {39m} Ruhland 22/3/45 w/Tappen; flak, cr Cottbus; crew headed for Russian lines; MACR 13243.MISS EMILIA.

44-6535 Del Hunter 31/8/44; Grenier 21/9/44; ass 483BG Sterparone 11/10/44; retUS 1103 BU Morrison 19/10/45; RFC Walnut Ridge 5/1/46.

44-6536 Del Hunter 1/9/44; Dow Fd 18/9/44; ass 347BS/99BG Tortorella 2/10/44; taxi acc 19/12/44; {18m} sal.

44-6537 Del Hunter 4/9/44; Grenier 22/9/44; ass 483BG Sterparone 9/10/44; retUS Bradley 25/7/45; Independence 27/7/45; RFC Kingman 21/12/45.

44-6538 Del Hunter 2/9/44; Grenier 22/9/44; ass 817BS/483BG Sterparone 28/9/44; MIA Ruhland 22/4/45 w/Bates; jet e/a, cr Opole, Pol.; 5POW 5RTD; MACR 13242. MISS PRISSY.

44-6539 Del Hunter 4/9/44; Grenier 22/9/44; ass 97BG Amendola 3/10/44; sal 9AF Germany 10/5/46.

44-6540 Del Hunter 1/9/44; Dow Fd 18/9/44; ass 463BG Celone 4/10/44; retUS 1377 BU Grenier 18/10/45; 1128 BU Grenier 10/2/46; Recl Comp 3/4/46.

44-6541 Del Hunter 2/9/44; Dow Fd 18/9/44; ass 340BS/97BG Amendola 9/10/44; MIA Bleckhammer 14/10/44 w/Boxell; no gas, cr Livno; MACR 12536.

44-6542 Del Hunter 4/9/44; Grenier 22/9/44; ass 429BS/2BG Amendola 3/10/44; b/d Maribor 1/4/45 w/Cope; three engines out, landed Prakos, Yugo (crew ret in C-47); a/c rep and flew back to base; retUS Bradley 12/7/45; Independence 6/8/45; RFC Kingman 21/12/45.

44-6543 Del Hunter 2/9/44; Grenier 22/9/44; ass 97BG Amendola 24/10/44; retUS Cincinnati 16/10/45; RFC Walnut Ridge 29/12/45.

44-6544 Del Hunter 4/9/44; Grenier 22/9/44; ass 414BS/97BG Amendola 11/10/44; retUS Bradley 24/7/45; Independence 26/7/45; RFC Kingman 7/1/46. KWITURBITCHIN II.

44-6545 Del Hunter 6/9/44; Grenier 22/9/44; ass 429BS/2BG Amendola 3/10/44; retUS Hunter 1/7/45; Sth Plains 3/7/45; RFC Kingman 13/12/45.

44-6546 Del Hunter 4/9/44; Grenier 21/9/44; ass 20BS/2BG Amendola 3/10/44; tran 32BS/301BG Lucera 29/10/44; MIA Vienna 12/2/45 w/Barnes; flak, cr Tapolza; 2KIA 8POW; MACR 12366.

44-6547 Del Hunter 4/9/44; Grenier 22/9/44; ass 772BS/463BG Celone 28/9/44; MIA Bolzano 16/2/45 w/Jones; mid air coll w/44-6684, ditched Adriatic; MACR 12098.

44-6548 Del Hunter 6/9/44; Dow Fd 12/10/44; ass 49BS/2BG Amendola 24/10/44; retUS Bradley 9/7/45; Sth Plains 11/7/45; RFC Kingman 18/12/45.

44-6549 Del Hunter 4/9/44; Grenier 22/9/44; ass 353BS/301BG Lucera 17/10/44; MIA Vienna 19/11/44 w/Luster; mid air coll w/42-9710, ditched Adriatic; 6KIA 3EVD & ret; MACR 10098.

44-6550 Del Hunter 5/9/44; Grenier 21/9/44; ass 49BS/2BG Amendola 28/9/44; MIA Brux 25/12/44 w/Myers; flak KO'd two engines; c/l Russian lines where crew used parts from crashed 44-6029 (301BG) for repairs before flying back to base 16/1/45. RetUS Bradley 3/7/45; Sth Plains 6/7/45; RFC Kingman 24/11/45. MACR 10703.

44-6551 Del Hunter 6/9/44; Grenier 25/9/44; ass 419BS/301BG Lucera 13/10/44; MIA Vienna 7/2/45 w/Fischer; mech fault, cr Vienna; 11POW; MACR 12375.

44-6552 Del Hunter 5/9/44; Grenier 23/9/44; ass 816BS/483BG Sterparone 3/10/44; MIA Vienna 21/3/45 w/Venable; flak, cr Breslau; 5KIA 5POW: MACR 13049.

44-6553 Del Hunter 4/9/44; Grenier 22/9/44; ass 97BG Amendola 17/10/44; retUS Bradley 25/7/45; Independence 29/7/45; RFC Kingman 22/12/45.

44-6554 Del Hunter 7/9/44; Grenier 22/9/44; ass 347BS/99BG Tortorella 17/10/44; {59m} RetUS Bradley 30/6/45; Sth Plains 4/7/45; RFC Kingman 28/11/45.

44-6555 Del Hunter 6/9/44; Grenier 21/9/44; ass 772BS/463BG Celone 11/10/44; MIA Ruhland 15/3/45 w/Griffeth; flak, cr Gorlitz; MACR 12999.

44-6556 Del Hunter 8/9/44; Grenier 21/9/44; ass 301BG Lucera 17/10/44; to depot 19/10/44; retUS 1945; to Bolivia as CP-624, sal 23/2/63 at Reyes, Bol.

44-6557 Del Hunter 6/9/44; Grenier 21/9/44; ass 97BG Amendola 17/10/44; depot 12/11/44; retUS, RFC Walnut Ridge 2/1/46.

44-6558 Del Hunter 6/9/44; Grenier 20/9/44; ass 463BG Celone 11/10/44; retUS, RFC Walnut Ridge 21/12/45.

44-6559 Del Hunter 6/9/44; Grenier 21/9/44; ass 325BS/92BG [NV-B] Podington 7/10/44; sal 9AF Germany 10/5/46.

44-6560 Del Patterson 4/9/44; Grenier 22/9/44; ass 730BS/452BG Deopham Green 25/10/44 PAPPY'S PRICE; retUS Bradley 3/7/45; Sth Plains 6/7/45; RFC Kingman 9/12/45. PUDDIN'S PRIDE.

44-6561 Del Patterson 7/9/44; Grenier 9/9/44; ass 379BG Kimbolton 28/10/44; retUS Bradley 5/7/45; Sth Plains 19/7/45; RFC Kingman 21/11/45.

44-6562 Del Lincoln 9/9/44; Grenier 18/9/44; ass 550BS/385BG Gt Ashfield 20/9/44; c/l, sal 30/10/44.

44-6563 Del Patterson 9/9/44; Grenier 18/9/44; ass 367BS/306BG [GY-N] Thurleigh 29/9/44; tran 533BS/381BG Ridgewell 5/45; retUS Bradley 9/6/45; Sth Plains 19/6/45; RFC Kingman 1/12/45.

44-6564 Del Lincoln 9/9/44; Grenier 30/9/44; ass 422BS/305BG Chelveston 18/10/44; MIA Berlin 18/3/45 w/?; MACR 13145.

44-6565 Del Lincoln 8/9/44; Dow Fd 24/10/44; 1379 BU Dow Fd 26/10/44; ass 511BS/351BG [DS-Q] Polebrook 9/2/45; 510BS[TU-Q]; retUS Bradley 23/5/45; Sth Plains 26/5/45; {26m} RFC Kingman 6/12/45.

44-6566 Del Lincoln 8/9/44; Grenier 24/9/44; ass 509BS/351BG [RQ-F] Polebrook 11/10/44; {68m} RetUS Bradley 13/6/45; Sth Plains 17/6/45; RFC Kingman 2/12/45.

44-6567 Del Lincoln 8/9/44; Dow Fd 27/10/44; ass 8AF 2/11/44; sal 9AF Germany 10/5/46.

44-6568 Del Lincoln 8/9/44; Dow Fd 15/10/44; ass 324BS/91BG [DF-G] Bassingbourn 29/11/44; MIA {55m} Dresden 17/4/45 w/Camp; jet e/a blew off wing tip, cr Dresden; 8KIA 1POW (tg); MACR 14111. SKUNFACE III.

44-6569 Del Lincoln 8/9/44; Dow Fd 25/9/44; ass 8AF 10/11/44; retUS Bradley 26/6/45; Sth Plains 28/6/45; RFC Kingman 27/11/45.

44-6570 Del Lincoln 9/9/44; Grenier 26/9/44; ass 836BS/487BG [2G-P] Lavenham 15/10/44; ct fire on take off for Hannover w/?; cr Grove Fm, Pakefield, UK; 2KIA 8 baled; sal.

44-6571 Del Lincoln 12/9/44; Grenier 26/9/44; ass 711BS/447BG Rattlesden 28/9/44; MIA Merseburg 2/11/44 w/Moses; mid air coll, cr Rheine; 8KIA 1POW; MACR 10312.

44-6572 Del Lincoln 9/9/44; Grenier 19/9/44; ass 562BS/388BG Knettishall 20/9/44; retUS Bradley 5/7/45; Sth Plains 7/7/45; RFC Kingman 27/11/45.

44-6573 Del Lincoln 12/9/44; Dow Fd 11/10/44; ass 603BS/398BG [N7-N] Nuthampstead 19/10/44; MIA Chemnitz 2/3/45 w/Christensen; e/a, cr Karlovary, Cz; 8KIA 1POW; MACR 12853.

44-6574 Del Lincoln 12/9/44; Grenier 1/10/44; ass 562BS/388BG Knettishall 3/10/44; MIA Neuburg 9/4/45 w/Berwick; flak, cr Landsberg; 3KIA 6POW; MACR 13871. SOLID SENDER.

44-6575 Del Lincoln 12/9/44; Grenier 26/9/44; ass 8AF 30/9/44; retUS, RFC Walnut Ridge 4/1/46.

44-6576 Del Lincoln 12/9/44; Grenier 9/9/44; ass 8AF 13/10/44; retUS Bradley 27/6/45; Sth Plains 2/7/45; RFC Kingman 30/11/45.

44-6577 Del Lincoln 12/9/44; Grenier 26/9/44; ass 652BS/25BG Watton 5/10/44; retUS, RFC Walnut Ridge 8/1/46.

Above: B-17G-55-DL 44-6566, F for Freddie of the 509th Bomb Squadron, a formation lead aircraft with three Fs to ensure visual identity. (John Greenwood)

44-6578 Del Lincoln 12/9/44; Dow Fd 25/9/44; ass 731BS/452BG Deopham Green 28/9/44; tran 332BS/91BG [LG-D] Bassingbourn 7/12/44; {17m} sal 4/4/45, after taxi coll w/43-38306. RUSTY DUSTY.

44-6579 Del Lincoln 12/9/44; Dow Fd 25/9/44; ass 511BS/351BG [DS-J] Polebrook 11/10/44; 508BS [YB-X]; tran 401BG Deenethorpe 30/5/45; {56m} RetUS Bradley 4/6/45; Sth Plains 10/6/45; RFC Kingman 1/12/45.

44-6580 Del Lincoln 15/9/44; Dow Fd 2/10/44; ass 832BS/486BG Sudbury 14/10/44 FLAK SAK; 834BS [2S-P]; MIA Brandenburg 10/4/45 w/Dolan; flak, cr Zeisar, Ger; 4KIA 5POW; MACR 14188, DREAM KING.

44-6581 Del Lincoln 16/9/44; Grenier 1/10/44; ass 711BS/447BG Rattlesden 6/10/44; MIA Weimar 9/2/45 w/Kuntz; e/a, cr Lochmuhle, Ger?; 3KIA 7POW; MACR 12242.

44-6582 Del Lincoln 13/8/44; Grenier 26/7/44; ass 561BS/388BG Knettishall 28/9/44; MIA Mannheim 21/1/45 w/Lenocker; flak, cr Heimerdingen, Ger; 9POW. MACR 11827.

44-6583 Del Lincoln 16/9/44; Dow Fd 2/10/44; ass 336BS/95BG [ET-Y] Horham 13/10/44; b/d Nuremberg 20/2/45 w/?; c/l Florrennes, Bel; 9RTD; sal 28/2/45.

44-6584 Del Lincoln 16/9/44; Grenier 1/10/44; ass 327BS/92BG [UX-D] Podington 9/2/45; b/d Chemnitz 3/3/45 w/?; mid air coll w/43-38675, c/l Florennes, Bel; 9RTD; sal.

44-6585 Del Lincoln 16/9/44; Dow Fd 2/10/44; ass 423BS/306BG [RD-K] Thurleigh 13/10/44; tran 535BS/381BG Ridgewell 5/45; COMMANDO CHIEF.

44-6586 Del Lincoln 16/9/44; Dow Fd 2/10/44; ass 652BS/25BG Watton 13/10/44; retUS, RFC Walnut Ridge 2/1/46.

44-6587 Del Lincoln 16/9/44; Grenier 1/10/44; ass 8AF HQ Widewing 3/11/44; sal 3/4/45.

44-6588 Del Lincoln 17/9/44; Grenier 16/10/44; ass 612BS/401BG [IN-D] Deenethorpe 6/12/44; retUS Bradley 6/6/45; Sth Plains 10/6/45; RFC Kingman 2/12/45.

44-6589 Del Lincoln 17/9/44; Grenier 1/10/44; ass 338BS/96BG [BX-P] Snetterton 3/10/44; b/d Hohenbudberg 28/1/45 w/?; flak, cr Catchi, Ger?; 8KIA 1MIA; sal 6/2/45.

44-6590 Del Lincoln 16/9/44; Grenier 1/10/44; ass 544BS/384BG [SU-J] Grafton Underwood 19/1/45; cr into tree 19/3/45 w/?; sal 20/3/45.

44-6591 Del Lincoln 17/9/44; Grenier 7/10/44; ass 322BS/91BG [LG-U] Bassingbourn 4/11/44; {34m} RetUS Bradley 11/6/45; Sth Plains 13/6/45; RFC Kingman 17/12/45. INCENDIARY BLONDE.

44-6592 Del Lincoln 16/9/44; Grenier 2/10/44; ass 547BS/384BG [SO-S] Grafton Underwood 28/10/44; MIA Berlin 3/2/45 w/Ruckman; flak, f/l Berlin; 9POW; MACR 12154; sal 9AF Germany 10/12/45. STARDUST.

44-6593 Del Lincoln 16/9/44 Grenier 1/10/44; ass 365BS/305BG Chelveston 17/10/44; MIA Oranienburg 10/4/45 w/Keene; mid air cioll, cr Wilsnack, Ger; 7KIA 1POW; MACR 13876.

44-6594 Del Lincoln 18/9/44; Grenier 7/10/44; ass 8AF 13/10/44; retUS Bradley 10/7/45; Sth Plains 11/7/45; RFC Kingman 22/11/45.

44-6595 Del Lincoln 18/9/44; Grenier 1/10/44; ass 710BS/447BG Rattlesden 6/10/44; b/d Bad Kreuznach 2/1/45 w/?; f/l Continent, sal 3/1/45.

44-6596 Del Lincoln 19/9/44; Grenier 7/10/44; ass 322BS/91BG [LG-L/P/F] Bassingbourn 4/11/44; b/d Berlin 5/12/44 w/Roach; flak, but ret base; 3POW 6RTD; 2 Rubberneck & 2 POW trips; {46m} RetUS Bradley 15/6/45; Sth Plains 21/6/45; RFC Kingman 6/12/45. SWEET DISH.

44-6597 Del Lincoln 18/9/44; Grenier 11/10/44; ass 561BS/388BG Knettishall 12/10/44; retUS Bradley 28/6/45; Sth Plains 1/7/45; RFC Kingman 17/12/45. SUPERMOUSE.

44-6598 Del Lincoln 17/9/44; Dow Fd 6/10/44; ass 335BS/95BG [OE-N] Horham 11/10/44; retUS Bradley 24/6/45; Sth Plains 28/6/45; RFC Kingman 26/11/45.

44-6599 Del Lincoln 19/9/44; Grenier 11/10/44; ass 833BS/486BG [4N-R] Sudbury 13/10/44; MIA Arnsbach 22/2/45 w/Ringler; mech fault, cr Vesoul, Fr; 9EVD 1RTD; MACR 12661.

44-6600 Del Lincoln 19/9/44; Grenier 7/10/44; ass 359BS/303BG [BN-B] Molesworth 28/10/44; MIA Gelsenkirchen 21/11/44 w/Virag; flak, cr Sangerhausen; 9POW; MACR 11198.

44-6601 Del Lincoln 21/9/44; Grenier 7/10/44; ass 728BS/452BG Deopham Green 13/10/44; MIA Heilbronn 20/1/45 w/Belton; flak, cr Midwound, Hol; 1EVD 8KIA; MACR 11796.

44-6602 Del Lincoln 18/9/44; Grenier 1/10/44; ass 379BG Kimbolton 18/10/44; retUS Bradley 9/7/45; Sth Plains 13/7/45; RFC Kingman 26/11/45. SLEW FOOT SUE.

44-6603 Del Lincoln 21/9/44; Dow Fd 15/10/44; ass 306BG Thurleigh 19/10/44 JAYNEE; tran 751BS/457BG Glatton 23/2/45 PRETTY BABY; 547BS/384BG [SO-J] Grafton Underwood 9/5/45; tran 9AF 14/2/46; re-ass ATC 7/4/47; 746 BU Vienna 18/1/48; 746 BU (NATO) Kaufber 19/1/48; Recl Comp 14/4/49. JAYHAWK.

44-6604 Del Lincoln 21/9/44; Dow Fd 8/10/44; ass 367BS/306BG [GY-A] Thurleigh 7/12/44; tran 381BG Ridgewell 5/45; 91BG Bassingbourn 30/5/45; Bradley 10/7/45; Sth Plains 13/7/45; RFC Kingman 29/11/45.

44-6605 Del Lincoln 21/9/44; Grenier 6/10/44; ass 305BG Chelveston 19/10/44; retUS Bradley 7/6/45; Sth Plains 12/6/45; RFC Kingman 30/11/45.

44-6606 Del Lincoln 21/9/44; Grenier 12/10/44; ass 20BS/2BG Amendola 19/10/44; c/l Rumania 21/1/45 w/Notheis; crew ret with a/c; retUS Bradley 12/7/45; Independence 16/7/45; RFC Kingman 7/1/46. MACR 11542.

44-6607 Del Lincoln 22/9/44; Grenier 7/10/44; ass 8AF 13/10/44; retUS Bradley 3/7/45; Sth Plains 4/7/45; RFC Kingman 4/12/45.

44-6608 Del Lincoln 19/9/44; Grenier 7/10/44; ass 349BS/100BG [XR-A] Thorpe Abbotts 11/10/44; retUS Bradley 24/6/45; Sth Plains 27/6/45; RFC Kingman 28/11/45.

44-6609 Del Lincoln 22/9/44; Grenier 11/10/44; ass 487BG Lavenham 11/10/44; b/d Frankfurt 17/2/45 w/?; flak, cr? ; sal 5 SAD.

44-6610 Del Lincoln 25/9/44; Grenier 7/10/44; ass 510BS/351BG [TU-B] Polebrook 7/12/44; {52m} RetUS Bradley 1/6/45; Sth Plains 6/6/45; RFC Kingman 17/12/45. MARTHA.

44-6611 Del Lincoln 22/9/44; Grenier 13/10/44; ass 561BS/388BG Knettishall 19/10/44; sal 19/5/45.

44-6612 Del Lincoln 21/9/44; Grenier 7/10/44; ass 337BS/96BG [AW-L] Snetterton 11/10/44; MIA Merseburg 25/11/44 w/Fischer; flak, cr Fladungen; 9POW; MACR 11196.

44-6613 Del Lincoln 22/9/44; Grenier 7/10/44; ass 100BG Thorpe Abbotts 11/10/44; b/d Nuremberg 20/2/45 w/?; sal 24/2/45.

44-6614 Del Lincoln 22/9/44; Grenier 11/10/44; ass 526BS/379BG [LF-D] Kimbolton 28/10/44; landing acc, nosed over 17/3/45; sal 18/3/45.

44-6615 Del Lincoln 22/9/44; Grenier 11/10/44; ass 324BS/91BG Bassingbourn 23/2/45; retUS Bradley 31/5/45; Sth Plains 4/6/45; RFC Kingman 17/12/45.

44-6616 Del Lincoln 22/9/44; Grenier 6/10/44; ass 833BS/486BG [4N-A]; 835BS [H8-B]; retUS Bradley 9/7/45; Sth Plains 11/7/45; RFC Kingman 13/12/45. SHORT ARM.

44-6617 Del Lincoln 25/9/44; Grenier 7/10/44; ass 332BS/94BG [XM-S] Rougham 11/10/44 SOUTHERN COMFORT; MIA Nuremberg 5/4/45 w/Dickerson; flak, cr Mainz; 9POW. AGONY WAGON.

44-6618 Del Lincoln 22/9/44; Grenier 11/10/44; ass 323BS/91BG [OR-U] Bassingbourn 4/11/44; retUS Bradley 31/5/45; Sth Plains 8/6/45; RFC Kingman 13/12/45.

44-6619 Del Lincoln 23/9/44; Grenier 7/10/44; ass 331BS/94BG [QE-S] Rougham 11/10/44 BIG GAS BIRD; MIA Kaiserlautern 23/12/44 w/Lander; e/a, cr Wolflingen, Ger?; 1KIA 6POW 2RTD; MACR 11346. DARLING DOT.

44-6620 Del Lincoln 25/9/44; Grenier 7/10/44; ass 20BS/2BG Amendola 16/10/44; retUS Bradley 10/7/45; Independence 13/7/45; RFC Kingman 13/12/45.

44-6621 Del Lincoln 25/9/44; Grenier 7/10/44; ass 349BS/100BG [XR-B] Thorpe Abbotts 11/10/44; tran 751BS/457BG Glatton 8/11/44; retUS Bradley 28/5/45; Sth Plains 7/6/45; RFC Kingman 8/12/45. TRIP'S TROUBLES.

44-6622 Del Lincoln 25/9/44; Grenier 7/10/44; ass 561BS/388BG Knettishall 11/10/44; retUS Bradley 28/6/45; Sth Plains 2/7/45; RFC Kingman 23/11/45. OUR LOVE.

44-6623 Del Lincoln 28/9/44; Grenier 7/10/44; ass 324BS/91BG [DF-B] Bassingbourn 24/10/44; retUS Bradley 31/5/45; Sth Plains 5/6/45; RFC Kingman

14/12/45.

44-6624 Del Lincoln 28/9/44; Grenier 11/10/44; ass 463BG Celone 17/10/44; retUS 1103 BU Morrison 3/10/45; RFC Walnut Ridge 12/12/45.

44-6625 Del Lincoln 27/9/44; Grenier 11/10/44; ass 534BS/381BG [GD-N] Ridgewell 4/11/44; {35+m} RetUS Bradley 9/6/45; Sth Plains 12/6/45; RFC Kingman 30/11/45. PEACEMAKER.

44-6626 Del Lincoln 25/9/44; Grenier 10/10/44; ass 563BS/388BG Knettishall 11/10/44; MIA Hamm 26/11/44 w/Daniels; flak & exploded, cr Eisleben; 4KIA 5POW; MACR 11207. THUNDERBIRD.

44-6627 Del Lincoln 28/9/44; Grenier 12/10/44; ass 96BS/2BG Amendola 19/10/44; engine trouble Bologna 16/4/45 w/Abbott; returned early, u/c collapsed; {45m} sal 16/4/45.

44-6628 Del Lincoln 28/9/44; Grenier 11/10/44; ass 96BS/2BG Amendola 21/10/44; {45m} RetUS Hunter 19/6/45; Sth Plains 21/6/45; RFC Kingman 13/12/45.

44-6629 Del Lincoln 27/9/44; Grenier 7/10/44; ass 560BS/388BG Knettishall 11/10/44; MIA Nuremberg 20/2/45 w/Ellis; flak, cr Nuremberg; 10POW; MACR 12551. KAREN W.

44-6630 Del Lincoln 3/10/44; Grenier 12/10/44; ass 97BG Amendola 3/11/44; MIA training op 6/11/44 w/Emerson; ditched Vis Island; cp KIA.

44-6631 Del Lincoln 30/9/44; Grenier 12/10/44; Fairfield 16/10/44; ass 773BS/463BG Celone 30/10/44; MIA Brux 25/12/44 w/Rains; flak, cr Bartelsdorf; MACR 10649.

44-6632 Del Lincoln 28/9/44; Grenier 12/10/44; ass 20BS/2BG Amendola 16/10/44; c/t/o Linz 3/12/44 w/Pilger (KIA) but crew safe; a/c sal.

44-6633 Del Lincoln 28/9/44; Grenier 11/10/44; ass 49BS/2BG Amendola 16/10; retUS Bradley 3/7/45; Sth Plains 6/7/45; RFC Kingman 17/12/45.

44-6634 Del Lincoln 28/9/44; Grenier 12/10/44; ass 97BG Amendola 3/11/44; c/l 16/2/45; sal.

44-6635 Del Lincoln 30/9/44; Grenier 15/10/44; ass 49BS/2BG Amendola 18/10/44; sal 30/11/45.

44-6636 Del Lincoln 30/9/44; Grenier 12/10/44; ass 347BS/99BG Tortorella 3/11/44; {46m} RetUS Morrison 5/10/45; RFC Walnut Ridge 4/1/46.

44-6637 Del Lincoln 30/9/44; Grenier 15/10/44; ass 49BS/2BG Amendola 18/10/44; retUS Bradley 13/7/45; Independence 18/7/45; RFC Kingman 21/12/45.

44-6638 Del Lincoln 2/10/44; Grenier 12/10/44; ass 49BS/2BG Amendola 16/10/44; retUS Bradley 12/7/45; Independence 14/7/45; RFC Kingman 18/12/45.

44-6639 Del Lincoln 30/9/44; Grenier 12/10/44; ass 96BS/2BG Amendola 26/10/44; tran 301BG Lucera 4/11/44; retUS Morrison 21/9/45; RFC Walnut Ridge 19/12/45.

44-6640 Del Lincoln 2/10/44; Dow Fd 13/10/44; ass 775BS/463BG Celone 24/10/44; MIA Berlin 24/3/45 w/Wilson; flak, cr Pilsen; MACR 13371. LAETITIA.

44-6641 Del Lincoln 2/10/44; Dow Fd 13/10/44; ass 817BS/483BG Sterparone 24/10/44; retUS 593 BU Charleston 28/10/45; RFC Walnut Ridge 28/10/45.

44-6642 Del Lincoln 2/10/44; Grenier 12/10/44; ass 49BS/2BG Amendola 30/10/44; MIA Ruhland 22/3/45 w/Forest; landed Russia and returned; retUS Bradley 14/7/45; Independence 17/7/45; RFC Kingman 21/12/45.

44-6643 Del Lincoln 2/10/44; Grenier 12/10/44; ass 96BS/2BG Amendola 20/10/44; {17m} cr mountains on practice mission w/Pinner; 4KIA out of five man crew, r/op survived.

44-6644 Del Lincoln 3/10/44; Grenier 13/10/44; ass 429BS/2BG Amendola 24/10/44; 483BG Sterparone 24/10/44; retUS Bradley 24/7/45; Independence 25/7/45; RFC Kingman 18/12/45.

44-6645 Del Lincoln 2/10/44; Dow Fd 13/10/44; ass 352BS/301BG Lucera 21/12/44; retUS Bradley 24/7/44; Independence 26/7/45; RFC Kingman 18/12/45.

44-6646 Del Lincoln 2/10/44; Grenier 15/10/44; ass 97BG Amendola 5/12/44; retUS Bradley 15/6/45; Sth Plains 19/6/45; RFC Kingman 1/12/45.

44-6647 Del Lincoln 3/10/44; Grenier 12/10/44; ass 340BS/97BG Amendola 3/12/44; MIA Augsburg 3/12/44 w/McGowan; flak, cr Augsburg; MACR 12667.

44-6648 Del Lincoln 4/10/44; Dow Fd 13/10/44; ass 97BG Amendola 5/12/44; retUS, RFC Walnut Ridge 14/12/45.

44-6649 Del Lincoln 4/10/44; Grenier 15/10/44; ass 97BG Amendola 6/12/44; retUS Morrison 28/9/45; RFC Walnut Ridge 13/12/45.

44-6650 Del Lincoln 5/10/44; Grenier 16/10/44; ass 20BS/2BG Amendola 24/10/44; retUS Bradley 15/6/45; Sth Plains 19/6/45; RFC Kingman 7/12/45.

44-6651 Del Lincoln 2/10/44; Grenier 19/10/44; ass 346BS/99BG Tortorella 20/12/44; {49m} RetUS Morrison 21/9/45; RFC Walnut Ridge 14/12/45.

44-6652 Del Lincoln 4/10/44; Grenier 10/10/44; ass 419BS/301BG Lucera 29/11/44; MIA Castelfranco Veneto 29/12/44 w/Pearson; flak, cr Brizen; 4KIA 6POW; MACR 10930.

44-6653 Del Lincoln 6/10/44; Grenier 16/10/44; ass 419BS/301BG Lucera 3/11/44; MIA Regensburg 13/2/45 w/Pilcher; flak, cr Vienna; 3KIA 7POW; MACR 12110.

44-6654 Del Hunter 4/10/44; Dow Fd 12/10/44; ass 20BS/2BG Amendola 30/10/44; retUS Morrison 7/10/45; RFC Walnut Ridge 18/1/46.

44-6655 Del Lincoln 3/10/44; Dow Fd 13/10/44; ass 96BS/2BG Amendola 30/10/44; {43m} RetUS Bradley 24/7/45; Independence 26/7/45; RFC Kingman 15/12/45.

44-6656 Del Hunter 7/10/44; Dow Fd 15/10/44; ass 96BS/2BG Amendola 30/10/44; {59m} nosed over at Naples after landing personnel 11/6/45 w/Dooley; no casualties.

44-6657 Del Hunter 6/10/44; Dow Fd 15/10/44; ass 429BS/2BG Amendola 19/11/44; retUS Morrison 18/9/45; RFC Walnut Ridge 19/12/45.

44-6658 Del Hunter 7/10/44; Dow Fd 15/10/44; ass 419BS/301BG Lucera 22/2/45; retUS Bradley 25/7/45; Independence 27/7/45; RFC Kingman 9/12/45.

44-6659 Del Hunter 5/10/44; Dow Fd 16/10/44; ass 429BS/2BG Amendola 30/10/44; MIA Vienna 14/2/45 w/Davis; flak, cr Boesing-Modra; MACR 12107. HELL'S ANGELS.

44-6660 Del Hunter 5/10/44; Dow Fd 15/10/44; ass 347BS/99BG Tortorella 13/12/44; to depot 18/12/44; {49m} RetUS Morrison 21/9/45; RFC Walnut Ridge 14/12/45.

44-6661 Del Hunter 5/10/44; Dow Fd 12/10/44; ass 347BS/99BG Tortorella 13/12/44; {17m} cr 19/2/45, sal.

44-6662 Del Hunter 6/10/44; Dow Fd 15/10/44; ass 347BS/99BG Tortorella 12/12/44; {54m} c/l base 22/6/45, sal.

44-6663 Del Hunter 7/10/44; Dow Fd 15/10/44; ass 46BS/99BG Tortorella 12/12/44; MIA {2m} Bleckhammer 26/12/44 w/Flake; flak & exploded, cr Marklowitz; 7 chutes seen; MACR 10939.

44-6664 Del Hunter 7/10/44; Dow Fd 15/10/44; ass 348BS/99BG Tortorella 12/12/44; {48m} RetUS Bradley 24/7/45; Independence 26/7/45; RFC Kingman 4/1/46.

44-6665 Del Hunter 9/10/44; Dow Fd 16/10/44; ass 348BS/99BG Tortorella 12/12/44; {52m} RetUS Bradley 26/7/45; Independence 3/8/45; RFC Kingman 20/12/45.

44-6666 Del Hunter 7/10/44; Dow Fd 16/10/44; ass 353BS/301BG Lucera 21/12/44; b/d Linz 26/4/45 w/?; sal.

44-6667 Del Lincoln 7/10/44; Grenier 16/10/44; ass 32BS/301BG Lucera 21/12/44; retUS Bradley 24/7/45; Independence 25/7/45; RFC Kingman 16/12/45.

44-6668 Del Lincoln 7/10/44; Grenier 16/10/44; ass 347BS/99BG Tortorella 20/12/44; {9m} caught fire 8/1/45, sal.

44-6669 Del Lincoln 7/10/44; Grenier 17/10/44; ass 347BS/99BG Tortorella 20/12/44; {36m} RetUS Morrison 19/10/45; RFC Walnut Ridge 2/1/46.

44-6670 Del Lincoln 7/10/44; Grenier 17/10/44; ass 416BS/99BG Tortorella 20/12/44; {45m} RetUS Morrison 18/9/45; RFC Walnut Ridge 19/12/45;

44-6671 Del Lincoln 9/10/44; Grenier 22/10/44; ass 20BS/2BG Amendola 6/11/44; MIA Ruhland 15/3/45 w/Stravers; fire on left wing, landed behind Russian lines; 1KIA (nav) 9RTD; MACR 12821. HOMESICK.

44-6672 Del Lincoln 11/10/44; Dow Fd 24/10/44; ass 419BS/301BG Lucera 22/2/45; retUS Bradley 24/7/45; Independence 26/7/45; RFC Kingman 25/12/45.

44-6673 Del Lincoln 10/10/44; Grenier 17/10/44; ass 416BS/99BG Tortorella 20/12/44; {53m} RetUS, RFC Walnut Ridge 18/12/45.

44-6674 Del Lincoln 11/10/44; Grenier 24/10/44; ass 96BS/2BG Amendola 6/11/44; MIA {12m} Ruhland 15/3/45 w/Good; landed Kielce, Pol; (classed as MIA because of inaccessability of field); crew safe.

44-6675 Del Lincoln 11/10/44; Grenier 22/10/44; ass 97BG Amendola 20/12/44; retUS Morrison 29/9/45; RFC Walnut Ridge 20/12/45.

44-6676 Del Lincoln 19/10/44; Dow Fd 26/10/44; ass 15AF 3/11/44; retUS Hunter 23/6/45; Sth Plains 25/6/45; RFC Kingman 17/12/45.

44-6677 Del Lincoln 17/10/44; Dow Fd 26/10/44; ass 96BS/2BG Amendola 11/11/44; {44m} RetUS Morrison 18/9/45; RFC Walnut Ridge 18/12/45.

44-6678 Del Lincoln 11/10/44; Dow Fd 26/10/44; ass 429BS/2BG Amendola 7/11/44; MIA Regensburg 5/2/45 w/Porter; no gas, cr Bludenz, Switz; MACR 12063.

44-6679 Del Lincoln 17/10/44; Dow Fd 26/10/44; ass 429BS/2BG Amendola 7/11/44; retUS Bradley 24/7/45; Independence 25/7/45; RFC Kingman 8/12/45.

44-6680 Del Lincoln 10/10/44; Grenier 18/10/44; ass 97BG Amendola 20/12/44; retUS Morrison 19/10/45; RFC Walnut Ridge 9/1/46.

44-6681 Del Lincoln 12/10/44; Grenier 22/10/44; ass 97BG Amendola 20/12/44; retUS Morrison 19/9/45; RFC Walnut Ridge 19/12/45.

44-6682 Del Lincoln 11/10/44; Grenier 22/10/44; ass 429BS/2BG Amendola 30/10/44; MIA {6m} Vienna 7/2/45 w/Gold; flak, two engines out, cr Papa; MACR 12086. LUCKY 7.

44-6683 Del Lincoln 11/10/44; Grenier 23/10/44; ass 483BG Sterparone 22/12/44; {41m} RetUS Morrison 31/3/45; RFC Walnmut Ridge 30/2/46. QUEENIE.

44-6684 Del Lincoln 12/10/44; Grenier 22/10/44; ass 414BS/97BG 772BS/463BG Celone 2/11/44; MIA Bolzano 16/2/45 w/Hatch; mid air coll w/44-6547, ditched Adriatic; MACR 12102. KWITURBITCHIN.

44-6685 Del Lincoln 14/10/44; Dow Fd 28/10/44; ass

352BS/301BG Lucera 1/1/45; retUS Bradley 25/7/45; Independence 27/7/45; RFC Kingman 14/12/45.

44-6686 Del Lincoln 14/10/44; Dow Fd 26/10/44; ass 774BS/463BG Celone 8/11/44; MIA Berlin 24/3/45 w/Giacopuzzi; flak, cr Pilsen; MACR 13208.

44-6687 Del Lincoln 14/10/44; Dow Fd 26/10/44; ass 20BS/2BG Amendola 8/11/44; retUS Bradley 4/8/45; Independence 8/8/45; RFC Kingman 14/12/45.

44-6688 Del Lincoln 16/10/44; Grenier 2/11/44; ass 429BS/2BG Amendola 3/11/44; sal 9AF Germany 11/7/46; retUS 19/11/46; Recl Comp 19/11/47.

44-6689 Del Lincoln 15/10/44; Dow Fd 26/10/44; ass 429BS/2BG Amendola 8/11/44; MIA Vienna 21/2/45 w/Bull; flak hit #4, cr Gyor; MACR 12099.

44-6690 Del Lincoln 14/10/44; Grenier 17/10/44; ass 772BS/463BG Celone 3/11/44; loaned to 2BG Amendola; retUS Morrison 28/9/45; RFC Walnut Ridge 13/12/45.

44-6691 Del Nashville 16/10/44; Dow Fd 27/12/44; ass 416BS/99BG Tortorella 11/1/45; MIA {7m} Graz 8/2/45 w/Reid; (top turret had radar gun sight) mid air coll w/42-32071, cr Mittelohming; 7KIA 3POW; MACR 12083.

44-6692 Del Nashville 14/10/44; Mobile 6/12/44; Hunter 19/2/45; Grenier 9/3/45; ass 2BG Amendola 17/3/45; retUS Morrison 7/10/45; RFC Walnut Ridge 9/1/46.

44-6693 Del Nashville 14/10/44; Hunter 6/11/44; Dow Fd 20/12/44; ass 20BS/2BG Amendola 18/1/45; retUS Morrison 16/9/45; RFC Walnut Ridge 14/12/45.

44-6694 Del Nashville 15/10/44; Hunter 8/12/44; Grenier 4/1/45; ass 416BS/99BG Tortorella 11/2/45; (top turret had radar gun sight); {35m} RetUS Bradley 15/7/45; Independence 17/7/45; RFC Kingman 21/12/45.

44-6695 Del Nashville 15/10/44; Hunter 2/12/44; Dow Fd 14/12/44; ass 347BS/99BG Tortorella 8/1/45; (top turret had radar gun sight); {28m} RetUS Hunter 18/6/45; Sth Plains 20/6/45; RFC Altus 21/11/45.

44-6696 Del Lincoln 15/10/44; Hunter 19/12/44; Grenier 20/1/45; ass 347BS/97BG Amendola 5/2/45; (top turret had radar gun sight) {28m} RetUS Bradley 18/8/45; Independence 20/8/45; RFC Kingman 20/12/45.

44-6697 Del Lincoln 20/10/44; Grenier 27/10/44; ass 429BS/2BG Amendola 8/11/44; MIA Ruhland 22/3/45 w/Pierik; flak, cr Ruhland; MACR 13245.

44-6698 Del Lincoln 18/10/44; Hunter 3/12/44; Grenier 14/12/44; ass 547BS/384BG [SO-H] Grafton Underwood 16/12/44; tran 346BS/99BG Tortorella 11/1/45; (top turret had radar gun sight); MIA {8m} Augsburg 27/2/45 w/Shields; flak, exploded; six chutes, seen, five burning; MACR 12512.

44-6699 Del Lincoln 18/10/44; Grenier 27/10/44; ass 346BS/99BG Tortorella 24/2/45; {30m} RetUS Bradley 19/8/45; 305 BU Biggs 30/4/46; 47 MSU Biggs 18/8/47; 4141 BU Pyote 14/9/47; Recl Comp 13/4/49.

44-6700 Del Lincoln 20/10/44; Dow Fd 29/10/44; ass 774BS/463BG Celone 8/11/44; retUS Morrison 23/10/45; RFC Walnut Ridge 21/1/46.

44-6701 Del Lincoln 19/10/44; Dow Fd 27/10/44; ass 346BS/99BG Tortorella 28/12/44; b/d Sopron, Hung 4/3/45 w/?; #3 & 4 out, landed Zara; {31m} RetUS Morrison 22/9/45; RFC Walnut Ridge 14/12/45.

44-6702 Del Lincoln 18/10/44; Dow Fd 26/10/44; ass 772BS/463BG Celone 8/11/44; MIA Berlin 24/3/45 w/Foster; flak, cr Pilsen; MACR 13271. UMBRIAGO.

44-6703 Del Lincoln 19/10/44; Grenier 27/10/44; ass 347BS/99BG Tortorella 24/2/45; {27m} sal 21/3/45.

44-6704 Del Lincoln 20/10/44; Grenier 4/11/44; ass 301BG Lucera 3/12/44; tran 348BS/99BG Tortorella 24/2/45; {24m} sal 9AF Germany 10/5/46.

44-6705 Del Lincoln 19/10/44; Dow Fd 26/10/44; ass 463BG Celone 16/11/44; b/d Szony, Hung 14/3/45 w/Gillos; sal 9AF Germany 23/9/46; Recl Comp 19/11/47.

44-6706 Del Lincoln 19/10/44; Dow Fd 29/10/44; ass 419BS/301BG Lucera 13/2/45; retUS, RFC Walnut Ridge 11/12/45.

44-6707 Del Lincoln 24/10/44; Grenier 28/10/44; W/O 2/11/44.

44-6708 Del Lincoln 21/10/44; Dow Fd 29/10/44; ass 772BS/463BG Celone 8/11/44; retUS Morrison 22/9/45; RFC Walnut Ridge 14/12/45.

44-6709 Del Hunter 23/10/44; Dow Fd 7/11/44; ass 483BG Sterparone 7/11/44; tran 97BG Amendola 15/3/45; loaned to 463BG Celone; retUS, RFC Walnut Ridge 4/1/46.

44-6710 Del Hunter 23/10/44; Dow Fd 1/11/44; ass 340BS/97BG Amendola 26/2/45; sal 9AF Germany 10/5/46.

44-6711 Del Hunter 24/10/44; Dow Fd 7/11/44; ass 301BG Lucera 16/3/45; retUS Morrison 29/9/45; RFC Walnut Ridge 8/10/45.

44-6712 Del Hunter 23/10/44; Dow Fd 30/10/44; ass 347BS/99BG Tortorella 28/12/44; b/d Maribor 1/4/44 w/Dodridge; {42m} RetUS Bradley 20/7/45; Love Fd 22/7/45; RFC Kingman 21/12/45.

44-6713 Del Hunter 20/10/44; Grenier 3/11/44; ass 97BG Amendola 26/2/45; sal 9AF Germany 23/5/46.

44-6714 Del Hunter 27/10/44; Grenier 5/11/44; ass 346BS/99BG Tortorella 8/11/44; {21m} sal 9AF Germany 10/5/46.

44-6715 Del Lincoln 23/10/44; Grenier 1/11/44; ass 97BG Amendola 12/11/44; sal 9AF Germany 23/5/46.

44-6716 Del Hunter 25/10/44; Grenier 2/11/44; ass 301BG Lucera 26/2/45; retUS Hunter 25/6/45; Sth Plains 27/6/45; RFC Kingman 27/11/45.

44-6717 Del Hunter 24/10/44; Grenier 5/11/44; ass 301BG Lucera 11/3/45; retUS Bradley 12/7/45; Independence 24/7/45; RFC Kingman 19/12/45.

44-6718 Del Hunter 23/10/44; Dow Fd 7/11/44; ass 20BS/2BG Amendola 4/12/44; MIA Berlin 24/3/45 w/Tappen; flak, cr Zossen; MACR 13374.

44-6719 Del Hunter 27/10/44; Dow Fd 12/11/44; ass 774BS/463BG Celone 3/12/44; retUS Morrison 4/12/45; RFC Walnut Ridge 5/1/46.

44-6720 Del Hunter 26/10/44; Grenier 6/11/44; ass 483BG Sterparone 5/12/44; sal 9AF Germany 10/5/46.

44-6721 Del Hunter 24/10/44; Dow Fd 7/11/44; ass 416BS/99BG Tortorella 17/3/45; {31m} sal 9AF Germany 10/5/46.

44-6722 Del Hunter 25/10/44; Dow Fd 7/11/44; ass 483BG Sterparone 8/12/44; retUS Morrison 19/9/45; RFC Walnut Ridge 5/1/46.

44-6723 Del Hunter 26/10/44; Grenier 6/11/44; ass 429BS/2BG Amendola 3/12/44; damaged in rough landing on return from gunnery range 31/3/45 w/Deadrick; sal.

44-6724 Del Hunter 24/10/44; Dow Fd 7/11/44; ass 97BG Amendola 6/3/45; sal 9AF Germany 10/5/46.

44-6725 Del Hunter 26/10/44; Grenier 5/11/44; ass 347BS/99BG Tortorella 7/3/45; {28m} tran 772BS/463BG Celone 5/45; {28m} sal 9AF Germany 23/5/46.

44-6726 Del Hunter 25/10/44; Grenier 6/11/44; ass 416BS/99BG Tortorella 3/12/44; {18m} tran 301BG Lucera 8/3/45; retUS Morrison 19/9/45; RFC Walnut Ridge 12/12/45.

44-6727 Del Hunter 27/10/44; Dow Fd 8/11/44; ass 463BG Celone 15/12/44; retUS Morrison 9/10/45; RFC Walnut Ridge 3/1/46.

44-6728 Del Hunter 25/10/44; Dow Fd 8/11/44; ass 483BG Sterparone 8/12/44; sal 9AF Germany 24/3/46.

44-6729 Del Lincoln 26/10/44; Grenier 15/12/44; ass 20BS/2BG Amendola 22/12/44; tran 99BG Tortorella 12/44; ret 2BG 14/1/45; {14m} RetUS, RFC Walnut Ridge 19/12/45.

44-6730 Del Lincoln 27/10/44; Grenier 7/11/44; ass 2BG Amendola 3/12/44; {0m} tran 97BG Amendola 8/3/45; sal 9AF Germany 10/5/46.

44-6731 Del Lincoln 28/10/44; Grenier 2/11/44; ass 773BS/463BG Celone 16/11/44; sal 9AF Germany 11/12/45.

44-6732 Del Hunter 10/11/44; Grenier 25/11/44; ass 483BG Sterparone 2/12/44; retUS Morrison 19/10/45; RFC Walnut Ridge 29/12/45. MARY WANNA.

44-6733 Del Lincoln 27/10/44; Dow Fd 2/11/44; ass 817BS/483BG Sterparone 14/11/44; MIA Campodazzo 8/4/45 w/Dexter; flak, cr Campodazzo; 10POW; MACR 13634.

44-6734 Del Lincoln 28/10/44; Dow Fd 2/11/44; ass 97BG Amendola 17/3/45; sal 9AF Germany 10/5/46.

44-6735 Del Lincoln 27/10/44; Dow Fd 2/11/44; ass 429BS/2BG Amendola 4/12/44; nosed over on arrival from Marrakesh 16/5/45 w/Dantonio; sal 18/5/45.

44-6736 Del Lincoln 30/10/44; Grenier 7/11/44; ass 772BS/463BG Celone 3/12/44; sal 9AF Germany 23/10/46; Recl Comp 19/11/47.

44-6737 Del Lincoln 28/10/44; Grenier 7/11/44; ass 32BS/301BG Lucera 18/11/44; MIA Vipiteno 20/4/45 w/Bowers; flak, cr Merano; MACR 14029.

44-6738 Del Lincoln 28/10/44; Grenier 7/11/44; ass 96BS/2BG Amendola 19/11/44; b/d Ruhland 22/3/45 w/?; landed behind Russian lines at Lodz, Pol; crew returned, a/c sal.

44-6739 Del Lincoln 28/10/44; Grenier 7/11/44; ass 775BS/463BG Celone 3/12/44; sal 9AF Germany 23/9/46; Recl Comp 19/11/47.

44-6740 Del Lincoln 30/10/44; Grenier 12/11/44; ass 815BS/483BG Sterparone 3/12/44; retUS Morrison 23/10/45; RFC Walnut Ridge 9/1/46.

44-6741 Del Lincoln 30/10/44; Grenier 7/11/44; ass 817BS/483BG Sterparone 3/12/44; MIA Ruhland 22/3/45 w/Skinner; jet e/a, cr Freiceburg; 2KIA 4POW 4RTD; MACR 13254. BEAT'S ME DOC.

44-6742 Del Lincoln 30/10/44; Grenier 12/11/44; ass 341BS/97BG Amendola 3/12/44; sal 9AF Germany 23/5/46.

44-6743 Del Lincoln 31/10/44; Grenier 26/11/44; ass 483BG Sterparone 14/12/44; retUS Morrison 2/11/45; RFC Walnut Ridge 12/12/45.

44-6744 Del Lincoln 3/11/44; Grenier 12/11/44; ass 2BG Amendola 3/12/44; retUS Morrison 3/11/45; RFC Walnut Ridge 3/1/46.

44-6745 Del Lincoln 30/10/44; Grenier 12/11/44; ass 815BS/483BG Sterparone 3/12/44; sal 9AF Germany 26/6/46. SWEET IRENE.

44-6746 Del Lincoln 1/11/44; Grenier 15/11/44; ass 301BG Lucera 14/3/45; retUS Morrison 18/9/45; RFC Walnut Ridge 19/12/45.

44-6747 Del Lincoln 1/11/44; Grenier 16/11/44; ass 483BG Sterparone 6/12/44; retUS, RFC Walnut Ridge 14/12/45.

44-6748 Del Lincoln 1/11/44; Grenier 13/11/44; ass 301BG Lucera 3/12/44; retUS Bradley 21/7/45; Independence 2/8/45; RFC Kingman 20/12/45. JUNE HAVER.

44-6749 Del Lincoln 2/11/44; Grenier 16/11/44; ass 463BG Celone 5/12/44; retUS, RFC Walnut Ridge 18/12/45.

44-6750 Del Lincoln 7/11/44; Dow Fd 26/11/44; ass 96BS/2BG Amendola 4/12/44; {20m} sal 9AF Germany 10/5/46.

44-6751 Del Lincoln 1/11/44; Grenier 3/12/44; ass 775BS/463BG Celone 15/12/44; on return from Pomigliano 26/5/45 w/Lowe; all three crew killed.

44-6752 Del Lincoln 1/11/44; Grenier 16/11/44; ass 772BS/463BG Celone 3/12/44; MIA Maribor 1/4/45 w/Adams; flak, cr Maribor; MACR 13378.

44-6753 Del Lincoln 2/11/44; Grenier 12/11/44; ass 772BS/463BG Celone 4/12/44; retUS Morrison 2/11/45; RFC Walnut Ridge 11/1/46.

44-6754 Del Lincoln 2/11/44; Dow Fd 12/11/44; ass 348BS/99BG Tortorella 5/12/44; {16m} sal 9AF Germany 23/5/46.

44-6755 Del Lincoln 3/11/44; Grenier 16/11/44; ass 2BG Amendola 3/12/44; retUS Morrison 29/9/45; RFC Walnut Ridge 14/12/45.

44-6756 Del Hunter 3/11/44; Grenier 14/11/44; ass 301BG Lucera 5/12/44; returning from Padua mission 12/4/45 w/?; hitting five C-47s on landing, burned out. CLANCY'S CREW.

44-6757 Del Hunter 4/11/44; Grenier 17/11/44; ass 342BS/2BG Amendola 3/12/44; MIA Vienna 16/3/45 w/Landa; mid air coll w/42-102939, ditched Adriatic; MACR 13051.

44-6758 Del Hunter 4/11/44; Grenier 14/11/44; ass 463BG Celone 3/12/44; retUS Morrison 19/10/45; RFC Walnut Ridge 4/1/46.

44-6759 Del Hunter 4/11/44; Grenier 14/11/44; ass 483BG Sterparone 7/12/44; sal 12/12/45.

44-6760 Del Hunter 2/11/44; Grenier 17/11/44; ass 346BS/99BG Tortorella 28/2/45; to depot 20/4/45; {24m} sal 9AF Germany 23/5/46. SWEET LORRAINE.

44-6761 Del Hunter 3/11/44; Grenier 17/11/44; ass 773BS/463BG Celone 7/12/44; MIA Berlin 24/3/45 w/Swan; jet e/a, cr Meissen; MACR 13274.

44-6762 Del Hunter 3/11/44; Grenier 12/11/44; ass 815BS/483BG Sterparone 3/12/44; sal 24/2/46. KANSAS CITY KITTY.

44-6763 Del Hunter 6/11/44; Dow Fd 15/11/44; ass 463BG Celone 3/12/44; retUS Morrison 19/10/45; RFC Walnut Ridge 20/12/45.

44-6764 Del Hunter 6/11/44; Grenier 22/11/44; ass 49BS/2BG Amendola 27/11/44; tran 483BG Sterparone; c/l 24/4/45, sal.

44-6765 Del Hunter 4/11/44; Grenier 14/11/44; ass 483BG Sterparone 7/12/44; cr in Alps 6//6/45 w/Mason; 16KIA plus 4WIA (crew + 10 pass); DOUGHBOY SPEED.

44-6766 Del Hunter 7/11/44; Grenier 23/11/44; ass 301BG Lucera 1/12/44; sal 26/3/46.

44-6767 Del Hunter 8/11/44; Grenier 17/11/44; ass 816BS/483BG Sterparone 7/12/44; retUS Morrison 22/10/45; RFC Walnut Ridge 4/1/46.

44-6768 Del Lincoln 7/11/44; Grenier 3/12/44; ass 463BG Celone 15/12/44; retUS Morrison 16/10/45; RFC Walnut Ridge 24/12/45.

44-6769 Del Lincoln 7/11/44; Grenier 3/12/44; ass 20BS/2BG Amendola 15/12/44; tran 483BG Sterparone 5/45; sal 9AF Germany 23/9/46; Recl Comp 19/11/47.

44-6770 Del Lincoln 6/11/44; Grenier 3/12/44; ass 774BS/463BG Celone 11/12/44; MIA Vienna 7/2/45 w/Rasmussen; flak, cr Keszthely; MACR 12492.

44-6771 Del Lincoln 6/11/44; Dow Fd 26/11/44; ass 347BS/99BG Tortorella 1/12/44; {15m} sal 9AF Germany 23/5/46.

44-6772 Del Lincoln 6/11/44; Dow Fd 23/11/44; ass 463BG Celone 4/1/45; retUS Morrison 19/10/45; RFC Walnut Ridge 3/1/46.

44-6773 Del Lincoln 6/11/44; Dow Fd 26/11/44; ass 463BG Celone 21/12/44; retUS, RFC Walnut Ridge 7/1/46.

44-6774 Del Lincoln 7/11/44; Grenier 15/12/44; ass 840BS/483BG Sterparone 22/12/44; retUS, RFC Walnut Ridge 9/1/46. COOKIE.

44-6775 Del Lincoln 6/11/44; Dow Fd 26/11/44; ass 2BG Amendola 6/12/44; retUS, RFC Walnut Ridge 14/12/45.

44-6776 Del Lincoln 7/11/44; Grenier 3/12/44; ass 817BS/483BG Sterparone 11/12/44; MIA Ruhland 22/3/45 w/Cobb; jet e/a, cr Cottbus; 1KIA (ettg) 9POW; MACR 13253.

44-6777 Del Hunter 10/11/44; Grenier 23/11/44; ass 97BG Amendola 11/12/44; c/l 25/5/45; sal.

44-6778 Del Hunter 10/11/44; Grenier 4/12/44; ass 96BS/2BG Amendola 1/1/45; {14m} sal 9AF Germany 23/5/46; Recl Comp 19/11/47.

44-6779 Del Hunter 10/11/44; Grenier 22/11/44; ass 463BG Celone 20/12/44; retUS Morrison 22/10/45; RFC Walnut Ridge 2/1/46.

44-6780 Del Hunter 8/11/44; Grenier 17/11/44; ass 773BS/463BG Celone 7/12/44; retUS, RFC Walnut Ridge 14/12/45.

44-6781 Del Hunter 9/11/44; Grenier 17/11/44; ass 97BG Amendola 7/12/44; sal 9AF Germany 23/5/46.

44-6782 Del Hunter 8/11/44; Grenier 22/11/44; ass 483BG Sterparone 11/12/44; retUS Charleston 28/10/45; RFC Walnut Ridge 21/1/46. THE TEXAN.

44-6783 Del Hunter 9/11/44; Grenier 22/11/44; ass 483BG Sterparone 8/12/44; retUS Morrison 4/10/45; RFC Walnut Ridge 12/12/45.

44-6784 Del Hunter 9/11/44; Grenier 17/11/44; ass 773BS/463BG Celone 23/12/44; retUS, RFC Walnut Ridge 8/1/46.

44-6785 Del Hunter 9/11/44; Grenier 22/11/44; ass 348BS/99BG Tortorella 30/11/44; {17m} sal 9AF Germany 23/5/46.

44-6786 Del Hunter 10/11/44; Grenier 19/11/44; ass 483BG Sterparone 7/12/44; retUS Morrison 18/9/45; RFC Walnut Ridge 17/12/45.

44-6787 Del Hunter 9/11/44; Grenier 19/11/44; ass 483BG Sterparone 7/12/44; retUS, RFC Walnut Ridge 17/12/45; later used as hack (VB-17G) for Gen Cannon.

44-6788 Del Hunter 10/11/44; Grenier 22/11/44; ass 429BS/2BG Amendola 11/12/44; sal 9AF Germany 23/5/46.

44-6789 Del Hunter 12/11/44; Grenier 26/11/44; ass 416BS/99BG Tortorella 11/1/45; {14m} sal 9AF

Below: B-17G-65-DL 44-6787 served with the 483rd Bomb Group in Italy and was later converted as a communications aircraft for General John Cannon—hence the name *Cannon Ball*. (Roger Besecker)

Germany 10/5/46.

44-6790 Del Hunter 11/11/44; Grenier 24/11/44; ass 96BS/2BG Amendola 4/12/44; {22m} sal 9AF Germany 23/5/46.

44-6791 Del Hunter 10/11/44; Dow Fd 24/11/44; ass 97BG Amendola 7/12/44; retUS Morrison 19/10/44; RFC Walnut Ridge 11/1/46.

44-6792 Del Hunter 11/11/44; Grenier 19/11/44; ass 2BG Amendola 7/12/44; retUS Morrison 29/10/45; RFC Walnut Ridge 21/1/46.

44-6793 Del Lincoln 14/11/44; Grenier 15/12/44; ass 816BS/483BG Sterparone 13/1/45; retUS Morrison 30/9/45; RFC Walnut 13/12/45.

44-6794 Del Lincoln 18/11/44; Grenier 15/12/44; ass 840BS/483BG Sterparone 13/1/45; MIA Ruhland 22/3/45 w/Bush; flak, cr Ruhland; MACR 13246. MY ROSE.

44-6795 Del Lincoln 15/11/44; Grenier 15/12/44; ass 49BS/2BG Amendola 31/12/44; cr 2/1/45 w/Abbey; sal.

44-6796 Del Lincoln 15/11/44; Grenier 15/12/44; ass 483BG Sterparone 20/12/44; re-ass AF 30/4/47; 43 HBS Erding 18/1/48; 7230 AB Gp Erding 18/7/48; 85 AB Erding 12/10/49; modified as VB-17G Erding 19/7/50.

44-6797 Del Lincoln 15/11/44; Dow Fd 15/12/44; ass 20BS/2BG Amendola 20/12/44; sal 9AF Germany 18/9/46; re-ass AF 30/4/47; Recl Comp 19/11/47.

44-6798 Del Lincoln 17/11/44; Dow Fd 15/12/44; ass 429BS/2BG Amendola 20/12/44; sal 9AF Germany 23/9/46; re-ass AF 30/4/47; Recl Comp 19/11/47.

44-6799 Del Lincoln 18/11/44; Grenier 15/12/44; ass 816BS/483BG Sterparone 22/12/44; MIA Linz 25/2/45 w/Kehr; flak, cr Hurm; 1KIA 9POW; MACR 12467.

44-6800 Del Lincoln 18/11/44; Dow Fd 17/12/44; ass 97BG Amendola 11/1/45; retUS Morrison 19/10/45; RFC Walnut Ridge 29/12/45.

44-6801 Del Hunter 14/11/44; Grenier 27/11/44; ass 412BS/95BG [QW-A] Horham 29/11/44; retUS Bradley 24/6/45; Sth Plains 26/6/45; RFC Kingman 9/12/45. UMBRIAGO.

44-6802 Del Hunter 16/11/44; Dow Fd 3/12/44; ass 509BS/351BG [RQ-X] Polebrook 17/12/44; 511BS [DS-X]; {17m} dec War Weary 18/5/45; tran 94 CBW 4/6/45; retUS Grenier 21/9/45; RFC Walnut Ridge 18/12/45. FEED 'EM.

44-6803 Del Hunter 16/11/44; Dow Fd 28/11/44; ass 562BS/388BG Knettishall 4/12/44; retUS, RFC Walnut Ridge 18/12/45.

44-6804 Del Hunter 15/11/44; Grenier 26/11/44; ass 306BG Thurleigh 3/1/45; b/d Ulm 4/3/45 w/?; f/l Continent; sal.

44-6805 Del Hunter 15/11/44; Dow Fd 28/11/44; ass 350BS/100BG Thorpe Abbotts 4/12/44; retUS Bradley 20/6/45; Sth Plains 25/6/45; RFC Kingman 7/12/45. FLAMIN' MAME.

44-6806 Del Hunter 17/11/44; Dow Fd 28/11/44; ass 8AF 12/12/44; retUS Bradley 3/7/45; Sth Plains 6/7/45; RFC Kingman 6/12/45.

44-6807 Del Hunter 17/11/44; Dow Fd 28/11/44; ass 423BS/306BG Thurleigh 11/12/44; b/d Siegen 7/3/45 w/?; f/l Continent; sal 14/3/45. DEAR MOM.

44-6808 Del Hunter 18/11/44; Grenier 24/11/44; ass 863BS/493BG Debach 29/11/44; retUS Bradley 6/7/45; Sth Plains 8/7/45; RFC Kingman 28/11/45.

44-6809 Del Hunter 17/11/44; Dow Fd 2/12/44; ass 535BS/381BG (MS-Y) Ridgewell 4/1/45; {45+m} RetUS Bradley 10/6/45; Sth Plains 12/6/45; RFC Kingman 27/11/45. PFC's LTD.

44-6810 Del Hunter 16/11/44; Grenier 2/12/44; ass 8AF 5/12/44; retUS Bradley 17/6/45; Sth Plains 21/6/45; RFC Kingman 14/12/45.

44-6811 Del Hunter 17/11/44; Grenier 3/12/44; ass 100BG Thorpe Abbotts 4/12/44; tran 482BG Alconbury 20/5/45; retUS Bradley 2/6/45; Sth Plains 6/6/45; RFC Kingman 17/12/45.

44-6812 Del Hunter 21/11/45; Grenier 1/12/44; ass 570BS/390BG [DI-O] Framlingham 3/12/44; retUS Bradley 2/7/45; Sth Plains 6/7/45; RFC Kingman 8/12/45.

44-6813 Del Hunter 18/11/44; Grenier 1/12/44; ass 305BG Chelveston 3/1/45; tran 384BG Grafton Underwood 9/5/45; sal 9AF Germany 29/12/45.

44-6814 Del Hunter 17/11/44; Grenier 1/12/44; ass 368BS/306BG [BO-G] Thurleigh 3/1/45; tran 533BS/381BG Ridgewell 5/45; retUS Bradley 23/6/45; Sth Plains 29/6/45; RFC Albuquerque 14/1/46. CHOO-Z-SUZY.

44-6815 Del Hunter 18/11/44; Dow Fd 25/11/44; ass 305BG Chelveston 3/1/45; b/d Chemnitz 3/3/45 w/?; f/l Continent, sal 5/3/45.

44-6816 Del Hunter 18/11/44; Dow Fd 28/11/44; ass 366BS/305BG [KY-B] Chelveston 1/12/44; tran 731BS/452BG Deopham Green 2/12/44; aborted Hamburg w/?, c/l Hilgay, UK 30/3/45; sal 24/4/45.

44-6817 Del Hunter 21/11/44; Grenier 6/12/44; ass 366BS/305BG [PU-F] Chelveston 12/12/44 OLD COCK; tran 418BS/100BG [LD-S] Thorpe Abbotts 13/12/44; taxi acc 19/4/45; sal 21/4/45.

44-6818 Del Hunter 20/11/44; Grenier 6/12/44; ass 493BG Debach 12/12/44; b/d Cottbus 15/2/45 w/?; f/l Continent, sal 12/3/45.

44-6819 Del Hunter 18/11/44; Grenier 1/12/44; ass 367BS/306BG [GY-Q] Thurleigh 3/1/45; 92BG Podington 9/5/45; sal 9AF Germany 25/7/46.

44-6820 Del Hunter 18/11/44; Dow Fd 24/12/44; ass 18BS/34BG Mendlesham 12/12/44; MIA Brandenburg 10/4/45 w/Roscher; flak, cr Brandenburg, Ger; 2EVD 7POW; MACR 14198. MISS PURTY.

44-6821 Del Lincoln 25/11/44; Dow Fd 15/12/44; ass 601BS/398BG [3O-Y] Nuthampstead 1/2/45; ATC 21/5/45; retUS Bradley 28/5/45; Sth Plains 31/5/45; RFC Kingman 28/11/45.

44-6822 Del Lincoln 21/11/44; Dow Fd 3/12/44; ass 413BS/96BG [MZ-N] Snetterton 12/12/44; tran 7BS/34BG Mendlesham 13/12/44; retUS Bradley 21/6/45; Sth Plains 22/6/45; RFC Kingman 30/11/45; BLIND DATE.

44-6823 Del Lincoln 20/11/44; Grenier 3/12/44; ass 8AF 7/12/44; retUS Bradley 6/7/45; Sth Plains 9/7/45; RFC Kingman 10/12/45.

44-6824 Del Lincoln 20/11/44; Dow Fd 18/12/44; ass 8AF 19/12/44; retUS Bradley 8/6/45; Sth Plains 13/6/45; RFC Kingman 30/11/45.

44-6825 Del Lincoln 22/11/44; Grenier 15/12/44; ass 8AF 19/12/44; retUS Bradley 8/6/45; Sth Plains 14/6/45; RFC Kingman 5/12/45.

44-6826 Del Lincoln 21/11/44; Grenier 6/12/44; ass 7BS/34BG Mendlesham 12/12/44; landing accident 4/2/45; sal 5/2/45.

44-6827 Del Hunter 23/11/44; Dow Fd 3/12/44; ass 730BS/452BG Deopham Green 12/12/44; retUS Bradley 28/6/45; Sth Plains 1/7/45; RFC Kingman 14/12/45; HI-BLOWER.

44-6828 Del Hunter 22/11/44; Grenier 4/12/44; ass 333BS/94BG [TS-T] Rougham 7/12/44; retUS Bradley 8/7/44; Sth Plains 10/7/45; RFC Kingman 29/12/45; JIMBO'S CIRCUS.

44-6829 Del Hunter 22/11/44; Grenier 13/12/44; ass 560BS/388BG Knettishall 15/12/44; sal 9AF Germany 23/5/46; KAREN W.

44-6830 Del Hunter 23/11/44; Grenier 13/12/44; ass 407BS/92BG [PY-H] Podington 4/3/45; b/d Berlin 18/3/45 w/?; f/l Poland; sal 26/3/45.

44-6831 Del Hunter 23/11/44; Grenier 6/12/44; ass 748BS/457BG Glatton 5/1/45; MIA Nordstern 16/32/45 w/Brazier; flak, cr Rauxel, Ger?; 6KIA 4POW; MACR 12437.

44-6832 Del Hunter 23/11/44; Grenier 16/12/44; ass 34BG Mendlesham 19/12/44; retUS Bradley 28/6/45; Sth Plains 2/7/45; RFC Kingman 23/11/45.

44-6833 Del Hunter 23/11/44; Grenier 2/12/44; ass 569BS/390BG [CC-T] Framlingham 7/12/44; retUS Bradley 3/7/45; Sth Plains 6/7/45; RFC Kingman 8/12/45.

44-6834 Del Hunter 23/11/44; Dow Fd 31/5/44; ass 603BS/398BG [N7-H] Nuthampstead 17/1/45; retUS Bradley 31/5/45; Sth Plains 3/6/45; RFC Kingman 18/12/45.

44-6835 Del Hunter 27/11/44; Grenier 5/12/44; ass 527BS/379BG [FO-A] Kimbolton 19/1/45; tran 839BS/487BG Lavenham 22/5/45; retUS Bradley 12/7/45; Independence 13/7/45; RFC Kingman 13/12/45. STARDUST.

44-6836 Del Hunter 23/11/44; Grenier 13/12/44; ass 332BS/94BG [XM-R] Rougham 15/12/44; b/d Dresden 17/4/45 w/?; c/l, sal.

44-6837 Del Hunter 25/11/44; Grenier 9/12/44; ass 390BG Framlingham 12/12/44; tran 418BS/100BG [LD-Z] Thorpe Abbotts 5/45; retUS, RFC Walnut Ridge 13/12/45.

44-6838 Del Hunter 27/11/44; Grenier 16/12/44; ass 335BS/95BG [OE-E] Horham 1/1/45; b/d Chemnitz 6/2/45 w/?; f/l Merville, rep; retUS Bradley 21/6/45; Sth Plains 23/6/45; RFC Kingman 19/12/45. CAL'S RASCALS.

44-6839 Del Hunter 24/11/44; Dow Fd 21/12/44; ass 8AF 3/1/45; retUS Bradley 9/7/45; Sth Plains 11/7/45; RFC Kingman 17/11/45.

44-6840 Del Hunter 25/11/44; Dow Fd 20/12/44; ass 18BS/34BG Mendlesham 23/12/44; retUS Bradley 21/6/45; Sth Plains 23/6/45; RFC Kingman 27/11/45. MARGE.

44-6841 Del Hunter 27/11/44; Grenier 7/12/44; ass 100BG Thorpe Abbotts 12/12/44; retUS Bradley 22/6/45; Sth Plains 24/6/45; RFC Kingman 20/12/45.

44-6842 Del Lincoln 25/11/44; Grenier 15/12/44; ass 613BS/401BG [IN-V] Deenethorpe 19/12/44; tran 384BG Grafton Underwood 10/5/45; sal 9AF Germany 31/5/46.

44-6843 Del Hunter 24/11/44; Dow Fd 15/12/44; ass 601BS/398BG [3O-P] Nuthampstead 17/1/45; b/d Dortmund 16/2/45 w/?; f/l Continent, sal.

44-6844 Del Lincoln 27/11/44; Dow Fd 15/12/44; ass 8AF 20/2/45; sal 9AF Germany 10/5/46.

44-6845 Del Lincoln 25/11/44; Dow Fd 15/12/44; ass 838BS/487BG [2G-J] Lavenham 5/2/45; retUS Bradley 12/7/45; Independence 13/7/45; RFC Kingman 13/12/45.

44-6846 Del Lincoln 27/11/44; Dow Fd 15/12/44; ass 8AF 17/12/44; retUS Bradley 8/7/45; Sth Plains 12/7/45; RFC Kingman 30/11/45.

44-6847 Del Lincoln 27/11/44; Dow Fd 17/12/44; ass 8AF 19/12/44; retUS Bradley 5/7/45; Sth Plains 6/7/45; RFC Kingman 25/11/45.

44-6848 Del Lincoln 28/11/44; Dow Fd 15/12/44; ass 398BG Nuthampstead 1/3/45; retUS Bradley 17/6/45; Sth Plains 21/6/45; RFC Kingman 18/12/45.

44-6849 Del Lincoln 27/11/44; Grenier 15/12/44; ass 341BS/97BG Amendola 11/1/45; MIA Linz 2/3/45 w/Gray; flak, cr Linz; MACR 12812.

44-6850 Del Lincoln 28/11/44; Grenier 15/12/44; ass 97BG Amendola 11/1/45; retUS Hunter 23/6/45; Sth Plains 25/6/45; RFC Kingman 17/12/45.

44-6851 Del Lincoln 1/12/44; Dow Fd 17/12/44; ass 347BS/99BG Tortorella 11/1/45; retUS Morrison 18/9/45; {43m} RFC Walnut Ridge 19/12/45.

44-6852 Del Lincoln 30/11/44; Dow Fd 15/12/44; ass 561BS/388BG Knettishall 17/12/44; tran 483BG Sterparone 20/2/45; retUS Morrison 18/9/45; RFC Walnut Ridge 19/12/45.

44-6853 Del Lincoln 30/11/44; Dow Fd 15/12/44; ass 97BG Amendola 11/1/45; retUS Bradley 12/7/45; Independence 20/7/45; RFC Kingman 20/12/45.

44-6854 Del Hunter 1/12/44; Grenier 9/12/44; ass 2BG Amendola 1/1/45; sal 9AF Germany 23/5/46.

44-6855 Del Hunter 1/12/44; Grenier 9/12/44; ass 97BG Amendola 11/1/45; sal 9AF Germany 23/5/46.

44-6856 Del Hunter 2/12/44; Grenier 13/12/44; ass 815BS/483BG Sterparone 20/12/44; sal 28/8/45. JACK OF HEARTS.

44-6857 Del Lincoln 2/12/44; Grenier 15/12/44; ass 429BS/2BG Amendola 18/12/44; retUS Bradley 10/7/45; Independence 13/7/45; RFC Kingman 19/12/45.

44-6858 Del Lincoln 1/12/44; Dow Fd 15/12/44; ass 97BG Amendola 26/3/45; retUS Morrison 9/10/45; RFC Walnut Ridge 8/1/46.

44-6859 Del Lincoln 2/12/44; Dow Fd 15/12/44; ass 483BG Sterparone 20/12/44; retUS Morrison 19/10/45; 593 BU Charleston 28/10/44; RFC Walnut Ridge 29/12/45.

44-6860 Del Lincoln 2/12/44; Grenier 15/12/44; ass 347BS/99BG Tortorella 11/1/45; {31m} sal 9AF Germany 10/5/46.

44-6861 Del Lincoln 4/12/44; Grenier 15/12/44; ass 840BS/483BG Sterparone 23/1/45; MIA Fortezza 20/4/45 w/Bissinger; flak between # 1 & 2, ditched Med; 1KIA 3POW 6RTD; MACR 13817.

44-6862 Del Lincoln 2/12/44; Dow Fd 14/12/44; ass 339BS/96BG [QJ-R] Snetterton 16/12/44; tran 2BG Amendola 20/12/44; retUS Morrison 8/10/45; RFC Walnut Ridge 14/1/46.

44-6863 Del Hunter 2/12/44; Grenier 16/12/44; ass 96BS/2BG Amendola 18/1/45; {36m} tran 483BG Sterparone 5/45; retUS 64 BU Andrews Fd 22/10/45; 4117 BU Robins 4/11/45; RFC Walnut Ridge 25/2/46.

44-6864 Del Hunter 7/12/44; Dow Fd 17/12/44; ass 2BG Amendola 23/12/44; Con FFC 30/9/46.

44-6865 Del Hunter 4/12/44; Grenier 15/12/44; ass 342BS/97BG Amendola 9/2/45; MIA Verona 6/4/45 w/Sabelman; ditched, 2KIA 8RTD.

44-6866 Del Lincoln 7/12/44; Dow Fd 22/12/44; ass 97BG Amendola 9/2/45; sal 9AF Germany 10/5/46.

44-6867 Del Lincoln 7/12/44; Dow Fd 22/12/44; ass 348BS/99BG Tortorella 4/1/45; {35m} RetUS Bradley 24/7/45; Independence 25/7/45; RFC Kingman 22/12/45.

44-6868 Del Lincoln 7/12/44; Dow Fd 27/12/44; ass 348BS/99BG Tortorella 9/2/45; {28m} RetUS Morrison 22/9/45; RFC Walnut Ridge 14/12/45.

44-6869 Del Lincoln 7/12/44; Dow Fd 22/12/44; ass 416BS/99BG Tortorella 9/2/45; {35m} RetUS Bradley 24/7/45; Independence 28/7/45; RFC Kingman 18/12/45.

44-6870 Del Hunter 7/12/44; Dow Fd 19/12/44; ass 416BS/99BG Tortorella 9/2/45; {34m} RetUS Morrison 2/10/45; RFC Walnut Ridge 2/1/46. JEANNIE.

44-6871 Del Hunter 7/12/44; Grenier 21/12/44; ass 353BS/301BG Lucera 10/2/45; cr 5/6/45.

44-6872 Del Hunter 7/12/44; Dow Fd 19/12/44; ass 419BS/301BG Lucera 9/2/45; retUS Bradley 24/7/45; Wright Fd 27/7/45; Cleveland 6/8/45; RFC Walnut Ridge 12/2/46.

44-6873 Del Lincoln 9/12/44; Dow Fd 22/12/44; ass 772BS/463BG Celone 23/1/45; b/d Linz 8/1/45 w/Johnson; burning engine drops off, a/c ditched, 9MIA; MACR 16474.

44-6874 Del Lincoln 9/12/44; Grenier 22/12/44; ass 463BG Celone 24/1/45; retUS Bradley 25/7/45; Independence 3/8/45; RFC Kingman 9/12/45.

44-6875 Del Lincoln 9/12/44; Dow Fd 22/12/44; ass 816BS/483BG Sterparone 28/12/44; sal 26/4/45.

44-6876 Del Lincoln 9/12/44; Dow Fd 3/1/45; ass 483BG Sterparone 7/2/45; retUS, RFC Walnut Ridge 3/1/46.

44-6877 Del Lincoln 9/12/44; Grenier 22/12/44; ass 840BS/483BG Sterparone 23/1/45; MIA Fortezza 20/4/45 w/Keen; flak, cr Maris Eland; 2KIA 8POW; MACR 13819.

44-6878 Del Hunter 9/12/44; Dow Fd 21/12/44; ass 463BG Celone 23/1/45; sal 11/8/45.

44-6879 Del Lincoln 9/12/44; Dow Fd 20/12/44; ass 483BG Sterparone 29/1/45; sal 10/5/45.

44-6880 Del Hunter 9/12/44; Dow Fd 20/12/44; ass 463BG Celone 23/1/45; retUS Morrison 28/9/45; RFC Walnut Ridge 14/12/45.

44-6881 Del Lincoln 9/12/44; Dow Fd 20/12/44; ass 463BG Celone 23/1/45; sal 9AF Germany 6/11/46.

44-6882 Del Hunter 28/12/44; Grenier 10/1/45; ass 546BS/384BG [BK-J] Grafton Underwood 31/1/45; sal 9AF Germany 29/12/45. BOOMERANG.

44-6883 Del Lincoln 9/12/44; Dow Fd 17/12/44; ass 535BS/381BG [MS-Q] Ridgewell 22/12/44; lost stabiliser in taxi acc 11/4/45 w/44-8826; {31+m} sal 9AF Germany 10/12/45. RAFAAF.

44-6884 Del Lincoln 9/12/44; Grenier 30/12/44; ass 401BS/91BG [LL-N] Bassingbourn 23/2/45; retUS Bradley 11/6/45; Sth Plains 14/6/45; RFC Kingman 6/12/45.

44-6885 Del Lincoln 9/12/44; Grenier 20/12/44; ass 600BS/398BG [K8-M] Nuthampstead 27/2/45; retUS Bradley 6/6/45; Sth Plains 9/6/45; RFC Kingman 10/12/45.

44-6886 Del Hunter 9/12/44; Grenier 23/12/44; ass 8AF 28/12/44; sal 9AF Germany 10/5/46.

44-6887 Del Hunter 9/12/44; Dow Fd 17/12/44; ass 391BS/34BG Mendlesham 21/12/44; retUS Bradley 20/6/45; Sth Plains 28/6/45; RFC Kingman 11/12/45.

44-6888 Del Hunter 9/12/44; Grenier 29/12/44; ass 337BS/96BG [AW-R] Snetterton 4/1/45; c/l 11/5/45; sal. SWEET CHARIOT.

44-6889 Del Lincoln 9/12/44; Dow Fd 17/12/44; ass 8AF 22/12/44; retUS Patterson 18/7/45; Independence 20/7/45; RFC Kingman 20/12/45.

44-6890 Del Lincoln 9/12/44; Grenier 22/12/44; ass 94BG Rougham 23/12/44; b/d Ruhland 7/3/45 w/?; c/l base and repaired with rear half of 42-97681; retUS Bradley 5/7/45; Sth Plains 7/7/45; RFC Kingman 10/12/45.

44-6891 Del Lincoln 11/12/44; Grenier 20/12/44; ass 8AF 24/12/44; retUS Bradley 6/7/45; Sth Plains 8/7/45; RFC Kingman 8/11/45.

44-6892 Del Lincoln 12/12/44; Grenier 20/12/44; ass 544BS/384BG [SU-D] Grafton Underwood 10/1/45; sal 9AF Germany 10/12/45.

44-6893 Del Lincoln 12/12/44; Grenier 20/12/44; ass 851BS/490BG Eye 7/1/45; retUS Bradley 12/7/45; Independence 18/7/45; RFC Kingman 21/12/45. LOOKY LOOKY.

44-6894 Del Lincoln 12/12/44; Grenier 20/12/44; ass 561BS/388BG Knettishall 24/12/44; retUS Bradley 3/7/45; Sth Plains 4/7/45; RFC Kingman 23/11/45.

44-6895 Del Hunter 13/12/44; Grenier 29/12/44; ass 325BS/92BG [NV-L] Podington 5/2/45; sal 9AF Germany 23/5/46.

44-6896 Del Hunter 12/12/44; Grenier 3/1/45; ass 600BS/398BG [N8-M] Nuthampstead 27/2/45; retUS Bradley 25/5/45; Sth Plains 29/5/45; RFC Kingman 8/12/45.

44-6897 Del Hunter 13/12/44; Grenier 30/12/44; ass 339BS/96BG Snetterton 4/1/45; MIA Frankfurt 9/3/45 w/Fechter; flak, cr Frankfurt; 9POW; MACR 12957.

44-6898 Del Lincoln 16/12/44; Grenier 22/12/44; ass 547BS/384BG [SO-H] Grafton Underwood 4/2/45; sal 9AF Germany 18/9/46; re-ass AF 30/4/47; Recl Comp 19/11/47.

44-6899 Del Lincoln 13/12/44; Grenier 20/12/44; ass 8AF 23/12/44; retUS Bradley 29/6/45; Sth Plains 1/7/45; RRFC Kingman 23/11/45.

44-6900 Del Lincoln 13/12/44; Grenier 20/12/44; ass 8AF 28/12/44; tran 1377 BU Grenier 28/12/44; 716 BU Westover 5/5/46; re-ass AF 30/4/47; 768 BU Narsars 1/1/48; 138 AC Narsars 1/6/48; AMC Olmstead 21/10/48; 1805 ACS Narsars 10/3/49; AMC Olmstead 16/3/49; 1932 ACS Goosebay 29/8/49; 2753 AST Pyote 30/3/50; AMC Hill Fd 13/4/50.

44-6901 Del Lincoln 13/12/44; Dow Fd 22/12/44; ass 571BS/390BG [FC-U] Framlingham 1/1/45; retUS Bradley 3/7/45; Sth Plains 7/7/45; RFC Kingman 23/11/45.

44-6902 Del Lincoln 13/12/44; Grenier 20/12/44; ass 335BS/95BG [OE-G] Horham 4/1/45; retUS Bradley 20/6/45; Sth Plains 23/6/45; RFC Kingman 15/12/45. MASON DIXON LINER.

44-6903 Del Lincoln 12/12/44; Dow Fd 22/12/44; ass 8AF 1/1/45; retUS Bradley 17/6/45; Sth Plains 21/6/45; RFC Kingman 10/12/45.

44-6904 Del Lincoln 13/12/44; Grenier 29/12/44; ass 749BS/457BG Glatton 6/2/45; retUS Bradley 4/6/45; Sth Plains 14/6/45; RFC Kingman 10/12/45. LADIES' DELIGHT.

44-6905 Del Hunter 15/12/44; Grenier 29/12/44; ass 452BG Deopham Green 4/1/45; retUS Bradley 29/6/45; Sth Plains 2/7/45; RFC Kingman 3/12/45. VIRGINIA.

44-6906 Del Hunter 14/12/44; Grenier 29/12/44; ass 570BS/390BG [DI-I] Framlingham 21/1/45; tran 525BS/379BG [FR-J] Kimbolton 20/2/45; retUS Bradley 28/6/45; Sth Plains 4/7/45; RFC Kingman 18/12/45. CONSTIPATED LADY.

44-6907 Del Hunter 14/12/44; Dow Fd 22/12/44; ass 509BS/351BG [RQ-P] Polebrook 1/1/45; {26m} RetUS Bradley 27/5/45; Sth Plains 30/5/45; RFC Kingman 24/11/45.

44-6908 Del Lincoln 16/12/44; Grenier 22/12/44; ass 306BG Thurleigh 4/2/45; tran 532BS/381BG Ridgewell 5/45; retUS Bradley 10/6/45; Sth Plains 12/6/45; RFC Kingman 1/12/45.

44-6909 Del Lincoln 16/12/44; Dow Fd 22/12/44; ass 731BS/452BG Deopham Green 7/1/45 ANNONY MISS; tran 546BS/384BG [BK-H] Grafton Underwood 4/2/45; sal 9AF Germany 29/12/45. ACHTUNG ADOLPH.

44-6910 Del Lincoln 16/12/44; Grenier 22/12/44; ass 571BS/390BG [FC-T] Framlingham 4/1/45; retUS Bradley 2/7/45; Sth Plains 4/7/45; RFC Kingman 25/11/45.

44-6911 Del Lincoln 16/12/44; Grenier 23/12/44; ass 560BS/388BG Knettishall 1/1/45; retUS Bradley 30/6/45; Sth Plains 2/7/45; RFC Kingman 23/11/45.

44-6912 Del Lincoln 16/12/44; Grenier 29/12/44; ass 332BS/94BG [XM-V] Rougham 1/1/45; 379BG Kimbolton 1/2/45; retUS, RFC Walnut Ridge 5/1/46.

44-6913 Del Lincoln 16/12/44; Grenier 3/1/45; ass 837BS/487BG Lavenham 5/2/45; MIA Brandenburg

10/4/45 w/Sell; jet e/a, cr Zobbenitz, Ger; 4EVD 6POW; MACR 13885. QUEEN OF HEARTS.
44-6914 Del Lincoln 16/12/44; Dow Fd 23/12/44; ass 568BS/390BG [BI-G] Framlingham 1/1/45; retUS Bradley 30/6/45; Sth Plains 3/7/45; RFC Kingman 24/11/45. THE FIGHTING LADY.
44-6915 Del Lincoln 16/17/44; Dow Fd 23/12/44; ass 524BS/379BG [WA-M] Kimbolton 28/1/45; retUS Bradley 3/7/45; Sth Plains 7/7/45; RFC Kingman 8/11/45.
44-6916 Del Lincoln 17/12/44; Dow Fd 23/12/44; ass 34BG Mendlesham 1/1/45; retUS Bradley 27/6/45; Sth Plains 30/6/45; RFC Kingman 19/12/45.
44-6917 Del Lincoln 16/12/44; Grenier 29/12/44; ass 8AF 1/1/45; retUS Bradley 3/7/45; Sth Plains 6/7/45; RFC Kingman 9/11/45.
44-6918 Del Lincoln 16/12/44; Grenier 29/12/44; ass 560BS/388BG Knettishall 1/1/45; retUS Bradley 30/6/45; Sth Plains 3/7/45; RFC Kingman 18/11/45. PISTOLAS JUANITA.
44-6919 Del Lincoln 17/12/44; Dow Fd 23/12/44; ass 407BS/92BG [PY-E] Podington 24/2/45; secret mission 1/6/45, ret 2/6/45; sal 9AF Germany 4//3/46.
44-6920 Del Hunter 15/12/44; Dow Fd 3/1/45; ass 34BG Mendlesham 7/1/45; retUS Bradley 21/6/45; Sth Plains 23/6/45; RFC Kingman 9/11/45.
44-6921 Del Hunter 18/12/44; Dow Fd 3/1/45; ass 427BS/303BG [GN-F] Molesworth 3/1/45; b/d Berlin 18/3/45 w/?; f/l Continent; sal 28/3/45.
44-6922 Del Lincoln 19/12/44; Grenier 24/12/44; ass 487BG Lavenham 1/1/45; retUS Bradley 12//6/45; Sth Plains 18/4/45; RFC Kingman 17/12/45.
44-6923 Del Lincoln 20/12/44; Dow Fd 3/1/45; ass 545BS/384BG [JD-J] Grafton Underwood 1/2/45; sal AFSC 6/4/45.
44-6924 Del Lincoln 20/12/44; Dow Fd 3/1/45; ass 836BS/487BG Lavenham 8/2/45; retUS Bradley 10/7/45; Independence 12/7/45; RFC Kingman 28/12/45.
44-6925 Del Lincoln 15/12/44; Dow Fd 23/12/44; ass 8AF 3/1/45; re-ass 30/4/47; 10 HBS Oberfaffenhofen 18/1/48; 7290 AB Oberpfaffenhofen 19/8/48; Recl Comp 11/2/49.
44-6926 Del Lincoln 20/12/44; Grenier 29/12/44; ass 8AF 3/2/45; retUS Bradley 17/6/45; Sth Plains 21/6/45; RFC Kingman 14/12/45.
44-6927 Del Hunter 20/12/44; Grenier 10/1/45; ass 8AF 22/1/45; retUS Bradley 28/6/45; Sth Plains 4/8/45; RFC Kingman 27/11/45.
44-6928 Del Hunter 20/12/44; Grenier 10/1/45; ass 368BS/306BG Thurleigh 1/2/45; retUS, RFC Kingman 8/12/45.
44-6929 Del Hunter 20/12/44; Dow Fd 3/1/45; ass 18BS/34BG Mendlesham 5/1/45; retUS Bradley 24/6/45; Sth Plains 26/6/45; RFC Kingman 8/12/45. EVADIN' MAIDEN.
44-6930 Del Hunter 20/12/44; Dow Fd 3/1/45; ass 8AF 24/1/45; sal 9AF Germany 31/5/46.
44-6931 Del Hunter 21/12/45; Dow Fd 3/1/45; ass 401BS/91BG [LL-K] Bassingbourn 7/2/45; (2 POW trips); {31m} RetUS Bradley 11/6/45; Sth Plains 15/6/45; RFC Kingman 20/12/45. RUGGED BUT RIGHT.
44-6932 Del Hunter 21/12/44; Dow Fd 2/1/45; ass 8AF 7/1/45; retUS Bradley 12/7/45; Independence 14/7/45; RFC Kingman 10/12/45.
44-6933 Del Lincoln 24/12/44; Dow Fd 2/1/45; ass 601BS/398BG [3O-H] Nuthampstead 7/2/45; 600BS [N8-H]; retUS Bradley 6/6/45; Sth Plains 7/6/45; RFC Kingman 8/11/45.
44-6934 Del Lincoln 22/12/44; Grenier 3/1/45; ass 8AF 7/2/45; re-ass 30/4/47; Belgian-Dutch coastal patrols 10/4/47; Recl Comp 17/2/48.
44-6935 Del Hunter 20/12/44; Grenier 3/1/45; ass 8AF 7/1/45; retUS Bradley 3/7/45; Ogden 6/7/45; 4135 BU Hill Fd 28/8/45; 4000 BU Patterson 5/7/46; re-ass AF 31/3/47; 4135 BU Hill Fd 8/4/47; 4141 BU Muroc 7/3/49; 4127 BU McClelland 1/9/49; 2759 EXPW Muroc 20/8/49.
44-6936 Del Hunter 27/12/44; Grenier 10/1/45; ass 8AF 25/1/45; re-ass AF 30/4/47; 2025 LS Templehof 18/1/48; 7908 BU Templehof 16/4/48; 7350 BU Templehof 1/7/48; 7160 BU Erben 16/11/48; 60 AB Weisbaden 1/6/49; 85 MAT Erding 14/10/49; Recl Comp 20/3/50.
44-6937 Del Hunter 26/12/44; Dow Fd 13/1/45; ass 8AF 22/1/45; retUS Bradley 9/6/45; Sth Plains 10/6/45; RFC Kingman 9/12/45.
44-6938 Del Hunter 22/12/44; Grenier 15/1/45; ass 18BS/34BG Mendlesham 22/1/45; retUS Bradley 21/6/45; Sth Plains 24/6/45; RFC Kingman 26/11/45. LITTLE GIZMO.
44-6939 Del Lincoln 26/12/44; Dow Fd 10/1/45; ass 7BS/34BG Mendlesham 21/1/45; retUS Bradley 24/6/45; Sth Plains 25/6/45; RFC Kingman 10/12/45. MIZPAH.
44-6940 Del Lincoln 22/12/44; Dow Fd 10/1/45; ass 731BS/452BG Deopham Green 22/1/45; sal 27/5/45.
44-6941 Del Lincoln 23/12/44; Dow Fd 3/1/45; ass 8AF 6/1/45; retUS Bradley 9/7/45; Sth Plains 11/7/45; RFC Kingman 17/12/45.
44-6942 Del Lincoln 23/12/44; Dow Fd 11/1/45; ass 8AF 24/1/45; sal 9AF Germany 6/11/46.
44-6943 Del Lincoln 23/12/44; Dow Fd 10/1/45; ass 8AF 14/1/45; retUS Bradley 9/7/45; Sth Plains 11/7/45; RFC Kingman 30/11/45.
44-6944 Del Hunter 26/12/44; Grenier 13/1/45; ass 551BS/385BG Gt Ashfield 22/1/45; MIA Berlin 18/3/45 w/?; MACR 13147.
44-6945 Del Hunter 23/12/44; Grenier 10/1/45; ass 8AF 22/1/45; retUS Bradley 3/7/45; Sth Plains 6/7/45; RFC Kingman 10/1/46.
44-6946 Del Lincoln 26/12/44; Grenier 3/1/45; ass 412BS/95BG [QW-F] Horham 7/1/45; retUS Bradley 22/6/45; Sth Plains 24/6/45; RFC Kingman 5/12/45. BLOOD AND GUTS.
44-6947 Del Hunter 27/12/44; Grenier 10/1/45; ass 614BS/401BG [IW-S] DeenEthorpe 10/3/45; tran 545BS/384BG [JD-J] Grafton Underwood 10/5/45; re-ass 30/4/47; 10 HB Oberpfaffenhofen 18/1/48; Recl Comp 7/1/49.
44-6948 Del Hunter 29/12/44; Grenier 10/1/45; ass 325BS/92BG [NV-M] Podington 4/2/45; secret mission 1/6/45, ret 2/6/45; sal 9AF Germany 10/12/45.
44-6949 Del Lincoln 29/12/44; Dow Fd 10/1/45; ass 8AF 24/1/45; retUS Bradley 12/7/45; Romulus 22/8/45; Independence 8/10/45; 593 BU Charleston 28/10/45; RFC Kingman 26/11/45.
44-6950 Del Lincoln 28/12/44; Grenier 25/1/45; ass 532BS/381BG [VE-M] Ridgewell 1/2/45 MELANCHOLY BABY; {16+m} RetUS Bradley 28/5/45; Sth Plains 30/5/45; RFC Kingman 9/11/45. ALABAMA GAL.
44-6951 Del Lincoln 28/12/44; Grenier 25/1/45; ass 368BS/306BG Thurleigh 19/3/45; tran 381BG Ridgewell 5/45; retUS Bradley 10/6/45; Sth Plains 13/6/45; RFC Kingman 27/11/45.
44-6952 Del Lincoln 29/12/44; Dow Fd 25/1/45; ass 509BS/351BG [RQ-H] Polebrook 1/2/45; {10m} RetUS Bradley 23/5/45; Sth Plains 26/5/45; RFC Kingman 14/12/45.
44-6953 Del Hunter 28/12/44; Grenier 6/1/45; ass 8AF 12/1/45; retUS Bradley 29/6/45; Sth Plains 3/7/45; RFC Kingman 25/11/45; to Alaskan Air Command 1949 as VB-17, with tail turret out and extra radio dept. window fitted; used as cargo/transport for troops; carried Arctic markings.
44-6954 Del Hunter 28/12/44; Grenier 6/1/45; ass 569BS/390BG [CC-F] Framlingham 12/1/45; retUS Bradley 2/6/45; Sth Plains 13/6/45; RFC Kingman 30/11/45. LIQUID 8 OR; HELL'S BELLE.
44-6955 Del Hunter 28/12/44; Grenier 6/1/45; ass 338BS/96BG [BX-D] Snetterton 22/1/45; retUS Bradley 2/6/45; Sth Plains 11/6/45; RFC Kingman 30/11/45.
44-6956 Del Hunter 31/12/44; Dow Fd 18/1/45; ass 8AF 5/2/45; sal 9AF Germany 23/5/45.
44-6957 Del Lincoln 31/12/44; Dow Fd 25/1/45; ass 427BS/303BG [GN-D] Molesworth 18/2/45; tran 457BG Glatton 22/5/45; sal 9AF Germany 10/5/46. EL SCREAMO.
44-6958 Del Lincoln 1/1/45; Grenier 25/1/45; ass 8AF 5/2/45; retUS Bradley 5/7/45; Sth Plains 8/7/45; RFC Kingman 13/12/45.
44-6959 Del Lincoln 1/1/45; Dow Fd 6/2/45; ass 8AF 14/2/45; re-ass 30/4/47; 10 HBS Oberpfaffenhofen 18/1/48; Recl Comp 7/1/49.
44-6960 Del Lincoln 31/12/44; Dow Fd 10/1/45; ass 8AF 21/1/45; retUS Bradley 20/6/45; Sth Plains 23/6/45; RFC Kingman 26/11/45.
44-6961 Del Lincoln 2/1/45; Dow Fd 25/1/45; ass 748BS/457BG Glatton 21/3/45; retUS Bradley 22/5/45; Sth Plains 24/5/45; RFC Kingman 9/12/45.
44-6962 Del –.
44-6963 Del Lincoln 2/1/45; Grenier 25/1/45; ass 326BS/92BG [JW-A] Podington 4/3/45; b/d Berlin 28/3/45 w/?; c/l, sal 2SAD 30/3/45.
44-6964 Del Lincoln 1//1/45; Dow Fd 25/1/45; ass 322BS/91BG [LG-Y] Bassingbourn 23/2/45; retUS Bradley 13/6/45; Sth Plains 17/6/45; RFC Kingman 30/11/45.
44-6965 Del Lincoln 2/1/45; Grenier 24/1/45; ass 524BS/379BG [WA-T] Kimbolton 5/2/45; retUS Bradley 6/7/45; Sth Plains 8/7/45; RFC Kingman 18/12/45.
44-6966 Del Hunter 3/1/45; Dow Fd 18/1/45; ass 34BG Mendlesham 1/2/45; retUS Bradley 30/6/45; Sth Plains 2/7/45; RFC Kingman 26/11/45.
44-6967 Del Hunter 3/1/45; Grenier 15/1/45; ass 8AF 25/1/45; sal 9AF Germany 10/5/46.
44-6968 Del Hunter 3/1/45; Grenier 15/1/45; ass 863BS/493BG Debach 22/1/45; retUS Bradley 3/7/45; Sth Plains 4/7/45; RFC Kingman 19/12/45.
44-6969 Del Hunter 3/1/45; Grenier 13/1/45; ass 493BG Debach 3/2/45; retUS Bradley 17/6/45; Sth Plains 18/6/45; RFC Kingman 18/12/45.
44-6970 Del Hunter 1/1/45; Dow Fd 13/1/45; ass 457BG Glatton 21/1/45; b/d Munich 25/2/45 w/?; f/l Continent, sal.
44-6971 Del Hunter 3/1/45; Grenier 13/1/45; ass 568BS/390BG [BI-M] Framlingham 21/1/45; retUS Bradley 30/6/45; Sth Plains 18/7/45; RFC Kingman 19/11/45. WHO DAT?
44-6972 Del Hunter 3/1/45; Dow Fd 13/1/45; ass 8AF 22/1/45; retUS Bradley 6/7/45; Sth Plains 7/7/45; RFC Kingman 10/12/45.
44-6973 Del Hunter 3/1/45; Dow Fd 18/1/45; ass 8AF 22/1/45; retUS Bradley 5/7/45; Sth Plains 7/7/45; RFC Kingman 20/2/46.
44-6974 Del Hunter 5/1/45; Grenier 13/1/45; ass 332BS/94BG [XM-S] Rougham 22/1/45; 331BS; retUS Bradley 3/7/45; Sth Plains 6/7/45; RFC Kingman 19/12/45.
44-6975 Del Hunter 5/1/45; Grenier 13/1/45; ass

535BS/381BG [MS-K] Ridgewell 1/2/45; {2m} modified as hack for CO of 1CBW, Gen Bill Gross, turrets removed and extra seats fitted, taking over 900 man hrs of 432nd SG to complete; tran 91BG Bassingbourn 15/4/45 flying two missions as scout; so 'christened' on 25/4/44 group's last combat mission; ret 381BG Ridgewell 20/5/45 as ETO transport for VIPs before returning US; ass USN as CB-17 in 1946. OUR BRIDGET.

44-6976 Del Hunter 5/1/45; Dow Fd 18/1/45; ass 407BS/92BG [PY-T] Podington 1/2/45; Istres Fd, France 5/6/45, ret 27/6/45; sal 9AF Germany 31/5/46.

44-6977 Del Hunter 5/1/45; Grenier 15/1/45; ass 427BS/303BG [GN-C] Molesworth 1/2/45; secret mission 28/3/45, ret 30/3/45; tran 457BG Glatton 23/5/45; retUS Bradley 9/6/45; Sth Plains 13/6/45; RFC Kingman 30/11/45. BETTER DO 'ER.

44-6978 Del Hunter 5/1/45; Dow Fd 18/1/45; ass 8AF 5/2/45; Re-ass 30/4/47; 10 HBS Oberpfaffenhofen 18/1/48; sal 1/7/49.

44-6979 Del ATC Oklahoma City 27/1/45; Dallas 24/3/45; Rome 26/5/45; Syracuse 12/10/45; RFC Altus 21/11/45.

44-6980 Del Hunter 11/1/45; Grenier 6/2/45; ass 8AF 8/2/45; retUS, RFC Walnut Ridge 12/12/45.

44-6981 Del Lincoln 6/1/45; Grenier 25/1/45; ass 20BS/2BG Amendola 31/1/45; sal 9AF Germany 6/11/46.

44-6982 Del Lincoln 5/1/45; Dow Fd 25/1/45; ass 2BG Amendola 31/1/45; retUS 1103 BU Morrison 16/10/45; 593 BU Charleston 28/10/45; RFC Walnut Ridge 21/12/45.

44-6983 Del Lincoln 6/1/45; Dow Fd 25/1/45; ass 20BS/2BG Amendola 31/1/45; sal 9AF Germany 17/7/46.

44-6984 Del Hunter 6/1/45; Grenier 15/1/45; ass 97BG Amendola 7/2/45; sal 10/2/46; retUS Morrison 19/2/45; RFC Walnut Ridge 23/2/45.

44-6985 Del Hunter 8/1/45; Grenier 19/1/45; ass 463BG Celone 7/2/45; retUS 2/10/45; RFC Walnut Ridge 12/12/45.

44-6986 Del Lincoln 6/1/45; Grenior 26/1/45; ass 463BG Celone 31/1/45; sal 9AF Germany 23/6/46; re-ass 30/4/47; Recl Comp 19/11/47.

44-6987 Del Lincoln 8/1/45; Dow Fd 25/1/45; ass 2BG Amendola 5/2/45; retUS Morrison 7/10/45; RFC Walnut Ridge 20/12/45.

44-6988 Del Lincoln 11/1/45; Dow Fd 25/1/45; ass 97BG Amendola 31/1/45; retUS 1103 BU Morrison 20/10/45; 593 BU Charleston 28/10/45; RFC Walnut Ridge 20/12/45.

44-6989 Del Oklahoma City 6/1/45; Boca Raton 15/2/45; Hunter 7/3/45; Grenier 24/3/45; ass 482BG Alconbury 4/4/45; tran 337BS/96BG [AW-V] Snetterton 5/4/45; sal 9AF Germany 6/11/46. RAGGED BUT RIGHT.

44-6990 Del Oklahoma City 12/1/45; Hunter 15/2/45; Boca Raton 4/3/45; Grenier 25/3/45; ass 813BS/482BG [PC-O] Alconbury 26/3/45; sal 9AF Germany 10/12/45.

44-6991 Del Oklahoma City 6/1/45; Boca Raton 25/2/45; Grenier 17/3/45; ass 482BG Alconbury 25/3/45; sal 9AF Germany 6/11/45.

44-6992 Del Oklahoma City 8/1/45; Boca Raton 24/2/45; Hunter 12/3/45; Grenier 18/3/45; ass 482BG Alconbury 1/4/45; tran 351BG Polebrook 10/5/45; 96BG Snetterton 28/5/45; sal 9AF Germany 6/11/45.

44-6993 Del Oklahoma City 8/1/45; Boca Raton 16/2/45; Hunter 17/3/45; Grenier 28/3/45; ass 482BG Alconbury 1/4/45; tran 338BS/96BG Snetterton 1/4/45; sal 9AF Germany 6/11/46.

44-6994 Del Oklahoma City 12/1/45; Boca Raton 19/2/45; Hunter 30/3/45; Grenier 12/4/45; ass 482BG Alconbury 14/4/45; sal 9AF Germany 6/11/46.

44-6995 Del Oklahoma City 13/1/45; Boca Raton 25/2/45; Hunter 17/3/45; Grenier 25/3/45; ass 482BG Alconbury 29/3/45; tran 351BG Polebrook 10/5/45; 96BG Snetterton 28/5/45; sal 9AF Germany 6/11/46.

44-6996 Del Oklahoma City 12/1/45; Boca Raton 19/2/45; Hunter 9/3/45; ass 482BG Alconbury 25/3/45; tran 351BG Polebrook 10/5/45; 96BG Snetterton 28/5/45; sal 9AF Germany 6/11/46.

44-6997 Del Oklahoma City 12/1/45; Boca Raton 23/2/45; Hunter 10/3/45; Grenier 20/3/45; ass 482BG Alconbury 25/3/45; tran 351BG Polebrook 10/5/45; 96BG Snetterton 28/5/45; sal 9AF Germany 23/8/46.

44-6998 Del Oklahoma City 13/1/45; Boca Raton 26/2/45; Hunter 15/3/45; Grenier 23/3/45; ass 482BG Alconbury 26/3/45; tran 351BG Polebrook 10/5/45; 96BG Snetterton 28/5/45; sal 9AF Germany 6/11/46.

44-6999 Del Oklahoma City 13/1/45; Boca Raton 25/2/45; Hunter 10/3/45; Grenier 20/3/45; ass 482BG Alconbury 26/3/45; tran 351BG Polebrook 10/5/45; 96BG Snetterton 28/5/45; sal 9AF Germany 6/11/45.

44-7000 Del Oklahoma City 13/1/45; Boca Raton 25/2/45; Hunter 16/3/45; Grenier 24/3/45; ass 482BG Alconbury 27/3/45; sal 9AF Germany 6/11/45.

B-17G-VE

44-8001 Del Dallas 10/5/44; Langley 27/6/44; Dow Fd 18/7/44; ass 32BS/301BG as PFF Lucera 30/7/44; b/d Linz 25/11/44 w/Johnson; cr Iesi, 8KIA 2RTD; MACR 7536.

44-8002 Del Dallas 11/5/44; Langley 24/6/44; Dow Fd 11/7/44; ass 401BG Deenethorpe 13/7/44; tran 833BS/487BG [4N-A] Lavenham 14/7/44; sal 9AF Germany 10/5/46.

44-8003 Del Dallas 11/5/44; Langley 24/6/44; Dow Fd 11/7/44; ass 816BS/483BG as PFF Sterparone 17/7/44; MIA Maribor 1/4/45 w/Lochansky; flak, cr Bihacue; 3POW (inc p) 7RTD; MACR 13472. SNOOPY III.

44-8004 Del Dallas 9/5/44; Langley 26/6/44; Dow Fd 16/7/44; ass 414BS/97BG PFF Amendola 21/7/44; MIA Bleckhammer 14/10/44 w/Bieniek; no gas, cr Oldrichevic; MACR 9592.

44-8005 Del Dallas 11/5/44; Langley 28/6/44; Grenier 27/7/44; ass 97BG PFF Amendola 6/8/44; retUS Morrison 25/3/45; 4100 BU Patterson 29/3/45; Recl Comp 2/5/46.

44-8006 Del Dallas 12/5/44; Langley 26/6/44; Dow Fd 18/7/44; ass 341BS/97BG PFF Amendola 26/7/44; blew up on take off for Linz 8/1/45 w/?; sal.

44-8007 Del Dallas 11/5/44; Langley 26/6/44; Grenier 11/7/44; ass 545BS/384BG [JD-Z] Grafton Underwood 3/8/44; tran 305BG Chelveston 9/5/45; SCREAMIN' EAGLE.

44-8008 Del Dallas 11/5/44; Langley 26/6/44; Grenier 9/7/44; ass 385BG Gt Ashfield 10/7/44; tran 544BS/384BG [SU-Y] Grafton Underwood 13/8/44; MIA Plauen 19/3/45 w/Kramer; flak, cr Ostend, Bel; 9KIA; MACR 13365.

44-8009 Del Dallas 11/5/44; Langley 19/6/44; Dow Fd 7/7/44; ass 95BG Horham 8/7/44; tran 349BS/100BG [XR-E] Thorpe Abbotts 9/7/44; retUS Charleston 2/10/44; RFC Walnut Ridge 5/1/46.

44-8010 Del Dallas 11/5/44; Langley 29/6/44; Dow Fd 15/7/44; ass 532BS/381BG [VE-J] Ridgewell 8/8/44; tran 91BG Bassingbourn 15/1/45; 306BG Thurleigh 23/5/45. Sal 9AF Germany 21/6/45; re-ass 30/4/47; Recl Comp 19/11/47.

44-8011 Del Dallas 14/3/44; Kearney 26/6/44; Grenier 6/7/44; ass 547BS/384BG [SO-J] Grafton Underwood 27/7/44; MIA Plauen 19/3/45 w/Capt Kelsay; flak, cr Liége, Bel; 1KIA 3POW 6RTD; MACR 10197. MISBEHAVIN'.

44-8012 Del Dallas 12/5/44; Langley 26/6/44; Dow Fd 15/7/44; ass 341BS/97BG PFF Amendola 21/7/44; sal 9AF Germany 10/5/46.

44-8013 Del Dallas 13/5/44; Langley 24/6/44; Dow Fd 15/7/44; ass 95BS Horham 16/7/44; tran 570BS/390BG [DI-P] Framlingham 17/7/44; retUS Bradley 5/7/45; Sth Plains 7/7/45; RFC Kingman 21/11/45. CHUG-A-LUG.

44-8014 Del Dallas 12/5/44; Langley 26/6/44; Grenier 21/7/44; ass 815BS/483BG PFF Sterparone 5/8/44; MIA Munich 14/10/44 w/McCann; flak, cr Otocac; 10EVD, ret 11/10/44; MACR 8974. BIG DEAL.

44-8015 Del Dallas 12/5/44; Langley 27/6/44; Dow Fd 9/7/44; ass 730BS/452BG Deopham Green 15/7/44; b/d Ansbach 22/2/45 w/Emmett; flak, c/l Pfafferhofen; 7KIA 3POW; sal 20/1/45; MACR 12657. JOHNNY REB.

44-8016 Del Dallas 12/5/44; Langley 27/6/44; Grenier 28/7/44; ass 774BS/463BG Celone 4/8/44; sal 9AF Germany 21/5/46.

44-8017 Del Dallas 16/5/44; Langley 29/6/44; Dow Fd 25/7/44; ass 527BS/379BG [FO-X] Kimbolton 13/8/44; MIA Zeitz 30/11/44 w/Maj Ramsdell; flak, cr Zeitz; 10POW; MACR 11125. THE SAD SACK.

44-8018 Del Dallas 14/5/44; Langley 26/6/44; Dow Fd 15/7/44; ass 840BS/483BG PFF Sterparone 4/8/44; cr 9/2/45 w/?; MARGE.

44-8019 Del Dallas 14/5/44; Langley 27/6/44; Dow Fd 18/7/44; ass 463BG PFF Celone 23/7/44; sal 6/10/44.

44-8020 Del Dallas 14/5/44; Langley 26/6/44; Dow Fd 17/7/44; ass 49BS/2BG PFF Amendola 23/7/44; retUS Hunter 31/5/45; RFC Kingman 28/12/45.

44-8021 Del Dallas 14/5/44; Langley 29/6/44; Dow Fd 20/7/44; ass 839BS/487BG [R5-W] Lavenham 30/10/44; tran 94BG Rougham 29/5/45; sal 9AF Germany 10/5/46.

44-8022 Del Dallas 16/5/44; Langley 28/6/44; Dow Fd 23/7/44; ass 925BS/92BG [NV-H] Horham 26/7/44; b/d Merzhausen 24/12/44 w/?; f/l Continent, sal 6/1/45.

44-8023 Del Dallas 14/5/44; Langley 29/6/44; Grenier 24/7/44; ass 837BS/487BG [4F-J] Lavenham 28/10/44; retUS Bradley 14/7/45; Independence 17/7/45; RFC Kingman 167/12/45.

44-8024 Del Dallas 14/5/44; Langley 29/6/44; Grenier 21/7/44; ass 534BS/381BG [GD-O] Ridgewell 15/8/44; {15+m} tran 306BG Thurleigh 23/5/45; re-ass 30/4/47; 10 HBS Oberpfaffenhofen 11/7/46; Recl Comp 7/1/49.

44-8025 Del Dallas 14/5/44; Langley 3/7/44; Dow Fd 24/7/44; ass 833BS/486BG [4N-B] Sudbury 26/7/44; sal 9AF 10/5/46.

44-8026 Del Tulsa 15/5/44; Dallas 12/6/44; Boca Raton 30/6/44; 3501 BU Boca Raton 5/7/44; 3539 BU Langley 30/6/44; W/O 8/6/44.

44-8027 Del Tulsa 16/5/44; Dallas 12/6/44; Boca Raton 1/7/44; 3501 BU Boca Raton 6/7/44; 110 BU Mitchell 23/9/44; 3501 BU Boca Raton 27/9/44; 3539 BU Langley 16/10/44; 334 BU Florence 26/1/45; 127 BU Florence 1/2/45; 3539 BU Langley 5/2/45; RFC Walnut Ridge 8/1/46.

44-8028 Del Tulsa 16/5/44; Dallas 13/6/44; Boca Raton 1/7/44; Key Fd 5/7/44; 3501 BU Boca Raton 7/7/44; 4006 BU Miami 18/8/44; 3501 BU Boca Raton 24/8/44; 3539 BU Langley 14/10/44; RFC Walnut Ridge 8/1/46.

44-8029 Del Tulsa 15/5/44; Dallas 13/6/44; Boca Raton 1/7/44; 3501 BU Boca Raton 7/7/44; 3539 BU Langley 14/10/44; RFC Walnut Ridge 7/1/46.

44-8030 Del Tulsa 16/5/44; Dallas 13/6/44; Boca Raton 3/7/44; 3501 BU Boca Raton 7/7/44; 3539 BU Langley 16/10/44; 4137 BU Hendricks 30/5/45; 2410 BU Smyrna 30/10/45; 554 BU Memphis 13/6/46; 4136 BU Tinker 16/6/46; 554 BU Memphis 26/6/46; Recl Comp 1/8/46.

44-8031 Del Tulsa 18/5/44; Dallas 13/6/44; Langley 2/7/44; Dow Fd 25/7/44; ass 447BS Rattlesden 28/7/44; tran 601BS/398BG [3O-Z] Nuthampstead 16/8/44; 603BS [N7-Z]; retUS Bradley 4/6/45; Sth Plains 8/6/45; RFC Kingman 17/12/45.

44-8032 Del Tulsa 16/5/44; Dallas 13/6/44; Langley 1/7/44; Dow Fd 25/7/44; ass 457BG Glatton 22/8/44, c/l on Greenland ice cap en route UK; sal 12/11/44. MY GAL SAL.

44-8033 Del Tulsa 17/5/44; Dallas 13/6/44; Langley 3/7/44; Dow Fd 24/7/44; ass 614BS/401BG [IW-C] Deenethorpe 18/8/44; 615BS [IY-C]; tran 305BG Chelveston 5/45; sal 9AF Germany 23/5/46.

44-8034 Del Tulsa 16/5/44; Dallas 13/6/44; Langley 5/7/44; Dow Fd 21/7/44; ass 379BG Kimbolton 21/1/45; retUS Morrison 22/10/45; RFC Walnut Ridge 21/1/46.

44-8035 Del Tulsa 17/5/44; Dallas 13/6/44; Langley 5/7/44; Dow Fd 26/7/44; ass 94BG Rougham 28/7/44; sal 9AF Germany 23/5/46.

44-8036 Del Tulsa 17/5/44; Dallas 14/6/44; Langley 7/7/44; Dow Fd 4/8/44; ass 534BS/381BG [GD-J] Ridgewell 31/8/44; tran 306BG Thurleigh 23/5/45; re-ass 30/4/47; Recl Comp 19/11/47.

44-8037 Del Tulsa 17/5/44; Dallas 24/6/44; Langley 3/7/44; Grenier 27/7/44; ass 838BS/487BG [2C-F] Lavenham 28/7/44; tran 94BG Rougham 29/5/45; retUS, RFC Walnut Ridge 9/1/46.

44-8038 Del Tulsa 17/5/44; Dallas 14/6/44; Langley 3/7/44; Grenier 1/8/44; ass 322BS/91BG Bassingbourn 2/8/44; tran 427BS/303BG [GN-Z] Molesworth 10/44; sal 9AF Germany 23/5/46.

44-8039 Del Tulsa 16/5/44; Dallas 14/6/44; Langley 3/7/44; Grenier 28/7/44; ass 836BS/487BG Lavenham 2/8/44; 837BS [4F-J]; tran 94BG Rougham 29/5/45; sal 9AF Germany 31/5/46.

44-8040 Del Tulsa 14/5/44; Dallas 14/6/44; Langley 6/7/44; Grenier 3/8/44; ass 335BS/95BG [OE-N] Horham 5/8/44; 412BS [QW-N]; sal 8/6/45. 13TH JINX.

44-8041 Del Tulsa 16/5/44; Dallas 13/6/44; Langley 21/7/44; Grenier 3/8/44; ass 305BG Chelveston 26/8/44; sal 2 SAD 8/9/44.

44-8042 Del Tulsa 20/5/44; Dallas 1/6/44; Langley 3/7/44; Grenier 3/8/44; ass 333BS/94BG Rougham 5/8/44; retUS, RFC Walnut Ridge 20/12/45.

44-8043 Del Tulsa 20/5/44; Dallas 14/6/44; Langley 6/7/44; Grenier 4/8/44; ass 429BS/2BG PFF Amendola 11/8/44; MIA Casarsa 4/10/44 w/Donovan; flak, blew off left wing tip and aileron, cr Giesing; MACR 8949.

44-8044 Del Tulsa 20/5/44; Dallas 6/6/44; Langley 6/7/44; Grenier 2/8/44; ass 603BS/398BG [N7-X] Nuthampstead 2/9/44; tran 306BG Thurleigh 23/5/45; sal 9AF Germany 10/5/46.

44-8045 Del Tulsa 22/5/44; Dallas 4/6/44; Langley 6/7/44; Dow Fd 2/8/44; ass 511BS/351BG [DS-L] as H2S a/c Polebrook 5/9/44; {48m} tran 305BG Chelveston 5/45; sal 9AF Germany 23/5/46. THE PATHFINDER.

44-8046 Del Tulsa 22/5/44; Dallas 10/6/44; Langley 6/7/44; Dow Fd 2/8/44; ass 351BG Polebrook 22/8/44; tran 750BS/457BG Glatton 24/8/44; MIA Politz 7/10/44 w/Capt Fischer; flak, cr Politz; 6KIA 5POW; MACR 9767.

44-8047 Del Tulsa 20/5/44; Dallas 17/6/44; Langley 8/7/44; Dow Fd 2/8/44; ass 547BS/384BG [SO-Z] Grafton Underwood 5/9/44; c/l 20/10/44, sal; rep tran 379BG Kimbolton 4/1/45; dec w/w 5/1/45; retUS, RFC Kingman 7/1/46.

44-8048 Del Tulsa 26/5/44; Dallas 5/6/44; Langley 10/7/44; Dow Fd 4/8/44; ass 346BS/99BG PFF Tortorella 14/8/44; {24m} sal 9AF Germany 10/5/46.

44-8049 Del Tulsa 20/5/44; Dallas 10/6/44; Langley 8/7/44; Grenier 8/8/44; ass 463BG PFF Celone 19/8/44; sal 9AF Germany 6/11/46.

44-8050 Del Tulsa 20/5/44; Dallas 16/6/44; Langley 15/7/44; Grenier 3/8/44; ass 326BS/92BG [JW-D/H] Podington 30/8/44; tran 306BG Thurleigh 8/5/45; sal 9AF Germany 23/5/46. CALAMITY JANE 2ND.

44-8051 Del Alexandra 23/5/44; 329 BU Alexandra 10/10/44; 330 BU Dyersburg 5/9/45; RFC Walnut Ridge 19/12/45.

44-8052 Del Alexandra 24/5/44; 221 BU Alexandra 16/10/44; 329 BU Alexandra 1/3/45; 330 BY Dyersburg 25/3/45; RFC Walnut Ridge 17/12/45.

44-8053 Del Alexandra 24/5/44; 221 BU Alexandra 17/1/45; 329 BU Alexandra 1/3/45; 325 BU Avon Park 29/6/45; RFC Walnut Ridge 20/8/45.

44-8054 Del Ardmore 20/5/44; Albuquerque 26/5/44; 222 BU Ardmore 18/6/44; 332 BU Ardmore 16/1/45; RFC Walnut Ridge 19/8/45.

44-8055 Del Ardmore 20/5/44; Amarillo 28/5/44; 222 BU Ardmore 19/6/44; 332 BU Ardmore 3/8/45; RFC Walnut Ridge 11/12/45.

44-8056 Del Dyersburg 21/5/44; Oklahoma City 28/5/44; 223 BU Dyersburg 23/8/44; 330 BU Dyersburg 1/3/45; RFC Walnut Ridge 17/12/45.

44-8057 Del Dyersburg 21/5/44; Oklahoma City 28/5/44; 330 BU Dyersburg 1/3/45; RFC Walnut Ridge 19/12/45.

44-8058 Del Sioux City 22/5/44; El Paso 26/5/44; 224 BU Sioux City 4/7/44; 236 BU Mt Home 1/7/45; 426 BU Mt Home 23/8/45; 237 BU Kirtland 20/9/45; RFC Walnut Ridge 14/2/45.

44-8059 Del Sioux City 24/5/44; Palm Springs 26/5/44; 224 BU Sioux City 4/7/44; 224 BU Pueblo 27/5/45; 203 BU Jackson 27/6/45; 242 BU Gr Island 24/10/45; RFC Walnut Ridge 14/2/45.

44-8060 Del Pyote 27/5/44; Coolidge 29/5/44; 237 BU Pyote 8/6/44; 235 BU Biggs 16/8/44; HHR Minneapolis 11/12/44; 235 BU Biggs 19/12/44; 222 BU Ardmore 4/3/45; 332 BU Ardmore 1/8/45; RFC Walnut Ridge 7/12/45.

44-8061 Del Rapid City 24/5/44; Ogden 1/6/44; 225 BU Rapid City 9/6/44; 203 BU Jackson 3/8/44; 233 BU Ft Worth 3/2/45; RFC Walnut Ridge 14/2/45.

44-8062 Del Rapid City 24/5/44; Albuquerque 28/5/44; ATS Burbank 2/11/44; 225 BU Rapid City 1/5/45; 239 BU March 9/7/45; 200 BU Peterson 15/10/45; RFC Altus 7/12/45.

44-8063 Del Pyote 27/5/44; 235 BU Biggs 17/1/45; 322 BU Ardmore 8/3/45; RFC Walnut Ridge 19/8/45.

44-8064 Del Hobbs 27/5/44; 3017 BU Hobbs 16/1/45; 3701 BU Amarillo 12/3/45; RFC Kingman 5/11/45.

44-8065 Del Hobbs 24/5/44; 3017 BU Hobbs 23/8/44; 3701 BU Amarillo 26/9/44; RFC Kingman 23/11/45.

44-8066 Del Hobbs 27/5/44; 3017 BU Hobbs 21/8/44; Recl Comp 28/12/45.

44-8067 Del Hobbs 27/5/44; 3017 BU Hobbs 4/8/44; 3701 BU Amarillo 17/3/45; RFC Kingman 23/11/45.

44-8068 Del Hobbs 28/5/44; Coolidge 30/5/44; 3017 BU Hobbs, W/O 5/8/44.

44-8069 Del Hobbs 2/6/44; 3017 BU Hobbs 4/6/44; 3021 BU Las Vegas 10/10/44; 4126 BU San Bernardino 15/12/44; 3022 BU Indian Springs 3/2/45; 3021 BU Las Vegas 23/3/45; 2126 BU Laredo 23/7/45; RFC Walnut Ridge 10/1/46.

44-8070 Del Hobbs 27/5/44; ATC Presque Is 23/7/44; 3017 BU Hobbs 2/12/44; HHR Minneapolis 10/12/44; 3017 BU Hobbs 13/12/44; Recl Comp 1/3/45.

44-8071 Del Hobbs 28/5/44; 3017 BU Hobbs 14/12/44; 3701 BU Amarillo 1/10/45; RFC Kingman 27/11/45.

44-8072 Del Hobbs 28/5/44; slated 836BS/487BG [2G-S], tran 3017 BU Hobbs 28/12/44; 3701 BU Amarillo 13/2/45; RFC Kingman 27/11/45.

44-8073 Del Denver 28/5/44; Dorval, Canada 7/6/44; slated RAF as HB 806; tran 332BS/94BG Rougham 3/8/44; sal 9AF Germany 23/5/46.

44-8074 Del Denver 28/6/44; Dorval 5/7/44; slated RAF HB 807; tran 94BG Rougham 8/44; sal 9AF Germany 23/5/46.

44-8075 Del Denver 29/5/44; Dorval 26/6/44; slated RAF HB 808, tran 8AF 8/44; sal 9AF Germany 23/5/44.

44-8076 Del Denver 30/5/44; Dorval 26/6/44; slated RAF HB 809, tran 369BS/306BG [WW-U] Thurleigh 11/10/44; 305BG Chelveston 5/45; sal 9AF Germany 23/5/46.

44-8077 Del Denver 31/5/44; Dorval 26/6/44; slated RAF HB 810; tran 8AF 3/8/44; retUS Morrison 1/10/45; RFC Walnut Ridge 3/1/46.

44-8078 Del Denver 6/6/44; Dorval 26/6/44; slated RAF HB 811, tran 560BS/388BG Knettishall 3/8/44; retUS Bradley 26/6/45; Sth Plains 29/6/45; RFC Kingman 11/12/45. ROUGH DARTS.

44-8079 Del Denver 2/6/44; Dorval 26/6/44; slated RAF HB 812, tran 511BS/351BG [DS-V] Polebrook 7/10/48; 510BS [TU-V]; {34m} 305BG Chelveston 23/5/46; 401BG Deenethorpe /45; sal 9AF Germany 23/5/46. JANET.

44-8080 Del Denver 2/6/44; Dorval 27/6/44; slated RAF HB 813, tran 385BG Gt Ashfield 4/8/44; 570BS/390BG Framlingham 5/8/44; MIA Merseburg 30/11/44 w/Capt Gray; mid air coll, cr Flur Oberklobikau; 10KIA; MACR 11131.

44-8081 Del Denver 6/6/44; Dorval 26/6/44; slated RAF HB 814, tran 731BS/452BG Deopham Green 4/8/44; retUS Bradley 28/6/45; Sth Plains 1/7/45; RFC Kingman 29/11/45.

44-8082 Del Denver 2/6/44; Dorval 6/6/44; RAF 214Sq HB 815, as [BU-J] at Oulton; shot down by intruder 8/3/45.

44-8083 Del Denver 2/6/44; Dorval 6/6/44; RAF 214Sq HB 816, as [BU-F] Oulton; SOC 11/3/47.

44-8084 Del Denver 6/6/44; Dorval 10/6/44; RAF 214Sq HB 817 as [BU-G] Oulton; SOC 11/3/47.

44-8085 Del Denver 2/6/44; Dorval 9/6/44; RAF 214Sq HB 818 as [BU-H] Oulton; SOC 11/3/47.

44-8086 Del Denver 2/6/44; Dorval 12/6/44; RAF 214Sq HB 819, as [BU-U] Oulton; SOC 11/3/47.

44-8087 Del Denver 1/6/44; Dorval 8/6/44; RAF 214Sq HB 820, as [BU-?] Oulton; c/l Manston, UK 15/2/45; sal 4/7/45.

44-8088 Del Roswell 2/6/44; 4121 BU Kelly 24/9/44; 3030 BU Roswell 20/1/45; 3502 BU Chanute 2/5/45; RFC Kingman 12/1/46.

44-8089 Del Roswell 2/6/44; 3018 BU Kingman 17/1/45; 3030 BU Roswell 22/4/45; RFC Walnut Ridge /45.

Above: B-17G-45-VE 44-8076, as HB809 for the RAF on a landing approach, displays a retracted H2X scanner in the ball turret well. For unrecorded reasons this aircraft was returned to the USAAF and served with the 306th Bomb Group in England. (W. T. Larkins)

44-8090 Del Roswell 6/6/44; 3018 BU Kingman 5/8/44; 3000 BU Orange 5/6/45; RFC Kingman 20/12/45.
44-8091 Del Roswell 9/6/44; 3030 BU Roswell 12/9/44; 4121 BU Kelly 10/6/45; 3030 BU Roswell 12/6/45; RFC Walnut Ridge /45.
44-8092 Del Roswell 6/6/44; 3021 BU Las Vegas 21/9/44; 3022 BU Indian Springs 24/9/44; 3021 BU Las Vegas 1/3/45; 3036 BU Yuma 14/3/45; 3017 BU Hobbs 4/6/45; 3701 BU Amarillo 5/8/45; RFC Kingman 28/12/45.
44-8093 Del Roswell 4/6/44; 3030 BU Roswell 26/12/44; 3502 BU Chanute 2/5/45; 4141 BU Pyote 14/4/47; Recl Comp 22/12/48.
44-8094 Del Roswell 6/6/44; 4126 BU San Bernardino 13/1/45; 3018 BU Kingman 14/1/45; 3030 BU Roswell 22/6/45; RFC Walnut Ridge /45.
44-8095 Del Roswell 7/6/45; 3030 BU Roswell 26/12/44; 3502 BU Chanute 2/5/45; 237 BU Kirtland 31/8/45; 3502 BU Chanute 30/9/45; 338 BU Keesler, Recl Comp 13/10/45.
44-8096 Del Chanute 7/6/44; 3502 BU Chanute 15/6/44; 4141 BU Pyote 14/4/47; Recl Comp 22/12/48.
44-8097 Del New Haven 6/6/44; 3501 BU Boca Raton 15/6/44; 3505 BU Scott 10/2/45; 3501 BU Boca Raton 4/3/45; 2144 BU Moody 6/3/45; 3501 BU Boca Raton 21/3/45; RFC Kingman 22/2/46.
44-8098 Del Dallas 23/6/44; Grenier 27/7/44; ass 381BG Ridgewell 1/8/44; tran 849BS 490BG Eye 2/8/44; c/l 27/12/44; sal 29/12/44.
44-8099 Del Dallas 7/6/44; Langley 27/6/44; Dow Fd 25/7/44; ass 423BS/306BG Thurleigh 24/8/44; MIA Hannover 22/10/44 w/Alvea; mid air coll, cr Nth Sea; 9KIA 1RTD; MACR 9655.
44-8100 Del Dallas 7/6/44; Hunter 17/6/44; Grenier 24/7/44; ass 511BS/351BG [DS-B] Polebrook 10/8/44; b/d Brux 12/9/44 w/Schmollinger; e/a, cr Tempelfelde, Ger; 9POW; MACR 8893; sal 9AF Germany 1/5/47.
44-8101 Del Dallas 6/6/44; W/O 10/6/44.
44-8102 Del Dallas 9/6/44; Hunter 20/7/44; Presque Is 8/8/44; ass 463BG Celone 16/8/44; sal 11/6/45.
44-8103 Del Dallas 9/6/44; Hunter 10/7/44; Grenier 4/8/44; ass 96BS/2BG Amendola 9/8/44; MIA Odertal 22/8/44 w/Cutler; flak hit #1, cr Clausenburg; MACR 7954.
44-8104 Del Dallas 7/6/44; Hunter 21/7/44; Dow Fd 3/8/44; ass 815BS/483BG Sterparone 10/8/44; sal 21/3/46. FLOOGIE BOO OLD WARHOSS.
44-8105 Del Dallas 5/6/44; Langley 3/7/44; Dow Fd 4/8/44; ass 353BS/301BG PFF Lucera 14/8/44; retUS, RFC Walnut Ridge 7/10/45.
44-8106 Del Dallas 7/6/44; Hunter 6/7/44; Dow Fd 4/8/44; ass 772BS/463BG PFF Celone 12/8/44; MIA Bleckhammer 13/9/44 w/Watson; flak, cr Gross Stohlitz; MACR 8345.
44-8107 Del Dallas 7/6/44; Hunter 26/7/44; Dow Fd 10/8/44; ass 419BS/301BG Lucera 18/8/44; MIA Regensburg 28/12/44 w/Hillyer; mech fault, cr Staubing; 1KIA(wg) 9POW; MACR 10894. JOSEPHINE.
44-8108 Del Dallas 7/6/44; Hunter 10/7/44; Dow Fd 4/8/44; ass 429BS/2BG Amendola 10/8/44; b/d Bologna 16/4/45 w/Underwood, who c/l, after rest of crew baled over friendly territory; sal; LINDA JANE, SIR JOHN WILCO.
44-8109 Del Dallas 16/6/44; Langley 19/7/44; Grenier 9/8/44; ass 338BS/96BG [BX-R] Snetterton 11/8/44; MIA Merseburg 30/11/44 w/Whaley; flak, cr Bebra, Ger; 1KIA 9POW; MACR 10832.
44-8110 Del Dallas 14/6/44; Langley 17/7/44; Grenier 8/8/44; ass 524BS/379BG [WA-F] Kimbolton 26/8/44; retUS Morrison 22/10/45; RFC Walnut Ridge 28/10/45.
44-8111 Del Dallas 13/6/44; Langley 8/7/44; Grenier 12/9/44; ass 817BS/483BG PFF Sterparone 15/9/44; MIA Vienna 11/12/44 w/Jarrett; mech fault, cr Szeged; 10EVD, ret 27/12/44; MACR 10129. KITTY ANN.
44-8112 Del Dallas 21/6/44; Langley 14/7/44; Presque Is 11/8/44; ass 4BS/34BG Mendlesham 19/8/44; retUS Morrison 29/10/44; RFC Walnut Ridge 7/1/46.
44-8113 Del Dallas 14/6/44; Langley 10/7/44; Dow Fd 9/8/44; ass 816BS/483BG PFF Sterparone 16/8/44; {52m} sal 9AF Germany 10/5/46. NO. 2 BANDWAGON.
44-8114 Del Dallas 14/6/44; Langley 11/7/44; Dow Fd 11/8/44; ass 341BS/97BG Amendola 11/9/44; retUS Independence; RFC Kingman 18/12/45.
44-8115 Del Dallas 15/6/44; Langley 10/7/44; Grenier 9/8/44; ass 97BG PFF Amendola 22/8/44; sal 9AF Germany 21/5/46.
44-8116 Del Dallas 15/6/44; Langley 17/6/44; Dow Fd 17/8/44; ass 347BS/99BG PFF Tortorella 31/8/44; {63m} sal 9AF Germany 10/5/46.
44-8117 Del Dallas 15/6/44; Langley 18/7/44; Dow Fd 17/8/44; ass 96BS/2BG PFF Amendola 28/8/44; c/l 11/2/45; sal.
44-8118 Del Dallas 14/6/44; Langley 6/7/44; Dow Fd 7/8/44; ass 772BS/463BG PFF Celone 11/8/44; MIA Bologna 12/10/44 w/Winters; flak, cr Ruffeld; 10POW; MACR 9080.
44-8119 Del Dallas 16/6/44; Langley 18/7/44; Dow Fd 8/8/44; ass 815BS/483BG PFF Sterparone 16/8/44; sal 9AF Germany 10/5/46.
44-8120 Del Dallas 28/6/44; Cheyenne 24/9/44; Hunter 3/10/44; Dow Fd 16/10/44; ass 815BS/483BG PFF Sterparone 3/11/44; MIA night mission to Salzburg 7/12/44 w/Cooper; flak, cr Fernhattal; 10POW; MACR 10219.
44-8121 Del Dallas 14/6/44; Langley 10/7/44; Grenier 7/8/44; ass 836BS/487BG Lavenham 10/8/44; b/d Darmstadt 24/12/44 w/?; f/l Continent; sal; MACR 11561.
44-8122 Del Dallas 15/6/44; Langley 14/7/44; Dow Fd 7/8/44; ass 816BS/483BG PFF Sterparone 10/8/44; sal 9AF Germany 10/5/46.
44-8123 Del Dallas 19/6/44; Langley 29/7/44; Grenier 8/9/44; ass 95BG Horham 9/9/44; tran 97BG PFF Amendola 17/9/44; sal 9AF Germany 10/5/46.
44-8124 Del Dallas 16/6/44; Langley 10/7/44; Grenier 6/8/44; ass 306BG Thurleigh 1/9/44; sal 9AF Germany 23/5/46.
44-8125 Del Dallas 16/6/44; Langley 19/7/44; Grenier 3/8/44; ass 360BS/303BG [PU-Y] Molesworth 5/8/44; sal 9AF Germany 31/5/46. SPARKY.
44-8126 Del Dallas 2/7/44; Grenier 13/8/44; ass 97BG PFF Amendola 13/4/45; tran 49BS/2BG Amendola 14/4/45; sal 9AF Germany 21/6/46.
44-8127 Del Dallas 16/6/44; Langley 2/7/44; Presque Is 7/8/44; ass 571BS/390BG [FC-G] Framlingham 15/8/44; retUS, RFC Walnut Ridge 8/1/46.
44-8128 Del Dallas 17/6/44; Langley 21/7/44; Grenier 7/9/44; ass 94BG Rougham 9/9/44; tran 97BG PFF Amendola 28/9/44; b/d Salzburg 11/11/44 w/Moore; c/l Rimini, burnt out; sal.
44-8129 Del Dallas 16/6/44; Langley 11/7/44; Dow Fd 7/8/44; ass 422BS/305BG [JJ-O] Chelveston 26/8/44; sal 9AF Germany 23/5/45. BANG AWAY LULU.
44-8130 Del Dallas 15/6/44; Langley 11/7/44; Dow Fd 9/8/44; ass 486BG Sudbury 11/8/44; b/d Berlin 3/2/44 w/?; c/l Rolozno, Pol; sal 14/2/45. BLUE STREAK.
44-8131 Del Dallas 17/6/44; Langley 18/7/44; Dow Fd 3/8/44; ass 333BS/94BG Rougham 6/8/44; tran

447BG Rattlesden 7/8/44; badly damaged by debris from exploding a/c while preparing for mission 21/2/45, sal.

44-8132 Del Dallas 19/6/44; Langley 10/7/44; Grenier 13/8/44; ass 94BG Rougham 21/8/44; sal 9AF Germany 23/5/46.

44-8133 Del Dallas 17/6/44; Langley 16/7/44; Dow Fd 3/8/44; ass 305BG Chelveston 26/8/44; sal 9AF Germany 18/4/46.

44-8134 Del Dallas 17/6/44; Langley 18/7/44; Grenier 15/8/44; ass 839BS/487BG Lavenham 15/8/44; tran 333BS/94BG [TS-U] Rougham 16/8/44; retUS, RFC Walnut Ridge 27/11/45. OUR BABY.

44-8135 Del Dallas 17/6/44; Langley 13/7/44; Dow Fd 7/8/44; ass 324BS/91BG [DF-A] Bassingbourn 27/8/44; b/d Hamburg 6/11/44 w/?; c/l Rackheath Afd, UK; sal 9/11/44.

44-8136 Del Dallas 22/6/44; Langley 21/7/44; Dow Fd 16/8/44; ass 379BG Kimbolton 6/9/44; b/d Cologne 14/10/44 ; f/l Continent, sal.

44-8137 Del Dallas 18/6/44; Langley 23/7/44; Grenier 11/8/44; ass 360BS/303BG [PU-Z] Molesworth 26/8/44; MIA Aschaffenburg 21/1/45 w/Duffield; mid air coll, cr Rottweil, Ger; 9KIA 1POW; MACR 11759.

44-8138 Del Dallas 18/6/44; Langley 20/7/44; Presque Is 13/8/44; ass 493BG Debach 15/8/44; sal 9AF Germany 29/12/45.

44-8139 Del Dallas 19/6/44; Ft Myers 24/7/44; as QB-17 110 BU Mitchell 23/8/44; 2 EEL Fort Dix 18/9/44; 1377 BU Grenier 21/9/44; 4149 BU Ft Dix 5/11/44; 110 BU Mitchell 27/1/45; 4149 BU Ft Dix 20/2/45; 139 BU Shaw Fd 1/5/45; 4121 BU Kelly 4/9/45; 4149 BU Ft Dix 22/10/45; ATS Dover 13/1/46; 4112 BU Olmstead 13/4/46; 4108 BU Newark 30/9/46; 110 BU Mitchell 10/2/47; 4000 BU Patterson 15/2/47; 4108 BU Newark 19/2/47; 4112 BU Olmstead 30/6/47; Recl Comp 7/1/49.

44-8140 Del Dallas 16/6/44; Langley 22/7/44; Dow Fd 12/8/44; ass 490BG Debach 18/8/44; tran 4BS/34BG Mendlesham 19/8/44; MIA Berlin 5/12/44 w/Capt Gregory; flak, cr Gross Zerlang, Ger; 10KIA 1POW; MACR 11046.

44-8141 Del Dallas 20/6/44; Langley 18/7/44; Grenier 13/8/44; ass 365BS/305BG Chelveston 8/9/44; MIA Bohlen 2/3/44 w/Lt Col Howell Clark; flak, cr Bohlen; 10KIA 1POW; MACR 12851.

44-8142 Del Dallas 20/6/44; Ft Dix 27/7/44; as QB-17 110 BU Mitchell 15/8/44; 2 EEL Ft Dix 19/9/44; 902 BU Orlando 9/10/44; 4112 BU Olmstead 1/11/44; 4149 BU Ft Dix 7/12/44; 1103 BU Morrison 25/1/45; 113 BU Charleston 25/2/45; 902 BU Orlando 27/2/45; 4149 BU Ft Dix 11/3/45; 1103 BU Morrison 20/4/45; 113 BU Charleston 20/5/45; 902 BU Orlando 4/7/45; 4149 BU Ft Dix 23/8/45; 4104 BU Rome 28/8/45; 4149 BU Olmstead 8/8/46; Recl Comp 24/10/47; AMC Columbus 1/1/48; 3203 MSU Eglin 14/3/49; 550 GM Eglin, W/O 3/1/50.

44-8143 Del Dallas 23/6/44; Langley 26/7/44; Dow Fd 13/8/44; ass 333BS/94BG Rougham 15/8/44; tran 548BS/385BG Gt Ashfield 19/8/44; MIA Berlin 6/10/44 w/Capt Batty; e/a, cr Senke, Ger; 7KIA 3POW; MACR 9516.

44-8144 Del Dallas 27/6/44; Langley 27/7/44; Dow Fd 4/8/44; ass 335BS/95BG [OE-O] Horham 10/8/44; b/d Hamburg 30/3/45 w/Parrish; f/l RAF Woodbridge (ELG), UK; 1WIA 8RTD; retUS Bradley 26/6/45; Sth Plains 29/6/45; RFC Kingman 29/11/45. HELL'S BELLE.

44-8145 Del Dallas 27/6/44; Langley 21/7/44; Grenier 17/8/44; ass 323BS/91BG [OR-C] Bassingbourn 15/9/44 TAILOR MADE; 324BS [DF-C]; tran 303BG Molesworth 4/12/44; 367BS/306BG Thurleigh 24/5/45; {24+m} sal 9AF Germany 26/7/46. AH'S AVAILBLE.

44-8146 Del Dallas 20/6/44; Langley 6/7/44; Dow Fd 7/9/44; ass 562BS/388BG Knettishall 9/9/44; sal 9AF Germany 28/2/46; retUS, 613 BU Phillips 29/4/46.

44-8147 Del Dallas 23/6/44; Langley 26/7/44; Dow Fd 18/8/44; ass 4BS/34BG Mendlesham 20/8/44; b/d Merseburg 30/11/44 w/?; f/l Continent; sal 13/12/44.

44-8148 Del Dallas 22/6/44; Langley 27/7/44; Grenier 11/8/44; ass 369BS/306BG [WW-K] Thurleigh 13/8/44; tran 95BG Horham 14/8/44; 100BG Thorpe Abbotts 30/8/44; b/d Hamm 26/11/44 w/?; f/l St Trond Afd, Bel; sal 5/1/45.

44-8149 Del Dallas 27/6/44; Langley 24/7/44; Dow Fd 18/8/44; ass 839BS/487BG Lavenham 29/10/44; tran 94BG Rougham 29/5/45; used for photography along Belgian-Dutch coasts (coded WIPE); sal 9AF Germany 20/2/47.

44-8150 Del Dallas 24/6/44; Langley 24/7/44; Presque Is 15/8/44; ass 490BG Debach 25/8/44; retUS, RFC Walnut Ridge 7/1/46.

44-8151 Del Dallas 29/6/44; Langley 16/7/44; Dow Fd 4/8/44; ass 569BS/390BG [CC-O] Framlingham 10/8/44; b/d Heilbronn 20/1/45 w/Greenstreet; flak, cr Ettenheim, Ger; 1KIA 9RTD; sal; MACR 11774. PRINCESS PAT.

44-8152 Del Dallas 23/6/44; Langley 28/7/44; Dow Fd 22/8/44; ass 748BS/457BG Glatton 22/9/44; exploded on base 5/4/45, sal. MISS IDA.

44-8153 Del Dallas 27/6/44; Langley 27/7/44; Dow Fd 17/8/44; ass 612BS/401BG [SC-Q] Deenethorpe 19/8/44; 615BS [IY-O]; tran 305BG Chelveston 20/5/45; sal 9AF Germany 23/5/46.

44-8154 Del Dallas 27/7/44; Langley 28/7/44; Grenier 2/9/44; ass 348BS/99BG PFF Tortorella 28/9/44; MIA {9m} Linz 25/11/44 w/Huff; e/a, cr San Marteu; 4KIA 4POW (only eight crew on each of four a/c on night mission); MACR 10012.

44-8155 Del Dallas 26/6/44; Langley 27/7/44; Dow Fd 23/8/44; ass 525BS/379BG [FR-Z] Kimbolton 16/9/44; sal 9AF Germany 31/5/46.

44-8156 Del Dallas 26/6/44; Langley 24/7/44; Dow Fd 5/8/44; ass 418BS/100BG [LD-U] Thorpe Abbotts 7/8/44; retUS, RFC Walnut Ridge 20/12/45.

44-8157 Del Dallas 25/6/44; Langley 26/7/44; Dow Fd 23/8/44; ass 359BS/303BG [BN-Z] Molesworth 25/8/44; tran 751BS/457BG Glatton 15/9/44; 305BG Chelveston 23/5/45; sal 9AF Germany 10/5/46.

44-8158 Del Dallas 24//6/44; Langley 27/7/44; Dow Fd 17/8/44; ass 4BS/34BG Mendlesham 18/4/44; tran 850BS/490BG Debach 20/8/44; 332BS/94BG [XM-Q] Rougham 5/45; retUS 593 BU Charleston 28/10/44; RFC Walnut Ridge 27/12/45. BOBBY SOX.

44-8159 Del Dallas 26/6/44; Hunter 28/7/44; Dow Fd 5/9/44; ass 817BS/483BG Sterparone 20/9/44; MIA Berlin 24/3/45 w/Dailey; jet e/a, cr Berlin; 10POW; MACR 13375.

44-8160 Del Dallas 26/6/44; Langley 27/7/44; Dow Fd 22/8/44; ass 4BS/34BG Mendlesham 26/8/44; retUS Bradley 12/7/45; Independence 16/7/45; RFC Kingman 28/12/45.

44-8161 Del Dallas 23/6/44; Hunter 27/7/44; Dow Fd 9/8/44; ass 353BS/301BG Lucera 15/8/44; MIA Bleckhammer 18/12/44 w/Keiser; baled Bihac, Yugo; 1POW(nav) 9EVD and ret; MACR 10893.

44-8162 Del Dallas 24/6/44; Hunter 24/7/44; Dow Fd 17/8/44; ass 429BS/2BG Amendola 28/8/44; MIA Berlin 24/3/45 w/Rapelyea; flak hit two engines, cr Gyor, Hung; MACR 13372.

44-8163 Del Dallas 27/6/44; Hunter 24/7/44; Dow Fd 8/8/44; ass 772BS/463BG Celone 15/8/44; MIA Vienna 13/2/45 w/Whitman; flak, cr Schuetzen; MACR 12109.

44-8164 Del Dallas 27/6/44; Hunter 28/7/44; Dow Fd 9/8/44; ass 348BS/99BG Tortorella 29/8/44; {47m} RetUS, RFC Kingman 17/12/45.

44-8165 Del Dallas 27/6/44; Cheyenne 31/6/44; Kearney 9/8/44; Grenier 25/8/44; ass 338BS/96BG [BX-R] Snetterton 27/8/44; sal n/b/d 9/5/45.

44-8166 Del Dallas 27/6/44; Hunter 27/7/44; Dow Fd 9/8/44; ass 340BS/97BG Amendola 16/8/44; MIA Bleckhammer 13/9/44 w/Knoblock; flak, cr Krakow; MACR 8726.

44-8167 Del Dallas 28/7/44; Hunter 29/7/44; Dow Fd 10/8/44; ass 96BS/2BG Amendola 17/8/44; {79m} RetUS Hunter 3/7/45; RFC Kingman 7/12/45.

44-8168 Del Dallas 29/6/44; Hunter 28/7/44; Dow Fd 15/8/44; ass 49BS/2BG PFF Amendola 29/8/44; MIA Regensburg 20/1/45 w/Wittlinger; flak hit two engines, cr Letten; MACR 11272. FLYING HOME.

44-8169 Del Dallas 28/6/44; Cheyenne 11/8/44; Hunter 22/8/44; Grenier 10/9/44; ass 570BS/390BG [DI-Q] Framlingham 13/9/44; retUS Bradley 2/7/45; Sth Plains 6/7/45; RFC Kingman 23/11/45.

44-8170 Del Dallas 29/6/44; Langley 24/7/44; Dow Fd 16/8/44; ass 4BS/34BG Mendlesham 26/8/44; retUS, RFC Walnut Ridge 5/1/46.

44-8171 Del Dallas 27/6/44; Langley 27/7/44; Dow Fd 20/8/44; ass 413BS/96BG [MZ-B] Snetterton 24/8/44; retUS Morrison 22/10/44; RFC Walnut Ridge 8/1/46.

44-8172 Del Dallas 28/6/44; Langley 24/7/44; Dow Fd 22/8/44; ass 327BS/92BG [UX-F] Podington 15/9/44; tran 381BG Ridgewell 7/5/45; 306BG Thurleigh 23/5/45; sal 9AF Germany 24/7/46.

44-8173 Del Dallas 28/6/44; Langley 22/7/44; Dow Fd 18/8/44; ass 322BS/91BG Bassingbourn 10/11/44; b/d Gelsenkirchen 22/11/44 w/?; f/l Continent, sal 3/12/44.

44-8174 Del Dallas 29/6/44; Langley 26/7/44; Dow Fd 17/8/44; ass 322BS/91BG [DF-E] Bassingbourn 18/11/44; aborted Mannheim mission, c/l base 20/1/45 w/?; sal 3/12/44.

44-8175 Del Dallas 30/6/44; Langley 28/7/44; Dow Fd 21/8/44; ass 533BS/381BG PFF [VP-N] Ridgewell 17/9/44; MIA {23m} Feldhausen 22/3/45 w/Fawcett (gp lead); flak hit #3, a/c exploded, tail broke off, cr Continent; 10KIA inc Capt Stone, only man in group with 50 missions. MACR 13605/13607.

44-8176 Del Dallas 29/6/44; Langley 30/7/44; Dow Fd 22/8/44; ass 34BG Mendlesham 30/8/44; retUS Morrison 29/10/44; RFC Walnut Ridge 8/1/46.

44-8177 Del Dallas 29/6/44; Langley 23/7/44; Dow Fd 27/8/44; ass 333BS/94BG [TS-O] Rougham 30/8/44; mid air coll w/42-97985 on approach, c/l base 30/11/44, rep; retUS Morrison 20/10/45; RFC Walnut Ridge 2/1/46.

44-8178 Del Dallas 29/6/44; Langley 20/7/44; Dow Fd 22/8/44; ass 413BS/96BG [MZ-D] Snetterton 24/8/44; b/d Ludwigshafen 6/1/45 w/?; f/l Continent, sal 22/2/45.

44-8179 Del Dallas 30/6/44; Langley 27/8/44; Dow Fd 22/8/44; ass 336BS/95BG [ET-L] Horham 25/8/44; b/d Cologne 17/10/44 w/Miller; c/l Belgium, 1KIA 4WIA 5RTD, rep; b/d Nuremberg 20/2/45 w/?; f/l Florennes, Bel; rep, sal 9AF Germany 10/5/46.

44-8180 Del Dallas 1/7/44; Langley 31/7/44; Dow Fd 24/8/44; ass 837BS/487BG [4F-N] Lavenham 28/10/44; tran 332BS/94BG [XM-K] Rougham 29/5/45; 410BS [GL-K]; sal 9AF Germany 10/5/46.

44-8181 Del Dallas 1/7/44; Langley 27/7/44; Dow Fd 22/8/44; ass 730BS/452BG Deopham Green

30/8/44; b/d Cologne 10/1/45 w/?; on return approach crew baled safely, but a/c cr on Thorpe Abbotts bomb dump, exploded, sal.

44-8182 Del Dallas 1/7/44; Langley 28/7/44; Grenier 16/9/44; ass 32BS/301BG PFF Lucera 17/10/44; b/d Bleckhammer 26/12/44 w/Kage; c/l Russian territory; sal 9AF Germany 10/5/46.

44-8183 Del Dallas 2/7/44; Langley 30/7/44; Dow Fd 23/8/44; ass 418BS/100BG [LD-Q] Thorpe Abbotts; b/d Hamm 26/11/44 w/?; f/l St Trond, Bel; retUS, RFC Walnut Ridge 8/1/46.

44-8184 Del Dallas 1/7/44; Langley 28/7/44; Grenier 9/9/44; ass 96BS/2BG Amendola 28/9/44; sal 9AF Germany 10/5/46.

44-8185 Del Dallas 5/7/44; Langley 31/7/44; Dow Fd 21/8/44; ass 4BS/34BG Mendlesham 30/8/44; MIA Ludwigshafen 27/9/44 w/Capt Blackburn; e/a, cr Stromberg, Ger; 11POW; MACR 9367.

44-8186 Del Dallas 2/7/44; Langley 3/8/44; Dow Fd 11/9/44; ass 32BS/301BG PFF Lucera 3/10/44; MIA Bleckhammer 26/12/44 w/Kagi; c/l Russian territory; 10EVD & ret; SUGAR REPORT.

44-8187 Del Dallas 1/7/44; Langley 29/7/44; Dow Fd 6/9/44; ass 346BS/99BG PFF Tortorella 17/10/44; MIA {20m} Augsburg 27/2/45 w/Smith; b/d, two engines out, f/l Switzerland; MACR 12513; sal 9AF Germany 10/12/45.

44-8188 Del Dallas 5/7/44; Langley 29/7/44; Grenier 16/9/44; ass 97BG PFF Amendola 3/10/44; retUS, RFC Walnut Ridge 9/12/45.

44-8189 Del Dallas 5/7/44; Langley 24/7/44; Grenier 23/9/44; ass 429BS/2BG PFF Amendola 11/11/44; bellied in Lake Lesina, nr Foggia 13/11/44 w/Trump; sal.

44-8190 Del Dallas 6/7/44; Langley 30/7/44; Dow Fd 18/9/44; ass 483BG PFF Sterparone 26/9/44; sal 9AF Germany 10/5/46.

44-8191 Del Dallas 5/7/44; Langley 28/7/44; Grenier 12/9/44; ass 429BS/2BG PFF Amendola 15/9/44; MIA Ruhland 22/3/45 w/Crane; flak, two engines out, cr Linz; MACR 13248.

44-8192 Del Dallas 6/7/44; Cheyenne 27/7/44; Grenier 7/9/44; ass 487BG Lavenham 10/9/44; MIA Darmstadt 24/12/44 w/?; hit by e/a while still over Belgium; MACR 11258.

44-8193 Del Dallas 6/7/44; Langley 30/7/44; Dow Fd 14/9/44; ass 773BS/463BG PFF Celone 21/9/44; MIA Regensburg 9/12/44 w/Jacobs; mech fault, #2 & 3 out; f/l Altenrhein, Switz; MACR 10130.

44-8194 Del Dallas 6/7/44; Langley 30/7/44; Grenier 3/9/44; ass 341BS/97BG PFF Amendola 17/10/44; retUS Bradley 12/7/45; Independence 16/7/45; RFC Albuquerque 6/2/46.

44-8195 Del Dallas 6/7/44; Langley 1/8/44; Grenier 2/9/44; ass 20BS/2BG PFF Amendola 13/11/44; MIA Bleckhammer 13/11/44 w/Pederson; no gas, ditched crew rescued by Italian fishing boats, inc Cpl George Barrett of Yank magazine.

44-8196 Del Dallas 7/7/44; Langley 7/8/44; Dow Fd 10/9/44; ass 533BS/381BG PFF [VP-U] Ridgewell 5/10/44; b/d {22+m} Berlin 29/3/45 w/Privett?; c/l base, sal 30/3/45.

44-8197 Del Dallas 8/7/45; Langley 6/8/44; Dow Fd 27/8/44; ass 367BS/306BG [GY-K] Thurleigh 15/9/44; sal 9AF Germany 26/7/46. PUNCHY.

44-8198 Del Dallas 7/7/44; Langley 5/8/44; Hunter 2/9/44; ass 379BG Kimbolton 5/10/44; mid air col w/44-8813 10/5/45 w/?; sal n/b/d 11/5/45.

44-8199 Del Dallas 7/7/44; Langley 4/8/44; Grenier 1/9/44; ass 603BS/398BG Nuthampstead 17/9/44; 601BS [3O-R]; MIA Münster 28/10/44 w/Sheely; flak, cr Emmerich; 10POW; MACR 10262.

44-8200 Del Dallas 8/7/44; Langley 3/8/44; Grenier 29/8/44; ass 861BS/493BG Debach 1/9/44; 863BS; tran 350BS/100BG [LN-D] Thorpe Abbotts 6/9/44; sal 9AF Germany 27/6/46.

44-8201 Del Dallas 7/7/44; Langley 9/8/44; Grenier 10/9/44; ass 731BS/452BG Deopham Green 12/9/44; 729BS; MIA Bad Kreuznach 2/1/45 w/McDougall; flak, cr Tier, Ger; 1KIA 8POW; MACR 11257.

44-8202 Del Dallas 8/7/44; Langley 8/8/44; Grenier 9/9/44; ass 570BS/390BG Framlingham 22/9/44; retUS, RFC Walnut Ridge 3/11/45.

44-8203 Del Dallas 8/7/44; Langley 8/8/44; Dow Fd 1/9/44; ass 306BG Thurleigh 21/9/44; tran 533BS/381BG Ridgewell 5/45; retUS Bradley 7/7/45; Sth Plains 13/7/45 RFC Kingman 1/12/45.

44-8204 Del Dallas 8/7/44; Langley 7/8/44; Grenier 18/9/44; ass 8AF 19/9/44; retUS Morrison 25/10/44; 593 BU Charleston 28/10/45; RFC Walnut Ridge 7/1/46.

44-8205 Del Dallas 10/7/44; Langley 5/8/44; Grenier 28/8/44; ass 305BG Chelveston 24/9/44; sal 1/6/45.

44-8206 Del Dallas, via 5rd FG, 11/7/44; Langley 8/8/44; Dow Fd 12/9/44; ass 571BS/390BG [FC-P] Framlingham 22/9/44; retUS Bradley 2/7/45; Sth Plains 8/7/45; RFC Kingman 17/12/45.

44-8207 Del Dallas 10/7/44; Langley 5/8/44; Grenier 29/8/44; ass 562BS/388BG Knettishall 2/11/44; 563BS; b/d Hamburg 31/12/44 w/Maj Harrell; flak, ditched off Borkum, Ger; 10POW; MACR 11241.

44-8208 Del Dallas 11/7/44; Langley 4/8/44; Dow Fd 12/9/44; ass 322BS/91BG [LG-Q] Bassingbourn 4/10/44; MIA Merseburg 2/11/44 w/Capt Hammer; e/a, cr Michelln, Ger?; 1KIA 8POW; MACR 10143. MY BABY II.

44-8209 Del Dallas 10/7/44; Langley 3/8/44; Dow Fd 12/9/44; ass 100BG Thorpe Abbotts 22/9/44; retUS 5693BU Charleston 28/10/44; RFC Walnut Ridge 27/10/45.

44-8210 Del Dallas 11/7/44; Langley 8/8/44; Dow Fd 12/9/44; ass 332BS/94BG [XM-Z] Rougham 14/9/44; tran 335BS/95BG [OE-J] Horham 11/44; retUS, RFC Walnut Ridge 19/10/45. SWEETHEART OF SEATTLE.

44-8211 Del Dallas 11/7/44; Langley 9/8/44; Dow Fd 18/9/44; ass 546BS/384BG [BK-Z] Grafton Underwood 30/9/44; tran 305BG Chelveston 9/5/45; sal 9AF Germany 10/5/46.

44-8212 Del Dallas 11/7/44; Langley 1/8/44; Grenier 18/9/44; ass 848BS/490BG Eye 26/9/44; ground accident, caught fire 15/2/45; sal 16/2/45.

44-8213 Del Dallas 11/7/44; Langley 31/7/44; Grenier 20/8/44; ass 338BS/96BG [BX-M] Snetterton 30/8/44; retUS Morrison 20/10/44; Charleston 28/10/44; RFC Walnut Ridge 26/11/45. HOOP'S SPOOKS.

44-8214 Del Dallas 17/7/44; Langley 3/8/44; Grenier 16/9/44; ass 379BG Kimbolton 12/9/44; tran 602BS/398BG [K8-B] Nuthampstead 11/10/44; 603BS [N7-S]; 306BG Thurleigh 27/5/45; sal 9AF Germany 31/5/46.

44-8215 Del Dallas 12/7/44; Langley 10/8/44; Grenier 14/9/44; ass 325BS/92BG [NV-M] Podington 4/10/44; b/d Merseburg 2/11/44 w/?; f/l Woodbridge ELG, UK; sal 3/11/44.

44-8216 Del Dallas 12/7/44; Langley 12/8/44; Grenier 18/9/44; ass 545BS/384BG [JD-Y] Grafton Underwood 4/11/44; 546BS [BK-Y]; MIA Cologne 10/1/45 w/Hicks; flak, cr Plum, Ger; 11KIA; MACR 11578.

44-8217 Del Dallas 9/7/44; Langley 15/8/44; Dow Fd 18/9/44; ass 100BG Thorpe Abbotts 19/9/44; tran 412BS/95BG [QW-X] Horham 20/9/44; retUS, RFC Walnut Ridge 20/20/44.

44-8218 Del Dallas 14/7/44; Langley 15/8/44; Dow Fd 18/9/44; ass 8AF 29/9/44; retUS, RFC Walnut Ridge 5/11/45.

44-8219 Del Dallas 14/7/44; Langley 14/8/44; Grenier 18/9/44; ass 749BS/457BG Glatton 4/10/44; tran 305BG Chelveston 5/45; sal 9AF Germany 10/5/46.

44-8220 Del Dallas 12/7/44; Langley 7/8/44; Hunter 27/8/44; Dow Fd 18/9/44; ass 350BS/100BG [XR-B] Thorpe Abbotts 20/9/44; MIA Brunswick 3/3/45 w/Thrasher; jet e/a, cr Dettum, Ger; 3KIA 6POW; MACR 12892.

44-8221 Del Dallas 14/7/44; Langley 8/8/44; Hunter 5/9/44; Dow Fd 18/9/44; ass 547BS/384BG [SO-X] Grafton Underwood 5/11/44; 545BS [JD-W]; tran 305BG Chelveston 9/5/45; sal 9AF Germany 18/4/46.

44-8222 Del Dallas 13/7/44; Langley 12/8/44; Grenier 12/9/44; ass 508BS/351BG [YB-A] Polebrook 23/9/44; 509BS [RQ-A]; b/d {4m} Politz 7/10/44 w/Lt Col Benoid Glawe; flak, f/l Sovde, Swed; 10INT; MACR 9565; Ret UK 29/5/45; retUS Bradley 3/7/45; Sth Plains 9/7/45; RFC Kingman 1/12/45.

44-8223 Del Dallas 15/7/44; Langley 14/8/44; Grenier 12/9/44; ass 562BS/388BG Knettishall 20/9/44; MIA Nuremberg 20/2/45 w/Capt Gaspard; flak, cr Ludwigsburg; 3KIA 8POW; MACR 12549. MISS KAREN K.

44-8224 Del Dallas 16/7/44; Langley 12/8/44; Dow Fd 12/9/44; ass 324BS/91BG Bassingbourn 14/9/44; ret 603BS/398BG Nuthampstead 11/10/44; MIA Neuss, Ger. 23/1/45 w/Col Frank Hunter (Gp CO); flak, cr Heerde, Hol; 10KIA; MACR 11799.

44-8225 Del Dallas 16/7/44; Langley 12/8/44; Dow Fd 12/9/44; ass 570BS/390BG [DI-L] Framlingham 29/9/44; MIA Kaltenkirchen 7/4/45 w/Kotta; jet e/a, cr Celle, Ger; 9POW; MACR 13891. HARD TO GET.

44-8226 Del Dallas 14/7/44; Langley 18/8/44; Grenier 14/9/44; ass 95BG Horham 25/9/44; tran 350BS/100BG [LN-B] Thorpe Abbotts 26/9/44; retUS Bradley 2/7/45; Independence 24/8/45; RFC Kingman 21/12/45. JIMBO (JUMBO?).

44-8227 Del Dallas 18/7/44; Langley 17/8/44; Dow Fd 18/9/44; ass 305BG Chelveston 6/10/44; c/t/o for Metz 9/11/44 w/?; sal.

44-8228 Del Dallas 24/7/44; Langley 17/8/44; Dow Fd 16/9/44; ass 418BS/100BG [LD-B] Thorpe Abbotts 18/9/44; tran 535BS/381BG [MS-L] Ridgewell 3/10/44; {7+m} 306BG Thurleigh 5/45; sal 9AF Germany 10/5/46. THE ALAMO.

44-8229 Del Dallas 16/7/44; Langley 18/8/44; Grenier 16/9/44; ass 333BS/94BG [TS-L] Rougham 18/9/44; b/d Kaiserlautern 18/1/45 w/?; f/l Continent; sal 25/2/45.

44-8230 Del Dallas 17/7/44; Langley 18/4/44; Hunter 10/9/44; Grenier 18/9/44; ass 334BS/95BG [BG-M] Horham 20/9/44; sal 6/5/45; retUS, RFC Walnut Ridge 19/10/45.

44-8231 Del Dallas 17/7/44; Langley 13/8/44; Dow Fd 10/10/44; ass 775BS/463BG PFF Celone 17/10/44; MIA Vienna 12/12/44 w/Wheeless; flak, cr Szolnok; 2KIA 8 in Bucharest; MACR 10892.

44-8232 Del Dallas 17/7/44; Langley 22/8/44; Dow Fd 5/10/44; ass 49BS/2BG PFF Amendola 10/10/44; {11m} tran 352BS/301BG Lucera 13/12/44; sal 9AF Germany 10/5/46.

44-8233 Del Dallas 9/7/44; Langley 4/8/44; Dow Fd 8/10/44; ass 483BG Sterparone 19/10/44; sal 9AF Germany 10/5/46. MISS CELLANEOUS.

44-8234 Del Dallas 17/7/44; Hunter 18/8/44; Dow Fd 18/9/44; ass 562BS/388BG Knettishall 20/9/44;

44-8235 Del Dallas 18/7/44; Hunter 22/8/44; Dow Fd 7/9/44; ass 4BS/34BG Mendlesham 26/9/44; retUS, RFC Walnut Ridge 7/1/46.

44-8236 Del Dallas 17/7/44; Hunter 25/8/44; Grenier 5/9/44; ass 332BS/94BG [XM-M] Rougham 12/9/44; retUS, RFC Walnut Ridge 2/1/46. MIKKEY.

44-8237 Del Dallas 19/7/44; Hunter 27/8/44; Grenier 8/9/44; ass 4BS/34BG Mendlesham 12/9/44; tran 333BS/94BG Rougham 13/9/44; sal 31/5/45; DALLAS DOLLIE.

44-8238 Del Dallas 19/7/44; Hunter 23/8/44; Grenier 2/9/44; ass 358BS/303BG [VK-Y] Molesworth 3/10/44; landing accident 6/5/45, sal.

44-8239 Dallas 19/7/44; Hunter 20/8/44; Grenier 18/9/44; ass 333BS/94BG [TS-W] Rougham 20/9/44; retUS, RFC Walnut Ridge 1/1/46.

44-8240 Del Dorval, Canada 18/7/44; ass RAF 223Sq [6G-C] Oulton, UK as KH 998; SOC 11/3/47.

44-8241 Del Dorval 18/7/44; ass RAF 214Sq [BU-W/M] as KH 999.

44-8242 Del Dorval 20/7/44; ass RAF 223Sq [6G-] Oulton as KJ 100; tran RWE (Radio Warfare Establishment) as [U3-A] 26/10/45; SOC 11/3/47.

44-8243 Del Dorval 18/7/44; ass RAF 214Sq [BU-M] as KJ 101; SOC 11/3/47.

44-8244 Del Dorval 19/7/44; ass RAF 223Sq [6G-] Oulton, UK as KJ 102; tran RWE as [U3-B] 20/10/45; SOC 3/11/47.

44-8245 Del Dallas 20/7/44; Langley 9/8/44; Dow Fd 2/9/44; ass 348BS/99BG PFF Tortorella 17/10/44; {24m} sal 21/3/46; sal 9AF Germany 10/5/46.

44-8246 Del Dallas 9/7/44; Hunter 22/7/44; Grenier 10/9/44; ass 861BS/493BG Debach 16/9/44; loaned 4BS/34BG Mendlesham, MIA Merseburg 2/11/44 w/Capt Alexander; flak, cr Sommerda, Ger; 4KIA 7POW; MACR 10169.

44-8247 Del Dallas 18/7/44; Langley 22/8/44; Dow Fd 30/9/44; ass 463BG PFF Celone 18/10/44; sal 9AF Germany 10/5/46.

44-8248 Del Dallas 21/7/44; Langley 25/8/44; Dow Fd 22/9/44; ass 414BS/97BG PFF Amendola 17/10/44; MIA Augsburg 27/2/45 w/Albin; mech fault, c/l Trumbach, Switz; all baled, POW; MACR 12515, 13051. DOTTIE.

44-8249 Del Dallas 27/7/44; Hunter 24/8/44; Grenier 13/9/44; ass 729BS/452BG Deopham Green 15/9/44; MIA Darmstadt 24/12/44 w/Kenworthy; flak, cr Prum, Ger; MACR 11229.

44-8250 Del Dallas 20/7/44; Langley 23/8/44; Dow Fd 3/9/44; ass 463BG PFF Celone 13/10/44; sal 9AF Germany 10/5/46.

44-8251 Del Dallas 26/7/44; Hunter 25/8/44; Grenier 16/9/44; ass 562BS/388BG Knettishall 19/9/44; retUS Bradley 20/6/45; Sth Plains 3/7/45; RFC Kingman 25/11/45.

44-8252 Del Dallas 27/7/44; Hunter 25/8/44; Dow Fd 18/9/44; ass 351BS/100BG [EP-F] Thorpe Abbotts 20/9/44; loaned 533BS/381BG [VP-Z] Ridgewell, {34m}, retUS, RFC Walnut Ridge 21/12/45.

44-8253 Del Dallas 24/7/44; Langley 21/8/44; Grenier 3/9/44; ass 773BS/463BG PFF Celone 12/10/44; MIA Vienna 15/2/45 w/Rohrs; hit by bombs from above, cr Vienna; 3POW 7KIA; MACR 12491.

44-8254 Del Dallas 25/7/44; Langley 21/8/44; Dow Fd 12/10/44; ass 348BS/99BG PFF Tortorella 5/11/44; {34m} sal 9AF Germany 23/10/46; re-ass AF 30/4/47; Recl Comp 19/11/47. JUDY ANN.

44-8255 Del Dallas 25/7/44; Hunter 23/8/44; Dow Fd 5/9/44; ass 751BS/457BG Glatton 3/10/44; MIA Soest, Ger 28/2/45 w/Kirk; mech fault, ditched Channel 10 miles off Nth Foreland, UK; 3KIA 6RTD; MACR 12802.

44-8256 Del Dallas 24/7/44; Hunter 22/8/44; Grenier 7/9/44; Slated 418BS/100BG [LD-R, switched 457BG Glatton 12/9/44; tran 359BS/303BG [BN-Y] Molesworth 2/10/44; 306BG Thurleigh 9/12/44; retUS, RFC Walnut Ridge 5/1/46.

44-8257 Del Dallas 26/7/44; Hunter 24/8/44; Dow Fd 8/9/44; ass 482BG Alconbury 9/9/44; retUS Morrison 21/10/45; RFC Walnut Ridge 2/1/46.

44-8258 Del Dallas 28/7/44; Hunter 29/8/44; Dow Fd 2/9/44; ass 615BS/401BG [IY-A] Deenethorpe 5/10/44; b/d Mannheim 11/12/44 w/Capt Chapman; f/l Melsbroek A/fd, Bel; dest on ground by e/a 1/1/45; sal 2/1/45.

44-8259 Del Dallas 26/7/44; Hunter 24/8/44; Grenier 9/10/44; ass 615BS/401BG [IW-K] Deenethorpe 18/11/44; 614BS [IW-G]; tran 305BG Chelveston 20/5/45; sal 9AF Germany 23/5/46.

44-8260 Del Dallas 26/7/44; Langley 19/9/44; Grenier 24/9/44; ass 335BS/95BG [OE-L] Horham 18/10/44; b/d Cologne 10/1/45 w/Hamilton; f/l Chievres A/fd, Bel; 7RTD 1WIA; sal & rep, tran 350BS/100BG [LN-E] Thorpe Abbotts 20/5/45; retUS, RFC Walnut Ridge 4/1/46.

44-8261 Del Dallas 24/7/44; Hunter 2/9/44; Dow Fd 18/9/44; ass 333BS/94BG Rougham 20/9/44; tran 92BG Podington 10/44; retUS, RFC Walnut Ridge 28/12/45.

44-8262 Del Dallas 26/7/44; Cheyenne 18/6/44; Dow Fd 2/10/44; ass 563BS/388BG Knettishall 17/10/44; tran 527BS/379BG [FO-C] Kimbolton 7/12/44; retUS Bradley 29/6/45; Sth Plains 1/7/45; 237 BU Kirtland 26/11/45; RFC Albuquerque 6/2/46.

44-8263 Del Dallas 27/7/44; Cheyenne 2/8/44; Kearney 10/8/44; Grenier 23/8/44; ass 7BS/34BG Mendlesham 30/8/44; MIA Derben 14/1/45 w/Carter; flak, cr Innien, Ger; 8KIA 1POW; MACR 11565.

44-8264 Del Dallas 26/7/44; Cheyenne 10/8/44; Grenier 17/8/44; ass 366BS/305BG Chelveston 27/8/44; MIA Kassel 1/1/45 w/Osborne; e/a, cr Boedexen, Ger; 3KIA 7POW; MACR 11355.

44-8265 Del Dallas 26/7/44; Cheyenne 4/8/44; Lincoln 16/8/44; Grenier 2/9/44; ass 570BS/390BG Framlingham 4/9/44; MIA Berlin 18/3/45 w/?; MACR 13149, 12351. RELUCTANT.

44-8266 Del Dallas 26/7/44; Cheyenne 3/8/44; Grenier 5/9/44; ass 97BG Amendola 28/9/44; retUS Hunter 26/5/45; Sth Plains 28/6/45; RFC Kingman 22/12/45.

44-8267 Del Dallas 27/7/44; Cheyenne 5/8/44; Lincoln 17/8/44; Dow Fd 5/9/44; ass 774BS/463BG Celone 19/9/44; retUS, RFC Walnut Ridge 14/12/45.

44-8268 Del Dallas 27/7/44; Cheyenne 6/8/44; Lincoln 17/8/44; Grenier 7/9/44; ass 366BS/305BG Chelveston 29/9/44; MIA Magdeburg 1/1/45 w/Soden; e/a, cr Magdeburg; 5KIA 5POW; MACR 11251.

44-8269 Del Dallas 28/7/44; Cheyenne 3/8/44; Grenier 8/9/44; ass 412BS/95BG [QW-K] Horham 10/9/44; 335BS [OG-K]; retUS Bradley 21/6/45; Sth Plains 24/6/45; RFC Kingman 2/12/45.

44-8270 Del Dallas 27/7/44; Cheyenne 3/8/44; Kearney 10/8/44; Grenier 5/9/44; ass 863BS/493BG Debach 7/9/44; retUS Bradley 3/7/45; Sth Plains 6/7/45; RFC Kingman 28/11/45.

44-8271 Del Dallas 27/7/44; Cheyenne 6/8/44; Grenier 25/8/44; ass 391BS/34BG Mendlesham 27/8/44; retUS Bradley 21/6/45; Sth Plains 23/6/45; RFC Kingman 2/12/45. BUTCH.

44-8272 Del Dallas 27/7/44; Lincoln 17/8/44; Grenier 3/9/44; ass 336BS/95BG [ET-P] Horham 5/11/44; b/d Frankfurt 5/1/45 w/Rose; f/l Laon A/fd, Fr; 8RTD 1WIA; rep & ret gp; retUS Bradley 24/6/45; Sth Plains 28/6/45; RFC Kingman 7/12/45.

44-8273 Del Dallas 29/7/44; Lincoln 17/8/44; Grenier 3/9/44; ass 570BS/390BG [DI-U] Framlingham 5/9/44; b/d Hamburg 1/1/45 w/?; c/l Parham A/fd, UK; 2WIA; sal 3/2/45. OLE BLOOD AND GUTS.

44-8274 Del Dallas 28/7/44; Cheyenne 4/8/44; Grenier 2/9/44; ass 602BS/398BG [K8-B] Nuthampstead 5/11/44; retUS Bradley 24/6/45; Sth Plains 26//6/45; RFC Kingman 19/12/45.

44-8275 Del Dallas 28/7/44; Cheyenne 4/8/44; Grenier 3/9/44; ass 338BS/96BG Snetterton 6/9/44; tran 379BG Kimbolton 26/9/44; c/t/o at Bozeat, UK 16/12/44 w/?; 9 baled, 1KIA; sal n/b/d 17/12/44.

44-8276 Del Dallas 27/7/44; Lincoln 10/8/44; Grenier 23/8/44; ass 837BS/487BG [4F-F] Lavenham 5/9/44; b/d Berlin 18/3/45 w/?; f/l Landsburg, Ger; sal 1/4/45.

44-8277 Del Dallas 27/7/44; Lincoln 17/8/44; Grenier 3/9/44; ass 379BG Kimbolton 27/9/44; retUS Bradley 30/6/45; Sth Plains 5/7/45; RFC Kingman 19/11/45. BUTCH.

44-8278 Del Dallas 29/7/44; Cheyenne 2/8/44; Hunter 4/9/44; ass 388BG Knettishall 6/9/44; b/d Cologne 10/1/45 w/?; c/l Abbeville, Fr; 9RTD; sal 28/1/45.

44-8279 Del Dallas 27/7/44; Cheyenne 22/8/44; Grenier 8AF 30/9/44; re-ass 30/4/47; 61 TC Rhine Main 1/1/48; 10 HBS Oberpfaffenhofen 19/9/48; Recl Comp 7/1/49.

44-8280 Del Dallas 27/7/44; Kearney 9/8/44; Grenier 23/8/44; ass 510BS/351BG [TU-H] Polebrook 10/9/44; {72m} landing accident, nosed over 13/5/45 w/?; sal 15/5/44. L'LLE BOY.

44-8281 Del Dallas 27/7/44; Cheyenne 1/8/44; Kearney 9/8/44; Grenier 21/8/44; ass 326BS/92BG [JW-A] Podington 9/9/44; during assembly for Münster 19/2/45 w/?, caught fire and abandoned; cr Temple Grafton, UK; sal.

44-8282 Del Dallas 23/7/44; Lincoln 4/8/44; Grenier 17/8/44; ass 18BS/34BG Mendlesham 20/8/44; RFC Kingman 12/45. AGETS.

44-8283 Del Cheyenne 2/8/44; Kearney 9/8/44; Grenier 17/8/44; ass 18BS/34BG Mendlesham 20/8/44 LUCKY 13; 7BS; MIA Nuremberg, Ger; 5/4/45 w/Mehling; flak, ditched Channel; 3KIA 6RTD. DINAH-MITE.

44-8284 Del Cheyenne 1/8/44; Kearney 13/8/44; Grenier 23/8/44; ass 350BS/100BG [LN-H] Thorpe Abbotts 30/8/44; b/d Leipzig 27/2/45 w/?; c/l Trimach, Switz; sal 31/10/45.

44-8285 Del Cheyenne 30/7/44; 4121 BU Kelly 1/9/44; 4100 BU Wright 27/2/45; 4142 BU Dayton 20/3/45; RFC Kingman /45.

44-8286 Del Cheyenne 30/7/44; 902 BU Orlando 19/8/44; 621 BU Pinecastle 7/7/46; (first Cheyenne turret) 62 BAS Aberdeen Proving Ground 25/7/46.

44-8287 Del Cheyenne 30/7/44; 902 BU Orlando 19/8/44; 903 BU Pinecastle 24/2/45; 62 BAS Aberdeen PG 25/7/46.

44-8288 Del Cheyenne 31/7/44; Lincoln 6/8/44; Grenier 19/9/44; ass 863BS/493BG Debach 5/9/44; b/d Neuss, Ger 23/1/45 w/?; f/l Continent, sal 28/1/45. HELL & BACK.

44-8289 Del Cheyenne 3/8/44; Gulfport 7/8/44; RFC Altus 29/10/45.

44-8290 Del Cheyenne 4/8/44; McDill 8/8/44; 4209 BU Des Moines 16/12/44; 325 BU Avon Park 3/1/45; RFC Walnut Ridge 2/8/45.

44-8291 Del Cheyenne 4/8/44; McDill 8/8/44; 325 BU Avon Park 31/45; re-ass as TB-17G Topeka 30/4/47 carrying propaganda for Army's re-enlistment campaign; 4119 BU Brookley 18/1/48; Recl Comp 14/9/48.

44-8292 Del Orlando 31/7/44; Tampa 7/8/44; W/O 11/47.

44-8293 Del Orlando 31/7/44; Gulfport 7/8/44; 3704 BU Keesler 13/8/44; 2137 BU Hendricks 23/5/45; 3704 BU Keesler 24/5/45; RFC Kingman 9/8/46.

44-8294 Del Orlando 31/7/44; 328 BU Gulfport 3/8/44; 4124 BU Altus 7/10/44; RFC Altus 29/1/45.

44-8295 Del Tampa 3/8/44; New Orleans 10/8/44; 326 BU McDill 19/1/45; ARL Dover 11/2/45; 1 BU Bolling 25/5/45; ATS Dover 28/5/45; 4000 BU Patterson 8/12/46; Re-ass 30/4/47; 4141 BU Pyote 29/8/45; Recl Comp 2/5/49.

44-8296 Del Gulfport 2/8/44; El Paso 5/8/44; 326 BU Gulfport 30/3/45; 329 BU Alexandra 6/4/45; 330 BU Dyersburg 4/9/45; RFC Walnut Ridge 18/12/45.

44-8297 Del Drew Fd 3/8/44; 327 BU Drew 4/5/45; 268 BU Peterson 30/10/45; RFC Kingman 27/12/45.

44-8298 Del Gulfport 2/8/44; 328 BU Gulfport 30/3/45; 329 BU Alexandra 24/6/45; 330 BU Dyersburg 4/9/45; RFC Walnut Ridge 18/12/45.

44-8299 Del Avon Park 5/8/44; 325 BU Avon Park 9/4/45; RFC Walnut Ridge 12/12/45.

44-8300 Del –.

44-8301 Del Hunter 3/8/44; Palm Springs 10/8/44; Hunter 15/9/44; Grenier 21/9/44; ass 560BS/388BG Knettishall 23/9/44; retUS Bradley 27/6/45; Sth Plains 17/7/45; RFC Kingman 26/11/45. SUSAN KAY.

44-8302 Del Hunter 3/8/44; Long Beach 10/8/44; Hunter 15/8/44; Dow Fd 1/9/44; ass 561BS/388BG Knettishall 14/9/44; MIA Saarbrücken 9/11/44 w/Panther; flak, cr Herne, Ger; 3KIA 6POW; MACR 10351. VAGABOND LADY.

44-8303 Del Lincoln 4/8/44; Bangor 20/8/44; Grenier 22/8/44; ass 4BS/34BG Mendlesham 24/8/44; MIA Nuremberg 5/4/45 w/Schwartz; e/a, cr Aachen; 7KIA 2POW; MACR 9368.

44-8304 Del Lincoln 8/8/44; Bangor 12/8/44; Grenier 18/8/44; ass 862BS/493BG Debach 20/8/44; cr Monewdon, UK en route Cologne 10/1/45 w/?; 4KIA 2WIA; sal 19/2/45.

44-8305 Del Hunter 5/8/44; Dallas 10/8/44; Grenier 6/9/44; ass 412BS/95BG [QW-Q] Horham 3/9/44; b/d Frankfurt 5/1/45 w/Painter; f/l Thionville A/fd, Fr; 8RTD 1WIA; sal 6/2/45.

44-8306 Del Hunter 5/8/44; Dallas 10/8/44; Grenier 6/9/44; ass 569BS/390BG [CC-H] Framlingham 9/9/44; b/d Chemnitz 14/2/45 w/?; f/l Continent; sal 9AF Germany 21/6/46.

44-8307 Del Lincoln 6/8/44; Bangor 12/8/44; Grenier 17/8/44; ass 325BS/92BG [NV-F] Podington 26/8/44; tran 838BS/487BG Lavenham 28/10/44; sal 9AF Germany 10/5/46.

44-8308 Del Lincoln 7/8/44; Long Beach 10/8/44; Grenier 2/9/44; ass 730BS/452BG Deopham Green 7/9/44; retUS Bradley 26/8/45; Independence 29/8/45; RFC Kingman 1/12/45.

44-8309 Del Lincoln 8/8/44; Grenier 18/8/44; ass 7BS/34BG Mendlesham 20/8/44; retUS Bradley 7/6/45; Sth Plains 12/6/45; RFC Kingman 26/11/45. OL' BUDDY.

44-8310 Del Hunter 7/8/44; Jacksonville 11/8/44; Grenier 5/9/44; ass 447BS Rattlesden 7/9/44; 524BS/379BG [WA-P] Kimbolton 10/9/44; retUS Bradley 12/6/45; Sth Plains 19/6/45; RFC Kingman 17/12/45.

44-8311 Del Hunter 7/8/44; Atlanta 13/8/44; Grenier 3/9/44; ass 324BS/91BG [DF-P] Bassingbourn 10/9/44; b/d {20m} Altenbeken 26/11/44 w/Martin; e/a hit #1 & 3, c/l Denain/Prouvy A/fd, Fr; as a/c bellied in killed woman and two children ran in panic; sal 11/12/44; TERRY'S TIGER.

44-8312 Del Hunter 9/8/44; Midland 12/8/44; Grenier 19/9/44; ass 862BS/493BG Debach 23/9/44; tran 836BS/487BG [2G-M] Lavenham 20/2/45; retUS Bradley 10/7/45; Independence 12/7/45; RFC Kingman 7/1/46.

44-8313 Del Hunter 7/8/44; Grenier 1/9/44; ass 561BS/388BG Knettishall 3/9/44; MIA Ludwigshafen 5/11/44 w/Esselmeyer; flak, cr Mannheim; 2KIA 7POW; MACR 10310. LADY ANNE.

44-8314 Del Hunter 8/8/44; Grenier 2/9/44; ass 863BS/493BG Debach 4/9/44; b/d Derben, Ger 14/1/45 w/Terry; mech fault, f/l Bulltofta, Swed; 9INT; MACR 11800; rep & ret gp 30/6/45; retUS Bradley 1/8/45; Independence 3/8/45; RFC Kingman 22/12/45. PAIR-A-DICE KIDS.

44-8315 Del Kearney 10/8/44; Grenier 22/8/44; ass 568BS/390BG [BI-P] Framlingham 24/8/44 I'LL BE AROUND; retUS Bradley 30/6/45; Sth Plains 4/7/45; RFC Kingman 25/11/45. MAIDEN'S PRAYER.

44-8316 Del Kearney 10/8/44; Grenier 27/8/44; ass 358BS/303BG [VK-C] Molesworth 25/8/44; b/d Berlin 26/2/45 w/?; f/l Continent; sal 1/3/45.

44-8317 Del Kearney 10/8/44; Grenier 21/8/44; ass 305BG Chelveston 4/9/44; retUS Bradley 7/6/45; Sth Plains 11/6/45; RFC Kingman 8/12/45.

44-8318 Del Kearney 11/8/44; Lincoln 15/8/44; Grenier 25/8/44; ass 360BS/303BG [PU-P] Molesworth 6/9/44; retUS Bradley 7/6/45; Sth Plains 14/6/45; RFC Kingman 1/12/45.

44-8319 Del Kearney 9/8/44; Lincoln 14/8/44; Grenier 3/9/44; ass 571BS/390BG [FC-L] Framlingham 5/9/44; MIA Mainz 4/12/44 w/Massa; flak, cr Simmern, Ger; 3KIA 6POW; MACR 11055.

44-8320 Del Lincoln 9/8/44; Long Beach 13/8/44; Grenier 27/8/44; ass 7BS/34BG Mendlesham 30/8/44; sal 9AF Germany 31/5/46. BOTTOMS UP.

44-8321 Del Kearney 8/8/44; Grenier 17/8/44; ass 18BS/34BG Mendlesham 20/8/44; retUS Bradley 25/6/45; Sth Plains 28/6/45; RFC Kingman 22/11/45.

44-8322 Del Kearney 9/8/44; Grenier 20/8/44; ass 563BS/388BG Knettishall 24/8/44; b/d Cologne 17/10/44 w/?; c/l Honington A/fd, UK sal; retUS Bradley 25/6/45; Sth Plains 29/6/45; RFC Kingman 21/11/45

44-8323 Del Kearney 11/8/44; Ogden 13/8/44; Grenier 21/8/44; ass 388BG Knettishall 26/8/44; tran 570BS/390BG [DI-N] Framlingham 28/8/44; MIA Kaiserlautern 25/12/44 w/Lee; flak, cr Bitburg, Ger; 6KIA 3POW; MACR 11115. BLONDE BOMBSHELL.

44-8324 Del Kearney 10/8/44; Albuquerque 15/8/44; Grenier 2/9/44; ass 401BS/91BG [LL-R] Bassingbourn 12/9/44 GYPSIE; {60+m} RetUS Bradley 11/6/45; Sth Plains 16/6/45; RFC Kingman 4/12/45. BLOOD 'N GUTS.

44-8325 Del Kearney 10/8/44; Long Beach 13/8/44; Grenier 2/9/44; ass 493BG Debach 4/9/44; tran 570BS/390BG [DI-T] Framlingham 6/9/44; MIA Merseburg 30/11/44 w/Harris; flak, cr Rittersheim, Ger; 9POW; MACR 11132. BOOGIE BABY.

44-8326 Del Kearney 10/8/44; Long Beach 13/8/44; Grenier 2/9/44; ass 358BS/303BG [VK-Y] Molesworth 10/9/44; f/l Honington 21/10/44; sal 25/10/44; tran 327BS/92BG Podington 4/11/44; MIA Kassel 9/3/45 w/Stewart; flak, cr Germany; 8KIA 2POW; MACR 12938.

44-8327 Del Kearney 10/8/44; Cheyenne 18/8/44; Grenier 22/8/44; ass 391BS/34BG Mendlesham 24/8/44; retUS Bradley 23/6/45; Sth Plains 30/6/45; RFC Kingman 20/11/45. GOOM-BAH!!

44-8328 Del Kearney 10/8/44; Ogden 13/8/44; Grenier 20/8/44; ass 391BS/34BG Mendlesham 22/8/44; 18BS; MIA Merseburg 7/10/44 w/Kiley; flak, cr Merseburg; 4KIA 5POW; MACR 9341.

44-8329 Del Hunter 12/8/44; Grenier 3/9/44; ass 407BS/92BG [PY-C] Podington 13/9/44; sal 9AF Germany 14/6/46. FORT SACK.

44-8330 Del Hunter 12/8/44; Dow Fd 3/9/44; ass 360BS/303BG Molesworth 24/9/44; MIA Magdeburg 28/9/44 w/Shields; e/a, cr Suepplingen; 7KIA 2POW; sal 9AF Germany 10/5/46. MACR 9404.

44-8331 Del Hunter 12/8/44; Amarillo 17/8/44; Dow Fd 3/9/44; ass 412BS/95BG [QW-G] Horham 9/9/44; b/d Hannover 28/3/45 w/Murphy; f/l Ashiet A/fd, Fr; 9RTD; retUS Bradley 21/6/45; Sth Plains 23/6/45; RFC Kingman 2/12/45.

44-8332 Del Hunter 12/8/44; Grenier 2/9/44; ass 837BS/487BG [4F-A] Lavenham 27/9/44; retUS Bradley 2/8/45; Independence 5/8/45; RFC Kingman 15/12/45.

44-8333 Del Hunter 13/8/44; Dow Fd 3/9/44; ass 837BS/487BG Lavenham 9/9/44; c/t/o for Münster 22/10/44 w/?; sal 25/10/44.

44-8334 Del Hunter 13/8/44; Grenier 2/9/44; ass 349BS/100BG [XR-M] Thorpe Abbotts 9/9/44; MIA Kaltenkirchen 7/4/45 w/?; jet e/a, cr Hannover; MACR 13716.

44-8335 Del Hunter 12/8/44; Grenier 29/8/44; ass 427BS/303BG Molesworth 26/9/44; MIA Magdeburg 28/9/44 w/Glasgow; e/a, cr Linden, Ger; 8KIA 1POW; MACR 9405.

44-8336 Del Dorval Fd, Montreal, Canada 13/8/44; ass RAF 214Sq [BU-M] Oulton, as {KJ 103}; c/l base, burned out 17/1/45.

44-8337 Del Dorval 13/8/44; ass RAF 214Sq [BU-D] Oulton as {KJ-104}; 1699 CU; 223Sq; SOC 11/3/47.

44-8338 Del Dorval 13/8/44; ass RAF 223Sq as {KJ 105}; RWE [U3-C]; F/Com [U3-6].

44-8339 Del Dorval 13/8/44; ass RAF 214Sq [BU-G] Oulton as {KJ-106}; SOC 8/3/45.

44-8340 Del Dorval 13/8/44; ass RAF 214Sq [BU-N] Oulton as {KJ 107}; SOC 11/3/47.

44-8341 Del Dorval 13/8/44; ass RAF No12 MU 3/9/44 as {KJ 108}; SOC 15/9/47.;

44-8342 Del Dorval 13/8/44; ass RAF 214Sq [BU-V] Oulton as {KJ 109}; 223Sq [6G-F]; 1699 CU [4Z-C]; SOC 11/3/47.

44-8343 Del Dorval 13/8/44; ass RAF 214Sq [BU-B] Oulton as {KJ 110}; 223SQ [6G-P]; SOC 11/3/47.

44-8344 Del Dallas 16/8/44; Scott Fd 2/9/44, Grenier 19/9/44; ass 100BG Thorpe Abbotts 11/10/44; b/d Havover 28/3/45 w/?; f/l St Trond A/fd, Bel; sal 30/3/45.

44-8345 Del Dallas 16/8/44; Langley 8/9/44; Dow Fd 15/10/44; ass 550BS/385BG Gt Ashfield 16/10/44; 549BS; tran 94BG Rougham 18/10/44; retUS Morrison 12/10/45; RFC Walnut Ridge 7/1/46.

44-8346 Del Dallas 18/8/44; Langley 5/9/44; Grenier 3/10/44; ass 305BG Chelveston 21/11/44; tran 384BG Grafton Underwood 9/5/45; sal 9AF Germany 14/9/46.

44-8347 Del Dallas 16/8/44; Langley 31/8/44; Grenier 11/10/44; ass 301BG PFF Lucera 20/3/45; sal 9AF Germany 1/5/47.

44-8348 Del Dallas 17/8/44; Langley 5/9/44; Grenier 21/9/44; ass 603BS/398BG Nuthampstead 2/11/44; 602BS [K8-A]; MIA Merseburg 21/11/44 w/Hastings; e/a, cr Hildburghausen, Ger; 1KIA 9POW; MACR 10412. NUTTY HUZZY.

44-8349 Del Dallas 14/8/44; Langley 5/9/44; Dow Fd 18/9/44; ass 532BS/381BG [VE-G] Ridgewell 2/11/44; tran 305BG Chelveston 5/45; sal 9AF Germany 23/5/46.

44-8350 Del Dallas 15/8/44; Hunter 5/9/44; Grenier 18/9/44; ass 381BG Ridgewell 20/10/44; tran 306BG

Thurleigh 4/44; sal 27/10/44.

44-8351 Del Dallas 18/8/44; Langley 2/9/44; Grenier 19/9/44; ass 358BS/303BG [VK-Z] Molesworth 2/11/44; tran 544BS/384BG [SU-P] Grafton Underwood 10/5/45; sal 9AF Germany 30/12/45.

44-8352 Del Dallas 17/8/44; Langley 2/9/44; Dow Fd 22/9/44; ass 4BS/34BG Mendlesham 1/10/44; tran 493BG Debach 3/10/44; MIA Hamburg 31/12/44 w/?; flak, exploded; MACR 11235.

44-8353 Del Dallas 21/8/44; Langley 2/9/44; W/O 24/9/44.

44-8354 Del Dallas 17/8/44; Langley 7/9/44; Grenier 11/10/44; ass 325BS/92BG [NV-A] Podington 8/11/44; tran 306BG Thurleigh 7/5/45; 29 TAC 27/5/45; sal 9AF Germany 31/5/46.

44-8355 Del Dallas 15/8/44; Langley 5/9/44; Dow Fd 10/10/44; ass 710BS/447BG Rattlesden 18/10/44; MIA Darmstadt 24/12/44 w/King; flak, cr Prum, Ger; 8KIA 2POW; MACR 11119.

44-8356 Del Dallas 17/8/44; Hunter 3/9/44; Grenier 27/9/44; ass 4BS/34BG Mendlesham 28/9/44; sal 27/10/44; retUS Morrison 9/10/45; RFC Walnut Ridge 9/1/46.

44-8357 Del Dallas 17/8/44; Keesler 9/9/44; Grenier 12/10/44; ass 401BS/91BG [LL-M] Bassingbourn 5/11/44 TENNESSEE TESS; tran {30+m} 306BG Thurleigh 1/5/45; sal 9AF Germany 24/6/46. TESS.

44-8358 Del Dallas 20/8/44; Langley 5/9/44; Dow Fd 8/10/44; ass 509BS/351BG [RQ-A] Polebrook 4/11/44; 511BS [DS-A]; {29m} tran 305BG Chelveston 5/45; sal 9AF Germany 6/11/46. LITTLE RUNT.

44-8359 Del Dallas 20/8/44; Langley 2/9/44; Dow Fd 16/10/44; ass 306BG Thurleigh 8/11/44; sal 9AF Germany 28/7/46.

44-8360 Del Dallas 21/8/44; Langley 7/9/44; Dow Fd 5/10/44; ass 305BG Chelveston 10/11/44; retUS 4000 BU Wright Fd 5/1/45; 4020 BU Nashville 12/1/45; 121 BU Bradley 14/1/45; 610 BU Eglin 21/1/45; Recl Comp 15/10/45.

44-8361 Del Dallas 20/8/44; Langley 11/9/44; Grenier 5/10/44; ass 550BS/385BG Gt Ashfield 17/10/44; sal 9AF Germany 23/5/46.

44-8362 Del Dallas 20/8/44; Langley 9/9/44; Dow Fd 4/10/44; ass 306BG Thurleigh 20/11/44; sal 9AF Germany 30/7/46.

44-8363 Del Dallas 20/8/44; Langley 27/9/44; Dow Fd 16/10/44; ass 601BS/398BG Nuthampstead 5/11/44; 603BS [N7-V]; tran 306BG Thurleigh 21/5/45; retUS, RFC Walnut Ridge 14/12/45.

44-8364 Del Dallas 25/8/44; Langley 4/9/44; Grenier 10/10/44; ass 335BS/95BG [OE-W] Horham 12/10/44; sal 9AF Germany 10/5/46.

44-8365 Del Dallas 22/8/44; Langley 5/9/44; Dow Fd 1/10/44; ass 731BS/452BG Deopham Green 14/10/44; retUS Morrison 8/10/45; RFC Walnut Ridge 25/10/45. VIRGINIA.

44-8366 Del Dallas 20/8/44; Langley 11/9/44; Dow Fd 12/10/44; ass 711BS/447BG Rattlesden 14/10/44; 711BS; tran 332BS/94BG [XM-P] Rougham 16/10/44; 548BS/385BG Gt Ashfield 18/10/44; retUS, RFC Walnut Ridge 8/1/46. ISLAND QUEEN.

44-8367 Del Dallas 23/8/44; Langley 28/8/44; Grenier 5/10/44; ass 327BS/92BG [UX-S] Podington 25/11/44; tran 306BG Thurleigh 7/5/45; sal 9AF Germany 23/5/46. OUR BABY.

44-8368 Del Dallas 22/8/44; Langley 20/9/44; Dow Fd 2/10/44; ass 385BG Gt Ashfield 14/10/44; tran 749BS/457BG Glatton 19/11/44; MIA Oranienburg 10/4/45 w/Capt Fox; jet e/a, cr Bernau, Ger; 1KIA 9POW; MACR 13882.

44-8369 Del Dallas 22/8/44; Langley 24/9/44; Dow Fd 4/10/44; ass 379BG Kimbolton 18/11/44; b/d Kassel 4/12/44 w/?; c/l Bolvoax, Bel; 4KIA; rep & ret gp 5/12/44; tran 601BS/398BG [3O-Z] Nuthampstead 5/1/45; retUS, RFC Walnut Ridge 8/1/46.

44-8370 Del Dallas 23/8/44; Langley 1/9/44; Dow Fd 25/9/44; ass 338BS/96BG Snetterton 17/10/44; retUS, RFC Walnut Ridge 20/12/45.

44-8371 Del Dallas 23/8/44; Langley 29/8/44; Dow Fd 20/10/44; ass 615BS/401BG [IY-M] 1/12/44 FRECKLES; MIA Minster Stein 16/2/45 w/Capt Lozinski; flak, cr Oschersleben; 8KIA 1POW; MACR 12445. BADLAND BAT II.

44-8372 Del Dallas 25/8/44; Langley 17/9/44; Grenier 19/10/44; ass 483BG Sterparone 30/10/44; sal 9AF Germany 10/5/46.

44-8373 Del Dallas 23/8/44; Langley 19/9/44; Dow Fd 3/10/44; ass 600BS/398BG [N8-K] Nuthampstead 5/11/44; tran 306BG Thurleigh 25/5/45; 1 BAD Burtonwood 18/6/45; retUS, RFC Walnut Ridge 14/1/46.

44-8374 Del Dallas 25/8/44; Langley 19/9/44; Dow Fd 13/10/44; ass 511BS/351BG [DS-U] Polebrook 5/11/44; {34m} tran 305BG Chelveston 23/5/45; sal 9AF Germany 5/11/46.

44-8375 Del Dallas 25/8/44; Langley 18/9/44; Dow Fd 12/10/44; ass 848BS/490BG Eye 14/10/44; tran 332BS/94BG [XM-S] Rougham 15/10/44; 398BG Nuthampstead 17/10/44; PHYLLIS JO.

44-8376 Del Dallas 25/8/44; Langley 17/9/44; Grenier 8/10/44; ass 508BS/351BG [YB-F] Polebrook 2/11/44; 511BS [DS-F]; {34m} tran 305BG Chelveston 23/5/45; sal 9AF Germany 5/7/46.

44-8377 Del Dallas 23/8/44; Langley 18/9/44; Dow Fd 15/10/44; ass 8AF, but c/l Ireland 22/10/44.

44-8378 Del Dallas 25/8/44; Langley 23/9/44; 334 BU Florence 25/1/45; 3539 BU Langley 5/2/45; RFC Walnut Ridge 7/1/46.

44-8379 Del Dallas 29/8/44; Hunter 25/9/44; Grenier 3/10/44; ass 351BS/100BG Thorpe Abbotts 12/10/44; MIA Berlin 3/2/45 w/Maj Rosenthal; flak, c/l Russia; 1KIA 10RTD; MACR 12046.

44-8380 Del Dallas 26/8/44; Langley 30/9/44; Grenier 10/10/44; ass 340BS/97BG PFF Amendola 25/10/44; MIA Landsberg 16/2/45 w/Foster; flak, cr Bozen; MACR 12106.

44-8381 Del Dallas 26/8/44; Langley 21/9/44; Grenier 1/10/44; ass 96BS/2BG PFF Amendola 24/10/44; MIA Linz 3/12/44 w/Pepperman; MACR 10031.

44-8382 Del Dallas 26/8/44; Hunter 25/9/44; Grenier 13/10/44; ass 413BS/96BG [MZ-V] Snetterton 18/10/44; retUS, RFC Walnut Ridge 20/12/45.

44-8383 Del Dallas 29/8/44; Langley 23/9/44; Grenier 12/10/44; ass 97BG PFF Amendola 31/10/44; tran 817BAS/483BG Sterparone 17/12/44; retUS, RFC Walnut Ridge 28/12/45. KITTY ANN II.

44-8384 Del Dallas 28/9/44; Langley 21/9/44; Grenier 12/10/44; ass 816BS/483BG PFF Sterparone 30/10/44; MIA night mission, Bleckhammer 13/11/44 w/Culpepper; no gas, cr Nevesinje; 1KIA (pilot) 9EVD & ret; MACR 9882.

44-8385 Del Dallas 27/8/44; Langley 21/9/44; Grenier 12/10/44; ass 463BG PFF Celone 25/10/44; sal 3/8/45.

44-8386 Del Dallas 27/7/44; Langley 23/9/44; 3539 BU Langley 7/10/44; 2140 BU Smyrna 31/1/45; 554 BU Memphis 1/6/45; 342 BU Smyrna 1/9/45; 554 BU Memphis 17/9/45.

44-8387 Del Dallas 26/8/44; Langley 22/9/44; Dow Fd 12/10/44; ass 429BS/2BG Amendola 1/11/44; sal 9AF Germany 10/5/46.

44-8388 Del Dallas 25/8/44; Langley 20/9/44; Grenier 12/10/44; ass 416BS/99BG PFF Tortorella 31/10/44; {45m} sal 9AF Germany 5/10/46.

44-8389 Del Dallas 29/8/44; Langley 23/9/44; 3539 BU Langley 24/10/44; RFC Walnut Ridge 9/1/46.

44-8390 Del Dallas 27/8/44; Langley 23/9/44; Grenier 12/10/44; ass 353BS/301BG PFF Lucera 1/11/44; MIA Brux 4/3/45 w/Sommers; flak, ditched Adriatic; 7KIA 3EVD & ret; MACR 12917. GARBAGE CANNIE.

44-8391 Del Dallas 29/8/44; Langley 22/9/44; Grenier 12/10/44; ass 774BS/463BG Celone 25/10/44; MIA Innsbruck 16/11/44 w/Young; flak, cr Conegliano, It; 10POW; MACR 9890.

44-8392 Del Dallas 25/8/44; Langley 25/9/44; 3539 BU Langley 3/1/45; RFC Walnut Ridge 3/1/46.

44-8393 Del Dallas 25/8/44; Hunter 29/9/44; Grenier 15/10/44; ass 709BS/447BG Rattlesden 18/10/44; retUS 15/10/45; RFC Walnut Ridge 29/12/45.

44-8394 Del Dallas 30/8/44; Hunter 27/9/44; Grenier 10/10/44; ass 333BS/94BG [TS-H] Rougham 12/10/44; retUS, RFC Walnut Ridge 20/12/45.

44-8385 Del Dallas 30/8/44; Hunter 26/9/44; Grenier 12/10/44; ass 347BS/99BG PFF Tortorella 31/10/44; {29m} RetUS Morrison 31/9/44; RFC Walnut Ridge 14/10/45.

44-8396 Del Dallas 30/8/44; Langley 23/9/44; 3539 BU Langley 18/10/44; RFC Walnut Ridge 5/1/46.

44-8397 Del Dallas 2/9/44; Hunter 28/9/44; Dow Fd 18/10/44; ass 4BS/34BG Mendlesham 20/10/44; b/d Darmstadt 24/12/44 w/?; sal.

44-8398 Del Dallas 30/8/44; Hunter 22/9/44; Grenier 19/10/44; ass 602BS/398BG [K8-Y/Q] Nuthampstead 26/11/44; tran 306BG Thurleigh 24/5/45; sal 9AF Germany 10/5/46.

44-8399 Del Dallas 2/9/44; Dayton 8/9/44; Hunter 9/12/44; Dow Fd 2/1/45; ass 337BS/96BG [AW-H] Snetterton 5/1/45; retUS, RFC Walnut Ridge 4/1/46.

44-8400 Del Dallas 5/9/44; Hunter 28/9/44; Grenier 12/10/44; ass 350BS/100BG [LN-W] Thorpe Abbotts 14/10/44; f/l Continent, sal 20/2/45.

44-8401 Del Dallas 3/9/44; Hunter 19/9/44; Dow Fd 13/10/44; ass 351BS/100BG [EP-N] Thorpe Abbotts 20/10/44; tran 544BS/384BG [SU-X] Grafton Underwood 5/11/44; 303BG Molesworth 8/5/45; retUS, RFC Walnut Ridge 20/12/45.

44-8402 Del Dallas 7/9/44; Hunter 21/10/44; Grenier 10/12/44; ass 535BS/381BG [MS-N] Ridgewell 19/1/45; {10+m} tran 306BG Thurleigh 5/45; sal 9AF Germany 10/5/46.

44-8403 Del Cheyenne 3/9/44; Hunter 2/10/44; Dow Fd 16/10/44; ass 429BS/2BG PFF Amendola 22/10/44; tran 305BG Chelveston 27/5/45; sal 9AF Germany 23/5/46.

44-8404 Del Cheyenne 5/9/44; Hunter 7/10/44; Grenier 22/10/44; ass 301BG PFF Lucera 17/11/44; tran 97BG Amendola 19/11/44; sal 9AF Germany 23/5/46.

44-8405 Del Cheyenne 5/9/44; Hunter 22/10/44; Dow Fd 31/10/44; ass 49BS/2BG PFF Amendola 11/11/44; sal 9AF Germany 5/7/46.

44-8406 Del Cheyenne 7/9/44; Hunter 24/10/44; Grenier 6/11/44; ass 96BS/2BG Amendola 8/12/44; burned out after collision w/97BG in landing acc 2/1/45 w/Lt Col Abbey; sal 10/1/45.

44-8407 Del Cheyenne 3/9/44; Hunter 15/10/44; Dow Fd 27/10/44; ass 97BG PFF Amendola 17/12/44; retUS Morrison 16/10/45; RFC Walnut Ridge 5/1/46.

44-8408 Del Patterson 5/9/44; Hunter 19/9/44; Dow Fd 27/9/44; ass 545BS/384BG [JD-C] Grafton Underwood 19/1/45; sal 9AF Germany 11/7/46.

44-8409 Del Patterson 5/9/44; Hunter 20/9/44; Grenier 2/10/44; ass 545BS/384BG [JD-N] Grafton Underwood 7/10/44; MIA Zeitz 30/11/44 w/Champ;

flak, cr Wuppertal; 5KIA 4POW; MACR 11128.

44-8410 Del Patterson 5/9/44; Hunter 18/9/44; Grenier 30/9/44; ass 447BG Rattlesden 1/10/44; tran 508BS/351BG [YB-A] Polebrook 7/10/44; {70m} RetUS Bradley 6/6/45; Sth Plains 14/6/44; RFC Kingman 5/12/45. MISS GLAMOUR PANTS.

44-8411 Del Patterson 5/9/44; Hunter 20/9/44; Grenier 23/10/44; ass 563BS/388BG Knettishall 25/10/44; b/d 24/12/44 w/?; flak, cr Leige, Bel; 9RTD; sal. BORROWED TIME.

44-8412 Del Patterson 5/9/44; Hunter 15/9/44; Grenier 16/10/44; ass 508BS/351BG [YB-H] Polebrook 18/10/44; {26m} tran 305BG Chelveston 26/5/45; retUS Bradley 31/5/45; Sth Plains 3/6/45; RFC Kingman 18/12/45.

44-8413 Del Patterson 6/9/44; Hunter 28/9/44; Grenier 12/10/44; ass 849BS/490BG Eye 20/10/44; retUS Bradley 15/7/45; Independence 17/7/45; RFC Kingman 8/12/45.

44-8414 Del Patterson 5/9/44; Hunter 18/9/44; Grenier 29/9/44; ass 750BS/457BG Glatton 5/10/44; b/d Plauen, Ger 19/3/45 w/?; f/l Continent; sal 26/3/45. G.I. VIRGIN III.

44-8415 Del Patterson 5/9/44; Hunter 21/9/44; Grenier 28/9/44; ass 548BS/385BG Gt Ashfield 28/9/44; tran 447BG Rattlesden 30/9/44; retUS Bradley 6/6/45; Sth Plains 11/6/45; RFC Kingman 8/12/45.

44-8416 Del Patterson 9/9/44; Hunter 20/9/44; Grenier 11/10/44; ass 8AF 16/10/44; retUS Bradley 5/7/45; Sth Plains 7/7/45; RFC Kingman 18/12/45.

44-8417 Del Patterson 7/9/44; Hunter 17/9/44; Grenier 25/9/44; ass 550BS/385BG Gt Ashfield 28/9/44; MIA Dresden 2/3/45 w/Tipton; e/a, cr Fictenburg, Ger?; 1KIA 8POW; MACR 12858.

44-8418 Del Patterson 6/9/44; Hunter 25/9/44; Grenier 25/9/44; ass 457BG Glatton 5/10/44; sal b/d 10/1/45. BAD TIME INC. II.

44-8419 Del Patterson 7/9/44; Hunter 18/9/44; Grenier 22/9/44; ass 711BS/447BG Rattlesden 26/9/44; 710BS; b/d Frankfurt 8/1/45 w/?; f/l Laon, Fr; sal 6/2/45.

44-8420 Del Patterson 7/9/44; Hunter 18/9/44; Grenier 22/9/44; ass 338BS/96BG [BX-F] Snetterton 26/9/44; retUS Bradley 1/6/45; Sth Plains 5/6/45; RFC Kingman 18/12/45.

44-8421 Del Lincoln 9/9/44; Hunter 16/9/44; Grenier 27/9/44; ass 384BG Grafton Underwood 8/12/44; c/l 16/12/44 w/?; sal 18/12/44.

44-8422 Del Patterson 7/9/44; Lincoln 17/9/44; Grenier 27/9/44; ass 360BS/303BG [PU-R] Molesworth 28/10/44; during assembly for Gelsenkirchen, cr Much Wenlock, UK 11/11/44 w/?; sal 14/11/44.

44-8423 Del Lincoln 11/9/44; Hunter 19/9/44; Grenier 27/9/44; ass 8AF 29/10/44; retUS Bradley 24/6/45; Sth Plains 27/6/45; RFC Kingman 27/12/45.

44-8424 Del Lincoln 6/9/44; Hunter 27/9/44; Grenier 29/9/44; ass 493BG Debach 30/9/44; b/d Dessau 16/1/45 w/?; f/l Continent; sal 26/1/45. LITTLE CLAMWINKLE.

44-8425 Del Lincoln 12/9/44; Hunter 16/9/44; Grenier 10/10/44; ass 379BG Kimbolton 14/10/44; b/d Desden 17/4/45 w/?; sal 18/4/45. CONNIE.

44-8426 Del Lincoln 11/9/44; Hunter 17/9/44; Grenier 19/9/44; ass 568BS/390BG Framlingham 21/9/44; MIA Derben 14/1/45 w/Norman; e/a, cr Nachow; 4KIA 5POW; MACR 11719.

44-8427 Del Lincoln 15/9/44; Hunter 17/9/44; Dow Fd 8/10/44; ass 358BS/303BG [VK-F] Molesworth 23/10/44; MIA Oranienburg 10/4/45 w/Murray; jet e/a, cr Oranienburg; 8KIA 1POW; MACR 13875. HENN'S REVENGE.

44-8428 Del Lincoln 12/9/44; Hunter 18/9/44; Dow Fd 27/9/44; ass 550BS/385BG Gt Ashfield 29/9/44; retUS Bradley 24/6/45; Sth Plains 27/6/45; RFC Kingman 2/12/45. MACK'S HACK.

44-8429 Del Lincoln 15/9/44; Hunter 19/9/44; Grenier 3/10/44; ass 401BS/91BG [LL-G] Bassingbourn 4/11/44; {50+m} RetUS Bradley 11/6/45; Sth Plains 14/6/45; RFC Kingman 16/12/45. BROAD MINDED.

44-8430 Del Lincoln 15/9/44; Hunter 17/9/44; Grenier 7/10/44; ass 547BS/384BG [SO-P] Grafton Underwood 16/10/44; 546BS [BK-P]; collision damage Ingolstadt 5/4/45 w/?; f/l Continent; sal 8/4/45.

44-8431 Del Lincoln 12/9/44; Grenier 6/10/44; ass 323BS/91BG [OR-W] Bassingbourn 4/11/44; {46m} RetUS Bradley 5/6/45; Sth Plains 8/6/45; RFC Kingman 14/12/45.

44-8432 Del Lincoln 15/9/44; Albuquerque 19/9/44; Grenier 16/10/44; ass 8AF 25/10/45; retUS Morrison 24/10/45; RFC Walnut Ridge 8/1/46.

44-8433 Del Lincoln 13/9/44; Grenier 24/9/44; ass 100BG Thorpe Abbotts 3/10/44; b/d Frankfurt 5/1/45 w/?; cr France, 10KIA; sal 30/1/45; MACR 11881.

44-8434 Del Lincoln 17/9/44; Grenier 7/10/44; ass 560BS/388BG Knettishall 12/10/44; retUS Bradley 26/6/45; Sth Plains 28/6/45; RFC Kingman 10/12/45.

44-8435 Del Lincoln 17/9/44; Grenier 7/10/44; ass 525BS/379BG [FR-N] Kimbolton 16/10/44; retUS Bradley 24/6/45; Sth Plains 28/6/45; RFC Kingman 14/12/45.

44-8436 Del Lincoln 16/9/44; Grenier 1/10/44; ass 326BS/92BG [JW-H] Podington 8/11/44; c/l base? 5/5/45, sal.

44-8437 Del Lincoln 18/9/44; Grenier 15/10/44; ass 563BS/388BG Knettishall 12/10/44; MIA Nuremberg 17/2/45 w/Capt Gladstone; flak, cr Prum, Ger; 9KIA 1POW; MACR 12414.

44-8438 Del Lincoln 12/9/44; Grenier 6/10/44; ass 334BS/95BG [BG-R] Horham 12/10/44; b/d Seelze, Ger 14/3/45 w/Brumbaugh; f/l Belgium; 1WIA 8RTD; rep & ret gp; retUS Bradley 21/6/45; Sth Plains 23/6/45; RFC Kingman 25/11/45.

44-8439 Del Dallas 12/9/44; Hunter 23/9/44; Dow Fd 16/10/44; ass 360BS/303BG [PU-Z] Molesworth 2/11/44; retUS Morrison 19/10/45; RFC Walnut Ridge 11/1/46.

44-8440 Del Dallas 8/9/44; Hunter 26/9/44; Dow Fd 16/10/44; ass 493BG Debach 18/10/44; tran 351BS/100BG [EP-Y] Thorpe Abbotts 20/10/44; retUS Morrison 24/10/45; RFC Walnut Ridge 8/1/46.

44-8441 Del Dallas 12/9/44; Hunter 26/9/44; Dow Fd 18/10/44; ass 4BS/34BG Mendlesham 20/10/44; tran 332BS/94BG [XM-L] Rougham 21/10/44; retUS Morrison 19/10/45; RFC Walnut Ridge 9/1/46.

44-8442 Del Dallas 12/9/44; Hunter 5/10/44; Dow Fd 23/10/44; ass 337BS/96BG [AW-K] Snetterton 26/10/44; retUS, RFC Walnut Ridge 5/1/46.

44-8443 Del Dallas 13/9/44; Dow Fd 27/10/44; ass 367BS/306BG [GY-M/A] Thurleigh 4/12/44; re-ass 30/4/47; Recl Comp 19/11/47.

44-8444 Del Dallas 14/9/44; Hunter 29/9/44; Dow Fd 16/10/44; ass 836BS/487BG [2G-N] Lavenham 20/11/44; b/d Darmstadt 24/12/44 w/Harriman; e/a hit #4, c/l Hods, Bel; 4KIA (inc Brig Gen Fred Castle, 94BG CO who took a/c down safely away from US troops below) 6RTD; sal 28/1/45; MACR 11552. TREBLE FOUR.

44-8445 Del Dallas 18/9/44; Hunter 5/10/44; Grenier 16/10/44; ass 8AF 7/11/44; sal n/b/d 25/11/44.

44-8446 Del Dallas 18/9/44; Hunter 9/10/44; Dow Fd 18/10/44; ass 369BS/306BG [GY-A] Thurleigh 26/11/44; MIA Euskirchen 10/1/45 w/Mattson; flak, cr Koeln-Kaln, Ger?; 2KIA 8POW; MACR 11746.

44-8447 Del Dallas 18/9/44; Hunter 6/10/44; Grenier 25/10/44; ass 569BS/390BG [CC-P] Framlingham 30/10/44; retUS, RFC Walnut Ridge 4/1/46. DOUBLE IN BRASS.

44-8448 Del Dallas 18/9/44; Hunter 5/10/44; Dow Fd 28/10/44; ass 351BS/100BG [EP-C] Thorpe Abbotts 30/10/44; retUS, RFC Walnut Ridge 2/1/46.

44-8449 Del Dallas 19/9/44; Hunter 15/10/44; Dow Fd 25/10/44; ass 615BS/401BG [IY-F] Deenethorpe 10/11/44; 613BS [IN-P]; tran 305BG Chelveston 19/4/45; sal 9AF Germany 23/5/46.

44-8450 Del Dallas 18/9/44; Hunter 10/10/44; Grenier 25/10/44; ass 322BS/92BG [NV-M] Podington 20/11/44; b/d Cologne 10/1/45 w/?; f/l Continent, sal 21/1/45.

44-8451 Del Dallas 21/9/44; Hunter 28/9/44; Dow Fd 26/10/44; ass 337BS/96BG [AW-D] Snetterton 30/10/44; tran 379BG Kimbolton 20/11/44; c/l base? 23/6/45, sal n/b/d. BUTCH.

44-8452 Del Dallas 17/9/44; Hunter 26/9/44; Grenier 28/10/44; ass 493BG Debach 30/10/44; tran 350BS/100BG [LN-V] Thorpe Abbotts 1/11/44; 568BS/390BG [BI-C] Framlingham; retUS, RFC Walnut Ridge 11/1/46. THE MAINLINER.

44-8453 Del Dallas 17/9/44; Hunter 16/10/44; Dow Fd 26/10/44; ass 833BS/486BG [4N-E] Sudbury 30/10/44; tran 2BG Amendola 29/5/45; sal 9AF Germany 30/3/48.

44-8454 Del Dallas 19/9/44; Hunter 16/10/44; Dow Fd 26/10/44; ass 613BS/401BG [IN-C] Deenethorpe 20/11/44; 615BS [IY-T]; tran 305BG Chelveston 20/5/45; sal 9AF Germany 5/7/46.

44-8455 Del Dallas 18/9/44; Hunter 16/10/44; Dow Fd 27/10/44; ass 510BS/351BG [TU-M] Polebrook 20/11/44; 511BS [DS-M]; {13m} tran 305BG Chelveston 20/5/45; sal 9AF Germany 18/4/46.

44-8456 Del Dallas 18/9/44; Hunter 16/10/44; Dow Fd 31/10/44; ass 837BS/487BG Lavenham 5/1/45; tran 94BG Rougham 22/5/45; retUS Morrison 19/10/45; RFC Walnut Ridge 5/1/46.

44-8457 Del Dallas 18/9/44; Hunter 16/10/44; Dow Fd 27/10/44; ass 4BS/34BG Mendlesham 30/10/44 RAPID CITY SPOOK; retUS Morrison 27/10/45; RFC Walnut Ridge 19/11/45 FALSE COURAGE.

44-8458 Del Dallas 18/9/44; Hunter 16/10/44; Dow Fd 26/10/44; ass 708BS/447BG Rattlesden 30/10/44; b/d Weimar 9/2/45 w/?; f/l Continent; sal 13/2/45. JEANNE E.

44-8459 Del Cheyenne 18/9/44; Hunter 27/10/44; Grenier 5/11/44; ass 429BS/2BG Amendola 22/11/44; tran 463BG Celone 2/45; 483BG Sterparone 2/45; retUS, RFC Walnut Ridge 5/1/46.

44-8460 Del Cheyenne 14/9/44; Langley 26/10/44; 3501 BU Boca Raton 31/10/44; 3539 BU Langley 10/6/45; RFC Walnut Ridge 3/1/46.

44-8461 Del Cheyenne 14/9/44; Hunter 27/9/44; Grenier 4/11/44; ass 20BS/2BG PFF Amendola 6/12/44; sal 9AF Germany 10/5/46.

44-8462 Del Cheyenne 14/9/44; Dow Fd 27/10/44; ass 483BG Sterparone 2/45; retUS Langley 20/6/45; RFC Walnut Ridge 4/1/46.

44-8463 Del Cheyenne 19/9/44; Langley 26/10/44; 3539 BU Langley 29/6/45; 554 BU Memphis 16/8/45.

44-8464 Del Cheyenne 17/9/44; Hunter 5/10/44; Dow Fd 6/11/44; ass 97BG Amendola 12/44; sal b/d Vienna 30/3/45; retUS, RFC Walnut Ridge 8/1/46.

44-8465 Del Cheyenne 23/9/44; Langley 27/10/44; 3539 BU Langley 29/6/45; RFC Walnut Ridge 8/1/46.

44-8466 Del Cheyenne 25/9/44; Hunter 28/10/44;

INDIVIDUAL B-17 HISTORIES 293

Grenier 5/11/44; ass 97BG PFF Amendola 12/12/44; retUS, RFC Walnut Ridge 8/1/46.
44-8467 Del Cheyenne 24/9/44; Langley 25/10/44; Dow Fd 7/11/44; 3539 BU Langley 29/6/45; RFC Walnut Ridge 8/1/46.
44-8468 Del Cheyenne 21/9/44; Hunter 31/10/44; Grenier 8/11/44; ass 510BS/351BG [TU-J] Polebrook 2/1/45; 511BS [DS-J]; {19m} tran 305BG Chelveston 23/5/45; sal 9AF Germany 10/5/46.
44-8469 Del Cheyenne 21/9/44; Hunter 26/10/44; Grenier 12/11/44; ass 527BS/379BG [FO-Z] Kimbolton 1/12/44; tran 838BS/487BG Lavenham 22/5/45; 94BG Rougham 29/5/45; retUS, RFC Walnut Ridge 18/1/46.
44-8470 Del Cheyenne 22/9/44; Hunter 27/10/44; Dow Fd 9/11/44; ass 349BS/100BG [XR-T] Thorpe Abbotts 11/11/44; tran 861BS/493BG Debach 13/11/44; 863BS; tran 15AF 20/5/45; 10HB Oberpfaffenhofen 30/4/47; Recl Comp 7/1/49.
44-8471 Del Cheyenne 21/9/44; Hunter 31/10/44; Dow Fd 8/11/44; ass 323BS/91BG [OR-C] H2X Bassingbourn 11/11/44; {26+m} tran 306BG Thurleigh 5/45; sal 9AF Germany 30/7/46. TOWER OF LONDON.
44-8472 Del Cheyenne 21/9/44; Hunter 21/10/44; Dow Fd 9/11/44; ass 94BG Rougham 11/11/44; retUS Morrison 7/10/45; RFC Walnut Ridge 7/1/46.
44-8473 Del Cheyenne 23/9/44; Hunter 5/11/44; Dow Fd 20/11/44; ass 493BG Debach 20/11/44; tran 351BS/100BG [EP-Q] Thorpe Abbotts 22/11/44; retUS, RFC Walnut Ridge 20/12/45.
44-8474 Del Cheyenne 25/9/44; Hunter 1/11/44; Dow Fd 12/11/44; ass 8AF 24/11/44; sal 9AF Germany 23/5/46.
44-8475 Del Cheyenne 25/9/44; Hunter 1/11/44; Dow Fd 16/11/44; ass 322BS/91BG [LG-C] Bassingbourn 11/12/44; {18m including a Rubberneck trip} tran 306BG Thurleigh 24/5/45; 1st BD 18/6/45; sal 9AF Germany 23/5/46. IRISH LASSIE.
44-8476 Del Cheyenne 23/9/44; Hunter 1/11/44; Dow Fd 18/11/44; ass 601BS/398BG [3O-X] Nuthampstead 8/12/44; 602BS [K8-X]; tran 396BG Thurleigh 5/45; retUS, RFC Walnut Ridge 10/1/46.
44-8477 Del Dallas 28/9/44; Hunter 15/10/44; Dow Fd 26/10/44; ass 305BG Chelveston 21/11/44; sal 9AF Germany 6/12/45. WINGED VICTORY.
44-8478 Del Dallas 26/9/44; Hunter 6/10/44; Dow Fd 26/10/44; ass 323BS/91BG [OR-G] Bassingbourn 20/11/44; tran 306BG Thurleigh 24/5/45; sal 9AF Germany 26/7/46.
44-8479 Del Dallas 26/9/44; Hunter 6/10/44; Dow Fd 25/10/44; ass 748BS/457BG Glatton 29/11/44; 750BS; tran 305BG Chelveston 23/5/45; re-ass 10HB Oberpfaffenhofen 30/4/47; sal 9AF Germany 9/4/48. SUZY SAG SUMP.
44-8480 Del Dallas 25/9/44; Hunter 20/10/44; Grenier 9/11/44; ass 418BS/100BG [LD-X] Thorpe Abbotts 11/11/44; tran 407BS/92BG [PY-N] Podington 30/11/44; 306BG Thurleigh 7/5/45; sal 9AF Germany 11/5/46.
44-8481 Del Dallas 25/9/44; Hunter 23/10/44; Grenier 10/11/44; ass 390BG Framlingham 20/11/44; tran 100BG Thorpe Abbotts 22/11/44; retUS, RFC Walnut Ridge 2/1/46.
44-8482 Del Dallas 25/9/44; Hunter 9/10/44; Dow Fd 26/10/44; ass 332BS/94BG [XM-N] Rougham 30/10/44; tran 4BS/34BG Mendlesham 1/11/44 HELLGATE LADY; retUS, RFC Walnut Ridge 6/1/46. GOLDEN GATE IN "48".
44-8483 Del Dallas 25/9/44; Hunter 20/10/44; Grenier 9/11/44; ass 600BS/398BG [N8-T] Nuthampstead 2/12/44; tran 91BG Bassingbourn 9/1/45; 306BG Thurleigh 5/45; retUS, RFC Walnut Ridge 4/1/46.
44-8484 Del Dallas 26/9/44; Hunter 26/10/44; Dow Fd 31/10/44; ass 358BS/303BG [VK-W] Molesworth 5/11/44; b/d Hamburg 30/3/45 w/?; f/l Continent; sal 22/4/45.
44-8485 Del Dallas 26/9/44; Hunter 27/10/44; Dow Fd 29/10/44; ass 482BG H2X Alconbury 2/11/44; tran 350BS/100BG [LN-X] Thorpe Abbotts 4/11/44; retUS, RFC Walnut Ridge 29/12/45.
44-8486 Del Dallas 25/9/44; Hunter 24/10/44; Dow Fd 31/10/44; ass 305BG Chelveston 1/11/44; tran 418BS/100BG [LD-P] Thorpe Abbotts 3/11/44; retUS, RFC Walnut Ridge 28/12/45.
44-8487 Del Dallas 26/9/44; Hunter 24/10/44; Grenier 9/11/44; ass 548BS/385BG Gt Ashfield 11/11/44; re-ass 10BH Oberpfaffenhofen 30/4/47; Recl Comp 5/8/48.
44-8488 Del Dallas 26/9/44; Hunter 17/10/44; Grenier 3/11/44; ass 8AF 14/11/44; retUS, RFC Walnut Ridge 20/12/45.
44-8489 Del Dallas 26/9/44; Hunter 25/10/44; Grenier 6/11/44; ass 337BS/96BG Snetterton 11/11/44; MIA Mainz 13/1/45 w/Capt Miller; flak, cr Ginsheim, Ger; 4KIA 6POW; MACR 11570.
44-8490 Del Dallas 26/9/44; Hunter 26/11/44; New Bedford 1/11/44; Hunter 5/1/45; Grenier 2/2/45; ass 482BG H2X Alconbury 4/2/45; retUS Morrison 29/10/45; RFC Walnut Ridge 4/1/46.
44-8491 Del Dallas 25/9/44; Hunter 27/10/44; Dow Fd 8/11/44; ass 452BG Deopham Green 10/11/44; retUS, RFC Walnut Ridge 27/12/45.
44-8492 Del Dallas 25/9/44; Hunter 2/10/44; Grenier 3/11/44; ass 418BS/100BG [LD-C] Thorpe Abbotts 10/11/44; tran 848BS/490BG Eye 11/11/44; retUS Morrison 16/10/45; RFC Walnut Ridge 10/1/46.
44-8493 Del Dallas 30/9/44; Hunter 1/11/44; Grenier 26/11/44; ass 305BG Chelveston 4/12/44; sal 9AF Germany 15/7/46.
44-8494 Del Dallas 30/9/44; Hunter 17/11/44; Grenier 9/11/44; ass 97BG PFF Amendola 3/12/44; tran 774BS/463BG Celone 12/12/44; retUS, RFC Walnut Ridge 7/1/46.
44-8495 Del Dallas 28/9/44; Hunter 27/11/44; Grenier 9/11/44; ass 427BS/303BG [GN-Y] Molesworth 4/12/44; b/d Ingolstadt 15/1/45 w/?; f/l Continent; sal 18/1/45.
44-8496 Del Dallas 25/9/44; Hunter 30/10/44; Grenier 12/11/44; ass 463BG PFF Celone 5/12/44; re-ass 10HBS Oberpfaffenhofen 30/4/47; Recl Comp 7/1/49.
44-8497 Del Dallas 27/9/44; Cheyenne 12/10/44; Eglin 9/11/44; re-claimed 621 BU Eglin 22/7/46.
44-8498 Del Dallas 21/9/44; Hunter 30/10/44; Dow Fd 10/11/44; ass 97BG Amendola 14/11/44; tran 772BS/463BG Celone 28/12/44; MIA Berlin 24/3/45 w/Hatcher; flak, cr Breslau; MACR 13258.
44-8499 Del Lincoln 26/9/44; Grenier 5/11/44; ass 832BS/486BG Sudbury 17/11/44; 832BS; b/d Merseburg 30/11/44 w/Heinz; flak, c/l Blofelden, Ger; 1EVD 4KIA 4POW; MACR 11152; sal 10/1/45 & ret UK; tran 305BS Chelveston 1/45; f/l Fritzlar A/fd, Ger 30/5/45.
44-8500 Del Lincoln 30/9/44; Grenier 2/10/44; Dow Fd 16/10/44; ass 602BS/398BG [K8-F] Nuthampstead 17/1/45; retUS Hobbs Fd 7/6/45; Lincoln 11/6/45; RFC Kingman 20/11/45.
44-8501 Del Lincoln 30/9/44; Fairfield 16/10/44; ass 526BS/379BG Kimbolton 13/11/44; MIA Cologne 6/1/45 w/McConnell; flak hit right wing, cr Plum, Ger; 4KIA 6POW; MACR 11568. JEANIE.
44-8502 Del Lincoln 1/10/44; Grenier 14/10/44; ass 8AF 16/10/44; retUS Bradley 6/7/45; Sth Plains 8/7/45; RFC Kingman 26/11/45.
44-8503 Del Lincoln 2/10/44; Grenier 14/10/44; ass 350BS/100BG [LN-A] Thorpe Abbotts 18/10/44; b/d Zwickau 19/3/45; f/l Le Culot A/fd, Bel; sal 1/4/45.
44-8504 Del Lincoln 4/10/44; Grenier 7/10/44; ass 561BS/388BG Knettishall 19/10/44; MIA Munich 9/4/45 w/Carroll; flak, cr Landsberg, Ger; 3KIA 7POW; MACR 13870.
44-8505 Del Lincoln 7/10/44; Grenier 12/10/44; ass 305BG Chelveston 5/12/44; tran 401BG Deenethorpe 25/5/45; retUS Bradley 7/6/45; Sth Plains 12/6/45; RFC Kingman 25/11/45.
44-8506 Del Lincoln 2/10/44; Grenier 16/10/44; ass 563BS/388BG Knettishall 18/10/44; retUS Bradley 17/6/45; Sth Plains 20/6/45; RFC Kingman 18/12/45. MISS MAC.
44-8507 Del Lincoln 2/10/44; Grenier 16/10/44; ass 8AF 18/10/44; retUS, RFC Walnut Ridge 16/12/45.
44-8508 Del Lincoln 3/10/44; Grenier 14/10/44; ass 325BS/92BG [NV-N] Podington 9/2/45; secret mission 28/5/45, ret 29/5/45; sal 9AF Germany 31/5/46.
44-8509 Del Lincoln 4/10/44; Grenier 27/10/44; ass 410BS/94BG [GL-L] Rougham 30/10/44; MIA Plauen 21/3/45 w/Nahrnstedt; flak, cr Poznan, Pol; 1POW 9RTD; MACR 13573. WAGON WHEELS.
44-8510 Del Lincoln 2/10/44; Grenier 23/10/44; ass 8AF 28/10/44; retUS Bradley 6/7/45; RFC Kingman 10/12/45.
44-8511 Del Lincoln 3/10/44; Grenier 22/10/44; ass 332BS/94BG [XM-Q] Rougham 25/10/44; retUS Bradley 7/6/45; Sth Plains 10/6/45; RFC Kingman 11/12/45.
44-8512 Del Lincoln 3/10/44; Grenier 26/10/44; ass 350BS/100BG [LN-E] Thorpe Abbotts 30/10/44; b/d Kollin 18/4/45 w/?; f/l Continent; rep & ret UK; retUS Bradley 21/6/45; Sth Plains 25/6/45; RFC Kingman 10/12/45.
44-8513 Del Hunter 3/10/44; Dow Fd 16/10/44; ass 8AF 18/10/44; sal 9AF Germany 22/5/46; retUS 4000 BU Patterson 23/5/46; 4000 BU Wright 30/6/46; re-ass 31/3/47; 4141 BU Pyote 25/5/47; Recl Comp 18/4/48.
44-8514 Del Lincoln 3/10/44; Grenier 19/10/44; ass 482BG H2X Alconbury 20/10/44; tran 452BG Deopham Green 21/10/44; 349BS/100BG [XR-R] Thorpe Abbotts 23/10/44; b/d Frankfurt 29/12/44 w/?; f/l Continent; rep & ret UK; MACR 11345; retUS Bradley 2/6/45; Sth Plains 9/6/45; RFC Kingman 30/11/45. LASSIE COME HOME.
44-8515 Del Hunter 7/10/44; Dow Fd 18/10/44; ass 563BS/388BG Knettishall 20/10/44; retUS Bradley 28/6/45; RFC Kingman 30/11/45.
44-8516 Del Hunter 7/10/44; Dow Fd 18/10/44; ass 423BS/306BG [RD-M] Thurleigh 3/1/45; tran 535BS/381BG Ridgewell 23/5/45; retUS Bradley 10/6/45; Sth Plains 13/6/45; RFC Kingman 1/12/45.
44-8517 Del Hunter 2/10/44; Dow Fd 16/10/44; ass 401BG Deenethorpe 1/1/45; tran 601BS/398BG [3O-J] Nuthampstead 9/2/45; retUS Bradley 25/5/45; Sth Plains 30/5/45; RFC Kingman 25/11/45.
44-8518 Del Hunter 3/10/44; Dow Fd 14/10/44; ass 729BS/452BG Deopham Green 26/10/44; MIA Ludwigshafen 5/12/44 w/Wagoner; mech fault, cr Talgewilsten, Ger?; 8KIA 1POW; MACR 11051.
44-8519 Del Lincoln 5/10/44; Grenier 20/10/44; ass 452BG Deopham Green 22/10/44; retUS Bradley 7/6/45; Sth Plains 5/6/45; RFC Kingman 16/12/45.
44-8520 Del Lincoln 9/10/44; Grenier 17/10/44; ass 535BS/381BG Ridgewell 1/45; retUS Morrison 19/10/45; RFC Walnut Ridge 5/1/46.
44-8521 Del Lincoln 3/10/44; Grenier 19/10/44; ass

562BS/388BG Knettishall 21/10/44; retUS Bradley 10/6/45; Sth Plains 16/6/45; RFC Kingman 17/11/45.

44-8522 Del Lincoln 3/10/44; Grenier 20/10/44; ass 452BG Deopham Green 22/10/44; tran 333BS/94BG [TS-D] Rougham 24/10/44; retUS Bradley 7/6/45; Sth Plains 9/6/45; RFC Kingman 16/11/45.

44-8523 Del Lincoln 5/10/44; Cooledge 12/10/44; Grenier 22/10/44; ass 331BS/94BG [QE-H] Rougham 25/10/44; tran 836BS/487BG Lavenham 20/3/45; retUS Bradley 11/6/45; Independence 14/6/45; RFC Kingman 16/12/45.

44-8524 Del Lincoln 5/10/44; Grenier 28/10/44; ass 487BG Lavenham 20/2/45; retUS, RFC Kingman 29/12/45.

44-8525 Del Lincoln 8/10/44; Grenier 19/10/44; ass 334BS/95BG [BG-U] Horham 21/10/44; tran 351BG Polebrook 29/5/45; retUS, RFC Kingman 9/11/45.

44-8526 Del Lincoln 8/10/44; Dow Fd 28/10/44; ass 533BS/381BG [VP-Q] Ridgewell 1/12/44; {39+m} RetUS Bradley 12/6/45; Sth Plains 16/6/45; RFC Kingman 14/12/45. ONE MEAT BALL.

44-8527 Del Lincoln 5/10/44; Dow Fd 25/10/44; ass 452BG Deopham Green 30/10/44; b/d Chemnitz 6/2/45 w/?; sal 9/2/45.

44-8528 Del Lincoln 5/10/44; Grenier 22/10/44; ass 834BS/486BG [2S-L] Sudbury 25/10/44; MIA Parchim 7/4/45 w/Krenz; flak, cr Seehausen, Ger; 1EVD 1KIA 8POW; MACR 11487. FLAK SACK.

44-8529 Del Lincoln 8/10/44; Grenier 23/10/44; ass 18BS/34BG Mendlesham 25/10/44; b/d Mainz, Ger 13/1/45 w/?; mid air coll w/44-8645; sal 21/2/45.

44-8530 Del Lincoln 8/10/44; Grenier 26/10/44; ass 836BS/487BG Lavenham 30/11/44; retUS, RFC Kingman 26/11/45.

44-8531 Del Lincoln 5/10/44; Palm Springs 12/10/44; Dow Fd 22/10/44; ass 728BS/452BG Deopham Green 26/10/44; MIA Parchim 7/4/45 w/Gill; e/a, cr Wandesbeck, Ger; 1KIA 8POW; MACR 13893.

44-8532 Del Lincoln 9/10/44; Grenier 23/10/44; ass 482BG H2X Alconbury 25/10/44; tran 349BS/100BG [XR-G] Thorpe Abbotts 27/10/44 KLEEN SWEEP; 482BG Alconbury 20/5/45; retUS Bradley 4/6/45; Sth Plains 8/6/45; RFC Walnut Ridge 26/11/44; CLEAN SWEEP.

44-8533 Del Lincoln 9/10/44; Dow Fd 22/10/44; ass 305BG Chelveston 4/12/44; tran 401BG Deenethorpe 22/5/45; retUS Bradley 7/6/45; Sth Plains 10/6/45; RFC Kingman 29/11/45.

44-8534 Del Dorval, Canada 12/10/44; ass RAF 214Sq [BU-C] Oulton as {KJ 111}; SOC 11/3/47.

44-8535 Del Dorval 10/10/44; ass RAF 214Sq [BU-P] Oulton as {KJ 112}; MIA 22/3/45.

44-8536 Del Dorval 12/10/44; ass RAF 223Sq as {KJ 113}; SOC 11/3/47.

44-8537 Del Dorval 12/10/44; ass RAF 214Sq [BU-B] Oulton as {KJ 114}; damaged by night fighter 3/4/45; SOC 11/3/47.

44-8538 Del Dorval 11/10/44; ass RAF 223Sq as {KJ 115}; tran RWE [U3-D]; SOC 11/3/47.

44-8539 Del Cheyenne 11/10/44; Hunter 1/11/44; Grenier 13/11/44; ass 327BS/92BG [UX-Q] Podington 30/12/44; tran 306BG Thurleigh 7/5/45; sal 9AF Germany 31/5/46.

44-8540 Del Cheyenne 11/10/44; Hunter 1/11/44; Dow Fd 20/1/45; ass 339BS/96BG [QJ-W] Snetterton 22/1/45; tran 562BS/388BG Knettishall /45; retUS, RFC Walnut Ridge 21/1/46. ROUND TRIP.

44-8541 Del Cheyenne 12/10/44; Hunter 18/11/44; Dow Fd 29/11/44; ass 546BS/384BG [BK-Y] Grafton Underwood 19/1/45; tran 305BG Chelveston 9/5/45; re-ass 30/4/47; Recl Comp 9/4/48; BUCKEYE BELLE.

44-8542 Del Cheyenne 12/10/44; Hunter 19/11/44; Dow Fd 4/1/45; ass 333BS/94BG Rougham 6/1/45; tran 349BS/100BG [XR-V] Thorpe Abbotts 8/1/45; retUS, RFC Walnut Ridge 19/10/45.

44-8543 Del All Weather Flying Centre Clinton 17/10/44; tran as ETB-17 on weather recon/electronic countermeasures at Wright Fd 1949; on a daily mission to Andrews Fd, recording weather; had red tails, engines cowls and noses; ass Federal telecommunications Corp, Teterboro, NJ mid 1950s with wing-tip antennas fitted; as N3710G Breckenridge, Tx 1986; Fort Worth 1988; livery now as 486BG; CHUCKIE.

44-8544 Del Cheyenne 15/10/44; Hunter 28/10/44; Dow Fd 10/12/45; ass 533BS/381BG [VP-V] Ridgwell 18/1/45; {8+m} c/l Gt Yeldham, sal n/b/d 14/3/45.

44-8545 Del Cheyenne 12/10/44; Hunter 24/11/44; Dow Fd 15/12/44; ass 427BS/303BG [GN-X] Molesworth 17/1/45; retUS, RFC Walnut Ridge 4/1/46.

44-8546 Del Cheyenne 12/10/44; Hunter 22/11/44; Dow Fd 3/12/44; ass 325BS/92BG [NV-H] Podington 28/1/45; tran 306BG Thurleigh 7/5/45; sal 9AF Germany 19/11/47. MISS COLUMBIA.

44-8547 Del Cheyenne 16/10/44; Hunter 19/11/44; Dow Fd 28/12/44; ass 836BS/487BG [2G-E] Lavenham 2/1/45; MIA Kiel 8/4/45 w/Milner; mid air coll w/43-38958; cr Neustadt, Ger; 5KIA 4POW; MACR 13742.

44-8548 Del Cheyenne 17/10/44; Hunter 2/11/44; Dow Fd 3/12/44; ass 351BS/100BG [EP-H] Thorpe Abbotts 6/12/44; tran 412BS/95BG [QW-K] Horham 8/12/44; retUS, RFC Walnut Ridge 18/1/46.

44-8549 Del Cheyenne 12/10/44; Hunter 5/11/44; Grenier 3/12/44; ass 562BS/388BG Knettishall 16/12/44; retUS, RFC Walnut Ridge 8/1/46. JUST JOYCE.

44-8550 Del Cheyenne 15/10/44; Hunter 5/11/44; Grenier 5/12/44; ass 613BS/401BG [IN-Q] Deenethorpe 2/1/45; 615BS [IY-D]; tran 305BG Chelveston 20/5/45; sal 9AF Germany 23/5/46.

44-8551 Del Cheyenne 15/10/44; Hunter 9/11/44; 621 BU Clinton 11/1/45 electronic warfare/weather recon; 4152 BU Clinton 4/7/50; Recl Comp.

44-8552 Del Cheyenne 11/10/44; Hunter 25/11/44; Dow Fd 16/12/44; ass 349BS/100BG [XR-D] Thorpe Abbotts 18/12/44; tran 360BS/303BG [PU-X] Molesworth 29/1/45; 92BG Podington 6/45; retUS, RFC Walnut Ridge 5/1/46.

44-8553 Del Cheyenne 16/10/44; Hunter 9/11/44; Dow Fd 3/12/44; ass 602BS/398BG [K8-Y] Nuthampstead 15/1/45; 601BS [3O-Y]; tran 306BG Thurleigh 5/5/45; sal 9AF Germany 14/3/47.

44-8554 Del Cheyenne 16/10/44; Hunter 4/11/44; Grenier 4/12/44; ass 325BS/92BG [NV-D] Podington 14/1/45; tran 306BG Thurleigh 7/5/45; sal 9AF Germany 6/11/46.

44-8555 Del Cheyenne 14/10/44; Hunter 11/11/44; Grenier 22/11/44; ass 482BG Alconbury 25/11/44; tran 338BS/96BG Snetterton 28/11/44; retUS, RFC Walnut Ridge 4/1/46.

44-8556 Del Cheyenne 17/10/44; Hunter 6/11/44; Dow Fd 2/12/44; ass 4BS/34BG Mendlesham 16/12/44; retUS Morrison 19/10/45; RFC Walnut Ridge 2/1/46. MISS PURDY.

44-8557 Del Cheyenne 17/10/44; Hunter 6/11/44; Dow Fd 3/12/44; ass 748BS/457BG Glatton 15/1/45; 751BS; b/d Rosenheim, Ger 18/4/45 w/Thistle; flak, c/l Freising, Ger; 1KIA 9POW; MACR 14183. Sal & rep 9AF, retUS 2/11/45; sal 10/6/46.

44-8558 Del Cheyenne 16/10/44; Hunter 24/10/44; Grenier 3/12/44; ass 8AF 13/12/44; retUS, RFC Walnut Ridge 20/12/45.

44-8559 Del Cheyenne 16/10/44; Hunter 29/11/44; Grenier 4/12/44; ass 7BS/34BG Mendlesham 16/12/44; tran 350BS/100BG [LN-Z] Thorpe Abbotts 18/12/44; 306BG Thurleigh /45; retUS, RFC Walnut Ridge 20/12/45.

44-8560 Del Cheyenne 10/10/44; Hunter 24/11/44; Grenier 29/11/44; ass 482BG H2X Alconbury 1/12/44; retUS, RFC Walnut Ridge 11/12/45.

44-8561 Del Cheyenne 16/10/44; Hunter 29/11/44; Lowry 2/12/44; Dow Fd 24/12/44; Hunter 20/1/45; Dow Fd 2/2/45; ass 49BS/2BG PFF Amendola 4/2/45; sal 24/12/46; re-ass 30/4/47; Recl Comp 11/1/47.

44-8562 Del Cheyenne 20/10/44; Hunter 6/12/44; Grenier 20/1/45; ass 483BG Sterparone 24/1/45; retUS, RFC Walnut Ridge 29/12/45.

44-8563 Del Cheyenne 21/10/44; Hunter 12/11/44; Grenier 5/12/44; ass 839BS/487BG Lavenham 30/12/44; MIA Derben 14/1/45 w/Stemple; flak, cr Gutenpaaren, Hol?; 2KIA 9POW; MACR 11731.

44-8564 Del Cheyenne 20/10/44; Hunter 16/11/44; Dow Fd 3/12/44; ass 359BS/303BG [BN-Z] Molesworth 21/1/45; retUS, RFC Walnut Ridge 7/1/46.

44-8565 Del Cheyenne 17/10/44; Hunter 27/11/44; Grenier 6/12/44; ass 349BS/100BG [XR-P] Thorpe Abbotts 8/12/44; retUS Morrison 22/10/45; RFC Walnut Ridge 28/1/46.

44-8566 Del Cheyenne 19/10/44; Hunter 17/11/44; Grenier 7/12/44; ass 571BS/390BG Framlingham 9/12/44; b/d Frankfurt 17/2/45 w/Kennedy; exploded 20m NW Ostend, Hol; 1RTD 8KIA; MACR 12321.

44-8567 Del Cheyenne 21/10/44; Hunter 27/10/44; Grenier 6/12/44; ass 8AF, but tran 4100 BU Patterson 7/12/44; 4168 BU Sth Plains 18/11/45; 4141 BU Pyote 1/1/46; sal 18/4/46.

44-8568 Del Cheyenne 20/10/44; Hunter 6/12/44; Grenier 20/12/44; ass 358BS/303BG [VK-X] Molesworth 22/1/45; retUS, RFC Walnut Ridge 28/12/45.

44-8569 Del Cheyenne 22/10/44; Hunter 29/11/44; Dow Fd 14/2/45; ass 839BS/487BG [R5-P] Lavenham 8/2/45; retUS, RFC Kingman 29/12/45.

44-8570 Del Cheyenne 20/10/44; Hunter 29/11/44; Dow Fd 7/12/44; ass 306BG Thurleigh 2/1/45; sal 9AF Germany 23/10/46.

44-8571 Del Cheyenne 20/10/44; Hunter 25/11/44; Dow Fd 12/12/44; ass 351BS/100BG [EP-X] Thorpe Abbotts 15/12/44; tran 570BS/390BG [DI-R] Framlingham 17/12/44; retUS Morrison 19/10/45, RFC Kingman 9/1/46.

44-8572 Del Cheyenne 22/10/44; Hunter 25/11/45; Dow Fd 7/2/45; ass 333BS/94BG Rougham 16/12/44; retUS, RFC Kingman 9/1/46.

44-8573 Del Cheyenne 22/10/44; Hunter 25/11/45; Dow Fd 17/12/44; ass 322BS/91BG Bassingbourn 29/1/45; 324BS; b/d Dresden 14/2/45 w/?; f/l Continent, sal 7/12/45.

44-8574 Del Cheyenne 22/10/44; Hunter 22/11/44; Grenier 26/12/44; ass 562BS/388BG Knettishall 31/12/44; caught fire & sal 7/4/45.

44-8575 Del Cheyenne 23/10/44; Hunter 29/11/44; Dow Fd 6/12/44; ass 452BG Deopham Green 18/12/44; sal 9AF Germany 1/9/46.

44-8576 Del Cheyenne 22/10/44; Hunter 25/11/44; Grenier 16/12/44; ass 303BG Molesworth 17/1/45; sal 19/11/47.

44-8577 Del Cheyenne 27/10/44; Hunter 28/11/44; Dow Fd 12/12/44; ass 325BS/92BG [NV-M]

Podington 20/1/45; 407BS [PY-M]; b/d Swinemünde, Ger 12/3/45 w/Ringsred; mech fault, f/l Bulltofta, Swed; 9INT; MACR 13093. Rep & ret UK 27/6/45; retUS Bradley 21/7/45; RFC Kingman 10/12/45.

44-8578 Del Cheyenne 27/10/44; Hunter 24/11/44; Dow Fd 8/12/44; ass 325BS/92BG [NV-G] Podington 28/1/45; tran 306BG Thurleigh 7/5/45; sal 9AF Germany 6/11/46.

44-8579 Del Cheyenne 23/10/44; Hunter 20/11/44; Dow Fd 5/12/44; ass 8AF 17/12/44; retUS, RFC Walnut Ridge 3/1/46.

44-8580 Del Cheyenne 20/10/44; Hunter 22/11/44; Dow Fd 2/12/44; ass 547BS/384BG [SO-Z] Grafton Underwood 28/1/45; 544BS [SU-Z]; tran 457BG Glatton 9/5/45; 305BG Chelveston 23/5/45; sal 9AF Germany 6/11/46.

44-8581 Del Cheyenne 27/10/44; Hunter 28/11/44; Dow Fd 22/2/45; ass 429BS/2BG PFF Amendola 28/12/44; Re-ass 30/4/47; Recl Comp 19/11/47.

44-8582 Del Cheyenne 28/10/44; Hunter 3/12/44; Dow Fd 13/12/44; ass 49BS/2BG PFF Amendola 24/12/44; sal 9AF 3/7/46.

44-8583 Del Cheyenne 29/10/44; Hunter 29/11/44; Dow Fd 15/12/44; ass 339BS/96BG [QJ-K] Snetterton 17/12/44; retUS Morrison 21/4/46; 613 BU Phillips PG 3/10/48.

44-8584 Del Cheyenne 28/10/44; Hunter 30/11/44; Dow Fd 23/12/44; ass 97BG Amendola 12/1/45; tran 816BS/483BG Sterparone 28/1/45; retUS, RFC Walnut Ridge 10/10/45. RUM & COKE.

44-8585 Del Cheyenne 26/10/44; Hunter 30/11/44; Grenier 10/12/44; ass 96BS/2BG PFF Amendola 19/12/44; {27m} sal 9AF Germany 10/5/46.

44-8586 Del Cheyenne 30/10/44; Hunter 3/12/44; Grenier 5/2/45; ass 32BS/301BG PFF Lucera 26/1/45; sal 9AF Germany 3/11/46.

44-8587 Del Cheyenne 27/10/44; Hunter 2/12/44; Grenier 18/12/44; ass 301BG PFF Lucera 31/1/45; sal 5/7/46.

44-8588 Del Cheyenne 27/10/44; Hunter 9/12/44; Grenier 22/12/44; ass 323BS/91BG [OR-E] Bassingbourn 23/1/45; 324BS [DF-E]; tran 369BS/306BG Thurleigh 24/5/45; sal 9AF Germany 7/11/46; KLETTE'S WILD HARES.

44-8589 Del Cheyenne 26/10/44; Hunter 9/12/44; Grenier 22/12/44; ass 332BS/94BG [XM-W] Rougham 24/1/45; tran 96BG Snetterton 28/12/44; 379BG Kimbolton 9/2/45; retUS, RFC Walnut Ridge 20/12/45. PRETTY OLGA.

44-8590 Del Cheyenne 29/10/44; Hunter 16/11/44; Grenier 20/12/44; ass 358BS/303BG [VK-Y] Molesworth 17/1/45; c/t/o for Dresden 15/2/45 w/?; crew OK; sal 16/2/45.

44-8591 Del Cheyenne 29/10/44; Hunter 26/11/44; Grenier 30/12/44; ass 817BS/483BG Sterparone 3/1/45; retUS, RFC Walnut Ridge 20/12/45.

44-8592 Del Cheyenne 30/10/44; Hunter 1/12/44; Grenier 30/12/44; ass 483BG Sterparone 4/1/45; retUS, RFC Walnut Ridge 10/1/46.

44-8593 Del Cheyenne 28/10/44; Hunter 2/12/44; Dow Fd 10/12/44; ass 301BG PFF Lucera 26/1/45; retUS Morrison 14/4/46; 613 BU Phillips PG 3/8/46.

44-8594 Del Lincoln 28/10/44; Grenier 29/11/44; ass 563BS/388BG Knettishall 9/12/44; MIA Oranienburg 15/3/45 w/Fehrman; mech fault, cr Ludwiglust, Ger; 5KIA 4POW; MACR 13094.

44-8595 Del Lincoln 29/10/44; Grenier 9/11/44; ass 8AF 11/11/44; retUS Bradley 10/6/45; Sth Plains 9/7/45; RFC Kingman 10/11/45.

44-8596 Del Lincoln 28/10/44; Grenier 9/11/44; ass 493BG Debach 11/11/44; b/d Cottbus, Ger 15/2/45 w/?; f/l Continent, sal 1/3/45.

44-8597 Del Lincoln 27/10/44; Grenier 10/11/44; ass 8AF 22/11/44.

44-8598 Del Lincoln 29/10/44; Grenier 12/11/44; ass 7BS/34BG Mendlesham 20/11/44; c/l 16/12/44; sal.

44-8599 Del Lincoln 28/10/44; Grenier 5/12/44; ass 533BS/381BG [VP-M] Ridgewell 4/1/45; {31+m} RetUS Bradley 28/5/45; Sth Plains 31/5/45; RFC Kingman 27/11/45.

44-8600 Del Lincoln 30/10/44; Dow Fd 26/11/44; ass 350BS/100BG [LN-X] Thorpe Abbotts 27/11/44; tran 331BS/94BG [QE-S] Rougham 28/1/45; c/t/o in heavy snow for Hohenbudberg 28/1/45 w/Weiss; 8KIA as a/c hit railway nr Thurston; sal 10/2/45.

44-8601 Del Lincoln 20/10/44; Dow Fd 26/11/44; ass 652BS/25BG Watton 12/12/44; MIA Atlantic weather mission 17/3/45 w/?; MACR 13856.

44-8602 Del Lincoln 28/10/44; Grenier 10/12/44; ass 731BS/452BG Deopham Green 22/1/45; b/d Hamburg 17/1/45 w/Smith; flak, f/l Bulltofta, Swed; 9INT; MACR 11728; rep & ret UK; retUS Bradley 1/8/45; Independence 3/8/45; RFC Kingman 10/12/45.

44-8603 Del Lincoln 30/10/44; Dow Fd 14/11/44; ass 551BS/385BG Gt Ashfield 26/11/44; tran 388BG Knettishall 28/11/44; retUS, RFC Walnut Ridge 1/2/46.

44-8604 Del Lincoln 31/10/44; Grenier 15/12/44; Dow Fd 15/12/44; ass 336BS/95BG [ET-X] Horham 17/12/44; b/d Holzwickede 23/3/45 w/Dunwoody; mid air coll w/44-8754; cr Campsea Ash, UK; 6KIA (inc on lost at sea) 4RTD; sal 26/3/45.

44-8605 Del Lincoln 31/10/44; Grenier 3/12/44; ass 18BS/34BG Mendlesham 20/12/44; b/d Operation 'Varsity' 24/3/45 w/?; mid air coll, sal 25/3/45.

44-8606 Del Lincoln 31/10/44; Grenier 4/12/44; ass 836BS/487BG [2G-C] Lavenham 1/2/45; b/d Chemnitz 6/2/45 w/?; c/l base, hit truck; sal.

44-8607 Del Lincoln 31/10/44; Grenier 20/11/44; ass 8AF 14/12/44; retUS Bradley 12/7/45; RFC Kingman 29/12/45.

44-8608 Del Lincoln 31/10/44; Dow Fd 16/12/44; ass 544BS/384BG [SU-B] Grafton Underwood 9/1/45; sal 9AF Germany 10/12/45.

44-8609 Del Lincoln 1/11/44; Grenier 3/12/44; ass 338BS/96BG [BX-N] Snetterton 7/12/44; tran 836BS/487BG Lavenham 9/2/45; 452BG Deopham Green 30/5/45; retUS Bradley 6/6/45; Sth Plains 11/6/45; RFC Kingman 4/12/45.

44-8610 Del Lincoln 1/11/44; Dow Fd 26/11/44; ass 493BG Debach 28/11/44; retUS Bradley 1/7/45; Sth Plains 4/7/45; RFC Kingman 24/11/45. PEORIA BELLE.

44-8611 Del Lincoln 1/11/44; Dow Fd 3/12/44; ass 836BS/487BG Lavenham 2/1/45; taxi acc 21/1/45 w/?; sal 22/1/45.

44-8612 Del Lincoln 1/11/44; Grenier 3/12/44; ass 407BS/92BG [PY-V] Podington 1/2/45; sal 9AF Germany 31/5/46. V-DAY.

44-8613 Del Hunter 1/11/44; Grenier 17/11/44; ass 350BS/100BG Thorpe Abbotts 19/11/44; MIA Plauen 21/3/45 w/Painter; e/a, cr Dobeln, Ger; 8KIA 1POW; MACR 13572.

44-8614 Del Hunter 2/11/44; Grenier 17/11/44; ass 836BS/487BG Lavenham 8/12/44; b/d Darmstadt, Ger 24/12/44 w/?; flak, f/l Continent; MACR 12207. Sal 28/1/45.

44-8615 Del Hunter 2/11/44; Grenier 19/11/44; ass 835BS/486BG [H8-G] Sudbury 21/11/44; retUS Bradley 9/7/45; RFC Kingman 7/12/45.

44-8616 Del Hunter 2/11/44; Grenier 23/11/44; ass 418BS/100BG [LD-Z] Thorpe Abbotts 25/11/44; retUS Bradley 3/7/45; Sth Plains 6/7/45; RFC Kingman 29/11/45.

44-8617 Del Hunter 2/11/44; Grenier 19/11/44; ass 509BS/351BG [RQ-G] Polebrook 20/2/45; {34m} RetUS Bradley 4/6/45; Sth Plains 7/6/45; RFC Kingman 6/12/45.

44-8618 Del Lincoln 5/11/44; Dow Fd 3/12/44; ass 413BS/96BG [MZ-Q] Snetterton 5/12/44; retUS Bradley 4/6/45; Sth Plains 7/6/45; RFC Kingman 29/12/45.

44-8619 Del Dorval, Canada 5/11/44; ass RAF RWE Sq [U3-F] as {KJ 116} 13/11/44; SOC 9/7/46.

44-8620 Del Dorval 5/11/44; ass RAF 223Sq, RWE Sq [U3-F] as {KJ 117} 13/11/44; SOC 11/3/47.

44-8621 Del Dorval 6/11/44; ass RAF 223Sq [6G-H], 214Sq Oulton; RWE Sq [U3-G] as {KJ 118}; SOC 11/3/47.

44-8622 Del Dorval 6/11/44; ass RAF 214Sq Oulton [BU-F] as {KJ 119}; SOC 11/3/47.

44-8623 Del Dorval 6/11/44; ass RAF 223Sq, RWE Sq [U3-H] as {KJ 120}; SOC 11/3/47.

44-8624 Del Dorval 6/11/44; ass RAF 223Sq [6G-B], 214Sq Oulton as {KJ 121}; SOC 11/3/47.

44-8625 Del Dorval 6/11/44; ass RAF 214BU Oulton as {KJ 122}; SOC 11/3/47.

44-8626 Del Dorval 6/11/44; ass RAF 51MU as {KJ 123}; SOC 11/3/47.

44-8627 Del Dorval 6/11/44; ass RAF 223Sq as {KJ 124}; SOC 11/3/47.

44-8628 Del Dorval 6/11/44; ass RAF 214Sq Oulton as {KJ 125}; W/O 19/4/45.

44-8629 Del Hunter 5/11/44; Dow Fd 27/11/44; ass 391BS/34BG Mendlesham 11/12/44; retUS Bradley 24/6/45; Sth Plains 28/6/45; RFC Kingman 4/12/45. PURTY CHILI.

44-8630 Del Hunter 9/11/44; Grenier 28/11/44; ass 603BS/398BG [N7-U] Nuthampstead 14/1/45; retUS Bradley 7/6/45; Sth Plains 10/6/45; RFC Kingman 27/12/45.

44-8631 Del Hunter 11/11/44; Grenier 3/12/44; ass 8AF 6/12/44; retUS Bradley 4/7/45; Sth Plains 7/7/45; RFC Kingman 14/12/45.

44-8632 Del Lincoln 9/11/44; Dow Fd 3/12/44; ass 351BS/100BG [EP-H] Thorpe Abbotts 12/12/44; c/l and struck tree 12/3/45; sal 16/3/45.

44-8633 Del Lincoln 9/11/44; Grenier 2/12/44; ass 568BS/390BG [BI-Z] 13/12/44 SWEET MARIE; retUS Bradley 9/7/45; RFC Kingman 27/11/45; THE SAINT.

44-8634 Del Lincoln 9/11/44; Grenier 3/12/44; ass 728BS/452BG Deopham Green 6/12/44; 731BS; MIA Kaltenkirchen 7/4/45 w/Sharp; e/a, cr Heide, Ger; 7KIA 3POW; MACR 14184. IDA WANNA.

44-8635 Del Lincoln 9/11/44; Dow Fd 3/12/44; ass 8AF 8/1/45; re-ass Europe 30/4/47; 605 BU Eglin 7/1/48; 1414 BU Dhahran 25/3/48; tran from MTO to AFE 20/4/49; sal 7210 BU Erding 22/6/49.

44-8636 Del Lincoln 14/11/44; Grenier 3/12/44; ass 601BS/398BG [3O-X] Nuthampstead 7/12/44; MIA Neumünster 13/4/45 w/Palant; exploded, cr Garbeck, Ger; 1EVD 9POW; MACR 13907.

44-8637 Del Lincoln 9/11/44; Dow Fd 3/12/44; ass 600BS/398BG [N8-A] Nuthampstead 3/1/45; 602BS [K8-X]; tran 390BG Framlingham 22/3/45; retUS Bradley 2/6/45; RFC Kingman 17/12/45.

44-8638 Del Hunter 14/11/44; Dow Fd 29/11/44; ass 305BG Chelveston 1/12/44; b/d Munich 25/2/45 w/?; f/l Continent; sal 19/4/45. OUR CHERRY.

44-8639 Del Hunter 10/11/44; Dow Fd 30/11/44; ass 305BG Chelveston 10/2/45; tran 351BG Polebrook 23/5/45; cr Barmouth, Wales, sal 8/6/45.

44-8640 Del Hunter 14/11/44; Dow Fd 3/12/44; ass 388BG Knettishall 4/12/44; tran 334BS/95BG [BG-D]

Horham 5/12/44; MIA Operation 'Chowhound' 7/5/44 w/Sceurman; flak, ditched Channel; 11KIA 2RTD. (Last 8AF a/c lost in WW II).

44-8641 Del Hunter 12/11/44; Grenier 2/12/44; ass 839BS/487BG Lavenham 7/3/45; retUS Bradley 12/7/45; Independence 15/7/45; RFC Kingman 14/12/45.

44-8642 Del Hunter 19/11/44; Grenier 2/12/44; ass 8AF 6/12/44; retUS Bradley 19/6/45; Sth Plains 21/6/45; RFC Kingman 14/12/45.

44-8643 Del Hunter 14/11/44; Grenier 2/12/44; ass 447BG Rattlesden 5/12/44; retUS Bradley 8/7/45; RFC Kingman 11/12/45.

44-8644 Del Hunter 16/11/44; Dow Fd 4/12/44; ass 602BS/398BG [K8-N] Nuthampstead 23/1/45; retUS Bradley 29/5/45; Sth Plains 30/5/45; RFC Kingman 18/12/45.

44-8645 Del Hunter 15/11/44; Grenier 3/12/44; ass 34BG Mendlesham 5/12/44; tran 838BS/487BG Lavenham 30/12/44; b/d Bischofsheim 13/1/45 w/?; mid air coll w/44-8529; sal 15/1/45.

44-8646 Del Hunter 14/11/44; Dow Fd 2/12/44; ass 8AF 3/12/44; retUS 4117 BU Robins 6/7/45; 4121 BU Kelly 2/10/45; re-ass 31/3/47; 4124 BU Kelly 6/11/47; sal 14/7/49.

44-8647 Del Hunter 12/11/44; Hunter 9/12/44; Dow Fd 9/12/44; ass 360BS/303BG [PU-M] Molesworth 17/12/44; MIA Lepizig 6/4/45 w/Lacker; mid air coll, cr Teplitz, Ger; 9KIA; MACR 13596.

44-8648 Del Cheyenne 15/11/44; Hunter 9/12/44; Dow Fd 22/12/44; ass 615BS/401BG [IY-N] Deenethorpe 21/5/45; 613BS [IN-M]; tran 305BG Chelveston 20/5/45; sal 9AF Germany 18/4/46.

44-8649 Del Cheyenne 15/11/44; Hunter 9/12/44; Dow Fd 22/1/45; ass 546BS/384BG [BK-X] 28/1/45 THE BOSS; tran 305BG Chelveston 9/5/45; became instrument trainer, sal 9AF Germany 18/4/46. TRAIL BLAZER.

44-8650 Del Cheyenne 16/11/44; Hunter 12/12/44; Grenier 22/1/45; ass 339BS/96BG Snetterton 24/1/45; b/d Arnsbach 23/2/45; c/l. Sal.

44-8651 Del Cheyenne 13/11/44; Hunter 9/12/44; Dow Fd 22/12/44; 324BS/91BG [DF-A] Bassingbourn 2/2/45; {21+m} tran 306BG Thurleigh 24/5/45; sal 9AF Germany 10/7/46. LORRAINE.

44-8652 Del Cheyenne 16/11/44; Hunter 12/12/44; Dow Fd 17/12/44; ass 369BS/306BG Thurleigh 6/1/45; sal 9AF 31/7/46. DRIVE IT HOME!

44-8653 Del Cheyenne 14/11/44; Hunter 16/12/44; Grenier 19/12/44; ass 615BS/401BG [IY-S] Deenethorpe 21/1/45; tran 305BG Chelveston 20/5/45; sal 9AF Germany 29/5/46.

44-8654 Del Cheyenne 14/11/44; Hunter 7/12/44; Grenier 20/12/44; ass 603BS/398BG [N7-M] Nuthampstead 8/2/45; retUS, RFC Walnut Ridge 5/1/46.

44-8655 Del Cheyenne 18/11/44; Hunter 9/12/44; Grenier 27/12/44; ass 331BS/94BG [QE-D] Rougham 29/12/44; 333BS [TS-D]; retUS, RFC Walnut Ridge 4/1/46.

44-8656 Del Cheyenne 17/11/44; Hunter 4/12/44; Grenier 26/12/44; ass 301BG PFF Lucera 14/1/45; tran 20BS/2BG Amendola 18/1/45; sal 9AF Germany 6/11/46.

44-8657 Del Cheyenne 18/11/44; Hunter 4/12/44; Dow Fd 27/12/44; ass 833BS/486BG [4N-T] Sudbury 3/1/45; retUS, RFC Walnut Ridge 8/1/46. LUSH THRUSH.

44-8658 Del Cheyenne 15/11/44; Hunter 9/12/44; Grenier 27/12/44; ass 333BS/94BG Rougham 29/12/44; retUS, RFC Walnut Ridge 21/1/46.

44-8659 Del Cheyenne 15/11/44; Hunter 14/12/44;
Grenier 24/12/44; ass 848BS/490BG Eye 3/1/45; tran 15AF 29/5/45; retUS, RFC Walnut Ridge 10/1/46.

44-8660 Del Cheyenne 15/11/44; Hunter 5/12/44; Grenier 23/12/44; ass 568BS/390BG [BI-L] Framlingham 25/12/44; tran 100BG Thorpe Abbotts 1/1/45; retUS Morrison 9/10/45; RFC Walnut Ridge 3/1/46.

44-8661 Del Cheyenne 15/11/44; Hunter 12/12/44; Dow Fd 21/12/44; ass 332BS/94BG [XM-G] Rougham 6/1/45; retUS Morrison 26/10/44; RFC Walnut Ridge 5/1/46.

44-8662 Del Cheyenne 22/11/44; Hunter 10/12/44; Dow Fd 3/1/45; ass 306BG Thurleigh 5/2/45; sal 9AF Germany 24/11/46.

44-8663 Del Cheyenne 22/11/44; Hunter 12/12/44; Grenier 20/12/44; ass 305BG Chelveston 6/1/45; tran 384BG Grafton Underwood 7/2/45; retUS Charleston 28/10/45; RFC Walnut Ridge 11/1/46.

44-8664 Del Cheyenne 20/11/44; Hunter 5/12/44; Dow Fd 2/1/45; ass 511BS/351BG [DS-D] Polebrook 14/2/45; tran 305BG Chelveston 23/5/45; sal 9AF Germany 18/4/46.

44-8665 Del Cheyenne 20/11/44; Hunter 9/12/44; Dow Fd 22/12/44; ass 305BG Chelveston 24/12/44; 547BS/384BG [SO-W] Grafton Underwood 28/1/45; 457BG Glatton 9/5/45; sal 9AF Germany 18/4/46.

44-8666 Del Cheyenne 20/11/44; Hunter 13/12/44; Grenier 29/12/44; ass 8AF 3/1/45; retUS, RFC Walnut Ridge 20/12/45.

44-8667 Del Cheyenne 20/11/44; Hunter 13/12/44; Dow Fd 22/12/44; ass 349BS/100BG [XR-H] Thorpe Abbotts 7/1/45; retUS, RFC Walnut Ridge 28/12/45.

44-8668 Del Cheyenne 21/11/44; Hunter 12/12/44; Grenier 20/12/44; ass 547BS/384BG [SO-V] Grafton Underwood 3/1/45; tran 305BG Chelveston 9/5/45; sal 9AF Germany 23/5/46.

44-8669 Del Cheyenne 20/11/44; Hunter 9/12/44; Dow Fd 31/12/44; ass 524BS/379BG [WA-H] Kimbolton 19/1/45; tran 457BG Glatton 9/5/45; sal 9AF Germany 10/5/46.

44-8670 Del Cheyenne 20/11/44; Hunter 9/12/44; Dow Fd 2/1/45; ass 350BS/100BG [LN-H] Thorpe Abbotts 6/1/45; tran 4BS/34BG Mendlesham 8/1/45; dam mid air coll w/44-8529 13/1/45 w/?; sal & rep; retUS, RFC Walnut Ridge 14/12/45. KERRY.

44-8671 Del Cheyenne 20/11/44; Hunter 12/12/44; Grenier 30/12/44; ass 390BG Framlingham 6/1/45; tran 423BS/306BG [RD-W] Thurleigh 5/2/45; sal 9AF Germany 30/1/46.

44-8672 Del Cheyenne 21/11/44; Hunter 12/12/44; Dow Fd 22/12/44; ass 838BS/487BG [2C-H] H2X Lavenham 20/1/45; taxi accident and caught fire 18/2/45; sal 20/2/45.

44-8673 Del Cheyenne 22/11/44; Hunter 12/12/44; Grenier 29/12/44; ass 365BS/305BG [XK-G] Chelveston 29/1/45; 422BS [JJ-G]; retUS 4000 BU Wright 14/7/45; 4020 BU Nashville 9/9/45; 601 BU Eglin 1/10/45; sal 611 BU Eglin 30/6/46.

44-8674 Del Cheyenne 22/11/44; Hunter 9/12/44; Grenier 2/1/45; ass 836BS/487BG [2G-S] Lavenham 20/2/45; b/d Oranienburg 15/3/45 w/?; f/l Poznan, Pol; sal 22/3/45.

44-8675 Del Cheyenne 22/11/44; Hunter 10/12/44; Grenier 21/12/44; ass 8AF 31/12/44; retUS, RFC Walnut Ridge 13/12/45.

44-8676 Del Cheyenne 22/11/44; Hunter 3/12/44; Grenier 30/12/44; ass 367BS/306BG [GY-G] Thurleigh 11/3/45; sal 9AF Germany 31/7/46. COL KEARNEY'S REBELS.

44-8677 Del Cheyenne 22/11/44; Hunter 2/12/44; Grenier 4/1/45; ass 326BS/92BG [JW-O] Podington
5/2/45; tran 306BG Thurleigh 7/5/45; sal 9AF Germany 23/10/46. DEANNA D.

44-8678 Del Hunter 22/11/44; Grenier 6/12/44; ass 8AF 8/12/44; retUS Bradley 26/6/45; Sth Plains 30/6/45; RFC Kingman 18/11/45.

44-8679 Del Hunter 23/11/44; Grenier 16/12/44; ass 545BS/384BG [JD-D] Grafton Underwood 28/1/45; sal 9AF Germany 20/12/45.

44-8680 Del Lincoln 23/11/44; Grenier 5/1/45; ass 482BG H2X Alconbury 7/1/45; tran 350BS/100BG [LN-X] Thorpe Abbotts 8/1/45; retUS Bradley 1/6/45; Sth Plains 4/6/45; RFC Kingman 18/12/45.

44-8681 Del Hunter 20/11/44; Grenier 6/12/44; ass 493BG Debach 20/12/44; retUS, RFC Walnut Ridge 12/12/45.

44-8682 Del Lincoln 23/11/44; Grenier 12/12/44; ass 8AF 31/12/44; sal 9AF Germany 11/5/46.

44-8683 Del Lincoln 23/11/44; Grenier 22/12/44; ass 306BG Thurleigh 24/12/44; tran 561BS/388BG Knettishall 26/12/44; while on navigation exercise c/l Gt Whernside, UK 17/5/45; sal 19/5/45. JUST JOYCE.

44-8684 Del Lincoln 23/11/44; Dow Fd 16/12/44; ass 8AF 18/12/44; retUS Bradley 2/7/45; 4136 BU Tinker 21/10/45; 4112 BU Olmstead 24/10/45; 4104 BU Rome 3/9/46; 1504 BU Fairfield 25/12/46; 4104 BU Rome 10/1/47; re-ass Pacific TSP 15/1/47; re-ass 30/4/47; PAC Hickam 1/1/48; Recl Comp 10/8/49.

44-8685 Del Lincoln 27/11/44; Dow Fd 16/12/44; ass 8AF 18/12/44; sal 9AF Germany 12/1/46.

44-8686 Del Lincoln 27/11/44; Grenier 17/12/44; ass 8AF 25/12/44; retUS Bradley 27/6/45; Sth Plains 31/6/45; RFC Kingman 10/11/45.

44-8687 Del Lincoln 23/11/44; Grenier 18/12/44; ass 486BG Sudbury 20/12/44; taxi accident 26/4/45; sal n/b/d 27/4/45.

44-8688 Del Lincoln 25/11/44; Dow Fd 26/12/44; ass 8AF 28/12/44; retUS Bradley 7/6/45; Sth Plains 9/6/45; RFC Kingman 10/12/45.

44-8689 Del Lincoln 22/11/44; Dow Fd 16/12/44; ass 8AF 20/12/44; sal 9AF Germany 17/5/46.

44-8690 Del Lincoln 22/11/44; Grenier 14/12/44; ass 332BS/94BG [XM-O] Rougham 30/12/44; tran 34BG Mendlesham /45; retUS Bradley 7/6/45; RFC Kingman 24/11/45.

44-8691 Del Lincoln 22/11/44; Grenier 14/12/44; ass 863BS/493BG Debach 16/12/44 BETSY; retUS Bradley 8/7/45; RFC Kingman 17/12/45. LITTLE WAMPUS.

44-8692 Del Lincoln 22/11/44; Grenier 25/12/44; ass 427BS/303BG [GN-A] Molesworth 27/12/44; tran 457BG Glatton 22/5/45; retUS Bradley 8/6/45; Sth Plains 10/6/45; RFC Kingman 10/12/45.

44-8693 Del Lincoln 20/11/44; Grenier 12/12/44; ass 533BS/381BG [VP-O] Ridgewell 11/2/45; 535BS [MS-O]; {26m} b/d Plauen 26/3/45 w/Hawley; c/l France & burned; sal 3/4/45.

44-8694 Del Lincoln 26/11/44; Dow Fd 16/12/44; ass 487BG Lavenham 2/2/45; retUS Bradley 12/6/45; Sth Plains 17/6/45; RFC Kingman 18/12/45.

44-8695 Del Lincoln 26/11/44; Grenier 16/12/44; ass 8AF 31/12/44; re-ass ETO mapping Belgian coast 30/4/47; 108HB Oberpfaffenhofen 18/1/48; Recl Comp 1/10/48.

44-8696 Del Lincoln 28/11/44; Grenier 26/12/44; ass 850BS/490BG Eye 28/12/44; retUS Bradley 7/7/45; Sth Plains 10/7/45; RFC Kingman 17/11/45.

44-8697 Del Hunter 30/11/44; Dow Fd 10/12/44; ass 413BS/96BG Snetterton 12/12/44; MIA Dresden 2/3/45 w/Stillwell; mid air coll w/43-37767 over sea; cr Channel; 9KIA; MACR 12846.

44-8698 Del Hunter 22/11/44; Dow Fd 20/12/44; ass

INDIVIDUAL B-17 HISTORIES **297**

751BS/457BG Glatton 23/12/44; tran 849BS/490BG Eye 2/1/45; 850BS; sal n/b/d 27/6/46. LOVE 'EM ALL!

44-8699 Del Lincoln 26/11/44; Grenier 20/12/44; ass 600BS/398BG [N8-J] Nuthampstead 1/2/45; retUS Bradley 1/6/45; Sth Plains 5/6/45; RFC Kingman 14/12/45.

44-8700 Del Lincoln 29/11/44; Dow Fd 28/12/44; ass 8AF 31/12/44; re-ass ETO 30/4/47; 10HB Oberpfaffenhofen 2/2/48; Recl Comp 1/12/48.

44-8701 Del Lincoln 29/11/44; Grenier 22/12/44; ass 8AF 228/12/44; retUS Bradley 28/6/45; Sth Plains 30/6/45; RFC Kingman 13/2/46.

44-8702 Del Lincoln 2/12/44; Dow Fd 16/12/44; ass 837BS/487BG Lavenham 20/2/45; 836BS [2G-S]; 838BS [2C-S]; MIA Magdeburg 10/4/45 w/Havenstein; jet e/a, cr Burg, Ger; 1EVD 1KIA 7POW; MACR 13884. FOREVER AMBER.

44-8703 Del Lincoln 3/12/44; Dow Fd 16/12/44; ass 452BG Deopham Green 18/12/44; retUS Bradley 28/6/45; Sth Plains 2/7/45; RFC Kingman 23/11/45.

44-8704 Del Cheyenne 30/11/44; Hunter 17/12/44; Dow Fd 5/12/44; ass 339BS/96BG Snetterton 22/11/45; MIA Jena Opt Wks 19/3/45 w/Capt Jones; flak, cr Scheiben, Ger; 8KIA 2POW; MACR 13571.

44-8705 Del Cheyenne 30/11/44; Hunter 14/12/44; Grenier 29/12/44; ass 351BS/100BG [EP-Z] Thorpe Abbotts 8/1/45; retUS Charleston 26/10/45; RFC Kingman 20/12/45.

44-8706 Del Cheyenne 30/11/44; Hunter 20/12/44; Grenier 2/2/45; ass 452BG Deopham Green 4/2/45; tran 750BS/457BG Glatton 14/2/45; 305BG Chelveston 23/5/45; sal 9AF Germany 30/10/45.

44-8707 Del Cheyenne 30/11/44; Hunter 16/12/44; Grenier 30/12/44; ass 615BS/401BG [IY-M] Deenethorpe 18/2/45; tran 305BG Chelveston 20/5/45; sal 9AF Germany 10/10/46.

44-8708 Del Cheyenne 30/11/44; Hunter 17/12/44; Dow Fd 13/12/44; ass 615BS/401BG [IY-M] Deenethorpe 18/2/45; tran 305BG Chelveston /45; sal 9AF Germany 6/11/46.

44-8709 Del Cheyenne 30/11/44; Hunter 20/12/44; Grenier 6/1/45; ass 350BS/100BG [LN-J] Thorpe Abbotts 8/1/45; tran 336BS/95BG [ET-F] Horham 23/1/45; retUS Morrison 20/10/45; RFC Walnut Ridge 20/12/45.

44-8710 Del Cheyenne 3/12/44; Hunter 16/12/44; Grenier 3/1/45; ass 332BS/94BG [XM-H] Rougham 22/1/45; tran 427BS/303BG [GN-Y] Molesworth 18/2/45; retUS Morrison 20/10/45; RFC Walnut Ridge 28/12/45. IDLE WHEEL.

44-8711 Del Cheyenne 3/12/44; Hunter 23/12/44; Grenier 20/1/45; ass 463BG PFF Celone 7/2/45; retUS, RFC Walnut Ridge 7/1/46.

44-8712 Del Cheyenne 3/12/44; Hunter 15/12/44; Dow Fd 3/1/45; ass 833BS/486BG [4N-S] Sudbury 8/1/45 (last a/c assgd to Grp); MIA Grafenwohr 8/4/45 w/Hohmann; flak, cr Rehau, Ger; 6KIA 3POW; MACR 13738. LONESOME POLECAT.

44-8713 Del Cheyenne 4/12/44; Hunter 16/12/44; Grenier 26/12/44; ass 94BG Rougham 1/1/45; tran 413BS/96BG [MZ-P] Snetterton 3/1/45; sal 9AF Germany 24/8/45; retUS Kingman /12/45.

44-8714 Del Cheyenne 4/12/44; Hunter 22/12/44; Grenier 3/1/45; ass 419BS/301BG PFF Lucera 10/2/45; retUS Morrison 2/10/45; RFC Walnut Ridge 9/1/46.

44-8715 Del Cheyenne 4/12/44; Hunter 16/12/44; Grenier 6/1/45; ass 306BG Thurleigh 8/1/45; tran 326BS/92BG [JW-O] Podington 3/2/45; 398BG Nuthampstead 7/5/45; sal 9AF Germany 30/10/46.

44-8716 Del Cheyenne 4/12/44; Hunter 20/12/44; Grenier 2/1/45; Barksdale 5/1/45; San Bernardino 30/1/45; Hunter 20/3/45; ass 1/4/45; sal 9AF Germany 31/7/46.

44-8717 Del Cheyenne 3/12/44; Hunter 23/12/44; Grenier 10/1/45; ass 418BS/100BG [LD-T] Thorpe Abbotts 12/1/45; MIA Berlin 18/3/45 w/Capt Swain; jet e/a, cr Kremmen, Ger; 1KIA 8POW; MACR 13142. PATHFINDER (MISS SWEETNESS).

44-8718 Del Cheyenne 5/12/44; Hunter 22/12/44; Dow Fd 11/1/45; ass 347BS/99BG Amendola 5/2/45; {27m} cr 28/3/45 w/?; sal 10/5/45.

44-8719 Del Cheyenne 4/12/44; Hunter 19/12/44; Grenier 22/1/45; ass 350BS/100BG [LN-W] Thorpe Abbotts 24/1/45; sal 9AF Germany 8/11/45.

44-8720 Del Cheyenne 5/12/44; Hunter 19/12/44; Dow Fd 3/1/45; ass 457BG Glatton 4/2/45; cr on test 6/2/45 w/?; sal 7/2/45.

44-8721 Del Cheyenne 6/12/44; Hunter 23/12/44; Grenier 20/1/45; ass 416BS/99BG PFF Tortorella 5/2/45; {19m} RetUS Morrison 21/9/45; RFC Walnut Ridge 14/12/45.

44-8722 Del Cheyenne 7/12/44; Hunter 22/12/44; Dow Fd 13/1/45; ass 346BS/99BG PFF Tortorella 5/2/45; {30m} RetUS, RFC Walnut Ridge 11/10/45.

44-8723 Del Cheyenne 6/12/44; Hunter 22/12/44; Grenier 30/1/45; ass 97BG PFF Amendola 18/2/45; retUS, RFC Walnut Ridge 4/1/46.

44-8724 Del Cheyenne 6/12/44; Oklahoma City 30/12/44; Hunter 29/1/45; Dow Fd 13/2/45; ass 423BS/306BG Thurleigh 19/3/45; sal 9AF Germany 6/11/46. UNDECIDED.

44-8725 Del Cheyenne 9/12/44; Hunter 26/12/44; Grenier 20/1/45; ass 463BG PFF Celone 7/2/45; retUS, RFC Walnut Ridge 8/1/46.

44-8726 Del Cheyenne 6/12/44; Hunter 27/12/44; Dow Fd 21/1/45; ass 350BS/100BG [LN-B] Thorpe Abbotts 23/1/45; tran 416BS/99BG Tortorella 5/2/45; {7m} RetUS Morrison 21/8/45; RFC Walnut Ridge 14/12/45.

44-8727 Del Cheyenne 5/12/44; Hunter 26/12/44; Dow Fd 22/1/45; ass 463BG Celone 1/2/45; retUS, RFC Walnut Ridge 5/1/46.

44-8728 Del Cheyenne 6/12/44; Hunter 22/12/44; Grenier 6/1/45; ass 8AF 8/1/45; retUS, RFC Walnut Ridge 14/12/45.

44-8729 Del Cheyenne 7/12/44; Hunter 26/12/44; Dow Fd 21/1/45; ass 91BG HSX Bassingbourn 23/1/45; tran 775BS/463BG PFF Celone 7/2/45; MIA Linz 25/2/45 w/Mateske; flak, cr Zheresienfeld; MACR 12716.

44-8730 Del Cheyenne 9/12/44; Hunter 16/1/45; Grenier 24/1/45; ass 341BS/97BG Amendola 6/2/45; MIA Linz 25/2/45 w/Koerwitz; flak, cr Linz; MACR 12715.

44-8731 Del Cheyenne 9/12/44; Hunter 23/12/44; Grenier 22/1/45; ass 332BS/94BG [XM-O] Rougham 24/1/44; tran 4BS/34BG Mendlesham 26/1/45; 391BS; retUS, RFC Walnut Ridge 21/12/45. KNOCKOUT DROPPER.

44-8732 Del Cheyenne 11/12/44; Burbank 31/12/44; Dallas 17/1/45; Hunter 17/2/45; ass 325BS/92BG [NV-C] Podington 29/3/45; tran 306BG Thurleigh 7/5/45; sal 9AF Germany 25/10/45.

44-8733 Del Cheyenne 11/12/44; Hunter 27/12/44; Grenier 20/1/45; ass 419BS/301BG PFF Lucera 7/2/45; retUS Morrison 27/9/45; RFC Walnut Ridge 12/12/45.

44-8734 Del Lincoln 12/12/44; Grenier 20/12/44; ass 359BS/303BG [BN-C] Molesworth 17/2/45; tran 457BG Glatton 22/5/45; retUS Bradley 27/6/45; Sth Plains 30/6/45; RFC Kingman 10/12/45. HELL'S CARGO.

44-8735 Del Lincoln 12/12/44; Dow Fd 6/1/44; ass 407BS/92BG [PY-C] Podington 4/3/45; tran 1BAD Burtonwood 12/6/45, ret 14/6/45; Istres Fd, Fr 19/6/45; sal 9AF Germany 25/7/46.

44-8736 Del Lincoln 12/12/44; Dow Fd 3/1/45; ass 385BG Gt Ashfield 5/1/45; tran 34BG Mendlesham 7/1/45; retUS Bradley 6/7/45; Sth Plains 8/7/45; RFC Kingman 25/11/45.

44-8737 Del Lincoln 12/12/44; Grenier 3/1/45; ass 8AF 24/1/45; re-ass 30/4/47; 10BH Oberpfaffenhofen 1/7/47; Recl Comp 3/8/49.

44-8738 Del Lincoln 14/12/44; Dow Fd 12/1/45; ass 8AF 14/1/45; retUS Bradley 28/6/45; Sth Plains 1/7/45; RFC Kingman 1/2/46.

44-8739 Del Lincoln 14/12/44; Dow Fd 3/1/45; ass 8AF 7/1/45; Recl Comp 17/7/45.

44-8740 Del Lincoln 16/12/44; Grenier 20/12/44; ass 837BS/487BG Lavenham 3/3/45; 838BS; retUS Bradley 5/7/45; Independence 10/7/45; RFC Kingman 11/12/45. ALUMINUM OVERCAST.

44-8741 Del Hunter 20/12/44; Dow Fd 29/12/44; ass 412BS/95BG [QW-M] Horham 5/1/45; retUS Bradley 5/6/45; RFC Kingman 15/12/45. WINGED WARRIORS.

44-8742 Del Hunter 13/12/44; Grenier 29/12/44; ass 562BS/388BG Knettishall 5/1/45; retUS, RFC Walnut Ridge 7/1/46.

44-8743 Del Lincoln 12/12/44; Grenier 6/1/45; ass 8AF 8/1/45; retUS Bradley 3/7/45; Newark 5/7/45; RFC Kingman 12/12/45.

44-8744 Del Lincoln 14/12/44; Grenier 22/12/44; ass 550BS/385BG Gt Ashfield 5/1/45; MIA Parchim 7/4/45 w/Burich; rammed by Sonderkammando FW190, cr Gifhorn, Ger, (in field, now 1994, used as a glider fd); 10KIA; MACR 13721.

44-8745 Del Lincoln 13/12/44; Dow Fd 31/12/44; ass 331BS/94BG [QE-W] Rougham 30/3/45; retUS Grenier 5/9/45; Independence 6/9/45; RFC Kingman 17/12/45.

44-8746 Del Cheyenne 13/12/44; Hunter 8/1/45; Grenier 2/2/45; ass 837BS/487BG Lavenham 20/2/45; 838BS; MIA Oranienburg 15/3/45 w/Conwill; flak, cr Benvenson?; 4KIA 6POW; MACR 13089.

44-8747 Del Cheyenne 13/12/44; Hunter 28/12/44; Grenier 2/2/45; ass 447BG Rattlesden 4/2/45; retUS, RFC Walnut Ridge 29/12/45.

44-8748 Del Cheyenne 13/12/44; Hunter 5/1/45; Grenier 2/2/45; ass 379BS Kimbolton 24/2/45; retUS, RFC Walnut Ridge 4/1/46.

44-8749 Del Cheyenne 13/12/44; Hunter 3/1/45; Grenier 7/2/45; ass 568BS/390BG [BI-N] Framlingham 9/2/45; tran 350BS/100BG [LN-P] Thorpe Abbotts 11/2/45; retUS RFC Walnut Ridge 8/1/46.

44-8750 Del Cheyenne 13/12/44; Hunter 25/12/44; Grenier 4/2/45; ass 390BG Framlingham 6/2/45; retUS, RFC Walnut Ridge 14/1/46.

44-8751 Del Cheyenne 15/12/44; Hunter 4/1/45; Dow Fd 11/1/45; ass 388BG Knettishall 13/1/45; retUS, RFC Walnut Ridge 12/12/45.

44-8752 Del Cheyenne 14/12/44; Hunter 2/1/45; Grenier 3/2/45; ass 349BS/100BG [XR-O] Thorpe Abbotts 5/2/45; retUS, RFC Walnut Ridge 2/1/46.

44-8753 Del Cheyenne 14/12/44; Hunter 3/1/45; Grenier 28/1/45; ass 482BG HSX Alconbury 8/2/45; tran 388BG Knettishall 10/2/45; retUS RFC Walnut Ridge 4/1/46.

44-8754 Del Cheyenne 12/12/44; Hunter 3/1/45; Grenier 3/2/45; ass 350BS/100BG [LN-Z] Thorpe Abbotts 4/2/45; tran 334BS/95BG [BG-Z] Horham 5/2/44; b/d Holzwickede, Ger 23/3/45 w/?; mid air coll w/44-8604; ret base & rep; retUS, RFC Walnut

Ridge 9/1/46.
44-8755 Del –.
44-8756 Del Hunter 9/12/44; Dow Fd 3/1/45; ass 8AF 14/2/45; RFC Kingman 7/12/45.
44-8757 Del Hunter 10/12/44; Dow Fd 2/1/45; ass 8AF 8/1/45; retUS Bradley 21/6/45; RFC Kingman 13/11/45.
44-8758 Del Hunter 17/12/44; Dow Fd 6/1/45; ass 8AF 10/1/45; sal n/b/d 19/3/45.
44-8759 Del Hunter 15/12/44; Grenier 4/1/45; ass 8AF 24/1/45; re-ass 30/4/47; 10HB Oberpfaffenhofen 19/7/47; Recl Comp 11/2/49.
44-8760 Del Hunter 14/12/44; Dow Fd 20/1/45; ass 8AF 24/1/45; re-ass 30/4/47; 10HB Oberpfaffenhofen 1/8/47; Recl Comp 16/12/48.
44-8761 Del Lincoln 18/12/44; Grenier 3/1/45; ass 8AF 12/1/45; re-ass 30/4/47; 10HB Oberpfaffenhofen -; Recl Comp 1/10/48.
44-8762 Del Lincoln 15/12/44; Grenier 29/12/44; ass 549BS/385BG Gt Ashfield 5/1/45; b/d Nuremberg 5/4/45 w/; f/l Continent, sal 27/6/45.
44-8763 Del Lincoln 15/12/44; Grenier 20/1/45; ass 8AF 22/1/45; retUS Bradley 26/6/45; RFC Kingman 1/11/45.
44-8764 Del Lincoln 15/12/44; Dow Fd 6/1/45; ass 326BS/92BG [JW-G] Podington 3/2/45; secret mission 28/5/45, ret gp 29/5/45; re-ass 30/4/47; 10HB Oberpfaffenhofen 1/1/48; Recl Comp 4/2/49.
44-8765 Del Lincoln 20/12/44; Grenier 6/1/45; ass 493BG Debach 8/1/45; retUS Bradley 6/7/45; RFC Kingman 16/12/45.
44-8766 Del Hunter 20/12/44; Dow Fd 6/1/45; ass 836BS/487BG Lavenham 8/1/45; retUS Bradley 10/7/45; RFC Kingman 21/12/45.
44-8767 Del Hunter 19/12/44; Grenier 5/1/45; ass 613BS/401BG [IN-W] Deenethorpe 8/3/45; retUS Bradley 7/6/45; Sth Plains 13/6/45; RFC Kingman 10/11/45.
44-8768 Del Lincoln 14/12/44; Dow Fd 3/1/45; ass 8AF 6/1/45; sal 14/4/45.
44-8769 Del Lincoln 17/12/44; Dow Fd 20/1/45; ass 8AF 24/1/45; re-ass 30/4/47; 10HB Oberpfaffenhofen 16/1/48; Recl Comp 7/1/49.
44-8770 Del Cheyenne 20/12/44; Hunter 1/1/45; Grenier 21/1/45; ass 837BS/487BG Lavenham 5/5/45; tran 15AF 29/5/45; sal 9AF Germany 6/11/46. GLORIA ANN.
44-8771 Del Cheyenne 20/12/44; Hunter 1/1/45; Grenier 20/1/45; ass 601BS/398BG [3O-B] Nuthampstead 3/2/45; tran 306BG Thurleigh 4/2/45; sal 9AF Germany 6/11/45.
44-8772 Del Cheyenne 21/12/44; Hunter 5/1/45; Grenier 21/1/45; ass 306BG Thurleigh 23/1/45; re-ass 30/4/47; 10HB Oberpfaffenhofen 14/1/48; Recl Comp 5/8/48. LOW AND SLOW.
44-8773 Del Cheyenne 21/12/44; Hunter 4/1/45; Dow Fd 31/1/45; ass 410BS/94BG [GL-W] Rougham 1/2/45; 332BS [XM-R]; retUS Morrison 3/10/45; RFC Walnut Ridge 5/1/46.
44-8774 Del Cheyenne 21/12/44; Hunter 2/1/45; Grenier 3//2/45; ass 511BS/351BG [DS-Z] Polebrook 20/2/45; {12m} tran 305BG Chelveston 23/5/45; sal 9AF Germany 21/5/46.
44-8775 Del Cheyenne 21/12/44; Hunter 1/1/45; Dow Fd 1/2/45; ass 748BS/457BG Glatton 8/3/45; tran 305BG Chelveston 23/5/45; sal 9AF Germany 6/11/45.
44-8776 Del Cheyenne 21/12/44; Hunter 4/1/45; Dow Fd 21/1/45; ass 350BS/100BG [LN-U] Thorpe Abbotts 23/1/45; retUS, RFC Walnut Ridge 5/1/46.
44-8777 Del Cheyenne 22/12/44; Hunter 4/1/45; Grenier 21/1/45; ass 339BS/96BG [QJ-J] Snetterton 23/1/45; tran 324BS/91BG [DF-J] Bassingbourn 5/2/45; 367BS/306BG Thurleigh 24/5/45; sal 9AF Germany 22/2/46.
44-8778 Del Cheyenne 22/12/44; Hunter 4/1/45; 302 BU Hunter 19/1/45; Recl Comp 29/1/45.
44-8779 Del Cheyenne 22/12/44; Hunter 5/1/45; Dow Fd 27/1/45; ass 532BS/381BG [VE-S] Ridgewell 21/2/45; {1+m} tran 367BS/306BG Thurleigh 5/45; re-ass 30/4/47; Recl Comp 19/11/47. EVELYN ANN.
44-8780 Del Cheyenne 22/12/44; Hunter 7/1/45; Grenier 4/2/45; ass 511BS/351BG [DS-H] Polebrook 24/2/45; {12m} tran 305BG Chelveston 23/5/45; sal 9AF Germany 18/4/46.
44-8781 Del Cheyenne 22/12/44; Hunter 4/1/45; Grenier 4/2/45; ass 8AF 8/2/45; retUS, RFC Walnut Ridge 29/12/45.
44-8782 Del Cheyenne 25/12/44; Hunter 5/1/45; Dow Fd 21/1/45; ass 412BS/95BG [QW-R] Horham 23/1/45 (last a/c assgd to grp); tran 100BG Thorpe Abbotts 20/5/45; retUS, RFC Walnut Ridge 7/1/46.
44-8783 Del Cheyenne 25/12/44; Hunter 5/1/45; Dow Fd 21/1/45; ass 709BS/447BG Rattlesden 22/1/45; tran 332BS/94BG [XM-X] Rougham 23/1/45; retUS, RFC Walnut Ridge 28/12/45.
44-8784 Del Cheyenne 25/12/44; Hunter 2/1/45; Grenier 4/2/45; ass 570BS/390BG [DI-Z] Framlingham 6/2/45; tran 351BS/100BG [EP-M] Thorpe Abbotts 8/2/45; retUS, RFC Walnut Ridge 9/1/46.
44-8785 Del Cheyenne 25/12/44; Hunter 5/1/45; Grenier 2/2/45; ass 457BG Glatton 8/3/45; tran 305BG Chelveston 23/5/45; sal 9AF Germany 23/5/46. CRACK UP.
44-8786 Del Cheyenne 24/12/44; Hunter 5/1/45; Dow Fd 2/2/45; ass 8AF 8/2/45; retUS, RFC Walnut Ridge 20/12/45.
44-8787 Del Cheyenne 26/12/44; Hunter 7/1/45; Dow Fd 21/1/45; ass 350BS/100BG [LN-C] Thorpe Abbotts 23/1/45; retUS, RFC Walnut Ridge 8/1/46.
44-8788 Del Cheyenne 26/12/44; Hunter 5/1/45; Dow Fd 21/1/45; ass 525BS/379BG [FR-Y] Kimbolton 3/2/45; rctUS, RFC Walnut Ridge 9/1/46.
44-8789 Del Cheyenne 26/12/44; Hunter 3/1/45; Grenier 4/2/45; ass 545BS/384BG [JD-X] Grafton Underwood 6/2/45; tran 401BG Deenethorpe 8/5/45; 305BG Chelveston 20/5/45; re-ass 30/4/47; Recl Comp 14/11/47.
44-8790 Del Cheyenne 29/12/44; Hunter 5/1/45; Grenier 4/2/45; ass 418BS/100BG [LD-V] Thorpe Abbotts 4/2/45; c/l on return from Holland food drop 5/5/45; sal n/b/d 12/5/45.
44-8791 Del Cheyenne 26/12/44; Hunter 9/1/45; Grenier 2/2/45; ass 751BS/457BG Glatton 1/3/45; tran 305BG Chelveston 23/5/45; sal 9AF Germany 18/4/46.
44-8792 Del Cheyenne 27/12/44; Hunter 4//1/45; Dow Fd 7/2/45; ass 401BS/91BG [LL-Q] Bassingbourn 26/2/45; tran 306BG Thurleigh 24/5/45; re-ass 30/4/47; Recl Comp 19/11/47.
44-8793 Del Cheyenne 27/12/44; Wright Fd 9/1/45; Hunter 1/3/45; ass 96BS/2BG PFF Amendola 20/3/45; retUS 902 BU Orlando 31/5/45; 621 BU Pinecastle 4/7/45; 613 BU Aberdeen PG 19/6/46.
44-8794 Del Cheyenne 27/12/44; Hunter 5/1/45; Dow Fd 27/1/45; ass 418BS/100BG [LD-B] Thorpe Abbotts 8/2/45; retUS, RFC Walnut Ridge 4/1/46.
44-8795 Del Cheyenne 29/12/44; Hunter 9/1/45; Dow Fd 4/2/45; ass 562BS/388BG Knettishall 6/2/45; sal 9AF Germany 6/11/46.
44-8796 Del Cheyenne 28/12/44; Hunter 11/1/45; Dow Fd 4/2/45; ass 305BG Chelveston 25/2/45; sal 9AF Germany 10/2/46. LAURA.
44-8797 Del Cheyenne 28/12/44; Hunter 12/1/45; Grenier 4/2/45; ass 305BG Chelveston 20/2/45; sal 9AF Germany 18/4/46.
44-8798 Del Cheyenne 28/12/44; Hunter 13/1/45; Grenier 6/2/45; ass 569BS/390BG H2X [CC-O] Framlingham 8/2/45; MIA Munich 9/4/45 w/Capt Slade; shot down by B-17, ditched Channel, 9RTD.
44-8799 Del Cheyenne 28/12/44; Hunter 12/1/45; Dow Fd 7/2/45; ass 452BG H2X Deopham Green 9/2/45; retUS, RFC Walnut Ridge 29/12/45. MANCHESTER MISSES.
44-8800 Del Cheyenne 31/12/44; Hunter 16/1/45; Grenier 2/2/45; ass 483BG Sterparone 6/2/45; retUS, RFC Walnut Ridge 9/1/46.
44-8801 Del Eglin Proving Ground 6/1/45; 610 BU Eglin 8/2/45; 611 BU Eglin 1/4/45; sal 9/7/46.
44-8802 Del Cheyenne 31/12/44; Hunter 16/1/45; Grenier 19/2/45; ass 487BG Lavenham 22/2/45; tran 96BS/2BG Amendola 23/2/45; sal 9AF Germany 6/11/46.
44-8803 Del Cheyenne 31/12/44; Hunter 17/1/45; Dow Fd 23/2/45; ass 301BG Lucera PFF 3/3/45; c/l 20/4/45; sal 30/4/45.
44-8804 Del Cheyenne 31/12/44; Hunter 6/1/45; Grenier 20/1/45; ass 15AF 1/2/45; retUS, RFC Walnut Ridge 11/12/45.
44-8805 Del Cheyenne 31/12/44; Hunter 27/1/45; Grenier 5/2/45; ass 482BG H2X Alconbury 15/2/45 (last assgd to grp); tran 413BS/96BG [MZ-0] Snetterton 17/2/45; 401BG Deenethorpe 26/5/45; retUS Morrison 3/10/45; RFC Walnut Ridge 7/1/46. SUGAR BABY.
44-8806 Del Cheyenne 1/1/45; Hunter 15/1/45; Grenier 31/1/45; ass 97BG PFF Amendola 18/2/45; retUS, RFC Walnut Ridge 20/12/45.
44-8807 Del Cheyenne 1/1/45; Hunter 12/1/45; Dow Fd 2/2/45; ass 8AF 9/2/45; retUS, RFC Walnut Ridge 9/1/46.
44-8808 Del Cheyenne 2/1/45; Hunter 13/1/45; Grenier 7/2/45; ass 837BS/487BG Lavenham 9/3/45; 838BS; MIA Brandenberg 10/4/45 w/McGinnes, jet e/a, cr Tangermünde, Ger; 2KIA 8POW; MACR 14196.
44-8809 Del Cheyenne 4/1/45; Hunter 15/1/45; Dow Fd 4/2/45; ass 422BS/305BG [JJ-S] Chelveston 16/2/45; sal 9AF Germany 23/5/46.
44-8810 Del Cheyenne 2/1/45; Hunter 15/1/45; Dow Fd 7/2/45; ass 349BS/100BG [XR-L] Thorpe Abbotts 9/2/45; retUS, RFC Walnut Ridge 20/12/46. TARGET FOR TONIGHT.
44-8811 Del Cheyenne 3/1/45; Hunter 16/1/45; Grenier 28/1/45; ass 600BS/398BG H2X [N8-C] Nuthampstead 30/3/45; b/d Halberstadt 8/4/45 w/?; sal 18/5/45.
44-8812 Del Cheyenne 3/1/45; Hunter 13/1/45; Grenier 7/2/45; ass 615BS/401BG [IY-A] Deenethorpe 20/2/45; tran 305BG Chelveston 20/5/45; re-ass 30/4/47; Recl Comp 7/11/47.
44-8813 Del Cheyenne 5/1/45; Hunter 12/1/45; Grenier 7/2/45; ass 379BG H2X Kimbolton 21/2/45; mid air coll w/44-8198 10/5/45 w/?; sal 11/5/45.
44-8814 Del Cheyenne 3/1/45; Hunter 16/1/45; Grenier 2/2/45; ass 96BS/2BG PFF Amendola 4/2/45; b/d Linz 2/3/45 w/Donnell; c/l nr Celone Fd (463BG); crew OK; sal 17/3/45.
44-8815 Del Cheyenne 4/1/45; Hunter 15/1/45; Dow Fd 2/2/45; ass 301BG PFF Lucera 22/2/45; retUS, RFC Walnut Ridge 10/1/46.
44-8816 Del Cheyenne 4/1/45; Hunter 10/1/45; Dow Fd 7/2/45; ass 816BS/483BG Sterparone 9/2/45; retUS, RFC Walnut Ridge 29/12/45.
44-8817 Del Cheyenne 4/1/45; Hunter 17/1/45; Dow

Fd 31/1/45; ass 418BS/100BG H2X [LD-S] Thorpe Abbotts 8/2/45; radio comp gun removed, tran 96BS/2BG Amendola 10/2/45; sal 24/9/45.

44-8818 Del Cheyenne 6/1/45; Hunter 17/1/45; Dow Fd 2/2/45; ass 97BG PFF Amendola 18/2/45; retUS, RFC Walnut Ridge 9/1/46.

44-8819 Del Cheyenne 4/1/45; Hunter 17/1/45; Dow Fd 31/1/45; ass 301BG PFF Lucera 22/2/45; retUS, RFC Walnut Ridge 12/10/45.

44-8820 Del Cheyenne 5/1/45; Hunter 17/1/45; Grenier 1/2/45; ass 49BS/2BG PFF Amendola 6/2/45; MIA Vienna 16/3/45 w/Col Waugh; c/l Hungary, 10RTD; MACR 13260.

44-8821 Del Cheyenne 7/1/45; Hunter 26/1/45; Dow Fd 7/2/45; ass 305BG Chelveston 6/3/45; retUS, RFC Walnut Ridge 2/1/46.

44-8822 Del Cheyenne 7/1/45; Hunter 24/1/45; Dow Fd 20/2/45; ass 413BS/96BG [MZ-N] Snetterton 25/2/45; RFC Walnut Ridge 2/1/45.

44-8823 Del Cheyenne 7/1/45; Hunter 27/1/45; Grenier 3/2/45; ass 351BS/100BG [EP-D] Thorpe Abbotts 17/2/45; retUS Morrison 10/10/45; RFC Walnut Ridge 9/1/46.

44-8824 Del Cheyenne 7/1/45; Hunter 26/1/45; Dow Fd 15/2/45; ass 349BS/100BG [XR-M] 16/2/45 MIKE; tran 91BG Bassingbourn 17/2/45; 427BS/303BG [GN-G] Molesworth 29/3/45; 457BG Glatton 23/5/45; RAF Valley 4/6/45; retUS, RFC Walnut Ridge 12/12/45.

44-8825 Del Cheyenne 7/1/45; Hunter 26/1/45; Dow Fd 1/2/45; ass 615BS/401BG [IY-J] Deenethorpe 20/2/45; tran 305BG Chelveston 20/5/45; sal 9AF Germany 6/11/45.

44-8826 Del Cheyenne 7/1/45; Hunter 26/1/45; Grenier 3/2/45; ass 535BS/381BG [MS-P] Ridgewell 27/3/45; {7m} tran 306BG Thurleigh 23/5/45; sal 9AF Germany 3/7/46.

44-8827 Del Cheyenne 8/1/45; Hunter 25/1/45; Dow Fd 1/2/45; ass 534BS/381BG [GD-B] Ridgewell 16/2/45; {13+m} tran 367BS/306BG Thurleigh 23/5/46; sal 9AF Germany 31/3/46; re-ass 30/4/47; Recl Comp 7/11/47. DUSTY GAY.

44-8828 Del Cheyenne 7/1/45; Hunter 27/1/45; Dow Fd 2/2/45; ass 493BG Debach 15/2/45 (last a/c assgd to grp); retUS, RFC Walnut Ridge 12/12/45.

44-8829 Del Cheyenne 8/1/45; Hunter 16/1/45; Grenier 4/2/45; ass 4BS/34BG Mendlesham 17/2/45; retUS Morrison 7/10/45; RFC Walnut Ridge 11/1/46.

44-8830 Del Cheyenne 8/1/45; Hunter 22/1/45; Grenier 3/2/45; ass 535BS/381BG [MS-S] Ridgewell 12/3/45; {4+m} tran 306BG Thurleigh 23/5/45; sal 9AF Germany 23/8/46. SOUTH BOSTON SHILLELAGH.

44-8831 Del Cheyenne 8/1/45; Hunter 22/1/45; Grenier 3/2/45; slated 381BG 5/2/45; trans All-Weather Flying Centre (Hurricane Hunters) w/red tail, nose & wingtips and yellow nacelles.

44-8832 Del Hunter 9/1/45; Grenier 3/2/45; ass 749BS/457BG Glatton 14/2/45; retUS Bradley 7/6/45; Sth Plains 13/6/45; RFC Kingman 7/12/45. BATTLE BABY.

44-8833 Del Hunter 9/1/45; Grenier 2/2/45; ass 8AF 12/2/45; re-ass 30/4/47; 10HB Oberpfaffenhofen 18/1/48; sal 17/6/49.

44-8834 Del Hunter 8/1/45; Dow Fd 6/2/45; ass 350BS/100BG [LN-G] Thorpe Abbotts 8/2/45; retUS Bradley 20/6/45; RFC Kingman 7/12/45. POO BAH.

44-8835 Del Hunter 12/1/45; Grenier 2/2/45; ass 379BG Kimbolton 4/2/45; retUS Bradley 17/6/45; Sth Plains 20/6/45; RFC Kingman 8/2/46.

44-8836 Del Hunter 10/1/45; Grenier 6/2/45; ass 351BS/100BG [EP-H] Thorpe Abbotts 8/2/45; retUS Bradley 3/6/45; RFC Kingman 17/12/45. ST LOUIS WOMAN.

44-8837 Del Hunter 13/1/45; Dow Fd 28/1/45; ass 525BS/379BG [FR-B] Kimbolton 20/2/45; retUS Bradley 14/7/45; Independence 20/7/45; RFC Kingman 21/12/45.

44-8838 Del Cheyenne 16/1/45; Hunter 27/1/45; Grenier 3/2/45; ass 306BG Thurleigh 15/2/45; re-ass 30/4/47; Recl Comp 19/11/47. BEAUTIFUL TAKEOFF.

44-8839 Del Cheyenne 16/1/45; Hunter 27/1/45; Dow Fd 7/2/45; ass 4BS/34BG Mendlesham 9/2/45; retUS, RFC Walnut Ridge 20/12/45.

44-8840 Del Cheyenne 16/1/45; Grenier 12/2/45; ass 323BS/91BG [OR-Q] Bassingbourn 30/3/45; tran 306BG Thurleigh 24/5/45; sal 9AF Germany 1/9/46.

44-8841 Del Cheyenne 13/1/45; Hunter 24/1/45; Dow Fd 12/2/45; ass 731BS/452BG Deopham Green 17/2/45; retUS, RFC Walnut Ridge 13/12/45.

44-8842 Del Cheyenne 12/1/45; Hunter 14/2/45; Grenier 16/2/45; ass 384BG Grafton Underwood 3/3/45; tran 511BS/351BG [DS-N] Polebrook 29/3/45; {3m} 305BG Chelveston 23/5/45; sal 9AF Germany 10/5/46.

44-8843 Del Cheyenne 16/1/45; Hunter 1/2/45; Dow Fd 5/2/45; ass 600BS/398BG [N8-T] Nuthampstead 15/2/45; tran 836BS/487BG Lavenham 19/4/45; tran 2BG Amendola 29/5/45; sal 9AF Germany 6/11/46.

44-8844 Del Cheyenne 12/1/45; Hunter 17/2/45; Grenier 25/2/45; ass 571BS/390BG [FC-E] Framlingham 27/2/45; retUS Morrison 29/9/45; RFC Walnut Ridge 14/12/45.

44-8845 Del Cheyenne 17/1/45; Hunter 12/2/45; Grenier 25/2/45; ass 379BG Kimbolton 30/3/45; retUS, RFC Walnut Ridge 5/1/46.

44-8846 Del Cheyenne 17/1/45; Hunter 12/2/45; Grenier 25/2/45; ass 511BS/351BG [DS-M] Polebrook 25/3/45; {6m} tran 305BG Chelveston 23/5/45; retUS, sold to French IGN as {F-BGSP} 7/12/54, then became {F-AZDX 5/85} and airshow circuit as LUCKY LADY.

44-8847 Del Cheyenne 17/1/45; Hunter 1/2/45; Grenier 25/2/45; ass 8AF 27/2/45; retUS Morrison 22/10/45; RFC Walnut Ridge 9/1/46.

44-8848 Del Cheyenne 24/1/45; Hunter 1/2/45; Grenier 27/2/45; ass 602BS/398BG [K8-L] Nuthampstead 29/2/45; tran 306BG Thurleigh 5/45; sal 9AF Germany 6/11/46.

44-8849 Del Cheyenne 16/1/45; Hunter 9/2/45; Grenier 23/2/45; ass 351BS/100BG [EP-J] Thorpe Abbotts 25/2/45; sal 11/10/45.

44-8850 Del Cheyenne 16/1/45; Hunter 7/2/45; Dow Fd 19/2/45; ass 562BS/388BG Knettishall 21/2/45; retUS, RFC Walnut Ridge 20/12/45.

44-8851 Del Cheyenne 16/1/45; Hunter 13/2/45; Grenier 25/2/45; ass 331BS/94BG [QE-K] Rougham 27/2/45; retUS Morrison 10/10/45; RFC Walnut Ridge 9/1/46.

44-8852 Del Cheyenne 16/1/45; Hunter 6/2/45; Dow Fd 12/2/45; ass 322BS/91BG [LG-V] Bassingbourn 9/3/45; tran 306BG Thurleigh 24/5/45; re-ass 30/4/47; Recl Comp 19/11/47.

44-8853 Del Cheyenne 16/2/45; Hunter 13/2/45; Grenier 16/2/45; ass 544BS/384BG [SU-Y] Grafton Underwood 25/2/45; tran 351BG Polebrook 9/5/45; 305BG Chelveston 23/5/45; sal 9AF Germany 23/5/46.

44-8854 Del Cheyenne 16/1/45; Hunter 14/2/45; Grenier 20/2/45; ass 333BS/94BG Rougham 22/2/45; retUS, RFC Walnut Ridge 8/1/46. "JUST ONCE MORE."

44-8855 Del Cheyenne 16/1/45; Hunter 9/2/45; Grenier 19/2/45; ass 533BS/381BG [VP-W] Ridgewell 21/2/45; {3+m} tran 306BG Thurleigh 5/45; sal 9AF Germany 23/5/46.

44-8856 Del Cheyenne 16/1/45; Hunter 10/2/45; Grenier 23/2/45; ass 8AF 27/2/45; retUS via RAF Valley 29/5/45, RFC Walnut Ridge 2/1/46.

44-8857 Del Cheyenne 16/1/45; Hunter 12/2/45; Grenier 20/2/45; ass 407BS/92BG [PY-M] Podington 22/3/45; tran 306BG Thurleigh 7/5/45; sal 9AF Germany 6/11/46.

44-8858 Del Cheyenne 17/1/45; Hunter 12/2/45; Dow Fd 20/2/45; ass 333BS/94BG [TS-G] Rougham 22/2/45; retUS Morrison 20/10/45; RFC Walnut Ridge 5/1/46.

44-8859 Del Cheyenne 17/1/45; Hunter 15/2/45; Grenier 20/2/45; ass 838BS/487BG Lavenham 16/3/45; tran 15AF 29/5/45; retUS Morrison 30/9/45; RFC Walnut Ridge 12/12/45.

44-8860 Del Cheyenne 17/1/45; Hunter 27/1/45; Grenier 25/2/45; ass 305BG Chelveston 30/3/45; re-ass 30/4/47; Recl Comp 19/11/47.

44-8861 Del Dorval, Canada 17/1/45; ass RAF 51MU as {KJ 126}; SOC 11/3/47.

44-8862 Del Dorval 17/1/45; ass RAF 12MU as {KJ 127}; SOC 15/9/47.

44-8863 Del Dorval 17/1/45; ass RCAF 51MU as {KL 830}; SOC 11/3/47.

44-8864 Del Dorval 17/1/45; ass RCAF 51MU as {KL 831}; tran Aeronautic College, Cranwell, UK; SOC 4/9/46.

44-8865 Del Dorval 17/1/45; ass RCAF 12MU as {KL 832}; SOC 15/9/47.

44-8866 Del Cheyenne 19/1/45; Hunter 4/2/45; Dow Fd 13/2/45; ass 533BS/381BG [VP-N] Ridgewell 17/2/45; {4+m} tran 306BG Thurleigh 5/45; sal 9AF Germany 1/4/46.

44-8867 Del Cheyenne 19/1/45; Hunter 6/2/45; Dow Fd 20/2/45; ass 511BS/351BG [DS-P] Polebrook 9/3/45 (last a/c ass grp); {7m} tran 305BG Chelveston 23/5/45; re-ass 30/4/47; mapping Dutch coast 15/5/47; Recl Comp 19/11/47.

44-8868 Del Cheyenne 20/1/45; Hunter 3/2/45; Grenier 22/2/45; ass 358BS/303BG [VK-X] Molesworth 28/2/45; tran 532BS/381BG Ridgewell 27/3/45; {2+m} 367BS/306BG Thurleigh 23/5/45; sal 9AF Germany 6/11/46. LON BOY.

44-8869 Del Cheyenne 19/1/45; Hunter 9/2/45; Grenier 23/2/45; ass 427BS/303BG [GN-W] Molesworth 30/3/45; retUS, RFC Walnut Ridge 15/1/46.

44-8870 Del Cheyenne 20/1/45; Hunter 8/2/45; Grenier 22/2/45; ass 8AF 27/2/45; retUS Morrison 29/10/45; RFC Walnut Ridge 7/1/46.

44-8871 Del Cheyenne 21/1/45; Hunter 7/2/45; Grenier 21/2/45; ass 413BS/96BG [MZ-K] Snetterton 2/3/45; retUS, RFC Walnut Ridge 14/1/46.

44-8872 Del Cheyenne 21/1/45; Hunter 6/2/45; Grenier 26/2/45; ass 490BG Eye 28/2/45; tran 2BG Amendola 30/5/45; retUS Morrison 1/10/45; RFC Walnut Ridge 12/12/45.

44-8873 Del Cheyenne 21/1/45; Hunter 7/2/45; Dow Fd 12/2/45; ass 749BS/457BG Glatton 30/3/45; tran 305BG Chelveston 23/5/45; re-ass 30/4/47; Recl Comp 19/11/47.

44-8874 Del Cheyenne 21/1/45; Hunter 17/2/45; Grenier 9/3/45; ass 815BS/483BG Sterparone 14/3/45; retUS, RFC Walnut Ridge 8/1/46.

44-8875 Del Cheyenne 21/1/45; Hunter 12/2/45; Dow Fd 16/2/45; ass 731BS/452BG Deopham Green 27/2/45; retUS, RFC Walnut Ridge 4/1/46.

44-8876 Del Cheyenne 22/1/45; Hunter 16/2/45;

Above: B-17G-85-VE 44-8889 went to the UK in 1945 and was purchased by IGN nine years later. Converted for high-altitude photographic work, the aircraft served IGN until September 1976. It now resides in Le Bourget Air Museum. (IGN)

Grenier 26/2/45; ass 418BS/100BG [LD-F] Thorpe Abbotts 28/2/45; tran 303BG Molesworth 2/4/45; retUS, RFC Walnut Ridge 8/1/46.
44-8877 Del Cheyenne 22/1/45; Hunter 15/2/45; Grenier 20/2/45; ass 339BS/96BG [QJ-T] Snetterton 22/2/45; retUS, RFC Walnut Ridge 5/1/46; sal 23/7/47.
44-8878 Del Cheyenne 22/1/45; Hunter 21/2/45; Grenier 1/3/45; ass 836BS/487BG Lavenham 16/3/45; retUS Morrison 24/10/45; RFC Walnut Ridge 3/1/46.
44-8879 Del Cheyenne 23/1/45; Hunter 5/2/45; Grenier 23/2/45; ass 562BS/388BG Knettishall 5/3/45; sal 9AF Germany 6/11/45.
44-8880 Del Cheyenne 27/1/45; Hunter 25/2/45; Grenier 4/3/45; ass 8AF 6/3/45; sal 14/1/46.
44-8881 Del Cheyenne 23/1/45; Hunter 28/2/45; Grenier 10/3/45; ass 8AF 14/3/45; re-ass 30/4/47; 10 HB Oberpfaffenhofen 2/2/48; Recl Comp 1/10/48.
44-8882 Del Cheyenne 23/1/45; Hunter 17/2/45; Grenier 20/2/45; ass 4BS/34BG Mendlesham 5/3/45; retUS, RFC Walnut Ridge 11/1/46.
44-8883 –.
44-8884 Del Lincoln 24/1/45; Grenier 12/2/45; ass 8AF 22/2/45; sal 9AF Germany 10/5/46.
44-8885 Del Lincoln 24/1/45; Grenier 17/2/45; ass 8AF 22/2/45; sal 9AF Germany 10/5/46.
44-8886 Del Hunter 22/1/45; Dow Fd 17/2/45; ass 8AF 7/3/45; Re-ass 30/4/47; 501 HB Eschaden 18/1/48; 7160 AB Oberpfaffenhofen 1/7/48; 7290 HB Oberpfaffenhofen 9/8/48; 1807 AC Weisbaden 26/4/49; sal 3/5/50.
44-8887 Del Hunter 27/1/45; Dow Fd 13/2/45; ass 8AF 15/2/45; sal 9AF Germany 23/5/46.
44-8888 Del Hunter 27/1/45; Grenier 13/2/45; ass 8AF 15/2/45; sal 9AF Germany 10/5/46.
44-8889 Ass 8AF, then sold to French IGN 12/8/54 as {F-BGSO}; Le Bourget Air Museum 8/9/76 - 1989.
44-8890 Del Hunter 27/1/45; Dow Fd 17/2/45; ass 333BS/94BG [TS-C] Rougham 17/2/45; retUS Bradley 8/7/45; Sth Plains 10/7/45; 613 BU Phillips 3/7/46.

44-8891 –.
44-8892 Del Hunter 26/1/45; Dow Fd 27/2/45; ass 325BS/92BG [NV-T] Podington 20/3/45; sal 9AF Germany 26/7/46.
44-8893 Del Hunter 26/1/45; Dow Fd 20/2/45; ass 8AF 22/2/45; retUS Bradley 22/5/45; RFC Walnut Ridge 14/2/46.
44-8894 Del Hunter 26/1/45; Dow Fd 11/2/45; ass 8AF 15/2/45; Re-ass 30/4/47; 10 HB Oberpfaffenhofen 18/1/48; Recl Comp 7/1/49.
44-8895 Del Hunter 26/1/45; Dow Fd 13/2/45; ass 8AF 15/2/45; retUS Bradley 3/7/45; Sth Plains 10/7/45; RFC Kingman 13/2/46.
44-8896 Del Lincoln 25/1/45; Grenier 15/2/45; ass 8AF 17/2/45; Re-ass 30/4/47; 10 HB Oberpfaffenhofen 18/1/48; Recl Comp 1/10/48.
44-8897 Del Lincoln 29/1/45; Grenier 12/2/45; ass 748BS/457BG Glatton 21/3/45; tran 547BS/384BG Grafton Underwood 9/5/45; sal 9AF Germany 11/5/46. BUGS BUNNY.
44-8898 Del Lincoln 29/1/45; Grenier 20/2/45; ass 8AF 22/2/45; sal 9AF Germany 11/5/46.
44-8899 Del Lincoln 29/1/45; Grenier 17/2/45; ass 8AF 21/2/45; mapping Dutch coast 2/7/45; Re-ass 30/4/47; Recl Comp 13/6/47.
44-8900 Del Lincoln 29/1/45; Dow Fd 13/2/45; ass 525BS/379BG Kimbolton 15/2/45; retUS Bradley 12/7/45; Independence 13/7/45; RFC Kingman 21/12/45. CARICO JO.
44-8901 Del Lincoln 29/1/45; Dow Fd 13/2/45; ass 333BS/94BG Rougham 15/2/45; retUS Bradley 8/7/45; RFC Kingman 9/12/45.
44-8902 Del Lincolon 29/1/45; Grenier 15/2/45; ass 748BS/457BG Glatton 21/3/45; retUS Bradley 25/5/45; RFC Kingman 16/12/45.
44-8903 Del Lincoln 20/1/45; Dow Fd 14/2/45; ass 327BS/92BG [UX-G] Podington 20/3/45; MIA Dresden 17/4/45 w/Huether; mid air coll w/43-39110, cr Dresden; 6KIA 2POW; MACR 14052.
44-8904 Del Lincoln 30/1/45; Grenier 18/2/45; ass 8AF 20/2/45; Re-ass 30/4/47; Recl Comp 14/11/47.
44-8905 Del Cheyenne 30/1/45; Hunter 3/2/45; Grenier 2/3/45; ass 8AF 4/3/45; retUS Morrison 19/10/45; RFC Walnut Ridge 2/1/46.
44-8906 Del Cheyenne 30/1/45; Hunter 3/3/45; ass 8AF 18/3/45; Re-ass 30/4/47; 2043 LS Tulln 18/1/48; 7909 BU Tulln 1/7/48; 7290 AB Oberpfaffenhofen 16/10/48.
44-8907 Del Cheyenne 3/2/45; Hunter 3/3/45; ass 8AF 16/3/45; sal 9AF Germany 22/5/46.
44-8908 Del Cheyenne 3/2/45; Hunter 3/3/45; Dow Fd 22/3/45; ass 452BG Deopham Green 27/3/45; tran 100BG Thorpe Abbotts 7/4/45; retUS Morrison 29/10/45; RFC Walnut Ridge 7/1/46.
44-8909 Del Cheyenne 3/2/45; Hunter 3/3/45; ass 8AF 22/3/45; retUS Morrison 29/10/45; RFC Walnut Ridge 5/1/46.
44-8910 Del Cheyenne 3/2/45; Hunter 3/3/45; Grenier 13/3/45; ass 390BG Framlingham 21/3/45 (last a/c assgd to grp); retUS Morrison 29/5/45; RFC Walnut Ridge 27/12/45.
44-8911 Del Cheyenne 3/2/45; Hunter 3/3/45; Grenier 14/3/45; ass 338BS/96BG Snetterton 21/3/45; retUS Charleston 28/10/45; RFC Walnut Ridge 7/1/46.
44-8912 Del Cheyenne 3/2/45; Hunter 3/3/45; Grenier 22/3/45; ass 351BS/100BG [EP-L] Thorpe Abbotts 14/3/45; retUS, RFC Walnut Ridge 2/1/46.
44-8913 Del Cheyenne 3/2/45; Hunter 3/3/45; Grenier 18/3/45; ass 8AF 27/3/45; sal 22/5/45.
44-8914 Del Cheyenne 3/2/45; Hunter 3/3/45; Grenier 18/3/45; ass 8AF 28/3/45; sal 9AF Germany 6/11/46.
44-8915 Del Cheyenne 2/3/45; Hunter 3/3/45; Grenier 27/3/45; ass 333BS/94BG Rougham 29/3/45; retUS Charleston 28/10/45; RFC Walnut Ridge 9/1/46.
44-8916 Del Cheyenne 5/2/45; Hunter 3/3/45; Grenier 22/3/45; ass 350BS/100BG [LN-R] Thoroe Abbotts 6/4/45; retUS Morrison 26/10/45; RFC Walnut Ridge 8/1/46.
44-8917 Del Cheyenne 5/2/45; Hunter 3/3/45; Grenier 17/3/45; ass 351BS/100BG [EP-K] Thorpe Abbotts 30/3/45; retUS, RFC Walnut Ridge 3/1/46.
44-8918 Del Cheyenne 5/2/45; Hunter 3/3/45; Grenier 26/3/45; ass 526BS/379BG [LF-D] Kimbolton 12/4/45; retUS, RFC Walnut Ridge 14/12/45.
44-8919 Del Cheyenne 5/2/45; Hunter 3/3/45; Dow Fd 21/3/45; ass 351BS/100BG [EP-G] Thorpe Abbotts 27/3/45 (last a/c assgd to grp); retUS Morrison 25/10/45; RFC Walnut Ridge 7/1/46. CANDY'S DANDY.
44-8920 Del Cheyenne 6/2/45; Hunter 3/3/45; Grenier 26/3/45; ass 8AF 28/3/45; retUS Morrison 28/10/45; RFC Walnut Ridge 2/1/46.
44-8921 Del Cheyenne 6/2/45; Hunter 3/3/45; Grenier 23/3/45; ass 4BS/34BG Mendlesham 26/3/45; retUS Charleston 28/10/45; RFC Walnut Ridge 21/12/45.
44-8922 Del Cheyenne 6/2/45; Hunter 5/3/45; Grenier 16/3/45; ass 838BS/487BG Lavenham 30/3/45; 837BS; caught fire 14/4/45; sal 22/5/45.
44-8923 Del Cheyenne 9/2/45; Hunter 5/3/45; Grenier 22/3/45; ass 544BS/384BG [SU-W] Grafton Underwood 12/4/45 TRAIL BLAZER; tran 369BS/306BG Thurleigh 9/5/45; sal 9AF Germany 18/2/46. THE BOSS.
44-8924 Del Cheyenne 9/2/45; Hunter 3/3/45; Grenier 12/3/45; ass 427BS/303BG Molesworth 18/3/45; retUS Morrison 8/10/45; RFC Walnut Ridge 21/12/45.
44-8925 Del Cheyenne 9/2/45; Hunter 5/3/45; Grenier 16/3/45; ass 388BG Knettishall 30/3/45; retUS, RFC Walnut Ridge 2/1/46.
44-8926 Del Cheyenne 9/2/45; Hunter 5/3/45; Grenier 27/3/45; ass 487BG Lavenham 23/4/45; retUS Charleston 26/10/45; RFC Walnut Ridge 8/1/46.

44-8927 Del Cheyenne 11/2/45; Hunter 3/3/45; Grenier 21/3/45; ass 457BG Glatton 12/4/45; tran 305BG Chelveston 23/5/45; sal 9AF Germany 23/5/46.

44-8928 Del Cheyenne 12/2/45; Hunter 5/3/45; Grenier 23/3/45; ass 388BG Knettishall 25/3/45; retUS Morrison 27/10/45; RFC Walnut Ridge 28/12/45.

44-8929 Del Cheyenne 9/2/45; Hunter 3/3/45; Grenier 22/3/45; ass 490BG Eye 28/3/45 (last a/c assgd to grp); tran 2BG Amendola 30/5/45; sal 9AF Germany 24/12/46; re-ass 30/4/47; Recl Comp 19/11/47.

44-8930 Del Cheyenne 9/2/45; Wright Fd 3/3/45; 4168 BU Sth Plains 25/4/45; re-ass 31/3/47; 4135 BU Hill Fd 3/4/47; 16 Ph Sq McDill 22/10/47; 4135 BU Hill 28/10/47; 7 GE McDill 30/3/48; 343 RVH Topeka 28/7/48; sal 8/3/49.

44-8931 Del Cheyenne 6/2/45; Hunter 3/3/45; Grenier 16/3/45; ass 8AF 18/3/45; sal 9AF Germany 6/11/46.

44-8932 Del Cheyenne 11/2/45; Hunter 25/3/45; Grenier 26/3/45; ass 8AF 28/3/45; re-ass 30/4/47; 10 HB Oberpfaffenhofen 18/1/48; Recl Comp 7/7/49.

44-8933 Del Dallas 14/2/45; Hunter 9/4/45; Grenier 13/4/45; ass 8AF 18/4/45; retUS, RFC Walnut Ridge 20/12/45.

44-8934 Del Dallas 13/2/45; Hunter 13/4/45; Grenier 16/4/45; ass 8AF 18/4/45; retUS, RFC Walnut Ridge 8/1/46.

44-8935 Del Dallas 16/2/45; Hunter 19/2/45; Grenier 15/4/45; ass 8AF 18/4/45; retUS, RFC Walnut Ridge 14/1/46.

44-8936 Del Dallas 12/2/45; Hunter 2/4/45; 4168 BU Sth Plains 27/4/45; re-ass 31/3/47; 4135 BU Hill 30/4/47; sal 4/5/49.

44-8937 Del Dallas 13/2/45; Hunter 12/4/45; Grenier 19/4/45; retUS, RFC Walnut Ridge 8/1/46.

44-8938 Del Dallas 13/2/45; Hunter 2/4/45; 91 RLP Waller (6AF) 15/3/48; 91 RLP McGuire 4/5/49.

44-8939 Del Dallas 13/2/45; Hunter 10/4/45; Grenier 18/4/45; ass 8AF 20/4/45; retUS Morrison 17/12/45; RFC Walnut Ridge 1/1/46.

44-8940 Del Dallas 14/2/45; Sth Plains 29/2/45; Syracuse 11/5/45; to storage RFC Altus 29/11/45.

44-8941 Del Dallas 17/2/45; Hunter 9/4/45; Grenier 15/4/45; ass 8AF 18/4/45; retUS Morrison 12/10/45; RFC Walnut Ridge 7/1/46.

44-8942 Del Dallas 13/2/45; Hunter 21/3/45; Grenier 28/3/45; ass 8AF 30/3/45; sal 9AF Germany 23/5/46.

44-8943 Del Dallas 19/2/45; Hunter 7/3/45; Grenier 19/3/45; ass 8AF 22/3/45; sal 9AF Germany 24/12/46; re-ass 30/4/47; Recl Comp 19/11/47.

44-8944 Del Dallas 17/2/45; Hunter 12/4/45; Grenier 23/3/45; ass 8AF 25/3/45; retUS Bradley 3/7/45; RFC Kingman 14/12/45.

44-8945 Del Dallas 17/2/45; Hunter 22/2/45; Grenier 30/3/45; ass 544BS/384BG [SU-F] Grafton Underwood 10/4/45 (last a/c assgd to grp); sal 9AF Germany 25/7/46.

44-8946 Del Dallas 16/2/45; Hunter 5/3/45; Grenier 29/3/45; ass 8AF 1/4/45; re-ass 30/4/47; 10 HB Oberpfaffenhofen 16/1/48; Recl Comp 7/1/49.

44-8947 Del Dallas 19/2/45; Hunter 23/2/45; Grenier 24/3/45; ass 8AF 26/3/45; retUS Bradley 6/6/45; RFC Kingman 14/2/46.

44-8948 Del Dallas 12/2/45; Hunter 4/3/45; Grenier 27/3/45; ass 8AF 29/3/45; sal 9AF Germany 6/11/46.

44-8949 Del Dallas 19/2/45; Hunter 7/3/45; Grenier 17/3/45; ass 385BG Gt Ashfield 21/3/45 (last a/c ass to grp); retUS Bradley 20/6/45; RFC Kingman 13/2/46.

44-8950 Del Dallas 15/2/45; Hunter 13/3/45; Grenier 26/3/45; ass 381BG Ridgewell 28/3/45; tran 306BG Thurleigh 21/5/46; retUS Bradley 24/5/45; RFC Kingman 21/2/46.

44-8951 Del Dallas 15/2/45; Hunter 27/2/45; Grenier 20/3/45; ass 8AF 22/3/45; retUS Bradley 7/6/45; Sth Plains 10/6/45; RFC Kingman 30/11/45.

44-8952 Del Dallas 16/2/45; Hunter 6/3/45; Grenier 29/3/45; ass 8AF 1/4/45; re-ass 30/4/47; 10 HB Oberpfaffenhofen 18/1/48; Recl Comp 3/8/47.

44-8953 Del Dallas 16/2/45; Hunter 7/3/45; Grenier 29/3/45; ass 1/4/45; retUS, RFC Kingman 15/2/46.

44-8954 Del Dallas 19/2/45; Hunter 7/3/45; Grenier 26/3/45; ass 8AF 28/3/45; retUS Bradley 25/6/45; Independence 27/6/45; RFC Kingman 22/12/45.

44-8955 Del Dallas 19/2/45; Hunter 7/3/45; Grenier 23/3/45; ass 96BG Snetterton 27/3/45; retUS Bradley 8/6/45; RFC Kingman 30/11/45.

44-8956 Del Cheyenne 19/2/45; Lincoln 4/3/45; Grenier 13/3/45; ass 8AF 16/3/45; retUS Bradley 4/6/45; Sth Plains 6/7/45; RFC Kingman 13/2/46.

44-8957 Del Cheyenne 20/2/45; Hunter 4/3/45; Grenier 27/3/45; ass 427BS/303BG [GN-D] Molesworth 30/3/45; retUS Bradley 7/7/45; RFC Kingman 14/2/46.

44-8958 Del Dallas 20/2/45; Hunter 5/3/45; Grenier 25/3/45; ass 8AF 27/3/45; re-ass 30/4/47; 10 BH Oberpfaffenhofen 18/1/48; Recl Comp 7/1/49.

44-8959 –. As CB-17 US Navy 1946.

44-8960 Del Cheyenne 14/2/45; Grenier 27/3/45; ass 8AF 29/3/45; retUS, RFC Walnut Ridge 4/1/46.

44-8961 Del Cheyenne 24/2/45; Hunter 6/3/45; Grenier 29/3/45; ass 8AF 30/3/45; sal 9AF Germany 23/5/46.

44-8962 Del Dallas 9/2/45; Hunter 22/2/45; Grenier 22/3/45; ass 306BG Thurleigh 20/5/45; sal 9AF Germany 24/12/46; re-ass 30/4/47; Recl Comp 19/11/47.

44-8963 Del Dallas 9/2/45; Hunter 27/2/45; Grenier 30/3/45; ass 8AF 1/4/45; retUS Bradley 7/6/45; 4168 BU Sth Plains 30/9/46; re-ass 31/3/47; 4141 BU Pyote 23/6/47; Recl Comp 11/2/49.

44-8964 Del Dallas 17/2/45; Hunter 7/3/45; Grenier 23/3/45; ass 8AF 26/3/45; sal 9AF Germany 6/11/46.

44-8965 Del Louisville 9/2/45; Hunter 27/2/45; Grenier 10/3/45; ass 8AF 12/3/45; re-ass 30/4/47; 10 HB Oberpfaffenhofen 18/1/48; 7290 BU Oberpfaffenhofen 1/7/47; Recl Comp 2/8/49.

44-8966 Del Dallas 15/2/45; tran Dorval, Canada 2/3/45; ass RCAF as {KL 833}; SOC 11/3/47.

44-8967 Del Dallas 16/2/45; tran Dorval 2/3/45; ass RCAF as {KL 834}; SOC 15/9/47.

44-8968 Del Cheyenne 19/2/45; tran Dorval 4/3/45; ass RCAF as {KL 835}; SOC 11/3/47.

44-8969 Del Cheyenne 24/2/45; tran Dorval 4/3/45; ass RCAF as {KL 836}; SOC?

44-8970 Del Cheyenne 24/2/45; tran Dorval 4/3/45; ass RCAF as {KL 837}; SOC 31/7/47.

44-8971 Del Dallas 17/2/45; Hunter 5/3/45; Grenier 30/3/45; ass 8AF 1/4/45; re-ass 30/4/47; 10 HB Oberpfaffenhofen 18/1/48; Recl Comp 7/1/49.

44-8972 Del Cheyenne 21/2/45; Hunter 4/3/45; Grenier 27/3/45; ass 8AF 29/3/45; retUS 4000 BU Wright Fd 27/8/45; re-ass 30/4/47; Recl Comp 9/4/48.

44-8973 Del Cheyenne 20/2/45; Hunter 4/3/45; Grenier 26/4/45; ass 28/4/45; sal 9AF Germany 22/5/46; retUS ATC Manchester 1/8/46; 613 BU Phillips 12/5/48.

44-8974 Del Louisville 20/2/45; Hunter 4/3/45; Grenier 2/5/45; ass 8AF 4/5/45; retUS Bradley 28/6/45; RFC Kingman 27/2/46.

44-8975 Del Cheyenne 20/2/45; Hunter 4/3/45; Grenier 10/3/45; ass 8AF 12/3/45; sal 9AF Germany 31/5/46.

44-8976 Del Cheyenne 20/2/45; Hunter 4/3/45; Grenier 2/5/45; ass 8AF 4/5/45; retUS Bradley 7/6/45; RFC Kingman 14/2/46.

44-8977 –.

44-8978 Del Cheyenne 20/2/45; Hunter 4/3/45; Grenier 28/3/45; ass 8AF 30/4/45; re-ass 30/4/47; 10 HB Oberpfaffenhofen 18/1/48; Recl Comp 7/1/49.

44-8979 Del Louisville 20/2/45; Hunter 4/3/45; Grenier 25/3/45; ass 8AF 27/3/45; retUS Bradley 25/5/45; RFC Kingman 27/12/45.

44-8980 Del Louisville 21/2/45; Hunter 4/3/45; Grenier 25/3/45; ass 8AF 27/3/45; retUS Bradley 21/6/45; 4168 BU Sth Plains 30/9/46; re-ass 31/3/47; 4141 BU Pyote 3/4/47; Recl Comp 11/2/49.

44-8981 Del Louisville 21/4/45; Hunter 5/3/45; Grenier 27/3/45; ass 8AF 29/3/45; sal 9AF Germany 10/8/46.

44-8982 Del Louisville 24/2/45; Hunter 6/3/45; Grenier 19/3/45; ass 8AF 21/3/45; retUS Bradley 19/5/45; RFC Kingman 25/2/46.

44-8983 Del Louisville 24/2/45; Hunter 6/3/45; Grenier 24/3/45; ass 8AF 26/3/45; re-ass 30/4/47; Recl Comp 19/11/47.

44-8984 Del Cheyenne 24/2/45; Hunter 4/3/45; Grenier 25/3/45; ass 8AF 27/3/45; retUS Bradley 7/6/45; RFC Kingman 22/11/45.

44-8985 Del Louisville 23/2/45; Hunter 4/3/45; Grenier 10/3/45; ass 8AF 12/3/45; retUS Bradley 17/6/45; re-ass 31/3/47; 4168 BU Sth Plains 13/6/47; 4141 BU Pyote 19/6/47; Recl Comp 11/2/49.

44-8986 Del Louisville 23/2/45; Hunter 27/2/45; Grenier 29/3/45; ass 8AF 1/4/45; retUS Bradley 12/6/45; Eglin 18/1/46; 3502 BU Chanute 30/9/46; re-ass 31/3/37; 2621 BU Barksdale 18/9/47; 3502 BU Chanute 18/1/48; 4117 BU Robins 18/3/48; Recl Comp 31/3/49.

44-8987 Del Cheyenne 24/2/45; Hunter 4/3/45; Grenier 19/3/45; ass 8AF 21/3/45; retUS Bradley 12/7/45; RFC Kingman 30/12/45.

44-8988 Del Cheyenne 23/2/45; Hunter 4/3/45; Grenier 20/3/45; ass 96BG Snetterton 27/3/45 (last a/c assgd to grp); sal 9AF Germany 23/5/46.

44-8989 Del Cheyenne 24/2/45; Hunter 5/3/45; Grenier 20/3/45; ass 8AF 22/3/45; sal 9AF Germany 23/5/46.

44-8990 –.To VIP transport. Used by Churchill as US; USN 1946; USAFE 6/54. Civil Reg 3678G; W/O Long Beach 1972.

44-8991 Del Cheyenne 22/2/45; Hunter 4/3/45; Grenier 22/3/45; ass 8AF 24/3/45; sal 9AF Germany 6/11/46.

44-8992 Del Cheyenne 23/2/45; Hunter 4/3/45; Grenier 22/3/45; ass 306BG Thurleigh 27/3/45; tran 457BG Glatton 8/5/45; 1 BAD Burtonwood 5/6/45; retUS 4100 BU Patterson 12/6/45; re-ass 8AF 20/4/47; 322 ASU Kadena, Japan 18/2/48; 13 ARE Tachikoa 29/5/48; 13 ARE Jama 13/7/48; 322 ASU Kadena 16/12/48; 332 MSU 7/4/49; Recl Comp 6/4/57.

44-8993 Del Cheyenne 25/2/45; Hunter 4/3/45; Grenier 23/3/45; ass 8AF 25/3/45; re-ass 30/4/47; 10 HB Oberpfaffenhofen 18/1/48; Recl Comp 7/1/49.

44-8994 Del Cheyenne 23/2/45; Hunter 4/3/45; Grenier 24/3/45; slated 381BG, tran 306BG Thurleigh 10/5/45 (last a/c asgd to grp); 92BG Podington 18/5/45; retUS, RFC Walnut Ridge 4/1/46.

44-8995 Del Cheyenne 25/2/45; Hunter 4/3/45; Grenier 27/3/45; ass 8AF 29/3/45; sal 9AF Germany 11/10/45; re-ass 30/4/47; 47 STG Rosten 18/1/48; 46 THP Furstnefeldbrück 26/5/48; 7499 AF Furstenfeldbrück 2/11/48; 7210 MAI Erding 11/11/48; Recl Comp Furstenfeldbrück 7/1/49.

44-8996 Del Cheyenne 25/2/45; Hunter 4/3/45; Grenier 26/3/45; ass 8AF 28/3/45; retUS Bradley 22/5/45; RFC Kingman 21/2/46.

44-8997 - To VIP transport. With USAFE 1950s.

44-8998 Del Cheyenne 26/2/45; Hunter 6/3/45; Grenier 26/3/45; ass 8AF 29/3/45; retUS Bradley 1/6/45; RFC Kingman 10/1/46.

44-8999 Del Cheyenne 26/2/45; Hunter 6/3/45; Grenier 27/3/45; ass 8AF 29/3/45; retUS Bradley 21/6/45; 4168 BU Sth Plains 31/1/46; Aberdeen PG 6/3/46.

44-9000 Del Dallas 26/2/45; Hunter 10/4/45; Sth Plains 2/5/45; 4168 BU Sth Plains 30/9/46; re-ass 31/3/47; 4136 BU Hill Fd 29/4/47; RFC Walnut Ridge 10/4/49.

B-17G-DL

44-83236 Del Hunter 8/1/45; Dow Fd 31/1/45; ass 15AF 5/2/45; re-ass 30/4/47; 10 HBS Oberpfaffenhofen 18/1/48; Recl Comp 7/1/49.

44-83237 Del Lincoln 8/1/45; Dow Fd 8/2/45; ass ETO 9/2/45; retUS Morrison 18/10/45; RFC Walnut Ridge 10/1/46. (Used by Gen Carl Spaatz 1946). BOOPS.

44-83238 Del Lincoln 8/1/46; Dow Fd 31/1/45; ass 483BG Sterparone 5/2/45; retUS Morrison 18/10/45; RFC Walnut Ridge 2/1/46.

44-83239 Del Lincoln 10/1/45; Grenier 6/2/45; ass 15AF 7/2/45; retUS, RFC Walnut Ridge 14/12/45.

44-83240 Del Hunter 10/1/45; Grenier 22/1/45; ass 483BG Sterparone 31/1/45; retUS, RFC Walnut Ridge 10/1/46.

44-83241 Del Hunter 10/1/45; Grenier 30/1/45; ass 96BS/2BG Amendola 5/3/45; {0m} retUS Morrison 25/9/45; RFC Walnut Ridge 13/12/45.

44-83242 Del Lincoln 10/1/45; Dow Fd 6/2/45; ass 96BS/2BG Amendola 5/3/45; {0m} tran 5th Bomb Wing pool 20/9/45; retUS Morrison 11/10/45; RFC Walnut Ridge 18/1/46.

44-83243 Del Lincoln 12/1/45; Grenier 6/2/45; ass 15AF 8/2/45; retUS, RFC Walnut Ridge 28/12/45.

44-83244 Del Lincoln 12/1/45; Dow Fd 8/2/45; ass 15AF 9/2/45; retUS Morrison 10/10/45; RFC Walnut Ridge 28/12/45.

44-83245 Del Lincoln 12/1/45; Dow Fd 6/2/45; ass 96BS/2BG Amendola 25/2/45; {0m} sal 9AF Germany 19/11/47.

44-83246 Del Hunter 12/1/45; Grenier 28/1/45; ass 483BG Sterparone 4/45; retUS Morrison 19/10/45; RFC Walnut Ridge 21/12/45.

44-83247 Del Lincoln 12/1/45; Dow Fd 6/2/45; ass 15AF 8/2/45; sal 9AF Germany 23/9/46; re-ass 30/4/47; Recl Comp 19/11/47.

44-83248 Del Lincoln 12/1/45; Grenier 6/2/45; ass 15AF 12/2/45; retUS Morrison 18/10/45; 593 BU Charleston 28/10/45; RFC Walnut Ridge 5/1/46.

44-83249 Del Lincoln 18/1/45; Dow Fd 6/2/45; ass 483BG Sterparone 8/2/45; retUS Morrison 17/10/45; retUS Walnut Ridge 2/1/46.

44-83250 Del Hunter 12/1/45; Dow Fd 1/2/45; ass 15AF 8/2/45; retUS Morrison 4/10/45; RFC Walnut Ridge 29/12/45.

44-83251 Del Hunter 15/1/45; Grenier 31/1/45; ass 8AF 2/2/45; sal 9AF Germany 10/5/46.

44-83252 Del Hunter 14/1/45; Grenier 2/2/45; ass 533BS/381BG [VP-Z] Ridgewell 24/2/45; retUS Bradley 28/5/45; Sth Plains 1/6/45; RFC Kingman 13/12/45.

44-83253 Del Hunter 14/1/45; Grenier 30/1/45; ass 8AF 8/2/45; retUS Bradley 10/7/45; Sth Plains 14/7/45; RFC Kingman 16/11/45.

44-83254 Del Hunter 14/1/45; Grenier 2/2/45; ass 8AF 15/2/45; retUS Bradley 9/7/45; Sth Plains 11/7/45; RFC Kingman 24/11/45.

44-83255 Del Hunter 14/1/45; Dow Fd 1/2/45; ass 8AF 8/2/45; retUS Bradley 17/6/45; Sth Plains 19/6/45; RFC Kingman 14/12/45.

44-83256 Del Lincoln 15/1/45; Grenier 6/2/45; ass 8AF 14/2/45; re-ass 30/4/45; mapping Belgian coast (Wipe) 5/6/47; Recl Comp 19/11/47.

44-83257 Del Lincoln 15/1/45; Dow Fd 12/2/45; ass 8AF 15/2/45; retUS Bradley 9/7/45; Sth Plains 12/7/45; RFC Kingman 23/11/45.

44-83258 Del Lincoln 15/1/45; Grenier 6/2/45; ass 8AF 15/2/45; re-ass 30/4/47; 10 HBS Oberpfaffenhofen 18/1/48; Recl Comp 7/1/49.

44-83259 –.

44-83260 Del Lincoln 15/1/45; Grenier 6/2/45; ass 327BS/92BG [UX-C] Podington 4/3/45; MIA Kassel 9/3/45 w/?; flak, cr Kassel. MACR 12938

44-83261 Del Lincoln 15/1/45; Grenier 6/2/45; ass 8AF 15/2/45; sal 9AF Germany 6/11/46.

44-83262 Del Lincoln 15/1/45; Dow Fd 6/2/45; ass 563BS/388BG Knettishall 16/2/45; retUS Bradley 28/6/45; Sth Plains 30/6/45; RFC Kingman 4/12/45.

44-83263 Del Lincoln 17/1/45; Dow Fd 6/2/45; ass 323BS/91BG [OR-J] Bassingbourn 20/2/45; 322BS [LG-J]; {24m plus two POW trips} retUS Bradley 31/5/45; Sth Plains 5/6/45; RFC Kingman 14/12/45. RAGAN'S RAIDERS.

44-83264 Del Lincoln 17/1/45; Dow Fd 8/2/45; ass 730BS/452BG Deopham Green 10/2/45; retUS Bradley 28/6/45; Sth Plains 1/7/45; RFC Kingman 5/12/45. SCRAPPY JR.

44-83265 Del Hunter 17/1/45; Dow Fd 1/2/45; ass 15AF 8/2/45; retUS Morrison 29/9/45; 593 BU Charleston 28/10/45; RFC Walnut Ridge 5/1/46.

44-83266 Del Lincoln 17/1/45; Grenier 6/2/45; ass 15AF 14/2/45; sal 9AF Germany 23/10/46; re-ass 30/4/47; Recl Comp 19/11/47.

44-83267 Del Lincoln 17/1/45; Dow Fd 6/2/45; ass 91BG Bassingbourn 23/2/45; retUS, RFC Walnut Ridge 14/12/45.

44-83268 Del Lincoln 17/1/45; Grenier 6/2/45; ass 15AF 14/2/45; retUS Morrison 30/9/45; RFC Walnut Ridge 13/12/45.

44-83269 Del Hunter 18/1/45; Grenier 3/2/45; ass 483BG Sterparone 8/2/45; tran 97BG Amendola; retUS Morrison 30/9/45; RFC Walnut Ridge 12/12/45.

44-83270 Del Hunter 15/1/45; Dow Fd 1/2/45; ass 96BS/2BG Amendola 25/2/45; {0m} tran 483BG Sterparone 4/45; 99BG Tortorella 20/9/45; retUS, RFC Walnut Ridge 5/1/46.

44-83271 Del Lincoln 22/1/45; Dow Fd 6/2/45; ass 15AF 10/2/45; sal 9AF Germany 23/5/46.

44-83272 Del Lincoln 15/1/45; Dow Fd 6/2/45; ass 15AF 15/2/45; retUS, RFC Walnut Ridge 3/1/46.

44-83273 Del Lincoln 18/1/45; Dow Fd 6/2/45; ass 15AF 10/2/45; re-ass 30/4/47; 501 SR Weisbaden 18/1/48; 10 HBS Oberpfaffenhofen 19/1/48; 501 SR Weisbaden 21/1/48; 37 BAS Turkey 27/5/48; 43 HBS Erding 27/6/48; 37 BAS Turkey 26/7/48; HQ Ankara 13/12/48; Recl Comp 7/4/49.

44-83274 Del Hunter 18/1/45; Grenier 4/2/45; ass 15AF 9/2/45; retUS, RFC Walnut Ridge 7/1/46.

44-83275 Del Hunter 18/1/45; Dow Fd 11/2/45; ass 15AF 14/2/45; re-ass 30/4/47; 10 HBS Oberpfaffenhofen 18/1/48; Recl Comp 16/12/48.

44-83276 Del Lincoln 17/1/45; Dow Fd 6/2/45; ass 600BS/398BG [N8-N] Nuthampstead 4/3/45; MIA Halberstadt 8/4/45 w/Wells; cr Plauen, 9KIA 1POW; MACR 13914.

44-83277 Del Lincoln 19/1/45; Grenier 17/2/45; ass 8AF 22/2/45; retUS Bradley 12/7/45; Independence 13/7/45; RFC Kingman 20/12/45.

44-83278 Del Lincoln 19/1/45; Grenier 6/2/45; ass 398BG Nuthampstead 15/2/45; tran 837BS/487BG Lavenham 12/4/45; retUS Bradley 13/7/45; Independence 15/7/45; RFC Kingman 18/12/45.

44-83279 Del Lincoln 19/1/45; Grenier 12/2/45; ass 8AF 22/2/45; retUS Bradley 8/7/45; Sth Plains 10/7/45; RFC Kingman 22/11/45.

44-83280 Del Lincoln 19/1/45; Dow Fd 6/2/45; ass 8AF 15/2/45; sal 9AF Germany 31/5/46.

44-83281 Del Lincoln 21/1/45; Grenier 6/2/45; ass 8AF 15/2/45; sal 9AF Germany 23/5/46.

44-83282 Del Lincoln 21/1/45; Grenier 6/2/45; ass 8AF 15/2/45; sal 9AF Germany 23/5/46.

44-83283 Del Lincoln 21/1/45; Grenier 12/2/45; ass 8AF 22/2/45; retUS Bradley 3/7/45; Sth Plains 6/7/45; RFC Kingman 6/12/45.

44-83284 Del Lincoln 21/1/45; Grenier 12/2/45; ass 8AF 22/2/45; sal 9AF Germany 10/5/46.

44-83285 Del Lincoln 21/1/45; Grenier 19/2/45; ass 8AF 22/2/45; retUS Bradley 5/7/45; Sth Plains 9/7/45; RFC Kingman 10/12/45.

44-83286 Del Lincoln 23/1/45; Grenier 17/2/45; ass 8AF 21/2/45; re-ass 30/4/47; 10 HBS Oberpfaffenhofen 18/1/48; Recl Comp 7/1/49.

44-83287 Del Lincoln 23/1/45; Grenier 6/2/45; ass 457BG Glatton 15/2/45; retUS Bradley 8/6/45; Sth Plains 12/6/45; RFC Kingman 27/11/45.

44-83288 Del Lincoln 23/1/45; Dow Fd 12/2/45; ass 527BS/379BG [FO-S] Kimbolton 14/2/45 LADY ANN (last a/c assgd to grp); tran 91BG Bassingbourn 25/5/45 (last a/c assgd to grp); retUS Bradley 11/6/45; Sth Plains 14/6/45; RFC Kingman 6/12/45. THE GRIM REAPER.

44-83289 Del Lincoln 23/1/45; Grenier 6/2/45; ass 8AF 15/2/45; retUS Bradley 29/6/45; sal 121 BU Bradley 17/7/45.

44-83290 Del Lincoln 23/1/45; Dow Fd 6/2/45; ass 8AF 15/2/45; retUS Bradley 12/7/45; Independence 13/7/45; RFC Kingman 20/12/45.

44-83291 Del Lincoln 23/1/45; Grenier 10/2/45; ass 8AF 22/2/45; sal 9AF Germany 31/5/46.

44-83292 Del Hunter 24/1/45; Love Fd 1/2/45; Grenier 11/2/45; Dow Fd 13/2/45; ass 560BS/388BG Knettishall 15/2/45; re-ass 30/4/47; 10 HBS Oberpfaffenhofen 18/1/48; Recl Comp 7/1/49. MISS BEA HAVEN.

44-83293 Del Hunter 24/1/45; Grenier 11/2/45; ass 19/2/45; retUS Bradley 5/7/45; Sth Plains 6/7/45; RFC Kingman 8/12/45.

44-83294 Del Hunter 24/1/45; Dow Fd 13/2/45; ass 8AF 15/2/45; retUS Bradley 29/6/45; Sth Plains 4/7/45; RFC Kingman 8/12/45.

44-83295 Del Hunter 24/1/45; Dow Fd 7/2/45; ass 8AF 22/2/45; sal 9AF Germany 18/9/46; re-ass 30/4/47; Recl Comp 19/11/47.

44-83296 Del Hunter 24/1/45; Dow Fd 13/2/45; ass 8AF 15/2/45; sal 9AF Germany 11/5/46.

44-83297 Del Hunter 25/1/45; Grenier 4/2/45; ass 365BS/305BG [KY-J] Chelveston 4/3/45 (last a/c assgd to grp); retUS Bolling 11/6/45; Sth Plains 14/6/45; RFC Kingman 10/12/45. ARLENE.

44-83298 Del Hunter 24/1/45; Dow Fd 11/2/45; ass 8AF 15/2/45; retUS Bradley 19/6/45; Sth Plains 21/6/45; RFC Kingman 4/12/45.

44-83299 Del Hunter 25/1/45; Dow Fd 11/2/45; ass

8AF 15/2/45; retUS Bradley 6/6/45; Sth Plains 9/6/45; RFC Kingman 18/12/45.

44-83300 Del Hunter 23/1/45; Dow Fd 7/2/45; ass 8AF 15/2/45; retUS Bradley 28/6/45; Sth Plains 30/6/45; RFC Kingman 17/12/45.

44-83301 Del Hunter 23/1/45; Dow Fd 7/2/45; ass 5 ASR Sq.

44-83302 Del Lincoln 25/1/45; Dow Fd 12/2/45; ass 15AF 18/2/45; retUS Morrison 6/10/45; RFC Walnut Ridge 28/12/45.

44-83303 Del Lincoln 26/1/45; Grenier 12/2/45; ass 15AF 20/2/45; retUS Morrison 9/10/45; RFC Walnut Ridge 7/1/46.

44-83304 Del Lincoln 26/1/45; Grenier 12/2/45; ass 15AF 20/2/45; retUS Morrison 4/10/45; 593 BU Charleston 28/10/45; RFC Walnut Ridge 29/12/45.

44-83305 Del Lincoln 26/1/45; Grenier 12/2/45; ass 8AF 2/3/45; re-ass 30/4/47; 10 HBS Oberpfaffenhofen 18/1/48; Recl Comp 16/12/48.

44-83306 Del Lincoln 26/1/45; Grenier 17/2/45; 4000 BU Wright 11/4/45; ass 9AF, retUS 11/4/46; Recl Comp 2/5/46.

44-83307 Del Lincoln 26/1/45; Dow Fd 13/2/45; ass 8AF 25/2/45; retUS Morrison 20/10/45; RFC Walnut Ridge 8/1/46.

44-83308 Del Hunter 26/1/45; Dow Fd 15/2/45; ass 8AF 21/2/45; retUS Morrison 22/10/45; 593 BU Charleston 28/10/45; RFC Walnut Ridge 21/1/46.

44-83309 Del Hunter 25/1/45; Grenier 12/2/45; ass 15AF 9/3/45; re-ass 30/4/47; 10 HBS Oberpfaffenhofen 18/1/48; 7290 AB Oberpfaffenhofen 19/7/48; Recl Comp 2/8/49.

44-83310 Del Hunter 28/1/45; Grenier 14/2/45; ass 15AF 28/2/45; retUS, RFC Walnut Ridge 4/1/46 (int Algeria while on ferry USA to Israel as N9814F).

44-83311 Del Hunter 30/1/45; Dow Fd 16/2/45; ass 15AF 21/2/45; retUS Morrison 3/10/45; RFC Walnut Ridge 21/12/45.

44-83312 Del Lincoln 30/1/45; Dow Fd 14/2/45; ass 15AF 20/2/45; retUS Morrison 29/10/45; RFC Walnut Ridge 20/12/45.

44-83313 Del Lincoln 30/1/45; Dow Fd 12/2/45; ass 15AF 16/2/45; retUS Morrison 2/10/45; RFC Walnut Ridge 10/1/46.

44-83314 Del Lincoln 30/1/45; Grenier 17/2/45; ass 96BS/2BG Amendola 11/3/45; {0m} retUS Morrison 26/9/45; RFC Walnut Ridge 14/12/45. HELL'S ANGELS.

44-83315 Del Lincoln 30/1/45; Grenier 17/2/45; ass 15AF 21/2/45; retUS Morrison 21/12/45.

44-83316 Del Lincoln 30/1/45; Grenier 15/2/45; ass 15AF 28/2/45; sal 9AF Germany 6/11/46; retUS Fairfax /52 then storage /56; Norton, Cal /59 as part of possible museum, but base CO scrapped idea; dismantled Chino, Cal 30/7/67; Spearfish, SD; Ocatillo, Cal 1988.

44-83317 Del Lincoln 30/1/45; Grenier 25/2/45; ass 15AF 28/2/45; sal 9AF Germany 6/11/46.

44-83318 Del Hunter 30/1/45; Dow Fd 11/2/45; ass 15AF 14/2/45; retUS Morrison 5/10/45; RFC Walnut Ridge 8/1/46.

44-83319 Del Hunter 29/1/45; Grenier 19/2/45; ass 8AF 22/2/45; retUS Morrison 18/10/45; RFC Walnut Ridge 2/1/46.

44-83320 Del Hunter 31/1/45; W/O 12/2/45; sal 24/2/45.

44-83321 Del Hunter 31/1/45; Dow Fd 15/2/45; ass 15AF 17/2/45; retUS, RFC Walnut Ridge 21/12/45.

44-83322 Del Lincoln 31/1/45; Bangor 1/3/45; ass 8AF 8/3/45; sal 9AF Germany 6/11/46.

44-83323 Del Lincoln 31/1/45; Grenier 1/3/45; ass 8AF 2/3/45; retUS Morrison 4/10/45; RFC Walnut Ridge 20/12/45.

44-83324 Del Lincoln 1/2/45; Grenier 1/3/45; ass 15AF 1/3/45; sal 9AF Germany 23/5/46.

44-83325 Del Lincoln 1/2/45; Grenier 17/2/45; ass 15AF 21/2/45; cr Beinn Edra, Skye, UK, 3/3/45; ex Meeks Fd en route Valley, UK. Sal 8/3/45.

44-83326 Del Lincoln 1/2/45; Grenier 1/3/45; ass 15AF 4/3/45; sal 9AF Germany 23/10/46; re-ass 30/4/47; Recl Comp 19/11/47.

44-83327 Del Lincoln 1/2/45; Grenier 17/2/45; ass 15AF 21/2/45; retUS Morrison 4/10/45; RFC Walnut Ridge 14/12/45.

44-83328 Del Hunter 1/2/45; Grenier 1/3/45; ass 15AF 4/3/45; retUS Morrison 9/10/45; RFC Walnut Ridge 11/1/46.

44-83329 Del Hunter 7/2/45; Grenier 16/2/45; ass 15AF 28/2/45; retUS, RFC Walnut Ridge 14/10/45.

44-83330 Del Hunter 2/2/45; Grenier 20/2/45; ass 15AF 22/2/45; mapping Dutch coast (Wipe) 2/12/46; re-ass 30/4/47; Recl Comp 13/6/47.

44-83331 Del Hunter 2/2/45; Grenier 19/2/45; ass 15AF 22/2/45; retUS Morrison 18/10/45; RFC Walnut Ridge 28/12/45.

44-83332 Del Hunter 2/2/45; Grenier 19/2/45; ass 15AF 22/2/45; retUS Morrison 11/10/45; RFC Walnut Ridge 15/1/46.

44-83333 Del Lincoln 2/2/45; Grenier 1/3/45; ass 483BG Sterparone 27/2/45; retUS Morrison 22/10/45; 593 BU Charleston 28/10/45; RFC Walnut Ridge 9/1/46.

44-83334 Del Lincoln 2/2/45; Grenier 17/2/45; ass 15AF 14/3/45; retUS Morrison 29/9/45; RFC Walnut Ridge 18/12/45.

44-83335 Del Lincoln 3/2/45; Grenier 17/2/45; ass 15AF 22/2/45; retUS, RFC Walnut Ridge 7/1/46.

44-83336 Del Lincoln 8/2/45; Grenier 1/3/45; ass 15AF 4/3/45; retUS Morrison 2/10/45; RFC Walnut Ridge 4/1/46.

44-83337 Del Lincoln 3/2/45; Grenier 17/2/45; ass 15AF 31/2/45; retUS, RFC Walnut Ridge 29/12/45.

44-83338 Del Lincoln 5/2/45; Grenier 17/2/45; ass 15AF 21/2/45; re-ass 30/4/47; 10 HBS Oberpfaffenhofen 18/1/48; Recl Comp 5/8/48.

44-83339 Del Hunter 5/2/45; Dow Fd 15/2/45; ass 15AF 21/2/45; sal 9AF Germany 23/6/46; re-ass 30/4/47; Recl Comp 19/11/47.

44-83340 Del Hunter 5/2/45; Grenier 15/2/45; ass 15AF 21/2/45; sal 25/2/46.

44-83341 Del Oklahoma City 7/2/45; Dallas 10/3/45; Rome 23/5/45; 4202 BU Syracuse 22/10/45; 593 BU Charleston 28/10/45; RFC Altus 7/11/45.

44-83342 Del Oklahoma City 7/2/45; Dallas 10/3/45; slated 7AF Hawaii, tran Syracuse 7/6/45; RFC Altus 28/11/45.

44-83343 Del Oklahoma City 7/2/45; Dallas 12/3/45; slated 7AF Hawaii, tran Rome 26/5/45; Syracuse 12/10/45; RFC Altus 28/11/45.

44-83344 Del Oklahoma City 7/2/45; Dallas 20/3/45; slated 7AF Hawaii, tran Rome 24/5/45; 4202 BU Syracuse 2/6/45; RFC Altus 7/11/45.

44-83345 –.

44-83346 Del Oklahoma City 7/2/45; Dallas 20/3/45; slated 7AF Hawaii, tran Rome 25/5/45; 4202 BU

Below: VB-17G-75-DL 44-83316 with 'picture windows' in waist and nose, a 'plush fittings' conversion for Headquarters officer use by the Central Air Defense Force in 1955. This aircraft was assigned to the Fifteenth Air Force in the spring of 1945 and later transferred to the Ninth Air Force in Germany. (R. Burgess)

Syracuse 31/5/45; RFC Altus 26/11/45.
44-83347 Del Oklahoma City 7/2/45; Dallas 12/3/45; slated 7AF Hawaii, tran Rome 28/5/45; 4202 BU Syracuse 29/5/45; RFC Altus 7/11/45.
44-83348 Del Oklahoma City 7/2/45; Dallas 20/3/45; Rome 31/5/45; AFSC Middletown 8/11/45; Morrison 3/1/46; ATC West Palm Beach 7/11/46; 2621 BU Barksdale 21/11/46; re-ass 31/3/47; 2621 BU Barksdale 29/7/47; 4112 BU Robbins 3/4/48; Recl Comp 13/4/49.
44-83349 Del Oklahoma City 8/2/45; Dallas 10/3/45; slated 7AF Hawaii, tran Rome 26/5/45; Syracuse 12/10/45; RFC Altus 29/11/45.
44-83350 Del Lincoln 8/2/45; Grenier 25/2/45; ass 8AF 27/2/45; re-ass 30/4/47; 10 HBS Oberpfaffenhofen 18/1/48; Recl Comp 1/10/48.
44-83351 Del Lincoln 8/2/45; Grenier 19/2/45; ass 8AF 22/2/45; retUS Bradley 9/6/45; Sth Plains 20/6/45; RFC Kingman 20/12/45.
44-83352 Del Lincoln 9/2/45; Grenier 1/3/45; ass 8AF 4/3/45; retUS Bradley 18/6/45; Sth Plains 21/6/45; RFC Kingman 7/12/45.
44-83353 Del Lincoln 9/2/45; Grenier 4/3/45; ass 8AF 8/3/45; sal 9AF Germany 10/5/46.
44-83354 Del Lincoln 9/2/45; Grenier 1/3/45; ass 8AF 4/3/45; sal 9AF Germany 31/5/45.
44-83355 Del Hunter 9/2/45; Grenier 24/2/45; ass 8AF 27/5/45; retUS Bradley 29/6/45; Sth Plains 2/7/45; RFC Kingman 23/11/45.
44-83356 Del Hunter 9/2/45; Grenier 25/2/45; ass 8AF 3/3/45; re-ass 30/4/47; 10 HBS Oberpfaffenhofen 18/1/48; Recl Comp 18/11/48.
44-83357 Del Hunter 9/2/45; Grenier 24/2/45; ass 8AF 27/2/45; retUS Bradley 1/7/45; Sth Plains 3/7/45; RFC Kingman 18/11/45.
44-83358 Del Hunter 9/2/45; Grenier 24/2/45; ass 8AF 27/2/45; retUS Bradley 10/7/45; Independence 12/7/45; RFC Kingman 21/12/45.
44-83359 Del Hunter 11/2/45; Grenier 26/2/45; ass 8AF 10/3/45; retUS Bradley 10/6/45; Sth Plains 13/6/45; RFC Kingman 1/12/45.
44-83360 Del Hunter 11/2/45; Grenier 25/2/45; ass 8AF 28/2/45; sal 9AF Germany 23/5/46.
44-83361 Del Hunter 11/2/45; Grenier 2/3/45; ass 8AF 7/3/45; retUS Bradley 6/6/45; Sth Plains 9/6/45; RFC Kingman 22/1/46.
44-83362 Del Hunter 11/2/45; Grenier 24/2/45; ass 8AF 28/2/45; re-ass 30/4/47; 10 HBS Oberpfaffenhofen 18/1/48; Recl Comp 1/10/48.
44-83363 Del Hunter 11/2/45; Grenier 24/2/45; ass 8AF 27/2/45; retUS Bradley 8/7/45; Sth Plains 11/7/45; RFC Kingman 10/12/45.
44-83364 Del Hunter 12/2/45; Grenier 24/2/45; ass 8AF 28/2/45; retUS Bradley 6/7/45; Sth Plains 9/7/45; RFC Kingman 21/2/46.
44-83365 Del Hunter 12/2/45; Grenier 2/3/45; ass 8AF 10/3/45; retUS Bradley 28/6/45; Sth Plains 1/7/45; 4168 BU Sth Plains 20/1/46; 4117 BU Robbins 24/2/46; 91 RC McDill 29/4/46; re-ass 30/4/47; 91 RLP Howard (Canal Zone) 18/1/48 (6AF); 91 RLP Waller 20/2/48 (Trinidad); 48 SR Ramey 22/6/48 (CZ); 91 RLP Allen 26/6/48 (CZ); 91 RLP Waller 30/11/49; Recl Comp 25/1/50.
44-83366 Del Hunter 12/2/45; Grenier 25/2/45; ass 325BS/92BG [NV-A] Podington 28/3/45 (last a/c assgd to grp); re-ass 30/4/47; 501 SR Weisbaden 18/1/48; 7290 AB Oberpfaffenhofen 1/7/48; 7160 AB Erben 27/7/48; 60 AB Weisbaden 1/6/49; Recl Comp 13/1/50.
44-83367 Del Hunter 12/2/45; Grenier 1/3/45; ass 8AF 7/3/45; retUS Bradley 29/7/45; Independence 2/8/45; RFC Albuquerque 7/2/46.

44-83368 Del Hunter 12/2/45; Grenier 1/3/45; ass 8AF 5/3/45; retUS Bradley 25/6/45; Sth Plains 27/6/45; RFC Kingman 5/11/45.
44-83369 Del Hunter 13/2/45; Grenier 26/2/45; ass 8AF 4/3/45; sal 9AF Germany 10/5/46.
44-83370 Del Hunter 13/2/45; Grenier 2/3/45; ass 8AF 7/3/45; sal 9AF Germany 23/5/46.
44-83371 Del Hunter 13/2/45; Grenier 2/3/45; ass 8AF 7/3/45; retUS Olmstead 3/8/47; 4112 BU Olmstead 20/8/47; 4141 BU Pyote 19/12/47; Recl Comp 18/4/50.
44-83372 Del Hunter 13/2/45; Grenier 26/2/45; ass 8AF 3/3/45; re-ass 30/4/47; 10 HBS Oberpfaffenhofen 18/1/48; Recl Comp 6/12/48.
44-83373 –.
44-83374 Del Lincoln 14/2/45; Grenier 1/3/45; ass 8AF 7/3/45; retUS Bradley 5/7/45; Sth Plains 9/7/45; RFC Kingman 9/12/45.
44-83375 Del Lincoln 14/2/45; Grenier 1/3/45; ass 8AF 4/3/45; re-ass 30/4/47; 10 HBS Oberpfaffenhofen 18/1/48; Recl Comp 7/1/49.
44-83376 Del Lincoln 14/2/45; Grenier 3/3/45; ass 8AF 12/3/45; retUS Bradley 7/6/45; Sth Plains 13/6/45; RFC Kingman 15/12/45.
44-83377 Del Topeka 14/2/45; Love Fd 23/2/45; Grenier 1/4/45; ass 8AF 5/4/45; retUS Bradley 23/5/45; Sth Plains 25/5/45; 613 BU Phillips 7/3/46.
44-83378 –.
44-83379 Del Lincoln 15/2/45; Grenier 1/3/45; ass 8AF 4/3/45; sal 9AF Germany 31/5/46.
44-83380 Del Lincoln 15/2/45; Grenier 1/3/45; ass 8AF 7/3/45; re-ass 30/4/47; 10 HBS Oberpfaffenhofen 18/1/48; Recl Comp 7/1/49.
44-83381 Del Lincoln 15/2/45; Grenier 4/3/45; ass 8AF 10/3/45; sal 9AF Germany 31/5/46.
44-83382 Del Hunter 16/2/45; Grenier 25/2/45; ass 8AF 28/2/45; re-ass 30/4/47; 10 HBS Oberpfaffenhofen 18/1/48; Recl Comp 5/8/49.
44-83383 Del Oklahoma City 16/2/45; Sth Plains 21/4/45; slated 8AF, tran Tinker 16/6/45; 200 BU Peterson 29/10/45; re-ass 31/3/47; 201 BU Peterson 29/6/47; 2621 BU Barksdale 22/7/45; 4117 BU Robins 30/4/48.
44-83384 Del Oklahoma City 16/2/45; Hunter 30/3/45; Grenier 15/4/45; slated 8AF, tran Sth Plains 30/6/45; 4168 BU Sth Plains 31/1/46; 4117 BU Robins 24/2/46; 554 BU Memphis 9/6/46; 65 BU Langley 13/6/46; 53 RCN Grenier 29/9/46; 53 RCN Morrison 10/10/46; 65 BU Morrison 13/11/46; 308 RCN Morrison 12/12/46; re-ass 31/3/47; 308 RCW Morrison 19/5/47; 308 RCW Fairfield 20/7/47; 4121 BU Kelly 23/11/47; 308 RCW Fairfield 8/12/47; 31 WEA Hickam 3/11/48; 2043 WEA Haneda 9/12/48; 2100 WEA Hickam 24/1/49; 2143 WEA Haneda 1/3/49; 1500 MSU Hickam 30/8/49; 31 WEA Hickam 7/9/49; sal 26/4/50.
44-83385 Del Oklahoma City 16/2/45; ass 8AF, tran Long Beach 22/5/45; Wright Fd 12/8/45; Recl Comp 21/1/46.
44-83386 Del Oklahoma City 16/2/45; Hunter 29/3/45; ass 8AF, tran Sth Plains 27/4/45; 200 BU Peterson 29/10/45; RFC Walnut Ridge 25/2/45.
44-83387 Del Oklahoma City 18/2/45; Tulsa 5/4/45; 4168 BU Sth Plains 14/8/45; re-ass 31/3/47; 4141 BU Pyote 30/6/47; Recl Comp 1/6/49.
44-83388 Del Oklahoma City 18/2/45; Sth Plains 29/4/45; 268 BU Peterson 21/6/45; 200 BU Peterson 29/10/45; 4104 BU Rome 4/8/46; 594 BU Topeka 15/8/46; 4104 BU Rome 20/8/46; re-ass 31/3/47; 4104 BU Rome 4/6/47; 4112 BU Olmstead 20/8/47; AMC Columbus 29/9/47; 3203 MSU Eglin 24/12/48; 1 EGM Eglin 27/12/48; Recl Comp 17/5/49.

44-83389 Del Oklahoma City 18/2/45; Hunter 5/4/45; Sth Plains 3/5/45; 246 BU Pratt 18/6/45; 2138 BU Alamogordo 14/8/45; 233 BU Davis Monthan 17/10/45; RFC Kingman 2/12/45.
44-83390 Del Oklahoma City 19/2/45; Hunter 5/4/45; slated 8AF, tran Sth Plains 3/5/45; 247 BU Smoky Hill 19/6/45; 244 BU Harvard 8/7/45; 233 BU Fort Worth 7/1/46; 613 BU Phillips 8/3/46; 233 BU Fort Worth 30/4/46; sal 8/5/46.
44-83391 Del Oklahoma City 19/2/45; slated 8AF, tran Sth Plains 27/4/45; 268 BU Peterson 21/6/45; 484 BU Topeka 22/10/45; 482 BU Merced 24/1/46; RFC Walnut Ridge 21/2/46.
44-83392 Del Oklahoma City 19/2/45; 246 BU Pratt 21/5/45; 231 BU Alamogordo 14/8/45; 236 BU Pyote 22/10/45; RFC Kingman 29/12/45.
44-83393 Del Hunter 19/2/45; Grenier 4/3/45; ass 8AF 6/3/45; re-ass 30/4/47; 10 HBS Oberpfaffenhofen 18/1/48; Recl Comp 10/10/48.
44-83394 Del Hunter 19/2/45; Grenier 8/3/45; ass 8AF 11/3/45; retUS Bradley 8/7/45; Sth Plains 10/7/45; RFC Kingman 21/2/46.
44-83395 Del Hunter 20/2/45; Grenier 2/3/45; ass 8AF 7/3/45; sal 9AF Germany 24/12/46; re-ass 30/4/47; Recl Comp 19/11/47.
44-83396 Del Lincoln 20/2/45; Grenier 4/3/45; ass 9/3/45; sal 9AF Germany 23/5/46.
44-83397 Del Lincoln 20/2/45; Grenier 4/3/45; ass 838BS/487BG Lavenham 15/4/45 (last a/c assgd to grp); retUS Bradley 13/7/45; Independence 15/7/45; RFC Kingman 31/12/45.
44-83398 Del Lincoln 20/2/45; Grenier 4/3/45; ass 15AF 9/3/45; retUS Morrison 19/2/46; 613 BU Phillips 9/4/46; 1103 BU Morrison 30/5/46.
44-83399 Del Lincoln 21/2/45; Grenier 23/3/45; ass 15AF 28/3/45; sal 9AF Germany 23/9/46; re-ass 30/4/47; Recl Comp 19/11/47.
44-83400 Del Hunter 21/2/45; Grenier 8/3/45; ass 15AF 14/3/45; retUS, RFC Walnut Ridge 12/12/45.
44-83401 Del Hunter 21/2/45; Grenier 10/3/45; ass 15AF 14/3/45; sal 9AF Germany 23/8/46.
44-83402 Del Hunter 21/2/45; Grenier 4/3/45; ass 15AF 14/3/45; retUS Morrison 9/10/45; RFC Walnut Ridge 29/12/45.
44-83403 Del Lincoln 21/2/45; Grenier 5/3/45; ass 483BG Sterparone 14/3/45; retUS Morrison 2/10/45; RFC Walnut Ridge 5/1/46.
44-83404 Del Lincoln 21/2/45; Grenier 12/3/45; slated 15AF, tran 34BG Mendlesham 14/3/44 (last a/c assgd to grp); retUS Bradley 28/6/45; Sth Plains 2/7/45; 4168 BU Sth Plains 31/1/46; 4117 BU Robins 3/3/46; 91 RCN McDill 29/4/46; re-ass 31/3/47; 91 RLP Howard (CZ) 6AF 18/1/48; 91 RLP Waller (Trinidad) 18/7/48; 91 RLP Sq McGuire 9/2/49; 3902 AB Offutt 23/3/49; sal 24/2/50.
44-83405 Del Hunter 22/2/45; Grenier 8/3/45; ass 15AF 11/3/45; retUS Morrison 9/10/45; RFC Walnut Ridge 20/12/45.
44-83406 Del Hunter 22/2/45; Grenier 8/3/45; ass 15AF 12/3/45; re-ass 30/4/47; 10 HBS Oberpfaffenhofen 18/1/48; Recl Comp 16/12/48.
44-83407 Del Hunter 22/2/45; Grenier 8/3/45; ass 815BS/483BG Sterparone 14/3/45; retUS Morrison 30/9/45; RFC Walnut Ridge 4/1/46.
44-83408 Del Lincoln 25/2/45; Grenier 12/3/45; ass 15AF 21/3/45; retUS Bradley 8/7/45; Sth Plains 12/7/45; 4168 BU Sth Plains 20/1/46; 4117 BU Robins 28/2/46; 91 RCN McDill 8/5/46; re-ass 31/3/47; 582 SR Howard (CZ) 18/1/48 (6AF); 91 RLP Waller (Trinidad) 18/2/48; 5904 AS Ramey 12/8/48; 91 RLP McGuire 9/2/49; 3902 AB Offutt 24/5/49; sal 24/2/50.

44-83409 Del Lincoln 26/2/45; Hunter 6/3/45; Grenier 27/3/45; ass 15AF 1/4/45; retUS Morrison 18/10/45; RFC Walnut Ridge 29/12/45.

44-83410 Del Hunter 26/2/45; Grenier 9/3/45; ass 815BS/483BG Sterparone 14/3/45; retUS Morrison 28/9/45; RFC Walnut Ridge 18/12/45.

44-83411 –. Used as CB-17 by 5AF HQ in Korea with radar dome for chin turret.

44-83412 Del Hunter 26/2/45; Grenier 12/3/45; ass 15AF 28/3/45; retUS Morrison 25/12/45; RFC Walnut Ridge 18/1/46.

44-83413 Del Lincoln 26/2/45; Grenier 27/3/45; ass 15AF 30/3/45; retUS, RFC Walnut Ridge 14/12/45.

44-83414 Del Lincoln 26/2/45; Grenier 13/3/45; ass 15AF 18/3/45; retUS Bradley 23/5/45; Sth Plains 26/5/45; RFC Kingman 26/2/46.

44-83415 Del Hunter 26/2/45; Grenier 11/3/45; ass 15AF 28/3/45; retUS Morrison 7/10/45; RFC Walnut Ridge 21/1/45.

44-83416 Del Hunter 26/2/45; Grenier 16/3/45; ass 15AF 28/3/45; re-ass 30/4/47; 10 HBS Oberpfaffenhofen 18/1/45; Recl Comp 7/1/49.

44-83417 Del Hunter 26/2/45; Grenier 9/3/45; ass 15AF 18/3/45; sal 25/6/45.

44-83418 Del Lincoln 26/2/45; Grenier 12/3/45; ass 15AF 21/3/45; re-ass 30/4//47; 10 HBS Oberpfaffenhofen 18/1/48; Recl Comp 7/1/49.

44-83419 Del Topeka 26/2/45; Grenier 6/3/45; ass 15AF 30/3/45; retUS, RFC Walnut Ridge 12/12/45.

44-83420 Del Hunter 28/2/45; Grenier 10/3/45; ass 15AF 14/3/45; retUS Morrison 7/10/45; RFC Walnut Ridge 20/12/45.

44-83421 Del Hunter 25/2/45; Grenier 9/3/45; ass 15AF 14/3/45; retUS Morrison 5/10/45; RFC Walnut Ridge 20/12/45.

44-83422 Del Lincoln 28/2/45; Hunter 9/3/45; Grenier 12/3/45; ass 15AF 18/3/45; retUS, RFC Walnut Ridge 4/2/46.

44-83423 Del Topeka 28/2/45; Grenier 8/3/45; ass 15AF 30/3/45; retUS, RFC Walnut Ridge 14/12/45.

44-83424 Del Topeka 28/2/45; Grenier 27/3/45; ass 15AF 2/4/45; retUS, RFC Walnut Ridge 2/1/46.

44-83425 Del Hunter 28/2/45; Grenier 9/3/45; ass 15AF 28/3/45; retUS Morrison 22/10/45; 594 BU Charleston 28/10/45; RFC Walnut Ridge 7/1/46.

44-83426 Del Hunter 1/3/45; Grenier 1/4/45; ass 15AF 5/4/45; retUS Morrison 5/10/45; RFC Walnut Ridge 27/12/45.

44-83427 Del Hunter 1/3/45; Grenier 10/3/45; ass 15AF 14/3/45; re-ass 30/4/47; 10 HBS Oberpfaffenhofen 18/1/48; Recl Comp 7/1/49.

44-83428 Del Hunter 1/3/45; Grenier 9/3/45; ass 483BG Sterparone 18/3/45; tran 97BG Amendola; retUS Morrison 2/10/45; RFC Walnut Ridge 20/12/45.

44-83429 Del Dallas 2/3/45; Syracuse (storage) 22/5/45; 4202 BU Syracuse 8/11/45; RFC Altus 15/11/45.

44-83430 Del Dallas 2/3/45; slated 7AF, tran Rome 25/5/45; Syracuse 12/10/45; RFC Altus 5/11/45.

44-83431 Del Dallas 2/3/45; Slated 7AF, tran Rome 24/5/45; Syracuse 12/10/45; RFC Altus 28/11/45.

44-83432 Del Hunter 2/3/45; Grenier 10/3/45; ass 8AF 17/3/45; sal 9AF Germany 10/5/46.

44-83433 Del Hunter 2/3/45; Grenier 13/3/45; ass 8AF 18/3/45; retUS Bradley 9/6/45; Sth Plains 13/6/45; 4168 BU Sth Plains 20/1/46; 4117 BU Robins 24/2/46; 91 RCN McDill 29/4/46; re-ass 30/4/47; 91 RLP Howard (CZ) 6AF 18/1/48; 91 RLP Waller (Trinidad) 3/2/48; Canal Zone 27/2/48; 91 RLP Waller 1/7/48; 91 RLP McGuire 9/2/49; 91 SRC Grp McGuire 4/5/49; 91 SRC Gp Barksdale 5/12/49; sal 16/2/50.

44-83434 Del Hunter 2/3/45; Grenier 17/3/45; ass 8AF 26/3/45; sal 9AF Germany 23/5/46.

44-83435 Del Hunter 2/3/45; Grenier 10/3/45; ass 8AF 14/3/45; sal 9AF Germany, retUS 20/10/46; re-ass 31/3/47; 4112 BU Olmstead 29/4/47; tran 23 PHR Momote (5AF) 18/1/48; 5 RVP Clark Fd 18/4/48; 9 SRGp Fairfield 2/6/49; sal 24/1/50.

44-83436 Del Hunter 2/3/45; Grenier 12/3/45; ass 8AF 18/3/45; re-ass 30/4/47; 10 HBS Oberpfaffenhofen 18/1/48; Recl Comp 1/10/48.

44-83437 Del Hunter 4/3/45; Grenier 18/3/47; ass 8AF 26/3/45; sal 9AF Germany 31/5/46.

44-83438 Del Hunter 4/3/45; Grenier 17/3/45; ass 27/3/45; sal 9AF Germany 6/11/46.

44-83439 –. US Civil 6180C (N131P), (5225V); at Miami 1963.

44-83440 Del Hunter 4/3/45; Grenier 15/3/45; ass 8AF 28/3/45; retUS 4100 BU Patterson 12/6/45; 1 BU Bolling 6/8/45; 1503 BU Hamilton 23/10/45; 1 BU Bolling 29/10/45; 902 BU Orlando 13/12/45; 621 BU Pinecastle 17/6/46; 554 BU Memphis 19/6/46; 613 BU Phillips 20/8/46.

44-83441 Del Hunter 4/3/45; Dallas 13/3/45; Grenier 17/3/45; ass 8AF 26/3/45; retUS Bradley 9/7/45; Sth Plains 15/11/45; RFC Kingman 24/11/45; (US Navy as CB-17 1946.)

44-83442 Del Hunter 5/3/45; Grenier 24/3/45; ass 8AF 28/3/45; retUS Bradley 29/5/45; Sth Plains 31/5/45; 4168 BU Sth Plains 7/2/46; 4117 BU Robins 24/2/46; 326 BU McDill 16/4/46; 91 RCN McDill 28/4/46; re-ass 30/4/47; 91 RLP Howard (CZ) 6AF 18/1/48; 91 RLP Waller (Trinidad) 18/7/48; 91 RLPSq McGuire 9/2/49; AMC Tinker 7/3/49; 91 RLPSq McGuire 18/3/49; SAC Peterson 20/9/49; 1 AB March 2/11/49; sal 6/3/50.

44-83443 Del Hunter 5/3/45; Grenier 13/3/45; ass 8AF 27/3/45; retUS Bradley 7/6/45; Sth Plains 14/6/45; sal 11/3/46.

44-83444 Del Hunter 5/3/45; Grenier 18/3/45; ass 8AF 26/3/45; re-ass 30/4/47; 10 HBS Oberpfaffenhofen 18/1/48; Recl Comp 1/10/48.

44-83445 Del Hunter 5/3/45; Grenier 18/3/45; ass 8AF 26/3/45; sal 9AF Germany 23/5/46.

44-83446 –.

44-83447 Del Hunter 6/3/45; Grenier 17/3/45; ass 427BS/303BG Molesworth 10/4/45; MIA Pilsen 25/4/45 w/Mauger; flak, cr Pilsen; 1EVD 3KIA 4POW; MACR 14223.

44-83448 Del Hunter 6/3/45; Grenier 17/3/456; ass 8AF 26/3/45; retUS Bradley 13/7/45; Independence 15/7/45; RFC Kingman 16/12/45.

44-83449 –.

44-83450 Del Hunter 6/3/45; Grenier 18/3/45; ass 8AF 28/3/45; retUS Bradley 31/5/45; Sth Plains 4/6/45; RFC Kingman 14/2/46.

44-83451 Del Hunter 7/3/45; Grenier 18/3/45; ass 8AF 27/2/45; retUS Bradley 1/6/45; Sth Plains 12/6/45; 613 BU Phillips 11/3/46.

44-83452 Del Hunter 7/3/45; Grenier 19/3/45; ass 8AF 27/3/45; retUS Bradley 8/6/45; Sth Plains 14/6/45; RFC Kingman 14/2/46.

44-83453 Del Hunter 7/3/45; Grenier 14/3/45; ass 8AF 27/3/45; retUS Bradley 5/7/45; Sth Plains 7/7/45; RFC Kingman 15/2/45.

44-83454 Del Hunter 8/3/45; Grenier 14/3/45; ass 8AF 27/3/45; RFC Kingman 28/2/46.

44-83455 Del Topeka 8/3/45; Grenier 13/3/45; ass 8AF 30/3/45; retUS Morrison 7/10/45; RFC Walnut Ridge 29/12/45.

44-83456 Del Topeka 8/3/45; Grenier 27/3/45; slated 8AF, tran 483BG Sterparone (Givia, It) 11/4/45; retUS Morrison 29/9/45; RFC Walnut Ridge 14/12/45.

44-83457 Del Topeka 8/3/45; Grenier 27/3/45; ass 8AF 30/3/45; retUS, RFC Walnut Ridge 12/12/45.

44-83458 Del Topeka 8/3/45; Grenier 27/3/45; ass 8AF 30/3/45; retUS Bradley 7/6/45; Sth Plains 9/6/45; RFC Kingman 21/2/46.

44-83459 Del Oklahoma City 9/3/45; slated 8AF, tran Hunter 21/4/45; Sth Plains 25/4/45; 248 BU Walker 18/6/45; 242 Gr Island 19/9/45; 4168 BU Sth Plains 30/9/46; re-ass 31/3/47; 4141 BU Pyote 25/6/47; Recl Comp 4/11/48.

44-83460 Del Tulsa 13/3/45; Sth Plains 28/4/45; 268 BU Peterson 21/6/45; 64 BU Andrews 3/10/45; 4100 BU Patterson 23/10/45; Recl Comp 2/3/46. Used as test a/c.

44-83461 –. Cloud Physics Project a/c Olmstead 1950; all armament removed and director's station installed at top turret position; nose revised with sensors and radar.

44-83462 Del Oklahoma City 9/3/45; Sth Plains 27/4/45; 268 BU Peterson 26/7/45; 427 BU Roswell 22/1/46; 4136 BU Tinker 17/6/46; 4168 BU Sth Plains 30/9/46; re-ass 31/3/47; 4141 BU Pyote 23/6/47; Recl Comp 18/4/50. (On display at Rio de Janiero 1985)

44-83463 Del Oklahoma City 9/3/45; slated 303BG, tran Sth Plains 27/4/45; 268 BU Peterson 22/6/45; 64 BU Andrews 1/3/46; NAMU Johnsville (for radar conversion) 5/46; 554 BU Memphis 6/8/46; 4149 BU

Above: B-17G-80-DL 44-83460 was used for experimental work at Patterson Field, Ohio, in 1946. It carried an aerofoil-shaped cover for the transverse scanner of an AN/APQ-7 Eagle radar and had 'bent' propeller tips. (W. T. Larkins)

Olmstead 7/8/46; re-ass 31/3/47; 4000 BU Wright 6/10/47; 4149 BU Olmstead 27/2/48; 4149 BU Griffiss 1/5/48; 4152 BU Clinton 26/7/48; 2750 AB Wright-Patterson 20/1/49 (to EB-17G); 2751 AB Griffiss 8/2/49; 5 AR McClelland 15/2/49; 2751 AB Griffiss 2/3/49; 3171 ERSq Griffiss 13/4/49; 373 RVWSq Kindley 7/9/49; 3171 ERSq Griffiss 8/12/49; tran US Navy as PB-1W {77137}, ass VC-11 San Diego 1/51; VW-1 Barbers Pt, Hawaii 2/51; retUS, NAS Norfolk, sal 10/7/56.

44-83464 Del Tulsa 13/3/45; Sth Plains 28/4/45; 268 BU Peterson 26/6/45; 484 BU Topeka 26/9/45; 482 BU Merced 15/10/45; 482 BU Castle 29/4/46; 556 BU Long Beach 18/6/46; 482 BU Castle 22/8/46; 4168 BU Sth Plains 30/9/46; re-ass 31/3/47; 4141 BU Pyote 30/6/47; Recl Comp 4/11/48.

44-83465 –.

44-83466 Del Oklahoma City 11/3/45; Sth Plains 24/4/45; 200 BU Peterson 29/10/45; sal Olmstead 15/2/46.

44-83467 Del Tulsa 13/3/45; Sth Plains 28/4/45; 200 BU Peterson 29/10/45; 326 BU McDill 31/12/46; 233 BU Fort Worth 16/1/47; re-ass 31/3/47; 39 BU Fort Worth 5/5/47; 4121 BU Kelly 7/5/47; 4136 BU Tinker 1/4/48; Recl Comp 23/3/49.

44-83468 Del Tulsa 13/3/45; Sth Plains 11/5/45; 248 BU Walker 18/6/45; 242 BU Gr Island 19/9/45; 246 BU Pratt 5/11/45; RFC Walnut Ridge 7/3/46.

44-83469 Del Hunter 11/3/45; Grenier 23/3/45; ass 8AF 28/3/45; retUS Bradley 9/6/45; Sth Plains 17/6/45; RFC Kingman 29/1/46.

44-83470 Del Hunter 12/3/45; Grenier 18/3/45; ass 8AF 30/3/45; retUS Bradley 6/6/45; 4104 BU Rome 28/6/45; Garden City 22/9/45; 4168 BU Sth Plains 18/1/46; 4136 BU Tinker 20/1/47; 4104 BU Rome 28/1/47; re-ass 31/3/47; 5 ASR Alaska 6/6/47; 10 RES Adak 18/1/48; 10 RES Davis 26/4/48 (Adak renamed Davis); ALA Elmendorf 23/6/48; 10 RES Davis 23/8/48; 10 RC Elmendorf 7/7/50; 10 RC Davis 13/9/50, Recl Comp 13/9/50.

44-83471 Del Hunter 12/3/45; Grenier 18/3/45; ass 8AF 30/3/45; retUS Bradley 17/6/45; Sth Plains 21/6/45; RFC Kingman 15/2/46.

44-83472 Del Hunter 12/3/45; Grenier 18/3/45; ass 8AF 27/3/45; retUS Bradley 7/5/45; Sth Plains 12/6/45; RFC Kingman 28/11/45.

44-83473 Del Hunter 12/3/45; Grenier 21/3/45; ass 731BS/452BG Deopham Green 23/3/45 (last a/c assgd to grp); retUS Bradley 3/7/45; Sth Plains 6/7/45; RFC Kingman 10/12/45.

44-83474 Del Hunter 13/3/45; Grenier 18/3/45; ass 8AF 27/3/45; retUS Bradley 8/6/45; 4132 BU Garden City 11/9/45; 4168 BU Sth Plains 20/1/46; 4134 BU Spokane 12/6/46; 594 BU Topeka 26/8/46; 4134 BU Spokane 30/9/46; re-ass Adak (11AF) 31/3/47; tran 1389 BU Bermuda 18/1/48; 522 AB Kindley 18/6/48; 1050 BU Kindley 18/8/48; 2152 RES Kindley 15/2/49; 6 RES Sq Kindley 25/4/49; 6 RES Sq Lagens 12/7/49; Recl Comp Olmstead 26/4/50.

44-83475 Del Hunter 13/3/45; Grenier 21/3/45; ass 8AF 30/3/45; retUS Bradley 25/5/45; Sth Plains 29/5/45; RFC Kingman 10/12/45.

44-83476 Del Hunter 13/3/45; Grenier 24/3/45; ass 8AF 27/3/45; retUS Bradley 9/6/45; Sth Plains 15/6/45; 613 BU Phillips 13/3/46.

44-83477 Del Hunter 13/3/45; slated 8AF, tran Wright Fd 15/3/45 (for Gen K.B.Wolfe); 4112 BU Olmstead 29/10/45; 648 BU Andrews 17/3/46; 4104 BU Rome 25/7/46; re-ass 31/3/47; 608 BU Andrews 4/11/47; 4112 BU Olmstead 15/3/48; 4 MSU Andrews 26/5/48; Recl Comp 3/9/48.(also used by Gen George Kenney 5AF in Pacific TO.)

44-83478 Del Hunter 13/3/45; Grenier 19/3/45; ass 8AF 25/3/45; retUS Bradley 31/5/45; Sth Plains 3/6/45; RFC Kingman 22/1/46.

44-83479 Del Hunter 14/3/45; Grenier 19/3/45; ass 8AF 27/3/45; retUS Bradley 23/5/45; Sth Plains 25/5/45; RFC Kingman 9/12/45.

44-83480 Del Hunter 14/3/45; Grenier 20/3/45; ass 8AF 30/3/45; retUS Bradley 1/6/45; Sth Plains 7/6/45; RFC Kingman 21/2/46.

44-83481 Del Hunter 14/3/45; Grenier 19/3/45; ass 8AF 27/3/45; retUS Bradley 5/6/45; Sth Plains 8/6/45; 4168 BU Sth Plains, sal 12/3/46.

44-83482 Del Hunter 14/3/45; Grenier 23/3/45; ass 8AF 1/4/45; retUS Bradley 9/7/45; Sth Plains 15/7/45; RFC Kingman 19/11/45.

44-83483 Del Hunter 14/3/45; Grenier 21/3/45; ass 303BG Molesworth 18/4/45; tran 457BG Glatton 22/5/45 (last a/c assgd to grp); retUS Bradley 7/6/45; Sth Plains 11/6/45; RFC Kingman 30/11/45.

44-83484 Del Topeka 12/3/45; Grenier 1/4/45; ass 8AF 5/4/45; retUS Bradley 22/5/45; Sth Plains 24/5/45; RFC Kingman 8/12/45.

44-83485 Del Hunter 14/3/45; Grenier 22/3/45; ass 8AF 1/4/45; retUS Independence 17/8/45; RFC Kingman 16/12/45.

44-83486 Del Hunter 15/3/45; Grenier 22/3/45; ass 8AF 30/3/45; retUS, 4000 BU Patterson 4/6/46; 4104 BU Rome 26/6/46; 554 BU Memphis 27/6/46; 4104 BU Rome 13/8/46; re-ass 31/3/47; 4104 BU Rome 1/6/47; 4112 BU Olmstead 27/10/47; BAL Columbus 27/11/47; 3203 MSU Gp Eglin 20/3/49; Recl Comp 1/3/50.

44-83487 Del Hunter 15/3/45; Grenier 21/3/45; ass 8AF 1/4/45; retUS Bradley 4/6/45; Sth Plains 9/6/45; RFC Kingman 27/2/46.

44-83488 Del Hunter 15/3/45; Grenier 20/3/45; ass 8AF 27/3/45; retUS Bradley 9/7/45; Sth Plains 10/7/45; RFC Kingman 7/11/45.

44-83489 Del Hunter 15/3/45; Grenier 22/3/45; ass 8AF 30/3/45; retUS Bradley 13/6/45; Sth Plains 18/6/45; RFC Kingman 22/1/46.

44-83490 Del Topeka 16/3/45; Grenier 1/4/45; ass 5/4//45; retUS Bradley 28/5/45; Sth Plains 30/5/45; RFC Kingman 11/2/46.

44-83491 Del Topeka 16/3/45; Grenier 1/4/45; ass 8AF 5/3/45; retUS Bradley 29/5/45; Sth Plains 31/5/45; RFC Kingman 7/2/46.

44-83492 Del Hunter 16/3/45 (via 5BG Dallas); Grenier 2/4/45; ass 8AF 5/4/45; retUS Bradley 25/5/45; Sth Plains 29/5/45; RFC Kingman 21/2/46.

44-83493 Del Hunter 16/3/45; Grenier 26/3/45; ass 8AF 1/4/45; retUS Bradley 13/6/45; Sth Plains 18/6/45; 613 BU Phillips, sal 13/3/46.

44-83494 Del Hunter 18/3/45; Grenier 22/3/45; ass 332BS/94BG [XM-H] Rougham 1/4/45 (last a/c assgd to grp); retUS 64 BU Andrews 20/9/45; re-ass 31/3/47; 4 MSU Andrews 21/8/47; 60 BU Andrews 4/11/47; 3902 AB Offutt 14/2/49; sal 7/4/49.

44-83495 Del Hunter 18/3/45; Grenier 23/3/45; ass 8AF 1/4/45; re-ass 30/4/47; 10 HBS Oberpfaffenhofen 18/1/48; Recl Comp 27/5/48.

44-83496 Del Hunter 18/3/45; Grenier 22/3/45; ass 8AF 30/3/45; retUS Bradley 6/6/45; Sth Plains 13/6/45; 613 BU Phillips, sal 13/3/46.

44-83497 Del Hunter 18/3/45; Grenier 26/3/45; ass 8AF 6/4/45; retUS Bradley 30/5/45; Sth Plains 31/5/45; 4134 BU Spokane 11/2/46; 65 BU Langley 1/4/46; 65 BU Andrews 26/9/46; 71 BU Robins 11/11/46; re-ass 31/3/47; 8 WEA Mitchell 7/5/47; 65 BU Robins 27/5/47; 4117 BU Robins 7/4/48; 2108 WEA Westover 14/12/48; 1600 MSU Westover 23/12/48; 2108 WEA Westover 4/3/47; AMC Olmstead 10/11/49; sal 19/5/50.

44-83498 Del Hunter 18/3/45; Grenier 29/3/45; ass 8AF 1/4/45; re-ass 30/4/47; 10 HBS Oberpfaffenhofen 18/1/48; Recl Comp 27/5/48.

44-83499 Del Topeka 19/3/45; slated 8AF, tran Sth Plains 15/4/45; Patterson 25/5/45; RFC Kingman 26/10/45.

44-83500 Del Topeka 19/3/45; Grenier 1/4/45; ass 8AF 5/4/45; retUS Bradley 25/5/45; Sth Plains 29/5/45; 4117 BU Robins 12/2/46; 311 RCN McDill 24/4/46 (6AF CZ); 91 RCN Rivra 28/4/46; 91 RCN McDill 26/5/46; Recl Comp 30/12/47.

44-83501 Del Topeka 19/3/45; slated 8AF, tran Sth Plains 18/4/45; Jackson 7/6/45; Patterson 10/6/45; RFC Kingman 25/10/46.

44-83502 –.

44-83503 Del Topeka 19/3/45; Grenier 25/3/45; ass 8AF 5/3/45; sal 9AF Germany 10/5/46.

44-83504 Del Hunter 20/3/45; Grenier 28/3/45; ass 8AF 6/4/45; retUS Bradley 29/5/45; Sth Plains 31/5/45; 4105 BU Davis Monthan 1/7/46; Recl Comp 3/8/46.

44-83505 Del Hunter 20/3/45; slated 8AF, tran Sth Plains 9/4/45; Patterson 4/6/45; 4117 BU Robins 14/11/45; 91 RCN Sq Buckley 11/2/46; 91 RCN McDill 6/5/46; 326 BU McDill 9/2/47; re-ass CZ 6AF 10/2/47; 91 RLP Sq Howard 18/1/48; 91 RLP Sq Waller (Trinidad) 20/2/48; 91 RLP Sq McGuire 9/2/49; 3902 AB Offutt 14/2/49; Recl Comp 21/4/50.

44-83506 Del Hunter 20/3/45; Grenier 27/3/45; ass 8AF 5/4/45; retUS Bradley 28/5/45; Sth Plains 30/5/45; 247 BU Smoky Hill 7/2/46; 4000 BU Patterson 14/5/46; 4000 BU Wright 19/5/46; 555 BU Love Fd 20/5/46; 4000 BU Wright 24/6/46; Recl Comp 22/7/46.

44-83507 Del Hunter 24/3/45; ass 8AF, tran Patterson 15/4/45; 4121 BU Kelly 20/2/46; 4117 BU Robins 25/2/46; 15 TSK Gp Clovis 25/3/46; 1503 BU Hamilton 16/6/46; 1504 BU Fairfield 20/8/46; 509 Comp Gp Roswell (Operation 'Crossroads') 21/8/46; 4104 BU Rome 4/11/46; re-ass 31/3/47; 4104 BU Rome 11/5/47; RRD Columbus 22/5/47; 1 EG Eglin 13/12/48; Recl Comp 17/5/49.

44-83508 Del Tulsa 21/3/45; 247 BU Salinas 25/5/45; 244 BU Harvard 10/10/45; 224 BU Sioux City 6/12/45; 233 BU Fort Worth 16/12/45; 613 BU Phillips, sal 5/5/46.

44-83509 –.

44-83510 Del Tulsa 21/3/45; Patterson 14/5/45; Grenier 29/6/45; 4200 BU Chicago Mun 25/11/45; 53 RCN Sq McChord 10/1/46; 503 BU Graves Pt 31/3/46; 53 RCN Sq Grenier 22/4/46; 53 RCN Sq Morrison 1/11/46; re-ass 30/4/47; 67 BU Robins 9/11/47; Recl Comp 15/10/48.

44-83511 –. To B-17H/SB-17; Japan 3ARS 1950; 57ARS Bovingdon, UK, 1955; Brookley, US, 7/5/76.

44-83512 Del Tulsa 22/3/45; Patterson 14/5/45; 53 RCN Sq McChord 10/1/46; 53 RCN Sq Buckley 11/3/46; 503 BU Grave Pt 31/3/46; 53 RCN Sq McChord 11/4/46; 62 BU McChord 30/5/46; 53 RCN Morrison 29/8/46; re-ass 31/3/47; 53 RV Morrison 2/6/47; 67 BU Robins 9/11/47; 4117 BU Robins 16/2/48; 535 BU Ft Peperel 9/7/48; 1225 AB Ft Peperel 1/10/48; AMC Olmstead 14/1/49; 1225 AB Ft Peperel 23/8/49; AMC Hill 6/6/50; 3700 IND Lackland 11/9/50; Recl Comp 26/9/50.

44-83513 Del Oklahoma City 22/3/45; Sth Plains 26/4/45; 268 BU Peterson 27/6/45; 200 BU Peterson 29/10/45; 4104 BU Rome 4/8/46; re-ass 31/3/47; 4104 BU Rome 8/6/47; 4112 BU Olmstead 2/9/47; 3203 MSU Eglin 18/1/49; Recl Comp 17/5/49.

44-83514 –. Once with Areo Unia, Chino, Cal (N9323Z); preserved in Boeing Museum as SENTIMENTAL JOURNEY.

44-83515 Del Oklahoma City 22/3/45; Sth Plains 29/4/45; 268 BU Peterson 19/7/45; 484 BU Topeka 20/8/45; WCW San Francisco 24/8/45; re-ass 31/4/47; 23 Ph RCN Momote 18/1/48; 5 RVP Gp Clark Fd 16/3/48; 358 SR Clark Fd 2/4/48; PAC Hickam 17/4/49; 5 RVP Gp Clark Fd 22/4/49; retUS 9 SRC Gp Fairfield 2/6/49; 9 MSU Fairfield 1/11/49; Recl Comp 5/5/50.

44-83516 Del Tulsa 22/3/45; El Paso 27/3/45; Patterson 17/5/45; Grenier 3/7/45; re-ass 30/4/47; Recl Comp 28/11/47.

44-83517 –.

44-83518 Del Hunter 23/3/45; Grenier 29/3/45; ass 8AF 4/4/45; retUS Bradley 22/5/45; Sth Plains 28/5/45; 242 Gr Island 7/2/46; 4168 BU Sth Plains 8/9/46; 4168 BU Sth Plains 30/9/46; re-ass 31/3/47; 4112 BU Olmstead 29/4/47; 2 RES Sq Kadena 18/1/48; 13 AR Jama 30/9/48; 2 RES Sq Kadena 21/10/48; Recl Comp 29/3/50.

44-83519 Del Hunter 23/3/45; Slated 8AF, tran Patterson 15/4/45; Sth Plains 6/11/45; Robins 15/11/45; 4121 BU Kelly 20/2/46; 4117 BU Robins 25/2/46; 15 TSK Gp Clovis 25/3/46; 1503 BU Hamilton 16/6/46; 1504 BU Fairfield 20/8/46; 509 Comp Gp Roswell (Operation 'Crossroads') 21/8/46; 1 EG Eglin 16/10/46; as TB-17G radio-controlled Drone at Stickell Fd, Eniwetok for A-Bomb testing; re-ass 31/3/47; 1 EG Eglin 1/6/48; AMC Brookley 16/9/48; Recl Comp 14/6/49.

44-83520 Del Hunter 23/3/45; Slated 8AF, tran Sth Plains 21/4/45; Patterson 25/5/45; 4117 BU Robins 5/2/46; 92 RCN Sq Buckley 11/4/46 as F-9; re-ass 30/4/47; 91 RLP Sq Howard, (CZ) 6AF 18/1/48; 4 SC France, CZ 1/7/48; 5621 MSU France 26/7/48; 91 RLP Sq Waller (Trinidad) 17/8/48; 91 RLP Sq McGuire 9/2/49; 91 AB Barksdale 30/9/49; 91 AB McGuire 11/10/49; Recl Comp 28/6/50.

44-83521 Del Hunter 23/3/45; Slated 8AF, tran Fairfield 14/4/45; Sth Plains 6/11/45; 4117 BU Robins 5/2/46; 91 RCN Sq Buckley 11/4/46 as F-9; re-ass 30/4/47; 91 RLP Sq Howard 18/1/48; 91 RLP Sq Waller 1/7/48; CAC Panama 9/12/48; 91 RLP Sq Waller 13/1/49; 91 RLP Sq McGuire 4/2/49; 91 RLP Sq Barksdale 30/9/49; AMC Brookley 7/10/49; Recl Comp 2/6/50.

44-83522 Del Topeka 26/3/45; Slated 8AF, tran Sth Plains 29/3/45; Patterson 25/5/45; 484 BU Topeka 21/9/45; Long Beach 3/10/45; sal Japan 13/6/47; Recl Comp 17/8/49.

44-83523 Del Topeka 26/3/45; Slated 8AF, tran Sth Plains 15/4/45; Patterson 25/5/45; RFC Kingman 3/11/45.

44-83524 Del Hunter 26/3/45; Slated 8AF, tran Fairfield 14/4/45; RFC Kingman 1/11/45.

44-83525 –. Last B-17 held at MASDC 1967; Civil 4250, at Tamiami, Fl 1989; Used in film *1000 Plane Raid*, as BALLS OF FIRE and SUZY Q.

44-83526 Del Hunter 26/3/45; Slated 8AF, tran El Paso 30/3/45; Patterson 17/4/45; RFC Kingman 31/10/45.

44-83527 Del Hunter 27/3/45; Slated 8AF, tran Dallas 3/4/45; Patterson 9/4/45; 4168 BU Sth Plains 7/11/45; re-ass 31/3/47; 4141 BU Pyote 23/7/47; 4117 BU Robins 19/3/48; 4112 BU Olmstead 30/6/48; 2 RES Sq Kadena 19/2/49; 4 RES Sq North Fd, Guam, 3/4/49; 2 RCU Sq North Fd, Guam, 31/5/49; 2 RCU Sq Anderson 30/8/50; 1503 TSP Haneda 27/11/50; Recl Comp 9/11/51.

44-83528 Del Hunter 27/3/45; Slated 8AF, tran Sth Plains 18/4/45; Patterson 25/5/45; 4121 BU Kelly 20/2/46; 4117 BU Robins 25/2/46; 15 TSK Gp Clovis 25/3/46; 556 BU Long Beach 9/6/46; 1503 BU Hamilton 16/6/46; 1504 BU Fairfield 20/8/46; 509 Comp Gp Roswell (Operation 'Crossroads') 21/8/46; 4104 BU Rome 16/10/46; AMC Columbus 27/11/46; 4000 BU Wright 22/5/47; 1 EG Eglin 28/5/47; 4168 BU Sth Plains 18/4/48; 609 BU Eglin 17/10/48; Recl Comp 30/1/49.

44-83529 Del Hunter 27/3/45; Slated 8AF, tran Sth Plains 24/4/45; Patterson 25/5/45; RFC Kingman 26/10/45.

44-83530 Del Hunter 27/3/45; Slated 8AF, tran Sth Plains, Patterson 25/5/45; RFC Kingman 27/10/45.

44-83531 Del Hunter 28/3/45; Slated 8AF, tran Sth Plains 23/4/45; Patterson 25/5/45; RFC Kingman 26/10/45.

44-83532 –.

44-83533 –.

44-83534 Del Hunter 29/3/45; Slated 15AF, tran Sth Plains 24/4/45; Patterson 25/5/45; 594 BU Topeka 26/8/46; 4112 BU Olmstead 22/9/46; 4168 BU Sth Plains 3/10/46; re-ass 31/3/47; AMC Olmstead 14/9/48; Recl Comp 10/11/49.

44-83535 Del Topeka 29/3/45; Slated 15AF, tran Sth Plains 15/4/45; Patterson 25/5/45; 129 BU Columbia for special weapon training 25/9/45; 139 BU Shaw 25/11/45; 2528 BU Midland 20/12/45; 2622 BU Mather 20/3/46; 556 BU Long Beach 31/5/46; 613 BU Phillips 3/6/46.

44-83536 –. As VB-17G used by Maj Gen Glenn O.Barcus, CO of 5AF Fighter Command in Korea.

44-83537 –.

44-83538 Del Hunter 30/3/45; Slated 15AF, tran Sth Plains 24/4/45; Patterson 25/5/45; ass US Navy, Johnsville 4/6/45 as PB-1W {34114}; then Civil 7726B; Peru {OB-SAC 576}.

44-83539 –. As CB-17 in Okinawa 1950, with H2X nose.

44-83540 Del Topeka 30/3/45; Slated 15AF, tran Sth Plains 15/4/45; Patterson 25/5/45; Long Beach 23/9/45; 4100 BU Patterson 19/9/46; sal Japan 18/4/47.

44-83541 Del Hunter 30/3/45; Slated 15AF, tran Sth Plains 20/4/45; Patterson 25/5/45; RFC Kingman 21/11/45.

44-83542 –. US Civil N9324Z; cr? 7/12/71; held dismantled Ocatillo, Cal 1988.

44-83543 Del Topeka 31/3/45; Slated 15AF, tran Sth Plains 15/4/45; Patterson 25/5/45; RFC Kingman 4/11/45.

44-83544 Del Topeka 31/3/45; Slated 15AF, tran Sth Plains 15/4/45; Patterson 25/5/45; Bolling 3/8/45; 1 BAS Bolling 13/6/46 prepared as CB-17 for Gen Sutherland in Manila, Pl; 4104 BU Rome 1/8/46; Recl Comp 24/7/47.

44-83545 Del Topeka 31/3/45; Slated 15AF, tran Sth Plains 15/4/45; Patterson 25/5/45; RFC Kingman 27/10/45.

44-83546 –. Ass Maj Gen Glenn O. Barcus, CO Fighter Command 5AF in Korea; Civil N3703G, first with TBM Inc as Tanker 78E with all-red tailpalne in 1974, Porterville. Cal; used as MEMPHIS BELLE in 1989 film. SQUARE DEAL.

44-83547 –. Ass 20AF HQ in Guam, used by Gen Walter Krueger; called BILLY.

44-83548 Del Topeka 2/4/45; Slated 15AF, tran Patterson 7/4/45; RFC Kingman 2/11/45.

44-83549 –.

44-83550 Del Hunter 2/4/45; Slated 15AF, tran Sth Plains 24/4/45; Patterson 25/5/45; 4168 BU Sth Plains 30/6/46; 594 BU Topeka 26/8/46; 4112 BU Olmstead 3/9/46 as VB-17G; 4136 BU Tinker 13/11/46; 4134 BU Spokane 25/12/46; re-ass 31/3/47; 4135 BU Hill Fd 24/8/47; Recl Comp 29/12/49.

44-83551 Del Topeka 2/4/45; Slated 15AF, tran Sth Plains 15/4/45; Patterson 25/5/45; RFC Kingman 26/10/45.

44-83552 –.

44-83553 Del Topeka 3/4/45; Slated 15AF, tran Sth Plains 20/4/45; Patterson 25/5/45; 4132 BU Garden City 1/10/45; San Antonio 5/2/46; 4121 BU Kelly 14/2/46; 15 TSK Gp Clovis 25/3/46; 556 BU Long Beach 9/6/46; 1503 BU Hamilton 16/6/46; ass 509 Comp Gp, Roswell (Operation 'Crossroads') 21/8/46; 1 EG Eglin 28/2/47; 605 BA Eglin 4/3/48; 4141 BU Pyote 29/3/48; Recl Comp 18/4/50.

44-83554 –.

44-83555 –. As QB-17N Holloman, NM 16/11/56;

44-83556 –.

44-83557 Del Topeka 3/4/45; Slated 15AF, tran Sth

Above: B-17G-85-DL 44-83514 has the look of a Fortress heading for battle, but in fact this is a display aircraft operated by the Arizona Wing of the Confederate Air Force in the 1980s. The clues to its peacetime status are the red navigation light on the upper fuselage and the distinctive Instrument Landing System antenna forward of the flight deck windshield. (Richard Bagg)

Plains 15/4/45; Patterson 25/5/45; 1 BU Bolling 4/8/45; Hickam Fd 30/12/45; sal 19/9/46.
44-83558 Del Topeka 3/4/45; Slated 15AF, tran Patterson 7/4/45; Sth Plains 6/11/45; 4168 BU Sth Plains 30/4/46; 594 BU Topeka 20/8/46; 4112 BU Olmstead 3/9/46; 4104 BU Rome 16/10/46; re-ass 31/3/47; 4104 BU Rome 8/6/47; 4152 BU Clinton 18/1/48; 2760 AB Clinton 7/9/49; Recl Comp 1/5/50.
44-83559 Del Hunter 4/4/45; Topeka 6/4/45; 4100 BU Patterson 8/4/45; 4168 BU Sth Plains 11/11/45; 4141 BU Pyote 16/7/46; 2753 AS Sq Pyote 17/2/50; AMC Olmstead 7/3/50 modify to DB-17G; 3200 Drone Sq Eglin 22/6/50; 3200 Drone Sq 58 BW Stickell Fd, Eniwetok 28/2/51; 3200 Drone Sq Eglin 31/5/51; 3205 Drone Gp Holloman 13/10/52; Eglin 16/10/52; 3310 TTW Scott 8/7/53; 3205 Drone Gp Eglin 26/7/53; 3205 Drone Gp Holloman 10/9/53; Recl Comp 5/58 as museum piece, Patrick; Offutt 5/60 still there in 1988; re-painted as KING BEE.
44-83560 –. As DB-17B 3235 Drone Sq 58 BW Stickell Fd, Enitewok.
44-83561 –.
44-83562 –.
44-83563 Del Hunter 7/4/45; Slated 447BG, tran Patterson and modified to CB-17G in Phillipines; used by Gen Jimmy Doolittle at Kadena, Okinawa 27/7/45 as BOOPS; also carried Gen Dwight D.Eisenhower; Civil N9563Z with AAC 9/5/60 Ryan Fd; new cargo doors fitted at Brownsville; now a Warbird, took part in films *The War Lover* and *Tora! Tora! Tora!*; repainted in 447BG configuration as FUDDY DUDDY.
44-83564 –.
44-83565 –.
44-83566 –.
44-83567 Del Tulsa 5/4/45; Patterson 17/5/45; 53 RCN Sq McChord 10/1/46; 53 RCN Sq Buckley 11/3/45; 503 BU Graves Pt 31/3/46; 53 RCN Sq McChord 11/4/46; 53 RCN Sq Morrison 12/5/46; 53 RCN Sq Grenier 3/10/46; re-ass 30/4/47; 67 BA Robins 9/11/47; 4117 BU Robins 17/12/47; 9 RES Biggs Fd 20/5/48; 4121 BU Kelly 4/8/48; 2151 RES Biggs 7/9/48; 2151 RES Lowry 25/10/48; Recl Comp 1/5/50.
44-83568 Del Tulsa 3/4/45; Patterson 26/5/45; 53 RCN Sq Grenier 25/8/45; Argentia, Nfld 1/12/45; re-ass 30/4/47; 1100 BU Morrison 8/10/47; Recl Comp 9/4/48.
44-83569 Del Tulsa 5/4/45; Patterson 26/5/45; 59 RCN McChord 3//6/46; 53 RCN Grenier 13/8/46; 59 RCN Castle 10/9/46; 53 RCN Morrison 8/12/46; 67 BU Robins 9/11/47; 1377 BU Westover 9/11/48; Recl Comp 25/4/49.
44-83570 Del Tulsa 5/4/45; Patterson 6/6/45; 53 RCN Sq Grenier 31/7/45; Argentia, Nfld 8/1/46; re-ass 30/4/47; 373 RV Kindley 18/1/48; 522 AB Kindley 14/9/48; 1604 AB Kindley 18/10/48; MTC Pope 8/11/48; 5 RCN Sq Maxwell 25/4/49; Recl Comp 8/12/49.
44-83571 Del Tulsa 6/4/45; Patterson 6/6/45; 53 RCN Sq Grenier 20/8/45; 53 RCN Sq McChord 10/1/46; 53 RCN Sq Buckley 11/3/46; 503 BU Graves Pt 31/3/46; 53 RCN Sq Morrison 12/5/46; 59 RCN Castle 11/8/46; 53 RCN Sq Morrison 1/12/46; re-ass 31/3/47; 4127 BU McClelland 20/4/47; 373 RV Kindley 18/1/48; AMC Olmstead 15/2/49; 375 RV Kindley 20/2/49; 1605 AB Lagens 23/2/49; Recl Comp 23/6/50.
44-83572 Del Tulsa 6/4/45; Patterson 6/6/45; 53 RCN Sq Grenier 25/7/45; ass Guam 11/3/46; re-ass 30/4/47; 373 RV Kindley 18/1/48; 523 AB Lagens 23/7/48; 1605 AB Lagens 18/12/48; 4 MSU Gp Andrews 2/4/49; 1600 MSU Gp Westover 30/8/49; AMC Olmstead 19/10/49; Recl Comp 13/6/50. PRINCESS PAT.
44-83573 Del Tulsa 6/4/45; Cheyenne 5/5/45; Hunter 23/5/45; Grenier 13/6/45; 1377 BU Grenier 28/1/46; 613 BU Phillips 15/7/46; 1377 BU Westover 30/8/46.
44-83574 Del Tulsa 6/4/45; Cheyenne 4/5/45; Hunter 22/5/45; Casablanca, Mor 3/6/45; re-ass 30/4/47; 61 TC Rheine-Main 18/1/48; 61 MSU Gp Rheine-Main 19/12/49; Recl Comp 26/4/50.
44-83575 - Ass 1 RS Puerto Rico (6AF) 1951; Civil N93012, at Stow, Mass, as MISS YUCCA; damaged at Beaver Co, PA 1987; re-painted as NINE-O-NINE.
44-83576 Del Tulsa 7/4/45; Cheyenne 4/5/45; Hunter 22/5/45; Casablanca, Mor 3/6/45; retUS 4112 BU Olmstead 7/7/47; 2621 BU Barksdale 14/9/47; 4117 BU Robins 27/3/48; Recl Comp 13/4/49.
44-83577 Del Tulsa 7/4/45; Cheyenne 5/5/45; Hunter 29/5/45; Grenier 17/6/45; sal 24/8/45.
44-83578 Del Cheyenne 13/4/45; Keesler 15/5/45; 3704 BU Keesler 21/5/45; 1377 BU Westover 21/5/46; re-ass 31/3/47; 1389 BU Bermuda 18/1/48; 522 AB Kindley 1/6/48; 1050 AB Kindley 18/8/48; 2152 RES Kindley 7/9/48; 2152 RES Lagens 28/3/49; AMC Olmstead 30/7/49; 3205 MSU Gp Eglin 17/9/49; Recl Comp 21/9/49.
44-83579 –. As TB-17G Chanute 1954.
44-83580 Del Tulsa 7/4/45; Cheyenne 5/5/45; Hunter 16/5/45; Natal, Brazil 26/5/45; Morrison 9/6/45; W/O 4/11/46.
44-83581 Del Cheyenne 12/4/45; Hunter 16/5/45; San Francisco 4/6/45; ass Manila, Pl. 31/12/45; Recl Comp 11/9/45.
44-83582 Del Cheyenne 12/4/45; Hunter 16/5/45; San Francisco 9/6/45; re-ass 30/4/47; 23 Ph RC Momote 1/1/48; 85 RVP RC Clark Fd 1/4/48; 5 RVP Gp Clark Fd 1/12/49; PAL Hickam 17/4/49; retUS 9 SRC Fairfield 27/9/49; AMC Hill Fd 21/10/49; Recl Comp 19/5/49.
44-83583 Del Tulsa 9/4/45; Cheyenne 5/5/45; Hunter 19/5/45; Natal, Brazil 29/5/45; Morrison 9/6/45; sal 29/12/45.
44-83584 Del Cheyenne 12/4/45; Hunter 16/5/45; San Francisco 31/5/45; re-ass 30/4/47; 23 Ph RC Momote 1/1/48; 5 RVP Gp Clark Fd 26/3/48; PAC Hickam 17/4/49; retUS 9 SRC Fairfield 27/9/49; AMC Hill Fd 7/11/49; Recl Comp 19/5/50.
44-83585 –. Civil N66573, as borate bomber, cr Cayuse Saddle, Montana 1979. BATMOBILE.
44-83586 Del Tulsa 10/4/45; Cheyenne 5/5/45; Hunter 23/5/45; San Francisco 15/6/45; re-ass 30/4/47; 358 SR Momote 1/1/48; 358 SR Clark Fd 11/1/48; 358 SR Momote 26/1/48; 5 RVP Gp Clark Fd 1/4/48; retUS 9 SRC Gp Fairfield 2/6/49; AMC Hill Fd 12/10/49; Recl Comp 19/5/50.
44-83587 –. Ass Cloud Physics Project Olmstead 1950; Civil N7046C; NANCY.
44-83588 Del Tulsa 10/4/45; Patterson 15/4/45; Sth Plains 6/11/45; 4121 BU Kelly 20/2/46; 15 TSK Gp Clovis 25/3/46; 556 BU Long Beach 9/6/46; 1503 BU Hamilton 16/6/46; 1 EG Eglin 15/8/46; 509 Comp Gp Roswell 21/8/46 Operation 'Crossroads'; re-ass 31/3/47; 1 EG Eglin 8/9/47; 605 BU Eglin 4/3/48; 4141 BU Pyote 17/3/48; Recl Comp 18/4/50.
44-83589 –.
44-83590 –.
44-83591 –.
44-83592 Del Tulsa 11/4/45; 4100 BU Patterson 21/9/45; 4168 BU Sth Plains 12/11/45; re-ass 31/3/47; 4141 BU Pyote 21/7/47; 4112 BU Olmstead 29/12/47; 605 BU Eglin 7/1/48; AMC Brookley 12/3/49; 3203 MSU Eglin 13/4/49; 1 EG Eglin 20/5/49; Recl Comp 17/10/49. (Used in crack-up scene in film *12 O'Clock High*.)
44-83593 Del Tulsa 11/4/45; Patterson 19/4/45; RFC Kingman 27/10/45.
44-83594 Del Tulsa 12/4/45; Patterson 19/4/45; RFC Kingman 3/11/45.
44-83595 –.
44-83596 –. Used as radar & electronics test a/c.
44-83597 –.
44-83598 Del Tulsa 12/4/45; Patterson 19/4/45; RFC Kingman 29/10/45.
44-83599 Del Tulsa 12/4/45; Patterson 17/4/45; RFC Kingman 6/11/45.
44-83600 –. Civil N7044C.
44-83601 Del Tulsa 12/4/45; Patterson 20/4/45; RFC Kingman 29/10/45.
44-83602 –.
44-83603 –. As TB-17P 58 BW Eniwetok, for atom bomb tests Bikini Atoll 1946, with yellow tailplane and black waist bands.
44-83604 –.
44-83605 –.
44-83606 Del Tulsa 13/4/45; Slated 8AF, tran Sth Plains 6/11/45; 4100 BU Patterson 20/4/46; re-ass 31/3/47; 4168 BU Sth Plains 23/6/47; 4141 BU Pyote 24/6/47; 4112 BU Olmstead 23/10/47; 1 EGM Eglin 17/1/48; HQ 11 MSU Bolling 20/9/48; 1 EGM Eglin 16/10/48; HQ 11 MSU Bolling 15/1/49.
44-83607 Del Tulsa 14/4/45; Patterson 31/4/45; RFC Kingman 14/11/45.
44-83608 Del Tulsa 14/4/45; Patterson 22/4/45; RFC Kingman 27/10/45.
44-83609 Del Patterson 16/4/45; ass 303BG Molesworth 24/5/45; retUS 4100 BU Patterson 12/9/45; RFC Altus 7/11/45.
44-83610 Del Patterson 16/4/45; Slated 8AF, tran Palm Springs 18/4/45; Sth Plains 6/11/45; 4100 BU Patterson 21/4/46; 4168 BU Sth Plains 30/4/46; re-ass 31/3/47; 4141 BU Pyote 29/6/47; 4112 BU Olmstead 20/10/47; 605 BU Eglin 6/1/48; 1 EGM Eglin 8/1/48; 3203 MSU Gp Eglin 24/11/48; AMC Brookley 1/12/48; 3203 MSU Gp Eglin 11/4/49; 550 GM Eglin 21/7/49; 2750 AB Gp Wright Fd 17/10/49; 3203 MSU Gp Eglin 15/5/50; Recl Comp 24/5/50.
44-83611 Del Patterson 16/4/45; Slated 8AF, tran El Paso 18/4/45; Patterson 20/4/45; RFC Kingman 2/11/45.
44-83612 Del Patterson 16/4/45; Slated 8AF, tran Love Fd 19/4/45; Sth Plains 6/11/45; 4100 BU Patterson 23/4/46; 4168 BU Sth Plains 30/4/46; re-ass 31/3/47; 4141 BU Pyote 22/4/47; 4112 BU Olmstead 25/12/47; 605 BU Eglin 22/1/48; 1 EGM Eglin 27/1/48; 3200 Drone Sq Eglin 15/6/50; 1100 AB Bolling 24/8/50; AMC Hill Fd 14/9/50; Recl Comp 26/2/51.
44-83613 –.
44-83614 Del Patterson 16/4/45; Slated 8AF, tran Tulsa 22/4/45; Patterson 23/4/45; RFC Kingman 31/10/45.
44-83615 Del Patterson 17/4/45; Slated 8AF, tran Love Fd 20/4/45; Patterson 21/4/45; RFC Kingman 1/11/45.
44-83616 –.
44-83617 –.
44-83618 Del Patterson 17/4/45; Slated 8AF, tran Love Fd 22/4/45; Patterson 27/4/45; RFC Kingman 29/10/45.
44-83619 Del Patterson 14/4/45; Slated 8AF, tran RFC Kingman 27/10/45.
44-83620 Del Patterson 17/4/45; Slated 8AF, tran RFC Kingman 3/11/45.
44-83621 –.
44-83622 Del Patterson 18/4/45; Sth Plains 6/11/45;

4100 BU Patterson 28/4/46; 4168 BU Sth Plains 30/4/46; re-ass 31/3/47; 4112 BU Olmstead 23/10/47; 4141 BU Pyote 27/7/47; 1 EGM Eglin 4/3/48; 550 GM Eglin 6/12/49; 3200 Drone Sq Eglin 15/6/50; Recl Comp 4/10/50.
44-83623 Del Patterson 15/4/45; Kirtland 21/4/45; 4100 BU Patterson 22/4/45; RFC Kingman 2/11/45.
44-83624 –. Ass 532BS/381BG [VE-F] Ridgewell 4/45 (last a/c assgd grp); 3205 Drone Sq in olive drab/grey; now Dayton Museum as PICADILLY LILY.
44-83625 Del Patterson 23/4/45; Slated 8AF, tran Love Fd 25/4/45; 4100 BU Patterson 26/4/45; RFC Kingman 31/10/45.
44-83626 Del Patterson 19/4/45; Sth Plains 6/11/45; 4117 BU Robins 5/2/46 as F-9C with chin and bonb-bay cameras; 16 Ph Sq Buckley 28/2/46; 16 Ph Sq McDill 9/5/46; 4104 BU Rome 9/10/46; 16 Ph Sq McDill 18/12/46; re-ass 31/3/47; 343 RV McDill 1/5/47; 343 SR Topeka 28/7/47; 55 MSU Gp Topeka 14/1/49; 55 AB Gp Topeka 14/2/49; AMC Hill Fd 12/10/49; Recl Comp 19/5/50.
44-83627 –.
44-83628 Del Patterson 19/4/45; Palm Springs 22/4/45; 4100 BU Patterson 25/4/45; RFC Kingman 30/10/45.
44-83629 Del Patterson 20/4/45; Slated 8AF, tran Coolidge 22/4/45; 129 BU Columbia 26/9/45 for special weapon training; 139 BU Shaw 25/11/45; 252 BU Midland 31/1/46; 2622 BU Mather 20/3/46; 3505 BU Scott 16/5/46; 556 BU Long Beach 31/5/46; 613 BU Phillips 12/6/46; 554 BU Memphis 13/6/46; 556 BU Long Beach 28/8/46.
44-83630 Del Patterson 20/4/45; Slated 8AF, tran Oklahoma City 26/4/45; RFC Kingman 27/10/45.
44-83631 Del Patterson 20/4/45; Slated 8AF, tran Oklahoma City 22/4/45; 4100 BU Patterson 24/4/45; RFC Kingman 29/10/45.
44-83632 Del Patterson 20/4/45; Slated 8AF, tran 4100 BU Patterson 25/4/45; RFC Kingman 2/11/45.
44-83633 Del Patterson 20/4/45; Slated 8AF, tran Albuquerque 24/4/45; 4100 BU Patterson 26/4/45; RFC Kingman 1/11/45.
44-83634 –. CB-17 US Navy 1946.
44-83635 Del Patterson 21/4/45; Slated 8AF, tran Sth Plains 6/11/45; 4100 BU Patterson 27/4/46; 4168 BU Sth Plains 30/9/46; re-ass 31/3/47; 4141 BU Pyote 17/6/47; 4000 BU Patterson 8/7/47; 4112 BU Olmstead 30/10/47; 605 BU Eglin 7/1/48; 1 EGM Eglin 18/1/48; 338 OTT Keesler 15/10/48; 2750 AB Wright 20/1/49; Recl Comp 5/4/50.
44-83636 –.
44-83637 –.
44-83638 Del Patterson 24/4/45; Slated 8AF, tran Palm Springs 27/4/45; Patterson 29/4/45; RFC Kingman 27/10/45.
44-83639 –.
44-83640 Del Patterson 23/4/45; Slated 8AF, tran RFC Kingman 31/10/45.
44-83641 Del Patterson 23/4/45; Slated 8AF, tran Tulsa 25/4/45; Sth Plains 6/11/45; 4100 BU Patterson 27/4/45; 4168 BU Sth Plains 30/9/46; re-ass 31/3/47; 4141 BU Pyote 15/6/47; ass 1 EGM Gp Eglin Project Sandstone; Kwajalein launching JB-2s, missiles similar to German V-1 (Doodlebug); 4112 BU Olmstead 17/11/47; 605 BU Eglin 15/2/49; 550 GM Sq Eglin 21/7/49; 3203 MSU Gp Eglin 28/10/49; 3200 Drone Sq Eglin 25/8/50; AMC Hill 13/9/50; Recl Comp 4/12/50. BABY 9.
44-83642 –.
44-83643 Del Patterson 25/4/45; Albuquerque 29/4/45; 4100 BU Patterson 30/4/45; RFC Kingman 31/10/45.
44-83644 –.
44-83645 Del Patterson 24/4/45; Slated 8AF, tran 4168 BU Sth Plains 6/11/45; re-ass 31/3/47; 4141 BU Pyote 25/6/47; 4112 BU Olmstead 23/10/47; 1 EGM Eglin 17/1/48; 3203 MSU Gp Eglin 18/10/48.
44-83646 Del Patterson 24/4/45; Slated 8AF, tran Sth Plains 6/11/45; 4121 BU Kelly 11/2/46; 4117 BU Robins 14/2/46; 4136 BU Tinker 7/4/46; 15 TSK Gp Clovis 11/4/47; 556 BU Long Beach 9/6/46; 1503 BU Hamilton 16/6/46; 509 Comp Gp Roswell 18/8/46 Operation 'Crossroads'; 1 EGM Eglin 28/2/47; re-ass 31/3/47; 1 EGM Eglin 8/9/47; 4112 BU Olmstead 11/1/48; 605 BU Eglin 8/3/48; 1 EGM Eglin 1/6/48; 3203 MSU Gp Eglin 24/11/48; AMC Brookley 8/4/49; Recl Comp 19/10/50.
44-83647 Del Patterson 25/4/45; Kirtland 28/4/45; 4100 BU Patterson 30/4/45; RFC Kingman 3/11/45.
44-83648 –.
44-83649 –.
44-83650 Del Patterson 27/4/45; RFC Kingman 27/10/45.
44-83651 Del Patterson 27/4/45; RFC Kingman 28/10/45.
44-83652 –.
44-83653 Del Cheyenne 27/4/45; Hunter 21/5/45; Mather 1/6/45; WCW San Francisco 12/6/45; re-ass 30/3/47; 338 RV Momote 1/1/48; 5 RVP Clark Fd 1/4/48; 567 BA Clark Fd 15/7/48; 1 RNS Clark Fd 18/8/48; 5 RVP Clark Fd 1/12/48; retUS 9 SRC Gp Fairfield 27/9/49; Recl Comp 18/1/50.
44-83654 –.
44-83655 Del Sth Plains 27/4/45; Patterson 25/5/45; 484 BU Topeka 20/9/45; Long Beach 2/10/45; Guam 3/10/45; cr Tacloban, Leyte, PI 22/4/46; sal 23/12/46; re-ass Guam 30/4/47; Recl Comp 29/4/48.
44-83656 –.
44-83657 –.
44-83658 –.
44-83659 –.
44-83660 Del Sth Plains 28/4/45; Patterson 25/5/45; 4132 BU Garden City 30/4/46; re-ass 31/3/47; 4141 BU Pyote 16/10/47; 4185 BU Independence 19/10/47; 4112 BU Olmstead 17/11/47; 605 BU Eglin 12/1/48; 1 EGM Gp Eglin 1/6/48; AMC Brookley 8/4/49; 3203 MSU Gp Eglin 11/4/49; 1 EGM Gp Eglin 5/7/49; AMC Brookley 30/8/49; Recl Comp 19/10/50.
44-83661 –. 19BG Commander's hack; 6319 ABW Anderson Fd, Guam 20AF as mobile office; (all turrets removed and celestial astrodome in top turret position. Seats for eight people installed, with galley in bomb bay and toilet near tail wheeel).
44-83662 Del Sth Plains 30/4/45; Patterson 25/5/45; 4132 BU Garden City 30/4/46; re-ass 31/3/47; 4141 BU Pyote 16/10/47; 4185 BU Independence 19/10/47; 4112 BU Olmstead 1/1/48; 1 EGM Gp Eglin 8/3/48; AMC Brookley 1/12/49; Recl Comp 19/10/50.
44-83663 –. 590 Comp Gp Roswell Operation 'Crossroads' 15/4/46; Brazilian AF Serial 5400; US Civil N47780; Chino 1975; Topeka 1980, then St Petersburg and painted O D; in 1983 flown in C-5 to Hill AFB Museum, on display as SHORT BIER.
44-83664 Del Sth Plains 30/4/45; Patterson 25/5/45; 4132 BU Garden City 7/3/46; re-ass 31/3/47; 4185 BU Independence 23/10/47; 4141 BU Pyote 19/11/47; 4112 BU Olmstead 1/1/48; 605 BU Eglin 8/3/48; 1 EGM Gp Eglin 10/3/48; Recl Comp 18/5/48.
44-83665 –.
44-83666 –.
44-83667 Del Sth Plains 1/5/45; Patterson 25/5/45; RFC Kingman 25/10/45.
44-83668 Del Sth Plains 1/5/45; Patterson 25/5/45; RFC Kingman 27/10/45.
44-83669 –. QB-17N Drone at Patrick Fd, 1954 in day-glo orange and three black diagonal stripes.
44-83670 Del Sth Plains 1/5/45; Patterson 25/5/45; RFC Kingman 26/10/45.
44-83671 –. As CB-17 US Navy 1946.
44-83672 Del Sth Plains 1/5/45; Patterson 25/5/45; RFC Kingman 27/10/45.
44-83673 Del Sth Plains 3/5/45; Patterson 25/5/45; RFC Kingman 27/10/45.
44-83674 –.
44-83675 Del Sth Plains 2/5/45; Patterson 25/5/45; Rome 17/7/45; 484 BU Topeka 5/8/45; 4000 BU Patterson 29/9/47; 807 BA Haneda, Japan 1/1/48; AMC Hill Fd 1/9/49; Recl Comp 20/10/50.
44-83676 Del Sth Plains 2/5/45; Patterson 25/5/45; RFC Kingman 27/10/45.
44-83677 Del Sth Plains 3/5/45; Patterson 25/5/45; RFC Kingman 26/10/45.
44-83678 Del Sth Plains 3/5/45; Patterson 25/5/45; 4132 BU Garden City 30/4/46; 4185 BU Independence 21/10/46; re-ass 31/3/47; 4141 BU Pyote 23/10/47; 4112 BU Olmstead 17/11/47; 605 BU Eglin 12/1/48; 1 EGM Gp Eglin 13/1/48; 3203 MSU Gp Eglin 19/7/48; Recl Comp 30/11/48.
44-83679 –.
44-83680 –.
44-83681 Del Sth Plains 4/5/45; Patterson 25/5/45; RFC Kingman 17/11/45.
44-83682 Del Sth Plains 4/5/45; Patterson 25/5/45; RFC Kingman 26/10/45.
44-83683 –.
44-83684 –. Ass 447BG Rattlesden 4/45 as PICCADILLY LILLY (last a/c assgd grp), tran to DB-17P Director for Drones at Air Defense Weapons Centre Eglin till 1960; Civil N3713G at Chino, Cal 1984; Used in film *12 O'Clock High*.
44-83685 Del Sth Plains 4/5/45; Patterson 11/5/45; RFC Kingman 28/10/45.
44-83686 Del Sth Plains 4/5/45; Patterson 9/5/45; WCW San Francisco 23/7/45; ass Okinawa 2/8/45; missing 25/7/46.
44-83687 –.
44-83688 Del Sth Plains 5/5/45; Patterson 10/5/45; RFC Kingman 4/11/45.
44-83689 –.
44-83690 –. At Grissom Fd, Ind 1988, painted as 305BG MISS LIBERTY BELLE.
44-83691 Del Sth Plains 5/5/45; Patterson 12/5/45; RFC Kingman 21/1/46.
44-83692 –.
44-83693 Del Sth Plains 7/5/45; Patterson 12/5/45; RFC Kingman 2/11/45.
44-83694 –.
44-83695 –.
44-83696 Del Sth Plains 8/5/45; Patterson 13/5/45; RFC Kingman 2/11/45.
44-83697 –.
44-83698 Del Sth Plains 8/5/45; Patterson 12/5/45; RFC Kingman 31/10/45.
44-83699 –.
44-83700 - Converted to B-17H.
44-83701 –. SB-17G; 2704 AFLC Davis Monthan 12/4/56.
44-83702 Del Cheyenne 7/5/45; Hunter 21/5/45; Natal, Brazil 29/5/45 (6AF); re-ass 30/4/47; Puerto Rico 6/11/47; Recl Comp 17/2/48.
44-83703 Del Cheyenne 9/5/45; Hunter 6/6/45; Grenier 22/6/45; re-ass 30/4/47; 1391 BU Azores 1/1/48; 523 AB Lagens 1/6/48; 1050 ARS Lagens

Above: B-17G-90-DL 44-83669 became a QB-17N radio-controlled target aircraft. Photographed here at Patrick AFB, Florida, in July 1954, it was painted dayglo yellow overall with black banding to be more easily seen by the crew of a directing aircraft. (G. S. Williams)

27/8/48; 2152 RES Lagens 2/9/48; 6 RES Sq Lagens 25/4/49; 1050 MSU Gp Amchitka 9/5/49; 6 RES Sq Lagens 1/6/49; AMC Olmstead 18/6/49; Recl Comp 4/11/49.

44-83704 –.

44-83705 –.

44-83706 –. ASR a/c with red tailplane and wing panels.

44-83707 Del Cheyenne 10/5/45; Hunter 22/5/45; Presque Is 9/6/45; 4136 BU Tinker 18/8/45; re-ass 30/4/47; ASR a/c Mediterranean; 61 TC Rheine Main 1/1/48; Recl Comp 9/6/48. PATTY ANN.

44-83708 Del Cheyenne 10/5/45; Hunter 29/5/45; WCW San Francisco 14/6/45; re-ass 30/4/47; 24 HBS Harmon 1/1/48; 64/0 AB Harmon 16/4/49; 4 RES Sq North Fd 12/7/49; 2 RCU Sq Anderson (Guam) 14/4/50; Recl Comp 12/10/50.

44-83709 Del Cheyenne 10/5/45; Hunter 6/6/45; Grenier 22/6/45; 1377 BU Westover 24/11/46; re-ass 31/3/47; 1100 BU Topeka 20/5/47; 4119 BU Brookley 21/5/47; Recl Comp 14/9/48.

44-83710 Del Cheyenne 8/5/45; Keesler 17/6/45; Grenier 22/6/45; 3704 BU Keesler 1/8/45; 484 BU Topeka 15/9/45; 146 BU Selfridge 30/9/45; 62 BU Selfridge 27/3/46 {BA-710}; re-ass 31/3/47; 62 BU Selfridge 1/1/48; 9 RES Selfridge 7/3/48; 2151 RES Lowry 21/10/48; Recl Comp 6/12/48.

44-83711 Del Cheyenne 11/5/45; Hunter 29/5/45; Grenier 13/6/45; 1377 BU Grenier 20/8/45; 1377 BU Westover 5/5/46; re-ass 30/4/47; Recl Comp 9/4/48.

44-83712 Del Cheyenne 11/5/45; Hunter 30/5/45; 4168 BU Sth Plains 16/11/45; 4104 BU Rome 19/1/47; Recl Comp 10/4/47.

44-83713 Del Cheyenne 12/5/45; Hunter 7/6/45; 1377 BU Grenier 4/7/45; 1379 BU Dow Fd 19/7/45; re-ass 30/4/47; 1391 BU Azores 1/1/48; 523 BU Lagens 1/6/48; 1050 BU Lagens 19/8/48; 2152 RES Lagens 23/9/48; AMC Olmstead 9/4/49; 6 RES Sq Kindley 13/6/49; 7 RCU Sq Weisbaden 22/11/49; Recl Comp 21/11/50.

44-83714 –.

44-83715 –.

44-83716 Del Cheyenne 12/5/45; Keesler 10/6/45; 484 BU Topeka 15/9/45; 110 BU Mitchell 30/9/45; 146 BU Selfridge 18/2/46; 62 BU Mitchell 25/3/46; 146 BU Selfridge 8/6/46; Recl Comp 10/6/46.

44-83717 –.

44-83718 –. In Air Museum Rio De Janiero, Brazil 1954-60.

44-83719 –.

44-83720 Del Cheyenne 14/5/45; Hunter 29/6/45; WCW San Francisco 13/7/45; re-ass 30/4/47; sal Manila, PI 6/8/47. Recl Comp 13/7/49.

44-83721 Del Cheyenne 14/5/45; Hunter 27/6/45; WCW San Francisco 13/7/45; re-ass 30/4/47; Manila, PI 15/2/48; Recl Comp 24/4/48.

44-83722 –. ASR a/c with H2X in nose turret with yellow nads and wing panels, Hamilton 4/46; Yucca Flats where badly damaged in ground atomic bomb tests; purchased by Aviation Specialties at Falcon Fd as hangar queen 5/65; then by Kermit Weeks in 10/85, still stored dismantled Borrego, Cal 1988.

44-83723 Del Cheyenne 15/5/45; Hunter 27/6/45; WCW San Francisco 13/7/45; re-ass 30/4/47; Brisbane, Aus 29/5/47; 3 ER Itazuke, Japan 1/1/48; 3 RES Itazuke 22/4/48; 13 ARE Tchkawa 8/5/48; 3 RES Itazuke 18/5/48; 3 RES Ashiya 11/1/49; 3 RES Johnson 24/9/50; 1500 TSP Hickam 20/11/50; Recl Comp 1/3/53.

44-83724 Del Cheyenne 15/5/45; Hunter 30/6/45; 1103 BU Morrison 21/7/45; 1105 BU Miami 2/1/46; re-ass 30/4/47; 1377 BU Westover 30/7/47; 1383 BU Goose Bay 8/3/48; 1003 AB Nabarsk 8/6/48; 2152 RES Goose Bay 19/11/48; 1231 AB Nabarsk 22/11/48; 2152 RES Goose Bay 21/12/48; Recl Comp 5/8/49.

44-83725 –.

44-83726 Del Cheyenne 16/5/45; Hunter 1/7/45; WCW San Francisco 15/7/45; re-ass 30/4/47; 338 RV Momote 1/1/48; 5 RVP Gp Clark Fd 1/4/48; PAC Hickam 17/4/49; 5 RVP Gp Clark 22/4/49; retUS 9 SRC Fairfield 2/6/49; 5 RVP Gp Mt Home 6/9/49; 9 SRC Fairfield 18/10/49; Recl Comp 5/1/50.

44-83727 Del Syracuse 16/5/45; Slated Oahu 7AF, tran Memphis 20/5/45; RFC Altus 7/11/45.

44-83728 Del Syracuse 16/5/45; Middletown 8/11/45; Morrison 17/12/45; 2621 BU Barksdale 13/3/47; re-ass 31/3/47; 4117 BU Robins 4/3/48; Recl Comp 14/9/48; purchased by Shah of Persia; to IGN France {F-BGOE} 12/7/52; sal 1970.

44-83729 Del Syracuse 17/5/45; Slated Oahu 7AF, tran Dallas 29/5/45; RFC Altus 21/11/45; to IGN France {F-BEED} 24/12/47; sal 1973. DENISE.

44-83730 –.

44-83731 Del Syracuse 17/5/45; Slated Oahu 7AF, tran Love Fd 20/5/45; RFC Altus 7/11/45.

44-83732 Del Syracuse 18/5/45; Middletown 8/11/45; Morrison 27/12/45; re-ass 30/4/47; 3 BC Albrook (CZ) 1/1/48; 5702 MA Albrook 26/7/48; 5701 MSU Gp Albrook 28/3/49; AMC Olmstead Recl Comp 8/9/49.

44-83733 Del Syracuse 18/5/45; Palm Springs 26/5/45; RFC Altus 15/11/45.

44-83734 Del Rome 18/5/45; 4202 BU Syracuse 26/9/45; RFC Altus 5/11/45.

44-83735 Del Rome 18/5/45; 4202 BU Syracuse 26/9/45; RFC Altus 5/11/45; Civil NL68269; owned by president of Phillipine Airlines named SAN MIGUEL; sold to IGN France as {F-BDRS} 23/8/52 named CHATEAU DE VERNEUIL; now at Duxford, UK Air Museum as MARY ALICE.

44-83736 Del Rome 19/5/45; 4202 BU Syracuse 20/9/45; RFC Altus 5/11/45.

44-83737 Del Rome 19/5/45; 4202 BU Syracuse 20/9/45; RFC Altus 28/11/45.

44-83738 –.

44-83739 Del Syracuse 19/5/45; Scott 31/5/45; RFC Altus 21/11/45.

44-83740 Del Rome 21/5/45; Middletown 8/11/45; Morrison 18/1/46; 2621 BU Barksdale 21/11/46; ass Caribbean, ret Barksdale 13/3/47; re-ass 31/3/47; 2621 BU Barksdale 29/7/47; 4117 BU Robins 4/3/48; Recl Comp 4/11/48.

44-83741 Del Rome 21/5/45; 4202 BU Syracuse 7/11/45; RFC Altus 15/11/45.

44-83742 Del Rome 21/5/45; Palm Springs 29/5/45; Buckley 19/9/45; 7 GES Sq Buckley 21/1/46; 7 GE McDill 10/6/46; re-ass 31/3/47; 7 GE McDill 10/7/47; 343 BU Topeka 28/7/48; 55 MSU Gp Topeka 1/4/49; 55 SRC Forbes 25/8/49; 3203 MSU Gp Eglin 6/9/49; Recl Comp 12/10/49.

44-83743 Del Rome 21/5/45; 4202 Syracuse 20/9/45; RFC Altus 15/11/45.

44-83744 Del Rome 22/5/45; Middletown 8/11/45; Morrison 11/1/46; 4 BU West Palm Beach 20/4/46; Caribbean, retUS 2621 BU Barksdale 8/12/46; re-ass 31/3/47; 4117 BU Robins 4/3/48; Recl Comp

14/6/49.

44-83745 Del Syracuse 22/5/45; Tulsa 30/5/45; 4202 BU Syracuse 20/9/45; RFC Altus 7/11/45.

44-83746 Del Syracuse 22/5/45; Middletown 8/11/45; Morrison 26/2/46; BAT W Palm Beach 3/3/46; re-ass 30/4/47; 6 BC Galapagos 1/1/48; 582 SR Howard (CZ) 14/1/48; 23 MSU Gp Howard 21/6/49; AMC Olmstead 13/9/49; Recl Comp 14/10/49.

44-83747 Del Rome 22/5/45; Middletown 8/11/45; Morrison 28/1/46; BAT W Palm Beach 12/2/46; Carribbean, retUS 2621 BU Barksdale 21/11/46; re-ass 31/3/47; 2621 BU Barksdale 29/7/47; 4117 BU Robins 1/1/48; Recl Comp 1/2/49.

44-83748 Del Rome 28/5/45; 4202 BU Syracuse 20/9/45; RFC Altus 7/11/45.

44-83749 Del Syracuse 28/5/45; Slated Oahu 7AF, tran Middletown 8/11/45; Morrison 24/2/46; 4112 BU Olmstead 27/3/46; re-ass 30/4/47; 91 RLP Sq Howard (CZ) 1/1/48; 91 RLP Sq Waller (Trinidad) 1/7/48; 91 RLP Sq Maguire 9/2/49; AMC Brookley 29/6/49; 1 AB March 9/11/49; Recl Comp 6/3/50.

44-83750 –. Bolivia Civil CP-623, sal La Paz 28/7/58.

44-83751 Del Rome 28/5/45; 4202 BU Syracuse 20/9/45; RFC Altus 21/11/45; purchased by US Navy 27/3/47 as [83993]; sal 6/47 NAS Corpus Christi, Tx and used for spares.

44-83752 Del Rome 28/5/45; 4202 BU Syracuse 20/9/45; Recl Comp 3/1/46.

44-83753 Del Rome 28/5/45; 4202 BU Syracuse 12/10/45; RFC Altus 7/11/45; Civil N5024, sold to Israel and sal 1958.

44-83754 –.

44-83755 –. SB-17G; 2704 AFLC Davis Monthan 22/3/56.

44-83756 –.

44-83757 Del Rome 27/5/45; 4202 BU Syracuse 31/10/45; RFC Altus 5/11/45; Civil N5198; to IGN France as {F-BDRR} 25/7/50; sal 1962, hulk existed 1972.

44-83758 Del Rome 29/5/45; Middletown 8/11/45; Morrison 12/1/46; Caribbean, retUS 2621 BU Barksdale 10/3/47; re-ass 31/3/47; 2621 BU Barksdale 8/7/47; 4117 BU Robins 4/3/48; Recl Comp 2/3/49.

44-83759 Del Syracuse 29/5/45; Middletown 20/10/45; Morrison 9/12/45; Caribbean, retUS 2621 BU Barksdale 13/3/47; re-ass 31/3/47; 2621 BU Barksdale 29/7/47; 4117 BU Robins 4/3/48; Recl Comp 14/9/48.

44-83760 Del Rome 29/5/45; 4202 BU Syracuse 23/10/45; RFC Altus 5/11/45.

44-83761 Del Cheyenne 30/5/45; Hunter 2/7/45; Barksdale 16/7/45; 4136 BU Tinker 16/7/46; re-ass 30/4/47; 8080 AD Futema 1/1/48; 13 ARE Tchkawa 11/3/48; 316 BVH Kanoya 1/6/48; 8080 AD Shanghai 1/6/48; 2 RES Kadena 23/6/48; 32 MSU Kadena 23/9/48; 374 TCH Harmon 16/11/48; 4 RES Sq Harmon 18/1/49;

4 RES Sq Northwest 19/3/49; 6332 AB Kadena 23/11/49; retUS, AMC Hill 16/1/50; Recl Comp 19/5/50.

44-83762 Del Cheyenne 30/5/45; Hunter 4/7/45; WSW San Francisco 18/7/45; re-ass 30/4/47; 24 HBS Harmon 1/1/48; 13 ARE Sq Jama 29/3/49; Recl Comp 21/12/49.

44-83763 Del Cheyenne 30/5/45; Hunter 6/7/45; Barksdale 17/7/45; re-ass 30/4/47; 338 RV Momote 1/1/48; 5 RVP Gp Clark Fd 23/3/48; 358 SR Clark Fd 1/4/48; 18 MSU Gp Clark Fd 6/10/48; 5 RVP Gp Clark Fd 15/5/49; retUS, 9 SRC Gp Fairfield 27/9/49; AMC Hill 21/10/49; Recl Comp 7/11/49; US Civil N7041C.

44-83764 –. US Civil N7042C.

44-83765 Del Cheyenne 1/6/45; Hunter 2/7/45; WSW San Francisco 17/7/45; re-ass 30/4/47; 23 Ph Rec Momote 1/1/48; 5 RVP Gp Clark Fd 1/4/48; 18 MSU Clark 30/9/48; 5 RVP Gp Clark 23/10/48; PAC Hickam 17/4/49; 5 RVP Gp Clark 22/4/49; retUS, 9 SRC Gp Fairfield 29/6/49; Recl Comp 13/1/50.

44-83766 Del Cheyenne 1/6/45; Hunter 30/6/45; WSW San Francisco 15/7/45; re-ass 30/4/47; 23 Ph Rec Momote 1/1/48; 5 RVP Gp Clark 1/4/48; retUS, 9 SRC Gp Fairfield 2/6/49; AMC Hill 13/10/49; Recl Comp 7/11/49.

44-83767 Del Cheyenne 1/6/45; Slated Oahu 7AF, tran Hunter 10/7/45; Long Beach 19/7/45; re-ass 30/4/47; 338 RV Momote 1/1/48; 5 RVP Gp Clark 1/4/48; 15 MSU Gp Clark 24/9/48; PAC Hickam 17/4/49; 5 RVP Gp Clark 22/4/49; retUS, 9 SRC Gp Fairfield 2/6/49; AMC Hill 21/10/49; Recl Comp 19/5/50.

44-83768 –.

44-83769 –.

44-83770 Del Cheyenne 2/6/45; Hunter 10/7/45; Long Beach 22/7/45; re-ass 30/4/47; sal Oahu (7AF) 13/5/47; Recl Comp 21/11/47.

44-83771 Del Cheyenne 2/6/45; Hunter 6/7/45; 1377 BU Grenier 10/2/46; 1128 BU Grenier 6/3/46; re-ass 30/4/47; Recl Comp 21/10/47.

44-83772 –.

44-83773 –.

44-83774 –.

44-83775 Del Cheyenne 5/6/45; Slated Brisbane 5AF, tran Hunter 11/7/45; Long Beach 11/9/45; 4168 BU Sth Plains 25/10/45; 4117 Robins 11/2/46; 550 BU Cincinnati 30/5/46; 1377 BU Westover 16/5/46; 765 BU Westover 10/9/45; re-ass 30/4/47; 765 BU Goose Bay 1/1/48; 716 BU McAndrews 11/3/48; 135 ACS Gp Goose Bay 1/6/48; 1932 ACS Gp Goose Bay 31/10/48; AMC Olmstead 9/3/49; 1805 ACS Gp McAndrews 29/7/49; 2753 AST Sq Pyote 30/3/50; AMC Hill 13/4/50; Recl Comp 28/6/50.

44-83776 Del Cheyenne 5/6/45; Hunter 12/7/45; Long Beach 24/7/45; ass Kanai, Tacloban, Pl; sal 25/6/46.

44-83777 –.

44-83778 Del Cheyenne 5/6/45; Hunter 5/7/45; Long Beach 19/7/45; re-ass 30/4/47; Guam 16/6/47; 338 RV Momote 1/1/48; 5 RVP Gp Clark 1/4/48; retUS, 9 SRC Gp Fairfield 2/6/49; AMC Hill 21/10/49; Recl Comp 7/11/49. Civil N3509G (7040C).

44-83779 Del Cheyenne 5/6/45; Hunter 14/7/45; Long Beach 26/7/45; Kanai, Tacloban, PI 1/8/45; sal 19/9/46.

44-83780 –.

44-83781 –.

44-83782 –.

44-83783 Del Cheyenne 6/6/45; Hunter 16/7/45; WCW San Francisco 23/8/45; Guam, accident, sal 28/5/46.

44-83784 –.

44-83785 –.

44-83786 Del Cheyenne 7/6/45; Hunter 4/7/45; re-ass 30/4/47; Oahu 7AF, 3 ER Itami 1/1/48; 3 RES Itami 18/5/48; 13 ARE Sq Jama 13/11/48; Recl Comp 6/6/49.

44-83787 –.

44-83788 Del Cheyenne 8/6/45; Hunter 18/7/45; WCW San Francisco 26/8/45; re-ass 30/4/45; Guam 5/12/47; 4 RES North West, Guam, 21/7/48; Recl Comp 7/1/49.

44-83789 Del Cheyenne 8/6/45; Hunter 16/7/45; WCW San Francisco 23/8/45; re-ass 30/4/47; sal Guam 2/5/47; Recl Comp 25/4/49.

44-83790 Del Cheyenne 8/6/45; Hunter 14/7/45; Slated Oahu 7AF, tran Sth Plains 25/10/45; 4168 BU Sth Plains 30/4/46; 4134 BU Spokane 11/9/46; 594 BU Topeka 15/9/46; re-ass 31/3/47; 1377 BU Westover 22/5/47; 1385 BU Nasasuak 1/1/48; 1383 BU Goose Bay 9/2/48; Recl Comp 10/6/48.

44-83791 –.

44-83792 Del Cheyenne 8/6/45; Hunter 14/7/45; Long Beach 5/9/45; re-ass 30/4/47; 338 RV Momote 1/1/48; 5 RVP Gp Clark 1/4/48; 18 MSU Gp Clark 17/3/49; retUS, 9 SRC Fairfield 26/4/49; AMC Hill 10/10/49; Recl Comp 19/5/50.

44-83793 –. ASR as TB-17H.

44-83794 –. ASR as TB-17H.

44-83795 Del Cheyenne 11/6/45; Hunter 18/7/45; WCW San Francisco 23/8/45; re-ass 30/4/47; 24 HBS Harmon 1/1/48; 4 RES Sq North West, Guam, 16/4/48; 2 RCO Sq Anderson (Guam) 14/4/50; Recl Comp 12/10/50.

44-83796 Del Cheyenne 11/6/45; Hunter 18/7/45; WCW San Francisco 23/8/45; re-ass 30/4/47; Guam, sal 13/10/47; Recl Comp 25/4/49.

44-83797 Del Cheyenne 12/6/45; Hunter 27/6/45; WCW San Francisco 16/7/45; re-ass 30/4/47; 24 HBS Harmon 1/1/48; 13 ARE Sq Jama 26/3/49; Recl Comp 6/12/49.

44-83798 –. Ass FEA Logistics Force in Korea as brigadier-general's hack; with white trim back to tail turret.

44-83799 –. SB-17 in ASR.

44-83800 Del Cheyenne 12/6/45; Hunter 28/6/45; San Francisco 13/7/45; re-ass 30/4/47; 3 RES Chitose 1/1/48; 3 RES Itami 1/7/48; 49 MSU Misawa 7/10/48; 3 RES Chitose 26/5/49; 3 RCU Sq Misawa 31/7/49; 1500 TSP Hickam 11/5/50; retUS, AMC Hill 29/5/50; Recl Comp 8/11/50.

44-83801 Del Cheyenne 12/6/45; Hunter 27/6/45; WCW San Francisco 16/7/45; Brisbane 19/7/45; damaged in parking accident Okinawa, sal 26/9/45.

44-83802 Del Cheyenne 12/6/45; Hunter 27/6/45; WCW San Francisco 17/7/45; re-ass 30/4/47; 6 ERS le Shima, Japan; 2 RES Sq Kadena 1/1/48; Recl Comp 8/3/49. PACIFIC TRAMP.

44-83803 Del Cheyenne 13/6/45; Hunter 17/7/45; WCW San Francisco 23/8/45; re-ass 30/4/47; 4 RES North West 1/1/48; 13 ARE Jama 15/1/49; Recl Comp 26/8/49.

44-83804 Del Drew Fd 31/7/45; Eglin 24/8/45; Nashville 30/9/45; RFC Kingman 26/10/45.

44-83805 Del Syracuse 14/6/45; Albuquerque 17/6/45; 4202 BU Syracuse 20/9/45; RFC Altus 7/11/45.

44-83806 Del Syracuse 14/6/45; RFC Altus 5/11/45.

44-83807 Del Syracuse 14/6/45; Las Vegas 16/46/45; 4202 BU Syracuse 20/9/45; RFC Altus 26/11/45.

44-83808 Del Syracuse 14/6/45; Middletown 8/11/45; Morrison 20/12/45; Caribbean, retUS 2621 BU Barksdale 13/3/47; re-ass 31/3/47; 2621 BU Barksdale 29/7/47; 4117 BU Robins 1/3/48; Recl Comp 18/2/49.

44-83809 Del Syracuse 18/6/45; Bermuda 11/45 for diplomatic mission; ret Bolling Fd, Washington, before another special mission to Russia 1/46; ass 1103 BU Morrison 5/46; Bolling 11/46; tran USCG 10/2/48 VIP transport [83809]; ret USAF 22/12/48, ass 1100 Special Air Mission Gp, Bolling; Davis Monthan, Az 11/7/56; sold Lloyd Aero Bolivianos 18/12/56 as CP-626, cr Caranavi, Bol 25/10/49.

44-83810 Del Syracuse 14/6/45; Amarillo 21/6/45; 4202 BU Syracuse 20/9/45; RFC Altus 5/11/45; US Navy PB-1 [83994]; scrapped NAS Corpus Christi, Tx 6/47 as spares.

44-83811 Del Syracuse 14/6/45; Tulsa 20/6/45; 4202 BU Syracuse 20/9/45; RFC Altus 5/11/45; Civil

N9814F to Israel; ended as fuselage in film *The War Lover* at Croydon, UK 8/61.

44-83812 Del Syracuse 14/6/45; RFC Altus 7/11/45; served in US CG as PB-1G; nose and tail at Grass Valley, Cal 1969, and fixed to 41-2451 fuselage.

44-83813 Del Syracuse 15/6/45; Columbus 20/6/45; 4202 BU Syracuse 20/9/45; RFC Altus 5/11/45.

44-83814 Del Syracuse 15/6/45; RFC Altus 5/11/45; Civil N66571; Mexico as XB-BEC; now at Pima Museum, Tucson, Az.

44-83815 Del Syracuse 15/6/45; RFC Altus 7/11/45.

44-83816 Del Syracuse 15/6/45; Chanute 18/6/45; 4202 BU Syracuse 12/10/45; RFC Altus 5/11/45.

44-83817 Del Syracuse 15/6/45; Middletown 30/10/45; Morrison 10/12/45; Caribbean 27/12/45; re-ass 30/4/47; 7 RUC Howard (CZ) 1/1/48; 6 Ph AD Howard 5/2/48; 582 SR Howard 5/6/48; 23 AB Howard 1/5/49; 23 MUS Gp Howard 20/6/49; AMC Olmstead 11/9/49; Recl Comp 14/10/49.

44-83818 Del Syracuse 21/6/45; RFC Altus 5/11/45.

44-83819 Del Syracuse 16/6/45; Las Vegas 20/6/45; 4202 BU Syracuse 20/9/45; RFC Altus 5/11/45.

44-83820 –.

44-83821 Del Syracuse 16/6/45; 35 BU Bolling Air Staff pool 12/10/45; 110 BU Mitchell 9/1/46; Recl Comp 24/5/46; in US CG 1946 as CB-17.

44-83822 Del Syracuse 15/6/45; Rome 30/9/45; RFC Kingman 26/10/45.

44-83823 Del Syracuse 18/6/45; Love 25/6/45; 4202 BU Syracuse 20/9/45; RFC Altus 21/11/45.

44-83824 –. ASR with ASV chin radar, 2704 AFLC Davis Monthan 20/2/56.

44-83825 Del Syracuse 21/6/45; Romulus 25/6/45; 4202 BU Syracuse 20/9/45; RFC Altus 5/11/45.

44-83826 Del Syracuse 19/6/45; Middletown 30/10/45; Morrison 12/12/45; Caribbean 25/12/45; re-ass 30/4/47; 24 CMP Borinquen (PR)1/1/48; 24 CMP Ramey 1/7/48; ANT Ramey 23/3/49; 5900 AB Ramey 1/5/49; AMC Olmstead 29/10/49; Recl Comp 22/11/49.

44-83827 Del Syracuse 19/6/45; Memphis 24/6/45; 4202 BU Syracuse 20/9/45; RFC Altus 15/11/45.

44-83828 Del Syracuse 20/6/45; RFC Altus 5/11/45.

44-83829 Del Syracuse 20/6/45; Love Fd 26/5/45; 4202 BY Syracuse 20/9/45; RFC Altus 5/11/45.

44-83830 Del Drew Fd 31/7/45; Fairfield 24/8/45; RFC Kingman 26/10/45.

44-83831 Del Drew Fd 31/7/45; Fairfield 24/8/45; 4100 BU Patterson 4/9/45; RFC Kingman 23/10/45; PB-1G in US CG.

44-83832 Del Drew Fd 10/8/45; Fairfield 24/8/45; RFC Kingman 20/10/45; PB-1G in US CG.

44-83833 Del Drew Fd 10/8/45; Fairfield 24/8/45; RFC Kingman 25/10/45. BLUE TWO.

44-83834 Del Drew Fd 11/8/45; Fairfield 24/8/45; RFC Kingman 26/10/45; PB-1G in US CG.

44-83835 Del Syracuse 21/6/45; RFC Altus 5/11/45.

44-83836 Del Syracuse 22/6/45; 593 BU Charleston 28/10/45; RFC Altus 5/11/45.

44-83837 Del Syracuse 22/6/45; RFC Altus 5/11/45.

44-83838 Del Syracuse 22/6/45; Patterson 28/6/45; 4202 BU Syracuse 20/9/45; RFC Altus 5/11/45; as PB-1G in US CG; Civil N7726B and 5235V.

44-83839 Del Syracuse 23/6/45; RFC Altus 5/11/45.

44-83840 Del Syracuse 23/6/45; RFC Altus 5/11/45.

44-83841 Del Syracuse 23/6/45; Nashville 30/6/45; 4202 BU Syracuse 20/9/45; RFC Altus 5/11/45; Civil N66572, to Canada as CF-HBP.

44-83842 Del Syracuse 23/6/45; RFC Altus 7/11/45; Civil 1212N and 7712M; interned Azores 1948 en route Israel; to Dominican Republic.

44-83843 Del Syracuse 25/6/45; Patterson 28/6/45; 4202 BU Syracuse 20/9/45; RFC Altus 5/11/45.

44-83844 Del Syracuse 26/6/45; RFC Altus 5/11/45.

44-83845 Del Syracuse 26/6/45; Romulus 2/7/45; 4202 BU Syracuse 20/9/45; RFC Altus 7/11/45; to US Navy [83995] 27/3/47; scrapped NAS Corpus Christi, Tx 6/47 for spares.

44-83846 Del Syracuse 26/6/45; Sth Bend 22/7/45; 4202 BU Syracuse 20/9/45; RFC Altus 5/11/45.

44-83847 Del Syracuse 27/6/45; RFC Altus 5/11/45.

44-83848 Del Syracuse 27/6/45; Middletown 8/11/.45; Morrison 26/2/46; Caribbean 11/3/46; retUS, 2621 BU Barksdale 16/12/46; re-ass 31/3/47; 2621 BU Barksdale 25/7/47; 4117 BU Robins 4/3/48; Recl Comp 15/10/48.

44-83849 Del Syracuse 26/6/45; Middletown 30/10/45; Morrison 16/12/45; Caribbean 29/12/45; retUS 2612 Barksdale 7/11/46; re-ass 31/3/47; 2621 BU Barksdale 29/7/47; 4117 BU Robins 4/3/48; Recl Comp 31/3/49.

44-83850 Del Syracuse 28/6/45; RFC Altus 5/11/45.

44-83851 Del Syracuse 29/6/45; RFC Altus 7/11/45; Civil N1098M; to Israel, sal 1962.

44-83852 –.

44-83853 Del Syracuse 30/6/45; RFC Altus 5/11/45.

44-83854 Del Syracuse 30/6/45; RFC Altus 26/11/45.

44-83855 Del Syracuse 30/6/45; US Navy Johnsville 11/7/45 as PB-1W {77225}; ass VX-4 Quonset Pt 8/47; Mustin Fd, Phil 5/48; Norfolk 6/50; San Diego 5/51; c/t/o San Diego 11/12/51, sal 13/12/51.

44-83856 Del Syracuse 2/7/45; RFC Altus 5/11/45.

44-83857 Del Syracuse 2/7/45; ass US Navy Johnsville 11/7/45 as PB-1W {77226}; ass VX-4 Quonset Pt 12/47; Squantum 6/48; Norfolk 2/50; ass VC-11 San Diego 12/50; Miramar 11/51; tran VW-1 Barbers Pt, Hawaii (early warning) 18/6/52; TD Atsugi, Japan; retUS Norfolk 8/53; VW-1 Barbers Pt 1/54; Litchfield Pk 17/1/55; SO 7/10/56; Aero Service Corp, Phil 1/10/57, as Civil N7228C 25/10/57; re-named ASC Inc 29/12/61; DBA Columbia Motive, Or 20/2/62; Aero Enterprises, Cal (tanker) 3/3/65; Aero Flite, Troutdale, Wyo (tanker) 5/3/66; cr 29/8/67.

44-83858 Del Syracuse 2/7/45; ass US Navy Johnsville 11/7/45 as PB-1W {77227}; ass VX-4 Quonset Pt 7/46; Norfolk, then Mustin Fd 5/48; Patuxent River 5/50; re-designated VW-2 18/6/52; Litchfield Pk 12/54; SO 10/7/56; AmCom Steel Corp, Dallas 2/12/57 as Civil N6461D and later N5226V; Carstedt Air, Long Beach (tanker/sprayer) 31/1/62; Zambrana AirCo, Miami, 14/5/64; to CRA, La Paz, Bolivia as CP-742 10/6/64; cr Santa Ana, Beni 21/2/65.

44-83859 Del Syracuse 3/7/45; ass US Navy Johnsville 11/7/45 as PB-1W {77228}; Squantum 8/46; Air Elec Lab, Johnsville 1/9/49; VW-1 Barbers Pt, Hawaii 5/53; TD Atsugi, Japan 2/54; Litchfield Pk 12/1/55; SO 10/7/56; AmComp Steel Corp, 2/12/57 as Civil N5228V; Beigert Bros Air Spray/Dusting Co, Phoenix 1/10/59; Wimaga Traders Inc, St Petersburg 2/12/59; Chas Pankow, Largo, Fl 18/7/60; Loffland Bros, Peru 10/11/60; Transair, Lima, Peru 22/12/61 as OB-LIN-623; two days later sold to Empress Andorient as OB-SAC-623; CRA, Bolivia as CP-767 17/4/65; cr Bolivia 4/67.

44-83860 Del Syracuse 3/7/45; Palm Springs 5/7/45; 4202 BU Syracuse 20/9/45; Ret Altus 7/11/45.

44-83861 Del Syracuse 3/7/45; ass US Navy Johnsville 11/7/45 as PB-1W {77229}; ass VPB-101 Floyd Bennett Fd late 1945; re-designated VX-4 Quonset Pt 9/46; AirDevel Ctr Johnsville 20/2/47; Litchfield Pk 20/12/54; SO 10/7/56; AmComp Steel Corp, Dallas 2/12/57, Civil N5227V; G.J. Towle, Alamo, Cal 25/3/58 as sprayer; Bellamy Avn, Miami 21/10/63; CRA, Bolivia as CP-714 1964; cr San Borja, Bol 30/10/64.

44-83862 Del Syracuse 4/7/45; ass US Navy Johnsville 11/7/45 as PB-1W {77230}; ass VPB-101 Floyd Bennett Fd 2/46; re-designated VX-4 Quonset Pt 9/46; VX-4 Patuxent River 2/50; VC-11 Miramar 31/3/50; San Diego 7/52; VW-2 Patuxent River 5/3/53; SO 21/12/53.

44-83863 Del Syracuse 4/7/45; ass US Navy Johnsville 11/7/45 as PB-1W {77231}; ass VX-4 Quonset Pt 2/47; Norfolk 2/50; Litchfield Pk 5/50; tran VC-11 Miramar 4/52; VC-11 Barbers Pt, Hawaii 6/52; re-designated VW-1 18/6/52; retUS, San Diego 5/54; Litchfield Pk 14/6/54; SO 10/7/56; AmComp Steel Corp, Dallas 2/12/57, Civil N5233V; Marson Equip/Sal Co, Tucson 26/2/60; AirUn, Anderson, Cal 27/9/61 (tanker); Rogue FlyServ, Medford, Or 3/1/62; Eglin AFB Museum 1975, displayed as 95BG, later as 388BG, WANDA THE WITCH.

44-83864 Del Syracuse 4/7/45; ass US Navy Johnsville 11/7/45 as PB-1W {77232}; ass VX-4 Quonset Pt 6/47; tran VPW-1 Ream Fd, Cal 4/48;

Below: B-17G-80-DL 44-83802 serving with the 6th Emergency Rescue Squadron in B-17H configuration. (USAAF)

Glenn Martin Co, Baltimore 2/50 (test prog); Norfolk 7/52; VW-1 Barbers Pt, Hawaii 15/9/53; duly armed, patrolled Kwajalein Atoll for Red subs; retUS Litchfield Pk 17/1/55; SO 10/7/56; AmComp Steel Corp, Dallas 2/12/57, Civil N5234V; AeroFoto, Mexico as XB-BOE 3/1/58; Hurd AirSurv, Goleta, Cal 2/3/64; a week later to CalNat Air, Grass Valley, Cal as tanker; Black Hills Avn, Alamogordo, NM 2/4/68; cr Silver City, NM 7/12/72.

44-83865 Del Syracuse 4/7/45; 4104 BU Rome 14/7/45; 593 BU Charleston 28/10/45; RFC Altus 5/11/45.

44-83866 Del Syracuse 5/7/45; Middletown 8/11/45; Morrison 6/12/45; Caribbean 12/3/47; re-ass 31/3/47; retUS 2621 BU Barksdale 3/11/47; 4117 BU Robins 4/3/48; Recl Comp 7/1/49.

44-83867 Del Syracuse 5/7/45; Topeka 27/8/45; Long Beach 21/9/45; re-ass 30/4/47; 338 RV Momote 1/1/48; 13 ARE Clark Fd 9/3/48; 5 Ph Recon Clark 9/3/48; 358 SR Clark 1/4/48; 567 BA Clark 16/7/48; 5 RVP Clark 18/7/48; Recl Comp 29/7/49.

44-83868 Del Syracuse 6/7/45; ass US Navy Johnsville 11/7/45 as PB-1W {77233}; ass VX-4 Quonset Pt 4/47; tran VPW-1 Ream Fd 4/48; Norfolk 2/50; VX-4 Patuxent River 21/7/50; Glenview 8/50; re-designated VW-2 18/7/52; TD Gardamoen, Norway 8/52; retUS, Norfolk 10/52; VW-2 Patuxent River 3/6/53; Litchfield Pk 26/5/55; SO 10/7/56; AmCom Steel Corp, Dallas 2/12/57, Civil N5237V; Ashland Corp, Tucson 26/2/60; Marson Equip/Sal Co, Tucson 7/7/60; AeroUn, Anderson, Cal 27/9/61 (tanker); Butler Avn, Redmond, Or 28/12/61 (tanker); TBM Inc, Tulare, Cal 1/2/83; to UK 1983, restored as 94BG in RAF Museum.

44-83869 Del & Ass US Navy Johnsville 11/7/45 as PB-1W {77234}; ass VX-4 Quonset Pt 4/47; tran VPW-1 Ream Fd 4/48; Norfolk 2/50; Litchfield Pk 13/4/50; re-ass USN Mustin Fd 5/5/50; ass VX-4 Patuxent River 20/3/51; re-designated VW-2 18/7/52; TD Gardamoen, Norway 8/52; retUS, Patuxent River 21/11/52; tran VW-1 Barbers Pt, Hawaii 11/2/53; TD Atsugi, Japan 9/3/53; ret Barbers Pt 4/53; retUS Norfolk 6/5/54; SO 30/7/56.

44-83870 Del Syracuse 6/7/45; Topeka 27/8/45; Long Beach 21/9/45; re-ass 30/4/47; 13 ARE Clark 5/2/48; 368 SR Clark 9/4/48; 6 SR Clark 1/7/48; Recl Comp 1/10/48.

44-83871 Del Syracuse 7/7/45; Albuquerque 10/7/45; 4202 BU Syracuse 20/9/45; RFC Altus 28/11/45.

44-83872 Del & Ass US Navy Johnsville 12/7/45 as PB-1W {77235}; ass VX-4 Quonset Pt 5/47; Norfolk 4/50; tran FAS 103 Quonset Pt 22/11/50; VX-4 Patuxent River 1/52; re-designated VW-2 18/6/52; Norfolk 6/53; VW-1 Atsugi, Japan 4/2/54; retUS, Litchfield Pk 15/1/55; SO 10/7/56; AeroServ Corp, Phil 1/10/57, Civil N7227C; ACS Inc 29/12/61; ConfedAF Mercedes, Tx 22/9/67; restored as 533BS/381BG [VP-X], performing at air shows, as TEXAS RAIDERS.

44-83873 Del & Ass US Navy Johnsville 10/7/45 as PB-1W {77236}; ass VPB-101 4/46; re-designated VX-4 6/46; Johnsville 6/47; Miramar 2/50; tran VC-11 San Diego 3/50; Norfolk 11/50; VW-2 Patuxent River 8/54; Litchfield Pk 2/55; SO 10/7/56; Kenting Avn, Toronto 6/57; Civil CG-JJH; WO for spares 2/62.

44-83874 Del & Ass US Navy Johnsville 13/7/45 as PB-1W {77237}; ass VX-4 Quonset Pt 6/47; tran VPW-1 Ream Fd 4/48; Norfolk 1/50; VX-4 Patuxent River 3/2/50; re-designated VW-2 18/7/52; Litchfield Pk 9/5/55; SO 10/7/56; AmComp Steel Corp, Dallas 2/12/57, Civil N5236V; Carstedt Air, Long Beach 31/1/62; WO Love Fd 1963.

44-83875 Del & Ass US Navy Johnsville 12/7/45 as PB-1W {77238}; ass VX-4 Quonset Pt 2/47; Norfolk 9/49; Johnsville 10/1/50; TD VX-1 Key West 1/50; Norfolk 27/12/51; Johnsville 22/7/53; Litchfield Pk 8/8/55; SO 10/7/56; Aerovias Tunari, Bolivia 1958, Civil CP-640; Comp/Boliv/Avn 23/12/64; cr La Paz 17/8/67.

44-83876 Del & Ass US Navy Johnsville 17/7/45 as PB-1W {77239}; ass VPB-101 Floyd Bennett Fd 2/46; tran VX-4 Patuxent River 1/50; overshot runway NAS Glenview, Ill 14/2/50, sal.

44-83877 Del & Ass US Navy Johnsville 10/7/45 as PB-1W {77240}; ass VPB-101 Floyd Bennett Fd 1/46; re-designated VX-4 6/46; Quonset Pt 9/46; Norfolk 5/47; Quonset Pt 8/47; Norfolk 10/51; VX-4 Roosevelt Roads, Puerto Rico 3/52; San Diego 31/7/53; tran VW-1 Barbers Pt, Hawaii 12/1/53; retUS San Diego 2/1/54; Litchfield Pk 8/12/54; SO 10/7/56; AmComp Steel Corp, Tucson 2/12/57, Civil N5232V; Aero AmCorp, Cincinnati 5/9/61; one of three a/c purchased by Columbia Pictures for film *The War Lover*, scrapped Bovingdon Airfield, UK 3/62. BLUE THREE.

44-83878 Del & Ass US Navy Johnsville 13/7/45 as PB-1W {77241}; Norfolk 20/9/45; ass VPB-101 Floyd Bennett Fd 10/45; re-designated VX-4 Quonset Pt 1948; NADS Norfolk for special AN/APS-35 radar trials 10/5/49; Patuxent River 27/9/52; Litchfield Pk 3/12/53; SO 1/55.

44-83879 Del & Ass US Navy Johnsville 11/7/45 as PB-1W {77242}; ass VPB-1-1 Floyd Bennett Fd 8/45; re-designated VX-4 6/46; after overhaul returned Patuxent River 1/50; Norfolk 4/51; re-designated VW-2 2/52; TD Gardamoen, Norway 8/52; retUS, Patuxent River; Norfolk 3/54; SO 30/7/56.

44-83880 Del Syracuse 29/8/45; RFC Kingman 20/10/45.

44-83881 Del Syracuse 29/8/45; RFC Kingman 20/10/45.

44-83882 Del Syracuse 29/8/45; Romulus 30/9/35; 4100 BU Patterson 7/10/45; RFC Kingman 21/10/45.

44-83883 Del & Ass US Navy Johnsville 12/7/45 as PB-1W {77243}; ass VX-4 Mustin Fd 6/46; tran VP-51 Miramar 1/50; VC-11 San Diego 31/3/50; VX-4 Patuxent River 7/4/52; re-designated VW-2 18/6/52; TD Gardamoen, Norway 8/52; retUS, Patuxent River 11/52; Litchfield Pk 26/7/55; SO 10/7/56; AmComp Steel Corp, Dallas 2/12/57, Civil N5229V; purchased by Columbia Pictures as one of three a/c for film *The War Lover* 1961; WO Bovingdon airfield, UK 1962.

44-83884 Del & Ass US Navy Johnsville 13/7/45 as PB-1W {77244}; ass VX-4 Quonset Pt 5/47; Norfolk 1/50; Patuxent River 29/9/50; re-designated VW-2 18/6/52; Norfolk 24/2/55; Litchfield Pk 12/3/55; SO 10/7/56; AmComp Steel Corp, Dallas 2/12/57, Civil N5230V; Marson Equip/Sal Co, Tucson 18/10/60; Aero Union Corp, Anderson, Cal 10/61 (tanker); Barksdale AFB 8AF Museum, restored as YANKEE DOODLE II.

44-83885 –. SB-17; used on first air-sea rescue mission of Korean War w/Scheib 25/6/50, taking top brass to Japan.

B-17G-VE
44-85492 –.
44-85493 Del Dallas 26/2/45; Sth Plains 24/4/45; re-ass 31/3/47; 343 RVM McDill 14/5/47; 343 RVM Topeka 28/7/48; 55 BSU Topeka 5/8/49; 3902 ABF Offutt 14/10/49; Recl Comp 24/2/50.

44-85494 –.
44-85495 Del Dallas 25/2/45; Sth Plains 24/4/45; 4136 BU Tinker 30/4/46; 4104 BU Rome 3/10/46; 4104 BU Mitchell 9/10/46; 4104 BU Rome 16/3/47; 16 Ph Gp McDill 31/3/47; re-ass 31/3/47; 343 RVM Topeka 28/7/48; 5 ABGp Mountain Home 17/5/49; 5 ABGp Fairfield 15/12/49; Recl Comp 24/2/50.

44-85496 Del Dallas 25/2/45; Sth Plains 27/4/45; re-ass 31/3/47; 343 RVM McDill 7/5/47; 343 RVM Topeka 28/7/48; 3415 IT Lowry 15/10/48; 55 SRGp Topeka 4/2/49; 5904 ABGp Ramey 4/5/49; 55 SRGp Topeka 5/4/49; Recl Comp 11/10/49.

44-85497 Del Dallas 25/2/45; Sth Plains 25/4/45; 4136 BU Tinker 30/6/46; 4104 BU Rome 3/10/46; 16 Ph Gp McDill 25/2/47; re-ass 31/3/47; 343 RVM McDill 1/7/47; 343 RVM Topeka 28/7/48; 343 RVM Ladd Fd 14/10/48; 55 SRGp Topeka 26/5/49; 55 SRGp Thule 8/8/49; 55 MSU Forbes 4/10/49; Recl Comp AMC Hill Fd 7/11/49.

44-85498 Del Dallas 25/2/45; Sth Plains 24/4/45; re-ass 31/3/45; 343 RVM McDill 14/5/47; 314 BU McChord 13/8/47; 343 RVM McDill 24/8/47; 91 ABG Maguire 4/3/49; 2750 ABG Wright-Patterson 12/4/49; 91 ABG Maguire 15/7/49; 91 ABG Barksdale 10/10/49; Recl Comp Brookley 17/10/49.

44-85499 –.
44-85500 –.
44-85501 Del Dallas 1/3/45; Sth Plains 28/4/45; 4136 BU Tinker 30/6/45; 4104 BU Rome 10/1/46; 16 Ph Gp McDill 20/2/47; re-ass 31/3/47; 343 RVM McDill 15/10/47; 4127 BU McClelland 14/9/48; 55 ABGp Topeka 11/3/49; 55 SRC Gp Thule 4/8/49; 55 MSU Forbes 8/8/49; Recl Comp AMC Hill Fd 19/5/50.

44-85502 Del Dallas 3/3/45; Syracuse 22/5/45; RFC Altus 7/11/45.

44-85503 Del Dallas 3/3/45; Syracuse 22/5/45; RFC Altus 5/11/45.

44-85504 Del Dallas 2/3/45; Syracuse 22/5/45; Patterson 21/12/45; 200 BU Peterson 26/2/46; 4121 BU Kelly 28/2/46; 15 TSK Clovis 9/5/46; 556 BU Long Beach 9/6/46; 1503 BU Hamilton 16/6/46; ass Crossroads 20/8/46; 509 RV Roswell 30/9/46; 4104 BU Rome 9/3/47; re-ass 31/3/47; AMC Columbus 21/8/47; 1 EG Eglin 1/10/47; Recl Comp 1/11/48.

44-85505 –.
44-85506 Del Dallas 2/3/45; Sth Plains 28/4/45; re-ass 31/3/47; 343 RVM McDill 14/5/47; 343 RVM Topeka 28/7/48; 55 MSU Topeka 14/3/49; Recl Comp 17/10/49.

44-85507 Del Dallas 3/3/45; Syracuse 19/5/45; RFC Altus 21/11/45; converted for Col Bob McCormick, editor of Chicago Tribune (Civil N5116N); Hurd Mapping Co 1952; crashed Nevada 10/11/52, used as spares for 44-83534.

44-85508 Del Louisville 7/3/45; Hunter 16/3/45; Grenier 28/3/45; ass 8AF 29/3/45; retUS Bradley 20/5/45; Sth Plains 4/6/45; re-ass 31/3/47; 4141 BU Pyote 2/6/47; Recl Comp 16/4/50.

44-85509 Del Louisville 3/3/45; Hunter 23/3/45; Grenier 30/3/45; ass 8AF 1/4/45; retUS Bradley 24/7/45; Independence 27/7/45; RFC Altus 16/12/45.

44-85510 Del Louisville 3/3/45; Hunter 16/3/45; Grenier 28/3/45; ass 8AF 29/3/45; retUS Bradley 22/5/45; Sth Plains 24/5/45; 247 BU Smoky Hill 17/2/46; 15 TSK Clovis 10/3/46; 234 BU Clovis 20/3/46; 401 BU Hamilton 6/8/46; Recl Comp 30/10/46.

44-85511 Del Louisville 6/3/45; Hunter 16/3/45; Grenier 24/3/45; ass 8AF 25/3/45; retUS Bradley 6/6/45; Sth Plains 9/6/45; RFC Kingman 10/12/45.

44-85512 Del Louisville 5/3/45; Hunter 16/3/45; Grenier 25/3/45; ass 8AF 26/3/45; re-ass 31/3/47;

10 HBS Oberpfaffenhofen 1/1/48; Recl Comp 7/1/49.

44-85513 Del Louisville 5/3/45; Syracuse 7/6/45; Middletown 8/11/45; Morrison 3/1/46; 2621 BU Barksdale 21/12/46; re-ass 31/3/47; 4117 BU Robins 4/3/48; Recl Comp 31/3/49.

44-85514 Del Louisville 6/3/45; Hunter 19/3/45; Grenier 30/3/45; ass 8AF 1/4/45; retUS 121 BU Bradley 10/6/46; 4168 BU Sth Plains 30/9/46; re-ass 31/3/47; 4112 BU Olmstead 25/5/47; 5 Ph Recon Clark Fd 1/1/48; 13 ARE Clark 9/3/48; retUS 375 OT Shephard 15/11/49; 9 SRC Gp Fairfield 19/12/49; Recl Comp 5/1/50.

44-85515 Del Louisville 5/3/45; Hunter 12/3/45; Grenier 28/3/45; ass 8AF 29/3/45; retUS Bradley 7/6/45; 4168 BU Sth Plains 7/2/46; 233 BU Forth Worth 19/2/46; 613 BU Phillips PG 29/4/46.

44-85516 Del Louisville 6/3/45; Hunter 16/3/45; Grenier 28/3/45; ass 8AF 29/3/45; retUS Bradley 22/5/45; Sth Plains 25/5/45; 242 BU Gr Island 21/2/46; 4104 BU Rome 2/10/46; re-ass 31/3/47; 4112 BU Olmstead 29/9/47; designated QB-17G Columbus 1/1/48; 55 CGM Eglin 21/7/49; Recl Comp 1/3/50.

44-85517 Del Louisville 6/3/45; Hunter 16/3/45; Grenier 28/3/45; ass 8AF 29/3/45; sal 9AF Germany 31/5/46.

44-85518 Del Louisville 6/3/45; Hunter 21/3/45; Grenier 31/3/45; ass 8AF 1/4/45; retUS Bradley 3/7/45; Sth Plains 11/7/45; 233 BU Ft Worth 5/2/46; 15 TSK Clovis 4/3/46; 4121 BU Kelly 9/4/46; Recl Comp 13/9/46.

44-85519 Del Louisville 7/3/45; Hunter 23/3/45; Grenier 4/4/45; Sth Plains 14/4/45; 2140 BU Smyrna 8/11/45; 342 BU Smyrna 5/5/46; 556 BU Long Beach 9/6/46; 594 BU Topeka 12/6/46; 4104 BU Rome 12/6/46; 554 BU Memphis 17/6/46; 4104 BU Rome 5/8/46; Recl Comp 10/4/47.

44-85520 Del Cheyenne 7/3/45; Hunter 25/3/45; Grenier 12/4/45; 1103 BU Morrison 9/10/45; RFC Walnut Ridge 21/1/46.

44-85521 Del Louisville 7/3/45; Hunter 29/3/45; Grenier 30/3/45; ass 8AF 31/3/35; re-ass 30/4/47; 10 HBS Oberpfaffenhofen 1/1/48; Recl Comp 7/1/49.

44-85522 Del Louisville 10/3/45; Hunter 21/3/45; Sth Plains 20/4/45; RFC Walnut Ridge 5/12/45.

44-85523 Del Cheyenne 13/3/45; Hunter 25/3/45; Grenier 12/4/45; 593 BU Charleston 28/10/45; 1103 BU Morrison 1/11/45; RFC Walnut Ridge 2/1/46.

44-85524 Del Louisville 13/3/45; Hunter 21/3/45; Grenier 30/3/45; ass 8AF 31/3/45; retUS Bradley 7/6/45; Sth Plains 13/6/45; 233 BU Ft Worth 3/2/46; 15 TSK Clovis 7/3/46; re-ass 31/3/47; 4168 BU Sth Plains 25/6/47; 4141 BU Pyote 26/6/47; Recl Comp 16/4/50.

44-85525 Del Cheyenne 13/3/45; Hunter 25/3/45; Grenier 15/4/45; 1103 BU Morrison 10/12/45; RFC Walnut Ridge 3/1/46.

44-85526 Del Cheyenne 15/3/45; Hunter 20/3/45; Grenier 30/3/45; ass 8AF 31/3/45; retUS Bradley 16/6/45; Sth Plains 1/7/45; RFC Kingman 26/11/45.

44-85527 Del Cheyenne 13/3/45; Hunter 21/3/45; Grenier 28/3/45; ass 8AF 29/3/45; Re-ass 30/4/47; 10 HBS Oberpfaffenhofen 1/1/48; Recl Comp 7/1/49.

44-85528 Del Cheyenne 13/3/45; Hunter 25/3/45; Grenier 12/4/45; ass 8AF 13/4/45; re-ass 30/4/47; 10 HBS Oberpfaffenhofen 1/1/48; Recl Comp 7/1/49.

44-85529 Del Cheyenne 13/3/45; Hunter 25/3/45; Grenier 12/4/45; 1103 BU Morrison 18/10/45; RFC Walnut Ridge 20/10/45.

44-85530 Del Cheyenne 13/3/45; Hunter 25/3/45; Grenier 13/4/45; RFC Walnut Ridge 14/12/45.

44-85531 Del Louisville 15/3/45; Topeka 25/3/45; Sth Plains 16/4/45; 2140 BU Smyrna 7/11/45; 4104 BU Rome 13/6/46; 554 BU Memphis 17/6/46; 342 BU Smyrna 17/9/46; re-ass 31/3/47; 4112 BU Olmstead 18/6/47; 338 RVM Momote 1/1/48; 5 RVP Clark Fd, Phil 1/7/48; 9 MSU Fairfield 25/6/49; AMC Hill Fd 21/10/49; Recl Comp 19/5/50; re-ass AF, painted all black for secret operations Vietnam; Civil N809Z, used by CIA during 50s & 60s from Marana, Az. fitted with forked pincers on nose to pick up agents; restored at McMinville, Or. 1987 as 490BG SHADY LADY.

44-85532 Del Cheyenne 15/3/45; Hunter 28/3/45; Sioux City 11/4/45; Grenier 16/4/45; ass 8AF 17/4/45; sal 9AF Germany 23/10/46; re-ass 30/4/47; recl Comp 19/11/47.

44-85533 Del Louisville 15/3/45; Topeka 25/3/45; Sth Plains 15/4/45; 2140 BU Smyrna 7/11/45; 342 BU Smyrna 30/4/46; 4104 BU Rome 13/6/46; 554 BU Memphis 16/6/46; 342 BU Smyrna 17/7/46; 4104 BU Rome 24/7/46; 594 BU Topeka 19/12/46; re-ass 31/3/47; 4112 BU Olmstead 18/6/47; 338 RVM Momote 1/1/48; 5 RVP Clark Fd 1/7/48; 9 SRGp Fairmont 20/10/49; AMC Hill Fd 25/10/49; Recl Comp 19/5/50.

44-85534 Del Cheyenne 13/3/45; Hunter 20/3/45; Grenier 30/3/45; ass 303BG Molesworth 10/4/45; retUS Bradley 9/6/45; Sth Plains 25/6/45; RFC Kingman 26/11/45.

44-85535 Del Louisville 15/3/45; Topeka 21/3/45; Grenier 1/4/45; Bradley 3/7/45; Sth Plains 5/7/45; RFC Kingman 7/12/45.

44-85536 Del Louisville 15/3/45; Syracuse 27/3/45; RFC Altus 28/11/45.

44-85537 Del Louisville 16/3/45; Hunter 24/3/45; Grenier 3/4/45; Bradley 6/6/45; Sth Plains 8/6/45; 247 BU Smoky Hill 17/2/46; re-ass 31/3/47; 4112 BU Olmstead 29/4/47; 5 PRR Clark Fd 1/4/48; 9 SRGp Fairmont 1/11/49; Recl Comp 5/1/50.

44-85538 Del Louisville 15/3/45; Hunter 21/3/45; Grenier 30/3/45; ass 8AF 31/3/45; retUS Bradley 21/5/45; Sth Plains 5/6/45; 247 BU Smoky Hill 17/2/46; 598 BU Topeka 25/6/46; 263 BU Geiger 30/9/46; 4134 BU Spokane 12/2/47; re-ass 31/3/47; 3705 BU Lowry 16/7/47; 2621 BU Barksdale 30/10/47; 4117 BU Robins 4/3/48; Recl Comp 15/10/48.

44-85539 Del Cheyenne 12/3/45; Hunter 25/3/45; Grenier 15/4/45; RFC Kingman 10/1/46.

44-85540 Del Cheyenne 14/3/45; Hunter 25/3/45; Grenier 12/4/45; 1103 BU Morrison 20/4/45; RFC Walnut Ridge 18/1/46.

44-85541 Del Louisville 13/3/45; Hunter 23/3/45; Grenier 1/4/45; ass 8AF 3/4/45; re-ass 10/4/47; 10 HBS Oberpfaffenhofen 1/1/48; Recl Comp 5/1/49.

44-85542 Del Louisville 13/3/45; Topeka 21/3/45; Sth Plains 15/4/45; 242 BU Gr Island 14/2/47; 4112 BU Olmstead 29/4/47; re-ass 31/3/47; 5 PR Gp Clark Fd 1/1/48; 5 RVPGp Clark 1/7/48; 9 MSU Fairmont 29/7/49; Recl Comp 21/2/50.

44-85543 Del Louisville 13/3/45; Hunter 25/3/45; Sth Plains 25/4/45; 611 BU Eglin, sal 13/2/46.

44-85544 Del Louisville 13/3/45; Hunter 24/3/45; Grenier 3/4/45; ass 8AF 4/4/45; retUS Bradley 31/5/45; Sth Plains 4/6/45; 247 BU Smoky Hill 17/2/46; 555 BU Love Fd 20/5/46; 4000 BU Patterson 28/5/46; 4000 BU 24/6/46; Recl Comp 22/7/46.

44-85545 Del Louisville 14/3/45; Hunter 29/3/45; Grenier 1/4/45; ass 8AF 2/4/45; retUS Bradley 29/5/45; Sth Plains 30/5/45; 234 BU Clovis 3/2/46; 408 BVM March 9/5/46; 248 BU Davis Monthan 22/5/46; re-ass 31/3/47; 4112 BU Olmstead 29/4/47; 5 PRGp Clark Fd 1/1/48; 5 RVPGp Clark Fd 15/5/49; 9 MSU Fairmont 2/8/49; AMC Hill Fd 7/12/49; Recl Comp 19/5/50.

44-85546 Del Louisville 14/3/45; Hunter 25/3/45; Sth Plains 23/4/45; 242 BU Gr Island 21/4/46; re-ass 31/3/47; 4104 BU Rome 19/5/47; AMC Columbus 22/5/47; 4112 BU Olmstead 2/10/47; AMC Columbus 22/11/47; 3203 MSUGp Eglin 7/4/49; Recl Comp 15/6/50.

44-85547 Del Louisville 14/3/45; Hunter 25/3/45; Grenier 1/4/45; ass 8AF 4/4/45; retUS Bradley 29/5/45; Sth Plains 21/5/45; 233 BU Ft Worth 27/3/45; 613 BU Phillips 3/5/46; 233 BU Ft Worth 30/5/46.

44-85548 Del Louisville 17/3/45; Hunter 23/3/45; Grenier 1/4/45; ass 8AF 2/4/45; retUS Bradley 6/6/45; 4104 BU Rome 25/6/45; 4168 BU Sth Plains 1/1/46; 4136 BU Tinker 8/12/46; 4104 BU Rome 26/2/47; re-ass 30/4/47; Recl Comp 15/5/47.

44-85549 Del Louisville 14/3/45; Hunter 24/3/45; Grenier 1/4/45; ass 2/4/45; retUS Bradley 25/5/45; Sth Plains 29/5/45; RFC Kingman 8/12/45.

44-85550 Del Cheyenne 15/3/45; Hunter 3/7/45; Grenier 13/4/45; ass 8AF 14/4/45; re-ass 30/4/45; 10 HBS Oberpfaffenhofen 1/1/48; Recl Comp 5/8/48.

44-85551 –.

44-85552 Del Louisville 15/3/45; Hunter 19/3/45; Grenier 1/4/45; ass 8AF 2/4/45; re-ass 30/4/47; 10 HBS Oberpfaffenhofen 1/1/48; Recl Comp 1/10/48.

44-85553 Del Cheyenne 15/3/45; Hunter 25/3/45; Grenier 15/4/45; ass 8AF 16/4/45; sal 29/10/45.

44-85554 Del Cheyenne 15/3/45; Hunter 20/4/45; Sth Plains 3/5/45; 4000 BU Wright 30/6/45; 610 BU Eglin 3/10/45; 4000 BU Patterson 13/5/46; 2759 ABGp Muroc 2/10/48; San Bernardino 8/2/49; Recl Comp 1/5/50.

44-85555 Del Cheyenne 16/3/45; Hunter 13/4/45; Grenier 19/4/45; ass 8AF 20/4/45; re-ass 30/4/47; 61 TC Rhine Main 1/1/48; 90 AB Oberpfaffenhofen 26/7/48; 7169 RCW Oberpfaffenhofen 2/2/49; 7210 MA Gp Erding 11/4/49; Recl Comp 20/3/50.

44-85556 Del Cheyenne 16/3/45; Hunter 2/4/45; Grenier 15/4/45; 1103 BU Morrison 10/10/45; RFC Walnut Ridge 2/1/46.

44-85557 Del Cheyenne 16/3/45; Hunter 6/4/45; Grenier 15/4/45; RFC Walnut Ridge 10/1/46.

44-85558 Del Cheyenne 13/3/45; Hunter 27/3/45; Sth Plains 25/4/45; 610 BU Eglin 12/7/45; 611 BU Eglin 2/2/46.

44-85559 Del Louisville 15/3/45; Hunter 30/3/45; Sth Plains 9/4/45; 2140 BU Smyrna 8/11/45; 342 BU Smyrna 30/4/46; 613 BU Phillips 19/6/46.

44-85560 –.

44-85561 Del Cheyenne 15/3/45; Hunter 26/3/45; Grenier 1/4/45; ass 8AF 2/4/45; retUS Bradley 6/6/45; Sth Plains 8/6/45; 233 BU Ft Worth 10/2/46; 15 TSK Clovis 30/4/46; re-ass 31/3/37; 4141 BU Pyote 19/6/47; Recl Comp 1/1/48.

44-85562 Del Louisville 13/3/45; Hunter 30/3/45; Sth Plains 19/4/45; RFC Walnut Ridge 7/1/46.

44-85563 Del Louisville 15/3/45; Topeka 26/3/45; Sth Plains 15/4/45; 2140 BU Smyrna 31/1/46; 342 BU Smyrna 10/4/46; 594 BU Topeka 18/6/46; 342 BU Smyrna 16/8/46.

44-85564 Del Louisville 19/3/45; Hunter 30/3/45; Sth Plains 20/4/45; RFC Walnut Ridge 5/12/45.

44-85565 Del Louisville 17/3/45; Sth Plains 6/4/45;

610 BU Eglin 19/7/45; 620 BU Muroc 26/7/45; re-ass 31/3/47; 4141 BU Pyote 1/1/48; Recl Comp 15/4/50.
44-85566 Del Cheyenne 19/3/45; Hunter 27/3/45; Sth Plains 19/4/45; 2140 BU Smyrna 12/11/45; 342 BU Smyrna 30/4/46; 594 BU Topeka 19/6/46; 613 BU Phillips 25/6/46; 594 BU Topeka 7/7/46.
44-85567 –.
44-85568 Del Cheyenne 19/3/45; Sth Plains 27/3/45; 611 BU Eglin 17/8/45.
44-85569 –.
44-85570 Del Cheyenne 19/3/45; Sth Plains 27/3/45; Wright Fd as test bed 5/49.
44-85571 Del Cheyenne 23/3/45; Hunter Fd, trans Sth Plains 27/4/45; 611 BU Eglin 11/7/45; trans USN 8/46 [85571] as test bed for Westinghouse J30 jet engine, later installed in FD-1 Phantom; Cornell Aero/Labs, Buffalo, NY as XPB-1 [83992]; (engine fitted under wing on external bomb shackles, but starter burned out as ignition switch was wired in reverse); 4104 BU Rome 21/2/47; project dropped and aircraft trans NAAF Mustin Fd 6/48; as 83992 ass VX-4 NAS Patuxent River 5/50 with TD Key West; sent for storage Litchfield Park 10/53, but scrapped for spares 24/11/54.
44-85572 Del Cheyenne 21/3/45; Hunter 25/3/45; Sth Plains 18/4/45; 2140 BU Smyrna 31/1/46; 342 BU Smyrna 30/4/46; 613 BU Phillips 18/6/46; 554 BU Memphis 23/6/46.
44-85573 –.
44-85574 Del Cheyenne 21/3/45; Sth Plains 3/5/45; re-ass 31/3/47; 343 BU McDill 7/6/47; 343 BU Topeka 28/7/48; 55 ABGp Topeka 10/2/49; 4205 ABGp Mt Home 12/10/49; 5 MSU Fairmont 15/12/49; Recl Comp 10/1/50.
44-85575 Del Cheyenne 22/3/45; Sth Plains 2/4/45; Mobile 22/8/45; Grenier 8/1/46; 4117 BU Robins 31/1/46; 503 BU Grave Pt 3/5/46; 53 RC Brookley 18/3/46; 53 CNSq McChord 11/6/46; re-ass 31/3/47; 53 RC Morrison 8/5/47; 373 RV Kindley 1/4/48; ATC Olmstead 18/10/48; 1805 HC McAndrews 18/10/48; 4 MSU Andrews 26/1/49; 1800 MS Tinker 18/5/49; 1600 MSU Westover 30/8/49; 1605 AB Lagens 23/3/50; 3200 PTSGp Eglin 15/6/50; AMC Hill 13/9/50; Recl Comp 24/1/51.
44-85576 –.
44-85577 Del Cheyenne 22/3/45; Hunter 27/3/45; Sth Plains 18/4/45; 3017 BU Hobbs 7/10/45; 2137 BU Hendricks 9/10/45; 2140 BU Smyrna 31/3/46; 342 BU Smyrna 5/5/46; 594 BU Topeka 12/6/46; 4104 BU Rome 18/6/46; re-ass 31/3/47; 10 RESq Ladd Fd 1/1/48; Elmendorf 20/7/48; 10 RES Davis (Adak) 24/8/48; Recl Comp 11/8/49.
44-85578 –.
44-85579 –.
44-85580 Del Louisville 27/3/45; Sth Plains 5/4/45; RFC Walnut Ridge 5/1/46.
44-85581 Del Louisville 24/3/45; Sth Plains 2/4/45; 3017 BU Hobbs 5/10/45; 2137 BU Hendricks 29/10/45; 2140 BU Smyrna 7/12/45; 342 BU Smyrna 5/5/46; 554 BU Memphis 12/6/46; 4104 BU Rome 18/7/46; re-ass 31/3/47; 10 RES Ft Randall 1/1/48; 10 RES Davis 31/3/48; 10 RES Elmendorf 1/10/49; 10 RES Davis 12/11/48; 10 RCU Elmendorf 7/7/50; Recl Comp Davis 14/11/50.
44-85582 Del Louisville 24/3/45; Sth Plains 4/4/45; RFC Walnut Ridge 7/1/46.
44-85583 –.
44-85584 –.
44-85585 Del Louisville 26/3/45; Sth Plains 4/4/45; Garden City 5/10/45; 4152 BU Lockburn 7/11/45; 4152 BU Clinton 5/5/46; 4112 BU Olmstead 10/7/46; re-ass 31/3/47; Recl Comp 11/8/49.

44-85586 Del Louisville 30/3/45; Sth Plains 5/4/45; RFC Walnut Ridge 5/1/46.
44-85587 Del Cheyenne 30/3/45; Sth Plains 6/4/45; RFC Walnut Ridge 5/1/46.
44-85588 Del Louisville 28/3/45; Sth Plains 4/4/45; Nashville 3/7/45; 4000 BU Wright 19/2/46; re-ass 31/3/47; Recl Comp 17/4/47.
44-85589 –.
44-85590 Del Cheyenne 30/3/45; Sth Plains 5/4/45; RFC Walnut Ridge 5/1/46.
44-85591 Del Cheyenne 30/3/45; Sth Plains 6/4/45; 2137 BU Hendricks 25/10/45; 2140 BU Smyrna 28/1/46; 342 BU Smyrna 5/5/46; 554 BU Memphis 1/6/46; 342 BU Smyrna 16/6/46.
44-85592 –.
44-85593 Del Cheyenne 30/3/45; Sth Plains 24/4/45; 4136 BU Tinker 5/10/46; 4104 BU Rome 9/10/46; 16 PhR McDill 25/2/47; re-ass 31/3/47; 343 RVM McDill 16/10/47; 594 BU Topeka 28/7/48; 4112 BU Olmstead 16/9/48; 16 PhR Maguire 24/6/49; 91 SRC Maguire 10/8/49; 91 SRC Barksdale 30/10/49; AMC Brookley 2/11/49; Recl Comp 2/6/50.
44-85594 –. Sold IGN, France as F-BGSQ 29/12/44; scrapped 1972.
44-85595 Del Cheyenne 30/3/45; Sth Plains 6/4/45; 233 BU Ft Worth 10/2/46; 613 BU Phillips 30/4/46.
44-85596 Del Cheyenne 30/3/45; Sth Plains 6/4/45; 234 BU Clovis 3/2/46; 40 RV March 7/5/46; 248 BU Davis Monthan 23/5/46; Recl Comp 20/11/46.
44-85597 –.
44-85598 Del Cheyenne 31/3/45; Sth Plains 6/4/45; 3017 BU Hobbs 2/10/45; 2137 BU Hendricks 28/10/45; 2140 BU Smyrna 31/1/46; 554 BU Memphis 19/6/46.
44-85599 –. Based Dyess AFB, Tx 1987 as BLACK HAWK.
44-85600 –. (US Civil N3696G)
44-85601 Del Cheyenne 4/4/45; Sth Plains 26/4/45; re-ass 31/3/47; 343 RVM McDill 14/5/47; 343 RVM Topeka 28/7/48; 55 MSU Topeka 23/3/49; 3902 ABGp Offutt 17/5/49; Recl Comp 2/3/50.
44-85602 –.
44-85603 Del Cheyenne 31/3/45; Sth Plains 6/4/45; re-ass 31/3/47; 343 RVM McDill 14/5/47; 343 SR Topeka 28/7/48; 91 ABGp Maguire 4/3/49; Recl Comp 14/12/49.
44-85604 Del Louisville 4/4/45; Sth Plains 15/4/45; 2140 BU Smyrna 8/10/45; 342 BU Smyrna 5/5/46; 594 BU Topeka 12/5/46; 4104 BU Rome 13/6/46; re-ass 31/3/47; 4112 BU Olmstead 18/6/47; 4 ER North West, Guam, 1/1/48; 4 RCU North West, Guam, 30/9/49; 2 RES Anderson 23/8/50; Recl Comp 16/2/51.
44-85605 Del Louisville 5/4/45; Sth Plains 10/4/45; 2137 BU Hendricks 25/10/45; 2140 BU Smyrna 19/12/45; 342 BU Smyrna 5/5/46; 594 BU Topeka 26/6/46.
44-85606 Del Louisville 4/4/45; Sth Plains 11/4/45; 3017 BU Hobbs 10/10/45; 2137 BU Hendricks 8/11/45; 2140 BU Smyrna 31/1/46; 594 BU Topeka 26/6/46.
44-85607 Del Louisville 31/3/45; Sth Plains 9/4/45; Brookley 24/8/45; 4132 BU Garden City 11/10/45; 4152 BU Lockburn 7/11/45; 4152 BU Clinton 13/5/46; 4112 BU Olmstead 13/6/46; re-ass 31/3/47; 4127 BU McClelland 29/4/47; Landing Aid Ex Station, All Weather Flying Centre, Arcata 1/1/48; Recl Comp 18/5/48.
44-85608 Del Louisville 31/3/45; Sth Plains 11/4/45; 2140 BU Smyrna 8/10/45; 342 BU Smyrna 10/4/46; 613 BU Phillips 19/6/46.
44-85609 Del Louisville 31/3/45; Patterson 10/4/45;

Hunter 1/5/45; 201 BU Peterson 13/3/46; 1 BU Bolling 31/3/46; 401 BU Hamilton 6/6/46; re-ass 31/3/47; 3 BC Albrook, CZ as CB-17 1/7/48 with extra radio compt windows, no chin or top turrets; 6702 MAT Albrook 26/7/48; 5701 MSU Albrook 23/3/49; Recl Comp 24/8/50.
44-85610 Del Louisville 6/4/45; Sth Plains 13/4/45; 2140 BU Smyrna 31/10/45; 2137 BU Hendricks 7/11/45; 342 BU Smyrna 5/5/46; 594 BU Topeka 18/6/46.
44-85611 Del Louisville 5/4/45; Sth Plains 11/4/45; RFC Walnut Ridge 25/2/46.
44-85612 –.
44-85613 Del Louisville 3/4/45; Sth Plains 11/4/45; 2140 BU Smyrna 31/10/45; 342 BU Smyrna 18/4/46; Recl Comp 15/7/46.
44-85614 Del Louisville 6/4/45; Sth Plains 19/4/45; RFC Walnut Ridge 3/1/46.
44-85615 Del Louisville 3/4/45; Sth Plains 11/4/45; 2519 BU Ft Worth 18/10/45; 2140 BU Smyrna 31/1/46; 342 BU Smyrna 5/5/46; 594 BU Topeka 16/6/46.
44-85616 Del Louisville 3/4/45; Sth Plains 11/4/45; 2519 BU Ft Worth 18/10/45; 2140 BU Smyrna 31/1/46; 342 BU Smyrna 30/4/46; 613 BU Phillips 25/6/46.
44-85617 Del Louisville 7/4/45; Sth Plains 13/4/45; 2137 BU Hendricks 25/10/45; 2140 BU Smyrna 31/1/46; 342 BU Smyrna 30/4/46; 4104 BU Rome 10/6/46; 4141 BU Pyote 30/6/46; re-ass 31/3/47; 4141 BU Pyote 1/1/48; Recl Comp 22/12/48.
44-85618 Del Louisville 7/4/45; Sth Plains 18/4/45; RFC Walnut Ridge 5/12/45.
44-85619 Del Louisville 6/4/45; Sth Plains 16/4/45; 2140 BU Smyrna 6/11/45; 342 BU Smyrna 5/5/46; 4104 BU Rome 10/6/46; 554 BU Memphis 12/6/46; 4104 BU Rome 30/9/46; Recl Comp 10/4/47.
44-85620 Del Louisville 6/4/45; Sth Plains 12/4/45; 2137 BU Hendricks 25/10/45; 2140 BU Smyrna 12/1/46; 613 BU Phillips 6/6/46; 342 BU Smyrna 30/6/46; 613 BU Phillips 8/6/46.
44-85621 Del Louisville 7/4/45; Rome 26/5/45; Middletown 8/11/45; Morrison 2/12/45; 2621 BU Barksdale 8/12/45; re-ass 31/3/37; 4117 BU Robins 4/3/48; Recl Comp 14/9/48.
44-85622 Del Louisville 10/4/45; Rome 2/5/45; Middletown 3/11/45; Morrison 6/12/45; West Palm Beach 9/1/46; re-ass 31/3/45; 2621 BU Barksdale 1/1/48; 4117 BU Robins 4/3/48; Recl Comp 2/3/49.
44-85623 Del Louisville 6/4/45; Rome 2/5/45; Syracuse 12/10/45; RFC Altus 26/11/45.
44-85624 Del Louisville 7/4/45; Rome 28/5/45; Middletown 8/11/45; West Palm Beach 17/12/45; re-ass 30/4/47; Recl Comp 6/10/47.
44-85625 Del Louisville 10/4/45; Rome 7/6/45; Middletown 8/11/45; Morrison 25/12/45; West Palm Beach 4/1/46; re-ass 31/3/47; 2621 BU Barksdale 11/8/47; 4117 BU Robins 4/3/48; Recl Comp 15/10/48.
44-85626 Del Dallas 15/4/45; Syracuse 22/5/45; Middletown 30/10/45; Morrison 6/12/45; West Palm Beach 23/2/46; re-ass 30/4/47; Recl Comp 6/10/47.
44-85627 Del Louisville 9/4/45; Rome 1/6/45; Middletown 6/11/45; West Palm Beach 9/1/46; re-ass 30/4/47; Canal Zone 1/1/48; 4141 BU Pyote 1/7/48; Recl Comp 18/4/50.
44-85628 Del Dallas 11/4/45; Rome 26/5/45; Middletown 8/11/45; Morrison 3/1/46; West Palm Beach 11/1/46; re-ass 30/4/47; 91 RLPSq Howard, CZ, 1/1/48; 91 RLPSq Waller, Trinidad, 27/5/48; 91 RLPSq Panama 12/6/48; 91 RLPSq Waller 1/7/48; 91 RLPSq Maguire 1/2/49; 3902 ABGp Offutt

14/2/49; Recl Comp 31/7/50.
44-85629 Del Dallas 10/4/45; Syracuse 23/5/45; Middletown 8/11/45; West Palm Beach 25/12/45; re-ass 30/4/47; Canal Zone 1/1/48; 91 RLPSq Waller 1/7/48; 91 RLPSq Panama 26/7/48; 91 RLPSq Maguire 9/2/49; Recl Comp 14/10/49.
44-85630 Del Dallas 11/4/45; Rome 22/5/45; RFC Altus 28/11/45.
44-85631 Del Dallas 11/4/45; Rome 31/5/45; Syracuse 12/10/45; RFC Altus 26/11/45.
44-85632 Del Dallas 12/4/45; Rome 29/5/45; Syracuse 12/10/45; RFC Altus 15/11/45.
44-85633 Del Dallas 11/4/45; Rome 26/5/45; Syracuse 12/10/45; RFC Altus 6/11/45.
44-85634 Del Dallas 13/4/45; Rome 5/6/45; Syracuse 12/10/45; RFC Altus 28/11/45.
44-85635 Del Dallas 12/4/45; Rome 28/5/45; Syracuse 12/10/45; RFC Altus 15/11/45.
44-85636 Del Dallas 13/4/45; Rome 15/5/45; Syracuse 12/10/45; RFC Altus 28/11/45.
44-85637 Del Dallas 12/4/45; Rome 29/5/45; Syracuse 12/10/45; RFC Altus 21/11/45.
44-85638 Del Dallas 13/4/45; Rome 4/6/45; Syracuse 12/10/45; RFC Altus 15/11/45.
44-85639 Del Dallas 13/4/45; Rome 26/5/45; Syracuse 12/10/45; RFC Altus 26/11/45.
44-85640 Del Dallas 13/4/45; Rome 5/6/45; Syracuse 12/10/45; RFC Altus 21/11/45.
44-85641 Del Dallas 14/4/45; Rome 4/6/45; Syracuse 12/10/45; RFC Altus 5/11/45.
44-85642 Del Dallas 14/4/45; Rome 1/6/45; Syracuse 12/10/45; RFC Altus 21/11/45.
44-85643 Del 21/4/45; Rome 14/6/45; Syracuse 20/6/45; RFC Altus 21/11/45; sold IGN, France 12/12/47 as F-BEEA; Barr Flood Fd, Port Moresby, PNG 1967; cr Binbrook, UK in filming of *Memphis Belle* 25/7/89, as AMELIA.
44-85644 Del Dallas 18/4/45; Rome 12/6/45; Middletown 8/11/45; Morrison 2/12/45; West Palm Beach 5/1/46; 2621 BU Barksdale 19/5/47; 4117 BU Robins 4/3/48; Recl Comp 31/3/49.
44-85645 Del Louisville 14/4/45; Sth Plains 19/4/45; 2519 BU Ft Worth 18/10/45; 3017 BU Hobbs 25/10/45; 2137 BU Hendricks 15/12/45; 2140 BU Smyrna 31/1/46; 342 BU Smyrna 30/4/46; 554 BU Memphis 12/8/46.
44-85646 Del Louisville 21/4/45; Sth Plains 30/4/45; RFC Walnut Ridge 3/1/46.
44-85647 Del Louisville 16/4/45; Sth Plains 23/4/45; 2519 BU Ft Worth 18/10/45; 3017 BU Hobbs 21/10/45; 2140 BU Smyrna 31/1/46; 342 BU Smyrna 30/4/46; 613 BU Phillips 26/6/46.
44-85648 Del Louisville 17/4/45; Sth Plains 21/4/45; 2519 BU Ft Worth 17/10/45; 3017 BU Hobbs 19/10/45; 2137 BU Hendricks 15/12/45; 2140 BU Smyrna 31/1/46; 342 BU Smyrna 30/4/46; 594 BU Topeka 12/6/46; 4104 BU Rome 18/6/46; Columbus 30/6/46; re-ass 31/3/47; 4104 BU Rome 29/6/47; 4112 BU Olmstead 6/7/47; 1 EG Eglin 13/1/49; ditched Adriatic, off Yugoslavia, in radio controlled ditching tests 17/5/49.
44-85649 Del Louisville 17/4/45; Sth Plains 25/4/45; RFC Walnut Ridge 3/1/46.
44-85650 Del Louisville 17/4/45; Sth Plains 23/4/45; 2140 BU Smyrna 5/11/45; 342 BU Smyrna 30/4/46; 613 BU Phillips 18/6/46.
44-85651 Del Louisville 17/4/45; Sth Plains 26/4/45; 2140 BU Smyrna 5/11/45; 342 BU Smyrna 30/4/46; 613 BU Phillips 26/6/46.
44-85652 Del Louisville 17/4/45; Sth Plains 27/4/45; Orlando 8/7/45; 611 BU Eglin 18/11/45; W/O 610 BU Eglin 11/4/46.

44-85653 Del Louisville 21/4/45; Grenier 26/4/45; Columbus 29/4/45; 1377 BU Grenier 2/6/45; 3 WER Grenier 6/6/45; 53 RCNSq Grenier 16/6/45; 112 BU Grenier 10/2/46; Recl Comp 5/8/46.
44-85654 Del Louisville 21/4/45; Grenier 26/4/45; 3 WER Grenier 30/4/45; 53 RCNSq Grenier 22/8/45; Buckley 11/3/46; 539 SC Morrison 14/5/46; 575 SR Andrews 7/5/47; 67 BU Robins 9/11/47; 5 RES McDill 12/11/48; 9 RES Biggs 7/7/48; 47 MSU Biggs 20/9/48; Recl Comp 16/12/48.
44-85655 Del Louisville 17/4/45; Sth Plains 19/4/45; 2140 BU Smyrna 8/11/45; 342 BU Smyrna 30/4/46; 613 BU Phillips 10/6/46; 594 BU Topeka 7/7/46.
44-85656 Del Louisville 23/4/45; Sth Plains 27/4/45; 2140 BU Smyrna 8/11/45; 342 BU Smyrna 30/4/46; 613 BU Phillips 18/6/46.
44-85657 Del Louisville 23/4/45; Syracuse 7/6/45; Middletown 6/11/45; Morrison 6/12/45; West Palm Beach 31/7/46; re-ass 30/4/47; 91 RLP Howard, CZ 1/1/48; 91 RLP Waller, Trinidad 3/7/48; 1 RLP Maguire 9/2/49; 4205 ABGp Mt Home 28/2/49; 91 RLP Maguire 1/4/49; 3902 ABGp Offutt 30/6/49; Recl Comp 18/1/50.
44-85658 Del Louisville 23/4/45; Rome 6/7/45; RFC Altus 7/12/45.
44-85659 –.
44-85660 Del Louisville 21/4/45; Sth Plains 25/4/45; 2140 BU Smyrna 8/11/45; 342 BU Smyrna 30/4/46; 594 BU Topeka 26/6/46.
44-85661 Del Cheyenne 23/4/45; Sth Plains 30/4/45; 4136 BU Tinker 22/10/45; 4104 BU Rome 9/10/46; 16 PhGp McDill 2/2/47; re-ass 31/3/47; 16 PhGp McDill 11/8/47; 343 BU Topeka 28/7/48; 91 ABGp Maguire 4/3/49; AMC Olmstead 26/6/49; 91 ABGp Ladd Fd 9/11/49; 91 SRC Barksdale 1/5/50; Recl Comp 18/5/50.
44-85662 Del Cheyenne 23/4/45; Sth Plains 30/4/45; re-ass 31/3/47; 343 RVM McDill 15/8/47; QB-17L as Drone in day-glo orange with three black stripes and silver rudder; 4135 BU Hill 7/8/48; 554 BU Topeka 16/11/48; 3345 TTW Chanute 10/6/49; 55 ABGp Topeka 20/6/49; 55 MSU Forbes 1/9/49; Recl Comp 19/5/50.
44-85663 Del Cheyenne 23/4/45; Sth Plains 1/5/45; re-ass 31/3/47; 343 RVM McDill 7/5/47; 343 BU Topeka 27/8/48; 7 GEO Dt Topeka 4/2/49; 55 MSU Topeka 17/3/49; Recl Comp 19/5/50.
44-85664 Del Louisville 23/4/45; Sth Plains 2/5/45; RFC Walnut Ridge 5/1/46.
44-85665 Del Cheyenne 23/4/45; Sth Plains 30/4/45; 4104 BU Rome 9/10/46; 16 PHSq McDill 1/2/47; re-ass 31/3/47; 343 RVM McDill 11/9/47; 201 BU Peterson 15/10/47; 343 BU Topeka 10/8/48; 55 MSU Gp Topeka 28/2/49; 3902 ABGp Offutt 22/4/49; Recl Comp 24/2/50.
44-85666 Del Louisville 23/4/45; Sth Plains 9/5/45; Vandalia 11/7/45; 4000 BU Patterson 25/11/45; re-ass 31/3/47; 4168 BU Sth Plains 24/6/47; 4141 BU Pyote 1/1/48; Recl Comp 13/4/49.
44-85667 –.
44-85668 Del Louisville 24/4/45; Sth Plains 2/5/45; 2140 BU Smyrna 8/11/45; 342 BU Smyrna 30/4/46; 613 BU Phillips 20/8/46.
44-85669 Del Louisville 23/4/45; Syracuse 6/6/45; Middletown 30/10/45; West Palm Beach 9/1/46; re-ass 30/4/47; 5828 RPG Howard, CZ 1/1/48; 6 BG Galapagos 25/2/48; 3 BG Albrook 20/3/48; 6 BG Galapagos 8/5/48; 5702 MSU Albrook 25/3/49; AMC Kelly 11/8/49; Recl Comp 14/10/49.
44-85670 Del Louisville 23/4/45; Sth Plains 2/5/45; RFC Walnut Ridge 7/1/46.
44-85671 Del Louisville 24/4/45; Sth Plains 14/6/45;

233 BU Ft Worth 27/2/46; 613 BU Phillips 1/5/46.
44-85672 Del Louisville 24/4/45; Rome 14/5/45; RFC Kingman 13/1/46.
44-85673 –.
44-85674 Del Louisville 26/4/45; Sth Plains 20/5/45; 3017 BU Hobbs 8/10/45; 2140 BU Smyrna 31/1/46; 342 BU Smyrna 30/4/46; 554 BU Memphis 12/6/46.
44-85675 Del Louisville 25/4/45; Syracuse 2/5/45; RFC Altus 21/11/45.
44-85676 –.
44-85677 Del Louisville 26/4/45; Sth Plains 9/7/45; RFC Walnut Ridge 5/12/45.
44-85678 Del Dallas 24/4/45; Sth Plains 13/5/45; 4150 BU Boca Raton 4/7/45; 4108 BU Newark 30/8/45; 4150 BU Boca Raton 20/11/45; re-ass 31/3/47; 4150 BU Robins 1/1/48; 4117 BU Robins 10/1/48; Recl Comp 28/4/48.
44-85679 Del Louisville 26/4/45; Chicago Mun. 8/5/45 for Bond Show; Sth Plains 23/6/45; 242 Gr Island 17/2/46; 4209 BU Des Moines 10/4/46; 242 BU Gr Island 17/4/46; 555 BU Love Fd 20/5/46; 4149 BU Olmstead 27/5/46; re-ass 31/3/47; USN for radar/electronics test bed Wright Fd 6/47 as [77138] and P-38 drop tanks fitted; AMC Muroc 5/2/49; Recl Comp 17/10/49; SOC 7/10/56; Lloyd Areos Bolivianos, cr Santo Domingo 6/3/64.
44-85680 –.
44-85681 Del Louisville 24/4/45; Syracuse 25/5/45; Middletown 8/11/45; Morrison 5/12/45; 4112 BU Olmstead 31/1/46; West palm Beach 3/3/46; 1103 BU Morrison 6/3/46; re-ass 30/4/47; 91 RLP Howard, CZ 1/1/48; 91 RLP Waller 1/7/48; 91 RLP Maguire 9/2/49; 91 SRC Barksdale 5/12/49; Recl Comp 16/2/50.
44-85682 Del Louisville 26/4/45; Rome 27/5/45; 4132 BU Garden City 27/9/45; 4000 BU Wright 24/2/46; 234 BU Clovis 4/3/46; 15 TSK Clovis 13/3/46; 4000 BU Patterson 18/4/46; 4135 BU Hill 11/7/46; 4145 BU Wendover 21/7/46; re-ass 31/3/47; 4104 BU Rome 11/8/47; AMC Columbus 25/9/47; 3203 MSU Eglin 28/4/49; 1 EG Eglin 21/7/49; Recl Comp 31/7/50.
44-85683 Del Louisville 26/4/45; Chicago Mun 8/5/45 for Bond Show; Sth Plains 16/6/45; NExAS Phildelphia 20/6/45; designated XPB-1 31/7/45 [77258] with experimental electronic equipment; ass VPB-101 Floyd Bennett Fd, NY 11/45; NAS Squantum 5/46; NAMU Johnsville 3/47; taxi accident NAS Mustin Fd with two other aircraft 29/12/49; became DPB-1 for drop tests at NAAS Chincoteague, Va 1950; NAAF Mustin Fd 9/50, scrapped for spares.
44-85684 Del Louisville 27/4/45; Sth Plains 9/5/45; Eglin 21/7/45; 620 BU Muroc 25/7/45; re-ass 31/3/47; 4141 BU Pyote 1/1/48; Recl Comp 1/6/49.
44-85685 Del Louisville 25/4/45; Rome 27/5/45; Middletown 8/11/45; Morrison 6/12/45; re-ass 30/4/47; Canal Zone 1/1/48; Panama Air Depot 26/7/48; Olmstead 22/10/49; Recl Comp 10/11/49.
44-85686 Del Louisville 27/4/45; Syracuse 25/5/45; RFC Altus 5/11/45.
44-85687 Del Louisville 30/4/45; Syracuse 24/5/45; Middletown 8/11/45; 4112 BU Olmstead 31/1/46; West Palm Beach 3/3/46; 2621 BU Barksdale 14/1/47; re-ass 31/3/47; 4117 BU Robins 4/3/48; Recl Comp 14/9/48.
44-85688 Del Louisville 29/4/45; Syracuse 1/6/45; Middletown 8/11/45; Morrison 17/1/46; West Palm Beach 2/1/47; 2621 BU Barksdale 23/6/47; re-ass 31/3/47; 4117 BU Robins 4/3/48; Recl Comp 14/9/48.
44-85689 Del Louisville 27/4/45; Syracuse 26/5/45;

INDIVIDUAL B-17 HISTORIES 317

Middletown 8/11/45; Morrison 18/1/46; West Palm Beach 23/1/46; re-ass 30/4/47; 2621 BU Barksdale 3/9/47; 7 MSU Ft Worth 8/1/48; 4117 BU Robins 27/3/48; Recl Comp 18/2/49.

44-85690 Del Louisville 28/4/45; Rome 27/5/45; major damage to wing in taxi accident with parked aircraft 30/5/45; Syracuse 20/6/45; Garden City 27/9/45; San Antonio 5/2/46; 4121 BU Kelly 13/2/46; 15 TSK Clovis 25/3/46; 1503 BU Hamilton 18/6/46; Pacific TSP 14/8/46, drone with 509 Comp Gp, Bikini Atoll A-bomb tests; 1 EG Eglin 28/2/47; re-ass 31/3/47; 605 BU Eglin 10/3/48; 4141 BU Pyote 17/3/48; Recl Comp 18/4/50. MISS LIBERTY BELLE.

44-85691 Del Louisville 30/4/45; Rome 27/5/45; Middletown 30/10/45; Morrison 6/2/46; 4202 BU Syracuse 30/9/46; 2621 BU Barksdale 13/11/46; re-ass 31/3/47; Robins 4/3/48; Recl Comp 15/10/48.

44-85692 Del Louisville 30/4/45; Syracuse 27/5/45; Middletown 8/11/45; Morrison 6/12/45; 4112 BU Olmstead 1/1/46; 2621 BU Barksdale 17/2/47; re-ass 31/3/47; Recl Comp 18/8/47.

44-85693 Del Louisville 1/5/45; Rome 25/5/45; Middletown 6/11/45; Morrison 6/12/45; West Palm Beach 17/12/45; re-ass 30/4/47; 5 BC Rio Hato, CZ 1/1/48; 4 BC France, CZ 8/1/48; Panama 1/6/48; 5621 MSU France 26/7/48; 5620 ABSq France 25/4/49; Panama 6/7/49; Eglin 26/8/49; Recl Comp 9/9/49.

44-85694 Del Louisville 1/5/45; Syracuse 24/5/45; Middletown 8/11/45; Morrison 11/1/46; West Palm Beach 31/7/46; re-ass 30/4/47; 5 BC Rio Hato 1/1/48; 3 BC Albrook 20/1/48; 6 BC Galapagos 16/5/48; 5701 MSUGp Albrook 23/2/49; AMC Olmstead 8/9/4/9; Recl Comp 14/10/49.

44-85695 Del Louisville 1/5/45; Rome 26/5/45; Middletown 8/11/45; Morrison 15/11/45; West Palm Beach 27/1/46; re-ass 30/4/47; 2621 BU Barksdale 29/7/47; 4117 BU Robins 4/3/48; Recl Comp 2/3/49.

44-85696 Del Louisville 2/5/45; Rome 28/5/45; 4202 BU Syracuse 20/9/45; RFC Altus 15/11/45.

44-85697 Del Louisville 2/5/45; Rome 27/5/45; Middletown 8/11/45; Morrison 6/12/45; 4112 BU Olmstead 1/3/46; West Palm Beach 3/3/46; re-ass 30/4/47; 4 BSR Borinquen, PR 1/1/48; 5904 ABGp Ramey 26/7/47; AMC Hill Fd 17/3/49; 5904 ABGp Ramey 1/5/49; AMC Olmstead 12/10/49; Recl Comp 25/10/49.

44-85698 Del Louisville 3/5/45; Syracuse 6/6/45; Middletown 8/11/45; Morrison 21/12/45; West Palm Beach 5/1/46; 2621 BU Barksdale 21/11/46; re-ass 31/3/47; 7 MSU Ft Worth 5/1/48; 4117 BU Robins 12/4/48; Recl Comp 15/10/48.

44-85699 Del Louisville 2/5/45; Syracuse 12/6/45; RFC Altus 7/11/45.

44-85700 Del Louisville 2/5/45; Rome 26/5/45; 4185 BU Independence 17/10/45; RFC Altus 5/11/45.

44-85701 Del Louisville 3/5/45; Syracuse 5/6/45; 593 BU Charleston 28/10/45; RFC Altus 5/11/45.

44-85702 Del Louisville 4/5/45; Syracuse 4/6/45; Middletown 8/11/45; Morrison 21/2/46; 4112 BU Olmstead 26/2/46; West Palm Beach 3/3/46; re-ass 30/4/47; 4 BC France 1/1/48; 319 FTR France 23/6/48; 3622 AB France 17/9/48; 5625 ABGp France 1/4/49; 5621 MSUGp France 22/4/49; 3203 MSUGp Eglin 5/8/49; 550 GM Eglin 7/11/49; Recl Comp 25/5/50.

44-85703 Del Louisville 5/5/45; Syracuse 8/6/45; RFC Altus 7/11/45.

44-85704 Del Louisville 5/5/45; Syracuse 4/6/45; RFC Altus 6/11/45.

44-85705 –.

44-85706 –. VB-17G with 6AF Caribbean, Canal Zone.

44-85707 Del Louisville 4/5/45; Syracuse 6/6/45; Middletown 6/11/45; Morrison 6/12/45; West Palm Beach 31/12/45; re-ass 30/4/47; 27 ADR Waller 1/1/48; 5922 MSU Waller 1/10/48; 5920 ABGp Waller 14/6/49; Panama AD 29/9/49; Recl Comp 25/10/49.

44-85708 Del Louisville 8/5/45; Syracuse 13/6/45; RFC Altus 29/11/45.

44-85709 Del Louisville 8/5/45; Syracuse 4/6/45; RFC Altus 7/11/45.

44-85710 Del Louisville 8/5/45; Syracuse 17/5/45; RFC Altus 29/11/45.

44-85711 Del Louisville 8/5/45; Syracuse 16/6/45; RFC Altus 15/11/45.

44-85712 Del Louisville 8/5/45; Syracuse 14/6/45; RFC Altus 5/11/45.

44-85713 Del Louisville 8/5/45; Syracuse 13/6/45; RFC Altus 28/11/45.

44-85714 Del Louisville 10/5/45; Syracuse 21/6/45; 593 BU Charleston 28/10/45; RFC Altus 5/11/45.

44-85715 –.

44-85716 Del Louisville 9/5/45; Rome 8/6/45; 593 BU Charleston 28/10/45; RFC Altus 7/11/45.

44-85717 Del Louisville 9/5/45; Rome 20/6/45; RFC Altus 7/11/45.

44-85718 Del Louisville 9/5/45; Rome 5/7/45; RFC Altus 21/11/45; IGN France [F-BEEC] 10/12/47 CHARLOTTE; Bitteswell, Leics, GB as G-FORT 12/6/84; US Civil N900RW; restored as 303BG Houston 1987 THUNDERBIRD.

44-85719 Del Louisville 8/5/45; Rome 21/6/45; RFC Altus 28/11/45.

44-85720 Del Louisville 12/5/45; Rome 5/7/45; RFC Altus 7/11/45.

44-85721 Del Louisville 12/5/45; Syracuse 7/6/45; RFC Altus 26/11/45.

44-85722 Del Louisville 12/5/45; Rome 6/7/45; RFC Altus 15/11/45.

44-85723 Del Louisville 14/5/45; Rome 4/7/45; RFC Altus 28/11/45.

44-85724 Del Louisville 14/5/45; Rome 6/7/45; RFC Altus 5/11/45.

44-85725 Del Louisville 14/5/45; Syracuse 7/7/45; RFC Altus 15/11/45.

44-85726 Del Louisville 14/5/45; Rome 8/7/45; Middletown 6/11/45; Morrison 6/12/45; West Palm Beach 5/1/46; re-ass 30/4/47; 91 RLP Howard, CZ 1/1/48; 91 RPL Waller 1/7/48; 91 SRCGp Maguire 9/2/49; Recl Comp 15/10/49.

44-85727 Del Louisville 14/5/45; Rome 9/7/45; RFC Altus 5/11/45.

44-85728 Del Louisville 14/5/45; Rome 10/7/45; 4202 BU Syracuse 20/10/45; RFC Altus 28/11/45; sal 15 TSK Clovis 30/4/46; sold TWA as 299AB 1947 (Civil NX4600) for Near East survey work; Converted for Shah of Persia 1947 [EP-HIM]; IGN France [F-BGOE]; scrapped France 1970s.

44-85729 Del Louisville 17/5/45; Rome 11/7/45; RFC Altus 28/11/45.

44-85730 Del Louisville 17/5/45; Rome 9/7/45; RFC Altus 5/11/45.

44-85731 Del Louisville 11/5/45; Syracuse 26/6/45; RFC Altus 7/11/45; tran USN 6/47 [83996]; NAS Corpus Christi, Tx, scrapped for spares.

44-85732 Del Louisville 15/5/45; Syracuse 22/6/45; RFC Altus 28/11/45.

44-85733 Del Dallas 17/5/45; Syracuse 23/6/45; RFC Altus 21/11/45; sold IGN France [F-BEEB] 12/2/48; cr Cameroons 11/3/49.

44-85734 Del Louisville 17/5/45; Syracuse 5/7/45; RFC Altus 15/11/45; Used as experimental Allison T-56 turbo-prop, Seattle with Buzz No BA-747B; Kissimee, Fl 1987. ANUDDERONE.

44-85735 Del Louisville 15/5/45; Syracuse 21/6/45; RFC Altus 7/11/45.

44-85736 Del Louisville 15/5/45; Syracuse 3/7/45; RFC Altus 5/11/45.

44-85737 Del Louisville 15/5/45; Syracuse 22/6/45; RFC Altus 29/10/45.

44-85738 Del Louisville 18/5/45; ass 509th Comp Gp, as drone, possibly last survivor of Operation 'Crossroads', A-bomb tests in Pacific; retUS 1946 for restoration at Tulare, Cal; sat at Arizona garage 1974; Tulare 1988, where damaged by vehicle collision 8/82 in USAF Museum.

44-85739 Del Louisville 15/5/45; Syracuse 23/6/45; RFC Altus 5/11/45. DENISE.

44-85740 Del Louisville 15/5/45; Syracuse 29/6/45; RFC Altus 7/11/45; (Civil N5015N) at Oshkosh 1987; sold Metal Products, to Universal Avn then Vero Beach, Fl Imp/Exp/Co as carrier for cattle to Puerto Rico; Aero Service, Phil and modified for high altitude mapping projects; now restored as ALUMINIUM OVERCAST.

44-85741 Del Louisville 21/5/45; Syracuse 27/6/45; RFC Altus 15/11/45. (?Civil N5011N?).

Above: B-17G-105-VE 44-85718 landing at Blackbushe, England, with No 1 feathered and the liferaft door sprung, both suggesting a troubled flight. Previously F-BEEC of IGN, the aircraft sports an unusual dome in the radio-compartment hatch.

44-85742 Del Louisville 22/5/45; Rome 11/7/45; RFC Altus 5/11/45.

44-85743 Del Louisville 22/5/45; Syracuse 9/7/45; RFC Altus 5/11/45.

44-85744 Del Louisville 22/5/45; Syracuse 30/6/45; RFC Altus 5/11/45.

44-85745 Del Louisville 21/5/45; Syracuse 30/6/45; RFC Altus 5/11/45.

44-85746 –.

44-85747 Del Louisville 22/5/45; Syracuse 10/5/45; Olmstead 11/45; ass Caribbean AC, Morrison Fd 26/2/46; Barksdale 26/3/47; Indianapolis 20/8/47; loaned to USN 5/9/47 [83999] as test bed for Allison engine and other turbo-props, some going on C-130 Hercules, P3V Orion etc; designated NB-17G, permanent test aircraft 1955; Eglin 4/58 and scrapped.

44-85748 Del Louisville 22/5/45; Syracuse 7/2/45; RFC Altus 7/11/45; tran USN 6/47 [83997]; NAS Corpus Christi, Tx, scrapped for spares.

44-85749 Del Dallas 24/5/45; Syracuse 21/6/45; Middletown 8/11/45; Morrison 6/12/45; 4112 BU Olmstead 31/1/46; West Palm Beach 27/2/46; 2621 BU Barksdale 16/3/47; re-ass 31/3/47; 4117 BU Robins 4/3/48; Recl Comp 31/3/49.

44-85750 Del Dallas 24/5/45; Syracuse 21/6/45; Middletown 8/11/45; Morrison 6/12/45; 4112 BU Olmstead 31/6/46; West Palm Beach 11/3/46; re-ass 30/4/47; 2621 BU Barksdale 3/9/47; 4117 BU Robins 4/3/48; Recl Comp 15/10/48.

44-85751 Del Dallas 24/5/45; Syracuse 21/6/45; RFC Altus 7/11/45.

44-85752 Del Dallas 24/5/45; Syracuse 23/6/45; Garden City 27/9/45; San Antonio 5/2/46; 4121 BU Kelly 18/2/46; 15 TSK Clovis 25/3/46; 4136 BU Tinker 3/4/46; 1503 BU Hamilton 16/8/46; 556 BU Long Beach 9/10/46; ass 509th Comp Gp Roswell for A-Bomb tests Drone in Pacific; 1 EG Eglin 28/2/47; re-ass 31/3/47; 605 BU Eglin 10/2/48; 4141 BU Pyote 7/3/48; Recl Comp 18/4/50.

44-85753 Del Dallas 25/5/45; Syracuse 23/6/45; RFC Altus 7/11/45.

44-85754 Del Dallas 24/5/45; Syracuse 26/6/45; RFC Altus 5/11/45.

44-85755 Del Dallas 24/5/45; Syracuse 25/6/45; RFC Altus 5/11/45.

44-85756 Del Dallas 25/5/45; Syracuse 26/6/45; RFC Altus 5/11/45.

44-85757 Del Dallas 25/5/45; Syracuse 25/6/45; 4124 BU Altus 16/10/45; Middletown 27/11/45; Morrison 6/12/45; 613 BU Phillips 23/1/46; 608 BU Phillips 13/7/46; re-ass 31/3/47; 609 BU Phillips 28/4/47; Recl Comp 19/7/48.

44-85758 Del Dallas 25/5/45; Syracuse 26/6/45; RFC Altus 7/11/45.

44-85759 Del Dallas 26/5/45; Syracuse 26/6/45; RFC Altus 5/11/45.

44-85760 Del Dallas 26/5/45; Syracuse 23/6/45; RFC Altus 29/10/45.

44-85761 Del Dallas 29/5/45; Syracuse 26/6/45; RFC Altus 5/11/45.

44-85762 Del Dallas 28/5/45; Syracuse 28/6/45; RFC Altus 7/11/45; tran USN 6/47 [83998]; NAS Corpus Christi, Tx, scrapped for spares.

44-85763 Del Dallas 26/5/45; Syracuse 27/6/45; RFC Altus 7/11/45.

44-85764 Del Dallas 26/5/45; Syracuse 26/6/45; RFC Altus 7/11/45.

44-85765 Del Dallas 29/5/45; Syracuse 31/5/45; RFC Altus 7/11/45.

44-85766 Del Dallas 31/5/45; Syracuse 28/6/45; RFC Altus 5/11/45.

44-85767 Del Dallas 31/5/45; Syracuse 24/6/45; RFC Altus 15/11/45.

44-85768 Del Dallas 1/6/45; Syracuse 28/6/45; RFC Altus 5/11/45.

44-85769 Del Dallas 4/6/45; Syracuse 4/7/45; RFC Altus 5/11/45.

44-85770 Del Dallas 4/6/45; Syracuse 10/7/45; RFC Altus 5/11/45.

44-85771 Del Dallas 4/6/45; Syracuse 30/6/45; RFC Altus 5/11/45.

44-85772 Del Dallas 4/6/45; Syracuse 30/6/45; RFC Altus 5/11/45.

44-85773 Del Dallas 4/6/45; Syracuse 7/7/45; RFC Altus 28/11/45.

44-85774 Del Seattle 14/6/45; 4000 BU Wright Fd 16/7/45; 4136 BU Tinker 25/4/46 as VB-17G; re-ass 31/3/47; AMC Tinker 1/7/48; Recl Comp 20/9/50; sold as tanker, cr Mesa, Az 1975 (remains of CP621 in Bolivia?).

44-85775 Del Dallas 6/6/45; Syracuse 2/7/45; RFC Altus 5/11/45.

44-85776 Del Dallas 6/6/45; Syracuse 6/7/45; RFC Altus 5/11/45.

44-85777 Del Dallas 7/6/45; Syracuse 4/7/45; RFC Altus 5/11/45.

44-85778 Del Dallas 6/6/45; Sth Plains 9/6/45; ass 48 SRGp and 24 Comp Gp in Caribbean Air Command; train Brazillian Air Command 1948 as VB-17G; retUS 1100 OpGp Bolling 1954; stored at Davis Monthan 1956; (Civil N3509G) restored to military configeration at Santa Monica, Cal 10/1991; MISS MUSEUM OF FLYING.

44-85779 Del Dallas 8/6/45; Rome 12/7/45; RFC Altus 5/11/45.

44-85780 Del Dallas 8/6/45; Rome 12/7/45; RFC Altus 5/11/45.

44-85781 Del Dallas 26/6/45; Rome 26/7/45; RFC Altus 5/11/45.

44-85782 Del Dallas 8/6/45; Syracuse 13/7/45; RFC Altus 5/11/45.

44-85783 Del Dallas 8/6/45; Rome 13/7/45; RFC Altus 5/11/45.

44-85784 Del Burbank 19/6/45; Rome 13/7/45; RFC Altus 5/11/45; designated EB-17G, then ETB-17G and used for man carrying wing tip pod tests 1949; sold IGN France as F-BGSR 31/10/54; sold to Ted White as N17TE in 1970; to UK as G-BEDF on airshow circuit as SALLY B (more latterly as MEMPHIS BELLE).

44-85785 Del Dallas 9/6/45; Rome 14/7/45; RFC Altus 5/11/45.

44-85786 Del Dallas 12/6/45; Rome 19/7/45; RFC Altus 5/11/45.

44-85787 Del Dallas 12/6/45; Rome 14/7/45; RFC Altus 5/11/45.

44-85788 Del Dallas 13/6/45; Rome 18/7/45; RFC Altus 5/11/45.

44-85789 Del Dallas 12/6/45; Rome 13/7/45; RFC Altus 5/11/45.

44-85790 Del Dallas 14/6/45; Rome 14/7/45; 4185 BU Independence 3/10/45; RFC Altus 5/11/45; ended up as Texaco gas station monument called The Bomb, at Milwaukee, Or.

44-85791 Del Dallas 14/6/45; Rome 21/7/45; RFC Altus 5/11/45.

44-85792 Del Dallas 16/6/45; Rome 22/7/45; 4185 BU Independence 7/10/45; 593 BU Charleston 28/10/45; RFC Louisville 12/6/45.

44-85793 Del Dallas 15/6/45; Rome 19/7/45; Topeka 4/9/45; WCW San Francisco 13/9/45; Leyte, PI 21/10/46; re-ass 30/4/47; sal 3 CON Manila, PI 5/5/47; Recl Comp 24/4/48.

44-85794 Del Dallas 15/6/45; Rome 25/7/45; RFC Altus 5/11/45.

44-85795 Del Dallas 16/6/45; Rome 30/7/45; Independence 28/9/45; RFC Kingman 4/11/45.

44-85796 Del Dallas 16/6/45; Rome 23/7/45; Independence 28/9/45; RFC Kingman 4/11/45.

44-85797 Del Dallas 19/6/45; Rome 20/7/45; Independence 2/10/45; RFC Kingman 26/10/45.

44-85798 Del Dallas 19/6/45; Rome 25/7/45; RFC Altus 5/11/45.

44-85799 Del Dallas 19/6/45; Rome 28/7/45; Independence 2/10/45; RFC Kingman 4/11/45.

44-85800 Del Dallas 23/6/45; Rome 28/7/45; RFC Altus 5/11/45.

44-85801 Del Dallas 31/6/45; Rome 27/7/45; Andrews Fd 2/10/45; re-ass 30/4/47; 3 BC Albrook, CZ 1/1/48; 5702 MAI Albrook 26/7/48; 5701 MSUGp Albrook 23/3/49; 5700 ABGp Albrook 1/5/49; AMC Olmstead 6/9/49; 3800 AU Maxwell 27/9/49; Recl Comp 25/10/49.

44-85802 Del Dallas 20/6/45; Rome 27/7/45; Walnut Ridge AD 15/10/45; Grenier 8/1/46; 4117 BU Robins 13/1/46; 304 BU Langley 17/1/46; 53 RCN Morrison 21/4/47; 1103 BU Morrison 31/7/47; Recl Comp 6/10/47.

44-85803 Del Dallas 23/6/45; Rome 30/7/45; Independence 28/9/45; RFC Kingman 26/10/45.

44-85804 Del Dallas 25/6/45; Rome 26//7/45; RFC Altus 5/11/45.

44-85805 Del Dallas 26/6/45; Rome 28/7/45; Independence 28/9/45; RFC Kingman 5/11/45.

44-85806 Del Dallas 27/6/45; Sth Plains 26/8/48; Rome 4104 BU 20/2/46; 1077 BU Bowman 25/2/46; Mustin Fd for conversion to PB-1G for US Coast Guard 15/8/46; del CG Elizabeth City 7/11/46; Spartan Aero, Tulsa for overhaul 10/49; CG Brooklyn 5/51; Delta Lease/Co, Charlotte, NC 26/10/56, Civil N117W; Biegert Bros, Shickley 7/2/57 (sprayer); Bolivian Air System 12/64, as CP-762; cr La Paz 16/6/64.

44-85807 Del Dallas 26/6/45; Rome 26/7/45; RFC Altus 5/11/45.

44-85808 Del Dallas 25/6/45; Rome 31/7/45; Independence 7/10/45; RFC Kingman 4/11/45.

44-85809 Del Dallas 29/6/45; Rome 28/7/45; Independence 4/10/45; RFC Altus 5/11/45.

44-85810 Del Dallas 26/6/45; Rome 26/7/45; RFC Altus 29/10/45.

44-85811 Del Dallas 27/6/45; Rome 27/7/45; RFC Altus 5/11/45.

44-85812 Del Dallas 26/6/45; Sth Plains 7/8/45; Rome 22/2/46; NAAF Mustin Fd 1/4/46 [77246]; to USCG Brooklyn 12/8/46; Elizabeth City 10/51; NAS Norfolk for overhaul 8/52; Port Angeles 10/53; Annette 9/54; Olmstead 11/55; Inter Ice Patrol, Argentia, Nfd /56; Elizabeth City 1/58; Delta Lease/Co, Charlotte, NC 16/5/58, Civil N4710C; Leroy Brown, Miami 23/1/59; wooden floor fitted for veg cargo to Bahamas; Challenger Lease/Co Ft Lauderdale 1/4/61; Dothan AvCo, Al 16/4/63 (sprayer); crashed Blakely, Ga 8/5/76.

44-85813 Del Wright Aero/Corp test a/c with XT-35 turbo-prop fifth engine, des JB-17G; Black Hills Av, (Civil N6694C) as tanker C12; c/t/o Bear Pen, NC 8/73; sal for spares.

44-85814 Del Dallas 30/6/45; Rome 31/7/45; Independence 28/9/45; RFC Altus 5/11/45.

44-85815 Del Dallas 29/6/45; Sth Plains 31/7/45; Walnut Ridge 24/8/45; Ft Worth 28/1/46; 4121 BU Kelly 18/2/46; 15 TSK Clovis 25/3/46; 556 BU Long Beach 9/6/46; 1503 BU Hamilton 16/6/46; 509 Comp Gp Roswell 21/8/46 Operation 'Crossroads'; 1

EG Eglin 28/2/47 MB-17 missile carrier JB-2; 609 BU Eglin 24/3/47; re-ass 31/3/47; 1 EG Eglin 1/1/48; 3203 MSU Eglin 18/8/48; 2753 ASTSq Pyote 4/4/50; Recl Comp 18/4/50.

44-85816 Del Dallas 29/6/45; Rome 2/8/45; RFC Altus 5/11/45.

44-85817 –. (Civil 31851), Bolivia CP-622; c/l and w/o Laja, Bol 18/12/57.

44-85818 Del Dallas 2/7/45; Sth Plains 6/8/45; Walnut Ridge 24/8/45; 233 BU Ft Worth 31/1/46; 4121 BU Kelly 18/2/46; 15 TSK Clovis 31/3/46; 556 BU Long Beach 9/6/46; 509 Comp Gp Roswell 18/8/46 Operation 'Crossroads'; 3235 Drone Sq Director at Eglin 1/47; 1 EG Eglin 9/8/47; Recl Comp 19/6/49.

44-85819 Del Dallas 5/7/45; Sth Plains 4/8/45; Walnut Ridge 24/8/45; 234 BU Clovis 31/1/46; 4121 BU Kelly 20/2/46; 15 TSK Clovis 25/3/46; 556 BU Long Beach 9/6/46; 1503 BU Hamilton 16/6/46; 509 Comp Gp Roswell 18/8/46 Operation 'Crossroads'; 4104 BU Rome 4/11/46; 4145 BU Wendover 15/12/46; 216 BU Wendover 23/3/47; re-ass 31/3/47; 4145 BU Alamogordo 16/4/47; 4121 BU Kelly 8/8/47; 4000 BU Patterson 4/9/47; 2750 AB Wright-Patterson 10/9/48; Recl Comp 15/12/49.

44-85820 –. Ass 58BW, used in Bikini Atoll A-Bomb tests; SUPER SPARE.

44-85821 Del Dallas 6/7/45; Sth Plains 9/8/45; Rome 23/2/46; NAAF Mustin Fd 2/4/46 as PB-1G [77247]; USCG Elizabeth City 29/7/45; SOC 31/7/46; Inter Ice Patrol, Argentia 9/46; Elizabeth City 1/47; CGAS Brooklyn 6/47; overhauled Spartan AR, Tulsa 5/49; CGAS San Francisco 10/49; CGAS Barbers Pt, Hawaii 2/50; NAS Norfolk 12/52; Elizabeth City 6/53; Annete, Port Angeles; Olmstead 10/55; Inter Ice Patrol, Argentia 1956-58; SOC Elizabeth City 29/7/58; sold Ace Smelting, Phoenix 1959 {N2873G}; Empressa Andoriente, Lima 18/11/60 as OB-SAA-532, then OB-R-532 in 1964; scrapped Pucalapa, Peru around 1965.

44-85822 Del Dallas 8/7/45; Sth Plains 9/8/45; Rome 26/2/46; NAAF Mustin Fd 2/4/46 [77248]; USCG Elizabeth City 11/9/46; San Diego 9/46; Elizabeth City 8/47; NAS Weeksville, NC 25/8/48; broken up and parts ferried to Mustin Fd and NAS Norfolk.

44-85823 Del Dallas 9/7/45; Sth Plains 25/8/45; Rome 26/2/46; NAAF Mustin Fd 28/3/46 [77249]; USCG Elizabeth City 17/7/46; Inter Ice Patrol, Nfd 31/7/46; Spartan Aero Repair, Tulsa 10/48; USCG Elizabeth City 6/49; Brooklyn 10/51; NAS Norfolk 4/42; Brooklyn 11/52; Ace Smelting, Phoenix /58 (Civil N3192G); Widtfelt & Biegert, Phoenix 30/1/59; Empressa Andrriente, Lima, Peru 25/2/60; c/l Tocumen Apt, Panama en route Lima 26/3/60 and scrapped.

44-85824 Del Dallas 10/78/45; Sth Plains 11/8/45; Rome 26/2/46; NAAF Mustin Fd 28/3/46 [77250]; USCG Brooklyn 29/6/46; Mustin Fd 12/49; Brooklyn 6/50; Inter Ice Patrol, Argentia, Nfd 1/53; Olmstead 9/55; Port Angeles 9/56; Elizabeth City 1/57; Delta Lease/Co 16/5/58 (Civil N4711C); Field AvCo, Oshawa, Ontario 29/1/59; re-reg N8055E; Air Int, Miami 27/5/60; L.B.Smith A/C Corp, Miami 30/4/62; Servicos Aereos, Cochabamba, Bolivia, Civil CP-694; cr El Alto, La Paz 18/12/63.

44-85825 Del Dallas 11/7/45; Sth Plains 24/8/45; Rome 4/3/46; NAAF Mustin Fd 28/3/46 [77251]; USCG Elizabeth City 4/10/46; NAS Johnsville 1/47; USCG Brooklyn 2/47; Spartan Aero Rep, Tulsa 6/49; San Francisco 2/50; Brooklyn 1/53; NAS Norfolk 7/53; USCG Annette 7/53; Port Angeles 3/55; Olmstead 11/55; Inter Ice Patrol Argentia, Nfd /56; USCG Elizabeth City 10/56; Fairchild Air/Surveys, LA 8/9/58 (Civil N7091C); photographic instruments were installed 4/59, but burned out at Kandahar, Afghanistan 1959.

44-85826 Del Dallas 12/7/45; Sth Plains 23/8/45; Rome 28/2/46; USN [77252]; USCG San Francisco 6/10/46; damaged in accident 10/10/46, sal.

44-85827 Del Dallas 13/7/45; Sth Plains 27/8/45; Rome 4/3/46; NAAF Mustin Fd 21/11/46 [77253]; USCG Elizabeth City 27/12/46; Inter Ice Patrol, Argentia, Nfd 1/47; USCG Elizabeth City 5/47; San Francisco 6/8/49; NAS Norfolk 9/52; USCG Port Angeles 5/4/53; overshot runway NAS Sand Point, ran into Lake Washington 26/8/53 and salvaged; sold to Columbia Airmotive, Troutdale, Or, for spares.

44-85828 Del Dallas 13/7/45; Sth Plains 31/8/45; Rome 2/46; NAF Johnsville 9/9/46 [77254]; converted into camera and survey ship for USCG; Elizabeth City 31/3/47 and operated these activities until 1959, the last mission from Alaska; USCG San Francisco 9/59; Elizabeth to retire, the last B-17 used by USAF with military crew on 14/10/59; Joe Marrs, Opa Locka, Fl 8/3/60 (Civil N9323R); Serv-Air, White Plains, NY 4/60; Tropical Export Tred/Co, Fort Lauderdale 23/5/62; Hugh Wheeless, Dothan, Al 17/7/62 (sprayer); Black Hills Avn. Spearfish, SD 4/10/62 (tanker B-30); Aero Flite, Cody, Wyo 3/1/64; Bruce Kinney, Richey, Mont 1975; Aircraft Spec. Mesa, Az 18/5/78; swapped for C-54 tanker and restored as 390BG at Pima Museum, Az. I'LL GET AROUND.

44-85829 Del Dallas 16/7/45; Sth Plains 3/9/45; Rome 1/3/46; NAAF Mustin Fd 6/46 [77255]; USCG Elizabeth City 6/12/46; Inter Ice Patrol, Argentia, Nfd 4/47; NAS Norfolk 4/52; USCG San Francisco 10/52; Elizabeth City 3/54; NAF Johnsville 10/55; Inter Ice Patrol, Argentia, Nfd 1956; Elizabeth City 9/58; Ace Smelt/Corp, Phoenix 11/5/59 (Civil N3193G); Fairchild Air/Surv, LA 16/11/59, modified with cameras and floors plus nine new crew positions; Aero Serv/Corp 2/8/65; Biegert Bros, Shickley, Neb 11/65 (sprayer); Air/Spec, Mesa, Az 3/66 (tanker 34); flew to Hawaii for film Tora! Tora! Tora!; owners re-named Globe Air; Yankee AF, Ypsilanti, Mich 7/68 and restored as 381BG, flying as YANKEE LADY.

44-85830 Del Dallas 17/7/45; Sth Plains 31/8/45; Rome 28/2/46; NAAF Mustin Fd 6/46 [77256]; USCG San Francisco 6/12/46; Port Angeles 6/50; NAS Norfolk 4/53; Port Angeles 9/53; Inter Ice Patrol, Argentia, Nfd 1955; Elizabeth City 12/55; c/l NAS Norfolk 29/5/56, scrapped for spares.

44-85831 Del Dallas 18/7/45; Sth plains 5/9/45; Rome 26/2/46; NAAF Mustin Fd 4/46 [77257]; USCG Elizabeth City 29/7/46; Inter Ice Patrol, Argentia, Nfd 2/49; Elizabeth City 12/49; c/l Goose Bay, Labrador 14/3/52, scrapped for spares.

44-85832 Del Dallas 19/7/45; Sth Plains 2/1/46; USCG Elizabeth City 5/47; probably serialled 85832 instead of ass USN 84000; one of four aircraft tran USN 25/8/48 to NAS Weeksville, NC, then NAS Mustin Fd; NAS Norfolk, scrapped for spares, when conversions proved uneconomical.

44-85833 Del Dallas 20/7/45; Sth Plains 8/45; damaged in taxi accident with 44-85835 in 2/46 in preparation for USN, then USCG; repairs uneconomical, scrapped 7/6/46.

44-85834 Del Dallas 21/7/45; Sth Plains 30/8/45; Rome 25/2/46; NAAF Mustin Fd 4/46 [82856]; USCG San Diego 25/8/46; Elizabeth City 8/8/47; NAS Weeksville, NC 10/6/48; NAS Norfolk for salvage, scrapped 1/50 for spares.

44-85835 Del Dallas 230/7/45; Sth Plains 8/45; damaged in taxi accident with 44-85833 in 2/46 in preparation for USN, then USCG; repairs uneconomical, scrapped 7/6/46.

44-85836 –.

44-85837 Del Dallas 25/7/45; Sth Plains 6/9/45; Rome 26/2/46; NAAF Mustin Fd 4/46 [82855]; USCG Elizabeth City 14/8/46; San Francisco 10/49; NAS Norfolk 11/52; USCG New York 3/54; Elizabeth City 8/55; NAS Norfolk 1/4/57, scrapped.

44-85838 Del Dallas 25/7/45; Sth Plains 9/45; Rome 25/2/46; NAAF Mustin Fd 4/46 [82857]; USCG San Diego 19/11/46; Elizabeth City 3/1/47; NAS Weeksville, NC 27/8/48; NAAF Mustin Fd, then NAS Norfolk and scrapped 1/50, for spares.

44-85839 Del Dallas 27/7/45; Sth Plains for storage before sent to Aberdeen Proving Grounds, Md 2/46, tested to destruction 6/3/46.

44-85840 Del Dallas 28/7/45; Sth Plains for storage, as one of 20 set for USCG; served with USAF as TB-17G and VB-17G; sold Lloyed Aeros Bolivianos 1956 as CP620; Aircraft Specialities, Mesa, Az 12/60 (Civil N620L) as tanker; took part in film Tora! Tora! 1969; dest in crash, Elko, Nev 12/7/73.

44-85841 Del Dallas 4/8/45; Sth Plains 1/9/45; 555 BU Love Fd 30/10/45; Recl Comp 13/2/46.

Below: B-17G-110-VE 44-85828 was the fourth from last Fortress produced at Burbank. Supplied to the US Navy, it became 77254 and was converted for US Coast Guard surveillance work. The last of its type retired from that service, it became a 'borate bomber' for fire-fighting before finally being restored to wartime configuration and exhibited at the Pima air museum, Arizona. (Via R. Besecker)

Select Bibliography

Andrews, Paul, *Bits & Pieces of the Mighty Eighth*
Anthoine, Roger, *Fortresses sur L'Europe*
Bell, Dana, *US Air Force Colors*, Vols I–III
Birdsall, Steve, *Winged Majesty: Hell's Angels*
Bishop, Cliff, *Fortresses of the Big Triangle First*
Bowden, Ray, *Named Planes of the 91st BG*
Caiden, Martin, *Flying Forts*
Chloe, John, *Aleutian Warriors: Top Cover*
Comer, John, *Combat Crew*
Drain, Richard, *5th Bomb Wing Aircraft*
Foreman, Wally, *B-17 Nose Art Directory*
Hagedorn, Dan, *Wings Over The Canal*
Hawkins, Ian, *Munster Raid: The Way It Was*
Hess, William, *B-17 Fortress*
Jablonski, Ed, *Flying Fortress*
Lande, David, *Somewhere In England*
Lloyd, Alwyn, *B-17 Fortress in Detail and Scale*, Vols I–III
McCarthy, Dave, *Fear No More*
Mitchell, John, *On Wings We Conquer*
Rust, Kenn, *7th, 8th, 12th, 15th AF Stories*
Scutts, Jerry, *USAAF Heavies in the ETO and MTO*
Slater, Harry, *Fortresses of the Big Square A*
Stapfer, Heinz, *Strangers in a Strange Land*, Vols I and II
Thole, Lou, *Forgotten Fields*
Thompson, Scott, *B-17 in Blue*